Contemporary Authors

Contemporary Authors

A Bio-Bibliographical Guide to
Current Writers in Fiction, General Nonfiction,
Poetry, Journalism, Drama, Motion Pictures,
Television, and Other Fields

FRANCES CAROL LOCHER
Editor

volumes 81-84

GALE RESEARCH COMPANY • BOOK TOWER • DETROIT, MICHIGAN 48226

CONTEMPORARY AUTHORS

Published by
Gale Research Company, Book Tower, Detroit, Michigan 48226
Each Year's Volumes Are Revised About Five Years Later

Frederick G. Ruffner, *Publisher*   James M. Ethridge, *Editorial Director*

Christine Nasso, *General Editor, Contemporary Authors*

Frances Carol Locher, *Editor, Original Volumes*

Victoria France Hutchinson, B. Hal May, Ann Factor Ponikvar,
Nancy M. Rusin, Leslie D. Stone, David Versical,
Barbara A. Welch, and Martha G. Winkel, *Assistant Editors*
Susan L. Rose, Norma Sawaya, Shirley Seip,
and Laurie M. Serwatowski, *Editorial Assistants*

Jane A. Bowden and Otto Penzler, *Contributing Editors*
Andrea Geffner, Carolyn Thomas, Arlene True,
and Benjamin True, *Sketchwriters*

Eunice Bergin, *Copy Editor*
Michaeline Nowinski, *Production Director*

Special recognition is given to the staffs of
Journalists Biographical Master Index
and
Yesterday's Authors of Books for Children

Questions and Answers About
Contemporary Authors

What types of authors are included in *Contemporary Authors*? Nearly 56,000 living authors of nontechnical works (and such authors who have died since 1960) are represented in the series. *CA* includes writers in all genres—fiction, nonfiction, poetry, drama, etc.—whose books are issued by commercial, risk publishers or by university presses. Authors of books published only by known vanity or author-subsidized firms are not generally included. Since native language and nationality have no bearing on inclusion in *CA*, authors who write in languages other than English are also included in *CA* if their works have been published in the United States or translated into English.

Although *CA* focuses primarily on persons whose work appears in book form, the series now also encompasses prominent writers of interest to the public whose work appears in other media: newspaper and television reporters and correspondents, columnists, newspaper and periodical editors, syndicated cartoonists, screenwriters, television scriptwriters, and other media people.

Among the authors of particular interest included in this volume are James Beard, Bruno Bettelheim, Mary Challans (best known for her writings under the pseudonym Mary Renault), Bill Cosby, Sara Davidson, Dorothy Eden, Lonne Elder III, Frederick Exley, William Faulkner, Germaine Greer, Dashiell Hammett, Martin Heidegger, S. E. Hinton, Pope John Paul I, Arthur Kopit, C. S. Lewis, Loretta Lynn, Groucho Marx, Colleen McCullough, Julia O'Faolain, Pope Paul VI, Norman Vincent Peale, Tom Robbins, Theodore Roethke, W. E. D. Ross, Tom Stoppard, David Storey, Theodore Sturgeon, Alice B. Toklas, Maria von Trapp, and Yevgeny Yevtushenko.

Prominent media writers represented in this volume include Ingmar Bergman, Carl Bernstein, Charlie Chaplin, Judith Crist, Blake Edwards, Frank D. Gilroy, Nunnally Johnson, Stanley Kubrick, Joan E. Murray, Sylvia Porter, Gaylord Shaw, Edgar Parks Snow, Josef von Sternberg, Garry Trudeau, and Luchino Visconti.

How is *Contemporary Authors* compiled? Most of the material in *CA* is furnished by the authors themselves. Questionnaires are sent regularly to authors as their new books appear and are reviewed as well as to prominent media personalities. Information provided by the authors in their questionnaires is then written in the distinctive *CA* format, and the proposed entries are sent to the authors for review and approval prior to publication.

How are entries prepared if authors do not furnish information? If authors of special interest to *CA* users fail to reply to requests for information, material is gathered from various other reliable sources. Biographical dictionaries are checked (a task made easier through the use of Gale's *Biographical Dictionaries Master Index* and *Author Biographies Master Index*), as are bibliographical sources, such as *Cumulative Book Index, The National Union Catalog,* etc. Published interviews, feature stories, and book reviews are examined, and often material is supplied by the authors' publishers.

As with entries prepared from questionnaires, sketches prepared through extensive research are also sent to the authors for approval prior to publication. If the authors do not respond, the listings are published with an asterisk (*) following them to indicate that the material has not been personally verified by the authors.

Why are obituary notices included in *Contemporary Authors*, and how can they be distinguished from full-length sketches? To be as timely and comprehensive as possible, *CA* publishes obituary notices on recently deceased authors. These notices provide date and place of birth and death, highlight the author's career and writings, and list other sources where additional biographical information and obituaries may be found. To distinguish them from full-length sketches, obituaries are now identified with the heading *Obituary Notice.*

CA includes obituary notices both for authors who already have full-length sketches in earlier *CA* volumes, thus effectively completing the sketches, and for authors not yet sketched in the series. Deceased authors of special interest presently represented in the series only by obituary notices are scheduled for full-length sketch treatment in forthcoming *CA* volumes.

Will you please explain the unusual numbering system used for *Contemporary Authors* volumes? The unusual four-volume numbering system used today reflects *CA*'s publication history. To meet the urgent need for information about authors as quickly as possible, *CA* began as a quarterly publication, with each book carrying a single volume number. The numbering system was changed to double-volume numbers when Volumes 5-6 was published with twice as many entries as a quarterly volume. With the appearance of Volumes 25-28, the numbering system was altered once more to indicate that each physical volume of *CA* represents four of the original quarterly volumes.

Now, all *CA* volumes are available as four-volume units, including the revised volumes. As early volumes of *CA* were revised, they were combined into the four-volume units presently being issued. For example, when Volumes 1, 2, 3, and 4 were revised, the material was updated, merged into a single alphabet, and is available today as Volumes 1-4, First Revision.

An unusual number of biographical publications have been appearing recently, and the question is now often asked whether a charge is made for listings in such publications. Do authors listed in *Contemporary Authors* make any payment or incur any other obligation for their listings? Some publishers charge for listings or require purchase of a book by biographees. There is, however, absolutely no charge or obligation of any kind attached to being included in *CA*.

Cumulative Index Should Always Be Consulted

Since *CA* is a multi-volume series which does not repeat author entries from volume to volume, the cumulative index published in alternate new volumes of *CA* should always be consulted to locate an individual author's listing. Each new volume contains authors not previously included in the series and is revised approximately five years after its original publication. The cumulative index indicates the original or revised volume in which an author appears. Authors removed from the revision cycle and placed in the *CA Permanent Series* are listed in the index as having appeared in specific original volumes of *CA* (for the benefit of those who do not hold *Permanent Series* volumes), *and* as having their finally revised sketches in a specific *Permanent Series* volume.

For the convenience of *CA* users, the *CA* cumulative index also includes references to all entries in two related Gale series—*Contemporary Literary Criticism,* which is devoted entirely to current criticism of major authors, poets, and playwrights, and *Something About the Author,* a series of heavily illustrated sketches on juvenile authors and illustrators.

As always, suggestions from users about any aspect of *CA* will be welcomed.

CONTEMPORARY AUTHORS

*Indicates that a listing has been compiled from secondary sources believed to be reliable, but has not been personally verified for this edition by the author sketched.

A

AALBEN, Patrick
    See JONES, Noel

*   *   *

ABERCROMBIE, Barbara (Mattes) 1939-

PERSONAL: Born April 6, 1939, in Evanston, Ill.; daughter of William F. (a businessman and writer) and Grace (a pianist; maiden name, Mann) Mattes; married Gordon E. Abercrombie (a stockbroker), March 8, 1964; children: Brooke Louise, Gillan Grace. *Education:* Attended Briarcliff College and Los Angeles Harbor College. *Residence:* Palos Verdes Estates, Calif. *Agent:* Aaron M. Priest Literary Agency, 150 East 35th St., New York, N.Y. 10016.

CAREER: Actress (on Broadway, in summer stock, on tour, and on television, including appearances on "Ironside" and "Route 66") and free-lance writer. Teacher of creative writing to children.

WRITINGS: (Editor) *The Other Side of a Poem,* Harper, 1977; *Connections* (novel), Harper, 1979. Contributor of poems to little magazines.

WORK IN PROGRESS: A book for children.

SIDELIGHTS: Barbara Abercrombie writes: "I write to make things clear to myself. This is especially true of the stories I write for children. I write about the things that happen in my own family from my own viewpoint, which, at age thirty-eight, I find not very different from the way I was in terms of thoughts and feelings at age ten."

*   *   *

ADAMS, Alice (Boyd) 1926-

PERSONAL: Born in Fredericksburg, Va., August 14, 1926; daughter of Nicholson (a professor) and Agatha (a writer; maiden name, Boyd); married in 1946 (divorced in 1958); children: Peter. *Education:* Radcliffe College, B.A., 1945. *Home:* 3904 Clay St., San Francisco, Calif. 94118. *Agent:* Lynn Nesbit, International Creative Management, 40 West 57th St., New York, N.Y. 10019.

CAREER: Writer. Has held various office jobs, including secretary, clerk, and bookkeeper.

WRITINGS: Careless Love, New American Library, 1966; *The Fall of Daisy Duke,* Constable, 1967; *Families and Survivors* (novel), Knopf, 1975; *Listening to Billie* (novel), Knopf, 1978; *Beautiful Girl* (short stories), Knopf, 1979.

Contributor of numerous short stories to periodicals, including *New Yorker, Atlantic Monthly, Redbook, McCalls,* and *Paris Review.*

WORK IN PROGRESS: A novel entitled *Rewards.*

SIDELIGHTS: Most reviewers agreed that *Families and Survivors* is a successful novel. Reviewing the book in *Newsweek,* Peter Prescott commented: "If it is a little difficult to keep the characters straight and a little hard to remember what happened when one puts the novel down, each scene is nonethless very sharp and the dialogue true." Adams "loves to jolt her readers," wrote a reviewer in the *New Yorker.* "Frequently, she interrupts her narrative to foretell disasters or twists of fate unforseen by a character. In a lesser writer this illusion-shattering prophesying might be annoying but Miss Adams' sense of timing is so acute and her eye for detail is so unvaryingly sensitive that it only enhances our pleasure in this excellent book." In *Book World* critic Jill Robinson's words, it is "a book to savor," and a "you-can't-put-it-down book, but unlike many of those it belongs to our permanent literature."

Adams's novel *Listening to Billie,* the title referring to legendary blues singer Billie Holiday, received more varied responses from reviewers than did *Families and Survivors.* *New Republic* critic Catherine O'Neill noted that "Adams has a sharp eye for character and place, and a gift for dialogue. Her characters really talk to each other." Susan Wood disagreed. She wrote in *Book World* that the "novel's weaknesses are not so easily apprehended; one finishes 'Listening to Billie' feeling vaguely unsatisfied," explaining that the "characters are not persuasive, one . . . does not know them as one still expects a good novelist to make us do."

In an interview with Patricia Holt in *Publishers Weekly,* Adams said that she sees "a movement among female writers, male or female, away from the conventional 'male stud novel' toward something far more diversified and exploratory." She added that she "very much admire[s] people like Laurie Colwin, Sheila Ballantyne, Margery Finn Brown, Ella Leffland and Diane Johnson, who are very professional writers of fiction—and very good women writers, too!"

BIOGRAPHICAL/CRITICAL SOURCES: Publishers Weekly, December 9, 1974, November 24, 1975, November 14, 1977, January 16, 1978; *New York Times,* January 30, 1975, January 10, 1978; *Harvard Magazine,* February, 1975; *Newsweek,* February 3, 1975; *New Yorker,* February 10,

1975; *Christian Science Monitor,* February 20, 1975; *Book World,* February 23, 1975, January 13, 1978, January 21, 1979; *New York Times Book Review,* March 16, 1975, February 26, 1978, January 14, 1979; *Contemporary Literary Criticism,* Volume 6, Gale, 1976; *Times Literary Supplement,* January 16, 1976; *New Statesman,* January 16, 1976; *Observer* (London), January 18, 1976; *Listener,* January 29, 1976; *Time,* December 26, 1977; *New Republic,* February 4, 1978; *New Leader,* March 27, 1978; *People,* April 3, 1978; *Rolling Stone,* April 20, 1978.

* * *

ADAMSON, Alan (Herbert)   1919-

PERSONAL: Born January 7, 1919, in Winnipeg, Manitoba, Canada; son of C.A. (a barrister) and Marguerite (Townsend) Adamson; married Judy Coull (a professor of English), December 9, 1968; children: Nicholas Patrick. *Education:* University of Manitoba, B.A. (honors), 1940; University of London, Ph.D., 1964. *Office:* Department of History, Concordia University, 1455 de Maisonneuve Blvd. W., Montreal, Quebec, Canada H3G 1M8.

CAREER: Department of Education, Winnipeg, Manitoba, director of audio-visual and radio education, 1940-41; National Film Board of Canada, Ottawa, Ontario, secretary and administrative assistant, 1941-44; Workers' Educational Association, Toronto, Ontario, research director, 1945-46; Voters' Research Institute, New York, N.Y., assistant director, 1946-47; independent political researcher in San Francisco, Calif., 1947-48; Institute of Modern Languages, Prague, Czechoslouakia, lecturer, 1949-52; Concordia University, Montreal, Quebec, member of department of history, 1964—. External adviser to University of the West Indies. *Member:* American Historical Association, Society for the Study of Labour History, Past and Present Society.

WRITINGS: Iceberg Politics: The Reserve Vote in San Francisco, Research Department, California Congress of Industrial Organizations, 1948; *Sugar Without Slaves: The Political Economy of British Guiana, 1838-1904,* Yale University Press, 1972. Contributor to *Europa.*

WORK IN PROGRESS: The Rulers and the Ruled: Aspects of Attitudes to Class in Industrial Britain; a series of studies examining the industrial revolution's impact on attitudes in nineteenth-century Britain.

* * *

ADISESHIAH, Malcolm S(athianathan)   1910-

PERSONAL: Born April 18, 1910, in Madras, India; son of Varanasi and Nesammah (Clarke) Adiseshiah; married Sanchu Pothan, December 26, 1951. *Education:* University of Madras, M.A., 1930; London School of Economics and Political Science, Ph.D., 1936. *Home:* 19 Cenotaph Rd., Madras, Tamil Nadu 600018, India. *Office:* Madras Institute of Development Studies, Madras, India.

CAREER: University of Calcutta, St. Paul's College, Calcutta, India, lecturer in economics, 1931-36; Madras Christian College, Tambaram, Madras, India, professor of economics, 1940-46; World University Service, Geneva, Switzerland, associate general secretary, 1946-48; UNESCO, Paris, France, department director of International Exchange Service, 1948-50, director of Department of Technical Assistance, 1950-54, assistant director general in charge of program, 1954-63, deputy director-general, 1963-71; Madras Institute of Development Studies, Madras, director, 1971-78, chairman, 1978—; University of Madras,

Madras, vice-chancellor, 1975-78. Member of development group for Ten Year Plan for Industrialization for India, 1940-46; member of government planning commissions; member of Rajya Sabha (upper house of Indian parliament). *Member:* International Social Science Council (president of World Social Science Development Committee), International Council of Adult Education (president), Family Planning Council of India (president), Indian Adult Education Association (president), Indian Council of Social Science Research, National Council of Educational Research and Training, National Council of Teacher Education, Indian Economic Association (president, 1973-74), Tamil Nadu Board of Continuing Education (president). *Awards, honors:* Honorary doctorates from University of Baghdad, 1965, University of Teheran, 1967, University of Santiago, 1968, University of Toronto, 1974, and University of Andhra, 1975.

WRITINGS: Education and National Development, Oxford University Press, 1967; *Let My Country Awake,* U.N.E.S.C.O., 1970; *It Is Time to Begin,* U.N.E.S.C.O., 1972. Also author of about ten government and university reports on agriculture, education, and economics.

SIDELIGHTS: Adiseshiah told *CA:* "Education has been and is a motor force for Indian development, both directly in enlarging political consciousness and participation and contributing to skills formation and application of science and technology, and indirectly by turning the search light on the lacks and defects of the educational system in its service of the country's development and showing how it can be restructured to contribute its share to people's happiness. My most exciting moments have been in this restructuration process."

* * *

ADLER, Irene
See PENZLER, Otto

* * *

AIMES, Angelica   1943-

PERSONAL: Born December 25, 1943, in Shanghai, China. *Education:* Attended Sorbonne, University of Paris and American University in Beirut. *Office:* 224 East 18th St., New York, N.Y. 10003.

CAREER: Writer, 1977—.

WRITINGS: Samantha (historical romance), Pinnacle Books, 1978; *Francesca* (historical romance), Pinnacle Books, 1978.

WORK IN PROGRESS: A historical romance/family saga, spanning nearly a hundred years and three generations in the life of an early American family.

SIDELIGHTS: Angelica Aimes told *CA:* "My extensive travels, my intense curiosity to discover how people live in other places and other times have drawn me to the realm of historic romance where adventure, fantasy, and wish fulfillment reign supreme and virtually anything is possible."

* * *

AIROLA, Paavo (Olavi)   1915-

PERSONAL: Born April 16, 1915, in Karelia, Finland; came to the United States in 1959; married Ruth-Eivor Persson, July 31, 1946 (divorced, 1976); children: Anni, Evi, Paul, Karen, Paula. *Education:* University of Leningrad, Ph.D., 1939; Brantridge Forest School, N.D., 1966. *Office address:* P.O. Box 22001, Phoenix, Ariz. 85028.

CAREER: Nutritionist, naturopathic physician, and biochemist. Researcher at European biological clinics and research centers. Lecturer at universities and colleges, including Stanford University Medical Center; conductor of educational seminars for physicians. Has made numerous appearances on television and radio programs. *Member:* International Society for Research of Civilization and Environment, International Naturopathic Association, International Institute of Arts and Letters (fellow), International Academy of Biological Medicine (president), Royal Canadian Academy of Fine Arts. *Awards, honors:* Award of Merit, 1971, from American Institute of Public Affairs.

WRITINGS: There Is a Cure for Arthritis, Parker Publishing, 1968; *Health Secrets From Europe,* Parker Publishing, 1970; *Sex and Nutrition: A Modern Study of Nutritional Aspects of Sexuality,* Information, Inc., 1970; *Are You Confused?: De-Confusion Book on Nutrition and Health, With the Latest Scientific Research and Authoritative Answers to the Most Controversial Question,* Health Plus, 1971; *How to Keep Slim, Healthy, and Young With Juice Fasting,* Health Plus, 1971; *Swedish Beauty Secrets,* Health Plus, 1971; *Cancer: Causes, Prevention, and Treatment—The Total Approach,* Health Plus, 1972; *Rejuvenation Secrets From Around the World—That Work,* Health Plus, 1973; *How to Get Well: Dr. Airola's Handbook of Natural Healing,* Health Plus, 1974; *The Miracle of Fasting,* Health Plus, 1978; *Everywoman's Book,* Health Plus, 1979. Also author of *Hypoglycemia: A Better Approach,* Health Plus. Contributing editor for *Let's Live* magazine, 1975-78, *Alive,* 1976, *New Realities,* 1978—, and *Health Street Journal,* 1978—.

*   *   *

ALBERY, Nobuko
(Nobuko Morris)

PERSONAL: Born in Ashiya, Japan; daughter of Keiji (a company chairman) and Sodako (Masutani) Uenishi; married Ivan Morris, December, 1967; married Sir Donald Albery (a theatrical producer), May, 1974. *Education:* Attended Waseda University, 1958-60, and New York University, 1961-63, received M.A. *Home:* 31 Ave. Princesse Grace, Monte Carlo, Monaco.

CAREER: Toho Co. (theater), Tokyo, Japan, representative, 1963—. Interpreter for U.S. State Department Protocol Agency, 1963-65. Producer for Wyndham Theatres (London), 1971-78.

WRITINGS: (Under name Nobuko Morris; with Ivan Morris and Paul Varley) *Samurai* (historical study), Weidenfeld & Nicolson, 1969; *Balloon Top* (novel), Pantheon, 1978. Contributor to *Mademoiselle.*

WORK IN PROGRESS: A novel about the life of a fourteenth-century Japanese actor.

SIDELIGHTS: Nobuko Albery writes: "I have had many wonderful friends, in particular Anais Nin and Robert Payne, who gave me constant and undaunted encouragement."

*   *   *

ALEXANDER, David M(ichael) 1945-

PERSONAL: Born August 21, 1945, in Rochester, N.Y.; son of Samuel (a postal worker) and Edna (Wellwood) Alexander. *Education:* Stanford University, B.A., 1967; University of California, Berkeley, J.D., 1970. *Agent:* Richard Curtis Literary Agency, 156 East 52nd St., New York, N.Y. 10022. *Office:* 2600 El Camino Real, #506, Palo Alto, Calif. 94306.

CAREER: Professional photographer in San Francisco, Calif., 1968-70; admitted to the Bar of California, 1971, and the Bar of the U.S. Supreme Court; DeCaro, Alexander & DeCaro (law corporation), Palo Alto, Calif., shareholder, 1971-74; attorney in private practice, Palo Alto, 1974—. Instructor at DeAnza Junior College and Foothill Junior College, 1974—. *Member:* Science Fiction Writers of America, California Bar Association, Santa Clara County Bar Association, San Mateo County Bar Association, Order of the Coif.

WRITINGS: The Chocolate Spy (science fiction), Coward, 1978.

WORK IN PROGRESS: Eagle Three Down!, a novel "about the crash of a fighter pilot behind enemy lines, the wife whom he left behind, the friend whom he betrays, and the half brother who damns him for ever having gone to war"; an adventure novel "about organized crime in the high technology electronics industry"; a fantasy novel; science fiction stories.

SIDELIGHTS: Alexander comments: "My background is varied; I have been an attorney at law, silkscreen artist, inventor, and businessman. I am an avid science fiction fan and count among my friends some of the top writers in that field.

"I enjoy writing about the adventure and excitement generated in society by rapidly advancing technology. I suppose this would be called 'soft science fiction'. *The Chocolate Spy* dealt with a cloned human organic computer—a protein computer instead of an electronic one. The fantasy novel I am writing deals with magic as a substitute for technology. The crime novel I am working on examines what would happen as a result of the combination of organized crime and high technology electronics. My science fiction stories deal with what a society would be like if criminals were imprisoned not in body but in mind—the idea of what a society might be like in which people could insure not against the expenses of being in an accident but against the fact of being in an accident itself. I have several other plots both for novels and short stories that basically deal with the kinds of adventures and excitement certain individuals in a society would be involved in if our present day world were changed with the addition of perhaps one major and possibly threatening advance in technology.

"I also enjoy writing about the changes in a character as a result of the events that he experiences. There is a change in Merriman in *The Chocolate Spy,* in Daniel Leighton in *Eagle Three Down!,* and also in the major characters of the two other books mentioned above. I like to see how adversity affects a character, if it makes him stronger or weaker."

*   *   *

ALEXANDER, Jan
See BANIS, Victor J(erome)

*   *   *

ALEXANDER, (Eben) Roy 1899(?)-1978

OBITUARY NOTICE: Born c. 1899 in Omaha, Neb.; died October 30, 1978, in Roslyn, N.Y. Journalist and editor. Alexander was managing editor of *Time* from 1949 to 1960, longer than anyone in the magazine's history. Obituaries and other sources: *Washington Post,* November 1, 1978; *Chicago Tribune,* November 2, 1978; *Time,* November 13, 1978.

ALLEN, Judson B(oyce) 1932-

PERSONAL: Born March 15, 1932, in Louisville, Ky.; son of Clifton Judson (a clergyman and editor) and Hattie Belle (a speech therapist and children's writer; maiden name, McCracken) Allen; married Jacqueline Johnson Hewitt (a realtor); children: Wade Cox, Rosalind Toy. *Education:* Baylor University, B.A., 1953; Vanderbilt University, M.A., 1954; further graduate study at Oxford University, 1960-62; Johns Hopkins University, Ph.D., 1963. *Politics:* Democrat. *Religion:* Baptist. *Residence:* Milwaukee, Wis. *Office:* Department of English, Marquette University, 635 North 13th St., Milwaukee, Wis. 53233.

CAREER: Southern Baptist Historical Commission, Nashville, Tenn., research assistant and editor, 1953-57; Southern Baptist Education Commission, Nashville, research assistant and staff writer, 1957; Johns Hopkins University, Baltimore, Md., junior instructor in English, 1957-60; Wake Forest University, Winston-Salem, N.C., instructor, 1962-63, assistant professor of English, 1964-69; Marquette University, Milwaukee, Wis., associate professor of English, 1969—. Visiting professor at University of Chicago, 1978. Member of advisory committee of Centre for Medieval and Renaissance Studies (Oxford, England), 1978—. Member of Baptist World Alliance Commission on Cooperative Christianity, 1969—.

MEMBER: American Association of University Professors, Modern Language Association of America, Medieval Academy of America, Northeast Modern Language Association (section head, 1974-76), Midwest Modern Language Association (section head, 1976). *Awards, honors:* Fellowships from Medieval-Renaissance Institute, summer, 1965, University of North Carolina, 1965-66, and National Endowment for the Humanities, 1969-70, for Italy, and 1975-76, for France; American Philosophical Society grant, 1969.

WRITINGS: The Friar as Critic: Literary Attitudes in the Later Middle Ages, Vanderbilt University Press, 1971. Contributor of over twenty articles and reviews to scholarly journals. Associate editor of *Encyclopedia of Southern Baptists,* 1957; member of editorial board of "Medieval Academy Reprints for Teaching."

WORK IN PROGRESS: A Typology of Tales, with Theresa Moritz; *Consideration, Custom, and Belief: The Ethical Poetic of the Later Middle Ages;* a book that will argue a connection between lyric and the medieval processes of role definition and personal role adoption; research on the city as a rhetorical system, drawing upon medieval theory as a matrix for solving problems of design, positional competition, hierarchy, and limited resources; studies in medieval lyric and verse translations.

SIDELIGHTS: Allen writes: "My work exists in the interface between fact and fiction, which the Middle Ages practiced as rhetoric, and which now may be dominated by anthropologists, since many literary critics cultivate the solipsism. Since I have lived in England, France, and Italy, as well as in the American South and Midwest, I have a lively awareness of the radical differences in sensibility which distinguish (and even alienate) people from one another. As a scholar, I am interested in understanding how a distinctive sensibility comes to be, and what various ones are (and may be) good for; I find literary processes powerful tools of explanation, and literary texts excellent moral and cultural evidence. My work so far has been the technical scholarship of the medievalist, but I achieved through it some positions and methods of more general significance, and I expect to begin now to work on more generally ethical problems, such as the urban studies book in progress."

ALLEN, Paul 1948-

PERSONAL: Born April 13, 1948, in Madison, W.Va.; married Susan Jacobs (a social worker), August, 1972. *Education:* University of South Florida, B.A., 1970, graduate study, 1970-71; University of Southern California, M.F.A., 1975. *Residence:* California. *Address:* c/o The Viking Press, 625 Madison Ave., New York, N.Y. 10022.

CAREER: Film editor, director of documentary and educational films, and screenwriter, 1976—. *Member:* Writers Guild (West).

WRITINGS: Apeland (novel), Viking, 1976.

WORK IN PROGRESS: A novel; a screenplay.

*   *   *

ALMAZ, Michael 1921-

PERSONAL: Born December 21, 1921, in Tel-Aviv, Israel; son of Yeruham Gabbai (in business) and Hannah (Kleinmann) Almaz; married Nitza Streit, 1944 (divorced, 1959); married June Kitty Thom, 1964 (divorced); married Pamela Jayne Wright, 1975; children: Basmat, Katya, Mahalia, Noam, Chris (stepson). *Education:* Attended Hebrew University of Jerusalem, 1939-42, Fordham University, 1947-48, and City College (now of the City University of New York), 1948-49. *Politics:* "Libertarian." *Home:* 182 Shaftesbury Ave., Covent Garden, London WC2H 8JJ, England. *Agent:* Jon Thurley, 78 New Bond St., London W.1, England.

CAREER: Playwright. Zira Theatre, Tel-Aviv, Israel, founder and literary/artistic director, 1949-58; British Broadcasting Corp., London, writer/director, 1958-68; Martef Theatre, Tel-Aviv, Israel, founder and literary/artistic director, 1968-69; worked as free-lance writer and broadcaster, 1969-71; Pool Theatre, Edinburgh, Scotland, associate director, 1971-74; Artaud Co., London, England, founder and resident dramatist, 1973—. Judge of All London Literary Competition, 1978. *Military service:* British Army, Infantry, 1942-46. Israeli Army, film unit, 1948-49. *Member:* British Actors Equity Association, Theatre Writers Union. *Awards, honors:* Fringe Award from Edinburgh Festival, 1973, for "Dreyfus on Devil's Island."

WRITINGS: In David's Schloss (one-act play; first produced in London, 1964), Kaiser Verlag, 1966, translation by Werner Simon published as *In the King's Bosom,* Evans Plays, 1968; "Every Number Wins" (one-act play; first produced in London, at Little Theatre, 1966), published in *The Best Short Plays of 1968,* edited by Stanley Richards, Chilton, 1968; *Verdammte Fussgaenger* (play; title means "The Bloody Pedestrians"; first produced in Tel-Aviv, Israel, at Martef Theatre, 1969), Kaiser Verlag, 1968; *Doppelspiel* (one-act play; title means "Duplex"; first produced in Bradford, England, at Bradford University, 1971), Baerenreiter Verlag, 1971.

Unpublished plays: "Wicked City" (two-act), first produced in London at Royal Academy of Dramatic Art, 1964; "Sign of the Fish" (two-act), first produced in London by British Broadcasting Corp. (BBC-Radio), 1965; "The Rasputin Show" (two-act), first produced in Brighton, England, 1968; "I Was Queen Victoria's Chauffeur" (one-act), first produced in Tel-Aviv, at Martef Theatre, 1969; "Monsieur Artaud" (two-act), first produced in London, at the Place, 1970; "Inquisition" (one-act), first produced in Glasgow, Scotland, at Close Theatre, 1970; "Santa Cruz" (one-act), first produced in Edinburgh, Scotland, at Edinburgh Festival, 1971; "Cut" (one-act), first produced in Edinburgh, at Pool Theatre, 1971; "The Port Said Performance" (one-act), first produced in Edinburgh, at Pool Theatre, 1971; "Anarchist" (two-act), first produced in London, at Royal Court Theatre, 1971; "The Tenor," first produced in Edinburgh, at Pool Theatre, 1972; "Paper Tiger" (one-act), first produced in London, at Soho Theatre, 1972; "Chicago Sunday School for Anarchists" (one-act), first produced in Edinburgh, at Pool Theatre, 1973; "The Moshe Dayan Extravaganza" (two-act), first produced in Bradford, at National Student Theatre Festival, 1973; "Dreyfus on Devil's Island" (one-act), first produced in Edinburgh, at Edinburgh Festival, 1973; "Letters from K." (one-act), first produced in Edinburgh, at Edinburgh Festival, 1974; "Story" (one-act), first produced in Edinburgh, at Edinburgh Festival, 1974; "Sailor" (two-act), first produced in Bracknell, England, at Bracknell Arts Centre, 1974; "Masoch" (two-act), first produced in Rotterdam, Netherlands, at De Lantaren, 1975; "Moments on a Jaffa Beach" (one-act), first produced in London, at Royal Court Theatre, 1976; "The Friend" (two-act), first produced in Edinburgh, at Traverse Theatre, 1977; "Diary of a Rat" (one-act), first produced in Edinburgh, at Traverse Theatre, 1977; "The F & H Show" (two-act), first produced in Edinburgh, at Traverse Theatre, November, 1978; "Rehearsing Stanislavsky Rehearsing" (two-act), first produced, 1978; "Smash Z" (two-act), first produced, 1979.

Creator of "The F & H Film," 1965.

WORK IN PROGRESS: A novel.

SIDELIGHTS: Almaz writes: "Although I have worked in the theatre, on radio, and even in film as a director, I see myself first as a writer—the originator of shows. I consider the live theatre to be not only the senior but also the most exciting, direct, and experimental of all the media. I object to those who misunderstand Artaud—who would rob the theatre of its verbal (literary) base. In this respect, I am anti-trendy.

"My main themes have been counter-politics (I am an anarchist), racism, the relation between art and life, the meaning of theatre, and what I call 'laff shows.'"

AVOCATIONAL INTERESTS: Travel, reading.

* * *

ALTER, Judith (MacBain) 1938-
(Judy Alter)

PERSONAL: Born July 22, 1938, in Chicago, Ill.; daughter of Richard Norman (a physician) and Alice (Peterman) MacBain; married Joel Alter (a physician), May 16, 1964; children: Colin, Megan, Jamie, Jordan. *Education:* University of Chicago, B.A., 1961; Northeast Missouri State University, M.A., 1964; Texas Christian University, Ph.D., 1970. *Residence:* Fort Worth, Tex. *Agent:* Patricia Falk Feeley Agency, Inc., 52 Vanderbilt Ave., New York, N.Y. 10017. *Office:* Texas College of Osteopathic Medicine, Camp Bowie at Montgomery, Fort Worth, Tex. 76107.

CAREER: Chicago Osteopathic Center, Chicago, Ill., typist and secretary, 1954-61; Kirksville College of Osteopathic Medicine, Kirksville, Mo., writer and editor in public relations, 1962-64; Fort Worth Osteopathic Hospital, Fort Worth, Tex., secretary, 1965-66, editor of employee publication, 1965-73, public relations consultant, 1971-73; free-lance writer, 1973-75; Texas Christian University, Fort Worth, instructor in English as a second language, 1975-76; Texas College of Osteopathic Medicine, Fort Worth, director of publications, 1972, acting director of public information, 1977-78, associate director of news and information, 1978—.

MEMBER: Western Writers of America (member of board of directors, 1976-77), Western American Literature Association, Southwestern American Literature Association.

WRITINGS—Under name Judy Alter: (With Phil Russell) *The Quack Doctor,* Branch-Smith, 1974; *Stewart Edward White* (pamphlet), Boise State University, 1975; *After Pa Was Shot* (juvenile), Morrow, 1978; (with Sam Pearson) *Single Again,* Branch-Smith. 1978. Author of book reviews and a column, "Along Publishers' Row," for *Roundup,* and "Women's Lit.," a review column in *Fort Worth Star Telegram,* 1974-75.

WORK IN PROGRESS: A juvenile novel; continuing research on the "Old West."

SIDELIGHTS: Judy Alter comments: "I always wanted to write—I feel as if publication has come after years of paying dues. I am very interested in the Old West as a viable subject for juvenile and adult fiction. I am most grateful to contacts made through Western Writers of America. I see discouragement for the new writer with no contacts, and wish the system could be changed.

"My interest in Western literature grew out of American literature studies in graduate school but gradually I have become more interested in popular literature rather than academic studies. My first juvenile novel, *After Pa Was Shot,* grew out of scraps of a story in the memoirs of a long-time Texas resident. It is, to me, the work which really justifies my calling myself a writer, and I am now deep into a second juvenile novel. But my writing began as strictly non-fiction, and it has been a long, slow transition. For a long time, I thought I simply couldn't write fiction and lots of short story manuscripts buried in my files seem to support that idea. But the idea for this novel just seemed suddenly right and I tried it. I was most fortunate to have an agent who encouraged me and who located an editor who really worked with me in revisions and rewrites."

BIOGRAPHICAL/CRITICAL SOURCES: Fort Worth Star Telegram, May 9, 1978.

* * *

ALTER, Judy
See ALTER, Judith (MacBain)

* * *

ALTMAN, Irwin 1928-
(Larry Altman)

PERSONAL: Born September 22, 1928, in New York, N.Y.; son of Morris Paul (a clothing designer) and Bertha (a business administrator; maiden name, Goldstein) Altman; married Sylvia Kavetsky, June, 1948 (died, 1951); married Marjorie Scheele (a communications specialist), April 26, 1954; children: Marcia Montoya, Jory Nanette. *Education:* Educated in New York, N.Y., and Los Angeles, Calif. *Politics:* "The person and what they stand for." *Religion:* "Yours and mine." *Residence:* San Francisco, Calif. *Office:* Teamwork Associates, 1005 Market St., San Francisco, Calif. 94103.

CAREER: Worked as lumper, 1942-45, and as bus boy, waiter, radio actor, comedian, hairdresser, salesman, inventor, teacher, and lecturer; writer. *Military service:* U.S. Navy, 1945-47.

WRITINGS—Under pseudonym Larry Altman: Song of Songs, Second Coming Press, 1976; *The Call of the Cricket,* Celestial Arts, 1978. Author of column, "Conning You," in *San Francisco Progress.*

WORK IN PROGRESS: Book of Crooks; Man of Wood, "contemporary Americana"; *Aleister,* on Aleister Crowley.

SIDELIGHTS: Altman told *CA:* "More and more I see myself as an insignificant player on an already too crowded field. I want to step away so that I can see clearly my love, my anger, my outrage, my standards (if any), and my laughter and my tears in relationship to yours. That's what I want to set upon paper."

BIOGRAPHICAL/CRITICAL SOURCES: San Francisco Progress, April, 1978; *San Francisco Examiner,* August 7, 1978.

* * *

ALTMAN, Larry
　　See ALTMAN, Irwin

* * *

AMES, Leslie
　　See ROSS, W(illiam) E(dward) D(aniel)

* * *

ANDERSON, Charlotte Maria 1923-

PERSONAL: Born July 7, 1923, in Vienna, Austria; came to the United States in 1935, naturalized citizen, 1939; daughter of William (an opera director) and Hilde (von Coelln) von Wymetal; married Carl Einar Anderson (a nuclear physicist), March 25, 1957. *Education:* University of California, Los Angeles, A.B., 1943, M.A., 1949; Yale University, Ph.D., 1954. *Residence:* Wayne, Pa. *Office:* Department of Foreign Studies, Montgomery County Community College, Blue Bell, Pa. 19422.

CAREER: Connecticut College, New London, assistant professor of German, 1953-58; Yale University, New Haven, Conn., instructor in German, 1958-59; Haverford College, Haverford, Pa., assistant professor of German, 1961-66; Montgomery County Community College, Blue Bell, Pa., associate professor, 1966-67, professor of German, 1967—, head of department of foreign studies, 1966—. *Member:* American Association of Teachers of German, Modern Language Association of America, Association of Departments of Foreign Languages (member of executive committee, 1970-72; president, 1973), Northeast Modern Language Association (member of executive council, 1975-78), Phi Beta Kappa, Delta Phi Alpha, Pi Delta Phi.

WRITINGS: (With Gerhard Weiss) *Begegnung mit Deutschland* (title means "Meeting Germany"), Dodd, 1970. Contributor of articles and reviews to foreign language journals. Associate editor of *Unterrichtspraxis;* member of editorial board of *German Quarterly.*

WORK IN PROGRESS: Research on eighteenth and nineteenth-century German literature.

SIDELIGHTS: Charlotte Anderson writes: "Aside from my teaching and research activities, I am committed to the propagation of the humanities in American schools and colleges. I feel that the stress on vocational training in our curricula has resulted in disastrous deficiencies in the students' reading, writing, and reasoning capabilities. We are, in effect, cheating our young people out of their Western heritage and depriving our country of well-educated and well-rounded college graduates.

"I am deeply concerned with the plight of animals—strays, animals used for senseless scientific experiments, and animals on the verge of extinction due to man's greed and lack

of planning. I devote as much time and money as possible to this pressing problem and try to win new supporters for the cause."

AVOCATIONAL INTERESTS: Painting abstractions, sewing, skiing, travel in Europe.

* * *

ANDERSON, Olive M(ary) 1915-

PERSONAL: Born May 2, 1915, in Dakota City, Neb.; daughter of Francis J. (a clergyman) and Olive Angeline (McKenzie) Aucock; married Fred N. Anderson (a clergyman), August 20, 1935; children: Mary Anderson Sarber, Francis Nels. *Education:* Nebraska Wesleyan University, A.B., 1937. *Religion:* Methodist. *Home:* 211 Seventh St., Pecatonica, Ill. 61063.

CAREER: Writer, 1947—. *Member:* North American Mycological Association, National Audubon Society, Michigan Botanical Club, Wisconsin Regional Writers, Upper Peninsula of Michigan Writers, Pecatonica Prairie Path (member of board of directors).

*WRITINGS—*All nonfiction: *A Wilderness of Wonder,* Augsburg, 1971; *Seeker at Cassandra Marsh,* Christian Herald Books, 1978; *A Land of Brooks and Water* (about Illinois), Douglas-West, Inc., 1979. Author of "Lizzie Hawkins Speaking," a column appearing in more than twenty weekly periodicals, 1955-71. Contributor of articles and stories to magazines.

WORK IN PROGRESS: Research for a book on the history of land use in Michigan's Upper Peninsula; a historical booklet with publication by Schoolcraft Historical Society expected in 1980; research on northern Illinois.

SIDELIGHTS: Olive Anderson writes: "I began serious nature study after we built our family cabin in the unfamiliar setting of the north woods. The story of this is told in *A Wilderness of Wonder.* My insatiable curiosity about the natural world and my observation of it led to *Seeker at Cassandra Marsh,* where I lived close to the earth and its Creator. My current writing concerns man's relationship to the earth on which he lives."

AVOCATIONAL INTERESTS: Nature photography, outdoor activities.

* * *

ANDREAS, Burton G(ould) 1921-

PERSONAL: Born April 6, 1921, in Rochester, N.Y.; son of Howard (a contractor) and Agnes (Gould) Andreas; married Janice Bessey (a retail proprietor), July 20, 1943; children: Cheryl. *Education:* University of Rochester, B.A., 1948; University of Iowa, M.A., 1950, Ph.D., 1951. *Residence:* Rochester, N.Y. *Office:* Department of Psychology, State University of New York College at Brockport, Brockport, N.Y. 14420.

CAREER: University of Rochester, Rochester, N.Y., assistant professor, 1951-58, associate professor of psychology, 1958-67; Eastern Regional Institute for Education, Syracuse, N.Y., program director, 1967-70; State University of New York College at Brockport, professor of psychology, 1970—. Consultant to Eastman Kodak Co. *Military service:* U.S. Army, 1942-46; served in Italy; became captain; received three battle stars. *Member:* American Psychological Association, Phi Beta Kappa.

WRITINGS: Experimental Psychology, Wiley, 1960, 2nd edition, 1972; *Psychological Science and the Educational*

Enterprise, Wiley, 1968; *Cast of Characters* (stories), Best Cellar Press, 1979. Contributor to psychology journals.

WORK IN PROGRESS: Castaway Characters, humorous stories, publication by Best Cellar Press expected in 1981.

SIDELIGHTS: Andreas comments: "Having published scientific books in psychology and a briefer monograph in education, I now intersperse writing in a lighter vein with my continuing scholarly efforts. I have discovered a new case of multiple personality—in myself. Rather than produce a weighty case study (as in *Sybil* or *Eve*), I examine my demons in punchy fun-filled interviews and sketches. My humorous fables of these figments of my right cerebral hemisphere should fill several small books."

* * *

ANDREWS, F(rank) Emerson 1902-1978

OBITUARY NOTICE—See index for *CA* sketch: Born January 26, 1902, in Lancaster, Pa.; died August 7, 1978, in Burlington, Vt. Foundation consultant and author of novels, children's books, and ten volumes on philanthropy. While serving as the director of publications and philanthropic research at the Russell Foundation, Andrews gained a reputation as an expert on foundations. In 1956 he helped organize the Foundation Center and became its director and president. In conjunction with that job, he edited *The Foundation Directory.* Andrews frequently testified at investigations into charity frauds, tax revision, and corporate charitable contributions. Obituaries and other sources: *Who's Who in America,* 40th edition, Marquis, 1978; *New York Times,* August 9, 1978; *Publishers Weekly,* August 28, 1978.

* * *

ANDREWS, Raymond 1934-

PERSONAL: Born June 6, 1934, in Madison, Ga.; son of George Cleveland (a sharecropper) and Viola (Perryman) Andrews; married Adelheid Wenger (an airline sales agent), December 28, 1966. *Education:* Attended Michigan State University, 1956-58. *Politics:* None. *Religion:* Baptist. *Home:* 78-19 46th Ave., Elmhurst, N.Y. 11373. *Agent:* Susan Anne Protter, 156 East 52nd St., New York, N.Y. 10022. *Office:* Archer Courier, 855 Ave. of the Americas, New York, N.Y. 10001.

CAREER: Worked as sharecropper, 1943-49, hospital orderly, 1949-51, variously as bartender, busboy, dishwasher, and stockroom worker, 1951-52, postal mail sorter, 1956, and stockroom clerk, 1957; Royal Dutch Airlines, New York City, airline employee, 1958-66; photograph librarian, 1967-72; Archer Courier, New York City, messenger, telephone operator, night dispatcher, and bookkeeper, 1972—. *Military service:* U.S. Air Force, 1952-56. *Awards, honors:* James Baldwin Prize for Fiction for *Appalachee Red.*

WRITINGS: Appalachee Red (novel), Dial, 1978; *Rosiebelle Lee Wildcat Tennessee* (novel), Dial, 1979. Contributor to *Sports Illustrated* and *Ataraxia.*

WORK IN PROGRESS: A third novel.

SIDELIGHTS: Andrews writes: "As children, my brother and I drew, with him continuing on and becoming an artist, while I stopped drawing and became more interested in reading. To me, there was nothing better than a *good* story. But in the farming—sharecropping—community I came from, most people couldn't read. This, along with a poor school system, did not encourage budding authors. Yet in the back of my head a writer was what I wanted to be most of all, and I couldn't help but feel that someday, *somehow,* I would write.

"It wasn't until the day of my thirty-second birthday that I finally got around to doing something about this nagging in the back of my head which down through the years had absolutely refused to shut up. At the time I was working for an airline, and was being given what I felt was an uncalled-for hard time over the telephone by a client. I told him to wait and put the call on hold. At precisely 12:36, after eight years, two months, two weeks and three days, I walked out never to return. I went home and had my telephone disconnected. The next morning upon rising at my usual early hour, I told myself, 'you *are* going to write.' And I've been at it ever since.

"My first book began as a poem, then became a short-short story, a short story, a long short story, finally, taking the easy way out, I wrote a novel. The book itself concerns the fictitious county of Muskhogean, Ga., centering mainly around the county seat of Appalachee and about the area's (mostly) black folks between 1918 and 1963. The book I'm currently writing also takes place in Muskhogean. And hopefully so will much more of my future work dealing with the daily social lives of Southern black folks.

"I love writing. I'm perhaps the world's slowest writer. But for years, while working for someone else, I was always told to rush, rush, rush—speed over accuracy. Being a born perfectionist, this went against my grain. I now feel that if in my writing it's going to be rush, rush, rush, then I may as well go back to my old airline job and pick up the telephone where my favorite travel agent might yet be waiting on hold."

BIOGRAPHICAL/CRITICAL SOURCES: Madisonian, June 8, 1978.

* * *

ANDRIC, Ivo 1892-1975

PERSONAL: Born October 10, 1892, in Docu, Bosnia, Austria-Hungary; married Milica Babic (a painter and theatre designer), 1959 (died). *Education:* Attended University of Zagreb, Yugoslavia, Vienna University, Austria, and University of Krakow, Poland; Graz University, Austria, doctorate in philosophy, 1923. *Politics:* Communist. *Home:* Proleterskih brigada 2a, Belgrade, Yugoslavia.

CAREER: Political prisoner during World War I; Yugoslav diplomatic service, 1919-1941, served in Rome, Geneva, Madrid, Bucharest, Trieste, Graz, Belgrade, and Berlin; full-time writer, 1941-49; Yugoslav Parliament, deputy and representative from Bosnia, 1949-55. *Member:* Federation of Writers of Yugoslavia (president, 1946-51), Serbian Academy. *Awards, honors:* Prize for Life Work from the Yugoslav Government, 1956; Nobel Prize for Literature, 1961; honorary doctorate, University of Krakow, 1964.

WRITINGS—In English; fiction: *Gospodjica,* [Yugoslavia], 1945, translation by Joseph Hitrec published as *The Woman From Sarajevo,* Knopf, 1965; *Travnicka hronika,* [Yugoslavia], 1945, translation by Kenneth Johnstone published as *Bosnian Story,* Lincolns-Prager, 1958, British Book Center, 1959, translation by Hitrec published as *Bosnian Chronicle,* Knopf, 1963; *Na Drini cuprija,* [Yugoslavia], 1945, translation by Lovett F. Edwards published as *The Bridge on the Drina,* Macmillan, 1959; *Prica o vezirovam slonu,* Nakladni Zavod (Zagreb), 1948, translation by Drenka Willen published as *The Vizier's Elephant: Three Novellas,* Harcourt, 1962; *Prokleta avlija,* [Yugoslavia], 1954, translation by Johnstone published as *Devil's Yard,* Grove, 1962; *Sabrana djela Ive Andrica* (also see below) Mladost (Zagreb), 1963, partial translation by Hitrec published as *The Pasha's Concubine and Other Tales*, Knopf, 1968; *Most na Zepi*, Svjetlost (Sarajevo), 1967, updated edition with text in Serbo-Croatian, English, German, and Italian published as *Most na Zepi/ The Bridge on the Zepa/Die Bruecke ueber die Zepa/Il ponte sulla Zepa*, Oslobodenje (Sarajevo), 1971.

Other: *Ex ponto* (prison meditations; title means "Restlessness"), Knjizevnog juga (Zagreb), 1918, reprinted, Univerzitetska biblioteka Svetozar Markovic, 1975; *Nemiri* (poems; title means "Disquietudes"), Naklada S. Kugli, 1920, reprinted, Univerzitetska biblioteka Svetozar Markovic, 1975; *Put Alje Djerzeleza*, [Yugoslavia], 1920; *Pripovetke* (short stories), [Yugoslavia], Volume I, 1924, Volume II, 1931, Volume III, 1936; *Nove pripovetka* (short stories), Kultura (Zagreb), 1949; *Prica o kmetu Simanu*, [Yugoslavia], 1950; *Novele*, Mladinska Knjiga (Ljubljana), 1951; *Pod grabicem: Pripovetke o zivotu bosanskog sela* (short stories), Seljacka knjiga (Sarajevo), 1952; *Panorama: Pripovetke* (short stories), Prosveta (Belgrade), 1958.

Lica (short stories), Mladost, 1960; *Izbor*, Svjetlost, 1961; *Sabrana djela Ive Andrica* (also see above; title means "Collected Works of Ivo Andric"), Volumes I-X, Mladost, 1963, Volumes XI-XVI, Svjetlost, 1976, Volume I: *Na Drini cuprija*, Volume II: *Travniska hronika*, Volume III: *Gospodicna*, Volume IV: *Prekleto dvorisce*, Volume V: *Nemirna godina*, Volume VI: *Zed*, Volume VII: *Jelena, zena koje nema*, Volume VIII: *Znakovi*, Volume IX: *Deca*, Volume X: *Staza. Lica. Predeli.*, Volume XI: *Ex ponto. Nemiri. Lirika.*, Volume XII: *Istorija i legenda*, Volume XIII: *Umetnik i njegova delo*, Volume XIV: *Znakovi pored puta*, Volume XV: *Kuca na osami*, Volume XVI: *Omerpasa Latas; Ljubav u Kasabi* (short stories), Branko Donovic (Belgrade), 1963; (contributor) *Nouvel essai yougoslave* (essays), compiled by Aleksandar V. Stefanovic, Zalozba Obzorja, 1965; *Anikina vremena* (short stories), Svjetlost, 1967; *Kula i druge pripovetke* (children's stories), Veselin Maslesa (Sarajevo), 1970; *Eseji i kritike* (essays), Svjetlost, 1976.

Poetry represented in *An Anthology of Modern Yugoslav Poetry*, edited by Janko Lavrin, J. Calder, 1963.

Member of editorial board of *Knjizevni jug*, a literary magazine.

SIDELIGHTS: In both his diplomatic and writing careers, Ivo Andric displayed a passion for politics and history. Andric was born in Bosnia, a region in Austria-Hungary that had been wracked by political turmoil for centuries. As a young man, he had joined the Mlada Bosna, a revolutionary Bosnian organization that sought the downfall of the Hapsburg regime and the establishment of an independent state for the South Slav peoples. A member of the Mlada Bosna shot and killed Archduke Ferdinand of Austria in 1914, an act that ignited World War I. Because of his association with the revolutionary group, Andric was imprisoned for three years.

Following the war, Andric entered his country's diplomatic service and continued in this capacity even after the Kingdom of the Serbs, Croats, and Slovenes became Yugoslavia in 1929. The last diplomatic post Andric held was ambassador to Nazi Germany. In 1941 he fled from Berlin only a few hours before the Germans began bombing Yugoslavia. After World War II, Andric resumed his career in politics. He joined the Communist party and became a deputy in the Yugoslav Parliament.

Andric's pen had not been idle during his years in the diplomatic service. His most fruitful creative periods, however,

occurred when he was in prison during World War I and when he was under virtual house arrest during World War II. When he was first incarcerated, Andric read the works of Soren Kierkegaard, a Danish philosopher and writer on religion. Kierkegaard's vision of the world as a place of fear, isolation, and irrationality had a permanent impact on Andric's writings. Andric stated his philosophy in *Ex ponto*, a collection of his prison meditations: "There is no other truth but pain, there is no other reality but suffering, pain and suffering in every drop of water, in every blade of grass, in every grain of crystal, in every sound of living voice, in sleep and in vigil, in life, before life and perhaps also after life."

Having forged such a philosophy, Andric found his native Bosnia the perfect setting for his fiction. The people of Bosnia had been oppressed and exploited throughout their history, and the resulting torment and gloom were explored in Andric's writings. "For Andric man, set against the vast panorama of history, is insignificant—fearful of external disaster and inwardly aware of his own insecurity in a world where everything is ephemeral, however much he may long for constancy," Konstantin Bazarov explained. "The particular history of old Turkish Bosnia, with its despotism and violence, thus portrays the broader theme of man's tragic struggle against the oncoming darkness of change and death."

Andric's most memorable novels about Bosnia were written during World War II. When the Germans occupied Belgrade, Andric refused to leave. He holed up in his apartment and wrote what has come to be known as the Bosnian trilogy—*Gospodjica* (*The Woman From Sarajevo*), *Travnicka hronika* (*Bosnian Story* or *Bosnian Chronicle*), and *Na Drini cuprija* (*The Bridge on the Drina*). In *The Woman From Sarajevo*, Andric portrayed the people of Sarajevo as "already burdened with the Turkish legacy of habitual indolence and with the Slavic hankering for excesses, having lately adopted the formal Austrian notions of society and social obligations, according to which one's personal prestige and the dignity of one's class were measured by a rising scale of senseless and non-productive spending." After reading the novel in translation, William Cooper remarked that *The Woman From Sarajevo* "is so fascinating and distinguished that one feels dismayed—and ashamed—to think of the writers in lesser-known languages whose work we have never read."

Even more highly acclaimed was *Bosnian Chronicle*. Set in Travnik during the Napoleonic era, *Bosnian Chronicle* focused on the conflicts that arose between the French and Austrian consulates as they vied to win the favor of the Turkish vizier and the support of the local townspeople. In his translator's note, Joseph Hitrec declared that Andric's principal themes—"causative interplay of guilt and human suffering, the individual versus tyranny, the warping of men's destinies through historic circumstance"—were masterfully combined in *Bosnian Chronicle*. Alan Ferguson saw two major themes in the novel, the first being the clash between the private individual and his public image. He pointed out that the Austrian and French consuls had much in common yet were prevented from becoming friends by their official duties. The second theme that Ferguson discerned in *Bosnian Chronicle* was the clash between East and West. Bosnia epitomized the struggle between these two cultures because the Christians and Moslems had been fighting over the territory since the fourteenth century.

Bosnian Chronicle covered only seven years in the history of Bosnia, but *The Bridge on the Drina* spanned three-and-a-half centuries. The Turks had constructed the bridge over the Drina River in the sixteenth century at the town of Visegrad. The novel recorded life in Visegrad from the time of the bridge's erection to shortly before World War I. Egon Hostovsky discussed the symbolic import of the bridge: "The ancient bridge is a piece of eternity, forged by human hands and baptized with the bold dreams of men. It has outlasted generations, invasions, wars, and peace. Everything around it was continually changing, rotting, dying, being reborn; but the bridge has stood immutable, the witness of values and efforts that do not pass."

The epic proportions of *The Bridge on the Drina* have prompted many critics to liken Andric to Tolstoy. Like Tolstoy, Andric was concerned with the inexorable flow of history, with the precedence that events take over the individual. Andric has also been compared to Herman Melville. Stoyan Christowe demonstrated that the elephant in "The Vizier's Elephant" was similar to Moby Dick because "both personify the universal, hostile forces against which man struggles."

Comparisons to writers of the caliber of Tolstoy and Melville suggest that Andric was not just a regional writer, but an artist whose work had universal implications. Alan Ferguson commented that Andric's works were not about foreign lands but "about the 'common course of all humanity'; its fundamental similarities rather than its superficial differences." The Swedish Academy attested to Andric's universality when it awarded him the Nobel Prize for Literature in 1961 "for the epic force with which he has depicted themes and human destinies drawn from the history of his country."

One mark of Andric's greatness was his devotion to truth and morality. Although Andric was involved in politics for many years, his writing was notably free of cant. He believed that fiction "should not be poisoned with hatred nor stifled by the din of lethal weapons. It should be motivated by love and guided by the breadth and serenity of the free human spirit. Because any storyteller and his work serve nothing if they do not, in one way or another, serve man and mankind."

Some of Andric's works have been translated into German, French, Russian, Spanish, and Italian.

BIOGRAPHICAL/CRITICAL SOURCES: Saturday Review, July 11, 1959; *Harvard Review,* autumn, 1959; *New York Times,* October 28, 1962; Ivo Andric, *Bosnian Chronicle,* translated by Joseph Hitrec, Knopf, 1963; *Slavonic and East European Review,* June, 1963, July, 1970; *Slavic Review,* September, 1964; *Times Literary Supplement,* May 20, 1965; *Literary Quarterly,* summer, 1965; *Listener,* August 11, 1966; *Slavic and East European Journal,* fall, 1972; *Books and Bookmen,* November, 1974; *Modern Language Review,* October, 1975; *Contemporary Literary Criticism,* Volume 8, Gale, 1978.

OBITUARIES: Washington Post, March 14, 1975; *New York Times,* March 14, 1975; *Newsweek,* March 24, 1975; *AB Bookman's Weekly,* April 7, 1975; *Current Biography,* May, 1975.*

(Died March 13, 1975, in Belgrade, Yugoslavia)

*   *   *

ANSON, Jay 1924(?)-

PERSONAL: Born in New York, N.Y. *Residence:* Roslyn, N.Y.

CAREER: Screenwriter of documentary motion pictures; writer, 1977—.

WRITINGS: The Amityville Horror: A True Story, Prentice-Hall, 1977. Also author of screenplays.

WORK IN PROGRESS: A screenplay, "The Amityville Horror."

SIDELIGHTS: The Amityville Horror is the story of a family of four who inhabited a home which was once the scene of a grisly multiple murder. Their account of what happened once they moved in, as noted in *People,* "made *The Exorcist* pale by comparison." The occupants claimed they levitated from their beds, a pig with eyes that glowed red played with their daughter, green slime oozed from cracks in walls, and flies hovered near windows in the winter.

Anson, who wrote *The Amityville Horror* from forty-five hours of taped interviews with the Lutz family and from talks with a priest who helped them, has refused to verify his own faith in the story. "I'm a professional writer," he said. "I don't believe and I don't disbelieve. I leave that to the reader."

One reader who doubted the story's credibility was *Washington Post* reviewer Curt Suplee. He cited a doctor's suspicion that there is a "very very strong possibility that the Lutzes invented much of their story because of financial worries" and gave evidence to dispute the book's claim that "the house was built on land used by the Shinnecock Indians 'as an enclosure for the sick, mad and dying.'" In addition, Suplee felt the story was contrived. "Among other things," he noted, "the demonic powers have been conducting themselves a little too carefully by William Friedkin/Universal City rules of diabolical etiquette—coming out at dramatic moments, but retiring modestly when the plot demands a quiet period of exposition, then building to a pleasing crescendo in the final 10 pages. . . . The more deeply one looks, the more like fiction—even fantasy—this 'true story' seems."

As for the home in Amityville, Long Island, new occupants have been so harrassed by sight-seers and tourists that they have sued the previous tenants for damages. "The book is completely untrue," claims Barbara Cromartys, one of the present dwellers. "This is a lovely home."

BIOGRAPHICAL/CRITICAL SOURCES: Washington Post Book World, December 9, 1977; *New York Times Book Review,* January 22, 1978; *People,* February 13, 1978.*

*   *   *

ANTREASIAN, Garo Z(areh) 1922-

PERSONAL: Born in 1922, in Indianapolis, Ind.; son of Zareh Minas and Takouhie (Daniel) Antreasian; married Jeanne Glascock (a weaver), 1947; children: David Garo and Thomas Bert. *Education:* Herron School of Art, B.F.A., 1948; studied with Will Barnet and Stanley William Hayter, 1948-49. *Home:* 1520 Los Alamos S.W., Albuquerque, N.M. 87104. *Office:* Department of Art, University of New Mexico, Albuquerque, N.M. 87131.

CAREER: Herron School of Art, Indianapolis, Ind., instructor of painting, design, composition, and printmaking, 1948-59; Tamarind Lithography Workshop, Inc., Los Angeles, Calif., technical director, 1960-61; Herron School of Art, instructor of painting, design, composition, and printmaking, 1961-64; University of New Mexico, Albuquerque, professor of art, 1964—; technical director of Tamarind Institute, 1970-72. Has had dozens of group and solo exhibitions in the United States, Italy, Quebec, Japan, and Hong Kong; work represented in collections all over the United States, including Boston Museum of Fine Arts, Chicago Art

Institute, Guggenheim Museum, Library of Congress, Metropolitan Museum of Art, and Smithsonian Institution. Lecturer at University of Michigan, 1975. Guest artist at California State College, Chico, 1976, East Texas State University, 1977, and University of Notre Dame, 1977. Teacher at summer workshops; juror for printmaking exhibitions. *Member:* College Art Association of America (member of board of directors, 1976-80). *Awards, honors:* Mary Milliken travel grant from Herron School of Art, 1948-49; D.F.A. from Purdue University, Indianapolis, 1972.

WRITINGS: (With Clinton Adams) *The Tamarind Book of Lithography: Art and Techniques,* Abrams, 1970; *The Works of Juergen Strunck,* Dallas Museum of Fine Arts, 1973. Contributor to museum bulletins.

WORK IN PROGRESS: Research on late nineteenth-century lithography in the United States and abroad.

* * *

APPLE, Max (Isaac) 1941-

PERSONAL: Born October 22, 1941, in Grand Rapids, Mich.; son of Samuel and Betty (Goodstein) Apple; married wife, Debra; children: Jessica, Sam. *Education:* University of Michigan, A.B., 1963, Ph.D., 1970; graduate study at Stanford University, 1964. *Agent:* Lyn Nesbit, International Creative Management, 40 West 57th St., New York, N.Y. 10019. *Office:* Department of English, Rice University, Houston, Tex. 77001.

CAREER: Reed College, Portland, Ore., assistant professor of literature and humanities, 1970-71; Rice University, Houston, Tex., assistant professor of English literature, 1972—. *Member:* Modern Language Association of America, PEN Club, Texas Institute of Letters. *Awards, honors:* National Endowment for the Humanities Younger Humanists fellowship, 1971; Jesse Jones Award from Texas Institute of Letters, 1976, for *The Oranging of America.*

WRITINGS: (Contributor) David Madden, editor, *Nathanael West: The Cheaters and the Cheated,* Everett/Edwards, 1972; (with others) *Studies in English,* Rice University, 1975; *The Oranging of America and Other Stories,* Grossman, 1976; *Zip: A Novel of the Left and the Right,* Viking, 1978. Contributor of stories to *Esquire, Mademoiselle, American Review, Georgia Review, Ohio Review,* and other periodicals.

WORK IN PROGRESS: A novel and a screenplay.

SIDELIGHTS: Max Apple's two full-length fictional works to date have been generally well received, but while he has been praised for his comic imagination, some reviewers have criticized him for his pop-art superficiality.

Amanda Heller called *The Oranging of America* "an irresistible collection of stories" marked by vitality, charm, and good humor. Carole Cook also acknowledged the fascination of Apple's lighthearted satire, but felt on the other hand that "his facility for playing cultural references off against each other approaches slickness." Both of these aspects of Apple's talent, however, satisfied Eliot Fremont Smith, who wrote: "Apple proves once again that literary delight may engage the current mind in a rewarding way even though it deliberately does not confront great issues of immediate consequence. This is healthy and always needed."

The *Newsweek* reviewer found that in *The Oranging of America* "Apple's principal asset is his startling imagination. Original, witty, writing deftly and economically, he translates the most battered of our cultural cliches into glistening artifacts. His inspiration is inconsistent—some of

these stories suffer from underdevelopment—but his purpose is enchanting: he means to make us feel a little better about ourselves, about American life, by polishing the rubble and hinting that man's spirit is frisky yet." "Much of his brilliance," assessed Celia Betsky, "lies in the versatile range of voices he is able to assume and in a talent for punning that leaps into a wonderful realm of linguistic high jinks and buffoonery. Apple pokes fun at high culture and appreciates low, but his own art shades more to the transcendental than the pop. It transforms while it impersonates, changing not only what we see but the way we see it."

Considered amusing yet lightweight, *Zip,* Apple's first novel, revealed Apple's "real comic talent. He has an eye for incongruity and an ear for intonation." To John Leonard, *Zip* "seems to me to be less a novel than a box of toys, epigrams, firecrackers, political pot shots, Talmudic maunderings, whistles and screams. What distinguishes it from other, similar exercises in Pop Modernism is its affection. Mr. Apple likes people, even crazy people." Leonard compares the writer of *Zip* to a host of contemporary authors, including Bernard Malamud, Philip Roth, Saul Bellow, E. L. Doctorow, Donald Barthelme, and Thomas Pynchon: "Mr. Apple reminds me at one time or another of all these writers. He is, however, kind. He is not a nag. You have only to compare his portrait of Debby Silvers in 'Zip' with Mr. Roth's portrait of Brenda Patimkin in 'Goodbye Columbus' to see what a difference two decades and a benign temperament can make. Inside Mr. Apple's cartoons of Bertha and Solomon are real people, with dimensions independent of politics and money and the mongering of a thesis. Mr. Apple uses a feather, not a blowtorch, on his characters. He would tickle politics out of business."

BIOGRAPHICAL/CRITICAL SOURCES: Newsweek, December 6, 1976; *Nation,* January 15, 1977; *Saturday Review,* January 22, 1977, July 22, 1978; *Atlantic Monthly,* February, 1977; *New York Times Book Review,* February 13, 1977, July 16, 1978; *Village Voice,* February 14, 1977; *New Republic,* June 24, 1978; *New York Times,* July 17, 1978; *Coda,* September/October, 1978; *Contemporary Literary Criticism,* Volume 9, Gale, 1978.

* * *

APPLEBEE, Arthur N(oble) 1946-

PERSONAL: Born June 20, 1946, in Sherbrooke, Quebec, Canada; born a U.S. citizen; son of Roger K. (a university dean) and Margaret (Aitken) Applebee; married Marcia Lynn Hull (a teacher), June 15, 1968. *Education:* Yale University, B.A. (cum laude), 1968; Harvard University, M.A.T., 1970; University of London, Ph.D., 1973. *Home:* 2418 East Elm, Urbana, Ill. 61801. *Office:* National Council of Teachers of English, 1111 Kenyon Rd., Urbana, Ill. 61801.

CAREER: National Council of Teachers of English, Urbana, Ill., part-time staff assistant, 1964-69; Massachusetts General Hospital, Child Development Laboratory, Boston, research assistant and psychologist, 1969-71; University of Lancaster, Lancaster, England, research associate at International Microteaching Unit, 1973-74; Tarleton High School, Tarleton, England, English and drama teacher, 1974-76; National Council of Teachers of English, staff associate, 1976—, and associate director of ERIC Clearinghouse on Reading and Communication Skills. *Member:* National Association of Teachers of English (England), National Conference on Research in English, International Reading Association, American Educational Research Association.

Awards, honors: Promising researcher award from National Council of Teachers of English, 1974.

WRITINGS: Tradition and Reform in the Teaching of English: A History, National Council of Teachers of English, 1974; *The Child's Concept of Story: Ages Two to Seventeen,* University of Chicago Press, 1978; *A Survey of Teaching Conditions in English, 1977,* National Council of Teachers of English, 1978. Contributor to psychology and education journals in England and the United States.

SIDELIGHTS: Applebee comments: "Five years of involvement, while a student, in various projects and activities of the National Council of Teachers of English, led to a continuing concern with educational issues, and a specific interest in language and language learning. This interest has had diverse manifestations, leading to studies in educational psychology, learning disabilities, educational history, and curriculum evaluation. Most recently, it has led to England, and five years of study, teaching, and research in British schools and universities."

* * *

APTEKAR, Jane 1935-

PERSONAL: Born June 9, 1935, in Prestwick, Scotland; came to the United States in 1959; daughter of Ian Hamilton (an army officer) and Christine (Judge) Reeve; married Bernard Aptekar, June 14, 1959 (divorced, 1977); children: Rachel, Alexander. *Education:* St. Hilda's College, Oxford, B.A., 1956, M.A., 1960; Columbia University, Ph.D., 1966. *Politics:* Socialist. *Religion:* Atheist. *Home:* 645 Water St., New York, N.Y. 10002.

CAREER: City University of New York, New York City, assistant professor of English, 1966-70; Rutgers University, New Brunswick, N.J., assistant professor of comparative literature, 1970-73; State University of New York College at Purchase, professor of literature, 1973-76; United Nations, Secretariat, New York City, editor for Economic and Social Council, 1976—. Vice-chairman of board of directors of Gouverneur Gardens Housing Corp., and of executive committee of United Nations Staff Union. *Member:* Modern Language Association of America. *Awards, honors:* Annesly Award from Columbia University, 1968, for *Icons of Justice.*

WRITINGS: Icons of Justice: Iconography and Thematic Imagery in Book V of "The Faerie Queene," Columbia University Press, 1969.

WORK IN PROGRESS: A study of Virginia Woolf; a study of paintings and poems dealing with the subject of Renaissance marriage.

SIDELIGHTS: Jane Aptekar comments: "Due to discrimination difficulties with advancing in academia, my scholarship has turned from the general topic of justice toward images of sex inequality in the Renaissance and toward research on Virginia Woolf."

* * *

ARCHAMBAULT, Paul 1937-

PERSONAL: Surname is pronounced *Ar*-shem-bo; born September 17, 1937, in Webster, Mass.; son of Joseph Alexis and Bernadette (Coderre) Archambault; divorced; children: Aude, Ellenore. *Education:* Assumption College, A.B., 1958; Yale University, Ph.D., 1963. *Politics:* Democrat. *Religion:* Roman Catholic. *Home:* 119 Dorset Rd., Syracuse, N.Y. 13210. *Office:* Department of Foreign Languages and Literatures, Syracuse University, Syracuse, N.Y. 13210.

CAREER: Amherst College, Amherst, Mass., assistant professor, 1964-68, associate professor of French, 1968-73; Syracuse University, Syracuse, N.Y., professor of French, 1973—, resident director of study programs in Poitiers and Strasbourg. *Member:* Modern Language Association of America, Mediaeval Academy of America. *Awards, honors:* National Institute for the Humanities junior fellow, 1969.

WRITINGS: Camus' Hellenic Sources, University of North Carolina Press, 1972; *Seven French Chroniclers,* Syracuse University Press, 1974.

WORK IN PROGRESS: Research on autobiography, from Augustine to Rousseau.

SIDELIGHTS: Archambault told *CA:* "I have come from a small textile town in Connecticut, and never had any love for big cities. My interest in French stems from my Canadian background. I was brought up blissfully and have raised my daughters to be blissful."

On the subject of writing, Archambault commented: "I have written books on both Albert Camus and medieval historiography, and find myself constantly bounding back and forth between the middle Ages and our own. In fact, the anxieties of our era have much in common with those of the late medieval period."

* * *

ARNOLD, Margot
See COOK, Petronelle Marguerite Mary

* * *

ARONSON, J(ay) Richard 1937-

PERSONAL: Born August 26, 1937, in New York, N.Y., married Judith L. Klein, September 13, 1959; children: Sarah, Miriam, Anne. *Education:* Clark University, A.B. (honors), 1959, Ph.D., 1964; Stanford University, M.A., 1961. *Politics:* Democrat. *Religion:* Jewish. *Home:* 1804 Jennings St., Bethlehem, Pa. 18017. *Office:* Department of Economics, Lehigh University, Bethlehem, Pa. 18015.

CAREER: Worcester Polytechnic Institute, Worcester, Mass., assistant professor of economics, 1961-65; Lehigh University, Bethlehem, Pa., faculty member, 1965-73, professor of economics, 1973—. Visiting lecturer at Clark University, 1964-65, summer, 1966; visiting scholar at University of York, spring, 1973. *Member:* American Economic Association, American Finance Association, National Tax Association, Royal Economic Society. *Awards, honors:* Ford Foundation grants, 1971-72, 1977; Fulbright scholar at University of York, spring, 1978.

WRITINGS: (With E. Schwartz and A. Weintraub) *The Economic Growth Controversy,* International Association of Scholarly Publishers, 1973; (with David Ott and J. Maxwell) *State and Local Finances in the Last Half of the 1970's,* American Enterprise Institute, 1975; (editor with Schwartz) *Management Policies in Local Government Finance,* International City Management Association, 1975; (contributor) *Economic Policies and Social Goals,* Martin Robinson, 1975; (with Maxwell) *Financing State and Local Governments,* Brookings Institution, 1977. Contributor of nearly thirty articles to economic and finance journals.

* * *

ARP, Hans
See ARP, Jean

ARP, Jean 1887-1966
(Hans Arp; Michel Seuphor, a pseudonym)

PERSONAL: Listed in some sources as Hans Arp; born September 16, 1887, in Strasbourg, Alsace; son of Pierre Guillaume (a merchant) and Josephine (Koeberle) Arp; married Sophie Henriette Gertrude Taeuber (an artist), 1921 (died, 1943). *Education:* Studied in Germany at Kunstakademie, 1905-07, and in France at Academie Julian, 1907-09. *Religion:* Roman Catholic. *Home:* 21 rue des Chataigniers, Meudon, Seine-et-Oise, France. *Office:* c/o Valentin Gallery, 32 East 57th St., New York, N.Y.

CAREER: Sculptor, painter, author, and poet. Works have been included in exhibitions at numerous galleries and museums, including Goltz Gallery, 1912, International Dada Exhibit in Berlin, 1920, Galerie Montaigne, 1922, Galarie Surrealiste, 1924, and Bucholz Gallery (now Curt Valentin Gallery), 1949. Paintings and sculptures are on permanent display in museums throughout the world. Member of Salon des Realities Nouvelles, 1946-48, and Salon de la Jeune Sculpture, 1950-52.

WRITINGS—In English: *Jours effeuilles: Poemes, essais, souvenirs, 1920-1965,* edited by Marcel Jean, Gallimard, 1966, translation by Joachim Neugroschel published as *Arp on Arp: Poems, Essays, Memories,* Viking, 1972, published in England as *Collected French Writings: Poems, Essays, Memories,* Calder & Boyars, 1974; (with Paul Klee and Kurt Schwitters) *Three Painter-Poets: Arp, Schwitters, Klee,* Penguin, 1974.

In French; all poetry: *Le siege de l'air: Poemes, 1915-1945,* Vrille, 1946; *Vers le blanc infini,* La Rose des vents, 1960; *L'ange et la rose,* Robert Morel, 1965.

In German; under name Hans Arp: (With Lazar' Markovich Lisitskii) *Die Kunstismen* (title means "The Isms of Art"), E. Rentsch, 1925; *Mondsand,* G. Neske, 1960; *Logbuch des Traumkapitaens,* Verlag die Arche, 1965.

Also author of a novel with Vicente Huidobro, *Tres Novelas Ejemplares,* 1935, and a monograph, "On My Way," 1948. Art work represented in numerous collections, including *Arp,* A. Zwemmer, 1961; *Arp Sculptures,* Tudor, 1964; *Hans Arp: Skulpturen, 1957-1966,* G. Hatje, 1968; and *Jean Arp: Exposition,* Le Havre Musee des beaux-arts, 1973. Listed in numerous U.S. and foreign catalogues, many with commentary by Arp under pseudonym Michel Seuphor.

SIDELIGHTS: Along with Hans Richter, Tristan Tzara, Marcel Duchamp, and Man Ray, Arp helped pioneer the art form known as Dadaism. Dada, a word chosen at random from a French dictionary, signified the irreverence with which Arp and his fellow artists approached their craft.

Arp's early years as an artist were marked by attempts to emphasize the objectivity in art. He worked in solitude from 1909 to 1911 trying to improve his technique. It was Wassily Kandinsky, the noted abstractionist painter, who confirmed Arp's first approach to art. Soon after meeting Kandinsky, Arp began to associate with expressionist artists, including Paul Klee and Franz Marc. When expressionism gave way to cubism, Arp again followed suit.

Up until the time he met his wife, Arp's art had not found a consistent frame of concept. Sophie Taeuber's art, however, exemplified simplicity. After their marriage, they both discarded their oils in favor of pursuing Taeuber's aims but with the use of fresh materials.

The couple produced several tapestries and collages over the next few years and much of their art was seen by critics as a more defined form of abstractness. In 1916, Arp and his wife met with Tzara and his fellow artists to form a united basis for dadaism. Rebelling against traditional art, Arp and the dadists provided the world of art with an innovative outlook which allowed for such styles as random art, in which one employed whatever was available to create with, and blank sketching, where the artist attempted to eliminate any conscious imposition in the act of creating art.

When dadism evolved into surrealism in the 1920's, Arp celebrated the new movement with his first solo exhibit. Several of Arp's best known works come from his surrealist period, including "Birds in an Aquarium" and "Overturned Shoe With Two Heels Under a Black Vault."

By the 1930's, Arp was working with three-dimensional concepts in sculpture. After suffering a brief bout of "artists block," Arp proceeded to produce several more well-known works, all in his new style of three-dimensional sculpturing. Several of these works, including "Cobra-Centaur" and "Configuration of a Serpent Movement," vaguely suggest a unified form and show Arp's keen eye for figure detail.

Aside from his work in sculpturing, Arp also produced woodcuts and tapestry designs. His poetry, largely ignored in comparison to his sculptings, has received high praise in recent years. Noting that Arp's poetry has "never been given more than a brief introduction or a rapid 'appreciation,' usually by other artists," Armine Kotin commented that the French poetry can be neatly divided in two. The surrealist poems appearing prior to 1957, according to Kotin, show no "radical experimentation with language." But, Kotin wrote, later poetry was "more obscure in the conventional modern manner," as opposed to the surrealism which marked the earlier material.

Roger Shattuck wrote that Arp's poetry in German, was "if not superior to, at least more interesting and varied than his French work." The German poetry is written "less rythmically" than the French. Shattuck felt that "Arp is forever looking for, or rather finding, verbal patterns in which sound and sense have approximately equal weight."

When Arp died in 1966, he left behind a variety of creations and styles. Critics have noted that Arp's art was almost all developed to a considerable degree of skill.

BIOGRAPHICAL/CRITICAL SOURCES: Forum, November, 1956; *New York Review of Books,* May 18, 1972; *Choice,* October, 1972; *Papers on Language and Literature,* spring, 1974; *New Statesman,* March 22, 1974; *Times Literary Supplement,* October 18, 1974, October 14, 1977; *Contemporary Literary Criticism,* Volume 5, Gale, 1976.

OBITUARIES: New York Times, June 8, 1966.*

(Died June 7, 1966)

*   *   *

ASCHER, Abraham 1928-

PERSONAL: Born August 26, 1928, in Breslau, Germany; came to the United States in 1943; naturalized citizen in 1950; son of Jakob (a store owner) and Feiga Ascher; married June 29, 1958; children: Deborah, Rachel, Stephen. *Education:* City College (now of the City University of New York), B.S.S., 1950; Columbia University, M.A., 1951, Ph.D., 1957. *Home:* 79 Vanderbilt Rd., Manhasset, N.Y. 11030. *Office:* Department of History, Brooklyn College of the City University of New York, Brooklyn, N.Y. 11210.

CAREER: Free-lance writer of radio scripts for Voice of America, 1952; Brooklyn College (now of the City University of New York), Brooklyn, N.Y., instructor in history,

1953-57; U.S. Department of State, Washington, D.C., research analyst of international Communism, 1957-58; State University of New York at Stony Brook, assistant professor of history, 1958-60; Brooklyn College of the City University of New York, assistant professor, 1960-64, associate professor, 1965-70, professor of history, 1970—, chairman of department, 1974-76. Instructor at Rutgers University (campus in Jersey City, N.J.), 1956-57. Director of National Endowment for the Humanities' Division of Education Programs, 1976—.

AWARDS, HONORS: Rockefeller Foundation fellow, 1963-64; Hoover Institution grants, summers, 1965-66; grant from Friedrich Ebert Stiftung, 1966; American Council of Learned Societies, 1968-69; fellow of Harvard University's Russian Research Center, 1968-69; American Philosophical Society grant, 1973; City University of New York grant, 1973; National Endowment for the Humanities senior fellow, 1974-75.

WRITINGS: Pavel Axelrod and the Development of Menshevism, Harvard University Press, 1972; *The Kremlin,* Newsweek, 1972; (editor and author of introduction) *The Mensheviks in the Russian Revolution,* Cornell University Press, 1976; (author of preface) Victor Muravin, *The Diary of Vikenty Angarov* (novel), Newsweek, 1978. Contributor of articles and reviews to history and foreign studies journals.

WORK IN PROGRESS: The Russian Revolution of 1905, publication expected in 1982.

* * *

ASHE, Douglas
See BARDIN, John Franklin

* * *

ATAMIAN, David 1892(?)-1978

OBITUARY NOTICE: Born c. 1892 in Behesni, Turkey; died October 26, 1978, in Arlington, Va. Interpreter, poet, diarist, and contributor of articles to newspapers. He served as an interpreter for the U.S. State Department. Atamian's twelve-volume diary was called a "valuable source" of Armenian history. Obituaries and other sources: *Washington Post,* October 28, 1978.

* * *

ATKIN, Mary Gage 1929-

PERSONAL: Born May 24, 1929, in Cleveland, Ohio; daughter of Charles G. and Winifred (Towne) Atkin; married Frederick Huchting, September 30, 1950 (divorced May 4, 1963); children: Amory Towne, Terence Gage. *Education:* Attended Connecticut College, 1947-50. *Politics:* "Conservative anarchist." *Home:* 243 East 52nd St., New York, N.Y. 10022. *Agent:* John Schaffner Literary Agency, 425 East 51st St., New York, N.Y. 10022.

CAREER: Actress, 1937-64; writer, 1977—.

WRITINGS: Paul Cuffe and the African Promised Land (young adult), Thomas Nelson, 1977.

WORK IN PROGRESS: The Man Who Impeached a President, a biography of Thaddeus Stevens, for young adults; *"Pap" Singleton: The Black Moses of the Western Exodus,* a biography, for young adults; *Fairfield the Abductor,* a fictionalized biography of John Fairfield, the American Scarlet Pimpernel.

SIDELIGHTS: Mary Atkin comments: "My career as an actress began when I was eight. I married a painter and hitchhiked around Europe while living as an expatriate in Paris. After I returned to the states, I became involved in the civil rights and anti-war movements. When my first son was born, I left the theater. I wanted an at-home occupation to support my babies, and started writing stories for my children to excite their interest in everything that interested me. I advanced to books for young adults and am now working on a fictionalized biography for adults."

* * *

AUBERT, Alvin (Bernard) 1930-

PERSONAL: Born March 12, 1930, in Lutcher, La.; son of Albert (a laborer) and Lucille (Roussel) Aubert; married second wife, Bernadine Tenant (a teacher and librarian), October 29, 1960; children: (first marriage) Stephenie; (second marriage) Miriam, Deborah. *Education:* Southern University, B.A., 1959; University of Michigan, A.M., 1960; further graduate study at University of Illinois, 1963-64, 1966-67. *Home:* 10 Georges Pl., Fredonia, N.Y. 14063. *Office:* Department of English, State University of New York College at Fredonia, Fredonia, N.Y. 14063.

CAREER: Southern University, Baton Rouge, La., instructor, 1960-62, assistant professor, 1962-65, associate professor of English, 1965-70; State University of New York College at Fredonia, associate professor, 1970-74, professor of English, 1974—. Visiting professor at University of Oregon, summer, 1970. Has given readings of his poems at educational institutions.

MEMBER: Modern Language Association of America, National Council of Teachers of English, African Heritage Studies Association, National Council for Black Studies. *Awards, honors:* Woodrow Wilson fellow, 1959; National Endowment for the Arts grant, 1973; scholarship for Bread Loaf Writers' Conference, Middlebury, Vt., 1978.

WRITINGS: Against the Blues (poems), Broadside Press, 1972; (contributor) James Vinson, editor, *Contemporary Novelists,* St. James Press, 1972; *Feeling Through* (poems), Greenfield Review Press, 1976; *A Noisesome Music* (poems), Blackenergy South Press, 1979; (contributor) Vinson, editor, *Writers of the English Language,* St. James Press, 1979.

Poems anthologized in six collections, including *Celebrations: An Anthology of Black Poetry,* edited by Arnold Adoff, Follett, 1979; *Contemporary Southern Poetry,* edited by Guy Owen, Louisiana State University Press, 1979; *A Geography of Poets,* edited by Edward Field, Bantam, 1979. Contributor of poems, articles, and reviews to literary journals, including *Nimrod, Black American Literature Forum, American Poetry Review,* and *Black World.* Advisory editor of *Drama and Theatre,* 1973-75, *Black Box,* 1974—, *Gumbo,* 1976—, and *Callaloo,* 1977—; founding editor of *Obsidian: Black Literature in Review,* 1975—.

WORK IN PROGRESS: A fourth collection of poems; a study of the fiction of Ernest J. Gaines.

SIDELIGHTS: Aubert wrote: "I grew up in a small Mississippi River town about midway between New Orleans and Baton Rouge, and this locale—particularly the river—nd the people, but especially the people; not to the extent of finding out exactly who and what they were (if that were possible), but of initiating and maintaining a spiritual connection. Most representative of this endeavor are poems of mine such as 'Baptism,' 'Remembrance,' 'Feeling Through,' 'Spring 1937,' 'Father, There,' and 'Fall of '43.' I like to think that all of my writings explore various aspects of the human situation and celebrate human existence at both a particualr and universal level.''

BIOGRAPHICAL/CRITICAL SOURCES: *Kliatt,* November, 1972; *Buffalo Courier-Express,* June 8, 1973.

*   *   *

AULT, Donald D(uane) 1942-

PERSONAL: Born October 5, 1942, in Canton, Ohio; son of Arthur Lewis (a machinist) and Lillian (in sales; maiden name, Morris) Ault; married Lynda Switzer, August 7, 1965; children: Lara Kristin, Jamie Alanna (daughter). *Education:* Kent State University, B.A., 1964, M.A., 1965; University of Chicago, Ph.D., 1968. *Home:* 2113 19th Ave. S., Nashville, Tenn. 37212. *Office:* Department of English, Vanderbilt University, Nashville, Tenn. 37235.

CAREER: Hoover Vacuum Cleaner Co., North Canton, Ohio, junior draftsman, 1959-61; E. W. Bliss Co., Canton, Ohio, assistant project engineer, 1962; General Tire & Rubber Co., Akron, Ohio, in equipment design, 1965-68; University of California, Berkeley, assistant professor of English, 1968-76, and Humanities Research Professor; Vanderbilt University, Nashville, Tenn., associate professor of English, 1976—.

WRITINGS: *Visionary Physics: Blake's Response to Newton,* University of Chicago Press, 1974.

WORK IN PROGRESS: *Perspective Ontology: Blake's Radical Narrative in "The Four Zoas"; The Contextual Eye: Essays on the Comic Book, Comic Strips, and Animation.*

SIDELIGHTS: Ault writes that his background in engineering and literature was a primary motivation for his first book, and that his writing on popular culture evolved from a lifelong hobby of collecting comics.

Visionary Politics: Blake's Response to Newton was described by *Choice* as ''an important and very likely a lasting contribution to Blake scholarship, to 19th century epistemology, and to intellectual history.'' D. R. Faulkner also had words of praise for the book: ''Ault thinks, and often writes, with great subtlety; and, having a background in physics and engineering, as well as a marked ability to comprehend the literature in the history of science, he appears to have a firm grasp on the scientific questions involved.''

BIOGRAPHICAL/CRITICAL SOURCES: *Times Literary Supplement,* June 20, 1975; *Choice,* July/August, 1975; *Yale Review,* winter, 1975.

*   *   *

AURTHUR, Robert Alan 1922-1978

PERSONAL: Born June 10, 1922, in New York, N.Y.; son of William and Margaret (Brock) Aurthur; married Jane Wetherell, May 27, 1966; children: Jonathan, Gretchen, Timothy, Kate. *Education:* University of Pennsylvania, B.A. (highest honors), 1946. *Home:* 968 Fireplace Rd., East Hampton, N.Y. 11937.

CAREER: Writer. Worked for ''Philco TV Playhouse'' television series as associate producer, 1955, producer, 1956, and writer, 1957-59; producer of ''NBC Sunday Showcase'' television series, 1959-60; vice-president of Talent Associates Ltd., 1961-62; producer of television projects for United Artists, 1963-64. *Military service:* U.S. Marine Corps Reserves, 1942-46; became first lieutenant. *Member:* National Association for the Advancement of Colored Peo-

ple, American Civil Liberties Union, Directors Guild of America, Writers Guild of America, West, Television Academy of Arts and Sciences (board of governors, 1958-59), Academy of Motion Picture Arts and Sciences, Actor's Studio, Sigma Nu. *Awards, honors:* Sylvania Award for best original television play, 1954, and 1955; Emmy Award from Television Academy of Arts and Sciences, 1955.

WRITINGS—Novels: *The History of the Third Marine Division,* Infantry Journal Press, 1948; *The Glorification of Al Toolum,* Holt, 1953.

Plays: ''A Very Special Baby,'' produced on Broadway, 1956; ''Kwamina,'' produced on Broadway, 1961; ''Carry Me Back to Morningside Heights,'' produced on Broadway, 1968.

Screenplays: ''The Edge of the City,'' Metro-Goldwyn-Mayer (MGM), 1957; ''Warlock'' (adapted from the novel by Oakley Hall), Twentieth Century-Fox, 1959; ''Grand Prix,'' MGM, 1966; ''For Love of Ivy,'' Cinerama, 1968; ''The Lost Man'' (adapted from the novel by Laurence Green, *Odd Man Out*), 1969.

SIDELIGHTS: In a review of ''Warlock,'' Bosley Crowther declared that Aurthur ''put the whole picture together in a straight, precise layout of plots and accumulating action that hold interest'' and also called the film ''good, solid, gripping Western fare.'' Paul V. Beckley disliked the film, noting that ''there isn't one situation or complication or characterization that isn't hackneyed.''

''Grand Prix,'' a film about cars, drivers and racing, received various positive and negative reviews. Judith Crist noted: ''This is the stuff of documentaries—and a pity it hasn't been saved for one instead of being jammed into the old hat that Robert Alan Aurthur has provided his scenario. We're back with the Grand Hotel syndrome, following the fate and sex life of four drivers.'' In contrast, a review for *Variety* stated: ''There is a curious thing . . . about the exposition of the characters in the screenplay. Under cold examination they are stock characters. Yet scenarist Robert Alan Aurthur has invested these individuals with distinctive personalities that are brought to meaningful life by the performers.''

Vincent Canby, in a critique of ''For Love of Ivy,'' focused on the inherent ''seething anger'' and stated that Aurther ''distilled from it a gentle satire designed to reinforce both white and black bourgeois dreams. . . . It's a slick funny tranquilizer.''

BIOGRAPHICAL/CRITICAL SOURCES: *New York Herald Tribune,* May 1, 1959; *New York Times,* May 1, 1959, July 18, 1968; *New York World Journal Tribune,* December 22, 1966; *Variety,* December 28, 1966.

OBITUARIES: *Time,* December 4, 1978.*

(Died in 1978 in New York, N.Y.)

*   *   *

AUSTIN, James Henry 1925-

PERSONAL: Born January 4, 1925, in Cleveland, Ohio; son of Paul W. (in advertising) and Bertha (Holtkamp) Austin; married Judith St. Clair (in real estate), February 7, 1948; children: Scott Whiting, Lynn Austin Manning, James Winslow. *Education:* Brown University, A.B., 1944; Harvard University, M.D., 1948. *Politics:* Independent. *Religion:* Unitarian-Universalist. *Home:* 128 South Fairfax, Denver, Colo. 80222. *Office:* Medical Center, University of Colorado, 4200 East Ninth Ave., Denver, Colo. 80220.

CAREER: Boston City Hospital, Boston, Mass., intern, 1948-49, assistant resident of neurology unit, 1949-50; Neurological Institute of New York, neurological resident, 1953-55; neurologist in private practice in Portland, Ore., 1955-67, and Denver, Colo., 1967—; University of Colorado Medical Center, Denver, professor and head of the division of neurology, 1967—, chairman of the department of neurology, 1974—. *Military service:* U.S. Naval Reserve, 1942-45. *Member:* United World Federalists, Sigma Xi, Delta Upsilon. *Awards, honors:* Kenny research fellow, 1959-63; Saul Korey Memorial lecturer, 1967; Alan Gregg fellow, 1974.

WRITINGS: Chase, Chance, and Creativity: The Lucky Art of Novelty, Columbia University Press, 1978.

SIDELIGHTS: Why did James Austin write *Chase, Chance, and Creativity?* He explained to *CA:* "I wrote this book to fill a need and to address the issue of how chance and creativity interact in biomedical research." According to Anthony Storr, Austin has achieved this goal. Storr praised Austin for setting forth a complex issue in terms comprehensible to a layman, and for conveying "some of the fascination and excitement of the hunt which accompanies research in any field." Storr recommended *Chase, Chance and Creativity* to both humanists and scientists: "Anyone engaged in any kind of original work will find the book rewarding."

AVOCATIONAL INTERESTS: Music and painting.

BIOGRAPHICAL/CRITICAL SOURCES: James Henry Austin, *Chase, Chance, and Creativity: The Lucky Art of Novelty,* Columbia University Press, 1978; *Washington Post Book World,* April 9, 1978; *Chicago Sun Times,* May 8, 1978.

*   *   *

AVENI, Anthony F(rancis)   1938-

PERSONAL: Born March 5, 1938, in New Haven, Conn.; son of Anthony M. (a restaurateur) and Frances (Cremonie) Aveni; married Lorrainê Reiner (a secretary), 1959; children: Patricia, Anthony F., Jr. *Education:* Boston University, A.B., 1960; University of Arizona, Ph.D., 1963. *Home address:* R.D. 2, Hamilton, N.Y. 13346. *Office:* Department of Physics and Astronomy, Colgate University, Hamilton, N.Y. 13346.

CAREER: Colgate University, Hamilton, N.Y., instructor, 1963-65, assistant professor, 1965-69, associate professor, 1969-75, professor of astronomy, 1975—, head of department, 1971-73. Visiting professor and acting director of observatory at University of South Florida, 1973-74. Conducted field studies in Mexico, Guatemala, Honduras, and Peru. Organized international gatherings of scientists.

MEMBER: American Astronomical Society, American Association for the Advancement of Science, American Association of University Professors, New York Academy of Sciences, Astronomical Society of New York State, Explorers Club. *Awards, honors:* National Science Foundation grants, 1963, 1965, 1968, 1969, 1971, 1973-75, 1975-76, 1977-78; Sigma Xi grant, 1971, to Mexico; OSCO Foundation grants, 1973, 1977; grants from Educational Expeditions International, 1976 and 1977, to Latin America.

WRITINGS: (With A. B. Meinel and M. W. Stockton) *Catalog of Emission Lines in Astrophysical Objects,* University of Arizona Press, 1968; (editor and contributor) *Archaeoastronomy in Pre-Columbian America,* University of Texas Press, 1975; (editor and contributor) *Native American Astronomy,* University of Texas Press, 1977; (contributor)

Edwin Krupp, editor, *In Search of Ancient Astronomies,* Doubleday, 1978; (with B. A. Collea) *A Selected Bibliography on Native American Astronomy,* Colgate University, 1978; (author of introduction) Travis Hudson and Ernest Underhay, *Crystals in the Sky: An Odyssey into Chumash Astronomy and Cosmology,* Ballena, 1978; *Sky Watchers of Ancient America,* University of Texas Press, 1979. Contributor of about twenty-five articles to anthropology, archaeology, and scientific journals.

WORK IN PROGRESS: Calendars of Cuzco, on Inca astronomy.

SIDELIGHTS: Aveni writes: "Archaeoastronomy is the study of ancient man's view of the cosmos. Its very name implies that such a field of inquiry is interdisciplinary. To know what the ancient Maya thought about the heavens we must understand both the workings of the celestial sphere and the Maya mind. Religion, astrology, architecture, and the structure of the ceremonial center, hieroglyphic writing, and mathematics—all are involved and integrated into the Maya 'cosmovision' in a way we can begin to comprehend only when we divest ourselves of our own western cultural presuppositions.

"Since 1970 much of my time has been occupied with a study of ancient manuscripts, along with expeditions and field trips to archaeological ruins in Mexico, Guatemala, Honduras, and Peru.

"When writing I try to fuse my traditional background and training in the field of astronomy with a knowledge of ancient native American cultures acquired since I began climbing the fence between physical science and cultural anthropology about a decade ago. By perching on the fencepost between these two disparate fields, perhaps one can see a wider horizon."

*   *   *

AVERY, Ira   1914-
(Mavis Hathaway)

PERSONAL: Born July 27, 1914, in Albany, N.Y.; son of Clarence L. (an office designer) and Elysabeth B. (Mowery) Avery; married Claire M. Gruber (an executive secretary), August 12, 1975; children: Jan Avery Frew, Devon Avery Supler. *Education:* University of Virginia, B.A., 1936; graduate study at Harvard University, 1952. *Politics:* Independent. *Religion:* "Unaffiliated." *Home and office:* 65 Glenbrook Rd., Stamford, Conn. 06902. *Agent:* International Creative Management, 40 West 57th St., New York, N.Y. 10019.

CAREER: WRVA-Radio, Richmond, Va., assistant program director, 1936-42; Office of War Information, New York City, program technician, 1943; National Broadcasting Co. (NBC), New York City, radio producer, 1943-45; Batten, Barton, Durstine & Osborn (advertising agency), New York City, 1945-62, began as staff member, became vice-president, 1959; free-lance writer, 1962—. Assistant program director for WOR-Radio, 1941-42; producer and director of radio and television programs; member of television advisory board at Stephens College. Official host of Richmond, Va., 1939-40. Consultant to ABC-TV, Henry Strauss Productions, and Channel 7, Sydney, Australia.

MEMBER: Authors League of America, Writers Guild of America, The Players. *Awards, honors:* Nominated for Italian Gold Medal, 1955; Christopher Award, 1955, for *Five Fathers of Pepi;* medals from Freedoms Foundation, 1958, for television economics education campaign, and 1965, for film "Beyond Three Doors"; citation from American Alumni Council for fund-raising album for Harvard University, 1958.

WRITINGS: (Contributor) E. B. Roberts, *Television Writing and Selling,* Writer, Inc., 1954; *The Five Fathers of Pepi* (novel; Catholic Book Club selection), Bobbs-Merrill, 1955; *Where Should I Eat in Italy?,* Macmillan, 1966; *The Miracle of Dommatina,* Putnam, 1978; (contributor) Judy Fireman, editor, *The TV Book,* Workman Publishing, 1978.

Gothic novels; all under pseudonym Mavis Hathaway: *What Evil Lurks?,* Curtis Books, 1975; *A Silence of Nightingales,* Popular Library, 1977.

Author of "Matilda" (three-act play) Samuel French, 1948. Author of scripts for industrial films, including work for Bell System and Armco Steel. Creator and writer for television and radio series, including "Armstrong Circle Theatre," "U.S. Steel Hour," "Dr. Kildare," and "Loretta Young Show"; head writer for "The Doctors," "The Guiding Light," "The Secret Storm," "Love of Life," and "Search for Tomorrow."

Columnist for *Richmond Times-Dispatch, Richmond News Leader, Indianapolis Star,* and *Arizona Gazette.*

Contributor to newspapers. Food editor of *Madison Avenue;* writer of travel articles for *Esquire* and *House & Garden;* editor of *Broadcasting.*

WORK IN PROGRESS: The Lovely Lady, a novel; *Targis,* a novel, *Post Scripts,* a novel; *Murder by the Script,* a novel; *The Living End Cookbook,* a book on gourmet diets; *How I Spent My Vacation,* an autobiography.

SIDELIGHTS: Avery writes: "Ask a writer to talk about himself and you will quickly learn more than you want to know.

"Motivation? God knows. It's apparently something I have to do, like drinking martinis and getting to Italy whenever possible. For as long as I can remember I have never been able to see a printed page without reading it or a blank page without writing on it. My childhood idol was Robert Louis Stevenson and I guess he still is, although he shares space today with a whole Valhalla of other gods from Homer and Proust to Robert Benchley, Mark Twain, Thornton Wilder, and Rex Stout. I was told Stevenson had been a frail kid (like me) and I suppose it established a bond, though they tried the same gimmick on me with Teddy Roosevelt and I don't think it took. My grandfather knew Roosevelt, and my mother saw him in their living room once when she was a girl and remembered only that his pants were baggy. Grandfather was the youngest Yankee soldier in the Civil War and answered a call for volunteers who could ride because, although he had never been in a saddle, he noticed that the horses knew all the bugle calls and did what they were supposed to do.

"I remember that when I was twelve I had read all the books in Grandfather's library including James Fenimore Cooper, *Pilgrim's Progress,* and *Little Dorrit,* stuff I could never negotiate today. I read *all* of Edgar Allan Poe, not just the poems and stories. I was writing stories when I was old enough to write, and later Dad would bring home rolls of adding machine paper from the office and I'd use them to make movies by drawing the action on panels and pulling the roll through a square opening in the back of a handmade stage. What motivated things like that? Spending most of the time in bed, I suppose, and running out of things to read.

"Circumstances? Mostly lack of cash, I guess. In 1962 my two careers were beginning to conflict and I left advertising to devote my full time to writing, unfortunately not having noticed that television had migrated to Hollywood, which to me is Quicksand, U.S.A. Nothing was left in the East but soap operas, and soap operas surprisingly proved to be lucrative as hell. But, to steal a phrase from Jim Elward, it was like writing in water. Periodically I resolved to wrench myself loose and write something reasonably permanent, and periodically I went broke. I'm still trying to master the formula that will give me the freedom of being poor with the security of being rich. I don't mind not having a power cruiser any more, or a house on an island in the Sound and a Mercedes and a villa in Italy, but I do mind being at the mercy of publishers who go out of business precisely when my book comes out, editors who have big promotional plans before publication date and the next day take a job with another publisher, and lovely young readers from Vassar whose image of the reading public is a cocktail party in Darien.

"Subjects I consider vital? Corruption in politics. War. Taxes paying for waste, graft, overruns, idiocy, and greed. Overcooked vegetables. Truck drivers who tailgate you into the slow lane, where you're delayed, or into the fast lane, where everybody else is going seventy-five. Women who block the aisles with their shopping carts and don't start writing their checks until they're at the checkout counter. Men who brag about sexual exploits in the bar car while their wives are trying to keep dinner warm. Bridge players who rap their fingers. Bridge players who lose interest when they have a bad hand. Crooks who make a fortune out of publishing their sins or their discovery of God. Book reviewers who tell the ending. Book reviewers who expound their superior knowledge of the subject.

"Major area of vocational interest? Writing. For itself, for catharsis, for profit. Avocational interests? Travel. I lived for a year in Italy, and a year in Australia. I love France. I once did an article for *Esquire* on the (then) twelve Michelin three-star restaurants. Of the great masters of *La Haute Cuisine,* only M. Point was missing. Now all are dead or retired but Claude Terrail. Wine. Not Bordeaux, they're too expensive a hobby. But Burgundies. And the much misunderstood, underestimated wines of Italy: Barolo, Valpolicella, Soave, Verdicchio, and a dozen others. Cooking. Curry, Imam Bayaldi, *Vitello tonnato, osso buco,* Boone County ham, key lime pie, Welsh rabbit made with Watney's Ale. Music. Opera, Benny Goodman, Wohumir Kryl, Hilda Gueden, Vladimir Horowitz, Red Nichols, Duke Ellington, Helen Reddy, Crosby, Wagner.

"And language. I speak only restaurant French, tourist German, and peasant Italian, and wish I had seven lifetimes to master English. I collect oddball reference books: *The Dictionary of Misinformation, Brewer's Dictionary of Fact and Fable, The Way Things Work, The Book of Surprises.* I started keeping a list of grammatical howlers on television and in the *New York Times* but ran out of paper. Things like 'congradulations,' 'negociate,' 'lugshury,' 'flaunt' for 'flout,' and a gem from Vincent Canby in which he devotes an entire article to excoriating somebody for writing *The Book of Revelations* instead of *Revelation* and in the exact same piece refers to 'the Court of St. James.'

"There are no illuminating personal data. The dearest friend I ever had beside my extraordinary wife was my father. The questions must often asked me are 'Do you write on a schedule?' (The answer is yes.) 'Where do you get your ideas?' (The answer is from everywhere.) 'Do your friends recognize themselves in your stories?' (Never. They recognize one another, but never themselves. Sometimes they think they see themselves in the good guys, but they're mistaken. The good guys are all me.)

"Incidentally, why is it that while almost nobody thinks he could design a World Trade Center, invent an incandescent bulb, or compose a symphony, everybody thinks 'if he had the time' he could write a novel? I find that most such people don't really want to write, they want to *be* writers."

* * *

AXELL, Herbert (Ernest) 1915-

PERSONAL: Surname is pronounced like "axle"; born July 1, 1915, in Rye, Sussex, England; son of Charles Henry (a photographer) and Bessie May (Rhodes) Axell; married Joan Mary Hamshire, December 5, 1938; children: Roderick Howard. *Education:* Attended elementary school in Rye, England. *Politics:* Conservative. *Religion:* Church of England. *Home:* Suffolk Punch, Westleton, Saxmundham, Suffolk IP17 3AZ, England. *Office:* Royal Society for the Protection of Birds, The Lodge, Sandy Bedfordshire SG19 2DL, England.

CAREER: General Post Office, London, England, post office clerk, 1931-46, assistant inspector of postal services, 1946-50; Dungeness Bird Reserve, Kent, England, warden, 1952-59; Minsmere Nature Reserve, Westleton, England, warden, 1959-65; Royal Society for the Protection of Birds, Sandy, England, land use adviser, 1965—. Member of board of governors of Lowestoft College of Further Education. *Military service:* British Army, Royal Horse Artillery, 1940-45; served in Africa and Europe; became lieutenant.

MEMBER: British Ornithologists Union, British Trust for Ornithology, Malta Ornithological Society, Suffolk Trust for Nature Conservation, Suffolk Ornithologists Group, Suffolk Naturalists Society. *Awards, honors:* Member of Order of the British Empire, 1965; Churchill Fellowship from Winston Churchill Memorial Trust, 1975, for a world tour.

WRITINGS: Minsmere: Portrait of a Bird Reserve, Hutchinson, 1977; *Birds of Britain,* Artus, 1978. Contributor to scientific journals and popular magazines.

WORK IN PROGRESS: British Bird Reserves, for Royal Society for the Protection of Birds; *A Place for Birds* (autobiography), for Hutchinson.

SIDELIGHTS: Axell writes: "I am concerned about communication with the public. I wanted to be a journalist and began publishing magazine articles when I was eighteen. Especially since World War II, I have been motivated by the need for painless, exciting, real education of the public in wildlife. Mainly I am involved with birds and their habitats, but necessarily other animals as well (their predators and prey).

"My work for the Royal Society for the Protection of Birds includes advising on the making of reserves for birds and birdwatchers in the United Kingdom and overseas. It also includes work on sites much affected by industry and people

at leisure. I like to work abroad, and have advised or lectured in Spain, France, Malta, Belgium, Kenya, Australia, New Zealand, the Philippines, Thailand, and Jamaica. I am currently making a large new reserve for wildlife and visitors in Donana, in Spain, and in Malta.

"While trying to extol the beauty of wildlife and our need of it, I believe that people have to matter most. I consider that Nature's best creation so far is *Homo sapiens.*"

Axell has traveled throughout Europe, Uganda, Nigeria, Hawaii, Fiji, India, and the Persian Gulf.

AVOCATIONAL INTERESTS: Wildlife photography.

* * *

AXELROD, Steven Gould 1944-

PERSONAL: Born May 15, 1944, in Los Angeles, Calif.; son of Bernard (a physician) and Martha (a writer; maiden name, Gould) Axelrod; married Rise Borenstein (a professor), August 27, 1966; children: Jeremiah. *Education:* University of California, Los Angeles, B.A., 1966, M.A., 1969, Ph.D., 1972. *Politics:* Democrat. *Religion:* Jewish. *Home:* 2944 Robin Rd., Riverside, Calif. 92506. *Office:* Department of English, University of California, Riverside, Calif. 92521.

CAREER: University of Missouri, St. Louis, assistant professor of English, 1972-73; University of California, Riverside, assistant professor, 1973-78, associate professor of English, 1978—. Visiting associate professor at University of Colorado, 1978-79. *Member:* National Council of Teachers of English, Modern Language Association of America, American Studies Association, Philological Association of the Pacific Coast, Phi Beta Kappa.

WRITINGS: Robert Lowell: Life and Art, Princeton University Press, 1978. Contributor to literature journals and literary magazines, including *American Quarterly* and *Bucknell Review.*

WORK IN PROGRESS: A biographical study of Hart Crane; a bibliography of Robert Lowell; writing on contemporary poetry.

SIDELIGHTS: Axelrod writes: "I always wanted to be a writer, but in the course of things found myself a teacher; now, with the publication of my book on Robert Lowell, I find myself a writer after all, a writer *too.* It is not entirely calming or usual to have one's hopes fulfilled, especially after one has consciously abandoned them, but the event is not displeasing either.

"My book is a biography of a great poet, which means that it is also a work of literary criticism, for great writers live part of their lives in their art. Indeed it is that part which matters most to us and makes us care about the whole. Writing the book was exciting to me, for in it I needed to imagine an imagination greater than my own. Perhaps my theme is the place the imagination makes for itself in America."

B

BABITZ, Eve 1943-

PERSONAL: Born May 13, 1943, in Hollywood, Calif.; daughter of Sol (a musician) and Mae (an artist; maiden name, Laviolette) Babitz. *Education:* Attended high school in Hollywood, Calif. *Agent:* Erica Spellman, International Creative Management, 40 West 57th St., New York, N.Y. 10019.

CAREER: Free-lance illustrator and designer of covers for record albums, 1967-72; office manager, *East Village Other,* 1966; office manager, *Ramparts,* 1967; writer, 1967—.

WRITINGS: Eve's Hollywood, Seymour Lawrence, 1974; (editor) *Los Angeles Manifesto* (stories), privately printed, 1976; *Slow Days, Fast Company* (fiction), Knopf, 1977; *Sex and Rage* (novel), Knopf, in press. Contributor of stories to popular magazines, including *Rolling Stone, Vogue, Viva, Cosmopolitan, Coast, Saturday Evening Post, Saturday Review of Literature, Crawdaddy,* and *New West.*

WORK IN PROGRESS: Screenplays.

SIDELIGHTS: Eve Babitz writes: "I became a writer when I felt I was too old to design rock'n'roll album covers any more. As I could no longer drink Southern Comfort till three o'clock A.M. with nineteen-year-old bass players from Mississippi, I felt that my days in rock'n'roll were numbered. I knew I'd be a writer eventually, and I decided to write stories about Los Angeles that weren't depressing. And I did."

AVOCATIONAL INTERESTS: Swimming, yoga.

BIOGRAPHICAL/CRITICAL SOURCES: Los Angeles Times, May 1, 1977.

* * *

BAER, Donald Merle 1931-

PERSONAL: Born October 25, 1931, in St. Louis, Mo.; son of George Eugene (a union organizer and manager) and Ida Sylvia (Feldman) Baer; married Ann M. Marshall, August 27, 1955 (divorced, 1977); married Stephanie B. Stolz (a division director for U.S. Department of Health, Education & Welfare), December 18, 1977; children: Ruth Alison, Miriam Jane, Deborah Margaret. *Education:* University of Chicago, A.B. (honors), 1950, Ph.D., 1957. *Religion:* Jewish. *Residence:* Lawrence, Kan. *Office:* Department of Human Development and Family Life, University of Kansas, Lawrence, Kan. 66045.

CAREER: University of Washington, Seattle, assistant professor, 1957-61, associate professor of psychology, 1961-65, acting director of Gatzert Institute of Child Development, 1961-62; University of Kansas, Lawrence, professor of human development, family life, and psychology, 1965—, Roy A. Roberts Distinguished Professor of Human Development and Family Life and Psychology, 1975—, head of Division of Child Development, research associate of Bureau of Child Research, and research director of Center for the Study of Human Development. Visiting associate professor at University of California, Los Angeles, summer, 1964; visiting professor at University of Hawaii, summers, 1967, 1971, Brigham Young University, summer, 1969, University of Western Australia, 1971-72, University of Sydney, 1972, Universidade de Sao Paulo, summer, 1975, and Drake University, summer, 1977; lecturer at San Francisco State University, summer, 1975; distinguished visiting professor at University of Manitoba, January, 1977, and University of Arizona, summer, 1977. Speaker at educational institutions and professional meetings; visiting scientist for National Science Foundation and American Psychological Association, 1963. Member of advisory board of Rainier State School for Retarded Children, 1961-62. Consultant to Veterans Administration, National Institute of Mental Health, National Institute of Child Health and Human Development, and Kansas Neurological Institute.

MEMBER: American Psychological Association (fellow; division vice-president, 1971-73), Society for Research in Child Development (fellow), American Association for the Advancement of Science, Association for Behavior Analysis, Association for the Advancement of Behavior Therapy, Society for Experimental Analysis of Behavior, Sigma Xi. *Awards, honors:* Grants from U.S. Public Health Service, 1958-64, 1964-68, 1965-70, State of Washington, 1960, 1962, 1963, U.S. Office of Education, 1967-71, State of Kansas Research Fund, 1969, 1970, National Institute of Mental Health, 1969-74, 1970—, and National Institute of Child Health and Human Development, 1970—.

WRITINGS: (With Sidney W. Bijou) *Child Development,* Appleton, Volume I, 1961, Volume II, 1965; (with Bijou) *Child Development: Readings in Experimental Analysis,* Appleton, 1967; (with Doug Guess and W. S. Sailor) *Functional Speech and Language Training for the Severely Handicapped,* Parts I-II, H & H Enterprises, 1976; (editor with B. C. Etzel and J. M. LeBlanc, and contributor) *New*

Developments in Behavioral Research: Theory, Method, and Applications, in Honor of Sidney W. Bijou, Lawrence Erlbaum Associates, 1977.

Contributor: Paul Mussen, editor, *Handbook of Research Methods in Child Development*, Wiley, 1960; Lewis Lippsitt and Charles Spiker, editors, *Advances in Child Development and Behavior*, Volume I, Academic Press, 1963; Lipsitt and D. S. Palermo, editors, *Research Readings in Child Psychology*, Holt, 1964; A. W. Staats, editor, *Human Learning Studies Extending Conditioning Principles*, Holt, 1964; R. E. Ulrich, T. J. Stachnik, and J. E. Mabry, editors, *The Control of Human Behavior*, Scott, Foresman, Volume I, 1966, Volume II, 1970; Werner Honig, editor, *Operant Conditioning: Areas of Research and Application*, Appleton, 1966; R. D. Hess and R. M. Baer, editors, *Early Education: Current Theory, Research, and Practice*, Aldine, 1968; C. M. Franks, editor, *Behavior Therapy: Appraisal and Status*, McGraw, 1969; W. J. Gagney, editor, *Readings in the Psychology of Classroom Learning*, Holt, 1969.

Charles Neuringer and Jack Michael, editors, *Behavior Modification in Clinical Psychology*, Appleton, 1970; H. W. Reese and Lipsitt, editors, *Experimental Child Psychology*, Academic Press, 1970; S. H. Osipow and W. B. Walsh, editors, *Behavior Change in Counseling: Readings and Cases*, Appleton, 1970; E. A. Ramp and B. L. Hopkins, editors, *A New Direction for Education: Behavior Analysis, 1971*, Volume I, University Press of Kansas, 1971; M. E. Meyer, editor, *Second Western Symposium on Learning: Early Learning*, Western Washington State College Press, 1971; W. C. Becker, editor, *An Empirical Basis for Change in Education*, Science Research Associates, 1971; Robert Silverman, editor, *Book of Readings*, New Century Press, 1971; J. G. Morrey, editor, *Learning and Behavior Management in Teacher Training*, Idaho State University Press, 1971; R. L. Schiefelbusch, editor, *Language of the Mentally Retarded*, National Institute of Child Health and Human Development, 1971; R. E. Ulrich and P. T. Mountjoy, editors, *The Experimental Analysis of Social Behavior*, Appleton, 1972; Joachim Wohlwill, editor, *The Study of Behavioral Development*, Academic Press, 1972; J. R. Nessleroade and H. W. Reese, editors, *Life-Span Developmental Psychology: Methodological Issues*, Academic Press, 1972; Benjamin Lahey, editor, *The Modification of Language Behavior*, C. C Thomas, 1972; (author of foreword) Beth Sulzer and G. R. Mayer, editors, *Behavior Modification Procedures for School Personnel*, Dryden, 1972; Paul Weisberg, editor, *The Applications of Psychological Principles*, Allyn & Bacon, 1972; B. A. Ashem and E. G. Poser, editors, *Adaptive Learning: Behavior Modification with Children*, Pergamon, 1973; Barbara Vance, editor, *Teaching the Pre-Kindergarten Child: Instructional Design and Curriculum*, Brooks/Cole, 1973; B. M. Caldwell and H. N. Ricciutti, editors, *Review of Child Development Research*, Volume III, University of Chicago Press, 1973; R. D. Klein, W. G. Hapkiewicz, and A. G. Roden, editors, *Behavior Modification in Educational Settings*, C. C Thomas, 1973; D. B. Gardner, editor, *Development in Early Childhood*, Harper, 1973; H. F. Clarizio, R. C. Craig, and W. A. Mehrens, editors, *Contemporary Issues in Educational Psychology*, Allyn & Bacon, 1973; W. G. Bounds, editor, *Understanding Statistics and Human Research Design*, Harper, 1974; R. L. Schiefelbusch and L. L. Lloyd, editors, *Language Perspectives: Acquisition, Retardation, and Intervention*, University Park Press, 1974; Norris Haring and Lou Brown, editors, *Teaching Severely and Profoundly Multi-Handicapped Children*, Grune, 1975; T. A.

Brigham, Robert Hawkins, John Scott, and T. F. McLaughlin, editors, *Behavior Analysis in Education: Self-Control and Reading*, Kendall/Hunt, 1976; Ann Pick, editor, *The Sixth Minnesota Symposium on Child Psychology*, Volumes I-II, University of Minnesota Press, 1976.

Contributor of about sixty articles to academic journals. Associate editor of *Journal of Experimental Child Psychology*, 1964-67, member of board of editors, 1967-70; associate editor of *Journal of Applied Behavior Analysis*, 1967-70, editor, 1970-71, member of board of editors, 1973-77; member of board of editors of *Journal of the Experimental Analysis of Behavior*, 1965-68, and *Behavior Modification*, 1976—; member of editorial board of *Psychotherapy*, 1972-76, and *Behaviorism*, 1973—; consulting editor of "Child Development Publications," Society for Research in Child Development, 1961-63.

AVOCATIONAL INTERESTS: Playing the flute, photography, tinkering, travel (Europe, Australia and New Zealand, Latin America, Barbados, Fiji, Dominican Republic).

* * *

BAER, Judith A(bbott) 1945-

PERSONAL: Born April 5, 1945, in Mount Kisco, N.Y.; daughter of Theodore S. (an economist) and Dorothy (an assistant comptroller; maiden name, Smith) Baer. *Education:* Bryn Mawr College, B.A., 1968; University of Chicago, A.M., 1971, Ph.D., 1974. *Home:* 58 Frost Pl., Albany, N.Y. 12205. *Office:* Department of Political Science, State University of New York at Albany, Albany, N.Y. 12222.

CAREER: University of Hawaii, Honolulu, assistant professor of political science, 1974-76; State University of New York at Albany, assistant professor of political science, 1976—. *Member:* American Political Science Association, National Organization for Women, National Women's Political Caucus, American Civil Liberties Union, Northeast Political Science Association.

WRITINGS: The Chains of Protection, Greenwood Press, 1978. Contributor to *Western Political Quarterly*.

WORK IN PROGRESS: Research on the legal and theoretical limitations of the idea of equality.

SIDELIGHTS: "*The Chains of Protection* is an analysis of state and federal court decisions on special labor legislation for women, from the 1870's up through the Equal Pay Act of 1963 and Title VII of the Civil Rights Act of 1964, which were interpreted to invalidate the earlier laws. I use these decisions as a way of getting at not only the legal problems but the larger issues of sexual equality. The analysis has a feminist perspective, and delves into psychology and political theory as well as the law.

"I am also exploring the history of the adoption of the Equal Protection Clause of the Fourteenth Amendment and its interpretation by the courts in cases of personal discrimination. Motivated by two recent developments in the law—the issue of reverse discrimination and the emergence of equal-protection claims from new groups—I am seeking to examine the relevance of this constitutional provision to these claims and to re-evaluate the judicial interpretations. I am concerned both with the aims of the writers of the Amendment and the normative issues involved. One part of this study will be a critique of the decision in University of California vs. Bakke.

"As a specialist in public law, I explore questions of constitutional interpretation, not only in the area of equality but also other issues pertaining to individual rights. I am concerned with the limits of, and gaps in, constitutional guarantees, as well as in what they do include. I try especially to bring political theory to my analyses of these problems."

AVOCATIONAL INTERESTS: Running, swimming, music, theatre, films.

* * *

BAER, Marianne 1932-

PERSONAL: Born July 5, 1932, in Elizabeth, N.J., daughter of Werner Curt (an engineer) and Anne (Holzer) Baer; married Robert Chambers (divorced). *Education:* Attended Pratt Institute, 1950-52. *Religion:* Moravian. *Residence:* New York, N.Y. *Agent:* Gloria Safier, Inc., 667 Madison Ave., New York, N.Y. 10021. *Office:* Conahay & Lyon, 380 Madison Ave., New York, N.Y. 10017.

CAREER: Ogilvy & Mather, Inc., New York City, vice-president and associate creative director, 1961-72; Botsford, Ketchum, Inc., San Francisco, Calif., associate creative director, 1972-75; Foote, Cone & Belding, Chicago, Ill. (and New York City), associate creative director, 1975-77; Conahay & Lyon, New York City, vice-president and associate creative director, 1977—. *Awards, honors:* Golden Lion award from the Venice Film Festival, 1965, for a Sears, Roebuck commercial; Gold medals from the Dublin, Cannes, and New York Film Festivals, 1969, all for commercials for International Paper; first prizes in all West Coast advertising competitions, 1975, for introductory campaign for Orville Redenbacher's Gourmet Popping Corn.

WRITINGS: A Man's Woman (novel), Putnam, 1978.

WORK IN PROGRESS: Another novel.

SIDELIGHTS: Marianne Baer told *CA:* "*A Man's Woman* is my first published novel. I burnt a number of earlier attempts, while trying to learn to deal with communications longer than the one-minute commercial. They deserved their Viking funeral, but I learned in the attempts. I found I could not deal with the commitment to four hundred pages of manuscript until I came upon a theme I truly needed to explore at length. That theme was the growing recognition of the support system provided by women friends. Until that day when I began work on *A Man's Woman,* I had accepted that men formed supportive bonding relationships with other men and that women were in competition with other women—largely over men, when not over career opportunities. I, upon realizing how misconceived that view was, set the protagonist of my book back into a more easily empathized and defined piece of my life—the knowledge and adjustment to a hysterectomy, the response of various friends at that time and the positive but unrealized growth that resulted.

"I submitted three chapters and an outline via an agent and was offered a contract six months later, by the first editor to whom it was submitted. I completed the first draft within six months, but had contract-completion difficulties with my agent, not my eventual publisher, and dismissed the agent, retaining an attorney to formalize the paperwork. During the next calendar year, I completed three revised drafts, with good, helpful, and insightful direction from the editor. The editor shortly thereafter moved to another publishing house and the book received minimal distribution, no publicity, and no promotional support. Too late, I realized that it was being sent into the market as an orphan and that my marketing background was of little use in this situation. I have since agreed to be represented by another agent, who has been highly recommended and whose 'selling' sense impresses me

after personal meetings, and I trust I will never commit two years of reclusive effort to an unmarketed volume again.

"If I have an axiom to offer other aspiring first novelists it is, Know thy agent. I found the business of breaking into print quite easy and gratifying. I find the business of selling books obscure, unbusinesslike, and frustrating. I might also suggest, that if a beginning writer feels compelled by a highly topical subject, as I did, he should work very fast. Risk everything. I might have done better if that excellent book *The Woman's Room,* had not taken a lot of the surprise out of my theme."

Any experience is good for a writer, Baer emphasized: "I continue to be astonished and delighted that nothing, however miserable it seems while in progress, is lost if you have a good relationship with your typewriter. The most boring as well as the most thrilling, the most heart-wrenching as well as the most happy moments all become a pleasure to be studied when you are working well. Writing is a way of living at least twice."

AVOCATIONAL INTERESTS: Sailing, tennis, cooking, travel, studying people.

* * *

BAIR, Deirdre 1935-

PERSONAL: Born June 21, 1935, in Pittsburgh, Pa.; married Lavon H. Bair (a museum administrator), May 29, 1957; children: Von Scott, Katherine Tracy. *Education:* University of Pennsylvania, B.A., 1957; Columbia University, M.A., 1968, Ph.D., 1972. *Politics:* Liberal. *Religion:* Roman Catholic. *Residence:* Woodbridge, Conn. *Agent:* Carl D. Brandt, Brandt & Brandt, 101 Park Ave., New York, N.Y. 10017. *Office:* Department of English, University of Pennsylvania, Philadelphia, Pa. 19104.

CAREER: Free-lance journalist, 1957-69; University of Pennsylvania, Philadelphia, Pa., assistant professor of English, 1976—.

WRITINGS: Samuel Beckett: A Biography, Harcourt, 1978. Contributor of journalism and scholarly articles to various publications.

WORK IN PROGRESS: A study of literary figures in New York during the 1930's, for Harcourt.

SIDELIGHTS: Bair's study of Samuel Beckett is most amazing in that the Irish author had never before permitted a biographer's inspection. Consequently, his promise to neither help nor hinder her efforts was all the encouragement Bair needed to embark on her task. For six years she probed into Beckett's life, corresponding with hundreds of his friends and acquaintances, to produce, in Paul Gray's terms, "a model of judicious, lively scholarship, an impressive translation of an enigma into a man."

One of Bair's intents, as written in her preface, was to offer a "factual foundation for all subsequent critical exegesis." Whether or not she succeeded in establishing such a groundwork has been debated by critics. Although her "diligent research" has been almost unanimously praised, some have contended her information is merely "hearsay" and "gossip." Others, like Kevin Flannery, believe "the book is fecund with fact, some important, some trivial yet memorable."

Much of Bair's focus on the mysterious Beckett surrounds his relationship with his mother. Benjamin DeMott wrote: "[Beckett's mother,] frozen in Anglo-Protestant propriety, was enraged, not disappointed, by her son's literary commitment. Hounding him ceaselessly in the name of respectability, she . . . occasionally feigned illness and breakdown with the intention of shaming him into repentance. . . . And the tormented relationship that developed never was worked through. . . . For decades he was racked, intermittently, by physical agony (cysts, boils, tremors), not to mention overwhelming assaults of guilt (his mother's single solace for his truancy). When the prime context of an alienated artist's anguish is familial, as in Beckett's case, the resonances are richly human; Ms. Bair's . . . [biography] does them proper justice."

Several critics have cited Bair's difficulty in establishing a relationship between Beckett's life and his works. John Leonard commented: "Miss Bair . . . lacks a critical theory or method to account for Beckett's art—unless that art is to be explained away as 'confession,' which is absurd, since such an explanation leaves out genius and humor, which means leaving out everything." Richard Ellmann voiced similar reservations: "Deirdre Bair prefers to consider that his fictional work is confessional, with *The Unnamable* as the ultimate confession. Yet the facts she has herself gathered defy this view." Conversely, William Kennedy felt Bair's biography revealed "that that old Bum Molloy, that nameless protagonist of *The Unnamable,* that sexless figure in *How It Is,* the Hamm and Clov of *Endgame,* and the Vladmir and Estragon of *Waiting for Godot* . . . are not only Beckett's psychic projections, but the full, transported actuality of this extraordinary man's extraordinary burden."

While objections to Bair's book range from her use of cliches to her presentation of "a simulacum," consistent praise has been given for at least letting us know "how it is with Samuel Beckett." *A Biography* might not "solve the 'mystery' of Beckett," but it is generally agreed that it shows "how rigorously and painfully Beckett earned his vision and with what heroism he prevailed over it."

BIOGRAPHICAL/CRITICAL SOURCES: Time, May 22, 1978; *New York Times,* May 30, 1978; *Newsweek,* June 5, 1978; *Book World,* June 11, 1978; *New York Review of Books,* June 15, 1978; *Atlantic,* July, 1978; *Psychology Today,* July, 1978; *New York Times Book Review,* July 2, 1978; *America,* July 15-22, 1978; *Saturday Review,* August, 1978; *New Republic,* September 1, 1978; *Christian Science Monitor,* September 18, 1978.*

* * *

BAKER, Allison
 See CRUMBAKER, Alice

* * *

BAKER, Nancy C(arolyn Moll) 1944-

PERSONAL: Born December 9, 1944, in Milwaukee, Wis.; daughter of Alvin Donald (a business executive) and Wilma (Robertson) Moll; married; children: Bradley. *Education:* University of Minnesota, B.A., 1965, M.A., 1974; University of Southern California, M.F.A., 1977. *Residence:* Santa Monica, Calif. *Agent:* Jean V. Naggar Literary Agency, 420 East 72nd St., New York, N.Y. 10021.

CAREER: St. Paul Dispatch, St. Paul, Minn., reporter, 1965-66; University of Minnesota, Minneapolis, editor in public relations, 1966-67; Northwest Airlines, Inc., St. Paul, editor in public relations, 1967-69; free lance writer, 1969-71; Control Data Corp., Edina, Minn., television scriptwriter, 1971-73; Metropolitan State University, St. Paul, director of communications, 1973-75; free-lance writer, 1975—; California State University, Northridge, assistant professor of journalism, 1977—.

WRITINGS: Babyselling: The Scandal of Black Market Adoption, Vanguard, 1978. Contributor to magazines and newspapers, including *Glamour, Parents Magazine,* and *Coronet.*

WORK IN PROGRESS: A book on mid-life career changers, for Vanguard; a book on displaced homemakers, for Anchor Books.

* * *

BALAGURA, Saul 1943-

PERSONAL: Born January 11, 1943, in Cali, Colombia; came to the United States in 1964, naturalized citizen, 1971; son of Isaac (in business) and Sara (Zighelboim) Balagura; married Ursula Loewy (an administrative secretary), August 15, 1964. *Education:* Universidad del Valle, M.D., 1964; Princeton University, Ph.D., 1967. *Religion:* Jewish. *Home:* 500 East 77th St., Apt. 1609, New York, N.Y. 10021. *Office:* Department of Neurosurgery, Albert Einstein College of Medicine, Bronx, N.Y. 10461.

CAREER: University of Chicago, Chicago, Ill., assistant professor of biopsychology, 1967-71; University of Masschusetts, Amherst, associate professor of biopsychology, 1971-74; State University of New York Downstate Medical Center, Brooklyn, resident in neurosurgery, 1974-76; Albert Einstein College of Medicine, Bronx, N.Y., resident in neurosurgery, 1976—. *Member:* American Physiological Society, Society for Neuroscience, American Psychological Association (fellow), American Medical Association.

WRITINGS: Hunger: A Biopsychological Analysis, Basic Books, 1973. Contributor of more than sixty articles to scientific journals.

WORK IN PROGRESS: Short Stories by My Father and I; Tales of Death and Life; research on the function of the brain.

SIDELIGHTS: Balagura comments: "As an author I search continually to communicate with the public. I have no difficulty publishing my scientific thoughts and work. On the other hand, I have had little success in publishing my literary work, consisting of *The Ivory Nest,* a novel about my experiences in the academic world, and *Ode to Ignorance,* a book of poems about poverty of wealth and thought."

* * *

BALLEM, John 1925-

PERSONAL: Born February 2, 1925, in New Glasgow, Nova Scotia, Canada; son of John Cedric and Flora Winnifred Ballem; married Grace Louise Flavelle, August 31, 1952; children: Flavelle Bishop, Mary Mercedes, John Flavelle. *Education:* Dalhousie University, B.A., 1946, M.A., 1948, LL.B., 1949; Harvard University, LL.M., 1950. *Religion:* Presbyterian. *Home:* 247 Eagle Ridge Dr. S.W., Calgary, Alberta, Canada T2V 2V6. *Office:* 3600 Scotia Centre, 700 Second St. S.W., Calgary, Alberta, Canada T2P 2W2.

CAREER: University of British Columbia, Vancouver, assistant professor of law, 1950-52; Imperial Oil Ltd., Toronto, Ontario, staff member of law department, 1952-56; Pacific Petroleums Ltd., Calgary, Alberta, general counsel, 1959-62; Ballem, McDill & MacInnes, Calgary, partner, 1962—. Appointed Queen's Counsel, 1966. *Military service:* Royal Navy, pilot in Fleet Air Arm, 1944-45. *Member:* Calgary Petroleum Club, Calgary Zoological Society (past president), Calgary Golf and Country Club. *Awards, honors:* Award from Canadian Petroleum Law Foundation, 1973, for *The Oil and Gas Lease in Canada.*

WRITINGS: The Devil's Lighter (novel), General Publishing, 1973; *The Oil and Gas Lease in Canada,* University of Toronto Press, 1973; *The Dirty Scenario* (novel), General Publishing, 1974; *The Judas Conspiracy* (novel), Musson, 1976; *The Moon Pool* (novel), McClelland & Stewart, 1978. Contributor to law journals and national magazines.

WORK IN PROGRESS: Novel with a Caribbean setting, tentatively entitled, *The Whistling Frog.*

SIDELIGHTS: John Ballem writes: "Much of my fiction writing has sprung from my work as an oil and gas lawyer. *The Devil's Lighter* deals with a wild well flaming out of control, which is something I have experienced in the course of my work; *The Moon Pool* involves native rights and drillships in the Arctic, both of which are matters I have dealt with as a lawyer."

* * *

BALSEIRO, Jose Agustin 1900-

PERSONAL: Born August 23, 1900, in Barceloneta, Puerto Rico; son of Rafael and Dolores (Ramos-Casellas) Balseiro; married Mercedes Pedreira, March 3, 1924; children: Yolanda Buchanon, Liliana Mees. *Education:* University of Puerto Rico, LL.B., 1921. *Address:* % E. A. Seeman Publishing, Box K, Miami, Fla. 33156.

CAREER: University of Illinois, Urbana, professor of Romance languages, 1930-33; University of Puerto Rico, Rio Piedras, visiting professor of Spanish literature, 1933-36; University of Illinois, professor of Romance languages, 1936-38; U.S. delegate to First International Congress on Teaching Iber-American Literature, 1938; U.S. representative to First International American Conference on Libraries and Publications, 1939; senator-at-large to Puerto Rican Senate, 1942-44; University of Miami, Coral Gables, Fla., professor of Hispanic literature, 1946-67; University of Arizona, Tucson, visiting professor of Spanish literature, 1967-72. Consultant on Hispanic literature at University of Miami. Summer lecturer, Northwestern University, 1937, Duke University, 1947, 1949, and 1950, Inter-American University, Puerto Rico, 1957-63, University of Mexico, 1959, University of North Carolina at Chapel Hill, 1973, Bryn Mawr College, 1973, Yale University, 1973, and Emory University, 1975. U.S. State Department, International Educational Exchange Program, lecturer in South America, 1954, in Spain and England, 1955-56, and in Puerto Rico, 1956; member of U.S. consultative committee of UNESCO, 1957; vice-president of Fourth Congress of the Academies of the Spanish Language, 1964.

MEMBER: International Institute of Ibero-American Literature (president, 1955-57), Modern Language Association of America (president of contemporary Spanish literature section, 1938), National Association of Authors and Journalists (honorary member, 1939), Spanish Royal Academy of Language (corresponding member), Spanish-American Academy of Sciences and Arts, Colombian Academy of Letters, Instituto Sarmiento of Argentina. *Awards, honors:* Spanish Royal Academy prize for best collection of essays of the year, 1925, for *El vigia,* Volume I; decorated commander of the Order of Queen Isabel of Spain; diploma of honor, Mexican Academy of Letters; honorary doctorate of letters, Polytechnic Institute of Puerto Rico; Litt.D., Inter-American University (Puerto Rico), 1950; Sc.D., Catholic University (Chile), 1954; L.H.D., Belmont Abbey, 1962; Letters D., Catholic University (Puerto Rico), 1972.

WRITINGS—In English: Eugenio Maria de Hostos: Hispanic America's Public Servant, [Coral Gables], 1949; *The Americas Look at Each Other,* translated by Muna Munoz Lee, University of Miami Press, 1969; (editor) *The Hispanic Presence in Florida,* E. A. Seeman, 1977.

Poetry: *Flores de primavera* (title means "Flowers of Spring"), [San Juan], 1919; *Las palomas de Eros* (title means "The Doves of Eros"), [Madrid], 1921; *Al rumor de la fuente* (title means "To the Murmur of the Fountain"), [San Juan], 1922; *La copa de Anacreonte* (title means "The Crown of Anacreon"), Editorial Mundo latino, 1924; *Musica cordial* (title means "Friendly Music), Editorial Lex, 1926; *Sonetos* (title means "Sonnets"), [San Juan], 1933; *La pureza cautiva* (title means "Captive Purity"), Editorial Lex (Havana), 1946; *Saudades de Puerto Rico* (title means "Homesickness for Puerto Rico"), Aguilar, 1957; *Visperas de sombras y otros poemas* (title means "Eves of Shadow and Other Poems"), Ediciones de Andre (Mexico), 1959.

Novels: *La maldecida* (title means "The Cursed Woman"), [Madrid], 1922; *La ruta eterna* (title means "The Eternal Way"), [Madrid], 1926; *En vela mientras el mundo duerme* (title means "Vigil While the World Sleeps"), Mnemosyne Press, 1969.

Other works: *El vigia* (title means "The Watchman), Volume I, Editorial Mundo latino (Madrid), 1925, Volume II, [Madrid], 1926, reprinted, Biblioteca de autores Puertorriquenas, 1956, Volume III, [San Juan], 1942; *Novelistas espanoles modernos* (title means "Modern Spanish Novelists"), Macmillan, 1933, reprinted, University of Puerto Rico, 1977; *El Quijote de la Espana contemporanea: Miguel de Unamuno* (title means "The Quixote of Contemporary Spain"), E. Gimenez, 1935; *Blasco Ibanez, Unamuno, Valle Inclan y Baroja, cuatro individualistas de Espana* (title means "Four Spanish Individualists"), University of North Carolina Press, 1949; *Mediciones fisicas: calculo de errores, approximaciones, metodos graficos* (title means "Physical Measurements: Calculation of Errors, Approximations, Graphic Methods"), Lebreria Machette (Buenos Aires), 1956; *Expresion de Hispanoamerica* (title means "Expression of Spanish America"), Instituto de Cultura Puertorriquena, Volume I, 1960, Volume II, 1963; *Seis estudios sobre Ruben Dario* (title means "Six Studies About Ruben Dario"), Editorial Gredos (Madrid), 1967.

Editor: (With J. Riis Owre, and others) Alejandro Casona, *La Barca sin pescador* (title means "The Boat Without a Fisherman"), Oxford University Press, 1955; (with Owre) Casona, *Corona de amor y muerte* (title means "Crown of Love and Death"), Oxford University Press, 1960; (with Eliana Suarez-Rivero) Casona, *El Cabellero de las espuelas de oro* (title means "The Cowboy of the Golden Spurs"), Oxford University Press, 1968.

Contributor to and editor of numerous Spanish language periodicals.

Also author of *El sveno de Manon* (novel), 1922.

SIDELIGHTS: Although trained for the law, a talented musician, and once asked to play professional baseball, Blaseiro set out at a young age to become a writer. While living in Spain, he was rewarded by the early publication of his first book of poems. Novels as well as works of criticism followed, and as his reputation grew, Balseiro's profession expanded to include the teaching of languages and literature. Eventually, he became known world-wide as a kind of cultural ambassador.

Since the 1930's, Balseiro has lectured on an international circuit. His topics have included the philosophies and biographies of poets, public leaders, artists, and musicians. His slant has always been the connections between Hispanic and American culture, and he once described his lectures and scholarly writings in this way: "Always I was trying to interpret the spirit of the U.S. to Spain and South America, and the spirit of the Hispanic world to the U.S."

From the beginning of his career, critics have acknowledged Balseiro's importance to peoples both within and without the Spanish-speaking world. In the 1920's, a writer for the *London Times* noted that "the originality of Senor Balseiro's criticism consists in the fact that it is both Spanish and international." Similarly, in the 1940's, the reviewer for the *South Atlantic Bulletin* remarked that Balseiro is not simply a "Spanish-American critic examining the works of Spanish writers; rather, he is an international scholar who knows no boundaries, and whose criterion is world literature."

During a lecture at the University of Miami in the 1950's, Balseiro explained the reason for his emphasis on internationalism. *Miami Herald* staff writer Sandy Flickner quotes him as saying: "The nearer we approach our neighbors by the disinterested paths of art, literature, scholarship, and open-hearted friendship, the sooner will we demolish the prejudices that hamper the constructive development of human nature." The university established the Jose A. Balseiro Award, an essay contest, in 1967.

Balseiro has kept alive his interest in music and some of his compositions have been performed at Carnegie Hall.

BIOGRAPHICAL/CRITICAL SOURCES: Miami Herald, April 29, 1974.*

*   *   *

BANIS, Victor J(erome)   1937-
(Jan Alexander)

PERSONAL: Born May 25, 1937, in Huntington County, Pa.; son of William (in construction) and Anna (Wing) Banis. *Education:* Attended Dayton Art Institute, 1959. *Politics:* "Register Republican, vote independent." *Religion:* "Religious Science." *Home and office address:* P.O. Box 4502, North Hollywood, Calif. 91607. *Agent:* Wieser & Wieser, Inc., Room 1402, 52 Vanderbilt Ave., New York, N.Y. 10017.

CAREER: Beerman's, Dayton, Ohio, in retail sales, 1956-57; Trotwood Trailers, Trotwood, Ohio, in travel trailer sales, 1958-60; writer, 1963—. President of Cross Sonnets, Inc. (literary service). Volunteer worker at Los Angeles Braille Institute.

WRITINGS: Men and Their Boys: The Homosexual Relationship Between Adult and Adolescent, Medco Books, 1966; *The Why Not* (novel), Greenleaf Classics, 1966; (editor and author of introduction) Prisoner X, *Prison Confidential,* Medco Books, 1969; *The Pussycat Man* (novel), Sherbourne, 1969; *Charms, Spells, and Curses for the Millions,* Sherbourne, 1970; *This Splendid Earth* (historical novel), St. Martin's, 1977; *The Sword and the Rose* (historical novel), Pyramid Publications, 1978.

Under pseudonym Jan Alexander; all suspense fiction: *Shadows,* Lancer Books, 1970; *The Wolves of Craywood,* Lancer Books, 1970; *Blood Moon,* Lancer Books, 1970; *White Jade,* Popular Library, 1971; *House of Fools,* Lancer Books, 1971; *The Second House,* Beagle Books, 1972; *House at Rose Point,* Avon, 1972; *The Devil's Dance,* Avon, 1972; *Moon Garden,* Popular Library, 1972; *The Glass House,* Popular Library, 1972; *The Glass Painting,* Popular Library, 1972; *The Girl Who Never Was,* Lancer Books, 1972; *The Bishop's Palace,* Popular Library, 1973;

The Jade Figurines, Curtis Books, 1973; *The Haunting of Helen Wren,* Pocket Books, 1975; *Blood Ruby,* Ballantine, 1975; *Darkwater,* Pocket Books, 1975; *The Lions Gate,* Berkley Medallion, 1976; *Green Willows,* Pocket Books, 1977.

WORK IN PROGRESS: A sequel to *This Splendid Earth;* a trilogy based on early California history.

SIDELIGHTS: Banis writes: "I am a professional story teller and a compulsive writer in the fortunate position of making money doing what I would be doing anyway. I suppose my chief motivation is to tell a good story as well as possible. I've spent a great deal of time coaching beginning writers and take pride in the fact that all of them went on to have their works published. I'm rather an old-fashioned writer, favoring well-structured plots and sound characterization, the latter being, in my opinion, the most important part of a fiction writer's craft. I believe strongly in practice; the more you write, the more you learn about writing.

"There are so many things I find interesting that it would hardly be practical to try to touch on them all; most of all, I find people infinitely interesting."

AVOCATIONAL INTERESTS: Reading, cooking.

*   *   *

BANNERMAN, Mark
See LEWING, Anthony Charles

*   *   *

BANNISTER, Pat
See DAVIS, Lou Ellen

*   *   *

BANTA, Martha   1928-

PERSONAL: Born May 11, 1928, in Muncie, Ind.; daughter of John Cullen (a merchant) and Irma (Purman) Banta. *Education:* Attended Western College, Oxford, Ohio, 1946-48; Indiana University, B.A. (high honors), 1950, Ph.D., 1964. *Residence:* Seattle, Wash. *Office:* Department of English, University of Washington, Seattle, Wash. 98195.

CAREER: L. S. Ayres, Indianapolis, Ind., copywriter, 1950-53; Hockaday Associates, New York City, copywriter and account executive, 1954-58; Batten, Barton, Durstine & Osborne, New York City, copywriter, 1958-59; *Harper's Bazaar,* New York City, copy editor, 1959-60; University of California, Santa Barbara, assistant professor of English, 1964-70; University of Washington, Seattle, associate professor, 1970-75, professor of English, 1975—. *Member:* Modern Language Association of America.

WRITINGS: Henry James and the Occult, Indiana University Press, 1972; *Failure and Success in America,* Princeton University Press, 1978. Contributor of numerous articles and reviews to academic journals.

WORK IN PROGRESS: Research on nineteenth-/and twentieth-century British literature, art history, history of science, and philosophy, with a book expected to result.

*   *   *

BANVILLE, Thomas G(eorge)   1924-

PERSONAL: Born June 7, 1924, in Brooklyn, N.Y.; son of Francis A. (a realtor) and Kathryn (a concert singer; maiden name Weigand) Banville; married Margaret Jacobs (a business manager), July 25, 1948. *Education:* California State University, Sacramento, B.A., 1963, M.A., 1966; National

University of Graduate Studies, Ph.D., 1974. *Home and office:* 2318 Homewood Way, Carmichael, Calif. 95608.

CAREER: Elementary school teacher in Carmichael, Calif., 1963-66; high school guidance consultant in Roseville, Calif., 1966-68; Washington Unified School District, West Sacramento, Calif., psychologist, 1968—, director of psychological and special services. Private practice in marriage and family counseling. *Military service:* U.S. Naval Reserve, active duty as aviation electronics technician, 1942-46. *Member:* Authors Guild, Sacramento Area School Psychologists Association (vice-president, 1970; president, 1971). *Awards, honors:* Distinguished achievement awards from Edpress, 1974, for a series of articles on communications and educational psychology, and 1975, for a series of articles on child growth and development.

WRITINGS: How to Listen, How to Be Heard, Nelson-Hall, 1978; *How to Get Your Child to Listen,* Condor Publishing, 1978; (contributor) John R. Hranitz and Ann Marie Noske, editors, *Working with the Young Child: A Text of Readings–II,* University Press of America, 1978.

Contributor to education journals and popular magazines, including *Family Digest, People,* and *Essence.*

WORK IN PROGRESS: A novel, tentatively entitled *The Seventh Incident.*

SIDELIGHTS: Banville writes: "There were two major influences in my life. The first was my family. I was born into a home in which literature was a part of daily life. I became a voracious reader at a very young age. The second great influence was my time in World War II. In spite of all the reading, I was an abysmally poor high school student. My experience in the Naval Reserve pointed out unmistakably that study was the sole key to the kinds of things I wanted to accomplish.

"Eventually I found my way into educational psychology. I also had a private practice in marriage and family counseling. In both areas I came to believe that all the problems I dealt with could be solved by improving communication skills.

"My first book is in the 'popular psychology' genre. It is interesting to the lay reader, but can also be used as a supplementary text for a college counseling course.

"I wanted parents to know how they could improve family relationships through better communication too. The second book came from that desire. What I hoped parents would learn is that in the final analysis, a child will do what he wants—he will listen to himself. All one can do is try to shape the kinds of messages he gets when he does listen to himself.

"Another concern I have is the poor job schools are doing in teaching children to communicate. There is a serious deficiency in the teaching of language. Before children can learn to read they have to learn to listen and talk. That isn't happening. In schools where there are concentrations of lower income families we find bilingual classes. Thus children who have poor skills in their native language are forced to learn a second one. So-called 'remedial reading' programs continue to proliferate in spite of their ineffectiveness and high cost."

*   *   *

BARCLAY, Hartley Wade 1903-1978

OBITUARY NOTICE: Born December 3, 1903, in Gladbrook, Iowa; died November 13, 1978, in Rye, N.Y. Manufacturing consultant, business writer, and author of technical books and articles. Wade founded the Management Research Institute in 1942, and was head of an industrial and aeronautical consulting firm. He was associated with several trade publications. Obituaries and other sources: *New York Times,* November 14, 1978; *Who's Who in America,* 40th edition, Marquis, 1978.

*   *   *

BARDIN, John Franklin 1916-
(Douglas Ashe, Gregory Tree)

PERSONAL: Born November 30, 1916, in Cincinnati, Ohio; son of Ernest Franklin (a merchant) and Mayrie Alberta Bardin; married Rhea Schooler Yalowich (divorced, 1964); married Phyllida Korman (an artist and writer), November 10, 1966; children: Judith Aycock, Franklin Clark. *Education:* Attended high school in Cincinnati, Ohio. *Politics:* Independent. *Religion:* None. *Residence:* New York, N.Y. *Agent:* Frank C. Bardin, 510-12 East Sixth St., New York, N.Y. 10009.

CAREER: Edwin Bird Wilson, Inc. (advertising agency), New York City, vice-president and member of board of directors, 1943-63; New School for Social Research, New York City, instructor at writers' workshop, 1961-66; *Coronet,* New York City, senior editor, 1968-72; *Today's Health,* Chicago, Ill., managing editor, 1972-73; American Bar Association, Chicago, Ill., managing editor of *Barrister* and *Learning and the Law,* 1973-74; free-lance writer, 1974—.

WRITINGS—Novels; under name John Franklin Bardin: *The Deadly Percheron,* Dodd, 1946; *The Last of Philip Banter,* Dodd, 1947; *Devil Take the Blue-Tail Fly,* Gollancz, 1948, Macfadden, 1967; *The Burning Glass,* Scribner, 1950; *Christmas Comes But Once a Year,* Scribner, 1953; *The John Franklin Bardin Omnibus* (contains his first three novels), Penguin, 1976; *Purloining Tiny,* Harper, 1978.

Under pseudonym Douglas Ashe: *A Shroud for Grandmama* (novel), Scribner, 1951 (published in England under pseudonym Gregory Tree), reprinted as *The Long-Street Legacy,* Paperback Library, 1970.

Novels; under pseudonym Gregory Tree: *The Case Against Myself,* Scribner, 1950; *The Case Against Butterfly,* Scribner, 1951; *So Young to Die,* Scribner, 1953.

WORK IN PROGRESS—Novels: *I Love You, Terribly,* a macabre love story; *The Eight Days of Merry; Seiglinde.*

SIDELIGHTS: Bardin comments: "There is only one motive for writing a novel: to be published and read. To me there is no distinction between the *mystery novel* and the novel, only between good books and bad books. A good book takes the reader into a new world of experience; it is an experiment. A bad book, unless the writing is inept, reinforces the intransigent attitude of the reader not to experiment with a new world. Since there are criminals and psychopaths and sociopaths in all my novels, they are in a way psychological thrillers.

"My first steady job was at a roller rink, where I was a ticket taker for four years. I believe that the social contact with thousands of people a night helped me to become a writer and possibly offset my lack of a college education."

*   *   *

BARDON, Edward J(ohn) 1933-

PERSONAL: Born May 19, 1933, in St. Paul, Minn.; son of Edward A. and Rosemarie (Kreyer) Bardon; married Jane

Scheer (a graphic designer), July 19, 1955; children: Athena, Lisa, Eric, Mark, Karl, Janie. *Education:* University of Minnesota, B.A. (summa cum laude), 1954, M.D., 1958. *Home:* 11 Pheasant Lane, St. Paul, Minn. 55110. *Office:* Student Health Service, University of Minnesota, Minneapolis, Minn. 55455.

CAREER: Veterans Administration Hospital, Minneapolis, Minn., psychiatry resident, 1958-62; University of Minnesota, Minneapolis, psychiatry resident, 1958-62, assistant professor of psychiatry, 1962—, assistant professor of psychiatry at Student Health Service, 1962—. Private practice of psychiatry in Minneapolis, 1962—. Consultant to U.S. Peace Corps and Hamm Memorial Psychiatric Clinic. *Member:* American Psychiatric Association, American Association of University Professors, Minnesota Psychiatric Association, Phi Beta Kappa.

WRITINGS: The Sexual Arena and Women's Liberation, Nelson-Hall, 1978. Contributor to medical journals.

WORK IN PROGRESS: "A book on how feminism in America is not fulfilling its inherent potential, but rather represents a victory for the male principle."

SIDELIGHTS: Bardon writes: "As a clinician, I spend many hours each week gaining a detailed understanding of individuals. This intimate knowledge of how people, within the context of a particular culture, meet or don't meet their basic human needs forms the cornerstone of my interest. Men and women have an amazing capacity to be led away from fulfillment by forces within a society. An understanding of these complicated pressures and expectations can help to gain control over one's own destiny.

"My goal as a writer is to produce entertaining works for the general audience which contain factual psychiatric knowledge on philosophic or controversial topics of current social interest.

"An undeveloped interest I have nourished is someday to explore the rich fantasy of psychiatric patients in a semi-fictionalized form."

*   *   *

BARKER, Larry L(ee) 1941-

PERSONAL: Born November 22, 1941, in Wilmington, Ohio; son of Milford (a teacher) and Ruth Maxine (a teacher) Barker; children: Theodore Allen, Robert Milford. *Education:* Ohio University, A.B., 1962, M.A., 1963, Ph.D., 1965. *Home:* 47 Ridgewood Village, Auburn, Ala. 36830. *Office:* Department of Speech Communication, Auburn University, Auburn, Ala. 36830.

CAREER: Southern Illinois University, Carbondale, assistant professor of speech, 1965-66; Purdue University, West Lafayette, Ind., assistant professor of speech, 1966-69; Florida State University, Tallahassee, associate professor, 1969-71, professor of communications, 1971-75; Auburn University, Auburn, Ala., alumni professor, 1975—. *Member:* International Communication Association, Speeech Communication Association of America, American Educational Research Association, American Psychological Association, Southern Speech Association, Tau Kappa Alpha, Phi Mu Alpha, Kappa Kappa Psi, Phi Delta Kappa.

WRITINGS: Speech: Interpersonal Communication, Chandler Publishing, 1967, revised edition, 1974; *Behavioral Objectives and Instruction,* Allyn & Bacon, 1970; *Listening Behavior,* Prentice-Hall, 1971; *Speech Communication Behavior: Perspectives and Principles,* Prentice-Hall, 1971; *Communication,* Prentice-Hall, 1978; *Groups in Process,* Prentice-Hall, 1978. Contributor to academic journals.

WORK IN PROGRESS: Research on nonverbal communication, interpersonal communication, and professional opportunities in the field of speech communication.

*   *   *

BARNABAS
See WEST, Charles Converse

*   *   *

BAROLSKY, Paul 1941-

PERSONAL: Born July 13, 1941, in Paterson, N.J.; son of Benjamin (a physician) and Eva (Kaiser) Barolsky; married Ruth Lassow, August 12, 1966; children: Deborah Eve, Daniel G. *Education:* Middlebury College, B.A., 1963; Harvard University, M.A., 1964, Ph.D., 1969. *Office:* Department of Art, University of Virginia, Fayerweather, Charlottesville, Va. 22903.

CAREER: Cornell University, Ithaca, N.Y., assistant professor of art history, 1968-69; University of Virginia, Charlottesville, associate professor of art, 1969—. *Member:* College Art Association of America, American Association of University Professors.

WRITINGS: Infinite Jest: Wit and Humor in Italian Renaissance Art, University of Missouri Press, 1978; *Daniele da Volterra: A Catalogue Raisonne,* Garland Publishing, 1979.

WORK IN PROGRESS: Research on Renaissance art and literature and on nineteenth-century art criticism.

SIDELIGHTS: Barolsky told *CA:* "*Infinite Jest* is the first general study of wit and humor in Italian Renaissance art. It is addressed to historians of art and literature and to non-specialists as well. The book treats satire, parody, irony, and caricature in the work of major artists such as Botticeli, Raphael, Michelangelo, and Titian and compares this humorous art to the comic or witty writings of the period by Aretino, Rabelais, Montaigne, and Shakespeare. As a polemic against the tendency of art historians to take an overly serious view of Renaissance art the book criticizes the exaggerated neoplatonic interpretations that modern scholars so often apply to Renaissance paintings. In addition, this study places emphasis on the erotic comedy in the nuptial art of the Renaissance.

"*Daniele de Volterra* is based on a doctoral dissertation. This study discusses the painting, sculpture, and drawings of the leading mannerist artist in Rome during the sixteenth century. The book includes an introductory essay surveying Daniele's artistic development and his relations to Michelangelo and mannerist art. The catalogue discusses a number of previously unpublished drawings by Daniele and analyzes in detail works by Daniele which have been little discussed in the previous scholarship."

*   *   *

BARRETT, Harold 1925-

PERSONAL: Born March 20, 1925, in Healdsburg, Calif.; son of Mathew Harold (a farmer) and Gladys (Parkerson) Barrett; married Carol Bliss, March 21, 1948; children: Joseph, Patrick, Edward, Lee, Jacob. *Education:* University of the Pacific, B.A., 1949, M.A., 1952; University of Oregon, Ph.D., 1962. *Politics:* Democrat. *Home:* 5126 Crane Ave., Castro Valley, Calif. 94546. *Office:* Department of Speech and Drama, California State University, Hayward, Calif. 94542.

CAREER: High school speech and English teacher in Lodi, Calif., 1950-54; Compton College, Compton, Calif., instructor in speech, 1954-59; University of Oregon, Eugene, instructor in speech, 1959-61; Southern Oregon College, Ashland, assistant professor of speech, 1961-63; California State University, Hayward, assistant professor, 1963-67, associate professor, 1967-72, professor of speech and rhetoric, 1972—. Director of Conference in Rhetorical Criticism. Has worked as farmer, longshoreman, and winery and lumberyard worker; interviewer for Gallup polls. *Military service:* U.S. Navy, Seabees, 1943-46. *Member:* Speech Communication Association of America, Western Speech Communication Association, United Professors of California, Pi Kappa Delta.

WRITINGS: Practical Methods in Speech, Holt, 1959, 4th edition published as *Practical Uses of Speech Communication,* 1977; (editor) *Rhetoric of the People,* Rodopi, 1974; *Daring to Be: Love and the Art of Rhetorical Intercourse,* Nelson-Hall, 1979. Contributor to speech journals.

WORK IN PROGRESS: Monograph on the Sophists in ancient Athens.

SIDELIGHTS: Barrett writes that his interests in the history and culture of Greece and Britain provide him with "numerous models to assist in understanding rhetorical interaction: What keeps people apart and how they discover ways of coming together."

AVOCATIONAL INTERESTS: Long-distance running, California wines, the historical, cultural, and democratic institutions of Greece and Britain.

* * *

BARRETT, James Lee 1929-

PERSONAL: Born November 19, 1929, in Charlotte, N.C. *Education:* Attended Anderson Junior College, Furman University, Penn State University, and Art Students League. *Address:* c/o Writers Guild of America, West, 8955 Beverly Blvd., Los Angeles, Calif. 90048.

CAREER: Screenwriter and journalist.

WRITINGS—Screenplays: "The D.I.," Warner Bros., 1957; "The Truth About Spring" (adapted from the novel by Henry de Vere Stacpoole, *Satan*), Universal, 1964; (with George Stevens) "The Greatest Story Ever Told," United Artists, 1965; "Shenandoah," Universal, 1965; "Bandolero!" (adapted from the story by Stanley L. Hough, "Mace"), Twentieth Century-Fox, 1968; "The Green Berets" (adapted from the novel by Robin Moore), Warner Bros., 1968; "The Undefeated," Twentieth Century-Fox, 1969; "Fools' Parade" (adapted from the novel by Davis Grubb), Columbia, 1971; "Something Big," National General Pictures, 1972. Also author of "tick . . . tick . . . tick," 1970, and "The Cheyenne Social Club," 1970.

* * *

BARRETT, Max
(Maye Barrett)

PERSONAL: Born in Sydney, Australia; son of Oliver John (an engineer) and Elsie (Liddle) Barrett. *Education:* Attended religious secondary school in East Melbourne, Victoria, Australia. *Home:* 26-A Hugh St., London SW1 V1RP, England. *Agent:* John Gibson Literary Agency, P.O. Box 173, London S.W.3, England.

CAREER: Actor on television, radio, and stage in Australia and England, 1946-56; theatrical manager, 1956-64; writer,

1966—. Art consultant on drawings of the "old masters." *Member:* Romantic Novelists Association.

WRITINGS—Romantic novels; all published in England under name Max Barrett and in the United States under pseudonym Maye Barrett: *Threat of Love,* John Gresham, 1967, Berkley, 1978; *The Changing Wind,* Hurst & Blackett, 1970, Berkley, 1978; *The Thorn in the Rose,* R. Hale, 1972, Berkley, 1978; *The House Across the Park,* R. Hale, 1977, published in the United States as *The Crystal Palace,* Berkley, 1978; *Wild Is the River,* Berkley, 1978; *Dark in the Morning,* Berkley, 1979. Contributor to *Woman's Realm* and *Woman's Mirror.*

SIDELIGHTS: Barrett writes: "'One man in a woman's world.' That is the tag the media have conveniently placed on me over the last ten years. I don't quite understand it—although I am told there are more female than male novelists writing my type of book—nor do I resent it. I suspect my writing has been influenced by women (it was writer Helga Moray who encouraged me to write my first novel) and I do consciously write with women in mind. My heroine is always the main character. Nevertheless, I do not write wholly romantic novels, which is something the media ignore, because if they didn't their tag wouldn't fit!"

BIOGRAPHICAL/CRITICAL SOURCES: "Television Profile," British Broadcasting Corp., August, 1970; *Sun,* November, 1972.

* * *

BARRETT, Maye
See BARRETT, Max

* * *

BARRIO-GARAY, Jose Luis 1932-

PERSONAL: Born March 17, 1932, in Zaragoza, Spain; son of Jose M. (in business) and Concepcion (Garay) Barrio; married Perry Lou Milner (a researcher), August 2, 1967. *Education:* Instituto de Ensenanza Media, B.S.L., 1949; University of Madrid, P.D., 1956; Columbia University, Ph.D., 1971. *Religion:* Roman Catholic. *Home:* 950 Woodhaven Court, London, Ontario, Canada N6H 4N5. *Office:* Department of Visual Arts, University of Western Ontario, London, Ontario, Canada N6A 5B7.

CAREER: University of Wisconsin, Milwaukee, assistant professor of art history, 1967-73; Ohio University, Athens, associate professor of art and director of School of Art, 1973-76; University of Western Ontario, London, professor of art history and head of department, 1976—, chairman of executive committee of McIntosh Gallery, 1978—. Member of advisory committee of London Regional Gallery, 1976—; co-chairman of Trisolini Gallery Committee, 1973-76; museum consultant.

MEMBER: International Association of Art Critics, University Art Association of Canada, Canadian Association of University Teachers, College Art Association of America, American Society for Hispanic Art Historical Studies, American Association of Teachers of Spanish and Portuguese, American Association of University Professors, Ontario Confederation of University Faculty Associations, Circulo de Bellas Artes de Madrid. *Awards, honors:* Traveling fellowships from city of Zaragoza, Spain, 1952, for Paris, and University of Madrid, 1956, for Rome; National Endowment for the Arts grant, summer, 1974.

WRITINGS: Tapies: Thirty-Three Years of His Work, Albright-Knox Art Gallery, 1977; *Jose Gutierrez-Solana:*

Paintings and Writings, Associated University Presses, 1978; *George Segal: Life and Work,* Ediciones Poligrafa, 1978. Author of exhibition catalogs. Foreign correspondent for *Goya.* Contributor of articles and reviews to journals of the arts. Editor of *Newsletter* of American Society for Hispanic Art Historical Studies, 1978—.

WORK IN PROGRESS: Another book on Jose Gutierrez-Solana.

SIDELIGHTS: Barrio-Garay comments: "From student days I have been interested in the arts and humanities and their interrelationships, and later became interested in interdisciplinary studies, including science and technology and the social sciences. As a result of these interests, I approach art history and criticism as broad areas of inquiry into cultural manifestations and history."

AVOCATIONAL INTERESTS: Travel (southern and central Europe, North Africa).

*   *   *

BARRON, Gloria Joan   1934-

PERSONAL: Born May 19, 1934, in Brooklyn, N.Y.; daughter of Maurice Lee and Irene (Levine) Barron. *Education:* Wellesley College, A.B., 1954; Columbia University, M.A., 1956, graduate study, 1958-59; further graduate study at University of Chicago, 1964-65; Tufts University, Ph.D., 1971. *Home:* 50 Park St., Brookline, Mass. 02146. *Office:* Department of History, Framingham State College, Framingham, Mass. 01701.

CAREER: Newton Junior College, Newtonville, Mass., registrar and teacher of history, 1956-58; high school history teacher at private school in Chestnut Hill, Mass., 1959--63; chairman of history department at Winthrop High School in Winthrop, Mass., 1963-64; U.S. Office of Education, Washington, D.C., education specialist, 1965-66; Framingham State College, Framingham, Mass., assistant professor of history, 1970—. *Member:* American Historical Association, Organization of American Historians. *Awards, honors:* American Association of University Women fellow, 1968-69.

WRITINGS: Leadership in Crisis: FDR and the Path to Intervention, Kennikat, 1973. Reviewer for *Journal of American History.*

SIDELIGHTS: Gloria Barron comments: "The years immediately preceding the entry of the United States into World War II were complicated and, of course, critical in the development of American foreign policy. I am pleased to feel I have made some contribution to the reassessment of this period with my book. In my research and teaching I continue to be concerned with the role of political leaders at vital turning points in American domestic affairs and foreign policy."

*   *   *

BARTEL, Pauline C(hristine)   1952-

PERSONAL: Born May 7, 1952, in Poughkeepsie, N.Y.; daughter of Joseph Anton (a butcher and cook) and Mary F. Bartel; married Hugh D. McAteer II (a state student loan control representative), August 16, 1975. *Education:* Albany Business College, A.A., 1972; student at College of St. Rose, 1979—. *Home:* 87-D Weis Rd., Albany, N.Y. 12208. *Office:* Edward A. Stasio, M.D., 662 Madison Ave., Albany, N.Y. 12208.

CAREER: Edward A. Stasio, M.D., Albany, N.Y., medical secretary, 1972—. Speaker at schools and workshops. *Member:* Society of Children's Book Writers.

WRITINGS: Biorhythm: Understanding Your Natural Ups and Downs (juvenile), F. Watts, 1978. Contributor of a story to *Villager* and about twenty-five puzzles to children's magazines and newspapers, including *Jack and Jill* and *Vine.*

WORK IN PROGRESS: Women Medical Pioneers; a book of Bible puzzles; a book of holiday puzzles; a mystery novel for teenagers; research for nonfiction books on the giraffe and on the cat family.

SIDELIGHTS: Pauline Bartel writes: "I have been interested in writing since high school, but did not seriously study the art until 1976, when I enrolled in a fiction workshop at State University of New York at Albany. As a result of the workshop, I had an adult short story, 'Premonition,' accepted for publication. I was pleased with my initial success and wanted to explore other areas of writing.

"I participated in a nonfiction workship. For a class assignment I submitted a list of five article ideas. The teacher thought one idea—biorhythm—lent itself more to a book than to a short article. He suggested I work up a nonfiction book proposal.

"At the time I received the contract for the book, I had been applying biorhythm to my life for more than a year. The biorhythm theory states that, from the moment of birth, each person is influenced by three separate rhythms: a twenty-three-day physical rhythm, a twenty-eight-day emotional rhythm, and a thirty-three-day intellectual rhythm. In each of the three rhythms, half of the days are plus days in which the individual is at his or her best. The remaining half of the days are minus days. During that portion of the cycle, efficiency is reduced. The theory worked so well for me that I followed the pattern of my biorhythms for the research and writing of the book. This method proved successful. I researched when my rhythms were in the minus phase. I, therefore, had a sense of accomplishment and avoided frustrating my creativity. I did the creative writing when my rhythms were in the plus phase. I was particularly conscious of the emotional rhythm which affects creativity. Writing was easier when I worked in harmony with my creative process.

"I enjoyed writing in the juvenile field so much that I enrolled in a third workshop, 'Writing for Children and Teenagers,' in 1978. I became aware of the market need for children's puzzles. I feel that children enjoy learning if the material is presented in an entertaining yet informative manner. That is the goal I strive for in creating my puzzles.

"I am earning my B.A. degree in English, and planning to continue my education beyond that degree. My long-range goals are to continue writing and eventually to teach creative writing at the college level. I was taught; therefore I will teach others. These goals, I feel, will make the best use of my talents.

"I consider the women's rights movement a vital issue today. As a woman, I want to be recognized as an individual with desires and goals of my own. These are exciting times for me because I have the freedom and opportunity to choose my life options."

Bartel added some words of advice to aspiring writers: "Read, study, and write. Read about writing technique in magazines and texts. Study the markets and the material other writers are producing. Write every day and constantly strive to improve your craft. And, no matter how discouraged you get or how many rejection slips you collect, don't give up."

AVOCATIONAL INTERESTS: Collecting Clark Gable and *Gone with the Wind* memorabilia, cooking and baking, needlepoint, music of the 1950's, old movies, reading, travel (especially Vermont; "I get such good feelings from the Green Mountain State that I'm sure I've lived a past life there"), psychic phenomena (especially ESP and psychometry), tennis, badminton, biking, volleyball, swimming.

*   *   *

BARTH, Richard 1943-

PERSONAL: Born March 27, 1943, in South Orange, N.J.; son of Otto (in business) and Felice (Lewin) Barth; married Ilene Kleinman (an editor), September 7, 1969. *Education:* Amherst College, B.A. (cum laude), 1964; Pratt Institute, M.F.A., 1973. *Agent:* Alphonso Tafoya, 655 Sixth Ave., New York, N.Y. 10010. *Office:* 655 Sixth Ave., New York, N.Y. 10010.

CAREER: Barth Smelting Corp. (scrap metal company), Newark, N.J., vice-president, 1964-71; goldsmith and sculptor, 1973—. Teacher at Fashion Institute of Technology, 1972—. Has had solo and group shows in the United States and England. *Military service:* U.S. Army Reserve, 1964-70.

WRITINGS: The Rag Bag Clan (novel), Dial, 1978.

WORK IN PROGRESS: A novel.

AVOCATIONAL INTERESTS: Travel (the South Pacific, Africa, India).

*   *   *

BARTON, John Bernard Adie 1928-

PERSONAL: Born November 26, 1928, in London, England; son of Harold Montagu and Joyce (Wale) Barton; married Anne Righter (a university lecturer), 1968. *Education:* King's College, Cambridge, B.A., 1951, M.A., 1955. *Home:* Hillborough Manor, Bidford-on-Avon, Warwickshire, England. *Agent:* Margaret Ramsay Ltd., 14-A Goodwin's Court, St. Martin's Lane, London WC2N 4LL, England. *Office:* Royal Shakespeare Theatre, Stratford-on-Avon, Warwickshire, England.

CAREER: University of California, Berkeley, lecturer in drama, 1953-54; Cambridge University, Cambridge, England, fellow of King's College, 1954-59, lay dean, 1956-59; Royal Shakespeare Company, Stratford-on-Avon, England, assistant director, 1959-64, associate director, 1964—, Stratford Company director, 1968-74.

WRITINGS: (Editor) *The Hollow Crown: An Entertainment by and About the Kings and Queens of England; Music, Poetry, Speeches, Letters, and Other Writings From the Chronicles, From Plays, and in the Monarch's Own Words, Also Music Concerning Them and by Them* (first produced in London, England, at Aldwych Theatre, March 19, 1961), Samuel French, 1962, new edition published as *The Hollow Crown: The Follies, Foibles, and Faces of the Kings and Queens of England,* Dial, 1971; (with Peter Hall) *The Wars of the Roses* (adapted from Shakespeare's plays), British Broadcasting Corp. (BBC), 1970.

SIDELIGHTS: The Hollow Crown was recorded by Argo in 1962. Barton also made "Le Morte d'Arthur," recorded by Argo in 1963. *Avocational interests:* Travel, chess.

*   *   *

BASSETT, James E(lias) 1912-1978

OBITUARY NOTICE—See index for *CA* sketch: Born October 18, 1912, in Glendale, Calif.; died September 26, 1978, in Malibu, Calif. Reporter and author of war novels. Bassett worked for forty-three years as a reporter and editor for the *Los Angeles Times* and the *Los Angeles Mirror.* In 1954 he was public relations director for the Republican National Committee, and he served in Richard Nixon's vice-presidential and presidential campaigns of 1952, 1956, and 1960. Bassett's best-known novel was *Harm's Way,* which was made into a motion picture. Obituaries and other sources: *Who's Who in America,* 40th edition, Marquis, 1978; *Washington Post,* September 29, 1978.

*   *   *

BASSETT, Ronald 1924-
(William Clive)

PERSONAL: Born April 10, 1924, in London, England; son of George William (a bank clerk) and Louisa (Vine) Bassett; married Ivy Owens, November 21, 1944 (deceased); married Sylvia Cruttwell (a wages clerk), November 6, 1956; children: Carole, Mark. *Education:* Attended high school in London, England. *Politics:* Conservative. *Religion:* Church of England. *Home:* 19 Binstead Dr., Blackwater, Camberley, Surrey, England. *Agent:* Brandt & Brandt, 101 Park Ave., New York, N.Y. 10017.

CAREER: British Army, rifleman and gunner in King's Royal Rifle Corps and Royal Artillery, 1938-40; Royal Navy, in communications branch, 1940-54, retiring as commander; Smith, Kline & French Laboratories Ltd., Welwyn Garden City, England, public relations officer, 1956-66; free-lance writer, 1966-69; E. R. Squibb & Sons, London, England, public relations officer, 1969-75; free-lance writer, 1975—.

MEMBER: Naval and Military Club, Picadilly Club. *Awards, honors*—Military: Distinguished Service Medal. Other: Silver medals from British Medical Association, 1964, for "Small Price to Pay," and 1965, for "Interuterine Contraception" and "Hypertension," gold medals, 1966, for "The Right to Work," and 1967, for "Seven Ages of Psychiatry"; Leopard d'Or from International Film Festival and British National Film Award, both 1965, both for "Triumph of Childbirth"; citations from American Medical Association and from Finnish Medical Association, both 1966, for services to postgraduate medical education.

WRITINGS—Naval books: *The Carthaginian,* Barrie & Jenkins, 1962; *The Pompeians,* Barrie & Jenkins, 1964; *Witchfinder General,* Barrie & Jenkins, 1966; *Amorous Trooper,* Barrie & Jenkins, 1967; *Rebecca's Brat,* Barrie & Jenkins, 1968; *Kill the Stuart,* Barrie & Jenkins, 1968; *The Tinfish Run,* Harper, 1977; *The Pierhead Jump,* Macmillan (England), 1978; *Neptune Landing,* Macmillan (England), 1978; *Equal Speed Charlie London,* Macmillan (England), 1979.

Military books; under pseudonym William Clive: *Dando on Delhi Ridge,* Putnam, 1971; *Dando and the Summer Palace,* Putnam, 1972; *The Tune That They Play,* Simon & Schuster, 1973; *Dando and the Mad Emperor,* Macmillan (England), 1974; *Blood of an Englishman,* Macmillan (England), 1975; *Fighting Mac,* Macmillan (England), 1977.

Films: "Emergency Ward Ten," Rediffusion TV, 1963; "Seven Ages," Smith, Kline & French, 1964; "Triumph of Childbirth," Smith; Kline & French, 1965; "The Right to Work," Smith, Kline & French, 1966; "Doctor on a Tightrope," Smith, Kline & French, 1966; "Stop the World I Want to Get off," Medical News, 1967; "Your Life in Their Hands," British Broadcasting Corporation, 1970. Also has created about forty single-reel films on medical and surgical techniques for professional distribution.

WORK IN PROGRESS: The Valiant Trumpeters, under pseudonym William Clive.

SIDELIGHTS: Bassett writes: "At the age of fourteen, during the Munich crisis, I falsified enlistment papers to become a rifleman in the King's Royal Rifle Corps. Following a period of active service, in which my battalion ceased to exist, I was transferred to the Royal Artillery, but was exposed and discharged, and my colonel noted: 'A good soldier. I am sorry to lose him.' Undismayed, I immediately joined the Royal Navy, in which I remained for fourteen years. I served as a radio operator on the cruiser *Norfolk* during the Bismarck action and for the North African landings, in a landing craft for the Normandy invasion, and later on an aircraft carrier in the Korean war zone. Most of my post-service life has been spent as a public relations writer for American pharmaceutical companies, the last of which made me redundant in 1975. I have been workless since, and the revenue from my books being inadequate for subsistence, I am supported by my wife, a wages clerk."

Bassett's book, *Witchfinder General,* was the basis of "The Conqueror Worm," a feature film starring Vincent Price, released by American International in 1968.

* * *

BATES, Jefferson D(avis) 1920-

PERSONAL: Born August 22, 1920, in Santa Fe, Mo.; son of Hugh Latham (a college professor) and Gladys Marian (Glascock) Bates; married Sarah Margaret Kemp (a hospital volunteer), October 21, 1949; children: William Loyd, Stacy Ellen. *Education:* Southeast Missouri State University, A.B. and B.S., 1942; Washington University, M.A., 1948; graduate study at American University, 1950. *Religion:* Presbyterian. *Home:* 4609 Village Dr., Fairfax, Va. 22030. *Office:* J. D. Bates Associates, Suite 79, 1121 Arlington Blvd., Arlington, Va. 22209.

CAREER: Teacher at high school in Clayton, Mo., 1948-49; U.S. Marine Corps, history division, Washington, D.C., military historian, 1950-51; U.S. Navy, bureau of personnel, Washington, D.C., education specialist, 1951-53; National Bureau of Standards, Washington, D.C., technical editor, 1953-55; U.S. Air Force, Washington, D.C., editorial director of effective writing program, 1955-57; U.S. Atomic Energy Commission, Washington, D.C., writer and editor, 1957-58; National Aeronautics and Space Administration (NASA), Washington, D.C., information specialist, 1959-61, communications bureau, writer and editor, 1962-66, public communications branch, chief, 1966-73; Reed Research, Inc., Washington, D.C., director of publications, 1961-62; Graduate School of the Agriculture Department, Washington, D.C., teacher of effective writing courses, 1969-72; J. D. Bates Associates, Arlington, Va., president, 1973—. *Military service:* U.S. Army, Signal Corps, 1942-47; became staff sergeant. U.S. Air National Guard, 1947-48; became second lieutenant. *Member:* Toastmasters International (vice-president of Fairfax chapter, 1976), National Association of Government Communicators, National Speakers Association, Authors Guild, Washington Area Writers, Washington Independent Writers, Writers Center, Sigma Tau Delta, Kappa Delta Pi, Potomac River Jazz Club. *Awards, honors:* Outstanding first-year speaker from Toastmasters International, Fairfax chapter, 1975; best club speaker of the year from Toastmasters International, Fairfax chapter, 1977; alumni merit award from Southeast Missouri State University, 1978.

WRITINGS: (Co-editor) *Presentation Books for the Second International Conference on Peaceful Uses of Atomic Energy, USAEC,* Addison-Wesley, 1958; *Writing With Precision: Effective Administrative Writing; A Systematic Approach,* Acropolis, 1977, published as *Writing With Precision: Zero Base Gobbledygook,* 1978. Chief ghostwriter at NASA headquarters during the Apollo and Skylab missions. Writer and editor of technical reports for government agencies.

WORK IN PROGRESS: The Professional Speechwriter (Backstage With a Washington Ghost); The Professional Editor, with James R. Atwell.

SIDELIGHTS: During his years as a ghostwriter, Jefferson Bates has written speeches and articles for many prominent men, including Presidents Kennedy and Johnson. He explains that these officials employ ghostwriters because "the demands of their positions don't allow them enough time to write their own speeches from scratch.

"The speech is not the ghostwriter's brainchild. The idea for the speech, the topic, the scope, the direction, are supplied by the person who will make the speech.

"What generally happens is that the ghostwriter and the speaker will get together for a preliminary conference. The writer might be required to supply input such as research, checking of technical data or statistics. On the basis of the discussion, a rough draft will be made. Later the two again collaborate on the finished speech or article. The ghostwriter doesn't just write a speech or article for the public figure."

While at NASA Bates wrote for every American astronaut who went to the moon, although he admits that he cannot take credit for Neil Armstrong's famous quotation "One small step for man; one giant leap for mankind."

In addition to speechwriting, Bates has dedicated his life to explaining "anything, no matter how technical, in clear straightforward language that anyone can understand." Part of his job at NASA involved describing the space missions in layman's language. He prepared a briefing for VIPs before the first moon landing, and wrote a glossary of space terms with simple definitions for the non-scientist.

After leaving NASA, Bates formed his own company, J. D. Bates Associates, and now he organizes writing seminars and classes where he teaches his pupils "professional tricks that help them to say what they mean and mean what they say."

BIOGRAPHICAL/CRITICAL SOURCES: Fairfax Journal, October 6, 1978.

* * *

BAUGHMAN, Urbanus E., Jr. 1905(?)-1978

OBITUARY NOTICE: Born c. 1905 in Camden, N.J.; died November 6, 1978, in Toms River, N.J. U.S. government employee and co-author of a book of memoirs. Baughman was Secret Service chief under Presidents Truman, Eisenhower, and Kennedy. Obituaries and other sources: *New York Times,* November 9, 1978.

* * *

BAXANDALL, Rosalyn Fraad 1939-

PERSONAL: Born June 12, 1939, in New York, N.Y.; daughter of Lewis Martin (a pediatrician) and Irma (a lawyer and art historian; maiden name, London) Fraad; married Lee Baxandall (a writer; divorced, 1978); children: Finney. *Education:* University of Wisconsin, Madison, B.A., 1961;

Columbia University, M.S.W., 1963. *Politics:* Socialist. *Home:* 2 Washington Square Village, New York, N.Y. 10012. *Office:* Department of American Studies, State University of New York College at Old Westbury, Box 210, Old Westbury, N.Y. 11568.

CAREER: Worked at Mobilization for Youth, 1963-67, and Hunter School of Social Work, 1967-70; State University of New York College at Old Westbury, assistant professor of women's studies, 1970—.

WRITINGS: America's Working Women, Random House, 1976.

WORK IN PROGRESS: Studying eroticism and feminism in the 1920's in the women of the Heterodoxy Club.

* * *

BAXTER, Valerie
See MEYNELL, Laurence Walter

* * *

BAY, Howard   1912-

PERSONAL: Born May 3, 1912, in Centralia, Wash.; son of William D. (a teacher) and Bertha A. (a teacher; maiden name, Jenkins) Bay; married Ruth Jonas, November 3, 1932; children: Ellen, Timothy. *Education:* Attended University of Washington, Seattle, 1928, Chappell School of Art, 1928, University of Colorado, 1929, Marshall College, 1929-30, Carnegie Institute of Technology (now Carnegie-Mellon University), 1930-31, and Westminster College, 1931-32; studied in Europe, 1939. *Home:* 345 West 58th St., New York, N.Y. 10019. *Office:* Department of Theater Arts, Brandeis University, Waltham, Mass. 02154.

CAREER: Set and lighting designer for Broadway plays, operas, touring companies, and film companies, 1933—. Producer and director for touring companies; art director for television productions. Professor at Brandeis University, 1965—, became Alan King Professor of Theatre Arts, head of department, 1966-69, and director of stage plays. Instructor at University of Michigan, summer, 1941; guest lecturer at Purdue University, 1962; Andrew W. Mellon guest director at Carnegie Institute of Technology (now Carnegie-Mellon University), 1963; lecturer at University of Oregon, 1963; director, designer, and instructor at Ohio University, 1964; visiting professor at Yale University, 1966-67; also taught at Cooper-Hewitt Museum. Member of national advisory board of International Theatre Institute.

MEMBER: United Scenic Artists (president, 1940-46, 1952-63), National Society of Interior Designers (member of board of directors, 1960-62), Society of Motion Picture Art Directors, Players Club. *Awards, honors:* Guggenheim fellowship, 1939-40; won New York Drama Critics Poll in *Variety,* 1942, for sets in "Brooklyn, U.S.A."; Donaldson Awards, 1944, for sets and lighting in "Carmen Jones," and 1945, for "Up in Central Park"; Antoinette Perry Awards (Tonys) from League of New York Theaters and Producers, 1960, for sets and lighting in "Toys in the Attic," and 1966, for "Man of La Mancha"; Maharam Award, 1966, for sets and lighting in "Man of La Mancha."

WRITINGS: Stage Design, Drama Book Specialists, 1974. Contributor to books, including *The Navy on Stage,* 1945, *Contemporary Stage Design, U.S.A.,* and *Scene Design for Stage and Screen,* 1961. Contributor to *Encyclopaedia Britannica.*

SIDELIGHTS: Bay's career in set and lighting design began in 1933 and gained momentum with a Works Progress Administration project at the Federal Theater in New York City in 1936. He stayed with the project through 1939, but began working on Broadway productions as early as 1937. His work includes designs for "Carmen Jones," "Show Boat," "The Would-Be Gentleman," "Come Back, Little Sheba," "Finian's Rainbow," "Pal Joey," "Music Man," and "Man of La Mancha."

Active off-Broadway as well, Bay's designs have been used for operas at Carnegie Hall, films for Universal-International Pictures, television productions, including "The Fred Waring Show," "Somerset Maugham Theatre," Hallmark's "Peer Gynt," "Mr. Broadway," and "The Pueblo Incident," a U.S. Department of Agriculture touring production, and a United Service Organizations tour.

* * *

BAYLOR, Byrd   1924-
(Byrd Baylor Schweitzer)

PERSONAL: Born March 28, 1924, in San Antonio, Tex. *Education:* Attended University of Arizona. *Residence:* Tucson, Ariz.; and New Mexico.

CAREER: Writer. Worked as a reporter for an Arizona newspaper. Former executive secretary for the Association for Papago Affairs. *Awards, honors:* Caldecott Medal from the American Library Association, 1973, for *When Clay Sings,* 1976, for *The Desert Is Theirs,* and for *Hawk, I'm Your Brother;* Catlin Peace Pipe Award, 1974, for *They Put on Masks;* Brooklyn art books for children citation, 1977, for *The Desert Is Theirs.*

WRITINGS—All for children, except as noted: (Under pseudonym Byrd Baylor Schweitzer) *Amigo,* illustrations by Garth Williams, Macmillan, 1963; (under Schweitzer pseudonym) *One Small Blue Bead,* illustrations by Symeon Shimin, Macmillan, 1965; (under Schweitzer pseudonym) *The Chinese Bug,* illustrations by Beatrice Darwin, Houghton, 1968; (under Schweitzer pseudonym) *The Man Who Talked to a Tree,* illustrations by Shimin, Dutton, 1968; *Before You Came This Way,* illustrations by Tom Bahti, Dutton, 1969; *Plink, Plink, Plink,* illustrations by James Marshall, Houghton, 1971; *Coyote Cry,* illustrations by Shimin, Lothrop, 1972; *When Clay Sings,* illustrations by Bahti, Scribner, 1972; *Sometimes I Dance Mountains,* illustrations by Ken Longtemps, photographs by Bill Sears, Scribner, 1973.

Everybody Needs a Rock, illustrations by Peter Parnell, Scribner, 1974; *They Put on Masks,* illustrations by Jerry Ingram, Scribner, 1974; *The Desert Is Theirs,* illustrations by Parnell, Scribner, 1975; (editor) *And It Is Still That Way: Legends Told by Arizona Indian Children,* Scribner, 1976; *We Walk in Sandy Places,* photographs by Marilyn Schweitzer, Scribner, 1976; *Hawk, I'm Your Brother,* illustrations by Parnell, Scribner, 1976; *Guess Who My Favorite Person Is,* illustrations by Robert Andrew Parker, Scribner, 1977; (for adults) *Yes Is Better Than No,* Scribner, 1977; *The Other Way to Listen,* Scribner, 1978; *The Way to Start a Day,* Scribner, 1978.

Contributor to *Redbook* and *Arizona Quarterly.*

SIDELIGHTS: Baylor grew up in the deserts of America's Southwest and spent many of her childhood summers in Mexico. Her familiarity with the area resulted in a variety of books for children. In *Before You Came This Way,* Baylor described what life in the southwestern canyons might have been like in the prehistoric ages. "It is not only the arts of brush and word that in this book evoke the sense of the past; it is above all the precision with which the authors have understood the unvoiced question with which children approach such novelty. . . . The explicit inspiration for the work is the American Southwest, but its impact is universal and intense,'' wrote a reviewer for *Scientific American*. ''The entire book is infused with a sense of wonder and quiet reverence. . . . Evocative and poetic, a distinguished book,'' Zena Sutherland commented.

BIOGRAPHICAL/CRITICAL SOURCES: Saturday Review, November 8, 1969; *Scientific American*, December, 1969; *New York Times Book Review*, November 13, 1977; *Children's Literature Review*, Gale, Volume 3, 1978.

* * *

BAZIN, Herve
  See HERVE-BAZIN, Jean Pierre Marie

* * *

BEARD, James (Andrews) 1903-

PERSONAL: Born May 5, 1903, in Portland, Ore.; son of Jonathan A. (a city official) and Mary Elizabeth (a hotel owner; maiden name, Jones) Beard. *Education:* Attended Reed College, 1920-21, University of Washington, Seattle, 1931, and Carnegie Institute of Technology (now Carnegie-Mellon University), 1931-32. *Address:* c/o Alfred A. Knopf, Inc., 201 East 50th St., New York, N.Y. 10022.

CAREER: Stage actor in New York City, appearing in productions of ''Cyrano de Bergerac'' and ''Othello,'' 1924-25; radio actor and announcer in food commercials in Portland, Ore., and San Francisco, Calif., 1927-32; private teacher of cooking in Portland, 1932-37; teacher of English and French at country day school in New Jersey, 1938; Hors d'Oeuvre, Inc. (catering business), New York City, co-owner, 1938-42; dairy and vegetable farmer in Reading, Pa., 1943; United Seaman's Service, director of clubs in Puerto Rico, Rio de Janerio, Cristobal, Naples, and Marseille, 1943-46; featured guest on television food programs, including ''Elsie Presents,'' 1946-55; lecturer and cooking demonstrator, 1949—; James Beard Cooking Classes, New York City, proprietor and teacher, 1955—; food consultant, 1965—. *Military service:* U.S. Army, 1942-43; served as cryptographer. *Awards, honors:* D.H.L. from Reed College, 1976.

WRITINGS: Hors d'Oeuvre and Canapes: With a Key to the Cocktail Party, Barrows, 1940, revised edition, 1963; *Cook It Outdoors*, Barrows, 1941; *Fowl and Game Cookery*, Barrows, 1944; *The Fireside Cookbook: A Complete Guide to Fine Cooking for Beginner and Expert* (illustrated), Simon & Schuster, 1949.

(With Alexander Watt) *Paris Cuisine* (illustrated), Little, Brown, 1952; *The Complete Book of Barbeque and Rotisserie Cooking* (illustrated), Bobbs-Merrill, 1954 (published in England as *Jim Beard's Complete Book of Barbeque and Rotisserie Cooking*, Maco Magazine Corp.); *Complete Book for Entertaining* (illustrated), Bobbs-Merrill, 1954; *Fish Cookery* (illustrated), Little, Brown, 1954 (published in England as *James Beard's Fish Cookery*, Faber, 1955); (with Sam Aaron) *How to Eat Better for Less Money*, Appleton, 1954, revised edition, Simon & Schuster, 1970; *The Casserole Cookbook*, Bobbs-Merrill, 1955; (with Helen Evans Brown) *The Complete Book of Outdoor Cookery*, Doubleday, 1955; (editor) Patrick G. Duffy, *Official Mixer's Manual*, Doubleday, 1956; *New Barbeque Cookbook*, Random House, 1958; (contributor) *House and Garden Cookbook*, Simon & Schuster, 1958; (with Isabel E. Callvert) *The James Beard Cookbook*, Dell, 1959, illustrated edition, Dutton, 1961, revised edition, 1970.

Treasury of Outdoor Cooking (illustrated), Golden Press, 1960; *Delights and Prejudices* (autobiographical), Atheneum, 1964; *James Beard's Menus for Entertaining*, Delacorte, 1965; *James Beard's Party Book*, Maco Magazine Corp., 1965; *Jim Beard's Barbeque Cookbook*, Maco Magazine Corp., 1966; *James Beard's Barbecue Cookbook: Over 200 Recipes for Every Taste, From Appetizers to Desserts*, Maco Publishing, 1967; *Casserole Cookbook*, Maco Publishing, 1968.

(With Gino P. Cofacci) *How to Eat (and Drink) Your Way Through a French (or Italian) Menu*, Atheneum, 1971; (consultant) Charlotte Adams, *The Four Seasons Cookbook*, Holt, 1971; *James Beard's American Cookery* (illustrated), Little, Brown, 1972; *Beard on Bread* (illustrated), Knopf, 1973; *Beard on Food*, Knopf, 1974; *The Best of Beard: Great Recipes From a Great Cook*, Western Publishing, 1974; (with others) *Great Cooks Cookbook*, Doubleday, 1974; *Penny-Wise Perfect Dinners* (illustrated), Doubleday, 1975; (editor with others, author of introduction, and contributor) *The Cooks' Catalogue: A Critical Selection of the Best, the Necessary, and the Special in Kitchen Equipment and Utensils* (illustrated), Harper, 1975; *James Beard's New Fish Cookery*, Little, Brown, 1976; (with others) *The International Cook's Catalogue* (illustrated), Random House, 1977; (with others) *The Great Cooks' Library*, separate volumes: *Breads, Clay Cookery, Crepes and Souffles, Fish Cookery, Salads*, and *Woks, Steamers, and Firepots*, Random House, 1977; *James Beard's Theory and Practice of Good Cooking*, Knopf, 1977. Also author, with Patrick G. Duffy, of *Standard Bartender's Guide*, Pocket Books.

Author of food columns for the Washington Star Syndicate, and in *House and Garden* and other magazines. Contributor of articles to *Harper's Bazaar, Vogue, Women's Day, Gourmet*, and other periodicals.

WORK IN PROGRESS: A companion volume to *James Beard's Theory and Practice of Good Cooking*.

SIDELIGHTS: Although he never studied cooking formally, James Beard is considered by many to be the foremost authority on American cooking and on food in general. He has produced numerous books on gastronomic subjects, ranging from barbeques and casseroles to French and Italian cuisines. Beard's cookbooks are unique in that they are not just collections of favorite recipes. He is also interested in the history of food and its preparation and includes sections devoted to these subjects in his books.

Beard's interest in cooking developed at an early age, largely as a result of his mother's expertise as a cook. A former hotel owner, Mrs. Beard supervised the family kitchen in a competent, businesslike manner. During the summers of his boyhood, the Beard family moved to the beach, where Mrs. Beard often cooked for the family and friends over driftwood fires. Outdoor cooking remains a favorite with Beard to this day, along with what has been called ''a passion for anything cold.''

In an article for *Newsweek*, Mary Rourke labeled Beard ''America's most sensuous cook.'' She went on to report that ''even his critics say he has more of a feel for food than Craig Claiborne or Julia Child. His patriotic passion for indigenous cooking has made him the acknowledged authority on American cuisine, and he promotes it like a proud grandparent.'' Beard's hearty defense of American cooking heritage is viewed with dismay by many who feel that American cookery is somewhat inferior to the European cuisines. Despite this opposition, Beard has been able to focus attention on simple home cooking in an era in which ''gourmet'' cooking is enjoying enormous popularity.

In his introduction to the revised edition of *How to Eat Better for Less Money*, Beard wrote: "A much misunderstood and misinterpreted word [is] 'gourmet.' It does not mean rich dishes from *haute cuisine*, Actually, the word can be applied to the simplest of food—nothing more than a potato cooked to the point at which it burst its tight skin and shows its snowy interior. It is not the basic cost of the food but the care with which it is selected and prepared that makes it gourmet rather than pedestrian." On another occasion, Beard commented, "I don't like gourmet cooking or 'this' cooking or 'that' cooking. I like *good* cooking."

Beard is always experimenting with different tastes and methods of food preparation. If some of his inventions and methods are unorthodox, Beard does not apologize. He urges cooks to make use of some convenience foods and new appliances, and publicly comes out in favor of the American hamburger, regarding it as the best in the world.

As an arbiter of tastes in food, Beard has been accused of helping to shape American cooking and eating habits without regard to nutritional considerations. James Hess, one of Beard's few critics, remarked, "He even admits he eats marshmallows." Beard himself admits that the menus he plans for himself "would shock people with an Edwardian background, the seven-course-dinner set—and the nutrition experts as well."

In the introduction to his popular book *Beard on Bread*, Beard discusses nutrition with regard to bread, which he considers "the most fundamentally satisfying of all foods." Of most breads available in markets, Beard says, "We are offered spongy, plasticised, tasteless breads, presliced, doctored with nutrients and preservatives, and with about as much gastronomic importance as cotton wool." He goes on to caution: "One doubtful fashion in breadmaking today . . . is the tendency to acquire as many different flours and meals as can be found and incorporate them all into a single loaf, without thought for texture, for crumb, or for any of the other attributes by which a fine loaf is judged. . . . The coarser it is, the healthier, some people think. To my mind, not only is this folly, but the result is also quite indigestible." Beard continues: "The irony of the health trend is that many of the coarse flours and meals found on the market, particularly in health food stores, are often quite dirty and, if anything, a risk to one's health."

American Cookery has been hailed as Beard's magnum opus, a masterwork, and as the authoritative sourcebook of American cuisine. *American Cookery* is not just a collection of favorite recipes. It is, in addition, a historical account of American food, with recipes gathered from old sources dating back to pioneering days. One reviewer noted that Beard discusses "the history of American food, its ties to other countries, the ways immigrants adapted their cooking to the very different resources of the new world, . . . the influence of social conditions, [and] in short the emergence of an American way of cooking."

William Rice notes that "James Beard's life-long examination of American cookery . . . has left no crumb unturned or untasted." He adds that "with the publication of . . . *American Cookery*, he has become a historian. . . . The book will surely stand as his chef d'oeuvre and should take a place on the narrow shelf reserved for major American culinary literature. . . . It is handsome enough for the coffee table, interesting enough to be bedtime reading and more than practical enough to be an asset in the kitchen."

Commenting on the historical aspect of *American Cookery*, William Rice continues: "Nostalgia is to be found along with

history as Beard recalls his early birthday cakes or baked apples served on the Union Pacific 'in the days when railroads catered to the public.' It is this marvelously personal point of view that transforms Beard's mosaic of American cookery from a worthy book of recipes into an exceedingly valuable historical record."

AVOCATIONAL INTERESTS: Travel, music, swimming, theatre.

BIOGRAPHICAL/CRITICAL SOURCES: New York Times, January 14, 1960; James Beard, *Delights and Prejudices,* Atheneum, 1964; *Newsweek,* January 13, 1969, April 11, 1977; *Redbook,* October, 1970; *Washington Post,* May 6, 1972; *Life,* June 16, 1972; *House and Garden,* February, 1977.*

* * *

BEATON, Cecil (Walter Hardy) 1904-

PERSONAL: Born January 14, 1904, in London, England; son of Ernest Walter Hardy (a timber merchant) and Esther (Sisson) Beaton. *Education:* Attended St. John's College, Cambridge, 1921-25. *Religion:* Church of England. *Home:* Reddish House, Broadchalke, Salisbury, Wiltshire, England. *Agent:* Rupert Crew Ltd., King's Mews, Gray's Inn Rd., London W.C.1, England.

CAREER: Worked as a clerk and as a typist before becoming a photographer in the late 1920's; photographer to British Royal Family, 1939—. Has also worked variously, and extensively, as an artist, writer, stage designer, and as a costume designer for theatre and films. *Military service:* British Ministry of Information, 1939-45, official photographer in all theatres of war. *Awards, honors:* Antoinette Perry (Tony) Award for costume design, 1956, for "My Fair Lady," and 1970, for "Coco"; Motion Picture Academy Award for costume design, 1958, for "Gigi," for set and costume design, 1964, for "My Fair Lady"; Commander of the Order of the British Empire, 1957; Legion d'Honneur, 1960; created Knight of the Order of the British Empire, 1972.

WRITINGS: Cecil Beaton's Scrapbook, Scribner, 1937; *Cecil Beaton's New York,* Lippincott, 1938 (revised edition published in England as *Portrait of New York,* Batsford, 1948); (by Baroness von Bulop as told to Beaton) *My Royal Past,* Batsford, 1939, revised edition, John Day, 1960; *Air of Glory* (wartime scrapbook), Her Majesty's Stationery Office, 1941; *Time Exposure,* Batsford, 1941; *Winged Squadrons,* Hutchinson, 1942; *Near East,* Batsford, 1943; *British Photographers,* Collins, 1944; *Far East,* Batsford, 1945; *Ashcombe,* Batsford, 1949.

Ballet, Doubleday, 1951; *Photobiography* (autobiographical), Doubleday, 1951; (with Kenneth Tynan) *Persona Grata,* Wingate, 1953, Putnam, 1954; *The Glass of Fashion,* Doubleday, 1954; *It Gives Me Great Pleasure,* Weidenfeld & Nicolson, 1955, published as *I Take Great Pleasure,* John Day, 1956; *The Face of the World,* John Day, 1957; *Japanese,* John Day, 1959; *The Wandering Years* (own diaries, 1922-39), Weidenfeld & Nicolson, 1961, Little, Brown, 1962; *Quail in Aspic* (biography of Count Charles Korsetz as tape-recorded to Cecil Beaton), Weidenfeld & Nicolson, 1962, Bobbs-Merrill, 1963; *Cecil Beaton's Fair Lady,* Holt, 1964; *The Years Between* (diaries, 1939-44), Holt, 1965.

My Bolivian Aunt (memoir), Weidenfeld & Nicolson, 1971; *Cecil Beaton: Memories of the 40's* (diaries, 1944-48) McGraw-Hill, 1972 (published in England as *The Happy Years,* Weidenfeld & Nicolson, 1972); *The Strenuous Years* (diaries, 1948-55), Weidenfeld & Nicolson, 1973; (with Gail

Buckland) *The Magic Image: The Genius of Photography From 1839 to the Present Day,* Little, Brown, 1975; *The Restless Years* (diaries, 1955-63), Weidenfeld & Nicolson, 1976; *The Parting Years* (diaries, 1963-74), Weidenfeld & Nicolson, 1978.

Books of photographs: *The Book of Beauty,* Duckworth, 1930; *History Under Fire,* Batsford, 1941; *Chinese Album,* Batsford, 1946; *Indian Album,* Batsford, 1946; *Royal Portraits,* Weidenfeld & Nicolson, 1963; *Beaton Portraits,* Her Majesty's Stationery Office, 1968; *The Best of Beaton,* Macmillan, 1968; *The Photographs of Sir Cecil Beaton,* York, 1973; (contributor of drawings) C. Z. Guest, *First Garden,* Putnam, 1976; (contributor) Colin Ford, editor, *Happy and Glorious: 130 Years of Royal Photographs,* Macmillan, 1977 (published in England as *Happy and Glorious: Six Reigns of Royal Photography,* Angus & Robertson, 1977).

Plays: "The Gainsborough Girls" (three-act), first produced in Brighton, England, at Theatre Royal, 1951.

SIDELIGHTS: "In choosing me to take her photographs," Beaton once wrote, "the Queen [Mother] made a daring innovation." Innovative, at least, is the multi-talented Beaton, whose unconventional photos of such personalities as Edith Sitwell, Greta Garbo, and the Duchess of Windsor brought him international attention in the 1930's. Yet his photographs exemplify only a fraction of his achievements. In addition to photographic exhibits at the Cooling Gallery (London, 1930) and the National Portrait Gallery (London, 1968), he has had a costume exhibit at the Victoria and Albert Museum (London, 1971), and painting and stage design exhibits at the Redfern Gallery (London, 1936, 1958, 1965), the Sagittarius Gallery (New York, 1956), and the Lefevre Gallery (London, 1966).

His many writings are highlighted by the six autobiographical books written from his lifelong diaries. George Cloyne wrote of the first, *The Wandering Years:* "The interest in his journal . . . lies in his ability to convey, beyond the glitter of a legendary career, the flavor of a genuine personality. . . . He noticed everything. That is what made him dangerous. Not a smut on the nose, not a crumb on the waistcoat escaped him. And if his photographs seem often charmingly romantic, his prose portraits are regularly needle-sharp." The latest in the series, *The Parting Years,* appeared in 1978.

AVOCATIONAL INTERESTS: Scrapbooks, decoration, traveling, gardening, collecting modern paintings.

BIOGRAPHICAL/CRITICAL SOURCES—All by Cecil Beaton: *Photobiography,* Doubleday, 1951; *The Wandering Years,* Weidenfeld & Nicolson, 1961, Little, Brown, 1962; *The Years Between,* Holt, 1965; *Memories of the 40's,* McGraw-Hill, 1972 (published in England as *The Happy Years,* Weidenfeld & Nicolson, 1972); *The Strenuous Years,* Weidenfeld & Nicolson, 1973; *The Restless Years,* Weidenfeld & Nicolson, 1976; *The Parting Years,* Weidenfeld & Nicolson, 1978.

Other sources: *Herald Tribune Book Review,* January 14, 1962; *New York Times,* December 23, 1971; Charles Spencer, *Cecil Beaton Stage and Film Designs,* St. Martin's, 1975.

* * *

BEATTIE, Ann 1947-

PERSONAL: Born September 8, 1947, in Washington, D.C.; daughter of James A. and Charlotte (Crosby) Beattie; married David Gates (a psychiatrist), 1972. *Education:* American University, B.A., 1969; University of Connecticut, M.A., 1970, further graduate study, 1970-72. *Address:* 279 Block Rock Tpke. RD1, West Redding, Conn. 06896. *Agent:* Lynn Nesbit, International Creative, Management, 40 West 57th St., New York, N.Y. 10019.

CAREER: Writer. University of Virginia, Charlottesville, visiting writer and lecturer, 1975-77; Harvard University, Cambridge, Mass., Briggs-Copeland Lecturer in English, 1977-78. *Awards, honors:* Guggenheim fellowship, 1978.

WRITINGS: Distortions (short stories), Doubleday, 1976; *Chilly Scenes of Winter,* Doubleday, 1976; *Secrets and Surprises* (short stories), Random House, 1979. Contributor of numerous short stories to *New Yorker.*

WORK IN PROGRESS: An untitled novel.

SIDELIGHTS: Beattie's novel, *Chilly Scenes of Winter,* is concerned with those people who came of age in the 1960's and find themselves lost and disillusioned in the 1970's. In an interview with Bob Miner Beattie said: "I *was* going out of my way in the novel to say something about the '60s having passed. It just seems to me to be an attitude that most of my friends and most of the people I know have. They all feel sort of let down, either by not having involved themselves more in the 60s now that the '70s are so dreadful, or else by having involved themselves to no avail. Most of the people I know are let down—they feel cheated—and these are the people I am writing about."

Critic Sheila Weller wrote that she had been waiting for a fictional account of the "turn-of-the-decade hero," and applauded Beattie's depiction of the novel's protagonist, Charles, which was accomplished with "sublime wit and humanity." Weller continued: ". . . Beattie has written a very sophisticated valentine to those young men who happened upon adulthood at a time when Love was all over postage stamps and placards and rock stations but was just about to be withdrawn by the culture, the economy, and the women they had innocently come to take for granted." David Thorburn also complimented Beattie on her portrait of Charles. He commented: "The hero himself is wonderfully alive: a gentle bewildered man, extravagantly loyal to old friends and to the songs of the sixties, drifting through a final nostalgia for the mythologies of adversary selfhood he absorbed in college and toward an embarrassed recognition of his hunger for such ordinary adventures as marriage and fatherhood. The unillusioned tenderness that informs Beattie's portrait of her central character is a rare act of intelligence and mimetic art."

But Beattie does not allow her characters to wallow in the decade's faded glory, as many of her contemporaries have done. As John Romano wrote: "She conveys adroitly the sensibility of After-the-Fall, without making fictive claims for the heights from which we fell. The Golden Age mythology and its attendant rhetoric will inevitably attach, for a while, to talk about the 60's. This represents, of course, a historical distortion, matched in its badness of fit only by the myth that the New Left was the Antichrist. Beattie's presentation of Charles's nostalgia for the 60's suggests that such longing has the limits of an elegy to lost innocence, and the advantages, too. It distorts, but it also provides, however disingenuously, the idea that things can be better than they are, because they have been better before now. As usual, the prospects for hope seem to depend upon some degree of mystification."

Beattie's style is characterized by simple declarative sentences and an accretion of detail—"an almost hallucinatory particularity of detail," Romano called it—that some reviewers have found distracting. Susan Horowitz was bothered by Beattie's "taste for the non sequitur." "The characters in both the novel and stories are fleshed out (or, rather, painted by number) in a collection of disjointed details, so that, although they are sometimes intriguingly eccentric, they lack an emotional core. Childhood histories, kinship patterns, recipes, and tastes in pop music do not necessarily add up to anyone we care about or remember."

Reviewers, such as Kristin Hunter, frequently mentioned that the stories in *Distortions* were comprised of "humorless still-lifes of people who do not have any meaningful connections to humanity and who do not move, feel or grow. The stylistic excellence of her writing is undeniable, but Beattie is unable to make us feel any empathy for most of the characters in *Distortions*—perhaps because they are too self-absorbed to feel anything for each other," Hunter continued. Anatole Broyard concurred and noted: "You never know what her people are going to say or do, surprise follows surprise. But, in the end, inscrutability proves to be boring. . . . And yet I am convinced that Ann Beattie is, potentially, a good writer. In spite of a style that virtually eliminates personality, she still manages to haunt the reader with her work. The things her characters say and do are rather like the inexplicable noises very old houses make in the middle of the night. You wake up in alarm when you hear them—what can *that* be?—then reason asserts itself and you go uneasily back to sleep."

Other reviewers have found Beattie's style praiseworthy. Romano wrote: "Her sentences are often plain, flat, their grammar exposed like the lighting fixtures in avant-garde furniture boutiques, and the effect is at first wearying. Only later does the sympathetic center of her work betray itself. We may feel misled by the outward reserve, but, again, her willingness to distort when necessary, her passion for the particular, is ultimately an index of her concern for the integrity of things and people in themselves." John Updike is another admirer of Beattie's style. "Her details—which include the lyrics of the songs her characters overhear on the radio and the recipes of the rather junky food they eat—calmly accrue," he wrote. "Her dialogue trails down the pages with an uncanny fidelity to the low-level heartbreaks behind the banal; her resolutely unmetaphorical style builds around us a maze of familiar truths that nevertheless has something airy, eerie, and in the end lovely about it. Her America is like the America one pieces together from the *National Enquirers* that her characters read—a land of pathetic monstrosities, of pain clothed in cliches, of extraterrestrial trivia. Things happen 'out there,' and their vibes haunt the dreary 'here' we all inhabit."

Beattie told Miner: "My stories are a lot about chaos . . . and many of the simple flat statements that I bring together are usually non sequiturs or bordering on being non sequiturs—which reinforces the chaos. I write in those flat simple sentences because that's the way I think. I don't mean to do it as a technique. It might be just that I am incapable of breaking through to the complexities underlying all that sort of simple statement you find in my work."

BIOGRAPHICAL/CRITICAL SOURCES: New York Times, July 24, 1976, January 3, 1979; *Saturday Review,* August 7, 1976; *Village Voice,* August 9, 1976; *New York Times Book Review,* August 15, 1976, January 14, 1979; *Newsweek,* August 23, 1976; *Christian Science Monitor,* September 29, 1976; *Book World,* October 3, 1976; *New Yorker,* November 29, 1976; *Ms.,* December, 1976; *Commentary,* February, 1977; *Hudson Review,* spring, 1977,

autumn, 1977; *Yale Review,* summer, 1977; *Contemporary Literary Criticism,* Volume 8, Gale, 1978.

* * *

BEAUSOLEIL, Beau 1941-

PERSONAL: Born September 27, 1941, in The Bronx, N.Y.; son of Frank (an auto mechanic) and Matilda (Jaeske) Beausoleil; children: Connolly. *Education:* Attended secondary school in New Rochelle, N.Y. *Home:* c/o 99 Sanchez St., San Francisco, Calif. 94114.

CAREER: Radio Corporation of America (RCA), cryptographic technician aboard ship in Pacific Ocean, 1966-68; currently employed in a used book store. Poet, 1968—. *Military service:* U.S. Army, 1960-65; became sergeant.

WRITINGS: Witness (poems), Panjandrum Press, 1976; (contributor of previously unpublished poems) Stephen Vincent, editor, *Five on the Western Edge,* Momo's Press, 1977; *What Happens* (poems), Cloud Marauder Press, 1978; *Red Light With Blue Sky* (poems), Five Trees Press, 1979. Contributor of poetry to various magazines, including *Beatitude, Abraxas,* and *Berkeley Poetry Review.*

WORK IN PROGRESS: A book, *Lascaux,* an eight-part poem, incorporating research in European prehistory, linguistic philosophy, the history of work in America, and language use of aphasia victims, completion expected in 1980.

SIDELIGHTS: In her notes on *Witness* Kay Boyle wrote: "The poetry of Beau Beausoleil is that rare quantity that comes unexpectedly out of the unknown. He is a 'you' poet, and in a time when the unhappiness of the 'I' poets is all too prevalent, his work is good to read." Lawrence Fixel commented in his notes on Beausoleil's first book: "What characterizes these poems is the steady level of looking at the self, recording its encounters with others with the phenomenal world. Difficult as this is, the poems retain their shape, their controlled force. Beside the gift of seeing; there is the courage to probe further. Beausoleil's *Witness* is the experience of poems that grow on and beyond the page."

Citing his indebtedness to Garcia Lorca, Beausoleil dedicated the poem "Your Thick Hair" (*Witness*) to the Spanish poet. "It's a poet's poem," Beausoleil told *CA,* "it was written at a point in my writing (after six years) when I knew I had to enter that 'forest of our poems.' Lorca helped me enter it."

Beausoleil added: "More and more I want to wrench something free from the language. I would like my poems to reveal something in the reader's life but not in any sequential order."

BIOGRAPHICAL/CRITICAL SOURCES: Beau Beausoleil, *Witness,* Panjandrum Press, 1976.

* * *

BELL, John Elderkin 1913-

PERSONAL: Born September 10, 1913, in Vancouver, British Columbia, Canada; came to the United States in 1939, naturalized citizen in 1945; son of William Robert (an engineer) and Bessie (Elderkin) Bell; married Elisabeth Anderson Samuel (a psychologist), May 31, 1941; children: Colin Elderkin. *Education:* University of British Columbia, B.A., 1933; Vancouver School of Theology, diploma, 1936; Columbia University, M.A., 1941, Ed.D., 1942. *Politics:* Independent. *Home and office:* 751 De Soto Dr., Palo Alto, Calif. 94303.

CAREER: Ordained minister of United Church of Canada,

1936; pastor of United Church of Canada in Barkerville, British Columbia, 1936-37; assistant pastor in Victoria, British Columbia, 1937-39; Park College, Parkville, Mo., professor of psychology, 1942-44; Clark University, Worcester, Mass., associate professor of psychology, 1944-56; National Institute of Mental Health, San Francisco, Calif., associate regional program director, 1956-68; Mental Research Institute, Palo Alto, Calif., director, 1968-73; Veterans Administration Hospital, Palo Alto, psychologist, 1973—. Lecturer at University of California, Berkeley, 1961-72, University of California, San Francisco, 1965—; and other universities and colleges in the United States, Canada, Great Britain, and Taiwan; associate clinical professor and senior social scientist at Stanford University, 1968—; adjunct professor at San Francisco Theological Seminary, 1970—. Visiting professor at Dalhousie University, 1946, Pennsylvania State University, 1949, University of British Columbia, 1959, University of Edinburgh, 1954-55, University of Arizona, 1962, and Union College of British Columbia, 1967. Member of California Task Force on Child Care in Industry, 1970-72.

MEMBER: National Council on Family Relations, American Psychological Association (fellow; past division president), American Association for the Care of Children in Hospitals, Society for Personality Assessment (fellow; past president), Association of Clinical Pastoral Education, British Association for Family Therapy, Royal Society of Health (fellow), Western Psychological Association, California State Psychological Association, Kappa Delta Pi, Phi Delta Kappa. *Awards, honors:* Silver award from Des Moines Child Guidance Center, 1966; distinguished service award from American Psychological Association, 1970.

WRITINGS: Projective Techniques: A Dynamic Approach to the Study of Personality, Longmans, Green, 1948; *Family Group Therapy* (monograph), U.S. Government Printing Office, 1961; *The Family in the Hospital: Lessons From Developing Countries,* U.S. Government Printing Office, 1970; *Family Therapy,* Jason Aronson, 1975.

Contributor: A. Weider, editor, *Contributions Toward Medical Psychology,* Volume II, Ronald, 1953; John G. Howells, editor, *Theory and Practice of Family Psychiatry,* Oliver & Boyd, 1968; N. W. Ackerman, editor, *Family Process,* Basic Books, 1970; H. E. Rie, editor, *Perspectives in Child Psychopathology,* Aldine-Atherton, 1971; M. F. Shore and S. E. Golann, editors, *Current Ethical Issues in Mental Health,* National Institute of Mental Health, 1973; B. S. Brown and E. D. Torrey, editors, *International Collaboration in Mental Health,* National Institute of Mental Health, 1973; Philip J. Guerin, Jr., editor, *Family Therapy,* Gardner Press, 1976; Max Rosenbaum and Milton M. Berger, editors, *Group Psychotherapy and Group Function,* Basic Books, 1976.

Contributor of more than thirty articles to psychology and social science journals. Chairman of editorial board of *Family Process,* 1969-73, member of board of advisory editors, 1973—; member of editorial advisory board of *Journal of Marriage and Family Counseling,* 1974—; member of editorial board of *Journal of the Association for the Care of Children in Hospitals,* 1975—, and *International Journal of Family Therapy,* 1977—.

WORK IN PROGRESS: Developing family context therapy, in which concepts of family therapy are expanded through attention to the family environment, and interventions are made to ameliorate family strains and promote family and personal well-being; studying the psychologist and other scientists as innovators; research on psychosocial studies of the family, family relations with cerebral-palsied children, therapy with total families, family relations with patients in hospitals and community institutions and services, family-focused training for health professionals, family context therapy; studying organization of community helping services and personality diagnosis.

SIDELIGHTS: Bell writes: "As a discoverer of family therapy, now a major form of psychologists' treatment, I have always felt an obligation to share my findings with professional persons and the literate public, but only when ideas were well-developed. Normally material was first presented in speeches and workshops, although that is less true now. It has always pleased me to reach out and invent new ideas, and to risk leaving behind current activities as I start to lose excitement. Thus I have had a varied career, mostly in exciting settings—in chemistry, the ministry, university teaching and counseling, as program director and administrator, consultant in program development, researcher, and writer.

"My Scottish wife has made our marriage a joy, and with our son has set an example for family living that allows me freedom to speak publicly and without embarrassment on family issues. We have worked together professionally—for example, in making the eight-month study of families in hospitals of Africa and Asia, the background for one of my books."

*   *   *

BELL, Michael Davitt   1941-

PERSONAL: Born March 30, 1941, in Pittsburgh, Pa.; son of Davitt Stranahan (in business) and Marian (Whieldon) Bell; married Claudia Swett, August 5, 1967 (divorced, 1975); children: Sophia Rutledge, Cathleen Davitt. *Education:* Yale University, B.A., 1963; Harvard University, M.A., 1968, Ph.D., 1969. *Home:* 200 The Knolls, Williamstown, Mass. 01267. *Office:* Williams College, Williamstown, Mass. 01267.

CAREER: Princeton University, Princeton, N.J., instructor, 1968-69, assistant professor of English, 1969-75; Williams College, Williamstown, Mass., associate professor of English, 1975—. *Member:* Modern Language Association of America, American Studies Association. *Awards, honors:* American Council of Learned Societies fellow, 1974-75.

WRITINGS: Hawthorne and the Historical Romance of New England, Princeton University Press, 1971; (with James M. McPherson, James M. Banner, Laurence Holland, and Nancy J. Weiss) *Blacks in America,* Doubleday, 1971; (editor) Hugh Henry Brackenridge and Philip Freneau, *Father Bombo's Pilgrimage to Mecca,* Princeton University, 1975.

WORK IN PROGRESS: Masks of Sincerity: Studies in the Development of American Romance.

*   *   *

BENNETT, Daniel
  See GILMORE, Joseph L(ee)

*   *   *

BENTLEY, Nicolas Clerihew   1907-1978

OBITUARY NOTICE—See index for *CA* sketch: Born June 14, 1907, in London, England; died August 14, 1978. Artist, publisher, and author of more than sixty books. Bentley illustrated books for such authors as Hilaire Belloc, Damon Runyon, T. S. Eliot, Roy Fuller, and Kingsley Amis. In addition to his activities as an illustrator and cartoonist, he wrote social and historical commentary on the Victorian period, poetry, an autobiography, and suspense novels. In 1951 Bentley co-founded the Andre Deutsch publishing company, where he served as director for many years. *Obituaries and other sources: Nicolas Clerihew Bentley, A Version of the Truth*, Deutsch, 1960; *The New Century Handbook of English Literature*, revised edition, Appleton, 1967; *Longman Companion to Twentieth Century Literature*, Longman, 1970; *Illustrators of Books for Young People*, 2nd edition, Scarecrow, 1975; *Who's Who in the World*, 3rd edition, Marquis, 1976; *Who's Who*, 130th edition, St. Martin's, 1978; *Publishers Weekly*, September 18, 1978.

* * *

BENTON, Richard G(lasscock) 1938-

PERSONAL: Born April 29, 1938, in San Antonio, Tex.; son of Jack (a rancher) and Birdie Elaine (a teacher; maiden name Glasscock) Benton; married Martha Eugenia Pena Ledesma (a school psychologist), January 22, 1966; children: Richard G., Martha Alexandra. *Education:* University of Houston, B.A., 1960, M.A., 1962, Ph.D., 1966. *Residence:* Houston, Tex. *Office:* 1213 Hermann Dr., Suite 440, Houston, Tex. 77004.

CAREER: University of Texas, Galveston, intern in psychology, 1962-63, assistant professor of psychology and research, 1966-71, director of Vocational REACT Center, 1968-71; Texas Tech University, Lubbock, research director at Research and Training Center in Mental Retardation, 1971-73, adjunct professor of psychology, 1973; University of Texas, Houston, associate professor of psychiatry, 1974—. Private practice in clinical psychology, 1973—; clinical psychologist at M. D. Anderson Hospital and Tumor Institute, 1974-76. Assistant professor at University of Houston, 1966-71, lecturer and instructor, 1975-76; member of reserve faculty at Galveston Community College, 1967-71. Team director of Vocational Rehabilitation of Open-Heart Surgery Patients, 1966-69; member of medical advisory committee of Texas Rehabilitation Commission, 1973-76; participant in workshops; consultant to St. Anthony Center.

MEMBER: International Society for Rehabilitation of the Disabled (U.S. Committee), Interamerican Psychological Association, American Psychological Association, American Association for the Advancement of Science, National Rehabilitation Association, Society for Psychophysiological Research, National Society for Programmed Instruction, Southwestern Psychological Association, Texas Psychological Association (head of Committee for Liaison with State Agencies in Texas, 1976), New York Academy of Science, Psi Chi (Houston president, 1964). *Awards, honors:* Postdoctoral fellowship from U.S. Department of Health, Education & Welfare, 1966-67, for Psychiatric and Psychosomatic Laboratory at Veterans Administration Hospital, Houston; National Science Foundation-National Institutes of Health grant, 1966; National Institutes of Health grant, 1968; Vocational Rehabilitation Facilities Establishment grant, 1968.

WRITINGS: (Contributor) Jan Van Eys, editor, *The Truly Cured Child*, International Universities Press, 1977; *Death and Dying: Principles and Practices in Patient Care*, Van Nostrand, 1978; *Contemporary Mental Health: An Individual and Family Resource*, Van Nostrand, in press. Contributor to *Handbook of Neurochemistry* and *M. D. Anderson Annual Yearbook*. Contributor to psychology and medical journals.

WORK IN PROGRESS: Psychiatric and Mental Health Nursing, publication by Van Nostrand expected in 1980; *The Workings of the Human Emotional System: A Fresh Approach with "How-to" Ideas; The Nature of Living: A Book on the Cycles of Life for Parents and Children*, with children, Richard and Alexandra Benton, for Tinker's Book Company, publication expected in 1980.

SIDELIGHTS: Benton told *CA:* "Although I had published research papers in professional journals, I had not given serious thought to publishing a book until *Death and Dying: Principles and Practice in Patient Care*. In fact, that topic was even foreign to me until deaths in my own family stirred my interest—an interest that was later enriched by experiences at M. D. Anderson Hospital and Tumor Institute. With the learning and effort that went into that book, I developed an interest in publishing in other areas of psychology. I find that writing is a good personal therapy. It forces me to clarify and pursue organizing those loose-ended "good ideas" that sometimes benefit my efforts with patients in a therapy situation. In essence, it has become my personal continuing education program."

BIOGRAPHICAL/CRITICAL SOURCES: Houston Post, September 28, 1969; *Shell News*, Volume 45, number 4, 1978; *Publishers Weekly*, February 6, 1978.

* * *

BERG, A(ndrew) Scott 1949(?)-

PERSONAL: Born in Norwalk, Conn.; son of Richard (a film producer) and Barbara Berg. *Education:* Graduated from Princeton University, 1971. *Residence:* Los Angeles, Calif. *Agent:* Russell & Volkening, Inc., 551 Fifth Ave., New York, N.Y. 10017.

CAREER: Writer.

WRITINGS: Max Perkins: Editor of Genius (biography), Dutton, 1978.

SIDELIGHTS: While still in high school, Berg became a devotee of F. Scott Fitzgerald. His enthusiasm for the spokesman of the Jazz Age prompted him to attend Princeton University, Fitzgerald's alma mater. At Princeton Berg noticed one name that surfaced repeatedly in discussions of twentieth-century literature, Maxwell Evarts Perkins. Perkins, who worked at Charles Scribner's Sons for more than thirty years, had been the editor of Fitzgerald, Ernest Hemingway, Thomas Wolfe, Ring Lardner, James Jones, Marjorie Kinnan Rawlings, and a host of other famous writers. Described as "the dean of American editors," Perkins was always quick to downplay his role. He once told a class of publishing students: "An editor does not add to a book. At best he serves as a handmaiden to an author. Don't ever get to feeling important about yourself, because an editor at most releases energy. He creates nothing." Encouraged by Carlos Baker (a biographer of Hemingway), Berg decided to write his senior thesis on Perkins. The thesis earned an A+ and won the English department's thesis prize.

After graduation, Berg set about converting his thesis into a book. In order to garner information about the elusive editor, Berg read tens of thousands of letters to and from Perkins, as well as conducting one hundred interviews with his family, friends, and colleagues. Among the people with whom Berg talked were James Jones, Alice Roosevelt Longworth, Martha Gellhorn, John Hall Wheelock, Malcolm Cowley, Matthew Josephson, and Perkins's daughters. A series of interviews with Elizabeth Lemmon yielded a treasure: one hundred letters that Perkins had written to Lemmon over a period of twenty-five years. Berg told an interviewer that the most important thing about these platonic love letters was "in them Max talked about what he did and what he believed. Wheelock had given me all the work data. . . . Miss Lemmon gave me the personal side."

The biography that emerged from Berg's research has been commended by numerous critics. "It is a pity that Perkins could not see the manuscript of his biography. He enjoyed finding promising young writers, and Berg . . . is one of that small group," Paul Gray observed. More praise was forthcoming from Peter Davison, who called *Max Perkins: Editor of Genius* "a highly readable work of literary history, also a fully achieved biography of a man whose career and life were marvels of self-effacement." According to Jack Beatty, the finest section of the book was that which dealt with the relationship between Perkins and Thomas Wolfe: "Berg's pages on the rift between the mercurial Wolfe and the stolid Yankee Perkins are his best, but his whole narrative is first-rate—filled with humor and feeling. Max would have published it in a minute."

Beatty did cite a deficiency in *Max Perkins;* he felt that Berg did not satisfactorily explain why Perkins dedicated his life to a "lot of rather ungrateful, occupationally self-centered people." Another criticism was voiced by Gray, who commented, "Berg includes far too many familiar anecdotes about the depressions and binges of Perkins's famous authors." Other readers, however, found the anecdotes intriguing. "Perkins's editorial friendships are absorbingly narrated by Mr. Berg," wrote Davison.

AVOCATIONAL INTERESTS: Pianist.

BIOGRAPHICAL/CRITICAL SOURCES: A. Scott Berg, *Max Perkins: Editor of Genius,* Dutton, 1978; *Publishers Weekly,* May 22, 1978; *New York Times,* July 24, 1978; *New York Times Book Review,* July 23, 1978; *Newsweek,* July 31, 1978; *Time,* August 7, 1978; *Detroit Free Press,* September 17, 1978.

*   *   *

BERGER, John (Peter) 1926-

PERSONAL: Born November 5, 1926, in London, England; son of S.J.D. and Miriam (Branson) Berger; married; children: two. *Education:* Attended Central School of Art and Chelsea School of Art, London. *Politics:* Marxist. *Address:* c/o Weidenfeld & Nicolson, 11 St. John's Hill, London S.W. 11, England.

CAREER: Worked as a painter and teacher of drawing; has exhibited his work at the Wildenstein, Redfern, and Leicester Galleries, London, England; art critic and writer. Has made numerous television appearances. *Military service:* British Army, 1944-46, served in the Oxford and Buckinghamshire Infantry. *Awards, honors:* Book Prize, 1972, and James Tait Black Memorial Prize, 1973, both for *G;* New York Critics Prize for the Best Scenario of the Year, 1976, for *Jonah;* Prize for Best Reportage from the Union of Journalists and Writers, Paris, 1977, for *The Seventh Man.*

WRITINGS—Novels: *A Painter of Our Time,* Secker & Warburg, 1958, Simon & Schuster, 1959; *The Foot of Clive,* Methuen, 1962; *Corker's Freedom,* Methuen, 1964; *G,* Viking, 1972.

Nonfiction: *Renato Guttuso,* translated from the original English manuscript by Wolfgang Martini, Verlag der Kunst, 1957; *Permanent Red: Essays in Seeing,* Methuen, 1960, published as *Toward Reality: Essays in Seeing,* Knopf, 1962; *The Success and Failure of Picasso,* Penguin, 1965;

(with Jean Mohr) *A Fortunate Man: The Story of a Country Doctor,* Holt, 1967; *Art and Revolution: Ernst Neizvestny and the Role of the Artist in the U.S.S.R.,* Pantheon, 1969; *The Moment of Cubism, and Other Essays,* Pantheon, 1969; Nikos Stangos, editor, *Selected Essays and Articles: The Look of Things,* Penguin, 1972, published as *The Look of Things: Essays,* Viking, 1974; *Ways of Seeing* (based on a television series), Penguin, 1972, Viking, 1973; *A Seventh Man: A Book of Images and Words About the Experience of Migrant Workers in Europe,* Penguin, 1975, published as *A Seventh Man: Migrant Workers in Europe,* Viking, 1975.

Poems: *Poems in Voix,* Maspero (Paris), 1977.

Translator: (From the German, with Anya Bostock) Bertolt Brecht, *Poems on the Theatre,* Scorpion, 1961, published as *The Great Art of Living Together: Poems on the Theatre,* Granville Press, 1972; (from the German, with Bostock) Bertolt Brecht, *Helene Weigel, Actress,* Veb Edition (Leipzig), 1961; (from the French, with Bostock) Aime Cesaire, *Return to My Native Land,* Penguin, 1969.

Also author of three screenplays, "La Salamandre," "Le Milieu du monde," and "Jonah Who Will Be 25 in the Year 2000," and of *Marcel Frishman.*

Contributor to periodicals, including *Nation* and *New Statesman.*

SIDELIGHTS: One of the most prominent Marxist art critics in the Western world, John Berger believes that art and art alone can "express and preserve the profoundest expectations of a period." Since Berger holds that the profoundest expectations in the twentieth century were aroused by socialism, he thinks that great art should mirror these changes in society. Of particular interest to him is cubism, a revolutionary art form that he contends presaged the political and economic revolution in Russia. In *The Moment of Cubism, and Other Essays,* Berger elaborates on his theories. He defines the "moment of cubism" as that brief period in which artists reached an understanding of the changes occurring in the outside world and reflected this understanding in their paintings.

One of the best-known cubists was Picasso, whose career Berger analyzes in *The Success and Failure of Picasso.* Berger believes that the most important periods in Picasso's career were his interlude with the cubists and the period in which Marie-Therese Walter modeled for him. According to Berger, the paintings that emerged from Picasso's cubist period were socially progressive, but much of his other work is "an example of a failure of revolutionary nerve." Berger argues that Picasso's art is a failure because it reflects the failure of Spanish anarchists to bring about a proletarian revolution. Although most reviewers did not agree with Berger's assessment of Picasso, they did find much of merit in *The Success and Failure of Picasso.* "Berger's fundamental mistake is to berate Picasso for what he is not (he is not, after all, Guttuso) and given his circumstances, never could have been. Still Berger emerges as one of the few writers equipped to make a constructive case for the prosecution," John Richardson remarked. Burton Silverman commented: "Despite ideological excesses, Berger makes cogent observations on Picasso's perpetual 'youth,' on his empty recapitulations of Velasquez and Delacroix and on Guernica. His book is a healthy antidote to the silliness of much contemporary art criticism."

In contrast to Picasso stands Ernst Neizvestny, a Russian sculptor. In *Art and Revolution: Ernst Neizvestny and the Role of the Artist in the U.S.S.R.,* Berger expresses an admiration for Neizvestny's work because it represents "a phase in the world struggle against imperialism.'' Although Neizvestny is a confirmed socialist, his work has not been accepted by the Soviet bureaucracy because his style is social expressionism rather than social realism. Rejecting the socially realistic, propagandistic work promoted by the Soviet establishment, Berger seeks to establish Neizvestny's ideological credentials. ''Berger's premises may be preposterous, his pompousness grating, his lack of objectivity extreme, but he has nevertheless produced a provocative, engrossing essay, if only because his very didacticism sparks such a broad dialogue of disagreement with the reader,'' Yorick Blumenfeld noted. ''It is unfortunate that this book is marred by such a fundamental theoretical confusion,'' Michael Harrington observed about *Art and Revolution.* ''But even so, I found it stimulating, exciting, and worthwhile.''

Berger's Marxist beliefs evolved because of circumstances in real life. In two of his books, *A Fortunate Man* and *A Seventh Man,* Berger documents actual situations with the help of photographer Jean Mohr. *A Fortunate Man* is about Dr. Sassall, a physician in rural England. The book consists of a series of sketches on Sassall's community, a description of Sassall's life and character, and some political and social deductions that Berger draws. A reviewer for the *Times Literary Supplement* complained that Berger does not portray Sassall in depth: ''Mr. Berger's text, then, is not basically about a human creature; it is a thinly disguised anti-capitalist argument. . . . and in politics the individual is apt to get overlooked.'' Other critics disagreed. ''Berger has been scrupulous in keeping to the facts, as well as illuminating in his interpretation of the facts,'' Philip Toynbee commented. George A. Silver, himself a doctor, was glowing in his praise. This is a beautiful book, beautifully written, and illustrated with striking, movingly apt photographs,'' Silver wrote. He recommended that *A Fortunate Man* be used as a text in medical course, and he definitely did not find the book didactic:''There is a world of difference between Berger's creative presentation and a sociological document.''

The plight of European migrant workers is examined in *A Seventh Man.* The rich industrial centers of northern and western Europe attract workers from the poorer countries to the south and east. According to Berger, in some countries the migrants number one in every seven manual workers. Many of these migrant workers are separated from their families, and many are never able to return to their homelands. Although a reviewer for *New Yorker* denigrated the book as ''a melange of enraged Marxism and doughy prose-poetry that evokes irritation with the writer rather than pity for his subjects,'' most readers were moved by *A Seventh Man.* ''It is one of the strengths of this book that Berger and Mohr do not confine themselves to 'the migrant as migrant,' to wringing their hands over the alienation of these men and women at their machines, in their hostels, loafing on foreign corners. They are almost more interested in the places they come from, where the worker can again be a husband, father, citizen, and patriot but cannot earn a living,'' wrote Neil Ascherson. Paul Delany asserted that ''Berger's tone is polemical rather than elegiac, and rightly so, since he speaks for men who come from marginal peasant cultures, but are not at all marginal in their function for the countries where they work.''

Berger's fascination with the impact that social structures have on the individual is reflected in his novels as well as his criticism and documentaries. G, the protagonist in the novel of the same name, is profoundly influenced by historical events although he is essentially apolitical himself. In an analysis of G's character, Leo Braudy likened him to Don Juan: ''Berger . . . makes his Don Juan more similar to Byron's—the boyish and fallible voyager after sexual adventure who sardonically but compassionately observes the shams and deceits of the societies he moves through.'' But the adolescent nature of G's observations annoyed Duncan Fallowell, who found the novel pretentious: ''Acne bursts from every page, in a series of subtle detonations designed to impress you with the enigmatic complexity of Berger's emotional insights. . . . An air of contrived import or significance hangs over much of it which often the content cannot justify.''

Even Fallowell, however, found much to commend in *G.* He thought that ''Berger's talent for invoking period is remarkable,'' and lauded the precision of his vignettes. Other critics were more generous with their praise. *G* ''is the most interesting novel in English I have read for a good many years,'' Arnold Kettle declared, while Braudy termed *G* an ''excellent and and fascinating'' novel. Both Kettle and Braudy were interested in defining *G*'s relationship to other English novels. Braudy placed it in ''the tradition of George Eliot, Tolstoy, D. H. Lawrence and Norman Mailer, the tradition of fallible wisdom, rich, nagging and unfinished. To read [*G*] is to find again a rich commitment to the resources and possibilities of the genre.'' Kettle stressed Berger's innovation, calling *G* ''one of the few serious attempts of our time to do for the novel what Brecht did for drama; to reshape it in the light of 20th-century experience and theory other than the purely subjective or self-analytical.''

Some of Berger's works have been translated into Spanish and French.

BIOGRAPHICAL/CRITICAL SOURCES: New York Review Of Books, April 6, 1967, February 5, 1976; *Observer Review,* April 30, 1967; *New Statesman,* May 5, 1967, February 28, 1969; *Times Literary Supplement,* May 25, 1967, June 12, 1969; *Nation,* September 4, 1967; *Washington Post Book World,* June 9, 1968; *Atlantic,* May, 1969; *Commonweal,* July 11, 1969; *New York Times Book Review,* November 6, 1969, September 10, 1972, January 11, 1976; *Books and Bookmen,* September, 1972; *New Republic,* October 7, 1972, March 15, 1975, July 26, 1976; *Contemporary Literary Criticism,* Volume 2, Gale, 1974; *New Yorker,* April 19, 1976.*

*   *   *

BERGIER, Jacques 1912(?)-1978

OBITUARY NOTICE: Born c. 1912 in Odessa, U.S.S.R.; died November 23, 1978, in Paris, France. Scientist, French resistance leader, and author of books on espionage, popular science, and science fiction. As a member of the French resistance during World War II, Bergier gathered data on the German V-2 rocket and was captured and tortured by the Gestapo. His co-written science fiction book, *Le Matin des magiciens,* was a best-seller in France. Obituaries and other sources: *New York Times,* November 25, 1978.

*   *   *

BERGMAN, (Ernst) Ingmar 1918-
(Buntel Eriksson, Ernest Riffe)

PERSONAL: Born July 14, 1918, in Uppsala, Sweden; married sixth wife, Ingrid von Rosen, 1971; children: eight. *Education:* Attended University of Stockholm.

CAREER: Writer, director, and producer of motion pictures, teleplays, and stage productions. Director with Maaster Olofsgaarden, 1938, Student Theater in Stockholm, 1941,

Haelsingborg City Theater, 1944-46, Gothenburg City Theater, 1947-52, Malmoe City Theater, 1952-59, and Royal Dramatic Theater in Stockholm, 1963-66; Associated with Svensk Filmindustri, 1942-69.

AWARDS, HONORS: Received numerous awards, including Grand Prix du Cinema from Cannes Film Festival, 1946, for "Hets"; prize from Sao Paolo Film Festival, 1954, for "Gycklarnas Afton"; prize for comedy from Cannes Film Festival, 1956, for "Sommarnattens leende"; special award from Cannes Film Festival, 1957, and Joseph Bernstein Award for best foreign import, 1958, both for "Det sjunde inseglet"; first prize award from International Berlin Film Festival, 1957, for "Smultronstaellet"; director's prize from Cannes Film Festival, 1958, for "Naera livet"; Academy Award for best foreign language film from Academy of Motion Picture Arts and Sciences, 1960, for "Jungfrukaellan"; Academy Award for best foreign language film from Academy of Motion Picture Arts and Sciences, 1961, for "Saasom i en Spegel"; award for best director and for best film from National Society of Film Critics, 1967, for "Persona"; award from National Society of Film Critics, 1968, for "Skammen"; Irving G. Thalberg Memorial Award from Academy of Motion Picture Arts and Sciences, 1971; award for best director from National Society of Film Critics, 1971, for "En Passion"; award for best screenwriter from National Society of Film Critics, awards for best screenwriter, best director, and best film from New York Film Critics, all 1972, all for "Viskningar och Rop"; and countless other film awards.

WRITINGS—Published screenplays: *Four Screenplays of Ingmar Bergman* (contains "Smiles of a Summer Night," "The Seventh Seal," "The Magician," and "Wild Strawberries"), translation from the Swedish by Lars Malmstrom and David Kushner, Simon & Schuster, 1960; *The Seventh Seal,* translation from the Swedish by Malmstrom and Kushner, Simon & Schuster, 1960; *En filmtrilogi: Saasom i en spegel, Nattvardsgaesterna, Tystnaden,* PAN/Norsted, 1963, translation by Paul Britten Austin published as *A Film Trilogy: Through a Glass Darkly, Winter Light, The Silence,* Orion Press, 1967; *Wild Strawberries,* translation by Malmstrom and Kushner, Simon & Schuster, 1969; *Three Films by Ingmar Bergman* (contains "Through a Glass Darkly," "Winter Light," and "The Silence"), translation by Austin, Grove, 1970; *Bergman: Persona and Shame,* translation by Keith Bradford, Penguin, 1972; *Filmberaettelser,* Volume I, II, and III, PAN/Norsted, 1973; *Scener ur ett iiktenshap,* Norsted, 1973, translation by Alan Blair published as *Scenes From a Marriage,* Pantheon, 1974; *Four Stories by Ingmar Bergman: The Touch, Cries and Whispers, The Hour of the Wolf, The Passion of Anna,* Doubleday, 1976; *Face to Face,* translation from the Swedish by Blair, 1976; *The Serpent's Egg,* Pantheon, 1977.

Screenplays; all released by Svensk Filmindustri; all as director, unless otherwise noted: (assistant director) "Hets" (released in U.S. as "Frenzy" and as "Torment"), 1944; "Kris" (released in U.S. as "Crisis"; adapted from the play by Leck Fisher, "Moderdyret"), 1945; (with Herbert Grevenius) "Det regnar paa vaar kaerlek" (released in U.S. as "It Rains Our Love"; adapted from the play by Oskar Braathen, "Bra mennesker"), Sveriges Folkbiografer, 1946; (writer only) "Kvinna utan ansikte" (released in U.S. as "Woman Without a Face"), 1947; "Skepp till Indialand" (released in U.S. as "A Ship to India" and as "Land of Desire"; adapted from the play by Martin Soederhjelm), Sveriges Folkbiografer, 1947; "Hamnstad" (released in U.S. as "Port of Call"; adapted from a story by Olle Laensberg),

1948; (writer only) "Eva," 1948; "Faengelse" (released in U.S. as "Prison" and as "The Devil's Wanton"), Terrafilm, 1949; "Till Glaedje" (released in U.S. as "To Joy"), 1949.

(With Grevenius) "Sommarlek" (released in U.S. as "Summer Interlude"), 1950; (writer only, with Grevenius) "Fraanskild" (released in U.S. as "Divorced"), 1951; "Kninnors Vantan" (released in U.S. as "Waiting Women" and as "Secrets of Women"), 1952; (with P. A. Fogelstroem) "Sommaren med Monika" (released in U.S. as "Summer With Monika"; adapted from the novel by Fogelstroem), 1952; "Gycklarnas Afton" (released in U.S. as "Sawdust and Tinsel" and as "The Naked Night"), Sandrews, 1953; "En Lektion i kaerlek" (released in U.S. as "A Lesson in Love"), 1954; "Kvinnodroem" (released in U.S. as "Journey Into Autumn" and as "Dreams"), Sandrews, 1955; "Sommarnattens leende" (released in U.S. as "Smiles of a Summer Night"), 1955; (writer only, with Alf Sjoeberg) "Sista paret ut" (released in U.S. as "The Last Couple Out"), 1956; "Det sjunde inseglet" (released in U.S. as "The Seventh Seal"; adapted from the play by Bergman, "Traemalning"), 1956; "Smultronstaellet" (released in U.S. as "Wild Strawberries"), 1957; (with Ulla Isaksson) "Nara Livet" (released in U.S. as "So Close to Life" and as "The Brink of Life"; adapted from the short story by Isaksson, "Det vanliga vardiga"), Nordisk Tomefilm, 1957; "Ansiktet" (released in U.S. as "The Face" and as "The Magician"), 1958.

"Djaevunes oega" (released in U.S. as "The Devil's Eye"; adapted from a Danish radio play), 1960; "Saasom i en spegel" (released in U.S. as "Through a Glass Darkly"), 1961; (with Erland Josephson, under joint pseudonym Buntel Eriksson) "Lustgaarden" (released in U.S. as "The Pleasure Garden"), 1961; "Nattvardsgaesterna" (released in U.S. as "Winter Light"), 1962; "Tystnaden" (released in U.S. as "The Silence"), 1963; (with Josephson, under pseudonym Eriksson) "Foer Att Inte Tala Om Alla Dessa Kvinnor" (released in U.S. as "Now About These Women"), 1964; "Persona," 1966; "Vargtimmen" (released in U.S. as "The Hour of the Wolf"), 1966; "Skammen" (released in U.S. as "Shame"), 1967; "Riten" (released in U.S. as "The Rite"), Svensk Filmindustri/Sveriges TV/Cinematograph, 1968; "En Passion" (released in U.S. as "A Passion of Anna"), Svensk Filmindustri/Cinematograph, 1969; "Faaroedokument" (released in U.S. as "Faro Document"), Cinematograph, 1969.

"The Touch," Cinematograph/ABC Pictures, 1970; "Viskningar och rop" (released in U.S. as "Cries and Whispers"), Cinematograph, 1972; "The Lie" (adapted from the play by Bergman), originally shown on British television, 1972; "Scener ur ett iiktenshap" (released in U.S. as "Scenes From a Marriage"), originally shown on Swedish television in six parts, 1973, edited version released as motion picture, 1975; "Ansikte mot ansikte" (released in U.S. as "Face to Face"), Cinematograph, 1976; "The Serpent's Egg," Parmount, 1978.

Published plays: *Jack hos skadespelarna* (title means "Jack Among the Actors"), Albert Bonniers, 1948; *Moraliteter* (title means "Morality Plays"; contains "Rachel och biografvaktmaestaren," "Dagen slutar tidget," and "Mig till skraeck"), Albert Bonniers, 1948. Contributor of "Staden" and "Traemalning" to *Svenska radiopjaeser.*

Plays: "Kaspers doed" (title means "Death of Punch"), first produced in 1942; "Rakel och biografvaktmaestaren" (title means "Rachel and the Cinema Doorman"), first produced in Gothenburg, Sweden, at Gothenburg City Theater, 1945; "Dagen slutar tidigt" (title means "The Day Ends Early"), first produced at Gothenburg City Theater, 1947; "Mig till skraeck" (title means "To My Terror"), first produced at Gothenburg City Theater, 1947; "Hets" (title means "Torment"; adapted from the screenplay), first produced in Oslo, Norway, 1948; "Staden" (title means "The City"), first produced for radio in 1951; "Mordet i Barjaerna" (title means "Murder at Barjaerna"), first produced in Malmoe, Sweden, at Malmoe City Theater, 1952; "Traemalning" (title means "Wood Painting"), produced in Stockholm, Sweden, at Royal Dramatic Theater, 1955. Also author of unproduced plays, including "Reskamrater" (title means "Travel Companions"), "Stationen" (title means "Station"), "De Ensamma" (title means "The Lonely Ones"), "Trivolet" (title means "The Fun Fair"), "Fullmanen" (title means "Full Moon"), "Dimman" (title means "The Fog"), and "Om en moerdare" (title means "About a Murder").

Contributor of essays to numerous film journals and periodicals, including *Cinemathek, Biografbladet, Tulane Drama Review,* and, under pseudonym Ernest Riffe, to *Chaplin.*

WORK IN PROGRESS: Directing the motion picture, "Autumn Sonata."

SIDELIGHTS: Despite a prolific dual-career as both filmmaker and playwright, Bergman was relatively unknown outside Sweden before 1956. His work was often characterized, as Brigitta Steene noted, by a "schematic conception of characterization and a verbose and overly rhetorical language." But Bergman worked constantly at overcoming his flaws. "For the most part, I was working like a galley-slave to get enough money to support two families," he remembered. "I didn't bother my head about anything except putting on plays and making films."

With the release of "The Seventh Seal," the hard work was justified. The critics' attention had been called to an earlier film, "Smiles of a Summer Night," and its popularity, coupled with the acclaim for "The Seventh Seal," thrust Bergman into the foreground of the film world. A complex tale of death and the search for religious truth, "The Seventh Seal" is regarded today as Bergman's first important effort as a religion-oriented filmmaker. "To me, religious problems are continuously alive," Bergman once said. "I never cease to concern myself with them; it goes on every hour of every day."

Bergman's probings into religious justification culminated in a highly regarded trilogy, "Through a Glass Darkly," "Winter Light," and "The Silence." "Through a Glass Darkly" is the most optimistic of the three films. Although the lead female character sees God as a giant spider and eventually succumbs to schizophrenia after an incestuous affair with her brother, the film seems positive because of the rapport between father and son which had not existed earlier. But Bergman was not happy with the film's progress. "When I wrote 'Through a Glass Darkly' I thought I had found a real proof of God's existence: God is love . . . and I let the whole thing emanate in that proof. . . . But it only seemed right until I started shooting the film. . . . For that reason I smash that proof of God in the new film."

"Winter Light" is largely concerned with the inability of people to communicate between themselves and with God: a minister is unable to prevent the suicide of one character consumed with the belief that nuclear holocaust is inevitable; another man idealizes his dead wife to the extent that he is blind to another woman's advances. Many critics have suggested that the final scene which takes place in an empty church implies that God must be contacted by the individual outside the institution of the church service.

It is the final film in the trilogy, "The Silence," that shows the futility of any method of contact. It is the story of two women who arrive in a country where the language is unfamiliar. One woman is sensual, the other is intellectual; both suffer from an inability to communicate. When one woman finally decides to leave the country, she leaves behind a list of words she's managed to define. When the other sister attempts to read the list aloud, however, a passing train drowns out her sounds. Steene described "The Silence" as "a film without any real character development. Rather, it is an attempt at an exact expression of a mood of isolation, death, and destruction. . . ." By the end of the trilogy, man is unable to communicate with God on any level. Bergman's search ends on a decidedly atheistic note. "Things are difficult enough without God," he conceded. "They were more difficult when I had to put God into it. But now it's finished, definitely, and I'm happy about it."

After his self-purging trilogy, Bergman shifted his emphasis to personal and interpersonal relationships. Films such as "Persona," "The Hour of the Wolf," "A Passion of Anna," and "Cries and Whispers" all provide an intense look into the psyche of the individual attempting to maintain a grasp on reality and the self. In these films, Bergman's aim is to "tell, to talk about, the wholeness inside every human being. It's a strange thing that every human being has a sort of dignity or wholeness in him, and out of that develops relationships to other human beings, tensions, misunderstandings, tenderness, coming in contact, touching and being touched, the cutting off of contact and what happens."

Many critics have suggested that "Persona," "The Hour of the Wolf," and "Shame" are a second trilogy in the Bergman canon. All three films are studies of artists coping with a world in which they realize little control. The actress-character of "Persona" shuts herself away from the world by refusing to talk and ultimately finds herself losing her identity with her nurse. Bergman playfully described the film as "about one person who talks and one who doesn't, and they compare hands and get all mingled up in one another." Bergman planned on following up "Persona" with "The Cannibals," which was a continuation of elements from the former, but chose instead to combine motifs from the two for "The Hour of the Wolf." "This cannibal motif, the hour-of-the-wolf motif, goes back a long way," he said. "The same applies to the other motifs in 'The Hour of the Wolf': the redistribution of power, the identification problem, the silent as against the speaking role." "The Hour of the Wolf" examines the life of a painter plagued by "demons." It is never clear whether the demons exist or not. As Bergman pointed out, "The boundary between dream and reality had been blurred." In "Shame," the hellish "blurred reality" implied in "Persona" and in "The Hour of the Wolf" becomes clear. Instead of characters agonized by a distorted sense of reality, the characters in "Shame" are tortured by a valid perception of their lives. In the film, a musician, Jan, and his wife, Anna, find their isolation and complacency threatened by the intimacy of war. "In some way the man is part and parcel of his instrument—the instant his instrument is smashed, his entire view of life crumbles too," Bergman said. "He is transformed." Shaken from his staid life, the musician eventually shoots his wife's lover and murders an enemy boy-soldier for his belongings. The film ends on a nihilistic note: a dream sequence featuring Jan and Anna in a rowboat, lost at sea and surrounded by floating dead bodies.

The films following "Shame" are almost exclusively devoted to the study of the female psyche. "A Passion of Anna," "Cries and Whispers," and "Face to Face" are all concerned with women victimized by guilt and isolation. Bergman told interviewers that the relationships in "A Passion of Anna" grew out of the setting of "The Shame." "I found the idea of Anna Fromm's experiences having a sort of secret background in the war in 'The Shame' stimulating." In "Cries and Whispers," Bergman expanded the themes of "A Passion of Anna" to include the sufferings of four women. Charles Champlin described it as a "truly overwhelming film.... No one, not even I think Bergman himself, has previously put the pain of living and the pain of dying onto the screen with such wrenching and inescapable force.... The abiding quality is loneliness, isolation and frustration amidst a yearning for tenderness." "Face to Face" was similarly reviewed by Jay Cocks who called it "an emotional descent into hell." In "Face to Face," as in "A Passion of Anna," emotional and psychological tension is observed through the actions of the female. But with "Face to Face," the critical response was not as complimentary. Cocks saw the film as a "transitional work.... It is a movie that bides time." Jack Kroll was less optimistic. He claimed that "the clinical quality" of "Face to Face" was "crowding out life and art." Bergman himself called the film merely an "investigation."

"The Serpent's Egg," is the story of an American in Berlin during the days preceeding Hitler's famous beer-hall putsche. After his brother's suicide, the American moves in with his sister-in-law, a prostitute and dance-hall performer. Soon afterward, a childhood acquaintance re-enters their lives under the guise of a concerned friend. The acquaintance is eventually discovered to be, as Vincent Canby pointed out, "a mad scientist ... B-movie creature" who injects kidnapped subjects with various serums and films their reactions. The film was an immense critical failure. Canby called it "full of dark portents ... dispossessed Bergman." Richard Schickel summed it up as "really quite a bad film."

Even after making more than forty films, the creative process still comes with difficulty for Bergman. "When I have to sit down, to start from the beginning and write script," Bergman told John Simon, "that is the hateful period—when I have to make up my mind about what I am going to do and actually write it.... It is a hard, painful time, and I don't like it, but I have to do it.... I am no improvisor; I must always prepare everything." Despite reviewers like John Simon who label him "the greatest filmmaker the world has seen so far," Bergman sees himself primarily as "just a professional; I'm a man who makes a table or something that is to be used. Whether it is good or bad, a masterpiece or a mess, has nothing to do with the making, with my creative mind.... I feel responsible only for the craftsmanship being good, for the thing having the moral qualities of my mind, and, if possible, for my not telling lies."

AVOCATIONAL INTERESTS: Listening to classical music, collecting films.

BIOGRAPHICAL/CRITICAL SOURCES—Books: Joern Donner, *The Personal Vision of Ingmar Bergman,* Indiana University Press, 1964, published as *The Films of Ingmar Bergman,* Dover, 1972; John Russell Taylor, *Cinema Eye, Cinema Ear,* Hill & Wang, 1964; Birgitta Steene, *Ingmar Bergman,* Twayne, 1968; Robin Wood, *Ingmar Bergman,* Studio Vista, 1969; John Simon, *Ingmar Bergman Directs,* Harcourt, 1972; Stig Bjoerkman, Torsten Manns, and Jonas Sima, editors, *Bergman on Bergman: Interviews With Ing-*mar Bergman, Simon & Schuster, 1973; Stuart M. Kaminsky and Joseph F. Hill, editors, *Ingmar Bergman: Essays in Criticism,* Oxford University Press, 1975.

Articles: *Cue,* December 28, 1968; *Time,* November 13, 1972; April 12, 1976, January 30, 1978; *Los Angeles Times,* January 15, 1974; *Newsweek,* November 24, 1975, April 12, 1976; *New York Times Magazine,* December 7, 1975; *New York,* April 12, 1976; *New York Times,* January 22, 1978, January 27, 1978.*

* * *

BERINGER, Richard E. 1933-

PERSONAL: Born December 29, 1933, in Madison, Wis.; married, 1964; children: two. *Education:* Lawrence College, B.A., 1956; Northwestern University, M.A., 1957, Ph.D., 1966. *Office:* Department of History, University of North Dakota, Grand Forks, N.D. 58201.

CAREER: Wisconsin State University (now University of Wisconsin), Oshkosh, instructor in history, 1963-64; California State College (now University), Hayward, assistant professor of history, 1965-69; University of North Dakota, Grand Forks, associate professor of history, 1970—. *Military service:* U.S. Air Force, 1957-60. *Member:* American Historical Association, Organization of American Historians, Southern Historical Association. *Awards, honors:* Editing fellow of National Historical Publishing Commission, 1969-70; National Endowment for the Humanities fellow, 1971-72.

WRITINGS: (With Thomas B. Alexander) *Anatomy of the Confederate Congress: A Study of the Influences of Member Characteristics on Legislative Voting Behavior, 1861-1865,* Vanderbilt University Press, 1972; *Historical Analysis: Contemporary Approaches to Clio's Craft,* Wiley, 1978. Contributor to history journals.

* * *

BERNSTEIN, Carl 1944-

PERSONAL: Born February 14, 1944, in Washington, D.C.; son of Alfred David and Sylvia (Walker) Bernstein; married Carol Ann Honsa (a reporter), April 28, 1968 (divorced); married Nora Ephron (a writer and editor), April 14, 1976; children: Jacob. *Education:* Attended University of Maryland, 1961-64. *Home:* 2853 Ontario Rd. N.W., Washington, D.C. 20005. *Agent:* David Obst, Room 1614, 525 Madison Ave., New York, N.Y. 10022. *Office:* 1150 15th St. N.W., Washington, D.C. 20005.

CAREER: Washington Star, Washington, D.C., began as copy boy, became city desk clerk, later became telephone dictationist, 1960-63, reporter, 1963-65; *Elizabeth Daily Journal,* Elizabeth, N.J., reporter and columnist, 1965-66; *Washington Post,* Washington, D.C., reporter, 1966-76; writer, 1976—. *Military service:* U.S. Army, 1968. *Awards, honors:* New Jersey Press Association first prize for general reporting, 1966; Drew Pearson Foundation Award, George Polk Memorial Award, Pulitzer Prize, Worth Bingham Prize, Heywood Broun Award, International Newspaper Guild Award, Sidney Hillman Foundation Award, and Sigma Delta Chi Award, all 1973, all for investigative reporting of Watergate scandal.

WRITINGS—Nonfiction; with Bob Woodward: *All the President's Men,* Simon & Schuster, 1974; *The Final Days,* Simon & Schuster, 1976. Contributor of articles to periodicals, including *New Yorker* and *Rolling Stone.*

WORK IN PROGRESS: A book about the witch-hunts of the Cold War.

SIDELIGHTS: At the time Carl Bernstein started working on what would become the most important news story of the decade, he had been on the metropolitan staff of the *Washington Post* for six years. Bernstein had covered local county and municipal governments, and liked to write long, colorful pieces about the capital city's people and neighborhoods. He was known around the newsroom as a capable, if undependable, reporter, who frequently went on "all-night prowls" of the city and didn't always bother to call in to the newsroom the next morning. A colleague, Leonard Downie, Jr., characterized him as "an iconoclastic throwback, cast in the reporter-as-social-misfit mold."

Bernstein also had a reputation for maneuvering his way into stories not originally assigned to him. Although he was not assigned to the story of the break-in at the Watergate complex headquarters of the Democratic National Committee on June 17, 1972, he wrote a sidebar story about the five burglary suspects to complement Bob Woodward's coverage of the break-in. He then persuaded the *Post* editors to let him cover leads Woodward was not following.

What at first appeared to be a routine burglary took on added dimensions when the *Post* reporters learned from a wire story that one of the burglars, James McCord, was the security coordinator for the Committee for the Re-election of the President (CRP) and that some of the burglars had ties to the CIA. Following other leads, Bernstein traveled to Miami at the end of July and was given a copy of a $25,000 check that had been deposited in the bank account of one of the Watergate burglars. The check was traced to CRP's Midwest finance chairman.

Until the August 1 story about the check appeared under Woodward and Berstein's joint by-line, the reporters had worked independently of each other, establishing their own sources and tips, which they only reluctantly shared. As their mutual distrust decreased, Woodstein (as they were known collectively in the newsroom) discovered advantages in working together. The writing method that evolved from their partnership was that Woodward, who wrote quickly and comprehensively, would write a first draft, and Bernstein would re-write the draft. As they admitted in *All the President's Men:* "To those who sat in the newsroom, it was obvious that Woodstein was not always a smoothly operating piece of journalistic machinery. The two fought, often openly. Sometimes they battled for fifteen minutes over a single word or sentence. Nuances were critically important; the emphasis had to be just right. The search for the journalistic mean was frequently conducted at full volume, and it was not uncommon to see one stalk away from the other's desk. Sooner or later (usually later), the story was hammered out."

Finding knowledgeable sources was the reporters' most difficult problem. Woodward and Bernstein quickly learned that people were likely to talk to them when the reporters approached them in their homes after working hours. They spent many evenings ringing doorbells of potential sources, trying to persuade them to be interviewed. Bernstein compared himself and Woodward to "magazine salesmen. For every sale, you had fifty rejects." He explained their strategy to Downie: "People come to perceive you as a friend if you come to see them at their homes. It really involved a different kind of relationship. If you think there is a chance of their agreeing to let you in by prearrangement, you call first. Otherwise, you just go and knock on the door. We went back to several places several times, were thrown out again and again, and then maybe on the fourth time, they will say, 'Okay, we'll talk to you.'"

Bernstein and Woodward were particularly successful in obtaining information from lower-level employees, who felt freer to talk than did their bosses. One conscience-stricken bookkeeper played an especially prominent part in steering the reporters in the right investigative direction. "Deep Throat" was their most infamous and mysterious source. A highly-placed administration official with ties to CRP, "Deep Throat" was an acquaintance of Woodward's before Watergate and has remained anonymous to date. Their clandestine meetings usually took place in the middle of the night in a parking garage. While "Deep Throat" was reluctant to provide primary information, he would often confirm information and would guide the reporters in fruitful directions.

Throughout the investigation, Bernstein and Woodward scrupulously collected information for their stories. While many interviews were conducted on background (the information could not be directly attributed to the source), information was confirmed by at least one other source before it was printed. As the Watergate stories began to implicate officials closer and closer to President Nixon, White House denials became more frequent and more caustic. Woodward and Bernstein were virtually alone in covering Watergate related stories for almost a year, and they and the *Post* were often accused of using third-hand information and of practicing shabby journalism, most audibly by presidential press secretary Ronald Ziegler.

Bernstein and Woodward made one major misstep which undermined their credibility. They reported that Hugh Sloan (a former aide to H. R. Haldeman) had testified before the grand jury investigating Watergate that Haldeman was one of five men with control over the secret slush fund that had financed the Watergate break-in and other campaign dirty tricks. Sloan's attorney immediately disclaimed the story and Ziegler issued a vehement denial.

The reporters were stunned. Because the story implied the president's involvement in the cover-up, the reporters had taken the extra precaution of confirming the information with four sources (including Sloan himself, who was one of their key sources throughout the investigation). Believing that one of their sources had knowingly given them faulty information and that they were therefore entitled to know the truth, they compromised their professional ethics by revealing him to his superior. Later, the reporters learned that although Sloan *would* have given the grand jury Haldeman's name, he was never asked: the reporters had misunderstood this point.

This was the low point of their Watergate investigation. Sources and new leads had seemingly dried up: no page one stories under their by-line appeared for five weeks. In their desperation, Bernstein and Woodward contacted members of the grand jury in an attempt to get information. While their actions were not specifically illegal, they later admitted that it was decidedly unethical to prod others into breaking the law. An enraged Judge Sirica censured them for their conduct. Bernstein commented afterwards: "I think we were wrong. Period."

In March, 1973, a letter from Watergate burglar James McCord to Judge Sirica implicated highly placed administration officials in perjury and use of political pressure, confirming much of what Bernstein and Woodward had written. Other reporters jumped into the Watergate investigation and scrambled with Woodward and Bernstein for scoops. Eventually, they lost the lead in evidence.

When the McCord letter was released by Judge Sirica, Woodward and Bernstein had already written four chapters of the book that was to be the culmination of their Watergate reporting. But rather than rehash events that would be common knowledge by the time the book was published, Woodward suggested that they write about their coverage of Watergate. Bernstein was at first opposed to the idea on the grounds that it would appear to be an ''ego trip.'' But Woodward began a first draft. As Bernstein recounted it: ''I looked at it, said, 'OK, it needs a lot of work, but it seems to me that if we're going to do this, there's only one way. . . . We have to be totally honest about what we did, including the mistakes we made and including the ethical problems that we had to deal with, and didn't always deal with very successfully.''

All the President's Men was well received by critics, who praised the book for its fast pace, historical value, and fascinating exposure of the inner workings of a large, metropolitan daily newspaper. Doris Kearns called the book ''a fast-moving mystery, a whodunit written with ease, if not elegance.'' Although Richard Rovere lauded the reporters for their ''unquestionable integrity,'' he found, contrary to the opinions of some other reviewers, that the book was ''barren of ideas, or imagination, or of a sense of either the tragic or comic aspects of the subject, and one that would be essentially boring if it were not for the historical importance of the events dealt with.''

Doris Kearns wrote that she was ''particularly impressed by their portrait of the White House staff.'' However, she was bothered that the reporters' ethical struggles are merely mentioned in the narrative and readers are not exposed to how they weighed their decisions. She wrote: ''The reporters apparently believed the government was so corrupted by the President's power that the press could justify morally dubious means to right the balance. . . . Woodward and Bernstein struck a right balance, but I think they failed to openly address the moral choices they made. . . . I would have preferred a slower, more introspective tale.''

Bernstein and Woodward began their next book, *The Final Days,* within a week of Nixon's resignation. They had originally planned to write an account of the President's impeachment and trial through the eyes of six senators, but when Nixon's resignation became imminent, ''people started telling us a truly incredible story, not just of those last couple of weeks but during the whole period,'' Bernstein said. They decided instead to chronicle the last fifteen months of Nixon's presidency, from the resignations of his chief aides in April, 1973, to his own resignation in August, 1974.

The reporters received a year's leave of absence from the *Post* and immediately began conducting interviews. ''We wanted to get to the people quickly, before hindsight changed any perceptions,'' Bernstein explained to a *Publishers Weekly* interviewer. They decided to conduct all interviews on background and to corroborate all facts with at least one other source. They collected notes, memoranda, letters, logs, calendars, and diaries, and with the help of two researchers, divided their material into twenty-two ''areas of inquiry,'' which were further divided chronologically into the last 100 days of the Nixon administration. Each reporter wrote first drafts for separate weeks. Woodward wrote the first half of the final draft and Bernstein wrote the second half.

Even before publication *The Final Days* had become a media event. *Newsweek*'s two 15,000 word pre-publication excerpts (the second of which was the fastest selling issue in *Newsweek*'s history), evoked accusations of inaccuracy,

shoddy methodology, and tastelessness. People who were quoted in the book were among the most vocally critical: Henry Kissinger, for example, complained of the book's ''inaccuracies, distortions, and misrepresentations.''

Bernstein vehemently defended the accuracy of the accounts. Noting that some sources had told the reporters in advance that they would publicly deny being interviewed, he told a *Newsweek* reporter: ''The fact is that the principals described in this book, the sources of information for this book, and those who are making comments about this book all know the accuracy of this account. . . . As for some statements people have made that they have never said things, in each of those instances we have confirmation of their actual statements by those to whom they spoke at the time—or in some cases from themselves.'' Most of the statements issued claiming inaccuracy rang hollow, and as Michael Janeway noted, none of the principals ever successfully refuted that their quotations were substantially inaccurate.

Some reviewers found fault with the reporters' decision to conduct all interviews on background. Using background interviews is an effective means of obtaining information if used judiciously, John Osborne contended. ''But the effect of piling statement upon statement for 450 pages is to give a good method a bad name,'' he wrote. Bernstein countered this criticism: ''I'd rather have somebody talk on background and know what I'm getting is true, than to have them on record, spinning out a bunch of B.S.'' Osborne also chided the reporters for their ''insecurity'' in not using information given to them by a single source. Because the quotes were unattributed, Max Lerner wrote, Bernstein and Woodward are ''asking us for blind trust. Not only must they have 'relations of trust' (as they put it) with their sources, but also they expect the reader to trust their assessments of the trustworthiness of the sources. It may have been the only way this particular kind of book could have been written, but the leap of faith it asks for is more of a jump than most of us can make.''

Objections were also voiced about the reporters' technique of describing thoughts of principals in the narrative. J. Fred Buzhardt complained: ''They write about my thought processes. I don't know how they derive that, for honestly I can't myself.'' John Hughes wrote, ''Woodward and Bernstein were not inside the heads of the participants at the moment crucial events took place, and yet the book unceasingly gives that impression.'' Nicholas von Hoffman defended their technique on the grounds that it ''may make the narrative flow more easily and there's no need to think history has to be dull to be good.''

The book received the most criticism for its heavy dose of ''backstairs gossip'' and what some considered to be a disregard for the privacy of Nixon and his family. Kissinger said that the reporters showed an ''indecent lack of compassion'' for Nixon. But as Janeway pointed out, if blame should be assigned, it was the principals' fault for breaking confidences, not Woodward and Bernstein's for reporting them.

Time addressed Woodward and Bernstein's problem in ''where to draw the line of discretion or taste. The fact is that Presidents and other major political figures to some extent forfeit their right to privacy by the career they have chosen. Their state of mind and their morals are subjects of legitimate concern to citizens and hence to journalists, even when the leaders are out of power or dead but especially in the case of a deep national crisis involving a President's character and personality.'' Bernstein told a reviewer for *Guardian* that to omit personal details ''would have been a tremendous abrogation of responsibility as reporters. When you start to understand how distant Nixon was from his own family, then it starts to make it more understandable why he was so distant from everything that was happening around him and from his staff. You can't divorce a man's personal life from his public behavior." And Bernstein told *Time,* "I'd be surprised if readers do not find the book not at all sympathetic to the former President of the United States."

But according to von Hoffman, the reporters' portrayal of Nixon as "basically a non-political figure," is precisely the problem. "If all they wanted to do was write the simple, human, and moving story of one man's family, they should have written a novel, because by giving us a depoliticized version of these momentously political events they're making a statement whether they're aware of it or not. . . . The answer to why this burglary should decapitate a president isn't to be found interviewing the White House butler or the Nixon children. It must lie in the domain of politics, in the hypothesis that a confluence of groups and individuals decided somewhere along the line to exploit Watergate and use the incident to rid themselves of a man who they'd come to think was either dangerous or dangerously incompetent."

Further controversy was engendered by critics who couldn't decide if the book should be considered journalism or history. P. S. Prescott termed it "instant history," and asserted that "the virtue of instant history is that evidence can be gathered while the participants' memories are fresh, relatively unreconstructed by hindsight. The liability is that the loss of the historian's perspective and accountability makes it impossible for the reader to assess the worth of what he's reading. Woodward and Bernstein can only say: trust us. I do, for their past courage and enterprise; still their book makes me nervous." Von Hoffman dissented, and called the book "pedestrian American journalism in the literal sense of that adjective. The foot replaces the brain as our reporters tumble about with great gumption and careful fidelity asking every and anyone whether he or she was at the scene of the crime, and what, perchance did they see? *The Final Days* is a splendid reportorial effort but no amount of energy expended can make up for the lack of thought." Janeway also dismissed the book's historical value. He wrote: "*The Final Days* . . . is meant for historians. It is daring and effective journalism. . . . But to qualify as history it ought to do more than redramatize a ghastly experience, in the course of which no viewer of nationwide television could have failed to suspect that the leading player was a broken and possibly unhinged man; to qualify as history, it would have to take one closer to, rather than further from, a sense of the whole truth. I don't think *The Final Days* does."

AVOCATIONAL INTERESTS: Bicycling.

BIOGRAPHICAL/CRITICAL SOURCES: Newsday, May 14, 1973; *National Observer,* May 19, 1973; Carl Bernstein and Bob Woodward, *All the President's Men,* Simon & Schuster, 1974; *Time,* April 22, 1974, December 30, 1974, April 12, 1976, May 3, 1976; *New York Times Book Review,* June 9, 1974, April 18, 1976; *New Yorker,* June 17, 1974; *Philadelphia Bulletin,* July 10, 1974; *Miami Herald,* July 17, 1974; Leonard Downie, Jr., *The New Muckrakers,* New Republic, 1976; Bernstein and Woodward, *The Final Days,* Simon & Schuster, 1976; *Newsweek,* April 12, 1976, May 3, 1976; *Parade,* April 18, 1976; *New Republic,* April 24, 1976; *New York Sunday News,* April 25, 1976; *Publishers Weekly,* April 26, 1976; *Christian Science Monitor,* May 19, 1976; *Saturday Review,* May 29, 1976; *Atlantic,* June, 1976; *Guardian,* June 7, 1976; *New York Review of Books,* June 10, 1976.*

BERTHRONG, Donald J(ohn) 1922-

PERSONAL: Born October 2, 1922, in LaCrosse, Wis.; son of LeRoy M. (a streetcar driver) and Viola (Ritter) Berthrong; married Edna Marr, December 21, 1942; children: John H., Sherri Lee. *Education:* University of Wisconsin, Madison, B.S., 1947, M.S., 1948, Ph.D., 1951. *Home:* 1005 Kenwood Dr., Lafayette, Ind. 47905. *Office:* Department of History, Purdue University, West Lafayette, Ind. 47907.

CAREER: University of Missouri, Kansas City, instructor in history, 1951-52; University of Oklahoma, Norman, assistant professor, 1952-58, associate professor, 1958-64, professor of history, 1964-70, head of department, 1966-70; Purdue University, West Lafayette, Ind., professor of history and head of department, 1970—. Consultant to U.S. Department of Justice and Cheyenne and Arapaho tribes of Oklahoma. *Military service:* U.S. Army Air Forces, 1942-44. U.S. Army, Signal Corps, 1944-46; became second lieutenant.

MEMBER: American Historical Association, American Association of University Professors, Organization of American Historians, Agricultural History Society, Western History Association, Oklahoma Historical Society. *Awards, honors:* Fulbright fellow in Hong Kong, 1965-66; award of merit from American Association for State and Local History, 1964, for *The Southern Cheyennes.*

WRITINGS: (editor) *Joseph Reddeford Walker and the Arizona Adventure,* University of Oklahoma Press, 1956; *The Southern Cheyennes,* University of Oklahoma Press, 1963; (editor) *A Confederate in the Colorado Goldfields,* University of Oklahoma Press, 1970; *Indians of Northern Indiana and Southwestern Michigan,* Garland Publishing, 1974; *The Cheyenne and Arapaho Ordeal: Reservation and Agency Life,* University of Oklahoma Press, 1976. Contributor to history and social science journals.

WORK IN PROGRESS: The Cheyennes and Arapahoes of Oklahoma in the Twentieth Century, publication by University of Oklahoma Press expected in 1982.

SIDELIGHTS: Berthrong comments: "During my residence in Oklahoma, I became aware that the state was a vast reservoir of the history of the American Indian. Concentrated in Indian Territory by the policies of the federal government, the Native Americans placed an indelible imprint upon the history of the Southern Plains. As a young historian, I was gradually attracted to the history of the Cheyennes and Arapahoes of Oklahoma. Few scholars have attempted to study Indian tribes in depth as those people have survived and died under the grinding ordeals imposed upon them by the policies of the United States Government. My hope is to continue to research and write a detailed study of the Cheyennes and Arapahoes down to the early 1950's, after which full archival sources and records are no longer available."

*   *   *

BETTELHEIM, Bruno 1903-

PERSONAL: Born August 28, 1903, in Vienna, Austria; came to United States in 1939, naturalized citizen in 1944; son of Anton and Paula (Seidler) Bettelheim; married Gertrud Weinfeld (a teacher and researcher), May 14, 1941; children: Ruth, Naomi, Eric. *Education:* University of Vienna, Ph.D., 1938. *Politics:* Democrat. *Religion:* Jewish. *Home:* 1 Sierra Lane, Portola Valley, Calif. 94025.

CAREER: Progressive Education Association, Chicago, Ill., research associate, 1939-41; Rockford College, Rockford, Ill., associate professor of psychology, 1942-44; University of Chicago, Chicago, Ill., assistant professor, 1944-

47, associate professor, 1947-52, professor of educational psychology, 1952-73, Stella M. Rowley Distinguished Service Professor of Education, and professor of psychology and psychiatry, 1963-73, head of Sonia Shankman Orthogenic School, 1944-73; writer, 1973—. Diplomate of American Psychological Association. Fellow of Center for Advanced Studies in the Behavioral Sciences, 1971-72. Former member of Chicago Council for Child Psychology.

MEMBER: American Psychological Association (fellow), American Orthopsychiatric Association (fellow), American Philosophical Association, American Association of University Professors, American Sociological Association, American Academy of Education (founding member), American Academy of Arts and Sciences, Chicago Psychoanalytical Society, Quadrangle Club. *Awards, honors:* D.H.L. from Cornell University.

WRITINGS: (With Morris Janowitz) *Dynamics of Prejudice: A Psychological and Sociological Study of Veterans,* Harper, 1950; *Love Is Not Enough: The Treatment of Emotionally Disturbed Children,* Free Press, 1950; *Overcoming Prejudice* (booklet), Science Research Associates, 1953; *Symbolic Wounds: Puberty Rites and the Envious Male,* Free Press, 1954, revised edition, Collier Books, 1962; *Truants From Life: The Rehabilitation of Emotionally Disturbed Children,* Free Press, 1955.

The Informed Heart: Autonomy in a Mass Age, Free Press, 1960; *Paul and Mary: Two Case Histories From "Truants From Life",* Doubleday-Anchor, 1961; (with others) *Youth: Change and Challenge* (proceedings of the American Academy of Arts and Sciences), American Academy of Arts and Sciences, 1961; *Dialogues With Mothers,* Free Press, 1962; *Child Guidance, a Community Responsibility: An Address, With a Summary of Public Provisions for Child Guidance Services to Michigan Communities,* Institute for Community Development and Services, Continuing Education Service, Michigan State University, 1962; (with Janowitz) *Social Change and Prejudice: Including Dynamics of Prejudice,* Free Press, 1964; *Art: As the Measure of Man,* Museum of Modern Art, 1964; *The Empty Fortress: Infantile Autism and the Birth of the Self,* Free Press, 1967; *Mental Health in the Slums: Preliminary Draft,* Center of Policy Study, University of Chicago, 1968; *The Children of the Dream,* Macmillan, 1969, reprinted as *The Children of the Dream: Communal Childrearing and American Education,* Avon, 1970, published in England as *The Children of the Dream: Communal Child-Rearing and Its Implications for Society,* Paladin, 1971.

Food to Nurture the Mind, Children's Foundation (Washington, D.C.), 1970; *Obsolete Youth: Toward a Psychograph of Adolescent Rebellion,* San Francisco Press, 1970; (with others) *Moral Education: Five Lectures,* Harvard University Press, 1970; *A Home for the Heart,* Knopf, 1974; *The Uses of Enchantment: The Meaning and Importance of Fairy Tales,* Knopf, 1976.

Columnist for *Ladies' Home Journal.* Contributor to professional and popular journals.

SIDELIGHTS: "Bruno Bettelheim stands as one of Freud's few genuine heirs in our time. Fearlessly independent and yet working within Freud's great discoveries, Bettelheim has sought to think through all of human psychology for himself," Paul Roazen declared in the *New York Times Book Review.* Bettelheim was inspired to begin his distinguished career in psychology after undergoing psychoanalysis during his adolescence. A harrowing personal experience provided him with important insights into his profession—shortly after he finished his education at the University of Vienna, Bettelheim was arrested by the Nazis and incarcerated in concentration camps at Dachau and Buchenwald from 1938 to 1939. While a prisoner Bettelheim took careful note of the actions and thoughts of his fellow captives. After being freed and moving to the United States, Bettelheim drew upon his observations in the concentration camps to write his famous article, "Individual and Mass Behavior in Extreme Situations." The essay attracted worldwide attention and became required reading for all United States military government officers in Europe.

Bettelheim's experiences as a prisoner of the Gestapo are explored in depth in *The Informed Heart: Autonomy in a Mass Age.* The first part of the book is devoted to his examination of the importance of maintaining individual freedom in a depersonalized society; the latter part examines how Hitler's concentration camps tried to destroy the autonomy of each inmate. Some commentators were disappointed with the generalities in the theoretical section of *The Informed Heart,* while others felt that the book did not provide any solutions to the problem of preserving personal autonomy. Overall assessments of the book, however, were glowing. Stirred by *The Informed Heart,* Franz Alexander remarked: "This is a dignified book, convincing because it is not derived from textbook knowledge, but from insights gained in the laboratory of the author's own life. In it reason and life experiences are closely integrated." Maurice Richardson wrote that Bettelheim's book "gives you the impression of being lit from within by a humanist glow. His clinical but by no means cold detachment from the horrors, both factual and social of the camps is moving and impressive."

Although Bettelheim's writings encompass a wide variety of concerns, his main interest is in working with children. His work with emotionally disturbed children at the Sonia Shankman Orthogenic School of the University of Chicago led him to write four books, *Love Is Not Enough, Truants From Life, The Empty Fortress,* and *A Home for the Heart. Love Is Not Enough* documents the story of the Orthogenic School and outlines the school's educational and therapeutic philosophy, whereas *Truants From Life* examines in detail the case histories of four children who attended the school and who learned to cope with the outside world. Both books were lauded for the insights they provided professionals and parents of emotionally disturbed children.

In *The Empty Fortress,* Bettelheim advances his theory of autism and reviews the case histories of three autistic children. According to Bettelheim, autistic behavior occurs when a child develops the belief that none of his acts have any effect on the outside world. Robert Coles stated that Bettelheim is "modest, sensible and unpretentious when he tries to specify the particulars that make for autism." A critic for *Scientific American* felt that Bettelheim's actions were even more convincing than his theory: "The pragmatic argument of successful therapy is generally powerful in medicine, but the humanity, intelligence, self-sacrifice and endurance of the therapy given by Dr. Bettelheim and his devoted staff seem to outweigh the specific content of any theory." The final book in the quartet about the Orthogenic School is *A Home for the Heart,* in which Bettelheim describes how to design and operate a mental hospital. Noting that Bettelheim had retired from the Orthogenic School a year before the book was published, J. A. Spiegel called *A Home for the Heart* "a fitting valedictory. He encourages us to live in dignity and hope—in fulfillment, commitment, seriousness. . . . It is a rich legacy he leaves to the field of mental health practitioners and to families with 'special' children everywhere.''

Bettelheim has not restricted his studies of children to the United States. In the spring of 1964, he traveled to Israel and spent seven weeks trying to understand the kibbutz system. His observations are recorded in *The Children of the Dream*. The kibbutzim (the word literally means *group*) were designed by the Israeli pioneers to banish the "ghetto Jew" mentality. By establishing a communal system of child rearing, they hoped to instill in their children an obligation to community rather than to family, to group goals rather than to personal achievements. Bettelheim discovered there were a number of advantages to this method of child rearing. Children raised in the kibbutz that he studied tended to be emotionally stable, responsible, and secure. They indicated a willingness to sacrifice their lives for their peers and for Israel. In addition, the kibbutz had a low crime rate and no incidences of drug abuse. But the emphasis on a group mentality also had its drawbacks. Youngsters brought up in the kibbutz were often unable to think independently. Many were unemotional, unimaginative, and incapable of intimacy. Nevertheless, Bettelheim found enough merit in the kibbutz system to recommend that a similar method be used to raise disadvantaged children in the United States.

Some of the limitations of Bettelheim's study include the brevity of his stay in the kibbutz, his confinement of the study to one kibbutz, and the fact that he knows no Hebrew. These are limitations that he freely acknowledges. *The Children of the Dream* ''is not ultimately of more than marginal interest. Many of Bettelheim's observations, however modestly advanced, will not bear the weight of the conclusions he draws,'' Naomi Sheperd remarked. Most commentators did not share this opinion. Paul Roazen noted that some ''may well challenge the particular assets and liabilities of group rearing that Bettelheim found in Israel, but they should be grateful for his clarity, lucidity, and boldness in stating an argument.'' It was generally agreed that the chief value of the book was its ability to stimulate discussion and to provoke a reassessment of American child-rearing methods. ''Bruno Bettelheim's account of child-rearing in an Israeli kibbutz is the kind of shrewd social reporting we need if we are going to renew a practical utopianism and revive our somewhat rusty national genius for building institutions,'' Joseph Featherstone asserted.

In *The Uses of Enchantment: The Meaning and Importance of Fairy Tales*, Bettelheim handles yet another aspect of child rearing. Although recently some parents have been hesitant to read fairy tales to their children, Bettelheim encourages them to do so. In response to those who claim that fairy tales are too frightening and violent for youngsters, Bettelheim argues that fairy tales do not precipitate violent behavior in children; rather, they serve as a safe outlet for violent tendencies already within the child. Neither does he heed those who claim that fairy tales, being fantasy, do not prepare a child for real life. Bettelheim believes that fantasy is necessary for children. Those youngsters deprived of the fantasy in fairy tales may search for it elsewhere, perhaps in drugs or in religious cults. He contends that fairy tales present universal human problems and thus help a child to deal with the real world. Reflecting the positive attitude of most reviewers, Alison Lurie found Bettelheim's approach to the fairy tale "far more thoughtful, humane, and sensitive" than those of other psychologists. John Updike hailed *The Uses of Enchantment* as ''a charming book about enchantment, a profound book about fairy tales. . . . What is new, and excit-

ing, is the warmth, humane and urgent, with which Bettelheim expounds fairy tales as aids to the child's growth.''

BIOGRAPHICAL/CRITICAL SOURCES: New York Times, February 12, 1950, September 17, 1950, May 29, 1955, March 24, 1969; *San Francisco Chronicle*, March 26, 1950, July 16, 1950; *Nation*, June 24, 1950, July 30, 1955, April 1, 1961; *American Academy of Political and Social Science. Annals*, July, 1950, November, 1950, September, 1961; *Chicago Sunday Tribune*, July 16, 1950; *American Sociological Review*, August, 1950, October, 1955, June, 1961; *Journal of Home Economics*, October, 1955, November, 1962; *New Statesman*, March 17, 1961, September 26, 1969, June 7, 1974; *American Journal of Sociology*, May, 1961, July, 1969; *New Republic*, May 22, 1961, March 4, 1967, May 24, 1969, May 29, 1976; *American Political Science Review*, June, 1961; *Saturday Review*, July 8, 1961, June 9, 1962, May 17, 1969, May 15, 1976; *New York Times Book Review*, October 8, 1961, February 26, 1967, April 6, 1969, March 17, 1974, May 23, 1976; *New York Review of Books*, May 4, 1967, May 30, 1974, July 15, 1976; *Scientific American*, July, 1967; *Harvard Educational Review*, fall, 1967; *Choice*, October, 1967, October, 1974, October, 1976; *Christian Century*, December 6, 1967, June 23-30, 1976; *New Leader*, March 31, 1969; *Washington Post Book World*, April 27, 1969, June 13, 1976; *Times Literary Supplement*, October 9, 1969, August 2, 1974; *New Yorker*, April 22, 1974; *National Review*, May 10, 1974, August 20, 1976; *Critic*, October-December, 1974; *Time*, May 3, 1976; *Harper's*, June, 1976; *Atlantic*, June, 1976; *America*, August 7, 1976.

*   *   *

BEVERIDGE, Meryle Secrest   1930-
(Meryle Secrest; June Doman, a pseudonym)

PERSONAL: Born April 23, 1930, in Bath, England; came to the United States in 1953, naturalized citizen, 1957; daughter of Albert Edward (a toolmaker) and Olive Edith May (Love) Doman; married David Waight Secrest, September 23, 1953 (divorced, 1965); married Thomas Gattrell Beveridge (a singer and composer), November 23, 1975; children: (first marriage) Cary Doman, Martin Adams, Gillian Anne. *Education:* Attended girls' high school in Bath, England. *Residence:* Chevy Chase, Md. *Agent:* Philip Spitzer, Philip G. Spitzer Literary Agency, 111-25 76th Ave., Forest Hills, N.Y. 11375.

CAREER: Hamilton News, Hamilton, Ontario, women's editor, wrote under pseudonym June Doman, 1949-50, *Bristol Evening Post*, Bristol, England, reporter, wrote under pseudonym June Doman, 1950-51; F&R Lazarus & Co., Columbus, Ohio, 1953-55; *Columbus Citizen*, Columbus, food editor, 1955-57; *Washington Post*, Washington, D.C., feature writer, 1961-69, cultural reporter, 1969-72, editor and art critic, 1972-75; free-lance writer, 1975—. *Member:* British Commonwealth Society of North America, Washington Independent Writers Association. *Awards, honors:* Award from Canadian Women's Press Club, 1950, for ''An interview with Barbara Ann Scott.''

WRITINGS—Under name Meryle Secrest: *Between Me and Life: A Biography of Romaine Brooks*, Doubleday, 1974; *Being Bernard Berenson*, Holt, in press. Contributor to American and British magazines; contributor of articles under pseudonym June Doman to *Hamilton News* and *Bristol Evening Post*.

WORK IN PROGRESS: A biography of British art historian Kenneth Clark.

SIDELIGHTS: Meryle Beveridge writes: "Biography seems to be the natural outgrowth of my journalistic experience, and skills acquired as a researcher and interviewer are particularly valuable in unearthing documentary information. Perhaps because of my training I attach particular importance to the interview as a source of information about my subject. Flawed though the human memory is, and biased as the reminiscence may be, colored by circumstance and prejudice, it is still a potentially rich source of information that can be obtained by no other means. However, I have changed my point of view about the form that a biography should take.

"Influenced by my reporting experience and also by the current vogue for the laundry-list biography, I began with the intention of reporting anything and everything that could be discovered about the personality and with the determination to keep my personality in the background. I completed the manuscript and realized that the biography simply didn't work. So I threw it away as a source and completely rewrote the book, taking another year to do it, and recasting it in the form which seemed much more sympathetic to my own assets as a writer. I eliminated extraneous detail and concentrated on developing and illustrating my own point of view about Romaine Brooks. Although the book had a small sale, it was well reviewed on both sides of the Atlantic and encouraged me to leave journalism to devote myself to biography.

"In the case of Bernard Berenson, I am studying the necessity to eliminate detail: A ridiculous amount of material exists, documenting almost every aspect of his life except his childhood and business dealings. So the challenge to present a coherent picture continues. I find myself unalterably opposed to the current vogue for biography which I find unreadable—and if I can't read it, why should I write it?"

AVOCATIONAL INTERESTS: European travel, foreign languages, painting, environmental problems (including air, water, and soil pollution and the acute problem of noise in twentieth-century America).

*   *   *

BEYERCHEN, Alan   1945-

PERSONAL: Surname is pronounced By-er-shen; born May 14, 1945, in Mt. Clemens, Mich.; son of Albert Ray (an electronics technician) and Eleanor (Sexton) Beyerchen; married Marila Stidham (an artist), August 3, 1974. Education: University of California, Santa Barbara, B.A. in German (summa cum laude), 1967, M.A., 1968, Ph.D. in history, 1973; also attended University of Goettingen, 1965-66. Office: Department of History, Ohio State University, Columbus, Ohio 43210.

CAREER: University of Florida, Gainesville, assistant professor of history, 1976-78; Ohio State University, Columbus, associate professor of history, 1978—. Military service: U.S. Army, 1974-76; became captain. Member: American Historical Association, History of Science Society, Conference Group on Central European History, Conference Group on German Politics.

WRITINGS: Scientists Under Hitler: Politics and the Physics Community in the Third Reich, Yale University Press, 1977, revised edition, 1978. Contributor to history journals.

WORK IN PROGRESS: A study of the post-World War II reconstruction of German science, from both Allied and German perspectives; research on relations among scientists of the belligerent nations during World War I.

SIDELIGHTS: Beyerchen writes: "I made my first brief trip to Europe in 1963, just prior to entering college as a physics major, and spent 1965-66 as a foreign student in Goettingen. While there I became intrigued by German history and the history of science, which led to graduate study in these fields. I returned to Germany in 1971 for dissertation research, living in Goettingen once again. My primary research interest is the study of science, technology, and politics in twentieth-century Germany; other interests include the contemporary Western transition from the modern to the post-modern world."

AVOCATIONAL INTERESTS: Chess, science fiction, tennis, theater.

*   *   *

BICHSEL, Peter   1935-

PERSONAL: Born March 24, 1935, in Lucerne, Switzerland; son of Willi (a painter) and Lina (Bieri) Bichsel; married Therese Spoerri, 1956; children: Christa, Matthias. Education: Attended teacher-training college in Solothurn, Switzerland. Home: CH-4512 Bellach, Nelkenweg Nr. 24, Switzerland.

CAREER: Teacher in primary schools in Zuchwil, Switzerland, and Solothurn, Switzerland, 1955-68; Literarischen Colloquium, West Berlin, West Germany, contributor, 1963-64; free-lance writer and journalist, 1968—. Awards, honors: Group 47 Prize, 1965; Lessing Prize of the City of Hamburg, 1965; Foerderungspreis of the City of Olten, 1966.

WRITINGS: Versuche ueber Gino (title means "Experiment Concerning Gino"), [Gigandet], 1960; Eigentlich moechte Frau Blum den Milchmann kennenlernen: 21 Geschichten, Walter, 1964, translation by Michael Hamburger published as And Really Frau Blum Would Very Much Like to Meet the Milkman, Calder & Boyars, 1968, Delacorte, 1969; Das Gaestehaus (novel; title means "The Guest House"), Literarisches Colloquium, 1965; Die Jahreszeiten (novel; title means "The Seasons"), Luchterhand, 1968; (with others) Tschechoslowakei 1968 (collected speeches), Verlag der Arche, 1968; (editor) Des Schweizers Schweiz (title means "A Swiss's Switzerland"), Die Arche, 1969; Kindergeschichten, Luchterhand, 1969, translation by Hamburger published as There Is No Such Place as America, Delacorte, 1970, (published in England as Stories for Children, Calder & Boyars, 1971). Author of column in Zuercher Woche. Contributor to periodicals.

SIDELIGHTS: Bichsel first attracted attention in 1964, when he read some of his short stories at a meeting of the influential German writers' association Group 47. A collection of twenty-one of his stories was published the same year, bringing him the Group's coveted annual literary prize.

Bichsel described his method as improvisational—a matter of discovery rather than the working out of a story already planned: "Language is never accidental.... One can find truths by varying language and by observing it." He said, for example, that he once became obsessed for a period of weeks by this sentence: "The milkman wrote on a piece of paper: 'No butter left today, sorry.'" From this developed the story which gave its title to his first collection, And Really Frau Blum Would Very Much Like to Meet the Milkman. The story is made up of an impersonal exchange of notes between Frau Blum and the milkman, together with her speculations about him as a person. The milkman does not speculate about her—he knows her: "She takes two litres, and has a dented milkpan." As Siegfried Mandel said, these two people "do not break through the anonymity of their relationship; modern life is caught here in a nutshell and *conjecture* becomes compensatory experience."

Mary Sullivan wrote that the "prose miniatures" in *Frau Blum,* few of them more than two pages long, "are less like short stories than those fragments of accuracy you sometimes recognise and remember forever in a novel whose plot you may forget in a week. Peter Bichsel sees everything that is contained in a simple situation and a short moment, and sets it down in utmost concentration. . . ." Sandra Schmidt Otto thought these pieces offered neither the pleasures of poetry nor the "explorative advantages of prose," but found that their effect was cumulative. "All of them," she wrote, "like glimpses through evening windows into the houses of strangers, carry a poignancy. . . . All of the people Bichsel sees are waiting—in cafes, in flower shops, up five flights of stairs unclimbed by passing acquaintances, in living rooms or in churches, beside the mailbox, in front of the desk, behind the door in the very early morning. And what they are waiting for is almost too simple, too literally perfect. They are waiting for life, or death, or for someone to speak to them. The three objects are really, in the end, synonymous to Bichsel. The lives of those waiting build toward a single, clear, limited view of the life they live in waiting."

The seven stories in *There Is No Such Place as America* were written, according to Rainer Schulte, "with the language of children for the minds of adults." Bichsel presents a man unable to accept that the world is round; another who seeks to remake the world he lives in by the simple but dangerous magic of swapping around the names of familiar objects. "Bichsel's imagination attacks the familiar to transform it into something unfamiliar and mysterious," Schulte wrote. "Bichsel challenges all beliefs and habits. . . . He rethinks himself, his ideas, his environment, and the man he sees next to him," seeking to restore the spontaneous responses of childhood to the adult mind. Another reviewer, discussing the "supremely deceptive simplicity" of Bichsel's style, said that "these plain, unadorned sentences embrace universal life and truth, describing attitudes and states of mind rather than events. . . . Bichsel is not interested in reality, but in the relationship individuals have to it. . . . Yet behind the charm, the softness, the simplicity, there is a highly conscious and skilled craftsman at work."

The most discussed of Bichsel's longer works is his experimental novel *Die Jahreszeiten,* "a novel about a man trying to write a novel." A critic for the *Times Literary Supplement* said that "in an irregular but persuasive rhythm he moves back and forth between descriptions of the house in which he lives and the degree to which the seasons alter its face, between quotations from documents such as insurance policies, painting manuals, household regulations and reminiscences, thoughts, epigrams, speculations about the fictitious entities that might serve him as raw materials of a narrative. This narrative, of course, never takes shape. But we participate in the shaping of it, we are presented with the alternatives of plot and character that occupy the author." It seemed to the reviewer that Bichsel's spare prose, with its "peculiar blend of melancholy and caprice," was reminiscent of Gertrude Stein's, and he concluded that Bichsel is a "genuine original . . . one of the few [German] writers who have explored the limits of the conventional novel without descending into the domain of mystification."

Some of Bichsel's ideas on language are illustrated in "Grammatik einer Abreise" ("Grammar of a Departure"), a magazine piece published in 1972 which is both a story and a commentary on the way in which the story is being written.

Siegfried Mandel explained that the story's "key sentence is, 'I am packing my trunk,' and Bichsel theorizes that here the grammatical present tense is an unstable tense in which a neurotic person tries to anchor herself; in the narration, her grammar of tenses, her spoken and unspoken thoughts, and her actions lack unity and thus identify her problems." Bichsel believes that all literature is political "in the sense that it holds a dialogue with men . . . and occupation with language in itself is always a form of one's occupation with humans." However, he has also written directly on political questions, national and international.

BIOGRAPHICAL/CRITICAL SOURCES: Listener, June 20, 1968; *Times Literary Supplement,* November 7, 1968, July 9, 1971; *Christian Science Monitor,* August 14, 1969; *Books Abroad,* winter, 1971; Siegfried Mandel, *Group 47,* Southern Illinois University Press, 1973.*

* * *

BIENEN, Henry Samuel 1939-

PERSONAL: Born May 5, 1939, in New York, N.Y.; son of Mitchell Richard and Pearl (Witty) Bienen; married Leigh Buchanan (a lawyer), April 24, 1961; children: Laura, Claire, Leslie. *Education:* Cornell University, B.A., 1960; University of Chicago, M.A., 1962, Ph.D., 1966. *Home:* 436 Prospect, Princeton, N.J. 08540. *Office:* Department of Politics, Princeton University, Corwin Hall, Princeton, N.J. 08540.

CAREER: University of Chicago, Chicago, Ill., assistant professor of politics, 1965-66; Princeton University, Princeton, N.J., assistant professor, 1966-68; associate professor, 1968-71, professor of politics and international affairs, 1972—, Oliver Ellsworth Bicentennial Preceptor, 1969-72. Fellow of Center for Advanced Study in the Behavioral Sciences, 1976-77. Director of Movement for a New Congress, 1970. Consultant to U.S. Department of State and National Security Council. *Member:* American Political Science Association, Inter-University Seminar on the Armed Forces and Society (member of executive committee, 1968-78). *Awards, honors:* Rockefeller Foundation grants, 1968-69, 1972-73.

WRITINGS: Tanzania: Party Transformation and Economic Development, Princeton University Press, 1967, revised edition, 1970; (editor and contributor) *The Military Intervenes,* Russell Sage Foundation, 1968; *Violence and Social Change,* University of Chicago Press, 1968; *The Military and Modernization,* Aldine, 1970; *Kenya: The Politics of Participation and Control,* Princeton University Press, 1974; *Armies and Parties in Africa,* Holmes & Meier, 1978.

WORK IN PROGRESS: Income Distribution in Nigeria; Comparative Urban Politics.

SIDELIGHTS: Bienen comments: "I started out interested in the Soviet Union and ended up interested in Africa. I am generally interested in politics and power. I have been studying the ways in which economic and political variables interact and the roles played by institutions in social and economic change. One important focus has been the role of the military in developing countries."

* * *

BIERMANN, Wolf 1936-

PERSONAL: Born in 1936, in Hamburg, Germany. *Education:* Attended Humboldt University, East Berlin.

CAREER: Berliner Ensemble, East Berlin, East Germany, assistant director, 1957-59; free-lance songwriter, ballad singer, poet, and playwright, 1959—. *Awards, honors:* Fontane Prize, West Berlin, West Germany, 1969.

WRITINGS: Die Drahtharfe: Balladen, Gedichte, Lieder, Verlag Klaus Wagenbach, 1965, translation by Eric Bentley published as *The Wire Harp: Ballads, Poems, Songs,* Harcourt, 1968; *Mit Marx und Engelszungen: Gedichte, Balladen, Lieder* (title means "With the Tongues of Marx and Engels: Poems, Ballads, Songs"), Wagenbach, 1968; *Der Dra-Dra: Die grosse Drachentoeterschau in acht Akten mit Musik* (title means "The Dra-Dra: The Great Dragon-Killer Show in Eight Acts With Music"), Wagenbach, 1970; *Deutschland: Ein Wintermaerchen* (title means "Germany: A Winter's Tale"), Wagenbach, 1972; *Fuer meine Genossen: Hetzlieder, Balladen, Gedichte* (title means "For My Comrades: Provocative Songs, Ballads, Poems"), Wagenbach, 1972; *Das Maerchen vom kleinen Herrn Moritz* (title means "The Story of Little Herr Moritz"), Parabel Verlag, 1972; *Nachlass I* (title means "Posthumous Remains I"), Kiepenheuer & Witsch, 1977; *Wolf Biermann: Poems and Ballads,* translated by Steve Gooch, Pluto Press, 1977.

SIDELIGHTS: Wolf Biermann's father, a Jew, was a member of the Communist resistance movement against the Nazis. He was arrested when Biermann was very young and remained in various concentration camps until he was killed in Auschwitz in 1941. Biermann has recalled how his mother taught him Communist workers' songs and "so far as my child's head could understand, she also taught me why I wasn't allowed to sing them." Nevertheless, Biermann did sing these songs—every morning from five (when his mother went off to her factory job) until seven (when his aunt fetched him to spend the day with her): "I lay in bed for two hours alone and was frightened and sang.... And these two hours a day were, so to speak, my singing academy, my ... training sessions, my time for practice, my education as a singer."

After the war, Biermann attended schools in Hamburg and, under his mother's influence, grew up as an idealistic Communist. In 1953, when thousands of East Germans were moving west after the ill-fated workers uprisings of that year, Biermann demonstrated his support for the Communist government of the German Democratic Republic by moving to East Berlin. There he attended Humboldt University, studying philosophy, economics, and mathematics, and worked in rural collectives. In 1957-59, he worked as an assistant director with Bertolt Brecht's famous Berliner Ensemble and it was then, under the influence of Brecht and of the composer Hanns Eisler, that he began to write his own songs and music. Brecht has remained the most obvious influence on his work, which also reflects his admiration for Francois Villon, Heinrich Heine, and Pierre-Jean de Beranger.

During the late 1950's Biermann's poems and ballads became immensely popular in East Germany, especially with young people. As John Flores noted, Biermann writes "in clear, straightforward language about problems affecting the widest contemporary audience.... Both 'partisan' and 'popular,' he meets precisely the qualifications of 'people's poet of the nation' set forth by East German cultural authorities." However, Biermann is also both honest and fearlessly outspoken, and his attacks on the East German bureaucrats—the "old guard" who refused to surrender power to younger men—became increasingly ferocious. The first crisis in his relations with the authorities came in 1961, during the rehearsals of his first play "Berliner Brauttag" ("Berlin Weddingday"), a savage satire on the theme of divided Germany. Biermann's candidate membership of the ruling Socialist Unity party was withdrawn, and he was forbidden

to perform anywhere in East Germany. This prohibition was relaxed in 1963, and the following year Biermann was allowed to make a concert tour of West Germany, where he was hailed as the leading East German poet of his generation (though his attacks on West German materialism and politics made him scarcely more popular with the authorities there than with those of his own country).

The Wire Harp, the first collection of Biermann's poems and songs, was published in West Berlin in 1965. It includes a number of love songs and other politically innocuous pieces, but also many of the poems that had most offended the East German authorities. Even the Brechtian "Buckower Balladen" ("Buckow Ballads"), Biermann's bittersweet vignettes of rural life, show the quality of that life being diminished in all kinds of ways by a clumsy and incompetent bureaucracy. "Ballade auf den Dichter Francois Villon," perhaps the most admired and discussed of all Biermann's poems, is a celebration of the French poet's anarchic, free, and creative spirit (as when Villon, visiting modern Berlin, strolls along the Wall playing tunes on the barbed wire—the wire harp—spitting out the bullets of the guards and bleeding red wine). John Flores called this ballad "a masterful parable which comments on its own social function. It provokes society by ridiculing its prudish intolerance and stands as proof of its own thesis because of the intolerance with which it was received." David Kleinbard said of the collection as a whole that "Biermann writes in a colloquial, hard-knuckled, vibrantly physical German.... The style itself laughs at the stuffy middle class and the *rigor mortis* of citizens who have lost all capacity for wit, love and play."

It was presumably the publication of *The Wire Harp* that ended Biermann's public career in East Germany. Already denied publication there, he was accused in December, 1965, of "bestial and frivolous attacks" on the Socialist Unity party, and forbidden to perform, record his songs, or travel abroad. In February, 1966, it was announced that authors could not sell their works to foreign publishers without government permission, a ruling that became popularly known as the "Biermann Law."

Nevertheless, in 1968, a new collection of Biermann's poems, ballads, and songs was published in West Berlin under the title *Mit Marx und Engelszungen* ("With the Tongues of Marx and Engels"). In this volume, wrote David Kleinbard, "the mood has become somber. Moments of desolation or intense bitterness prevail. 'Balancesheet Ballad in the Thirtieth Year' portrays the poet as cut off from all means of livelihood by the government. For Biermann at thirty both parts of Germany have become a rats' nest in which men sell themselves for communist or capitalist money. The poem also reveals the struggle in Biermann between his passionate hope for a liberated, more humane communism and his somber vision of human history." The same is true of Biermann's next collection, "For My Comrades," in which he expresses his solidarity with geniune socialists everywhere. The poem-cycle "Germany: A Winter's Tale" derives its form from Heine's "A Winter's Tale," and bitterly satirizes life in a divided Germany.

In happier days, Biermann had been invited to write the songs for an East German production of Yevgeny Shvarts's Communist fairy-tale, *Der Drache.* Biermann's songs were dropped for political reasons, and he later wrote his own play to go with them, making different use of the same story. This has been published as *Der Dra-Dra,* and tells the story of Hans Folk's battle to save the city from the despotic dragon Dra-Dra. The citizens are so resigned to tyranny that they refuse to help their would-be savior, who has to rely on the assistance of animals (representing the oppressed workers). The play caused a scandal when it was performed in Munich because its director had sought to show a connection between the wicked Dra-Dra and local politicans. A reviewer in the *Times Literary Supplement* found the work extremely witty, with "some delightful mimicry of party jargon," but dark and scatalogical in its humor, showing "the extremes to which such a creative talent can be pushed by being repressed."

In 1971, in an interview in the West German magazine *Der Spiegel,* Biermann said that his status in East Germany was that of "a nationally recognized enemy of the state." A year later, in the same magazine, he spoke of his fear of being exiled from his country, saying that this might be the end of him as a writer. Elsewhere, in an October, 1974, letter to Stuart Hood, Biermann sought to explain his feelings about the country to which he had committed himself in "the decisive step of my life, the first step I really made on my own responsibility.... Here, particularly in the early years, I experienced a downright joyous, fervent unity with society. I was, as the romantic saying goes, at home in my fatherland, in the land for which my father fought and died. This was very good for me; but for this very same reason, because of this same political passion, I came into conflict with this same land.... The harshness of the tone of my songs reflects nothing more nor less than the harshness of the political confrontation between progress and reaction in our society."

In 1976, Biermann was allowed to go to West Germany for a concert tour. On November 16, when the tour had just begun, he was informed that he was no longer a citizen of the German Democratic Republic and could not return there. In East Germany, waves of protest, by workers as well as intellectuals, greeted this decision. In fact, Biermann's worst fears have not been realized: he has not ceased to write, and in 1977, he published his first collection of work produced in exile. In it, wrote Philip Brady, "the poet himself is waiting and seeing, a posture cleverly captured in the title.... 'Posthumous Remains I,' a title which manages to look backwards, to death, and forward to a work-in-progress."

For political as well as aesthetic reasons, Biermann has chosen to write not in literary German but in the language of the people. Jack Zipes, in his introduction to Biermann's *Poems and Ballads,* stresses this aspect of his work and goes on to describe "his original use of music which he composes *against* the text. Biermann maintains that the music should not be a mere vehicle for carrying the text. The music attacks the lyrics which make an incomplete statement about the subject matter being treated, and in this sense the music serves as a critique of the text. This antithetical tension in Biermann's ballads and poems which allows for abrupt changes of mood is necessary since he often writes about his personal problems, and he consciously uses the music and text to achieve an ironical stance."

Philip Brady is one of a number of critics who have pointed out that reading Biermann gives only a very imperfect understanding of "what all the fuss is about," urging the reader to listen to one of the several recordings Biermann has made: "The voice—and here indeed there is not even an echo of Brecht—ranges from snarl to sweet falsetto with astonishing versatility, and neither text ... nor musical notation can convey the gasping shifts of tone and volume, the telling changes of tempi and the bittersweet guitar ornaments." David Kleinbard, similarly, wrote that Biermann's "exuberant performances are astonishing in their range, agility and sensitivity. It is understandable that he has ignited the spirits

of stifled young people in both Germanys; he satirizes the most fearful aspects of war and tyranny with an extravagance of imagination reminiscent of Swift and Rabelais. His lyrical moods of tenderness and sadness are no less stirring."

BIOGRAPHICAL/CRITICAL SOURCES: Theater Heute, Volume VII, number 2, 1962; *Times Literary Supplement,* December 2, 1965, March 19, 1971, April 28, 1978; *Partisan Review,* winter, 1966; *Der Zeit,* June 9, 1967; *Atlas,* October, 1967; *Nation,* November 20, 1967, April 7, 1969; August Closs, editor, *Twentieth Century German Literature,* Cresset Press, 1969; *Deutschunterricht,* October, 1969; *Time,* January 18, 1971, October 3, 1977; John Flores, *Poetry in East Germany,* Yale University Press, 1971; Robert Havemann, *Questions, Answers, Questions,* translated by Salvator Attanasie, Doubleday, 1972; Siegfried Mandel, *Group 47,* Southern Illinois University Press, 1973; *Newsweek,* February 11, 1974; Heinz Ludwig Arnold, editor, *Wolf Biermann,* Text und Kritik, 1975; Thomas Rothschild, editor, *Wolf Biermann: Liedermacher und Sozialist,* Rowohlt, 1976; *Economist,* November 20, 1976; Wolf Biermann, *Poems and Ballads,* Pluto Press, 1977; *Index on Censorship,* March-April, 1977; *New York Times Magazine,* October 23, 1977.*

*   *   *

BIHALJI-MERIN, Oto   1904-
(Peter Merin, Peter Thoene)

PERSONAL: Born January 3, 1904, in Belgrade, Yugoslavia; son of David (a painter) and Clara (a teacher; maiden name, Schoenman) Bihalji; married Elizabeth Asher (an author under name Liza Bihalji-Merin and a librarian), 1938; children: Mirjana Bihalji Schoenberner. *Education:* Attended Academy of Fine Arts, Belgrade, Yugoslavia, 1922-24, and Academy of Fine Arts, Berlin, Germany, 1924-27. *Politics:* Socialist. *Home:* YU-11000 Beograd, Nemanjina 3, Belgrade, Yugoslavia.

CAREER: Artist, journalist, art critic, and writer. Former editor of *Linkskurve,* Berlin, Germany; Yugoslavija (publisher), Belgrade, Yugoslavia, art director, beginning 1948; Mladinska knjiga (publisher), Ljubljana, Yugoslavia, art director, beginning 1968; currently free-lance writer. Lecturer in art in Vienna, Austria, 1960, Berlin, West Germany, 1964, Graz, Austria, 1965-69, Munich, West Germany, 1969. Member of exhibition committees; creator of television art films. *Military service:* Yugoslavian Air Force, 1929—. Interned in German prison camps, 1941-45; became captain first class. Yugoslavian Air Force Reserves, 1945—. *Member:* Association Internationale de Critiques d'Art, P.E.N., Writers Organization of Yugoslavia, Institute of Modern Art (Nuremberg, West Germany), Academy of Sciences, Letters, and Fine Arts (Brussels, Belgium). *Awards, honors:* Ordre Jugoslav, 1941-45; Gottfried von Herder prize, 1964; Ordre de Leopold (Belgium); Grand Cross of Distinguished Service of Federal Republic of Germany.

WRITINGS—In English: (Under pseudonym Peter Thoene) *Eroberung des Himmels: Geschichte des Fluggedankens,* E. P. Tal, 1937, translation by Charles Fullman published under pseudonym Peter Merin as *Conquest of the Skies: The Story of the Idea of Human Flight,* John Lane, 1938; (under Merin pseudonym) *Spanien Swischen tod und Gebert,* Christophe & Buechergilde Gutenberg, 1937, translation by Fullman published as *Spain Between Death and Birth,* Dodge, 1938; (under Thoene pseudonym) *Modern German Art,* Penguin, 1938.

Jugoslawische Skulptur des XX. Jahrhunderts, Jugoslavija, 1955, translation published as *Yugoslav Sculpture in the Twentieth Century,* Jugoslavija, 1955; (editor) *Contemporary Yugoslav Painting,* Jugoslavija, 1957; (editor) *Macedonia, Yugoslavia,* Jugoslavija, 1957; *Das naive Bild der Welt,* DuMont Schauberg, 1959, translation by Norbert Guterman published as *Modern Primitives: Masters of Naive Painting,* Abrams, 1961 (translation by Russell M. Stockman published in England as *Modern Primitives: Naive Painting From the Late Seventeenth Century Until the Present Day,* Thames & Hudson, 1971), new German edition published as *Die Malerei der Naiven,* DuMont Schauberg, 1975; (editor) *Yugoslavia Primitive Art,* Jugoslavija, 1959; (editor) *Umetnost naivnih u Jugoslaviji,* Jugoslavija, 1959, translation published as *Naive Art in Yugoslavia,* Jugoslavija, 1959.

(Editor) *Croatia, Yugoslavia,* Jugoslavija, 1961; (editor) *Montenegro, Yugoslavia,* Jugoslavija, 1961; (editor) *Serbia, Yugoslavia,* Jugoslavija, 1961; (editor) *Yugoslavia, Tracks and the Present,* Jugoslavija, 1961; (editor) *Adriatic Islands,* Jugoslavija, 1961; (editor) *Jugoslavija danas, 1941-1961,* Jugoslavija, 1961, translation published as *Yugoslavia Human Stories, 1941-1961,* Jugoslavija, 1962; (with Alojz Benac) *Stecci,* Jugoslavija, 1962, translation published as *The Bogomils,* Thames & Hudson, 1962, published as *Bogomil Sculpture,* Harcourt, 1963; *Primitive Artists of Yugoslavia,* McGraw, 1964; (editor with J. Ribnikar) *Savremeno slikarstvo u Jugoslaviji,* Jugoslavija, 1965, translation by Marija Stansfield-Popovic published as *Modern Yugoslav Painting,* Jugoslavija, 1965.

(Contributor) Hanns Reich, *Die Welt von oben,* Reich, 1966, translation published as *The World From Above,* Hill & Wang, 1968; *Adventures of Modern Art,* Abrams, 1966; (editor) *Umetnicko blago Jugoslavije,* Jugoslavija, 1969, translation published as *Art Treasures of Yugoslavia,* Abrams, 1972; *Masken der Welt: Verzauberung,* Bertelsmann Kunstverlag, 1970, translation by Herma Plummer published as *Masks of the World,* Thames & Hudson, 1971, published as *Great Masks,* Abrams, 1972; *Masters of Naive Art: A History and Worldwide Survey,* translated by Stockman from original manuscript, McGraw, 1974.

Other works: *Do videnja u oktobru* (novel; title means "Au Revoir in October"), Zagreb Hrvatske, 1948; *Misli i boje* (essays; title means "Thoughts and Colors"), Prosveta, 1950; (with wife, Liza Bihalji-Merin) *Mala zemlja izmedju svetova* (title means "A Small Country Among Worlds"), Prosveta, 1954; *Susreti sa mojim vremenom* (essays; title means "Encounters With Our Time"), Prosveta, 1957; (editor) *Sovremennaia iugoslavskaia zhivopis,* [Belgrade], 1957; (editor) *Mala enciklopedija Prosveta,* [Belgrade], 1959.

Abenteuer der modernen Kunst (title means "Adventure of Modern Art"), DuMont Schauberg, 1962; *Prodori moderne umetnosti: Utopija i nove stvarnosti,* Nolit, 1962; (editor) *Savremena jugoslovenska grafika* (title means "Contemporary Yugoslav Graphics"), Jugoslavija, 1963; *Graditelji moderne misli u literaturi i umetnosti,* Prosveta, 1965; (contributor) Toso Dabac, *Toso Dabac,* Foto-Savez Jugoslavije, 1967; *Ende der Kunst im Zeitalter der Wissenschaft?* (title means "The End of Art in the Era of Science?"), Kohlhammer, 1969.

(With Vasko Pregelj) *Marij Pregelj,* Obzorja, 1970; (editor with Liselotte Hansmann and Claus Hansmann) *Bruecken der Welt* (title means "Bridges of the World"), Bucher, 1971; *Die Naiven der Welt,* Kohlhammer, 1971; (with L. Bihalji-Merin) *Leben und Werk des Malers Henri Rousseau*

(title means "Life and Work of the Painter Henri Rousseau"), Verlag der Kunst, 1971, 2nd edition, 1973; (editor) *Mala splosna enciklopedija,* Prosveta, 1973; *Jedinstvo sveta u viziji umetnosti* (title means "Unity of the World in the Vision of Art"), Nolit, 1974; *Bild und Imagination* (title means "Image and Imagination"), Bucher, 1974; (with L. Bihalji-Merin and Ingrid Krause) *Die Kunst der Naiven* (title means "Art of the Naives"), Ausstellungsleitung Haus der Kunst Muenchen, 1974. Contributor to periodicals.

WORK IN PROGRESS: A three volume series on Francisco Goya.

SIDELIGHTS: Bihalji-Merin told *CA:* "Very early I left the small town where I was born to travel as far as I could. I was curious and impatient. Berlin became an important place for me with modern art, expressionism, first plays by Bertolt Brecht, and the 'Sturm' gallery of Herwart Walden.

"Sometimes people ask me if I am the 'father' of the naive artists! I organized the first exhibitions and wrote about primitive and naive arts in the world. That was an important experience in my life.

"During my long life, I met Maxim Gorki, Pablo Picasso, Kandinsky, and Brecht. In the United States I visited Alexander Calder, Ben Shahn, and William Faulkner, the ingenious romancer of our days."

*   *   *

BISCHOFF, David F(redrick) 1951-

PERSONAL: Born December 15, 1951, in Washington, D.C.; son of Herman (a fireman) and Betty Mae (Fesler) Bischoff. *Education:* University of Maryland, B.A., 1973. *Politics:* "Variable." *Religion:* Christian. *Home and office:* 2004 Erie St., Adelphi, Md. 20783. *Agent:* Henry Morrison Inc., 58 West Tenth St., New York, N.Y. 10011.

CAREER: Has worked variously as dishwasher, soda-jerk, salesman, clerk, and collection department operative; National Broadcasting Co. (NBC), Washington, D.C., employed in various positions, 1974—. *Member:* Science Fiction Writers of America (secretary, 1978—), Civil Air Patrol.

WRITINGS: (With Chris Lampton) *The Seeker,* Laser, 1976; *Phantom of the Opera* (juvenile), Scholastic Book Services, 1976; (editor) *Quest* (juvenile anthology), Raintree, 1977; *Strange Encounters,* Raintree, 1977; (with Ted White) *Forbidden World,* Popular Library, 1978; *Nightworld,* Del Ray, 1979; (with Dennis Bailey) *Tin Woodman,* Doubleday, 1979; *Star Fall,* Harcourt, 1979. Contributor of over thirty short stories to various publications, including *Thrust Science Fiction.* Associate editor of *Amazing Science Fiction.*

WORK IN PROGRESS—All fiction books: *Night Mayor; The Vampires of Nightworld; Changewinds; The Saved and the Damned.*

SIDELIGHTS: "I am a writer now," Bischoff told *CA,* "because I was first a fanatical devotee of science fiction. Much of what I write now is science fiction, but I have worked with historical fiction, detective and mystery stories, and fantasy and suspense. I shall never stop writing science fiction, but I hope to spread out further."

Bischoff sees an encouraging trend surrounding science fiction. "The important fact," he said, "is that it is diffusing into the rest of modern literature, as, at the same time, the general stream of modern literature is influencing science fiction.... Books, after all, are examples of the thoughts and lives of various people, different people. It's all part of communication, and communication has got to get mixed up together in order that the maximum possible amount of communication can be achieved. Otherwise it's no good.''

BIOGRAPHICAL/CRITICAL SOURCES: Fanny Hill, summer, 1978.

*   *   *

BISHOP, Robert 1938-

PERSONAL: Born August 25, 1938, in Readfield, Me; son of Charles H. and Muriel (Webber) Bishop. *Education:* University of Michigan, Ph.D., 1974. *Home:* 213 West 22nd St., New York, N.Y. 10011. *Office:* Museum of American Folk Art, 49 West 53rd St., New York, N.Y. 10019.

CAREER: Antique Shop, Readfield, Me., owner, 1956; Robert Bishop Gallery, New York City, owner, 1957-59; American Heritage Antiques, New York City, owner, 1959-63; Les Trois Provinces, New York City, artistic director, 1963-69; Henry Ford Museum, Dearborn, Mich., curator of furniture in department of decorative arts, 1968-73, museum editor, 1973-77, manager of publications, 1970-71; Museum of American Folk Art, New York City, director, 1977—. Guest lecturer at University of Michigan, 1972-74. Lecturer at museums and art conferences; appraiser of European and American furniture, folk art, and decorative art. Performer on Broadway and television programs, including ''Ed Sullivan,'' ''Carol Burnett,'' and ''Bell Telephone Hour''; performed with Metropolitan Opera; participated in European tour with Igor Stravinsky; New England regional dance director for Fred Astaire Studios. Registered representative of New York Stock Exchange, 1956-58; registered for real estate sales in New York, 1957-58; member of board of directors of Peace Realty Co. (past vice-president).

MEMBER: American Association of Museums, Arts Appraisal Assocation (president), Heritage Antique Appraisal Association of America (chairman), Antique Appraisal Association of America, National Trust for Historic Preservation, Smithsonian Institution, Victorian Society, Midwest Museums Conference, Impresario Cultural Society (past honorary president), Friends of Greenfield Village and Henry Ford Museum (life member), Connoisseur Club (Metropolitan Museum).

WRITINGS: (Editor) *Greenfield Village and Henry Ford Museum: Preserving America's Heritage,* Edison Institute, 1972; (with Dean Fales) *American Painted and Decorated Furniture,* Dutton, 1972; *Centuries and Styles of the American Chair, 1640-1970,* Dutton, 1972; (with Carleton Safford) *America's Quilts and Coverlets,* Dutton, 1972; *How to Know American Antique Furniture,* Dutton, 1973; *Guide to American Antique Furniture,* Edison Institute, 1973; *American Folk Sculpture,* Dutton, 1974; *New Discoveries in American Quilts,* Dutton, 1975; (with Elizabeth Safanda) *A Gallery of Amish Quilts,* Dutton, 1976; (with William Distin) *The American Clock,* Dutton, 1976; *The Borden Limner and His Contemporaries,* University of Michigan, Museum of Art, 1976; *American Victorian Art, Architecture, and Antiques,* Dutton, 1978.

Editor of catalogs and pamphlets. Editor of *Gray Letter;* associate editor of *Antique Monthly;* picture editor for American Heritage Publishing, 1963-69; Midwest editor of *Top Dobe,* 1969-73, and *Art Gallery,* 1970-72; Contributing editor of *Arts and Antiques.*

BISSELL, Elaine

PERSONAL: Born in Chicago, Ill.; daughter of Harold Whitney (a manufacturer) and Edwinna (Biederman) Faulkner; married John C. McMahon (an artist), May, 1941 (divorced); married Nicol Bissell (an architect), December, 1965; children: (first marriage) Mary Jane McMahon Christofferson, Kathleen McMahon Conroy, Susan. *Education:* Attended Goodman Theater School of Drama, 1936-39, and New York University, 1969-70. *Politics:* Republican. *Religion:* Protestant. *Home:* 9 Manchester Rd., Eastchester, N.Y. 10709. *Agent:* Meredith Bernstein, Henry Morrison, Inc., 58 West 10th St., New York, N.Y. 10011. *Office:* Gannett-Westchester Newspapers, 1 Gannett Dr., White Plains, N.Y. 10604.

CAREER: Free-lance radio and television writer, 1951-56; *Mamaroneck Daily Times,* Mamaroneck, N.Y., assistant women's editor, 1956-61; *New Rochelle Standard-Star,* New Rochelle, N.Y., editor of women's page, 1961-74; Gannett-Westchester Newspapers, White Plains, N.Y., social editor of ''Lifestyles,'' 1974-77, editor of ''Lifestyles'' and author of column, ''Three-Time Loser,'' and a rock-pop column, 1977—. Member of board of directors of Iona College Institute for the Arts and of Guidance Center of New Rochelle. *Member:* Dramatists Guild, Authors League of America. *Awards, honors:* Citations from city of New Rochelle, 1974, and Westchester Against Cancer; Penney-Missouri Award from University of Missouri School of Journalism and J. C. Penney Foundation, 1978, for ''Lifestyles'' section of Gannett-Westchester Newspapers, Inc.

WRITINGS: Women Who Wait (novel), M. Evans, 1978. Radio scriptwriter for ''Grand Central Station,'' ''Stars Over Hollywood,'' and ''Family Theater.'' Television scriptwriter for Columbia Broadcasting System (CBS-TV) and American Broadcasting Companies (ABC-TV).

WORK IN PROGRESS: A novel.

SIDELIGHTS: Elaine Bissell told *CA:* ''My first novel, *Women Who Wait,* started from a newspaper series I wrote on women in the Bedford Hills Correctional Facility in Bedford Hills, N.Y. I wanted to write a documentary book, but the inmates refused permission, so I turned the idea to fiction. The book concerns four women, three of them serving long minimum sentences for 'crimes of passion,' murdering their husbands, and the fourth one, an attorney, who believes they should receive full pardons and works toward that goal.

''In the newspaper series, as in the book, I brought the fact that in New York there is no review system for prisoners, and that a person serving a twenty-year minimum sentence would have to serve nineteen years before being reviewed by the parole board. And yet, penologists believe that if rehabilitation is going to take place, it will occur within the first three years of incarceration. They also believe that persons who perform 'crimes of passion' will not commit another major crime. All this is brought out in *Women Who Wait,* but in a fictionalized account. The climate now in this country is for tougher sentencing, meaning, of course, that prisoners who are no threat to society, such as the women in my book, cost $13,000 a year to keep in prison, but would only cost $500 a year if released and monitored by a parole officer—while many incorrigibles will continue to walk the streets and perform acts of violence and aggression.''

Bissell's favorite writers include Edith Wharton, Sinclair Lewis, F. Scott Fitzgerald, Jane Austen, Irwin Shaw, Herman Wouk, Anne Edwards, Jean Rhys, and Theodore Dreiser. She noted: ''I'm an old-fashioned novelist—at least

I've been told this—and I cling to my favorite authors, because they tell a marvelous story and tell it beautifully. I become easily bored with the gimmicky contemporary novelists; I think a lot of their work is pretentious junk. But there are many very good ones, too, including Joyce Carol Oates, Mary Gordon, Judith Guest and Joan Didion. There are more good women writers than ever, I think—in fiction, at least."

*   *   *

BLACKBURN, Paul 1926-1971

PERSONAL: Born November 24, 1926, in St. Albans, Vt.; son of William Gordon Blackburn and Frances Frost (a poet); married Winifred Gray (marriage ended); married Joan Miller; children: Carlos T. *Education:* Attended New York University; University of Wisconsin, B.A., 1950; attended University of Toulouse, 1954-55. *Home:* 60 Prospect Ter., Cortland, N.Y.

CAREER: Poet, translator, and editor. University of Toulouse, Toulouse, France, lecturer, 1955-56; Funk & Wagnalls, New York, N.Y., assistant editor of *New International Yearbook,* 1959-60. Taught writing at City College (now of the City University of New York); assistant professor of English at State University of New York, Cortland. *Awards, honors:* Fulbright fellow, 1954-55; Guggenheim fellow in poetry, 1967.

WRITINGS: The Dissolving Fabric (poems), Divers Press, 1955; *Brooklyn-Manhattan Transit: A Banquet for Flatbush* (poems), Totem Press, 1960; *The Nets* (poems), Trobar, 1961; *Sing-Song* (poems), Asphodel Bookshop (Cleveland), 1966; *Sixteen Sloppy Haiku and a Lyric for Robert Reardon,* 400 Rabbit Press (Cleveland), 1966; *The Cities* (poems), Grove, 1967; *The Reardon Poems,* Perishable Press, 1967; *In, On, or About the Premises: Being a Small Book of Poems,* Grossman, 1968; *Two New Poems,* Perishable Press, 1969; *Three Dreams and an Old Poem,* University Press at Buffalo, 1970; *Gin: Four Journal Pieces,* Perishable Press, 1970; *The Assassination of President McKinley: A Poem,* Perishable Press, 1970; *The Journals: Blue Mounds Entries,* Perishable Press, 1971; *Early Selected Y Mas: Collected Poems, 1949-1966,* Black Sparrow Press (Los Angeles), 1972; *The Journals,* edited by Robert Kelly, Black Sparrow Press, 1975; *Halfway Down the Coast: Poems and Snapshots,* Mulch Press (Northampton, Mass.), 1975.

Translator: *Proensa: An Anthology of Troubador Poetry,* Divers Press, 1953, reprinted, University of California Press, 1978; (editor and translator from the Spanish) El Cid Campeador, *Poems of the Cid,* American R.D.M. Corp., 1966; (from the Portugese with others) Elizabeth Bishop and Emanuel Brasil, editors, *An Anthology of Twentieth-Century Brazilian Poetry,* Wesleyan University Press, 1972; (from the Spanish) Julio Cortazar, *Cronopios and Famas,* Pantheon, 1978; (from the Spanish), Cortazar, *End of the Game, and Other Stories,* Harper, 1978. Also translator of works by Pierre Vidal and Guillaume IX, Duke of Aquitaine.

Contributor of poems to numerous magazines and literary journals, including *Black Mountain Review, Hudson Review, Partisan Review,* and *Nation.* Poetry editor of *Nation,* 1962.

SIDELIGHTS: Often associated with the Black Mountain poets of the 1950's, Blackburn has been compared to such poets as Robert Creeley, Charles Olson, Ezra Pound, and William Carlos Williams. His work has frequently been identified as "Projective" verse. "Blackburn's version of the style features, besides such familiar surface mannerisms as a mixing of high and low vernaculars, eccentric punctuation and clumping of words about the page—a kind of easy lope through all sorts of sense impressions, stray thoughts, bits of booklearning, bursts of emotion," Peter Schjeldahl wrote.

If, as Schjeldahl noted, Blackburn "seems at times to turn everything into poetry," he is usually quite successful at creating lyric poetry out of seemingly banal subjects. Ross Feld wrote: "Blackburn is one of those poets who gives you to believe he can write about anything, and do a half-way credible job of it, too. As a result we sometimes even mistrust him for a while, until we begin to catch sight of the poet in his poem, well armored with his hard-metal belief that poetry is the one thing that always remains. In a review of *The Journals,* William Heath commented: "Obviously this kind of poetry is often risky, and probably a majority of the poems don't quite come off, the fragments don't cohere . . . , the music doesn't make it through, the images don't earn their attention." Nonetheless, Heath contended, "He is one of the finest poets of his generation."

The strength of Blackburn's work is generally acknowledged to be his poetic voice. Blackburn's poetry, Gilbert Sorrentino asserted, "is at once a triumph of voice and a triumph over it, a total mastery of his endless and variegated materials in a form that allowed him complete flexibility." Sorrentino continued: "At that moment, in his poems, when we think we will, finally, be allowed to see the poet, he magically fades away into his voice, a protean voice so perfectly under control that we think it is telling us something true. [*The Journals*] is the work of a man who had come to a perfect sense of his own powers. He had done what all poets who have tried to remain faithful to the lyric must envy. His ego has been disguised, not revealed, by his voice, it has been subsumed. To come to this expertise within a poetic structure that we may call, for want of a better word, closed, is an enormous achievement. To arrive at this position in the poem as 'journal,' the open poem, is mastery."

Charles Stein was also impressed with this aspect of Blackburn's work. He wrote: "Blackburn assumes a number of voices in his poems which realize a compassion that is at once generous and alarming. The poems' matter-of-fact diction and the poet's suggested identification with his characters save him from self-congratulation and make his material potent and immediate."

The Journals was written from 1967 to 1971, when Blackburn died of cancer. Michael Stephens' praise is typical of the reception the book received. "This book is remarkable for many reasons," he wrote," among which are the maturity of Blackburn's poetry and poetics, the energy and intelligence of the writing, and the human courage informing every utterance. *The Journals* presents consummate Blackburn. The book culls deep intelligence, vast energy which refuses to wane with cancer, experience, and boldface originality. As the book presents new hope for poetry, it simultaneously breaks new ground for prose. Novelists of the future should read this work."

BIOGRAPHICAL/CRITICAL SOURCES: Times Literary Supplement, October 24, 1968; *Nation,* February 17, 1969, September 4, 1976; *Virginia Quarterly Review,* summer, 1973; *Parnassus: Poetry in Review,* spring/summer, 1974, spring/summer, 1976; *New York Times Book Review,* May 1, 1977; *Open Places,* spring/summer, 1977; *Contemporary Literary Criticism,* Volume 9, Gale, 1978.*

(Died September 13, 1971, in Cortland, N.Y.)

BLACKWELL, (Samuel) Earl (Jr.) 1913-

PERSONAL: Born May 3, 1913, in Atlanta, Ga.; son of Samuel Earl (a cotton broker) and Carrie (Lagomarsino) Blackwell. *Education:* Oglethorpe University, B.A., 1933; attended Columbia University. *Politics:* Republican. *Religion:* Roman Catholic. *Home and office:* Celebrity Service, Inc., 171 West 57th St., New York, N.Y. 10019. *Agent:* Irving Paul Lazar Agency, 211 South Beverly Dr., Beverly Hills, Calif. 90212.

CAREER: Previously worked in Hollywood, Calif., as an actor, and in New York, as a playwright; Celebrity Service, Inc., New York City, co-founder and president, 1939—, owner and publisher of *Celebrity Bulletin, Theatrical Calendar,* and *Contact Book,* publisher and co-editor of *Celebrity Register,* president of Celebrity Register Ltd., 1957—. Celebrity director for New York World's Fair, 1939-40; commentator of radio program, "Celebrity Table," 1955-56. Founder and first director of Theater Hall of Fame; president of Embassy Foundation, Inc., 1958-67. Director of New York City mayor's committee for scholastic achievement, 1957-65. *Member:* Pi Kappa Phi, Soldiers, Sailors & Airmen's Club (member of board of directors), Tamboo Club (Bahamas; president of board of governors, 1972—), Doubles Club (founder and chairman, 1975—), Raffles Club (founder; past chairman of board of directors), Nine O'-Clocks of New York (founder; past president), Boars Head Club, New York Athletic Club, Knights of Malta.

WRITINGS: (With Eugenia Sheppard) *Crystal Clear* (fiction), Doubleday, 1978. Author of "Aries Is Rising" (three-act play), first produced on Broadway at John Golden Theatre, 1939. Contributor to popular magazines. *Town and Country,* contributing editor, 1964—, and editorial consultant.

WORK IN PROGRESS: A novel; a screen adaptation of *Crystal Clear.*

SIDELIGHTS: Blackwell's clients are most often entertainers, but he also keeps files on businessmen, government officials, newspaper, radio, and television personalities, nonprofit organizations, and famous people in other fields all over the world. He has offices in Hollywood, London, Paris, and Rome. But his work goes beyond that of an editor. He produced President Kennedy's birthday celebration in Madison Square Garden in 1962, and in 1972, he organized Israel's twenty-fifth anniversary celebration in Jerusalem.

*   *   *

BLANCHARD, Paula (Barber) 1936-

PERSONAL: Born December 2, 1936, in Flushing, N.Y.; daughter of Roscoe Hall (an engineer) and Mildred C. (Hansen) Barber; married Byron E. Blanchard (an engineer), December 7, 1963. *Education:* Attended University of New Hampshire, 1953-55; Harvard University, B.A., 1964; Tufts University, M.A., 1969. *Politics:* Liberal. *Religion:* "Complicated." *Residence:* Lexington, Mass. *Office:* c/o Seymour Lawrence, Inc., 90 Beacon St., Boston, Mass.

CAREER: Writer, 1965—.

WRITINGS: Margaret Fuller: From Transcendentalism to Revolution, Seymour Lawrence, 1978. Contributor to *New Hampshire Profiles.*

WORK IN PROGRESS: Research on Emily Carr.

SIDELIGHTS: Blanchard told *CA:* "I have good reason to know how thin is the line separating the writer who is able to write from the one who is not, and I know that for many women our society makes that line almost impossible to cross. My interest in Margaret Fuller and Emily Carr stems from my own experience of the obstacles women face—not only the external ones, but the inner ones of which we have only recently become aware."

*   *   *

BLISS, George William 1918-1978

OBITUARY NOTICE: Born July 21, 1918, in Denver, Colo.; died September 11, 1978. in Oak Lawn, Ill. A three-time Pulitzer Prize-winning investigative reporter for the *Chicago Tribune,* Bliss was well known for exposing a fraudulent election and a federal housing program scandal. Obituaries and other sources: *Newsweek,* September 25, 1978; *Time,* September 25, 1978; *Who's Who in America,* 40th edition, Marquis, 1978.

*   *   *

BLUEBOND-LANGNER, Myra 1948-

PERSONAL: Born June 29, 1948, in Philadelphia, Pa.; daughter of Mahlon (a wholesaler) and Claire (a secretary; maiden name, Schulman) Bluebond; married Richard Woods Langner, June 9, 1972; children: Rachel Olga. *Education:* Temple University, B.A., 1969; University of Illinois, M.A., 1971, Ph.D., 1975. *Home:* 2505 Panama Mall, Philadelphia, Pa. 19103. *Office:* Department of Sociology and Anthropology, Rutgers University, Camden Campus, Camden, N.J. 08102.

CAREER: Rutgers University, Camden Campus, Camden, N.J., assistant professor, 1974-78, associate professor of anthropology, 1978—. Instructor for Hebrew school, 1965-67, 1967-68, and for preschool reading readiness program, 1969; guest lecturer at colleges and universities. Guest on television and radio programs, including "Not for Women Only." Conducted field research all over the United States; expert witness for Federal Trade Commission. Member of advisory board of Term-Care, Inc., 1975-77; vice-president of Ars Moriendi, 1976-77; member of international advisory council for National Institute for the Seriously Ill and Dying, 1976—. Principal of Rodeph Shalom Religious School, 1974-75.

MEMBER: American Anthropological Association (fellow), Society for Applied Anthropology (fellow), Society for Medical Anthropology, American Association for the Advancement of Science, American Association of University Professors (member of local executive committee, 1975—), Philadelphia Anthropological Society, Sigma Xi, Phi Kappa Phi.

WRITINGS: (Contributor) Bernard Schoenberg and other editors, *Anticipatory Grief,* Columbia University Press, 1974; (contributor) Harry Brendt and William Lutz, editors, *Rhetorical Consideration,* Winthrop Publishing, 1976; (contributor) Herman Feifel, editor, *New Meanings of Death,* McGraw, 1977; *The Private Worlds of Dying Children,* Princeton University Press, 1978. Contributor to *Current Anthropology.* Member of editorial board of *Journal of the Julian Steward Society,* 1969-71.

WORK IN PROGRESS: The World of the Preschool Child, with David Rosen.

*   *   *

BLUESTEIN, Gene 1928-

PERSONAL: Born May 1, 1928, in Bronx, N.Y.; son of Jack (a furrier) and Masha (Oysher) Bluestein; married Eleanore Bisberg, June 12, 1949; children: Joel, Avrom, Jeremy, Frayda. *Education:* Brooklyn College (now of the City University of New York), B.A., 1950; University of Minnesota, M.A., 1952, Ph.D., 1959. *Home:* 4414 East Alamos, Fresno, Calif. 93726. *Office:* Department of English, California State University, Fresno, Calif. 93740.

CAREER: Michigan State University, East Lansing, instructor, 1960-62, assistant professor of American thought and language, 1962-63; California State University, Fresno, associate professor, 1963-65, professor of English, 1965—. Fulbright professor at University of Helsinki, 1967-68; distinguished visiting professor at Brooklyn College of the City University of New York, 1978. Director of University of Southern California's Idyllwild School of Music and the Arts folk music program, 1967—; resident folklorist at Pinewoods Folk Music Camp, 1970-71; presented folklore and folk music programs on University of Minnesota's educational television network and folk music special on Nordic Television. *Member:* American Studies Association. *Awards, honors:* Carnegie Foundation fellowship, 1955, 1957; James J. Hill Family Foundation fellowship, 1958; California State Colleges and Universities Creative Research grant, 1966; distinguished lecturer award, 1974, from California State University, Fresno.

WRITINGS: (Contributor) Jules Chametzky, editor, *Black and White in American Culture,* Viking, 1970; *The Voice of the Folk: Folklore and American Literary Theory,* University of Massachusetts Press, 1972. Contributor of more than a dozen articles to academic journals and popular magazines, including *New Republic* and *Progressive.*

WORK IN PROGRESS: Research on Yiddish in American literature, folklore and the American experience, and "Literary Calvinism: The Brotherhood of Sinners."

SIDELIGHTS: Bluestein told *CA:* "My main interest is in American Studies, which gives me an opportunity to bring together ideas from literature, music, and popular culture. My activity as a performing artist of folk music is an attempt to preserve me from hardening of the academic arteries. In recent years I have been working with the National Endowment for the Arts to bring traditional performers to California State University, Fresno, as resident artists. It gives students as well as the general community an opportunity to discover that our folk heritage is alive and well and will continue so if we pay attention to it."

His recordings, all for Folkways Records, include "Songs of the North Star State," "Songs of the Holidays," "Bamboushay Steel Band," "Buell Kazee Plays and Sings," and "California's a Garden of Eden: The Bluestein Family."

* * *

BOGDANOR, Vernon 1943-

PERSONAL: Surname is accented on first syllable; born July 16, 1943, in London, England; son of Harry (a pharmacist) and Rosa (Weinger) Bogdanor; married Judy Evelyn Beckett (a doctor), July 27, 1972; children: Paul Simon Rupert, Adam Mark Daniel. *Education:* Queen's College, Oxford, B.A. (first class honors), 1964; Nuffield College, Oxford, M.A., 1968. *Agent:* Caradoc King, A. P. Watt & Son, 26/28 Bedford Row, London WC1R 4HL, England. *Office:* Department of Politics, Brasenose College, Oxford University, Oxford, England.

CAREER: Oxford University, Oxford, England, tutor in politics and fellow of Brasenose College, 1966—, university lecturer in politics, 1967—.

WRITINGS: (Editor and contributor) *The Age of Affluence, 1951-1964,* Macmillan, 1970; (editor) *Disraeli: Lothair,* Oxford University Press, 1975; *Devolution,* Oxford University Press, 1979. Contributor to British periodicals, including *Spectator, Encounter,* and *Times Literary Supplement.*

WORK IN PROGRESS: Research on modern British government and on the nature of federalism.

* * *

BOSLOOPER, Thomas 1923-

PERSONAL: Born December 30, 1923, in Grand Rapids, Mich.; son of Peter and Gertrude (DeVries) Boslooper; married Lois Taylor, August 31, 1948; children: Peter, Jonathan. *Education:* Attended Calvin College, 1941-44; Hope College, A.B., 1945; Western Theological Seminary, B.D., 1947; attended Union Theological Seminary, New York, N.Y., 1948-49; Columbia University, Ph.D., 1954. *Politics:* Independent. *Office address:* Box 130, Closter, N.J. 07624.

CAREER: Ordained minister of Reformed Church in America, 1947; minister in Closter, N.J., 1949-55 and 1965-76, Pella, Iowa, 1955-60, and Schenectady, N.Y., 1960-65. Teacher of religion in New York, N.Y., at Marymount, 1968-73, and at Notre Dame Academy, 1972-75; professor of Biblical studies at Unification Seminary, Barrytown, N.Y., 1975—.

WRITINGS: The Virgin Birth, Westminster, 1962; (with Marcia Hayes) *The Feminity Game,* Stein & Day, 1973. Contributor of articles to *Christian Century, Religion in Life, WomenSports, Journal of Physical Education,* and *Saturday Evening Post.*

WORK IN PROGRESS: A book entitled *The Image of Woman in Classical and Biblical Tradition;* research on the Unification Church.

SIDELIGHTS: Boslooper believes that girls and women should engage in sports and other forms of physical activity, and has been lecturing on the subject since 1962. He told *CA* he has given major presentations at the American Association for the Advancement of Science and the World Congress on Sport.

BIOGRAPHICAL/CRITICAL SOURCES: WomenSports, July, 1974.

* * *

BOWERSOCK, G(len) W(arren) 1936-

PERSONAL: Born January 12, 1936, in Providence, R.I.; son of Donald Curtis (an insurance executive) and Josephine (Evans) Bowersock. *Education:* Harvard University, A.B. (summa cum laude), 1957; Oxford University, B.A. (first class honors), 1959, M.A., 1962, D.Phil., 1962. *Home:* 5 Brewster St., Cambridge, Mass. 02138. *Office:* Department of Classics, 319 Boylston, Harvard University, Cambridge, Mass. 02138.

CAREER: Oxford University, Balliol College and New College, Oxford, England, lecturer in ancient history, 1960-62; Harvard University, Cambridge, Mass., instructor, 1962-64, assistant professor, 1964-67, associate professor, 1967-69, professor of Greek and Latin, 1969—, chairman of department of classics, 1972-77, associate dean of Faculty of Arts and Sciences, 1977—. Visiting professor at Oxford University, 1966, and Australian National University, 1972; lecturer in the United States, Canada, England, Germany, France, Switzerland, Italy, Greece, Turkey, Jordan, Israel, New Zealand, and Australia. Co-chairman of International

Conference on Pre-Islamic Arabia, 1972; consultant to National Endowment for the Humanities.

MEMBER: American Philological Association, Archaeological Institute of America, American Academy of Arts and Sciences (fellow), Society for the Promotion of Roman Studies (England), Society for the Promotion of Hellenic Studies (England), Phi Beta Kappa. *Awards, honors:* Rhodes Scholar at Balliol College, Oxford, 1957-61; senior fellow of Center for Hellenic Studies, 1976—.

WRITINGS: Augustus and the Greek World, Oxford University Press, 1965; *Ps.-Xenophon: Constitution of the Athenians,* Loeb Library, 1968; *Greek Sophists in the Roman Empire,* Oxford University Press, 1969; (editor) *Apollonius of Tyana,* translation by C. P. Jones, Penguin, 1970; (editor) *Approaches to the Second Sophistic,* American Philological Association, 1974; (editor with John Clive and Stephen Graubard) *Edward Gibbon and the Decline and Fall of the Roman Empire,* Harvard University Press, 1977; *Julian the Apostate,* Harvard University Press, 1978.

Contributor to *Encyclopaedia Britannica* and *Cambridge History* of *Classical Literature.* Contributor of about seventy articles to scholarly journals. Member of editorial board of "Provinces of the Roman Empire," Routledge and Kegan Paul, 1967—. Corresponding member of editorial board of *Phoenix,* 1978—.

WORK IN PROGRESS: Rome and the Arabs, publication by Harvard University Press expected in 1981.

SIDELIGHTS: Bowersock commented briefly: "I believe that an author can be best understood through his writings, through the choices he has seen fit to make in his life, and through unselfconscious *obiter dicta* which some Boswell may have chanced to record."

* * *

BOYER, Elizabeth (Mary) 1913-

PERSONAL: Born November 12, 1913, in Fremont, Ohio; daughter of Clyde S. and Lydia (Miller) Boyer; divorced. *Education:* Bowling Green State University, B.S.; Cleveland-Marshall Law of School, J.D.; Western Reserve University (now Case Western Reserve University), LL.M., 1957. *Politics:* Independent. *Religion:* Presbyterian. *Home:* 7657 Dines Rd., Novelty, Ohio 44072. *Agent:* H. N. Swanson, Inc., 8523 Sunset Blvd., Los Angeles, Calif. 90069.

CAREER: Attorney in private practice of law, 1947—; Cuyahoga Community College, Cleveland, Ohio, faculty member, 1966—.

MEMBER: Zonta International, National Association of Women Lawyers, Writers Guild of America, Authors Guild, Authors League of America, American Association of University Professors, American Association of University Women, Women's Equity Action League (founder), Business and Professional Women's Club, Ohio Bar Association, Cuyahoga County Bar Association, Women's City Club of Cleveland, Pi Kappa Delta, Sigma Tau Delta, Delta Gamma. *Awards, honors:* Named woman of achievement by Cleveland Interclub Council, 1973.

WRITINGS: Marguerite de la Roque: A Story of Survival (historical novel), Veritie Press, 1975; *Freydis and Gudrid* (historical novel), Veritie Press, 1976. Contributor to law journals.

WORK IN PROGRESS: A contemporary suspense novel, *The Scratching Inside the Wall.*

SIDELIGHTS: Elizabeth Boyer comments: "I am interested in historical achievements of little-recognized women whose exploits have been notable but largely forgotten. My interest in historical research (largely in medieval French) led to the writing of *Marguerite.*"

AVOCATIONAL INTERESTS: Ecology, sailing, survival in the wild.

* * *

BOYLAN, Brian Richard 1936-

PERSONAL: Born December 11, 1936, in Chicago, Ill.; son of Francis T. (a principal) and Mary (an educator; maiden name, Kane) Boylan; divorced; children: Rebecca Boylan Wold, Gregory, Ingrid. *Education:* Attended Loyola University, Chicago, Ill. *Politics:* "Indifferent." *Religion:* None. *Home and office:* 1530 South Sixth St., Minneapolis, Minn. 55454. *Agent:* Timothy Seldes, Russell & Volkening, Inc., 551 Fifth Ave., New York, N.Y. 10017.

CAREER: Photographer, 1965—. Film director and producer, 1967—; theatrical director in New York and New Jersey, 1969—.

WRITINGS: The New Heart (nonfiction), Chilton, 1969; *Infidelity* (nonfiction), Prentice-Hall, 1971; *Benedict Arnold: The Dark Eagle* (biography), Norton, 1973. Also author of "The Trial of Major Andre" (play), "The Dark Eagle" (filmscript), and "The Wonderful World of Smoking" (screenplay).

WORK IN PROGRESS: Satan's Moon; Getting in Shape; The Angel of Death, a biography of Dr. Josef Mengele.

SIDELIGHTS: Boylan remarks that one of his main interests has been "history, especially the darker side. My current interest in surviving Nazi war criminals has led me throughout South America, and shortly will take me to Europe. Other than this interest, my writing now is exclusively in fiction, drama, and screenplay form. For me, this is the most creative medium."

* * *

BRACE, Gerald Warner 1901-1978

OBITUARY NOTICE—See index for *CA* sketch: Born September 23, 1901, in Islip, N.Y.; died July 20, 1978, in Blue Hill, Me. Educator and author of novels and criticism. A professor of English at Boston University, Brace wrote about New England life. In his books he advocated such traditional virtues as moderation, self-control, and reason. His last novel, *The Department,* was lauded for its discerning portrayal of academic life. Obituaries and other sources: *Current Biography,* Wilson, 1947, September, 1978; *The Oxford Companion to American Literature,* 4th edition, Oxford University Press, 1965; *The Author's and Writer's Who's Who,* 6th edition, Burke's Peerage, 1971; *Directory of American Scholars,* Volume II: *English, Speech, and Drama,* 6th edition, Bowker, 1974; *The Writers Directory, 1976-78,* St. Martin's, 1976; *Who's Who in America,* 40th edition, Marquis, 1978; *New York Times,* July 22, 1978; *Publishers Weekly,* July 31, 1978; *Time,* July 31, 1978.

* * *

BRANCH, William Blackwell 1927-

PERSONAL: Born September 11, 1927, in New Haven, Conn.; son of James Matthew (a minister) and Iola (Douglas) Branch; divorced; children: Rochelle Ellen. *Education:* Northwestern University, B.S., 1949; Columbia University,

M.F.A., 1958, graduate study, 1958-60; additional study at Yale University, 1965-66. *Home and office:* 53 Cortlandt Ave., New Rochelle, N.Y. 10801.

CAREER: Has worked as an actor in theatre, films, radio, and television; field representative, *Ebony* magazine, 1949-50; free-lance producer, writer and director of plays, films, and news documentaries, 1950—; president of William Branch Associates (development, production and consulting firm), 1973—. Director of "The Jackie Robinson Show," NBC-Radio, 1959-60; staff producer, contributing writer, and director of documentary films for "The City" series, Educational Broadcasting Corp., 1962-64; writer and director of "The Alma John Show," 1963-65; writer and producer of television documentary programs for NBC, 1972-73. Associate in film, Columbia University, 1968-69; visiting playwright at Smith College, summer, 1970, and North Carolina Central University, spring-summer, 1971; lecturer at colleges and universities, including Harvard University, University of Ghana, Fisk University, and University of California, Los Angeles. *Military service:* U.S. Army, 1951-53; served as educational instructor in Germany.

AWARDS, HONORS: Robert E. Sherwood Television Award and National Council of Christians and Jews citation, 1958, both for television drama "Light in the Southern Sky"; Hannah del Vecchio Award from Columbia University, 1958; John Simon Guggenheim fellowship for creative writing in drama, 1959-60; American Film Festival award and "Emmy" award nomination, 1969, both for television documentary "Still a Brother: Inside the Negro Middle Class."

WRITINGS—Plays: "A Medal for Willie," first produced in New York City at Club Baron, 1951; "In Splendid Error," first produced in New York City at Greenwich Mews Theatre, 1955; "To Follow the Phoenix," first produced in Chicago at Civic Opera House, 1960; "A Wreath for Udomo" (based on novel by Peter Abrahams), first produced on the West End at Lyric Theatre, 1961; "Baccalaureate," first produced in Hamilton, Bermuda, at City Hall Theatre, 1975. Work represented in anthologies, including *Black Scenes,* edited by Alice Childress, Doubleday, 1971; *Black Drama Anthology,* edited by Woodie King and Ron Milner, Columbia University Press, 1972; and *Black Theatre U.S.A.,* edited by James V. Hatch and Ted Shine, Free Press, 1974.

Screenplays and documentary dramas: "Fifty Steps Toward Freedom," National Association for the Advancement of Colored People (NAACP), 1959; "The Man on Meeting Street," Alpha Kappa Alpha Sorority, 1960; "Judgement!," Belafonte Enterprises, 1969; "Together for Days," Olas Corp., 1971.

Television documentaries and dramas: "The Way," American Broadcasting Co., 1955; "Let's Find Out" series, National Council of Churches, 1956; "What is Conscience?," Columbia Broadcasting System, 1955; "Light in the Southern Sky," National Broadcasting Co., 1958; "Legacy of a Prophet," Educational Broadcasting Corp., 1959; "Still a Brother: Inside the Negro Middle Class," National Educational Television, 1968; "The Case of the Non-Working Workers," National Broadcasting Co., 1972; "The 20 Billion Dollar Rip-Off," National Broadcasting Co., 1972; "No Room to Run, No Place to Hide," National Broadcasting Co., 1972; "The Black Church in New York," National Broadcasting Co., 1973.

Author of a filmstrip, screenplay outlines, and radio scripts; also author of syndicated newspaper column with Jackie

Robinson, 1958-60. Contributor to *The American Negro Writer and His Roots,* edited by Alice Childress, American Society of African Culture, 1960; also contributor to periodicals.

WORK IN PROGRESS: A play and a screenplay, both untitled.

SIDELIGHTS: Loften Mitchell wrote of Branch's first play, "A Medal for Willie," that it "posed in strong dramatic terms the question: should the Negro soldier fight and die abroad or should he take up arms against the prejudiced southland?" Mitchell noted that the play "didn't only shock white people. It shocked Negroes." On the day following the successful opening of "A Medal for Willie," Branch was inducted into the Army.

During his tour of service in Germany, Branch wrote "In Splendid Error," a play concerning the historical characters John Brown and Frederick Douglass. The play was produced in New York in 1954, and despite production problems enjoyed a successful run.

"Light in the Southern Sky" was written as a television drama rather than for the stage. The drama is the story of Mary McLeod Bethune, a pioneering black educator. For this production, Branch was the recipient of the Robert E. Sherwood Television Award which was presented to him by Eleanor Roosevelt.

William Branch told *CA:* "Though considerable progress, relatively, seems to have been made in the past quarter-century in mainstream utilization of Black Americans as subject matter in the arts and the media, and of Black American writers and other creative professionals in these fields, my concern continues to be focused upon how much further there is yet to go before racism no longer constitutes the unspoken barrier which must almost constantly be overcome before we can then move on to more basic and realistic *curriculum vitae,* such as talent, craft and creative vision."

BIOGRAPHICAL/CRITICAL SOURCES: Freedomways, Summer, 1963; Loften Mitchell, *Black Drama: The Story of the American Negro in the Theatre,* Hawthorne, 1967; *Negro Digest,* January, 1968; Doris E. Abramson, *Negro Playwrights in the American Theatre, 1925-1959,* Columbia University Press, 1969.

* * *

BRAND, Stewart 1938-

PERSONAL: Born December 14, 1938, in Rockford, Ill.; son of Arthur Barnard (in advertising) and Julia (Morley) Brand; married Lois Jennings, December, 1966 (divorced, 1972). *Education:* Stanford University, B.S., 1960; studied design and photography at San Francisco Art Institute College and San Francisco State College (now University). *Politics:* Conservative. *Religion:* "Quasi Buddhist." *Office:* c/o *CoEvolution Quarterly,* Box 428, Sausalito, Calif. 94965.

CAREER: Researcher in the office of Gordon Ashby, San Francisco, Calif., 1963-64; artist and performer in "America Needs Indians," San Francisco, 1963-66; organizer, Trips Festival, San Francisco, 1966; organizer, New Games Tournament, San Francisco, 1973; *CoEvolution Quarterly,* Sausalito, Calif., editor and publisher, 1973—. Member, Merry Pranksters, 1964-69; special consultant to California Governor Jerry Brown, 1976—. *Military service:* U.S. Army, 1960-62, served in infantry; became first lieutenant. *Member:* Point Foundation (president, 1972-74), Neighborhood Foundation, Magic Theater, Bread and Roses. *Awards, honors:* National Book Award in Contemporary Affairs,

1972, for *The Last Whole Earth Catalog;* Lindisfarne fellow, 1975.

WRITINGS: (Editor) *The Last Whole Earth Catalog: Access to Tools,* Random House, 1971, 16th edition, 1975; (editor) *Whole Earth Epilog,* Penguin, 1974; *Two Cybernetic Frontiers,* Random House, 1974; (editor) *Space Colonies,* Penguin, 1977; (editor with J. Baldwin) *Soft Tech,* Penguin, 1978.

WORK IN PROGRESS: A book entitled *Tree Life.*

SIDELIGHTS: The Last Whole Earth Catalog has been praised by many critics as a cleverly annotated listing of tools for the self-sufficient person; a reviewer for the *Virginia Quarterly Review* described it as "a combination of many unlikely and often hard-to-find items laced with pithy comments and lively asides." In addition to listing the necessary implements for an independent life, *The Last Whole Earth Catalog* also lists the titles of hundreds of useful books. But according to *Economist,* the book is more than an entertaining catalog and bibliography: "It is a philosophical tract that endeavours to make shopping via catalogue a spiritual experience . . . It has become the bible of the commune and the creator of the cults. Earth is the theme throughout."

Brand's other books also reflect his interest in science, technology, and individual education. *Two Cybernetic Frontiers* recounts "much of what is going on in the artificial intelligence branch of computing—computer music, games, and the wild, active, computer-oriented pranks that computer bums and hacks play on each other and on the world—all in informal, nontechnical prose." *Space Colonies* has been lauded by *Book World* as a book which "does not so much discuss as surround the subject, looking at it from dozens of angles and giving room to a variety of apparently conflicting views. Anyone who is turned on by the concept of space colonization will want to examine these ideas."

Brand told *CA* that there are certain people whose ideas and activities he watches closely: Steve Durkee, Steve Baer, Ken Kesey, Richard Baker-Roshi, Jerry Brown, Buckminster Fuller, Phillip Morrison, and Gregory Bateson.

BIOGRAPHICAL/CRITICAL SOURCES: Virginia Quarterly Review, spring, 1972; *Economist,* December 30, 1972; *Choice,* November, 1974; *Book World,* January 8, 1978.

*   *   *

BRAND, Susan
     See ROPER, Susan Bonthron

*   *   *

BREDEMEIER, Mary E(lizabeth)   1924-

PERSONAL: Born September 4, 1924, in Cascade, Va.; daughter of W. T. (a builder) and Cora (Lewis) Robertson: married Harry Charles Bredemeier (a professor), November 16, 1953; children: Suzanne. *Education:* Madison College, B.S., 1944; Columbia University Teachers College, M.A., 1946; Rutgers University, Ed.D., 1973. *Politics:* Democrat. *Religion:* Unitarian Universalist. *Home:* 150 Emerson Rd., Somerset, N.J. 08873.

CAREER: Finch College, New York, N.Y., instructor in home economics, 1945-46; teacher of home economics in Yonkers, N.Y., 1948-53; Rutgers University, Douglass College, New Brunswick, N.J., instructor in home economics, 1953-54; teacher of social studies and guidance counselor in Woodbridge, N.J., 1954-67; Montclair State College, Upper Montclair, N.J., assistant professor, 1967-72, associate pro-

fessor of education, 1972—, president of faculty senate, 1977—. *Member:* American Association of University Professors (president of New Jersey conference, 1978—), American Personnel and Guidance Association, Eastern Sociological Society.

WRITINGS: The Worker in Modern Society, N.J. State Department of Education, 1973; (with husband, Harry Charles Bredemeier) *Social Forces in Education,* Alfred Publishing, 1978. Contributor of numerous articles to various professional journals. Associate editor of *Teaching Sociology,* 1978—.

WORK IN PROGRESS: Social and Philosophical Foundations of Counseling, a textbook for introduction to counseling.

SIDELIGHTS: Bredemeier told *CA:* "One of my main purposes in writing and teaching is to help educators learn to think more sociologically than they presently do. I teach graduate students, primarily—most of them educators. Their educational backgrounds reflect little or no awareness of the impact of social structure on personality development. Rather, they tend to interpret behavior and events in personal terms. To put it differently: One may ask, 'What can I do to the psyche of this child to help him/her run this maze (school)?' *Or,* one may ask, 'What can I do to this maze to help this child run it?' I encourage educators to ask the second question more often."

*   *   *

BREGGIN, Peter R(oger)   1936-

PERSONAL: Born May 11, 1936, in Brooklyn, N.Y.; son of Morris Louis (an accountant) and Jean (Weinstein) Breggin; married Sally Ann Friedman, 1960 (divorced, 1970); married Phyllis Lundy, October 13, 1972; children: Linda Karen, Sharon Jane, Benjamin Jay. *Education:* Harvard University, B.A., 1958; Case Western Reserve University, M.D., 1962. *Politics:* Libertarian. *Home and office:* 4628 Chestnut St., Bethesda, Md. 20014.

CAREER: State University of New York Upstate Medical Center, Syracuse, intern, 1962-63; Massachusetts Mental Health Center, Boston, Mass., resident in psychiatry, 1963-64; State University of New York Upstate Medical Center, resident in psychiatry, 1964-66; National Institute of Mental Health, Charlottesville, Va. and Rockville, Md., consultant, 1966-68; Washington School of Psychiatry, Washington, D.C., faculty member, 1968-73, and director of project to examine psychiatric technology, 1972-73; Center for the Study of Psychiatry, Bethesda, Md., founder and executive director, 1973—. Licensed in New York, Washington, D.C., Virginia, and Maryland; diplomate of National Board of Medical Examiners. Private practice of psychiatry, 1968—. Guest on television and radio programs in the United States, Canada, and Europe. *Military service:* U.S. Public Health Service, 1966-68; became lieutenant commander.

MEMBER: American Psychiatric Association, American Association for the Abolition of Involuntary Mental Hospitalization, Authors Guild of the Authors League of America, Libertarian Health Association, District of Columbia Psychiatric Association.

WRITINGS: (With Carter Umbarger, James Dalsimer, and Andrew Morrison) *College Students in a Mental Hospital,* Grune, 1962; *The Crazy From the Sane* (novel), Lyle Stuart, 1971; *After the Good War: A Love Story* (novel), Stein & Day, 1972; *Electroshock as Brain-Disabling Therapy,*

Springer Publishing, 1979. Also author of "Johnson versus Goldman," a three-act play, as yet neither published nor produced. Contributor of more than twenty articles and reviews to medical and law journals and popular magazines and newspapers, including *Penthouse.*

WORK IN PROGRESS: Liberty and Love as a Way of Life, a book which "develops in plain English a personal psychology based on the exercise of free will, courage, and reason"; *The Menace of Psychiatry to You; Psychiatric Drugs as Brain-Disabling Therapy; When I See a Duck,* with wife, Phyllis L. Breggin, a three-volume series for preschoolers; *A Letter to Benjamin,* a book "reminding him of his joyful individuality at the age of one."

SIDELIGHTS: Breggin writes: "The Center for the Study of Psychiatry is a non-profit research and educational foundation devoted to examining psychiatry against the values of personal freedom, civil liberties, and the well-being of the individual. The board of directors includes Congressmen, noted lawyers, psychiatrists, and individuals from across the political spectrum. Our main achievement has been drawing attention to the psychiatric abuse of individuals subjected to involuntary drug therapy, psychosurgery, electroshock, and other oppressive technologies.

"In my private practice of psychotherapy I use no drugs and refuse to participate in involuntary treatment. My emphasis is upon the individual's personal responsibility for overcoming his failures and for learning to fulfill his dreams and aspirations.

"My two novels, many of my professional and popular publications, and most of my public appearances have dealt in part with examining and criticizing psychiatry from the viewpoint of libertarian ethics and politics. But I am devoting an increasing amount of time to my positive ideals about individual liberty and life. Above all, I love to write fiction."

BIOGRAPHICAL/CRITICAL SOURCES: Human Behavior, November, 1973.

* * *

BRENNAN, Maeve 1917-

PERSONAL: Born January 6, 1917, in Dublin, Ireland; came to United States in 1934; daughter of Robert and Anastasia (Bolger) Brennan. married St. Clair McKelway (a writer; divorced). *Education:* Attended a convent school in Ireland. *Agent:* Russell & Volkening, Inc., 555 Fifth Ave., New York, N.Y. 10017. *Office:* 25 West 43rd St., New York, N.Y. 10036.

CAREER: Harpers Bazaar, New York City, copywriter, 1943-49; *New Yorker,* New York City, writer, 1949—.

WRITINGS: In and Out of Never-Never Land (short stories), Scribner, 1969; *The Long-Winded Lady,* Morrow, 1969; *Christmas Eve* (short stories), Scribner, 1974.

SIDELIGHTS: Brennan's books are collections of short stories or other writings, most of which have been published in the *New Yorker* through the years. Critics have generally agreed with Joyce Carol Oates' description of Brennan's writing as "polished gentle, highly feminine," and that her talent is in transforming the commonplace into something quite meaningful.

Out of Never-Never Land is a collection of twenty-two tales, many based on every-day middle-class life in Dublin, Ireland. "They are conventional short stories, expertly realized, expertly controlled and very moving," commented Anne O'Neill-Barna in the *New York Times Book Review.*

Oates wrote in *Saturday Review* that, despite the book's merits, "one does expect from fiction something more than the carefully controlled 'cute' dullness of *In and Out of Never-Never Land.*"

Brennan's vignettes are based on "the overheard and the glimpsed and the guessed at," wrote John Updike in a review of *The Long-Winded Lady.* The author "is constantly alert, sharp-eyed as a sparrow for the crumbs of human event." W. G. Rogers observed: "The pieces all together give a clearer understanding of her feminine aptitude for proving that what looks unimportant is often very important. Her speciality is the stuff of New York City itself . . ." Disagreeing, a *New York* reviewer said simply that reading it "is like being trapped with a dread dinner companion on a 21-day cruise."

Christmas Eve contains both stories set in a working-class area of Dublin, Ireland, and in an affluent New York City suburb. In critic Robert Kiely's opinion, "the Irish stories, though unsensational, have a fine, mature, well-knit quality to them," while the American tales are "shallow, obvious, ill-composed and all but devoid of fresh observation, intellectual subtlety and emotional depth." Helen Rogan wrote in *Time* that Brennan's stories are marked by a "steady accumulation of detail and alternate flashes of passionate statement and raw insight. The accomplishment is formidable—something few writers attempt without sounding precious, dull, or both."

BIOGRAPHICAL/CRITICAL SOURCES: Saturday Review, March 22, 1969, March 23, 1974; *New York,* September 15, 1969; *Atlantic,* October, 1969; *New York Times Book Review,* November 6, 1969, August 4, 1974; *Best Sellers,* November 15, 1969, April 15, 1974; *Publishers Weekly,* February 4, 1974; *New Republic,* April 27, 1974; *Village Voice,* May 16, 1974; *Choice,* June, 1974; *Time,* July 1, 1974; *Contemporary Literary Criticism,* Volume 5, Gale, 1976.*

* * *

BRICKMAN, Marshall 1941-

PERSONAL: Born August 25, 1941, in Rio de Janeiro, Brazil; son of Abram and Pauline (Wolin) Brickman; married Anita Feinberg (a filmmaker), 1973. *Education:* University of Wisconsin, B.M. and B.S., 1962. *Religion:* "Druid." *Residence:* New York, N.Y. *Agent:* William Morris Agency, 1350 Avenue of the Americas, New York, N.Y. 10019.

CAREER: Writer; screenwriter and director of motion pictures. Worked as head writer of television series "The Tonight Show," 1968-70; producer of television series "The Dick Cavett Show," 1970-72. *Member:* Writers Guild. *Awards, honors:* Emmy Award for best producer from Academy of Television Arts and Sciences, 1971-72, for "The Dick Cavett Show"; co-winner of Academy Award for best screenplay from Academy of Motion Picture Arts and Sciences, best screenplay award from New York Film Critics Circle, and Stella Award for best screenplay from British Society of Film and Television Arts, all 1977, all for "Annie Hall."

WRITINGS—Screenplays: (With Woody Allen) *Sleeper* (produced by United Artists, 1973), Random House, 1978; (with Woody Allen) *Annie Hall* (produced by United Artists, 1977), Random House, 1978; (and director) "Simon," in production.

Also author of recordings. Contributor to *New Yorker.*

WORK IN PROGRESS: Directing the motion picture "Simon," which Brickman called, "A comedy about the end of the world more or less."

SIDELIGHTS: Brickman's screenplays done in collaborations with Woody Allen often address his own frustrations and concerns. What worries him? "The fact that you're going to die, loneliness, alienation, disappointment, not being able to get to sleep." Brickman and Allen work well as a team dealing with the anxieties of existence. They "wrote" many portions of "Annie Hall" while walking the Manhattan streets attempting to top each other's jokes. "Marshall makes my game better," Allen told an interviewer. "It's like playing tennis with a pro." Taking the success of "Sleeper" and "Annie Hall" in stride, Brickman said, "All I can say is that when you collaborate, you are both responsible for everything." Brickman and Allen share a subtle ambiguity in their humor. Allen's one regret in life is that he is not someone else. Brickman told *CA* that "the first rule of life is that you always want the other thing."

AVOCATIONAL INTERESTS: Playing the banjo.

BIOGRAPHICAL/CRITICAL SOURCES: New York Times, August 21, 1977.

*　　*　　*

BRODIE, Bernard 1910-1978

OBITUARY NOTICE—See index for *CA* sketch: Born May 20, 1910, in Chicago, Ill.; died November 24, 1978. Educator and writer best known for his books on modern warfare, including *The Absolute Weapon, From Crossbow to H-Bomb, War and Politics,* and *Escalation and the Nuclear Option.* Henry Kissinger noted that Brodie "early saw the paradox that every increase in our destructive ability had a tendency to paralyze the will to resort to it." Brodie was also revered for his knowledge of international politics. Obituaries and other sources: *New York Times,* November 27, 1978; *Washington Post,* December 4, 1978.

*　　*　　*

BROOKS, H(arold) Allen 1925-

PERSONAL: Born November 6, 1925, in New Haven, Conn.; son of Harold A. and Mildred (McNeill) Brooks. *Education:* Dartmouth College, B.A., 1950; Yale University, M.A., 1955; Northwestern University, Ph.D., 1957. *Religion:* Protestant. *Residence:* Toronto, Ontario, Canada. *Office:* Department of Fine Art, University of Toronto, Toronto, Ontario, Canada M5S 1A1.

CAREER: W. J. Negin Construction Co., Naugatuck, Conn., apprentice, 1950-52; University of Illinois, Urbana, assistant professor of architecture, 1957-58; University of Toronto, Toronto, Ontario, lecturer, 1958-61, assistant professor, 1961-64, associate professor, 1964-71, professor of fine art, 1971—. Mellon Professor at Vassar College, 1970-71; visiting professor at Dartmouth College, 1969, and Architectural Association School of Architecture, London, England, 1977, 1978; guest lecturer at schools in the United States, Canada, England, France, Germany, Scotland, and Switzerland.

MEMBER: Society for the Study of Architecture in Canada, Canadian Association for American Studies, Society of Architectural Historians (president, 1964-66; past member of board of directors), Victorian Society in America, College Art Association of America, Society of Architectural Historians of Great Britain. *Awards, honors:* Canada Council fellowships, 1962-63, 1975-76, 1977-79; Guggenheim fellowship, 1973; Alice Davis Hitchcock Book Award from

Society of Architectural Historians, 1973, for *The Prairie School.*

WRITINGS: (Contributor) *Studies in Western Art: Acts of the Twentieth International Conference of the History of Art,* Volume IV, Princeton University Press, 1963; (contributor) H. D. Bullock and Terry B. Norton, editors, *The Pope-Leighey House,* National Trust for Historic Preservation, 1970; *The Prairie School: Frank Lloyd Wright and His Midwest Contemporaries,* University of Toronto Press, 1972, 2nd edition, 1975, Norton, 1976; (editor) *Prairie School Architecture: Studies from the "Western Architect",* University of Toronto Press, 1975; (contributor) Paul E. Sprague, *Guide to Frank Lloyd Wright and Prairie School Architecture in Oak Park,* privately printed, 1976. Contributor to *Encyclopedia of World Art.* Contributor of articles and reviews to art and architecture journals.

WORK IN PROGRESS: Charles Edouard Jeanneret: The Formative Years, publication expected in 1982; editing *Writings on Wright: Collected Writings Concerning Frank Lloyd Wright.*

SIDELIGHTS: Brooks writes: "I am especially concerned with the psychological importance of architecture (and our built environment) as it affects our mental health and well-being. Too many people, I believe, take architecture for granted and are not sufficiently aware of the impact which it has upon us. These concerns surface more frequently in my lectures than in my publications."

AVOCATIONAL INTERESTS: The outdoors, skiing, canoeing.

*　　*　　*

BROUGHTON, Diane 1943-

PERSONAL: Born June 20, 1943, in Detroit, Mich.; daughter of William Haydn (a musician) and Edith (a bookkeeper; maiden name, Hemmingway) Broughton. *Education:* Occidental College, B.A., 1965. *Politics:* "Kennedy Democrat in mourning." *Residence:* Los Angeles, Calif. *Office:* c/o Laurence Frank Co., 1801 Avenue of the Stars, Suite 900, Century City, Calif. 90067.

CAREER: Worked as high school teacher in Hollywood, Calif., and Los Angeles, Calif., 1966-68; KFWB-Radio, Los Angeles, news writer, editorial assistant, and secretary, 1969-71; David Wolper Productions, Los Angeles, researcher, writer, and associate producer, 1971-73; free-lance writer, 1973—.

WRITINGS: Confessions of a Compulsive Eater, Thomas Nelson, 1978. Contributor to local magazines and newspapers.

WORK IN PROGRESS: Another book, the life story of an animal lover; "Tararath," a screenplay based on a true incident that occurred in Newfoundland in 1904.

SIDELIGHTS: Diane Broughton writes: "My father—musician and pioneer in going-for-yourself—worked the music business while my mother, sister, and I lived in Los Angeles boarding and apartment houses that catered to single working mothers. Mom compensated with multiple desserts. Yet neither my sister nor I has ever been obese. Chunky, yes.

"At college, I was conservative, sensible, and dieting. Then John Kennedy died and a little nihilism crept in. I began cutting classes and gave up plans to teach history. I gorged and gained with each term paper, delivering them past the deadline in a tent dress.

"After graduation I walked out of graduate class at Los Angeles State and never returned. I tried for a job in news—I was told there were no women's bathrooms in the news department, sorry, I was ahead of my time. So I taught medieval history and dancing at a Catholic high school. When I invited hairy, sandaled draft-dodgers into the cloistered classrooms one day for a debate, the Mother Superior decided I didn't fit in.

"Then Robert Kennedy announced his candidacy and I became a substitute teacher at the black high schools and worked in his campaign. Later I found myself moving into the Beverly Hills Hotel to be live-in babysitter to Senator Kennedy's six children the week he died.

"After the second Kennedy shooting, psychological recovery came slowly. I ate nothing but miniature Tootsie Rolls and Reeds cinnamon. I returned to the black schools but found myself seconding their bitter comments. So I took a job at KFWB. At the all-news station, I learned to type in a crowd of thirty obscenity-shouting men and to drive home in a straight line after two drinks. And I went on the Stillman diet.

"From there I took a job at David Wolper Productions. It got hectic. I accidently dumped borscht on Mr. Wolper, backed my Thunderbird into the executive producer's car, slammed a door on Perle Mesta, and fought with every executive in the building. Finally I filed a claim with the Writers Guild for writing credit. My last day there I was threatened with physical violence if one of the executives saw me in the hallway. I picked up my lamp and left.

"The Stillman diet had caused minor strokes from cholesterol. I went off all animal fats and haven't been overweight since, but the obsession to eat remains, and for my sister the obsession and its physical damage have been much worse.

"As I recovered from the strokes and learned to like soybeans, I wrote a few free-lance things, scripted the two-hour special for ABC's network pilot of 'AM America,' and finally talked my sister into telling me her own quite bizarre story of compulsive eating. I sold the book across the transom.

"If there is a theme to my writing, it's to make people see familiar things, the universal things in our society, in a new way. My first book is terribly, urgently important in this respect because it involves the life struggle of my sister, and if compulsive eating is not soon seen in a new way, my sister will die. The next projected book will deal with the emotional anguish that comes with having empathy for animals' suffering, on a planet that is largely abusive of them. There are more books to come, all dealing with the misunderstood."

* * *

BROWN, Ronald 1900-

PERSONAL: Born October 4, 1900, in Chicago, Ill.; son of Charles (a merchant) and Florence (a writer; maiden name, Cohen) Brown; married Isabelle Gup (a management trainer for volunteer organizations), February 24, 1933; children: Bennett, Barrett. *Education:* Attended Dartmouth College, 1918-19. *Home:* 13435 North Park Blvd., Cleveland Heights, Ohio 44118.

CAREER: Tremco Co., Cleveland, Ohio, and Tremco Co. Ltd. of Canada, Toronto, Ontario, co-founder, officer and board member, 1928-60; management consultant, 1960—. Conductor of seminars for American Management Association. Founder of Skills Available (employment agency for older people). Past chairman of Ohio Commission on Aging; delegate to White House Conference on Aging; past vice-chairman of advisory board of Cuyahoga County Juvenile Court; former vice-president of Jewish Community Center; former board member, Juvenile Community Federation.

WRITINGS: From Selling to Managing, American Management Association, 1968; *The Practical Manager's Guide to Excellence in Management,* American Management Association, 1979. Contributor to *AMA Management Handbook.* Contributor to magazines.

WORK IN PROGRESS: A book containing "charming anecdotes" based on travel experiences.

SIDELIGHTS: Ronald Brown describes his latest book as "a book for managers who do not have time to read books for managers." *From Selling to Managing* has been published in German, Italian, and Spanish.

* * *

BROWN, Warren 1894(?)-1978

OBITUARY NOTICE: Born c. 1894; died November 19, 1978, in Forest Park, Ill. As a sportswriter and columnist for more than sixty years, Brown covered almost every important sports event during that time for several newspapers. Obituaries and other sources: *Chicago Tribune,* November 22, 1978.

* * *

BROWNE, Theodore R. 1911(?)-1979

OBITUARY NOTICE: Born c. 1911 in Suffolk, Va.; died January 1, 1979, in Boston, Mass. Browne was a playwright whose works include "A Black Woman Called Moses" and "Natural Man." Obituaries and other sources: *Chicago Tribune,* January 5, 1979.

* * *

BUCHHEIT, Lee C(harles) 1950-

PERSONAL: Born August 25, 1950, in Pittsburgh, Pa.; son of Charles Robert, Jr. (an insurance executive) and Helen (a librarian; maiden name, Wheeler) Buchheit. *Education:* Middlebury College, A.B., 1972; University of Pennsylvania, J.D., 1975; Cambridge University, diploma, 1976. *Home:* 7070 Skyles Way, Springfield, Va. 22151. *Office:* Cleary, Gottlieb, Steen & Hamilton, 1250 Connecticut Ave. N.W., Washington, D.C. 20036.

CAREER: Cleary, Gottlieb, Steen & Hamilton, Washington, D.C., attorney, 1976—. Member of bar in Pennsylvania and District of Columbia. *Member:* American Society of International Law, Phi Beta Kappa, Coif.

WRITINGS: (Contributor) R. B. Lillich, editor, *Economic Coercion and the New International Economic Order,* Michie Co., 1976; *Secession: The Legitimacy of Self-Determination,* Yale University Press, 1978.

* * *

BUCK, Paul H(erman) 1899-1978

OBITUARY NOTICE: Born August 25, 1899, in Columbus, Ohio; died December 23, 1978, in Cambridge, Mass. Educator and author. A professor of history, Buck won a Pulitzer Prize in 1939 for *The Road to Reunion,* a book about the South during Reconstruction. Obituaries and other sources: *Current Biography,* Wilson, 1955; *The Oxford Companion to American Literature,* 4th edition, Oxford University Press, 1965; *Directory of American Scholars,*

Volume 1: *History,* 6th edition, Bowker, 1974; *Who's Who in America,* 39th edition, Marquis, 1976; *Washington Post,* December 29, 1978.

* * *

BUCKLEY, Priscilla 1921-

PERSONAL: Born August 13, 1921, in Everett, Mass.; daughter of Robert Parker (an accountant) and Gertrude (a secretary; maiden name, Crowley) Zanes; married William R. Buckley (a physician), February 22, 1949; children: Priscilla Buckley Kelley, Kathryn, William R., Jr. *Education:* Attended high school in Malden, Mass. *Home:* 170 Coniston Dr., Rochester, N.Y. 14610.

CAREER: Bank clerk in Boston, Mass., 1938-49; writer, 1965—. Lecturer at high schools. *Member:* Genesee Valley Writers' Association (president, 1975-76).

WRITINGS: Turia (historical novel), Pyramid Publications, 1977.

WORK IN PROGRESS: Valeria, a novel set in the time of Julius Caesar and the Roman civil war; *Hanah,* a novel covering three generations of one family, 1880-1940.

SIDELIGHTS: Priscilla Buckley writes: "Unable to go to college, I decided to educate myself. I concentrated on the English language, which was practical, and ancient Roman life, which intrigued me. I am curious about everything, which leads me to pursue my research farther than is necessary. This is a pleasure in itself. In the course of it I have come across numerous women who have overcome enormous social, legal, and physical barriers to achieve their goals. These are the stories I would like to tell, given the time."

AVOCATIONAL INTERESTS: Travel (especially throughout the Roman world).

* * *

BULL, Odd 1907-

PERSONAL: Born June 28, 1907, in Oslo, Norway; son of Gjert and Sigrid (Oddvin) Bull; married Inga-Lisa Furugaard, November 28, 1953; children: Odd, Jr. *Education:* Attended Norwegian Army Academy, 1925-28, and Army Flying School, 1929-30. *Home:* Nedre Baastad Vei 48, 1370 Asker, Norway.

CAREER: Norwegian Army, infantry officer, 1928-30, Army Flying Corps, 1930-40; Royal Norwegian Air Force, 1940-63, deputy chief of air staff, 1948-51, deputy chief of staff operations with Allied Air Forces of Northern Europe, 1951-53, air commander of northern Norway, 1953-56, commander of Tactical Air Forces, 1956-60, chief of air staff, 1960, retiring as lieutenant general; United Nations Truce Supervision Organization (UNTSO), chief of staff for Palestine, 1963-70. Executive member of United Nations observation group in Lebanon, 1958; special representative of United Nations secretary-general to British air evacuation of troops from Jordan to Cyprus, 1958; worked with governments of Israel and Jordan to secure Pope Paul's pilgrimage to the Holy Land, 1964. *Member:* Norwegian Geographical Society, Norske Selskab, Clipper Club. *Awards, honors:* Grand cross of Order of St. Olav, 1970; two United Nations medals in the service of peace, 1958, 1963; named honorary citizen of several states, including Texas, 1960.

WRITINGS: Paa post i Midt-Oesten: I FN's fredsbevarende tjenesta, Gyldendal, 1973, translation published as *War and Peace in the Middle East: The Experiences and*

Views of a UN Observer, Leo Cooper, 1976. Also editor, with Bjorn Christophersen, of book in Norwegian, "Norway During World War II: The Participation of the Norwegian Air Force Outside Norway."

SIDELIGHTS: Bull believes in human rights—"not used politically, but from a really humane point of view."

AVOCATIONAL INTERESTS: Skiing, swimming, reading.

* * *

BURDEN, William Douglas 1898-1978

OBITUARY NOTICE: Born September 24, 1898, in Troy, N.Y.; died November 14, 1978, in Charlotte, Vt. Naturalist, explorer, and book author. Burden's best known expedition was to the Island of Komodo in the Dutch East Indies, the home of a fierce lizard directly descended from the dinosaur. He trapped several of the lizards but they soon died in captivity. He wrote a book about the expedition in 1927; he also wrote *Look to the Wilderness* in 1960. Obituaries and other sources: *New York Times,* November 16, 1978; *Who's Who in America,* 40th edition, Marquis, 1978.

* * *

BURGER, Angela Sutherland (Brown) 1936-

PERSONAL: Born July 9, 1936, in Charlotte, N.C.; daughter of John Bass (an electrical engineer) and Angela (a volunteer worker with the blind; maiden name, Whitley) Brown; married Josef Burger (a professor of politcal science), January 23, 1960; children: Josef Thomas, Katherina Dewetter, John Bass, Charles Sutherland, Victoria Whitley. *Education:* Furman University, B.A. (magna cum laude), 1958; University of Wisconsin—Madison, M.A., 1960, Ph.D., 1966. *Religion:* Presbyterian. *Home:* 501 La Salle St., Wausau County, Wis. 54401. *Office:* University of Wisconsin—Marathon City Campus, Wausau, Wis. 54401.

CAREER: University of Wisconsin—Marathon City Campus, Wausau, instructor, 1965-66, assistant professor, 1966-71, associate professor, 1972-77, professor, 1977—. *Member:* United Nations Association, Wisconsin Political Science Association, Wisconsin South Asian Center.

WRITINGS: Opposition in a Dominant Party System, University of California Press, 1969; *Benchmarks in Wisconsin Politics,* Institute of Governmental Affairs, University of Wisconsin Extension, 1972.

WORK IN PROGRESS: A Himalayan Miscalculation: Analysis of Elite Control in the 1977 Indian Parliamentary Elections; Coming to Power: A Janata Perspective; Civil, Military, and Paramilitary Relations: Congress to Janata.

* * *

BURGER, Jack
See BURGER, John R(obert)

* * *

BURGER, John R(obert) 1942-
(Jack Burger)

PERSONAL: Born January 25, 1942, in Concord, Mass.; son of Arthur Taylor (a social worker) and Grace Kathryn (Fanning) Burger; married Sylvia Rubin, 1965; children: Timothy, Peter, Nathaniel. *Education:* Columbia University, A.B., 1966; Michigan State University, M.S., 1970. *Politics:* Independent. *Religion:* "Searching." *Home and office:* 14 Capricorn Lane, Monsey, N.Y. 10952.

CAREER: International Paper Co., New York, N.Y., exploration and staff geologist, 1970-75; Dames & Moore, Cranford, N.J., staff geologist, 1976-77; consulting geologist, 1977; *Backpacker,* Bedford Hills, N.Y., circulation manager, 1978—. Consultant to General Crude Oil Co. Registered geologist in state of Georgia. *Member:* Society of Mining Engineers.

WRITINGS: (With Lewis Gardner) *Children of the Wild,* Messner, 1978. Contributor of stories, articles, and reviews, sometimes under name Jack Burger, to magazines, including *Backpacker, Science World, Scholastic Scope,* and *Stained Glass Quarterly.*

WORK IN PROGRESS: A book on automobile repair; a children's novel; an adult novel.

SIDELIGHTS: Burger participated in Lamont-Doherty Geological Observatory's International Indian Ocean Expedition in 1963, spent three months on Fletcher's Ice Island (T-3) in the Arctic Ocean, and was a member of National Science Foundation's Juneau Icefield Research Project.

He writes: "I want, through fiction, to introduce people to new visions of reality. *Children of the Wild* attempts to teach the young reader to sift fact from fiction using the subject of feral children as an example, while at the same time being entertaining reading on a fascinating subject."

* * *

BURGESS, Ann Marie
See GERSON, Noel Bertram

* * *

BURGESS, Michael
See GERSON, Noel Bertram

* * *

BURGESS, W(arren) Randolph 1889-1978

OBITUARY NOTICE—See index for *CA* Sketch: Born May 7, 1889, in Newport, R.I.; died September 16, 1978, in Washington, D.C. Banker, economist, diplomat, and author of books in his field. Burgess worked at the Federal Reserve Bank of New York and the National City Bank of New York before going into government service. As deputy to the secretary of the treasury and later undersecretary during the Eisenhower administration, he played an important part in formulating America's foreign and domestic economic policies. From 1957 to 1961 Burgess was U.S. ambassador to the North Atlantic Treaty Organization (NATO); he also served as U.S. representative to the Organization for European Economic Cooperation (OEEC). His book, *The Reserve Banks and the Money Markets,* is a standard reference work. Obituaries and other sources: *Current Biography,* Wilson, 1949; *American Men and Women of Science: The Social and Behavioral Sciences,* 12th edition, Bowker, 1973; *Washington Post,* September 18, 1978.

* * *

BURNS, Alma 1919-
(Claire Dalton)

PERSONAL: Born March 29, 1919, in Poplar, Minn.; daughter of Walter Leighton (a farmer) and Nora (Scott) Smith; married Chester D. Burns (an engineer), September 15, 1945; children: Penny Jean (Mrs. Dennis J. Hansen). *Education:* Attended University of Washington, Seattle, 1937-39. *Politics:* Moderate. *Religion:* Protestant. *Home:* 56 South Second St., Roslyn, Wash. 98941. *Agent:* Lisa Collier, Collier Associates, 280 Madison Ave., New York, N.Y. 10016. *Office: Ellensburg Daily Record,* Fourth & Main Sts., Ellensburg, Wash. 98926.

CAREER: Secretary and bookkeeper, 1939-46, 1957-63; *Ellensburg Daily Record,* Ellensburg, Wash., reporter, photographer, and author of weekly column, "News From the Upper County," 1974—. *Member:* National Federation of Press Women, Washington Press Women. *Awards, honors:* Journalism awards from Washington Press Women, 1974, 1975, 1977.

WRITINGS: (Under pseudonym Claire Dalton) *The Second Life of Cecily Pride* (novel), Beagle Books, 1973; *The Witches of Turnstone Bay* (novel), Zebra Publications, 1977. Contributor to popular journals and magazines.

WORK IN PROGRESS: Yesterday's Shadow, a historical romance set in a coal mining town in the 1880's; *Other Lifetimes, Other Loves.*

SIDELIGHTS: Alma Burns writes: "I do not consider myself a serious writer. I write to entertain and write the kinds of books that I find entertaining to read. My novels are fantasies and deal primarily with the occult. I am fascinated by the concept of reincarnation and have used this theme in more than one book.

"I am a journalist more by accident and necessity than by design or good judgment. The pay is certain but the work lacks the challenge of creating a novel from the smallest germ of an idea. Writing a novel is fun.

"My greatest single interest is people. Without them, I would never have an idea for a story or a character. People stimulate and solve."

AVOCATIONAL INTERESTS: Mycology, canoeing, hiking, golf, studying wildflowers, watching birds.

* * *

BURROWS, Millar 1889-

PERSONAL: Born October 26, 1889, in Wyoming, Ohio; son of Edwin Jones (in business) and Katharine (Millar) Burrows; married Irène Gladding, July 6, 1915 (died January 15, 1967); children: Edwin Gladding. *Education:* Cornell University, B.A., 1912; Union Theological Seminary, New York, N.Y., M.Div., 1915; Yale University, Ph.D., 1925. *Home:* 1670 Woodland Ave., Winter Park, Fla. 32789.

CAREER: Ordained Presbyterian minister, 1915; pastor of Presbyterian churches in rural Texas, 1915-19; Interchurch World Movement, New York, N.Y., rural survey supervisor for Texas, 1919-20; Tusculum College, Greenville, Tenn., professor of Bible and college pastor, 1920-23; Brown University, Providence, R.I., assistant professor, 1925-29, associate professor, 1929-32, professor of Biblical literature and history of religions, 1932-34; Yale University, New Haven, Conn., professor of Biblical theology, 1934-58; writer and researcher. Visiting professor at American University of Beirut, 1930-31; director of American School of Oriental Research in Jerusalem, 1931-32, 1947-48; president of American Schools of Oriental Research, 1934-48. Member of American Middle East Relief, 1954.

MEMBER: American Academy of Religion, American Oriental Society, Society of Biblical Literature (president, 1954), American Academy of Arts and Sciences (fellow emeritus), Society for Old Testament Study (England; honorary member).

WRITINGS: Founders of Great Religions, Scribner, 1931;

What Mean These Stones?, American Schools of Oriental Research, 1941; *Outline of Biblical Theology*, Westminster, 1946; *Palestine Is Our Business*, Westminster, 1949; *The Dead Sea Scrolls*, Viking, 1955; *More Light on the Dead Sea Scrolls*, Viking, 1958; *Diligently Compared*, Thomas Nelson, 1964; (contributor) Harry Thomas Frank and William L. Reed, editors, *Translating and Understanding the Old Testament: Essays in Honor of Herbert Gordon May*, Abingdon, 1970; (contributor) James L. Crenshaw and John T. Willes, editors, *Essays in Old Testament Ethics*, Ktav, 1974; *Jesus in the First Three Gospels*, Abingdon, 1977. Contributor to numerous journals in his field.

* * *

BUSH, Lewis William   1907-

PERSONAL: Born May 6, 1907, in London, England; son of Charles (a businessman) and Esther Elizabeth Bush; married Kane Tsujimura, August 10, 1931 (died, 1965); married Hideko Kubo, August, 1966; children: (second marriage) David Sazo Charles Jerome. *Education:* Educated privately. *Home:* Inamura, 33 Savill Rd., Lindfield, Sussex RH16 2NW, England.

CAREER: Lecturer in English literature and Japanese in secondary schools and universities, 1934-40; representative of British film producers in Japan, 1947-56; broadcaster for Japan Broadcasting and adviser for Uni Japan Films, 1956-74. *Military service:* Royal Naval Volunteer Reserve, 1940-47; became lieutenant. *Member:* Japan Society, Royal Naval Volunteer Reserve Officer Association, Tokyo Club, Nippon Ocean Racing Club, Enoshima Yacht Club. *Awards, honors:* Member, Order of the British Empire, and Order of the Rising Sun (Japan).

WRITINGS: (With Yoshiyuki Kagami) *Japanalia: Reference Book to Things Japanese*, Gifford, 1938, published as *Japan Dictionary: Japanalia* (sole author), Philosophical Library, 1957, 5th edition published as *Japanalia*, McKay, 1959, 6th edition published as *Japanalia: A Concise Cyclopaedia*, Tokyo News Service, 1965; *Clutch of Circumstance*, Okuyama, 1956; *Bath House Nights*, Okuyama, 1958; *Land of the Dragonfly*, R. Hale, 1959; *The Road to Inamura* (autobiography), R. Hale, 1961; *Habakari Hankin*, Tokyo News Service, 1961; *Japanalia: Past and Present*, Japan Times, 1967; *The Life and Times of the Illustrious Captain Brown: A Chronicle of the Sea and of Japan's Emergence as a World Power*, Tuttle, 1969; *77 Samurai: Japan's First Embassy to America*, Kodansha International, 1968. Contributor to *Japan Times*.

WORK IN PROGRESS: Research on Japanese history and folklore; work on maritime history.

* * *

BUTLER, Nathan
   See SOHL, Jerry

* * *

BUTTITTA, Anthony   1907-
   (Tony Buttitta)

PERSONAL: Born July 26, 1907, in Chicago, Ill.; son of Giacomo (in business) and Nina (a teacher) Buttitta; married Remy Horton (an artist), 1932 (marriage ended, 1941); married Monica Hannasch (a batik artist). *Education:* Attended Normal College, Natchitoches, La., 1926-28; University of Texas, B.A., 1929; graduate study at University of North Carolina. *Politics:* Democrat. *Home:* 28 Jones St., New

York, N.Y. 10014; and 84070 Scario, Salerno, Italy. *Agent:* Audrey Wood, International Creative Management, 40 West 57th St., New York, N.Y. 10019.

CAREER: Free-lance newspaper correspondent, 1932-35; North Carolina Symphony Orchestra, Chapel Hill, press representative, 1935; Federal Theater Project, New York, N.Y., staff member, 1936-38; Broadway press agent, 1939-45; San Francisco Civic Light Opera, San Francisco, Calif., press representative, 1931-62; free-lance writer, 1962—. Press representative for Lost Colony (Roanoke Island, N.C.), 1938-40. *Military service:* U.S. Army, in public relations, 1943-44. *Member:* Authors Guild of Authors League of America, Actors Fund. *Awards, honors:* Louisiana state award, 1927, for play "Barataria"; North Carolina state prize, 1931, for play "Playthings."

WRITINGS—All under name Tony Buttitta: *After the Good Gay Times: A Season with Scott Fitzgerald*, Viking, 1974. Also author of an unpublished novel, *No Resurrection*.

Plays: "Barataria" (one-act), first produced in Natchitoches, La. at State Normal College, 1927; "Playthings" (three-act), first produced in Chapel Hill, N.C., at University of North Carolina, 1931; "Singing Piedmont" (one-act), first produced in Detroit, Mich., at Labor Stage Co., 1937.

Contributor to magazines. Founder and editor of *Contempo*, 1931-33.

WORK IN PROGRESS: There Were No Elephants, a memoir of the Federal Theater Project, publication expected in 1980; *Young Man with a Promising Past*, an autobiographical novel.

SIDELIGHTS: Buttitta writes: "The summer of 1935, in Asheville, when I met Scott Fitzgerald, was instrumental in helping me to decide to become a serious writer, primarily because Scott saw plenty of material in my personal background as an Italo-American. I am interested in the theater but not as entertainment, though I spent years promoting such a theater; I am interested in the theater of ideas, represented by Shaw, Pirandello, Brecht, and many plays done by the Federal Theater Project, such as 'The Living Newspaper,' a relevant theater for the changing world of today."

* * *

BUTTITTA, Tony
   See BUTTITTA, Anthony

* * *

BUTTON, James W(ickham)   1942-

PERSONAL: Born February 5, 1942, in Rochester, N.Y.; son of Frederick W. (a teacher) and Marion (Case) Button; married Christine Bennett, July 2, 1966 (divorced, May, 1977); children: Matthew, Adam. *Education:* Colgate University, B.A., 1964; Stanford University, M.A., 1965; University of California, Los Angeles, M.A., 1969; University of Texas, Ph.D., 1975. *Politics:* "Liberal Democrat." *Religion:* "Unitarian-Universalist." *Home:* 4736 Northwest 28th Ter., Gainesville, Fla. 32605. *Office:* Department of Social Science, University of Florida, Gainesville, Fla. 32611.

CAREER: High school teacher of government in Sunnyvale, Calif., 1965-68; University of Florida, Gainesville, assistant professor of social science, 1973—. Local director of Department of Housing and Urban Development; member of governing board of Community Action Agency of Alachua County. Lecturer on power and violence in America;

participant in symposia. *Member:* American Political Science Association, Midwest Political Science Association, Southern Political Science Association.

WRITINGS: Black Violence: The Political Impact of the 1960's Riots, Princeton University Press, 1978. Contributor to *Theory into Practice.*

WORK IN PROGRESS: Research on the impact of the civil rights movement in Florida.

*   *   *

BYRNE, James E. 1945-

PERSONAL: Born December 6, 1945, in Detroit, Mich.; son of John F. (a chemical engineer) and Grace P. Byrne; married Maria T. Difato, November 24, 1973; children: John, Michael, Mary Catherine. *Education:* University of Notre Dame, B.A., 1968; Stetson University, J.D., 1977; University of Pennsylvania, LL.M., 1978. *Religion:* Roman Catholic. *Home:* 2305 Harn Blvd., Clearwater, Fla. 33516. *Office:* 601 Federal Office Building, St. Petersburg, Fla. 33701.

CAREER: Charismatic Renewal Services, Notre Dame, Ind., president, 1968-73; writer and lecturer in Largo, Fla., 1973-74; law clerk in St. Petersburg, Fla., 1978—.

WRITINGS: (Contributor) *As the Spirit Leads Us,* Paulist Press, 1971; *Threshold of God's Promise,* Ave Maria Press, 1971; *Living in the Spirit,* Paulist Press, 1975; *The Charismatic Experience of the Holy Spirit,* Dove Publications, 1976.

*   *   *

BYRON, William J(ames) 1927-

PERSONAL: Born May 25, 1927, in Pittsburgh, Pa.; son of Harold J. (a physician) and Mary I. (Langton) Byron. *Education:* Attended St. Joseph's College, Philadelphia, Pa., 1947-50, and Jesuit Novitiate, Wernersville, Pa., 1950-53; St. Louis University, A.B., 1955, Ph.L., 1956, M.A., 1959; Woodstock College, Woodstock, Md., S.T.B., 1960, S.T.L., 1962, University of Maryland, Ph.D., 1969; Harvard University, postdoctoral certificate, 1974. *Office:* University of Scranton, Scranton, Pa. 18510.

CAREER: Entered Society of Jesus (Jesuits), 1950, ordained Roman Catholic priest, 1961; teacher of mathematics at private school in Scranton, Pa., 1956-58; Loyola College, Baltimore, Md., assistant professor of economics, 1967-69; Woodstock College, New York, N.Y., associate professor of social ethics, director of field education, and rector of Jesuit community, 1969-73; Loyola University, New Orleans, La., associate professor of economics and dean of College of Arts and Sciences, 1973-75; University of Scranton, Scranton, Pa., president of university and member of board of trustees, 1975—. Adjunct professor at Woodstock College (Woodstock, Md.), 1967-69; lecturer at Union Theological Seminary (New York, N.Y.), 1969-73. Director of social ministries for Maryland Province of Society of Jesus, 1969-73. Member of board of directors of St. Joseph's College (Philadelphia, Pa.), 1969-78, Scranton Home Health Maintenance Organization, 1976—, Scranton Community Medical Center, 1977—, Economic Development Council of Northeastern Pennsylvania, 1975—, Scranton-Lackawanna Industrial Building Co., 1977—, Morningside Heights, Inc., 1969-73, Bread for the World, 1973—, Lackawanna County Planning Council for Social Services, 1976—, Scranton Neighbors, 1977—, MetroAction, Inc. (also vice-chairman), 1977—, and Northeastern Bank of Pennsylvania, 1978—. Member of board of trustees of St. Joseph's Preparatory School, 1968-70, Woodstock College, 1970-73, Xavier University, 1974-77, Carlow College, 1975-78, and Georgetown University, 1978—. Member of advisory board or council of New Orleans Institute of Politics, 1973-75, Harvard University's Institute for Educational Management, 1974-77, and University of Notre Dame's Center for Constitutional Studies, 1977—; member of Public Committee for the Humanities in Pennsylvania, 1976—; member of consumer advisory council of Blue Shield of Pennsylvania, 1977—. *Military service:* U.S. Army, Parachute Infantry, 1945-46.

MEMBER: American Economic Association, American Society of Christian Ethics, American Council on Education, American Association of University Professors, Association of Jesuit Colleges and Universities (member of board of directors, 1975—), Association of Catholic Colleges and Universities (member of board of directors, 1978—), Visiting Nurses Association (Scranton; member of board of directors, 1976—), Greater Scranton Chamber of Commerce (member of board of directors, 1977—), Alpha Sigma Nu.

WRITINGS: (Contributor) F. X. Quinn, editor, *The Ethical Aftermath of Automation,* Paulist/Newman, 1962; (with Raymond Baumhart and John E. McMillan) *Ethics of the Businessman,* America Press, 1963; (contributor) William C. Bier, editor, *Alienation: Plight of Modern Man?,* Fordham University Press, 1972; *Toward Stewardship: An Interim Ethic of Poverty, Pollution, and Power,* Paulist/Newman, 1975; *Words of Inauguration* (pamphlet), University of Scranton, 1975. Contributor of more than thirty articles to religion and education journals and national magazines, including *America, Commonweal,* and *Today.* Member of editorial staff of *America,* 1962; consulting editor for Paulist/Newman, 1973—.

WORK IN PROGRESS: Education for Justice.

SIDELIGHTS: Byron told *CA:* "Since 1973, when I went into academic administration full time, writing has been a sideline. I am grateful that my interests range from both economic and ethical theory to contemporary social issues, thus providing me with much to write about whenever the opportunity presents itself."

C

CABOT, Tracy 1941-

PERSONAL: Born March 4, 1941, daughter of Ben (a real estate broker) and Ruth (a real estate broker; maiden name, Burston) Blank. *Education:* Attended Long Beach City College, Bryn Mawr College, and Pennsylvania State University; Whittier College, received B.A. *Politics/Religion:* "I'm a Republican Jew by heritage, a liberal agnostic by choice." *Residence:* Van Nuys, Calif. *Agent:* Barbara Lowenstein, 8608 Holloway Dr., Los Angeles, Calif. 90069; and 250 West 57th St., New York, N.Y. 10019.

CAREER: Universal Studios, Universal City, Calif., worked in publicity, 1964-65; assistant casting director of "Get Smart" television show, 1965-66; *Overdrive* magazine, Los Angeles, Calif., editorial supervisor, 1966-67; editor of *Confidential* magazine, 1968-71, and of *American Art,* 1971-73; *National Enquirer,* Hollywood, Calif. bureau, reporter, 1975-76. Public relations work for Impact Enterprises, and public relations consultant to San Fernando Valley homeowner groups.

WRITINGS: The Parkhursts (nonfiction), Transamerican Press, 1967; *Inside the Cults* (nonfiction) Holloway 1971; (with Zev Wanderer) *Letting Go: A Twelve Week Personal Action Program to Overcome a Broken Heart,* Putnam, 1978. Columnist for *Hollywood Citizen News* and *Los Angeles Free Press.* Contributor to *Playgirl, Cosmopolitan, Forum, Penthouse, Viva,* and *Los Angeles Magazine.*

WORK IN PROGRESS: Gentle Passage, featuring new ways of looking at and predicting your own death; *Unmarried by Choice,* about people who are divorced or prefer to remain single by first choice; *The Princess,* fiction, about a fashion designer; a television situation comedy based on Cabot's own experiences at the Hollywood bureau of the *National Enquirer.*

SIDELIGHTS: Cabot has free-lanced, edited pornographic magazines, and collected unemployment checks in between her various reporting, editing, and public relations jobs. Although she had written professionally for ten years, Cabot told *CA* that *Letting Go* "was the first thing I'd ever done without any sure indication that a publisher or anyone else was interested.

"The reason I was willing to go out on a limb for this project is because I had personally suffered so much in my life over terminated relationships. The pain was real enough to drive me into analysis, voodoo dolls, sensitivity sessions, or anything else I thought might help. None of them ever did.

"Eventually I would recover, but it would seem that I couldn't wait to get involved in the same kind of destructive relationship again. I wrote about it for magazines, but still that didn't help. Each time when the relationship fell apart, so did I. When I discovered the behavioral methods for overcoming a broken heart, I couldn't believe it. Best of all, it worked. Years of therapy and depression could be replaced simply and rationally and I didn't have to make the same mistake over and over again.

"*Letting Go* can give everyone that same opportunity to get over old pain from old relationships and avoid future traumas."

Cabot is "happily unmarried" ("not divorced") and lives with "a devoted doberman and two cats."

* * *

CAHN, Rhoda 1922-

PERSONAL: Born March 29, 1922; daughter of Israel and Gertrude Lipofsky; married William Cahn (a free-lance writer), 1943 (died October 13, 1976); children: Susan Cahn Krieger, Kathe Cahn Morse, Daniel. *Education:* Southern Connecticut State College, B.S., 1942, M.S., 1971; further study at Banks Street College and Brooklyn College (now of the City University of New York). *Home:* 488 Norton Pkwy., New Haven, Conn. 06511.

CAREER: Affiliated with Cahn Associates (public information service), New Haven, Conn., 1963—. Editor of newsletter and member of board of directors of Connecticut Association of School Psychologists, 1973-76. Founding member of Arts Council of Greater New Haven, 1964—.

WRITINGS—With husband, William Cahn: *The Story of Writing: From Cave Art to Computer,* Harvey House, 1963; *No Time for School, No Time for Play: The Story of Child Labor in America* (juvenile), Messner, 1972; *The Great American Comedy Scene,* Messner, 1977.

WORK IN PROGRESS: A book on the diagnosis, research, and treatment of blood diseases; *Blood Lines and Life Lines,* for teenagers; a biography, *Augusta Lewis Troup.*

* * *

CALDER, C(larence) R(oy), Jr. 1928-

PERSONAL: Born October 7, 1928, in Lynn, Mass.; son of

Roy Clarence and Helen (Smtih) Calder; married Rose D. Vasilakopoulos (a researcher), June 22, 1958; children: George, Christine. *Education:* Fitchburg State College, B.S.Ed., 1952; Northeastern University, M.Ed., 1957; University of Connecticut, Ph.D., 1964. *Home address:* R.F.D.3, Stearns Rd., Willimantic, Conn. 06226. *Office:* School of Education, University of Connecticut, U-33, Storrs, Conn. 06268.

CAREER: Fitchburg State College, Fitchburg, Mass., instructor in education, 1957-61; University of Connecticut, Storrs, 1961—, currently professor of education. *Member:* Council for Exceptional Children, American Industrial Arts Association, Phi Delta Kappa, Epsilon Pi Tau.

WRITINGS: (With E.M. Antan) *Techniques and Activities to Stimulate Verbal Learning,* Macmillan, 1970; (with J. Shivers) *Recreational Crafts,* McGraw, 1974; (with J.F. Cawley) *Behavior Resource Guide,* Educational Progress Corp., 1975, new edition, 1978. Contributor of about thirty-five articles to education journals.

WORK IN PROGRESS: Industrial Arts for the Handicapped Learner; Elementary Industrial Arts, a monograph.

AVOCATIONAL INTERESTS: Woodcrafts, gardening.

* * *

CAMERON, Harold W. 1905-

PERSONAL: Born January 27, 1905, in Russelville, Mo.; son of Arthur W. (a clergyman) and Laura (a writer; maiden name, Enloe) Cameron; married wife, Laurene; married wife, Dorothy; married wife, Shirley; married Molly Green, 1978; children: Harold, Robert, Carroll, Janet, Michael. *Education:* Montezuma Baptist College, B.A., 1924; attended Silver City Normal University, 1926; graduate study at Kansas State University, 1929. *Home:* 1765 Spruce Dr., Helena, Mont. 59601.

CAREER: Teacher at public schools in Kentucky Valley and House, N.M., 1922-25; Baptist minister in Moriarty, N.M., 1925; sales manager in Chicago, Ill., 1931-49, and in Canada, 1949-50; Ben Franklin Institute, Philadelphia, Pa., teacher of human relations, 1949; pastor of Church of Religious Science in Paradise, Calif., 1972-77. State price coordinator for Oregon, 1941-43. *Military service:* U.S. Army, Cavalry, 1922-23. *Member:* Psychic Research Federation, New Thought, Unity, Research on Meditation.

WRITINGS: (With Constance Westbie) *Night Stalks the Mansion,* Stackpole, 1978.

WORK IN PROGRESS: Adventures in Self Discovery; Reflections on Reality; a book on psychic phenomena, *Living With the Supernatural.*

SIDELIGHTS: Cameron told *CA:* "I have lived a very active and exciting life. I am now at seventy-three in my fourth career, which I anticipate will be the most rewarding of all. I live in the Montana mountains where quiet, tranquility and inspiration prevail. I have chosen this place intentionally for its creative vibrations."

* * *

CAMMARATA, Jerry F(rank) 1947-

PERSONAL: Born March 14, 1947, in New York, N.Y.; son of Jerome (a plumber) and Mary (Peccorale) Cammarata; married Margaret Pucciorelli (a secretary), October 12, 1968; children: Elizabeth, Michelle. *Education:* Hofstra University, B.A., 1968, M.A., 1969; graduate study at New York University, City University of New York, 1970, and

California Western University, 1976—. *Religion:* Catholic. *Home:* 185 Maryland Ave., Staten Island, N.Y. 10305. *Agent:* Lou Reda, 44 North Second St., Easton, Pa. 18042.

CAREER: Wagner College, Staten Island, N.Y., lecturer, 1970—; U.S. Public Health Hospital, Staten Island, speech pathologist and audiologist, 1970—. Director, Richmond County Speech and Hearing Rehabilitation Center, 1969—. Vice-president of faculty family fellowship of St. Joseph Hill Academy of Staten Island, 1977—. *Member:* International Association of Laryngectomees, American Speech and Hearing Association, American Association of University Professors, New York Speech and Hearing Association, Long Island Speech and Hearing Association, Italian Club of Staten Island (sergeant at arms and editor of newsletter).

WRITINGS: The Fun Book of Fatherhood; or, How the Animal Kingdom Is Helping to Raise the Wild Kids at Our House, Corwin, 1978. Also researcher for *Moments: The Pulitzer Prize Photographs,* by Sheryle Leekley and John Leekley, Crown, 1978.

WORK IN PROGRESS: Kids Are Consumers Too, a book to help children buy more wisely; *First Aid for Kids; Portrait of a Father,* about celebrity dads and their families, publication expected in 1982.

SIDELIGHTS: "Parents are losing control of their kids," Jerry Cammarata has said, "because they are relying on child psychologists to do their thinking." He made sure, however, that he would do his own thinking in his children's upbringing when he was granted an unprecedented four year paternity leave from the New York City school system. "Human fathers," he says, "are best able to provide leadership for their sons, just as fathers do among the lower species. . . . If Congress really wants to do something about crime in the streets, I am more convinced than ever that paternity leave is the answer, not just when a child is born, but sporadically during the early impressionable years."

Subtitled *How the Animal Kingdom is Helping to Raise the Wild Kids at Our House, The Fun Book of Fatherhood* relies on animals as role models for parenting. He notes that some different species of animals have either males or females caring for their offspring: "They know that not everybody is meant to be a parent. . . . Sometimes fathers make the best mothers." The examples of animal parents have helped Cammarata and his wife ignore many child psychologists' advice to leave crying babies alone. "No monkey or chimp would be so cruel as to desert its baby at night," Cammarata maintains. He also feels animals are far more successful at parenting than humans, as "few human parents can match their record . . . or end up with fewer emotionally crippled offspring and juvenile delinquents." Animal parents "do what comes naturally," he says. "Sometimes they make a mistake, but they pick up and keep on going."

Known as "super pop," Cammarata has held three places in the *Guinness Book of World Records*—for a seventy-five hour bathtub singing marathon, a ninety-five hour subway singing marathon, and for "composing" the worlds's longest silent musical piece, (fifty-two minutes to let his children's imaginations run wild). Despite these efforts, he remains no less than devoted to his premier concern—family unity. He told *CA:* "The family is the unit of survival if we are to preserve our kind. In my work with adults and children as a speech and language pathologist and audiologist, I have developed a sense of understanding for how people should interact, particularly kids and parents. My life work will revolve around this."

BIOGRAPHICAL/CRITICAL SOURCES: New York

Daily News, November 20, 1974, November 13, 1975, *Sunday News,* January 4, 1976; *Seattle Post-Intelligencer,* March 4, 1975; *Houston Post,* November 30, 1975; *Charleston Evening Post,* June 18, 1978; *Detroit Free Press,* September 21, 1978.

* * *

CAMPBELL, R. T.
See TODD, Ruthven

* * *

CANBY, Vincent 1924-

PERSONAL: Born July 27, 1924, in Chicago, Ill.; son of Lloyd and Katharine Anne (Vincent) Canby. *Education:* Dartmouth College, B.A., 1947. *Home:* 215 West 88th St., New York, N.Y. 10024. *Agent:* Robert Lescher, 155 East 71st St., New York, N.Y. 10021. *Office: New York Times,* 229 West 43rd St., New York, N.Y. 10036.

CAREER: Chicago Journal of Commerce, Chicago, Ill., assistant to drama editor, 1949-51; critic and reporter, *Motion Picture Herald-Motion Picture Daily,* 1951-58; *Variety,* New York City, movie, theater, and television reporter and critic, 1959-67; *New York Times,* New York City, member of film and theater criticism staff, 1967-69, film critic, 1969—. *Military service:* Served in U.S. Navy during World War II.

WRITINGS: Living Quarters (novel), Knopf, 1975; "End of the War" (play), produced at Ensemble Studio Theatre, 1978; *Unnatural Scenery* (novel), Knopf, 1979.

SIDELIGHTS: Although he is chiefly known as a film critic, Canby has also written a well-received novel. *Living Quarters* "is told in language that shimmers," wrote Webster Schott. "It's a story that emerges from plots that explore human longing, suffering and pleasure among the civilized on three continents as though seeking a statement about a condition beyond articulation."

"Mr. Canby's prose is flat and dry, glinting now and then with satiric, disenchanted humor," Hollis Alpert commented. "The book's method is that of remembered gossip, told in monotone, but not monotonously. Little in the way of sympathy is allowed any of the characters—so careful is the author in keeping any sentiment or unseemly emotion from coloring the tale. All incidents of the past, he seems to be saying, have the same weight in memory, whether it be a failed movie actress who takes her life or a jaded Frenchman who suffers the embarassment of a dog's suddenly urinating against his leg."

Schott concluded: "Vincent Canby's film criticism in the *Times* shows that he was born to think and to write. This first novel says that he may have been born to write fiction."

BIOGRAPHICAL/CRITICAL SOURCES: Newsweek, March 10, 1969; *Variety,* March 11, 1970, October 25, 1972; *Saturday Review,* March 8, 1975; *New York Times Book Review,* April 13, 1975; *New Statesman,* February 21, 1976.

* * *

CANEMAKER, John 1943-

PERSONAL: Born May 28, 1943, in Waverly, N.Y.; son of John F. and Rose (Laux) Cannizzaro. *Education:* Marymount Manhattan College, B.A., 1974; New York University, M.F.A., 1976. *Residence:* New York, N.Y. *Agent:* Susan Ann Protter, 156 East 52nd St., New York, N.Y. 10022.

CAREER: Worked as actor, singer, and dancer on televi-

sion commercials and on stage, 1961-71; WCBS-TV, New York City, teacher, cartoonist, and performer on "Patchwork Family" series, 1972-75; animation teacher at workshops in New York City, 1973-76, and Nassau County Arts Development Center, Long Island, 1976; William Paterson College, Wayne, N.J., instructor in animation techniques, 1978—; Adelphi University, Garden City, N.Y., instructor in animation history, 1978—. Lecturer in animation at School of Visual Arts, New York City, 1976, New York University, 1977-78, Adelphi University, 1978, and Los Angeles International Film Exposition (Filmex), 1978. Host for CBS Camera Three, 1975-77; artistic director and master of ceremonies at New York International Animation Festival, 1975; coordinated the first U.S. retrospectives of the classic animated films of Winsor McCay, 1975; arranged the first U.S. retrospective "Felix the Cat" tribute to Otto Messmer at Whitney Museum of American Art, 1976. Held drawing exhibition in 1978; held cartoon screenings at New York Film Festival, Museum of Modern Art, Carpenter Center for Visual Arts, and John F. Kennedy Center. Freelance animator for producers of "Sesame Street," "Electric Company," "Captain Kangaroo," "Patchwork Family," American Broadcasting Co. (ABC)-TV's special "Days of Liberty," and in-house video for Merrill Lynch Pierce Fenner & Smith, Inc. *Military service:* U.S. Army, 1965-67. *Awards, honors:* Award for best film in nostalgia category from Association of Animators, 1973, for "Lust"; third prize from Association of Animators, 1973, for "Greed"; grant from American Film Institute to produce, write, and direct "Remembering Winsor McCay," 1976; "The 40's" was selected for 1977 New York Film Festival American Program.

WRITINGS: The Animated Raggedy Ann & Andy: An Intimate Look at the Art of Animation; Its History, Techniques and Artists, Bobbs-Merrill, 1977.

Television programs: "The Boys From Termit Terrance," Columbia Broadcasting System (CBS)-TV, 1975; "The Animated Art of Oskar Fischinger," CBS-TV, 1977.

Short subject films: "Animation: Its History and Uses," 1959; "Lust," 1973; "The 40's," 1974; "Street Freaks," 1974; "Remembering Winsor McCay," 1976; "Otto Messmer and Felix the Cat," 1977; "Confessions of a Stardreamer," 1978.

Contributor of articles to periodicals, including *Film Comment, Filmmakers Newsletters, Variety,* and *Cinefantasique.* Animation editor of *Millimeter,* 1975—.

WORK IN PROGRESS: Researching two books about the art of animation; another animation documentary film; a new animated short.

BIOGRAPHICAL/CRITICAL SOURCES: Film News, November and December, 1976, summer, 1977; *Hollywood Reporter,* August 12, 1977; *Los Angeles Times,* May 26, 1978; *Atlanta Journal-Constitution,* November 18, 1978.

* * *

CANOVAN, Margaret 1939-

PERSONAL: Born April 25, 1939, in England; daughter of Walter (in the nursery business) and Evelyn (Routledge) Leslie; married James Canovan, March 24, 1971; children: Cherry. *Education:* Earned M.A. and Ph.D. from Girton College, Cambridge. *Home:* 1 Moorsfield Ave., Audlem, near Crewe, Cheshire, England. *Office:* Department of Politics, University of Keele, Keele, Staffordshire, England.

CAREER: University of Lancaster, Lancaster, England,

lecturer in politics, 1965-71; University of Keele, Keele, England, lecturer in politics, 1971—.

WRITINGS: The Political Thought of Hannah Arendt, Harcourt, 1974, revised edition, Methuen, 1977; *G. K. Chesterton, Radical Populist*, Harcourt, 1977. Contributor to political and European studies journals.

WORK IN PROGRESS: A book on populism, for Harcourt.

BIOGRAPHICAL/CRITICAL SOURCES: Washington Post Book World, October 9, 1977; *New York Times Book Review*, October 9, 1977.

*   *   *

CANTWELL, Robert Emmett 1908-1978

OBITUARY NOTICE—See index for *CA* sketch: Born January 31, 1908, in Little Falls, Wash.; died December 8, 1978, in New York, N.Y. Editor and author best known for his short stories and novels written during the early 1930's, including *Land of Plenty* and *Laugh and Lie Down.* Cantwell worked as literary editor of *New Outlook* before serving at the same position for *Time* and eventually *Newsweek.* While with *Time,* Cantwell specialized in stories on Europe during World War II. His most recent years were spent as a contributor to *Sports Illustrated.* Obituaries and other sources: *The Oxford Companion to American Literature*, 4th edition, Oxford University Press, 1965; *Twentieth Century Writing: A Reader's Guide to Contemporary Literature*, Transatlantic, 1969; *The Author's and Writer's Who's Who*, 6th edition, Burke's Peerage, 1971; *Contemporary Novelists*, 2nd edition, St. Martin's, 1976; *The Writer's Directory, 1976-78*, St. Martin's, 1976; *Who's Who in America*, 40th edition, Marquis, 1978; *Washington Post*, December 10, 1978; *New York Times*, December 10, 1978.

*   *   *

CAPP, Richard 1935-

PERSONAL: Born November 19, 1935, in Atlantic City, N.J.; son of Joseph (a shoemaker) and Anna (Williams) Capp; married Helene Branca (a representative of a cosmetic firm), March 4, 1972; children: Dawn, Richard Paul. *Education:* Attended high school in Atlantic City, N.J. *Politics:* "Neutral." *Home:* 408 East 4th St., National City, Calif. 92050.

CAREER: Writer, 1955—; *Atlantic City Press,* Atlantic City, N.J., district manager, 1972-73; National Aviation Facilities Experimental Center, Pomona, N.J., general worker, 1973.

WRITINGS: Crown of Thorns (novel), Ashley Books, 1978. Contributor to *Coronet* and *Pageant.*

WORK IN PROGRESS: Research for another novel; a science fiction screenplay.

SIDELIGHTS: Capp writes: "The specific motivation for my novel came from many years of personal experience in and out of religion. Actually, I was born and raised a Catholic. Certainly, I met my share of rebel priests similar to those in my novel and Vance Catanese, the central character, is more or less a composite of these. Further education and some personal study of religion, philosophy, and the Bible led to my complete separation from the Catholic faith, but I am far from being an atheist. My personal religious beliefs are not important in relation to the novel as I was not trying to grind any axes or topple any towers, although there are valid points made in the novel that I think are long overdue

in regard to the human condition of those whom society chooses to castrate in one form or another. But essentially, as with all my writings, I wrote a story that appealed to me and about characters that were 'real.' In a sense, I've met these men and women in my novel. I've talked with them, read about them, grown up with them. So YES, Virginia, there is a Vance Catanese, and disillusioned Taylors, and bigoted Monsignors and perhaps even a tortured soul or two out there in the darkness. Perhaps."

AVOCATIONAL INTERESTS: Science, history, the Bible, music.

*   *   *

CAREY, Mary (Virginia) 1925-

PERSONAL: Born May 19, 1925, in New Brighton, England; came to the United States in 1925, naturalized citizen, 1955; daughter of John Cornelius (an engineer) and Mary (Hughes) Carey. *Education:* College of Mount St. Vincent, B.S., 1946. *Religion:* Roman Catholic. *Home and office:* 11960 Moorpark St., Studio City, Calif. 91604.

CAREER: Coronet, New York, N.Y., editorial associate, 1948-55; Walt Disney Productions, Burbank, Calif., assistant editor of publications, 1955-69; free-lance writer, 1969—. Editorial consultant to Oak Tree Publications. *Member:* Women in Communications.

WRITINGS—Novelizations of Walt Disney motion pictures; juvenile: (With George Sherman) *Walt Disney's Babes in Toyland*, Golden Press, 1961; *Walt Disney's The Sword in the Stone*, Whitman Publishing, 1963; *The Story of Walt Disney's Motion Picture Mary Poppins*, Whitman Publishing, 1964; *Walt Disney's The Misadventures of Merlin Jones*, Whitman Publishing, 1964; *Walt Disney's Donald Duck and the Lost Mesa Ranch*, Whitman Publishing, 1966; *The Story of Walt Disney's Motion Picture Jungle Book*, Whitman Publishing, 1967; *The Story of Walt Disney's Motion Picture Blackbeard's Ghost*, Whitman Publishing, 1968.

The Mystery of the Flaming Footprints (juvenile), Random House, 1971; *The Mystery of the Singing Serpent* (juvenile), Random House, 1972; *Step-by-Step Candlemaking*, Golden Press, 1972; *Raggedy Ann and the Glad and Sad Day* (juvenile), Golden Press, 1972; *The Mystery of Monster Mountain* (juvenile), Random House, 1973; *Step-by-Step Winemaking*, Golden Press, 1973; *The Secret of the Haunted Mirror* (juvenile), Random House, 1974; *The Tawny, Scrawny Lion and the Clever Monkey* (juvenile), Golden Press, 1974; *Alonzo Purr, the Seagoing Cat* (juvenile), Western Publishing, 1974; *The Mystery of the Invisible Dog* (juvenile), Random House, 1975; *Love Is Forever* (collection of prose and poetry), C. R. Gibson, 1975; *The Mystery of Death Trap Mine* (juvenile), Random House, 1976; (with George Sherman) *A Compendium of Bunk*, C. C Thomas, 1976; (editor) *Grandmothers Are Very Special People*, C. R. Gibson, 1977; *The Owl Who Loved Sunshine* (juvenile), Golden Press, 1977; *The Mystery of the Magic Circle* (juvenile), Random House, 1978.

WORK IN PROGRESS: The Mystery of the Sinister Scarecrow, for Random House; *Allie's Year*, a novel for young adults; *Sidney and the Silver Streak*, for children.

SIDELIGHTS: Mary Carey comments: "I began writing late; my first articles and stories were published after I was thirty, and I was motivated by money. Money is not a bad motivation. The need to eat keeps us from laziness, and the fact that someone is willing to pay to read what we write assures us that we have indeed written.

"I think that writing should be honest and simple, and it should say something about what it means to be a person. When God is good to us, we write in such a way that the act of reading becomes a pleasure to those who buy our books. This experience doesn't happen all the time, but when it does it is at least as heady as winning the Irish sweepstakes. It makes mere competence seem dull. It is probably also what makes writing a compulsive occupation; some of us are uncomfortable when we are away from our typewriters for any length of time.

"My lifelong ambition, aside from writing, is to finish exploring the American West. This should keep me busy for at least another thirty years, since there is a great deal of space here and we have always attracted great individualists."

* * *

CARNEGY, Patrick 1940-

PERSONAL: Born September 23, 1940, in Leeds, England; son of P.C.A. (a clergyman) and Joyce Eleanor (Townsley) Carnegy. *Education:* Trinity Hall, Cambridge, M.A., 1965. *Home:* 5 The Causeway, Elsworth, Cambridgeshire, England.

CAREER: Times Literary Supplement, London, England, assistant editor, 1968-1978; Faber & Faber, London, music books editor, 1978—. Has also worked as broadcaster and lecturer.

WRITINGS: Faust as Musician: A Study of Thomas Mann's Novel "Dr. Faustus", New Directions, 1973. Opera critic for *Times Educational Supplement.* Contributor of articles on music, literature, and art for various publications.

* * *

CARR, Terry (Gene) 1937-
(Norman Edwards, a joint pseudonym)

PERSONAL: Born February 19, 1937, in Grants Pass, Ore.; son of Leslie Clarence (a machinist) and Marcella (Drummond) Carr; married Miriam Dyches, January 31, 1959 (divorced, 1961); married Carol Newmark (a secretary), September 7, 1961. *Education:* City College of San Francisco, A.A., 1957; attended University of California, Berkeley, 1957-59. *Home and office:* 11037 Broadway Ter., Oakland, Calif. 94611. *Agent:* Henry Morrison, Inc., 58 West 10th St., New York, N.Y. 10011.

CAREER: Scott Meredith Literary Agency, Inc., New York City, associate editor, 1962-64; Ace Books, Inc., New York City, editor, 1964-71, founding editor of "Ace Science Fiction Specials," 1968-71; free-lance writer and editor, 1971—. Lecturer on science fiction at universities and colleges. *Member:* Science Fiction Writers of America (charter member). *Awards, honors:* Hugo Award from World Science Fiction Convention, 1959, for best fan magazine, *Fanac,* and 1973, for best fan writer.

WRITINGS: Warlord of Kor (novella), Ace Books, 1963; (with Theodore Edwin White under joint pseudonym Norman Edwards) *Invasion From 2500* (novel), Monarch, 1964; *The Light at the End of the Universe* (stories), Pyramid Publications, 1976; *Cirque* (novel), Bobbs-Merrill, 1977.

Editor: *Science Fiction for People Who Hate Science Fiction,* Doubleday, 1966; *The Others,* Fawcett, 1969; *On Our Way to the Future,* Ace Books, 1970; *This Side of Infinity,* Ace Books, 1972; *Into the Unknown,* Thomas Nelson, 1973; *An Exaltation of Stars,* Simon & Schuster, 1974; *Worlds Near and Far,* Thomas Nelson, 1974; *Creatures From Beyond,* Thomas Nelson, 1975; *Planets of Wonder: A Treasury*

of Space Opera, Thomas Nelson, 1976; *The Ideas of Tomorrow,* Little, Brown, 1976; *The Infinite Arena,* Thomas Nelson, 1977; *To Follow a Star,* Thomas Nelson, 1977; *The Year's Finest Fantasy,* Putnam, 1978; *Classic Science Fiction: The First Golden Age,* Harper, 1978.

Editor of science anthology series, "Universe": *Universe One,* Ace Books, 1971, . . . *Two,* Ace Books, 1972, . . . *Three,* Random House, 1973, . . . *Four,* Random House, 1974, . . . *Five,* Random House, 1974, . . . *Six,* Doubleday, 1976, . . . *Seven,* Doubleday, 1977, . . . *Eight,* Doubleday, 1978.

Work represented in about twenty anthologies, including *Nebula Award Series Four,* edited by Paul Anderson, Doubleday, 1969, *Again, Dangerous Visions,* edited by Harlan Ellison, Doubleday, 1972, and *Science Fiction: Contemporary Mythology,* edited by Patricia Warrick, Martin Harry Greenberg, and Joseph Olander, Harper, 1978.

Contributor of stories, articles, and reviews to mystery, science fiction, and popular magazines, including *Esquire, Realist, Galaxy,* and *Fantasy and Science Fiction.* Editor of *Science Fiction Writers of America Bulletin,* 1967-68; founding editor of *Science Fiction Writers of America Forum,* 1967-70.

WORK IN PROGRESS: A novel, *Who Speaks for the Dead?*

SIDELIGHTS: Carr commented: "The focus of my career has always been science fiction and fantasy, though I've done some writing in other fields, too. Most of my published work has been anthologies I've edited, but I intend to spend more time writing in the future, achieving a balance between writing and editing.

"Science fiction writing affords me the opportunity to speculate on the experiences and relationships between people that may be possible in the future but haven't come to pass yet; since the focus of my thinking is on future possibilities rather than matters of the past, this is a comfortable medium for me. I like to think about the future because I'm an optimist; and I feel it's valuable to do so because even the problems we may have to face some day can tell us a great deal about who and what we are today. My own writing tends to center around questions of communications, which I believe is the heart of human experience; a secondary theme in my writing is self-knowledge, which we have to attain before we can communicate with anyone."

* * *

CARROLL, Anne Kristin
See DENIS, Barbara J.

* * *

CARROLL, James P. 1943(?)-

PERSONAL: Born in Chicago, Ill.; married Alexandra Marshall (a novelist). *Education:* Studied poetry with Allen Tate at the University of Minnesota, 1965. *Residence:* Boston, Mass. *Address:* c/o Little, Brown & Co., 34 Beacon St., Boston, Mass. 02106.

CAREER: Entered Missionary Society of St. Paul the Apostle (Paulists), ordained Roman Catholic priest, left the priesthood, 1974; Boston University, Boston, Mass., chaplain, 1969-74; full-time writer, 1974—. Playwright-in-residence at the Berkshire Theater Festival, Stockbridge, Mass., 1974.

WRITINGS—Religious works: *Feed My Lambs: A Begin-*

ner's Guide for Parents Who Want to Prepare Their Children for the Eucharist and Penance, Pflaum/Standard, 1967; *Tender of Wishes: The Prayers of a Young Priest,* Paulist/Newman Press, 1969; *Wonder and Worship,* Paulist/Newman Press, 1970; *Prayer From Where We Are: Suggestions About the Possibility and Practice of Prayer Today,* Pflaum/Standard, 1970; *Elements of Hope,* Pastoral Educational Services, 1971; *Contemplation: Liberating the Ghost of the Church, Churching the Ghost of Liberation,* Paulist/Newman Press, 1972; *A Terrible Beauty: Conversions in Prayer, Politics, and Imagination,* Paulist/Newman Press, 1973; *The Winter Name of God,* Sheed, 1975.

Other: *Forbidden Disappointments* (poems), Paulist/Newman Press, 1974; *Madonna Red* (novel), Little, Brown, 1976; *Mortal Friends* (novel; Book-of-the-Month Club selection), Little, Brown, 1978.

Plays: "O, Farrell! Oh Family!," produced in showcase in New York, N.Y.

Contributor of articles and poetry to journals, including *Catholic World, Poetry,* and *Christian Century.*

SIDELIGHTS: For several years James Carroll worked at two jobs—being a priest and being a writer. In 1965, when he went to the University of Minnesota to study poetry with Allen Tate, Carroll had his first inkling that he could not meet the demands of both careers forever. After finishing the poetry course, Carroll requested that Tate autograph a book of his poetry. Tate scrawled across the page: "'Inscribed to James Carroll, with best wishes for his two vocations.'" Then Tate looked up at Carroll and warned him: "'You know, you're not going to be able to have them both.'" Tate's prediction proved true: in 1974 Carroll left the priesthood to devote himself to writing.

All of Carroll's writings are infused with religious and moral concerns. *Forbidden Disappointments,* his volume of poetry, deals with the difficulties of being a priest as well as with the problems of maintaining faith in an increasingly secular world. David Lehman felt the confessions in the book were too personal: "There is . . . a line separating frankness from self-indulgent indiscretion, and Carroll, poor fellow, crosses it often." Other commentators, however, found merit in the book. Gerard Reedy praised Carroll's "bursts of power and fresh perception," although he found that some of the poems lacked "sustained discipline of thought and form, ironic rejection of stock situations, and attention to certain generally accepted rules of good writing." The tone and style of the poems aroused Frances Sullivan's admiration. "It is an amiable poetry, James Carroll's small book, partly because the language of it is uniformly simple and self-giving, partly because the vision of each poem is like a recovered boyishness with the motes and beams of adult wickedness stuck in its eye," she commented.

Ostensibly a suspense novel, *Madonna Red* also examines religious issues, as the *New York Times Book Review* emphasized: "'Madonna Red' is a very up-to-date book about the problems of Catholicism in the modern world; about the role of women in the church; about the obligations of priesthood and the doctrine of unfaltering obedience to the bishop." In writing this novel about the attempted assassination of a British ambassador, Carroll threw a red herring across the reader's path early in the book, a ploy which the *New York Times Book Review* found particularly clever: "At the beginning of the book there is as neat a piece of misdirection as one is going to come across in any crime novel anywhere." In contrast, a critic for *Newsweek* was quite disdainful of this misleading clue: "The foundation for this

trick is laid early in the book and in such a self-conscious manner that no reader with an IQ above 79 can possibly fail to catch it." The book as a whole was panned by other commentators. Tim Murray dismissed *Madonna Red* as a "potboiler," while J. G. Murray described it as "a mishmash of bad story-telling and worse theology."

Mortal Friends met with greater critical approval. The novel revolves around the life of Colman Brady, an Irish rebel who is compelled to flee to America with his infant son. Brady lands in Boston, where he becomes involved in a stream of shady political intrigues, underworld activities, and bloody schemes for vengeance. Reflecting the favorable opinions of many others, Webster Schott wrote: "'Mortal Friends' is a serious work of fiction intended for a wide audience. It informs, entertains, and does so without abandoning intellectual standards. James Carroll has observed life carefully, and thought about what he saw." Schott remarked that the plot too often relies upon chance and that the book is humorless; nonetheless he considered *Mortal Friends* an impressive work, declaring Carroll to be "a novelist of consequence."

Carroll's intermingling of historical and fictional characters in *Mortal Friends* was a subject that attracted much comment. Among the real people who appear in the novel are Senator Estes Kefauver, Boston mayor James Michael Curley, Richard Cardinal Cushing, and Joseph, John, and Robert Kennedy. Curt Suplee praised the "deft characterizations" and observed that "the keenly distinct voices give the story plausibility." In keeping with Carroll's philosophy that "all historical figures in some way are unsavory, and all in some way merit respect," the depictions of the authentic people are neither entirely flattering nor entirely disparaging. While Mayo Mohs found the portraits of these historical figures "intriguing," he could not refrain from asking, "Are they real?"

The themes of defeat, betrayal, and revenge pervade *Mortal Friends.* The lack of remorse in the vengeful characters disturbed Suplee, but many readers perceived a moral lesson in the novel. Christopher Lehmann-Haupt compared *Mortal Friends* to a Greek tragedy. He asserted that the denouement of the book, in which Colman Brady finally decides to end the cycle of gory retaliation, "is a resolution that was first worked out over two-and-a-half millennia ago in Aeschylus's Oresteian trilogy, but [it also] is a lesson that must somehow be impressed on our increasingly archaic contemporary society, where cries for revenge seem to grow louder with each passing day." Mohs attributed the ultimate triumph of virtue in the novel to Carroll's "priestly sense of morality, his conviction that not even a life of deepening compromise can ultimately elude the Hound of Heaven."

BIOGRAPHICAL/CRITICAL SOURCES: James Carroll, *The Winter Name of God,* Sheed, 1975; *America,* May 10, 1975, August 7, 1976; *Commonweal,* March 26, 1976; *Poetry,* April, 1976; *Newsweek,* June 21, 1976, July 3, 1978; *New York Times Book Review,* July 11, 1976, April 30, 1978, August 6, 1978; *Bestsellers,* September, 1976; *Critic,* fall, 1976; *Washington Post,* April 21, 1978; *Christian Science Monitor,* May 18, 1978; *New Yorker,* May 22, 1978; *New York Times,* May 25, 1978; *Time,* June 12, 1978.*

*   *   *

CARROLL, Loren   1904-1978

OBITUARY NOTICE: Born March 5, 1904, in Scanlon, Minn.; died October 21, 1978, in Chevy Chase, Md. Foreign service officer and newspaper and magazine editor. As a reporter for a Chicago newspaper, he covered the Leopold and Loeb murder trial. Carroll was a foreign correspondent in Paris and served for a time as chief of *Newsweek's* bureau there. He was public affairs officer for the U.S. mission to the North Atlantic Treaty Organization (NATO). Obituaries and other sources: *Washington Post,* October 27, 1978; *Who's Who in America,* 40th edition, Marquis, 1978.

*   *   *

CARTER, Carolle J(ean) 1934-

PERSONAL: Born July 25, 1934, in Spokane, Wash.; daughter of Raymond E. and Rose Dias; married David A. Carter (a real estate broker), June 9, 1963; children: Craig James, Daniel Philip. *Education:* Attended University of Washington, Seattle, 1951-54; University of Southern California, B.A., 1955; graduate study at Los Angeles State College of Applied Arts and Sciences (now California State University, Los Angeles), 1956-57; San Jose State College (now San Jose State University), M.A., 1965. *Office:* Department of Social Science, Menlo College, Menlo Park, Calif. 94025.

CAREER: Pacific Telephone, service representative in Seattle, Wash., 1955-56, and Van Nuys, Calif., 1956-57; junior high school teacher of social studies, English, and reading in Milpitas, Calif., 1963-68; San Jose State University, San Jose, Calif., lecturer in history, 1968-69; Foothill Community College, Los Altos Hills, Calif., assistant professor of American history, 1969-70; San Jose State University, lecturer in history, 1971-75; Menlo College, Menlo Park, Calif., professor of history and political science, 1976—. Part-time instructor of American history at San Jose City College, 1966-73, and assistant professor of California history at Foothill Community College, 1976—; lecturer at West Valley College, 1975-76. Member of Commission on the Status of Women, 1976-80, Santa Clara County Grand Jury, 1974-75, and Brandeis University National Women's Committee.

MEMBER: American Historical Association, American Political Science Association, Oral History Association, British Studies Association, Irish Literary and Historical Society, League of Women Voters, West Coast Association of Women Historians, Wedgwood Society of Northern California, 101 Association.

WRITINGS: The Shamrock and the Swastika: German Espionage in Ireland in World War II, Pacific Books, 1977. Contributor of about a dozen articles and reviews to magazines. Book review editor of local *Jewish Community News,* 1972-73.

WORK IN PROGRESS: American Intelligence With the Communist Chinese During World War II, "a study of a special military group sent to Yenan in 1944 to act in a liaison capacity with the Chinese Communists and assess the possibilities of augmenting a united effort to defeat the Japanese via increased cooperation with the Chinese Communists," completion expected in 1981; research on industrial espionage among the potteries of eighteenth- and nineteenth-century England and on Irish-American relations in World War II.

SIDELIGHTS: Carolle Carter told *CA:* "The obligation of the historian is to write history and continually update human knowledge of the past. The social scientist is obliged to apply academics to the current human condition. My career, writing, and community involvement reflect my attempts to interweave these elements in order to make a creative contribution to learning and to our society."

Carter added some comments about her book: "*The Shamrock and the Swastika* deals with Irish neutrality in World War II and includes a study of British-Irish, United States-Irish, and German-Irish relations. The Irish Republican Army's (IRA) role is also covered as well as the perspective that German military intelligence had on Ireland's potential value to the German war effort and the steps taken to realize that potential. Among other things, the latter involved two types of espionage activities: sending German agents on missions to Ireland, and utilizing Irishmen who happened to be in England during the war due to a variety of circumstances. The book is a reassessment of Ireland's true position with respect to the belligerents and makes extensive use of documentary and governmental sources that have not been available to scholars previously."

*   *   *

CARTWRIGHT, Rosalind Dymond 1922-
(Rosalind Dymond)

PERSONAL: Born December 20, 1922, in New York, N.Y.; daughter of Henry O. and Stella H. (a writer) Falk; married Desmond Cartwright (a psychologist), March 21, 1953 (divorced, November 26, 1961); children: Christine Cartwright Khalsa, Carolyn. *Education:* University of Toronto, B.A., 1945, M.A., 1946; Cornell University, Ph.D., 1949. *Politics:* Democrat. *Religion:* None. *Home:* 706 Forest Ave., Evanston, Ill. 60202. *Office:* Rush-Presbyterian-St. Lukes Medical Center, Chicago, Ill. 60612.

CAREER: Mount Holyoke College, South Hadley, Mass., assistant professor of psychology, 1949-51; University of Chicago, Chicago, Illinois, research associate, 1951-60; University of Colorado, Boulder, research associate, 1960-61; University of Illinois College of Medicine, Chicago, 1961-69, began as associate professor, became professor of psychology and director of division; University of Illinois at Chicago Circle, Chicago, professor of psychology, 1969-77; Rush-Presbyterian-St. Lukes Medical Center, Chicago, Ill., chairman of department of psychology, 1977—. Director of Sleep Disorder Service and Research Center. Member of board of directors of Midwest School of Professional Psychology. *Member:* American Psychological Association (fellow; member of council of representatives), American Association for the Advancement of Science (fellow), Association for the Psychophysiological Study of Sleep (member of board of directors). *Awards, honors:* Outstanding awards from American Personnel and Guidance Association, 1955, 1958; research grants from National Science Foundation, National Institute of Mental Health, and Illinois Department of Mental Health.

WRITINGS: (Editor with Carl Rogers; under name Rosalind Dymond) *Psychotherapy and Personality Change,* University of Chicago Press, 1954; *Nightlife,* Prentice-Hall, 1977; *Primer on Sleep and Dreaming,* Addison-Wesley, 1978.

Contributor: A. P. Hare, E. Borgatta, and R. F. Bales, editors, *Small Groups,* Knopf, 1955; D. Byrne and M. Hamilton, editors, *Personality Research: A Book of Readings,* Prentice Hall, 1966; G. Stollack, B. Guerney, Jr., and M. A. Rothberg, editors, *Psychotherapy Research,* Rand McNally, 1966; L. A. Gottschalk and A. H. Aurback, editors, *Methods of Research in Psychotherapy,* Appleton, 1966; H. Toch and H. C. Smith, editors, *Social Perception,* Van Nostrand, 1968; M. Kramer, editor, *Dream Psychology and the New Biology of Dreaming,* C. C Thomas, 1969; E. Hartmann, editor, *Dreams and Sleeping,* Little, Brown, 1970; S.

Brown and D. Brenner, editors, *Science, Psychology and Communication,* Teachers College Press, 1972; M. Chase, editor, *The Sleeping Brain,* Brain Information Service Press, 1973.

Contributor to professional journals and to conference proceedings. Member of editorial boards of *Psychiatry* and *Psychotherapy: Theory, Research and Practice.*

WORK IN PROGRESS: Research on dreams of depressed divorced women, and their reshaping.

* * *

CASHMAN, John
See DAVIS, Timothy Francis Tothill

* * *

CASTLE, Mort 1946-

PERSONAL: Born July 8, 1946, in Chicago, Ill.; son of Sheldon H. (in sales) and Lillian (a nutritionist; maiden name, Marcus) Castle; married Jane Potts (a high school French teacher), July 4, 1971. *Education:* Illinois State University, B.S.E., 1968. *Politics:* "Democrat/Monarchist." *Religion:* Jewish. *Home:* 402 Stanton Lane, Crete, Ill. 60417. *Agent:* Porter, Gould & Dierks, 215 West Ohio, Chicago, Ill. 60610. *Office:* Crete-Monee High School, West Exchange St., Crete, Ill. 60417.

CAREER: Entertainer (singer, musician, comedian, and hypnotist, including television and radio work), 1965-68; Crete-Monee High School, Crete, Ill., English teacher, 1968—. Editor and publisher of Eads Street Press, 1975—. Co-chairman of local annual writer's conference, 1972—; judge of Northwoods Press Poetry Quarto Contest, 1977; public lecturer. *Member:* National Education Association, Illinois Education Association, Crete-Monee Education Association.

WRITINGS: Mulbray (short stories), Samisdat Associates, 1976; *The Deadly Election* (novel), Major Books, 1976. Writer of advertising copy, musical continuity, and cartoon captions. Contributor of more than sixty stories, poems, and articles to popular and literary journals, including *Cavalier, New Infinity Review, Nitty-Gritty, Riverside Quarterly,* and *Fireland Arts Review.*

WORK IN PROGRESS: Fire Melody, a suspense novel; "Space Opera," a musical comedy; "Danny Gulf," a detective drama series for radio.

SIDELIGHTS: Castle writes: "I was fortunate to have been friends with Bill Wantling, one of our most gifted poets, during our undergrad days. I was a jerky suburban kid, dreaming of being show biz boffo, and he was a genuine! writer! It was good to sit on his living room floor, ugly central Illinois wind growling outside, strumming guitar, trying to look/sound like Bob Dylan, while Wantling made poems happen. Initial inspiration, experiences that made me think I might someday toss a line in literary waters? I think so. Thanks Bill, and thanks to Miss Ryan, my kindergarten teacher, who kept telling me someday I'd be writing for television.

"I became serious about writing in 1971, at age twenty-five, with certain intimations about my own mortality clobbering me. My first submitted story sold to a men's magazine, *Mr.*—thanks, Everett Myers, editor—and I figured I had it made. Write it up, send it out, get the money. *Hubris.* One hundred fifty rejections later, I had the realization it might not be that easy. It still isn't. One persists and hopes and dreams.

"My major complaint regarding the Human Condition: not enough time! I want hours to make music on the guitar, mandolin, banjo, harmonica. I want hours to read every darn book in my comic book collection. Hours to listen to all the great radio shows I've got on tape. I dream of seeing the most magnificent places on earth—Japan, Ireland, Disneyland. And is there anyone in the south suburbs of Chicago who would like to spend an afternoon talking Yiddish with me, assuming I ever can find a free afternoon?

"Complaint aside, I think myself a lucky person. The high school kids I teach in our writer's workshop for the gifted student program are the best people one could want to know. Ten years from now, this high school will have sent up a bunch of blazing skyrockets into the literary skies. I love my wife, she loves me, and she writes good poems, too. Lewis, our fox terrier, has a marvelously square head and a keen sense of humor.

"I do hope there comes a time, though, when my writing, or my teaching, starts bringing in a decent wage!"

BIOGRAPHICAL/CRITICAL SOURCES: Chicago Sun-Times, March 1, 1977; *Suburban Tribune,* June 10, 1977; *Inside,* September 25, 1977.

* * *

CATTON, (Charles) Bruce 1899-1978

OBITUARY NOTICE—See index for *CA* sketch; Born October 9, 1899, in Petoskey, Mich.; died August 28, 1978, in Frankfort, Mich. Journalist and author of historical works on the Civil War and an autobiography. As a boy, Catton listened with fascination to the yarns of Civil War veterans. The Civil War was a lifelong interest, but Catton embarked on a career in journalism and government service and did not begin writing about his favorite subject until the age of fifty. *Mr. Lincoln's Army* was the first of thirteen books he wrote on the War Between the States, all of which were acclaimed for their historical accuracy and vivid descriptive passages. *A Stillness at Appomattox* won the National Book Award and the Pulitzer Prize in 1954. Catton was an editor at *American Heritage* magazine from 1954 until the time of his death. Obituaries and other sources: *Current Biography,* Wilson, 1954, October, 1978; *The Oxford Companion to American Literature,* 4th edition, Oxford University Press, 1965; *The Reader's Encyclopedia,* 2nd edition, Crowell, 1965; *The Penguin Companion to American Literature,* McGraw, 1971; Bruce Catton, *Waiting for the Morning Train: An American Boyhood,* Doubleday, 1972; *Authors in the News,* Volume I, Gale, 1976; *Who's Who in America,* 40th edition, Marquis, 1978; *Detroit News,* August 29, 1978; *Publishers Weekly,* September 11, 1978; *Newsweek,* September 11, 1978; *Time,* September 11, 1978; *AB Bookman's Weekly,* November 6, 1978.

* * *

CHAIKIN, Miriam 1928-

PERSONAL: Born December 8, 1928, in Jerusalem, Palestine (now Israel); brought to the United States in 1929; daughter of Abraham and Leah (Tikochinsky) Chaikin. *Education:* Attended high school in Brooklyn, N.Y. *Politics:* Democrat. *Religion:* Jewish. *Home:* 107 Waverly Pl., New York, N.Y. 10011. *Agent:* Dorothy Markinko, McIntosh & Otis, Inc., 475 Fifth Ave., New York, N.Y. 10017. *Office:* Holt, Rinehart & Winston, Inc., 383 Madison Ave., New York, N.Y. 10017.

CAREER: Anna M. Rosenberg Associates, New York

City, in public relations, 1957-60; World Publishing Co., Cleveland, Ohio, subsidiary rights director, 1961-66; Bobbs-Merrill Co., Inc., New York City, editorial director, 1969-73; Holt, Rinehart & Winston, Inc., New York City, editorial director, 1973—. *Member:* International P.E.N., Authors Guild, Authors League of America, Women's National Book Association.

WRITINGS—All juveniles: *Ittki Pittki,* Parents' Magazine Press, 1971; *The Happy Pairr,* Putnam, 1972; *Hardlucky,* Lippincott, 1973; *I Should Worry, I Should Care,* Harper, 1979; *The Seventh Day,* Doubleday, 1979.

WORK IN PROGRESS: The Cheese Stands Alone, for children; a novel, for children.

* * *

CHALLANS, Mary   1905-
(Mary Renault)

PERSONAL: Born September 4, 1905, in London, England; emigrated to South Africa in 1948; daughter of Frank (a doctor) and Clementine Mary (Baxter) Challans. *Education:* St. Hugh's College, Oxford, M.A.; Radcliffe Infirmary, Oxford, S.R.N., 1936. *Politics:* Progressive. *Address:* 3 Atholl Rd., Camps Bay, Cape Town 8001, South Africa.

CAREER: Writer, 1938—. Worked as a nurse in England. *Member:* P.E.N. Club of South Africa (past president), Royal Society of Literature (fellow). *Awards, honors:* MGM award, 1946, for *Return to Night;* National Association of Independent Schools Award, 1963; Silver Pen Award, 1971, for *Fire From Heaven.*

WRITINGS—All under pseudonym Mary Renault; novels: *Promise of Love,* Morrow, 1939, reprinted, Queens House, 1976 (published in England as *Purposes of Love,* Longmans, Green, 1939); *Kind Are Her Answers,* Morrow, 1940, reprinted, Queens House, 1976; *The Friendly Young Ladies,* Longmans, Green, 1944, published as *The Middle Mist,* Morrow, 1945, reprinted, Queens House, 1976; *Return to Night,* Morrow, 1947, reprinted, Queens House, 1976; *North Face,* Morrow, 1948, reprinted, Queens House, 1976; *The Charioteer,* Longmans, Green, 1953, reprinted, Bantam, 1974; *The Last of the Wine,* Pantheon, 1956, reprinted, Random House, 1975; *The King Must Die* (Book-of-the-Month-Club selection), Pantheon, 1958, reprinted, Bantam, 1974; *The Bull From the Sea,* Pantheon, 1962, reprinted, Vintage Books, 1975; *The Mask of Apollo,* Pantheon, 1966; *Fire From Heaven,* Pantheon, 1969; *The Persian Boy,* Pantheon, 1972; *The Praise Singer,* Pantheon, 1978.

Other; under pseudonym: *The Lion in the Gateway: Heroic Battles of the Greeks and Persians at Marathon, Salamis, and Thermopylae* (juvenile; illustrated by C. Walter Hodges), Harper, 1964; *The Nature of Alexander,* Pantheon, 1975.

SIDELIGHTS: Mary Challans decided at an early age that she wanted to be a writer. Because Challans felt that a writer must participate actively in life, she enrolled in a nursing school. Her experiences as a nurse provided material for her first novel, *Promise of Love,* which she wrote under the pseudonym Mary Renault. *Promise of Love* was well-received by critics. A reviewer for the *New York Times* stated: "One a double count *Promise of Love* strikes me as an unusually excellent first novel. There is a fusion between background and personal drama, between inner and outer reality, which enriches and dignifies both. The story of Mic and Vivian would not be nearly so arresting as it is if one were not so sharply aware of the pressure of their environ-

ment. . . . When one adds to this that Mary Renault's style has a sure, fluid quality, that she possesses humor as well as sensitiveness, that even her minor characters are shrewdly drawn—the sum total is quite impressive."

Buoyed by the success of her first novel, Challans planned to become a full-time writer, but World War II interfered with her plans. She continued her nursing career and wrote in her spare time. A novel that appeared after the war, *Return to Night,* brought her name to the attention of the American reading public because it received the MGM prize, the largest financial award in the field of literature. Echoing the enthusiasm of many other critics, a *New Yorker* reviewer described *Return to Night* as "an expert, vivid novel," explaining that "Miss Renault sets forth the characters of three extremely complex people with a penetrating lucidity and a certain moderate reasonableness, making this not just an impassioned love story but a novel of considerable depth."

Following the end of World War II, Mary Challans traveled extensively in France, Italy, Africa, Greece, and the Aegean Islands. She was most impressed with Greece, and it became the setting for many of her historical novels. The first of these novels, *The Last of the Wine,* concerns the Theseus myth and takes place during the Third Peloponnesian War. "To read *The Last of the Wine,*" wrote a critic in *New York Herald Tribune Book Review,* "is to walk for a while in the shadow of the Acropolis with Plato and his friends." Observed the *Times Literary Supplement: "The Last of the Wine* is a superb historical novel. The writing is Attic in quality, unforced, clear, delicate. The characterization is uniformly successful and, most difficult of all, the atmosphere of Athens is realized in masterly fashion. Miss Renault is not only obviously familiar with the principal sources. She has disciplined her imagination so that the reader ceases to question the authenticity of her fiction."

Challans discovered her metier in the historical novel. *The Bull From the Sea,* a sequel to *The King Must Die,* also earned accolades from critics. Moses Hadas wrote that *The King Must Die* "is brilliantly and convincingly imagined, artistically presented, at once mind-stretching and deeply moving." In *The Mask of Apollo,* Challans describes Syracuse and Athens in the fourth century B.C. Two subsequent novels, *Fire From Heaven* and *The Persian Boy,* thoroughly examine the life of Alexander the Great. The appearance of each book helped enhance her reputation as the foremost historical novelist of our time.

Striving to explain why Challans's work is so highly esteemed, a commentator for *New York Herald Tribune Book Review* stated: "Miss Renault's historical novels are excellent. They hold their own as artistically wrought and moving stories and they are rich in the adult entertainment which is the special province of historical fiction. They are particularly welcome because they illuminate uncharted but essential passages and epochs in the formative stages of our civilization. . . . Her narrative is not, nor does it claim to be, history; but it is a well-considered suggestion of how things may have happened, and for the personality and culture with which she deals we have nothing more plausible."

BIOGRAPHICAL/CRITICAL SOURCES: Times Literary Supplement, February 25, 1939, June 29, 1956, September 19, 1958, March 16, 1962, December 15, 1966, December 11, 1970, November 3, 1972; *New York Times,* March 12, 1939, April 20, 1947, July 13, 1958; *Books,* March 12, 1939; *New Yorker,* April 19, 1947; *New York Herald Tribune Book Review,* October 14, 1956, July 13, 1958, February 18, 1962; *Booklist,* June 15, 1958; *Saturday Review,* July 12, 1958, February 17, 1962, October 1, 1966, December 9, 1972; *Christian Science Monitor,* July 17, 1958, November 6, 1975; *Commonweal,* August 1, 1958; *New York Times Book Review,* February 18, 1962, October 30, 1966, December 14, 1969, December 31, 1979; *Book Week,* November 6, 1966; *New Republic,* November 19, 1966; Peter Wolfe, *Mary Renault,* Twayne, 1969; *Washington Post Book World,* November 23, 1969; *Best Sellers,* December 15, 1969; *Catholic World,* September, 1970; Bernard F. Dick, *The Hellenism of Mary Renault,* Southern Illinois Press, 1972; *Atlantic,* December, 1972; *Virginia Quarterly Review,* summer, 1973; *Sewanee Review,* autumn, 1973; *Contemporary Literary Criticism,* Volume 3, Gale, 1975; *Economist,* October 4, 1975.*

*   *   *

CHAMBERLIN, Judi   1944-

PERSONAL: Born October 30, 1944, in New York, N.Y.; daughter of Harold and Shirley (Jaffe) Ross; married Robert Chamberlin, April 17, 1965 (divorced, February, 1972); children: Julie Ross. *Education:* Attended Hunter College of the City University of New York, 1965-66, and Kutztown State College, 1967-68. *Home:* 14 Evergreen Ave., Somerville, Mass. 02145. *Agent:* Ellen Levine, Curtis Brown Ltd., 575 Madison Ave., New York, N.Y. 10022. *Office:* Mental Patients' Liberation Front, P.O. Box 156, West Somerville, Mass. 02144.

CAREER: Former legal secretary; currently staff member of Mental Patients' Liberation Front, West Somerville, Mass. Chairwoman of National Committee on Patients' Rights; member of President's Commission on Mental Health task panel on legal and ethical issues; member of bar funding management board of American Bar Association Commission on the Mentally Disabled. Consultant to National Institute of Mental Health.

WRITINGS: (Contributor) *Women Look at Psychiatry,* Press Gang Publishers, 1975; *On Our Own: Patient-Controlled Alternatives to the Mental Health System,* Hawthorn, 1978.

WORK IN PROGRESS: A book on the mental patients' liberation movement, including information on the harmfulness of much psychiatric treatment, and interviews with movement activists.

SIDELIGHTS: Judi Chamberlin writes: "I have been a full-time activist in the mental patients' liberation movement since 1971. I have worked with a number of groups who are trying to gain rights for mental patients, publicize the need for involvement of present and former patients in evaluating, planning, and delivering mental health services, and combat the stigma of being a mental patient, by showing the public that mental patients can be competent and articulate."

*   *   *

CHAPLIN, Bill
See CHAPLIN, W. W.

*   *   *

CHAPLIN, Charles Spencer   1889-1977
(Charlie Chaplin)

PERSONAL: Born April 16, 1889, in London, England; came to United States, 1914; son of Charles Spencer (a singer) and Hannah (singer, pianist, and actress under stage name Lily Harley) Chaplin; married Mildred Harris, 1918

(divorced, 1920); married Lolita McMurray (an actress under stage name Lita Grey), 1924 (divorced, 1927); married Pauline Levy (an actress under stage name Paulette Godard), 1936 (divorced, 1942); married Oona O'Neill, 1943; children: Charles Spencer, Jr., Sydney Earl, Geraldine, Michael, Josephine, Victoria, Eugene O'Neill, Jane, Annette-Emilie, James. *Residence:* Vevey, Switzerland.

CAREER: Actor and vaudeville performer; screenwriter, producer, and director of motion pictures; author. Vaudeville performer with Fred Karno troupe, 1906-14; actor in motion pictures for Keystone Films, including "Making a Living," 1914, "Kid Auto Races at Vienna," 1914, "Mabel's Strange Predicament," 1914, "Between Showers," 1914, "A Film Johnnie," 1914, "Tango Tangles," 1914, "His Favorite Pastime," 1914, "Cruel, Cruel Love," 1914, "The Star Boarder," 1914, "Mabel at the Wheel," 1914, and "Twenty Minutes of Love," 1914. Co-founder of United Artists Releasing Corp., 1919. *Awards, honors:* Received special Academy Award, and nominations for Academy Awards for best actor and best comedy director, all from Academy of Motion Picture Arts and Sciences, all 1928, all for "The Circus"; nominations for Academy Awards for best actor, best screenplay, and best film, all 1940, all for "The Great Dictator"; nomination for Academy Award for best screenplay, 1947, for "Monsieur Verdoux"; special Academy Award, 1972; knighted, 1975.

WRITINGS: Charlie Chaplin's Own Story: Being the Faithful Recital of a Romantic Career, Beginning With Early Recollections of Boyhood in London and Closing With the Signing of His Latest Motion-Picture Contract, Bobbs-Merrill, 1916; *My Trip Abroad,* Harper, 1922; *"The Great Dictator": Synopsis of the Film,* Charles Chaplin Film Corp., 1941; *Les Feux de la rampe* (screenplay; title means "Limelight"), Gallimard, 1953; *My Autobiography,* Simon & Schuster, 1964; *My Life in Pictures,* Bodley Head, 1974.

Screenplays; all as director, unless otherwise noted; released by Keystone Films, 1914: (Co-director with Mabel Normand) "Caught in a Cabaret"; "Caught in the Rain"; "A Busy Day"; "Laughing Gas"; "The Property Man"; "Recreation"; "The Masquerader"; "His New Profession"; "The Rounders"; "The New Janitor"; "Those Love Pangs"; "Gentlemen of Nerve"; "His Musical Career"; "His Trysting Place"; "Getting Acquainted"; "His Prehistoric Past."

Released by Essanay: "His New Job," 1915; "A Night Out," 1915; "The Champion," 1915; "In the Park," 1915; "A Jitney Elopement," 1915; "The Tramp," 1915; "By the Sea," 1915; "Work," 1915; "A Woman," 1915; "The Bank," 1915; "Shanghaied," 1915; "A Night in the Show," 1915; "Charlie Chaplin's Burlesque on Carmen," 1915, revised, 1916; "Police," 1916; (with Leo White) "Triple Trouble," 1916; "The Essanay-Chaplin Revue of 1916" (contains "The Tramp," "His New Job," and "A Night Out"), 1916.

Released by Mutual: "The Floorwalker," 1916; "The Fireman," 1916; "The Vagabond," 1916; "One A.M.," 1916; "The Count," 1916; "The Pawnshop," 1916; "Behind the Screen," 1916; "The Rink," 1916; "Easy Street," 1917; "The Cure," 1917; "The Immigrant," 1917; "The Adventurer," 1917.

Released by First National: "A Dog's Life," 1918; "Shoulder's Arms," 1918; "Sunnyside," 1919; "A Day's Pleasure," 1919; "The Kid," 1921; "The Idle Class," 1921; "Pay Day," 1922; "The Pilgrim," 1923.

Released by United Artists: "A Woman of Paris," 1923; "The Gold Rush," 1925; "The Circus," 1928; "City Lights," 1931; "Modern Times," 1936; "The Great Dictator," 1940; "Monsieur Verdoux," 1947; "Limelight," 1952.

Other: "A King in New York," Archway, 1957; "A Countess From Hong Kong," Universal, 1967.

SIDELIGHTS: Few entertainers have received more recognition in their time than Chaplin. He was lovingly known the world over as "the tramp," an impoverished "never say die" hero of more than eighty films. For over thirty years he was a major force in comedy. He wrote, directed, and acted in the vast majority of his films, most of which are now considered classics. "His films, always modern, are eternal," said French comedian Jacques Tati, "and his contribution to the cinema and to his century irreplaceable." He was "the original great one in our business," noted Bob Hope. "We're fortunate to have been alive in his time."

Chaplin's early life was that of the struggling entertainer. He was placed in an orphanage in 1894 when his parents, both hard-luck vaudeville performers, became unable to support their family of five. When he left the orphanage, Chaplin earned money as an extra in small vaudeville shows. Soon he was playing major parts in touring productions, and in 1906 he joined Fred Karno's vaudeville troup. Chaplin rose to star billing within four years as a comedian in Karno's company and one night, during a performance of "A Night in an English Music Hall," his acting drew the attention of Hollywood film mogul Mack Sennett. Sennett was impressed with Chaplin's performance and offered him a weekly salary of $150 to appear in three shorts for Keystone Films. Chaplin replied by demanding $200 although Sennett's offer was twice what he was making with Karno. They eventually agreed on terms of $150 for three months and $175 for nine months thereafter.

When Chaplin arrived in Hollywood in 1914, he was given the star dressing room, the same one used previously by Roscoe "Fatty" Arbuckle and also by Sennett. But despite the star treatment, Chaplin worked only sporadically, often going an entire week with no assignments. Then one day Chaplin spied Sennett in conversation with a fellow actor. Impatient with inactivity, Chaplin persistently placed himself in Sennett's line of vision in order to gain the filmmaker's attention. Sennett eventually spotted Chaplin, though apparently unaware of the ploy, and told him to dress for a comedy sequence. As Chaplin recalled: "I had no idea what make-up to put on. . . . However, on the way to the wardrobe I thought I would dress in baggy pants, big shoes, a cane and a derby hat. I wanted everything a contradiction: the pants baggy, the coat tight, the hat small and the shoes large." After adding a small moustache to the disguise, he went to meet Sennett. "I had no idea of the character," Chaplin said. "But the moment I was dressed, the clothes and the make-up made me feel the person he was. I began to know him, and by the time I walked onto the stage he was fully born." The guise proved so successful that Chaplin was to adopt it as his exclusive on-camera garb for the next twenty years.

Chaplin soon found himself under the direction of Mabel Normand, a top comedy actress but a novice director. Chaplin immediately began plaguing her with countless suggestions on how to improve their film. Normand disagreed and the confrontation resulted in Chaplin's refusal to perform in a specific scene unless his ideas were implemented. Normand stalked off to Sennett for arbitration. His immediate reaction was to fire Chaplin. However, that very day he'd

received a demand from New York distributors for more Chaplin films. Sennett conferred with Chaplin and asked for his cooperation. Chaplin replied that if Sennett were to let him direct, there would be no problem. After some consternation, Sennett agreed to let Chaplin direct a film provided he cover for any financial loss.

Buoyed by the prospect of directing his own films, Chaplin returned to the set where Normand and crew waited. He immediately noticed a new attitude on Normand's part and responded by turning in a string of admirable performances. Normand and Chaplin created several successful films together, including "Caught in a Cabaret," "Mabel's Busy Day," and "Mabel's Married Life." However, Chaplin felt himself better suited to working under his own direction. "Tillie's Punctured Romance," co-starring Normand and Chaplin and directed by Sennett in 1914, was his last film under another director. Sadly, Normand's career declined with the advent of sound.

Chaplin's contract with Keystone Films expired in 1915, whereupon he joined the Essanay Company. He made fifteen short films for Essanay before signing with Mutual Film Company in 1916. There he made twelve more two-reelers, including the popular "Easy Street" in which Chaplin, in his tramp guise, plays a policeman who overcomes his assailant by placing his head in a gas street lamp.

Upon expiration of his agreement with Mutual, Chaplin signed an eight-film pact with First National Exhibitors' Circuit which netted him more than one million dollars and made him one of the highest paid entertainers in the world. Some of Chaplin's most acclaimed films were made for First National. "A Dog's Life," "Shoulders Arms," and "The Idle Class" are all highly regarded films, as are "The Pilgrim" and "Pay Day." But Chaplin's biggest success up to that time came with his first full-length film, "The Kid." The story of a tramp's relationship with an abandoned child was much praised for its blend of humor and pathos. Looking back, one critic remarked that "The Kid" "would have won many awards had they been as prevalent then as they are now." Chaplin himself was so inspired by the film's popularity that after completing his contractual obligations with First National, he never again made a film of less than feature length.

With completion of "The Kid," Chaplin felt drained. Chaplin's first divorce coincided with the film's release. His uncertainty of the film's potential, coupled with his disintegrating marriage, forced Chaplin into taking a much needed vacation. In 1921, he went to Europe. There he was greeted by enthusiastic crowds in Paris, Berlin, and London. The trip seemed to rejuvenate him. "I was reluctant to leave England," he remembered. "But celebrity could give me no more. I was returning with complete satisfaction—though somewhat sad, for I was leaving behind not alone the noise of acclaim or accolades of the rich and celebrated who had entertained me, but the sincere affection and enthusiasm of the English and the French crowds that had waited to welcome me. . . . I was also leaving behind my past. . . ." He felt that a visit to his old home "had completed something within me; I was satisfied to return to California and get back to work. . . ."

Upon returning from Europe, Chaplin made three more shorts, thus ending his contract with First National. He then began working for United Artists, a releasing company he co-founded in 1919. Chaplin's first film for his own company was a marked departure from what the public had come to expect. The film was "A Woman of Paris." It was not a comedy but a serious study of upper-class life in Paris. It did not star Chaplin. He made the film as a vehicle for his long time co-star Edna Purviance with the hope that she could start her own career as a "serious" actress. Although it received critical praise, the film was met with ambivalence by Chaplin's followers and was rarely seen in the United States following its initial release. However, the film underwent a revival in 1977, in New York City, and was considered by many critics as one of the best films shown that year. "A Woman of Paris" is now a highly regarded film in its own right although it failed as a showcase for Purviance's talents. Later, Chaplin commissioned Joseph von Sternberg to direct Purviance in an adaptation of Chekhov's *The Sea Gull*. But despite claims by viewers that "The Sea Gull" contained an excellent performance by Purviance, Chaplin refused to release the film. She did remain under contract to Chaplin until her death in 1958, but aside from appearing as an extra in two later films, she made only "The Education of a Prince," a French film never released in the United States.

Chaplin followed "A Woman of Paris" with what is generally acknowledged as his finest comedy, "The Gold Rush." Released in 1925, the movie contains some of Chaplin's best known scenes: the tramp eating a boot and later using a dog leash to tie his pants up, a cabin that almost falls over a cliff, and a delirious fellow prospector imagining the tramp to be a chicken. Called "the outstanding gem of all Chaplin's pictures" by Mordaunt Hall, "The Gold Rush" was the one film Chaplin hoped to be remembered by. It was selected as the best motion picture comedy in a recent polling of national critics.

After "The Gold Rush," Chaplin made "The Circus," a film in many ways reminiscent of his early two-reelers. The film was another success and was nominated for several awards in the first year of the Academy of Motion Picture Arts and Sciences.

It took almost three years for Chaplin to make his next movie, "City Lights." Like "The Gold Rush," "City Lights" was warmly received by both critics and the public but, unlike the former, "City Lights" contained a serious and more sentimental theme; in its pathos, it is often compared to "The Kid." The movie is about the tramp's affections for a blind girl. He takes care of her and when he learns an operation can restore her sight, he obtains the money from a millionaire friend. Unfortunately, the police believe the tramp stole the money and he is put in prison. When he gets out, he meets the girl and she realizes who he is. One critic called the final scene "the most moving he [Chaplin] ever created." Another critic, James Agee, said that "it is enough to shrivel the heart to see and it is the greatest piece of acting and the highest moment in movies." Though "The Gold Rush" is referred to as Chaplin's best comedy, "City Lights," with its pathos, is widely considered his greatest film.

Chaplin had taken a chance with "City Lights." By the time of its release in 1931, sound had been incorporated into the movies. He chose to make "City Lights" as a silent picture anyway and the film proved to be one of the top box-office winners that year. With the release of "Modern Times" in 1936, Chaplin again refused to use sound. However, the lack of sound did not keep "Modern Times" from being a resounding success. Chaplin called the film "a story of industry, of individual enterprise—of humanity crusading in pursuit of happiness." Like "The Gold Rush," "Modern Times" too contains some of Chaplin's most classic sequences. Most notable are the first scenes when the tramp, as an assembly line worker, goes crazy from the monotony

of the job and dives into the mechanisms of the line. After being rescued, he attempts to tighten anything which will fit his wrenches, including the buttons on a woman's dress. Other famous gags include the tramp being mistaken as the leader of a demonstration when he retrieves a red flag, and a scene where cocaine is used by prison inmates. However, despite the popularity of "Modern Times," it was Chaplin's last film without spoken dialogue and, more importantly, it marked his last appearance as the tramp.

"The Great Dictator" was released in 1940 amid great controversy. Chaplin's first sound film was a parody of Adolf Hitler, whose tyranny Chaplin could not imagine when he began production in 1937. As one critic pointed out, "Chaplin did not know that Hitler's racist policies included the mass slaughter of Jews; if he had, 'The Great Dictator' probably would never have been made as a comic satire." Nonetheless, "The Great Dictator" was as popular with his followers as the previous films and it too contained many timeless moments: the dictator Adenoid Hynkel dancing with the globe and sliding up the curtain, the Jewish barber fighting off Hynkel's henchmen, and Hynkel's confrontations with fellow dictator Napaloni. Although Chaplin received some criticism for the excessive dialogue which ends the film, most critics applauded his decision to abandon the tramp character in favor of the demanding dual role. Bosley Crowther called the movie "a truly superb accomplishment by a truly great artist—and, from one point of view, perhaps the most significant film ever produced."

With "Monsieur Verdoux," Chaplin continued the bold approach to characterization he began in "The Great Dictator." The movie is a black comedy about a fashionable socialite who marries rich women and then murders them. Eventually, he is caught and put on trial. The end sequence is similar to the speech that closes "The Great Dictator" but without the grand gestures for freedom. In "Monsieur Verdoux," Chaplin justifies the murders by rationalizing that Verdoux is no less a killer than a ruler who plunges his country into war. Verdoux suggests that these rulers cause more deaths than he has. With such a radical theme, Chaplin began to lose his following. One critic noted that "'Monsieur Verdoux' was made, perhaps, before audiences were ready to contemplate such a thesis." Another critic, Howard Barnes, called it "an affront to the intelligence." Kate Cameron was equally negative, saying that the joke was on Chaplin. But the film has grown in stature over the years. It is shown frequently at art houses and film festivals and many critics today rate "Monsieur Verdoux" as one of Chaplin's finest works.

"Limelight" proved to be an apt title for Chaplin's last film in the United States. The sentimental story of an aging music hall comedian whose greatest triumph is followed by his death typified Chaplin's own feelings on life. Bosley Crowther wrote: "Out of his knowledge of the theatre and his sense of the wistfulness of man in the ever-repeating cycle of youth taking over from age, Charlie Chaplin has drawn the inspiration and the poignantly sentimental theme." And critics were universal in their praise of the scene in which Chaplin and Buster Keaton perform at a benefit show.

Chaplin, however, had little opportunity to rejoice over the reviews of "Limelight.' In 1952, Chaplin vacationed in England. Owing to two scandalous marriages, a paternity suit, and various political stands, Chaplin was informed by the attorney general that he would have to prove his "moral worth" before he could be allowed back in the United States. Insulted, Chaplin went back to England and later settled in Switzerland.

Chaplin made two more films before he died. "A King in New York" was generally viewed as a swipe at McCarthyism without the subtle humor Chaplin was known for. Made in 1957, the film was not released in the United States for almost twenty years. In 1967, Chaplin directed his own screenplay, "A Countess From Hong Kong," but despite commendable performances by Sophia Loren and Marlon Brando, it too is regarded as an inferior film.

In 1972, Chaplin was allowed to return to the United States to accept a special Academy Award for his contributions to cinema. It was an emotional situation for Chaplin, who expressed himself by saying: "Words are so futile, so feeble. I can only say thank you for the honor of inviting me here. You're wonderful, sweet people. Thank you."

BIOGRAPHICAL/CRITICAL SOURCES—Books: Theodore Huff, *Charlie Chaplin,* Arno, 1951; Charles Chaplin, *My Life,* Simon & Schuster, 1964; Michael Conway, Gerald D. McDonald, and Mark Ricci, editors, *The Films of Charlie Chaplin,* Citadel, 1965; Parker Tyler, *Chaplin: Last of the Clowns,* Horizon, 1972; Blythe F. Finke, *Charlie Chaplin: Famous Silent Movie Actor and Comic,* edited by D. Steve Rahmas, SamHar Press, 1973; W. Dodgson Bowman, *Charlie Chaplin: His Life and Art,* Haskell House, 1974; Roger Manvell, *Chaplin,* Little, Brown, 1974; David Jacobs, *Chaplin: The Movies and Charlie,* Harper, 1975; Robert Moss, *Charlie Chaplin,* Harcourt, 1975; Uno Asplund, *Chaplin's Films,* A. S. Barnes, 1976.

Articles: *Films and Filming,* August, 1957, September, 1958, November, 1964; *Sight and Sound,* autumn, 1957; *Film Culture,* January, 1958, spring, 1966, spring, 1972; *Film Quarterly,* fall, 1959; *Film Comment,* winter, 1969, fall, 1970.

Obituaries: *New York Times,* December 26, 1977; *Washington Post,* December 26, 1977; *Newsweek,* January 9, 1978.*

(Died December 25, 1977, in Vevey, Switzerland)

*   *   *

CHAPLIN, Charlie
See CHAPLIN, Charles Spencer

*   *   *

CHAPLIN, W. W.   1895(?)-1978
(Bill Chaplin)

OBITUARY NOTICE: Born c. 1895 in New York, N.Y.; died August 18, 1978, in Bradenton, Fla. Chaplin was a radio news commentator for National Broadcasting Co. (NBC) and covered World War II and the White House. Obituaries and other sources: *Washington Post,* August 22, 1978.

*   *   *

CHAPMAN, Vera   1898-
(Belladonna Took)

PERSONAL: Born May 7, 1898, in Bournemouth, England; daughter of John Frederick (an architect) and Kate Isabella Veronica (Morse) Fogerty; married Charles Sydney Chapman (a clerk in holy orders), April 23, 1924 (deceased); children: William Denis, Mary Veronica Chapman Terberg. *Education:* Lady Margaret Hall, Oxford, B.A. (second class honors), 1921. *Religion:* Church of England. *Home:* 21 Harrington House, Stanhope St., London NW1 3RB, England.

CAREER: Her Majesty's Colonial Office, London, England, student welfare officer, 1945-63; writer, 1963—. *Member:* Tolkien Society (founder; uses name Belladonna Took).

WRITINGS—Novels: *The Green Knight,* Rex Collings, 1975, Avon, 1978; *The King's Damosel,* Rex Collings, 1976, Avon, 1978; *King Arthur's Daughter,* Rex Collings, 1976, Avon, 1978; *Judy and Julia* (juvenile), Rex Collings, 1977; *The Wife of Bath,* Rex Collings, 1978. Also author of *Blaedud the Birdman,* 1978. Contributor of stories to *Fantastic Imagination.*

WORK IN PROGRESS: Another Arthurian romance; her autobiography; short stories about the Crusades.

SIDELIGHTS: Vera Chapman writes: "My books are written purely as romances, to be read for pleasure; but in them I have interwoven many scraps of mythology, philosophy, and mysticism gathered from many sources. I am said to have a 'flypaper mind,' and it seems that a few colorful butterflies have stuck on it here and there.

"I have been trying to gain recognition as a writer for many years. I hope to amuse and perhaps thrill with a few good stories, and to convey a little of the pleasure I myself have felt in life and literature. I am a very irregular writer, and find it hard to keep to any routine. Mostly I carry my stories in my head and polish them there, perhaps over years. When there is time I scribble them out, and after that comes the real hard work of typing them.

"I have been much influenced by the romantic writers of the nineteenth and early twentieth century, and must acknowledge a special debt to Tennyson, Rudyard Kipling, T. H. White, and J.R.R. Tolkien. I am not very much attracted to the contemporary science, literature or music. It is hardly to be wondered at if I am old-fashioned, though I hope I am not rigidly so.

"My advice to young (or not so young) aspiring authors is this: Don't try to make a living by writing. But keep on at it. Hit the contemporary wavelength if you can, but if not, wait for the turn of the wheel."

Chapman's Arthurian trilogy has been published in Dutch, and *The Green Knight* was made into a noncommercial film by West Surrey College of Art and Design.

*   *   *

CHARLTON, James (Mervyn)   1939-

PERSONAL: Born November 1, 1939, in New York, N.Y.; son of James M. (a glassblower) and Mary L. Charlton; married wife, Patricia; children: Kevin, Anne, Tim. *Education:* Attended Western Michigan University, 1957-62, and Wayne State University, 1964. *Home:* 7 Evans Court, Huntington, N.Y. 11746. *Agent:* Elaine Markson Literary Agency, Inc., 44 Greenwich Ave., New York, N.Y. 10011. *Office:* Quick Fox, 33 West 66th St., New York, N.Y. 10023.

CAREER: Worked as managing editor for Doubleday & Co., Inc., Garden City, N.Y.; Quick Fox, New York, N.Y., editor-in-chief, 1978—. *Member:* Coffee House Club, Editors Club (New York City), Players Club, New York Croquet Club.

WRITINGS: (Editor with Barbara Gilson) *The Christmas Feast: A Delightful Treasury of Yuletide Stories and Poems for the Whole Family,* Doubleday, 1976; (with William Thompson) *Croquet,* Scribner, 1977. Also author of *The Handbook* (on gestures), Prentice-Hall.

SIDELIGHTS: Charlton comments briefly: "'Anyone who writes for reasons other than money is a blockhead.' Samuel Johnson, 1709-1784." *Avocational interests:* Slow-pitch softball.

CHARNEY, David H.   1923-

PERSONAL: Born July 30, 1923, in New York, N.Y.; son of Boris and Frances (Mink) Charney; married Claire Ackerman, August 1, 1944 (divorced, 1964); married Louise Verrette (a dance teacher), April 30, 1965; children: Beth, Steven, Kenneth. *Education:* Cooper Union, certificate, 1949, B.F.A., 1977. *Home:* 341 Scarsdale Rd., Crestwood, N.Y. 10707. *Office:* Robert A. Becker, Inc., 622 Third Ave., New York, N.Y. 10016.

CAREER: Daniel & Charles (advertising agency), New York City, art director, 1955-61; Robert A. Becker, Inc. (advertising agency), New York City, art director, 1961—, vice-president, 1965—. *Military service:* U.S. Army Air Forces, 1942-46; became first lieutenant; received Air Medal with two oak leaf clusters.

WRITINGS: Magic, Quadrangle, 1975.

Work represented in anthologies, including *Tomorrow's Alternatives,* edited by Roger Elwood, Macmillan, 1973, and *Science Fiction Tales,* edited by Elwood, Rand McNally, 1973.

WORK IN PROGRESS: Behind the Victorian Curtain, a history of special effects and spectaculars in Victorian theater; *As Dust Before Wind,* a novel set in twelfth-century Japan; *Death on a Peak in Darien,* a novel of exploration for the Panama Canal.

SIDELIGHTS: Charney writes: "I became interested in writing at age fifty, and drew on my varied life experiences to furnish my material. By then, I had worked as a machinist, draftsman, illustrator, and art director, in fields as diverse as engineering, high fashion, and pharmaceuticals. Before that, I had spent four years in the Air Force and had ratings as a navigator, radar bombardier, gunner, and meteorologist. I had won medals as a gymnast, and had been nationally ranked as a table tennis player. On my fiftieth birthday, I was working as a karate instructor (fourth degree black belt), and flamenco guitarist in addition to my full-time job with a medical advertising agency.

"My first pieces were short stories based on my experiences with Spanish gypsies in the world of flamenco. They were okay but I found, to my surprise, that I enjoyed it more when I wrote about things outside of my personal experience. The research, study, and learning about different ways of life gives me as much pleasure as the actual writing.

"Thus, stimulated by a childhood interest in the subject, I went back to study magic for a year before writing *Magic.* I spent a year studying the Victorian theater for a book on special effects and Victorian spectacles, and for the past year and a half I have been researching twelfth-century Japan for a novel."

*   *   *

CHATTERJI, Suniti Kumar   1890-

PERSONAL: Born November 26, 1890, in Sibpur Howrah, Bengal, India; son of Haridas (a government clerk) and Katyayani (Devi) Chatterji; married Kamal Devi Mukherji, April 17, 1914 (died December 8, 1964); children: Suman (son), Ruchi, Rama, Nila, Sati, Suchi (all daughters). *Education:* Attended Presidency College (Calcutta), 1909-13; University of Calcutta, B.A. (first in honours), 1911; University of London, M.A. (first in honours), 1913, also earned Ph.D. degree. *Home:* Sudharma, 16 Hindustan Park, Calcutta 29, India. *Office:* University of Calcutta, Calcutta 12, India.

CAREER: University of Calcutta, Calcutta, India, lecturer, 1914-22, professor of comparative philology, 1922-52, professor emeritus, 1952—; West Bengal State Legislature, chairman of the Upper House, 1952-65; National Professor of India in Humanities, 1965—. Visiting professor, University of Pennsylvania, 1951-52.

MEMBER: Sahitya Academy (president, 1969—), International Phonetic Association (president, 1969—), Bangiya Sahitya Parishad (former president), Linguistic Society of India (former president), Societe Asiatique of Paris (honorary member), American Oriental Society (honorary member), Norwegian Academy of Sciences (honorary member), Royal Siam Society (honorary member), Ecole Francaise de l'Extreme Orient (honorary member), Linguistic Society of America (honorary member), Indian Council for Cultural Relations (fellow, 1961—). *Awards, honors:* Padma-Vibhushana (Order of the Republic of India); D.Litt., University of Rome, University of Delhi, Visva-Bharati University, Osmania University, Rabindra-Bharati University, and University of Calcutta.

WRITINGS: The Origin and Development of the Bengali Language, United Press (Calcutta), 1926, reprinted, three volumes, Allen & Unwin, 1970-72; *Bengali Self-Taught by the Natural Method, With Phonetic Pronunciations,* Marlborough, 1927; *Bengali Phonetic Reader,* University of London Press, 1928; (editor, translator and author of introduction with Priyaranjan Sen) Manoel da Assumpcam, *Manoel da Assumpcam's Bengali Grammar,* United Press, 1931; *Two New Indo-Aryan Etymologies,* Sonderabdruck (Leipzig), 1932; *A Roman Alphabet for India,* University of Calcutta, 1935; *Indo-Aryan and Hindi* (eight lectures delivered in 1940), Firma K. L. Mukhopadhyay, 1942, revised and enlarged 2nd edition, 1969; *Languages and the Linguistic Problem,* Oxford University Press (Bombay), 1943, 2nd edition, 1944; *The National Flag: A Selection of Papers Cultural and Historical,* Mitra & Ghosh (Calcutta), 1945.

The Place of Assam in the History and Civilisation of India (Banikanta Kakati Memorial Lectures, 1954), University of Gouhati, 1955; (contributor) *Suniti Kumar Chatterji Jubilee Volume: Presented on the Occasion of His Sixty-Fifth Birthday* (collection of essays), Linguistic Society of India (Madras), 1955; *Africanism: The African Personality,* Publishers Private (Calcutta), 1960; (with Sukumar Sen) *A Middle Indo-Aryan Reader* (two volumes in one), University of Calcutta, 3rd revised edition, 1960; *Indianism and the Indian Synthesis,* University of Calcutta, 1962; *Languages and Literatures of Modern India* (transliterated text), Bengal Publishers, 1963; *Dravidian: A Course of Three Lectures on Dravidian Origins and on Modern Dravidian Literature,* Annamalai University, 1965.

(With Bhikhan Lal Atreya and Alain Danielou) *Indian Culture,* Universal Book and Stationery Co., 1966; *The People, Language, and Culture of Orissa,* Orissa Sahitya Akademi, 1966; *Religious and Cultural Integration of India: Atombapu Sarma of Manipur,* Atombapu Research Centre (Imphal, India), 1967; *Balts and Aryans in Their Indo-European Background,* Indian Institute of Advanced Study, 1968; *India and Ethiopia, From the Seventh Century B.C.,* Asiatic Society (Calcutta), 1968; *India: Ghose Languages,* Publications Division, Ministry of Information and Broadcasting, 1970; *The Place of Assam in the History and Civilisation of India,* Department of Publication, University of Gauhati, 1970.

Also author of *World Literature in Tajore,* 1971, and *Kiratojana krta or The Indo-Mongoloids* (text in Hindi and English), 1951, of books in Hindi, including a collection of essays entitled *Ritambhara*, and *Rajasthani Bhasha*, and of books in Bengali, including *Jati, Sahitya o Samskriti*, 1938, *Bharat Samskriti*, 1945, *Bharater Bhasha o Bhasha Samasya*, 1945, and *Vaidesiki*, 1947.

WORK IN PROGRESS: Hindus and Turks: India-Central Asia Contacts From Prehistoric Times to the Present Day; Iranianism; a book on his travel experiences; an autobiography.

AVOCATIONAL INTERESTS: Studying and collecting art, listening to music, traveling.

BIOGRAPHICAL/CRITICAL SOURCES: Suniti Kumar Chatterji Jubilee Volume: Presented on the Occasion of His Sixty-Fifth Birthday, Linguistic Society of India, 1955; *Suniti Kumar Chatterji: The Scholar and the Man* (in English, Bengali, Hindi, and Sanskrit), Jijnasa, 1970.

* * *

CHEATHAM, K(aryn) Follis   1943-
(Long-Neck Woman)

PERSONAL: Born January 30, 1943, in Oberlin, Ohio; daughter of Benjamine Curtis (in U.S. Air Force) and Elizabeth (a secretary; maiden name, Blackburn) Follis; married Eugene C. Cheatham (president of an audio-visual marketing company), July 17, 1965; children: Nisah (son), Onika (daughter). *Education:* Attended Ohio State University, 1960-66. *Religion:* "Native American." *Residence:* Nashville, Tenn. *Agent:* Jean Naggar, Manuscripts Unlimited Literary Agency, 420 East 72nd St., New York, N.Y. 10021.

CAREER: Battelle Memorial Institute, Columbus, Ohio, research analyst, 1965-69; University of Michigan, Ann Arbor, administrative secretary at Environmental Simulation Laboratory, 1969-70; American Indians Unlimited, Ann Arbor, founding member, 1970-73, executive officer, 1970, 1972, editor of newsletter, 1971, 1972; Brotherhood of Southern Indians, Nashville, Tenn., co-director, 1973; freelance writer, 1973—. Tutor and counselor for Prevent High School Drop Outs (Raleigh, N.C.), 1975-76; lecturer on Native American history; adviser on Indian recruitment for colleges and universities. *Member:* National American Indian Movement, Tennessee Artist/Craftsman Association, Longview Writers.

WRITINGS: Spotted Flower and the Ponokomita, Westminster, 1977; (contributor) Jane B. Katz, editor, *I Am the Fire of Time: The Voices of Native American Women,* Dutton, 1977; *Life on a Cool Plastic Ice Floe,* Westminster, 1978; *Time Out for Trouble* (juvenile adventure novel), Westminster, 1979. Author of a review column in *Carolina Indian Voice,* 1975-76. Contributor to magazines (sometimes under name Long-Neck Woman), including *Six Nations, Webster Review, Lutheran,* and *Messenger.*

WORK IN PROGRESS: U.S. Route 2 and Vicinity, poems; *Range War,* a novel; *Bring Home the Ghost,* a historical novel; *Things Yet to Come,* a science fiction novel; *City Says,* poems; *Forts, Blankets, and Sellouts,* a novel; *Patch Basin Getaway,* a juvenile adventure novel; *Cycles,* an occult novel; short stories.

SIDELIGHTS: K. Follis Cheatham writes: "I consider myself a communicator to children and other free beings, one who harmonizes with all creation and who also finds expression through writing. I have wanted to be a professional writer since I was six, but never gained that status until I was thirty-three. Perhaps it took that long to establish an order to my own mind so that I could clearly express things to others.

"My life situations have been varied. I was raised by my grandparents during my formative years. There are many musicians and artists in my family. I attended the Oberlin Conservatory of Music at age five; took years and years of piano and dance lessons; was encouraged in artistic endeavors, but that area has only developed after I recognized myself. I struggled with personal religious upheavals from devout Catholicism to Judaism before I finally returned to the ways I was taught as a child. I survived a traumatic adolescence: family problems, a private predominantly-white school, prejudice and reverse prejudice at the university. It wasn't until I began raising my children that I realized my own potential and my 'personal universe.'

"Writing is just a natural extension of the verbal and mental communication I have with all things around me. I talk to butterflies and families of thistles, to people—big and little. But neither butterflies nor people listen well in this fast-paced society, so the written word is important. Much of my writing has been to convey information to my readers, information they have overlooked, ignored, or of which they have been deprived. My first book developed because I learned that most people believe the horse has always been a part of this country and were ignorant of the culture of indigenous peoples who have populated this hemisphere for countless centuries. The book tells how the Blackfeet Nation (the strongest part of my own heritage) first encountered this new animal in 1736.

"That was the beginning of my interest in historical fiction. Not only did I feel right about what I was communicating, but I also enjoyed the research that included re-remembering old stories I had heard, and reading new materials to give the story and characters vivid imagery.

"Then a thought emerged: when dealing with young people, history does not necessarily mean one or two centuries ago. The only time reference for history is that the events are in the past. *Life on a Cool Plastic Ice Floe* is modern historical fiction. It deals with adoption problems of Native American children in Michigan in 1970. I worked with Native American rights groups in Michigan and was a member of the Michigan Indian Adoption Council; also, one of my own children is adopted, and I know the workings and hang-ups of the courts.

"Not all of my writing is for teens or about history, but even in these other manuscripts I have tried to give realism to people's inner spirit, fears, and momentum. I hope that good characterization can give others greater insight into their own lives, and produce a better understanding of all things around them.

"The majority of my life's energies will always be for people to have a better understanding of their world. My primary thoughts are based on my Native American heritage and are perpetually focused toward the young. I have yet to complete a fictional piece where there is not a major character of teen age. At this age most people are more creative, open, and eager to learn, and I've always had good rapport with them. I also try to retain in my own life the spontaneity I see in young people. Because of this I believe I have absorbed realistic responses to the places in which I have lived (Ohio, Michigan, North Carolina, Tennessee) and traveled (the northwest Rockies—especially Montana—California, Canada, and points between).

"The ability to see all aspects of the environment is a necessity not only to my writing, but to any true communication.

Communication requires both a giver and a receiver. I receive from my surroundings and at the same time am giving. Like musical notes, this communication works best when the giver and receiver are in harmony. Therefore each occurrence and being I experience is a part of my learning to harmonize. Each moment I can remember, translate, decipher, and live is another note in my communication and I continually remember that everything on this Earth is unique. Through my writing I hope that others may read my thoughts and blend them with their own life experiences to lead them toward their own holistic identity, just as I am growing toward mine.''

AVOCATIONAL INTERESTS: Beadweaving, photography, art (water colors, pen and ink), music (composing; playing piano, flute, and autoharp; singing and teaching children to sing).

BIOGRAPHICAL/CRITICAL SOURCES: Nashville Banner, May 2, 1973; *Review for Religious,* September, 1975; *Christian Century,* September 24, 1975; *Kirkus Reviews,* August 1, 1977; *Social Education,* April, 1978.

* * *

CHEETHAM, Nicholas (John Alexander) 1910-

PERSONAL: Born October 8, 1910, in London, England; son of Sir Milne (a diplomat) and Anastasia (Muraviev) Cheetham; married Jean Evison Corfe, 1937 (marriage ended, 1960); married Mabel Kathleen Jocelyn Brooke, June 18, 1960; children: (first marriage) two sons. *Education:* Christ Church, Oxford, M.A. (first class honors), 1933. *Religion:* Church of England. *Home:* 50 Cadogan Sq., London SW1X 0JW, England.

CAREER: British Diplomatic Service, London, England, diplomat, 1934-68, at Foreign Office, 1934-36, 1944-46, 1951-54, in Athens, Greece, 1936-37, in Buenos Aires, Argentina, 1938-41, in Mexico City, Mexico, 1941-44, in Vienna, Austria, 1946-50, deputy permanent representative to North Atlantic Council, 1954-59, minister to Hungary, 1959-61, assistant under-secretary at Foreign Office, 1961-64, ambassador to Mexico, 1964-68. *Member:* Travellers Club. *Awards, honors:* Named companion of the Order of St. Michael and St. George, 1953, named knight commander, 1964.

WRITINGS: History of Mexico, Hart-Davis, 1970, published as *Mexico: A Short History,* Crowell, 1971; *New Spain: The Birth of Modern Mexico,* Gollancz, 1974.

WORK IN PROGRESS: The Feudal Age of Greece: A History of Greece in the Middle Ages.

AVOCATIONAL INTERESTS: Travel, shooting.

* * *

CHOUCRI, Nazli 1943-

PERSONAL: Born April 1, 1943, in Cairo, Egypt; came to the United States in 1962, naturalized citizen, 1969; daughter of Mustafa Choucri; married John Osgood Field (a researcher), 1969; children: Allyson. *Education:* American University, Cairo, Egypt, B.A. (high honors), 1962; Stanford University, M.A., 1964, Ph.D., 1967. *Office:* Department of Political Science, Massachusetts Institute of Technology, E53-490, Cambridge, Mass. 02139.

CAREER: Queen's University, Kingston, Ontario, assistant professor of political science, 1967-69; Massachusetts Institute of Technology, Cambridge, assistant professor, 1969-72, associate professor, 1972-78, professor of political science, 1978—, research associate at Center for International Studies, 1969, associate director of technology adaptation program, 1976—. Co-chairman of National Academy of Science Middle East Workshop, 1973; member of International Social Science Documentation Committee, 1976—. Consultant to United Nations, U.S. Department of State, Agency for International Development, and Inter-American Development Bank.

MEMBER: International Political Science Association, International Peace Research Society, International Committee for Social Science Information, International Studies Association, American Political Science Association, American Association for the Advancement of Science, Population Association of America, Institute for Strategic Studies (England). *Awards, honors:* Fulbright fellow, 1962-63; National Science Foundation grants, 1972-75, 1972-76; National Institute of Mental Health grant, 1978-81.

WRITINGS: (With Michael Laird and Dennis Meadows) *Resource Scarcity and Foreign Policy: A Simulation Model of International Conflict* (monograph), Center for International Studies, Massachusetts Institute of Technology, 1972; *Population Dynamics and International Violence: Propositions, Insight and Evidence,* Heath, 1974; *Energy Interdependence* (monograph), Center for International Studies, Massachusetts Institute of Technology, 1974; *Population Dynamics and Local Conflict: A Cross-National Study of Population and War—A Summary* (monograph), Center for International Studies, Massachusetts Institute of Technology, 1974; (with W. Parker Mauldin, Frank W. Notestein, and Michael Teitelbaum) *A Report on Bucharest: The World Population Conference and the Population Tribune* (monograph), Population Council, 1974; (with Robert C. North) *Nations in Conflict: National Growth and International Violence,* W. H. Freeman, 1975; (with Vincent Ferraro) *The International Politics of Energy Interdependence,* Heath, 1976; *The Pervasiveness of Politics: Political Definitions of Population Issues* (monograph), Institute of Society, Ethics and the Life Sciences, 1976; (editor with Thomas W. Robinson, and contributor) *Forecasting in International Relations: Theory, Methods, Problems, Prospects,* W. H. Freeman, 1978.

Contributor: Bruce Russett, editor, *Peace, War, and Numbers,* Sage Publications, 1972; Michael Haas, editor, *International Systems: A Behavioral Approach,* Chandler Publishing, 1974; James N. Rosenau, editor, *In Search of Global Patterns,* Free Press, 1976; *The Population Debate: Papers of the World Population Conference,* Volume II, United Nations, 1976; Dennis Clark Pirages, editor, *The Sustainable Society,* Praeger, 1977. Contributor of more than a dozen articles to political science and international studies journals.

WORK IN PROGRESS: Energy Exchange and International Relations: A Simulation Model of Price, Exchange, and Control, with David Scott Ross; continuing research on international relations and international political economy, public policy in developing areas, and politics of international trade in natural resources.

* * *

CHRISTIANSON, Gale E. 1942-

PERSONAL: Born June 29, 1942, in Charles City, Iowa; son of John Edward and Donna Jean (Lester) Christianson: married wife, Terry Diane (divorced, April, 1974); married Brenda Pell (a teacher), November 26, 1974. *Education:* University of Iowa, B.A., 1964; University of Northern

Iowa, M.A., 1966; Carnegie-Mellon University, D.Arts, 1971. *Residence:* Terre Haute, Ind. *Agent:* Gerard Mc-Cauley, P.O. Box AE, Katonah, N.Y. 10536. *Office:* Department of History, Indiana State University, Terre Haute, Ind. 47809.

CAREER: North Iowa Area Community College, Mason City, instructor in history, 1966-69; Indiana State University, Terre Haute, associate professor of history, 1971—. Adjunct professor at Rose-Hulman Institute of Technology, 1977. *Member:* American Association of University Professors, American Committee of Irish Scholars, Phi Alpha Theta. *Awards, honors:* Fellow of Hunt Institute for Botanical Documentation, 1971; American Philosophical Society grant, 1973.

WRITINGS: The Wild Abyss: The Story of the Men Who Made Modern Astronomy, Macmillan, 1978. Contributor to history, science, education, and science fiction journals, and to *Commonweal.*

WORK IN PROGRESS: Research for a biography of Sir Isaac Newton, for Macmillan, completion expected in 1980.

SIDELIGHTS: Christianson writes: "My primary interest as a historian is the early modern period of European history, 1500-1750. More specifically, I am interested in the history of discovery, particularly in the science of astronomy. During the winter of 1978 I spent my sabbatical at Cambridge University working on the papers of Isaac Newton. I teach a broad range of courses at Indiana State University, but my favorite is a course of my own, 'Science and Society.' Drawing students from a broad range of academic disciplines, the course traces the development of modern science from the Egyptians and Greeks through the Middle Ages, Renaissance, and modern period."

* * *

CHU, Arthur (T. S.) 1916-
(W. R. Chu)

PERSONAL: Original name, Tsung Shou Chu; born March 19, 1916, in Wusih, China; came to the United States in 1949, naturalized citizen, 1955; son of T. H. (an educator) and C. Y. (Chen) Chu; married Grace Goodyear (a teacher and writer), 1946; children: Ted. *Education:* National Central University, China, A.B., 1938; graduate study at Stanford University. *Home and office:* 14670 Midland Rd., San Leandro, Calif. 94578.

CAREER: Researcher, translator, and writer. Served as community chairperson for Nelson Rockefeller in 1964, and was an alternate delegate to the Republican national convention. *Military service:* Chinese Air Force, Flying Tigers, 1940; became captain.

WRITINGS—All with wife, Grace Chu: *Oriental Antiques and Collectibles: A Guide* (Better Homes and Gardens Book Club selection), Crown, 1973; *Oriental Cloissone and Other Enamels,* Crown, 1976; *The Collector's Book of Jade,* Crown, 1978. Contributor of articles to periodicals, under name W. R. Chu, including *American Mercury* and *Catholic World.*

WORK IN PROGRESS: The Centipede, a historical novel of the Japanese-Chinese War, 1937-45, with wife, Grace Chu.

SIDELIGHTS: Chu writes: "As we went around to antique stores and shows for a few years, we were amazed by the misinformation or lack of information among collectors and dealers in Oriental antiques and collectibles. We felt a book in the field was in order."

CHU, Grace (Goodyear) 1916-

PERSONAL: Born January 15, 1916, in Scottsbluff, Neb.; daughter of Wesley and Sallie (Emerson) Goodyear; married Arthur Chu (a writer), March, 1946; children: Ted. *Education:* Colorado State College (now Northern Colorado State University), B.A., Mills College, M.Ed.; graduate study at University of Denver, 1944-45, and Stanford University, 1953-58; University of California, Berkeley, Ed.D., 1966. *Home and office:* 14670 Midland Rd., San Leandro, Calif. 94578.

CAREER: Teacher in one-room schoolhouse on Colorado prairie, 1938; former kindergarten teacher in Denver (Colo.) Public Schools; demonstration teacher at nursery school, Colorado State College (now Northern Colorado State University), 1945-46; Kindergarten and primary school teacher in Oakland (Calif.) Public Schools, 1947-67; former vice-principal and teacher in San Leandro (Calif.) Unified School District; California State University, Hayward, assistant professor of education in department of continuing education, 1967-70. *Member:* Pi Lambda Theta.

WRITINGS—All with husband, Arthur Chu: *Oriental Antiques and Collectibles: A Guide* (Better Homes and Gardens Book Club selection), Crown, 1973; *Oriental Cloisonne and Other Enamels,* Crown, 1976; *The Collector's Book of Jade,* Crown, 1978.

WORK IN PROGRESS: The Centipede, a historical novel of the Japanese-Chinese War, 1937-45, with husband, Arthur Chu.

SIDELIGHTS: Grace Chu writes: "As we went around to antique stores and shows for a few years, we were amazed by the misinformation or lack of information among collectors and dealers in Oriental antiques and collectibles. We felt a book on the field was in order."

* * *

CHU, W. R.
See CHU, Arthur (T. S.)

* * *

CLAGUE, Maryhelen 1930-

PERSONAL: Born April 4, 1930, in Lakeland, Fla.; daughter of Paul Alber (a building contractor) and Christie (Wright) Ellis; married William James Clague (a clergyman), February 22, 1965; children: William James Ellis, Sarah Pauline. *Education:* Florida State University, B.Mus., 1952; Union Theological Seminary, New York, N.Y., M.R.E., 1956. *Politics:* Democrat. *Religion:* Episcopalian. *Home and office:* St. Mary's Church Rectory, Albany Post Rd., Scarborough, N.Y. 10510. *Agent:* Clyde Taylor, 34 Perry St., New York, N.Y. 10514.

CAREER: Elementary school music teacher in Ruskin, Fla., 1952-54; director of religious education at churches in New York, N.Y., 1956-57, and Larchmont, N.Y., 1957-65; Public School #41, Staten Island, N.Y., teacher, 1966; writer, 1975—. Substitute teacher, church organist, and choir director. Member of board of directors of Staten Island Family Service.

WRITINGS: So Wondrous Free (historical romance), Stein & Day, 1978.

WORK IN PROGRESS: A family story set in Westchester County, N.Y., between 1760 and 1830.

SIDELIGHTS: Maryhelen Clague writes: "I read historical fiction avidly for many years before I ever tried writing it.

History fascinates me—not political trends or treaties and dates, but the everyday life and hopes and passions of people now dead. I think it recalls for us a time very different from our own and sometimes gives us insights into why we are as we are. A good story is important, but above all, the author should be true to the times. That is what makes them really live again.''

* * *

CLARK, Clifford E(dward), Jr. 1941-

PERSONAL: Born July 13, 1941, in Bay Shore, N.Y.; son of Clifford Edward (a teacher) and Helen (a teacher; maiden name, Lapan) Clark; married Grace Williams (an occupational therapist), August 20, 1966; children: Cynthia Williams, Christopher Allen. *Education:* Yale University, B.A., 1963; Harvard University, Ph.D., 1967. *Religion:* Episcopalian. *Home:* 718 East Fourth St., Northfield, Minn. 55057. *Office:* Department of History, Carleton College, Northfield, Minn. 55057.

CAREER: Amherst College, Amherst, Mass., assistant professor of American studies, 1967-70; Carleton College, Northfield, Minn., associate professor of history and director of American studies program, 1970—. *Member:* American Historical Association, Organization of American Historians, American Studies Association, Minnesota School Board Association. *Awards, honors:* National Endowment for the Humanities younger humanist award, 1972.

WRITINGS: Henry Ward Beecher: Spokesman for a Middle-Class America, University of Illinois Press, 1978. Contributor of articles and reviews to history journals.

WORK IN PROGRESS: A book on architecture and social history.

SIDELIGHTS: Clark told *CA:* "I have a particular interest in the relationship between intellectual and social and cultural history. The study of American material culture, the examination of artifacts and architecture as reflections of social values, and an analysis of the physical environment as an index to cultural assumptions—these are all areas that presently fascinate me. They also reflect my own love for physical work, wood-working, and house construction and modification."

* * *

CLARK, Mary Higgins 1931-

PERSONAL: Born December 24, 1931, in New York, N.Y.; daughter of Luke Joseph (a restaurant owner) and Nora C. (a buyer; maiden name, Durkin) Higgins; married Warren F. Clark (an airline executive), December 26, 1949 (died, September 26, 1964); married Raymond Charles (an attorney), August 8, 1978; children: Marilyn, Warren, David, Carol, Patricia. *Education:* Attended Villa Maria Academy and Ward Secretarial School; Fordham University, B.A., 1978. *Religion:* Roman Catholic. *Home:* 2508 Cleveland Ave., Washington Township, N.J. 07675; and 200 Central Park South, New York, N.Y. 10019. *Agent:* Patricia Myrer, McIntosh & Otis, 475 Fifth Ave., New York, N.Y.

CAREER: Writer. Worked for Remington Rand and as stewardess for Pan American Airlines. Partner and vice-president of Aerial Communications. *Member:* Mystery Writers of America (member of board of directors), Authors Guild, American Society of Journalists and Authors. *Awards, honors:* New Jersey Author Award, 1969, for *Aspire to the Heavens,* 1977, for *Where Are the Children,* and 1978, for *A Stranger Is Watching.*

WRITINGS: Aspire to the Heavens (biography of George Washington), Meredith Press, 1969; *Where Are the Children?,* Simon & Schuster, 1975; *A Stranger Is Watching,* Simon & Schuster, 1978; (contributor) *I, Witness,* Times Books, 1978. Work anthologized in *The Best Saturday Evening Post Stories,* 1962. Also author of syndicated radio dramas. Contributor of stories to periodicals, including *Saturday Evening Post, Redbook, McCall's,* and *Family Circle.*

WORK IN PROGRESS: Remember House and *Through a Glass Darkly.*

SIDELIGHTS: Clark told *CA:* "I feel a good suspense novel can and should hold a mirror up to society and make a social comment. For this reason, I've used the death penalty issue in *A Stranger Is Watching.*" Elsewhere, Clark has commented on her work and her desire to provide in them entertainment and romance. But, she noted: "I would like to get across a sense of values. I like nice, strong people confronting the forces of evil and vanquishing them."

AVOCATIONAL INTERESTS: Traveling, skiing, tennis, playing piano.

BIOGRAPHICAL/CRITICAL SOURCES: People, March 6, 1978; *New York Times Book Review,* May 14, 1978.

* * *

CLARK, Thomas Willard 1941-
(Tom Clark)

PERSONAL: Born March 1, 1941, in Chicago, Ill.; son of Arthur Willard (an artist) and Rita Mary (Kearin) Clark; married Angelica Louise Heinegg, March 22, 1968; children: Juliet. *Education:* Attended John Carroll University, 1959-60; University of Michigan, B.A., 1963; graduate study at Cambridge University, 1963-65, and University of Essex, 1965-67. *Address:* P.O. Box 155, Nederland, Colo. 80466. *Agent:* Gerard McCauley, P.O. Box AE, Katanoh, N.Y. 10536. *Office: Boulder Monthly,* 1200 Pearl, Boulder, Colo. 80466.

CAREER: Poet and writer. *Awards, honors:* Fulbright Fellowship, 1963-65; Bess Hopkins Prize from *Poetry,* 1966; National Endowment for the Arts grant, 1966, 1968; Rockefeller Fellowship, 1967-68; Poets Foundation Award, 1967; George Dillon Memorial Prize from *Poetry,* 1968; Guggenheim Fellowship, 1970-71.

WRITINGS—Under name Tom Clark; poetry: *Airplanes,* Once Press, 1966; *The Sand Burg: Poems,* Ferry Press, 1966; (with Ron Padgett) *Bunn,* Angel Hair Books, 1968; *Stones,* Harper, 1969; *Air,* Harper, 1970; *Green,* Black Sparrow Press, 1971; *John's Heart,* Grossman, 1972; (with Padgett and Ted Berrigan) *Back in Boston Again,* Telegraph Books, 1972; *Smack,* Black Sparrow Press, 1972; *Suite,* Black Sparrow Press, 1974; *Blue,* Black Sparrow Press, 1974; *Chicago,* Black Sparrow Press, 1975; *When Things Get Tough on Easy Street: Selected Poems, 1963-73,* Black Sparrow Press, 1978.

Other: "The Emperor of the Animals" (play; three-act), first produced in London, 1966; *Neil Young* (biography), Coach House Press, 1972; *At Malibu,* Kulchur Books, 1975; *Champagne and Baloney: The Rise and Fall of Finley's A's,* Harper, 1976; (with Mark Fidrych) *No Big Deal,* Lippincott, 1977; *The World of Damon Runyon,* Harper, 1978; *How I Broke in/Five Modern Masters,* Tombouctou Books, 1978; *35,* Poltroon Press, 1978; *A Conversation With Hitler* (stories), Black Sparrow Press, 1978; *The Mutabilitie of the*

English Lyric, Poltroon Press, 1979; *One Last Round for the Shuffler: A Blacklisted Ballplayer's Story*, Truck Books, 1979; *Who Is Sylvia?* (novel), Blue Wind Press, 1979; *The Master*, Truck Books, 1979.

Poetry editor of *Paris Review*, 1963-73; senior writer for *Boulder Monthly*, 1978—.

WORK IN PROGRESS: The Cold Execution, a novel about Hollywood screenwriters and politics, 1936-55; *Incident at Basecamp*, a science-fiction novel set in Colorado.

SIDELIGHTS: Clark told *CA:* "How did I come to be both a poet and an author of sports books? These are two fields that I think have a natural relationship. The best poems and the best baseball games share a dramatic tension you can't find in very many other places.

"What prompted me to write on Damon Runyon? I believe Runyon to be one of our great American writers—a pioneer sportswriter, a brilliant short story writer, and perhaps our finest columnist. I wanted to write a book to do justice to Runyon the writer."

* * *

CLARK, Tom
See CLARK, Thomas Willard

* * *

CLAY, Lucius D(uBignon) 1897-1978

PERSONAL: Born April 23, 1897, in Marietta, Ga.; son of Alexander Stephen (a senator) and Sarah (Francis) Clay; married Marjorie McKeown, September 21, 1918; children: Lucius, Jr., Frank Butner. *Education:* United States Military Academy, B.S., 1918. *Religion:* Methodist. *Residence:* Cape Cod, Mass.

CAREER: U.S. Army, career officer, 1918-49, retiring as four-star general; chairman of the board and chief executive of Continental Can Co., 1950-62; diplomat, 1961-62; chairman of Republican Party National Finance Committee, 1965-68. Coordinated airport construction program, 1940-41, director of material for Army Service Forces, 1942-44, also worked as production engineer; military governor of Germany and commander of U.S. armed forces in Europe, 1945-49. Senior partner in Lehman Brothers, 1963-73; head of public development program in New York City, 1966, member of New York City charter revision commission, 1972; associated with numerous corporations. *Awards, honors:* Legion of Merit, 1942; Distinguished Service Medal, 1944, later received Oak Leaf Cluster.

WRITINGS: Decision in Germany, Doubleday, 1950; *The Papers of General Lucius D. Clay: Germany, 1945-49*, edited by Jean Edward Smith, Indiana University Press, 1974.

SIDELIGHTS: Clay's military career encompassed a variety of activities but he never commanded in combat. Thus he was one of a select few to rise to the rank of four-star general without serving on the battlefield.

Clay received his greatest recognition during the late 1940's when he was military governor of Germany. When the Communists enforced a blockade of the Western sector, Clay devised a means of beating the cordon by using airlifts. Claiming that he would do battle rather than depart from Germany, Clay conferred with President Truman on how best to deal with the Communist blockade. In *Decision in Germany*, Clay declared that the airlift was instrumental in maintaining the U.S. position in Berlin. "I asserted my confidence that given the planes, we could remain in Berlin in-

definitely without war," he wrote, "and that our departure would be a serious, if not disastrous, blow to the maintenance of freedom in Europe." The airlifts were so successful that in 1949, the Communists put an end to the blockade.

Clay returned from Berlin a national hero. While settling into a life befitting one whose primary duties now included assisting and managing various companies, Clay eventually found himself in the political forum. In 1961, Clay served as ambassador in Berlin at the request of President Kennedy. He once again proved to the Communists that the U.S. was firm in its plans to remain in Berlin. In 1963, Clay was being touted as a possible candidate for the presidency on the Republican ticket. Although a committee to draft him was formed, Clay solemnly declared he would not seek the nomination. Clay remained prominent on the business scene, even after retiring from public life. In 1973, he was mentioned, according to *New York Times,* as "a director or member of the board of eighteen major corporations."

It was his extreme intelligence and ability to create order from chaos which had attracted businesses to him initially. He was known for his powers of concentration and his ability to rise to the occasion. In 1944, General Eisenhower summoned Clay to France and explained to him that one of the important ports for shipping had become impossibly entangled. In one day, Clay not only stabilized the situation but doubled the amount of shipping. Within weeks, the port was functioning with speed and efficiency.

Clay's manner was best described as one befitting a man who insisted on order and organization. Unlike his ancestor Henry Clay, he was known as "the great uncompromiser." As one bargaining opponent said, "He looks like a Roman emperor—and acts like one."

AVOCATIONAL INTERESTS: Horseback riding, fishing.

BIOGRAPHICAL/CRITICAL SOURCES: Lucius D. Clay, *Decision in Germany*, Doubleday, 1950; Red Reeder, *Heroes and Leaders of West Point*, Nelson, 1970; Lloyd C. Gardner, *Architects of Illusion*, Quadrangle, 1970.

OBITUARIES: New York Times, April 18, 1978.*

(Died April 17, 1978, in Cape Cod, Mass.)

* * *

CLAYTON, Jo 1939-

PERSONAL: Born February 15, 1939, in Modesto, Calif.; daughter of Howard Garland (a farmer) and Bessie (a farmer; maiden name, Jones) Clayton. *Education:* Attended University of California, Berkeley, 1956-58, and Modesto Junior College, 1958-59; University of Southern California, A.B., 1962; graduate study at University of New Orleans, 1977—. *Home:* 4239 Iris, New Orleans, La. 70122.

CAREER: Teacher in public schools in Los Angeles, Calif., 1962-68; Orleans Parish School Board, New Orleans, La., high school teacher of English, 1971—. Portrait artist in New Orleans, summer, 1972. *Member:* National Education Association, Science Fiction Writers of America.

WRITINGS—Science fiction novels: *Diadem From the Stars*, DAW Books, 1977; *La Marchos*, DAW Books, 1978; *Irsud*, DAW Books, 1978; *Maeve*, DAW Books, 1979. Contributor to *Isaac Asimov's Science Fiction Magazine*.

WORK IN PROGRESS—All tentative titles: *Sunguralingu*, a novel; "Shadows in Broken Water," a story; "Looking Out," a story.

SIDELIGHTS: Jo Clayton comments: "In addition to my commitment to writing, I am an artist. I find the two interests reinforce each other, as both demand intense attention to physical detail and general observation. In both aspects of my work, I am concerned with the human being who manages to gain a measure of self-respect and self-reliance in spite of manifold difficulties—especially women.''

* * *

CLEARY, Florence Damon   1896-

PERSONAL: Born November 1, 1896, in Livonia, N.Y.; daughter of Daniel Lyman (a farmer) and Jennie (Disbrow) Damon; married Edmund Zwielser Cleary, August 24, 1921 (deceased); children: Elizabeth Cleary Fickes, Justine Cleary Johnston. *Education:* Attended State College of Arts and Sciences, Geneseo, N.Y., 1913-15, and Columbia University, 1915; Wayne State University, M.A., 1938, further graduate study, 1939-45. *Religion:* Episcopalian. *Home and office:* 17 Spanish Main, Tampa, Fla. 33609.

CAREER: Assistant librarian in Geneseo, N.Y., 1919-21; Detroit Public Schools, Detroit, Mich., supervising librarian, 1921-45; Wayne State University, Detroit, 1921—, began as instructor, became professor emeritus of library science, 1965—, coordinator of citizenship education study, 1945-50, chairman of department, 1950-64; University of South Florida, Tampa, professor and chairman of department of library science, 1964-68; writer, 1968—. Librarian at State Teachers College, Bridgewater, Mass., 1919-21. *Member:* National League of American Pen Women (president, 1972-74), Women's National Book Association, Tampa Women's Club, Friends of the Public Library (Tampa). *Awards, honors:* Grants from Voelker Foundation, 1945-50, and U.S. Department of Health, Education & Welfare, 1970-72; Athena award from Theta Sigma Phi, 1962.

WRITINGS: Learning to Use the Library, H. W. Wilson, 1936; *A Curriculum for Citizenship,* Wayne State University Press, 1953; *Blueprints for Better Reading,* H. W. Wilson, 1957, 2nd edition, 1976; (with Arnold Meres) *Discovering Books and Libraries: A Handbook for the Upper Elementary and Junior High School Grades,* H. W. Wilson, 1966, 2nd edition, 1977; *Blueprints for Better Learning,* Scarecrow, 1969, 2nd edition, 1978. Contributor of more than twenty-five articles to education journals.

* * *

CLEMENT, Herbert F(lint)   1927-

PERSONAL: Born February 24, 1927; son of Floyd Sherman (in sales) and Dorothy (a teacher; maiden name, Flint) Clement. *Education:* Attended New England Conservatory of Music. *Residence:* New York, N.Y. *Office:* Central Park Zoo, 830 Fifth Ave., New York, N.Y. 10021.

CAREER: Franklin Park Zoo, Boston, Mass., assistant director, 1960-64; Harvard University, Museum of Comparative Zoology, Cambridge, Mass., zoologist, 1964-65; Staten Island Zoo, New York, N.Y., keeper and lecturer, 1965-71; Central Park Zoo, New York City, instructor, 1971—. Member of board of advisers of Vansaun Park Zoo. *Military service:* U.S. Army. *Member:* American Association of Zoological Parks and Aquariums (fellow).

WRITINGS: Zoo Man (nonfiction), Macmillan, 1969; *The Circus: Bigger and Better than Ever,* A. S. Barnes, 1974; (author of revision) John Stidsworthy, *Snakes of the World,* Grosset, 1976. Author of "The Nature of Things," a weekly column in *Staten Island Register,* 1968—.

WORK IN PROGRESS: Elephants; Small Zoos.

SIDELIGHTS: Clement comments: "Natural history, con-

servation, animals, zoos, circuses, animal experiments of all sorts, are the laboratories for my work. I visit reservations, wildlife preserves, zoos, and museums everywhere, but mainly in the United States.''

BIOGRAPHICAL/CRITICAL SOURCES: Georg Zappler and Geary, *Behind the Scenes at the Zoo,* Doubleday, 1977.

* * *

CLERK, N. W.
See LEWIS, C(live) S(taples)

* * *

CLINTON, Jon
See PRINCE, J(ack) H(arvey)

* * *

CLIVE, William
See BASSETT, Ronald

* * *

COBLEIGH, Ira U(nderwood)   1903-

PERSONAL: Born December 25, 1903, in Derby, Conn.; son of Irving Vas (a teacher) and Elizabeth L. (Cone) Cobleigh; married Dorothy H. Cobb, April 11, 1929; children: Ronald G., Gordon U. *Education:* Columbia University, A.B., 1923, A.M., 1950. *Politics:* Republican. *Religion:* Episcopalian. *Home:* 46-41 Hanford St., Douglaston, N.Y. 11362. *Agent:* Albert Zuckerman, 131 West 31st St., New York, N.Y. 10036. *Office:* 17 Battery Pl., New York, N.Y. 10004.

CAREER: Economist and author. Worked for Halsey Stuart & Co., New York City, 1923-29; Wright & Cobb Lighterage Co., New York City, officer and director, 1930-56, president, 1947-60; vice-president and economist of DeWitt Conklin Organization, 1961-77. Consultant to Dowbeaters, an investment advisory service; economist for Providence Fund for Income, 1962-74. Member of faculty at New School for Social Research, 1977-78. Member of board of directors of Harbor Carriers of New York, 1947-60 (president of board, 1948-49). *Member:* Whitehall Club (member of board of governors, 1952—).

WRITINGS: Expanding Your Income; Many Happy Returns on Your Investment Dollar, McKay, 1951; *Winning in Wall Street,* McKay, 1953; *A Killing in Uranium,* Duval's Consensus, 1954; (with James H. Durgin) *How to Gain Security and Financial Independence,* Hawthorn, 1956; *How to Make a Killing on Wall Street and Keep It,* McKay, 1961; (editor) *Guide to Success in the Stock Market,* Avon, 1961, revised edition, 1962; *Life Insurance Stocks for Lifetime Gains,* Cobleigh & Gordon, 1963; *How and Where to Borrow Money,* Avon, 1964; *$100 Billion Can't Be Wrong! Savings and Loan Associations for Safety, Income, Market Gain,* Cobleigh & Gordon, 1964; *Happiness Is a Stock That Doubles in a Year,* Geis, 1967; *Building a Successful Family Investment Program,* Association Press, 1967; *The $2 Window on Wall Street,* Toucan Press, 1968; *Live Young as Long as You Live,* Association Press, 1969; *All About Stocks: A Guide to Profitable Investing in the '70's,* Weybright, 1970; *All About Investing in Real Estate Securities,* Weybright, 1971; *Gold, the $, and You,* Goldfax, 1972; *How to Find a Growth Stock,* U.S. News & World Report, 1973; (with others) *What Everyone Should Know About Credit Before Buying,* U.S. News & World Report, 1975; *Speculat-*

ing in Rare Minerals, Crown, 1979; (with Bruce Dopfman) *Dowbeaters,* Macmillan, 1979.

Contributor to *U.S. News & World Report, Mademoiselle, Parade,* and *Medical Economics.* Feature editor of *Commercial and Financial Chronicle,* 1950-72; associate editor of Market Chronicle, 1950—; editor of *Physicians' Financial Review,* 1971-72.

AVOCATIONAL INTERESTS: Tennis.

BIOGRAPHICAL/CRITICAL SOURCES: Harper's, August, 1967; *New York Times,* October 8, 1967; *Saturday Review,* January 11, 1969.

* * *

COFFIN, Geoffrey
See MASON, F(rancis) van Wyck

* * *

COHEN, George Michael 1931-

PERSONAL: Born September 24, 1931, in Brookline, Mass.; son of Jack M. (in hardware business) and Sadie (Eilenberg) Cohen; married Charlene Rona Glassman, June 21, 1964; children: Louis Henry, Ronn Victor. *Education:* Harvard University, A.B. (cum laude), 1955, A.M., 1958; Boston University, Ph.D., 1962. *Home:* 80 Wintercress Lane, East Northport, N.Y. 11731. *Office:* Department of Art History and Humanities, Hofstra University, Axinn House, Hempstead, N.Y. 11550.

CAREER: Massachusetts College of Art, Boston, assistant professor of art history, 1963-68; Long Island University, C. W. Post College, Greenvale, N.Y., associate professor of art history, 1968-69; Newark State College, Union, N.J., associate professor of art history, 1969-70; Hofstra University, Hempstead, N.Y., associate professor of art history and humanities, 1970—. *Member:* Authors Guild of Authors League of America, American Association of University Professors, College Art Association of America, American Society of Appraisers, Appraisers Association of America, National Association of Review Appraisers.

WRITINGS: Ancient Art, Hymarx, 1966; *A History of American Art,* Dell, 1971; *Art History,* two volumes, University College Tutors, 1977. Contributor to *McGraw-Hill Dictionary of Art* and *Encyclopedia of Southern History.* Contributor to art and art history journals, including *College Art Journal, American Artist, Art Voices, Arts, Continental,* and *Valuation.*

WORK IN PROGRESS: A book on American genre and Amerind painters of the nineteenth century.

SIDELIGHTS: Cohen's specialty is nineteenth and twentieth century American painting.

* * *

COHEN, Sarah Blacher 1936-

PERSONAL: Born June 13, 1936, in Appleton, Wis.; daughter of Louis and Mary (Kaminsky) Blacher; married Gary Cohen (a mental health administrator), June 13, 1965. *Education:* University of Illinois, B.A. (summa cum laude), 1958, M.A., 1961; Northwestern University, Ph.D., 1969. *Religion:* Jewish. *Home:* 60 Buckingham Dr., Albany, N.Y. 12208. *Office:* Department of English, State University of New York, Albany, N.Y. 12222.

CAREER: High school English teacher in Skokie, Ill., 1959-64; University of Illinois at Chicago Circle, Chicago, instructor, 1965-69, assistant professor of English, 1969-72;

State University of New York at Albany, assistant professor, 1972-76, associate professor of English, 1976—. *Member:* Modern Language Association of America, Multi-Ethnic Literature Society of America, Northeastern Modern Language Association, Phi Beta Kappa.

WRITINGS: Saul Bellow's Enigmatic Laughter, University of Illinois Press, 1974; (editor) *Comic Relief: Humor in Contemporary American Literature,* University of Illinois Press, 1978. Contributor to literature journals. Member of editorial board of State University of New York Press and *Studies in American Jewish Literature.*

WORK IN PROGRESS: Editing a collection of essays on Jewish-American drama; a book on the city in contemporary American literature; articles on Saul Bellow's *To Jerusalem and Back* and on comedy and survivor guilt in Bellow's *Humboldt's Gift.*

SIDELIGHTS: Sarah Cohen writes: "Humor in modern literature is a most complex and baffling subject and it is especially elusive and protean in Saul Bellow's Nobel-Prize-winning fiction. While many critics have generally recognized the antic nature of Bellow's muse, in my book, *Saul Bellow's Enigmatic Laughter,* I provide the first systematic and extended analysis of his novels' comedy: its 'suffering joker' characters, its mingled situations of laughter and trembling, its wide-ranging ideological wit, and its drolly prolix rhetoric. I trace this peculiar brand of mirth to the comic traditions of Russian, Jewish, and American culture.

"Believing comedy to be a profound means of expressing things that vitally matter, I also consider the interplay between the comic mode and its ultimately serious intention. I explore the influence Bellow's comedy has on his larger vision and note its function in the development of his particular characterizations and themes. Treating his novels separately and chronologically, I find in his canon a progressively sophisticated and versatile use of the comic mode.

"Like Saul Bellow, I was born of Jewish Russian immigrants in a home where broken English, snatches of Russian, and fluent Yiddish were spoken. From my junk-dealer father, who was my Judaic studies instructor, and my solicitous mother, who embodied all the values of Judaism, I developed my love of Yiddish culture. From my father I also acquired my comic sense. He would regale me with his calamitous 'greenhorn' adventures among the *goyim* and his unending battle of wits with the not-too-wise rabbi at the local synagogue. From my two older brothers, who were masters of dialect and off-color comedy, and from my two older sisters, who were often characters of domestic comedy, I received further training. Growing up Jewish in the Christian Midwest, in Appleton, Wisconsin, Joe McCarthy's hometown no less, I was able to appreciate the risible incongruities of both worlds. Like the title of my new collection of essays, I find my hyphenated sense of humor a *Comic Relief.*"

* * *

COLBY, William Egan 1920-

PERSONAL: Born January 4, 1920, in St. Paul, Minn.; son of Elbridge (an army officer and educator) and Margaret (Egan) Colby; married Barbara Heinzen, September 15, 1945; children: Jonathan, Catherine (deceased), Carl, Paul, Christine. *Education:* Princeton University, A.B., 1940; Columbia University, LL.B., 1947. *Religion:* Catholic. *Home:* 5317 Briley Place, Washington, D.C. 20016. *Agent:* Morton L. Janklow, 375 Park Ave., New York, N.Y. 10021.

Office: Colby, Miller & Hanes, 1625 I St. N.W., Washington, D.C. 20006.

CAREER: Admitted to the Bar of New York State, 1947, and the Bar of Washington, D.C., 1976; Donovan, Leisure, Newton & Irvine (law firm), New York City, attorney, 1947-49; National Labor Relations Board, Washington, D.C., attorney, 1949-50; Central Intelligence Agency (CIA), Washington, D.C., intelligence officer in Stockholm, 1951-53, and Rome, 1953-58, station chief in Saigon, 1959-62, chief of Far East division in Washington, D.C., 1962-67, director of pacification effort and Phoenix program in Saigon, 1968-71, executive director, 1972-73, deputy director for operations, 1973, director of agency, 1973-76; Colby, Miller & Hanes (law firm), Washington, D.C., partner, 1977—. Lecturer for Harry Walker, Inc., 1976—. *Military service:* U.S. Army, 1941-45; became major; received Silver Star and Bronze Star. *Member:* Council on Foreign Relations, Federal City Club, Cosmos Club. *Awards, honors:* Distinguished Intelligence Medal, 1975; National Security Medal, 1976; Distinguished Honor Award of Department of State.

WRITINGS: (With Peter Forbath) *Honorable Men: My Life in the CIA,* Simon & Schuster, 1978.

SIDELIGHTS: When William Colby took over the directorship of the Central Intelligence Agency (CIA) in 1973, he appeared bent on cooperating as fully as possible with official investigations of possible wrongdoing by the CIA. After hearing Colby's testimony on the agency's involvement in Chile before the overthrow of Allende, Tad Szulc remarked that "Colby seems to be turning into the most candid CIA director in a quarter of a century." On subsequent occasions Colby divulged information about the CIA's role in Watergate, in an unsuccessful attempt on Cuban Premier Fidel Castro's life, in opening domestic mail, and in a plan to illegally contribute six million dollars to Italian anti-Communist parties. Colby's decision to cooperate with investigators embroiled him in controversy. While some observers were enraged by his frankness, others accused him of being a liar, and still others were appalled by the immorality of some of the CIA's activities.

Within the CIA, many of Colby's colleagues considered his testimony traitorous, feeling he betrayed his fellow intelligence officers and unnecessarily exposed CIA secrets to the scrutiny of enemy intelligence agencies. According to *Time* magazine, some government officials were also alarmed by Colby's exposure of spying secrets, among them Secretary of State Henry Kissinger, Vice-President Nelson Rockefeller, and President Gerald R. Ford. *Time* suggested that Colby was fired because Ford was annoyed by the director's forthrightness: "Publicly, Ford claimed that Colby was carrying out his directions, as befits an 'open' Administration; privately, Ford was irritated." In his memoirs, *Honorable Men: My Life in the CIA,* Colby corroborated this viewpoint. Colby stated that the Ford administration's "preferred approach, bluntly put, would have been to stonewall."

Others were not distressed by Colby's decision to testify; rather, they believed his testimony was evasive or mendacious. In 1974, an observer at the Washington Conference on the CIA and Covert Action felt that "the only thing of any real value that occurred at the conference was the demonstration—if such is still needed—that unless of bureaucrat of Colby's steel is threatened at least with firing, and preferably with jail, he simply will not reveal his dirty work." Colby justified his refusal to answer some questions put to him by explaining that secrets are unavoidable in the operation of an intelligence agency: "There are some 'bad' secrets—mistakes we've made, things that have gone wrong, sure. But there are some 'good' secrets, necessary secrets.... We have people whose lives and reputations depend on our secrecy. We have technical systems whose effectiveness can be anulled if it comes out we are doing a particular thing."

But there is a difference between refusing to give out information to questioners and in giving out false answers, which is what ex-CIA officer John Stockwell accused Colby of. In his book, *In Search of Enemies,* Stockwell charged that Colby lied to Congress about the extent of CIA involvment in Angola. Colby's *Honorable Men* maintained that "no CIA officers were permitted to engage in combat or train [in Angola]," whereas Stockwell's book alleged that American military advisers with large sums of money at their disposal were dispatched to the African nation to hire French and Portuguese mercenaries. Stockwell and Colby appeared on different segments of "Sixty Minutes," a Columbia Broadcasting System (CBS) televison program, to defend their positions.

CIA activities in Angola and elsewhere have raised questions about the morality of covert operations. One critic, Richard N. Gardner of Columbia University, remarked that covert operations are neither ethical nor practical: "Dirty tricks have always been immoral and illegal. Now they have also outlived their usefulness." Colby himself termed the CIA preparation of a psychological profile on Daniel Ellsberg as "deplorable," and held that the agency should not attempt to assassinate foreign leaders: "I am opposed to assassinations because I think they're wrong and because I think they frequently bring about absolutely uncontrolled and unforeseeable results."

Nonetheless, Colby thinks that doing away completely with clandestine activities would endanger the security of the United States, for it would "leave us with nothing between a diplomatic protest and sending in the Marines." When asked how he could insure the CIA would not commit any atrocities in the name of national security, Colby replied, "As for disclosure, the press does a good job of catching us when they can." Furthermore, he declared that the conscience of the CIA would also prevent such things from occurring: "If anyone tried to use the CIA against the U.S.A., the CIA would explode from within." Despite his belief in the morality as well as the necessity of secret operations, during his term as CIA director Colby attempted to curtail covert actions and to channel CIA efforts into gathering, evaluating, and analyzing information.

Questions about the morality of CIA operations have inevitably led to questions about Colby's personal character. Those who admire him cite the remarkable bravery he displayed while working as an espionage agent behind German lines in France and Norway during World War II. His devotion to family, friends, and country has also been praised. While conceding that Colby is incapable of performing dirty tricks, one CIA officer said, "I'd call him an enlightened cold warrior.... But remember that this business is cold." Others would reject even the term "enlightened," pointing out that Colby headed the Phoenix program in Vietnam, which aimed to wipe out Vietcong infiltration in South Vietnamese villages. By Colby's own admission, between 1968 and 1971 the program was responsible for the deaths of 20,587 Vietnamese (some possibly innocent), but he estimated that eighty-seven per cent of the victims were slain by the regular military in skirmishes.

Colby's work with the CIA in South Vietnam is covered in *Honorable Men*. Thomas Powers pointed out that "Vietnam absorbs the largest part of his [Colby's] book, as it did his life, and one is tempted to linger over his astonishing (to me) inability to notice any but the most particular causes of failure.... I kept expecting Mr. Colby to conclude that we'd have done better if we had done less, but his style of post-mortem is maddeningly narrow." Although he was disappointed with Colby's discussion of Vietnam, Powers concluded that the book as a whole "is important, a serious treatment of a serious subject."

One of the serious subjects that Colby addressed in *Honorable Men* was why he decided to cooperate with the commissions conducted by Vice-President Rockefeller and Senator Frank Church. He wrote that he was motivated by his belief that the CIA should be subject to the constitution, and that if the bad secrets of the agency were brought to light the public would not consider them so terrible. In an article in *Commentary*, Edward Jay Epstein rejected Colby's high-sounding reasons for aiding investigators. Epstein charged that Colby himself created the leaks that lead to the presidential committee's probe of the CIA. Furthermore, he claimed that Colby's actions were essentially self-serving, for the exposure brought about the resignation of James Angleton and the junking of the troublesome counterintelligence program that Angleton had developed.

Colby offered *CA* a different explanation for his revelation of CIA secrets: "I am a man accustomed to being shot at from the rear as well as the front—from the right as well as the left. In World War II behind German lines in France and Norway, I learned to depend on my own judgment, to reach out to friends for help and to avoid the extremes. During my middle years as a CIA operations officer in Italy and Vietnam, I applied the same techniques. I was heavily involved in a program to strengthen the center democratic parties in Italy through covert financial and political support. In Vietnam, I advocated and finally directed the support of villagers to fight for their own security and future, rather than relying on regular military forces or pushing for more refined constitutional procedures in the Saigon political arena.

"But my most intensive application of this technique occurred when CIA and American intelligence became the subject of sensational accusations and revelations. I rejected the traditional tight-lipped image of the 'secret service' and revealed in excruciating detail to investigating committees and to TV interrogators such events as CIA's attempts to assassinate Fidel Castro, its collection of information on the anti-war movement, and its experimentation with mind-controlling drugs. I did this because it was the only way to bring out the true and small proportion of these missteps and misdeeds over the quarter century history of an organization ordered in the early 1950's to be 'more ruthless' than its adversaries, and to protect the identities of the individuals who worked with CIA over these years."

About his memoirs, Colby added: "In *Honorable Men*, I describe my turbulent path through various guerrilla-like campaigns. I assert that my guiding stars during this trek through our post-war history were my opposition to totalitarianism of the right or the left and my belief in the American Constitution and its separation of powers. I do not link my title *Honorable Men* to my predecessor Richard Helms's statement that 'the nation must take on faith that we too are honorable men devoted to its service' nor to the remark of Nathan Hale, our nation's first spy, that 'every kind of service, necessary to the public good, becomes honorable by being necessary.' Nor do I associate it with Marc Anthony's

famous sarcastic praise of Brutus and his fellow-conspirators against Caesar. Rather I insist that the title is a straightforward statement that the 'men and women of CIA had been honorable to themselves and in their service to their nation, with the very few exceptions that occur in any collection of fallible human beings.' But I then go beyond that defense of CIA to say that 'Americans have long looked to a government of laws and not merely of men, and the CIA must fit within this if it is to continue.' I thus call for a new and American intelligence to be conducted under the law and our Constitution's discipline. I also look ahead to a new role for this modern version of intelligence—that the knowledge now available from its fantastic technology, from its legion of scholars and analysts, and yes, from its spies, can be used to solve the problems of the world ahead rather than allowing them to surprise us."

BIOGRAPHICAL/CRITICAL SOURCES: New Republic, December 8, 1973, September 21, 1974, March 13, 1976; *Time,* September 30, 1974, March 31, 1975, November 17, 1975, January 19, 1976; *Nation,* October 5, 1974; *U.S. News and World Report,* December 2, 1974, April 7, 1975, August 25, 1975; William Colby and Peter Forbath, *Honorable Men: My Life in the CIA,* Simon & Schuster, 1978; John Stockwell, *In Search of Enemies: A CIA Story,* Norton, 1978; *Newsweek,* January 20, 1975, May 15, 1978; *New York Times Book Review,* May 21, 1978; *Commentary,* August, 1978.

*   *   *

COLE, Leonard A(aron) 1933-

PERSONAL: Born September 1, 1933, in Paterson, N.J.; son of Morris and Rebecca (Harelick) Cohen; married Ruth L. Gerber, July 7, 1957; children: Wendy Marcia, Philip Arthur, William Edward. *Education:* Attended Indiana University, 1951-53; University of Pennsylvania, D.D.S., 1957; University of California, Berkeley, B.A. (highest honors), 1961; Columbia University, M.A., 1965, Ph.D., 1970. *Home:* 381 Crest Rd., Ridgewood, N.J. 07450. *Office:* 723 Lafayette Ave., Hawthorne, N.J. 07506.

CAREER: Children's Hospital of East Bay, Oakland, Calif., dental extern, 1960; private dental practice in Hawthorne, N.J., 1961—. Lecturer in political science at William Paterson College, 1970—. President of Glen Rock Human Rights Council, 1969-70. *Military service:* U.S. Air Force, Dental Corps, 1957-59; became captain. *Member:* American Dental Association, American Society of Dentistry for Children, American Political Science Association, Academy of Political Science, Americans for Democratic Action (member of state board of directors, 1965-70), Phi Beta Kappa, Alpha Omega (president, 1956-57).

WRITINGS: Blacks in Power, Princeton University Press, 1976. Contributor to political science and urban affairs journals.

*   *   *

COLEMAN, Arthur 1924-

PERSONAL: Born June 29, 1924, in New York, N.Y.; married wife, June, February 8, 1946; children: Geoffrey, Hildy. *Education:* Manhattan College, B.A., 1946; New York University, M.A., 1948, Ph.D., 1953. *Politics:* None. *Religion:* None. *Home:* 104 Searingtown Rd., Albertson, N.Y. 11507. *Office:* Department of English, C. W. Post College, Long Island University, Greenvale, N.Y. 11548.

CAREER: Bennett College, Greensboro, N.C., instructor

in English, 1952-53; Iona College, New Rochelle, N.Y., instructor in English, 1953-54; Hofstra University, Hempstead, N.Y., instructor in English, 1954-57; free-lance writer, 1957-61; Long Island University, C. W. Post College, Greenvale, N.Y., professor of English, 1961—, chairman of department.

WRITINGS: (With Gary R. Tyler) *Drama Criticism,* Swallow Press, Volume I: *A Checklist of Interpretation Since 1940 of English and American Plays,* 1968, Volume II: *A Checklist of Interpretation Since 1940 of Classical and Continental Plays,* 1970; (compiler) *Epic and Romance Criticism,* Watermill Publishers, Volume I: *English and American,* 1972, Volume II: *Classical and Continental,* 1973; *Petals on a Wet Black Bough* (novel), Watermill Publishers, 1973; *A Case in Point* (novel), Watermill Publishers, 1978. Contributor to *Sherlock Holmes Journal, Baker Street Journal,* and *Wellsian.*

WORK IN PROGRESS: Sinclair Lewis: The Early Years; a novel; scholarly papers on Paul Bunyan, Sherlock Holmes, *Sir Gawain and the Green Knight,* and Ernest Hemingway's *The Spanish Earth.*

SIDELIGHTS: Coleman writes that his motivation is "simply the idea of being productive in areas and with projects of moderate value."

* * *

COLEMAN, Vernon 1946-
(Edward Vernon)

PERSONAL: Born May 18, 1946, in Walsall, England; son of Edward (an engineer) and Kathleen (a company director; maiden name, Lloyd) Coleman; married Margaret Barton, June 23, 1975; children: Helen, Neil. *Education:* University of Birmingham, M.B.Ch.B., 1970. *Residence:* Leamington Spa, England. *Agent:* Harold Ober Associates, Inc., 40 East 49th St., New York, N.Y. 10017.

CAREER: Chilton Designs Ltd., Kintbury, England, secretary, 1970—. General practitioner of medicine, 1974—. *Member:* Royal Society of Medicine, Society of Authors, British Medical Association, Marylebone Cricket Club, National Liberal Club, Warwickshire County Cricket Club.

WRITINGS: The Medicine Men (nonfiction), Temple Smith, 1975, Transatlantic, 1977; *Everything You Want to Know About Ageing,* Atheneum, 1976; *Paper Doctors* (nonfiction), Transatlantic, 1977; *Stress Control,* Temple Smith, 1978.

Under pseudonym Edward Vernon: *Practice Makes Perfect,* Macmillan (England), 1977, St. Martin's, 1978; *Practice What you Preach,* Macmillan (England), 1978, St. Martin's,1979; *Getting Into Practice,* Macmillan, 1979. Author of "Your Family's Health," a column syndicated by Features International (London) to about twenty newspapers, 1971—. Contributor of more than a thousand articles to magazines. Executive editor of *British Clinical Journal,* 1971-72.

WORK IN PROGRESS: Social History of Medicine, nonfiction; other fiction and nonfiction.

AVOCATIONAL INTERESTS: Cricket, European cities, books.

* * *

COMAN, Dale Rex 1906-

PERSONAL: Born February 22, 1906, in Hartford, Conn.; son of Edward Lokker (in business) and Florence Marguerite (a teacher; maiden name, Rex) Coman; married Mona Charity Segal (an artist), December 22, 1937; children: Michael Dale, Charity Beth Coman Sledge. *Education:* Attended University of Rhode Island, 1924-26; University of Michigan, B.A., 1928; McGill University, M.D., C.M., 1933. *Politics:* Independent Liberal. *Religion:* None. *Home address:* Sand Point Rd., Bar Harbor, Maine 04609.

CAREER: McGill University, Montreal, Quebec, assistant in Pathologic Institute, 1933-34; University of Pennsylvania Hospital, Philadelphia, resident in pathology, 1934-35; Massachusetts State General Hospital, Pondville, resident in pathology, 1935-36; New York University, New York, N.Y., instructor in pathology, 1936-37; University of Pennsylvania, Philadelphia, instructor, 1937-42, assistant professor to associate professor, 1942-54, professor of experimental pathology, 1954-72, professor emeritus, 1972—, chairman of department of pathology, 1954-67. Diplomate of American Board of Pathology Research associate of Jackson Laboratory Past member of board of directors of College of the Atlantic, Coastal Resource Center, and Nature Conservancy. Bar Harbor conservation commissioner.

MEMBER: International Society of Cell Biology, American Association for the Advancement of Science (fellow), American Association of Pathologists and Bacteriologists, American Society for Experimental Pathology and Medicine, American Society for Cell Biology, American Association for Cancer Research, Tissue Culture Association (past vice-president), New York Academy of Sciences, Sigma Xi, Alpha Omega Alpha.

WRITINGS: Pleasant River (self-illustrated), Norton, 1967; *The Endless Adventure* (self-illustrated), Regnery, 1972. Also author of *The Technique of Postmortem Examination,* 1934. Columnist for *Philadelphia Bulletin.* Contributor of articles to medical and scientific journals, conservation and natural history magazines, and newspapers.

WORK IN PROGRESS: Our Bay, about Frenchman Bay, Maine; *Swamp Yankee,* a novel based on research.

SIDELIGHTS: Coman writes: "I have had a lifetime love affair with Earth, and beguilement with its living forms." *Avocational interests:* Nature study, sailing, flyfishing, oil painting, illustration.

BIOGRAPHICAL/CRITICAL SOURCES: Maine Life, February, 1978.

* * *

CONNABLE, Alfred 1931-

PERSONAL: Born December 26, 1931, in Ann Arbor, Mich.; married Roma Lipsky (a writer), May 6, 1962; children: Benjamin, Joel. *Education:* University of Michigan, A.B., 1953; Yale University, M.F.A., 1958. *Agent:* Lynn Nesbit, International Creative Management, 40 West 57th St., New York, N.Y. 10019.

CAREER: Writer. *Military service:* U.S. Army, 1953-55.

WRITINGS: (With Edward Silberfarb) *Tigers of Tammany: Nine Men Who Ran New York,* Holt, 1967; *Twelve Trains to Babylon* (spy novel), Little, Brown, 1971.

* * *

CONNELLAN, Leo 1928-

PERSONAL: Born November 30, 1928, in Portland, Maine; son of James (a postmaster) and Ida Elizabeth (a teacher; maiden name, Carey) Connellan; married Nancy Anderson (a state social worker), February 21, 1961; children: Amy

Charlotte. *Education:* University of Maine, B.A., 1951. *Politics:* "No preference." *Religion:* "No preference." *Agent:* Samuel J. Mandelbaum, Maurice Mandelbaum Associates, East 84th St., Brooklyn, N.Y.

CAREER: Poet. Old Town Corp., Brooklyn N.Y., manager of New York retail branch, 1965-68; Addressograph-Multigraph Corp., New York, N.Y., in sales, 1968-70; Annhurst College, Woodstock, Conn., special lecturer in creative writing and poet-in-residence, 1971-73; associate with Kores Manufacturing Corp., 1973-75; Bee Chemical Co., Fairfield, N.J., in sales for New England region, 1975-77; Southern Connecticut State College, New Haven, special lecturer and poet-in-residence, 1977-78. *Military service:* Served in U.S. Army.

MEMBER: International P.E.N., Poetry Society of America. *Awards, honors:* National Endowment for the Arts grant, 1969; grants from State of Connecticut, 1974, and Main Commission on the Arts, 1978.

WRITINGS—All poetry: *Penobscot Poems,* New Quarto Editions, 1974; *Another Poet in New York,* Living Poets Press, 1975; *First Selected Poems,* University of Pittsburgh Press, 1976; *Crossing America* (foreword by Richard Eberhart), Penman Press, 1976; *Death in Lobster Land* (foreword by Herbert Selby, Jr.), Great Raven Press, 1978; *Seven Short Poems,* Western Maryland College Press, 1978; *The Gunman and Other Poems,* Seven Buffalos Press, 1979. Also author of screenplays, including "Leo Connellan and Walter Lowenfels," TruPix Films, 1969; "Leo Connellan at Fifty," Eikon Films, 1978. Editor of *Dasein,* 1965-69.

WORK IN PROGRESS: Massachusetts Poems.

SIDELIGHTS: Connellan writes: "I am trying to become a good lyric narrative poet in the tradition of Robert Penn Warren's *Democracy and Poetry,* Delmore Schwartz's *In Dreams Begin Responsibilities,* Karl Shapiro's *V-Letter and Other Poems,* Richard Wilbur's *Walking to Sleep,* Francois Villon's *The Legacy—The Testament,* and John Milton's *Paradise Lost.* I want to convey the futility of poor working people who get up and go to work knowing each day before they start that they cannot ever earn enough.

"The trick of writing is to include the reader. Writing is done either out of brilliance or because something disturbs the writer."

* * *

CONSTABLE, John W. 1922-

PERSONAL: Born March 20, 1922, in Baltimore, Md.; son of Leroy M. and Bessie (Bessling) Constable; married Anna M. Saggau, August 16, 1947; children: Barbara Constable Schaper, Kathryn Constable Ahrens, James, Patricia, Joel. *Education:* Received degrees from Concordia College, Bronxville, N.Y., 1943; Concordia Seminary, St. Louis, Mo., 1949; Iowa State University, M.A., 1960; Ohio State University, Ph.D., 1967. *Home:* 7285 Princeton, St. Louis, Mo. 63130. *Office:* Christ Seminary, 607 North Grand, St. Louis, Mo.

CAREER: Ordained Lutheran Minister; pastor of Lutheran university chapel in Columbus, Ohio, 1949-56, and church in Iowa City, Iowa, 1956-64; Concordia Seminary, St. Louis, Mo., professor of history, 1964-74; Christ Seminary, St. Louis, professor of history, 1974—. *Member:* American Historical Association, American Society of Church History, American Association of University Professors. *Awards, honors:* Danforth scholarship, 1962-63.

WRITINGS: Church Since Pentecost, Concordia, 1969. Editor of *Concordia Institute Quarterly.*

WORK IN PROGRESS: An oral history project.

AVOCATIONAL INTERESTS: World travel, including the Soviet Union.

* * *

CONSTANTINE, Larry L(eRoy) 1943-

PERSONAL: Born February 14, 1943, in Minneapolis, Minn.; son of Philip Francis (a mechanic) and L. Loraine (a secretary and newspaper writer; maiden name, Hack) Constantine; married Joan Marie Kangas (a family therapist), March 7, 1964; children: Joy Marie, Heather Ellen. *Education:* Massachusetts Institute of Technology, S.B., 1967, graduate study, 1967-68; Boston Family Institute, certificate in family therapy, 1973. *Religion:* "Humanist." *Home:* 22 Bulette Rd., Acton, Mass. 01720.

CAREER: C-E-I-R, Inc., Washington, D.C. (and Boston, Mass.), programmer and analyst, 1963-67; Information & Systems Institute, Inc., Cambridge, Mass., president, 1967-69; International Business Machines, Systems Research Institute, New York, N.Y., adjunct member of faculty, 1968-72; Tufts University, School of Medicine, Boston, Mass., assistant clinical professor of psychiatry, 1973—. Family therapist in private practice in Acton, Mass., 1973—. Independent consultant in general systems theory applied to systems design, 1968-76. Member of Groves Conference on Marriage and the Family. *Member:* National council on Family Relations (head of Alternative Lifestyles Task Force, 1972—), American Orthopsychiatric Association, Society for Family Therapy and Research.

WRITINGS: (With wife, Joan M. Constantine) *Group Marriage: A Study of Contemporary Multilateral Marriages,* Macmillan, 1973; (with Ed Yourdon) *Structured Design: Fundamentals of a Discipline of Computer Program and Systems Design,* Yourdon Press, 1975, revised edition, Prentice-Hall, 1978; (with J. M. Constantine) *Treasures of the Island: Children in Alternative Families* (monograph), Sage Publications, 1976; (with Alvin K. Swonger) *Drugs and Therapy: The Psychotherapist's Handbook of Psychotropic Drugs,* Little, Brown, 1976; (editor with Floyd Martinson) *Children and Sex: New Findings and Perspectives,* Little, Brown, 1979. Contributor of more than fifty articles to family counseling journals and popular magazines, including *Penthouse Forum.* Member of editorial board of *Alternative Lifestyles* and *Sage Families Abstracts.* Research for *Human Process: Elements of a Unified Theory of Behavior and Development of Individuals and Social Systems.*

SIDELIGHTS: Constantine writes: "I never considered becoming a writer until my freshman humanities professor, Emmett Larkin, pronounced me hopelessly illiterate and incapable of constructing a coherent sentence. With the tenacity of scum in a bathtub, I clung to this challenge, determined to learn to write a readable, informative sentence. I advanced to striving for interesting sentences and hope someday to graduate to writing short paragraphs.

"Technical themes were my first literary drills, and my first technical article was published during my sophomore year. I wrote at first to give permanence to otherwise fleeting technical notions and out of unabashed careermanship. Alas, my theories and techniques were largely ignored during my tenure in information sciences, becoming recognized and accepted only after I switched my allegiance to family studies and human relations. There I found the purpose absent in my first career.

"I write not to write but to reach. Writing still does not come easily for me, consisting largely of repeated revision and self-inflicted editing. The work is only the vehicle for the idea, which is, in turn, the servant of the intent, for all my writing is intentioned, part of my drive to be cause, to contribute substantively to human progress. Will evolution's forward thrust outrun the forces of decay or our potential for self-destruction? I know not, but only that I wish to be on one side and not the other.

"In this epoch, human survival will depend on the continued evolution of social forms to fit accelerating conditions of change in a universe of new rules, new constraints, new potentials. We need tolerance of differences, support of variation, and expanded self-understanding if the necessary social innovations are to emerge. Alternatives must be allowed to flourish and to fail freely, to be sifted for new institutions, values, and lifestyles to supplant those which once served us well but now lead us to the very edge of oblivion.

"Social change and alternatives pervade my life. My own family is open, egalitarian, a place of generous freedom and easy affection. We are staunch supporters of the Equal Rights Amendment and advocates of children's rights."

AVOCATIONAL INTERESTS: "In spare moments I play electronic synthesizer and compose songs (part of our oral tradition), write science fiction short stories (still unpublished), and make slow but visible progress on the house we have been building for six years."

*   *   *

COOK, Marjorie 1920-

PERSONAL: Born April 21, 1920, in California; daughter of Elvis E. (a clergyman and professor) and Ruth (a teacher; maiden name, Logan) Cochrane; married Harlow William Cook (a high school teacher), March 21, 1946; children: Marilee Cook Shaner, Kristine Cook Nelson, Karen Cook Smee. *Education:* Seattle Pacific University, B.A., 1941. *Religion:* First Covenant Church. *Residence:* Federal Way, Wash.

CAREER: Former elementary school teacher in Arcadia, and Hawthorne, Calif., and in Elma, and Montasano, Wash.; elementary school librarian in Fife, Wash., 1960-74; free-lance writer, 1974—. *Member:* National Writers Club, Pacific Northwest Writers Club, Pacific Northwest Association of Church Libraries (local president).

WRITINGS: To Walk on Two Feet (juvenile novel), Westminster, 1978. Contributor of articles and stories to newspapers.

WORK IN PROGRESS: Build for Tomorrow; His Approval; Road's End; six juvenile books, *Something to Love, Ghost Music, Secret Doors, Bird Brain, Reading Can Be Trouble,* and *Jebuel, Son of Joshua.*

SIDELIGHTS: Marjorie Cook comments: "I am vitally interested in communicating Christian values." *Avocational interests:* Reading, crafts, knitting, storytelling.

*   *   *

COOK, Petronelle Marguerite Mary 1925-
(Margot Arnold)

PERSONAL: Born May 16, 1925, in Plymouth, England; came to United States, 1950; naturalized U.S. citizen, 1953; daughter of Harry Alfred (a communications engineer) and Ada Wood (Alford) Crouch; married Philip Remington Cook, Jr. (a diplomat), July 20, 1949 (divorced, 1978); children: Philip Remington III, Nicholas Edward Ariel, Alex-

andra Mary Louise. *Education:* Oxford University, B.A., 1946, M.A., 1950; graduate study at University of Chicago, 1952. *Politics:* "Independent." *Home:* 11 High School Rd., Hyannis, Mass. 02601. *Agent:* Lisa Collier, Collier Associates, 280 Madison Ave., New York, N.Y. 10016.

CAREER: Archaeologist. University of Maryland, College Park, instructor in anthropology and archaeology with foreign program in Rome, Italy, 1971; Cape Cod Community College, West Barnstable, Mass., instructor in anthropology and archaeology, 1972-78; writer, 1972—. Curator for Sussex Archaeological Society, 1947-49; staff assistant of University of Chicago Oriental Institute, 1950-52. *Member:* Archaeological Institute of America, Prehistoric Society (England), Society of Authors (England), New England Genealogical and Historic Society, Boston Authors's Club, Twelve O'Clock Scholars. *Awards, honors:* Ryerson fellowship, University of Chicago, 1952.

WRITINGS—Under pseudonym Margot Arnold: *The Officer's Woman,* Wingate, 1972, Fawcett-Crest, 1973; *The Villa on the Palatine,* Wingate, 1975, Berkeley, 1978; *Exit Actors Dying,* Playboy Press, 1979; *Voodoo Marie,* Simon & Schuster, 1979; *Murder–Cape Cod Style,* Playboy Press, 1979. Work anthologized in *Eighth Armada Book of Short Stories, Frighteners No. 2,* and *Fontana, Great Horror Stories.*

WORK IN PROGRESS: Zodok's Treasure, publication by Playboy Press.

SIDELIGHTS: Cook was attracted to archaeology at an early age when she viewed the remains of an ancient Roman city. Fascinated by the marble floors and central heating, Cook went on to study at Oxford where she participated in several "rescue digs," expeditions where development locales are carefully searched for artifacts before work begins.

Upon graduation, Cook acquired a job making her the youngest museum curator in Europe, but she left the position in favor of an expedition to Turkey. She returned with a greater knowledge of the submissive role of women in foreign countries. Soon after that, Cook embarked on a series of excavation trips to Africa. Working with such noted archaeologists as Merrit Posnansky, Desmond Clark, and Revell Mason, Cook was able to make some interesting discoveries. "We made a particularly good find at a site near Johannesburg while I was digging with Revell Mason," she recalled. "When we removed the initial layer of dirt we found an area literally covered with hand axes. . . ."

A main concern of Cook's regarding her African journeys was that she never did field work with the revered archaeologist Louis Leakey. "When I was in Africa he had run out of funds," she noted sadly. "I did spend two years putting together his old friends the Australopithecine though, in Nairobi and Pretoria.

Although her role as the wife of a diplomat afforded her the opportunity to participate in several research trips, the same position also had its disadvantages. On one particular occasion, her findings from a recent trip were discarded by a secretary. However, she has managed to salvage numerous items, including Ugandan drums and Turkish milk jugs.

Aside from her considerable reputation as both an archaeologist and anthropologist, Cook has acquired some notoriety as a writer. Her books are often quite the opposite of what would be expected from one with her background. For instance, *The Villa of the Palatine* is an historical-romance about English folk swept up in the Italian rebellion of 1847. Of course, her primary interests are not totally subordinated. A prospective mystery series lists both an archaeologist and an anthropologist among its characters.

Cook also plans on incorporating her knowledge of the occult into future books. "One plot I have in mind is a loving, wry look at a terribly efficient American woman," she mused, "who goes into a town full of vampires and just cleans things up." But her interest in the occult is not all tongue-in-cheek. "I'm a Cornish Celt," she commented. "I've always been interested in the occult. Of course, living in countries where these things are a normal part of people's lives has probably predisposed me in that direction too." Cook also recently discovered that four women in her ex-husband's family fell victim to the Salem witch hunts.

Summing up her knowledge and skills, Cook told CA: "As you can see . . . I started life as an archaeologist, was a diplomat's wife for twenty-nine years, traveled widely in the Middle East (two years), Africa (six years), and Europe. . . . I can speak French, Italian, and some Turkish and Swahili. My writing interests are multiple. I hope to continue my mystery series but also hope to write historical and contemporary novels."

Cook's first book, *The Officers' Woman*, has also been published in France, Holland, and Brazil.

AVOCATIONAL INTERESTS: Genealogy, the occult.

BIOGRAPHICAL/CRITICAL SOURCES: Rand Daily Mail, January 15, 1960; *Pretoria News,* April 25, 1960; *Cape Cod Times,* December 26, 1976.

*   *   *

COREA, Gena
See COREA, Genoveffa

*   *   *

COREA, Genoveffa   1946-
(Gena Corea)

PERSONAL: Born July 18, 1946, in Weymouth, Mass.; daughter of Edward Vitaliano (an electrical engineer) and Marie (a teacher; maiden name, Daugherty) Corea; married Thomas E. Marlin (a chemical engineer), May 22, 1971. *Education:* University of Massachusetts, B.A., 1971. *Residence:* Madison, N.J.

CAREER: Peter Bent Brigham Hospital, Boston, Mass., nurse's aide, 1964; *Berkshire Eagle,* Pittsfield, Mass., reporter, 1967-68; teacher of English at a school in Athens, Greece, 1968-69; *Holyoke Transcript,* Holyoke, Mass., reporter and editor of column, "Tomorrow's Woman," 1971-73; New Republic Feature Syndicate, Washington, D.C., author of syndicated column, "Frankly Feminist," 1973-74; free-lance writer, 1974—. *Member:* Women's Institute for Freedom of the Press, Authors Guild.

WRITINGS—Under name Gena Corea: *The Hidden Malpractice,* Morrow, 1977, reprinted as *The Hidden Malpractice: How American Medicine Mistreats Women as Patients and Professionals,* Jove, 1978. Contributor to magazines, including *Ms., Glamour,* and *Seminar,* and newspapers.

WORK IN PROGRESS—All under name Genoveffa Corea: A series of articles on the lives of women in Northern Ireland; writing about the male obstetrician's technological takeover of childbirth.

SIDELIGHTS: Genoveffa Corea wrote that she did not begin her career as a feminist, but added "I would have to be a cretin not to be one now." Her work as an investigative journalist led her to research in schools and hospitals, mu-

nicipal governments and business corporations, day care centers and welfare offices, newspaper offices themselves, stores, military and police recruiting centers, and even churches.

With regard to her work, Corea told *CA:* "I explore obstetrics and gynecology because it is a field which cries out for investigation. Though many people believe the speciality was formed to help women, my research proves that to be a myth. The history of obstetrics and gynecology is, in large part, a history of violence against women—from the days when Dr. J. Marion Sims, the 'Father of Modern Gynecology,' kept black female slaves in a building behind his house and repeatedly performed experimental, unanesthetized surgery on them, to the present, when doctors commit unnecessary hysterectomies, ovariectomies and 'prophylactic' mastectomies against women. When doctors take their knives to women's bodies—cutting out their uteri, ovaries and breasts—for reasons which have nothing to do with improving the health or well-being of these women, then they are committing acts of violence comparable to rape and wife-battering."

BIOGRAPHICAL/CRITICAL SOURCES: Seminar Quarterly, June, 1972.

*   *   *

COSBY, Bill
See COSBY, William Henry, Jr.

*   *   *

COSBY, William Henry, Jr.   1937-
(Bill Cosby)

PERSONAL: Born July 12, 1937, in Philadelphia, Pa.; son of William Henry (a U.S. Navy mess steward) and Anna Cosby; married Camille Hanks, January 25, 1964; children: Erika Ranee, Erinn Chalene, Ennis William, Ensa Camille, Evin Harrah. *Education:* Attended Temple University, 1961-62; University of Massachusetts, M.A., 1972, Ph.D., 1976. *Office:* c/o Jemmin Inc., 1900 Avenue of the Stars, Suite 1929, Century City, Calif. 90067.

CAREER: Comedian, actor, and recording artist. Performer in nightclubs, including Gaslight Cafe, New York City, Gate of Horn, Chicago, Ill., Shadows Club, Washington, D.C., Bitter End, New York City, Hungry i, San Francisco, and various nightclubs in Las Vegas, Nev., 1962—; performer in television series' for National Broadcasting Co. (NBC-TV), including "I Spy," and "The Bill Cosby Show," 1965-71, for Columbia Broadcasting System (CBS-TV), "The Bill Cosby Show," 1971, and American Broadcasting Co. (ABC-TV), "Cos," 1976; actor in motion pictures, including "Hickey and Boggs," 1972, "Man and Boy," 1972, "Uptown Saturday Night," 1974, "Let's Do It Again," 1975, "Mother, Jugs, and Speed," 1976, and "California Suite," 1978. Performer on radio program, "The Bill Cosby Radio Program." Member of Carnegie Commission for the Future of Public Broadcasting, board of directors of National Council of Crime and Delinquency, Mary Homes College, and Ebony Showcase Theater, advisory board of Direction Sports, communications council at Howard University, and steering committee of American Sickle Cell Foundation. *Military service:* U.S. Navy Medical Corps, 1956-60.

Awards, honors: Grammy Award for best comedy album from National Academy of Recording Arts and Sciences, 1964, for "Bill Cosby Is a Very Funny Fellow . . . Right?,"

1965, for ''I Started Out as a Child,'' 1966, for ''Why Is There Air?,'' 1967, for ''Revenge,'' and 1969, for ''To Russell, My Brother, Whom I Slept With''; Emmy Award for best actor in a dramatic series from Academy of Television Arts and Sciences, 1966-68, for ''I Spy''; Emmy Award, 1969, for ''The First Bill Cosby Special''; named ''most promising new male star'' by *Fame* magazine, 1966; selected number one comedy artist in campus poll, 1968.

WRITINGS—Under name Bill Cosby: *The Wit and Wisdom of Fat Albert,* Windmill Books, 1973; *Bill Cosby's Personal Guide to Tennis Power; or, Don't Lower the Lob, Raise the Net,* Random House, 1975. Author of recordings, including ''Bill Cosby Is a Very Funny Fellow . . . Right?,'' 1964, ''I Started Out as a Child,'' 1965, ''Why Is There Air,'' 1966, ''Wonderfulness,'' 1967, ''Revenge,'' 1967, ''To Russell, My Brother, Whom I Slept With,'' 1969, ''Bill Cosby Is Not Himself These Days, Rat Own, Rat Own, Rat Own,'' 1976, ''My Father Confused Me . . . What Must I Do? What Must I Do?,'' 1977, ''Disco Bill,'' 1977, ''Bill's Best Friend,'' 1978, and also ''200 MPH,'' ''Silverthroat,'' ''Hoorah for the Salvation Army Band,'' ''8:15, 12:15,'' ''For Adults Only,'' ''Bill Cosby Talks to Kids About Drugs,'' ''Inside the Mind of Bill Cosby.''

SIDELIGHTS: ''When I was a kid I always used to pay attention to things that other people didn't even think about,'' claimed Cosby. ''I'd remember funny happenings, just little trivial things, and then tell stories about them later. I found I could make people laugh, and I enjoyed doing it because it gave me a sense of security. I thought that if people laughed at what you said, that meant they like you. Telling funny stories became, for me, a way of making friends.

''My comedy routines come from this storytelling knack . . . I never tell jokes. I don't think I could write an out and out joke if my life depended on it. Practically all my bits deal with my childhood days back in Philadelphia where the important thing on the block was how far you could throw a football.''

In his youth, Cosby was equally adept at throwing either a punchline or a football. While Cosby was making his schoolmates and, later, his shipmates, laugh with his humorous stories, he was also developing into an impressive athlete. He played football and learned physical therapy during his stint in the navy. Upon discharge, he enrolled at Temple University with an athletic scholarship. But Cosby soon grew tired of the academic and athletic life and began appearing as a comedian in local coffeehouses.

By 1962, Cosby had dropped out of Temple University and was devoting full-time to honing his skills as an entertainer. He played at various coffeehouses in Greenwich Village and, although the beatnik movement was still popular, Cosby began to gather a large audience. ''I think what people like most about my stories is that they can identify,'' he commented. ''The situations I talk about people can find themselves in . . . it makes them glad to know they're not the only ones who have fallen victim to life's little ironies. For example, how many of us have put the ice water bottle back in the refrigerator with just enough water left so we won't have to refill it? Be honest now.

''That's how I got involved in comedy . . . it just sort of happened. Once I decided it was a way to make a living, the struggle was on. Breaking into show business is one of the hardest . . . longest . . . most discouraging things you can do. If you want to make the old school try, you better have plenty of guts and determination 'cause you'll need all you can muster up.''

Cosby's success in coffeehouses led to bookings in nightclubs which only served to broaden his following. Eventually, Cosby received a recording contract and he quickly became the best-selling comedian on records. From 1964 to 1969, Cosby's albums were a mainstay of the record charts with several of his recordings selling over $1 million each.

By 1965, Cosby was enjoying popularity on both stage and record. But there was still another talent of his to be displayed: acting. With ''I Spy,'' Cosby revealed an acting ability which brought him three Emmy Awards successively for best actor. On the show, he played a multi-lingual Rhodes scholar working as part of a spy team. Together with fellow actor Robert Culp, Cosby made the show one of the most watched on television in the late 1960's. Cosby recalled: ''I was quite satisfied with my work after I got going. Nightclubs were good to me . . . and television suddenly started opening up. It wasn't until 'I Spy' came along that I really felt established . . . at least to a certain degree. It was so completely different from anything I had ever known. Storytelling is one thing, but playing a definite character . . . and serious yet . . . that's something else. . . . I must admit I was nervous in the beginning, but the experience has really been great for me. I know it's hard to keep pushing yourself into different areas, but you have to if you want to be around in a few years. In this business, if you stand still, you disappear.''

But Cosby's career was still developing. In 1972, he also began making motion pictures. His first film, ''Hickey and Boggs,'' was an adaptation of the television series ''I Spy'' with Cosby and Culp playing the same characters they'd portrayed in the show. 1972 also saw the release of ''Man and Boy,'' Cosby's first drama outside the ''I Spy'' world. ''I really enjoyed it,'' he remembered.

Cosby's success in motion pictures has been remarkable. At a time when most of the films for black audiences were oriented to violence, Cosby teamed with Sidney Poiter and several other black actors to make a highly successful series of comedies, including ''Uptown Saturday Night,'' ''Let's Do It Again,'' and ''A Piece of the Action.'' Critics have been especially generous in their praise of Cosby's acting. Tom Allen noted Cosby's ''free-wheeling, jiving, put-down artistry,'' and Alvin H. Marill wrote that, in ''Let's Do It Again,'' Cosby ''breezes through the outrageous antics.''

Through a variety of media, Cosby has proven to be one of the funnier men in entertainment. ''What I do with humor is to have three levels hitting all at the same time. There is the middle level which is the total laughter itself, but there is also an overcurrent and an undercurrent. For instance, in 'my monologues the humor itself goes straight down the middle because of identification. Then the overcurrent is the fact that rather than trying to bring the races of people together by talking about the differences, let's try to bring them together by talking about the similarities. Then there is also the undercurrent that makes an appeal for an understanding of the gap between the ages.''

AVOCATIONAL INTERESTS: Tennis.

BIOGRAPHICAL/CRITICAL SOURCES: National Observer, January 6, 1964; *New York Post,* February 23, 1964; *Ebony,* May, 1964; *New York Times Magazine,* March 14, 1965; *Village Voice,* November 3, 1975; *Films in Review,* November, 1975.

* * *

COSSI, Olga 1921-

PERSONAL: Born January 28, 1921, in St. Helena, Calif.;

daughter of Orlando (in olive oil manufacturing) and Filomena (Michelli) Della Maggiora; married Don Cossi, July 29, 1939; children: Tamara Cossi Frishberg, Caren Cossi Franci, Donald. *Education:* Attended Palmer Institute of Authorship. *Religion:* "Non-denominationalism." *Home and office address:* Highway I N., Gualala, Calif. 95445. *Agent:* Carol Mann, Carol Mann Literary Agency, 519 East 87th St., New York, N.Y. 10028.

CAREER: Staff correspondent for *Santa Rosa Press Democrat,* Santa Rosa, Calif.; staff member of *Mendocino Beacon,* Mendocino, Calif., author of column, "Barnacles Around the Bay"; free-lance writer and photographer. Head of 5th district, Mendocino County Republican Central Committee. Vice-president and later president of Gualala Community Center. *Member:* Society of Children's Book Writers, Gualala Arts.

WRITINGS: Robin Deer (juvenile), Naturegraph, 1967, revised edition, 1968; *Fire Mate* (juvenile novel), Independence Press (Independence, Mo.), 1977; (contributor) *Voices of the Wineland,* AITA Napa Press, 1978. Also editor of *The Star and the Sixth,* Eldridge Publishing. Contributor to newspapers.

WORK IN PROGRESS: The Gospel According to Me, on linguistic archaeology; *Learning About Harp Seals,* juvenile; *My Friend the Witch,* juvenile, on water-witching; *The Girl Who Laid, She Thought, an Egg,* juvenile.

SIDELIGHTS: Olga Cossi writes: "What I term 'linguistic archaeology' resulted from a deeply-felt interest in metaphysics and a life-long study of languages, which culminated in a five-year study of original Hebrew and Greek scripture. Linguistic archaeology re-affirms subjective pacifism and joy as natural to being. Because of my studies of words, I feel my stories are the kind of which childhood memories are made. They are not easily forgotten reading. My writings are quietly revolutionary! My writings and my studies confirm and reflect the individualism of Stella Warner, an unpublished writer and philosopher."

AVOCATIONAL INTERESTS: Whitewater rafting, backpacking, tennis, most sports.

*   *   *

COSTLEY, Bill
    See COSTLEY, William K(irkwood), Jr.

*   *   *

COSTLEY, William K(irkwood), Jr. 1942-
   (Bill Costley)

PERSONAL: Born May 21, 1942, in Salem, Mass.; son of William Kirkwood (a factory worker) and Mary Stefania (Kulik) Costley; married Joan Helen Budyk (an educational consultant), June 6, 1964; children: Maya, Alex William. *Education:* Boston College, A.B., 1963; graduate study at Boston University, 1967-68. *Politics:* "Anti-fascist, etc." *Religion:* "Ex-Roman Catholic." *Home:* 126 Thorndike St., Apt. 2, Brookline, Mass., 02146. *Office:* Redbridge Collective, P.O. Box 33, Allston, Mass. 02134.

CAREER: Harvard University Medical School, Boston, Mass., medical technician, 1966; Massachusetts Institute of Technology, Cambridge, Mass., engineering periodical librarian, 1967; National Aeronautics and Space Administration, Cambridge, librarian and book acquisitioner, 1967; Boston College, Boston, associate editor of *Institute of Human Sciences Review* (now *Urban and Social Change Review*), 1968; Grahm Junior College, Boston, instructor in

English, 1968; Model Cities program and City Demonstration Agency, Inc. (CDA), Cambridge, newspaper editor and public information officer, 1969-73; free-lance journalist, Cambridge, 1969-73; free-lance writer and editor, Brookline, Mass., 1973—. Consultant to Cambridge Civic Association and C.I.T.Y. high school alternative. *Member:* 100 Flowers Bookstore Cooperative, Redbridge Collective, Central 4 Tenant Union (secretary, 1969-72).

WRITINGS—Under name Bill Costley: *RAG(a)S* (poems), Ghost Dance Press, 1978; *Knosh I Cir* (poems) Ghost Dance Press, 1978; *The War Stories (of Lewis H. Stone)* (chapbook of poems), Nostoc, 1979; (with Peter T. Bates and Arnold S. Trachtman) *Lynn Voices* (poems), BLT Press, 1979; (author of introduction) Vincent Ferrini, *Know Fish* (poems), University of Connecticut, 1979. Work represented in *The Movement Toward a New America,* edited by Mitchell Goodman, Knopf, 1970; *The Living Underground: An Anthology of Contemporary American Poetry,* edited by Hugh Fox, Whitston Publishing, 1973; *Eleven Young Poets,* edited by Harry Smith, Horizon Press, 1975. Contributor of poetry to numerous magazines and journals, including *Arts in Society, Aspect,* and *West End.* Editor of various publications, including *Communicator, Observer,* and *Nostoc.*

SIDELIGHTS: Costley wrote in 1969: "I went through Zen/romanticism and language reduction until 1963-64 when my wife and working gradually woke me up. Since then I've broken ambiguity addictions and unwound. Jeffers, Mayakovsky, and Brecht did things for me at each stage; now I think I'm almost on my own. I write almost every poem in one draft in fifteen minutes. I learned to make my poems readable and alive by giving public readings—anywhere: on church steps, at meetings, in schoolrooms, on ladders, at gallery openings, on sidewalks, over the radio. I plan to keep it up and develop politically—with or without my generation."

He later stated (in 1977): "Education and the events of the past ten years only convince me of two facts: my working class ethnicity (I grew up in Lynn, Massachusetts, in a Scot/Polish family) and that north-northeast small General Electric factory city cannot be ignored or disguised in my work. I see myself as representing a denial of the rural cultural-oligarchic New England literary cultures of Frost and the Lowells, using an urban dialectical-realism based on oral history. But this is a means, not an end, and the work is only just begun; a twentieth-century school of working class urban, realistic, oral poetry is collecting, witnessing the twentieth century's continual fascist outbursts, and our contrary motions."

Bibliographical collections of Costley's papers, letters, and other writings have been established at the Northwestern University Library and in the Charles Olson Collection at the Wilbur Cross Library, University of Connecticut. Recordings of Costley reading his early poems and *Knosh I Cir* are kept at Harvard University's Lamont Library.

BIOGRAPHICAL/CRITICAL SOURCES: Margins, January, 1975; *Suffolk University Journal,* November 9, 1978.

*   *   *

COTT, Nancy F. 1945-

PERSONAL: Born November 8, 1945, in Philadelphia, Pa.; daughter of Max E. (a textile manufacturer) and Estelle (Hollander) Falik; married Leland Cott (an architect), August 31, 1969; children: Joshua. *Education:* Cornell University, B.A. (magna cum laude), 1967; Brandeis University, Ph.D., 1974. *Home:* 172 Hancock St., Cambridge, Mass.

02139. *Office:* American Studies Program, Yale University, New Haven, Conn. 06520.

CAREER: Wheaton College, Norton, Mass., part-time instructor in history, 1971; Clark University, Worcester, Mass., part-time instructor in history, 1972; Wellesley College, Wellesley, Mass., part-time instructor in history, 1973-74; Yale University, New Haven, Conn., assistant professor of history and American studies, 1975—, co-chairwoman of Women's Studies Task Force, 1976—. Lecturer at Boston Public Library, spring, 1975, and at colleges and universities. Member of advisory board of Arthur and Elizabeth Schlesinger Library on the History of Women in America, at Radcliffe College, 1977—.

MEMBER: American Historical Association, American Studies Association, Berkshire Conference of Women Historians, Coordinating Committee of Women in the Historical Profession, Phi Beta Kappa, Phi Kappa Phi. *Awards, honors:* Rockefeller Foundation humanities fellow, 1978-79; fellow in law and history at Harvard University, School of Law, 1978-79.

WRITINGS: Root of Bitterness: Documents of the Social History of American Women, Dutton, 1972; *The Bonds of Womanhood: "Woman's Sphere" in New England, 1780-1835,* Yale University Press, 1977. Contributor of articles and reviews to history and women's studies journals. Member of editorial board of *American Quarterly* and *Feminist Studies,* both 1977—, *Journal of Social History,* 1978—; member of editorial advisory board of *The Correspondence of Lydia Maria Child,* University of Massachusetts, 1977—.

WORK IN PROGRESS: Research on women and feminism in the United States, 1920-1970.

*   *   *

COTTAM, Keith M. 1941-

PERSONAL: Born February 13, 1941, in St. George, Utah; son of Von Bunker (a plumber) and Adrene (McArthur) Cottam; married Laurel Springer, June 16, 1961; children: Mark Patrick, Lisa Diane, Andrea Jill, Brian Lowell. *Education:* Utah State University, B.S., 1963; Pratt Institute, M.S., 1965; further graduate study at Brigham Young University, 1967-72. *Religion:* Church of Jesus Christ of Latter-day Saints (Mormons). *Home:* 528 Idlewood Lane, Knoxville, Tenn. 37919. *Office:* Undergraduate Library, University of Tennessee, Knoxville, Tenn. 37916.

CAREER: Brooklyn Public Library, Brooklyn, N.Y., trainee, 1963-65, assistant instructor and adult services librarian, 1965; Southern Illinois University, Edwardsville, assistant social science librarian, 1965-67; Brigham Young University, Provo, Utah, social sciences librarian and head of Social Sciences Library, 1967-72, supervisor of library technician program, 1969-72; University of Tennessee, Knoxville, 1972—, currently assistant director of libraries for Undergraduate Library and associate professor of library and information science. Member of management team and executive committee of General Oil Tools, Inc., 1969-73. Adviser to National Institute of Administration (Saigon, Vietnam), 1971. Conducts and participates in workshops; information resources consultant.

MEMBER: American Library Association, Tennessee Library Association, East Tennessee Library Association, Phi Kappa Phi, Beta Phi Mu. *Awards, honors:* Fellowship from Council on Library Resources, 1975-76.

WRITINGS: Health, Physical Education, and Recreation: A Guide to Research in the Brigham Young University Library (monograph), Brigham Young University Press, 1971; (with Robert W. Pelton) *Writer's Research Handbook: A Guide to Sources,* A. S. Barnes, 1977. Contributor to *American Biking Atlas and Touring Guide.* Contributor of more than twenty-five articles and reviews to professional journals and to *Bike World.* Associate editor of *News and Views* (at Brigham Young University), 1968-69, editor, 1969-70; member of editorial board of *Utah Libraries,* 1970-72, assistant editor, 1970-71, editor, 1971-72; editor of *Newsletter* (of East Tennessee Library Association), 1974—.

SIDELIGHTS: Cottam writes: "My career progress as a librarian and my modest success as a writer are firmly rooted in family heritage. My ancestors were Mormon pioneers—industrious, rugged, and committed to principles. I try not to waver from that heritage. I have deep respect for the knowledge and wisdom born of experience, and no matter how successful or ambitious I think I am, I still have mountains to climb. I'm a loner, but conscious of it."

*   *   *

COURTHION, Pierre (Barthelemy) 1902-

PERSONAL: Born January 14, 1902, in Geneva, Switzerland; son of Louis (a journalist) and Elisa (Bocquet) Courthion; married Pierrette Karcher, April 26, 1927; children: Sabine (Mrs. Tristan d'Oelsnitz). *Education:* Attended University of Geneva, 1920, Ecole des Beaux Arts, Paris, 1921, and Ecole du Louvre, 1923. *Home:* 11 rue des Marronniers, 75016 Paris, France.

CAREER: L'Eclair, Paris, France, editor, 1923-25; League of Nations, International Institute for Intellectual Cooperation, Geneva, Switzerland, joint chief of arts section, 1928-32; Cite Universitaire de Paris, Paris, France, director of Swiss foundation, 1933-39; director of literary collections "Le Cri de la France," 1940-45, and "Les Grandes Artistes racontes par euxmemes et leurs amis," 1940-46; Association Internationale des Critiques d'Art, Paris, vice-president, 1945-61, member of administrative council, 1962; Syndicat de la presse artistique de France, Paris, vice-president, 1965-78. Archaeologist for Valais canton, 1933-37; director of Archaeological Museum of Valere, 1933-37; member of international jury for the Auschwitz monument, 1959, and jury of International Guggenheim Prize, 1960; lecturer at Princeton University, Yale University, New York University, and other American universities; director of missions under direction of French ministries of culture and foreign affairs to Brazil, 1963, Venezuela, 1965, the United States, 1967, Canada, 1969, and Japan and the Republic of Korea, 1973. Producer of films on art and artists, "Ingres peintre du nu," "Ingres portraitiste," and "Georges Rouault."

WRITINGS—In English: (Author of introduction) *Gauguin (1848-1903),* Volume II, Faber, 1949; (editor with Pierre Cailler) *Manet raconti par lui-meme et par ses amis,* two volumes, Cailler, 1953, translation by Michael Ross published as *Portrait of Manet by Himself and His Contemporaries,* Roy, 1960; *Montmartre,* Skira, 1955, translation by Stuart Gilbert published under same title, Skira, 1956; *Paris d'autrefois: De Fouquet a Daumier,* Skira, 1957, translation by James Emmons published as *Paris in the Past: From Fouquet to Daumier,* Skira, 1957; *Paris des temps nouveaux: De l'impressionisme a nos jours,* Skira, 1957, translation by Gilbert published as *Paris in Our Time: From Impressionism to the Present Day,* Skira, 1957; *La Peinture flamande, de Van Eyck a Bruegel,* Somogy, 1958, translation by Jonathan Griffin published as *Flemish Painting,* Thames & Hudson, 1958.

Le Romantisme, Skira, 1961, translation by Gilbert published as *Romanticism*, Skiva, 1961; *Georges Rouault*, Flammarion, 1962, translation published under same title, Abrams, 1962; *Edouard Manet*, Abrams, 1962; *Georges Seurat*, Editions Cercle d'art, 1969, translation by Norbert Guterman of original French manuscript published under same title, Abrams, 1968; *Impressionism*, translated by John Shepley from original French manuscript, Abrams, 1972, abridged edition, 1977.

Other works: *La Vie de Delacroix* (title means ''The Life of Delacroix''), Gallimard, 1927; *Panorama de la peinture contemporaine* (title means ''Panorama of Contemporary Painting''), Kra, 1927; *Nicolas Poussin*, Plon, 1929; *Courbet*, two volumes, Floury & Cailler, 1931; *Claude Lorrain*, Floury, 1932; *Henri Matisse*, Rieder, 1934; *Geneve; ou, Le Portrait des Toepffer*, Grasset, 1936; *Delacroix*, Skira, 1940; *Henri Rousseau: Le Douanier*, Skira, 1944; *Bonnard: Peintre du merveilleux*, Marguerat, 1945; *Gericault*, Cailler, 1947; *Peintres d'aujourd'hui* (title means ''Painters of Today''), Cailler, 1952; (with Maurice Herzog and others) *La Montagne* (title means ''The Mountain''), Librairie Larousse, 1956; *L'Art independant: Panorama international de 1900 a nos jours* (title means ''Independent Art: International Panorama From 1900 to Our Time''), Albin-Michel, 1958.

Leon Zack, G. Fall, 1961; *Autour de l'impressionnisme*, Nouvelles Editions Francaises, 1964; *Paris: De sa naissance a nos jours* (title means ''Paris: From Her Birth to Our Time''), Somogy, 1966; *Paris: Histoire d'une ville* (title means ''Paris: History of a City''), Somogy, 1966; *Elisabeth Kaufmann*, Kossodo, 1967; *Debre*, G. Fall, 1967; *Utrillo et Montmartre*, Fabbri, 1967; *Charles Rollier*, Editions Ides et Calendes, 1969; (author of introduction) *Felice Filippini*, I.L.T.E., 1971; *Soutine peintre du dechirant*, Denoel, 1973; *Pablo Gargallo*, Vingtieme Siecle, 1973; *Artigas et la ceramique d'aujourd'hui* (title means ''Artigas and Ceramics Today''), Poligrafa, 1977. Writer and compiler of a text with slides, *L'Ecole de Paris, de Picasso a nos jours.*

WORK IN PROGRESS: Vision d'un demi-siecle (memoires; title means ''Vision of Half a Century''); *Bizarreries.*

* * *

COURTINE, Robert 1910-
(La Reyniere, Savarin)

PERSONAL: Born May 16, 1910, in Paris, France; son of Benjamin (a manufacturer's agent) and Marthe (Julien) Courtine; married Elisabeth Mauron, November 10, 1936. *Education:* Attended public schools in Paris, France. *Home:* 49 rue Raspail, 92270 Bois-Colombes, France.

CAREER: Journalist, writer, and composer. Gourmet columnist for French newspapers and magazines, including *Le Monde*, beginning 1949, *La Vie francaise*, beginning 1960, *Depeche du Midi*, beginning 1961, *Jours de France*, beginning 1970, and *Touring Club*, beginning 1972. *Member:* Societe des gens de lettres, Academie Rabelais, Societe des auteurs, compositeurs et editeurs, Association des critiques de music-hall, Academie Malt Whisky. *Awards, honors:* Prize from International Association of Gourmet Journalists, 1954, for *Le Plus doux des peches;* Prix Rabelais, 1960; Prix Epicure, 1977; Officier du merite agricole, 1978; member of various other orders of knighthood, including Commanderie des cordons bleus, Commanderie du Bontemps, and Jurade de Saint-Emilion.

WRITINGS—In English: (Under pseudonym La Reyniere) *Cent Merveilles de la cuisine francaise*, Seuil, 1971, translation by Derek Coltman published as *The Hundred Glories of French Cooking*, Farrar, Straus, 1973; (compiler; under pseudonym La Reyniere) *Mes Repas les plus etonnants*, Laffont, 1973, translation by Jane Guicharnaud published as *Feasts of a Militant Gastronome*, recipes translated by Madelaine Damman, Morrow, 1974; (under pseudonym La Reyniere) *Le Cahier de recettes de Madame Maigret*, preface by Georges Simenon, Laffont, 1974, translation by Mary Manheim published as *Madame Maigret's Recipes*, illustrations by Nikolaus E. Wolff, Harcourt, 1975; *Guide Courtine: Bon Appetit a Paris*, Lyle Stuart, 1976, translation by Rose L. H. Finkenstaedt published as *Guide Courtine: A Guide to Paris Restaurants*, Lyle Stuart, 1976.

Other works: *Un Gourmand a Paris*, B. Grasset, 1959; *Un Nouveau savoir manger*, Grasset, 1960; (under pseudonym Savarin) *La Vraie Cuisine francaise simple et anecdotique, avec quelques-unes des meilleures recettes etrangeres*, Collection Marabout, 1960, new edition, 1967; *Les Dimanches de la cuisine*, La Table ronde, 1962; (under pseudonym Savarin) *La Cuisine du monde entier*, Gerard, 1963; *Goncourt a table*, Fayard, 1963; *Quatre Cent Cinquante Recettes originales a base de fruits*, Editions de la Pensee moderne, 1963; *Mangez-vous francais?*, SEDIMO (Paris), 1965; (with Henry Clos-Jouve) *Ou manger quoi*, Hachette, 1967; (with Prosper Montagne) *Nouveau Larousse gastronomique*, Larousse, 1967; *Toutes les boissons et les recettes au vin*, Larousse, 1968; *L'Assassin est a votre table*, La Table ronde, 1969; *Cinq Mille Recettes, cuisine de France et du monde entier*, Centre national du livre familial, 1969; *La Cuisine des fleurs*, illustrations by Henri Samouilov, D. Halevy, 1969.

(With Jean Desmur) *Anthologie de la litterature gastronomique*, Trevise, 1970; (with Desmur) *Anthologie de la poesie gourmande*, Trevise, 1970; *La Gastronomie*, Presses universitaires de France, 1970; (with Francoise Condat) *Guide de l'homme arrive*, illustrations by Jean-Denis Malcles, La Table ronde, 1970; (with Celine Vence) *La Cuisine au fromage*, Denoel, 1971; *Les Vacances dans votre assiette*, Fayard, 1971; (with Vence) *Les Fruits de mer*, Denoel, 1972; *Dictionnaire des fromages*, Larousse, 1972, new edition published as *Larousse des fromages*, Larousse, 1973; (with Vence) *Les Poissons de mer*, Denoel, 1972; *Poulardes et poulets*, Denoel, 1972; (with Pierre Jean Vaillard) *L'Escargot est dans l'escalier*, La Table ronde, 1972; (with Vence) *La Cuisine au vin*, Denoel, 1972; (compiler with Vence) *Les Grands maitres de la cuisine francaise du Moyen Age a Alexandre Dumas*, Bordas, 1972; (with Vence) *Grillades et barbecue*, Denoel, 1972; (with Vence) *Les Salades*, Denoel, 1972; *Un Cognac, un cigare, une histoire*, illustrations by Alde, Editions de la Pensee moderne, 1973; (editor with Maurice Edmond Suilland) *Cuisine et vins de France*, new edition, Larousse, 1974; *Deux Cent Recettes des meilleurs cuisiniers de France*, Michel, 1976; *Balzac a Table*, Laffont, 1976; *Zola a Table*, Laffont, 1978; (with Vence) *The Grand Masters of French Cuisine: Five Centuries of Great Cooking*, Putnam, 1978.

Also author of introductions to cookbooks and *Le Plus doux des peches*, 1952.

SIDELIGHTS: When Robert Courtine, France's leading gourmet, began his career as a political writer, he discovered he was more interested in describing what the politicians ate than what they had to say, according to Sanche de Gramont in *New York Times Magazine.* He had found his *metier.*

It is Courtine's conviction that ''only gourmets can be great novelists,'' he told de Gramont. ''Balzac, Proust, and Simenon prove that the greatest novelists are the greatest eaters, for the mind's roots are in the stomach." He chose the pseudonym La Reyniere in honor of Grimod de la Reyniere, the eighteenth-century French gourmet.

Courtine's style of writing has been called "vitriolic." Reviewing *The Hundred Glories of French Cooking,* Phyllis Hanes wrote: "It is a knowledgeable, opinionated, and thoroughly entertaining book. Although it is organized by menu, I found the reading better than the recipes."

BIOGRAPHICAL/CRITICAL SOURCES: New York Times Magazine, July 6, 1967; *Saturday Review,* November 20, 1973; *Christian Science Monitor,* December 27, 1973; *Time,* January 1, 1979.

* * *

COX, Joseph W(illiam) 1937-

PERSONAL: Born May 26, 1937, in Hagerstown, Md.; son of Joseph F. and Ruth (Silvers) Cox; married Regina M. Bollinger, 1963; children: Matthew, Andrew, Abigail. *Education:* University of Maryland, B.A., 1959, Ph.D., 1967. *Office:* Department of History, Towson State University, Baltimore, Md. 21204.

CAREER: Towson State University, Baltimore, Md., instructor, 1964-67, assistant professor, 1967-69, associate professor, 1969-72, professor of history, 1972—, dean of social sciences, 1969-72, dean of continuing education, 1972-75, vice-president for academic affairs, 1977—.

WRITINGS: Champion of Southern Federalism: Robert G. Harper of South Carolina, Kennikat, 1972; *The Corps of Engineers: The Early National Experience, 1783-1812,* Department of the Army, Government Printing Office, 1978. Member of board of editors of *Maryland Historical Magazine.*

WORK IN PROGRESS: The Maryland Historical Society: A Case Study in Cultural Philanthropy.

SIDELIGHTS: Cox comments: "I am interested in Canadian history, the history of higher education, and the history of technology."

* * *

COZZENS, James Gould 1903-1978

OBITUARY NOTICE—See index for *CA* sketch: Born August 19, 1903, in Chicago, Ill.; died August 9, 1978, in Stuart, Fla. Educator and author of novels and short stories. Cozzens was a traditional writer whose precise style and rigid moral outlook earned him praise from some critics and the disdain of others. *Guard of Honor* won the Pulitzer Prize in 1948, but his best-known work was probably *By Love Possessed,* a runaway bestseller. *By Love Possessed* received the William Dean Howells Medal in 1960 and was made into a motion picture. Cozzens contributed short stories to magazines, including *Saturday Evening Post, Scribner's, Collier's,* and *Woman's Home Companion.* Obituaries and other sources: *Current Biography,* Wilson, 1949, October, 1978; *The Oxford Companion to American Literature,* 4th edition, Oxford University Press, 1965; *The Reader's Encyclopedia,* 2nd edition, Crowell, 1965; *Encyclopedia of World Literature in the Twentieth Century,* updated edition, Ungar, 1967; *The Penguin Companion to American Literature,* McGraw, 1971; *Cassell's Encyclopedia of World Literature,* revised edition, 1973; *Who's Who in America,* 40th edition, Marquis, 1978; *Washington Post,* August 19, 1978; *Newsweek,* August 28, 1978; *Time,* August 28, 1978; *Publishers Weekly,* September 4, 1978.

CRAIG, H(enry) A(rmitage) L(lewellyn) 1921(?)-1978

OBITUARY NOTICE: Born c. 1921 in West Cork, Ireland; died October 24, 1978, in Rome, Italy. Screenwriter and author. Among his best known filmscripts are "Anzio," "The Charge of the Light Brigade," and "Barry Lyndon." Craig also wrote a book, *Bilal,* and collaborated on a series of ballad-operas. Obituaries and other sources: *New York Times,* November 17, 1978.

* * *

CRAIG, Robert D(ean) 1934-

PERSONAL: Born April 16, 1934, in Hamilton, Ohio; son of Orville and Leona (Thomas) Craig; married Judith Blackwelder; children: Larry, Lisa, Tim, Cathy, David, Jenny. *Education:* University of Cincinnati, B.A., 1962, M.A., 1964; further graduate study at University of Innsbruck, 1964; University of Utah, Ph.D., 1966. *Religion:* Church of Jesus Christ of Latter-day Saints (Mormons). *Home:* 55-474 Moana St., Laie, Hawaii 96762. *Office:* Brigham Young University—Hawaii Campus, Box 44, Laie, Hawaii 96762.

CAREER: Atomic Energy Commission, Cincinnati, Ohio, office manager, 1952-58; Texas A & M University, Bryan, assistant professor, 1966-67; Brigham Young University—Hawaii Campus, Laie, professor of history, 1967—, David O. McKay Lecturer, 1969. *Military service:* U.S. Army, 1956-58; became sergeant. *Member:* American Historical Association, Mediaeval Academy of America, Cincinnati Historical Association, Phi Alpha Theta. *Awards, honors:* Poetry awards include award from National Canticle Society, 1964, for "My Sunday Walk."

WRITINGS: Revolutionary Soldiers in Hamilton County, Ohio, Ohio Historical Association, 1965; *An Old-French Workbook,* Brigham Young University—Hawaii Campus Press, 1965, 2nd edition, 1978; *The Life of St. Alexis,* Gallic Press, 1975; (translator) Edmond de Bovis, *Tahitian Culture Before the Arrival of the Europeans,* Brigham Young University—Hawaii Campus Press, 1976; *Index au Bulletin de la Societe des Etudes Oceaniennes* (title means "Index to Bulletin of the Society of Oceanic Studies"), Brigham Young University—Hawaii Campus Press, 1977; *Captain Cook in the Pacific,* Brigham Young University—Hawaii Campus Press, 1978; (editor) Robert Thomson, *The Marquesas: Their Description and Early History,* Brigham Young University—Hawaii Campus Press, 1978; *History of Tahiti,* Brigham Young University—Hawaii Campus Press, 1979. Editor of *Pacific Studies: A Journal Devoted to the Pacific—Its Islands and Adjacent Countries.*

SIDELIGHTS: Craig writes: "I have had extensive travel in Europe, researching materials in the British Museum, Bibliotheque Nationale, and others. I am interested in Classical and Medieval studies as well as Polynesian culture, and have presented numerous talks before various groups on genealogical research, as a result of the 'Roots' phenomenon. I have contributed poetry to various groups and have won national poetry awards."

* * *

CRANE, Robert Dickson 1929-

PERSONAL: Born March 26, 1929, in Cambridge, Mass.; son of John Bever (an economics educator) and Catherine (a book seller; maiden name, Dickson) Crane; married Sigrid Ruedel (a parliamentarian), March 5, 1951; children: Marietta, Hanns, Mark. *Education:* Northwestern University,

B.A. (summa cum laude), 1956; graduate study at University of Munich, 1955-56; Harvard University, J.D., 1959. *Politics:* Independent conservative. *Religion:* Independent Roman Catholic. *Home and office:* 511 Kramer Dr., Vienna, Va. 22180.

CAREER: Admitted to the Bar of Washington, D.C.; U.S. Air Force, Defense Research division, China affairs, department deputy head, 1959-61; Georgetown University Center for Strategic Studies, Washington, D.C., research principal, 1962-66; Hudson Institute, Croton-on-Hudson, N.Y., project director, 1966-69; U.S. Department of State, Washington, D.C., policy planner and systems analyst, 1969-73; independent investment banking consultant, 1973—. Co-founder, corporate secretary, and director, American Indian National Bank, Washington, D.C. Chairman, Fairfax County Civil Rights Committee, 1964-66. *Military Service:* U.S. Army, 1950-53. *Member:* Phi Beta Kappa. *Awards, honors:* American Institute of Aeronautics and Astronautics fellowship, 1961; American Society of International Law fellowship, 1961.

WRITINGS: (Editor) *Soviet Nuclear Strategy: A Critical Appraisal,* Center for Strategic Studies, 1963; *Detente: Cold War Strategies in Transition,* Praeger, 1965; *The Crane Report: Building Native American Self-Determination,* Office of Management and Budget, The White House, 1971; *Planning the Future of Saudi Arabia: A Model for Achieving National Priorities,* Holt, 1978.

Contributor: Hans Baade, editor, *The Soviet Impact on International Law,* Oceana, 1965; F. R. Barnett, Mott, and Neff, editors, *Peace and War in the Modern Age: Premises, Myths and Realities,* Doubleday, 1965; John Erickson, editor, *The Military-Technical Revolution: Its Impact on Strategy and Foreign Policy,* Praeger, 1966; James Dougherty and John Lehman, editors, *Prospects for Arms Control,* MacFadden-Bartell, 1966; Denis Dirscherl, editor, *The New Russia: Communism in Evolution,* Pflaum/Standard, 1968; Wilhelm Cornides, editor, *Die Internationale Politik, 1962,* Verlag Oldenbourg (Munchen-Wien), 1968; *Assessing the Future and Policy Planning,* Gordon & Breach, 1972; Lorna Demidoff and Michael Jennings, editors, *The Complete Siberian Husky,* Howell, 1978. Contributor of over forty-five articles to magazines and professional journals, including *Fortune, Reporter, Federal Bar Journal,* and *American Journal of International Law.*

WORK IN PROGRESS: The Profit Makers: Building a Quadrilateral World, completion expected in 1980.

SIDELIGHTS: Crane writes: "My background as a Cherokee Indian with an inherited responsibility to the tribe has produced a lifelong interest in the dynamics of civilization as a guarantor of justice. At the age of eleven, I wrote 150 pages of an intended one thousand-page book, entitled *From Savagery to Civilization.* The book ended when the budding civilization abandoned its culture and reverted to savagery. The next ten years I spent studying the intellectual dynamics of resistance against the worst perversions of Western civilization. As a result, I was imprisoned once in Mexico in 1944 and twice in Eastern Europe in Communist concentration camps. The decade of the 1950's was devoted largely to acquiring a bilingual command of Russian and the first degree ever issued in the United States on combined Soviet and Chinese area studies.

"A decade in American think tanks during the 1960's convinced me that Communist global strategies of political and military expansion can be countered best by positive strategies to build capitalism. Since capitalism is nothing but the economic dimension of liberty, its power requires that the citizens abide by the principles of liberty. Foremost among these is the responsibility of each individual to produce as much as he consumes. The power of voting blocs organized to rip off the producers in society will destroy the profit incentives that power capitalist production. This is another way of saying that if there are solutions to injustice in this world, they lie not in economic or political systems but in the moral sensitivities and discipline of each individual human being. Someday I will say this more fully in a series of novels patterned after Tolkien's *Lord of the Rings* and based in ancient Arabia."

* * *

CRAWFORD, Kenneth G(ale) 1902-

PERSONAL: Born May 27, 1902, in Sparta, Wis.; son of Robert Levy (a dentist and bacteriologist) and Madge (Gale) Crawford; married Elisabeth Bartholomew, July 21, 1928; children: William, Gale. *Education:* Beloit College, B.A., 1924. *Politics:* None. *Religion:* None. *Home:* 1412 30th St. N.W., Washington, D.C. 20007.

CAREER: United Press (now United Press International), New York City, reporter and bureau manager for the midwest region, 1924-27, Washington correspondent, 1927-29; *Buffalo Times,* Buffalo, N.Y., author of column "Politics," 1929-32; *New York Post,* New York City, Washington bureau chief, 1932-40; *P.M.* (newspaper), New York City, Washington bureau chief, 1940-43; *Newsweek,* Washington, D.C., war correspondent from North Africa, Italy, the Middle East, England, and France, 1943-44, Washington correspondent, 1944-49, contributing editor, 1949-50, national affairs editor, 1950-55, Washington bureau chief, 1955-60, author of column, "Washington," 1960-70, senior editor, 1970; free-lance writer, 1971—. *Member:* American Newspaper Guild (president, 1939-40), National Press Club, Overseas Writers (Washington, D.C.), Washington Press Club, Federal City Club, Players Club. *Awards, honors:* LL.D. from Olivet College, 1940; Commendations from U.S. Army, and U.S. Navy, 1944, for war correspondence; French Liberation Medal, 1944; Litt. D. from Beloit College, 1954.

WRITINGS: The Pressure Boys: The Inside Story of Lobbying in America, Messner, 1939, reprinted, Arno, 1974; *Report on North Africa,* Farrar & Rinehart, 1943. Contributor to national magazines and newspapers, including *Nation, New Republic,* and *Saturday Evening Post.*

SIDELIGHTS: Crawford was the first correspondent to land with the first infantry attack during the D-Day offensive.

* * *

CRAY, Ed(ward) 1933-

PERSONAL: Born July 3, 1933, in Cleveland, Ohio; son of Max (a laundry owner) and Sara (a teacher; maiden name, Shaffer) Cray; married Marjorie Best, 1963 (divorced, 1966); children: Jennifer. *Education:* University of California, Los Angeles, B.A., 1957, graduate study, 1958-59. *Politics:* Democrat. *Religion:* Jewish. *Home:* 10436 Kinnard Ave., Los Angeles, Calif. 90024. *Agent:* Michael Hamilburg, 10840 Lindbrook Ave., #2, Los Angeles, Calif. 90024. *Office:* 10906 Rochester Ave., Los Angeles, Calif. 90024.

CAREER: University of California, Los Angeles, instructor in folklore and folksong, 1958-60; *Frontier,* Los Angeles, Calif., associate editor and business manager, 1961-64; free-lance writer, 1964-65; American Civil Liberties Union of Southern California, Los Angeles, director of publications, 1965-70; Southern California Symphony-Hollywood Bowl Association, Los Angeles, director of publicity and public relations, 1970-71; free-lance writer, 1971—. Senior lecturer at University of Southern California, 1976—; consultant to President's Commission on the Causes of Violence. *Military service:* U.S. Army, 1952-54. *Member:* American Folklore Society, American Civil Liberties Union, California Folklore Society.

WRITINGS: (Editor) *The Anthology of Erotic Restoration Verse,* Brandon House, 1965; (editor) *The Fifteen Plagues of Maidenhead, and Other Forbidden Verse,* Brandon House, 1966; *The Big Blue Line: Police Power Versus Human Rights,* Coward, 1967; (editor) *The Erotic Muse,* Oak Publications, 1967; *Law Enforcement: The Matter of Redress* (monograph), Institute of Modern Legal Thought, 1969; (editor) *Bawdy Ballads,* Anthony Blond, 1970; *In Failing Health: The Medical Crisis and the A.M.A.,* Bobbs-Merrill, 1971; *The Enemy in the Streets,* Doubleday, 1972; *Burden of Proof: The Trial of Juan Corona,* Macmillan, 1973; *Levi's: The History of Levi Strauss & Co.,* Houghton, 1978; *Kodak,* Houghton, 1980.

Has written instructional filmscripts, including "All Bottled Up," 1975, "Teenagers Talk: Getting Through Adolescence," 1976, and "Joey and Me," 1977. Contributor of articles and reviews to folklore, musicology, and law journals, to popular magazines, including *New West, Nation, Change,* and *Viva,* and to newspapers. Copy editor for *Hollywood Reporter,* summer, 1972; editor for City News Service, Los Angeles, 1972-73.

WORK IN PROGRESS: The Chrome Colossus: A History of General Motors.

SIDELIGHTS: Cray writes: "After a frustrating effort in academe—where narrow specialization was demanded—I gratefully turned back to the freedom of news reporting and writing, free-lanced, then took a new direction as director of publications for the American Civil Liberties Union, then as publicity director for the Los Angeles Philharmonic. I am now writing general nonfiction, largely dealing with social issues. The law is a specialty of sorts, though I also review classical music for sundry publications. In the main, I write to effect change in social institutions."

AVOCATIONAL INTERESTS: Model trains, photography.

*   *   *

CREW, Louie 1936-

PERSONAL: Born December 9, 1936, in Anniston, Ala.; son of Erman (a government worker) and Lula (Hagin) Crew. *Education:* Baylor University, B.A., 1958; Auburn University, M.A., 1959; University of Alabama, Ph.D., 1971. *Politics:* Democrat. *Religion:* Episcopalian. *Home:* 701 Orange St., Fort Valley, Ga. 31030. *Office address:* P.O. Box 5203, Fort Valley, Ga. 31030.

CAREER: Master of English and religion at private and public schools in the United States and England, 1959-66; University of Alabama, Tuscaloosa, instructor in English, 1968-70; Experiment in International Living, Putney, Vt., director of independent study in England program, 1970-71; Emory University, Atlanta, Ga., instructor in Upward Bound program, summer, 1971; Chaflin College, Orangeburg, S.C., professor of English, 1971-73; Fort Valley State College, Fort Valley, Ga., associate professor of English,

1973—. Guest professor at Lavender University, 1974. Founder of Integrity (national organization of gay Episcopalians), 1974. Consultant to church sexuality commissions. *Member:* National Council of Teachers of English (member of board of directors), South Atlantic Modern Language Association, National Gay Task Force (board member), Fort Valley Writers (founder). *Awards, honors:* Writing fellow at Wurlitzer Foundation, 1963; National Endowment for the Humanities fellow, 1974, 1977; Fulbright award, 1974-75; Integrity award for outstanding contributions to the Christian understanding of sexuality, 1975.

WRITINGS: (Contributor) W. F. Smith and R. D. Liedlich, editors, *From Thought to Theme,* 4th edition, Harcourt, 1974; (contributor) Karla Jay and Allen Young, editors, *After You're Out: A Gay Survival Book,* Douglas Books, 1975; (contributor) Jim Wickliff, editor, *In Celebration,* Integrity Publications, 1975; "Mister Jones" (one-act play), published in *GPU News,* Volume 4, number 8, June, 1975; (contributor) Lenore Hoffman and Gloria DeSole, editors, *Couples and Careers,* Modern Language Association, 1976; *Sunspots* (poems), Lotus Press, 1976; (editor) *The Gay Academic,* ETC Publications, 1977.

Work represented in anthologies, including *Unexpected: An Anthology,* edited by Jene Ballentine and Nadra Ballentine, Otherworlds Media, 1976; *Human Sexuality: Contemporary Perspectives,* edited by Elanor Morrison and Vera Borosage, Mayfield, 1977. Contributor of more then one hundred stories, poems, and articles to periodicals, including *College English, Christianity and Crisis, Saturday Review,* and *Mid-West Quarterly.* Reading editor of *Notes on Teaching English,* 1973—; founding editor of *Integrity: Gay Episcopal Forum,* 1974-77; guest editor of *College English,* fall, 1974; contributing editor of *Barb,* 1975—, *Margins,* 1975—, and *Journal of Homosexuality,* 1978—.

WORK IN PROGRESS: Black Parables; Queers! For Christ's Sake, poetry.

SIDELIGHTS: Crew writes: "As an academician, I am a generalist with special skills in composition and other forms of applied linguistics. I have written widely about opportunities of minority education (racial, sexual minorities), and the specialized skills required there. I consider myself principally an essayist and a poet, and I frequently address national audiences of linguists, Episcopalians, poetry enthusiasts, and all sorts and conditions of other persons."

*   *   *

CRIST, Judith 1922-

PERSONAL: Born May 22, 1922, in New York, N.Y.; daughter of Solomon and Helen (Schoenberg) Klein; married William B. Crist, 1947; children: Steven Gordon. *Education:* Hunter College (now of the City University of New York), B.A., 1941; Columbia University, M.S., 1945. *Home:* 180 Riverside Dr., New York, N.Y. 10024.

CAREER: State College of Washington (now Washington State University), Pullman, instructor, 1942-44; *New York Herald Tribune,* New York City, reporter, 1945-60, associate drama critic, 1957-60, arts editor, 1960-63, film critic, 1963-66; National Broadcasting Co. (NBC), New York City, "Today Show" film commentator, 1963-73; *New York World Journal Tribune,* New York City, film critic, 1966-67; *T.V. Guide,* New York City, film critic, 1966—. Adjunct professor of critical writing and journalism, Columbia University, 1959—; associated with Education for the arts, 1960-63.

MEMBER: New York Film Critics (past chairman), Society of Film Critics, Columbia University School of Journalism Alumni Association (president, 1967-1969). *Awards, honors:* George Polk Award, 1951; Education Writers Association award, 1952; New York Newspaper Guild award, 1955; New York National Writers Club awards, 1955, 1959, 1963, 1965, 1967.

WRITINGS: The Private Eye, the Cowboy, and the Very Naked Girl: Movies from Cleo to Clyde (nonfiction), Holt, 1968; (contributor) H. H. Hart, editor, *Censorship: For and Against,* Hart, 1971; (contributor) Hart, editor, *Marriage: For and Against,* Hart, 1972; (contributor) P. Nobile, editor, *Favorite Movies,* Macmillan, 1972; *Judith Crist's T.V. Guide to the Movies,* Popular Library, 1974. Contributing editor and film critic for periodicals, including *Playgirl, Saturday Review,* and *New York.* Contributor of articles and reviews to periodicals.

SIDELIGHTS: In an interview with David Paletz in *Film Quarterly,* Judith Crist explained her approach to movie reviewing: "To me movies are very much a mass medium. I do not think that as a whole they can be regarded as an art form because most movies are not art, so why be concerned with the form when you haven't got any art to put into it? And they are one of the most important social factors in our society, and even more important, they are to me the one medium that is an intellectually international medium. . . . And when you say, what do you look for in a movie, I could say you look for quality. I look for content. I am rather old-fashioned. I think that a movie has to say something. . . . I don't think my being a woman makes any difference because, well certainly not in my case because I was a newspaper man and I feel now like a critic. . . . The more you know, the better critic you can be."

Crist further presented her theories in a *TV Guide* article: "Anyone who is a movie critic can't 'hate' movies. He has, in fact, not merely to 'like' movies but to love them with a fanatic's passion. . . . And obviously, to subject yourself to film after film . . . you either have to be the world's foremost masochist—or else you have to be the movie-lover that any film critic worth the label is. . . . Why bother to criticize if you don't care?. . . Critics are people; their opinions are personal. But their subjectivity is, hopefully, tempered by a background, an experience, a knowledge that broadens the value of their viewpoint. . . . We're all critics—but what separates us from the other animals is that our discriminatory reactions go beyond taste, smell and instinct and involve a bit of gray matter. And what separates the professional critic from the other reactors is essentially that he articulates the reactions that the layman is, alas, prone to put in a succinct 'Wow!' or 'Yuch!'. . . Hard to believe, but a critic's major goal is to share the good things, to advocate what he considers quality stuff, to urge others to see what has pleasured or enriched him. There's little joy in negativism, even though, alas, it attracts the most attention."

In a review of *The Private Eye, the Cowboy, and the Very Naked Girl,* Richard R. Lingeman labeled Crist a "good, gutsy critic, a self-styled 'preacher' with a tendency to moralize, who keeps her built-in bunk dectector, zap-the-producer gun, parody-the-plot knife and other critical weapons in fine condition. . . . Her thinking is grooved down the middle of the intellectual road, which means it is on the *Consumer Reports,* rather than the *Partisan Review,* level of discourse." Of her book Lingeman noted that, "taken in well-spaced doses . . . these collected reviews are an often sprightly running commentary on our cinematic times, of

special interest to the presumably numerous movie-goers who are disciples of Crist."

BIOGRAPHICAL/CRITICAL SOURCES: Film Quarterly, winter, 1968; *New York Times Book Review,* December 29, 1968; *TV Guide,* August 29, 1970.

*   *   *

CROFT, Sutton
See LUNN, Arnold

*   *   *

CRONLEY, Jay 1943-

PERSONAL: Born November 9, 1943, in Lincoln, Neb.; son of John Wilson (a writer and sports editor) and Bess (Pock) Cronley; married Elizabeth Reger (divorced); married Connie Condray (a university teacher and writer), July 30, 1971; children: (first marriage) Cinnamon. *Education:* University of Oklahoma, B.A., 1966. *Residence:* Tulsa, Okla. *Agent:* Mel Berger, William Morris Agency, 1350 Ave. of the Americas, New York, N.Y. 10019. *Office:* *Tulsa Tribune,* P.O. Box 1770, Tulsa, Okla. 74102.

CAREER: Merrill, Lynch, Pierce, Fenner & Smith, Tulsa, Okla., stockbroker, 1968-70; *Tulsa Tribune,* Tulsa, Okla., author of column "Cronley at Large," 1970—. Faculty member at University of Tulsa. *Awards, honors:* Nonfiction awards from *Playboy,* 1975, for a story about Houston, and 1977, for a camping story.

WRITINGS: Fall Guy (novel), Doubleday, 1978; *Good Vibes* (novel), Doubleday, 1979. Contributor of about twenty articles to *Playboy, Esquire,* and *Sports Illustrated.*

WORK IN PROGRESS: Another novel.

SIDELIGHTS: Cronley writes: "My career has been a fairly normal progression, I think. You read five years, then work for a newspaper, then write for magazines, and then you write a book.

"I like to write about serious things with a little smile. I am not a bad writer when I'm hungry—starvation is the only motivation I know of.

"*Fall Guy* was about a kid who went off to college to play football. It's a funny book about a grim subject. If a kid doesn't produce, the hell with him. It's condensed life. The point is, life shouldn't be condensed. The other book, *Good Vibes,* is about a fairly grim subject, gambling, but I think the seriousness comes out only between the lines. I think it's a funny novel. There's not much humor writing being done any more, except nonfiction. I wonder why."

BIOGRAPHICAL/CRITICAL SOURCES: Tulsa, April, 1978.

*   *   *

CROXFORD, Leslie 1944-

PERSONAL: Born August 10, 1944, in Alexandria, Egypt; came to the United States in 1978; son of Frank S. F. (a British Army officer) and Rosette (Yerouchalmi) Croxford. *Education:* Selwyn College, Cambridge, B.A., 1966, M.A., 1970; Clare College, Cambridge, Ph.D., 1971. *Home:* 420 Riverside Dr., #1-H, New York, N.Y. 10025. *Agent:* Harold Matson Co., Inc., 22 East 40th St., New York, N.Y. 10016. *Office:* Department of English, Douglass College, Rutgers University, New Brunswick, N.J. 08903.

CAREER: Cambridge University, Cambridge, England, supervisor in history at Selwyn College, 1968-72; Eton College, Windsor, England, history teacher, 1969; free-lance writer, 1972-77; Brookside College, Cambridge, head of academic department, 1977; Rutgers University, New Brunswick, N.J., assistant professor of English at Douglass College, 1978—. *Awards, honors:* Harper-Wood creative writing student at St. John's College, Cambridge, 1971-72; British Arts Council grant, 1974.

WRITINGS: Solomon's Folly (novel), Chatto & Windus, 1974, Vanguard, 1977.

WORK IN PROGRESS: Another novel.

SIDELIGHTS: Croxford writes: "I agree with W. H. Auden's remark that the relationship between an author's work and his life is either so obvious as to require no comment, or so complex as to preclude comment. All I want to say about myself is that I write novels; and all I want others to know about me is that I write novels—I hope good ones."

*   *   *

CRUMBAKER, Alice 1911-
(Allison Baker)

PERSONAL: Born September 13, 1911, in Pittsburgh, Pa.; daughter of John (an insurance company president) and Anne (Feidt) Eibeck; married Herbert Crumbaker (a dentist), June 15, 1937; children: Barbara (Mrs. Vicente Teves), Susan (Mrs. Robert Maloney), Gregory, Jeffrey. *Education:* University of Pittsburgh, B.S., 1932; also attended Western Pennsylvania School for the Deaf, 1932-33. *Religion:* Roman Catholic. *Home:* 822 Center Ave., Pittsburgh, Pa. 15202. *Agent:* Henry Morrison, Inc., 58 West 10th Ave., New York, N.Y. 10011.

CAREER: Florida State School for the Deaf and the Blind, St. Augustine, classroom teacher of the deaf and physical education instructor, 1933-37.

WRITINGS: (Under pseudonym Allison Baker) *Asya* (historical romance), Dell, 1978. Contributor to *Volta Review* and *Extension.*

WORK IN PROGRESS: A novel set in the Philippines at about the time of Ferdinand Marcos's takeover as dictator.

SIDELIGHTS: Alice Crumbaker comments: "I have traveled extensively in the Philippines, the Caribbean, and Europe. When I visited Haiti, nobody could answer any of my questions except to say the French were thrown out about 1793 and Haiti became the first black republic in the new world. So, curious, I went home and spent years in research and found its history so fascinating that I had to write *Asya.* Since history repeats itself, if the powers that be had delved into some of Haiti's history, they never would have sent our army into Vietnam, for they would have known we didn't have a chance to win."

AVOCATIONAL INTERESTS: Classical music, cooking, swimming, tennis, ballroom dancing.

*   *   *

CUFF, Barry
See KOSTE, Robert Francis

*   *   *

CULLIGAN, Joe
See CULLIGAN, Matthew J(oseph)

CULLIGAN, Matthew J(oseph) 1918-
(Joe Culligan)

PERSONAL: Born June 25, 1918, in New York, N.Y.; son of Matthew and Sarah J. (Hogan) Culligan; married Doris Dernberger, May, 1946 (divorced); children: Kerry Matthew, Susan, Carolyn, Eileen. *Education:* Attended Columbia University, 1945. *Home and office:* 160 East 38th St., New York, N.Y. 10016. *Agent:* William Morris Agency, 1350 Ave. of the Americas, New York, N.Y. 10019.

CAREER: Hearst Magazines, New York City, in advertising sales, 1945-50; advertising director, Ziff-Davis Publications, 1951-52; National Broadcasting Corp. (NBC), New York City, sales manager, NBC-TV, 1952-53, national sales manager, 1954-55, vice-president and sales director, 1955-56, executive vice-president, NBC-Radio, 1956-62; president, Curtis Publishing, 1962-64, chairman of board of directors, 1964-65; president, Mutual Broadcasting System, 1966-68; founder and president, Culligan Communications Corp., 1968-70; president, Diebold Group, 1970-71; Teletape Corp., New York City, president, 1970—. Member of board of directors of Chemway Corp. Associated with U.S. Information Agency, 1969; chairman of Phaedra Publishers. *Military service:* U.S. Army, Infantry, 1943-45; served in Europe; became first lieutenant. *Member:* Apawamis Club, Pine Valley Golf Club, Key Largo Anglers Club, Sky Club.

WRITINGS: The Curtis-Culligan Story: From Cyrus to Horace to Joe, Crown, 1970; *How to Kill Stress Before It Kills You,* Grosset, 1977; *Horrid Horoscopes,* Crown, 1977; *How to Be a Billion-Dollar Persuader,* St. Martin's, 1979; *Quest for the Galloping Hogan,* Newsweek, 1979. Editorial chairman of *Town Crier.*

WORK IN PROGRESS: How to Prepare Your Mind, Body, and Emotions for Surgery, The Suicide of the Competitive EDT System, and *I Could Have Loved You, Roundeye,* all to be completed in 1980.

SIDELIGHTS: Culligan writes: "I became a writer, after twenty years as a communications executive, to establish a new base of credibility for later expressions on the failures of our system to provide for the dependent young and indigent old."

AVOCATIONAL INTERESTS: Golf, horseback riding, fishing, trap shooting, swimming.

BIOGRAPHICAL/CRITICAL SOURCES: Nation, June 26, 1978.

*   *   *

CUMBERLEGE, Vera 1908-

PERSONAL: Born February 18, 1908, in Stanwell, England; daughter of Sir Alexander and Gladys (Watkins) Gibbons; married Geoffrey F. J. Cumberlege (a publisher), November 30, 1927; children: four. *Education:* Attended private school in England. *Religion:* Church of England. *Residence:* Horsted Keynes, Sussex, England.

CAREER: Writer, 1965—. Justice of the peace for East Sussex, 1952-67.

WRITINGS—For children: The Grey Apple Tree, Deutsch, 1965; *Carry a Long Knife,* Deutsch, 1969; *Shipwreck,* Deutsch, 1974; *Trapped by the Tide and Other Stories,* Deutsch, 1977.

Also author of religious plays published by Oxford University Press, including *Come and Behold Him, He Came Unto His Own,* and *Crown of Glory.*

SIDELIGHTS: Vera Cumberlege comments: "My first

book was written for a grandson, after historical and archaeological research on our village of Horsted Keynes, which is mentioned in *Domesday Book*. It was an imaginary account of the village and its people at the time of the Norman Conquest. The second book covered an earlier period, about 460 A.D., and the massacre of the local people by the Saxons. *Shipwreck* was based on a wreck I had seen in childhood. The religious plays were written to suit the people who lived in the village."

* * *

CUNNINGHAM, Noble E., Jr. 1926-

PERSONAL: Born July 25, 1926, in Evans Landing, Ind.; son of Noble E. and Mary Cunningham; married Dana Gulley, August 20, 1954. *Education:* University of Louisville, B.A., 1948; Duke University, A.M., 1949, Ph.D., 1952. *Home:* 2012 Evans Rd., Columbia, Mo. 65201. *Office:* Department of History, University of Missouri, Columbia, Mo. 65211.

CAREER: Wake Forest College, Wake Forest, N.C., instructor in history, 1952-53; University of Richmond, Richmond, Va., assistant professor, 1953-58, associate professor of history, 1958-64; University of Missouri, Columbia, associate professor, 1964-66, professor of history, 1966—, chairman of department, 1971-74. *Military service:* U.S. Army, 1944-46. *Member:* American Historical Association, Organization of American Historians (member of executive board, 1971-74), Southern Historical Association, Phi Beta Kappa. *Awards, honors:* Guggenheim fellow, 1959-60; National Endowment for the Humanities senior fellow, 1970-71.

WRITINGS: The Jeffersonian Republicans, 1789-1801, University of North Carolina Press, 1957; *The Jeffersonian Republicans in Power, 1801-1809,* University of North Carolina Press, 1963; (editor) *The Making of the American Party System,* Prentice-Hall, 1965; (editor) *The Early Republic, 1789-1828,* Harper, 1968; *The Process of Government Under Jefferson,* Princeton University Press, 1978; (editor) *Circular Letters of Congressmen to Their Constituents, 1789-1829,* three volumes, University of North Carolina Press, 1978. Contributor to history journals. Member of editorial board of *Journal of Southern History,* 1974-78.

WORK IN PROGRESS: The Image of Thomas Jefferson.

SIDELIGHTS: Cunningham told *CA:* "Perhaps the most intellectual of all American presidents, Thomas Jefferson was not a visionary philosopher lost in the realm of practical politics. Rather, he was a successful party leader, a capable administrator, and a president who effectively exercised strong presidential leadership."

* * *

CUTT, W(illiam) Towrie 1898-

PERSONAL: Born January 26, 1898, in Orkney, Scotland; son of John (a fisherman) and Betsy (Muir) Cutt; married Margaret Nancy Davis, (a university lecturer and writer), May, 1948. *Education:* Attended University of Edinburgh; University of Alberta, B.A., 1942, B.Ed., 1947, M.A., 1950. *Politics:* "Neither Right nor Left." *Religion:* Anglican Church of Canada. *Home:* 624 Cornwall St., Victoria, British Columbia, Canada V8V 4L1.

CAREER: Teacher; writer. *Military service:* British Army, 1916-18; served with Gordon Highlanders in France.

WRITINGS: (Contributor) *The New Orkney Book,* Thomas Nelson, 1966; *On the Trail of Long Tom,* Collins, 1970; *Message From Arkmae,* Collins, 1972; *Seven for the Sea,* Collins, 1972, Follett, 1974; *Carry My Bones Northwest,* Collins, 1973; *Faraway World* (autobiography), Deutsch, 1977; (with wife, Margaret Nancy Cutt) *The Hogboon of Hell and Other Strange Orkney Tales,* Deutsch, 1978.

WORK IN PROGRESS: Research on Orkneymen and Orkney folklore; a fictional story of vanishing islands in the North Atlantic.

SIDELIGHTS: Cutt writes: "In my second and third books, I wanted to get children interested in sea mammals, seals and porpoises, as I am against seal slaughter and against experiments with porpoise and dolphin. I also wished to comment upon Indian-white half-breed problems and to outline something of the history here in Canada in my first and fourth books, showing in the first a Metis boy choosing his white heritage and in the fourth a boy choosing to follow his Indian people. In *Faraway World* I wanted to show a boyhood that I myself found happy, and a way of life now lost.

"If there is anything of interest about me, it is probably that my books were published when I was in my seventies. My prescription for the elderly retired: *Make something.* A garden is not subject to the frustrations of a book in progress, which gives joy only when the story pulls instead of being pushed. Publication is hard to attain and when it happens, so slow that it is almost an anticlimax."

D

DAHINDEN, Justus 1925-

PERSONAL: Born May 18, 1925, in Zurich, Switzerland; son of Josef (a writer) and Eugenie (Kraus) Dahinden; and married Marta Arquint, 1950; children: Zeno, Ivo, Delia. *Education:* Federal Institute of Technology, Zurich, Switzerland, diploma in architecture, 1949, Dr. sc. techn., 1956. *Office:* Heuelstrasse 21, Zurich, Switzerland.

CAREER: Independent practice of architecture in Zurich, Switzerland (with offices in Germany, Austria, Italy, Egypt, and Uganda), 1955—. Professor at Technical University (Vienna, Austria), 1973—, also director of its Institute for Environmental International Congress of Religion, Architecture, and the Visual Arts, 1967—, and Zurich Town Planning Commission; jury member for national and international architectural and town planning competitions. *Military service:* Swiss Army, 1958—; present rank, sergeant.

MEMBER: International Group of Prospective Architecture, International Society of Food Service Consultants, International Society of Christian Artists (honorary president, 1976), American Institute of Architects (honorary fellow). *Awards, honors:* Prizes include honor awards from Guild for Religious Architecture, 1969, for excellence in design; awards from *Institutions'* annual food service contest, 1969, for superlative achievement in interior design; Grand Prix International d'Urbanisme et d'Architecture from Association pour la Promotion de l'Urbanisme et de l'-Architecture, 1969.

WRITINGS: Standortbestimmung der Gegenwartsarchitektur (title means "Theoretical Research on Modern Architecture"), Girsberger, 1956; *Bauen fuer die Kirche in der Welt,* NZN Buchverlag (Zurich), 1966, translation by Cajetan J. B. Baumann published as *New Trends in Church Architecture,* Universe Books, 1968; *Stadtstrukturen fuer morgen: Analysen, Thesen, Modelle,* Verlag Gerd Hatje (Stuttgart), 1971, translation by Gerald Onn published as *Urban Structures for the Future,* Praeger, 1972; *Denken, Fuehlen, Handeln/Penser, sentir, agir/Thinking, Feeling, Acting* (biography; text in English, French, and German), English text translated by Ann Hadfield and Susan Russel, Karl Kraemer Verlag (Stuttgart), 1973; *Projekt 18 Akro-Polis Frei-Zeit-Stadt/Leisure City* (text in English and German), English text translated by J. Hull, Karl Kraemer Verlag, 1974. Contributor to architectural journals in Switzerland, Germany, France, England, and the United States.

WORK IN PROGRESS: Building new urban structures, including AKRO-Polis, a leisure city, and housing developments for the Third World.

SIDELIGHTS: Dahinden writes: "As director of the Institute for Environmental Design at the Technical University of Vienna, I work on the following topics: creative perceptive contents transmitted from the manmade environment; architecture as a phenomenon of appearance named *gestalt,* getting its own function as an information medium and motivating the practical purposes; meaningful signs and symbols in architecture, giving a message of what happens with it and stimulating its use; the influence of gestalt upon the behavior of man; and the anthropological aspects of the archetypes."

*   *   *

DALLAS, Athena Gianakas
   See DALLAS-DAMIS, Athena G(ianakas)

*   *   *

DALLAS-DAMIS, Athena G(ianakas) 1925-
   (Athena Gianakas Dallas)

PERSONAL: Born October 20, 1925, in Baltimore, Md.; daughter of James (a steelworker) and Angeliki (Andreadis) Gianakas; married Tom Dallas, April, 1950 (divorced); married George Damis (a painter and decorator), December 31, 1964; children: (first marriage) Peter. *Education:* Attended Queen's College of City University of New York, 1975-76. *Politics:* Democrat. *Religion:* Greek Orthodox. *Home and office:* 230-30 58th Rd., Bayside, N.Y. 11364. *Agent:* Weiser & Weiser, Inc., 60 East 42nd St., Suite 902, New York, N.Y. 10017.

CAREER: Western Union Telegraph Co., Steubenville, Ohio, and Weirton, W.Va., began as teletype operator, became district cashier, then branch manager, 1943-56; St. Basil's Girls' Academy, Garrison, N.Y., assistant supervisor, 1956-57; Greek Archdiocese of North and South America, New York City, public relations secretary and translator of religious books and pamphlets, 1957-58; McCann-Erickson, New York, N.Y., in market research, 1960; Encyclopaedia Britannica Films, New York City, secretary to the president, 1961-62; free-lance journalist, 1962-64; *Hellenic-American,* New York City, co-editor and publisher, 1964-67; free-lance writer, editor, and translator, 1967—. Head of little theater group for children and young adults in Steubenville, 1948-55; co-producer of "The Virginia Griffin Hour" on WSTV-TV, 1954-55; host of "Greek Radio Hour" on WKWK-Radio, Wheeling, W. Va., 1955. Journalistic liaison with Greek consulate during the 1960's. Teacher of Greek in Steubenville, 1948; Greek-English interpreter and translator, including work for U.S. Supreme Court, 1962— . Executive secretary of United Greek Orthodox Charities, 1969. Lecturer for universities and organizations.

AWARDS, HONORS: Literature award from *Greek World,* 1977, for *Island of the Winds;* journalism-literature award from Widener College, 1977; award from Chios Society of Delaware, 1977, for service to Greek-Americans; Nikos Kazantzakis Award for Literature and the Arts from American-Hellenic Educational Progressive Association, 1978, for *Island of the Winds.*

WRITINGS: Religious Poems for Children (bilingual), H. D. Mann, 1959; (translator; under name Athena Gianakas Dallas) Nikos Kazantzakis, *The Fratricides* (novel), Simon & Schuster, 1964; (translator; under name Athena G. Dallas) Kazantzakis, *Three Plays: Christopher Columbus, Melissa, Kouros,* Simon & Schuster, 1969; *Islands of the Winds* (historical novel), Caratzas Brothers, 1976; (translator) Rozanna Mouzaki, *Greek Dances in America,* Doubleday, 1979; *Windswept* (historical novel), Caratzas Brothers, 1979.

Co-author of "Once Upon a Bus" (bilingual comedy screenplay), John Christian Productions, 1961. Author of "News of the Archdiocese," a column in the bilingual *National Herald,* 1957-58, and "Hellenic-American Scenes," a column appearing in six Greek-American newspapers in major U.S. cities, 1960-64. Contributor to Greek-American magazines and *Film Comment.* English editor of *To Ellinoamerikanopoulo* (bilingual children's magazine; title means "The Greek-American Child"), 1961-62; contributing editor of *Hellenic Times,* 1973— .

WORK IN PROGRESS: A historical novel, the last volume of the "Island" trilogy; translating "Buddha," a play by Nikos Kazantzakis, with Kimon Friar.

SIDELIGHTS: The Turkish massacre of the Greek island of Chios is the subject of Athena Dallas-Damis's historical novel, *Island of the Winds.* Dallas-Damis has a personal interest in this era of history, for her great grandfather, John Fatouros, played an important role in defending Chios from the Turks. On Easter Day of 1822, two thousand Chiote women and children sought shelter from the invading Turks at the monastery of St. Menas. Repulsed by the monastery's heavy steel gate, the Turks dug a hole beneath the wall and crept inside the walls, one by one. Fatouros, who was serving as night watchman, killed each man as he crawled to the surface. After slaughtering almost two hundred Turks in this manner, Fatouros was finally slain. The remaining Turks entered the monastery and massacred the women and children. Before writing about this event in her novel, Dallas-Damas visited Chios. Afterwards she described her reactions to the scene of the carnage: "This whole episode not only stirred me . . . it shattered me. . . . And then I looked at the glass-enclosed bones in the small mausoleum at St. Menas—they were white and clean, the bones of my ancestors. I went inside and touched them, without horror. I stroked them without cringing . . . I felt only sadness and love."

Dallas-Damis told *CA* more about her Greek heritage: "I was an 'ethnic' before it was chic to be ethnic. Though born in the United States, I have been steeped in Greek tradition and customs and have made the study of my people my life's work. I have always been interested in and concerned about

their struggle, from the Revolution of 1821 against the Turks when Greece became a new nation, to their struggle for survival and success as immigrants in America. I have watched their growth with pride and witnessed the children of those early settlers—dishwashers, steelworkers, hot dog vendors—growing into successful individuals in all fields of endeavor, particularly in the arts. I was once fondly called a 'professional Greek' by an executive at Encyclopaedia Britannica Films, and indeed my work has encompassed all things Greek. I believe my writing is my personal contribution, however small, to my forefathers and to the parents who loved Greece—the land that gave light to the world—deeply. They taught me that being a good American encompasses an active pride in one's heritage."

BIOGRAPHICAL/CRITICAL SOURCES: New York World-Telegram, June 5, 1961; *Chicago Greek Press,* March 29, 1963; *Hellenic Times,* February 13, 1975, August 12, 1976.

* * *

DALTON, Claire
See BURNS, Alma

* * *

DALZELL, Robert (Fenton), Jr.   1937-

PERSONAL: Born April 28, 1937, in Cleveland, Ohio; son of Robert F. (a business executive) and Lucile C. (an art teacher) Dalzell; married Lee Baldwin (a librarian), June 18, 1960; children: Frederick, Jeffrey, Victoria, Alex. *Education:* Amherst College, B.A., 1959; Yale University, M.A., 1962, Ph.D., 1966. *Home:* 123 Park St., Williamstown, Mass. 01267. *Office:* Department of History, Williams College, Williamstown, Mass. 01267.

CAREER: Yale University, New Haven, Conn., acting instructor, 1962-66, assistant professor of history, 1966-70; Williams College, Williamstown, Mass., associate professor, 1970-75, professor, 1975-77, Ephram Williams Professor of History, 1977— . Member of advisory committee for Historic Deerfield. *Member:* Berkshire County Historical Society (vice-president; member of board of directors). *Awards, honors:* Guggenheim fellow, 1973-74; Charles Warren fellow at Harvard University, 1973-74.

WRITINGS: American Participation in the Great Exhibition of 1851, Amherst College, 1960; *Daniel Webster and the Trial of American Nationalism,* Houghton, 1973.

WORK IN PROGRESS: A book on the Boston Associates.

* * *

D'AMATO, Alex   1919-

PERSONAL: Born February 4, 1919, in Italy; son of Luigi (a stone cutter) and Raffaela D'Amato; married Janet Potter (a writer and artist), February 28, 1949; children: two daughters. *Education:* Attended art schools. *Home and office:* 32 Bayberry St., Bronxville, N.Y. 10708.

CAREER: Free-lance writer and illustrator. *Military service:* Served in U.S. Army.

WRITINGS—With wife, Janet D'Amato; all self-illustrated: Animal Fun Time (juvenile), Doubleday, 1964; *Cardboard Carpentry,* Lion Press, 1966; *Handicrafts for Holidays,* Lion Press, 1967; *Indian Crafts,* Lion Press, 1968; *African Crafts for You to Make,* Messner, 1969; *African Animals Through African Eyes,* Messner, 1971; *American Indian Craft Inspirations,* M. Evans, 1972; *Gifts to Make for Love or Money: A How-to Book of Imaginative Ideas for Fun-Giving or Fund-Raising,* Golden Press, 1973; *Colonial Crafts for You to Make* (juvenile), Messner, 1975; *Quillwork: The Craft of Paper Filigree,* Messner, 1975; *Italian Crafts: Inspirations From Folk Art,* M. Evans, 1977.

Illustrator: Mary Elting, *Water Come, Water Go,* Harvey House, 1964; Evelyn L. Fiore, *The Wonder Wheel Book of Birds,* Thomas Nelson, 1965; Arthur Liebers, *Fifty Favorite Hobbies,* Hawthorn Books, 1968; Iris Vinton, *The Folkways Omnibus of Children's Games,* Stackpole, 1970.

* * *

DAMORE, Leo 1929-

PERSONAL: Born October 20, 1929, in Port Colbourne, Ontario, Canada; came to United States in 1947, naturalized citizen, 1968; son of Nick (a barber) and Carmen (DeAngelo) Damore; married Dorothea Bush, October 15, 1955 (divorced, April, 1969); married June King Davison (a high school English teacher), August 11, 1973; children: Leslie Joy, Charles Edward. *Education:* Kent State University, B.A., 1952. *Politics:* Independent. *Religion:* Roman Catholic. *Home address:* P.O. Box 37, Centerbrook, Conn. 06409. *Agent:* Craig Virden, Curtis Brown Ltd., 575 Madison Ave., New York, N.Y. 10022. *Office:* TRG Communications Consultants, Fowler Rd., North Branford, Conn. 06471.

CAREER: Cape Cod News, Hyannis, Mass., reporter, 1969-74, author of column "Current Events," 1976—; TRG Communications Consultants, North Branford, Conn., communications consultant. Also worked as bank clerk, menswear buyer and mason tender. *Awards, honors:* Best editorial of the year award from New England Newspaper Alliance, 1974, for "Epitaph for Carrol Fonseca."

WRITINGS: The Cape Cod Years of John Fitzgerald Kennedy, Prentice-Hall, 1967; *The "Crime" of Dorothy Sheridan,* Arbor House, 1978; *Found Money* (novel), Arbor House, 1979. Contributor of stories to *Cosmopolitan, Redbook,* and *Ellery Queen Mystery Magazine.*

WORK IN PROGRESS: In His Garden, a book about the case of Cape Cod murderer Antone Costa, with publication by Arbor House; "A Long Weekend," a three-act play; "Resurrection and the Life," a film script.

SIDELIGHTS: Leo Damore told *CA:* "My career as a writer has been a very difficult one. From 1967 when I published *The Cape Cod Years of John Fitzgerald Kennedy* to 1978 when *The "Crime" of Dorothy Sheridan* appeared, I published nothing, although I was agented and writing well. The singular accomplishment here is not finally publishing, but rather, perservering in the face of overwhelming discouragement to continue writing. I learned a valuable lesson from those years: every career is self-generating. One cannot depend on the encouragement of others to make a career viable. Once the commitment is made, the writing should be enough. To publish is, of course, the goal of every writer, but it cannot be the only goal.

"In particular this was true of *The "Crime" of Dorothy Sheridan* . . . an enormously difficult work of eight years and five complete rewrites. The book deals with a Christian Science mother accused of involuntary manslaughter in the death of pneumonia of her six-year-old daughter by reason of her failure to provide the child 'proper' medical care. Among the issues the case confronted were several of the utmost seriousness and importance and revealed, through the ordeal of the defendant, many of the flaws in the fabric of American justice (i.e., the rights of parents to raise their children, the freedom of religious practice versus the interests of the state in the welfare of children, the efficacy of healing by prayer, the roles imposed upon women by laws created by men, etc.).

"Roberston Davies, the Canadian man of letters, told me a strong moral backbone supports my work, that I write of the moral choices people must make in their lives and the consequences of these choices . . . made or not made . . . and on examination of my work I find his judgment to be correct, although I do not consciously point to any moral, or seek to 'preach' in my work."

* * *

DANA, Rose
See ROSS, W(illiam) E(dward) D(aniel)

* * *

DANIELS, Randy (Allan) 1949-

PERSONAL: Born November 30, 1949, in Chicago, Ill.; son of William Lloyd and Ophelia (Johns) Daniels; married Jacqueline Hurd (a florist), June 22, 1974. *Education:* Southern Illinois University, B.S. *Politics:* Independent. *Religion:* Muslim. *Office:* CBS News, 630 North Mc Clurg Ct., Chicago, Ill. 60611.

CAREER/WRITINGS: WVON-Radio, Chicago, Ill., reporter, 1969-71; WSIV-TV, Carbondale, Ill., producer, 1971-72; Columbia Broadcasting System (CBS), New York, N.Y., news correspondent in Chicago, 1972—. Notable assignments include coverage of both Republican and Democratic national conventions, and special reports on Jesse Jackson, Anwar Sadat, Ronald Reagan, Nelson Rockefeller, and Shiek Amad I' amani. Master of public affairs lecturer at Southern Illinois University. *Member:* National Association of Black Journalists, National Association of Television and Radio Artists. *Awards, honors:* Powell Scholar, Southern Illinois University.

SIDELIGHTS: Daniels told *CA:* "I have an irrepressable desire to reflect life via television the way it really is. Politics, social issues, problems of everyday life, I view my role and responsibility [as] to tell it like it is."

* * *

DARKE, Marjorie 1929-

PERSONAL: Born January 25, 1929, in Birmingham, England; children: two sons, one daughter. *Education:* Attended Leicester College of Art and Central School of Art, London. *Residence:* Coventry, England.

CAREER: Writer. Worked as textile designer in London, England, 1951-54. *Member:* Society of Authors.

WRITINGS: Ride the Iron Horse (illustrated by Michael Jackson), Longman Young, 1973; *The Star Trap* (illustrated by Jackson), Longman Young, 1974; *Mike's Bike* (illustrated by Jim Russell), Kestrel, 1974; *What Can I Do?* (illustrated by Barry Wilkinson), Kestrel, 1975; *A Question of Courage* (illustrated by Janet Archer), Crowell, 1975; *Kipper's Turn* (illustrated by Mary Dinsdale), Blackie & Son, 1976; *The Big Brass Band* (illustrated by Charles Front), Kestrel, 1976; (contributor) M. R. Hodgkin, editor, *Young Winter's Tales,* Macmillan (London), 1976; (contributor) Dorothy Edwards, editor, *The Read-Me-Another-Story Book,* Methuen, 1976; (contributor) Edwards, editor, *Once Twice Thrice and Then Again,* Lutterworth, 1976; *The First of Midnight* (illustrated by Anthony Morris), Kestrel, 1977; *My Uncle Charlie* (illustrated by Janat Houston), Kestrel, 1977.

SIDELIGHTS: Marjorie Darke writes: "As far back as I can remember I have been a kind of dipsomaniac where words are concerned. A solitary child, reading was a major source of pleasure to me, becoming almost an obsession in my teens when I devoured a novel a day. At this point my father objected, book lover though he was, as my school work was suffering. He rationed me severely I thought, allowing me no more than two books a week. Was this a blueprint for authorship? If it was, it did not bear fruit until long after I had left school, been to art college and to work, married and had a family. By the time my children were going to school I felt a real need to swim out of the pleasurable but self-effacing seas of motherhood and do something totally different; something creative and personal. Writing seemed a natural answer and fitted easily into family life.

"A ten year apprenticeship followed when I tried my hand at innumerable forms of writing—thrillers, adult novels, short stories for young and old, television plays. Writing for children evolved out of these years of trial and error, and for the first time I found I was really happy; slotting without difficulty into this particular genre, perhaps because my own childhood and adolescence have remained very clear in my mind. The first novel I felt to be worthy of publication was born—*Ride the Iron Horse,* a story of the coming of an early railway to a remote part of England. It was a success and gave me the much needed encouragement to continue.

"To date my novels for young adults all have historical settings, which may seem strange when one considers the fact that I found school history extremely dull. Acts of Parliament, foreign policies, battle strategy bored me into near sleep. My interest lay in ordinary people, their loves, trials, everyday lives. As a child I often begged my mother and grandmother: 'Tell me about when you were a little girl!'

"Their answers are with me still, so that I feel strongly linked to the past as I do to the present and future. I love to sink myself into a chosen period, feel it in my bones, try to reproduce it so that the reader too, may know what it was like to be a Victorian actress, a Suffragette, a slave. . . .

"Ideas for my stories usually originate at unexpected moments—a chance remark in conversation; something I see in the street or on television; a phrase I read in a book, or a newspaper item. Any of these and many others may spark off a train of thought which I like to jot down straight away because they are rare treasures and easily lost. Once an idea takes hold I have a marvellous time letting my mind rove freely, even wildly, as the story begins to take shape, but before it evolves too far I begin research into the particular background. Much of this research is from books, but I find it equally important to visit places and talk to people connected with my current interest. In this way I can begin to experience the period within myself, and in doing so inadvertantly have a lot of fun. There was the time I drove a steam traction engine at a rally, and another time when I crawled up and up alarmingly vertical ladders in an old water mill, peering down on the great cogs of wood and iron and the flat milling stones which once had pounded wheat into flour, worked by the mill race I could still hear thundering way beneath my feet. For the sake of *A Question of Courage* I spent a fascinating afternoon with a lady whose sheltered cousin defied her family, went to London and smashed a window because she believed in the Suffragette Cause. A deed which put her in prison. Holding the badges Mrs. Pankhurst had presented to her, was for me a very poignant moment. There are, of course, details which defy capture. I never did discover whether Bathbrick was in use as a pan scourer in the late eighteenth century, when researching for

The First of Midnight. Neither did I find out whether charcoal irons were used by dressmakers in 1912, in the case of *A Question of Courage.* When this happens the only course left open to me is to ruthlessly discard any material where there is the smallest element of doubt. It is only fair to the reader.

"Not all my books require this same intensive research. I like to alternate with stories for very young children which can be read aloud. It is a refreshing change playing with the words, building and developing the sounds as well as the story line. These stories are closely bound to the pictures decorating the book, and I have always been most fortunate in the excellent and sympathetic artists chosen to illustrate them.

"Ultimately there are the sheets of blank paper beside my typewriter, a stack of notes and my head filled with broken jigsaw pieces. I know that the story is hovering there, already independent of me but hidden. Before other people can see it, there is an elusive wall of fog to be pushed away—and that is my job for the next few weeks or months. It is not easy and sometimes it is exasperating, but the moment when my characters begin to direct their own lives and I am merely a recorder of events, then there is an exhilaration, a joy in the writing, which is impossible to define."

*   *   *

DAVIAU, Donald G(eorge)   1927-

PERSONAL: Born September 30, 1927, in West Medway, Mass.; son of George (a spinner) and Jennie (Burbank) Daviau; married Patricia Edith Mara (a teacher), August 20, 1950; children: Katherine Ann, Robert Laurence, Thomas George, Julie Marie. *Education:* Clark University, B.A., 1950; University of California, Berkeley, M.A., 1952, Ph.D., 1955; also attended University of Vienna, 1953-54. *Politics:* Independent. *Religion:* Congregationalist. *Home:* 184 Nisbet Way, Riverside, Calif. 92507. *Office:* Department of Literatures and Languages, University of California, Riverside, Calif. 92521.

CAREER: University of California, Riverside, instructor, 1955-56, assistant professor, 1957-63, associate professor, 1964-70, professor of German, 1971—, head of department of German and Russian, 1969-75. *Military service:* U.S. Naval Reserve, active duty, 1945-46. *Member:* International Arthur Schnitzler Research Association (president, 1978—), Modern Language Association of America, American Association of Teachers of German. *Awards, honors:* Fulbright scholarship for Vienna, 1953-54; Ehrenkreuz fuer Wissenschaft und Kunst from Government of Austria, 1977.

WRITINGS: (Editor with Jorun B. Johns) *The Correspondence of Arthur Schnitzler and Raoul Auernheimer: With Raoul Auernheimer's Aphorism,* University of North Carolina Press, 1972; (with George J. Buelow) *The "Ariadne auf Naxos" of Hugo von Hofmannsthal and Richard Strauss,* University of North Carolina Press, 1975; (editor) *The Letters of Arthur Schnitzler to Hermann Bahr,* University of North Carolina Press, 1978. Contributor to professional journals. Editor of *Modern Austrian Literature,* 1971—.

WORK IN PROGRESS: A critical biography of Austrian writer, Hermann Bahr.

*   *   *

DAVIDSON, Sara   1943-

PERSONAL: Born February 5, 1943, in Los Angeles, Calif.; daughter of Marvin H. (a realtor) and Alice S. (Wass)

Davidson; married Jonathan Schwartz (a disc jockey and author), January 26, 1968 (divorced, 1975). *Education:* University of California, B.A., 1964; Columbia University, M.S., 1965. *Residence:* Venice, Calif. *Agent:* Lynn Nesbit, International Creative Management, 40 West 57th St., New York, N.Y. 10019.

CAREER: Boston Globe, Boston, Mass., reporter, 1965-67, correspondent in New York City, 1967-69; free-lance writer, 1969—. Notable assignments include coverage of youth and the counterculture, rock groups, radical activists, the Robert Kennedy assassination, and the 1968 political conventions.

WRITINGS: Loose Change: Three Women of the Sixties, Doubleday, 1977. Contributor to periodicals, including *Harper's, Atlantic, Life, Rolling Stone, Esquire, Ms., New York Times* Magazine, and *New York Times Book Review.*

WORK IN PROGRESS: "Wolfe & Rose," a filmscript for United Artists; a novel, untitled, for Doubleday.

SIDELIGHTS: "In the Sixties, I often felt that I was caught between two worlds: the Establishment and the counterculture," Davidson wrote. "In the first, I was viewed as a youth spokesman and in the second, I was seen as a representative of the bourgeois capitalist press. I could move in both worlds, but I did not fit in either.

"In 1972, I had a chance meeting in an elevator with a young woman I had known at Berkeley. It was this meeting which led me to seek out others from my past, to see if, by tracing our stories, I might piece together a social history of the Sixties and gain an understanding of what happened to us—and our country—in this time."

After the surprise reunion with her former apartment-mate, Davidson sought out the other woman who had lived with them at Berkeley, and convinced the two to tell their stories. Davidson spent six months interviewing Natasha in New York and six months interviewing Susie in Berkeley (their names are fictional).

"We would meet once a week and spend all day," Davidson wrote. "Often I would ask them to go very deep. For instance I'd ask Susie to reconstruct the time she and Jeff broke up. All she could say was: 'I remember we had a terrible fight and then he left.'

"I would ask her: 'What was the fight about? Who said what? What were you wearing?' She kept saying: 'I don't remember.' So I had to invent it, invent all that texture, from what I knew of Susie at the time, and what I knew of Berkeley.

"Which gets to the question of: is it still nonfiction? I decided it was, if you were using the facts and details that were real and if you were taking the plot from history. But I was certainly filling it out, filling in the skeleton, with my memory."

Malcolm Cowley called *Loose Change* "the liveliest account of the era" yet written and found that "the mood of the times is vividly suggested." However, some critics complained that the book did little to elucidate the meaning of the Sixties. While many reviewers were impressed by Davidson's journalistic skills, they were bothered by her lack of insight into the social and political upheavals of the decade. "It is as if the author expected the mere invocation of the events to carry their own emotional weight," Erica Jong noted. Jong admired Davidson's attempt to be "descriptive rather than judgmental," and praised Davidson for her "engaging sense of adventure, a willingness to try anything once, a real lust for life. She is a risk-taker, willing to be a fool if in the process she may find enlightenment."

Time judged Davidson "an acute observer and ironist," but decried the book's confusion of sex and politics, which it termed "countercultural soap opera." Other reviewers, however, found that she handled the subject of sex with honesty and delicacy.

"Sara Davidson's book is like a loaf that has been taken out of the oven too soon—crisp and brown on the outside, rather runny and shapeless within," commented Lucinda Franks. "There is no doubt that Davidson is a fine reporter: she paints a colorful era in broad, bright strokes; she has an eye for the bizarre, the ironic, the tiny detail," Franks continued. "Her fundamental problem lies in her failure, after four years of researching and writing the book, to discover the inner logic to analyze the meaning of an event."

In anticipation of the criticism *Loose Change* would receive, Davidson wrote in the epilogue: "I'm afraid I will be criticized for copping out. . . . But the truth is, I have not found answers and I'm not sure I remember the questions."

"If you follow the book, people in it learn no answers," she told Barry Siegel. "There are just different interpretations. If you asked me why my marriage broke up when it was happening, I'd have said one thing; a year later, something else.

"The point is, we all used to believe in certain interpretations that explained everything. When one interpretation wouldn't work, we'd change and get another. I've grown wary of explanations. No explanation ever closes all accounts."

Loose Change has been adapted as a miniseries on NBC-TV, 1978.

BIOGRAPHICAL/CRITICAL SOURCES: Los Angeles Times, March 24, 1977; *New Times,* May 13, 1977; *New York Times,* May 15, 1977, June 1, 1977; *New York Post,* May 21, 1977; *New York Times Book Review,* May 21, 1977; *Chicago Tribune Book World,* May 22, 1977; *Saturday Review,* May 28, 1977; *Newsweek,* May 30, 1977; *Atlantic,* June, 1977; *New Yorker,* July 11, 1977; *Time,* July 11, 1977; *Rolling Stone,* July 28, 1977; *Commentary,* August, 1977; *New Republic,* August 20, 1977; *Mademoiselle,* October, 1977; *Contemporary Literary Criticism,* Volume 9, Gale, 1978.

*   *   *

DAVIES, Rhys   1903-1978

OBITUARY NOTICE—See index for *CA* sketch: Born November 9, 1903, in Rhondda Valley, Wales; died in 1978, in London, England. Author of novels, short stories, and nonfiction books on Wales. Most of Davies's work took Wales for its background, but he strove to make his writing universal. His short stories, many of which appeared in *New Yorker* magazine, were praised for their elegant prose and keen sense of humor. "The Chosen One" received an Edgar Allan Poe Award. Obituaries and other sources: *Longman Companion to Twentieth Century Literature,* Longman, 1970; *Penguin Companion to English Literature,* McGraw, 1971; *The Author's and Writer's Who's Who,* 6th edition, Burke's Peerage, 1971; *Cassell's Encyclopaedia of World Literature,* revised edition, Morrow, 1973; *Who's Who in America,* 40th edition, Marquis, 1978; *Who's Who,* 130th edition, St. Martin's, 1978; *AB Bookman's Weekly,* November 6, 1978.

*   *   *

DAVIS, Elizabeth
See DAVIS, Lou Ellen

DAVIS, Lou Ellen 1936-
(Pat Bannister, Elizabeth Davis)

PERSONAL: Born November 9, 1936, in Pittsburgh, Pa.; daughter of Stanley Alfred and Mary Lee (Starr) Orr; married Perry J. Davis (a business executive), July 3, 1957; children: Michael Scott, David Perry, Leslie Elizabeth. *Education:* Attended New York University, New School for Social Research, and Dartmouth Alumni College. *Religion:* Unitarian-Universalist. *Residence:* Skillman, N.J. *Agent:* Richard Curtis Literary Agency, 156 East 52nd St., New York, N.Y. 10022.

CAREER: Village Voice, New York City, reporter and feature writer, 1958-60; *Villager,* New York City, staff writer, 1960-61; free-lance writer, 1961—. Actress for major radio and television networks, for commercials, and in summer stock. *Member:* Authors Guild of Authors League of America, Mystery Writers of America.

WRITINGS: (With Leo Barnett) *Careers in Computer Programming,* Walck, 1967; *Clouds of Destiny* (historical romance), Putnam, 1978.

Under pseudonym Pat Bannister: *Seven Votes for Death* (mystery novel), Gold Medal, 1964.

Under pseudonym Elizabeth Davis: *Suffer a Witch to Die* (suspense novel), Signet, 1969; *My Soul to Keep* (suspense novel), Pyramid Publications, 1970; *Along Came a Spider* (suspense novel), Signet, 1970; *There Was an Old Woman* (mystery novel), Doubleday, 1971. Contributor of stories and verse to mystery, computer programming, and women's magazines.

WORK IN PROGRESS: A historical novel set in Europe during the reign of Henry VIII, completion expected in 1980.

SIDELIGHTS: Lou Ellen Davis writes: "I enjoy meeting new people. I enjoy being very much involved with life. I would like to work with ceramics, paint, pursue assorted academic subjects, and possibly participate in a Little Theater group—all interests which have had to step aside for the time demands of continuing to write while caring for a family."

There Was an Old Woman was made into the television movie "Revenge!," released by American Broadcasting Companies (ABC-TV), in 1972.

*　　*　　*

DAVIS, Olivia 1922-

PERSONAL: Born December 4, 1922, in Leeds, Yorkshire, England; naturalized U.S. citizen, 1956; daughter of Henry Marvell (a painter) and Olive Frances Kate (Rumble) Carr; married Tom Lucian Davis (a lawyer), October 14, 1943; children: Sebastian, Miranda Rose, Olivia Penelope. *Education:* Attended girls' school in London, England, and was privately tutored. *Politics:* "I vote for the person rather than the party, but the person invariably turns out to be a Democrat." *Home:* 6828 Floyd Ave., Springfield, Va. 22150. *Agent:* Curtis Brown Ltd., 575 Madison Ave., New York, N.Y. 10022.

CAREER: British Intelligence, secretary in Oxford and London, 1940-44; writer. Active with London's Theatre Arts Club, 1943-44, Frankfurt's Anglo-American Little Theatre, 1949-51, and Springfield Little Theatre, 1956—. *Member:* Authors Guild, National Trust for Historic Preservation, Smithsonian Resident Associates. *Awards, honors:* Emily Clark Balch Short Story Award (first prize) from

Virginia Quarterly Review of Literature, 1968, for "Girl Bathing."

WRITINGS: The Last of the Greeks (novel), Houghton, 1968; *The Steps of the Sun* (novel), Houghton, 1972; *The Scent of Apples* (stories), Houghton, 1972. Work represented in anthologies, including *Reality in Conflict,* Scott, Foresman, 1976, and in *Winter's Tales,* Macmillan. Contributor of stories to literary journals in the United States, England, Sweden, Czechoslovakia, and Germany, including *Kenyon Review, Prairie Schooner,* and *Western Humanities Review.*

WORK IN PROGRESS: Three novels, *Voices, Weapons,* and one as yet untitled; a collection of short stories; research on guerrilla and terrorist activities (past and present); research on physical and mental aging.

SIDELIGHTS: Olivia Davis wrote: "My father, a landscape, portrait, and figure painter, was a collateral descendant of Andrew Marvel, one of England's finest metaphysical poets, a fact which denotes an artistic heritage.

"I attended Camden School for Girls, founded by Frances Mary Buss, one of the two pioneers for higher education for women in England in the nineteenth century. I matriculated for university with honors in history of art, English literature, and French, but my education was interrupted by World War II.

"My deepest interest is in the literary form of 'landscape with figures'—people who belong in an essential way to their background, and conversely, in those who obviously do not—the Boudin-like strollers on the beach. The sea has always fascinated me and figures in a number of my stories.

"I read a great deal—fiction, biography, history—for life is too short for one to be able to meet all those thousands of people personally; and all those fascinating places they live in can only be fractionally known except as other writers have revealed them.

"Travel has played an important part in my life. I have traveled extensively in Italy and France, and lived in Germany, 1946-51. I have also traveled in Mexico, and have a great affection for that country—its people, its history, its scenery."

AVOCATIONAL INTERESTS: Tent camping, watching point-to-point races in Virginia hunt country, birdwatching.

BIOGRAPHICAL/CRITICAL SOURCES: Saturday Review, October 26, 1968.*

*　　*　　*

DAVIS, Timothy Francis Tothill 1941-
(John Cashman)

PERSONAL: Born January 14, 1941, in Simla, India; married wife, Susan Mary; children: three. *Education:* Graduated from Beaumont College. *Politics:* None. *Religion:* Roman Catholic. *Home:* Briar House, Briar Rd., Twickenham, Middlesex, England. *Agent:* A. M. Heath & Co., William IV St., London, England. *Office:* Queen Elizabeth Building, Temple, London, England.

CAREER: Barrister-at-law in London, England. *Military service:* British Army, Airborne Forces, Parachute Regiment, 1963-66; became captain. *Member:* Honorary Society of Gray's Inn, Crime Writers Association, Mystery Writers of America, British Alpine Club, Swiss Alpine Club, Mexican Alpine Club, United Services Club.

WRITINGS—All under pseudonym John Cashman: *The Gentleman From Chicago,* Harper, 1973; *The Cook-General,* Harper, 1975; *Kid Glove Charlie,* Harper, 1978.

WORK IN PROGRESS: The Chapman Case, a book on the chief suspect in the "Jack the Ripper" murders.

AVOCATIONAL INTERESTS: Mountaineering, Victorian crime, history, military studies.

* * *

DAVIS, W(illiam) N(ewell), Jr. 1915-

PERSONAL: Born January 29, 1915, in Kingsburg, Calif.; son of William Newell (an educator) and Elizabeth A. (a teacher; maiden name, Glenn) Davis; married Ruth A. Maudlin (a piano teacher), September 30, 1948; children: Carol, Ann, Jane. *Education:* Fresno State College, A.B., 1936; University of California, Berkeley, M.A., 1938, Ph.D., 1942. *Politics:* Democrat. *Religion:* Presbyterian. *Home:* 4440 Sycamore Ave., Sacramento, Calif. 95841. *Office:* California State Archives, 1020 O St., Room 130, Sacramento, Calif. 95814.

CAREER: High school teacher of social science and mathematics in Bieber, Calif., 1938-40; San Francisco Junior College, San Francisco, Calif., instructor in history, 1946; University of Missouri, Columbia, assistant professor of history, 1946-47; University of California, Berkeley, assistant professor of history, 1947-55; California State Archives, Sacramento, historian, 1955-66, chief of archives, 1966—. Member of California State Bar. Member of California Heritage Preservation Commission; California state historical records coordinator for National Historical Publications and Records Commission, 1977—. *Military service:* U.S. Army Air Forces, 1942-46; became captain.

MEMBER: American Bar Association, American Historical Association, Organization of American Historians, Society of American Archivists (fellow), American Society for Legal History, Selden Society, Hakluyt Society, Forest History Society, Western History Association, California Historical Society, Commonwealth Club of California. *Awards, honors:* Oscar Winther Award from Western History Association, 1972.

WRITINGS: Sagebrush Corner: The Opening of California's Northeast, Garland Publishing, 1974. Contributor to *Encyclopedia Americana.* Contributor to history journals and *American Archivist.*

* * *

DAY, Price 1907-1978

OBITUARY NOTICE: Born November 4, 1907, in Plainview, Tex.; died December 9, 1978, in Baltimore, Md. Reporter and editor. Day was a foreign correspondent for fifteen years and covered World War II, the Potsdam Conference, and the Nuremberg Trials. In 1948 he was awarded the Pulitzer Prize for distinguished international reporting for his correspondence from India. Day was the last interviewer of Mahatma Gandhi in 1947. Obituaries and other sources: *Washington Post,* December 11, 1978; *Who's Who in America,* 40th edition, Marquis, 1978.

* * *

DAYANANDA, James Yesupriya 1934-

PERSONAL: Born October 27, 1934, in Bangalore, India; came to the United States in 1964; son of Daniel Yesupriya (a teacher) and Kamalamma Dayananda; married Vanitha Shadrach, July 17, 1969; children: Priyalatha, Souymalatha. *Education:* University of Mysore, B.A. (honors), 1956; Central Institute of English, Hyderabad, India, certificate, 1958; Temple University, Ph.D., 1969. *Home:* 140 Cardinal Dr., Lock Haven, Pa. 17745. *Office:* Department of English and Philosophy, Lock Haven State College, Lock Haven, Pa. 17745.

CAREER: University of Madras, Madras, India, lecturer in English, 1956-64; Lock Haven State College, Lock Haven, Pa., associate professor, 1969-72, professor of English, 1972—, head of department of English and philosophy. *Member:* Modern Language Association of America, African Studies Association, Asian Studies Association, American Association of University Professors, Association of Commonwealth Literature, Association of Pennsylvania State College and University Faculty.

WRITINGS: Manohar Malgonkar, Twayne, 1974. Contributor of more than a dozen articles to literature journals and literary magazines.

WORK IN PROGRESS: Four books on the Phillpotts family: "(1) a definitive critical biography of Eden Phillpotts, generously illustrated with photographs, facsimiles, and maps; (2) a critical study of Eden Phillpotts for the Twayne 'English Authors' series; (3) *The Eden Phillpotts Dictionary of Characters and Places,* with maps and topographical illustrations; (4) a critical study of Adelaide Phillpotts Ross. She is eighty-one years old and lives alone near Bude, Cornwall, England. I visited her in July, 1976, and in August, 1977, to record interviews with her."

* * *

DeANDREA, William L(ouis) 1952-

PERSONAL: Born July 1, 1952, in Port Chester, N.Y.; son of William Nicholas (an engineering assistant) and Mary Agnes (a registered nurse; maiden name, Morabito) DeAndrea. *Education:* Syracuse University, B.S., 1974. *Religion:* Roman Catholic. *Home:* 330 South Regent St., Port Chester, N.Y. 10573. *Agent:* Lynn Roberts, P.O. Box 23040, San Jose, Calif. 95153.

CAREER: Writer. Worked as reporter, laborer, and brickcutter. *Member:* Mystery Writers of America.

WRITINGS: Killed in the Ratings, Harcourt, 1978.

WORK IN PROGRESS: A Tainted Soul; The Hog Murders; Talking Shadows.

SIDELIGHTS: DeAndrea told *CA:* "I began writing for a reason that I found compelling and insistent: I had failed at everything else, or rather hadn't been able even to get started. The greatest compensation of being a writer (though this opinion may change if I start to make money) is that no one has to let you do it—if you own a pencil and a blank surface, you can be a writer.

"I have concentrated (so far) on crime fiction for several reasons. The most basic is that it's what I find most entertaining, and it's my opinion that if a work of fiction hasn't entertained, it hasn't done anything. I'm very suspicious of anyone who says he's going to sit down and produce a work of art. All you can do is write a story—when it's *finished,* then it's art or it's not.

"At the same time, it's possible in crime fiction to deal with any important question—the form, in fact, imposes important questions on the writer. Any crime story is automatically concerned with good versus evil, order versus chaos, and illusion versus reality, whether the writer chooses to stress them or not.

"My basic concern is with illusion, which is part of the reason, no doubt, my published book (which I hope to make into a series) has to do with television—the ultimate fantasyland which, paradoxically, is the means by which most people in this country shape their opinions of reality—whatever *that* is.

"I also love paradox, and read and reread the masters of paradox—Lewis Carroll, G. K. Chesterton, Jerome K. Jerome, Will Rogers, and others. My characters run up against human frailty and downright evil but just as often, they're up against what Sir Henry Merrivale called 'the blinkin' awful cussedness of things in general.'

"Sir Henry's creator, John Dickson Carr, is one of my favorite writers, but I came to him late, so I doubt he had an influence on my style, assuming I have one. If the most likely influences are those writers I spent the most time reading, and enjoyed most thoroughly, I'd have to write like (though not so well, of course) a combination of Ellery Queen, Rex Stout, Ed McBain, Ross Macdonald, and the four fellows I mentioned before.

"I was born just after television, and I've never lived in a place without one. I can't perceive TV as the monster the PTA and various nervous others say it is. I always have watched a lot of TV (I never miss "The Muppets"), and I have never committed a violent crime. For this I thank my parents, who were kind enough to accept the responsibility for me themselves, and not foist it off on an electric appliance. When we'd see a violent or antisocial act committed on the tube, my parents would say, 'See that? That's bad. If you ever do anything like that, I'll beat you senseless.' Voila! With the addition of one parental admonition, the monster became a fount of moral instruction.

"Similarly, I don't believe television keeps children from reading. It didn't keep me from reading. And authors know (and have known for generations) that so pitifully few *adults* read anything more profound than Ann Landers that it's silly to blame anything other than the comforts of ignorance. To sum up this part of the program: If thine eye offends thee, pluck out the plug, and leave the rest of us alone. Better yet, let them go read a book, especially mine."

*   *   *

DEANE, Dee Shirley 1928-

PERSONAL: Original name, Dee Shirley Brass; name legally changed; born October 8, 1928, in New York, N.Y.; daughter of Nathaniel and Lennie (Silverman) Brass; married Joseph Arbeit, July 10, 1949 (divorced, 1952). *Education:* Attended New York University, 1945-49, and 1954-55, University of Munich, Munich, Germany, 1957, and London School of Tropical Medicine and Hygiene, 1961; studied at the Divine Life Society, Yoga/Vedanta Academy, Rishikesh, India, 1963. *Religion:* "Born Jewish, converted to Roman Catholicism in 1963, but I'm no longer church oriented. I prefer the experience, the esoteric to ritualistic exoteric." *Address:* P.O. Box 2369, Durban 4000, South Africa.

CAREER: Accordionist, composer, arranger, and interviewer for radio and television stations in New York, N.Y., and Chicago, Ill., and theatre and night club entertainer, 1944-56; musician and entertainer on cruise ship to Caribbean Islands, South America, and Scandinavia, 1955-56; musician and entertainer for television, night clubs, and U.S. Air Force and Army installations in Europe and Africa, 1956-61; voluntary worker on kibbutz farm in Israel, 1959; traveled alone in Land Rover from London, England, to Rishikesh, India, working as writer of travel articles and musician and entertainer, 1961-63; Divine Life Society, Rishikesh, voluntary secretary to chief administrator, 1963; worked for Swiss Red Cross and Swiss Association for

Technical Assistance as manager of a Tibetan refugee camp and director of its school, Trisuli, Nepal, 1964-65; Divine Life Society, worked in voluntary capacity as editor, secretary, toilet cleaner, and assistant in mobile clinic, 1966-67; Inanda Seminary (boarding high school for black girls), Durban, South Africa, English teacher, school secretary, and fund raiser, 1967-73; private secretary, liaison officer, and public relations officer for KwaZulu Prime Minister Gatsha Buthelezi, 1971-73; researcher and writer, 1974—. Has made numerous television appearances.

WRITINGS: Black South Africans: 57 Profiles of Natal's Leading Blacks; A Who's Who, Oxford University Press, 1978. Editor for books published by Divine Life Society.

WORK IN PROGRESS: Research on ways to achieve "a life focused on output rather than intake, on expression and full development of faculties rather than acquisition," and on a "de-institutionalized" city in India.

SIDELIGHTS: In 1956 Dee Shirley Deane left America "because the value system was so alien." As Deane roved about the world, she developed a value system of her own. "I feel morally responsible to identify the forest among the trees I've lived with all my life, and once identified, to improve upon that forest to the best of my ability," she told *CA.* "Above all, I can only act in a manner and do only those things that are consonant with my highest understanding of reality. That understanding is that life is an educative process, an exercise in becoming, a gradual evolvement of higher levels of consciousness. Life is not a race against time or neighbor, nor a struggle to triumph."

In the course of her travels, Deane also learned to distrust institutions. "I'm too de-institutionalized to be categorized by labels," she commented. "I prefer working alone, freely, independently, apart from predetermined scope and orientation. I'm eager to motivate people to examine and question the institutions and conventions they have lived with all their lives: institutions they have accepted unconditionally as right and good, and not to be challenged."

One of the institutions that Deane has challenged is the South African policy of apartheid. After she started to compile material for *Black South Africans*, she became the victim of a terror campaign. Her apartment was ransacked, and the tapes she had amassed for her project were destroyed. Deane began receiving threatening telephone calls, and someone tampered with her car. Undiscouraged, Deane persevered with her book. She explained that she was motivated to write *Black South Africans* by "the enriching proximity to black South Africans, and the lack of white South African exposure to them, their consequent ignorance of what black South Africans are and have, and painful white amorphous view of blacks. To most whites in South Africa, whites are people, and blacks are black. Yet whites are more deprived by lack of interracial contact than are blacks, as this book shows. The chief criterion for inclusion was willingness to sacrifice self in the interest of others. I suppose *Black South Africans* is important because it reveals the moral fiber, character, responsibility, integrity, and leadership qualities in our black community. Quite frankly, I have never met whites who have what these blacks have, and are what these blacks are. But will it really matter to South African whites who still say, 'I know them!' "

When asked by *CA* if she intended to stay in South Africa or if she now sees her mission as taking place elsewhere, Deane replied: "Writing a book on black South Africans was once the most important thing in my life: that is, to show white South Africans and people abroad the humanity behind the pigmentation. But even if the book were to have enormous impact and even perform the impossible, such as a change in government with some of those blacks in decision-making positions, it would still be but a drop in the bucket. Cosmetic change, that's all. So I'm off to India to see (and experience osmotically) a city that has changed from the roots up. I would then like to establish a similar city in South Africa, which to me is one of the most magnificent countries in the world today. The city would be multi-racial, multi-national, and nondenominational.''

It seems unlikely that Deane will ever return permanently to the United States. The American value system that she eschewed in 1956 has grown even worse, she contended: "It's ten times worse! The technology is much more advanced, life more sophisticated, people more demanding, more distractions from distractions by distractions. Americans are that much further away from themselves, always outward bound, outward oriented, less and less free. And they don't know it. They don't know that they are manipulated without force, prompted without aim. They don't know that life is more than a consumer exercise.''

"I cannot live one way and dream another," Deane concluded.

Deane speaks German and French "and can get along in almost every country. All languages come easily—except one: Afrikaans.''

AVOCATIONAL INTERESTS: "I used to love chess, flying a Piper Cub, and composing symphonic suites—but there are only twenty-four hours a day and I now have higher priorities.''

* * *

DeCARL, Lennard 1940-

PERSONAL: Born January 21, 1940, in New York, N.Y.; son of William and Adele DeCarl. *Education:* Hofstra University, B.A., 1961. *Politics:* Democrat. *Religion:* Roman Catholic. *Home:* 484 West 43rd St., Apt. 21-T, New York, N.Y. 10036.

CAREER: Actor, 1945—; theatrical director, 1971—. Performed with National Shakespeare Company and the national company for "Cactus Flower," as well as dinner theaters, summer stock, films ("You're a Big Boy Now," "Reflections in a Golden Eye," "Three," and "Bananas"), and television (including "The Doctors"). *Awards, honors:* Dan H. Lawrence Award, 1960, for playing Mercutio in "Romeo and Juliet."

WRITINGS: (With James Robert Parish) *Hollywood Players: The Forties,* Arlington House, 1976. Contributor to *Films in Review.*

SIDELIGHTS: DeCarl writes: "I am primarily interested in writing about films and film performers. I have one of the most extensive files on film performers' careers, which I started when I was eight years old.

"I am of Spanish, Italian, and French descent, and spoke Spanish before English. I spend as much time as possible in Spain.''

* * *

de CHIRICO, Giorgio 1888-1978

OBITUARY NOTICE: Born July 10, 1888, in Volos, Greece; died November 20, 1978, in Rome, Italy. Painter, sculptor, and author of a novel, an autobiography, and art criticism. De Chirico has been called the father of the sur-

realist school of art. His early, highly praised paintings were often of Italian city squares and featured faceless mannequins. He sought to make his an "art of dreamed sensation," and, in 1917, de Chirico founded the metaphysical school of art with Carlo Carra. In 1919 he abruptly abandoned this art to paint in the manner of nineteenth-century French romantic painters, and he became a vocal critic of modernism. De Chirico wrote an important surrealist novel, *Hebdomeros,* in 1929, several books of art criticism, including *Commedia dell'arte moderna* with his wife in 1945, and an autobiography, *Memorie della mia vita,* also in 1945. Obituaries and other sources: *Current Biography,* Wilson, 1956; *Who's Who in the World,* 2nd edition, Marquis, 1973; *Washington Post,* November 22, 1978.

* * *

De CHRISTOFORO, Ron(ald) 1951-

PERSONAL: Born June 24, 1951, in Philadelphia, Pa.; son of Rudolph (a grocer) and Rita (a beautician; maiden name, Matura) De Christoforo; *Education:* Temple University, B.A., 1974; Columbia University, M.F.A., 1976. *Residence:* New York, N.Y. *Agent:* Virginia Barber, 44 Greenwich Ave., New York, N.Y. 10011.

CAREER: Writer.

WRITINGS: The One and Only (based on screenplay of the same name by Steve Gordon), Pocket Books, 1978; *Grease* (based on screenplay of the same name by Bronte Woodard), Pocket Books, 1978. Contributor of fiction to *City* magazine.

WORK IN PROGRESS: A novel, set in the 1930's, for Simon & Schuster; editing *Strange Actions: An Anthology of Fantastic Fiction in the Twentieth Century.*

SIDELIGHTS: De Christoforo told *CA:* "Writing for a living (paying the damn bills) is often a thankless and ungratifying job, yielding, for the most part, little financial retribution and even less aesthetic satisfaction. But for a young writer, writing anything at all is better than not writing. For me, publishing two novels (adapted from screenplays) provided an opportunity to be discovered as a writer. After finishing my second book, I was contracted to write an original novel. In short, it was a way of breaking-in.

"The difficulties and contradictions of being a working writer (similar to those of a working mother) were best explained by Stephen Crane, when he commented on his own similar situation: 'It is hopeless work. Of all human lots for a person of sensibility, that of an obscure free lance in literature or journalism is, I think, the most discouraging. It was during this period that I wrote *The Red Badge of Courage.*'"

* * *

DeGARMO, Kenneth Scott 1943-

PERSONAL: Born September 3, 1943, in Miami, Fla.; son of Kenneth (an artist) and Elizabeth (Madden) DeGarmo; married Barbara Johnson, August 31, 1968; children: Madden Eileen, Julie Elizabeth. *Education:* University of Florida, B.A., 1968. *Home:* Nash Rd., Purdys, N.Y. 10578. *Office: Family Weekly,* 641 Lexington Ave., New York, N.Y. 10022.

CAREER/WRITINGS: Florida Observer, Daytona Beach, editor, 1969-70; *St. Petersburg Times,* St. Petersburg, Fla., editor of *Floridian* Sunday magazine, 1970-73; *Philadelphia Inquirer,* Philadelphia, Pa., editor of *Today* Sunday magazine, 1973-76; *Family Weekly* Sunday magazine, New York, N.Y., staff member, 1976—. *Member:* Sigma Delta Chi.

Awards, honors: Sidney Hillman Foundation Prize Award; John Hancock Award; Carl M. Loeb, Jr. Award from National Council on Crime and Delinquency.

* * *

DEGUINE, Jean-Claude 1943-

PERSONAL: Born October 31, 1943, in Agen, France; son of Jean Baptiste (a civil servant) and Felinda Deguine; married Annyck Lagier, December 21, 1964 (died December 7, 1965). *Education:* French Air Force Technical School, diploma, 1964.

CAREER: Member of meteorological department of a French expedition to Antarctica, 1967-69; computer engineer in Australia and Europe, 1970-77; free-lance writer and photographer, 1977—. *Military service:* French Air Force, electronic service engineer, 1960-67; became sergeant. *Awards, honors:* Award from New York Academy of Sciences, 1976, for best science book for children, *Emperor Penguin.*

WRITINGS: Emperor Penguin (juvenile science book; with own photographs), Stephen Greene Press, 1975.

WORK IN PROGRESS: A book on Southeast Asia, with own photographs; a book on his travels, with his photographs; research on audio-visual shows, especially those on Antarctica.

SIDELIGHTS: Deguine writes: "*Emperor Penguin* was made after my sixteen months in Antarctica, where I was very impressed by the penguin. I traveled alone through South and Central America (via local transport) in 1972-73, to accumulate enough material and experience to make an interesting book on Latin America, but the slides and notes were lost in the United States. Then I traveled extensively in Europe and am now leaving for Southeast Asia with my camera. I plan to stay in Australia, and to establish myself permanently after this trip. I plan to work in the computer field and also continue as a photographer-writer."

* * *

DEINDORFER, Scott 1967-

PERSONAL: Born October 4, 1967, in New York, N.Y.; son of Robert G. (a writer) and Joan Deindorfer. *Education:* Attends elementary school in New York, N.Y. *Religion:* Episcopal. *Home:* 114 East 71st St., New York, N.Y. 10021.

CAREER: Elementary school student.

WRITINGS: Dear Scott, Workman Publishing, 1978.

WORK IN PROGRESS: Another book.

SIDELIGHTS: A published author at age eleven, Scott Deindorfer told *CA* how he set about writing his first book: "I wrote to more than six hundred famous Americans like President Carter, John Wayne, Roger Staubach, Dr. Menninger, Mary Tyler Moore, Senator Kennedy, and others asking for their favorite quotations. Then I picked out the best answers, from these and other people, and wrote a long introduction that my teacher at school said was very good. I wrote the book because I was interested in quotations famous Americans say helped them become successful. The publisher just told me that more than 20,000 copies have sold. I didn't like it much, but I was interviewed on radio and newspapers, and they had a big autograph party for me at Womraths when the book came out."

AVOCATIONAL INTERESTS: Soccer, baseball, tennis, swimming, fishing, chess.

DELANY, Samuel R(ay), Jr. 1942-

PERSONAL: Born April 1, 1942, in New York, N.Y.; son of Samuel R. (a funeral director) and Margaret Carey (a library clerk; maiden name, Boyd) Delany; married Marilyn Hacker (a poet), August 24, 1961 (separated, 1974); children: Iva Alyxander. *Education:* Attended City College (now of the City University of New York), 1960 and 1962-63. *Residence:* New York City. *Agent:* Henry Morrison, Inc., 58 West 10th St., New York, N.Y. 10011.

CAREER: Writer. Butler Professor of English, State University of New York at Buffalo, 1975; senior fellow at the Center for Twentieth Century Studies, University of Wisconsin—Milwaukee, 1977. *Awards, honors:* Nebula Award from Science Fiction Writers of America, 1967, for *Babel-17,* 1968, for "Aye, and Gomorrah" and *The Einstein Intersection,* and 1970, for "Time Considered as a Helix of Semi-Precious Stones"; Hugo Award from the World Science Fiction Conventions, for "Time Considered as a Helix of Semi-Precious Stones."

WRITINGS—Science fiction, except as noted: *The Jewels of Aptor,* Ace Books, 1962, revised edition, 1968; *Captives of the Flame* (first novel in trilogy; also see below), Ace Books, 1963, revised edition published as *Out of the Dead City,* Sphere Books, 1968; *The Towers of Toron* (second novel in trilogy; also see below), Ace Books, 1964; *City of a Thousand Suns* (third novel in trilogy; also see below), Ace Books, 1965; *The Ballad of Beta-2,* Ace Books, 1965; *Empire Star,* Ace Books, 1966; *Babel-17,* Ace Books, 1966; *The Einstein Intersection,* Ace Books, 1967; *Nova,* Doubleday, 1968.

The Fall of the Towers (trilogy; includes *Captives of the Flame, The Towers of Toron, City of a Thousand Suns*), Ace Books, 1970; *Driftglass: Ten Tales of Speculative Fiction,* New American Library, 1971; *The Tides of Lust,* Lancer Books, 1973; *Dhalgren,* Bantam, 1975; *Triton,* Bantam, 1976; *The Jewel-Hinged Jaw: Notes on the Language of Science Fiction,* Dragon Press, 1977; *Empire,* Putnam, 1978; *The American Shore* (criticism), Dragon Press, 1978; *Tales of Neveryon,* Bantam, 1979; *The Heavenly Breakfast,* Bantam, 1979.

Editor: *Quark, No. 1,* Popular Library, 1970; (with Marilyn Hacker) *Quark, No. 2,* Popular Library, 1971; *Quark, No. 3,* Popular Library, 1971; *Quark, No. 4,* Popular Library, 1971.

Work represented in anthologies, including *Dangerous Visions,* edited by Harlan Ellison, 1967; *The Best From Fantasy and Science Fiction,* edited by Edward L. Ferman, Doubleday, 1968; *SF 12,* edited by Judith Meril, Delacorte, 1968; *The Shores Beneath,* edited by James Sallis, Avon, 1971. Contributor to periodicals, including *Fantasy and Science Fiction* and *Worlds of Tomorrow.*

SIDELIGHTS: Samuel R. Delany has helped raise science fiction from the lowly status of light reading to the rank of a respected genre. Because Delany's *Dhalgren* is written on such a high level of sophistication, Gerald Jonas predicted that even academia would consider the novel worthy of comment and criticism. A year later, Jonas named Delany "the most interesting author of science fiction writing in English today," explaining that "no one else has managed to put the space-defying, time-denying adventure story to such high purpose . . . without sacrificing the narrative drive that made such stories appealing in the first place."

Delany's most pervasive theme is the rationale behind human myth-making. Ronald M. Jacobs observed that Delany is more interested in men than ideas, so he allows his "characters to create mythos out of other characters, and then proceed[s] to show the human truth that is masked by the mythic facade." This concern with myth-making, Jacobs pointed out, is the reason that many of Delany's heroes are poets, musicians, and singers (seer-like figures) who encounter mythical creatures. Delany has not tried to hide his fascination with legend. An author's note in *The Einstein Intersection* stated that "the central subject of the book is myth." Numerous legends crop up in Delany's novels, including the Orpheus and Eurydice myth in *The Einstein Intersection* and the legend of the Holy Grail in *Nova*.

BIOGRAPHICAL/CRITICAL SOURCES: Books and Bookmen, June, 1968, July, 1969; *The CEA Critic*, March, 1974; *Washington Post Book World*, January 19, 1975; *New York Times Book Review*, February 16, 1975, March 28, 1976; *Contemporary Literary Criticism*, Volume 8, Gale, 1978.

*   *   *

DeLILLO, Don 1936-

PERSONAL: Born in 1936. *Address:* c/o Alfred A. Knopf, Inc., 201 East 50th St., New York, N.Y. 10022.

CAREER: Writer.

WRITINGS—Novels: *Americana*, Houghton, 1971; *End Zone*, Houghton, 1972; *Great Jones Street*, Houghton, 1973; *Ratner's Star*, Knopf, 1976; *Players*, Knopf, distributed by Random House, 1977; *Running Dog*, Knopf, 1978. Contributor of short stories to periodicals, including *New Yorker, Esquire, Sports Illustrated*, and *Atlantic*.

SIDELIGHTS: DeLillo made an auspicious literary debut with his novel, *Americana*. Although critics who praised DeLillo's work had some qualifications, they were impressed that he overcame the overworked subject he chose—the discontent of an American television executive—with the freshness of his writing. Terming *Americana* "very much a first novel," Christopher Lehmann-Haupt wrote, "It is a loose-jointed, somewhat knobby novel, all of whose parts do not fit together and some of whose parts may not belong at all." Still, the novel had virtues, Lehmann-Haupt declared, and they had "mostly to do with DeLillo's ability to write. . . . DeLillo made me the willing victim of his verbal assaults. He rearranged my brain cells to think the world his way and to continue composing DeLillo-like phrases long after I had laid his book aside. He had me soaring on his moods, scarcely caring about meaning at all."

DeLillo's next novel, *End Zone*, was almost universally acclaimed for the author's skillful evocation of football as American ritual. As the reviewer for *Time* wrote, "The gear, mechanics and incantations of American football would challenge a Claude Levi-Strauss. Confronting them as a novelist, Don DeLillo shows a touch of the structuralist anthropologist too. *End Zone* is a cool, plotless, witty novel of football as technology and necessary ritual." DeLillo's facility with language is the central point of praise from reviewers. G. M. Knoll wrote: "Through the religious, psychological, and absurdly humorous themes of the narrative, language itself merges as a major concern. It is as if the book were an attempt to compile a last repository of a lost language and simplicity of life. DeLillo's success in dealing with such a vast thematic scope makes this a visionary novel and a major triumph of the imagination."

The reviewer for *Times Literary Supplement*, however, criticized the novelist's "view of football as a microcosm of the holocaust." "All in all," he wrote, "the parallels seem self-defeatingly tenuous, with the attempts to mythologize the game sounding like an academic's apologia for leaving the library." He found the book "most successful and enjoyable when the narrative is forced to be straight about football and characters alike." On the other hand, Lehmann-Haupt greatly admired the novel and listed "everything that makes his novel wonderful—the craft with which he builds the scenes that make the . . . lines seem funny; the grace and humor of his own narrative voice; the football game told in pure jargonese that makes up the exciting centerpiece of the novel; a pick-up game played in the snow that ought to be placed in all textbooks on creative writing to demonstrate the art of building a scene—simply everything."

The next American milieu DeLillo tackled was the world of rock stars and the drug culture in the novel *Great Jones Street*. Walter Clemons's assessment of the novel as an "in-between book," was representative of critical opinion, and while critics realized that DeLillo was extending himself as a writer, they weren't completely satisfied with the result. Although Sara Blackburn described the book as "full of beautiful writing," she felt that it didn't "save the book from being more of a sour, admirably written lecture than a novel, a book that is always puffing to keep up with the power and intensity of its subject." Clemons compared *Great Jones Street* to its predecessor, *End Zone*, which he called "brilliant": "The worst of *Great Jones Street* is that it become portentous, as *End Zone* never did. On the other hand, there is moving evidence of a writer stretching himself, accomplishing things he hasn't done before. A girl's death occurs with stunning hush and shock; deep-city crime and fear are laceratingly evoked. At such moments, even in this unsuccessful book, DeLillo is a powerfully disturbing writer."

DeLillo turned to the genre of science fiction for his next work, *Ratner's Star*, which is about a fourteen year-old mathematical genius and Nobel laureate. "There is no easy way to describe *Ratner's Star*, a cheerfully apocalyptic novel," Amanda Heller wrote. "Imagine *Alice in Wonderland* set at the Princeton Institute for Advanced Studies." A reviewer from *New Yorker* called it "a whimsical, surrealistic excursion into the modern scientific mind." George Stade described the book as "not only interesting, but funny (in a nervous kind of way). From it comes an unambiguous signal that DeLillo has arrived, bearing many gifts. He is smart, observant, fluent, a brilliant mimic and an ingenious architect."

While reviewers found much to admire in the brilliant and ruthless parody of the cult of science, as Heller noted, many considered the book to be lacking in its depiction of characters. Knoll wrote: "It is in this architecturally symmetrical rendering of the novel's form that DeLillo scores a major triumph, rather than in the sustained development of characters. For the ideas of the book turn back on themselves and create a constantly shifting ground of reality. Anything can happen in this book, and the result is not so much confusion as exhilaration. . . . But without consistently developed characters in action, this brilliant, truly amazing, but finally frustrating book rings a bit hollow."

Despite finding the novel derivative of Thomas Pynchon's *Gravity's Rainbow*, Paul Gray commented, "Still, *Ratner's Star*, for all of its monotonic monologues, often displays impressive erudition and the same inebriated infatuation with language that worked so well in DeLillo's *End Zone*, his surrealistic send-up of football and warfare." Several reviewers compared DeLillo to Pynchon, but J. D. O'Hara found another comparison to be more apt. He wrote: "Don

DeLillo writes the American version of a European novel of ideas. Perhaps he most resembles Thomas Mann, lacking Mann's mysticism and long-windedness but sharing his remarkable ability to evoke and evaluate the ideas, language and attitudes of a wide range of intellectual disciplines.'' O'Hara, though, was disappointed with DeLillo's choice of the form of science fiction, which, he wrote, ''obliges him to reach answers and to impose a dramatic conclusion on his discrete materials. The plot may be intended to appease those hominids still longing for the reassurance of cause and effect, but the many ideas so satisfyingly raised, developed, and clarified in this fine novel deserve a better fate. Still, what a mind-expanding trip to the finish line, and full of wit and slapstick as well.''

Peter Prescott, also appreciative of DeLillo's effort while not finding it totally artistically satisfying, commented: ''To be really disappointing a novel cannot be really bad. What's needed is a developing tension between the author's talent and reader's hopes on the one hand and the author's performance and reader's frustration on the other. *Ratner's Star* provides such exquisite tension in large measure. DeLillo knows how to write brilliantly, even movingly, but he doesn't know when he's writing dully, doesn't know when his book has started to die in his typewriter. *Ratner's Star* is twice too long; as its terminal signs (failing inspiration, metastasis of exhausted ideas and dialogue) progress in the second half it becomes virtually unbearable. There are too many cartoon characters, too many familiar situations and too much talk without insights, without any real *vision* at all.''

In *Players* DeLillo takes on another contemporary American subject—terrorism. But as John Updike wrote, ''Terrorism of an attenuated, urbane sort; the book is really about sophistication, or at least nothing is as clear about it as the sophistication of the author, who combines a wearily thorough awareness of how people pass their bored-silly lives in New York City with a (in this novel) lean, slit-eyed prose and a pseudo-scientific descriptive manner. He slices up ordinary experience into paper-thin transparencies and feeds it back in poetic printout.'' The book's central characters are an urbane, seemingly model married couple—Lyle, a broker on the stock exchange who becomes involved in a terrorist scheme, and Pammy, who works for the Grief Management Council. ''They are also zombies,'' John Leonard wrote. ''*Players* is a willful book. The will belongs to Mr. DeLillo, who is too smart to let his characters get away with anything or out of control. Consciousness in this novel is a disease, a pathological condition. Emotions and events are not experienced; they are reviewed, as though they were programs or ritual urns. Esthetically, life leaves a lot to be desired, but it's a good excuse for wit, and Mr. DeLillo—with his 'per diem rates for terminal illness counseling'—is extremely witty. He may be our wittiest writer.''

Thomas LeClair praised DeLillo's fresh approach to his subject. He declared: ''What makes this familiar material fascinating is DeLillo's dual perspective: he is a sensor inside the characters and a distant scientist converting signals into information. While Lyle and Pammy process (and reduce) a world they're trying to enlarge with adventure, DeLillo decodes both action. The prose knows how experience turns into abstraction and how people become channels, how plot fades to probabilities and place empties into space, how little becomes less. DeLillo isn't writing sociology or satire, but the equations for what one character calls 'the sensual pleasures of banality.' His is no easy investigation, yet *Players* is both original and final, a new formula for the

familiar.'' Updike echoed that sentiment: ''Don DeLillo has, as they used to say of athletes, class. His is original, versatile, and, in his disdain of last year's emotional guarantees, fastidious. He brings to human phenomena the dispassionate mathematics and spatial subtleties of particle physics. Into our technology-riddled daily lives he reads the sinister ambiguities, the floating ugliness of America's recent history.''

One dissenting view was heard from Amanda Heller who chided DeLillo for adopting a ''sterile vision.'' She complained, ''Chic despair just isn't DeLillo's style. He has put his wicked wit and imagination to better use in the past.''

DeLillo's mastery of language in *Players* was praised by a majority of its reviewers. Leonard wrote: ''As Mr. DeLillo in the last several years has gone about demystifying—or alchemizing, or eviscerating—such abstract ambiguities as sports, advertising, rock culture and science . . . he has developed a prose style that amounts to incantation. It is full of stops and magic, an abrupt keening, here and there glissando, crazy syllogisms, rogue puns. It thumps, winds, foreshortens, slides.''

''DeLillo's attention to detail is masterful,'' Diane Johnson declared. ''He suggests that though freedom is what people ostensibly want, too naive a definition of it brings a reaction as frightening as chaos. This is not a fashionable idea, but DeLillo convinces you that it is true. The discoveries of artists do not always—perhaps seldom—corroborate political fashions. But the wit, elegance and economy of Don DeLillo's art are equal to the bitter clarity of his perceptions.''

BIOGRAPHICAL/CRITICAL SOURCES: New York Times, May 6, 1971, March 22, 1972, April 16, 1973, May 27, 1976, July 30, 1976, August 11, 1977; *New York Times Book Review,* May 30, 1971, April 22, 1973, December 2, 1973, June 20, 1976, September 4, 1977, November 12, 1978; *Time,* April 17, 1972, April 23, 1973, June 7, 1976; *New Yorker,* May 6, 1972, July 12, 1976, March 27, 1978; *Antioch Review,* spring, 1972; *New York Review of Books,* June 29, 1972; *America,* July 22, 1972, August 7, 1976; *Saturday Review,* December 2, 1972, September 3, 1977, September 16, 1978; *Newsweek,* April 23, 1973, June 7, 1976, August 29, 1977; *National Review,* June 8, 1973, October 28, 1977; *Times Literary Supplement,* September 14, 1973; *Book World,* June 13, 1976, August 21, 1977, December 11, 1977; *Atlantic,* August, 1976, September, 1977; *Nation,* September 17, 1977; *Virginia Quarterly Review,* spring, 1978; *New Republic,* October 7, 1978; *Crawdaddy,* October, 1978; *Contemporary Literary Criticism,* Volume 8, Gale, 1978.*

* * *

DELL, Roberta E(lizabeth) 1946-

PERSONAL: Born January 15, 1946, in Philadelphia, Pa.; daughter of Walter J. (a government worker) and Marie (Cavalier) Cropper; married Ronald William Dell (a data processing manager), July 20, 1963; children: Ronald William, Jr., Gwendolynne Suzanne. *Politics:* Republican. *Religion:* Atheist. *Home:* 318 Second Ave., Newtown Square, Pa. 19073. *Agent:* Ronald William Dell, 318 Second Ave., Newtown Square, Pa. 19073.

CAREER: Bell Telephone Co., Lansdowne, Pa., long distance operator, 1963-64; writer, 1972—.

WRITINGS: The United States Against Bergdoll: How the Government Spent Twenty Years and Millions of Dollars to Capture and Punish America's Most Notorious Draft Dodger (biography), A. S. Barnes, 1977.

WORK IN PROGRESS: Two mysteries, *Red Litten Windows* and *Mark of the Beast;* a historical novel set in Philadelphia; research on the witchcraft mass murders in Philadelphia in the 1930's.

SIDELIGHTS: A wealthy American playboy of German descent, Grover Bergdoll chose to evade the draft during World War I. He amused himself with sports cars and private planes while other men joined the military, and the public became so infuriated by Bergdoll's escapades that he was forced to flee to Germany after the Armistice. Even there Bergdoll was not safe, for some vengeful Americans threatened to kidnap or kill him. With the coming of Hitler and the Nazis into power, Bergdoll voluntarily returned to the United States to be prosecuted so that his children might grow up in a free country. Raised in the same area where the Bergdoll family lived, Roberta Dell first heard the story of the infamous draft dodger from her father-in-law. She was intrigued and did some research at a local library. Astonished by the amount of information available about the case, Dell decided to write a book on the subject. The result was *The United States Against Bergdoll.*

Dell told *CA:* "Neither church, home, nor school had any positive effect upon me. My husband has always been the greatest influence upon my life. I write to please him. I am most proud of the fact that I taught both of my children to read before they were two."

About the problems of being an author, Dell said: "I don't believe there is anything known as writer's block. I can write about anything—any time, anywhere. The only writing difficulty I have is detaching myself from my work. I was so obsessed with the incredible Bergdoll family in my first book that I dreamed about them almost every night for five years."

AVOCATIONAL INTERESTS: Traveling (Canada, Morocco, Italy, Germany, Spain, France, Switzerland), swimming, biking, oil painting, cooking, dancing, reading.

* * *

DEMBY, William 1922-

PERSONAL: Born December 25, 1922, in Pittsburgh, Pa.; son of William and Gertrude (Hendricks) Demby; married Lucia Drudi (a novelist); children: James. *Education:* Attended West Virginia State College; Fisk University, B.A., 1947; additional study at University of Rome, Italy. *Residence:* New York, N.Y. *Office:* College of Staten Island of the City University of New York, Staten Island, N.Y.

CAREER: Has worked as jazz musician and screenwriter in Rome, Italy, and as advertising agent in New York, N.Y.; currently associate professor at College of Staten Island of the City University of New York. Novelist. *Military service:* Served in North Africa during World War II. *Member:* European Community of Writers, Alpha Phi Alpha.

WRITINGS—Novels: *Beetlecreek,* Rinehart, 1950; *The Catacombs,* Pantheon, 1965; *Love Story Black,* Reed, Cannon & Johnson, 1978; *Blueboy,* Pantheon, 1979. Work represented in anthologies, including *Soon One Morning: New Writing by American Negroes, 1940-1962,* edited by Herbert Hill, Knopf, 1963; *A Native Sons Reader,* edited by Edward Margolies, Lippincott, 1970; *Cavalcade: Negro American Writing From 1760 to the Present,* Houghton, 1971.

SIDELIGHTS: In an interview with John O'Brien in *Studies in Black Literature,* William Demby spoke of writing and the novelist's function: "It must be very, very difficult not to write because there's certainly plenty of things to write, but the whole context of the novel seems to have moved into another ball field. You can do almost anything you want . . . yet, you have to remain in contact with the consciousness of your reader, at the same time you are seeing things yourself. . . . How much can we feed back, how much should we feed back . . . ? The novelist must have this function of seeing connections." Demby assessed that "he also has the responsibility (and this may be true for all artists), to make some connection with the past. That is, to illustrate how much of the past is living in the present and how much of the present is only the future and the past. All these things he must bring to life, all the connections, or 'myths' if you will, by which people will imagine things to survive. I suppose that that may be the artist's function, as you say, to make all the connections," he concluded, "because if we disavow the chronological progression idea of history, then it must be something like that tapestry, it must be made up at the same moment of the past, present and future."

Nancy Y. Hoffman wrote: "Demby re-creates himself as a descendant of Michelangelo, of the Renaissance man, whose goal is to be that most elusive of human beings, a whole man—or even in Demby's terms, the Yang-Yin of the whole man-woman. While Demby writes in an age where the anti-hero is king, he himself writes in the Michelangelo tradition of the artist as hero. . . ."

BIOGRAPHICAL/CRITICAL SOURCES: New York Times Book Review, July 11, 1965; Edward Margolies, *Native Sons: A Critical Study of Twentieth Century Negro American Authors,* Lippincott, 1968; *TriQuarterly 15,* 1969; *Studies in Black Literature,* Number 2, 1972, Number 3, 1972; Roger Whitlow, *Black American Literature,* Nelson Hall, 1973; John O'Brien, *Interviews With Black Writers,* Liveright, 1973.*

* * *

DENIS, Barbara J. 1940-
(Anne Kristin Carroll)

PERSONAL: Born September 6, 1940, in Houston, Tex.; daughter of Ed C. (a business executive) and Reba (Barnett) Jones; married Ronald E. Wilson, 1958 (divorced, 1962); married Michael R. Denis (a sales manager), April, 1962; children: Ronald E., Michael W. *Education:* Attended University of Houston, Gulf Coast Bible College, and Houston Baptist University. *Politics:* "Right Wing Conservative Constitutionalist." *Religion:* "Fundamental, evangelical Christian." *Home:* 3090 Rivermont Pkwy., Alpharetta, Ga. 30201. *Office:* Live's Outreach, P.O. Box 888312, Atlanta, Ga. 30338.

CAREER: Writer. Formerly a reservationist for Pan American Airways and Texas International Airways; free-lance model in Houston, Tex. *Member:* Freedom Foundation, Campus Crusade for Christ, National Right to Life, Christian Right to Life, Women Who Want to Be Women.

WRITINGS—Under pseudonym Anne Kristin Carroll: (With Darien B. Cooper) *We Became Wives of Happy Husbands,* Victor, 1976; *From the Brink of Divorce: An Evangelical Marriage Counselor Advises How to Save Your Marriage,* Doubleday-Galilee, 1978. Also author of cassette tape recordings and workbooks "Marital Dynamics" and "Children: Heartbreak or Happiness."

WORK IN PROGRESS: "A nonfiction Christian book which relates to children."

SIDELIGHTS: Denis recovered from a traumatic second divorce to remarry her second husband and to write two books based on that experience. She told *CA:* "My driving motivation is to share Jesus Christ with others. My vocation will first and foremost be to be a wife and mother. My avocation, I pray both now and in the future, will be a continuing, in-depth study of God's Word, and as important, the daily application of God's truths to my own personal life, marriage, and family. Personally, I believe that between the pages of the book called the Holy Bible can be found all the insights and directions for living life to its fullest, understanding man in every situation, the solutions to *all* of man's heartbreak and problems, and the clear promise of life eternal to all who accept Jesus Christ's substitutionary death at Calvary.

"I believe God's Word is real, alive, and contemporary. I feel it contains clear, vital statements and postions on current issues such as marriage, divorce, the nurture and discipline of children, sex, homosexuality, government, finances, and life after death."

BIOGRAPHICAL/CRITICAL SOURCES: Atlanta Constitution Journal, September 2, 1978; *Christian Review,* September, 1978.

* * *

DENNISTON, Elinore ?-1978
(Rae Foley)

OBITUARY NOTICE: Born in North Dakota; died May 24, 1978, in Phoenix, Ariz. Author. Denniston wrote more than forty suspense novels under the pseudonym Rae Foley. Her most recent works include *The Slippery Step, The Girl Who Had Everything,* and *Where Helen Lies.* She also wrote children's books under her own name. Obituaries and other sources: *Publishers Weekly,* August 28, 1978.

* * *

DENT, Harry (Shuler) 1930-

PERSONAL: Born February 21, 1930, in St. Matthews, S.C.; son of Hampton N. and Sallie (Prickett) Dent; married Elizabeth Francis, August 16, 1951; children: Harry Shuler, Jr., Dolly N., Virginia M. Dent Brant, John R. *Education:* Presbyterian College, B.A. (cum laude), 1951; George Washington University, J.D., 1957; Georgetown University, LL.M., 1959. *Religion:* Southern Baptist. *Home:* 2030 Bermuda Hills Rd., Columbia, S.C. 29204. *Office:* P.O. Box 528, Columbia, S.C. 29202.

CAREER: Washington correspondent for South Carolina newspapers, 1954; chief assistant to U.S. Senator Strom Thurmond, 1955-65; practicing attorney in Columbia, S.C., 1965—. Special counsel to President Richard Nixon, 1968-72. Southern campaign manager for Republican presidential candidates Barry Goldwater, Richard Nixon, and Gerald Ford. Chairman of South Carolina Republican Party, 1965-68; general counsel for Republican National Committee, 1973-74. Member of board of trustees of Freedoms Foundation. *Military service:* U.S. Army, 1951-53; became first lieutenant. U.S. Army Reserve, 1953-68; became major. *Awards, honors:* Distinguished achievement award from Presbyterian College and Pi Kappa Alpha, 1970; D.Pol.Sci. from Baptist College at Charleston, 1971; LL.D. from Presbyterian College, 1971.

WRITINGS: The Prodigal South Returns to Power, Wiley, 1978.

SIDELIGHTS: Dent writes that his book "is concerned with the rise and development of two-party presidential politics in the South and the election of the first Southerner as president in a century. The book covers all presidential campaigns from 1964-1976, with inside accounts."

* * *

D'ERASMO, Martha 1939-

PERSONAL: Born December 6, 1939, in Newark, N.J.; daughter of Harry Eugene and Phellis (Wing) Aldrich; married Joseph J. D'Erasmo (an attorney), September 14, 1959; children: Stacey, Nancy. *Education:* St. Luke's Hospital School of Nursing, R.N., 1961; graduate study at Antioch College, 1976-77. *Politics:* Democrat. *Home:* 5916 Kirby Rd., Bethesda, Md. 20034. *Office:* Legal Research and Services for the Elderly, 1511 K St. N.W., Washington, D.C. 20005.

CAREER: St. Luke's Hospital, New York, N.Y., general staff nurse, 1962-63; East Orange General Hospital, East Orange, N.J., general staff nurse, 1964-65; MarSalle Convalescent Center, Washington, D.C., assistant director of nursing services, 1966-68; Holy Cross Hospital, Silver Spring, Md., pediatric nurse, 1968-70; Washington Home for Incurables, Washington, D.C., director of nursing services, 1971-74; Kensington Georgetown Medical Center, Kensington, Md., nursing coordinator, 1975-77; Legal Research and Services for the Elderly, Washington, D.C., project coordinator, 1977—. *Awards, honors:* Grant from U.S. Administration on Aging, 1977.

WRITINGS: (With Sarah Greene Burger) *Living in a Nursing Home: A Guide to the Nursing Home Experience for Patient, Family, and Friends,* Seabury, 1976.

WORK IN PROGRESS: A textbook on primary care in nursing, with publication by Duxbury.

SIDELIGHTS: Martha D'Erasmo writes: "Much of my work in nursing has involved chronic care for disabled young adults and senior citizens. Having witnessed the same problems occurring over and over in nursing homes, I felt the need to write a book aimed specifically at helping some families and nursing home residents to avoid the painful situations so often witnessed."

Her present work, on a nursing home advocacy project, is designed to test the efficacy of utilizing volunteer groups to work under supervision as advocates for nursing home residents.

* * *

DESAI, Anita 1937-

PERSONAL: Born June 24, 1937, in Mussoorie, India; daughter of D. N. (a businessman) and Toni (Nime) Mazumdar; married Ashvin Desai (an executive), December 13, 1958; children: Rahul, Tani, Arjun, Kiran. *Education:* Delhi University, B.A., 1957. *Address:* c/o Hind Pocket Books, G. T. Rd., Shahdara, New Delhi 32, India.

CAREER: Writer. Member of Advisory Board for English, Sahitya Akademi, New Delhi, India, 1972—.

WRITINGS: Cry, The Peacock (novel), P. Owen, 1963; *Voices in the City* (novel), P. Owen, 1965; *Bye-Bye, Blackbird* (novel), Hind Pocket Books, 1968; *The Peacock Garden* (juvenile), India Book House, 1974; *Where Shall We Go This Summer?* (novel), Vikas Publishing House, 1975; *Cat on a Houseboat* (juvenile), Orient Longmans, 1976; *Fire on the Mountain* (novel), Harper, 1977. Contributor of short stories to periodicals, including *Thought, Envoy, Writers Workshop, Quest, Indian Literature, Illustrated Weekly of India, Femina,* and *Harper's Bazaar.*

WORK IN PROGRESS: Games at Twilight, a collection of short stories, and an untitled novel.

BIOGRAPHICAL/CRITICAL SOURCES: K. R. Srinivasa Iyengar, *Indian Writing in English,* Asia Publishing House, 1962; Paul Verghese, *Indian Writing in English,* Asia Publishing House, 1970; Meena Bellioppa, *The Fiction of Anita Desai,* Writers Workshop, 1971; Meenakshi Mukherjee, *The Twice-Born Fiction,* Arnold Heinemann, 1972; *New York Times Book Review,* November 20, 1977.

*　　*　　*

DESCHNER, John 1923-

PERSONAL: Born October 23, 1923, in Stillwater, Minn.; son of John (a clergyman) and Eleanor (Rieke) Deschner; married Margareta Neovius (a professor), March 19, 1949; children: Martin, Paul, Thomas. *Education:* University of Texas, B.A., 1944; Yale University, B.D., 1947; University of Basel, D.Th., 1960. *Politics:* Democrat. *Religion:* United Methodist. *Home:* 3211 Drexel Dr., Dallas, Tex. 75205. *Office:* Perkins School of Theology, Southern Methodist University, Dallas, Tex. 75275.

CAREER: United Student Christian Council, New York City, general secretary, 1946-52; World University Service, New York City, vice chairman, 1952-53; World Student Christian Federation, Geneva, Switzerland, staff member, 1953-56; Southern Methodist University, Dallas, Tex., assistant professor, 1956-58, associate professor, 1958-62, professor of theology, 1962—. Vice-chairman of World Council of Churches Faith and Order Commission. *Member:* Amnesty International, American Theological Society (fellow), American Association of University Professors.

WRITINGS: Wesley's Christology: An Interpretation, Southern Methodist University Press, 1960; (editor with Leroy T. Howe and Klaus Cenzel) *Our Common History as Christians: Essays in Honor of Albert C. Outler,* Oxford University Press, 1975. Contributor to theology journals.

WORK IN PROGRESS: Research on ecclesiology, practical theology, and ecumenical theology.

*　　*　　*

DEVINE, Donald J. 1937-

PERSONAL: Born April 14, 1937, in Bronxville, N.Y.; son of John (in sales) and Frances (Phelan) Divine; married Ann Smith (an educator), August 29, 1956; children: William, Patricia, Joseph. *Education:* St. John's University, Jamaica, N.Y., B.B.A., 1959; City University of New York, M.A., 1965; Syracuse University, Ph.D., 1967. *Politics:* Republican. *Religion:* Roman Catholic. *Home:* 3311 Camden St., Wheaton, Md. 20902. *Agent:* Jameson G. Campaigne, Jr., 236 Forest Park Pl., Ottawa, Ill. 61350. *Office:* Department of Government, University of Maryland, College Park, Md. 61350. *Office:* Department of Government, University of Maryland, College Park, Md. 20742.

CAREER: University of Maryland, College Park, associate professor of government and politics, 1967—. *Military service:* U.S. Army Reserve, 1960-66. *Member:* American Political Science Association, American Association for Public Opinion Research, Southern Political Science Association, Midwestern Political Science Association.

WRITINGS: The Attentive Public, Rand McNally, 1970; *The Political Culture of the United States,* Little, Brown, 1972; *Does Freedom Work?,* Caroline House, 1978.

WORK IN PROGRESS: Traditional Americans in a Postindustrial Era, on public opinion and public policy.

DEW, Edward MacMillan 1935-

PERSONAL: Born June 10, 1935, in Burbank, Calif.; son of Edward M. and Mary (Wages) Dew; married Anke Van Dijk (a demographer), December 27, 1960; children: Edward M., Ian M. *Education:* Pomona College, B.A., 1957; George Washington University, M.A., 1958; Yale University, M.A., 1960; University of California, Los Angeles, Ph.D., 1966. *Home:* 1102 Stillson Rd., Fairfield, Conn. 06430. *Office:* Department of Politics, Fairfield University, Fairfield, Conn. 06430.

CAREER: U.S. Peace Corps, Washington, D.C., associate representative in Peru, 1966-67; Fairfield University, Fairfield, Conn., assistant professor, 1967-74, associate professor of politics, 1974—. Lecturer for U.S. State Department Foreign Service Institute. *Member:* Latin American Studies Association, Caribbean Studies Association. *Awards, honors:* Research grants from Ford Foundation and Rockefeller Foundation, 1973-74, and Netherlands Institute for Advanced Study, 1975-76.

WRITINGS: Politics in the Altiplano: The Dynamics of Change in Rural Peru, University of Texas Press, 1969; *The Difficult Flowering of Surinam: Ethnicity and Politics in a Plural Society,* Nijhoff, 1978. Contributor to politics and foreign studies journals.

WORK IN PROGRESS: An introductory textbook in comparative politics.

SIDELIGHTS: Dew writes: "The Peruvian study deals with political development in the department of Puno (on Lake Titicaca), while the Surinam book traces that country's history from Dutch colony to independent nation. Both deal with the phenomenon of ethnic politics: the Puno study shows the paralytic effects of ethnic cleavages reenforced by socio-economic stratification, while the experience of Surinam shows that ethnic conflict may be accommodated where all groups share to some extent in the society's opportunities and resources. Indeed, Surinam's achievements offer hope to racially-divided societies everywhere!"

*　　*　　*

DEXTER, (Ellen) Pat(ricia) Egan

PERSONAL: Born in Oak Park, Ill.; daughter of Joseph James (a butcher) and Katherine (a bookkeeper; maiden name, Arado) Egan; married Ralph Dexter (a systems analyst); children: Carla, John, David. *Education:* Phoenix College, A.A., 1973; attended Grand Canyon College, 1978—. *Residence:* Phoenix, Ariz. *Agent:* Ruth Cantor, 156 Fifth Ave., New York, N.Y. 10010.

CAREER: Writer. Also worked as bookkeeper, teacher, and secretary, and in data processing field. *Member:* Phoenix Writers Club, Desert Toastmasters Club. *Awards, honors:* Awards from Phoenix Writers Club national fiction contest, 1972, for "Attack on the Old Age Syndrome of Jack." and from *Guidepost's* workshop contest, 1976, for "After the Party Is Over."

WRITINGS: The Emancipation of Joe Tepper (fiction), Thomas Nelson, 1976; *Arrow in the Wind* (fiction), Thomas Nelson, 1978; *The Boy Who Snuck In* (juvenile picture book), Concordia, 1978. Contributor of articles and stories to magazines.

WORK IN PROGRESS: How to Use the Magic in Your Mind; Shifting Mountain, a novel.

SIDELIGHTS: Pat Dexter writes: "Basically I consider myself a fiction writer, and my stories are meant to be interesting tales, nothing more. But I also write articles about incidents that move me, touch my soul, and make me want to say, 'Listen, everyone, you know what. . . .'

"I am interested in psychology, and have spent four or five years studying, researching, and experimenting with methods of meditation. From this came *How to Use the Magic in Your Mind.* I am a perpetual student, and expect at a later date to be teaching Western meditation."

* * *

DIAL, Joan 1937-
(Katherine Kent, Amanda York)

PERSONAL: Born November 9, 1937, in Liverpool, England; came to the United States in 1956, naturalized citizen, 1973; daughter of Edwin (a police officer) and Sarah G. Rogers; married Paul E. Dial (a supervisor), February 10, 1956; children: Criag Edwin, Gary William, Sharon Lisa. *Education:* Attended public schools in Liverpool, England. *Politics:* Democrat. *Home:* 25191 Sea Vista Dr., Dana Point, Calif. 92629. *Agent:* Richard Huttner Agency, Inc., 330 East 33rd St., New York, N.Y. 10016.

CAREER: Writer, 1975—. Also worked as secretary and editorial assistant.

WRITINGS—Under name Joan Dial: *Susanna* (novel), Fawcett, 1978; *Lovers and Warriors* (novel), Fawcett, 1978; *Deadly Lady* (novel), Fawcett, 1979.

Under pseudonym Katherine Kent: *Druid's Retreat* (novel), Pinnacle Books, 1979.

Under pseudonym Amanda York: *Beloved Enemy* (novel), Pocket Books, 1978; *Somewhere in the Whirlwind* (novel), Pocket Books, 1979.

WORK IN PROGRESS: Inn of the Blue Lantern, a historical romance; *This Very Midnight Cease,* a contemporary novel.

SIDELIGHTS: Joan Dial writes: "I spent my childhood surrounded by colorful characters—from aristocrats to gypsies—growing up in England. An early and precocious reader, I was frequently disappointed that storytellers often tossed aside a potentially exciting thread of their plots without fully exploring all of the possibilities. I wanted to do better—I still do. As a child I would study my parents' rather exotic friends and ask myself: 'What if that man had met this woman (instead of that one) earlier in his life—how would their lives have been different?' 'What if that woman had been born into the upper class instead of the working class?' 'What if . . . ?' *'What if . . . ?'* My mind reeled with the endless possibilities for drama in even the most mundane of lives.

"I knew I'd be a writer when I read my first book. I didn't know I would marry, travel extensively, and have three children first.

"The most mystical metamorphosis of my life was when I married an American, came to live here, and—slowly—fell in love with a country."

When asked her opinion on other contemporary writers, Dial responded: "This country has a tremendous pool of writing talent and a steadily growing number of readers. In my opinion, American writers now lead the world in sheer innovative genius. (Since I am only an American by adoption, I feel objective enough to arrive at this conclusion.)"

Dial advises aspiring writers to "write, don't talk about it. Remember that your readers want to be entertained (and try not to bore them!)." She herself writes for a minimum of

eight hours a day, Monday through Friday, "more when I'm researching as well as writing. Weekends are for outdoor activities."

Reviewing *Beloved Enemy* for the *Santa Ana Register,* Diane Hoyle called it a "heart pounding love story." "Its suspense," she added, "is a literary bribe that hastens one to the last stirring page." *Lovers and Warriors* is a "neat blending of fact and fiction . . . bound to hold the interest of devotees to the genre," wrote a *Publishers Weekly* critic.

BIOGRAPHICAL/CRITICAL SOURCES: Santa Ana Register, May 7, 1978, October 1, 1978; *Publishers Weekly,* July 3, 1978.

* * *

DIAMOND, I(sidore) A. L. 1920-

PERSONAL: Born June 27, 1920, in Ungheni, Rumania; came to United States, 1929; son of David and Elca (Waldeman) Diamond; married Barbara Bentley; children: Ann Cynthia, Paul Bentley. *Education:* Columbia University, B.A., 1941. *Residence:* Beverly Hills, Calif. *Agent:* Irving Paul Lazar Agency, 211 South Beverly Dr., Beverly Hills, Calif. 90212.

CAREER: Screenwriter. Associated with Paramount Pictures Corp., 1941. *Awards, honors*—All with Billy Wilder: Writers Guild Award from Writers Guild of America, 1957, for "Love in the Afternoon"; Writers Guild Award and nomination for best screenplay from Academy of Motion Picture Arts and Sciences, both 1959, both for "Some Like It Hot"; Writers Guild Award, Oscar from Academy of Motion Picture Arts and Sciences for best screenplay, and New York Film Critics award, all 1960, all for "The Apartment"; nominations from Academy of Motion Picture Arts and Sciences, 1966, for "The Fortune Cookie."

WRITINGS—Screenplays: (With Stanley Davis) "Murder in the Blue Room" (adapted from a story by Erich Philippi), Universal, 1944; (with James V. Kern) "Never Say Goodbye," Warner Bros., 1946; (with Eugene Conrad and Francis Swann) "Love and Learn," Warner Bros., 1946; (with Charles Hoffman) "Two Guys From Milwaukee," Warner Bros., 1946; (author of additional dialogue) "Romance on the High Seas," Warner Bros., 1948; (with Henry Ephron and Phoebe Ephron) "Always Together," Warner Bros., 1948; (with Allen Boretz) "Two Guys From Texas" (adapted from the play by Robert Sloan and Louis Pelletier, "Howdy, Stranger"), Warner Bros., 1948; (author of screen story) "It's a Great Feeling," Warner Bros., 1949; "The Girl From North Beach," Warner Bros., 1949.

"Love Nest" (adapted from the novel by Scott Corbett, *The Reluctant Landlord),* Twentieth Century-Fox, 1951; (with F. Hugh Herbert) "Let's Make It Legal," Twentieth Century-Fox, 1951; (with Ben Hecht and Charles Lederer) "Monkey Business," Twentieth Century-Fox, 1952; (with Boris Ingster) "Something for the Birds," Twentieth Century-Fox, 1952; (with William Altman, Melvin Frank, and Norman Panama) "That Certain Feeling" (adapted from the play by Jean Kerr and Eleanor Brooke, "The King of Hearts"), Paramount, 1956; (with Isobel Lennart) "Merry Andrew" (adapted from the novel by Paul Gallico, *The Romance of Henry Menafee),* Metro-Goldwyn-Mayer (MGM), 1958; "Cactus Flower," Columbia, 1969.

With Billy Wilder: "Love in the Afternoon" (adapted from the novel by Claude Anet, *Ariane),* Allied Artists, 1957; "Some Like It Hot" (adapted from the film by Robert Thoeren and M. Logan, "Fanfare of Love"), United Artists,

1959; "The Apartment," United Artists, 1960; "One, Two, Three" (adapted from the play by Ferenc Molnar), United Artists, 1961; "Irma La Douce" (adapted from the musical play by Alexandre Breffort), United Artists, 1963; "Kiss Me Stupid" (adapted from the play by Anna Bonacci, "L'Ora della Fantasia"), Lopert, 1964; "The Fortune Cookie," United Artists, 1966; "The Private Life of Sherlock Holmes," United Artists, 1970; *Two Screenplays: The Apartment and The Fortune Cookie,* Praeger, 1971; "Avanti" (adapted from the play by Samuel Taylor), United Artists, 1972; "The Front Page," Universal-CIC, 1974; "Fedora," Allied Artists, 1979.

WORK IN PROGRESS: Screenplay entitled "Around the World in Eighty Hours."

SIDELIGHTS: Diamond has shared credit with Billy Wilder on a number of successful film ventures. "Some Like It Hot," their second screenplay, was called a "rare, rib-tickling lampoon" by A. H. Weiler who added that the film was a "broad farce in which authentically comic action vies with snappy and sophisticated dialogue."

Diamond and Wilder followed the successful "Some Like It Hot" with "The Apartment," a more serious film about a lonely office worker who lets his co-workers use his apartment to carry out their romantic flings. Bosley Crowther deemed it "gleeful, tender and even sentimental. . . ."

BIOGRAPHICAL/CRITICAL SOURCES: New York Times, March 30, 1959, June 16, 1960, June 6, 1963, December 23, 1964, October 20, 1966, December 17, 1969.

* * *

DICKERSON, Martha Ufford 1922-

PERSONAL: Born March 16, 1922, in Bellow Falls, Vt.; daughter of Lucien Henry (a contractor) and Marjorie (Carroll) Ufford; married Wade Dickerson, February 15, 1944; children: Marjori Dickerson Rynberg, Forrest. *Education:* Green Mountain Junior College, A.A., 1941; Eastern Michigan University, B.S., 1960; Wayne State University, M.S.W., 1967, further graduate study, 1968. *Home:* 33620 Grand River, Farmington, Mich. 48024. *Office:* Institute for the Study of Mental Retardation and Related Disabilities, University of Michigan, 130 South First St., Ann Arbor, Mich. 48104.

CAREER: Center director of several retired workers centers in Detroit, Mich., 1960-69; Wayne Region Service and Training Center for the Retarded, Detroit, clinical social worker, 1969-73; University of Michigan, Ann Arbor, Institute of Gerontology, instructor, 1969—, Institute for the Study of Mental Retardation and Related Disabilities, lecturer in the School of Social Work, 1973—, program associate in social work, 1973-76, acting director of social work, 1976-77, director of human fulfillment project, 1977—. Therapist at Parent/Youth Developmental Services, Farmington, Mich., 1972-73. Workshop conductor and lecturer, 1974—. *Member:* National Association of Social Workers, National Council on the Aging, American Association of Retired Persons, American Association of Mental Deficiency, Academy of Certified Social Workers, Michigan Foster Parents Association, Wayne State University School of Social Work Alumni Association.

WRITINGS: (With P. Barnard, M. Demery, A. Kambouris, and E. W. Lynch) *You and Me,* with companion volume, Wayne County Intermediate School District, 1977; *Fostering Children With Mental Retardation* (instructor's manual and trainee's workbook), Foster Parenting Training Program, Eastern Michigan University, 1977. *Our Four Boys: Foster Parenting Retarded Teenagers,* Syracuse University Press, 1978.

WORK IN PROGRESS: Social Work Practice and Mental Retardation.

SIDELIGHTS: Martha Dickerson writes: "As I reflect upon the unfoldment of my life, I recognize how much I value human dignity and respect for self. Much of my personal commitment and public involvement has been based on my belief that each person has an inherent right to respect himself and demand or earn respect from others. Down through the years I have often become involved in situations where a person or group of persons was in jeopardy of losing those basic human rights. I have come to know that I care profoundly about the dignified survival or life experience of other people because my own dignity, self-worth, and survival are at stake.

"Life has been good to me, and I've attempted to be a contributor to my own good life and the lives of others. My parents, husband, children, friends, and colleagues have provided me with acceptance, support, encouragement, and frequent constructive confrontation which has helped me to sustain a love of life, a respect for self, and a concern for others. I have practiced, trained, and taught, but mostly I have learned, from those close to me as much or more than from the scholars and professors. My writing has been and will be primarily based upon the experiences I have had with the people from whom I have learned the most—my family (husband, biological children, foster children), clients and students."

* * *

DICKINSON, William B(oyd) 1908-1978

OBITUARY NOTICE: Born May 18, 1908, in Kansas City, Mo.; died September 12, 1978, in Philadelphia, Pa. Newspaper reporter, foreign correspondent, and editor. Dickinson was a correspondent for United Press International for nineteen years and covered the Japanese surrender of World War II. After the war he became a news editor of the *Philadelphia Bulletin;* in 1969, he was named executive editor of the paper. Obituaries and other sources: *Washington Post,* September 13, 1978; *Who's Who in America,* 40th edition, Marquis, 1978.

* * *

DILLER, Phyllis (Ada) 1917-

PERSONAL: Born July 17, 1917, in Lima, Ohio; daughter of Perry Marcus (an insurance sales manager) and Frances Ada (a secretary; maiden name, Romshe) Driver; married Sherwood Anderson Diller, November 4, 1939 (divorced September 3, 1965); married Warde Donovan, October 7, 1965; children: (first marriage) Peter, Sally, Suzanne Diller Mills, Stephanie Diller Waldron, Perry. *Education:* Attended Sherwood Music School, Chicago, Ill., 1935-38; Bluffton College, B.A., 1941. *Home and office:* 163 South Rockingham Ave., Los Angeles, Calif. 90049.

CAREER: Comic and actress. Prior to show business career, worked as columnist for *San Leandro News-Observer,* copy writer for Kahn's Department Store in Oakland, Calif., writer for KROW-Radio, Oakland, and as staff member of the merchandising and press relations office of KSFO-Radio, San Francisco, Calif. Made professional comic debut on March 7, 1955, at the Purple Onion, San Francisco; has headlined shows at major nightclubs in New York City,

Chicago, and Las Vegas, including The Tropicana and Caesar's Palace. Made television debut on "The Jack Paar Show," 1959; appeared as a guest on variety shows and specials, including "Hollywood Palace," "The Flip Wilson Show," "The Muppets," "Chips," and "America 2-Night"; star of "The Phyllis Diller Special," ABC-TV, 1963, "Show Street," 1965, "An Evening With Phyllis Diller," 1966, "The Phyllis Diller Show," ABC-TV, 1966, "The Beautiful Phyllis Diller Show," NBC-TV, 1968, and "Phyllis Diller's 102nd Birthday Party," ABC-TV, 1974. Made motion picture debut in "Splendor in the Grass," Warner Bros., 1961; appeared in motion pictures, including "Boy, Did I Get a Wrong Number," United Artists, 1966, "Eight on the Lam," United Artists, 1967, and "The Sunshine Boys," Metro-Goldwyn-Mayer, 1975. Concert pianist, making more than fifty guest appearances as a piano soloist, 1971—.

Member: American Guild of Variety Artists, American Federation of Television and Radio Artists, Screen Actors Guild, Actors' Equity Association, American Society of Composers, Authors and Publishers. *Awards, honors:* Numerous citations from national associations, mostly for humanitarian work, including awards from Veterans Assistance League, Jewish Foundation for Retarded Children, U.S. Department of the Army, and Hemophilia Foundation of Southern California; doctorate of humane letters, National Christian University, 1977; USO Liberty Bell Award, 1978.

WRITINGS: Phyllis Diller's Housekeeping Hints, Doubleday, 1966; *Phyllis Diller's Marriage Manual,* Doubleday, 1967; *The Complete Mother,* Doubleday, 1969. Also author of lyrics to song "My Prayer."

SIDELIGHTS: Phyllis Diller began her show business career at the age of thirty-seven. Prior to her success as a comedian, Diller worked at various jobs in order to contribute to the support of her five children. Her life as a mother and homemaker has provided Diller with much of her comedic material. Usually Diller's routine includes a discussion of her "stage" family with emphasis on her husband, Fang, mother-in-law, Moby Dick, and sister-in-law, Captain Bligh. Diller also uses outlandish and exotic costumes and hairdos as part of her comedy act. Her comedic success was, perhaps, forecasted by the overwhelming success of that first engagement; booked for two weeks at the Purple Onion, Diller stayed on for eighty-nine!

In her private life Diller remains distant from her stage character. While Diller on stage carries a long cigarette holder, in private she does not smoke. An accomplished comedian, Diller is also a serious musician who has made over fifty guest appearances with national symphonies. Her house is filled with musical instruments, all of which she plays.

In addition to her appearances on variety shows, Diller also takes part in charity functions. She accompanied Bob Hope on his annual Christmas USO shows. Diller has received numerous citations for her contributions to humanitarian causes, and was named "Miss 101st" by the U.S. Army 101st Division.

AVOCATIONAL INTERESTS: Cooking, painting, music, and writing.

*   *   *

DISPENZA, Joseph Ernest 1942-

PERSONAL: Born September 14, 1942, in Ashtabula, Ohio; son of Joseph Frank and Margaret (Savarise) Dis-

penza. *Education:* St. Edward's University, B.A., 1968; University of Texas, M.A., 1970. *Home:* 622 Alto St., Santa Fe, N.M. 87501. *Agent:* Elaine Markson Literary Agency, Inc., 44 Greenwich Ave., New York, N.Y. 10011.

CAREER: Entered Roman Catholic Congregation of the Holy Cross, 1960, teaching brother (monk), 1960-68, legally released from obligations of the brotherhood, 1968; Center for Social Communication, San Antonio, Tex., director of Film & Television Division, 1968-69; American Film Institute, Washington, D.C., director of education, 1970-73; freelance writer, 1974—. High school teacher and social worker in Terre Haute, Ind. 1963-66, and Chicago, Ill., 1966-67. Lecturer at American University, 1970-73. Lecturer at colleges and universities; conducted seminars and workshops; consultant to U.S. Information Agency, Action for Children's Television, and film companies. *Member:* Society for Cinema Studies, Institute for Environmental Response (Canada; fellow), University Film Association. *Awards, honors:* Grant from U.S. Information Agency, 1974, for Latin American tour.

WRITINGS: Forgotten Patriot, Dujarie Press, 1966; *Re-Runs* (analysis of feature films), Benziger, 1970; (contributor) Kathleen Karr and Sali Ann Knegsman, editors, *The American Film Heritage,* Acropolis Books, 1972; *Freeze Frame: A History of the American Film,* with filmstrips, Pflaum/Standard, 1973; *Advertising the American Woman,* Pflaum/Standard, 1974; *The House of Alarcon* (novel), Coward, 1978.

Other: "The Death and Trial of Pope Formosus" (three-act play), first produced in Austin, Tex., at St. Edward's University, March, 1968; "Juarez" (screenplay), Capricorn Productions, 1975; "Washington Story" (screenplay), 1976. Author of teleplays for University of Texas. Member of editorial board of *Journal of Popular Film* and *Journal of Aesthetic Education.*

WORK IN PROGRESS: A novel, a historical family saga.

SIDELIGHTS: Dispenza comments: "It seems to me that there is a difference between writers and serious writers. I have decided to devote the rest of my life to being a serious writer, one who is interested in depicting the fullness of the human condition in order to elevate, enlighten, and instruct. Human emotions are infinite in their complexity, and I am intent upon examining them. The novel is still the best form for this kind of examination."

*   *   *

DOBSON, Terry 1937-

PERSONAL: Born June 9, 1937, in Cambridge, Mass.; son of Walter N. and Janet (Bissell) Dobson. *Education:* Attended private school in Deerfield, Mass. *Home address:* Box A-268, Peek Slip Station, New York, N.Y. 10038.

CAREER: Pergamon Press Ltd., Oxford, England, Far East regional manager in Tokyo, Japan, 1963-65; Think, Inc., Tokyo, vice-president, 1968-70; writer, 1969—. Associate faculty member at City College of the City University of New York and Wesleyan University, Middletown, Conn. *Military service:* U.S. Marine Corps, 1957-59. *Member:* Bond Street Dojo (co-founder).

WRITINGS: (With Victor Miller) *Giving in to Get Your Way,* Delacorte, 1978. Contributor to *Esquire.*

WORK IN PROGRESS: Research on non-violent responses to conflict situations.

SIDELIGHTS: Dobson's career has included work as a

mechanic, cowboy, seaman, carnival worker, carpenter, photographer and photographer's model, bodyguard, and political speechwriter.

He writes: "My view of man's nonviolent tendencies was informed chiefly by my eight-year apprenticeship to Japan's Moirbei Ueshiba, founder of Aikido. *Giving in to Get Your Way* seeks to appraise the conflicts of daily American life from a tactical reference. The principles which are inherent in the order and motion of men in masses are the same principles which govern individuals. Ueshiba taught me benevolent, individual tactics, and I have tried to explain what I learned in the current American idiom."

* * *

DOESER, Linda (Ann) 1950-

PERSONAL: Born May 5, 1950, in London, England; daughter of Hendrikus Jacobus and Margaret (O'Donnell) Doeser; married Robert James Burroughs (an art director), September 23, 1978. *Education:* Royal Holloway College, London, B.A. (honors), 1973. *Home:* 80 Iffley Rd., London W.6, England. *Office:* Octopus Books Ltd., 59 Grosvenor, London W1X 9DA, England.

CAREER: Marshall Cavendish Books Ltd., London, England, editor, 1973-77; Hestair Kiddicraft Publishing Co., Kenley, England, publishing manager, 1977; Octopus Books Ltd., London, editor, 1977—. Volunteer teacher of English to speakers of other languages.

WRITINGS: Ballet and Dance, St. Martin's, 1977.

WORK IN PROGRESS: A critical study of the works of Malcolm Lowry, completion expected in 1980.

SIDELIGHTS: Linda Doeser writes: "An abiding—even obsessive—interest in words led me naturally to a career in publishing and a desire to write. A fascination with language (I speak French and Spanish) and a formal education in English literature inclines me toward literary study. Possibly, if I study in depth the skill of novelists I admire, I may one day develop sufficient technique to write a readable novel myself."

* * *

DOIG, Ivan 1939-

PERSONAL: Born June 27, 1939, in White Sulphur Springs, Mont.; son of Charles Campbell (a ranch worker) and Berneta (Ringer) Doig; married Carol Muller (a professor), April 17, 1965. *Education:* Northwestern University, B.S., 1961, M.S., 1962; University of Washington, Seattle, Ph.D., 1969. *Home:* 17021 10th Ave. NW, Seattle, Wash. 98177.

CAREER: Lindsay-Schaub Newspapers, Decatur, Ill., editorial writer, 1963-64; *Rotarian,* Evanston, Ill., assistant editor, 1964-66; free-lance writer, 1969—. *Military service:* U.S. Air Force Reserve, 1962-68; became sergeant. *Member:* American Society of Journalist and Authors, Authors Guild of Authors League of America.

WRITINGS: (With wife, Carol M. Doig) *News: A Consumer's Guide,* Prentice-Hall, 1972; *The Streets We Have Come Down* (textbook), Hayden, 1975; *Utopian America: Dreams and Realities,* Hayden, 1976; *Early Forestry Research,* U.S. Forestry Service, 1976; *This House of Sky: Landscapes of a Western Mind* (memoir), Harcourt, 1978. Contributor to periodicals, including *Modern Maturity, New York Times, Editor and Publisher,* and *Writer's Digest.*

WORK IN PROGRESS: A book on the past and present of the Pacific Northwest.

SIDELIGHTS: Doig comments: "For ten years, and several hundred thousand published words, I wrote primarily for magazines and was tagged as a free-lance writer. With the critical success of *This House of Sky,* I've been elevated to author—which is somewhat strange to me, in that I use the same typewriter and seem to be the same person sitting down to it day after day. Anyway, my theme will remain what it has been—the American people and the westering expanse of this continent they happened to come to."

AVOCATIONAL INTERESTS: Reading, hiking.

BIOGRAPHICAL/CRITICAL SOURCES: Time, September 11, 1978; *Los Angeles Times,* September 13, 1978; *Chicago Tribune,* September 17, 1978; *Seattle Post-Intelligencer,* October 1, 1978.

* * *

DOLAN, Jay P(atrick) 1936-

PERSONAL: Born March 17, 1936, in Bridgeport, Conn.; son of Joseph T. (in business) and Margaret (Reardon) Dolan; married Patricia McNeal (a professor), May 25, 1973; children: Patrick Joseph, Mark McNeal. *Education:* Gregorian University, S.T.L., 1962; University of Chicago, Ph.D., 1970. *Religion:* Roman Catholic. *Home:* 16130 Brockton Ct., Granger, Ind. 46530. *Office:* Department of History, University of Notre Dame, Notre Dame, Ind. 46556.

CAREER: University of San Francisco, San Francisco, Calif., assistant professor of history, 1970-71; University of Notre Dame, Notre Dame, Ind., assistant professor, 1971-77, associate professor of history, 1977—, director of Center for the Study of American Catholicism, 1977—. *Member:* Organization of American Historians, American Church History Society, American Catholic Historical Association. *Awards, honors:* Fellowship from Shelby Cullom Davis Center at Princeton University, 1973-74; John Gilmary Shea Award from American Catholic Historical Association, 1975, for *The Immigrant Church;* fellowship from American Council of Learned Societies, 1978-79.

WRITINGS: The Immigrant Church: New York's Irish and German Catholic, 1815-1865, Johns Hopkins Press, 1975; (editor) *Heritage of '76,* University of Notre Dame Press, 1976; (editor) *The American Catholic Tradition,* Arno, 1978; *Catholic Revivalism: The American Experience, 1830-1900,* University of Notre Dame Press, 1978. Contributor to history and religious studies journals. Editor of *American Catholic Studies Newsletter,* 1975—.

WORK IN PROGRESS: A social history of American Catholicism.

SIDELIGHTS: Dolan comments: "I love to write, but I find it very frustrating at times. I am a different personality when doing serious and prolonged writing; my mind is in another world. Basically, I flip out during these periods.

"A personal goal is to promote the study of American Catholicism, an area too long neglected by scholars and in need of competent creative study."

* * *

DOMAN, June
   See BEVERIDGE, Meryle Secrest

* * *

DONNELLY, John Patrick 1934-

PERSONAL: Born September 23, 1934, in Milwaukee,

Wis.; son of John Patrick (a lawyer) and Margaret (a nurse; maiden name, O'Neill) Donnelly. *Education:* St. Louis University, B.A., 1958; St. Mary's College, St. Marys, Kan., S.T.L., 1967; University of Wisconsin—Madison, Ph.D. *Home and office:* 1404 West Wisconsin Ave., Milwaukee, Wis. 53233.

CAREER: Entered Society of Jesus (Jesuits), 1952, ordained Roman Catholic priest, 1965; Marquette University, Milwaukee, Wis., assistant professor, 1972-76, associate professor of history, 1977—. *Member:* American Historical Association, American Catholic Historical Association, American Society for Reformation Research, Italian Historical Association, Sixteenth Century Studies Conference (president, 1977).

WRITINGS: Calvinism and Scholasticism in Vermigli's Doctrine of Man and Grace, E. J. Brill, 1976; *Reform and Renewal,* Consortium, 1977.

WORK IN PROGRESS: A bibliography of Vermigli works, with publication by Corpus Reformatorum Italicorum; a biography of Antonio Possevino.

AVOCATIONAL INTERESTS: Golf, bridge, Renaissance painting.

*   *   *

DONNELLY, Joseph P(eter) 1905-

PERSONAL: Born September 20, 1905, in O'Connor, Neb.; son of Peter Thomas and Bridget Ann (Mawe) Donnelly. *Education:* St. Louis University, A.B., 1928, M.A., 1929, Ph.D., 1940; St. Mary College, Leavenworth, Kan., S.T.L., 1937. *Home and office:* 3601 Lindell Blvd., St. Louis, Mo. 63108.

CAREER: Entered Society of Jesus (Jesuits), 1923, ordained Roman Catholic priest, 1936; Regis College, Denver, Colo., associate professor of history, 1940-43; St. Louis University, St. Louis, Mo., associate professor of history, 1943-55, director of libraries, 1946-55; Marquette University, Milwaukee, Wis., associate professor, 1955-56, professor of history, 1956-74, chairman of department, 1960-72. *Member:* American Historical Association, American Catholic Historical Association, Missouri Historical Association.

WRITINGS: Old Cahokia, St. Louis Historical Documents Foundation, 1959; *The French in the Mississippi Valley,* University of Illinois Press, 1965; *Thwaites' Jesuit Relations: Errata and Addenda,* Loyola University Press, 1967; (translator and author of introduction) Nicolas Point, *Wilderness Kingdom: Indian Life in the Rocky Mountains 1840-1847,* Holt, 1967; *Jacques Marquette, S.J., 1637-1675,* Loyola University Press, 1968; *Pierre Gibault, Missionary, 1737-1802,* Loyola University Press, 1971; *Jean de Brebeuf, 1593-1649,* Loyola University Press, 1975. Also author of *The Parish of the Holy Family at Cahokia.*

*   *   *

DONOSO, Jose 1924-

PERSONAL: Born October 5, 1924, in Santiago, Chile; son of Jose (a physician) and Alicia Donoso; married Maria del Pilar Serrano (a translator) 1961; children: Maria. *Education:* Attended Instituto Pedagogico, 1947; Princeton University, A.B., 1951. *Politics:* "Anti-authoritarian." *Religion:* Atheist. *Residence:* Calaceite, Teruel, Spain. *Agent:* Carmen Balcells, Generalisimio 580, Barcelona 11, Spain.

CAREER: Writer. Worked as shepherd in Patagonia; professor of conversational English at Catholic University of

Chile, 1954; taught techniques of expression at University of Chile; journalist for *Revista Ercilla* in Santiago, Chile, 1959-64; taught writing and modern Spanish-American literature at University of Iowa Writer's Workshop, 1965-67, and in Fort Collins, Colo., 1969. *Awards, honors:* Premio Municipal de Santiago, 1955; Chile-Italia Prize for journalism, 1960; William Faulkner Foundation Prize, 1962, for *Coronacion;* Guggenheim fellowship.

WRITINGS: Veraneo y otros cuentos (short stories; title means "Summertime and Other Stories"), Santiago, 1955; *Coronacion* (novel), Nascimento, 1957, translation from the Spanish by Jocasta Goodwin published as *Coronation,* Knopf, 1965; *El charleston* (short stories; title means "The Charleston"), Nascimento, 1960, abridged edition published as *Cuentos,* Seix Barral, 1971, translation published as *Charleston and Other Stories,* David R. Godine, 1977; *Los mejores de Jose Donosco,* (title means "The Major Stories of Jose Donoso"), Zig-Zag, 1966; *El lugar sin limites* (novel), J. Moritz, 1966, translation published as "Hell Has No Limits" in *Triple Cross,* Dutton, 1972; *Este domingo* (novel), Zig-Zag, 1966, translation by Lorraine O'Grady Freeman published as *This Sunday,* Knopf, 1967; (co-editor with William A. Henkin and others) *The Tri-Quarterly Anthology of Contemporary Latin American Literature,* Dutton, 1969; *El obsceno pajaro de la noche* (novel), Seix Barral, 1970, translation by Hardie St. Martin and Leonard Mades published as *The Obscene Bird of Night,* Knopf, 1973; *Historia personal de "boom",* Anagrama, 1972, translation by Gregory Kolovakos published as *The Boom in Spanish American Literature: A Personal History,* Columbia University Press, 1977; *Tres novelitas burguesas* (novellas), Seix Barral, 1973, translation by Andree Conrad published as *Sacred Families,* Knopf, 1977. Literary critic for *Siempre* magazine, 1964-66.

SIDELIGHTS: Although he is now regarded as one of the premier writers to emerge from South America in this century, Donoso labored for years in relative obscurity. His first book, *Veraneo y otros cuentos* was published only after Donoso had guaranteed sales of one hundred copies via subscriptions. After that, he enlisted his friends to help sell copies on streetcorners throughout Santiago. In 1965, Donoso was forced to sell his first novel, *Coronacion,* in similar fashion.

Before the publication of *Coronacion,* Donoso had written another collection of stories in the same vein as *Veraneo y otros cuentos.* The second collection was entitled *El charleston* and, although it too met with little success, it contained suggestions of what Donoso would later accomplish. Many of the tales show a preoccupation with childhood and growing up. But even with his early stories, Donoso displayed his obsessions with isolation and madness which would come to the fore in his masterpiece, *The Obscene Bird of Night.* Still, Donoso had written the short stories in a fairly realistic style; he had not yet mastered his unique "hallucinogenic" approach, yet the stories in which he attempted his own style were appreciated more than the conventional ones. Robert Maurer wrote: "What is clear . . . is that, in pursuit of his own demons, his agile, sometimes hypertrophied imagination was off and running in the morning. After his first three novels . . . Donoso was pegged as a *criollista,* a writer in the tradition of Chilean regional realism." Maurer believed even Donoso's early experiments with style were superior to his realist narratives.

In 1962, Donoso received the William Faulkner Foundation Prize for his first novel, *Coronacion.* Though the novel established him as a writer outside his native Chile, it too was written in the realist manner. The following two novels, "Hell Has No Limits" and *This Sunday* began to deal more intimately with themes closely associated with Donoso—self-disintegration and eventual madness. Z. Nelly Martinez wrote that "the abundance of costumes and disguises in Donoso's novels marks this process of disintegration and emphasizes the many personalities or symbolic masks that the characters assume in their futile attempts at self-integration." In the same article, Martinez also observed, "The tragic nature of Donoso's characters stems from their inability to alter their condition.... The only alternative to this helplessness is 'to join the cosmic madness.' Thus we perceive a glorification, a symbolic crowning of insanity."

The Obscene Bird of Night is widely considered to be Donoso's greatest work and the culmination of his thematic obsessions. "It is as though reality mirrored dreams," declared Wolfgang A. Luchting, "history showed us legend or myth, as if each were a form of all others. People change into each other, into animals, and back. The whole novel strikes one as the delirium of a physical and metaphysical hypochondriac, almost a schizophrenic." Robert Coover noted: "*The Obscene Bird of Night* is a dense and energetic book, full of terrible risk-taking, populated with legendary saints and witches, mad old crones and a whole estate-full of freaks and monsters, and narrated by a disturbed deaf-mute, many times disguised. The story line is like a great puzzle...."

The Boom in Spanish American Literature is a marked departure from Donoso's typical writing. The book traces the rise of Spanish-American literature during the 1960's, a movement in which Donoso played a large part. Aside from tracing Donoso's evolution from realist to avant-garde writer, the book also comments on the rise of other noted Latin American writers, including Jorge Luis Borges, Carlos Fuentes, and Mario Vargas Llosa. And most critics compare Donoso's acknowledged masterpiece, *The Obscene Bird of Night*, favorably to any literary work derived from that movement. As Luchting remarked, *The Obscene Bird of Night* is "unquestionably one of the most skillful works that continent and a half has produced."

BIOGRAPHICAL/CRITICAL SOURCES: Books Abroad, spring, 1972, winter, 1972, spring, 1975; *Contemporary Literary Criticism*, Gale, Volume 4, 1975, Volume 8, 1978; *New York Times Book Review*, June 26, 1977; *Saturday Review*, July 9, 1977.

* * *

DORSET, Ruth
  See ROSS, W(illiam) E(dward) D(aniel)

* * *

DOSSICK, Philip 1941-
PERSONAL: Born May 29, 1941, in Brooklyn, N.Y.; son of Jesse (a history professor) and Sarah (a teacher of the deaf; maiden name, Berman) Dossick; married Jane Kolbert (a physical therapist); children: Stephen. *Education:* New York University, B.A., 1967; studied classical piano with Lillian Reznikoff-Wolff. *Residence:* New York, N.Y. *Agent:* Peter Skolnik, Sanford Greenburger Associates, 825 Third Ave., New York, N.Y. 10022. *Office:* 305 West 72nd St., New York, N.Y. 10023.

CAREER: Pianist for a jazz trio in Greenwich Village, New York, N.Y., 1959-62; writer and director, 1963—. Producer and director of the award-winning Barry Farber talk show, Mutual Broadcasting System, 1967-68.

WRITINGS: Transplant: A Family Chronicle, Viking, 1978.

Other: (And director) "The P.O.W." (screenplay; based on original unpublished novel, "The Puppet"), 1973; (and director) "Field of Honor" (teleplay; adapted from the motion picture, "The P.O.W."), American Television Theatre, 1976.

WORK IN PROGRESS: A novel and a screenplay based on the book, *Transplant: A Family Chronicle*, for Columbia Broadcasting System.

SIDELIGHTS: Concerning his best-selling book, *Transplant: A Family Chronicle*, Dossick told *CA:* "I've always been interested in how people *cope*, how they manage to keep things together in the face of catastrophe, when their backs are against the wall and everything looks hopeless. *Transplant* is the true story of how a New Jersey couple endured and ultimately triumphed over an agonizing encounter with heart disease. The man was only thirty-five when he suffered a massive coronary. He was a top executive with a large shipping firm. The 'experts' told the family that he would not survive the night. But four years later he was still marching around, giving orders, being the 'General' around the house. This was due entirely to his incredible will to live and the equally incredible support of his wife and three children. Plus, I might add, an unshakeable religious faith."

Similarly, his film "The P.O.W." released in 1973 dealt with the theme of survival in the face of almost overwhelming odds. It is the story of a young, paralyzed Vietnam veteran named Howie Kaufman, and traces his life for the first few weeks after his discharge from the hospital. With little money and fewer prospects he is forced to fend for himself and put some kind of productive life together for himself before giving way to depression and despair. And with the help of his friends and family, he succeeds in doing just that. Roger Greenspun of the *New York Times* wrote of it: "You don't go out smiling from a movie about a paraplegic. But you may go out admiring the skill, the tact, the instincts of a new director who has made an impressive debut."

BIOGRAPHICAL/CRITICAL SOURCES: New York Times, May 11, 1973; *Wall Street Journal*, May 4, 1973; *Playboy*, July, 1973; *Village Voice*, May 3, 1973, May 10, 1973, June 7, 1973; *Independent Film Journal*, May 14, 1973; *Newsday*, May 11, 1973; *Publishers Weekly*, Dec. 26, 1977; *New York Post*, April 19, 1978; *Cleveland Plain Dealer*, April 23, 1978; *Boston Globe*, July 16, 1978.

* * *

DOUGLAS, George H(alsey) 1934-
PERSONAL: Born January 9, 1934, in East Orange, N.J.; son of Halsey M. (a journalist) and Harriet (Goldbach) Douglas; married Rosalind Braun (an artist), June 19, 1961; children: Philip. *Education:* Lafayette College, A.B., 1956; Columbia University, M.A., 1966; University of Illinois, Ph.D., 1968. *Home:* 1514 Grandview, Champaign, Ill. 61820. *Office:* Department of English, University of Illinois, 911 South Sixth St., Champaign, Ill. 61820.

CAREER: Bell Telephone Laboratories, Whippany, New Jersey, technical writer, 1958-59; University of Illinois at Urbana-Champaign, Urbana, technical writer at Agricultural Experiment Station, 1961-66, instructor, 1966-68, assistant professor, 1968-77, associate professor of English, 1977—. *Member:* Modern Language Association of America, American Society for Aesthetics, American Studies Association, Popular Culture Association.

WRITINGS: H. L. Mencken: Critic of American Life, Archon Books, 1978. Contributor to academic journals.

WORK IN PROGRESS: A book on Edmund Wilson as an observer of the American scene, publication expected in 1980; a book on Chicago as a railroad town, publication expected in 1981.

SIDELIGHTS: Douglas writes: "I am mainly interested in American culture and American life. My chief concerns are with shifts in style and ways of doing things. I write both nostalgically and critically about the American past and its relation to the present. My great interest is popular culture—railroads, local history, old-time radio, movies, maps, printing, ferry boats, and maritime history."

* * *

DOUGLASS, Elisha Peairs 1915-

PERSONAL: Born November 23, 1915, in New York, N.Y.; son of Earl L. (a clergyman) and Lois (Haler) Douglass; married Louisa MacIsaac (a teacher), March 30, 1959; children: Adaire, Earl. *Education:* Princeton University, A.B., 1939; Columbia University, M.S., 1941; Yale University, Ph.D., 1949. *Home:* 711 Bradley Rd., Chapel Hill, N.C. 27514. *Office:* 410 Hamilton Hall, University of North Carolina, Chapel Hill, N.C. 27514.

CAREER: Elon College, Elon College, N.C., professor of history, 1949-52; University of North Carolina, Chapel Hill, associate professor, 1955-59, professor of history, 1959—. *Military service:* U.S. Navy, 1941-45; became lieutenant commander. *Member:* American Historical Association, Organization of American Historians, Southern Historical Association.

WRITINGS: Rebels and Democrats: The Struggle for Political Equality and Majority Rule in the American Revolution, University of North Carolina Press, 1955; *The Coming of Age of American Business: Three Centuries of Enterprise, 1600-1900,* University of North Carolina Press, 1973.

WORK IN PROGRESS: The Image of the Businessman in American Fiction, completion expected in 1981.

* * *

DOWNS, James Francis 1926-

PERSONAL: Born December 20, 1926, in Pasadena, Calif.; son of James G. and Martha (Switzer) Downs; married Sabra Farwell Woolley (an anthropologist), November 25, 1970; children: Christian J., Martha Joy, Mark Christopher. *Education:* University of California, Berkeley, B.A., 1958, M.A., 1960, Ph.D., 1961. *Home:* 1855-B Biltmore N.W., Washington, D.C. 20009. *Office:* U.S. Navy, PERS-62, Washington, D.C. 20370.

CAREER: Los Angeles Herald Express, Los Angeles, Calif., reporter, 1948-50; worked in advertising and journalism, 1950-56; R. H. Lowie Museum of Anthropology, Berkeley, Calif., preparator, summer, 1958; University of Washington, Seattle, assistant professor of anthropology, summer, 1962; University of Rochester, Rochester, N.Y., assistant professor of anthropology and East Asian studies, 1962-64; University of Wyoming, Laramie, assistant professor of anthropology, summer, 1964; California State College, Los Angeles, associate professor of anthropology, 1964-65; University of Arizona, Tucson, associate professor of anthropology, 1965-69; University of Hawaii, Honolulu, visiting associate professor, 1969-70, professor of anthropology at Hilo College, 1970, chairman of cross-cultural studies at Center for Cross-Cultural Training and Research, 1970-

72. Consultant to U.S. Navy and various governmental and private agencies. *Military service:* U.S. Navy, 1944-47, 1950-51. U.S. Naval Reserve, 1974-75, 1977—.

MEMBER: American Anthropological Association (fellow), Society for Applied Anthropology, Tibet Society. *Awards, honors:* Research scholarship from Institute for International Studies at University of California, Berkeley, 1968-69; National Institute of Education fellowship for University of Hawaii, 1972-73.

WRITINGS: Two Worlds of the Washo, Holt, 1963; *Human Nature: Introduction to Cultural Anthropology,* Glencoe Press, 1964; (with H. K. Bliebtreu) *Human Variation,* Glencoe Press, 1968; *Cultures in Crisis,* Glencoe Press, 1969; *The Navajo,* Holt, 1970; *The Tibetans of Lhasa,* HRFLX Books, 1972; *Making Anthropology Work,* Holt, in press. Contributor to anthropology journals.

WORK IN PROGRESS: A novel, *The Sea Divided;* continuing research on military organization and warfare; application of anthropology to modern organizational problems.

SIDELIGHTS: Downs has conducted research among Washo-Navajo American Indians, Tibetan refugees in India, and junior high school children in Hawaii.

* * *

DOWNS, William Randall, Jr. 1914-1978

PERSONAL: Born August 17, 1914, in Kansas City, Kan.; son of William R. and Katherine Lee (Tyson) Downs; married Rosalind Gerson, December 18, 1946; children: William Randall III, Karen Louise Downs Smith, Adam Michael. *Education:* University of Kansas, A.B., 1937. *Home:* 5535 Warwick Pl., Chevy Chase, Md. 20015.

CAREER/WRITINGS: Reporter for newspapers and the United Press in Kansas City, Kan., 1937-39; United Press, London, England, foreign correspondent, 1939-42; reporter with Columbia Broadcasting System (CBS), 1942-62, war correspondent in Europe and the Far East, 1944-46, diplomatic correspondent in Rome, 1956-62; free-lance writer, 1962-63; American Broadcasting Companies (ABC), Washington, D.C., network correspondent, 1964-78. Notable assignments include coverage of the battle of Stalingrad, the D day landings in Normandy, the surrender of German forces to Field Marshall Montgomery, the surrender of Japan, the atomic tests at Bikini Atoll, the Berlin airlift, and several presidential campaigns. Contributor to magazines, including *Newsweek* and *This Week. Member:* National Press Club, Overseas Press Club. *Awards, honors:* National Headliners Club award, 1945, for exclusive coverage of the German surrender to Montgomery; Overseas Press Club award for best foreign radio reporting, 1949.

OBITUARIES: Washington Post, May 4, 1978.*

(Died May 3, 1978, in Bethesda, Md.)

* * *

DOYLE, Charlotte Lackner 1937-

PERSONAL: Born June 25, 1937, in Vienna, Austria; came to the United States in 1939, naturalized citizen, 1955; daughter of George (a restaurant worker) and Mary (a writer; maiden name, Meisel) Lackner; married Jim Doyle (a playwright), August 20, 1959. *Education:* Temple University, A.B., 1959; University of Michigan, M.A., 1961, Ph.D., 1965. *Home:* 293 Bronxville Rd., Bronxville, N.Y. 10708. *Office:* Department of Psychology, Sarah Lawrence College, Bronxville, N.Y. 10708.

CAREER: Cornell University, Ithaca, N.Y., assistant professor of psychology, 1964-66; Sarah Lawrence College, Bronxville, N.Y., faculty member, 1966—. *Member:* American Psychological Association, American Association for the Advancement of Science. *Awards, honors:* Woodrow Wilson fellow, 1959-60.

WRITINGS: (With W. J. McKeachie) *Psychology,* Addison-Wesley, 1966, 3rd edition (with McKeachie and M. M. Moffatt), 1976. Contributor to psychology journals.

WORK IN PROGRESS: An innovative introduction to psychology, publication by Brooks-Cole expected in 1980; studying the psychology of the creative process.

SIDELIGHTS: Charlotte Doyle comments: "My new book is an exploration into the changing visions of human nature that psychologists have put forward and the resulting many-faced self-portrait. It is a text, a progress report for the field, and a personal intellectual journey."

* * *

DOYLE, Don H(arrison) 1946-

PERSONAL: Born February 23, 1946, in Long Beach, Calif.; son of Leo Walter (a physician) and Barbara (Ferron) Doyle; married Marilyn Dunn (a health administrator), 1967; children: Caroline Ruth, Kelly Lynn. *Education:* University of California, Davis, B.A., 1968; Northwestern University, Ph.D., 1973. *Home:* 221 Leonard Ave., Nashville, Tenn. 37205. *Office:* Department of History, Vanderbilt University, Nashville, Tenn. 37235.

CAREER: University of Michigan, Dearborn, assistant professor of history, 1971-74; Vanderbilt University, Nashville, Tenn., assistant professor of history, 1974—. *Member:* Organization of American Historians, Social Science History Association, Southern Historical Association. *Awards, honors:* Woodrow Wilson fellowship, 1970; American Philosophical Society grant, 1977-78; American Council of Learned Societies grant, 1978.

WRITINGS: The Social Order of a Frontier Community: Jacksonville, Illinois, 1825-70, University of Illinois Press, 1978; (contributor) Vernon Burton and Robert C. McMath, editors, *Southern Communities in the Nineteenth Century,* Greenwood Press, 1979.

WORK IN PROGRESS: Urbanization and Southern Culture: Economic Elites in Four New South Cities (Atlanta, Nashville, Charleston, Mobile), 1865-1910.

SIDELIGHTS: Doyle writes: "My interest in frontier community building derived to a large extent from my family's background in California, which goes back to the Gold Rush days. Jacksonville's founding and its struggle for urban success seems to embody a fundamental recurring theme in American culture—the effort to build a community amid a society that exalts individualism, mobility, egalitarianism. My current work in the South explores the persistence of traditional regional values in an urban world."

* * *

DRACHMAN, Theodore S(olomon) 1904-

PERSONAL: Born August 31, 1904, in New York, N.Y.; son of Bernard and Sarah (Weil) Drachman; married Grace Loesser, May 14, 1933; children: Mary Margaret, Chaffee, Theodore Loesser. *Education:* City College (now of the City University of New York), B.S., 1924; University of Minnesota, M.B., 1937, M.D., 1938; Columbia University, M.S.P.H., 1941; also attended University of Santo Tomas.

Politics: "Independent Democrat." *Home:* Eagle St., Philmont, N.Y. 12565. *Office:* Columbia County Department of Health, 363 Allen St., Hudson, N.Y. 12534.

CAREER: Specialist in preventive medicine, epidemiologist, and public health servant. Worked as health commissioner in New Rochelle, N.Y., 1941-42; chief of labs and communicable diseases in Colombia, 1943-44; director of preventive medicine in South Korea, 1945-46; first deputy health commissioner in Westchester County, N.Y., 1946-58; health commissioner in Columbia County, N.Y., 1958-63; health commissioner in Ulster County, N.Y., 1963-65; health commissioner in Columbia County, 1977—. Consultant to World Health Organization, Columbia Memorial Hospital, and organizations in Colombia, Peru, Mexico, Korea, Philippines, Indonesia, and other countries. *Member:* American Public Health Association (fellow), American College of Preventive Medicine, Pan American Medical Association, Mystery Writers of America, Alpha Omega Alpha, New York State Public Health Association, New York State Medical Society, Columbia County Medical Society, Association of County Health Officers. *Awards, honors:* Received Riggs Medal from City College (now of the City University of New York), 1924, for English; scholarship from University of Minnesota, 1937; *Cry Plague* was named by *New York Times* as one of the three best first mysteries, 1953.

WRITINGS: False Faces, Newland Press, 1931; *Cry Plague,* Ace Books, 1953; *Something for the Birds,* Crown, 1958; *Addicted to Murder,* Avon, 1960; *Reason for Madness,* Abelard-Schuman, 1970; *The Grande Lapu-Lapu,* Abelard-Schuman, 1972.

WORK IN PROGRESS: The Deadly Dream, a novel about a real disease which kills only Filipino males.

SIDELIGHTS: Drachman told *CA:* "Public health comes first, but I like to write medical mysteries. I speak several languages, including Spanish, French, German, and Japanese. I have worked, lived, and traveled a great deal, mostly as a public health consultant or administrator in many parts of the world."

* * *

DRAGER, Marvin 1920-

PERSONAL: Born May 10, 1920, in New York, N.Y.; son of Harry and Fannie (Katzman) Drager; married Lenore Schwam (in public relations), June 27, 1943; children: Sharon Drager Katler, Laura, Iris. *Education:* St. John's University, Jamaica, N.Y., B.S.S., 1940; Columbia University, M.A., 1942. *Home:* 40 West 86th St., New York, N.Y. 10024. *Office:* Marvin Drager, Inc., 420 Madison Ave., New York, N.Y. 10017.

CAREER: New York Post, New York City, reporter, 1942-44; Associated Press, New York City, picture editor, 1944-46; Columbia Records, New York City, in public relations, 1946-47; Marvin Drager, Inc., New York City, in public relations, 1947—.

WRITINGS: The Most Glorious Crown (nonfiction), Winchester Press, 1975. Contributor to magazines, including *New York, Dogs,* and *Seventeen.*

SIDELIGHTS: Drager told *CA:* "*The Most Glorious Crown* is a book of nine chapters dealing with the stories of the nine Triple Crown Champions of thoroughbred racing, from Sir Barton in 1919 to Secretariat in 1973. There is also an introduction tracing the establishment of the Triple Crown races—the Kentucky Derby, Preakness, and Belmont Stakes. What made the stories of the book so fascinating is the horses in question betrayed so many human qualities. They seemed to recognize their sudden success and, like humans, reacted accordingly. They developed traits of importance as well as idiosyncrasies that are aborning of success. They, in effect, became characters. And these are the factors that made the research so interesting and the stories such a pleasure to relate.''

He added: ''I love good human interest stories, and love to research them. I also like good crisp fast-paced copy.''

*   *   *

DREXLER, Rosalyn 1926-
(Julia Sorel)

PERSONAL: Born November 25, 1926, in New York; married Sherman Drexler, 1946; children: one daughter, one son. *Home:* 131 Greene St., New York, N.Y. 10012. *Agent:* Georges Borchardt, 136 East 57th St., New York, N.Y. 10022.

CAREER: Playwright, novelist, and painter. Taught at Writer's Workshop, University of Iowa, 1976-77; taught art at University of Colorado. Has held one woman art shows at galleries in New York City, Boston, and Provincetown, R.I.; her work has been included in group shows at Martha-Jackson, Pace Gallery, Washington Gallery of Modern Art, Guggenheim Museum, and Whitney Museum. *Member:* New Dramatists, New York Theatre Strategy, Dramatists Guild, P.E.N., Actors Studio. *Awards, honors:* Obie Award from *Village Voice,* 1964, for ''Home Movies''; MacDowell fellowship, 1965; Rockefeller grants, 1965, 1968, and 1974; humor prize from *Paris Review,* 1966, for short story, ''Dear''; Guggenheim fellowship, 1970-71; Emmy Award for writing excellence from Academy of Television Arts & Sciences, 1974, for ''The Lily Show.''

WRITINGS—Novels: *I Am the Beautiful Stranger,* Grossman, 1965; *One or Another,* Dutton, 1970; *To Smithereens,* New American Library, 1972; *The Cosmopolitan Girl,* M. Evans, 1974; *Starborn: Story of Jenni Love,* Simon & Schuster, 1979.

Novels under pseudonym Julia Sorel; all published by Ballantine: *Dawn: Portrait of a Teenage Runaway,* 1976; *Alex: Portrait of a Teenage Prostitute,* 1977; *Rocky,* 1977; *See How She Runs,* 1978.

Plays: *The Line of Least Existence and Other Plays,* introduction by Richard Gilman, includes ''Home Movies'' (first produced in New York City at Judson Poets' Theatre, 1964), ''Hot Buttered Roll'' (first produced in New York City at New Dramatists Committee, 1966; also see below), ''The Investigation'' (first produced in Boston at Theatre Co. of Boston; first produced in New York City at New Dramatists Committee, 1966; also see below), ''The Bed Was Full'' (first produced at New Dramatists Committee, 1967), ''The Line of Least Existence'' (first produced at Judson Poets' Theatre, March 15, 1968), and ''Softly, and Consider the Nearness'' (first produced in New York City at St. Luke's Church, 1969), Random House, 1967; (with others) *Collision Course* (twelve plays; includes ''Skywriting'' by Drexler; first produced together in New York City at Cafe au Go Go, May 8, 1968), Random House, 1968; *The Investigation* [and] *Hot Buttered Roll* (also see above), Methuen (London), 1969; ''Was I Good?'' first produced by New Dramatists Committee, 1972; ''The Ice Queen,'' first produced in Boston at The Proposition, 1973; ''She Who Was He,'' first produced in Richmond, Va., at Virginia Commonwealth University, 1974; ''Travesty Parade,'' first

produced in Los Angeles at Center Theatre Group, 1974; ''Vulgar Lives,'' first produced in New York City at Theatre Strategy, 1979; ''Writer's Opera,'' first produced in New York City at TNC, 1979.

Work represented in anthologies, including *The Bold New Women,* Fawcett, 1966; *New American Review,* New American Library, 1969; *The Off-Off Broadway Book,* 1972. Author of screenplay for ''Naked Came the Stranger.'' Contributor of articles and reviews to periodicals, including *Esquire, Village Voice,* and *Mademoiselle.* Film reviewer for *Vogue.*

SIDELIGHTS: Critics have almost unanimously praised Rosalyn Drexler for the several plays she has written. ''Few contemporary playwrights can equal her verbal playfulness, fearless spontaneity, and boundless irreverance,'' Michael Smith wrote. ''Few in fact, share her devotion to pure writing, preferring their language functional, meaningful, or psychologically 'real.' Jack Kroll was similarly impressed with her playwriting skills. He commented, ''Drexler presents the spectacle of a playwright with a brilliant gift, not only for language, but for making language work on many levels with the ease and excitement of a Cossack riding his horse everywhere but in the saddle.''

''The Line of Least Existence,'' which Kroll found to be ''about the total dissonance that occurs whenever living creatures find themselves in any sort of relationship,'' was deemed by him to be evidence of Drexler's ''sweet shrewdness that seems to be talking straight to the most hidden part of you. She has the great and necessary gift of fashioning a new, total innocence out of the total corruption that she clearly sees. With lots of laughs.''

In viewing the London productions of ''The Investigation'' and ''Hot Buttered Roll,'' Benedict Nightingale was impressed with Drexler's achievement in taking her preoccupation ''with sterile hedonism and dead feelings,'' and translating it into ''arresting dramatic terms.''

Some reviewers, however, have mentioned that Drexler's timeliness might prove to be a disadvantage in the long run. Smith commented: ''Whether her plays amount to anything, whatever that means, is hard to say: hers is obviously an up-to-date sensibility, and I read considerable off-hand, tough, supercool wisdom about human relationships into her fantastications, knowing all the time that they may be as frivolous as they look.''

Drexler's novels have been more unevenly received. William Hjortsberg noted that Drexler's second novel, *One or Another,* ''is a very funny book; moreover, it is both funny 'ha-ha' and funny 'weird,' an observation Melissa Johnson, the novel's heroine-narrator, would be likely to make herself.'' ''Rosalyn Drexler may very well be the first Marx Sister,'' Christopher Lehmann-Haupt wrote. ''Her new novel, *One or Another,* has no more plot than 'Horse Feathers' (far less, in fact), but she has filled it up with so many sight, sound and word gags, so many sillinesses and surrealities—not to mention little grinning obscenities—that the reader soon begins to flinch in anticipation of the next verbal skit and to bark with relieved laughter when it works.'' But Lehmann-Haupt found that, ''It is by no means unpleasant, the shower of absurdities. It is like being pelted with toy balloons and an occasional mud-pie. Mrs. Drexler has a determined inventiveness and complete control of her language, and it becomes clear very early that she is not going to repeat herself or slip into predictable patterns. The only trouble is that her material evaporates as quickly as it spills out. One is left at the end with the feeling that one has just consumed a meal of odorless gas or listened to a disembodied giggle in the dark.''

Hjortsberg thought that Kafka was an ''accurate reference-point'' for the understanding of Drexler's work. He cited comparisons between the authors' ''spare, clean style, the bizarre juxtaposing of abnormalities, the hard edges and latent guilt.'' ''But,'' he continued, ''here it is Kafka as interpreted by the Marx Brothers, with all the pratfalls and raised eyebrows intact. *One or Another* is as immediate as a pie in the face.''

Jack Kroll contended that Drexler belongs with Donald Barthelme and Thomas Pynchon as representatives of the ''new literary voice.'' He wrote: ''The new literary voice comes from some odd and perilous psychic area still being charted, some basic metabolic flashpoint where the self struggles to convert its recurrent breakdowns into new holds on life and reality.... There can be, Mrs. Drexler knows, no psychic or social resolution of all this. What counts now is the delicate new apotheosis, a new transcendence that accepts the mad world as the only human habitat, while plotting shrewdly against its madness. Few writers have been able to suggest this new transcendence. Mrs. Drexler is one of them; funny, scary, preternaturally aware she is at the exact center where the new sensibility is being put together cell by cell.''

Drexler's next novel, *To Smithereens*, fared less well with critics. Michael Wood was impressed with the humor and intelligence of the novel and noted that the language ''has confidence in its capacity to render precisely the perceptions it is supposed to render.'' But Anatole Broyard wrote: ''Rosalyn Drexler has written well enough in some of her other books to make us wish to inquire patiently what went wrong with this one. The feeling one gets is that of an irrepressibly healthy woman trying to force a freakiness that does not come naturally to her. She seems almost to strain for irrelevancy, to struggle through a strenuous willed-free association in search of a fashionable zaniness.'' Calling the book ''a series of gratuitous acts,'' he further commented, ''It is not that she is being ironical or toying with that old standby, the absurd. Rather, it seems as if she is avoiding the notion of causation, of one action being related to another.'' The *Times Literary Supplement* explained its failure to be totally satisfied with the book: ''The strength of Miss Drexler's writing is in the energy of her prose: every joke is clean-cut. And yet she refuses to go inside, to go deeper into her characters' psyches. She has a natural eye and ear but her mistake is in assuming that the number of empty gaps, the things *not* said, will indicate, or evoke, the emptiness of the lives she has created. Everyone plays cool, acts hard, and packs those punches, but the 'smithereens' of the novel are the fragments of their world.''

Drexler was back on her feet with the publication of *The Cosmopolitan Girl*, an outrageous love story about a girl and her dog. ''The raunchy and the ridiculous are Drexler's home territory,'' Sara Sanborn wrote. ''You feel she spends a lot of time in all-night cafeterias. Her word-play is like swordplay—with rubber swords that still deliver a stinging slap. Her set pieces—newspaper clippings, radio interviews, beauty advice—are among the delights of [*The Cosmopolitan Girl*]; her one-liners are memorable: 'Most of Daddy's friends were young and in an advanced state of inner peace.' She weaves a seamy web of parodies that covers the situation perfectly. Moving back and forth between the absurd and the everyday, Drexler puts both in their place—on the same plane.'' Jane Shapiro noted: ''Not surprisingly, the jacket of *The Cosmopolitan Girl* describes the story as

'zany' and full of 'madcap humor,' which I suppose it is; it isn't *normally* zany and madcap. It is also wonderfully satirical about fine art and popular culture; stylish feminism and standard versions of femininity and masculinity; the occult, herbal cures, crankiness between the generations, psychological self-help, the sexual revolution, Las Vegas, and other signs of modern life. I have been asked to say what, exactly, Rosalyn Drexler is *doing* with all of this. Merciless Rosalyn Drexler is giving us the elbow.''

Sara Blackburn offered this assessment of Drexler: ''She's an absolute original who can take all of the ingredients that usually characterize 'serious' fiction about her concerns here—identity as a woman, emptiness, the insanity of daily life in America, hypocrisy, the absence of love—and use them with inventiveness, playfulness, and even hilarity. Wonderfully, it works, and the result is admirable not only for its style and wit, but for its lack of pretense, for the respect it grants its reader in not straining beyond its materials, and for what it achieves; art which is also high entertainment.''

BIOGRAPHICAL/CRITICAL SOURCES: Books and Bookmen, June, 1967; *Village Voice,* March 28, 1968; *Newsweek,* April 1, 1968, February 9, 1970, June 1, 1970, March 10, 1975; *New Statesman,* February 27, 1969; *New York Times,* June 5, 1970, February 21, 1972; *New York Times Book Review,* June 28, 1970, March 30, 1975; *Nation,* August 31, 1970; *Book World,* March 19, 1972; *New York Review of Books,* August 10, 1972; *Times Literary Supplement,* September 14, 1973; *Contemporary Literary Criticism,* Gale, Volume 2, 1974, Volume 6, 1976; *Ms.,* July, 1975.

* * *

DREYER, Peter (Richard) 1939-

PERSONAL: Born November 15, 1939, in Caledon, South Africa; came to United States, 1972; son of Basil Melt (a hotelier) and Greta Edna (Less) Dreyer. *Education:* Attended school at De Aar, South Africa, until age fourteen. *Residence:* Oakland, Calif. *Agent:* Robert Briggs, 2154 Filbert St., San Francisco, Calif. 94123.

CAREER: Journalist. Worked at a variety of jobs after leaving school; joined the South African Liberal party at Kimberly, 1956; member of the Cape Provincial committee of the Liberal party, 1957, and Bus Apartheid Resistance Committee, 1959; writer for *Contact* (Liberal party fortnightly), 1958-59; lived in England, 1962-66, and Greece, 1966-72; founding editor of *Omphalos: A Mediterranean Review,* 1971; expelled from Greece by order of the military junta's security police, 1972; free-lance writer and editor, 1972—.

WRITINGS: A Beast in View (novel), Andre Deutsch, 1969; *The Future of Treason* (autobiographical), Ballantine, 1973; *A Gardener Touched With Genius: The Life of Luther Burbank,* Coward, 1975. Literary editor, *San Francisco* magazine, 1973-75; contributing editor, *San Francisco Review of Books,* 1977-78. Contributor of Greek translations to *Omphalos,* original poetry to *De Arte,* and articles and reviews to *City, Prose, California Living, This World, San Francisco Fault, San Francisco Bay Guardian, Nation, San Francisco Chronicle,* and other publications.

WORK IN PROGRESS: Victims, Martyrs, and Fanatics, a nonfiction work dealing with contemporary South Africa.

SIDELIGHTS: Dreyer told *CA:* ''The focus of my writing and thinking at present is the human predicament in South Africa, which I see as a microcosm of the relations between the 'have' nations of the West and the impoverished people of the unindustrialized world. Apartheid is at base a failure of the imagination, the consequence of greed and myopia. I believe there are lessons here for humanity and seek to draw them.''

BIOGRAPHICAL/CRITICAL SOURCES: Peter Dreyer, *The Future of Treason,* Ballantine, 1973.

* * *

DRUCKER, Malka 1945-

PERSONAL: Born March 14, 1945, in Tucson, Ariz.; daughter of William (a clothing manufacturer) and Francine (a writer; maiden name, Epstein) Chermak; married Steven Drucker (a certified public accountant), August 20, 1966; children: Ivan, Max. *Education:* University of California, Los Angeles, B.A., 1967; University of Southern California, teaching credential, 1968. *Religion:* Jewish. *Home:* 863 Manning Ave., Los Angeles, Calif. 90024. *Agent:* Curtis Brown Ltd., 575 Madison Ave., New York, N.Y. 10022.

CAREER: Writer, 1975—. *Member:* Society of Children's Book Writers, Association of Jewish Librarians.

WRITINGS: (With Tom Seaver) *Tom Seaver: Portrait of a Pitcher* (juvenile; *Sports Illustrated* Book-of-the-Month Club alternate selection), Holiday House, 1978; *The George Foster Story* (juvenile), Holiday House, 1979.

SIDELIGHTS: A critic for the *New York Times Book Review* praised Malka Drucker's biography of Tom Seaver for providing the reader with insights into Seaver's home life and the adjustments that the family of a major league baseball player must make. Although *Tom Seaver: Portrait of a Pitcher* does recount some of Seaver's better games and keeps track of the baseball records that Seaver has set, the same reviewer felt that ''this is a fairly flat portrait. . . . There is more both to the athlete and to the man than is recounted here.''

The majority of reviews, however, were positive. A commentator for *Booklist* described *Tom Seaver* as an ''exciting sports biography'' filled with fascinating anecdotes. ''The play-by-play accounts of key moments in Seaver's career are well done—not boringly detailed—while most of the author's fictionalization is realistic enough not to threaten the book's credibility,'' he observed.

Malka Drucker told *CA* her purpose in writing *Tom Seaver:* ''This was not to be a book about baseball; it was to be about a man who happened to play the game and what the game meant to him.''

BIOGRAPHICAL/CRITICAL SOURCES: New York Times Book Review, April 30, 1978; *Kirkus Reviews,* June 1, 1978; *Best Sellers,* June, 1978; *Booklist,* July 1, 1978.

* * *

DRUMMOND, Jack 1923(?)-1978
(George Redder)

OBITUARY NOTICE: Born c. 1923; died June 15, 1978, in Columbus, Ohio. Crime novelist. A struggling writer, Drummond planned to research his third book by robbing a Columbus, Ohio, bank. He was slain before he commited the crime when he pulled a gun on suspecting police. His one published novel, *The Flight Instructor Murders,* appeared under the pseudonym George Redder. Obituaries and other sources: *New York Times,* July 22, 1978.

* * *

DRUTMAN, Irving 1910(?)-1978

OBITUARY NOTICE: Born c. 1910 in New York City; died September 20, 1978, in New York City. Theatrical journalist, editor, and author. Drutman wrote the memoir *Good Company* and edited several of Janet Flanner's books. He contributed articles on theatre and film personalities to newspapers and periodicals, including regular *New York Herald Tribune* and *New York Times* features. Drutman also worked as a free-lance publicist, translator, and songwriter for Hollywood films. Obituaries and other sources: *The ASCAP Biographical Dictionary of Composers, Authors, and Publishers,* American Society of Composers, Authors, and Publishers, 1966; *Publishers Weekly,* October 9, 1978.

* * *

DUGAN, Alan 1923-

PERSONAL: Born February 12, 1923, in Brooklyn, N.Y.; married Judith Shahn. *Education:* Attended Queens College (now of the City University of New York) and Olivet College; received B.A. from Mexico City College. *Address:* Box 97, Truro, Mass. 02666.

CAREER: Poet. Worked in advertising and publishing and as a model maker for a medical supply house in New York, N.Y.; Sarah Lawrence College, Bronxville, N.Y., member of the faculty, 1967-71; Fine Arts Work Center, Provincetown, Mass., member of the faculty, 1971—. *Military service:* Served in United States Army Air Forces during World War II. *Awards, honors:* Award from *Poetry* magazine, 1946; Yale Series of Younger Poets Award, 1961; National Book Award, 1961, for *Poems;* Pulitzer Prize for poetry, 1962, for *Poems,* and 1967, for *Poems 3;* Rome fellowship from the American Academy of Arts and Letters, 1962-63; Guggenheim fellow, 1963-64; Rockefeller Foundation fellow, 1966-67; Levinson poetry prize from *Poetry* magazine, 1967.

WRITINGS: General Prothalamion in Populous Times, privately printed, 1961; *Poems* (also see below), Yale University Press, 1961, reprinted as *Poems of Alan Dugan,* Atlantic; *Poems 2* (also see below), Yale University Press, 1963; *Poems 3* (also see below), Yale University Press, 1967; *Collected Poems* (contains *Poems, Poems 2,* and *Poems 3*), Yale University Press, 1969; *Poems 4,* Little, Brown, 1974. Contributor of poetry to magazines, including *New Yorker, Atlantic, Harper's,* and *Poetry.*

SIDELIGHTS: First books, especially volumes of verse, are often relegated to obscurity, but Alan Dugan's *Poems* was greeted with enthusiasm. Philip Booth saluted *Poems* as ''the most original first book that has appeared on any publisher's poetry list in a sad long time,'' and the awards the book later received bore out Booth's appraisal. *Poems* was awarded the National Book Award and the Pulitzer Prize. Many commentators feel that Dugan has maintained this high level of excellence in his subsequent volumes of verse. ''Never a 'promising young poet,' Dugan showed what he could do, which was considerable, in his first book,'' Helen Chasin commented in a review of *Poems 4.* ''And he has simply kept on writing strong, skillful, interesting poems.''

Dugan's style and tone have remained consistent throughout his career. Concise and brusque, his language is close to everyday speech. X. J. Kennedy described Dugan's style as ''a plain stodgy no-nonsense American prose, like that of your nearest bartender.'' The low-keyed humor and the strains of satire that underpin Dugan's poems have frequently attracted comment. Some of Dugan's strongest effects, R. J. Mills observed, are gained ''through mockery, invective, sudden reversal, and exposure.'' His poetry is typically ironic and unsentimental.

For subject matter, Dugan turns to the commonplace. "A confirmed angel-wrestler, Dugan is beset by the facts of life, such as the need to make money and the unpleasant nature of the job that makes it, or the simple problem of how much to drink, or not to drink," Richmond Lattimore explained. Dugan's examination of daily life leads him to feelings of alienation, defeat, and despair. His disenchantment with society is reflected in his attacks on sacred cows, including the Statue of Liberty and Joyce Kilmer's "Trees." Dugan "seems more than a little fearful of life in general, for he speaks of getting up in the morning and walking out into the 'daily accident,'" Stephen Stepanchov noted. "He distrusts all slogans, prophecy, and questions all received values."

Dugan's predictable style and subject matter have led some to accuse him of stagnation. "The sameness of [Dugan's] poems suggests someone who is concerned not to seek variety or development, and continue working the same weirdly attractive yet essentially limited vein," Alan Brownjohn remarked. Taking the opposite tack, Robert Boyers argued that Dugan's limited range is a virtue: "By cultivating what is by any standard a confining style, and by exercising his caustic intelligence on a relatively narrow range of subjects, Dugan has created a significant body of work that speaks with authority to a variety of modern readers. One does not get terribly excited about Alan Dugan's work, but one nevertheless returns to it with increasing regularity, for it successfully inhabits that middle ground of experience which our best poets today seem loathe to admit."

BIOGRAPHICAL/CRITICAL SOURCES: Nation, May 13, 1961; *Poetry,* July, 1961, March, 1964, July, 1968, February, 1972, February, 1975; *Saturday Review,* July 22, 1961; *Times Literary Supplement,* August 18, 1961, March 19, 1964, January 22, 1971; *Atlantic,* November, 1961; *New York Times Book Review,* December 22, 1963; *Book Week,* March 1, 1964; Stephen Stepanchev, *American Poetry Since 1945,* Harper, 1965; *New York Review of Books,* November 23, 1967, May 7, 1970; *Salmagundi,* spring-summer, 1968; Richard Howard, *Alone With America,* Atheneum, 1969; *New Statesman,* January 1, 1971; *Observer Review,* January 3, 1971; *Christian Science Monitor,* April 27, 1971; *Partisan Review,* spring, 1972; *Contemporary Literary Criticism,* Gale, Volume 2, 1974, Volume 6, 1976; *Christian Science Monitor,* May 1, 1974; *Village Voice,* August 22, 1974; *Hudson Review,* autumn, 1974.*

* * *

DUHAMEL, Georges 1884-1966
(Denis Thevenin)

PERSONAL: Born June 30, 1884, in Paris, France; married Blanche Albane (an actress); children: three sons. *Education:* University of Paris, M.D., 1907. *Residence:* Paris, France.

CAREER: Writer. Physician in private practice; worked as laboratory researcher, 1909-14. Co-founder and member of L'Abbaye (an artists' colony), 1906-07; director of French Radio Broadcasting during World War II. *Military service:* Military surgeon during World War I. *Member:* National Committee of Authors, French Academy (former acting secretary), Academy of Medicine. *Awards, honors:* Prix Goncourt, 1918, for *Civilization.*

WRITINGS—"Vie et aventures de Salavin" series; novels; published by Mercure de France: *La Confession de Minuit* (translation by Gladys Billings published in *Salavin* as *Confession at Midnight;* also see below), 1920; *Deux Hommes* (title means "Two Men"), 1924; *Journal de Salavin* (transla-tion by Billings published in *Salavin* as *Salavin's Journal;* also see below), 1927; *Le Club de Lyonnais* (translation by Billings published in *Salavin* as *The Lyonnais Club;* also see below), 1929; *Tel qu'en lui-meme* (translation by Billings published in *Salavin* as *End of Illusion;* also see below), 1932; translation of series by Billings published as *Salavin* (contains *Confession at Midnight, Salavin's Journal, The Lyonnais Club, End of Illusion*), Putnam, 1936, reprinted, Morley-Baker, 1969.

"La Chronique des Pasquier" series; novels; all originally published by Mercure de France, except as noted: *Le Notaire du Havre* (also see below), 1933, translation by Beatrice de Holthoir published as *News From Havre,* Dent, 1934, published as *Papa Pasquier,* Harper, 1934; *Le Jardin des betes sauvages* (also see below), 1934, translation by de Holthoir published as *Young Pasquier,* Dent, 1935, translation by de Holthoir in *The Pasquier Chronicles* published as *Caged Beasts; Vue de la terre promise* (also see below), 1934, translation by de Holthoir published as *The Sight of the Promised Land,* Dent, 1935; *La Nuit de la Saint Jean* (translation by de Holthoir published in *The Pasquier Chronicles* as *St. John's Eve;* also see below), 1935; *Le Desert de Bievres* (translation by de Holthoir published in *The Pasquier Chronicles* as *The House in the Desert;* also see below), 1937; partial translation of series by de Holthoir published as *The Pasquier Chronicles* (contains *News From Havre, Caged Beasts, In Sight of Promised Land, St. John's Eve, The House in the Desert*), Dent, 1937, Holt, 1938; *Les Maitres* (translation by de Holthoir published in *Cecile Among the Pasquiers* as *Pastors and Masters;* also see below), 1937; *Cecile parmi nous* (translation by de Holthoir published in *Cecile Among the Pasquiers* as *Cecile;* also see below), 1938; *La Combat contre les ombres* (translation by de Holthoir published in *Cecile Among the Pasquiers* as *The Fight Against the Shadows;* also see below), 1939; partial translation of series by de Holthoir published as *Cecile Among the Pasquiers* (contains *Pastors and Masters, Cecile, The Fight Against the Shadows*), Dent, 1940, published as *Cecile Pasquier,* Holt, 1940; *Suzanne et les jeunes hommes* (translation by de Holthoir in *Suzanne and Joseph Pasquier* published as *Suzanne and the Young Men;* also see below), [Paris], 1940; *La Passion de Joseph Pasquier* (translation by de Holthoir in *Suzanne and Joseph Pasquier* published as *The Passion of Joseph Pasquier*), [Paris], 1941; partial translation of series by de Holthoir published as *Suzanne and Joseph Pasquier* (contains *Suzanne and the Young Men* and *The Passion of Joseph Pasquier*), Dent, 1946; series reprinted as *Chronique des Pasquier,* ten volumes, French and European Publications, 1957-63.

Poetry: *Des Legendes, des batailles,* Abbaye Press, 1907; *L'Homme en tete,* [France], 1908; *Selon ma loi,* [France], 1910; *Compagnons,* [France], 1912; *Elegies,* Mercure de France (Paris), 1920; *Voix du vieux monde,* [France], 1925.

Plays: *La Lumiere* (four-act; first produced at the Odeon in 1911), translation by Sasha Best published as *The Light,* [Boston], 1914; *Dans l'ombre des statues* (three-act; first produced at the Odeon in 1912), translation by Best published as *In the Shadow of Statues*), R. G. Badger, 1914; *Le Combat* (five-act; first produced at Theatre des Arts in 1913), [Paris], 1913, translation by Best published as *The Combat,* R. G. Badger, 1915; *L'Oeuvre des athletes* (four-act; first produced at the Vieux Colombier, April 10, 1920), Editions de la nouvelle revue francaise, 1920; *La Journee des aveux* (three-act; first produced at the Comedie des Champs-Elysees in 1923), Mercure de France, 1924; *Quand vous voudrez,* [France], 1924.

"Lumieres sur ma vie" series (memoirs): *Inventaire de l'abime 1884-1901* (also see below), P. Hartmann, 1944; *Biographie de mes fantomes 1901-1906* (also see below), P. Hartmann, 1944; *Le Temps de la recherche,* P. Hartmann, 1947; partial translation of series by Basil Collier published as *Light on My Days* (contains *Inventaire de l'abime 1884-1901* and *Biographie de mes fantomes 1901-1906*), Dent, 1948; *La Pesee des ames 1914-1919,* Mercure de France, 1949; *Les Espoirs et les epreuves 1919-1928,* Mercure de France, 1953.

Other; all originally published by Mercure de France, except as noted: (With Charles Vildrac) *Notes sur la technique poetique* (nonfiction), [Paris], 1910; *Propos critiques* (literary criticism), [France], 1912; *Paul Claudel* (literary criticism), [France], 1913, 9th edition, Mercure de France, 1924; *Les Poetes et la poesie, 1812-1913,* [Paris], 1914; (under pseudonym Denis Thevenin) *Vie des martyrs 1914-1916* (war stories), 1917, reprinted, 1966, translation by Florence Simmonds published as *New Book of Martyrs,* George H. Doran, 1918; *Civilisation 1914-1917* (war stories), 1918, translation by Eleanor Stimson Brooks published as *Civilization 1914-1917,* Century Co., 1919, reprinted, Richard West, 1978; *Entretiens dans le tumulte: Chronique contemporaine 1918-1919* (essays), 1919; *Elevation et mort d'Armand Branche* (fiction), B. Grasset (Paris), 1919; *La Possession du monde* (essays), 1919, reprinted, 1964, translation by Brooks published as *The Heart's Domain,* Century Co., 1919.

Guerre et litterature, [Paris], 1920; *Les Hommes abandonnes* (short stories; title means "The Abandoned Men"), 1921; *Les plaisers et les jeux,* 1922, reprinted, 1946, translation by R. Wills Thomas published as *Days of Delight,* Andrew Dakers, 1939; *Lettres d'Auspasie,* Sablier (Paris), 1922; (editor) *Anthologie de la poesie lyrique francaise de la fin du xv siecle a la fin du xix siecle,* Insel Verlag (Leipzig), 1923; *Le Miracle: Suivi de la chambre de l'horlage,* Stock (Paris), 1923; *Le Prince Jaffar* (novel; title means "The Prince of Jaffar"), 1924; *La Belle-Etoile,* A l'Enseigne de la porte etroite, 1925; *Suite Hollandaise,* Sablier, 1925; *Deliberations,* Les Cahiers de Paris, 1925; *Essai sur le roman* (literary criticism), M. Lesage (Paris), 1925; *Essai sur une renaissance dramatique* (literary criticism), Les Editions Lapina (Paris), 1926; *Lettres au Patagon,* 1926; *Lettre sur les malades,* [Paris], 1926; *La Pierre d'Horeb* (novel; title means "Horeb's Stone"), 1926, reprinted, Vialetay (Paris), 1973; *Le Voyage de Moscou* (nonfiction), 1927; *Memorial de Cauchois,* Editions de la belle page, 1927; *Hommages et souvenirs,* [Liege], 1928; *Les Sept Dernieres Plaies* (title means "The Last Seven Wounds"), 1928; *Entretien sur l'esprit europeen* (essays), Aux Editions des Cahiers libres, 1928; *La Nuit d'orage* (novel; title means "The Stormy Night"), 1928, reprinted, Harper, 1953.

Scenes de la vie future (essays), 1931, translation by Charles Miner Thompson published as *America: The Menace,* Houghton, 1931, reprinted, Arno, 1974; *L'Alsace entrevue,* Librairie de la Mesange (Strasbourg), 1931; *Geographie cordiale de l'Europe* (nonfiction), 1931; *Pages de mon carnet* (nonfiction), Aux Editions des Cahiers libres, 1931; *Les Jumeaux de Vallangoujard,* P. Hartmann, 1931; *Mon Royaume,* [Paris], 1932; *Querelles de famille* (essays), 1932, reprinted, 1959; *L'Humaniste et l'automate* (nonfiction), P. Hartmann, 1933; *Remarques sur les memoires imaginaires* (literary criticism), 1934; *Discours aux nuages,* Editions du siecle, 1934; (with Charles Jules Henri Nicolle and others) *Responsabilites de la medecine,* [Paris], 1935; *Fables de mon jardin* (nature studies), 1936; *Defense des lettres,* 1936,

translation by Ernest Franklin Bozman published as *In Defence of Letters,* Dent, 1938, Greystone Press, 1939, reprinted, Richard West, 1973; *Discours de reception de m. Georges Duhamel a l'Academie francaise,* 1936; *Deux patrons, suivi de vie et mort d'un heros de roman,* [Paris], 1937; *Memorial de la guerre blanche,* 1938, translation by N. Hoppe published as *The White War of 1938,* Dent, 1939; *Au chevet de la Civilisation* (essays), Flammarion (Paris), 1938.

Positions francaises: Chronique de l'annee 1939, 1940, translation by Basil Collier published as *Why France Fights,* Dent, 1940, published as *The French Position,* Dent, 1940; *Les Confessions sans penitence, suivi de trois autres entretiens: Rousseau, Montesquieu, Descartes, Pascal,* Plon (Paris), 1941; *Chronique des saisons ameres 1940-43,* P. Hartmann, 1944; *Civilisation francaise,* Librairie Hachette (Paris), 1944; *La Musique consolatrice,* Editions du Rocher (Monaco), 1944; *Lieu d'asile,* 1945; *Souvenirs de la vie du paradis,* 1946; *Paroles de medecin,* Editions du Rocher, 1946; *Semailles au vent,* Editions du Rocher, 1947; (with Henri Mondor) *Entretien au bord du fleuve: Discours de reception a l'Academie francaise de Henri Mondor et reponse de Georges Duhamel,* Editions du Rocher, 1947; *Consultation aux pays d'Islam,* 1947; *Tribulations de l'esperance,* 1947; *Homere au xx siecle,* Union latine d'editions (Paris), 1947; *Le bestiaire et l'herbier,* 1948.

(Author of preface) *Paris,* M. J. Challamel, 1950; *Le Voyage de Patrice Periot* (novel), 1951, translation by Bozman published as *Patrice Periot,* Dent, 1952; *Cri de profondeurs* (novel), 1951, translation by Bozman published as *Cry Out of the Depths,* Dent, 1953, Little, Brown, 1954; *Manuel du protestataire,* 1952; *Le Japon entre le tradition et l'avenir,* 1953; *La Turquie nouvelle, puissance d'occident,* 1954; *Refuges de la lecture,* 1954; *L'Archange de l'aventure* (novel), 1955; *Croisade contre le cancer,* Jeheber (Geneve), 1955; *Les Compagnons de l'apocalypse* (novel), 1956; *Les Voyageurs de "L'Esperance",* Gedalge (Paris), 1956; *Israel, clef de l'Orient,* 1957; *Les Livres du bonheur,* 1957; *Problemes de l'heure,* 1957; *Le Complexe de Theophile* (novel), 1958; (author of introduction) Georges Poisson, *Histoire et histoires de Sceaux,* Les Amis du Musee de l'ile de France, 1959; *Travail, mon seul repos!,* Editions Wesmael-Charlier, 1959.

Nouvelles du sombre empire, 1960; *Traite du depart, suivi de Fables du ma vie,* 1961; *Problemes de civilisation,* 1962.

Director of *Mercure de France,* a literary magazine, 1935-37.

SIDELIGHTS: While studying to be a doctor at the University of Paris, Georges Duhamel began developing an interest in literature. With several other young men, including Jules Romains, Rene Arcos, Charles Vildrac, Albert Gleizes, and Henri Martin, Duhamel founded an artists' colony, L'Abbaye. The experimental community was located in an old house on the shore of the Marne. Its members shared a belief in unanimism, a philosophy developed by Romains which held that the spirit of a group lends direction and energy to an individual's life. The community published several books as a joint venture but was forced to disband after fourteen months for economic reasons. After the failure of L'Abbaye, Duhamel worked as a researcher in a laboratory and wrote poetry and plays in his spare time. It was his plays that first brought him public recognition.

Duhamel's literary aspirations were temporarily shoved aside when World War I broke out. Duhamel worked as a military surgeon at the front for over four years. During that time he performed 2300 operations and took care of 4000 wounded soldiers. Having witnessed the ravages of war firsthand, Duhamel yearned for a world in which compassion and tolerance would prevail over the baser instincts of mankind. This longing for a better world was to guide his future writing. Boyd G. Carter noted that Duhamel's canon "demonstrates the continuity of his interest in permanent human values and his anxiety concerning their survival in an age of mechanical acceleration, fantastic destruction, and epochal transformation."

In *The New Book of Martyrs* and *Civilization,* written when Duhamel could snatch time from his duties at the front, he describes the anguish of the wounded and dying as well as the insensitivity of those who ran the military hospitals. "In the spiritual sense, the author of *Civilisation* is a great war casualty: he is a man who has never recovered from what he saw every day for four years," Francois Mauriac observed. "The essential gift of the man who wrote *Vie des Martyres* is imagination of the heart; he had the ability to share the suffering of others, to relive it in himself."

Following the war, Duhamel began work on his two famous novel cycles, "Salavin" and "The Pasquier Chronicles." The five novels that make up the "Salavin" series are now regarded as classics of world literature. Salavin is a mediocre yet introspective man who works for a pasteurized milk company. Although he wishes to improve himself and his circumstances, Salavin fails in most of his endeavors. Nonetheless, he is a likable character because he remains aware of his potential even though he never achieves it. Critics have praised Duhamel for the subtlety and psychological depth with which he portrays Salavin. Salavin, who searches for salvation outside of religion, is considered by many to be the prototype of the ordinary man of the twentieth century.

The "Salavin" cycle focuses on an individual, but "The Pasquier Chronicles" give a broader picture of French middle class life from the 1880's to World War I. The saga of the Pasquier family is based on Duhamel's own family. The head of the Pasquier clan, like Duhamel's father, studied medicine in middle age and became a practicing physician. Of the five Pasquier children, Duhamel most closely resembles Laurent, an urbane, successful, and stable man. "The Pasquier Chronicles" are not so highly regarded as the "Salavin" series. Some commentators found the long series boring, while others faulted Duhamel's subjective promotion of his own values. "Duhamel's humanism is sincere and his concern with the frustrations and joys of the man in the street is real, but the rather facile sentimentality of his approach, the naive ethical evangelism of his attitude, based on vague spiritual values, hamper the creative artist he might have been," Germaine Bree and Margaret Guiton wrote in *An Age of Fiction.*

For a man who had devoted his life and work to promoting harmony between people, Duhamel was forced to view an excessive amount of violence and suffering. Duhamel stayed in Paris during the German occupation in World War II, even though he had openly announced his opposition to Hitler. Duhamel's books were banned, three of his relatives were arrested, but he himself managed to evade the Nazi persecutors. Extremely proud of the French resistance movement, Duhamel contributed to *Les Lettres francaises,* an underground publication.

Duhamel's experiences in World War II did not drive him to despair; rather, they reinforced his belief in humanism. In a review of the French author's work, Henri Peyre remarked that Duhamel "is not blind to the disappointments that an optimist must endure, and all his novels display the gradual collapse of a rosy dream. He will not seek a solution in an easy catchword, tendered by Christianity, which he respected but never professed, or in science, which he always admired, though he was aware of its limitations. Friendship is the feeling of which he spoke most nobly (in *Deux Hommes* especially); like Romains, Vildrac, and later Malraux and Saint-Exupery, he would have liked to build a virile and warm regeneration of mankind upon friendship, that is, upon the most beautiful of all words and ideals proposed by humanism and by Christianity—fraternity."

Some of Duhamel's works have been translated into German, Spanish, Polish, and Arabic.

AVOCATIONAL INTERESTS: Flutist.

BIOGRAPHICAL/CRITICAL SOURCES: Regis Michaud, *Modern Thought and Literature in France,* Funk, 1934; *Books Abroad,* winter, 1946; *Contemporary Review,* April, 1948; *National Review of Literature,* July, 1948; Helmut Hatzfeld, *Trends and Styles in Twentieth Century French Literature,* Catholic University, 1957; Germaine Bree and Margaret Otis Guiton, *An Age of Fiction: The French Novel From Gide to Camus,* Rutgers University Press, 1957, published as *The French Novel: From Gide to Camus,* Harcourt, 1962; Francois Mauriac, *Second Thoughts,* World, 1961; Louis Clark Keating, *Critic of Civilization: Georges Duhamel and His Writings,* University of Kentucky Press, 1965; Henri Peyre, *French Novelists of Today,* Oxford University Press, 1967; Bettina L. Knapp, *Georges Duhamel,* Twayne, 1972; *Contemporary Literary Criticism,* Volume 8, Gale, 1978.

OBITUARIES: New York Times, April 14, 1966; *Publishers' Weekly,* April 25, 1966; *Antiquarian Bookman,* May 2, 1966; *Books Abroad,* spring, 1967; *Britannica Book of the Year,* 1967.*

(Died April 13, 1966, in Valmondois, France)

*   *   *

DUMAS, Claire
See Van WEDDINGEN, Marthe

*   *   *

DUNCAN, Archibald A(lexander) M(cBeth)   1926-

PERSONAL: Born October 17, 1926, in Pitlochry, Perthshire, Scotland; son of Charles G. and Christina H. (McBeth) Duncan; married Ann H. Sawyer, August 21, 1954; children: Beatrice, Alastair, Ewen. *Education:* University of Edinburgh, M.A. (honors), 1948; Oxford University, B.A., 1950. *Religion:* Church of Scotland. *Home:* 17 Campbell Dr., Bearsden, Glasgow G61, Scotland. *Office:* University of Glasgow, 9 University Gardens, Glasgow G12, Scotland.

CAREER: Oxford University, Balliol College, Oxford, England, lecturer in history, 1950-51; Queen's University of Belfast, Belfast, Northern Ireland, lecturer in medieval history, 1951-53; University of Edinburgh, Edinburgh, Scotland, lecturer in medieval history, 1953-62; University of Glasgow, Glasgow, Scotland, professor of Scottish history and literature, 1962—, dean of Faculty of Arts, 1974-76, clerk of Senate, 1978—. Member of Royal Commission on Ancient and Historical Monuments of Scotland. *Member:* Royal Historical Society (fellow), Scottish History Society (president, 1977—).

WRITINGS: Scotland: The Making of the Kingdom, Oliver & Boyd, 1975, revised edition, 1978; (editor) W. Croft

Dickinson, *Scotland From the Earliest Times to 1603,* 3rd edition (Duncan was not associated with earlier editions), Oxford University Press, 1977.

WORK IN PROGRESS: Acts of Robert I, King of Scots, 1306-29; a study of Bede's sources for his account of St. Columba and the Picts.

SIDELIGHTS: Duncan writes: "I enjoy university affairs too much, and should spend less time on them and more on what I do better—evaluation of historical sources—which has more enduring value. I find the vanities of my colleagues an unending source of entertainment and should like to write *the* university novel. But I never shall. I suspect they'll find 'A Short-Story Man' graven on my heart when I die."

*   *   *

DUNKLING, Leslie Alan   1935-

PERSONAL: Born June 24, 1935, in London, England; son of William Joseph George and Ethel (Johnson) Dunkling; married Nicole Germaine Tripet, December 30, 1961; children: Stephen, Catherine, Laurence. *Education:* University of London, teaching certificate, 1961, B.A. (honors), 1965; University of Stockholm, M.A., 1967. *Home:* 7 Aragon Ave., Thames Ditton, Surrey KT7 0PY, England.

CAREER: Teacher of English and French at Bordetsone Secondary School in Hanwell, England, 1961-62; University of Stockholm, Stockholm, Sweden, lecturer in English, 1965-67; associated with British Broadcasting Corp. (BBC), 1971—, senior producer of "English by Radio," 1977—. Public lecturer; guest on television and radio programs.

WRITINGS: When They Were Young, Svenska Bokforlaget, 1967; *English House Names,* Names Society, 1971; *Kate and the Clock,* Longman, 1971; *The Battle of Newton Road,* Longman, 1972; *The Guinness Book of Names,* Guinness Superlatives, 1974; *First Names First,* Universe Books, 1977; *Scottish Christian Names,* Johnston & Bacon, 1978, *The Loch Ness Monster,* Longman, 1978; *What's in a Name?,* Ventura, 1978; *Everyman's Dictionary of Christian Names,* Dent, 1980.

Author of about five hundred radio plays, including two full-length plays, and thirty-six television scripts, including "Off We Go," a series to teach English to German children.

Author of "The Names Game," a column syndicated by Central Press Features to about fifty periodicals, 1974-78. Editor of *VIZ.* (journal of Names Society), 1969-71.

WORK IN PROGRESS: The Name Givers, with Catherine Cameron.

SIDELIGHTS: Dunkling writes: "I am committed at the moment to the study of personal names; I also write in the field of teaching English as a foreign language."

BIOGRAPHICAL/CRITICAL SOURCES: Times Literary Supplement, March 10, 1972, August 5, 1977.

*   *   *

DUNN, Nell
See SANDFORD, Nell Mary

*   *   *

DYE, Margaret   1932-

PERSONAL: Born April 30, 1932, in Norfolk, England; daughter of James and Edna (a teacher; maiden name, Scott)

Bidwell; married Frank Dye (a business manager), December 21, 1975. *Education:* Attended Keswick Training College, 1951-53. *Politics:* Conservative. *Religion:* Church of England. *Home address:* Runton Hill, West Runton, Cromer, Norfolk, England.

CAREER: Teacher in grammar schools in Norfolk and Cheshire, England, 1952-78; Runton Hill Private School, West Runton, England, teacher of biology and environmental sciences, 1978—. Violinist for orchestras and opera companies.

WRITINGS: (With husband, Frank Dye) *Ocean Crossing Wayfarer,* David & Charles, 1977; *Dinghy Cruising,* Spurbooks, 1977. Contributor to boating magazines in England.

WORK IN PROGRESS: Withie Ways, "a smuggling book based on love of waterways of Norfolk"; children's books on sailing and smuggling in Norfolk; a book on sailing in Greece.

SIDELIGHTS: Margaret Dye writes: "I am a biologist and environmentalist, combining a teaching career with a wide variety of semi-professional occupations, in sailing, music, and natural sciences. I also teach survival skills for the Duke of Edinburgh Award Scheme. I enjoy seeing young people reach self-realization through struggle and independent thought.

"I am very interested in travel, and would like to sail to lonely islands everywhere. I have already sailed an open Wayfarer dinghy to Arctic Norway, St. Kilda, and the Outer Hebrides. I find the challenges of survival very stimulating. I love the simple life and avoid materialism. Communication with like-minded people is more important than a high salary or status."

AVOCATIONAL INTERESTS: Music of Mozart and Britten, horticulture, wine making, country living.

*   *   *

DYER, George Bell   1903-1978

OBITUARY NOTICE: Born April 12, 1903, in Washington, D.C.; died November 8, 1978, in New Hope, Pa. Teacher, political historian, and author. Dyer worked as a newspaper reporter for several years before writing seven mystery novels between 1931 and 1940. After service in World War II, he resumed writing with an interest in political-warfare themes. Founder of the Dyer Institute of Interdisciplinary Studies in 1951, he later taught political science at University of Pennsylvania and Yale University. His works include *A Century of Strategic Intelligence, Estimating National Power and Intentions,* and his last book, *On Ritualization of War.* Obituaries and other sources: *American Men and Women of Science: The Social and Behavioral Sciences,* 12th edition, Bowker, 1973; *Who's Who in America,* 40th edition, Marquis, 1978; *New York Times,* November 11, 1978.

*   *   *

DYMOND, Rosalind
See CARTWRIGHT, Rosalind Dymond

E

EASON, Ruth P.   1898(?)-1978

OBITUARY NOTICE: Born c. 1898 in Glen Burnie, Md.; died November 28, 1978, in Gaihtersburg, Md. Teacher, school administrator, and author. After serving as teacher and principal of a one-room school for ten years, Eason became supervisor of Maryland's Anne Arundel County schools in 1925. In 1947, she left that post to do experimental teaching with handicapped children and later spent ten years directing the county's special education program. Her published work includes a guide list for Anne Arundel facilities for the handicapped and *History of the Town of Glen Burnie.* Eason won the Pioneer Woman in Education Award in 1956. Obituaries and other sources: *Washington Post,* December 1, 1978.

*   *   *

EDEN, Dorothy (Enid)   1912-

PERSONAL: Born April 3, 1912, in Canterbury, New Zealand; came to England in 1954; daughter of John (a farmer) and Eva Natalie Eden. *Education:* Attended public schools in New Zealand. *Residence:* London, England. *Agent:* David Higham Associates, 5-8 Lower John St., London W1R 4HA, England.

CAREER: Writer. Worked as a legal secretary in New Zealand.

WRITINGS—All fiction: *Singing Shadows,* Stanley Paul, 1940; *The Laughing Ghost,* Macdonald & Co., 1943, Ace Books, 1976; *We Are for the Dark,* Macdonald & Co., 1944; *Summer Sunday,* Macdonald & Co., 1946; *Walk Into My Parlour,* Macdonald & Co., 1947; *The Schoolmaster's Daughters,* Macdonald & Co., 1948.

Crow Hollow, Macdonald & Co., 1950, Ace Books, 1977; *Voice of the Dolls,* Macdonald & Co., 1950, Ace Books, 1973; *Cat's Prey,* Macdonald & Co., 1952, Ace Books, 1975; *Lamb to the Slaughter,* Macdonald & Co., 1953; *Bride by Candelight,* Macdonald & Co., 1954, Ace Books, 1975; *Darling Clementine,* Macdonald & Co., 1955; *Death Is a Red Rose,* Macdonald & Co., 1956, Ace Books, 1976; *The Pretty Ones,* Macdonald & Co., 1957, Ace Books, 1976; *Listen to Danger,* Macdonald & Co., 1958, Ace Books, 1976; *Deadly Travellers,* Macdonald & Co., 1959, Ace Books, 1975; *The Sleeping Bride,* Macdonald & Co., 1959, Ace Books, 1976.

Samantha, Hodder & Stoughton, 1960, published as *Lady of Mallow,* Coward, 1962; *Sleep in the Woods,* Hodder & Stoughton, 1960, Coward, 1961; *Afternoon for Lizards,* Hodder & Stoughton, 1961; *Whistle for the Crows,* Hodder & Stoughton, 1962, Ace Books, 1971; *The Bird in the Chimney,* Hodder & Stoughton, 1963; *Bella,* Hodder & Stoughton, 1964; *Darkwater,* Coward, 1964; *The Marriage Chest,* Hodder & Stoughton, 1965, Coward, 1966; *Ravenscroft,* Coward, 1965; *Never Call It Loving: A Biographical Novel of Katherine O'Shea and Charles Stewart Parnell,* Coward, 1966; *Siege in the Sun,* Coward, 1967; *Winterwood,* Coward, 1967; *The Shadow Wife,* Coward, 1968; *Yellow Is for Fear, and Other Stories,* Ace Books, 1968; *The Vines of Yarrabee,* Coward, 1969.

Melbury Square, Coward, 1970; *Waiting for Willa,* Coward, 1970; *An Afternoon Walk,* Coward, 1971; *Bridge of Fear,* Ace Books, 1975; *The Brooding Lake,* Ace Books, 1972; *Shadow of a Witch,* Ace Books, 1972; *Speak to Me of Love,* Coward, 1972; *The Millionaire's Daughter,* Coward, 1974; *Night of the Letter,* Ace Books, 1976; *The Time of the Dragon,* Coward, 1975; *The Daughters of Ardmore Hall,* Ace Books, 1976; *Face of an Angel,* Ace Books, 1976; *The House on Hay Hill and Other Romantic Fiction,* Fawcett, 1976; *The Salamanca Drum,* Coward, 1977.

Contributor of short stories to magazines, including *Redbook* and *Good Housekeeping.*

SIDELIGHTS: "From the first pages of all her books Dorothy Eden never fails to intrigue," Anne Britton asserted in *Books and Bookmen.* Apparently many other readers share this sentiment, for since 1970 more than five million copies of Eden's books have been sold, and she now numbers more than thirty books in print. A reviewer for the *Washington Post* named Eden, along with Daphne du Maurier, Georgette Heyer, Victoria Holt, Mary Stewart, and Norah Lofts, as among the best-known contemporary Gothic novelists.

Growing up in a remote area helped to nourish Eden's creativity, as she herself explained: "My childhood on a lonely New Zealand farm was the most invaluable background for developing imagination." With few other diversions to occupy her time, the young Eden read voraciously and at an early age decided to become a writer. While she was working as a legal secretary, Eden churned out manuscripts and mailed them to publishers. After a few of her manuscripts were accepted for publication, she packed up for London and became a full-time writer.

Eden's novels are set in such locations as Australia, Peking, and Denmark, and she has no intention of abandoning exotic settings in her future works: "I don't particularly want to write about squalor, or poor people. I enjoy glamourous backgrounds—they give me vicarious pleasure, and I think that's what readers want to enjoy too. I don't mean I want to write only about millionaires—just people who are comfortably off and who are articulate."

Some commentators point to *Never Call It Loving* as evidence of Eden's talent for painstakingly researching her backgrounds. The book is a fictionalized account of the real love affair between Charles Stewart Parnell, leader of the Irish Party at the turn of the century, and Katherine O'Shea, the wife of a dissolute politician. Their passion ruined Parnell's reputation, destroyed his chance to get the Irish Home Rule Bill passed, and drove him to an early grave. A reviewer for *Books and Bookmen* wrote of the novel: "There is nothing mawkish about Miss Eden's reconstruction of this Victorian *cause celebre*. Working from good source material, she has allied the available facts with her undoubted storytelling abilities to produce a tale which is at once romantic and infinitely pathetic."

In *The Vines of Yarrabee,* perhaps the most popular of her novels, Eden spins a yarn about the Australian outback in the early nineteenth century. Gilbert Massingham, an ambitious Australian vintner, imports a well-bred woman from England to be his wife so that his Yarrabee mansion may become a center of culture. Shady financial schemes and love triangles serve to complicate the plot. Lucille G. Crane admired *The Vines of Yarrabee* for its "maturity in organization and a smoothness of writing. The story is plausible. The atmosphere of Australia authentic. The background of wine growing and wine making is interesting." Joining in the praise, Anne Britton commented: "Miss Eden has done her research thoroughly. Because of her gift for story telling and her knowledge of the country, she is able to transport her readers back to the days when all labour stemmed from the convicts and violence was just a part of life."

Eden also has her detractors. While many commentators consider her to be a superb storyteller, others find her plots unoriginal and artificial. In a critique of *Winterwood,* P. J. Earl remarked, "The various twists and turns made by the plot are not unusual and I am sure most readers will work them out at least five pages before they happen." Similar complaints were lodged by other reviewers about *Shadow Wife*—"the situation is too contrived, the plot unsatisfactory"—and *Waiting for Willa*—" a poor plot which never really mystifies and a solution that can hardly be acceptable."

Of her work habits, Eden told an interviewer: "I have to know the end before I start writing. I love to write about families, then you can have characters coming in later and surprising you, people you didn't know about when you started writing. And I like to write about children, too. I feel they're waiting for me to write about them."

Eden's books have been translated into eighteen languages, including German, French, and Finnish.

BIOGRAPHICAL/CRITICAL SOURCES: Best Sellers, April 1, 1967, March 15, 1969, March 1, 1970; *New York Times Book Review,* April 16, 1967, December 13, 1970; *Books and Bookmen,* May, 1968, August, 1968, March, 1969; *Washington Post,* November 14, 1970; *Publishers Weekly,* March 28, 1977; *Washington Post Book World,* May 22, 1977.

EDWARDS, Audrey 1947-

PERSONAL: Born April 21, 1947, in Tacoma, Wash.; daughter of Cyril Alfred (a writer) and Bertie (a director of a senior citizens' center) Edwards. *Education:* University of Washington, Seattle, B.A., 1969; Columbia University, M.A., 1974. *Home:* 195 Claremont Ave., New York, N.Y. 10027. *Office: Family Circle,* 488 Madison Ave., New York, N.Y. 10017.

CAREER: Redbook, New York City, associate editor, 1970-72; Columbia University, New York City, editor for Urban Center, 1972-73; Fairchild Publications, New York City, promotion editor, 1974-77; *Black Enterprise,* New York City, senior editor, 1977-78; *Family Circle,* New York City, senior editor, 1978—. *Member:* National Association of Black Journalists (New York program chairman). *Awards, honors:* Coretta Scott King Fellowship from American Association of University Women, 1969.

WRITINGS—Children's books: (With Gary Wohl) *The Picture Life of Muhammad Ali,* F. Watts, 1976; (with Wohl) *The Picture Life of Bobby Orr,* F. Watts, 1976; (with Wohl) *The Picture Life of Stevie Wonder,* F. Watts, 1977; *Muhammad Ali, the People's Champ,* Little, Brown, 1977. Contributor to popular magazines, including *Redbook, Essence,* and *Your Place.*

SIDELIGHTS: Audrey Edwards writes: "Writing takes many shapes, moods, and routes, touching us in places we know and recognize. As a black writer I attempt to strike the note that is universal, explore the experience which is common, and give expression to the black aesthetic. My writing necessarily reflects a black perspective, and should be about the business of education, informing illuminating, and transmitting. I strive, always, to be responsible.

"Travels have taken me to Africa (which revealed more about me than about Africans), Japan, the Caribbean, and throughout the United States, and I consider traveling to be the next best thing to reading."

* * *

EDWARDS, Blake 1922-

PERSONAL: Born July 26, 1922, in Tulsa, Okla.; married Julie Andrews (an actress and entertainer), 1969. *Office:* c/o Directors Guild of America, 7950 West Sunset Blvd., Hollywood, Calif. 90046.

CAREER: Writer; actor, director, and producer of motion pictures. Actor in motion pictures, including "Ten Gentlemen From West Point, " 1942, "Strangler of the Swamp," 1945, "Leather Gloves," 1948, "Panhandle," 1948, and "Stampede," 1949. Director of motion pictures, including "Breakfast at Tiffany's" 1961, and "The Days of Wine and Roses," 1962. Creator of television series, including "Dante's Inferno," "Peter Gunn," and "Mr. Lucky." Cofounder of production company with Harold Robbins and Alden Schwimmer. *Military service:* Served in U.S. Coast Guard. *Member:* Directors Guild of America. *Awards, honors:* Co-nominee for best screenwriting from Writers Guild of America, 1957, for "Operation Mad Ball," 1962, for "The Notorious Landlady," 1964, for "The Pink Panther," and 1965, for "The Great Race."

WRITINGS—Screenplays: (With John C. Champion) "Panhandle," Allied Artists, 1948; (with Champion) "Stampede" (adapted from the novel by Edward Beverly Mann), Allied Artists, 1949; (with Richard Quinn) "Sound Off," Columbia, 1952; (with Quinn) "Rainbow 'round My Shoulder," Columbia, 1952; (with Quinn and Robert Welles)

"All Ashore," Columbia, 1953; (with Quinn) "Cruisin' Down the River," Columbia, 1953; "Drive a Crooked Road," Columbia, 1954; (screen story) "The Atomic Kid," Republic, 1954; (with Quinn) "My Sister Eileen" (adapted from the earlier film of the same title, the play by Joseph Fields and Jerome Chodorov, and stories by Ruth McKenney), Columbia, 1955; (with Quinn, and director) "Bring Your Smile Along," Columbia, 1955; (with Quinn; and director) "He Laughed Last," Columbia, 1956; (and director) "Mister Cory" (adapted from a story by Leo Rosten), Universal, 1957; (with Arthur Carter and Jed Harris) "Operation Mad Ball" (adapted from the play by Carter), Columbia, 1957; (and director) "This Happy Feeling" (adapted from the play by F. Hugh Herbert, "For Love or Money"), Universal, 1958.

(Screen story, with Owen Crump) "The Couch," Warner Bros., 1962; (with Larry Gelbart) "The Notorious Landlady" (adapted from the short story by Margery Sharp, *Notorious Tenant*), Columbia, 1962; (with Maurice Richlin; and director) "The Pink Panther," United Artists, 1964; (with William Peter Blatty; and director) "A Shot in the Dark" (adapted from the play by Harry Kurnitz), United Artists, 1964; (with Richlin) "Soldier in the Rain" (adapted from the novel by William Golden), Allied Artists, 1964; (with Arthur Ross; and director) "The Great Race," Warner Bros., 1965; (screen story, with Richlin; and director) "What Did You Do in the War, Daddy?," United Artists, 1966; (with Blatty) "Gunn," Paramount, 1967; (with Tom Waldman and Frank Waldman; and director) "The Party," United Artists, 1968; (with Blatty; and director) "Darling Lili," Paramount, 1969.

(And director) "Wild Rovers," Metro-Goldwyn-Mayer (MGM), 1972; (and director) "The Tamarind Seed" (adapted from the novel by Evelyn Anthony), Scotia-Barber, 1974; (with Frank Waldman, and director) "The Return of the Pink Panther," United Artists, 1975; (with Waldman) "The Pink Panther Strikes Again," United Artists, 1976; (with Waldman and Ron Clark; and director) "The Revenge of the Pink Panther," United Artists, 1978.

Contributor of scripts to radio programs, including "Johnny Dollar," "Line-Up," and "Richard Diamond."

SIDELIGHTS: Edwards is best known as the writer and director of the "Pink Panther" films, all of which chronicle the misadventures of Inspector Clouseau. Clouseau is a bungling French investigator who achieved notoriety in "The Pink Panther" when he deduced who had stolen the jewel of the same name. Oddly enough, none of the later films have anything to do with the fictitious gem. In reviewing the first "Pink Panther" film, Hollis Alpert referred to Edwards' brand of humor as "anti-slapstick" and declared that the film "has been made exquisitely funny by Mr. Edwards' ability to set up a situation expected by the audience and to then counter the situation."

Edwards returned to Clouseau in "A Shot in the Dark" and, although it was not met with the same critical acclaim as "The Pink Panther," it was popular enough with film audiences to merit three more Clouseau films. The most recent Clouseau movie, "The Revenge of the Pink Panther," received consistent praise from critics who noted the film's riotous slapstick." It is to Edwards' credit that the "Pink Panther" films have endured so well. As one critic observed, "It's the kind of movie series there is no real reason to discontinue."

BIOGRAPHICAL/CRITICAL SOURCES: Variety, September 30, 1959, January 15, 1964, June 24, 1964; *New York Times*, December 4, 1959, October 6, 1961, June 24, 1964; *Time*, December 24, 1959, February 1, 1963; *Saturday Review*, September 30, 1961, February 2, 1963, April 18, 1964; *New York Herald Tribune*, June 24, 1964; *Washington Post*, July 19, 1978.*

* * *

EDWARDS, Norman
    See CARR, Terry (Gene)

* * *

EDWARDS, Samuel
    See GERSON, Noel Bertram

* * *

EEKMAN, Thomas   1923-

PERSONAL: Born May 20, 1923, in Middelharnis, Netherlands; came to United States in 1966; son of Thomas Adam (a high school teacher) and Anna (a nurse; maiden name, De Kruyff) Eekman; married Tine De Jong, May 2, 1946; children: Menno, Roeland, Ivo, Milja (daughter). *Education:* University of Amsterdam, M.A., 1946, Ph.D., 1951. *Politics:* "Socialist idealist." *Religion:* "Humanist." *Home:* 1035 Centinela Ave., Santa Monica, Calif. 90403. *Office:* Department of Slavic Languages, University of California, Los Angeles, Calif. 90024.

CAREER: University of Amsterdam, Amsterdam, Netherlands, research fellow, 1947-60; University of California, Los Angeles, visiting professor of Slavic languages, 1960-61; University of Amsterdam, docent, 1960-66; University of California, Los Angeles, professor of Slavic languages and literatures, 1966—. Visiting professor at University of Hamburg, 1972-73. *Member:* Association Internationale des Langues et Litteratures Slaves, Association of Southeast European Studies, Western Slavic Association, Philological Association of the Pacific Coast (vice-president, 1972; president, 1973), Netherlandic Studies Group (University of California, Los Angeles), Medieval and Renaissance Studies Center (University of California, Los Angeles). *Awards, honors:* Order of the Yugoslav Flag, 1965.

WRITINGS: Anton Tsjechov en de Russische intelligentsia (title means "Anton Chekhov and the Russian Intelligentsia"), Van Loghum Slaterus, 1951; *Tussen twee oevers: A. Herzen* (title means "Between Two Shores: A. Herzen"), Van Loghum Slaterus, 1953; (editor) *Anton Chekhov (1860-1960): A Symposium*, E. J. Brill, 1960; *Zes Russische klassieken* (title means "Six Russian Classics"), De Bussy, 1963; *The Realm of Rime: A Study of Rime in the Poetry of the Slavs*, Hakkert, 1974; (editor with Ante Kadic) *Juraj Krizanic (1618-1683): Russophile and Ecumenic Visionary*, Mouton, 1976; *Thirty Years of Yugoslav Literature, 1945-1975*, University of Michigan Press, 1978; (editor with Paul Debreczeny) *Chekhov's Art of Writing*, Slavica, 1978. Contributor to literature, language, and foreign studies journals. Co-editor of *California Slavic Studies*.

WORK IN PROGRESS: Research for *"Free Verse" in the Slavic Literatures* and *Russian-Dutch Contacts in the Seventeenth and Eighteenth Centuries*.

SIDELIGHTS: Eekman writes: "I miss the imagination to become a fiction writer and the original, deep mind to become a poet; but I love literature and believe that literary works, even the minor ones, reveal a great deal about the human condition, about culture, history, psychology, human relations. Literature is one of the great arenas of human creativity; therefore it is very worthwhile to study its formal aspects, too. I am competent in Dutch, English, French, German, and the main Slavic literary languages: Russian, Polish, Czech, Serbo-Croatian (with a reading knowledge of the other Slavic and the Scandinavian languages); this has considerably widened my view and taught me that each nation through its writers expresses universal values.''

* * *

EGYPT, Ophelia Settle   1903-

PERSONAL: Born February 20, 1903, in Clarksville, Tex.; daughter of Green Wilson (a teacher) and Sarah (a teacher; maiden name, Garth) Settle; married Ivory Lester Egypt (a waiter), June, 1940 (died, November, 1953); children: Ivory Lester, Jr. *Education:* Howard University, B.A., 1925, M.S., 1944; University of Pennsylvania, M.A., 1926, further graduate study, 1949-50; attended Columbia University. *Home:* 1933 Alabama Ave. S.E., Washington, D.C. 20020.

CAREER: Orange County Training School, Chapel Hill, N.C., teacher, 1925-26; Fisk University, Nashville, Tenn., researcher and instructor in social sciences, 1928-33; St. Louis Provident, St. Louis, Mo., assistant consultant, 1933-35; Flint Goodridge Hospital, New Orleans, La., director of social service department, 1939; Howard University, Washington, D.C., assistant professor and field work supervisor in medical school, 1939-51; Juvenile Court, Washington, D.C., probation officer, 1950-52; Iona R. Whipper Home, executive director, 1952-54; case worker for unmarried mothers in Washington, D.C., 1954-56; Planned Parenthood of Metropolitan Washington, D.C., founder and director of Parklands Neighborhood Clinic, 1956-68; writer, 1968—. Consultant to government agencies and social service organizations. *Member:* Garfield Douglas Civic Association, Anacostia Historical Society. *Awards, honors:* Named Iota Phi Lambda Sorority's woman of the year, 1963; Club Twenty International Women's Year Award, 1975.

WRITINGS: James Weldon Johnson (biography for children), Crowell, 1974. Contributor of articles to periodicals.

WORK IN PROGRESS: A story for children; interviews with ex-slaves, entitled *Unwritten History of Slavery.*

SIDELIGHTS: Ophelia Egypt told *CA:* "I've been scribbling little jingles since elementary school days but it was in high school that I wrote my first poem. I didn't like what my history book said about Dred Scott, the slave who took his case to the Supreme Court to prove that he should be free since he had lived outside slave territory. My poem said that the Court was wrong when it decided that he was *not* free and that he had no right to freedom since a slave could not be a citizen. It wasn't a very good poem but it made my point. I read it proudly in class and my teacher and classmates liked it.

"Most of my writing began like the poem about Dred Scott. Some incident in my life or in my family or work starts ideas moving around in my head and the first thing I know, I'm dreaming about that subject and thinking about it more and more. That's the way I started writing the story about my early childhood. One day, at work, after I had become a professional social worker, I was helping a young mother who wanted to give up her baby for adoption. She loved him very much but she knew she could not take care of him or give him the kind of life she wanted him to have. But she had a hard time making up her mind. After many discussions, she decided to give him up. After he left the office with his new parents, his mother wept as she talked with me about her feeling of loss and aloneness and her firm conviction that she had done the right thing.

"Somehow, that mother's experience started me thinking about my own mother who had died before my fifth birthday. I began wondering how she had felt about me and my younger brothers as she became aware of the nearness of her death. My own feeling of loss overwhelmed me and before the day ended, I sat down to the typewriter and tried to put my feeling on paper. Often that is the way I begin, but I do have to sit at my typewriter and struggle for hours day after day. Incidently, that story is still unpublished.

"I had to work even harder on *James Weldon Johnson.* It was almost three years from the time I selected his name from a list of biographies the publisher wanted done. I had known him and his wife personally and had loved listening to him talk about his experiences and read from his writings. Doing a biography about him was much harder than I thought because so many things had to be left out and so much research had to be done. Hardest of all, I had to learn to write short sentences and use words that had meaning for young children.

"Fortunately, other members of the Black Writers Workshop of Washington, D.C. were experiencing similar problems and we had the expert leadership of two beautiful writers, Sharon Bell Mathis and Eloise Greenfield, who gave me invaluable assistance and encouragement. My editor also provided skilled, understanding guidance. Earlier influences include my English teachers, friends and family and such writers as Charles S. Johnson under whom I worked at Fisk University when I interviewed more than one hundred former slaves and Langston Hughes who was always willing to read my material and encourage me to keep writing. More recently, another poet and writer, Sterling Brown, has helped me in countless ways with my ex-slave manuscript.

"My favorite work, based on interviews with men and women who had been slaves is still unpublished but I hope that it will be available in a few years. Those aged men and women reminded me of my own grandparents who had been slaves. I remember how we used to sit around the fireplace spellbound listening to their stories of life in slavery. So talking to men and women who had been children during slavery, was like having my grandparents come alive again. Now I am trying to make these old people's stories come alive for children. I hope I can help youngsters feel the pride and excitement I experienced as I listened to my own grandparents.

"To the children who want to become writers, I'd like to say begin now. Write about your own experiences and feelings, the people you see every day, and all the world around you. There is beauty there as well as ugliness, joy as well as sorrow and pain. I also want my writing to say to children, especially black children, life can be hard and discouraging, but never as bad as slavery. If slave parents could find a way to survive and make good lives for themselves and their children, surely you can do it. Work and stick together. Love and help each other. No matter how poor or how rich or successful you become, always reach out to those around you. Lend a helping hand, even to those who seem hopeless, remembering always that 'There but by the grace of God, go I.' ''

* * *

EHRENFELD, David W(illiam)   1938-

PERSONAL: Born January 15, 1938, in New York, N.Y.; son of Irving (a physician) and Anne (Shapiro) Ehrenfeld; married Joan Gardner (a plant ecologist), June 28, 1970; children: Kate, Jane. *Education:* Harvard University, B.A.,

1959, M.D., 1963; University of Florida, Ph.D., 1966. *Religion:* Jewish. *Residence:* Middlesex, N.J. *Office:* Cook College, Rutgers University, P.O. Box 231, New Brunswick, N.J. 08903.

CAREER: Columbia University, Barnard College, New York, N.Y., assistant professor, 1967-70, associate professor of biological science, 1970-74; Rutgers University, Cook College, New Brunswick, N.J., professor of biology, 1974—.

WRITINGS: Biological Conservation, Holt, 1970; *Conserving Life on Earth,* Oxford University Press, 1972; *The Arrogance of Humanism,* Oxford University Press, 1978. Contributor to scientific journals.

WORK IN PROGRESS: With C. K. Mack, "a popular novel with a scientific base."

*   *   *

EIDENBERG, Eugene 1939-

PERSONAL: Born October 5, 1939, in New York, N.Y.; son of Nathan (a certified public accountant) and Eve (Rosenbaum) Eidenberg; married Susan Zox (an educator), January 28, 1961; children: Danielle, Elizabeth. *Education:* University of Wisconsin—Madison, B.A., 1961; Northwestern University, M.A., Ph.D. *Home:* 3210 34th St. N.W., Washington, D.C. 20008. *Office:* U.S. Department of Health, Education & Welfare, 200 Independence Ave. S.W., Washington, D.C. 20201.

CAREER: University of Minnesota, Minneapolis, professor of political science, 1965-70, assistant vice-president in administration, 1970-72; University of Illinois at Chicago Circle, Chicago, vice-chancellor, 1972-76; U.S. Department of Health, Education & Welfare, Washington, D.C., executive assistant, 1977, deputy under-secretary for intergovernmental affairs, 1977—. Deputy mayor of Minneapolis, 1968-69. Past chairman of Illinois Law Enforcement Commission. *Member:* American Political Science Association. *Awards, honors:* Congressional fellow of American Political Science Association, 1964-65.

WRITINGS: (With Roy D. Morey) *An Act of Congress: The Legislative Process and the Making of Education Policy,* Norton, 1969. Contributor of articles to academic journals.

*   *   *

EISENBERG, Gerson G. 1909-

PERSONAL: Born March 5, 1909, in Baltimore, Md.; son of Abram (an art collector and merchant) and Helen (Gutman) Eisenberg; married Sadie Frenkl (active in civic affairs), September 15, 1967. *Education:* George Washington University, B.A., 1930; graduate study at Johns Hopkins University, 1936-37; New York University, M.B.A., 1944. *Religion:* Jewish. *Home:* 7940 Stevenson Rd., Baltimore, Md. 21208. *Office:* Eisenberg Educational Enterprises, Inc., 2 Hamill Rd., #327, Baltimore, Md. 21210.

CAREER: U.S. Government, Washington, D.C., economist for state and local government census bureau and War Department, 1944-45; Eisenberg Educational Enterprises, Inc., Baltimore, Md., president, 1945—. Vice-president of Robinson's Department Store in Glen Burnie, Md., 1949-62; vice-president of Plastic & Metal Products in Linthicum, Md., 1962-70. President of Gerson G. Eisenberg Foundation; member of board of directors of Maryland Conference of Social Concern, Baltimore Museum of Art, Associated Jewish Charities & Welfare Fund, American Jewish Committee, Hebrew Immigrant Aid Society, and Ecumenical Institute of St. Mary's Seminary.

MEMBER: American Academy of Political and Social Science, American Economic Association, American Historical Association, Jewish Historical Society of Maryland (member of board of directors).

WRITINGS: Learning Vacations, Eisenberg Educational Enterprises, 1977, new edition, Acropolis Books, 1978. Contributor to *Maryland Historical Magazine.*

WORK IN PROGRESS: 1917 Russian Revolutions and American Reaction; an economic study of 1917 Russia.

SIDELIGHTS: Eisenberg writes: "I wrote *Learning Vacations* after thirty years of attending alumni seminars and public affairs conferences in the United States and abroad. I was asked for information and found no central source.

"I have a continued interest in social and economic history and social reformers (Robert Owen, Robert Dale Owen, Frances Wright, etc.). I have a great interest in 'New Harmony' and other 'utopias.'"

AVOCATIONAL INTERESTS: Stereo-photography, operettas (including composition).

BIOGRAPHICAL/CRITICAL SOURCES: Baltimore Sun Magazine, December 14, 1975.

*   *   *

EISENBERGER, Kenneth 1948-

PERSONAL: Born March 20, 1948, in Bronx, N.Y.; son of Irving (an investor) and Ruth (Segal) Eisenberger. *Education:* Santa Monica College, A.A., 1968; University of California, Santa Barbara, B.A., 1970; University of Southern California, M.S.W., 1977. *Residence:* Los Angeles, Calif. *Agent:* Collier Associates, 280 Madison Ave., New York, N.Y. 10016. *Office:* 6399 Wilshire Blvd., Suite 1007, Los Angeles, Calif. 90048.

CAREER: St. Joseph Medical Center, Burbank, Calif., clinical social worker, 1977—. Member of health and welfare committee of Los Angeles County Commission for the Handicapped. *Member:* National Association of Social Workers, Society for Clinical Social Work, Council of Nephrology Social Workers, National Association of Patients on Hemodialysis and Transplantation, Consumers Union, American Council on Consumer Interests, American Civil Liberties Union, Council for Economic Survival, Writers Guild of America (West), Academy of Television Arts and Sciences, California Association of Marriage and Family Counselors, Consumers Federation of California, Nephrology Social Workers of Southern California (vice-president).

WRITINGS: The Expert Consumer: A Complete Handbook, Prentice-Hall, 1977. Editor of *Hemodialysis Newsletter.*

WORK IN PROGRESS: A children's consumer action book; an adult book on personality exploration and development; a screenplay for a comedy feature film.

SIDELIGHTS: Eisenberger writes: "My first published work is a complete handbook on consumer rights and protection, a subject I have been exploring for a number of years. A consumer is anyone who purchases or consumes goods and services, from an infant in a crib to an elderly person who is hospitalized. We consumers form the largest special interest group of any in existence. We have enormous power if only we will work together and harness that power for mutual benefit.

"My parents taught me much about assertiveness, a key factor in getting satisfaction in the marketplace. Becoming an expert consumer, like so many things, is easy when you know how. Once we utilize an optimum system of buying, understand our consumer rights, complain effectively, learn and make use of our avenues of help, become conscientious about following through, and make our needs known to companies, government agencies, legislative bodies, and consumer groups, we will see better laws to protect us and we will derive much more satisfaction from our purchases.

"Being a new author, I have had a lot to learn. I thought once the contract was signed and the final manuscript submitted, all I had to do was sit back and wait for my royalty checks. To my great surprise, it was only the beginning. Even with such a large publisher, most of the actual work in promoting the book to the fullest extent seems to have been mine. I appeared on about thirty television and radio shows in five states, and secured numerous magazine and newspaper reviews by assertively telephoning and writing media bookers and book reviewers. I visited countless book store managers, letting them know of my interviews and securing commitments for orders. All of the intense, prolonged efforts I have made have been worth it, however, because I feel certain that thousands of people will now benefit from my research and experiences."

*   *   *

ELA, Jonathan P(ell) 1945-

PERSONAL: Born October 7, 1945, in New York, N.Y.; son of Walter Pell (an attorney) and Janet (Smith) Ela. *Education:* Harvard University, A.B., 1967; graduate study at Columbia University, 1967-68, and University of Wisconsin—Madison, 1968-69. *Home:* 4541 Crescent Rd., Madison, Wis. 53711. *Office:* Sierra Club, 444 West Main, Madison, Wis. 53703.

CAREER: U.S. Senate, Washington, D.C., legislative aide to Senator Gaylord Nelson from Wisconsin, 1967-68; Sierra Club, Madison, Wis., regional environmental representative for the Midwest, 1969—.

WRITINGS: The Faces of the Great Lakes, Sierra Club Books, 1977.

*   *   *

ELDER, Lonne III 1931-

PERSONAL: Born December 26, 1931, in Americus, Ga.; son of Lonne Elder, Jr.; married Judith Ann Johnson (an actress), February 14, 1969; children: David DuBois, another son. *Education:* Attended Yale University School of Drama. *Agent:* Bart/Levy Associates, 280 South Beverly Dr., Beverly Hills, Calif. 90212.

CAREER: Playwright, screenwriter, and freelance writer. Has worked as a waiter, professional gambler, and dock worker; actor in "A Raisin in the Sun" in New York City, 1959, and on tour, 1960-61; actor in "A Day of Absence" in New York City, 1965; Negro Ensemble Company, New York City, coordinator of playwrights and directors unit, 1967-69; Talent Associates, New York City, writer, 1968; Cinema Center Films, Hollywood, Calif., writer and producer, 1969-70; Universal Pictures, Hollywood, writer, 1970-71; Radnitz/Mattel Productions, Hollywood, writer, 1971; Talent Associates, Hollywood, writer and producer, 1971; Metro-Goldwyn-Mayer Pictures, Hollywood, writer, 1971; Columbia Pictures, Hollywood, writer, 1972; American Broadcasting Co. (ABC), New York City, script writer. *Military service:* Served in U.S. Army.

MEMBER: Black Academy of Arts and Letters, Writers' Guild of America, West, New Dramatists, Harlem Writers' Guild. *Awards, honors:* Stanley Drama Award, 1965; John Hay Whitney Fellowship, 1965-66; ABC Television fellowship, 1965-66; Hamilton K. Bishop Award in playwriting; American National Theatre Academy award, 1967; Joseph E. Levine Fellow in film making, 1967; John Golden Fellow, 1967; Award of Merit from University of Southern California Film Conference, 1971; Academy award nomination from Academy of Motion Picture Arts and Sciences, 1972, for "Sounder"; Award of Merit from California Association of Teachers of English, 1973. Pulitzer prize nomination, 1969, Outer Critics Circle award, 1970; Vernon Rice Drama Desk award, 1970, Stella Holt Memorial Playwriting Award, 1970, and Los Angeles Drama Critics award, 1970, all for "Ceremonies in Dark Old Men."

WRITINGS—Plays: *Ceremonies in Dark Old Men* (two-act; first produced in New York City at Wagner College, July, 1965, revised version produced in New York City at St. Mark's Playhouse, February 4, 1969), Farrar, Straus, 1969; "Charades on East 4th Street" (one-act), first produced in Montreal, Quebec, 1967. Also author of a "A Hysterical Turtle in a Rabbit Race," 1961; "Kissing Rattlesnakes Can be Fun" (one-act), 1966; and "Seven Comes Up, Seven Comes Down" (one-act), 1966.

Screenplays and television dramas: "Sounder," Twentieth Century-Fox, 1972; "Melinda," Metro-Goldwyn-Mayer, 1972; "Sounder, Part II," Twentieth Century-Fox, 197?. Author of television dramas, including "Deadly Circle of Violence" and "The Terrible Veil," 1964. Contributor of television scripts to "NYPD" series, 1968, and "McCloud" series, 1970-71.

Work has been represented in anthologies, including *Black Drama Anthology,* edited by Ron Milner and Woodie King, New American Library, 1971. Contributor of articles to *New York Times* and *Black Creation.*

SIDELIGHTS: Elder began writing at the age of six or seven, but at that time he had no idea of making writing his career. Elder said, "I don't think I even knew what a writer was. I just liked the idea of writing to myself; it was a way of expressing feelings that I didn't know how to express in other ways, like talking. There was no one to whom I could convey those kinds of thoughts and emotions in the environment I grew up in."

In his early adult years, Elder's writing was influenced by the poet and teacher Robert Hayden. While in the army, Elder was stationed near Fisk University where Hayden taught. During this time, Elder was able to spend a great deal of time working on his poems and short stories with Hayden, who, Elder says, was "very, very encouraging.... [Hayden] helped me to handle and structure the things I was trying to write.... He really made a tremendous impact on my life that has lasted up to this day."

Elder describes his early writings as "basically a direct expression of my own anguish about the race situation. They made for great politics, but they were bad art ... as I look back on them, basically they were demeaning of the people I was trying to write about rather than taking situations, very common and very simple situations of people ... and exhalting them to a place of nobility. That's not very easy to do and I just hope that I can do it." He adds: "I am a perfectionist. But, contrary to what a lot of Black artists say, I don't think you have to create new standards and values. They're already there, on anybody's terms. But structure and craftsmanship are all-important.... I intend for whatever I write to be excellent."

Elder was first exposed to drama by Douglas Turner Ward, with whom he shared an apartment at one time. Ward, an actor and playwright, wrote his first play during their time together. Elder's first reaction to the play was disbelief. He said: "He wrote the whole thing! And he was one of my peers. . . . If he had been an older person, it would've been different. The most I had ever written was maybe a fifteen-page short story or a one-page poem. So I said, well, I can do that too! And that's when I started writing plays." To Elder, the most impressive aspect of drama was "the immediacy of the whole thing, the immediacy of expressing a feeling or an emotion."

Elder began taking acting lessons and was invited by Lorraine Hansberry to audition for a role in her play, "A Raisin in the Sun." He was given a part which he played for two years, both in New York and on tour. During that time he was able to concentrate on writing in his free time. The acting experience was helpful to Elder, who believes that acting sharpens the playwright's ability to write for the stage.

"Ceremonies in Dark Old Men," perhaps Elder's best known work, was hailed by many critics as "the most interesting new American play of the season." Richard Watts, Jr. considered the play "absorbing, moving, comic, committed, and remarkably objective in its viewpoint. . . ." He went on to term it "a drama of power and importance." James Davis described it as "an extraordinarily well-written play."

Women's Wear Daily reported that in Lonne Elder, "it looks as if the Negro Ensemble Company has found itself what every resident theatre dreams of—a playwright suited in purpose and style to its own." "Ceremonies in Dark Old Men" was the first full-length play presented by the Negro Ensemble Company that was entirely set in Harlem. Martin Gottfried added that the play has "a persuasive warmth and understanding of the Negro situation that only a black man could have. The combination of love and perception is what makes the play."

The few faults critics found in "Ceremonies in Dark Old Men" included the opinion of one reviewer that the play is "overlong" and that the "final moments are anticlimactic." The *Wall Street Journal* felt that the "play's major fault is that it is constructed just a bit too well" so that it was occasionally predictable. However, the same reviewer also felt that Elder displayed "a formidable talent for saying some things about black life that should be heard."

Lonne Elder's writing is mainly concerned with questions of Negro identity. When the movie "Sounder," for which Elder wrote the screenplay, premiered in 1972, the *Chicago Sun-Times* called the film a "story simply told and universally moving. . . . It is one of the most compassionate and truthful of movies, and there's not a level where it doesn't succeed completely. . . . The story is so simple because it involved, not so much what people do, but how they change and grow. Not a lot happens on the action level, but there's tremendous psychological movement in 'Sounder,' and hardly ever do movies create characters who are so full and real, and relationships that are so loving. . . .'"

Gary Arnold of the *Washington Post* called "Sounder" a "remarkably touching and heartening film." He wrote: "The screenplay . . . is based on a Newberry prizewinning novella. It's an exceedingly spare, stark book . . . and Elder has done a superb job of fleshing out and dramatizing the basic material. . . . They [Elder and director Martin Ritt] have given three dimensions and depth of feeling to an intriguing but rather one-dimensional book."

In an interview for *Black World* Elder said he had been told that people were amazed at his ability to write competently about life in the rural South, having grown up in the New York/New Jersey area. He explains his ability in this way: "From my standpoint as a Black artist, I think much of what we know about each other, no matter where we're from, comes from the institution of being Black. And secondly, and more importantly, in the ghettos of Harlem and Jersey City which I grew up in, those communities were basically made up of immigrants from the rural South."

Elder wrote the screenplay for another film, "Melinda," which was received with less than favorable reviews. One critic wrote: "The screenplay was allegedly written by Lonne Elder, III, and it's more than a little difficult to reconcile his name with this material." Elder, who had been writing for movies and television for several years, claimed to have written the script for "Melinda" in less than two weeks. He is still interested in films and says that his "whole objective is to write, produce, and direct my own pictures."

A collection of Elder's manuscripts is maintained by Boston University.

BIOGRAPHICAL/CRITICAL SOURCES: New York Post, February 6, 1969; *New York Daily News,* February 6, 1969; *Women's Wear Daily,* February 6, 1969; *Wall Street Journal,* February 19, 1969; *Washington Post,* September 23, 1972; *Village Voice,* November 12, 1972; *Chicago Sun-Times,* December 18, 1972; *Black World,* April, 1973.*

* * *

ELIAS, Albert J. 1920-

PERSONAL: Born September 21, 1920, in New York, N.Y.; son of Albert I. (an architect) and Helen (Cassett) Elias; married wife Rea, January 28, 1945; children: Albert L., William D. *Education:* Attended University of Virginia, 1938-41. *Politics:* Republican. *Religion:* Unitarian. *Home:* Oakley Lane, Greenwich, Conn. 06830. *Agent:* Harvey Klinger, 250 West 57th St., New York, N.Y. 10019.

CAREER: R. H. Macy & Co., New York City, buyer, 1941-52; Vick Chemical Co., New York City, vice-president, 1957-66; Pharmaco Co., Schering Division, Kenilworth, N.J., president, 1966-72; writer, 1976—. Director of North Shores Hospital, 1956-62. *Military service:* U.S. Army, First Engineers Amphibious Brigade, 1942-46; became captain; received five battlestars and two invasion arrowheads. *Member:* United Cerebral Palsy Association (vice-president).

WRITINGS: The Bowman Test (novel), Dell, 1977; *The Sonora Mutation* (novel), Avon, 1978.

WORK IN PROGRESS: Three novels, *Barstoe's Brain* and *The Sprug Experiment,* both completed, and *Encore.*

SIDELIGHTS: After two D day invasions (Normandy and Okinawa), his oldest son's cerebral palsy (1947), and his wife's polio (1949), Elias "knew the shortness, if not the meaning, of life. My first book (*The Bowman Test*) reflected this. I never wrote until 1976—it has added much to our lives." Elias changed careers and became a writer after his youngest son completed college.

* * *

ELIOT, Sonny 1926-

PERSONAL: Birth given name, Marvin; born December 5, 1926, in Detroit, Mich.; son of Jacob and Jennie (Schlossberg) Eliot; married Annette Gaertner, May 19, 1962. *Education:* Wayne State University, B.A., 1959, M.A., 1960.

Home: 1417 Nicolet St., Detroit, Mich. 48207. *Office:* WDIV-TV, 622 West Lafayette St., Detroit, Mich. 48231.

CAREER: WWJ radio and WDIV television, Detroit, Mich., performer, program host, and weather broadcaster, 1950—, television public relations director. Commissioner, Detroit Aviation Commission; vice-president, Lindell Aviation Co.; co-owner, Sonny's Weather Station Restaurant. *Military Service:* U.S. Army Air Forces, environments and threats directorate, 1942-47; received Distinguished Flying Cross and Purple Heart. *Member:* American Meteorological Society, American Federation of Television and Radio Artists, Screen Actors Guild, Actors' Equity Association, Adcraft Club of Michigan (member of board of directors), Sigma Delta Chi. *Awards, honors:* National Association of Television Program Executives award; National Safety award; News Media award from Midwestern Aviation Conference; Michigan School Bell award.

WRITINGS: Eliot's Ark (collection of columns), Wayne State University Press, 1972. Former weekly columnist, *Detroit News.*

SIDELIGHTS: During World War II, Eliot was a bomber pilot flying missions from England over Germany. "The day my plane was hit," he told *Detroit News* columnist Pete Waldmeir, "I remember sitting in the bomb bay door before I bailed out and trying to decide whether or not to throw away my identification tags. The choice was between having proof that I was an officer and getting preferential treatment in the prison camp or revealing the fact that I was a Jew and being sent to a concentration camp. It wasn't much of a decision. I ripped the dogtags off and threw them away." After parachuting, Eliot was sent to a prisoner of war camp where it was later discovered that he was Jewish. The deadline for shipment to death camp was over by that time, however, and he was set free a few days later.

Now a celebrated Detroit media personality, Eliot is best known for his clever and quick-witted television weather reports. This same style characterized his performances as host of the local television program "At the Zoo."

BIOGRAPHICAL/CRITICAL SOURCES: Detroit News, April 21, 1978.

*   *   *

ELLIS, Peter Berresford   1943-
(Peter Tremayne)

PERSONAL: Born March 10, 1943, in Coventry, Warwickshire, England; son of Alan J. (a journalist) and Eva Daisy (Randell) Ellis; married Dorothea P. Cheesmur, September, 1966. *Education:* Studied at Brighton College of Art. *Politics:* Marxist. *Religion:* "Humanity." *Residence:* London, England. *Agent:* A. M. Heath & Co. Ltd., 40-42 William IV St., London WC2N 4DD, England.

CAREER: Junior reporter on *Brighton Herald* (weekly newspaper), 1960-62; held various jobs including reporter, bus conductor, rifle range attendant, and dishwasher; assistant editor on publishing trade weeklies; deputy editor of *Irish Post,* 1970; editor of *Newsagent & Bookshop,* 1974-75; full-time writer, 1975—.

WRITINGS: Wales—A Nation Again: The Nationalist Struggle for Freedom, Tandem Books, 1968; *The Creed of the Celtic Revolution* (pamphlet), Medusa, 1969; (with Seumas Mac a'Ghobhainn) *The Scottish Insurrection of 1820,* Gollancz, 1970; (with Mac a'Ghobhainn) *The Problem of Language Revival,* Club Leabhar, 1971; *A History of the Irish Working Class,* Gollancz, 1972, Braziller, 1973; (editor

and author of introduction) *James Connolly: Selected Writings,* Penguin, 1973; *The Cornish Language and Its Literature,* Routledge & Kegan Paul, 1974; *Hell or Connaught!: The Cromwellian Colonisation of Ireland 1652-1660,* St. Martin's, 1975; *The Boyne Water: The Battle of the Boyne 1690,* St. Martin's, 1976; *The Great Fire of London: An Illustrated Account,* New English Library, 1977; *Caesar's Invasion of Britain,* Orbis, 1978; *A Voice From the Infinite: The Life of Sir Henry Rider Haggard 1856-1925,* Routledge & Kegan Paul, 1978; *MacBeth: High King of Scotland 1040-57 A.D.,* Orbis, 1979.

Under pseudonym Peter Tremayne: *The Hound of Frankenstein,* Venture Books, 1977; *Dracula Unborn,* Bailey Bros. & Swinfen, 1977; (editor and author of introduction) *Masters of Terror: William Hope Hodgson,* Volume I, Corgi Books, 1977; *The Vengeance of She,* Sphere Books, 1978; *The Revenge of Dracula,* Bailey Bros. & Swinfen, 1978; *Mandibles,* Sphere Books, 1979; *The Curse of Loch Ness,* Sphere Books, 1979.

Contributor of articles on the problems of national minorities to English, Irish, French, Spanish, Italian, and other journals.

WORK IN PROGRESS: Research for a biography of the writer Talbot Mundy; a serious historical novel; the first title in a fantasy trilogy, *The Fires of Lan Kern,* for Bailey Bros. & Swinfen/Magnum, under pseudonym Peter Tremayne.

SIDELIGHTS: Ellis writes: "The Irish descent on my father's side made me particularly interested in Irish problems, spending a lot of time in that country and in Northern Ireland. This interest created a concern for the problems of other national minorities struggling to retain their individuality against the tremendous weight of the twentieth-century conformity machine from as far afield as North American Indians to the Georgians in the U.S.S.R. My particular concern is the Celtic nationalities in the United Kingdom and France. A confirmed socialist, I preach that national independence and social independence are two sides of one great democratic principle (a fact rejected by many dogmatic Marxists), but I am too much of an individualist to join one particular party or group. Instead, I struggle against injustices on many fronts."

The impact of popular literature on the mind of the reader is another of Ellis's interests. He told *CA:* "Popular literature fascinates me, particularly science fiction and fantasy, and its effect on creating and confirming the prejudices of people. I collect books by certain late Victorian and early twentieth-century writers. My biography of Haggard was inspired by the fact that Haggard was one of the few Victorian English writers who, in contrast to Kipling and others, wrote about Africans and natives of other countries without prejudice—portraying them as real people instead of racial caricatures. Such racial caricatures have done much harm to generations of young readers.

"My interest in science fiction and fantasy evolve from my interest in the mythologies of various nations. Sometimes it is easier to put over social concepts and ideas in the medium of a fantasy novel, and to do it with more clarity, than to do so in a realistic novel or a great sociological tome."

*   *   *

ELLISON, William McLaren   1919(?)-1978

OBITUARY NOTICE: Born c. 1919 in New York City; died December 21, 1978, in New York City. Caseworker and free-lance writer. Ellison served in World War II as a

Marine captain and dive-bomber pilot and later published collections of his Pacific war letters in books and newspapers. After spending several years employed in *Newsweek* magazine's advertising department, he turned to free-lancing and for fifteen years contributed diaries and travel stories to various magazines and the North American Newspaper Alliance. From 1964 until early 1978, Ellison was a caseworker for the New York City Department of Social Services. Obituaries and other sources: *New York Times,* December 23, 1978.

*   *   *

ELLUL, Jacques 1912-

PERSONAL: Born January 6, 1912, in Bordeaux, France; son of Joseph and Marthe (Mendes) Ellul; married Yvette Lensvelt, July 31, 1937; children: Jean, Yves, Dominique. *Education:* Earned licence from University of Bordeaux; earned doctorat en droit and agregation from University of Paris,. *Religion:* Reformed. *Home:* 29 Avenue A. Danglade, 33600 Pessac, France. *Office:* Faculte de Droit, University of Bordeaux I, Bordeaux, France.

CAREER: University of Montpellier, Montpellier, France, lecturer, 1937; University of Strasbourg, Strasbourg, France, lecturer, 1938; University of Bordeaux, Bordeaux, France, professor of the history of law, 1946—; Institute of Political Studies, Bordeaux, professor of social history, 1947—. Deputy mayor of Bordeaux, 1944-47. Consultant to Ecumenical World Council of Churches, 1947-53. *Member:* National Council of the Reformed Church. *Awards, honors:* Officier de la Legion d'honneur; Officier de l'ordre du Merite; grand croix des Palmes Academiques; prize in history from l'Academie Francaise, 1942, for *Histoire comparative du recrutement militare en France;* prix Rancheron, 1955; Docteur honoris causa from University of Amsterdam, 1965; prix Veillon, 1975, for best European essay.

WRITINGS—In English: *Le Fondement theologique du droit,* Delachaux, 1946, translation by Marguerite Wieser published as *The Theological Foundation of Law,* S.C.M. Press, 1960, Seabury, 1969; *Presence au monde moderne,* Labor & Fides, 1948, translation by Olive Wyon published as *The Presence of the Kingdom,* Westminster, 1951; *Le Livre de Jonas,* Foi & Vie, 1951, translation by Geoffrey W. Bromiley published as *The Judgment of Jonah,* Eerdmans, 1971; *La Technique; ou, L'Enjeu du siecle,* A. Colin, 1954, translation by John Wilkinson published as *The Technological Society,* Knopf, 1964, revised edition, 1967; *Propagandes,* A. Colin, 1954, translation by Konrad Kellen and Jean Lerner published as *Propaganda: The Formation of Men's Attitudes,* Knopf, 1965.

Fausse presence au monde moderne, Les Bergers & les Mages, 1963, translation by G. Edward Hopkin published as *False Presence of the Kingdom,* Seabury, 1972; *Le Vouloir et le faire: Recherches ethiques pour les chretiens,* Labor & Fides, 1964, translation by Hopkin published as *To Will and to Do: An Ethical Research for Christians,* Pilgrim Press, 1969; *L'Illusion politique,* Laffont, 1964, translation by Kellen published as *The Political Illusion,* Vintage Books, 1967; *Politique de Dieu, politiques de l'homme,* Editions Universitaires, 1966, translation by Bromiley published as *The Politics of God and the Politics of Man,* Eerdmans, 1972; *Exegese des nouveaux lieux communs,* Calmann-Levy, 1966, translation by Helen Weaver published as *A Critique of the New Commonplaces,* Knopf, 1968; *Autopsie de la revolution,* Calmann-Levy, 1969, translation by Patricia Wolf published as *Autopsy of Revolution,* Knopf, 1971.

Contre les violents, Le Centurion, 1970, translation by Cecelia Gaul Kings from original French manuscript published as *Violence: Reflections from a Christian Perspective,* Seabury, 1969; *L'Impossible Priere,* Le Centurion, 1971, translation by Hopkin from original French manuscript published as *Prayer and Modern Man,* Seabury, 1970; *L'Esperance oubliee,* Gallimard, 1972, translation by Hopkin published as *Hope in Time of Abandonment,* Seabury, 1973; *Les Nouveaux Possedes,* Fayard, 1973, translation by Hopkin published as *The New Demons,* Seabury, 1975; *Ethique de la liberte,* Labor & Fides, 1973, translation by Bromiley published as *The Ethics of Freedom,* Eerdmans, 1976; *Sans feu ni lieu: Signification biblique de la grande ville,* Gallimard, 1975, translation by Dennis Pardee from original French manuscript published as *The Meaning of the City,* Eerdmans, 1970; *L'Apocalypse: Architecture en Mouvement,* Desclee, 1975, translation by George W. Schreiner published as *Apocalypse: The Book of Revelation,* Seabury, 1977; *Trahison de l'occident,* Calmann-Levy, 1976, translation by Matthew J. O'Connell published as *The Betrayal of the West,* Seabury, 1978.

Other works: *Etude sur l'evolution et la nature juridique du Mancipium* (title means "A Study of the Evolution and Judicial Nature of the 'Mancipium'"), Delmas, 1936; (with Paul Tournier and Rene Gillouin) *L'Homme mesure de toute chose,* Centre Protestant d'Etudes, 1947; *Histoire des Institutions de l'Antiquite* (title means "History of the Institutions of Antiquity"), two volumes, Presses Universitaires de France, 1951-52, 4th edition, revised and augmented, 1972; *L'Homme et l'argent* (title means "Man and Money"), Delachaux, 1953; *Histoire des institutions, de l'epoque franque a la Revolution* (title means "History of French Institutions from the Frankish Era to the Revolution"), three volumes, Presses Universitaires de France, 1953-56, 5th edition, 1967.

Les Relations publiques (title means "Public Relations"), Presses Universitaires de France, 1963; *Histoire de la Propagande* (title means "History of Propaganda"), Presses Universitaires de France, 1966; (with Pierre Huillier and Jacques Jullien) *Les Chretiens et l'etat* (title means "Christians and the State"), Mame, 1966; *Metamorphose du bourgeois* (title means "Metamorphosis of the Bourgeois"), Calmann-Levy, 1967; (contributor) *Dynamique de la guerison* (title means "Dynamics of Healing"), Delachaux & Niestle, 1967; (with Yves Charrier) *Jeunesse delinquante* (title means "Juvenile Delinquency"), Gallimard, 1971; *De la revolution aux revoltes* (title means "From Revolution to Revolt"), Calmann-Levy, 1972; *Le Systeme technicien* (title means "The Technician System"), Calmann-Levy, 1977. Also author of *Histoire comparative du recrutement militaire en France* (title means "A Comparative History of Military Recruitment in France"), 1941, and *Introduction a l'histoire de la discipline des eglises reformees de France* (title means "An Introduction to the History of Discipline in the Reformed Churches of France"), 1943.

WORK IN PROGRESS: L'Art dans la societe technicienne (title means "Art in the Technological Society").

SIDELIGHTS: Ellul told *CA:* "My principal effort is to bring a new interpretation of the whole of modern society and to determine whether the Christian faith still has power in this society. I have not always been a Christian; I was converted rather late in life and this is the most important event for me."

Ellul's principle works of socio-political analysis (*The Technological Society, The Political Illusion,* and *Propaganda:*

The Formation of Men's Attitudes) established his reputation as a social critic, and led Saul Padover to describe him as "a fresh political thinker, something of a cross between an academic Eric Hoffer and a French *enfant terrible*." Padover added, "His analysis of modern society reminds one of the child who blurted out that the emperor was naked." Ellul's efforts to create a "composition in counterpoint" by balancing a searing socio-political analysis with an often contradictory biblical-theological analysis have evoked responses ranging from sharp criticism to admiration from an audience that cannot long remain neutral to his challenge.

In *The Technological Society* Ellul indicted the concept of "technique" as the force which would ultimately destroy humanity by completely overpowering man, taking him for its object, and thus becoming the center of society. Defining technique as "the totality of methods rationally arrived at and having absolute efficiency in every field of human activity," Ellul proceeded to analyze the effects of a social mindset devoted to developing and executing the "one best way of doing things." His pessimistic description of technical civilization provoked a barrage of criticism from reviewers who rejected his thesis of the inevitability of man's destruction by technology. Mocking the view that technology had not improved man's living conditions throughout the centuries, A. Rupert Hall wrote that Ellul failed to "differentiate between the role of tolerable techniques in a good society and the predominance of malicious techniques in a diseased one." Though Ellul had argued that man's inability to foresee the secondary effects of his use of technology nullified his ability to direct "neutral" techniques to "good" ends, Hall maintained his optimism, contending: "Is not the tool or machine indifferent as to ends and purposes, which are determined by human will?" H. H. Ransom concurred in affirming man's freedom to control technology, declaring, "Man need not allow technology to enslave him in a concentration camp run by technicians if he can adapt his institutions to modern realities and thereby transcend the technological prison."

While critics such as Hall condemned Ellul for failing to propose any positive means of averting the disaster he predicted, Robert Theobald pointed out that Ellul had originally included a section dealing with means of releasing man from technology's death grip but had chosen to eliminate it from the published edition of *The Technological Society*. Christopher Walters-Bugbee explained that Ellul countered his socio-political analysis of technology with a theological analysis in other works. "Ellul's sociology is fueled by a theologically-based pessimism which finds little cause for hope in humanity's unceasing efforts to justify itself by works apart from God's redemptive grace," he wrote. "The current ascendance of technique to its position of unparalleled dominance is merely the latest, most progressive manifestation of the Fall's consequences. Only the biblical revelation of humanity's true potential illumines and reveals the extent of our actual depravity, as well as the specific nature of the only effective cure."

Ellul pursued his critique of society in *The Political Illusion*, exposing the growing trend towards "politization" or man's tendency to depend completely upon the state for the solutions to all of his problems. He expressed his concern that man was losing control over the political mechanisms as the state grew into an "overpowering leviathan," and that the idea of "government by the people" was fast becoming an illusion. Walters-Bugbee summarized Ellul's analysis, declaring: "Ellul suggests that in the absence of moral determinants sufficiently strong to resist the encroachment of technology's needs, necessity and efficiency have become the dominating criteria of political life. Spurred by the constant growth of the technology that it serves, the state has assumed its place at the center of human life and has in the process been invested with a religious faith and trust by its citizens." Having identified the illusory effects of politization, Ellul called for a "repolitization" which depended upon "a profound change in the citizen." He added: "As long as he is preoccupied with only his security, the stability of his life, his material well-being, we should have no illusion; he will certainly not find the civic virtue necessary to make democracy live. . . . What is needed is a conversion of the citizen, not to a certain political ideology, but at the much deeper level of his conception of life itself, his presuppositions, his myths. If this conversion fails to take place, all the constitutional devices, all studies on economic democracy, and all reassuring sociological inquiries on man and society are vain efforts at justification."

Because Ellul sought particularly to describe the effects of technology and politization in modern society, offering his balancing theological analysis in other works, most critics found his assertions pessimistic and refused to assent to his conclusions. Responding to Ellul's use of historical examples to show man's inability to control political decisions, Anthony LeJeune countered: "I believe man can still choose, that France was driven from Algeria and that Britain's Conservative Government failed to dismantle the welfare state, not because of any historical determinism, but through sheer lack of will. Things could have turned out otherwise; they could turn out otherwise tomorrow when we try the game again. And even if this isn't true, I believe that, for sanity's sake and to give us the heart for another fight, we ought to believe that it is." Oscar Handlin concluded that Ellul's book "leaves unanswered the basic question an American asks, What better means than democratic politics are available for organizing intelligently the life of a complex modern society?"

The comments of Handlin and LeJeune reveal the conflict in levels of analysis between Ellul and his secular critics. While the critics examine society and Ellul's critique in terms of the pragmatic concerns of autonomous man within his society, Ellul's perspective revolves around biblical revelation and acknowledges the transcendent God as the one who has the final word about man and his society. Walters-Bugbee graphically sketched the conflict, declaring, "Both Ellul's evangelical and his liberal detractors stumble on the same rock of offense, the Christocentric nature of his thought." Though Ellul's works of sociological analysis only allude to his biblical convictions, this perspective pervades his other works, in which he addresses nonbelievers about the nature of society's ills and Christians about their role in that society.

Perhaps a critique of one of Ellul's latest books, *The Ethics of Freedom*, best summarizes the implications of his thought for modern man. David Gill wrote: "Ellul removes our commonplaces and securities, destroys our idols, crutches, and supports, ruthlessly strips away our justifications, and attacks our conformity to the world and lack of faith in Christ. Both through sociological criticism and through biblical exposition, he leaves us with no way out, with the exits sealed off, with no hope. But wait! . . . After everything has been closed off, *The Ethics of Freedom* throws open the doors, batters down the walls, and opens out on a whole new life of freedom in service of God and our neighbor."

BIOGRAPHICAL/CRITICAL SOURCES: Saturday Review, September 26, 1964, April 29, 1967; *Nation*, October

19, 1964; *Scientific American,* February, 1965; *Atlantic,* May, 1967; *National Review,* July 11, 1967; *Christianity Today,* September 10, 1976; *Sojourners,* June, 1977.

* * *

EMECHETA, (Florence Onye) Buchi   1944-

PERSONAL: Born July 21, 1944, in Lagos, Nigeria; daughter of Jeremy Nwabudike (a railway worker and molder) and Alice Ogbanje (Okwuekwu) Emecheta; separated, 1966; children: Florence, Sylvester, Jake, Christy, Alice. *Education:* University of London, B.Sc., 1972. *Religion:* Anglican. *Agent:* Curtis Brown Ltd., 1 Craven Hill, London W.1, England.

CAREER: British Museum, London, England, library officer, 1965-69; Inner London Education Authority, London, youth worker and sociologist, 1969—; writer.

WRITINGS: In the Ditch, Barrie & Jenkins, 1972; *Second Class Citizen,* Allison & Busby, 1975; *The Bridge Price,* Allison & Busby, 1976; *The Slave Girl,* Allison & Busby, 1977. Also author of two television scripts, "A Kind of Marriage" and "The Juju Landlord."

WORK IN PROGRESS: The Plight of the Black Youth in London; The Joys of Motherhood.

SIDELIGHTS: Buchi Emecheta writes historical novels set in Nigeria, both before and after independence. She notes that "some of them seem from a female point of view." She also writes political history in the form of fiction.

* * *

ENDY, Melvin B(ecker), Jr.   1938-

PERSONAL: Born April 27, 1938, in Pottstown, Pa.; son of Melvin Becker and Virginia (Myers) Endy; married Susan Craig (a music teacher), September 7, 1962; children: Michael Becker, Margaret Gordon. *Education:* Princeton Univeristy, B.A., 1960; Yale University, B.D., 1963, received M.A., Ph.D., 1969. *Religion:* Society of Friends (Quakers). *Home:* 1 Griffin Rd., Clinton, N.Y. 13323. *Office:* Department of Religion, Hamilton College, Clinton, N.Y. 13323.

CAREER: Hamilton College, Clinton, N.Y., 1966—, currently professor of religion. *Member:* American Society of Church History, American Academy of Religion (co-chairman of American religion), Organization of American Historians, Friends Historical Association. *Awards, honors:* National Endowment for the Humanities fellowship, 1975-76.

WRITINGS: William Penn and Early Quakerism, Princeton University Press, 1973. Contributor to history and religious history journals.

WORK IN PROGRESS: Attitudes Toward War in Colonial America, completion expected in 1980.

SIDELIGHTS: Endy told CA: "I expect to write a popular history of American cultural attitudes toward war and a more definitive history of American religious thought."

* * *

ENGEL, Peter H.   1935-

PERSONAL: Born February 4, 1935, in Germany; son of Walter Hans and Illse (Griep) Engel; married first wife, Jane (divorced); married Patricia Burbridge Schreiner (a psychologist), September 1, 1974; children: Mark, Kirsten, Andrew, Karin, Melissa. *Education:* McGill University, B.Comm., 1956. *Home address:* West Lane, Revonah Woods, Stamford, Conn. 06905. *Agent:* Jay Acton, Edward J. Acton,

Inc., 17 Grove St., New York, N.Y. 10014. *Office:* Helena Rubinstein, Inc., 300 Park Ave., New York, N.Y. 10022.

CAREER: Proctor & Gamble, marketing trainee and executive in Toronto, Ontario, 1956-61, marketing executive in Frankfort, Germany, 1961-64, and Cincinnati, Ohio, 1964-65; Philip Morris, New York City, director of marketing, 1966-68; Lehigh Coal & Navigation, Bethlehem, Pa., president and member of board of directors, 1969-71; Colgate-Palmolive Co., New York City, vice-president, 1971—. President of Helena Rubinstein, Inc., 1974—.

WRITINGS: The Overachievers, Dial, 1976. Also author of *The Power Seekers* (novel), 1979.

SIDELIGHTS: The Overachievers, Engel's defense of business and "the movers and shakers of industry," was fueled by an antibusiness remark he heard at a party. *Booklist* said "Engel sets forth with authority and conviction the common attributes of overachievers, and copiously illustrates with examples from the lives of highly motivated people." The book also tells what the overachiever is attracted to in a business and how employers can identify one.

According to *Book World,* "the author . . . is a member of the group he describes in this book: aggressive, nonconformist business executives who have done the most to make our economy (for better *and* for worse) what it is. His orientation is, perhaps unfortunately, how-to rather than critical."

BIOGRAPHICAL/CRITICAL SOURCES: Kirkus Reviews, January 15, 1976; *Booklist,* April 1, 1976; *Christian Science Monitor,* June 2, 1976; *Washington Post Book World,* June 6, 1976.

* * *

ERIKSSON, Buntel
See BERGMAN, (Ernst) Ingmar

* * *

ESEKI, Bruno
See MPHAHLELE, Ezekiel

* * *

ESMAN, Milton J.   1918-

PERSONAL: Born September 15, 1918, in Pittsburgh, Pa.; son of Mayer (a merchant) and Hermoine (Bernstein) Esman; married Janice Newman (an office manager), October 23, 1949; children: Michael, Oliver, Judith. *Education:* Cornell University, A.B., 1939; Princeton University, Ph.D., 1942. *Home:* 903 Triphammer Rd., Itahca, N.Y. 14850. *Office:* Center for International Studies, Cornell University, Ithaca, N.Y. 14853.

CAREER: U.S. Civil Service Commission, Washington, D.C., planning officer, 1947-51; U.S. Department of State, Washington, D.C., foreign affairs officer, beginning 1951; International Cooperation Agency, Saigon, Vietnam, former foreign affairs officer; University of Pittsburgh, Pittsburgh, Pa., professor of public and international affairs, 1959-69; Cornell University, Ithaca, N.Y., professor of government, 1969—, director of Center for International Studies. Research director of Inter-University Research Program in Institution Building, 1964-66; senior adviser to Government of Malaysia, 1966-68; *Military service:* U.S. Army, 1942-46, civil affairs officer at headquarters of U.S. Occupation of Japan, 1945-46; became first lieutenant.

MEMBER: American Political Science Association, American Society for Public Administration, Society for International Development, International Studies Association.

WRITINGS: (With Daniel S. Cheever) *The Common Aid Effort,* Ohio State University Press, 1967; *Administration and Development in Malaysia,* Cornell University Press, 1972; (with Norman Uphoff) *Local Organization for Rural Development: Analysis of Asian Experience,* Rural Development Committee, Cornell University, 1974; (editor) *Ethnic Conflict in the Western World,* Cornell University Press, 1977.

WORK IN PROGRESS: Research on ethnic conflict, the politics of Canadian pluralism, the politics of Scottish nationalism, rural development, local organization, and local administration in developing countries.

*   *   *

ETON, Robert
See MEYNELL, Laurence Walter

*   *   *

ETZOLD, Thomas H(erman)   1945-

PERSONAL: Born June 2, 1945, in St. Clair County, Ill.; son of Herman A. (a professor and minister) and Mabel M. (a nurse; maiden name, Traugott) Etzold; married Suzanne E. Burdick, June 12, 1965; children: Klaus C., Ingrid A. *Education:* Indiana University, B.A., 1967, M.A., 1968; Yale University, M.Phil., 1969, Ph.D., 1970. *Office:* Department of Strategy, Naval War College, Newport, R.I. 02840.

CAREER: Yale University, New Haven, Conn., instructor in history, 1970-71; Miami University, Oxford, Ohio, assistant professor of history, 1971-74; Naval War College, Newport, R.I., associate professor, 1974-77, professor of strategy, 1977—. *Member:* Society for Historians of American Foreign Relations, U.S. Naval Institute, U.S. Strategic Institute, Royal United Services Institute for Defence Studies.

WRITINGS: (With F. G. Chan) *China in the 1920's: Nationalism and Revolution,* F. Watts, 1976; *The Conduct of American Foreign Relations: The Other Side of Diplomacy,* F. Watts, 1977; *Aspects of Sino-American Relations Since 1784,* F. Watts, 1978; (with John Lewis Gaddis) *Containment: Documents on American Policy and Strategy, 1945-1950,* Columbia University Press, 1978. Contributor to history and military journals and newspapers.

WORK IN PROGRESS: A book on strategic theory for Indiana University Press, publication expected in 1980; a book on statecraft.

SIDELIGHTS: Etzold wrote to *CA:* "Francois de Callieres once wrote that, 'A diplomat's speeches should contain more sense than words.' That observation is just as useful to writers as to diplomats. The marks of good prose, carefully crafted, are brevity, clarity, and felicity of expression. Without these, great ideas may go unappreciated; with them, even medicore thoughts can gain at least as much attention as they may deserve.

"As for the literary scene, no matter what the fads of style or the lack of it, or the fads of topics and stances, basic good paragraphing and good topic sentence writing will always carry. Readers are grateful for prose that permits them to grapple with ideas rather than with syntax.

"When writing, I compose in the morning and edit and do library follow-up work in the afternoon and evening. Most people have a time of the day, a portion of it, when they are at their best for a few hours in terms of creativity. A consistent writer needs to figure out what his or her best composition hours are, and, when writing, ruthlessly guard them from trivial interference."

*   *   *

EVANS, Joseph S., Jr.   1909(?)-1978

OBITUARY NOTICE: Born c. 1909 in Quincy, Mass.; died September 12, 1978, in Washington, D.C. Foreign correspondent and Foreign Service officer. Evans began his career as a *New York Herald-Tribune* reporter and later served as a member of *Newsweek* magazine's European staff, a Columbia Broadcasting Service (CBS) correspondent, and a Marshall Plan spokesman. In the 1950's he directed information and cultural affairs activities for the U.S. Embassy in London. After working for the U.S. Information Agency in Tokyo and Buenos Aires, Evans became its inspector general from 1957 to 1962. He finished his career as public affairs director for the U.S. civil administration of the Ryukyu Islands. Obituaries and other sources: *Washington Post,* October 6, 1978.

*   *   *

EVANS, William   1895-

PERSONAL: Born November 24, 1895, in Tregaron, Wales; son of Ebenezer (a farmer) and Elinor (Jenkins) Evans; married Christina Downie (died, 1964). *Education:* Attended University of Wales College at Aberystwyth; University of London, B.Sc. (honors), 1925, M.D., 1927, D.Sc., 1944. *Politics:* Conservative. *Religion:* Church of Wales. *Home:* Bryndomen, Tregaron, Cardiganshire, West Wales.

CAREER: Physician, farmer, and writer. Consulting cardiologist for London Hospital, National Heart Hospital, Institute of Cardiology, and Royal Navy; honorary consulting cardiologist for Royal Society of Musicians and Lloyds of London. Strickland Goodall Lecturer, 1942; Finlayson Lecturer, 1947; St. Cyres Lecturer, 1952; Gerrick Milligan Lecturer at University of Pennsylvania, 1954; Rufus Stolp Memorial Lecturer at Northwestern University, 1954; Casbult Memorial Lecturer, 1957; Schorstein Lecturer, 1961; Wiltshire Lecturer, 1961; Leonard Abrahamson Lecturer, 1963; Dixon Memorial Lecturer, 1965. High sheriff of Cardiganshire, 1959. *Military service:* British Army, Lancashire Fusiliers, 1914-19; served in France; became first lieutenant.

MEMBER: Royal Society of Medicine (fellow), Royal College of Physicians (fellow), British Cardiac Society (fellow), Australian Cardiac Society (fellow), Order of Druids (honorary member). *Awards, honors:* Hutchinson Triennial Prize in Clinical Surgery, 1920; Payne Prize in Pathology, 1927; Liddle Triennial Prize in Pathology, 1931; Strickland Goodall Gold Medal, 1942; Sydney Body Gold Medal, 1954; D.Sc. from University of Wales, 1961.

WRITINGS: Student's Handbook of Electrocardiography, H. K. Lewis, 1934; *Cardioscopy,* Butterworth & Co., 1952; *Cardiography,* Butterworth & Co., 2nd edition, 1954; *Cardiology,* Butterworth & Co., 1956; *Diseases of the Heart and Arteries,* E. & S. Livingstone, 1964; *Journey to Harley Street* (memoirs), Reidel, 1968; *Diary of a Welsh Swagman,* Macmillan (Australia), 1975. Contributor of more than a hundred articles to British medical journals.

WORK IN PROGRESS: Back Home, memoirs; *Treasury of Sayings; The Trecefel Diaries.*

SIDELIGHTS: Evans comments: "I was destined as a

youth to enter the church, and I took a scholarship in Greek at a divinity college, but when the Welsh Church was disestablished, I did not proceed. I entered Lloyds Bank as a clerk, then enlisted in military service during the war, then pursued medical studies after demobilization in 1919. Now I am retired to the place of my birth; hence, my book, *Back Home.*

"In *Journey to Harley Street*, I record my consultation in the case of Stanley Baldwin when he was Prime Minister. He was alleged to have 'heart trouble' and steps were afoot to retire him, supposedly on that account, but really because of his opposition to Edward VIII's courtship with Mrs. Simpson. I declared his heart to be healthy, so the plot failed."

AVOCATIONAL INTERESTS: Gardening, fishing.

* * *

EVTUSHENKO, Evgenii Aleksandrovich
See YEVTUSHENKO, Yevgeny (Alexandrovich)

* * *

EWING, Donald M.   1895(?)-1978

OBITUARY NOTICE: Born c. 1895 in Asheville, N.C.; died September 2, 1978, in Shreveport, La. Journalist. While covering the Chicago Black Sox scandal for the Associated Press in 1919, he witnessed the famous "Say it ain't so, Joe" incident when a small boy approached Shoeless Joe Jackson outside the Chicago Criminal Courts building. Jackson and seven teammates had thrown the 1919 World Series. Ewing also witnessed the 1922 Herring, Ill., coal mine massacre in which nineteen strike-breakers were killed. He later testified at the trial. Ewing spent the last five years as associate editor emeritus of the *Shreveport Times*. Obituaries and other sources: *Washington Post*, September 4, 1978.

* * *

EWING, Frederick R.
See STURGEON, Theodore Hamilton

* * *

EWTON, Ralph W(aldo), Jr.   1938-

PERSONAL: Born January 4, 1938, in Shawnee, Okla.; son of Ralph Waldo Ewton; married; children: two. *Education:* Rice University, B.A., 1959, M.A., 1961, Ph.D., 1966. *Office:* Department of Modern Languages, University of Texas, El Paso, Tex. 79968.

CAREER: Rice University, Houston, Tex., instructor in German, 1965-66; University of Texas, El Paso, assistant professor, 1966-68, associate professor of German, 1968—, head of department of modern languages, 1977—. *Member:* Modern Language Association of America, American Association of Teachers of German, South Central Modern Language Association, Phi Beta Kappa. *Awards, honors:* Fulbright grant for Germany, 1968.

WRITINGS: (With Jacob Ornstein) *Studies in Language and Linguistics*, Texas Western Press, 1969-70 edition, 1970, 1972-73 edition, 1972; (with Ornstein and Theodore H. Mueller) *Programmed Instruction and Educational Technology in the Language Teaching Field*, Center for Curriculum Development, 1971; *The Literary Theories of August Wilhelm Schlegel*, Mouton, 1972. Contributor of articles and reviews to language journals.

EXLEY, Frederick (Earl)   1929-

PERSONAL: Born in Watertown, N.Y.; married and divorced twice; children: two. *Education:* Attended Hobart College; University of Southern California, B.A., 1953. *Residence:* Alexandria Bay, N.Y. *Agent:* Lynn Nesbit, International Creative Management, 40 West 57th St., New York, N.Y. 10019.

CAREER: Writer. Has been employed as an editor, publicist, and English teacher; taught at Iowa Writers Workshop, University of Iowa. *Awards, honors:* William Faulkner Award, nomination for National Book Award, and Rosenthal Award from National Institute of Arts and Letters, 1969, all for *A Fan's Notes; Playboy* silver medal, 1974, for article "St. Gloria and the Troll." Rockefeller Foundation grant; Harper-Saxton fellowship.

WRITINGS: A Fan's Notes (fictional memoir), Harper, 1968; *Pages From a Cold Island* (novel), Random House, 1975.

WORK IN PROGRESS: Last Notes From Home, the final volume in the autobiographical trilogy.

SIDELIGHTS: Exley has been extremely candid in discussing the events of what he describes as "that long malaise, my life." Alcoholism, two broken marriages, a string of sexual encounters, a brush with suicide, and three stays in mental hospitals have marked Exley's life and his writing. Although he called *A Fan's Notes* a fictional memoir, the book is admittedly based largely on Exley's own life: he has explained that some characters and the portrait of his first wife are fictionalized.

Despite the apparent bleakness of Exley's life, *A Fan's Notes*, as Christopher Lehmann-Haupt has written, is "a singularly moving, entertaining, *funny* book." The appeal of the book, Lehmann-Haupt remarked, is partly "the writing, which is wise and subtle—a courtly prose verging on the sort that drunks and clowns employ to dignify their pratfalls. Mostly, it's because Exley's character and experience are familiar enough to identify with (and therefore to fear) and at the same time mad and extreme and bizarre enough to separate him from us (and therefore to pity). One gets involved without getting hurt."

Lucy Rosenthal was impressed by the honesty of Exley's book. She wrote: "For all the imaginative license Frederick Exley may have taken in this fictional memoir, billed as a first novel, the book is more impressive as a human document than as an artistically achieved work. It is overcrowded and overwritten; it has the sweat of the author's labors on it. But it has a fierce honesty."

"Frederick Exley's book is a beautiful attempt to tell the truth," Jack Kroll wrote. "He calls the book a 'fictional memoir' and points out that many of the characters are imaginary, but that only sharpens the nature of the gallant enterprise: Exley knows that truth is in good part a function of the imagination. What counts, and where the difficulty lies, is the psychic, the emotional, the spiritual truth." "Apart from anything else," the reviewer for *Times Literary Supplement* wrote, "Mr. Exley writes well—a faintly mocking (usually self-mocking) eloquent style provides the essential distance between Exley as author and Exley as star performer, a stratagem which has the paradoxical effect of assuring the truth while reminding us of the fictional part of 'fictional memoir.' The ability of Exley the writer to distance himself in this way proves invaluable: the wry, sometimes painfully funny events are kept from becoming maudlin, but retain the poignancy of a confession which, told solely to amuse, gains sympathy for that very reason."

Stanley Reynolds, however, complained that "as a work of art [*A Fan's Notes*] is rambling, unclear, repetitious, and written in that curious overblown American style.... The effect here is rather like getting button-holed by a drunk in a bar who grips you by both lapels, breathing whisky and polysyllables into your face, and never uses two words where he can possibly find 10 that'll do."

Most critics found *A Fan's Notes* to be surprisingly devoid of self-pity. John Dorschner commented: "His subject is the dark, bizarre meanderings of his own life, but his writing is noted for its lack of self-pity, its absence of bitterness, its unmitigated refusal to conform or give false hope. He writes with restraint: a brush with suicide consumes only a page and a quarter."

A Fan's Notes is, in fact, a "romantic book," Rudolph Wurlitzer remarked. Despite Exley's shattered dreams, "hope is never really forgotten, and that is perhaps the real source of despair. With a kind of fantastic innocence, Exley manages to draw humor from his defeats and humiliations, and this in turn increases the anguish. And, all through, his embrace of himself is illumined with grace and an almost mandarin sense of literary timing, of when to move on to the next event, the next nightmare."

Several critics have compared Exley's work to that of Fitzgerald, finding comparisons between Exley and Jay Gatsby and between Exley's love Bunny Sue and Daisy Buchanan to be particularly apt. Kroll discussed the similarities between the two writers: "[Exley] has the Fitzgerald-like gift to wrap up the aching vision of beauty (usually in a young girl), the funnily maladroit failure to possess that beauty, and the overwhelming despair that follows the entire process—all in a single tone of narrative accuracy whose authentic sweetness is the measure of truth-telling."

Exley's enthusiasm for the New York Giants football team and for running-back Frank Gifford in particular is central to the book. Gifford is practically Exley's alter ego in *A Fan's Notes,* as several reviewers have noted. (After reading the book Gifford called Exley and invited him to a Giants game; the two are now friends.) Exley's status as a fan is long-standing. His father was the star athlete in the town where Exley grew up; but however much Exley yearned for athletic stardom, he was never successful. In *A Fan's Notes,* he wrote: "Other men might inherit from their fathers a head for figures, a gold pocket watch all encrusted with the oxidized green of age, or an eternally astonished expression; from mine I acquired this need to have my name whispered in reverential tones." By the end of the book he has reconciled himself to a life as a fan rather than as a participant. "I fought because I understood, and could not bear to understand, that it was my destiny—unlike that of my father, whose fate it was to hear the roar of the crowd—to sit in the stands with most men and acclaim others. It was my fate, my destiny, my end, to be a fan."

In his next book, *Pages From a Cold Island,* Exley once again undertook the task of ruthless self-examination. Jack Kroll commented that in this book, "Exley evokes the world as a pop shambles, a mad morass of media monsters with no moral center. His symbol for this is the death of Edmund Wilson in 1972, which sends him off on a year of spasmodic encounters and confrontations." Jonathan Yardley remarked, "The subject of *A Fan's Notes* was, in large measure, the kinds and varieties of American success and failure. The subject of *Pages From a Cold Island* is the 'literary life,' as exemplified by Wilson, as occasionally practiced by Exley himself, and as mocked by the literary personalities of the media fame."

Douglas J. Maloney called Exley "a writer of incomparable skill and a scintillating genius," and termed the book a work of "stunning brilliance." "Throughout both books he maintains an infectious Rabelaisian humor," Maloney continued, "skillfully averting the confessional sump which has pervaded recent literature. Most importantly, his writing is so beautifully structured that its effect is almost hypnotic. It has a rhythmic cadence which beggars description—almost a feeling of sensuousness—despite the usually raunchy import of the test. Perhaps he is an intuitive genius who can blithely fire these superbly formulated little gems out at typing speed."

However, not all reviewers praised the book. Roger Sale found that *Pages From a Cold Island* was "mostly an anguished mess born of a terrible need to write *some* book, *any* book." Alfred Kazin's assessment of Exley's work is similarly negative. He commented: "Although he tries to be the last word in total horrendous honesty and is so total in recalling every shake in his innards that reading him is like being married to him, Exley cares for nothing but storytelling, has evidently read nothing but novels, and wouldn't recognize the unfabled, unvarnished, non-smart truth if it hit him. Like so many new American writers, he grew up on 20th-century novels, he would rather be Nick Carraway than anyone else, he often confuses himself with Herzog. Through such a film of famous characters, scenes, narrative techniques, he no longer knows his life from the book he has made of it."

"Readers who aren't interested in the workings of [Exley's] mind probably won't be interested in his books," Yardley concluded, "but what strikes me as singularly impressive in both of them is that he *makes* the reader interested. The true subject of *Pages From a Cold Island* is not Edmund Wilson or Gloria Steinem or Norman Mailer, but Frederick Exley, and he makes Exley matter. He matters, I think, because beneath the sad surface of a life seemingly given over to too much booze and too much random sex and too much aimlessness, there is a true writer, an artist unseduced by fad and fashion, pressing on to the fulfillment of his vision. *Pages From a Cold Island* is real progress toward that goal, the work of a writer we will no longer have to 'rediscover.'"

BIOGRAPHICAL/CRITICAL SOURCES: Frederick Exley, *A Fan's Notes,* Harper, 1968; *New York Times Book Review,* October 6, 1968, April 20, 1975; *Book World,* October 6, 1968; *Time,* October 25, 1968, April 28, 1975; *New Republic,* November 2, 1968, May 31, 1975; *New York Times,* December 23, 1968; *Newsweek,* January 21, 1969, May 12, 1975; *Times Literary Supplement,* January 29, 1970; *New Statesman,* January 30, 1970; *Mademoiselle,* July, 1974, June 1976; *Literary Quarterly,* May 15, 1975; *New York Review of Books,* June 26, 1975; *Miami Herald,* April 4, 1976; *Contemporary Literary Criticism,* Volume 6, Gale, 1976; *Authors in the News,* Volume 1, Gale, 1976.

F

FABIAN, Robert (Honey) 1901-1978

PERSONAL: Born January 31, 1901, in Ladywell, England; son of Andrew Pinwill (a seagoing engineer) and Ada Eliza (Taggart) Fabian; married Letitia Stockwell, May 9, 1925; children: Peter Robert. *Education:* Attended Detective Training School at Herndon, England. *Politics:* Conservative. *Religion:* Church of England. *Home:* 13 Bramlet Way, Ashstead, Surrey, England.

CAREER: Worked as an engineering draftsman; London Metropolitan Police, London, England, police constable, 1921-23, with the Criminal Investigation Department of Scotland Yard, 1923-1949, began as plain-clothes detective, became detective-superintendent, chief of flying squad, 1943-45. Lecturer; crime feature writer for Kemsley Newspapers, Ltd. *Awards, honors:* King's Medal for Gallantry from King George VI, 1939, for dismantling a bomb planted by the Irish Republican Army in Piccadilly Circus.

WRITINGS: Fabian of the Yard: An Intimate Record (autobiography), Naldrett Press, 1950, British Book Centre, 1953; *London After Dark: An Intimate Record of Night Life in London, and a Selection of Crime Stories From the Case Book of Ex-Superintendent Robert Fabian,* Naldrett Press, 1954, published as *London After Dark,* British Book Centre, 1954; *The Anatomy of Crime,* Pelham, 1970.

SIDELIGHTS: Considered the foremost sleuth in Great Britain, Robert Fabian solved a succession of major crimes during his years with Scotland Yard. One of his most famous cases occurred in 1946, when the body of an unidentified girl was discovered on Wrotham Hill in Kent. A hair net tangled in some underbrush was his first clue, and with that evidence he began a reconstruction of the crime, eventually identifying both the victim and the murderer. Shortly after Fabian had solved that murder, he became involved in another heralded investigation. Alec de Antiquis had been slain when he had tried to stop some jewel thieves in April, 1947. Through a label sewn in the lining of a raincoat, Fabian was able to trace the killers. The famous detective solved his last murder case two years before his death. While in retirement, he came up with the solution to a homicide which had baffled him when he investigated it thirty-one years before.

There were many reasons for Fabian's success. One advantage was that he built up a network of underworld contacts who would turn information over to him. Fabian also carefully studied criminal psychology, as he explained in *Fabian of the Yard:* "I soon realized that if I was to beat the crook, I would have to study his methods and follow the reasonings of his warped mind." In the same book, Fabian outlined the qualities that a good detective should possess: "He must be tactful, courageous, painstaking and vigilant . . . and should be a wizard at jigsaws." Fabian's colleagues felt that he epitomized all these qualities.

Several movies were inspired by Fabian's cases, and *Fabian of the Yard* served as the basis for a series of television shorts for British Broadcasting Corporation (BBC-TV).

AVOCATIONAL INTERESTS: Shooting, golf, gardening, swimming, chess, cricket, rugby, boxing.

BIOGRAPHICAL/CRITICAL SOURCES: Robert Fabian, *Fabian of the Yard: An Intimate Record,* Naldrett Press, 1950, British Book Centre, 1953; Leonard Gribble, *Great Manhunters of the Yard,* Roy, 1968. Obituaries: *New York Times,* June 15, 1978; *Washington Post,* June 17, 1978; *Time,* June 26, 1978.*

(Died June 14, 1978, in Epsom, Surrey, England)

*   *   *

FAGG, John (Edwin) 1916-

PERSONAL: Born November 21, 1916, in San Saba, Tex.; son of Edwin Earl (a realtor) and Bessie May (Sanderson) Fagg. *Education:* Attended Schreiner Institute, 1934-35; University of Texas, B.A., 1938; University of Chicago, M.A., Ph.D., 1942. *Religion:* Episcopal. *Office:* Department of History, New York University, 19 University Pl., New York, N.Y. 10003.

CAREER: New York University, New York, N.Y., 1946—, began as instructor, became professor of history, chairman of department, and director of Ibero-American Language and Area Center. Visiting professor of history at University of Virginia, 1976-77. *Military service:* U.S. Army Air Forces, 1942-46; became captain. *Member:* American Historical Association, Conference on Latin American Studies, Society for Spanish and Portuguese Studies, Center for Inter-American Relations.

WRITINGS: (Contributor) *The Army Air Forces in World War II,* University of Chicago Press, Volume III, 1952, Volume VII, 1958; *Latin America: A General History,* Macmillan, 1963, 3rd edition, 1977; *Cuba, Haiti, and the Dominican Republic,* Prentice-Hall, 1965. Also author of

History of the Church of the Holy Innocents, 1972. Contributor to history journals.

WORK IN PROGRESS: A history of St. Luke's Church; studying nineteenth-century Spain.

AVOCATIONAL INTERESTS: Travel, especially in Europe, Asia, Latin America.

* * *

FAIRMAN, Honora C.   1927(?)-1978

OBITUARY NOTICE: Born c. 1927 in Binghamton, N.Y.; died July 30, 1978, in Washington, D.C. Journalist and editor. She worked on newspapers in Binghamton and Rochester, N.Y., before becoming assistant fiction editor for *Redbook* magazine in 1950. Fairman retired in 1977 from her editorship of the *Journal of Home Economics.* Active in civil service groups, she worked on school programs for dependents of military families stationed abroad and helped establish day care centers in Arlington, Va. Obituaries and other sources: *Washington Post,* July 31, 1978.

* * *

FAKINOS, Aris   1935-

PERSONAL: Born January 1, 1935, in Athens, Greece; son of Dimitrios (an engineer) and Agheliki Fakinos. *Education:* Attended University of Lausanne. *Home:* 191 Rue de l'Universite, 75007 Paris, France. *Agent:* Georges Borchardt, Inc., 136 East 57th St., New York, N.Y. 10022.

CAREER: Institut Francais d'Athenes, Athens, Greece, professor of French literature, 1960-65; *Allaghi* (daily newspaper), Crete, Greece, editor, 1965-67; Radio France, Paris, journalist, 1967-74, producer of musical programs, 1974—. *Military service:* Greek Army, 1957-59; became lieutenant.

WRITINGS: Les Derniers Barbares (novel), translated by Sophie Le Bret from the original Greek, Editions du Seuil, 1969, translation by Jacqueline Lapidus published as *The Marked Men,* Liveright, 1971; (editor) *Le Livre noir de la dictature en Grece* (title means "The Black Book of the Dictatorship in Greece"), Editions du Seuil, 1969; *Zone de surveillance* (novel; title means "The Restricted Zone"), Editions du Seuil, 1972; *Les Rats de Hambourg* (novel; title means "The Rats of Hamburg"), Editions du Seuil, 1976. Also author of a Greek novel, title means "I Cried Out," Fexis, 1964. Greek press correspondent.

WORK IN PROGRESS: A novel about Greeks in exile, title means "Scaffolding"; a nonfiction work, *Athens.*

* * *

FANNING, Charles (Frederick, Jr.)   1942-

PERSONAL: Born November 11, 1942, in Norwood, Mass.; son of Charles Frederick (a janitor) and Frances P. (Balduf) Fanning; married Jane Frances Purcell (a clerk-typist), June, 1974. *Education:* Harvard University, B.A., 1964, M.A.T., 1966; University of Pennsylvania, M.A., 1968, Ph.D., 1972. *Home:* 26 Hale St., Bridgewater, Mass. 02324. *Office:* Department of English, Bridgewater State College, Bridgewater, Mass. 02324.

CAREER: Bridgewater State College, Bridgewater, Mass., instructor, 1966-67, 1970-72, assistant professor of English, 1972—. *Member:* Modern Language Association of America, American Studies Association, American Committee for Irish Studies.

WRITINGS: (Editor) *Mr. Dooley and the Chicago Irish,* Arno, 1976; (contributor) Blanche Touhill, editor, *Varieties*

of Ireland: Varieties of Irish-America, University of Missouri, St. Louis, 1976; (contributor) Daniel J. Casey, editor, *Irish-American Fiction: Essays in Criticism,* AMS Press, 1978; *Finley Peter Dunne and Mr. Dooley: The Chicago Years,* University Press of Kentucky, 1978. Contributor to scholarly journals.

WORK IN PROGRESS: The Irish Voice in American Literature; research on American immigrant writing, especially Irish.

SIDELIGHTS: Fanning comments: "My own background led me to my first researches into the Irish immigrant experience. I have traveled extensively in Ireland, and continue to be interested in the immigrant experience as it affects people who express themselves in literature. Finley Peter Dunne was the first important writer to deal realistically with the Irish immigrant experience in America. My work on him has led me to pursue the theme further."

AVOCATIONAL INTERESTS: Painting, especially watercolor, writing poems, "making box-collages, in the tradition of Joseph Cornell."

* * *

FARINA, Richard   1936(?)-1966

PERSONAL: Born in Brooklyn, N.Y.; married first wife Carol Hester; married second wife Mimi Baez, 1963. *Education:* Attended Cornell University.

CAREER: Songwriter, folksinger, playwright, and novelist.

WRITINGS: Been Down So Long It Looks Like Up to Me, Random House, 1966; *Long Time Coming and a Long Time Gone,* foreword by Joan Baez, Random House, 1969. Author of "Pack Up Your Sorrows," 1966, "Hard Lovin' Loser," 1969, and other songs. Recordings include "Celebrations for a Grey Day," and "Reflections in a Crystal Wind," both Vanguard.

SIDELIGHTS: A gifted songwriter and novelist and an important figure in the folk music period of the sixties, Richard Farina was an American of Irish and Cuban heritage. During the middle fifties, he fought with the Irish Republican Army in Northern Ireland and was later forced to leave the country. He moved on to Cuba and supported the revolution while Castro was fighting in the mountains. He finally left Cuba as Castro's guerrillas were entering the city of Havana. In addition to his songs, Farina wrote two novels which have drawn diverse criticism. Praised by many critics for his imaginative and free style, Farina also was criticized for shallow writing.

A *Partisan Review* critic noted that the value of his first novel, *Been Down So Long It Looks Like Up to Me,* "as a literary work . . . is slight. . . . But as an expression, highly personal and honest, of the outcome of those feelings of disinterested virtue and existential autonomy once encouraged by universities, and later condemned as 'apathy,' Mr. Farina's book deserves some serious attention." Maybelle Lacey of *Library Journal* praised Farina for his style: "the story rolls with its own momentum, carrying the reader from page to page," and called him "a gifted writer with free expression."

However, a *Time* reviewer stated that the book created "nothing more than a pot mood: airless self-satisfaction," and described it as "fashionably incoherent." Bernard Bergonzi of the *New York Review of Books* agreed: "There isn't much to it except for a forceful facility in the writing and a horribly accurate ear for the inanities of hipster speech. . . . Mr. Farina keeps it all going wildly on, in the accepted manner of comic-strip fiction. . . . For all its souped-up gaiety I found it depressing: a bright, cold, cruel, empty book.''

Farina, a contemporary of Thomas Pynchon at Cornell University, has long been compared to Pynchon, Brautigan, and other writers of the 1960's. Gene Bluestein summarized: ''*Been Down So Long* is in the classic tradition of American literature—a comic quest by a young hero, 'the keeper of the flame,' obssessed by intimations of death and loneliness, but with a fine seriousness underlying the often fantastic episodes. . . . Farina provides a complex vision—he has written an 'autobiographical chronicle of personal catastrophe expressed lyrically,' and in a framework that encompasses some uniquely American materials, ranging from folklore to the mass media. But despite some fantastic episodes, his plot line is linear and we can see in clearer outline some central themes which are more obscurely developed by a writer like Pynchon who, like Farina, shows us a devastated spiritual landscape, lighted by explosions of mad, pop humor and similarly destined for television.'' Pynchon, who dedicated *Gravity's Rainbow* to Farina, wrote: ''This book [*Been Down So Long*] comes on like the Hallelujah Chorus done by 200 kazoo players with perfect pitch, I mean strong, swinging, skillfull, and reverent—but also with the fine brassy buzz of irreverence in there too. Farina has going for him an unerring and virtuoso instinct about exactly what, in this bewildering Republic, is serious and what cannot possibly be.''

Richard Farina died in a motorcycle accident only two days after the publication of his first novel. ''His was an intensely colorful and eclectic life while it lasted,'' wrote Henry S. Resnik, ''a continual assertion of individuality and creative strength. Farina was so aggressively himself, in fact, that he probably had too much 'ego' for most of today's teeny-boppers; he was more tuned in to the beat generation than to the McLuhanized 'post-literates' who succeeded them, for, above everything else, he was relentlessly articulate.''

BIOGRAPHICAL/CRITICAL SOURCES: Kirkus Reviews, February 15, 1966; *Library Journal,* April 1, 1966; *Time,* May 6, 1966; *Saturday Review,* May 28, 1966, July 5, 1969; *New York Times,* June 4, 1966; *Partisan Review,* summer, 1966; *National Review,* August 9, 1966; *Yale Review,* autumn, 1966; *New York Review of Books,* October 6, 1966; *Journal of Popular Culture,* spring, 1976; *Contemporary Literary Criticism,* Volume 9, Gale, 1978.

OBITUARIES: New York Times, May 2, 1966; *Publishers Weekly,* May 9, 1966.*

(Died April 30, 1966, near Carmel, Calif.)

*   *   *

FARNSWORTH, James
   See POHLE, Robert W(arren), Jr.

*   *   *

FAULKNER, William (Cuthbert)   1897-1962

PERSONAL: Surname originally Falkner, later changed to Faulkner; born September 25, 1897, in New Albany, Miss.; son of Murry Cuthbert (a railroad worker, owner of a cotton-seed oil and ice plant, livery stable operator, hardware store employee, secretary and business manager at University of Mississippi) and Maud (Butler) Falkner; married Lida Estelle Oldham Franklin, June 20, 1929; children: Alabama (died, 1931), Jill (Mrs. Paul Dilwyn Summers, Jr.); (stepchildren) Victoria, Malcolm Argyle. *Education:* Attended University of Mississippi, 1919-1920. *Residence:* Rowan Oak, Oxford, Miss.

CAREER: First National Bank, Oxford, Miss., clerk, 1916; Winchester Repeating Arms Co., New Haven, Conn., ledger clerk, 1918; Lord & Taylor, New York, N.Y., bookstore clerk, 1921; University of Mississippi, Oxford, postmaster, 1921-24; worked as roof painter, carpenter, and paper hanger, New Orleans, La., 1925; deckhand on Genoa-bound freighter, 1925; full-time writer, 1925-62. Coal shoveler at Oxford Power Plant, 1929. Screen writer for Metro-Goldwyn-Mayer, 1932-33, and for Warner Bros., 1942-45, 1951, 1953, and 1954. Chairman of Writer's Group People-to-People Program, 1956-57. Writer-in-residence, University of Virginia, 1957-62. *Military service:* British Royal Air Force, cadet pilot, 1918; became honorary second lieutenant. *Member:* American Academy of Arts and Letters, Sigma Alpha Epsilon. *Awards, honors:* Elected to National Institute of Arts and Letters, 1939; O. Henry Memorial Short Story Awards, 1939, 1940, and 1949; elected to American Academy of Arts and Letters, 1948; Nobel Prize for Literature, 1949; William Dean Howells Medal from American Academy of Arts and Letters, 1950; National Book Award, 1951, for *Collected Stories;* Legion of Honor of Republic of France, 1951; National Book Award and Pulitzer Prize, both 1955, both for *A Fable;* Silver Medal of the Greek Academy, 1957; gold medal for fiction from National Institute of Arts and Letters, 1962.

WRITINGS: The Marble Faun (poems), Four Seas, 1924, reprinted with *A Green Bough,* Random House, 1965; (with William Philip Spratling) *Sherwood Anderson and Other Famous Creoles: A Gallery of Contemporary New Orleans,* Pelican Bookshop Press, 1926; *Soldiers' Pay* (novel), Boni & Liveright, 1926, new edition, 1970; *Mosquitoes* (novel), Boni & Liveright, 1927, Dell, 1965; *Sartoris* (abridged version of *Flags in the Dust;* also see below), Harcourt, 1929, Random House, 1966; *The Sound and the Fury* (novel), Cape & Smith, 1929, Modern Library, 1967.

As I Lay Dying (novel), Cape & Smith, 1930, Modern Library, 1967; *Sanctuary* (novel), Cape & Smith, 1931, New American Library, 1968; *These Thirteen* (stories), Cape & Smith, 1931; *Light in August* (novel), Smith & Haas, 1932, reprinted, Random House, 1972; *A Green Bough* (poems), Smith & Haas, 1933, reprinted with *The Marble Faun,* Random House, 1965; *Doctor Martino and Other Stories,* Smith & Haas, 1934; *Pylon* (novel), Smith & Haas, 1935, New American Library, 1968; *Absalom, Absalom!* (novel), Random House, 1936, reprinted, 1972; *The Unvanquished* (fiction), Random House, 1938, reprinted, 1965; *The Wild Palms* (novel) Random House, 1939, New American Library, 1968.

The Hamlet (novel), Random House, 1940, Vintage, 1964; *Go Down, Moses and Other Stories,* Random House, 1942, reprinted, 1973; *The Portable Faulkner,* edited by Malcolm Cowley, Viking, 1946, revised edition, 1967; *Intruder in the Dust* (novel), Random House, 1948, reprinted, 1972; *Knight's Gambit* (stories), Random House, 1949; *Collected Stories of William Faulkner,* Random House, 1950; *Requiem for a Nun* (stage version first produced on Broadway, January 30, 1959), Random House, 1951, revised edition, 1975; *Mirrors of Chartres Streets* (stories and sketches), Faulkner Studies, 1953, reprinted, Folcroft, 1977; *A Fable* (novel), Random House, 1954, reprinted, 1978; (and author of foreword) *The Faulkner Reader,* Random House, 1954; *Big Woods* (stories), Random House, 1955; *The Town* (novel), Random House, 1957, reprinted, 1961; *New Orleans Sketches,* edited by Carvel Collins, Rutgers University Press, 1958, Random House, 1968; *The Mansion* (novel), Random House, 1959, Vintage, 1965; *Faulkner in the Uni-*

versity (interviews and conversations), edited by Frederick L. Gwynn and Joseph L. Blotner, University Press of Virginia, 1959.

The Reivers (novel), Random House, 1962, New American Library, 1969; *Early Prose and Poetry,* edited by Collins, Little, Brown, 1962; *Selected Short Stories,* Modern Library, 1962; *Faulkner at West Point* (interviews), edited by Joseph L. Fant and Robert Ashley, Random House, 1964; *The Faulkner-Cowley File,* edited by Malcolm Cowley, Viking, 1966; *Essays, Speeches and Public Letters,* edited by James B. Meriwether, Random House, 1966; *The Wishing Tree* (children's fiction), Random House, 1967; *Flags in the Dust* (uncut version of *Sartoris*), edited by Douglas Day, Random House, 1973.

Screenplays: "Today We Live," 1933; "Lazy River," 1934; (with Joel Sayre) "The Road to Glory," Twentieth Century-Fox, 1936; (with Nunnally Johnson) "Banjo on My Knee," Twentieth Century-Fox, 1936; (with Sam Hellman, Lamar Trotti, and Gladys Lehman) "Slave Ship," Twentieth Century-Fox, 1937; (with Joel Sayre, Fred Guiol, and Ben Hecht) "Gunga Din," 1939; (with Jean Renoir) "The Southerner," Universal, 1945; (with Jules Furthman) "To Have and Have Not," Warner Bros., 1945; (with Leigh Brackett and Jules Furthman), "The Big Sleep," Warner Bros., 1946; (with Harry Kurnitz and Harold Jack Bloom) "Land of the Pharoahs," Warner Bros., 1955.

Contributor of poems, short stories, and articles to magazines and newspapers, including *New Orleans Times-Picayune, New Republic, Saturday Evening Post, Scribner's,* and *Sports Illustrated.*

SIDELIGHTS: "I hope to be the only unregimented and unrecorded individual left in the world," William Faulkner once announced. In order to protect his privacy, the famous Southern novelist often resorted to telling whoppers or to greeting questions with stony silence. He delighted in using his abundant imagination to embroider upon the facts of his own life as well as upon the lives of his fictional characters. Some of Faulkner's stories about himself were clearly tall tales, as when he claimed that he was "born in 1826 of a negro slave and an alligator." At other times, his yarns were told so convincingly that they circulated for years before they were proved to be untrue. For instance, a story that Faulkner had crashed in France while serving with the Canadian Royal Air Force during World War I was later demonstrated to be a patent lie. Faulkner had never even been in France until 1925.

Faulkner was reluctant to talk about himself because he thought that what was significant was not an author's personality or his habits but his writing. In a well-known essay, "Lion in the Garden," Madeleine Chapsal recorded her realization of this simple fact. After watching even the boldest reporters being squelched by Faulkner's terse replies and long periods of silence, Chapsal observed: "There is no use looking at Faulkner. You must read him. To someone who has read him, Faulkner has given all that he has, and he knows it. . . . What Faulkner wants one to be interested in are his books." Later in his career, Faulkner became more willing to talk about his moral vision and to discuss his books. But even if he had never uttered a word, there would have been no lack of commentary on his work. To date only William Shakespeare, John Milton, and the Bible have received more critical attention than Faulkner. Faulkner's desire that people be interested first and foremost in his books has certainly been realized, but he would have been chagrined by the attention that has also been paid to his personal life.

By this time most of the biographical facts about Faulkner have been thoroughly documented. He was born into a genteel Southern family that had played a significant part in the history of Mississippi. His great-grandfather, William Clark Falkner, was a colorful figure who had built railroads, served in the Confederate Army, and written a popular novel, *The White Rose of Memphis.* An indifferent student, Faulkner dropped out of Oxford High School in 1915 and then worked for a time as a clerk in his grandfather's bank. During this period he wrote bad imitative verse and contributed drawings to the University of Mississippi's yearbook, *Ole Miss.* When the United States declared war on Germany, Faulkner tried to enlist but was rejected because of his small stature.

Instead of going to war, Faulkner went to New Haven, Connecticut, to visit his friend Phil Stone, then a student at Yale. Stone had recognized Faulkner's talent early on and had encouraged his literary bent. The two men read and discussed Balzac and the French Symbolist poets. Although some critics have pointed to Stone as the determining factor in Faulkner's success, Michael Millgate theorized that the "apparent passivity of the younger man [Faulkner], his willingness to accept the position of listener, learner, recipient, and protege, undoubtedly led Stone to exaggerate in his own mind, and in public and private statements, the real extent of his influence. . . . Inevitably, Faulkner grew beyond Stone." At this time, however, Stone and Faulkner were still close friends. With Stone's help, Faulkner hatched a scheme to get admitted into the Royal Canadian Air Force. By affecting a British accent and forging letters of recommendation from nonexistent Englishmen, Faulkner was accepted into the RAF.

The war ended before Faulkner saw combat duty. He returned to his hometown, where he intermittently attended Ole Miss as a special student. His dandified appearance and lack of a stable job led townspeople to dub him "Count No'Count." On August 6, 1919, he surprised them when his first poem, "L'Apres-midi d'un faune," was published in *New Republic;* later in the same year the *Mississippian* published one of his short stories, "Landing in Luck." After Faulkner dropped out of Ole Miss, he went to New York City at the invitation of Stark Young, a Mississippi novelist and drama critic. While he was there, Faulkner worked for Elizabeth Prall as a bookstore clerk.

Back at Oxford, Faulkner was hired as university postmaster, but his mind was rarely on his duties. Before putting magazines into the proper subscriber's post office box, he read through the issues. He brought his writing to the post office with him and became so immersed in what he was doing that he ignored patrons. Eventually his laxness came to the attention of the postal inspector, and he resigned rather than be fired. Faulkner remarked that he quit the job because he "didn't want to be at the beck and call of every son-of-a-bitch with the price of a two-cent stamp."

His career in the postal service over, Faulkner called on Elizabeth Prall in New Orleans. She was now married to novelist Sherwood Anderson, and the two men struck up a friendship. The association with Anderson helped Faulkner realize that his true metier was not poetry but the novel. Faulkner's first book, *The Marble Faun,* a collection of verse, was published after he arrived in New Orleans in 1924. Sales were so poor that most of the five hundred copies were sold to a bookstore for a mere ten cents a volume. Acting upon Anderson's advice, Faulkner wrote a novel and set it in the South. Anderson told Faulkner he would recommend the book, entitled *Soldiers' Pay,* to a publisher as long as he didn't have to read it. Although the two men were very close for several months, a rift developed between them. Millgate postulated that "Faulkner's early realisation that Anderson's way was not to be his way must always have been a source of strain in their relationship." During this period in New Orleans, Faulkner also contributed short stories and sketches to the *Times-Picayune.*

In 1925, Faulkner joined the American literary expatriates and went to Europe. He did not remain there long, however, and after a brief stay in New Orleans, he returned to Oxford, where he finally settled down. While he had been in Europe, *Soldiers' Pay* had appeared on the bookstands. It attracted some favorable notices but was not a commercial success. Years later, Robert Penn Warren, also a Southern writer, remembered his own reactions when he first read *Soldiers' Pay* in the spring of 1929: "As a novel, *Soldiers' Pay* is no better than it should be, but it made a profound and undefinable impression on me." *Mosquitoes,* a mildly satirical novel on literary life in New Orleans, came out in 1927. Faulkner then penned *Flags in the Dust,* the first of his novels to be set in Yoknapatawpha County.

Early in 1928 *Flags in the Dust* was being shuffled from one publisher to another without success, and Faulkner had grown disgusted with the entire publication process. Abruptly, he decided to stop worrying about whether or not others liked his manuscripts. "One day I seemed to shut a door," he recalled, "between me and all publishers' addresses and book lists. I said to myself, Now I can write. Now I can make myself a vase like that which the old Roman kept at his bedside and wore the rim slowly away with kissing it. So I, who never had a sister and was fated to lose my daughter in infancy, set out to make myself a beautiful and tragic little girl." The story that Faulkner sat down to write was, of course, *The Sound and the Fury,* and "the beautiful and tragic little girl" was Caddy Compson. It was *The Sound and the Fury* that helped Faulkner establish a solid reputation among critics. Stirred by Faulkner's novel, Lyle Saxon wrote, "I believe simply and sincerely this is a great book." A reviewer for the *Boston Evening Transcript* called *The Sound and the Fury* a novel "worthy of the attention of a Euripides."

When writing his next novel, *As I Lay Dying,* Faulkner did not experience the same rapture he had felt when he was working on *The Sound and the Fury. As I Lay Dying* was written in a six-week period while Faulkner was working the night shift at a powerhouse. The constant humming noise of a dynamo serenaded him while he wrote his famous *tour de force* on the nature of being. By the time *As I Lay Dying* came out in 1930, John Bassett observed that "Faulkner's name, if not a household word, was at least known to many critics and reviewers, who spoke of him no longer as a neophyte, or a new voice in fiction, but as one either continuing his development in fruitful ways or floundering after several attempts, in either case as a writer known to the literary world."

Faulkner was not recognized by the general public until *Sanctuary,* one of his most violent and shocking novels, appeared in 1931. When he wrote *Sanctuary,* Faulkner later admitted, he had one purpose in mind: to make money. By this time he had a family to support, and out of desperation he concocted a book he thought would sell to the masses. Faulkner was ashamed when he saw the printer's galleys of the book and extensively rewrote his potboiler so that it would have a more serious intent. The scandalous subject matter of *Sanctuary* appealed to the reading public, and it sold well. For a brief time Faulkner became a minor celebri-

ty, but the rest of the decade did not go as well. Many reviewers had favorable comments to make about *Sanctuary*—Andre Malraux declared it "marks the intrusion of Greek tragedy into the detective story"—but in the view of others, the novel proved that Faulkner was merely a purveyor of the monstrous, the gory, and the obscene, and they judged his subsequent books in the same light. Faulkner was also a victim of the times. The Depression caused book sales in general to plummet, but his novels were particularly unpopular because they were not in keeping with the nation's mood. Warren speculated that critics and the public became disenchanted with Faulkner because his books offered no practical solutions to the pressing problems of the day—feeding the hungry and providing jobs for the millions of unemployed. Some readers were offended by Faulkner's novels because they were not written in the optimistic spirit of the New Deal, while still others discerned fascist tendencies in his work.

During the 1930's and 1940's Faulkner wrote many of his finest books, including *Light in August, Absalom, Absalom!, The Wild Palms, The Hamlet,* and *Go Down, Moses.* They brought in very little revenue, however, and he was forced to work in Hollywood as a screenwriter. Faulkner worked on and off in Hollywood for a number of years, but he was never happy there. He fled from the movie capital as soon as he had amassed enough money to pay his bills. Few people in Hollywood were appreciative of Faulkner's genius. At one time Faulkner and Howard Hawks paid a visit to movie star Clark Gable. Hawks and Faulkner were carrying on a discussion about literature when Gable interrupted.

"Mr. Faulkner," Gable inquired, "what do you think somebody should read if he wants to read the best modern books? Who would you say are the best living writers?"

Faulkner replied, "Ernest Hemingway, Willa Cather, Thomas Mann, John Dos Passos, and William Faulkner."

"Oh," Gable said. "Do you write?"

"Yes, Mr. Gable," Faulkner answered. "What do you do?"

It should not be assumed, however, that Faulkner was completely unappreciated during this time period. Bassett pointed out that the majority of reviews were positive, and that between 1939 and 1942 several important examinations of Faulkner appeared in literary journals and in literary histories. Although hardly noticed by the public, Faulkner was esteemed by many of his fellow writers. His work had also attracted a substantial following in France. Maurice Coindreau translated several of Faulkner's novels and short stories into French, and his fiction received perceptive treatment from such critics as Andre Malraux, Maurice LeBreton, Jean Pouillon, and Jean-Paul Sartre.

Despite Faulkner's stature in literary circles at home and abroad, in the 1940's his books gradually began dropping out of print, partly because of lack of popular interest, partly because of the war effort. By 1945 all seventeen of his books were out of print. In 1946 the publication of *The Portable Faulkner,* edited by Malcolm Cowley, created a resurgence of interest in Faulkner. Cowley's introduction to the volume, with its emphasis on the Southern legend that Faulkner had created in his works, served as a springboard for future critics. "Faulkner performed a labor of imagination that has not been equaled in our time, and a double labor," Cowley asserted. "First, to invent a Mississippi county that was like a mythical kingdom, but was complete and living in all its details; second, to make his story of Yoknapatawpha County stand as a parable or legend of all the Deep South."

Fifteen of Faulkner's novels and many of his short stories are set in Yoknapatawpha County, which bears a close resemblance to the region in northern Mississippi where Faulkner spent most of his life. Faulkner defined Yoknapatawpha as an "Indian word meaning water runs slow through flat land." The county is bounded by the Tallahatchie River on the north and by the Yoknapatawpha River on the south. Jefferson, the county seat, is modeled after Oxford. Up the road a piece is Frenchman's Bend, a poverty-stricken village. Scattered throughout the countryside are ramshackle plantation houses, farmhouses, and the hovels of tenant farmers. Depicted in both the past and the present, Yoknapatawpha is populated with a vast spectrum of people—the Indians who originally inhabited the land, the aristocrats, those ambitious men who fought their way into the landed gentry, yeoman farmers, poor whites, blacks, carpetbaggers, and bushwhackers. Faulkner was proud of the kingdom he had erected in his imagination. On a map of Yoknapatawpha County he prepared for the first edition of *Absalom, Absalom!*, he wrote, "William Faulkner, Sole Owner & Proprietor."

Following Cowley's lead, critics began examining the Yoknapatawpha legend. Although Faulkner took the trouble to make maps of his county and genealogies of his characters, it is not clear whether he had a well-conceived plan of the community in mind when he wrote his first Yoknapatawpha novel, *Flags in the Dust,* originally published as *Sartoris.* Most commentators have argued that Faulkner's vision of Yoknapatawpha evolved as his writing career progressed. "This saga seems to be as unplanned as life itself," William Barrett wrote of the Yoknapatawpha novels. "It buds and grows organically from work to work, altering a character here and changing a perspective there, but always returning to the soil from which it grows." When *Flags in the Dust* was first published in its entirety in 1973, some seized upon it as evidence that Faulkner had originally had a much clearer notion of the Yoknapatawpha cycle than previously thought. Jonathan Yardley commented: "*Flags in the Dust,* because it is so much more intricate than *Sartoris,* makes clear that everything that would engage Faulkner for three and a half decades had formed in his imagination at the outset."

Although there are some inconsistencies in the Yoknapatawpha novels and although the books are certainly not arranged in a neat chronological order, the saga does have unity. Millgate called this unity "a unity of inspiration, of a single irradiating tragi-comic vision." In order to appreciate Faulkner's vision fully, one must read the entire saga, which Yardley described as "a tapestry of incomparable intricacy, past and present woven together in a design that can be comprehended through one book but that gains astonishing richness when seen as a whole." The greatness of Faulkner's design led critics to recognize that he was not just a provincial writer. Like the works of such famous regional authors as Robert Frost, Thomas Hardy, and William Butler Yeats, Faulkner's novels have a universal appeal. Faulkner created, Arthur Edelstein remarked, a "hallucinated version of the Deep South which has escaped its local origins to become a region of the modern consciousness."

Those who investigated the Yoknapatawpha legend began exploring other aspects of Faulkner's fiction. The resulting criticism exploded two myths that had persisted about him: that his style was the result of incompetence and that his writing promoted immorality. Faulkner's prose often seems like a morass of words to the uninitiated, and the difficulty of his style prevented his being read by the general public for a long time. The defects in Faulkner's prose probably resulted

from his isolation in the South. Faulkner had no mentors. He shunned literary society and often described himself as a farmer rather than a writer. Cowley compared Faulkner to Nathaniel Hawthorne: "Like Hawthorne, Faulkner is a solitary worker by choice, and he has done great things not only with double the pains to himself that they might have cost if produced in more genial circumstances, but sometimes also with double the pains to the reader." Even Faulkner's most loyal admirers admit that some of his writing is careless or downright bad, but they also contend that the majority of his prose is more than worth the effort of reading. Evidently Faulkner felt this way too, for when a student asked him what he would advise a person who had read his books and didn't understand them, he responded, "Read them again."

Some of the stylistic techniques that have puzzled readers include the repetition of words, the absence of punctuation, vague pronoun references, and the use of long, convoluted sentences, flashbacks, and multiple viewpoints. As Conrad Aiken pointed out, Faulkner was perfectly capable of writing straightforward prose when he wished; thus, he must have had some purpose in mind when he employed techniques that confused readers. Warren Beck observed that Faulkner's reiteration of certain words and his habit of piling one adjective upon another sometimes help to create a mood or to accentuate a particular character trait. For examples, Beck turned to *Absalom, Absalom!* In that novel, Miss Rosa's persistent use of the word "demon" indicates her crazed obsession, while the description of the "long still hot weary dead September afternoon" when Quentin hears Miss Rosa's story emphasizes not only the muggy weather but also the spiritual malaise of the characters. Joseph Blotner noted that sometimes Faulkner followed James Joyce's lead and "would omit all punctuation to denote the flowing stream of consciousness." This technique was used in Benjy's and Quentin's sections in *The Sound and the Fury.* As for Faulkner's vague pronoun references, Helen Swink surmised that he used them because he wanted to adapt the art of the oral storyteller to the written page. In attempting to sound like he was spinning yarns aloud, Faulkner used vague pronoun references because this is a characteristic of oral speech.

Most often, Faulkner's style is keyed to his themes. One of Faulkner's chief thematic preoccupations is the past, and this theme is also reflected in his form. In a famous analogy, Jean-Paul Sartre compared the Faulknerian character's point of view to that "of a passenger looking backward from a speeding car, who sees, flowing away from him, the landscape he is traversing. For him the future is not in view, the present is too blurred to make out, and he can see clearly only the past as it streams away before his obsessed and backward-looking gaze." Faulkner's pages are filled with characters who are fettered to the past. Millgate pointed out that in *The Sound and the Fury* the suicidal Quentin Compson searches "for a means of arresting time at a moment of achieved perfection, a moment when he and Caddy could be eternally together in the simplicity of their childhood relationship." The Reverend Gail Hightower in *Light in August* is also locked in the past, endlessly reliving the glory of his grandfather's cavalry charge. Robert Hemenway believed that in *As I Lay Dying* Faulkner is showing "that the South, like the Bundrens, must bury the past; that it cannot remain true—without courting tragedy or absurdity—to the promises given to dead ancestors or to the illusions of former glory." In "A Rose for Emily," Emily Grierson's embracing of her dead lover becomes a gruesome symbol of what happens when one clings to the past.

According to J. W. Dunne, Faulkner's own concept of time seems to be that the "present, the past, and the future coexist." Cleanth Brooks pointed out that Faulkner's view of time as a continuum is similar to the understanding of time that Dilsey, the faithful old black servant in *The Sound and the Fury,* has. Dilsey has a broken kitchen clock, but she always knows the correct time. "Her ability to make sense of the clock is simply one aspect of her ability to make sense of past, present, and future," Brooks wrote. "All are aspects of eternity, and Dilsey, in her simple religious faith, believes in an order that is grounded in eternity."

The stylistic methods most closely associated with Faulkner's treatment of the past are his use of long sentences, flashbacks, and multiple viewpoints. Aiken suggested that Faulkner utilizes complicated sentence structures because he wants "a medium without stops or pauses, a medium which is always *of the moment,* and of which the passage from moment to moment is as fluid and undetectable as in the life itself which he is purporting to give." Swink posited that the confusing sentences that withhold meaning from the reader "intensify the emotional experience," while Millgate claimed that these sentences enable Faulkner "to hold a single moment in suspension while its full complexity is explored." The flashbacks are even more clearly related to Faulkner's interest in the past. Edward Murray pointed out that in *Light in August* the minds of Joe Christmas, Gail Hightower, Joanna Burden, and Lena Grove frequently revert back to the past, but "the flashbacks are not there merely to supply expository material for the actions in the present that need further explanation. Since the past is Faulkner's subject—or a large part of it—the flashbacks are not simply 'functional': they are thematically necessary."

By telling a story from several points of view, Faulkner adds a further dimension to his concept of time. The past is part of the present; thus, it is subject to re-evaluation and re-interpretation. Depending on his biases, a character may either distort or illuminate certain aspects of the past. In *The Sound and the Fury* the history of the Compson family is related alternately through the eyes of Benjy, Quentin, and Jason Compson, and then from the viewpoint of an omniscient narrator. Each narrator's perspective is different from the last. Olga Vickery commented that this use of alternating viewpoints reveals the theme of the novel to be "the relation between the act and man's apprehension of the act, between the event and the interpretation." A similar process takes place in *Absalom, Absalom!* Faulkner emphasizes his theme of the mutability of time by having Rosa Coldfield, Jason Compson, Quentin Compson, and Shreve McCannon all give their own differing versions of Thomas Sutpen's story. Brooks observed that the use of multiple perspectives makes *Absalom, Absalom!* "a persuasive commentary upon the thesis that much of 'history' is really a kind of imaginative construction."

Faulkner's view of time as a continuum has certain moral implications, Millgate explained: "The all-important point consisted in the idea that there could be no such thing as 'was': since time constituted a continuum the chain of cause and effect could never be broken, and every human action must continue to reverberate, however faintly, into infinity. Hence the all-importance of conduct, of personal responsibility for all one's actions." This belief partially accounts for Faulkner's frequent allusions to the Bible. "Faulkner's true domain is that of the eternal myths, particularly those popularized by the Bible," Maurice Coindreau observed. "The themes that he prefers, his favorite images and metaphors, are those which ornament the fabric of the Old Testament."

Like the writers of the Old Testament, Faulkner believes that the sins of the fathers are visited upon their children. Many of his characters are plagued by guilt, precipitated by their own sins as well as by the actions of their forefathers, who had callously shoved aside the Indians, enslaved the blacks, and laid waste the land.

Perhaps the greatest moral burden borne by Southerners was slavery. Much of Faulkner's fiction shows the evil that results from the failure to recognize the humanity of black people. Certainly many of the slave owners he depicts are cruel to their human property. In *Go Down, Moses,* Carothers McCaslin seduces Eunice, one of his Negroes. Years later he seduces the daughter who resulted from that union, thus driving Eunice to suicide. One of the reasons that Thomas Sutpen's grand design fails in *Absalom, Absalom!* is his acceptance of racism. When Sutpen leaves Haiti to found a dynasty in Mississippi, he abandons his black wife and infant son because their color would not be acceptable to Southerners. That deed comes back to haunt Sutpen and the children from his second marriage, Judith and Henry. Sutpen's mulatto son shows up and wants to marry Judith. As horrified by the thought of miscegenation as he is by the possibility of incest, Henry guns down his half brother. This is only one incident in *Absalom, Absalom!* that demonstrates, as John V. Hagopian pointed out, how "the novel as a whole clearly repudiates Southern racism."

But even after slavery had been abolished, racism lingered on, in fact and in Faulkner's novels. Carothers McCaslin's white progeny spurn their black relatives. The black Lucas Beauchamp and his white cousin Zack Edmonds grew up together, fishing and hunting together and even sharing the same blanket when they slept out in the woods, but as Zack grows older he sets himself above Lucas. The older Lucas Beauchamp reappears in *Intruder in the Dust,* where he is accused of murder and is in danger of being lynched because of his race. In *Light in August,* Joe Christmas commits a murder but does not receive a fair trial. Instead, Christmas is killed and castrated by Percy Grimm, a murder justified in Grimm's eyes because Christmas is believed to be a Negro.

Men do not only exploit one another, Faulkner points out; they also exploit the earth. Cleanth Brooks noted that "Faulkner seems to accept the Christian doctrine of original sin. Men are condemned to prey upon nature. The only question is whether in doing so they will exercise some kind of restraint and love the nature that they are forced to use, or whether they will exploit nature methodically and ruthlessly, in a kind of rape." Faulkner's most in-depth exploration of the rape of the wilderness occurs in *Go Down, Moses.* In that novel, the young Ike McCaslin learns some important lessons by hunting for Old Ben, a legendary bear who has eluded hunters for years. "Old Ben is the wilderness, the mystery of man's nature and origins beneath the forms of civilization," William Van O'Connor explained. "And man's proper relationship with the wilderness teaches him liberty, courage, pride, and humility." In his long life, Ike lives to see the wilderness he so loved destroyed. Lumbermen chop down the trees, and railroad tracks crisscross the territory where once Old Ben reigned supreme.

Although Ike rejected his inheritance, choosing to live in the wilderness and live out the values he learned there, it would be wrong to view him as a completely admirable character. He cut himself off from other human beings, thus rendering himself ineffectual. Ike lacked an ability to love and a sense of community, both values that Faulkner regards highly. Love between family members is particularly important to Faulkner. Cowley observed that Faulkner's books "have what is rare in the novels of our time, a warmth of family affection, brother for brother and sister, the father for his children—a love so warm and proud that it tries to shut out the rest of the world." In *The Sound and the Fury,* Caddy loves and watches out for her brother Benjy even though he is retarded. When Caddy leaves town, Dilsey assumes primary responsibility for Benjy. In his later years Faulkner said that Dilsey was one of his favorite characters, and what he admired most about her was her outgoing love: "Dilsey . . . had taken care of a family who were decaying, going to pieces before her eyes. She held the whole thing together, with no hope of reward, except she was doing the best she could because she loved that poor, otherwise helpless, idiot child."

If family life has eroded in Faulkner's fiction, it is at least partially because society is debilitated. "Faulkner's recurrent dramatization of the decay of families," Philip Momberger reflected, "e.g., the deterioration of the Compson, Sutpen, and Sartoris lines—is an expression in the domestic sphere of a more general, public disintegration: the collapse of the ideal of 'human family' in the modern world and the resulting deracination of the individual." Momberger went on to say that the social ideal that underpins Faulkner's work is "a state of communal wholeness within which, as within a coherent and loving family, the individual's identity would be defined, recognized, and sustained." *Pylon,* one of Faulkner's few novels not set in Yoknapatawpha County, shows that a sense of communal wholeness is almost impossible to achieve in modern society. According to Hyatt H. Waggoner, the novel states in symbolic form "the loss of true community; the dwindling significance of the traditional family and home; the relaxing grip or embrace of institutions that embodied and supplied meaning and a sense of stability and permanence."

Although a person's ties to the community are important, Faulkner suggests that men must never let the community become the sole arbiter of their values. Brooks stated that the "community is at once the field for man's action and the norm by which his action is judged and regulated" and further indicated that Faulkner's "fiction also reveals keen awareness of the perils risked by the individual who attempts to run counter to the community. The divergent individual may invite martyrdom; he certainly risks fanaticism and madness." For examples of divergent individuals, Brooks turned to *Light in August.* In that novel, many of the characters are social outcasts—Joe Christmas because of his suspected Negro blood, Joanna Burden because of her abolitionist background, Gail Hightower because he does not conform to the conventional behavior of a minister, Percy Grimm because he did not serve in World War I. In *The Town,* Eula Varner Snopes is rejected by Jefferson society when her affair with Manfred De Spain comes out in the open. "And in the repudiation of Eula as sinner, Jefferson also repudiates its own roots in the physical and emotional world which is the source of its strength," Vickery commented. "Even though social forms and conventions have a very real value in regulating behavior, the healthy society is the one that dares to flout its own prescriptions."

Many of society's prescriptions have been laid down by the established religion. Faulkner's characters are often deeply disturbed by the rigid attitudes of the church-going populace. In *Sanctuary,* Horace Benbow is taken aback when the Christian community refuses to help a man who is falsely accused of murder. Waggoner declared that in that novel "Southern fundamentalist Protestantism is pictured as self-righteous moralism." Calvinist righteousness is also at-

tacked in *Light in August,* where Hightower comes to realize that rigid religious attitudes encourage people to crucify themselves and others. One of the people they feel compelled to crucify is Joe Christmas, who is clearly an outcast in the community. The major significance in Christmas's name, O'Connor noted, "is the irony of Joe Christmas' being pursued and harassed throughout his life by voices of Christian righteousness."

Allied with the theme of the individual running counter to the community and its values is the theme of a young boy's initiation into manhood. This initiation process usually involves some ritualistic gesture or task that a youth must perform in order to achieve knowledge and manhood, and a choice, as Brooks observed, "between a boy's ties with his community—his almost fierce identification with it—and his revulsion from what the community seems committed to do." After he kills his first deer, Ike McCaslin is initiated into manhood by Sam Fathers, who anoints his forehead with the deer's blood. This initiation process is the first step in Ike's decision to eschew the values of society. *The Unvanquished* consists of a series of short stories recounting the growth of Bayard Sartoris. In the final story, Bayard refuses to avenge the death of his father. By so doing, he defies the community, for the townspeople think vengeance is honorable. Chick Mallison in *Intruder in the Dust* is another sensitive adolescent who is forced to choose between the community's standards and what his heart tells him is right. Faulkner's last novel, *The Reivers,* also deals with a young boy's initiation into manhood. When he runs away to Memphis with Boon Hogganbeck and Ned McCaslin, Lucius Priest is forced to grow up. "Lucius experiences pain and suffering and the trauma of his first encounter with sex, with violence, and with crime, but his initiation into human identity and his discovery of the essential truths of life take place under the guidance of reliable protectors," Sally R. Page asserted.

M. E. Bradford pointed out that the thematic corollary to Faulkner's consideration of a young man's coming into his majority is the question of pride, "or pride's proper role in the formation of good character and of its necessary limitation in contingency. . . . The gentleman, the exemplar of ordinate pride and enactor of a providentially assigned place, sums up in his person the possibility of a civil and religiously grounded social order. In him either presumption or passivity is communal and spiritual disaster." In part it was Thomas Sutpen's presumption, his arrogance, that created communal and spiritual disaster in *Absalom, Absalom!* As Dan Vogel demonstrated, Sutpen is a tragic hero who is afflicted by what the Greeks termed hubris, or overweening pride. "The hubris in Sutpen makes him grotesque, a demon . . . , a victim of his own obsession of dynastic design, and a symbol of guilt," Vogel explained.

Closely linked to pride is the Faulknerian concept of honor, the need for a man to prove himself. In Faulkner's novels, exaggerated notions of honor lead to trouble. Quentin Compson's fanatic defense of his sister's honor is narcissistic; his "insistence upon honor and dignity have become extreme, forms of self love," O'Connor noted. In *As I Lay Dying,* the Bundren family's attempt to honor Addie's dying wish is ludicrous, yet Brooks pointed out that Cash and Jewel "exhibit true heroism—Cash in his suffering, Jewel in his brave actions." The scruple of honor is also of great significance in *The Hamlet.* After Eula Varner becomes pregnant, her honor is ironically preserved when her father pays Flem Snopes to marry her. Even Mink Snopes has a warped sense of honor that compels him to kill Zack Houston. But

Mink discovers that his cousin Flem is so devoid of honor that he won't even help Mink when he is arrested. Mink evens this score in a later novel, *The Mansion*. When he is released from prison, Mink kills Flem for the sake of honor.

When Faulkner's characters are initiated into manhood, they lose their innocence and are forced to face reality. The world they discover is one in which good and evil are intermingled. The nature of good and evil is examined in detail in *Sanctuary* and the Snopes trilogy. Vickery observed that in *Sanctuary* violence is used to compel a re-evaluation of self and society. As he struggles to help his client beat a murder rap, Horace Benbow becomes disillusioned by the evil that lurks in society, in the courts, and in religion. In that same novel Popeye is often interpreted as emblematic of the evil in a materialistic society, but Faulkner told a group at the University of Virginia that to him Popeye was "another lost human being. He became a symbol of evil in modern society only by coincidence."

It is the Snopes trilogy, Stanley Edgar Hyman claimed, that is "Faulkner's fullest exploration of natural evil." In *The Hamlet,* the heartless Flem Snopes is pitted against V. K. Ratliff, an itinerant sewing machine salesman. Flem is almost the perfect embodiment of evil, whereas Ratliff, John Lewis Longley demonstrated, is a man "who is willing to actively commit himself against evil, but more important, to form actions of positive good." Although Flem is depicted as the incarnation of evil in *The Hamlet*, commentators have noted that he is portrayed more sympathetically in the succeeding two books in the trilogy. This treatment is in keeping with Faulkner's view of the nature of man. "I think that you really can't say that any man is good or bad. I grant you there are some exceptions, but man is the victim of himself or his fellows, or his own nature, or his environment, but no man is good or bad either. He tries to do the best he can within his rights," the novelist once said.

Although Faulkner believed that men are a combination of good and evil, many scholars feel that his women characters tend to be more evil than good. Brooks explained that "in nearly every one of Faulkner's novels, the male's discovery of evil and reality is bound up with his discovery of the true nature of women." Far from being the romantic creatures men suppose them to be, Faulkner's women are dispassionate, practical, sometimes even wicked. Some argue that even those of his women with praiseworthy traits are stupid—Lena Grove is cited frequently as an example. Leslie Fiedler expounded upon this problem: "[Faulkner] reminds us (again and again!) that men are helpless in the hands of their mothers, wives, and sisters; that females do not think but proceed from evidence to conclusions by paths too devious for males to follow; that they possess neither morality nor honor; that they are capable, therefore, of betrayal without qualm or quiver of guilt but also of inexplicable loyalty; that they enjoy an occasional beating at the hands of their men; that they are unforgiving and without charity to other members of their own sex; that they lose keys and other small useful articles with maddening regularity but are quite capable of finding things invisible to men; that they use their sexuality with cold calculation to achieve their inscrutable ends, etc., etc."

In a review of *A Loving Gentleman,* Meta Carpenter Wilde's book about her love affair with Faulkner, Cowley suggested that Faulkner's view of women was quite ambivalent. "He was female-intoxicated and adoring, but he was also female-suspicious, fearful of being dominated, almost a misogynist; and he was cynical too, not only about women but also about his own motives," wrote Cowley. For Cow-

ley, Faulkner's schizophrenic view of women is best embodied in his use of counterpoint in *The Wild Palms*. The two unrelated stories in the novel show two diametrically opposed attitudes toward women. On the one hand there is Harry, a doctor who performs an abortion on his lover. When she dies, Harry is sentenced to fifty years of hard labor. Rather than kill himself, Harry decides that "between grief and nothing I will take grief." On the other hand is the convict, who is willing to go back to jail to rid himself of love. According to Cowley, the convict's final words, "Women,——t," express Faulkner's negative feelings about women.

Faulkner did not feel that his depictions of women were entirely negative. When a student in Japan asked him how he felt about women, he responded: "I don't think that I would make any generalization about an opinion of women—some of the best people are women, and I'm inclined to think that every young man should know one old woman, that they can talk more sense—they'd be good for any young man—well, an old aunt, or an old school teacher, just to listen to." Faulkner also pointed out that many of his most noble characters are women; he referred to Dilsey and her capacity to endure. Another of Faulkner's most admirable creations is Judith Sutpen. Brooks pronounced Judith to be "one of Faulkner's finest characters of endurance—and not merely through numb, bleak stoicism but also through compassion and love. Judith is doomed by misfortunes not of her making but she is not warped and twisted by them. Her humanity survives them."

From today's perspective, it is difficult to understand the outcry that arose when Faulkner was awarded the Nobel Prize in 1949. The preponderance of criticism has shown that his concerns are ultimately moral, but at that time many readers still considered Faulkner a naturalistic monster. Reflecting the views of many other small-town newspapers, the editor of the *North Mississippi Herald* declared that Faulkner was a member of the "privy school of literature." Even the *New York Times* expressed the fear that the rest of the world might consider Yoknapatawpha County an accurate depiction of life in America. Faulkner's reply to those who accused him of promoting immorality was contained in his acceptance speech. He explained that it is the writer's duty and privilege "to help man endure by lifting his heart, by reminding him of the courage and honor and hope and pride and compassion and pity and sacrifice which have been the glory of his past. The poet's voice need not merely be the record of man, it can be one of the props, the pillars, to help him endure and prevail."

Faulkner's stirring acceptance speech caused many to change their opinion of him overnight. Suddenly he became a moral hero. As Herman Spivey pointed out, the truth is that Faulkner's outlook had undergone no dramatic change; from the beginning of his writing career he had concerned himself with "the old verities and truths of the heart, the old universal truths lacking which any story is ephemeral and doomed." One reason why some perceived Faulkner's moral vision as altering was that he became more vocal after receiving the Nobel Prize. In 1954 the U.S. Supreme Court struck down the separate-but-equal clause, and many Mississippians vowed they would never comply with orders to integrate their schools. Faulkner stated publicly that he believed in integration but felt it should proceed slowly. This position aroused the ire of both sides. Conservatives lambasted him for accepting integration, while liberals were disturbed by his advice to go cautiously. Faulkner did not back down from his position. He told students in Japan he felt the most practical way to achieve integration was for people to be calm: "the victims of the injustice . . . must be the ones that will have the most patience . . . they must be capable of waiting rather than to be frightened into taking irrecoverable steps."

Another reason why people thought Faulkner's moral position had changed was because his later books became didactic, often seeming to be mere echoes of his Nobel Prize acceptance speech. Spivey contended that in Faulkner's later novels "there is a major and regrettable shift from mythic and symbolic and implicit communication to allegorical and explicit communication." In *A Fable,* which Faulkner hoped would be his masterpiece, allegory is used to convey a moral message. Few critics were happy with the book's general and abstract statements. Brendan Gill called *A Fable* "a calamity," while Charles Rolo termed it "a heroically ambitious failure."

Rolo's words recall some of Faulkner's own thoughts on the nature of literary achievement. Although Faulkner had once told Clark Gable that the five finest contemporary writers were Hemingway, Cather, Mann, Dos Passos, and himself, he later changed his mind. This time he named the greatest writers as Thomas Wolfe, himself, Dos Passos, Erskine Caldwell, and Hemingway. When asked the rationale behind this ranking, he explained: "We were all failures. All of us had failed to match the dream of perfection and I rated the authors on the basis of their splendid failure to do the impossible. I believe Wolfe tried to do the greatest of the impossible, that he tried to reduce all human experience to literature. And I thought after Wolfe I had tried the most. I rated Hemingway last because he stayed within what he knew. He did it fine, but he didn't try for the impossible."

If Faulkner failed greatly, he also succeeded mightily. Whatever the faults of his later books, few would dispute the general excellence of his canon. Even Faulkner seemed overwhelmed by his achievement. Toward the end of his life, he wrote to a friend: "And now I realize for the first time what an amazing gift I had: uneducated in every formal sense, without even very literate, let alone literary, companions, yet to have made the things I made. I don't know where it came from. I don't know why God or gods or whoever it was, elected me to be the vessel. Believe me, this is not humility, false modesty: it is simply amazement." Many others have expressed amazement that Faulkner, in many ways such an isolated and provincial artist, was able to imbue his work with universal meaning. Perhaps John W. Aldridge put it best when he wrote, "Working alone down there in that seemingly impenetrable cultural wilderness of the sovereignly backward state of Mississippi, he managed to make a clearing for his mind and a garden for his art, one which he cultivated so lovingly and well that it has come in our day to feed the imagination of literate men throughout the civilized world."

Each of Faulkner's novels has been translated into at least one other language, and several have been translated into as many as thirteen languages. *Light in August* can be read in all the Slavic languages, Finnish, Spanish, Italian, Hebrew, Danish, German, Swiss-German, French, Portuguese, Hungarian, and Swedish. *The Reivers* has been translated into Slovenian and Croatian, and "The Bear" can be read in Serbian, East Indian, and Japanese, among others.

The following novels by Faulkner have been adapted for movies: "Intruder in the Dust," Metro-Goldwyn-Mayer, 1949; "Tarnished Angels" (based on *Pylon*), Universal, 1957; "The Long, Hot Summer" (based on *The Hamlet*),

Twentieth Century-Fox, 1958; "The Sound and the Fury," Twentieth Century-Fox, 1959; "Sanctuary" (also includes parts of *Requiem for a Nun*), Twentieth Century-Fox, 1961; "The Reivers," Cinema Center Films, 1969.

The Sound and the Fury was adapted for television in 1955, and several of Faulkner's short stories have been adapted for television, including "An Error in Chemistry" and "The Brooch."

AVOCATIONAL INTEREST: Aviation, raising and training horses, hunting, sailing.

BIOGRAPHICAL/CRITICAL SOURCES—Selected periodicals: *Southern Review,* summer, 1968, autumn, 1972; *Sewanee Review,* winter, 1970, autumn, 1971; *Georgia Review,* summer, 1972; *American Literature,* May, 1973; *Twentieth Century Literature,* July, 1973; *Modern Fiction Studies,* summer, 1973, winter, 1973-74, summer, 1975; *Journal of Popular Culture,* summer, 1973; *New Republic,* September 8, 1973; *Studies in Short Fiction,* summer, 1974.

Selected books: William Faulkner, *The Portable Faulkner,* edited by Malcolm Cowley, Viking, 1946; Harry M. Campbell and Reuel M. Foster, *William Faulkner: A Critical Appraisal,* University of Oklahoma Press, 1951, reprinted, Cooper Square, 1971; Frederick J. Hoffman and Olga W. Vickery, editors, *William Faulkner: Two Decades of Criticism,* Michigan State University Press, 1951; Ward L. Miner, *The World of William Faulkner,* Duke University Press, 1952; Irving Howe, *William Faulkner: A Critical Study,* Random House, 1952; William Van O'Connor, *The Tangled Fire of William Faulkner,* University of Minnesota Press, 1954; Robert Humphrey, *Stream of Consciousness in the Modern Novel,* University of California Press, 1954; Louis Untermeyer, *Makers of the Modern World,* Simon & Schuster, 1955; John Lewis Longley, Jr., *The Tragic Mask: A Study of Faulkner's Heroes,* University of North Carolina Press, 1957; Hyatt H. Waggoner, *William Faulkner: From Jefferson to the World,* University of Kentucky Press, 1959; Faulkner, *Faulkner in the University,* edited by Frederick L. Gwynn and Joseph L. Blotner, University Press of Virginia, 1959; Vickery, *The Novels of William Faulkner: A Critical Interpretation,* Louisiana State University Press, 1959, revised edition, 1964.

Walter J. Slatoff, *Quest for Failure: A Study of William Faulkner,* Cornell University Press, 1960; Hoffman and Vickery, editors, *William Faulkner: Three Decades of Criticism,* Michigan State University Press, 1960; James B. Meriwether, *The Literary Career of William Faulkner: A Bibliographical Study,* Princeton University Press, 1961; Hoffman, *William Faulkner,* Twayne, 1961; Warren Beck, *Man in Motion: Faulkner's Trilogy,* University of Wisconsin Press, 1961; Michael Millgate, *William Faulkner,* Grove, 1961; Stanley Burnshaw, editor, *Varieties of Literary Experience,* New York University Press, 1962; Cleanth Brooks, *The Yoknapatawpha Country,* Yale University Press, 1963; John Faulkner, *My Brother Bill: An Affectionate Reminiscence,* Trident, 1963; Hoffman, *The Modern Novel in America,* Regnery, 1963; Louis D. Rubin, Jr., *Writers of the Modern South: The Faraway Country,* University of Washington Press, 1963; Edmond Volpe, *Reader's Guide to William Faulkner,* Farrar, Straus, 1964; Faulkner, *Faulkner at West Point,* edited by Joseph L. Fant and Robert Ashley, Random House, 1964; W. M. Frohock, *The Novel of Violence in America,* Beacon Press, 1964; Meriwether, *Faulkner and the South,* University Press of Virginia, 1964.

Stanley Edgar Hyman, *Standards: A Chronicle of Books for Our Time,* Horizon Press, 1966; Melvin Backman, *Faulk-*

ner, The Major Years: A Critical Study, Indiana University Press, 1966; Cowley, editor, *The Faulkner-Cowley File: Letters and Memories,* Viking, 1966; Leslie A. Fiedler, *Love and Death in the American Novel,* Stein & Day, 1966; Joseph Gold, *William Faulkner: A Study in Humanism From Metaphor to Discourse,* University of Oklahoma Press, 1966; Millgate, *The Achievement of William Faulkner,* Random House, 1966; Murry C. Falkner, *Falkners of Mississippi: A Memoir,* Louisiana State University Press, 1967; Robert Penn Warren, editor, *Faulkner: A Collection of Critical Essays,* Prentice-Hall, 1967; Lawrence Roger Thompson, *William Faulkner: An Introduction and Interpretation,* Holt, 1967; Conrad Aiken, *Collected Criticism,* Oxford University Press, 1968; Jonathan Baumbach and Arthur Edelstein, editors, *Moderns and Contemporaries: Nine Masters of the Short Story,* Random House, 1968; Meriwether and Millgate, *Lion in the Garden: Interviews With William Faulkner,* Random House, 1968; Richard P. Adams, *Faulkner: Myth and Motion,* Princeton University Press, 1968; Harold Edward Richardson, *William Faulkner: The Journey to Self-Discovery,* University of Missouri Press, 1969; Bernard Dekle, *Profiles of Modern American Authors,* Tuttle, 1969.

Maurice Edgar Coindreau, *The Time of William Faulkner,* University of South Carolina Press, 1971; William Barrett, *Time of Need: Forms of Imagination in the Twentieth Century,* Harper, 1972; Edward Murray, *The Cinematic Imagination: Writers and the Motion Pictures,* Ungar, 1972; John W. Aldridge, *The Devil in the Fire,* Harper's Magazine Press, 1972; Cowley, *The Second Flowering: Works and Days of the Lost Generation,* Viking, 1973; Linda Welshimer Wagner, *William Faulkner: Four Decades of Criticism,* Michigan State University Press, 1973; *Contemporary Literary Criticism,* Gale, Volume 1, 1973, Volume 3, 1975, Volume 6, 1976, Volume 8, 1978, Volume 9, 1978; Dan Vogel, *The Three Masks of American Tragedy,* Louisiana State University Press, 1974; Panthea Reid Broughton, *William Faulkner: The Abstract and the Actual,* Louisiana State University Press, 1974; Blotner, *Faulkner: A Biography,* two volumes, Random House, 1974.

Kenneth H. Baldwin and David K. Kirby, *Individual and Community: Variations on a Theme in American Fiction,* Duke University Press, 1975; John Bassett, editor, *William Faulkner: The Critical Heritage,* Routledge & Kegan Paul, 1975; Warren Beck, *Faulkner,* University of Wisconsin Press, 1976; George H. Wolfe, editor, *Faulkner: Fifty Years After ''The Marble Faun'',* University of Alabama Press, 1976; Meta Carpenter Wilde and Orin Borsten, *A Loving Gentleman: The Love Story of William Faulkner and Meta Carpenter,* Simon & Schuster, 1976; *Authors in the News,* Volume 1, Gale, 1976; David Williams, *Faulkner's Women: The Myth and the Muse,* McGill-Queens University Press, 1977; Blotner, editor, *Selected Letters of William Faulkner,* Random House, 1977; Barbara Fried, *The Spider in the Cup: Yoknapatawpha County's Fall Into the Unknowable,* Harvard University Press, 1978; Cleanth Brooks, *Toward Yoknapatawpha and Beyond,* Yale University Press, 1978.*

(Died July 6, 1962, in Byhalia, Miss.)

* * *

FAUX, Marian 1945-

PERSONAL: Surname is pronounced "fox"; born July 2, 1945, in Norfolk, Va.; daughter of Donald E. (in business) and Lilliam (Walsh) Faux. *Education:* Purdue University, B.A., 1967; graduate study at Roosevelt University. *Home*

and office: 123 West 95th St., New York, N.Y. 10025. *Agent:* Dominick Abel Literary Agency, 498 West End Ave., Apt. 12-C, New York, N.Y. 10024.

CAREER: Robert Snyder Associates, Chicago, Ill., editorial assistant, 1967-68; Douglas Dunhill, Inc., Chicago, editor, 1968-70; Follett Publishing Co., Chicago, senior editor for social science, 1970-74; Henry Regnery Co., Chicago, senior editor, 1973-75; free-lance editor and writer, 1975—. *Member:* Freelance Editor's Association.

WRITINGS: Drying, Curing, and Smoking Food, Grosset, 1977; (with Marjabelle Stewart) *The Top: Getting There and Staying There,* St. Martin's, 1979.

WORK IN PROGRESS: A business book, for Monarch; research for a book on social issues concerning women.

AVOCATIONAL INTERESTS: Reading, collecting American first editions, ballet, theater, travel (Western Europe, Mexico, Virgin Islands).

* * *

FEARS, Gerald

PERSONAL: Born in Kokomo, Ind.; son of Clifton (a laborer) and Marguerita (Jones) Fears; married Francisca Madayag Balagot (a department store manager), May 9, 1953; children: Clarita Ysias, Vilma, Noel. *Education:* Attended secondary schools in Marion, Ind. *Politics:* Independent. *Religion:* Catholic. *Home address:* 1/4-Mile Badger Rd., Fairbanks, Alaska 99707. *Office:* KFAR Radio-TV, P.O. Box 910, Fairbanks, Alaska 99707.

CAREER: U.S. Air Force, career officer, 1947-74; retiring as master sergeant; KFAR Radio-TV, Fairbanks, Alaska, news director, 1974—. Advisory board member of Fairbanks Comprehensive Alcoholism Program; member of Fairbanks Council on Alcoholism. *Member:* Farthest North Press Club, Lions Club. *Awards, honors:* Commendation Medal.

WRITINGS: Boom, Cash, and Balderdash: A Different Look at Fairbanks During Pipeline Construction, foreword by Lowell Thomas, Jr., That New Publishing Co., 1978. Contributor of articles to *Tundra Times, Goldpanner,* and other newspapers and magazines. Editor, *Goldpanner.*

WORK IN PROGRESS: How Much Time for a Lost Soul?, a book on alcoholism.

SIDELIGHTS: Fears had always planned on becoming a journalist. During his high school days he wrote his first story on the death of black musician Fats Waller, and later earned money by publishing a community paper. After graduation, Fears enlisted in the Air Force and became a military journalist in Fairbanks, Alaska.

Boom, Cash, and Balderdash, a collection of his commentaries describing Fairbanks, and its history and industrial development, was written after Fears decided to make Fairbanks his home. "It's ugly, but sometimes it's beautiful," Fears said of Fairbanks. "It's cold but sometimes it's pleasant. . . . It's a town full of villagers, but sometimes it's a village full of townfolk," he continued. These contrasts are also evident in the history of Fairbanks. "It's as old as yesterday, but often it's as young as day after tomorrow," Fears noted. He explained that although Fairbanks is seventy years old, "and that's considered old in Alaska," the city is still relatively "young" in terms of industrial development.

According to Fears, Fairbanks lacks major industry; the majority of available jobs are in construction, government, and the military. The Alaskan pipeline, Fears explained initially, seemed to offer potential for long-term industrial growth. Construction of the pipeline brought "boom times," a large number of high-paying construction and engineering jobs, and also an influx of people into the city. The population of Fairbanks grew from 18,000 people in 1970 to 50,000 inhabitants in 1978. Inflation increased also. After the pipeline construction ended, Fears noted, the number of people in Fairbanks remained high, but few new industries were present as a result of the pipeline to support the population and the vast economic growth of the city. Looking at the twenty percent unemployment rate and recessionary trends that followed completion of the pipeline, Fears concluded that the pipeline produced more long-ranging economic problems than benefits.

BIOGRAPHICAL/CRITICAL SOURCES: Fairbanks News-Miner, June 25, 1977, April 16, 1978, April 17, 1978, April 18, 1978; *Kokomo Tribune,* May 14, 1978, *Marion* (Ind.) *Chronicle Tribune,* April 16, 1978.

* * *

FECHER, Charles A(dam) 1917-

PERSONAL: Surname rhymes with "stretcher"; born November 1, 1917, in Baltimore, Md.; son of Adam (a laborer) and Elizabeth (Hanna) Fecher; married Muriel Burmeister, September 19, 1953; children: Mary Elizabeth, Charlotte Ann. *Politics:* Democrat. *Religion:* Roman Catholic. *Home:* 5625 Ready Ave., Baltimore, Md. 21212. *Office:* Archdiocese of Baltimore, 320 Cathedral St., Baltimore, Md. 21201.

CAREER: Globe Venetian Blind Corp., Baltimore, Md., service manager, 1946-52; General Automatic Products (manufacturers), Baltimore, Md., advertising manager, 1953-61; Foremost Graphic Services (printers), Baltimore, Md., office manager, 1961-63; Archdiocese of Baltimore, Baltimore, Md., administrator, 1963—. *Awards, honors:* Awards from Catholic Press Association, 1977 and 1978, for weekly column, "Books in Review."

WRITINGS: The Philosophy of Jacques Maritain, Newman Press, 1953; *Parish Council Committee Guide,* National Council of Catholic Men, 1970; *Mencken: A Study of His Thought,* Knopf, 1978. Contributor of articles and reviews to religious magazines. Book editor and author of column "Books in Review" for *Baltimore Catholic Review,* 1969—.

WORK IN PROGRESS: A novel.

SIDELIGHTS: Fecher comments: "The nature of my job has involved me very much locally—and to some degree nationally—with all the changes that have taken place in the Catholic church since the Second Vatican Council, and much of my writing has dealt with this. The Second Vatican Council had the effect of dividing the church into two armed camps, liberals and conservatives, and I belong very definitely in the liberal camp. That is to say, I am in favor of most (though not all) of the changes and believe that they were long overdue. Unfortunately they also brought a lot of clowns and zanies out of the woodwork, and some of their nonsensical ideas are still with us; it will take a long time to live them down."

AVOCATIONAL INTERESTS: English literature, philosophy, classical music.

BIOGRAPHICAL/CRITICAL SOURCES: New York Times, May 16, 1978.

FEDIN, Konstantin A(lexandrovich) 1892-1977

PERSONAL: Born February 27, 1892, in Saratov, Russia. *Education:* Attended Moscow Commercial Institute. *Office:* U.S.S.R. Writers' Union, 52 Ul. Vorovskogo, Moscow, U.S.S.R.

CAREER: Interned in Germany, 1914-18; employed by Commissariat of Education; journalist and war correspondent during Russian civil war; full-time writer, 1921-77. Deputy to U.S.S.R. Supreme Soviet. *Member:* Writers' Union of U.S.S.R. (first secretary, 1959-71; chairman, 1971-77), Union of Soviet Writers (member of Secretariat, 1953-77), U.S.S.R. Academy of Sciences, Soviet-German Cultural and Friendship Society (chairman), Deutsche Akademie der Kuenste, Moscow Union of Soviet Writers (chairman, 1955-59). *Awards, honors:* Received Order of Lenin and Order of Red Banner of Labor; named Hero of Socialist Labor, 1967; honorary doctorate from Humbolt University; awarded Silver Medal of World Peace Council.

WRITINGS—In English: *Goroda i gody,* [Moscow], 1924, translation by Michael Scammell published as *Cities and Years,* Dell, 1962; *Sanatorii Arktur,* [Moscow], 1940, translation by O. Shartse published as *Santorium Arktur,* Foreign Language Publishing (Moscow), 1957; *Pervye radosti,* [Moscow], 1946, translation by Hilda Kazanina published as *Early Joys,* Foreign Language Publishing, 1948, Vintage Books, 1960; *Neobyknovennoe leto,* [Moscow], 1949, translation by Margaret Wettlin published as *No Ordinary Summer,* Foreign Language Publishing, 1950; (with others) *Maxim Gorky, Vladimir Mayakovsky, Alexei Tolstoy, Konstantin Fedin on the Art and Craft of Writing,* translated by Alex Miller, Progress Publishing (Moscow), 1972.

Other works: *Pustyr* (stories; title means "The Wasteland"), [Moscow], 1923; *Bratya* (title means "The Brothers"), [Moscow], 1928; *Povesti i rasskazy,* [Moscow], 1936; *Gorkii sredi nas* (title means "Gorky Among Us"), two volumes, [Moscow], 1943-44; *Izbrannye proizvedeniia,* [Moscow], 1947; *Carp,* edited by G. A. Birkett, Oxford University Press, 1950; *Ia byl akterom,* [Moscow], 1956; *Pisatel, iskusstvo, vremia* (essays), [Moscow], 1957, 3rd edition, 1973; *Fedin und Deutschland,* Aufbau-Verlag, 1962; *Koster,* [Moscow], 1962; *Kak my pishem,* Moscow, 1966; *Malenkie romany, povesti, rasskazy,* [Moscow], 1975; (contributor) *Slovo k molodym,* [Moscow], 1975. Also author of *Anna Timofsevna,* 1922; *Narovcatskaja chronika,* 1926; *Transvaal,* 1927; *Bakunin v Drezdene,* 1928; *Pokhishchenie Evropy* (title means "The Rape of Europe"), two volumes, 1933-35; *Ispytanie,* 1942; *Davno i nedavno,* 1947; *Rasskazy mnogikh let,* 1957; *Sobranii sochinenii* (collected works).

Work represented in anthologies, including *Great Soviet Short Stories,* 1962. Contributor to *Atlantic* and other periodicals.

SIDELIGHTS: Martin Weil discussed Fedin's contribution to Soviet literature: "While living under a system not known for fostering artistic freedom, [Fedin] succeeded in creating works of widely recognized artistic merit. . . . While evincing the optimism about Soviet life that characterized members of [the] officially approved school [of Soviet Realism], Mr. Fedin avoided the sentimentalism and woodenly simplistic psychology that plagued the work of many of them."

OBITUARIES: New York Times, July 18, 1977; *Washington Post,* July 18, 1977.*

(Died July 15, 1977, in the Soviet Union)

FEELEY, Pat(ricia Falk) 1941-

PERSONAL: Born January 31, 1941, in San Francisco, Calif.; daughter of Mark M. (an aviator and engineer) and Ina (Wilson) Falk; married Peter James Feeley, October 16, 1965 (divorced, 1967); children: Mary Carole. Education: Stanford University, A.B., 1963. Politics: "Disillusioned Democrat." Religion: "Christian, I hope." Home address: Morehouse Lane, Darien, Conn. 06820. Agent: Hy Cohen Literary Agency Ltd., 111 West 57th St., New York, N.Y. 10019. Office: Patricia Falk Feeley, Inc., 52 Vanderbilt Ave., New York, N.Y. 10017.

CAREER: Editor, associated with Sunset, Menlo Park, Calif., 1964-66, National Academy of Sciences, Washington, D.C., 1966-68, American University, Washington, D.C., 1968-69, Oxford University Press, New York City, 1969-71, Sports Illustrated, and Fortune Book Clubs, New York City, 1972-73, Ballantine Books, Inc., New York City, 1973, and Harper Magazine Press, New York City, 1974; Patricia Falk Feeley, Inc., New York City, literary agent, 1975—. Member: Independent Literary Agents Association, Authors Guild, Authors League of America.

WRITINGS: Best Friend (novel), Dutton, 1977; (with Katherine B. Archer) Perfect Needlepoint Projects, St. Martin's, 1977.

WORK IN PROGRESS: Cautionary Tales, essays.

SIDELIGHTS: Pat Feeley remarks: "I wrote Best Friend when the client for whom I'd devised the plot angrily declined to do it. I wrote Needlepoint because I needed it, and nothing like it was available. I am writing essays because I'm interested in the confusion that's resulted from the decline of manners." Avocational interests: Gardening.

*   *   *

FEENEY, Leonard 1897-1978

PERSONAL: Born February 15, 1897, in Lynn, Mass. Education: Woodstock College, M.A., 1927; further graduate study at Weston College, 1927-29, Wadham College and Campion Hall, Oxford, and the Sorbonne, University of Paris. Home and office: St. Benedict Center, Still River, Mass. 01467.

CAREER: Entered Society of Jesus (Jesuits), 1914, ordained Roman Catholic priest, 1928, excommunicated, 1953, excommunication removed, 1972; served tertianship at St. Beuno's College, North Wales; Boston College, Boston, Mass., 1931-36, began as lecturer, became professor of English; America magazine, New York, N.Y., literary editor, 1936-40; St. Benedict Center, Cambridge, Mass., director, 1939-41; founder and superior of Slaves of the Immaculate Heart of Mary, Cambridge and Still River, Mass., 1949-78. Lecturer. Instructor at Weston College. Member: Catholic Poetry Society of America (president, 1940-42).

WRITINGS—Poetry: (Editor) Poems for Memory: An Anthology for High School Students, Loyola University Press, 1925; In Towns and Little Towns: A Book of Poems, America Press, 1927, 4th edition, 1943; Riddle and Reverie, Macmillan, 1933; Boundaries, Macmillan, 1935; Song for a Listener, Macmillan, 1936; Your Second Childhood: Verses, Bruce Publishing Co., 1945.

Other: Fish on Friday, and Other Sketches, Sheed, 1934; Elizabeth Seton: An American Woman, America Press, 1938, published as Mother Seton: An American Woman, Dodd, 1947, revised edition published as Mother Seton: Saint Elizabeth of New York (1774-1821), Ravengate, 1975; You'd Better Come Quietly: Three Sketches, Some Outlines and Additional Notes, Sheed, 1939, reprinted, 1970; Survival Till Seventeen: Some Portraits of Early Ideas, Sheed, 1941; The Leonard Feeney Omnibus: A Collection of Prose and Verse, Old and New, Sheed, 1943; London Is a Place, Ravengate, 1951; Bread of Life, St. Benedict Center, 1952. Also co-author with Nathalia Crane of The Ark and the Alphabet, 1939.

Contributor to magazines.

SIDELIGHTS: Leonard Feeney's belief that only Roman Catholics could achieve salvation embroiled him in controversy. Prior to the Second Vatican Council, the Roman Catholic church had officially taught that salvation was limited to members of their faith, but even conservative clergymen granted that there were exceptions. After the church hierarchy had repudiated the hard-line doctrine, Feeney continued to cling to it, thus angering religious officials. In 1949 Archbishop Richard Cushing suspended him, and the Vatican excommunicated him in 1953 for refusing to meet with the Pope.

After he was excommunicated, Feeney maintained his ties with St. Benedict Center, a gathering place for Catholic students, and founded a religious order, The Slaves of the Immaculate Heart of Mary. Feeney lived with his followers at a farm commune, established in 1958 in Stillwater, Massachusetts. His adherents were called Feeneyites. Attired in black and white, they journeyed around the country, preaching and selling literature and books written by Feeney. The Feeneyites were often treated scornfully because some of the handbills and placards they distributed were anti-Semitic in tone.

During the sixties and seventies, the Roman Catholic church became more tolerant of both its liberal and conservative wings. Acting on a plea from Cardinal Humberto Medeiros, Pope Paul VI secretly removed Feeney's excommunication on November 22, 1972. There is no indication that Feeney ever changed his position that non-Catholics were damned. A year after the excommunication had been revoked, he said: "We wish to inform our spiritual fathers and our fellow Catholics that there can be no compromise. We still profess the same faith, out of which no one at all can be saved, as we did a quarter-century ago."

Writing after Feeney's death, Avery Dulles described the priest's early career. Dulles, who had worked with Feeney at the St. Benedict Center in 1946, called him a superb orator, a brilliant conversationalist, and a sound theologian. Although he could not understand why Feeney later committed himself to such a rigid stand, Dulles did make some speculations: "Perhaps Father Feeney was somewhat embittered by his encounters with the non-Catholic universities about him; perhaps he was fatigued by his arduous apostolate and overtaxed by his poor health; perhaps, also, he was led into doctrinal exaggeration by his own mercurial poetic temperament. Then again, he and others may have been somewhat intoxicated by the dramatic successes of the Center and too much isolated from opinions coming from outside their own narrow circle. It occurs to me also that the religious enthusiasm of some of Father Feeney's convert disciples may have led him further than he would have gone on his own."

Whatever the reasons for Feeney's dogmatic stand, Dulles regretted that obituaries had focused only on the controversy that had surrounded him. Dulles offered these words in eulogy: "In an age of accommodation and uncertainty, he went to extremes in order to avoid the very appearance of compromise. With unstinting generosity he placed all his talents and energies in the service of the faith as he saw it."

BIOGRAPHICAL/CRITICAL SOURCES: Time, October 14, 1974; *Commonweal,* January 7, 1977.

OBITUARIES: New York Times, February 1, 1978; *Washington Post,* February 3, 1978; *America,* February 25, 1978.*

(Died January 30, 1978, in Ayer, Mass.)

* * *

FEINBERG, Bea
(Cynthia Freeman)

PERSONAL: Born in New York, N.Y.; married; children: one son, one daughter. *Education:* Attended the University of California. *Residence:* San Francisco, Calif. *Address:* c/o Arbor House Publishing Co., Inc., 641 Lexington Ave., New York, N.Y. 10022.

CAREER: Writer. Worked as an interior designer.

WRITINGS—Under pseudonym Cynthia Freeman: *A World Full of Strangers* (novel), Arbor House, 1975; *Fairytales* (novel), Arbor House, 1977.

WORK IN PROGRESS: A novel.

SIDELIGHTS: Bea Feinberg's first novel, *A World Full of Strangers,* related the story of a Jew from New York's Lower East Side who goes to great lengths to conceal his ethnic background—including such measures as changing his name, forbidding his wife to tell their son about his heritage, and even indulging in some anti-Semitism himself. Dubbing the book a "Jewish soap opera," Gilbert Millstein dismissed the plot as "preposterous": "Many Jews have, indeed, changed their names and concealed the fact that they are Jewish. But I never heard of one carrying on against Jews in the manner of David Resinetsky-Reid." Of the book's mood and style, Millstein wrote: "It is a novel of singular, if not intentional, innocence. Its writing is of a primitive directness—lush here, bromidic there and so heartfelt that it wore me out."

In *Fairytales,* Feinberg switches to the political milieu and spins the tale of Dominic Rossi, whose ambition to be senator from California is wrecked by a wife who yearns for all his attention. A reviewer for *Publishers Weekly* described the book as "long, maudlin, strewn with familial contretemps," and noted that *Fairytales* "plays on our sympathy for the emotionally abandoned in general and political wives in particular."

BIOGRAPHICAL/CRITICAL SOURCES: New York Times Book Review, November 14, 1976; *Publishers Weekly,* May 30, 1977.*

* * *

FELDMAN, Abraham J(ehiel)   1893-1977

PERSONAL: Born June 28, 1893, in Kiev, Ukraine; came to United States in 1906; son of Jehiel and Elka (Rubin) Feldman; married Helen Bloch, June 2, 1918; children: Daniel Bloch, Joan Helen (Mrs. Jerome W. Mecklenburger), Ella (Mrs. Charles Norwood). *Education:* Hebrew Union College (now Hebrew Union College—Jewish Institute of America), B.H.L., 1913, Rabbi, 1918; University of Cincinnati, A.B., 1917. *Home:* 145 Ballard Dr., Hartford, Conn. 06119. *Office:* 701 Farmington Ave., Hartford, Conn. 06119.

CAREER: Rabbi of Free Synagogue, New York, N.Y., 1918-19, Congregation Children of Israel, Athens, Ga., 1919-20, and Reform Congregation Keneseth Israel, Philadelphia, Pa., 1920-25; Congregation Beth Israel, Hartford, Conn., rabbi, 1925-68, rabbi emeritus, 1968-77. Lecturer in

Old Testament, Hartford Theological Seminary, beginning 1954. National co-chairman, Consultative Council on Desegregation, 1957-59; chairman of Connecticut Advisory Committee to U.S. Commission on Civil Rights, 1958-60. Incorporator, United War and Community Funds of Connecticut; director of Jewish Social Services of Mt. Sinai Hospital, Julius Hartt Musical Foundation and Hartt College of Music, Hebrew Home for the Aged, Hartford Jewish Foundation, and Hartford Jewish Community Center. Member of executive board, Union of American-Hebrew Congregations, 1945-48, 1958; member of board of directors and executive committee, National Jewish Welfare Board; member of executive board, American Jewish Committee; trustee and national co-chairman on religious groups, People to People Federation. Founder and regent of University of Hartford.

MEMBER: Central Conference of American Rabbis (president, 1947-49), B'nai B'rith, Masons, Phi Epsilon Pi (national chaplain, 1938). *Awards, honors:* D.D., Hebrew Union College, 1944; S.T.D., Trinity College, 1953; LL.D., Hillyer College, 1953; H.H.D., Hartt College of Music, 1953; Americanism and Civic Award, Connecticut Valley Council of B'nai B'rith, 1955; George Washington Medal of Honor, Freedoms Foundation, 1956; university medal, University of Hartford, 1968; City of Hartford Medal, 1968; National Human Relations Award, National Conference of Christians and Jews, 1969; D.Litt., Parsons College, 1969.

WRITINGS: God's Fools: Sixteen Discourses, Bloch Publishing, 1924; *The Faith of a Liberal Jew,* Beth Israel Pulpit (Hartford, Conn.), 1931; *"Hills to Climb": Eight Discourses,* Beth Israel Pulpit, 1931; *Sources of Jewish Inspiration,* [Hartford], 1934; *The Adventure of Judaism: Three Confirmation Services,* Behrman's Jewish Book House, 1937; *The American Jew: A Study of Backgrounds,* Bloch Publishing, 1937, revised edition, 1959; *A Companion to the Bible,* Behrman's Jewish Book House, 1939; *The Rabbi and His Early Ministry* (collected lectures), Bloch Publishing, 1941; *Confirmation: Twenty-Five Confirmation Services,* Bloch Publishing, 1948; (compiler) *Choice Passages in the Holy Scriptures: A Teacher's Guide,* [Hartford], 1965; *The American Reform Rabbi: A Profile of a Profession,* Bloch Publishing, 1965; *Words of My Mouth, Being Excerpts From a Rabbi's Messages to His Congregation at Annual Meetings, 1926-1968,* Bloch Publishing, 1969. Also author of *Remember the Days of Old: An Outline History of the Congregation Beth Israel,* 1943. Writer of pamphlets on religious topics and temple reports. Contributor to *Universal Jewish Encyclopedia* and *The Twentieth Century Encyclopedia of Religious Knowledge.* Founder, 1929, and editor of *Jewish Ledger.*

SIDELIGHTS: Feldman once stated that, as a rabbi, he believed his mission was "to speak the word of God and the message of religion in the hope of influencing human behavior in every sphere."

OBITUARIES: New York Times, July 23, 1977.*

(Died July 21, 1977, in West Hartford, Conn.)

* * *

FENN, Henry Courtenay   1894-1978

OBITUARY NOTICE: Born February 26, 1894, in Peiping (now Peking), China; died July 22, 1978, in Kennett Square, Pa. Sinologist, educator, and author. Best known for helping originate the "blitz" method of teaching Chinese, Fenn taught at several schools before joining the Yale Institute of Far Eastern Languages. He directed there from 1952 to 1962. Later he established the Chinese language department at Dartmouth University and served as acting chairman of the department of Chinese and Japanese at Washington University in St. Louis. His books include *Syllabus of Chinese History and Culture* and the widely used *Speak Mandarin.* Obituaries and other sources: *Who's Who in America,* 39th edition, Marquis, 1976; *New York Times,* July 26, 1978.

* * *

FERMOR, Patrick Leigh 1915-

PERSONAL: Born February 11, 1915, in London, England; son of Lewis Leigh and Muriel Eileen Taaffe (Ambler) Fermor; married Joan Eyres-Monsell. *Education:* Attended boys' school in Canterbury, England. *Address:* c/o John Murray, 50 Albemarle St., London W.1, England.

CAREER: Writer; world traveler. Traveled extensively in Europe, Greece, and Balkans, 1935-39; enlisted in Irish Guards, 1939; served as second lieutenant in Intelligence Corps in Middle East and liaison officer in Greek headquarters in Albania; officer of British Military Mission stationed in Greece and Crete, 1940; commander of guerilla operations in German-occupied Crete, 1942-44, disguised as shepherd, led successful expedition to capture German general; became Major in 1943; team commander of Special Allied-Airborne Reconnaissance Force in North Germany, 1945; deputy director of British Institute in Athens, 1945-46; traveled in Caribbean, Central America, Africa, India, and Far East. *Member:* Travellers' Club, White's Club, Pratt's Club, Special Forces, Cercle Huysmans. *Awards, honors:* Officer of the Order of the British Empire, 1943; Distinguished Service Order, 1944; Heineman Foundation Prize for literature, 1950, and Kemsley Prize, 1951, both for *The Traveller's Tree;* Duff Cooper Prize, for *Mani.*

WRITINGS—All published by J. Murray, except as indicated: *The Traveller's Tree,* 1950; (translator) Colette, *Chance Acquaintances,* 1952; *A Time to Keep Silence,* 1953; *The Violins of St. Jacques,* 1953; (translator) George Psychoundakis, *The Cretan Runner,* 1955; *Mani* (Book Society's Choice), 1958; *Roumeli,* 1966; *A Time of Gifts,* 1977. Also author, with Stephen Spender, of *The Paintings of Niko Ghika,* and translator of *Forever Ulysses* (Book-of-the-Month-Club selection), 1937. Contributor of articles to various periodicals, including *Atlantic, Reader's Digest,* and *Holiday.*

WORK IN PROGRESS: A sequel to *A Time of Gifts,* describing a journey on foot from Rotterdam to Constantinople, from 1933-35.

SIDELIGHTS: A Time of Gifts was written from notes made by Fermor during his travels in the 1930's. Reviewing the book, Raymond A. Sokolov commented that Fermor's keen sense of observation came through in his "long breath imagery." The reviewer wrote: "The dialogue captures with wonderful economy the feel of cross-cultural misunderstanding familiar to everyone who travels. Leigh Fermor also records similarly direct and historically irreplaceable impressions of Central European Jews waking up to Hitler's menace, of the last days of the charming, Hapsburgian petty nobility and of the pre-Communist landscape of Hungary and Rumania."

AVOCATIONAL INTERESTS: Ancient and modern history and languages, religion, painting, architecture.

BIOGRAPHICAL/CRITICAL SOURCES: New York Times Book Review, November 27, 1977.

FERRIER, Lucy
See PENZLER, Otto

* * *

FERRIS, Norman (Bernard) 1931-

PERSONAL: Born November 29, 1931, in Richmond, Va.; son of Paul Whyte (a newspaper editor) and Elizabeth (Gillette) Ferris; married Frances Ragsdale, September, 1951 (divorced, June, 1960); married Kathleen Richard (a teacher), February 21, 1961; children: Allison, Cheryl, Adrienne Ferris Sartain, Kennedy, Julie. *Education:* Lamar College, A.A., 1951; George Washington University, B.A., 1953; Emory University, M.A., 1957, Ph.D., 1962. *Religion:* Unitarian-Universalist. *Home address:* Route 8, Box 178, Compton Rd., Murfreesboro, Tenn. 37130. *Office:* Box 187, Middle Tennessee State University, Murfreesboro, Tenn. 37132.

CAREER: Middle Tennessee State University, Murfreesboro, assistant professor, 1962-65, associate professor, 1965-69, professor of history, 1969—. Secretary of Rutherford County Democratic Party Executive Committee, 1972-78. *Military service:* U.S. Naval Reserve, 1953-69, active duty, 1953-56; became lieutenant commander.

MEMBER: American Historical Association, Organization of American Historians, National Historical Society, American Association of University Professors (president of Tennessee conference, 1978-80), American Civil Liberties Union, Society for Historians of American Foreign Relations, Southern Historical Association. *Awards, honors:* Pulitzer Prize nomination, 1977, for *The Trent Affair.*

WRITINGS: (Contributor) James I. Robert, Allan Nevins, and B. I. Wiley, editors, *Civil War History: A Bibliography,* two volumes, Louisiana State University Press, 1967; (contributor) Richard M. McMurray and James I. Robertson, editors, *Rank and File,* Presidio Press, 1976; *Desperate Diplomacy: William H. Seward's Foreign Policy, 1861,* University of Tennessee Press, 1976; *The Trent Affair: A Diplomatic Crisis,* University of Tennessee Press, 1977.

WORK IN PROGRESS: The third volume in a series on Seward's diplomacy during the American Civil War, University of Tennessee Press, 1980; a biography of William H. Seward; a novel dealing with the late 1940's.

SIDELIGHTS: Ferris told *CA:* "While working on my doctoral dissertation during the late 1950's, I learned some things about the brilliant nineteenth-century humanitarian statesman William Henry Seward that impelled me to embark on a study of his life and work. Although most historians who deal with Seward tend to treat him as a supporting actor in a drama which features Abraham Lincoln in the 'star' role, it became apparent to me from my work with historical sources that Seward was a far more important figure in the development of American civilization during the era in which both men lived.

"I wrote my first book-length historical narrative, *Desperate Diplomacy,* for the purpose of demonstrating that the traditional historical accounts of Seward's early diplomacy, while he served as Lincoln's secretary of state at the start of the American Civil War, were inaccurate and incomplete. Although I was, in effect, suggesting that specialists in the field were, almost without exception, wrong in their interpretations of Seward's early diplomacy, reviewers were surprisingly receptive to my message. Having spent over ten years working on the book, mainly in the evenings and during vacations, I was gratified that most reviewers considered the book an important contribution to the history of American diplomacy, and I was even happier that most commentators thought it was well written.

"By the time *Desperate Diplomacy* was ready for a publisher, I had also done most of the research necessary to bring out a sequel to that volume. My second book, *The Trent Affair,* was published in 1977. Less revisionary than its predecessor, it was designed to show how a serious diplomatic crisis, one in which the United States almost went to war with Great Britain, came about and how it was resolved through adroit diplomacy, mostly by W. H. Seward. The University of Tennessee Press nominated the book for a Pulitzer Prize. I was encouraged to continue writing.

"The third volume in the series treating Seward's Civil War diplomacy will probably be ready for publication in about two more years. It will be written, as were the other two, on weekends, sometimes in the evenings, and mainly during academic vacation periods. Most of the necessary research for this book has been done, so that what remains is almost entirely literary composition.

"While continuing the story of Seward's work as secretary of state, which will probably run to five volumes, I am beginning a far more ambitious project—a full-scale biography, which I hope will capture Seward's elusive but rewarding personality and recall his important ideas on such subjects as human rights, international relations, the development of economic and social institutions, and the future of democratic politics."

AVOCATIONAL INTERESTS: Operating his small cattle farm.

*   *   *

FICKEN, Frederick A(rthur)   1910-1978

OBITUARY NOTICE: Born August 13, 1910, in Moore's Hill, Ind.; died December 20, 1978, in New York, N.Y. Educator and author. Ficken was a professor at the University of Tennessee before he came to New York University in 1959. He served as chairman of the mathematics department there until his retirement in 1973. Ficken authored two books in his field and edited *American Mathematical Monthly* from 1962 to 1966. Obituaries and other sources: *American Men and Women of Science: The Physical and Biological Sciences,* 12th edition, Bowker, 1971-73; *Who's Who in America,* 39th edition, Marquis, 1976; *New York Times,* December 23, 1978.

*   *   *

FIELDS, Howard K(enneth)   1938-

PERSONAL: Born March 11, 1938, in Jenkins, Ky.; son of William G. (a miner) and Cordia A. (Knight) Fields; married Cheryl M. Beatty (a journalist), May 20, 1967. *Education:* Bradley University, B.A., 1961. *Home and office:* 716 South Wayne St., Arlington, Va. 22204.

CAREER: Farmington Bugle, Farmington, Ill., owner and publisher, 1961-64; United Press International, reporter in Minneapolis, Minn., 1964-65, Detroit, Mich., 1965-66, Chicago, Ill., 1966-69, and Washington, D.C., 1969-76; freelance writer, 1976—. Reporter for *Peoria Journal Star,* 1961-62.

WRITINGS: High Crimes and Misdemeanors (nonfiction), Norton, 1978. Contributor to *Kitchens and Bathrooms* of "Home Repair and Improvement" series, Time-Life. Contributor of articles and photographs to national magazines and newspapers, including *Nation's Business, Washingtonian, Congressional Quarterly,* and *Washington Post.*

WORK IN PROGRESS: Perqs, on Congressional perquisites and their effect on the ability of members of Congress to function effectively.

SIDELIGHTS: Fields told *CA:* "I am a free-lance writer specializing in Congress, travel, consumer affairs, the environment, and politics. I have a desire to write political novels, when I can afford to be that frivolous.

"*High Crimes and Misdemeanors* focuses solely on the inquiry into the impeachment of President Nixon, which, regardless of all else written, was the single activity that drove him from office. The book describes the approach to the House Judiciary Committee's conclusion that Nixon should be impeached, concluding that the conduct of the inquiry was rancorous, haphazard and almost failed several times, but that its conclusion nonetheless was justified. The inquiry proved that the Constitution still works. Strangely enough, the book is the only readily available source for the wording of the articles of impeachment and the breakdown of the votes cast on them."

Of his background, Fields wrote: "I was born number eight of eleven children in the mountains of eastern Kentucky. My father went blind when I was thirteen. I suppose that background is responsible for whatever motivation I have."

AVOCATIONAL INTERESTS: Foreign travel, flying, most participation sports.

*   *   *

FINLAY, Ian Hamilton   1925-

PERSONAL: Born October 28, 1925, in Nassau, Bahamas; married; children: Keck, Ailie. *Residence:* Stonypath, Dunsyre, Lanarkshire, Scotland.

CAREER: Writer of poetry, concrete poetry, and short stories; creator of poem-objects; Wild Hawthorn Press, Dunsyre, Lanarkshire, Scotland, publisher, 1961—. Exhibited concrete poetry at Axiom Gallery, London, 1968, Scottish National Gallery of Modern Art, 1972, and National Maritime Museum, Greenwich, 1973. *Awards, honors:* Scottish Arts Council bursary, 1966, 1967, 1968; Atlantic-Richfield Award, 1968.

WRITINGS—All poetry, except as indicated: *The Sea-Bed and Other Stories* (short stories), Castle Wynd Printers (Edinburgh), 1958; *The Dancers Inherit the Party: Selected Poems,* Migrant Press (Worcester), 1960, enlarged edition, Fulcrum Press, 1969; *Glasgow Beasts, an a Burd Haw, an Inseks, an, a Fush,* Wild Hawthorn Press, 1961; *Telegrams From my Windmill,* Wild Hawthorn Press, 1964; *Earthship,* Wild Hawthorn Press, 1965; *Headlines, Eavelines,* Openings Press (Corsham, Wiltshire), 1966; *6 Small Songs in 3's,* Wild Hawthorn Press, 1966; *Tea-Leaves and Fishes,* Wild Hawthorn Press, 1966; *Stonechats,* Wild Hawthorn Press, 1967; *Canal Game,* Fulcrum Press, 1967; *Air Letters,* Tarasque Press (Nottingham), 1968; *Lanes,* Wild Hawthorn Press, 1969.

30 Signatures to Silver Catches, Tarasque, 1971; *Poems to Hear and See* Macmillan (New York), 1971; (with Gordon Huntly) *A Sailor's Calendar: A Miscellany,* Something Else (New York), 1971; *The Olsen Excerpts,* U. Breger (Goettingen), 1971; *Honey by the Water,* Black Sparrow Press, 1973; (with Martin Fidler) *The Wild Hawthorn Wonder Book of Boats,* Wild Hawthorn Press, 1975.

Other ("standing poems," cards, broadsides, portfolios, pamphlets, visual poems, and poem-objects); all published by Wild Hawthorn Press, except as noted: *Rapel: Ten Fauve and Suprematist Poems,* 1963; *Concertina,* 1963;

Formal Poem, 1963; *Standing Poems 1, 2, 3*, 1963, 1965; *Poster Poem (Le Circus)*, 1964; *Fish-Sheet One*, c. 1964; *Opening Number 3*, Glevum Press (Woodchester), 1965; *First Suprematist Standing Poem*, 1965; *Summer Poem*, 1966; *Autumn Poem*, 1966; *Acrobats*, Tarasque, 1966; *5 Poems*, H. Mayer (Stuttgart), 1966; *Star/Steer* (poem/print), Tarasque, 1966; *Six Small Pears for Eugen Gomringer*, 1966; *Sea-Poppy 1* (poem/print), Tarasque, 1966; *How Blue!*, 1966.

I Lo Lov Love, c. 1967, *Three Blue Lemons*, 1967; *Ajar*, 1967; *La Belle Hollandaise*, 1967; *Land/Sea*, 1967; *Two From the Yard of . . .* , 1967; *The Collected Coaltown of Challenge Tri-kai*, Screwpacket Press, 1968; *The Blue and the Brown: Poems*, Atlantic Richfield and Graphic Arts Typographers, 1968; *Arcady*, Tarasque, 1968; *Marine*, 1968; *Sea-Poppy 2*, 1968; *The Land's Shadow*, 1968; *From "The Analects of 'Fishing News,'"* 1968; *From "Illuminations of 'Fishing News,'"* 1969; *From "Ta Myoika of 'Fishing News,'"* 1969; *A Boatyard*, 1969; *3/3's*, 1969; *Wave*, 1969; (with John Furnival) *After the Russian*, Openings, 1969; *Net/Planet*, 1969; *Point-to-Point*, 1969; *Xmas Star*, 1969; *Poem/Print No. 11*, 1969; *Seams*, 1969; *Four Sails*, 1969.

"Fishing News" News, 1970; *From "The Metamorphoses of 'Fishing News,'"* 1970; *Skylarks*, 1970; *Valses pour Piano*, 1970; *Arcadian Sundials*, 1970; (with Stuart Mills and Simon Cutts) *Allotments*, Tarasque, 1970; *A Waterlily Pool*, 1970; *Still Life With Lemons*, 1970; *Les Hirondelles*, 1970; *A Patch . . .* , 1970; *Sheaves*, 1970; *A Use for Old Beehives*, 1970; *Xmas Rose*, 1970; *The Little Seamstress*, 1970; *Homage to Mozart*, 1970; *Scottish Zulu*, 1970; *The Press*, 1970; (with David Button) *Errata*, 1970; *Evening/Sail*, 1970; *Catameringue*, 1970; *Poem/Print No. 14*, 1970; (with Richard Demarco) *Glossary*, c. 1970; *Boats of Letters*, 1970; *Ian Hamilton Finlay*, with photographs by Diane Tammes, Ceolfrith Press (Sunderland, Scotland), 1970; *Ceolfrith 5*, Ceolfrith Press, 1970; *The Weed Boat Masters Ticket*, Preliminary Test, two parts, Tarasque, 1970-71.

(With Michael Harvey) *Interior/Interieur: Homage to Vuillard*, 1971; *Zulu "Chieftan,"* 1971; *A Memory of Summer*, 1971; *A Sea Street Anthology*, 1971; *Homage to Donald McGill*, 1971; *Flags*, 1971; *The Sign of the Nudge*, 1971; *The Harbour*, 1971; *The Old Nobby*, 1971; *Sail/Waves 1, 2*, 1971; *I Saw Three Ships*, 1971; *Is There A Ship . . .* , 1971; *A Heart Shape*, 1971; *Birch-Bark*, 1971; *Daisies*, 1971; *Book-Flag*, 1971; *The Land's Shadow*, 1971; *Kite*, 1971; *Tree-Shells*, 1971; *Catches*, 1971; *Unicorn*, 1971; *Elegy for "Whimbrel" and "Petrel,"* Sepia Press (Wilsden, Yorkshire), 1971; *Xmas Morn*, 1971; *Street Handout*, Ceolfrith Press, 1971; *Shenval Christmas Poem/Print*, 1971; (with Ian Gardner) *A Rock Rose*, 1971; *Archangel*, 1971; *Seashells*, 1971; *The Little Drummer Boy*, 1971; *Evening/Sail 2*, 1971; *From "An Inland Garden,"* 1971.

Sail/Sundial, 1972; *Prinz Eugen*, 1972; *Sail Wholemeal*, 1972; *Homage to Modern Art*, 1972; *Illustrious*, 1972; *Jibs*, 1972; *The Washington Fountain*, 1972; *Topiary Aircraft Carrier*, 1972; *Homage to E. A. Hormel*, 1972; *F1*, 1972; *The End . . .* , 1972; *Homage to Seurat*, 1972; *Homage to Walter Reekie's Ring Netters*, 1972; *Kite–Estuary Model*, 1972; *Iron Ship*, 1972; *Homage to Jonathan Williams*, 1972; *Blue/Water's/Bark*, 1972; *Spiral Binding*, 1972; *D1*, 1972; *The Sea's/Waves'/Sheaves*, 1972; *Der Tag*, 1972; *Christmas Card*, 1972; *Estuary Cupboards*, 1972.

Neck Tank, 1973; *Arcadia*, 1973; *Butterflies*, 1973; *Trim Here*, 1973; *Mid-Pacific Elements*, 1973; *Bath Roundels*, 1973; *Mower Is Less*, 1973; (with George L. Thompson)

Exercise X, 1973; *Homage to Pop Art*, 1973; *Tea-Card Series*, 1973; *Copyright*, 1973; *Stationary*, 1973; (with Ron Costley) *Schiff*, 1974; (with Simon Cutts and Sydney McK. Glen) *Straiks*, 1974; *Three Sundials*, Rougemont Press (Exeter), 1974; *A Pretty Kettle of Fish*, 1974; (with Karl Torok) *Family Group*, c. 1974; (with Costley) *Airs, Waters, Graces*, 1975; (with Laurie Clark) *So You Want to Be a Panzer Leader*, 1975.

Also author or co-author of *Homage to Robert Lax, Silhouettes, A Calm in a Tea-Cup: After Kate Greenaway, Snow Sail Drop Flake, The Sea's Waves, Rhymes for Lemons, Imitations, Variations, Reflections, Copies, Definitions of Lawns (2): Plan for Projected U-Boat Sculpture, Homage to Malevich, Norfolk Woods, Sailing Barge Redwing, Gourd*, and *Mast of Hankies*. Author of "Ocean Stripe" series and "Canal Stripe" series; editor of *Poor. Old. Tired. Horse.*

SIDELIGHTS: "Finlay is a poet whose experiments in permutations of typography and word combinations have earned him an international reputation with the Concrete poetry movement," said *New York Times Book Review*. Dale McConathy called him "the major concrete poet in English" and credited him with introducing to England and America the Brazilian and German poets who were the chief originators of concrete poetry. Finlay has done this through his magazine, *Poor. Old. Tired. Horse.*, and his Wild Hawthorn Press, founded in 1960 and used for most of his own typographical experimentation.

Jonathan Raban recalled a Sunday supplement story on poets which featured a photograph of Finlay "looking wary and disturbed as he was getting into a rowing boat surrounded by mountains and Scotch mist. His poems are like that," Raban continued, "full of a circumspect, private wit that resists condensation into fulsome generalizations about 'the poet' or into the slick ideologies of movement, underground or otherwise." The poems from *The Dancers Inherit the Party*, a collection written before Finlay's move into concretism, were described by Raban: "Again and again his poems rise to the Alice-like logic of the nursery rhyme; the words take over with a euphoric life of their own, speeded by puns and games and fragments of pure lyrical nonsense."

Finlay's shift to concretism grew in some ways out of this linguistic playfulness, Raban feels. "His fascination with the aural and metrical qualities of the words themselves, his readiness to give language its head and find out where the poem takes him, his discovery of the poem as an area of sheer libidinous play, provide the basic foundations for concrete poetry." Concrete poetry, strictly speaking, conveys its meaning by the placement of words, letters, or symbols in graphic patterns instead of conventional arrangements such as phrases. Finlay's concern for words as entities with their own values may be seen in such works as *Star/Steer*, with the word "star" repeatedly etched on glass to form a curved line from top to bottom, ending in a single etching of the word "steer." He has done the same poem on slate. The use of glass, stone, wood, and other natural elements grew out of his love of nature and resulted in the creation of "Poem-objects." His work has been exhibited at Axiom Gallery in London, the Scottish National Gallery of Modern Art, and the National Maritime Museum at Greenwich. He has sundials at the University of Kent, Canterbury, and in Biggar, Lanarkshire, and has designed poems for the Max Planck Institute in Stuttgart.

Visiting the poet several years ago at Stonypath, his home two hours from Edinburgh, Dale McConathy found the buildings and grounds enlivened by Finlay's poem-objects.

A sign beside the pond where his small son sailed a miniature sailboat read, "Please don't feed the boats." The building housing Wild Hawthorn Press contained a trough of water with the names of different kinds of boats floating in it. A small stone pool had a slab behind it bearing the engraved word "cloud," with a hand pointing up and one pointing down—the reflection of sky, slab, and word creating a kind of poem. McConathy explained: "Somewhere in that relationship—the word—and what it represents is the strength and contradiction of *concrete poetry* that Finlay is exploring."

BIOGRAPHICAL/CRITICAL SOURCES: Times Literary Supplement, June 8, 1967; *Poetry*, May, 1968; *Books and Bookmen*, September, 1968; *Harper's Bazaar*, April, 1969; *London Magazine*, December, 1969; *New York Times Book Review*, April 11, 1971.*

*   *   *

FINLAYSON, Roderick (David) 1904-

PERSONAL: Born April 26, 1904, in Auckland, New Zealand; son of John McLennan (a bank clerk) and Mary Milliken (Cargo) Finlayson; married Ruth Evelyn Taylor, June 3, 1936; children: Mary, Antony, Janice, Denis, Alan, Kathleen. *Education:* Seddon Memorial Technical College, diploma in engineering, 1922; attended Auckland University School of Architecture, 1922-24. *Politics:* "Radical, i.e., grass roots." *Religion:* Roman Catholic. *Home:* 46 McLeod Rd., Weymouth, Manurewa, New Zealand. *Agent:* Dennis McEldownery, Auckland University Press, Auckland, New Zealand.

CAREER: Writer. Architect's assistant in Auckland, New Zealand, 1922-27; worked variously as tobacco grower, seasonal worker, salesman, and free-lance journalist; Department of Education, School Publications Branch, Wellington, New Zealand, writer of school bulletins, 1950-60; Auckland City Council, Auckland, printing assistant, 1958-67; part-time work at Auckland Regional Authority, Auckland. *Military service:* New Zealand Home Guard, 1940-45. *Member:* P.E.N. *Awards, honors:* New Zealand Centennial Prize for short story, "The Totara Tree," 1940.

WRITINGS: Brown Man's Burden (short stories), Unicorn Press, 1938, enlarged edition published as *Brown Man's Burden and Later Stories*, edited and introduced by Bill Pearson, Oxford University Press, 1973; *Our Life in This Land* (essay), Griffin Press, 1940; *Sweet Beulah Land* (short stories), Griffin Press, 1942; *Tidal Creek* (novel), Angus & Robertson, 1948; *The Schooner Came to Atia* (novel), Griffin Press, 1952; (with Joan Smith) *The Maoris of New Zealand* (nonfiction), Oxford University Press, 1959; *The Springing Fern* (juvenile historical fiction), Whitcome & Tombs, 1965, Ocean Books, 1967; *D'Arcy Cresswell* (literary study), Twayne, 1972; *Other Lovers* (three novellas), John McIndoe, 1976.

Work represented in anthologies, including *New Zealand Short Stories*, edited by D. M. Davin, Oxford University Press, 1953; *New Zealand Short Stories*, second series, edited by C. K. Stead, Oxford University Press, 1966. Contributor of short stories to various periodicals, including *Landfall, New Zealand Listener, Auckland Star, Arena*, and *Bulletin*.

WORK IN PROGRESS: A novel, *Letters in an Unknown Code*.

SIDELIGHTS: Roderick Finlayson told *CA:* "My writing centers around the Maori people of New Zealand and all those who reject—or are rejected by—the Big Organisation of modern science with its destructiveness and greedy materialism. As D. H. Lawrence said, 'Make any people mainly rational in their life, and their inner activity will be the activity of destruction.' In 1972 I made a pilgrimage to Europe and Greece, to the sources of former civilization. Now I am active in advocating undisputed Maori control of the remaining tribal lands in the interests of a more civilized society."

Finlayson's early years at his grandmother's house were characterized chiefly by a more-than-tolerant, egalitarian attitude toward people of other races, the sincerity of which is attested to by his prevailing literary theme: The oppression of the Maoris by the *pakeha's* materialism and misplaced values. Frequent visitors to the Cargo home included a black American singer and a Chinese laundryman, observed Bill Pearson, who theorized that Finlayson's resulting approach to writing about the Maoris involved their simpler, "truer" values in contrast to the greedy capitalism of the *pakeha,* the New Zealander of European descent. Pearson praised Finlayson's depiction of "the dignity, humour, and emotional richness of Maori rural life being corroded by . . . the calculator and the clock" and observed that, similar to the Victorian essayists such as Carlyle and Ruskin, Finlayson felt that "salvation would come from the reunion of intellect with intuition and its agent would be the poet, whose appeal to the poetic spirit would awaken a properly religious attitude to Nature and to the land." It was Robert Chapman's feeling that Finlayson, "à la Jean-Jacques Rousseau," portrayed the Maori as a noble savage, while Pearson criticized such an assessment because of the patronization he felt to be basic to this attitude.

Pearson noted the "litheness of style" and "the swift movement" of Finlayson's phraseology which, in a manner similar to Sicilian writer Giovanni Verga, ultimately emphasizes content rather than technique, and also pointed to the comedic elements which Finlayson had so much admired in Pirandello's stories.

"At present I am giving talks on literature and readings to pupils in schools and am planning my 'Memoirs'," Finlayson told *CA.*

AVOCATIONAL INTERESTS: Vegetable gardening, swimming.

BIOGRAPHICAL/CRITICAL SOURCES: Landfall, March, 1953; *Journal of the Polynesian Society,* September, 1958; E. H. McCormick, *New Zealand Literature: A Survey,* Oxford University Press, 1959; Joan Stevens, *The New Zealand Novel 1860-1965,* A. H. & A. W. Reed, 1966; H. Winston Rhodes, *New Zealand Fiction Since 1945,* John McIndoe, 1968; Erik Schwimmer, editor, *The Maori People in the Nineteen-Sixties,* Hurst Publishing, 1968; Wystan Curnow, editor, *Essays on New Zealand Literature,* Heinemann Educational Books, 1973; Roderick Finlayson, *Brown Man's Burden and Later Stories,* edited and introduced by Bill Pearson, Oxford University Press, 1973.

*   *   *

FINNERTY, Adam Daniel 1944-
(A. Daniel McKenna)

PERSONAL: Born May 27, 1944, in Chautauqua, N.Y.; son of John Charles (in U.S. Air Force) and Frances (a teacher; maiden name, Mapes) Finnerty. *Education:* University of Pennsylvania, B.A., 1967, M.A., 1968; Bryn Mawr College, M.S.S., 1972. *Religion:* "Quaker-Catholic." *Home:* 120 West Mt. Airy, Philadelphia, Pa. 19119. *Office:*

Liberty to the Captives, P.O. Box 12236, Philadelphia, Pa. 19144.

CAREER: Horizon House, Philadelphia, Pa., assistant group work supervisor, 1968-69; Horizon House-Jefferson Community Mental Health Center, Philadelphia, group work specialist, 1969-70; City of Philadelphia, intern under deputy health commissioner, 1970-71; Eagleville Drug and Alcohol Rehabilitation Center, Eagleville, Pa., member of school consultation team, 1971-72; Kirkridge Retreat Center, Bangor, Pa., assistant to program director, 1973-74; Shakertown Pledge Group, Philadelphia, director, 1974-75; free-lance writer and consultant, 1975—. Staff director of Liberty to the Captives; co-director of Krowten Associates (consultants). Assistant to director of Montgomery County Opportunity Board, 1966; member of Churchmouse Collective, 1974-77. Conducts workshops and seminars. *Member:* Mental Health Advocacy Association (founder and president, 1970-72).

WRITINGS: (With Charles Funnell) *Exiled: A Draft Counselor's Handbook for the Draft-Age Emigrant,* Resistance Press, 1968; *No More Plastic Jesus: Global Justice and Christian Lifestyle,* Orbis, 1977; *Action for Global Justice,* Orbis, 1979. Contributor to magazines, including *Fellowship, Win, Friends Journal,* and *National Guardian.* Editor of *Mental Health Advocacy Newsletter,* 1970-72, and *Shakertown Pledge Newsletter,* 1974-75.

WORK IN PROGRESS: O'Ryan, M.A., a "thriller-spoof," under pseudonym A. Daniel McKenna; "Henry the Last," a comic play; "Melody," a biographical play.

SIDELIGHTS: Finnerty wrote: "I guess I have to identify myself as very much the 'sixties' activist. I first got involved in social change by going to participate in the Selma to Montgomery march in 1965. From there, I became involved in the Civil Rights and Peace movements—primarily in the Philadelphia area. Concern about Vietnam led me into a deeper understanding of Third World problems. Seeing that many Third World nations cut their own throats by jailing some of their most creative people (often with help from the United States in the form of training and military aid to the dictators), I have recently been most concerned with human rights.

"I started off at age eighteen as an 'Air Force brat' (father was a career enlisted man) who expected to go into corporate management. Then I hit the big city (Philadelphia), got 'radicalized' by the war in Vietnam, and haven't yet recovered. My religious journey has taken me from mainstream Protestantism into a Jesus-freak phase, then an 'esoteric' phase, then a renewal of interest in my Catholic heritage and a discovery that I think like a Quaker (and enjoy silent worship).

"My nonfiction is all directed at a concerned-but-not-too-well-informed Middle American audience—in other words *me,* before I started research in any particular field. My fiction is much crazier, free-wheeling, and immoral—a release for that side of my personality."

* * *

FIRMIN, Peter 1928-

PERSONAL: Born December 11, 1928, in Harwich, England; son of Lewis Charles (a railway telegrapher) and Lila (Burnett) Firmin; married Joan Ruth Clapham (a bookbinder), July 29, 1952; children: Charlotte, Hannah, Josephine, Katharine, Lucy, Emily. *Education:* Colchester Art School, diploma, 1947; Central School of Art, diploma, 1952. *Poli-*

tics: Socialist. *Home:* Hillside Farm, 36 Blean Hill, Blean, Canterbury, Kent, England.

CAREER: Free-lance book illustrator, puppet maker, and cartoon film artist, 1952—. *Military service:* Royal Navy, 1947-49. *Member:* Canterbury Art Society.

WRITINGS—For children: "Basil Brush" series; all self-illustrated; all published by Kaye & Ward: *Basil Brush Goes Flying,* 1969, Prentice-Hall, 1977; ... *Goes Boating,* 1969, Prentice-Hall, 1976; ... *in the Jungle,* 1970; ... *at the Seaside,* 1970, Prentice-Hall, 1976; ... *and a Dragon,* 1971; ... *Finds Treasure,* 1971; ... *Builds a House,* 1973, Prentice-Hall, 1977; ... *Gets a Medal,* 1973.

Illustrator of numerous children's books, including the "Noggin" series and "Ivor the Engine" series, both by Oliver Postgate. Also illustrator of *The "Blue Peter" Book of Limericks,* Pan Books, 1972, and *the "Blue Peter" Book of Odd Odes,* BBC Publications, 1976, both by Biddy Baxter.

WORK IN PROGRESS: Illustrating more books for the "Ivor the Engine" series.

SIDELIGHTS: Firmin writes: "Most of my work results from the partnership with Oliver Postgate. We have made films, including cartoon and puppet films. I also made various puppets for live television programs, one of which was Basil Brush. I did not write for him for television, but the 'Basil Brush' books are my sole venture so far into writing.

"My family and I have dogs, donkeys, chickens, tortoises, a cat, rabbits, gerbils, ducks, and hamsters on the farm, which is no longer a real farm, but forms the studios in which the films are made."

AVOCATIONAL INTERESTS: Walking, sailing, birds, books.

* * *

FISCHER, John 1910-1978

OBITUARY NOTICE—See index for *CA* sketch: Born April 27, 1910, in Texhoma, Okla.; died August 18, 1978, in New Haven, Conn. Journalist, editor, and author. Fischer worked for both United Press International and Associated Press before accepting government posts during World War II. He became associate editor of *Harper's* in 1944 and later rose to chief editor of Harper & Brothers. When he returned to *Harper's* as editor-in-chief, according to Michael Bessie, he introduced "a strong element of native-American, Western thinking." Fischer's books include *Why They Behave Like Russians, The Stupidity Problem,* and *From the High Plains.* Obituaries and other sources: *Current Biography,* Wilson, 1953, October, 1978; *Who's Who,* 130th edition, St. Martin's, 1978; *Who's Who in America,* 40th edition, Marquis, 1978; *The International Who's Who,* Europa, 1978; *Washington Post,* August 21, 1978; *Publishers Weekly,* September 4, 1978; *Time,* September 4, 1978; *AB Bookman's Weekly,* January 8, 1979.

* * *

FISHER, Gene L(ouis) 1947-
(Gene Lancour)

PERSONAL: Born June 15, 1947, in Chicago, Ill.; son of Leonard and Marilynn (Hanson) Fisher. *Education:* Chicago City Colleges, A.A. (high honors), 1970; Lewis University, B.A. (high honors), 1972; Northern Illinois University, M.A., 1976. *Politics:* Independent. *Religion:* "Really?" *Home address:* P.O. Box 138, DeKalb, Ill.

60115. *Agent:* Writer's House, Inc., 132 West 31st St., New York, N.Y. 10001. *Office: Consumer Guide,* 3841 West Oakton, Skokie, Ill. 60076.

CAREER: Free-lance writer, 1976-77; Northern Illinois University, DeKalb, administrative assistant, 1977-78; *Consumer Guide,* Skokie, Ill., managing editor, 1978—. *Member:* Science Fiction Writers of America, Writers Guild.

WRITINGS—All under pseudonym Gene Lancour: *The Lerios Mecca* (science fantasy), Doubleday, 1972; *The War Machines of Kalinth* (science fantasy), Doubleday, 1977; *Sword for the Empire* (science fantasy), Doubleday, 1978; *Globes of Llarm* (science fiction), Doubleday, 1979.

WORK IN PROGRESS: A three-volume fantasy series consisting of *The Emeralds of Ruerc, The Belt of Aldia,* and *Wine, Wine–Hot Spiced Wine;* a science fiction novel about genetic research; historical novels set in medieval times.

SIDELIGHTS: Fisher comments: "Most of my writing centers on historical subjects and fantasy, which I consider to be the only sane literature left in a world full of doom and nay-sayers. I write because I enjoy it. It is pleasing to think that I may give some enjoyment to others, and hopefully tear them away from the staring eye in the living room.

"Fantasy, in particular, is one of the few genres left that has a sense of wonder. The hard and soft sciences, technology, and the fortunes of politics and war are all grand subjects—and all too real. It is difficult to hold Coleridge's 'suspension of disbelief' in anything after reading a daily newspaper. Wizards, goblins, and dragons, on the other hand, can be incredibly horrifying, yet disappear with a flick of the wrist that closes the book's cover. That's true entertainment, when you want it.

"Most fiction writers are dreamers, endlessly populating a world full of their own ideals. Unfortunately I can't picture any of my ideals living in this reality. And, if I think real hard about it, I have trouble picturing *myself* in it—the rudest laugh of all."

*   *   *

FISHER, James R(aymond), Jr.   1937-

PERSONAL: Born April 29, 1937, in Clinton, Iowa; son of James R. (a brakeman for the railroad) and Dorothy C. (Eckland) Fisher; married Patricia A. Zimmerman (a hospital administrator), February 11, 1956; children: Robert Joseph, Laura Ann, Jeanne Marie, Michael John. *Education:* University of Iowa, B.A. (biology), 1956, B.S. (chemistry), 1956, M.S. (biochemistry), 1958; University of South Florida, M.A. (social psychology), 1976; Walden University, Ph.D. (social and industrial psychology), 1977. *Home and office:* 312 Cedar Lane, Harbor Bluffs, Largo, Fla. 33540.

CAREER: Nalco Chemical Co., Chicago, Ill., 1958-68, began as chemical sales engineer, became corporate executive in international division; free-lance writer, 1969-70; Industrial Chemicals & Dye, Inc., New York, N.Y., management consultant, 1970-72; St. Petersburg Junior College, St. Petersburg, Fla., instructor in applied sales psychology, 1972-73; University of South Florida, Tampa, research assistant, 1973-74; American Management Association, director of management relations and training program in St. Petersburg, 1973-74, project manager and resident consultant to Fairfax County, Va., 1974-75; North Carolina Police Department for Public Safety Research Institute, Raleigh, senior consultant and project manager for police management study, 1975-76; Psyche-ology, Inc. (manpower development and consulting firm), Largo, Fla., president and

managing director, 1977—. Adjunct professor of social and criminal psychology at several colleges and universities, including Nova University, Florida Institute of Technology, and Golden Gate University; instructor in development programs for police administrators at Florida universities; instructor at Police Academy of Hillsborough and Pinellas County. Consultant to national firms, management institutes, and research organizations. Guest lecturer at colleges and universities. *Military service:* U.S. Navy, 1956-57; hospital corpsman assigned to U.S.S. *Salem. Member:* American Chemical Society, Phi Beta Kappa, Omicron Delta Kappa, Phi Eta Sigma, Phi Kappa Phi.

WRITINGS: Sales Training and Technical Development, Nalco Chemical Co., 1968; *Confident Selling,* Prentice-Hall, 1971; *A Social Psychological Study of the Police Organization: The Anatomy of a Riot,* Free Press, 1978. Contributor of more than one hundred articles to journals and newspapers. Contributing editor, *Lawrence Journal.*

WORK IN PROGRESS: The Police Paradox; Confident Managing: A Guide to the Humanistic Managing of Today; Time Out for Sanity: Blueprint for Coping in a Sick Society.

SIDELIGHTS: James Fisher wrote: "I have learned that a lot of garbage is printed but, by the same token, you would be hard pressed to convince me that many gems of wisdom are overlooked. As a matter of fact, of my some one hundred or so articles and pieces which have been published, I think better than half of them are space wasters. This notwithstanding, I consider myself a writer. A novel I have been working on—off and on—for nine years might still come together for me. The influence of James Joyce, Herman Melville, August Strindberg and Fyodor Dostoyevsky, along with Alan W. Watts and Krisnarmurti, among others, is still too obvious to me. I still lack the authority of my own voice.

"Work, quite frankly, has never been like one expects work to be. I have elsewhere defined work as 'what we have to do' whereas play carries the definition of 'what we like to do.' My work and play, then, have been the same. For I never do what I do not want to do. Just as I have seldom written what does not please me to write."

*   *   *

**FISHER, John (Oswald Hamilton)   1909-
  (Roger Piper)**

PERSONAL: Born in 1909, in Surrey, England; married Phyllis Parsons-Smith; children: one son, one daughter. *Education:* Balliol College, Oxford, B.A. *Residence:* London, England.

CAREER: Diplomatic correspondent, Thomas Newspapers Ltd.; author.

WRITINGS—Nonfiction: (For children) *The True Book About the Civil War,* illustrations by N. G. Wilson, Muller, 1958; (for children) *The True Book About the Russian Revolution,* illustrations by N. G. Wilson, Muller, 1960; (editor) *Eye-Witness: An Anthology of British Reporting,* Cassell, 1960; *1815: An End and a Beginning,* Harper, 1963 (published in England as *Eighteen Fifteen: An End and a Beginning,* Cassell, 1963); (for children; under pseudonym Roger Piper) *The Big Dish: The Fascinating Story of Radio Telescopes,* Harcourt, 1963; (for children; under pseudonym R. Piper) *The Story of Computers,* Harcourt, 1964; (under pseudonym R. Piper) *The Story of Jodrell Bank,* Hutchinson, 1965; *Six Summers in Paris, 1789-1794,* Harper, 1966 (published in England as *The Elysian Fields: France in Ferment, 1789-1794,* Cassell, 1966); *The Australians From*

1788 to Modern Times, Hale, 1968; *The Afrikaners*, Cassell, 1969; *That Miss Hobhouse*, Secker & Warburg, 1971; *Paul Kruger: His Life and Times*, Secker & Warburg, 1974; *What a Performance: The Life of Sid Field*, Seeley, 1975; *The World of the Forsytes*, Universe Books, 1976.

Sailing: How to Sail, Eyre & Spottiswoode, 1952, revised edition, 1959; *Sailing Dinghies*, R. Ross, 1952, 4th edition, J. de Graff, 1961; *Better Small-Boat Sailing*, J. de Graff, 1955; (with Adland Coles and Douglas Phillips-Birt) *Sailing: Handling and Craft*, J. de Graff, 1958; *Starting to Sail*, illustrated by Roy Glanville, J. de Graff, 1958; *Storms*, J. de Graff, 1958; *Catamarans*, illustrations by Glanville, Adlard Coles, 1959, revised edition, 1962; *The New Small Boat Sailing*, J. de Graff, 1959; *Starting to Race*, J. De Graff, 1959.

BIOGRAPHICAL/CRITICAL SOURCES: New York Herald Tribune Books, May 12, 1963; *New York Times Book Review*, March 26, 1967; *Christian Science Monitor*, May 6, 1967.*

* * *

FISHER, Roy 1930-

PERSONAL: Born June 11, 1930, in Birmingham, England; son of Walter (a jeweler's journeyman) and Emma (Jones) Fisher; married Barbara Venables (a lecturer), June 20, 1953; children: Joel, Benjamin. *Education:* University of Birmingham, B.A., M.A. *Office:* Department of American Studies, University of Keele, Keele, Staffordshire ST5 5BG, England.

CAREER: Poet. Teacher at schools and colleges, beginning 1953; Dudley College of Education, Worcestershire, England, began as lecturer, senior lecturer, 1958-63; Bordesley College of Education, Birmingham, England, principal lecturer and head of department of English and drama, 1963-71; University of Keele, Keele, England, began as lecturer, senior lecturer in American studies, 1972—. Jazz pianist, 1946—; director of Migrant Press; chairman of literature advisory panel, West Midlands Arts, 1977—.

WRITINGS: City (poetry), Migrant Press, 1961; *Then Hallucinations: City 2*, Migrant Press, 1962; *The Ship's Orchestra* (prose poem), Fulcrum Press, 1966; *Ten Interiors With Various Figures* (poetry), Tarasque Press, 1967; *The Memorial Fountain* (poetry), Northern House, 1967; *Collected Poems 1968: The Ghost of a Paper Bag*, Fulcrum Press, 1969; (with Tom Phillips) *Correspondence* (poetry), Tetrad Press, 1970; *Metamorphoses* (prose poems), Tetrad Press, 1970; *Matrix* (poems), Fulcrum Press, 1971; *The Cut Pages* (prose poems), Fulcrum Press, 1971; *Bluebeard's Castle* (poetry), Circle Press, 1972; *Also There* (poetry), Tetrad Press, 1972; *Nineteen Poems and an Interview*, Grosseteste, 1975; (with J. William Jones, Peter Jones, Stephen Morris, and Bryan Walters) *Widening Circles: Five Black Country Poets*, West Midlands Arts, 1976; *Neighbors*, Circle Press, 1977; *Barnardine's Reply*, Sceptre Press, 1977; *The Thing About Joe Sullivan* (poetry collection), Carcanet Press, 1978; *4974*, Circle Press, 1979. Contributor of poems to periodicals, including *Stand, Migrant, Kulchur, Poetry Review*, and *Antaeus*.

SIDELIGHTS: Many of Fisher's writings are about Birmingham, England. Critic Donald Davies found the temperament of Fisher's characterization of the city "profoundly Hardyesque." Ronald Hayman, writing in *Encounter*, noted: "In the pictures of Birmingham, his [Fisher's] strong sense of place works hand in hand with his affectionate awareness of people.... By a careful descriptive focus on parts of the city, Roy Fisher creates an impression of it as a whole, rooting the human lives into the individual landscape."

Asked by *CA* whether he regarded himself as part of a literary counterculture in England, Fisher replied: "Is there still a literary counterculture in England? I don't know. If there is, it doesn't make itself recognizable to me, nor did it ever. I have probably always belonged to the 'counterculture,' assuming that it was the culture. The thing commonly regarded as the literary culture here (certain writers and texts and the debate about them) is not a thing to be taken seriously."

Fisher also told *CA* that his poetry is more influenced by music and art than by literature.

BIOGRAPHICAL/CRITICAL SOURCES: Kulcher, Volume VII, 1962; *Spectator*, October 27, 1967; *New Statesman*, November 14, 1969, October 1, 1971; *Encounter*, February, 1970; *Poetry*, April, 1970; Donald Davies, *Thomas Hardy and British Poetry*, Oxford University Press, 1972.

* * *

FISHER, Sterling Wesley 1899(?)-1978

OBITUARY NOTICE: Born c. 1899; died December 1, 1978, in Santa Monica, Calif. Broadcaster and journalist. Fisher worked for the *New York Times* during the 1930's as an editor. He covered stories in China, Manchuria, and Korea. Fisher also spent seventeen years with *Reader's Digest* for which he served as general manager in the Far East and director of public affairs. In the 1940's, Fisher worked for National Broadcasting Co. as director of public affairs. Obituaries and other sources: *Who's Who in the East*, 14th edition, Marquis, 1973; *New York Times*, December 4, 1978.

* * *

FITCH, Willis Stetson 1896(?)-1978

OBITUARY NOTICE: Born c. 1896, in West Medford, Mass; died August 9, 1978, in Washington, D.C. Military officer, banker, and author of a book of memoirs. Fitch served in World War I as a fighter pilot. In 1941, he enlisted in the U.S. Army Air Force after the attack on Pearl Harbor. He attained the rank of colonel. After World War II, Fitch joined the Federal Renegotiation Board which regulated agreements between business and the government. *Wings in the Night*, Fitch's memoirs of World War I, was published in 1938. Obituaries and other sources: *Washington Post*, August 12, 1978.

* * *

FITTING, Greer A. 1943-

PERSONAL: Born October 22, 1943, in New York, N.Y.; daughter of H. Oscar (an editor and literary agent) and Gertrude (an artist; maiden name, Barrer) Collier; married Kim Woodruff (divorced, 1970); married Melvin C. Fitting (a mathematician and writer), January, 1971; children: Miriam, Rebecca. *Education:* Attended City College of the City University of New York. *Home address:* Star Route, Stephentown Center, N.Y. 12169. *Agent:* Collier Associates, 280 Madison Ave., New York, N.Y. 10016.

CAREER: Writer. Has worked as editor, historical researcher, and civil rights worker. Has taught art classes to children and participated in workshops.

WRITINGS: (With husband, Melvin C. Fitting) *In Praise of Simple Things: A Young Couple's Guide to Joyous Self-Sufficiency* (self-illustrated), McKay, 1975.

WORK IN PROGRESS: Children's books; research on British history, for a novel set in Manchester, England in 1847, on vampirism, for a novel set in contemporary upstate New York, and on early English "poor law," for a historical monograph.

SIDELIGHTS: Greer Fitting comments: "I left college one credit short of an honor's degree, because I found academia too appealing: I felt a need to be a writer rather than an academic hack. I have an interest in country arts and homesteading. I live on a farm, grow my own food, make maple syrup, et cetera."

*   *   *

FLACH, Frederic F(rancis) 1927-

PERSONAL: Born January 25, 1927, in New York, N.Y.; son of George R. (a business executive) and Margaret (Donovan) Flach; married Joyce Rasmussen; children: Frederica, Christopher, Geraldine, Andrew, Winifred. *Education:* St. Peter's College, B.A. (summa cum laude), 1947; Cornell University, M.D., 1951. *Religion:* Christian. *Agent:* Sterling Lord Agency, Inc., 660 Madison Ave., New York, N.Y. 10022. *Office:* 420 East 51st St., New York, N.Y. 10022.

CAREER: Bellevue Hospital, New York City, intern, 1951-52; New York Hospital, New York City, resident in psychiatry at Payne Whitney Clinic, 1953-58; private practice of psychiatry in New York City, 1958—. Clinical associate professor of psychiatry at Cornell University, 1962—. Attending psychiatrist at Payne Whitney Clinic of New York Hospital, 1964—; associate attending psychiatrist at St. Vincent Hospital and Medical Center of New York. *Military service:* U.S. Naval Reserve, active duty as pharmacist's mate, 2nd class, 1945-46; became lieutenant, 1947-51. *Member:* American Psychiatric Association (fellow), Alpha Omega Alpha.

WRITINGS: (With P. F. Regan) *Chemotherapy in Emotional Disorders: The Psychotherapeutic Use of Somatic Treatments,* McGraw, 1960; *The Secret Strength of Depression,* Lippincott, 1974; (with Suzanne Draghi) *The Nature and Treatment of Depression,* Wiley, 1975; *The Creative Process in Psychiatry* (monograph), Life Sciences Advisory Group, 1976; *Choices: Coping Creatively With Personal Change,* Lippincott, 1977; *A New Marriage, a New Life,* McGraw, 1978.

Co-author of "The Language of Depression" (film), Life Sciences Advisory Group, 1976. Editor of "Creativity in Psychiatry," a monograph series, Life Sciences Advisory Group, 1975—.

WORK IN PROGRESS: A novel.

SIDELIGHTS: Flach comments: "I have felt drawn to writing since my early high school years, even then working on fiction and plays. For many years my writing was devoted to scientific and medical work, and I have recently returned to more creative forms. I am especially interested in translating psychiatric concepts into sound, meaningful language which can be used constructively by people attempting to develop healthier life styles."

Flach is considered one of the nation's experts on the subject of depression. His unique approach to this is to regard the experience of depression itself as a normal phenomenon, becoming a problem when it is too much or lasts too long. With this viewpoint, he sees resilience—the ability to renew oneself after the impact of stress—as the critical factor in health. Such resilience is practically synonomous with the term 'creativity' and the ability of an individual to engage in

renewal depends upon his mental attitudes, his environment, and his physiological systems. In his books for the public, Flach has approached the subject of depression and creativity and, more recently, examined this in the specific concept of marriage, divorce, and remarriage. His view of the human's response to stress not only permits new ways to deal with psychotherapy and research, but also offers a more sensible and effective philosophy for the individual dealing with life changes.

*   *   *

FLADER, Susan L. 1941-

PERSONAL: Born April 29, 1941; daughter of Milton W. (in business) and Dolores C. (Becker) Flader. *Education:* University of Wisconsin—Madison, B.A., 1963, graduate study, 1967-69; Stanford University, M.A., 1965, Ph.D., 1971. *Home:* 917 Edgewood Ave., Columbia, Mo. 65201. *Office:* Department of History, University of Missouri, Columbia, Mo. 65201.

CAREER: University of Wisconsin—Madison, instructor in environmental studies and fellow of Institute for Research in the Humanities, 1970-71, lecturer at Institute for Environmental Studies, beginning 1971, visiting assistant professor; University of Missouri, Columbia, assistant professor, 1973-75, associate professor of history, 1975—. Member of Wisconsin Resource Conservation Council (member of board of directors), 1970-73, and Wisconsin Historic Preservation Review Board, 1972-73; assembly member of Institute of Ecology, 1974—.

MEMBER: Organization of American Historians, Forest History Society (member of board of directors, 1972—), National Audubon Society (member of board of directors, 1974—), Phi Beta Kappa, Phi Kappa Phi. *Awards, honors:* Frederick K. Weyerhaeuser Award, 1973, for introductory chapter of *Thinking Like a Mountain;* University of Missouri Curators' Publication Award, 1974, for *Thinking Like a Mountain;* Theodore C. Blegen Award, 1976, for article, "Scientific Resource Management: An Historical Perspective"; National Endowment for the Humanities fellowship for University of Wisconsin—Madison, 1977-78.

WRITINGS: (With Charles Steinhacker) *The Sand Country of Aldo Leopold,* Sierra Club Books, 1973; *Thinking Like a Mountain: Aldo Leopold and the Evolution of an Ecological Attitude Toward Deer, Wolves, and Forests,* University of Missouri Press, 1974. Contributor of articles and reviews to professional journals.

WORK IN PROGRESS: Toward a Land Ethic: A Biography of Aldo Leopold.

*   *   *

FLANNER, Janet 1892-1978
(Genet)

OBITUARY NOTICE—See index for *CA* sketch: Born March 13, 1892, in Indianapolis, Ind.; died November 7, 1978, in New York, N.Y. Writer best known for her column "Letter From Paris" which appeared in *New Yorker* for more than fifty years. The column was a bi-weekly insight into what the French were doing. "Don't write about France," she'd been told. "Write about the French." And so Flanner devised a style for her column in the form of a letter. Flanner also contributed profiles of famous personalities to *New Yorker.* Later, these were collected and published as *An American in Paris* and *Men and Monuments.* Among Flanner's other writings are *The Cubical City, Cheri, The*

Pure and the Impure, and *Master.* Obituaries and other sources: *Current Biography,* Wilson, 1943; *The Oxford Companion to American Literature,* 4th edition, Oxford University Press, 1965; *Celebrity Register,* 3rd edition, Simon & Schuster, 1973; *World Authors, 1950-1970,* Wilson, 1975; *The Writers Directory, 1976-78,* St. Martin's, 1976; *Who's Who in America,* 40th edition, Marquis, 1978; *New York Times,* November 8, 1978; *Washington Post,* November 8, 1978; *Chicago Tribune,* November 12, 1978; *AB Bookman's Weekly,* December 4, 1978.

* * *

FLEMING, Joan Margaret 1908-

PERSONAL: Born March 27, 1908, in Horwich, Lancastershire, England; daughter of David and Sarah Elizabeth (Sutcliffe) Gibson; married Norman Bell Beattie Fleming (an eye doctor), June, 1932; children: Penelope, Lalage, David, Rowan Whitfield. *Education:* Attended University of Lausanne. *Politics:* "Free thinker." *Religion:* Church of England. *Home:* Kylsant House, Broadway, Worcestershire, England. *Agent:* David Higham Associates, Ltd., 5-8 Lower John Street, London, W1R 4HA, England.

CAREER: Writer, 1949—. *Awards, honors:* Crime Writers Association critics award, 1962, for *When I Grow Rich,* 1970, for *Young Man, I Think You're Dying.*

WRITINGS—All novels, except as noted: *The Jackdaw's Nest,* Hammond, Hammond, 1949; *A Daisy Chain for Satan,* Doubleday, 1950; *The Man Who Looked Back,* Hutchinson, 1951; *Polly Put the Kettle On,* Hutchinson, 1952; *The Good and the Bad,* Doubleday, 1953; *He Ought to Be Shot,* Doubleday, 1953; *The Deeds of Dr. Deadcert,* Hutchinson, 1955, Washburn, 1957; *You Can't Believe Your Eyes,* Washburn, 1957; *Maiden's Prayer,* Collins, 1957, Washburn, 1958; *Malice Matrimonial,* Washburn, 1959; *Miss Bones,* Collins, 1959, Washburn, 1960.

The Man From Nowhere, Collins, 1960, Washburn, 1961; (author of introduction and notes on the illustrations) *Shakespeare's Country in Colour: A Collection of Colour Photographs* (nonfiction), Batsford, 1960; *In the Red,* Washburn, 1961; *When I Grow Rich,* Washburn, 1962; *The Chill and the Kill,* Washburn, 1964; *Death of a Sardine,* Washburn, 1964; *Nothing Is the Number When You Die,* Washburn, 1965; *Midnight Hag,* Washburn, 1966; *No Bones About It,* Washburn, 1967; *Hell's Belle,* Collins, 1968, Washburn, 1969; *Kill or Cure,* Washburn, 1968.

Young Man, I Think You're Dying, Putnam, 1970; *Be a Good Boy,* Putnam, 1971 (published in England as *Grim Death and the Barrow Boys,* Collins, 1971); *Screams From a Penny Dreadful,* Hamish Hamilton, 1971; *Dirty Butter for Servants,* Hamish Hamilton, 1972; *Alas Poor Father,* Collins, 1972, Putnam, 1973; *You Won't Let Me Finish,* Collins, 1973, published as *You Won't Let Me Finnish,* J. Curley & Associates, 1977; *How to Live Dangerously,* Collins, 1974, Putnam, 1975; *The Gallows in My Garden,* Hamish Hamilton, 1974; *Too Late! Too Late the Maiden Cried,* Putnam, 1975; *To Make an Underworld,* Putnam, 1976; *Every Inch a Lady: A Murder of the Fifties,* Putnam, 1977; *The Day of the Donkey Derby,* Putnam, 1978.

SIDELIGHTS: Joan Fleming told *CA:* "I have led an extremely happy life with four lovely and loving children and four dogs (Yorkshire terriers)."

Acclaimed by critics for her wit, sensitivity, and versatility, Joan Fleming says she gets her ideas for plot and characters by "looking at people." Although Fleming has written four historical romances, she prefers her usual mysteries because "the work time taken up by research at the London Library is too much and makes my life far too difficult." Her only nonfiction work, *Shakespeare's Country in Colour,* caused less difficulty than the historical novels since Fleming lives only fifteen miles from Stratford-on-Avon, the subject of the book.

Fleming's *The Deeds of Dr. Deadcert* was made into a motion picture with the title "Family Doctor," released by Twentieth Century-Fox in 1957, directed by Derek Twist.

AVOCATIONAL INTERESTS: Photography, gardening, travel.

* * *

FLEMING, Oliver
See MacDONALD, Philip

* * *

FLEMING, Susan 1932-

PERSONAL: Born June 12, 1932, in Eliot, Maine; daughter of Maynard F. (a rural mail carrier) and Marjorie (Fernald) Douglas; married Donald Fleming, Jr. (an administrative assistant), April 17, 1965; children: Eric, Gregory. *Education:* Emerson College, A.B. (high honors), 1953; Harvard University, Ed.M., 1960; Boston University, certificate, 1966. *Home:* 22 Morton St., Needham, Mass. 02194.

CAREER: Teacher at state school in Wrentham, Mass., 1953-54, and at public elementary schools in Ossining, N.Y., 1955-57, Lexington, Mass., 1957-58, and Arlington, Mass., 1958-65; Houghton Mifflin Co., Boston, Mass., editor in elementary reading department, 1966-67; free-lance writer, 1967—. Reporter for *Needham Reporter,* 1975.

WRITINGS: Trapped on the Golden Flyer (Junior Literary Guild selection), Westminster, 1978. Contributor to magazines and newspapers, including *American Baby, Instructor, Christian Home,* and *Boston Herald-American.*

WORK IN PROGRESS: Another book for young people.

SIDELIGHTS: Susan Fleming writes: "I don't know how anyone can get through this world without books. I hide behind them when I need to escape, I lean on them when I need inspiration. For many years I enjoyed teaching children to read. Now I enjoy even more the process of writing a book for them. I love to read tales of triumphant struggle or the little person who wins the big prize. I suspect that these themes will appear in my books as long as I continue to write."

* * *

FLETCHER, John (Walter James) 1937-

PERSONAL: Born June 23, 1937, in Barking, England; son of Roy Arthur (an engineer) and Eileen (a telephonist; maiden name, Beane) Fletcher; married Beryl S. Connop (an editor), September 14, 1961; children: Harriet, Hilary, Edmund. *Education:* Attended Nancy University, 1956; Cambridge University, B.A., 1959, M.A., 1963; University of Toulouse, M.A., 1961, Ph.D., 1964. *Politics:* Social Democrat. *Religion:* None. *Home:* 16 Mill Hill Rd., Norwich NR2 3DP, England. *Office:* Department of Comparative Literature, University of East Anglia, University Plain, Norwich NR4 7TJ, England.

CAREER: University of Toulouse, Toulouse, France, lector in English, 1961-64; University of Durham, Durham, England, lecturer in French, 1964-66; University of East

Anglia, Norwich, England, lecturer, 1966-68, reader in French, 1968-69, professor of comparative literature, 1969—, pro-vice-chancellor of university, 1974-79. *Member:* International Comparative Literature Association (member of executive committee), International Association of University Professors of English, British Comparative Literature Association (member of executive committee), Association of University Teachers, Modern Humanities Research Association, Modern Language Association of America.

WRITINGS: The Novels of Samuel Beckett, Barnes & Noble, 1964, 2nd edition, 1970; *Samuel Beckett's Art,* Barnes & Noble, 1967; *A Critical Commentary on Flaubert's "Trois Contes,"* St. Martin's, 1968; *New Directions in Literature: Critical Approaches to a Contemporary Phenomenon,* Calder & Boyars, 1968.

(With Raymond Federman) *Samuel Beckett: His Works and His Critics, an Essay in Bibliography,* University of California Press, 1970; (editor with wife, Beryl S. Fletcher) Beckett, *Fin de Partie* (title means "Endgame"), Methuen, 1970; (editor) Beckett, *Waiting for Godot,* Faber, 1971; (with John Spurling) *Beckett: A Study of His Plays,* Hill & Wang, 1972, 2nd edition, 1978; (editor and contributor) *Forces in Modern French Drama: Studies in Variations on the Permitted Lie,* Ungar, 1972; *Claude Simon and Fiction Now,* Humanities, 1975; (with B. S. Fletcher, Barry Smith, and Walter Bachem) *A Student's Guide to the Plays of Samuel Beckett,* Faber, 1978; *Novel and Reader: Fiction and Its Forms,* Marion Boyars, 1979. General editor of "Critical Appraisals Series," Marion Boyars.

WORK IN PROGRESS: Iris Murdoch: A Study of Her Work, completion expected in 1982.

SIDELIGHTS: Fletcher writes: "I speak and write fluent French; I know France very well, the rest of Europe pretty well, the United States somewhat, the rest of the world not at all. My ambition is to travel widely before I die, especially in the west of North America, in Central and South America, Africa, Asia, and the central Australian plain which haunts me as a result of reading Patrick White, especially *Voss.*

"I admire Beckett as the greatest living writer but I am totally unlike him and don't presume to imitate him at all.

"I am a slow, meticulous reader, so I am not well-read and in fact am not interested in becoming so since there are relatively few books I can bear reading, preferring films or recorded music (Monteverdi, Bach, Mozart, chamber Beethoven and Schubert, Berlioz, Verdi, and chamber Bartok) to reading most of the time.

"On the other hand, some writers I can read obsessively: Swift, Henry James, Pauline Reage and Iris Murdoch, for example, and certain works, like *Hamlet,* Dante's *Inferno,* and the *Odyssey.*

"I suffer chronically from boredom but not insomnia, from asthma and hay fever in summer but rarely indigestion, so I consider myself reasonably fortunate. I am not always what I appear to others: I seem like Henry VIII or Falstaff but am in fact more like Hamlet, though thankfully not like Macbeth and even less like Lear. I earn my living as a university teacher and administrator and on the whole enjoy my work."

AVOCATIONAL INTERESTS: "My only hobbies are reading and writing, and food (all cuisines, even American) and wine (to the exclusion of that abomination, sweet red or pink table wine), and meeting and talking to women (I find few men very interesting)."

BIOGRAPHICAL/CRITICAL SOURCES: New York Times Book Review, November 12, 1967; *Listener,* July 4, 1968; *New Republic,* July 11, 1970; *Times Literary Supplement,* October 3, 1975; *Modern Language Journal,* November, 1976.

*   *   *

FLETCHER, William W(higham) 1918-

PERSONAL: Born November 9, 1918, in Airdrie, Scotland; son of Gavin (in insurance) and Jeannie (Whigham) Fletcher; married Elizabeth Kennedy (a radiographer), August 3, 1963; children: Marion Jane, Gavin Carmichael. *Education:* University of Glasgow, B.Sc. (first class honors), 1946, Ph.D., 1952. *Home:* 128 Dowanhill St., Glasgow, Scotland. *Office:* Department of Biology, University of Strathclyde, Glasgow Gl 1XW, Scotland.

CAREER: University of Glasgow, Glasgow, Scotland, 1948-52, began as assistant lecturer, became lecturer in botany; West of Scotland Agricultural College, professor of botany and department head, 1962; University of Strathclyde, Glasgow, Scotland, senior lecturer, 1962-64, reader, 1964-66, professor of botany and department head, 1966—. Gives popular lectures to general audiences; prepared and performed in "Science, Technology, and Modern Life," 1971, and "Great Scots: A Guid Conceit of Ourselves," 1973, television series for Scottish television. *Military service:* British Army, 1939-45. *Member:* Royal Philosophical Society (Glasgow; past president), Royal Society of Edinburgh (fellow; member of council), Botanical Society of Edinburgh (past president), Commonwealth Club, Buchanan Castle Golf Club.

WRITINGS: Modern Man Looks at Evolution, Collins, 1974; *The Pest War,* Basil Blackwell, 1974; (editor with J.M.A. Lenihan) *Environment and Man,* Blackie & Son, Volume I, 1975, Volume II, 1975, Volume III, 1976, Volume IV, 1976, Volume V, 1977, Volume VI, 1977, Volume VII, 1978. Author of "Science," a science column in *Glasgow Herald.* Editor of *Proceedings* of the Royal Society of Edinburgh.

WORK IN PROGRESS: Editing additional volumes of *Environment and Man,* with J.M.A. Lenihan, for Blackie & Son; biological research.

SIDELIGHTS: Fletcher writes: "I am very interested in interpreting science for the general public. My book, *Modern Man Looks at Evolution,* grew out of a series of lectures that I gave at the American summer school for American ministers in 1972 and 1973. The book deals with evolution right through from the evolution of the plant and animal kingdoms, evolution of man, evolution of society, and a look ahead. *The Pest War* grew out of my research into pesticides when it became clear that the public in general was unaware of the enormous benefits gained by mankind due to the use of pesticides. It was a counter balance to *Silent Spring.*"

*   *   *

FLOYD, Lois Gray 1910(?)-1978

OBITUARY NOTICE: Born c. 1910 in Larrabee, Wyo.; died December 22, 1978, in Woodland, Calif. Educator and author. A specialist in Spanish gypsy culture, Floyd was professor emeritus of both psychology and anthropology at Montclair State College in New Jersey. Her 1972 book, *Que Gitano,* dealt with her specialty. Obituaries and other sources: *New York Times,* December 25, 1978.

FOGELSON, Robert M(ichael) 1937-

PERSONAL: Born May 19, 1937, in New York, N.Y.; son of Nathan B. (a lawyer) and Gussie (Richman) Fogelson. *Education:* Columbia University, B.A., 1958; Harvard University, M.A., 1959, Ph.D., 1964. *Home:* 41 Linnaean St., Cambridge, Mass. 02138. *Office:* Department of Urban Studies and Planning, Massachusetts Institute of Technology, 3-411, Cambridge, Mass. 02139.

CAREER: Columbia University, New York, N.Y., assistant professor of history, 1964-68; Massachusetts Institute of technology, Cambridge, associate professor, 1968-76, professor of urban studies and history, 1976—, faculty associate of Joint Center for Urban Studies, 1968-76. *Awards, honors:* Guggenheim fellow, 1973-74.

WRITINGS: The Fragmented Metropolis: Los Angeles, 1850-1930, Harvard University Press, 1967; *Violence as Protest: A Study of Riots and Ghettos,* Doubleday, 1971; *Big-City Police,* Harvard University Press, 1977.

WORK IN PROGRESS: A study of the public employee pension problem in American cities.

*   *   *

FOLEY, Rae
See DENNISTON, Elinore

*   *   *

FOLLETT, Ken(neth Martin) 1949-
(Symon Myles)

PERSONAL: Born June 5, 1949, in Cardiff, Wales; son of Martin D. (a lecturer) and Lavinia C. (Evans) Follett; married Mary Emma Ruth Elson, January 5, 1968; children: Emanuele, Marie-Claire. *Education:* University College, London, B.A., 1970. *Religion:* Atheist. *Home:* 4 Bayford Cease Hawley, Camberley, Surrey GU17 9HQ, England. *Agent:* Writers House, Inc., 132 West 31st St., New York, N.Y. 10001.

CAREER: Rock music columnist at *South Wales Echo,* 1970-73; *Evening News,* London, England, reporter, 1973-74; Everest Books Ltd., London, editorial director, 1974-76, deputy managing director, 1976-77; full-time writer, 1977—.

WRITINGS—All novels, except as indicated: *Secret of Kellerman's Studio,* Grasshopper Books, 1976; *Bear Raid,* Harwood-Smart Publishing, 1976; *The Shakeout,* Harwood-Smart Publishing, 1976; *Eye of the Needle* (Literary Guild selection), Arbor House, 1978; (with Rene Louis Maurice) *Heist of the Century* (nonfiction), Fontana, 1978.

Under pseudonym Symon Myles: *The Big Needle,* Everest Books Ltd., 1973.

Also author of filmscripts, "Fringe Banking," British Broadcasting Corp. (BBC), 1978, and "A Football Star," with John Sealy, 1979.

WORK IN PROGRESS: A novel, *Triple,* for Arbor House.

SIDELIGHTS: A highly successful marketing campaign enabled *Eye of the Needle,* Ken Follett's first novel published in the United States, to be on the best-seller list for weeks before its publication date actually arrived. Follett explained how he was inspired to write his popular spy thriller: "In November, 1976, in my capacity as deputy managing director of Everest Books, I attended a sales conference held by their distributors, Futura Publications. Futura's managing director, Anthony Cheetham, asked me to write him a best seller: 'An open-air adventure story having

something to do with the war.' I spent that night painting the town red with assorted publishing executives and book salesmen, but the following morning—without having slept—I wrote a three-paragraph summary of a story about a German spy in England who discovers the deception plan for the Normandy invasion. I gave the summary to Anthony, who lost it. Fortunately, I still remembered the story when I sobered up, and Futura commissioned it. When I completed the book, I liked it so much that I resigned my job and became a full-time writer."

Eye of the Needle "is rubbish, but it is rubbish of the very best sort," Peter S. Prescott declared. Despite the abundance of cliches in the book, Prescott praised *Eye of the Needle* as "a triumph of invention over convention" and admired "its remarkable pace, its astute use of violence, its sense of particular environments and its occasionally felicitous prose." Roderick MacLeish compared Follett to some contemporaries when he wrote: "If Frederick Forsyth could write as well as he can plot and if John le Carre could plot as well as he can write, one of them might have produced 'Eye of the Needle.'"

Follett remarked that he loves to read fiction but wrote: "I have no interest in what, in England, passes for serious literature. I'd swap Kingsley Amis for Robert Ludlum any day of the week."

United Artists has puchased the motion picture rights for *Eye of the Needle.*

AVOCATIONAL INTERESTS: Contemporary fiction, music, medieval cathedrals.

BIOGRAPHICAL/CRITICAL SOURCES: Washington Post, July 2, 1978; *New York Times Book Review,* July 16, 1978; *Newsweek,* August 7, 1978.

*   *   *

FONTAINE, Joan 1917-

PERSONAL: Original name Joan de Beauvoir de Havilland; born October 22, 1917, in Tokyo, Japan; came to United States in 1919, naturalized citizen, 1943; daughter of Walter Augustus (a patent attorney) and Lilian (Ruse) de Havilland; married Brian Aherne (an actor), August 20, 1939 (divorced June 2, 1944); married William Dozier (a film director and producer), May 2, 1946 (divorced January 25, 1951); married Collier Hudson Young (a film producer), November 10, 1952 (divorced January 3, 1961); married Alfred Wright, Jr. (a writer and editor), January 27, 1964; children: (second marriage) Deborah Leslie Dozier, Martita Valentina Caideron. *Education:* Attended schools in California, and Tokyo, Japan; studied acting with Max Reinhardt. *Home:* 160 East 72nd St., New York, N.Y. 10021. *Agent:* International Creative Management, 40 West 57th St., New York, N.Y. 10019.

CAREER: Actress. Lecturer and author. Made film debut in "No More Ladies," Metro-Goldwyn-Mayer, 1935; subsequently appeared in more than fifty films, including: "Rebecca," United Artists, 1940; "Suspicion," RKO, 1941; "Jane Eyre," Twentieth Century-Fox, 1944; "Frenchman's Creek," Paramount, 1944; "Letter From an Unknown Woman," 1947; and "Tender Is the Night," Twentieth Century-Fox, 1962. Made stage debut in touring company production of "Kind Lady," 1935; made Broadway debut in "Tea and Sympathy," Ethel Barrymore Theatre, May 31, 1954. Has appeared in television dramas and performed in more than forty radio dramas. *Member:* Academy of Motion Picture Arts and Sciences, Actors' Equity Association,

American Federation of Television and Radio Artists, Screen Actors Guild. *Awards, honors:* Academy of Motion Picture Arts and Sciences, Academy Award nomination for performances in "Rebecca," 1940, and "The Constant Nymph," 1943, Academy Award, 1941, for "Suspicion"; Canadian Critics Award, 1940, for "Rebecca"; New York Critics Award, 1941; Eleanor Roosevelt Award, 1966.

WRITINGS: No Bed of Roses, Morrow, 1978.

SIDELIGHTS: Joan Fontaine won an Academy Award, in 1941, for her performance in Alfred Hitchcock's "Suspicion"; she was twenty-three. During the previous year, she had been nominated for the same award for her portrayal of Mrs. de Winter in du Maurier's best-selling book, *Rebecca.* In her book, *No Bed of Roses,* Fontaine describes her life as Joan de Beauvoir de Havilland and her life as one of Hollywood's top actresses. She frankly discusses her own family: a father who could trace his English ancestry back to the Plantagenets; a mother whom she describes as an "artistic, flirtatious, Victorian snob"; her relationship with her sister, actress Olivia de Havilland; and a childhood filled with illness.

When asked about her stage name, Fontaine told *People* magazine she had not kept her original surname because "professionally de Havilland was Olivia's; she was the first-born and I was not to disgrace *her* name." After going by the theatrical names Joan Burfield and Joan St. John, she finally chose her stepfather's name, Fontaine, "at the urging of a fortune teller.... 'Take that,' she advised, 'Joan Fontaine is a success name.' She was right."

Book World critic Faiga Levine described Fontaine as a woman who "seems to possess abundant wit, resiliency and intelligence to carry her through most situations." He continued: "Fontaine writes with a mixture of candor and lady-like reserve. The first half of *No Bed of Roses,* being more descriptive and introspective, is exceptionally readable.... Fontaine has memories that span some of Hollywood's greatest years. Neither scandal nor pique figures in any of her anectdotes. Rather, she displays a decided reportorial flair in her discussions about film studio life, and the rampant insecurity and fear she observed on every level.... Because Joan Fontaine is a literate and witty woman, her book is a better than average Hollywood autobiography."

AVOCATIONAL INTERESTS: Needlework, fishing, golf, flying, oil painting, gardening, and cooking.

BIOGRAPHICAL/CRITICAL SOURCES: Joan Fontaine, *No Bed of Roses,* Morrow, 1978; *Kirkus Reviews,* July 1, 1978; *Publishers Weekly,* July 10, 1978; *Good Housekeeping,* August, 1978; *Book World,* September 28, 1978; *People,* November 20, 1978.

*   *   *

FOONER, Michael

PERSONAL: Born in London, England; married; children: two. *Education:* Earned B.Sc. from City College (now of the City University of New York), and M.A. from University of Wisconsin—Madison. *Residence:* New York, N.Y. *Office:* New York Institute for Advanced Studies.

CAREER: Employed as an economist in Washington, D.C.; reporter for *U.S. News & World Report;* member of sociology faculty of Hunter College of the City University of New York, New York City; professor of criminology at New York Institute for Advanced Studies; faculty member of New School for Social Research, New York City. Visiting professor at University of London; lecturer at colleges and universities. Consultant to Presidential commissions, police agencies, and business corporations. *Member:* American Association for the Advancement of Sciences (fellow).

WRITINGS: Interpol: The Inside Story of the International Crime-Fighting Organization, Regnery, 1973; *Inside Interpol: Combatting World Crime Through Science and International Police Cooperation,* Coward, 1975; *Women in Policing: Fighting Crime Around the World,* Coward, 1976; *Smuggling Drugs: The Worldwide Connection,* Coward, 1977; *Blue Domino,* Putnam, 1978.

Film scripts: "The Family Man," "The League of Red-Heads," "Man in the Glass Booth," "Georgie Girl."

Author of material for television and radio. Contributor to scientific journals, law and police journals, and popular magazines, including *Penthouse, Saturday Review, Argosy, Nation,* and *Family Circle,* and to newspapers.

WORK IN PROGRESS: A suspense series, describing contemporary international conspiracies concerned with drugs, forgery, financial fraud, and white slavery.

*   *   *

FORD, George Barry   1885-1978

OBITUARY NOTICE: Born October 28, 1885, in Utica, N.Y.; died August 1, 1978, in New York, N.Y. Roman Catholic priest, pastor, activist, and author. Ford retired from New York City's Church of Corpus Christi in 1958 after forty-four years of priesthood there, twenty-three of them as pastor. Often the center of controversy for his unbending liberalism, Ford advocated the ordination of women as priests and favored a more democratic pope-electing process. In the 1940's, he campaigned for the rights of blacks, labor, and Soviet Jews and continued to involve himself in debate into the 1970's. A friend of Protestants and Jews, Ford's awards include the Stephen Wise Award from the Free Synagogue and other awards from Temple Israel and Congregation B'nai Jeshurun. His book, *A Degree of Difference,* appeared in 1969. Obituaries and other sources: *New York Times,* August 3, 1978.

*   *   *

FORRESTER, Leland S.   1905(?)-1978

OBITUARY NOTICE: Born c. 1905 in Neodesha, Kan.; died November 8, 1978, in Virginia Beach, Va. Journalist. Forrester was the news editor of the *Chicago Tribune's* Washington bureau. He covered the first atomic bomb test in Almagordo, N.M., in 1945, and was among the first reporters to warn of its destructive powers. Obituaries: *Washington Post,* November 11, 1978.

*   *   *

FOSTER, Robert A(lfred)   1949-

PERSONAL: Born September 6, 1949, in Brooklyn, N.Y.; son of Alfred F. and Eleanor (Feipel) Foster. *Education:* Columbia University, B.A. (cum laude), 1970; University of Pennsylvania, M.A., 1974, Ph.D., 1974. *Mailing address:* 312 11th St., Brooklyn, N.Y. 11215.

CAREER: Writer. Pennsylvania State University, Delaware County Campus, Media, lecturer in English, 1974-75; Rutgers University, New Brunswick, N.J., assistant professor of English, 1975-78. *Member:* Modern Language Association of America, Mediaeval Academy of America, Mythopoeic Society.

WRITINGS: A Guide to Middle-Earth, Mirage Press,

1971; *The Complete Guide to Middle-Earth,* Del Rey Books, 1978. Contributor to language and literature journals.

WORK IN PROGRESS: Fulk Fitz Warin, a medieval fantasy novel; a critical study of Tolkien; a dialect survey of New Jersey; a medieval romance; science fiction and fantasy stories; studying commercial and audience factors in the literary development of science fiction.

SIDELIGHTS: Foster writes: "My early interest in Tolkien led me to linguistics and medieval literature, specifically medieval romance and the Welsh March. Now I am trying to combine my interest in narrative (in the basic sense of stories) with my medievalism. All stories should be entertaining, but also they inevitably try to teach something; I see my own writing as a realization, more than an invention. I suppose readers react differently, but for me writing fiction and nonfiction are very similar processes. In both cases there is a group of ideas, images and connections (which I fondly claim possess some sort of validity) which must be coordinated and then transferred into words."

* * *

FRAGER, Robert 1940-

PERSONAL: Born June 20, 1940, in New York, N.Y.; son of Solomon G. (in business) and Doris (Levin) Frager; married Lya Hirth, August 24, 1968; children: Ariel, Edward. *Education:* Reed College, B.A., 1961; Harvard University, Ph.D., 1967. *Home:* 1478 Richardson Ave., Los Altos, Calif. 94022. *Office:* 250 Oak Grove Ave., Menlo Park, Calif. 94025.

CAREER: University of California, Santa Cruz, assistant professor of psychology, 1969-75; California Institute of Transpersonal Psychology, Menlo Park, Calif., founder and director, 1975—. *Member:* American Psychological Association, Association for Transpersonal Psychology (head of education committee).

WRITINGS: (With James Fadiman) *Personality and Personal Growth,* Harper, 1976.

Contributor: C. Garfield, editor, *Rediscovery of the Body,* Dell, 1977; L. Austin, editor, *Japan by 1980,* Yale University Press, 1976. Contributor to psychology journals.

WORK IN PROGRESS: Research on theory and practical exercises for improved mental and physical functioning, balance, and concentration.

SIDELIGHTS: Frager writes: "The writing of my book was motivated by a desire to expand the literature in the area of transpersonal psychology, and to provide a new approach to personality theory, a focus on human growth and development, and practical conceptual tools for readers to improve their understanding of self and others. We also needed new conceptual material—chapters on the psychology of consciousness, on Eastern psychology, and the psychology of the body.

"My current project is motivated by a desire to promote practical psychology, to provide effective techniques (physical, mental, emotional, and spiritual) that enhance one's functioning and enjoyment of work and leisure in daily life.

"I lived in Japan for almost three years, and speak, read, and write Japanese fairly fluently."

AVOCATIONAL INTERESTS: Aikido, body alignment and therapy work, Eastern psychology (particularly Yoga and Zen Buddhism).

FRANCKE, Donald Eugene 1910-1978

OBITUARY NOTICE: Born August 28, 1910, in Athens, Pa.; died November 6, 1978, in Washington, D.C. Pharmacist, educator, and author. Francke was the editor of several pharmaceutical publications and was the founder and president of Drug Intelligence Publications. He wrote more than two hundred articles and edited or wrote more than a dozen books in his field. Obituaries and other sources: *American Men and Women of Science: The Physical and Biological Sciences,* 12th edition, Bowker, 1971-73; *Who's Who in America,* 40th edition, Marquis, 1978; *Washington Post,* November 11, 1978.

* * *

FRANK, John G. 1896(?)-1978

OBITUARY NOTICE: Born c. 1896 in Blankenburg, West Germany; died November 1, 1978, in Washington, D.C. Educator and author. Fluent in more than twelve languages, Frank was a professor of modern languages. Because he was held prisoner in Russia during World War I, he was particularly interested in the language and literature of that country. Frank wrote German-language college textbooks. Obituaries and other sources: *Washington Post,* November 4, 1978.

* * *

FRANK, Peter (Solomon) 1950-

PERSONAL: Born July 3, 1950, in New York, N.Y.; son of Reuven (a journalist) and Bernice (a librarian; maiden name, Kaplow) Frank. *Education:* Columbia University, B.A., 1972, M.A., 1974. *Politics:* "Left—liberal—cynical." *Religion:* Jewish by cultural identification." *Home:* 80 North Moore St., Apt. 12-C, New York, N.Y. 10013.

CAREER: SoHo Weekly News, New York City, art critic, 1973-76; *Village Voice,* New York City, art critic, 1977—. Visiting assistant professor at Pratt Institute, 1975-76; adjunct associate professor at Columbia University, 1978. Member of board of directors of Franklin Furnace Archive and Institute for Advanced Studies in Contemporary Art; member of board of advisers of Center for Book Arts. *Member:* International Association of Art Critics, Poets and Writers. *Awards, honors:* National Endowment for the Arts traveling fellow, 1978.

WRITINGS: The Travelogues VI: Lady Be Good (poetry), Nobodaddy Press, 1976. Co-editor of *Columbia Review,* 1970-72; associate editor of *Tracks,* 1974-76; editor of *Collation Newsletter,* 1977—.

WORK IN PROGRESS: Compiling material on artists' publications, including books, magazines, records, and ephemera.

SIDELIGHTS: Frank comments: "My professional role as an art critic—and all the attendant functions and perceptions it might entail—overlaps with, even orders, my activity as a 'creative' writer; the art forms of the twentieth century inform my writing, even unto format (poetry, performance notation, et cetera). I am most concerned with intermedia, interfacing areas between the art forms."

AVOCATIONAL INTERESTS: Travel in Western Europe and North America.

BIOGRAPHICAL/CRITICAL SOURCES: Detroit Artists Monthly, May, 1978; *Print Collectors Newsletter,* May-June, 1978.

FRANK, Reuven 1920-

PERSONAL: Born December 7, 1920, in Montreal, Quebec; came to United States in 1940; naturalized U.S. citizen in 1943; son of Moses Zebi Reichenstein and Anna (Rivenovich) Frank; married Bernice Kaplow, June 9, 1946; children: Peter Solomon, James Aaron. *Education:* Attended University College, Toronto, and University of Toronto; City College of the City University of New York, B.S., 1942; Columbia University, M.S., 1947. *Office:* 30 Rockefeller Plaza, New York, N.Y. 10020.

CAREER/WRITINGS: Newark Evening News, Newark, N.J., reporter, 1947-49, night city editor, 1949-50; National Broadcasting Co., NBC News, staff member, 1950-67, executive vice-president, 1967-68, president, 1968-72, senior executive producer, 1972—. News editor, Camel News Caravan, 1951-54; Huntley-Brinkley Report, producer, 1956-62, executive producer, 1963-65; producer of television coverage of conventions, 1956, of conventions and elections, 1960, of elections, 1962, executive producer of television coverage of conventions and elections, 1964. Writer and producer of television specials for NBC-TV, including "Berlin-Window on Fear," 1953, "The Road to Spandau," 1954, "The S-Bahn Stops at Freedom," 1958, "The Requiem for Mary Jo," 1959, "Our Man in the Mediterranean," 1959, "Where is Abel, Your Brother?," 1960, "The Many Faces of Spain," 1962, and "A Country Called Europe," and of the television news series, "Chet Huntley Reporting," 1960-63. Trustee of Edwin E. Aldrin Fund, State of New Jersey, 1970-73.

MEMBER: National Academy of Television Arts and Sciences, Writers Guild of America (member of organizing committee, 1954-56), American Newspaper Guild (member of Newark News organizing committee), Radio and Television Correspondents Association. *Awards, honors:* Sigma Delta Chi television newswriting award, 1955; Robert E. Sherwood Award, 1958, 1959; George Polk award, Long Island University, 1961; Columbia Journalism Alumni award for distinguished service, 1961; First Person award, Ohio State University Institute of Education by Radio-TV, 1963; Emmy Award from Academy of Television Arts and Sciences, 1958, 1959, 1960, 1961, 1962, 1964, all for best news program, and 1963, for best documentary program and for program of the year; Poynter fellow, Yale University, 1970.

*   *   *

FRANKFORTER, A(lbertus) Daniel (III) 1939-

PERSONAL: Born May 17, 1939, in Waynesboro, Pa.; son of A. Daniel II (a photographer) and Louise (a guidance counselor; maiden name, Flickinger) Frankforter; married Karen Keene (a musician), May 26, 1973. *Education:* Franklin & Marshall College, A.B., 1961; Drew University, M.Div., 1965; Pennsylvania State University, M.A., 1969, Ph.D., 1971. *Religion:* Protestant. *Home:* 521 Rankine Ave., Erie, Pa. 16511. *Office:* Department of History, Behrend College, Pennsylvania State University, Station Rd., Erie, Pa. 16510.

CAREER: Ordained minister of United Methodist Church, 1965; Pennsylvania State University, Behrend College, Erie, assistant professor, 1970-78, associate professor of history, 1978—. *Member:* American Historical Association, Mediaeval Academy of America, American Society for Church History, American Catholic Historical Association.

WRITINGS: A History of the Christian Movement, Nelson-Hall, 1978. Contributor to history and religious studies journals.

WORK IN PROGRESS: Images of Women From Medieval Sources; A History of Medieval Europe.

SIDELIGHTS: Frankforter writer: "*A History of the Christian Movement* is a non-sectarian attempt to describe the influence of Christian institutions on Western civilization. It is written from a detached historical perspective which enables persons of many theological persuasions to use it as a means for setting their personal opinions in broader contexts. It is one in a series of several books that I hope to publish, which will be designed to present technical historical data to intelligent lay persons. I feel that it is important for scholars to make more of their work available in a form which will meet the needs and interests of the university trained public."

*   *   *

FREELAND, Richard M. 1941-

PERSONAL: Born May 13, 1941, in Orange, N.J.; son of Harry Middleton (a statistician) and Margaret (Child) Freeland. *Education:* Amherst College, B.A., 1963; graduate study at University of Bristol, 1963-64; University of Pennsylvania, Ph.D., 1968. *Home:* 255 Beacon St., Boston, Mass. 02116. *Office:* College of Professional Studies, University of Massachusetts, Boston, Mass. 02125.

CAREER: Model Cities Program, Trenton, N.J., program developer, 1968-69; University of Massachusetts, Boston, assistant professor, 1973-74, associate professor of history, 1974—, director of educational planning, 1972-74, dean of College of Professional Studies, 1974—. *Member:* Organization of American Historians.

WRITINGS: The Truman Doctrine and the Origins of McCarthyism, Knopf, 1972.

WORK IN PROGRESS: Research on higher education in the United States, particularly social functions of higher education.

*   *   *

FREEMAN, Cynthia
   See FEINBERG, Bea

*   *   *

FREVERT, Peter 1938-

PERSONAL: Born April 3, 1938, in Newark, N.J.; son of William and Harriett (Jones) Frevert; married Anna M. Reder, March 28, 1959; children: Elizabeth, Laura, Benjamin, Mary Ann. *Education:* Otterbein College, B.S., 1959; Purdue University, Ph.D., 1964. *Home address:* R.R. 1, Pomona, Kan. 66076. *Office:* Department of Economics, University of Kansas, Lawrence, Kan. 66044.

CAREER: DePauw University, Greencastle, Ind., instructor in economics, 1961-63; State University of New York at Buffalo, assistant professor of economics, 1964-67; University of Kansas, Lawrence, faculty member in department of economics, 1967—.

WRITINGS: Production and Trade, Holt, 1971. Contributor to economic journals.

*   *   *

FRIEDMAN, Leon 1933-

PERSONAL: Born February 6, 1933, in New York, N.Y.;

son of Morris and Fannie (Shawes) Friedman; married Patricia Welles, 1963 (marriage ended, 1966); married Gail Marks (an artist), 1974; children: Michael. *Education:* Harvard University, A.B., 1954, LL.B., 1960. *Home:* 103 East 86th St., New York, N.Y. 10028. *Agent:* Claire Degener, 666 Madison Ave., New York, N.Y. 10022. *Office:* School of Law, Hofstra University, Hempstead, N.Y. 11550.

CAREER: Chelsea House Publishers, New York City, general counsel, 1968-70; New York City Bar Association, New York, project director, 1970-72; American Civil Liberties Union, New York City, staff attorney, 1972-74; Hofstra University, Hempstead, N.Y., currently faculty member in School of Law. *Military service:* U.S. Army, 1954-56; became sergeant. *Member:* New York City Bar Association, Committee for Public Justice. *Awards, honors:* Scribes Award, 1970, for *The Justices of the Supreme Court, 1789-1969*.

WRITINGS: The Justices of the Supreme Court, 1789-1969, Chelsea House, 1970; *The Wise Minority*, Dial, 1971; (editor) *Obscenity*, Chelsea House, 1972; (with Neuborne) *Unquestioning Obedience to the President*, Norton, 1973; (with N. Dorsen) *Disorder in the Court*, Pantheon, 1974; (editor) *The United States Versus Nixon*, Chelsea House, 1975. Author of play, "The Trial of Lee Harvey Oswald," first produced in New York, N.Y., 1967. Contributor to magazines.

* * *

FROMM, Lilo 1928-

PERSONAL: Born December 27, 1928, in Berlin, Germany; daughter of Hugo (a merchant) and Ida (Koslowski) Fromm. *Education:* Studied at colleges of art in Freiburg, Munich, and Hamburg. *Home:* Brunnhildestrasse 3, D-7000 Berlin 4A, Germany.

CAREER: Worked as advertising artist and illustrator for newspapers, 1951-56; free-lance painter, illustrator, and author, 1956—. *Awards, honors:* German Children's Book Prize and Bratislava Gold Medal, both 1967, both for *Der Goldene Vogel*.

WRITINGS—All self-illustrated: (With Tilde Michels) *Karlines Ente*, G. Lentz (Munich), 1960, translation published as *Karline's Duck*, Oxford University Press, 1961; *No Zoo Without Mumba*, translated from German by Anne Marie Jauss, Norton, 1962; *Gusti Sucht die Eisenbahn*, Georg Lentz Verlag, 1962; *Pumpernick und Pimpernell*, H. Ellerman (Munich), 1967, translation by Sophie Wilkins published as *Pumpernick and Pimpernell*, Doubleday, 1970. Also author of *Geburtstag* (title means "The Birthday"), 1969, and *Wenn Du Einen Drachen Hast*, 1973.

Illustrator of more than forty books, including: Christa Duchow, *Oberpotz und Hoppelhans*, Obpacher Buch und Kunstverlag, 1962; Jakob Ludwig Karl Grimm, *Der Goldene Vogel*, H. Ellerman, 1966, translation published as *The Golden Bird*, Doubleday, 1970; Grimm, *Sechse Kommen Durch die Ganze Welt*, translation by Katya Sheppard published as *Six Companions Find Their Fortune*, Macdonald & Co., 1970, Doubleday, 1971; Gerlinde Schneider, *Mein Onkel Harry*, H. Ellermann, 1971, translation by Elizabeth Shub published as *Uncle Harry*, Macmillan, 1972. Also creator of story book of pictures only, *Muffel und Plums*, H. Ellermann, 1972, American edition published as *Muffel and Plums*, Macmillan, 1972.

BIOGRAPHICAL/CRITICAL SOURCES: Kirkus Reviews, July 15, 1970, January 1, 1973; *New York Times Book Review*, April 1, 1973; *Christian Science Monitor*, May 2, 1973; *New Statesman*, November 9, 1973.

* * *

FRONCEK, Thomas (Walter) 1942-

PERSONAL: Born July 30, 1942, in Milwaukee, Wis.; son of Walter Thomas (a teacher and draftsman) and Alice (a librarian; maiden name, Raniszewski) Froncek; married Ellen Kahn (a teacher and potter), April 16, 1966; children: Jesse Thomas. *Education:* University of Wisconsin—Madison, B.S., 1964; University of Kent, M.A., 1967. *Home:* 63 Elysian Ave., Nyack, N.Y. 10960. *Agent:* Paul R. Reynolds, Inc., 12 East 41st St., New York, N.Y. 10017. *Office:* Reader's Digest, Pleasantville, N.Y. 10570.

CAREER: Tablet, London, England, reporter and reviewer, 1964-65; *Life*, New York City, reporter, 1965-66; *American Heritage*, New York City, editor of Horizon Books, 1967-70; free-lance writer and editor in New York City and Princeton, N.J., 1970-77; Newsweek Books, New York City, associate editor, 1977-78; Reader's Digest Condensed Books, Pleasantville, N.Y., associate editor, 1978—.

WRITINGS: (Editor) *The Arts of China*, Horizon Books, 1969; (editor) *The Arts of Russia*, Horizon Books, 1970; *Voices from the Wilderness: The Frontiersman's Own Story*, McGraw, 1974; *The Northmen*, Time-Life, 1974; (editor) *Sail, Steam and Splendour*, Times Books, 1977; (editor) *Washington, D.C.: A Pictorial History*, Knopf, 1977. Contributor to popular magazines including *American Heritage, Country Journal*, and *Americana*.

WORK IN PROGRESS: A book-length, nonfiction suspense narrative.

SIDELIGHTS: Froncek told *CA:* "Writing is the most difficult thing I do—and the most satisfying. I write to learn, to find out what I think, where I am, where I've been.

"I have always been drawn to the outdoors: to the freedom I find there, to the adventure of finding out what's around the next bend or over the next ridge. For me, writing about America's wilderness frontier has been a way of enlarging that adventure beyond my own place and time, of sharing the thrill of discovery with those who first followed the animal traces into the unknown.

"America's frontier history is a great epic of discovery, full of marvelous stories and characters, full of gritty conflicts, deep emotions, high aspirations, meanness, greed, suffering, delight, and savagery: a treasure trove for anyone who enjoys telling or hearing a good story. On a deeper level, the confrontation between 'civilized' men and the raw wilderness also provides a powerful metaphor for the most basic human conflicts—conflicts that rage within us still: the ongoing war between our civilized and our wild selves, between our urge to build and our lust to destroy, between our need for human companionship and our will to live free."

* * *

FRUCHTER, Norman D.

PERSONAL: First syllable of surname rhymes with "look"; son of Lewis Arthur (a factory worker) and Betty (Levin) Fruchter; married Rachel Gillett (a medical researcher); children: Lev, Chenda. *Education:* Attended Rutgers University, 1959, and Columbia University, 1963; also attended Harvard University. *Home:* 577 Sixth St., Brooklyn, N.Y. 11215.

CAREER: Kingsway College (for adult further education),

London, England, instructor, 1960-62; University Settlement, New York City, street worker with youth gang, 1962-63; Free University of New York, New York City, instructor, 1964-66; British Film Institute, London, lecturer, 1966-68; Newsreel (filmmaking collective), New York City, organizer and member, 1968-70; Independence High School (alternative school for dropouts), Newark, N.J., organizer, teacher, and administrator, 1970—. Lecturer at University of London and Workers Educational Association, 1960-62; member of adjunct faculty at Essex County College, 1970-72, and St. Peter's College, 1970—; high school teacher at experimental school in New York City, 1971-72. Co-founder of Blue Van Films (documentary filmmaking cooperative), 1965—. Street worker with New York State Division for Youth, 1963; rent-strike organizer and researcher, Mobilization for Youth, 1963-64; researcher for HARYOU-ACT, 1963; organizer of Ironbound Youth Project, 1970—; founder and member of board of directors of Resource Center for Community Action. Member of Artist Civil Rights Assistance Fund; member of board of directors of New York City Teachers and Writers Collaborative.

WRITINGS: Coat Upon a Stick (novel), Simon & Schuster, 1963; *Single File* (novel), Knopf, 1970. Also author of screenplays, including "Had Us a Time," 1965, "We Got to Live Here," 1965, "Troublemakers," 1966, "Summer '68," 1968, and "People's War". Contributor of articles and reviews to popular magazines in the United States and England, including *Nation, Partisan Review, Monthly Review, Liberation,* and *Film Quarterly.* Editor of *New Left Review,* 1960-62, and *Studies on the Left,* 1964-66.

WORK IN PROGRESS: A novel.

* * *

FUCHS, Daniel 1909-

PERSONAL: Born June 25, 1909, in New York, N.Y.; son of Jacob (a newsstand owner) and Sara (Cohen) Fuchs; married Susan Hessen, 1932; children: Jacob, Thomas. *Education:* City College (now of the City University of New York), B.A., 1930. *Residence:* Los Angeles, Calif. *Agent:* Irving Paul Lazar Agency, 211 South Beverly Dr., Beverly Hills, Calif. 90212.

CAREER: Elementary teacher at public schools in New York, N.Y., 1930-37; scriptwriter in Hollywood, Calif., 1937—. *Awards, honors:* Academy Award for best original story from Academy of Motion Picture Arts and Sciences, 1956, for "Love Me or Leave Me"; National Institute of Arts and Letters grant, 1962.

*WRITINGS—*Fiction: *Summer in Williamsburg* (first novel in trilogy; also see below), Vanguard, 1934; *Homage to Blenholt* (second novel in trilogy; also see below), Vanguard, 1936; *Low Company* (third novel in trilogy; also see below), Vanguard, 1937 (published in England as *Neptune Beach,* Constable, 1937); (with others) *Stories,* Farrar, Straus, 1956 (published in England as *A Book of Stories,* Gollancz, 1957); *Three Novels: Summer in Williamsburg, Homage to Blenholt, and Low Company,* Basic Books, 1961, reprinted as *The Williamsburg Trilogy: Summer in Williamsburg, Homage to Blenholt, and Low Company,* Avon, 1972; *West of the Rockies,* Knopf, 1971.

Screenplays: (With Peter Viertel) "The Hard Way," Warner Bros., 1942; "Hollow Triumph," Eagle Lion, 1948; "Love Me or Leave Me," Metro-Goldwyn-Mayer, 1955; (with Franklin Coen) "Interlude," Universal, 1957; (with Sonya Levien and John Fante) "Jeanne Eagels," Columbia, 1957; "Panic in the Streets," Twentieth Century-Fox, 1957.

Short stories represented in anthologies.

Contributor of short stories to magazines, including *New Yorker, Esquire, Collier's, Saturday Evening Post,* and *New Republic.*

SIDELIGHTS: "I know of few novelists in America today of Fuchs's age who possess his natural talent and energy or his sense of life," James T. Farrell wrote in 1937. Although Daniel Fuchs was held in high esteem by Farrell, Alfred Kazin, and other critics, his three novels on Jewish ghetto life were a commercial failure. Discouraged, Fuchs went to Hollywood and became a screenwriter. It was not until *Summer in Williamsburg, Homage to Blenholt,* and *Low Company* were reissued in a single volume in 1961 that Fuchs achieved widespread critical recognition. Reading Fuchs's novels for a second time in the sixties, Hollis Alpert observed: "I was fearful that they might not hold up, but time has neither dimmed nor darkened them, and I suspect they are more readable and compelling today, if only because the problems are different now, and we can meet all of the author's wonderful people simply as people and not as representatives of a condition. They are fixed now, the nice ones, the evil ones, the old, the young, as a wonderful tapestry of 'low life' captured with unsentimental warmth."

The novels that Alpert so admired are all set in the Jewish slum in Brooklyn at the foot of the Williamsburg Bridge. Fuchs, who grew up in Brooklyn, drew upon his own experiences to write about immigrant life. Noting that Fuchs's writing is firmly rooted in the Jewish ghetto, Irving Howe wrote: "Rarely does his horizon extend beyond the slum: it is there that he finds his truth and his sadness. All of Fuchs's novels are dominated by a sense of place as it grasps a man's life and breaks him to its limits."

Circumscribed as their lives are by the ghetto, Fuchs's characters are often sustained by their sense of humor. Many critics have labelled Fuchs's comic sense as distinctly Jewish. Kazin pointed out, however, that Fuchs does not merely guffaw at funny situations: "In Mr. Fuchs' hands the humor retains its extravagance and its crude vitality, but it is a humor that is pointed to indicate the desperation that so often lies behind it." It is this sense of humor, along with Fuchs's vivid depictions of ghetto life, his realistic dialogue, and his unsentimental yet humane treatment of his characters, which have spurred commentators to compare him to other Jewish authors. Similarities have been cited between his writing and that of Nathanael West, Henry Roth, Saul Bellow, and Bernard Malamud.

Perhaps the critical welcome that *Three Novels* received encouraged Fuchs to return to that genre, for in 1971 *West of the Rockies* appeared. The book is concerned with the relationship between a Hollywood star and a man who works for her agency. "Masterly" was John Updike's description of the portrait of the star, and a reviewer for *Times Literary Supplement* was equally admiring of the skill with which Fuchs develops the "notion of dependence and muted anguish." Stanley Kauffman had a lower estimation of *West of the Rockies.* "Some of the writing is beautiful, but the book's depth is questionable," he remarked. "The lovely phrases, the sharp precepts, as they occur, are almost like reminders to him and us that this is not just more Hollywood fiction, this is serious."

But Howe needed no reminder that the novel deals with serious matters. Although *West of the Rockies* is set in Hollywood rather than Brooklyn, Howe perceived that the same grim sense of the power of environment infuses this book as infused Fuchs's earlier novels: "He [Fuchs] writes from a persuasion that, when all is said and done, the vision that more than three decades ago had led him to weary silence was an accurate assessment of the way men live. It is a persuasion of the essential bleakness of existence, a somber despair that makes the noisier antics of our 'black humorists' seem like childish innocence.''

Some of Fuchs's works have been translated into Polish and Swedish.

BIOGRAPHICAL/CRITICAL SOURCES: New York Times, November 18, 1934, September 10, 1961; *New Republic,* April 1, 1936, February 24, 1937, May 15, 1971; *New York Herald Tribune,* February 14, 1937; *Nation,* February 27, 1937; *Saturday Review,* September 23, 1961; *New York Times Book Review,* June 13, 1971, July 18, 1971; *Harper's,* July, 1971; *Times Literary Supplement,* October 15, 1971; *New Yorker,* October 23, 1971; *Partisan Review,* No. 1, 1974; John Updike, *Picked-Up Pieces,* Knopf, 1975; Irving Howe, *World of Our Fathers,* Harcourt, 1976; *Contemporary Literary Criticism,* Volume 8, Gale, 1978.

* * *

FUCHS, Roland J(ohn)   1933-

PERSONAL: Born January 15, 1933, in Yonkers, N.Y.; son of Alois L. and Elizabeth (Weigand) Fuchs; married Gaynell R. McAuliffe (a teacher), June 15, 1957; children: Peter K., Christopher K., Andrew K. *Education:* Columbia University, B.A., 1954, graduate study, 1956-57; Clark University, M.A., 1957, Ph.D., 1959; postdoctoral study at Moscow State University, 1960-61. *Home:* 5136 Maunalani Circle, Honolulu, Hawaii 96816. *Office:* Department of Geography, University of Hawaii at Manoa, 445 Porteus Hall, 2424 Maile Way, Honolulu, Hawaii 96822.

CAREER: University of Hawaii, Honolulu, assistant professor of geography, 1958-63; Clark University, Worcester, Mass., visiting associate professor of geography, 1963-64; University of Hawaii, associate professor, 1964-68, professor of geography, 1968—, chairman of department, 1964—. Visiting professor at National Taiwan University, 1974. Member of National Academy of Sciences and National Research Council committees and boards; chairman of U.S. national committee for International Geographical Union and National Academy of Sciences, 1973—.

MEMBER: Association of American Geographers, American Association for the Advancement of Slavic Studies (member of board of directors, 1977—), Population Association of America, American Geographical Society, Pacific Science Association (member of council, 1978—). *Awards, honors:* Award from inter-university committee for travel grants for the Soviet Union, 1960-61; National Science Foundation grant for Ohio State University, summers, 1963-65, 1967-69, 1970-71, 1976-78; Fulbright scholar at Tribhuvan University, 1966-67; National Science Council grant for Republic of China, 1973-74; Rockefeller Foundation grant, 1975.

WRITINGS: (Editor with George Demko, and contributor) *Geographical Perspectives in the Soviet Union,* Ohio State University Press, 1974; (editor with John Street, and contributor) *Geography in Asian Universities: Current Status and Needs,* Oriental Press, 1975; (editor with Demko) *Theoretical Problems in Geography,* Ohio State University

Press, 1977; (contributor) H. L. Kostanick, editor, *Population and Migration Trends in Eastern Europe,* West View, 1977; (editor with Street) *Report of the United States-China Workshop on Land Use Planning,* National Science Council, 1978. Contributor of about twenty-five articles and reviews to academic journals. Assistant editor of *Economic Geography,* 1963-64; member of editorial advisory committee of *Soviet Geography: Review and Translation,* 1966—.

WORK IN PROGRESS: Studying population distribution and redistribution policies in the socialist countries of eastern Europe; research on population growth, modernization, land use change, and environmental degradation.

SIDELIGHTS: Fuchs comments: "My major interest is in problems of economic development with particular reference to settlement systems and land use issues in the socialist countries and Asian countries. I have resided in the U.S.S.R., Nepal, and China, and have traveled extensively in Eastern Europe and Southeast Asia. My language competencies include Russian, German, and Chinese (spoken Mandarin)."

* * *

FUSERO, Clemente   1913-1975

PERSONAL: Born February 21, 1913, in Caramagna, Italy; son of Matteo and Lucia (Ingaramo) Fusero; married Lucrezia Pipino, 1936; children: Sergio, Giuliana, Luciana. *Education:* Teacher's Training School, Turin, teaching certificate, 1931. *Religion:* Roman Catholic. *Residence:* Cherasco, Italy.

CAREER: Teacher in elementary schools in Cherasco and Milan, Italy, 1933-58; writer, journalist, and literary critic. *Military:* Italian Army, 1940-44; became lieutenant. *Awards, honors:* Recipient of Premio della Cultura award from the Italian Government.

WRITINGS—In English: *I Borgia,* Dall'Oglio (Milan), 1966, 2nd edition, 1976, translation published under same title, Praeger, 1972.

Other; all published by Dall'Oglio, except as noted: *Leonardo,* 1939, 7th edition, 1966; *Raffaello,* 1939, 3rd edition, 1963; *Mozart,* S.E.I. (Societa Editrice Internazionale; Turin, Italy), 1941, 4th edition, 1958; *Stendhal,* Mondadori (Milan), 1949; *Bargellini,* Vallecchi (Florence), 1950; *L'artefice bizzarro,* (Benvenuto Cellini), Vallecchi, 1951; *Vita e poesia di Rimbaud,* 1951; *Daniele Comboni,* Nigrizia (Bologna), 1953, 4th edition, 1967; *I poeti maledetti,* 1955, 3rd edition, 1963; *Opere di Baudelaire,* 1957, 2nd edition, 1967; *Il romanzo di Modigliani, 1958, 2nd edition, 1966;* Cesare Borgia, *1958, 5th edition, 1974;* Poesie di Apollinaire, *1959, 2nd edition, 1968;* Tutta la poesia di Oscar Wilde, *1962;* Giulio II, *1965, 2nd edition, 1974;* Josephine, plus que reine, *Waleffe (Paris), 1967;* Gandhi, *1968, 2nd edition, 1977;* Garcia Lorca, *1969;* Antonio Vignato nell' Africa di ieri, *Nigrizia, 1970;* Eleonora Duse, *1971;* I Doria, *1973.*

Also translator of over fifty books into Italian. Contributor to numerous literary journals.

SIDELIGHTS: Some of Fusero's books have been translated into foreign languages, including French, Portuguese, Spanish, German, and Czechoslovakian.

(Died May 10, 1975, in Cherasco, Italy)

[Sketch verified by son, Sergio Fusero]

G

GAAN, Margaret 1914-

PERSONAL: Born August 18, 1914, in Shanghai, China; came to the United States in 1977; daughter of Antonio Martins (an accountant) and Marie (Lubeck) d'Oliveira; married E. Reginald Gaan, February 12, 1945 (died February 23, 1976). *Education:* Attended convent schools in Shanghai, China. *Politics:* None. *Religion:* Roman Catholic. *Home:* 3325 Northrop Ave., Sacramento, Calif. 95825. *Agent:* William Reiss, Paul R. Reynolds, Inc., 12 East 41st St., New York, N.Y. 10017.

CAREER: United Nations Children's Fund (UNICEF), Bangkok, Thailand, program officer for Asia region, 1950-65, chief of Asia Desk in New York, 1965-68, program officer in Bangkok, 1968-72, deputy regional director in Bangkok, 1972-74; writer, 1974—.

WRITINGS: Last Moments of a World (recollections of Shanghai), Norton, 1978.

WORK IN PROGRESS: White Poppy (tentative title), a novel based on life in Shanghai in the early 1930's; a sequel to *Last Moments of a World.*

SIDELIGHTS: Margaret Gaan told *CA:* "I have always liked to write. One of my vivid childhood memories is of the stationery shop opposite my school in Shanghai, with its stacks of paper, all beautifully blank, just waiting for me to buy it and write on it. But, until I retired, I never had time to write. I was too busy working for UNICEF, mainly traveling in Asia, helping to build programs in Pakistan, Bangladesh, Burma, Thailand, Malaysia, Vietnam, Cambodia, Laos, Indonesia, the Philippines, Korea (South), Singapore, Hongkong.

"As soon as I was settled after retirement, I began to write. I think there is no 'best' time of life for a writer; in fact, perhaps writing is one of the few occupations in which age is an advantage—it enables one to write with compassion as well as passion."

AVOCATIONAL INTERESTS: Contract bridge—Gaan participated for Thailand in Far East Bridge Championships.

*   *   *

GABOR, Mark 1939-

PERSONAL: Born August 12, 1939, in New York, N.Y.; son of Louis D. and Rose (Astor) Gabor; married Nancy Greenstein, May 30, 1964 (divorced, 1978); children: Julia Shami. *Education:* Reed College, B.A., 1960; New York University, M.A., 1962. *Home and office:* 317 East Fifth St., New York, N.Y. 10003.

CAREER: Pitman Publishing Corp., New York City, editor of art series, 1961-63; Dell Publishing Co., Inc., New York City, coordinator of book department, 1963-65; Harry N. Abrams, Inc., New York City, managing editor, 1965-70; Flatsfixed Art Gallery, New York City, director, 1970-72; free-lance writer, 1972—.

WRITINGS: The Pin-Up: A Modest History, Universe Books, 1972; *Art of the Calendar,* Crown, 1976; *Vans: And the Truckin' Life,* Abrams, 1977; *Houseboats: Living on the Water Around the World,* Ballantine, 1978.

WORK IN PROGRESS: Skin: A Visual History of the Body in Advertising, for Reed Books.

SIDELIGHTS: Gabor comments: "I don't particularly enjoy writing, per se. My interest is in putting together visual books, with supplemental text. My interest focuses on popular culture, treated in terms of historical development. I am most rewarded (and productive) when travel is involved with a given project. I enjoy most dealing with subcultures and foreign cultures—meeting strangers and relating to other ways of life. I could do this vocationally or avocationally forever."

*   *   *

GALAMBOS, Louis (Paul) 1931-

PERSONAL: Born April 4, 1931, in Fostoria, Ohio; son of Louis Paul (a shop superintendent) and Elizabeth (Himburg) Galambos; married Margaret Ann Miller, June 7, 1956; children: Denise, Jennifer. *Education:* Indiana University, B.A., 1955; Yale University, M.A., 1957, Ph.D., 1960; also attended Harvard University, 1960. *Home:* 2 Millbrook Rd., Baltimore, Md. 21218. *Office:* Department of History, Johns Hopkins University, Baltimore, Md. 21218.

CAREER: Rice University, Houston, Tex., assistant professor, 1960-66, associate professor, 1966-69, professor of history, 1969-70; Rutgers University, New Brunswick, N.J., professor of history, 1970-71; Johns Hopkins University, Baltimore, Md., professor of history, 1971—. *Military service:* U.S. Navy, 1951-52. *Member:* American Economic Association, Economic History Association, Business History Conference (member of board of trustees, 1977—).

WRITINGS: Competition and Cooperation: The Emergence of a Modern Trade Association, Johns Hopkins Press, 1966; The Public Image of Big Business in America, 1880-1940, Johns Hopkins Press, 1975; (editor) The Papers of Dwight David Eisenhower, Volumes VII-IX: The Chief of Staff, Johns Hopkins Press, 1979. Co-editor of Journal of Economic History, 1975-78.

WORK IN PROGRESS: Studying organizational change in modern America, and changes in the American economy, 1870—.

SIDELIGHTS: Galambos writes: "My major interest is in achieving a better understanding of how the rise of modern, large-scale organizations has changed our society and our lives.

"I feel strongly that American history can be revitalized if we will begin to stress new themes, such as the evolution of bureaucracies in the modern United States. I am convinced that bureaucracies, both private and public, have done more to change America in the recent past than any other single institution. Hence all of my writings explore some aspect of organizational change, and my current work traces the change into the post-World War II period when our bureaucracies achieved their greatest power."

AVOCATIONAL INTERESTS: Playing squash and tennis.

* * *

GALLAGHER, Edward J. 1892(?)-1978

OBITUARY NOTICE: Born c. 1892; died July 19, 1978, in Laconia, N.H. Newspaper publisher. He owned and published the Concord (N.H.) Patriot, which later merged with the Concord Monitor. Later Gallagher founded the Laconia Evening Citizen in 1925 and remained publisher for fifty years. Obituaries and other sources: New York Times, July 20, 1978.

* * *

GAMMOND, Peter 1925-

PERSONAL: Born September 30, 1925, in Northwich, Cheshire, England; son of John Thomas (a clerk) and Dorothy (Heald) Gammond; married Elizabeth Ann Hodgson (a teacher), July 31, 1954; children: John Julian, Stephen. Education: Attended Wadham College, Oxford, 1943, 1947-50. Politics: Socialist. Religion: Church of England. Home and office: Craven Cottage, Dunboe Pl., Shepperton, Middlesex, England.

CAREER: Decca Record Co., London, England, editor, 1953-60; free-lance writer, 1960—. Military service: British Army, Royal Armoured Corps, 1943-47; became sergeant. Member: National Union of Journalists, Rotary International (president), Savile Club.

WRITINGS: (Editor and contributor) The Decca Book of Jazz (Jazz Book Club selection), Muller, 1958; (editor and contributor) Duke Ellington: His Life and Music (Jazz Book Club selection), Roy, 1958.

(With Peter Clayton) A Guide to Popular Music, Phoenix House, 1960, Philosophical Library, 1961; Terms Used in Music, Phoenix House, 1960; (with Charles Fox, Alexis Korner, and Alun Morgan) Jazz on Record, Hutchinson, 1960, Greenwood Press, 1978; (with Burnett James) Music on Record, Hutchinson, Volume I, 1962, Volume II, 1962, Volume III, 1963, Volume IV, 1963, Greenwood Press, 1978; (with Clayton) Know About Jazz, Blackie & Son,

1963; (with Clayton) Fourteen Miles on a Clear Night (Jazz Book Club selection), P. Owen, 1966; Bluff Your Way in Music, Wolfe Publishing, 1966; The Meaning and Magic of Music, Hamlyn, 1968, Golden Books, 1970.

Your Own, Your Very Own (music hall scrapbook), Allan, Shepperton, 1971; One Man's Music, Wolfe Publishing, 1971; (editor) Best Music Hall and Variety Songs, Wolfe Publishing, 1972; Scott Joplin and the Ragtime Era, St. Martin's, 1975; (editor) Music Hall Songbook, David & Charles, 1975; Musical Instruments in Colour, Blandford, 1975, published in the United States as Musical Instruments in Color, Macmillan, 1976; The Brass Band World, Stephens, 1978; The Music Goes Round and Round, Quartet Books, 1978; (editor) The Good Old Days, British Broadcasting Corp. Publications, 1979; The Oxford History of Popular Music, Oxford University Press, 1980.

Composer of "Trial and Error," a one-act operetta, and of songs. Contributor to music and recording industry journals and newspapers. Editor of Audio Record Review, 1966-70; music editor of Hi-Fi News and Record Review, 1970—.

SIDELIGHTS: Gammond writes: "My ambition to be a creative writer was sidetracked, after a period with Decca Record Co., into writing about music and records. It is sometimes frustrating, but at least it is a source of constant commissions. I have always attempted to write about music in understandable terms, and have become increasingly interested in the field of popular music, though I am still reviewing in classical areas. I am also trying to give more time to writing music."

AVOCATIONAL INTERESTS: Tennis, badminton, golf.

* * *

GANS, Bruce Michael 1951-

PERSONAL: Born August 23, 1951, in Chicago, Ill.; son of Benjamin J. (an oral surgeon) and Dorothy (Marcus) Gans. Education: University of Wisconsin—Madison, B.A., 1973; University of Iowa, M.F.A., 1975. Home and office: 1635 Pratt St., Apt. 2-N, Chicago, Ill. 60626.

CAREER: Chicago Daily News, Chicago, Ill., assistant to columnist Mike Royko, 1969, 1970; Southeast Economist, Chicago, general assignment reporter, 1970; Michael Reese Hospital, Chicago, associate editor for in-house publications, summer, 1971; primary reporter for Independent Bulletin, summers, 1973-74; editor of Story Quarterly, 1976-77; free-lance writer, 1977—; taught at Lake Forest College, summer, 1978. Free-lance public relations consultant for Ruder & Finn. Has given readings from his works. Member: Authors Guild.

AWARDS, HONORS: College fiction prize from Mademoiselle, 1972; George B. Hill Memorial Award from University of Wisconsin, 1972, for short story "Leslie Anderson and the Chinese Over the Wall"; National Endowment for the Arts grant, 1974.

WRITINGS: (With Stephen Z. Cohen) The Other Generation Gap: The Middle-Aged and Their Aging Parents, (nonfiction), Follett, 1978. Contributor of short stories to numerous literary journals; also contributor of articles and reviews to magazines and newspapers, including New Times, Seventeen, Chicago Magazine, and Apocalypse.

WORK IN PROGRESS: Sweet Home Chicago, stories; a novel, Acquired Taste; Customs in Limbo, nonfiction.

SIDELIGHTS: Gans told CA: "No one can see into the heart [or] into the mind of another. Novels and short stories are the most intimate, perhaps the only, means we have of learning and conveying what we think, how we feel, and how we live. It is also true that writing holds out the *illusory* possibilities of a) horsewhipping your enemies, b) achieving universal admiration, especially from women, [and] c) imposing your will upon all those men-of-action who appear a little frightening and whose life's work is of no lasting, intrinsic, permanent value. In reality, of course, writing does no such thing. But it does force you, or free you, into self reliance and a sound idea of who you are—an issue by the way of absolutely no consequence to anyone else, which is, I suppose, as it should be.''

AVOCATIONAL INTERESTS: Classical music, modern painting, canoeing.

*		*		*

GARAB, Arra M. 1930-

PERSONAL: Born May 24, 1930, in Woodcliff, N.J.; son of Garaud (an insurance executive) and Varsenig (Kiremidjian) Garab; married Suzanne Anderson, June 16, 1956; children: Varsenig Ann, Elisabeth Araxie, Gary Anderson. *Education:* Swarthmore College, B.A. (high honors), 1951; Columbia University, M.A., 1952, Ph.D., 1962; postdoctoral study at Seabury Western Theological Seminary, 1968-70. *Home:* 8 Evergreen Circle, DeKalb, Ill. 60115. *Office:* Department of English, Northern Illinois University, DeKalb, Ill. 60115.

CAREER: Columbia University, New York, N.Y., lecturer in English, summer, 1954; City College (now of the City University of New York), New York City, lecturer in English, 1954-57; Colby College, Waterville, Maine, assistant professor of English, 1957-63; Northern Illinois University, DeKalb, associate professor, 1966-71, professor of English, 1971—, chaplain for department of security and safety, 1972. Lecturer at Loyola University (Chicago, Ill.), 1972—. Ordained Episcopal minister, 1970; assistant at St. Paul's Episcopal Church. *Military service:* U.S. Army, 1952-54. *Member:* DeKalb Ministerial Association, Northern Illinois University Campus Ministers Association.

WRITINGS: (With A. D. Raisner) *Teaching English to Spanish Speakers,* Adjutant General's Office, U.S. Army, 1953; *A New University,* Northern Illinois University Press, 1968; (with Russel S. Nye) *Modern Essays,* 4th edition, Scott, Foresman, 1969; *Beyond Byzantium: The Last Phase of Yeats's Career* (Scholarls Library selection), Northern Illinois University Press, 1969, 2nd edition, 1971; (editor) *Hovhannes Toumanian: A Selection of Stories, Lyrics, and Epic Poems,* T & T Publishers, 1971. Contributor to numerous periodicals and literary and theology journals.

WORK IN PROGRESS: *Theology of Hope and Despair in British and American Poetry of the Nineteenth and Twentieth Centuries* (tentative title).

SIDELIGHTS: Garab comments: ''I am a scholar-teacher who, having been called to the ministry of the Church, sees all his doings (wherever they occur) as forming a united proclamation to the greater glory of God. Because of the Incarnation and the Resurrection, any wall dividing 'spiritual' from 'secular' is not authentic.''

*		*		*

GARDIOL, Rita M(azzetti)

PERSONAL: Born in Pittsburgh, Pa.; married Rene Gardiol. *Education:* Mount Mercy College (now Carlow College), B.A., 1959; Middlebury College, M.A., 1964; Indiana University, Ph.D., 1968. *Office:* Department of Spanish, Ball State University, Muncie, Ind. 47306.

CAREER: Teacher in parochial schools in Pittsburgh, Pa., 1950-52, 1959-63, and San Juan, P.R., 1952-59; Mount Mercy College (now Carlow College), Pittsburgh, Pa., assistant professor of Spanish, 1968-69; Ball State University, Muncie, Ind., assistant professor, 1969-73, associate professor, 1973-77, professor of Spanish, 1977—, chairperson of department of foreign languages, 1978—, coordinator of Spanish, 1970-73, administrative assistant, 1973-78. *Member:* Modern Language Association of America, American Association of Teachers of Spanish and Portuguese, Indiana Foreign Language Teachers Association. *Awards, honors:* Fulbright scholarship, University of Madrid, 1963-64.

WRITINGS: Ramon Gomez de la Serna, Twayne, 1975. Contributor to language journals.

WORK IN PROGRESS: Spanish Through Cognates—The Easy Way, a language book for beginners.

*		*		*

GARLINGTON, Phil 1943-

PERSONAL: Born October 24, 1943; son of Philip C. Garlington. *Office: Los Angeles Times,* Times-Mirror Sq., Los Angeles, Calif.

CAREER: San Francisco Examiner, San Francisco, Calif., reporter, 1968-72; *San Diego Evening Tribune,* San Diego, Calif., reporter, 1973; *National Enquirer,* Lantana, Fla., reporter, 1974; *Los Angeles Times,* Los Angeles, Calif., currently reporter. *Military service:* U.S. Army, 1961-64.

WRITINGS: Aces and Eights, M. Evans, 1975.

*		*		*

GARRARD, Gene
See GARRARD, Jeanne Sue

*		*		*

GARRARD, Jeanne Sue
(Gene Garrard)

PERSONAL: Surname is pronounced Jar-*rard;* born in Birmingham, Ala.; daughter of Oscar Julian (in real estate) and Jeanne (Holoman) Garrard; married Huber S. Ebersole, October 1, 1957 (divorced November, 1960). *Education:* Attended Stetson University, 1940-42, and Lindsey Hopkins Hotel School, 1959. *Politics:* Democrat. *Religion:* Congregationalist. *Home:* 5768 Pine Tree Dr., Miami Beach, Fla. 33140. *Office:* 924 Lincoln Road Mall, Miami Beach, Fla. 33139.

CAREER: Director, writer, and commentator for WDBO-Radio and WLOF-Radio, both in Orlando, Fla., 1942-43; *Orlando Sentinel-Star,* Orlando, reporter and author of column ''Shop Talk,'' 1943; Burdine's, radio writer and commentator in Palm Beach, Fla., 1943, and Miami, Fla., 1943-44; WKAT-Radio, Miami Beach, Fla., writer and commentator, 1944-45; WIOD-Radio, Miami, commentator, 1944; WGBS-Radio, Maimi, writer and commentator, 1944-48; Melody, Inc., Miami Beach, program director, 1945-48; Grant Advertising, Inc., Miami, free-lance commentary and advertising writer, 1946; *Miami Beach Sun Star,* Miami Beach, author of columns ''Shop Talk'' and ''Personality Parade,'' 1946; WVCG-Radio, Coral Gables, Fla., writer, 1949-50; *Coral Gables Riviera Times,* Coral Gables, author of columns ''Shop Talk'' and ''Personality Parade,'' 1950; *Miami Daily News,* Miami, author of column ''Personality Parade,'' 1950-51; WIOD-Radio, Miami, writer, 1951; Miami Visitor Publishing Co., Miami Beach, feature editor, 1952-55, managing editor, 1955-56, editor, 1956-58; free-lance writer and photographer, 1958—. Scout assistant for *Better Homes and Gardens,* 1959—; photographer and assistant to editor of Meredith Corp., 1961; editorial assistant for *Ortho Garden Guide,* 1964; business manager and executive editor of *Beach and Town,* 1964—. Executive editor of Visitor Publishing Co., Miami Beach. Instructor for adult high school courses in North Miami, Fla., 1956—; owner and manager of local apartment building. Public relations counselor. Member of board of directors of Miami Beach Garden Center and Conservatory.

MEMBER: Gold Coast Unlimited Orchid Society (honorary life member), Naples Orchid Society (honorary member), Southern Florida Orchid Society, Metropolitan Miami Flower Show Association, Advertising Federation of Greater Miami, Miami Beach Garden Club (president, 1966-68), Theta Sigma Phi (local president, 1966-67), Pi Beta Phi. *Awards, honors:* National horticulture award from National Council of Garden Clubs, 1967, for *Growing Orchids for Pleasure.*

WRITINGS: Growing Orchids for Pleasure, A. S. Barnes, 1966; *Potted* (cartoons), Beach & Town Press, 1967; *Tropical Flowers of Florida,* Argos, 1970; *Flowers of the Caribbean,* Argos, 1970; *Flowers of the Bahamas,* Argos, 1970; *Flowers of Bermuda,* Argos, 1970; *Fairchild Tropical Garden,* Sun Publishing, 1971; *Tropical Flowers,* Doubleday, 1973. Contributor of columns, articles, and photographs to national magazines and newspapers, including *American Home* and *Stag* (under pseudonym Gene Garrard). Southern Florida editor of *Flower and Garden.*

WORK IN PROGRESS: Two books.

SIDELIGHTS: Jeanne Garrard writes that her first book came about because previous books on growing orchids were too difficult to understand. "I wanted to 'translate' then current data and add unrevealed data." Later writings were intended to "add fun to information on flowers, airboats, swamp buggies, boats, diving, et cetera."

Growing Orchids for Pleasure earned this praise from the *American Orchid Society Bulletin:* "[This book] is almost a story book—a love story, if you will—with growing orchids as its plot. Like a good novel, it captures the reader's interest from the first page and holds it through to the postscript, 282 pages later. In the process, it not only introduces the reader to a host of fascinating characters (human and otherwise), all sharply illuminated in the glow of the author's own enthusiasm, but it reveals a solid, professional grasp of the background information typical of the novelist who has 'lived there.'"

BIOGRAPHICAL/CRITICAL SOURCES: American Orchid Society Bulletin, April, 1966.

* * *

GARRETT, Richard 1920-

PERSONAL: Born January 15, 1920, in London, England; son of Victor (in business) and Gladys (Fisher) Garrett; married Anne Selves, August 20, 1945; children: Anthony, Simon, Jane. *Education:* Attended school in Berkshire, England. *Politics:* "Middle of the road." *Religion:* Christian. *Home and office:* White Cottage, 27-A Broadwater Down, Tunbridge Wells, Kent TN2 5NL, England.

CAREER: Has worked in journalism, public relations, and advertising. Owner of an industrial book and magazine publishing company in England, 1958-69; free-lance writer, 1969—. Broadcaster of weekly general interest shows for British Broadcasting Corp. (BBC); guest on radio and televi-

sion programs. *Military service:* British Army, 1939-45; served as officer in Norway; prisoner-of-war in Italy and Germany, 1943-45; became captain; staff writer for *Soldier.* *Member:* Society of Authors, National Union of Journalists.

WRITINGS: Fast and Furious: The Story of the World Championship of Drivers, foreword by Graham Hill, Stanley Paul, 1968, Arco, 1969; *The Motor Racing Story,* Stanley Paul, 1969, A. S. Barnes, 1970; *Anatomy of a Grand Prix Driver,* Arthur Barker, 1970; *The Rally-Go-Round: The Story of International Rallying,* Stanley Paul, 1970; *Motoring and the Mighty,* Motorbooks International, 1971; *Cross-Channel,* Hutchinson, 1972; *The Search for Prosperity: Emigration From Britain, 1815-1930,* Wayland, 1973; *Stories of Famous Ships,* Arthur Barker, 1974; *General Gordon,* Arthur Barker, 1974; *The British Sailor,* Wayland, 1974; *General Wolfe,* Arthur Barker, 1975; *Famous Characters of the Wild West,* Arthur Barker, 1975, St. Martin's, 1977; *Stories of Famous Natural Disasters,* Arthur Barker, 1976; *Clash of Arms: The World's Great Land Battles,* Weidenfeld & Nicolson, 1976; *Robert Clive,* Arthur Barker, 1976; *Submarines,* Little, Brown, 1977; *Famous Rescues at Sea,* Arthur Barker, 1977; *Scharnhorst and Gneisenau: The Elusive Sisters,* Hippocrene, 1977. Also author of *That's Odd,* 1979.

Children's books; all published by Piccolo, except as indicated: *Great Sea Mysteries,* 1971; *Atlantic Jet,* Hutchinson, 1971; *Hoaxes and Swindles,* 1972; *True Tales of Detection,* 1972; *Narrow Squeaks,* 1973; *Heroines,* 1974; *Queen Victoria,* Hutchinson, 1974; *They Must Have Been Crazy,* 1977; *Dangerous Journeys,* 1978; *Great Air Adventures,* 1978; *In the Nick of Time,* 1979.

Editor of *Shellman* (of Shell United Kingdom Oil Co.).

WORK IN PROGRESS: A book with a war theme ("it's a tremendous idea"), for David & Charles.

SIDELIGHTS: Garrett writes: "I see my writing very much as a job of work. I try to write at least three thousand words a day when I am not carrying out research. Professionalism is, I believe, maintaining a constant and consistent output no matter what the circumstances. 'Not feeling like it' can usually be overcome by doing it.

"My basic aim is to tell a story (I suspect a novelist screaming to get out, but since I have no talent in this area, he remains inside). I attempt to explore history, to experience the feeling of the times, and, in the case of children's books, to pass on this excitement. I suspect that history is taught without much imagination in the schools—there is little attempt to show what tremendous stories history contains. My books concentrate on entertainment—easy to read books which could happily occupy a long train journey."

AVOCATIONAL INTERESTS: Walking, the countryside, watching the sea.

* * *

GARSKOF, Michele Hoffnung
See HOFFNUNG, Michele

* * *

GATES, David Murray 1921-

PERSONAL: Born May 27, 1921, in Manhattan, Kan.; son of Frank Caleb and Margaret Henry (Thompson) Gates; married Marian Francis Penley, June 4, 1944; children: Murray, Julie, Heather, Marilyn. *Education:* University of Michigan, B.S., 1942, M.S., 1944, Ph.D., 1948. *Politics:* Independent. *Religion:* Protestant. *Home:* 442 Huntington

Pl., Ann Arbor, Mich. 48104. *Office:* Biological Station, University of Michigan, Ann Arbor, Mich. 48104.

CAREER: University of Denver, Denver, Colo., member of faculty, 1948-57; American Embassy, London, England, scientific director and liaison officer with Office of Naval Research, 1955-57; National Bureau of Standards, Boulder Laboratories, Boulder, Colo., assistant chief of upper atmosphere and space physics division, 1957-64; University of Colorado, Boulder, professor of natural history, 1964-65; Washington University, St. Louis, Mo., professor of biology and director of biology station, 1965-71; University of Michigan, Ann Arbor, professor of botany and director of biology station, 1971—. Dalgary Distinguished Lecturer at University of Manitoba, 1977-78. Director of Missouri Botanical Garden, 1965-71. Member of National Science Board, 1970-76.

MEMBER: Ecological Society of America, American Meteorological Society, American Association for the Advancement of Science, National Audubon Society (member of board of directors, 1972-78), Cosmos Club. *Awards, honors:* Award from American Meteorological Society, 1975, for outstanding achievements in biometeorology.

WRITINGS: Energy Exchange in the Biosphere, Harper, 1962; (with Papian) *Atlas of Energy Budgets of Plant Leaves,* Academic Press, 1971; *Man and His Environment: Climate,* Harper, 1972; (editor with R. B. Schmerl) *Perspectives of Biophysical Ecology,* Springer-Verlag, 1975. Contributor to scientific journals.

WORK IN PROGRESS: Biophysical Ecology, for Springer-Verlag.

*   *   *

GAWTHROP, Louis C. 1930-

PERSONAL: Born October 27, 1930, in Baltimore, Md.; son of Louis (an electrician) and Claudia (Smith) Gawthrop; married Virginia L. Bonelli, May 31, 1958; children: Tracy M., Nicholas A., Anne E. *Education:* Franklin and Marshall College, B.A., 1958; Johns Hopkins University, M.A., 1960, Ph.D., 1962. *Office:* School of Public and Environmental Affairs, Indiana University, Bloomington, Ind. 47401.

CAREER: University of Pennsylvania, Philadelphia, instructor, 1962-63, assistant professor of political science, 1963-67; State University of New York at Binghamton, associate professor, 1967-72, professor of political science, 1972-77, acting chairman of department, 1976-77; Indiana University, Bloomington, professor of public and environmental affairs, 1978—. Visiting professor at Syracuse University, spring, 1973; visiting fellow at Netherlands Institute for Advanced Study in the Humanities and Social Sciences, 1973-74. *Military service:* U.S. Air Force, 1951-54; became staff sergeant. *Member:* American Political Science Association, American Society for Public Administration, Phi Beta Kappa, Phi Sigma Alpha, Pi Alpha Alpha.

WRITINGS: The New Mayor Council Cities: A Redistribution of Administrative and Legislative Powers, Department of Internal Affairs, Commonwealth of Pennsylvania, 1965; (contributor) Edward Janosik and Garold Thumn, editors, *Parties and the Governmental System,* Prentice-Hall, 1967; *Bureaucratic Behavior in the Executive Branch: An Analysis of Organizational Change,* Free Press, 1969; *The Administrative Process and Democratic Theory,* Houghton, 1970; *Administrative Politics and Social Change,* St. Martin's, 1971; (contributor) Anant R. Negandhi, editor, *Mod-*

ern Organization Theory, Kent State University Press, 1973; (contributor) George Frederickson and Charles Wise, editors, *Public Policy and Public Administration,* Lexington Books, 1977; (contributor) Susan Welch and John Peters, editors, *Legislative Reform and Public Policy,* Praeger, 1977. Editor-in-chief of *Public Administration Review.* Contributor to political science journals.

WORK IN PROGRESS: An analysis and evaluation of organizational ethics as related to environmental forces of change; a comparative analysis of the operational strategies and tactics of selected decision-making models; an evaluation of responsive and anticipatory planning capacities of organizations; a theoretical consideration of the organizational, socio-political, and ethical implications of a progressive deterioration of our traditional notions of time and space.

*   *   *

GAY, John E(dward) 1942-

PERSONAL: Born October 21, 1942, in Pa.; son of John Edward (an engineer) and Louise (a nurse; maiden name, Johnson) Gay; married Katrina Judson (a teacher), October 1, 1977. *Education:* State University of New York College at Buffalo, B.S., 1965; San Diego State University, M.S., 1972; West Virginia University, Ed.D., 1974. *Politics:* None. *Religion:* Roman Catholic. *Home:* 19 Stoneridge Ct., Baltimore, Md. 21239. *Office:* Department of Health Science, Towson State University, Towson, Md. 21204.

CAREER: Towson State University, Towson, Md., assistant professor of health science, 1974—. Member of U.S. Department of Health, Education, and Welfare's Blue Ribbon Commission on Aging; consultant to International Business Machines and Black & Decker Corp. *Military service:* U.S. Navy, pilot, 1965-68; served in Vietnam; received Bronze Star and Purple Heart. *Member:* Association for the Advancement of Medical Education, American Association for Health, Physical Education and Recreation, American Public Health Association, American Medical Association, American School Health Association, American Alliance for Health Education; Association of American University Professors, Royal Society for the Preservation of Health, Phi Delta Kappa.

WRITINGS: (With Neil E. Gallagher) *Drugs in Our Culture,* Kendall-Hunt, 1976; (with Clint E. Bruess) *Implementing Comprehensive School Health,* Macmillan, 1978; (with W. Boskin, M. S. Wantz, H. Sloboff, and C. Hooper) *Current Health Problems,* Saunders, 1979; (contributor with Carl Willgoose) *Environmental Health,* Saunders, 1979; (with Wantz) *The Aging Process: A Health Perspective,* Saunders, 1980. Contributor to school health, drug education, and medical journals.

SIDELIGHTS: Gay comments: "As a member of Olympic, Pan-American, and World Cup teams, I have found this to have absolutely *NO* impact on my professional growth or career. Although such activities do not reflect one's professional spiral, it is necessary to experience all facets of one's inner mobility to experience optimal well being. Academic writing should not be a publish-or-perish syndrome, but a labor of love for the particular area to which one is committed. It seems a crime to see articles and texts written for the sake of promotion or tenure; especially when individuals often replicate prior research or frame of thought.

"I consider myself an educator first and foremost and ponder the often talked about grade inflation. Today's students are pampered, coddled, and given academic achievements that in some cases are not deserved. Sometime, somewhere, this will end—most assuredly with future ramifications.''

* * *

GAYA-NUNO, Juan Antonio 1913-1975

PERSONAL: Born in 1913, in Soria, Spain. *Education:* Earned Ph.D. from University of Madrid. *Residence:* Madrid, Spain.

CAREER: Writer. Member of Coimbra Institute. *Member:* Spanish Art Critics Association (vice-president), Art Critics Academy, Hispanic Society of America.

WRITINGS—In English: *Juan Gris,* Ediciones Poligrafa, 1974, translation by Kenneth Lyons published under same title, New York Graphic Society, 1975.

Other works: *Madrid,* Editorial Aries, 1944, 2nd edition, 1950; *El romanico en la provincia de Soria,* Instituto Diego Velazquez, 1946; *Historia del arte espanol* (title means "History of Spanish Art"), Editorial Plus-Ultra, 1946, 4th edition, 1968; *El Escorial,* Editorial Plus-Ultra, 1947; *Zurbaran,* Ediciones Aedos, 1948; *Burgos,* Editorial Aries, 1949; *El arte espanol en sus estilos y en sus formas,* Ediciones Omega, 1949.

Autorretratos de artistas espanoles, Argos, 1950; *Salvadore Dali,* Ediciones Omego 1950; *Francisco Cossio,* Ediciones Sagitario, 1951; *La pintura espanola en el medio siglo,* Ediciones Omega, 1952; *El santero de San Saturio,* Castalia, 1953; *Pancho Cossio: Estudio,* Gallades, 1954; *Historia y guia de los museos de Espana* (title means "History and Guide of the Museums of Spain"), Espasa-Calpe, 1955, 2nd edition, 1968; *La pintura,* Ediciones Pegaso, 1955; *Escultura espanola contemporanea* (title means "Contemporary Spanish Sculpture"), Ediciones Guadarrama, 1957; *El arte en su intimidad,* Aguilar, 1957; *La pintura espanola fuera de Espana: Historia y catalogo,* Espasa-Calpe, 1958; *Entendimiento del arte,* Taurus, 1959.

Un conflicto: Literatura y arte, Taurus, 1960; *La arquitectura espanola en sus monumentos desaparecidos,* Espasa-Calpe, 1961; *Francisco Arias,* Direccion General de Bellas Artes, 1961; *Teoria del romanico,* Publicaciones Espanolas, 1962; *Tratado de mendicidad,* Taurus, 1962; *La pintura y la lirica de Cristobal,* Ponce de Leon, 1963; *Bibliografia critica y antologica de Velazquez,* Fundacion Lazaro Galdiano, 1963; *Escultura iberica* (title means "Iberian Sculpture"), Aguilar, 1964; *Pequenas teorias de arte,* Taurus, 1964; *La pintura espanola en los museos provinciales* (title means "Spanish Painting in Provincial Museums"), Aguilar, 1964; *Pintura europea perdida por Espana, de Van Eyck a Tiepolo,* Espasa-Calpe, 1964; *El arte europeo en peligro, y otros ensayos,* Editora y Distribuidora Hispano Americana, 1964.

Sentido de la filosofia contemporanea, Universidad Central de Venezuela, 1965; *Museo del Louvre* (title means "The Louvre Museum"), Aguilar, 1965; *La espeluznante historia de la calavera de Goya,* Edizioni dell'Elefante, 1966; *Historia del cautivo: Episodios nacionales,* Mexico, 1966; *Arte del siglo decimonono* (title means "Nineteenth Century Art"), Editorial Plus-Ultra, 1966; *Bibliografia critica y antologica de Picasso,* Universidad de Puerto Rico, 1966; (contributor) Javier Rubio, *Formas de la escultura contemporanea,* Aguado, 1966; (with Jose Pijoan y Soteras) *Arte europeo de los siglos XIX y XX* (title means "European Art of the Nineteenth and Twentieth Centuries"), Espasa-Calpe, 1967; *Los gatos salvajes y otras historias,* Taurus, 1968; *Historia del Museo del Prado (1819-1969),* Editorial Everest, 1969.

Velazquez: Biografia ilustrada, Ediciones Destino, 1970; *La Espana de los museos,* Direccion General de Promocion del Turismo, 1970; (with Jose Caso Gonzalez and Joaquin Arce) *Los conceptos de rococo, neoclasicismo y prerromanticismo en la literatura espanola del siglo XVIII* (title means "The Concepts of Rococo, Neoclassicism, and Pre-Romanticism in Eighteenth Century Spanish Literature"), Universidad de Oviedo, 1970; *Museos de Madrid* (title means "Museums of Madrid"), Editorial Everest, 1970; *El Museo del Prado,* Editorial Everest, 1970; *La pintura espanola del siglo XX* (title means "Twentieth Century Spanish Painting"), Iberico Europea de Ediciones, 1970, 2nd edition, 1972; *Sartre,* Ediciones de la Biblioteca, Universidad Central de Venezuela, 1971; (with Concha de Marco) *Soria,* Editorial Everest, 1971; *Francisco Gutierrez Cossio: Vida y obra,* Iberico Europea de Ediciones, 1973; *Diego Velazquez,* Publicaciones Espanolas, 1974; *Historia del arte universal* (title means "History of World Art"), Editorial Everest, 1974; *Historia de la critica de arte en Espana* (title means "History of Art Criticism in Spain"), Iberico Europea de Ediciones, 1975.*

(Died in 1975)

* * *

GEASLAND, Jack
See GEASLAND, John Buchanan, Jr.

* * *

GEASLAND, John Buchanan, Jr. 1944-
(Jack Geasland)

PERSONAL: Born September 9, 1944, in Kingsport, Tenn.; son of John Buchanan and Virginia (Littleton) Geasland. *Education:* Georgetown University, B.S.F.S., 1966; attended University of Fribourg, Fribourg, Switzerland, 1964-65, Defense Language Institute West Coast, 1967-68, and Gwang Chi Institute, Quezon City, Philippines, 1970. *Residence:* Roxbury, Conn.

CAREER: Writer. Worked as proofreader for a medical publication and as a columnist for *Drug Therapy* magazine. *Military service:* U.S. Naval Reserve, 1967-70, served in South Vietnam; became lieutenant.

WRITINGS—Under name Jack Geasland: (With Bari Wood) *Twins* (novel: Literary Guild selection), Putnam, 1977.

WORK IN PROGRESS: San Miguel, a novel.

SIDELIGHTS: Carol Eisen Rinzler felt the storytelling in *Twins* was absorbing: "Wood's and Geasland's reconstruction may well appear hogwash to anyone with a grounding in psychology, but if one is mercifully ignorant of such matters—and if one is able to suspend as well any faculties critical of literature—one is left with a good read of the first order, a gripping, stunningly paced novel, a first-rate entertainment with which to while away a few hours." Ted Morgan disagreed, saying, "Contrary to the usual encomium, this is a book that I could have put down." He went on to declare that "the book as a whole is too gratuitous and mechanical to make one feel anything stronger than a shudder of distaste."

The numerous parallels between the plot of *Twins* and a real case that received a large amount of attention from the press in 1975 have been pointed out by a number of commentators. Cyril and Stewart Marcus were twin brothers, both doctors and drug addicts, whose dead bodies were discovered in their littered Manhattan apartment. The main characters in

Twins are also twin brothers in medical practice. They, too, are hooked on Seconal and die under mysterious circumstances. Julian Baines dismissed the book as a money-making enterprise: "*Twins* is a good example of the latest American way to make $1 million (the price of paperback rights). You take a spectacular newspaper story . . . and ease it into fiction. The actual details of the messy end you keep nudgingly close to the real case, hitching as much of a ride from authenticity as you can, and then work backwards, inventing motive, childhood, and the current market level of sex."

AVOCATIONAL INTERESTS: Travel (Manila, Malaysia, India, Tibet, Europe).

BIOGRAPHICAL/CRITICAL SOURCES: Washington Post Book World, April 24, 1977; *New York Times Book Review,* May 1, 1977; *New Statesman,* July 1, 1977.

* * *

GEIST, Kenneth L(ee) 1936-

PERSONAL: Born May 13, 1936, in New York, N.Y.; son of Irving (in business) and Sydell (Bloomfield) Geist. *Education:* Haverford College, B.A. (high honors), 1958; attended London Academy of Music and Dramatic Art, 1958-59, and Yale University, 1959-60. *Home:* 37 West 12th St., New York, N.Y. 10011.

CAREER: Affiliated with Barr & Wilder, 1961; production stage manager of Cherry Lane Theatre, New York City; Theatre Guild, New York City, head of play department, 1962-63; Columbia Broadcasting System (CBS), Hollywood, Calif., television program executive, 1965-66. *Member:* Phi Beta Kappa.

WRITINGS: Pictures Will Talk: The Life and Films of Joseph L. Mankiewicz, Scribner, 1978. Contributor of articles and reviews to magazines and newspapers, including *Film Comment* and *Show.* Contributing editor of *Interview.*

WORK IN PROGRESS: "Confidential."

SIDELIGHTS: Geist comments on *Pictures Will Talk:* "In celebrating the life and work of a noted iconoclast, I attempted to break with the conventions of a typical scholarly biography or critical study. The sometimes ribald footnotes and humorous photo captions are as unusual as my relating an incident from multiple points-of-view, which is the mosaic technique of Mankiewicz's fictional film biographies.

"In an era of the big, dumb, blockbuster movie, I wanted to draw attention to the work of a highly literate, sophisticated, and adult filmmaker—a vanished breed in the American cinema."

BIOGRAPHICAL/CRITICAL SOURCES: Washington Post Book World, October 15, 1978.

* * *

GELMAN, Rita Golden 1937-

PERSONAL: Born July 2, 1937, in Bridgeport, Conn; daughter of Albert (a pharmacist) and Frances (an artist and a Zionist; maiden name, Friedman) Golden; married Steve Gelman (an editor and writer), December 11, 1960; children: Mitchell, Jan. *Education:* Brandeis University, B.A., 1958; additional study at Northeastern University, Yeshiva University, New York University, and University of California, Los Angeles. *Politics:* Populist. *Religion:* Jewish. *Residence:* Los Angeles, Calif. *Agent:* Marilyn Marlow, Curtis Brown Ltd., 575 Madison Ave., New York, N.Y. 10022.

CAREER: Young Americans magazine, New York City, staff writer, 1958-60; Crowell-Collier Publishing Co., New

York City, editor, 1961-62; Book-of-the-Month Club, New York City, juvenile consultant, 1972—; Macmillan Publishing Co., New York City, editor, 1973-74; free-lance writer, 1974—. Guest lecturer, University of California, Los Angeles, 1976-78; faculty member, Sixth Annual Writers' Conference in Children's Literature, Los Angeles, 1977; faculty member in extension program, California State University at Northridge, 1978-79. *Member:* Society of Children's Book Writers, Southern California Council on Literature for Children and Young People.

WRITINGS—Juvenile; all published by Scholastic Book Services, except as indicated: *Dumb Joey,* Holt, 1973; *The Can,* Macmillan, 1975; *Fun City,* Macmillan, 1975; *The Me I Am,* Macmillan, 1975; *Comits, a Book of Comic Skits,* Macmillan, 1975; (with husband, Steve Gelman) *Great Quarterbacks of Pro Football,* 1975; *Why Can't I Fly,* 1977; *More Spaghetti, I Say,* 1977; *Hey Kid!,* F. Watts, 1977; (with Joan Richter) *Professor Coconut and the Thief,* Holt, 1977; (with Susan Buxbaum) *OUCH!: All About Cuts and Other Hurts,* Harcourt, 1977; (with Warner Friedman) *Uncle Hugh, A Fishing Story,* Harcourt, 1978; *Cats and Mice,* 1978; (with S. Gelman) *America's Favorite Sports Stars,* 1978; (with Marcia Seligson) *UFO Encounters,* 1978; *The Biggest Sandwich Ever,* 1979.

WORK IN PROGRESS: Hats, Favorite Riddles, and *The Hippo Must Go,* all for Scholastic Book Services.

* * *

GEMME, Leila Boyle 1942-

PERSONAL: Born November 29, 1942, in Philadelphia, Pa.; daughter of Thomas Edward (in sales) and Virginia (a legal secretary; maiden name, Antisdale) Boyle; married Francis R. Gemme (a publisher), August 20, 1964; children: Michael Antisdale, Ellen Martin, Abigail Berkeley. *Education:* Newton College of the Sacred Heart, B.A., 1964; University of Connecticut, M.A., 1966; further graduate study at Smith College, 1967, and Chicago-Kent College of Law, 1978—. *Religion:* Roman Catholic. *Home and office:* 147 Birch St., Winnetka, Ill. 60093.

CAREER: Teacher in public schools in Milford, Conn., 1964-65, Franklin, Conn., 1965-66, and Granby, Mass., 1966-68; writer.

WRITINGS: Complete Crossword Puzzle Dictionary, Grosset, 1971; *New Breed of Athlete,* Pocket Books, 1972; *New Breed of Performer,* Pocket Books, 1973; *King on the Court: Billie Jean King,* Raintree, 1976; *Spinoffs From Space,* Childrens Press, 1977; *True Book of the Mars Landing,* Childrens Press, 1977; *T-Ball Is Our Game,* Childrens Press, 1978; *Ten-Speed Taylor,* Albert Whitman, 1978.

WORK IN PROGRESS: Hockey Is Our Game; Basketball Hall of Fame; Baseball Hall of Fame; Football Hall of Fame.

* * *

GENET
See FLANNER, Janet

* * *

GERSON, Noel Bertram 1914-
(Ann Marie Burgess, Michael Burgess, Samuel Edwards, Paul Lewis, Leon Phillips, Carter A. Vaughan)

PERSONAL: Born November 6, 1914, in Chicago, Ill.; son

of Samuel Philip and Rosa Anna (Noel) Gerson; married Cynthia Ann Vautier; married second wife Marilyn Allen Hammond; children: (first marriage) Noel Anne Gerson Brennan; stepchildren: Michele, Margot, Paul. *Education:* University of Chicago, A.B., 1934, M.A., 1935. *Address:* 63 Pratt Ave., Clinton, Conn. 06413.

CAREER: Chicago Herald-Examiner, Chicago, Ill., reporter and rewriteman, 1931-36; WGN-Radio, Chicago, executive, 1936-41; radio and television scriptwriter for national networks, 1936-51; writer. President, Goodspeed Opera House Foundation, Haddam, Conn.; member of board of directors, Connecticut Advocates of Arts. *Military service:* U.S. Army, Military Intelligence, World War II. *Member:* P.E.N., Authors Guild, Centro Studi E Scambi Internazionali (Rome, Italy), American Academy of Political and Social Sciences, American Historical Association, Mississippi Valley Historical Association, Phi Beta Kappa, Kappa Alpha, Linguanea Club (Jamaica, W.I.), Players Club (New York City).

WRITINGS—Fiction; all published by Doubleday, except as noted: *Savage Gentleman,* 1950; *The Mohawk Ladder,* 1951; *The Cumberland Rifles,* 1952; *The Golden Eagle,* 1953; *The Impostor,* 1954; *The Forest Lord: A Romantic Adventure of 18th Century Charleston,* 1955; *The Highwayman,* 1955; *That Egyptian Woman,* 1956; *The Conqueror's Wife,* 1957; *Daughter of Eve,* 1958; *The Emperor's Ladies,* 1959; *The Yankee From Tennessee,* 1960; *The Hittite,* 1961; *The Land Is Bright,* 1961; *The Trojan,* 1962; *The Golden Lyre,* 1963; (under pseudonym Michael Burgess) *Mister,* New Authors Ltd., 1964; *Old Hickory,* 1964; *The Slender Reed: A Biographical Novel of James Knox Polk,* 1965; *Yankee Doodle Dandy: A Biographical Novel of John Hancock,* 1965; *Give Me Liberty: A Novel of Patrick Henry,* 1966; *I'll Storm Hell: A Biographical Novel of 'Mad Anthony' Wayne,* 1967; *The Swamp Fox: Francis Marion,* 1967; *Jefferson Square: A Novel,* M. Evans, 1968; *Sam Houston: A Biographical Novel,* 1968; *The Golden Ghetto: A Novel,* M. Evans, 1969; *P. J., My Friend,* illustrations by Patricia Coombs, 1969.

Clear for Action!, 1970; *The Crusader: A Novel on the Life of Margaret Sanger,* Little, Brown, 1970; *Mirror, Mirror,* Morrow, 1970; *TR,* 1970; *Warhead,* 1970; *Island in the Wind: A Novel,* 1971; *Talk Show,* Morrow, 1971; *Double Vision: A Novel,* 1972; *The Sunday Heroes,* Morrow, 1972; *Temptation to Steal: A Novel,* 1972; *State Trooper,* 1973; *All That Glitters,* 1975 (published in England under pseudonym Samuel Edwards, Heinemann, 1976); *Neptune,* Dodd, 1976; *Special Agent,* Dutton, 1976; *Liner: A Novel About a Great Ship,* 1977.

Nonfiction: (Under pseudonyms Ann Marie Burgess and Michael Burgess) *Neither Sin nor Shame,* Belmont-Tower Books, 1961; (under pseudonyms Ann Marie Burgess and Michael Burgess) *The Girl Market,* Monarch Books, 1963; *Belgium,* Macmillan, 1964; *Kit Carson: Folk Hero and Man,* Doubleday, 1964; (with Louis P. Saxe) *Sex and the Mature Man,* Gilbert Press, 1964; *Food,* Doubleday, 1965; (with Ellen F. Birchall) *Sex and the Adult Woman,* Gilbert Press, 1965; *Light-Horse Harry: A Biography of Washington's Great Cavalryman,* Doubleday, 1966; *The Anthem,* M. Evans, 1967; *Franklin: America's "Lost State",* Crowell-Collier Press, 1968; *The Edict of Nantes,* illustrations by Bob Pepper, Grosset, 1969; *Because I Loved Him: The Life and Loves of Lillie Langtry,* Morrow, 1971 (published in England as *Lillie Langtry: A Biography,* R. Hale, 1972); *The Prodigal Genius: The Life and Times of Honore de Balzac,* Doubleday, 1972; *Daughters of Earth and Wa-*

ter: A Biography of Mary Wollstonecraft Shelley, Morrow, 1973; *The Velvet Glove,* Thomas Nelson, 1975; *Harriet Beecher Stowe: A Biography,* Praeger, 1976; *Sad Swashbuckler: The Life of William Walker,* Thomas Nelson, 1976; *Statue in Search of a Pedestal: A Biography of the Marquis de Lafayette,* Dodd, 1976; *Trelawny's World: A Biography of Edward John Trelawny,* Doubleday, 1977; *The Trial of Andrew Johnson,* Thomas Nelson, 1977.

For children: *Nathan Hale: Espionage Agent,* Doubleday, 1960; *Rock of Freedom: The Story of the Plymouth Colony,* illustrations by Barry Martin, Messner, 1964; *The Last Wilderness: The Saga of America's Mountain Men,* illustrations by Martin, Messner, 1966; *Mr. Madison's War: 1912, The Second War for Independence,* illustrations by Martin, Messner, 1966; *Survival: Jamestown; First English Colony in America,* illustrations by Martin, Messner, 1967; *Passage to the West: The Great Voyages of Henry Hudson,* illustrations by Martin, Messner, 1968; *James Monroe: Hero of American Diplomacy,* illustrations by Tommy Upshur, Prentice-Hall, 1969; *Free and Independent: The Confederation of the United States,* Thomas Nelson, 1970.

Under pseudonym Samuel Edwards: *The Scimitar,* Farrar, Straus, 1955; *The King's Messenger,* Farrar, Straus, 1956; *The Naked Maja,* McGraw, 1959; *The Queen's Husband,* McGraw, 1960; *The White Plume,* Morrow, 1961; *Master of Castile,* Morrow, 1962; *Daughter of Gascony,* Macrae, 1963; *55 Days at Peking: A Novel* (based on the screenplay by Philip Yordan and Bernard Gordon), Bantam, 1963; *The Magnificent Adventures of Alexander Mackenzie,* Redman, 1965; *Barbary General: The Life of William H. Eaton,* Prentice-Hall, 1968; *Theodora: A Novel,* Prentice-Hall, 1969; *The Divine Mistress,* McKay, 1970; *Victor Hugo: A Tumultuous Life,* McKay, 1971, reprinted as *Victor Hugo: A Biography,* New American Library, 1975; *The Double Lives of Francisco de Goya,* Grosset, 1973; *Peter Paul Rubens: A Biography of a Giant,* McKay, 1973; *George Sand: A Biography of the First Modern, Liberated Woman,* McKay, 1973; *The Exploiters,* Praeger, 1974; *Rebel! A Biography of Tom Paine,* Praeger, 1974; *The Caves of Guernica: A Novel,* Praeger, 1975; *The Vidocq Dossier: The Story of the World's First Detective,* Houghton, 1977.

Under pseudonym Paul Lewis: *The Nelson Touch,* Holt, 1960; *The Gentle Fury,* Holt, 1961; *Queen of Caprice: A Biography of Kristina of Sweden,* Holt, 1962; *Lady of France: A Biography of Gabrielle d'Estrees,* Funk, 1964 (published in England under pseudonym Samuel Edwards, Redman, 1964); *Queen of the Plaza: A Biography of Adah Issacs Menken,* Funk, 1964 (published in England under pseudonym Samuel Edwards, Redman, 1965); *The Great Rogue: A Biography of Captain John Smith,* McKay, 1966; *Yankee Admiral: A Biography of David Dixon Porter,* McKay, 1968; *The Grand Incendiary: A Biography of Samuel Adams,* Dial, 1973; *The Man Who Lost America: A Biography of Gentleman Johnny Burgoyne,* Dial, 1973.

Under pseudonym Leon Phillips: *When the Wind Blows,* Farrar, Straus, 1956; *Split Bamboo,* Doubleday, 1966; *The Fantastic Breed: Americans in King George's War* (juvenile), Doubleday, 1968; *First Lady of America: A Romanticized Biography of Pocahontas,* Westover, 1973.

Under pseudonym Carter A. Vaughan; all published by Doubleday: *The Devil's Bride,* 1956; *The Invincibles,* 1958; *The Charlatan,* 1959; *The Wilderness,* 1959; *The Yankee Brig,* 1960; *Scoundrel's Brigade,* 1962; *The Yankee Rascals,* 1963; *Dragon Cove,* 1964; *Roanoke Warrior,* 1965; *Fortress Fury,* 1966; *The Silver Saber,* 1967; *The River Devils,* 1968; *The Seneca Hostage,* 1969.

SIDELIGHTS: Gerson has written over a hundred books, many of which have been published in foreign countries. The author combines fact and fiction in his novels, which frequently receive mixed reviews from literary critics who either praise or question the credibility of the book's historical aspects. Gerson's first historical novel, *Savage Gentleman*, was set in the eighteenth century during the French and Indian wars. A critic for the *Chicago Sunday Tribune* noted: "*Savage Gentleman* has the merit of restraint and spare writing, though not at the expense of color or action. Its movement is rapid and steady, and no reader will find the novel dragging at any time. Mr. Gerson's historical research seems to have been adequate, and he has indeed re-created a little known period of American history. . . ."

In reviewing Gerson's novel, *Mohawk Ladder,* a critic for the *Saturday Review of Literature* wrote: "Mr. Gerson's kind is the tale with action, plenty of it, a fast-moving plot with enough intricacies to baffle us agreeably, a sympathetic hero, a villanous villain, and somewhat perfunctory characterization." In reviewing the same book a reviewer for the *New York Herald Tribune* commented that "the narrative may not be history, but it is certainly a lusty package of entertainment."

Gerson used the Mexican War as a backdrop for his book *The Golden Eagle.* "Seldom does a historical adventure novel combine the elements of authenticity, readability and suspense as convincingly as does *The Golden Eagle,*" observed a critic for the *Springfield Republican.* A *New York Times* reviewer noted, "The Mexican War has figured too seldom in historical fiction; Mr. Gerson's novel rouses that somewhat torpid conflict from its long siesta and puts zip and vinegar in it."

In *The Highwayman* Gerson told a tale based upon America's colonial lifestyle in 1745. "The author displays, as in earlier books, a writing style that depends for suspense on the devices of posing threats which are never quite fulfilled, [and] raising impossibilities that are always overcome. . . . The result is that *The Highwayman* builds up to an exciting tale, mellerdrammerish in tone. It provides pleasant, light entertainment for a quiet evening. . . . But it carries little conviction that here is life as it may have been lived at a crucial period in history," wrote a reviewer for the *Chicago Sunday Tribune.* In contrast a critic for the *San Francisco Chronicle* noted that "the author takes his history seriously enough to insist on accuracy of detail, and he has skill enough to create believable people who speak in a most plausible way."

AVOCATIONAL INTERESTS: Gardening and swimming.

BIOGRAPHICAL/CRITICAL SOURCES: Chicago Sunday Tribune, June 11, 1950; *Saturday Review of Literature,* July 7, 1951; *New York Herald Tribune Book Review,* July 8, 1951; *New York Times,* June 14, 1953; *Springfield Republican,* August 9, 1953; *Chicago Sunday Tribune,* November 20, 1955; *San Francisco Chronicle,* December 11, 1955; *Kirkus Reviews,* March 15, 1957; *Saturday Review,* July 6, 1957; *Christian Science Monitor,* January 31, 1973; *New York Times Book Review,* February 11, 1973; *Book World,* July 4, 1976; *Booklist,* May 1, 1977.*

* * *

GERTH, Hans Heinrich   1908-1978

OBITUARY NOTICE: Born April 24, 1908, in Kassel, Germany; died December 29, 1978, in Frankfurt, West Germany. Educator, scholar, and author best known for his English translations of Max Weber's *Sociology on Hinduism*

in India and the *Sociology of Judaism,* and as the co-author, with C. Wright Mills, of *Character and Social Structure.* During World War II, after his expulsion from Nazi Germany, Gerth wrote for several German periodicals, including the daily newspaper *Berliner Tageblatt.* Obituaries and other sources: *American Men and Women of Science: The Social and Behavioral Sciences,* 12th edition, Bowker, 1973; *New York Times,* January 4, 1979, January 5, 1979.

* * *

GERZON, Mark

PERSONAL: married; children: Shane, Ari. *Education:* Harvard University, B.A., 1970; University of Chicago, further study, 1971.

CAREER: Journalist.

WRITINGS: The Whole World Is Watching, Viking, 1962; *A Childhood for Every Child,* Dutton, 1973; *The Young Internationalists,* University Press of Hawaii, 1973. Contributor to magazines and newspapers, including *New Age.*

* * *

GETTINGS, Eunice J.   1901(?)-1978

OBITUARY NOTICE: Born c. 1901, in Suffolk, Va.; died October 10, 1978, in Washington, D.C. Gettings worked for the Census Bureau as a government editor for thirty years before retiring in 1962. Obituaries and other sources: *Washington Post,* October 12, 1978.

* * *

GILMAN, J. D.
   See ORGILL, Douglas

* * *

GILMAN, James
   See GILMORE, Joseph L(ee)

* * *

GILMER, Ann
   See ROSS, W(illiam) E(dward) D(aniel)

* * *

GILMORE, Joseph L(ee)   1929-
   (Daniel Bennett, James Gilman)

PERSONAL: Born January 31, 1929, in Portsmouth, Ohio; son of Joseph P. (an editor) and Vesta (Reynolds) Gilmore; married Dona Lee Hanes, July 4, 1952; children: James Lee, Billie (Mrs. David Anderson), Jody (Mrs. Antonio Ospina). *Education:* Ohio State University, B.A., 1952. *Home:* 928 Valleyview Dr., Bellevue, Ohio 44811. *Agent:* Dominick Abel Literary Agency, 498 West End Ave., Apt. 12-C, New York, N.Y. 10024. *Office:* Literary Associates, 5220 East 52nd St., Indianapolis, Ind. 46406.

CAREER: Lorain Journal, Lorain, Ohio, reporter, 1952-56; *TV Guide,* Cleveland, Ohio, editor, 1956-57; *Toledo Blade,* Toledo, Ohio, reporter, 1957-61; Goodyear Tire & Rubber Co., Akron, Ohio, public relations manager, 1961-70; Literary Associates, Indianapolis, Ind., president, 1969—. *Military service:* U.S. Navy, 1946-48; became seaman first class.

WRITINGS: Vendetta (novel), Pinnacle Books, 1973, revised edition, 1976; (with E. A. Komorowski) *Night Never Ending* (nonfiction), Regnery, 1974; *View from Renner's Corners* (biography), Charter Publications, 1976; (under pseudonym James Gilman) *Multiple Kill: Operation Nazi* (novel), Award Books, 1976; *Rattlers* (novel), Signet, 1979; *Blue Flame* (novel), Fawcett, 1979; (under pseudonym Daniel Bennett) *Ask No Mercy* (novel), Ace Books, 1979. Contributor to magazines, including *Redbook*.

WORK IN PROGRESS: A novel probing cryonics, *Morpheos Cold;* research on "total civilization for a Year Two Thousand series."

SIDELIGHTS: Gilmore writes: "My greatest motivating factor is a desire to learn; in writing, one must read incredible amounts and find it entertaining and instructive. Research on a specific project, such as a book, is perhaps the most gratifying kind of reading for me—it is sheer pleasure. One tenet I follow and advise others to follow is: if you do not read, you cannot write. I have no vocational interest other than writing."

AVOCATIONAL INTERESTS: Golf, travel (especially overseas), collecting antiques, decorating, cooking, boating.

* * *

GILMOUR, H. B. 1939-

PERSONAL: Born November 24, 1939, in Brooklyn, N.Y.; child of Sydney Bindler (a pharmacist) and Sara (Middleberg) Weissman. *Education:* University of Florida, B.A., 1961. *Home:* 314 West 89th St., New York, N.Y. 10024.

CAREER: Bantam Books, Inc. (publishing house), New York, N.Y., 1963-76, worked as secretary, staff member in promotion and editorial departments, associate editor on youth-oriented projects, copy writer, and copy chief; writer, 1976—.

WRITINGS: The Trade (novel), Warner Paperback, 1973; *Saturday Night Fever* (novelization based on the screenplay of the same name), Bantam, 1977; *Eyes of Laura Mars* (novelization based on the screenplay of the same name), Bantam, 1978.

WORK IN PROGRESS: A novel, for Morrow; "All That Jazz" and "Rich Kids," novelizations of screenplays.

* * *

GILROY, Frank D(aniel) 1925-

PERSONAL: Born October 13, 1925, in New York, N.Y.; son of Frank B. (a coffee broker) and Bettina (Vasti) Gilroy; married Ruth Dorothy Gaydos (a secretary), February 13, 1954; children: Anthony, John, Daniel. *Education:* Dartmouth College, B.A. (magna cum laude), 1950; graduate study at Yale University. *Residence:* Monroe, N.Y. *Office:* Dramatists Guild, 234 West 44th St., New York, N.Y. 10036.

CAREER: Playwright and author of scripts for television and motion pictures; director of motion pictures. Worked as messenger for Young and Rubicam, New York, N.Y.; beach cabana renter in Atlantic City, N.J. *Military service:* U.S. Army, 1943-46. *Member:* Writers Guild of America, Dramatists Guild (president 1969-71), Directors Guild of America. *Awards, honors:* Obie Award for best play from *Village Voice*, 1962, for "Who'll Save the Plowboy?"; Outer Circle Award for outstanding new playwright, 1964; Drama Critics Circle Award, New York Theatre Club Award, Antoinette Perry Award from League of New York Theatres and Producers, and Pulitzer Prize for Drama, all 1965, all for "The Subject Was Roses"; Silver Bear Award from Berlin Film Festival, 1971, for "Desperate Characters."

WRITINGS: About Those Roses; Or, How Not to Do a Play and Succeed (journal), Random House, 1965; *Private* (novel), Harcourt, 1970; (with Ruth G. Gilroy) *Little Ego* (juvenile), Simon & Schuster, 1970; *From Noon Till Three: The Possibly True and Certainly Tragic Story of an Outlaw and a Lady Whose Love Knew No Bounds* (novel), Doubleday, 1973 (published in England as *For Want of a Horse*, Coronet, 1975).

Plays: *Who'll Save the Plowboy?* (three-act; first produced Off-Broadway at Phoenix Theater, January 9, 1962), Random House, 1962; *The Subject Was Roses* (two-act; first produced on Broadway at Royale Theater, May 26, 1964), Samuel French, 1962; *That Summer–That Fall; and, Far Rockaway* first produced in 1967; latter first produced for television in 1965), Random House, 1967; *The Only Game in Town* (two-act; first produced in 1968), Random House, 1968; *A Matter of Pride* (first produced for television in 1957; adapted from the story by John Langdon, "The Blue Serge Suit"), Samuel French, 1970; *Present Tense* (includes "Come Next Tuesday," "Twas Brillig," "So Please Be Kind," and "Present Tense"; first produced in 1972), Samuel French, 1973.

Screenplays: (With Russell Rouse) "The Fastest Gun Alive" (adapted from the play and short story by Gilroy), Metro-Goldwyn-Mayer (MGM), 1956; (with Beirne Lay, Jr.) "The Gallant Hours," United Artists, 1960; "The Subject Was Roses" (adapted from the play by Gilroy), MGM, 1968; "The Only Game in Town" (adapted from the play by Gilroy), Twentieth Century-Fox, 1969; (and director) "Desperate Characters" (adapted from the novel by Paula Fox), ITC and TDJ, 1971; (and director) "From Noon Till Three" (adapted from the novel by Gilroy), 1976; (and producer-director) "Once in Paris," 1978.

Also contributor of teleplays to various programs, including "U.S. Steel Hour," "Kraft Theatre," "Playhouse 90," "Studio One," "Lux Video Theatre," and "Omnibus." Author of scripts for series, including "The Rifleman," "Have Gun, Will Travel," "Burke's Law," and "Gibbsville."

SIDELIGHTS: The success of "Who'll Save the Plowboy" in 1962 established Gilroy as a major new talent in play writing. Earlier, he'd churned out numerous plays and scripts for a variety of television programs, ranging from "Playhouse 90" to "The Rifleman." But he regarded his work for television as an occupational duty while his plays, he felt, contained his real work.

Gilroy wrote "Who'll Save the Plowboy" in 1957 but encountered difficulties in finding an obliging producer. Time after time, Gilroy endured the enthusiasm of directors only to be informed by producers that the play lacked an audience. Finally the play opened Off-Broadway under the direction of Daniel Petrie, who later gained recognition for his own work in television and film. The grim tale of two ex-G.I.'s reunion met with reasonable reviews. Critics unaccustomed to the stark realism of the play implied that it was "crude," but others praised its "sympathy" and its fresh approach.

Gilroy followed "Who'll Save the Plowman" with his most popular work, "The Subject Was Roses." The story of a World War II veteran's return home to parent's vying for his affection received numerous awards. Oddly enough, Gilroy kept the play from being produced for two years after completion. He'd demanded that the play be performed on his conditions, one of which was that Jack Albertson, an unknown performer who later appeared in the television series

"Chico and the Man," be cast as the father. Discouraged because no producers would handle the play under his stipulations, Gilroy approached his friends, Edgar G. Lansbury and Ulu Grossbard, for help. Lansbury became both investor and producer while Grossbard agreed to direct.

After the success of "Who'll Save the Plowboy" and "The Subject Was Roses," Gilroy went on to write several more plays but also acquired an appreciative audience as both a novelist and filmmaker. His novel *Private* harkens back to the settings of both the plays mentioned. Phoebe Adams called *Private*, "A war novel, reduced to brainlessly simple terms. . . . It is only at the end that one realizes how subtly the author has presented the transformation of his hero from amiable, homesick civilian to wary, surly combat veteran."

"Desperate Character" was Gilroy's first film as director. Although he was praised for his faithfulness to the original novel by Paula Fox, Gilroy was also criticised by Vincent Canby for his disinclination to invest artistic properties into the film. Wrote Canby, "'Desperate Characters' left me, if not unmoved, then unenriched. It's as if cheerlessness had been bottled straight, without the additive that transforms recognizable experience into art." However, the film also received good reviews from several critics who noted the realistic atmosphere and sense of characterizations. "Desperate Characters" also won top honors at the Berlin Film Festival, a remarkable feat for a directorial debut.

Gilroy's next two films were a disappointment. "From Noon Till Three," one of Charles Bronson's few unprofitable films, was downplayed by distributors. In an effort to prevent the same thing from happening to "Once in Paris," Gilroy himself took over its distribution. Unfortunately, this did little to aid the movie. Critics tended to agree with Vincent Canby that "'Once in Paris' is not a mistake, but it's too innocent and too without guile for its own good. . . . The film means to be a romantic lark, but this lark seldom becomes airborne."

BIOGRAPHICAL/CRITICAL SOURCES: New York Times, January 28, 1962, September 23, 1974, November 9, 1978; *New York Post,* June 7, 1964; *Atlantic,* December, 1970; *Contemporary Literary Criticism,* Volume 2, Gale, 1974.*

*   *   *

GILSON, Etienne Henri   1884-1978

OBITUARY NOTICE: Born June 13, 1884, in Paris, France; died September 19, 1978, in Cravant, France. Historian, philosopher, educator, and author best known as an authority on the lives and works of St. Thomas Aquinas and St. Augustine. He was a professor of medieval philosophy at the Sorbonne and held the chair of the history of philosophy in the Middle Ages at the College de France. Though he lectured at universities throughout France, Great Britain, and the United States, he taught primarily at the Pontifical Institute of Medieval Studies in Toronto, Ontario, which he helped to establish in 1929. In 1950 and 1951, Gilson became involved in a stormy political controversy when he advocated a policy of neutrality to keep Europe out of any future war. He urged France to remain politically neutral when the United States took a firm stand against the Soviet Union, and to dramatize his position, he resigned his chair at the College de France, stating that he would rather live in North America than remain to see Europe devastated by another war. Some of his writings include *The Philosophy of St. Thomas Aquinas, Reason and Revelation in the Middle Ages, Christianity and Philosophy, God and Philosophy,*

and *A History of Christian Philosophy in the Middle Ages.* Obituaries and other sources: *The Oxford Companion to French Literature,* corrected edition, Oxford University Press, 1966; *The Canadian Who's Who,* Volume 12, Who's Who Canadian Publications, 1972; *Who's Who in the World,* 2nd edition, Marquis, 1973; *Who's Who,* 126th edition, St. Martin's, 1974; *Washington Post,* September 22, 1978; *Time,* October 2, 1978; *AB Bookman's Weekly,* January 8, 1979.

*   *   *

GIRODO, Michel   1945-

PERSONAL: Born February 3, 1945, in Farges (L'Ain), France; son of Victor and Juliette (Savisky) Girodo; married Barbara J. Haines, November 11, 1971; children: Paul. *Education:* Sir George Williams University, B.A., 1966; University of New Brunswick, M.A., 1968; Carleton University, Ph.D., 1970; postdoctoral study at Royal Ottawa Hospital, 1970-71. *Home:* 8 Garden Pl., Ottawa, Ontario, Canada K2H 6M3. *Office:* School of Psychology, University of Ottawa, Ottawa, Ontario, Canada.

CAREER: University of Ottawa, Ottawa, Ontario, assistant professor, 1972-75, associate professor of psychology, 1975—, director of clinical psychology, 1978—. Lecturer at Carleton University, 1970-72. Member of publications board of Social Science Federation of Canada, 1977—; consultant to Public Service Commission. *Military service:* Royal Canadian Navy, 1963-67; became lieutenant. *Member:* Canadian Psychological Association, American Psychological Association, American Society for Clinical Hypnosis, Association for the Advancement of Behaviour Therapy, Society for Research in Social Issues, Ontario Psychological Association, Ontario Society for Clinical Hypnosis.

WRITINGS: (Contributor) Charles Speilberger and I. G. Sarason, editors, *Stress and Anxiety,* Volume IV, Hemisphere, 1977; *Shy? You Don't Have to Be,* Pocket Books, 1978. Contributor to journals in the behavioral sciences. Editorial consultant to *Canada's Mental Health,* 1975—; member of editorial board of *Canadian Journal of Behavioural Science,* 1978—.

WORK IN PROGRESS: Research on shyness and mental bias, the effects of contracting and communication skills training on disturbed marital relations, and managing interpersonal relations through self-awareness strategies.

SIDELIGHTS: Girodo told *CA* how he overcame his own battle with shyness: "Eleven years in boarding school failed to equip me with the skills for dealing effectively with the opposite sex. In college I developed a severe case of shyness and went to a guidance clinic for help. I told the counselor I wanted help on academic matters, since I thought shyness was a silly complaint. His message to me was 'if you try hard enough, you can succeed.' I applied this advice to social situations, tasks, and interpersonal relations. I set out graduated goals and assignments to get me out of my shell and tried hard at each endeavor. It worked. The book now casts this 'try hard and you'll succeed' formula in the context of psychological theory."

According to information supplied by the publisher, *Shy? You Don't Have to Be* "is the product of five years of social research on the problem of shyness and how to overcome it. The nature of these investigations ranged from: (1) the study of social life, rituals, and reactions of people in singles bars, discotheques, and organized 'singles vacations' in the United States and several countries in Europe; (2) the study of the problems caused by shyness in children, adolescents, married people, and among the elderly; (3) to an extensive clinical survey of styles that cope best with social stress; and (4) to the analysis of shyness components and the application of a variety of psychological strategies for altering these. Findings from these studies led to the development of a 'Shyness Clinic' where the use of these procedures and principles were developed, tried out, refined, and finally spelled out in a series of step-by-step social learning exercises.''

Among other conclusions, Girodo's research revealed that ''when shyness is prolonged it produces social isolation and loneliness accompanied by feelings of boredom, aimlessness, and social exclusion.'' In addition, ''it has become clear that the number of social contacts and friendships a person has is very much related to his emotional well being.'' Finally, ''marriage will not prevent feelings of isolation, social loneliness and depression.''

''A large portion of the book,'' says the publisher, ''is devoted to teaching specific psychological methods for overcoming shyness reactions. These are based upon the successful operation of the author's Shyness Clinic, and guide the reader in a step-by-step self-paced program that covers all shyness components. The last chapter deals with preventing shyness tomorrow and focuses upon a description of a psychological and social life style designed to help people cope with stresses caused by social change.''

* * *

GIROUD, Francoise 1916-

PERSONAL: Born September 21, 1916, in Geneva, Switzerland; daughter of Salih (a journalist) and Elda (Faragi) Gourdji; married Anatole Eliacheff, June 25, 1946 (divorced, 1961); children: Alain Danis (died, 1972), Caroline Eliacheff. *Education:* Educated in France. *Politics:* Radical Party. *Religion:* Catholic. *Agent:* Max Becker, 115 East 82nd St., New York, N.Y. 10028. *Office:* c/o Editions Fayard, 75 rue des Saints-Peres, Paris 75007, France.

CAREER: Script-girl in cinema productions with Marc Allegret (''Fanny''), 1932, and Jean Renoir (''La Grande Illusion''), 1936; assistant producer, 1937; *Elle* (women's magazine), Paris, France, editor-in-chief, 1946-53; *L'Express* (news magazine), co-founder and editor-in-chief, 1953-74, president of Express-Union, 1970-74; served as French minister of women, 1974-76, and minister of culture, 1976-77; writer. Press consultant to Hachette (publishers). Vice-president of Parti Radical. *Wartime service:* Member of French Resistance. *Awards, honors:* Received Merite Civil decoration from Spain; Ordre du Drapeau decoration from Yugoslavia; D.H.L. from University of Michigan, 1976, and Goucher College, 1977.

WRITINGS: Le Tout Paris, Gallimard, 1952; *Nouveaux Portraits,* (title means ''New Portraits''), Gallimard, 1953; *La Nouvelle Vague* (title means ''The New Wave''), Gallimard, 1958; *Si je mens . . . ,* Stock, 1971, translation by Richard Seaver published as *I Give You My Word,* Houghton, 1974; *Une poignee d'eau* (title means ''A Handful of Water), Laffont, 1972; *La Comedie du pouvoir* (title means ''The Comedy of Power''), Fayard, 1977.

Also author of dialogue and adaptations for numerous films, including ''Antoine et Antoinette,'' 1947; ''La Belle que voila,'' 1950; ''L'Amour, Madame,'' 1951; and ''Julietta,'' 1953. Regular contributor to *Le Monde.*

WORK IN PROGRESS: Memoire de femme, a book on women; *Ce que je crois* (title means ''What I Believe'').

SIDELIGHTS: As secretary of the world's first ministry for the feminine condition, recently created by French President Valery Giscard D'Estaing, Francoise Giroud captured the world's attention by her attempts to meet the ministry's stated goal of ''overseeing the integration of women into contemporary French society.'' In a society still largely dominated by the sexist Napoleonic Code and traditional views of women's roles, French women have continued to fill low-status, low-paying jobs and to endure discrimination because of their sex. Giroud viewed her task primarily as one of ''[changing] the mentality of the people'' in order to facilitate the adoption of various reform measures. High on the list of her priorities were the special problems of older women, who often lacked skills necessary for entering the work force because of the years they had spent in child-rearing. Giroud also sought to encourage the development of day-care centers and the institution of more flexible working hours to enable women with families to pursue jobs outside their homes. Despite the visible accomplishments of women in French national life, Giroud remained concerned with the *average* level of women in the society and endeavored to upgrade their status by such measures as urging professional schools to admit more women. Determined to find ways of enforcing the already-existing legislation guaranteeing women equal pay for equal work, she also strove for more stringent legislation banning discrimination in hiring practices. Besides the issue of employment, Giroud also concentrated on other concerns of women such as the liberalization of abortion laws and the banning of exploitative television advertising.

Though she has forcefully denounced sexism in French society, both as editor of the popular magazine *L'Express* and as minister of women, Giroud has refused to ally herself with feminists or the women's liberation movement. In an interview with Sally Quinn of the *Washington Post* she once declared: ''I have no interest in 'women' as such. I can't stand this idea that there is a world plot by men to subjugate women. If it is true, and the men have succeeded, then women really are stupid.'' She told *CA* that she is reluctant, or more exactly, *refractaire,* towards radical feminism.

When asked about the phenomenon of reverse discrimination, Giroud told *CA:* ''The problem of 'reverse discrimination' doesn't exist in France—or perhaps I should say, not yet. But I believe that we are far from it, even if it should come about some day. The economic crisis and the accompanying unemployment are in the process of seriously slowing down things, for one thing. Besides that, it seems to me that discrimination is felt much less in France than in the United States.''

BIOGRAPHICAL/CRITICAL SOURCES: Time, July 29, 1974; *Ms.,* January, 1975; *Saturday Review,* June 14, 1975; *Newsweek,* September 22, 1975.

* * *

GLASS, David Victor 1911-1978

OBITUARY NOTICE: Born January 2, 1911, in London, England; died September 23, 1978, in London. Educator and author best known for his fifty year association with the London School of Economics and Political Science. Glass held several government positions in London, particularly with the Ministry of Supply, and in Washington, D.C. He served as United Kingdom representative to the United Nations and various UNESCO conferences. His research and writings concerned current and historical population trends, and among his publications are the influential *Town in a Changing World* and *Population Policies and Movements in*

Europe. Obituaries and other sources: *The Author's and Writer's Who's Who,* 6th edition, Burke's Peerage, 1971; *Who's Who,* 126th edition, St. Martin's, 1974; *The International Who's Who,* Europa, 1974; *AB Bookman's Weekly,* October 23, 1978.

*   *   *

GLASS, Joanna (McClelland) 1936-

PERSONAL: Born October 7, 1936, in Saskatoon, Saskatchewan, Canada; daughter of Morrell MacKenzie and Katharine (Switzer) McClelland; divorced; children: Jennifer, Mavis, Lawrence. *Education:* Attended Saskatoon Collegiate, Saskatoon, Saskatchewan. *Residence:* Canada. *Agent:* Lucy Kroll Agency, 390 West End Ave., New York, N.Y. 10024.

CAREER: Writer.

WRITINGS: Reflections on a Mountain Summer (novel), Knopf, 1974; *Canadian Gothic/American Modern* (two one-act plays; first produced in New York, N.Y. at Manhattan Theatre Club, in 1973); (contributor) James Wright, editor, *Winter's Tales, 22,* St. Martin's, 1976; (contributor) Stanley Richards, editor, *Best Short Plays, 1978,* Chilton, 1978.

Unpublished plays: "Artichoke" (two-act), first produced in New Haven, Conn. at Long Wharf Theatre, 1975; "The Last Chalice" (two-act), first produced in Winnipeg, Manitoba at Manitoba Theatre Centre, October, 1977.

SIDELIGHTS: Reflections on a Mountain Summer was read in ten segments on BBC-Radio in 1975. A ninety-minute television adaptation of "Artichoke" was broadcast in 1977 on CBC-TV.

*   *   *

GLIMCHER, Arnold B. 1938-

PERSONAL: Born March 12, 1938, in Duluth, Minn.; son of Paul and Eva (Fishman) Glimcher; married Mildred L. Cooper, December 20, 1959; children: Paul W., Marc C. *Education:* Massachusetts College of Art, B.F.A., 1960; graduate study at Boston University, 1961-62. *Office:* Pace Gallery, 32 East 57th St., New York, N.Y. 10022.

CAREER: Pace Gallery, New York, N.Y., president, 1960—.

WRITINGS: Louise Nevelson, Praeger, 1972, revised edition, Dutton, 1976; *Lucas Samaras: Photo-Transformations,* Dutton, 1975; *Parallelism in Visual Sciences and Visual Arts,* Dutton, in press.

*   *   *

GODFREY, Lionel (Robert Holcombe) 1932-
(Elliot Kennedy, Scott Mitchell)

PERSONAL: Born April 26, 1932, in Mansfield, England; son of Reginald Thomas (a postmaster) and Kathleen (a pianist; maiden name, Holcombe) Godfrey; married Sylvia Eve Christy, 1954 (divorced, 1969); married Maureen Anderson Hendry (a legal executive), July 30, 1969. *Education:* Attended University of Freiburg, 1951; University of Nottingham, B.A. (honors), 1954. *Home:* 9 Aldwick Close, Leamington Spa, Warwickshire CV32 6LP, England. *Agent:* Hughes Massie Ltd., 69 Great Russell St., London WC1B 3DH, England.

CAREER: Writer, 1963—.

WRITINGS: The Life and Crimes of Errol Flynn, R. Hale, 1977; *Paul Newman, Superstar,* R. Hale, 1978.

Suspense novels under pseudonym Elliot Kennedy: *The Big Loser,* R. Hale, 1972; *Bullets Are Final,* R. Hale, 1973; *That Fatal Feeling,* R. Hale, 1974; *Never Say Dead,* R. Hale, 1974; *The Dead Sleep Late,* R. Hale, 1975; *No Love in a Bullet,* R. Hale, 1976.

Suspense novels under pseudonym Scott Mitchell: *Sables Spell Trouble,* Hammond, 1963; *Some Dames Play Rough,* Hammond, 1963; *Deadly Persuasion,* Hammond, 1964; *The Lonely Shroud,* Hammond, 1964; *Come, Sweet Death,* Hammond, 1967; *Double Bluff,* Jenkins, 1968; *A Knife-Edged Thing,* Cassell, 1969; *A Haven for the Damned,* R. Hale, 1971; *You'll Never Get to Heaven,* R. Hale, 1972; *Rage in Babylon,* R. Hale, 1972; *The Girl in the Wet-Look Bikini,* R. Hale, 1973; *Dead on Arrival,* R. Hale, 1974; *Nice Guys Don't Win,* R. Hale, 1974; *Over My Dead Body,* R. Hale, 1974; *Death's Busy Crossroads,* R. Hale, 1975; *Obsession,* R. Hale, 1976.

Author of "Filmusic," a column in *Films and Filming,* 1966-69. Contributor to cinema journals.

WORK IN PROGRESS: The Rise and Fall of the Hollywood Stars; a biography of an expatriate American star.

SIDELIGHTS: Godfrey writes: "Although I have written for private pleasure for as long as I can remember, my public career as an author has been shaped largely by a series of accidents. It to be mindful of practical exigencies and thus to tailor one's writing to a market smacks of hack-work, I take comfort in the reflection that Bach and Mozart were in a sense glorious hacks. These prefatory remarks may explain many facts, not least how I came to create two series of mystery novels. I am by instinct an iconoclastic novelist, deeply absorbed in style and psychology, and I have written many 'straight' novels; but my first published work, a mystery novel, was composed as a joke—an affectionate parody of a forties gangster movie. Later works were written more seriously but never, I hope, solemnly—and always with the aim of finding room within a restrictive genre for wit, civilised expression, and literate notions. I see no reason why entertainment has to be sedative.

"My novels have been interspersed with critical writings on the cinéma, and in 1975 I was commissioned to write a biography of Errol Flynn. This work came conveniently after a fifteen-year period in which I had published twenty-two mystery novels and had come to believe (if only temporarily) that I had exhausted the possibilities of the genre. I have since, with greater creative freedom, written a critical biography of Paul Newman, and I am at present working on a more general critical volume about the nature of stardom.

"In many ways, I regard myself as an American author. My novels are American both in setting and ethos, but my deep interest in Americana is a matter of critical affection rather than adulation. Among the authors who have probably influenced me are Henry David Thoreau, Scott Fitzgerald, Robert Penn Warren, Raymond Chandler, Flaubert, and Turgenev."

AVOCATIONAL INTERESTS: Music, cinema, good food.

*   *   *

GODFREY, Michael A. 1940-

PERSONAL: Born June 29, 1940, in Washington, D.C.; son of Arthur M. (an entertainer) and Mary (Bourke) Godfrey. *Education:* University of North Carolina, earned B.S. degree. *Religion:* "Nature." *Home:* 210 High St., Carrboro, N.C. 27510. *Agent:* George F. Scheer, Kings Mill Rd., Chapel Hill, N.C. 27514.

CAREER: Air-Care, Inc., Rocky Mount, N.C., manager and commercial pilot, 1967; Peat, Marwich, Mitchell & Co., Washington, D.C., financial consultant, 1969-70; University of North Carolina, Chapel Hill, director of systems design, 1970-76; free-lance writer and nature photographer, 1976—. *Military service:* U.S. Air Force, 1963-66; served in Asia.

WRITINGS: A Closer Look, Sierra Club Books, 1975; *Winter Birds of the Carolinas and Nearby States,* Blair, 1976. Contributor to wildlife and gardening magazines.

WORK IN PROGRESS: Field Guide to the Life Systems of the Piedmont, publication by Sierra Club Books.

SIDELIGHTS: Godfrey writes: "My personal and professional orientation is toward seeing and expressing the life processes which are close at hand, accessible, but easily overlooked."

AVOCATIONAL INTERESTS: White-water canoeing, rock climbing, running, American literature.

* * *

GOLDBERG, Norman L(ewis) 1906-

PERSONAL: Born February 10, 1906, in Nashville, Tenn.; son of Sam (a merchant) and Theresa (Cronstine) Goldberg; married Roselea Jonas, February 17, 1946. *Education:* University of Toledo, B.S., 1926; Vanderbilt University, M.D., 1930. *Politics:* Independent. *Religion:* Jewish. *Home and office:* 721 Brightwaters Blvd., St. Petersburg, Fla. 33704.

CAREER: University Hospital, Iowa City, Iowa, intern and resident in surgery, 1930-32; Mt. Sinai Hospital, New York City, general surgeon, 1932-53; art historian, lecturer, and writer in St. Petersburg, Fla., 1954—. *Military service:* U.S. Army, Medical Corps, 1942-45; became captain. *Member:* College Art Association of America. *Awards, honors:* Millard Meiss Publication Award from College Art Association of America, 1976, for *John Crome the Elder.*

WRITINGS: Landscapes of the Norwich School, Cummer Gallery of Art, 1967; *John Crome the Elder,* New York University Press, 1978. Contributor to art and medical journals.

WORK IN PROGRESS: The Etchings of John Sell Cotman, publication expected in 1985; *The Promenade Tradition in Art,* publication expected in 1986.

SIDELIGHTS: Goldberg comments: "I am a connoisseur of art works of the Old Masters: British and Dutch. The purchase of an unsigned painting, presumably by John Crome, in 1951, sparked my interest in art and fueled all subsequent research, extending up to the present time."

BIOGRAPHICAL/CRITICAL SOURCES: Journal of the American Medical Association, June, 1959; *The Connoisseur,* December, 1960, "Year Book," 1962, November, 1963, February, 1967; *New York Times,* March 18, 1967; *Antiques,* March, 1967; *Times Literary Supplement,* February 27, 1969; *Medical Economics,* July 31, 1972; *Art News,* May, 1978; *St. Petersburg Times,* May 21, 1978; *Vanderbilt Alumnus,* summer, 1978.

* * *

GOLDEN SILVER
See STORM, Hyemeyohsts

* * *

GOLDMAN, Frederick 1921-

PERSONAL: Born January 2, 1921, in Philadelphia, Pa.; son of William and Fanny Goldman; married; children: one. *Education:* Attended Pennsylvania State University, University of Pennsylvania, and International University, Rome, Italy. *Residence:* Philadelphia, Pa. *Office:* 725½ North 24th St., Philadelphia, Pa. 19130.

CAREER: Creative director at Werman & Schorr Advertising Agency in Philadelphia, Pa.; vice-president of Bauer & Tripp Advertising Agency; president of Frederick Goldman Advertising Agency, Penn Holding Corp., Warwick Terrace Corp., Aurora Associates, and Turet Importers; town manager of Maplewood, La., and Bantam Heights, Conn.; promotion director and member of board of directors of Hilco Homes Corp. Consultant to brokerage firms and real estate agencies. Import/export representative (educational and art films and books) of Netherlands Information Agency, Belgian Ministry of Culture and Education, Film Polski, governments of India and Israel, and port authorities of New York and London. Co-founder and president of International Festival of Short Films; organizer of film festivals at Philadelphia Museum of Art; director of Hedgerow Theatre Corp. (and co-producer); co-founder of Theatre of the Living Arts (and co-producer of plays). Adjunct instructor at high schools, colleges, and universities in the Pennsylvania and New Jersey area; director of seminars at Community College of Philadelphia, Drexel University, and other institutions. Founding director of Middle Atlantic Film Board; first president of Philadelphia Council for the Performing Arts (also vice-chairman of board of directors); member of jury (and sometimes administrator) of American Film Festival and Academy of Motion Picture Arts and Sciences National Student Film Competition. *Military service:* U.S. Navy; received Medal for Exceptional Service.

MEMBER: American Federation of Film Societies (past president; past international vice-president), Exceptional Films Society (founder; member of board of directors, 1950—). *Awards, honors:* Academy Award for best documentary from Academy of Motion Picture Arts and Sciences, 1963, for "Black Fox," which Goldman produced.

WRITINGS: Tribute to Buster Keaton (monograph), Philadelphia Museum of Art, 1966; *Five Decades of Soviet Cinema* (monograph), Philadelphia Museum of Art, 1967; *Highlights in the American Musical Film* (monograph), Philadelphia Museum of Art, 1970; *Need Johnny Read?,* Pflaum, 1971. Work anthologized in *The Documentary Tradition* and *Film News Omnibus.* Contributor to magazines and newspapers, including *Preview, Saturday Review/World,* and *Film News.*

WORK IN PROGRESS: Two books; a proposal for tandem-teaching, linking schools and libraries with public television programming; a pilot program to use retired people as part-time volunteer high school teachers of trades and skills.

* * *

GOLDOVSKY, Boris 1908-

PERSONAL: Born June 7, 1908, in Moscow, Russia; naturalized United States citizen, 1937; son of Onesim and Lea (Luboshutz) Goldovsky; married Margaret Codd, 1933; children: Michael, Marina. *Education:* Liszt Academy, graduate, 1930; Curtis Institute of Music, graduate, 1932. *Home:* 183 Clinton Rd., Brookline, Mass. 02146. *Office:* Goldovsky Opera Institute, Inc., 154 West 57th St., New York, N.Y. 10019.

CAREER: Pianist and composer (beginning with Berlin Philharmonic in 1921); Cleveland Institute of Music, Cleveland, Ohio, assistant to Artur Rodzinski and head of opera department, 1936-42; New England Conservatory of Music, Boston, Mass., director of opera department, 1942—. Founder and organizer of New England Opera Theater (known on tour as Goldovsky Opera Theater), 1946—; head of opera department of Berkshire Music Festival, 1946-61. Broadcast "Opera News on the Air," on Metropolitan Opera Saturday afternoon program, 1946—. Faculty member at Stanford University, Northwestern University, and Oglebay Park.

MEMBER: American Academy of Arts and Sciences (fellow). *Awards, honors:* George Foster Peabody Award from University of Georgia's School of Journalism, 1954, for contributions to radio music; named man of the year by *Good Listening,* 1955; D.Mus. from Bates College, 1956, and Cleveland Institute of Music, 1969; citation from National Federation of Music Clubs, 1959; D.F.A. from Northwestern University, 1972.

WRITINGS: (With Mary Ellis Peltz) *Accents on Opera,* Farrar, Straus, 1953; *Bringing Opera to Life,* Appleton, 1968; (with Arthur Schoep) *Bringing Soprano Arias to Life,* Schirmer Books, 1973.

* * *

GOLDSTEIN, Jeffrey H(askell) 1942-

PERSONAL: Born August 11, 1942, in Norwalk, Conn.; son of Robert and Sylvia (Schwartz) Goldstein; married Helene Feinberg, August 22, 1973 (divorced). *Education:* University of Connecticut, B.A., 1964; Boston University, M.S., 1966; Ohio State University, Ph.D., 1969. *Religion:* Jewish. *Home:* 649 Henderson Rd., King of Prussia, Pa. 19406. *Office:* Department of Psychology, Temple University, Philadelphia, Pa. 19122.

CAREER: Temple University, Philadelphia, Pa., assistant professor, 1969-72, associate professor, 1972-78, professor of psychology, 1978—. Visiting associate professor at University of Massachusetts, 1973-74. Consultant to National Science Foundation, U.S. Department of Labor, and Canada Council. *Member:* International Society for Research on Aggression (fellow), American Psychological Association (fellow), Society of Experimental Social Psychology, Society for the Psychological Study of Social Issues, Authors League of America.

WRITINGS: (Editor with Paul E. McGhee, and contributor) *The Psychology of Humor,* Academic Press, 1972; *Aggression and Crimes of Violence,* Oxford University Press, 1975; (contributor) Patricia Golden, editor, *The Research Experience,* F. T. Peacock, 1976; (contributor) Antony J. Chapman and Hugh C. Foot, editors, *It's a Funny Thing, Humor,* Pergamon, 1977; (editor and contributor) *Sports, Games, and Play,* Wiley, 1977; *Social Psychology,* Academic Press, 1978. Contributor to more than a dozen psychology, sociology, anthropology, and communications journals. Member of editorial board of *Journal of Applied Social Psychology.*

WORK IN PROGRESS: Funny Business, completion expected in 1980.

SIDELIGHTS: Goldstein writes: "As an experimental social psychologist, I believe my work should deal with important aspects of behavior, such as aggression and positive emotions, and some effort should be made by scientists to communicate their work to the interested public. Therefore I have written, and continue to write, trade books as well as textbooks."

GONZALEZ-ALLER, Faustino 1922-

PERSONAL: Born March 2, 1922, in Gijon, Spain; married second wife, Margaret Mahoney (an art dealer), July 15, 1961; children: (first marriage) Faustino, Casilda, Luis; (second marriage) J. Christopher. *Education:* University of Salamanca, doctor of law, 1944; Escuela Official, Madrid, graduate study in journalism, 1945. *Home:* 80 North Moore St., Apt. 26-H, New York, N.Y. 10013. *Agent:* Elaine Markson Literary Agency, Inc., 44 Greenwich Ave., New York, N.Y. 10011. *Office:* Agencia Efe, United Nations Bldg., New York, N.Y.

CAREER: Radio Nacional de Espana, Madrid, Spain, journalist, 1945-53; cinematographic scriptwriter, 1953-56; Channel 4, Havana, Cuba, scriptwriter, 1956-58; Channel 13, Havana, editorial director, writer and host of program, "De balcon a balcon," 1956-58; United Nations, New York City, Department of Information, writer, 1959-66, Department of Radio/Television, chief of Latin American and Iberian section, 1966-73; full-time novelist, 1973-77; Agencia Efe (Spanish news agency), New York City, correspondent, 1977—. *Member:* Press Association of Madrid, Madrid Bar Association. *Awards, honors:* Premio Lope de Vega, 1950, for "La Noche no se acaba"; first prize, Film Festival of San Sebastian, 1956, for "Todos somos necessarios."

WRITINGS—Plays: (With Armando Ocano) *La Noche no se Acaba* (three-act; first produced in Madrid, Spain, at Teatro Espanol, 1951), Editorial Esceliser, 1975; (with Ocano) *La Estatua fue....* (three-act; first produced in Madrid, Spain, at Teatro Infanta Beatriz, 1952), Editorial Alfil, 1952; "Menta" (three-act), first produced in Madrid, Spain, at Teatro Infanta Beatriz, 1953; *El Taxidermista* [and] *La Flauta en Flor* (both two-act), Editorial Literoy, 1972.

All novels, except as indicated: *El Yugo* (novella), Doubleday, 1960; *Nina Huanca,* Seix Barral, 1974, translation by Margaret Penden published under same title, Viking, 1977; *Orosia,* Editorial Euros, 1975; *Via Gala,* Editorial Argos, 1977.

Screenplays include "El puente de diablo," "Ha pasado un hombre," and "Todos somos necesarios." Contributor of articles to *Informacion, Avance, Ya,* and *El Alcazar;* also contributor of short stories to *Bohemia* and *Carteles.*

WORK IN PROGRESS: Two plays; the first part of a trilogy on the periods before, during, and after the Spanish Civil War.

SIDELIGHTS: La noche no se acaba was translated into German and performed at the State Theatre of Kassel and in many other German cities.

BIOGRAPHICAL/CRITICAL SOURCES: Time, May 23, 1977; *Times Literary Supplement,* August 5, 1977.

* * *

GOODELL, Charles E(llsworth) 1926-

PERSONAL: Born March 16, 1926, in Jamestown, N.Y.; son of Charles Ellsworth and Francesca (Bartlett) Goodell; married Jean Rice, August 28, 1954 (marriage ended, 1978); married Patricia Goldman, July 1, 1978; children: William Rice, Timothy Bartlett, Roger Stokoe, Michael Charles Ellsworth, Jeffrey Harris. *Education:* Williams College, A.B., 1948; Yale University, LL.B., 1951, M.A., 1952. *Politics:* Republican. *Religion:* Episcopalian. *Home:* 5022 V St. N.W., Washington, D.C. 20007. *Office:* 1220 19th St. N.W., Suite 700, Washington, D.C. 20036.

CAREER: Admitted to the Bar of Connecticut, 1951, to the

Bar of New York State, 1954, and to the Bar of the District of Columbia, 1974; Quinnipiac College, New Haven, Conn., instructor in chemistry and natural sciences, 1950-52; U.S. Department of Justice, Washington, D.C., congressional liaison assistant, 1954-55; Van Vlack, Goodell & McKee (law firm), Jamestown, N.Y., partner, 1955-59; U.S. House of Representatives, Washington, D.C., representative, 1959-68; U.S. Senate, senator from New York, 1968-71; Roth Carlson, Kwit, Spengler & Goodell (law firm), attorney, New York, N.Y., 1971-72; Hydeman, Mason & Goodell (law firm), Washington, D.C., partner, 1974—. Chairman of Chautauqua County Republican Committee, 1958-59, and of Presidential Clemency Board, 1974-75. Chairman of the board of DGA International. Director of Jamestown Chamber of Commerce. *Military service:* U.S. Naval Reserve, 1944-45; U.S. Air Force, 1952-53, served in Korea; became first lieutenant. *Member:* American Bar Association, District of Columbia Bar Association, Capitol Hill Club, Phi Beta Kappa, Gamma Sigma Chi. *Awards, honors:* Ford Foundation faculty fellow, 1952; honorary degrees from Houghton College, Alfred University, and St. Bonaventure University.

WRITINGS: Political Prisoners in America, Random House, 1973; *Doing Justice,* Hill & Wang, 1976.

SIDELIGHTS: Charles E. Goodell was appointed in 1968 to succeed Robert F. Kennedy as U.S. senator from New York. While in the Senate, Goodell received a long letter from Philip Berrigan, who was serving time at the Lewisburg Penitentiary for having poured blood and napalm over draft board records. The two men became friends, and Goodell spent many hours talking to Berrigan and Berrigan's brother Dan, also a prisoner. Finding the brothers to be virtuous men distressed about the situation in Vietnam, Goodell was troubled. As a lawyer, he did not want to countenance lawbreaking, but as a man concerned about ethics, he realized that at times civil disobedience might be necessary.

Several other experiences intensified Goodell's concern about political prisoners. With Senator Alan Cranston, Goodell investigated the case of the Presidio 27, in which twenty-seven men were court-martialed for mutiny and sentenced to up to sixteen years of hard labor for participating in a ten-minute, nonviolent sit-down demonstration at the Presidio stockade. The case of Roger Priest, a sailor who faced court-martial for writing and distributing a humorous but insulting anti-war newsletter, further dismayed Goodell. The culmination of Goodell's involvement with civil liberties cases occurred when he became one of the defense lawyers in Daniel Ellsberg's trial.

Having become involved in such cases, Goodell was compelled to dig into U.S. history and to reexamine the American criminal process. The result of his research was *Political Prisoners in America.* In the introduction to that book, Goodell writes: "The reality of our political life is not so easily brought into line with the ideal. I have come to acknowledge that we *do* have, and that we always have had, political prisoners in America. In the perennial struggle for political power and in the inevitable conflicts that accompany change, dissenters and government alike have manipulated America's criminal process for political ends. It is through this intercourse of the political and criminal systems that 'political prisoners' are born."

Goodell does not identify himself with those who claim that all laws are instruments of political repression and that all criminals are political prisoners. He is proud of the American democratic system, but maintains that Americans should be aware of the failures in their system as well as its strengths. He explains: "We tend to forget the difficult circumstances of our birth as a nation and some of the sordid events marking our passage to the present. I confess that in writing this book I have been astonished at how much there is on the darker side of American history that I either never knew, or had too quickly forgotten."

BIOGRAPHICAL/CRITICAL SOURCES: Charles E. Goodell, *Political Prisoners in America,* Random House, 1973; *New York Review of Books,* July 19, 1973; *Commonweal,* July 27, 1973.

* * *

GOODHART, Arthur Lehman 1891-1978

OBITUARY NOTICE: Born March 1, 1891, in New York, N.Y.; died November 10, 1978, in London, England. Educator, lawyer, and author best known as one of the most distinguished Americans in British university circles and the British bar. He was a former master of University College at Oxford University (the first American to hold that position), a leading authority on international law, and one of the few Americans to become a Queen's counselor. Though ineligible for knighthood, he received the grade of knight commander of the Order of the British Empire in 1948. Goodhart was a former editor of the *English Quarterly Review,* author of several books and essays on jurisprudence, and the biographer of five widely-known Jewish lawyers. Obituaries and other sources: *New York Times,* November 11, 1978.

* * *

GOODMAN, Rubin Robert 1913-1978

OBITUARY NOTICE: Born June 3, 1913, in Brooklyn, N.Y.; died December 22, 1978, in Hyattsville, N.Y. Lawyer and author. Goodman served with the Civil Aeronautics Board as an attorney-examiner for twenty-five years. After his retirement in 1965, he devoted himself to writing. His published work includes *The Liberal Faith,* a critical study of economics and politics in modern life; *Nibur and the Sick Sixties,* a novel; and *Poetic Snippets.* Obituaries and other sources: *Who's Who In Finance and Industry,* 18th edition, Marquis, 1973; *Washington Post,* December 24, 1978.

* * *

GOODRICH, Leland Matthew 1899-

PERSONAL: Born September 1, 1899, in Lewiston, Me.; son of Fred Bartlett and Alice May (Tibbetts) Goodrich; married Eleanor Allen, June 30, 1928; children: Richard Allen, John Bradbury. *Education:* Bowdoin College, A.B., 1920; Harvard University, A.M., 1921, Ph.D., 1925; additional graduate study at University of Brussels, 1923-25. *Home:* 460 Riverside Dr., New York, N.Y. 10027. *Office:* School of International Affairs, Columbia University, New York, N.Y. 10027.

CAREER: Lafayette College, Easton, Pa., instructor in government and law, 1925-26; Brown University, Providence, R.I., assistant professor, 1926-31, associate professor, 1931-46, professor of political science, 1946-50; Columbia University, New York, N.Y., professor of international organization and administration, 1950-70, professor emeritus, 1970—, special lecturer, 1971-72. World Peace Foundation, director, 1942-46, trustee; member of international secretariat of United Nations Conference on International Organization, 1945; director of Belgian-American Educational Foundation, 1953—; member of United Nations Secretary General's Committee to Review Organization and Activities, 1961; trustee overseer of Bowdoin College Memorial Foreign Policy Association. Professor at Fletcher School of Law and Diplomacy, 1943-50; visiting lecturer in government at Harvard University, 1949-50; visiting professor at University of Toronto, 1969-71.

MEMBER: American Society of International Law (member of executive council, 1940-43), American Political Science Association, American Academy of Arts and Sciences, Academy of Political Scientists, Council on Foreign Relations, Phi Beta Kappa. *Awards, honors:* C.R.B. fellowship, 1923-25; Sc.D. from Bowdoin College, 1952; LL.D. from Columbia University, 1972.

WRITINGS: (Co-editor) *Documents on American Foreign Relations,* World Peace Foundation, Volumes IV-VII, 1942-47; (with Edvard Hambro) *Charter of the United Nations: Commentary and Documents,* World Peace Foundation, 1946, revised edition, 1949, new revised edition (with Anne P. Simons), Columbia University Press, 1969; *Development of the General Assembly,* Carnegie Endowment for International Peace, 1951; *Korea: Collective Measures Against Aggression,* Carnegie Endowment for International Peace, 1953; (with Simons) *The United Nations and the Maintenance of International Peace and Security,* Brookings Institution, 1955; *Korea: A Study of United States Policy in the United Nations,* Council on Foreign Relations, 1956; *The United Nations,* Crowell, 1959.

New Trends in Narcotics Control, Carnegie Endowment for International Peace, 1960; (editor with Norman J. Padelford) *The United Nations in the Balance,* Praeger, 1965; *International Sanctions,* Columbia University Institute of War and Peace Studies, 1968; (editor with David A. Kay) *International Organization: Politics and Process,* University of Wisconsin Press, 1973; (editor with Kay) *The Politics of International Organization,* University of Wisconsin Press, 1973; *The United Nations in a Changing World,* Columbia University Press, 1974.

Contributor of articles to journals. Member of editorial board of *International Organization,* chairman, 1947-54.

* * *

GORDON, Margaret T(aber) 1939-

PERSONAL: Born May 8, 1939, in Rockford, Ill.; daughter of Joseph Taber and Gwen (Bardwell) Johnson; married Andrew C. Gordon; children: Sarah, Seth. *Education:* Northwestern University, B.S.J., 1961, M.S.J., 1962, Ph.D., 1972. *Home:* 1120 Asbury, Evanston, Ill. 60202. *Office:* Center for Urban Affairs, Northwestern University, 2040 Sheridan Rd., Evanston, Ill. 60201.

CAREER: University of Nigeria, Nsukka, lecturer in journalism, 1962-64; *Chattanooga Times,* Chattanooga, Tenn., copy editor, 1967-68; *St. Petersburg Times,* St. Petersburg, Fla., copy editor, 1968-69; Northwestern University, Evanston, Ill., evening instructor in sociology, 1970; Institute for Juvenile Research, Chicago, Ill., research scientist and fellow, 1972-73; University of Illinois at Chicago Circle, Chicago, assistant professor of sociology and urban sciences, 1973-75; Northwestern University, assistant professor, 1975-77, associate professor of journalism and sociology, 1977—, assistant director of Center for Urban Affairs, 1975—. Stringer for Associated Press in Chattanooga, 1967-68.

MEMBER: Association for the Education of Journalists, American Sociological Association (member of national

council, social psychology section, 1974-77), Society for the Study of Social Problems, Association of Public Opinion Researchers, Sociologists for Women in Society, Midwest Sociological Society, Midwest Sociologists for Women in Society. *Awards, honors:* Research grants from Department of Health, Education & Welfare's Office of Child Development, 1972, Law Enforcement Assistance Act, 1975, and National Institute of Mental Health, 1977.

WRITINGS: (With Robert F. Winch) *Familial Structure and Function as Influence,* Heath, 1974; (contributor) Winch and Graham B. Spanier, editors, *Selected Studies in Marriage and the Family,* Holt, 4th edition (Gordon was not included in earlier editions), 1974; *Involving Paraprofessionals in the Helping Process: The Case of Federal Probation,* Ballinger, 1976; (editor with Winch, and contributor) *Familial Organization: A Quest for Determinants,* Free Press, 1977. Contributor of articles and reviews to sociology, education, and law journals. Consulting editor of *Social Problems, Sociology of Education, Sociology of Work and Occupations, Urban Affairs Quarterly,* and *Federal Probation.*

WORK IN PROGRESS: A report of the content analysis of crime stories appearing in metropolitan daily newspapers during a two-month period in three cities; research projects of fear of rape and reactions to crime.

SIDELIGHTS: Margaret Gordon told *CA:* "As a sociologist I am concerned about the nature and control of the forces that shape people's behavior and result in patterns of behavior engaged in by a wide variety of people. I believe that the mass media are such a force. And as a journalist, I am concerned about the nature and consequences of routines of work and other dynamics that shape decisions about news. And finally, as a teacher of future journalists, I am concerned that they leave the university having been forced to think through some of the implications of their profession.

"I am currently involved in two large-scale research projects which I expect to result in book-length manuscripts. In the Fear of Rape Project, funded by the National Center for the Prevention and Control of Rape, NIMH, my co-principal investigator (Stephanie Riger, Lake Forest College) and I are studying how women cope with their fears of being assaulted. We have interviewed women and men in Philadelphia, Chicago and San Francisco. One of our aims is to identify preventative measures which do not further limit women's freedom.

"In the second project (Reactions to Crime, funded by the Law Enforcement Assistance Administration), I am one of several faculty investigators studying the responses to crime of citizens in the same three cities. My component of that research is focussed on the role of the media (especially metropolitan newspapers) in influencing citizen's perceptions of crime and their own safety. We have therefore analyzed the crime content of the metropolitan papers in those three cities, and in addition have interviewed citizens about their reading and viewing habits as well as their assessments of the crime news coverage by the media, facts they would like to know (and why) when they read a crime story, and recollections of the crime content of the papers they read. I expect to use these data for a second purpose—for illustrating to journalism students the dynamics of news decision making and its consequences."

* * *

GORDON, Nancy
See HEINL, Nancy G(ordon)

GORDON, Ruth (Jones) 1896-

PERSONAL: Born October 30, 1896, in Wollaston, Mass.; daughter of Clinton (a sea captain) and Annie Tapley (Ziegler) Jones; married Gregory Kelly (an actor), 1921 (died, 1927); married Garson Kanin (a director and playwright), 1942; children: Jones Harris. *Education:* Attended American Academy of Dramatic Arts, 1914-15; studied singing with Keith Davis. *Office:* Suite 1203, 200 West 57th St., New York, N.Y. 10019.

CAREER: Actress and writer. Began her acting career as an extra in silent films, Fort Lee, N.J.; made her Broadway debut in "Peter Pan," 1915; has made numerous stage performances, including roles in "Seventeen," 1917, "Tweedles," 1923, "Saturday's Children," 1928, "Ethan Frome," 1935, "The Country Wife," 1936, "A Doll's House," 1937, "The Three Sisters," 1942, "Over Twenty-One," 1944, "The Matchmaker," 1954, "My Mother, My Father and Me," 1963, "A Very Rich Woman," 1965, and "Mrs. Warren's Profession," 1976; has made film appearances, including performances in "Abe Lincoln in Illinois," 1939, "Edge of Darkness," 1943; "Rosemary's Baby," 1967, "Whatever Happened to Aunt Alice?," 1968, "Where's Poppa," 1970, "Harold and Maude," 1971, "The Big Bus," 1976, and "Every Which Way But Loose," 1978; has also made television performances. *Member:* Dramatists Guild, Actors' Equity Association, Theatre Hall of Fame, Authors League of America. *Awards, honors:* Writers Guild nomination for "The Actress"; Academy Award and Writers Guild nominations for "Pat and Mike"; Writers Guild nomination for "The Marrying Kind"; Academy Award and Writers Guild nominations and Box Office Ribbon award for "Adam's Rib," 1949; Academy Award nomination for "A Double Life"; Academy Award nomination for role in "Inside Daisy Clover," 1966; Academy Award for supporting actress in "Rosemary's Baby," 1968.

WRITINGS—Memoirs: *Myself Among Others,* Atheneum, 1971; *My Side: The Autobiography of Ruth Gordon,* Harper, 1976.

Plays: *Over Twenty-One* (first produced in 1943), Random House, 1944; *Years Ago* (first produced in 1947), Viking, 1947; "The Leading Lady," (first produced in 1948); (adaptor of Philippe Heriat's play "Les Joies de Famille") "A Very Rich Woman" (three-act comedy), first produced in New York City at Belasco Theatre, 1965; "Ho, Ho, Ho" (two-act), first produced in Stockbridge, Mass. at Berkshire Theatre Festival, 1976.

Screenplays: (With husband, Garson Kanin) "A Double Life," Universal, 1947; (with Kanin) "Adam's Rib," Metro-Goldwyn-Mayer, 1950; (with Kanin) "The Marrying Kind," Columbia, 1952; (with Kanin) "Pat and Mike," Metro-Goldwyn-Mayer, 1952; "The Actress" (adapted from own play *Years Ago*), Metro-Goldwyn-Mayer, 1953.

Play represented in anthology, *Best Plays of 1943/44,* 1944; contributor of a play to *Atlantic.*

SIDELIGHTS: Ruth Gordon didn't win an Oscar until she was seventy-two. It finally came for her portrayal of Minnie Castevet, the nosy neighbor in Roman Polanski's "Rosemary's Baby" (1968). When she accepted the award, she told the Academy, "I can't tell you how encouraging a thing like this is"; and while there is irony in her remark, there is sincerity, too. For Gordon's career has not been a steady climb to stardom. Rather, it has been an uneven effort punctuated by moments of great success and recognition, as well as by times of failure.

Much of Ruth Gordon's recognition has come from writers. For example, her long-time friend Alexander Woollcott of the *New York Times* called her version of Margery Pinchwife, in the 1936 production of Wycherley's "The Country Wife," "the most richly comic performance [he had] ever seen given by any actress in any country at any time in any play." Other writers offered a different kind of praise. Booth Tarkington created several roles for her, including the lead in "Tweedles" (1923). Similarly, in 1938 Thorton Wilder wrote "The Merchant of Yonkers," creating for Gordon the role of Dolly Gallagher Levy, but she declined it and the play folded. Sixteen years later it was revised and successfully produced as "The Matchmaker," with Ruth Gordon as Dolly. Later it became the musical "Hello, Dolly!" with such leading ladies as Carol Channing, Pearl Bailey, and Barbra Streisand following in Gordon's footsteps.

Since receiving the Oscar in 1968, Ruth Gordon's position as grand dame of the theater has solidified. In 1976, for example, on the occasion of her eightieth birthday, she was honored by the town of Quincy, Massachusetts, whose mayor announced the plans for a $4 million Ruth Gordon Center for the Performing Arts.

BIOGRAPHICAL/CRITICAL SOURCES: Pageant, March, 1949; *Saturday Review,* June 12, 1971; *New York Times Book Review,* August 15, 1971, October 10, 1976; *New York Times,* October 21, 1974, August 8, 1976, January 26, 1977; Ruth Gordon, *My Side: The Autobiography of Ruth Gordon,* Harper, 1976.*

* * *

GORMLEY, Gerard (Joseph) 1931-

PERSONAL: Born June 15, 1931, in Boston, Mass.; son of James Joseph (an automobile dealer) and Helen L. (Eagan) Gormley; married Patricia M. Cieminski, November, 1953 (divorced, 1971); children: Pamela K. Gormley Ropi, Patrick G., Sean J. *Education:* Northeastern University, A.E.E., 1961. *Politics:* "Independent (moderate conservative)." *Religion:* "Independent (moderate agnostic)." *Home and office:* 7 Washington St., Manchester-by-the-Sea, Mass. 01944. *Agent:* Boston Literary Agency, P.O. Box 1472, Manchester, Mass. 01944.

CAREER: Ewen Knight Corp., Natick, Mass., publications manager, 1955-61; Impact Advertising, Inc., Boston, Mass., founder and president, 1961-70; Gerard J. Gormley Advertising, Inc., Manchester, Mass., president, 1970—. *Military service:* U.S. Navy, submarine duty, 1951-55. *Member:* Authors Guild, Authors League of America, National Geographic Society, Whale Protection Fund. *Awards, honors:* National Advertising effectiveness award from United Technical Publishers, 1968.

WRITINGS: The Doll (novel), Pinnacle Books, 1977.

WORK IN PROGRESS: The Dogs (tentative title), a novel of terror and suspense in a small town ravaged by packs of wild dogs; *Swiftly Swim My Brothers, Laughing,* a fictional account of life in a free dolphin tribe; *A Man Among Dolphins,* a novel about an ocean swimmer who denounces humanity and lives with a tribe of dolphins; *The Summoning of Marin Darby,* a tale of events which could be reincarnation or schizophrenia.

SIDELIGHTS: Gormley writes: "Those who have judged my work to date invariably cite compelling narrative style and unique plotting as my major strengths. Without weakening these aspects of my writing, I am striving with each manuscript I write, to enhance my lyric strength as well. I greatly admire writers such as Updike, Bellow, and Thomas Wolfe, but they could all use some of the yarn-spinning genius of Ray Bradbury.

"My work pace tends to approach the maniacal. It is not unusual for me to work ten to twelve hours a day when a novel has me in its grip. Writing is the most grueling work I have ever done, but I cannot conceive of a more gratifying occupation.

"My interests are eclectic. The topics of my novels to date have been feral dog packs, obsessive love, dolphins from the dolphins' viewpoint, dolphins from the human viewpoint, and the boundary layer separating reincarnation and schizophrenic psyche-splitting. The on-going education which I derive from my frenetic research is another aspect of writing which gives me great enjoyment. My current project is another novel, which started out to present a broadbrush portrait of married mid-life in middle class, late 70's America. This novel has been stirring crazily in my mind since its inception, but that has not disturbed me much, because my other novels took me through similar wanderings. I have decided to focus this current work on problems of sexuality and near-incest in a contemporary American family. The story is told through the experiences of a mid-life man whose recurring attempts to rediscover the young beauty who was once his mother had led him (subconsciously) into strange relationships with his sister, his wife, and now his daughter. His struggle to avoid incest leads him into a further strange relationship with a very young woman. The story is based on a composite of actual case histories reported by psychiatric counselors and social workers. The novel attempts to illustrate how incest can pose a threat to many otherwise normal families, and to show that the total suppression of sexuality between parents and children can often have the reverse of the desired effect. I am holding the explicit sex to an absolute minimum; however, some sex is prerequisite to the proper establishment of the protagonist's psychosexual make-up.

"Writers are asked repeatedly (by themselves if by no one else) why they write. For me, writing is the ideal medium through which an introvert can be a performing artist. I live every minute of my characters' roles, and love every moment of applause. Then again, even if I had not sold a single manuscript, I would still be writing."

AVOCATIONAL INTERESTS: Studying marine mammals.

*   *   *

GOTT, K(enneth) D(avidson) 1923-
(Sebastian Hogbotel)

PERSONAL: Born February 22, 1923, in Melbourne, Australia; son of John (a ship engineer) and Jessie Miller (a saleswoman; maiden name, Davidson) Gott; married Margaret Beth Noye (a biology teacher), October 16, 1948; children: Margaret Janine, James Davidson, Miranda Helen. *Education:* University of Melbourne, B.A., 1947, diploma in journalism, 1959. *Home:* 65 Chapel St., St. Kilda, Victoria 3182, Australia. *Agent:* Curtis Brown Ltd., 575 Madison Ave., New York, N.Y. 10022.

CAREER: Economic researcher for labor unions, 1947-48; British Broadcasting Co. (BBC) news service, London, England, staff member, 1949; International Union of Students, Prague, Czechoslovakia, chief of weekly news service, 1950-52; Pacific Merchandise Agency, Melbourne, Australia, manager, 1953-55; Western Australia Newspapers Ltd., Perth, staff member and Melbourne bureau chief, 1955-64;

Austalian, Canberra, national feature writer, 1964-65; *Business International,* New York, N.Y., Asian editor, 1965-67, editor, 1967-70; *Business Asia,* Hong Kong, editor, 1970-76; *Business International,* editor, 1976-78; free-lance writer, 1978—. Co-managing director of Business International Asia/Pacific Ltd., Hong Kong, 1970-76. Lecturer for American Management Association, 1965-70, and various business groups, chambers of commerce, and trade societies, 1965-76. *Member:* World Trade Writers Association, Overseas Press Club, Australian Journalists' Association (member of federal executive committee, 1958-64), Asia Society, Japan Society, Foreign Correspondents' Club (Hong Kong), Press Club (Hong Kong and Melbourne), Hong Kong Journalists Association. *Awards, honors:* Distinguished service award from American Asiatic Association, 1970.

WRITINGS: (Editor under pseudonym Sebastian Hogbotel, with Stephen Murray-Smith) *Snatches and Lays* (song collection), Boozy (Melbourne), 1962, 4th edition, Sun Books, 1977; *Voices of Hate,* Dissent Press (Melbourne), 1965; *Japan: Meeting the Challenge of Asia's Richest Market,* Business International, 1966; *Australia: New Business Power in the Pacific,* Business International, 1968; *Japan's New Era,* Business International, 1971; *Business Strategies for Developing Asia, 1975-85,* Business International, 1976. Editor of *Farrago,* 1942-43, and *Melbourne University Magazine,* 1947.

WORK IN PROGRESS: Studies on the multinational company, and the Australian economy in a world context; autobiographical material on years in student movement and left-wing groups in Australia, Prague, Berlin, etc.

SIDELIGHTS: Gott resigned from his position as editor of *Business International* in January, 1978, after he learned that the publication had provided cover for four C.I.A. agents during the late 1950's. Though in subsequent interviews he conceded the need for the C.I.A., he protested, "It is deplorable that the C.I.A., formed to defend democratic ways, should have cast doubts on one of the most important and distinctive Western institutions—our free, though certainly not flawless, Press." Gott's resignation demonstrated his desire to disassociate himself from any involvement in C.I.A. activities.

When asked about how his association with left-wing movements during his student days had influenced his approach to social questions and his decision to join the staff of Business International, Gott told *CA:* "A main legacy of my years in left-wing movements was adherence to internationalism and an abhorrence of chauvinism and destructive forms of nationalism. Business International's unspoken credo favors the free movement of men, capital, goods, ideas, and technology."

BIOGRAPHICAL/CRITICAL SOURCES: Patrick O'Brien, *The Saviours: An Intellectual History of the Left in Australia,* Drummond, 1977; *Melbourne Age,* January 18, 1978; *New York Post,* January 18, 1978; *Washington Star,* January 19, 1978.

*   *   *

GOTT, Richard (Willoughby) 1938-

PERSONAL: Born October 28, 1938, in Aston Tirrold, England; married Josephine Ann Zammit; children: one son. *Education:* Attended Corpus Christi College, Oxford, 1958-61. *Home:* 21 Priory Grove, Stockwell, London S.W.8, England.

CAREER: Royal Institute of International Affairs, London,

England, research assistant, 1962-65; University of Chile, Santiago, research fellow at Institute of International Studies, 1966-69; *Standard,* Dar es Salaam, Tanzania, foreign editor, 1970-72; free-lance writer, 1972—. *Member:* Royal United Services Institution.

WRITINGS: (With Martin Gilbert) *The Appeasers,* Weidenfeld & Nicolson, 1963; *Mobuto's Congo,* Fabian Society, 1968; *Guerrilla Movements in Latin America,* Thomas Nelson, 1970. Also co-editor of *Documents on International Affairs,* 1960, *NATO's Final Decade,* 1964, and *The End of the Alliance,* 1965. *London Guardian,* leader writer, 1964-66, and foreign news editor. Contributor to magazines, including *Nation, World Today,* and *International Affairs.*

AVOCATIONAL INTERESTS: Travel, politics.

* * *

GOTTSCHALK, Elin Toona   1937-

PERSONAL: Born July 12, 1937, in Tallinn, Estonia; came to the United States in 1968; daughter of Enn (a theater director) and Liki (an actress) Toona; divorced; children: Timothy-Rein. *Education:* "Extremely unusual circumstances and varied." *Religion:* Lutheran. *Home:* 1805 Cathedral Rd., Huntingdon Valley, Pa. 19006; and Flat 10, 29 Finborough Rd., London S.W.10, England. *Agent:* Ann Elmo Agency, Inc., 52 Vanderbilt Ave., New York, N.Y. 10017.

CAREER: Worked as secretary; actress in London, England, 1960-65; writer, 1960—. Has given readings on Philadelphia radio programs. *Member:* International P.E.N. (Estonian writers section). *Awards, honors:* Certificate of merit from *Storyteller,* 1962, for "The Old Farm"; first prize from *Writer's Review,* 1966; H. Visnapuu Literary Award from World Association of Estonians, 1966, for novel, *Puuingel;* certificate of commendation from Radio Nederland Wereldomroep, 1971.

WRITINGS: In Search of Coffee Mountains (novel), Thomas Nelson, 1977. Also author of historical sagas.

In Estonian: *Puuingel* (novel; title means "Wooden Angel"), Estonian Writers Kooperative, 1965; *Lotukata* (novel; title means "The Kate in the Funny Hat"), Estonian Writers Kooperative, 1968; *Sipelgas Sinise Kausi All* (novel; title means "The Ant Under the Blue Glass Bowl"), Estonian Writers Kooperative, 1973.

Author of "The Amateurs" (radio play), for British Broadcasting Corp., 1966. Contributor of poems and stories in Estonian and English to magazines and newspapers, including *Coastal Illustrated, Coastal Quarterly,* and *Indian River Life.*

WORK IN PROGRESS: A sequel to *In Search of Coffee Mountains,* for Thomas Nelson; a novel in Estonian.

SIDELIGHTS: Gottschalk told *CA:* "Because of the quirks of history during my early years, I never experienced a 'normal life' as most people understand it. From age two onwards, the continual occupation of Estonia by the Russians or Germans, until 1944 when we became refugees, made 'normal life' for me a kaleidoscope of changing countries, languages, and war situations. My life depended upon instant adaptation (such as passing as a German in Germany). From a D.P. camp in Germany to a Quaker Orphanage in England was a major step. There I had my ears boxed for not holding a teacup properly, when I had never seen a teacup before or a properly laid out table for tea!

"The rigid class system of the fifties also denied me an edu-cation and I was put into a textile mill when I was fifteen. My mother and grandmother had spent the five years I was in the orphanage (we were separated) as indentured servants in hospitals despite the fact that they were highly educated. Under the same system doctors, lawyers, professors, and a judge or two were weaving carpets in other parts of Yorkshire. Under the class discrimination (as rigid as any caste system in India) one becomes what one does. And I was not just weaving for a living, but I had *become* a weaver.

"I started to read insatiably not only to perfect my English but to educate myself beyond the weaving shed. In effect 'getting ideas above my station in life.' Outside the mill I was treated as a weaver. At home I was the child of prominent and educated Estonians, although we lived in one room in a slum. Classical music, good books, art, poetry and European events were the insulation with which the refugee communities isolated themselves from their supposed 'class peers' in the mills and factories. All my Estonian books have dealt with these problems of the emotionally and physically displaced in the English class system.

"As soon as I realized that [the] game of fancy dress and scenery was the way the world operated, I made it my business to learn the rules. I dropped the label weaver and took on secretary. I dropped the heavy Yorkshire brogue and foreign accent and adopted a BBC tone of voice. The world saw cleaner clothes, cleaner fingernails and immediately assumed that I had become a better person because of it."

BIOGRAPHICAL/CRITICAL SOURCES: New York Times Book Review, November 13, 1977.

* * *

GOUDSMIT, Samuel A(braham)   1902-1978

OBITUARY NOTICE: Born July 11, 1902, in the Hague, Holland; died December 4, 1978, in Reno, Nev. Physicist, educator, and writer best known as the co-discoverer of the electron's spin in the hydrogen atom and as a leading figure in American physics. Goudsmit became widely known after World War II when it was disclosed that he had been scientific director of Alsos, the secret wartime effort to learn if the Germans were making an atomic bomb. He was also a staff member from 1941 to 1946 at the radiation laboratory of the Massachusetts Institute of Technology, which was the center of wartime research on radar. Goudsmit was designated an officer of the Order of the British Empire and was the recipient of the Max Planck Medal, the Medal of Freedom, and the National Medal of Science. His writings include a book co-authored with Linus Pauling, *The Structure of Line Spectra,* and another, *Atomic Energy States,* as well as his popular books, *Alsos* and *Time.* Obituaries and other sources: *Current Biography,* Wilson, 1954; *American Men and Women of Science: The Physical and Biological Sciences,* 12th edition, Bowker, 1971-73; *The International Who's Who,* Europa, 1974; *Who's Who in America,* Marquis, 1974; *New York Times,* December 6, 1978.

* * *

GOULD, Shirley (Goldman)

PERSONAL: Born in Chicago, Ill.; daughter of Abraham (a shopkeeper) and Rose (a shopkeeper; maiden name, Mesigal) Goldman; married Joseph E. Gould (an executive), June 30, 1940; children: Ruth Jessica Gould Kurlandsky, Arthur Edwin, Shepard Saul. *Education:* University of Illinois at Chicago Circle, B.A., 1967, M.S.W., 1969; Alfred Adler Institute, certificate in psychotherapy, 1975. *Politics:* Independent. *Religion:* Jewish. *Home and office:* 8944 Kilbourn

Ave., Skokie, Ill. 60076. *Agent:* Dominick Abel Literary Agency, 498 West End Ave., Apt. 12-C, New York, N.Y. 10024.

CAREER: Worked as a legal secretary, 1934-45; administrative assistant for village of Skokie, Ill, 1959-61; American Red Cross, Chicago, Ill., social worker, 1969-70; Jewish Family & Community Service, Highland Park, Ill., social worker, 1970-71; private practice of psychotherapy in Skokie, 1971—. *Member:* North American Society of Adlerian Psychology.

WRITINGS: (With Rudolf Dreikurs and Raymond Corsini) *Family Council: The Dreikurs Technique,* Regnery, 1974; *Teenagers: The Continuing Challenge,* Hawthorn, 1977; *The Challenge of Achievement: Helping Your Child Succeed,* Hawthorn, 1978; *How to Raise Your Child to Be Independent,* St. Martin's, 1979. Contributor to *Journal of Individual Psychology* and *Chicago Sunday Tribune.* Women's editor, *The Life of Nile's Township* (weekly), 1960-61.

WORK IN PROGRESS: A book for St. Martin's.

SIDELIGHTS: Shirley Gould writes: "My first published writing was in 1960, the result of the urging of the late Dr. Rudolf Dreikurs, my friend and teacher, who saw me as a writer when I did not. Writing books did not begin until I had undertaken (for the first time) and completed a university education, and then worked in a new profession for a few years. The major part of my working time is devoted to writing; I see clients in the practice of psychotherapy, helping individuals, couples, families, and groups. I also do some public speaking and teaching."

*   *   *

GOWING, Margaret (Margaret Mary)   1921-

PERSONAL: Born April 26, 1921, in London, England; daughter of Ronald (a motor engineer) and Mabel (a teacher; maiden name, Donaldson) Elliott; married Donald James Graham Gowing, July 6, 1944 (deceased); children: Nicholas, James. *Education:* Studied at Christ's Hospital, 1931-38; London School of Economics and Political Science, B.Sc., 1941. *Office:* Faculty of History, Indian Institute, Oxford University, Broad St., Oxford, England.

CAREER: Civil servant on board of trade, London, England, 1941-45; Cabinet Office, London, historian, 1945-59; United Kingdom Atomic Energy Authority, London, historian and archivist, 1959-66; University of Kent, Canterbury, England, reader in contemporary history, 1966-72; Oxford University, Oxford, England, professor of history of science, 1972—. Member of Public Records Advisory Council and British Broadcasting Corp. Archives Advisory Committee. Member of board of trustees of National Portrait Gallery. *Awards, honors:* M.A. from Oxford University, 1973; British Academy fellow, 1975; D.Litt. from University of Leeds, 1976.

WRITINGS: (With W. K. Hancock) *British War Economy,* H.M.S.O., 1949; (with E. L. Hargraves) *Civil Industry and Trade,* H.M.S.O., 1952; *Britain and Atomic Energy, 1939-1945,* Macmillan, 1964; *Independence and Deterrence,* two volumes, Macmillan, 1975.

WORK IN PROGRESS: Books on atomic energy history.

SIDELIGHTS: Gowing writes that she "is concerned with nineteenth- and twentieth-century history of science, especially in its economic, social, and political context. [My] atomic energy history includes, for example, diplomatic, strategic, administrative, economic and technological, as well as scientific history."

BIOGRAPHICAL/CRITICAL SOURCES: New Scientist, Volume XXVIII, number 11, 1975.

*   *   *

GRABER, Gerry S(amuel)   1928-

PERSONAL: Born June 10, 1928, in London, England; son of Alex and Diana (Boxer) Graber; married Phyllis Fraser (a marriage guidance counselor), March 11, 1953; children: Paul, David. *Education:* London School of Economics and Political Science, B.Sc. (honors), 1947, M.Sc., 1949; graduate study at University of Basel, 1949-50. *Home:* 28A Thurlow Rd., London NW3 5PP, England. *Agent:* Bolt & Watson, 12 Old Queen St., London S.W.1, England.

CAREER: Worked as assistant editor of *European Digest,* 1950-52; free-lance writer, 1952-54; Society for Education Through Travel, London, England, founder and academic administrator, 1954—; writer, 1973—. *Member:* International P.E.N.

WRITINGS: Stauffenberg (biography; Military Book Club selection), Ballantine, 1973; *History of the SS* (Military Book Club selection), McKay, 1978.

WORK IN PROGRESS: A historical novel about seventeenth-century Messiah Sabbatai Zevi; *Rodney Cooper Talks to Himself,* a novel on suburban manners; *Reinhard Heydrich,* a biography.

SIDELIGHTS: Graber comments: "I write because this activity generates more excitement than anything else for me, with the possible exception of playing tennis. I am basically an historian and direct my efforts at 'popularizing' the study of history. I believe writers are born. I am against all 'writers training courses' and the concept of courses in English (or any other) 'literature' irritates me beyond belief. I have lectured on this theme and am happy to sound off on it at any opportunity."

*   *   *

GRAHAM, Virginia
See GUTTENBERG, Virginia

*   *   *

GRANT, Gerald   1938-

PERSONAL: Born February 3, 1938, in Syracuse, N.Y.; son of G. Edward (in sales) and Ruth (Smith) Grant; married Judith Dunn (a teacher), July 22, 1961; children: Susan, Sarah, Robert. *Education:* John Carroll University, S.S.B., 1959; Columbia University, M.S., 1960; Harvard University, Ed.D., 1972. *Politics:* Democrat. *Religion:* Roman Catholic. *Office:* Department of Cultural Foundations of Education, Syracuse University, 305 Comstock Ave., Syracuse, N.Y. 13210.

CAREER: Washington Post, Washington, D.C., staff education editor, 1961-67; Syracuse University, Syracuse, N.Y., associate professor, 1972-77, professor of sociology and education, 1977—. *Military service:* U.S. Marine Corps, 1960-61. *Member:* American Sociological Association, American Educational Research Association, American Association of University Professors. *Awards, honors:* Nieman fellow at Harvard University, 1967-68; research fellow at Harvard University, 1971-72.

WRITINGS: (With David Riesman) *The Perpetual Dream: Reform and Experiment in the American College,* University of Chicago Press, 1978; *On Competence,* Jossey-Bass, 1979. Contributor to education journals and popular magazines, including *New Republic, Commonweal, Daedalus,* and *Progressive.*

WORK IN PROGRESS: What Makes a Good School.

SIDELIGHTS: In *The Perpetual Dream,* Gerald Grant and David Riesman examine recent educational trends in the United States and argue for further experiments which can benefit from the failures and successes of the 1960's. George Levine praised the authors for achieving "the kind of detached, yet compassionate vision necessary if the newest reforms are to be anything but ignorant backlash." Levine also found admirable the authors' "obvious commitment to intellectual rigor and a healthy resistance to the sort of jargon and moral bullying that sometimes make it difficult to distinguish a serious reform from self-indulgence or frightened capitulation."

BIOGRAPHICAL/CRITICAL SOURCES: New York Times Book Review, May 7, 1978.

*   *   *

GRANT, Mary Kathryn   1941-

PERSONAL: Born July 24, 1941, in Brooklyn, N.Y.; daughter of John T. (a general traffic manager) and Mary Linus (Guerin) Grant. *Education:* Mercy College of Detroit, B.A., 1964; University of Notre Dame, M.A., 1968; Indiana University, Ph.D.,1974. *Home:* 10800 Rose, Apt. 1, Los Angeles, Calif. 90034. *Office:* 12001 Chalon Rd., Los Angeles, Calif. 90049.

CAREER: Teacher of English and journalism in high schools in Iowa and Michigan, 1964-68; Mercy College of Detroit, Detroit, Mich., assistant professor of English, 1969-76; Detroit Area Consortium of Catholic Colleges, Detroit, executive director, 1976-77; Mount St. Mary's College, Los Angeles, Calif., associate academic dean, 1977—. *Member:* American Studies Association, American Association of Higher Education, Modern Language Association of America (member of women's caucus), American Conference of Academic Deans. *Awards, honors:* Modern Language Association of America regional women writers award, 1978.

WRITINGS: The Tragic Vision of Joyce Carol Oates, Duke University Press, 1978; (with Daniel Hoeber) *Basic Skills Programs: Are They Working?,* Educational Resources Information Center, American Association for Higher Education, 1978. Also author of a history of a health corporation. Editorial consultant for numerous educational reports. Contribut0r of articles to journals, including *Catholic Educational Review* and *Arizona Quarterly.*

WORK IN PROGRESS: The Image of the Working Woman in America: Literature From 1900; An Evaluation of the Role and Function of Value Education in Postsecondary Institutions.

SIDELIGHTS: Grant wrote: "My current literary and professional interest is in career development: re-entry programs for older women; career and life planning; seminars related to internships and pre-work experiences for the younger woman; adult developmental cycles as related to work and career." *Avocational interests:* Cross country skiing, photography.

*   *   *

GRAY, Bettyanne   1934-

PERSONAL: Born October 8, 1934, in Philadelphia, Pa.; daughter of Israel (a businessman) and Manya (a factory sewing machine operator; maiden name, Polevoi) Abram-

son; married Donald Gray (a mechanical contractor), June 2, 1957; children: Ellis, Heidi, Debra. *Education:* Attended Temple University, 1953-54; Gratz College, received certificate, 1978. *Religion:* Jewish. *Home and office:* 9004 Cargill Lane, Philadelphia, Pa. 19115.

CAREER: Legal secretary in Philadelphia, Pa., 1952-57; free-lance writer and lecturer, 1975—. Adult education lecturer, Congregation Shaare Shamayim, Philadelphia, 1977-78; lecturer in Holocaust studies, Traditional Hebrew High School, Philadelphia, 1977-78. Board member of Adath Tikvah Sisterhood, and Henrietta Szold Hadassah. Volunteer for several Jewish organizations, including Jewish Family Service, Soviet Jewry Committee, and Federation of Jewish Agencies. *Member:* Hadassah (life member; study group adviser), Pioneer Women, Deborah (life member), Friends of Dropsie University. *Awards, honors:* Marcia Sheinman Memorial Prize for History, Gratz College, 1976; Lewis Carroll Shelf Award, University of Wisconsin—Madison, 1978, for *Manya's Story.*

WRITINGS: Manya's Story, Lerner, 1978. Contributor of articles and essays to Jewish newspapers and periodicals. Former editor of *Scroll* (congregational monthly).

WORK IN PROGRESS: A book on present day Jewish customs; a novel dealing with Soviet Jewish immigration to the United States in the 1970's.

SIDELIGHTS: Bettyanne Gray writes: "I am a first generation American whose parents were survivors of two pogroms in the Ukraine during the Russian Revolution. As a child, I listened to the grim tales of Jewish slaughter in tzarist Russia. Each time, I hoped the vivid details would be less gruesome. But time could not alter the facts; could not mute the monstrous realities.

"And so as a pre-teen in south Philadelphia, I reacted with terror to the whispered rumors of the Holocaust. My parents spoke of it in tones of veiled mystery. I recall the ashen faces of my parents as they spoke. They were consumed with anguish by the legacy they left for those who remained in the Ukraine.

"Since that time, I have been drawn to whatever I could learn about the Holocaust. For two semesters, I studied the Nazi debacle with Nora Levin, eminent historian and authority on the Holocaust. I followed this with a year-long course on Russian Jewish history so that I might more fully understand the experiences of my brethren.

"But researching my roots has been very disquieting. I am becoming consumed with an intensity that feels as if it will rupture my soul. I have developed a compulsion to discuss my courses with everyone; demanding as it were, that they immerse themselves in the European Jewish tragedy and become sensitized; and I feel compelled to keep that sensitivity floating on the surface of their consciousness.

"And so I have written *Manya's Story.* My mother's story. It is about life in the shtetlach of the Ukraine before they were destroyed by the final solution of the Jewish problem. It is about a uniquely Jewish world which even in the 1920's faced partial destruction at the hands [of] another lethal enemy.

"My mother's reminiscenses of that earlier time have painted a portrait of that world which disappeared. During our lifetime of intimate companionship, she told me vivid stories of the joy of traditional shtetl life and of the agonies that followed.

"However, *Manya's Story* reflects the joy and heartache of not only her own family, but of all shtetl Jews—for the special value of my mother's memoirs, beyond their personal impact is that her experiences represent what millions lived through in Eastern Europe.

"I wrote [*Manya's Story*] for my family and for Jews everywhere who share an interest in discovering their own Jewish roots, and to give new insight to all Americans of the continuing Jewish struggle to live in peace among our neighbors."

BIOGRAPHICAL/CRITICAL SOURCES: Jewish Exponent, March 3, 1978; *Philadelphia Inquirer,* August 15, 1978.

* * *

GRAYMONT, Barbara

EDUCATION: Columbia University, Ph.D., 1969. *Office:* Department of History, Nyack College, Nyack, N.Y. 10960.

CAREER: Nyack College, Nyack, N.Y., professor of history. *Member:* American Historical Association, Organization of American Historians.

WRITINGS: The Iroquois in the American Revolution, Syracuse University Press, 1972; (editor) *Fighting Tuscarora: The Autobiography of Chief Clinton Rickard,* Syracuse University Press, 1973.

* * *

GREALEY, Thomas Louis 1916-
(Louis Southworth)

PERSONAL: Born June 12, 1916, in Lancanshire, England; son of Thomas (a railwayman) and Annie (Southworth) Grealey; married Hilda Forrest, May 2, 1938; children: Patricia Mary, Christine Ann. *Education:* Educated in Lancanshire, England. *Politics:* Conservative. *Home:* 6 Derby Rd., Luton, Bedfordshire, England. *Agent:* Curtis Brown Ltd., 1 Craven Hill, London, England. *Office:* Food Securities Ltd., The Broadway, Stanmore, Middlesex, England.

CAREER: City of London Police, London, England, became detective chief inspector, 1936-68; Food Securities Ltd., Middlesex, England, chief security officer, 1968-76. *Military service:* British Army, 1942-45; received Civil Defence Medal, Africa Star, and Italy Star. *Member:* (British) Crime Writers' Association. *Awards, honors:* Third Prize in short story competition from *Police Review;* Police Long Service Medal.

WRITINGS: (Under pseudonym Louis Southworth) *Felon in Disguise,* R. Hale, 1966; (under pseudonym Louis Southworth) *Corpse on London Bridge,* R. Hale, 1968. Also author of television script, "Dixon of Dock Green." Contributor to *Police Review, London Mystery Magazine, John Creasey Mystery Magazine, Criminologist,* and *Weekend* magazine.

* * *

GREEN, George MacEwan 1931-

PERSONAL: Born September 9, 1931, in Nairn, Scotland. *Education:* Attended Webster's Commercial College. *Residence:* Inverness, Scotland.

CAREER: Playwright; member of staff, Highland Fuels Ltd., Inverness, Scotland.

WRITINGS—One-act plays: *One Season's King,* Evans Plays, 1972; *Sequence of Events,* Evans Plays, 1974. Also author of *Terrace Talk,* Evans Plays, and *Ritual for Dolls,* Evans Plays.

SIDELIGHTS: Green writes: "In my plays I am mainly preoccupied with attempting to capture certain moments when ritualised or structured behaviour breaks down and there is an escape of pent-up humanity, resulting sometimes in enlightenment, sometimes in tragedy."

* * *

GREEN, Susan 1941-

PERSONAL: Born April 5, 1941, in New York, N.Y.; daughter of Irving L. (a physician) and Naomi (a pianist; maiden name, Koplin) Kohn; married Oscar Green (divorced); children: Elizabeth. *Education:* University of Colorado, B.A., 1964; also attended Art Students League, 1968-72. *Agent:* Robert Lantz, Lantz Office, Inc., 114 East 55th St., New York, N.Y. 10022.

CAREER: Receptionist, secretary, and researcher, 1965-70; illustrator and painter, 1968—.

WRITINGS: (Self-illustrated) *Gentle Gorilla: The Story of Patty Cake* (nonfiction), Richard Marek, 1978.

WORK IN PROGRESS: The Adventures of Samuel Z, a self-illustrated children's book; *Songs for Elizabeth,* a self-illustrated book of children's songs.

SIDELIGHTS: Susan Green told *CA:* "It is simply that so many things are beautiful or interesting and I want to find out why—so I draw or write about them. Discovery of beauty is always reaffirmed if you keep looking for it. For some reason I must do it. Writing makes thoughts reality and creates excitement. Insofar as my children's books are concerned: they come from love and pure pleasure. My mind can move freely, with no restraints on imagination."

BIOGRAPHICAL/CRITICAL SOURCES: New York Times, July 16, 1978.

* * *

GREENFELD, Howard

EDUCATION: Attended University of Chicago, New York University, and Columbia University; received M.A. *Residence:* Camaiore, Italy.

CAREER: Taught English in Rome, Italy; worked under Bennett Cerf at Random House, New York City; founder of Orion Press (publishing company; now part of Viking Press), Florence, Italy; editor, J. Philip O'Hara (publishing company), Chicago, Ill., beginning 1971; author of books for young people. *Awards, honors:* Follett Award, 1968, for *Marc Chagall.*

WRITINGS—Nonfiction: *Marc Chagall* (illustrated with reproductions of the artist's work), Follett, 1967; *The Waters of November,* Follett, 1969; *Pablo Picasso: An Introduction,* Follett, 1971; *The Impressionist Revolution* (juvenile), Doubleday, 1972; *Gertrude Stein: A Biography* (juvenile), Crown, 1973; *F. Scott Fitzgerald* (juvenile), Crown, 1974; *They Came to Paris* (juvenile), Crown, 1975; *Books: From Writer to Reader* (juvenile), Crown, 1976; *Chanukah,* Holt, 1976; *Gypsies,* Crown, 1977; *Summer Is Icumen in: Our Ever-changing Language,* Crown, 1978.

SIDELIGHTS: In writing biographies for young people, Howard Greenfeld researched his subjects throughly—reading everything he could find about the noted person and talking with anyone associated with the individual. "I have to know the people I'm writing about and to care about them," revealed Greenfeld in an interview for *Publishers Weekly,* "I couldn't do it any other way."

Marc Chagall was the result of Greenfeld's first effort in saturating himself in the life and times of a well-known person. A critic for *Young Readers' Review* noted: "Mr. Greenfeld loves his subject; that is evident on every page. He wants his readers to appreciate the genius of Chagall and this book will certainly set them on the right road. . . . Young people should appreciate the beauty of this book—the illustrations, the painter himself, and the author's warm style."

One of Greenfeld's more recent biographical studies is *They Came to Paris*. In this book the author focuses on Americans living in Paris during the 1920's. A reviewer for *Booklist* wrote: "In what he calls 'a collage of events and portraits,' the author . . . affords a real sense of the colorful decade of the twenties. . . . Although not all the personalities will be familiar to teenagers, this is a vivid overview that complements standard biographies of the major figures of the period."

The author did not restrict himself to writing biographies, however, and in *The Waters of November*, Greenfeld gave an account of the flood that struck Florence, Italy, in 1966. "[The story is] vividly told and illustrated with stunning pictures of the flood. . . . Almost as moving is the description of the restoration now . . . in progress," commented Zena Sutherland in a *Saturday Review* article. "A large, fascinating book with numerous, beautifully printed photographs," wrote a critic for *Commonweal*.

BIOGRAPHICAL/CRITICAL SOURCES: Young Readers' Review, March, 1968; *Book World*, June 2, 1968; *Saturday Review*, November 8, 1969; *Commonweal*, November 21, 1969; *Publishers Weekly*, September 3, 1973; *Booklist*, November 15, 1975.*

*   *   *

GREER, Art(hur Ellis, Jr.)   1929-

PERSONAL: Born June 10, 1929, in Detroit, Mich.; son of Arthur E. (a tool and die machinist) and Edna (Bornefeld) Greer; married Barbara Wahl (a minister of Disciples of Christ), June 6, 1954 (divorced, 1978); children: Daniel Scott, Julia Louise. *Education:* Elmhurst College, B.A., 1951; Eden Theological Seminary, M. Div., 1955; University of Houston, M.Ed., 1971. *Politics:* Democrat. *Home and office:* 3230 South Gessner, Suite 1312, Houston, Tex. 77063.

CAREER: Ordained minister of United Church of Christ, 1955; pastor of United Church of Christ in Mineral City, Ohio, 1955-56; U.S. Air Force, chaplain, 1956-66, leaving service as major; pastor of United Church of Christ in Houston, Tex., 1966-69; University of Houston, Houston, Tex., campus minister, 1969-72; private practice of psychotherapy in Houston, Tex., 1972—. Clinical transactional analyst and social psychotherapist. *Member:* International Transactional Analysis Association (clinical member), American Association of Marriage and Family Therapists, Masons.

WRITINGS: No Grown-Ups in Heaven Hawthorn, 1975; *The Sacred Cows Are Dying: Exploding the Myths We Try to Live By*, Hawthorn, 1978. Contributor to magazines. Editor-in-chief of *Elm Bark*, 1950-51.

WORK IN PROGRESS: Ten Roads to Freedom, publication expected in 1980; *Life Is a Trade-Off*, publication expected in 1981.

SIDELIGHTS: Greer writes: "My work centers around the interface of theology and psychology. The books are written to be enjoyed rather than 'labored over.' For the reader, if I do well, the laboring comes later.

"Both theology and psychotherapy deal with complex issues. The author's task, as I see it (unless s/he writes for colleagues), is to unravel these issues in ways that are immediately useful to the reader. This means translating concepts into situations that most readers have experienced, and *then* showing the reader what s/he might possibly *do* with the idea. I'm convinced that this happens most easily when the reader is enjoying what s/he reads. My favorite compliment, and the one I most frequently get, is hearing that my books are read twice, first for fun and secondly to nail down the ideas. (This conforms to Ornstein's notion of our brains working in two different fashions—the Right Brain, which tends to control our behaviors, does not think logically, or linearly. The Left Brain does. For my readers to be helped, I *want* them to read it first as an experience—a fun thing to do. And the second reading won't hurt them, either.

"I first really fell in love with writing as a columnist for my college newspaper. Seeing my words in print under a by-line was glory enough for a while. Seeing those words stir the imaginations of my readers, or better yet, subtly change the campus scene proved to be addictive. Writing books was a natural progression. It took me twenty-four years to get around to it, though.

"I wish I could report that I wrote stereotypically: pipe, dog, fireplace, foolscap or legal-sized pads, four hours each day at the same time. (Like J. D. MacDonald's hero, Travis McGee, this author continues to have a 'lingering nostalgia for the lives he had never lived.') The fact is that I deliver books the way I hear women do babies: in great agony, and with much boiling of water (into which is poured instant coffee). Starting either at 10 a.m. or 4 p.m., I literally crank up, stall and re-crank for two or three hours to get the Muse persuaded. Once it comes, it comes full-blast, and I bang keys almost without ceasing for the next two to eight hours until the section or chapter is finished. It then takes another two hours to quiet everything down inside so I can sleep or re-enter society with some degree of civility. While the start-up is painful, the writing itself is feverishly gleeful. Since editing (my own and my editor's) will come later, I can let the words fly, much as when I talk. The writing then becomes a genuine conversation, one-sided though it may be. Ultimately, that's what both theology and psychotherapy are all about—the sharing of one's personhood with another. Words and ideas are a dime a dozen. So are people, I guess, but the difference is remarkable. A new idea will possibly change how I think; being touched by a person tends to change *me*, and that's a significant difference.

"What led to my writing books? When I started my first book, I wrote the following in my journal: '1973 seems to be the time when many "preparations" come together like the vectors on a navigator's map—the years of writing columns and sermons; the years of secular experience (taxi driving, mortician's assistant, milkman, etc.); the years of faith (pastor, preacher); the years of training; the years of humor and joy; the years of knowing what it means to be human and to struggle; the years filled with friends who brought grace into my life; the years of lecturing to Joe Average; the dissatisfaction with Christianity as most folk know it.' A book is simply a place to put all of that."

AVOCATIONAL INTERESTS: Sailing his twenty-seven-foot sloop, camping, leatherwork, woodwork.

*   *   *

GREER, Germaine   1939-

PERSONAL: Born January 29, 1939, near Melbourne, Australia; daughter of Eric Reginal (a newspaper advertising manager) and Margaret May Mary (Lanfrancan) Greer; married Paul de Feu (a newspaperman), 1968 (divorced, 1973). *Education:* University of Melbourne, B.A., 1959; University of Sydney, M.A., 1961; Newnham College, Cambridge, Ph.D., 1967. *Politics:* Anarchist. *Religion:* Atheist. *Residence:* Tuscany, Italy. *Agent:* Curtis Brown Ltd., 1 Craven Hill, London W2 3EP, England.

CAREER: Taught at a girls' school in Australia; University of Warwick, Coventry, England, lecturer in English, 1967-73; free-lance writer, 1973—. Has been an actress on a television comedy show in Manchester, England.

WRITINGS: The Female Eunuch, MacGibbon & Kee, 1970, McGraw, 1971. Columnist, *London Sunday Times,* 1971-73. Contributor to periodicals, including *Listener, Spectator, Oz,* and *Esquire.* Co-founder of *Suck.*

WORK IN PROGRESS: The Obstacle Race: The Story of Women in Painting.

SIDELIGHTS: Germaine Greer became a media success upon the American publication of *The Female Eunuch* in 1971. Such celebrity was consistent with her roles as a television performer and as a self-avowed London "groupie" (her enthusiasm for jazz and popular music had brought her into contact with musicians and other members of Britain's underground culture); but critics seized upon her slick and frankly sexual image as counterproductive to the feminist cause she espoused. While her book climbed the bestseller charts in both the United States and England and *Vogue* magazine hailed her as "a super heroine," hard-line members of the women's liberation movement questioned her authority. While *Newsweek* described her as "a dazzling combination of erudition, eccentricity and eroticism," some feminist writers wondered whether an undisputably attractive Shakespearean scholar could speak with understanding about the plight of women in general.

Nevertheless, *The Female Eunuch* sold. It was made a Book-of-the-Month Club alternate and a Book Find Club selection and was ultimately translated into twelve languages. During a United States promotional tour in the spring of 1971, Greer furthered her message on television and radio talk shows, in *Life* magazine, and in a well publicized debate with Norman Mailer, the novelist and self-confirmed "male chauvinist."

Greer's basic argument, as explained in the book's introduction, is that women's "sexuality is both denied and misrepresented by being identified as passivity." She explains that women, urged from childhood to live up to an "Eternal Feminine" stereotype, are valued for characteristics associated with the castrate—"timidity, plumpness, languor, delicacy and preciosity"—hence the book's title. From the viewpoint of this primary assumption, Greer examines not only the problems of women's sexuality, but their psychological development, their relationships with men, their social position, and their cultural history. What most struck early critics of the book was that she considered "the castration of our true female personality . . . not the fault of men, but our own, and history's." Thus *Newsweek* could consider Greer's work "women's liberation's most realistic and least anti-male manifesto"; and Christopher Lehmann Haupt could call it "a book that combines the best of masculinity *and* feminity."

BIOGRAPHICAL/CRITICAL SOURCES: Observer, October 11, 1970; *Listener,* October 22, 1970; *Newsweek,* March 22, 1971; *New York Times,* April 20, 1971; *Life,* May 7, 1971; *Detroit News,* May 9, 1971.*

GREGG, Charles T(hornton)   1927-

PERSONAL: Born July 27, 1927, in Billings, Mont.; son of Charles Thornton (a broker) and Gertrude (Hurst) Gregg; married Elizabeth Whitaker (an operating room nurse), December 20, 1957; children: Paul, Diane (Mrs. John Gregg-Stohler), Brian, Elaine. *Education:* Attended Reed College, 1948-50; Oregon State University, B.S., 1952, M.S., 1955, Ph.D., 1959. *Politics:* Liberal. *Religion:* Unitarian-Universalist. *Home:* 2460-A 35th St., Los Alamos, N.M. 87544. *Office:* Los Alamos Scientific Laboratory, MS890, P.O. Box 1663, Los Alamos, N.M.

CAREER: Oregon State University, Corvallis, instructor in agricultural chemistry, 1955-59; Johns Hopkins University, Baltimore, Md., research fellow in physiological chemistry, 1959-63; University of California, Los Alamos Scientific Laboratory, Los Alamos, N.M., biochemist, 1963—. Visiting professor at Free University of Berlin, 1973-74. *Military service:* U.S. Navy, 1944-46; served in Pacific theater. *Member:* American Association for the Advancement of Science (fellow), American Society for Microbiology, Authors Guild of Authors League of America, American Society of Biological Chemists (fellow). *Awards, honors:* U.S. Public Health Service fellowship, 1959-63.

WRITINGS: Plague!, Scribner, 1978. Also author of an unproduced play, "Patriots/Traitors."

Contributor: Ronald W. Estabrook and Maynard E. Pullman, editors, *Methods in Enzymology,* Volume 10: *Oxidation and Phosphorylation,* Academic Press, 1967; George H. Rothblat and Vincent J. Cristafalo, editors, *Growth, Nutrition, and Metabolism of Cells in Culture,* Volume I, Academic Press, 1972; Diether Neubert and Hans-Jochen Merker, editors, *New Approaches to the Evaluation of Abnormal Embryonic Development,* George Thieme (Stuttgart), 1975; Rudoph Weber, editor, *The Biochemistry of Animal Development,* Volume III: *Molecular Aspects of Animal Development,* Academic Press, 1975.

Contributor to *Proceedings* of the British Pharmacology Society Symposium on Stable Isotopes, 1978, and to *Proceedings* of the Third International Conference on Stable Isotopes, in press; contributor of about forty articles to scientific journals.

WORK IN PROGRESS: A novel; a nonfiction book on the invasion of Tarawa.

SIDELIGHTS: Gregg writes: "I considered myself a writer for a very long time before I had anything published. I wrote short stories, a two-act play, magazine articles and queries, and half of a novel, and I accumulated a stack of rejection slips to attest to my status as a writer.

"I finally concluded that first I had to get a publisher's attention and I could do that best by using my technical background to write on a subject that would be difficult for someone without my training (or the genius of Camus) to handle. It worked—hence the book *Plague!*. My next book will also be nonfiction, though not biomedical, since I don't want to be typecast. Then I would like to complete the novel that I turned away from some years ago when I lost control of it. Ideally, I would like to move back and forth between fiction and nonfiction, but it remains to be seen whether or not I can write salable fiction at all."

AVOCATIONAL INTERESTS: Reading, sailing, hiking, playing squash.

*   *   *

GREGORY, Stephen
See PENZLER, Otto

GREGSTON, Gene 1925-

PERSONAL: Born May 19, 1925, in Marlow, Okla.; son of Roy Lee (employed in a shoe store) and Elsie (Lamb) Gregston; married Donna Patricia Bettis (a nurse), June 3, 1945; children: Donna Gene Gregston Rahilly, Richard Patrick. *Education:* Attended University of Missouri, 1943, and University of Oklahoma, 1946-47. *Home and office:* 4899 Atlanta Dr., San Diego, Calif. 92115. *Agent:* Paul Sutherland, 2612 Burgener Blvd., San Diego, Calif. 92115.

CAREER: Odessa American, Odessa, Tex., sports editor, 1947-48; *Topeka Daily Capital,* Topeka, Kan., sports editor, 1949; *Fort Worth Star-Telegram,* Fort Worth, Tex., sports writer, 1949-58; *San Diego Evening Tribune,* San Diego, Calif., sports editor, 1958-64, managing editor, 1965-70, editor, 1970; *San Diego Union,* San Diego, editor, 1971-75; free-lance writer, 1975—. Member of board of directors of San Diego Natural History Museum and San Diego Convention-Visitors Bureau. *Military service:* U.S. Army Air Forces, pilot and advanced flying instructor, 1943-45. *Member:* Authors Guild, Sigma Delta Chi. *Awards, honors:* News writing award from Golf Writers Association of America, 1957, for coverage of Doug Ford's victory in the Masters Golf Tournament.

WRITINGS: Hogan, the Man Who Played for Glory, Prentice-Hall, 1978. Also author of syndicated sports column.

WORK IN PROGRESS: S Is for Snitch, a novel about drug trafficking from Mexico to California; *Red, White, and Black,* a novel about black cavalrymen in west Texas in 1879; *The Arizona Ringer,* nonfiction about horse race fraud.

SIDELIGHTS: Gregston told *CA:* "Writing has been my first love in the field since I was fifteen years old.... The challenge of leaving sports writing to manage major metropolitan newspapers was too great to resist. As an editor, I learned much about writing. When I decided to write full-time I felt I was much better prepared for it. The fiction I have done generally would be described as 'adventure.' There are personal messages expressed through the characters but I could not pinpoint each."

*   *   *

GRENFELL, Joyce (Irene) 1910-

PERSONAL: Born February 2, 1910, in London, England; daughter of Paul (an architect) and Nora (Langhorn) Phipps; married Reginald Pascoe Grenfell (an accountant and mine director), December 12, 1928. *Education:* Educated in England. *Address:* c/o Christopher Mann Ltd., 140 Park Lane, London W. 1, England.

CAREER: Actress, author, and entertainer. Worked as designer of Christmas cards, 1929; radio critic for *London Observer,* 1935-38; British quiz master on television series, "Trans-Atlantic Quiz"; panelist on radio program "We Beg to Differ," 1949-50; actress in stage reviews, including "The Little Review," 1939, "Diversion," 1940, "Diversion No. 2," 1941, in stage productions, including "Sigh No More," 1945, "Tuppence Coloured," 1947-48, "Penny Plain," 1951-52, and "Joyce Grenfell Requests the Pleasure ...," 1954-72, and in motion pictures, including "The Happiest Days of Your Life," 1950, "Man With a Million," 1954, "Pure Hell at St. Trinians," 1961, and "The Old Dark House," 1963. Appeared on numerous television shows, including "Ed Sullivan Show," "David Susskind's Festival Performing Arts Television Hour," "Dick Cavett," and "David Frost." Toured battle areas in Europe, Asia, and Africa, 1944. Former president of North Islington Nursery School; member of Pilkington Committee on Broadcasting, 1960-62, and general advice council of British Broadcasting Corp. (BBC). *Member:* Society of Women Writers and Journalists (president, 1957). *Awards, honors:* Order of the British Empire, 1946, for services during World War II; honorary fellow at Manchester Polytechnic and Lucy Cavendish Collegiate Society, Cambridge.

WRITINGS: (Contributor) Edward R. Murrow, *This I Believe,* Simon & Schuster, 1952; *Joyce Grenfell Requests the Pleasure,* Macmillan, 1976; *George, Don't Do That,* Macmillan, 1977; *Stately as a Galleon,* Macmillan, 1978; *In Pleasant Places,* Macmillan, 1979. Also author of sketches and song lyrics for stage production, "Joyce Grenfell Requests the Pleasure...." Contributor to periodicals, including *Vogue, Spectator, London Observer,* and *Punch.*

SIDELIGHTS: Grenfell came into entertaining by chance. At a dinner party, she met Stephen Potter, a noted British humorist, and impressed him with her delivery of a story she'd created, "How to Make a Boutonniere Out of Empty Beech Nut Husk Clusters." Potter convinced Grenfell to repeat the story for a friend of his, Herbert Farjeon. Farjeon, too, was charmed by Grenfell's style and invited her to join the cast of "The Little Review." In the next few years, Grenfell appeared in two more reviews of Farjeon's, "Diversion," and "Diversion No. 2." Both reviews were tailored as entertainment for Londoners during the air raids. She then performed in another Farjeon production, "Light and Shade," and soon after that toured various battle sites with another troupe.

Upon return from the war, Grenfell branched out into theater and radio. Her work in both began to earn her a wide and appreciative audience. In 1949, she made her first appearance in a motion picture, "Letter to America." She then went on to portray a variety of background characters in films such as "Poets and Pals," "While the Sun Shines," and Alfred Hitchcock's "Stage Fright," where she played a woman at a shooting gallery.

By the early 1950's, Grenfell had developed into an impressive character actress but lead roles had eluded her. So, in 1954, she developed her own stage show, "Joyce Grenfell Requests the Pleasure...." The production, which consisted of songs and monologues written by Grenfell, was such a success that it played consistently, with revisions, for the next eighteen years. A forerunner of such entertainers as Jonathan Winters and Lily Tomlin, Grenfell paraded a variety of characters through her show. Among the most popular ones she played were a nursery-school teacher, the dissatisfied mother-of-the-bride, and a bubbly woman at a literary party. She also created more serious characters, including characters drawn from English literature, the wife of the vice-chancellor of "Oxbridge" University, and Lolly Tullett, an old Virginian woman. Later, Grenfell repeated highlights of her review on various television shows.

Grenfell's memoirs, *Joyce Grenfell Requests the Pleasure,* were graciously reviewed in *New Yorker:* "The book takes us through the war, when she entertained the troops, and on to the triumphs of her stage, cinema, and broadcasting career. It is full of her friends—many of them famous, many not—and full of herself: an ebullient, thoughtful, sharply observant (naturally) woman who is a delight to read, and to read about."

AVOCATIONAL INTERESTS: Reading, collecting flowers, chamber music, jazz, and needlepoint.

BIOGRAPHICAL/CRITICAL SOURCES: New Yorker, October 31, 1977.

* * *

GRESHAM, Elizabeth (Fenner) 1904-
(Robin Grey)

PERSONAL: Born December 20, 1904, in Plainfield, N.J.; daughter of David Colton (an engineer) and Gertrude (Smith) Fenner; married Thomas Baxter Gresham (a gunsmith and ballistics expert), July 23, 1932 (died, 1949). *Education:* Vassar College, A.B., 1926; American Laboratory Theatre School, certificate, 1927. *Politics:* Independent. *Religion:* Presbyterian. *Home:* 942 Rosser Lane, Charlottesville, Va. 22903. *Agent:* Frances Collin, 141 East 55th St., New York, N.Y. 10022.

CAREER: Writer, actress, and director of stage productions. Dallas Little Theatre, Dallas, Tex., actress, 1927-28; McKinney Little Theatre, McKinney, Tex., director of stage productions, 1927-28; teacher of speech and drama at private school in Dallas, 1927-29; actress and director with University Players in West Falmouth, Mass., and Baltimore, Md., 1928-32; University of Virginia Players, Charlottesville, Va., actor and director, 1932-39; teacher of speech and drama in Virginia for St. Anne's School, 1932-34, Sweet Briar College, 1940-42, and Roanoke College, 1944-45; Lynchburg Little Theatre, Lynchburg, Va., director of stage productions, 1939-42, 1963. Director of University of Virginia Players, summer, 1950 and 1951. *Member:* Mystery Writers of America, Fortnightly Club.

WRITINGS—Novels; "Puzzle" series: (Under pseudonym Robin Grey) *Puzzle in Porcelain,* Duell, Sloan & Pearce, 1945; (under Grey pseudonym) *Puzzle in Pewter,* Duell, Sloan & Pearce, 1947; *Puzzle in Paisley,* Curtis Books, 1972; *Puzzle in Parquet,* Curtis Books, 1973; *Puzzle in Patchwork,* Curtis Books, 1973; *Puzzle in Parchment,* Curtis Books, 1973.

Other: *The World of the Aztecs* (nonfiction), Walker & Co., 1961; *Lucifer Was Tall* (novel), Popular Library, 1976; *Pawn in Jeopardy* (novel), Popular Library, 1977; *Daughter of Darkness* (novel), Popular Library, 1977. Contributor of serialized novel, "Masquerade for Murder," to *Everywoman's,* 1948.

Plays: "Murder for Two," first produced in Charlottesville at the University of Virginia, 1934; "Detour to Success," first produced in Charlottesville at the University of Virginia, 1935; "That Lesser Aphrodite," first produced in Charlottesville at the University of Virginia, 1936; "The Lady Was a Stranger," first produced in Charlottesville at the University of Virginia, 1937; "Siesta in Shakespearia," first produced in Salem, Va., at Roanoke College, 1945.

WORK IN PROGRESS: Poisoner's Base, a novel, for Popular Library.

SIDELIGHTS: Gresham told *CA:* "I am most alive when I have a story or book 'growing' on my desk. When it is unfolding and hinting at bloom, I can write all day. When it is attacked by insects, or begins to wilt, I take pleasure in fighting for its life.

"My favorite mystery writers are those who depend on wit to outwit: those who introduce me to three-dimensional characters and make me care what happens to them and who accomplish this without excessive violence and explicit sex. Outstanding authors would certainly include Josephine Tey, Manning Coles, Margery Allingham, Rex Stout, Dorothy L. Sayers, and Ngaio Marsh. All of these but Marsh are dead now, and it is said that their type of book is dying—or dead—too. I haven't talked with anyone in the last few years who does not regret this, and this response covers readers from sixteen to sixty. So, I write—and read—on, hopefully."

BIOGRAPHICAL/CRITICAL SOURCES: Joshua Logan, *Josh: My Up and Down, In and Out Life,* Delacorte, 1976.

* * *

GREY, Robin
See GRESHAM, Elizabeth (Fenner)

* * *

GRIMSLEY, Linda 1940-

PERSONAL: Born April 3, 1940, in Staunton, Va.; daughter of Samuel A. (a manufacturer's consultant) and Saral (Dickerson) Cravotta; married Joseph W. Grimsley (a member of the North Carolina governor's cabinet), December 22, 1962; children: Wayne, Julie, Christie. *Education:* Attended University of Richmond, 1958-59, and American University, 1959-60; University of North Carolina, B.A., 1962; North Carolina State University, M.S., 1977, doctoral study, 1977—. *Home:* 3119 Birnamwood, Raleigh, N.C. 27607. *Agent:* Mary Ann Colas and Jean Naggar, Manuscripts Unlimited Literary Agency, 229 East 79th St., New York, N.Y. 10021. *Office:* Department of Continuing Education, Meredith College, Raleigh, N.C. 27611.

CAREER: U.S. Department of the Navy, Bureau of Naval Personnel, Washington, D.C., secretary to research psychologists, summer, 1958; U.S. Information Agency, Washington, D.C., television production assistant, summers, 1959-61; *Northern Virginia Sun,* Alexandria, Va., reporter, 1962; *Foreign Agriculture,* Washington, D.C., public information specialist, 1963; *New Orleans States-Item,* New Orleans, La., reporter, 1963; free-lance writer and public relations consultant, 1964-71; North Carolina Museum of Art, Raleigh, N.C., editor, 1971-73; WUNC-TV, Chapel Hill, N.C., assistant producer and feature reporter for "The General Assembly Today," 1973-74; Meredith College, Raleigh, N.C., instructor in education, 1975—, director of enrichment program, 1978—. Instructor for writers' workshop; guest on television programs. Member of North Carolina governor's Business Council on the Arts and Humanities, Cultural Advisory Council, and Women's Political Caucus.

MEMBER: American Psychological Association, American Personnel and Guidance Association, League of Women Voters.

WRITINGS: Guerrilla in the Kitchen (novel), Liveright, 1974. Also editor of *The Peace Corps in Honduras,* a booklet, and author of museum catalogs.

WORK IN PROGRESS: A book on risk-taking in personal development and leadership.

SIDELIGHTS: Linda Grimsley writes: "I am interested in the rapid change in society as it relates to personal development."

* * *

GRINSPOON, Lester 1928-

PERSONAL: Born June 24, 1928, in Newton, Mass.; son of Simon (a lawyer) and Sally (Rose) Grinspoon; married Evelyn Popky (a professor of mathematics), June 19, 1954; children: David, Joshua, Peter. *Education:* Tufts University, B.S., 1951; Harvard University, M.D., 1955; also graduated from Boston Psychoanalytic Institute. *Home:* 35 Skyline Dr., Wellesley, Mass. 02181. *Office:* 74 Fenwood Rd., Boston, Mass. 02115.

CAREER: Beth Israel Hospital, Boston, Mass., intern, 1955-56; National Cancer Institute, Los Angeles, Calif., field investigator, 1956-58; Massachusetts Mental Health Center, Boston, Mass., resident in psychiatry, 1958-59, chief of drug unit, 1959-60, chief of service, 1960-61, senior research psychiatrist, 1961-64, research director of psychiatry, 1964—, director of Clinical Research Center, 1961-68. Diplomate of National Board of Medical Examiners and American Board of Psychiatry and Neurology; licensed to practice in Massachusetts and California. Lecturer at Harvard University, 1961-63, instructor, 1962-64, assistant clinical professor, 1965-68, associate clinical professor, 1968-73, associate professor, 1973—, clinical associate in psychiatry, 1964-65; director of American Academy of Arts and Sciences Summer Institute on Alternative Ways of Handling Conflict, 1962. Executive director of Massachusetts Mental Health Research Corp., 1973—. Examiner for American Board of Psychiatry and Neurology; member of advisory board of Center for the Study of Non-Medical Drug Use, 1976—; has testified before National Marihuana Commission and U.S. Congress.

MEMBER: World Federation of Mental Health, American Psychiatric Association (fellow; chairman of Council on Research and Development, 1977-79), American Association for the Advancement of Science, Society of Biological Psychiatry, Group for the Advancement of Psychiatry, National Organization for the Reform of Marijuana Laws (member of advisory board), Boylston Society, Massachusetts Medical Society, Columbia University Seminar (associate member), Phi Beta Kappa, Alpha Omega Alpha.

WRITINGS: Marihuana Reconsidered, Harvard University Press, 1971, 2nd edition, 1977; (with J. R. Ewalt and R. I. Shader) *Schizophrenia: Pharmacotherapy and Psychotherapy,* Williams & Wilkins, 1972; (with Peter Hedblom) *The Speed Culture: Amphetamine Use and Abuse in America,* Harvard University Press, 1975; (with J. B. Bakalar) *Cocaine: A Drug and Its Social Evolution,* Basic Books, 1976.

Contributor: Milton Greenblatt, D. J. Levinson, and G. L. Klerman, editors, *Mental Patients in Transition,* C. C Thomas, 1961; Seymour Melman, editor, *No Place to Hide,* Grove, 1962; Greenblatt, G. Grosser, and H. Wechsler, editors, *The Threat of Impending Disaster: Contribution to the Psychology of Stress,* M.I.T. Press, 1964; R. D. Fisher, editor, *International Conflict and Behavioral Science: The Craigville Papers,* Basic Books, 1964; D. V. Siva Sankar, editor, *Schizophrenia: Current Concepts and Research,* PJD Publications, 1969; M. E. Adelstein and J. G. Pival, editors, *Drugs,* St. Martin's, 1972; Carl Sagan and Thornton Page, editors, *UFO's: A Scientific Debate,* Cornell University Press, 1972; M. S. Weinberg and E. Rubington, editors, *The Solution of Social Problems: Five Perspectives,* Oxford University Press, 1973; Stella Chess and Alexander Thomas, editors, *Progress in Child Psychiatry and Child Development, 1974,* Brunner, 1975; Alfred M. Freedman, Harold I. Kaplan, and Benjamin J. Sadock, editors, *Comprehensive Textbook of Psychiatry,* Volume II, Williams & Wilkins, 1975; Milton Greenblatt, editor, *Drugs in Combination With Other Therapies,* Grune, 1975; Siva Sankar, editor, *Psychopharmacology of Childhood,* PJD Publications, 1976; Colette Chiland, editor, *Long-Term Treatments of Psychotic States,* Human Sciences Press, 1977; William H. Reid, editor, *The Psychopath: A Comprehensive Study of Socio-*

pathic Disorders and Behaviors, Brunner/Mazel, 1978. Also contributor to *Anthology of Selected References From the Balanced Service System,* Division of Mental Health, State of New York Department of Mental Hygiene, 1974, and John Paul Brady and H. Keith Brodie, editors, *Controversy in Psychiatry,* Saunders.

Contributor to *Encyclopedia of Science and Technology.* Contributor of about seventy-five articles and reviews to scientific and popular journals, including *New Republic, Science Digest, Scientific American, Mademoiselle, Saturday Review,* and *Parents' Magazine.*

WORK IN PROGRESS: A book on psychedelic drugs.

* * *

GROLLMAN, Sharon Hya 1954-

PERSONAL: Born July 12, 1954, in Boston, Mass.; daughter of Earl Alan (a rabbi and writer) and Netta (an artist; maiden name, Levinson) Grollman; married Nathaniel Novod (a computer scientist and photographer), June 18, 1978. *Education:* Attended Brandeis University, 1974; Union College, Schenectady, N.Y., B.S. (magna cum laude), 1976; graduate study at Tufts University, 1977—. *Home:* 36 Carver St., Cambridge, Mass. 02138.

CAREER: Union College, Schenectady, N.Y., tutor and counselor for academic opportunity program, 1975-76; Reading International, Belmont, Mass., book clerk, 1976-77; Children's Hospital Medical Center, Boston, Mass., intern in children's activities therapy, 1977-78. Counseling intern at private school in Marlborough, Mass., 1977-78, and at Tri-City Mental Health Center in Malden, Mass., 1978—. Volunteer worker with mentally retarded children and adults. *Awards, honors:* Scholarship for Bread Loaf Writer's Conference, 1976.

WRITINGS: More Time to Grow: Explaining Mental Retardation to Children, Beacon Press, 1977; (with father, Earl A. Grollman) *Caring for Your Aged Parents,* Beacon Press, 1978. Contributor to psychology and medical journals.

SIDELIGHTS: Sharon Grollman, whose current studies are aimed at a career in clinical psychology, comments: "I have always been interested in writing. Until several years ago, I wrote only fiction; however, as a result of my continuing fascination with psychology, the content of my work has changed. It is my hope that through my writing I can help others come to terms with themselves in moments of crisis, and better understand and accept individuals with special needs."

* * *

GROSS, Sheldon H(arvey) 1921-
(Shelly Gross)

PERSONAL: Born May 20, 1921, in Philadelphia, Pa.; married Joan Seidel (a psychiatric social worker), May 1, 1946; children: Byron J., Frederick O., Daniel Ben. *Education:* University of Pennsylvania, A.B.; Northwestern University, M.S.J. *Religion:* Jewish. *Home:* Fairmont, Apt. 504, Bala Cynwyd, Pa. 19004. *Agent:* Henry Morrison, Inc., 58 West 10th St., New York, N.Y. 10011. *Office:* Music Fair Enterprises, 555 City Line, Bala Cynwyd, Pa. 19004.

CAREER: WFIL-AM and FM Radio and TV, Philadelphia, Pa., commercial announcer, newsman, special events director, and master of ceremonies for variety shows, 1949-58; Music Fair Enterprises, Bala Cynwyd, Pa., co-founder and co-producer, 1955—. President of Tract Advertising Agency. Operator of Jones Beach Theatre and Pop Arts

Festival of Radio City Music Hall. Member of board of directors of American-Israeli Cultural Foundation. *Military service:* U.S. Navy, communications officer, 1942-46; served in the South Pacific; became lieutenant senior grade. *Member:* Musical Arena Theatre Association (vice-president), Phi Beta Kappa, Sigma Delta Chi, Pi Gamma Mu.

WRITINGS: (Under name Shelly Gross) *The Crusher* (novel), Curtis Books, 1973; (under name Shelly Gross) *Havana X* (novel), Arbor House, 1978.

WORK IN PROGRESS: Research for a novel dealing with an attempt by five Russian dissidents to escape the Soviet Union.

SIDELIGHTS: Gross has been a journalist, broadcaster, concert impresario, and theatrical producer. But he is best-known for presenting live talent and producing Broadway shows, including "The King and I," and national theatrical tours, including "Lorelei," "Li'l Abner" and "A Thurber Carnival." His Music Fair Enterprises has grown to include operation of the largest chain of theaters-in-the-round in the United States.

*   *   *

GROSS, Shelly
  See GROSS, Sheldon H(arvey)

*   *   *

GRUBBS, Donald H.   1936-
PERSONAL: Born December 14, 1936, in Miami, Fla.; son of Donald H. (a teacher) and Ruth (a teacher; maiden name, Franks) Grubbs; children: Donald H. III. *Education:* University of Florida, B.A., 1958, M.A., 1959, Ph.D., 1963; attended Vanderbilt University, 1959-60. *Home:* 1040 West Willow, Stockton, Calif. 95203. *Office:* University of the Pacific, Stockton, Calif. 95211.

CAREER: Miami-Dade Junior College, Miami, Fla., instructor, 1961-62; University of the Pacific, Stockton, Calif., 1963—, began as assistant professor, became associate professor.

WRITINGS: Cry From the Cotton: The STFU and the New Deal, University of North Carolina Press, 1971. Contributor to history and political science journals.

WORK IN PROGRESS: "History of the National Farmers' Organization," for national public television series, "The American Labor History Series."

SIDELIGHTS: Grubbs writes: "Because of the current uninspiring condition of American agriculture and labor, public interest in these fields has declined noticeably. Yet the history of, say, miners or sharecroppers in our country reveals dramatic parallels with the experience of humanity in general—more, perhaps, than can be found in any other branches of history than those of diplomacy and warfare. Through the struggles of farmers and workers we can approach the most universal human problems."

*   *   *

GUDIOL, Jose
  See GUDIOL i RICART, Josep

*   *   *

GUDIOL i RICART, Josep   1904-
  (Jose Gudiol, Josep Gudiol Ricart, Jose M. Gudiol Ricart)
PERSONAL: Born July 4, 1904, in Barcelona, Spain. *Edu-*

cation: Attended University of Barcelona and New York University. *Home:* Corcega, 317, Barcelona, Spain. *Office:* Instituto Amatller de Arte Hispanico, paeio de Gracia, 41, Barcelona 7, Spain.

CAREER: Art historian and writer. Worked as architect in Spain; University of Toledo, Toledo, Ohio, Carnegie Professor, 1939-40; New York University, New York, N.Y., professor of fine arts, 1940-41; currently director of Instituto Amatller de Arte Hispanico (Institute of Hispanic Art), Barcelona, Spain. *Member:* Real Academia de Bellas Artes de San Jorge, Real Academia de San Carlos, Real Academia de Bellas Artes de Santa Isabel de Hungria, Real Academia de San Fernando.

WRITINGS—In English: (Under name Jose Gudiol) *Goya,* Hyperion Press, 1941; *Spanish Painting,* Toledo Museum of Art, 1941; (under name Jose Gudiol) *The Arts of Spain,* Doubleday, 1964; (with Enzo Carli and Genevieve Souchal; under name Josep Gudiol Ricart) *La Peinture gothique,* Editions du Pont Royal, 1964, translation by Michael Raeburn and William Harris published as *Gothic Painting,* Viking, 1965; (under name Josep Gudiol Ricart) *Goya,* translated by Priscilla Muller, Abrams, 1965; (under name Josep Gudiol Ricart) *Arte romanico catalan: Pinturas murales,* G. Gili, 1965, translation by Bettina Wadia published as *Romanesque Catalan Art: Mural Painting,* Methuen, 1965; *Goya, 1764-1828,* four volumes, Editiones Poligrafa, 1969; translation by Kenneth Lyons published under same title, Editiones Poligrafa, 1971; (under name Jose Gudiol) *Domenikos Theotokopoulos: El Greco, 1541-1614,* Editiones Poligrafa, 1971, translation by Lyons published under same title, Viking, 1973; (under name Jose Gudiol) *Velazques, 1599-1660,* Ediciones Poligrafa, 1973, translation by Lyons published under same title, Viking, 1974.

Other: *La Catedral de Toledo* (title means "The Cathedral of Toledo"), Editorial Plus-Ultra, 1947; (with Juan Ainuad de Lasarte) *La Ciudad de Barcelona* (title means "The City of Barcelona"), Instituto Diego Velazquez, 1947; (with Jose Pijoan y Soteras) *Las pinturas murales romanicas de Cataluna* (title means "The Romanesque Mural Paintings of Catalonia"), Alpha, 1948; *Borrassa,* Instituto Amatller de Arte Hispanico, 1953; *Museo Episcopal de Vich* (title means "Episcopal Museum of Vich"), Aries, 1954; *Tarragona y su provincia* (title means "Tarragona and Its Province"), Aries, 1957; (editor) *Badajoz y su provincia* (title means "Badajoz and Its Province"), Aries, 1964; (with Julian Gallego) *Zurbaran, 1598-1664,* Ediciones Poligrafa, 1976; *Les Natures mortes de Sanchez Cotan* (title means "The Still Lifes of Sanchez Cotan"), Pantheon, 1977.

Under name Josep Gudiol Ricart: (With P. M. de Artinano) *Vidrio: Resumen de la historia del vidrio* (title means "Glass: A Summary of the History of Glass"), Tipografia Casulleras, 1935; *Els Vidres catalans,* Editorial Alpha, 1936; *Barcelona,* Aries, 1946, 3rd edition, 1954; (with Santiago Alcolea Gil and Juan Dias de Budalles) *Provincia de Barcelona* (title means "Province of Barcelona"), Aries, 1954; *Cataluna,* Seix Barral, 1955.

Under name Jose Gudiol: *Historia de la Pintura Gotica en Cataluna,* A.D.A.C., 1938; *El retablo del "Sant Esperit" de la Seo de Manresa,* Manresa, 1954; (with Gil) *Hispania: Guia general de arte espanol* (title means "Hispania: General Guide to Spanish Art"), Argos, 1962; (with J. Valenti and Juan Regla) *Tierras de Espana: Cataluna I* (title means "Lands of Spain: Catalonia"), Fundacion Juan March, 1974. Also author of *Pintura medieval en Aragon* (title means "Medieval Painting in Aragon"), 1971.

Under name Jose M. Gudiol Ricart: (With Juan-Eduardo Cirlot and Gil) *Historia de la pintura en Cataluna*, Editorial Tecnos, 1956.

* * *

GUDIOL RICART, Jose M.
See GUDIOL i RICART, Josep

* * *

GUDIOL RICART, Josep
See GUDIOL i RICART, Josep

* * *

GUGGENMOS, Josef 1922-

PERSONAL: Born July 2, 1922, in Irsee, Germany; son of Ignaz and Theresia (Maierhauser) Guggenmos; married Therese Wild, June 23, 1959; children: Ruth, Vera, Bettina. *Education:* Attended University of Marburg, University of Erlangen, and University of Bonn. *Religion:* Roman Catholic. *Home:* Am Staffel 21, D-8951 Irsee bei Kaufbeuren, Germany.

CAREER: Publisher's reader. *Member:* P.E.N., Rotary. *Awards, honors:* Premium of the German Youth Book Prize, 1968; named to honorary list of the European Youth Book Prize Citta di Caorle, 1968; honorary award from Bavarian Academy of Fine Arts, 1975.

WRITINGS—Juvenile works in English: *Gugummer geht ueber den See, Gedichte*, Mitteldeutscher Verlag, 1957, translation by Alvin Tresselt published as *Wonder-Fish From the Sea*, Parents' Magazine Press, 1971; (with Ursula Konopka) *Dragon Franz*, adapted by Elizabeth Shub from original German version, *Franz, der Drache*, Greenwillow Books, 1976.

Other; all juvenile: (Editor) Hans Jacob Christoffel von Grimmelshausen, *Der abenteuerliche Simplizissimus*, Bertelsmann Lesering, 1958; (with Rudolf Hautzinger) *Wir gehen mit Waldi spazieren*, Verlag fuer Jugend und Volk, 1963; *Die Schatzkiste*, Oesterreichischer Bundesverlag, 1967; *Der junge Naturforscher*, Ueberreuter, 1967; *Was denkt die Maus am Donnerstag? 123 Gedichte fuer Kinder*, Paulus Verlag, 1967, 4th edition, G. Bitter, 1969; *Ein Elefant marschiert durchs Land: Geschichten und Gedichte fuer Kinder*, Paulus Verlag, 1968; *Hunde*, Ueberreuter, 1968; *Voegel*, Ueberreuter, 1968; *Warum die Kaeuze grosse Augen machen*, Paulus Verlag, 1968; *Wer nie ein Nilpferd gaehnen sah*, G. Bitter, 1969.

Ein Koernchen fuer den Pfau, Kaufmann, 1970; (adapter) Edward Lear, *Die vergnuegte Reise*, Berliner Handpresse, 1970; (with Irmgard Lucht) *Alle meine Blaetter*, Middlehauve, 1970; *Gorilla, aergere dich nicht!*, Beltz & Gelberg, 1971; *Sieben kleine Baeren: Geschichten und Gedichte fuer Kinder*, G. Bitter, 1971; (with Johannes Grueger) *Auf einem Stern, der Moritz heisst*, Herder, 1972; *Ich hab's mit eigenen Ohren gesehn: Geschichten und Gedichte fuer Kinder*, O. Maier, 1973; *Theater, Theater!* (children's plays), G. Bitter, 1974; (with Heide Mayr-Pletschen) *Der kleine Springinsfeld: Ein Bilderbuch*, Kaufmann, 1975; *Das Knie aus der Wand: Unglaubliche Geschichten*, Stalling, 1975. Also author of a radio drama, and translator of works from English and Finnish into German.

SIDELIGHTS: Guggenmos told *CA* that he had lived for a year in Finland, and that he had traveled to southwest Africa and Arizona. *Avocational interests:* Art, zoology, botany, modeling.

GUGGISBERG, C(harles) A(lbert) W(alter) 1913-

PERSONAL: Born February 27, 1913, in Berne, Switzerland; son of Karl Wilhelm (a teacher) and Paula (Schanfelberger) Guggisberg; married Rosanne Leclere (a linguist), June 4, 1946. *Education:* Attended Imperial College of Science and Technology, London, 1935-36; University of Berne, earned B.S. degree, M.Sc., 1938. *Home and Office Address:* P.O. Box 45882, Nairobi, Kenya. *Agent:* Bruce Coleman, Windsor Street, Uxbridge UB8 1AB, England.

CAREER: High school teacher in Berne, Switzerland, 1939-46; moved to East Africa, 1946; traveled in Tanganyika, Tanzania, 1947; Medical Research Laboratory, Nairobi, Kenya, zoologist, 1948-69; full-time writer, photographer, and lecturer, 1970—. Member of many natural history expeditions in Kenya, Uganda, Tanzania, Congo, Zambia, Rhodesia, and South Africa, 1948—; consultant on plague and plague reservoirs in East Africa for World Health Organization, 1966-71; consultant on plague research for Lesotho Government, 1968. *Member:* East African Wildlife Society, National Geographic Society, Authors Guild (United States), Swiss Society for the Study and Protection of Birds, British Ornithological Union, Berne Authors' Association, Swiss Alpine Club. *Awards, honors:* Literary Prize from the city of Berne, 1963; honorary doctorate of science, University of Berne.

WRITINGS—All published by Hallwag Taschenbuecher, 1943-52: *Unsere Voegel I* (title means "Our Birds I"); *Unsere Voegel II* (title means "Our Birds II"); *Tiere in Feld und Wald* (title means "Animals of Field and Forest"); *Alpenfibel* (title means "Guide to the Alps"); *Schmetterlinge und Nachfalter* (title means "Butterflies and Moths"); *Kaefer und andere Insekten* (title means "Beetles and Other Insects"); *Kleine Erdgeschichte* (title means "Little Earth History"); *Exotische Tiere* (title means "Exotic Animals"); *Die Menschenrassen* (title means "The Human Races"); *Exotische Voegel* (title means "Exotic Birds").

Other: *Game Animals of Eastern Africa*, [Nairobi], 1949; *Unter Loewen und Elefanten* (title means "Amidst Lions and Elephants"), Hallwag Taschenbuecher, 1953; *Das Tierleben der Alpen* (title means "Animal Life of the Alps"), Hallwag Taschenbuecher, volume I, 1954, volume II, 1955; *Riesentiere und Zwergmenschen* (title means "Giant Animals and Dwarf People"), Hallwag Taschenbuecher, 1956.

Simba: Eine Loewenmonographie, Hallwag Taschenbuecher, 1960, translation by Guggisberg published as *Simba: The Life of the Lion*, Chilton, 1961; *The Wilderness Is Free*, [London], 1963; *Die Tierwelt der Schweiz: Saeugetiere, Kriechtiere, Lurche* (title means "Animals of Switzerland: Mammals, Reptiles, Amphibians"), [Neuchatel], 1965; *S.O.S. Rhino*, Andre Deutsch, 1967; *Tierwelt Afrikas*, [Neuchatel], 1967, translation by Guggisberg published as *Animals of Africa*, [Nairobi], 1972; *Giraffes*, Arthur Barker, 1969.

Man and Wildlife, Arco, 1970; *Mammals of East Africa: Ungulates, Carnivores, Primates*, [Nairobi], 1970; (with wife, Rosanne Guggisberg) *Touring East Africa*, [Nairobi], 1971; *Crocodiles: Their Natural History, Folklore and Conservation*, Newton Abbot, 1972; *Wild Cats of the World*, Taplinger, 1975; (with R. Guggisberg) *Der Grosse Polyglott: Ostafrika* (title means "The Great Polyglott: East Africa"), [Munich], 1975, revised edition, 1979; *Early Wildlife Photographers*, Taplinger, 1977; *The African Elephant*, Sapra, 1978; *A Guide to the Brids of East Africa*, [Nairobi], in press; (with R. Guggisberg) *Little Polyglott: Kenya and Northern Tanzania*, [Munich], in press; (with R. Guggisberg) *A Guide to Kenya and Northern Tanzania*, [Nairobi], in press.

Translator from the English: Gordon C. Aymar, *Herrlicher Vogelflug*, [Thun], 1949; Ivan T. Sanderson, *Dynastie of Abu: Geschichte und Etnwicklung der Elefanten und Ihrer Verwandten*, [Berne], 1966.

Contributor to *Der Durchsug der Limicolenarten am Fanalstrand, Jahrbuch des Naturhistorischen Museums der Stadt Bern 1966-68* (title means "Yearbook of the Natural History Museums for the City of Berne, 1966-68"), and numerous professional journals and yearbooks.

WORK IN PROGRESS: Research on various groups of animals and on historical and biographical subjects connected with exploration in general and Africa in particular.

SIDELIGHTS: C.A.W. Guggisberg commented to *CA:* "I've been interested in animals as far back as I can remember. Ever since reading H. M. Stanley's *In Darkest Africa* at the age of ten, I wanted to go to Africa." After translating *Simba: Eins Loewenmonographie* from the German original into English, Guggisberg began writing in both languages. Some of his books have been translated into French, Swedish, and Italian.

* * *

GUILLEMIN, Henri 1903-

PERSONAL: Born March 19, 1903, in Macon, France; son of Philippe and Louise (Thenoz) Guillemin; married Jacqueline Rodel, May 24, 1928; children: Philippe, Francoise, Marianick, Michel. *Education:* Ecole Normale Superieur, Paris, agrege des lettres, 1927, docteur es lettres, 1936. *Politics:* "Republican on the far left." *Religion:* Catholic. *Home:* 58 faubourg de l'Hopital, 2000 Neuchatel, Switzerland.

CAREER: Teacher of French literature at various schools in France, 1928-36; University of Cairo, Cairo, Egypt, professor of French literature, 1936-38; University of Bordeaux, Bordeaux, France, professor of French language and literature, 1938-42; French Embassy, Berne, Switzerland, cultural counselor, 1945-62; University of Geneva, Geneva, Switzerland, professor of French literature, 1963—. *Awards, honors:* Chevalier de la Legion d'honneur, 1948; Grand Prix de la Critique, Paris, 1965.

WRITINGS—In English: *Jeanne dite Jeanne d'Arc*, translation by Harold J. Salemson published as *Joan, Maid of Orleans*, Saturday Review Press, 1970 (translation by William Oxferry published in England as *The True History of Joan "of Arc"*, Allen and Unwin, 1972).

Other works: *Le Jocelyn de Lamartine: Etude historique et critique*, Boivin et cie, 1936, reprinted, 1967; *Flaubert devant la vie et devant Dieu*, preface by Francois Mauriac, Plon, 1939; *Lamartine, l'homme et l'oeuvre* (title means "Lamartine: The Man and His Works"), Boivin et cie, 1940; *"Cette affaire infernale," l'affaire J.-J. Rousseau—Hume, 1766*, Plon, 1942; *Connaissance de Lamartine*, Editions de la librairie, l'Universite de Fribourg, 1942; *Un Homme, deux ombres (Jean Jacques, Julie, Sophie)*, Editions du milieu du monde, 1943; *La Bataille de Dieu*, Editions du milieu du monde, 1944; *Histoire des catoliques francais au XIXe siecle, 1815-1905* (title means "History of the French Catholics of the Nineteenth Century, 1815-1905"), [Geneva], 1947; *Cette nuit-la, conte de Noel* (booklet; title means "Tonight: The Story of Christmas"), illustrations by Andre Rosselet, Editions au Griffon, 1948.

Le Coup du 2 decembre, [Paris], 1951; *L'Humour de Victor Hugo* (title means "The Humor of Victor Hugo"), La Baconniere, 1951; *Hugo et la sexualite* (title means "Hugo and Sexuality"), Gallimard, 1954; *Claudel et son art d'ecrire*, [Paris], 1955; *M. de Vigny, homme d'ordre et poete*, Gallimard, 1955; *Claudel et son art d'ecrire*, Gallimard, 1955; *A vrai dire*, Gallimard, 1956; *Cette curieuse guerre de 70: Thiers, Trochu, Bazaine*, Gallimard, 1956; *Lamartine: Documents iconographiques*, P. Cailler, 1958; *Madame de Stael, Benjamin Constant et Napoleon*, Plon, 1959; *Les Origines de la commune*, Gallimard, 1959; *L'Heroique defense de Paris, 1870-1871*, Gallimard, 1959.

La Capitulation, 1871 (title means "The Capitulation: 1871"), Gallimard, 1960; *Zola, legende et verite*, R. Julliard, 1960; *Eclaircissements*, Gallimard, 1961; *L'Enigme Esterhazy*, Gallimard, 1962; *Presentation des Rougon-Macquart*, Gallimard, 1964; *L'Homme des "Memoires d'outre-tombe,"* Paris, 1965; *Madame de Stael et Napoleon ou Germaine et le caid ingrat*, Bienne, 1966; *L'Arriere-pensee de Jaures* (essays), 1966; *La Premiere resurrection de la Republique: 24 fevrier 1848*, Gallimard, 1967; *Le "Converti" Paul Claudel*, Gallimard, 1968; *Napoleon tel quel*, Editions de Trevise, 1969; *Pas a pas*, Gallimard, 1969.

L'Avenement de M. Thiers, et Reflexions sur la Commune, Gallimard, 1971; *Emile Zola: Sa vie, le sens de son oeuvre*, Les Editions du cercle d'education populaire (Brussels), 1971; *La Liaison Musset-Sand*, Gallimard, 1972; *Precisions*, Gallimard, 1973; *Henri Guillemin parle de Jean-Jacques Rousseau, Voltaire, Rimbaud, Valles* (title means "Henri Guillemin Talks About . . ."), Cercle d'education populaire, 1974; *Nationalistes et "nationaux," 1870-1940*, Gallimard, 1974; *Regards sur Bernanos*, Gallimard, 1976; *Sulivan; ou, La Parole liberatrice*, Gallimard, 1977.

Editor: Alphonse Marie Louise de Lamartine, *Lettres inedites, 1821-1851* (title means "Unpublished Letters, 1821-1851"), Aux Portes de France, 1944; Victor Marie Hugo, *Hugo par lui-meme* (title means "Hugo, by Himself"), Seuil, 1951; Hugo, *Strophes inedites* (title means "Unpublished Verses"), Editions Ides et calendes, 1952; Jean Jacques Rousseau, *Du contrat social*, Union general d'-editions, 1963; Alfred de Musset, *Theatre complet*, Editions Rencontre, 1964; Hugo, *Romans* (title means "Novels"); Emile Zola, *Germinal*, Garnier-Flammarion, 1968.

Also author of introduction of works of Emile Zola, Victor Hugo, Sainte-Beuve, and others.

WORK IN PROGRESS: Regards sur Peguy.

SIDELIGHTS: Guillemin told *CA* that he has been most influenced by the writings of nineteenth-century French author Sainte-Beuve. He writes for approximately six hours daily, a process he describes as "slow and difficult."

* * *

GUPTARA, Prabhu S(iddhartha) 1949-

PERSONAL: Born February 9, 1949; son of Murli Manohar (a professor) and Chinnamma (a nurse; maiden name, Nainan) Guptara; married Philippa Mary Rann (a secretary), January 15, 1976. *Education:* University of Delhi, B.A. (honors), 1968, M.A., 1970; doctoral study at University of Stirling, 1976—. *Politics:* "Interested, but belong to no party." *Religion:* "Hindu follower of Jesus Christ." *Home address:* c/o North-Eastern Hill University, Shillong 793 003, India. *Agent:* Arts Centre Group, 21 Short St., London SE1 8LJ, England. *Office:* Department of English, University of Stirling, Stirling FK9 4LA, England.

CAREER: Associated with University of Delhi, St. Stephen's College, Delhi, India, 1970-73, and North-Eastern Hill University, Shillong, India, 1973-76. Has given poetry readings and lectures at universities in Edinburgh, Glasgow, Paris, and Stirling; participant in seminars and conferences. Member of national board of directors and executive committee of National Council of the Young Men's Christian Associations of India, 1973-76.

MEMBER: Indian P.E.N., Asiatic Society (Calcutta), Royal Commonwealth Society, Arts Centre Group, Association for Commonwealth Literature and Language Studies, Conference on Christianity and Literature. *Awards, honors:* Received scholarship, 1974, for Farel House (Switzerland); Oxford University bursary, 1977.

WRITINGS: Beginnings (poems), Writers Workshop (Calcutta, India), 1975; (editor) *Selected Poems of Leela Dharmaraj,* Writers Workshop (Calcutta, India), 1977. Editor of *An Anthology of Contemporary Indian Religious Poetry in English.* Contributor of poems, articles, and reviews to language and literature journals, including *World Literature Today.*

WORK IN PROGRESS: India and France: The Literary Traffic; The Impact of India on American Literature; research on the impact of India on the literature of the old British colonies (Canada, Australia, New Zealand); studies in literature and religion.

SIDELIGHTS: Guptara writes: "I started (mainly journalistic) writing in 1966, an interest which continues; my critical work (commencing in 1971) concentrates on revaluation; in my poetry, which I started writing in 1972, I seek to share a feeling, a doubt, a thought, a joke, a sensation, or an affirmation in as succinct as possible a pattern and combination of word-sound and word-content, rhythm, allusion, and image.

"I consider my life-work to be the twin task of helping to have India's very substantial contribution to world culture and civilization more justly appreciated than it has been; and grafting into our now stratified, fossilized, and somnolent culture that which will produce life in place of all that has produced death (disease, discrimination, and deprivation)."

*   *   *

GUTEK, Gerald L(ee)   1935-

PERSONAL: Born July 10, 1935, in Streator, Ill.; son of Albert T. and Irene (Novotney) Gutek; married Patricia Ann Egan, June 12, 1965; children: Jennifer Ann, Laura Lee. *Education:* University of Illinois, B.A., 1957, M.A., 1959, Ph.D., 1964. *Religion:* Roman Catholic. *Residence:* LaGrange, Ill. *Office:* Department of Foundations of Education, Loyola University, 820 North Michigan Ave., Chicago, Ill. 60611.

CAREER: Loyola University, Chicago, Ill., instructor, 1963-65, assistant professor, 1965-68, associate professor, 1968-72, professor of education and history, 1972—, chairman of department of foundations of education, 1969—. Visiting professor at Loyola University (Los Angeles, Calif.), summer, 1965, University of Illinois, summer, 1966, and Michigan State University, summer, 1969; visiting professor at Loyola University in Rome, Italy, 1974-75.

MEMBER: American Educational Studies Association, American Studies Association, Comparative Education Society, History of Education Society, National Council for the Social Studies, Organization of American Historians, Philosophy of Education Society, Society for Professors of Education, Midwest Comparative Education Society, Midwest History of Education Society (president, 1970-71),

Midwest Philosophy of Education Society, Illinois Council for the Social Studies, Phi Delta Kappa. *Awards, honors:* American Philosophical Society grant, 1968; National Endowment for the Humanities grant, 1970.

WRITINGS: Pestalozzi and Education, Random House, 1968; *The Educational Theory of George S. Counts,* Ohio State University Press, 1970; *An Historical Introduction to American Education,* Crowell, 1970; *A History of the Western Educational Experience,* Random House, 1972; *Philosophical Alternatives in Education,* C. E. Merrill, 1974; (contributor) Elmer L. Towns, editor, *A History of Religious Educators,* Baker Book, 1975; *Joseph Neef: The Americanization of Pestalozzianism,* University of Alabama Press, 1978; (contributor) Allan C. Ornstein, editor, *An Introduction to the Foundations of Education,* Rand McNally, 1978. Contributor of about twenty articles and reviews to academic journals.

WORK IN PROGRESS: An Educational History of the New Harmony Committee: Robert Owen and William Maclure.

SIDELIGHTS: Gutek has visited schools and colleges in India and in the Soviet Union.

*   *   *

GUTTENBERG, Virginia   1914-
(Virginia Graham)

PERSONAL: Born July 4, 1914, in Chicago, Ill.; daughter of David Stanley (a businessman) and Bessie Jane (Feiges) Komiss; married Harry William Guttenberg (a theatrical costumer and businessman), May 2, 1935; children: Lynn Karen (Mrs. Seymour M. Boffrer). *Education:* University of Chicago, B.A., 1931; Northwestern University, M.A. *Home:* 1025 Fifth Ave., New York, N.Y. 10028. *Agent:* Julian Bach Literary Agency, Inc., 3 East 48th St., New York, N.Y. 10017.

CAREER: Television commentator, charity organizer, and author. Worked briefly as photographer's model; fashion reporter for WBBM-Radio, Chicago, Ill., 1934; scriptwriter for WMCA-Radio, New York City, 1936-38; commentator for television variety programs, "Zeke Manners Show," 1950-51, and "Food for Thought," Channel 5, New York City, 1951-57; co-host of radio program, "Weekday," National Broadcasting Co., 1956; goodwill ambassador for Clairol Co., 1961; host of television programs, "Girl Talk," 1961-70, and "The Virginia Graham Show," RKO, 1970-74. Co-founder of Cerebral Palsy Foundation, 1947; active member of numerous charity and health organizations, including the American Cancer Society, March of Dimes, and the Kidney Foundation; has appeared on many fund-raising telethons. *Wartime service:* American Red Cross, volunteer during World War II; became master sergeant in the motor corps. *Awards, honors:* Named International Woman of the Year, 1959; named Woman of the Year by the American Cancer Society, 1961; numerous citations for civic and charitable activities.

WRITINGS—Under name Virginia Graham: (With Jean Black) *There Goes What's Her Name,* Prentice-Hall, 1965; *Don't Blame the Mirror,* Meredith, 1967; *The Tonite or Never Cook Book,* Avon, 1968; (with Ionescu-Tulcea) *A Book of Casino Gambling,* Van Nostrand, 1976; *If I Made It, So Can You,* Bantam, 1978. Contributor of articles to popular magazines, including *Good Housekeeping* and *TV Guide.*

WORK IN PROGRESS: Battered Parents; Big Business

Makes Whores and Widows; for television, "The Insatiable Appetite."

SIDELIGHTS: Virginia Guttenberg told *CA:* "I talk my writings into a tape because my mental agility is faster than my muscular dexterity. I believe in simplistic descriptions largely colored with humor and basic truths about my life. I am a 'first person' writer and am a firm believer in only telling what I want to tell—my private life will always be my own."

H

HAAS, Ernst B(ernard) 1924-

PERSONAL: Born March 31, 1924, in Frankfurt, Germany; came to the United States in 1938, naturalized citizen, 1943; son of Fritz (a zoologist) and Helene (Ganz) Haas; married Hildegarde Vogel (a painter), May 1, 1945; children: Peter. *Education:* Attended University of Chicago, 1942-43; Columbia University, B.S., 1948, M.A., 1950, Ph.D., 1952. *Office:* Department of Political Science, University of California, Berkeley, Calif. 94720.

CAREER: University of California, Berkeley, instructor, 1951-53, assistant professor, 1953-58, associate professor, 1958-62, professor of political science, 1962—, Robson Research Professor of Government, 1974—, director of Institute of International Studies, 1969-73. Member of Commission to Study the Organization of Peace, 1960-77; member of Social Science Research Council committee on international organization, 1963-68; member of Murphy Commission Task Force on International Institutions, 1975; consultant to U.S. Department of State and Arms Control and Disarmament Agency. *Military service:* U.S. Army, Military Intelligence Service, 1943-46. *Member:* American Academy of Arts and Sciences (fellow). *Awards, honors:* Social Science Research Council grants, 1955-56, 1960-61; Rockefeller Foundation grants, 1955-63, 1974-78; Guggenheim fellow, 1973-74.

WRITINGS: (With A. S. Whiting) *Dynamics of International Relations,* McGraw, 1956; *International Conciliation* (monograph), Carnegie Endowment for International Peace, 1957; *The Uniting of Europe,* Stanford University Press, 1958; *Consensus Formation in the Council of Europe* (monograph), University of California Press, 1960; *Beyond the Nation-State: Functionalism and International Organization,* Stanford University Press, 1964; (with Philippe C. Schmitter) *Mexico and Latin-American Economic Integration* (monograph), Institute of International Studies, University of California, Berkeley, 1964; (with Schmitter) *The Politics of Economics in Latin-American Regionalism: The Latin-American Free Trade Association After Four Years of Operation* (monograph), Social Science Foundation, University of Denver, 1965; *Collective Security and the Future International System* (monograph), Social Science Foundation, University of Denver, 1968; *Tangle of Hopes: American Commitments and World Order,* Prentice-Hall, 1969.

Human Rights and International Action: The Case of Free-dom of Association, Stanford University Press, 1970; (with R. L. Butterworth and J. S. Nye) *Conflict Management by International Organizations* (monograph), General Learning Press, 1972; *The Obsolescence of Regional Integration Theory* (monograph), Institute of International Studies, University of California, Berkeley, 1975; (editor with J. G. Ruggie) *International Responses to Technology,* International Organization, 1975; (with M. P. Williams and Don Babai) *Scientists and World Order: The Uses of Knowledge in International Organizations,* University of California Press, 1977.

Contributor: Norman Padelford, editor, *Contemporary International Relations Readings,* 3rd series, Harvard University Press, 1954; C. O. Lerche and M. E. Lerche, editors, *Readings in International Politics,* Oxford University Press, 1958; Stanley Hoffmann, editor, *Readings in the Theory of International Relations,* Prentice-Hall, 1959; James Rosenau, editor, *International Politics and Foreign Policy,* Free Press, 1961; Morton Kaplan, editor, *The Revolution in World Politics,* Wiley, 1962; Stichting Grotius Seminarium, editor, *Limits and Problems of European Integration,* Nijhoff, 1963; Stephen R. Graubard, editor, *A New Europe?,* Houghton, 1964; David A. Kay, editor, *The United Nations Political System,* Wiley, 1967; Paul Deabury and Aaron Wildavsky, editors, *U.S. Foreign Policy: Perspectives and Proposals for the 1970's,* McGraw, 1969.

Naomi Rosenbaum, editor, *Readings on the International Political System,* Prentice-Hall, 1970; Louis B. Sohn, editor, *The United Nations: The Next Twenty-Five Years,* Oceana, 1970; R. S. Wood, editor, *The Process of International Organization,* Random House, 1971; Leon Lindberg and Stuart Scheingold, editors, *Regional Integration: Theory and Research,* Harvard University Press, 1971; Kenneth Twitchett, editor, *The Evolving United Nations,* Europa, 1971; Gary C. Byrne and K. S. Pederson, editors, *Politics in Western European Democracies,* Wiley, 1971; R. Romani, editor, *The International Political System,* Wiley, 1972; Richard Rosecrance, editor, *The Future of the International Strategic System,* Chandler, 1972; Geoffrey L. Goodwin and Andrew Linklater, editors, *New Dimensions of World Politics,* Croom Helm, 1975.

Contributor to *Encyclopaedia Britannica, Encyclopedia Americana,* and *International Encyclopedia of the Social Sciences.* Contributor of more than thirty articles to political science journals. Member of board of editors of *International Organization* (chairman of board, 1977-79).

WORK IN PROGRESS: Studying the origin and likely evolution of international arrangements for managing science and technology collaboratively.

BIOGRAPHICAL/CRITICAL SOURCES: Henry Mason, *Modern Constitutionalism and Democracy,* Mohr, 1966; J. E. Dougherty and R. L. Pfaltzgraff, *Contending Theories of International Relations,* Lippincott, 1971; J. K. De Vree, *Political Integration,* Mouton, 1972.

* * *

HAGAN, Patricia
See HOWELL, Patricia Hagan

* * *

HAGELSTANGE, Rudolf 1912-

PERSONAL: Born January 14, 1912, in Nordhausen, Harz, Germany; son of Wilhelm (a merchant) and Helene (Struchmann) Hagelstange; married Karola Dittel, 1939; children: five. *Education:* Studied German philology in Berlin, 1931-33. *Religion:* Roman Catholic. *Home:* 6122 Erbach, Am Schlehdorn, West Germany.

CAREER: Held various jobs, 1936-39; worked as feuilleton editor of *Nordhaeuser Zeitung,* 1939; war correspondent, 1940-45; free-lance writer, 1945—. *Military service:* German army, serving in France and Germany, 1940-45; held prisoner-of-war by Americans, 1945. *Member:* Bavarian Academy of Fine Arts, Darmstadt Academy for Language and Poetry (vice-president, 1966), German P.E.N. Center (vice-president, 1968-70). *Awards, honors:* Suedverlag Prize for Lyric Poetry, 1950; Berlin Critics' Prize, 1952; award from Schiller Foundation, 1955; Villa Massimo Prize, 1957; Julius Campe Prize, 1958; Grosses Bundesverdienstkreuz, 1959; Olympic Diploma, 1964.

WRITINGS—In English: *Ballade vom Verschuetteten Leben* (poetry), Insel, 1952, translation by Herman Salinger published as *Ballad of the Buried Life,* University of North Carolina Press, 1952; *Griechenland,* Rembrandt-Verlag, 1957, published as *Greece,* Rembrandt-Verlag, 1957.

In German; poetry: *Es Spannt sich der Bogen* (title means "The Bow Tightens Itself"), Rupert Verlag, 1943; *Venezianisches credo* (title means "The Venetian Creed"), Editiones Officianae Bodoni, 1945; *Strom der Zeit* (title means "Stream of Time"), Insel, 1948; *Mein Blumen-ABC* (title means "My Flower ABC"), illustrated by Jochen Specht, EOS Verlag, 1949.

Meersburger Elegie (title means "Meersburg Elegy"), Tschudy Verlag, 1950; *Die Elemente: Gedichte zu den Mosaiken von Frans Masereel* (title means "The Elements: Poems on the Mosaics of Frans Masereel"), Officina Bodoni (Verona), 1950; *Zwischen Stern und Staub* (title means "Between Star and Dust"), Insel, 1953; *Die Beichte des Don Juan* (title means "Don Juan's Confession"), illustrated by Gunter Boehmer, Oltner Buecherfreunde, 1954.

Die schwindende Spur (title means "The Disappearing Trail"), Josef Keller, 1961; *Lied der Jahre: Gesammelte Gedichte 1931-1961* (title means "Song of the Years: Collected Poems 1931-1961"), Insel, 1961; *Corazon: Gedichte aus Spanien* (title means "Corazon: Poems From Spain"), Hoffmann & Campe, 1963; *Der Krak in Prague: Ein fruhlingsmaerchen* (title means "The Kraken in Prague: A Springtime Fable"), Hoffmann & Campe, 1969; *Gast der Elemente: Zyklen und Nachdichtungen 1944-1972* (title

means "Guest of the Elements: Poem Cycles and Translations 1944-1972"), Kiepenheuer & Witsch, 1972.

Fiction: *Ich bin die Mutter Cornelias* (title means "I Am Cornelias's Mother"), Haacke, 1939; *Balthasar, eine Erzaehlung* (title means "Balthasar: A Story"), woodcuts by Frans Masereel, Insel, 1951; *Wo bleibst du, Trost: eine Weihnachtserzaehlung* (title means "Where Are You, Consolation: A Christmas Story"), Hegner, 1958; *Die Nacht Mariens: Ein Weihnachtsbuch* (title means "Mary's Night: A Christmas Book"), illustrated by Carlos Duss, Verlag der Arche, 1959, published as *Stern in der Christnacht* (title means "Star on Christmas Eve"), Verlag der Arche, 1965.

Spielball der Goetter: Aufzeichnungen eines trojanischen Prinzen (novel; title means "Plaything of the Gods: Notes of a Trojan Prince"), Hoffman & Campe, 1960; *Viel Vergnuegen* (title means "Many Pleasures"), illustrated by Helmut Bibow, Fackeltraeger Verlag, 1960; *Altherrensommer* (novel; title means "Indian Summer"), Hoffmann & Campe, 1969; *Es war im Wal zu Askalon: Dreikoenigslegende* (title means "It Was in the Whale at Askalon: Epiphany Legends"), linocuts by Eduard Pruessen, Piper, 1971; *Venus im Mars: Liebesgeschichten* (title means "Venus in Mars: Love Stories"), Kiepenheuer & Witsch, 1972; *Der General und das Kind* (novel; title means "The General and the Child"), Kiepenheuer & Witsch, 1974; *Der grosse Filou* (title means "The Great Trickster"), List, 1976.

Other works: *Es steht in unserer Macht: Gedachtes und Erlebtes* (essays; title means "It Rests in Our Power: Things Thought and Experienced"), Piper, 1953; *Die Nacht: Die 37 Holzschnitte schuf Frans Masereel* (title means "The Night: The 37 Wood Engravings by Frans Masereel"), Europa Verlag, 1955; (editor and translator) Angelo Poliziano, *Die Tragoedie des Orpheus* (title means "The Tragedy of Orpheus"), [Germany], 1956; *Verona,* photographs by Gerhard Kerff, Knorr & Hirth, 1957; *How Do You Like America?: Impressionen eines Zaungastes* (title means "How Do You Like America?: Impressions of an Outsider"), Piper, 1957; (editor) *Ein Licht scheint in die Finsternis: Ein Weihnachtsbuch* (title means "A Light in the Darkness: A Christmas Book"), illustrated by Albrecht Appelhaus, Rufer, 1958; *Das Lied der Muschel* (Aegean Islands travel and description; title means "The Song of the Mussel"), Piper, 1958; *Offen gesagt: Aufsaetze und Reden* (title means "Frankly Speaking: Essays and Lectures"), Ullstein Taschenbuecher Verlag, 1958; (translator) Giovanni Boccaccio, *Die Nymphe von Fiesole* (title means "The Nymph of Fiesole"), Trojanus-Presse, 1958.

Huldigung: Droste, Eichendorff, Schuller (title means "Homage to Annette von Droste-Huelshoff, Joseph Freiherr von Eichendorff, Johann Christoph Friedrich von Schuller"), Insel, 1960; *Roemische Brunnen* (title means "Roman Fountains"), Knorr & Hirth, 1960; *Roemisches Olympia: Kaleidoskop eines Weltfestes* (title means "Rome Olympics: Kaleidoscope of a World Festival"), illustrated by Helmut Bibow, Piper, 1961; (editor with Jens Carstensen) *Phantastische Abenteuererzaehlungen: Eine Sammlung der spannendsten Erzaehlungen aus aller Welt* (title means "Fantastic Adventure Stories: A Collection of the Most Thrilling Stories in the World"), R. Bardtenschlager, 1961; (translator) Pablo Neruda, *Die Hoehen von Macchu Picchu* (title means "The Heights of Macchu Picchu"), Hoffmann & Campe, 1961; *Reise nach Katmandu* (title means "Journey to Katmandu"), illustrated by Helmut Bibow, Vereinigung Oltner Buecherfreunde, 1962; *Die Puppen in der Puppe: Eine Russlandreise* (title means "The Dolls

Inside the Doll: A Russian Journey''), Hoffmann & Campe, 1963.

(Editor) Kurt Craemer, *Mein Panoptikum* (title means "My Waxworks''), Hoffmann & Campe, 1965; (translator) *Fabeln des Aesop* (title means "The Fables of Aesop''), Otto Maien Verlag, 1965; *Zeit fuer ein Laecheln: Heitere Prosa* (title means "Time for a Smile: Good-Humored Prose''), Hoffmann & Campe, 1966; *Der schielende Loewe oder How Do You Like America?* (title means "The Squinting Lion; or, How Do You Like America?''), Hoffmann & Campe, 1967; *Aegaeischer Sommer* (title means "Aegean Summer''), Hoffmann & Campe, 1968; *Ein beispielhaftes Lebenswerk: Laudatio auf Giovanni Mardersteig* (title means "An Exemplary Life-Work: Eulogy on Giovanni Mardersteig''), Gutenberg-Gesellschaft, 1968; (compiler with Monika Achtelik) *Das grosse Weihnachtsbuch fuer die Familie* (title means "The Big Christmas Book for the Family''), Moderne Verlags, 1969.

Alleingang: 6 Schicksale (title means "Solitary Path: Six Destinies''), Hoffmann & Campe, 1970; *Fuenf Ringe: Vom Oelzweig zur Goldmedaille* (title means "Five Rings: From the Olive Branch to the Gold Medal''), Bruckmann, 1972; *Die Weihnachtsgeschichte* (title means "The Christmas Story''; retold for children), Fabbri & Praeger, 1974; *Reisewetter* (title means "Traveling Weather''), List, 1975.

SIDELIGHTS: Hagelstange traveled in Italy and the Balkans from 1933 to 1936 and subsequently began his career as a journalist. He wrote his first poems during World War II, when he was serving in the German army. He first made his mark with the sonnet sequence "The Venetian Creed,'' which was secretly circulated among members of the *Wehrmacht* towards the end of the war. These rigorously formal sonnets present a powerful indictment of totalitarianism and war and are an eloquent plea for human freedom and dignity.

Hagelstange's reputation as one of the most important poets of his generation was confirmed with the publication of *Ballad of the Buried Life*. This is a long narrative poem based on an Associated Press report of June 17, 1951, which later turned out to be a hoax (fortunately, this didn't diminish the poem). According to the Associated Press story, Polish workmen clearing away the remains of a huge food storage bunker near Gdingen had discovered two German soldiers—the surviving members of a party of six trapped in the storehouse by an explosion six years earlier, just before the fall of Germany. Hagelstange turned this story into what August Closs called "one of the most important literary achievements in present-day German lyrical poetry.'' The six soldiers are subtly differentiated in the poem, Closs said: "There is the dreamer Benjamin who later commits suicide, then the sergeant with the symbolic name Wenig—a penitent sinner who shoots himself, the third is the Schreiber—a clerk who perishes 'sans grace,' and finally Christof who dies as a steadfast Christian; the two survivors are a carpenter and The Other.'' The Other, who has remained nameless, but has shared and survived the death-in-life of the soldiers is, we are told at last, the reader himself. This somber poem ends with the Christian promise "that they finally witness out of a thousand dark silences a single shining child.'' Charles W. Hoffmann has shown that the poem is more than a grim tale about six soldiers—more even than a portrait of postwar Germany; it is "actually an expression of the tensions and emotions and paradoxes of man's being and specifically of modern man's being.'' According to Patrick Bridgwater, all of Hagelstange's poetry, "informed by a love of freedom and a sense of the values of Western civilization, has a strong religious basis; but he is no less a master of the

modern idiom.'' Another critic has described him as "the representative poet of a generation which views the war not merely as a tragedy but as a moral challenge.''

Hagelstange has also written a number of travel books, including two recording his impressions of the United States, and several volumes of essays. He has translated Boccaccio, Pablo Neruda, and Aesop, among others, and compiled some popular anthologies. Hagelstange's novel *Plaything of the Gods* is an invented biography of Paris, centering on his life during the siege of Troy. The book was generally admired for its originality and charm, and for some "social criticism pointedly applicable to the present.'' *Altherrensommer*, a later novel, is an account of the friendship that grows up between a middle-aged journalist and an aging writer during an ocean voyage from Europe to the Far East. A reviewer in the *Times Literary Supplement* found it hardly a novel at all, but "rather an elegant dovetailing of duologue and travelogue'' with "amusing and believably grotesque characters'' and an unexpectedly powerful conclusion.

AVOCATIONAL INTERESTS: Travel, canoeing, music.

BIOGRAPHICAL/CRITICAL SOURCES: Times Literary Supplement, August 19, 1949, October 16, 1969, June 4, 1970; *Catholic World*, April 1956; August Closs, *Medusa's Mirror*, Cresset Press, 1957; *Germanic Review 2*, 1958; August Closs, editor, *Twentieth Century German Literature*, Cresset Press, 1969.*

*   *   *

HALDEMAN, H(arry) R(obbins)   1926-

PERSONAL: Born October 27, 1926, in Los Angeles, Calif.; son of Harry F. and Katherine (Robbins) Haldeman; married Jo Horton (in real estate), February 19, 1949; children: Susan Ward, Harry Horton, Peter Robbins, Ann Kurtz. *Education:* Attended University of Redlands, 1944-45, University of Southern California, 1945-46; University of California, Los Angeles, B.S., 1948. *Politics:* Republican. *Religion:* Christian Scientist. *Residence:* Newport Beach, Calif. *Agent:* Ronald Konecky, Harder, Barovich, Konechy, and Braun, 1 Dag Hammerskjold Plaza, New York, N.Y. 10017.

CAREER: J. Walter Thompson Co., New York, N.Y., account executive, 1949-59, vice-president and manager of Los Angeles office, 1960-68; assistant to U.S. president and chief of White House staff, 1969-73; writer, 1978—. Chief of staff of Richard Nixon presidential campaign, 1968. Member of University of California board of regents, 1965-67, 1968-69; California Institute of Arts, trustee, 1966-68, chairman of board, 1968; chairman of board of trustees, Nixon Foundation, 1969—; member of White House Fellows, 1969-73; member of executive committee and trustee, Kennedy Center for Performing Arts, 1970—. *Military service:* U.S. Naval Reserve, 1944-46. *Member:* Beta Theta Pi, Pi Delta Epsilon.

WRITINGS: (With Joseph DiMona) *The Ends of Power*, Time-Life, 1978.

WORK IN PROGRESS: More memoirs.

SIDELIGHTS: Haldeman's position as a top government aide afforded him the rare opportunity to work with the president on a daily basis. Commenting on his association with Richard Nixon, he noted: "[Nixon] didn't see me as a person or even, I believe, as a human being. I was a machine. A robot. Shortly after it came out, I saw the movie 'Star Wars.' There is a robot, a metal machine clanking along doing what it's told by a computer-like mind. From Nixon's standpoint, that's what I was.''

Upon request of the president, Haldeman and Ehrlichman submitted their resignations after they became implicated in the "supposed hanky-panky concerning cash paid to Watergate defendants. . . ." Later, Haldeman recalled an ironic exchange with Nixon. "Let me ask you this, to be quite candid," Haldeman quoted Nixon as saying. "Is there any way you can use *cash*?" According to Haldeman, both he and Ehrlichman declined the monetary offer.

Once a key member of an administration that could boast among its accomplishments the pursuit of peace in the Middle East, the withdrawal of U.S. troops from Vietnam, and the re-establishment of communications with China, Haldeman, upon resigning, found himself abandoned by his associates in the capital and a target of the Senate investigation. He was ultimately found guilty of perjury in connection with the Watergate scandal and served a brief sentence at California's Lompoc prison farm. Later Haldeman reflected: "My part in this program was wrong. I am deeply sorry for every act of mine that furthered this effort."

While in prison, Haldeman had an opportunity to watch David Frost's televised interviews with Nixon. According to *Time*, "Haldeman had fumed as he watched his former chief imply . . . that he might have saved his presidency if he had just had the heart to fire earlier his two closest aides, Haldeman and domestic adviser John Ehrlichman. Haldeman vowed then and there to turn his pro-Nixon memoirs into a stinging expose of 'the truth' about Watergate."

Haldeman's "stinging expose," *The Ends of Power*, is regarded by many as something less than the "truth" Haldeman had "vowed" to tell. *Time* deemed it "badly flawed, frustratingly vague and curiously defensive. Many key sections were promptly denied; others are clearly erroneous." And former associate Ehrlichman wrote of the book's "material, factual errors which impeach its substance."

However, despite some harsh criticism, Ehrlichman nurtures some hope for Haldeman and his literary future. "Bob Haldeman was in a unique position to write a truly valuable book about Richard Nixon. I hope that *The Ends of Power* is not his last word."

BIOGRAPHICAL/CRITICAL SOURCES: H. R. Haldeman and Joseph DiMona, *The Ends of Power*, Time-Life, 1978; *New York Times*, February 20, 1978; *Newsweek*, February 27, 1978, March 6, 1978; *Time*, February 27, 1978, March 6, 1978.

* * *

HALLIBURTON, Rudia, Jr. 1929-

PERSONAL: Born December 31, 1929, in McAlester, Okla.; son of Rudia H. and Oral (Cable) Halliburton; married Helen LaVonne McCollum (a teacher of English), February 14, 1949; children: Janet Diane, Judith Elaine Halliburton Colburn. *Education:* Phillips University, B.S., 1957; Oklahoma State University, M.A., 1959; further graduate study at University of Oklahoma, 1960. *Politics:* Democrat. *Religion:* Christian Church (Disciples of Christ). *Home:* 408 Jamestown, Tahlequah, Okla. 74464. *Office:* Department of History, Northeastern Oklahoma State University, Tahlequah, Okla. 74464.

CAREER: High school history teacher in Garnett, Kan., 1957-58; Cameron State College, Lawton, Okla., instructor in history, 1959-61, chairman of social sciences division, 1960-61; Northeastern Oklahoma State University, Tahlequah, assistant professor, 1962-65, associate professor of history, 1965—, chairman of department, 1971—. Visiting

scholar at Smithsonian Institution, 1973; guest lecturer at University of Winnipeg, 1975. Member of Oklahoma Consortium on Research Development, 1967.

MEMBER: American Association of University Professors (local vice-president, 1967), Great Plains Historical Association (member of board of governors and advisory council, 1961), Southern Historical Association, Oklahoma Academy of Science, Oklahoma College History Professors Association (president, 1960), Oklahoma Historical Society, Oklahoma Education Association (local president, 1961-62), Kansas State Teachers Association, Eastern Oklahoma Education Association, Phi Alpha Theta, Pi Gamma Mu. *Awards, honors:* National Science Foundation fellow in history, summer, 1960; Lilly Endowment grant, 1975.

WRITINGS: Seminary Hall of Northeastern State College, Northeastern State College Press, 1973; *The Tulsa Race War of 1921*, Research Associates, 1975; *Red Over Black: Black Slavery in the Cherokee Nation*, Greenwood Press, 1977; *America's First Anti-Darwin Law*, Greenwood Press, 1977. Author of catalogs and brochures. Contributor to *Encyclopedia of Southern History*. Contributor of about fifty articles and reviews to professional journals and newspapers. Book review editor of *Junior College Journal*, 1960; associate editor of *Proceedings* of the Oklahoma Academy of Science, 1963; founding editor of *Northeastern State College Social Science Newsletter*, 1971.

WORK IN PROGRESS: Black Slavery Among the American Indians; The Cherokee National Female Seminary; Black Slavery in the Choctaw Nation.

* * *

HALSEY, Margaret (Frances) 1910-

PERSONAL: Born February 13, 1910, in Yonkers, N.Y.; daughter of Reinhold Henry Francis (an architect) and Annie Shelton (a teacher; maiden name, Braithwaite) Halsey; married Henry V. Simon (a professor of English), 1935 (divorced, 1944); married Milton R. Stern (a professor of education), 1944 (divorced, 1970); children: (second marriage) Deborah Halsey. *Education:* Skidmore College, B.S., 1930; Columbia University, M.A., 1936. *Politics:* Democrat. *Religion:* Unitarian-Universalist. *Home:* 33 Greencroft Gardens, London NW6 3LN, England. *Agent:* Roberta Pryor, International Creative Management, 40 West 57th St., New York, N.Y. 10019.

CAREER: Secretary, 1930-35; writer, 1938—. *Awards, honors: With Malice Toward Some* was named most original book of the year by American Booksellers Association, 1939; award from Council Against Intolerance, 1946, for *Color Blind*.

WRITINGS: With Malice Toward Some (Book-of-the-Month Club selection), Simon & Schuster, 1938; *Some of My Best Friends Are Soldiers*, Simon & Schuster, 1944; *Color Blind*, Simon & Schuster, 1946; *The Folks at Home*, Simon & Schuster, 1952; *This Demi-Paradise: A Westchester Diary*, Simon & Schuster, 1960; *The Pseudo-Ethic: A Speculation on American Politics and Morality*, Simon & Schuster, 1963 (published in England as *The Corrupted Giant*, Macmillan, 1963); *No Laughing Matter: The Autobiography of a WASP*, Lippincott, 1977. Contributor to magazines, including *New Yorker* and *New Republic*.

WORK IN PROGRESS: "A few ideas for another book are swirling around in my head, but I always just have to sit and wait until the concept for a new book occurs to me."

SIDELIGHTS: Margaret Halsey writes: "My first book

was a funny book about the English, which came out just before World War II and was a runaway best-seller. It is still quoted by people writing about the British.

"But after the war, life in America got to be full of new and dismaying problems—McCarthyism and the anti-Communist hysteria, conformity in the 1950's, relentlessly expanding consumerism, the Vietnam war, Watergate, et cetera. I have always reacted with intensity to the life of my time, and in response to the foregoing phenomena, I wrote several serious books on subjects like racism or the neglect of women and children by a business society.

"These books have been said by critics to have been rather ahead of their time in pinpointing social problems and the moral implications they carried with them. In 1958, in fact, I had an article in *New Republic* which was revived and much-quoted at the time of Watergate. I had said, more than a decade before it happened, that if we ever had a Nixon Administration, that administration would be staffed by other Nixons and would be *Walpurgisnacht* on the Potomac.

"Social and political institutions in a time of great flux have been my deep concern, particularly in their ethical aspects, but I believe that people can best be influenced if here and there, amidst all the earnestness, is a mocking and really on-target phrase that makes them chuckle. Were I to sum up my writing in a single sentence, perhaps I could say that I am at once a humorist and a moral positivist.

"However, I am one who just naturally enjoys life, and my serious books were interrupted, just for the fun of it, by an amusing one about life in the suburbs. My humor remains old-fashioned, somewhat Mark Twainish humor, rather than 'sick' or 'black' comedy."

AVOCATIONAL INTERESTS: Reading, exploring the antiquities and ancient monuments of London.

BIOGRAPHICAL/CRITICAL SOURCES: New York Times, October 26, 1977; *New York Times Book Review,* November 13, 1977.

* * *

HAMILTON, Clive
See LEWIS, C(live) S(taples)

* * *

HAMMACK, James W., Jr. 1937-

PERSONAL: Born April 5, 1937, in Scooba, Miss.; son of James W. and Marie Katherine (Wofford) Hammack; married Charlotte Lynn Mills, August, 1963; children: Amanda Jane, James W. III. *Education:* Attended Southwestern at Memphis, 1955-57, and University of Arkansas, 1956-58; Memphis State University, B.S., 1961, M.A., 1962; University of Kentucky, Ph.D., 1974. *Religion:* Presbyterian. *Office:* Department of History, Murray State University, Murray, Ky. 42071.

CAREER: Junior Military Academy, Chicago, Ill., instructor in history, spring, 1962; Louisiana Tech University, Ruston, instructor in history, 1962-63; Murray State University, Murray, Ky., associate professor of history, 1968—. Director of Forrest C. Pogue Oral History Institute. *Member:* Oral History Association, Coal Miners Research Project Consortium (president, 1977-78), Southern Historical Association, Kentucky Historical Society, Phi Alpha Theta.

WRITINGS: Kentucky and the Second American Revolution: The War of 1812, University Press of Kentucky, 1976.

WORK IN PROGRESS: Kentucky's Jackson Purchase: A

Regional Study; editing *The Public Papers of Earle C. Clements;* continuing research on the War of 1812.

* * *

HAMMER, David Harry 1893(?)-1978

OBITUARY NOTICE: Born c. 1893 in England; died October 13, 1978, in Washington, D.C. Stock broker, navy captain, Veterans Administration official, and author of a book, *Lion Six,* which examined the development of a military base on Guam, and several articles on the subject of yachting. Obituaries and other sources: *Washington Post,* October 31, 1978.

* * *

HAMMETT, (Samuel) Dashiell 1894-1961

PERSONAL: Born May 27, 1894, in St. Mary's County, Md.; son of Richard Thomas (a farmer and politician) and Annie (Bond) Hammett; married Josephine Dolan, July 6, 1921 (separated, 1927); children: Mary Jane, Josephine. *Education:* Attended Baltimore Polytechnic Institute. *Politics:* Marxist. *Residence:* Katonah, N.Y.; and New York, N.Y.

CAREER: Writer, 1921-61. Worked as freight clerk, stevedore, timekeeper, yardman, and railroad worker; operative with Pinkerton National Detective Agency, c.1914-18, 1919-21; advertising copywriter, Albert S. Samuels Jewelers, San Francisco, Calif., 1922-27; worked sporadically as screenwriter for various motion picture studios from 1930 until after World War II; active in various left-wing organizations, beginning 1937; member of Civil Rights Congress, New York state president, 1946, national vice-chairman, 1948, New York state chairman, 1951; Jefferson School of Social Sciences, faculty member, 1946-47, 1949-56, member of board of trustees, 1948. *Military service:* U.S. Army Ambulance Corps, 1918-19, became sergeant; U.S. Army Signal Corps, 1942-45, became sergeant.

WRITINGS: Red Harvest (novel), Knopf, 1929, reprinted, Vintage Books, 1972; *The Dain Curse* (novel), Knopf, 1929, reprinted, Vintage Books, 1972; *The Maltese Falcon* (novel), Knopf, 1930, reprinted, Vintage Books, 1972; *The Glass Key* (novel), Knopf, 1931, reprinted, Vintage Books, 1972; (editor) *Creeps by Night* (stories), John Day, 1931 (published in England as *Modern Tales of Horror,* Gollancz, 1932; selections published in England as *The Red Brain and Other Thrillers,* Belmont, 1961, and as *Breakdown and Other Thrillers,* New English Library, 1968); *The Thin Man* (novel), Knopf, 1934, reprinted, Vintage Books, 1972; *Secret Agent X-9* (comic strip), McKay, 1934, reprinted, Nostalgia Press, 1976; *Dashiell Hammett Omnibus: "Red Harvest," "The Dain Curse," "The Maltese Falcon,"* Knopf, 1935.

The Complete Dashiell Hammett (contains *The Thin Man, The Glass Key, The Maltese Falcon,* and *Red Harvest*), Knopf, 1942; *$106,000 Blood Money* (stories), Spivak, 1943, published as *Blood Money,* Dell, 1944, and as *The Big Knockover,* Jonathan Press, 1948; *The Battle of the Aleutians* (history), U.S. Army, 1944; *The Adventures of Sam Spade* (stories), Spivak, 1944, published as *They Can Only Hang You Once,* Spivak, 1949; *The Continental Op* (stories), Spivak, 1945; *A Man Called Spade* (stories), Dell, 1945; *The Return of the Continental Op* (stories), Spivak, 1945; *Hammett Homicides* (stories), Spivak, 1946; *Dead Yellow Women* (stories), Spivak, 1947; *Nightmare Town* (stories), Spivak, 1948; *Creeping Siamese* (stories), Spivak, 1950; *Woman in the Dark* (stories), Spivak, 1951.

A Man Named Thin (stories), Ferman, 1962; "*The Maltese Falcon*" and "*The Thin Man*," Vintage Books, 1964; *Novels* (contains *Red Harvest, The Dain Curse, The Maltese Falcon, The Glass Key,* and *The Thin Man*), Knopf, 1965; *The Big Knockover* (stories), edited by Lillian Hellman, Random House, 1966 (published in England as *The Dashiell Hammett Story Omnibus,* Cassell, 1966); *The Continental Op: More Stories From "The Big Knockover,"* Dell, 1967; *The Continental Op* (stories; different from two collections above with same title), edited by Steven Marcus, Random House, 1974.

Screen stories, except as indicated: "City Streets," Paramount, 1931; "Mister Dynamite," Universal, 1935; "Satan Met a Lady," Warner Bros., 1936; "After the Thin Man," Metro-Goldwyn-Mayer, 1936; "Another Thin Man," Metro-Goldwyn-Mayer, 1939; "Watch on the Rhine" (screenplay; adapted from the play by Lillian Hellman), Warner Bros., 1943.

Works represented in numerous anthologies of detective fiction.

Contributor of stories and articles to over thirty magazines, including *Smart Set, Brief Stories, Black Mask, True Detective Stories, Argosy All-Story Monthly, Saturday Review, Bookman, American Magazine, Collier's, Liberty, Redbook,* and *Ellery Queen's Mystery Magazine.*

SIDELIGHTS: Dashiell Hammett is widely considered the father of hard-boiled detective fiction. Along with those of Caroll John Daley, Hammett's stories in *Black Mask* helped to bring about a major movement in detective fiction away from the genteel detectives solving crimes perpetrated by masterminds, to rough, believable private eyes dealing with common crooks. In the words of Raymond Chandler, "Hammett took murder out of the Venetian vase and dropped it into the alley.... Hammett gave murder back to the kind of people that commit it for reasons, not just to provide a corpse; and with the means at hand, not with hand-wrought duelling pistols, curare, and tropical fish."

Hammett's importance as a writer lies in his influence as an innovator, his impact as a stylist, and his skill in characterization. In 1948, Raymond Chandler wrote in a letter to fellow crime-fiction writer Cleve F. Adams: "I did not invent the hard boiled murder story and I have never made any secret of my opinion that Hammett deserves most or all of the credit." Along with Chandler, Hammett is the most imitated writer of the genre. Erle Stanley Gardner declared: "I think of all the early pulp writers who contributed to the new format of the detective story, the word 'genius' was more nearly applicable to Hammett than to any of the rest. Unfortunately however, because Hammett's manner was so widely imitated it became the habit for the reviewers to refer to 'the Hammett School' as embracing the *type* of story as well as the *style*."

Hammett was important as more than simply a genre writer. As Howard Haycraft observed, Hammett's novels "are also character studies of close to top rank in their own right, and are penetrating if often shocking as novels of manners as well. They established new standards for realism in the genre. Yet they are as sharply stylized and deliberately artificial as Restoration Comedy, and have been called an inverted form of romanticism."

In one sense Hammett's detectives are romantics. They dare to believe in and hold firmly to a strict code of behavior which is in opposition to that of the world in which they move. Realistic and resourceful enough to be able to operate effectively among thieves, murderers, kidnappers, and blackmailers, Hammett's Continental Op, Sam Spade, Ned Beaumont, and Nick Charles are incorruptible in their belief that criminals ought to pay for their acts. When the unnamed Continental Op is tempted with money and sex to let a Russian princess guilty of murder and theft go free, he explains: "You think I'm a man and you're a woman. That's wrong. I'm a manhunter and you're something that's been running in front of me. There's nothing human about it. You might just as well expect a hound to play tiddly-winks with the fox he's caught." That sentiment presages the famous farewell of Sam Spade to Brigid O'Shaughnessy, the murderess he loves but turns over to the police: "I'm going to send you over. The chances are you'll get off with life. That means you'll be out again in twenty years. You're an angel. I'll wait for you.... If they hang you I'll always remember you." Ellery Queen noticed the seeming paradox of Hammett's romanticism early on: "The skin of realism hides the inner body of romance. All you see at first glance is that tough outer skin. But inside—deep in the core of his plots and counterplots—Hammett is one of the purest and most uninhibited romantics of all."

But Hammett was most of all a realist, and he was successful because, unlike his predecessors, he knew so well the world about which he wrote. When he was an operative for the Pinkerton National Detective Agency, Hammett "rated at the very top." As a detective, Hammett searched for accused securities thief Nick Arnstein; he worked for the defense during Fatty Arbuckle's celebrated trial for rape and murder; and he once found $125,000 in stolen gold stuffed down the smoke stack of a ship about to embark for Australia. In 1921, tuberculosis contracted during World War I forced Hammett to give up detective work for a more sedate occupation. He apparently was determined to be a poet and sought to support himself by writing detective stories. In 1922, he began writing about the characters and the life he had been forced to abandon. Hammett remarked in 1929: "The 'op' I use ... is the typical sort of private detective that exists in our county today. I've worked with half a dozen men who might be he with a few changes."

Black Mask magazine, begun by H. L. Mencken and George Jean Nathan, was the most important forum for writers of the hard-boiled school, and Hammett quickly became the most popular of the *Black Mask* writers with the magazine's readership. Between 1923 and 1927, thirty-two of his stories were published there. *Black Mask* editors took their work and their writers seriously; they demanded quality material and freely suggested new avenues for their writers' work. In 1926, Captain Joseph T. Shaw became editor of *Black Mask* and encouraged Hammett to write longer fiction. As a result, in November, 1927, the first installment of the four-part *Red Harvest,* Hammett's first novel, was published in *Black Mask.*

The opening lines of *Red Harvest* illustrate well the major elements of Hammett's style: "I first heard Personville called Poisonville by a red-haired mucker named Hickey Dewey in the Big Ship in Butte. He also called a shirt a shoit. I didn't think anything of what he had done to the city's name. Later I heard men who could manage their r's to give it the same pronunciation." Careful attention to vernacular speech, use of criminal argot, and a knowledgeable, objective point of view characterize Hammett's fiction.

In *Red Harvest* the unnamed Continental Op tells the story of one of his cases. Typically, he goes into Personville, a totally lawless community, and by manipulating one group of criminals against another causes them to kill off each other. William F. Nolan pointed out that by the end of the novel "more than thirty deaths are toted up, a total which includes twelve of the nineteen main characters." During the course of the novel, the op breaks some laws, tells some lies, betrays some confidences, but he does so in a criminal environment where, he is realist enough to know, an honest man wouldn't stand a chance.

Red Harvest was a critical success. Herbert Asbury in *Bookman* declared: "It is doubtful if even Ernest Hemingway has ever written more effective dialogue than may be found within the pages of this extraordinary tale of gunmen, gin and gangsters. The author displays a style of amazing clarity and compactness, devoid of literary frills and furbelows, and his characters, who race through the story with the rapidity and destructiveness of machine guns, speak the crisp hard-boiled language of the underworld." W. R. Brooks in *Outlook* echoed those remarks: "It is written by a man who plainly knows his underworld and can make it come alive for his readers."

Those comments are typical, and they forecast a success for which Hammett would have to wait until the publication in 1930 of his third novel, *The Maltese Falcon. The Dain Curse,* published in 1929, was not up to Hammett's standards. Though it received a share of reviewers' compliments, most contemporary readers might agree with William Nolan's description: "Lacking the cohesive element of a single locale, this story jumps from seacoast to city to country, while the reader is forced to cope with over thirty characters." Based on Hammett's short story "The Scorched Face," *The Dain Curse* is the story of a family curse caused by incest which links the op's client's daughter with her blackly religious captor. The story is of drugs and, most of all, murder in a gothic setting. Elizabeth Sanderson reported that Hammett considered *The Dain Curse* "a silly story."

If *The Dain Curse* was Hammett's least successful novel, *The Maltese Falcon* ranked with his very best. The novel brought Hammett instant fame and prosperity. Sam Spade, the novel's protagonist, has served as a standard of hard-boiled characterization. Tough, calloused, competent, and operating according to his own code of justice, Sam Spade is the epitome of the lone detective working without reward to make things right. When Spade was accused of murder by an incompetent district attorney, the private eye explained his position: "As far as I can see my best chance of clearing myself of the trouble you're trying to make for me is by bringing in the murderers—all tied up. And my only chance of ever catching them is by keeping away from you and the police, because neither of you show any signs of knowing what in hell it's all about." Spade perhaps best illustrates the emotional callous characteristic of Hammett's detectives. Somerset Maugham complained that Spade was hardly recognizable from the crooks he chased. That observation is critical to an understanding of Spade and his work. As Spade tells Brigid O'Shaughnessy: "Don't be too sure I'm as crooked as I'm supposed to be. That kind of reputation might be good business ... making it easier to deal with the enemy." Good men can't deal with bad ones because being good, they obey a different set of rules. Spade deals with the enemy on his own terms.

In 1930, W. R. Brooks wrote in *Outlook* that "this is not only probably the best detective story we have ever read, it is an exceedingly well written novel." That opinion has worn well over the past forty-five years. *The Maltese Falcon* is widely considered a standard by which American mysteries are judged.

Hammett is said to have liked *The Glass Key* best among his novels. As Oliver Pilat has suggested, Ned Beaumont, the protagonist of *The Glass Key,* is "closer to the character of the author than some of Hammett's brassier detectives." Beaumont is tubercular, a gambler, a man with an intense sense of loyalty to his friend, yet a man who lives by a private code. Like Sam Spade, he is not impervious to human relationships, but he will not allow his personal feelings to blind him to the truth. When a U.S. senator, father of the woman Beaumont respects, if not loves, is proven to have murdered his son, he asks Beaumont for "the return of my revolver and five minutes—a minute—alone in this room" so that he may take the honorable way out. Beaumont's reply has the force of unrefined justice about it: "You'll take what's coming to you." As Hammett's plots got less complex, his characters more realistic, his writing more mature, the heroes of his fiction continued to see that people got what they deserved. *The Glass Key* is a novel about justice, friendship, and priorities. Ned Beaumont's friend, Paul Madvig, is a political boss who very nearly lets his attraction to Senator Ralph B. Henry's daughter, Janet, ruin him. Beaumont serves his friend well by saving him, against Madvig's will, from a murder charge by exposing Senator Henry as his son's murderer and by saving Madvig from Janet Henry, who "hates him like poison." Madvig is unwilling to face the truth and Beaumont is too good a friend to allow him not to. Beaumont serves to make people accept reality—whether it be to take what's coming to them or to give up what they have no claim to.

M. I. Cole writing in *Spectator* called *The Glass Key* "the work of a man who knows exactly what he means to do, and who knows, also, why the current tradition of English detective fiction cannot be translated into American. . . . His people are violent, grafty, and full of sex appeal and responsiveness thereto: he is a clever writer."

After *The Glass Key,* it was three years before Hammett's next—and last—novel was written. Five years earlier he had literally been a starving writer. In 1931, his income was estimated at over $50,000; it would soon double. He rode in a chauffer-driven Rolls Royce (he was said to have refused to drive after he dumped an ambulance load of wounded soldiers during World War I) and tipped his barber twenty-dollar bills. He had become a celebrity—and he had met perhaps the most influential woman in his life who was to be his companion until his death, Lillian Hellman.

The Maltese Falcon was shocking to the readers of its day because it featured a homosexual villain. But one line in *The Thin Man* which referred to a man's sexual arousal while wrestling with a young girl created such a furor that the publisher felt obliged to run an ad in the *New York Times Book Review* defending the book's popularity: "Twenty thousand people don't buy a book within three weeks to read a five-word question." The sex in Hammett's work is very mild by today's standards; what is more interesting about *The Thin Man* is the change of tone and the change in the character of the detective. Nick Charles hates his work. A former detective, he has married a rich woman and wants to enjoy liquor and leisure. In many ways Hammett was, in 1934, much like Nick Charles. He was wealthy, an alcoholic, and his interest in his work was waning. Curiously *The Thin Man,* a light mystery with a self-indulgent hero, was Hammett's best-selling and most lucrative book. The movie starring William Powell and Myrna Loy was so successful that five sequels were made. Hammett no longer had to write to survive.

Hammett wrote *The Thin Man* at a hotel run by Nathanael West. Lillian Hellman recalled the process: "I had known Dash when he was writing short stories, but I had never been around for a long piece of work. Life changed: the drinking stopped; the parties were over. The locking-in time had come and nothing was allowed to disturb it until the book was finished. I had never seen anyone work that way: the care for every word, the pride in the neatness of the typed page itself, the refusal for ten days or two weeks to go out even for a walk for fear something would be lost.''

Later, in a letter to Hellman, who served as the model for Nora Charles, Hammett wrote: ''Maybe there are better writers in the world, but nobody ever invented a more insufferably smug pair of characters. They can't take that away from me, even for $40,000.'' The $40,000 referred to the money he made from one of the *Thin Man* sequels.

After 1934, movies played an important part in Hammett's life. F. Scott Fitzgerald called Hammett one of the good writers ''ruined'' by Hollywood. Raymond Chandler concurred: ''He was one of the many guys who couldn't take Hollywood without trying to push God out of the high seat.''

For whatever reason, Hammett stopped writing after *The Thin Man*. All of the books which appeared under his name after 1934 are simply collections by someone else of stories written earlier. The extent of his literary activities appears to have been as a screenwriter—including the only screenplay for which he was credited, the adaptation of Lillian Hellman's *Watch on the Rhine*—script doctor for stage plays, consultant for radio scripts, and occasional book reviewer. He did attempt a novel, but returned the advance he had accepted from Random House when it became clear that the novel would never be completed (the unfinished novel, *Tulip,* appears in *The Big Knockover*). William Nolan suggested that one clue to Hammett's silence lies in the words of Pop, *Tulip'*s Hammett-like narrator: ''If you are tired you ought to rest, I think, and not try to fool yourself and your customers with colored bubbles.''

Though Hammett's writing career effectively ended in 1934, he remained a nationally-prominent man until his death. About 1937, Hammett apparently joined the Communist Party and he figured in Communist Party affairs for the next twenty years. At the height of the paranoia which accompanied McCarthyism, the FBI reported that Hammett was a sponsor, member, or supporter of over forty organizations sympathetic to communism; in 1948 he served as national vice-chairman of the Civil Rights Congress (CRC), declared by the U.S. Attorney General to be a subversive organization. Lillian Hellman faced squarely the subject of Hammett's politics: ''I don't know if Hammett was a Communist Party member: most certainly he was a Marxist. But he was a very critical Marxist, often contemptuous of the Soviet Union in the same hick sense that many Americans are contemptuous of foreigners. He was often witty and bitingly sharp about the American Communist Party, but he was, in the end, loyal to them.'' On February 23, 1955, testifying before the joint legislative committee Investigation of Charitable and Philanthropic Agencies and Organizations at the Supreme Court—New York City, Hammett testified: ''Communism to me is not a dirty word. When you are working for the advance of mankind it never occurs to you whether a guy is a Communist.''

In 1951, Hammett was called to testify before the New York State Supreme Court as a trustee of the Bail Bond Committee of CRC in the wake of the violation of bail by eleven members of the Communist Party for whom the CRC had posted bond, four of whom could not be located. When Hammett refused to testify—even to identify his signature—he was sentenced to six months in federal prison for

contempt of court. He served his term between July and December, 1951.

In April, 1953, Hammett was called to testify before the Senate Permanent Subcommittee on Investigations of the Committee on Government Operations, chaired by Joseph McCarthy. His testimony before that committee is often quoted. Asked by McCarthy if he would ''purchase the works of some seventy-five Communist authors and distribute their works throughout the world,'' Hammett replied, ''If I were fighting communism, I don't think I would do it by giving people any books at all.''

Royalties from Hammett's work supported him well into the 1950's. Before he was jailed, Hammett still earned $1000 per week from royalties. But after his release, the Internal Revenue Service took an increasing interest in his affairs, resulting in February, 1957, in a $140,796 default judgment for tax deficiencies. Tubercular and physically exhausted, Hammett was unable to pay the judgment and his income was attached for the rest of his life. In 1957, he listed his income as less than $30. In November, 1960, he was found to have cancer of the lungs. He died on January 10, 1961.

At his funeral Lillian Hellman said of Dashiell Hammett: ''He never lied, he never faked, he never stooped. . . . He seemed to me a great man.''

BIOGRAPHICAL/CRITICAL SOURCES—Books: Howard Haycraft, *Murder for Pleasure,* Appleton-Century, 1941; Dashiell Hammett, *They Can Only Hang You Once,* introduction by Ellery Queen, Spivak, 1944; Haycraft, editor, *The Art of the Mystery Story,* Simon & Schuster, 1946; Dorothy Gardiner and Katherine Sorley Walker, editors, *Raymond Chandler Speaking,* Houghton, 1962; E. H. Mundell, *A List of the Original Appearances of Dashiell Hammett's Magazine Work,* Kent State University Press, 1968; Lillian Hellman, *An Unfinished Woman,* Little, Brown, 1969; William F. Nolan, *Dashiell Hammet: A Casebook,* McNally & Loftin, 1969; Hellman, *Pentimento,* Little, Brown, 1973; Hammett, *The Continental Op,* edited by Steven Marcus, Random House, 1974; Joe Gores, *Hammett,* Putnam, 1975; *Contemporary Literary Criticism,* Gale, Volume 3, 1975, Volume 5, 1976; Hellman, *Scoundrel Time,* Little, Brown, 1976.

Periodicals: *Outlook,* February 13, 1929, February 26, 1930; *Bookman,* March, 1929; *Spectator,* February 14, 1931; *Esquire,* September, 1934; *Atlantic Monthly,* December, 1944; *New York Times,* January 11, 1961; *Baltimore News-American,* August 19, 1973; *Miami Herald,* March 17, 1974; *City of San Francisco,* November 4, 1975.*

(Died January 10, 1961, in New York, N.Y.)

*   *   *

HAMMOND, Lawrence 1925-

PERSONAL: Born May 26, 1925, in London, England; son of Walter Francis (a legal executive) and Margaret (Hespe) Hammond; married Maria Somersalo; children: Dona Haycraft. *Education:* Educated in England. *Residence:* Suffolk, England. *Agent:* A. M. Heath, 40-42 William IV St., London, WC2N 4DD, England.

CAREER: Former features editor for *London Daily Express;* managing editor of Fleetway Publications Ltd., London; editor of various International Publishing Co. magazines in London; director of Curtis Brown Ltd. (literary agency), London; currently head of public relations for W. H. Smith Group (bookseller), London. *Member:* Writers' Guild of Great Britain, National Union of Journalists,

Crime Writers' Association (Great Britain), Writers' Action Group.

WRITINGS: A Life to Lose, W. H. Allen, 1966, Four Square Books, 1967; *Deny the Stranger*, Popular Library, 1967; *Thriller Movies*, Octopus Books, 1975. Writer for British Broadcasting Co. radio and television. Contributor to magazines.

* * *

HAMPTON, David R(ichard)   1933-

PERSONAL: Born April 4, 1933, in Detroit, Mich.; son of William John and Alice L. (McLaughlin) Hampton; married Dorothy Ann Bender (a clerk), June, 1962; children: David R., Jr. *Education:* University of Michigan, B.A., 1955; University of Southern California, M.B.A., 1960; Columbia University, Ph.D., 1964. *Home:* M5 North Lane, Del Mar, Calif. 92014. *Office:* Department of Management, San Diego State University, San Diego, Calif. 92182.

CAREER: San Diego State University, San Diego, Calif., assistant professor, 1964-66, associate professor, 1967-69, professor of management, 1970—. *Member:* Academy of Management.

WRITINGS: Organizational Behavior and the Practice of Management, Scott, Foresman, 1968, 3rd edition, 1978; *Behavioral Concepts in Management*, Wadsworth, 1968, 3rd edition, 1978; *Modern Management*, Dickenson, 1969, 2nd edition, 1974; *Black Americans and White Business*, Dickenson, 1971; *Management Today*, Wiley, 1975; *Contemporary Management*, McGraw, 1978. Contributor to professional journals.

WORK IN PROGRESS: A revised edition of *Contemporary Management*.

* * *

HANE, Mikiso   1922-

PERSONAL: Surname is pronounced *Hah*-neh; born January 16, 1922, in Hollister, Calif.; son of Ichitaro (a farmer) and Hifuyo (Taoka) Hane; married Rose Kanemoto (a secretary), September 19, 1948; children: Laurie Shizuye, Jennifer Kazuko. *Education:* Yale University, B.A., 1952, M.A., 1953, Ph.D., 1957; attended University of Munich, 1958-59. *Religion:* Buddhist. *Home:* 2285 North Broad, Galesburg, Ill. 61401. *Office:* Department of History, Knox College, Galesburg, Ill. 61401.

CAREER: Yale University, New Haven, Conn., part-time instructor in Japanese, 1948-54, 1956-57; University of Toledo, Toledo, Ohio, assistant professor of history, 1959-61; Knox College, Galesburg, Ill., assistant professor, 1961-67, associate professor, 1967-71, professor of history, 1972—. *Member:* American Historical Association, Association for Asian Studies, American Association of University Professors. *Awards, honors:* Fulbright research grant, 1957-58.

WRITINGS: Japan: A Historical Survey, Scribner, 1972; (translator) Masao Maruyama, *Studies in the Intellectual History of Tokugawa Japan*, Princeton University Press, 1974.

WORK IN PROGRESS: Translating the diary of General Honjo Shigeru; research on modern Japanese social history.

SIDELIGHTS: Hane writes: "Because I am a Japanese-American citizen who was raised in Japan, I have developed a special interest in Japanese history and culture. Currently I am interested in trying to look at modern Japanese history from the bottom up: how things may have looked to the peasants in particular, what 'modernization' meant to them, and how the war years affected their lives and thoughts. Having grown up as a 'peasant,' I hope to bring the peasants' perspective to the task of examining rural Japan in the prewar years. What I have learned in studying and teaching history is the enormous impact that Western civilization, especially science and technology, has had on non-Western societies, but at the same time I have been struck by the resiliency of traditional attitudes and values which have survived the onslaught of Western science, logic, and rationalism."

* * *

HANFORD, S. A.   1898-1978

OBITUARY NOTICE: Born in 1898, in Manchester, England; died October 10, 1978, in England. Classical scholar, educator, and author. A translator of Xenophon, Caesar, and Sallust, he published a work entitled *The Latin Subjunctive* and edited a pocket Latin-English dictionary. Obituaries and other sources: *AB Bookman's Weekly*, January 8, 1979.

* * *

HARCOURT, Peter   1931-

PERSONAL: Born July 26, 1931, in Toronto, Ontario, Canada; son of John Adam A. (a physician) and Constance (Watson) Harcourt; divorced; children: Jennifer, John. *Education:* University of Toronto, B.Mus., 1951; Cambridge University, M.A., 1957. *Politics:* "Canadian!" *Religion:* "Canadian!" *Home:* 45 MacPherson Ave., Toronto, Ontario, Canada M5R 1W7. *Office:* Department of Film, York University, Downsview, Ontario, Canada M3J 2R6.

CAREER: British Film Institute, London, assistant education officer, 1962-67; Queen's University, Kingston, Ontario, assistant professor, 1967-70, associate professor, 1970-74, chairman of department of film, 1967-74; York University, Downsview, Ontario, associate professor of film, 1974—. Producer and director of films, "Vaghy," Quarry Films, 1971, and "Production: Dance," CFDC, 1977. Member of board of directors of Canadian Film Institute. Broadcaster for Canadian Broadcasting Corp. *Member:* Society for Cinema Studies, Film Studies Association of Canada, University Film Association. *Awards, honors:* Canada Council grants, 1973-74.

WRITINGS: Six European Directors, Penguin, 1974; *Movies and Mythologies*, Canadian Broadcasting Corp., 1977.

Films: "Antonioni" (documentary), BBC-TV, 1967; "Bieter," CFDC, 1973. Contributor to film journals. Member of editorial board of *Sight and Sound*.

WORK IN PROGRESS: Research on Canadian cinema.

SIDELIGHTS: Harcourt told *CA:* "The most pressing need for Canadian film makers is to free themselves from dependence on the international (read: American) market. There are a lot of tears still to be shed."

* * *

HARDAWAY, Francine   1941-

PERSONAL: Born May 14, 1941, in New York, N.Y.; daughter of Chauncey S. (an attorney) and Sybil Olman (a stockbroker; maiden name, Rosen); married John Hardaway (a professor), April 6, 1971; children: Samantha, Chelsea. *Education:* Cornell University, B.A. (with distinction), 1962; Columbia University, M.A. (high honors), 1963; Syracuse University, Ph.D., 1968. *Home:* 1758 East Sunnyslope Lane, Phoenix, Ariz. 85020.

CAREER: Macmillan Publishing Co., Inc., New York City, promotion copywriter, 1962-63; J. Walter Thompson, New York City, copy trainee, 1963; Columbia University Press, New York City, promotion copywriter, 1963; Syracuse University Press, Syracuse, N.Y., promotion copywriter, 1963-64; Syracuse University, Syracuse, N.Y., instructor in English, 1965-67; Le Moyne College, Syracuse, assistant professor of English, 1967-68; Phoenix College, Phoenix, Ariz., instructor in English, 1968-69; Scottsdale Community College, Scottsdale, Ariz., professor of communications, 1970-78; Rio Salado College, Phoenix, in program development, 1978—. Visiting lecturer at Arizona State University, 1973-74. Head of Maricopa County Community College district committee on non-traditional education, 1975-76, administrative intern, 1975. Leader and participant in workshops and seminars.

MEMBER: Modern Language Association of America, National Council of Teachers of English, Conference on College Composition and Communication, American Association of University Professors, Popular Culture Association, National Academy of Television Arts and Sciences, American Film Institute, Rocky Mountain Modern Language Association, Pacific Coast Conference on English in the Two-Year College, Phi Beta Kappa, Phi Kappa Phi, Alpha Lambda Delta. *Awards, honors:* National Endowment for the Humanities fellowship, summer, 1974.

WRITINGS: (Co-editor) *Freshman English at Syracuse,* Wadsworth, 1966; *Creative Rhetoric,* Prentice-Hall, 1976; (with husband, John Hardaway) *Writing Through Reading,* Winthrop Publishing, 1976; (contributor) Dan Dieterich, editor, *Doublespeak and Teaching,* National Council of Teachers of English, 1976; (with J. Hardaway) *Thinking Into Writing: The Basics and Beyond,* Winthrop Publishing, 1978. Investigative reporter and film reviewer for *New Times, Phoenix,* and *Nickel Review,* 1968—. Contributor to education journals. Co-editor of *Doublespeak Newsletter;* member of editorial board of *Teaching English in the Two-Year College* and *Open Door.*

SIDELIGHTS: Francine Hardaway writes: "It may be impossible to teach critical skills in the way we did before the ascendency of the mass media. To make students aware of the need for reading and writing skills is a new consciousness-raising task teachers have to face. Television teaches an over-simplified problem-solution way of looking at the world, that is reinforced by political doublespeak. Students have to be made aware of popular culture's ubiquitous impact before they can be expected to value the critical skills of reading and writing. All my work is currently focused on these themes."

* * *

HARRIS, Sara Lee
See STADELMAN, S(ara) L(ee)

* * *

HARTMAN, Mary S(usan) 1941-

PERSONAL: Born June 25, 1941, in Minneapolis, Minn.; daughter of Kenneth W. (an engineer) and Dorothy (Morris) Robertson; married Edwin M. Hartman (a management consultant), September 2, 1966. *Education:* Swarthmore College, B.A. (magna cum laude), 1963; Columbia University, M.A., 1964, Ph.D., 1969. *Home:* 16 Perdicaris Pl., Trenton, N.J. 08618. *Office:* Department of History, Douglass College, Rutgers University, New Brunswick, N.J. 08903.

CAREER: Rutgers University, Douglass College, New

Brunswick, N.J., instructor, 1968-69, assistant professor, 1969-75, associate professor of history, 1975—, director of Women's Studies Institute, 1975-77. Jacobus Visiting Lecturer at University of Virginia, spring, 1978; lecturer at universities. *Member:* American Historical Association, Berkshire Conference of Women Historians (president, 1977-79), Northeastern Victorian Studies Association, Coordinating Committee for Women in the Historical Profession, Phi Beta Kappa. *Awards, honors:* Woodrow Wilson fellowships, 1963-64, 1966-67; Fulbright fellowship for study in France, 1965-67; National Endowment for the Humanities grant, 1972.

WRITINGS: (Editor with Lois W. Banner, and author of introduction) *Clio's Consciousness Raised: New Perspectives on the History of Women,* Harper, 1974; *Victorian Murderesses: A True History of Thirteen Respectable French and English Women Accused of Unspeakable Crimes* (Literary Guild alternate selection), Schocken, 1977; *The Sex Factor in History: Women, Men, and Modernity,* Doubleday, 1979. Contributor of about a dozen articles and reviews to history and feminist studies journals. Associate history editor of *Feminist Studies,* 1977—.

SIDELIGHTS: Hartman told *CA:* "*Victorian Murderesses* presents accounts of twelve cases of middle class women who murdered husbands, lovers, and assorted others. It argues that far from being freaks, lunatics, or rebels, these troubled accused murderesses were ordinary women who found extreme solutions to ordinary problems.

"*The Sex Factor in History* considers the differential impact of change on men and women in Western societies in the past 250 years. It argues that contrary to prevailing views, the transition to modernity has been kinder to women than to men, contending that for the first time in history, women's lives are changing faster than men's. It explores how this happened and suggests what future sexual arrangements are possible. The book was motivated by concern over the historical vacuum in which the current debate over our troubled sexual arrangements is being conducted."

* * *

HARTNOLL, Phyllis 1906-

PERSONAL: Born September 22, 1906, in London, England; daughter of Herbert Nicholas (an army officer) and Hetty Kate (a headmistress; maiden name, Roberts) Hartnoll. *Education:* University of France, Lyons, Certificat d'etudes superieur, 1923-24; University of France, Algiers, Licence-es-lettres, 1924-26; St. Hugh's College, Oxford, M.A., 1926-29. *Home and office:* Hill Crest, Ware Lane, Lyme Regis, Dorsetshire DT7 3EL, England.

CAREER: Countryman (quarterly review), Idbury, England, secretary, 1930; B. H. Blackwell (bookshop), Oxford, England, foreign correspondent, 1931-33; Rehavia Girl's School, Jerusalem, Palestine (now Israel), teacher and secretary, 1933-34; held various positions at Macmillan Publishers Ltd., London, England, 1934-69; writer. Lecturer at Royal Academy of Dramatic Art, London, 1950-54; visiting lecturer at many universities in the United States, including Princeton, Yale, and Purdue. *Member:* International Federation for Theatre Research (founding member), Society for Theatre Research (founding member), Societe d'Histoire du Theatre. *Awards, honors:* Newdigate Prize for English Verse, 1929; Prize for Poem on a Sacred Subject, 1947 and 1964; Gold Medal for the Speaking of Poetry from Poetry Society, 1963.

WRITINGS: Sands of Egypt (poems), Basil Blackwell,

1929; *Twenty Poems,* Basil Blackwell, 1931; (translator from the German) Hege-Rodenwaldt, *The Acropolis,* Basil Blackwell, 1931; *The Dancer and Other Poems,* Macmillan, 1935; (translator from the Italian) Collodi, *Pinocchio,* Macmillan, 1937; (translator from the French) *Fairytales From France,* Macmillan, 1938; *The Maid's Song and Other Poems,* Macmillan, 1938; *St. Luke* (poetry), Basil Blackwell, 1947; *The Grecian Enchanted* (novel), Golden Cockerel Press, 1952; (translator from the Spanish) Fernando de Rojas, *Celestina,* Dent, 1959; *The Mammon of Unrighteousness* (poetry), Macmillan, 1964; *The Concise History of the Theatre,* Thames & Hudson, 1968; *The Concise Oxford Companion to the Theatre,* Oxford University Press, 1972; *Who's Who in Shaw,* Hamish Hamilton, 1975, Taplinger, 1977; *Winter War and Other Poems,* Epworth Press, 1977; *Who's Who in George Eliot,* Taplinger, 1977.

Editor: John Gielgud, *Brief Stages,* Macmillan, 1939; J. J. Jefferson, *Rip Van Winkle,* new edition, Bodley Head, 1949; *Oxford Companion to the Theatre,* Oxford University Press, 1951, 3rd edition, 1967; Kenneth Barnes, *Welcome, Good Friends,* Peter Davies, 1958; *Shakespeare in Music* (essays and music catalog), Macmillan, 1964; Massine, *My Life in Ballet,* Macmillan, 1968.

Plays: "Peter Peppercorn" (3-act; based on "Le Medicin malgre lui" by Moliere), first produced by Taverners theatre company, 1937; "Day Before Dawn," first produced in London, Ontario, 1947; "Lady of Camellias" (3-act; new adaptation), first produced in Northampton at Northampton Repertory Theatre, 1955; "The Family First" (3-act; adapted from the play, "The Swedenhjelms," by Bergman), first produced in Birmingham at Birmingham Repertory Theatre, 1960; "The Jealous Wife" (new adaptation of Colman's play), first produced in Dorsetshire at Lyme Regis Festival, 1974. Also author of other unproduced plays.

Translator of stories for "Children's Classics" series. Author of fifteen episodes adapted from *Old London* for BBC-Radio program, "Book at Bedtime," 1952. Contributor to *American Encyclopaedia of the Arts, Everyman's Encyclopaedia,* and *Enciclopedia della Spettacola.* Contributor of articles and reviews on theatre to many magazines, including *Times Literary Supplement,* and of stories to children's magazines. *Theatre Research/Recherches Theatrales* (bilingual journal for theatre students), first editor, 1958-61, reviewer.

WORK IN PROGRESS: A fourth edition of *Oxford Companion to the Theatre;* research on symbolism in costume and on Queen Victoria at the theatre.

SIDELIGHTS: Phyllis Hartnoll is, to date, the only member of Oxford University, male or female, to have won Oxford's Newdigate Prize for English Verse and twice won Oxford's Prize for a Poem on a Sacred Subject. She told *CA:* "I was the third woman at Oxford to win the Newdigate and the first woman to win the Prize for Sacred Verse. Both these are awards of long standing, previously open to men only." She also reported that "no one is allowed to enter for the Sacred Verse Prize after winning it twice."

Hartnoll has traveled in the United States and throughout Europe and North Africa. She is fluent in French and has a working knowledge of Spanish, German, and Italian.

AVOCATIONAL INTERESTS: Crossword puzzles, television quiz programs (has appeared on several).

BIOGRAPHICAL/CRITICAL SOURCES: Observer Review, October 8, 1967; *Cue,* December 14, 1968; *Spectator,* December 20, 1968; *Saturday Review,* March 8, 1969.

HASENCLEVER, Herbert Frederick   1924-1978

OBITUARY NOTICE: Born April 1, 1924 in Fort Madison, Iowa; died September 21, 1978, in Corvallis, Mont. Scientist and author. Hasenclever, a former scientist-director at the National Institute of Allergy and Infectious Diseases, specialized in research on fungus diseases. He was the author or co-author of more than 60 technical publications in the field of microbiology. Obituaries and other sources: *American Men and Women of Science: The Physical and Biological Sciences,* 12th edition, Bowker, 1971-73; *Washington Post,* September 30, 1978.

* * *

HASTINGS, (Macdonald) Max   1945-

PERSONAL: Born December 28, 1945, in London, England; son of Macdonald (a writer) and Anne (a writer; maiden name, Scott-James) Hastings; married Patricia Mary Edmondson, May 27, 1972; children: Charles, Charlotte. *Education:* Attended University College, Oxford, 1964-65. *Religion:* Church of England. *Home:* Jerpoint House, Thomastown, County Kilkenny, Ireland. *Agent:* Curtis Brown Ltd., 1 Craven Hill, London W.2, England.

CAREER: British Broadcasting Corp., London, England, researcher for television historical documentaries, 1963-64; *Evening Standard,* London, reporter, 1965-67, foreign correspondent, 1968-70; British Broadcasting Corp., current affairs commentator for television program "Twenty-Four Hours" (covering southeast Asia, the Middle East, southern Africa, China, and India), 1970-73; free-lance foreign correspondent for television and newspapers, 1973—. *Military service:* British Army, Parachute Regiment, 1963. *Member:* Beefsteak Club. *Awards, honors:* Fellowship from World Press Institute, St. Paul, Minn., 1967; British Press Award, 1973, for coverage of "Yom Kippur War."

WRITINGS: The Fire This Time: America in 1968, Taplinger, 1968; *Barricades in Belfast: The Struggle for Civil Rights in Northern Ireland,* Taplinger, 1970; *Montrose: The King's Champion,* Gollancz, 1977; *Yoni: The Hero of Entebbe,* Dial, 1979; *Bomber Command: The British Bombing of Germany in World War II,* Dial, 1979. Author of scripts for television reports and special programs. Contributor to magazines, including *Field, Spectator,* and *Economist.*

SIDELIGHTS: Hastings writes: "I am a passionate traveler, especially in the Far East and Africa. I am also devoted to field sports like fishing and shooting. I am delighted to be paid for doing what I like doing best: e.g., traveling, meeting people, and writing about it."

* * *

HATHAWAY, Mavis
See AVERY, Ira

* * *

HAVERSTOCK, Mary Sayre   1932-

PERSONAL: Born June 24, 1932, in Cambridge, Mass.; daughter of Daniel Clemens (an aeronautical engineer) and Rosamond (a pianist; maiden name, Foster) Sayre; married Nathan A. Haverstock (a consultant), May 22, 1954; children: Rosamond, Daniel, Julia, John, Gwendolyn. *Education:* Radcliffe College, B.A., 1954. *Home:* 1122 South 22nd St., Arlington, Va. 22202. *Agent:* Maxine Groffsky, 2 Fifth Ave., New York, N.Y. 10011.

CAREER: Corcoran Gallery of Art, Washington, D.C., secretary, 1955-58; *Art in America,* New York, N.Y., member of editorial staff, 1958-69; free-lance writer, 1969—. Film consultant.

WRITINGS: Indian Gallery: The Story of George Catlin, Four Winds Press, 1974; *An American Bestiary,* Abrams, 1979. Contributor of articles and stories to magazines, including *American Heritage, National Wildlife,* and *Smithsonian.*

WORK IN PROGRESS: By the People, a juvenile book on American folk art, publication by Four Winds Press.

SIDELIGHTS: Mary Haverstock writes: "I concentrate on nineteenth-century America, as reflected in art, popular culture, and attitudes toward nature. Though I devote most of my time to rather scholarly art-historical subjects, I also enjoy the challenge of writing for younger readers about the ideas and the images that have shaped the present. Young poeple have very good vision; they should be helped to 'see'."

*   *   *

HAYS, H(offmann) R(eynolds) 1904-

PERSONAL: Born March 25, 1904, in New York, N.Y.; son of Hoffmann Reynolds and Martha (Stark) Hays; married Juliette Levine (an interior designer), 1934; children: Daniel, Henry, Penelope, Martha (Mrs. Hugh Brown). *Education:* Cornell University, B.A., 1925; Columbia University, M.A., 1928; attended University of Liege, 1930-31. *Politics:* "Left—Liberal." *Religion:* Atheist. *Home address:* P.O. Box 22, East Hampton, N.Y. 11937. *Agent:* Oliver Swan, Collier Associates, 280 Madison Ave., New York, N.Y. 10016.

CAREER: City College (now of the City University of New York), New York, N.Y., instructor in English, 1928-29; University of Minnesota, Minneapolis, instructor in English, 1929-33; Wagner College, Staten Island, N.Y., teacher of drama and playwriting for New York Writers Conference, 1950-55; Fairleigh Dickinson University, Rutherford, N.J., associate professor of English, 1955-59; former faculty member at Southampton College, Southampton, N.Y. Organizer of poetry readings and chairman of literary committee, East Hampton's Guild Hall, 1975-77. *Member:* International P.E.N., Writers Guild (East). *Awards, honors:* Nonfiction award from Putnam, 1963, for *In the Beginnings.*

WRITINGS: (Translator) Bertolt Brecht, *The Trial of Lucullus,* New Directions, 1943; *Stranger on the Highway* (novel), Little, Brown, 1943; (editor and translator) *Twelve Spanish American Poets,* Yale University Press, 1943, reprinted, Beacon Press, 1972; *Lie Down in Darkness* (novel; Crime Book Club selection), Reynal, 1944; *The Takers of the City* (novel), Reynal, 1946; (editor and translator) Brecht, *The Selected Poems of Bertolt Brecht,* Reynal, 1947, reprinted, Harcourt, 1972; (translator) Jose Revueltas, *The Stone Knife* (novel), Reynal, 1947; *The Envoys* (novel), Crown, 1955; (translator) *Selected Writings of Juan Ramon Jimenez,* Farrar, Straus, 1957; *From Ape to Angel* (nonfiction; selection of Hudson Book Club and Midcentury Book Club), Knopf, 1958.

In the Beginnings (Hudson Book Club selection), Putnam, 1963; *The Kingdom of Hawaii* (juvenile), New York Graphic Society, 1964; *Charley Sang a Song* (juvenile), Harper, 1961; *The Dangerous Sex: The Myth of Feminine Evil* (Hudson Book Club selection), Putnam, 1964; *Selected Poems, 1933-1967,* Kayak Books, 1968; *Explorers of Man* (juvenile), Macmillan, 1971; (editor and translator) *Selected*

Poems of Jorge Carrera Andrade, State University of New York Press, 1972; *Birds and Beasts and Men* (Saturday Review Book Club selection), Putnam, 1972; *Children of the Raven,* McGraw, 1975. Also writer of about twenty-five television plays.

WORK IN PROGRESS: A biography of anthropologist Franz Boas, for Prentice-Hall; poems.

SIDELIGHTS: Hays's books have been translated into Arabic, Spanish, Italian, Dutch, French, Portuguese, German, and Japanese. *Stranger on the Highway* was purchased by Twentieth Century Film Co.; *Lie Down in Darkness* by Charles Feldman Film Co.

BIOGRAPHICAL/CRITICAL SOURCES: Street, October, 1977.

*   *   *

HAYWARD, Brooke 1937-

PERSONAL: Born July 5, 1937, in Los Angeles, Calif.; daughter of Leland Hayward (a theatrical agent and producer) and Margaret Sullavan (an actress); married Michael Thomas (a stockbroker), 1956 (marriage ended, 1960); married Dennis Hopper (an actor and director), 1961 (marriage ended, 1968); children: (first marriage) Jeffrey, William; (second marriage) Marin. *Education:* Attended Vassar College; studied acting with Lee Strasberg. *Residence:* Beverly Hills, Calif.

CAREER: Writer. Formerly an actress and a model.

WRITINGS: Haywire (Book-of-the-Month Club selection), Knopf, 1977.

SIDELIGHTS: Brooke Hayward is the daughter of actress Margaret Sullavan and top theatrical and movie agent Leland Hayward, sometimes referred to as the "Toscanini of the telephone." Always making big deals over the telephone, Hayward used "Haywire" as his cable address. His daughter used it as the title for her best-selling chronicle of the tragedy of her family. She witnessed and experienced the bitter divorce of her parents, the years that her brother spent in and out of mental institutions, the untimely deaths of both her sister and mother, and finally the death of her father.

In an interview with *W* Magazine about *Haywire,* Brooke Hayward stated: "Part of the reason I wrote this book is a feeling of guilt—that I, as a survivor, had to chart the history of those in my family who didn't survive to find out why I'm here and they're not." She continued: "I led into this project with a definite unresolved feeling of anger toward my father because I believed he . . . failed me most. He was the glamorous one who'd abandoned me and mother was a martyred saint. But as I wrote it, I discovered the reverse was the case. . . . The quality I most admire in people is their ability to survive, and I think father did with grace, enthusiasm and light-heartedness. He was the gentleman who went the distance. My mother didn't."

People magazine reported that "to help her memory, Brooke interviewed some thirty family friends including three Fondas, Jimmy Stewart and Josh Logan. Most of them are quoted at length in the book." Hayward told *People:* "My parents were very unusual people, but it was more valuable to have others say that than me. . . . The moral of my book is that you pay for everything. They were rich, accomplished, famous and beautiful. We were drowned in privilege, yet it ended in all this hideous tragedy."

John Leonard wrote that *Haywire* "unblinkingly reports on the end of a joyride. It is an account of beauty and talent so extravagent, of a mismanagement of emotions and responsibilities so stupid and unrelenting, that one stares at the evidence as though it were some surreal smear: arbitrary, sullen, inexplicable, parodic. *Haywire* is also, I hope, an exorcism.''

In his review of *Haywire*, Peter Prescott of *Newsweek* stated: "To write a memoir is to impose a deliberate and healing order on a life that may have hitherto seemed singularly lacking in structure. For Brooke Hayward, writing *Haywire* became a kind of therapy; the wonder is not that she wrote it but that she has written it so well. Organizing her material deftly by theme and character, advancing her narrative through a series of overlapping flashbacks, and bearing always in mind that this is a book about how the five of them affected each other, Brooke has wisely omitted all information about her life as a wife, divorcee and mother. It is . . . a brave, honest, intelligent and deeply moving book.''

Haywire is presently being adapted for television.

BIOGRAPHICAL/CRITICAL SOURCES: W Magazine, October 1-8, 1976; Brooke Hayward, *Haywire*, Knopf, 1977; *New York Times*, February 28, 1977; *New York Times Book Review*, March 6, 1977; *Newsweek*, March 14, 1977; *Time*, March 28, 1977; *People*, May 23, 1977.*

* * *

HAZLITT, Joseph
See STRAGE, Mark

* * *

HEFFERNAN, Thomas (Patrick Carroll) 1939-

PERSONAL: Born August 19, 1939, in Hyannis, Mass.; son of Thomas Carroll (a lawyer and educator) and Mary E. (a lawyer; maiden name, Sullivan) Heffernan; married Nancy Elizabeth Iler (a medical systems director), July 15, 1972. *Education:* Boston College, A.B., 1961; University of Manchester, M.A., 1963. *Home:* 413 Guilford Ave., Greensboro, N.C. 27401. *Office:* Guilford Technical Institute, P.O. Box 309, Jamestown, N.C. 27282.

CAREER: University of Manchester, Manchester, England, assistant lecturer in English literature, 1964-65; University of Bristol, Bristol, England, assistant lecturer in poetry, 1965-66; University of Hartford, West Hartford, Conn., instructor in literature, 1967-70; North Carolina State University, Raleigh, instructor in literature, 1971-73; poet-in-residence for "Poetry in the Schools" program in North Carolina, 1973-77; Central Piedmont Community College, Charlotte, N.C., visitng artist (poet), 1977-78; Guilford Technical Institute, Jamestown, N.C., visiting artist (poet), 1978—. Director of Martha's Vineyard Writers' Workshop, 1973—. Member of board of directors of Yorick Books, New House Publishers, 1969—.

MEMBER: Modern Language Association of America, Poetry Society of America, Committee of Small Magazine Editors and Publishers, American Committee for Irish Studies, Associated Writing Programs, Poetry Society of Virginia. *Awards, honors:* Second prize from *Atlantic* National Collegiate Essay Contest, 1960, for "A Bridge of Sade"; Editors' Honorary Poetry Prize from *The Whole Thing*, 1973, for "The Sadness of Cerberus and the Bitch"; Dillard Award from Poetry Society of Virginia, 1973, for "A Narrative Poem Which Concerns an Incident that Occurred at the Clifton Suspension Bridge," and 1975, for "Liam on the Fringe of the Dark Wood"; award from *St. Andrews Review*, 1974, for "Old Julia"; first Poetry Award from *Cruci-*

ble, 1977, for "The Great Bog"; fellowship from Southern Federation of State Arts Agencies, 1977; Gordon Barber Memorial Award from Poetry Society of America, 1978, for "Thanksgiving Parade."

WRITINGS: Mobiles and Other Poems, St. Andrews Press, 1974; (editor) *A Poem Is a Smile You Can Hear,* North Carolina Department of Public Instruction, 1976; *A Narrative of Jeremy Bentham* (poem), New House Publishers, 1978; *The Liam Poems,* Green River Review Press, 1979. Author of "Some Rise, Some Fall" (one-act play), first produced in Chestnut Hill, Mass., at Boston College, 1959.

Poems represented in anthologies, including *North Carolina Poetry: The Seventies,* edited by Sam Ragan, 1975; *White Trash,* edited by Nancy Stone and Robert Waters Grey, New South Publishing, 1976; and *Contemporary Poetry of North Carolina,* edited by Guy Owen and Mary C. Williams, Blair, 1977. Editor of *International Poetry Review,* spring, 1979.

WORK IN PROGRESS: A novel; *Charlotte Poems.*

SIDELIGHTS: Heffernan writes: "I lived as a student and university lecturer in England for more than five years, with much time spent in other countries, particularly Ireland and Italy.

"The written art-work, to me, is something fitted together—made—to communicate: feeling, thought, how it was or might be, or is. Writing as a process is a social act. Artists live and participate in the world, respond to it, and to themselves and other people in it, and write in the developing idiom of their art: they take in, form, and give back.''

* * *

HEIDEGGER, Martin 1889-1976

PERSONAL: Born September 26, 1889, in Messkirch, Germany; son of Friedrich (a sexton) and Johanna (Kempf) Heidegger; married Elfride Petri, 1917; children: Joerg, Hermann, Erika. *Education:* Received doctorate from University of Freiburg. *Home:* Roetebuckweg 47, Freiburg im Breisgau, West Germany.

CAREER: Philosopher. University of Freiburg, Freiburg, Germany, *Privatdozent,* 1915, seminar leader, 1916-20, assistant to Edmund Husserl, 1920-23; University of Marburg, Marburg, Germany, professor ordinarius, 1923-28; University of Freiburg, Freiburg, professor ordinarius, 1928-33, rector, 1933-34; lecturer, 1945-50; University of Freiburg, Freiburg, professor emeritus, 1951-57; lecturer. *Member:* Academy of Fine Arts of Berlin, Academy of Sciences of Heidelberg, Bavarian Academy of Fine Arts. *Awards, honors:* Named honorary citizen of Messkirch, 1959; Hebel prize of Baden-Wuerttemberg, 1960.

WRITINGS—In English: *Sein und Zeit,* Halle, 1927, translation by John Macquarrie and Edward Robinson published as *Being and Time,* Harper, 1962; *Kant und das Problem der Metaphysik,* F. Cohen, 1929, translation by James S. Churchill published as *Kant and the Problem of Metaphysics,* Indiana University Press, 1962; *Existence and Being* (contains "Remembrance of the Poet," "Hoelderlin and the Essence of Poetry," "On the Essence of Truth," and "What Is Metaphysics"; also see below), edited by Edward Brock, Regnery, 1949.

Einfuehrung in die Metaphysik, M. Niemeyer, 1953, translation by Ralph Manheim published as *An Introduction to Metaphysics,* Yale University Press, 1959; *Was Heisst Denken?,* M. Niemeyer, 1954, published as *What Is Called*

Thinking?, Harper, 1968; *Zur Seinsfrage*, [Frankfurt], 1955, translation by William Kluback and Jean T. Wilde published as *The Question of Being*, Twayne, 1958; *Was Ist das—die Philosophie?*, [Pfullingen], 1956, translation by Kluback and Wilde published as *What Is Philosophy?*, Twayne, 1958; *Identitaet und Differenz*, G. Neske, 1957, translation by Kurt F. Leidecker published as *Essays in Metaphysics: Identity and Difference*, Philosophical Library, 1960; *Gelassenheit*, G. Neske, 1959, translation by John M. Anderson and E. Hans Freund published as *Discourse on Thinking*, Harper, 1966; *Unterwegs zur Sprache*, G. Neske, 1959, translation by Peter D. Hertz published as *On the Way to Language*, Harper, 1971.

Die Frage nach dem Ding, M. Niemeyer, 1962, translation by W. B. Barton, Jr., and Vera Deutsch published as *What Is a Thing?*, Regnery, 1967; *German Existentialism*, translated by Dagobert D. Runes, Wisdom Library, 1965; *Vom Wesen des Grundes*, M. Klostermann, 1965, translation by Terrence Malick published with German text as *The Essence of Reasons*, Northwestern University Press, 1969; *Zur Sache des Denkens*, Niemeyer, 1969, translation by Joan Stambaugh published as *On Time and Being*, Harper, 1972.

Hegel's Concept of Experience, Harper, 1970; *Poetry, Language, Thought*, translated by Albert Hofstadter, Harper, 1971; *The End of Philosophy* (contains excerpts from *Nietzche* and *Vortraege und Aufsatze*), translated by Stambaugh, Harper, 1973; *Early Greek Thinking*, translated by David Farrell Krell and Frank A. Capuzzi, Harper, 1975.

Other: *Die Kategorien und Bedeutungslebre des Duns Scotus*, Mohr, 1916; *Platons Lehre von der Wahrheit*, A. Francke, 1947; *Holzwege* (title means "Woodpaths"), V. Klostermann, 1950; *Erlaeuterungen zu Hoelderlins Dichtung* (translation by D. Scott published as "Hoelderlin and the Essence of Poetry" in *Existence and Being* [see above]), V. Klostermann, 1951; *Vortraege und Aufsatze* (title means "Lectures and Essays"), G. Neske, 1954; *Der Satz vom Grund* (title means "The Law of Explanation"), G. Neske, 1957.

Der Ursprung des Kunstwerkes, P. Reclam, 1960; *Was Ist Metaphysiks?* (translation by R.F.C. Hull and A. Crick published as "What Is Metaphysics" in *Existence and Being* [see above]), M. Klostermann, 1962; *Vermittlung und Kehre*, K. Alber, 1965; *Wegmarkea* (title means "Trail Marks"), M. Klostermann, 1967; *Der Europaeische Nihilismus*, G. Neske, 1967; *Zur Sache des Denkens* (title means "In the Matter of Thinking"), M. Niemeyer, 1969; *Martin Heidegger*, V. Klostermann, 1969; *Heraklit: Seminar Wintersemester 1966-1967*, V. Klostermann, 1970; *Schellings Abhandlung*, M. Niemeyer, 1971; *Fruehe Schriften*, V. Klostermann, 1972; *Die Grundprobleme der Phaenomenologie*, V. Klostermann, 1975; *Logik: Die Frage nach der Wahrheit*, V. Klostermann, 1976.

Also author of *Die Selbstbehauptung der Deutschen Universitaet* (title means "Self-Determination of the German University"), 1933, and *Die Technik und die Kehre* (title means "Technology and the Turning Point"), 1962.

SIDELIGHTS: Heidegger is regarded by many scholars as one of the most innovative and inquisitive thinkers concerned with the posing of philosophical questions. Living at a time when the nihilism coined by Turgenev had blossomed into a movement, Heidegger chose to question the definition of "existence," rather than apply the term to refute other concepts. His major asset lay, according to Edward B. Fiske, in his ability to "rethink the entire history of Western philosophy and to restore confidence in man's ability to ask the big questions."

Heidegger felt that it was man's primary duty to define the word "being." "Do we have an answer today to the question, what do we really mean by the word 'being' . . .," he asked in *Being and Time*. "By no means, and it behooves us to pose anew the question. . . ."

Heidegger was driven to "pose anew the question" by his belief that man—in the classical Greek period—had hastily applied the assumption that truth was whatever was intellectually perceived as correct. He interpreted the classical Greek scholars' definition as a distortion of reality. For Heidegger, it was not enough to say simply that something existed. He devoted most of his lifetime to addressing this difficult problem of metaphysics.

Although the bulk of Heidegger's writings deal obsessively with the term "being," he defined it for himself in his first major work, *Being and Time*. After an interminable amount of philosophical diatribes (Heidegger was known as an excessive and wordy writer), he resolved in *Being and Time* that "being," for man, was an endless quest to define that very term. Put simply, Heidegger had, through complex and highly evolved concepts, reduced the incomprehensible act of being to a finite state. If the act of being is to ceaselessly attempt to define the term, then being must be finite, for all those that exist die. Heidegger termed this cycle of life-quest-death *Dasein* or "being there." Heidegger separated man from all else by claiming only those who experienced *Dasein* could exist. Cleverly, Heidegger had used the principle of the opposite to define: in order to exist, one must cease to exist.

Heidegger proposed his complex philosophy at a time when existentialism was also taking a hold among European scholars. By concerning himself with the definition of being as it applies to man, Heidegger was incorrectly associated with other existentialists, notably Jean Paul Sartre, whose own work was heavily influnced by Heidegger's. Heidegger argued that, unlike the existentialists, he was not concerned with man but with being. His own conclusions had forced him to accept man as an integral part of his concept, but his major concern was with existence and the finiteness of being.

Heidegger had made a sufficient name for himself by 1930 and was periodically offered positions outside the one he held with the University of Freiburg. However, after taking a new position at Freiburg, Heidegger spoke about the obligations of the German race to history. Soon after, he embraced a neo-Nietzschean stance and frequented Nazi rallies. After declaring that Adolf Hitler "alone is the German reality," Heidegger even denied one of his former teachers, a Jew, access to the university. "Heidegger behaved disgracefully," wrote Sidney Hook, "towards his teacher and other Jewish colleagues. . . ."

Many scholars and critics were stung by Heidegger's bizarre political stance, though it noticeably cooled towards the late 1930's. He became disillusioned by Hitler and resigned from his position at Freiburg. Still, the association with Nazism had been established and it haunted him for many years. After the war, a tribunal ruled that Heidegger was merely a sympathizer and, though his colleagues protested, he returned to teach at Freiburg.

While he never abandoned his pursuit of being, Heidegger's later years were devoted more to hermeneutics, defined by Fiske as an approach to linguistics that "focuses on language as revelational and conceives of words as events." He saw language as essential to being and wrote that "only where there is language is there world."

Working essentially from the poetry of Hoelderlin, Heidegger determined that "to write poetry is to make a discovery." As Alvin Rosenfeld observed, "The poem enacts a reality which has no existence prior to language but rises contemporaneously with it. What is manifest in the poem is the real: poetry is 'the transmutation of the world into word.'" Heidegger saw language as a proof of existence. "Language is the house of Being," he wrote, "the whole sphere of presence is present in saying."

The relation between language and being was a preoccupation with Heidegger in his last years. Aside from giving occasional lectures at Freiburg, he rarely wandered from his home in the Black Forest. But his works, long slighted because of his past association with Nazism, regained the attention that had been deprived them by vindictive scholars. "Even when we say that we greet him with gratitude and reverence, we do not know exactly what that means," acknowledged Karl Rahner. "But certainly he has taught us this: that in any and every unutterable mystery we can and should seek what holds sway over us, even when we can hardly express it in words."

BIOGRAPHICAL/CRITICAL SOURCES: Martin Heidegger, *Being and Time,* Harper, 1962; Manfred S. Frings, *Heidegger and the Quest for Truth,* Time Books, 1968; Henri Decleve, *Heidegger und Kant,* Kluwer, 1970; John Sallis, editor, *Heidegger and the Path of Thinking,* Duquesne University Press, 1970; Werner Marx, *Heidegger and the Tradition,* Northwestern University Press, 1971; Charles M. Sherover, *Heidegger, Kant, and Time,* Indiana University Press, 1971; L. M. Vail, *Heidegger and Ontological Difference,* Pennsylvania State University Press, 1972.

American Poetry Review, January/February, 1974; James L. Perotti, *Heidegger on the Divine: The Thinker, the Poet, and God,* Ohio University Press, 1974; Thomas Aquinas Fay, *Heidegger: The Critique of Logic,* Kluwer, 1977; Thomas Sheehan, editor, *Heidegger: The Man and the Thinker,* Precedent Publishing, 1978; David A. White, *Heidegger and the Language of Poetry,* University of Nebraska Press, 1978; Michael Murray, *Heidegger and Modern Philosophy,* Yale University Press, 1978.

OBITUARIES: Detroit Free Press, May 27, 1976; *New York Times,* May 27, 1976; *Washington Post,* May 27, 1976; *Newsweek,* June 7, 1976; *Time,* June 7, 1976; *Current Biography,* July, 1976.*

(Died May 26, 1976, in Messkirch, West Germany)

* * *

HEIMBERG, Marilyn Markham
See ROSS, Marilyn Heimberg

* * *

HEINL, Nancy G(ordon) 1916-
(Nancy Gordon)

PERSONAL: Born June 12, 1916, in London, England; daughter of Charles J. and Phyllis (Langlois) Wright; married Robert Debs Heinl, Jr. (a writer), September 23, 1939; children: Pamela Gordon Burdick, Michael Charles. *Education:* Attended St. Margaret's College, London, Cours de Parc Monceau, and College Marie-Jose. *Religion:* Episcopalian. *Home and office:* 2400 California St. N.W., Washington, D.C. 20008.

CAREER: Library of Congress, Washington, D.C., 1937-

39; free-lance writer, 1939—. Volunteer hospital worker and fund-raiser. *Member:* Women's National Democratic Club.

WRITINGS: (With husband, Robert D. Heinl) *Written in Blood,* Houghton, 1978. Author of newspaper column (under name Nancy Gordon), syndicated by North American Newspaper Alliance. Contributor to foreign service and armed forces magazines and to *Cathedral Age* (under name Nancy Gordon).

WORK IN PROGRESS: Research on China.

SIDELIGHTS: Nancy Heinl writes: "I started writing in 1939 in Parris Island, S.C., following my marriage. My husband was in the Marine Corps, making a hundred-twenty-five dollars a month, so writing gossip columns for local and service papers helped put food on the table. My interest in Haiti stems from more than four years spent in Port-au-Prince and my in-depth study of voodoo."

AVOCATIONAL INTERESTS: Travel (including People's Republic of China).

BIOGRAPHICAL/CRITICAL SOURCES: Washington Post, September 23, 1978.

* * *

HEISSENBUETTEL, Helmut 1921-

PERSONAL: Born June 21, 1921, in Ruestringen, Germany; son of Hans (a court bailiff) and Klara (Lorenz) Heissenbuettel; married Ida Warnholz, 1954; children: Ruth, Dietrich, Esther. *Education:* Attended Technische Hochschule, Dresden, University of Leipzig, and University of Hamburg. *Home:* Donizettistrasse 21, 7 Stuttgart-Botnang, West Germany.

CAREER: Poet, novelist, radio dramatist, and critic. Claassen Verlag (publisher), Hamburg, West Germany, reader, 1955-57; Sueddeutscher Rundfunk (South German radio service), Stuttgart, West Germany, contributor, 1957-58, chief editor of literary programs, 1959—. Lecturer at University of Frankfurt, 1963. *Military service:* German Army, 1940-41; served on Eastern Front. *Member:* German Academy for Language and Literature (Darmstadt), Academy of Arts (Berlin), Academy of Science and Literature (Mainz). *Awards, honors:* Lessing Prize, 1956; Hugo Jacobi Prize, 1960; Buechner Prize, 1969.

WRITINGS—In English: *Texts,* selected and translated by Michael Hamburger, M. Boyars, 1977.

Other works: *Kombinationen: Gedichte 1951-1954* (title means "Combinations: Poems 1951-1954"), Bechtle, 1954; *Topographien: Gedichte 1954-1955* (title means "Topographies: Poems 1954-1955"), Bechtle, 1956; *Textbuch 1* (title means "Textbook 1"), Walter Verlag, 1960; *Textbuch 2,* Luchterhand, 1961; *Textbuch 3,* Luchterhand, 1962; *Textbuch 4,* Luchterhand, 1964; *Mary McCarthy: Versuch eines Portraets, Mit einem interview der "Paris Review"* (title means "Mary McCarthy: Sketch for a Portrait, With a 'Paris Review' Interview"), Knaur, 1964, published as *Versuch eines Portraets,* Droemer, 1964; *Textbuch 5,* Luchterhand, 1965; *Ueber Literatur* (essays; title means "About Literature"), Walter Verlag, 1966; *Textbuch 6,* Luchterhand, 1967; (editor) *Rudolf Borchardt: Auswahl aus dem Werk* (title means "Rudolf Borchardt: Selected Works"), Klett, 1968; *Was ist das Konkrete an einem Gedicht?* (title means "What Is Concrete in a Poem?"), Hansen & Hansen, 1969; (with Heinrich Vormweg) *Briefwechsel ueber Literatur* (title means "Correspondence About Literature"), Luchterhand, 1969.

234 CONTEMPORARY AUTHORS • Volumes 81-84

Projekt Nr. 1: D'Alemberts Ende (novel; title means "Project Number One: D'Alembert's End"), Luchterhand, 1970; *Das Texbuch* (contains Textbooks 1-6 in one volume), Luchterhand, 1970; *Zur Tradition der Moderne* (essays; title means "On the Modern Tradition"), Luchterhand, 1972; *Geiger*, G. Hatje, 1972; *Gelegenheitsgedichte und Klappentexte* (title means "Occasional Poems and Blurbs"), Luchterhand, 1973; *Das Durchhaven des Kohlhaupts: Projekt 2* (poems and radio plays; title means "The Splitting of the Cabbage: Project Number Two"), Luchterhand, 1974.

SIDELIGHTS: Heissenbuettel has been called one of the most controversial and influential of Germany's postwar avant-garde writers. He has not published his early poems, and when his work began to appear in the mid-1950's he had already chosen his path as a writer. He works, he says, within "a tradition of experimental writing" in which his recent ancestors include Mallarme, the surrealist Apollinaire, the Dadaists, Gertrude Stein, and the futurist Marinetti. His work also reflects his interest in the philosophy of Ludwig Wittgenstein and others who have explored the relationship between language and thought. Heissenbuettel became a member of the influential writers' association Gruppe 47 (Group 47) in May, 1955, and his readings at the Group's regular meetings soon established him, according to Siegfried Mandel, "as the most intelligible representative of the new avant-garde."

In fact, his first two books retained some of the forms and concerns of traditional poetry, but showed a progressive rejection of punctuation, of grammar, and of anything resembling romanticism. Heissenbuettel's experiments were conducted primarily in the six so-called "textbooks" he published between 1960 and 1967. They included "concrete" or visual poems, "quasi-stories," poems that depend on Joycean puns, word associations, and other verbal games, collages of quotations, all kinds of lists and catalogs, and parodies of political manifestos and logical propositions ("If I were not only I but we I would be you he she it. Because I am I and not we I am I and can only talk about myself"). Perhaps the most admired of Heissenbuettel's poems, "Gedicht ueber die Ubung zu sterben" (Poe on Practice in Dying), combines personal recollections with scraps of conversation and bits of advertising copy; it seemed to Peter Demetz that in this poem "a modern consciousness . . . reveals experience totally made up of speech, at once infinitely rich and extremely limited." Demetz added, "It is one of the rare German poems that can compete with Ezra Pound's finest."

Mandel wrote that Heissenbuettel's "skeletonized word-algebra erases the line between poetry and prose and most often withdraws commentary and continuity from his writing to render a pure 'happening,' past or present, and to demonstrate the 'happenable' as might a chemical scientist." But Mandel found "Heissenbuettel's mechanics of massive concern with techniques . . . close to preciosity or pedantry," and he is not alone in this opinion. On the other hand, critics like Demetz took Heissenbuettel's experiments very seriously. Demetz suggested that he and other such contemporary experimental writers "combat the rules of grammar because these imply an ordered world which has long since ceased to exist. For Heissenbuettel, the antigrammatical resistance is preparing the second revolution against the establishment in literature." Peter Bridgwater called him "one of the most original poets of his generation, a master of 'discontinuous consciousness'." Some critics, bewildered by Heissenbuettel's experiments, preferred his essays on literature, and on painting, sculpture, photography, and the cinema.

Demetz wrote that the essays collected in *Ueber Literatur* "are of absolutely key importance for our critical understanding of future developments in the arts."

Heissenbuettel himself has explained that he is not interested in giving aesthetic pleasure or the simple satisfactions of narrative, but in exploring the limits of language and the conventions of literature for what they reveal about the nature of reality. This is obviously his intention in his long novel *D'Alemberts Ende*, which is as much a discussion of what is involved in the writing of a novel as a work of fiction, and which reminded many reviewers of the French "new novel."

BIOGRAPHICAL/CRITICAL SOURCES: Hilde Domin, editor, *Doppelinterpretationen*, Athenaeum Verlag, 1966; Heinrich Vormweg, *Die Woerter und die Welt*, Luchterhand, 1968; Michael Hamburger, *The Truth of Poetry*, Harcourt Brace, 1970; Peter Demetz, *Postwar German Literature*, Pegasus, 1970; Siegfried Mandel, *Group 47*, Southern Illinois University Press, 1973; *Times Literary Supplement*, August 17, 1973.*

* * *

HELFGOTT, Roy B. 1925-

PERSONAL: Born October 27, 1925, in New York, N.Y.; son of Moses N. (an attorney) and Dorothy (a teacher; maiden name, Levine) Helfgott; married Gloria Wolff (an artist), July 4, 1948; children: Daniel A. *Education:* City College (now of City University of New York), B.S. (cum laude), 1948; Columbia University, M.A., 1949; New School for Social Research, Ph.D., 1957. *Residence:* Warren, Conn. 06754. *Office:* Department of Organization and Social Science, New Jersey Institute of Technology, 323 High St., Newark, N.J. 07102.

CAREER: International Ladies' Garment Workers' Union, Coat Joint Board, New York City, director of research, 1949-57; New York Metropolitan Region Study, New York City, economist, 1957-58; Pennsylvania State University, University Park, assistant professor of economics, 1958-60; Industrial Relations Counselors, Inc., New York City, chief economist, 1960-66, director of research, 1967-68; New Jersey Institute of Technology, Newark, professor, 1968-75, distinguished professor of economics, 1975—, head of department of organization and social science, 1968—. Lecturer at City College (now of City University of New York), 1948-58; adjunct associate professor at City University of New York, Graduate Division, 1961-68. Industrial relations analyst for Wage Stabilization Board, 1952; economist for Pittsburgh Economic Study, 1960; industrial development officer for United Nations, 1966-67, head of mission to Lower Mekong Basin, 1967; consultant with Organization Resources Counselors, Inc., 1968—. *Military service:* U.S. Army, 1944-46; served in European theater; received Bronze Star and Combat Infantry Badge with two battle stars.

MEMBER: American Economic Association, Industrial Relations Research Association, Metropolitan Economic Association (president, 1978-79), Phi Beta Kappa. *Awards, honors:* Fulbright senior scholar in England, 1955-56; fellow of Inter-University Institute in Social Gerontology (Berkeley, Calif.), 1959.

WRITINGS: Made in New York, edited by Max R. Hall, Harvard University Press, 1959; (with Richard A. Beaumont) *Management, Automation, and People*, Industrial Relations Counselors, 1964; (with Salvatore Schiavo-Campo) *Industrial Planning*, United Nations, 1969; *Labor Economics*, Random House, 1974, 2nd edition, 1980.

Contributor: Aaron Antonovsky and Lewis L. Lorwin, editors, *Discrimination and Low Incomes,* Interdepartmental Committee on Low Incomes, State of New York, 1959; *Region in Transition,* University of Pittsburgh Press, 1963; Solomon Barkin, editor, *Technical Change and Manpower Planning,* Organization for Economic Co-Operation and Development, 1967; Beaumont, editor, *People, Programs, and Employee Relations,* University Press of Virginia, 1976. Contributor of more than fifteen articles to scholarly journals and to *Challenge.*

SIDELIGHTS: Helfgott comments: "I have had three decades of experience in industrial relations and labor economics as a student, researcher, teacher, and consultant, working both with labor and management. I have also had a subsidiary interest in regional economics, which was applied to the problems of the New York and Pittsburgh metropolitan areas, as well as to those of developing countries (during my service with the United Nations). I do not consider myself an ideologist (except for my firm belief in the values of a free society), but an analyst, having recognized many years ago that slogans do not solve socio-economic problems."

BIOGRAPHICAL/CRITICAL SOURCES: Town and Country, April, 1960.

* * *

HELPRIN, Mark   1947-

CAREER: Writer.

WRITINGS: A Dove of the East and Other Stories, Knopf, distributed by Random House, 1975; *Refiner's Fire: The Life and Adventures of Marshall Pearl, a Foundling* (novel), Knopf, distributed by Random House, 1977. Contributor of numerous short stories to *New Yorker.*

SIDELIGHTS: Helprin's collection of short stories, *The Dove of the East,* impressed critics with its wide range of story settings and characters and its gracefully crafted prose. Dorothy Rabinowitz commented that the stories are "immensely readable" and that some are "quite superb." She wrote: "Mr. Helprin's old-fashioned regard shines through all his characters' speeches, and his endorsement gives them eloquent tongues. Now and again the stories lapse into archness, and at times, too, their willed drama bears down too heavily. But these are small flaws in works so estimably full of talent and—the word must out—of character."

However, Amanda Heller, as a result of what she called Helprin's "dreamy, antique style," was fatigued by the "sameness of tone" throughout the stories. "It appears that Helprin is striving for loveliness above all else," she commented, "a tasteful but hardly compelling goal for a teller of tales." Duncan Fallowell allowed that some of the stories are "unbeatably vague," but praised Helprin for "recognising the intrinsic majesty" of seemingly meaningless events, because, as Fallowell wrote, "he is also a seeker after truth. Bits of it are squittering out all over the place, sufficiently to fuse into a magnetic centre and make one recognise that the book is not written by a fool."

Dan Wakefield was even more appreciative of Helprin's work. He wrote: "The quality that pervades these stories is love—love of men and women, love of landscapes and physical beauty, love of interior courage as well as the more easily obtainable outward strength. The author never treats his subjects with sentimentality but always with gentleness of a kind that is all too rare in our fiction and our lives."

Helprin's novel, *Refiner's Fire: The Life and Adventures of Marshall Pearl, a Foundling,* further delighted critics. The reviewer for *New Yorker* found that Helprin described the protagonist's boyhood "lyrically and gracefully," and proved himself to be "a writer of great depth and subtle humor." For Joyce Carol Oates the problem was "where to begin" in admiring the novel she described as a "daring, even reckless, sprawling and expansive and endlessly inventive 'picaresque' tale." She wrote: "At once we know we are in the presence of a storyteller of seemingly effortless and artless charm; and if the exuberant, extravagant plotting of the novel ever becomes tangled in its own fabulous inventions, and its prodigy of a hero ever comes to seem more allegorical than humanly 'real,' that storytelling command, that lovely voice is never lost."

BIOGRAPHICAL/CRITICAL SOURCES: Saturday Review, September 20, 1975; *Atlantic,* October, 1975; *New York Times Book Review,* November 2, 1975, January 1, 1978; *New Statesman,* February 13, 1976; *Spectator,* April 24, 1976; *New Yorker,* October 17, 1977; *Harper's,* November, 1977; *Contemporary Literary Criticism,* Volume 7, Gale, 1977; *New York Review of Books,* February 23, 1978.*

* * *

HENDERSON, Lois T(hompson)   1918-

PERSONAL: Born October 14, 1918, in Coraopolis, Pa.; daughter of John R. (in personnel) and Freda S. Thompson; married Albert J. Henderson (a chemical engineer), September 26, 1941; children: David, Mary Sue (Mrs. James Nichols). *Education:* Grove City College, B.A., 1940; graduate study at University of Pittsburgh, 1949-51. *Politics:* Republican. *Religion:* United Methodist. *Home:* 1315 Ridge Ave., Coraopolis, Pa. 15108.

CAREER: Montour High School, McKees Rocks, Pa., teacher of political science, 1960-64; writer, 1949—. *Member:* Pittsburgh Poetry Society (president, 1970-74).

WRITINGS: The Opening Doors (non-fiction), John Day, 1955; *The Holy Experiment* (novel), Exposition Press, 1974; *Hagar* (novel), Christian Herald Books, 1978. Contributor of stories and articles to magazines and newspapers, including *Reader's Digest, Redbook, Woman's Day, Alfred Hitchcock's Mystery Magazine,* and *Christian Home.*

WORK IN PROGRESS: A biblical novel about Lydia, the seller of purple, whose story appears in the Book of Acts.

SIDELIGHTS: Lois Henderson writes: "My son was born blind, and my serious writing stemmed from a need to share our experiences with others. My first book deals with the first eight years of David's life. Our second child is adopted and some of my writing has dealt with our conviction that an adopted child is as dear to the heart as a child born to us."

* * *

HENDRICK, Irving G(uilford)   1936-

PERSONAL: Born August 30, 1936, in Los Angeles, Calif.; son of Guilford (employed in an oil refinery) and Ingeborg (a registered nurse; maiden name, Eid) Hendrick; married Sandra Lee Scheer (an artist), August 16, 1958; children: Julie Lynn, Maralene Ayn, Stephanie Lee. *Education:* Mount San Antonio Junior College, A.A., 1956; Whittier College, A.B., 1958, M.A., 1960; University of California, Los Angeles, Ed.D., 1964. *Politics:* Democrat. *Religion:* Lutheran. *Home:* 1355 Iverson Pl., Riverside, Calif. 92506. *Office:* School of Education, University of California, Riverside, Calif. 92521.

CAREER: Social studies teacher in junior high schools in

Montebello, Calif., 1959-62; University of Michigan, Flint campus, assistant professor of education, 1964-65; University of California, Riverside, assistant professor, 1965-69, associate professor, 1969-75, professor of education, 1975—, chairman of department, 1970-75, associate dean of School of Education, 1975—. Member of California Commission for Teacher Preparation and Licensing, 1977—. *Member:* American Historical Association, History of Education Society, American Educational Research Association, National Society for the Study of Education, Phi Delta Kappa. *Awards, honors:* Grant from National Institute of Education, 1973-74.

WRITINGS: Academic Revolution in California, Dawson's Book Shop, 1968; (editor with Reginald L. Jones) *Student Dissent in the Schools,* Houghton, 1972; *Public Policy Toward the Education of Non-White Minority Group Children in California, 1849-1970,* School of Education, University of California, Riverside, 1975; (contributor) Harold B. Gerard and Norman Miller, editors, *Desegregation in Riverside, California: A Longitudinal Study,* Plenum, 1975; *The Education of Non-Whites in California, 1849-1970,* R & E Research Associates, 1977; *An Educational History of California,* Boyd & Fraser, 1979. Contributor of about twenty articles and reviews to academic journals.

WORK IN PROGRESS: An analysis of federal and state policies affecting the education of American Indians.

SIDELIGHTS: Hendrick writes: "Like my writings, my career has focused on an integration of education and history. As a native Californian, most of my work has centered on the history of education in that state, with subthemes emphasizing the education of minority group children, the education of teachers, and the politics of education."

*   *   *

HENNIG, Margaret (Marie)   1940-

PERSONAL: Born April 2, 1940, in Paterson, N.J.; daughter of Paul A. and Hazel (Hess) Hennig. *Education:* Simmons College, B.S., 1962; Radcliffe College, certificate in business administration, 1963; Harvard University, M.B.A., 1964, D.B.A., 1971. *Religion:* Episcopalian. *Office:* 300 The Fenway, Boston, Mass. 02115.

CAREER: Harvard University, Cambridge, Mass., research assistant, 1964-65, associate in research, 1965-66; Simmons College, Boston, Mass., assistant professor, 1966-71, associate professor of management and director of Prince retailing program, 1971—, co-founder and joint director of graduate program in management for women, 1973—. Visiting professor at Harvard University. Business consultant in general management and organizational behavior. *Member:* American Marketing Association, Massachusetts Consumer Council Association, Harvard Business School Association, Doctoral Association of Harvard Business School.

WRITINGS: (With Anne Jardim) *The Managerial Woman* (nonfiction), Anchor Books, 1977. Contributor to journals.

WORK IN PROGRESS: A book, written in collaboration with Anne Jardim, about businessmen who feel threatened by women executives.

SIDELIGHTS: Of the 500,000 officials and managers in the United States who earn more than $25,000 annually, only 12,500—2.5 percent—are women. In their book, *The Managerial Woman,* Margaret Hennig and Anne Jardim examine why only a minuscule percentage of women command large salaries. They discovered that women tend to have a differ-

ent frame of mind about careers than men do. Women lack a team spirit, while men have been inculcated since childhood to work with others. Women consider their careers and personal lives to be separate, whereas men do not separate the two. For women, risk equals danger; for men, risk spells opportunity. Women see a job as a daily chore, while men view a job as part of a career.

In what Anthony Astrachan described as "the most interesting section of their book," Hennig and Jardim analyze the lives of twenty-five successful women executives. Material from Hennig's doctoral thesis served as the basis for this section. The authors note that this elite group of women have several factors in common: all were first-born or only children, all were extremely close to fathers who encouraged them to engage in traditionally male activities, and all had a strong sense of self-esteem and team spirit. In middle age, these women all went through a crisis stage in which they were torn between their desire to advance their careers and their desire to have a more fulfilling personal life. This conflict was eventually resolved when the women came to terms with their sexual identity and learned to develop better relationships with their friends and co-workers. At this point, many of the women got married, often to older men with families.

For those women eager to climb the corporate ladder, Hennig and Jardim offer some advice. Future managers should define their career goals clearly and should be willing to take risks. While they should acquire technical competence, they should be wary of overspecialization. Finally, aspiring women should seek out a mentor already in a high-level position. Although *The Managerial Woman* counsels women to adapt themselves to the male-dominated power structure, it also suggests ways that business could adjust to changing patterns in male and female roles. Among the suggestions are paternity leave, voluntary rather than compulsory transfers, and creation of a new work atmosphere that fosters individual growth rather than corporate conformity.

Although M. S. Strobel objected to the "overuse of sociological jargon and frequent references to Freudian psychology" in *The Managerial Woman,* he nonetheless felt that "to the woman interested in working her way up through the ranks of the American corporate structure, this volume can prove invaluable." Astrachan commented that the book "shine[s] with intelligence," and noted that it "should be required reading for future bosses, male and female, and for present feminists, male and female."

BIOGRAPHICAL/CRITICAL SOURCES: Time, May 2, 1977; *Best Sellers,* August, 1977; *New York Times Book Review,* September 18, 1977, October 23, 1977.*

*   *   *

HEPPLE, Peter   1927-

PERSONAL: Born January 2, 1927, in London, England; son of William (an executive) and Margery (Mays) Hepple; married Josephine Barnette (a teacher), July 22, 1954; children: Clare Ruth, Julia Diane. *Education:* Attended City of London School, 1940-44. *Home:* 12 Minchenden Crescent, Southgate, London N14 7EL, England. *Office: The Stage,* 19-21 Tavistock St., London W12E 7PA, England.

CAREER/WRITINGS: Member of editorial staff, *Burkes Peerage and Burkes Landed Gentry* (reference book), 1948-51; Institute of Petroleum, London, member of editorial staff, 1952-72, editor of *Journal of the Institute of Petroleum* and *Institute of Petroleum Review,* 1965-72; *The Stage* (weekly journal of British theatrical and entertainment industry), London, editor, 1972—. Theatre critic for *Where to Go in London*, 1966-77. Contributor to periodicals, including *Record Mirror*, *Show Pictorial*, *In Town Tonight*, *What's on in London*, *Plays and Players*, and *Theatre World*. Publicist for entertainers and for clubs and restaurants. *Military service:* British Army, Corps of Royal Engineers, 1945-48.

WORK IN PROGRESS: Research for a book on the history of London and British nightlife entertainment.

SIDELIGHTS: Peter Hepple is a leading authority on the theatre and entertainment industry, with an emphasis on popular entertainment rather than the arts. He told *CA* that he has a particular interest in the British nightlife scene and is often consulted in this capacity by the press and television.

* * *

HERBERT, James 1943-

PERSONAL: Born April 8, 1943, in London, England; son of Herbert (a street trader) and Kitty (Riley) Herbert; married Eileen O'Donnell, August 26, 1967; children: Kerry Jo, Emma Jane. *Education:* Attended Hornsey College of Art, 1959. *Politics:* None. *Religion:* Roman Catholic. *Home and office:* Hunter's View, Woodmancote, near Henfield, Sussex, England. *Agent:* Paul Gitlin, Ernst, Cant, Berner & Gitlin, 7 West 51st St., New York, N.Y. 10019.

CAREER: John Collings Advertising, London, England, member of staff, 1963-66; Ayer, Barker, Hegemann (advertising agency), London, art director, 1966-69, group head, 1969-71, associate director, 1971-77; full-time writer, 1977—.

WRITINGS—Novels: *The Rats*, New American Library, 1974; *The Fog*, New American Library, 1975; *The Survivor*, New English Library, 1976, New American Library, 1977; *Fluke*, New English Library, 1977.

WORK IN PROGRESS: A sequel to *The Rats;* a novel, *The Spear.*

* * *

HERSHATTER, Richard Lawrence 1923-

PERSONAL: Born September 20, 1923, in New Haven, Conn.; son of Alexander C. and Belle (Blenner) Hershatter; married Evelyn Chohat, April 4, 1948 (divorced August, 1975); children: Gail Brook, Nancy Jill, Bruce Warren. *Education:* Yale University, B.A., 1948; University of Michigan, J.D., 1951. *Home:* 29 D Stonegate, Branford, Conn. 06405. *Agent:* Jay Garon-Brook Associates, Inc., 415 Central Park W., New York, N.Y. 10024. *Office:* 35 Center St., New Haven, Conn. 06510.

CAREER: Attorney in private practice, New Haven, Conn., 1951—. Connecticut Council of School Attorneys, president, 1977—, and director. *Military service:* U.S. Army, 1941-46; became second lieutenant. *Member:* Mystery Writers of America, Connecticut Bar Association, New Haven County Bar Association.

WRITINGS: *The Spy Who Hated Licorice*, New American Library, 1966; *Fallout for a Spy*, Ace Books, 1969; *The Spy Who Hated Fudge*, Ace Books, 1970.

WORK IN PROGRESS: Another spy novel, *The Casselman Channel Is Open.*

AVOCATIONAL INTERESTS: Skiing and flying.

* * *

HERSKOWITZ, Mickey

CAREER: Writer.

WRITINGS: *Letters From Lefty* (baseball anecdotes), Houston Post Co., 1966; (with Howard Cosell) *Cosell*, Playboy Press, 1973; *Golden Age of Pro Football*, Macmillan, 1974; (with Steve Perkins) *The Greatest Little Game: A Complete How-To Book for the Coaches, Parents, Boys, and Girls in Kid Baseball*, Sheed, 1975; (with Dan Rather) *The Camera Never Blinks: Adventures of a TV Journalist*, Morrow, 1977; (with Steve Perkins) *Everything You Always Wanted to Know About Sports (But Didn't Know Where to Ask)*, New American Library, 1977; (with Walter Cunningham) *The All-American Boys*, Macmillan, 1977; (with Gene Autry) *Back in the Saddle*, Doubleday, 1978; (with George Blanda) *Over Forty, Feeling Good and Looking Great*, Simon & Schuster, 1978; (with Gene Tierney) *Self Portrait*, Wyden, in press. Also author, with Leon Jaworski, of *Days in Court.*

Contributor to periodicals, including *Ladies Home Journal* and *Good Housekeeping.*

SIDELIGHTS: Most of Mickey Herskowitz's books have been collaborations, but having a well-known co-author receive most of the attention does not disturb him. He explained to an interviewer: "I feel if I have a chance to do a book with a Dan Rather or a Gene Tierney or a Leon Jaworski or a Gene Autry, those names are going to sell a lot better than Mickey Herskowitz. It just makes sense to do their books instead of mine. I think anyone who does this would rather be doing his own work, but I don't have any false pride about it. I don't consider it stealing and I don't consider it demeaning. I find it interesting and I like the people."

BIOGRAPHICAL/CRITICAL SOURCES: *Bookviews*, October, 1978.

* * *

HERVE-BAZIN, Jean Pierre Marie 1911-
(Herve Bazin)

PERSONAL: Born April 17, 1911, in Angers, France; son of Jacques (a government official) and Paule (Guilloteaux) Herve-Bazin; married Monique Serre-Gray (a writer), May 9, 1967; children: Jacques, Jean-Paul, Maryvonne, Catherine, Cominique, Claude. *Education:* Sorbonne, University of Paris, licence es lettres, 1934. *Home:* Le Grand Courtoiseau, 45220 Trigueres, France; and 46 rue Benard, 75014 Paris, France. *Agent:* Georges Borchard, Inc., 136 East 57th St., New York, N.Y. 10022.

CAREER: Editions Grasset, Paris, France, staff member, 1953-61; *L'Information* (newspaper), Paris, critic, 1954; Editions Seuil, Paris, 1967—. President of Academie Goncourt, 1973—, and of Aide a la Creation (foundation for aiding young writers), 1974—; administrator, Centre National des Lettres, 1974—. *Military service:* French Infantry, 1940-44. *Member:* Association of Writers (vice-president), P.E.N. Club, Societe des Gens de Lettres, Societe des Auteurs Dramatiques. *Awards, honors:* Recipient of many awards, including Prix des Lecteurs, Gazette des Lettres, 1948, for *Vipere au point*, and Grand Prix de Monaco, 1967, for *Qui j'ose aimer;* Officier du Merite National, 1948; Chevalier de la Legion d'Honneur, 1970; Commander des Arts et Lettres, 1976.

*WRITINGS—*All novels, except as noted; in English: *Vipere au poing* (also see below), Odege, 1948, illustrations by Madelaine Chapsal, translation by W. J. Strachan published as *Viper in the Fist*, Prentice-Hall, 1951; *La Tete contre les murs*, Grasset, 1949, translation by Strachan published as *Head Against the Wall*, Prentice-Hall, 1952; *Leves toi et* *marche,* Grasset, 1952, translation by Herma Briffault published as *Constance,* Crown, 1955; *Qui j'ose aimer,* Le Cercle du livre de France, 1956, translation by Richard Howard published as *Tribe of Women,* Simon & Schuster, 1958, published as *An End to Passion,* Hilman Books, 1960; *Au nom de fils* (foreword and introduction in English), Seuil, 1960, translation by Howard published as *In the Name of the Son,* Simon & Schuster, 1962; *Les Bienheureux de la desolation,* Seuil, 1970, translation by Derek Coltman published as *Tristan,* Simon & Schuster, 1971.

Other: *Jours* (poetry; title means "Days"), Editions des Iles de Lerins, 1947; *A la poursuite d'Iris,* 1948; *La Mort du petit cheval* (novel; sequel to *Vipere au poing;* also see below), 1950; *Le Bureau des mariages* (collection of short stories), Grasset, 1951; *Humeurs* (poetry), Grasset, 1953; *L'Huile sur le feu* (novel), Grasset, 1954; *La Fin des asiles* (essays), Grasset, 1959; *La Clope* (novel), Marie-Claire, 1960; *La Mansarde* (novel), Fayard, 1963; *Chapeau bas* (collection of short stories), Seuil, 1963; *Plumons l'oiseau* (essays), illustrations by J. B. Fourt, Grasset, 1966; *Le Matrimoine* (novel), Le Cercle du livre de France, 1967; *Cri de la chouette* (novel; sequel to *La Mort du petit cheval*), La Presse, 1972; *Madame Ex* (novel; title means "Madame X"), Seuil, 1975; *Traits* (poetry), Seuil, 1976; *Ce que je crois* (poetry), Seuil, 1977; *Un Feu devore un autre feu* (novel), Seuil, 1978.

Contributor of articles to numerous periodicals and journals.

WORK IN PROGRESS: Three novels.

SIDELIGHTS: Herve-Bazin told *CA:* "I am primarily an author of private life and of social evolution. Although my works have been translated into twenty-six languages, I have relatively few readers in the United States. My novels are most popular in other countries, where my readers number twenty-five million." He added, "As president of the Academie Goncourt, I have had the opportunity to travel widely, including in Canada, the United States, Europe, and Africa."

Several screenplays have been adapted from Herve-Bazin's novels, including *Vipere au poing, Qui j'ose aimer,* and *Madame Ex.*

BIOGRAPHICAL/CRITICAL SOURCES: French Review, Volume XLVII, 1974.

* * *

HESS, Karl 1923-

PERSONAL: Born May 25, 1923, in Washington, D.C.; son of Carl (a broker) and Thelma (Snyder) Hess; married Yvonne Cahoon, 1943 (divorced, 1966); married Therese Machotka (an editor), January 22, 1970; children: (first marriage) Karl IV, Eric Callan. *Education:* Attended public school in Washington, D.C. *Politics:* "Libertarian." *Religion:* None. *Home address:* Kearneysville, W.Va. 25430.

CAREER: Formerly affiliated with *Aviation Week and Space Technology, Pathfinder* Magazine, and *Newsweek;* American Enterprise Institute for Public Policy Research, Washington, D.C., director of special projects, 1961-64; Republican National Committee, Washington, D.C., speech writer, 1963-64; Institute for Policy Studies, Washington, D.C., associate fellow, 1966-70; Goddard College, Plainfield, Vt., member of social ecology program faculty, 1975—. Founder of Community Technology, Inc., 1972, and of Panhandle Appropriate Technology Group, 1976. Member of Appropriate Technology Task Force of the U.S. Congress Office of Technology Assessment, 1977.

WRITINGS: In a Cause That Will Triumph: The Goldwa-

ter Campaign and the Future of Conservatism, Doubleday, 1967; (with Thomas Reeves) *The End of the Draft,* Random House, 1970; (with David Morris) *Neighborhood Power: The New Localism,* Beacon Press, 1975; *Dear America,* Morrow, 1975. Contributor to *Playboy, Penthouse, New York Times, Quest,* and other periodicals.

WORK IN PROGRESS: Community Technology, for Harper.

SIDELIGHTS: Hess told *CA:* "After becoming a successful political speechwriter (Goldwater, Ford, most Republican leaders, two Republican platforms), I moved in a direction which the FBI choses to call 'leftward.' What I actually did was go to work as a commerical welder, get arrested for demonstrating against the Indo-China war, work with Black Panthers, and teach a course on anarchism."

Hess is perhaps best known as the author of the Barry Goldwater campaign slogan: "Extremism in the defense of liberty is no vice. Moderation in the pursuit of justice is no virtue." While it appears that Hess has moved from one political extreme to its opposite, he denies that this is so. He finds more parallels between libertarian thinking and conservative belief than between traditional Republicanism or liberalism. The former have in common the "antipathy for the disutility of large organizations, such as government, which enables Hess to remain perfectly at ease with his past," Nicholas Wade explained.

Now Hess advocates "a free society in which people, without any help from city hall or Congress, organize at a local level to run their own schools, businesses and neighborhoods." He was recently involved with a community group which utilized such "soft" technology as home fish growing, hydroponic gardening on rooftops, and sewage and junk reclamation and recycling, to realize community self-sufficiency.

Because Hess is a tax resister, the Internal Revenue Service has a lien on any money he earns or property he acquires. He lives mainly by barter, a means of exchange he discussed recently in the *New York Times* Magazine. Hess wrote: "With barter, the symbol can never outpace the source. Work is exchanged for work, value is exchanged for value. Furthermore, if freely given to someone, work, or an object, represents a true transfer of something of value. Sharing your food with a neighbor (barter-charity) is an act both personal and understandable—and expectantly reciprocal, should you sometime be the needy one. There is no hint of undignified pleading as with a person facing a welfare bureaucrat. But in money-charity, say, involving the impersonal billions of the government welfare system, values are hard to keep straight."

BIOGRAPHICAL/CRITICAL SOURCES: New York Times, December 6, 1970, November 9, 1975, November 7, 1976; *Science,* January 31, 1975; *Publishers Weekly,* April 14, 1975; *Time,* May 19, 1975.

* * *

HESS, Thomas B(aer) 1920-1978

PERSONAL: Born July 14, 1920, in Rye, N.Y.; son of Gabriel Lorie and Helen (Baer) Hess; married Audrey Stern, June 29, 1944 (died, 1974); children: William, Helen, Philip. *Education:* Yale University, B.A., 1942. *Home:* 19 Beckman Pl., New York, N.Y. 10022.

CAREER: Worked at the Museum of Modern Art, New York City, 1942; *Art News* magazine, New York City, associate editor, 1946-49, executive editor, 1949-65, editor, 1965-

72; Metropolitan Museum of Art, New York City, consultative chairman of the department of twentieth-century painting, 1978. Art critic for *Le Monde,* 1967-72, and *New York* magazine, 1972-78. Director of exhibitions at the Museum of Modern Art, the New York Cultural Center, the New York State Museum in Albany, the Tate Gallery in London, England, and the Grand Palais in Paris, France. President of Longview Foundation, 1958-78. *Military service:* U.S. Army Air Forces, pilot, 1942-45. *Member:* Phi Beta Kappa.

WRITINGS: Abstract Painting: Background and American Phase, Viking, 1951; *Willem de Kooning* (monograph), Braziller, 1959; (contributor) Nathan Lyons, editor, *Aaron Siskind, Photographer,* George Eastman House, 1965; *De Kooning: Recent Paintings* (catalog), Walker, 1968; *Barnett Newman* (monograph), Walker, 1969; *Dali: Paintings and Drawings, 1965-70,* M. Knoedler, 1970; *Willem de Kooning: Drawings,* New York Graphic Society, 1972; *The Art Comics and Satires of Ad Reinhardt,* Marlborough, 1975; (contributor) *Cleve Gray: Paintings, 1966-77,* Albright-Knox Art Gallery, 1977.

Editor: (With John Ashbery) *The Grand Eccentrics: Five Centuries of Artists Outside the Main Currents of Art History,* Macmillan, 1966; (with Ashbery) *The Academy: Five Centuries of Grandeur and Misery From the Carracci to Mao Tse-tung,* Macmillan, 1967; (with Ashbery) *The Avant-Garde,* Macmillan, 1968, published as *Avant-Garde Art,* 1968; (with Ashbery) *Light, From Aten to Laser,* Macmillan, 1969, published as *Light in Art,* Collier Books, 1971; (with Ashbery) *Narrative Art,* Macmillan, 1970; (with Ashbery) *Academic Art,* Macmillan, 1971; (with Ashbery) *Painterly Painting,* Newsweek, 1971; (with Linda Nochlin) *Woman as Sex Object: Studies in Erotic Art, 1730-1970,* Newsweek, 1972; (with Elizabeth C. Baker) *Art and Sexual Politics: Women's Liberation, Women Artists, and Art History,* Macmillan, 1973.

Also author of books on Willem de Kooning's and Barnett Newman's retrospective exhibitions.

SIDELIGHTS: A highly regarded art critic, Thomas B. Hess was a booster of contemporary American painting and sculpture. His interest in abstract expressionism, particularly in the works of Willem de Kooning and Barnett Newman, spurred him to write *Abstract Painting: Background and American Phase,* considered the first serious assessment of the topic. Although Hess's enthusiasm for abstract expressionism diminished as the years went by, he still championed many of the younger artists of the sixties and seventies.

Many major exhibitions were organized by Hess. He directed the exhibitions of de Kooning and Newman, which were seen first at the Museum of Modern Art and then toured in the United States and Europe. His most highly acclaimed exhibition was "The New York School," organized for the New York State Museum at Albany. A lavish representation of the artists with whom Hess had associated, the exhibition was described by the *New York Times* as "the most spectacular display of its kind ever brought together."

Shortly before his death, Hess had accepted a post at the Metropolitan Museum of Art in New York City. As consultative chairman of the department of twentieth-century painting, he had hoped to assemble a great modern collection, and had proposed several large exhibitions. After Hess died, museum officials promised that his projects would be continued. Harold Rosenberg, also an early supporter of abstract expressionism, had died just a few days before Hess did. In a joint obituary on the two famous art critics, Mark

Stevens wrote: "Both men . . . shared the two principal traits of an important critic. They were never dull, and they were passionate advocates who helped define the art of their time."

BIOGRAPHICAL/CRITICAL SOURCES: New York Review of Books, March 9, 1967; *Book Week,* March 19, 1967; *Washington Post Book World,* October 22, 1972, December 10, 1972; *New York Times Book Review,* March 25, 1973, February 15, 1976; *New Yorker,* March 31, 1973; *Times Literary Supplement,* November 9, 1973; *New Statesman,* December 7, 1973; *New Republic,* November 20, 1976.

OBITUARIES: New York Times, July 14, 1978; *Time,* July 24, 1978; *Newsweek,* July 24, 1978.*

(Died July 13, 1978, in New York, N.Y.)

* * *

HESSELGRAVE, David J(ohn) 1924-

PERSONAL: Born January 3, 1924, in New Freedom, Wis.; son of Elbertus Leroy (a merchant) and Selma (Johnson) Hesselgrave; married Gertrude Swanson, September 16, 1944; children: David Dennis, Ronald Paul, Sheryl Ann. *Education:* Trinity Evangelical Divinity School, dipl.theol., 1944; University of Minnesota, B.A. (cum laude), 1955, M.A., 1956, Ph.D., 1965. *Home:* 2570 Hickory Lane, Deerfield, Ill. 60015. *Office:* Trinity Evangelical Divinity School, Bannockburn, Deerfield, Ill. 60015.

CAREER: Ordained minister, 1950; pastor in Radisson, Wis., 1945-47, and St. Paul, Minn., 1947-50; Evangelical Free Church of America, missionary in Japan, 1950-62; University of Minnesota, Minneapolis, instructor in speech, 1963-65; Trinity Evangelical Divinity School, Deerfield, Ill., associate professor, 1965-69, professor of mission, 1970—, director of School of World Mission of Evangelism, 1970—. Visiting professor at Evangel Theological College, 1972, and Asian Theological Seminary (Manila), 1973. First president of Japan Council of Evangelical Missions.

MEMBER: Evangelical Association of Professors of Missions (past vice-president), American Society of Missiology, Evangelical Theological Society, Pacific Broadcasting Association (vice-president). *Awards, honors:* Academia Prize from University Alumni Association of Japan, 1958.

WRITINGS: (Contributor) *Studies on Asia, 1966,* University of Nebraska Press, 1966; (editor and contributor) *Theology and Mission: Papers Given at Trinity Consultation, Number I,* Baker Book, 1978; (editor and contributor) *Dynamic Religious Movements: Case Studies of Rapidly Growing Religious Movements Around the World,* Baker Books, 1978; *Communicating Christ Cross-Culturally: An Introduction to Mission Communicating,* Zondervan, 1978. Also co-author of *I Believe: Studies in Christian Doctrine–Evangelical Free Church History and Missions,* Ministerial Association of the Evangelical Free Church of America. Contributor to *Dictionary of Ethics.* Contributor to periodicals.

WORK IN PROGRESS: A book on church development.

SIDELIGHTS: Hesselgrave writes: "My most important motivation has been my interest in, and study of, the communication of the Christian faith as contained in the Scriptures to those of other faiths or no faith." *Avocational interests:* Music (plays saxophone), photography, preparing multi-media presentations.

HESSION, Roy 1908-

PERSONAL: Born April 10, 1908, in London, England; *Religion:* Protestant. *Home:* North Dene, Beckenham Place Park, Beckenham, Kent BR3 2BS, England.

CAREER: Itinerant evangelist and Bible teacher, 1926—.

WRITINGS: (With Revel Hession) *The Calvary Road,* Christian Literature Crusade, 1950; *We Would See Jesus,* Christian Literature Crusade, 1958; *Be Filled Now,* Christian Literature Crusade, 1968; *The Way of the Cross,* Christian Literature Crusade, 1974; *When I Saw Him,* Christian Literature Crusade, 1975; *Our Nearest Kinsman,* Christian Literature Crusade, 1976; *Forgotten Factos,* Christian Literature Crusade, 1976; *From Shadow to Substance: A Rediscovery of the Inner Message of the Epistle to the Hebrews Centered Around the Words "Let Us Go On",* Zondervan, 1977; *My Calvary Road: One Man's Pilgrimage* (autobiography), Zondervan, 1978.

*   *   *

HETZELL, Margaret Carol 1917-1978

OBITUARY NOTICE: Born July 9, 1917, in Vineland, N.J.; died September 2, 1978, in Washington, D.C. Hetzell, director of communications in the public relations department of the Seventh-day Adventist Church, conducted writing workshops for the church in Africa, Borneo, Cyprus, India, Iran, the Holy Land, Canada, and the United States. She wrote scripts and directed films for the church and was the author of many religious articles and books, including *The Undaunted* and *Church PR Workbook.* Obituaries and other sources: *Who's Who in Public Relations (International),* 4th edition, PR Publishing, 1972; *Washington Post,* September 6, 1978.

*   *   *

HEWISON, Robert 1943-

PERSONAL: Born June 2, 1943, in Surrey, England; son of Robert J. P. (a civil servant) and Nancy (Henderson) Hewison. *Education:* Brasenose College, Oxford, M.A., 1965, B.Litt., 1972. *Home:* 82 Fetter Lane, London E.C.4, England. *Agent:* Michael Sissons, A. D. Peters & Co., 10 Buckingham St., London WC2N 6BU, England.

CAREER: Free-lance radio journalist, 1967—. Part-time lecturer at Winchester School of Art, 1976-77; guest curator at J. B. Speed Art Museum in Kentucky, 1977-78. *Member:* Writers' Guild of Great Britain.

WRITINGS: John Ruskin: The Argument of the Eye, Princeton University Press, 1976; (with Chris Orr) *Chris Orr's John Ruskin,* Signford, 1976; *Under Siege: Literary Life in London, 1939-45,* Oxford University Press, 1977; *Ruskin and Venice,* Thames & Hudson, 1978. Author of "The Gentle Art of Making Enemies" (documentary), British Broadcasting Corp., 1969.

WORK IN PROGRESS: In Anger: The Arts in Britain, 1945-63, publication by Oxford University Press expected in 1980; a book on the arts in Britain during the 1960's, for Oxford University Press.

SIDELIGHTS: Hewison writes: "As a professional writer, I am very concerned that all authors should be properly rewarded for their work, by the granting of a payment through the Public Lending Right for the free use of their work in the public library system. Hence my firm belief in the value of the Writers' Guild of Great Britain. Although the study of Ruskin has been (and will continue to be) a speciality, I find it helpful to alternate this with work in a more contemporary field. There is nonetheless a connection between the two areas of study, since Ruskin was one of the pioneers of the genre of cultural history which I am trying to develop."

BIOGRAPHICAL/CRITICAL SOURCES: Washington Post, December 26, 1977; *New York Times,* July 21, 1978.

*   *   *

HEWITT, Philip Nigel 1945-

PERSONAL: Born November 28, 1945, in Bicester, England; son of Jack (an electrical engineer) and Margaret (Williams) Hewitt; married Ilse Schulz, February 4, 1967; children: Madeleine, Tania, David. *Education:* Lincoln College, Oxford, B.A. (honors), 1968. *Home:* Blumenstrasse 6, Pfaffenhofen/Wuerttemberg, West Germany. *Office:* Ludwigstrasse 124, 7000 Stuttgart 1, West Germany.

CAREER: Royal Merchant Navy School, Wokingham, England, teacher of German, 1968-70; Benedict Language School, Hannover, Germany, teacher of English, 1970-71; Ernst Klett Publishing House, Stuttgart, Germany, English-language editor, 1971-77; free-lance writer, translator, and interpreter, 1977—. Co-founder and director of Lingua Travel Educational Holidays.

WRITINGS: Sudden Death (stories), Ernst Klett, 1974; *Looking at Russia* (juvenile; with own photographs), Lippincott, 1977; (with Derrick P. Jenkins) *English Conversation for All,* Ernst Klett, 1978.

WORK IN PROGRESS: Life in an East German Town, for English students, for Harrap; *Women Without Men,* a collection of stories.

SIDELIGHTS: Hewitt writes: "I had working-class parents (an Irish father and Welsh mother) and lower middle-class upbringing. I have spent most of my working life in Germany, and met my wife while working as a volunteer on a rebuilding project in Dresden. I have also traveled widely in eastern Europe."

Besides English and German, Hewitt speaks Russian, French, and some Polish.

AVOCATIONAL INTERESTS: Photography, classical music.

*   *   *

HICKEY, Edward Shelby 1928(?)-1978

OBITUARY NOTICE: Born c. 1928 in San Benito, Tex.; died November 14, 1978, in Alexandria, Va. Hickey was a foreign correspondent and news writer for Voice of America since 1956. He covered several space events and was an anchorman for coverage of the first lunar landing. He was stationed in Lagos, Nigeria, and Vietnam for extended assignments. Obituaries and other sources: *Washington Post,* November 17, 1978.

*   *   *

HIGGINS, Ronald 1929-

PERSONAL: Born July 10, 1929, in London, England; son of Robert Mold (a detective) and Jean (a dressmaker; maiden name, Richmond) Higgins; married Mary Holland (a writer), April 2, 1966 (divorced, 1971); married Elizabeth Mary Bryan (a pediatrician), September 16, 1978. *Education:* London School of Economics and Political Science, B.Sc. (first class honors), 1953; graduate study at Magdalen College, Oxford, 1953-54. *Politics:* "Social Democrat with ecological variations." *Religion:* "Post-Christian." *Home:*

40 Ripplevale Grove, London N.1, England. *Agent:* Curtis Brown Ltd., 1 Craven Hill, London W.2, England. *Office:* Richmond Fellowship, 8 Addison Rd., London W.14, England.

CAREER: British Diplomatic Service, foreign office based in London, England, 1954-56, third secretary in Tel Aviv, Israel, 1956-58, second secretary in Copenhagen, Denmark, 1958-60, private secretary to the Lord Privy Seal, 1961-63, foreign office, 1963-66; head of Chancery, Jakarta, Indonesia, 1966-67; *London Observer,* London, special adviser to editor, 1968-75; full-time writer, 1975-78; Richmond Fellowship (therapeutic communities), London, assistant director for residential services, 1978—. Head of Champernowne Trust (for psychotherapy); member of board of directors of Earth Resources Ltd.; member of board of governors of London School of Economics and Political Science. *Military service:* British Army, 1947-48; became sergeant. *Member:* Turning Point.

WRITINGS: The Seventh Enemy: The Human Factor in the Global Crisis, McGraw, 1978. Contributor to British magazines, including *Development Forum,* and newspapers.

WORK IN PROGRESS: Studying relevance of individual and group psychology to politics, therapeutic methods, and ''psycho-spiritual questions.''

SIDELIGHTS: Higgins comments: ''International experience made me gloomy about the responsiveness and far-sightedness of government. Journalism and background research impressed on me the scale and seriousness of the converging global crisis of our era. A flood of reader response to an article of mine in the *Observer* in 1975 precipitated commissions from a publisher to expand it. Three years of isolation in my Welsh border cottage finally produced the book along with a passionate intention to continue thinking and campaigning—by writing and lecturing—for global sanity.

''In the book, as in my own life, I have found myself changing focus from the general to the particular, the abstract to the immediate, the great cause to the magic (or terror) of the moment. In trying to diagnose the ills of our time I moved my main focus from the technical to the political and then, after much inward struggle, to the personal. The main threat to mankind's future is the human factor, the 'Seventh Enemy' and if collective or political inertia is one of its faces, the other is yet more significant—our individual blindness. Both as politicians and individuals we seem unwilling to acknowledge the gravity of our situation. Only a radical change in our perception could now save us from multiple calamity.

''To speak of the need for a new consciousness is not enough. In *The Seventh Enemy* I have explored seven specific directions in which we most need to develop our awareness of ourselves and our world. These include the need for rational fear, self-awareness, visionary awareness, a revaluation of the feminine, an ethic of wholeness, and a revived awareness of the transcendent. But most of all we must welcome tensions in both action and thought. There are no simple answers. Everything—even love—has its price. Mankind now walks a tightrope. Yet perhaps each of us has always done so, must always do so. And perhaps there is joy to be found in that vulnerability, as well as danger and a reconciling laughter within that joy.''

BIOGRAPHICAL/CRITICAL SOURCES: Vole, June, 1978.

HIGMAN, B(arry) W(illiam)   1943-

PERSONAL: Born September 30, 1943, in Wagga Wagga, Australia; son of William James (a farmer) and Ida (a teacher and writer; maiden name, Jordan) Higman. *Education:* University of Sydney, B.A., 1967; University of the West Indies, Ph.D. (history), 1969; University of Liverpool, Ph.D. (geography), 1971. *Office:* Department of History, University of the West Indies, Kingston 7, Jamaica.

CAREER: University of the West Indies, Kingston, Jamaica, lecturer in history, 1971—. Owner of Caldwell Press. Research fellow at Princeton University, 1976-77. *Member:* Economic History Society, Economic History Association, Caribbean Historians Association, American Archaeological Society, Society for Historical Archaeology. *Awards, honors:* Bancroft Prize in American History from Columbia University, for *Slave Population and Economy in Jamaica, 1807-1834.*

WRITINGS: The Caribbean 1975, Social Development Commission of Jamaica, 1975; *Slave Population and Economy in Jamaica, 1807-1834,* Cambridge University Press, 1976. Contributor to history, geography, Caribbean studies, and population studies journals.

WORK IN PROGRESS: Slave Society in the Caribbean.

AVOCATIONAL INTERESTS: Papermaking experiments.

* * *

HILL, Geoffrey   1932-

PERSONAL: Born June 18, 1932, in Bromsgrove, Worcestershire, England; *Education:* Graduated from Keble College, Oxford. *Residence:* Leeds, Yorkshire, England. *Office:* Department of English Literature, University of Leeds, Leeds LS2 9JT, England.

CAREER: Poet. Senior lecturer in English at University of Leeds, Leeds, Yorkshire, England. *Member:* Royal Society of Literature (fellow, 1972). *Awards, honors:* Gregory Award, 1961, for *For the Unfallen;* Hawthornden Prize, 1969, and Geoffrey Faber Memorial Prize, 1970, both for *King Log;* Whitbread Award, 1971, Alice Hunt Bartlett Prize from the Poetry Society, 1971, and Heinemann Award from the Royal Society of Literature, 1972, all for *Mercian Hymns.*

WRITINGS—Poetry: Poems (pamphlet), Oxford University Poetry Society, 1952; *For the Unfallen: Poems 1952-1958* (also see below), Deutsch, 1959, Dufour, 1960; *Preghiere* (pamphlet), Northern House, 1964; (with Edwin Brock and Stevie Smith) *Penguin Modern Poets 8,* Penguin, 1966; *King Log* (also see below), Dufour, 1968; *Mercian Hymns* (also see below), Deutsch, 1971; *Somewhere Is Such a Kingdom: Poems 1952-1971* (includes *For the Unfallen, King Log,* and *Mercian Hymns*), Houghton, 1975; *Tenebrae,* Deutsch, 1978.

Plays: *Brand* (five-act version of Henrik Ibsen's play of the same name; first produced in London at the National Theatre, April, 1978), Heinemann, 1978.

SIDELIGHTS: The past is Geoffrey Hill's domain. ''More than any modern poet in English Hill feels a deep responsibility to address the reality of history,'' explained Robert Morgan. ''Where most of his contemporaries stay with their personal experience for subject matter, or play with fantastic and vague textures, practicing an emotional nominalism, Hill works with the biography of state and race, language, the neuroses of empires, the actuality of war.'' Hill's preoccupation with history does not mean that he should be shunned by modern readers. His poetry is concerned with universal themes: war, death, suffering, God, and love.

As Hill examines history, he discovers both the brutal and the beautiful, with the emphasis upon the brutal. Although some commentators have faulted him for his obsession with violence, it is Hill himself who seems most concerned that he may be exploiting cruel incidents that have occurred in the past. According to Morgan, Hill is "suspicious, even ashamed, of art which cultivates and feeds on the violence, waste, and suffering of human experience." Indeed, Hill grows to distrust the very words he uses to depict savagery and suffering. Edward Hirsch pointed out the paradox at the center of Hill's work: "the apparent meaninglessness of sacrifice, the abandonment of those who suffer, the erosion of logos, in fact the impotence and impossibility of speech in the face of wholesale destruction seem to undercut the very possibility of poetry."

Hill's interest in history is reflected in his traditional style. Unlike many modern poets, Hill does not shy away from regular rhyme schemes or metric patterns. His style is usually described as powerful, formal, and controlled. "In most of his poems Hill tries to convey extreme emotions by opposing the restraint of established form to the violence of his insight or judgment," observed Irvin Ehrenpreis. "He uses savage puns, heavy irony, and repeated oxymorons. He uses bold, archetypal images and religious symbols while complaining of their inefficacy." Calvin Bedient noted that a strain of sensuality counterbalances the strict control of Hill's verse: "The writing is at once austere and passionately sensuous, the two qualities coming together in a kind of menace."

The reader who turns to Hill's poetry must be prepared to work. Roger Hecht remarked that many of Hill's poems are "made brilliant by a fury a great part of which is suppressed. That means that the reader must, alas, work and work as hard as Mr. Hill has done and does in order to supply to the occasions all that the poet has omitted." Despite the difficulty of Hill's verse, few readers would deny its significance. Hill's talent for using the oblique to illuminate, for writing in a traditional yet original manner, and for making the past meaningful to the present, has caused many to consider him one of the finest British poets writing today.

BIOGRAPHICAL/CRITICAL SOURCES: Poetry, May, 1967, September, 1969, June, 1972, July, 1976; *Observer Review,* August 25, 1968; *Listener,* September 5, 1968; *London Magazine,* December, 1968; *Times Literary Supplement,* August 27, 1971, June 16, 1978; Michael Schmidt and Grevel Lindop, editors, *British Poetry Since 1960: A Critical Survey,* Carcanet, 1972; *Parnassus: Poetry in Review,* spring/summer, 1973, spring/summer, 1976; *Contemporary Literary Criticism,* Gale, Volume 5, 1976, Volume 8, 1978; *New York Times Book Review,* January 11, 1976; *New York Review of Books,* January 22, 1976; *Christian Science Monitor,* February 11, 1976; *Yale Review,* spring, 1976; *Sewanee Review,* summer, 1976.

*   *   *

HILL, James
    See JAMESON, (Margaret) Storm

*   *   *

HILTON, Conrad N(icholson)   1887-1979

OBITUARY NOTICE: Born December 25, 1887, in San Antonio, N.M.; died January 3, 1979, in Santa Monica, Calif. Hotel executive and author. Hilton's initial investment of $5,000 in a hotel chain sixty years ago burgeoned into a fortune of more than one-half billion dollars by the time of his death. There are presently 185 Hilton Hotels in the United States and 75 abroad. Hilton also established the Carte Blanche credit card company. His autobiography, *Be My Guest,* was distributed in his hotel rooms. Obituaries and other sources: Max Gunther, *The Very, Very Rich and How They Got That Way,* Playboy Press, 1972; *Celebrity Register,* 3rd edition, Simon & Schuster, 1973; *The International Who's Who,* Europa, 1974; *Who's Who,* 128th edition, St. Martin's, 1976; *Who's Who in America,* 40th edition, Marquis, 1978; *Newsweek,* January 15, 1979.

*   *   *

HINTON, S(usan) E(loise)   1950-

PERSONAL: Born in Tulsa, Okla.; married David Inhofe, September, 1970. *Education:* Graduated from University of Tulsa, 1970. *Residence:* Tulsa, Okla.

CAREER: Began writing at the age of sixteen; lived for six months in southern Spain. *Awards, honors: That Was Then, This Is Now* was chosen as a notable book by the American Library Association; *The Outsiders* was chosen by the *New York Herald Tribune* as one of the best teen-age books for 1967, and received the *Media & Methods* Maxi Award in 1975; both books were selected as Honor Books in the *Chicago Tribune Book World's* Children's Spring Book Festival.

*WRITINGS—*Fiction: *The Outsiders,* Viking, 1967; *That Was Then, This Is Now,* Viking, 1971; *Rumble Fish,* Delacorte, 1975.

SIDELIGHTS: Hinton enjoyed reading books as an adolescent, but was dismayed to find only a small segment of a teen-ager's life depicted in literature. To remedy this oversight, the young author began to write about teens in a setting she felt would be familiar to her contemporaries. Ms. Hinton's *The Outsiders* was loosely based on the gang-oriented life-style of her fellow high school classmates. In reviewing the book, a critic for the *New York Times* commented: "Can sincerity overcome cliches? In this book by a now 17-year-old author, it almost does the trick. By almost any standard, Miss Hinton's performance is impressive. . . ." A *Saturday Review* critic expressed a similar view, noting that *The Outsider* is "written with distinctive style by a teen-ager who is sensitive, honest and observant. . . ."

While Hinton's first book was acclaimed by book critics and applauded by the younger generation, many parents objected to the characters' unruly and often violent nature. Some adults became concerned that the storyline might encourage teens to idolize a life of lawlessness and destruction, while others felt it was wrong for young people to be exposed to violence in literature under any circumstances. Nevertheless, it was the publication and success of *The Outsider* that enabled Hinton to attend the University of Tulsa.

Hinton's latest book, *Rumble Fish,* continues the theme of delinquent youths. A reviewer for *Horn Book* observed, "The dialogue and the boy's monologue are vibrant and authentic, and the narrative moves quickly and dramatically from one event to another." In addition however, the critic noted, Hinton's "writing has the same style and the same perception as it had when she was seventeen. Instead of becoming a vehicle for growth and development, the book, unfortunately, simply echoes what came before. . . ."

BIOGRAPHICAL/CRITICAL SOURCES: New York Times Book Review, May 7, 1967; Saturday Review, May 13, 1967, January 27, 1968; Horn Book, December, 1975; Children's Literature Review, Gale, Volume 3, 1978.*

* * *

HISAMATSU, (Hoseki) Shin'ichi 1889-

PERSONAL: Born June 5, 1889, in Gifu City, Japan. Education: Kyoto Imperial University (now Kyoto University), M.A., 1915. Home: 228, 3 Chome, Takami, Nagara, Gifu City, Japan 502.

CAREER: Kyoto University, Kyoto, Japan, lecturer, 1932-37, assistant professor of science of religion and of Buddhism, 1937-46, professor of Buddhism, 1946-49; Kyoto Municipal University of Fine Arts, professor of science of religion and chief librarian, 1953-63. Lecturer at Rinzaishu-Hanazono College, Ryukoku University, University of Ohtani, Bukkyo University, and Kyushu University. Vice-chairman of Suzuki Research Foundation, Tokyo; adviser to Institute of Zen Studies and Eastern Buddhist Association of Religious Studies. Member: Nihon-Shukyo-Gaku-Kai (honorary member). Awards, honors: Senior Grade of the Fifth Court Rank, 1946; Purple Ribbon Medal, 1961; Third Order of Merit with the Order of the Sacred Treasure; Tantansai Prize for Tea Art Culture, 1975.

WRITINGS: Zen to Bijutsu (text in English), Bokubisha (Kyoto), 1958; (editor with Keiji Nishitani), Zen no honshitsu to ningen no shinri (title means "The Essence of Zen and the Truth of Man"), Sobunsha (Tokyo), 1969; Hisamatsu shin'ichi chosakushu (title means "Collection of Writings"), Risosha (Tokyo), Volume I: Toyoteki mu (title means "Oriental Nothingness"), 1969, Volume II: Zettai shutai do (title means "The Way of the Ultimately Fundamental Subject"), 1972, Volume III: Kaku to sozo (title means "Awakening and Creation"), 1971, Volume IV: Sado no tetsugaku (title means "The Philosophy of the Art of Tea"), 1973, Volume V: Zen to geijutsu (title means "Zen and Art"), 1970, Volume VI: Kyorokusho (title means "Selections From Lectures on Buddhist Scriptures and Zen Texts"), 1973, Volume VII: Nin-in-shu (title means "Resting in My Destiny"; collection of aesthetic works and pictures), in press, Volume VIII: Ha-soai (title means "Broken Straw Sandals"; collection of character sketches, letters from travels abroad, and comments on current events), 1974; Die Fulle des nichts, translation by Takashi Hirata and Johanna Fisher from original Japanese manuscript, Neske, 1971; Zen and the Fine Arts, Kodansha International (Tokyo), 1975. Contributor of articles to periodicals in his field.

WORK IN PROGRESS: Philosophy of Postmodernist World History.

SIDELIGHTS: Brought up as a devout Buddhist, Hisamatsu began questioning his faith when in his teens. He explains, "It was because the free, critical mind and the spirit of autonomy which had begun to awaken within me, coupled with the scientific knowledge I had been acquiring more and more, quickly developed my awareness of modern humanism." He found himself drawn to the field of philosophy where he felt free "to question and criticize religions, scriptures, dogmas, churches, and even God or Buddha...." Hisamatsu was influenced by the works of Kitaro Nishida, a "genius philosopher of unearthly temperment" who taught at Kyoto University.

BIOGRAPHICAL/CRITICAL SOURCES: Alcopley, Listening to Heidegger and Hisamatsu, Bokubi Press (Kyoto), 1963; Asahi Shinbun, July, 1966.

HITE, Shere D. 1942-

PERSONAL: Born November 2, 1942, in St. Joseph, Mo. Education: University of Florida, B.A. (cum laude), 1964, M.A., 1968; further graduate study at Columbia University, 1968-69. Home: New York, N.Y., and Laffont, 6 Place St., Sulpice, Paris 75006, France. Office: 47 East 19th St., New York, N.Y. 10003.

CAREER: National Organization for Women (NOW), New York City, director of Feminist Sexuality Project, 1972—. Instructor in female sexuality at New York University, 1977—; lecturer at Harvard University, McGill University, Columbia University, and for numerous women's groups. Member: National Organization for Women (NOW), Society for the Scientific Study of Sex, Women's Health Network.

WRITINGS: Sexual Honesty By Women For Women, Warner, 1974; The Hite Report: A Nationwide Study of Female Sexuality, Macmillan, 1976.

WORK IN PROGRESS: A study of "male sexuality and the politics of private life," publication by Knopf expected in 1980.

SIDELIGHTS: Hite was a doctoral candidate in the history of ideas when she began distributing questionnaires on female sexuality. The questionnaires were advertised in magazines (Village Voice, Brides, Mademoiselle, Oui, and Ms.), in her first book, church newsletters, and through certain chapters of the National Organization for Women (NOW). Of the 100,000 questionnaires distributed, 3,019 were returned and 1,844 responses of women aged fourteen to seventy-eight were tabulated statistically. (The remaining questionnaires were received too late to be tabulated, although many of the responses are quoted in the text.)

The Hite Report was an immediate bestseller and was placed in the company of such classic works on sexuality as the Kinsey report and the Masters and Johnson reports. Although statistical analyses are included and conclusions are drawn by the author, the bulk of the The Hite Report is quotations from women who answered the questionnaire on a variety of sexual topics. "Reading The Hite Report," Karen Durbin wrote, "is rather like sitting in on a mass-consciousness raising session about female sexuality. Women talk in unusual detail about their sexual experiences and feelings—graphically, factually, rapturously, glumly, and sometimes brutally . . ." The book, Erica Jong explained, can be seen as the "culmination of the trend" to let women "speak in their own words about what they liked, felt, thought . . ."

The conclusion Hite draws is that a revision of current notions of sexuality is necessary for women to achieve sexual fulfillment. She faults the male-oriented, reproductive pattern of sexual expression for many of women's sexual difficulties: "There has rarely been any acknowledgement that female sexuality might have a complex nature of its own which would be more than just the logical counterpart of (what we think of as) male sexuality."

Some reviewers have been put off by what they regard as Hite's feminist bias. Others have found the study based on shaky scientific ground. James Wolcott, who called the book "a 478-page bull session," thought it was "dubious as sociology, drear and dry as literature, and hopelessly muddled as polemic." (Durbin wrote in response: "The book is like a bull session, but that's precisely what I found valuable about it and what I suspect may be a major reason for its popularity. Perhaps he doesn't realize women rarely have bull sessions about sex.") Carol Tavris, writing in Psychology To-

day, said that "Hite's real mistake was to try to make an unscientific study seem scientific." On the first questionnaire (there were four different questionnaires used), Hite didn't ask for demographic information from respondents because she didn't want researchers' categories to interfere with the stories women had to tell. But in the text of the book, complained Tavris, "Hite proceeded to construct categories. Masturbation, it seems, can be broken into six types. . . . But this effort at 'statistical' precision, which borders on the comical, advances neither sexual liberation nor sex research."

Wolcott found what he called Hite's "pleasure-lobbying" depressing. Durbin, however, wrote: "Whatever the limitations of *The Hite Report,* its intentions are more than mechanistic hedonism. If it lobbies for anything, it's for illumination and understanding of a dimension of women's experience that may always remain somewhat mysterious but has so far only been needlessly mystified." Jong predicted that *The Hite Report* "could have as much impact on sexual mores in this country as the Kinsey reports. Women who read it will feel enormously reassured about their own sexuality and if enough men read it, the quality of sex in America is bound to improve."

AVOCATIONAL INTERESTS: Vintage movies and opera.

BIOGRAPHICAL/CRITICAL SOURCES: New York Times Book Review, October 3, 1976; *Newsweek,* October 18, 1976; *Time,* October 25, 1976; *Village Voice,* November 1, 1976; *Psychology Today,* December, 1976; *Mademoiselle,* January, 1977; *Book World,* March 13, 1977.

*　　　*　　　*

HITTI, Philip K(huri) 1886-1978

OBITUARY NOTICE—See index for *CA* sketch: Born June 24, 1886, in Shimlan, Lebanon; died December 24, 1978, in Princeton, N.J. Educator and author. Hitti was regarded by many as an expert in Arabic and Islamic culture and was instrumental in encouraging recognition of Arab culture in the United States. Among his many works on Arab culture are *History of the Arabs, Arabs: A Short History, Lebanon in History,* and *The Near East in History.* Obituaries and other sources: *Current Biography,* Wilson, 1947; *Directory of American Scholars,* Volume I: *History,* 6th edition, Bowker, 1974; *The International Who's Who,* Europa, 1978; *Who's Who in America,* 40th edition, Marquis, 1978; *New York Times,* December 28, 1978; *Washington Post,* December 30, 1978.

*　　　*　　　*

HOBBS, (Carl) Fredric 1931-

PERSONAL: Born December 30, 1931, in Philadelphia, Pa.; son of Robert Frederic and Gertrude (Madison) Hobbs; children: Leslie Newbold, Mary Alison. *Education:* Cornell University, B.A., 1953; attended Academie de San Fernando de Belles Artes, Madrid, 1955-56. *Politics:* Democrat. *Religion:* Episcopalian. *Home:* Box 334, Los Altos, Calif. 94022.

CAREER: Artist, filmmaker, writer. Fredric Hobbs Films, Inc., San Francisco, Calif., president, 1971-75; Madison Hobbs Companies, Inc., San Francisco, president, 1975-78. President of Virginia City Restoration Corp. in Nevada, 1976-79. Has been commissioned to create art works by Big Sur Redwoods Episcopal Church, 1962, and Hall of Spirits, 1972-73. One-man shows have been held at California Palace

Legion of Honor, San Francisco, 1958, and Museum of Science and Industry, Los Angeles, 1976. Exhibits have been held at various institutes, including Pennsylvania Academy of Fine Arts, Philadelphia, 1964, Smithsonian Institution, Washington, D.C., 1964, and Institute of Contemporary Art, Philadelphia, 1970. Permanent collections of his work are housed at Museum of Modern Art, Metropolitan Museum of Art, Finch College Museum, Oakland Museum of Art, and Spencer Memorial Church, Brooklyn, N.Y. *Military service:* U.S. Air Force, 1953-55; became lieutenant. *Member:* Commodore Club, Virginia City Yacht Club.

WRITINGS: (With Warren Hinckle III, and illustrator) *Richest Place on Earth: The Story of Virginia City, Nevada, and the Heyday of the Comstock Lode,* Houghton, 1978; *Paradise on Earth: An Illustrated History of the Monterey Coast,* California Living Books, in press. Author, producer and director of six screenplays, including "The Monster and Mr. Hughes," Troika Emerson, 1970, "Roseland," Boxoffice International, 1971, "Alabama's Ghost," Ellman Enterprises, 1972, and "The Richest Place on Earth," 1979. Contributor of numerous articles to periodicals.

WORK IN PROGRESS: Eat Your House: An Art Eco Guide to the Future.

SIDELIGHTS: Hobbs told *CA:* "It is the responsibility of the enlightened individual to change his environment into an art form."

*　　　*　　　*

HOBBS, Williston C. 1925(?)-1978

OBITUARY NOTICE: Born c. 1925 in Washington, D.C.; died November 12, 1978, in Largo, Md. Hobbs was a professor of mathematics and the author of textbooks in his field. Obituaries and other sources: *Washington Post,* November 16, 1978.

*　　　*　　　*

HOBBY, Oveta Culp 1905-

PERSONAL: Born January 19, 1905, in Killeen, Tex.; daughter of I. W. and Emma (Hoover) Culp; married William P. Hobby, February 23, 1931 (died, 1964); children: William, Jessica (Mrs. Henry E. Catto, Jr.). *Education:* Attended Mary Hardin-Baylor College. *Religion:* Episcopalian. *Residence:* Houston, Tex. *Office:* Houston Post, 4747 Southwest Frwy., Houston, Tex.

CAREER: Texas House of Representatives, Austin, parliamentarian, 1926-31; *Houston Post,* Houston, Tex., 1931—, began as research editor, became literary editor, assistant editor, vice-president, executive vice-president, editor, and publisher, president and editor, 1955-65, editor and chairman of board of directors of Houston Post Co., 1965—. Director of KPRC-Radio and TV, 1945-53; chairman of board of directors of Channel II TV Co., 1970—; chairman of KPRC Radio Co., 1970—. Chief of woman's interest section of War Department's Bureau of Public Relations, 1941-42; member of Federal Security Administration, 1953; secretary of U.S. Department of Health, Education, and Welfare, 1953-55. Member of board of directors of National Conference of Christians and Jews, Advisory Committee for Economic Development, 1956—, Houston Symphony Society, General Aniline & Film Corp., 1965-67, General Foods Corp., Corp. for Public Broadcasting, 1968-72; member of board of trustees of American Assembly, 1957-66, Eisenhower Birthplace Memorial Park, Eisenhower Exchange Fellowships, Mutual Insurance Co. of New York, 1956-72, Eleanor Roosevelt Memorial Foundation, Rice University, 1967-75; member of advisory board of George C. Marshall Research Foundation; member of national board of development of Sam Rayburn Foundation. Member of Carnegie Commission on Educational Television, 1965-67, National Advisory Commission on Selective Service, 1966-67, and Health, Education, and Welfare Education Task Force, 1966; member of President's Committee on Employment of the Physically Handicapped and Committee on Civilian National Honors. Member of national committee of American Museum of Immigration, 1956, and national advisory board of Navy-Marine Corps Memorial Stadium, 1957-58; member of American Design Awards Committee and Business Committee for the Arts, 1967—; sponsor of Clark School for the Deaf. *Military service:* Women's Army Auxiliary Corps, 1942-45, director, 1942, commander, 1943-45; served in the Philippines; became colonel.

MEMBER: Institute of International Education (member of regional advisory board), Society for Rehabilitation of the Facially Disfigured (member of board of trustees), Crusade for Freedom, Cuban Freedom Committee, Texas Heart Association (member of board of directors), University of Texas Committee of Seventy-Five, Gamma Alpha Chi (honorary vice-chairman), Houston Country Club, Bayou Club, Ramada Club, Junior League Club. *Awards, honors:* Honorary degrees include: LL.D. from Baylor University, Sam Houston State Teachers College, and University of Chattanooga, 1943, Bryant College and Ohio Wesleyan University, 1953, Columbia University, Smith College, and Middlebury College, 1954, University of Pennsylvania and Colby College, 1955, and Fairleigh Dickinson University and Western College, 1956; D.H.L. from Bard College, 1950, and Lafayette College, 1954; D.Litt. from Colorado Women's College, 1947, and C. W. Post College of Long Island University, 1962; D.H. from Mary Hardin-Baylor College, 1956. Honor award for journalism from University of Missouri, 1950; publisher of the year award from Headliners Club, 1960; Living History Award from Research Institute of America, 1960; honor award from National Jewish Hospital, 1962; award from Carnegie Corp., 1967, for advancement and diffusion of knowledge and understanding.

WRITINGS: Mr. Chairman: Rules, and Examples in Story Form, of Parliamentary Procedure Written Expressly for Use in the Elementary Schools and the Junior High Schools, Economy Co., 1936. Author of "Mr. Chairman," a syndicated newspaper column.

* * *

HOBSON, Harold 1904-

PERSONAL: Born August 4, 1904, in Sheffield, England; son of Jacob (an insurance agent) and Minnie (McKegg) Hobson; married Gladys Bessie Johns, July 13, 1935; children: Margaret (Mrs. N.A.O. Lyttelton). *Education:* Oriel College, Oxford, B.A., 1928, M.A., 1935. *Politics:* "Pragmatic." *Religion:* Christian Scientist. *Home:* 905 Nelson House, Dolphin Sq., London S.W.1, England. *Office:* 200 Gray's Inn Rd., London W.C.1, England.

CAREER: Christian Science Monitor, London, England, drama critic, 1933-42; *Sunday Times,* London, England, assistant literary editor, 1942-48, assistant drama critic, 1944-47, drama critic, 1947-76; free-lance writer, 1976—. Member of board of governors of National Theatre, 1976—. *Member:* Critics Circle (president, 1955; member of council), Beefsteak Club, Garrick Club, Athenaeum Club. *Awards, honors:* Chevalier, French Legion of Honor, 1959; commander,

Order of the British Empire, 1971, knighted, 1977; honorary fellow of Oriel College, Oxford, 1974; D.Litt. from University of Sheffield, 1977.

WRITINGS: The First Three Years of the War: A Day-by-Day Record, Hutchinson, 1942; *The Devil in Woodford Wells* (novel), Longmans, Green, 1946; *Theatre,* Longmans, Green, 1948; *Verdict at Midnight: Sixty Years of Dramatic Criticism,* Longmans, Green, 1952; *The Theatre Now,* Longmans, Green, 1953; *French Theatre Today: An English View,* Arno, 1953; *Ralph Richardson: An Illustrated Study of Sir Ralph's Work, With a List of His Appearances on Stage and Screen,* Macmillan, 1958; (with Phillip Knightley and Leonard Russell) *Pearl of Days: Intimate Memoir of the "Sunday Times," 1822-1972,* Hamish Hamilton, 1972; *Indirect Journey* (autobiography), Weidenfeld & Nicolson, 1978; *The French Theatre Since 1830,* J. Calder, 1978. Also author of *Theatre II,* 1950. Television critic for *Listener,* 1947-51. Contributor to magazines. Editor of *International Theatre Annual,* 1956-60.

SIDELIGHTS: Hobson told *CA:* "I write in order to earn a living. I have no lofty motivation or high-falutin' purpose. My main, indeed exclusive, area of vocational interest is the theatre. I have traveled in the United States, Spain, Italy, and (extensively) in France." *Avocational interests:* Watching cricket, playing bridge.

* * *

HOCKS, Richard A(llen) 1936-

PERSONAL: Born June 30, 1936, in Cincinnati, Ohio; son of Harry Joseph and Marie (Meinhart) Hocks; married Elaine Dowling, August 3, 1957; children: Richard A., Jr., Robert, Stephen, Mary. *Education:* University of Notre Dame, B.A., 1957; University of North Carolina, Ph.D., 1965. *Religion:* Roman Catholic. *Home:* 401 South Glenwood, Columbia, Mo. 65201. *Office:* Department of English, University of Missouri, Columbia, Mo. 65201.

CAREER: University of Missouri—Columbia, assistant professor, 1965-71, associate professor, 1971-76, professor of English, 1976—. *Member:* International Institute of Philosophy and Literature, Modern Language Association of America. *Awards, honors:* National Book Award nomination from American Academy and Institute of Arts and Letters, 1974, for *Henry James and Pragmatistic Thought.*

WRITINGS: Henry James and Pragmatistic Thought, University of North Carolina Press, 1974; (contributor) Shirley Sugarman, editor, *The Evolution of Consciousness: Studies in Polarity,* Wesleyan University Press, 1976; (with J. Donald Crowley) *The Wings of the Dove,* critical edition, Norton, 1978.

WORK IN PROGRESS: A book on the nature of transition in literary history.

* * *

HODGES, Louis W. 1933-

PERSONAL: Born January 24, 1933, in Eupora, Miss.; son of John Calvin (a mail carrier) and Lorene (Phillips) Hodges; married Helen Elizabeth Davis, June 6, 1954; children: John David, George Kenneth. *Education:* Millsaps College, B.A., 1954; Duke Divinity School, B.D., 1957; Duke University, Ph.D., 1970. *Politics:* Democrat. *Religion:* Methodist. *Home address:* Route 5, Box 334, Lexington, Va. 24450. *Office:* Department of Religion, Washington and Lee University, Lexington, Va. 24450.

CAREER: Washington and Lee University, Lexington,

Va., assistant professor, 1960-64, associate professor, 1964-68, professor of religion, 1968—, director of "Society and the Professions: Studies in Applied Ethics," 1974—. Visiting professor at University of Virginia, summers, 1966-73. President of Rocibridge Area Housing Corp., 1968-75. *Member:* American Society of Christian Ethics, National Rifle Association.

WRITINGS: (With Harmon L. Smith) *The Christian and His Decisions: An Introduction to Christian Ethics,* Abingdon, 1969; (editor) *Social Responsibility,* Washington and Lee University, Volume I: *Journalism,* 1975, Volume II: *Law,* Volume III: *Medicine,* 1977.

WORK IN PROGRESS: Ethics and Journalism.

SIDELIGHTS: Hodges writes: "My initial interest in ethics grew from concern with treatment blacks typically received in Mississippi during my childhood. A liberal Democrat politically and an orthodox Christian theologically, I am influenced heavily by Reinhold Niebuhr and Walter Rauschenbusch." *Avocational interests:* Beekeeping, gunsmithing, the outdoors.

*   *   *

HOFFENBERG, Jack   1906-1977

PERSONAL: Born February 8, 1906, in Baltimore, Md.; son of Bernard and Faye (Buch) Hoffenberg; married Mary Joel Kramer (a public information officer), October 5, 1939. *Education:* Attended Baltimore City College and University of Maryland; studied sculpture under Reuben Kramer. *Politics:* Democrat.

CAREER: Kaufman Advertising Agency, Washington, D.C., account executive, 1937-40; Jack Hoffenberg Advertising, Baltimore, Md., owner, 1945-54; writer, 1954-77. *Military service:* U.S. Army, 1942-45; became major.

WRITINGS: Sow Not in Anger (Doubleday Book Club selection), Dutton, 1961; *A Hero for Regis,* Dutton, 1963; *A Thunder at Dawn,* Dutton, 1965; *Forge of Fury,* Avon, 1967; *Reap in Tears,* Avon, 1969; *Anvil of Passion,* Avon, 1971; *A Time for Pagans,* Avon, 1971; *A Raging Talent,* Avon, 1973; *The Desperate Adversaries,* Crown, 1975; *Seventeen Ben Gurian,* Putnam, 1977. Also author of teleplay, "The Powers," and unpublished manuscript, "The Inheritors."

SIDELIGHTS: All of Hoffenberg's books have been published abroad.

(Died March 23, 1977)

*   *   *

HOFFMAN, Jo Ann S.   1942-

PERSONAL: Born November 19, 1942, in Toledo, Ohio; daughter of James George (in industrial relations) and Mary Margaret (a teacher; maiden name, Hunt) Steger; married William Hubert Hoffman (a physician), June 26, 1965; children: Martin, Emily. *Education:* Mary Manse College, B.A., 1964; attended Marygrove College, University of Louisville, and University of Windsor. *Residence:* Grosse Pointe Park, Mich.

CAREER: Teacher in Indianapolis, Ind., and Louisville, Ky.; free-lance journalist in Detroit, Mich., 1976—. *Awards, honors:* First prize from Poetry Society of Michigan, 1978, for juvenile poem.

WRITINGS: Martin's Invisible Invention (juvenile), Judson, 1977. Contributor to automobile dealer publications.

WORK IN PROGRESS: A novel for young adults.

HOFFMANN, Peter (Conrad Werner)   1930-

PERSONAL: Born August 13, 1930, in Dresden, Germany; son of Wilhelm (a librarian) and Elfriede Frances (a sculptor; maiden name, Mueller) Hoffmann; married Helga Luise Hobelsberger (a teacher), July 22, 1959; children: Peter Friedrich Georg Wilhelm, Susan Judith Gudula. *Education:* Attended University of Stuttgart, 1953-54, University of Tuebingen, 1954-55, University of Zurich, 1955, and Northwestern University, 1955-56; University of Munich, Ph.D., 1961. *Home:* 4332 Montrose Ave., Montreal, Quebec, Canada H3Y 2A9; and Rosshaustrasse 4, Stuttgart 70, Germany. *Agent:* Niedieck Linder Aktien—Gesellechaft, Gerechtigkeitgasse 23, 8039 Zurich, Switzerland. *Office:* Department of History, McGill University, 855 Sherbrooke St. W., Montreal, Quebec, Canada H3A 2T7.

CAREER: University of Maryland, Heidelberg, Germany, lecturer in history, 1961-65; University of Northern Iowa, Cedar Falls, assistant professor, 1965-68, associate professor of history, 1968-70; McGill University, Montreal, Quebec, professor of history, 1970—. Lecturer at Schiller College, 1964-65. *Member:* Canadian Committee for the History of the Second World War, American Committee for the History of the Second World War, Wuerttembergischer Geschichtskund Altertumsverein, Deutsche Schillergesellschaft, Sigma Alpha Epsilon.

WRITINGS: Die diplomatischen Beziehungen zwischen Wuerttemberg und Bayern im Krimkrieg und bis zum Beginn der Italienischen Krise 1853-1858 (title means "Diplomatic Relations Between Wuerttemberg and Bavaria During the Crimean War and to the Beginning of the Italian Crisis, 1833-1858"), W. Kohlhammer Verlag, 1963; *Widerstand, Staatsstreich, Attentat: Der Kampf der Opposition gegen Hitler* (title means "Resistance, Coup d'Etat, Assassination: The Struggle of the Opposition to Hitler"), R. Piper, 1969, 3rd edition, 1977, translation by Richard Barry published as *The History of the German Resistance 1933-1945,* M.I.T. Press, 1977; *Die Sicherheit des Diktators: Hitlers Leibwachen, Schutzmassnahmen, Residenzen, Hauptquartiere* (title means "The Security of the Dictator: Hitler's Bodyguards, Protective Measures, Residences, Headquarters"), R. Piper, 1975; *Hitler's Personal Security,* M.I.T. Press, 1979.

Contributor: Franklin H. Littell and Hubert G. Locke, editors, *The German Church Struggle and the Holocaust,* Wayne State University Press, 1974; Hans Juergen Schultz, editor, *Der zwanzigste Juli: Alternative zu Hitler?* (title means "The Twentieth of July: Alternative to Hilter?"), Kreuz Verlag, 1974; George L. Mosse, editor, *Police Forces in History,* Sage Publications, 1975. Contributor to German, Canadian, and American history journals.

WORK IN PROGRESS: Studying the intellectual background of the Stauffenberg brothers and the correspondence of William I of Wuerttemberg.

BIOGRAPHICAL/CRITICAL SOURCES: Washington Post, May 15, 1977; *New York Times,* June 13, 1977.

*   *   *

HOFFMANN, Stanley (H.)   1928-

PERSONAL: Born November 27, 1928, in Vienna, Austria; came to United States, 1955, naturalized citizen, 1960; married Inge Schneier. *Education:* Institut d'Etudes Politiques, diploma, 1948; Harvard University, M.A., 1952; University of Paris, Ph.D., 1953. *Home:* 91 Washington Ave., Cambridge, Mass. 02140. *Office:* Department of Political Science, Harvard University, Cambridge, Mass.

CAREER: French Political Science Association, Paris, France, assistant, 1952-53; Harvard University, Cambridge, Mass., instructor, 1955-57, assistant professor, 1957-59, associate professor, 1959-63, professor of government, 1963—, chairman of Center for European Studies. Member: American Academy of Arts and Sciences, American Political Science Association, American Society of International Law, Council on Foreign Relations, Association Francaise de Science Politique. Awards, honors: Carnegie Prize in International Organization, 1955.

WRITINGS: Organisations internationales et pouvoirs politiques des etats (title means "International Organizations and Political Powers of States"), A. Colin, 1954; Le Mouvement poujade (title means "The Poujade Movement"), A. Colin, 1956; Contemporary Theory in International Relations, Prentice-Hall, 1960; (with Robert Richardson Bowie) In Search of France, Harvard University Press, 1963; The State of War, Praeger, 1965; Gulliver's Troubles; or, The Setting of American Foreign Policy, McGraw, 1968; (editor) Conditions of World Order, Houghton, 1968; (editor) The Relevance of International Law, Schenkman, 1968; Decline or Renewal?: France Since the 1930's, Viking, 1974; Sur la France (title means "On France"), Editions du Seuil, 1976; Primacy or World Order, McGraw, 1978. Contributor to Foreign Policy, Foreign Affairs, and Daedalus.

WORK IN PROGRESS: Studies of the French Fifth Republic and of France, 1934-44.

BIOGRAPHICAL/CRITICAL SOURCES: New York Times Book Review, June 18, 1978.

*   *   *

HOFFNUNG, Michele   1944-
(Michele Hoffnung Garskof)

PERSONAL: Born April 10, 1944, in New York, N.Y.; daughter of Abraham and Peninah (Hoffmann) Hoffnung; married Bertram E. Garskof, 1966 (divorced, 1975); children: Joshua, Jesse. Education: Rutgers University, B.A. (honors), 1965; University of Michigan, Ph.D., 1969. Home: 34 Ellsworth Ave., New Haven, Conn. 06511. Office: Department of Psychology, Quinnipiac College, P.O. Box 119, Hamden, Conn. 06518.

CAREER: University of Virginia, Mary Washington College, Fredericksberg, assistant professor of psychology, 1969-70; Quinnipiac College, Hamden, Conn., assistant professor, 1970-73, associate professor of psychology, 1973—. Organizer of several cooperative childcare centers, 1969-75; member of Childcare Organizing Committee, New Haven, 1973-75; member of board of directors, Hamden Community Childcare Center.

WRITINGS: (Editor, under name Michele Hoffnung Garskof) Roles Women Play, Brooks/Cole, 1971; (with John M. Faragher and Bertram Garskof) Parent Cooperative Group Child Care, Educational Resources Information Center/ Early Childhood Education, 1975. Contributor to academic journals, and Off Our Backs and New American Movement. Co-editor, People About Children, 1974-75.

WORK IN PROGRESS: A book on motherhood in America.

SIDELIGHTS: Michele Hoffnung writes: "My interests, professional and personal, center on the issues of women's liberation. It is my belief that sex-role stereotyping and sex-defined personalities are formed early; that nurturing must be done by men as well as women; that men, women, and children benefit from parent-run and controlled-group child-care." The psychology courses that Hoffnung teaches are in the areas of the psychology of women and motherhood and maternal behavior.

*   *   *

HOGAN, James P(atrick)   1941-

PERSONAL: Born June 27, 1941, in London, England; came to the United States in 1977; son of James (a factory worker) and Agnes (Dragon) Hogan; married Iris Crossley, May 27, 1961 (divorced, 1977); married Lynda Shirley Dockerty (a secretary); children: (first marriage) Debbie and Jane (twins), Tina. Education: Royal Aircraft Establishment Technical College, certificates, 1963; Reading Technical College, Certificate, 1965. Home: 174 Main St., Acton, Mass. 01720. Office: Digital Equipment Corp., Main St., Maynard, Mass. 01720.

CAREER: Racal Electronics, Bracknell, England, electronics designer, 1962-65; International Telephone & Telegraph, Harlow, England, electronics designer, 1965-68; Honeywell, in computer sales in London, England, 1968-70, and Leeds, England, 1970-72; Sun Life of Canada, Leeds, in insurance sales, 1972-74; Digital Equipment Corp., in computer sales and training in Leeds, 1974-77, and Maynard, Mass., 1977—.

WRITINGS: Inherit the Stars (novel), Ballantine, 1977; The Genesis Machine (novel), Ballantine, 1978; Assassin (novelette), Ballantine, 1978; The Gentle Giants of Ganymede (novel), Ballantine, 1978.

WORK IN PROGRESS: A novel, tentatively entitled Microplanet Janus, dealing with a global computer system that begins to acquire independent intelligence.

SIDELIGHTS: Hogan writes: "I was born with deformities in both feet which required something like thirteen years of fairly regular surgery to put right. Hence I was always six months behind everybody else at school and in the process of 'catching up.' That got me into the habit of reading a lot and relying more on self-teaching than on teachers—something that has proved invaluable since, both in terms of developing the self-discipline that writing demands and in conducting research. Also it meant that I never became very much involved with things like football, sports, or any of the other team-activities that are normal for most boys. I suspect that this lack of early conditioning to group expectations and pressures had a lot to do with my preference to do my own things in my own way and in my own time today; that's probably why I don't belong to any political parties or institutional religions. It's probably also the reason why the prospect of living as a full-time writer appeals strongly to me.

"Why write science fiction? A lot of popular misunderstanding exists today of what science is fundamentally all about, resulting in the familiar hysterical articles seen in magazines and newspapers and much needless irrational argument. Science is simply a formalized methodology for distinguishing between what's true and what isn't, and as such is without doubt the most powerful technique that the human race has so far devised. It works! Its end-product is accurate information; i.e., knowledge. How that knowledge is applied is another issue, for example technology, which is continually confused with science. Advocates of anti-'science' are really arguing that problems can be solved by the opposite of knowledge, which is ignorance. Ignorance, of course, can help solve nothing.

"In writing I try to combine entertainment and a little mystery with backgrounds of science as it is and scientists as they are. If in doing this I can contribute something toward improving the general level of awareness and appreciation of such matters, I'll be more than satisfied.

"I wanted to write when I left school but couldn't think of anything I knew enough about. Later, after many years of selling in electronics, computers, and systems to all areas of industry, research, and government, I found I'd absorbed details of countless people, places, projects, how they ticked, how they worked, what motivated them and so on. This has proved a rich source of material."

*   *   *

HOGBOTEL, Sebastian
See GOTT, K(enneth) D(avidson)

*   *   *

HOLLAND, Jack H. 1922-

PERSONAL: Born October 31, 1922, in San Diego, Calif.; son of Henry Joseph (an engineer) and Hazel M. (a registered nurse; maiden name, Mitchell) Holland. *Education:* San Diego State University, A.B., 1942; Stanford University, M.B.A., 1948; Faith Seminary, Ph.D., 1967; Divine Science College, D.D., 1977. *Home:* 1604 Hillsdale Ave., San Jose, Calif. 95118. *Office:* 3535 Ross Ave., Suite 301-A, San Jose, Calif. 95124.

CAREER: San Jose State University, San Jose, Calif., instructor, 1948-51, assistant professor, 1951-53, associate professor, 1953-56; professor of management, 1956—, head of department, 1956-68. Minister of Divine Science church (Denver, Colo.), 1969—; director of Divine Science Federation International; vice-president of Divine Science College. President of Institute for Human Growth and Awareness, 1976—. Lecturer in the United States and abroad; consultant. *Military service:* U.S. Navy, 1942-46; received Purple Heart, Bronze Star, and Presidential Unit Citation.

MEMBER: International New Thought Alliance (first vice-president), Academy of Management, Society for the Advancement of Management (past vice-president), National Association of Purchasing Management, Commonwealth Club of California, Alpha Tau Omega, Phi Kappa Phi, Beta Gamma Sigma. *Awards, honors:* Leadership awards from California Bankers Association, 1967, and National Association of Purchasing Management, 1978; named Distinguished Professor by California State Legislature, 1967.

WRITINGS: An Outline of Materials Management, Spartan Books, 1956, 9th edition, 1977; *An Annotated Bibliography for Parapsychology,* Spartan Books, 1967; (editor) Thomson J. Hudson, *The Law of Psychic Phenomena,* Hudson-Cohan, 1970; *Man's Victorious Spirit: How to Release the Victory Within You,* Hudson-Cohan, 1971; *Your Freedom to Be,* Hudson-Cohan, 1978. Contributor to *Science of Mind, Aspire, Unity, Successful Living,* and *New Thought.*

WORK IN PROGRESS: Research on human motivation and ways to activate man's dormant qualities.

SIDELIGHTS: Holland wrote: "An 'unexplained retrogression' in regard to a serious illness made me look beyond the ordinary channels and forced me to look at the 'total man' (holistic concept). Having traveled in foreign countries (with teaching and lecturing there) I also became aware of the 'oneness' of the world's religions."

HOLLINGS, Michael 1921-

PERSONAL: Born December 30, 1921, in England; son of Richard Eustace (an officer in the Royal Navy) and Agnes Mary (Hamilton-Dalrymple) Hollings. *Education:* Earned M.A. at Beaumont College, Oxford; also attended St. Catherine's, 1939, Sandhurst, 1941, and Beda College, 1946-50. *Home:* St. Anselm's Rectory, Green, Southall, Middlesex, England.

CAREER: Ordained Roman Catholic priest, 1950; assistant priest of Roman Catholic church in London, England, 1950-54; chaplain of Westminster Cathedral, 1954-58; religious adviser for Associated Television Ltd., 1958-59, Rediffusion, 1959-68, and Thames Television, 1968; St. Anselm's Parish, Southall, England, parish priest, 1970—. Assistant chaplain at University of London, 1958-59; chaplain at Oxford University, 1959-70, National Council of Lay Apostolate, 1970-74, and Catholic Institute of International Relations. Member of National Catholic Radio and Television Commission, 1968; lay member of Press Council, 1969-75; executive member of Council of Christians and Jews, 1971—, Ealing Community Relations Council, 1973—, and National Conference of Priests Standing Committee, 1974—. *Military service:* British Army, 1939-45, commander of Coldstream Guards, 1941; served in North Africa, Italy, and Palestine; became major. *Member:* Southall Chamber of Commerce, Athenaeum Club. *Awards, honors:* Chaplain to Sovereign Military Order of Malta, 1957.

WRITINGS: Hey You!: A Call to Prayer, Burns & Oates, 1954, Newman Press, 1955; *Purple Times,* Burns & Oates, 1956; (with Etta Gullick) *The One Who Listens: A Book of Prayer,* Morehouse, 1971; *The Pastoral Care of Homosexuals,* Church Classics, 1971; (with Gullick) *It's Me, O Lord!: New Prayers for Every Day,* Mayhew-McCrimmon, 1972, Doubleday, 1973; (with Gullick) *Day by Day: An Encouragement to Pray,* Mayhew-McCrimmon, 1972, Doubleday, 1973; *The Shade of His Hand,* Abbey Press, 1973; (with Ann Dummett) *Restoring the Streets,* Catholic Committee for Racial Justice, Conference of Bishops of England and Wales, 1974; *Living Priesthood,* Mayhew-McCrimmon, 1977, Our Sunday Visitor, 1978. Also author of *Chaplaincraft,* 1963, *I Will Be There,* 1975, *You Must Be Joking, Lord,* 1975, and *The Catholic Prayer Book,* 1976. Contributor to religious periodicals.

WORK IN PROGRESS: Studying prayer, the Virgin Mary, and community and race relations.

SIDELIGHTS: Hollings writes: "Readers will learn most about me from *Living Priesthood.* At present I am living in an area of poverty. I am much concerned with this issue—also the multiracial area, race relations, etc. I have specifically traveled to the Caribbean and India to study the people there."

AVOCATIONAL INTERESTS: Reading, walking, people.

*   *   *

HOLLINGSWORTH, Kent 1929-

PERSONAL: Born August 21, 1929, in St. Louis, Mo.; son of Denzil M. (in oil industry) and Thelma (Parrott) Hollingsworth; married Betty Boggess, December 17, 1951; children: Val, Randolph, Amery, Letitia, Wright. *Education:* University of Kentucky, A.B., 1950, LL.B., J.D., 1959. *Religion:* Episcopal. *Home address:* Eclipse Place, Georgetown, Ky. 40324. *Office: Blood-Horse,* P.O. Box 4038, Lexington, Ky. 40504.

CAREER: Attorney in Lexington, Ky., 1959-63; *Blood-*

Horse, Lexington, Ky., editor, 1963—. Member of board of trustees of National Museum of Racing, 1973—; member of Grayson Foundation. *Military service:* U.S. Army, Armor, 1952-54; became captain. *Member:* Thoroughbred Club of America (member of board of directors, 1962, 1971, 1972, 1976; vice-president, 1973; president, 1974-75), National Turf Writers Association (president, 1968-70; member of board of directors, 1974-76), Rotary International.

WRITINGS: John E. Madden, Blood-Horse, 1965; (editor) *A Quarter-Century of American Racing and Breeding,* Blood-Horse, 1967; *The Great Ones,* Blood-Horse, 1970; *The Kentucky Thoroughbred,* University Press of Kentucky, 1976. Contributor to magazines, including *Sports Illustrated* and *Newsweek,* and newspapers.

SIDELIGHTS: Hollingsworth comments: "I fell off my first horse at the age of six, and have been off and on ever since. I am a farmer with vast unwanted experience in water pumps, fence repair, fragile tractors and ancillary equipment, and steeplechasing cattle."

* * *

HOLT, Michael F(itzgibbon) 1940-

PERSONAL: Born July 8, 1940, in Pittsburgh, Pa.; son of Henry Whiting (in business) and Jane (Orr) Holt; married Joyce Gentry, June 17, 1967; children: Adam Hathaway, Erin Gentry. *Education:* Princeton University, B.A., 1962; Johns Hopkins University, Ph.D., 1967. *Religion:* Presbyterian. *Home:* 620 Preston Pl., Charlottesville, Va. 22903. *Office:* Department of History, University of Virginia, Charlottesville, Va. 22903.

CAREER: Yale University, New Haven, Conn., acting instructor, 1965-67, assistant professor, 1967-72, associate professor of history, 1972-73; Stanford University, Stanford, Calif., visiting associate professor of history, 1973-74; University of Virginia, Charlottesville, associate professor of history, 1974—. *Member:* Phi Beta Kappa. *Awards, honors:* Morse fellow at Yale University, 1970-71; National Endowment for the Humanities senior fellow, 1976-77.

WRITINGS: Forging a Majority: The Formation of the Republican Party in Pittsburgh, 1848-1860, Yale University Press, 1969; (contributor) Arthur M. Schlesinger, Jr., editor, *History of U.S. Political Parties,* Chelsea House, 1973; *The Political Crisis of the 1850's,* Wiley, 1978. Contributor to history journals.

WORK IN PROGRESS: Research on the collapse of the American Whig party, 1844-1856.

* * *

HOOKS, William H. 1921-

PERSONAL: Born November 14, 1921, in Whiteville, N.C.; son of Ulysses G. (a farmer) and Thetis (Rushing) Hooks. *Education:* University of North Carolina, B.A., 1948, M.A., 1950; also attended American Theatre Wing, New School for Social Research, and Bank Street College. *Home:* 387 Bleecker St., New York, N.Y. 10014. *Office:* Publications Division, Bank Street College, 610 West 112th St., New York, N.Y. 10025.

CAREER: High school teacher of history and social studies in Chapel Hill, N.C., 1949; associated with Hampton Institute, Hampton, Va., 1950; Brooklyn College of the City University of New York, Brooklyn, N.Y., choreographer at Opera Workshop, 1960-64; owner of dance studio in New York City, 1965-70; Bank Street College, New York City, member of staff in Publications Division, 1970-72, chairman

of division, 1972—. Vice-president of Ballet Concepts, Inc.; choreographer for New Jersey Opera Guild, Paramount Pictures, outdoor dramas, and off-Broadway productions; also choreographer for his own dance company. Managing editor of Bank Street College's "Bank Street Readers," revised edition, "Discoveries: An Individualized Approach to Reading," "Tempo Series," and "Education Before Five." *Military service:* U.S. Army, Medical Corps, 1942-46; became technical sergeant. *Member:* Phi Beta Kappa.

WRITINGS: The Seventeen Gerbils of Class 4A (juvenile), Coward, 1976; *Maria's Cave* (juvenile), Coward, 1977; *Doug Meets the Nutcracker* (juvenile), Warne, 1977; (with Ellen Galinsky) *The New Extended Family: Day Care That Works,* Houghton, 1977. Also author of *Come Out,* for Macmillan, *What Color Is This?, You Come Too,* and *Open It.* Contributor to *Discoveries,* for Houghton. Reviewer for *Dance Digest.* Associate editor of "U.S.R.D. Readers," "Bank Street Unit Readers," and "Captain Kangaroo" television scripts.

WORK IN PROGRESS: A book for middle-years children, based on his own childhood in rural North Carolina.

* * *

HOPE, Jack 1940-

PERSONAL: Born April 22, 1940, in Middletown, N.Y.; son of Paul (an electrician) and Dorothy (a medium; maiden name, Avery) Hope. *Education:* Cornell University, B.A., M.A. *Religion:* Episcopalian. *Home:* 740 West End Ave., New York, N.Y. 10025.

CAREER: Marine Midland Trust Co., Syracuse, N.Y., management trainee, 1963-65; Michigan Department of Social Services, Lansing, public information specialist, 1967; senior editor, *Natural History,* 1967-70; writer, 1970—. Member of county Democratic committee. *Member:* American Society of Journalists and Authors.

WRITINGS: A River for the Living, Crown, 1975; *Yukon,* Prentice-Hall, 1976. Contributor to magazines and newspapers, including *New York, Harper's* and *Smithsonian.* Contributing editor of *Audubon, Backpacker,* and *Mountain Gazette.*

WORK IN PROGRESS: A novel.*

* * *

HOPPE, Joanne 1932-

PERSONAL: Born January 10, 1932, in Worcester, Mass.; daughter of Albert (a construction superintendent) and Mary (Calvert) San Antonio; married Edward Hoppe (a writer and producer), August 22, 1958; children: Lisa, Lynn, Beth. *Education:* University of Maine, B.A., 1952; University of North Carolina, M.A., 1954. *Politics:* Independent. *Religion:* Catholic. *Home:* 9 Shore Rd., Old Greenwich, Conn. 06870. *Agent:* Warren Bayless, 145 East 52nd St., New York, N.Y. 10022. *Office:* Greenwich High School, Greenwich, Conn. 06873.

CAREER: "Who Do You Trust?" television quiz show, New York, N.Y., question writer, 1956-59; Greenwich High School, Greenwich, Conn., teacher of English, 1966—. *Member:* National Education Association, Connecticut Education Association, Greenwich Education Association.

WRITINGS: The Lesson Is Murder (novel), Harcourt, 1976; *April Spell* (young adult novel), Warne, 1979.

SIDELIGHTS: The Lesson Is Murder is set in a modern

high school of affluent Scarborough, Conn. "It appears that Mrs. Hoppe's experience at GHS [Greenwich High School] has influenced her writing," remarked Iain Bruce. "One can see resemblances between the Scarborough High and GHS, both architecturally and socially.... But Mrs. Hoppe has done more than merely create a believable high school. She has created believable characters." By using familiar surroundings, her story has come alive.

The story is about a series of slayings and the trail of puzzling clues left behind by the murderer. In the novel, the killer chooses the members of a select humanities class to become the murder victims. "The murderer leaves perplexing clues to his identity in small quotes from the likes of Nietzsche and Sophocles," using the same reading material the students were assigned to discuss, which bring every member of the class, including the teacher, under suspicion. "The clues challenge the reader to take part in the mystery and to solve the crime.... Mrs. Hoppe has not only provided her readers with a good mystery, but she has worked in a few thoughts on varying attitudes toward education in recent years," Bruce stated.

Raymond G. Cushing described the novel, initially written for young readers, as a 'genuine' mystery story. Cushing commented: "We're talking about the good old-fashioned puzzler, which is solved in the end by someone's superior intellect—someone like Hercule Poirot, Nero Wolfe, or Lord Peter Wimsey.... Youth market or not, 'The Lesson is Murder' assumes more intelligence on the part of the reader than do most crime shows on television."

Gloria Levitas wrote in *New York Times Book Review:* "Joanne Hoppe set out to write a classic whodunit—but 'The Lesson Is Murder' succeeds primarily in proving that a little learning is a dangerous thing.... Hoppe writes primly—and her lofty sociological jargon suggests that life in an elite suburban school is quite as deadly as she images...."

BIOGRAPHICAL/CRITICAL SOURCES: New York Times Book Review, June 12, 1977; *Stamford Advocate,* June 18, 1977.

* * *

HORAN, Francis Harding   1900-1978

OBITUARY NOTICE: Born May 18, 1900, in Saxtons River, Vt.; died December 31, 1978, in New York, N.Y. Lawyer and author. A former assistant chief with the Department of Justice and general counsel for the Liggett & Meyers Tobacco Co., Horan wrote a book, *Bad Housekeeping,* on the subject of a simplified, statewide court system for New York. Obituaries and other sources: *Who's Who in America,* 38th edition, Marquis, 1974; *New York Times,* January 1, 1979.

* * *

HORNER, Althea (Jane)   1926-

PERSONAL: Born January 13, 1926, in Hartford, Conn.; daughter of Louis (a tobacco wholesaler) and Celia (Newmark) Greenwald; married Edward Horner, 1945 (divorced, 1970); married David Doroff, 1972 (died, 1978); children: (first marriage) Martha Horner Hartley, Anne, David, Kenneth. *Education:* University of Chicago, B.S., 1952; University of Southern California, Ph.D., 1965. *Home address:* Route 23, Great Barrington, Mass. 01230. *Agent:* Bertha Klausner International Literary Agency, Inc., 71 Park Ave., New York, N.Y. 10016. *Office:* 445 East 86th St., New York, N.Y. 10028.

CAREER: Los Angeles Psychiatric Service, Los Angeles, Calif., clinical psychology intern, 1962-63; University of Southern California, Psychological Service Center, Los Angeles, intern, 1963-64; Pasadena Child Guidance Clinic, Pasadena, Calif., staff psychologist, 1964-66; private practice in clinical psychology in Arcadia, Calif., 1965-70, and New York, N.Y., 1970—. Member of faculty at Pasadena City College, 1965-67; assistant professor at Los Angeles College of Optometry, 1967-68, associate professor, 1968-70; associate clinical professor at Mount Sinai School of Medicine, 1977—. Supervisor of psychology interns at Pasadena Child Guidance Clinic, 1969-70; supervising psychologist and director of group therapy training at Beth Israel Medical Center, 1972—.

MEMBER: American Psychological Association, American Association for the Advancement of Science, American Academy of Psychotherapists, American Women in Science, American Group Psychotherapy Association, New York Society of Clinical Psychologists.

WRITINGS: (With Garlie A. Forehand) *Psychology for Living,* McGraw, 1957, 4th edition, 1977; (contributor) Charlotte Buhler and Fred Massarik, editors, *The Course of Human Life,* Springer Publishing, 1968; (contributor) Charles Frederick, editor, *The Future of Psychotherapy,* Little, Brown, 1969; *Being and Loving,* Schocken, 1978. Contributor to psychology journals.

WORK IN PROGRESS: An Introduction to Object Relations Theory and Its Application to Clinical Practice, publication by Jason Aronson expected in 1979; *Douglas: The Biography of a Six-Year-Old,* with Martha J. Hartley, completion expected in 1981.

SIDELIGHTS: Horner told *CA:* "As a child and adolescent I loved to read mystery books. I find the study of the human mind has the same challenge and excitement. I must look for clues, derive a hypothesis, and then put that hypothesis to the test. I feel fortunate that I can experience this kind of intellectual gratification and, at the same time, do useful work.

In my recent book I have tried to make a body of important psychological information available to the average reader. Hopefully the reader will be able to use this information to better her or his life. Just as it is important to me to feel that I make a contribution to my profession with my theoretical papers, I like to feel that I am also making a contribution on this wider scale.

The field of psychotherapy is both an expression of and vehicle for social change. Social values are an intrinsic aspect of goal setting in the therapeutic process. I hope that my writing will lend support to certain values which I believe to be important for the life of the individual and to the society in which we live."

* * *

HOROVITZ, Michael   1935-

PERSONAL: Born April 4, 1935, in Frankfurt, Germany; immigrated to England in 1937; son of Abraham (a lawyer) and Rosi Relina (Feist) Horovitz; married Frances Margaret Hooker (a poet and actress), June 16, 1964; children: Adam Albion. *Education:* Brasenose College, Oxford, B.A., 1959, M.A., 1964. *Religion:* "Born Jewish, now agnostic." *Agent:* Amy Page, Aitken/Page Associates, 15 East 48th St., New York, N.Y. 10016. *Office: New Departures* magazine, Bisley, Stroud, Gloucestershire GL6 7BU, England.

CAREER: New Departures magazine, London, England

(now Bisley, Gloucestershire), founder, editor, and publisher, 1959—, director and performer in more than two thousand "Live New Departures" road shows, 1959—. University of Maryland Overseas Program, lecturer in English grammar and literature, 1961-64; Royal College of Art, London, tutor, 1966-69. *Awards, honors:* Translator's Award from Arts Council of Great Britain, 1967, for *The Egghead Republic;* Writer's Award from Arts Council of Great Britain, 1977.

WRITINGS—All poetry, except as indicated: (Translator from the Polish, with Stefan Themerson) Anatol Stern, *Europa,* Gaberbocchus, 1962; *Alan Davie* (monograph), Methuen, 1963; *Declaration,* New Departures, 1963; *Strangers,* New Departures, 1965; *Nude Lines for Barking (in Present Night Soho),* Goliard Press, 1965; *High Nights From When I Was Rolling in Moss,* New Departures, 1966; *Poetry for the People: A Verse Essay in "Bop" Prosody,* Latimer Press, 1966; *Bank Holiday,* Latimer Press, 1967; *The Wolverhampton Wanderer: An Epic of Britannia in Twelve Books With a Resurrection and a Life,* Latimer Press, 1969; (editor) *Children of Albion: Poetry of the "Underground" in Britain,* Penguin, 1969; *Love Poems,* New Departures, 1971; (translator from the German) Arno Schmidt and Marion Boyars, *The Egghead Republic,* Marion Boyars, 1979; *Growing Up: Selected Poems 1953-1978,* Allison and Busby, 1979.

Contributor to numerous periodicals, including *Times Literary Supplement, New York Quarterly, Akzente, Ukrainian Review, Vogue,* and *City Lights Journal.*

WORK IN PROGRESS: Voices and Visions, a sequel to *Children of Albion,* for Penguin; an anthology of North American and British verse tentatively entitled *Transatlantic Voices;* an anthology of poems about soccer; two records, "Michael Horovitz Reads Poems," and "MH Faces the Music."

SIDELIGHTS: Horovitz's *New Departures* is a poetry magazine in the bohemian tradition whose contributors have included such notables as Jack Kerouac, John Cage, Gregory Corso, Yevtushenko, Ted Hughes, Heathcote Williams, and R. D. Laing. Despite the magazine's popularity, Horovitz was not content with allowing verse to be confined to the written page. He decided to put the magazine on the stage in the form of a traveling "Live New Departures" show. The programs are a potpourri of poetry readings, jazz playing, singing, and acting. Self-described troubadours, since 1959 Horovitz and his troupe have given more than two thousand performances in Great Britain and the United States.

Horovitz not only serves as organizer and ringmaster of "Live New Departures," he also performs—reading, singing, gesticulating, ad libbing, and playing the kazoo with gusto. According to Adrian Mitchell, Horovitz's oral presentations are particularly effective because of the nature of his verse: "Mike's poems are written to be read aloud, chanted, sung, even danced." After attending one of Horovitz's shows, Christopher Logue of the *London Times* applauded the poet's acting abilities and wit: "He waves his arms about as he reads—something the mawkish psychopath, Hamlet, would dislike; he imitates the voices that surface in his lines; he does not stand on his jokes; his subjects are almost all didactic, rabbinical-lyrical; his humor is sly."

Determined to popularize poetry by means of his road show, Horovitz told an interviewer that "younger people get their poetry by ear and regard it as just as valid as any other method." Jeff Nuttall, a fellow performer and reviewer for

Ambit, stated that Horovitz's goal is "to see the arts reinstated as public festival—gay, simple, stripped of obscurity and stripped of sour perverse overtones." Mitchell believes that Horovitz has come close to achieving his aim of making poetry accessible to the masses. He claimed that "Horovitz has done one hundred times more than the Arts Council to encourage poetry in this country [Great Britain]. The informality and excitement of these concerts has brought into the open a huge new audience for poetry, as well as many other new poets."

BIOGRAPHICAL/CRITICAL SOURCES: Listener, May 14, 1970; *Ambit,* Volume 48, 1971; *International Herald Tribune,* November 28, 1975; *London Times,* May 21, 1977.

* * *

HORVATH, Joan 1944-

PERSONAL: Born April 24, 1944, in Budapest, Hungary; daughter of John (a violinist) and Valeria (Buzas) Horvath. *Education:* Columbia University, earned B.F.A. degree; graduate study at New School for Social Research. *Agent:* Jo Stewart, 201 East 66th St., New York, N.Y. 10021.

CAREER: Film writer and director in New York, N.Y., 1966—. *Member:* Actors Studio (charter member of Directors Unit). *Awards, honors:* Received Academy Award nomination from Motion Picture Academy of Arts and Sciences, blue ribbon from American Film Institute, and Chris Award.

WRITINGS: Filmmaking for Beginners, Thomas Nelson, 1974; *What Boys Want to Know About Girls/What Girls Want to Know About Boys,* Thomas Nelson, 1976. Author of several dozen scripts for television, documentary, educational, and industrial films. Film critic for *Report* and *Films in Review.*

WORK IN PROGRESS: Three feature-length film scripts, including "Somebody's Children" and "My Fair Share."

SIDELIGHTS: Joan Horvath comments: "I am primarily a film director—all other endeavors are simply a means to that end."

* * *

HOWELL, Patricia Hagan 1939-
(Patricia Hagan)

PERSONAL: Born August 19, 1939, in Atlanta, Ga.; daughter of Garrett (an attorney) and Lavinia (Wright) Hagan; married Jerry K. Howell (a technician), July 20, 1972; children: Don Walker. *Education:* Attended University of Alabama, 1957-58. *Politics:* Republican. *Religion:* Protestant. *Home:* 303 Wendy Cir., Goldsboro, N.C. 27530. *Agent:* Donald MacCampbell, Inc., 12 East 41st St., New York, N.Y. 10017. *Office address:* P.O. Box 1375, Goldsboro, N.C. 27530.

CAREER: Legal secretary, 1961-65; motorsports correspondent for WNCT-TV, Greenville, N.C., 1976—, North Carolina Radio News Network, 1978—, and Associated Press, 1978—. Teacher of creative writing, Wayne Community College, Goldsboro, N.C., 1972-75. *Member:* American Auto Racing Writers and Broadcasters Association, National Motorsports Press Association (secretary-treasurer, 1977—), North Carolina Writers Conference, North Carolina Literary and Historical Society, Goldwayne Writers Guild (president, 1972-75).

WRITINGS: (Under name Patricia Hagan) *Invitation to the Wedding,* Bantam, 1973; *Dark Journey Home,* Avon, 1974;

Winds of Terror, Avon, 1975; (under name Patricia Hagan) *Love and War,* Avon, 1978; *The Raging Hearts* (sequel to *Love and War*), Avon, 1979. Contributor to *Southern Motorsports Journal, Grand National Scene,* and of our twenty-five hundred short stories to miscellaneous romance magazines. Contributing editor, *Stock Car Racing* magazine, 1973—.

WORK IN PROGRESS: Souls Aflame, a historical romance dealing with blockade runners in the Civil War, for Avon.

SIDELIGHTS: Howell writes: "I began writing in 1961, doing confession stories. In 1972, I sold my first book, and since then have worked primarily on novels. I have a deep interest in the Civil War period, but I would also like to do contemporary novels. My interest in stock car racing gives me the needed outlet away from the lonely, often confining life of a writer. I spend approximately fifteen weekends a year covering Grand National stock car racing.

"I believe the prime ingredient necessary to become a successful writer is that of self-discipline, for there is no one around to stand over a writer and make him remain at his typewriter. And I do not believe in inspiration. A writer should never wait for inspiration. If he is dedicated, he will learn to summon inspiration at will and command the production of creativity. If a writer does not learn to do this, then he will never master his art. His art will master him, making him a slave and blocking his path to success."

*   *   *

HUBLEY, Faith Elliot 1924-

PERSONAL: Born September 16, 1924, in New York, N.Y.; daughter of Irving and Sally (Rosenblatt) Chestman; married John Hubley (a film producer), June 24, 1955 (died, 1977); children: Mark, Ray, Emily, Georgia. *Education:* Attended Actor's Lab in California. *Home:* 923 Fifth Ave., New York, N.Y. 10021. *Office:* Hubley Studio, Inc., 971 Madison Ave., New York, N.Y.

CAREER: Worked as editor, script supervisor, and music editor of motion pictures in Hollywood, Calif., and New York City, 1944-55; animated motion picture producer, 1955—, writer and director, 1975—. Producer with husband, John Hubley, of animated motion pictures, including "Adventures of an *," 1956, "Moonbird," 1959, "The Hole," 1963, "The Hat," 1964, "Windy Day," 1968, "Of Men and Demons," 1969, "Voyage to Next," 1974, "People People People," 1975, and "A Doonesbury Special," 1977; producer of animated motion picture "Whither Weather," 1977. Founder with John Hubley of production company, Storyboard (now Hubley Studio, Inc.), 1955. Visiting lecturer at Yale University, 1972-77. Artist; paintings displayed in over twenty exhibits in New York, California, and Europe. *Member:* International Animated Film Society, Motion Picture Editors, Art Students League of New York.

AWARDS, HONORS—All with husband, John Hubley, except as indicated: Diploma Speciale, 1956, for "Adventures of an *," honorable mention, 1957, for "Harlem Wednesday," Grand Prize, 1958, for "Tender Game," and Special Jury Prize, 1964, for "The Hat," all from Venice Film Festival; Academy Award from Academy of Motion Picture Arts and Sciences, 1959, for "Moonbird," 1963, for "The Hole," 1966, and for "Tijuana Brass Double Feature"; first prize award from Venice Documentary Festival, 1960, for "Children of the Sun"; Prix Special du Jury from Annecy Film Festival, 1962, for "Of Stars and Men"; CINE Golden Eagle award, 1966, for "Urbanissimo," 1970,

for "Eggs," 1972, for "Dig," 1975, for "People People People," (sole winner), 1975, for "WOW (Women of the World)," and (sole winner), 1976, for "Second Chance: Sea"; nomination from Academy of Motion Picture Arts and Sciences, 1968, for "Windy Day," 1969, for "Men and Demons," and 1974, for "Voyage to Next"; Blue Ribbon Award from American Film Festival, 1975, for "Everybody Rides the Carousel."

WRITINGS—All adapted from screenplays; with husband, John Hubley: *Dig: A Journey Under the Earth's Crust,* Harcourt, 1973; *The Hat,* Harcourt, 1974. Also author of *Zuckerkandl.*

Screenplays: "Adventures of an *," first produced for Solomon R. Guggenheim Foundation, 1956; "Harlem Wednesday," 1957; "Tender Game," 1958; (creator) "Moonbird," 1959; "Children of the Sun," 1960; "Of Stars and Men" (adapted from the book by Harlow Shapley), 1962; "The Hole," 1963; "The Hat," first produced for the World Law Fund, Institute for World Order, 1964; "Urbanissimo," 1966; "Tijuana Brass Double Feature," 1966; "Zuckerkandl," first produced for Center for the Study of Democratic Institutions, 1968; (creator) "Windy Day," 1968; "Eggs," 1970; "Dig," 1972; "Cockaboody," 1973; "Voyage to Next," first produced for Institute for World Order, 1974; "People People People," first produced for American Revolution Bicentennial Administration, 1975; "WOW (Women of the World)," first produced for World Council of Churches, 1975; (with J. Hubley) "Everybody Rides the Carousel," 1975; "Second Chance: Sea," first produced for Board of Global Ministries of United Methodist Church, 1976; (with Gary Trudeau) "A Doonesbury Special," first produced for National Broadcasting Co., 1977.

AVOCATIONAL INTERESTS: Painting, playing the cello.

*   *   *

HUCHEL, Peter 1903-

PERSONAL: Born April 3, 1903, in Lichterfelde, Berlin, Germany; son of Friedrich (a civil servant) and Marie (Zimmermann) Huchel; married Monica Nora Rosenthal, 1953; children: one son, one daughter. *Education:* Attended Humboldt University, University of Freiburg, and University of Vienna. *Office:* c/o Suhrkamp Verlag, Postfach 4229, 6000 Frankfurt am Main, West Germany.

CAREER: Free-lance writer and translator, 1925-40; Berliner Rundfunk (the East Berlin Radio service), 1945-48, began as editor and producer of radio plays, became artistic director; *Sinn und Form* (magazine), chief editor, 1949-62; free-lance writer and translator, 1962—. *Military service:* German Army, 1940-45. *Member:* German Academy of Arts, Free Academy of Arts (honorary member), Gruppe 47 (Group 47). *Awards, honors:* Die Kolonne prize for lyric poetry, 1932; National Prize, 1955; plaquette of the Free Academy of Arts, Hamburg, 1959; Fontane Prize, 1963; Young Generation's Prize, Hamburg, 1965; Nordrhein-Westfalen Grand Prize for Art, 1968.

WRITINGS: Gedichte (title means "Poems"), Aufbau Verlag, 1948; *Chausseen, Chausseen: Gedichte* (title means "Roads, Roads: Poems"), S. Fischer, 1963; *Die Sternenreuse: Gedichte 1925-1947* (title means "Grid of Stars: Poems 1925-1947"), Piper, 1967; *Gezaehlte Tage: Gedichte* (title means "Numbered Days: Poems"), Suhrkamp, 1972; *Ausgewaehlte Gedichte* (title means "Selected Poems"), Suhrkamp, 1973; (with Hans Henny Jahnn) *Ein Briefwechsel: 1951-1959* (tittle means "A Correspondence: 1951-

1959''), Hase & Koehler, 1974; *Selected Poems,* translated by Michael Hamburger, Carcanet Press, 1974; (editor) *Gedichte: Marie Luise Kaschnitz* (title means ''Poems of Marie Luise Kaschnitz''), Suhrkamp, 1975. Contributor to *Das innere Reich* and other periodicals.

SIDELIGHTS: Though Huchel was born in Berlin, and has traveled a great deal in the course of his life, the experience that has counted for most in his poetry was the time he spent during his childhood on his grandfather's farm in Mark Brandenburg. After studying literature and philosophy at universities in Germany and Austria, he went in 1928 to Paris, working as a translator, and then spent some time in Brittany and the South of France, earning his living as a farm laborer. Further wanderings followed in Turkey and the Balkans (1930-32), after which Huchel returned to Germany, living in Berlin and later in the country.

The poems Huchel wrote as a young man began to appear in periodicals in the mid-1920's. Simple but rich in language and traditional in form, they revealed from the beginning a mastery of rhythm. These early poems, concerned mostly with the rural scenes and peasant life of Mark Brandenburg, are seen by some West German critics as examples of modern ''Naturlyrik,'' whose exponents seek to deal both lovingly and knowledgeably with the concrete details of nature (and whose opponents speak of ''village-pond poetry''). Many of these poems also reflect Huchel's concern for the poor of Brandenburg, the exploited farm laborers and migrant workers, the servants and the vagrants. As he wrote many years later, ''I wanted to make visible in the poem a deliberately ignored, suppressed class, the class of the people.'' This element in his work has been claimed by East German critics as evidence of his socialist leanings, though Huchel has always refused to join any political party.

John Flores found some justification for both the East and the West German views of Huchel's work, but maintained that his early verse expresses ''a class-consciousness which is at the same time consciousness of a more fundamental relationship between man and his environment. . . . a 'version of pastoral,' a kind of personal idyll. . . . Its two major components are . . . the sense of continuity . . . between past, present and future activity . . . and the seemingly magical harmony between productive human activity and the processes of nature.''

Huchel's first poetry collection won a prize from the literary journal *Die Kolonne* in 1932. It was to have been published the following year as *Der Knabenteich* (''The Boy's Pond''), but Huchel withdrew it when the Nazis came to power, fearing that it would be confused with the kind of nature poetry associated with National Socialism. Between 1933 and 1945 Huchel wrote a number of apolitical radio plays but published no poems, apart from a few in the periodical *Das innere Reich.* Most of the grim and wintry verse written in reaction to Nazism and the war was destroyed by Allied bombs, though some of it was later reconstructed and published.

From 1940 to 1945 Huchel served as a conscript in the German army. He was sent to the Eastern Front, where he was eventually captured by the Russians. In 1945 he was taken to the Soviet Zone of Berlin, where for the next three years he worked for the local radio station. His first volume of verse, which appeared in 1948, consisted mainly of early work, with only a few of the generally inferior poems written during the Nazi years.

In 1949, Huchel became editor of the East German quarterly *Sinn und Form* (''Meaning and Form''). He turned it into the best cultural periodical in East Germany and one of the best in Europe, a ''bridge between East and West.'' Huchel published in *Sinn und Form* only work that he admired for its literary quality, offending the East German literary establishment by ignoring every other consideration, including the author's nationality, political views, and literary orthodoxy. His contributors included Pablo Neruda and Bertolt Brecht, Thomas Mann and Nathalie Sarraute, Johannes Bobrowski and Jean-Paul Sartre, to name only a few of the most illustrious. Huchel resumed his travels during this period, visiting the Soviet Union, England, the Netherlands, Italy, Bulgaria, Czechoslovakia, and Poland.

In the years just after the war Huchel's own poetry took on a more optimistic tone, reflecting his hope that the Communist government of East Germany might achieve a more just society there. His verse at this time approached the ''socialist realism'' urged on East European writers. ''Das Gesetz'' (''The Law''), the best-known product of this phase of Huchel's work, is an uncompleted and generally rather uninspired verse chronicle in praise of the program of land reform announced in 1945. This hopeful interlude ended with the decision in 1952 to collectivize the land which had been given to the peasants. Huchel's poetry since then has been for the most part a somber meditation on the pain and uncertainty of human existence, with no suggestion that this condition might be alleviated by any kind of political development. His style has also altered, becoming more cryptic and abstract.

Huchel's disenchantment with socialism and his eschewal of socialist realism did not, of course, pass unnoticed in East Germany. His refusal to toe the party line either as a poet or as an editor brought him increasingly into conflict with the authorities. At last, in 1962, Huchel was dismissed from the editorship of *Sinn und Form* and publicly disgraced. Unable to publish in East Germany (though he was by then widely regarded as his country's most eminent poet), he retired into complete seclusion in his house near Potsdam. This state of affairs continued until 1971, when he was allowed to leave East Germany with his family. He went first to Italy and then to West Germany, where he has remained.

In 1963, meanwhile, Huchel's second volume of poetry had appeared in West Germany as *Chausseen, Chausseen.* ''This poetry of disenchantment,'' John Flores wrote, ''is dominated by embittered reflections; an abstract, fragmented style; and images of an icy, static landscape. . . . Nature itself is dead . . . leaving only silence, blindness, and icy treachery. Poetry . . . still lives in nature, as though communing with the dead, drawing utterance from its silence and vision from its blindness, and announcing the lurking danger to all who read.'' This hopeless mood of tired aloofness persists in Huchel's subsequent work. A *Times Literary Supplement* reviewer compared *Gezaehlte Tage* to the work of Robert Frost, and wrote: ''Unlike Frost, Huchel has become alienated from nature by his experience of man's inhumanity and his subsequent creative isolation; he finds himself cast into a spiritual winter from which nature has withdrawn into itself and refuses to reveal itself to him any more.'' What he shares with Frost, according to this critic, ''is the fact that he is a major poet. . . . *Gezaehlte Tage* may well be the most important volume of poetry to emerge from Germany for some time.'' Another critic in the same journal has described Huchel as ''certainly one of the most courageous and humane of living contemplative poets.''

BIOGRAPHICAL/CRITICAL SOURCES: *Neue Deutsche Literatur* 1, 1953; *Akzente,* XII 1965; Brian Keith-Smith, editor, *Essays on Contemporary German Lit-*

erature (Volume 4 of "German Men of Letters"), Oswald Wolff, 1966; *Times Literary Supplement,* September 28, 1967; *Hummage fuer Peter Huchel,* Piper, 1968; John Flores, *Poetry in East Germany,* Yale University Press, 1971; *Deutsche Dichter der Gegenwart,* Erich Schmidt Verlag, 1973; Hans Mayer, editor, *Ueber Peter Huchel,* Suhrkamp, 1973; Peter Huchel, *Selected Poems,* translated and introduced by Michael Hamburger, Carcanet Press, 1974.*

*   *   *

HUGHES, Jonathan R(oberts) T(yson) 1928-

PERSONAL: Born April 23, 1928, in Wenatchee, Wash.; son of Benjamin Bartholomew (a bricklayer) and Rachel (Ward) Hughes; married Mary Gray Stilwell (a writer), December 19, 1953; children: Benjamin, Margaret, Charis. *Education:* Utah State University, B.S., 1950; graduate study at University of Washington, Seattle, 1950-52; Oxford University, D.Phil., 1955. *Home:* 1016 Ridge Ave., Evanston, Ill. 60202. *Agent:* McIntosh & Otis, Inc., 475 Fifth Ave., New York, N.Y. 10017. *Office:* Department of Economics, Northwestern University, Evanston, Ill. 60201.

CAREER: Economist with Federal Reserve Bank, N.Y., 1955-56; associated with Purdue University, Lafayette, Ind., 1956-66; Northwestern University, Evanston, Ill., professor of economics, 1966—. *Military service:* U.S. Army, 1946-47. *Member:* American Economic Association, Economic History Association, Economic History Society (England). *Awards, honors:* Rhodes scholar, 1952; visitor at Nuffield College, Oxford, 1962; Guggenheim fellow, 1971; fellow of All Souls College, Oxford, 1971.

WRITINGS: Fluctuations in Trade, Industry and Finance, Oxford University Press, 1960; *The Vital Few,* Houghton, 1966; *Industrialization and Economic History: Theses and Conjectures,* McGraw, 1970; *Social Control in the Colonial Economy,* University Press of Virginia, 1976; *The Governmental Habit,* Basic Books, 1977. Contributor to journals.

WORK IN PROGRESS: A study of American capitalism.

*   *   *

HULKE, Malcolm 1924-

PERSONAL: Born November 21, 1924, in London, England; son of Elsie Marian (Ainsworth) Hulke. *Home:* 45 Parliament Hill, London NW3 2TA, England. *Agent:* Harvey Unna & Stephen Durbridge Ltd., 14 Beaumont Mews, Marylebone High St., London W1N 4HE, England.

CAREER: Employed as office clerk, charity appeals organizer, and advertising staff member, 1941-59; full-time writer, 1959—. *Military service:* Royal Navy, 1945-46. *Member:* Writers Guild of Great Britain, Australian Writers Guild.

WRITINGS: Writing for Television in the '70s, A. & C. Black, 1974; (editor) *Cassell's Parliamentary Directory,* Cassell, 1975; *The Siege,* Everest Books, 1977; *Bring Your Own Towel: A Guide to Inexpensive Conference Centres,* Edford Square Press, 1977; (editor) *The Encyclopedia of Alterative Medicine and Self Help,* Rider & Co., 1978.

"Crossroads" series: *New Beginning,* White Lion Publishers, 1974; *Warm Breeze,* Everest Books, 1975; *Something Old, Something New,* White Lion Publishers, 1976; *Time for Living,* Everest Books, 1976.

"Doctor Who" series; all published by Tandem Books, except as indicated: *Doctor Who and the Cave Monsters,* 1974; . . . *and the Sea Devils,* 1974; . . . *and the Green Death,* 1975; . . . *and the Dinosaur Invasion,* 1976; . . . *and the Space War,* Wingate, 1976.

Also editor of *The Writer's Guide* for Writers' Guild of Great Britain, 1968, 1970. Writer of numerous television and radio scripts. Contributor of articles and stories to newspapers and magazines.

WORK IN PROGRESS: Doctor Who and The War Games; The Airship; Absolutely New You, a nonfiction book on total self-improvement; *Crime Writing;* a directory about the U.S. Congress.

SIDELIGHTS: Malcolm Hulke told *CA:* "We moved a lot when I was a child so I never went to school. Uneducated, I had little to offer the world; yet I had this obsession to achieve. So I trained myself to become a writer, a profession requiring no formal qualifications. At some time I have written almost everything—romantic short stories for a women's monthly, horror for late-night radio, strip cartoons, thrillers, social drama, children's books, adult novels. I have written for print, television, radio, stage. For a while as a sideline I was a joke-broker, buying jokes in Britain for a big American television comedy show. I codified my writing knowledge into a course of lessons; these form the basis of a correspondence course business run by other people. Writing has taken me to Australia, all over Western Europe, and to many parts of the United States. I enjoy lecturing on writing techniques.

"I have tried to educate myself and know a little French, German and Russian. For relaxation I read history. My hobby is organizing things. I am now creating and organizing Bognor Writers' Weekend—lectures, debates and fun for about 180 people. I will fight authority when it is stupid: after a two-year battle I got a much-needed pedestrian crossing put up in my part of London. I don't think anyone now remembers who initiated that crossing, but it gives me a childish pleasure to see people using it."

*   *   *

HURTGEN, Andre O(scar) 1932-

PERSONAL: Born March 29, 1932, in Brussels, Belgium; came to the United States in 1955, naturalized citizen, 1964; son of Pierre (in business) and Leona (Danneau) Hurtgen; married Barbara Whitney, August 23, 1958; children: Lisa, Ann-Marie. *Education:* Universite Catholique de Louvain, licence es lettres, 1955; University of Vermont, M.A., 1957; further graduate study at University of Mexico, 1956, 1961, University of Colorado, 1960, 1962, Harvard University, 1966, University of Brussels, 1969, University of New Hampshire, 1970, and Goethe Institute, 1970. *Home and office:* St. Paul's School, Concord, N.H. 03301.

CAREER: St. Paul's School, Concord, N.H., teacher of French and Spanish, 1960—, head of department of modern languages, 1969—. *Military service:* Belgian Army, Ordnance Corps, 1957-59; became second lieutenant. *Member:* American Association of Teachers of French, American Association of Teachers of Spanish and Portuguese, American Council of Teachers of Foreign Languages. *Awards, honors:* Fulbright fellowship, 1955-57.

WRITINGS: (With John G. Boucher and Robert L. Paris) *Reprise* (textbook), Allyn & Bacon, 1975; (with Boucher) *Encore* (textbook), Allyn & Bacon, 1976; (with Boucher) *La Famille Martin* (reader), Holt, 1977; (with Boucher) *En visite chez la Martin* (reader; title means "Visiting the Martin Family"), Holt, 1977; (editor) *Poemes pour le cours avance* (title means "Poetry for the Advanced Placement Course"), Independent School Press, 1979.

WORK IN PROGRESS: An annotated edition of Camus's

Les Justes, publication by Independent School Press expected in 1981.

SIDELIGHTS: Hurtgen writes: "Writing textbooks and literary explications is an adjunct of my teaching. I am first a teacher. I write books because I believe there is a need for specific works. If they cannot be found on the market, I put pen to paper to produce what I deem useful. I am very interested in the developing field of black writers in the French language, and hope sometime to be able to put together an anthology of their works suitable for students of French at the secondary and college levels."

*   *   *

HUSAR, John   1937-

PERSONAL: Born January 29, 1937, in Chicago, Ill.; son of John Z. (a public servant) and Kay Husar; married Louise K. Lewis (a school board member); children: Kathy, Laura. *Education:* University of Kansas, B.S., 1962; Dodge City College, A.A., 1975. *Politics:* Independent. *Religion:* Catholic. *Office:* 435 North Michigan, Chicago, Ill. 60611.

CAREER/WRITINGS: *Okinawa Morning Star,* Naha, night wire editor, 1962; *Pasadena Daily Citizen,* Pasadena, Tex., city editor, 1962-63; *Topeka Capital-Journal,* Topeka, Kan., business editor, 1963-64; *Wichita Beacon,* Wichita, Kan., regional editor, 1964-66; *Chicago Tribune,* Chicago, Ill., sports columnist, 1966—. Correspondent for *Golf World, Golf Digest,* and *Golf* Magazine. Consultant to State University of New York College at Brockport for sports journalism program. Lecturer. Chairman of zoning committee commission for Village of Willow Springs, Ill. *Member:* Golf Writers Association of America (former director), Baseball Writers Association, Professional Football Writers of America, Football Writers Association of America.

*   *   *

HUSBAND, William Hollow   1899(?)-1978

OBITUARY NOTICE: Born c. 1899 in St. Ives, Cornwall, England; died September 21, 1978, in Washington, D.C. Banker, educator, and author of two books, *Modern Corporation Finance* and *Real Estate.* Obituaries and other sources: *Washington Post,* September 28, 1978.

*   *   *

HUSTED, Darrell   1931-

PERSONAL: Born February 24, 1931, in Pampa, Tex.; son of Clayton A. (a trucking contractor) and Lucille (Keim) Husted. *Education:* Attended University of Oklahoma, 1950-53; Sorbonne, University of Paris, diploma, 1957; Columbia University, B.S., 1959. *Politics:* Democrat. *Religion:* None. *Home:* 39 West 76th St., New York, N.Y. 10023. *Agent:* Lisa Collier, Collier Associates, 280 Madison Ave., New York, N.Y. 10016.

CAREER: Prentice-Hall, Inc., Englewood Cliffs, N.J., assistant production editor, 1959, production editor, 1959-61, editor of "Spectrum Paperbacks," 1961-63, senior editor, 1963; Fleet Publishing Corp., New York City, managing editor, 1963-65; Charles Scribner's Sons, New York City, associate editor in science book department, 1965-68; Corinthian Editions, Inc., New York City, managing editor, 1969-70; free-lance editor and writer, 1970—. *Military service:* U.S. Army, 1953-55. *Member:* International P.E.N., Gay Independent Democrats.

WRITINGS: *A Country Girl,* Popular Library, 1978; *Miss Cordelia Harling,* Popular Library, 1978.

WORK IN PROGRESS: A historical novel about a ballerina, set in nineteenth-century Copenhagen and London; a nonfiction book on self-esteem.

SIDELIGHTS: Husted comments: "My two published books have been Regency romances, types of works that usually appear under the names of women writers. I refused to use a pseudonym because I think such a conception is foolish and insulting to both men and women.

"I have particularly enjoyed researching and writing about the Regency era (1811-20) in England because in many ways it was a period very similar to our own. England was the most powerful nation the world had ever seen up to that time, yet she was wracked by dissension and threat of revolution. The contrast between the great wealth and power of the ruling class and the misery and discontent of the working class created a dynamic out of which a glittering and volatile society arose. It was one of the most brilliant social periods that ever existed."

*   *   *

HUTCHINS, Pat   1942-

PERSONAL: Born June 18, 1942, in Yorkshire, England; daughter of Edward (a soldier) and Lilian (Crawford) Goundry; married Laurence Hutchins (a film director), July 21, 1965; children: Morgan, Sam. *Education:* Attended Darlington School of Art, 1958-60, and Leeds College of Art, 1960-62. *Home:* 89 Belsize Lane, London N.W.3, England.

CAREER: J. Walter Thompson (advertising agency), London, England, assistant art director, 1963-65; free-lance writer and illustrator, 1965—. *Awards, honors:* Kate Greenaway Award from Library Association (England), 1974, for *The Wind Blew.*

WRITINGS:—Self-illustrated books for children, except as indicated: *Rosie's Walk,* Macmillan, 1968; *Tom and Sam,* Macmillan, 1968; *The Surprise Party,* Macmillan, 1969; *Clocks and More Clocks,* Macmillan, 1970; *Changes, Changes,* Macmillan, 1971; *Titch,* Macmillan, 1971; *Goodnight, Owl,* Macmillan, 1972; *The Wind Blew,* Macmillan, 1974; *The Silver Christmas Tree,* Macmillan, 1974; *The House That Sailed Away,* illustrated by husband, Laurence Hutchins, Greenwillow, 1975; *Don't Forget the Bacon,* Greenwillow, 1976; *Follow That Bus,* illustrated by L. Hutchins, Greenwillow, 1977; *The Best Train Set Ever,* Greenwillow, 1978; *Happy Birthday, Sam,* Greenwillow, 1978.

WORK IN PROGRESS: A picture book sequel to *Follow That Bus!,* for Greenwillow.

SIDELIGHTS: Pat Hutchins writes: "To me, the most important thing about a children's picture book is that it should be logical, not only the story, but the layout, too. To a very small child, an opened book is one page, not two—he doesn't see the gutter as a dividing line.

"I like to build my stories up, so the reader can understand what is happening and, in some cases, anticipate what is likely to happen on the next page. I think one can get quite complicated ideas across to small children as long as they are presented in a simple, satisfying way."

BIOGRAPHICAL/CRITICAL SOURCES: Barbara Bader, *A History of American Picture Books: From Noah's Ark to the Beast Within,* Macmillan, 1976.

*   *   *

HUTSCHNECKER, Arnold A.   1898-

PERSONAL: Born May 13, 1898, in Austria; came to the

United States in 1936, naturalized citizen, 1946; son of David (an interior designer) and Laura Hutschnecker; married Florita Platting, September, 1934 (deceased). *Education:* University of Berlin, M.D. (magna cum laude), 1925. *Home and office:* 829 Park Ave., New York, N.Y. 10021. *Agent:* Alexandra Hatcher, 150 West 55th St., New York, N.Y. 10019.

CAREER: University of Berlin Hospital, Berlin, Germany, specialist in internal medicine, 1929-55; private practice in psychotherapy, 1955—. Consultant to President Nixon's Action Office of Drug Abuse Prevention. Member of advisory board, Foundation of Thanatology. *Member:* American Association of Psychoanalytic Physicians (fellow), American Medical Association, Academy of Psychosomatic Medicine (fellow), Authors Guild, Academy of Political and Social Science, Royal Society of Health (England), New York Academy of Science (fellow), New York Medical Society.

WRITINGS: The Will to Live, Crowell, 1951; *Love and Hate in Human Nature,* Crowell, 1955; (contributor) *The Meaning of Death,* McGraw, 1959; *The Will to Happiness,* Prentice-Hall, 1964; *The Drive for Power,* edited by Jeanne Bernkopf, M. Evans, 1974. Contributor to scientific and popular journals, including *Look* and *Vogue,* and to newspapers.

WORK IN PROGRESS: A book on psycho-dynamics; an autobiography.

SIDELIGHTS: A tragedy in his own life motivated Hutschnecker to write his first book, *The Will to Live.* In addition, he felt "a need to present [his] own views on the then new concept of psychosomatic medicine since [he] experienced many physical illnesses of psychogenic origin." Hundreds of positive letters he received commenting on *The Will to Live* have given him "proof of the great value a book can have to people in the grips of acute conflict."

Hutschnecker told *CA:* "The following three books aimed at clarifying the psychodynamics in human interaction and from a point of therapy how people can learn to extricate themselves from their own, often unconscious, self-destructive drives. The theme in these books is to live naturally and that 'happiness is a natural state,' while unhappiness is caused, for the most part, by the confusions and inconsistencies in values of our early environment and of unresolved conflict situations.

"While *The Will to Happiness* deals with the experimental psychology of Pavlovian work on conditioning and methods of reconditioning, *The Drive for Power* shows the motivation and unconscious 'overdrive' not merely to win but to gain control over other people, caused by a need to overcome feelings of inferiority and lack of self worth or a need to take vengeance on early rejections and painful hurts. My experience with political leaders and their human frailties caused me to introduce a new term, 'psychopolitics': the need to evaluate the mental stability of leaders before they can assume a position of power, such as the presidency of the United States. As the former physician of President Nixon, I could gain insight to the power play of politics.

"*The Drive for Power* contains references to my appearance before the House and Rules Committee of the U.S. Senate and the House Judiciary Committee of the U.S. Congress to testify, under oath, whether or not I treated Gerald Ford before his nomination to the vice-presidency of the United States. The question of professional confidentiality was under strong debate. The book also contains a program on the prevention of crime, a project President Nixon had asked me to present to him which was sabotaged by a member of his own White House staff."

The Will to Live, a bestseller with twenty printings, has been translated into French, Dutch, Italian, Polish, Spanish, and Portuguese. It is required reading at many college and training hospitals.

BIOGRAPHICAL/CRITICAL SOURCES: Bruce Mazlich, *In Search of Nixon,* Penguin, 1972; *Washington Post,* November 20, 1973; *People,* October 7, 1974; Roger Rapoport, *The Superdoctors,* Playboy Press, 1975; Osborn Segerberg, Jr., *Living with Death,* Dutton, 1976.

* * *

HUWS, Daniel 1932-

PERSONAL: Born June 28, 1932, in London, England; son of Richard Llywelyn and Edrica (Tyrwhitt) Huws; married Helga Kobuszewski; children: Madelin, Lucy, Hanna, Louisa, Andreas. *Education:* Peterhouse, Cambridge, B.A., 1955. *Home:* Tyddyn Seilo, Penrhyncoch, Dyfed, Wales.

CAREER: National Library of Wales, Aberystwyth, assistant keeper of manuscripts, 1961—.

WRITINGS: Noth (poems), Secker & Warburg, 1972; *Buzzards* (poems), Sceptre Press, 1974; *From an Old Book of Riddles* (poems), Sceptre Press, 1974; (editor with Maldwyn Mills) *Fragments of an Early Fourteenth Century "Guy of Warwick",* Basil Blackwell, 1974. Contributor of articles on medieval manuscripts and Welsh folk music to journals.

SIDELIGHTS: Huws comments: "Academic pursuits are bad for poets."

* * *

HUYGEN, Wil(librord Joseph) 1922-

PERSONAL: Born June 23, 1922, in Amersfoort, Netherlands; son of Frederique Constant and Catarina (Woltring) Huygen; married Anne-Marie Arts, September, 1950; children: Alexander, Tijl Uilenspiegel, Agnes, Pieter Bas, Jochem. *Education:* University of Utrecht, M.D., 1949. *Politics:* None. *Religion:* None. *Home and office:* Berg en Dalse weg 110, Nijmegen, Holland.

CAREER: Practitioner of general medicine in Nijmegen, Holland, 1952—; writer. *Military service:* Royal Dutch Navy, 1949-51; served as health officer; became major. *Member:* Royal Dutch Sportsmen's Society. *Awards, honors:* Golden Book Award, 1977, for *Gnomes.*

WRITINGS—In English: *Leven en werken van de Kabouter,* illustrated by Rien Poortvliet, Unieboek, 1976, translation published as *Gnomes,* Abrams, 1977.

Other: *Jagersland* (title means "Sportsmen's Land"), illustrated by Poortvliet, Thieme-Zutphen, 1964; *Dokter en Diana* (title means "Doctor and Diana"), Ambo, 1966; *Alleen voor jagers* (title means "For Sportsmen Only"), illustrated by Poortvliet, Fontein, 1967, published as *Niet alleen voor jagers* (title means "Not Only for Sportsmen"), Luitingh, 1975; *Met een kluitje in het riet* (title means "Sent Out on a Silly Errand"), illustrated by Poortvliet, Fontein, 1968.

En buiten lag het paradijs (juvenile; title means "And Paradise Laid Outside"), illustrated by Poortvliet, Unieboek, 1970; *Op schootsafstand* (title means "At Shooting Range"), illustrated by Poortvliet, Unieboek, 1970; *De Geheime nachten van jochem* (juvenile; title means "The Secret Nights of Jochem"), Unieboek, 1972; *Scholletje* (juvenile; title means "Scholletje"), Unieboek, 1974; *Op reeen nit* (title means "Watching Roe Deer"), Government of Holland, 1974.

WORK IN PROGRESS: Waarnemer gevraagd (title means "Stand-In Asked"), a story of all the troubles of a young doctor in a large countryside practice.

SIDELIGHTS: "With exhilarating wit and tongue-in-cheek charm, Dutch physician Wil Huygen and illustrator Rien Poortvliet put together a mock sociological history of the gnome that is proving to be an astonishing money spinner," observed *Time* magazine of the best-selling book, *Gnomes.* Richard R. Lingeman added: "Huygen's text is in the spirit of physiological whimsy; while his quasi-scientific tone also avoids cuteness, there is a stolid Dutch thoroughness running through, a determined jolliness, without the least trace of leavening wit or satire."

When asked about his motivation for writing, Huygen told *CA:* "I seek to write as much as possible for my brothers and sisters about our common youth and the beautiful, though very poor years we spent together. Writing allows me to express my love for nature, for animals of any kind, and for big or small game hunting.

"As an average child I became interested in gnomes from my very early years," he added. "Maybe it is because my mother used to read to us the book *Niels Holgersson's Wonderful Journey* by Selma Lagerloef time and again. I am firmly convinced that character, personality, and interests are born or at least founded when sitting on your mother's lap, while she sings little songs to you or reads books, even if you don't understand a single word of it.

"Niels Holgersson may not be a typical gnome, but he fits in. Gnomes are the personification of reverence for nature and things without violence. They are even our alter ego, although I cannot understand why they are so small in that case. But they certainly are a happy projection of ourselves.

"The book *Schollentje* (which is the name of a small girl) contains large parts about a gnome, who helps Scholletje (bedridden by a badly broken leg with infection) to do things for her outside the house and later outside the hospital, to which she is transferred. With the help of a second gnome he even fetches wonder herbs for her in the end to save her life, when she is on the verge of dying. Of course the doctors think that they have done the job with antibiotics, but Schollentje and the two gnomes know better.

"At Christmas in 1975 Rien Poortvliet called me on the phone and said, 'We must make a book about gnomes and gnomes alone.' After two hours I knew what he meant, and after that we worked like mad to get it ready, which was a bad time for my patients. Four times we stopped, because we were certain that it was going to be a flop. The ridiculous success of the book in Holland and America I can only explain by guessing that the book fills in something which mankind thought was lost, or at least should or could not be spoken of any longer in these days. Suddenly it was there again and you were allowed to give your time to a book which was not for children alone but for children from eight to eighty, taking you back to happy times in early childhood."

BIOGRAPHICAL/CRITICAL SOURCES: New York Times Book Review, December 25, 1977, January 1, 1978; *Time,* April 3, 1978.

*   *   *

HUYGHE, Rene   1906-

PERSONAL: Surname is pronounced "Yoog"; born May 3, 1906, in Arras, France; son of Louis (a journalist) and Marie (a professor; maiden name, Delvoye) Huyghe; married second wife, Lydie Bouthet (a museum curator); children: (first marriage) Claire Helene; (second marriage) Francois-Bernart. *Education:* Attended Ecole du Louvre and Sorbonne, University of Paris. *Home:* 3 rue Corneille, 75006 Paris, France.

CAREER: Louvre Museum, Paris, France, staff member, 1927-30, assistant curator, 1930-37, chief curator, beginning 1937, became honorary chief curator of paintings and drawings; College of France, Paris, professor of psychology of plastic arts, 1950-76, honorary professor, 1976—, also served as chairman of department; Jacquemart-Andre Museum, Paris, director, 1974—. Coordinator of art expositions, conferences, and art films. Council of National Museums, member, 1952—, vice-president, 1964, president, 1975—; member of Academie Francaise, 1960—. *Member:* International Association of Art Films (founder; president, 1958), Amis des Arts (honorary chairman), Amis de Delacroix (vice-president). *Awards, honors:* Prix europeen Erasme, La Haye, 1966; Grand Officer of the Legion of Honor; Commander of the Order of Leopold; Knight of the Order of Danebrog; Knight of Isabel the Catholic.

WRITINGS—In English: *Cezanne,* Plon, 1936, reprinted, Somogy, 1961, translation by Kenneth Martin Leake published under same title, Abrams, 1961; *La Peinture francaise: Les Contemporains,* P. Tisne, 1939, new edition published as *Les Contemporains,* 1949, translation by Paul C. Blum of first edition published as *French Painting: The Contempories,* New York, French, and European Publications, 1939; *La Peinture italienne: XIIIe-XVIIIe siecle* (text in French, English, and German), Braun, 1948; *Le Dessin francais au XIXe siecle,* Mermod, 1948, translation published as *French Drawing of the Nineteenth Century,* Vanguard Press, 1956; *Art Treasures of the Louvre,* Abrams, 1951.

Le Louvre: Les Chefs-d'oeuvre de la peinture du XVe au XXe siecle (text in French and English), Editions Nomis, 1953; *Dialogue avec le visible,* Flammarion, 1955, translation by Norbert Guterman published as *Ideas and Images in World Art,* Abrams, 1959 (published in England as *Discovery of Art,* Thames & Hudson, 1959); *Van Gogh,* Flammarion, 1958, translation by Helen C. Slonim published under same title, Crown, 1958; *Gauguin,* Flammarion, 1959, translation by Slonim published under same title, Crown, 1959; (author of introduction) *Francis Gruber, 1912-1948,* Art Council of Great Britain (London), 1959.

(Author of introduction) *Gustave Courbet, 1819-1877,* Philadelphia Museum of Art, 1960; *L'Art et l'ame,* Flammarion, 1960, translation by Guterman published as *Art and the Spirit of Man,* Abrams, 1962; *Delacroix ou le combat solitaire,* Hatchette, 1963, translation by Jonathan Griffin published as *Delacroix,* Abrams, 1963; *Trois conferences sur l'art,* National Bank of Egypt, 1965, translation by Magdi Wahba published as *Three Lectures on Art,* 1965; *L'Univers de Watteau,* illustrations by Helene Adhemar, H. Screpel, 1968, translation by Barbara Bray published as *Watteau,* Pall Mall Press, 1970.

Editor: *L'Art et l'homme,* three volumes, Larousse, 1957-61, translation by Dennis Gilbert, Michael Heron, and others published as *Art and Mankind,* Prometheus Press, Volume I: *Larousse Encyclopedia of Prehistoric and Ancient Art: Art and Mankind,* 1962, Volume II: *Larousse Encyclopedia of Byzantine and Medieval Art,* 1963, Volume III: *Larousse Encyclopedia of Renaissance and Baroque Art,* 1964, Volume IV: *Larousse Encyclopedia of Modern Art From 1800 to the Present Day,* 1965.

Other works: (Contributor) Ary Bob de Vries, *La Poetique de Vermeer*, P. Tisne, 1948; (contributor) Paul Gauguin, *Ancien Culte mahorie*, La Palme, 1951; *Cent chefs-d'oeuvre du musee du Louvre*, Nouvelles Editions francaises, 1952; *Le Carnet de Paul Gauguin*, two volumes, Quatre Chemins-Editart, 1952; *Henri Matisse, 1869-1954*, Flammarion, 1953; *Discours prononces dans la seance publique tenue par l'Academie francaise*, Firmin-Didot, 1961; *Baudelaire*, Hachette, 1961; *Discours de reception a l'Academie francaise . . .*, Flammarion, 1962; *La Peinture francaise des XVIIe et XVIIIe siecle*, Flammarion, 1962; *L'Universalite de Delacroix*, Union general d'editons, 1963; *Les Puissances de l'image: Bilan d'une psychologie de l'art*, Flammarion, 1965; *Sens et destin de l'art*, two volumes, Flammarion, 1965. *L'Art et le monde moderne*, Larousse, Volume I, 1970, Volume II, 1971; *Hommage a Frits Lugt*, Institut neerlandais, 1971; *Formes et forces: De l'atome a Rembrandt*, Flammarion, 1971; (with Gaston Palewski) *Hommage solonnel a Paul Valery, 1871-1971*, Firmin-Didot, 1972; *Leonard de Vinci, La Jaconde: Musee du Louvre*, Office du livre, 1974; *La Releve du reel: La Peinture francaise au XIXe siecle*, Flammarion, 1974; *La Releve de l'imaginaire: La Peinture francaise au XIXe siecle*, Flammarion, 1976; *Ce que je crois*, Grasset, 1976.

Editor, *Amour de l'Art*, 1930—, and *Quadrige*, 1945.

SIDELIGHTS: Rene Huyghe was called "one of the most prolific and dazzling writers on art in France today," by Hilton Kramer in *Nation*. His book *Watteau* was described in *Best Sellers* as "excellent and perceptive."

A reviewer wrote of *Art and the Spirit of Man* in *Times Literary Supplement:* "There are . . . several illuminating observations, especially on contemporary art, but they are difficult to discover among the overburdened, diffuse and in part rather chatty text." Another *Times Literary Supplement* reviewer commented that the *Larousse Encyclopedia of Byzantine and Medieval Art* is "both readable and informative. It has its faults, but they do not seriously detract from its very considerable merits."

BIOGRAPHICAL/CRITICAL SOURCES: Times Literary Supplement, November 23, 1962, November 21, 1963, February 8, 1963; *Nation*, December 15, 1962; *New Yorker*, November 23, 1963; *Saturday Review*, December 7, 1963, March 19, 1966; *New York Times Book Review*, December 22, 1963; *Best Sellers*, June 1, 1970.

*   *   *

HYNEK, J(osef) Allen 1910-

PERSONAL: Born May 1, 1910, in Chicago, Ill.; son of Josef (a cigar maker) and Bertha (Waska) Hynek; married Miriam Curtis, May 31, 1942; children: Scott, Roxanne, Joel, Paul, Ross. *Education:* University of Chicago, B.S., 1931, Ph.D., 1935. *Politics:* Independent. *Religion:* Theosophist. *Home:* 2623 North Ridge, Evanston, Ill. 60201. *Office:* Center for UFO Studies, 1609 Sherman, Suite 207, Evanston, Ill. 60201.

CAREER: Astronomer and astrophysicist. Ohio State University, Columbus, assistant professor, 1935-41, astronomer and assistant dean of graduate school, 1935-56, associate professor of physics and astronomy, 1946-50; director of National Science Foundation astro-science workshop and associate director of Smithsonian Astrophysics Observatory, 1956-60; director of department of astronomy of Dearborn Observatory, 1960-75; Northwestern University, Evanston, Ill., director of center for UFO studies, 1973—, professor emeritus, 1978—. Director of McMillin Observa-

tory, 1946-53; supervisor of technical reports with Applied Physics Laboratory, Johns Hopkins University, 1942-45; scientific consultant to U.S. Air Force blue book project, 1948-59; visiting lecturer, Harvard University, 1956-60; director of Lindheimer Astronomical Research Center and Corralitos Observatory, 1967-75; technical consultant on motion picture, "Close Encounters of the Third Kind," 1976-77. *Member:* International Astronomical Union, American Astronomical Society (secretary, 1953-58), Royal Astronomical Society (fellow).

WRITINGS: A Quantitative Study of Certain Phases of F-type Spectre, University of Chicago Press, 1935; (editor) *Astrophysics: A Topical Symposium Commemorating the Fiftieth Anniversary of the Yerkes Observatory and a Half Century of Progress in Astrophysics*, McGraw, 1951; (with Leon Campbell, Jr.) *Visual Observations of Alpha One Made by Moonwatch Stations During the Lifetime of the Objects*, Smithsonian Institution Press, 1957; (with G. F. Schilling) *Observational Information on Artificial Earth Satellites*, Smithsonian Institution Press, 1958; *Challenge of the Universe*, Scholastic Book Services, 1962; (with Jacques Vallee) *The UFO Experience: A Scientific Inquiry*, Regnery, 1972; (with Necia H. Apfel) *Astronomy One*, Benjamin, W. A., 1972; *The Edge of Reality: A Progress Report on Unidentified Flying Objects*, Regnery, 1975; *The Hynek UFO Report*, Dell, 1977; (with Apfel) *The Architecture of the Universe*, Benjamin, W. A., 1978. Also author of numerous technical papers. Editor-in-chief of *International UFO Reporter*.

WORK IN PROGRESS: Articles.

SIDELIGHTS: In 1948, when the U.S. Air Force first approached Hynek to act as consultant to a group studying unidentified flying objects (UFOs), he was skeptical. Over the years, however, he has come to believe that there are sightings which are, at present, inexplicable, and he believes that such cases should be studied in detail. His Center for UFO Studies is a scientific clearinghouse for data which makes it possible for members of the public to report sightings without fear of ridicule.

Hynek's knowledge of UFOs has made him indispensable to others interested in establishing the validity of their sightings. In 1966, Hynek was summoned to Michigan after a rash of suspected UFO sightings. Hynek was not swayed by the publicity regarding the incidents though and his own conclusion was that the citizens had seen glowing swamp gas. Hynek brought the UFO inquiry into full focus that same year when he harangued the nation's scientists for refusing to pursue the issue of UFOs for fear of public humiliation. Evidently, the statement had some effect. Shortly afterward, the Air Force established an investigative committee to research UFO data. Hynek expressed doubt, though, that the committee's findings would differ substantially from previous committee's summations.

Hynek has also complained that this fear of embarrassment frequently stops private citizens from reporting UFO sightings. "When I lecture around the country," he said. "I frequently ask how many in the audience think they have had a UFO experience. Ten to twenty percent raise their hands. But when I ask how many reported it, I get very few hands."

Hynek compares the disregard for UFO research to the firm, but misconceived, faith ancient scientists held. "It reminds me of the old days of Galileo," he commented, "when he was trying to get people to look at sunspots. They would say that the sun is the visible symbol of God; God is perfect; therefore there's no point in looking."

Hynek's association with UFO investigations has obscured his work outside the popular subject. During the 1950's, Hynek was instrumental in the U.S. satellite program. He trained others to track the satellites and was in charge of both the tracking and the distributing of information. He organized Operation Moonwatch, an international network whose purpose was to chart the satellites and calculate their orbits.

BIOGRAPHICAL/CRITICAL SOURCES: Christian Science Monitor, August 27, 1963; *Newsweek,* November 21, 1977.

I

IBBOTSON, Eva 1925-

PERSONAL: Born January 21, 1925, in Vienna, Austria; daughter of B.P. (a physiologist) and Anna (a writer; maiden name, Gmeyner) Wiesner; married Alan Ibbotson (a university lecturer), June 21, 1948; children: Lalage Ann, Tobias John, Piers David, Justin Paul. *Education:* Bedford College, London, B.Sc., 1945; attended Cambridge University, 1946-47; University of Durham, diploma in education, 1965. *Politics:* "Wavering." *Religion:* None. *Home:* 2 Collingwood Ter., Jesmond, Newcastle-upon-Tyne NE2 2JP, England. *Agent:* Curtis Brown, 1 Craven Hill, London W.2, England; and John Cushman Associates Inc., 25 West 43rd St., New York, N.Y. 10036.

CAREER: Former research worker, university teacher, and school teacher; now full-time writer.

WRITINGS: The Great Ghost Rescue, Walck, 1975. Also author of "Linda Came Today" (television drama), ATV, 1965. Contributor to *Yearbook of the American Short Story.* Contributor of over one hundred articles and stories to periodicals.

WORK IN PROGRESS: The Siege of Vienna, a novel about the siege by the Turks and their Hungarian allies in 1683; a children's book about the kidnapping of zoo animals for use as familiars by a group of witches; various short stories.

AVOCATIONAL INTERESTS: Ecology and environmental preservation, music, continental literature, history ("My favorite period is 1904!").

*   *   *

IRVINE, R(obert) R(alstone) 1936-

PERSONAL: Born March 16, 1936, in Salt Lake City, Utah; son of Garner Davis (a businessman) and Stacie (Ellsworth) Irvine; married Angela Prata (an engineer), January 31, 1959. *Education:* University of California, A.B., 1959. *Home:* 5461 La Forest Drive, La Canada, Calif. 91011. *Agent:* Dorothy Pittman, Illington Rd., Ossining, N.Y. 10562.

CAREER: Daily Signal, Huntington Park, Calif., reporter, 1962-63; *Citizens News,* Hollywood, Calif., reporter and Los Angeles City Hall bureau chief, 1963-64; KTLA-TV, Los Angeles, Calif., worked as newswriter, producer, assistant assignments editor, and secretary, 1964-65; KNX-Radio, Los Angeles, writer, producer, and news director, 1966-68; KABC-TV, Los Angeles, news director, 1968-71; writer. Teacher at University of Southern California, 1977. *Military service:* U.S. Army, 1959-61; became first lieutenant. *Member:* Mystery Writers of America (director of Southern California chapter). *Awards, honors:* Received two Emmy Awards from Academy of Television Arts and Sciences, 1969, for documentaries on battered children and rat epidemics; nominations for Edgar Allan Poe Awards from Mystery Writers of America, 1975, for *Jump Cut,* and 1977, for *Freeze Frame.*

WRITINGS—All novels: *Jump Cut,* Popular Library, 1974; *Freeze Frame,* Popular Library, 1976; *The Face Out Front,* Popular Library, 1977; *Horizontal Hold,* Popular Library, 1978. Contributor of short stories to *Ellery Queen's Mystery Magazine.*

WORK IN PROGRESS: Two novels.

SIDELIGHTS: Irvine told *CA:* "My writing career began in 'the classical manner,' as a reporter assigned to obituaries on a small daily newspaper. Three years later, I was with a large newspaper on the day John Kennedy was shot. The story bewildered my boss, who turned on his television set to see what was happening. In that instant I decided I was in the wrong business. I wanted to be where the action was—in television.

"I joined a local television station. At that point, however, the station changed anchormen, opting for a ratings-grabber who was part politician, part actor, but never a journalist. I had to flee, landing at KNX-Radio, where I worked my way to the top job and planned the station's transition to an all-news format.

"But television was still my first love, or so I thought. So when the chance came to make the switch, I jumped, this time landing with KABC-TV. Thus, within the space of seven years, I had risen from the dead (obituaries) to news director of one of country's biggest television stations.

"But, by then, television news had become big business, too important to be trusted to the journalists. The salesman saw to it that show business was substitued for journalism, money for integrity, and power—corrupting power—for sanity. I took refuge in fiction."

*   *   *

IRVING, Henry
    See KANTER, Hal

ISAACS, Norman Ellis 1908-

PERSONAL: Born March 28, 1908, in Manchester, England; naturalized U.S. citizen; son of Rufus and Esther (Simon) Isaacs; married Dorthy Ritz, March 21, 1932; children: Roberta (Mrs. John F. Mathews III), Stephen. *Education:* Attended Montreal and Indianapolis public schools. *Home:* 45 East 89th St., New York, N.Y. 10028. *Office:* Graduate School of Journalism, Columbia University, New York, N.Y. 10027.

CAREER: Indianapolis Star, Indianapolis, Ind., reporter, 1925; *Indianapolis Times,* Indianapolis, reporter, 1926-36, managing editor, 1936-43; *Indianapolis News,* Indianapolis, editorial director, 1943-45; *St. Louis Star-Times,* St. Louis, Mo., managing editor, 1945-51; *Louisville Times,* Louisville, Ky., managing editor, 1951-61; *Courier-Journal* and *Louisville Times,* Louisville, vice-president and executive editor, 1962-71; Columbia University, New York, N.Y., associate dean and editor-in-residence, 1971—; News-Journal Co., Wilmington, Del., president and publisher, 1975—. President, director of Courier-Journal and Louisville Times Co., Educational Broadcasting Corp., and Roper Organization; chairman, University of California Campus Press Commission, 1970; vice-chairman, Twentieth Century Fund task force on government and press; member of Stanford journalism fellowship board; Harvard Nieman Fellowship selection committee; Pulitzer Prize advisory board; Edward Murrow Fellowship Committee; U.S. Department of State mission to India, 1958, to Yugoslavia, 1959. President, Louisville Philharmonic, 1956-66, Louisville Fund, 1958-59.

MEMBER: International Press Institute, National News Council (adviser, 1973; chairman), American Society of Newspapers Editors (president, 1969-70), Council on Foreign Relations, Associated Press Managing Editors Association, (president, 1953), Sigma Delta Chi (chairman of committee to review press, 1954, national chairman of ethics committee, 1955-56). *Awards, honors:* William A. White award; Southern Methodist University medal, 1955.

WRITINGS: Student Newspaper: Report of the Special Committee on the Student Press to the President and the University of California, Ace, 1970.

* * *

ISAACS, Stephen D(avid) 1937-

PERSONAL: Born December 8, 1937, in Indianapolis, Ind.; son of Norman Ellis (an editor) and Dorothy (a columnist; maiden name, Ritz) Isaacs; married Diane Scharfeld (a teacher), June 8, 1963; children: Deborah, David, Sharon. *Education:* Harvard University, B.A., 1959. *Home:* 4521 East Lake Harriet Blvd., Minneapolis, Minn. 55409. *Agent:* Sterling Lord Agency, Inc., 466 Madison Ave., New York, N.Y. 10022. *Office: Minneapolis Star,* 425 Portland Ave., Minneapolis, Minn. 55488.

CAREER: Louisville Times, Louisville, Ky., staff member, 1954-60; staff reporter and editor for periodicals in London, England, 1960-61; *Washington Post,* Washington, D.C., reporter, 1961-62, assistant city editor and day city editor, 1962-63, city editor and metropolitan editor, 1963-70, editor of magazine section, 1970-71, chief of New York bureau, 1971-74, national correspondent, 1974-76; Los Angeles Times-Washington Post News Service, Washington, D.C., director, 1976-78; *Minneapolis Star,* Minneapolis, Minn., editor, 1978—.

WRITINGS: Jews and American Politics, Doubleday, 1974; (contributor) Laura Longley-Babb, editor, *Of the*

Press, By the Press, For the Press, Houghton, 1974. Contributor to magazines.

* * *

ISRAEL, Gerard 1928-

PERSONAL: Born November 24, 1928, in Oran, Algeria; French citizen by birth; son of Prosper (a business manager) and Elise (Haziza) Israel; married Danielle Rondolat (a mounter of films), April 23, 1967; children: Nicolas. *Education:* Sorbonne, University of Paris, licence, 1953, diplome d'etudes superieures, 1955. *Office:* Alliance Israelite Universelle, 45 rue La Bruyere, 75009 Paris, France.

CAREER: Alliance Israelite Universelle, Paris, France, deputy secretary general, 1957—, manager of *Les Nouveaux Cahiers* (Jewish quarterly). Member of council of International Human Rights Institute; deputy secretary general to French Committee of Non-Governmental Organizations for the Liaison of the United Nations. *Military service:* French Army, 1955-57; served in Algeria.

WRITINGS: (With Jacques Lebar) *Quand Jerusalem brulait,* Laffont, 1970, translation by Alan Kandall published as *When Jerusalem Burned,* Morrow, 1973; *JID.: Les Juifs en U.R.S.S.,* Lattes, 1971, translation by Sanford L. Chernoff published as *Jews in Russia,* St. Martin's, 1975; *Le Dernier Jour de l'Algerie francaise* (title means "The Last Day of French Algeria"), Laffont, 1973; *Heureux comme Dieu en France* (title means "Happy as God in France"), Laffont, 1975. Contributor of articles to *Le Monde.*

WORK IN PROGRESS: Human Rights and Detente; Second World War.

SIDELIGHTS: Israel spent his childhood in Algeria where he learned very early the meaning of anti-Semitism. Recalling the taunts of "dirty Jew" he endured from his schoolmates during the Petain regime, he described how the Petain ideology "fit the inhabitants of Oran like a glove," and pointed out that the antipathy came much more from the Europeans than the Moslems. After pursuing university studies in Paris, Israel was drafted into the French Army and sent to Algeria to do his military service. Assigned to a rural outpost there, he began to understand the importance of culture and came to believe that "the more men were 'instructed,' the less they would participate in deeds of repression and torture." Thus, he has devoted his career to defending human rights through his association with the cultural organization Alliance Israelite Universelle.

Israel's writings deal with the destruction of the Jewish temple in 70 A.D., the tragedy of Jews in Russia, the bloody decolonization of Algeria, and the persecution of Jews in France during World War II. When an interviewer commented upon his "morbid taste for catastrophe," Israel protested: "I believe myself to be an optimist. These events have molded my conscience, and what's more, they are poorly analyzed by historians. One forgets that the Jews were a nation and had a state in the first century. The violation of human rights in Russia is quite underestimated. Under the cover of a pre-existing injustice, one fails to recognize the injustice which the politics of decolonization in Algeria represented. The persecution of Jews in France during World War II is hidden away."

When asked about his views of France from his perspective as an Algerian-born Jew, Israel replied: "A just conception of France leads to the love of justice for all peoples enamored of liberty, and even to fighting for them, without losing one's allegiance to France. Of course, like all rich societies,

French society is selfish and conservative, but it is not the worst. I believe that France is truly a liberal country, but perhaps it is still a monarchy. The effects of the Revolution of 1789 have not yet reached all parts of French society."

BIOGRAPHICAL/CRITICAL SOURCES: L'Arche, September-October, 1976.

* * *

IVANOV, Miroslav 1929-

PERSONAL: Born April 10, 1929, in Jaromer, Czechoslovakia; son of Antonin (a military officer) and Marie (Subrtova) Ivanov; married Hana Klugova (a teacher), December 30, 1952; children: Klara (Mrs. Oldrich Riha). *Education:* Charles University, Ph.D., 1953. *Politics:* None. *Religion:* None. *Home:* Pred Cibulkami 8, 150 00 Prague 5-Kosire, Czechoslovakia. *Agent:* Dilia, Vysehradska 28, Prague 2-Kosire, Czechoslovakia.

CAREER: Charles University, Prague, Czechoslovakia, scientific assistant in philosophy, 1953-60; *Hlas revoluce* (anti-fascist journal), Prague, Czechoslovakia, managing editor, 1960-67; free-lance writer, 1967—. *Member:* Czechoslovak Writers Union, Society for Historic Literature, Academy of Sciences (Prague). *Awards, honors:* Received awards from the mayor of Prague, the committee of the Antifascist Movement, and Czechoslovak Writers Union.

*WRITINGS—*In English: *Lenin v Praze,* Svobodne Slovo, 1960, 3rd edition, 1973, translation by Marian Wilbraham published as *Lenin and Prague,* Orbis, 1967; *Nejen cerne uniformy: Monology o atentatu na Reinharda Heydricha,* Nase Vojsko, 1963, 4th edition, 1978, translation by Patrick O'Brian published as *The Assassination of Heydrich, 27 May, 1942,* Hart-Davis, 1973, translation published as *Target: Heydrich,* Macmillan, 1974.

Other: *Historia skoro detektivni: Po stopach literarnich zahad* (title means "Almost a Detective Story"), Mlada fronta, 1961, 2nd edition, Orbis, 1973; *Slunce zaslo za mraky,* Nase Vojsko, 1963; *Modra ozvena,* Vychodoceske, 1963; *Noc hnedych stinu,* Ministerstva Narodni Obrany, 1966; *Cerny dostal mat: Zprava o ctyrech pripadech z historie protispionazniho oddeleni generalniho stabu,* Nase Vojsko, 1967; *Tajemstvi RKZ,* Mlada fronta, 1969.

Smrt na cekane, Nase Vojsko, 1970; *Zahada rukopisu kralovedvorskeho,* Novinar, 1970; *Labyrint* (title means "Labyrinth"), Severoceske, 1970; *Bohove odesli: Reportaze o Recku a Italii,* Olympia, 1973; *Martova pole: Svedectvi bojist* (title means "Fields of Mars"), Orbis, 1974; *Akce Tetrev: Svedectvi o partyzanske skupine,* Spisovatel, 1974; *Vrazda Vaclava: Knizete ceskeho k niz udajne doslo na dvore bratra*

jeho Boleslava v pondeli po svatku svateho Kosmy a Damiana (title means "The Regicide of Good King Wenceslas"), Spisovatel, 1975, 2nd edition, in press; *Cesky pitaval: Aneb, Kralovrazdy* (title means "The Czech Regicides"), Orbis, 1976, 2nd edition, 1977; (author of preface) *Karlovy Vary,* Orbis, 1977; *A Confidential Report on K. H. Macha* (in Czechoslovakian), Spisovatel, 1978.

Children's books (in Czechoslovakian): *Bengt, Your Friend From Sweden,* Albatros, 1964; *Gaston, Your Friend From France,* Albatros, 1965, 2nd edition, 1969; *Adventures Wait Everywhere,* Albatros, 1975; *How the Kingfisher Boniface Lost His Way in Prague,* Albatros, 1978.

Also author of and contributor to many other books and textbooks in Czechoslovakian. Author of three film scripts, eight television scripts, and four radio scripts. Contributor of about eight hundred articles to journals.

WORK IN PROGRESS: Curious Stories: Seven Stories from Czech History; How a Commander in Chief Dies, about fourteenth-century warrior John Zizka.

SIDELIGHTS: Ivanov's books cover a wide variety of subjects. He has written about the mysteries of Czech literature from the eleventh century to the present day, about the world's battlefields, and about the Czech village of Lidice, destroyed by Nazis in 1942.

About "The Secret of the Manuscripts" he wrote: "Fourteen scrolls of parchment, discovered in 1817, contained allegedly medieval Czech poetry. Their romantic spirit, characteristic of the beginning of the nineteenth century, gave some clues about their falsification. The problem consisted of solving the mystery by means of modern up-to-date techniques, such as the laser. The investigation of the authenticity of the documents resulted in perfect proofs that the parchments were a genial forgery."

On "The Regicide of Good King Wenceslas" he commented: "The regicide was allegedly committed at the court of his brother, Boleslav, on Monday after St. Cosmas & Damian's Eve. Two retired men—a criminologist and a historian—started an inquiry into the assassination. New facts about his death in the year 935 were brought to light, resulting in a new concept of historic evaluation."

His confidential report on Macha is a reconstruction of the last thirteen days of the Czech poet, based on his own unpublished diary, written in code.

"The motivation for my literary work can be characterized by an old Latin proverb," Ivanov told *CA.* 'Amicus Plato, amicus Aristoteles, sed magis amica veritas,' or 'My friend is Plato, my friend is Aristotle, but the best friend is the truth.'"

J

JACKSON, Dave 1944-

PERSONAL: Born July 16, 1944, in Glendale, Calif.; son of L.B. (a manufacturing supervisor in the aircraft industry) and Helen N. (Miller) Jackson; married Neta J. Thiessen (a writer), October 5, 1966; children: Julian David, Rachel Joy. *Education:* Multnomah School of the Bible, diploma, 1965; attended Portland State University, 1966-67; Judson College (Elgin, Ill.), B.A., 1969. *Religion:* Christian. *Home and office:* 810 Reba Pl., Evanston, Ill. 60202.

CAREER: David C. Cook Publishing Co., Elgin, Ill., assistant editor, 1967-70; *Campus Life,* Carol Stream, Ill., associate editor, 1970-71; free-lance writer, 1972-74; Reba Place Fellowship, Evanston, Ill., writer, 1974—. Coordinator of Urban Life Center (Chicago, Ill.), 1969. *Military service:* Army National Guard, 1966-71. *Awards, honors:* First place award from Evangelical Press Association, 1970, for photographic feature, "What Could Be More Natural."

WRITINGS: (With wife, Neta Jackson) *Living Together in a World Falling Apart,* Creation House, 1970; (editor with George White) *National Concrete Technology Reference Shelf,* five volumes, Wiley, 1975; *Coming Together,* Bethany Fellowship, 1978. Contributor to religious periodicals.

WORK IN PROGRESS: A book about an urban-pacifist community dealing with neighborhood violence; a science fiction novel.

SIDELIGHTS: Jackson comments: "Reba Place Fellowship is an intentional Christian community of about three hundred people. Our family has been here since 1972. My Christian commitment and my life in this charismatic community play largely in the things I write."

Living Together in a World Falling Apart has been translated and published in Swedish.

AVOCATIONAL INTERESTS: Fishing, tropical fish, reading science fiction.

* * *

JACKSON, George D. 1929-

PERSONAL: Born August 25, 1929, in Woburn, Mass.; son of George D. and Zella (Welton) Jackson; married Marianne Quinn Whitfield; children: Jeanne, Benjamin, Alexander, Anthony. *Education:* Harvard University, A.B., 1951; Columbia University, M.A., 1953, Ph.D., 1961. *Home:* 416 Archer St., Freeport, N.Y. 11520. *Office:* Department of History, Hofstra University, Hempstead, N.Y. 11550.

CAREER: Hofstra University, Hempstead, N.Y., 1958—, currently professor of history, chairman of department, 1971-77. *Military service:* U.S. Army, 1951-53. *Member:* American Historical Association, American Association for the Advancement of Slavic Studies.

WRITINGS: Comintern and Peasant in East Europe, 1919-1930, Columbia University Press, 1966; (contributor) Henry Adolf Landsberger, editor, *Rural Protest: Peasant Movements and Social Change,* Harper, 1974. Contributor to *The Russian Revolution Reconsidered,* 1977; also contributor to academic journals.

WORK IN PROGRESS: Dictionary of the October Revolution; A Short History of the October Revolution; a biography of Lenin; *The October Revolution in Moscow.*

SIDELIGHTS: Jackson comments: "I have been inspired, by the drama and quest for social justice evident in the October Revolution, to make that event the focal point of most of my research and writing. I read Russian and French, spent the years 1953-55 in Europe as a member of the U.S. Army, and visited Russia and Eastern Europe in 1970."

* * *

JACKSON, Jon A(nthony) 1938-

PERSONAL: Born November 5, 1938, in Royal Oak, Mich.; son of Jabe Cook (a machine repairer) and Grace (Goodwin) Jackson; married Ruth Baum, September 30, 1968 (marriage ended, 1977); married Cinda L. Purdy (a communication consultant), September 3, 1977; children: Sarah Rachel, Devin Purdy. *Education:* Attended Wayne State University, 1961-65; University of Montana, B.A., 1970; University of Iowa, M.F.A., 1973. *Politics:* Democrat. *Religion:* None. *Residence:* Helena, Mont. *Agent:* Henry Morrison, Inc., 58 West 10th Ave., New York, N.Y. 10011.

CAREER: Carpenter, 1965-76; writer, 1976—.

WRITINGS: The Diehard, Random House, 1977; *The Blind Pig,* Random House, 1979. Contributor to popular magazines, including *Sports Illustrated* and *Saturday Review,* and newspapers. Editor of *Iowa Review.*

WORK IN PROGRESS: Prime Evil (tentative title), a novel; with Tracy Kidder, a nonfiction book dealing with the medical examiner of New York City; *Queensleap,* a novel.

SIDELIGHTS: Jackson writes: "I always thought I wanted

to be a writer (or, more accurately, a storyteller), but it wasn't until I left Detroit in 1965, to return to my boyhood home near Traverse City, Mich., that I began seriously to work at it. I started out in poetry, which I never mastered, but which gave me the confidence and courage to continue in fiction. I owe a lot to teachers at Montana and the Iowa Writer's Workshop.

"I always felt that my proper medium was the novel, but I couldn't figure out how to write a novel. Then I read a *Paris Review* interview with Georges Simenon. He claims that he taught himself how to write by writing 'penny dreadfuls' (not his phrase, actually, but it's apt). He also said that he'd taken some short stories to Colette, then the editor of a prestigious Parisian journal. She liked the stories, but refused to print them, advising the young Simenon to 'ruthlessly expunge all trace of literariness' from his writing. He did so, with wonderful results. I've tried to follow his example.

"*The Diehard* and *The Blind Pig* are both detective novels, and the book I'm writing now is, too. The mystery field is a fine place to start writing, and to continue to write. The writer is enjoined simply to tell a story and is discouraged from attempting 'great lit.' I think that's just what a starting writer should do, generally. In time, like Simenon, one might find his or her powers developing so that more serious work may be attempted. I think this is the direction I'm moving in with my as-yet-unfinished novel, *Queensleap*. But I'm chiefly a storyteller, not a *litterateur*. For a long time I cluttered my writing with literary references and devices, hoping that would give it weight. It certainly did. Now I'm content to tell the story. All the writers I admire today are storytellers, from Cheever to Simenon. Bill Fox tried to get this through my thick head, at Iowa, and I guess it finally penetrated."

At this point, critical reception would seem to suggest that Jackson's efforts have been successful. A *New York Times Book Review* critic found that Jackson's first book, *The Diehard,* has a plot elaboration and writing quality that would put the book "pretty close to the top of its class." The reviewer continued: "Jackson's prose is clear and alert. There is nothing fancy about his style. Characters in his book talk as they would talk in real life. There are no high-flown metaphors, and everything is concentrated on the story line.... The plot hangs together beautifully. The characters are well motivated and there is no straining for effect.... Chances are we will be hearing from him [Jackson] again."

BIOGRAPHICAL/CRITICAL SOURCES: New York Times Book Review, March 13, 1977.

*   *   *

JACKSON, Mae 1946-

PERSONAL: Born January 3, 1946, in Earl, Ark.; children: Njeri Cruse. *Education:* Study at New School for Social Research, 1966-67, 1974— . *Politics:* "The struggle for human rights." *Home:* 165 Clinton Ave., Brooklyn, N.Y. 11205.

CAREER: Member of national staff, Student Nonviolent Coordinating Committee (SNCC), 1966-70; substitute nursery and kindergarten teacher in Brooklyn, N.Y., 1971-72; junior high school creative writing teacher, 1972-75; Brooklyn Family Court, Family Reception Center, Brooklyn, court social worker, 1975— . Member of field faculty at Goddard College, 1973-74; instructor at Cell Block Theatre, Bronx Men's House of Detention, Queens Men's House of Detention, Metropolitan Correctional Facilities, Loft Film

and Theatre Center, and South Jamaica Senior Citizens Center. Member of Brewery Puppet Troupe, 1974-75, and Negro Ensemble Company Playwrights Workshop. Has given dramatic readings, and appeared on television and radio programs.

MEMBER: National Association of Black Students, Poets and Writers, Associated Writing Programs, Sisterhood of Black Single Mothers, Museum of Natural History. *Awards, honors:* Conrad Kent Memorial Award from *Negro Digest,* for *Can I Poet With You.*

WRITINGS: Can I Poet With You (poems), Black Dialogue Press, 1969. Also author of children's plays, "The Harriet Tubman Story," "When Kawanza Comes," "The Jackson Five Meets Malcolm X," and "When I Grow Up I Want to Be . . . ," and a documentary, "The Prison Movement," for Pacifia Radio.

Work represented in anthologies, including *Black Spirits,* Random House, 1971, *Black Out Loud,* Macmillan, 1971, *The Poetry of Black America,* Macmillan, 1974. Contributor to magazines and newspapers, including *Black World, Essence, Black Creation,* and *Black Scholar.*

SIDELIGHTS: Mae Jackson writes: "I am interested in traveling abroad to meet other people of interest, to exchange ideas and spiritual values."

*   *   *

JAMESON, (Margaret) Storm 1891-
(James Hill, William Lamb)

PERSONAL: Born January 8, 1891, in Whitby, Yorkshire, England; daughter of William Storm (a sea captain) and Hannah Margaret (Gallilee) Jameson; married second husband Guy Patterson Chapman (a writer and historian), February 1, 1926 (died June 20, 1972); children: (first marriage) C. W. Storm Clark. *Education:* Leeds University, B.A. (first class honors), 1912; King's College, London, M.A., 1914. *Residence:* Cambridge, England.

CAREER: Novelist, playwright, and literary critic. *New Commonwealth,* London, England, editor, 1919-21; Alfred A. Knopf, Inc., New York, N.Y., English representative and later co–manager of London office, 1925-28; *New English Weekly,* London, reviewer, 1934. Also worked as a copywriter for the Carlton Agency, London. *Member:* English Centre of International P.E.N. (president, 1938-45). *Awards, honors:* John Ruteau fellowship, 1912-13; D.Litt., Leeds University, 1948; English Centre of International P.E.N. award, 1974, for *There Will Be A Short Interval.*

WRITINGS—All fiction, except as indicated: *The Pot Boils,* Constable, 1919; *The Happy Highways,* Century, 1920; *Modern Drama in Europe* (nonfiction), Collins, 1920; *The Clash,* Little, Brown, 1922; *The Pitiful Wife,* Constable, 1923, Knopf, 1924; *Lady Susan and Life: An Indiscretion,* Chapman & Dodd, 1924; (translator from the French) Guy de Maupassant, *Mont-Oriol,* Knopf, 1924; (translator) Maupassant, *Horla and Other Stories,* Knopf, 1925; *Three Kingdoms,* Knopf, 1926; *The Lovely Ship,* Knopf, 1927, reprinted, Berkeley Publishing, 1975; *Farewell To Youth,* Knopf, 1928; *Full Circle* (one-act play), Basil Blackwell, 1929; *The Georgian Novel and Mr. Robinson* (nonfiction), Morrow, 1929.

The Decline of Merry England (nonfiction), Bobbs-Merrill, 1930; (translator with Ernest Boyd) de Maupassant, *Eighty-Eight Short Stories,* Knopf, 1930; *The Voyage Home,* Knopf, 1930, reprinted, Berkeley Publishing, 1975; *A Richer Dust,* Knopf, 1931, reprinted, Berkeley Publishing, 1975;

The Triumph of Time: A Trilogy (includes *The Lovely Ship, A Voyage Home, A Richer Dust*), Heinemann, 1932; *That Was Yesterday*, Knopf, 1932, reprinted, Berkeley Publishing, 1976; *The Single Heart*, Benn, 1932; *A Day Off*, Nicholson & Watson, 1933; *Women Against Men* (includes *A Day Off, Delicate Monster, The Single Heart*), Knopf, 1933; *No Time Like the Present* (autobiography), Knopf, 1933; *Company Parade*, Knopf, 1934; (editor) *Challenge to Death*, Constable, 1934, Dutton, 1935.

The Soul of Man in the Age of Leisure (nonfiction), Nott, 1935; *Love in Winter*, Knopf, 1935; *In the Second Year*, Macmillan, 1936; *None Turn Back*, Cassell, 1936; *Delicate Monster*, Nicholson & Watson, 1937; (under pseudonym William Lamb) *The World Ends*, Dent, 1937; (under pseudonym James Hill) *Loving Memory*, Collins, 1937; *The Moon Is Making*, Cassell, 1937, Macmillan, 1938; (under Hill pseudonym) *No Victory for the Soldier*, Collins, 1938; *The Novel in Contemporary Life* (nonfiction), The Writer (Boston), 1938; *Here Comes a Candle*, Cassell, 1938, Macmillan, 1939; *Civil Journey* (essays), Cassell, 1939; *The Captain's Wife*, Macmillan, 1939 (published in England as *Farewell, Night; Welcome, Day*, Cassell, 1939), reprinted, Berkeley Publishing, 1975.

Europe To Let: The Memoirs of an Obscure Man, Macmillan, 1940; *Cousin Honore*, Cassell, 1940, Macmillan, 1941; *The End of This War* (nonfiction), Allen & Unwin, 1941; *The Fort*, Macmillan, 1941; (editor) *London Calling*, Harper, 1942; *Then Shall We Hear Singing: A Fantasy in C Major*, Macmillan, 1942; *Cloudless May*, Macmillan (London), 1943, Macmillan (New York), 1944; *The Journal of Mary Hervey Russell*, Macmillan, 1945; *The Other Side*, Macmillan, 1946; *Before the Crossing*, Macmillan, 1947; *The Black Laurel*, Macmillan (London), 1947; *The Moment of Truth*, Macmillan, 1949.

The Writer's Situation and Other Essays (nonfiction), Macmillan (London), 1950, reprinted, Greenwood Press, 1977; *The Green Man*, Macmillan (London), 1952, Harper, 1953; *The Hidden River*, Harper, 1955 (published serially under title *The House of Hate*); *The Intruder*, Macmillan/St. Martin's Press (London), 1956; *A Cup of Tea for Mr. Thorgill*, Harper, 1957; *One Ulysses Too Many*, Harper, 1958 (published in England as *A Ulysses Too Many*, Macmillan, 1958); *A Day Off: Two Short Novels and Some Stories*, Macmillan (London), 1959.

Morley Roberts: The Last Emminent Victorian (nonfiction), Unicorn Press, 1961; *Last Score; Or, The Private Life of Sir Richard Ormston*, Harper, 1961 (published serially under title *The Lion and the Dagger*); *The Road from the Monument*, Harper, 1962; *A Month Soon Goes*, Harper, 1963; *The Blind Heart*, Harper, 1964 (published in England as *The Aristide Case*, Macmillan, 1964); *The Early Life of Stephen Hind*, Harper, 1966; *The White Crow*, Harper, 1968.

Journey from the North: Autobiography of Storm Jameson, Collins, two volumes, 1969-70, Harper, 1970; *Parthian Words* (literary criticism), Collins, 1970, Harper, 1971; *There Will Be a Short Interval*, Harper, 1973; (editor) *A Kind of Survivor: The Autobiography of Guy Chapman*, Gollancz, 1975.

Author of television plays including "William the Defeated" (published in *The Book of P.E.N.*, edited by Hermon Ould, Barker, 1950), and "The Commonplace Heart," 1953; contributor of short stories, articles, and prefaces to numerous publications.

WORK IN PROGRESS: *Speaking of Stendhal*, for Gollancz.

SIDELIGHTS: At a dinner meeting with Storm Jameson to discuss the manuscript of her first novel, the amused publisher said to his wife, "She is the first author I ever knew to let herself be hacked to pieces without a murmur." But, Jameson explained in her autobiography: "What he took for submissiveness or timidity was nothing of the sort. It was a deep unrealized contempt for novel-writing as a serious use for energy and intellect." Despite this attitude and the fact that the ten-pound advance Constable gave her on *The Pot Boils* "meant that their loss on the book was precisely ten pounds heavier than it would have been," Jameson now has more than forty-five novels to her credit. Literary criticism, translations of de Maupassant, articles, short stories, and plays add further to the large body of work she has produced in some fifty years of writing.

Wary all her life of settled domesticity, Jameson said in *Journey from the North*, "Writing is only my second nature. I would infinitely rather write than cook, but I would rather run around the world, looking at it, than write." She has traveled extensively in Europe, especially in France, a country for which she feels a fondness "peculiarly English, a store of humble love." In the years preceding World War II, her work as a P.E.N. official with exiled writers took her to Germany, Austria, Poland, Hungary, and Czechoslovakia. Returning to Poland and Czechoslovakia in 1945, she observed Warsaw in ruins and the internment camps which now housed German prisoners of war, but also a strong spirit of renaissance among the artists of those countries.

In 1948, teaching positions at Pittsburgh University brought Jameson and her husband, Guy Chapman, to the United States. Although Jameson found the country "oppressively large," she described Pittsburgh, to the surprise of many Americans, as a "splendid city" which still retained its European elements. With a small group of friends there, she experienced a rare sense of community in which she was "perfectly at ease, perfectly light-hearted."

In addition to its detailed descriptions of the writer's travels, *Journey From the North* is enhanced by a number of character sketches. A chapter of the autobiography was reprinted in *Books* as "That Old Captain, My Father." The account of a P.E.N. dinner party in London contains lively sketches of Jan Masaryk, H. G. Wells, and Baroness Moura Budberg.

Ambitious from childhood, Jameson seems to have been driven to write the novels she herself describes as "too many," sometimes recording personal family details for later use in her fiction. The European landscapes she knows well provide settings for some of her best novels. Though most of her fiction has received mixed critical attention, she early commanded the sort of respect V. S. Pritchett paid her in the *Christian Science Monitor:* "Miss Jameson is one of the intelligent novelists. She can always be relied upon not to outrage our judgment. She is shrewd and is intensely interested in character not only for its own amusing or tragic sake but because of a very pleasant seriousness of temperament." Twenty-four years later, W. S. White said in a review of *The Road from the Monument* (1962), "The present, mature Storm Jameson is a social satirist of a keen perception, a skillful writer, who has an ability to comment with ironic detachment, a figure of literary distinction and integrity which makes the merely angry young British writers seem pallid and puerile."

In *Parthian Words* (1970), a collection of historical and critical essays on the novel, Jameson takes much modern fiction to task for its lack of clarity and its emphasis on pornography, which she distinguishes from eroticism. In *Journey From the North* she said, "I am genuinely puzzled by the indifference, even hostility, so many writers (critics and others) feel for clear writing. I am prepared to work hard and loyally to find my way in the deeper, less readily intelligible levels in a work, but only if I can believe in the writer's good faith. Only if I can believe that he at least tried to be accessible."

In an article for *Writer*, Jameson quoted Coleridge's remark as advice to the aspiring novelist: "Never pursue literature as a trade." She spoke of the "intolerable anguish of being forced to succeed, year in year out, as a public entertainer, spinning my verbal webs, going through my tricks, perhaps with diminishing intellectual and financial returns, again and again and again, with the agility of a street acrobat." She would wait, she said further, until her early thirties before attempting a novel: "Not too long, not so long that the terrible sharpness of young senses—like the sharpness of sensual excitement which makes a traveller's first moments in a foreign country worth more to him in insight and emotion than a year's stay—had lost their acuteness, but long enough to be able to see myself with a margin of detachment . . . and long enough for my relationship with my fellowmen to begin, at least to begin, to be unclouded by vanity, diffidence, greed."

BIOGRAPHICAL/CRITICAL SOURCES: Christian Science Monitor, September 29, 1937, July 19, 1969; *New York Herald Tribune Books*, April 8, 1962; *Spectator*, October 25, 1969; *Books*, April, 1970; Storm Jameson, *Journey From the North*, Harper, 1970; *Books and Bookmen*, May, 1970; *Bookseller*, September 19, 1970; *New Republic*, March 13, 1971; *Best Sellers*, April 1, 1971; *Writer*, April, 1971; *New York Times Book Review*, May 9, 1971.

* * *

JANSEN, Robert B(ruce) 1922-

PERSONAL: Born December 14, 1922, in Spokane, Wash.; son of George Martin (a logger) and Pearl M. (Kent) Jansen; married Barbara Mae Courtney, September 18, 1943. *Education:* University of Denver, B.S., 1949; University of Southern California, M.S., 1955. *Home:* 6084 South Coventry Lane W., Littleton, Colo. 80123. *Agent:* Vance Halloway, P.O. Box 518, Pearlblossom, Calif. 93553. *Office:* U.S. Bureau of Reclamation, Denver Federal Center, Denver, Colo.

CAREER: Bonneville Power Administration, engineering assistant in Portland, Ore. and Spokane, Wash., 1941-42; Bureau of Reclamation, Denver, Colo., engineering assistant, 1945-47; California Department of Water Resources, Sacramento, assistant civil engineer, 1949-50; City of Los Angeles, Calif., civil engineer associate, 1950-52; Morrison-Knudsen Co., Lima, Peru, hydraulic engineer, 1952-54; California Department of Water Resources, San Bernardino, associate engineer, 1954-55; Colorado River Board, Los Angeles, senior engineer, 1955-56; California Department of Water Resources, worked in various engineering positions in Sacramento, Glendale, and Fresno, 1956-71, deputy director, 1971-75; executive director of Independent Panel to Review the Teton Dam Failure, 1976-77; U.S. Bureau of Reclamation, assistant commissioner of engineering and research, 1977—. Registered civil engineer in California, Washington, and Colorado. Head of engineering board of inquiry on Baldwin Hills Dam failure; head of California governor's Interagency Earthquake Committee and secretary of Earthquake Council; member of executive committee and vice-chairman of U.S. Committee on Large Dams. *Member:* American Society of Civil Engineers.

WRITINGS: The ABC's of Bureaucracy, Nelson-Hall, 1978. Contributor to technical journals.

WORK IN PROGRESS: A History of Dams and Their Failures.

SIDELIGHTS: Jansen told *CA:* "As a professional engineer who believes in getting a job done, I have found my strongest challenges in the bureaucratic labyrinth. Governmental systems have an intrinsic resistance to fast action. They appear to be designed to discourage the achiever. The government's stifling of initiative and catering to mediocrity have undermined the country's footings. This destruction should not go unannounced. That is why I write about it."

* * *

JANZEN, John M(arvin) 1937-

PERSONAL: Born October 28, 1937, in Newton, Kan.; son of Louis A. (a farmer) and Hilda (Neufeldt) Janzen; married Reinhild Kauenhoven (an art historian), September, 1963; children: Bernd Gunnar, Gesine Sara, Marike Sophie. *Education:* Bethel College, North Newton, Kan., B.A., 1961; graduate study at Sorbonne, University of Paris, 1962-63; University of Chicago, M.A., 1964, Ph.D., 1967. *Religion:* Mennonite. *Office:* Department of Anthropology, University of Kansas, Lawrence, Kan. 66045.

CAREER: Bethel College, North Newton, Kan., assistant professor of anthropology, 1967-68; McGill University, Montreal, Quebec, assistant professor of anthropology, 1969-72; University of Kansas, Lawrence, associate professor, 1972-78, professor of anthropology, 1978—. Member of Social Science Research Council's Africa committee; member of board of directors of Bethel College. *Member:* American Anthropological Association, Medical Anthropology Association, Current Anthropology (associate member). *Awards, honors:* Social Science Research Council fellow in central Africa, 1968-69; Alexander von Humboldt fellowship from the Federal Republic of Germany Humboldt Foundation, 1977; National Endowment for the Humanities fellow, 1978; Wellcome Medal from Royal Institute of Anthropology, 1978, for *The Quest for Therapy in Lower Zaire.*

WRITINGS: (With Wyatt MacGaffey) *Anthology of Kongo Religion: Primary Texts From Lower Zaire*, University of Kansas, 1974; *The Quest for Therapy in Lower Zaire*, University of California Press, 1978; *The Development of Health* (monograph), Mennonite Central Committee, 1979. Contributor to anthropology and social studies journals.

WORK IN PROGRESS: Lemba: Government and Healing in African Segmentary Society; editing *A Reader in Medical Semiotics.*

SIDELIGHTS: Janzen writes: "My writing has been mostly 'academic' thus far, based on my interest in clarifying the nature of medical or healing systems in several social traditions. Central Africa has been my focus, and this is an area of importance to the Western world which requires scholarly interpretation. Unique contributions to the nature of medical organization, and to the very conceptualization of health, may be found in African culture. *Anthology of Kongo Religion* sought to bring together primary texts from the transition to literacy in one major African society. The book on Lemba will combine the interest in therapeutics with textual analysis. *The Quest for Therapy in Lower Zaire* examines the contemporary reality of the developing world medical situation in which a society has its own therapeutic system and people decide daily how to use it alongside modern medicine, imported from the outside. In *The Develop-*

ment of Health I am finally getting around to a popular level of writing, combining the scholarly research of the other books and articles with an interpretive approach in which I assess the leading problems in world health and suggest how health workers in development organizations might meet them most directly.''

* * *

JARRELL, John W. 1908(?)-1978

OBITUARY NOTICE: Born c. 1908 in Kansas; died December 8, 1978, in Santa Fe, N.M. Journalist. Jarrell was the Washington bureau chief of the *Omaha World-Herald* for twenty-five years and had worked for papers in Kansas, Salt Lake City, and China. He covered World War II for the old International News Service and was aboard General Omar Bradley's command ship when American forces landed in Normandy on D-Day. Obituaries and other sources: *Washington Post,* December 10, 1978.

* * *

JEFFERIS, Barbara (Tarlton) 1917-

PERSONAL: Born March 25, 1917; daughter of Tarlton (a scientist) and Lucy (Smythe) Jefferis; married John Hinde (a film critic), April 1, 1939; children: Rosalind Tarlton. *Education:* Attended University of Adelaide. *Home:* 63 Point Rd., Woolwich, New South Wales 2110, Australia. *Agent:* Laurence Pollinger Ltd., 18 Maddox St., Mayfair, London, England.

CAREER: Newspaper journalist in Sydney, Australia, 1939-44; staff member of Australian Broadcasting Commission, 1944-61; free-lance writer, 1961—. *Member:* International P.E.N., Australian Society of Authors (vice-president, 1966-73; president, 1973-76; honorary life member, 1977—).

WRITINGS: Undercurrent (novel), Morrow, 1953; *Beloved Lady* (novel), Morrow, 1955; *Half Angel* (novel), Morrow, 1959; *Solo for Several Players* (novel), Morrow, 1961; *The Wild Grapes* (novel), Morrow, 1963; *One Black Summer* (novel), Morrow, 1967; *Time of the Unicorn* (novel), Morrow, 1974; *The Tall One* (novel), Morrow, 1977. Also author of *A Guide to Book Contracts.*

Author of more than a hundred documentaries, plays (both adult and juvenile), and children's serials for Australian Broadcasting Commission. Book critic for *Sydney Morning Herald* and *National Times.*

WORK IN PROGRESS: Ark (tentative title), a novel.

SIDELIGHTS: Barbara Jefferis writes: ''My work for the Society of Authors is concerned mainly with writer-publisher relations, the protection of an author's copyright, the awful menace to writers' rights and incomes of multiple copying in schools, et cetera. I recently visited the Soviet Union on a writers' exchange program.

''My last two published novels have dealt with the early medieval period. The novel in progress goes so far back in time that after it there's nowhere to go except forward.''

* * *

JELLINEK, J(oseph) Stephan 1930-

PERSONAL: Born October 1, 1930, in Holzminden, Germany; son of Paul (a perfumer and author) and Lisa (Furth) Jellinek; divorced. *Education:* Cornell University, B.A., 1951; University of Wisconsin, Madison, Ph.D., 1955. *Home:* Am Hungerborn 22a, 3450 Holzminden, West Ger-

many. *Office:* i. Fa. Dragoco, 3450 Holzminden, West Germany.

CAREER: Perfumer at Polak's Frutal Works (perfume and flavor manufacturer) in Amersfoort, Netherlands, 1955-59, and in Middletown, N.Y., 1959-63; General Foods Corp., Tarrytown, N.Y., manager of flavor research, 1963-66; manager of marketing research in White Plains, N.Y., 1966-69; Elizabeth Arden, New York, N.Y., director of research and development, 1969-70; Sensory Signals Corp. (consultants on new consumer product development), Irvington, N.Y., president, 1970-73; Dragoco GmbH, Holzminden, West Germany, marketing director, 1973—. Organized and taught perfumery course at New York Institute for the Blind. *Member:* American Society of Perfumers (past vice-president; past member of board of directors), American Chemical Society, Society of Cosmetic Chemists, Gesellschaft deutscher Kosmetik-Chemiker, Phi Beta Kappa.

WRITINGS: Kosmetologie, Huethig Verlag, 1959, 3rd edition, 1976, translation published as *The Function and Formulation of Cosmetics,* Wiley, 1969; *The Use of Fragrance in Consumer Products,* Wiley, 1975; *The Inner Editor: The Offence and Defense of Communication,* Stein & Day, 1978. Contributor of about thirty articles to American, German, French, and English cosmetics and perfumery journals.

SIDELIGHTS: Jellinek writes: ''Although *The Inner Editor* may appear to be totally unrelated to anything I have previously done or written, it is not. My interest in communication in its broadest sense comes from my conviction that perfumes and flavors are best understood as forms of communication. Volney Stefflre's ideas on language and behavior naturally became part of my thinking in the course of my work with him on market research and product development, and my work on advertising research led to the central ideas of the book. My ongoing attempts to understand the tumultuous times into which I was born, and my fate of knowing intimately three Western cultures (Austrian, Dutch, American) and not being totally part of any of them—these are the main roots of the book.''

* * *

JENKINS, Simon 1943-

PERSONAL: Born June 10, 1943, in Birmingham, England. *Education:* Attended St. John's College, Oxford, 1961-64, and University of Sussex, 1965. *Office: Evening Standard,* Shoe Lane, London E.C.4, England.

CAREER: Country Life, London, England, editorial assistant, 1965; *Times Educational Supplement,* London, news editor, 1966-68; *London Evening Standard,* London, author of column, ''Living in London,'' 1968-74, features editor, 1972-74; *London Times,* London, editor of ''Insight,'' 1975-76; *London Evening Standard,* deputy editor, 1976, editor, 1977—.

WRITINGS: City at Risk, Hutchinson, 1970; *Landlords to London,* Constable, 1975; (editor) *Insight on Portugal,* Deutsch, 1976. Editor of *Crossbow,* 1968-70.

* * *

JENNINGS, Ted C(harles) 1949-

PERSONAL: Born June 29, 1949, in Au Gres, Mich.; son of Fred Charles and Mary (Snellgrove) Jennings; married B. Renee Rupp, August 19, 1972; children: Emily Rae. *Education:* University of Michigan, B.A., 1971, M.A., 1972, D.Arts, 1977. *Religion:* Atheist. *Agent:* Barbara Rhodes

Literary Agency, 140 West End Ave., New York, N.Y. 10023.

CAREER: Teacher of English at middle school in Union City, Mich., 1972-74, and high school in Beaverton, Mich., 1974—. *Awards, honors:* Avery Hopwood Award from University of Michigan, 1975, for *Take a Sad Song.*

WRITINGS: Take a Sad Song (novel), University of Michigan Press, 1977.

WORK IN PROGRESS: Plastic Flowers, "a novel of hopelessness and wasted, empty lives, a book peopled with immature characters who never find Godot."

SIDELIGHTS: Jennings writes: "At the moment my career alternates between teaching (gotta pay for the refrigerator, you know) and writing. Too much for the former and not enough of the latter, unfortunately. Any of you folks out there discovered how to grade a hundred godforsaken tenth-eleventh-twelfth grade compositions a week and still write the great American novel? I know, don't assign them. Somebody has to educate America, after all. Too bad it's me instead of you.

"Anyway, my career budded somewhere in 1972 when I needed a thesis for an M.A. (Never go to graduate school; they're crazy there. They still ask people to write about the 'Importance of Nightingales in Shelley's Poesy!') Figuring I'd take the easy way out, I slapped together a play and immediately addicted myself to writing—which in turn led to a Hopwood Award.

"Why am I writing, you ask? Can't be the bucks, that's obvious. The old love-hate relationship, I guess. Nothing I hate more than starting a nice summer morning with a bitter cup of instant coffee and a Bic pen. Two, three hours later, though, I'm euphoric.

"I can say to myself: 'Hey, Ted old buddy, you wrote some decent stuff today. Congrats. You can go cut grass like the rest of America and not feel guilty.'

"Driven's the word for it.

"Anyway, writing gives me a chance to splatter all the sickness in me onto a page. On the order of taking out the garbage—routine disgust but necessary to survival. Not that I expect my writing to change the world. No more than my teaching does. But it changes me into a better person. That's enough for now."

*   *   *

JENSEN, Marlene   1947-

PERSONAL: Born April 16, 1947, in Aurora, Ill.; daughter of Ben W. (an attorney) and Sylvia (Brott) Fann; married Raymond N. Jensen (a movie studio technician), September 11, 1970 (divorced, September, 1975). *Education:* Attended Denver University, 1965-66, and New York University, 1969; California State University, Los Angeles, B.A., 1972.

CAREER: Worked as a model, road manager for a rock group, publicity director, copywriter, and photographer; *Movie Life* magazine, New York, N.Y., editor, 1967-69; *Sportswoman* magazine, Culver City, Calif., publisher and editor, 1972-77. *Member:* International Mensa Society, National Organization for Women's California Task Force on Women in Sports (chairperson).

WRITINGS: Improve Your Figure Through Sports, Books for Better Living, 1975. Scriptwriter for television pilot films.

SIDELIGHTS: When Marlene Jensen was in high school, she loathed sports. Gym classes did not inspire any ardor,

for students were graded not on their athletic prowess but on cleanliness. "A girl could get an A for clean socks," Jensen explained to an interviewer. After marrying a sports enthusiast, Jensen became a confirmed athlete. Her interest in sports led her to found *Sportswoman* magazine, in which she battled for the rights of female athletes. *Avocational interests:* Skiing, golfing, tennis, and scuba diving.

BIOGRAPHICAL/CRITICAL SOURCES: Los Angeles Times, November 25, 1973; *Denver Post,* July 28, 1974.

*   *   *

JENSI, Muganwa Nsiku
See SHORTER, Aylward

*   *   *

JEWELL, Edmund F.   1896(?)-1978

OBITUARY NOTICE: Born c. 1896, in Danville, Ill.; died August 3, 1978, in Laconia, N.H. Former newspaper executive and publisher. Jewell served as general manager of the *Washington Times* (1931-33) and in 1940 became publisher of the *Manchester Union Leader.* Obituaries and other sources: *New York Times,* August 5, 1978.

*   *   *

JOHN PAUL I, Pope   1912-1978

PERSONAL: Birth-given name, Albino Luciani; born October 17, 1912, in Forno di Canale, Italy; son of Giovanni (a bricklayer and glassworker) and Bertola (a scullery maid) Luciani. *Education:* Belluno Seminary, degree in philosophy and theology, 1935; Pontifical Gregorian University, Rome, graduate study, 1936, laureate in theology, 1947. *Residence:* Vatican City, Italy.

CAREER: Ordained Roman Catholic priest, July 7, 1935; assistant parish priest, Canale d'Agordo (formerly Forno di Canale), Italy, 1935-37; teacher in mining technicians school, Canale d'Agordo, 1935-37; Belluno Seminary, Belluno, Italy, professor of dogmatic theology and deputy director, 1937-47; deputy to bishop of Belluno, 1948-54; Belluno diocese, director of catechism teaching, 1948-54, vicar general, 1954-58; appointed bishop of Vittorio Veneto diocese, Venice, Italy, December 27, 1958; named patriarch of Venice, December 15, 1969; named cardinal of Vittorio Veneto, March 5, 1973; elected pope, August 26, 1978, coronation ceremony, September 3, 1978, papal reign, until September 28, 1978. Metropolita of Ecclesiastical Province of Venice; president of Episcopal Conference Triveneta; vice-president of Episcopal Conference in Italy; named by Pope Paul VI to participate in third synod of bishops, 1971.

WRITINGS: Catechism Crumbs, [Italy], 1949; *L'origine dell'anima umana secondo Antonio Rosmini: Esposizione e critica,* Tip. Vescovile, 1950; *Illustrissimi,* Edizioni Messaggero di S. Antonio, 1976, translation by William Weaver published under same title, Little, Brown, 1978. Contributor of numerous articles on church affairs to the press and Italian journals.

SIDELIGHTS: Despite the brevity of his reign as "the September pope," John Paul I made a great impact on the world. Officially, he had little time to affect the dogma or policy of the Catholic church. He signed only one major decree, dealing with seminary reform, which was nullified because it had been post-dated to December, 1978. But John Paul I will be remembered for his human qualities. In his fleeting thirty-four days as pope, he won the hearts of people the world over with his kindness, humility, warmth, and winning smile.

Albino Luciani grew up in a tiny town in the Dolomite Alps of northeastern Italy. This rural area had been ravaged by fighting during World War I, and life was difficult for the Luciani family. They wore wooden clogs instead of shoes and often dined on stews made of grass and nettles, and on birds which Albino skipped school in order to catch.

Young Albino was the center of many religious discussions at home. His mother was a strong and devout Catholic, but his father was a committed socialist, who once burned a crucifix in the kitchen stove. Giovanni finally put aside his antipathy to the church, however, and allowed his eleven-year-old son to attend the seminary.

By escalating his studies, Luciani was able to finish college and be ordained at the unusually early age of twenty-two. At twenty-four he was the youngest staff member at Belluno Seminary. He was considered so valuable in his post there that he later obtained a Vatican dispensation to earn a diploma from the Pontifical Gregorian University in Rome without ever attending a class.

During his years as priest, bishop, and cardinal, Albino was known for his simplicity. No matter how high his rank, he was always a pastor, a concerned and compassionate shepherd to his flock. Albino loved to ride his bicycle or walk through the city to visit his parishioners. A champion of the poor, he urged the local parishes in Venice to sell their jewels and give the proceeds to the needy and handicapped, "the true treasures of the church." When he was named Patriarch of Venice he refused the traditional grand procession of gondolas and would not wear the precious ring of his office.

Although highly respected in his own diocese, Albino Luciani was barely considered as a candidate for pope after Pope Paul VI's death on August 6, 1978. He was not a part of the Curia, the Vatican's powerful advisory council. He had never drafted any Vatican documents or served overseas in the papal diplomatic service. Many church leaders had never even heard of him. Luciani himself told reporters: "There is a Class A list of candidates, a Class B list of candidates, and a Class C list of candidates. I am surely on the Class C list." Only his cousin, Silvio Luciani, from Marysville, Michigan, was confident that Albino would be the next pope: "I've been telling people around here that for the last two years, but nobody would take me seriously."

Neither Albino Cardinal Luciani nor any of his peers were favored as the conclave settled to vote for the new pope on August 26, 1978. But after just a morning's deliberation Albino emerged as a favorite, and by 6 P.M. was chosen almost unanimously as the 263rd pope. The elated electors felt that their swift and unexpected choice had been divinely influenced.

Most of the cardinals had been searching for similar qualities in the new pope, and Albino had them all. He was Italian, which they felt would enable him to more easily handle the delicate role of the papacy in Italian politics. He was a pastoral leader, a humble man who could touch the average parishioner with his deep faith. He was not controversial, but quite conservative on doctrinal issues. Although the Curia sought a non-pastoral pope whom they could more readily influence, and the ultraconservatives favored Giuseppi Siri of Genoa, Italy, the left and right factions converged to elect Albino Luciani as the inevitable choice for pope.

During his month as pope, Albino seemed to rekindle single-handedly some half-lost feeling of goodness about Catholicism. He signaled a fresh leadership for the Catholic church by choosing "John Paul I" as his papal name. He was the first pope in over a millennium to choose a first-of-its-kind name and the only one to ever adopt a double name. His choice was a tribute to his immediate predecessors John XXIII and Paul VI, but it was evident from the beginning that he meant to set his own style.

At his coronation, which he chose to call simply a "solemn Mass to mark the start of his ministry as Supreme Pastor," John Paul I walked in procession rather than being carried on the usual portable throne, and refused to be crowned with a tiara. Said John Jay Hughes, a St. Louis church historian: "He abolished the one-thousand-year-old ceremony with the tiara and relegated it permanently to the trash heap. It will be impossible to go back to this triumphalism of the past."

John Paul often dispensed with the royal "we" in his speeches and changed the formal audiences into more casual conversations. Even little children loved him because they could understand everything he said. This occasionally worried the church officials, who were used to Paul VI's "grand theological flights of oratory."

Most of John Paul's views were quite traditional. He opposed marriage for priests, ordination for women, abortion, and divorce. He disapproved of homosexuality and the modernization of nuns' habits, and opposed Communism adamantly. He was very stern with those in positions of responsibility who openly questioned church teachings. Undoubtedly John Paul I would not have made any sudden, drastic changes in the church since he believed that "it is necessary to know how to build on top of what exists, often being content with what we already have."

Pope John Paul I was more open on scientific issues than some of his predecessors. When the first test tube baby was born in July, 1978, Luciani said: "I extend the warmest wishes to the English girl. As for the parents, I have no right to condemn them. Subjectively, if they acted in good faith and with good intentions, they could even gain great merit before God.

"Progress is a great thing, but not all progress is good for man. Will not science bear the appearance of the Sorcerer's Apprentice, who scatters mighty forces without, however, being able to dam or dominate them? Could there not be danger of a new industry arising, that of manufacture of children? The individual conscience must always be followed, but the individual must make an effort to have a well-formed conscience. Conscience, indeed, does not have the duty of creating law, but of informing itself first on what the law of God dictates."

Luciani was an avid reader, and it seemed he could never get his fill of literature. John Cardinal Wright described him as "a witty pontiff who delights in combining love of literature with love of the words of God." John Paul was also a fine writer. He once told an interviewer, "If I hadn't been a bishop, I would have wanted to be a journalist." His book *Illustrissimi* is a compilation of imaginary letters to illustrious people through the ages, including some of his favorite authors such as Charles Dickens and Sir Walter Scott. To Mark Twain he wrote: "My students were always excited when I told them 'now I will tell you another story about Mark Twain.' However, I fear that my superiors were scandalized—'A bishop who quotes Mark Twain!' Perhaps one should explain to them that bishops are as varied as books are."

Catechism Crumbs, Luciani's earlier book, is an account of his experiences during the 1940's trying to explain catechism simply enough for illiterate mountain people to understand.

Offering advice to religious educators, he wrote: "Michelangelo was asked, How do you produce statues that are so full of life? He responded: The marble already contains the statues; it is just a matter of extracting them. Like marble, children are rough material: you can extract gentlemen, heroes, even saints."

Pope John Paul I died unexpectedly only thirty-four days after his reign had begun. He had been in his Vatican bed chambers reading Thomas a Kempis's *Imitation of Christ* when he suffered a fatal heart attack or stroke. Health had not been considered an important factor in Luciani's election, despite the fact that he had been in frail health all his life. He was so weak at birth that his parents had had him baptized the same day for fear he might not live. As a teenager he contracted tuberculosis and twice spent time in a TB sanatorium. But Albino's doctor had given him a complete examination only three weeks before his election and found no sign of trouble.

The new pope's death stunned and shocked the world, leaving even Carlo Confalonieri, dean of the College of Cardinals, to wonder "about the inscrutable designs of God." Millions of people had been touched by John Paul I's radiance and humility, and had felt him a friend even though their only contact with him had been through mass media. He will long be remembered, for "he only had time to be loved."

BIOGRAPHICAL/CRITICAL SOURCES—All published in 1978: *Maclean's*, September 4, October 9, October 16; *Time*, September 4, September 11; *Newsweek*, September 4, September 11; *America*, September 9, September 16, September 23, October 14; *Christian Century*, September 13; *Commonweal*, September 15; *National Review*, September 15; *Christianity Today*, September 22; *Four Popes: Keepers of the Faith Since 1958*, souvenir issue number 12, Ideal Publishing Corp., 1978.

OBITUARIES: Washington Post, September 30, 1978; *Time*, October 9, 1978; *Newsweek*, October 9, 1978; *U.S. News & World Report*, October 9, 1978, October 16, 1978; *Christian Century*, October 11, 1978; *Commonweal*, October 13, 1978.

(Died September 28, 1978, in Vatican City, Italy)

[Sketch reviewed by a cousin, Mrs. Dolly Nutt]

*　　*　　*

JOHNSON, Benton 1928-

PERSONAL: Born August 19, 1928, in Burlington, N.C.; son of Guy Benton (a teacher) and Guion (a writer; maiden name, Griffis) Johnson; married Miriam Massey (a teacher), July 21, 1951; children: Frank Shannon, Rebekah Paullin. *Education:* University of North Carolina, B.A., 1947; Harvard University, A.M., Ph.D. *Politics:* Democrat. *Religion:* None. *Home:* 2410 Spring Blvd., Eugene, Ore. 97403. *Office:* Department of Sociology, University of Oregon, Eugene, Ore. 97403.

CAREER: University of North Carolina, Woman's College, Greensboro, assistant professor of sociology, 1955-56; University of Texas, Austin, assistant professor of sociology, 1956-57; University of Oregon, Eugene, 1957—, began as assistant professor, then associate professor, currently professor of sociology. *Military service:* U.S. Army, 1953-55. *Member:* American Sociological Association, Society for the Scientific Study of Religion (vice-president, 1976-77), Pacific Sociological Association (vice-president, 1968-69).

WRITINGS: (Editor with Phillip E. Hammond) *American Mosaic*, Random House, 1971; *Functionalism in Modern Sociology: Understanding Talcott Parsons*, General Learning Corp., 1975. Contributor to scholarly journals. Associate editor of *American Sociological Review*, 1964-67; editor of *Journal for the Scientific Study of Religion*, 1971-74.

WORK IN PROGRESS: Research on the historical development of American Protestantism, theoretical issues in the sociology of religion, and issues in general sociological theory.

*　　*　　*

JOHNSON, James P(earce) 1937-

PERSONAL: Born August 20, 1937, in Birmingham, Ala.; son of James B. (a salesman) and Ella Louise (a teacher; maiden name, Pearce) Johnson; married Carolyn Brown (a secretary), October 24, 1959; children: Deborah, Katherine. *Education:* Attended Harvard University, summers, 1957-58; Duke University, A.B., 1959; graduate study at Union Theological Seminary, 1959-60; Columbia University, M.A., 1962, Ph.D., 1968. *Politics:* Independent. *Religion:* Unitarian. *Home:* 716 Clark St., Westfield, N.J. 07090. *Office:* Department of History, Brooklyn College of the City University of New York, Brooklyn, N.Y. 11210.

CAREER: Teacher at day school in Brooklyn, N.Y., 1960-61; Pace University, New York, N.Y., instructor, 1965-66; Brooklyn College of the City University of New York, Brooklyn, instructor, 1966-67, assistant professor, 1967-75, associate professor of history, 1975—, deputy chairman of department, 1972-78. *Member:* International Psychohistorical Association, American Historical Association, Organization of American Historians, Society for Values in Higher Education, Society for History Education, Social Science History Association, Group for the Use of Psychology in History, Phi Beta Kappa, Phi Eta Sigma. *Awards, honors:* Danforth graduate fellow, 1961-66, associate, 1976; Louis B. Pelzer Prize from the Organization of American Historians, 1966.

WRITINGS: Westfield: From Settlement to Suburb, Westfield Bicentennial Committee, 1977; *The Politics of Soft Coal: From the First World War Through the New Deal*, University of Illinois Press, in press. Contributor of articles to *Smithsonian* and other journals.

WORK IN PROGRESS: Articles on Herbert Hoover and Richard Nixon.

SIDELIGHTS: Johnson told *CA:* "Having undergone a 'conversion' experience during high school, I was determined to become a minister in the Methodist church. I went to Duke with this in mind and entered Union Theological Seminary in 1959, but left after one year to teach in a private country day school. I found my vocation as a teacher there and won a Danforth fellowship to attend Columbia for a history doctorate.

"At Columbia under William E. Leuchtenburg, I developed my interest in writing, although it did not lead to significant publication for several years. I have now shifted my interests more and more toward writing and toward writing of a popular as well as a scholarly nature. I am now a dedicated believer in the psychodynamic character of an individual's historical development and have been writing about historical figures whose childhoods lend themselves to analysis."

*　　*　　*

JOHNSON, Lincoln F., Jr. 1920-

PERSONAL: Born May 21, 1920, in Lynn, Mass.; son of

Lincoln F. (a diemaker) and Theresa (Mc Gowan) Johnson; married Rodica Helena Isaila (a publicist), August 10, 1974; children: Christopher F., Michael D. *Education:* Bowdoin College, A.B., 1942; Harvard University, M.A., 1947, Ph.D., 1956. *Home:* 1611 Templeton Rd., Towson, Md. 21204. *Office:* Department of Fine Arts, Goucher College, Towson, Md. 21204.

CAREER: Goucher College, Towson, Md., 1950—, professor of art, 1963—, chairman of department, 1959-69. Visiting lecturer at Wellesley College, 1949-50. Member of board of trustees of Maryland Institute College of Art, 1956—. Member of visual arts panel of Maryland Arts Council, 1969—; program chairman for Baltimore Film Forum, 1976-77; member of advisory panel of Baltimore Inner Harbor Project, 1976—; member of local Municipal Arts Commission, 1960-71, 1977—. *Military service:* U.S. Army Air Forces, 1942-45; became sergeant.

MEMBER: American Association of University Professors, College Art Association of America, Film Study Association, University Film Association. *Awards, honors:* Award from Art Directors Club; Longfellow fellow, 1942; Bacon fellow, 1948-49; Fulbright fellowship, 1962; Ford Foundation fellowship, 1970-71; award of merit from Artists Equity Association, 1976.

WRITINGS: Amalie Rothschild: Drawings, Goucher College, 1968; *Film: Space, Time, Light, Sound,* Holt, 1974. Author of an art column in *Baltimore Sun,* 1971—. Contributor to art journals.

WORK IN PROGRESS: Research on the art of fin-de-siecle and on Alain Robbe-Grillet.

* * *

JOHNSON, Nunnally 1897-1977

PERSONAL: Born December 5, 1897, in Columbus, Ga.; son of James Nunnally and Pearl (Patrick) Johnson; married third wife, Doris Bowdon, February 4, 1940; children: Marjorie, Nora, Gene Fowler, Christie, Roxanna, Scott Bowdon. *Education:* Educated in Columbus, Ga. *Residence:* Beverly Hills, Calif.

CAREER: Screenwriter, director, and producer of motion pictures. Worked as reporter for *Columbus Enquirer Sun, Brooklyn Daily Eagle, New York Herald Tribune,* and *New York Post* during 1920's and 1930's. *Military service:* U.S. Army, 1916-18. *Member:* Writers Guild of America, West. *Awards, honors:* Nominations for Academy Awards from Academy of Motion Picture Arts and Sciences, 1940, for "The Grapes of Wrath," and 1943, for "Holy Matrimony"; Laurel Award for screenwriting from Writers Guild of America, West, 1959; nominations from Writers Guild, 1953, for "How to Marry a Millionaire," 1962, for "Mister Hobbs Takes a Vacation," and 1964, for "The World of Henry Orient."

WRITINGS: There Ought to be a Law and Other Stories, Doubleday, 1931; "The World of Henry Orient" (adapted from the novel by Nora Johnson), first produced in New York at Palace Theatre, October, 1967.

Screenplays; released by Twentieth Century-Fox, unless otherwise indicated: (With Henry Lehrman) "Moulin Rouge," 1934; (with Arthur Sheekman and Nat Perrin) "Kid Millions," United Artists, 1934; "Thanks a Million," 1935; (with Howard Ellis Smith) "The Man Who Broke the Bank at Monte Carlo" (adapted from the play by Ilia Surgutchoff and Frederick Albert Swann), 1935; "The Prisoner of Shark Island," 1936; "Banjo on My Knee" (adapted from

the novel by Harry Hamilton), 1936; "Jesse James," 1939; "Wife, Husband and Friend," 1939; "Rose of Washington Square," 1939.

"The Grapes of Wrath" (adapted from the novel by John Steinbeck), 1940; "Chad Hanna" (adapted from the novel by Walter D. Edmonds, *Red Wheels Rolling*), 1940; "Tobacco Road" (adapted from the play by Jack Kirkland based on the novel by Erskine Caldwell), 1941; "Roxie Hart" (adapted from the play by Maurine Watkins, "Chicago"), 1942; "Life Begins at Eight-thirty" (adapted from the play by Emlyn Williams, "The Light of Heart"), 1942; "The Pied Piper" (adapted from the novel by Nevil Shute), 1942; "Holy Matrimony" (adapted from the novel by Arnold Bennett, *Buried Alive*), 1943; "The Moon Is Down" (adapted from the novel by John Steinbeck), 1943; "Casanova Brown" (adapted from the play by Floyd Dell and Thomas Mitchell, "The Little Accident"), RKO, 1944; "The Woman in the Window" (adapted from the novel by J. G. Wallis, *Once Off Guard*), RKO, 1944; (with Joseph L. Mankiewicz) "The Keys of the Kingdom" (adapted from the novel by A. J. Cronin), 1945; "Along Came Jones" (adapted from the novel by Alan LeMay, *Useless Cowboy*), RKO, 1945; "The Dark Mirror," Universal, 1946; "Mr. Peabody and the Mermaid" (adapted from the novel by Constance Jones and Guy Jones, *Peabody's Mermaid*), Universal, 1948; "Everybody Does It," 1949.

"Three Came Home" (adapted from nonfiction by Agnes Newton Keith), 1950; "The Mudlark" (adapted from the novel by Theodore Bonnet), 1951; "The Desert Fox" (adapted from the autobiography of Desmond Young), 1951; "The Long, Dark Hall" (adapted from the novel by Edgar Lustgarten, *A Case to Answer*), Eagle Lion, 1951; "Phone Call From a Stranger" (adapted from the novella by I.A.R. Wylie), 1952; "We're Not Married," 1952; "My Cousin Rachel" (adapted from the novel by Daphne du Maurier), 1952; (and director) "How to Marry a Millionaire" (adapted from the play by Zoe Akins, "The Greeks Had a Word for It," and the play by Dale Eunson and Katharine Albert, "Loco"), 1953; (and director) "Night People," 1954; (and director) "Black Widow" (adapted from the novel by Patrick Quentin), 1954.

(And director) "How to Be Very, Very Popular" (adapted from the novel by Edward Hope, *She Loves Me,* and the play by Lyford Moore, "Sleep It Off"), 1955; (and director) "The Man in the Grey Flannel Suit" (adapted from the novel by Sloan Wilson), 1956; (and director) "The Three Faces of Eve" (adapted from nonfiction by Corbett H. Thigpen and Hervey M. Cleckley, *A Case of Multiple Personality*), 1957; (and director) "The Man Who Understood Women" (adapted from the novel by Romain Gary, *The Colors of the Day*), 1959.

"The Angel Wore Red" (adapted from the novel by Bruce Marshall, *The Fair Bride*), Metro-Goldwyn-Mayer (MGM), 1960; (with Clair Huffaker) "Flaming Star" (adapted from the novel by Huffaker, *Flaming Lance*), 1960; "Mister Hobbs Takes a Vacation" (adapted from the novel by Edward Streeter, *Mr. Hobbs' Vacation*), 1962; "Take Her, She's Mine" (adapted from the play by Phoebe Ephron and Henry Ephron), 1963; (with Nora Johnson; and director) "The World of Henry Orient" (adapted from the novel by Nora Johnson), United Artists, 1964; (with Lukas Heller) "The Dirty Dozen" (adapted from the novel by E. M. Nathanson), MGM, 1967. Contributor to periodicals, including *Saturday Evening Post.*

SIDELIGHTS: In reviewing *There Ought to be a Law and*

Other Stories, a critic noted that "the manner is agreeably carefree and the morals none the less effective for their burlesque slant." A *New York Times* critic was similarly complimentary, writing that the "yarns are funny and crackle with wisecracks.... When Mr. Johnson writes with less strain and less overstatement, his irony is going to be finer and his humor likewise. Now he is just robustly funny."

Despite such praise for his stories, Johnson is best known for his screenplays. His two adaptations of novels by John Steinbeck, "The Grapes of Wrath" and "The Moon Is Down," were highly acclaimed upon release of the respective films. Frank S. Nugent was especially impressed by Johnson's adaptation of *The Grapes of Wrath.* He wrote that the screenplay "followed the book; has followed it closely, but not with blind, undiscriminating literalness; has followed it so well that no one who has read and admired it should complain of the manner of its screen telling."

BIOGRAPHICAL/CRITICAL SOURCES: New York Times, April 12, 1931, November 14, 1935, May 6, 1939, January 25, 1940, February 21, 1941, March 27, 1943, October 19, 1946, December 25, 1950, December 26, 1952, April 13, 1956, September 27, 1957, June 16, 1962, March 26, 1977; *Books,* August 23, 1931. *Obituaries: New York Times,* March 26, 1977.*

(Died in Los Angeles, Calif., March 25, 1977)

*   *   *

JOHNSON, Paul C(ornelius)   1904-

PERSONAL: Born August 17, 1904, in Lakeville, Minn.; son of Peter C. (a farmer) and Ingeborg (Alfson) Johnson; married Eveline Ellingson (a teacher and editorial assistant), August 5, 1931; children: David, Linda (Mrs. Ralph Carpenter). *Education:* St. Olaf College, B.A., 1928. *Religion:* Lutheran. *Home:* 1115 South Maple, Northfield, Minn. 55057.

CAREER: St. Olaf College, Northfield, Minn., instructor in English, 1930-31; editor of *Bellingham Times,* 1931-32, *Madison Western Guard,* 1933-34, and *Grant County Herald,* 1934; *Worthington Daily Globe,* Worthington, Minn., editor, 1935-40; University of Minnesota, Minneapolis, instructor, 1941-43, associate professor of communications, 1944-47; *Prairie Farmer,,* Chicago, Ill., editor-in-chief, 1947-70; Farm Progress Publications, Chicago, Ill., contributing editor, 1970—. Lecturer on agriculture and humor in literature. Head of board of directors of Lutheran General Hospital, 1955-70. Editorial consultant to Wallace-Homestead Book Co.

MEMBER: American Agricultural Editors Association (president, 1953), American Country Life Association (president, 1954), Farm Foundation (head of board of directors, 1953-70), Phi Beta Kappa. *Awards, honors:* Named honorary American farmer by National Future Farmers of America, 1951; Freedoms Foundation medal, 1951; D.H.L. from St. Olaf College, 1953; Reuben Brigham Award from American Association of Agricultural College Editors, 1954; Soil Builders Award from National Plant Food Institute, 1955; Asta Award for Farm Writers from American Seed Trade Association, 1965, for general excellence as a farm writer; golden anniversary medal from Land Bank Association, 1967; Oscar in Agriculture from DeKalb Agricultural Association, 1969, for "long time editorial contribution to American agricultural philosophy and practice."

WRITINGS: John Turnipseed's Four Seasons Almanac, Wallace-Homestead, 1973; *Farm Animals in the Making of America,* Wallace-Homestead, 1975; *Farm Inventions in the Making of America,* Wallace-Homestead, 1976; *Farm Power in the Making of America,* Wallace-Homestead, 1978; *John Turnipseed Speaks His Piece,* Wallace-Homestead, 1978. Author of columns in *Prairie Farmer,* including "Prairie Farmer Says," 1947-70, "John Turnipseed," 1948-76, "This Business of Farming," 1949-62, and "Editor's Viewpoint," 1962-70. Contributor to magazines.

WORK IN PROGRESS: Research and writing on agricultural history and antiques.

SIDELIGHTS: Paul C. Johnson told *CA:* "My editorial stance throughout my career may best be described as conservative. With respect to agriculture, my position was that there should be a minimum of governmental control or subsidy. My humor column, "John Turnipseed," carried out simultaneously with other editorial writings, was somewhat more liberal. It was devoted to reminding rural people that there are human values in farming aside from technological and financial success."

*   *   *

JOHNSON, Ronald C.   1927-

PERSONAL: Born July 18, 1927, in Duluth, Minn.; son of Bror A. and Mabel (Carlson) Johnson; married Carol Anderson (a researcher), November 1, 1953; children: Roni, Steven, Christopher. *Education:* University of Minnesota, Duluth, B.A. (cum laude), 1949, Ph.D., 1959; University of Denver, M.A., 1950. *Home:* 23 Kalaka Pl., Kailua, Hawaii 96734. *Office:* Department of Psychology, University of Hawaii, 2430 Campus Rd., Honolulu, Hawaii 96822.

CAREER: University of Minnesota, Minneapolis, instructor in psychology, 1956-57; San Jose State College (now University), San Jose, Calif., 1957-62, began as assistant professor, became associate professor of psychology; University of Hawaii, Honolulu, associate professor of psychology, 1962-65; University of Colorado, Boulder, 1965-70, began as associate professor, became professor of psychology; University of Hawaii, professor of psychology, 1970—. *Military service:* U.S. Naval Reserve, active duty, 1944-46. *Member:* American Psychological Association (fellow), Society for Research in Child Development, American Association for the Advancement of Science (fellow), American Association on Mental Deficiency, Behavior Genetics Association, Sigma Xi. *Awards, honors:* Distinguished visiting fellow at Australian National University, summer, 1978.

WRITINGS: (With W. N. McBain) *The Science of Ourselves,* Harper, 1962; (co-author) *Child Psychology: Behavior and Development,* Wiley, 1965, 3rd edition, 1974; (co-author) *Child and Adolescent Psychology,* Wiley, 1969, 2nd edition, 1976; (editor with P. R. Dokecki and O. H. Mowrer) *Conscience, Contrast, and Social Reality,* Holt, 1970; (with Linda K. Dixon) *Roots of Individuality,* Brooks-Cole, 1978. Consulting editor of *American Journal of Mental Deficiency,* 1971-74.

WORK IN PROGRESS: Research on cerebral lateralization and cognitive functioning, and on conscience and adjustment.

*   *   *

JOHNSON, Sam Houston   1914(?)-1978

OBITUARY NOTICE: Born c. 1914, in Texas; died December 11, 1978, in Austin, Tex. Former presidential aide and author. A non-practicing lawyer, Johnson worked for his brother, the late President Lyndon Baines Johnson, for thirty years. As his brother's employee, Johnson once described himself as "babysitter, chauffeur, political trouble shooter, administrative aide and general adviser," and commented that "there were a lot of people who never knew Lyndon Johnson had a brother." His book, *My Brother Lyndon,* was published in 1970. Obituaries and other sources: *Look,* December 16, 1969; *Newsweek,* January 12, 1970; *Harper's,* April, 1970; *Washington Post,* December 12, 1978; *Chicago Tribune,* December 12, 1978; *Time,* December 25, 1978.

* * *

JOHNSTONE, Lammy Olcott 1946-

PERSONAL: Born January 23, 1946, in New York, N.Y.; daughter of Edmund Frank (in advertising) and Janet (Olcott) Johnstone; married Walter J. Carlson (a public relations company president), December 3, 1971. *Home:* 390 West End Ave., New York, N.Y. 10024. *Office:* The *Trib,* 711 Third Ave., New York, N.Y. 10017.

CAREER/WRITINGS: Beverly Hills Times, Beverly Hills, Calif., feature editor, 1964-66; reporter in society department for *New York Daily News; Advertising News of New York,* New York City, associate editor, 1968-72, managing editor, 1972-77; *Trib,* New York City, senior editor, 1977-78. Notable assignments include an interview with Martin Luther King and coverage of the Watts riots. On-air reporter for "Grandstand," a nationally televised weekly sports/news program. U.S. correspondent for *Campaign* (British business journal); contributor to consumer and business publications, and to popular magazines including *Ladies' Home Journal* and *American Home.*

SIDELIGHTS: Lammy Johnstone commented on her position as senior editor covering communications for the *Trib:* "There is no other city that can claim it is the home for as many media, advertising agency, marketing and public relations facilities as New York can. The *Trib,* in its decision to provide extensive coverage to communications five days a week, is the first New York City newspaper to recognize the magnitude and power of this industry—an industry that has matured to that level where it now affects each one of us every moment of the day.... Both the entertainment and the business sectors of the field will be covered in an informative, lively manner. To my knowledge this is the first time that both portions of the industry will be incorporated under the guidance of one editor."

* * *

JOHNSTONE, Robert Morton, Jr. 1939-

PERSONAL: Born December 20, 1939, in Nashville, Tenn.; son of Robert Morton (a commercial artist) and Georgia B. Johnstone; married Linda Lazenby, 1962; children: Gwyneth Owen. *Education:* Vanderbilt University, B.A., 1962; Cornell University, M.A., 1970, Ph.D., 1972. *Politics:* Democrat. *Religion:* Protestant. *Home:* 204 South 16th St., Richmond, Ind. 47374. *Office:* Department of Political Science, Earlham College, Richmond, Ind. 47374.

CAREER: Wilson College, Chambersburg, Pa., assistant professor of political science, 1972-75; Earlham College, Richmond, Ind., associate professor of political science, 1975—. Director of Whitewater Opera Company. *Military service:* U.S. Navy, 1962-67; became lieutenant senior grade. *Member:* American Political Science Association, American Historical Association.

WRITINGS: Jefferson and the Presidency: Leadership in the Young Republic, Cornell University Press, 1978.

WORK IN PROGRESS: Research for a biography of John Randolph of Roanoke, Va.

SIDELIGHTS: Johnstone writes: "My scholarly interests include research on the American presidency, executive politics, and political leadership."

AVOCATIONAL INTERESTS: Singing, both solo and choral.

* * *

JONES, Arthur F(rederick) 1945-

PERSONAL: Born December 20, 1945, in New York, N.Y.; son of Arthur F. (a policeman) and Theresa (Schnabel) Jones; married Janice Sieman (a registered nurse), May 11, 1968; children: Mark, Meredith. *Education:* State University of New York College at New Paltz, B.A. (cum laude), 1967; Case Western Reserve University, M.A., 1970, Ph.D., 1974. *Home:* 204 Lackawanna Rd., Lexington, Ky. 40503. *Office:* Department of Art, University of Kentucky, Lexington, Ky. 40506.

CAREER: John Carroll University, Cleveland, Ohio, lecturer in art history, 1970-71; University of Kentucky, Lexington, instructor, 1971-74, assistant professor, 1974-77, associate professor of art history, 1977—. Lecturer at Case Western Reserve University and Cleveland State University, summer, 1970, and Cleveland Museum of Art, summer, 1971. Has had exhibitions of his sculpture in Kentucky. *Member:* College Art Association.

WRITINGS: The Art of Paul Sawyier, University Press of Kentucky, 1976. Author of exhibition catalogs. Contributor to *Antiques.*

WORK IN PROGRESS: Research on artists of Kentucky, Indiana, and Ohio, on the role of women in the arts of those areas, and on art patronage, with publications expected to result.

SIDELIGHTS: Jones writes: "As an art historian I am particularly interested in communicating how major European trends have effected the cultural activities of people in my own neighborhood—so-to-speak—who, yet, may not even be aware of the major world trends in fine art. I view regional study in art history as a practical, non-snob, non-elitist alternative for art historians who desire to combine academic activity with the real world. I am also interested in expressing myself in visual terms, and my own visual work has been treated in regional publications as genuine 'folk art' even though it is produced by an art historian with a Ph.D. I am not sure about such an assessment, but there appears to exist a state of harmony between my visual expressions and the topics that motivate my interest as an academic writer on art. I have not forgotten my background as the son of a 'cop,' rather than that of a professor or a physician. I am not ashamed to say that the world of art, and art history, had no 'noticeable' value for me as a child, or for my parents—nor did it have to at the time. Such an attitude has strongly affected the direction of my work as a writer."

* * *

JONES, Barbara (Mildred) 1917(?)-1978

OBITUARY NOTICE—See index for *CA* sketch: Born c. 1917 in Croydon, Surrey, England; died August 28, 1978. Painter, illustrator, mural and exhibition designer, and author. Jones wrote and illustrated several books, including *The Isle of Wight, The Unsophisticated Arts,* and *Follies and Grottoes.* Her best-known book was *Design for Death,* an examination of burial and memorial customs. Obituaries and other sources: *The Author's and Writer's Who's Who,* 6th edition, Burke's Peerage, 1971; *The Writers Directory, 1976-78,* St. Martin's, *AB Bookman's Weekly,* October 23, 1978.

* * *

JONES, Craig 1945-

PERSONAL: Born December 4, 1945, in San Diego, Calif.; son of Melvin Elbert (a salesman) and Marianne (a secretary; maiden name, Langdon) Jones. *Education:* Michigan State University, B.A., 1967; New York University, M.A., 1968. *Politics:* Independent. *Religion:* Presbyterian. *Home:* 108 West 15th St., New York, N.Y. 10011.

CAREER: New York Public Schools, Brooklyn, N.Y., English teacher, 1968-78; full-time writer, 1978—.

WRITINGS: Blood Secrets, Harper, 1978.

WORK IN PROGRESS: A play, "Boxcar," with Frank Moore.

SIDELIGHTS: Jones told *CA:* "I intend to be a full-time writer of novels, short stories, plays and hopefully screenplays. I am particularly attracted to emotionally controversial subjects and plots which center around family situations. My interest in writing was spawned by 'excessive' movie-going since childhood. As a writer, I feel the greatest offering I can give a reader is 'surprise.' My first love is satire, a genre I intend to pursue at length."

BIOGRAPHICAL/CRITICAL SOURCES: Publishers Weekly, May 29, 1978.

* * *

JONES, Garth N(elson) 1925-

PERSONAL: Born February 25, 1925, in Salt Lake City, Utah; son of Harry H. and Sophronia (Nielsen) Jones; married Verda Marie Clegg (a librarian), September 29, 1950; children: Edward Hood, Garth Kevin, Drew Luke. *Education:* Utah State University, B.S., 1947; University of Utah, M.S., 1948, Ph.D., 1954. *Religion:* Church of Jesus Christ of Latter-day Saints (Mormons). *Office:* University of Alaska, 3221 Providence Dr., Anchorage, Alaska 99504.

CAREER: U.S. Department of the Interior, Washington, D.C., assistant to the district administrator, 1951-52; U.S. Department of State, Washington, D.C., chief of the public administration division, 1956-61; Brigham Young University, Provo, Utah, assistant professor of political science, 1953-56; University of Southern California, Los Angeles, associate professor of public administration, 1961-67; U.S. Department of State, member of AID mission to Pakistan, 1967-70; Colorado State University, Fort Collins, professor of political science, 1970-72; United Nations, New York, N.Y., senior consultant on population, 1972-73; University of Alaska, Anchorage, professor of public policy and administration and dean, 1973—. *Member:* American Public Administration Society, American Political Science Association, American Society for Applied Anthropology, Western Political Science Association.

WRITINGS: Planned Organizational Change: A Study Using an Empirical Approach, Routledge & Kegan Paul, 1968, Praeger, 1969. Contributor to academic journals.

WORK IN PROGRESS: Short stories based on western history; research on organizational change and population growth.

SIDELIGHTS: Jones told *CA:* "I have a strong interest in the impact of law and social institutions on the shape and conduct of human behavior and affairs. To what extent can human beings take destiny in their own hands and shape their future?"

* * *

JONES, Hettie 1934-

PERSONAL: Born July 16, 1934, in Brooklyn, N.Y.; daughter of Oscar and Lottie (Lewis) Cohen; married LeRoi Jones (now Amiri Baraka; a writer), October 13, 1958 (divorced, 1966); children: Kettie, Lisa. *Education:* University of Virginia, Fredericksburg, B.A., 1955; attended Columbia University, 1955-56. *Residence:* New York, N.Y. *Agent:* Elaine Markson, 44 Greenwich Ave., New York, N.Y. 10011.

CAREER: Columbia University Press, Center for Mass Communication, New York City, staff writer, 1956-57; *Partisan Review,* New York City, managing editor, 1957-61; Mobilization for Youth, New York City, 1967-69, began as staff writer, became director of educational after-school program; free-lance writer, 1970—. Day care worker and substitute teacher. Church of All Nations Day Care Center, community representative and president of board of directors. *Awards, honors: The Trees Stand Shining* was chosen as notable children's book by American Library Association, 1971; *Big Star Fallin Mama* was featured by New York Public Library as young adult best book, 1975.

WRITINGS: (Editor) *Poems Now* (anthology), Kulchur Press, 1966; (compiler) *The Trees Stand Shining* (selected Indian poems), Dial, 1971; (adaptor) *Longhouse Winter* (Iroquois transformation tales), Holt, 1972; *Coyote Tales,* Holt, 1974; *Big Star Fallin Mama* (biographies of women jazz musicians; for young adults), Viking, 1974; *How to Eat Your ABC's: A Book About Vitamins,* Four Winds Press, 1976; *I Hate to Talk About Your Mother* (novel), Viking, 1979. Also author of "Action" series, Scholastic Books, 1977.

SIDELIGHTS: Hettie Jones writes: "Since 1957 I've been involved with literature and writers one way or another. I owned (with my husband) a samll press (Totem), which published Ginsberg, Corso, O'Hara, Dorn, Gary Snyder, etc., and a magazine called *Yugen.* When I have time I like to write short stories for slow readers, textbook stories for kids. Interest and competence: avant-garde jazz. I write novelizations to support my children and my writing habit. Have been totally self-employed since 1970, but am POOR." Jones also mentioned that she enjoys writing for children because "it's a challenge to simplify and clarify."

* * *

JONES, Kathleen 1922-

PERSONAL: Born April 7, 1922, in London, England; daughter of William Robert and Kate Lilian (Barnard) Savage; married David Gwyn Jones, July 22, 1944 (deceased); children: Stephen Gwyn. *Education:* University of London, B.A., 1943, Ph.D., 1953. *Politics:* "Christian Socialist." *Religion:* Anglican. *Home:* Woodlands Cottage, Barton-le-Willows, North Yorkshire, England. *Office:* Goodricke College, University of York, York YO1 5DD, England.

CAREER: University of Manchester, Manchester, England, research assistant, 1952-54, assistant lecturer in history, 1954-55; Victoria Institution, Kuala Lumpur, Malaysia, senior historian, 1956-58; University of Manchester, lecturer, 1958-62, senior lecturer in history, 1962-65; University of York, York, England, professor of history and head of department, 1965—. Chairwoman of United Kingdom Commission for UNESCO social sciences committee, 1968-72. Maudsley Lecturer for Royal College of Psychiatrists, 1977. *Military service:* Auxiliary Territorial Service, welfare worker, 1946-47; became junior commander. *Member:* Association of Psychiatric Social Workers of Great Britain (president, 1968-70), Social Administration Association, Royal College of Psychiatrists (fellow), University Women's Club.

WRITINGS: Lunacy Law and Conscience, Routledge & Kegan Paul, 1955; *Mental Health and Social Policy*, Routledge & Kegan Paul, 1960; (with R. Sidebotham) *Mental Hospitals at Work*, Routledge & Kegan Paul, 1962; *The Teaching of Social Studies in British Universities*, Bell & Son, 1965; *The Compassionate Society*, S.P.C.K., 1965; *A History of the Mental Health Services*, Routledge & Kegan Paul, 1972; *Opening the Door: A Study of New Policies for the Mentally Handicapped*, Routledge & Kegan Paul, 1975; (with J. Brown and J. R. Bradshaw) *Issues in Social Policy*, Routledge & Kegan Paul, 1978. General editor of "International Library of Social Policy." Contributor to medical and health services journals. Editor of *Yearbook of Social Policy in Britain*, 1971-76.

WORK IN PROGRESS: A book of documents on nineteenth-century social policy; a study of creativity in administration; research on social stress and industrialization.

SIDELIGHTS: Kathleen Jones writes: "All my writing relates to my professional field of social policy and administration. My values are those of the Declaration of Human Rights, 1948: I am against racism, sexism, and ageism, and in favour of liberty, equality, and fraternity (though the three are unfortunately not always compatible, hence the need for the academic study of social policy and administration). These I believe to be the values of the Gospel."

*   *   *

JONES, Noel   1939-
(Patrick Aalben)

PERSONAL: Born December 1, 1939, in Dublin, Ireland; son of Thomas Anthony (a bank clerk) and Margaret (Lane) Jones; married Margaret Graham (a marketing consultant), December 24, 1970; children: Graham, Mark. *Education:* Attended National University of Ireland, 1957-59. *Religion:* Quaker. *Home:* 16 Mountpleasant Sq., Dublin 6, Ireland. *Agent:* Campbell Thompson and McLaughlin, 31 Newington Green, London N16 9PU, England.

CAREER: Worked in Dublin, Ireland, as free-lance journalist and radio producer, 1957-60, and advertising copywriter, 1960-63; publicity manager of Irish Peat Development Authority, 1963-65; writer, 1965—. Editor of "Lookaround" and script editor of "Harbour Hotel," both for RTE-Radio, Ireland, 1973—. *Member:* Society of Irish Playwrights (council member), Society of Irish Playwrights Limited (board member), P.E.N., Society of Authors, Crime Writers' Association (Great Britain).

WRITINGS: (Under pseudonym Patrick Aalben) *The Grab*, R. Hale, 1977. Also writer of radio plays broadcast in Ireland, Great Britain, Sweden, Yugoslavia, Australia, New Zealand, and South Africa.

WORK IN PROGRESS: Radio plays.

SIDELIGHTS: Noel Jones writes: "I have a special interest in and knowledge of France, where I spend several months each year."

JONES, Penelope   1938-

PERSONAL: Born February 17, 1938, in Rochester, N.Y.; daughter of Gikas (in business) and Metaxia (Jebeles) Critikos; married Graham Starr Jones II (a patent attorney), July 5, 1959; children: Candida Starr, Kimberley Jebeles. *Education:* Smith College, B.A., 1959. *Home:* 8 Jeffrey Lane, Chappaqua, N.Y. 10514.

CAREER: Camp counselor in Algonquin Park, Ontario, summer, 1955; secretary, 1959-60; writer, 1976—; Country Day Nursery, Chappaqua, N.Y., teacher, 1977—. Actress with Southbury Playhouse, summer, 1974; member of Dobbs Ferry Village Players; member of board of directors, past president, and casting director and producer of Chappaqua Drama Group. Volunteer remedial reading teacher at Children's Village, 1963-65; volunteer reader for Chappaqua Library. *Member:* Chappaqua Garden Club.

WRITINGS: I Didn't Want to Be Nice (juvenile), Bradbury, 1977; *I'm Not Moving* (juvenile picture book), Bradbury, 1979.

WORK IN PROGRESS: A juvenile reader.

SIDELIGHTS: Penelope Jones writes: "I feel very strongly about the importance of children learning to love books at the preschool level. In addition to the boundless possibilities for developing the imagination, being read to gives the young child an enormous amount of assurance, understanding, and sheer pleasure, which will have positive effects throughout his life. Having this conviction, I am particularly interested in helping young children to understand that their feelings of hostility, jealousy, and fear are legitimate—everyone has them."

*   *   *

JONSSON, Snaebjorn   1888(?)-1978

OBITUARY NOTICE: Born c. 1888; died in 1978 in Reykjavik, Iceland. Publisher, bookseller, poet, author, and translator of English literature into Icelandic. Jonsson, founder of the renowned English Bookshop in Reykjavik, was best known for his positive influence on Iceland's book production industry. Obituaries and other sources: *AB Bookman's Weekly*, September 4, 1978.

*   *   *

JOSEFSBERG, Milt   1911-

PERSONAL: Born June 29, 1911, in New York, N.Y.; son of Jacob (a merchant) and Dinah (Fruchter) Josefsberg; married Hilda Wolarsky, January 26, 1936; children: Alan Roy, Steven Kent. *Education:* Attended City College of the City University of New York. *Religion:* Jewish. *Residence:* Encino, Calif. *Agent:* Scott Meredith Literary Agency, Inc., 845 Third Ave., New York, N.Y. 10022. *Office:* Tandem Productions, "All in the Family," 5752 Sunset Blvd., Los Angeles, Calif. 90078.

CAREER: Worked as press agent, 1933-38; writer for radio for "The Bob Hope Show," 1938-43; writer for radio and television for "The Jack Benny Show," 1943-55; National Broadcasting Corp., New York, N.Y., programming executive, 1955-57; script consultant for television for "The Bob Hope Show," 1957-59; writer for television for "The Milton Berle Show," 1959-60; script consultant for television for "The Danny Thomas Show," 1960-61; script consultant for television for "Joey Bishop," 1962-63; head writer and script consultant for television for "The Lucy Show" and "Here's Lucy," 1964-73; writer for various televised specials, 1973-75; writer, script supervisor, and producer for television for "All in the Family," 1975—. Script consultant for television for "The Odd Couple," 1972-73. Creator of television series, "Here's Lucy." *Awards, honors:* Received nominations for awards from Academy of Television Arts and Sciences, Critics Circle Award, and Writers Guild of America; received nominations for Humanities Award and Population Zero Award.

WRITINGS: The Jack Benny Show: The Life and Times of America's Best Loved Entertainer, Arlington House, 1977. Also author of scripts for television series, including "The Bob Hope Show," "The Jack Benny Show," "The Milton Berle Show," "The Danny Thomas Show," "The Lucy Show," "Here's Lucy," "Joey Bishop," and "All in the Family," and radio series, including "The Bob Hope Show," and "The Jack Benny Show."

*   *   *

JOSEPHSON, Matthew   1899-1978

PERSONAL: Born February 15, 1899, in Brooklyn, N.Y.; son of Julius (a banker) and Sarah (Kasindorf) Josephson; married Hannah Geffen, May 6, 1920 (died, 1976); children: Eric Jonathan, Carl Philip Emmanuel. *Education:* Columbia University, B.A., 1920. *Home:* New York, N.Y.; and Sherman, Conn.

CAREER: Financial and literary editor for *Newark Ledger;* co-founder and editor of *Secession* (literary magazine), 1922-24; associate editor of *Broom* (literary magazine), 1922-24; account representative for brokerage firms in New York City, 1924-26; American editor for *transition* (literary magazine), 1928-29; Macaulay Co., New York City, book editor, 1929; *New Republic,* Washington, D.C., assistant editor, 1931-32; writer. Special lecturer at the University of California, Irvine, 1968-69; visiting professor at University of California, Santa Cruz, 1977-78. *Member:* Authors Guild, Authors League of America. *Awards, honors:* Guggenheim traveling fellowship for creative literature, 1933-34; elected to the National Institute of Arts and Letters, 1948; Francis Parkman prize from the Society of American Historians, 1960, for *Edison: A Biography;* Van Wyck Brooks prize for biography and history, 1969, for *Al Smith: Hero of the Cities.*

WRITINGS: Zola and His Time: The History of His Martial Career in Letters, Macaulay, 1928, reprinted, Russell, 1969; *Portrait of the Artist as American,* Harcourt, 1930, reprinted, Octagon, 1964; *Jean-Jacques Rousseau,* Harcourt, 1931, reprinted, Russell, 1970; *Nazi Culture: The Brown Darkness Over Germany,* John Day Co., 1933; *The Robber Barons: The Great American Capitalists, 1861-1901,* Harcourt, 1934, reprinted, 1962; *The Politicos, 1865-1896,* Harcourt, 1938, reprinted, 1963.

The President Makers: The Culture of Politics and Leadership in an Age of Enlightenment, 1896-1919, Harcourt, 1940, reprinted, Ungar, 1964; *Victor Hugo: A Realistic Biography of the Great Romantic,* Doubleday, 1942; *Empire of the Air: Juan Trippe and the Struggle for World Airways,* Harcourt, 1944, reprinted, Arno, 1972; *Stendhal: or, The Pursuit of Happiness,* Doubleday, 1946, reprinted, Russell, 1969; (editor, author of introduction, and translator from French with wife, Hannah Josephson) Marie Henri Beyle, *Memoirs of Egotism,* Lear, 1949.

Sidney Hillman: Statesman of American Labor, Doubleday, 1952; *Union House, Union Bar: The History of the Hotel and Restaurant Employees and Bartenders International Union, AFL-CIO,* Random House, 1956; *Edison: A Biography,* McGraw, 1959; *Life Among the Surrealists: A Memoir,*

Holt, 1962; *Infidel in the Temple: A Memoir of the Nineteen-Thirties,* Knopf, 1967; (with H. Josephson) *Al Smith: Hero of the Cities,* Houghton, 1969; (author of introduction) Ruth Gikow, *Ruth Gikow,* Random House, 1970; *The Money Lords: The Great Finance Capitalists, 1925-1950,* Weybright, 1972. Also author of *Galimathias, and Other Poems,* 1923.

Contributor to *New Yorker, Saturday Evening Post, Nation,* and *Outlook.*

SIDELIGHTS: Tolerance and objectivity are perhaps the most characteristic traits of Matthew Josephson's life and work. Although outwardly an orthodox individual, he consorted with Bohemians and unconventional literary lights. A Communist sympathizer in the 1930's, Josephson nevertheless had a certain admiration for the American capitalists whose lives he documented. Always he was willing to listen to views different from his own, and this spirit of fair play infused his books. His accurate, unbiased descriptions of historical figures and events earned him accolades from numerous critics.

Josephson's chief concerns were nineteenth-century French literature and twentieth-century American capitalism. He had studied French literature at Columbia University, and this interest was intensified when he joined other American expatriates in the 1920's and traveled to Paris. There he became friends with such people as Paul Eluard, Andre Breton, Louis Aragon, and Max Ernst. These friendships enabled him to become an eyewitness to the development of surrealism, as he explains in *Life Among the Surrealists.* Harold Clurman called the book a combination of high-brow gossip and American cultural history, noting that it "is written without malice and with . . . optimism and enthusiasm." Although Andre Ferrier found the anecdotes in *Life Among the Surrealists* entertaining, he complained that Josephson "hardly ever refers to the works of the painters or poets he has known. So in reading him, one gets the impression that they were just charming and tiresome young people, noisy and harmless cafe anarchists, engaging in practical jokes of dubious taste in dubious haunts."

Josephson brought an understanding of the French character to his biographies of Zola, Rousseau, Hugo, and Stendhal. When *Zola and His Time* appeared, critics were generous with their praise. Malcolm Cowley declared the biography to be "vigorous, absorbing, hastily written, superbly documented, and rich, amazingly rich." *Jean-Jacques Rousseau* was equally well-received. "In this all but monumental book which Mr. Josephson has composed with so much careful and painstaking study, perhaps a truer picture of Rousseau appears than any that has gone before," H. J. Forman asserted. Although most commentators felt that *Victor Hugo* was a well-balanced account of Hugo's life, it was generally conceded that it did not measure up to Josephson's previous biographies. Several critics pointed out historical errors in the text. The last biography that Josephson wrote about a Frenchman was *Stendhal.* Described by a *Time* reviewer as "the best and most comprehensive English study of its subject," Josephson's book is credited with creating a resurgence of interest in Stendhal's life and works.

But Josephson did not confine his scholarly pursuits to French writers and literature. After graduating from Columbia, he had lived for a time in Greenwich Village, where he met many of the leading American writers of the day. While in Paris he was a crony of William Carlos Williams, E. E. Cummings, Kenneth Burke, and Malcolm Cowley. His editorial work on *Secession, Broom,* and *transition,* avant-garde literary magazines, also brought him into contact with many aspiring American authors. Josephson had met Hart Crane while he was still struggling for recognition and had urged the poet to continue writing.

The onset of the Depression in 1929 shifted Josephson's thinking from literary concerns to economic issues. As a member of the editorial staff of the *New Republic,* he wrote of the problems facing the country: poverty, labor conditions, government controls, and individual freedom. *New Republic* reflected the intelligentsia's growing belief that left-wing politics could cure the nation's economic ills. Although Josephson never joined the Communist party, he supported the cause and helped to draft the Communists' manifesto in the election year of 1932. Josephson's account of this period in history is set forth in *Infidel in the Temple.* A reviewer for *New Yorker* called the book "perhaps the most cogent informal history of the Depression that we have had." Commenting about Josephson's detachment, Daniel Aaron wrote: "Throughout the period that he describes and analyzes so brilliantly, he enjoyed the role of the disengaged and prescient fellow-traveler . . . making good use of his connections with power and opinion centers and objectively studying a society in 'chronic cataclysm.'" Wilson C. McWilliams disagreed with such an assessment, contending that *Infidel in the Temple* "is not a history of the 1930's: it is a chronicle, a tale of *nemesis.* He has, in fact, set out to *un-write* a revisionist history which sees the intellectuals of the thirties as 'dupes' of a super-cunning 'Communist conspiracy.'" Opinions like McWilliams's were in the minority.

Josephson's interest in politics and economics provoked him to delve into the American past. He wrote several books about U.S. politicians and captains of industry, the most famous of which is *The Robber Barons.* Now regarded as a classic, the book traced the careers of well-known capitalists, including Jay Gould, John D. Rockefeller, Andrew Carnegie, J. P. Morgan, E. H. Harriman, and Henry Clay Frick. Josephson's thesis was that "the captains or barons of industry were agents of progress [and] under their command our mainly agrarian-mercantile society was swiftly transformed into a mass-production economy."

The Robber Barons won the admiration of nearly all who read it. A. B. Miller termed it "an adroit and thrilling account," while Robert Cantwell declared it "the best, the liveliest and most illuminating of the works on this subject." Plaudits were also forthcoming from the *New York Times:* "What he [Josephson] has written is not a mere series of biographies but a genuine history, with the stories of the great American capitalists skillfully interwoven, and with an eye always on the broader social background." Some commentators, however, discerned a bias in *The Robber Barons.* Allan Nevins noted that "this interesting book is a pamphlet or polemic as well as a vivid picture. It bears a direct relationship to our own time. Anyone who believes in the New Deal must wish it the widest possible reading. It shows how evil the worst side of the Old Deal, the Raw Deal, actually was."

Working in collaboration with his wife, Josephson wrote his final biography, *Al Smith: Hero of the Cities.* A former New York governor and the 1928 Democratic presidential candidate, Smith worked for—and won—liberal labor, housing, and welfare legislation. Josephson told an interviewer, "Al Smith is very much a meaningful politician for modern America, for he was a brave liberal in very dark times in the 1920's." Critics lauded the Josephsons' portrait of Al Smith. A reviewer for *Atlantic* considered it "a lively, sympathetic account," and Francis Russell observed, "The publisher's

claim that this is the definitive biography—a well-worked adjective—seems in this case justified."

In his later years, Josephson reflected on the American scene. He pointed out that current entrepreneurs are not nearly so colorful as the great financiers of the past: "Today's Horatio Alger capitalists just go out and get a contract from the military-industrial complex. They're virtually faceless partisans of state capitalism. Even the conglomerateurs—those who put one and one companies together and come out with three, four or five—are awfully tame compared with such flamboyant characters as Jay Gould or J. P. Morgan."

Although Josephson was concerned about the gargantuan federal bureaucracy and the tendency for large corporations to work in league with the government, he told an interviewer in 1972 that he could not think of a satisfactory alternative to the free enterprise system. "We could turn to a socialist state, or a dictatorship," he said. "When I was younger, I used to consider the possibility. Now, I wouldn't enjoy it. Suppose you had an authoritarian state run by Nixon or Hoffa?"

Some of Josephson's books have been translated into Spanish and Italian.

BIOGRAPHICAL/CRITICAL SOURCES: Books, October 14, 1928, January 24, 1932, March 4, 1934, April 10, 1938, November 10, 1940, October 25, 1942; *New York Times,* October 28, 1928, January 24, 1932, March 4, 1934, April 10, 1938, October 18, 1942, October 20, 1946, December 7, 1952, January 25, 1968, December 1, 1969, December 31, 1972; *Times Literary Supplement,* December 6, 1928, April 14, 1932, May 5, 1961; *Saturday Review of Literature,* January 30, 1932, March 3, 1934, April 9, 1938; *New Republic,* February 10, 1932, March 14, 1934, May 4, 1938, December 16, 1940, November 4, 1946, December 22, 1952, November 11, 1967; *Nation,* February 10, 1932, March 7, 1934, May 14, 1938, October 12, 1940, November 28, 1942, March 3, 1962, November 6, 1967; Malcolm Cowley, *Exile's Return: A Literary Odyssey of the 1920's,* Viking, 1934, revised edition, Penguin, 1976; *Yale Review,* summer, 1934; *American Academy of Political and Social Science Annals,* July, 1934; *Time,* October 19, 1942, October 21, 1946, October 20, 1967, January 19, 1970; *New Yorker,* October 19, 1946, November 4, 1967, November 8, 1969; *New Statesman,* April 14, 1961; Matthew Josephson, *Life Among the Surrealists: A Memoir,* Holt, 1962; *New York Times Book Review,* February 4, 1962, November 26, 1967, February 1, 1970, November 5, 1972; *Christian Science Monitor,* February 8, 1962, December 24, 1969; Matthew Josephson, *Infidel in the Temple: A Memoir of the Nineteen-Thirties,* Knopf, 1967; *Harper's,* January, 1968; *Vogue,* January 15, 1968; *Best Sellers,* January 15, 1968, November 15, 1969, December 15, 1972; *Commonweal,* January 19, 1968; *Saturday Review,* January 27, 1968, March 7, 1970; *Atlantic Monthly,* November, 1969; *Washington Post Book World,* March 8, 1970.

OBITUARIES: New York Times, March 14, 1978; *Time,* March 27, 1978.*

(Died March 13, 1978, in Santa Cruz, Calif.)

*   *   *

JUSSIM, Estelle 1927-

PERSONAL: Born March 18, 1927, in New York, N.Y.; daughter of Boris Ossipovich (a photographer) and Manya Aaronovna (Glusker) Jussim. *Education:* Queens College (now Queens College of the City University of New York), B.A., 1947; Columbia University, M.S., 1963, D.L.S., 1970. *Home address:* P.O. Box 132, Granby, Mass. 01033. *Office:* Graduate School of Library Science, Simmons College, 300 Fenway, Boston, Mass. 02115.

CAREER: Free-lance art director and graphic designer in New York City, 1948-60; Columbia University libraries, New York City, member of staff, 1963-65; Borough of Manhattan Community College, New York City, executive assistant director of educational resources, 1965-66; Hampshire College, Amherst, Mass., assistant professor of communications media, 1969-72; Simmons College, Boston, Mass., associate professor of film and visual communication, 1972—. Lecturer on history of photography and visual communications theory. Member of board of trustees of Massachusetts State Library, 1971-73, and of Visual Studies Workshop, Rochester, N.Y.; member of visiting committee of International Museum of Photography.

MEMBER: Popular Culture Association, Society for Photographic Education, Deutsches Gesellschaft fuer Photographie (honorary member). *Awards, honors:* Award for distinguished achievement in the history of photography from New York Photographic Historical Society, 1974, for *Visual Communication and the Graphic Arts.*

WRITINGS: Visual Communication and the Graphic Arts: Photographic Technologies of the Nineteenth Century, Bowker, 1974; (contributor) Susan R. Channing, editor, *The Art of the State, the State of the Art: Fourteen Massachusetts Photographers, 1975-77,* Addison House, 1978; (contributor) Kelly Wise, editor, *Appraisals,* Addison Press, in press.

Work anthologized in *Expanding Media,* edited by Deirdre Boyle, Oryx Press, 1977, and *Women in Architecture,* edited by Susan Torre, Whitney Library of Design (New York), 1977. Contributor to photographic history and communications media journals, and to *Massachusetts Review.* Member of international advisory board, *History of Photography* (London).

WORK IN PROGRESS: Research for a monograph on photographer F. Holland Day, for Camera Graphic Press.

SIDELIGHTS: Estelle Jussim writes: "My work on the theory of the graphic arts was undoubtedly made possible by years of practical experience with the printing industries. My father was a studio photographer, and so I seem to have come by my interest in visual communication 'legitimately,' as a bewildered colleague once remarked. My lectures and writing seem to be intimately connected, and a student once put the ultimate curse on me by saying that I spoke just as I wrote.

"I consider that much of my life has been dominated by the thinking of two philosophers with whom I had the good fortune to study: Carl Hempel, a logical positivist, and Arnold Isenberg, an aesthetician. I have been trying to synthesize the logic of one with the logic of the other, and have been discovering that 'history' grips me because it represents similar struggles to synthesize conflicting ideological position. I admire the work of Morse Peckham most enthusiastically. While my first book was an attempt to investigate the possibility that Marshall McLuhan's hypotheses might be valid (concerning photography and media in general), my next book is more in the nature of art historical and biographical writing, with an emphasis on the influence of poetic imagery and literary themes on the visual arts. Walter Pater may have thought that all the arts aspire to the condition of music; I suggest that all the arts, including music, aspire to the condition of poetry."

AVOCATIONAL INTERESTS: Airedales, architecture, wild birds.

K

KAISER, Harvey H. 1936-

PERSONAL: Born July 8, 1936, in New York, N.Y.; son of Jerome (a carpenter) and Rachel T. (a bookkeeper) Kaiser; married Linda Pembroke (a physical therapist), September 20, 1960; children: Sven-Erik, Robert, Christina. *Education:* Rensselaer Polytechnic Institute, B.Arch., 1959; Syracuse University, M.Arch., 1965, Ph.D., 1975. *Home:* 304 Brookford Rd., Syracuse, N.Y. 13224. *Office:* Syracuse University, Syracuse, N.Y. 13210.

CAREER: Architect in Goteborg, Sweden, 1960-61; Sargent, Webster, Crenshaw & Foley, Syracuse, N.Y., associate partner, 1962-72; Syracuse University, Syracuse, associate professor of architecture, 1972—, and vice-president. Private architecture practice in Syracuse, 1970-72. President of Urbanistics, Inc.; member of board of trustees of Everson Museum of Art and of Russell Sage College. *Military service:* U.S. Army Reserve, 1959-67; became captain.

MEMBER: American Institute of Architects, American Institute of Planners, Association of University Architects, Association for the Protection of the Adirondacks, National Trust for Historic Preservation, National Association of College and University Business Officers, National Council of Architecture Registration Boards, Association of Physical Plant Administrators of Universities and Colleges. *Awards, honors:* American-Scandinavian fellow, 1960-61; National Endowment for the Arts fellow, 1978-79.

WRITINGS: The Building of Cities, Cornell University Press, 1978.

WORK IN PROGRESS: Adirondack Architecture, completion expected in 1980; *Architecture of Syracuse University,* 1980.

SIDELIGHTS: Kaiser writes: "My active practice as an architect and city planner was directed by earlier travel and study in Sweden. My need to solve environmental problems on a comprehensive basis led to doctoral studies in social science and ongoing study of physical development. I expect to combine my career as a university administrator with my practice and writing on environmental design."

*　　*　　*

KALLIR, Otto 1894-1978

OBITUARY NOTICE—See index for *CA* sketch: Born April 1, 1894, in Vienna, Austria; died November 30, 1978, in New York, N.Y. Art dealer, publisher, and author of biographies, art books, and works on aviation. Kallir founded his own publishing company and operated art galleries in Austria and Paris before coming to the United States at the onset of World War II. In America, Kallir specialized in exhibiting the work of German and Austrian expressionists. His gallery, the Galerie St. Etienne, gave Grandma Moses her first one-woman show, which helped launch her career. Kallir became Moses' representative. He wrote her biography and compiled a book on her paintings. Obituaries and other sources: *Who's Who in American Art,* Bowker, 1973; *Who's Who in the World,* 3rd edition, Marquis, 1976, *New York Times,* December 1, 1978.

*　　*　　*

KALME, Egils 1909-

PERSONAL: Born August 16, 1909, in Latvia; came to the United States in 1951, naturalized citizen, 1957; son of Janis (a musician) and Anna (Evelons) Ozolins; married Eva Lopez (a cook), August 8, 1957. *Education:* Graduated from State Technical School, Riga, Latvia, 1933; attended City College of the City University of New York, 1954-66. *Politics:* "Not interested in politics." *Office:* Department of Physical Plant, Manhattan College, Riverdale, Bronx, N.Y. 10471.

CAREER: VEF Factory, Riga, Latvia, engineer, 1934-44; Manhattan College, Riverdale, N.Y., member of physical plant and property staff, and artist, 1951-75, emeritus chief of college artists, 1975—. Has exhibited paintings in both group and solo shows. *Member:* Latvian Artists and Writers Associations of America.

WRITINGS: Between Two Midsummer Nights (novel), Branden Press, 1976.

In Latvian: *Sava Dzive* (novel; title means "Own Life"), Riga, 1944; *Zelts* (three-act play; title means "The Gold"; first produced in Bruges, Belgium at P.O.W. Camp of Zedelgem, November 23, 1945), [Hamburg], 1950; *Tiksanas* (three-act play; title means "Meeting"; first produced in Grossenbrode, West Germany, October 30, 1946), [Neustadt, West Germany], 1946; *Devitais Vilnis* (novel; title means "The Ninth Billow"), [Oldenburg, West Germany], 1951. Contributor of stories and reviews to Latvian periodicals and to *Religious Media Today.*

WORK IN PROGRESS: In the Shadow of Freedom, a his-

279

torical novel; translating his English-language novels into Latvian.

SIDELIGHTS: Kalme left Latvia during the 1945 Russian invasion. He writes: "I'm grateful for the opportunity to live and work in the United States, because here is freedom—the most important thing for artists and writers. Peace without freedom is worthless.

"I am not writing for profit. I even do not think if I can get some money out of it. I am writing only when I have something to say that seems to me is important. For example, in my novel *Between Two Midsummer Nights* I am touching the roots of the contemporary counterculture with questions whether a high standard of living would always raise the quality of life, showing that our industrial society creates loneliness and despair."

AVOCATIONAL INTERESTS: Photography.

BIOGRAPHICAL/CRITICAL SOURCES: Riverdale Press, March 17, 1977.

*   *   *

KALPAKIAN, Laura Anne 1945-

PERSONAL: Born June 28, 1945, in Long Beach, Calif.; daughter of William J. (a technical representative) and Peggy K. (a secretary) Johnson; married Julian P. McCreary (an oceanographer), March 18, 1977. *Education:* University of California, Riverside, B.A., 1967; University of Delaware, M.A., 1970; further graduate study at University of California, San Diego, 1972-77. *Residence:* Encinitas, Calif. *Agent:* Toni Strassman, 130 East 18th St., #7-D, New York, N.Y. 10003.

CAREER: Citrus Experiment Station, Riverside, Calif., clerical worker, 1962-66; County of San Bernardino, Calif., social worker, 1969; Lincoln University, Lincoln University, Pa., instructor in English and humanities, 1970-72; University of California, San Diego, teacher of English, 1973-77; writer, 1973—.

WRITINGS: Beggars and Choosers (novel), Little, Brown, 1978.

WORK IN PROGRESS: These Latter Days, a novel about three generations of a Mormon family, for Little, Brown.

SIDELIGHTS: Charles Larson praised Laura Kalpakian's *Beggars and Choosers* for its accurate depiction of academic life. He commented: "What distinguishes Kalpakian's fast-paced and humorous novel is the author's gift for plotting (including the elements of surprise) coupled with her sense of perspective (she realizes, after all, that most of this is pretty insignificant stuff). In the most ironic sections, 'Beggars and Choosers' reminds one of Alison Lurie's 'The War Between the Tates,' though Kalpakian could learn a thing or two from Lurie's brevity. More importantly, Kalpakian realizes that humor is all that will save one of our stuffiest professions."

Kalpakian told *CA:* "I began writing for publication many years before I was published. I took to the typewriter seriously in 1973, primarily writing short stories. Both of my novels began life masquerading as short stories. Most of my work is quite long and my next professional project will be to take one of those short stories and try to make a short novel of it. Both *Beggars and Choosers* and *These Latter Days* are long complicated books, told in a circular rather than linear manner; the past not only shapes and forms the present and the characters' lives, but intrudes into the narrative as well. Generally, however, the two are quite different works. *Beg-*

gars and Choosers takes place in three months in a small California college town and *These Latter Days* moves from Liverpool to Idaho, California, and Utah from 1893 to 1972. Both novels reflect my observations rather than my immediate experience. (The major character in both books is a middle-aged man.)"

BIOGRAPHICAL/CRITICAL SOURCES: Washington Post, May 30, 1978.

*   *   *

KALUGER, Meriem Fair 1921-

PERSONAL: Born October 27, 1921, in Butler, Pa.; daughter of Julian Harvey and Frances (Reynders) Fair; married George Kaluger (a professor), June 11, 1947. *Education:* Slippery Rock State College, B.S.Ed., 1943; University of Pittsburgh, Litt.M., 1946. *Home:* 625 Brenton Rd., Shippensburg, Pa. 17257.

CAREER: Teacher in public elementary school in Butler, Pa., 1943-47, substitute teacher, 1947-53; substitute teacher in elementary schools in Shippensburg, Pa., 1953-64; Shippensburg State College, Shippensburg, assistant professor of geography, 1955-56, assistant professor in laboratory school, 1963-64, adjunct assistant professor in special education, 1975-77; Bureau of Vocational Rehabilitation, Harrisburg, Pa., psychologist, 1967-69; Learning Disabilities Center for Cumberland County, Carlisle, Pa., program coordinator, 1970-73; Capital Area Intermediate Unit, Camp Hill, Pa., program coordinator, 1970-73, psycho-educational consultant in Lemoyne, Pa., 1973-74; Lincoln Intermediate Unit, Greencastle, Pa., psycho-educational consultant, 1974-76; clinical psychologist in private practice, Shippensburg, Pa., 1977—. Gives workshops.

MEMBER: National Association of School Psychologists, Association for Children with Learning Disabilities, Council of Exceptional Children (Division for Children with Learning Disabilities), Orton Society, Pennsylvania Psychological Association, Shippensburg Civic Club (president, 1966-67), Shippensburg State College Faculty Wives (president, 1957-59, 1974-75).

WRITINGS: (With husband, George Kaluger) *Human Development: The Span of Life,* Mosby, 1974, 2nd edition, 1979; (with G. Kaluger) *Profiles of Human Development,* Mosby, 1976. Author of brochures, diagnostic materials, and informal tests.

WORK IN PROGRESS: Human Behavior: A Developmental Approach, for Mosby, and *The Inefficient Learner: Learning Disabilities,* both with husband, George Kaluger.

SIDELIGHTS: Kaluger told *CA:* "My husband and I share an educational and teaching background, psychological and clinical experiences, and research interest in three fields: human development, human behavior, and learning dysfunctions in individuals with normal or above average intelligence.

"*Human Development: The Span of Life* covers the life span of development by chronological stages, from 'womb to tomb.' *Profiles of Human Development* presents approximately 120 personal living accounts in keeping with the life span format. *Human Behavior: A Developmental Approach* will be based on psychological principles and determinants of development. It will contain some cross-cultural implications that we have garnered from our world-wide travels and studies. *The Inefficient Learner: Learning Disabilities* will be a practical book on working with children and adults who, in spite of good intelligence, cannot learn efficiently and effectively."

AVOCATIONAL INTERESTS: Writing poetry, photography and photojournalism, painting (oils and watercolors), music (piano), aerobic dance, international travel (including New Guinea, Africa, the Galapagos Islands).

*   *   *

KANSIL, Joli 1943-

PERSONAL: Original name, Joel Dennis Gaines; name legally changed; born January 27, 1943, in New York, N.Y.; son of Sam (restaurateur) and Marie (Orlove) Gaines; married Carla Mengko (a model), March 27, 1971; children: Melanie. *Education:* Rutgers University, B.A., 1964; University of the Americas, M.A., 1966; further graduate study at University of Hawaii, 1967, 1968, 1969. *Politics:* Libertarian. *Religion:* Atheist. *Home and office address:* Xanadu Leisure Ltd., P.O. Box 10-Q, Honolulu, Hawaii 96816. *Agent:* Michael Larsen/Elizabeth Pomada, 1029 Jones St., San Francisco, Calif. 94109.

CAREER: National Lexicographic Board, New York, N.Y., writer and editor, 1964-65; teacher of English at a junior high school in Honolulu, Hawaii, 1966-71; Gamut of Games, Inc., New York City and Honolulu, president, 1970-76; Xanadu Leisure Ltd., Honolulu, president of Honolulu Backgammon Club, 1974—. *Member:* Mensa, Explorers Club, Pips Backgammon Club, Outrigger Canoe Club.

WRITINGS: A Guide to Backgammon (booklet), Gamut of Games, 1973; *Backgammon!,* Victoria Publishers, 1974; *The Backgammon Quiz Book,* Playboy Press, 1978. Author of "Points and Blots," a backgammon newsletter.

WORK IN PROGRESS: More backgammon material.

SIDELIGHTS: Kansil comments: "I am primarily a games creator. I invented 'Bridgette,' a two-handed bridge game, and several word games and board games that have been marketed nationally. I have written numerous crosswords for the *New York Times,* and have invented a script phonetic alphabet, a reform calendar, and a reform system of music notation. I also have traveled in 112 foreign countries. Life is just a game—don't take it so seriously."

*   *   *

KANTER, Hal 1918-
(Henry Irving)

PERSONAL: Born December 18, 1918, in Savannah, Ga.; son of Albert L. (a publisher) and Rose (Ehrenreich) Kanter; married Doris Prudowsky (a writer), September 5, 1941; children: Lisa Kanter Shafer, Donna, Abigail. *Politics:* "Usually Democrat." *Religion:* Jewish. *Agent:* Marvin Moss, 9200 Sunset Blvd., Los Angeles, Calif. 90069. *Office:* Savannah Productions, 13063 Ventura Blvd., Studio City, Calif. 91604.

CAREER: Writer for radio, television, motion pictures, and comedians. Worked as cartoonist during 1930's. Producer of television series, including "The George Gobel Show," 1954-57, "Kraft Music Hall," 1958-59, "Valentine's Day," 1964-65, "Julia," 1968-71, "All in the Family," 1975-76, and "Chico and the Man," 1976-77. Guest lecturer at University of Southern California, University of California, Los Angeles, and University of Colorado. *Military service:* U.S. Army, 1941-45; served in infantry, and in Pacific Theater as broadcaster and combat correspondent for Armed Forces Radio Service. *Member:* Writers Guild of America, West, Directors Guild, Producers Guild, American Federation of Television and Radio Artists (AFTRA), Academy of Motion Picture Arts and Sciences, National Academy of Tele-

vision Arts and Sciences, Pacific Pioneer Broadcasters, Friars. *Awards, honors:* Received Emmy Award from National Academy of Television Arts and Sciences, 1954, for "The George Gobel Show"; nomination for best screenplay from Writers Guild, 1960, for "Let's Make Love," and 1961, for "Blue Hawaii."

WRITINGS: (Contributor) *Television and Screen,* University of California Press, 1958; *Snake in the Glass* (novel), Delacorte, 1971.

Screenplays: (Author of additional dialogue) "My Favorite Spy," Paramount, 1951; (with Sid Solvers) "Two Tickets to Broadway," RKO, 1951; (with Jack Sher) "Off Limits," Paramount, 1952; (with Frank Butler and William Morrow) "Road to Bali," Paramount, 1952; (with Edmund L. Hartmann) "Here Come the Girls," Paramount, 1953; (with James Allardice) "Money From Home" (adapted from a short story by Damon Runyon), Paramount, 1954; (with Hartmann) "Casanova's Big Night," 1954; (with Ketti Frings) "About Mrs. Leslie" (adapted from the novel by Vina Delmar), Paramount, 1954; (with Frank Tashlin and Herbert Baker) "Artists and Models" (adapted from the play by Michael Davidson and Norman Lessing), Paramount, 1955; "Once Upon a Horse" (adapted from the novel by Henry Gregor Felsen, *Why Rustlers Never Win*), Universal, 1958; (with Baker) "Loving You" (adapted from the short story by Mary Agnes Thompson, *A Call From Mitch Miller*), Paramount, 1957; (with Winston Miller) "Mardi Gras," Twentieth Century-Fox, 1958; (author of additional dialogue) "Let's Make Love," Twentieth Century-Fox, 1960; (with Harry Tugend) "Pocketful of Miracles" (adapted from the screenplay by Robert Riskin, "Lady for a Day"), United Artists, 1961; (with Valentine Davies) "Bachelor in Paradise," Metro-Goldwyn-Mayer, 1961; (with Harry Allan Weiss) "Blue Hawaii," Paramount, 1961; (with Sher) "Move Over Darling" (adapted from a screen story by Bella Spewack, Samuel Spewack, and Leo McCarey), Twentieth Century-Fox, 1963; "Dear Brigitte" (adapted from the novel by John Haase, *Erasmus With Freckles*), Twentieth Century-Fox, 1965.

Contributor to radio shows, including "Amos 'n' Andy," and "Grand Central Station," and television shows, sometimes under pseudonym Henry Irving, including "Shower of Stars," "The Bing Crosby Show," "The George Gobel Show," and "Kraft Music Hall." Author of comedy material for numerous performers, including Jack Haley, Danny Kaye, Jack Benny, and Bob Hope. Contributor to periodicals.

SIDELIGHTS: At a roundtable of comedy writers, Kanter once said: "An observation that I made some time ago, primarily to myself, is that there are three bands in the spectrum of laughter. These three bands are generally wit and humor and comedy. Now surely all of us would agree that wit is the champagne of laughter, and I think it's only fair to admit that those of us here on this panel tonight are involved in dispensing beer, which is what comedy is on the spectrum. It's some comfort to me to note, that there is more beer sold in this country than champagne or whiskey."

Kanter said that he has learned from and been influenced by many of the people and situations he has encountered in his career. "I learned more about comedy from Ed Wynn than almost anyone else," said Kanter. "More about style from Bing Crosby. "Amos 'n' Andy" taught me the importance of characterization. From Fred Allen, I learned the importance of words and grammar. Olsen and Johnson taught me the value of tempo. From George Gobel I discovered the humor that can be found in small truths. If you don't learn as you go along, you're wasting time."

AVOCATIONAL INTERESTS: Deep sea fishing, travel, talk show appearances, philately, public speaking.

BIOGRAPHICAl/CRITICAL SOURCES: New York Morning Telegram, June 4, 1964, January 20, 1965; *New York Daily News,* June 27, 1971; *New York Times,* June 29, 1971.

* * *

KANTOR, Seth 1926-

PERSONAL: Born January 9, 1926, in New York, N.Y.; son of Arvid (in advertising) and Ella (Reisman) Kantor; married Anne Blackman (an advertising business operator), June 7, 1952; children: Susan Kantor Bank, Amy Joan. *Education:* Attended Wayne State University, 1946-48. *Politics:* Independent. *Religion:* Jewish. *Home:* 5115 Wessling Lane, Bethesda, Md. 20014. *Office: Atlanta Constitution,* Washington Bureau, Suite 501, 1901 Pennsylvania Ave., Washington, D.C. 20006.

CAREER: Reporter for dailies in Lamar, Pueblo, and Denver, Colo., 1948-50; magazine editor and free-lance writer in Fort Worth, Tex., and New York City, 1950-57; *Press,* Fort Worth, Tex., police reporter, 1957-60; *Times Herald,* Dallas, Tex., general assignments reporter, 1960-62; Scripps-Howard Newspapers, New York City, Washington bureau, Capitol Hill and White House correspondent, 1962-72; *Detroit News,* Detroit, Mich., Washington bureau, investigative reporter, 1972-78; *Atlanta Constitution,* Atlanta, Ga., Washington bureau, national investigative reporter, 1978—. Member of board of directors, National Press Foundation, 1978—; secretary of standing committee of correspondents of U.S. Capitol Press Galleries, 1966-67. *Military service:* U.S. Marine Corps, 1943-46. *Member:* National Press Club (chairperson of professional issues committee, 1976; member of board of governors, 1976-79), White House Press Correspondents Association. *Awards, honors:* Texas Headliners award, 1960; several UPI and AP statewide reporting awards for Texas newspapers, 1961; National Sigma Delta Chi-Professional Journalism Society award for distinguished Washington correspondence, 1974.

WRITINGS: Who Was Jack Ruby?, Everest House, 1978. Author of column syndicated by North American Newspaper Alliance, 1972—. Contributor to numerous national periodicals, including *Collier's, Sports Illustrated, Coronet, Pageant, Look,* and *Better Homes and Gardens.*

Work represented in numerous anthologies, including *Best Sports Stories of the Year,* Dutton, 1949; *Combat,* 1954; *The Best of Sport,* 1957; *Swords and Plowshares,* 1964; *The Lobbyists,* 1969.

WORK IN PROGRESS: A novel, *King of the Hill.*

SIDELIGHTS: Kantor's notable assignments include "breaking the TFX warplane scandal story in 1962, which led to a lengthy U.S. Senate probe and hearings; was a member of the traveling party of Kennedys as White House correspondent when the president was killed in 1963; covered the Johnson White House and broke the national story of Johnson speeding down Texas highways at up to 90 mph in 1964; writing a series on FEDNET, a federal computer system, which led to a congressional crackdown on the General Services Administration in 1974; a 1975 series which led Congress to write new laws blocking foreign contributions to major U.S. political campaigns; and a 1975-77 series on the interstate shipment of welfare children to pri-

vately run human 'warehouses', which made national headlines."

* * *

KANTROWITZ, Joanne Spencer 1931-

PERSONAL: Born December 6, 1931, in Marquette, Mich.; daughter of Robert S. (a railroad worker) and Doris (a railroad worker; maiden name, Jorgensen) Spencer; married Nathan Kantrowitz (a sociologist), June 2, 1958; children: Alexander, Edward. *Education:* University of Michigan, B.A., 1953; University of Chicago, M.A., 1957, Ph.D., 1967; postdoctoral study at Oxford University, 1969-70. *Politics:* Democrat. *Religion:* "Judaeo-Christian." *Home and office:* 122 McKeel Ave., Tarrytown, N.Y. 10591.

CAREER: Vassar College, Poughkeepsie, N.Y., lecturer in English, 1965-67; Marymount College, Tarrytown, N.Y., assistant professor of English, 1967-69; Kent State University, Kent, Ohio, visiting assistant professor of English, 1972-76; writer, 1976—. *Member:* Modern Language Association of America, Mediaeval Academy of America, National Organization for Women. *Awards, honors:* American Council of Learned Societies grant, 1971-72.

WRITINGS: Dramatic Allegory, University of Nebraska Press, 1975; (editor with S. J. Kahrl) *The Medieval Adventure,* Braziller, 1979; (with husband, Nathan Kantrowitz) *Stateville Names,* Maledicta Press, 1979. Work represented in *Rocking the Boat: Academic Women in Protest,* Modern Language Association of America, 1978. Contributor to scholarly journals.

WORK IN PROGRESS: Editing academic prose in humanities and social sciences; continuing research on medieval and Renaissance drama and allegory; studying women and part-time work in America.

SIDELIGHTS: Joanne Kantrowitz is currently involved in a feminist lawsuit against Kent State University. Her earlier interests have included rent strikes and work in slum housing in Chicago.

Kantrowitz commented: "Like other women in the field, my career has been hampered by professional restrictions versus marriage and children. I am currently taking time to fight for 'the new woman' who is wife, mother, and professional. As such, I remain outside the educational institutions, despite the quality of my work. There are thirty-three thousand women in a comparable position in academia *now.*"

BIOGRAPHICAL/CRITICAL SOURCES: Chronicle of Higher Education, December, 1974, January, 1975.

* * *

KAPLAN, Eugene H(erbert) 1932-

PERSONAL: Born June 26, 1932, in Brooklyn, N.Y.; son of Jacob (in sales) and Lea (an office manager; maiden name, Gerstler) Kaplan; married Breena Lubow, August 25, 1957; children: Julie, Susan. *Education:* Brooklyn College (now of the City University of New York), B.S., 1954; Hofstra University, M.A., 1957; New York University, Ph.D., 1963. *Home:* 148 West Waterview St., Northport, N.Y. 11768. *Office:* Department of Biology, Hofstra University, Hempstead, N.Y. 11550.

CAREER: Hofstra University, Hempstead, N.Y., lecturer, 1957-59, instructor, 1959-63, assistant professor, 1963-69, associate professor, 1969-74, professor of biology, 1974—. Expert for United Nations Educational, Scientific & Cultural Organization (UNESCO). Associate director of Tel

Aviv Elementary School science program. *Member:* National Association for Research in Science Teaching, American Society of Parasitologists. *Awards, honors:* National Science Foundation fellow, 1963-64; Wright fellowship from Bermuda Biological Laboratory, 1976.

WRITINGS: Problem Solving in Biology, with teacher's edition, Macmillan, 1968, 2nd edition, 1976; *Experiences in Life Science,* with teacher's edition, Macmillan, 1969, 2nd edition, 1976; *Teaching Children Science,* Israel Ministry of Education, 1972; *A Guide to the Seashores and Coral Reefs of Florida and the Caribbean,* Houghton, 1979. Contributor to biology, parasitology, and education journals.

* * *

KARAGEORGHIS, Vassos 1929-

PERSONAL: Born April 29, 1929, in Trikomo, Cyprus; son of George Georghiou (a mason) and Panayiota (Georghiou) Karageorghis; married Jacqueline Girard (a teacher), March 21, 1953; children: Clio, Andreas. *Education:* University of London, B.A. (honors), 1952, certificate in archaeology, 1952, Ph.D., 1957. *Religion:* Greek Orthodox. *Home:* 12 Kastorias St., Nicosia 110, Cyprus. *Office:* Department of Antiquities, Ministry of Communications and Works, Republic of Cyprus, Nicosia, Cyprus.

CAREER: Cyprus Museum, Nicosia, Cyprus, assistant curator, 1952-60, curator, 1960-63; Republic of Cyprus, Department of Antiquities, Nicosia, acting director, 1963-64, director of antiquities, 1964—. Regents Lecturer at University of California, Berkeley, 1967; visiting professor at Universite Laval, 1968, 1971; adjunct professor at State University of New York at Albany, 1973—; Geddes Harrower Professor of Classical Archaeology at University of Aberdeen, 1975. Member of governing body of Cyprus Research Centre. Participant in excavations at Salamis, 1952-73, the Necropolis at Akhere and Pendayia, 1960, the Necropolis at Salamis, 1962-67, and Kition, 1962-77.

MEMBER: Society for Cypriot Studies (vice-president of council), Greek Archaeological Society (honorary member of council), Society of Antiquaries of London (fellow), British Academy (corresponding fellow), Royal Society of Arts (fellow), German Archaeological Institute, Academie des Inscriptions et Belles Lettres (corresponding member), Royal Society for Humanistic Studies (Lund; fellow), Royal Swedish Academy, Austrian Academy of Sciences (corresponding member), Archaeological Society of Athens (corresponding member), Academy of Athens (corresponding member). *Awards, honors:* Prize from Societe des Etudes Grecques, Sorbonne, University of Paris, 1966; chevalier de l'Ordre National de la Legion d'Honneur, 1971; honorary doctorates from University of Lyon and University of Goeteborg, 1972, University of Athens, 1973, and University of Birmingham, 1974; fellow of University of London, 1975; R. B. Bennett Commonwealth Prize, 1978.

WRITINGS: Treasures in the Cyprus Museum, Department of Antiquities, Ministry of Communications and Works, Republic of Cyprus, 1962; *Cyprus Museum (Nicosia), Larnaca District Museum,* Department of Antiquities, Ministry of Communications and Works, Republic of Cyprus, 1963; (with Cornelius C. Vermeule) *Sculptures From Salamis,* Department of Antiquities, Ministry of Communications and Works, Republic of Cyprus, Volume I, 1964, Volume II, 1966; *Salamis,* Department of Antiquities, Ministry of Communications and Works, Republic of Cyprus, 1964; *Private Collections,* Department of Antiquities, Ministry of Communications and Works, Republic of Cyprus,

1965; *Nouveaux Documents pour l'Etude du Bronze Recent a Chypre, recueil critique et commente,* E. de Boccard, 1965; *Anaskaphai Salaminos, 1964-1966,* Department of Antiquities, Ministry of Communications and Works, Republic of Cyprus, 1966; *Excavations in the Necropolis of Salamis,* Department of Antiquities, Ministry of Communications and Works, Republic of Cyprus, Volume I, 1967, Volume II, 1970, Volume III, 1974, Volume IV, 1978; *Mycenaean Art From Cyprus,* Department of Antiquities, Ministry of Communications and Works, Republic of Cyprus, 1968; *Cyprus,* Hippocrene, 1968; *Zypern,* Nagel, 1968; *Salamis: Recent Discoveries in Cyprus,* McGraw, 1969 (published in England as *Salamis in Cyprus: Homeric, Hellenistic, and Roman,* Thames & Hudson, 1969); *The Ancient Civilization of Cyprus,* Cowles Education Corp., 1969.

(With Hans-Guenter Buchholz) *Altaegaeis und Altkypros,* E. Wasmuth, 1971, translation by Francisca Garvie published as *Prehistoric Greece and Cyprus: An Archaeological Handbook,* Phaidon, 1973; *Cypriote Antiquities in the Pierides Collection, Larnaca, Cyprus,* privately printed, 1973; (with Jean Des Gagniers) *La ceramique Chypriote de style figure: Age du fer, 1050-500 av.J.C.,* two volumes, Consiglio nazionale della ricerche, Istituto per gli studi micenei ed egeo-anatolici, 1974; (with Darrell A. Amyx and others) *Cypriote Antiquities in San Francisco Bay Area Collections,* Soedra Vaegen, 1974; (with Manolis Andronikos and Manolis Chatzidakis) *Ta hellenika mouseia,* 1974, translation published as *The Greek Museums,* Ekdotike Athenon, 1975; *Kition, Mycenaean and Phoenician,* Oxford University Press, 1974; *Cyprus Museum and Archaeological Sites of Cyprus,* translated by Kay Cicellis, new edition, Caratzas Brothers, 1975; *Kition: Mycenaean and Phoenician Discoveries in Cyprus,* Thames & Hudson, 1976; *Ho politismos tes prolstorikes Kyprou,* Ekdotike Athenon, 1976; *View from the Bronze Age: Mycenaean and Phoenician Discoveries at Kition,* Dutton, 1976; (with Jean Des Gagniers) *Vases et figurines de l'age du bronze ancien et du bronze moyen a Chypre,* International Scholastic Book Service, 1977.

Also author of *Corpus Vasorum Antiquorum,* Volume I, 1964, Volume II, 1965, *Excavations at Kition,* Volume I: *The Tombs,* 1974, *Alaas: A Protogeometric Necropolis in Cypris,* 1975, *The Civilization of Prehistoric Cypris,* 1975, *Fouilles de Kition,* with G. Clerc, E. Lagarce, and J. Leclant, Volume II: *Objets egyptiens et egyptisants,* 1976, *Cypriote Antiquities in the Medelhavsmuseet, Stockholm* with C. G. Styrenius and M. G. Winbladh, Volume II: *Memoirs,* 1977, *Two Cypriote Sanctuaries of the End of the Cypro-Archaic Period,* 1977, *The Goddess With Uplifted Arms in Cyprus,* 1977, and *Fouilles de Kition,* with M. G. Guzzo Amadasi, Volume III: *Inscriptions Pheniciennes.* Contributor to English, French, Greek, and German periodicals.

* * *

KARP, Naomi J. 1926-

PERSONAL: Born October 17, 1926, in New York, N.Y.; daughter of Nathan I. (an attorney) and Jennie (a teacher; maiden name, Friedman) Kaplan; married Martin E. Karp (a business executive), March 14, 1948; children: Betsy (Mrs. Jeffrey J. Davis), Leslie (Mrs. David Goldenberg), Jonathan. *Education:* Attended University of Wisconsin, Madison, 1946; Queens College (now of the City University of New York), B.A., 1948. *Politics:* Democrat. *Religion:* Jewish. *Home:* 12 Ave. Bel Air, 1180 Brussels, Belgium.

CAREER: Westport News, Westport, Conn., political reporter, 1964-69; Capitol Correspondent, Hartford, Conn., owner of syndicate, 1969-71; Chatham Press, Riverside, Conn., public relations director, 1971-73; free-lance writer, 1973—. Member of board of trustees of Norwalk Public Library, 1972-77. *Member:* Authors League of America.

WRITINGS: Nothing Rhymes With April (juvenile), Harcourt, 1974; *The Turning Point* (juvenile; selection of Junior Literary Guild and Jewish Book Club), Harcourt, 1976.

WORK IN PROGRESS: A novel, *The Bystander.*

SIDELIGHTS: Naomi Karp writes: "Obviously, growing up in the 1930's had a profound effect on me, for these years are the source of material for my two children's books. Although neither is autobiographical, much of the background and characters are related to events about which I was concerned, more deeply than I knew at the time. What I have written about is the effects of outside forces on this most sensitive period of childhood."

The Turning Point deals with a young Jewish girl who moves from the Bronx, in 1938, to an anti-Semitic suburb.

*   *   *

KASHIMA, Tetsuden   1940-

PERSONAL: Born September 5, 1940, in Oakland, Calif.; son of Tetsuro (a priest) and Yoshiko (Murata) Kashima. *Education:* University of California, Berkeley, B.A., 1963; San Francisco State University, M.A., 1968; University of California, San Diego, Ph.D., 1975. *Home:* 4611 149th Ave. S.E., Bellevue, Wash. 98006. *Office:* Asian American Studies Program, University of Washington, GN-80, Seattle, Wash. 98195.

CAREER: University of California, Santa Barbara, acting assistant professor of sociology, head of department and head of Asian American studies program, 1971-76; University of Washington, Seattle, adjunct lecturer in sociology and director of Asian American studies program, both 1976—. *Military service:* U.S. Army, Intelligence, 1963-65; became captain. *Member:* American Sociological Association, Association for Asian Studies, American Association for the Advancement of Science, Pacific Sociological Association.

WRITINGS: Buddhism in America: The Social Organization of an Ethnic Religious Organization, Greenwood Press, 1977.

WORK IN PROGRESS: Research on concentration camps for the Japanese in the United States, 1941-46; an article for *Phylon* journal on the return to society and readjustment of Japanese-Americans in the United States after World War II.

SIDELIGHTS: Kashima told *CA:* "There are two factors that continue to influence my writing and research orientation. First, along with 117,000 other Japanese and Japanese Americans during World War II, our family spent some three years in an American concentration camp. Although I was only a year old when we went in, I still retain memory traces of that incarceration. My interest in the sociological study of race relations, thus, had a very early genesis. Second, our family has long been involved in Jodo Shinshu Buddhism. The Kashima family temple, in Japan, has existed for more than 300 years and as a boy growing up in that tradition, the Japanese and Buddhist roots are strong and pervasive. What I hope to continue to do, then, is to explore the meaning of being an Asian American."

KASSON, John F(ranklin)   1944-

PERSONAL: Born October 20, 1944, in Muncie, Ind.; son of Robert Edwin and Mary Louise (Shirk) Kasson; married Joy Schlesinger (a university professor), December 22, 1968; children: Peter. *Education:* Harvard University, B.A. (magna cum laude), 1966; Yale University, Ph.D., 1971. *Home:* 206 Hillcrest Circle, Chapel Hill, N.C. 27514. *Office:* Department of History, University of North Carolina, Chapel Hill, N.C. 27514.

CAREER: University of North Carolina, Chapel Hill, assistant professor, 1971-76, associate professor of history, 1976—. *Member:* American Historical Association, American Studies Association, Society for the History of Technology. *Awards, honors:* National Endowment for the Humanities fellowship, 1974.

WRITINGS: Civilizing the Machine: Technology and Republican Values in America, 1776-1900, Grossman, 1976; *Amusing the Million: Coney Island at the Turn of the Century,* Hill & Wang, 1978.

*   *   *

KATZ, Mickey
See KATZ, Myron Meyer

*   *   *

KATZ, Myron Meyer   1909-
(Mickey Katz)

PERSONAL: Born June 15, 1909, in Cleveland, Ohio; son of Max (a tailor) and Johanna (Herzberg) Katz; married Grace Epstein (an artist), March 15, 1930; children: Joel Grey, Ronald. *Education:* Attended secondary school in Cleveland, Ohio. *Religion:* Jewish. *Home:* 10366 Wilshire Blvd., Los Angeles, Calif. 90024. *Agent:* Jane Jordan Browne, 170 South Beverly Dr., Suite 314, Beverly Hills, Calif. 90212.

CAREER: Musician, 1924—; recording artist, 1947—; comedian, 1948—. *Member:* Friars Club of California, Musicians Union.

WRITINGS—Under name Mickey Katz: *Nonsense on Who's Who end Wat's Wat* (bedtime story parodies), Spear & Gilpin, 1929; (with Hannibal Coons) *Papa Play for Me: The Hilarious, Heartwarming Story of Comedian and Bandleader Mickey Katz,* Simon & Schuster, 1977.

SIDELIGHTS: Mickey Katz made his "show business" debut when he was twelve, playing local amateur night acts, and "three times out of four" gaining a tie for first prize with his younger sister. A poor child, the young clarinetist often returned his winnings to his needy Jewish parents. Though Katz has always maintained his faith, this strong Jewish background provided him with a wealth of material for comedy later in his career.

After an infamous one night stint as half of the "Louis & Kay" stage act, as well as several other more prosperous clarinet and saxaphone playing performances in New York, Katz returned to Cleveland in the early 1930's. Main jobs in that decade included extended bookings with Maurice Spitalny at Loew's State Theater and five years as orchestra leader on the then prosperous Lake Erie excursion boats.

In a chapter from *Papa Play for Me,* "What Did You Do in the War, Daddy?," Katz recounts with humor his "military service." "When I got my draft notice and proudly reported for my preinduction physical in the early stages of World War II," he laughs, "the examining doctors greeted me with mirth. My small stature, my big glasses, . . . my flat feet, the problem of finding a rifle small enough for me to carry—everything about me aroused them to almost open hilarity. . . . I was rejected for the Army, the Navy, the Air Force, the Boy Scouts, the Girl Scouts, the Brownies, and the Junior B'nai B'rith.'' Few rejected him towards the end of the war when he toured Europe, giving ''an endless succession of USO camp shows'' for receptive GI audiences.

Katz's reputation continued to grow after the war. ''Life for me didn't really begin at forty,'' he claims. ''It began at thirty-eight. . . . I left Spike Jones [with whom he played for over a year], faced starvation, decided not to starve, and a month later recorded my first English-Yiddish comedy record. Continuing where his first book, English-Yiddish parodies of well-known bedtime stories, left off, this popular release featured ''Haim afen Range'' [''Home on the Range''] and ''Yiddish Square Dance,'' an impersonation of ''an Arkansas hog caller calling a square dance in Yiddish.'' Katz scoffed at critics of his new genre, especially reluctant production managers and disc jockeys, claiming his records were ''harmless and well-meaning fun.'' Over the years these parody hits have included ''Davey Crockett,'' ''Come Ona My Hois,'' and ''How Much Is That Pickle in the Window?'' His first album, ''Mish Mosh,'' featured many of his ''hit'' singles.

In the 1950's Katz led a host of American Jewish singers and comedians, including his son Joel Grey, to form the immensely popular Borscht Capades. Playing to capacity audiences in Los Angeles and later in Chicago, Katz's greatest moments in show business, ironically, brought him his greatest personal despair. As he recounts in his autobiography: ''I developed a case of stage fright that would have destroyed Milton Berle. My emotional problem . . . was that I was suddenly too successful. . . . I got to the point where I thought that the next time I walked out on that stage I'd die out there. . . . Stage fright turns your blood to water and your bones to Jell-o. It's sheer terror.'' Happily for the lonely family man, when his wife joined him in Chicago ''all the panic and misery went away.''

In his later performing years Katz played his ''informal'' and ''often spicy'' mix of music and comedy in France, England, South Africa, and Australia, as well as throughout the United States. His own success, however, has not dwindled his pride in the accomplishments of his two sons. Ron and a partner patented the Telecredit computerized cash checking system, which his dad calls ''steady as the Rock of Gilbrator.'' Actor Joel Grey is ''an international superstar.'' True to his own exuberance though, Katz's great love of his work prevents him from being a doting father. ''I'm only sixtynine,'' he concludes in his book. ''I still love to play my clarinet. I still love to make people laugh. I can still fit into my size 37 tuxedo, and I'm still available for weddings, bar mitzvahs, and brisses.''

BIOGRAPHICAL/CRITICAL SOURCES: Mickey Katz and Hannibal Coons, *Papa Play for Me,* Simon & Schuster, 1977.

*   *   *

KAUFMANN, John   1931-
(David Swift)

PERSONAL: Born in New York, N.Y.; married wife, Alicia; children: two sons. *Education:* Attended Pennsylvania Academy of Fine Arts, Art Students League, and Instituto Statale d'Arte in Florence, Italy. *Residence:* Fresh Meadows, N.Y.

CAREER: Author and illustrator of books for children. Has also worked in an aircraft factory and has also done technical illustrations.

WRITINGS—All for children; all self-illustrated: *Fish Hawk,* Morrow, 1967; *Wings, Sun, and Stars,* Morrow, 1969; *Birds in Flight,* Morrow, 1970; *Robins Fly North, Robins Fly South,* Crowell, 1970; *Winds and Weather,* Morrow, 1971; *Chimney Swift,* Morrow, 1971; *Bats in the Dark,* Crowell, 1972; *Insect Travelers,* Morrow, 1972; *Flying Hand-Launched Gliders,* Morrow, 1974; *Streamlined,* Crowell, 1974; (with Heinz Meng) *Falcons Return: Restoring an Endangered Species,* Morrow, 1975; *Flying Reptiles in the Age of Dinosaurs,* Morrow, 1976; *Little Dinosaurs and Early Birds,* Crowell, 1977; (under pseudonym David Swift) *Animal Travelers,* Morrow, 1977.

Illustrator: Bernice K. Hunt, *Our Tiny Servants: Molds and Yeasts,* Prentice-Hall, 1962; Philip B. Carona, *Things That Measure,* Prentice-Hall, 1962; Eric Windle, *Sounds You Cannot Hear,* Prentice-Hall, 1963; Betty Baker, *Killer-of-Death,* Harper, 1963; Penelope Farmer, *The Magic Stone,* Harcourt, 1964; Lenore Sander, *The Curious World of Crystals,* Prentice-Hall, 1964; Millicent E. Selsam, *Courtship of Animals,* Morrow, 1964; Kai Soderhjelm, *Free Ticket to Adventure,* Lothrop, 1964; Natalie S. Carlson, *Letter on the Tree,* Harper, 1964; Patrick Young, *Old Abe: The Eagle Hero* (a Junior Literary Guild selection), Prentice-Hall, 1965; Lace Kendall, *Rain Boat,* Coward, 1965; Susan E. F. Welty, *Birds With Bracelets: The Story of Bird-Banding,* Prentice-Hall, 1965; Carlson, *Empty Schoolhouse,* Harper, 1965; Selsam, *Animals as Parents,* Morrow, 1965; Selsam, *When an Animal Grows,* Harper, 1966; Erick Berry, *The Springing of the Rice: A Story of Thailand,* Macmillan, 1966; Joseph Cottler, *Alfred Wallace: Explorer-Naturalist,* Little, Brown, 1966; Robert Murphy, *Wild Geese Calling,* Dutton, 1966; Jocelyn Arundel, *Little Stripe: An African Zebra,* Hastings House, 1967; Jean C. George, *The Moon of the Salamanders,* Crowell, 1967; Selsam, *How Animals Tell Time,* Morrow, 1967; Selsam, *The Bug That Laid the Golden Eggs,* Harper, 1967; Andre Norton, *Fur Magic,* World Publishing, 1968; Delia Goetz, *Rivers,* Morrow, 1969; Peter Sauer, *Seasons,* Coward, 1969; Bertha S. Dodge, *Potatoes and People: The Story of a Plant,* Little, Brown, 1970; Margaret F. Bartlett, *Rock All Around,* Coward, 1970; Alfred Slote, *The Moon in Fact and Fancy,* World Publishing, 1971.

SIDELIGHTS: John Kaufmann believes that quality children's books are in direct opposition to the construction of missiles and the manipulation of public opinion; thus, he places a high value on his work.

The *Christian Science Monitor* called *Wings, Sun, and Stars: The Story of Bird Migration* ''a technical book written simply and entertainingly. The author has drawn over 75 maps, diagrams, and sketches illustrating various experiments and theories attempting to ascertain how birds find their way across vast distances. . . .'' Zena Sutherland wrote the following about *Robins Fly North, Robins Fly South:* ''Sharp, clear, delicately detailed pictures of robins fill these pages with movement. . . . Migration, while discussed in detail, is treated as part of the robin's life cycle and its relationship to the environment, all in the simplest of terms in straightforward style.''

Most of Kaufmann's illustrations are in black and white, which allows him to work over an area without picking up what is underneath. If this is done well, he feels it can match any more complex illustrating technique.

BIOGRAPHICAL/CRITICAL SOURCES: Christian Science Monitor, May 1, 1969; Saturday Review, November 4, 1970.*

*   *   *

KAVANAGH, P(atrick) J(oseph Gregory)   1931-

PERSONAL: Born January 6, 1931, in Worthing, Sussex, England; son of H. E. (a radio writer) and Agnes (O'Keefe) Kavanagh; married Sally Philipps, 1956 (died, 1958); married Catherine Ward, 1965; children: (second marriage) Cornelius, Bruno. Education: Merton College, Oxford, M.A., 1954. Religion: Roman Catholic. Agent: A. D. Peters, 10 Buckingham St., Adelphi, London W.C.2, England.

CAREER: Actor (on stage and television, and in films) and writer, 1960-70. Lecturer at University of Indonesia, 1957-58. Awards, honors: Richard Hillary Memorial Prize, 1966, for The Perfect Stranger; fiction prize from Guardian, 1969, for A Song and Dance.

WRITINGS: One and One (poems), Heinemann, 1960; The Perfect Stranger (autobiography), Chatto & Windus, 1966; On the Way to the Depot (poems), Chatto & Windus, 1967; A Song and Dance (novel), Chatto & Windus, 1968; About Time (poems), Chatto & Windus, 1970; A Happy Man (novel), Chatto & Windus, 1972; Edward Thomas in Heaven (poems), Chatto & Windus, 1974; Scarf Jack (juvenile novel), Bodley Head, 1978, published as The Irish Captain, Doubleday, 1979; People and Weather (novel), Calder & Boyars, 1979; Life Before Death (poems), Chatto & Windus, 1979.

Documentary television plays: "William Cowper Lived Here," 1971; "Journey Through Summer," 1973. Contributor of feature articles to London Daily Telegraph Colour Supplement, and to magazines, including New Yorker, Transatlantic Review, Encounter, and New Statesman.

WORK IN PROGRESS: Poems; a sequel to The Irish Captain.

AVOCATIONAL INTERESTS: Walking.

*   *   *

KAYE, Buddy   1918-

PERSONAL: Born January 3, 1918, in New York, N.Y.; son of Samuel (a house painter) and Ethel (a business person; maiden name, Goldstein) Kaye; married Lillian Kipp, June 27, 1942; children: Richard, Barbara, Ronnie. Education: "Mostly self-taught after high school." Residence: Tarzana, Calif. Office: c/o American Society of Composers, Authors, and Publishers, 6430 Sunset Blvd., Los Angeles, Calif. 90028.

CAREER: Songwriter, musician, and record producer. Teacher at University of California, Los Angeles (UCLA), 1976—. Conductor of numerous seminars. Member: American Society of Composers, Authors, and Publishers (ASCAP), Academy of Motion Picture Arts and Sciences, American Guild of Composers and Authors, National Academy of Recording Arts and Sciences, Nashville Songwriters Association. Awards, honors: Grammy Award, 1976, for production of recording "The Little Prince."

WRITINGS: (With Og Mandino) The Gift of Acabar, Lippincott, 1978; The Complete Songwriter, Budd Music, 1978. Lyricist for television theme songs, including "The Cross Wits," "I Dream of Jeannie," "Richard the Lionhearted," and "Little Lulu and Little Audrey"; motion picture theme songs, including "Change of Habit," "The Trouble With

Girls," "Hurry Sundown," "Not as a Stranger," "Twist Around the Clock," "Fun and Fancy Free," and "The Treasure of the Sierra Madre"; and numerous other songs, including "Till the End of Time," "Full Moon and Empty Arms," "Speedy Gonzalez," "Little Boat," "Quiet Nights," and "A—You're Adorable."

WORK IN PROGRESS: A musical; Luna Prince, a novel; Happiness—You Can't Sprinkle It Around Without Getting Some On Yourself, for Bantam.

SIDELIGHTS: "Kaye told CA: "My motivation is the excitement of achievement—'making the impossible dream possible.' I function on many different levels and with various projects simultaneously. I like the challenge of turning negatives into positives to prove to myself and to the young people around me (my children and students) that it can be done."

Kaye has contributed lyrics to songs used in films by many noted directors, including Otto Preminger and John Huston. His songs have been recorded by such singers as Perry Como, Frank Sinatra, Sarah Vaughn, Cleo Laine, Tony Bennett, Elvis Presley, and Pat Boone.

*   *   *

KEARNEY, Robert N(orman)   1930-

PERSONAL: Born January 20, 1930, in Exira, Iowa; son of John Thomas (a pharmacist) and Genevieve (a schoolteacher; maiden name, Gamber) Kearney; divorced; children: Diane Lynn, Andrea Marie, Paul Brian. Education: University of Iowa, B.A. (highest distinction), 1953, M.A., 1954; further graduate study at School of Oriental and African Studies, London, 1960-61; University of California, Los Angeles, Ph.D.,1963. Office: Foreign and Comparative Studies Program, Maxwell School, Syracuse University, 119 College Pl., Syracuse, N.Y. 13210.

CAREER: Duke University, Durham, N.C., assistant professor of political science, 1963-66; University of California, Santa Barbara, assistant professor of political science, 1966-68; Syracuse University, Syracuse, N.Y., associate professor, 1968-73, professor of political science, 1973—, director of foreign and comparative studies program, 1975—, resident director of program in New Delhi, India, 1970-71. Member of board of trustees of American Institute of Indian Studies, 1971-73, 1975—, chairman of board, 1978—, member of executive committee, 1976-78. Military service: U.S. Air Force, 1947-50. Member: International Society of Political Psychology, American Political Science Association, Association for Asian Studies, Phi Beta Kappa.

WRITINGS: Communalism and Language in the Politics of Ceylon, Duke University Press, 1967; Trade Unions and Politics in Ceylon, University of California Press, 1971; The Politics of Ceylon (Sri Lanka), Cornell University Press, 1973; (editor and contributor) Politics and Modernization in South and Southeast Asia, Schenkman, 1975.

Contributor: Ralph Braibanti, editor, Asian Bureaucratic Systems Emergent From the British Imperial Tradition, Duke University Press, 1966; Nimrod Raphaeli, editor, Readings in Comparative Public Administration, Allyn & Bacon, 1967; Robert A. Scalapino, editor, The Communist Revolution in Asia, 2nd edition, Prentice-Hall, 1969; Paul R. Brass and Marcus F. Franda, editors, Radical Politics in South Asia, M.I.T. Press, 1973; Maureen L. P. Patterson and Martin Yanuck, editors, South Asian Library Resources in North America, Inter Documentary Co., 1975; Robert I. Crane, editor, Aspects of Political Mobilization in South

Asia, Maxwell School, Syracuse University, 1976; Michael Roberts, editor, *Collective Identities, Nationalism, and Protest in Sri Lanka During the Modern Era,* Marga Institute (Sri Lanka), 1978. Contributor of about twenty articles to foreign studies journals.

WORK IN PROGRESS: Research on generations and politics in Sri Lanka, and on political socialization and the political career in Sri Lanka.

SIDELIGHTS: Kearney told *CA:* "When, nearly two decades ago, I first developed an interest in Sri Lanka, I did not imagine the extent to which my professional career and, to a not insignificant degree, my personal identity would be linked with that nation. Almost all of my serious writing has grown out of research conducted during the course of eleven visits to the island. My concern throughout has been contemporary politics, particularly political phenomena related to modernization and social change, a field which is unendingly interesting because it is perpetually changing."

* * *

KEES, Beverly (Ann) 1941-

PERSONAL: Born July 4, 1941, in Minneapolis, Minn.; daughter of Burton J. and Dorothy (White) Kees. *Education:* University of Minnesota, B.A., 1963. *Politics:* Independent. *Religion:* Episcopalian. *Home:* 15 South First St., Minneapolis, Minn. 55401. *Office: Minneapolis Tribune,* 425 Portland Ave., Minneapolis, Minn. 55488.

CAREER: Minneapolis Star, Minneapolis, Minn., woman's reporter, 1963-66, suburban reporter, 1966-67, business reporter, 1967-69, editor of Taste section, 1969-73, editor of special sections, 1971-73; Minneapolis Star & Tribune Co., Minneapolis, research planning analyst, 1973-74; *Minneapolis Tribune,* Minneapolis, assistant managing editor, 1974—. Member of faculty at College of St. Thomas, 1974. *Member:* Minnesota Alumni Association (member of board of directors, 1975—; member of executive committee, 1976—), Minnesota Alumnae Club (president, 1977).

WRITINGS: (With Donnie Flora) *Fondue on the Menu,* Golden Press, 1971; *Wonderful Ways With Chicken,* Stephen Greene Press, 1972; *Cook With Honey,* Stephen Greene Press, 1973; *Basic Breads Around the World,* Stephen Greene Press, 1977.

SIDELIGHTS: Beverly Kees writes: "I like to eat. Compiling cookbooks gives me a professional reason not to stay on a diet. And I can eat my work, which makes it more economical than most research."

* * *

KEIL, (Harold) Bill 1926-

PERSONAL: Born April 11, 1926, in Portland, Ore.; son of Harry G. (a musician) and Elizabeth M. (Kussmann) Keil; married Gloria Trantenella (a teacher), February 27, 1959; children: Richard T., Gregory H. *Education:* Oregon State University, B.S., 1950. *Religion:* Presbyterian. *Home and office:* 6306 Southwest 39th Ave., Portland, Ore. 97221.

CAREER: U.S. Forest Service, Portland, Ore., timber cruiser, 1950-51; City of Portland, Ore., park forester, 1952-56; *Forest Industries,* Portland, Ore., associate editor, 1956-61; *World Wood,* Portland, Ore., editor, 1961-71; free-lance writer, 1971-75; Bureau of Land Management, Portland, Ore., in public affairs, 1975—. Vice-president of Forest Park Committee of Fifty. Member of Mountain Rescue and Safety Council of Oregon. Past president, vice-president, and patrol chief of Mount Hood Ski Patrol. *Military service:*

U.S. Army, 1944-46; served in the Philippines; became staff sergeant.

MEMBER: Society of American Foresters, U.S. Ski Writers Association (northwestern president, 1971-76; member of national board of directors, 1963-76), Outdoor Writers Association of America, Commonwealth Forestry Association (England). *Awards, honors:* Award from Pacific Northwest Ski Writers Association for best coverage in Pacific Northwest, 1965; second place from U.S. Ski Writers Association, for best ski coverage, 1965, 1975.

WRITINGS: Guide to Roads and Trails of Forest Park, Westrails Press, 1973. Author of "Northwest Ski Tips" and Northwest Trail Trips," series on KOIN-TV, 1968-74. Author of "Ski Tips," a column in *Oregonian,* 1951. Contributor to sport and outdoor magazines, including *Skiing, Sports Afield,* and *Sports Illustrated.* Editor of *American Ski Annual,* 1956; field editor of *Timberman,* 1956-57, associate editor, 1957-58; field editor of *Lumberman,* 1957-58; editor of *Logging and Forestry,* 1958-68; western editor of *Plywood and Panel,* 1974—.

WORK IN PROGRESS: Research on contemporary history of Mount Hood, Ore.

SIDELIGHTS: Keil told *CA:* "Nearly all my work is in writing and photography covering aspects of the outdoors, mountains, and forests. This includes not only recreation, but also the important forest industry. Wood is one of our few renewable resources—a new crop soon replaces the crop harvested. It's an important building material as well as a source of other raw materials necessary for man's existence and comfort. Wood is unlike oil, coal, steel, and plastics . . . once they are gone, they are gone. I have found writing covering these activities through the medium of trade journals is satisfying both as a full-time staffer and as a free-lancer. There are real satisfactions in chronicling the progress of these industries. The trade journals, in general, are no longer the domain of the hack writer. There are opportunites for imaginative work, both in writing and in editing. The same holds true for sports publications. Some of the better outdoor writing today is appearing in some of the ski magazines.

"Free-lance writing (I comment with the background of having been both a full-time free-lancer and part-timer) is an activity that can continue as a writer advances in years, taking not only the place of the 'make work hobbies' of some retirees, but also as a cash generator. If I should ever retire (and I seriously question if I ever will), I'll still be pounding the typewriter keys."

AVOCATIONAL INTERESTS: Hiking, backpacking, natural history, geology, canoeing, photography.

* * *

KELEMAN, Stanley 1931-

PERSONAL: Born November 17, 1931, in Brooklyn, N.Y.; son of Joe and Rose (Cohen) Keleman; married Gail Hughes; children: Leah, Robert. *Education:* Attended Adelphi University, 1950; Chiropractic Institute of New York, D.C., 1954; attended Alfred Adler Institute, 1960-62. *Office:* 2045 Francisco St., Berkeley, Calif. 94709.

CAREER: Psychologist and bio-energetic trainer in private practice, Berkeley, Calif., 1968—. Lecturer at colleges and associations.

WRITINGS: Sexuality, Self, and Survival, Lodestar, 1970, 2nd edition published as *The Human Ground: Sexuality, Self, and Survival,* 1975; *Your Body Speaks Its Mind: The*

Bio-Energetic Way to Greater Emotional and Sexual Satisfaction, Simon & Schuster, 1975; *Living Your Dying,* Random House, 1976.

WORK IN PROGRESS: The Life of Your Body.

AVOCATIONAL INTERESTS: Metal sculpting, public speaking, swimming.

* * *

KELLER, Frances Richardson 1914-

PERSONAL: Born August 14, 1914, in Lowville, N.Y.; daughter of Stephen Brown (a cheese producer and merchant) and Sarah Eliza (Bell) Richardson; married Chauncey A. R. Keller, June 10, 1938 (divorced, 1963); married William P. Rhetta (an attorney), May 10, 1969; children: (first marriage) Reynolds, Stephen, Julia, William. *Education:* Sarah Lawrence College, B.A., 1935; University of Toledo, M.A., 1964; University of Chicago, Ph.D., 1973. *Home:* 835 Junipero Serra Blvd., San Francisco, Calif. 94127. *Office:* Department of History, San Jose State University, San Jose, Calif. 95192.

CAREER: Indiana University, Northwest Campus, Gary, lecturer in history, 1966-67; University of Illinois at Chicago Circle, Chicago, lecturer in history, 1967-68; Chicago City College, Chicago, Ill., assistant professor of history, 1968-70; San Francisco State University, San Francisco, Calif., lecturer in history, 1972-74; San Jose State University, San Jose, Calif., lecturer in history, 1974—. Lecturer at University of California, Berkeley extension, 1972-74. Associate member of board of directors of *Media Report to Women,* 1976—; past member of board of directors of Toledo Symphony Orchestra; narrator for concerts and television and radio programs, including "Six Major Interpretations of American History," on KCBS-Radio, 1974.

MEMBER: American Historical Association, Organization of American Historians, American Studies Association, National Women's Studies Association, Western Society for French History, West Coast Association of Women Historians, Berkshire Conference.

WRITINGS: An American Crusade: The Life of Charles Waddell Chesnutt, Brigham Young University Press, 1978. Contributor of about a dozen articles and reviews to journals, including *North American Review,* and newspapers.

WORK IN PROGRESS: Translating from the French, *Slavery and the French Revolution;* a book on social mobility, comparing responses of women and blacks, from the 1860's to the 1960's.

SIDELIGHTS: Frances Keller writes: "A preoccupation with American and world history began I know not when, but it was nourished by my aunt, and my friend, Francis D. Wormuth, and my teachers at college. I married, raised four children, then returned to study at the brilliantly-staffed University of Chicago in the 1960's. There a general social unrest and an acute racial dissatisfaction were daily fare. I faced decisions involving racial difficulties and the sexual prejudices of our society. My interests began to focus on slavery and its consequences and, later, on women's histories. From a village background in northern New York where neither problem seemed present, I have traveled to an understanding of the depths of both."

BIOGRAPHICAL/CRITICAL SOURCES: San Francisco Examiner, August 25, 1975; *New York Times,* June 12, 1976, January 18, 1977, January 23, 1977; *Media Report to Women,* January 1, 1977; *Woman's Paper,* February, 1977.

KELLEY, Alice van Buren 1944-

PERSONAL: Born September 26, 1944, in Abilene, Texas; daughter of Francis Reid and Edith (Pardee) van Buren; married Richard Ian Kelley (a physician), October 13, 1969; children: Ian Andrews, Nathan Ross. *Education:* Smith College, B.A., 1966; City University of New York, Ph.D., 1971. *Residence:* Philadelphia, Pa. *Office:* Department of English, University of Pennsylvania, Philadelphia, Pa. 19104.

CAREER: University of Pennsylvania, Philadelphia, lecturer, 1971-72, assistant professor, 1972-74, associate professor of English, 1974—. *Member:* Modern Language Association of America.

WRITINGS: The Novels of Virginia Woolf: Fact and Vision, University of Chicago Press, 1973. Contributor of articles and reviews to literature journals and newspapers.

WORK IN PROGRESS: A study of the novels of Anthony Trollope.

SIDELIGHTS: Commenting on her studies of Woolf and Trollope, Kelley told *CA:* "It is a long stretch from Woolf, a modern experimentalist, to Trollope, a Victorian realist, but a mind left flaccid grows dull, and a bored teacher is a boring one. So although it may take me some time to move from one century to another, I am finding the experience exhilarating."

* * *

KELLEY, Dean M(aurice) 1926-

PERSONAL: Born June 1, 1926, in Cheyenne, Wyo.; son of Mark M. (a civil engineer) and Irena (a music teacher; maiden name, Lancaster) Kelley; married Maryon Hoyle (an administrator of a state institution for the mentally retarded), June 9, 1946; children: Lenore Hoyle. *Education:* University of Denver, A.B., 1946; Iliff School of Theology, Th.M., 1949; further graduate study at Columbia University, 1949-50. *Politics:* Independent. *Home:* 122 Old East Neck Rd., Melville, N.Y. 11746. *Office:* 475 Riverside Dr., New York, N.Y. 10027.

CAREER: Ordained Methodist minister; pastor of Methodist churches in Oak Creek, Colo., 1946-49, East Meadow, N.Y., 1950-52, Westhampton Beach, N.Y., 1952-55, Queens, N.Y., 1955-56, and Bronx, N.Y., 1957-60; National Council of Churches, New York, N.Y., executive for religious and civil liberty, 1960—. *Member:* American Civil Liberties Union.

WRITINGS: Why Conservative Churches Are Growing, Harper, 1972; *Why Churches Should Not Pay Taxes,* Harper, 1976. Editor of *Annals* of Academy of Social and Political Science, autumn, 1979.

WORK IN PROGRESS: Research for a book, *New Frontiers of Religious Liberty.*

* * *

KELLEY, Kitty 1942-

PERSONAL: Born April 4, 1942, in Spokane, Wash.; daughter of William V. (an attorney) and Adele (Martin) Kelley; married Michael Edgley (a media director), August 28, 1976. *Education:* University of Washington, Seattle, B.A. (cum laude), 1964. *Home and office:* 1636-D Beekman Pl. N.W., Washington, D.C. 20009.

CAREER: World's Fair, New York, N.Y., hostess for General Electric exhibit, 1964-65; press secretary to U.S. Senator Eugene McCarthy in Washington, D.C., 1966-69;

Washington Post, Washington, D.C., member of editorial page staff, 1969-71; *Washingtonian,* Washington, D.C., contributing editor, 1971-73; free-lance writer, 1973—. Member of board of directors of Richmund Fellowship. *Member:* American Newspaperwomen's Club, Washington Press Club, Washington Independent Writers (member of board of directors).

WRITINGS: The Glamour Spas, Simon & Schuster, 1975; (co-author) *The Marriage Maintenance Manual,* Dial, 1976; *Jackie Oh!,* Lyle Stuart, 1978. Editor of "Today Is Sunday," appearing weekly in *Chicago Sun Times* and *Philadelphia Bulletin,* 1978. Contributor to magazines, including *Newsweek, McCall's, Ladies Home Journal, Cosmopolitan,* and *Family Circle,* and newspapers. Assistant editor of *The Berkshires,* 1976.

SIDELIGHTS: Kitty Kelley wrote: "Words are more important to me than anything else in the world. I write fulltime, which means I'm in constant agony until a project is finished. There is nothing I'd rather do, and just as soon as I summon the nerve, I'll try a novel."

*   *   *

KELLOGG, Marjorie   1922-

PERSONAL: Born July 17, 1922, in Santa Barbara, Calif.; *Education:* Attended University of California, Berkeley; Smith College, B.A., 1952, M.A., 1953. *Agent:* The Lantz Office, Inc., 114 East 55th St., New York, N.Y. 10022.

CAREER: Writer. Worked on copy desk for *San Francisco Chronicle,* San Francisco, Calif.; writer for *Salute* magazine. Hospital social worker.

WRITINGS: Tell Me That You Love Me, Junie Moon (novel), Farrar, Straus, 1968; *Like the Lion's Tooth* (novel), Farrar, Straus, 1972.

Screenplays: "Tell Me That You Love Me, Junie Moon," 1970.

SIDELIGHTS: Kellogg received much encouragement to write a novel from Paula Fox, a friend with whom she had previously collaborated on a television play. Fox suggested that Kellogg write about hospital patients, since that was an area Kellogg knew well. Kellogg's protest that she did not know *how* to write a novel brought this response from Fox: "Just sit there at the typewriter until you do." Following that order, Kellogg began getting up at five o'clock every morning and writing until almost nine a.m., when she had to leave for work. "After the first hundred pages," she recalled, "I began to work nights and weekends." Kellogg's efforts resulted in her highly praised first novel, *Tell Me That You Love Me, Junie Moon.*

Junie Moon is the story of three physically handicapped people who meet in a hospital and later take up housekeeping together. Junie, horribly disfigured by acid burns, Arthur, afflicted with a progressive neurological disease which causes involuntary flailings, and Walter, a paraplegic, learn to live with and care for each other. But the process is a painful one. The three fight: "At first it was because they were afraid of having to tend to their ailments themselves without Miss Oxford picking at them. Without knowing it, they missed the lack of privacy at the hospital. Their bodies and thoughts had been exposed for so long for many and all to see, it was hard to stitch them up again into belonging only to them."

Many critics have commented on Kellogg's sensitive handling of the difficult subject matters in *Junie Moon.* Bruce Cook stated: "Given the same situation and characters, Marjorie Kellogg could have been pietistic, clinical, or surrealistic. She could consciously have imitated any of the writers with whom she has been compared. But she has mostly managed to resist such temptations, has kept her eye directly on her characters, and has written her own book." Eliot Fremont-Smith described the novel as "funny, sardonic, occasionally biting, more often tender, even sentimental, and, to my surprise, the most affecting work of fiction I have read in quite some time." Piers Brendon's review of the book was equally enthusiastic: "The tensions between the characters are superbly maintained.... The dialogue is witty and bitter even when the mutual hostility finally softens into dependence and love." Brendon found thematic similarities between Kellogg's writing and that of Flannery O'Conner and Carson McCullers. He said, "If not yet quite their stature, Marjorie Kellogg can certainly stand beside them without being dwarfed."

Some reviewers found *Junie Moon* to be overly simplistic in its dealings with serious emotional matters. Edmund White noted that as the characters in the novel get accustomed to each other and begin to forget each other's deformities, the reader begins to do the same. This creates a credibility problem for White: "The symbolic magic of the written word has transported us out of the world of appearances into the realm of sentiments. Perhaps the victory has come a little too easily. I, for one, find it hard to believe that people who suffered as much as Miss Kellogg's trio would be so likeable, gallant, and childlike." White also found Kellogg's style to be too "well-crafted." He explained: "What's annoying about Miss Kellogg's book is its craftmanship. Her novel is, in effect, a well-made play, replete with easy motivations, tidy psychological summations and mechanically developed details." Too many details can be oppressive, White found: "If she mentions an owl early in the book, she feels obliged to turn the poor bird into a *motif.*"

Shaun O'Connell found stylistic problems with *Junie Moon,* which he called "an artful, but artificial, novel." The artificiality, he explained, is due to the fact that "Miss Kellogg overcontrols, overdirects the counters in her pattern. Throughout, we remain conscious of those things she is trying to do—move beyond the grotesque mode and move us—and the way she does them. We would be more moved ... if she were a bit less concerned with contriving a pattern—juxtaposing the normal with the freakish, the sentimental with the horrible—to move us."

In writing *Like the Lion's Tooth,* which concerns the lives of three emotionally disturbed children, Kellogg drew once more upon her experiences as a hospital social worker. Christopher Lehmann-Haupt found the book to be overly sentimental: "It is all very compelling the way Marjorie Kellogg has jig-sawed her picture to bits and slipped us the pieces. She does it well. But what was not worth doing was painting the picture in the first place. For when all the pieces are finally in place, what we see is a sentimental story about the cruelty of grown-ups to children—a story whose heavily weighted message has nothing whatever to do with the tricky form in which it is told—and we can't help feeling we've been had."

Other reviews of Kellogg's second novel, however, have been far more favorable. Several have compared it to *Junie Moon,* noting that *Like the Lion's Tooth* is an improvement, stylistically. Josephine Hendin, for example, called the second novel a "wrenching tale," and further stated: "Kellogg achieves the extraordinary feat of writing about atrocities with her eye fixed on love, infusing into the mutilation of innocents the sense that, even if parents use and wreck them, the young can keep each other whole and alive. . . . Miss Kellogg's school is filled with the loving, needing, damaged young. Through their yearning for each other she achieves a hard optimism more moving than anything in her first novel, *Tell Me That You Love Me, Junie Moon*. [This] is a stark, passionate book, pure in its belief that the tenderest victims of human cruelty and inhuman social forces can love sublimely, can be overpoweringly humane.''

BIOGRAPHICAL/CRITICAL SOURCES: Life, October 4, 1968; *New York Times Book Review,* October 6, 1968, November 5, 1972; *New York Times,* October 18, 1968, December 14, 1968, November 4, 1972; *New Republic,* November 23, 1968; *National Observer,* December 23, 1968; *Village Voice,* February 6, 1969; *New York Review of Books,* February 27, 1969; *Yale Review,* spring, 1969; *Books and Bookmen,* July, 1969; *Saturday Review,* October 14, 1972; *Newsweek,* October 16, 1972; *Atlantic,* November, 1972; *Contemporary Literary Criticism,* Gale, Volume 2, 1974.*

*   *   *

KELLOGG, Mary Alice 1948-

PERSONAL: Born June 6, 1948, in Tucson, Ariz.; daughter of Katherine (a placement officer) Kellogg. *Education:* University of Arizona, B.A. (cum laude), 1970. *Residence:* New York, N.Y. *Agent:* Timothy Seldes, Russell & Volkening, Inc., 551 Fifth Ave., New York, N.Y. 10017. *Office: Parade,* 750 Third Ave., New York, N.Y. 10017.

CAREER: Newsweek, New York City, researcher and reporter, 1970-71, correspondent from Chicago, 1971-73, and San Francisco, 1973-75, associate editor, 1975-77; WCBS-TV, New York City, correspondent, 1977-78; *Parade,* New York City, senior editor, 1978—. *Member:* American Federation of Television and Radio Artists, Society of Professional Journalists, Women in Communications, Kappa Tau Alpha. *Awards, honors:* National communications award from Easter Seal Society, 1977, for article ''The Next Minority.''

WRITINGS: (Editor with Min S. Yee and contributor) *The Great Escape,* Bantam, 1974; *Fast Track: The Superachievers and How They Make It to Early Success, Status, and Power,* McGraw, 1978. Contributor to national magazines, including *Glamour, Nation, Saturday Review, Travel and Leisure,* and *Working Woman.* Member of editorial board of *Chicago Journalism Review,* 1971-73.

WORK IN PROGRESS: A novel.

BIOGRAPHICAL/CRITICAL SOURCES: Glamour, February, 1976.

*   *   *

KELLY, Gail P(aradise) 1940-

PERSONAL: Born June 14, 1940, in New York, N.Y.; daughter of Joseph L. (a lawyer) and Lillian (a lawyer; maiden name, Liss) Paradise; married David H. Kelly (a professor), August 17, 1964; children: Jennifer Ann, Elizabeth Ella. *Education:* University of Chicago, A.B., 1962; Indiana University, M.S.Ed., 1970; University of Wisconsin—Madison, Ph.D., 1975. *Home:* 131 Greenfield St., Buffalo, N.Y. 14214. *Office:* Department of Social Foundations of Education, State University of New York at Buffalo, 432 Baldy Hall, Amherst, N.Y. 14216.

CAREER: Indiana University, Bloomington, editorial associate for *Reading Research Quarterly,* 1965-68, publications editor for ERIC Clearinghouse on Reading, 1968-70; Coop-

erative Education Services Agency, Waupan, Wis., project director, 1973-74; Wisconsin Department of Health and Social Services, Madison, planning analyst, 1974-75; State University of New York at Buffalo, Amherst, assistant professor, 1974-78, associate professor of foundations of education, 1978—. *Member:* Comparative and International Education Society (member of board of directors, 1974—), French Colonial History Society, Society for Asian Studies.

WRITINGS: (Editor with P. G. Altbach, and contributor) *Colonialism and Education,* Longman, 1977; *From Vietnam to America: A Chronicle of the Vietnamese Immigration to the United States,* Westview Press, 1978; *Feminism: Its Impact on the Disciplines,* University of Illinois Press, in press. Contributor to history and education journals. Associate editor of *Comparative Education Review.*

*   *   *

KELLY, Laurence 1933-

PERSONAL: Born April 11, 1933, in Brussels, Belgium; son of Sir David (an ambassador) and Lady Marie Noel (de Jourda de Vaux) Kelley; married Alison Linda McNair Scott (a writer); children: Rosanna, Rachel, Nicholas. *Education:* Attended New College, Oxford, 1952-55, and Harvard University, 1958-59. *Religion:* Christian. *Home:* 44 Ladbroke Grove, London W11 2PA, England. *Agent:* A.M. Heath & Co., 40 William IV St., London W.C.2, England.

CAREER: Northern Ireland Development Agency, Belfast, member of board of directors, 1972-78. Vice-chairman of British Iron and Steel Consumers' Council, 1975—. *Member:* Royal Geographical Society (fellow).

WRITINGS: Lermontov: Tragedy in the Caucasus, Constable, 1977, Braziller, 1978.

WORK IN PROGRESS: Research on Russian subjects.

*   *   *

KELLY, Rita Mae 1939-

PERSONAL: Born December 10, 1939, in Waseca, Minn.; daughter of John Francis and Agnes (Lorentz) Cawley; married Vincent Peter Kelly (a college professor), June 2, 1962; children: Patrick Joseph, Kathleen Theresa. *Education:* University of Minnesota, B.A. (magna cum laude), 1961; Indiana University, M.A., 1964, Ph.D., 1967; graduate study at University of Southern California, 1966. *Religion:* Roman Catholic. *Residence:* Moorestown, N.J. *Office:* Department of Urban Studies and Community Development, Rutgers University, Camden, N.J. 08102.

CAREER: Indiana University at Bloomington, counselor and instructor at Institute for International Education, summers, 1962-64; University of Maryland, European Division, Heidelberg, Germany, lecturer in political science and history, 1965-67; American University, Center for Research in Social Systems, Washington, D.C., assistant professor, 1968-69, research associate professor, 1969-70; American Institutes for Research, Kensington, Md., senior research scientist, 1970-72; U.S. Office of Economic Opportunity, Washington, D.C., consultant to Office of Economic Development and Office of Program Development, 1972-73; Center for Community Economic Development, Cambridge, Mass., staff research analyst, 1973; Seton Hall University, South Orange, N.J., adjunct associate professor of government and politics, 1974-75; Rutgers University, Camden, N.J., associate professor of urban studies and community development, 1975—. Special adviser to Institute of American Government, 1970-71. Speaker at professional gatherings; guest on radio and television programs in New York and New Jersey. Member of religious folk singing groups in Maryland, 1969-73, and New Jersey (also director), 1973-75. Member of board of directors of Cabin John preschool program, 1973, and Rutgers-Camden County Day Care Center, 1975-76; co-planner and producer of public service programs for distribution by New Jersey county public libraries, 1977-78; adviser to Respond, Inc.; consultant to Parity Development Corp.

MEMBER: International Public Policy Institute (member of board of advisers, 1975—), International Association of Applied Psychology, International Association of Political Psychology, American Political Science Association, Women's Caucus for Political Science, American Sociological Association, Policy Studies Organization, Society for the Psychological Study of Social Issues, Institute of Comparative Social and Cultural Studies (member of board of directors, 1975—), Northeast Women's Caucus for Political Science (president, 1978-79), Northeastern Political Science Association (member of executive council, 1977—), New Jersey Political Science Association (member of executive council, 1976-78; second vice-president, 1977-78; first vice-president, 1978-79), Phi Beta Kappa. *Awards, honors:* Member of first United States-Soviet Union student exchange program, 1959.

WRITINGS: The Pilot Police Project: A Description and Assessment of an Experiment in Police-Community Relations, U.S. Government Printing Office, 1972; *Expression of Training Needs by CDC Boards of Directors* (monograph), Center for Community Economic Development, 1974; *The Executive Directors of Community Development Corporations: Their Backgrounds, Job Satisfaction, and Use of Work Time* (monograph), Center for Community Economic Development, 1974; *Community Participation in Directing Economic Development,* Center for Community Economic Development, 1976, reprinted as *Community Control of Economic Development: A Study of the Boards of Directors of Community Development Corporations,* Praeger, 1977; (with Mary Boutilier) *The Making of Political Women: A Study of Socialization and Role Conflict,* Nelson-Hall, 1978.

Contributor: Erik Hoffman and Frederic J. Fleron, Jr., editors, *The Conduct of Soviet Foreign Policy,* Aldine, 1971; Richard L. Merritt, editor, *Communication in International Politics,* University of Illinois Press, 1972; John and Homa Snibbe, editors, *The Urban Policemen in Transition,* C. C Thomas, 1973; Alvin W. Cohn and Emilio C. Viano, editors, *Police-Community Relations: Images, Roles, Realities,* Lippincott, 1976; Judith V. May and Aaron B. Wildavsky, editors, *The Policy Cycle,* Sage Publications, 1978. Contributor of more than twenty articles to scholarly journals and newspapers. Editor of *New Jersey Political Science Association Newsletter,* 1976-78; member of editorial board of *Journal of International and Comparative Public Policy,* 1975—, and *Evaluation Quarterly: A Journal of Applied Social Research,* 1978—.

WORK IN PROGRESS: Editing a book of readings on citizen participation and criminal justice, with Richard Rich and Jon Van Til, publication expected in 1980; editing a book of readings on productivity, urban services, and human satisfaction; a test of her theory on female political achievement; contributing to *Methodological Issues in the Study of Women and Politics,* edited by Sarah Slavin Schramm.

SIDELIGHTS: Rita Kelly writes: "I am interested in social change and greater participation by all human beings in so-cial and political life. This interest undergirds all my research and writing. The book *The Making of Political Women* reflects a direct concern for the types of social change needed for greater female participation. Clearly, the political importance of mothers and of being a mother has been underestimated. The book states how and why mothers are important for female development."

AVOCATIONAL INTERESTS: Playing classical and folk guitar, piano, and accordian, bicycling, swimming, hiking.

* * *

KEMP, Edward C.   1929-

PERSONAL: Born October 3, 1929, in Boston, Mass.; son of Edward Clark (an attorney) and Alice Marie (Graham) Kemp; married Elaine Long Baker, July 29, 1971; children: (previous marriage) Edith M. and Susan A. (twins); Jennifer E. *Education:* Harvard University, A.B. (cum laude), 1951; University of California, Berkeley, M.L.S., 1955. *Home:* 3237 Onyx Pl., Eugene, Ore. 97405. *Office:* Library, University of Oregon, Eugene, Ore. 97403.

CAREER: University of Oregon, Eugene, reference and acquisitions librarian, 1955-56, acquisitions and special collections librarian, 1957—. *Member:* American Library Association, Society of American Archivists, Pacific Northwest Library Association, Northwest Archivists, Oregon Library Association.

WRITINGS: Manuscript Solicitation for Libraries, Special Collections, Museums, and Archives, Libraries Unlimited, 1978. Contributor of articles and reviews to library journals. Editor of *Imprint Oregon,* 1957—.

WORK IN PROGRESS: Bibliography and biography of Edward A. Wilson, Kurt Wiese, and Kurt Werth.

SIDELIGHTS: Kemp's special interests include manuscript collections created by transportation, forestry, fishing, political leaders, missionaries from the Orient, South America, and Africa, writers and illustrators of children's books, and regional historical figures. He believes that too many valuable materials are lost to natural disasters and human carelessness before the owners think to make a donation to a library or museum, and feels that special attention should be given to active solicitation of manuscript collections. His book is a detailed practical approach to planning and carrying out programs that will enhance the holdings of libraries and museums in the most effective and economic ways.

* * *

KENDALL, Elizabeth B(emis)   1947-

PERSONAL: Born April 7, 1947, in St. Louis, Mo.; daughter of Henry C. (a commodity broker) and Elizabeth (Conant) Kendall. *Education:* Radcliffe College, B.A. (cum laude), 1969; Harvard University, M.A.T., 1971. *Politics:* Democrat. *Home:* 400 West 43rd St., Apt. 2L, New York, N.Y. 10036. *Agent:* Maxine Groffsky, 2 Fifth Ave., New York, N.Y. 10011.

CAREER: High school teacher of English in Brookline Mass., 1971-72; substitute teacher in Newton, Mass., 1972-73; free-lance writer. Member of Manhattan Plaza dance committee; consultant to Ford Foundation.

WRITINGS: Where She Danced: American Dancing, 1880-1930, Knopf, 1979. Also author of television scripts, for WNET-TV, "Dance in America: Pilobolus," 1977, and "Trailblazers of Modern Dance," 1977. Contributor to dance magazines and newspapers.

WORK IN PROGRESS: A novel; research on Ford Foundation's dance funding since 1959.

SIDELIGHTS: Elizabeth Kendall writes: "I began dancing late, after having been very well-educated in the English language. Dance is very healthy for writers: it removes one's mind completely from words, yet it is a complete discipline itself. Ultimately the wordless language feeds back into the prose. I usually take a dance class every day."

* * *

KENDRICK, Thomas Downing 1895-

PERSONAL: Born April 1, 1895, in Handsworth, Birmingham, England; son of Thomas Henry (in the brass industry) and Fanny Susan (Downing) Kendrick; married Helen Martha Kiek, 1920 (died, 1955); married Katharine Elizabeth Wrigley, October 14, 1957; children: (first marriage) Helen Frances Kendrick Atkin. *Education:* Oriel College, Oxford, M.A., 1919. *Politics:* Conservative. *Religion:* Church of England. *Home:* Old Farm, Organford, near Poole, Dorsetshire BH16 6EU, England.

CAREER: British Museum, London, keeper of British antiquities, 1938-50, director and principal librarian, 1951-59; writer, 1959—. Member of Royal Commission of 1851. *Military service:* British Army, Royal Warwickshire Regiment.

MEMBER: British Academy (fellow), Society of Antiquaries (fellow), Royal Institute of British Architects (fellow), Royal Swedish Academy of Letters, History, and Antiquities (foreign member), German Archaeological Institute, Athenaeum Club. *Awards, honors:* Knight commander of Order of the Bath, 1951; D.Litt. from University of Durham, and Oxford University; Litt.D. from University of Dublin; honorary fellow of Oriel College, Oxford.

WRITINGS: The Druids, Methuen, 1927, reprinted, 1966; *The Archaeology of the Channel Islands: Guernsey,* Methuen, 1928; *A History of the Vikings,* Methuen, 1930, reprinted, 1968; *Anglo-Saxon Art to A.D. 900,* Methuen, 1938, reprinted, 1972; *Late Saxon and Viking Art,* Methuen, 1949, reprinted, 1974; *British Antiquity,* Methuen, 1950, reprinted, 1970; *The Lisbon Earthquake,* Methuen, 1956; *Saint James in Spain,* Methuen, 1960; *Great Love for Icarus* (novel), Methuen, 1962; *Mary of Agreda,* Routledge & Kegan Paul, 1967.

WORK IN PROGRESS: Philip IV of Spain.

* * *

KENNEDY, Elliot
See GODFREY, Lionel (Robert Holcombe)

* * *

KENNEDY, James G(ettier) 1932-

PERSONAL: Born May 30, 1932, in New York, N.Y.; son of Durward Bellmont (a mechanical engineer) and Kathryn Gettier (a teacher; maiden name, Herrman) Kennedy; married Winona Ann Saunders (a home economist), August 28, 1954; children: Candace Ann Kennedy Boyd, Pamela Kathryn, James Frederick. *Education:* Kenyon College, A.B. (summa cum laude), 1954; University of Minnesota, M.A., 1955, Ph.D., 1961. *Politics:* Marxist. *Home:* 1018 South Second St., DeKalb, Ill. 60115. *Office:* Department of English, Northern Illinois University, DeKalb, Ill. 60115.

CAREER: Hofstra College (now University), Hempstead, N.Y., lecturer in English, 1957-58; Upsala College, East Orange, N.J., instructor, 1958-60, assistant professor, 1960-64, associate professor of English, 1964-69; Northern Illinois University, DeKalb, associate professor of English, 1969—. Public speaker; guest on television programs. *Member:* Midwest Victorian Studies Association, Phi Beta Kappa. *Awards, honors:* Woodrow Wilson fellowship, 1954-55.

WRITINGS: (Contributor) James G. Hepburn, editor, *Letters of Arnold Bennett,* Volume I: *Letters to J. B. Pinker,* Oxford University Press, 1966; (editor and contributor) *Stories East and West,* Scott, Foresman, 1971; (contributor) Bruce E. Teets and Helmut E. Gerber, editors, *Joseph Conrad: An Annotated Bibliography of Writings About Him,* Northern Illinois University Press, 1971; *Herbert Spencer,* Twayne, 1978. Contributor of articles and reviews to literature journals.

WORK IN PROGRESS: Victorian Syntax, completion expected in 1982.

SIDELIGHTS: Kennedy writes: "The necessary sense of literature and writing is social, and teaching must reflect this fact. A freshman student introduced me to Herbert Spencer in 1957; radical students introduced me to Marxism in the late 1960's; an in-law confirmed me in Marxism in 1968 by breaking my left humerus in anger at my views; the King and Kennedy assassinations, the police riots of the summer of 1967, the police riot in Chicago in 1968, the martyrs of Kent State University, the writings of G. William Domhoff, Noam Chomsky, and Victor Perlo, and *The Pentagon Papers* confirmed my distrust of government in the United States; five months in Cambridge, England in 1967 confirmed my sense that one might live a decent life in some other society as well as in our own.

"American blacks and whites can find one common ground in understanding *Native Son.* I read and teach fiction, poetry, and plays from anyplace but the U.S., and avoid fiction by contemporary mainstream authors. I emphasize cultural differences as explanations for differences in works on similar topics. I use the tutorial method to teach business writing to one hundred women and men majoring in computer science."

* * *

KENRICK, Donald Simon 1929-

PERSONAL: Born June 6, 1929, in London, England; son of Mack (a furrier) and Gertrude (Levy) Kenrick; married Bente Hansen (a designer); children: Timna (daughter). *Education:* University of London, earned B.A., M.A., and Ph.D. *Home:* 61 Blenheim Cres., London W11 2EG, England. *Agent:* A. D. Peters, 10 Buckingham St., London W.C.2N., England.

CAREER: Taught in schools in London, England, Morocco, Switzerland, and Bulgaria; lecturer at colleges and non-vocational adult institutes in London and Kent, England; writer. Secretary of Language Commission of World Romani Congress. *Member:* Association of Gypsy Organizations.

WRITINGS: (With Grattan Puxon) *The Destiny of Europe's Gypsies,* Basic Books, 1972. Contributor to gypsy and linguistic journals.

WORK IN PROGRESS: A semi-fictional book on English gypsies; research on the Romani language.

SIDELIGHTS: Kenrick writes: "I first became interested in the social problems of the gypsies while studying the Romani language. Now I am engaged in civil rights work for gypsies on a national and international level, but continue to support myself by teaching and lecturing.

"Ever since the gypsy people came to Europe, writers have been predicting the end of their culture, yet they still survive. It's my belief that instead of trying to assimilate them into society we should learn from them. There is more to their way of life than the caravan and ethnic dress. There are the virtues of the extended family network, an attitude which limits the time devoted to work to that which produces enough money for basic needs, and a wealth of music and tales that has barely been tapped."

* * *

KENT, Frank (Richardson, Jr.) 1907(?)-1978

OBITUARY NOTICE: Born c. 1907; died December 2, 1978, in Washington, D.C. Journalist. Kent worked as a police reporter, war correspondent, and Washington bureau chief of the *Baltimore Sun*. He later became a member of the *Washington Post* news staff and then Central Intelligence Agency (CIA) editor based in Europe and the Far East. Obituaries and other sources: *Washington Post,* December 4, 1978.

* * *

KENT, Katherine
See DIAL, Joan

* * *

KERNAN, Michael 1927-

PERSONAL: Born April 29, 1927, in Utica, N.Y.; son of Michael J. (a state senator) and Katharine K. (Clarke) Kernan; married Margot S. Starr (a professor of film), September 5, 1949; children: Nathan M., Lisa D. Kernan Medina, Nicholas G. *Education:* Harvard University, A.B. (cum laude), 1949. *Agent:* William Reiss, Paul R. Reynolds, Inc., 12 East 41st St., New York, N.Y. 10017. *Office:* *Washington Post,* 1150 15th St. N.W., Washington, D.C. 20005.

CAREER: Worked for *Watertown Times,* Watertown, N.Y., 1949-53; *Redwood City Tribune,* Redwood City, Calif., writer, 1953-62, news editor, 1962-63, city editor, 1963-66; *Washington Post,* Washington, D.C., assignment editor, 1967-68, reporter, 1968—. *Awards, honors:* Investigative writing award from American Political Science Association, 1958, for articles on city politics; feature award from Associated Press, 1959, for an article on the aftermath of an auto accident.

WRITINGS: The Violet Dots (nonfiction), Braziller, 1978. Contributor of articles and fiction to popular magazines, including, *Life, Look, Saturday Evening Post, Reader's Digest,* and *Ladies Home Journal,* and newspapers.

WORK IN PROGRESS: A novel.

SIDELIGHTS: Kernan wrote that *The Violet Dots* "started to be an account of the first day of the battle of the Somme, July 1, 1916, when nearly 60,000 British soldiers were lost in a foolish daylight charge. But my subject, an eighty-year-old English coal miner, interested me so much that my wife said, 'You're in love with that old man. You should write a book about him.' So I did. It is done in mosaic form: bits of diary, interviews, letters, plus contemporary accounts on British life during the war, song excerpts, news items, etc."

* * *

KERNS, Frances Casey 1937-

PERSONAL: Born February 22, 1937, in Marion County, Ark.; daughter of Melvin Leslie and Verna Lessie (Richardson) Casey; married Jack Kerns, February 14, 1971; children: Alan Lee Jobe, Mary Reyna. *Education:* University of Colorado, Denver, B.S., 1971. *Politics:* Independent. *Home address:* P.O. Box 645, Walden, Colo. 80480. *Agent:* David Hull, James Brown Associates, Inc., 25 West 43rd St., New York, N.Y. 10036.

CAREER: Writer, 1971—. Proof-reader of braille books. *Member:* Authors Guild, Authors League of America, Colorado Authors League.

WRITINGS—All novels: *The Stinsons,* Curtis Books, 1972; *A Cold Wild Wind,* Crowell, 1974; *This Land Is Mine,* Crowell, 1974; *The Winter Heart,* Warner, 1978; *Cana and Wine,* Warner, 1979; *Dark Places,* Warner, 1979.

SIDELIGHTS: Frances Kerns writes: "My first years were spent in the Arkansas Ozarks. Perhaps my greatest love, aside from my family and books, is our mountains. I first knew them at the age of fifteen and they called to me constantly through the seven remaining years before I became a Colorado resident. Now, the western country and people's feelings for or against it play large parts in my books.

"There was a time when I thought of going into family counseling, thus my degree in sociology. Matters of sociology and psychology are still of great interest to me, partly because they are very relevant to the kind of writing I do.

"All my books are novels, set in the west, but not 'westerns.' It is long past time that people in other states and other countries knew the west as it really was, and is now. Two of my books are historical novels (not historical romances), well and deeply researched. My chief purpose in all the books is character study and development. My subjects are ordinary people, whoever they may be, and my aim is to set them forth to readers as honestly as I possibly can. I have been interested in telling stories since my earliest memory, and have 'played' at writing since I learned how to put words on paper. If I have a philosophy in life, it is to go on learning."

AVOCATIONAL INTERESTS: Folk music, driving, walking, horseback riding and bicycling in the mountains.

* * *

KERR, Joan P. 1921-

PERSONAL: Born November 8, 1921, in New Jersey; daughter of David A. (a broker) and Marjorie (Sclater) Paterson; married Edwin S. Mills, Jr., July 14, 1946 (divorced, August, 1960); married Chester B. Kerr (a director of a publishing company), June 30, 1964; children: (first marriage) Tony, Hilary P., Alison. *Education:* Vassar College, B.A., 1942; Mills College, M.A., 1943. *Home:* 421 Humphrey St., New Haven, Conn. 06511.

CAREER: Life, New York City, researcher, 1944-49; Picture Press, New York City, picture editor, 1952-54; *American Heritage,* New York City, assistant editor, 1954-58, associate editor, 1958-66, art editor, 1966-68, consulting editor, 1968-76, contributing editor, 1976—.

WRITINGS: (Editor with Oliver Jensen and Murray Belsky) *American Album,* American Heritage Publishing, 1968; (editor with Scottie Fitzgerald Smith and Matthew J. Bruccoli) *The Romantic Egoists,* Scribner, 1974. Contributor to *American Heritage.*

WORK IN PROGRESS: Romance in America.

* * *

KESSLER, Walter R. 1913-1978

OBITUARY NOTICE: Born in 1913; died December 22,

1978, in New York, N.Y. Doctor of medicine, children's allergy specialist, and author. Kessler's most notable achievement was the development of allergy medicine for children and of diagnostic tests used to determine the presence of cystic fibrosis. He is author, with Dr. William Sherman, of *Allergy in Pediatric Practice,* published in 1957. Obituaries and other sources: *New York Times,* December 26, 1978.

* * *

KEZYS, Algimantas 1928-

PERSONAL: Born October 28, 1928, in Vistytis, Lithuania; came to the United States in 1950, naturalized citizen, 1956; son of George (a government employee) and Eugenija (Kolytaite) Kezys. *Education:* Loyola University, Chicago, Ill., M.A., 1956. *Home and office:* 5620 South Claremont Ave., Chicago, Ill. 60636.

CAREER: Entered Society of Jesus (Jesuits), 1950, ordained Roman Catholic priest, 1961; editor in Chicago, Ill., 1964-67, founder of Lithuanian Photo Library in Chicago, 1966—, director of Lithuanian Youth Center in Chicago, 1974-77, founder and director of *Lithuanian Ethnic Encyclopedia,* 1976—. Director of "Lithuanian Television Hour" in Chicago, 1976-78. Photographer; first one-man show, 1963; exhibitions held at Art Institute of Chicago, 1965, and at other institutions in the United States and abroad.

WRITINGS: Sventoji auka (with own photographs; title means" The Holy Sacrifice"), Jesuit Fathers of Della Strada, 1965; (photographer) Bruno Markaitis, *Photographs: Algimantas Kezys,* Loyola University Press, 1966; (with William M. Barbieri) *Sidewalk: Reflections and Images,* photographs by Aligmantas Zezysist, Maryknoll Publications, 1969.

(Editor and photographer) Francis Thompson, *I Fled Him, Down the Nights and Down the Days,* Loyola University Press, 1970; *Form and Content* (photographs), M. Morkunas, 1972; (editor and photographer) *A Lithuanian Cemetery: St. Casimir Cemetery in Chicago, Ill.,* Lithuanian Photo Library, 1976; (photographer) Tom Collins, *The Search for Jimmy Carter,* Word Books, 1976; *Posters: Algimantas Kezys,* Volume I and Volume II, Loyola University Press, 1978.

Contributor of photographs to *Famous Photographers Annual* and to various magazines, including *Camera.*

WORK IN PROGRESS: Posters, Volumes III and IV.

AVOCATIONAL INTERESTS: Artist.

* * *

KILLINGER, John 1933-

PERSONAL: Born June 12, 1933, in Germantown, Ky.; son of John Raymond and Jessie Frances Killinger; married Anne Katherine Waddle (a composer), June 12, 1952; children: John Eric, Paul Krister. *Education:* Baylor University, A.B., 1953; University of Kentucky, M.A., 1954, Ph.D.,1957; Harvard University, S.T.B., 1959; Princeton Theological Seminary, Th.D., 1963. *Politics:* Democrat. *Home:* 805 Clearview Dr., Nashville, Tenn. 37205. *Agent:* Joan Raines, Raines & Raines, 475 Fifth Ave., New York, N.Y. 10017. *Office:* Vanderbilt Divinity School, Nashville, Tenn. 37240.

CAREER: Ordained Baptist minister, 1952; pastor of Baptist church in North Reading, Mass., 1957-59; Georgetown College, Georgetown, Ky., associate professor of English,

1959-61; Princeton Theological Seminary, Princeton, N.J., instructor in homiletics, 1961-63; Kentucky Southern College, Louisville, academic dean, 1963-65; Vanderbilt Divinity School, Nashville, Tenn., professor of preaching, worship, and literature, 1965—. Visiting professor at University of Chicago, 1965. Theologian-in-residence at American Church in Paris, 1967-68. Ecumenical Council on Drama and the Other Arts, member, vice-president, 1976-77. *Member:* American Academy of Religion, American Academy of Homiletics, Societas Liturgica.

WRITINGS: Hemingway and the Dead Gods, University Press of Kentucky, 1960; *The Failure of Theology in Modern Literature,* Abingdon, 1963; *The Thickness of Glory,* Abingdon, 1965; *The Word Not Bound: A One-Act Play,* Word Books, 1968; *The Centrality of Preaching in the Total Task of the Ministry,* Word Books, 1969.

For God's Sake, Be Human, Word Books, 1970; *Leave It to the Spirit,* Harper, 1971; *World in Collapse: The Vision of Absurd Drama,* Dell, 1971; *The Salvation Tree,* Harper, 1973; *The Fragile Presence: Transcendence in Modern Literature,* Fortress, 1973; (editor) *Experimental Preaching,* Abingdon, 1973; *All You Lonely People, All You Lonely People,* Word Books, 1973; *The Second Coming of the Church,* Abingdon, 1974; (editor) *The Eleven O'Clock News and Other Sermons,* Abingdon, 1975; *Bread for the Wilderness, Wine for the Journey,* Word Books, 1976; *A Sense of His Presence,* Doubleday, 1977; *His Power in You,* Doubleday, 1978; *A Little Primer on Prayer,* Word Books, 1979.

WORK IN PROGRESS: Gentle, My Love, a novel; a book on children's loneliness.

AVOCATIONAL INTERESTS: Art, theater.

* * *

KILPATRICK, Terrence 1920-

PERSONAL: Born May 9, 1920, in Portland, Ore.; son of William (a union official) and Ruth (Mendenhall) Kilpatrick; married Marilyn Stenson, September 9, 1948 (marriage ended); married Helen Peterson (a symphony conductor), June 17, 1977; children: Teresa Hodges, Kelly Stern, Connie. *Education:* Attended University of San Francisco, 1940-41, and Webber College, 1942-43; San Francisco State University, A.B., 1947, M.A., 1955. *Home:* 2612 Ponce Ave., Belmont, Calif. 94002. *Agent:* Richard Parks, Curtis Brown, Ltd., 575 Madison Ave., New York, N.Y. 10022. *Office:* City College of San Francisco, #50 Phelan Ave., San Francisco, Calif. 94112.

CAREER: Writer. Worked as journalist for *San Francisco Chronicle, Virginia Beach Daily,* and *Atlantic City Daily World;* San Francisco City College, San Francisco, Calif., professor, 1968; University of San Francisco, San Francisco, currently professor. *Military service:* U.S. Navy during World War II. *Member:* Authors Guild, Western Writers of America, American Federation of Teachers, Screenwriter's Guild West, California Teachers Association. *Awards, honors:* Pasadena One-Act Play Award, 1951, for "Strike Four," and 1953, for "Fool Kid"; second place for Sylvania Award for best television play, 1958, for "Drop on the Devil"; Spur Award for best western novel, 1977-78, for *Swimming Man Burning.*

WRITINGS: Swimming Man Burning (western novel), Doubleday, 1977.

Other: "Strike Four" (play; one-act), first produced at San Francisco University, 1951; "Fool Kid" (play; one-act), first produced at San Francisco State College, 1953; "Out of Context" (play), first produced in San Francisco at Actor's Workshop, 1955; "Barricade on the Big Black" (screenplay), Paramount, 1959.

Also author of teleplays, 1958-70, including "Drop on the Devil," "Honest Cop," "Out of Nowhere," "I'll Die Tomorrow," "Dark Night," "Outlaw's Spurs," "Towerman," "Hutch," "Pompeii In an Elevator," "Deception," "The Whip," "Angry Town," "He's Only a Boy," "You Steal My Eyes," "The Pit," "Satan In Saffron," "Walker Without Light," "The Liberators," "Walk the Killer," "The Saintsburg Bagman," and "Moira McCarthy's Miracle."

WORK IN PROGRESS: A novel, *Play the Fife Lowly.*

SIDELIGHTS: Kilpatrick told *CA:* "I write, I think, to show what I'm made of. And what is that? Nothing, perhaps. But perhaps, just perhaps, there is something there. I'd like to find out. I write to find out."

* * *

KIMBERLY, Gail

PERSONAL: Born in New York, N.Y.; daughter of Wilbert R. (an architect) and Evelyn (in real estate sales; maiden name, Cox) Kimberly; married Antonius J. Van Achthoven, February 8, 1951 (divorced, 1973); children: Leslie (Mrs. Edward Cordova, Jr.), Eric N. *Education:* Attended Pasadena City College. *Home:* 270 East Alegria Ave., Sierra Madre, Calif. 91024. *Agent:* Kirby McCauley Ltd., 310 East 46th St., New York, N.Y. 10017.

CAREER: Columbia Broadcasting System, Television City, Los Angeles, Calif., secretary, 1957-60; Brown Brothers Adjusters, Pasadena, Calif., secretary, 1963-67; University of California, College of Medicine, Orange, secretary, 1967-69; Milliman & Robertson (actuarial consultants), Pasadena, secretary, 1971-74; writer, 1974—. *Member:* International P.E.N., Science Fiction Writers of America, Mystery Writers of America, Los Angeles Science Fantasy Society, Lunch Bunch Writers.

WRITINGS: Flyer (science fiction novel), Popular Library, 1975; *Dracula Began* (horror novel), Pyramid Publications, 1976; *Skateboard* (adapted from the feature film), Tempo Books, 1978; *Star Jewel* (juvenile science fiction), Sprint Books, 1979; *Pavan for a Dead Marriage* (novel), Zebra Publications, 1979.

Work represented in ten anthologies, including: *The Other Side of Tomorrow,* Random House, 1973; *The Far Side of Time,* Dodd, 1974; *Dystopian Visions,* Prentice-Hall, 1975. Contributor of stories to adult and juvenile magazines in the United States and England, including *Galaxy, Alfred Hitchcock's Mystery Magazine,* and *Gothic Stories.*

WORK IN PROGRESS: A novel about a divorced woman; research for a book about telepathy; research on life in seventeenth-century Transylvania for a historical romance.

SIDELIGHTS: Gail Kimberly writes: "I started writing when I was seven years old, turning out poetry and fantastic tales with wild abandon. My parents thought they were great, but nobody else seemed interested in my writing until high school.

"When my two children were small, I wrote during their nap time, one to two hours every afternoon. When they were in school, I usually held down full-time jobs and wrote evenings and weekends. After I had sold several science-fiction short stories to one editor, he requested that I write a novel

for him. His request came at the same time as my separation from my husband, and although I had six months to write the novel, I found my personal life interfering so much with my writing time that I had to ask for an extension. He gave me three weeks. *Flyer* was written in those three weeks, and while it was subsequently published, I'd hate to try doing that again.

"Since I was raised in Canada, many of my stories have a Canadian background. I've traveled across Canada and the United States, and made a camping tour of Europe that lasted six months. I lived for a year in Hawaii, on the island of Oahu, and wrote a science fiction novel there, set in the Hawaii of the future.

"I've written both juvenile and adult stories, and my favorite genre, to read and write, is science fiction/fantasy, although I love mysteries, occult stories, and adventure yarns."

BIOGRAPHICAL/CRITICAL SOURCES: Pasadena Star-News, June 25, 1975.

* * *

KING, Edward L. 1928-

PERSONAL: Born November 7, 1928, in Fort Worth, Tex.; son of Edgar L. and Zula (Burch) King; married Lourdes Miranda (a company president), April 16, 1962; children: Edward, Glen, Cristina. *Education:* University of Nebraska, B.S., 1960; University of Madrid, licenciatura, 1963. *Residence:* Chevy Chase, Md. *Office:* U.S. Senate, 248 Russell Senate Office Building, Washington, D.C. 20510.

CAREER: U.S. Army, career officer, 1945-47, 1950-69, general staff officer with U.S. European headquarters in France, 1960-62, military adviser to Spanish Armed Forces, 1962-66, general staff officer with joint chiefs of staff, 1966-69, retired as lieutenant colonel; free-lance writer, 1969-71; national security adviser for Senator George McGovern's presidential campaign, 1972; executive director of Coalition on National Priorities and Military Policy, 1973-76; executive assistant to Senator William D. Hathaway of Maine, 1976—. Lecturer at University of Maryland, European Division, 1963-65. Radio commentator for "In the Public Interest." Consultant to U.S. Congress.

WRITINGS: The Death of the Army: A Premortem, Dutton, 1972.

Film scripts: "Thin Red Line," Warner Bros., 1965; "Battle of the Bulge," Panavision, 1966. Contributor to national magazines and newspapers, including *New York Times, Saturday Review, New Republic,* and *World.*

SIDELIGHTS: King wrote: "*The Death of the Army* was an outgrowth of years of concern about what I had seen happening within and to the Army from the end of World War II to the Vietnam War. It was an early call for sweeping reform of an institution that had drifted far from its original purpose. I hoped that the book could be a catalyst to cause a critical examination of policies by Army leaders before it was too late for the Army and the nation.

"After publication I spent the next four years working through the 1972 McGovern campaign, and later lobbying in Congress to try and bring about some of the reforms I had recommended. This was an extremely challenging period. Some reforms have occurred, but for the most part we continue to spend billions on military forces that are neither adequately trained, positioned, nor equipped to defend the country effectively.

"These years of public advocacy have given me many personal insights into what befalls a citizen who attempts to challenge and bring change in any of our large institutions.

"My book was begun while I was living in Spain, 1969-70. I speak Spanish and am intrigued by Spanish history and culture."

AVOCATIONAL INTERESTS: Hiking, reading, international travel.

*   *   *

KING-STOOPS, Joyce 1923-

PERSONAL: Born January 25, 1923, in Lancastershire, England, came to the United States in 1924, naturalized citizen, 1956; daughter of James and Elizabeth (Williams) Barlow; married Emery Stoops (a professor), July 3, 1968; children: Amy Joyce King Dundon. *Education:* Northern Illinois University, B.S., 1954; California State University, Long Beach, M.S., 1957; University of Southern California, Ed.D., 1967. *Residence:* Los Angeles, Calif. *Office:* School of Education, University of Southern California, University Park, Los Angeles, Calif. 90007.

CAREER: University of Southern California, Los Angeles, assistant professor, 1967-72, associate professor of education, 1972—, coordinator and director of teacher assistantship program, 1967-72, special administrative assistant, 1977—. Director of National Science Foundation marine education program, 1977—; national lecturer for Phi Delta Kappa, 1978. Member of board of directors of local Young Men's Christian Association (YMCA). *Member:* Individualized Instruction Association, Phi Delta Kappa (faculty sponsor), Delta Kappa Gamma, Phi Kappa Phi (vice-president, 1977-78), Alpha Delta Kappa.

WRITINGS: (With James Marks and husband, Emery Stoops) *Handbook of Educational Supervision,* Allyn & Bacon, 1973, revised edition, 1978; (with E. Stoops) *Discipline or Disaster?,* Phi Delta Kappa, 1974; (contributor) E. Stoops, Russ Johnson, and Max Rafferty, editors, *Handbook of Educational Administration,* Allyn & Bacon, 1974; *The Child Wants to Learn: Elementary Teaching Methods,* Little, Brown, 1977; *Educating the Wanderer: Migrant Education,* Phi Delta Kappa Educational Foundation, 1979. Contributor to education journals.

WORK IN PROGRESS: A bilingual (Spanish-English) film for young people on marine education.

SIDELIGHTS: Joyce King-Stoops writes: "The responsibilities of the American public school in today's society have become so numerous and varied that schools are not functioning as well as might be expected in teaching basic needed coping skills—reading, writing, and mathematics. Parents need to remember their responsibilities in teaching citizenship, values, and such, and schools need to emphasize these areas and work closely with parents."

AVOCATIONAL INTERESTS: Travel (away from usual tourist spots).

*   *   *

KINNEY, James R(oser) 1902(?)-1978

OBITUARY NOTICE: Born c. 1902, in Netcong, N.J.; died November 23, 1978, in Bronx, N.Y. Veterinarian, author. Before entering private practice, Kinney was chief veterinarian and director of Manhattan's Ellin Prince Speyer Animal Hospital. James Thurber illustrated Kinney's successful book, *How to Raise a Dog: In the City, In the Sub-* *urbs,* published in 1938. Obituaries and other sources: *New York Times,* November 25, 1978.

*   *   *

KIRKPATRICK, Jean 1923-

PERSONAL: Born March 2, 1923, in Quakertown, Pa.; daughter of Peter C. (in business) and Helen (Spangler) Romig; divorced. *Education:* Moravian College, B.A., 1950; Lehigh University, M.A., 1954, postdoctoral study, 1971-72; University of Pennslyvania, Ph.D., 1970. *Politics:* Independent. *Religion:* Lutheran. *Home:* 344 Franklin, Quakertown, Pa. 18951. *Office:* Women for Sobriety, P.O. Box 618, Quakertown, Pa. 18951.

CAREER: Educational Computer Corp., King-of-Prussia, Pa., writer, editor, and counselor, 1967-70; Women for Sobriety, Quakertown, Pa., founder and executive director, 1972—. Teacher at Rutgers University, summer, 1976—; speaker at colleges and universities. Has appeared on national television programs, including "The Today Show," "The Phil Donahue Show," "Good Morning America," and "To Tell the Truth." *Member:* Alcohol and Drug Problem Association of North America, American Psychological Association, American Association for Rehabilitative Therapy, Academy of Political and Social Science, American Association of University Women, Daughters of the American Revolution.

WRITINGS: The Social and Political Implications of the Nineteenth-Century Temperance Literature, University of Pennsylvania Press, 1970; *The Woman Who Drinks Too Much* (pamphlet), Cortland Press, 1976; *Turnabout: Help for a New Life,* Doubleday, 1978. Contributor to sociology and medical journals. Editor and publisher of *Sobering Thoughts* (newsletter), 1976—.

WORK IN PROGRESS: Another book.

SIDELIGHTS: An alcoholic herself, Jean Kirkpatrick has devoted herself to helping women alcoholics with her national and international program, Women for Sobriety. She gives credit to other established programs for helping alcoholics, but feels that women have special needs that cannot be met by other existing facilities. Women alcoholics, she writes, experience more guilt (rather than remorse), more boredom, and more loneliness than men, and her organization was designed specifically to deal with these needs and to provide support and build self-esteem. Her most recent book is based on her own experiences as an alcoholic, her recovery, and her commitment to other women through Women for Sobriety, which now has chapters all over the United States, in Canada, and abroad.

*   *   *

KIRSHENBLATT-GIMBLETT, Barbara 1942-

PERSONAL: Born September 30, 1942, in Toronto, Ontario, Canada; daughter of Meyer Makhl (a merchant) and Dora (Shushanoff) Kirshenblatt; married Maxwell Gimblett (a painter), September 4, 1964. *Education:* Attended University of Toronto, 1962-65; University of California, Berkeley, A.B., 1966, M.A., 1967; Indiana University, Ph.D., 1972. *Residence:* New York, N.Y. *Office:* Department of Folklore and Folklife, University of Pennsylvania, Box 13, 404 Logan Hall, Philadelphia, Pa. 19174.

CAREER: University of Texas, Austin, assistant professor of anthropology, 1970-71, 1972-73, assistant professor of English, 1971-73, assistant director of Center for Intercultural Studies in Folklore and Oral History, 1970-73, archivist, 1971-73; University of Pennsylvania, Philadelphia, associate professor of folklore and folklife, 1973—. Visiting assistant professor at Columbia University, 1972-73, visiting associate professor, 1973—, member of executive board of Max Weinreich Center for Advanced Jewish Studies, 1974—; visiting assistant professor at Indiana University, summer, 1976. Guest curator of New York's Jewish Museum, 1976-77; instructor at Royal Ontario Museum, 1962-64. Researcher and performer for Canadian Broadcasting Corp., 1962-64. Participant in conferences.

MEMBER: World Union of Jewish Studies, American Folklore Society (member of executive board, 1976-77), American Anthropological Association, Association for the Anthropological Study of Play, Oral History Association, Maledicta: Society for the Study of Verbal Aggression (member of board of directors), Association of Jewish Studies, Association for the Sociological Study of Jewry, American Association of Professors of Yiddish, American Society for Jewish Music, Adelantre: Judezmo Society, Folklore Studies Association of Canada (Pennsylvania representative, 1977-79), Canadian Folklore Society, Canadian Folk Music Society, Association of Canadian Radio and Television Artists, Pennsylvania Folklore Society (president, 1975-76; member of executive board, 1976—), California Folklore Society. *Awards, honors:* National Endowment for the Humanities grants, 1973-75, 1975-76; grant from Memorial Foundation for Jewish Culture, 1973-75; National Endowment for the Arts grant, 1976-77.

WRITINGS: (Contributor) R. Bauman and J. Sherzer, editors, *Explorations in the Ethnology of Speaking,* Cambridge University Press, 1974; (contributor) Dan Ben-Amos and Kenneth Goldstein, editors, *Folklore: Performance and Communication,* Mouton, 1975; (editor and contributor) *Speech Play: Research and Resources for Studying Linguistic Creativity,* University of Pennsylvania Press, 1976; (contributor) R. M. Dorson, editor, *Folktales Told Around the World,* University of Chicago Press, 1976; *Fabric of Jewish Life: Textiles From the Jewish Museum Collection,* Volume I, Jewish Museum, Jewish Theological Seminary, 1977; (with Lucjan Dobroszycki) *Image Before My Eyes: A Photographic History of Jewish Life in Poland, 1864-1939,* Schocken, 1977; (contributor) Dorson, editor, *Folklore in the Modern World,* Mouton, 1978. Contributor of about twenty-five articles to scholarly periodicals. Member of editorial board of "Folklore and Folklife" series, University of Pennsylvania Press, 1973—. Member of editorial board of *Jewish Folklore and Ethnology Newsletter,* 1970, *Field of Yiddish,* 1975—, and *Southern Folklore Quarterly,* 1975—.

WORK IN PROGRESS: Fabric of Jewish Life: Textiles From the Jewish Museum Collection, Volume II; folklore for children; a semiotic analysis of Jewish artifacts; studying Jewish photography in Poland, ethnogastronomy of East European Jews, and more generally, folklore, culture, and aging; studying bibliographies of Yiddish folklore, in English, French, German, Yiddish, Hebrew, and East European languages.

* * *

KITTRIE, Nicholas N(orbert Nehemiah) 1928-

PERSONAL: Born March 26, 1928, at sea, aboard a Polish ship; came to the United States in 1944, naturalized citizen, 1950; son of S. K. Kronenbergh and Perla F. (Ver Standig) Kittrie; married Sara Yudovic de Burak, June 1, 1962; children: Orde Felicien, Norda Nicole, Zachary McNair. *Education:* Attended University of Cairo, 1946, and University

of London, 1947; University of Kansas, LL.B., 1950, M.A., 1951; further graduate study at University of Chicago, 1954-55; Georgetown University, LL.M., 1963, S.J.D., 1968. *Home:* 6908 Ayr Lane, Bethesda, Md. 20034. *Office:* School of Law, American University, Washington, D.C. 20016.

CAREER: University of Kansas, Lawrence, instructor in Western civilization, 1948-50; legal analyst at Kansas Government Research Center, 1951-54; American Bar Association, Chicago, Ill., assistant to director of legislative service, 1955-56; American Bar Foundation, Chicago, Ill., project director, 1956-58; U.S. Senate, Washington, D.C., legal assistant to Senator Wiley, 1959, counsel to antitrust and monopoly subcommittee, 1959-62; American University, School of Law, Washington, D.C., member of faculty, 1963-67, professor of criminal and comparative law, 1967—, director of research, 1968—, director of Institute for Advanced Studies in Justice, 1970—, dean, 1977—. Admitted to bars of Kansas, 1953, District of Columbia, 1958, and U.S. Supreme Court; member of firm of De Grazia & Kittrie, 1962-67. Lecturer at University of Ottawa, summer, 2966; visiting professor at London School of Economics and Political Science and fellow of its Institute for Advanced Legal Research, 1973-74. Research associate of University of Chicago's Center for Studies of Criminal Justice, 1967-68; director of Center for the Administration of Justice, 1969-71; director of Law and Policy Institute (Jerusalem), summers, 1970-75; vice-chairman of University of Messina's scientific committee, 1977—. Vice-chairman of United Nations Alliance for Crime Prevention and Criminal Justice, 1976—. Member of board of directors of First Washington Development Corp. and Bank of Chios (Athens); member of board of directors and general counsel of Avoca Publishing Corp.; consultant to President's Commission on Marijuana and Drug Abuse. *Military service:* British Army, Middle East Command, 1944-45.

MEMBER: International Association of Penal Law (American vice-president, 1975—; permanent representative to the United Nations), International Association of Comparative Public Law (member of board of directors, 1976—), International Institute for Space Law, Inter-American Bar Association, American Society of Criminology (president, 1975), American Association for the Advancement of Science (member of council, 1972—), American Society for Public Administration, American Judicature Society, American Sosiety of International Law, American Bar Association, Kansas Bar Association, District of Columbia Bar Association, Phi Delta Phi, Pi Sigma Alpha. *Awards, honors:* Research scholarships to universities in Warsaw and Berlin, 1967, 1968; National Endowment for the Humanities senior fellowship, 1973-74.

WRITINGS: The Right to Be Different: Deviance and Enforced Therapy, Johns Hopkins Press, 1971; (editor) *Comparative Law of Israel and the Middle East,* Lerner Law Book Co., 1971; (editor) *Crescent and Star: Arab-Israeli Perspectives on Middle East Conflict,* AMS Press, 1973; (editor) *Medicine, Law, and Public Policy,* AMS Press, 1975. Contributor to learned journals. Chairman of editorial board of *Journal of Criminology,* 1973—, and *Justice,* 1973-75.

WORK IN PROGRESS: Rebellion in Eden: Political Crime and Criminals in America; Sentencing and Corrections, a textbook; editing *From Political Crime to Terrorism.*

KLERMAN, Lorraine V(ogel) 1929-

PERSONAL: Born July 10, 1929, in New York, N.Y.; daughter of Jacob (a real estate Broker) and Ethel (Hamburger) Vogel; married Gerald L. Klerman (a psychiatrist), November 28, 1954; children: Jacob Alex, Elizabeth Beryl, Karen Paula, Daniel Marc. *Education:* Cornell University, B.A. (with distinction), 1950; Harvard University, M.P.H., 1953, Dr.P.H., 1962. *Home:* 7509 Marburg Rd., Bethesda, Md. 20034. *Office:* Florence Heller Graduate School for Advanced Studies in Social Welfare, Brandeis University, Waltham, Mass. 02154.

CAREER: Passaic County Voluntary Health Associations, Paterson, N.J., staff member, 1952-56; Brandeis University, Waltham, Mass., research associate, 1962-65; Yale University, New Haven, Conn., assistant professor of public health, 1965-70, research associate, 1970-71; Brandeis University, Florence Heller Graduate School for Advanced Studies in Social Welfare, lecturer, 1971-73, associate professor of public health, 1973—.

MEMBER: American Public Health Association (fellow), Society of Public Health Educators (fellow), National Alliance Concerned with School-Age Parents, Massachusetts Public Health Association, Phi Beta Kappa, Delta Omega. *Awards, honors:* Doctoral fellowships and grants from Public Health Service and National Tuberculosis Association.

WRITINGS: (With J. F. Jekel) *School-Age Mothers: Problems, Programs, and Policy,* Shoe String, 1973; (contributor) Jack Zackler and William Brandstadt, editors, *The Teenage Pregnant Girl,* C. C Thomas, 1974. Contributor of about twenty-five articles to public health and medical journals.

WORK IN PROGRESS: Research on services to handicapped children and deviant behavior in adolescents, including pregnancy, alcoholism, and delinquency.

SIDELIGHTS: Klerman told *CA:* "Like most individuals who choose a career in public health, I basically want to use my skills to assist people in need. For this reason I do research and then try to disseminate the results of my studies as widely as possible in an attempt to affect policies and programs. This can be done through teaching, addressing groups, and writing. The last probably reaches the largest audience and, therefore, demands and receives a large portion of my professional time."

* * *

KLINE, Nathan S. 1916-

PERSONAL: Born March 22, 1916, in Philadlephia, Pa.; son of Ignatz and Flora (a physician; maiden name, Schellenberg) Kline; married Margot Hess, June 29, 1942 (divorced, 1976); children: Marna Kline Anderson. *Education:* Swarthmore College, B.A. (honors), 1938; graduate study at Harvard University, 1938-39, and New School for Social Research, 1940-41; New York University, M.D., 1943; postdoctoral study at Washington School of Psychiatry, 1943-44, Princeton University, 1947, and Rutgers University, 1947-48; Clark University, M.A., 1951. *Politics:* "Tired Democrat." *Religion:* Jewish. *Residence:* New York, N.Y. *Office:* Rockland Research Institute, Orangeburg, N.Y. 10962.

CAREER: St. Elizabeth's Hospital, Washington, D.C., intern, 1943, resident, 1944; Veterans Administration Hospital, Lyons, N.J., staff physician, 1946-50; Worcester State Hospital, Worcester, Mass., director of research, 1950-52; Rockland State Hospital, Orangeburg, N.Y., director of Research Center, 1952-75; Rockland Research Institute,

Orangeburg, director of research, 1975—. Child psychiatrist at Union County Mental Hygiene Society Clinic, 1946-47; private practice in New York, N.Y., 1953—; director of psychiatric services at Bergen Pines County Hospital, 1963—; attending physician at Lenox Hill Hospital, 1974—. Diplomate of American Board of Psychiatry and Neurology; licensed to practice in Maryland, District of Columbia, New Jersey, and New York. Research assistant at Columbia University, 1948-50, research associate, 1952-57, assistant clinical professor, 1957-69, associate clinical professor, 1969-73, clinical professor, 1973—; permanent visiting professor at University of California, San Diego, 1972—. Member of clinical advisory panel of National Institute of Mental Health's Psychopharmacology Service Center, 1957-59; cofounder and research director of Centre de Psychiatrie et Neurologie (Port-au-Prince, Haiti), 1959—; member of medical advisory council of CARE-Medico, 1962—; member of Nepal's Psychiatric Hospital Board, 1968—; member of scientific advisory board of Yerkes Regional Primate Research Center, 1972-75. Has testified before U.S. Congressional committees; consultant to World Health Organization. *Military service:* U.S. Public Health Service Reserve, 1944-50, active duty, 1944-46.

MEMBER: Collegium Internationale Neuropsychopharmacologicum (charter fellow; head of committee on reorganization, 1972—), International Committee Against Mental Illness (president), World Federation for Mental Health (associate), International Psychiatric Research Foundation, Pan American Medical Association, American Psychiatric Association (fellow; head of research committee, 1956-57; head of task force on liaison with international and foreign psychiatric organizations, 1973—), American Psychological Association (fellow), Association for Research in Nervous and Mental Disease, American Association for the Advancement of Science (fellow), American College of Physicians (fellow), Society for Biological Psychiatry, Society for Experimental Biology and Medicine, American Medical Association, American Chemical Society (associate), National Committee Against Mental Illness (sponsoring member), American Society for Clinical Pharmacology and Therapeutics, American College of Neuropsychopharmacology (charter fellow; president, 1966-67; head of constitutional committee, 1968-71), American Public Health Association (fellow), Drug Information Association (charter member), American Psychopathological Association, American Geriatrics Society, Royal Society of Medicine (fellow), Indian Psychiatric Association (corresponding member), Societe Moreau de Tours (France), Royal College of Psychiatrists (foundation fellow), Royal Medico-Psychological Association (corresponding member), Sociedad Colombiana de Psiquiatria (honorary member), Sociedad Mexicana de Psiquiatria Biologica (honorary associate), New York Academy of Sciences (fellow), New York Academy of Medicine (fellow), Medical Society of the County of New York, Manhattan Society for Mental Health, Sigma Xi, Circumnavigators Club, Explorers Club, Atrium Club. *Awards, honors:* Page One Award in Science from Newspaper Guild of New York, 1956; Adolf Meyer Award from Association for the Improvement of Mental Health, 1956; Albert Lasker Award from American Public Health Association, 1957; named commander of Haiti's Order Toussaint-Louverture and grand officer of Legion d'Honneur et Merite, both 1959; named knight great cross, Serenissimi Military Order of Saint Mary the Glorious, 1961; Henry Wisner Miller Award from Manhattan Society for Mental Health, 1963; named knight grand commander of Liberian Humane Order of African Redemption, 1963; Albert Lasker Clinical Research Award, 1964; certificate of appreciation from Japanese Society of Psychiatry and Neurology, 1965; certificate of recognition from University of Indonesia, 1965; Taylor Manor Award, 1970; distinguished service citation from New York State Department of Mental Hygiene, 1973.

WRITINGS: Synopsis of Eugen Bleuler's Dementia Praecox: Or, The Group of Schizophrenias, International Universities Press, 1952; (editor and contributor) *Psychopharmacology*, American Association for the Advancement of Science, 1956; (editor and contributor) *Psychopharmacology Frontiers*, Little, Brown, 1959; (editor and contributor) *Psychiatry in the Underdeveloped Countries*, American Psychiatric Association, 1960; (editor with D. H. Efron and B. Holmstedt, and contributor) *Ethnopharmacologic Search for Psychoactive Drugs*, U.S. Government Printing Office, 1967; (editor with E. Laska, and contributor) *Computers and Electronic Devices in Psychiatry*, Grune, 1968; (editor with W. O. Evans, and contributor) *The Psychopharmacology of the Normal Human*, C. C Thomas, 1969; (editor with Evans, and contributor) *Psychotropic Drugs in the Year 2000*, C. C Thomas, 1971; *Drugs: To Use, Not Abuse–You and Your Health*, Council on Family Health, 1974; (editor and contributor) *Factors in Depression*, Raven Press, 1974; *From Sad to Glad: Kline on Depression*, Putnam, 1974; (with S. Alexander and A. Chamberlain) *A Manual of Overdoses with Psychotropic Drugs*, Medical Economics, 1974.

Contributor: G. G. Killinger, editor, *The Psychobiological Program of the War Shipping Administration*, Stanford University Press, 1947; *Ships Medicine Chest and First Aid at Sea*, U.S. Government Printing Office, 1947; W. H. Soden, editor, *Rehabilitation of the Handicapped*, Ronald, 1949; F. A. Mettler, editor, *Selective Partial Ablation of the Frontal Cortex: A Correlative Study of Its Effects on Human Psychotic Subjects*, Paul B. Hoeber, 1949; Mettler, editor, *Psychosurgical Problems*, Blakiston, 1952; W. T. Lhamon, editor, *Pharmacologic Products Recently Introduced in the Treatment of Psychiatric Disorders*, American Psychiatric Association, 1955; N. D. C. Lewis, H. E. King, and C. Landis, editors, *Studies in Topectomy*, Grune, 1956; H. E. Himwich, editor, *Tranquilizing Drugs*, American Association for the Advancement of Science, 1957; (author of foreword) Robert S. deRopp, *Drugs and the Mind*, St. Martin's, 1957; M. Greenblatt, editor, *Research in Psychiatry with Special Reference to Drug Therapy*, American Psychiatric Association, 1958; R. A. Cleghorn, editor, *Research in Affects*, American Psychiatric Association, 1958; S. O. Waife and A. P. Shapiro, editors, *Clinical Evaluation of New Drugs*, Paul B. Hoeber, 1959; R. M. Featherstone and A. Simon, editors, *A Pharmacologic Approach to the Study of the Mind*, C. C Thomas, 1959; F. Braceland, editor, *Effect of Pharmacologic Agents on the Nervous System*, Association for Research in Nervous and Mental Diseases, 1959.

B. E. Flaherty, editor, *Psychophysiological Aspects of Space Flight*, Columbia University Press, 1961; (author of foreword), *Miltown Behind the Iron Curtain*, Wallace Laboratories, 1962; (author of introduction) James G. Miller, *The Golden Adventure Book of the Human Mind*, Capitol Publishing, 1962; J. T. Freeman, editor, *Clinical Principles and Drugs in the Aging*, C. C Thomas, 1963; B. Kissin, editor, *Evaluation of Present Day Treatment Modalities in the Long Term Rehabilitation of Alcoholics*, Downstate Medical Center, State University of New York, 1965; J. Wortis, editor, *Recent Advances in Biological Psychiatry*, Volume VII, Plenum, 1965; H. L. P. Resnick, editor, *Suicidal Be-*

haviors, Little, Brown, 1968; E. Harms, editor, *Pathogenesis of Nervous and Mental Diseases in Children*, Libra, 1968; P. Black, editor, *Drugs and the Brain*, Johns Hopkins Press, 1969.

Lithium: The History of Its Use in Psychiatry, Brunner, 1969; F. J. Ayd, Jr. and B. Blackwell, editors, *Discoveries in Biological Psychiatry*, Lippincott, 1970; A. B. Tulipan and D. W. Heyder, editors, *Outpatient Psychiatry in the 1970's*, Brunner, 1970; W. G. Clark and J. del Giudice, editors, *Principles of Psychopharmacology*, Academic Press, 1970; H. I. Kaplan and E. J. Sadock, editors, *Comprehensive Group Psychotherapy*, Williams & Wilkins, 1971; *Advances in Biochemical Psychopharmacology*, Raven Press, 1973; B. S. Brown and E. F. Torrey, editors, *International Collaboration in Mental Health*, U.S. Government Printing Office, 1973; J. Angst, editor, *Classification and Prediction of the Outcome of Depression*, F. K. Shattauer Verlag, 1974; J. D. Sinclair and K. Kiianmaa, editors, *The Effects of Centrally Active Drugs on Voluntary Alcohol Consumption*, Satellite Symposium, Sixth International Congress of Pharmacology, 1975; F. N. Johnson, editor, *Lithium Research and Therapy*, Academic Press, 1975; S. Arieti and G. Chrzanowski, editors, *New Dimensions in Psychiatry: A World View*, Wiley, 1975; J. Meislin, editor, *Rehabilitation Medicine and Psychiatry*, C. C Thomas, 1976; O. Lee McCabe, editor, *Psychotherapy and Behavior Change Trends: Innovations and Future Direction*, Grune, 1977.

Contributor to *Handbook of Psychiatric Treatment in Medical Practice*. Contributor of more than three hundred articles and reviews to medical journals, popular magazines, and newspapers, including *Rotarian, Vogue, Science Teacher, Image*, and *U.S. News and World Report*. Co-editor of *Foreign Psychiatry*, 1971-75; member of international board of editors of *Excerpta Medica*, 1966—; member of editorial board of *Research Communications in Chemical Pathology and Pharmacology*, 1969—; member of advisory editorial board of *International Journal of Social Psychiatry* and *Psychopharmacologia*, both 1958—.

BIOGRAPHICAL/CRITICAL SOURCES: New York Times, April 6, 1969.

* * *

KLUGE, Alexander 1932-

PERSONAL: Born February 14, 1932, in Halberstadt, Germany; son of Ernst Kluge (a general practitioner). *Education:* Educated in Germany, received Dr. jur., 1956. *Home:* 38 Elisabethstrasse, 8 Munich 40, Germany.

CAREER: Attorney in Germany, 1958—; novelist and short story writer. Honorary professor at Frankfort on the Main University; director, Ulm Institute of Film Arts.

WRITINGS: Lebenslaufe, Henry Goverts Verlag, 1962, translation by Leila Vennewitz published as *Attendance List for a Funeral* (short stories), McGraw, 1966; *Schlachbeschreibung*, Walter Verlag, 1962, translation by Vennewitz published as *The Battle*, McGraw, 1967. Also author of *Artisten in der Zurkuskuppel: ratlos*, 1968; *Der grosse Verhau*, 1971; *Lernprozesse mit toedl Ausgang* (short story), 1973; *Gelegenheits arbeit einer Sklavin*, 1973.

Filmscript: "Abschied von gestern," 1966.

SIDELIGHTS: Although Kluge is a lawyer by training, he is considered by some to be among Europe's most controversial writers. He has also been credited with giving the novel of protest new dimensions by stripping it of pleas and morals, and substituting a documentary style.

Kluge's collection of short stories, *Attendance List for a Funeral*, one of his two works available in English translation, was described by Joseph Bauke as full "of the language of the Hitler period, with its white lies, hypocricies, and bureaucratic euphemisms." Bauke went on to say that Kluge "writes with a precision and detachment rather rare in German tradition. There are no verbal cascades, no intellectual fireworks, no expressionist flights into the absolute. Instead we have a prose as reasoned and as dispassionate as a lawyer's brief. . . ."

BIOGRAPHICAL/CRITICAL SOURCES: Saturday Review, October 8, 1966, September 30, 1967; *New York Times Book Review,* November 20, 1966; *Best Sellers,* September 15, 1967; *Book World,* September 17, 1967.*

*   *   *

KNAPP, Mark L(ane)   1938-

PERSONAL: Born July 12, 1938, in Kansas City, Mo.; son of Herbert H. and Mary Ellen (Coleman) Knapp; married Cynthia L. Lackie, January 27, 1963 (divorced, 1974); married Lillian J. Davis (a corporation manager), August 12, 1975; children: Hilary A., Eric C. *Education:* University of Kansas, B.S., 1962, M.A., 1963; Pennsylvania State University, Ph.D., 1966. *Politics:* None. *Religion:* None. *Home:* 17631 Stonebridge, Hazel Crest, Ill. 60429. *Office:* Department of Communication, Purdue University, West Lafayette, Ind. 47907.

CAREER: University of Wisconsin, Milwaukee, assistant professor of communication, 1965-70; Purdue University, West Lafayette, Ind., associate professor, 1970-75, professor of communication, 1975—. Consultant to business, civic, and government agencies. *Military service:* U.S. Army, 1957-59. U.S. Army Reserve, 1959-63. *Member:* International Communication Association (president, 1975-76), Speech Communication Association of America, Central States Speech Association, Phi Kappa Phi. *Awards, honors:* Outstanding young teacher award from Central State Speech Association, 1969; Leather Medal from Sigma Delta Chi, 1972-73; golden anniversary award from Speech Communication Association of America, 1974, for a monograph.

WRITINGS: (With J. C. McCroskey and C. E. Larson) *An Introduction to Interpersonal Communication,* Prentice-Hall, 1971; *Nonverbal Communication in Human Interaction,* Holt, 1972, 2nd edition, 1978; *Social Intercourse: From Greeting to Goodbye,* Allyn & Bacon, 1978. Also author of a monograph, *The Rhetoric of Goodbye: Verbal and Nonverbal Correlates of Human Leave-Taking.* Author of audio-visual materials. Contributor of more than thirty articles and reviews to academic journals. Member of editorial board of *Journal of Communication, Human Communication Research, Speech Teacher, Communication,* and *Sign Language Studies.*

WORK IN PROGRESS: Several articles.

SIDELIGHTS: Knapp told *CA:* "The subjects I research and write about arise out of questions and observations related to my daily interactions with other people. Some of these include: body language, lying, greetings, goodbyes, taking turns in conversations, and communication in developing and deteriorating relationships. For me, scholarly writing can be accurate and precise without overdosing on jargon; it can be interesting and fun to read without losing its scientific value; and common sense and a sense of humor are not incompatible with scientific writing."

KNIGHT, Alanna

PERSONAL: Born in County Durham, England; daughter of Herbert William Farrar (a businessman) and Gladys Lyall (Allan) Cleet; married Alexander Harrow Knight (a scientist), August 6, 1951; children: Christopher, Kevin. *Education:* Educated privately. *Religion:* Christian. *Home:* 374 Queen's Rd., Aberdeen AB1 8DX, Scotland. *Agent:* Jo Stewart, 66 101st St., New York, N.Y. 10021.

CAREER: Secretary, 1949-51; writer, 1964—. *Member:* Society of Antiquaries (Scotland; fellow), Society of Authors (Scotland), Scottish P.E.N., Writers Guild, Crime Club, Romantic Novelists Association, Society of Women Writers and Journalists, Radiowriters Association. *Awards, honors:* First novel award from Romantic Novelists Association, 1968, for *Legend of the Loch.*

WRITINGS—Novels: *Legend of the Loch,* Hurst & Blackett, 1969, Lancer Books, 1970; *The October Witch,* Lancer Books, 1971; *Castle Clodha,* Avon, 1972; *Lament for Lost Lovers,* Avon, 1973; *The White Rose,* Avon, 1974; *A Stranger Came By,* Avon, 1975; *The Passionate Kindness,* Milton House, 1975; *A Drink for the Bridge,* Macmillan (England), 1976, Corgi, 1977; *The Wicked Wynsleys,* Leisure Books, 1977; *The Black Duchess,* Macdonald & Jane's, in press.

Plays: "The Private Life of Robert Louis Stevenson" (two-act; based on *The Passionate Kindness),* first produced at Edinburgh Festival of Arts, 1974; *Girl on an Empty Swing* (one-act), New Playwrights Network, 1978. Work represented in *Scottish Short Stories,* Collins, 1978. Contributor of articles and short stories to magazines and newspapers all over the world.

WORK IN PROGRESS: Colla's Children, a historical novel of life in the Scottish Hebridean Islands, 1852-1919; a Victorian thriller, *The Balmoral Foxes; A Place Called Always.*

SIDELIGHTS: Alanna Knight told *CA:* "Hobbies are reading, historical research—and writing. Interested in teaching creative writing. Lectured for four years in Aberdeen. Member of Scottish Arts Council 'Directory of Scottish Writers' and 'Writers in Schools' teams. Enjoy greatly this activity of talking to groups, clubs, and school-children as it is beneficial to author and writing to be taken out of isolation occasionally."

AVOCATIONAL INTERESTS: Travel in Europe, the Middle East, and the United States.

*   *   *

KNIGHT, Alice Valle   1922-

PERSONAL: Born March 3, 1922, in Bryn Mawr, Pa.; daughter of Paul Barbeau and Alice (English) Valle; married Robert H. Knight, December 14, 1940 (divorced, 1975); children: Robert H., Jr., Jessie V. Knight Schmidt, Patricia W. Knight Cluett, Alice I. Knight Price, Eli Whitney. *Education:* Attended Finch College, 1939-40, Corcoran School of Fine Arts, 1961-62, and National Academy School of Fine Arts, 1962-65, 1968, 1970. *Religion:* Episcopalian. *Home:* 50 East 89th St., New York, N.Y. 10028.

CAREER: Painter, specializing in portraits, 1968—. *Awards, honors:* Painting awards from Corcoran School of Fine Arts, 1962, and National Academy School of Fine Arts, 1968, 1970.

WRITINGS: The Meaning of Teilhard de Chardin: A Primer, Devin-Adair, 1974; (translator) Pierre Leroy, *Lettres familieres de mon ami, Teilhard de Chardin* (title means "Personal Letters From My Friend, Tielhard de Chardin"), Paulist Press, 1978.

WORK IN PROGRESS: Another book on Teilhard de Chardin, publication expected in 1980.

SIDELIGHTS: Alice Knight writes: "My encounter with the writings of Teilhard de Chardin has had such a profound effect on my life that I wrote the primer in order to spread his thought and vision to people who might find his own books too difficult to read. As a result I have become somewhat of a cosmologist and Teilhard scholar."

She also states that she is "presently working on a series of watercolors of the Rargeley Lake area in northwestern Maine."

* * *

KNOWLES, Clayton   1908-1978

PERSONAL: Born April 27, 1908, in Brooklyn, N.Y.; married Ruth Richards; children: Clayton Jr., Jeffrey, Laurie Knowles McCord. *Education:* Graduated from Columbia University, 1931. *Residence:* Largo, Fla.

CAREER/WRITINGS: After college graduation worked briefly as staff member of the *Commercial and Financial Chronicle,* New York City; S. I. Newhouse Newspapers, *Long Island Daily Press,* Jamaica, N.Y., general staff member, 1931-38, Albany correspondent for all newspapers, 1938-42, *Long Island Star Journal,* Long Island City, N.Y., night city editor, 1942; writer of daily roundup of World War II news, for International News Service; *New York Times,* New York City, 1943-71, began as political and governmental reporter in Albany, N.Y., became reporter in Washington, D.C., city staff member, 1954-71, City Hall bureau chief, 1963. Notable assignments include an on-the-spot report of the 1954 attack on the U.S. House of Representatives by four Puerto Rican nationalists, coverage of Adam Clayton Powell's surrender to authorities in 1968, and a survey of railroad problems in the New York Metropolitan area. Member of Standing Committee of Correspondents, Washington, D.C. *Member:* Newspaper Guild (charter member; chairman of *Long Island Daily Press* chapter), Albany Legislative Correspondents Association (president, 1945-46).

SIDELIGHTS: Being present at the House of Representatives on March 1, 1954, resulted in one of Clayton Knowles's biggest scoops. When four Puerto Rican nationalists fired at representatives, Knowles dashed to the floor and ministered to the injured before beginning his news coverage.

Arthur Gelb, deputy managing editor of the *New York Times,* spoke of Knowles's passion for politics: "I have never known anyone to live, think, breathe, enjoy politics the way Clay did. He would go to every political dinner, table-hop and next morning write memos to the editor that would go to sometimes a half dozen other reporters for stories."

AVOCATIONAL INTERESTS: Golfing.

OBITUARIES: New York Times, January 5, 1978.*

(Died January 4, 1978, in Largo, Fla.)

* * *

KNOX, Alexander   1907-

PERSONAL: Born January 16, 1907, in Strathroy, Ontario, Canada; son of William John and Jean (Crozier) Knox; married Doris Nolan; children: Andrew Joseph. *Education:* Attended University of Western Ontario. *Address:* Actors Equity Association, 1500 Broadway, New York, N.Y. 10036.

CAREER: Actor; has appeared in over thirty plays in England and the United States, including "Anna Christie," 1937, "The King of Windsor," 1938, "Romeo and Juliet," 1940, and "The Three Sisters," 1942; has appeared in over thirty films including "Wilson," 1944, "Khartoum," 1966, "Accident," 1967, and "Nicholas and Alexander," 1971; has made several television appearances, including "The Hidden Truth," 1964, "The Saint," and "The Vise." *Member:* Actors Equity Association, Screen Actors Guild, Players. *Awards, honors:* Recipient of Critics Choice Award, Best Actor Award from Foreign Correspondents, and an Academy Award nomination from Academy of Motion Picture Arts and Sciences.

WRITINGS—Novels: *Bride of Quietness,* Macmillan, 1933; *Night of the White Bear,* Viking, 1971; *The Enemy I Kill,* Macmillan, 1972, published as *Totem Dream,* Viking, 1973; *Raider's Moon,* Macmillan, 1975; *The Kidnapped Surgeon,* Macmillan, 1976.

Plays: *Old Master* (first produced in Malvern, England, at the Malvern Festival, 1939), Constable, 1940; "The Closing Door," first produced in New York at the Empire Theatre, 1949, shown on National Educational Television (NET), 1964; "Red on White," first produced in Windsor at the Theatre Royal, 1959.

Screenplays: (With Dudley Nichols) "Sister Kenny," RKO, 1946; (with Charles Bennett) "Sign of the Ram," Columbia, 1948; (with Boris Inkster) "Judge Steps Out," RKO, 1948.

Contributor to numerous newspapers and periodicals, including *Times Literary Supplement, Boston Post, Toronto Star, Hollywood Quarterly, London Free Press,* and *Willison's Monthly.*

SIDELIGHTS: Alexander Knox's *Night of the White Bear* recounts the dangerous journey that three Eskimos make across the polar sea. The realism of the Arctic setting has been viewed favorably by critics. Martin Levin commented: "The novel—at least to this non-Eskimo—seems utterly authentic." Echoing his opinions, Sara Blackburn wrote, "What [Knox] gives us is a remarkably detailed version of Eskimo life that includes methods for fighting, hunting, killing, butchering, and cooking; the building and maintenance of an igloo; sexual mores; and the basis for social status and respect." Of the book's structure, Levin noted, "The fluctuating emotional balance among the three travelers, as they struggle for survival in an Arctic winter, gives the novel a powerful centrifugal coherence." Blackburn found Knox's characters "believable and appealing" and his storytelling "skillful," but observed that *Night of the White Bear* "peaks a bit too often, and both its length and its general design . . . make the narrative secondary to . . . the 'sociological or ecological significance' which is its major interest."

BIOGRAPHICAL/CRITICAL SOURCES: New Statesman, April 30, 1971; *New York Times Book Review,* September 19, 1971; *Book World,* January 2, 1972.

* * *

KOENIG, Rene   1906-

PERSONAL: Born July 5, 1906, in Magdeburg, Germany; son of Gustav (an engineer) and Marguerite (a teacher; maiden name Godefroy-Leboeuf); married Irmgard Till-manns, February 27, 1947; children: Mario Rene, Oliver Manuel. *Education:* Attended University of Vienna, 1926; University of Berlin, Ph.D., 1930; additional study at University of Paris, 1930-34. *Home:* Marienstrasse 9, 5000 Cologne 40, Widdersdorf, Germany. *Office:* University of Cologne, 5000 Cologne 40, Widdersdorf, Germany.

CAREER: University of Zurich, Zurich, Switzerland, lecturer, 1938; University of Cologne, Cologne, Germany, professor of sociology, 1949-74, professor emeritus, 1974—. Visiting professor at University of Michigan, 1957, 1975, at University of California, 1957, 1959-1960, and 1964-65, at Columbia University, 1959, at University of Colorado, 1962, at University of Kagul (Afghanistan), 1963, 1977, at University of Arizona, 1968-69, and at College de France, 1969. Secretary of First World Congress of Sociology in Zurich, 1950; director of Sociological Research Institute, 1953. *Member:* International Sociological Association (president, 1962-66), Association Internationale des Sociologue de Langue Francaise (Paris), Royal Academy of Sciences (Netherlands), P.E.N. Club (Germany), German Sociological Association (honorary member), Turkish Sociological Association (honorary member). *Awards, honors:* Rockefeller Foundation fellow, 1952-53; Commendatore al Ordine di Merito della Republica Italiana, 1966; Beccaria Gold Medal from German Criminological Association, 1966; Gold Medal from German Engineers Association, 1966; Premio Verga, 1967; Medal for Education from Afghanistan, 1972.

WRITINGS—In English: *Grundformen der Gesellschaft: die Gemeinde,* Rowohlt (Hamburg), 1958, 2nd edition, 1974, translation by Edward Fitzgerald published as *The Community,* Schocken, 1968; *Macht und Reiz der Mode: verstaendnisvolle Betrachtungen eines Soziologen* (also see below), Econ Verlag, 1971, translation by F. Bradley, with introduction by Tom Wolfe, published as *A La Mode: On the Social Psychology of Fashion,* Seabury Press, 1973 (published in England as *The Restless Image: A Sociology of Fashion,* Allen & Unwin, 1973).

Other works: *Die naturalistische Aesthetik in Frankreich und ihre Aufloesung: ein Beitrag zur Systemwissenschaftlichen Betrachtung der Kuenstleraesthetik* (title means "Naturalistic Esthetics in France and Its Dissolution: A methodological Interpretation of Artists' Esthetics"), R. Noske, 1931; *Vom Wesen der deutschen Universitaet* (title means "The Nature of the German University"), Verlag die Runde, 1935, reprinted, 1970; *Niccolo Machiavelli: zur Krisenanalyse einer Zeitenwende* (title means "Niccolo Machiavelli: A Theory of Crisis"), E. Rentsch, 1941, new edition, 1979; *Sizilien: ein Buch von Staedten und Hoehlen, von Fels und Lava, und von der grossen Freiheit des Vulkans* (title means "Sicily: A Book of Cities and Caves, of Rocks and Lava, and the Great Liberty of the Volcano"), Buechergilde Gutenberg (Zurich), 1943, new edition, Nymphenburger Verlagshadlung, 1957; *Materialien zur Soziologie der Familie* (title means "Materials for a Sociology of the Family"), A. Francke, 1946, revised and enlarged edition, Kiepenheuer & Witsch 1974; *Soziologie heute* (title means "Sociology Today"), Regio-Verlag, 1949; *Das Interview: Formen, Technik, Auswertung* (title means "The Interview. Forms, Techniques, and Evaluation"), Verlag fuer Politik und Wirtschaft, 1957; *Soziologie* (title means "Dictionary of Sociology"), Fischer Verlag, 1958, 17th edition, 1977.

(With Alphons Silbermann) *Der unversorgte, selbstaendige Kuenstler: ueber die wirtschaftliche und soziale Lage der selbstaendigen Kuenstler in der Bundesrepublik* (title means "Old Age Pensions for Independent Artists in the Federal Republic of Germany"), Deutscher Aerzte-Verlag, 1964; (with Guenther Lueschen) *Jugend in der Familie* (title means "Youth and the Family"), Juventa, 1965; *Soziologische Orientierungen: Vortraege und Aufsaetze* (title means "Sociological Orientations: Essays"), Kiepenheuer & Witsch, 1965, 2nd edition, 1973; *Kleider und Leute* (title means "Clothes and People"), Fischer Buecherei, 1967; (with Fritz Sack) *Kriminalsoziologie* (title means "Criminal Society"), Academische Verlagsgesellschaft, 1968, 3rd edition, 1979.

Studien zur Soziologie (title means "Studies in Sociology"), Fischer Buecherei, 1971; (with Axel Schmalfuss) *Kulturanthropologie* (title means "Cultural Anthropology"), Econ, 1972; *Indianer-wohin? Alternativen in Arizona: Skizzen zur Entwicklungssoziologie* (title means "Quo Vadis Red Man? Alternatives in Arizona"), Westdeutscher Verlag, 1973; *Die Familie der Gegenwart: ein interkultureller Vergleich* (title means "Contemporary Family: An Intercultural Comparison"), Beck, 1974, 3rd edition, 1979; (with Silbermann) *Kuenstler und Gesellschaft* (title means "Artists and Society"), Westdeutscher Verlag, 1974; (with Nico Stehr) *Wissenschaftsoliologie. Studien u. Materialien* (title means "Sociology of Science"), Westdeutscher Verlag, 1975; *Kritik der historisch-existenzialistischen Soziologie* (title means "A Critical Analysis of Historistic and Existentialistic Sociology"), Piper, 1975; *Emile Durkheim zur Diskussion. Jenseits von Dogmatismas und Skepsis,* Carl Hanser Verlag, 1978.

Author and editor: *Koelner Zeitschrift fuer Soziologie und Sozialpsychologie* (title means "Cologne Journal of Sociology and Social Psychology"), Westdeutscher Verlag, 1948; *Praktische Sozialforschung* (title means "Applied Social Research"), Ardey Verlag, 1952, new edition published in two volumes as *Das Interview. Formen Technik Auswertung,* Kiepenheuer & Witsch, 1957; *Beobachtung und Experiment in der Sozialforschung* (title means "Observation and Experiment in Social Research"), Verlag fuer Politic und Wirtschaft, 1956, 8th edition, 1978; *Soziologie der Gemeinde* (title means "Sociology of the Community"), Westdeutscher Verlag, 1957, 4th edition, 1972; (with Peter Heintz) *Soziologie der Jugendkriminalitaet* (title means "Sociology of Juvenile Delinquency"), Westdeutscher Verlag, 1957, 6th edition, 1974; (with Margaret Toennesman) *Probleme der Medizin-Soziologie* (title means "Sociology of Medicine"), Westdeutscher Verlag, 1958, 4th edition, 1970; (with Peter W. Schuppisser) *Die Mode in der menschlichen Gesellschaft* (title means "Fashion in Human Society"; also includes *Macht und Reiz der Mode),* Modebuch-Verlagsgesellschaft, 1958; *Handbuck der empirischen Sozialforschung* (title means "Handbook of Empirical Social Research"), Enke, Volume I, 1962, Volume II, 1969, new edition, 14 volumes, 1973-79; (with Johannes Winckelmann) *Max Weber zum Gedaechtnis: Materialien und Dokumente zur Bewertung von Werk und Persoenlichkeit* (title means "In memoriam Max Weber: Documents and Materials"), Westdeutscher Verlag, 1963; (with Klaus Roghmann and others) *Beitraege zur Militaersoziologie* (title means "Contributions to Military Sociology"), Westdeutscher Verlag, 1968; (with Guenther Albrecht and others), *Aspekte der Entwicklungssoziologie,* Westdeutscher Verlag, 1969; (with Reuben Hill) *Families in East and West,* Mouton, 1970. Also author, with David Glass, of *Soziale Schichtung und sociale Mobilitaet* (title means "Social Stratification and Social Mobility"), 1962, 5th edition, 1974.

Contributor of approximately three hundred and fifty articles to professional and literary journals in Germany, England, France, Spain, Italy, and other countries.

WORK IN PROGRESS: An autobiography.

SIDELIGHTS: In a review of *The Community* in *American Anthropology,* S. T. Kimball recommended that the book be "valued as a serious and on the whole successful attempt to assess critically the respective contributions of European and American social scientists to the growth of community sociology."

Besides German, Koenig is fluent in French, English, Italian, and Spanish. He has some knowledge of Slavic languages, Turkish, Persian, and Arabic.

BIOGRAPHICAL/CRITICAL SOURCES: American Anthropology, December, 1969; *American Sociology Review,* December, 1969; *Observer,* February 10, 1974; *Times Literary Supplement,* April 12, 1974; *Esquire,* July, 1974; L. Rademaker, *Hoofdfiguren mit de Sociologie,* Hef Spectrum, 1978.

* * *

KOEPF, Michael 1940-

PERSONAL: Born March 14, 1940, in San Mateo, Calif.; son of Ernest (a fisherman) and Ursula (a bookkeeper; maiden name, Kane) Koepf; married Mary Frucht, September 3, 1972; children: Michele, Ehren. *Education:* San Francisco State College, B.A., 1966, M.A., 1968. *Politics:* "Government in conscious exile." *Home address:* P.O. Box 1055, Elk, Calif. 95432.

CAREER: Captain of a commercial fishing vessel in Half Moon Bay, Calif., 1963-69; English teacher and principal of one-room schoolhouse in Hillsbourgh, Calif., and Big Sur, Calif., 1969-72; captain of commercial fishing vessel in Elk, Calif., 1972—.

WRITINGS: Save the Whale (novel), McGraw, 1978. Contributor of stories to magazines, including *100 Flowers* and *Redneck Review.*

WORK IN PROGRESS: A novel, *All Men Are Sailors,* about the commercial fishing industry.

SIDELIGHTS: Koepf told *CA:* "Americans have always been a culture in search of all things great and elusive. *Save the Whale* is a novel about three poor people who tow a dead and rotting killer whale through a sea of environmental, political, and economic hype trying to parlay grand ideals into hard cash.

"On the personal side, all I can say is that I have been a fisherman most of my life and got tired of measuring my life in fish so I turned to writing. I think writers should be outlaws and bandits using their novels to rob us of our smug prejudices, expectations, and certainties. I believe in three things in general and one specifically: One, life is great and terrible. Two, most men function like snails secreting a protective covering of illusion to hide the entrances of their shells. Three, man will not be rescued by flying saucers. The specific thing is I would make a rotten poet."

AVOCATIONAL INTERESTS: Fly fishing, television, road maps, Irish music and whiskey.

* * *

KOO, V(i) K(yuin) Wellington 1888-

PERSONAL: Name originally Ku Wei-chun; born in 1888, in Shanghai, China; son of Koo Hsiung (a banker) and Ching Ting-an; married Oei Hui-lan (marriage ended); married Juliana Young, September 3, 1959; children: T. C., Yu-chang

(deceased), Mrs. K. C. Tsien, Freeman (deceased). *Education:* Columbia University, A.B., 1908, M.A., 1909, Ph.D., 1912. *Home:* 1185 Park Avenue, New York, N.Y. 10028.

CAREER: Secretary of the Chinese Cabinet, to Chinese President Yuan Shihkai, to the Ministry of Foreign Affairs, and councillor in the Foreign Office, 1912-15; minister to Mexico and the United States, 1915; China's plenipotentiary and later head of Chinese delegation at the Paris Peace Conference, 1919; minister to Great Britain, 1920-22; president of the Commission for the Discussion of National Financial Questions, 1922; chief of the Preparations Bureau for the Special Tariff Conference, 1922-23; Minister of Foreign Affairs, Peking, 1922-24, 1926-27, 1931; president of the Customs Tariff Commission, 1926; minister of finance, 1926; prime minister, 1926-27; minister to France, 1932-35; ambassador to France, 1936-41; ambassador to the United States, 1946-56; senior adviser to General Chiang Kai-shek, 1956-57; 1967-74; senior adviser to President Yen Chia-kan, 1975—.

The League of Nations, Geneva, Switzerland, representative on the administrative council, 1920-22, 1932-34, 1937-39, assessor to the Lytton Commission of Inquiry, 1932, delegate to the assemblies, 1920-22, 1932-33, chief delegate to the assemblies, 1935-36 and 1938, president of the 96th assembly, 1922; The United Nations, New York, N.Y., delegate and acting chief delegate to San Francisco Conference to draft a United Nations charter, 1945, delegate to the United Nations Relief and Rehabilitation Administration and Food and Agriculture Organization, 1946-49, International Court of Justice, judge, 1957-67, vice-president, 1964-67. Served as delegate to the International Labor Conference, 1919, the conference on the Limitation of Naval Armaments, Washington, D.C., 1921-22, the World Monetary and Economic Conference, London, 1933, the Conference for Reduction and Limitation of Armaments, Geneva, 1933, the Brussels Conference, 1937, and the Dumbarton Oaks Conference. Special envoy to coronation of His Holiness Pius XII and to the accession of Leopold to the throne of Belgium, 1938; ambassador extraordinary to eight-hundredth anniversary of foundation of Portugal, 1940; representative on War Crimes Commission, London. Member of International Court of Arbitration, The Hague, 1927-57, and Far Eastern Commission, 1946-49. *Awards, honors:* LL.D. from Yale University, Columbia University, Saint John's University (Shanghai), University of Birmingham, University of Aberdeen, and University of Manchester; L.H.D., Rollins College; honorary degrees from Bowdoin College, Williams College, and Colgate University.

WRITINGS: The Status of Aliens in China, Columbia University, 1912, reprinted, 1968. Author of numerous official reports for the League of Nations.

BIOGRAPHICAL/CRITICAL SOURCES: Richard Dean Burns and E. M. Bennett, editors, *Diplomats in Crisis,* ABS-Clio Press, 1974; Hui-lan Koo and Isabella Taves, *No Feast Lasts Forever,* Quadrangle, 1975; William L. Tung, *V. K. Wellington Koo and China's Wartime Diplomacy,* St. John University Press, 1977.

* * *

KOPIT, Arthur (Lee) 1937-

PERSONAL: Born May 10, 1937, in New York, N.Y.; son of George (a sales manager) and Maxine (Dubin) Kopit; married Leslie Ann Garis, 1968. *Education:* Harvard University, B.A. (cum laude), 1959. *Agent:* Audrey Wood, International Creative Management, 40 West 57th St., New York, N.Y., 10019.

CAREER: Free-lance playwright, writer, and director. *Member:* Phi Beta Kappa. *Awards, honors:* Vernon Rice Award and Outer Circle Award, 1962, both for "Oh Dad, Poor Dad, Mamma's Hung You in the Closet and I'm Feelin' So Sad"; Guggenheim Fellowship, 1967; Rockefeller grant, 1968; National Institute of Arts and Letters award, 1971; National Endowment for the Arts grant, 1974; Wesleyan University Center for the Humanities fellowship, 1974.

WRITINGS—Published plays: *Oh Dad, Poor Dad, Mama's Hung You in the Closet and I'm Feelin' So Sad: A Tragifarce in a Bastard French Tradition* (first produced in Cambridge, Mass., 1960, produced in New York City, 1962), Hill & Wang, 1960; *The Day the Whores Came Out to Play Tennis, and Other Plays* (contains "The Questioning of Nick," first produced in Cambridge, Mass., 1957, produced in New York City, 1974; "Sing to Me Through Open Windows," produced in Cambridge, Mass., 1959, revised version produced in New York City, 1976; "Chamber Music," first produced in New York City as "And as for the Ladies," 1963, produced in London, 1971; "The Hero," produced in New York City, 1964; "The Conquest of Everest," produced in New York City, 1964; "The Day the Whores Came Out to Play Tennis," produced in New York City, 1965), Hill & Wang, 1965, (published in England as *Chamber Music and Other Plays,* Methuen, 1969); *Indians* (first produced in London, 1968, produced in New York City, 1969), Hill & Wang, 1969; *Wings* (first broadcast on National Public Radio, 1978; first produced in New York at the New York Shakespeare Festival, 1978), Hill & Wang, 1978.

Unpublished plays: "Gemini," produced in Cambridge, Mass., 1957; (with Wally Lawrence) "Don Juan in Texas," produced in Cambridge, Mass., 1957; "On the Runway of Life, You Never Know What's Coming Off Next," produced in Cambridge, Mass., 1957; "Across the River and into the Jungle," produced in Cambridge, Mass., 1958; "Aubade," produced in Cambridge, Mass., 1959; "Mhil'daim," produced in New York City, 1963; "Asylum; or, What the Gentlemen Are Up To, and as for the Ladies," produced in New York, 1963; "What's Happened to the Thorne's House," produced in Peru, Vt., 1972; "Louisiana Territory; or, Lewis and Clark—Lost and Found," produced in Middletown, Conn., 1975. Also author of "An Incident in the Park."

Also author of teleplay "The Questioning of Nick," 1959, and "Promontory Point Revisited," a segment of "Foul," on the New York Television Theatre, 1969. Contributor to *Harvard Advocate.* Work represented in *Pardon Me, Sir, But Is My Eye Hurting Your Elbow?,* edited by Bob Booker and George Foster, Geis, 1968.

SIDELIGHTS: After writing several successful plays while still a student at Harvard, Kopit gained public attention and critical acclaim with his "Oh Dad, Poor Dad, Mamma's Hung You in the Closet and I'm Feelin' So Sad." Commenting on Kopit's view of life, George Wellwarth cited a passage of dialogue from the play: "Life is a lie, my sweet. Not words but Life itself. Life in all its ugliness. It builds green trees that tease your eyes and draw you under them. Then when you're there in the shade and you breathe in and say, 'Oh God, how beautiful,' that's when the bird on the branch lets go his droppings and hits you on the head. Life, my sweet, beware. It isn't what it seems. I've seen what it can do." Wellwarth continued: "Like most modern playwrights . . . Kopit has a distinct tendency to view the rotting underside of life from below. . . . There is nothing particu-

larly new about this—Kopit's contribution lies in the wry imagination he brings to his description of life as he sees it."

Unlike many writers who apparently flourish in a cosmopolitan setting, Kopit prefers to write in isolation. "Vermont in the winter . . . any holiday resort in the off season . . . Majorca . . . [in] a huge hotel almost empty" have been among his choices. *Antiquarian Bookman* noted Kopit's response to a particularly productive weekend of writing: "'The Conquest of Everest' and 'The Hero' were both written in 1964 on a pleasant March weekend. 'The Hero' has no dialogue because I was struck dumb by the prospect of writing two plays in a single day."

A few days after the New York opening of "Indians," Lewis Funke discussed the origin of the play with Kopit. Funke reported, "Such are the quirks of the creative process that if General Westmoreland had not made some remarks about the accidental tragedies of the war in Vietnam, which Arthur Kopit read as he listened to Charles Ives's 'Fourth Symphony,' he might never have written 'Indians.'" "For a long time I had wanted to do a play dealing with the subject. I knew it would have to be epical in scope. But I didn't know how to do it," recalled Kopit. After the experience of reading Westmoreland's remarks and hearing the music, Kopit remembered, "I knew almost instantly that I would write a play that would explore what happens when a social and political power imposes itself on a lesser power and creates a mythology to justify it, as we did with the Indians, as we have tried to do in Vietnam, what others have done elsewhere. And, in the manner of the symphony it would be a kind of mosaic, a counterpoint of memory and reality."

Credited by such critics as Clive Barnes with successfully avoiding the use of "those old linear guidelines of a beginning, a middle, and an end" in favor of a less structured style, Kopit openly appreciates the efforts of other playwrights who try bold, innovative methods. "There's a new vitality returning to [the theatre], which curiously enough hasn't much to do with the writers. I mean activities like Peter Brooke's experiments at the Round House, with a flexible audience. I think flexibility about what the theatre is, that's important," Kopit told Brendan Hennessy.

Kopit seems to be more comfortable writing when he is able to maintain a certain distance between himself and his characters. In his interview with Hennessy, he said he left a novel unfinished to do "Indians," because "the pose is so different. The playwright is at a distance from his characters. I find the narrator's role, getting inside his characters, intimidating." As for directing his own plays, Kopit told Hennessy he prefers to delay the decision and "after seeing one or two productions" perhaps take over the production as he did in Paris with "Oh Dad, Poor Dad."

In answer to Hennessy's questions about his hopes for the future and his ambitions, Kopit replied: "I'd like to write a play a year, I admire those who write a lot: Osborne, Albee, and others. You're less vulnerable to critics that way—no matter how one play is received, you've always got another on the way. In any case, the important plays come by accident. You can't sit down and write an important play."

BIOGRAPHICAL/CRITICAL SOURCES: George Wellwarth, *Theatre of Protest and Paradox,* New York University Press, 1964; *Antiquarian Bookman,* March 22, 1965; *Time,* March 3, 1967, April 5, 1968, June 6, 1969, October 24, 1969; *Village Voice,* March 9, 1967; *Books,* June, 1967; *Transatlantic Review,* April, 1968; *Observer Review,* July 7, 1968; *New York Times,* July 9, 1968, July 21, 1968, May 18, 1969, October 14, 1969, November 9, 1969, November 15,

1969, November 19, 1969, December 30, 1970; *Spectator,* July 12, 1968; *Punch,* July 17, 1968; *London Magazine,* October, 1968; *Washington Post,* November 23, 1968, May 11, 1969, October 15, 1969; *Prompt,* Number 12, 1968; *Variety,* March 7, 1969, May 14, 1969, October 15, 1969, October 22, 1969, April 1, 1970; *Christian Science Monitor,* May 23, 1969, March 16, 1970; *Saturday Review,* June 7, 1969; *Evergreen Review,* October, 1969; *New Yorker,* October 18, 1969; *National Observer,* October 20, 1969; *Cue,* October 25, 1969; *New York,* October 27, 1969; *Nation,* November 3, 1969; *Commonweal,* November 7, 1969; *New Republic,* November 8, 1969; *Vogue,* November 15, 1969; *New Leader,* November 24, 1969; *Newsweek,* November 27, 1969, December 22, 1969; *Contemporary Literary Criticism,* Volume 1, Gale, 1973.*

*　　*　　*

KOSTE, Robert Francis 1933-
(Barry Cuff)

PERSONAL: Born November 23, 1933, in New York, N.Y.; son of William Frederick (an engineer) and Dorothy (Kozma) Koste; married Leone Ludlam (a bookkeeper and secretary), April 26, 1962. *Education:* Attended University of Kansas, 1951, University of Miami, 1952-53, and University of Missouri, 1953. *Home address:* P.O. Box 999, Yucca Valley, Calif. 92284.

CAREER: Employed as general construction contractor or construction manager in both commercial and residential fields in Kansas City, Mo., 1958-60, and in California, 1960—. *Member:* American Society of Professional Estimators, Mystery Writers of America, Alpha Tau Omega.

WRITINGS—Under pseudonym Barry Cuff: *The Right Fuse,* Holloway House, 1968; *Damned Spot,* Holloway House, 1968.

WORK IN PROGRESS: A mystery-adventure novel.

SIDELIGHTS: Koste told *CA:* "I have always been strongly motivated to write. I have completed six novels: two were published, two are still making the rounds, and the first two are, actually, pretty bad. In positions of management in the construction industry, with the attendant demands, it is difficult to 'let it all go' and concentrate on a full-time writing career, even though it is what I will probably do within the next few years."

*　　*　　*

KOTRE, John N(icholas) 1940-

PERSONAL: Born April 4, 1940, in Evanston, Ill.; son of John F. (an electrician) and Elizabeth L. (Dyker) Kotre; married Ann Marie Wenthe (a microbiologist), August 18, 1965; children: Stephen, David, My-Linh (adopted daughter). *Education:* Xavier University, Litt. B. (magna cum laude), 1962; graduate study at Loyola University, Chicago, Ill., 1962-64; University of Chicago, Ph.D., 1970. *Home:* 114 Grandview Dr., Ann Arbor, Mich. 48103. *Office:* Department of Behavioral Science, University of Michigan—Dearborn, 4901 Evergreen Rd., Dearborn, Mich. 48128.

CAREER: American Bar Association Foundation, Chicago, Ill., assistant project director, summer, 1967; DePaul University, Chicago, part-time instructor in psychology, 1968; Lake Forest College, Lake Forest, Ill., instructor in psychology, 1968-69; University of Michigan—Ann Arbor, lecturer in psychology and project director at Center for Research on the Utilization of Scientific Knowledge and

Institute for Social Research, 1969-71; Eastern Michigan University, Ypsilanti, part-time lecturer in psychology, 1971-72; University of Michigan—Dearborn, assistant professor, 1972-75, associate professor of psychology, 1975—. Part-time instructor at University of Chicago Extension, 1968; part-time lecturer at University of Michigan Extension, 1971-72.

WRITINGS: The View from the Border: A Social Psychological Study of Current Catholicism, Aldine-Atherton, 1971; (contributor) William C. Rhodes and Michael Tracy, editors, *A Study of Child Variance,* University of Michigan Press, 1972; *The Best of Times, The Worst of Times: Andrew Greeley and American Catholicism, 1950-1975,* Nelson-Hall, 1978; (contributor) David Tracy, editor, *Towards Vatican III: The Work that Needs to Be Done,* Seabury, 1978; *Dance, Then, Wherever You May Be: The Lives of Pat and Patty Crowley,* Sheed, Andrews, & McMeel, in press. Contributor of more than fifteen articles and reviews to professional journals and popular magazines, including *America* and *Commonweal.*

*　　*　　*

KOTZ, David M(ichael) 1943-

PERSONAL: Born June 19, 1943, in Philadelphia, Pa.; son of Jerry (in sales) and May (Gippa) Kotz. *Education:* Harvard University, A.B., 1965; Yale University, M.A., 1966; University of California, Berkeley, Ph.D., 1975. *Office:* Department of Economics, University of Massachusetts, Amherst, Mass. 01003.

CAREER: University of California, Berkeley, acting instructor in economics, 1973-74; American University, Washington, D.C., assistant professor of economics, 1974-78; U.S. Federal Trade Commission, Washington, D.C., visiting staff economist, 1977-78; University of Massachusetts, Amherst, assistant professor of economics, 1978—. *Member:* Union for Radical Political Economics, Association for Evolutionary Economics. *Awards, honors:* Woodrow Wilson fellow, 1965-66; National Science Foundation trainee, 1967-68.

WRITINGS: Bank Control of Large Corporations in the United States, University of California Press, 1978. Member of board of editors of *Review of Radical Political Economics,* 1974-76.

WORK IN PROGRESS: Research on bank influence over corporate merger activity.

AVOCATIONAL INTERESTS: Tennis.

*　　*　　*

KRAMER, Leonie Judith 1924-

PERSONAL: Born October 1, 1924, in Melbourne, Australia; daughter of Alfred Leonard (a banker) and Gertrude Isobel (Walker) Gibson; married Harold Kramer (a pathologist), April 2, 1952; children: Jocelyn Anne, Hilary Lorraine. *Education:* University of Melbourne, B.A., 1945; Oxford University, D.Phil., 1953. *Office:* Department of English, University of Sydney, Sydney, New South Wales 2006, Australia.

CAREER: Canberra University College (now Australian National University), Canberra, Australia, lecturer in English, 1954-56; University of New South Wales, Sydney, Australia, 1958-68, began as lecturer, then senior lecturer, became associate professor of English; University of Sydney, Sydney, Australia, professor of English, 1968—. President of Australian Council for Educational Standards; member of Universities Council; member of board of trustees of Australian Museum; member of council of National Library of Australia and interim council of Alexander Mackie College of Advanced Education.

MEMBER: Australian College of Education (fellow), Australian Society of Authors (fellow), Australian Academy of the Humanities (fellow), English Teachers Association, Royal Historical Society of Victoria.

WRITINGS: Henry Handel Richardson and Some of Her Sources, Melbourne University Press, 1954; *James McAuley: Tradition in Australian Poetry* (bound with *The Misfortunes of Henry Handel Richardson,* by T. Inglis Moore), Canberra University College, 1957; (editor) *Australian Poetry,* Angus & Robertson, 1961; *A Companion to Australia Felix,* Heinemann (Australia), 1962; (editor) *Coast to Coast, 1963-64,* Angus & Robertson, 1965; *Myself When Laura: Fact and Fiction in Henry Handel Richardson's School Career,* Heinemann (Australia), 1966; *Henry Handel Richardson,* Oxford University Press, 1967; (editor) Hal Porter, *Selected Stories,* Angus & Robertson, 1971; (with Robert D. Eagleson) *Language and Literature: A Synthesis,* Thomas Nelson, 1976; (with Eagleson) *A Guide to Language and Literature,* Thomas Nelson, 1977. Editorial adviser for *Quadrant, Poetry Australia,* and *Australian Literary Studies.*

*   *   *

KRANTZ, Judith 1932-

PERSONAL: Born January 9, 1932, in New York, N.Y.; daughter of Jack D. (an advertising executive) and Mary (an attorney; maiden name, Braeger) Tarcher; married Stephen Krantz (an independent film producer); children: Nicholas, Anthony. *Education:* Wellesley College, B.A., 1952. *Residence:* Beverly Hills, Calif. *Agent:* Morton Janklow, 375 Park Ave., New York, N.Y. *Address:* c/o Stephen Krantz, 6290 Sunset Blvd., Hollywood, Calif.

CAREER: Writer, free-lance journalist. Fashion publicist in Paris, France, 1952-53; *Good Housekeeping,* New York City, fashion editor, 1953-56; contributing writer, *McCall's* magazine and *Ladies Home Journal,* 1957-67; *Cosmopolitan,* New York City, contributing West Coast editor, 1967-77.

WRITINGS: Scruples (novel), Crown, 1978. Contributor of articles to magazines.

SIDELIGHTS: Krantz's first novel, *Scruples,* is the story of a woman who sets out to build the most glamorous and luxurious store in the world. Her name is Billy Ikehorn Orsini, and she ultimately finds happiness as the wife of a movie producer, and as the founder of the ultra-chic store, "Scruples." This is a world that Krantz knows well. She told *Los Angeles Times* reporter, Pat Nation: "I didn't really have to research it. Fashion is one of the things I have always been interested in. A lot of my friends are retailers. I like to talk to sales people in the stores. I had been living and shopping in Beverly Hills for six years with the eye of a New Yorker."

When questioned about the possible resemblance of characters in *Scruples* to real-life acquaintances and friends, Krantz replied: "A novelist has to be schizophrenic without being mentally ill. You draw on lots of facets of your life for characters and then fictionalize. Of course, I know what it's like to be the wife of a producer, how you have to spend your time. And there's a sliver of myself in all the female characters."

With regard to *Scruples,* Krantz stated that she has no illusions about her book being great literature. "I wrote it because I realized that no one was writing the big, fun, entertainment book for women. I'm a storyteller. This book is not a magnificent work of art. Art is reserved for the really great writers. If I can't be a Doris Lessing or an Iris Murdoch, it doesn't depress me. What I do is entertainment and I do it as well as I can."

Krantz has done it as well or better than anyone could. Robert Friedman of the *New York Post* wrote: "[*Scruples*] has more inside information about the worlds of high fashion and Hollywood than you'd find in a dozen manuals. . . . It's all thoroughly explicit and, after Judith Krantz, the only way for men writers now to blaze new trails is to reinvest a decent Victorian reticence."

BIOGRAPHICAL/CRITICAL SOURCES: New York Post, February 27, 1978; *Washington Post,* March 3, 1978; *New York Times Book Review,* March 19, 1978; *Los Angeles Times,* May 19, 1978.

*   *   *

KRAUSS, Rosalind E(pstein) 1940-

PERSONAL: Born November 30, 1940, in Washington, D.C.; daughter of Matthew M. (a lawyer) and Bertha (Luber) Epstein; married Richard I. Krauss, September 17, 1962 (divorced, 1971). *Education:* Wellesley College, A.B., 1962; Harvard University, M.A., 1963, Ph.D., 1969. *Home:* 12 Greene St., New York, N.Y. 10013 *Agent:* Maxine Groffsky, 2 Fifth Ave., New York, N.Y. 10011. *Office:* Department of Art, Hunter College of City University of New York, 695 Park Ave., New York, N.Y. 10021.

CAREER: Princeton University, Princeton, N.J., lecturer and director of visual arts program, 1972-74; Hunter College of City University of New York, New York, N.Y., associate professor of art, 1974—. Guest curator for exhibitions at Guggenheim and Whitney Museums. *Awards, honors:* Mather Award for Criticism from College Art Association, 1972.

WRITINGS: Terminal Iron Works: The Sculpture of David Smith, M.I.T. Press, 1971; *Joan Miro: Magnetic Fields,* Guggenheim Museum, 1972; *Line as Language,* Princeton University Museum, 1974; *Passages in Modern Sculpture,* Viking, 1977. Contributor to *Artforum, Art in America, October,* and *Partisan Review.* Associate editor of *Artforum,* 1972-75; editor of *October,* 1976—.

*   *   *

KREEFT, Peter 1937-

PERSONAL: Surname is pronounced Krayft; born March 16, 1937, in Paterson, N.J.; son of John (an engineer) and Lucy (Comtobad) Kreeft; married Maria Massi, August 18, 1962; children: John, Jennifer, Katherine, Elizabeth. *Education:* Calvin College, A.B., 1959; graduate study at Yale University, 1959-60; Fordham University, M.A., 1961, Ph.D., 1965. *Religion:* Roman Catholic. *Home:* 44 Davis Ave., West Newton, Mass. 02165. *Office:* Department of Philosophy, Boston College, Chestnut Hill, Mass. 02167.

CAREER: Villanova University, Villanova, Pa., instructor in philosophy, 1961-65; Boston College, Chestnut Hill, Mass., assistant professor, 1965-69, associate professor of philosophy, 1969—. *Awards, honors:* Woodrow Wilson fellowship, 1959-60; Danforth fellowship, 1966-67.

WRITINGS: C. S. Lewis, Eerdmans, 1969; *The Five Faces of Death,* Harper, 1978.

WORK IN PROGRESS: A book on life after death.

SIDELIGHTS: Kreeft writes that his main interests are philosophy in literature, philosophy of religion, East-West dialogue, mysticism, and existentialism. He himself is actively involved in the Roman Catholic charismatic movement. He would someday like to write books on philosophy of human sexuality and philosophy of chess.

*   *   *

KREIDL, John Francis 1939-

PERSONAL: Born July 13, 1939, in Vienna, Austria; came to United States, 1940; naturalized U.S. citizen, 1945; son of Norbert J. Kreidl (a physicist) and Melanie (a raiser of cats; maiden name, Schreiber) Kreidl. *Education:* Attended University of Vienna, 1957-58; University of Rochester, B.S., 1960; further study at Harvard University, 1974-75. *Politics:* Democrat. *Religion:* Catholic. *Home and office:* 560 Green St., Cambridge, Mass. 02139. *Agent:* Alice Phalen, 107 Myrtle St., Boston, Mass.

CAREER: Writer. Engelhard Industries, Newark, N.J., research chemist, 1960-62; Air Reduction Inc., Murray Hill, N.J., research chemist, 1962-63; Harvard University, Cambridge, Mass., cinema researcher, 1973-76.

WRITINGS: Nicholas Ray (critical biography), Twayne, 1977; *Alain Resnais* (critical biography), Twayne, 1978. Contributor to *Quincy Patriot-Ledger.*

WORK IN PROGRESS: Two critical biographies, *Jean-Luc Godard* and *Orson Welles;* a study of Russia as depicted in American film, tentatively entitled *Red Star Over Hollywood.*

SIDELIGHTS: Kreidl told *CA:* "I am interested primarily in writing about the genesis of something, how it came about, how it came to be made, how it represents itself socially.

"My father engineered the first CinemaScope lenses. I always thought still photography was boring because it didn't recreate time-space like projected film images. I love film because it is 'suspended' between life and art, and gives an alternative reality rather than the iconic sign of itself, like still photography. There is no such thing as bad photography; there are bad films, good films, marvelous films, indifferent films."

CA asked Kreidl why his first book was on Nicholas Ray. "I like American outsiders," he replied. "They are the best Americans because they are the least security conscious Americans. They risk. I also wondered why he made the best of the three James Dean films. Ray's films weren't nihilistic; they were very positive, even romantic. Perhaps, in the year 2100, the 1950's will be seen as having belonged to the nineteenth century and individualism."

Kreidl also offered his opinions on Jean-Luc Godard. "Godard's decline is only relative," he said. "He doesn't make commercial films anymore, but even if he did have distribution, his college audience is gone. Godard was associated with the 1960's, perhaps too heavily, as he himself realizes. But, in "Numero Deux," Godard tries hard to address himself with new vigor and tactics to showing how images shape our lives."

*   *   *

KREUGER, Miles 1934-

PERSONAL: Born March 28, 1934, in New York, N.Y.; son of Louis Jules (a furrier) and Helene Anita (a fashion buyer; maiden name, Friedman) Kreuger. *Education:* Bard College, B.A., 1954. *Home:* 220 West 93rd St., New York, N.Y. 10025.

CAREER: Musical theatre and motion picture researcher and archivist; author. Director of dramatic programs, WEOK, Poughkeepsie, N.Y., 1952; record librarian, WNEW, New York City, 1954-55; production assistant, stage manager, or scenic designer for Broadway and Off-Broadway shows, 1955-57; producer of "The Mime Theatre of Etienne Decroux," 1959-60; director of "Fun and Games in the Living Room," 1961. Producer, Decca Records, 1958-59; Columbia Records, associate producer, 1961, producer of reissues from early recordings, 1967-69; director of publicity for Alan Jay Lerner, 1963-64. Founder and president, Institute of the American Musical, 1972—. New York University, instructor, 1965-66; Columbia University, adjunct associate professor of film, 1975—. Producer of film retrospectives, "The Roots of the American Musical Film (1927-1932)," "Gershwin on Film," and "The 50th Anniversary of Vitaphone, 1926-1976"; conducted interviews on "Voice of America," 1975. Frequent radio and television guest and lecturer; actor. *Military service:* U.S. Army Reserves, 1954-57. *Member:* National Academy of Recording Arts & Sciences (member of hall of fame elections committee, 1975—). *Awards, honors:* Grammy nomination for best album notes, 1968, from National Academy of Recording Arts & Sciences, for "Ethel Waters on Stage and Screen."

WRITINGS: (Contributor of discography) *Cole,* Holt, 1971; (contributor) *United Artists 16mm Film Library,* United Artists, 1972; (contributor of discography) *The Gershwins,* Atheneum, 1973; (editor and author of introduction) *The Movie Musical From Vitaphone to 42nd Street,* Dover, 1975; (author of introduction) *At Long Last Love,* Chappell, 1975; (author of introduction) *Kurt Weill in America,* Chappell, 1975; (editor and author of introduction) *Souvenir Programs of Twelve Classic Movies, 1927-1941,* Dover, 1977; *Show Boat: The Story of a Classic American Musical,* Oxford University Press, 1977. Also contributor of a discography to the unpublished book, "The Business of Rainbows."

Author and conductor of radio program, "Opening Night," broadcast on WBAI-FM, 1958-60. Author of souvenir programs and of numerous record album liner notes for musicals. Author of column, "In the Limelight," in *American Record Guide,* 1966-68. Contributing editor, *The World of Music* (four volume encyclopedia), Abradale, 1963; contributing editor and author of introduction to *Popular Music,* Volume 5, 1964—. Contributing editor, *33 Guide,* 1961, *High Fidelity,* 1972-74. Contributor of numerous articles to periodicals, including *Performing Arts, Billboard, Film Comment,* and *Insight.*

WORK IN PROGRESS: The American Musical Film (a critical history), *Chronology of American Film,* and *Chronology of the American Musical Theatre* ("including complete casts, production staffs, musical numbers, and discography from inception to present"), all to be published by Oxford University Press.

SIDELIGHTS: Kreuger, who has assembled the world's largest private archives of research materials and recordings on American musical theatre and motion pictures, commented to *CA:* "Ever since attending my first Broadway musical, "Knights of Song," at the age of four, I have been fascinated by the American musical theatre, which I regard as this country's principal contribution in form to theatre history. As there was almost no available literature on this subject during my childhood, I began quite young to collect recordings, playbills, and other materials on musical theatre, with my interests in time expanding to include film. Through my nonprofit organization, The Institute of the American Musical, these materials are available to scholars who are preparing books and theses. We also produce exhibitions, film series, etc., and plan to begin a quarterly periodical. In the early 1950's, my interest in the musical was regarded with ridicule or at least suspicion: today the subject is studied on college campuses all across the nation.''

BIOGRAPHICAL/CRITICAL SOURCES: Harper's Bazaar, January, 1967; *FM Guide,* May, 1967; *Sales Management,* June 15, 1971; Don Dunn, *The Making of No, No, Nanette,* Citadel, 1972; *High Fidelity,* February, 1973; *New Yorker,* September 17, 1973; Jon Tuska, *The Films of Mae West,* Citadel, 1973; *New York Daily News,* November 6, 1975; Tuska, *The Filming of the West,* Doubleday, 1976; *Publishers Weekly,* January 2, 1978; *Variety,* January 4, 1978.

* * *

KRIEG, Saul 1917-

PERSONAL: Born September 15, 1917, in Chicago, Ill.; son of Abraham (in food business) and Beatrice (Beichman) Krieg; married Helen Cohen, January 25, 1941; children: Bonnie Krieg Feldman, Andrew G., Robin V. Krieg Nevins. *Education:* Attended City College (now of the City University of New York), 1936-39. *Politics:* Democrat. *Home:* 875 Park Ave., New York, N.Y. 10021. *Office:* Saul Krieg Associates, Inc., 633 Third Ave., New York, N.Y. 10017.

CAREER: Saul Krieg Associates, Inc. (public relations), New York, N.Y., president, 1946—. Publicity director and script editor for television and radio shows; guest on radio and television programs. *Member:* Culinary Association, Navy League, Friars Club. *Awards, honors:* Awards from American Cancer Society, 1948, for a radio show, from conference of Christians and Jews, 1949, for a radio show, and from Professional Chefs Guild, 1973, for culinary writing.

WRITINGS: The Spirit of Grand Cuisine, Macmillan, 1969; *The New Spirit of Grand Cuisine,* Macmillan, 1971; *The Alpha and Omega of Greek Cooking,* Macmillan, 1973; *What's Cooking in Portugal,* Macmillan, 1974; *The Spirited Taste of Italy,* Macmillan, 1975. Author of "The Wine Rack," a column in *New York Post,* 1975-77. Contributor to magazines, including *Finance* and *National Culinary Review,* and newspapers. Wine editor of *New York Post,* 1975-77.

WORK IN PROGRESS: They Never Caught the Murderer, a novel, publication expected in 1980; *The Beer Drinker's Guide,* completion expected in 1980; *We Made the Headlines,* an autobiography, completion expected in 1981; research for *The Gourmands and Gourmets of the World,* completion expected in 1981.

SIDELIGHTS: Krieg writes: "My interest in cookbooks stems from the age of thirteen, when I apprenticed to the Ritz in Paris as a chef's helper. I learned cooking in great style in Europe, and both food and wines became more than a hobby. I have traveled, and continue to travel every year, in Europe and America, visiting the great chefs and eating palaces. I entertain well, and love to cook the great dishes I learned during my travels. I know wines, having worked as a youngster in the vineyards, am knowledgable about beer and all the liqueurs, which I like to write about. Writing comes easily for me, and since I have had a full career in television

and radio (with 'Gangbusters,' 'Mr. and Mrs. North,' and 'Counterspy'), I come naturally to crime stories."

* * *

KRIER, James E(dward) 1939-

PERSONAL: Surname is pronounced Kreer; born October 19, 1939, in Milwaukee, Wis.; son of Ambrose E. (in business) and Genevieve (Behling) Krier; married Gayle Grimsrud, March 22, 1962 (divorced, June, 1973); married Wendy L. Wilkes (a legal assistant), April 20, 1974; children: Jennifer, Amy. *Education:* University of Wisconsin, Madison, B.S., 1961, J.D., 1966. *Residence:* Stanford, Calif. *Office:* School of Law, Stanford University, Stanford, Calif. 94305.

CAREER: California Supreme Court, San Francisco, law clerk, 1966-67; Arnold & Porter, Washington, D.C., associate attorney, 1967-69; University of California, Los Angeles, acting professor, 1969-72, professor of law, 1972-78; Stanford University, Stanford, Calif., professor of law, 1978—. Consultant to government agencies. *Military service:* U.S. Army, 1961-63; became first lieutenant. *Member:* Wisconsin Bar Association, Phi Kappa Phi, Artus, Order of the Coif.

WRITINGS: Environmental Law and Policy, Bobbs-Merrill, 1971; (with Edmund Ursin) *Pollution and Policy,* University of California Press, 1977. Contributor to law journals.

WORK IN PROGRESS: Research on property law and environmental law.

SIDELIGHTS: Krier told *CA:* "My major concern in the environmental law area is to see to it that we do not waste resources in ill-conceived attempts to conserve resources. Our history to date has been rather to the contrary."

* * *

KRIPPNER, Stanley (Curtis) 1932-

PERSONAL: Born October 4, 1932, in Edgerton, Wis.; son of Carroll Porter (a farmer) and Ruth (Volenberg) Krippner; married Lelie Harris, June 25, 1966; children: Caron Harris, Robert Harris. *Education:* University of Wisconsin, Madison, B.S., 1954; Northwestern University, M.A., 1958, Ph.D., 1961. *Politics:* Independent. *Religion:* Presbyterian. *Home:* 79 Woodland Rd., Fairfax, Calif. 94930. *Agent:* Ruth Hagy Brod Literary Agency, 15 Park Ave., New York, N.Y. 10016. *Office:* Humanistic Psychology Institute, 325 Ninth St., San Francisco, Calif. 94103.

CAREER: Speech therapist for city of Warren, Ill., 1954-55, and for public schools of Richmond, Va., 1955-56; Kent State University, Kent, Ohio, director of Child Study Center, 1961-64; Maimonides Medical Center, Brooklyn, N.Y., director of Dream Laboratory, 1964-73, senior research associate in psychiatry, 1964—; Humanistic Psychology Institute, San Francisco, Calif., professor of psychology and program planning coordinator, 1973—. Lecturer at Fordham University, 1967, University of California, Los Angeles, 1968; U.S.S.R. Academy of Pedagogical Sciences, 1971, Brooklyn College of the City University of New York, 1972, and Ontario Curriculum Institute, 1975; adjunct associate professor at Yeshiva University, 1974; adjunct professor at Wagner College, 1967-72; Rosary Hill College, 1973, St. John's University of Staten Island, 1973-74, and West Georgia College, 1976; visiting professor at University of Puerto Rico, 1972-73, California State College, Sonoma, 1972-73, College of Life Sciences (Bogota, Colombia), 1974, and Institute for Psychodrama and Humanistic Psychology (Caracas, Venezuela), 1975. Member of board of directors of National Foundation for Gifted and Creative Children and of Gardner Murphy Research Institute; member of advisory boards of foundations, schools, and health centers, including Foundation for Mind Research, National Council on Drug Abuse, Center for Attitudinal Healing, and Association for the Rights of Disabled Consumers; member of Menninger Foundation. Consultant to New York Institute for Child Development.

MEMBER: International Association for Psychotronic Research (vice-president, 1973-77), International Reading Association, International Society for General Semantics, InterAmerican Psychological Association, National Society for the Study of Education, National Association for Gifted Children (vice-president, 1968-74), National Gay Task Force, American Society for Clinical Hypnosis (fellow), American Society for Psychical Research, American Psychological Association (member of executive board), American Association for the Advancement of Science, American Academy of Social and Political Science, American Educational Research Association, American Personnel and Guidance Association, American Society of Psychosomatic Dentistry and Medicine, Association for Humanistic Psychology (president, 1974-75), Association for the Psychophysiological Study of Sleep, Biofeedback Research Society, Council for Exceptional Children, College Reading Association, Parapsychological Association, Psychologists for Social Action, Society for Clinical and Experimental Hypnosis, Society for the Scientific Study of Sex, Society for the Scientific Study of Religion, Albert Schweitzer Cultural Association (honorary vice-president), New York Speech and Hearing Association, New York Society of Clinical Psychologists. *Awards, honors:* Service to Youth Award from Young Men's Christian Association, 1959; citations of merit from National Association for Gifted Children, 1972, and National Association for Creative Children and Adults, 1975; certificate of recognition from U.S. Office of the Gifted and Talented, 1976.

WRITINGS: (With Montague Ullman) *Dream Studies and Telepathy* (monograph), Parapsychological Foundation, 1970; (editor with Daniel Rubin) *Galaxies of Life: The Human Aura in Acupuncture and Kirlian Photography,* Gordon & Breach, 1973; (with Ullman and Alan Vaughan), *Dream Telepathy: Experiments in Nocturnal E.S.P.,* Macmillan, 1973; (editor with Rubin) *The Kirlian Aura,* Doubleday, 1974; (editor with Rubin) *The Energies of Consciousness: Explorations in Acupuncture, Auras, and Kirlian Photography,* Gordon & Breach, 1975; *Song of the Siren: A Parapsychological Odyssey,* Harper, 1975; (with Alberto Villoldo) *The Realms of Healing,* Celestial Arts, 1976; (with Roy Dreistadt) *The Psychology of Societies* (monograph), Kishkam Press, 1976; (with Eleanor Criswell) *Physiology of Consciousness* (monograph), Kishkam Press, 1976; (editor) *Advances in Parapsychological Research,* Plenum, Volume I: *Psychokinesis,* 1977, Volume II: *Extrasensory Perception,* 1978; (editor with John White) *Future Science: Life Energies and the Physics of Paranormal Phenomena,* Doubleday-Anchor, 1977; (with Dreistadt and Judith Malamud) *The Measurement of Behavior* (monograph), Kishkam Press, 1977; (with Dreistadt) *Cognitive Functions of Human Intentionality* (monograph), Kishkam Press, 1977; (with Brian Leibovitz) *Drug-Related Altered States of Consciousness* (monograph), Kishkam Press, 1978; (editor with Sidney Cohen) *LSD Revisited,* Unity Press, 1978.

Editor of "Psychic Studies" series for Gordon & Breach. Contributor of more than three hundred articles to journals in psychology, education, psychiatry, and parapsychology. Editor emeritus of *Psychoenergetic Systems: An International Journal* and editor-in-chief of *Advances in Parapsychological Research: A Biennial Review;* member of editorial board or advisory board of *Gifted Child Quarterly, Journal of Altered States of Consciousness, Journal of the American Society of Psychosomatic Dentistry and Medicine, International Journal of Paraphysics, Journal of Humanistic Psychology,* and *Journal of Transpersonal Psychology.*

SIDELIGHTS: In 1971 Krippner gave the first lecture of parapsychology ever presented at the U.S.S.R. Academy of Pedagogical Sciences in Moscow, and in 1972 in Tokyo he read the first paper on parapsychology ever accepted by the International Congress of Psychology. His main research interest has been the understanding of psychic ability and the function of psychic ability in different altered states of consciousness. He has also studied gifted and exceptional children, with an interest in the relationship between creativity and psychic phenomena.

AVOCATIONAL INTERESTS: Cinema, theater, jogging.

* * *

KROCH, Adolph A. 1882-1978

OBITUARY NOTICE: Born January 7, 1882, in Austria; died November 19, 1978, in Tucson, Ariz. Bookseller and author. Kroch established his first bookstore in 1907 and in 1955 created Kroch's & Brentano's Inc., the largest bookstore in the world. He wrote *A Great Book Store in Action* in 1939. Obituaries and other sources: *Chicago Tribune,* November 21, 1978; *Who's Who in America,* 40th edition, Marquis, 1978.

* * *

KROEPCKE, Karol
See KROLOW, Karl (Gustav Heinrich)

* * *

KROLOW, Karl (Gustav Heinrich) 1915-
(Karol Kroepcke)

PERSONAL: Born March 11, 1915, in Hanover, Germany; son of Albert (an administrative official) and Christine (Lange) Krolow; married Luzie Gaida, 1941; children: one. *Education:* Attended University of Goettingen and University of Breslau, 1935-41. *Home:* 6100 Darmstadt, Park Rosenhoehe 5, West Germany.

CAREER: Poet, translator, critic, and essayist, 1942—. Visiting lecturer in poetry at University of Frankfurt, 1960-61, and at University of Munich, 1964. Town clerk of Bergen-Enkheim, 1975-76. *Member:* German Academy of Speech and Poetry (vice-president, 1966-75; president, 1972-75), Mainz Academy of Science and Literature, Bavarian Academy of Fine Arts, German P.E.N. Center. *Awards, honors:* Georg Buechner Prize, 1956; Grosse Niedersaechsischer Kunstpreis, 1965; Grosse Bundesverdienstkreuz, 1975; Goethe-Plak, Hessen, 1975; Silver Verdienstplak, City of Darmstadt, 1975; Rilke Prize, 1975; Honorary Doctorate, Technical University of Darmstadt, 1975.

WRITINGS—All poetry, except as noted; in English: *Fremde Koerper,* Suhrkamp, 1959, translation by Michael

Bullock published as *Foreign Bodies,* Ohio University Press, 1969; *Unsichtbare Haende: Gedichte 1959-62,* Suhrkamp, 1962, translation by Bullock published as *Invisible Hands,* Cape Goliard Press, 1969; *Leave-Taking and Other Poems,* translation by Herman Salinger, Austin, 1968; *Poems Against Death: Selected Poems,* translation by Salinger, Charioteer Press, 1969; *The Human Soul,* new edition, Anthroposophic, 1973.

In German: *Heimsuchung* (title means "Affliction"), Volk & Welt, 1948; *Gedichte* (title means "Poems"), Sued Verlag, 1948; *Auf Erden* (title means "On Earth"), Ellermann, 1949; *Die Zeichen der Welt* (title means "The Signs of the World"), Deutsche Verlags-Anstalt, 1952; *Wind und Zeit: Gedichte 1950-54* (title means "Wind and Time: Poems 1950-54"), Deutsche Verlags-Anstalt, 1954; *Tage und Naechte* (title means "Days and Nights"), E. Diederich, 1956; (editor) Paul Verlaine, *Gedichte: ausgewaehlt von Karl Krolow* (title means "Poems: Selected by Karl Krolow"), Insel, 1957.

Ausgewaehlte Gedichte (title means "Selected Poems"), Suhrkamp, 1962; *Reise durch die Nacht* (title means "Journey Through the Night"), J. G. Blaeschke, 1964; *Gesammelte Gedichte* (title means "Collected Poems"), Suhrkamp, 1965; *Landschaften fuer mich* (title means "My Landscapes"), Suhrkamp, 1966; *Alltaegliche Gedichte* (title means "Everyday Poems"), Suhrkamp, 1968; *Minuten-Aufzeichnungen* (title means "Minute Sketches"), Suhrkamp, 1968.

(Under pseudonym Karol Kroepcke) *Buergerliche Gedichte* (title means "Bourgeois Poems"), illustrations by Arno Waldschmidt, Merlin, 1970; *Nichts weiter als Leben* (title means "Nothing More than Life"), Suhrkamp, 1970; *Zeitvergehen* (title means "Passing of Time"), Suhrkamp, 1972; *Gesammelte Gedichte 2* (title means "Collected Poems 2"), Suhrkamp, 1975; *Ein Lesebuch* (title means "A Reader"; selected poetry and prose), Suhrkamp, 1975; *Der Einfachheit halber* (title means "On Behalf of Simplicity"), Suhrkamp, 1977. Also author of *Hochgelobles gutes Leben* (title means "The High-Praised God Of Life"), 1943.

Other: (With others) *Das Gedicht in unserer Zeit* (title means "The Poem in Our Time"), Sponholtz, 1946; (translator) *Nachdichtungen aus fuenf jahrhunderten franzoesischer lyrik* (title means "Translation from Five Centuries of French Lyric Poetry"), R. Beeck, 1948; *Von nahen und fernen Dingen: Betrachtungen* (title means "Of Near and Distant Things: Reflections"), illustrations by Fritz Fischer, Deutsche Verlags-Anstalt, 1953; (translator) *Die Barke Phantasie: Zeitgenoessische franzoesische Lyrik* (title means "The Barque Fantasy: Contemporary French Lyric Poetry"), Diederich, 1957; Guillaume Apollinaire, *Bestiarium: Fuenfundzwanzig Gedichte nach Guillaume Apollinaire's "Le Bestiaire ou Cortege d'Orphee"* (title means "Bestiary: Twenty-five Poems After Guillaume Appollinaire's 'Le Bestiaire . . .'"), Walltor Verlag, 1959; *Tessin* (title means "Ticino"), with photographs by Fritz Eschen, Knorr & Hirth, 1959; *Schatten eines Manns: Rudolf Schoofs Gravueren* (title means "Shadow of a Man: Rudolf Schoofs's Engravings"), Schoofs-Heiderhoff, 1959.

Aspekte zeitgenoessischer deutscher Lyrik (title means "Aspects of Contemporary German Lyric Poetry")' Mohn, 1961; *Die Rolle des Autors im experimentellen Gedicht* (title means "The Role of the Author in the Experimental Poem"), Akademie der Wissenschaften und der Literatur, Mainz, 1962; (and editor) *Spanische Gedichte des XX. Jahrhunderts* (title means "Spanish Poems of the Twentieth

Century"), Insel, 1962; *Schattengefecht* (title means "Shadow Boxing"), Suhrkamp, 1964; *Corrida de toros* (title means "Bullfight"), photographs and illustrations by Helmut Landers, Verlag der Peter-Presse, Christoph Kreickenbaum, 1964; *Poetisches Tagebuch* (title means "Poetic Diary"), Suhrkamp, 1966; *Das Problem des langen und kurzen Gedichte-heute* (title means "The Problem of the Long and the Short Poem Today")' Wiesbaden, Akademie der Wissenschaften und der Literatur, 1966; *Flug ueber Heide, Moor und gruen Berge: Niedersachsen, Nordhessen, Ostwestfalen* (title means "Flight Over Heath, Fen and Green Mountains: Lower Saxony, North Hesse, East Westphalia"), Westermann, 1969.

Deutschland deine Niedersachsen: Ein Land, das es nicht gibt (title means "Germany, Your Lower Saxony: A Country That Doesn't Exist"), illustrations by Heinz Knoke, Hoffmann & Campe, 1972; *Zu des Rheins gestreckten Huegeln* (title means "To the Rolling Hills of the Rhine"), Grotesche, Verlagsbuch-handlung, 1972; *Ein Gedicht entsteht: Selbstdeutungen, Interpretationem, Aufsaetze* (title means "A Poem Begins: Self-explanations, Interpretations, Essays"), Suhrkamp, 1973.

SIDELIGHTS: Krolow's first collection of poems appeared in 1943, and showed the influence of the mystical nature lyrics of Wilhelm Lehmann and Oskar Loerke. Krolow made a greater impact with the more exact and sober poems that appeared in Friedrich Rasche's important postwar anthology *Gedicht in unserer Zeit* ("Poetry in Our Time," 1946), and with his introduction to that collection. According to August Closs, Krolow maintained that "amidst the barrenness of a world politically and morally bankrupt the countryside should be won back again for poetry, that the rivers, trees, fields, flowers, the stars themselves should speak once more through poetry. Thus the intimate relations between Nature and mankind, between God and man, should once more be kindled or awakened. Moreover, the tendency toward 'intellectual' poetry, towards vague mysticism and a guilt-laden consciousness should yield to a new mode of poetic form. . . . The poet's deepest concern should be the creation of a lyric poetry expressive of *our* present age and *our* generation." The modern lyric, Krolow added, should be religious in the deepest sense, without being limited to any particular creed, and it should demonstrate a serious concern for poetic form. A few years later, in an essay published in 1955, Krolow called for "intellectual cheerfulness," implying his dissatisfaction with poets who agonize over the inadequacy of language or of poetry itself. He recommended that poetry should be objective, intelligible, and elegant, conveying emotion and sensation with the greatest possible immediacy through metaphors of maximum precision and evocativeness. Krolow's conscious artistry and refinement, the "delicate nervous coloration" of his poetry and its absence of "hard contours," did not please everyone: in 1956 Peter Ruehmkopf described him as a "master perfumer."

The elegant, rhymed, and rather mannered poetic style Krolow evolved during the 1940's and early 1950's was modified by his involvement as a translator with modern French and Spanish verse. Surrealism in particular became an element in his work. Under these influences he concluded that nature poetry suffered from "excessive weightiness of meaning." According to Siegfried Mandel, "the remedies he wished to apply would create a poem lighter in words and movement, with 'geometric clarity, algebraic sureness,' surprise, and sudden illumination of meaning." Beginning in the late 1950's, all this was reflected in his own verse, in which the imagery became less dense and less logical, rhyme was abandoned, and the diction became sparer and simpler. Nevertheless, Mandel says, "the mellifluous tone remained as did the basic ideas that self-knowledge comes through understanding of nature and that experience is visual rather than metaphysical."

Though Krolow is primarily a nature poet, not all of his work is on this theme. He has written some notable love poems and—especially during the 1960's—some powerful or ironic pieces on social and political themes. However, in the opinion of Michael Hamburger, "the everyday life that dominates his later work is that of a highly civilized and fastidious cultivator of his own garden," whose characteristic manner is now remarkable for coolness, an almost throwaway casualness of diction and stance, the deliberate avoidance of pathos and soulfulness." A critic in the *Times Literary Supplement* noted in 1973 that Krolow writes "with all the power and authority of a true poet. His is a distinguished voice, melancholy but not self-pitying, elegiac without in any way being morbid." Siegfried Mandel has written that Krolow's "blend of aesthetic and moral observations without glaringly abrasive social criticism puts him close to the public pulse," and he is "the most widely read" of modern German poets.

AVOCATIONAL INTERESTS: Ancient music, rambling.

BIOGRAPHICAL/CRITICAL SOURCES: Hans Egon Holthusen, *Ja und Nein,* Piper, 1954; Karl Krolow, *Ausgewaehlre Gedichte,* Suhrkamp, 1962; *Times Literary Supplement,* May 3, 1963, January 12, 1973, September 5, 1975; Artur Ruemmler, *Die Entwicklung der Metaphorik in der lyrik Karl Krolows, 1942-1962,* Lang, 1972; Rolf Paulus, *Karl-Krolow-Bibliographie,* Athenaeum, 1972; Siegfried Mandel, *Group 47,* Southern Illinois University Press, 1973.

* * *

KUBRICK, Stanley 1928-

PERSONAL: Born July 26, 1928, in Bronx, N.Y.; son of Jacques L. (a doctor) and Gertrude (Perveler) Kubrick; married Toba Metz (divorced, 1952); married Ruth Sobotka (a dancer; marriage ended); married Suzanne Christiane Harlan (an actress), April, 1958; children: Anya, Vivian. *Education:* Attended City College (now of the City University of New York). *Address:* P.O. Box 123, Boreham Wood, Hertfordshire, England.

CAREER: Worked as free-lance photographer, 1945-46; *Look* magazine, New York, N.Y., staff photographer, 1946-50; screenwriter, producer and director of motion pictures, 1951—. *Awards, honors:* Best director award from New York Film Critics, 1964, for "Dr. Strangelove; or, How I Learned to Stop Worrying and Love the Bomb"; co-nominee for best screenplay from Academy of Motion Picture Arts and Sciences, 1968, for "2001: A Space Odyssey"; best director award and best film award from New York Film Critics, nominations for best director and best film from Academy of Motion Picture Arts and Sciences, all 1971, all for "A Clockwork Orange"; co-winner of best director award and best English language film award from National Board of Review of Motion Pictures, nominations for best director and best film from Academy of Motion Picture Arts and Sciences, all 1975, all for "Barry Lyndon."

WRITINGS—All screenplays, all as director: "Day of the Fight," RKO, 1951; "Flying Padre," RKO, 1952; "Killer's Kiss," United Artists, 1955; "The Killing" (adapted from the novel by Lionel White, *Clean Break*), Harris-Kubrick, 1956; (with Calder Willingham) "Paths of Glory" (adapted from the novel by Humphrey Cobb), United Artists, 1957;

(with Peter George and Terry Southern) "Dr. Strangelove; or, How I Learned to Stop Worrying and Love the Bomb" (adapted from the novel by George, *Red Alert*), Columbia, 1964; (with Arthur C. Clarke) "2001: A Space Odessey," Metro-Goldwyn-Mayer, 1968; *A Clockwork Orange* (produced by Warner Brothers, 1971; adapted from the novel by Anthony Burgess), Abelard, 1972; "Barry Lyndon" (adapted from the novel by William Makepeace Thackeray), Warner Brothers, 1975.

WORK IN PROGRESS: Directing the motion picture "The Shining."

SIDELIGHTS: "I have always enjoyed dealing with a slightly surrealistic situation and presenting it in a realistic manner," declared Kubrick to an interviewer. "I've always liked fairy tales and myths, magical stories, supernatural stories, ghost stories, surrealistic and allegorical stories. I think they are somehow closer to the sense of reality one feels today than the equally stylized 'realistic' story in which a great deal of selectivity and omission has to occur in order to preserve its 'realistic' style." Kubrick's finest efforts are examples of his "surrealism as realism" approach. "2001" is shrouded in technical space jargon that paves the way for the ambigious final sequence in which a giant fetus floats through outer space. Similarly, "A Clockwork Orange" is the often humorous narrative of a futuristic hoodlum's thoughts and actions. "There is a very wide gulf between reality and fiction," Kubrick commented, "and when one is looking at a film the experience is much closer to a dream than anything else. In this daydream, if you like, one can explore ideas and situations which one is not able to do in reality."

Kubrick's concept of film as a dream is exemplified in his trilogy of films set in the future. "Dr. Strangelove" was Kubrick's initial attempt at "realistic surrealism" and it contains some of the finer elements of that particular style, including bizarre people in bizarre, but realistic, situations. Kubrick played on the public's post-cold war paranoia by revealing a world whose fate lies in the hands of madmen: an ex-Nazi whose right hand perpetually rises in salute to the Fuehrer, and American general whose first instinct is always to declare war, and an extremist patriot who rides an earthward atom bomb like a cowboy. With its threats of total annihilation and political chaos, "Dr. Strangelove" is the dark side of Kubrick's dream film-philosophy. He once said that many of the characters in "Dr. Strangelove" are "straight out of a nightmare."

"2001" is the opposite of "Dr. Strangelove." Whereas "Dr. Strangelove" forecasts the destruction of humanity by its own inept use of knowledge, "2001" celebrates the rebirth of man as he forges past the insignificance of what he does know into the greater realm of what is still to be discovered. The film is extremely complex and does not lend itself easily to interpretation after one viewing; co-author Arthur Clarke claimed, "If anyone understands it on the first viewing, we've failed in our intention." Many critics responded unfavorably to the combination of symbolism, scientific data, and abstract conception comprising "2001": John Simon called it "pretentious" and "a shaggy God story"; Andrew Sarris claimed that the movie was "anti-human, anti-science, and anti-progress...." Kubrick, though, stood fast in the wake of negative reviews. Although he insisted that "the nature of the visual experience in '2001' is to give the viewer an instantaneous, visceral reaction," he also implied that repeated viewings would enhance the audience's appreciation when he said, "We don't believe that we should hear a great piece of music only once, or see a great painting once, or even read a great book once." He noted that "film has until recent years been exempted from the category of art," but added that, with the release of "2001," the situation "is finally changing."

"A Clockwork Orange" is widely considered to be Kubrick's finest film. It is a skillful blend of the technical and visual artistry evident in "2001" with the apocalyptic theme of "Dr. Strangelove." But whereas "Dr. Strangelove" is concerned with the self-destructive power of the political machinery, "A Clockwork Orange" is dually concerned with both the destructive power and those that exist beneath it. Alex, the lead character in the film, inhabits a world whose political status is described by Vincent Canby as "a kind of weary socialism." In a world which encourages conformity, Alex establishes his own identity by leading a gang in nightly ventures of rape, mugging, and murder. Harkening back to his dream concept, Kubrick stated that "the film communicates on a subconscious level, and the audience responds to the basic shape of the story on a subconscious level, as it responds to a dream." Earlier he had stated, "What we respond to subconsciously is Alex's guiltless sense of freedom to kill and rape, and to be our savage natural selves, and it is in this glimpse of the true nature of man that the power of the story derives." Though Alex is eventually captured and brainwashed into passivity, the government realizes the folly of displacing one's identity and restores Alex to his normal self. "Alex symbolizes man in his natural state," remarked Kubrick, "the way he would be if society did not impose its 'civilizing' processes upon him." Kubrick makes plausible his suggestion that individuals are more important than the society they inhabit, even when they threaten that society, by telling the story from Alex's standpoint. "Alex is a character who by every logical and rational consideration should be completely unsympathetic," he said, "and possibly even abhorrent to the audience. And yet in the same way that Richard III gradually undermines your disapproval of his evil ways, Alex does the same thing and draws the audience into his own vision of life. This is the phenomenon of the story that produces the most enjoyable and surprising artistic illumination in the minds of an audience."

Kubrick's other films have been ambiguously received by critics. "Lolita" was praised by Arthur Schlesinger as "a brilliant and sinister film," but was panned in some quarters for the liberties it took with Nabokov's novel. Similarly, "Barry Lyndon" was mentioned on many top film lists although more than one critic agreed with Jack Kroll's summation when he called it "an epic of self-indulgence, beautiful but empty."

Oddly enough, Kubrick has reached a plateau of respectability in his field at a time when originality and auteurship inspire particular acclaim. Almost all of Kubrick's films have been adaptations from other sources. After "2001," one must go back to "Killer's Kiss" to find an original screenplay and that film has been largely forgotten. How does Kubrick achieve such success adapting other material? "A great narrative is like a miracle," he related. "It's not something that can be forced. At the same time, I trust that I shall never be tempted to become an alchemist and believe that I can turn lead into gold. I might try to make something of an imperfect story with my efforts as a writer, but I would never attempt a film story that I was not finally in love with."

AVOCATIONAL INTERESTS: Reading, listening to classical music.

BIOGRAPHICAL/CRITICAL SOURCES: Playboy, September, 1968; *New York Times,* December 20, 1971, January 4, 1972; *Time,* December 20, 1971, December 15, 1975; *Saturday Review,* December 25, 1971; Alexander Walker, *Stanley Kubrick Directs,* Harcourt, 1971; *Newsweek,* December 22, 1975; Gene Phillips, *Stanley Kubrick,* Popular Library, 1975, revised edition, 1977.

*　　*　　*

KUHN, Ferdinand 1905-1978

OBITUARY NOTICE—See index for *CA* sketch: Born April 10, 1905, in New York, N.Y.; died October 17, 1978, in Washington, D.C. Journalist and author. Kuhn worked as a foreign correspondent for the *New York Times* and the *Washington Post.* During World War II, he served as an assistant to the secretary of the treasury and then became deputy director of the Office of War Information. In 1953, Kuhn and his wife became free-lance writers on world affairs. They wrote three books about their extensive travels. Obituaries and other sources: *International Who's Who,* Europa, 1978; *Who's Who in America,* 40th edition, Marquis, 1978; *Washington Post,* October 18, 1978.

*　　*　　*

KURZ, Ron 1940-

PERSONAL: Born November 27, 1940, in Baltimore, Md.; son of Gordon L. and Dorothy (Driver) Kurz; married Darlene M. Sweet, January 16, 1965 (divorced, 1975); children: Scott Nelkens. *Education:* Attended high school in Baltimore County, Md. *Politics:* Liberal Independent. *Religion:* None. *Home address:* P.O. Box 164, Antrim, N.H. 03440. *Agent:* Alex Jackinson, 55 West 42nd St., New York, N.Y. 10036.

CAREER: Maryland Department of Corrections, Baltimore, Md., and Jessup, Md., correctional officer, 1963-69; theater manager in Baltimore, Md., 1970-74; free-lance writer, 1975—. *Military service:* U.S. Army, 1958-61; served in Germany; became sergeant. *Member:* Writers Guild of America (East).

WRITINGS: Lethal Gas (novel), M. Evans, 1974; *Black Rococo* (novel), M. Evans, 1976.

WORK IN PROGRESS: Two novels, tentatively entitled *Pont St. Michel* and *Nukus Interruptus.*

SIDELIGHTS: Kurz writes: "I wish I could chuck all this literary falderal, but if I'm away from my typewriter for more than twenty-four hours, my toes tingle and I get woozy in the head. I would like to be a movie director; I am just going about getting there the long way. It's probably a cliche by now, but I find that talking or writing about my writing makes me ill (really!). I just like to get on with it."

*　　*　　*

KUSHNER, Howard Irvin 1943-

PERSONAL: Born July 21, 1943, in Camden, N.J.; son of Samuel and Gertrude (Slotnikoff) Kushner; married Carol Rubin (a teacher), August, 1965; children: Peter Evan. *Education:* Rutgers University, A.B. (cum laude), 1965; Cornell University, M.A., 1968, Ph.D., 1970. *Home:* 4415 Hingston Ave., Montreal, Quebec, Canada H4A 2J8. *Office:* Department of History, Concordia University, 7141 Sherbrooke St. W., Montreal, Quebec, Canada H4B 1R6.

CAREER: State University of New York College at Fredonia, assistant professor, 1970-74, associate professor of history, 1975-76; Cornell University, Ithaca, N.Y., visiting associate professor of history, 1976-77; Concordia University, Montreal, Quebec, associate professor of history, 1977—. Visiting assistant professor at San Francisco State University, 1973-74. *Member:* Canadian Association of American Studies, American Studies Association, American Historical Association, Organization of American Historians, Inter-University Centre for European Studies.

WRITINGS: Conflict on the Northwest Coast: American-Russian Relations in the Pacific Northwest, 1790-1867, Greenwood Press, 1975; (with Anne H. Sherrill) *John Milton Hay: The Union of Poetry and Politics,* Twayne, 1977. Contributor to history and American studies journals.

WORK IN PROGRESS: Myth and Expansion: A Psychoanalytic Approach to American Expansion, 1600-1860.

* * *

KYEMBA, Henry 1939-

PERSONAL: Born December, 1939, in Masese, Uganda; son of Suleman Nabeta (a chief) and Babi Kisajja; married Theresa Mwewulize Bagenda, 1970; children: Henry Nabeta, Susan Muwanse. *Education:* Received degree from Makerere University College, 1962. *Religion:* Anglican.

CAREER: Government of Uganda, Kampala, principal private secretary to President Milton Obote, 1963-71, and Idi Amin, 1971-72, minister of culture, 1972-74, minister of health, 1974-77; World Health Assembly, London, England, vice-president, 1977—. Chairman of African Health Ministers, 1976-77. Has appeared on the "Today Show," "Sixty Minutes," and "World in Action" (Great Britain). *Awards, honors:* Awarded Order of St. Sylvester by Pope Paul VI, 1969.

WRITINGS: (With John Man) *A State of Blood: The Inside Story of Idi Amin,* Grosset, 1977.

WORK IN PROGRESS: Black on Black, "working title of a book on world failure to deal with Uganda's Amin, the Organization of African Unity's skeleton in the cupboard and the shame of double standard."

SIDELIGHTS: Kyemba told *CA:* "As a senior civil servant in Amin's Uganda, I have seen Africa's image brought close to ruin by the failure of the African and black leaders to come to terms with the reality of the Amin murders. Attempts have been made to justify the application of double standards in dealing with Amin, Vorster and Smith, and an African, black voice is highly desirable at this critical time of the genocide going on in Uganda."

Kyemba fled from Uganda in May, 1977, when he learned that he was marked for elimination by the Amin regime, and his expose of the atrocities in Uganda was published soon afterward in England and the United States. *New York Times* reporter John Darnton observed: "*A State of Blood* . . . stands above the pulp thrillers and satirical concoctions; it is the most important book on Amin since David Martin's *General Amin.* . . . It is a self-serving account but under the circumstances probably the most reliable we are like to have of how Amin thinks, acts, and squirms to stay in power."

Kyemba's close relationship with Amin uniquely qualified him to produce such an account as *A State of Blood.* He himself admitted, "I have worked intimately with the man who gradually revealed himself to be Africa's most ruthless killer." Questioning Kyemba's continued service to Amin, even after learning of the atrocities, Darnton wrote: "He is at pains to explain it, and his rationalizations thrad the narrative from start to finish. . . . Kyemba's capacity to close his eyes to the horrors inflicted upon others around him . . . undercuts a moral tone he strives vainly to impress upon the reader and makes his plea for international sanctions against Uganda something of a hollow call." But Crawford Young explained the plight of Ugandan officials more sympathetically, declaring: "For many, flight is simply not a feasible alternative: doctors and academicians have internationally transferable credentials, but administrators are unlikely easily to find employment in neighboring countries, much less in Europe. Relatives of exiles are potential victims of regime vengeance; those tempted by conspiracy must reckon with likely retaliation visited upon their entire community in the event of failure."

Kyemba defended himself during an interview with Genevieve Stuttaford: "If I'm told that a minister is part of the regime of terror, I answer back that Amin has also killed many of his ministers. People put too much weight on association with the regime. I would not have left unless I had to. Uganda is my home. But I had to ensure I was not killed at the hands of Amin."

BIOGRAPHICAL/CRITICAL SOURCES: Book World, September 18, 1977; *Publishers Weekly,* October 3, 1977; *New York Times Book Review,* November 6, 1977.

L

LACEY, Louise 1940-

PERSONAL: Born May 17, 1940, in San Antonio, Tex.; daughter of Lewis Lawrence (a radio commentator) and Alice (a registered nurse; maiden name, Freiermuth) Lacey. *Education:* Attended San Francisco State University, 1957-66. *Politics:* "Libertarian." *Residence:* Kensington, Calif. *Agent:* Candida Donadio & Associates, Inc., 111 West 57th St., New York, N.Y. 10019. *Office: Woman's Choice,* P.O. Box 489, Berkeley, Calif. 94701.

CAREER: Executive secretary for a chain of retail stores in San Francisco, Calif., 1961-63; Novel Books and Specialty Books, Chicago, Ill., editor and staff writer, 1963-65; *Ramparts,* San Francisco, Calif., research coordinator, 1966-67; buyer for bookstores in Berkeley and San Francisco, Calif., 1967-69; free-lance writer, 1969—; *Woman's Choice* (monthly letter), Berkeley, editor and publisher, 1978—. Member of board of directors of Marin Alternative Community Training.

WRITINGS: Lunaception (nonfiction), Coward, 1975; *Drug Use in San Jose,* Project DARE, 1978. Contributor to magazines and journals.

WORK IN PROGRESS: Editing a book about the beliefs and development of nine spiritually-evolved women; studying Mayan history and religion.

SIDELIGHTS: Louise Lacey writes: "*Woman's Choice* is the ultimate realization of a twenty-plus year-old dream whereby people would pay me to write to them. My curiosities are so omnivorous that I could never write a book about each subject which fascinates me. *Woman's Choice* is an intimate monthly letter by subscription. Thus I have a vehicle with which to write about things as diverse as dependency, the rhythms of life, and traveling alone. My purpose is to give a mental, emotional, and spiritual goosing to the reader on a new subject each month. No dogmas, just intriguing ideas and a fresh perspective in a personal but non-sentimental style."

*   *   *

LADD, John 1917-

PERSONAL: Born June 24, 1917, in Middletown, Conn.; son of William P. and Ailsie (Taylor) Ladd; married Hylda Higginson, January, 1943 (divorced, 1959); married Rosalind Ekman, July 8, 1963; children: (first marriage) Mary Madeleine; (second marriage) Sarah, Deborah. *Education:* Harvard University, A.B. (magna cum laude), 1937, A.M., 1941, Ph.D., 1948; University of Virginia, M.A., 1941; Brown University, M.A., 1957. *Home:* 72 Taber Ave., Providence, R.I. 02906. *Office:* Department of Philosophy, Brown University, Providence, R.I. 02906.

CAREER: University of Goettingen, Goettingen, Germany, guest lecturer, 1948-49; Harvard University, Cambridge, Mass., instructor in philosophy, 1949-50; Brown University, Providence, R.I., staff member, 1950-62, professor of philosophy, 1962—. Visiting professor at Harvard University, spring, 1961; visiting lecturer at Smith College, 1961-62. *Military service:* U.S. Naval Reserve, active duty, 1942-46; became lieutenant. *Member:* American Society for Political and Legal Philosophy (president, 1976-78), American Philosophical Association (member of executive committee, 1962-64; chairman of committee on philosophy and medicine, 1975—). *Awards, honors:* Rockefeller Foundation fellow, 1948-49; Guggenheim fellow, 1958-59.

WRITINGS: The Structure of a Moral Code, Harvard University Press, 1957; (translator) Immanuel Kant, *Metaphysical Elements of Justice,* Bobbs-Merrill, 1965; (editor and author of introduction) *Ethical Relativism,* Wadsworth, 1973; (editor) *Ethical Issues Relating to Life and Death,* Oxford University Press, 1979; (with wife, Rosalind Ekman and Robert P. Davis) *Philosophy of Medicine,* Prentice-Hall, 1979. Contributor to scholarly journals.

*   *   *

LAERTES, Joseph
See SALTZMAN, Joseph

*   *   *

LA FARGE, Oliver (Hazard Perry) 1901-1963

PERSONAL: Born December 19, 1901, in New York, N.Y.; son of Christopher Grant (an architect and lecturer) and Florence Bayard (a worker in nursing training schools; maiden name Lockwood) La Farge; married Wanden E. Mathews, September 28, 1929 (divorced, 1937); married Consuelo O. C. de Baca (a literary agent), October 14, 1939; children: (first marriage) Povy (daughter), Oliver Albee; (second marriage) John Pendaries. *Education:* Harvard University, B.A., 1924, M.A., 1929. *Religion:* Roman Catholic. *Residence:* Santa Fe, N.M.

CAREER: Tulane University, New Orleans, La., assistant

professor of ethnology, 1926-28; Columbia University, New York, N.Y., research fellow in anthropology, 1931-33; teacher of the technique of writing, 1936-41; director of Eastern Association in Indian Affairs, 1930-32, and of Intertribal Exhibitions of Indian Arts, 1931; field representative for United States Indian Service, 1936; editorial adviser, Alliance Book Corp., 1940-41; appointed to ten-man advisory committee to the Government on Indian Affairs, 1949; member of U.S. Department of Interior's Committee on Indian Arts and Crafts; official adviser to the Hopi Indians. Trustee for W.E.B. DuBois prize for Negro Literature, 1932-34; member of advisory board of the Laboratory of Anthropology, Santa Fe, N.M., 1935-41, 1946-63; member of committee of awards of Opportunity Fellowships of John Hay Whitney Foundation. Participant in archaelogy exhibitions to Arizona, Mexico, and Guatemala. *Military Service:* Served in U.S. Army Air Forces, 1942-45; became lieutenant colonel; received Legion of Merit award.

MEMBER: National Association on Indian Affairs (president, 1933-37), Association on American Indian Affairs (president, 1937-42, 1946-63), American Association for the Advancement of Science (fellow), American Anthropological Association, National Insitutute of Arts and Letters, P.E.N., Authors' League (New York City), Century Club, Coffee House Club. *Awards, honors:* Hemenway fellow, 1924-26; Pulitzer Prize for fiction, 1929, for *Laughing Boy;* O. Henry Memorial Prize, 1931, for *Haunted Ground;* M.A., 1932, from Brown University; Guggenheim fellowship for writing, 1941.

WRITINGS: Laughing Boy (novel), Houghton, 1929, reprinted, Barrie & Jenkins, 1972; (with Douglas Byers) *The Year Bearer's People,* Tulane University Press, 1931; *Sparks Fly Upward* (novel), Houghton, 1931, reprinted, Popular Library, 1959; *Long Pennant* (novel), Houghton, 1933; *All the Young Men* (short stories; includes *Haunted Ground*), Houghton, 1935, reprinted, AMS Press, 1976; *The Enemy Gods* (novel), Houghton, 1937, reprinted, University of New Mexico Press, 1975; *As Long as the Grass Shall Grow* (nonfiction), Longmans, Green, 1940; (editor) *The Changing Indian,* University of Oklahoma Press, 1942; *The Copper Pot* (novel), Houghton, 1942; *Raw Material* (autobiography), Houghton, 1945; *Santa Eulalia: The Religion of a Cuchumatan Indian Town,* University of Chicago Press, 1947; *The Eagle in the Nest,* Houghton, 1949, reprinted, Arno, 1972.

Cochise of Arizona: The Pipe of Peace Is Broken (juvenile), illustrations by L. F. Bjorklund, Aladdin Books, 1953; *The Mother Ditch* (juvenile) illustrations by Karl Larsson, Houghton, 1954; *Behind the Mountains,* Houghton, 1956; *A Pictorial History of the American Indian,* Crown, 1956, revised edition, 1974, special edition for young readers published as *The American Indian,* Golden Press, 1960; *A Pause in the Desert* (short stories), Houghton, 1957; (with Arthur N. Morgan) *Santa Fe: The Autobiography of a Southwestern Town,* University of Oklahoma Press, 1959; *The Door in the Wall* (short stories), Houghton, 1965; Winfield Townley Scott, editor, *The Man with the Calabash Pipe: Some Observations* (selections from the author's weekly newspaper column from 1950-63), Houghton, 1966.

Author of a weekly newspaper column in the *Santa Fe New Mexican,* 1950-63; contributor of articles and book reviews to many periodicals, including the *New York Times Book Review.*

SIDELIGHTS: Former Secretary of the Interior Stewart L. Udall once described Oliver La Farge as knowing "more about the American Indian than any non-Indian."

A descendent of Benjamin Franklin and Commodore Oliver Hazard Perry, and a grandson of John La Farge, the famous painter and artist in stained glass, and brother of poet and novelist Christopher La Farge, Oliver La Farge maintained an interest in the American Indian that began during his youth when he nicknamed himself "Indian Man." During his life, La Farge championed numerous Indian causes. When Congress passed an $88 million Navajo-Hopi rehabilitation bill in 1949, La Farge urged President Truman to veto it on the premise that two of the bill's amendments destroyed Indian rights and jeopardized their land. Through La Farge's insistence the bill was reworked, and when passed by Congress in 1950, the new legislation supported a ten-year expenditure of $88 million to alleviate poverty, illiteracy, and high incidence of disease among the Navajo and Hopi Indian populations in the United States.

La Farge's first literary effort, the Pulitzer Prize winning *Laughing Boy,* was regarded by a critic in *Bookman* as "an almost perfect specimen of the sustained and tempered, the lyrical, romantic idyll." He continued: "It moves among conceptions of life so foreign to those of our naturalistic fiction that it would seem to belong to a different kind of writing. It is filled with love, with nature; it is also filled with morals and religion. The love and nature are ours, as they are anybody's; the morals and religion are those of the Indian. We are thus transported into a strange, foreign, and rather pleasant civilization. . . ." "Oliver La Farge is a welcome addition to the ranks of our younger fictionists," wrote a *New York Post* reviewer, adding: "His first novel reveals an ability considerably out of the ordinary. It reveals a style devoid of stylism, a gift of simple, straightforward statement which is at the same time lyrical and colorful, and a quite adequate inventive power. . . ." A critic for the *New York Times* also observed: "Mr. La Farge has infused the romance of *Laughing Boy* with a lucid beauty, with a vital, artistic imagination and clear, almost hypnotic style." A film version of the book was produced in 1934 by Metro-Goldwyn-Mayer.

BIOGRAPHICAL/CRITICAL SOURCES: New York Post, September 7, 1929; *New York Times,* November 24, 1929; *Bookman,* January, 1930; Oliver La Farge, *Raw Material,* Houghton, 1945; Everett A. Gillis, *Oliver La Farge,* Steck-Vaughn, 1967; D'Arcy McNickle, *Indian Man: A Life of Oliver La Farge,* Indiana University Press, 1971; Thomas M. Pearce, *Oliver La Farge,* Twayne, 1972.

Obituaries: *New York Times,* August 3, 1963; *Time,* August 9, 1963; *Newsweek,* August 12, 1963; *Publishers Weekly,* August 12, 1963; *Americana Annual,* 1964; *American Antiquity,* January, 1966.*

(Died August 2, 1963)

*   *   *

LAMB, William
See JAMESON, (Margaret) Storm

*   *   *

LAMB, William Kaye   1904-

PERSONAL: Born May 11, 1904, in New Westminster, British Columbia, Canada; son of Alexander and Barbara (McDougall) Lamb; married Wessie M. Tipping, May 15, 1939; children: Barbara Elizabeth. *Education:* University of British Columbia, B.A., 1927, M.A., 1930; graduate study at University of Paris, 1928-29, 1930-32; University of London, Ph.D., 1933. *Home:* 2055 Pendrell St., Vancouver, British Columbia, Canada V6G 1T9.

CAREER: Provincial Library and Archives, Victoria, British Columbia, librarian and archivist, 1934-40; University of British Columbia, Vancouver, librarian, 1940-48; Public Archives of Canada, Ottawa, dominion archivist, 1948-69; writer, 1969—. National librarian for National Library of Canada, 1953-68.

MEMBER: Royal Society of Canada (fellow; past president), Canadian Library Association (past president), Canadian Historical Association (past president), Champlain Society (past president), Society of American Archivists (past president), American Antiquarian Society, Society of Archivists (London; past president), Massachusetts Historical Society, Rideau Club. *Awards, honors:* LL. D. from University of British Columbia, 1948, University of Manitoba, 1953, University of Toronto, 1954, University of Saskatchewan, 1956, Assumption University, 1958, University of Victoria, 1964, McMaster University, 1966, University of New Brunswick, 1967, and York University, 1968; D.S.Litt. from Victoria University, 1961; Tyrrell Medal from Royal Society of Canada, 1965; officer of Order of Canada, 1969.

WRITINGS: (Author of introduction) *The Letters of John McLoughlin, 1825-1846,* three volumes, Champlain Society, 1941-44; (author of introduction and notes) *Sixteen Years in the Indian Country: The Journal of Daniel Williams Harmon, 1800-1815,* Macmillan (Canada), 1957; (author of introduction and notes) *The Letters and Journals of Simon Fraser, 1806-1808,* Macmillan (Canada), 1960; *The Hero of Upper Canada* (about Sir Isaac Brock), Rous & Mann, 1962; (author of introduction and notes) *The Journal of Gabriel Franchere,* Champlain Society, 1969; (author of introduction and notes) *The Journals and Letters of Sir Alexander Mackenzie,* Cambridge Press (London, England), 1970; *Canada's Five Centuries,* McGraw (Canada), 1971; (with Norman R. Hacking) *The Princess Story: A Century and a Half of West Coast Shipping,* Mitchell Press, 1974; *History of the Canadian Pacific Railway,* Macmillan, 1976.

Contributor to history, marine, and library journals. Editor of *British Columbia Historical Quarterly,* 1937-46.

WORK IN PROGRESS: Editing *Voyage of Discovery to the North Pacific Ocean,* three volumes, by George Vancouver for Hakluyt Society.

AVOCATIONAL INTERESTS: The history of western Canada, the fur trade, transportation, marine history, especially of the West Coast and the Pacific, and exploration of the West Coast.

*   *   *

LANCASTER, Evelyn
See SIZEMORE, Chris(tine) Costner

*   *   *

LANCE, LaBelle D(avid)   1931-

PERSONAL: Born May 8, 1931, in Dalton, Georgia; daughter of Claude Barker (a banker) and Ruth (McConnell) David; married Thomas Bertram Lance (a banker), September 9, 1950; children: Thomas Bertram, Jr., David J., Stuart Austin, Claude Beverly. *Education:* Attended Agnes Scott College, 1948-49, and University of Georgia, 1950-51. *Politics:* Democrat. *Religion:* Methodist. *Residence:* Calhoun, Ga.; and Atlanta, Ga. *Office:* P.O. Box 637, Calhoun, Ga. 30701.

CAREER: Speaker at numerous local and national meetings; co-chairman, with husband, Bert Lance, of Friendship Force.

WRITINGS: (With Gary Sledge) *This Too Shall Pass* (autobiography), Christian Herald Books, 1978.

SIDELIGHTS: In *This Too Shall Pass,* LaBelle Lance recounts a host of family problems, ranging from her late father's alcoholism to the resignation of her husband, Bert Lance, from President Jimmy Carter's cabinet. What has sustained her throughout all her difficulties, Mrs. Lance avers, is her religious faith. She believes that even her husband's decision to leave Washington was a part of ''God's plan.'' When an interviewer for the *New York Times* asked her if she still thinks everything in life happens for the best, she reaffirmed her piety: ''Yes . . . I believe strongly in the scriptures, which say that all things work for good for those who wait upon the Lord.''

While conceding that Mrs. Lance is ''a very devout Christian,'' Larry L. King finds her book disappointing because it sheds no light on Bert Lance's complicated financial affairs. Among other things, he says that *This Too Shall Pass* ignores or does not satisfactorily explain how Bert Lance accrued his wealth, why he was able to use questionable banking practices at his bank in Calhoun, Ga., or how much money he lent to Jimmy Carter during his presidential campaign. In his final assessment of the book, King concludes: ''Almost every page of this volume, as thin in appearance as it is in substance, offers sugar-candy coating of the spiritual or the 'inspirational'. . . . She [Mrs. Lance] alludes to prayer so often it makes the reader dizzy. One who hungers for news of this world, and not the next, will find her book full of cliches and empty of merit.''

BIOGRAPHICAL/CRITICAL SOURCES: LaBelle D. Lance and Gary Sledge, *This Too Shall Pass,* Christian Herald Books, 1978; *New York Times,* April 1, 1978; *New York Times Book Review,* April 30, 1978.

*   *   *

LANCOUR, Gene
See FISHER, Gene L(ouis)

*   *   *

LAND, Barbara (Neblett)   1923-

PERSONAL: Born July 11, 1923, in Hopkinsville, Ky.; daughter of Robert Trawick and Jacqueline (Barbour) Neblett; married Myrick Ebben Land (a writer and teacher), February 26, 1949; children: Robert Arthur, Jacquelyn Myrick (Mrs. Pierre LaRamee). *Education:* University of Miami, B.A., 1944; Columbia University, M.S., 1946, further study, 1959. *Politics:* Democrat. *Religion:* Episcopalian. *Home:* 100 North Arlington Ave., Reno, Nev. 89501. *Agent:* Sterling Lord Agency, 660 Madison Ave., New York, N.Y. 10021.

CAREER: Miami Herald, Miami, Fla., reporter, 1940-47; *Life* magazine, New York City, reporter, 1948-49; *New York Times,* New York City, reporter, 1955-57; Columbia University, Graduate School of Journalism, 1962-65, began as lecturer, became instructor in journalism; Book-of-the-Month Club, New York City, reader and editor, 1969-72; University of Queensland, Brisbane, Australia, tutor in journalism, 1973-75; full-time writer, 1975—. Conducted a series of interviews with scientists for Columbia University Oral History collection, 1960-65. Gave broadcasts for Australian Broadcasting Corp., Armed Forces Network (Germany), and Municipal Broadcasting. *Member:* Authors Guild. *Awards, honors:* Pulitzer travel scholarship, 1946; Sloan-Rockefeller fellowship for advanced science writing program, 1959.

WRITINGS—Juvenile: (With husband, Myrick Land) *Jungle Oil*, Coward, 1957; (with M. Land) *The Changing South*, Coward, 1958; (with M. Land) *The Quest of Isaac Newton*, Doubleday, 1960; *The Quest of Johannes Kepler*, Doubleday, 1963; (with M. Land) *Lee: A Portrait of Lee Harvey Oswald*, Coward, 1967; *The Telescope Makers*, Crowell, 1968; *Evolution of a Scientist*, Crowell, 1973.

WORK IN PROGRESS: Women of the Antarctic, publication expected in 1979.

SIDELIGHTS: Land writes: "My father always told me, when I was a child, 'You can do anything you really want to do. Just make up your mind and *do* it.'

"Not quite believing it could be that easy for a girl, I used to test him with questions about unlikely activities.

'Could I be a doctor?'
'Of course.'
'A fireman?'
'If you want to.'
'Could I go to the moon?'
'If anybody can.'
'Well, how about being . . . a football player?'

"I never really wanted to be a football player, but I did want to go to the South Pole with Admiral Richard E. Byrd. He had taken a Boy Scout with him in 1928. By 1933, when I was old enough to read about Byrd's adventures in the Antarctic, it seemed to me only fair that a girl should be included next time around. It didn't work out that way, but nearly thirty years later I interviewed Byrd's Boy Scout for *Science World* magazine. He had grown up to be Dr. Paul Siple, leader of the team of scientists who manned the first permanent research station at the very bottom of the world. As he described to me the all-male world of Antarctic science, I felt again my childhood fascination with ice and snow—anything polar. Still, it seemed unlikely that I—or any other woman of my generation—would be allowed to work at the South Pole. I was wrong. All over the world there were women, in various fields of science, determined to show that they could survive the hostile Antarctic climate and make valuable contributions. Some of these women are working in Antarctica right now—but only since 1969. I am currently talking with them and writing about their experiences. I remember my father's encouraging words, now repeated by my husband and children, and am still trying to visit Antarctica myself."

* * *

LANDEIRA, Ricardo L(opez) 1917-

PERSONAL: Born July 20, 1917, in El Ferrol, Spain; son of Ricardo Lopez (a naval engineer) and Josefa Landeira (Fernandez) Alvarino; married Harmony Filgueira, December 10, 1941; children: Richard Lopez, Carmen, Mary Jo. *Education:* Ferrol Instituto-Nacional, Bachillerato Universitario, 1935; Santiago Escuela Normal, Maestro, 1941; University of Colorado, Ph.D., 1965. *Home:* 3315 South La Corta Dr., Tempe, Ariz. 85282.

CAREER: Writer.

WRITINGS: La saudade en el renacimiento de la literatura gallega, Galaxia, 1970; (editor with Ronert J. Bininger) *El conde Don Sancho Nino*, Galaxia, 1970; (with H. A. Van-Scoy) *Mosaico hispanico*, Van Nostrand, 1971. Contributor to Spanish and American newspapers.

LANDRUM, Phil 1939-

PERSONAL: Born January 28, 1939, in Lost Creek, Ky.; son of Clyde Kermit (a clergyman) and Ruby Ansena (a nurse; maiden name, Larson) Landrum; married Lois Jane Nagel (a teacher); children: Anita Kay, Valerie Ann. *Education:* Grace College, Winona Lake, Ind., A.B., 1960; graduate study at Indiana University, 1960-61; Moody Bible Institute, diploma, 1965; Northwestern University, M.S.J., 1967. *Religion:* Grace Brethren. *Home and office:* 1308 Santa Rosa, Wheaton, Ill. 60187.

CAREER: Warsaw Times-Union, Warsaw, Ind., reporter, 1961-62; *Moody Monthly*, Chicago, Ill., editorial assistant, 1962-66, news editor, 1962-66, youth editor, 1963-66; Medill News Service, Washington, D.C., Washington correspondent, 1967; Christian Businessmen's Committee International, Glen Ellyn, Ill., director of publications, 1967-71; free-lance writer, 1971—. Reporter for WRSW-Radio, 1961-62. Director of literature, Christian Businessmen's Committee of U.S.A., 1976—. Member of board of directors of Wheaton Christian Grammar School, 1976-79.

MEMBER: Evangelical Press Association, Association of American Universities (central region), National Association of Christian Schools (member of board of directors, 1970-74), National Fellowship of Grace Brethren Men (member of board of directors, 1969-71), Sigma Delta Chi. *Awards, honors:* More than twenty-five awards from Evangelical Press Association since 1963, including editor-of-the-year award, 1970 and 1978.

WRITINGS: (With Bob Stultz) *White Black Man*, Creation House, 1972; (with Henry Brandt) *I Want to Enjoy My Children*, Zondervan, 1975; (with Margaret Laird) *They Called Me Mama*, Moody, 1975; (with Brandt) *I Want My Marriage to Be Better*, Zondervan, 1976; (with Brandt) *I Want Happiness—Now*, Zondervan, 1978; *God's School System*, Tyndale House, in press. Editor of *CBMC Contact*, 1967-71, 1976—, and of *Christian Teacher*, 1971-75.

WORK IN PROGRESS: A book on culture concerning the problem of television and rock and roll, for Good News Publishers.

SIDELIGHTS: Landrum told *CA:* "I work in the area of Christian journalism, which I enjoy, because in that field you can do more than react to what is happening. You can actually deal with the problems of the world today by bringing in Biblically-based solutions to these questions."

* * *

LANHAM, Charles Trueman 1902-1978

OBITUARY NOTICE: Born in 1902, in Washington, D.C.; died July 20, 1978, in Chevy Chase, Md. Major general, military scholar, poet, and author. In 1944, during World War II, Lanham and his troops were among the first to break out from Normandy, France, enter Paris, and attack the Siegfried line in Germany. He and his regiment also formed a strong line of defense in the Battle of the Bulge. The unit was awarded two citations as a result of its efforts. For his heroic actions, Lanham received seventeen decorations and was promoted from colonel to general. During the war, Lanham became friends with writer Ernest Hemingway with whom he corresponded regularly for the next seventeen years. The character of Colonel Cantwell of Hemingway's *Across the River and Into the Trees* is said to be based on Lanham. After World War II, Lanham became chief of troop information and education under Army chief of staff, General George C. Marshall. Later, Lanham was appointed first director of publications for Supreme Headquarters Allied Powers in Europe (SHAPE) by General Dwight D. Eisenhower. After his retirement from the Army, Lanham became vice-president of government relations, then consultant, for Xerox Corp. Lanham also taught military history at Fort Benning, Ga., and was associate editor of *Infantry Journal*. He wrote and directed the well-known "Fighting Men" series and other training films. Lanham also wrote poetry and books on military subjects, and co-authored *Ernest Hemingway: A Life Story* with Carlos Baker. Obituaries and other sources: *New York Times*, July 22, 1978; *Washington Post*, July 22, 1978.

* * *

LANSBURY, Angela 1946-

PERSONAL: Born March 16, 1946, in London, England; daughter of Albert (an opthalmic optician) and Netta (Geduld) Lansbury; married Trevor Sharot (a statistician and company director), April 11, 1976. *Education:* University of London, B.A. (honors), 1967. *Politics:* "No prejudices." *Religion:* "Jewish Humanist Atheist." *Home:* Colman Court, Flat 23, Rosedale Close, Gordon Ave., Stanmore, Middlesex HA7 3QF, England. *Agent:* Janet Freer, 118 Tottenham Court Rd., London W1P 9HL, England.

CAREER: Writer, 1975—. Public lecturer. *Member:* National Union of Journalists, Women in Media, Society of Women's Writers and Journalists. *Awards, honors:* Grant from United Nations Student Association, 1968, for travel in Japan.

WRITINGS: Enquire Within Upon Travel and Holidays, Barrie & Jenkins, 1976; *See Britain at Work*, Two Continents Publishing, 1977, revised edition, 1979; *The A to Z of Shopping by Post*, Exley Publications, revised edition, 1979. Contributor to children's encyclopedias and women's magazines, including *What Holiday?* Sub-editor of *Woman*, of *Woman's Realm*, 1974, and of the European edition of *How It Works*, 1978.

WORK IN PROGRESS: A novel based on the biblical story of Samson and Delilah; a book of biographies of children's authors; a consumer handbook; a book of British recipes.

SIDELIGHTS: Angela Lansbury comments: "I have always wanted to be a writer. Authors fascinate me. I started my career as personal assistant to the late Eric Webster, author of the humorous Penguin book, *How to Win the Business Battle*. When he died I became an advertising copywriter at the firm where he worked. Since then I've had various jobs in magazine and book publishing, on the staff or as a free-lancer, and have broadcast on radio and television about my travels and books.

"I like to present practical information and fascinating facts in a style which anyone can read. I don't believe people who say that they can't explain skills, techniques, and theories or describe their experiences. These people must be lazy, dishonest, or simply inarticulate. If somebody can explain the theory of relativity in an encyclopedia so that children can follow it, then surely a person who makes the effort can make anything easy-to-understand and interesting.

"In my second book, *See Britain at Work*, I combined two of my great interests: travel and shopping. I gave information about factories, glassworks, potteries, and craftshops where you could see goods being made and buy seconds, and I described the methods used in manufacturing and gave details of the careers and philosophies of the company directors and craftsmen. This led to my consumer books, and tied in with my interest in explaining processes so that I and my readers can make more sense of the world."

Lansbury added: "After I left the university I felt intellectually starved. I founded and organized the Graduates' Music and Literature Society and later a postgraduate discussion group. I have vague plans for starting a society for out-of-town authors. American authors visiting London are welcome to call me."

AVOCATIONAL INTERESTS: Travel (United States, Soviet Union, Tunisia, Morocco, Europe, Japan, India, Israel), exotic foods, dining out.

* * *

LANSKY, Vicki 1942-

PERSONAL: Born January 6, 1942, in Louisville, Ky.; daughter of Arthur and Mary Rogosin; married Bruce Lansky (a publisher and literary agent), 1967; children: Douglas, Dana. *Education:* Connecticut College, B.A., 1963. *Home and office:* 16648 Meadowbrook Lane, Wayzata, Minn. 55391. *Agent:* Bruce Lansky, Lansky & Associates, 16648 Meadowbrook Lane, Wayzata, Minn. 55391.

CAREER: Lord & Taylor, New York, N.Y., sportswear buyer, 1965-69; Childbirth Education Association, Minneapolis, Minn., teaching assistant, 1971-74; Meadowbrook Press, Wayzata, Minn., founder, treasurer, and executive vice president in charge of operations, 1975—; writer.

WRITINGS: (With others) *Feed Me! I'm Yours*, Meadowbrook Press, 1975; *The Taming of the C.A.N.D.Y. (Continuously Advertised Nutritionally Deficient Yummies) Monster*, Meadowbrook Press, 1978.

WORK IN PROGRESS: Working on starting a parenting newsletter.

SIDELIGHTS: What do you do when you have important ideas to communicate to the American public, but publishers show no interest in your book? Vicki Lansky faced this dilemma in 1974 when she and several other mothers from a local Childbirth Education Association chapter wrote a baby food cookbook for new mothers. Undaunted, Lansky and her husband turned their back porch into their own publishing company and began producing *Feed Me! I'm Yours* for commerical distribution. Their creative promotional efforts and appearances on television talk shows made *Feed Me! I'm Yours* America's best selling baby food and toddler cookbook.

As her children grew older, Lansky found the struggle to maintain good nutritional habits intensifying. Saturday morning television commercials for junk food permeated her children's minds along with their fare of cartoons, and she perceived the need to counter this offensive with tasty alternative recipes for young children. In *The Taming of the C.A.N.D.Y. Monster* she sought to provide parents with practical ideas to improve their children's eating habits. The book rose quickly to the number one spot on the *New York Times* Trade Paperback Bestseller list, and Meadowbrook Press is struggling to meet the demand for it.

When an interviewer for *Us* magazine asked Lansky how she had broken her own children of the sugar habit, she replied: "I don't know if I have, but if I have cured them, it's because they didn't have any choice; I don't keep any sugar around the house. That makes it easier to say no to the kids without fear of repercussions. They're not going to move out. I told them: 'I don't want you to have it because I want you to grow up to be strong and healthy, and all this sugar is not going to help you. I'm not doing this to punish you, I'm doing it because I love you.' I think that kids are willing to accept that.'' Her idea of a good diet involves ''a greater emphasis on vegetables and fruits, . . . a switch from meats into poultry and fish. . . . less emphasis on the simple carbohydrates, the sugars and flours, and more on the complex carbohydrates, the whole grains and rices,'' but she admitted: ''It's going to be a long time before Americans can achieve this diet. I'm not into supernutrition or supervitamins, just eating better with what we've got.''

AVOCATIONAL INTERESTS: Tending plants and children.

BIOGRAPHICAL/CRITICAL SOURCES: New York Times Book Review, April 2, 1978; *Us* magazine, June 27, 1978.

*   *   *

LAPP, Ralph Eugene   1917-

PERSONAL: Born August 24, 1917, in Buffalo, N.Y.; son of Henry R. and Lilly E. (Grammel) Lapp; married Jeannette F. DeRome (a secretary-treasurer), September 6, 1956; children: Christopher Warren, Nicholas DeRome. *Education:* University of Chicago, B.S., 1940, Ph.D., 1945. *Home:* 7215 Park Terrace Dr., Alexandria, Va. 22310. *Office:* 1028 Connecticut Ave., Washington, D.C. 20036.

CAREER: Manhattan Project, Chicago, Ill., associate physicist and assistant laboratory director at Metallurgy Laboratory, 1943-45; Argonne National Laboratory, Chicago, assistant director, 1945-46; U.S. War Department, Washington, D.C., scientific adviser to general staff, 1946-47; Research and Development Board, Washington, D.C., executive director for atomic energy, 1947-48; Office of Naval Research, Washington, D.C., head of nuclear physics branch, 1949; Nuclear Science Service, Washington, D.C., consulting physicist, 1950—. Senior member and partner of Quadri-Science, Inc. (in energy management systems); president of Lapp, Inc. Member of U.S. Senate Public Works Committee; scientific adviser to the Pentagon; consulting scientist for Bikini bomb tests, 1946; consultant to U.S. Government General Accounting Office.

MEMBER: American Association for the Advancement of Science, American Institute of Physics, American Geophysical Union, Phi Beta Kappa, Sigma Xi. *Awards, honors:* Award from Atomic Industrial Forum, 1972; award from American Physical Society Forum, 1974, for promoting public understanding of the relation of physics to society.

WRITINGS: (With H. L. Andrews) *Nuclear Radiation Physics,* Prentice-Hall, 1948, new edition, 1973; *Must We Hide?,* Addison-Wesley, 1949; *The New Force,* Harper, 1953; *Atoms and People,* Harper, 1956; (with Jack Schubert) *Radiation: What It Is and How It Affects You,* Viking, 1957; *The Voyage of the Lucky Dragon,* Harper, 1958.

Roads to Discovery, Harper, 1960; *Man and Space: The Next Decade,* Harper, 1961; *Kill and Overkill,* Basic Books, 1962; *Matter,* Time-Life, 1963; *The New Priesthood,* Harper, 1965; *The Weapons Culture,* Norton, 1968; *Arms Beyond Doubt: The Tyranny of Weapons Technology,* Cowles Book Co., 1970; *The Logarithmic Century,* Prentice-Hall, 1973; *The Nuclear Controversy,* Fact Systems, 1974; *Nader's Nuclear Issues,* Fact Systems, 1975; *America's Energy,* Reddy Communications, 1976; *Radioactive Waste: Society's Problem Child,* Reddy Communications, 1977. Contributor to scientific and popular journals and newspapers, including *Fortune, New Republic, Harper's, Collier's,* and *Saturday Evening Post.* Guest editor of *Bulletin of Atomic Scientists.*

WORK IN PROGRESS: The Radiation Controversy, for Reddy Communications.

SIDELIGHTS: Lapp has been associated with nuclear energy development, and its problems, since World War II. His views, however, do not coincide with some other scientists in the field. His writings, based on knowledge and personal experience, consistently point out the dangers of radiation, of uncontrolled arms proliferation, and other negative aspects of what has grown into a vastly profitable operation, in contrast to the publicized views of military, industrial, and political leaders.

*   *   *

La REYNIERE
See COURTINE, Robert

*   *   *

LARNER, John (Patrick)   1930-

PERSONAL: Born March 24, 1930, in London, England; son of William John (a park keeper) and Gladys (Painter) Larner; married Christina Ross (a sociologist), March 4, 1960; children: Gavin, Patrick. *Education:* New College, Oxford, B.A., 1954, M.A., 1957; attended British School at Rome, 1954-57. *Home:* 24 Hamilton Dr., Glasgow G12 8DR, Scotland. *Office:* Department of History, University of Glasgow, Glasgow, Scotland.

CAREER: Teacher at Westbourne Primary School in London, England, 1950-51; University of Glasgow, Glasgow, Scotland, lecturer, 1957-66, senior lecturer, 1966-71, reader, 1971-78, professor of history, 1978—. *Military service:* British Army, 1948-50. *Awards, honors:* Rome medieval scholar at British School at Rome, 1954-57.

WRITINGS: The Lords of Romagna, Macmillan (England), 1965; *Culture and Society in Italy,* Batsford, 1971; *Commune and Signoria, 1216-1380,* Longman, 1979.

Author of ''The Building of Florence Cathedral,'' a television presentation, released by Open University in 1970.

WORK IN PROGRESS: A translation of *Chronicle,* by Salimbene de Adam.

BIOGRAPHICAL/CRITICAL SOURCES: Speculum, April, 1973.

*   *   *

LARSON, Peggy (Ann Pickering)   1931-

PERSONAL: Born June 26, 1931 in North Platte, Neb.; daughter of Leo (a county official) and Marguerite (a teacher) Pickering; married Mervin W. Larson (a designer and builder of natural history exhibits), July 7, 1951; children: Lane, Lynn. *Education:* University of the Pacific, B.A., 1952; University of Arizona, M.Ed., 1965, M.L.S., 1978. *Home:* 4918 East Glenn St., Tucson, Ariz. 85712. *Agent:* Donald MacCampbell, Inc., 12 East 41st St., New York, N.Y. 10017.

CAREER: Tucson Unified School District, Tucson, Ariz., children's librarian, 1960—. Instructor at University of Arizona, Tucson.

WRITINGS: (Contributor) William Burns, editor, *The Natural History of the Southwest,* Watts, 1960; (with husband, Mervin W. Larson) *Ants Observed,* R. Hale, 1961, published as *All About Ants,* World Publishing, 1965; *Life in the Desert* (juvenile), Children's Press, 1967; (with M. W. Larson) *Lives of Social Insects*, World Publishing, 1968; *Deserts of America*, Prentice-Hall, 1970; (with Lane Larson) *A Sierra Club Naturalist's Guide: The Deserts of the Southwest*, illustrated by Lynn Larson, Sierra Books, 1977. Contributor to *Collier's Encyclopedia Year Book*, 1973 and 1974. Contributor of fiction to *Scholastic* magazine and articles to *Junior Natural History* and *Nature*.

SIDELIGHTS: Larson is especially interested in the deserts of the world. In addition to living in the Sonoran Desert for more than twenty years, she has traveled in the Nambi, Sahara, Kalahari, Patagonian, and North American deserts. *Avocational interests:* Hiking, camping, animals, ecology, and southwestern American history.

*   *   *

LAWLESS, Anthony
See MacDONALD, Philip

*   *   *

LAWRENCE, George H(ill Mathewson)   1910-1978

OBITUARY NOTICE: Born June 19, 1910, in East Greenwich, R.I.; died June 11, 1978. Bibliographer, administrator, and author. Lawrence was a professor of botany at Cornell University and director of Barley Horatorium before becoming director of Hunt Botanical Library at Carnegie Institute of Technology (now Carnegie-Mellon University) in Pittsburgh. He was a principal founder of Hunt Institute for Botanical Documentation. An editor of works on various aspects of botany, Lawrence also wrote several books on the subject, and was author of scientific papers. Obituaries and other sources: *New York Times*, June 20, 1978, June 21, 1978; *AB Bookman's Weekly*, September 4, 1978; *Who's Who in America*, 40th edition, Marquis, 1978.

*   *   *

LAWRENCE, John (Waldemar)   1907-

PERSONAL: Born May 27, 1907, in Eastbourne, England; son of Alexander Waldemar (fourth Baronet Lawrence; a lawyer) and Anne Elizabeth Le Poer (Wynne) Lawrence; married Jacynth Mary Ellerton, 1948. *Education:* New College, Oxford, M.A., 1925. *Politics:* "Non-party." *Religion:* Church of England. *Home:* 24 St.Leonard's Ter., London SW3 4Q6, England. *Agent:* Curtis Brown Ltd., 1 Craven Hill, London W2 3EW, England.

CAREER: Sixth Baronet Lawrence of Lucknow. Admitted solicitor, 1933; German Jewish Aid Committee, London, England, personal assistant to the director, 1938-39; British Broadcasting Corp., London, European intelligence officer, 1939-40, European services organiser, 1940-41; British Embassy in the Soviet Union, Moscow and Kuibyshev, press attache, 1942-45; free-lance writer, 1946—. Member of Church Assembly of the Church of England and General Synod of the Church of England, 1960-75; observer to the Vatican Council for the Anglican Communion; chairman of Veston College (formerly Centre for the Study of Religion and Communism), 1969—. *Member:* Great Britain-U.S.S.R. Association (chairman, 1970), Athenaeum Club. *Awards, honors:* Officer of Order of the British Empire, 1945; officer of Order of Orange Nassau, 1950.

WRITINGS: Life in Russia, Allen & Unwin, 1947, 2nd edition, 1948; *Russia in the Making*, Allen & Unwin, 1957; *Hard Facts: A Christian Looks at the World*, S.C.M. Press, 1958; *A History of Russia*, Farrar, Straus, 1960, 6th edition,

New American Library, 1978; *The Hard Facts of Unity: A Layman Looks at the Ecumenical Movement*, S.C.M. Press, 1961; *Russia*, Roy, 1965; *Soviet Russia*, Benn, 1967, David White, 1968; *Russians Observed*, Hodder & Stoughton, 1969, University of Nebraska Press, 1971; *Take Hold of Change: Alternatives for Society at the End of the Second Millennium*, S.P.C.K., 1975. Editor of *Christian News Letter*, 1953-57, and *Frontier*, 1958—.

WORK IN PROGRESS—For Hodder & Stoughton: A biography of great-grandparents, Sir Henry Lawrence of Lucknow and his wife, Honona; editing, with Audrey Woodiwiss, the journals of Honona Lawrence, 1837-52.

SIDELIGHTS: Sir John Lawrence writes: "I read ten languages for pleasure and my interests are very varied. I am especially interested in religion and its interaction with society, in the Indian sub-continent and in the Soviet Union and Eastern Europe generally. My training is first that of a classical scholar and then that of a lawyer.

"I wrote my history of Russia because I found that I could not work effectively in the Soviet Union without understanding the Russian past and because I wished to pass on to others what I had myself discovered. In my historical writing I seek to show the interaction of outstanding personalities, the circumstances of their times, and the effect of the past on the present. I try to enter into the feelings of all the actors in history, both great and small, and to see what was possible for them and what was not. I am not a determinist. Therefore, I believe that the future can be shaped but that we are all conditioned by a past, which is important for us to understand.

"My work on India is occasioned by the fact that I own an exceptionally rich volume of unpublished historical manuscript (now on permanent deposit at the India Office Library). These relate to my ancestors who played a central part in the formative period of British rule in India. It is now possible to consider the 'Raj' more objectively than was possible at any earlier period, but memories and a tradition are still alive. In another generation they will be lost. On any showing the 'Raj' was one of the most extraordinary episodes in history and it is important to understand it.

"As a writer I aim at clarity and economy above all. Color comes, if it comes at all, of its own accord when the structure is right. My models of style are Thucydides, Pushkin's prose, and Stendahl."

AVOCATIONAL INTERESTS: Travel.

*   *   *

LAWRENCE, Thomas
See ROBERTS, Thom(as Sacra)

*   *   *

LAYMAN, Emma McCloy   1910-

PERSONAL: Born February 25, 1910, in Danville, Va.; daughter of Charles Harold and Anna (Fisher) McCloy; married James Walter Layman, December 12, 1936 (died May 4, 1978). *Education:* Oberlin College, A.B., 1930; New York University, M.A., 1931; University of Iowa, Ph.D., 1937; postdoctoral study at University of Colorado and Sophia University. *Politics:* Democrat. *Religion:* Episcopalian. *Home:* 403 South Walnut St., Mount Pleasant, Iowa 52641.

CAREER: Iowa Psychopathic Hospital, Iowa City, psychological examiner, 1934-35; Michigan Children's Institute, Ann Arbor, clinical psychologist, 1935-36; Iowa Psychopathic Hospital, psychological examiner, 1937; Iowa Board of Social Welfare, Des Moines, supervisor of psychological services, 1937-41; private practice in clinical psychology, 1941-47; University of North Carolina, Woman's College, Greensboro, associate professor of psychology, 1947-52; Brooke Army Hospital, Fort Sam Houston, Tex., clinical psychologist, 1952-54; Children's Hospital, Washington, D.C., chief psychologist, 1954-60; Iowa Wesleyan College, Mount Pleasant, associate professor, 1960-61, professor of psychology, 1961-75, professor emeritus, 1975—, head of department, 1960-75, chairman of Social Science Division, 1969-75, director of East Asian Insitute, 1963—, director of international studies, 1970-75. Diplomate of American Board of Examiners in Professional Psychology; private practice in clinical psychology. Lecturer at University of Chattanooga, 1946-47, and Howard University, 1956-60; adjunct professor at American University, 1954-60. Consultant to Walter Reed Army Hospital. *Military service:* U.S. Naval Reserve, active duty as Japanese language officer, 1943-46; became lieutenant senior grade.

MEMBER: International Council of Psychologists (past president; member of board of directors), Inter-American Psychological Association, American Psychological Association (fellow), American Psychopathological Association, Association for Asian Studies, Phi Beta Kappa, Sigma Xi, Clio Club, Mount Pleasant Women's Investment Club (president, 1970-71).

WRITINGS: Mental Health Through Physical Education and Recreation, Burgess, 1955; *Airesboro Castle,* Lenox Hill, 1974; *Buddhism in America,* Nelson-Hall, 1976.

Contributor to academic journals. Editor of newsletter of International Council of Psychologists, 1956-58.

WORK IN PROGRESS: Three mystery novels, including *Z Is for Zen;* a Gothic novel, *Ghoulies and Ghosties; Prayer Without Words: A Guide for the Christian Yogi.*

SIDELIGHTS: Emma Layman writes: "As an undergraduate I majored in physical education, and taught it briefly before shifting to psychology. My background in these two fields was utilized in my first book, and many of my articles have dealt with sport psychology.

"I grew up in China. During those thirteen years I also traveled in Japan. My postdoctoral study was in East Asian history and culture, and for some years I taught courses in Asian studies as well as psychology. I also conducted several student tours in Asia. All of this is related to my interest in Buddhism. While teaching a course on Buddhism in the modern world, I became aware of Buddhist groups in America and decided to spend a sabbatical leave researching this in depth. The result was *Buddhism in America.*

"I have always been an avid reader of detective stories and gothic novels and planned to spend my retirement years writing mysteries. I've also always been an avid traveler. *Airesboro Castle* was researched during a summer vacation in Yorkshire. Of my unpublished novels, one was based on experiences during a summer in Japan; one made use of historical material on seventeenth-century England obtained at the Oxford University Library; one was based on campus disturbances in the United States during the late 60's; and one utilized my studies of Zen. Background material obtained last summer in Cornwall is being used in a gothic which I'm currently working on."

AVOCATIONAL INTERESTS: Painting, crafts, playing the organ, photograpy.

LEAVENWORTH, Carol 1940-

PERSONAL: Born December 5, 1940, in Oak Park, Ill.; daughter of Frank Gates (in business) and Audrey (a designer; maiden name, Melum) Leavenworth; married Vernon Vobejda (divorced, 1975); married Carroll Gaylord Hendricks (a psychologist), April 1, 1978; children: (first marriage) Susan Marie, Steven Edward. *Education:* University of Minnesota, B.A., 1965; University of Wisconsin, M.S., 1974. *Residence:* Colorado Springs, Colo. *Office:* Career Center, Colorado College, Colorado Springs, Colo. 80903.

CAREER: Virginia Neal Blue Center (social service agency), Colorado Springs, Colo., director, 1974-75; Integral Therapy Associates, Colorado Springs, psychotherapist, 1975—. Colorado College, Colorado Springs, director of career center, 1976—. Member of College Placement Council. *Member:* Rocky Mountain College Placement Association, Colorado Collegiate Career Planning Association, Colorado College Personnel Association, Phi Beta Kappa.

WRITINGS: (With husband, Gay Hendricks) *How to Love Every Minute of Your Life,* Prentice-Hall, 1978; (with Hendricks) *Cool and Creamy: The Ice Cream and Frozen Yogurt Cookbook,* Prentice-Hall, 1979.

WORK IN PROGRESS: A book on love and marriage; articles on problem solving in everyday life.

SIDELIGHTS: Leavenworth comments on her development as a writer: "Three years before the publication of *How to Love Every Minute of Your Life,* Gay Hendricks asked me to work with him on a book for the lay audience about personal growth and problem solving. I didn't have much confidence in myself as a writer, but I agreed because I knew we had something fresh and helpful to say on the subject. I was excited by the challenge of sharing our ideas in writing. I wasn't surprised that starting the book was easier than finishing it. At the time I found working against a deadline to be the strongest motivator in completing the work I had begun. In the process I learned that writing for others about growth and problem solving enhances my own growth as a person and as a psychotherapist. Right now the thing I like most about writing is that it helps me organize my thoughts while looking at ordinary problems in new ways. It keeps me excited about what I am doing."

*   *   *

LEBOWITZ, Fran 1951(?)-

PERSONAL: Born in Morristown, N.J.; daughter of furniture store proprietors. *Residence:* New York, N.Y. *Office:* c/o E. P. Dutton, 2 Park Ave., New York, N.Y. 10016.

CAREER: Writer. Previously worked at a number of "colorful and picturesque" jobs in New York City, including bulk mailing, taxi driving, apartment cleaning, poetry reading, and selling advertising for *Changes* magazine.

WRITINGS: Metropolitan Life (humorous essays), Dutton, 1978. Author of columns, "I Cover the Waterfront," in *Interview,* and "The Lebowitz Report," in *Mademoiselle.* Contributor of book and film reviews to *Changes* magazine.

WORK IN PROGRESS: Social Studies, another book of essays.

SIDELIGHTS: When Fran Lebowitz complains, people listen. *Metropolitan Life,* her book of satirical essays on trendy urban (specifically, New York) life, is a tremendous bestseller, and Lebowitz is in great demand as a talk show guest. She loves the celebrity. "Listen, what would I rather be doing than being mobbed by people who love what I do? I consider autographing books the ultimate human activity," she told *New Times.*

Lebowitz's fame has a strong critical base, as well as a popular one. Lauded by critics as an important humorist, she has been compared to everyone from Erma Bombeck to Dorothy Parker to Oscar Wilde. John Leonard, who found her book an "enormous amount of fun," described the recipe for Lebowitz's success: "To a base of Huck Finn, add some Lenny Bruce and Oscar Wilde and Alexis de Tocqueville, a dash of cab driver, an assortment of puns, minced jargon, and top it off with smarty pants. Serve without whine. This is the New York style, and I for one am glad that it survives and prospers because otherwise we might as well grow moss in unsurprising Omaha. Against such a wiseguy scourge, nothing in the culture is safe, not art, science, literature, food or children."

The essays in *Metropolitan Life* are "designed to offend almost everyone," Pete Axthelm noted. But trendiness deserves "powerful countermeasures. We have waited too long for a writer who is willing to point at her reader and warn: 'You are under arrest for being boring.'" In one piece originally published as a *Mademoiselle* column (Axthelm called it the "gem" of the collection), Lebowitz unleashed her wit on houseplants. "I can't stand plants in New York City," she wrote. "I don't think you should go up to someone's thirty-eighth-floor apartment and feel as if you were walking into a forest or a jungle, any more than I would want to walk into a forest and see a Breuer chair. I think it's exceedingly pious to treat plants like children or animals, and I find it a terrifying thought that people think plants have feelings. It's irritating enough to contend with people's feelings." She received hate mail when that column was published.

Also inspiring her crankiness are early rising, physical fitness, and t-shirts with printed messages. Winning her approval are sleep, smoking, and certain traits of children. ("They either sleep alone or with small toy animals. The wisdom of such behavior is unquestionable, as it frees them from the immeasurable tedium of being privy to the whispered confessions of others. I have yet to run across a teddy bear who is harboring the secret desire to wear a maid's uniform.").

"Fran Lebowitz wears life like an itchy muffler," Jill Robinson wrote. "She braids its fringes, flings it over her shoulder and savors its discomforts . . ." Paul Rudnick commented: "Lebowitz promotes the paradox of maliciousness and popularity. She revels in her crankiness, and feels that 'almost all good humor is negative—what's funny about a cheery person?' Simple grouchiness, or mere adolescent sneering, is not really amusing. Style, a reverence for language and a worship of the well-turned phrase, are the fundamentals of Lebowitz's craft. This worship can result in the seemingly effortless cutting delight found in the work of Lebowitz's idol, Oscar Wilde: the exhilaration of a mathematically concise slur."

Lebowitz's most admirable quality, according to Axthelm, is her refusal to cope. "She has spent most of her life not coping with school and assorted jobs. . . . Truly, the woman deserves a place of honor in a troubled time. I wish there were a Nobel Prize for Not Coping, so she could win it."

BIOGRAPHICAL/CRITICAL SOURCES: Newsweek, April 10, 1978; *New York Times Book Review,* March 26, 1978; *New York Times,* March 31, 1978; *Washington Post,* June 5, 1978; *New Times,* July 10, 1978; *Bookviews,* September, 1978; *People,* September 4, 1978.*

LEE, Devon
See POHLE, Robert W(arren), Jr.

*   *   *

LEE, H. Alton   1942-

PERSONAL: Born June 23, 1942, in Raleigh, N.C.; son of H. A. (a printer) and Helen Leota Lee; married Paula Cameron (a teacher), August 4, 1968. *Education:* Attended North Carolina State University, 1960-62, Atlantic Christian College, 1962-64, and Union Theological Seminary, 1965-68. *Home and office:* 5813 19th Ave. S., Gulfport, Fla.

CAREER: WKIX-Radio, Raleigh, N.C., announcer and copywriter, 1960-63; Presbyterian Church in the United States, Richmond, Va., church relations associate, 1965-66; Creative Services, Richmond, Va., writer, 1966; managing editor of *Richmond Trade Magazine,* 1966-68; United Presbyterian Church in the United States of America, Philadelphia, Pa., associate editor of "Approach," 1968-70, director of information for Board of Christian Education, 1971-73; Eckerd College, St. Petersburg, Fla., information specialist, 1973-74; free-lance writer, 1974—. *Member:* International Bromeliad Society, International Aroid Society, International Begonia Society, International Marantha Society, Florida West Coast Bromeliad Society (president), Florida West Coast Gesneriad Society.

WRITINGS: Seven Feet Four and Growing (fiction), Westminster, 1978. Author of "Entertainment Unlimited," film column, 1968-72. Contributor to *International Bromeliad Journal.*

WORK IN PROGRESS: A novel set in southern Florida's farming area, for Westminster; a mystery novel; research for a book on teenage marriages and a fictional book about wolves.

SIDELIGHTS: Lee writes: "Writing is inescapable for me, a necessary release, something I have to do, and which I do for my own satisfaction, with the subsequent hope that someone else will like what I have written. I have done lots of nonfiction for religious, horticultural, and entertainment periodicals, but fiction has always been my main interest." In writing fiction, one also gets to act, playing all the roles in a scenario. But sometimes—almost always—the outcome of work is much different from what was first anticipated.

AVOCATIONAL INTERESTS: Tropical horticulture, astronomy, cinema and theater, art, reading mysteries, travel.

*   *   *

LEE, Helen Jackson   1908-

PERSONAL: Born July 23, 1908, in Richmond, Va.; daughter of Charles N. (a building superintendent) and Nannie (Brisby) Jackson; married Robert E. Lee, November 1, 1930 (deceased); children: Barbara Nan, Robert E., Jr. *Education:* Virginia State College, B.A., 1930. *Politics:* Democrat. *Religion:* Roman Catholic. *Home:* 316 Brinton Ave., Trenton, N.J. 08618.

CAREER: Worked as clerk-typist for New Jersey Unemployment Commission, 1942-47; New Jersey Department of Institutions & Agencies, Trenton, senior clerk-stenographer, 1947-67, public information assistant, 1967-70; social worker, 1971-73; writer, 1973—. *Member:* National Association for the Advancement of Colored People, Urban League, Alpha Kappa Alpha (local historian). *Awards, honors:* Golden Girl Award from Alpha Kappa Alpha, 1978.

WRITINGS: Nigger in the Window (autobiography), Doubleday, 1978.

Co-author of "The Unfinished Revolution" (two-act musical), first produced in Trenton, N.J. at War Memorial Building, 1976. Part-time reporter for *New Jersey Afro-American, Philadelphia Independent, Pittsburgh Courier,* and *Chicago Defender* (Philadelphia edition). Feature writer for *Christian Review.*

WORK IN PROGRESS: A novel.

SIDELIGHTS: Helen Lee comments: "I was motivated to write by listening to stories told me as a child by my foster grandmother and my own mother, especially those centered around ghosts and spirits. My mother read to me every evening at supper time. I fell in love with words very early and my devotion has never flagged during the years. I consider it vital that black people should write down the rich store of folk stories and legends of our people. Too many good stories about blacks are written by white writers."

BIOGRAPHICAL/CRITICAL SOURCES: Washington Post, May 18, 1978.

* * *

LeFEVRE, Adam 1950-

PERSONAL: Born August 11, 1950, in Albany, N.Y.; son of Ira Deyo (a physician) and Helen (a hospital's patient representative; maiden name, Rhodes) LeFevre. *Education:* Williams College, B.A., 1972; University of Iowa, M.F.A., 1976. *Home:* 18 Cherry St., Somerville, Mass. 02144.

CAREER: Writer, 1965—. Actor and director for Eastern Slope Playhouse, summers, 1974—. *Member:* Phi Beta Kappa.

WRITINGS: Everything All at Once (poems), Wesleyan University Press, 1978.

Plays: "Yucca Flats" (two-act), first produced at Manhattan Theater Club, September, 1973; "Phil Gafney" (two-act), first produced in Iowa City at University of Iowa, April, 1976; "The Window Washer" and "In the Meat District" (both one-acts), produced together at Eastern Slope Playhouse, August, 1977.

WORK IN PROGRESS: Another book of poems; "The Crashing of Moses Flying-By," a three-act play.

* * *

LEHMAN, Harold D(aniel) 1921-

PERSONAL: Born January 26, 1921, in Millersville, Pa.; son of Daniel W. and Ada (Neff) Lehman; married Ruth Krady (a college registrar), December 30, 1944; children: Kenneth, Daniel, David, Larry. *Education:* Madison College, B.S., 1942; Pennsylvania State University, M.Ed., 1949; University of Virginia, Ed.D., 1961. *Religion:* Mennonite. *Home:* 1068 College Ave., Harrisonburg, Va. 22801. *Office:* Department of Education, James Madison University, Harrisonburg, Va. 22801.

CAREER: Elementary teacher at public schools in Rockingham County, Va., 1939-41; teacher of the mentally retarded at Vineland Training School, N.J., 1943-46; Eastern Mennonite College, Harrisonburg, Va., assistant professor of physical education, 1946-56; Eastern Mennonite High School, Harrisonburg, principal, 1957-62; Eastern Mennonite College, professor of education and registrar, 1962-67; James Madison University, Harrisonburg, professor of secondary education, 1967—. Member of Mennonite Secondary Education Advisory Council, 1970—. Vice chairman of Mennonite Commission on Christian Education, 1968-72; chairman of Rockingham Council on Human Relations,

1970-71; chairman of local Red Cross, 1970-74. *Member:* National Education Association, Virginia Education Association, Provident Readers Club, Phi Delta Kappa, Kappa Delta Pi.

WRITINGS: In Praise of Leisure, Herald Press, 1974. Author of Christian education curriculum material for Herald Press. Member of editorial council of "Foundation Series."

WORK IN PROGRESS: Education for Lifetime Leisure.

SIDELIGHTS: Lehman writes: "I have traveled in Western Europe (including the Soviet Union and Czechoslovakia), Bolivia, and Cuba. I spent the 1979-80 school term at Woodbrooke College in Birmingham, England, for study and professional renewal. I am interested in the study of comparative education, especially in Socialist countries."

* * *

LEIDER, Emily Wortis 1937-

PERSONAL: Surname pronounced *Ly*-der; born December 23, 1937, in New York, N.Y.; daughter of Joseph (a psychiatrist) and Helen (a social worker; maiden name, Zunser) Wortis; married William Leider (a pediatrician), December 22, 1957; children: Jean, Richard. *Education:* Barnard College, B.A., 1959; Columbia University, M.A., 1961. *Religion:* Jewish. *Home:* 1520 Lake St., San Francisco, Calif. 94118. *Office: San Francisco Review of Books,* 2140 Vallejo, San Francisco, Calif. 94123.

CAREER: Northwestern University, Evanston, Ill., instructor in English literature and writing, 1964-66; Antioch College West, San Francisco, Calif., instructor in poetry and women's studies, 1973-76; *San Francisco Review of Books,* San Francisco, associate editor, 1977—. *Member:* Poets and Writers.

WRITINGS: Rapid Eye Movement and Other Poems, Bay Books, 1976; (editor and author of postscript) Miriam Shomer Zunser, *Yesterday: The Memoir of a Russian Jewish Family,* Harper, 1978.

WORK IN PROGRESS: Poems.

SIDELIGHTS: Leider told *CA:* "My poems tend to be concise and imagistic lyrics with narrative and dramatic leanings. *Rapid Eye Movement* contains a sequence of poems based on characters and events in my grandmother's memoir, *Yesterday.*"

* * *

LEIGH, Susannah 1938-

PERSONAL: Born December 4, 1938, in Minneapolis, Minn.; daughter of Arthur W. (a personnel manager) and Eliane (a purchasing agent; maiden name, Rainville) Smith; divorced. *Education:* University of Minnesota, B.A. (cum laude). *Address:* c/o New American Library, 1301 Avenue of the Americas, New York, N.Y. 10019.

CAREER: Worked at a variety of jobs, including tour guide for a radio and television station, writer for Minnesota School of the Air, administrative assistant for advertising agencies, exhibition secretary for the New York Art Directors Club, assistant for an art gallery, and actress, 1958-66; worked for a publishing house, 1966-71; free-lance editor and technical writer, 1972-75; writer, 1975—.

WRITINGS—Novels: Dark Labyrinth, Fawcett, 1976; *Winter Fire,* New American Library, 1978; *Glynda,* New American Library, 1979.

WORK IN PROGRESS: An untitled historical novel, "set

in Egypt, both in ancient times and during the nineteenth century, exploring the romance and adventures of a young woman who accompanies archaeologists searching for an unplundered tomb in the valley of the dead, near the ancient city of Thebes.''

AVOCATIONAL INTERESTS: Travel (Morocco, East Africa, Egypt, Jordan, Israel, Greece, Iran, Afghanistan, India, Burma, Indonesia, Taiwan, Korea, and Japan).

* * *

LEIGHTON, Frances Spatz

PERSONAL: Born in Thompson, Ohio. Education: Attended Ohio State University. Home: 3636 16th St. N.W., Washington, D.C. 20010. Agent: Ruth Hagy Brod, 15 Park Ave., New York, N.Y. 10016. Office: Metropolitan Sunday Newspapers, 1035 National Press Bldg., Washington, D.C. 20004.

CAREER: Washington correspondent, American Weekly, 1950-63, This Week magazine, 1963-69, and Metropolitan Sunday Newspapers, Washington, D.C., 1965—. Member: National League of American Pen Women, Women's National Press Club, American Newspaper Women's Club, Art League. Awards, honors: Edgar Allen Poe award from the Mystery Writers of America, 1961.

WRITINGS—Autobiography: (With Francois Rysavy) White House Chef: As Told to Frances Spatz Leighton, Putnam, 1957; (with Jane Rucker Barkley) I Married the Veep, Vanguard, 1958; (with Louise Pfister) I Married a Psychiatrist, Citadel, 1961; (with David Greer) Bum Voyage, Citadel, 1961; (with Mini Rhea) I Was Jacqueline Kennedy's Dressmaker, Fleet Publishing, 1962; (with Lillian Rogers Parks) It Was Fun Working at the White House, Fleet Press, 1969; (with Traphes Bryant) Dog Days at the White House: The Outrageous Memoirs of the Presidential Kennel Keeper, Macmillan, 1975; (with William Miller) Fishbait: The Memoirs of the Congressional Doorkeeper, Prentice-Hall, 1977; (with Jerry Cammarata) The Fun Book of Fatherhood; or, How the Animal Kingdom Is Helping To Raise the Wild Kids at Our House, Corwin, 1978.

Other: (With Deborah Pierce) I Prayed Myself Slim: The Prayer-Diet Book, Citadel, 1960; (with Rysavy) White House Menus and Recipes (cookbook), Avon, 1962; (with Helen Baldwin) They Call Her Lady Bird (biography), Macfadden-Bartell, 1964; (editor) The Johnson Wit, Citadel, 1965; The Memoirs of Senator Brown, a Capitol Cat, as Told to Frances Spatz Leighton (satire), Fleet Publishing, 1965; (with Frank Samuel Caprio) How To Avoid a Nervous Breakdown, Meredith Press, 1969; (with Rhea) Sew Simply, Sew Right, Fleet Press, 1969; (with Rysavy) A Treasury of White House Cooking, Putnam, 1972; (with John D. Dahlinger) The Secret Life of Henry Ford (biography), Bobbs-Merrill, 1978.

Contributor to journals, including McCall's, Ladies Home Journal, and Good Housekeeping.

SIDELIGHTS: Leighton has often been interviewed on radio and television.*

* * *

LEISHMAN, Thomas L. 1900-1978

OBITUARY NOTICE: Born in 1900, in Scotland; died November 12, 1978, in Bronx, N.Y. Lecturer and author. Leishman lectured on religious topics throughout the United States and in other countries. Author of The Continuity of the Bible: Joshua to Elisha, The Continuity of the Bible:

Paul, the Missionary Apostle, and other books on the Bible, Leishman also contributed to the Christian Science Monitor. Obituaries and other sources: New York Times, November 15, 1978.

* * *

LEONARD, Elmore 1925-
(Emmett Long)

PERSONAL: Born Oct. 11, 1925, in New Orleans, La.; son of Elmore John (a salesman) and Flora (Rive) Leonard; married Beverly Cline, July 30, 1949 (divorced May 24, 1977); children: Jane Freels, Peter, Christopher, William, Katherine. Education: University of Detroit, Ph.B., 1950. Religion: Catholic. Home: 211 East Merrill, Birmingham, Mich. 48011. Agent: H. N. Swanson, 8523 Sunset Blvd., Los Angeles, Cal. 90069.

CAREER: Copywriter for Campbell-Ewald Advertising Agency, Detroit, Mich., 1950-61; free-lance writer of industrial and educational motion pictures, many for Encyclopaedia Britannica Films, 1961-63; head of Elmore Leonard Advertising company, 1963-66; free-lance writer, 1967—. Military Service: U.S. Naval Reserve, 1943-46. Member: Writers Guild of America, West, Mystery Writers of America, Western Writers of America, Authors Guild. Awards, honors: Hombre was selected as one of twenty-five best Western novels of all time by Western Writers of America, 1977.

WRITINGS—Novels: The Bounty Hunters, Houghton, 1953; The Law at Randado, Houghton, 1955; Escape From 5 Shadows, Houghton, 1956; Last Stand at Saber River, Dell, 1957; Hombre, Ballantine, 1961; The Big Bounce, Gold Medal, 1969; The Moonshine War, Doubleday, 1969; Valdez Is Coming, Gold Medal, 1970; Forty Lashes Less One, Bantam, 1972; Mr. Majestyk, Dell, 1974; Fifty-Two Pickup, Delacorte, 1974; Swag, Delacorte, 1976; Unknown Man No. 89, Delacorte, 1977; The Hunted, Dell, 1977; The Switch, Bantam, 1978; Ryan's Rule, Dell, 1978.

Screenplays: "The Moonshine Wars," (adapted from the novel), Metro-Goldwyn-Mayer, 1970; "Joe Kidd," Universal, 1973; "Mr. Majestyk," United Artists, 1974.

WORK IN PROGRESS: Three novels, The Juvenal Touch, Seascape, and Fox Hunt, a crime story set in Miami Beach; a television play, "Jesus Saves"; Gunsight, under pseudonym Emmett Long.

SIDELIGHTS: Reviewing Unknown Man No. 89, Newgate Callendar of the New York Times Book Review commented: "Leonard bows to no one in plot construction. Yet there is never the feeling of gimmickry in his plots; events follow a natural course. Above all, there is Leonard's style. He has a wonderful ear, and his dialogue never has a false note. He avoids artiness, writes clear expository prose and has the ability to create real people. It is not High Literature, nor does it pretend to be. Leonard is primarily an entertainer. But he is one with enormous finesse, and he can write circles around almost anybody active in the crime novel today."

Leonard told CA: "I've been wanting to write and tell stories since the fifth grade when I wrote a play in school. After 'writing to order' for a good many years, I'm now writing exactly what I want (on my own since 1961; full-time fiction since 1967) and I've never been happier. I learned to write by reading Hemingway."

Other films based on Leonard's work include "3:10 to Yuma," Columbia Pictures, 1957, "Hombre," Twentieth

Century-Fox, 1961, "The Big Bounce," Warner Bros., 1969, and "Valdez Is Coming," United Artists, 1971.

AVOCATIONAL INTERESTS: Travel.

BIOGRAPHICAL/CRITICAL SOURCES: New York Times Book Review, May 22, 1977.

* * *

Le PELLEY, Guernsey 1910-
(Kerry Norman, Lee Richard)

PERSONAL: Born May 14, 1910, in Chicago, Ill.; son of Franklin (a banker) and Ardria (Miner) Le Pelley; married Maxine Gillis, September 11, 1938; children: Lynn, Richard. *Education:* Principia College, Elsah, Ill., A.A.; Harvard University, B.A. *Politics:* "As a cartoonist I became an Independent." *Religion:* Christian Scientist. *Home address:* Amenia Union Rd., Sharon, Conn. 06069. *Office: Christian Science Monitor,* 1 Norway St., Boston, Mass. 02115.

CAREER: Highland Park Press, Highland Park, Ill., writer, 1930-33; WFAA-radio, Dallas, Tex., writer, 1933-34, free-lance writer and artist in Sharon, Conn., 1940-60; *Christian Science Monitor,* Boston, Mass., author of daily comic strip, "Tubby." 1935—; editorial cartoonist, 1961—. Gives public lectures. *Military service:* Served in World War II. *Member:* International Twin-Engine Society, Association of American Editorial Cartoonists, National Pilots Association, Aircraft Owners and Pilots Association, Canadian Aircraft Owners and Pilots Association, Harvard Club, Quiet Birdmen.

WRITINGS—Three-act plays; all published by Harper: *Love Is Too Much Trouble,* 1946; *To Blush Unseen,* 1951; *Absolutely Murder,* 1954. Also author of *The Zoozah, In Spring the Sap, When I Was Green, Ghost Wanted, Maybe Love, Second Fiddle,* and *Mistakes at the Blakes.*

Author of one-act plays; all published by Harper: *Another Beginning, Nobody Sleeps, Cracked Ice,* and *Tell Dory Not to Cry.*

Writes occasionally under pseudonyms Kerry Norman and Lee Richard. Contributor of articles to aviation magazine and children's stories to newspapers.

WORK IN PROGRESS: Skeleton in the Water, a suspense novel; *Flying Is for the Birds,* a novel, completion expected in 1980; "Corpus Delectable," a play.

SIDELIGHTS: Le Pelley comments: "Although my interest in cartooning and playwriting continues, I hope to extend my work into novels, especially suspense novels; I am also given to humorous writing in various forms. My work is more and more intertwined with flying. I own a Twin Comanche, and have a commercial multi-engine license with instrument rating."

* * *

LeROY, Dave
See LeROY, (Lemuel) David

* * *

LeROY, (Lemuel) David 1920-
(Dave LeRoy)

PERSONAL: Born January 2, 1920, in Tignall, Ga.; son of Lansing B. (a postmaster) and Glennie D. LeRoy; married Mary M. Pridgeon (a real estate broker), September 2, 1945; children: David C., Gregory A. *Education:* University of Georgia, A.B., 1941. *Religion:* Presbyterian. *Home:* 4404

North 36th St., Arlington, Va. 22207. *Office:* National Press Foundation, National Press Building, Washington, D.C. 20045.

CAREER: Air Force Times, Washington, D.C., associate editor, 1950-51, managing editor, 1951-53; *U.S. News & World Report,* Washington, D.C., copy editor, 1953-64, member of Capitol Hill staff, 1964-70; Republican Congressional Committee, Washington, D.C., in public relations, 1970-74, director of public relations, 1974-76; National Press Foundation, Washington, D.C., executive director, 1977—. Past member of board of directors of National Press Building Corp. *Military service:* U.S. Army, 1941-46; served in Europe and North Africa; became captain; received Purple Heart. *Member:* National Press Club (president, 1967), National Rifle Association, National Republican Club of Capitol Hill (life member), Sigma Delta Chi.

WRITINGS—Under name Dave LeRoy: *Gerald Ford—Untold Story* (biography), R. W. Beatty, 1974, revised edition, 1974; (with Jack Brosius) *Building and Repairing Canoes and Kayaks,* Contemporary Books, 1978; *Outdoorsman's Guide to Government Surplus,* Contemporary Books, 1978; (with Brosius) *Canoes and Kayaks: A Complete Buyer's Guide,* Contemporary Books, 1979. Contributor of articles and photographs to magazines, including *Consumers Digest,* and newspapers.

WORK IN PROGRESS: Feature articles on senior citizens and other topics for the Virginia weekly edition of the *Washington Post.*

SIDELIGHTS: LeRoy comments: "I believe in good English and a return to basics by copydesks that spend too much time seeking to 'jazz up' copy and too little removing errors of fact and grammar. Book writing is great fun. The aspiring author—even a talented one—seeking to get his or her first book in print faces a very tough market today." *Avocational interests:* European travel, outdoor activities.

* * *

LESLIE-MELVILLE, Betty 1929-

PERSONAL: Born March 7, 1929, in Baltimore, Md.; daughter of Richard A. (a doctor) and Ida (Tomlinson) McDonnell; married F. Dancy Bruce, August 31, 1951 (divorced, June, 1964); married Jock Leslie-Melville (a writer), July 7, 1964; children: Dancy Bruce, McDonnell Bruce, Rick Anderson. *Education:* Attended Johns Hopkins University. *Politics:* "Democrat and filthy capitalist." *Religion:* "Christian, sort of." *Address:* Box 15004, Langata, Nairobi, Kenya. *Agent:* Gloria Safier, Inc., 667 Madison Ave., New York, N.Y. 10021.

CAREER: President of Uplands Nursery School, 1950-53; fashion model, 1953-60; co-owner of Bruce Safaris, 1960-65; lecturer, 1964—; writer, 1974—. Cameraperson for documentary filmed in Tanzania; assistant producer of a documentary filmed in Ethiopia. Founder and president, African Fund for Endangered Species; board member, African Student Aid Fund. *Member:* Friends of the Earth (executive board member).

WRITINGS: (With husband Jock Leslie-Melville) *Elephants Have Right Away,* Doubleday, 1974; *There's a Rhino in the Rosebud, Mother,* Doubleday, 1975; *That Nairobi Affair,* Doubleday, 1976; (with J. Leslie-Melville) *Raising Daisy Rothschild,* Simon & Schuster, 1977. Board member, *Africana* Magazine.

WORK IN PROGRESS: Will Success Spoil Daisy Rothschild?; a children's book on Daisy Rothschild; a historical novel on Kenya.

SIDELIGHTS: Leslie-Melville told *CA:* "I moved to East Africa in 1960 and was the first American to organize non-hunting safaris (Bruce Safaris). I write together with my husband. Our writing is always 'Africa oriented'—because it is a subject we know. I speak Swahili and never think of myself as a 'writer'—we talk books more than write them."

* * *

LESLIE-MELVILLE, Jock 1933-

PERSONAL: Born February 28, 1933, in London, England; son of David William (a farmer) and Eleanor Mary (a farmer; maiden name, Abrahall) Leslie-Melville; married Lady Zinnia Denison, July 14, 1961 (divorced); married Betty McDonnell (a writer), July 7, 1964. *Education:* Attended Sandhurst Military Academy, 1952-53. *Politics:* Liberal. *Religion:* "Agnostic, inclining to atheism." *Home address:* P.O. Box 15004, Nairobi, Kenya. *Agent:* Gloria Safier, Inc., 667 Madison Ave., New York, N.Y. 10021.

CAREER: Farmer in Gloucestershire, England, 1954-57; government of Kenya, aide to colonial governor, 1957-59; executive officer of first non-racial political party in Kenya, 1959; speech writer and press officer for African political leaders, including Daniel arap Noi, 1961-63; writer and public speaker, 1963-78. Director of Marco Surveys Ltd. (marketing research company), 1960-64; operator of safaris in East Africa, 1964-69; head of Percival Tours, 1969—. Organized African Fund for Endangered Wildlife, 1977. *Military service:* British Army, Coldstream Guards, 1951-52. *Member:* Royal Geographical Society (fellow).

WRITINGS—All with wife, Betty Leslie-Melville: *Elephant Have Right of Way,* Doubleday, 1974; *There's a Rhino in the Rosebed, Mother,* Doubleday, 1975; *Raising Daisy Rothschild,* Simon & Schuster, 1977.

WORK IN PROGRESS: Collecting African writing on politics, wildlife, and tribal customs.

SIDELIGHTS: Leslie-Melville writes: "We live in Africa and undertake extensive lecture tours throughout the United States each winter. From answering questions about Africa came the thought, 'why not write about it?' Having started, the very act of writing is enormously satisfying and pleasant to do, providing needed contrast to the hassle of administering safari arrangements for thousands a year, or traversing the States in the winter to lecture. We write intensively—twelve hours a day—at a beach house on the Indian Ocean, undistracted by anything—immersed. I have been fluent in Swahili since childhood, and have travelled widely in eastern Africa and visited remote and almost inaccessible places. Explaining Africa and Africans to a world that knows little of the continent is most rewarding."

BIOGRAPHICAL/CRITICAL SOURCES: New York Times Book Review, November 13, 1977; *People,* December 5, 1977.

* * *

LESLY, Philip 1918-

PERSONAL: Born May 29, 1918, in Chicago, Ill.; married Ruth Edwards, October 17, 1940 (divorced December 3, 1971); children: Craig. *Education:* Northwestern University, B.A. (honors), 1940. *Home:* 155 Harbor Dr., Chicago, Ill. 60601. *Office:* Philip Lesly Co., 130 East Randolph St., Chicago, Ill. 60601.

CAREER: Philip Lesly Co. (public relations counsel), Chicago, Ill., owner, 1949—. Director of National Safety Council, 1967-70. *Military service:* U.S. Navy, 1944. *Member:*

International Public Relations Association, Public Relations Society of America, Phi Beta Kappa, Mid-America Club. *Awards, honors:* Silver Anvil awards from Public Relations Society of America, 1946, 1963, 1965.

WRITINGS: Public Relations: Principles and Procedures, Irwin, 1945; *Public Relations in Action,* Ziff-Davis, 1947; *Public Relations Handbook,* Prentice-Hall, 1950, third edition, 1967; *Everything AND the Kitchen Sink,* Farrar, Straus, 1955; *Lesly's Public Relations Handbook,* Prentice-Hall, 1971, second edition, 1978; *The People Factor,* Dow Jones-Irwin, 1974. Also author of bimonthly, *Managing the Human Climate.* Contributor to business and public relations journals. Member of editorial advisory board of *Public Relations Quarterly, Public Relations Review, PR Reporter,* and *International Public Relations Review.*

WORK IN PROGRESS: How We Discommunicate.

SIDELIGHTS: Lesly writes: "I believe only concentration on excellence can bring about the high standards needed to improve any human activity or society. We must encourage the excellent. I concentrate on gaining satisfaction from what is achieved for my clients, my staff, my readers, my family, my friends.

"The writer, even more than other people, must focus on what he or she can uniquely offer, not following what others have done, or what has been proved popular. The way to be recognized for one's special abilities, ideas, and contributions is to focus on what others have not done and cannot do as well. This is especially important if the writer is dealing with an area of expertness aside from writing, such as a professional who is conveying his knowledge and judgment.

"I sold my first writing at the age of eight (to a children's page of a newspaper) because I had a good deal of time to myself and I was allowed to use an old typewriter. Ever since, blank paper has been a lure to me, calling out to be filled with new thoughts and challenging ideas. I've built my career around communication, with my books and other writing (other than work for clients) being projections of what I've learned and the insights I've gained.

"My influences on national affairs and ways of life have been through invisible works (on behalf of clients), as well as visible (under my name)."

* * *

LEVIN, Bob
See LEVIN, Robert A.

* * *

LEVIN, Robert A. 1942-
(Bob Levin)

PERSONAL: Born March 14, 1942, in Philadelphia, Pa.; son of Herbert S. (a lawyer and judge) and Rebecca (Katz) Levin; married August 2, 1971, wife's name Adele (a psychologist). *Education:* Brandeis University, B.A., 1964; University of Pennsylvania, LL.B., 1967; San Francisco State University, M.A., 1975. *Agent:* Evelyn Singer Agency, Inc., P.O. Box 163, Briarcliff Manor, N.Y. 10510. *Office:* 722 Montgomery, San Francisco, Calif. 94111.

CAREER: Admitted to the Bar of California; attorney in San Francisco, Calif., 1969—. President of board of directors of Center for Responsive Health Policy. *Member:* California Bar Association, California Applicants Attorneys Association. *Awards, honors:* Pushcart Prize, for story, "Best Ride from New York."

WRITINGS: (Under name Bob Levin) *The Best Ride to New York* (novel), Harper, 1978.

Contributor of articles and stories to literary journals and popular magazines, including *New Republic, Massachusetts Review,* and *Folio.*

* * *

LEVITH, Murray J(ay) 1939-

PERSONAL: Born November 8, 1939, in Pittsburgh, Pa.; son of Nathan (an accountant) and Vivian (a secretary; maiden name, Schaffer) Levith; married Christina Ladd, December 29, 1972; children: Nathaniel Albert. *Education:* Washington and Jefferson College, B.A., 1961; University of Nebraska, M.A., 1962; Syracuse University, Ph.D., 1970. *Office:* Department of English, Skidmore College, Saratoga Springs, N.Y. 12866.

CAREER: Clarion College, Clarion, Pa., instructor in English, 1962; Syracuse University, Syracuse, N.Y., part-time instructor in English, 1962-66; Cazenovia College, Cazenovia, N.Y., instructor in English, 1966-67; Skidmore College, Saratoga Springs, N.Y., instructor, 1967-69, assistant professor, 1969-77, associate professor of English, 1977—. Violinist for symphony orchestras; violin teacher. *Member:* Modern Language Association of America, American Association of University Professors, American Federation of Musicians.

WRITINGS: (Editor) *Renaissance and Modern,* Skidmore College, 1976; *What's in Shakespeare's Names,* Archon Books, 1978; (editor) *Fiddlers in Fiction,* T.F.H. Publications, 1978. Contributor of articles and reviews to magazines, including *Explicator* and *Salmagundi.*

WORK IN PROGRESS: Dads Have Babies Too! (tentative title), on childbirth from a male point of view; studying Shakespeare, Vaughan, and Traherne.

SIDELIGHTS: Levith writes: "I consider myself a humanist and a scholar. Thus, I teach, play the violin, and write—on wide-ranging topics. I am interested in Shakespeare and fatherhood, names and the concerto in the thirties, Faulkner and Venice. And I guess I am now, and always will be, a student."

* * *

LEVITT, Saul 1911-1977

PERSONAL: Born March 3, 1911, in Hartford, Conn.; son of Max and Leah (Migdal) Levitt; married Dena Glanz (a film editor), October 8, 1949; children: Dan. *Education:* Attended City College (now of the City University of New York), 1931-33. *Home:* 320 Riverside Dr., New York, N.Y. 10025.

CAREER: Playwright and author. Correspondent for *Yank* (U.S. Army weekly newspaper), 1944-45. *Member:* Writers Guild of America, Dramatists Guild. *Military service:* Served in U.S. Army Air Force and Express Transportation Order during World War II. *Awards, honors:* Emmy Award from Academy of Television Arts and Sciences, 1971, for "The Andersonville Trial."

WRITINGS: The Sun Is Silent (novel), Harper, 1951; *The Andersonville Trial* (two-act play; first produced on Broadway at Henry Miller's Theatre, December 29, 1959), Random House, 1960; (co-author) "The Trial of the Catonsville Nine" (play), first produced on the West End at Phoenix Theatre, February 7, 1971, produced in New York City, 1971.

Screenplays: "Last Frontier," Columbia, 1955; (with Larry Marcus) "Covenant With Death," Warner Bros., 1967. Also author of "The Major and the Private," Chislaw.

Writer for television programs, including "Danger," CBS-TV, 1952-53; "You Are There," CBS-TV, 1953-54; "Wide Wide World," NBC-TV, 1955; "Climax," CBS-TV, 1957; "Westinghouse Theatre," CBS-TV, 1960; "Judd for the Defense," ABC-TV. Also author of television specials, including "Dispossessed," CBS-TV, 1960; "Seaway," CBS-TV, 1966; "The Andersonville Trial," PBS-TV, 1971; "Shepherd Murder Case," UHF, 1973.

Contributor of short stories and articles to *Harper's, Atlantic Monthly, American Mercury, Fortune,* and *Nation.*

WORK IN PROGRESS: A four-part television series on crises in the life of George Washington.

SIDELIGHTS: Saul Levitt based his writings on the morality of war. He is best known for his Broadway play, "The Andersonville Trial." Levitt was deeply influenced by military life. His novel, *The Sun Is Silent,* traced the military careers of its characters from the final stages of their military training through the completion of their missions over Europe and World War II.

OBITUARIES: New York Times, October 1, 1977.*

(Died September 30, 1977, in New York, N.Y.)

* * *

LEVY, Babette May 1907-1977

PERSONAL: Born December 24, 1907, in New York, N.Y. *Education:* Hunter College (now of the City University of New York), A.B., 1928; Columbia University, A.M., 1929, Ph.D., 1942; earned M.A. (librarianship) from University of Colorado.

CAREER: Hunter College (now of the City University of New York), New York, N.Y., tutor, 1929-32, instructor, 1932-45, assistant professor, 1945-54, associate professor, 1954-60, professor of English, beginning 1960; distinguished visiting professor at Morehouse College; lecturer at Rutgers University and Marymount Manhattan College; Sweet Briar College, Sweet Briar, Va., Charles A. Dana Professor, 1968-73; lecturer in American literature at University of Coimbra, Portugal. *Member:* American Society of Church History, American Antiquarian Society, Modern Language Association, College English Association. *Awards, honors:* Grants from Institute of Early American History and Culture, 1948, 1949; Brewer prize from American Society of Church History, 1949; Fulbright-Hays award at University of Coimbra.

WRITINGS: Preaching in the First Half Century of New England History, American Society of Church History, 1945, reprinted, Russell, 1967; *Milton's Paradise Lost, and Other Works,* Barrister, 1966.

OBITUARIES: New York Times, December 23, 1977.*

(Died December 21, 1977, in Huntington, N.Y.)

* * *

LEWINE, Richard 1910-

PERSONAL: Born July 28, 1910, in New York, N.Y.; son of Irving I. (a real estate investor) and Jane (Weinberg) Lewine; married Mary Haas, September 28, 1945 (died December, 1968); married Elizabeth Rivers, November 27, 1972; children: (first marriage) Peter Emmett, Cornelia Mary. *Education:* Attended Columbia University, 1927-30. *Home:* 352 East 69th St., New York, N.Y. 10021.

CAREER: Composer and lyricist; producer and musical director of Broadway plays. Composer for "Fools Rush In," 1934, "Naughty Naught," 1937, "The Fireman's Flame," 1938, and "It's All Yours," 1942; producer and musical director of "Two Weeks With Pay," 1940, "It's All Yours," 1942, and "Look to the Lilies," 1970; composer of theatrical scores, including "Make Mine Manhattan," 1948, "Ziegfeld Follies," 1956, and "Girls Against the Boys," 1959. Originator of concept for Broadway production, "Rodgers and Hart," 1975. Television producer of the "Noel Coward-Mary Martin Special," 1955, Rodgers and Hammerstein's "Cinderella," 1957, "Hootenanny" series, 1963, "My Name is Barbra," 1964, and "Pinocchio," 1968. Director of special programs for Columbia Broadcasting System (CBS) television network, 1952-61; network executive producer for Ringling Brothers Circus, Sarasota, Fla., 1956, and Madison Square Garden, 1957; executive producer for "Crescendo," 1957, New York Philharmonic "Young People's Concerts," with Leonard Bernstein, 1957-61, and "Fabulous Fifties," 1960; co-producer and composer of a short subject film, "The Days of Wilfred Owen," 1964. Military service: U.S. Army, 1942-46; became captain. Member: American Society of Composers, Authors, and Publishers (ASCAP), Authors League of America, Dramatists Guild (vice president; member of council, 1950—), Coffee House (New York City). Awards, honors: Screen Producers Guild award for best program, 1964, and Emmy award from National Academy of Television Arts and Sciences, 1964-65, both for "My Name is Barbra."

WRITINGS: (With Alfred Simon) Encyclopedia of Theater Music, Random House, 1964; (with Simon) Songs of the American Theater, Dodd, 1973; (contributor) Playwright, Lyricists, Composers on Theater, Dodd, 1975. Contributor of articles to Glamour, Variety, and Dramatists Guild Quarterly.

*   *   *

LEWING, Anthony Charles 1933-
(Mark Bannerman)

PERSONAL: Born July 12, 1933, in Colchester, England; son of Herbert Charles (a British Army officer) and Gladys (Matthews) Lewing; married Francoise Faury (a teacher); children: Coralie, Benjamin. Education: Educated in England. Religion: Church of England. Agent: Winant, Towers Ltd., 14 Cliffords Inn, London EC4A 1DA, England.

CAREER: Officer in Royal Army Pay Corps, 1958—. Member: Crime Writers' Association (Great Britain).

WRITINGS—Under pseudonym Mark Bannerman: Gunsmoke Valley, Zavallis Press, 1976; Year of the Lance, Zavallis Press, 1976. Contributor of short stories to magazines throughout the world.

SIDELIGHTS: Lewing commented: "I am particularly interested in the history of the American West."

*   *   *

LEWIS, Archibald Ross 1914-

PERSONAL: Born August 25, 1914, in Bronxville, N.Y.; son of Burdett Gibson and Pearl Merriam (Archibald) Lewis; married Elizabeth Z. Cutler, December 27, 1954; children: David Adelbert, Allyson Cutler. Education: Princeton University, A.B., 1936, M.A., 1939, Ph.D., 1940. Religion: Presbyterian. Home: 42 Hitching Post Rd., Amherst, Mass. 01002. Office: Department of History, University of Massachusetts, Amherst, Mass. 01003.

CAREER: University of South Carolina, Columbia, adjunct professor, 1940-42, associate professor, 1947-48, professor of history, 1948-51; University of Texas, Austin, associate professor, 1951-55, professor of history, 1955-59, 1961-69, head of department, 1955-59, 1963-69; Munson-Maritime Institute, Mystic, Conn., co-director, 1959-61; University of Massachusetts, Amherst, professor of history, 1969—, head of department, 1969-71. Fulbright professor in the United Arab Republic, 1964-65. Member of New England Medieval Conference; secretary-general of International Congress of Historians of the United States and Mexico, 1958. Military service: U.S. Army, 1942-46; became major; received Bronze Star and French Croix de Guerre.

MEMBER: American Historical Association, Mediaeval Academy of America (fellow and member of council, 1970—), Middle East Studies Association (fellow), Royal Historical Society (fellow), Phi Beta Kappa. Awards, honors: Ford Foundation fellow in Europe, 1954-55; American Council of Learned Societies fellowship, 1959-60.

WRITINGS: Naval Power and Trade in the Mediterranean, A.D. 500-1100, Princeton University Press, 1951; The Northern Seas: Shipping and Commerce in Northern Europe, A.D. 300-1100, Princeton University Press, 1958; (editor with Thomas F. McGann) The New World Looks at Its History (proceedings), University of Texas Press, 1963; The Development of Southern French and Catalan Society, 718-1050, University of Texas Press, 1965; Emerging Medieval Europe, A.D. 400-1000, Knopf, 1967; (editor) Aspects of the Renaissance (symposium), University of Texas Press, 1967; (editor) The Islamic World and the West, A.D. 662-1492, Wiley, 1970; (editor) The High Middle Ages, 814-1300, Prentice-Hall, 1970; Knights and Samurai: Feudalism in Northern France and Japan, Temple Smith, 1974; The Sea and Comparative Civilization, Variorum Reprints, 1978.

Contributor of numerous articles and reviews to professional journals.

WORK IN PROGRESS: Nomads and Crusaders, on comparative civilizations, 1000-1500, publication expected in 1980.

SIDELIGHTS: Lewis told CA: "I believe comparative history is the most exciting present field of historical writing. It and archaeology are throwing the most light upon the past, especially the exciting new field of underwater archaeology."

*   *   *

LEWIS, C(live) S(taples) 1898-1963
(N. W. Clerk, Clive Hamilton)

PERSONAL: Born November 29, 1898, in Belfast, Ireland; son of Albert James (a solicitor) and Flora Augusta (Hamilton) Lewis; married Joy Gresham Davidman, 1956 (died, 1960). Education: University College, Oxford, A.B. (classics; first class honors), 1922, A.B. (English; first class honors), 1923. Home: Magdalen College, Cambridge, England.

CAREER: Oxford University, Oxford, England, lecturer, University College, 1924, fellow and tutor in English literature, Magdalen College, 1925-54; Cambridge University, Cambridge, England, professor of medieval and Renaissance English, 1954-63. Ballard Matthews Lecturer at University of Wales, 1941; Riddell Lecturer at University of Durham, 1942; Clark Lecturer at Trinity College, Cambridge, 1944. Military service: British Army, Somerset Light Infantry, 1918-19; became second lieutenant.

MEMBER: British Academy (fellow, 1955), Royal Society

of Literature (fellow, 1948), Athenaeum, Sir Walter Scott Society (president, 1956). *Awards, honors:* Hawthornden prize, 1936, for *The Allegory of Love;* Gollancz Memorial Prizeman, 1937; D.D. from St. Andrews University, 1946; Docteur es Lettres from Laval University, 1952; honorary fellow of Magdalen College, Oxford, 1955, University College, Oxford, 1958, and Magdalen College, Cambridge, 1963; Carnegie Medal, 1957, for *The Last Battle;* D.Litt. from University of Manchester, 1959; Lewis Carroll Shelf Award, 1962, for *The Lion, the Witch, and the Wardrobe;* honorary doctorate from University of Dijon, 1962, and University of Lyon, 1963.

WRITINGS—All novels, except as noted: (Under pseudonym Clive Hamilton) *Dymer* (poem), Dutton, 1926, reprinted, Macmillan, 1950; *Out of the Silent Planet*, John Lane, 1938, reprinted, Macmillan, 1970; *Perelandra: A Novel*, John Lane, 1943, reprinted, Macmillan, 1968, new edition published as *Voyage to Venus*, Pan Books, 1960; *That Hideous Strength: A Modern Fairy-Tale for Grownups*, John Lane, 1945, reprinted, Macmillan, 1968; (editor) *George MacDonald: An Anthology*, Centenary Press, 1945; *The Great Divorce: A Dream*, Bles, 1945; *Till We Have Faces: A Myth Retold*, Bles, 1956.

For children; all illustrated by Pauline Baynes: *The Lion, the Witch, and the Wardrobe: A Story for Children*, Macmillan, 1950; *Prince Caspian: The Return to Narnia*, Macmillan, 1951; *The Voyage to the Dawn Treader*, Macmillan, 1952; *The Silver Chair*, Macmillan, 1953; *The Horse and His Boy*, Macmillan, 1954; *The Magician's Nephew*, Macmillan, 1955; *The Last Battle*, Macmillan, 1956; *The Complete Chronicles of Narnia*, seven volumes (a collection of the above books), Penguin, 1965.

Theological works: *The Pilgrim's Regress: An Allegorical Apology for Christianity, Reason and Romanticism*, Dent, 1933, reprinted, Eerdmans, 1958; *The Problem of Pain*, Centenary Press, 1940, reprinted, Macmillan, 1968; *The Screwtape Letters*, Bles, 1942, new edition, with the addition of *Screwtape Proposes a Toast*, Macmillan, 1964; *Broadcast Talks: Reprinted With Some Alterations From Two Series of Broadcast Talks*, Bles, 1942, published as *The Case for Christianity*, Macmillan, 1943, reprinted, 1968; *Christian Behaviour: A Further Series of Broadcast Talks*, Macmillan, 1943; *Beyond Personality: The Christian Idea of God*, Bles, 1944, Macmillan, 1945; *Miracles: A Preliminary Study*, Macmillan, 1947; *The Weight of Glory, and Other Addresses*, Macmillan, 1949 (published in England as *Transposition, and Other Addresses*, Bles, 1949).

Surprised by Joy: The Shape of My Early Life (autobiographical), Bles, 1955, Harcourt, 1956; *Reflections on the Psalms*, Harcourt, 1958; *Shall We Lose God in Outer Space?*, S.P.C.K., 1959; *The Four Loves*, Harcourt, 1960; *The World's Last Night, and Other Essays*, Harcourt, 1960; (under pseudonym N. W. Clerk) *A Grief Observed*, Faber, 1961, Seabury, 1963; *Beyond the Bright Blur*, Harcourt, 1963; *Letters to Malcolm: Chiefly on Prayer*, Harcourt, 1964; *Christian Reflections*, edited by Walter Hooper, Eerdmans, 1967; *God in the Dock: Essays on Theology and Ethics*, edited by Hooper, Eerdmans, 1970; *Undeceptions: Essays on Theology and Ethics*, edited by Hooper, Bles, 1971.

Literary criticism: *The Allegory of Love: A Study in Medieval Tradition*, Clarendon Press, 1936, reprinted, Oxford University Press, 1959; (with Eustace M. W. Tillyard) *The Personal Heresy: A Controversy*, Oxford University Press, 1939, reprinted, 1965; *Rehabilitations and Other Essays*, Oxford University Press, 1939, reprinted, Folcroft, 1973; *A*

Preface to 'Paradise Lost': Being the Ballard Matthews Lectures, Delivered at University College, North Wales, 1941, Oxford University Press, 1942, reprinted, 1970; *Hamlet: The Prince or the Poem?*, H. Milford, 1942, reprinted, Folcroft, 1973; *The Abolition of Man; or, Reflections on Education*, Oxford University Press, 1943, reprinted, Macmillan, 1967.

The Literary Impact of the Authorized Version, Athlone Press, 1950, revised edition, Fortress, 1967; *English Literature in the Sixteenth Century, Excluding Drama*, Clarendon Press, 1954; *Studies in Words*, Cambridge University Press, 1960, 2nd edition, 1967; *An Experiment in Criticism*, Cambridge University Press, 1961; *The Discarded Image: An Introduction to Medieval and Renaissance Literature*, Cambridge University Press, 1964; *Spenser's Images of Life*, edited by Alastair Fowler, Cambridge University Press, 1967; *Selected Literary Essays*, edited by Hooper, Cambridge University Press, 1969; (author of commentary) Charles W. S. Williams, *Taliessin Through Logres*, [and] *The Region of the Summer Stars*, [and] *Arthurian Torso*, Eerdmans, 1974.

Collected works: *Mere Christianity* (contains revised and enlarged versions of *The Case for Christianity, Christian Behaviour*, and *Beyond Personality*), Macmillan, 1952; *They Asked for a Paper: Papers and Addresses*, Bles, 1962; *Poems*, edited by Hooper, Bles, 1964, Harcourt, 1965; *Letters of C. S. Lewis*, edited by W. H. Lewis, Harcourt, 1966; *Of Other Worlds: Essays and Stories*, Bles, 1966; *Studies in Medieval and Renaissance Literature*, edited by Hooper, Cambridge University Press, 1966; *Letters to an American Lady*, edited by Clyde S. Kilby, Eerdmans, 1967, Hodder & Stoughton, 1969; *A Mind Awake: An Anthology of C. S. Lewis*, edited by Kilby, Bles, 1968, Harcourt, 1969; *C. S. Lewis: Five Best Books in One Volume*, Iversen Associates, 1969; *Narrative Poems*, edited by Hooper, Bles, 1969, Harcourt, 1972; *Space Trilogy* (contains *Out of the Silent Planet, Perelandra*, and *That Hideous Strength*), Macmillan, 1975; *The Joyful Christian* (readings), Macmillan, 1977.

Contributor to the proceedings of the British Academy and to *Essays and Studies by Members of the English Association*. Author of the recording "Love," Creative Resources, 1971.

SIDELIGHTS: Whether one approaches the thought of C. S. Lewis through his childhood fantasyland of Narnia, the mythical worlds of Malacandra and Perelandra, the playfully satirical letters of the senior devil Screwtape to his nephew, Wormwood, the witty but thoroughly logical theological works, or the critical literary studies which established him as a noted scholar in his field, one finds that each path leads to an encounter with the faith that thoroughly shaped Lewis's life and writing. Phrases such as "apostle to the skeptics" and "defender of the faith," which serve as subtitles for critical studies of his work, testify to the influence of Lewis's thought upon readers in the mid-twentieth century. Best known as the "unorthodox defender of the orthodoxy," Lewis sought to communicate the essentials of "mere Christianity" to the masses through the various literary genres in which he excelled. "Accepting the fundamental truth in his guts, he set his intellect—and, more important, his common sense—to work on the ramification of that truth, in other words, on exegesis of Holy Writ," wrote Anthony Burgess. "He became a very notable popular exegete, a theologian for Everyman."

Critics point out that Lewis's own journey from atheism to a vital Christian faith uniquely qualified him to defend that faith against its severest opponents. Though brought up in a nominally Christian home, Lewis rejected any belief in God when he was at boarding school. In his autobiography, *Surprised by Joy*, he described his intellectual and spiritual development from childhood through adolescence and early adulthood. Richard Cunningham summarized his journey: "Reason and imagination, beginning early in his life and often pulling in opposite directions, were the controlling elements in Lewis' intellectual and spiritual pilgrimage. Imaginative life came natural to Lewis: the *Sehnsucht*, the longing and desire for Joy, fairyland, and Norse and Celtic mythology. Reason was forced on him by his early tutors, so that he demanded evidence for truth and logically consistent thought. . . . After a period of years in which reason and imagination alternated in dominating him, the two faculties began to work in harmony, first one and then the other forging ahead. . . . His imagination and reason converged at the point of revelation; and for him revelation pointed to where myth had become fact: the Incarnate God Jesus Christ." Describing the moment of his conversion to theism, which came more as a necessary submission to indisputable evidence than as a voluntary choice, Lewis wrote: "You must picture me alone in that room in Magdalen, night after night, feeling, whenever my mind lifted even for a second from my work, the steady, unrelenting approach of Him whom I so earnestly desired not to meet. . . . In the Trinity Term of 1929 I gave in, and admitted that God was God, and knelt and prayed: perhaps, that night, the most dejected and reluctant convert in all England. . . . Who can duly adore that Love which will open the high gates to a prodigal who is brought in kicking, struggling, resentful, and darting his eyes in every direction for a chance of escape?"

Just as the interplay of reason and imagination was instrumental in Lewis's conversion to theism and subsequently to Christianity, so it characterized the body of writings which flowed forth from his pen in the years which followed. Defining his understanding of the relationship between the two faculties, Lewis wrote: "Reason is the natural organ of truth; but imagination is the organ of meaning." Propelled by this conviction, he communicated his ideas in myth, satire, and fantasy, which appealed to the imagination, and in didactic logical treatises, whose arguments addressed the mind. And even though critics distinguished between these genres and assigned his works to one category or another, many acknowledged the interplay within individual works. Edward Ericson noted: "Lewis is always lucid, even in his mythmaking works; he is far from the haziness of expression and the general minimizing of argument characteristic of Romantic works." From the other perspective, Cunningham observed: "His literary technique, even in his didactic writing where he relies so heavily on reason and logic, also depends for its impact on the myths, allegories, metaphors, analogies, epigrams, and illustrations provided by his imagination."

In his discussion of the space trilogy (*Out of the Silent Planet, Perelandra*, and *That Hideous Strength*), R. J. Reilly isolated one of the elements which has made Lewis's works so powerful. "The whole trilogy is full of the old Chestertonian device of making something marvelous by describing it in terms that we never use for it, of making us see something as if for the first time," he declared. Indeed, Lewis specialized in translating orthodox Christian dogma into fresh new terms, or, in Reilly's words, "into mythology in order that Christianity may seem more wonderful (not more wonderful than it is, perhaps, but more wonderful than we ordinarily conceive it)." Lewis himself explained his aim in writing the tales of Narnia: "I thought I saw how stories of this kind could steal past a certain inhibition which had paralysed much of my own religion in childhood. Why did one find it so hard to feel as one was told one ought to feel about God or about the sufferings of Christ? I thought the chief reason was that one was told one ought to. . . . But supposing that by casting all these things into an imaginary world, stripping them of their stained-glass and Sunday school associations, one could make them for the first time appear in their real potency? Could one not thus steal past those watchful dragons? I thought one could."

Though many critics focused primarily upon Lewis's literary contributions, finding his didactic works less satisfying, Ericson contended: "It is the clarity of his argument which has captured the minds of so many of his readers. . . . Whether those who have made Lewis one of their academic specialties are comfortable with the fact or not, those treatises which are in cold prose apologetics for the Christian faith are the ones which have carried Lewis to the farthest corners of the earth." Calvin Linton lauded Lewis's scholarly merits, declaring: "A major, if not the chief, service he performed was to demonstrate that the Christian faith need fear no intellectual assault. . . . Trained in the debating arenas of Oxford and Cambridge, where, in cuts and parries with the finest verbal swordsmen of the world, the dueler whose blade slips on the form of a Greek verb or on an infelicitous use of a Latin quotation is quickly bled, Lewis was a feared and respected warrior."

Of course Lewis had his enemies as well. Ericson admitted that Lewis has been "a source of . . . irritation, of exasperation, of hostility" as well as "of solace, of challenge, of inspiration." Some critics accused him of "brittle dogmatism" in the radio talks which later became part of *Mere Christianity*, and others found his defense of Christianity unconvincing. "The Chronicles of Narnia" came under attack by critics such as Penelope Lively, who rebuked Lewis for "the cardinal error of condescension towards children" which he allegedly committed by writing "with a 'message.'" But the tributes have far outweighed the assaults upon Lewis's work. *The Screwtape Letters*, perhaps his best known book, has not failed to live up to the *Manchester Guardian*'s prediction in 1942 that "it should become a classic." Roger Lancelyn Green expressed his confidence that the tales of Narnia would "live to take their permanent place among the great works of children's literature." Other words of praise abound, but perhaps Linton paid Lewis the highest homage when he exclaimed: "Lewis has altered our sensibility, the *way* we think about things; he has given us words and phrases by which we grasp vital ideas; he has given us a pattern of feeling within which we better comprehend artistic and Christian truths. He is one of those rare writers who leave us different from what we were before we read him."

BIOGRAPHICAL/CRITICAL SOURCES: Manchester Guardian, February 24, 1942; Chad Walsh, *C. S. Lewis: Apostle to the Skeptics*, Macmillan, 1949, reprinted, Folcroft, 1974; C. S. Lewis, *Surprised by Joy: The Shape of My Early Life*, Harcourt, 1956; Clyde S. Kilby, *Christian World of C. S. Lewis*, Eerdmans, 1964; H. H. Kruener, *Religion in Life*, Summer, 1965; Jocelyn Gibb, editor, *Light on C. S. Lewis*, Harcourt, 1965; W. H. Lewis, editor, *Letters of C. S. Lewis*, Harcourt, 1966; Richard B. Cunningham, *C. S. Lewis: Defender of the Faith*, Westminster Press, 1967; David C. Hill, *Messengers of the King*, Augsburg, 1968; Kilby, editor, *Letters to an American Lady*, Eerdmans, 1967; Peter Kreeft, *C. S. Lewis*, Eerdmans, 1969.

Douglas Gilbert, *C. S. Lewis: Images of His World*, Eerdmans, 1973; *Contemporary Literary Criticism,* Gale, Volume 1, 1973, Volume 3, 1975, Volume 6, 1976; *Christianity Today,* November 9, 1973; Corbin S. Carnell, *Bright Shadow of Reality: C. S. Lewis and the Feeling Intellect,* Eerdmans, 1974; Roger L. Green and Walter C. Hooper, *C. S. Lewis: A Biography,* Harcourt, 1974; Carolyn Keefe, *C. S. Lewis: Speaker and Teacher,* Zondervan, 1974; Anne Arnott, *Country of C. S. Lewis,* Eerdmans, 1975; R. P. Tripp, editor, *Essays on C. S. Lewis,* Society for New Language Study, 1975; *New York Times Book Review,* December 25, 1977; Gilbert Meilander, *The Taste for the Other: The Social and Ethical Thought of C. S. Lewis,* Eerdmans, 1978; *Children's Literature Review,* Volume 3, Gale, 1978.*

(Died November 22, 1963)

*　　*　　*

LEWIS, David Kellogg 1941-

PERSONAL: Born September 28, 1941, in Oberlin, Ohio; son of John Donald (a college professor) and Ewart (a college professor; maiden name, Kellogg) Lewis; married Stephanie Robinson (a university teacher), September 5, 1965. *Education:* Swarthmore College, B.A., 1962; Harvard University, M.A., 1964, Ph.D., 1967. *Politics:* Democrat. *Religion:* None. *Residence:* Princeton, N.J. *Office:* Department of Philosophy, Princeton University, Princeton, N.J. 08540.

CAREER: University of California, Los Angeles, assistant professor of philosophy, 1966-70; Princeton University, Princeton, N.J., associate professor, 1970-73, professor of philosophy, 1973—. Fulbright lecturer in Australia, 1971. *Member:* American Association of University Professors. *Awards, honors:* Matchette Prize for philosophical writing, from Franklin J. Matchette Foundation, 1972, for *Convention.*

WRITINGS: Convention: A Philosophical Study, Harvard University Press, 1969; *Counterfactuals,* Harvard University Press, 1973. Contributor to philosophy journals.

WORK IN PROGRESS: Research on philosophy of science, metaphysics, and semantics.

*　　*　　*

LEWIS, Paul
See GERSON, Noel Bertram

*　　*　　*

LIANG, Chin-tung 1893-

PERSONAL: Born May 24, 1893, in Foochow, China. *Education:* National University of Peking, LL.B., 1915; graduate study at London School of Economics and Political Science, 1920-23, and Literary Academy (Taiwan), 1972. *Home:* 425 Riverside Dr., New York, N.Y. 10025.

CAREER: Professor of comparative criminal law at National University of Peking, Peking, China; director of Institute of Modern History, Academia Sinica, Nankang, Taipei, Taiwan.

WRITINGS: The Crisis of September 18, 1931, World's Book Store (Taipei, Taiwan), 1970; *General Stilwell in China,* St. John's University Press, 1972; *The Cairo Conference and China,* Commercial Press (Taipei, Taiwan), 1973.

*　　*　　*

LIBBEY, James K(eith) 1942-

PERSONAL: Born May 16, 1942, in Holden, Mass.; son of Russell James (an engineer) and Narcissa (an English teacher; maiden name, Gleason) Libbey; married Joyce Holmes (a secretary), December 28, 1963. *Education:* Miami University, Oxford, Ohio, B.A., 1964, B.S.Ed., 1967; Eastern Kentucky University, M.A., 1971; University of Kentucky, Ph.D., 1976. *Politics:* Democrat. *Religion:* Roman Catholic. *Home:* 937 Vickers Village, Richmond, Ky. 40475. *Office:* Central University College, Eastern Kentucky University, Richmond, Ky. 40475.

CAREER: Teacher at Roman Catholic school in Brookville, Ind., 1964-67; University of Kentucky, Lexington, instructor in Russian history, 1973-74; Eastern Kentucky University, Richmond, assistant professor of learning skills, 1974-78, associate professor of humanities and associate dean of College of Arts and Humanities, 1978—. Member of Richmond Food Bank Committee and Newman Center Committee of Faculty and Friends. *Military service:* U.S. Army, 1968-69. *Member:* American Association for the Advancement of Slavic Studies, Organization of American Historians, Society for Historians of American Foreign Relations, Phi Alpha Theta, Phi Delta Kappa.

WRITINGS: Alexander Gumberg and Soviet-American Relations, 1917-1933, University Press of Kentucky, 1977; *'Dear Alben': Mr. Barkley of Kentucky,* University Press of Kentucky, 1978. Contributor to *The Modern Encyclopedia of Russian and Soviet History.* Contributor to magazines and newspapers, including *Journalism Quarterly* and *Foreign Affairs Newsletter.*

WORK IN PROGRESS: A biography, tentatively entitled *Alben W. Barkley: Democracy's Defender.*

SIDELIGHTS: Libbey writes: "My youthful disappointment with America's response to the Hungarian Revolt of 1956 helped launch me on a life-long search for an explanation for the weaknesses of American foreign policy. Although a penchant for biography has led me into pleasant sidestreets called Humanities, my initial conclusion from my search is that ideologues and moralists should never be allowed to enter the realm of foreign affairs."

*　　*　　*

LIEDLOFF, Jean

PERSONAL: Born in New York, N.Y.; daughter of James E. (a sculptor) and Helen (a sculptor; maiden name, Willard) Liedloff. *Education:* Attended Cornell University, Florida Southern College, and New School for Social Research. *Home:* 11 St. George's Ter., London NW1, England.

CAREER: Writer. Columnist for *Il Borghese* (magazine), Milan, Italy; editor-writer for *Ecologist,* London, England; copywriter for McCann Erickson, New York City; broadcaster and interviewer for British Broadcasting Corporation (BBC-TV). Foreign language interpreter. Explorer in the Venezuelan jungle near the Brazilian border. Lecturer. *Awards, honors:* Best book award from *Psychology Today,* 1975, and annual award from Transcendental Meditation program, 1977, both for *The Continuum Concept.*

WRITINGS: The Continuum Concept, Duckworth, 1975, published as *The Continuum Concept: A Rediscovery of Man's Capacity for Happiness From the Critical First Months of Life,* Knopf, 1977. Contributor of articles to *Esquire, Saturday Evening Post,* and *Populi* (UN publication).

WORK IN PROGRESS: The Continuum Sense.

SIDELIGHTS: Jean Liedloff, a native New Yorker who speaks Italian, Spanish, and French fluently, prefers to spend her time in foreign countries. Liedloff's first expedition to the Venezuelan jungle was a twenty-minute decision on a last minute invitation. Liedloff explained: "In Florence, on my first trip to Europe, I was invited to join two Italian explorers on a diamond hunting expedition in the region of Venezuela's Caroni River, a tributary of the Orinoco. It was very dramatic, but rather frightening when the action suddenly subsided and I saw our compartment piled with suitcases reflected in the light through the dusty window, and I realized I was on my way to a genuine jungle."

It was during the first month of exploring that Liedloff realized that "The Glade" had brought back all of the excitement that she experienced when she was eight and at summer camp. Liedloff recalled that camp experience: "I was the last in line, I had fallen back a bit and was hurrying to catch up when, through the trees, I saw a glade. The whole picture had completeness, an all-there quality of such dense power that it stopped me in my tracks." Liedloff had recaptured that feeling through this expedition. She was experiencing a "grown-up glade," the biggest jungle on earth. This rediscovery of "The Glade" would not be forgotten. Liedloff said: "It was the 'rightness' I had tried to discern through the bafflements of my childhood and in the talks, discussions, arguments, often pursued until dawn, in the hope of a glimpse of it in the following years. It was 'The Glade,' recognized, this time forever."

After seven and a half months of exploration, Liedloff had formed a clear view of things as they were. She was able to pacify her curiosity about the Indians. Liedloff considered the Tauripan Indians to be the most interesting and happiest people she had ever become acquainted with. They had adapted and lived the life of a species in its habitat. Liedloff described the Indian children as being "uniformly well-behaved," never fighting or giving reason to be punished.

Liedloff's second expedition was also led by an Italian, a professor who believed that women did not belong in the jungle. Liedloff was accepted through the arrangement of one of her former partners. During this expedition she became acquainted with the Yequana and Sanema tribes. She found the personalities of the men, women, and children to be more individual, not like the defensive "blank-face-for-strangers" personalities projected by the Tauripans. Liedloff lived three weeks alone with the Yequana. She stated: "In that short time I unlearned more of the assumptions upon which I was reared than I had on the entire expedition. And I begin to see the value of the unlearning process." The fifth expedition confirmed Liedloff's interpretation of the behavior of the Indians supported by the reality and unaccountable actions of both tribes.

BIOGRAPHICAL/CRITICAL SOURCES: Jean Liedloff, *The Continuum Concept,* Knopf, 1977; *New Age,* February, 1978.

*   *   *

LIGHTFOOT, Neil R(oland) 1929-

PERSONAL: Born September 22, 1929, in Waco, Tex.; son of W. D. (a realtor) and Minnie Lee (Crow) Lightfoot; married Ollie Robinson (an elementary school teacher), April 7, 1951; children: Donna Lynn, Lu Anne, Michelle. *Education:* Baylor University, B.A., 1952, M.A., 1955; Duke University, Ph.D., 1958. *Home:* 1093 Cedar Crest Dr., Abilene, Tex. 79601. *Office:* Department of Religion, Abilene Christian University, Abilene, Tex. 79601.

CAREER: Abilene Christian University, Abilene, Tex., assistant professor, 1958-61, associate professor, 1961-67, professor of New Testament, 1967—. *Member:* Society of Biblical Literature.

WRITINGS: How We Got the Bible, Sweet Publishing, 1962, revised edition, Baker Book, 1963; *The Parables of Jesus,* Sweet Publishing, 1963; *Lessons From the Parables,* Baker Book, 1965; *Jesus Christ Today: A Commentary on the Book of Hebrews,* Baker Book, 1976; *The Role of Women: New Testament Perspectives,* Student Association Press, 1978. Author of narration for filmstrip series, "How We Got the Bible," produced by Gospel Services.

SIDELIGHTS: Lightfoot writes: "*How We Got the Bible* and *Lessons From the Parable* were written especially for use in Bible classes in various churches. Both books have been used widely and have had an extraordinary circulation. In writing *Jesus Christ Today,* I sought to write a scholarly and yet interesting commentary. The book seeks to bring out the contemporary message of Hebrews: in the midst of much language of ritual, Hebrews has a vital message of exhortation for Christians today. *The Role of Women: New Testament Perspectives* is the publication of four lectures I gave at the Harding Graduate School of Religion in September, 1977. The occasion was the second annual W. B. West Lectures for the Advancement of Christian Scholarship. I propose in all of my writings to present sound biblical scholarship in a practical and understandable way."

*   *   *

LINKS, J(oseph) G(luckenstein) 1904-

PERSONAL: Born December 13, 1904, in London, England; son of Calman and Katey (Symons) Links; married Mary Lutyens (a writer), June 6, 1946. *Education:* Attended high school in London, England. *Home:* 2 Hyde Park St., London W2 2JN, England. *Office:* 149 Brompton Rd., London SW3 1QX, England.

CAREER: Former director of Calman Links Ltd., London, England; director of Hudson's Bay Co. in London and Winnipeg, Manitoba, 1946-75; writer, 1975—. *Military service:* Royal Air Force, 1939-46; became wing commander; received Order of the British Empire. *Member:* British Fur Trade Association (president), Savile Club, Beefsteak Club.

WRITINGS: (With Dennis Wheatley) *Murder Off Miami,* Hutchinson, 1936; (with Wheatley) *Who Killed Robert Prentice?,* Hutchinson, 1937; (with Wheatley) *The Malinsay Massacre,* Hutchinson, 1938; (with Wheatley) *Herewith the Clues!,* Hutchinson, 1939.

The Book of Fur, J. Barrie, 1956; *How to Look at Furs,* Bodley Head, 1959; (editor) John Ruskin, *The Stones of Venice* (abridged edition), Hill & Wang, 1960; *Venice for Pleasure* (travel book), Bodley Head, 1966, revised edition, 1973, Dufour, 1968, revised edition, Norton, 1973; *Venice,* Lutterworth, 1967; *The Ruskins in Normandy: A Tour in 1848 with Murray's Handbook,* J. Murray, 1968.

(Author of introduction and commentary) Antonio Canal, *Views of Venice,* Dover, 1971; *Townscape Painting and Drawing,* Harper, 1972; (author of introduction and commentary) *Canaletto: Thirty Etchings,* Brandon Press, 1976; *Canaletto and His Patrons,* New York University Press, 1977; (author of revision) William George Constable, *Canaletto: Giovanni Antonio Canal, 1697-1768,* two volumes, Clarendon Press, 1977. Contributor to magazines, including *Burlington* and *Apollo.*

WORK IN PROGRESS: European Travellers; Venice for Pleasure, third edition; lectures on Canaletto.

*   *   *

LIPHAM, James Maurice 1927-

PERSONAL: Born August 10, 1927, in Fyffe, Ala.; son of

William Herbert and Ava Frances (Gilley) Lipham; married Charlotte Kight, June 10, 1956; children: Mary Elizabeth, William James. *Education:* Tennessee Wesleyan College, A.A., 1948; University of Georgia, B.S., 1951, M.Ed., 1953; University of Chicago, Ph.D., 1960. *Religion:* Baptist. *Home:* 6318 Old Sauk Rd., Madison, Wis. 53705. *Office:* Department of Educational Administration, University of Wisconsin, 1025 West Johnson St., Madison, Wis. 53706.

CAREER: High school teacher of science in Tifton, Ga., 1953-55, and Upper Arlington, Ohio, 1955-56; superintendent of schools in DeGraff, Ohio, 1956-58; University of Chicago, Chicago, Ill., staff associate, 1958-60; University of Wisconsin—Madison, assistant professor, 1960-62, associate professor, 1963-65, professor of educational administration, 1966—. *Military service:* U.S. Army, 1946-48, 1951-52. *Member:* National Education Association, American Educational Research Association, Wisconsin Education Association, Wisconsin Association of School Administrators, Phi Beta Kappa, Phi Kappa Phi, Phi Delta Kappa, Kappa Delta Pi, Gamma Sigma Epsilon, Masons, Kiwanis.

WRITINGS: Educational Administration as a Social Process, Harper, 1968; *The Principalship: Foundations and Functions,* Harper, 1974; *The Principal and Individually Guided Education,* Addison-Wesley, 1976; *Individually Guided Secondary Education,* Wisconsin Research and Development Center, 1980; *Organizational Relationships in Schools,* Wisconsin Research and Development Center, 1980. Contributor to professional journals. Associate editor of *School Review,* 1959-60, and *Administrator's Notebook,* 1959-60.

SIDELIGHTS: Lipham writes: "The principal fulfills a crucial and significant leadership role in the improvement of education. Much of my writing is devoted to improving the conceptual, technical, and human skills required of the school principal. In implementing a major educational innovation, such as 'Individually Guided Education,' the principal must understand the nature of the change process and be skilled in involving staff, students, parents, citizens, and others in planning, decision making, implementing, and evaluating educational processes, programs, and outcomes."

*   *   *

LITOWINSKY, Olga (Jean) 1936-

PERSONAL: Born February 9, 1936, in Newark, N.J.; daughter of Zachary (a tailor) and Helen (Bazyk) Litowinsky. *Education:* Latin American Institute, diploma, 1955; Columbia University, B.S., 1965. *Politics:* "Sympathetic to current national and international liberation movements." *Religion:* Agnostic ("former Catholic and atheist"). *Residence:* Brooklyn, N.Y. *Office:* Viking Press, Inc., 625 Madison Ave., New York, N.Y. 10022.

CAREER: Columbia University Forum, New York City, assistant editor, 1958-63; Charles Scribner's Sons, New York City, assistant editor of trade science books, 1965-67; Crowell-Collier Press, New York City, associate editor, 1967-70; Viking Press, Inc., New York City, editor of children's books, 1971—. Spanish-English secretary to Intercontinental Hotels and Pan American Airways. *Member:* Society of Children's Book Writers, Children's Artists and Writers Collaborative.

WRITINGS: The High Voyage (juvenile), Viking, 1977; (with Bebe Willoughby) *The Dream Book* (juvenile), Coward, 1978; (editor and contributor) *The New York Kid's Catalog,* Doubleday, 1979. Contributor to *SCBW Bulletin* and *Atlas.*

WORK IN PROGRESS: A novel about contemporary teenagers; picture books for children.

SIDELIGHTS: Olga Litowinsky writes: "I've been a voracious reader since childhood and, like most editors, I've longed to write for a long time, but did not take myself seriously until I joined the Children's Artists and Writers Collaborative, a group of published and unpublished writers and illustrators of children's books. With their support, my collaborator and I managed to submit a proposal to Coward for *The Dream Book,* the notes for which had been sitting in our desk drawers for about four years. Once the contract was a reality, so was the thought of considering myself a writer. I've just begun, and I have a lot to say. All I need now is time.

"I want to write for children because I want to write honestly. We are surrounded by lies and soft thinking these days, and it's important to get to young people with the truth before they become corrupted by the easy lies of the media and exploitative adult publishing. I am an incurable romantic about people and their possibilities."

AVOCATIONAL INTERESTS: Travel (Europe, Latin America).

*   *   *

LITTLE, Loyd (Harry), Jr. 1940-

PERSONAL: Born September 12, 1940, in Hickory, N.C.; son of Loyd Harry (in sales) and Reba (Bailey) Little; married Drena Edwards (a realtor), December 23, 1963. *Education:* University of North Carolina, B.A., 1962, graduate study, 1967-68. *Home address:* Route 3, Box 91, Hillsborough, N.C. 27278. *Agent:* Roberta Pryor, International Creative Management, 40 West 57th St., New York, N.Y. 10019.

CAREER: Editor of newspaper in Pembroke, N.C., 1966; *Winston-Salem Journal,* Winston-Salem, N.C., reporter, 1966-67; *Raleigh News & Observer,* Raleigh, N.C., business editor, 1969-70; *Carolina Financial Times,* Raleigh, editor and publisher, 1970-76; *Durham Morning Herald,* Durham, N.C., investigative reporter, 1977—. *Military service:* U.S. Army, Special Forces, 1962-65; served in Vietnam; became staff sergeant; received Bronze Star. *Awards, honors:* Ernest Hemingway Foundation Award, 1976, for *Parthian Shot.*

WRITINGS: Parthian Shot (novel), Viking, 1975; *In the Village of the Man* (novel), Viking, 1978. Contributor of a short story to *Playboy.*

*   *   *

LITTMAN, Robert J. 1943-

PERSONAL: Born August 23, 1943, in N.J.; son of Maxwell L. (a physician) and Mildred (Geist) Littman; married Bernice Fingerhut (a lawyer), August 29, 1966. *Education:* Columbia University, B.A., 1964, Ph.D., 1970; Oxford University, B.Litt., 1968. *Home:* 1541 Kalaniwai Pl., Honolulu, Hawaii 96821. *Office:* Department of European Languages, University of Hawaii, Honolulu, Hawaii 96822.

CAREER: Rutgers University, New Brunswick, N.J., instructor in history, 1967-68; Brandeis University, Waltham, Mass., instructor in classics, 1968-70; University of Hawaii, Honolulu, assistant professor, 1971-75, associate professor of classics, 1975—. *Awards, honors:* Herodotus fellowship for Princeton's Institute for Advanced Study, 1977.

WRITINGS: The Greek Experiment: Imperialism and So-

cial Conflict, 800-400 B.C., Harcourt, 1974. Contributor of articles on ancient history, literature, and Biblical studies to scholarly journals.

* * *

LIVINGSTON, Bernard 1911-

PERSONAL: Born February 6, 1911, in Baltimore, Md.; son of Benjamin N. (a theater owner) and Bertha (Mogul) Livingston; married Nina G. Martin, November 26, 1935 (divorced March 28, 1942); married Dori Sarin (a fashion consultant), April 1, 1942 (divorced, 1958). *Education:* University of Baltimore, LL.B., 1931. *Residence:* New York, N.Y. *Agent:* Maxmillian Becker, 115 East 82nd St., New York, N.Y. 10028.

CAREER: United Press International, New York City, staff photographer, 1944-46; independent documentary film producer in New York City, 1945-55; public relations executive in New York City, 1955-70; writer, 1970—. Once managed a burlesque theater. *Military service:* U.S. Army, 1941-43; became technical sergeant. *Awards, honors:* Award from Scholastic Magazines, 1953, for best documentary film of the year, "Greentree Thoroughbred."

WRITINGS: Papa's Burlesque House (novel), William-Frederick, 1971; *Their Turf: America's Horsey Set and Its Princely Dynasties,* Arbor House, 1973; *Zoo: Animals, People, Places* Arbor House, 1974.

WORK IN PROGRESS: Manhattan Odyssey, nonfiction; *The Survivor,* a novel.

AVOCATIONAL INTERESTS: Mozart.

* * *

LLERENA, Mario 1913-
(Ara Niemoller)

PERSONAL Born March 5, 1913, in Placetas, Las Villas, Cuba; came to the United States in 1960, naturalized citizen, 1971; son of Rafael (a laundry worker) and Maria (a teacher; maiden name, Rodriguez) Llerena; married Laura Hernandez, December 21, 1946 (divorced, December, 1966); married Victoria Galvez (a seamstress), June 17, 1967; children: Mario A., Stella Llerena Portada. *Education:* University of Havana, D.Phil., 1940; Princeton Theological Seminary, B.Th., 1947. *Politics:* Conservative Democrat. *Religion:* Christian. *Home:* 3211 West Flagler, #12, Miami, Fla. 33135. *Office:* LOGOI, Inc., 4100 West Flagler, Miami, Fla. 33134.

CAREER: Elementary and high school teacher in Cuba, 1934-42; Duke University, Durham, N.C., instructor in Spanish, 1948-52; free-lance writer in Havana, Cuba, 1952-56, and in New York, N.Y., and Miami, Fla., 1960-66; University of Miami Press, Miami, Fla., assistant editor, 1967-72; free-lance writer, 1972-75; LOGOI, Inc., Miami, Fla., chief editor, 1975—.

WRITINGS: (Under pseudonym Ara Niemoller) *Drogas* (title means "Drugs"), LOGOI, 1976; *The Unsuspected Revolution,* Cornell University Press, 1978; *A Manual of Style for the Spanish Language,* LOGOI, 1979. Contributor to Hispanic studies journals.

SIDELIGHTS: Llerena writes: "During the 1940's and 1950's I worked for several Cuban newspapers and weeklies, writing mostly on political and educational subjects. From 1952 to 1957 I was actively involved in the anti-Batista struggle in Cuba, and in 1957, I was appointed delegate abroad of the Castro movement in New York, from which I resigned publicly on August 14, 1958.

"Two leading factors have played a determining role in my life: my conversion to evangelical Christianity in my late teens and my interest in the political development of Cuba. I can definitely say that my political ideology has been the result of and shaped my Christian faith.

"I write in response to an inner urge for self-expression. Since I found myself not precisely cut to be a preacher or a missionary, writing became both a dear vocation and a means to achieving some sense of a constructive purpose in life.

"However, much as writing is for me a form of expression directly influenced by my personal faith, I don't find myself writing on religious subjects in the strict sense of the word.

"I should add here that for all that writing means to me (my greatest ambition since earliest childhood was to become and to be known of as a 'writer'), writing is an almost painful activity for me. I can only write about something that I deeply feel about, but I have to work very hard to achieve a readable style. I write and rewrite and rewrite some more. In this I am an incurable 'perfectionist'—which doesn't at all mean that the finished product ever comes near perfection.

"Most of my writing has been in the form of articles for the press, and appeared in a variety of Cuban and a few American publications (newspaper, weeklies, journals, etc.) from approximately 1939 through the present day.

"For what should be obvious reasons, I admire writers who have suffered political disillusionment and have had both the capacity and the courage to write about it—Arthur Koestler, Milovan Djilas, among others."

* * *

LLYWELYN, Morgan 1937-

PERSONAL: Born December 3, 1937, in New York, N.Y.; daughter of Joseph John (an attorney) and Henri Llywelyn (a secretary; maiden name, Price) Snyder; married Charles Winter (a professional pilot), January 1, 1957; children: John Joseph. *Education:* Attended high school in Dallas, Tex. *Residence:* Annapolis, Md. *Agent:* Richard Curtis Literary Agency, 156 East 52nd St., New York, N.Y. 10022.

CAREER: Fashion model and dance instructor in Dallas, Tex., 1954-56; secretary in Denver, Colo., 1956-59; riding instructor in Denver, 1959-61; amateur equestrian, training and showing her own horses, 1961-76; writer, 1974—. *Member:* United States Dressage Federation, American Horse Shows Association, Mensa, National Geographic Society.

WRITINGS: The Wind from Hastings (historical novel), Houghton, 1978; *Boru* (fictionalized biography), Houghton, in press.

WORK IN PROGRESS: Research for a novel "set in pre-Roman Britain, dealing with Druidic and pre-Druidic beliefs and their relationship to the ancient wisdom of the lost civilizations."

SIDELIGHTS: Morgan Llywelyn writes: "Since becoming a writer, I have become an impassioned student of history as well, particularly the earliest history of what we now call the English-speaking peoples.

"History is cyclical. That era which seems most distant may return again, and yet again; our past may be our future. The Dark Ages of a thousand years ago may not be the first, nor yet the last, in mankind's story, but they are a region I intend to explore. In my writing I move backward through time, retelling the legends and investigating the lives of our remote ancestors, and offering my readers a chance to ride a time machine into their own pasts.

"By writing real history in a fictional style I hope to make it familiar and interesting territory, full of lessons that are applicable today and people that have something in common with us—perhaps more than we know.

"Our roots go all the way back to the dawn of civilization, and in every generation there have been lives of high adventure and great drama, many of them unfortunately forgotten. I want to bring them to light again."

BIOGRAPHICAL/CRITICAL SOURCES: Classic, January, 1977.

* * *

LOCHHEAD, Liz 1947-

PERSONAL: Born December 26, 1947, in Motherwell, Scotland; daughter of John (a local government official) and Margaret (Forrest) Lochhead. *Education:* Glasgow School of Art, diploma, 1970. *Home:* 356 West Princes St., Glasgow, Scotland.

CAREER: Teacher of art at schools in Glasgow, Scotland, and Bristol, England; lecturer at University of Glasgow. *Member:* Poetry Society (England). *Awards, honors:* Scotland Prize from British Broadcasting Corp., 1971; new writing award from Scottish Arts Council, 1972, for *Memo for Spring.*

WRITINGS: Memo for Spring (poems), Reprographia, 1972. Also author of a book of poems, *The Grimm Sisters,* and a screenplay, "Now and Then," 1972. Work represented in *Seven New Voices: Made in Scotland,* Carcanet Press, 1974.

SIDELIGHTS: Liz Lochhead writes: "*The Grimm Sisters* includes a large section of retellings of old ballads, old stories, and poems about storytelling itself. I am becoming more and more interested in the ancient border ballads, old religions, and folklore, especially of Scotland."

* * *

LOEOEF, Jan 1940-

PERSONAL: Born May 30, 1940, in Trollhaettan, Sweden; son of Hilding Emanuel and Kerstin (Wennerberg) Loeoef. *Education:* Attended Konstfackskolan, Stockholm, Sweden, 1959-64. *Politics:* Social-democrat. *Religion:* Protestant. *Home:* Renstiernasgata 41A, Stockholm, Sweden. *Office:* Carlsen if, Kobmagergade 9, Copenhagen, Denmark.

CAREER: Free-lance writer and illustrator, 1964—.

*WRITINGS—*For children: *Min morfar er soeroever* (self-illustrated), translation by Else Holmelund Minarik published as *My Grandpa Is a Pirate,* Harper, 1968; *Historien om det roede aeble,* translation by Ole Risom and Linda Hayward published as *Who's Got the Apple?,* Random House, 1975; *Skrot-nisse,* translation published as *Junk Jimmy's African Trip,* A. & C. Black, 1976.

Not published in English: *En trollkari i Stockholm,* Raben & Sjoegren, 1966; *Sagan om den flygande hunden,* Carlsen/Illustrations foerlaget, 1967.

* * *

LOEVINGER, Lee 1913-

PERSONAL: Born April 24, 1913, in St. Paul, Minn.; son of Gustavus (a judge) and Millie (a teacher; maiden name, Strouse) Loevinger; married Ruth E. Howe (a nurse), March 4, 1950; children: Barbara Lee, Eric Howe, Peter Howe. *Education:* University of Minnesota, B.A. (summa cum laude), 1933, J.D., 1936. *Politics:* Democrat. *Religion:* Unitarian-Universalist. *Home:* 5669 Bent Branch Rd.,

Washington, D.C. 20016. *Office:* Hogan & Hartson, 815 Connecticut Ave., Washington, D.C. 20006.

CAREER: Admitted to bar in Minnesota, District of Columbia, U.S. Supreme Court, and U.S. Tax Court; Watson, Ess, Groner, Barnett & Whittaker, Kansas City, Mo., associate, 1936-37; National Labor Relations Board, Washington, D.C., trial attorney and regional attorney, 1937-41; U.S. Department of Justice, Washington, D.C., attorney in Antitrust Division, 1941-46; Larson, Loevinger, Lindquist, Freeman & Fraser, Minneapolis, Minn., partner, 1946-60; Minnesota Supreme Court, St. Paul, associate justice, 1960-61; U.S. Department of Justice, assistant attorney general in charge of Antitrust Division, 1961-63; Federal Communications Commission, Washington, D.C., commissioner, 1963-68; Hogan & Hartson, Washington, D.C., partner, 1968—. General counsel to General Securities, Inc. (mutual fund), 1951-60; special counsel to U.S. Senate subcommittee on small business, 1951-52; vice-president and member of board of directors of Craig-Hallum Corp. and Craig-Hallum, Inc. (investment bankers), 1968-73; member of Administrative Council of the United States, 1972-74. Lecturer at University of Minnesota, 1953-60, visiting professor, 1961; professorial lecturer at American University, 1968-70. Chairman of Minnesota Atomic Development Problems Committee, 1957-59. U.S. delegate to international conferences. *Military service:* U.S. Naval Reserve, active duty, 1942-46; served in European theater; became lieutenant commander.

MEMBER: American Bar Association (member of House of Delegates, 1974—; chairman of committee on uniform rules, 1969-70), Federal Communications Bar Association, Federal Bar Association, American Judicature Society, American Association for the Advancement of Science, Broadcast Pioneers, National Lawyers Club, Minnesota Bar Association, Bar Association of the District of Columbia (chairman of antitrust committee, 1969-70), Hennepin County Bar Association, Phi Beta Kappa, Sigma Xi, Delta Sigma Rho, Sigma Delta Chi, Phi Delta Gamma, Tau Kappa Alpha, Alpha Epsilon Rho, International Club (Washington, D.C.), Sycamore Island Club, Rehoboth Bay Sailing Association. *Awards, honors:* Outstanding achievement medal from University of Minnesota, 1968.

WRITINGS: The Law of Free Enterprise, Funk, 1949; (editor and contributor) *Basic Data Regarding Atomic Development Problems in Minnesota,* Minnesota State Publications Office, 1958; *Jurimetrics: The Methodology of Legal Inquiry, Law, and Contemporary Problems,* Basic Books, 1963. Also author of *The Morality of Mergers: The Antitrust Trip From Economics to Ecclesiastics and Back,* 1974.

Contributor: R. D. Henson, editor, *Landmarks of Law,* Harper, 1960; *Law and Electronics: The Challenge of a New Era,* Matthew Bender, 1962; *Understanding the Antitrust Laws,* Practising Law Institute, 1963; Michael D. Reagan, editor, *Politics, Economics, and the General Welfare,* Scott, Foresman, 1965; (author of introduction) Glendon Schubert, *Judicial Policy-Making,* Scott, Foresman, 1965; (author of foreword) James Marshall, *Law and Psychology in Conflict,* Bobbs-Merrill, 1966; David M. White and Richard Averson, editors, *Sight, Sound, and Society,* Beacon Press, 1968; Walter B. Emery, editor, *National and International Systems of Broadcasting,* Michigan State University Press, 1969; Pennypacker and Braden, editors, *Broadcasting and the Public Interest,* Random House, 1969; M.A. Duggan and other editors, *The Computer Utility,* Heath, 1970; Voelker, editor, *Mass Media: Forces in Our Society,* Harcourt, 1972; *Computers and the Legal Profession,* American Bar Association, 1973; Backman, editor, *Business*

Problems of the Seventies, New York University Press, 1973; Divita, editor, *Advertising and the Public Interest*, American Marketing Association, 1974; Nicosia, editor, *Advertising, Management, and Society*, McGraw, 1974; Thomas, editor, *Scientists in the Legal System*, Ann Arbor Science Publishers, 1974. Also contributor to *The Sociology of Law*, edited by Rita J. Simon, 1968, and *Problems and Controversies in Television and Radio*, 1968.

Contributor of more than a hundred articles and reviews to a variety of scholarly journals and popular magazines and newspapers, including *TV Guide*. Member of advisory board of *Antitrust Bulletin, Performing Arts Review*, and *Duke Law Journal*. Editorial adviser for *Jurimetrics Journal*.

WORK IN PROGRESS: Defending Antitrust Lawsuits.

SIDELIGHTS: Loevinger writes: "My major areas of interest have been science and the law. In 1949 I first used the term 'jurimetrics' in a publication, for the intersecting area of science and law. I have published numerous articles on the subject and the term is now in general use. My second area of interest is economics and the law."

* * *

LONG, Emmett
    See LEONARD, Elmore

* * *

LONG, Frank Belknap 1903-

PERSONAL: Born April 27, 1903, in New York, N.Y.; son of Frank (a dentist) and May (Doty) Long; married Lyda Arco, August 19, 1960. *Education:* Attended New York University, 1920-21. *Home and office:* 421 West 21st St., New York, N.Y. 10011.

CAREER: Free-lance writer. Associate editor of such publications as *Mike Shayne Mystery Magazine*, Renown Publications, New York, N.Y., 1953-61. *Member:* Science Fiction Writers of America. *Awards, honors:* Hall of Fame Award, World Science Fiction Convention, 1977.

WRITINGS: A Man From Genoa, and Other Poems, W. P. Cook, 1926; *The Goblin Tower* (poems), Dragonfly Press, 1935; *Howard Phillips Lovecraft: Dreamer on the Nightside* (biography), Arkham, 1975.

Science fiction and fantasy: *The Hounds of Tindalos*, Arkham, 1946, reprinted with *The Black Druid*, Panther, 1975; *John Carstairs, Space Detective*, Fell, 1949; *Space Station 1*, Ace Books, 1957; *Woman From Another Planet*, Chariot Books, 1960; *Mars Is My Destination: A Science-Fiction Adventure*, Pyramid Books, 1962; *Three Steps Spaceward*, Avalon Books, 1963; *It Was the Day of the Robot*, Belmont Books, 1963; *The Horror From the Hills*, Arkham, 1963; *The Dark Beasts, and Eight Other Stories From The Hounds of Tindalos*, Belmont Books, 1964; *The Martian Visitors*, Avalon Books, 1964; *Mission to a Star*, Avalon Books, 1964; *Odd Science Fiction*, Belmont Books, 1964; *This Strange Tomorrow*, Belmont Books, 1966; *Lest Earth Be Conquered*, Belmont Books, 1966; *Journey Into Darkness*, Belmont Books, 1967; (with Lin Carter) *Two Complete Science Fiction Novels: The Thief of Thoth*, by Lin Carter, *And Others Shall Be Born*, by Frank Belknap Long, Belmont Books, 1968; *The Three Faces of Time*, Tower, 1969; *Monster From Out of Time*, Popular Library, 1970; *Survival World*, Lancer Books, 1971; *The Night of the Wolf*, Popular Library, 1972; *The Rim of the Unknown* (short stories), Arkham, 1972; *The Early Long: Frank Belknap Long*

(stories), Doubleday, 1975; *In Mayan Splendor* (poetry), Arkham, 1977.

Work represented in many anthologies, including *Sleep No More: Railway, Canal, and Other Stories of the Supernatural*, International Publications Service, 1975, *Strange Gifts*, Thomas Nelson, 1975, and *Dying of Fright*, Scribner, 1976.

WORK IN PROGRESS: A new fantasy novel.

SIDELIGHTS: Several of Long's short stories have been dramatized on radio, and one, "Guest in the House" (not to be confused with the play of the same title), appeared on television. His stories have been widely reprinted in England, France, Italy, Spain, and West Germany. Long was nominated for lifetime achievement awards in the genre at the First, Second, and Third World Fantasy Conventions, 1975 to 1977. Other nominees and previous winners of this award included Robert Bloch and Ray Bradbury.

Long told *CA:* "For many years the mystery story, despite its preoccupation with the darker aspects of human experience, was thought of as a form of light, popular entertainment, and unworthy to be taken seriously as an important literary genre. But few critics of stature would embrace such a view today, for the psychological insight, and stylistic brilliance of a round dozen mystery fiction writers have made a re-evaluation mandatory. In the realm of science fiction a similar re-evaluation is now taking place. The prophetic nature of science fiction and the emphasis it places on *tomorrow*—both in a terrestrial utopian, and space-travel sense—makes it even more important, in some respects, than mystery fiction at its best. Whether or not it will become the 'main stream' literature of the future may still be a moot point. But it will certainly continue to be, more and more, a germinal influence in the shaping of the major aspects of a new world outlook."

* * *

LONGHURST, Henry Carpenter 1909-1978

OBITUARY NOTICE: Born March 18, 1909; died July 23(?), 1978, in Sussex, England. Golf commentator, journalist, and author. Longhurst was best known for his dry wit and, with his candid literary style, bringing culture to television commentaries on major golf tournaments. He often spoke at such championships as the British Open, the Masters, and the U.S. Open. Beginning in 1932 Longhurst also was golf correspondent for the Sunday *London Times*. A golfer in his own right, he was awarded the German amateur title in 1937. He later received the Journalist of the Year Special Award and the Walter Hagen Award for his contribution to English-American golf relations. Longhurst authored *Golf, It was Good While It Lasted, Only on Sundays*, and other books, including an autobiography entitled *My Life and Soft Times*. Obituaries and other sources: *The Author's and Writer's Who's Who*, 6th edition, Burke's Peerage, 1971; *New York Times*, July 24, 1978; *Who's Who*, 130th edition, St. Martin's, 1978.

* * *

LONG-NECK WOMAN
    See CHEATHAM, K(aryn) Follis

* * *

LOPEZ, Ella B. 1900(?)-1978

OBITUARY NOTICE: Born c. 1900, in Virginia; died October 23, 1978, in Washington, D.C. School administrator, teacher, and author. Lopez taught home economics before becoming a science teacher and head of the science department at Takoma Park Junior High School in Maryland. She received a National Science Foundation award for organizing outstanding community science fairs. Lopez wrote a book for children entitled *Croakie Goes West.* Obituaries and other sources: *Washington Post,* October 26, 1978.

* * *

LoPICCOLO, Joseph 1943-

PERSONAL: Born September 13, 1943, in Los Angeles, Calif.; son of Joseph E. (in business) and Adeline (Russo) LoPiccolo; married Leslie J. Matlen (a research associate), June 25, 1964; children: Joseph T. *Education:* University of California, Los Angeles, B.A. (highest honors), 1965; Yale University, M.S., 1967, Ph.D., 1969. *Politics:* None. *Religion:* None. *Home address:* P.O. Box 456, Stony Brook, N.Y. 11790. *Office:* Department of Psychiatry and Behavioral Science, Health Sciences Center, State University of New York at Stony Brook, Stony Brook, N.Y. 11794.

CAREER: Yale University, New Haven, Conn., intern in psychology at Connecticut Mental Health Center, 1967-68; University of Oregon, Eugene, assistant professor of psychology, 1969-73, director of University Psychology Clinic, 1972-73; University of Houston, Houston, Tex., associate professor of psychology and director of undergraduate affairs, 1973-74; State University of New York at Stony Brook, associate professor, 1974-77, professor of psychiatry and behavioral science, 1977—. Clinical associate professor at Baylor University, 1973-74. Participant in workshops; consultant to Veterans Administration. *Member:* American Psychological Association, Phi Beta Kappa, Sigma Xi. *Awards, honors:* Woodrow Wilson fellowship, 1965; National Institutes of Health biomedical science grant, 1969-72; National Institute of Mental Health grants, 1974-76, 1976-79, 1976-81.

WRITINGS: (Contributor) L. A. Hammerlynck, L. C. Handy, and E. J. Mash, editors, *Behavior Change: Methodology, Concepts, and Practice,* Research Press, 1973; (contributor) H. J. Eysenck, editor, *Case Studies in Behavior Therapy,* Routledge & Kegan Paul, 1976; (with Julia R. Heiman and wife, Leslie LoPiccolo) *Becoming Orgasmic: A Sexual Growth Program for Women,* Prentice-Hall, 1976; (contributor) John Money and Herman Musaph, editors, *Textbook of Sexology,* Elsevier North-Holland, 1977; (contributor) Gloria Harris, editor, *The Group Treatment of Human Problems: A Social Learning Approach,* Grune, 1977; (contributor) Brandon Qualls, John Wincze, and David Barlow, editors, *The Prevention of Sexual Disorders: Issues and Approaches,* Plenum, 1978; (contributor) Richard Green and Jack Weiner, editors, *Methodological Issues in Sex Research,* U.S. Government Printing Office, 1978; (contributor) Green, editor, *Human Sexuality: A Health Practitioners Text,* Williams & Wilkins, 2nd edition (LoPiccolo was not included in 1st edition), 1978, (with L. LoPiccolo) *Handbook of Sex Therapy,* Plenum, 1978; (contributor) Ovine Pomerlieu and J. P. Brady, editors, *Behavioral Medicine,* Williams & Wilkins, in press.

Contributor of about twenty-five articles to scholarly journals. Member of editorial board of *Archives of Sexual Behavior, Behavior Therapy,* and *International Journal of Marriage and Family Counseling;* advisory editor of *Contemporary Psychology;* consulting editor of *Journal of Sex and Disabilities.*

WORK IN PROGRESS: Research on assessment and treatment of sexual dysfunction, enhancement of the sexual relationship in normal couples, determinants of sexual function and dysfunction, and predictors of response to therapy.

* * *

LORD, Mary Stinson Pillsbury 1904-1978

OBITUARY NOTICE: Born November 14, 1904, in Minneapolis, Minn.; died July 21, 1978, in New York, N.Y. Civic worker, organization official, and author. Appointed by President Dwight D. Eisenhower, Lord succeeded Eleanor Roosevelt as U.S. representative to the United Nations Commission on Human Rights, a position she held for eight years. Lord, heir to the Pillsbury fortune, had been an active participant in developing numerous organizations based in New York, most notably the National Council of Women, the New York World's Fair, the Community Service Society, and the United Nations International Children's Emergency Fund. She traveled widely in Europe during World War II as chairman of the Civilian Advisory Committee for the Women's Army Corps, setting up camps for the troops. Lord held twelve honorary degrees. With her husband, Oswald Bates Lord, she authored *Exit Backward Bowing,* published in 1970. Obituaries and other sources: *Current Biography,* Wilson, 1952; *Who's Who of American Women,* 10th edition, Marquis, 1977; *New York Times,* July 23, 1978; *Time,* August 7, 1978; *Who's Who in America,* 40th edition, Marquis, 1978.

* * *

LOSANG, Rato Khyongla Ngawang 1923-

PERSONAL: Khyongla is pronounced "chungla"; born July 4, 1923, in Dayab, Kham, Tibet; son of Trinley (an administrative secretary) and Lhamo Tenzin. *Education:* Rato College, Central Tibet, Doctor of Buddhism (highest honors), 1947; Gyudto Tantric College, Tibet; Tantric Buddhism Degree (highest honors), 1948. *Religion:* Buddhist. *Home:* Apt. C5, 220 East 36th St., New York, N.Y. 10016. *Agent:* Russell and Volkening, Inc., 551 Fifth Ave., New York, N.Y. 10017. *Office:* The Tibet Center, Inc., 114 East 28th St., Rm. 405, New York, N.Y. 10017.

CAREER: Private teacher in Lhasa, Tibert, 1948-59; Ethnological Museum of Leiden, Leiden, Holland, cataloguer of Tibetan books and objets d'art, 1962-66; University of Minnesota, Minneapolis, teaching assistant in Tibetan, 1966-67; Crowell Collier Institute of Continuing Education, Arlington, Va., teacher of Tibetan, 1967-68; John D. Rockefeller III Foundation, New York City, historian and writer, 1971; The Tibet Center, Inc., New York City, founder, president and teacher, 1975—. Officer of religious affairs of Gyaltse District in Tibet, 1955; writer of text books, Tibetan Text Committee for the Council for Tibetan Education in Dharmsala, Himachal Pradesh, India, 1959; lecturer in Argentina on Buddhism and the Tibetan refugee situation, government of Tibet, 1966.

WRITINGS: My Life and Lives (autobiography), Dutton, 1977. Also author of *Summary of Pramana Logic* and *Summary of 'Bodhicaryavatara' by Santideva,* both in Tibetan.

WORK IN PROGRESS: A book on the stages of the path to enlightenment, entitled *A Commentary of the Lam Rim; A History of the Major Gelugpa Monasteries of Tibet; Tsong Kha Pa's Life Story,* a book on the founder of the Gelugpa Tibetan Buddhist Sect.

BIOGRAPHICAL/CRITICAL SOURCES: My Life and Lives, Dutton, 1977.

LOSSY, Rella 1934-

PERSONAL: Born June 26, 1934, in Chicago, Ill.; daughter of Arnold (in business) and Flora (in business; maiden name, Rand) Berk; married Frank T. Lossy (a psychiatrist), May 13, 1956; *children:* Panna, David. *Education:* Attended University of Iowa, 1952-53, and Northwestern University, 1953-54; University of California, Berkeley, A.B., 1956; San Francisco State University, M.A., 1965. *Home:* 96 Highland Blvd., Kensington, Calif. 94708.

CAREER: High school English teacher in Martinez, Calif., 1958-61; East Bay Center for the Performing Arts, Berkeley, Calif., head of dramatic arts department, 1974-75, theater editor of *East Bay Review of the Performing Arts,* 1976—. Guest lecturer at Golden Gate University, 1978. Performer with Makeshift Mysteries, 1969-74, and Elizabethan Trio, 1971—; choreographer of musical plays: producer, writer, and interviewer for KPFA-FM Radio, 1958-65. Teacher of drama to children in Richmond, Calif., 1974-75. *Member:* Poets and Writers, American Theatre Critics Association, Bay Area Theater Critics Circle (vice-president, 1978-79), Phi Beta Kappa.

WRITINGS: Audible Dawn (poems), Holmgangers, 1975. Editor of poetry supplement to *Critical Quarterly,* 1965.

WORK IN PROGRESS: A play; a radio drama.

AVOCATIONAL INTERESTS: Travel (eastern and western Europe, Australia and New Guinea, the Caribbean, Greece and the Middle East, Mexico).

*   *   *

LOTZ, Wolfgang 1912-

PERSONAL: Born April 19, 1912, in Heilbronn, Germany; son of Hermann and Clara (Meyer) Lotz; married Hilde Bauer, August 5, 1941. *Education:* Attended University of Freiburg, 1932-33, and University of Munich, 1934-35; University of Hamburg, Ph.D., 1937. *Home and office:* 28 Via Gregoriana, Rome, Italy 00187.

CAREER: German Institute for Art History, Florence, Italy, research fellow, 1937-39; Central Institute for Art History, Munich, Germany, curator of photographs, 1939-42, deputy director, 1946-52; Vassar College, Poughkeepsie, N.Y., professor of fine arts, 1952-58; New York University, New York, N.Y., professor of fine arts, 1959-62; Max-Planck Institut, Rome, Italy, director of Bibliotheca Hertziana, 1963—. Kress Professor at National Gallery of Art (Washington, D.C.), 1976-77. Member of Institute for Advanced Study (Princeton, N.J.), 1966. *Military service:* German Army, 1943-45. *Member:* College Art Association of America, Renaissance Society of America, Society of Architectural Historians.

WRITINGS: (With L. H. Heydenreich)*Architecture in Italy, 1400-1600,* Pelican, 1974; (with J. Coolidge, C. Thoenes, and others)*Jacopo Barozzi da Vignola,* Vignola, 1974; *Studies in Italian Renaissance Architecture,* M.I.T. Press, 1977. Contributor to scholarly journals in the United States, Italy, and Germany.

WORK IN PROGRESS: Iconoclasm and sacred images in fifteenth and sixteenth century Europe.

*   *   *

LOVE, Richard S. 1923-

PERSONAL: Born March 29, 1923, in Utica, N.Y.; son of Thomas W. and Helen E. (Mainwaring) Love; married Hazel Scott Bayne (a librarian), February 19, 1955. *Education:*
University of Rochester, B.A., 1947; graduate study at Columbia University, 1947-48, and George Washington University, 1952-53. *Home:* 13775E Flora Pl., Delray Beach, Fla. 33445. *Agent:* Collier Associates, 280 Madison Ave., New York, N.Y. 10016.

CAREER: U.S. Department of Commerce, Washington, D.C., geographer, 1948-51; U.S. Air Force, headquarters, Arlington, Va., civilian photographic intelligence specialist for guided missiles, 1951-63; Defense Intelligence Agency, Arlington, branch chief in Photographic Intelligence Office, 1963-73; writer, 1973—. *Military service:* U.S. Army, Special Troops, 1943-45; served in European theater; received five battle stars. *Member:* Association of American Geographers, Sigma Chi.

WRITINGS: Superformance Stocks: An Investment Strategy for the Individual Investor Based on the Four-Year Political Cycle, Prentice-Hall, 1977.

WORK IN PROGRESS: Strategic Deception, a novel about a future world military crisis.

SIDELIGHTS: Love writes: "Most of my professional career has been in military intelligence, primarily in photographic analysis. Since my service in the Army during World War II I have been deeply concerned about the approach of another large-scale war which would involve the United States. A major avocation since 1950 has been the analysis of economic and political trends and their effects on security prices. I am registered as an investment adviser with the Securities Exchange Commission."

*   *   *

LOVE, Sydney F(rancis) 1923-

PERSONAL: Born June 10, 1923, in Winnipeg, Manitoba, Canada; son of Francis Henry (an electrician) and May Eliza (a secretary; maiden name, Smith) Love; married Marian Irene Southern, June 2, 1953 (divorced, 1976); children: Rodney, Kevin, Brian. *Education:* University of Toronto, B.A.Sc., 1947, M.A., 1948; University of Waterloo, M.A.Sc., 1970. *Home:* 327 Batavia Pl., Waterloo, Ontario, Canada N2L 3W1. *Agent:* Hy Cohen Literary Agency Ltd., 111 West 57th St., New York, N.Y. 10019. *Office:* Advanced Professional Development, Inc., 1888 Century Park E., Suite 10, Century City, Los Angeles, Calif. 90067.

CAREER: Canadian General Electric Co. Ltd., Toronto, Ontario, supervisor of applications, 1952-59; Electrohome Ltd., Kitchener, Ontario, manager of television and organ engineering, 1959-66; Designectics International, Inc., Waterloo, Ontario, consultant, 1966—. President of Advanced Professional Development, Inc., 1974—. Registered professional engineer; participant in and director of workshops and seminars. *Member:* Canadian Authors Association, Project Management Institute, Institute of Electrical and Electronics Engineers (senior member), Engineering Management Society.

WRITINGS: Mastery and Management of Time, Prentice-Hall, 1978; *Time Mastery Workbook,* Designectics International, 1978; *Planning and Creating Successful Engineered Designs,* Van Nostrand, 1979; *Successful Project Management,* Designectics International, 1979. Author of columns, including "Time Management," 1976-78, and "Time Tips for Technical Types," 1977-78. Contributor of more than a hundred articles to trade journals and newspapers.

WORK IN PROGRESS: Time Management for Working Mothers; Cover Your Ass.

SIDELIGHTS: Love writes: "My father was a writer with a modest record, and while I was a young lad I tried to write some short vignettes. Nothing much was written for the next thirty years, except for a few technical papers. At the age of forty-six I went back to the university and got recharged with new ideas. This started my first major effort, a series of twelve articles which has grown into the material for my second book. I have learned how to travel and write. This enables me to be where I want to be and during this time my writing productivity is high. I expect to do much more of it. Currently I am conducting seminar-workshops on time mastery and on project management.''

BIOGRAPHICAL/CRITICAL SOURCES: Kitchener-Waterloo Record, March 13, 1976.

* * *

LOWITZ, Anson C.   1901(?)-1978

PERSONAL: Married Sadyebeth Heath (died, 1969); married Marion Leland; children: (first marriage) Mrs. John Ross Hamilton. *Education:* Graduated from Wesleyan University. *Residence:* Pebble Beach, Calif.; and Greenwich, Conn.

CAREER: J. Walter Thompson Co. (advertising agency), New York City, vice-president, 1937-51; Foote, Cone & Belding (advertising agency), Chicago, Ill., vice-president, 1951-53; Ted Bates & Co. (advertising agency), New York City, vice-president, 1953-59. *Wartime service:* During World War II helped develop the Cadet Nursing Corps.

WRITINGS—All with wife, Sadyebeth Lowitz; all ''Really Truly Story'' juvenile series; all originally published by Stein & Day: (Self-illustrated) *The Pilgrims' Party,* 1931, revised edition, Lerner, 1967; *General George the Great,* 1932, revised edition, Lerner, 1967; (self-illustrated) *The Cruise of Mr. Christopher Columbus,* 1932, revised edition, Lerner, 1967; *The Magic Fountain,* 1936, revised edition, Lerner, 1967; *Mr. Key's Song,* 1937, revised edition, Lerner, 1967; (self-illustrated) *Barefoot Abe,* 1938, revised edition, Lerner, 1967; (self-illustrated) *Tom Edison Finds Out,* 1940, revised edition, Lerner, 1967.

OBITUARIES: New York Times, January 25, 1978.*

(Died January 22, 1978, in Pebble Beach, Calif.)

* * *

LOWTHER, Kevin G(eorge)   1941-

PERSONAL: Born April 16, 1941, in Yonkers, N.Y.; son of George F. (a radio and television writer) and Florence (Wagner) Lowther; married Patricia Mitchell (a teacher), June 10, 1967; children: Allison, Andrea. *Education:* Dartmouth College, B.A., 1963; graduate study at University of Michigan, 1976-77. *Office:* Africare, 1601 Connecticut Ave. N.W., Washington, D.C. 20009.

CAREER: U.S. Peace Corps, Washington, D.C., volunteer teacher in Sierra Leone, 1963-65, administrator in Washington, 1965-71; *Keene Sentinel,* Keene, N.H., editor of editorial page, 1971-78; Africare, Washington, D.C., field representative in Lusaka, Zambia, 1978—. *Awards, honors:* National Endowment for the Humanities fellowship in journalism, 1976-77.

WRITINGS: (With C. Payne Lucas) *Keeping Kennedy's Promise: The Peace Corps–Unmet Hope of the New Frontier,* Westview Press, 1978.

WORK IN PROGRESS: A historical novel examining race relations in the early decades of American independence.

SIDELIGHTS: Lowther told *CA:* ''I write from a fascination with human relations: how it is that some people tran-

scend cultural, racial, and other barriers, and others do not. I am an optimist. It is difficult to be a human being and not believe in higher possibilities. At the same time, I am all too personally aware that there is no nastier or ignorant or fellow-fearing creature on earth than *homo sapiens*. To be optimistic about human nature, then, you have to concede and know the evil within us. You have to know the enemy, so to speak. And knowing that enemy, you are better able to devise a strategy for combatting it. My strategy, simply, is knowledge and spreading that knowledge.

''In *Keeping Kennedy's Promise,* my co-author and I have sought to explain why so many Peace Corps volunteers—indeed, most—have been too culturally inhibited, too lacking in curiosity, in effect too ignorant, to experience the fulfillment possible in giving oneself over to an alien society. In the historical novel now in progress, I hope to show how and why certain whites and blacks came to know one another and, through that knowledge, blazed the high road of non-racialism in the early years of American independence. Both works are based on some very depressing documented evidence of human frailities; but both point toward higher ground, an eminence which is visible, and perhaps even attainable.''

* * *

LUCAS, Marion B(runson)   1935-

PERSONAL: Born September 9, 1935, in Ward, S.C.; son of Charles M. and Frances (Joyner) Lucas; married Italene Glascock, May 28, 1957; children: Amy, Susan, Scott. *Education:* University of South Carolina, B.A., 1959, M.A., 1962, Ph.D., 1965. *Politics:* Democrat. *Home:* 1749 Karen Circle, Bowling Green, Ky. 42101. *Office:* Department of History, Western Kentucky University, Bowling Green, Ky. 42101.

CAREER: Western Kentucky University, Bowling Green, Ky., assistant professor of history, 1964-66; Morehead State University, Morehead, Ky., associate professor of history, 1966-74; Western Kentucky University, professor of history, 1974—. *Member:* Southern Historical Association.

WRITINGS: Sherman and the Burning of Columbia, Texas A&M University Press, 1976.

WORK IN PROGRESS: Kentucky Blacks, 1865-1900, publication by University of Kentucky Press, expected in 1983.

SIDELIGHTS: In reference to his book, *Sherman and the Burning of Columbia,* Lucas wrote: ''It was maintained for a century that Sherman's march was the most devastating of all American wars. A close study, however, reveals that Sherman's activities in South Carolina were far less destructive than previously believed. Indeed, it seems clear that the burning of Columbia was the result of an accident of war rather than deliberate destructiveness on the part of Sherman.''

''*Kentucky Blacks, 1865-1900,*'' Lucas continued, ''is an attempt to write a history of blacks during that period emphasizing, as much as possible, black sources. That is, I hope to make the book more than 'what whites have said about blacks.'''

* * *

LUCAS, N. B. C.   1901-

PERSONAL: Born January 2, 1901, in Newbury, Berkshire, England; son of Alan (a solicitor's clerk) and Norah Evelyn (a book buyer; maiden name, Brooks) Lucas; married Vera Agnes Douglas, August 2, 1934 (deceased); married Doreen Mary Bassett, July 25, 1972. *Education:* Emmanuel College, Cambridge, B.A. (first class honors), 1922. *Politics:* "No party." *Religion:* "Not specific." *Home:* Coombe Cottage, Grayswood Rd., Haslemere, Surrey GU2 72BU, England.

CAREER: Teacher in Paris, France, Cairo, Egypt, and England; teacher of art history in Newcastle, England, 1933-38; school headmaster in Midhurst, England, 1938-67; writer, 1967—. *Member:* Historical Association, Contemporary Art Society.

WRITINGS: An Experience of Teaching, Weidenfeld & Nicolson, 1975. Also author of *A Search for Meaning.* Contributor to *Studio* and *Journal of Aesthetics.*

SIDELIGHTS: Lucas writes: "An unusual record of changing circumstances in my boyhood when I had many different homes and little contact with my parents led me later to be deeply concerned with emotional deprivation and personal security.

"I was much influenced in my twenties by working under a headmaster who was a friend of Homer Lane, an American who came to England about 1912 to found a settlement for deprived and delinquent children.

"After leaving Cambridge in order to break with restrictive home circumstances I took a teaching post near Paris for one year and then a post in Egypt for two years where I was considerably affected by my experience of imperial control.

"About 1928-29 I was influenced by reading Henri Bergson, which led to the French historian, Elie Halevy, persuading me to study the work of the founder of Syndicalism, Georges Sorel, who was one of Bergson's keenest followers. I wrote a treatise which led Halevy to write, to say that he considered [me to be] the first man to have understood Sorel. I was unable to complete my research, first through illness and then through lack of money. So I returned to England and again took a teaching post.

"My work on Sorel led me indirectly to form a particular idea of the concept of myth which I believe to be the basis of both personal and collective attitudes. I had become deeply interested in art, and this was much affected by the meaning I attached to my view of myth. All this became the basis of my teaching of history which I think I may claim to have been unusually successful. But besides the academic side of my work I used a comparable approach to enable me to help pupils who were frustrated or depressed by personal circumstances and neurotic difficulties.

"When I became a headmaster, a post I held for thirty years, all this was fundamental to my attitude. I was concerned with academic achievement, but equally with the 'problem' pupil. Every year I took in boys (and later girls when the school became co-educational) who had failed at other schools. I not only hoped to liberate them, but also got my more normal pupils to help me in this work. I believe that this increased the understanding of all my pupils and that this considerably raised the general level of achievement.

"After my retirement I summed up my work in *An Experience of Teaching.* I had originally entitled it *God Smiles: An Essay on Order and Sensitivity* (using the term God to express the concept of ultimate authority). I had a most appreciative editor—an American! I quote from her comments on the cover of the book: 'Problems of community, of acceptance and rejection, are the starting points of these absorbing reflections on the nature of personality.... In looking back upon his work with boys and girls at both ends of the educational spectrum Mr. Lucas takes the reader into fascinating and controversial areas of modern doctrine which he brilliantly illuminates. The scope of the book ranges from the motivation of the habitual rule-breaker to the relevance of the Christian myth in a post-Christian era. He tackles head-on the related problems of community, authority, and discipline, of learning to dispense with punishment; his approach is not utopian but individualistic and eminently practical. The author's delicacy of touch, his unpedantic originality and above all his humane wisdom make this remarkable book not only a great pleasure to read, but a fundamental process of renewal, causing the reader to view his own formative experience in a new light and with vastly increased understanding.'

"I should add that I have worked in Paris, Florence, Cairo, and London, which has helped me in my understanding of art. I have a collection of pictures, pottery, and some sculpture."

* * *

LUCKERT, Karl W(ilhelm) 1934-

PERSONAL: Born November 18, 1934, in Winnenden-Hoefen, Germany; came to the United States in 1955, naturalized in 1961; son of Wilhelm Gottlob (a farmer) and Emilie (Hilt) Luckert; married Dora M. Laemmle, September, 1957; children: Ursula Dorothea, Martin Karl, Heidi Marie. *Education:* University of Kansas, B.A. (honors), 1963; graduate study at Evangelical Theological Seminary, Naperville, Ill., 1963-64; University of Chicago, M.A., 1967, Ph.D., 1969. *Religion:* United Methodist. *Home:* 1915 North Marion Dr., Flagstaff, Ariz. 86001. *Office:* Department of Humanities, Northern Arizona University, Box 6031, Flagstaff, Ariz. 86011.

CAREER: Painter and decorator in Germany, 1949-55, and Abilene, Kan., 1955-56, 1958-59; North Central College, Naperville, Ill., visiting lecturer in religion, 1968-69; Northern Arizona University, Flagstaff, assistant professor of humanities, 1969—. *Military service:* U.S. Army, 1956-58. *Awards, honors:* National Endowment for the Humanities fellowship, 1972-73; grants from Smithsonian Institution and Wenner-Gren Foundation, 1974-75, and People's Legal Services and Rockefeller Brothers Fund, 1976-77; honorary research associate of Museum of Northern Arizona, 1977; Rockefeller Foundation fellowship, 1977-78.

WRITINGS: (Contributor) J. M. Kitagawa, editor, *History of Religions,* University of Chicago Press, 1967; (contributor) Kitagawa and C. H. Long, editors, *Myths and Symbols: Studies in Honor of Mircea Eliade,* University of Chicago Press, 1969; *The Navajo Hunter Tradition,* University of Arizona Press, 1975; *Olmec Religion: A Key to Middle America and Beyond,* University of Oklahoma Press, 1976; *Navajo Mountain and Rainbow Bridge Religion,* Museum of Northern Arizona Press, 1977; *A Navajo Bringing-Home Ceremony: The Claus Chee Sonny Version of Deerway "Ajilee",* Museum of Northern Arizona Press, 1978; (editor) Berard Haile, *Love-Magic and Butterfly People: The Slim Curly Version of the "Ajilee" and Mothway Myths* (monograph), Museum of Northern Arizona Press, 1978; *Coyoteway: A Navajo Holyway Healing Ceremonial,* University of Arizona Press, 1979. Contributor to scholarly journals.

WORK IN PROGRESS: A history of religion, from Australopithecus to Homo Scientificus.

SIDELIGHTS: Luckert described himself as "a historian of religions who came to the Southwest in 1969 and stayed." He continued: "I soon began collecting my own ethnological field data. Wherever in Southwestern religions a scholar touches ground, he finds himself at a frontier. My first hope of writing a full history of Navajo religion was soon abandoned as an impossibility. In this part of the world not enough of the available data have been collected to justify comprehensive ambitions of that sort, and not enough field evidence has gotten lost yet, to make historical summaries sufficiently simple and plausible. I am therefore satisfied with saving smaller portions of Navajo tradition from oblivion and extinction. When I began my field work, the Navajo hunter tradition and the Rainbow Bridge religion were nearly unknown; the Deerway *ajilee* and the Coyoteway ceremonials were believed extinct. I regard *Coyoteway* as my best salvage job, to date.

"According to a number of well-established scholars in Olmec religion, I have turned Middle American religious history upside down—rightside up, as I see things. Why do I express my new-fangled ideas so boldly? Too many scholars nowadays are intimidated by their own disciplines. I guess this comes from taking graduate schools and academic degrees too seriously. Any kind of research, undertaken by finite minds, is of necessity hypothetical. This is a truism that should not need to be mentioned at every step or even in every book. As far as I am concerned, I shall be happy, if twenty years from now eighty percent of my conclusions will have withstood bickering. I shall even be happier, if by then someone can brighten my armchair years and come forth with better interpretations. Somehow, I feel that I ought to understand some of these things a little better by the time I get ready to die."

* * *

LUDLOW, Geoffrey
See MEYNELL, Laurence Walter

* * *

LUDWIG, Jerry 1934-

PERSONAL: Born January 23, 1934, in New York, N.Y.; son of Isidor (an electrician) and Rose (Spivack) Ludwig; married Barbara Goldberg, November 23, 1954; children: Carey, Scott, Laura. *Education:* City College (now of the City University of New York), B.A., 1955. *Religion:* Jewish. *Residence:* Pacific Palisades, Calif. *Agent:* Leonard Hanzer, Major Talent, 12301 Wilshire Blvd., Los Angeles, Calif. 90025.

CAREER: New York Herald-Tribune, New York, N.Y., college reporter, 1954-55; *Neosho Daily News,* Neosho, Mo., reporter, 1955; worked as motion picture specialist for Hecht-Lancaster, for Paramount Pictures, and for Mirisch Co., all in Hollywood, Calif.; free-lance writer, 1965—. *Member:* Writers Guild of America (West), Academy of Motion Picture Arts and Sciences, Television Academy of Arts and Sciences, Producers Guild of America. *Awards, honors:* Nominated for best television dramatic episode, by Writers Guild of America, 1971, for "Hawaii Five-O" script; special award from Mystery Writers of America, 1978, for television film, "In the Glitter Palace."

WRITINGS: Little Boy Lost, Delacorte, 1977. Author of television film scripts.

WORK IN PROGRESS: A novel for Delacorte.

* * *

LUKE, Peter (Ambrose Cyprian) 1919-

PERSONAL: Born August 12, 1919, in St. Albans, Hertfordshire, England; son of Harry (a writer) and Joyce (Fremlin) Luke; married June Tobin (an actress), 1963; children: four daughters, three sons. *Education:* Attended Byam

Shaw School of Art and Andre Lhote Studio. *Home:* La Almona, El Chorro, Malaga, Spain; and The Dower House, EMO, County Laois, Ireland. *Agent:* Harvey Unna Ltd., 14 Beaumont Mews, Marylebone High St., London W.1, England.

CAREER: Reuters Ltd., London, England, sub-editor, 1947; worked in wine trade in Portugal, Spain, and France, 1947-57; *Queen* magazine, London, book critic, 1957-58; American Broadcasting Companies (ABC-TV), London, drama and story editor, 1958-60, *Bookman* editor, 1960-61, *Tempo* arts program editor, 1961-63; British Broadcasting Corp. (BBC-TV), London, drama producer, 1963-67; freelance playwright and short-story writer, 1967—; Dublin Gate Theatre, Dublin, Ireland, director, 1977—. Has also worked as a diamond-point glass engraver. *Military service:* Royal Rifle Brigade, 1940-46; received Military Cross. *Member:* Writers Guild of Great Britain, Society of Authors, Eton Viking Rowing Club, Kildare Street and University Club. *Awards, honors:* Italia Prize, 1967, for "Silent Song"; Antoinette Perry Award ("Tony") nomination for best play, 1969, for "Hadrian VII."

WRITINGS: Sisyphus and Reilly: An Autobiography, Deutsch, 1972; (editor) *Enter Certain Players* (festschrift), Dolmen Press, 1978; *Collected Short Stories,* Goldsmith Press, 1979. Has also done translations from the Spanish.

Plays: "Hadrian VII" (based on *Hadrian the Seventh* and other works by Frederick Rolfe; produced in London at Mermaid Theatre, April 18, 1965, produced on Broadway at Helen Hayes Theatre, January 8, 1969), published as *The Play of Hadrian VII,* Deutsch, 1968, Knopf, 1969; "Bloomsbury," first produced in the West End at Phoenix Theatre, July, 1974.

Teleplays, except as noted: "Small Fish Are Sweet," 1959; "Pig's Ear With Flowers," 1960; "Roll On, Bloomin' Death," 1961; (with William Sansom) "A Man on Her Back," 1966; "The Devil a Monk Wou'd Be," 1967; (also director) "Anach Cuan: The Music of Sean O'Riada" (television film), BBC-TV, 1967; (also director) "Black Sound—Deep Song: The Andalusian Poetry of Federico Garcia Lorca" (television film), BBC-TV, 1968.

Work represented in various anthologies. Contributor to periodicals, including *Envoy, Cornhill, Vogue, Queen, New Statesman, Times Literary Supplement,* and *Listener.*

WORK IN PROGRESS: A play, "Proxopera," based on the novel of the same title by Benedict Kiely, to be produced at Dublin Gate Theatre; a play, "Mr. Darwin's Fancy," contracted for production by Bill Freedman Ltd. and Richard Homer Associates.

SIDELIGHTS: "Hungarian chromosomes, of which Peter Luke has plenty, are supposed to make for success in show-business," reported the *Observer Review.* Yet, Luke's tutors at Eton never expected success from their wayward pupil in spite of his Hungarian grandfather from Detroit. Luke's school reports, some of which were quoted in a *Times Literary Supplement* review of *Sisyphus and Reilly,* show the unanimous disapprobation of his tutors: "Many of my pupils are incompetent at managing their own affairs but Luke is far the most incompetent. . . . He has the ability to appear awake and actually to be asleep." Luke's reputation as "dreadfully backward," "lazy," and "naturally idle" provoked one tutor to say, "I cannot prophesy anything but failure."

Despite these less than encouraging reports, Luke's tutors admitted, "He is quite willing and cheerful in spite of misfortunes." That virtue was still an obvious part of Luke's philosophy even after his stage success spared him from depending on his cheerful disposition to live. "So, looking back (from a mountain in Spain) I see that I've been rather lucky. I've been in the right place at the right time," wrote Luke in *Listener*. When a television drama editor told Luke that he would no longer assign work to someone living so far away, Luke had an answer typical of his attitude: "I replied that I would rather die of starvation in Spain than of bronchitis in London."

Luke had planned a career as an artist, but his studies were interrupted by the war. After leaving the military, Luke worked as a journalist before assuming an apprenticeship in the wine trade which took him to Portugal, France, and Spain. "The brush, the diamond-point, the typewriter have been the tools of my trade to date," Luke told *Listener*. "Tomorrow they may be a hammer and chisel or a pick and shovel. But it was the former ones—or rather the attitudes engendered by them—that I have brought with me to television. Once within, I learned, more or less by accident, something of the craft of creating drama. Now I am saddled with it—for the time being, at least," he reflected.

Luke's adaptation of Rolfe's *Hadrian the Seventh* for the stage brought him international success. *National Observer* declared: "Mr. Luke's play is good, at times fascinating. But it is essentially a one-character evening, though its author does go at that one character as a surgeon doing very delicate work. Carefully he peels away Rolfe's facade to reveal the confused, tortured dreamer at the core." Several critics noted that it was to Luke's credit that actors playing the title role of Hadrian were critically acclaimed for their performances. When the play production crossed the Atlantic and opened in New York, the reviews were equally positive. *Show Business* observed, "Without any gimmicks, courting of the sensational, or attempts at innovation, 'Hadrian VII' is quite simply the best play on Broadway this season."

The *Times Literary Supplement* discussed the common life patterns that run through Luke's autobiography, *Sisyphus and Reilly,* concluding: "Familiar this may be: but Mr. Luke has an original talent for writing of the blank spaces between the incidents of life, the grey times of waiting and inertia. He can write gaily of unhappiness, ironically of success, shyly of his own courage, bravely of his fears. Perhaps only another Etonian will understand how typically Etonian is his attitude to everything that ought to be taken seriously."

AVOCATIONAL INTERESTS: Andalusian horses, country life, tauromachia.

BIOGRAPHICAL/CRITICAL SOURCES: Listener, September 12, 1968; *Variety,* January 15, 1969; *National Observer,* January 20, 1969; *Show Business,* January 25, 1969; *Commonweal,* February 7, 1969; *Washington Post,* March 4, 1970; *Books and Bookmen,* May, 1970; Peter Luke, *Sisyphys and Reilly: An Autobiography,* Deutsch, 1972; *Observer Review,* January 16, 1972; *Times Literary Supplement,* September 29, 1972.

*   *   *

LUNDBORG, Louis B(illings) 1906-

PERSONAL: Born March 31, 1906, in Billings, Mont.; son of Andrew John (an engineer) and Emma Louise (Karlsson) Lundborg; married Barbara Ann Wellington, June 25, 1926; children: Bradford Wellington. *Education:* Attended Stanford University, 1923-26. *Politics:* Republican. *Religion:* Congregationalist. *Home:* 95 West Shore Rd., Belvedere, Calif. 94920. *Office:* Bank of America Center, P.O. Box 37000, San Francisco, Calif. 94137.

CAREER: Research chemist, California & Hawaiian Sugar Refining Corp., 1926-27; California Chamber of Commerce, member of research department, 1927-29, district manager for San Joaquin Valley in Fresno, 1929-32, and for Central Coast in San Francisco, 1932-39, assistant general manager, 1939-43; San Francisco Chamber of Commerce, San Francisco, Calif., general manager, 1943-48; Stanford University, Stanford, Calif., vice-president of the university, 1948-49; Bank of America, San Francisco, Calif., vice-president, 1949-59, executive vice-president, 1959-65, chairman of board of directors, 1965-71, member of managing committee and advisory council to directors, 1957-71; writer, 1971—. Chairman of board of directors of Bank of America International, Bamerical International Finance Corp., 1965-71, and Bank of America Corp., 1968-71; member of board of directors of MCA, Inc., 1970—, Envirotech Corp., 1971-77, General Automation, Inc., L. B. Nelson Corp., Getty Oil Co., 1968-71, and Stanford Research Institute, 1948—; member of board of trustees of Los Angeles World Affairs Council, 1947-63 (president of board, 1969-70), Pomona College, and Huntington Library (chairman of board, 1970-72); consultant to National Park Service.

MEMBER: Public Relations Society of America, American Bankers Association (president of Savings & Mortgaging Division, 1958-59), U.S. Chamber of Commerce (member of board of directors, 1955-60; vice-president, 1960-63; head of Mexico-United States committee, 1957-61, 1965-66), American Management Association (member of board of directors), Newcomen Society, Association of Reserve City Bankers, Cercle de l' Union, Pacific Union Club, Bohemian Club, California Club, Links Club, Stock Exchange Club, Los Angeles Country Club. *Awards, honors:* LL.D. from Rocky Mountain College, 1965, Occidental College, 1971, and California Lutheran College.

WRITINGS: Public Relations in the Local Community, Harper, 1951; *Future Without Shock,* Norton, 1974; (with Glover and Simon) *Chief Executives Handbook,* Dow Jones-Irwin, 1976; *Up to Now,* Norton, 1978; (with W. H. Baughn and C. E. Walker) *Bankers Handbook,* Dow Jones-Irwin, 1978. Also author of *Practical Psychology for the Organization Executive.* Author of column in *Industry Week,* 1978—.

*   *   *

LUNN, Arnold 1888-1974
(Sutton Croft, Rubicon)

PERSONAL: Born April 18, 1888, in Madras, India; son of Henry (a Methodist minister, later owner of a travel and tourist agency) and Ethel Kingsmill (Moore) Lunn; married Mabel Northcote, December, 1913 (died, 1959); married Phyllis Holt-Needham, 1961; children: (first marriage) Peter, John, Jaqueta. *Education:* Attended Balliol College, Oxford, 1907-11. *Religion:* Roman Catholic. *Address:* 118 Eaton Square, London SW1, England.

CAREER: Notre Dame University, Notre Dame, Ind., assistant professor of apologetics, 1936-37; war correspondent, in Spain, 1937-38, for *America,* 1939; writer. Lecturer. *Wartime service:* Attached to the British War Office, 1941. *Member:* Oxford Union Society (past secretary), Alpine Club, Ski Club of Great Britain (past president), Kandahar Ski Club, Athenaeum (honorary). *Awards, honors:* Knighted, 1952; named citoyen d'honneur, Chamonix, France, 1952; Ph.D., University of Zurich, 1954.

WRITINGS—Skiing and mountaineering: (Editor) *Oxford Mountaineering Essays,* Edward Arnold, 1912; *The Explor-*

ation of the Alps, Holt, 1914; Cross Country Skiing, Methuen, 1920; Alpine Skiing at All Heights and Seasons, Methuen, 1921; Skiing for Beginners, Methuen, 1924; The Mountains of Youth, Oxford University Press, 1925; A History of Skiing, Oxford University Press, 1927; The Complete Ski Runner, Methuen, 1930; Skiing in a Fortnight, Methuen, 1933; Mountain Jubilee, Eyre & Spottiswoode, 1943; Switzerland and the English, Eyre & Spottiswoode, 1944; Mountains of Memory (autobiographical), Hollis & Carter, 1948, Macmillan, 1949; The Story of Skiing, Eyre & Spottiswoode, 1952; A Century of Mountaineering, 1857-1957, Allen & Unwin, 1957; The Swiss and Their Mountains: A Study of the Influence of Mountains on Man, Rand McNally, 1963; (editor) The Englishman on Ski, Museum Press, 1964; Matterhorn Centenary, Rand McNally, 1965; The Kandahar Story: A Tribute on the Occasions of Mueren's Sixtieth Skiing Season, Allen & Unwin, 1969.

Travel and description: Switzerland: Her Topographical, Historical, and Literary Landmarks, Doubleday, 1928; Venice: Its Story, Architecture, and Art, Harrap, 1932, Farrar & Rinehart, 1935; The Italian Lakes and Lakeland Cities, Harrap, 1932; The Cradle of Switzerland, Hollis & Carter, 1952; Zermatt and the Valais, Hollis & Carter, 1955; The Bernese Oberland, Eyre & Spottiswoode, 1958, reprinted, Allen & Unwin, 1973.

Christianity and philosophy: Roman Converts, Chapman & Hall, 1924, reprinted, Books for Libraries, 1966; The Flight from Reason, Dial, 1931; Is Christianity True?, Eyre & Spottiswoode, 1933; (editor) Public School Religion, Faber, 1933; Now I See (partially autobiographical), Sheed & Ward, 1934, reprinted, 1960; Science and the Supernatural, Sheed & Ward, 1935; A Saint in the Slave Trade: Peter Claver, Sheed & Ward, 1935; Within That City, Sheed & Ward, 1936; The Good Gorilla (essays), Hollis & Carter, 1944; The Third Day, Newman Book Shop, 1945; (with George G. Coulton) Is the Catholic Church Anti-Social?, Burns & Oates, 1946; The Revolt Against Reason, Eyre & Spottiswoode, 1950, Sheed & Ward, 1951, reprinted, Greenwood Press, 1971; Enigma: A Study of Moral Rearmament, Longmans, Green, 1957; And Yet So New (autobiographical), Sheed & Ward, 1958; (with Ronald A. Knox) Difficulties, Dufour, 1952, Eyre & Spottiswoode, 1958; (with Garth Lean) The New Morality, Blandford, 1964, revised edition, 1967; (with Lean) The Cult of Softness, Blandford, 1965; (with Lean) Christian Counter-Attack, Arlington House, 1969; Come What May (autobiographical), Eyre & Spottiswoode, 1940, Little, Brown, 1941.

Other: The Harrovians, Methuen, 1919; Loose Ends (novel), Hutchinson, 1919; (under pseudonym Rubicon) Auction Piquet, Methuen, 1920; (under pseudonym Sutton Croft) Was Switzerland Pro-German?, Hazell, Watson, 1920; Things That Have Puzzled Me, Benn, 1927; John Wesley, Dial, 1929; Family Name, Methuen, 1931, Dial, 1932; "Within the Precincts of the Prison", Hutchinson, 1932; The Unpopular Front, Burns & Oates, 1937; Spanish Rehearsal, Sheed & Ward, 1937, reprinted, Devin-Adair, 1975; The Science of World Revolution, Sheed & Ward, 1938; Revolutionary Socialism in Theory and Practice, Right Book Club, 1939; Communism and Socialism: A Study in the Technique of Revolution, Eyre & Spottiswoode, 1939; Whither Europe?, Sheed & Ward, 1940; And the Floods Came (autobiographical), Eyre & Spottiswoode, 1942; (editor) Switzerland in English Prose and Poetry, Eyre & Spottiswoode, 1947, reprinted, Gordon Press, 1976; (editor and author of introduction) Is Evolution Proved?, Hollis & Carter, 1947; Memory to Memory (autobiographical), Hollis &

Carter, 1956; (author of introduction) John Ruskin, The Seven Lamps of Architecture, Dutton, 1956, 2nd edition, Dent, 1969; Unkilled for So Long (autobiographical), Allen & Unwin, 1968.

Also author of Guide to Montana, 1907; editor of Isis, 1909-10, and British Ski Year Book; contributor of articles to America and the London Tablet.

SIDELIGHTS: Although Arnold Lunn's writings cover a diverse range of subjects from skiing to Christian apologetics, the author admitted that his legacy would probably be that he invented the slalom ski race rather than any of his literary efforts. Between the ages of four and eight, when every summer and almost every winter were spent in the Alps, Lunn's interst in skiing and mountain climbing developed. He was the first to attempt ski ascents of several Alpine peaks, and was instrumental in getting downhill ski racing included as an event of the Olympic Games. He was a referee at the first slalom race in the 1948 Winter Olympics held in St. Moritz, Switzerland. As a study of snow and avalanche craft, his book, Alpine Skiing at All Heights and Seasons, has been recognized as a classic.

BIOGRAPHICAL/CRITICAL SOURCES: Arnold Lunn, Mountains of Memory, Macmillan, 1949; New Yorker, December 20, 1952; Lunn, Memory to Memory, Hollis & Carter, 1958; Lunn, And Yet So New, Sheed & Ward, 1959; Lunn, Unkilled for So Long, Allen & Unwin, 1968.

OBITUARIES: New York Times, June 3, 1974; Time, June 17, 1974; National Review, July 5, 1974.*

(Died June 2, 1974)

*　　*　　*

LYKIARD, Alexis (Constantine) 1940-
(Celeste Piano)

PERSONAL: Born January 2, 1940, in Athens, Greece; son of Anthony (a bank clerk) and Maria (Casdagli) Lykiard. Education: King's College, Cambridge, B.A. (first class honors), 1962, M.A., 1966. Politics: "Agnostic Surrealism." Religion: "Agnostic Surrealism." Home: Tillworth Cottage, Hawkchurch, near Axminster, Devonshire, England. Agent: A. D. Peters & Co., 10 Buckingham St., London W.C.2, England.

CAREER: Writer, 1963—. Has worked as teacher, publisher's reader, scriptwriter, and film extra. Member of literature panel of Arts Council of Great Britain, 1974-76; tutor at Arvon Foundation centers, 1974—; writer-in-residence at Sutton Central Library, 1977; judge of All-London Literary Competition, 1978. Has given poetry readings and lectures in England and abroad, including Romania and Mauritius. Member: Society of Authors, Writers Guild of Great Britain, Poets' Conference, Writers Action Group, South West Arts Association (member of literature panel, 1977—), Association of Cinematograph Television and Allied Technicians. Awards, honors: Grants from Arts Council of Great Britain, 1973, 1978; C. Day Lewis Fellowship from Greater London Arts Association, 1977.

WRITINGS: Lobsters (poems), Carter, 1961; Journey of the Alchemist (poems), Carter, 1963; The Summer Ghosts (novel), Anthony Blond, 1964, Tower Books, 1966; Zones (novel), Anthony Blond, 1966; A Sleeping Partner (novel), Weidenfeld & Nicolson, 1967; Paros Poems, Diphros, 1967; Robe of Skin: Poems, 1958-68, Allison & Busby, 1969.

Strange Alphabet (novel), Weidenfeld & Nicolson, 1970, Stein & Day, 1971; Eight Lovesongs (poems), Trans-Gravity, 1972; The Stump (novel), Hart-Davis, 1973; Greek

Images (poems), Second Aeon, 1973; *Lifelines* (poems), Arc, 1973; *Instrument of Pleasure* (novel), Panther, 1974; *Milesian Fables* (poems), Arc, 1976; *Last Throes* (novel), Panther, 1976; *The Drive North* (novel), Allison & Busby, 1977; (with Vernon Scannell) *A Morden Tower Reading* (poems), Morden Tower Books, 1977.

Editor and author of introduction: *Wholly Communion,* Lorrimer, 1965, Grove, 1967; *Best Ghost Stories of Sheridan Le Fanu,* Sphere Books, 1970; *The Horror Horn: Best Ghost Stories of E. F. Benson,* Panther, 1974; (with Derwent May) *New Stories 2,* Arts Council of Great Britain, 1977; *Six Greek Poets Writing in English,* Quill Books, 1979; *Collected Poems, 1958-79,* Allison & Busby, 1979.

Translator from French: Le Comte de Lautreamont, *Maldoror,* Allison & Busby, 1970, Crowell, 1972; Charles Cros, Jules Supervielle, and Blaise Cendrars, *The Piano Ship* (poems), Platform, 1974; (under pseudonym Celeste Piano) Emmanuelle Arsan, *Laure,* Mayflower, 1977; Lautreamont, *Poesies Et Cetera,* Allison & Busby, 1978; (under pseudonym Celeste Piano) Emmanuelle Arsan, *Nea, a Young Emmanuelle* (novel), Mayflower, 1978.

Poems represented in more than a dozen anthologies, including *New Poems: P.E.N. Anthology,* Hutchinson, 1975; *Poetry Dimension Annual 5,* Robson Books, 1978; *The Puffin Book of Salt Verse,* Penguin, 1978. Contributor to magazines in England and abroad, including *Transatlantic Review, Adam,* and *Samphire.*

WORK IN PROGRESS: A novel, as yet untitled, for Allison & Busby; a book on jazz, completion expected in 1980.

SIDELIGHTS: Lykiard told *CA:* "Since English is my adopted rather than native tongue, I particularly admire authors such as Conrad, Nabokov, and Jerzy Kosinski—masters of style all the more remarkable in that English has been their adopted writing language also.

"Yet all authors, however original, absorb, reject, learn from influences. No writer is suddenly a master of the craft without having read intelligently: one becomes, first, a creative reader, and this involves sympathy, persistence, and an open mind. With this in view, I have organized and tutored creative writing workshops in the United Kingdom and elsewhere (for the Arvon Foundation, the British Council, etc.) because I believe writing is a skill which must be carefully acquired and cherished. This sort of teaching context helps professional and tyro alike, and is vital in an age so dominated by the mass media and one in which words are being so rapidly devalued and willfully misused. I'm not implying that tradition is better than experiment, nor extolling elitism above the popular: but the writer *does* need to recognize some heritage or chain of continuity before he or she can rebel against it, modify it, use it, or even render it obsolete!

"I have always wanted to be a writer more than anything else and consider writing a privilege, a responsibility, and a pleasure, while at the same time hard and generally underpaid work. Most writers, and I am no exception, have held a wide variety of part-time jobs and at some point or other have gravitated like myself towards teaching and giving readings of their work. This I have always found enjoyable, as communication is, after all, the writer's *raison d'etre.*

"I am against obscurity, lack of humor, and pretentiousness—a Fascist trinity, come to think of it!

"I see no basic differences between working in prose or in poetry: the one should be quite as well written as the other. Both are essentially storytelling techniques and in both I try to explore my main preoccupation/theme, which is, as suc-

cinctly as possible, the struggle between flesh and spirit, and man's search for his simple yet elusive union. This also seems to me to be a kind of definition of freedom."

Adding a plug for free expression, Lykiard wrote: "All censorship of any kind should be abolished. The Public Lending Right in the United Kingdom should be implemented—and soon! Otherwise creative writers will not be able to afford the luxury of writing *books* (as opposed to scripts and articles)."

Lykiard's books have been translated into Romanian and Japanese.

AVOCATIONAL INTERESTS: "I like travel, food, wine, women, music, films, poetry—in no particular order, but in abundance."

BIOGRAPHICAL/CRITICAL SOURCES: Orizont, 1977; *Journal of the Hellenic Diaspora,* winter-spring, 1978.

*   *   *

LYNEIS, Richard George   1935-

PERSONAL: Born September 12, 1935, in Fond du Lac, Wis.; son of Roman E. and Wilhemine (Kramer) Lyneis; married Mary Kay (a physical therapist), September 23, 1961; children: Susan, Lynn, Paul. *Education:* Attended St. Norbert College, 1953-54, Marquette University, 1956-58, and Stanford University, 1966-67. *Home:* 3415 Bahia Pl., Riverside, Calif. 92507. *Office: Press-Enterprise,* Box 792, Riverside, Calif. 92502.

CAREER/WRITINGS: Post-Crescent, Appleton, Wis., reporter, 1961-67, city editor, 1967-69; *Press-Enterprise,* Riverside, Calif., city editor, 1969-71, investigative reporter, 1971—. Member of executive committee of Investigative Reporters and Editors (IRE), 1977—, and national director, 1976—. Notable assignments include coverage of California farm labor dispute, Arizona organized crime for I.R.E., and a wide variety of stories on land fraud, labor union corruption, and political corruption. *Member:* Sigma Delta Chi. *Awards, honors:* Ford Foundation Professional Journalism fellowship, 1966-67; Award from the California Associated Press, 1977, for investigative reporting; recipient, with others, of Public Service Award from Sigma Delta Chi, 1977, American Society of Authors Award, 1977, and John Peter Zenger Award from the University of Arizona, 1977, all for work on IRE's Arizona Project reporting team.

SIDELIGHTS: Lyneis told *CA:* "My fields of investigative reporting have been labor unions, political corruption, organized crime, and international land fraud. Other than that, my principal activity has been in educational and public speaking efforts aimed at developing more reporters into investigative reporters . . . a great need for our society."

*   *   *

LYNN, Elizabeth A.   1946-

PERSONAL: Born June 8, 1946, in New York, N.Y.; daughter of Richard Nathan (an accountant) and Winifred (an artist; maiden name, Null) Lynn. *Education:* Case Western Reserve University, B.A., 1967; University of Chicago, M.A., 1968. *Agent:* Richard Curtis Agency, 156 East 52nd St., New York, N.Y. 10022. *Office address:* P.O. Box 14107, San Francisco, Calif. 94114.

CAREER: Teacher in public schools, Chicago, Ill., 1968-70; St. Francis Hospital, Evanston, Ill., unit manager, 1970-72; French Hospital, San Francisco, Calif., unit manager, 1972-75; teacher in women studies program at San Francisco

State University. Medical secretary in San Francisco, 1974-75. *Member:* Mystery Writers of America, Science Fiction Writers of America, Feminist Writers Guild. *Awards, honors:* Woodrow Wilson fellowship, 1967-68.

WRITINGS: A Different Light, Berkley Publishing, 1978. Work represented in anthologies, including: *Tricks and Treats,* edited by Joe Gores and Bill Pronzini, Doubleday, 1976; *Dark Sins, Dark Dreams,* edited by Barry Malzberg and Pronzini, Doubleday, 1978; and *Millennial Women,* Delacorte, edited by Virginia Kidd, 1978. Contributor of stories to science fiction magazines.

WORK IN PROGRESS: Chronicles of Tornor: A Fantasy Trilogy; The Sardonym Net, a novel.

AVOCATIONAL INTERESTS: Aikodo; Lynn holds a first kyu (brown belt) and is registered with the World Aikido Federation in Tokyo, Japan.

*   *   *

LYNN, Loretta (Webb)   1932(?)-

PERSONAL: Born in Butcher Hollow, Ky.; daughter of Melvin (a coal miner) and Carla (Butcher) Webb; married Oliver Vanetta Lynn (a business manager), January 10, 1948; children: Betty Sue (Mrs. Paul Markworth), Jack Benny, Carla (Mrs. Gary Lyell), Ernest Ray, Peggy and Patsy (twins). *Education:* Attended public schools in Van Lear, Ky. *Home:* Hurrican Mills, Tenn. 37078. *Agent:* Jimmy Jay United Talent, Inc., 1907 Division, Nashville, Tenn. 37203. *Office:* 903 16th Ave. S., Nashville, Tenn. 37213.

CAREER: Professional country and western vocalist and composer with MCA Recording Co., 1963—; guest on various television programs, including "Bobby Lord Show," "Flatt and Scruggs Show," "Eddie Hill Show," "Ralph Emery Show," "Porter Wagoner Show," "Today Show," "Dinah Shore Show," "David Frost Show," "To Tell the Truth," "Hee Haw," "Dean Martin's Music Country," and NBC's "Midnight Special." Organized her own ensemble, Blue Kentuckians; founder and secretary-treasurere of Loretta Lynn Enterprises, and Loretta Lynn Championship Rodeo; founder and vice-president of United Talent Inc.; founder and honorary board chairman of Loretta Lynn Western Stores; founder of Loretta Lynn Dude Ranch, and Loretta Lynn Museum. *Awards, honors:* Country Music Association Grammy Award, 1972, for entertainer of the year and for vocal duo of the year; earned gold album for "Don't Come Home A-Drinkin (With Lovin on Your Mind),"; named top country female vocalist by *Record World,* favorite female vocalist by *Billboard,* female country singer of the year by *Music Business,* and most programmed female vocalist by *Cash Box;* twice voted number one female country singer in Europe.

WRITINGS: (With George Vecsey) *Loretta Lynn, Coal Miner's Daughter: An Autobiography,* Regnery, 1976.

Songs: "I'm a Honky Tonk Girl," Doggone Blues," "The World of Forgotten People," "I've Cried the Blue Right Out of My Eyes," and "Coal Miner's Daughter."

SIDELIGHTS: Known in the music industry as the "Country Queen," Loretta Lynn grew up in the poverty stricken hills of the Appalachia where she married Oliver Lynn a few weeks before her fourteenth birthday. Doolittle, as Lynn prefers to call her husband, was responsible for her career. "As you can tell, I've always liked to sing. But the singing career was Doolittle's idea. . . . He had got me this seventeen dollar Harmony guitar at Sears and Roebuck . . .: he told me I could do it. I'd still be a housewife today if he didn't bring that guitar home and then encourage me to be a singer," explained Lynn.

By the time she was eighteen, Lynn had four children. In the midst of raising her family, she began to write songs and taught herself to play her guitar. "When the kids were in school or asleep at night, I'd sit in my front room, learning how to play . . . better. I never took no lessons or nothing—I just played," recalled Lynn.

Lynn wrote and recorded her first song, "I'm a Honky Tonk Girl" under Zero, a West Coast record company, for a small recording company in Vancouver, British Columbia. "Honky Tonk Girl" hit the top ten record charts across the country. Lynn and her husband tried to promote the record themselves. They toured the country and contacted every country music disc jockey they could find. "We didn't care if it was a 500-watt local station or a 50,000-watt clear channel station, we'd hit 'em all," said Lynn.

Lynn's primary objective was to reach Nashville, Tenn., and appear on the Grand Ole Opry, the oldest and most popular of the country radio shows. "Nothing could stop us from trying to make it in Nashville. I guess I went at it like a bull in a china shop. . . . I'd be on people's doorsteps at eight in the morning, holding copies of my first record and of new songs I'd written," remarked Lynn.

Lynn made her first appearance on the Opry in the latter part of 1960. She was well received and invited to come back. Lynn's lifetime recording contract with MCA came shortly after.

To date, Loretta Lynn has given over one hundred concerts a year, has released more than twenty-two albums for MCA, and has turned out numerous hit singles (some of which she composed herself). Her autobiography was also a 1976 bestseller and a movie version is underway.

BIOGRAPHICAL/CRITICAL SOURCES: Newsday, March 6, 1971; *National Observer,* April 26, 1971; *New York Times,* October 25, 1972; *News,* January 19, 1973; *Newsweek,* June 18, 1973; *Newsday,* October 7, 1973; *People,* June 5, 1975, *Book Digest,* December, 1976; *Loretta Lynn; Coal Miner's Daughter: An Autobiography,* Regnery, 1976.*

M

MacARTHUR, John F., Jr. 1939-

PERSONAL: Born June 19, 1939, in Los Angeles, Calif.; son of John F. (a clergyman) and Irene (Dockendorf) Mac-Arthur; married Patricia Sue Smith, August 30, 1973; children: Matthew, Marcy, Mark, Melinda. *Education:* Los Angeles Pacific College, B.A., 1961; Talbot Theological Seminary, M.Div., 1964, D.D., 1977. *Office:* Grace Community Church, Sun Valley, Calif. 91352.

CAREER: Talbot Theological Seminary, La Mirada, Calif., representative, 1966-69; Grace Community Church (non-denominational), Sun Valley, Calif., pastor, 1969—. Faculty member at Talbot Theological Seminary, 1976—. Speaker on national radio and at conferences; seminar leader. Chaplain for Los Angeles police department.

WRITINGS: The Church: The Body of Christ, Zondervan, 1973; *Found: God's Will,* Victor, 1973, revised edition, 1977; *Keys to Spiritual Growth,* Revell, 1976; *Liberated for Life,* Regal Books (Glendale), 1976; *Focus on Fact,* Revell, 1977; *Giving: God's Way,* Tyndale, 1978. Contributor to magazines.

WORK IN PROGRESS: Interpreting biblical passages for practical application, with special emphasis on spiritual ethics.

SIDELIGHTS: MacArthur writes: "The motivating force behind all my writing is a personal, vital, real relationship with the God man, Jesus Christ. My life is committed to service to Him and building His kingdom."

*   *   *

MacBRIDE, Roger Lea 1929-

PERSONAL: Born August 6, 1929, in New York; son of William Burt (an editor) and Elise (Lea) MacBride; married Susan Ford, September, 1961 (divorced, July, 1972); children: Abigail Adams. *Education:* Princeton University, A.B., 1951; Harvard University, J.D., 1954. *Religion:* Deist. *Agent:* Collier Associates, 280 Madison Ave., New York, N.Y. 10016. *Office:* 2401 Arlington Blvd., Suite 14, Charlottesville, Va. 22903.

CAREER: Practicing attorney in New York, N.Y. and Brattleboro, Vt., 1955-68; assistant creator of "Little House on the Prairie," NBC-TV, 1974—, and "Young Pioneers," ABC-TV, 1978. Active in local government; Libertarian Party Presidential candidate, 1976. *Member:* Mont Pelerin Society, Racquet and Tennis Club.

WRITINGS: The American Electoral College, Caxton, 1952; *Treaties Versus the Constitution,* Caxton, 1956; *The First Four Years* (nonfiction), Harper, 1971; *The Lady and the Tycoon* (nonfiction), Caxton, 1972; *A New Dawn for America,* Green Hill, 1976; *Rose Wilder Lane,* Stein & Day, 1978. Contributor to magazines.

WORK IN PROGRESS: Discovery of Liberty, a posthumous collection, with Rose Wilder Lane.

SIDELIGHTS: MacBride told *CA:* "My first two books were technical analyses of aspects of American government which interested me. *The First Four Years* was a posthumous editing of Laura Ingalls Wilder's draft of the ninth book in the "Little House" series, which was not published in her lifetime. *The Lady and the Tycoon* was a condensation of 4,000 pages of correspondence between Rose Wilder Lande and Jasper Crane to about one tenth of that length, a labor of love as Mrs. Lane was my adopted grandmother. And of course my 1978 book is the story of her early life. *A New Dawn for America* describes the Libertarian philosophy in less than a hundred pages, and applies it to specific issues in contemporary America. My views have not changed in the slightest from those expressed in that book, and it's possible that I will be the Libertarian party candidate again in 1980."

*   *   *

MacCAFFREY, Isabel Gamble 1924-1978

PERSONAL: Born August 2, 1924, in Baltimore, Md.; daughter of Thomas Owen and Isabel (Davidson) Gamble; married Wallace T. MacCaffrey (a history professor at Harvard University), June 16, 1956. *Education:* Swarthmore College, B.A., 1946; Radcliffe College, M.A., 1947, Ph.D., 1954. *Residence:* Acton, Mass.

CAREER: Bryn Mawr College, Bryn Mawr, Pa., instructor, 1949-50, 1952-54, assistant professor, 1954-60, associate professor, 1960-66, professor of English, 1966-69; Tufts University, Medford, Mass., professor of English, 1969-71; Harvard University, Cambridge, Mass., William R. Kenan Professor of History and Literature, 1971-78, chairman of department of history and literature, beginning 1972. *Member:* Modern Language Association of America, Renaissance Society of America, English Institute (member of executive committee, 1967-70). *Awards, honors:* Fulbright Scholar, Cambridge University, 1950-51; Guggenheim fellowship, 1971-72; D. Litt., Holy Cross College, 1972.

WRITINGS: Paradise Lost as Myth, Harvard University Press, 1959; (contributor) *The Lyric and Dramatic Milton,* Columbia University Press, 1965; (editor) John Milton, *Samson Agonistes and the Shorter Poems,* New American Library, 1966; (editor with Robert Hodge) John Milton, *Paradise Lost: Books V-VI,* Cambridge University Press, 1975; *Spenser's Allegory: The Autonomy of Imagination,* Princeton University Press, 1976. Contributor to scholarly journals.

SIDELIGHTS: An authority on English Renaissance literature, MacCaffrey was the first woman to chairman Harvard's department of history and literature.

OBITUARIES: New York Times, May 21, 1978.*

(Died May 19, 1978, in Acton, Mass.)

* * *

MacDONALD, Philip　1896(?)-
(Anthony Lawless, Martin Porlock, W. J. Stuart, Warren Stuart; Oliver Fleming, a joint pseudonym)

PERSONAL: Born in Scotland; son of Ronald MacDonald (a playwright and novelist); married Mona Ventris (divorced); married Florence Ruth Howard (a novelist), 1944; children: one daughter. *Education:* Educated in England. *Residence:* Woodland Hills, Calif.

CAREER: Novelist, short story writer, and author of screenplays. Began motion picture writing career as a scenarist for RKO Pictures, Hollywood, Calif., 1931; has also worked as a private secretary and civil servant. *Military service:* British Army, 1915-19. *Awards, honors:* Edgar Allan Poe Award of Mystery Writers of America for best short stories, 1952, for *Something to Hide;* has also received five second prize awards for short stories from *Ellery Queen's Mystery Magazine.*

WRITINGS—Novels: (With father, Ronald MacDonald, under joint pseudonym Oliver Fleming) *Ambrotox and Limping Dick,* Ward, Lock, 1920; (under Fleming pseudonym) *The Spandau Squid,* Cecil Palmer, 1923; *Gentleman Bill: A Boxing Story,* Herbert Jenkins, 1923; *The Rasp,* Collins, 1924; *Patrol,* Collins, 1927, published as *The Lost Patrol,* Novel Library, 1934; *The White Crow,* Collins, 1928; *Likeness of Exe,* Collins, 1929; *Rynox,* Collins, 1930, published as *Rynox Murder Mystery,* Doubleday, 1931, Avon, 1965; *The Link,* Collins, 1930; *The Noose,* Collins, 1930; (under pseudonym Anthony Lawless) *Harbour,* Collins, 1931, Doubleday, 1932; *The Wraith,* Collins, 1931; *Persons Unknown: An Exercise in Detection,* Doubleday, 1931; *Murder Gone Mad,* Collins, 1931; *Crime Conductor,* Doubleday, 1931; *Moonfisher,* Collins, 1931; (under pseudonym Martin Porlock) *Mystery at Friar's Pardon,* Collins, 1931, Doubleday, 1932; *The Polferry Riddle,* Doubleday, 1931; *The Choice,* Collins, 1931; *The Polferry Mystery,* Collins, 1932; *The Maze,* Collins, 1932; *Escape,* Doubleday, 1932; (under Porlock pseudonym) *Mystery in Kensington Gore,* Collins, 1932; *Rope to Spare,* Doubleday, 1932; *Death on My Left,* Doubleday, 1933; *Menace,* Doubleday, 1933; *R.I.P.,* Collins, 1933; (under Porlock pseudonym) *X. v. Rex,* Collins, 1933, published as *Mystery of the Dead Police,* Doubleday, 1933; *The Mystery of Mr. X,* Collins, 1934; *"Glitter,"* Collins, 1934; *Warrant for X,* Doubleday, 1938, Avon, 1973; *The Nursemaid Who Disappeared,* Collins, 1938; (under pseudonym Warren Stuart) *The Sword and the Net,* Morrow, 1941; (with A. Boyd Correll) *The Dark Wheel,* Morrow, 1948, published as *Sweet and Deadly,* Zenith, 1959; *Guest in the House,* Doubleday, 1955, published

as *No Time for Terror,* Bestseller, 1956; (under pseudonym W. J. Stuart) *Forbidden Planet,* Farrar, Straus, 1956; *The List of Adrian Messenger,* Doubleday, 1959.

Short stories: *Queen's Mate,* Collins, 1926; *Something to Hide,* Doubleday, 1952; *Fingers of Fear,* Collins, 1953; *The Man Out of the Rain,* Doubleday, 1955; *Death and Chicanery,* Doubleday, 1962.

Collected works: *The Philip MacDonald Omnibus* (includes *The Rasp, The White Crow, The Link, Murder Gone Mad*), Collins, 1932; *Triple Jeopardy* (includes *Warrant for X, Escape, The Polferry Riddle*), Doubleday, 1962; *Three for Midnight* (includes *The Rasp, Murder Gone Mad, The Rynox Murder*), Doubleday, 1963.

Screenplays: "The Lost Patrol," RKO, 1934; "The Menace," Paramount, 1934; "The Mystery of Mr. X," Metro-Goldwyn-Mayer, 1934; "Yours for the Asking," Paramount, 1936; "The Princess Comes Across," Paramount, 1936; "Mysterious Mr. Moto," Twentieth Century-Fox, 1938; "Mr. Moto's Last Warning," Twentieth-Century-Fox, 1938; "Mr. Moto Takes a Vacation," Twentieth Century-Fox, 1938; "Blind Alley," Columbia, 1939; "Rebecca," United Artists, 1940; "Whispering Ghosts," Twentieth Century-Fox, 1942; "Street of Chance," Paramount, 1942; "Sahara," Columbia, 1943; "Action in Arabia," RKO, 1944; "The Body Snatcher," RKO, 1945; "Strangers in the Night," Republic, 1945; "Dangerous Intruder," Producers Releasing Corp., 1945; "Love from a Stranger," Eagle Lion, 1947; "The Dark Past," Columbia, 1949; "The Man Who Cheated Himself," Twentieth Century-Fox, 1951; "Circle of Danger," United Artists, 1951; "Ring of Fear," Warner Bros., 1954; "Tobor the Great," Republic, 1954.

Columnist, *Laguna Beach Post.* Contributor of short stories to periodicals, including *Saturday Evening Post.*

SIDELIGHTS: Several of MacDonald's novels have been made into motion pictures, including *Patrol,* which was originally produced by RKO as "The Lost Patrol" in 1934 and has since been remade several times. "Nightmare," made by Universal in 1942, is based on *Escape,* and "The Hour of 13," Metro-Goldwyn-Mayer, 1952, is based on *Mystery of the Dead Police.* In 1963, Universal produced "The List of Adrian Messenger," directed by John Huston.

MacDonald has maintained a lifelong interest in horses, ranging from his work training horses imported from Argentina for use in the British Army to his raising and training horses for fancy riding and jump shows. In 1931, he and his wife moved to Hollywood, where he works as a scenarist and raises Great Danes.*

* * *

MacKAY, Alistair McColl　1931-

PERSONAL: Born January 6, 1931, in Niagara Falls, N.Y.; son of Alex and Helen (Hay) MacKay; married Elizabeth MacDonald, December 6, 1949; children: Stuart Alexander, Elizabeth Saville. *Education:* Attended secondary school in Glasgow, Scotland. *Home:* Ocean Towers, 201 Ocean Ave., Santa Monica, Calif. 90402. *Agent:* Stiefel Office, 9255 Sunset Blvd., Los Angeles, Calif. 90069.

CAREER: Sterling Value Fare, supermarket manager in Glasgow, Scotland, and London, England, 1954-60; Product Development Corp., San Francisco, Calif., sales promotion executive, 1960-61; Merchandising Manpower Ltd., London, marketing executive, 1961-67; public relations and marketing consultant, 1967-74; free-lance writer, 1974—.

Military service: British Army, Royal Army Service Corps, 1952-54; served in Malaysia; became staff sergeant. *Member:* Institute of Marketing, Institute of Public Relations, Institute of Industrial Editors.

WRITINGS—All novels: *The Triad Conspiracy,* Bantam, 1978; *The Triad Conspiracy, Part Two,* Bantam, 1979. Contributor to magazines and newspapers.

WORK IN PROGRESS: The Triad Conspiracy, Part Three; a novel concerning the supernatural.

SIDELIGHTS: MacKay writes that his first book "was inspired by evidence of Triad activity in London. The evidence was unearthed while [I] was researching a routine article for a magazine and, recalling encounters with the Triad Society when serving with army in the Malaysia, [I] became fascinated with the subject. Research yielded a rich vein of material and it became obvious that a series of books could be written in the form of novels. The novels are based on documented facts and are intended to bring to the attention of the general public a criminal organization which has existed for centuries." MacKay also told *CA* that his other interest is research into the supernatural.

*   *   *

MACKENDRICK, John 1946-

PERSONAL: Born January 23, 1946, in Ware, England; son of William (a physician) and Violet Mackendrick. *Education:* University of Nottingham, B.A., 1967; Bretton Hall College, certificate in education, 1974; University of Leeds, M.A.,1975. *Agent:* Michael Imison, Van Loewen Ltd., 81-3 Shaftsbury Ave., London W1V 8BX, England.

CAREER: Family caseworker for Nottinghamshire County Council, England, 1967-68; teacher of English and drama in secondary schools in Yorkshire and Wilshire, both England, 1968, 1970, 1973; child care officer in London, England, 1969; writer, 1973—; resident dramatist at National Theatre, 1977-78. *Member:* Theatre Writers Union, Society of Authors. *Awards, honors:* Yorkshire Arts Association fellowship, 1975-76.

WRITINGS—Plays: "Doctor Struensee," first produced in Dublin, Ireland, at Abbey Theatre, summer, 1974; "Who'll Be Next and Who'll Be Lucky?," first produced in London, England, at Soho Poly, summer, 1974; "Ludd!," first produced at Ilkley Literature Festival, summer, 1975; *Woyzeck* (translation and adaptation of Georg Buechner's work of the same title; first produced in Leeds, England, at Workshop Theatre, 1975), published in *Methune Theatre Classics,* Methuen, 1979; "Cain" (translation and adaptation of *Mactatio Abel*), first produced at Workshop Theatre, 1976; *Lavender Blue* (first produced on the West End at National Theatre, November, 1977), published in *Methuen New Theatrescript,* Methuen, 1977; "Canticle," first produced at Keele University, January, 1977. Also author of "No Hands," "Rules," and a translation of *Weitere Aussichten* by Franz Xaver Kroetz.

Other works: *Pickles Hill Music* (poetry), Byron Press, 1977; *Noli Me Tangere,* published with *Lavender Blue* in *Methuen New Theatrescript* (also see above), Methuen, 1977; *Big Fish, Little and Lady Lie Easy,* Poet & Printer, 1978; *Prophets,* Faber, 1978. Contributor of poetry to such magazines as *New Statesman, Poetry Review, Stand,* and *Samphire.*

WORK IN PROGRESS: A collection of fables, *Cautionary Tales;* a play, "Azimuth."

SIDELIGHTS: Mackendrick told *CA:* "Works exist in

their own world and their own right. I have never found it possible either to talk about them or assist in bringing them into the world in any way. I am a poet, which is why I write plays: a play is a big poem. The naturalist tradition of theatre hold no interest for me whatsoever. If my output resembles anyone else's that person would be John Arden. Like him, I am without faith in contemporary theatre. A play is an entire world with its own language, feel and spiritual location; inevitably, then, they are so different, one from another, as to make generalities impossible. I have never written "about" anything in my life; that function is reserved for academics and journalists. The two poles of poetry are love and death; which is all that can be said, if something has to be. Information on my work may just possibly be had from the First Circle Theatre, Manhattan, who may or may not be going to do some of it, but certainly have acquaintance. Scripts can be had from my agent. I don't take commissions any more, have as little as possible to do with established theatres and have no interest in talking about things I have written."

*   *   *

MacLEISH, Kenneth 1917-1977

PERSONAL: Born February 24, 1917, in Cambridge, Mass.; son of Archibald (a poet) and Ada (Hitchcock) MacLeish; married Carolyn Elisabeth de Chadenedes, September 7, 1938 (divorced, December, 1973); married Roslyn Clarry Ker, July, 1974 (separated, April, 1975); children: (first marriage) Martha Lane, Archibald Bruce, Ellen Ishbel, Kenneth Ian. *Education:* Harvard University, B.S. (cum laude), 1938, M.A., 1939. *Home:* 1889 Governor Ritchie Hwy., Annapolis, Md. 21401. *Office:* National Geographic Society, 17th and M Sts. N.W., Washington, D.C. 20036.

CAREER/WRITINGS: U.S. Department of Agriculture, Washington, D.C., social scientist, 1939-41; Office of Strategic Services, Washington, D.C., staff member, 1941-42; *Life* magazine, Chicago, Ill., assistant science editor, 1946-48, science editor, 1948-53, director of special projects, 1953-55, assistant to managing editor, 1955-56, senior editor, 1956-63; *National Geographic* magazine, Washington, D.C., assistant editor, 1963-69, senior assistant editor, 1969-77. Regular contributor to *Life* and *National Geographic.* Member of the editorial staff of many Time-Life series books, including *The World We Live in* and *The Epic of Man. Military service:* U.S. Naval Reserve, 1942-46; became lieutenant.

AVOCATIONAL INTERESTS: Pilot and diver. At one time shared the record for the world's deepest underwater dive of 724 feet.

OBITUARIES: New York Times, August 7, 1977.*

(Died August 6, 1977, in Annapolis, Md.)

*   *   *

Mac LOW, Jackson 1922-

PERSONAL: Born September 12, 1922, in Chicago, Ill.; son of Jackson (a salesperson) and Fannie (Baskin) Mac Low; married Iris Lezak (a painter; separated); children: Mordecai-Mark, Clarinda. *Education:* University of Chicago, A.A., 1941; Brooklyn College (now of the City University of New York), A.B., 1958; has studied music privately. *Politics:* "Long-term anarchist; short-term radical-liberal pacifist." *Home:* 42 North Moore St., New York, N.Y. 10013.

CAREER: Poet, playwright, editor, teacher, and composer and performer of verbal and theatrical works. Funk & Wagnalls, New York City, editorial assistant, 1957-58, 1961-62;

Standard Reference Works, New York City, editor in humanities, 1958-59; Alfred A. Knopf, New York City, copy editor, 1964-66; poetry editor, *WIN* Magazine, 1966—. New York University, American Language Institute, instructor, 1966-73. *Member:* Amnesty International, P.E.N., American Civil Liberties Union, New York Civil Liberties Union, War Resisters League. *Awards, honors:* American Academy of Arts and Sciences grant, 1971; Creative Artists Public Service (CAPS) fellowship in multimedia, 1973-74, and in poetry, 1976-77; Madeline Sadin Award for the poem, "27th Ode for Iris," 1974; P.E.N. American Center grant, 1974.

WRITINGS—Poetry: *Manifestos,* Something Else, 1966; *August Light Poems,* C. Eshelman, 1967; *22 Light Poems,* Black Sparrow Press, 1968; *23rd Light Poem: For Larry Eigner,* Tetrad Press, 1969; *Stanzas for Iris Lezak,* Something Else, 1970; *4 Trains,* Burning Deck, 1974; *36th Light Poem: In Memorian Buster Keaton,* Permanent Press, 1975; *21 Matched Asymmetrics,* Aloes Books, 1976; *3 Light Poems for 3 Women,* Station Hill Press, 1977; *First Book of Gathas,* Membrane Press, 1978.

Published plays: *Verdurous Sanguinaria* (six-act; first produced in New York City, 1961), Southern University, 1967; *The Twin Plays: Port-au-Prince and Adams County Illinois* (first produced in New York City, 1963), Something Else, 1966; *The Pronouns: A Collection of 40 Dances—For the Dancers,* Tetrad Press, 1971.

Unpublished plays: "Biblical Play," first produced in New York City, 1955; "The Marrying Maiden: A Play of Changes," first produced in New York City at Living Theatre, 1961; "Thanks: A Simultaneity for People," first produced in Wiesbaden, Germany, 1962; "Letters for Iris, Numbers for Silence," first produced in Wiesbaden, 1962; "A Piece of Sari Dienes," first produced in 1962; "Thanks II," first produced in Paris, 1962; "Questions and Answers: A Topical Play," first produced in New York City, 1963; "Play," first produced in New York City, 1965; "Asymmetrics No. 408, 410, 485," first produced in New York City, 1965; "Asymmetrics, Gathas, and Sounds From Everywhere," first produced in New York City, 1966.

Contributor to numerous periodicals in the United States and abroad, including, *Nation, Hudson Review, American Poetry Review,* and *Times Literary Supplement.*

Work represented in numerous anthologies, including *Chicago Review Anthology,* edited by David Ray, University of Chicago Press, 1959; *Notations,* edited by John Cage and Alison Knowles, Something Else, 1969; *The American Experience,* edited by Harold Jaffe and John Tytell, Harper, 1970; *A Big Jewish Book,* edited by Jerome Rothenberg, Doubleday, 1977.

Composer of incidental music for *The Age of Anxiety* by W. H. Auden and *The Heroes* by John Ashberry. Several of Mac Low's poems and musical compositions are included on records and tapes.

SIDELIGHTS: According to *Nation,* in *22 Light Poems* "Mac Low seems primarily concerned with the registration of precise physical, psychic or social events, within a musical structure that crisply articulates that precision."

BIOGRAPHICAL/CRITICAL SOURCES: Nation, May 12, 1969.

* * *

MACY, Helen 1904(?)-1978

OBITUARY NOTICE: Born c. 1904 in New York City; died July 14, 1978, in New York City. Publisher who became president and treasurer of both the Limited Editions Club and the Heritage Press in 1956. Macy was a fellow of Timothy Dwight College of Yale University and former president of the Associates of the Hofstra University Library. Obituaries and other sources: *New York Times,* July 20, 1978; *Publishers Weekly,* July 31, 1978.

* * *

MADARIAGA (Y ROJO), Salvador de 1886-1978

OBITUARY NOTICE—See index for *CA* sketch: Born July 23, 1886, in La Coruna, Spain; died December 14, 1978, in Locarno, Switzerland. Diplomat and writer of novels, poetry, plays, essays, biographies, and historical works. One of Spain's leading intellectuals, Madariaga served in the 1930's as Spanish ambassador to the United States and France and delegate to the League of Nations. After the Spanish Civil War broke out in 1936, he fled to Great Britain. Madariaga was one of the foremost critics of the Franco regime and did not return to Spain until after Franco's death in 1975. During his years in exile, Madariaga wrote prolifically. His output included *Spain,* a history of his native country; and a trilogy on South America, consisting of *Columbus, Cortes,* and *Bolivar. Bolivar* aroused the ire of many South Americans because it claimed the famous liberator was "nothing but a vulgar imitator of Napoleon." Obituaries and other sources: *Current Biography,* Wilson, 1964; *Longman Companion to Twentieth Century Literature,* Longman, 1970; *The International Who's Who,* Europa, 1978; *Washington Post,* December 15, 1978; *New York Times,* December 15, 1978; *Chicago Tribune,* December 15, 1978; *Time,* December 25, 1978.

* * *

MADDEN, Carl H(alford) 1920-1978

OBITUARY NOTICE—See index for *CA* sketch: Born February 14, 1920, in Baltimore, Md.; died October 8, 1978, in Pittsburgh, Pa. Educator, economist, and author of books in his field. After a career in teaching and college administration, Madden went to Washington, where he served as chief economist of the U.S. Chamber of Commerce from 1963 to 1976. At the time of his death, he was a professor at American University. His books include *The Money Side of the Street* and *Clash of Culture.* Obituaries and other sources: *American Men and Women of Science: The Social and Behavioral Sciences,* 12th edition, Bowker, 1973; *Who's Who in America,* 40th edition, Marquis, 1978; *Washington Post,* October 11, 1978.

* * *

MADDOCK, Brent 1950-

PERSONAL: Born May 29, 1950, in St. Louis, Mo.; son of S. Dean, Jr. and Joan (Ritter) Maddock. *Education:* Colgate University, B.A., 1972; University of Southern California, M.A., 1977. *Home:* 839 North Kenwood, Burbank, Calif. 91505.

CAREER: Free-lance film editor, educational film writer, and educational filmmaker in Los Angeles, Calif., 1975—.

WRITINGS: The Films of Jacques Tati, Scarecrow, 1977. Also author of film scripts. Contributor to magazines and newspapers, including *Take One.*

SIDELIGHTS: Maddock writes that his special interests include children's films and comedies, especially silent comedies.

MADDOCK, Reginald (Bertram) 1912-

PERSONAL: Born in 1912, in Warrington, England; married Louisa S. Hawthorn. *Residence:* High Legh, Knutsford, Cheshire, England.

CAREER: Headmaster; writer. *Member:* Society of Authors, P.E.N.

WRITINGS—Juvenile; all published by Thomas Nelson, except as noted: *Rocky and the Lions,* illustrated by Robert Hodgson, 1957; *The Time Maze,* illustrated by Hodgson, 1960; *The Last Horizon,* illustrated by Douglas Relf, 1961; *Rocky and the Elephant,* illustrated by Hodgson, 1962; *The Willow Wand,* illustrated by Hodgson, 1962; *The Tall Man From the Sea,* illustrated by Hodgson, 1962; *One More River,* illustrated by A. S. Douthwaite, 1963; *The Great Bow,* Collins, 1964; *The Widgeon Gang,* illustrated by Dick Hart, 1964; *The Pit,* illustrated by Douglas Hall, Little, Brown, 1966; *Danny Rowley,* Little, Brown, 1969; *The Dragon in the Garden,* Little, Brown, 1969; *Sell-Out,* Collins, 1969; *Northmen's Fury,* illustrated by Graham Humphreys, Macdonald & Co., 1970; *Thin Ice,* Little, Brown, 1971.

"Corrigan" series; all illustrated by Hodgson; all published by Thomas Nelson: *Corrigan and the White Cobra,* 1956; *. . . and the Black Riders,* 1957; *. . . and the Tomb of Opi,* 1957; *. . . and the Yellow Peril,* 1957; *. . . and the Golden Pagoda,* 1958; *. . . and the Dream-Makers,* 1959; *. . . and the Blue Crater,* 1960; *. . . and the Green Tiger,* 1961; *. . . and the Red Lions,* 1962; *. . . and the Little People,* 1963.

SIDELIGHTS: Reginald Maddock's *The Pit* told the story of Butch Reece and how he improved his self-image and his tough kid reputation. *The Pit* "is full of exciting incident and good dialogue and does not dawdle in the narration. Underprivileged American adolescents will readily understand Butch Reece's attitudes, which are not unlike their own," commented a critic for *Book World.* A commentator for *Young Readers' Review* wrote: "Mr. Maddock does an outstanding job in bringing this youth to life. . . . Incorporated into this good adventure story is a fine study of character and reputation that will interest, intrigue, and enlighten readers. This is a very good book with solid substance."

In *Northmen's Fury,* Maddock wove a tale set during the time of the Danish invasion and King Alfred. "It is a straight historical adventure, only saved from mediocrity by the excellent portrayal of its chief character. . . . The book as a whole fails to convey a proper sense of period. . . . Change the names and these people could be fighting invaders at any time in history," commented a reviewer for *Books and Bookmen.* A critic for the *Times Literary Supplement* also noted that Maddock failed to provide any "sense of period." However, he observed other commendable qualities about the book. *Northmen's Fury* has "a good climax; it is all plausible, possible and fast-moving. The interests and doings of the little band are woven quite deftly into the larger Alfredian heroic picture."

BIOGRAPHICAL/CRITICAL SOURCES: Young Readers' Review, April, 1968; *Book World,* May 5, 1968; *Times Literary Supplement,* April 16, 1970; *Books and Bookmen,* May, 1970.*

*   *   *

MAGEE, David (Bickersteth) 1905-1977

PERSONAL: Born in 1905, in West Riding, Yorkshire, England; came to United States in 1925; married wife, Dorothy. *Education:* Attended public school in Sussex, England. *Residence:* San Francisco, Calif.

CAREER: Clerk for an exporting and importing firm in London, England, 1922-24; bookseller's assistant for John Howell, San Francisco, Calif., 1925-28; rare book dealer and owner of his own bookshop, San Francisco, 1928-77. *Member:* Antiquarian Booksellers Association of America (president, 1966-68), Grolier Club, Book Club of California (former president), Roxburghe Club of San Francisco (former president), Bohemian Club.

WRITINGS: (Compiler with Elinor Raas Heller) *Bibliography of the Grabhorn Press, 1915-1940,* Grabhorn Press, 1940; *Jam Tomorrow* (novel), Houghton, 1941; (compiler with wife, Dorothy Magee) *Bibliography of the Grabhorn Press, 1940-56,* Grabhorn Press, 1957; (compiler) *The Hundredth Book: A Bibliography of the Publications of the Book Club of California and a History of the Club,* Grabhorn Press, 1958; (compiler) *A Catalogue of Some Five Hundred Examples of the Printing of Edwin and Robert Grabhorn, 1917-60; and Two Gentlemen From Indiana, Now Resident in California,* [San Francisco], 1961; (compiler) *Victoria R.I.: A Collection of Books, Manuscripts, Autograph Letters, Original Drawings, etc., by the Lady Herself and Her Loyal Subjects, Produced During Her Long and Illustrious Reign,* three volumes, Grabhorn-Hoyem, 1969-70; *Infinite Riches: The Adventures of a Rare Book Dealer* (autobiography), Paul Eriksson, 1973. Writer of plays for the San Francisco Bohemian Club; also author of pamphlets on cataloging techniques. Contributor of numerous articles to *AB Bookman's Weekly.*

SIDELIGHTS: Book collecting was in David Magee's blood: a great-great aunt, Frances Mary Richardson Currer, was a prominent English book collector in the nineteenth century. Among his personal collections, Magee counted a complete collection of P. G. Wodehouse and an assemblage of books on the literature of murder.

BIOGRAPHICAL/CRITICAL SOURCES: David Magee, *Infinite Riches: The Adventures of a Rare Book Dealer* (autobiography), Paul Eriksson, 1973. Obituaries: *AB Bookman's Weekly,* August 1, 1977.*

(Died July 17, 1977, in San Francisco, Calif.)

*   *   *

MAGUIRE, Anne
See NEARING, Penny

*   *   *

MAGUIRE, Gregory 1954-

PERSONAL: Born June 9, 1954, in Albany, N.Y.; son of John (a journalist) and Marie (McAuliff) Maguire. *Education:* State University of New York at Albany, B.A., 1976; Simmons College, M.A., 1978. *Religion:* Roman Catholic. *Home:* 9 Avon St., Cambridge, Mass. 02138.

CAREER: Vincentian Grade School, Albany, N.Y., teacher of English, 1976-77; writer, 1977—. Director of contemporary music at Roman Catholic church in Albany, N.Y., 1972-77. *Awards, honors:* Fellow at Bread Loaf Writers' Conference, summer, 1978.

WRITINGS: The Lightning Time (novel for children), Farrar, Straus, 1978.

WORK IN PROGRESS: The Daughter of the Moon, a novel for children.

SIDELIGHTS: Maguire writes briefly: "All I can say is: 'The earth is full of the goodness of the Lord.' And having remembered that, I rest, silent."

MAGUIRE, Jack 1920-

PERSONAL: Born April 10, 1920, in Denison, Tex.; son of Jeff Edward (a railroad engineer) and Elizabeth (Russell) Maguire; married Pat Horton (an editor and public relations executive), August 11, 1946; children: Jack, Jr., Kevin. *Education:* Attended North Texas State University, 1940-42; University of Texas, B.J., 1944. *Politics:* Independent. *Religion:* Presbyterian. *Home address:* P.O. Box 2282, San Antonio, Tex. 78294. *Office address:* P.O. Box 1226, San Antonio, Tex. 78294.

CAREER: Denison Herald, Denison, Tex., reporter, 1944-45; Missouri-Kansas-Texas Railroad, St. Louis, Mo., public relations representative, 1945-50; Texas Insurance Advisory Association, Austin, public relations director, 1950-56; University of Texas, Austin, executive director of Ex-Students' Association, 1956-76; Institute of Texas Cultures, San Antonio, executive director, 1976—. Member of board of directors of Texas Commerce Bank; past president of Longhorn Travelers, Inc.; past chairman of Highland Lakes Council. *Member:* Public Relations Society of America, Philosophical Society of Texas, Sigma Delta Chi, Rotary International, Chamber of Commerce.

WRITINGS: (Editor) *A President's Country,* Shoal Creek Publishers, 1964; *Talk of Texas,* Shoal Creek Publishers, 1973; *Texas: Amazing, but True,* Shoal Creek Publishers, 1979. Author of "Talk of Texas," a column syndicated by Pat-Jack Enterprises, San Antonio, 1963—, and "This Is T.I. Territory," in *Texas Flyer* (Texas International Airlines magazine), and "Profiles of Texas," in *Southwest Airlines Magazine,* both 1978—. Contributor of more than four hundred articles to magazines.

WORK IN PROGRESS: Another "This Is Texas" book, due in late 1979 or 1980.

SIDELIGHTS: Maguire writes: "I decided at age twelve that I wanted to be a writer. My parents encouraged the idea by buying me a used typewriter for ten dollars. As a high school junior I really got launched with the help of the president of the United States. It happened this way:

"That spring, I had dropped into the editorial office of my hometown paper, the *Denison Herald,* and asked the editor for a summer job. Depression was abroad in the land and he could hire experienced reporters for twenty dollars a week. He appreciated my ambition, but gave me a gentle 'No.'

"'O.K.' I said. 'But if I can find a news story so important that you'll have to print it on page one, will you give me a job?' He was a sporting fellow and agreed that he would.

"It happened that 1936 was Texas' centennial year and President Roosevelt had accepted an invitation to come to Dallas and open the world's fair that was to highlight the celebration. In those days, presidents traveled by train, and to get into Texas F.D.R. had to enter either through Texarkana or through Denison. So I wrote the President a letter, explained my bet and asked him to stop off and make a speech in Denison so I would get my story. About eleven thousand of my high school classmates signed the letter also. F.D.R. must have been a sporting man too. He accepted the invitation, made a rear platform speech in Denison and I got the job.

"Later, in journalism school at the University of Texas, a wonderful professor of feature writing used to tell our class: 'If you want to write and sell what you write, pick out a specialty. Find the one subject that interests you most, learn all you can about it and don't write about anything else. Soon editors will be asking you for material because you will be a specialist in your field.'

"It sounded like a good idea. Having grown up in a railroad town, I had always like transportation. I decided this field would be my specialty. By the middle 1950's I had a large file of more than fifty thousand clippings on railroads and railroading and a large library of books on the subject. But the industry was changing. Passenger trains were being lopped off, the diesel was replacing the steam engine and much of the romance of railroading was gone. I knew it was time to find another specialty. I selected Texas.

"And with good reason. Much of my railroad material already concerned Texas and Texas personalities. As a native, I knew the state well. And as an amateur historian, I had long collected some of the unique, unusual, odd and human interest stories from Texas history. Soon editors were calling me to give me assignments just as they did when I specialized in railroads. Now, I write and sell about one hundred thousand words a year, on average, and every work is sold before it is written.

"In 1963, my long-time friend, President Lyndon Johnson, dropped in on a party my wife and I were giving for some close friends. At the party, he told me that he was concerned that the Washington press corps needed a more detailed briefing on Texas than most of them had ever had. He asked me to get together for him 'some mimeographed stuff that I can hand them.' I agreed. By July, with the help of some friends who were experts on Johnson's Hill Country, I had put together a manuscript. President Johnson personally gave it a final reading, approved it, and *A President's Country* was published. He ordered one thousand copies and handed them out to distinguished visitors during his years in the White House. The book still sells in Texas.

"And so it goes. Writing, to me, has always been a marvelous way to express one's self and get paid for doing it. Though I haven't made a lot of money as a writer, to know that my columns and articles still are reaching over 1.5 million readers a month is satisfying to one's ego. Even more satisfying is the number of doors that have been opened to me as a writer, even though I'm only a regional writer and, I suppose, more of a journalist than anything else. But I have interviewed five presidents of the United States, have dined with prime ministers, count hundreds of people throughout the world as friends, and have had one hell of an interesting life.

"And all because of a president who wanted to help a high school kid win a bet, and a professor who knew that the 'Open Sesame' to the writing game is one word: Specialize."

*   *   *

MAHONEY, Patrick 1927-

PERSONAL: Born September 16, 1927, in Portsmouth, England; son of Patrick and Doris (Parker) Mahoney. *Education:* Attended evening school in London, England. *Politics:* "Right wing." *Religion:* "Ex-Roman Catholic." *Home:* 127 Christie Gardens, Chadwell Heath, Romford, Essex RM6 4SD, England. *Agent:* A.P. Watt & Sons, 26-28 Bedford Row, London WC1R 4HL, England. *Office:* Electra House, Victoria Embankment, London W.C.2, England.

CAREER: Cable & Wireless Ltd., London, England, messenger, 1941-46; overseas telegraphist, 1948—. *Military service:* British Army, Highland Brigade, 1946-48; served in Germany. *Member:* Masons, Ilford Conservative Club.

WRITINGS: (With Martin Middlebrook) *Battleship* (nonfiction), Penguin, 1976.

SIDELIGHTS: Mahoney comments: "I have a morbid fascination with war. I am considered an expert on Napoleon, the war in France (1914-48), and war in the Far East (1941-45). I have visited battlefields at Waterloo, Ypres, Loos, Vimy Ridge, Somme, Arnhem, Nijmagen, Singapore, and Malaya. I have worked at overseas stations in Bermuda, Aden, Amman, Jerusalem, Geneva, and Ndola.''

*   *   *

MALEK, Frederic Vincent 1937-

PERSONAL: Born December 22, 1937, in Oak Park, Ill.; son of Fred W. and Martha (Smickilas) Malek; married Marlene McArthur (a nurse), August 5, 1961; children: Frederic W., Michelle A. *Education:* U.S. Military Academy, B.S., 1959; Harvard University, M.B.A., 1964. *Politics:* Republican. *Religion:* Episcopalian. *Home:* 6709 Lupine Lane, McLean, Va. 22101. *Office:* Marriott Corp., 5161 River Rd., Washington, D.C. 20016.

CAREER: Triangle Corp., Columbia, S.C., chairman, 1967-69; U.S. Department of Health, Education, and Welfare, Washington, D.C., deputy under-secretary, 1969-70; assistant to U.S. president in Washington D.C., 1970-72; U.S. Office of Management and the Budget, Washington, D.C., deputy director, 1973-75; Marriott Corp., Washington, D.C., executive vice-president, 1975—. Member of board of directors of Sargent Welch Scientific Co., Sun Line Greece, and Sun Line Special Shipping Co. Past member of President's Commission on White House Fellows, Council on Personnel Interchange, and Domestic Council. *Military service:* U.S. Army, 1959-62; became first lieutenant. *Member:* American Management Association. *Awards, honors:* D.Hum. from St. Leo College, 1970; man of the year award from Bohemian Lawyers Association, 1973.

WRITINGS: Washington's Hidden Tragedy: The Failure to Make Government Work, Free Press, 1978. Contributor to business magazines and newspapers.

SIDELIGHTS: Malek told *CA:* "When I entered the government from the business world, I found that government lacked strong, effective management. This existed from top to bottom with most government officials caring more about how well the government appeared to be working than how well it actually was working. After my six years of wrestling with these problems, I felt I had learned a great deal about the hidden tragedy of government's failure to deliver upon its promises to the American people as well as solid practical guidelines to deal with this problem. This led to my decision to write this book.

"The book draws upon a rich variety of case examples outlining basic inadequacies in the way that the government selects its top officials, organizes and reorganizes, evaluates programs, and plans for the future. It demonstrates the successes and failures of government, takes a critical look at the practices and attitudes that lead to both, and shows how enlightened management can make a recognizable and major difference in helping the government work more effectively for the people.

"It is my contention as stated in the book that it is possible to make government work despite the frustrations involved: the glare of publicity, divided loyalties, and the pervasive influence of political pressures. Each chapter raises problems, but it also provides answers. In my view, the solutions must start at the top in the Oval Office, but every level of government below the president must also become involved in the management process if the bureaucracy is ever to be molded into an effective force.''

MALIK, Yogendra K(umar) 1929-

PERSONAL: Born May 24, 1929, in India; son of K. R. and D. (Lajwanti) Malik; married Usha (a teacher), April, 1959; children: Sunita, Arvind, Rajiv. *Education:* Punjab University, B.A., 1949; University of Florida, M.A., 1963, Ph.D., 1966. *Home:* 4190 Bobolink Circle, Stow, Ohio 44224. *Office:* Department of Political Science, University of Akron, Akron, Ohio 44325.

CAREER: Southwest Texas State University, San Marcos, assistant professor of political science, 1966-69; University of Akron, Akron, Ohio, professor of political science, 1969—. Visiting professor at Nehru University of India, 1974.

MEMBER: American Political Science Association, American Association for Asian Studies, Canadian Association for South Asian Studies, Southern Political Science Association. *Awards, honors:* Indian Council of Social Science Research senior fellowship, 1974.

WRITINGS: East Indian in Trinidad, Oxford University Press, 1971; *Asian Studies,* Volume VI, E. J. Brill, 1975; *The Political Novel in India,* Orient Longman, 1978; *North Indian Intellectuals,* E. J. Brill, 1978. Contributor to political science and Asian studies journals, including *Journal of Politics, Western Political Quarterly, Asian Studies,* and *Asian Survey.*

WORK IN PROGRESS: Intellectuals and Social Change in South Asia; research on the development of partisanship and political attitudes among secondary-school students.

AVOCATIONAL INTERESTS: Travel (Middle East, England, the Caribbean).

*   *   *

MALLOWAN, Max (Edgar Lucien) 1904-1978

OBITUARY NOTICE—See index for *CA* sketch: Born May 6, 1904, in London, England; died August 19, 1978, in London. Educator, archaeologist, and author of works in his field. Mallowan received recognition for his discovery of the Eye Temple of Tell Brak and the Akkadian Palace of Naram-Sim. His book *Nimrud and Its Remains* chronicles his activjties in Mesopotamia. Mallowan also wrote an autobiography, *Mallowan's Memoirs,* which takes into account his forty-six year marriage to mystery writer Agatha Christie. Obituaries and other sources: Lynn Poole and Gray Poole, *Men Who Dig Up History,* Dodd, 1968; *Who's Who in the World,* 2nd edition, Marquis, 1973; *The Writers Directory, 1976-78,* St. Martin's, 1976; *Who's Who,* 130th edition, St. Martin's, 1978; *The International Who's Who,* Europa, 1978; Max Mallowan, *Mallowan's Memoirs,* Dodd, 1978; *Publishers Weekly,* September 18, 1978.

*   *   *

MALOCSAY, Zoltan 1946-

PERSONAL: Born June 28, 1946, in Miami, Okla.; son of Nelson (in aircraft business) and Eloese Malocsay; married Dolores Arnold. *Education:* University of Oklahoma, B.A., 1968; graduate study at University of Iowa, 1968-69. *Residence:* Colorado Springs, Colo.

CAREER: Northeastern Agricultural & Mechanical College, Miami, Okla., newspaper editor and public relations representative, 1964-65; *Miami Daily News-Record,* Miami, Okla., general reporter, 1966-71; free-lance writer, 1971—. Instructor at University of Iowa, 1968-69; technical editor for University of Oklahoma Research Institute, 1969-70. *Member:* Phi Beta Kappa.

WRITINGS: Galloping Wind (novel), Putnam, 1978; *Official Pikes Peak Area Guide to Hiking and Horse Trails,* Pikes Peak Area Council of Governments, 1978.

Work represented in anthologies, including *Forerunners,* Economy Co., 1978.

Contributor to *Boy's Life.* Contributing editor of *Westerner, Rock and Gem,* and *Old Trails.*

WORK IN PROGRESS: A flying novel, for Unicorn Books; a historical novel about Opothle-Yahola and Indians who fought against the Confederacy in the Civil War.

SIDELIGHTS: Malocsay writes: "I want to write the kind of books and stories that are of lasting value, that never go out of date. *Galloping Wind* is an attempt to show how exciting and beautiful a Western adventure can be without gunfights, fistfights, lynchings—in other words, without the usual dose of sex and violence that is thought necessary to make a Western thrilling. I am frustrated because the current definition of an adult book (and only adult books are bought in large numbers) holds that it must be unsuitable for kids. I want to show that an adult book should be any book that adults like, even if it is also wholesome enough for kids. The best 'juvenile' material is sophisticated enough for the entire family. My problem is that my publisher refuses to allow my book on the adult list because it has no sex and brutality, and only adults and teenagers buy books for their own entertainment, so my book is doomed as a gift item."

*   *   *

MAMET, David   1947-

PERSONAL: Surname pronounced *Mam*-it; born November 30, 1947, in Chicago, Ill.; son of Bernard (an attorney) and Lenore (a teacher; maiden name, Silver) Mamet; married Lindsay Crouse (an actress), December 21, 1977. *Education:* Attended Neighborhood Playhouse School of the Theater, 1968-69; Goddard College, B.A., 1969. *Politics:* "The last refuge of the unimaginative." *Religion:* "The second-to-last." *Agent:* Howard Rosenstone, 850 Seventh Ave., New York, N.Y. 10019. *Office:* St. Nicholas Theater Co., 2851 North Halstead St., Chicago, Ill. 60657.

CAREER: Playwright. St. Nicholas Theater Co., Chicago, Ill., artistic director, 1973-76, member of board of directors, 1973—; Goodman Theater, Chicago, associate artistic director, 1978—. Artist-in-residence in drama, Goddard College, 1971-73; visiting lecturer in drama, University of Chicago, 1975-76; teaching fellow, Yale University, 1976-77. Has also worked at a canning plant, a truck factory, a real estate agency, and as a window washer, office cleaner, and taxi driver. *Member:* Dramatists Guild, Writers Guild of America, Actors Equity Association, P.E.N., United Steelworkers of America, Randolph A. Hollister Association, *Awards, honors:* Joseph Jefferson award, 1975, for *Sexual Perversity in Chicago;* Obie Award for best new American plays from *Village Voice,* 1976, for *American Buffalo* and *Sexual Perversity in Chicago;* CBS fellowship in creative writing, 1976; New York Drama Critics Circle Award for best American play, 1977, for *American Buffalo;* Outer Critics Circle Award, 1978, for contributions to the American theater.

WRITINGS—Plays; all published by Grove, except as indicated: *Sexual Perversity in Chicago* [and] *Duck Variations* ("Sexual Perversity in Chicago" [one-act], first produced in Chicago, Ill. at Organic Theater, 1974; "Duck Variations" [one-act], first produced in Chicago at St. Nicholas Theater, 1976, produced in New York City at St. Clement's, 1976), 1977; *American Buffalo* (two-act; first produced in Chicago

at Goodman Theater, 1977, produced in New York City at Ethel Barrymore Theater, February 16, 1977), 1977; *The Revenge of the Space Pandas, or Binky Rudich and the Two-Speed Clock* (one-act for children; first produced in New York City at Flushing Town Hall, 1977), Sergel, 1978; *The Water Engine* (two-act; first produced at St. Nicholas Theater, 1977, produced in New York City at Public Theater, February 28, 1978, produced on Broadway at Plymouth Theater, 1978), 1978; *A Life in the Theater* (one-act; first produced at Goodman Theater, 1977, produced in New York City at Theater de Lys, 1978), 1978.

Unpublished plays: "Lakeboat" (one-act), first produced in Marlboro, Vt. at Marlboro Theater Workshop, 1970; "Squirrels" (one-act), first produced at St. Nicholas Theater, 1974; "The Woods" (two-act), first produced at St. Nicholas Theater, November 16, 1977, produced in New York City at Public Theater, 1979; "Reunion" and "Dark Pony" (both one-act), first produced together in New Haven, Conn., at Yale Repertory Theater.

Contributing editor, *Oui* magazine, 1975-76.

WORK IN PROGRESS: "Lone Canoe," a musical with Rokko Jans; a screenplay adaptation of "Sexual Perversity in Chicago"; a television situation comedy.

SIDELIGHTS: Critics are applauding the extraordinary use of speech in Mamet's plays. "To congratulate David Mamet upon his ear for speech is to miss the main thing about him," reviewer Richard Eder wrote. "His is no ear, but a stethoscope. His characters' words are heartbeats—evidence of their state of life and its constant fibrillating transformations.

"The evidence is not always direct," Eder continued. "For Mr. Mamet, speech can testify in its awkwardnesses and silences to the opposite of what it seems to say. The gun flash is precisely not where the bullet lodges. Mr. Mamet's extraordinary talent is to report the flash and show us where the wound really is."

Agreeing that the language of his plays is extremely important, Mamet told Steven Dzielak that "what the characters say to each other must contain and give birth to what they do to each other." And to explain his play *Sexual Perversity in Chicago,* he once commented: "Voltaire said words were invented to hide feelings. That's what the play is about, how what we say influences what we think."

A Life in the Theater is Mamet's current and very successful New York production. Edith Oliver wrote: "Mr. Mamet has written—in gentle ridicule; in jokes, broad and tiny; and in comedy, high and low—a love letter to the theater. It is quite a feat, and he has pulled it off." According to Mel Gussow, with this play, Mamet has proven that "he is an eloquent master of two-part harmony. An abundantly gifted playwright, he brings new life to the theater."

"You know, I don't have any theories about how to write plays," Mamet told Dzielak, "that's something you can't possibly learn from reading a book of plays. You do it by doing it. You can sort of be guided in the pursuit of this knowledge by what other people have done, and by what you see happening on the stage, but you have to teach yourself. I mean, if the technique in Beckett were so blatant as to be abstractable upon reading, it couldn't possibly be that beautiful."

As for the future, Mamet says "I'm going to keep writing. I'd like to write a really good play sometime. Like O'Neill, Odets, Chekhov, something the way it really is, capture the action of the way things really go on."

BIOGRAPHICAL/CRITICAL SOURCES: New York

Times, July 5, 1976, February 5, 1977, February 13, 1977, February 18, 1977, October 21, 1977, June 24, 1977, November 30, 1977; *New Yorker,* October 31, 1977; *US,* January 10, 1978; *New York Arts Journal,* February/March, 1978; *New York Times* Magazine, March 12, 1978; *Contemporary Literary Criticism,* Volume 9, Gale, 1978.

*   *   *

MANCKE, Richard B(ell)   1943-

PERSONAL: Surname is pronounced Mank; born January 11, 1943, in Bethlehem, Pa.; son of Donald B. and Elizabeth (Schlottman) Mancke; married Barbara Hobbie (a writer and poet). *Education:* Colgate University, B.A., 1965; Massachusetts Institute of Technology, Ph.D., 1969. *Residence:* Medford, Mass. *Office:* Fletcher School of Law and Diplomacy, Tufts University, Medford, Mass. 02155.

CAREER: University of Chicago, Chicago, Ill., assistant professor of business economics, 1969-71; University of Michigan, Ann Arbor, assistant professor of economics, 1971-74, and law, 1973-74; Tufts University, Fletcher School of Law and Diplomacy, Medford, Mass., associate professor of international economic relations, 1974—. Staff economist for U.S. Cabinet task force on oil import controls, 1969-70; research director of Twentieth Century Fund task force on U.S. energy policy; testified before U.S. Senate committees; expert witness for Environmental Protection Agency; consultant to Federal Trade Commission, Center for Law and Social Policy, Institute for Defense Analyses, and several law firms.

WRITINGS: The Failure of U.S. Energy Policy, Columbia University Press, 1974; *The Performance of the Federal Energy Office,* American Enterprise Institute, 1975; *Squeaking By: U.S. Energy Policy Since the Embargo,* Columbia University Press, 1976; (editor and contributor) *Providing for Energy,* McGraw, 1977; *Mexican Oil and Natural Gas: Political, Strategic, and Economic Implications,* Praeger, 1979.

Contributor: Joseph Szliowicz and Bard O'Neill, editors, *The Energy Crisis and U.S. Foreign Policy,* Praeger, 1975; Patricia Markun, editor, *The Future of American Oil: The Experts Testify,* American Petroleum Institute, 1976; A. Lawrence Chickering, editor, *The Politcs of Planning,* Institute for Contemporary Studies, 1976; Edward Mitchell, editor, *Vertical Integration in the Oil Industry,* American Enterprise Institute, 1976; Mitchell, editor, *Perspectives on U.S. Energy Policy: A Critique of Regulation,* Praeger, 1976; (author of foreword) Barbara Hobbie, *Oil Company Divestiture and the Periodical Press,* Praeger, 1977. Contributor of more than twenty-five articles and reviews to professional and popular journals, including *New Republic.* Member of editorial advisory board of *Energy Economics,* 1978—.

WORK IN PROGRESS: Writings on U.S. and Western Hemispheric energy policies; on-going studies of the U.S. electronic data processing industry.

SIDELIGHTS: Mancke wrote in the preface to his first book: "The United States is in the midst of a well-publicized but very real energy crisis. The crux of this crisis lies in the contradiction between economic, political, and technological realities and our policymakers' inappropriate responses. Energy policy has historically been hit and miss, partially because of the complexity of comprehensive policy formulation and partially because those who make decisions are not usually allowed to view the situation in a comprehensive framework. Whatever the reasons, we are now shackled with a frequently contradictory set of policies designed for a world our policymakers have misperceived." His subsequent writings and current research elaborate upon this theme.

*   *   *

MANDER, Jerry   1936-

PERSONAL: Born May 1, 1936, in New York, N.Y.; son of Harry and Eva (Weissman) Mander; married Anica Vesel (a writer), November 27, 1965; children: Yari, Kai. *Education:* University of Pennsylvania, B.S., 1958; Columbia University, M.S., 1959. *Residence:* San Francisco, Calif. *Agent:* John Brockman Associates, 241 Central Park W., New York, N.Y.

CAREER: Writer. Worked as assistant director of San Francisco International Film Festival, 1961-62; president of public relations firm, Jerry Mander & Associates, 1962-65; president of Freeman, Mander & Gossage Advertising, 1965-72. Member of Public Interest Communications, 1972-74.

WRITINGS: (With George Dippel and Howard Gossage) *The Great International Paper Airplane Book,* Simon & Schuster, 1967; *Four Arguments for the Elimination of Television,* Morrow, 1978. Contributor of articles to periodicals, including *Co-Evolution Quarterly, City* magazine, *San Francisco Chronicle, Mother Jones, Ramparts, Scanlan's Monthly,* and *Penthouse.*

SIDELIGHTS: Critics did not know quite how to take Mander's first book, *The Great International Paper Airplane Book.* S. V. Jones gave it a straight-faced review, noting the variety of contestants (including scientists in aerodynamics as well as practitioners of the oriental art of origami), the statistics of record flights, and the appendix (a collection of twenty "tear-out-fold-and-fly" paper airplane designs).

However, J. V. Brian saw through the volume's academic facade: "Masquerading as a book, this essay in promotion is, in fact, an elaborate spoof with tongue in cheek scholarly apparatus that raises trivia to a fine art." James Wolcott called it "an amusing put-on entertainment."

In his review of Mander's solo effort, *Four Arguments for the Elimination of Television,* Wolcott was less generous. He called the book a "visionary manifesto" and explained that Mander's thesis concerns the dangers of television as both a cultural phenomenon and an artistic medium. Wolcott acknowledged that "the special value of Mander's call-to-arms is that by dedicating himself to a concrete destructive end he can more effectively marshal his facts." But Wolcott criticized the scope of those facts; he claimed that Mander ignores not only the incidence of artistically successful TV programming but the work of such serious television critics as Gilbert Seldes, John Leonard, Reed Whittemore, and Arthur Asa Berger.

BIOGRAPHICAL/CRITICAL SOURCES: New York Times Book Review, January 28, 1968, February 25, 1968; *Library Journal,* February 15, 1968; *New York Review of Books,* April 6, 1978.

*   *   *

MANGUM, Garth L(eroy)   1926-

PERSONAL: Born July 23, 1926, in Delta, Utah; son of James L. (a farmer) and Golda (Elder) Mangum; married Marion Poll (a writer and publisher), November 20, 1953; children: Stephen, Mary, David, Susan. *Education:* Brigham Young University, B.S., 1956; Harvard University, M.P.A., 1958, Ph.D., 1960. *Politics:* Democrat. *Religion:* Church of Jesus Christ of Latter-day Saints (Mormons). *Home:* 4316 Adonis Dr., Salt Lake City, Utah 84117. *Office:* Human Resources Institute, College of Business, University of Utah, Salt Lake City, Utah 84112.

CAREER: Brookings Institution, Washington, D.C., research assistant, 1957-59; Harvard University, Cambridge, Mass., instructor in economics, 1959-60; Brigham Young University, Provo, Utah, associate professor of economics, 1960-63; U.S. Senate, Washington, D.C., executive director of subcommittee on employment and manpower, 1963-64; National Commission on Technology, Automation & Economic Progress, executive secretary, 1965-66; Appalachian Regional Commission, member of education advisory committee, 1966-68; University of Utah, Salt Lake City, McGraw Professor of Economics and professor of management, 1968—, director of Human Resources Institute. Member and past chairman of National Council on Employment Policy; chairman of advisory board of National Institute for Career Education; arbitrator for Federal Mediation and Conciliation Service and American Arbitration Association; adviser to federal and state agencies and foreign governments. Research professor and co-director for Manpower Policy Studies at George Washington University, 1966-72; guest lecturer at University of Tel Aviv, 1969, and University of South Africa, 1977; visiting lecturer at American Seminar (Salzburg, Austria), 1975.

Senior staff analyst for Presidential Railroad Commission, 1961; mediator for U.S. Department of Labor and Atomic Energy Commission, 1962-63; member of Presidential Board of Inquiry for Union Carbide Corp.-United Steelworkers of America dispute, 1966; member of President Lyndon Johnson's Advisory Council on Vocational Education, 1967-68. U.S. Information Agency lecturer in Saudi Arabia, Kuwait, and Jordan, 1972; Ford Foundation lecturer in Bahrain, Yemen, Saudi Arabia, and Jordan, 1975; World Bank adviser to United Arab Emirates, 1978; participant in international conferences; consultant to U.S. Department of Labor and Organization for Economic Co-Operation and Development. *Military service:* U.S. Army Air Forces, 1944-45. *Awards, honors:* Ford Foundation research professorship, 1962-63.

WRITINGS: (With R. Joseph Monsen) *The Investment of Idle State Funds* (monograph), Utah Bankers Association, 1962; *The Operating Engineers: Economic History of a Trade Union,* Harvard University Press, 1964; *Wage Incentive System* (monograph), Institute of Industrial Relations, University of California, Berkeley, 1964; *The Manpower Revolution: Its Policy Consequences,* Doubleday, 1965; (with Howard R. Bowen) *Automation and Economic Progress,* Prentice-Hall, 1966; (with Sar A. Levitan) *Making Sure of Federal Manpower Policy* (monograph), Institute of Labor and Industrial Relations, University of Michigan, 1967; *Contributions and Costs of Manpower Development and Training* (monograph), Institute of Labor and Industrial Relations, University of Michigan, 1967; (with Lowell M. Glenn) *Vocational Rehabilitation and Federal Manpower Policy* (monograph), Institute of Labor and Industrial Relations, University of Michigan, 1968; *Reorienting Vocational Education* (monograph), Institute of Labor and Industrial Relations, University of Michigan, 1968; *MDTA: Foundation of Federal Manpower Policy,* Johns Hopkins Press, 1968; (with Arnold L. Nemore) *Reorienting the Public Employment Service* (monograph), Institute of Labor and Industrial Relations, University of Michigan, 1968; (with Glenn) *Employing the Disadvantaged in the Federal Civil*

Service (monograph), Institute of Labor and Industrial Relations, University of Michigan, 1969; (with Levitan) *Federal Work and Training Programs in the Sixties,* Institute of Labor and Industrial Relations, University of Michigan, 1969; *The Emergence of Manpower Policy,* Holt, 1969; (with Rupert Evans and Otto Pragen) *Education for Employment: The Background and Potential of the 1968 Vocational Education Amendments* (monograph), Institute of Labor and Industrial Relations, University of Michigan, 1969.

(With Sar A. Levitan and Robert Taggert III) *Economic Opportunity in the Ghetto: The Partnership of Government and Business,* Johns Hopkins Press, 1970; (with Levitan and Ray Marshall) *Human Resources and Labor Markets,* Harper, 1971, 2nd edition, 1976; (with Kenneth Hoyt, Rupert Evans, and Edward Mackin) *Career Education: What It Is and How to Do It,* Olympus, 1972; (with R. Thayne Robson) *Metropolitan Impact of Manpower Programs,* Olympus, 1973; (with John Walsh) *A Decade of Manpower Development and Training,* Olympus, 1973; (with Hoyt, Nancy Pinson, and Darryl Laramore) *Career Education and the Elementary School Teacher,* Olympus, 1973; (with Hoyt and Evans) *Career Education in the Middle School and Junior High,* Olympus, 1973; (with David Snedeker) *Manpower Planning for Local Labor Markets,* Olympus, 1974; (with D. and Bonnie Snedeker) *Self-Evaluation of CETA Manpower Programs: A Guide for Prime Sponsors* (monograph), Olympus, 1975; (editor with James Becker, Garn Coombs, and Pat Marshall) *Career Education in the Academic Classroom,* Olympus, 1975; *Employability, Employment, and Income: A Reassessment of Manpower Policy,* Olympus, 1976; (with Ella Bowen, Don Gale, and others) *Career Education in the High School,* Olympus, 1976; (with Gale, Mary L. Olson, and others) *Your Child's Career: A Guide to Home-Based Career Education,* Olympus, 1977; (with Arvil V. Adams) *The Lingering Crisis of Youth Unemployment,* W. E. Upjohn Institute for Employment Research, 1978; (with Stephen F. Seninger) *Coming of Age in the Ghetto: A Dilemma of Youth Unemployment,* Johns Hopkins Press, 1978; (co-author) *Planning and Managing Local Manpower Programs,* Olympus, 1978; *Employment and Training Programs for Youth: What Works Best for Whom?,* Office of Youth Programs, 1978. Contributor of more than sixty-five articles to professional journals and government publications.

*   *   *

MANHEIM, Michael 1928-

PERSONAL: Born March 4, 1928, in New York, N.Y.; son of Leonard F. (a professor) and Eleanor (a teacher; maiden name, Blackman) Manheim; married Martha Bradshaw (a lecturer), March 6, 1955; children: James, Daniel. *Education:* Columbia University, A.B., 1949, M.A., 1951, Ph.D., 1961. *Politics:* Democrat. *Home:* 3426 Kirkwall Rd., Toledo, Ohio 43606. *Office:* Department of English, University of Toledo, Toledo, Ohio 43606.

CAREER: University of Delaware, Newark, instructor in English, 1953-61; University of Toledo, Toledo, Ohio, assistant professor, 1961-63, associate professor, 1963-67, professor of English, 1967—, chairman of department, 1966-72. Member of summer faculty at Dartmouth College, 1972. Project director of WGTE-TV, 1976—. *Member:* Modern Language Association of America, Shakespeare Association of America, Midwest Modern Language Association (member of executive committee). *Awards, honors:* Danforth

Foundation teaching award, 1959-60; Huntington Library research fellowship, 1974.

WRITINGS: The Weak King Dilemma in the Shakespearean History Play, Syracuse University Press, 1973. Contributor to language, literature, and education journals.

WORK IN PROGRESS: Eugene O'Neill's New Language of Kinship, a critical study of his life and works; *Thomas Dekker and the Rhapsodical Strain.*

SIDELIGHTS: Manheim writes: "I consider myself primarily a student of human beings and the nature of life, secondarily a scholar. I believe man's function in the universe may be measured only by what he does in clarifying human relationships, and that clarification may be much aided by the study of great literature." *Avocational interests:* European travel, tennis.

* * *

MANNING, Sylvia 1943-

PERSONAL: Born December 2, 1943, in Montreal, Quebec, Canada; came to the United States in 1963; daughter of Bruno and Lea (Rosenbaum) Bank; married Peter J. Manning (a professor of English), August 20, 1967; children: Bruce David, Jason Maurice. *Education:* McGill University, B.A., 1963; Yale University, M.A., 1964, Ph.D., 1967. *Residence:* Los Angeles, Calif. *Office:* Department of English, University of Southern California, Los Angeles, Calif. 90007.

CAREER: California State University, Hayward, assistant professor, 1968-71, associate professor of English, 1971-75, associate dean of arts and letters, 1972-75; University of Southern California, Los Angeles, associate professor of English, 1975—, associate director of Humanities Center, 1975-77, head of freshman writing program, 1977—. *Member:* Modern Language Association of America, Dickens Society.

WRITINGS: Dickens as Satirist, Yale University Press, 1971. Contributor to *Dickens Studies, Dickensian,* and *Options in the Teaching of English.*

WORK IN PROGRESS: Research on nineteenth-century novelist W. M. Thackeray.

SIDELIGHTS: Sylvia Manning writes: "I was led to Dickens because I was fascinated by his novels. With Thackeray it is more the presence of the man behind the novels that holds me. I spend most of my work days now administering a writing program for college freshmen because I enjoy difficult tasks and because I really believe in the value of writing as mental exercise."

* * *

MARGOLD, Stella

PERSONAL: Born In New York, N.Y.; daughter of Morris (a manufacturer) and Anna (Persen) Kaplan; married Charles Margold; children: David Persen, William Persen. *Education:* University of Michigan, B.A. (summa cum laude), 1931, M.A. and doctoral study, 1932; also attended University of Southern California, London School of Economics and Political Science, London, and Columbia University. *Politics:* Republican. *Home:* 765 Amsterdam Ave., New York, N.Y. 10025. *Office:* United Nations, Press Section, New York, N.Y. 10017.

CAREER: Reconstruction Finance Corporation (RFC), Washington, D.C., research specialist on foreign and export matters, 1932-34; U.S. Department of Commerce, Washington, D.C., research specialist on business exports, 1934-40; columnist on Poland during mid-1940's for *Cleveland News* and *Philadelphia Dispatch; Hartford Times,* Hartford, Conn., Columnist on Middle East, 1946; contributor of articles on foreign affairs to *Boston Globe,* 1946-51, *Christian Science Monitor,* 1950-54, and Women's News Service and North American Newspaper Alliance, 1946-75; presently ghostwriter for a former U.S. ambassador (work appears in seventy-five newspapers). Former contributor to *Syracuse Herald-Journal* and Spadea. Covered Paris Peace Conference, 1946, and events in the Middle East, Far East, Western, Central, and Eastern Europe, and North and West Africa. Has done public relations work for foreign governments. Has been interviewed on radio programs. Scholar at Harvard University's Widener Library.

MEMBER: Overseas Press Club, Foreign Press Club, United Nations Correspondents Association, United Nations Foreign Press Association, Phi Kappa Phi. *Awards, honors:* Honored by *American Import and Export Bulletin,* 1963, for contributions on international trade and finance.

WRITINGS: Export Credit Insurance, U.S. Government Printing Office, 1934; *Housing Abroad up to World War II,* M.I.T. Press, 1942; *Let's Do Business with Russia: How We Can,* Harper, 1948. Contributor to national and international magazines, including *Current History, World Affairs, American City, Middle East,* and *Viewpoints.*

WORK IN PROGRESS: Magazine articles.

SIDELIGHTS: Stella Margold writes: "My first article, on the origins of World War I, appeared in *Current History* in 1930. A subject which is vital to me is understanding the Russians and their government policies, and U.S. reluctance to defer necessary reaction. We have known what might eventually happen in the Horn of Africa and other areas in Southeast Asia and Africa since the early 1950's, but took no action to prevent it."

AVOCATIONAL INTERESTS: Music (especially classical).

* * *

MARGOLIS, Susan Spector 1941-

PERSONAL: Born July 7, 1941, in Springfield, Ohio; daughter of Louis Bernard (a department store executive) and Sylvia (Kane) Margolis; married Richard Winter (a textile executive), October 16, 1977. *Education:* Attended Syracuse University, 1959-60; Ohio State University, B.A., 1964; attended University of California, Berkeley, 1964; Exeter College, Oxford, certificate, 1966; San Francisco State University, M.A., 1967. *Home:* 372 Central Park West, New York, N.Y. 10025. *Agent:* Elaine Markson, 44 Greenwich Ave., New York, N.Y. 10011.

CAREER: Ohio State University, Columbus, instructor in English, 1963-64; U.S. Department of Justice, San Francisco, Calif., researcher in probation office, 1964-65; Pierce College, Athens, Greece, instructor in literature, psychology, and foreign languages, 1969-70; San Mateo Jr. College District, San Mateo, Calif., instructor in English, 1968-73; free-lance writer, 1973—. Instructor in English, San Francisco State University, 1965-73.

WRITINGS: Fame, San Francisco Book Co., 1977. Contributor of articles to periodicals, including *New York, Rolling Stone, Ms., New Times, New West,* and *New York Times.*

WORK IN PROGRESS: A novel; a screenplay; a book about pleasure; and a book about bio-ethics.

SIDELIGHTS: In her book *Fame,* Susan Margolis examines America's fascination with fame and the phenomenon of celebrity-watching. Focusing on three "arenas of fame," New York, Los Angeles, and Washington, D.C., she considers the effects of fame on real people.

Speaking with Patricia Burstein, Margolis defined "fame": "In its loftiest sense fame is immortality. [But] right now it is at a lower standard." She explained its function in the United States: "We don't have royalty in America. And we are always looking for heroes and saints. Fame makes people bigger than life and thus gives us something to believe in." On the other hand, she continued, fame has its dangers: "It can dry us—the unfamous—out. Our intimacy energy goes into relationships with images instead of people.... Fame drains emotionally and gives us shallow feedback. It distracts us from our own reality. Someone kills herself because Freddie Prinze is dead. Or a man gets divorced because his wife no longer looks like Marilyn Monroe."

BIOGRAPHICAL/CRITICAL SOURCES: People, January 23, 1978.

* * *

MARK, Julius   1898-1977

PERSONAL: Born December 25, 1898, in Cincinnati, Ohio; son of David and Ida (Tanur) Mark; married Margaret Corinne Baer, June 30, 1924; children: James Berthold David, Peggy (Mrs. Martin F. Heller). *Education:* Hebrew Union College—Jewish Institute of Religion, Cincinnati, Ohio, B.H.L., 1917, Rabbi, 1922; University of Cincinnati, A.B., 1921; graduate study at the University of Chicago. *Home:* 575 Park Ave., New York, N.Y. 10021. *Office:* 1 East 65th St., New York, N.Y. 10021.

CAREER: Temple Beth-El, South Bend, Ind., rabbi, 1922-26; Vine Street Temple, Nashville, Tenn., rabbi, 1926-48; Temple Emanu-El, New York City, senior rabbi, 1948-68, rabbi emeritus, 1968-77. Visitng professor of homiletics and practical theology at Hebrew Union College-Jewish Institute of Religion, New York City, 1949-63. Conductor of preaching missions for U.S. Armed Forces in Hawaii, Johnson Island, Guam, and Japan, 1956. Chairman of Chicago Institute on Judaism, Managment and Labor, 1947, and St. Louis Institute on Judaism and Civil Rights, 1948; co-convener, National Conference on Religion and Race, Chicago, 1963; member of Advisory Committee on Chaplains' Service, Board of Chaplains, and New York Board of Rabbis; member of the board of directors, Hillel Foundation Building Corp.; member of the board of governors, Hebrew Union College—Jewish Institute of Religion, Cincinnati, Ohio; trustee of Federation of Jewish Philanthropies, Union of American Hebrew Congregations, National Conference of Christians and Jews, and Hebrew Union School of Education and Sacred Music; special adviser, Interfaith, Inc.; honorary president, American Jewish Encyclopedia Society; chairman, Board Overseers, Hebrew Union College-Jewish Institute of Religion, New York City, 1964-68. Director, New York World's Fair, 1964-65; colonel, staffs of the governors of Kentucky and Tennessee; member of Armed Forces Advisory Committee of the Northeast Area, New York State Civil Defense Commission, Mayor's Committee of Citizens of Juvenile Delinquency Evaluation Project of New York City, and Mayor's Committee for Better Public Housing; member of the board of directors, Association for New Americans, Welfare and Health Council of New York, Housing and Planning Council of New York, and American Red Cross (New York City chapter); president, Metzger-Price Fund; honorary vice-chairman, Lighthouse of New York Association for the Blind, 1952-77. *Wartime service:* U.S. Navy, Chaplains' Corps, 1942-45; became lieutenant commander.

MEMBER: World Union for Progressive Judaism (member of American board of governors), United States National Commission for the United Nations Educational, Scientific and Cultural Organization (UNESCO), American Jewish Committee, Jewish Conciliation Board of America, Synagogue Council of America (president, 1961-63), Central Conference of American Rabbis (chairman of Commission on Justice and Peace, 1946-49), Anti-Defamation League of B'nai B'rith, Army and Navy Chaplains Association, Conference on Jewish Material Claims Against Germany, Foreign Policy Association, Interfaith Committee, Association of Reform Rabbis of New York and Vicinity, Alumni Association of Hebrew Union College—Jewish Institue of Religion, Cincinnati (president, 1948-50), The Judaeans, Theta Phi, Zeta Beta Tau, Shamus, Harmonie Club. *Awards, honors:* Man of the Year Award from Zeta Beta Tau, 1959; Human Relations Award from the Methodist Church, 1963; Gold Medallion from National Conference of Christians and Jews, 1966, for courageous leadership; Israel Bond Plaque, 1967, 1968, and 1969, in recognition of devoted support of Israel; Israel Tower of David Award, 1968; Clergyman of the Year award from Religious Heritage of America, 1969; Wisdom Award of Honor. LL.D., Cumberland University, 1936; honorary D.D., Hebrew Union College, 1949; H.H.D., University of Tampa, 1955; S.T.D., New York University, 1959; D.H.L., Long Island University, 1967, Dropsie University, 1975.

WRITINGS: Reaching for the Moon and Other Addresses, Farrar, Straus, 1959. Also author of *The Art of Preaching, Behaviorism and Religion,* 1930, and *The Rabbi Meets Some Big Dilemmas,* 1956. Contributing editor to the *Observer,* 1934-38. Contributor to *The Universal Jewish Encyclopedia.*

OBITUARIES: New York Times, September 8, 1977.*

(Died September 7, 1977, in New York, N.Y.)

* * *

MARKIDES, Kyriacos (Costa)   1942-

PERSONAL: Born November 19, 1942, in Nicosia, Cyprus; came to United States in 1960, naturalized citizen, 1978; son of Kostas K. (a shopkeeper) and Melpo (Nicolaou) Markides; married Emily Joannides, August 19, 1972; children: Constantine. *Education:* Youngstown State University, B.A., 1964; Bowling Green State University, M.A., 1966; Wayne State University, Ph.D., 1970. *Home:* 30 Free St., Stillwater, Maine 04489. *Office:* Department of Sociology, University of Maine, Orono, Maine 04469.

CAREER: Youngstown State University, Youngstown, Ohio, assistant professor of sociology, 1970-71; University of Maine, Orono, assistant professor, 1972-76, associate professor of sociology, 1977—. *Member:* American Sociological Association, Cyprus Sociological Association (co-founder). *Awards, honors:* Ford Foundation grant for study at Cyprus Social Research Centre, 1973-74.

WRITINGS: The Rise and Fall of the Cyprus Republic, Yale University Press, 1977; (with Eleni Niketa and Elengo Rangou) *Lysii: Social Change in a Cypriot Village,* Cyprus Social Research Centre, 1978.

WORK IN PROGRESS: The Phenomenon of International Terrorism: A Search for Causes and Cures.

SIDELIGHTS: Markides comments: "The tragedy of Cyprus in 1974—the conquest of half the island by Turkey—was the most painful experience of my life. This led to the writing of my first book. It also intensified my concern with the problem of human survival in the nuclear age. I am deeply interested in questions of consciousness, humanistic psychology, and its application to social concerns in general."

AVOCATIONAL INTERESTS: Running, swimming, fishing in the Mediterranean.

* * *

MARKOE, Karen 1942-

PERSONAL: Surname is pronounced *Mar*-ko; born May 21, 1942, in New York, N.Y.; daughter of Charles (in sales) and Hannah (a teacher; maiden name, Solon) Fox; married Arnold Markoe (a historian and college administrator), August 20, 1966; children: Lauren, Nancy. *Education:* Hunter College of the City University of New York, B.A., 1962; Columbia University, M.A., 1963, Ph.D., 1971. *Residence:* Bronx, N.Y. *Office:* Department of Humanities, State University of New York Maritime College at Fort Schuyler, Bronx, N.Y. 10465.

CAREER: Brooklyn College of the City University of New York, Brooklyn, N.Y., adjunct lecturer in history, 1964-65; Hunter College of the City University of New York, New York, N.Y., lecturer, 1965-66, lecturer in history, 1966-68; Bronx Community College of the City University of New York, Bronx, N.Y., adjunct assistant professor of history, 1972-74; State University of New York Maritime College at Fort Schuyler, Bronx, associate professor of history, 1974—. *Member:* North American Society for Oceanic Historians, American Historical Association, Phi Beta Kappa, Phi Alpha Theta. *Awards, honors:* National Endowment for the Humanities grant, 1978.

WRITINGS—All with Louis Phillips; all for children: *Super Duper American History Fun Book,* F. Watts, 1978; *Word Puzzlers,* Xerox Publishing Co., 1979; *Funtime Puzzles,* Scholastic Book Services, 1979; *Sneakers,* Lippincott, 1979; *The Handy Book of Women's Sports, Records, Stars and Feats,* Harcourt, 1979. Contributor to *Search.*

WORK IN PROGRESS: Editing *Readings in Maritime History,* with husband, Arnold Markoe; *In Their Own Words,* and *Nobody Ever Explained It That Way,* both with Louis Phillips.

SIDELIGHTS: Karen Markoe writes: "I wear two hats. I teach history to college students; maritime history is a new interest. But I am particularly interested in writing children's history and puzzle books, so that children can learn and have fun simultaneously. Without books, children have a terrible sense of the past. Ask them to name two presidents, and they will immediately say George Washington and Abraham Lincoln. Ask them if Lincoln and Washington were friends and most assuredly they will say yes."

* * *

MARR, John S(tuart) 1940-

PERSONAL: Born April 22, 1940, in New York, N.Y.; son of James Pratt and Anne (Johnson) Marr; married. *Education:* Yale University, B.A., 1962; Harvard University, M.P.H., 1972. *Home:* 430 East 86th St., New York, N.Y. 10028. *Office address:* Bureau of Preventable Diseases, Box 46, 125 Worth, New York, N.Y.

CAREER: Metropolitan Hospital, New York City, resident in internal medicine, 1968-71; Bureau of Preventable Diseases, New York City, director, 1974—. *Military service:* U.S. Army, Health Environment Division, 1972—; currently major. *Member:* American College of Preventive Medicine (fellow), American Society of Tropical Medicine and Hygiene, American College of Physicians, American Public Health Association, New York City Academy of Medicine, New York City Tropical Medicine Society, New York Mycological Society, Alpha Omega Alpha, Explorers Club (New York City).

WRITINGS: The Good Drug and the Bad Drug, with teacher's manual, M. Evans, 1970; *Breath of Air and a Breath of Smoke* (juvenile), M. Evans, 1971; *The Food You Eat,* (juvenile), M. Evans, 1973; (with Gwyneth Cravens) *The Black Death* (novel), Dutton, 1976. Contributor of articles on infectious and tropical diseases to medical journals.

SIDELIGHTS: Reviewing Marr's latest book, *The Black Death,* a *Times Literary Supplement* critic pointed out that "the authors' anger is one of the book's strengths: another is that the medical data are fascinating, authoritative and clear." A reviewer from *Newsweek* commented: "Admirers of Albert Camus's moral parable about an outbreak of pestilence may want to leave this novel alone. It's subliterary stuff, overlong and burdened with an outrageous love story, but for what is is, it's first rate: on par with *Seven Days in May,* for instance, or *The Andromeda Strain.* The authors are knowledgeable about the plague; and their grim insistence that it's only a matter of time before their story comes true may make some of us regret having passed up our swine-flu shots."

A critic from the *New York Times Book Review* also agreed and observed: "The epidemiology has an authentic ring. So has the crowded, festering New York scene, which the authors depict with ripe imagery, and which could be a superb host for any pandemic. The corpse-by-corpse timing of the book is good too, as the death rate multiplies in geometric progression. When they come to causality, however, the authors project a touch of Dr. Strangelove paranoia that is a bit much."

BIOGRAPHICAL/CRITICAL SOURCES: New York Times, February 13, 1971; *Publishers Weekly,* November 1, 1976; *Newsweek,* January 10, 1977; *New York Times Book Review,* January 30, 1977; *Times Literary Supplement,* May 6, 1977.

* * *

MARROW, Alfred J. 1905-1978

PERSONAL: Born March 8, 1905, in New York, N.Y.; son of Isidore and Rebecca (Green) Marrow; married Monette Courod, May 2, 1934; children: Paul, Marjorie Marrow Sandberg. *Education:* New York University, B.S., 1926, Ph.D., 1937; Columbia University, M.A., 1928. *Residence:* Palm Beach, Fla.

CAREER: Psychologist, author, and business leader. President and chairman of board of Harwood Manufacturing Corp., 1940-76. Field collaborator at Massachusetts Institute of Technology, Cambridge, Mass., beginning 1944; New School for Social Research, New York City, lecturer, beginning 1947, member of board of trustees, beginning 1954; chairman of Commission on Intergroup Relations, New York City, 1955-60; member of board of trustees of Institutional Office of Behavioral Sciences, 1964-70; consultant to U.S. Department of State, Washington, D.C., beginning 1964; chairman of American Council for Behavioral Sciences in Kibbutz Management. Member of board of trustees of Marshall Fund, beginning 1964, and National Training Laboratories.

MEMBER: American Psychological Association (fellow), American Sociological Association, American Board of Professional Psychology (president, 1967-70), American Association for the Advancement of Science, Society for the Psychological Study of Social Issues, National Training Laboratory in Group Development, Society of Industrial Psychologists, American Parents Committee (consultant, beginning 1964), American Jewish Congress (chairman of national executive committee), Authors Guild, Eastern Psychological Association, New York State Psychological Association, New York Academy of Science (fellow). *Awards, honors:* Kurt Lewin Memorial Award from American Psychological Association, 1964.

WRITINGS: Living Without Hate: A Scientific Approach to Human Relations, Harper, 1951; *Making Management Human,* McGraw, 1957; *Changing Patterns of Prejudice: A New Look at Today's Racial, Religious, and Cultural Tensions,* Chilton, 1962; *Behind the Executive Mask: Greater Managerial Competence Through Deeper Self-Understanding,* American Management Association, 1964; (with David G. Bowers and Stanley E. Seashore) *Management By Participation: Creating a Climate for Personal and Organizational Development,* Harper, 1967; *The Practical Theorist: The Life and Work of Kurt Lewin,* Basic Books, 1969; (editor) *The Failure of Success* (case studies), AMACOM, 1972; *Making Waves in Foggy Bottom: How a New and More Scientific Approach Changed the Management System at the State Department,* National Training Laboratory Institute, 1974; *The T-Group Experience: An Encounter Among People for Greater Self-Fulfillment,* Paul Eriksson, 1975. Contributor to professional journals.

SIDELIGHTS: An authority on industrial psychology and group dynamics, Marrow's 1955 appointment as chairman of New York City Mayor Robert F. Wagner's Commission on Intergroup Relations was in recognition of his talent for making practical application of his scholarly expertise. Dr. Allen Ross, a professor of psychology with the State University of New York, emphasized this skill when he remarked: "The key ingredient in his philosophy, which he applied to all of his endeavors, was a knowledge of how to achieve participatory democracy in groups of people with whom he worked."

Marrow's co-authored *Management By Participation* is considered a classic in the study of industrial relations.

OBITUARIES: New York Times, March 4, 1978.*

(Died March 3, 1978, in New York, N.Y.)

*   *   *

MARSHALL, S(amuel) L(yman) A(twood)   1900-1977

PERSONAL: Born July 18, 1900, in Catskill, N. Y.; son of Caleb Carey (a brickmaker) and Alice Medora (Beeman) Marshall; married Ruth Elstner (deceased); married Edith Ives Westervelt (died, 1952); married Catherine Finnerty, March 10, 1954; children: (first marriage) Samuel Lyman Atwood, Jr.; (third marriage) Sharon, Catherine, Bridget; (stepdaughter) Mrs. Pat Troiano. *Education:* Attended Texas College of Mines (now Texas Western University). *Religion:* Episcopalian. *Residence:* 2909 Stone Edge, El Paso, Tex. 79904.

CAREER: Writer. Actor, Western Essanay Co., 1913-15; U. S. Army, enlisted June 11, 1917, World War I, participant in campaigns in the Soissons, St. Mihiel, Meuse-Ar-

gonne, and Ypres-Lys, and instructor in grenades, gas warfare, bayonets, demolitions, and minor tactics; commissioned first lieutenant, 1921; served in Texas National Guard, 1922-27; *El Paso Herald,* El Paso, Tex., 1923-27, began as sports editor, became city editor; North American Newspaper Alliance, foreign correspondent, 1927-35; *Detroit News,* Detroit, Mich., editorial writer, military critic, and foreign correspondent, 1927-62; war correspondent during Spanish Civil War, 1936-37; consultant to Secretary of War, 1942; U.S. Army, major; chief of Orientation during World War II; transferred to Historical Division of War Department; appointed Chief Combat Historian, served in Central Pacific, 1943, participant in invasions of Gilbert and Marshall Islands; transferred to Europe, 1944, covered all airborne operations of Normandy invasion; named Chief Historian of European Theater of Operations, staff member under supreme commander, 1945-46; participant in campaigns of Normandy and Brittany, Siege of Brest, Airborne Invasion of Holland, Ruhr Encirclement, and battles in East Germany; researched formation of North Atlantic Alliance, 1946; served in Korea, 1950-51, as an infantry operations analyst with the Eighth Army, and with Operations Research Office; commissioned as Brigadier General, 1951; retired, 1960; war correspondent, Korea, 1953, Sinai War, Israel-Egypt, 1956, Lebanon, 1958, and South Vietnam; correspondent in Middle East and Congo, 1961; affiliated with U. S. Army in Vietnam, 1966-67, and consultant to Pentagon during the Vietnam War. Lecturer at National War College, Air University, Armed Service Information School, Infantry School, and Armored School. Member of U. S. Army Historical Advisory Commission, Public Relations Commission, Michigan Civil Defense Commission, Chancellor's Council of University of Texas, and trustee of Detroit chapter of American Red Cross.

MEMBER: Sons of the American Revolution, Society of American Historians, Military Order of World Wars, Association of the U. S. Army, American Legion, Veterans of Foreign Wars, Coffee House Club (New York City), Detroit Press Club, Bloomfield (Mich.) Hunt Club. *Awards, honors*—Military; U.S.: Distinguished Service Medal, Legion of Merit, Bronze Star medal with oak leaf cluster, Citation Medal with oak leaf clusters, Combat Infantry Badge, German Occupation World War I award, German Occupation World War II award, Pacific Theater award, Vistory, Pacific, Africa-Middle East-European, Korean, and United Nations Korean medals; France: Legion of Honor; Croix de Guerre with Palm; Ordre d'Armee; Belgium: Order d'Leopold with Palm; Croix de Guerre with Palm; Ardennes medal; Italy: Croci di Guerra; Fatigue di Guerra; Ethiopia: Infantry Combat medal; Israel: Medallion of Valor. Civilian: Elected to National Cowboy Hall of Fame, 1972; honorary fellow, Bar Ilan University; L.H.D., Wayne State University; LL. D., St. Bonaventure University.

WRITINGS: Blitzkrieg: Its History, Strategy, Economics, and the Challenge to America, Morrow, 1940; *Armies on Wheels,* Morrow, 1941; *Island Victory,* Penguin, 1944; *Bastogne: The Story of the First Eight Days in Which the 101st Airborne Division was Closed Within the Ring of German Forces,* Infantry Journal Press, 1946; *Men against Fire: The Problem of Battle Command in Future War,* Infantry Journal Press, 1947; (contributor) Leonard Rapport, *Rendezvous with Destiny,* Infantry Journal Press, 1947; *The Price of Peace,* Washington and Jefferson College Press, 1948; *The Soldier's Load and the Mobility of a Nation,* Combat Forces Press, 1950; *The Armed Forces Officer,* Department of Defense, 1950, reprinted as *The Officer as a Leader,*

Stackpole Books, 1966; *The River and the Gauntlet: Defeat of the Eighth Army by the Chinese Communist Forces, November, 1950, in the Battle of the Chongchon River,* Morrow, 1953; *Pork Chop Hill: The American Fighting Men in Action, Korea, Spring, 1953,* Morrow, 1956; *Sinai Victory: Command Decisions in History's Shortest War, Israel's Hundred-Hour Conquest of Egypt East of Suez, Autumn, 1956,* Morrow, 1958.

Night Drop: The American Airborne Invasion of Normandy, preface by Carl Sandburg, illustrations by H. Garver Miller, Little, Brown, 1962; (with Al Hine) *D-Day: The Invasion of Europe* (juvenile), Harper, 1962; *The Military History of the Korean War,* F. Watts, 1963; *Battle at Best,* illustrations by H. G. Miller, Morrow, 1964; *The American Heritage History of World War I,* American Heritage Press, 1964, reprinted as *World War I,* 1971 (edition adapted by Robert Leckie for young people published as *The Story of World War I,* Random House, 1965); *The War to Free Cuba: The Military History of the Spanish-American War,* F. Watts, 1966; *Sinai Victory: Command Decisions in History's Shortest War,* Morrow, 1967; *A Special Study of South Africa: The Strategic View,* American-African Affairs Association, 1967; *Swift Sword: The Historical Record of Israel's Victory, June, 1967,* American Heritage Press, 1967; *Battles in the Monsoon: Campaigning in the Central Highlands, Vietnam, Summer, 1966,* Morrow, 1967; *West to Cambodia,* Cowles, 1968; *Bird: The Christmastide Battle,* Cowles, 1968; *Ambush: The Battle of Dau Tieng,* Cowles, 1969; (with Stephen Sears) *The Battle of the Bulge* (juvenile), American Heritage Press, 1969; *The Fields of Bamboo: Dong Tre, Trung Luong, and Hoa Hoi, Three Battles Just Beyond the South China Sea,* Dial, 1971; *Crimsoned Prairie: The Wars Between the United States and the Plains Indians During the Winning of the West,* Scribner, 1972.

Also author of *Makin,* 1947; *The Mobility of One Man,* 1949; *Critique of Weapons and Tactics in Korea,* 1952; *Hill 440,* 1952; *Tactics in Defense Against Atomic Attack,* 1954; *First Book on Korea,* 1964; *Vietnam Primer,* 1967; *History of World War II,* 1969; and *On Urban Warfare,* 1973; and numerous military texts and manuals.

Syndicated newspaper columnist, with articles appearing in the *Washington Post, Los Angeles Times,* and others. Military contributor to *American College Dictionary, Crowell-Collier Encyclopaedia, Encyclopaedia Britannica,* and *U.S. Navy Annual Review.* Contributor of articles on technical studies to *Combat Forces Journal, Marine Corps Gazette, Military Quarterly,* and other military periodicals; also contributor to *Reporter, New York Times Book Review, Collier's,* and *Harper's.*

SIDELIGHTS: It seems ironic that S. L. A. Marshall's two careers were soldiering and writing since his only training in English was a high school sophomore class and he failed both of the history classes he took. As a soldier, he operated the combat forces for nineteen campaigns in every American war since World War I. As a correspondent, he has reported twenty-one wars, and written nearly thirty books.

Marshall developed the technique of doing battlefield history by interviewing survivors about its operations soon after an encounter. "Marshall specialized in the small-unit type of action where he would talk to the people involved and elicit the details of what had happened," explained Brigadier General James L. Collins, Jr. to the *Washington Post.* "He was very good at putting it down in a vivid way, and made people read things that professional historians might make dry as dust." According to *Time,* "his writing was distin-

guished by narrative drive, a gritty attention to the details of combat, and a plain-spoken sympathy for the men who suffered on the front lines."

Pork Chop Hill, Marshall's account of the Korean War is probably his best known work. Called a "moving and stirring record," by a *Kirkus Reviews* critic, a *New York Times* reviewer went on to describe it as "a distinguished contribution to the literature of war. It may be doubted whether Stephen Crane or Ambrose Bierce have ever written with such sustained realism about combat. . . ." Gregory Peck starred in the movie version of the book produced by United Artists in 1959.

In critiquing *Battle at Best,* a *Reporter* reviewer made the following observations, which can also apply to Marshall's intentions in all of his books: "What S. L. A. Marshall writes about is rarely to be found in legend, traditional history, or fiction. His soldiers are not protagonists who inferentially represent all who fight in a war or battle. Marshall fills the gap between the impersonality of history and the over-personality of fiction. He writes not of representative heroes but of all the soldiers in thier own terms. He records deeds of heroism and acts of cowardice, and the far more common combat situation of inexplicable inactivity and misdirected overactivity. . . ."

AVOCATIONAL INTERESTS: Polo, horse show judging, music, and collecting porcelains.

BIOGRAPHICAL/CRITICAL SOURCES: Newsweek, June 13, 1955, August 15, 1960; *Kirkus Reviews,* October 1, 1956; *New York Times,* November 18, 1956; *Reporter,* May 7, 1964; *Esquire,* May, 1970.

Obituaries: *New York Times,* December 18, 1977; *Washington Post,* December 18, 1977; *Time,* December 26, 1977; *Newsweek,* January 2, 1978.*

(Died December 17, 1977)

*   *   *

MARTIN, George R(aymond) R(ichard)   1948-

PERSONAL: Born September 20, 1948, in Bayonne, N.J.; son of Raymond Collins and Margaret (Brady) Martin; married Gale Burnick, November 15, 1975. *Education:* Northwestern University, B.S.J., 1970, M.S.J., 1971. *Religion:* None. *Home:* Burnick and Martin Manor, 2266 Jackson, Dubuque, Iowa 52001. *Agent:* Kirby McCauley Ltd., 310 East 46th St., New York, N.Y. 10017.

CAREER: Volunteers in Service to America (VISTA), Cook County Legal Assistance, Chicago, Ill., communications coordinator, 1972-74; Continental Chess Association, Chicago, tournament director, 1973-75; Clarke College, Dubuque, Iowa, instructor in journalism, 1976—. *Member:* Science Fiction Writers of America (member of regional board of directors). *Awards, honors:* Hugo Award from World Science Fiction Society, 1975, for "A Song for Lya," Hugo Award nominations, 1974, for "With Morning Comes Mistfall," 1976 (with Lisa Tuttle), for "Storms of Windhaven," and 1978, for *Dying of the Light;* Nebula Award nominations from Science Fiction Writers of America, 1974, for "With Morning Comes Mistfall," 1975, for "A Song for Lya," 1976, for "Storms of Windhaven," and 1978, for "The Stone City."

WRITINGS: A Song for Lya (science fiction stories), Avon, 1976; (editor) *New Voices in Science Fiction,* Volume I, Macmillan, 1977, Volume II, Harcourt, 1979, Volume III, 1980; *Songs of Stars and Shadows* (science fiction stories), Pocket Books, 1977; *Dying of the Light* (novel),

Simon & Schuster, 1978. Contributor of more than thirty-five stories to various anthologies and science fiction magazines, including *Analog Science Fiction* and *Science Fact*.

WORK IN PROGRESS: With Lisa Tuttle, a three-part novel, *Windhaven;* various short fiction stories.

SIDELIGHTS: Many of Martin's works have seen publication in French, German, Spanish, and Italian. Some individual short stories have appeared in magazines in Spain, Germany, and Australia.

* * *

MARTIN, J(ohn) P(ercival)   1880(?)-1966

PERSONAL: Born in Scarborough, Yorkshire, England; *Religion:* Methodist. *Home:* Timberscombe, Somerset, England.

CAREER: Entered the Methodist ministry in 1902; served as a missionary in South Africa; became chaplain during World War I and worked mainly in Palestine; went into semi-retirement at the end of World War II and served the chapel in Timberscombe, Somerset, England, until 1966; author of books for children.

WRITINGS—All illustrated by Quentin Blake: *Uncle,* J. Cape, 1964, Coward-McCann, 1966; *Uncle Cleans Up,* J. Cape, 1965, Coward-McCann, 1967; *Uncle and His Detective,* J. Cape, 1966; *Uncle and the Treacle Trouble,* J. Cape, 1967; *Uncle and Claudius the Camel,* J. Cape, 1969.*

(Died March, 1966, in Timberscombe, England)

* * *

MARTIN, James L.   1948-

PERSONAL: Born January 14, 1948, in Brockton, Mass.; son of Morrill O. (a clergyman) and Jennyvee (McBride) Martin. *Education:* Colby College, B.A., 1970; Boston University, Th.M., 1973, Ph.D., 1978. *Home:* 311 Swanee Dr., North Dighton, Mass. 02764. *Office:* Department of English, Suffolk University, Boston, Mass. 02114.

CAREER: Ordained Methodist minister, 1973; University of Lowell, Lowell, Mass., instructor in English, 1975; Suffolk University, Boston, Mass., instructor in English, 1976—. Organizer of rare book exhibits, specializing in modern first editions. *Awards, honors:* National Endowment for the Arts creative writing fellowship, 1976-77.

WRITINGS: A Reunion and Other Poems, Copper Beech Press, 1975. Work represented in *Ten American Poets,* 1973. Contributor of poems and articles to literary journals and popular magazines, including *Esquire, Harper's, New American Review,* and *Poetry.*

WORK IN PROGRESS: A book of poems; a play based on the life of John Berryman.

* * *

MARTIN, Malachi
(Michael Serafian)

PERSONAL: Born in Kerry, Ireland; came to United States, 1965, naturalized citizen, 1970. *Education:* Attended Oxford University and Hebrew University of Jerusalem; earned Ph.D. from University of Louvain.

CAREER: Roman Catholic priest of Society of Jesus (Jesuits), until 1964, laicized, 1964; professor at Pontifical Biblical Institute in Rome; associate of Cardinal Augustine Bea and Pope John XXIII; worked as waiter, taxi driver, longshoreman, painter, and public relations firm employee, beginning

1965; editor of *Encyclopaedia Britannica,* New York City; co-founder of Collector's Funding (antiques firm). *Awards, honors:* Awarded Guggenheim fellowship twice.

WRITINGS: (Under pseudonym Michael Serafian) *The Pilgrim,* Farrar, Straus, 1964; *The Encounter: Religions in Crisis,* Farrar, Straus, 1969; *Three Popes and the Cardinal,* Farrar, Straus, 1972; *Jesus Now,* Dutton, 1973; *The New Castle: Reaching for the Ultimate,* Dutton, 1974; *Hostage to the Devil,* Reader's Digest Press, 1976; *The Final Conclave,* Stein & Day, 1978. Also author of *The Scribal Character of the Dead Sea Scrolls.* Columnist for *National Review.* Contributor to periodicals, including *Harper's* and *New York Daily News.*

SIDELIGHTS: Eileen Biro called Martin "a study in contrasts—intellectual-optimist, conservative critic of conservatism, youth of fifty," adding: "Unlike many of the seceding clerics, he adheres to the basic principles of Roman Catholicism. At the same time he is vehement in his criticism of the church as an organization, vocal on his opinion of the Pope and pulls no punches when he discusses the state of the church today." Since Martin left the Jesuits in 1964, he has expressed his convictions in several books which have received a wide variety of responses from critics in the United States.

In *The Encounter,* Martin analyzed the historical development of the three major religions, Judaism, Christianity, and Islam, concluding that they had become virtually irrelevant to modern man because their institutionalization had suffocated the spark of life which had glowed during their early "priceless moments." Melvin Maddocks explained the gist of his argument: "He describes how, in all three cases, the truth-in-the-desert—the vision that transcended history—hardened into a dogma and grew gross as a worldly power among worldly powers. . . . All orthodoxies, whether political or religious, tend to play the same game, which Dr. Martin calls 'dominance.' At some point, he assumes, the second, third, or fortieth generation of a religion lose [sic] sight of that vision-in-the-desert and become machineries for their own self-perpetuation. . . . The self-perpetuation of that 'wealth, power, and influence,' he believes, has become of profound insignificance to modern man. The phenomenon of change—radical, breath taking change—has undermined authority, making strange and difficult the common religious premises of 'final revelation,' 'permanent truth,' and 'ethical absolutes.'"

Several critics questioned Martin's characterization of "modern man" as a being "intent on encountering himself in the raw, not through the colored glasses of ancient mythologies or modern ideological presuppositions." Michael J. Rush protested: "His depiction of modern man is degrading, superficial and, I dare say, false. . . . The members of the new generation may not be engaged in a search for the traditional God of Judaism, Christianity, and Islam, but neither are they settling for a purely scientific or mechanical explanation for man's wealth of capacities." Eugene Fontinell added: "There is the flavor of an outmoded positivism in the assertion that 'Western man's sociology is completely value-free.'" While other critics found fault with Martin's "bog of historical minutiae," historical speculation, and "glibly stated reasoning," Maddocks emphasized the spirit of the work, declaring: "What gives Dr. Martin's book its special force is the evident agony with which he has conducted his investigation. He is as sorrowfully angry as he is erudite, and his book, consequently, turns out to be a spiritual autobiography as well as a work of scholarship."

Three Popes and a Cardinal revealed many of Martin's views on the Roman Catholic church and the "high places" in Rome to which he enjoyed intimate access during Vatican II. Robert McAfee Brown observed: "His book is by turns brash, tender, impudent, caring, arrogant, brilliant and muddled. It is inspired by a passionate love of man and an equally passionate hatred of individual men. It implies a latent and wistful hope for what modern Catholicism might have become, and therefore expresses a patent repugnance for what it has in fact become." Most critics, including Brown, did not share Martin's pessimism about the Vatican Council or his belief that the church was fast approaching its demise.

An interview with Martin further illuminated his views on the church. "That organization (the Catholic Church and other high churches) is going to fade away because it's an organization created by men who were power brokers and still are," he maintained. "They tied it to an economic system and they tied it to political big deals, and now that's all over. It's good that it's happening because dignity, rings, hand kissing and satin slippers and Latin have nothing to do with the spirit whatever." In *Jesus Now,* Martin continued his attack on the subordination of religious truth to the world's power structures. D. A. Boileau noted: "You find first a destroying of the images of Jesus, as lived in the Church and the world. Martin is hacking idols, laying bare the good conscience of Catholics, Protestants, and orthodoxes, the infantileness or dishonesty of revolutionaries, gay people, and charismatics. . . . Martin is rejecting the narrow search of the historical Jesus and is bringing some incisive correctives and criticisms."

Martin's latest book, *The Final Conclave,* elaborated upon this theme of the church's involvement in the world's power struggle, making some startling claims about the internal politics of the Vatican. He declared: "The Church was allied with Western European governments when those governments exercised power and influence over the rest of the world. Now that influence, some Cardinals believe, is gone. They believe that new governments in France and Italy may be led by Communists. Important Churchmen are convinced that Latin America will go the way of Southeast Asia. These Cardinals believe the Church must ally itself with the next world empire, which will be Communist-dominated. . . . I see two great institutions in danger, the Roman Catholic Church and the United States. The electioneering now going on for a new Pope involves five factions, at least one of which clearly favors a Rome-Moscow axis and wants to see a new Pope elected who will support such an alliance. A Pope cannot be impeached. Once he is elected, he and the faction he represents will use the might and power of the Church not to minister to souls but to effect an alliance that will isolate the United States and put its institutions in great jeopardy. It was my duty as a Catholic and an American to reveal the secret negotiations now going on. Silence would have been the highest treason."

BIOGRAPHICAL/CRITICAL SOURCES: Saturday Review, February 28, 1970, April 8, 1972; *New York Times,* March 9, 1970, April 11, 1972; *Christian Science Monitor,* March 26, 1970; *New York Times Book Review,* April 19, 1970; *Commonwealth,* May 29, 1970; *Christian Century,* June 24, 1970; *National Review,* November 9, 1973; *Baltimore News-American,* October 20, 1974.*

* * *

MARTINES, Julia
    See O'FAOLAIN, Julia

MARTINEZ, S(ally) A.   1938-

PERSONAL: Born April 16, 1938, in Philadelphia, Pa.; daughter of Joseph E. (a teacher) and Virginia (a teacher; maiden name, Crisp) Trendall; married Joel Martinez (a consultant), November 8, 1958; children: Donna, Jill. *Education:* Attended University of California, Los Angeles, 1968. *Politics:* Democrat. *Home:* 24654 Malibu Rd., Malibu, Calif. 90265.

CAREER: Writer. Worked as dance teacher and photographer. *Member:* Mystery Writers of America.

WRITINGS: Target for Terror, Major Books, 1976; *Nashville Babylon,* Major Books, 1977. Contributor of short stories to *London Mystery Magazine.*

WORK IN PROGRESS: A novel on contemporary life in Malibu, California.

SIDELIGHTS: Martinez told *CA:* "I speak 'survival' Spanish, have traveled extensively in England, am a serious—though amateur—photographer, and enjoy performing Greek dances."

* * *

MARX, Arthur   1921-

PERSONAL: Born July 21, 1921, in New York, N.Y.; son of Groucho (a comedian) and Ruth (a dancer; maiden name, Johnson) Marx; married Irene Kahn, February 27, 1943 (divorced June 26, 1961); married Lois Goldberg (an interior decorator), June 27, 1961; children: Steven, Andy. *Education:* Attended University of Southern California, 1939-40. *Politics:* "That depends on who's running." *Religion:* Jewish. *Residence:* Los Angeles, Calif. *Agent:* Scott Meredith Literary Agency, Inc., 835 Third Ave., New York, N.Y. 10022.

CAREER: Tournament tennis player, 1934-51; advertising copy writer, 1941; joke writer for Milton Berle's radio programs, 1942; Metro-Goldwyn-Mayer, Culver City, Calif., reader, 1948, writer of "Pete Smith Specialties," 1949-50; free-lance magazine writer, 1950-58; television writer, 1958—. Executive story consultant and script writer for "Alice," a series on CBS-TV, 1977—. Producer and writer of Mickey Rooney's television show, 1964. *Military service:* U.S. Coast Guard, 1942-45; served in Pacific theater. *Awards, honors:* Straw Hat Award from Council of Stock Theatres, 1970, for best new play of the summer season, "The Chic Life."

WRITINGS: The Ordeal of Willie Brown (novel), Simon & Schuster, 1950; *Life with Groucho* (biography), Simon & Schuster, 1954; *Not as a Crocodile* (family stories), Harper, 1958; *Son of Groucho* (autobiography), McKay, 1972; *Everybody Loves Somebody Sometime* (about Dean Martin and Jerry Lewis), Hawthorn, 1974; *Goldwyn* (biography), Norton, 1976.

Feature films (co-author): "Blondie in the Dough," Columbia, 1947; "Global Affair," Seven Arts, 1964; "I'll Take Sweden," United Artist, 1965; "Eight on the Lam," United Artists, 1967; "Cancel My Reservation," Warner Bros., 1972. Also co-wrote twelve "Pete Smith Specialties" for Metro-Goldwyn-Mayer, 1949-50.

Plays (co-author): "The Impossible Years" (two-act comedy), produced on Broadway at the Playhouse, October 13, 1965; "Minnie's Boys" (two-act musical), first produced in New York City at Imperial Theater, March 26, 1970.

Television writer for major network series, including "All in the Family," "Maude," "The Jeffersons," and "McHale's

Navy.'' Contributor of articles and photographs to popular national magazines, including *Saturday Evening Post, Esquire, Redbook, Cosmopolitan,* and *Good Housekeeping.*

WORK IN PROGRESS: Research for a biography of Robert Ripley, creator of ''Believe It Or Not''; a biography of Red Skelton.

SIDELIGHTS: Marx told *CA:* ''My first novel, *The Ordeal of Willie Brown,* was drawn directly from my experiences as an amateur tennis player during my high school and college years before going into the service in 1943. I was ranked as high as number five in the eighteen and under category, holding a major victory over the then current boy wonder, Jack Kramer. My novel attempted to expose the corrupt world of 'amateur' tennis, where the players were allegedly amateurs, but were actually taking great sums, in the form of expense money, under the table. The books suggested, in a comic way, that there should be an open tennis tournament, where the players could make an honest living doing what they did best. The open tennis tournament eventually came to pass, and I consider myself partially responsible for it.

''In my biographies of show business figures I felt it important to show them as real people and not the cardboard cutouts of publicity men's imaginations.''

''My biography of my father, *Life With Groucho,* which was serialized in eight parts in the *Saturday Evening Post,* was one of the first of the biographies of show business luminaries to attract important critical acclaim. *New York Times* labeled it 'great,' and *New Yorker* called it 'an excellent piece of work.' I believe it started the trend of relatives writing objective biographies of famous figures.

''My current job of writing the 'Alice' television program is one of the most satisfying experiences I've ever had in television, because the show is so popular and the people so easy and pleasant to work with. But another play, which is Broadway bound, is also in the works, and I am looking forward to having another hit in that medium, too.''

*   *   *

MARX, Groucho
  See MARX, Julius Henry

*   *   *

MARX, Julius Henry   1890-1977
  (Groucho Marx)

PERSONAL: Born October 2, 1890, in New York, N.Y.; son of Samuel (a tailor) and Minnie (Schoenberg) Marx; married Ruth Johnson, 1920 (divorced, 1942); married Catherine Gorcey, 1945 (divorced, 1950); married Eden Hartford (a model), 1953 (divorced, 1969); children: Miriam, Arthur, Melinda. *Home:* Beverly Hills, Calif.

CAREER: Comedian; actor in vaudeville, on stage, and in motion pictures; writer. Actor in vaudeville shows, including ''Fun in Hi Skule,'' ''Home Again,'' 1919, and ''On the Mezzanine,'' 1922; in stage productions, including ''I'll Say She Is,'' 1924, and ''Animal Crackers,'' 1929; and in motion pictures, including ''The Cocoanuts,'' 1929, ''Animal Crackers,'' 1930, ''Horse Feathers,'' 1932, ''A Night at the Opera,'' 1935, ''A Day at the Races,'' 1937, ''Love Happy,'' 1949, ''The Story of Mankind,'' 1957, and ''Skidoo,'' 1968; appeared on radio in ''Flywheel, Shyster, and Flywheel,'' 1934, in a variety show for Columbia Broadcasting System (CBS), 1943-44, and as quizmaster on game show ''You Bet Your Life,'' 1947-50; appeared on television as quizmaster of series ''You Bet Your Life,'' 1950-61, and

''Tell It to Groucho,'' 1962; toured United States as solo performer in concert, 1972. *Awards, honors:* Peabody Award, 1948, for radio version of ''You Bet Your Life''; Emmy award from Academy of Television Arts and Sciences, 1951, for television version of ''You Bet Your Life''; named Commander of the French Order of Arts and Letters, 1972; special Emmy award, 1975; and numerous other awards.

WRITINGS—All under pseudonym Groucho Marx: (With Will Johnstone) ''I'll Say She Is'' (musical play), first produced in Philadelphia at the Walnut Street Theatre, produced in New York City at the Casino Theatre, May 19, 1924; *Beds,* Farrar & Rinehart, 1930, reprinted, Bobbs-Merrill, 1976; *Many Happy Returns: An Unofficial Guide to Your Income Tax Problems,* Simon & Schuster, 1942; (with Norman Krasna) *Time for Elizabeth* (play), Dramatists Play Service, 1949; *Groucho and Me,* Simon & Shcuster, 1959; *Memoirs of a Mangy Lover,* Geis, 1963; *The Groucho Letters: Letters From and to Groucho Marx,* Simon & Schuster, 1967; (with Richard J. Anobile) *The Marx Brothers Scrapbook,* Crimson Press, 1974; (with Hector Arce) *The Secret Word Is Groucho,* Putnam, 1976; *Grouchophile,* Bobbs-Merrill, 1976.

SIDELIGHTS: Marx was regarded as one of the ultimate wits of his age. He was, according to fellow comedian George Burns, ''one of the great original funny men.'' George Bernard Shaw called him ''the world's greatest living actor.'' But Marx refrained from taking himself seriously. Once, when introduced to someone who commented on what a pleasure it was to meet the infamous Groucho Marx, Marx replied, ''I've known him for years and I can tell you it's no pleasure.''

Marx entered the entertainment world when he was still in his teens. His mother, a stage-struck woman with several children to care for, encouraged Groucho and his brothers to be actors and even created shows for them. An early act featured Groucho, his brothers Adolph (Harpo) and Milton (Gummo), a soprano singer, his mother, and her sister. The show, ''Six Musical Mascots,'' was less than a critical success. The brothers themselves performed admirably but the women, particularly Mrs. Marx and her sister, left much to be desired. To save the show, they withdrew and changed the act to ''The Marx Brothers and Company.''

Touring the South and Midwest in their revised format, Groucho and his brothers performed a basic vaudeville show with lots of harmony singing and some skits. Unfortunately, like their previous incarnation, they were not doing well. ''Our act was so lousy,'' recalled Groucho, ''that when word passed through the audience of numbskull Texans that a mule had run away, they got up en masse to go out and see something livelier.'' Ironically, this very incident inspired the brothers to invoke the style which later became their trademark. When the distracted Texans returned to their seats, Groucho unleashed a few one-liners. ''It wasn't the best line I ever ad-libbed, but I recall I told them 'Nacagdoches [the town where they were performing]—is full of roaches.' And—ultimate insult—I called those Texans 'damn yankees.''' But the audience enjoyed the spontaneity of the insults and soon the act shifted its emphasis towards plots around which ad-libbing could be used.

Two of Groucho's other brothers, Chico and Zeppo, joined the act and all the brothers refined their new style by touring steadily for many years. In 1924, they played Broadway in ''I'll Say She Is.'' On the strength of their second hit, ''The Cocoanuts,'' they were signed to a film contract. The brothers worked hard in New York City. The film version of "The Cocoanuts" was shot during the day, and every night they performed in "Animal Crackers," their third consecutive Broadway success.

In "Animal Crackers," Groucho gave one of his most heralded performances. He played Captain Jeffrey T. Spaulding, a famous African explorer. As an actor, Groucho was always comfortable within the chaos that typified most storylines in his films. The anarchy inspired him with some of his best lines: when Spaulding arrives at a women's party, he says, "One morning I shot an elephant in my pajamas. How he got in my pajamas, I don't know. . . . But that's entirely irrelephant. . . ." At another point in the film, Spaulding confides to a wealthy woman, "You're the most beautiful woman I've ever met, which doesn't say much for you."

Marx was equally zany in "Horse Feathers" in the role of Professor Quincey Adams Wagstaff. When told that his rival, Jennings, was "waxing wroth" outside the door, Wagstaff replies, "Tell Roth to wax Jennings for a change." The line, like most of Marx's clever comments, was spontaneous. In fact, Marx so deviated from scripts that during a performance of "Animal Crackers," the author, George S. Kauffman, asked for a moment of silence from those sitting near him because he thought he'd heard one of the play's original lines.

Although "Duck Soup" was a disappointment in comparison to their first three films, it too contains some fine examples of Groucho's wit. While Groucho and his brothers ward off a woman's enemies, he cracks, "Remember, we're fighting for her honor—which is probably more than she ever did."

The Marx Brothers reached their zenith with "A Night at the Opera" and "A Day at the Races." Groucho played Otis P. Driftwood in the former and his favorite role was in the latter, as Doctor Hackenbush. These two films, true to the anarchy of the previous films but more refined technically (due, probably, to Irving Thalberg's production), remain the most popular of all those the brothers made together.

Groucho went on to make several more films with his brothers but by 1939, the enthusiasm was gone. He noted that "the fun had gone out of picture-making. I was like an old pug, still going through the motions, but now doing it solely for the money."

So Groucho turned to radio. After some intermittent appearances on several shows, including two of his own, he took the advise of John Guedel, the originator of shows featuring Art Linkletter, and introduced a new quiz show with himself as quizmaster. With "You Bet Your Life," the emphasis was not on contestants or prizes but on Groucho's wit; he reveled under the attention. Several of his most famous quips originate from the show, which later transferred to television where it achieved the number one rating. On one show, a contestant gave her age as "approaching forty." "From which direction?," asked Groucho. On another, Marx handled a contestant who'd developed stage fright by announcing, "Either this man is dead or my watch is stopped." He asked another contestant, a tree surgeon, "Have you ever fallen out of any of your patients?"

In 1963, "the man with the grease-paint moustache" and ever-present cigar retired to a life of golf (which he misplayed to such an extent that on one occasion he actually hurled his equipment over a cliff) and tennis. Frequently, however, he did appear in public. He finished behind Jesus Christ and Albert Schweitzer in a 1969 poll asking college students whom they most admired. Accepting the honor at an awards ceremony, he said, "I'm sorry Jesus Christ couldn't be here. He had to be in Philadelphia." On another occasion, he received a prestigious award in France. "Can it be hocked?," he asked.

By 1970, Marx was showing signs of his age. His sight had noticeably declined and he also wore a hearing aid. He did perform in a series of solo shows in 1972, but critics took note of his aged appearance. Marx was semi-reclusive up until his death. He endured a hip operation in 1976, but finally succumbed after a lengthy bout with pnuemonia.

"We're going to miss him a lot," commented George Burns, "but the things Groucho said will always be with us." He said many things worth remembering him by. Once, when asked for an autograph, Groucho answered, "No, but you can have my footprints. They're upstairs in my socks." Many of Marx's declarations have even been used by other comedians. In "Annie Hall," Woody Allen reiterated Groucho's sentiments when he remarked, "I wouldn't belong to any club that would have me for a member." He will long be remembered by those who appreciate his brand of humor. Of the man who once said, "Three years ago I came to Florida and I didn't have a nickel. Now I have a nickel," Red Skelton declared, "He was one of the greatest of all the clowns. He'll go on forever as a great legend."

AVOCATIONAL INTERESTS: Tennis, golf.

BIOGRAPHICAL/CRITICAL SOURCES: Groucho Marx, *Groucho and Me,* Simon & Schuster, 1959; Marx, *Memoirs of a Mangy Lover,* Geis, 1963; Allen Eyles, *Marx Brothers: Their World of Comedy,* A. S. Barnes, 1966; Marx, *The Groucho Letters: Letters From and to Groucho Marx,* Simon & Schuster, 1967; Joe Adamson, *Groucho, Harpo, Chico, & Sometimes Zeppo,* Simon & Schuster, 1973; Marx and Richard J. Anobile, *The Marx Brothers Scrapbook,* Crimson Press, 1974; William Wolf, *Marx Brothers,* Harcourt, 1975; Marx and Hector Arce, *The Secret Word Is Groucho,* Putnam, 1976; Marx, *Grouchophile,* Bobbs-Merrill, 1976; Arce, *Groucho: The Authorized Biography,* Putnam, 1978.

OBITUARIES: New York Times, August 20, 1977; *Washington Post,* August 21, 1977; *Newsweek,* August 29, 1977; *Time,* August 29, 1977.*

(Died August 19, 1977, in Los Angeles, Calif.)

*   *   *

MARX, Werner 1910-

PERSONAL: Born September 19, 1910, in Muelheim/Ruhr, Germany; came to the United States in 1938, naturalized citizen, 1944; son of Karl and Emilie (Kann) Marx; married Hilde Ritter, 1937. *Education:* University of Bonn, LL.D., 1933; New School for Social Research, M.Sc., 1944, Ph.D., 1953. *Office:* Philosophy Seminar I, University of Freiburg, 7800 Freiburg im Breisgau, West Germany.

CAREER: New School for Social Research, New York, N.Y., lecturer, 1953-55, assistant professor, 1955-60, adjunct associate professor, 1960-62, adjunct professor of philosophy, 1962; University of Freiburg, Freiburg, Germany, professor of philosophy and head of philosophy seminar, 1964—. Visiting professor at University of Heidelberg, 1958, Fulbright professor, 1962. *Member:* Internationale Hegel-Vereinigung, Institut International de Philosophie, American Philosophical Association, Allgemeine Gesellschaft fuer Philosophie in Deutschland, Deutsche Gesellschaft fuer phaenomenologische Forschung, Collegium Phaenomenologicum Monteripido (Italy).

WRITINGS: The Meaning of Aristotle's "Ontology", Nijhoff, 1954; *Heidegger und die Tradition,* Kohlhammer, 1961, translation by Theodore Kisiel and Murray Greene published as *Heidegger and the Tradition,* Northwestern University Press, 1971; *Die Bestimmung der Philosophie im Deutschen Idealismus* (title means "The Role of Philosophy in German Idealism"), Kohlhammer, 1965; *Das Spiel, Wirklichkeit und Methode* (title means "The Play: Its Reality and Method"), Klostermann, 1967; *Absolute Reflexion und Sprache* (title means "Absolute Reflection and Language"), Klostermann, 1967.

Vernunft und Welt: Zwischen Tradition und anderem Anfang, Nijhoff, 1970, translation by Thomas V. Yates and Joseph P. Fell published as *Reason and World: Between Tradition and Another Beginning,* Nijhoff, 1971; *Hegel's Phaenomenologie des Geistes: Die Bestimmung ihrer Idee in Vorrede und Einleitung,* Klostermann, 1971, translation by Peter Heath published as *Hegel's Phenomenology of Spirit, Its Point and Purpose: A Commentary on the Preface and Introduction,* Harper, 1975; *Einfuehrung in Aristoteles' Theorie vom Seienden,* Rombach, 1972, translation by Robert S. Schine published as *Introduction to Aristotle's Theory of Being as Being,* Nijhoff, 1977; *Schelling: Geschichte, System, Freiheit* (title means "Schelling's Conception of History, System and Freedom"), Alber, 1977; (contributor) *Heidegger: Freiburger Universitaetsvortraege zu seinem Gedenken* (title means "Heidegger: Lectures Delivered at a Memorial Celebration at the University of Freiburg"), Alber, 1977; (contributor) *Die Sterblichen* (title means "The Mortals"), Gerstenberg, 1978.

WORK IN PROGRESS: Thought and Its Issue; The Function of the Evil in History.

*   *   *

MARZOLLO, Jean   1942-

PERSONAL: Born June 24, 1942, in Manchester, Conn.; daughter of Richard (a town manager) and Ruth (a teacher; maiden name, Smith) Martin; married Claudio Marzollo (a sculptor), March, 1969; children: Daniel, David. *Education:* University of Connecticut, B.A., 1964; Harvard University, M.A.T., 1965. *Residence:* Cold Spring, N.Y. *Agent:* Sheldon Fogelman, 10 East 40th St., New York, N.Y. 10016.

CAREER: Teacher in Arlington, Mass., 1965-66; Harvard University, Cambridge, Mass., assistant director of Project Upward Bound, 1967; General Learning Corp., New York City, 1967-69; National Commissional Resources for Youth, New York City, director of publications, 1970-71; Scholastic Magazines, Inc., Englewood Cliffs, N.J., editor of *Let's Find Out* (magazine for kindergarten children), 1971—.

WRITINGS: Learning Through Play, Harper, 1972; *Nine Months, One Day, One Year,* Harper, 1975; *Supertot,* Harper, 1978; *Close Your Eyes* (juvenile), Dial, 1978.

WORK IN PROGRESS: A book on education; children's books.

SIDELIGHTS: Jean Marzollo writes: "I am interested in children and families. I like to write books that support families."

*   *   *

MASCOTT, Trina

PERSONAL: Born in Chicago, Ill.; married Laurence Mascott (a film writer and producer); children: Holly, Cynthia, T. Owen. *Education:* Attended Black Mountain College and Northwestern University. *Home:* 6784 Shearwater Lane, Malibu, Calif. 90265. *Agent:* Robert P. Mills Ltd., 156 East 52nd St., New York, N.Y. 10022.

CAREER: Editor for *Edison-Norwood Review,* Edison Park, Ill.; reporter for *Arkansas Gazette,* Little Rock, Ark.; radio announcer and writer for station KGKB, Tyler, Tex.; radio news writer at Associated Press, New York, N.Y.; television writer and producer in Hollywood, Calif.; writer, 1973—.

WRITINGS—Novels: *The Wife Who Ran Away,* Dell, 1975; *Bella Figura,* St. Martin's, 1977, reprinted as *Love at Noon,* Dell, 1978.

WORK IN PROGRESS: Two novels and a television movie.

SIDELIGHTS: Trina Mascott told *CA:* "I'm a great believer in change. To quote one of my own characters, Joella, in *Bella Figura:* "I don't care how good today is, I want tomorrow to be different." This, my philosophy, is based not on restlessness, but on boundless curiosity. Thus, when my heroine, Marty, in *The Wife Who Ran Away,* decides to leave her husband and home in Pasadena, her first impulse is to GO, anywhere, not only to run *away,* but simply to *run.* I had a wonderful time exploring California's Gold Rush country, where Marty finally stops running. Even more exciting was my historical research on the area which enabled me to write the journal Marty finds, written by a woman named Katie who lived there a hundred years earlier.

"I am fascinated by history, despite its male-oriented, violent nature and, even more, by archaeology, where imagination can fill in the unknown facts. To satisfy these interests I am indeed fortunate that my husband and I are able to travel for three or four months each year in Europe and the U.S.; when our children were younger we lived for a wonderful while in Rome, which I still consider my 'home town' even though I'm not Italian.

"In my books I try to show that place often molds people. If the same three women (American) in *Bella Figura* had spent the summer in, say, England, instead of Italy, I would have written an entirely different story. When I visit an appealing new area, in Europe or America, I begin to feel how it would be to live there; then I wish I could spend the next five hundred years writing novels about all the places I love."

*   *   *

MASON, F(rancis) van Wyck   1901-1978
(Van Wyck Mason; pseudonyms: Geoffrey Coffin, Frank W. Mason, Ward Weaver)

OBITUARY NOTICE—See index for *CA* sketch: Born November 11, 1901, in Boston, Mass.; died August 28, 1978, in Bermuda. Writer best known for his numerous mysteries and historical novels. Mason had considered a diplomatic career but switched to importing in 1925. In 1928, he ventured into writing and it became his full-time occupation. He wrote *Three Harbours, Blue Hurricane, Seeds of Murder, The Bucharest Ballerina Murders,* and many other novels. Obituaries and other sources: *The Author's and Writer's Who's Who,* 6th edition, Burke's Peerage, 1971; *Authors of Books for Young People,* 2nd edition, Scarecrow, 1971; *Who's Who in America,* 40th edition, Marquis, 1978; *Washington Post,* August 30, 1978; *Time,* September 11, 1978; *Publishers Weekly,* September 11, 1978; *AB Bookman's Weekly,* November 6, 1978.

*   *   *

MASON, Frank W.
See MASON, F(rancis) van Wyck

MASON, Van Wyck
See MASON, F(rancis) van Wyck

*   *   *

MASSIE, Diane Redfield

PERSONAL: Born in Los Angeles, Calif.; daughter of James Gilbert (an insurance agent) and Marion (a teacher; maiden name, Haskell) Redfield; married David M. Massie (a professor); children: Caitlin, Tom. *Education:* Attended Los Angeles City College and Occidental College. *Residence:* Hunterdon County, N.J.

CAREER: Author and illustrator of books for children. Professional oboist with Honolulu Symphony for five seasons. *Awards, honors:* Honor Book Award from Book Week Children's Spring Book Festival, 1965, for *A Turtle and a Loon;* design award from Chicago's Book Clinic, 1966, for *A Birthday for Bird.*

WRITINGS—All juvenile; all self-illustrated: *The Baby Bee Bee Bird,* Harper, 1963; *Tiny Pin,* Harper, 1964; *A Turtle and a Loon,* Atheneum, 1965; *A Birthday for Bird,* Parents' Magazine Press, 1966; *Cockle Stew,* Atheneum, 1967; *King Henry the Mouse,* Atheneum, 1968; *Dazzle,* Parents' Magazine Press, 1969; *Walter Was a Frog,* Simon & Schuster, 1970; *The Monstrous Glisson Glop,* Parents' Magazine Press, 1970; *Zigger Beans,* Parents' Magazine Press, 1971; *Good Neighbors,* McGraw, 1972; *Briar Rose and the Golden Eggs,* Parents' Magazine Press, 1973; *Turtle's Flying Lesson,* Grosset, 1973; *The Lion's Bed,* Weekly Reader Children's Book Club, 1974; *The Komodo Dragon's Jewels,* Macmillan, 1975; *The Thief in the Botanical Gardens,* Weekly Reader Children's Book Club, 1975; *Sloth's Birthday Party,* Weekly Reader Children's Book Club, 1976; *Brave Brush-Tail Possum,* Weekly Reader Children's Book Club, 1978.

Also author of several one-act plays. Contributor of poems to *Humpty Dumpty.*

WORK IN PROGRESS: Muskrat's Hotel.

SIDELIGHTS: MacGregor Was a Dog and *The Baby Bee Bee Bird* were selected and read by Captain Kangaroo on television.

*   *   *

MASTERSON, Dan 1934-

PERSONAL: Born February 22, 1934, in Buffalo, N.Y.; son of Stephen Vincent (a buyer) and Kathleen (a teacher; maiden name, Fitzpatrick) Masterson; married Janet Rae Travis (a registrar at a private school), June 22, 1957; children: Martha McCarrick, Stephen Vincent. *Education:* Attended Canisius College, 1953; Syracuse University, B.S., 1956. *Home:* 41 Fisher Ave., Pearl River, N.Y. 10965. *Office:* Department of English, Rockland Community College, 145 College Rd., Suffern, N.Y. 10901.

CAREER: WBNY-Radio, Buffalo, N.Y., newscaster, disc jockey, and announcer, 1956-57; free-lance broadcast announcer and actor, 1959-60; Martin Tahse Productions, Inc., New York City, public relations director, 1961-65; lay missionary and public relations director, New York City, 1965; Rockland Community College of State University of New York, Suffern, instructor, 1966-68, associate professor, 1968-71, professor of English, 1971—, director of the writing program. *Military service:* U.S. Army, Signal Corps, 1958; became second lieutenant. U.S. Army Reserve, 1959-64; became first lieutenant.

AWARDS, HONORS: Bullis Prize from *Poetry Northwest,* 1975, for "Blizzard"; poetry prize from Coordinating Council of Literary Magazines, 1975, for "Blizzard"; Borestone poetry prize, 1977, for "A Child Going Blind"; Pushcart poetry prize, 1977, for "The Survivor"; award from New York state chancellor, 1977, for excellence in teaching.

WRITINGS: On Earth As It Is (poems), University of Illinois Press, 1978. Contributor of poems to literary journals and popular magazines, including *Paris Review, New Yorker, Esquire, Poetry,* and *Yankee.*

WORK IN PROGRESS: A long narrative poem on the last years of Shelley.

SIDELIGHTS: Masterson wrote to *CA:* "I remember writing poems in grade school and hiding them away in an orangewood box under my bed. I also recall hopping the back fence from the schoolyard and having lunch alone with my mother—and how she got me involved with words, making a game of it, the dictionary never far from hand. And my dad's fast wit and funny rhymes. That all had to help. In high school, I found a copy of Shelley's collected poems in a study hall cupboard; I was so bored, I read it. That started something; I was astonished that language could be handled that way.

"My own writing started to matter at Syracuse University when the late Norman Whitney sat me down after class and told me that I could be a writer if I worked hard. I wish he could read my work now; maybe he is. After college, and the army, I hired out as a copywriter at a slave-labor agency in the garment district of Manhattan and pushed shopping carts of film down Fifth Avenue, when the garbage can spray ads were finished for the day. The following year, I began writing publicity blurbs for a Broadway theatrical producer. But no poetry.

"The poems returned when my wife and I left our careers in New York, stumbling briefly through a five month stint as lay missionaries. I started substitute teaching across the Hudson and Janet stayed home with our brand new daughter. I had time to think again, write again. A colleague, Gust Babalis, kept after me to show some poems to professionals. Finally I agreed; Gust knew that Horace Gregory and Marya Zaturenska, the award-winning poets, would read my work kindly. They did, commenting that I may have learned my Frost too well. I defrosted my style and kept on writing. Within the year I sent five poems off to James Dickey at the Library of Congress, hoping for a word from the poet whose work I read with awe. He wrote back within the week, saying some good things and offering some sound revisional advice. He continued to encourage me, predicting in 1967 that I'd have a volume of poems in ten years. He was correct! I placed *On Earth As It Is* with The University of Illinois Press in 1977.

"There were hard years, but then there are supposed to be hard years. I never thought I'd really have a book; yes I did. Something way back in the head told me it would happen; it had to. But I learned this year that it is frightening to go public with a book. That old orangewood box is out from under the bed for everyone to see. There have been some awards, some good letters from fellow poets, offers to read and teach. The waiting seems less important than I tried to make it. There must have been a schedule to things. I needed time to learn the craft, the art, just as a pianist and dancer must.

"It's a good life; writing, teaching. I'm trying to turn people on to poetry, in my classes and at readings. There are four elements I look for and try for in a poem: they are memorable language, remarkable images, engaging storylines, and residue of pain or experience. I spend a great deal of time (sometimes 200 hours) finishing a poem. The idea arrives like a chicken bone caught in the throat and it takes a long while to write it out of there. Much of my writing happens at our mountain cabin hidden away, like that orangewood box, in the high peak region of New York State's Adirondacks.''

* * *

MATHEWSON, Rufus Wellington, Jr. 1919(?)-1978

OBITUARY NOTICE: Born c. 1919; died August 2, 1978, in Blue Hill, Me. Educator and author. Mathewson was professor of Russian and comparative literature at Columbia University. He wrote *The Positive Hero in Russian Literature.* Obituaries and other sources: *New York Times,* August 4, 1978.

* * *

MATTHEWS, Ralph 1904(?)-1978

OBITUARY NOTICE: Born c. 1904 in Hartford County, Md.; died August 30, 1978, in Washington, D.C. Editor and reporter for Afro-American newspaper chain. Matthews began his journalism career as a reporter for the *Baltimore Afro-American* in 1924, and retired in 1968 as associate editor of the *Washington Afro-American.* He was also affiliated with sister newspapers in Newark, N.J., and Philadelphia, Pa., in addition to his five-year editorship of the *Cleveland Call and Post.* During the forty-four year span of his career, Matthews covered such international events as the coronation of Britain's King George VI in 1936, and the Korean conflict, as well as national political and civil rights problems. He was also a charity organizer for the newspaper chain for sixteen years. Obituaries and other sources: *Washington Post,* September 2, 1978.

* * *

MAULTSBY, Maxie C(larence), Jr. 1932-

PERSONAL: Born April 24, 1932, in Pensacola, Fla.; son of Maxie Clarence and Valdee (a teacher; maiden name, Campbell) Maultsby; married Rita Oliveras; children: Maxie Clarence III, Evalina Nahir, David Alan. *Education:* Talladega College, B.A., 1953; Case Western Reserve University, M.D., 1957; special study with Joseph Wolpe and Albert Ellis, 1968, and Wolfgang Luthe, 1969. *Politics:* Democrat. *Agent:* Arthur Pine Associates, Inc., 1780 Broadway, New York, N.Y. 10019. *Office:* Department of Psychiatry, University of Kentucky, Lexington, Ky. 40506.

CAREER: Philadelphia General Hospital, Philadelphia, Pa., intern, 1957-58; general practice of medicine in Cocoa, Fla., 1958-62; University of Wisconsin—Madison, resident in adult psychiatry, 1966-68, and child psychiatry, 1968-70, assistant professor of medicine and clinical researcher in psychophysiology, both 1970-71; University of Kentucky, Lexington, assistant professor, 1971, associate professor of psychiatry, 1973—, director of Training Center for Rational Behavior Therapy and Emotional Self-Help, 1973—. Diplomate of National Board of Examiners; certified by American Board of Psychiatry; licensed in Florida, Ohio, California, Wisconsin, Michigan, and Kentucky; trained at Center for Marital and Sexual Studies, 1975. Visiting professor at Western Michigan University, 1970; permanent member of counseling practicum faculty at Institute for Rational Living, 1968—. Conducts frequent workshops for mental health professionals. *Military service:* U.S. Air Force, Medical Corps, 1962-66, chief of outpatient departments at Clark Air Force Base and Tachikawa Air Force Base.

MEMBER: Association for the Advancement of Behavior Therapy, American Association for Group Psychotherapists, American Personnel and Guidance Association, American School Health Association, American Psychiatric Association (fellow), American Association of Psychotherapists, American Association of Sex Educators, Counselors and Therapists, Association for Rational Thinking (executive director), Wisconsin State Medical Society. *Awards, honors:* National Institute of Mental Health grants, 1973-77; Social Science Research Council grant, 1972; National Institute of Drug Abuse grant, 1972; U.S. Department of Health, Education & Welfare grant, 1977.

WRITINGS: A Handbook of Rational Self-Counseling, Rational Self-Help Aids, Inc., 1971; (contributor) *Growth Through Reason,* Science & Behavior Books, 1971; (with A. Hendricks) *You and Your Emotions,* Rational Self-Help Aids, 1974; *More Personal Happiness Through Rational Self-Counseling,* Training Center for Rational Behavior Therapy and Emotional Self-Help, University of Kentucky, 1974; (with David Goodman) *Emotional Well-Being Through Rational Behavior Training,* C. C Thomas, 1974, 3rd edition, 1977; *Introduction and Summary for Rational Behavior Therapy: The Art and Science,* University of Northern Colorado Press, 1976; *Help Yourself to Happiness Through Rational Self-Counseling,* Institute for Rational Living, 1977; (contributor) Charles Zastrow and Dae Chang, editors, *The Personal Problem Solver,* Spectrum, 1977; (contributor) Russell Grieger, editor, *Rational Emotive Psychotherapy: Handbook of Theory and Practice,* Springer Publishing, 1978. Contributor to Outward Bound of America student and instructor training manuals. Contributor of more than thirty articles to medical, social science, and education journals.

WORK IN PROGRESS: Research on the elderly, on effective low-cost mass school and community mental health program techniques, on application of rational behavioral psychotherapy in psychosomatic disease management, and application of rational behavioral self-help concepts and techniques for use by the elderly and underserviced minorities.

SIDELIGHTS: Maultsby has involved himself in high-school-level mental health programs, and university and minority student counseling problems. In 1969 he formulated and supervised a program for the successful solution of Wisconsin's "black athletic players' rebellion."

He writes that one of his current interests is "self-help techniques in the field of mental health. I am executive director of the Association for Rational Thinking, a nonprofit, self-help corporation founded at University of Wisconsin in 1970. ART is dedicated to exploring practical means of·enabling interested lay people to improve their mental and emotional fitness according to valid principles of human behavior, without professional help."

AVOCATIONAL INTERESTS: Flying (licensed pilot), horseback riding.

* * *

MAYES, Frances

PERSONAL: Born in Fitzgerald, Ga.; daughter of Garbert (a cotton mill manager) and Frankye (Davis) Mayes; married William Frank King (a computer research scientist); children: Ashley. *Education:* Attended Randolph-Macon Woman's College; earned B.A. from University of Florida; San Francisco State University, M.A., 1975. *Home:* 1518 Hamilton Ave., Palo Alto, Calif. 94303. *Office:* 514 Bryant St., Palo Alto, Calif. 94301.

CAREER: Former free-lance copywriter for cookbook publishers and newspapers; currently member of department of English, San Francisco State University, San Francisco, Calif. Teacher at writing workshops at Foothill College and Canada College. *Awards, honors:* Award from Academy of American Poets, 1975.

WRITINGS: Sunday in Another Country, Heyeck Press, 1977; *Climbing Aconcagua* (pamphlet), Seven Woods Press, 1977. Work anthologized in *Contemporary Women Poets.* Contributor of poems to literary journals, including *Epoch, Ascent, Mother Jones,* and *Carolina Quarterly.*

WORK IN PROGRESS: A book, tentatively entitled *House in the Palm of My Hand.*

*   *   *

MBERI, Antar Sudan Katara   1949-

PERSONAL: Original name, Thomas Louis Henderson; name changed in 1967; born May 14, 1949, in Bronx, N.Y.; son of Calvin Vernon and Izetta (Boone) Henderson; children: Yvonne Louise Benjamin, Izetta Loretta Henderson. *Education:* Ohio University, B.A., 1971, M.A., 1972. *Home and office:* 2155 Seventh Ave., Apt. 7, New York, N.Y. 10027. *Office:* Young Workers Liberation League, 235 West 23rd St., New York, N.Y. 10011.

CAREER: Ohio University, Athens, instructor of Afro-American studies, 1971-75; Young Workers Liberation League, New York, N.Y., staff member, 1976-77. Director of W.E.B. DuBois Harlem Community Center, 1977-78. National coordinator of U.S. National Preparatory Committee for World Festival of Youth and Students (Havana, Cuba), 1969-78. Public lecturer on Afro-American subjects; has given dramatic presentations, sometimes with dance performances, on television, radio, and stage. *Awards, honors:* Second prize from *Cultural Reporter*'s national poetry contest, 1975, for "The Soil of Georgia Is Red as Blood"; National Endowment for the Arts grant, 1977.

WRITINGS: Bandages and Bullets: In Praise of the African Revolution (poems), West End Press, 1977; (editor with Cosmo Pieterse) *Speak Easy, Speak Free* (poems), International Publishers, 1977.

Work anthologized in *For Neruda, for Chile,* edited by Walter Lowenfels, Beacon Press. Contributor of more than forty poems and reviews to magazines, including *Obsidian, Freedomways, Young Worker,* and *African Agenda,* and newspapers. Assistant editor of *Confrontation: Third World Literary Journal,* 1974-75.

WORK IN PROGRESS: Two books of poems, *I Look to Your Lips for Wine,* and *Platts;* "Suite of the Singing Mountain: For Paul Robeson," a blues-jazz cantata.

*   *   *

Mc ADAM, Robert E(verett)   1920-

PERSONAL: Born November 20, 1920, in Chicago, Ill.; son of Walter (an architect) and Irene (Lussier) McAdam; married Grace Ford (a registered nurse), August 16, 1947; children: Patrick, Gary, William, Tom, Brian, Michael, Diane. *Education:* De Paul University, B.S; University of Illinois, M.S., Ph.D. *Home:* 201 Concord Dr., Normal, Ill. 61761. *Office:* 310 Hovey Hall, Illinois State University, Normal, Ill. 61761.

CAREER: Northern Illinois University, DeKalb, assistant professor of physical education, 1955-62; University of Minnesota, Minneapolis, 1962-70, began as associate professor,

became professor of physical education; Illinois State University, Normal, professor of physical education, chairperson of department of health education physical education, and athletics, and director of research, 1972—. Member of board of directors of St. Joseph's Hospital. *Military service:* U.S. Air Force, 1954; became major. *Member:* American Alliance for Health, Physical Education & Recreation, College of Physical Education (Men), National Council of University Research Administrators, Phi Delta Kappa.

WRITINGS—All published by Bowmar: *Forty for Sixty,* 1971; *Viva Gonzales,* 1971; *Chief Cloud of Dust,* 1971; *Bull on Ice,* 1971, teacher's guide, 1971; *Climb Any Mountain,* 1976; *The Skillful Rider,* 1976; *Holdup at the Crossover,* 1976; *More Than Speedy Wheels,* 1976, teacher's guide, 1976. Associate editor of *Research Quarterly,* of American Alliance for Health, Physical Education & Recreation.

WORK IN PROGRESS: Concepts and Practices in Elementary Physical Activity Programs.

SIDELIGHTS: McAdam writes: "My primary interest is in improvement of the quality of human life through exploring human activity and sport."

*   *   *

McAULIFFE, Kevin Michael   1949-

PERSONAL: Born September 9, 1949, in Bronx, N.Y.; son of Daniel Joseph (a physician) and Ethel (a teacher; maiden name, Dierks) McAuliffe. *Education:* Fairfield University, B.A., 1971; Columbia University, M.S., 1975. *Home:* 339 East 90th St., #3-C, New York, N.Y. 10028. *Agent:* Roberta Kent, WB Agency, 145 East 52nd St., New York, N.Y. 10022.

CAREER: Milford Citizen, Milford, Conn., news writer, 1971-73; free-lance writer, 1973—. Instructor at Fairleigh Dickinson University, 1975-78. Speechwriter and press secretary for Insurance Crime Prevention Institute, 1972; speechwriter for political figures, including the mayor of New York City, 1978.

WRITINGS: (With Alan Jeffry Breslau) *The Time of My Death,* Dutton, 1977; *The Great American Newspaper,* Scribner, 1978. Contributor to magazines, including *Nation, New Republic, Progressive,* and *Sport,* and newspapers. Contributing editor of *Fusion: New England Business Journal.*

WORK IN PROGRESS: Charro (tentative title), about rodeo entertainer Francisco Zamora; *Shattered* (tentative title), an American's adventure in guerrilla warfare among tribes of the Sahara.

SIDELIGHTS: McAuliffe writes: "Long ago I decided I wanted to live my life outside any institutional framework and without any long-range one-job life plan. I wanted to be a writer, to have many jobs, to live by my wits and my words, to be doing different things and sampling the maximum number of experiences my whole life long. To have that freedom I have had to do without security, economic and otherwise. I have been broke many times and starving almost as many, but I would not have had it any other way. I do not know, when asked, what I will wind up doing—editing a newspaper, writing novels or plays or political speeches (as I am doing now), or radio and television work—but I know what I will not do: lead a safe, dull life or do any one thing too long."

AVOCATIONAL INTERESTS: Law, politics, sports, media, urban issues, books, theater, movies.

McAULIFFE, Mary Sperling 1943-

PERSONAL: Born September 25, 1943, in Orlando, Fla.; daughter of Godfrey, Jr. (a journalist) and Betty Louise (Feldmann) Sperling; married John Herbert McAuliffe (a university administrator), 1970; children: Mavyn. *Education:* Principia College, B.A., 1965; University of Maryland, M.A., 1967, Ph.D., 1972. *Office:* Department of History, Iowa State University, Ames, Iowa 50011.

CAREER: Executive Office of the President, Council on Environmental Quality, Washington, D.C., research assistant, 1970-71; Iowa State University, Ames, assistant professor of history, 1973—. *Member:* American Historical Association, Organization of American Historians, Phi Alpha Theta, Phi Alpha Eta.

WRITINGS: (contributor) Robert Griffith and Athan Theoharis, editors, *The Specter,* F. Watts, 1974; *Crisis on the Left: Cold War Politics and American Liberals, 1947-1954,* University of Massachusetts Press, 1978. Contributor to *Journal of American History.*

WORK IN PROGRESS: Research on American liberals.

* * *

McBRIDE, Chris(topher James) 1941-

PERSONAL: Born May 6, 1941, in Johannesburg, South Africa; son of Cyril James (a company director) and Patricia (Brady) McBride; married Charlotte Mason, July 23, 1971; children: Tabitha Catherine, Robert Charles. *Education:* University of the Witwatersrand, B.A., 1961; Johannesburg College of Education, Transvaal Teachers Higher Diploma, 1965; Humboldt State University, graduate study in wildlife management, 1972—. *Address:* P.O. Box 80, Pilgrims Rest, 1290, Transvaal, South Africa.

CAREER: Secondary school teacher in Rhodesia, 1962-64, 1967-72, and in Transvaal, South Africa, 1966; acting warden for Timbavati Private Nature Reserve, South Africa, 1975; manager of Tanda Tula Game Lodge, South Africa, 1976-77; consultant for documentary film on white lions, Alan Landsburg Productions Ltd. and Paddington Press, 1977; speaker on basic conservation principles.

WRITINGS: The White Lions of Timbavati, Paddington Press, 1977.

WORK IN PROGRESS: A sequel to *The White Lions of Timbavati,* entitled *Operation White Lion,* for Paddington Press; further research on predators, with possible publication in scientific journals.

SIDELIGHTS: In 1975, Chris McBride was studying a pride of lions, specifically the Machaton pride in the Timbavati Nature Reserve in South Africa, for his masters thesis in wildlife management. He had observed two of the lions mating and was familiar enough with pride members to identify these two as Tabby and Agamemnon. The result of their mating was the unprecedented birth of white lions. Tabby gave birth to three cubs, two of which were completely snow white; the other being the natural tawny color. White lions have always existed in African legends, but the unexpected arrival of these two white cubs with their tawny-colored brother was an exciting event. *An* exciting event, that is, until a third white cub appeared with the Machaton pride almost twelve months later, probably sired again by Agamemnon. McBride's book, *The White Lions of Timbavati,* is proof of the existence of the legendary white lion of Africa and a chronicle of the growth of these special creatures.

McBride provides extensive information about the cubs,

noting that they are not albinos since they have the same eye color and markings as a tawny lion. In addition, he gives his own explanation for the appearance of such phenomena: "If a white recessive gene exists among these lions and you have the situation of a father mating with his own daughter or granddaughter, the chances of the white strain appearing are naturally increased." It is thought that Agamemnon carried this recessive white gene.

But the birth of such extraordinary creatures carried with it an added burden and in his book, McBride showed genuine concern for them: "From the moment we discovered the white lions everything changed.... I felt from the outset a growing sense of responsibility toward them. If they were going to survive, it was probable that at some stage they would need human assistance." The mortality rate of lion cubs, as noted in the book, is about seventy percent. However, it was most likely higher for the white cubs, because they did not have the help of their tawny color as camouflage, and also might face rejection from other pride members because of their snow white color. McBride, at one point, did feed the white cubs because he alarmingly noticed their protruding ribs.

McBride's concern isn't restricted only to the white lions. Rather, his book is a statement of his beliefs in conservation and wildlife management. It is also a record of his feelings, his love for Africa and its lands, and his concern about the future. While studying in California, a homesick McBride observed that the bush is "something in your blood. A combination of the climate, the landscape, the wildlife, the whole atmosphere. You somehow feel that you're missing everything when you're not there."

About his concern for Africa and its wildlife, McBride wrote: "I only hope that the ever more pressing demands of Africa's human population will not result in the place being given over to some sort of 'progress.' It would be tragic if mere expediency resulted in the obliteration of what were among man's first footprints on this earth. Even more important, we must try to preserve what remains of the environment that existed in perfect stability before his arrival, and before the subsequent arrival of language, thought, invention and ultimately civilization and industrialization upset the working of the entire ecosystem."

BIOGRAPHICAL/CRITICAL SOURCES: Chris McBride, *The White Lions of Timbavati,* Paddington Press, 1977; *Newsweek,* May 9, 1977; *Washington Post,* October 20, 1977.

* * *

McCAMMON, Robert R(ick) 1952-

PERSONAL: Born July 17, 1952, in Birmingham, Ala.; son of Jack (a musician) and Barbara (Bundy) McCammon. *Education:* University of Alabama, B.A., 1974. *Religion:* Methodist. *Home:* 8912 Fourth Ave. S., Birmingham, Ala. 35206. *Agent:* Michael Larsen/Elizabeth Pomada, 1029 Jones St., San Francisco, Calif. 94109. *Office:* 4321 Fifth Ave. S., Birmingham, Ala. 35214.

CAREER: Loveman's Department Store, Birmingham, Ala., in advertising, 1974-75; B. Dalton Booksellers, Birmingham, in advertising, 1976; *Birmingham Post-Herald,* Birmingham, copy editor, 1976—.

WRITINGS—Horror novels; all published by Avon: *Baal* 1978; *Diana's Daughters,* 1979; *The Hungry,* 1980. Contributor to local newspapers.

WORK IN PROGRESS: The Night-Boat, a horror novel for Avon.

SIDELIGHTS: McCammon comments: "I'm interested in fear: the things that go bump in the night, that leer from the realm of dreams, that slither behind our backs on the stairway when we're not looking. Why? Because probing the counterfeit fears, the fun fears, can tell us a lot about how we tick and define the things that really make us afraid. Horror fiction is one of the oldest of literary forms—if not the oldest—and it relates to the psychology of man as surely as our dreams relate to our waking hours. Nothing makes me feel better than getting a good scare out of a novel, or putting a good scare into a novel."

*   *   *

McCARDLE, Dorothy   1904-1978

OBITUARY NOTICE: Born July 25, 1904, in Jonesboro, Tenn.; died November 1, 1978, in McLean, Va. Journalist. A Washington Post reporter, McCardle became known worldwide in the early 1970's when President Richard Nixon excluded her from White House social events to which she was assigned. She was forced to wait in the White House press room until she could obtain details from the other reporters. Although Nixon never explained the reason for McCardle's banishment, it was speculated that the president was perturbed with the Washington Post for its coverage of the Watergate break-in. Art Buchwald and other nationally syndicated columnists wrote about her plight and stories were sent overseas by wire. A reporter for over half a century, McCardle covered such major assignments as the kidnapping of the Lindbergh baby and the explosion of the Hindenburg airship. She also contributed articles to the Saturday Review of Literature and McCall's magazine. Obituaries and other sources: Who's Who in America, 40th edition, Marquis, 1974; Washington Post, November 3, 1978; Newsweek, November 13, 1978.

*   *   *

McCLURE, Hal   1921-

PERSONAL: Born March 9, 1921, in Indianapolis, Ind.; son of Harold Alonzo (an engineer) and Betty (Hays) McClure; married Dorothea Millar (a secretary), January 15, 1949. Education: Los Angeles City College, A.A., 1941. Home address: P.O. Box 213, San Marcos, Calif. 92069. Agent: Foley Agency, 34 East 38th St., New York, N.Y. 10016.

CAREER: Reporter and editor for various California newspapers, 1948-56; Associated Press, newsman with Los Angeles bureau, 1956-58, and New York bureau, 1959-60, foreign correspondent in Far East, 1961-62, chief of bureau for Turkey, Cyprus, and Israel, 1962-67, chief of Israel bureau, 1967-76, chief of New Jersey bureau, 1976-77; Seton Hall University, South Orange, N.J., instructor in journalism, 1977; owner and head of Hal McClure Productions (production company of travel-adventure films). Military service: U.S. Air Force, 1942-48; pilot and instructor; became captain. Member: International Motion Picture and Lecturers Association, International Travel-Adventure Film Guild, American Film Institute, Mystery Writers of America, Middle East Institute, Sigma Delta Chi. Awards, honors: Ogden Reid fellowship for study in North Africa and the Middle East, 1959.

WRITINGS: (Contributor) Lightning Out of Israel, Associated Press, 1967; (English editor) Fire Over Suez, Schocken Books, 1970. Senior editor, Performer.

WORK IN PROGRESS: A mystery novel, The Cutout Man; two films, "The Gates of Jerusalem" and "Jordan the Desert Kingdom."

McCORDUCK, Pamela   1940-

PERSONAL: Born October 27, 1940, in Liverpool, England; came to the United States in 1946, naturalized citizen, 1955; daughter of William John and Hilda May (Bond) McCorduck; married Joseph E. Traub (a professor of computer science), December 6, 1969. Education: University of California, Berkeley, A.B., 1961; Columbia University, M.F.A., 1970. Home: 5391 Northumberland, Pittsburgh, Pa. 15217. Agent: Al Hart, Fox Chase Agency, 419 East 57th St., New York, N.Y. 10022. Office: Department of English, University of Pittsburgh, Pittsburgh, Pa. 15260.

CAREER: University of California, Berkeley, textbook assistant, 1961-63; Athena Beauty Colleges, Berkeley, business manager, 1963-65; Stanford University, Computation Center, Stanford, Calif., staff assistant and technical writer, 1965-67; Seattle Community College, Seattle, Wash., instructor in English, 1971-72; University of Pittsburgh, Pittsburgh, Pa., assistant professor of English, 1972—. Director of Allegheny County Women's Political Caucus, 1973-75. Public lecturer. Member: Modern Language Association of America, American Association of University Professors, Feminist Writers Guild. Awards, honors: Yaddo Foundation fellowship, 1972; grants from Massachusetts Institute of Technology, 1974-76, Carnegie-Mellon University, 1974-76, and National Humanities Faculty, 1976-77.

WRITINGS: Familiar Relations (novel), M. Joseph, 1971; Working to the End (novel), M. Joseph, 1972; (contributor) J. W. Sire, editor, How to Read Slowly, Inter-Varsity Press, 1978; Machines Who Think: A Personal Inquiry Into the History and Prospects of Artificial Intelligence, W. H. Freeman, 1979. Contributor of numerous articles to education journals and newspapers.

WORK IN PROGRESS: Two novels, one entitled Three Rivers; a book on fear; short stories.

SIDELIGHTS: Pamela McCorduck writes: "My aim is always to make connections, to see the similarities in apparently disparate human endeavors. Though I think of myself primarily as a fiction writer, two major themes recur in my writing: women in society, and the great intellectual adventure of the twentieth-century science. This latter led to my third book, about computers which, by human standards, behave intelligently. I aimed to show that science is as much a part of our cultural heritage as literature is, that, indeed, the two are intimately interwoven. But then I don't like ghettos of any kind, which accounts for my militant feminism. I expect these themes will continue to dominate my writing for a long time to come."

McCorduck has made several television appearances.

*   *   *

McCOY, Kathleen   1945-
(Kathy McCoy, Kaylin McCoy)

PERSONAL: Born April 25, 1945, in Dayton, Ohio; daughter of James Lyons (an engineer) and Caron (a nurse; maiden name, Curtis) McCoy; married Robert Miles Stover (a production manager), May 28, 1977. Education: Northwestern University, B.S., 1967, M.S., 1968. Home and office: 439 West Stocker St., #312, Glendale, Calif. 91202. Agent: Susan Ann Protter, 156 East 52nd St., New York, N.Y. 10022.

CAREER: Free-lance writer, 1965-68; 'Teen magazine, Los Angeles, Calif., feature editor, 1968-77; free-lance writer, 1977—. Actress, using stage name Kaylin McCoy, 1968—. Adjunct member of faculty at Antioch College (West), 1973; guest lecturer at California State University, Los Angeles,

1974. Guest on radio and television talk shows. *Member:* American Guild of Variety Artists, Society of Professional Journalists, Women in Communications (central area representative, 1975-76), Screen Actors Guild. *Awards, honors:* Eddie Award from Western Magazine Association, 1975, for a sex-education/body awareness article in *'Teen.*

WRITINGS—All under name Kathy McCoy: *Discover Yourself* (juvenile), Petersen, 1976; (contributor) Judith D. Houghton, Bonnie Piedmonte, and Judy Thomas, editors, *Make the Good Things Happen,* Abelard, 1976; *Discover Yourself II* (juvenile), Petersen, 1978; (with Charles Wibbelsman) *The Teenage Body Book,* Pocket Books, 1979. Author of educational scripts for Walt Disney Studio. Contributor to *Clinical Child Psychology* and *TV Guide.* Contributing editor of *'Teen,* 1978.

WORK IN PROGRESS: A novel, *The Twelve Days of Christmas,* set in Vietnam; *Marriage Shock,* nonfiction.

SIDELIGHTS: Kathleen McCoy writes: "My primary orientation as a writer is in the areas of health maintenance and psychological self-help. A look at my early background explains some of this interest. I had polio as a child and spent most of the elementary school years in hospitals and at home, isolated from my peers. I returned to school a shy and awkward adolescent with two passionate interests: acting and writing. I felt most confident on the stage when I could become someone else, if only for a few moments. Naturally, I thought that acting would be my primary vocation. I did study theatre in college, but my father insisted that I major in journalism so that I would have 'a steady, sensible career' once my infatuation with show business waned.

"I pursued both careers professionally for several years and enjoyed both, but as time went on, I found that writing is my first love. Beginning as I did in the teen market, I began to realize that there are so many young people who are troubled, lonely, shy, awkward, or otherwise in need of compassionate, non-judgmental information about their feelings, options, physical and mental health. Memories of my own painful, troubled youth have helped me to write to this audience with compassion and understanding. I feel a deep commitment to help people who are in pain, and great joy in being able to offer support and ideas to young people struggling to help themselves."

*   *   *

McCOY, Kathy
See McCOY, Kathleen

*   *   *

McCOY, Kaylin
See McCoy, Kathleen

*   *   *

McCOY, Ronald   1947-

PERSONAL: Born August 12, 1947, in Abington, Pa.; son of Tim (an actor, ethnologist, and writer) and Inga (a newspaper columnist; maiden name, Arvad) McCoy; married Elizabeth Borland, December 29, 1976. *Education:* Arizona State University, B.S., 1971. *Politics:* "As little as possible since working for Nixon." *Religion:* "Complex and personal." *Residence:* Nogales, Ariz.

CAREER: Free-lance writer. Has worked as circus clown, meat cutter, turquoise dealer, and substitute teacher.

WRITINGS: (With father, Tim McCoy) *Tim McCoy Remembers the West,* Doubleday, 1977.

WORK IN PROGRESS: The Buffalo Stone, North American Indian legends, with father, Tim McCoy; research for a historical novel about the fight of the Northern Plains Indians to save their homelands.

SIDELIGHTS: McCoy comments: "I am intrigued by any people or peoples confronted with degrees of change unprecedented in their experience. In such a situation there is gallantry, sadness, desperation, optimism, and an underpinning notion that, somehow, there is a 'message' to be gotten across. This is what interests me."

*   *   *

McCOY, Tim(othy John Fitzgerald)   1891-1978

PERSONAL: Born April 10, 1891, in Saginaw, Mich.; son of Timothy Henry (a police chief) and Cathrine (Fitzpatrick) McCoy; married Agnes Miller (divorced, 1932); married Inga Arvad (a newspaper columnist), February 14, 1946 (died, 1973); children: Gerald Miller, Marguritte McCoy Dudley-Smith, D'Arcy Miller, Terrence, Ronald. *Education:* Attended St. Ignatius College, 1908-09.

CAREER: State adjutant general, Wyoming, Cheyenne, 1918-21; film star (including roles in "The Thundering Herd," "War Paint," "Below the Border," "Ghost Town Law," and "West of the Law"), 1926-42; performed in Ringling Brothers Barnum & Bailey Circus tours during the 1930's; participant in personal appearance tours, 1956-74. *Military service:* U.S. Army, Cavalry; U.S. Army Air Forces; became colonel; received Bronze Star and Legion of Honor. *Awards, honors:* Inducted into National Cowboy Hall of Fame, 1974; Buffalo Bill Western Heritage Award from Nebraskaland Days, 1977; Emmy award for "The Tim McCoy Show."

WRITINGS: (With son, Ronald McCoy) *Tim McCoy Remembers the West,* Doubleday, 1977.

Author of "Injun Talk," a documentary film on Plains Indian sign language.

WORK IN PROGRESS: The Buffalo Stone, on American Indian myths, legends, and stories, with son, Ronald McCoy.

SIDELIGHTS: McCoy wrote, just before his death: "I consider myself fortunate in that there is nothing I ever wanted to be or do that I have not been or done. The most significant factor in my entire life was my association as a young cowboy with the last of the buffalo-hunting Indians of the Great plains; old warriors who had lived in tepees, counted coups, fought for their homes and, most important, understood the world. I knew them not as an anthropologist would, as subjects to be studied. I knew them, rather, as friends."

BIOGRAPHICAL/CRITICAL SOURCES: William K. Everson, *A Picture History of the Western Film,* Citadel, 1969; James Horowitz, *They Went Thataway,* Citadel, 1969; Jon Tuska, *The Filming of the West,* Doubleday, 1975; *American Heritage,* Volume XXVIII, number 4. *Obituaries: New York Times,* January 31, 1978.*

(Died January 29, 1978, in Nogales, Ariz.)

*   *   *

McCULLOUGH, Colleen

PERSONAL: Born in Wellington, New South Wales, Australia; came to United States. *Education:* Attended University of Sydney. *Office:* c/o Harper & Row, Ten East 53rd St., New York, N.Y. 10022.

CAREER: Worked as a teacher in Australia's Outback, as a library worker, and as a journalist; Yale University, School of Internal Medicine, New Haven, Conn., associate in research neurology department, 1967-76; writer, 1976—.

WRITINGS—Novels: *Tim,* Harper, 1974; *The Thorn Birds* (Literary Guild selection), Harper, 1977.

WORK IN PROGRESS: A cookbook of traditional Australian recipes, with Jean Easthope; a war novel; a contemporary novel.

SIDELIGHTS: McCullough's three-generation, 280,000 word saga, *The Thorn Birds,* has been described as an Australian *Gone With the Wind.* Indeed, the character who has received the most critical and popular attention, the uncelibate priest Ralph de Bricassart, was called "one of the greatest fictional males since Rhett Butler," by Robert D. Hale.

The book, which is set largely on an Australian sheep ranch and chronicles the lives of members of the Cleary family from 1915 to 1969, satisfies the need for "predictability in our popular escape fiction," according to Christopher Lehmann-Haupt. It is nothing, he continued, "if not good old fashioned story-telling."

The faults of the book are its "stock characters, plot contrivances, and so forth," Alice K. Turner commented. "But to dismiss it would also be wrong. On its own terms, it is a fine, long, absorbing, popular book. It offers the best heart-throb since Rhett Butler, plenty of exotic color, plenty of Tolstoyan unhappiness and a good deal of connivance and action. Of its kind, it's an honest book."

Amanda Heller declared the book "awesomely bad," but added that, "to its credit, *The Thorn Birds* is as easy to absorb as an hour of 'The Bionic Woman' and as addictive as popcorn." Walter Clemons was similarly unimpressed with McCullough's literary accomplishments, while noting that the book does offer "big simplified emotions, startling coincidences and thumping hammer blows of fate."

A more positive assessment of the novel was made by Webster Schott. He wrote: "While Miss McCullough's vocabulary isn't any wider than her reservoir of ideas, her memories of Australia and her imagination never run dry. She reads easily. Her characters are credible, if interchangeable. She writes as if to improve on life. And if we read fiction to fill the boring spaces left by reality, then *The Thorn Birds* fits our need. It runs like a dream factory."

The author herself has no pretentions to artistry. "I think of myself as a glorified typist who pounds along, chasing my characters to find out what happens," McCullough told Fred Hauptfuhrer. On her best evening, she typed 30,000 words.

In hardcover, the book has sold over one-half million copies. The paperback rights were sold to Avon for $1.9 million, the highest price ever paid for paperback rights to a book. Warner Brothers has purchased the film rights. The book will be translated into fifteen languages.

BIOGRAPHICAL/CRITICAL SOURCES: Publisher's Weekly, March 7, 1977; *People,* March 14, 1977; *Village Voice,* March 28, 1977; *Saturday Review,* April 16, 1977; *Book World,* April 24, 1977; *Newsweek,* April 25, 1977; *New York Times,* May 2, 1977; *New York Times Book Review,* May 8, 1977, September 18, 1977; *Time,* May 9, 1977; *Atlantic,* June, 1977; *Detroit News,* July 22, 1977.

*   *   *

McCULLY, Helen   1902(?)-1977

PERSONAL: Born in Amherst, Nova Scotia, Canada.

Education: Educated in Canada. *Home:* 414 East 52nd St., New York, N.Y.

CAREER: Editor and writer. Former advertising copywriter at Lord & Taylor, New York City; Bloomingdale's, New York City, food editor, 1947-60; *House Beautiful,* New York City, columnist and food editor, 1968-77.

WRITINGS: (With Eleanor Noderer) *Just Desserts,* Obolensky, 1961; (with Dorothy Crayder) *The Christmas Pony,* Bobbs-Merrill, 1967; *Nobody Ever Tells You These Things About Food and Drink,* Holt, 1967; (with William North Jayme and Jacques Pepin) *The Other Half of the Egg; or, 180 Ways to Use Up Extra Yolk or White,* Barrows, 1967; (editor with Noderer) *The American Heritage Cookbook,* American Heritage Press, 1969; *Cooking With Helen McCully Beside You,* Random House, 1970; *Roasted and Braised Dishes,* Doubleday, 1972; *Things You've Always Wanted to Know About Food and Drink,* Holt, 1972; *Waste Not Want Not,* Random House, 1975.

SIDELIGHTS: Helen McCully, born to a prominent family, was honored in her hometown for her successful achievements. She was an ambitious energetic woman, and one of the world's best known food editors and authors of cookbooks. McCully was highly respected by her friends and colleagues for her professionalism.

OBITUARIES: New York Times, August 25, 1977; *AB Bookman's Weekly,* October 7, 1977.*

(Died August 24, 1977, in New York, N.Y.)

*   *   *

McCURDY, Howard E(arl)   1941-

PERSONAL: Born December 18, 1941, in Atascadero, Calif.; son of Howard E. (a chemist) and Jo (an office manager; maiden name, Test) McCurdy; married Margaret M. Hurley (a teacher), June 27, 1970. *Education:* Attended Oregon State University, 1959-61; University of Washington, Seattle, B.A., 1962, M.A., 1965; Cornell University, Ph.D., 1969. *Residence:* Brookmont, Md. 20016. *Office:* School of Government and Public Administration, American University, Washington, D.C. 20016.

CAREER: American University, Washington, D.C., assistant professor, 1968-72, associate professor, 1972-78, professor of public administration, 1978, director of public administration, 1976—, director of key executive program, 1978—. Conductor of study on administration of national park system in Kenya, 1975; Fulbright-Hays lecturer in management and public administration at University of Zambia, 1978. *Member:* American Society for Public Administration.

WRITINGS: Public Administration: A Bibliography, College of Public Affairs, American University, 1972; *An Insider's Guide to the Capitol,* College of Public Affairs, American University, 1977; *Public Administration: A Synthesis,* Cummings, 1977. Contributor to business and public administration journals.

WORK IN PROGRESS: Gathering materials on teaching public administration and the different approaches to management used in government agencies.

SIDELIGHTS: McCurdy told *CA:* "I would like to see my professional colleagues break away from their conventional views of public administration as policy-making, staffing, and budgeting and acquire a broader view of the types of management problems encountered in government agencies and the fields of study that contribute strategies to these problems.

"The generalist approach to public administration is going to be outstripped by the contributions made by more technical and sophisticated fields of study and we had better be prepared to absorb these contributions into our profession or face the prospect of losing our relevance in the eyes of students and public managers."

*   *   *

McDANIEL, Walton Brooks   1871-1978

OBITUARY NOTICE—See index for CA sketch: Born March 4, 1871, in Cambridge, Mass.; died September 16, 1978, in Camden, N.J. Educator, author, and expert in the field of ancient Roman culture. He wrote Roman Private Life and Its Survivals and Riding a Hobby in the Classical Lands. As an educator, McDaniel counted Thornton Wilder, Ezra Pound, and Franklin Delano Roosevelt among his students. He was also Harvard's oldest alumnus. Obituaries and other sources: Washington Post, September 20, 1978.

*   *   *

McDARRAH, Fred W(illiam)   1926-

PERSONAL: Born November 5, 1926, in Brooklyn, N.Y.; son of Howard Arthur and Elizabeth (Swahn) McDarrah; married Gloria Schoffel, November 5, 1960; children: Timothy Swann, Patrick James. Education: New York University, B.A., 1954. Home: 505 LaGuardia Pl., New York, N.Y. 10012. Office: 80 University Pl., New York, N.Y. 10003.

CAREER: Writer and photojournalist. Worked for advertising and publishing firms during 1950's; Village Voice, New York, N.Y., staff photographer, 1958-71, picture editor, 1971—. Photographs have been exhibited at galleries and museums, including Soho Photo Gallery, 1973, Whitney Museum, 1974, and Dallas Museum, 1974. Military service: U.S. Army, paratrooper, 1944-47; became staff sergeant. Member: American Society of Magazine Photographers, Authors Guild, American Society of Photographers in Communication. Awards, honors: Awards from New York Press Association, 1964, 1965, 1967, 1968, 1970, all for spot news photography, 1965 and 1967, both for feature photography, and 1969 and 1970, both for picture stories; first place awards from National Newspaper Association, 1966, for best pictorial series, and 1971, for spot news photography; Page One Award from New York Newspaper Guild, 1971, for best spot news photography; John Simon Guggenheim Memorial Foundation Award, 1972; second place for Edward Steichen Memorial Award in newspaper photography, 1976.

WRITINGS—All as photographer: (With others) The Beat Scene, Corinth Books, 1960; (with wife, Gloria Schoffel McDarrah) The Artist's World in Pictures, Dutton, 1961; Greenwich Village, Corinth Books, 1963; New York, New York: A Photographic Tour of Manhattan Island From Battery Park to Spuyten Duyvil, Corinth Books, 1964; (with John Gruen) The New Bohemia, Shorecrest, 1966; Museums in New York, Dutton, 1967, revised edition, Quick Fox, 1978; (with James J. Young) Guide for Ecumenical Discussion, Paulist Press, 1970; Photography Marketplace (reference), Bowker, 1975, revised edition, 1977; Stock Photo and Assignment Sourcebook (reference), Bowker, 1977. Contributor of articles and picture stories to periodicals, including Art News, Cosmopolitan, Esquire, Newsweek, Playboy, Time, and many others. Editor of Executive Desk Diary for Saturday Review, 1962-64.

McDarrah also published a book, Sculpture in Environment, for New York City Parks Department in 1967.

BIOGRAPHICAL/CRITICAL SOURCES: Time, February 15, 1960; Cue, March 5, 1960; New York Times Magazine, April 17, 1960; Village Voice, May 14, 1970; Camera 35, November, 1972.

*   *   *

McDONALD, Archie P(hilip)   1935-

PERSONAL: Born November 29, 1935, in Beaumont, Tex.; married Judith Barrett (a city commissioner), December 21, 1957; children: Tucker Barrett, Christopher Lee. Education: Lamar University, B.S., 1958; Rice University, M.A., 1960; Louisiana State University, Ph.D., 1965. Religion: Baptist. Home: 1615 Redbud, Nacogdoches, Tex. 75961. Office: Department of History, Stephen F. Austin State University, Nacogdoches, Tex. 75961.

CAREER: Murray State University, Murray, Ky., assistant professor of history, 1963-64; Stephen F. Austin State University, Nacogdoches, Tex., assistant professor, 1964-67, associate professor, 1967-72, professor of history, 1972—, Alumni Distinguished Professor, 1976. Visiting professor at Central Washington State College, 1970. Member of Nacogdoches County Historical Survey Committee, 1971—, head of committee, 1971. Public speaker. Member: Southern Historical Association, Texas State Historical Association (member of executive council, 1975-78), Texas Lodge of Research, Texas Folklore Society, Louisiana Historical Association, East Texas Historical Association, Confederate Historical Society (London), Phi Alpha Theta. Awards, honors: National Endowment for the Humanities younger humanist grant, 1971, 1979; Kempner Grant from Kempner Foundation, 1971; Tenneco Grant from Tenneco Foundation, 1972.

WRITINGS: By Early Candelight: The Story of Old Milam, Masonic Home Press, 1967; Hurrah for Texas!: The Diary of Adolphus Sterne, Texian Press, 1969; The Mexican War: Crisis for American Democracy, Heath, 1969; Fighting Men: The Western Military Heritage, Kendall-Hunt, 1970; Make Me a Map of the Valley: The Journal of Jedediah Hotchkiss, 1862-1865, Southern Methodist University Press, 1974; Recollections of a Long Life, Blue & Gray Press, 1974; First United Methodist Church, San Augustine, Texas, 1837-1976, Henington Publishing Co., 1976; Travis, Pemberton Press, 1977; (editor) An East Texas Anthology, Pemberton Press, 1978. Contributor of about fifty articles and reviews to southern history and military journals and newspapers.

WORK IN PROGRESS: Editing The Inaugural Addresses of Texas Governors, Texas State Library, 1979; a biography of Jedediah Hotchkiss; research on the oil industry's first texas well.

SIDELIGHTS: McDonald writes: "As a native Texan and Southerner, I have naturally gravitated to those subjects in historical studies. I am a humanist, in that I believe man the motivating factor of earthly progress, and I believe in hard work."

AVOCATIONAL INTERESTS: Music (choir), gardening.

*   *   *

McDOUGALL, Donald   1907-

PERSONAL: Born October 11, 1907, in Glasgow, Scotland; son of Alexander (an engineer) and Marion (Gilmour) McDougall; married Williamina Henney, June 6, 1933; children: Alisin Marion. Education: Attended private academy in Broughty Ferry, Scotland. Politics: Labour. Religion:

Protestant. *Home:* 40 Dundee St., Carnoustie, Angus, Scotland. *Agent:* Patricia Falk Feeley, 52 Vanderbilt Ave., New York, N.Y. 10017.

CAREER: Worked as retail shop manager from depression until 1939; factory worker during World War II; traveler for engineering supply firm, 1947-51; director for engineering firm, 1951-62; retailer for sports firm, 1962-77; writer. *Military service:* Royal Air Force, Royal Observer Corps., 1944-70; became chief observer.

WRITINGS: Davie (novel), St. Martin's, 1977; *Boswell and Son* (novel), St. Martin's, 1978. Author of "A Logan Bridge Log," a radio play, aired by British Broadcasting Corp. (BBC), 1950. Contributor to stories and articles to Scottish journals.

WORK IN PROGRESS: Crombie's Lass, a sequel to *Davie; Barney Baxter,* a novel set in present-day Glasgow and the highlands; *The Rainbow Days,* sketches from boyhood.

SIDELIGHTS: McDougall writes: "I was a late developer. I didn't start writing till I was nearly fifty, but I love writing above all things. A good piece of work is my greatest satisfaction. My two books were written years ago, and gathered dust till my agent got them. I have another half-dozen novels in mind, and hope I live long enough to write them—even if they're never published."

AVOCATIONAL INTERESTS: Painting (water colors and acrylics), "touring by car in remote parts of Ireland, England, and the Scottish highlands."

* * *

McFARLANE, Bruce John 1936-

PERSONAL: Born July 1, 1936, in Mudgee, New South Wales, Australia; son of William (a pharmacist) and Iris (Jeffrey) McFarlane. *Education:* University of Sydney, B.Econ. (honors), 1956, M.Econ., 1961. *Politics:* Socialist. *Home:* 12 Park Rd., Kensington Park, South Australia 5068, Australia.

CAREER: University of Queensland, Brisbane, Australia, lecturer in economic development, 1961-62; Australian National University, Canberra, research fellow and senior lecturer in economic policy, 1963-72; University of Adelaide, Adelaide, Australia, reader in politics, 1972-76, professor of politics, 1976—. Consultant to Indian Planning Commission, 1959-60.

WRITINGS: (With M. Gough) *Queensland: Industrial Enigma,* Melbourne University Press, 1964; *Economic Policy in Australia,* F. W. Cheshire, 1968; *The Chinese Road to Socialism,* Penguin, 1971; *Tweedledum to Tweedledee,* ANZ Book Co., 1973.

WORK IN PROGRESS: Marx as an Economist, for Penguin.

SIDELIGHTS: McFarlane told *CA:* "Most of the writings listed have been based on extensive periods of research and living in the Communist bloc countries: Yugoslavia (two years); U.S.S.R. (one-half year); Poland (one-half year); as well as China (one-half year) and India (one year). The aim has been to bring into the analysis the peculiarities of the societies involved, and the goals they have set for themselves, rather than being judgmental through a prism of Western economic and political theory."

* * *

McFEE, June King 1917-

PERSONAL: Born June 3, 1917, in Seattle, Wash.; daughter of L. P. (a lawyer) and Betty (a musician; maiden name, Smith) King; married Malcolm McFee (an anthropologist), September 27, 1941; children: John King. *Education:* Attended Whitman College, 1935-37; University of Washington, Seattle, B.A., 1939; Central Washington College, M.Ed., 1954; Stanford University, Ed.D., 1957. *Home:* 2375 Bailey Hill Rd., Eugene, Ore. 97402. *Office:* Department of Art Education, School of Architecture and Allied Arts, University of Oregon, Eugene, Ore. 97403.

CAREER: Yakima Valley Junior College, Yakima, Wash., instructor in art education, 1952-54; Stanford University, Stanford, Calif., assistant professor of art education, 1955-63; Arizona State University, Flagstaff, visiting associate professor of art education, 1964-65; University of Oregon, Eugene, associate professor, 1965-71, professor of art education and education, 1971—, head of department of art education, 1977—, director of Institute for Community Art Studies. Visiting faculty member at colleges and universities all over the United States and Canada. Work exhibited in Seattle and Stanford. Consultant to National Park Service.

MEMBER: National Art Education Association (member of national board of directors; president of Pacific region), Seminar for Research in Art Education.

WRITINGS: Preparation for Art, Wadsworth, 1961, 2nd edition, 1970; (contributor) Elliot W. Eisner and David W. Ecker, editors, *Readings in Art Education,* Blaisdell, 1966; (editor) *Oregon Communities: Visual Quality and Economic Growth,* Institute for Community Art Studies, University of Oregon, 1968; (contributor) Raymond V. Wiman and Wesley C. Meierhenry, editors, *Educational Media: Theory Into Practice,* C. E. Merrill, 1969; (contributor) George Pappas, editor, *Concepts in Art and Education: An Anthology of Current Issues,* Macmillan, 1970; (with Rogena Degge) *Art Culture and Environment: A Catalyst for Teaching,* Wadsworth, 1977; (editor) *Elementary Art Education,* Oregon State Department of Education, 1977. Also contributor to 9th yearbook of National Art Education Association and to 64th yearbook of National Society for the Study of Education. Contributor to numerous periodicals, including *Everyday Art, Art Education, Studies in Art Education,* and *The Instructor.*

SIDELIGHTS: McFee told *CA:* "We must help school decision-makers recognize that designed objects have as great an impact on peoples lives as what they read. The design of everything in the day from toothbrushes to bed linens, from food packaging, clothing, furnishings, cars, city and street design, to mass media advertising, films and television, are all designed to influence peoples concepts of themselves, their ideas about others, the quality of their lives, and their hopes and aspirations.

"This is only one aspect of art that influences people—but it is the most pervasive. For this reason learning to read the ways design is used to communicate ideas and impressions is as important as learning how words convey ideas.

"Everyone needs to be a designer in a world shrinking in the relation of space to people, and in the supply of basic resources. Our responsibility for what we do to other environments becomes more acute as space and resources decrease. Short supplies require we all become more creative in reusing and redesigning the resources that are left.

"Good design comes when the qualities of art are used to serve the needs of people. People who can draw have learned to see and analyze the essential nature of their environment. Thus art education should be a part of the basic skills taught in any educational program."

McGRAW, Walter John, Jr. 1919(?)-1978

OBITUARY NOTICE: Born c. 1919, in Boston Mass.; died November 18, 1978, in New York, N.Y. Director, producer, and writer known primarily for his contributions to radio. Early in his career McGraw wrote and directed a series of documentaries for Columbia Broadcasting System (CBS-Radio) and National Broadcasting Corp. (NBC-Radio). He was producer of screenplays, including "New York Confidential," and worked more recently as a free-lance writer. McGraw wrote *Prison Riots* with his wife, Peg McGraw, and *The World of the Paranormal.* Obituaries and other sources: *New York Times,* November 22, 1978.

* * *

McINTYRE, Vonda N(eel) 1948-

PERSONAL: Born August 28, 1948, in Louisville, Ky.; daughter of H. Neel (an electrical engineer) and Vonda Kieth (a volunteer worker) McIntyre. *Education:* University of Washington, Seattle, B.S., 1970, graduate study, 1970-71. *Home:* 4121 Interlake N., Seattle, Wash. 98103. *Agent:* Frances Collin, Marie Rodell-Frances Collin Literary Agency, 141 East 55th St., New York, N.Y. 10022.

CAREER: Writer, 1969—. *Member:* Authors Guild of Authors League of America, Science Fiction Writers of America, National Organization for Women, Cousteau Society. *Awards, honors:* Nebula Award from Science Fiction Writers of America, 1973, for best science fiction novelette, "Of Mist, and Grass, and Sand."

WRITINGS: The Exile Waiting (science fiction novel), Fawcett, 1975; (editor with Susan Janice Anderson) *Aurora: Beyond Equality,* Fawcett, 1976; *Dreamsnake* (science fiction novel), Houghton, 1978. Contributor to science fiction magazines, including *Analog.*

WORK IN PROGRESS: Two novels.

SIDELIGHTS: Vonda McIntyre writes: "I write science fiction because its boundaries are the only ones wide enough for me to explore experiences people have not had—*yet*; and because it allows my characters to develop as far as their abilities will take them, unlimited by the crippling demands and unambitious expectations our society puts on us."

BIOGRAPHICAL/CRITICAL SOURCES: Pacific Northwest Review of Books, June, 1978.

* * *

McKAY, Derek 1942-

PERSONAL: Born February 2, 1942, in Altrincham, Cheshire, England; son of Konrad (a farm worker) and Ada (Landsborough) Kirby; married Frances Raymond (a junior high school teacher), December 28, 1963; children: Louise, Katharine. *Education:* London School of Economics and Political Science, B.A., 1963, Ph.D., 1971. *Office:* Department of International History, London School of Economics and Political Science, University of London, Houghton St., London W.C.2, England.

CAREER: University of York, York, England, lecturer in history, 1965-68; University of London, London School of Economics and Political Science, London, England, lecturer, 1968-78, senior lecturer in international history, 1978—.

WRITINGS: Prince Eugene of Savoy, Thames & Hudson, 1977; *War and Society in the Seventeenth and Eighteenth Centuries,* Fontana, in press.

WORK IN PROGRESS: History of the Austrian Monarchy, 1526-1918, publication by Longman expected in 1982; a history of the foreign policy of George I, 1714-27.

SIDELIGHTS: McKay writes: "I have been trained primarily as a diplomatic historian and am now trying to broaden my whole approach to history. This is not easy, given the present financial restraints on research abroad. I write slowly and painfully but try to keep in mind the adage of my friend and ex-teacher R. Halton: 'The better is the enemy of the good.'"

* * *

McKENNA, A. Daniel
See FINNERTY, Adam Daniel

* * *

McKENNA, George 1937-

PERSONAL: Born March 2, 1937, in Chicago, Ill.; son of Robert Emmet (a steel mill worker) and Helen (Norton) McKenna; married Sylvia Iafolla, August 29, 1964; children: Laura, Maria, Christopher. *Education:* Attended University of Illinois at Chicago Circle, 1955-57, University of Chicago, 1957-59, University of Massachusetts, 1959-60, and Fordham University, 1961-66. *Home:* 162 Newcombe Rd., Tenafly, N.J. 07670. *Office:* City College of the City University of New York, New York, N.Y. 10031.

CAREER: Associated with City College of the City University of New York, New York, N.Y.

WRITINGS: (Editor and contributor) *American Populism,* Putnam, 1974; *American Politics: Ideals and Realities,* McGraw, 1976; (editor with Stanley Feingold) *Taking Sides,* Dushkin, 1978.

WORK IN PROGRESS: Research on politics and religion.

SIDELIGHTS: McKenna writes: "My motivation flows in some measure from fear of having to return advances."

* * *

McLANATHAN, Richard 1916-

PERSONAL: Born March 12, 1916, in Methuen, Mass.; son of Frank Watson (in business) and Helen (a pianist; maiden name, Kennedy) McLanathan; married Jane Fuller, 1942. *Education:* Harvard University, A.B., 1938, Ph.D., 1951. *Home:* 2737 Devonshire Pl. N.W., Washington, D.C. 20008. *Agent:* McIntosh & Otis, Inc., 475 Fifth Ave., New York, N.Y. 10017.

CAREER: Teacher of English and history at private school in New York, N.Y., 1938-43, head of Lower School, 1941-43; Museum of Fine Arts, Boston, Mass., assistant curator of paintings, 1946-48, secretary of museum and host of its television program, "Open House at the Museum," 1952-56, editor of museum publications, 1952-57, associate curator of sculpture and decorative arts, 1954, curator, 1954-57; Munson-Williams-Proctor Institute, Utica, N.Y., director of Museum of Art, 1957-62; writer, lecturer, and consultant, 1963-76; American Association of Museums, Washington, D.C., director, 1976-78; writer, lecturer, and consultant, 1978—. Faculty member at Harvard University, 1952-56; lecturer at schools, colleges, and museums. American specialist for U.S. Department of State in West Germany, Poland, and Denmark, 1959, and Yugoslavia, 1961; curator of art exhibit for American National Exhibition in Moscow, 1959. Presented "Looking at Art" on WQXR-Radio; guest on television and radio programs. Member of Society of Fellows, Harvard University, 1943-46; member of executive committee and board of trustees of Boston Arts Festival, 1951-59; member of New York State Council on the Arts, 1960-64; consultant to International Business Machines, Xerox, and National Gallery.

AWARDS, HONORS: Prix de Rome and senior fellow at American Academy in Rome, 1948; distinguished service award from U.S. Information Agency, 1959, for Moscow art exhibit; Rockefeller senior fellow at Metropolitan Museum of Art, 1976.

WRITINGS: (Editor) Agnes Baldwin Bratt, *Classical Coins,* Museum of Fine Arts (Boston, Mass.), 1949; (with John I. H. Baur and others) *The M. and M. Karolik Collection of American Paintings, 1815-1865,* Museum of Fine Arts, 1949; *Art Across America,* Museum of Art (Utica, N.Y.), 1960; *Images of the Universe: Leonardo da Vinci, the Artist as Scientist,* Doubleday, 1966; *The Pageant of Medieval Art and Life,* Westminster, 1966; (contributor) Warren Weaver, editor, *U.S. Philanthropic Foundations,* Harper, 1967; *The American Tradition in the Arts,* Harcourt, 1968; *A Guide to Civilisation: The Kenneth Clark Films on the Cultural Life of Western Man,* Time-Life, 1970; *The Brandywine Heritage,* New York Graphic Society, 1971; *Art in America: A Brief History,* Harcourt, 1973; *The Art of Marguerite Stix,* Abrams, 1977; *East Building, National Gallery of Art: A Profile,* National Gallery of Art, 1978. Advisory editor for *The Great Contemporary Issues: The Arts.* Contributor to *Encyclopedia of World Art* and *Encyclopaedia Britannica;* also contributor to journals of the arts. Decorative arts editor of *Webster's Unabridged Dictionary;* consulting editor of *Art and Man,* 1969-73.

WORK IN PROGRESS: Research on poetry, medieval bridges, and American art and architecture.

SIDELIGHTS: McLanathan writes: "I have always been deeply interested in both the arts and education, and have been associated with art museums as curator, director, and trustee, as well as serving as a consultant on artistic and educational matters. I am pleased that three of my books have been used as textbooks, though none was written as such. After serving three years as director of the American Association of Museums, to rehabilitate it as a professional association, I am grateful to return to writing and consulting, and perhaps, hopefully, to teaching as well."

*   *   *

McLAURIN, Melton Alonza 1941-

PERSONAL: Born July 11, 1941, in Fayetteville, N.C.; son of A. Merrill (an insurance agent) and Thelma (Melton) McLaurin; married Sandra Cockrell (a teacher), November 23, 1961; children: Natasha Olivia, Shena Nicole. *Education:* East Carolina University, B.S., 1962, M.A., 1964; University of South Carolina, Ph.D., 1967. *Religion:* Unitarian-Universalist. *Home:* 6241 Teal St., Wilmington, N.C. 28403. *Office:* Department of History, University of North Carolina, Wilmington, N.C. 28403.

CAREER: University of South Alabama, Mobile, assistant professor, 1967-72, associate professor, 1972-76, professor of history, 1976-77; University of North Carolina, Wilmington, professor of history and chairman of history department, 1977—. *Member:* Organization of American Historians, Southern Historical Association, North Carolina Historical Society.

WRITINGS: Paternalism and Protest: Southern Cotton Mill Workers and Organized Labor, 1875-1905, Greenwood Press, 1971; (with Michael Thomason) *Mobile: American River City,* Easter Publishers, 1975; *The Knights of Labor in the South,* Greenwood Press, 1978. Contributor to *Phylon, Labor History, Southern Exposure, South Today, North Carolina Historical Review,* and *South Carolina Historical Magazine.*

WORK IN PROGRESS: A biography of Mobile civil rights leader John LeFlore; research on black-white political reform efforts of the nineteenth century.

SIDELIGHTS: McLaurin told *CA:* "My major motivation is to probe the past of the southern United States, the region in which I live. Some subjects which I feel need to be explored are the life of the southern Negro after slavery and before the second Reconstruction, the uses of photography in history, and the use of the photograph as a historical document."

*   *   *

McNAUGHTON, Frank 1906(?)-1978

OBITUARY NOTICE: Born c. 1906; died October 30, 1978, in Evanston, Ill. Journalist, businessman, and writer. McNaughton was a former panel member of the National Broadcasting Co. (NBC-TV) program "Meet the Press," and had been a reporter for United Press International (UPI). He later became chief congressional correspondent for *Time* and *Life* magazines, during which time he was responsible for nearly forty cover stories. McNaughton formed a consulting company in 1957 which he operated for eighteen years. He also acted as speech writer and publicity agent for Paul Douglas, late U.S. democratic senator from Illinois. Obituaries and other sources: *Chicago Tribune,* November 1, 1978.

*   *   *

McQUADE, De Rosset Morrissey 1934(?)-1978

OBITUARY NOTICE: Born c. 1934 in Rye, N.Y.; died October 23, 1978, in New York, N.Y. Journalist for *Life* Magazine who covered the White House from 1963 to 1970. Obituaries and other sources: *Washington Post,* October 26, 1978.

*   *   *

MEAD, Margaret 1901-1978

OBITUARY NOTICE—See index for *CA* sketch: Born December 16, 1901, in Philadelphia, Pa.; died November 15, 1978, in New York, N.Y. Educator, anthropologist, lecturer, and author of works in her field. Mead was known throughout the world as a humanitarian and expert in numerous categories, including family structure, mental health, ecology, and growth, change, and structure of culture. Although much of her life was spent researching foreign cultures, Mead was able to anticipate many of the changes in American culture by projecting data. She was also a prolific and diverse lecturer. During one year's time, she delivered 110 lectures on different topics, including alcoholism, architecture, drugs, family structure, health, environmental problems, and women's role in society. Among her more popular books are *Coming of Age in Samoa, The Study of Culture at a Distance, The Golden Age of American Anthropology,* and *Continuities in Cultural Evolution.* Obituaries and other sources: *Current Biography,* Wilson, 1940, 1951; *The Author's and Writer's Who's Who,* 6th edition, Burke's Peerage, 1971; *Authors of Books for Young People,* 2nd edition, Scarecrow, 1971; *The Writers Directory, 1976-78,* St. Martin's, 1976; *International Who's Who,* Europa, 1978; *Who's Who,* 130th edition, St. Martin's, 1978; *Chicago Tribune,* November 16, 1978; *New York Times,* November 16, 1978; *Washington Post,* November 16, 1978; *Publishers Weekly,* November 27, 1978; *Newsweek,* November 27, 1978; *Time,* November 27, 1978; *AB Bookman's Weekly,* December 4, 1978.

MEDVEDEV, Roy (Alexandrovich) 1925-

PERSONAL: Born November 14, 1925, in Tbilisi, U.S.S.R.; son of Alexander Romanovich (a philosopher) and Yulia Isaakovna (a musician; maiden name, Reiman) Medvedev; married Galina Gaidina (a physiologist), September, 1956; children: Alexander. *Education:* Leningrad State University, B.Sc., 1951; Moscow Academy of Pedagogical Sciences, Ph.D., 1958. *Address:* P.O. Box 45, Moscow G-19, Soviet Union. *Agent:* Zhores A. Medvedev, National Institute for Medical Research, Mill Hill, London NW7 1AA, England.

CAREER: Teacher of history at a high school in Sverdlovsk, U.S.S.R., 1951-54; director of a high school in Leningrad, U.S.S.R., 1955-56; Publishing House of Educational Literature, Moscow, U.S.S.R., deputy to editor-in-chief, 1957-61; Research Institute of Vocational Education, Moscow, division head, 1962-71; free-lance writer, 1971—.

WRITINGS: Professional'noe obuchenie shkol'nikov na promyshlennom predpriiatii: nekotorye vyvody iz opyta raboty eksperimental'nykh shkol v RSFSR (volume of pamphlets; title means "Vocational Education of Schoolchildren at the Industrial Enterprises: Some Results and Conclusions from the Work of Experimental Schools of the Russian Federation"), Uchpegiz (Moscow), 1960; *Voprosy organizatsii professional'nogo obucheniia shkol'nikov* (title means "Problems of Organization of Vocational Education in Schools"), Academy of Pedagogical Sciences (Moscow), 1963; *Faut-il rehabiliter Staline?* (title means "Is It Possible to Rehabilitate Stalin?"), translated by François Oliver from the Russian, Seuil (Paris), 1969; David Joravsky and Georges Haupt, editors, *Let History Judge: The Origins and Consequences of Stalinism,* translation by Colleen Taylor from the original Russian manuscript, Knopf, 1971, revised edition published in Russian as *K sudy istorri,* Knopf, 1974; (with brother, Zhores Medvedev) *Kto sumasshedshii?,* Macmillan, 1971, translation by Ellen de Kadt published as *A Question of Madness,* Knopf, 1971; *Kniga o sotsialisticheskoi demokrattii,* B. Grasset (Paris), 1972, translation by Ellen de Kadt published as *On Socialist Democracy,* Knopf, 1975; (editor) *Politicheskii dnevnik* (title means "Political Diary"), A. Herzen Foundation (Amsterdam), Volume I, 1972, Volume II, 1975.

Qui a ecrit "Le Don paisible?", translated from the original Russian manuscript, C. Bourgois (Paris), 1975, translation by A.D.P. Briggs from the revised Russian manuscript published as *Problems in the Literary Biography of Mikhail Sholokhov,* Cambridge University Press, 1977; (with Z. Medvedev) *Khrushchev. gody u vlasi,* Xerox University Microfilm, 1975, translation by Andrew R. Durkin published as *Khrushchev: The Years in Power,* Columbia University Press, 1976; *Solschenitzyn und die Sowjetische Linke* (collection of essays), translated from the Russian, Verlag Olle & Wolter (Berlin), 1976; *La revolution d'octobre etait-elle ineluctable?* (title means "Was the October Revolution Inevitable?"), translated by Jean Chantal from the Russian, A. Michel (Paris), 1976; *Political Essays,* translated by Brian Pearce and others from the Russian, Spokesman Books, 1976, R. Enslow, 1977.

Intervista sul dissenso in URSS, translated by P. Ostellino from the Russian, Laterza (Rome), 1977, translation of the revised edition published as *Interview on Dissension in the U.S.S.R.,* Columbia University Press, 1979; (editor) *The Samizdat Register* (collection of essays), translated by Brian Pearce and others from the Russian, Norton, Volume I, 1977, Volume II, 1979; (with Sergei Starikov) *Philip Mi-*

ronov and the Russian Civil War, translated by Guy Daniels from the Russian, Knopf, 1978; *La revolution d'octobre,* translated by Michele Kahn from the Russian, F. Maspers Ed. (Paris), 1978, translation by G. Saunders published as *The October Revolution,* Columbia University Press, 1979; *Stalin and Stalinism,* translated by Ellen de Kadt from the Russian, Oxford University Press, 1979; *The Last Years of Nikolai Bukharin,* translated from the Russian, Riuniti (Rome), 1979.

SIDELIGHTS: Despite persecution by Soviet authorities, Roy Medvedev remains a Marxist and a staunch believer in socialist democracy. Medvedev's problems with the Communist bureaucracy first became publicized in 1970 when his twin brother, Zhores, an eminent biologist and author, was held against his will for nineteen days in a psychiatric clinic. Medvedev launched a publicity campaign to free his brother, eliciting the support of many world notables, among them Andrey Sakharov. After Zhores was conditionally released, the brothers collaborated on a book about the affair, *A Question of Madness.* Their charges that the U.S.S.R. uses punitive psychiatry to discredit dissidents so worried Soviet officials that they took the highly unusual step of printing a long denial in a government newspaper. Susan Jacoby conjectured that Communist leaders were alarmed by the book because "the patriotism, integrity, and—hardly a non sequitur in this case—sanity of the authors are evident in every line."

This incident was only the beginning of the harassment of the Medvedev brothers. While Zhores was working as an attached scientist at the National Institute for Medical Research in England in 1973, his passport was confiscated and his Soviet citizenship revoked. Roy Medvedev has remained in the U.S.S.R., but his existence there has been plagued by trouble. After the publication of *Faut-il rehabiliter Staline?,* Medvedev was expelled from the Communist party and fired from his job as a division head for the Research Institute of Vocational Education. In 1971, the KGB (secret police) searched his apartment and seized his archives and the manuscript of *Let History Judge: The Origins and Consequences of Stalinism.*

Fortunately, a copy of the manuscript had already been dispatched to the West, for when *Let History Judge* was published it was hailed by R. C. Tucker as a "monumental achievement," and Strobe Talbott proclaimed it to be "the most comprehensive and revealing investigation of Stalinism ever to appear anywhere." The fact that this study of Stalin came from within Russia impressed most critics. "What is most exciting about it is that Medvedev is doing all this as a Russian, as a Marxist, and that he is giving us Stalin and Russia *from the inside,*" H. E. Salisbury observed. Medvedev's position as an insider enabled him to unearth many previously unknown facts. When writing about Stalin's infamous purges, Medvedev obtained much of his information from sources unavailable in the West, including official reports, eyewitness accounts, personal memoirs, and previously unpublished letters from Lenin and Stalin.

Medvedev compares Stalin unflatteringly with Lenin, scoffs at the contention that purges were necessary to protect the Stalinist regime from conspirators, and reviles Stalin's abilities as a military leader. Stalin is depicted as an innately evil man who was not even a true Communist, but rather an opportunist who saw the revolution as a chance to wrest power. Some commentators found the portrayal of Stalin disappointing, particularly the examination of his motivations. Medvedev "does not explain Stalin the man," Paul Wohl remarked. R. C. Tucker commented: "Stalin emerges in this work as a consciously demonic figure, hypocritically pretending to be the Marxist and Communist that he knew himself not to be. Such a picture of him is not, I believe, a true description of Stalin's sense of identity.''

Although Medvedev denounces Stalinism in *Let History Judge,* he is not disillusioned with socialism. Roger Jellinek thought Medvedev's faith in socialism was ''the most remarkable aspect of his book.'' The brand of socialism which Medvedev adheres to was described by Jellinek as ''a quite special idea of Lenin and Leninism, a Jeffersonian Leninism, decentralized, unmanipulative and sweetly reasonable, with an open society accepting dissent and valuing criticism, balancing the good of society with the good of the individual.'' Reflecting the views of many other commentators, Strobe Talbott observed that Medvedev's ''reiteration of faith in Lenin pales ... next to his more powerful and persuasive indictment of the man whom Lenin himself tolerated and whom a whole generation of loyal Leninists continued to serve.''

Medvedev's biographies of Nikita Khruschchev and Philip Mironov are further efforts in his continuing campaign to illuminate those areas of Russian history which the Communist regime has wiped out or misrepresented. *Khrushchev: The Years in Power* was lauded by Joshua Rubinstein as ''a fair-minded, incisive account,'' but he modified his approval by adding: ''As a piece of scholarship, the book has certain limitations. While it is the first study of Khrushchev's regime by a Soviet author, it does not add considerably to what western scholars ... have reported for some time.'' Although Philip Mironov is a much lesser-known figure than Khrushchev, his biography is also of significance. H. E. Salisbury praised *Philip Mironov and the Russian Civil War* as ''a story of importance, for it lifts one little corner of the veil that hides one of the great tragedies of the Revolution, the decimation of Russia's Cossack population.... This book recaptures one small part of that story and tells it simply and well.''

In *On Socialist Democracy,* Medvedev analyzes the development of the U.S.S.R. during the post-Stalin period. Medvedev is confident that democracy and socialism can mix; in his book he argues for the gradual introduction of democracy to the Soviet system. ''Everyone interested in Soviet and world affairs should read 'On Socialist Democracy,''' S. F. Cohen declared. ''Plainly written, devoid of eloquence or bombast, it gives Western readers a truer understanding of Medvedev's special Marxism-Leninism and compels us to rethink the potential of Soviet Communism.'' However, Jane Majeski found Medvedev's advocacy of democratization suspect: ''Medvedev's constant insistence on the practicality of freedom and democracy gives the impression that ultimately he is most concerned with governmental efficiency and the upholding of the Soviet Union's global position, and democracy represents little more than the means by which he can achieve this end.''

As a democratic socialist, Medvedev belongs to an extremely small ideological group. The opinions of other democratic socialists appear in *The Samizdat Register,* a collection of essays which Medvedev edited. The essays, all taken from *XX Century* journal, cover a number of subjects, ranging from alcoholism in the U.S.S.R. to Solzhenitsyn's historical ignorance. ''This volume is remarkable,'' Susan Jacoby noted, ''not only because it attests to the continued existence of sophisticated political discourse within the Soviet Union but because it represents a serious dialogue encompassing both the dissidents who have left their country and those who have remained behind.''

When *CA* asked Zhores Medvedev how it was possible for his brother Roy to write so many books in such inimical surroundings, he explained: ''The productivity of many authors declined when they emigrated from the U.S.S.R. Solzhenitsyn is a good example; most of his recent publications were written in the U.S.S.R. The immediate surroundings are usually very friendly. Roy has many supporters—friends, assistants, and people who give him their memoirs. Solzhenitsyn had an even wider circle of supporters. Although the hostile bureaucracy is not in immediate contact, the author feels he is in a sort of confrontation, with his books and essays serving as weapons. Because the author believes his works are important and must survive, he writes intensively. He uses his unpleasant experiences with officials either as a case for research, or as a topic for literary works.''

With the exception of Medvedev's works on education, none of his books have been published in the U.S.S.R., although they have been distributed in *samizdat* (unofficial circulation). Some of his works have been translated into French, German, Spanish, Japanese, and Italian.

BIOGRAPHICAL/CRITICAL SOURCES: Saturday Review, November 20, 1971, January 8, 1972, September 17, 1977; *Time,* December 13, 1971, January 17, 1972; *New York Times Book Review,* December 26, 1971, July 13, 1975, July 9, 1978; *New York Times,* December 28, 1971; *Christian Science Monitor,* January 6, 1972; *National Review,* August 1, 1975; *New Yorker,* September 22, 1975; Ken Coates, editor, *Detente and Socialist Democracy: A Discussion With Roy Medvedev,* Monad Press, 1976; *Commentary,* February, 1977; *New Statesman,* May 6, 1977; *Times Literary Supplement,* September 30, 1977.

*   *   *

MEIR, Golda   1898-1978

OBITUARY NOTICE: Born May 3, 1898, in Kiev, Russia (now U.S.S.R.); died December 8, 1978, in Jerusalem, Israel. Fourth prime minister of Israel, member of parliament, zionist, and author of autobiography *My Life.* Meir was one of the original signers of Israel's proclamation of independence and statehood. An ardent zionist, Meir spoke about the need for a Jewish state even at the age of seventeen. Although she was born in the Ukraine, Meir grew up in Milwaukee, Wis., after her family immigrated to the United States in the early 1900's. However, memories of her father barricading the family's home entrance before an impending cossack raid remained with her always. Meir arrived in Palestine in 1921 and became a member of a kibbutz. Later she worked for labor organizations and, after World War II, Meir helped Jewish immigrants enter Palestine against the dictates of the British rule. In 1948, Meir was named minister to the Soviet Union and a year later she became a member of the Israeli parliament. Meir was minister of labor from 1949 until 1956, when she became foreign minister under the leadership of Ben-Gurion. Later Ben-Gurion was to remark that Meir was ''the only man in my Cabinet,'' an opinion that was attributed to her support of his policy of tough retaliation for any Arab raid or terrorist activity. Prime minister from 1969 to 1973 when she resigned after her government failed to detect the signs of the upcoming war, Meir remained firm about the survival of the Jewish state. She once stated, ''I have never believed in inflexibility except when Israel is concerned.'' Obituaries and other sources: *Current Biography,* Wilson, 1970; *Who's Who,* 130th edition, St. Martin's, 1978; *New York Times,* December 9, 1978; *Washington Post,* December 9, 1978; *Time,* December 18, 1978; *Newsweek,*

MEJIA, Arthur, Jr. 1934-

PERSONAL: Born May 8, 1934, in San Francisco, Calif.; son of Arthur (a broker) and Anne (Dibblee) Mejia. *Education:* Stanford University, A.B., 1956, LL.B., 1959, Ph.D., 1968. *Politics:* Republican. *Religion:* Episcopalian. *Home:* 2105 Bush St., San Francisco, Calif. 94115. *Office:* Department of History, San Francisco State University, San Francisco, Calif. 94132.

CAREER: San Francisco State University, San Francisco, Calif., instructor, 1965-68, assistant professor, 1968-71, became associate professor, 1971, currently professor of history. *Member:* American Historical Association, Society for French Historical Studies, Conference on British Studies.

WRITINGS: (With Gordon Wright) *An Age of Controversy,* Harper, 1963, alternate edition, 1973; (with J. A. Thompson) *The Modern British Monarchy,* St. Martin's, 1971.

*   *   *

MELCHINGER, Siegfried 1906-

PERSONAL: Born November 22, 1906, in Stuttgart, West Germany; son of August (a postman) and Gerda (Keyn) Melchinger; married Maria Novottny, May 30, 1934; children: Ulrich. *Education:* Attended University of Munich; University of Tuebingen, Dr.phil., 1927. *Home:* 7821 Strittberg, Hochenschwand, Schwarzwald, West Germany.

CAREER: Critic for *Stuttgarten Neues Tagblatt,* Stuttgart, Germany, for *Frankfurter General Anzeiger,* Frankfurt, Germany, for *Neues Wiener Tagblatt,* Vienna, Austria, and for *Munchen Illustrierte,* Stuttgart, 1930-60; Academy of Music and Representational Art, Stuttgart, professor of theatre theory, 1960-69. *Member:* P.E.N. Club (German), Deutscher Schriftsteller-Verband. *Awards, honors:* Sigmund Freud Preis, 1978.

WRITINGS: Modernes Welttheater: Lichter und Reflexe, Schuenemann, 1956; *Theater der Gegenwart,* Fischer Buecherei, 1956; *Drama zwischen Shaw und Brecht: Ein Leitfaden durch das zeitgenoessische Schauspiel,* Schuenemann, 1957, translation by George Wellwarth published as *Concise Encyclopedia of Modern Drama,* edited by Henry Popkin, Horizon Press, 1964; *Harlekin: Bilderbuch der Spassmacher,* Basilius Presse, 1959; *Keine Masstaebe? Kritik der Kritik,* Artemis, 1959; *Gruendgens Faust,* Suhrkamp, 1959.

(With Walter Felsenstein) *Musiktheater,* Schuenemann, 1961; *Das Aergernis Brecht,* Basilius Presse, 1961; (with Henning Rischbieter) *Welttheater, Buehnen, Autoren, Inszenierungen,* Westermann, 1962; *Sphaeren und Tage: Staedte, Spiele, Musik,* Leibniz, 1962; *Shakespeare auf dem modernen Welttheater,* Friedrich, 1964; (contributor) Juergen Fehling, *Die Magie des Theaters, Ausserungen und Aufzeichnungen,* Friedrich, 1965; (with Rosemarie Clausen) *Schauspieler* (title means "Actor"), Friedrich, 1965.

Sophokles, Friedrich, 1966, translation by David A. Scrase published as *Sophocles,* Ungar, 1974; (editor with Gottfried von Einem) *Casper Neher,* Freidrich, 1966; *Euripedes,* Friedrich, 1967, translation by Samuel Rosenbaum, Ungar, 1973; *Rolf Hochhuth,* Friedrich, 1967; *Anton Tschechow,* Friedrich, 1968, translation by Edith Turcov published as *Anton Chekhov,* Ungar, 1972; (editor with Roman Clemens) *Theater auf Buehnen deutscher Sprach,* [Munich], 1969, translation by Barbara von Waldstein published as *Theatre on the German-Speaking Stage,* Goethe-Institute (Munich), 1971; *Geschichte des politischen Theaters,* two volumes, Friedrich, 1971; *Das Theater der Tragoedie: Aischylos,*

Sophokles, Euripides auf d. Buehne ihrer zeit, Beck, 1974; *Die Welt als Tragoedie,* two volumes, Beck, 1979.

Co-editor, *Theater Heute,* 1960-68.

*   *   *

MELDER, Keith E(ugene) 1932-

PERSONAL: Born May 13, 1932, in Seattle, Wash.; son of Frederick Eugene (a college professor) and Eleanor (Morrill) Melder. *Education:* Williams College, B.A., 1954; Yale University, M.A., 1958, Ph.D., 1964. *Politics:* Independent Democrat. *Home:* 334 South Carolina Ave. S.E., Washington, D.C. 20003.

CAREER: Case Institute of Technology (now Case Western Reserve University), Cleveland, Ohio, instructor in humanities and social studies, 1958-61; Smithsonian Institution, Washington, D.C., assistant curator, 1961-65, associate curator of Division of Political History, 1966-71; writer and consultant (clients include Old Sturbridge Village and Essex Institute), 1971—. Lecturer at Catholic University of America, 1964-66. Member of Capitol Hill Community Council, 1962-69 (president, 1966-67). Member of board of directors of City Museum Project (Washington, D.C.).

MEMBER: American Association of Museums, American Association for State and Local History, American Historical Association, American Studies Association, Phi Beta Kappa. *Awards, honors:* Lena Lake Forrest Fellowship from Business and Professional Women's Foundation, 1964-65.

WRITINGS: (Contributor) Peter C. Marzio, Carl H. Scheele, and others, editors, *A Nation of Nations,* Harper, 1976; *The Village and the Nation,* Old Sturbridge, 1976; *Beginnings of Sisterhood: The American Woman's Rights Movement, 1800-1850,* Schocken, 1977. Contributor to history journals.

WORK IN PROGRESS: Research for a biography of feminist abolitionist Abby Kelley Foster, completion expected in 1981; historical studies of Washington, D.C. for museum exhibitions; research for a museum exhibition on the shoe industry in Lynn, Mass.

SIDELIGHTS: Melder writes: "During the last twenty-five years my research interests have centered on American social history of the nineteenth century: subjects such as the history of women and women's movements, the changing roles of ethnic groups in American life, education and the communications media, American attitudes toward social change, urbanism and regionalism in this country. My major writing has dealt with nineteenth-century women's movements. Personally I am a moderate feminist and believe that male chauvinism and bravado are clear and present dangers to all of us, indeed, probably a threat to human survival.

"My applications of academic interests have evolved over a quarter century from fairly traditional forms of teaching and college involvement. An excursion into museum work turned into what appears to be a lifetime trip. I now see myself as a translator of academic research into 'living history' made available to the understanding of a mass audience by means of museum technique. Therefore, the bulk of my every-day writing goes into museum exhibitions. However trivial such writing may seem to most academic historians, it has a chance to reach average people in large numbers. I would defend the need to popularize academic history, because unless we do so, we may not have an economically-viable discipline left. It's fun to do this sort of work, also, with its multi-media presentations and the constant challenge of new subjects. By occasional lectures and classroom appearances, along with participation in scholarly meetings, I try to keep a toe in the academic whirlpool.''

AVOCATIONAL INTERESTS: Old trains (''I wish I could afford to buy a personal private railroad car'').

* * *

MELLY, George 1926-

PERSONAL: Born August 17, 1926, in Liverpool, England; son of Francis Heywood (a wool broker) and Maud (Isaac) Melly; married Diana Margaret Campion Dawson (a writer), May 4, 1962; children: Tom. *Education:* Attended private school in Buckingham, England. *Politics:* ''Confused, vote Labour, idealistically anarchist.'' *Religion:* None. *Home:* 102 Savernake Rd., London NW3 2JR, England. *Agent:* A. M. Heath & Co. Ltd., 40-42 William IV St., London WC2N 4DD, England.

CAREER: Writer. London Gallery, London, England, assistant 1948-50; Mick Mulligan's Jazz Band, London, vocalist, 1949-61; free-lance journalist, 1961-65; music critic for *Observer,* 1965-67, television critic, 1967-71, film critic, 1971-73. Vocalist for John Chilton's Feetwarmers, 1971—. *Military service:* Royal Navy, 1944-47. *Member:* National Union of Journalists, Equity Union, Musicians Union, Colony Room. *Awards, honors:* Named critic of the year by Independent Publishing Corp., 1971.

WRITINGS: I Flook (fantasy), Macmillan, 1962; *Owning Up* (autobiography), Weidenfeld & Nicolson, 1965; *Revolt into Style* (sociology), Alan Laine, 1970; *Flook by Trog* (fantasy), Faber, 1970; *Rum Bum and Concertina* (autobiography), Weidenfeld & Nicolson, 1977. Contributor to magazines and newspapers, including *Punch, New Statesman, New Society,* and *Observer.*

WORK IN PROGRESS: Editing conversations with Edward James, for Duckworth.

* * *

MEMMI, Albert 1920-

PERSONAL: Born December 15, 1920, in Tunis, Tunisia; son of Francois (an artisan) and Marguerite (Sarfati) Memmi; married Germaine Dubach; children: Daniel, Dominique, Nicolas. *Education:* University of Algiers, licence en philosophie, 1943; Sorbonne, University of Paris, Dr. es lettres, 1970. *Home:* 5 rue St. Merri, 75004 Paris, France. *Office:* University of Paris, 92 Nanterre, France.

CAREER: High school teacher of philosophy in Tunis, Tunisia, 1953-56; Center of Educational Research, Tunis, director, 1953-57; National Center of Scientific Research, Paris, France, researcher, 1958-60; University of Paris, Sorbonne, Ecole pratique des hautes etudes, assistant professor, 1959-66, professor of social psychology, 1966-70; University of Paris, Nanterre, France, professor of sociology, 1970—. School of Higher Studies in Social Sciences, conference director, 1958, director of department of social sciences, 1975-78; Walker Ames Professor, University of Seattle, 1972. *Member:* Societe des Gens de Lettres, P.E.N. Club (France; vice-president), Academie des Sciences d'Outremer. *Awards, honors:* Commander of Ordre de Nichan Iftikhar (Tunisia); Prix Carthage, 1953; Prix Feneon, 1954.

WRITINGS—In English: *La Statue du sel* (novel), introduction by Albert Camus, Correa, 1953, translation by Edouard Roditi published as *Pillar of Salt,* Criterion, 1955; *Agar* (novel), Correa, 1955, translation by Brian Rhys published as *Strangers,* 1958, Orion Press, 1960; *Portrait du colonise precede du portrait du colinisateur,* introduction by Jean-Paul Sartre, Buchet/Chastel, 1957, translation by Howard Greenfield published as *The Colonizer and the Colonized,* Orion Press, 1965; *Portrait d'un Juif,* Gallimard, 1962, translation by Elisabeth Abbott published as *Portrait of a Jew,* Orion Press, 1962; *La Liberation d'un Juif,* Gallimard, 1962, translation by Judy Hyun published as *The Liberation of a Jew,* Orion Press, 1966; *L'Homme domine,* Gallimard, 1968, new edition, Payot, 1973; translation published as *Dominated Man: Notes Towards a Portrait* (collection of essays), Orion Press, 1968; *Le Scorpion ou la confession imaginaire* (novel), Gallimard, 1969, translation by Eleanor Levieux published as *The Scorpion or the Imaginary Confession,* Grossman, 1971, 2nd edition, J. Philip O'Hara, 1975; *Juifs et Arabes,* Gallimard, 1974, translation by Levieux published as *Jews and Arabs,* J. Philip O'Hara, 1975.

Other works: *La Poesie algerienne de 1830 a nos jours: approches socio-historiques,* Mouton, 1963; (editor) *Anthologie des ecrivains maghrebins d'expression francaise,* two volumes, Presence africaine, 1964, revised and updated edition, 1965; (with Paul Hassan Maucorps) *Les Francais et le racisme,* Payot, 1965; *Ecole pratique des hautes etudes,* Mouton, 1965; *Albert Memmi: un entretien avec Robert Davies suivi d'intineraire de l'experience vecue a la theorie de la domination,* Reedition Quebec, 1975; *La Terre interieure entretiens avec Victor Malka,* Gallimard, 1976; *Le Desert* (title means ''The Desert''), Gallimard, 1977.

Work represented in textbooks and in numerous anthologies.

SIDELIGHTS: The English translations of Memmi's works have been well-received in the United States. In his autobiographical novels *The Pillar of Salt* and *Strangers,* Memmi, who grew up in a traditional Jewish household in Tunisia, colorfully describes life in North Africa. ''But these novels are far more than exotic Durrellian travel guides,'' a *New York Times* critic wrote; ''for Memmi, like a Tunisian Balzac graced with Hemingway's radical simplicity and sadness, gave us this world through the voice of a quiet, well-behaved, quite charmingly sad but earnest young man who was slowly disintegrating before our eyes.'' These novels ''today remain two of the best works to appear in Europe after the war,'' he concluded, comparing them to Albert Camus's *The Stranger* and *The Plague.*

Man's alienation from himself and from others is a major theme in Memmi's novel *The Scorpion.* In the story, the protagonist, Emile Memmi, expresses the self-doubts that Memmi sees as a part of the human condition. Reviewer Gerard E. Grealish called the novel a philosophical ''parallel'' to Camus's *The Myth of Sysyphus.* Although the *New York Times* critic did not consider *The Scorpion* to be completely successful as a novel, he did comment that ''the audacious form and technique of the book are totally unprecedented in Memmi: a richly interwoven net of autobiography, diary, commentary, aphorism, parable, *faux memoire* and novel-within-the-novel. . . .''

In *Portrait du colonise, Portrait d'un Juif,* and some of his other books, Memmi explores the theories of colonization and rule and the exploitation of minorities, concluding that once the exploited gain their freedom, they become like those who ruled them.

Translations of Memmi's books have been published in Israel, Italy, Germany, England, Spain, Argentina, Yugoslavia, Japan, and other countries.

BIOGRAPHICAL/CRITICAL SOURCES: Nation, May 22, 1967; *Research in African Literatures,* Volume I, number 1, University of Texas, spring, 1970; *New York Times,* May 22, 1971; *Best Sellers,* July 1, 1971.

*   *   *

MENDES-FRANCE, Pierre   1907-

PERSONAL: Born January 11, 1907, in Paris, France; son of Cerf (a merchant) and Palmyre (Cahn) Mendes-France; married Lily Cicurel (a portrait-painter), December 26, 1933 (deceased); married Marie-Claire Servan-Schreiber, January 2, 1971; children: (first marriage) Bernard, Michel. *Education:* University of Paris, Docteur en droit, 1928, diploma in political science, 1928. *Home:* 23 rue du Conseiller Collignon, Paris, France.

CAREER: Lawyer and politician. Admitted to the Bar, 1927; lawyer in France, 1927-67; deputy from Eure in French National Assembly, 1932-40; commissioner of finance for Committee of National Liberation, 1943-44; minister of national economy, 1944-45; deputy from Eure in National Assembly, 1945-58; minister of foreign affairs and prime minister, 1954-55; minister without portfolio, 1956; president of editorial committee of *Cahiers de la Republique* until 1963; deputy from Isere in National Assembly, 1967-68; writer. Mayor of Louviers, France, 1934-58. Undersecretary of state for Department of the Treasury, 1938; governor for France of the International Monetary Fund and International Bank for Reconstruction and Development, 1946-58; permanent French representative to the Economic and Social Council of the United Nations (ECOSOC), 1947-50. Visiting professor at Ecole National d'Administration. *Military service:* French Air Force, 1939-40; entered as lieutenant, tried by Vichy government for desertion; escaped to serve with De Gaulle's Free French forces in London, 1940-43; received Legion of Honor, War Cross, Medal of the Resistance, Medal of Escaped Prisoners; named Grand Officer of the Order of Leopold.

WRITINGS—In English: *Liberte, liberte cherie,* Didier, 1943, translation by Terence Kilmartin published as *The Pursuit of Freedom,* Longmans, Green, 1956, French edition reprinted, Fayard, 1977; (with Gabriel Ardant) *La Science economique et l'action,* Unesco-Julliard, 1954, translation published as *Economics and Action,* Columbia University Press, 1955; *La Republique moderne: Propositions,* Gallimard, 1962, translation by Anne Carter published as *A Modern French Republic,* Hill & Wang, 1963, new French edition, 1966; *Dialogues avec l'Asie d'aujourd'hui,* Gallimard, 1972, translation by Susan Danon published as *Face to Face With Asia,* Liveright, 1974.

Other: *La Banque internationale* (title means "The International Bank"), Librairie Valois, 1930; *Gouverner, c'est choisir* (title means "To Govern Is to Choose"), Julliard, Volume I: *Discours d'investiture et reponses aux interpellateurs* (title means "Investiture Discourse and Responses to Interpellators"), 1953, Volume II: *Sept mois et dix-sept jours* (title means "Seven Months and Seventeen Days"), 1955, Volume III: *La Politique et la verite* (title means "Politics and the Truth"), 1958; (with Pietro Nenni and Aneurin Bevan) *Rencontres: Nenni, Bevan, Mendes France* (discussions organized by *L'Express),* Julliard, 1959.

(Contributor) Alfred Sauvy, *Le Plan Sauvy,* Calmann-Levy, 1960; (author of introduction) Georges Boris, *Servir la Republique* (title means "To Serve the Republic"), Julliard, 1963; (with Michel Debre) *Le Grand Debat* (title means "The Great Debate"), Gonthier, 1966; *Pour preparer l'avenir* (title means "Preparing for the Future"), Denoel, 1968; (with Ardant) *Science economique et lucidite politique* (title means "Economic Science and Political Lucidity"), Gallimard, 1973; *Choisir* (title means "To Choose"), Stock, 1974; *La Verite guidait leurs pas* (title means "The Truth Guided Their Steps"), Gallimard, 1976.

Contributor to periodicals. Editor-in-chief of *Le Courrier de la Republique.*

SIDELIGHTS: After a distinguished career in French politics, including a period of service as prime minister, Mendes-France discussed the "mission of politics" in *Saturday Review:* "In my opinion, politics is not what one calls a vocation or a profession, even if a man devotes all his time and all his trouble to it. It is a mission, with its greatness and with its demands, which can be burdensome. For if there are several ways, both good and bad, to approach politics, those which most effectively serve or guarantee a man's personal ambitions are not necessarily the best, as far as the general interest is concerned. . . . To young people who are thinking of a political career, I want to say this: if you dread those struggles in which you are sustained only by the conviction that the great causes to which you are attached will win out irresistably one day, with you or without you or after you; if you dread confrontation that will go on for years, marked by discouragement and reverses, until the moment when the facts and history at last render their verdict; if you prefer to avoid a life richer in uncertainties than in triumphs, in disappointments than in rewards—then I advise you without hesitation, to stay out of politics. But if you like the invigorating sensation of striving for what you believe in, in behalf of noble convictions, then enter the arena without fear, for men like you are needed."

When asked about the current political situation in France, Mendes-France told *CA:* "I believe that the situation in France today is unstable and uncertain due to the malaise which reigns in many people. I wish with all my heart that those in positions of responsibility—in the administration, the political parties, the unions, cultural organizations and others—will occupy themselves in bringing the necessary improvements to fruition. If not, they risk condemning many, especially young people, to becoming discouraged, pouring themselves into scepticism, and renouncing their best aspirations, while others, even only a minority, will seek in violence the means of achieving a new sort of life better adapted to their impatience. The duty of the politician is to work without respite for that which can make a better future, in order to spare his country from the most dangerous tensions and convulsions. For that, he must be capable of devoting himself to the projects of the future and, little by little, of assuring their success, in spite of the resistance from routines, vested interests, privilege, and selfishness."

BIOGRAPHICAL/CRITICAL SOURCES: Donald McCormick, *Mr. France,* Jarrolds, 1955; Alexander Werth, *Lost Statesman: The Strange Story of Pierre Mendes-France,* Abelard, 1958; *Saturday Review,* May 31, 1969.

*   *   *

MENZIES, Robert Gordon   1894-1978

PERSONAL: Born December 20, 1894, in Jeparit, Victoria, Australia; son of James (a storekeeper and legislator) and Kate (Sampson) Menzies; married Pattie Maie Leckie, 1920; children: Kenneth, Ian, Heather. *Education:* Graduated from Wesley College and Melbourne University. *Politics:* Liberal. *Religion:* Presbyterian. *Home:* 2 Haverbrack Ave., Malvern, Victoria, Australia 3144. *Office:* 95 Collins St., Melbourne, Victoria, Australia 3000.

CAREER: Called to the Bar, Victoria County and High

Court of Australia, 1918; lawyer in private practice; Victoria Legislative Council, representative from East Yarra, 1928-29; honorary minister of Victoria, 1928-29; appointed King's Counsel, 1929; Victoria Legislative Assembly, representative from Nunawading, 1929-34; attorney general, minister of railways, and deputy premier of Victoria, 1932-34; Australian Federal Parliament, representative from Kooyong, 1934-66; attorney general of Australia and minister for industry, 1934-39; deputy leader of United Australian Party, 1936-39, and leader, 1939-41; made a privy councilor, 1937; prime minister of Australia, 1939-41; minister for defense coordination, 1939-41, for information and munitions, 1940, and for trade and customs, 1940; leader of the Liberal party, 1943-49; prime minister of Australia, 1949-66; University of Melbourne, Melbourne, Australia, chancellor, 1967-72. Opposition member of the advisory war council, 1941-44; chairman of committee to discuss nationalization of the Suez Canal with Nasser, 1956. President of Dover College, 1966-78. Trustee of Melbourne Cricket Ground. Lord Warden of the Cinque Ports, 1965-78.

MEMBER: Royal Society of Arts (fellow); honorary fellow of Australian Academy of Science, Royal Australasian College of Physicians, 1955, Royal Australian Institute of Architects, 1956, the Institute of Marketing, 1957, Royal College of Physicians of Edinburgh, 1960, Royal College of Obstetricians and Gynaecologists, 1961, and Royal College of Surgeons of England, 1965. *Awards, honors:* Knighted by Queen Elizabeth, 1963; LL.D. from Melbourne University, Queen's University, Belfast, University of Bristol, University of British Columbia, University of Sydney, McGill University, University of Laval, University of Montreal, Harvard University, Royal University of Malta, University of Tasmania, Cambridge University, University of Leeds, University of Adelaide, University of Edinburgh, University of Birmingham, Australian National University, and University of Sussex; D.C.L. from Oxford University and University of Kent at Canterbury; D.Sc. from University of New South Wales; honorary fellow at Worcester College, Oxford, 1968.

WRITINGS: "To the People of Britain at War" From the Prime Minister of Australia (speeches), Longmans, Green, 1941; *The Forgotten People, and Other Studies in Democracy* (broadcast addresses), Angus & Robertson, 1943; *Speech Is of Time* (speeches and writings), Cassell, 1958; (with others) *The Challenge to Australian Education,* F. W. Chesire, 1961; *The Wit of Sir Robert Menzies,* compiled by Raymond Robinson, Frewin, 1966; *Central Power in the Australian Commonwealth: An Examination of the Growth of Commonwealth Power in the Australian Federation,* University Press of Virginia, 1967; *Afternoon Light: Some Memories of Men and Events,* Cassell, 1967, Coward, 1968; *The Measure of the Years,* Cassell, 1970. Also author of booklets and pamphlets on politics and higher education.

SIDELIGHTS: Sir Robert Menzies was a key figure in modern Australian politics. When Prime Minister Joseph Lyons died in 1939, the United Australia and Country parties coalition government collapsed. Menzies reorganized the United Australia party, became its leader, and was chosen prime minister. During his first term as prime minister, Menzies concentrated primarily on the war effort. He declared war on Germany, began a nationwide war program, and represented Australia at the London war conferences. While in England, Menzies met such famous figures as Winston Churchill, Earl Atlee, Lloyd George, and Neville Chamberlin. He was later to record his observations of these men in *Afternoon Light: Some Memories of Men and*

Events. But Menzies's position at home was insecure because of dissension in the United Australia party and the growing strength of the Labor party. He was forced to resign in 1941.

While the Labor party was in power from 1943 to 1949, the alliance between the United Australia and Country parties dissolved. By helping to revive an old party, the Liberals, Menzies staged a dramatic political comeback. In 1949 the Liberals campaigned on a platform calling for a halt to governmental controls and socialism, an increase in industrial production, and a cut in taxes. They also wanted to outlaw Communism and remove its members from public office. After the Liberals and their allies, the Country party, gained a majority in parliament in 1949, Menzies returned to the office of prime minister, a position that he was to hold for seventeen more years. Perhaps Menzies's greatest domestic achievement during the years was his expansion of university facilities in Australia. His most prominent international role was serving as chairman of a committee that went to Cairo, Egypt to discuss nationalization of the Suez Canal with Nasser.

A superb orator and witty conversationalist, Menzies had many of his speeches recorded in books. He also wrote two volumes of memoirs, the aforementioned *Afternoon Light* and *The Measure of the Years.* After reading *Afternoon Light,* Sylvia Wain gave her impressions of Menzies: "He is essentially an 'English' Australian, a convinced monarchist and upholder of the older concept of the Commonwealth.... 'Old Bob' comes out tough, hard and practical. He is also didactic and has a ponderous sense of humor."

BIOGRAPHICAL/CRITICAL SOURCES: Robert Gordon Menzies, *Afternoon Light: Some Memories of Men and Events,* Cassell, 1967, Coward, 1968; *Listener,* October 26, 1967; *Times Literary Supplement,* November 30, 1967, December 25, 1970; Kevin Perkins, *Menzies: Last of the Queen's Men,* Rigby, 1968; *Books and Bookmen,* January, 1968; *Pacific Affairs,* fall, 1968; Edgar Holt, *Politics Is People: The Men of the Menzies Era,* Angus & Robertson, 1969; Robert Gordon Menzies, *The Measure of the Years,* Cassell, 1970; Don Whitington, *Twelfth Man?,* Jacaranda Press, 1972.

OBITUARIES: Time, May 29, 1978.*

(Died in 1978, in Melbourne, Australia)

* * *

MERCIER, Vivian (Herbert Samuel) 1919-

PERSONAL: Born April 5, 1919, in Dublin, Ireland; came to the United States in 1946; son of William Cochrane (a sales manager) and Charlotte Olivia (Abbott) Mercier; married Lucy Bronson Glazebrook, 1940 (divorced, 1949); married Gina di Fonzo, August 15, 1950 (died, 1971); married Eilis Dillon (a novelist and children's book writer), April 5, 1974; children: Vivian Allan Ciaran, Christine Lucy Renee Mercier Wooding, William Cochrane. *Education:* Trinity College, Dublin, B.A. (honors), 1940, Ph.D., 1945. *Religion:* Church of Ireland. *Home:* Los Robles, Apt. 42, 1 El Vedado Lane, Santa Barbara, Calif. 93105. *Agent:* Georges Borchardt, Inc., 136 East 57th St., New York, N.Y. 10022. *Office:* Department of English, University of California, Santa Barbara, Calif. 93106.

CAREER: Bennington College, Bennington, Vt., instructor in English, 1947-48; City College of the City University of New York, New York, N.Y., instructor, 1948-53, assistant professor, 1953-60, associate professor of English, 1961-65;

University of Colorado, Boulder, professor of English and comparative literature, 1965-74; University of California, Santa Barbara, professor of English, 1974—. Visiting lecturer at University of California, Berkeley, 1959-60. *Military service:* Irish Army, 1940-45.

MEMBER: International Association for the Study of Anglo-Irish Literature, Modern Language Association of America, American Association of University Professors, American Committee for Irish Studies, Samuel Beckett Society. *Awards, honors:* Ford Fund for the Advancement of Education fellowship, 1955-56; American Council of Learned Societies fellowship, 1964-65; Guggenheim fellowship, 1972-73.

WRITINGS: (Editor with David H. Greene) *1,000 Years of Irish Prose: The Literary Revival,* Devin-Adair, 1952; *The Irish Comic Tradition,* Clarendon Press, 1962, revised edition, Oxford University Press, 1969; (editor) *Great Irish Short Stories,* Dell, 1964; *The New Novel: From Queneau to Pinget,* Farrar, Straus, 1971; *A Reader's Guide to the New Novel,* Noonday, 1971; *Beckett/Beckett,* Oxford University Press, 1977.

Contributor: Seon Givens, editor, *James Joyce: Two Decades of Criticism,* Vanguard Press, 1948; John Gassner, editor, *Ideas in the Drama: Selected Papers From the English Institute,* Columbia University Press, 1964; Ray B. Browne, William John Roscelli, and Richard Loftus, editors, *The Celtic Cross: Studies in Irish Culture and Literature,* Purdue University, 1964; James V. Logan, John E. Jordan, and Northrop Frye, editors, *Some British Romantics: A Collection of Essays,* Ohio State University, 1966; Norman Jeffares, editor, *Fair Liberty Was All His Cry: A Tercentenary Tribute to Jonathan Swift, 1667-1745,* Macmillan, 1967; Douglas A. Hugher, editor, *Perspectives on Pornography,* St. Martin's, 1970; Kathleen McGrory and John Unterecker, editors, *Yeats, Joyce, and Beckett: New Light on Three Modern Irish Writers,* Bucknell University Press, 1976.

Co-author of "Books in Brief," a column in *World,* 1972-73. Contributor of articles and reviews to popular and academic journals in the United States and abroad, including *Saturday Review, Shenandoah, Commonweal, Nation,* and *New Republic.* Former member of editorial staff of *Church of Ireland Gazette* and *Literary Digest;* advisory editor for *James Joyce Quarterly.*

WORK IN PROGRESS: Anglo-Irish Literature, 1878-1978: A Critical History (tentative title), two volumes, for Oxford University Press, completion expected in 1982.

SIDELIGHTS: Mercier writes: "As an Irish citizen of French Protestant descent on my father's side, with several Episcopal clergymen as ancestors on my mother's side, I made the most of the excellent education available to me at boarding school and university. If World War II had not broken out, I would have gone to France for graduate work in 1940. Instead, I married an American girl in Ireland and entered the United States as a permanent resident.

"When my first marriage ended, I stayed in New York to be near my children, remarried, and made the teaching of English my career. Although I had entered Trinity College, Dublin, with a Sizarship in Latin and Greek, my specialization in Anglo-Irish literature made me feel more and more ashamed of knowing almost no Gaelic. Thanks to the Ford Foundation, I spent a year in Ireland studying the earlier forms of Gaelic, known as Old and Middle Irish. As a result of this study, I was able to trace the famous Irish gift for wit and humor back to at least 800 A.D. in my second book.

"After that, it seemed time to pay my debt to my French heritage. The result was *The New Novel,* a study of seven French writers, most of whom are still alive, who were associated with the movement known in the 1950's and 1960's as *le nouveau roman.* Not surprisingly, perhaps, the book's most important conclusion proved to be that all of these writers had in some way been influenced by a single Irish writer, James Joyce.

"Samuel Beckett, also of Huguenot descent, had attended Portora and Trinity some years before I did: I first became aware of him as a writer-alumnus in 1934, and by 1938 I was a keen admirer of his first novel, *Murphy.* An editor at Oxford University Press in New York was about to write to me suggesting a short book on Beckett when I submitted *The Irish Comic Tradition* to her in 1960. Because my second wife had developed unmistakable symptoms of multiple sclerosis in 1958, I was in no mood to write about Beckett's cripples. Only after Gina's death in 1971 did I finally tackle a critical study of Beckett. Since Beckett has written so much in French, my knowledge of that language again proved useful, as did my Irish background and education. Having studied Racine under the same professor as Beckett, I suggested that the influence of the French classical dramatist on the supposedly 'absurdist' plays of the Irishman was very strong indeed. The reviewers of *Beckett/Beckett* found this the most startling and yet the most believable paradox in the whole book.

"Although America has been very good to me—and I hope I have served her conscientiously in return—I seem to have been trying to get back to Ireland ever since I arrived here. Since I married Eilis Dillon—an old friend, widowed like myself, who is both Irish and Catholic—we spend half the year in Santa Barbara and the rest with Dublin as our base. It's time to write that long history of Irish literature in the English language that I have had on my mind for many years. After spending so long in America writing and teaching about Ireland and France, I hope to retire permanently to Ireland in another ten years. Then it will be the right time and place in which to write about the America and the Americans I have learned to love."

* * *

MERIN, Oto Bihalji
   See BIHALJI-MERIN, Oto

* * *

MERIN, Peter
   See BIHALJI-MERIN, Oto

* * *

MERRILL, Robert 1919-

PERSONAL: Birth-given name, Morris Miller; later changed to Merrill Miller; then changed to Robert Merrill; born June 4, 1919, in Brooklyn, N.Y.; son of Abraham (a tailor) and Lillian (a singer; maiden name, Balaban) Miller; married Roberta Peters (a singer), March 30, 1952 (divorced, June 24, 1952); married Marion Machno (a pianist), May 30, 1954; children: David R., Lizanne. *Education:* Attended public schools in Brooklyn, N.Y. *Agent:* David Hill, 22 East 60th St., New York, N.Y. 10022. *Office:* 79 Oxford Rd., New Rochelle, N.Y. 10804.

CAREER: Metropolitan Opera Association, New York, N.Y., baritone, 1945-76. Won Metropolitan Auditions of the Air, 1945; made debut as Germont in "La Traviata," 1945;

has made appearances in operas, including "Carmen," "Faust," "La Boheme," "La Forza del Destino," "Lucia de Lammermoor," "Un Ballo in Maschera," "Barber of Seville," "Rigoletto," "Tosca," "Otello," "Il Trovatore," and "Andrea Chenier"; appeared in the Broadway musical, "Fiddler on the Roof," 1970; has made frequent radio and television performances; has performed throughout the United States, Europe, and Asia; has made recordings for RCA-Victor, Angel, London, and Columbia. Member of National Council of the Arts, 1968-74. *Member:* American Federation of Radio Artists, American Guild of Variety Artists, Opera Guild, Actors Equity, Friars Club (monk, 1968—). *Awards, honors:* Music Annual Award from Record Industry, 1946, for best classical vocal recording; Harriet Cohen International Music Award, 1961; Grammy Awards from National Academy of Recording Arts & Sciences, 1962 and 1964; Handel Medal from New York City, 1970; Mus.D. from Gustavus Adolphus College, 1971.

WRITINGS: Once More From the Beginning, Macmillan, 1965; *Between Acts: An Irreverent Look at Opera* (memoirs), McGraw, 1976; *The Divas* (fiction), Simon & Schuster, 1978.

SIDELIGHTS: Robert Merrill is said to possess one of the great baritone voices of the century. He has sung almost every baritone role in the operatic repertoire, and, in 1973, he was recognized as the first American opera singer to sing 500 performances at the Metropolitan Opera.

"The secret," Merrill told Michael Redmond, "is knowing how to conserve your energy. And you need a certain amount of healthy self-confidence, which comes through practicing and working hard. Then you know you're going to walk out there and do a really good job.

"Opera is the toughest art of all," he continued. "It's a human instrument. I heard Rubenstein play with a 104-degree fever—it was beautiful! But a singer couldn't do that, no way. Your voice, so many words, so much music, your colleagues—you've got to be in form. There's a lot of emotion."

Merrill is also well known to New York Yankee fans for his taped rendition of "The Star Spangled Banner" that is the standard game opener. He has also made appearances for Presidents Roosevelt, Truman, Eisenhower, Kennedy, and Johnson, and was the only singer to perform at the Roosevelt Memorial before both houses of the U.S. Congress.

Merrill told *CA:* "I heartily endorse government subsidy to the arts in this country. Arts have long been subsidized in Europe and Canada. We are long overdue here but have made strides in recent years. Young singers today are greatly talented and well schooled but are in a hurry to make successes rather than letting their careers unfold and develop naturally. Consequently, they are having shorter careers. Televised opera is a great way to bring the art to the masses but I would like to see studio performances that would be geared to the camera for greater visual viewing rather than to live audiences."

AVOCATIONAL INTERESTS: Golf and art collecting.

BIOGRAPHICAL/CRITICAL SOURCES: Christian Science Monitor, December, 1965, January 24, 1977; *Opera News,* April 16, 1966, January 9, 1971; *High Fidelity,* October, 1970; Stephen E. Rubin, *New Met in Profile,* Macmillan, 1974; *Newark Star-Ledger,* December 22, 1974; Robert Merrill and Robert Saffron, *Between Acts: An Irreverent Look at Opera and Other Madness,* McGraw, 1976; *New York Times Book Review,* December 12, 1976.

MESSNER, Reinhold 1944-

PERSONAL: Born September 17, 1944, in Bressanone, Italy; son of Josef (a teacher) and Maria (Troi) Messner; married Ursula Demeter, June 24, 1972 (divorced, June 22, 1977). *Education:* Attended the Universita Degli Studi, Padua, Italy, 1967-69. *Home:* St. Magdalena 52, Funes, Italy.

CAREER: Surveyor in Boczano, Italy, 1960-66; Alpine School, Funes, Italy, instructor, 1970—. Lecturer. *Member:* Omicron Delta Upsilon. *Awards, honors:* Prima Mouti, 1968; received award, 1975, for *Der Siebte Grad,* and 1976, for *Bergvoelker der Erde.*

WRITINGS: Zurueck in die Berge, Athesia, 1970; *Die Rote Raketa am Nanga Parbat,* Nymphenburger Verlagshandlung, 1971; (with Vittorio Valare and Domenico A. Rudatis) *Sesto Grado,* Longanesi, 1971; *Sturm am Manaslu: Himalaya-Expeditions-Report,* BLV, 1972; *Aufbruch ins Abenteuer,* Athesia, 1972; *Der Siebte Grad: Extremstes Bergsteigen,* BLV, 1973, translation published as *The Seventh Grade: Most Extreme Climbing,* Oxford University Press, 1974; *Dolomiten Klettersteige: 35 Versicherete Hohenwege Zwischen Brenta und Drei Zinnen,* Athesia, 1974; *Bergvoelker der Erde,* Athesia, 1975; *Arena der Einsamkeit,* Athesia, 1976; *The Challenge,* translation from the German by Noel Bowman and Audrey Salkeld, Oxford University Press, 1977. Contributor to magazines, including *Geo, Alpinism, Bergwelt,* and *Bergsteiger.*

WORK IN PROGRESS: More books about Alpinism.

SIDELIGHTS: One of the world's noted solo free climbers, Reinhold Messner told *CA:* "For me mountaineering is discovering the man, not the mountain." *Zurueck in der Berge* has been adapted for television.

*　　　*　　　*

MEYNELL, Laurence Walter 1899-
(Valerie Baxter, Robert Eton, Geoffrey Ludlow, A. Stephen Tring)

PERSONAL: Born August 9, 1899, in Wolverhampton, England; son of Herbert and Agnes Meynell; married Shirley Darbyshire (a novelist), 1932 (died, 1955); married Joan Henley, 1956; children: (first marriage) one daughter. *Education:* Attended private schools in England. *Address:* 9 Clifton Terrace, Brighton, Sussex BN1 3HA, England.

CAREER: Worked as schoolmaster and estate agent; writer, 1924—. *Military service:* Served in the Honourable Artillery Company during World War I and in the Royal Air Force during World War II. *Member:* Johnsonian Society (past president), Author's Club, Savage Club, Paternosters.

*WRITINGS—*All novels except as noted: *Mockbeggar,* Harrap, 1924, Appleton, 1925; *Lois,* Appleton, 1927; *Bluefeather,* Appleton, 1928; *The Shadow and the Stone,* Appleton, 1929; *Camouflage,* Harrap, 1930; *The Mystery at Newton Ferry,* Lippincott, 1930; *Asking for Trouble,* Ward, Lock, 1931; *Consummate Rose,* Hutchinson, 1931; *Storm Against the Wall,* Lippincott, 1931; *The House on the Cliff,* Lippincott, 1932; *Watch the Wall,* Harrap, 1933; *So Many Doors,* Lippincott, 1933; *Paid in Full,* Harrap, 1933; *Odds on Bluefeather,* Harrap, 1934, Lippincott, 1935; *The Gentlemen Go By,* Lippincott, 1934; *Third Time Unlucky,* Harrap, 1935; "On the Night of the 18th . . . ", Harper, 1936; *The Door in the Wall,* Harper, 1937; *The House in the Hills,* Nicholson & Watson, 1937, Harper, 1938; *The Hut,* Nicholson & Watson, 1938; *Palace Pier,* Nicholson & Watson, 1938; *The Dandy,* Nicholson & Watson, 1938; *And Be a Vil-*

lain, Nicholson & Watson, 1939; *His Aunt Came Late,* Nicholson & Watson, 1939; *Death's Eye,* Withy Grove Press, 1939.

The Dark Square, Collins, 1941; *The Creaking Chair,* Collins, 1941; *Strange Landing: A Tale of Adventure,* Collins, 1946; *The Evil Hour: A Chronicle of Our Days,* Collins, 1947; *The Bright Face of Danger,* Collins, 1948; *The Echo in the Cave,* Collins, 1949; *The Lady on Platform One,* Collins, 1950; *Party of Eight,* Collins, 1950; *Bedfordshire* (travel and description), R. Hale, 1950; *The Man No One Knew,* Collins, 1951; *'Plum' Warner,* Phoenix House, 1951; *Famous Cricket Grounds* (history), Phoenix House, 1951; *Smoky Joe* (illustrated by Charlotte Hough), Bodley Head, 1952; *Danger Round the Corner,* Collins, 1952; *The Frightened Man,* Collins, 1952; *Builder and Dreamer: A Life of Isambard Kingdom Brunel* (biography; illustrated by Ley Kenyon), Bodley Head, 1952; *Smoky Joe in Trouble* (illustrated by C. Hough), Bodley Head, 1953; *Exmoor* (travel and description), R. Hale, 1953; *Rolls: Man of Speed: A Life of Charles Stewart Rolls* (biography), Bodley Head, 1953; *Policeman in the Family* (illustrated by Neville Dear), Oxford University Press, 1953; *Too Clever by Half,* Collins, 1953; *Give Me the Knife,* Collins, 1954; *Under the Hollies* (illustrated by Ian Robbins), Oxford University Press, 1954; *Where Is She Now?,* Collins, 1955; *Great Men of Staffordshire* (biography), Bodley Head, 1955; *First Men to Fly* (biography), Laurie, 1955; *Bridge Under the Water* (illustrated by J. S. Goodall), Phoenix House, 1955, Roy, 1957.

Smoky Joe Goes to School (illustrated by C. Hough), Bodley Head, 1956; *Saturday Out,* Walker, 1956; *Animal Doctor* (illustrated by Raymond Sheppard), Oxford University Press, 1956; *James Brindley: The Pioneer of Canals* (biography), Laurie, 1956; *The Sun Will Shine,* Transworld, 1956; *Our Patron Saints* (biography; illustrated by John Turner), Acorn Press, 1957; *Thomas Telford: The Life Story of a Great Engineer* (biography; illustrated by Donald Forster), Bodley Head, 1957; *Sonia Back Stage,* Chatto & Windus, 1957; *The Breaking Point,* Collins, 1957; *Nurse Ross Takes Over,* H. Hamilton, 1958; *Farm Animals* (illustrated by Jennifer Miles), E. Ward, 1958; *The Young Architect* (illustrated by David Knight), Oxford University Press, 1958; *District Nurse Carter,* Chatto & Windus, 1958; *One Step From Murder,* Collins, 1958; *Nurse Ross Shows the Way,* H. Hamilton, 1959; *Monica Anson, Travel Agent,* Chatto & Windus, 1959; *The Haunted King,* Bodley Head, 1959.

Nurse Ross Saves the Day, H. Hamilton, 1960; *Baudaberry,* Bodley Head, 1960; *The Abandoned Doll,* Collins, 1960, new edition, H. Hamilton, 1971; *The House on Marsh Road,* Collins, 1960; *The Pit in the Garden,* Collins, 1961; *Moon Over Ebury Square,* R. Hale, 1962; *Nurse Ross and the Doctor,* H. Hamilton, 1962; *Airmen on the Run: True Stories of Evasion and Escape by British Airmen of World War II* (personal narratives), Odhams Press, 1963; *Sleep of the Unjust,* Collins, 1963; *The Dancers in the Reeds,* H. Hamilton, 1963; *Good Luck, Nurse Ross,* H. Hamilton, 1963; *Virgin Luck,* Collins, 1963, Simon & Schuster, 1964; *Scoop,* H. Hamilton, 1964; *More Deadly Than the Male,* Collins, 1964; *Double Fault,* Collins, 1965; *Break for Summer,* H. Hamilton, 1965; *The Empty Saddle,* H. Hamilton, 1965.

Die by the Book, Collins, 1966; *Shadow in the Sun,* H. Hamilton, 1966; *The Imperfect Aunt,* R. Hale, 1966; *The Suspect Scientist,* H. Hamilton, 1966; *The Man in the Hut* (illustrated by Tony Hart), Kaye & Ward, 1967; *The Mauve Front Door,* Collins, 1967; *Weekend in the Scampi Belt,* R. Hale, 1967; *Bessie Scudd: Fifty Years of a Woman's Life,*

R. Hale, 1968; *Death of a Philanderer,* Collins, 1968, Doubleday, 1969; *Of Malicious Intent,* Collins, 1969; *Peter and the Picture Chief* (illustrated by Hart), Kaye & Ward, 1969; (with Colin Pickles) *The Beginning of Words: How English Grew* (history; for children), Blond, 1970, Putnam, 1971; *The Curious Crime of Miss Julia Blossom,* Macmillan, 1970; *Jimmy and the Election* (illustrated by Hart), Kaye & Ward, 1970; *The Shelter,* R. Hale, 1970; *Troy Trotter and the Kitten,* Kaye & Ward, 1970; *The End of the Long Hot Summer,* R. Hale, 1972; *Death by Arrangement,* McKay, 1972; *A View From the Terrace,* R. Hale, 1972; *A Little Matter of Arson,* Macmillan, 1972; *The Fatal Flaw,* Macmillan, 1973; *The Fortunate Miss East,* R. Hale, 1973; *The Thirteen Trumpeters: A Hooky Hefferman Story,* Macmillan, 1973; *The Fairly Innocent Little Man,* Macmillan, 1974; *The Great Cup-Tie* (illustrated by Gareth Floyd), Kaye & Ward, 1974; *The Woman in Number Five,* R. Hale, 1974; *Burlington Square,* Coward, 1974; *The Footpath,* R. Hale, 1975; *Hooky and the Crock of Gold,* Macmillan, 1975; *Don't Stop for Hooky Hefferman,* Macmillan, 1975; *The Folly of Henrietta Dale,* R. Hale, 1976; *The Lost Half Hour,* Macmillan, 1976; *The Vision Splendid,* R. Hale, 1976.

Under pseudonym Valerie Baxter; all published by Bodley Head: *Jane: Young Author,* 1954; *Elizabeth: Young Policewoman,* 1955; *Shirley: Young Bookseller,* 1956; *Hester: Ship's Officer,* 1957.

Under pseudonym Robert Eton; all novels and all published by Nicholson & Watson, unless otherwise noted: *The Pattern,* Harrap, 1934; *The Dividing Air,* Harrap, 1935; *The Bus Leaves for the Village,* 1936; *Not in Our Stars,* 1937; *The Journey,* 1938; *The Legacy,* 1939; *The Faithful Years,* 1939; *The Corner of Paradise Place,* 1940; *St. Lynn's Advertiser,* 1947; *The Dragon at the Gate,* 1949.

Under pseudonym Geoffrey Ludlow; all novels: *Inside Out!; or, Mad as a Hatter!,* Harrap, 1934; *Women Had to Do It!,* Nicholson & Watson, 1936.

Under pseudonym A. Stephen Tring; all fiction for children and all published by Oxford University Press, unless otherwise noted: *The Old Gang* (illustrated by John Camp), 1947; *The Cave by the Sea* (illustrated by T. R. Freeman), 1950; *Barry's Exciting Year* (illustrated by C. Hough), 1951; *Barry Gets His Wish* (illustrated by Hough), 1952; *Young Master Carver: A Boy in the Reign of Edward III* (illustrated by Alan Jessett), Phoenix House, 1952; *Penny Penitent* (illustrated by Freeman), 1953; *Penny Dreadful* (illustrated by Freeman), 1953, reissued; *Penny Triumphant* (illustrated by Freeman), 1953; *Barry's Great Day* (illustrated by Hough), 1954; *The Kite Man,* B. Blackwell, 1955; *Penny Puzzled* (illustrated by Freeman), 1956; *Frankie and the Green Umbrella* (illustrated by Richard Kennedy), H. Hamilton, 1957; *Penny in Italy* (illustrated by Freeman), 1957; *Pictures for Sale* (illustrated by Christopher Brookes), H. Hamilton, 1958; *Peter's Busy Day* (illustrated by Raymond Briggs), H. Hamilton, 1959; *Penny and the Pageant* (illustrated by Kathleen Gell), 1959; *Ted's Lucky Ball* (illustrated by J. Russell), H. Hamilton, 1961; *Penny Says Good-Bye* (illustrated by Gell), 1961; *The Man with the Sack* (illustrated by Peter Booth), H. Hamilton, 1963; *Chad* (illustrated by Joseph Acheson), H. Hamilton, 1966.

SIDELIGHTS: Laurence Meynell's writings have received satisfactory reviews. Of his first book, *Mockbeggar,* a *New York Tribune* critic wrote, "Mr. Meynell writes with undoubted facility and he has his moments." Another early book, *Bluefeather,* was reviewed in the *Boston Transcript:* "The author's style fits his story, and the result is a smoothly written mystery yarn."

Later efforts included *Saturday Out,* critiqued in the *New York Herald Tribune Books:* "Laurence Meynell has assembled a thriller that makes its way with some dexterity and a rather cool air of improvisation while discovering unseemly horrors in a Cotswold village near an atomic installation. . . ." And in reviewing *Death by Arrangement,* a *New York Times Book Review* critic commented, "For a traditional type of mystery, sans sociology, sans heroic action, take a look at *Death by Arrangement.* Meynell, who has been turning 'em out since 1924, is in the main line of the British school. . . . There is no great puzzle here; Meynell puts all of his cards on the table. But his happy-go-lucky investigator is a pleasant chap, [and] the dialogue is urbane."

The film, "The Price of Silence," was based on Meynell's novel, *One Step From Murder.*

BIOGRAPHICAL/CRITICAL SOURCES: New York Tribune, May 3, 1925; *Boston Transcript,* November 3, 1928; *New York Times,* December 23, 1928; *New York Times Book Review,* May 27, 1962, March 29, 1964, November 19, 1972; *New York Herald Tribune Books,* June 3, 1962; *Book Week,* April 19, 1964.*

*   *   *

MICHAELS, Joe
See SALTZMAN, Joseph

*   *   *

MICHEL, Walter   1922-

PERSONAL: Born in 1922, in Cologne, Germany; son of Friedrich (a businessman) and Aennie (Simons) Michel; married Harriet Fleck (a student). *Education:* McGill University, Ph.D., 1948; New York University, M.A., 1961.

CAREER: National Research Council, Ottawa, Canada, physicist working on radioactivity, 1948-55; associated with General Hospital in Boston, Mass., 1954-55; physicist in communications industry, 1956—.

WRITINGS: (Editor with C. J. Fox) *Wyndham Lewis on Art,* Funk, 1969; (contributor) P. Adam Sitney, editor, *Film Culture Reader,* Praeger, 1970; *Wyndham Lewis: Paintings and Drawings,* University of California Press, 1971. Contributor to scientific journals and journals of the arts, including *Film Culture, Apollo,* and *Poetry National Review.*

WORK IN PROGRESS: The Life and Writings of Gottfried Benn.

SIDELIGHTS: Michel writes: "I plan to write a book on the relation between science and art, and a book on the German silent film which, in the hands of certain directors, I consider was a major art form. I plan to retire soon from my job in communications and devote myself to writing full-time."

*   *   *

MIDDLEBROOK, Diane Wood   1939-

PERSONAL: Born April 16, 1939, in Pocatello, Idaho; daughter of Thomas Isaac (a pharmacist) and Helen (a nurse; maiden name, Downey) Wood; married Jonathan Middlebrook (divorced, 1972); children: Leah Wood. *Education:* University of Washington, Seattle, B.A., 1961; Yale University, M.A., 1962, Ph.D., 1968. *Home:* 1101 Green St., San Francisco, Calif. 94109. *Office:* Department of English, Stanford University, Stanford, Calif. 94305.

CAREER: Olympic College, Bremerton, Wash., instructor in English, 1961-62; Stanford University, Stanford, Calif.,

assistant professor, 1966-73, associate professor of English, 1973—, director of Center for Research on Women, 1977-79. *Member:* Modern Language Association of America, Wallace Stevens Society.

WRITINGS: Walt Whitman and Wallace Stevens, Cornell University Press, 1974; *Completing the Creation: Reading Modern Poems,* Stanford Alumni Association, 1978. Contributor to poetry magazines.

WORK IN PROGRESS: A Contagion of Dreams, poems, 1963-77.

*   *   *

MIDDLETON, O(sman) E(dward)   1925-

PERSONAL: Born March 25, 1925, in Christchurch, New Zealand; son of Walter Maitland (in business) and Dorothy (Benson) Middleton; married wife, Maida Edith (marriage ended, January, 1970); children: two. *Education:* Attended University of Auckland, 1946, 1948, and Sorbonne, University of Paris, 1955-56. *Home:* 20 Clifford St., Dalmore, Dunedin, New Zealand. *Agent:* David Bolt, Bolt & Watson Ltd., 8 Storey's Gate, London S.W. 1, United Kingdom.

CAREER: Writer. Has worked variously as a farm worker, clerk, seaman, construction worker, adult education tutor, telephonist, and landscape gardener. *Military service:* Royal New Zealand Air Force, 1944, leading aircraftsman. New Zealand Army, 1945. *Member:* P.E.N. International, New Zealand Foundation for the Blind and Partially Blind. *Awards, honors:* New Zealand government bursary for study in France, 1955-56; New Zealand Literary Fund Award of Achievement, 1959, scholarship, 1965; Hubert Church Memorial Award, 1965, for *A Walk on the Beach;* Robert Burns fellow at Otago University, 1970-71; New Zealand Prose Fiction Award joint winner, 1976.

WRITINGS: Six Poems (poetry), Handcraft Press, 1951; *Short Stories,* Handcraft Press, 1953; *The Stone and Other Stories,* Pilgrim Press-Paul, 1959; *A Walk on the Beach* (short stories), M. Joseph, 1964; *From the River to the Tide* (juvenile), School Publications Branch, New Zealand Department of Education, 1964; *The Loners* (short stories), Square & Circle, 1972; *Selected Stories,* John McIndoe, 1975, International Publications Service, 1976; *Confessions of an Ocelot* [and] *Not for a Seagull,* John McIndoe, 1978.

Work represented in anthologies, including *New Zealand Short Stories,* edited by D. M. Davin, Oxford University Press, 1953; *Coast to Coast,* edited by Clement Semmler, Angus & Robertson, 1966; *New Zealand Short Stories 2,* edited by C. K. Stead, Oxford University Press, 1966; *Headway,* edited by Lois A. Michel, Holt, 1970; *New Zealand Short Stories 3,* edited by Vincent O'Sullivan, Oxford University Press, 1975. Contributor to periodicals, including *Landfall* and *Islands.*

WORK IN PROGRESS: Novels and stories.

SIDELIGHTS: Middleton told *CA:* "Although my chief interest is in English I have an abiding fascination for French language and culture. The plight of the inarticulate interests me keenly and I have sometimes tried to give them a voice."

Several prominent New Zealand writers were invited to respond to a *Landfall* questionnaire about their writing. When O. E. Middleton was asked what, if any, effect his other jobs had had on his writing, he replied: "All have enriched my understanding of fellow-workers, fellow-human-beings. I consider my working background inseparable from my development as a writer."

Jim Williamson noted that Middleton's style of writing, "apparently the record of ordinary, even insignificant events," is responsible for Middleton's "reputation for realism." Williamson observed that "Middleton does not describe things: he handles them with delight." Because of Middleton's obvious pleasure in his work, Williamson felt that the audience was "able to feel the 'thing-ness' of the life, [and be] drawn to participate in it because the writing does so."

Reviewing *The Stone and Other Stories*, R. A. Copland commented that Middleton's "interest centres not on the complexity and variety of the human mind or of human motivation but upon the simple impulses and the nearly inarticulate emotions of uncultivated people." This assessment seemed to be in keeping with Middleton's expressed concern for his "fellow-human-beings." Copland added that Middleton's "close fidelity to idiom and to topography [is due to] a prose . . . built out of Maori borrowings, occupational slang and native plant-names [creating] a necessarily disinfected vernacular which asserts . . . the Kiwi provenance of these stories."

Bill Manhire agreed with Copland's opinion of Middleton's humanism. Calling Middleton "one of our most moral writers," Manhire said, "Middleton has always been able to discover and render the human worth of individuals." Copland added, "His real quest is for the gleam of the human spirit where it breaks out (sometimes improbably) *above* the crude creature movements."

Noting that Middleton's "fictional world is a narrow one," Williamson saw Middleton as a champion of the "'outsiders'; the drifters, the jobless, the displaced and exiled: children, prisoners, sailors, Maoris, artists, immigrants." "As he records their lives," Williamson continued, "Middleton loves them: he is a committed writer whose radical social viewpoint springs from an instinctive identification with the dispossessed."

BIOGRAPHICAL/CRITICAL SOURCES: Landfall, March, 1960, March, 1967; H. Winston Rhodes, *New Zealand Fiction Since 1945*, John McIndoe, 1968; *Islands*, winter, 1973, September, 1976.

* * *

MIGLIS, John 1950-

PERSONAL: Born May 29, 1950, in Brooklyn, N.Y.; married Ernestine Galassi (a dancer), January 2, 1971; children: Jennifer. *Education:* Miami-Dade Community College, A.A., 1972; University of Florida, B.A., 1974, M.A., 1976. *Agent:* John Hawkins, Paul R. Reynolds, Inc., 12 East 41st St., New York, N.Y. 10017.

CAREER: Technical writer, Water and Air Research, Inc., 1976; group manager of technical writing staff, Environmental Science and Engineering, Inc., 1976-77; free-lance writer, 1977—. Visiting instructor at University of Florida, autumn, 1976, adjunct assistant professor, autumn, 1977.

WRITINGS: Not a Bad Man (novel), Morrow, 1978. Author of "Ars Poetica," WPBS-TV, and a screenplay, "Sand." Work represented in *Space Behind the Clock*, Anhinga Press, 1975; *Cafe at St. Mark's*, Anhinga Press, 1976.

WORK IN PROGRESS: Sand, a novel; "Least Resistance," a short story; *The Nightwatch of Pieter Beckum*.

AVOCATIONAL INTERESTS: Karate, wildlife conservation, art restoration, ballet.

MILES, Matthew B(ailey) 1926-

PERSONAL: Born November 3, 1926, in Kentung, Burma; son of Max D. (a physician) and Margaret (a social worker; maiden name, Bailey) Miles; married Elizabeth Baker, 1949; children: Sara, David, Ellen. *Education:* Antioch College, A.B., 1950, M.A., 1951; Columbia University, Ed.D., 1954. *Home:* 94 Sparkill Ave., Tappan, N.Y. 10983. *Office:* Center for Policy Research, 475 Riverside Dr., New York, N.Y. 10027.

CAREER: Columbia University, Teachers College, New York City, assistant professor, 1954-56, associate professor, 1956-61, professor of psychology and education, 1954-71; Center for Policy Research, New York City, senior research associate, 1970—. Adjunct professor at Case Institute of Technology (now Case Western Reserve University), 1964-66; lecturer at University of Leeds, summer, 1967; adjunct professor at Union Graduate School, 1970—. Certified psychologist. Research associate of Horace Mann-Lincoln Institute of School Experimentation, 1955-66; senior research associate at State University of New York at Albany's program in humanistic education, 1971-73. Special adviser in management development for Philips Electrical Co., 1961-62; member of summer staff and conference director for National Training Laboratories, 1954-70, member of board of directors, 1958-61, 1965-68; member of New York Organization Development Network; consultant to educational, industrial, and non-profit organizations. *Military service:* U.S. Army, 1945-46.

MEMBER: European Association for Transnational Studies in Group and Organization Development (fellow), American Psychological Association (fellow), American Sociological Association, American Educational Research Association (head of committee on research utilization, 1964-67), Society for the Psychological Study of Social Issues, Council for Applied Social Research, Eastern Psychological Association, Midwest Group for Human Resources (member of board of directors, 1967-68). *Awards, honors:* U.S. Office of Education senior postdoctoral research fellow, 1968-69; National Institute of Mental Health grants, 1972-74; Fulbright scholar at University of Nijmegen, 1978.

WRITINGS: (With A. H. Passow, S. M. Corey, and D. C. Draper) *Training Curriculum Leaders for Cooperative Research*, Teachers College Press, 1955; *Learning to Work in Groups*, Teachers College Press, 1959, revised edition, 1979; (editor and contributor) *Innovation in Education*, Teachers College Press, 1964; (editor with R. O. Carlson, E. M. Rogers, and others, and contributor) *Change Processes in the Public Schools*, Center for the Advanced Study of Educational Administration, 1965; (with W. W. Charters) *Learning in Social Settings: New Readings in the Social Psychology of Education*, Allyn & Bacon, 1970; (editor with R. A. Schmuck, and contributor) *Organization Development in Schools*, Mayfield, 1971; (with Morton A. Lieberman and I. D. Yalom) *Encounter Groups: First Facts*, Basic Books, 1972; (with Dale G. Lake and Ralph B. Earle) *Measuring Human Behavior: The Assessment of Social Functioning*, Teachers College Press, 1972; (with Amitai Etzioni) *Comparing Psychosocial and Behavior Modification Approaches to Social Casework: A Design and Feasibility Study*, Center for Policy Research, 1974; *The Teacher Center: Educational Change Through Teacher Development*, Syracuse University Research Corp., 1974; *Planning and Implementing New Schools: A Conceptual Framework*, Center for Policy Research, 1977; *On Networking*, National Institute of Education, 1978.

Contributor: L. P. Bradford, editor, *Issues in Training,* National Training Laboratories, 1962; Bradford, K. D. Benne, and J. R. Gibb, editors, *T-Group Therapy and Laboratory Method: Innovation in Re-Education,* Wiley, 1964; M. G. Abbott and J. T. Lowell, editors, *Change Perspectives in Educational Administration,* Auburn University, 1965; Goodwin Watson, editor, *Change in School Systems,* National Training Laboratories, 1967; W. G. Bennis, Benne, and Robert Chin, editors, *The Planning of Change,* Holt, revised edition (Miles was not included in 1st edition), 1969; *Process Education: Its Meaning and Merit,* Eastern Regional Institute for Education, 1971; S. V. Temkin and M. V. Brown, editors, *What Does Research Say About Getting Innovations into Schools?: A Symposium,* Research for Better Schools, 1974; A. E. Adams, editor, *In-Service Education and Teachers' Centres,* Pergamon, 1975; Warner Burke, editor, *The Cutting Edge: Theory and Practice in OD,* University Associates, 1978. Also contributor to *Organization Development: Theory and Practice,* edited by D. E. Zand.

Contributor to education and psychology journals. Editor of *Journal of Applied Behavioral Science,* 1971-73 (member of board of directors, 1965-70); member of editorial board of *Interpersonal Development,* 1971—, *Journal for the Study of Planned Change,* 1972—, and *Educational Change and Development,* 1978—; member of board of directors of *Journal of Social Issues,* 1965-68; consulting editor of *Journal of Applied Social Psychology,* 1970-78, *Social Psychology,* 1976—, and National Press Books, 1970-71.

SIDELIGHTS: Miles writes that his areas of professional specialization include social psychology, small groups, and organization change processes. He told *CA:* "My current topics of primary concern are: organization design and creation; implementation of educational innovations; knowledge utilization; organization development as a change strategy; consequences of feedback of qualitative data."

*   *   *

MILLER, E. F.
    See POHLE, Robert W(arren), Jr.

*   *   *

MILLER, Neal E(lgar)   1909-

PERSONAL: Born August 3, 1909, in Milwaukee, Wis.; son of Irving E. (a university professor) and Lily (Fuenfstueck) Miller; married Marion Edwards, June 30, 1948; children: York, Sara Miller Mauch. *Education:* University of Washington, Seattle, B.S., 1931; Stanford University, M.A., 1932; Yale University, Ph.D., 1935. *Home:* 500 East 77th St., Apt. 1423, New York, N.Y. 10021. *Office:* Laboratory of Physiological Psychology, Rockefeller University, 1230 York Ave., New York, N.Y. 10021.

CAREER: Yale University, New Haven, Conn., research assistant in psychology, 1933-35; Vienna Psychoanalytic Institute, Vienna, Austria, council fellow, 1935-36; Yale University, New Haven, research assistant, 1936-41, research associate, 1941-42, 1946-50, professor, 1950-52, James Rowland Angell Professor of Psychology, 1952-66; Rockefeller University, New York, N.Y., professor of psychology and head of Laboratory of Physiological Psychology, both 1966—. *Military service:* U.S. Army Air Forces, 1942-46; became major.

MEMBER: National Academy of Sciences, American Philosophical Society, American Psychological Association (president, 1960-61), Society for Neuroscience (president,

1971-72), Academy of Behavioral Medicine Research (president, 1978-79). *Awards, honors:* Warren Medal from Society for Experimental Psychology, 1956; Newcomb Cleveland Prize from American Association for the Advancement of Science, 1959; distinguished scientific contribution award from American Psychological Association, 1964, national medal of science, 1964; D.Sc., University of Michigan, 1965, University of Pennsylvania, 1968, and St. Lawrence University, 1973; gold medal from American Psychological Foundation, 1975; Ph.D., University of Uppsala, 1977. McAlpin Award from National Mental Association, 1978.

WRITINGS: (With L. W. Doob, O. H. Mowrer, and others) *Frustration and Aggression,* Yale University Press, 1939; (with J. Dollard) *Social Learning and Imitation,* Yale University Press, 1941; (editor) *Psychological Research on Pilot Training,* U.S. Government Printing Office, 1947; (with Dollard) *Personality and Psychotherapy,* McGraw, 1950; *Graphic Communication and the Crisis in Washington,* National Education Association, 1957; *Neal E. Miller: Selected Papers,* Aldine-Atherton, 1971. Contributor of more than one hundred fifty articles to scientific journals.

WORK IN PROGRESS: Research on biofeedback, the effects of learning on visceral responses, the effects of learning on homeostasis, and the effects of stress on the immune system.

*   *   *

MILLER, Randall Martin   1945-

PERSONAL: Born April 16, 1945, in Chicago, Ill.; son of Richard A. (a real estate investor) and Irma (a secretary and urban planner; maiden name, Jockwig) Miller; married Linda Rae Patterson (a professor of American literature), August 3, 1968. *Education:* Hope College, A.B., 1967; Ohio State University, M.A., 1968, Ph.D., 1971. *Politics:* "Jeffersonian, with a tinge of John Adams." *Religion:* Presbyterian. *Home:* 244 Sagamore Rd., Havertown, Pa. 19083. *Office:* Department of History, St. Joseph's College, Philadelphia, Pa. 19131.

CAREER: Otterbein College, Westerville, Ohio, counselor and resident dormitory supervisor, 1968-69; Ohio State University, Columbus, lecturer in history, 1970-71; Wesley College, Dover, Del., assistant professor of history, 1971-72; St. Joseph's College, Philadelphia, Pa., assistant professor, 1972-78, associate professor of history, 1978—. Consultant to Balch Institute. *Member:* American Historical Association, American Studies Association, Organization of American Historians, Ethnic Studies Association, Society of Architectural Historians, Southern Historical Association. *Awards, honors:* American Philosophical Society grant, 1973; American Council of Learned Societies fellowship, 1974; Robert Starobin Memorial Library fellowship, 1975; National Endowment for the Humanities fellowship, 1976.

WRITINGS: (Editor with Thomas Marzik) *Immigrants and Religion in Urban America,* Temple University Press, 1977; *"Dear Master": Letters of a Slave Family,* Cornell University Press, 1978; (editor) *Ethnic Images in American Film and Television,* Balch Institute, 1978; *The Cotton Mill Movement in Alabama,* Arno, 1978; (editor) *"A Warm and Zealous Spirit": John J. Zubly and the Revolution in Georgia,* Beehive Press, 1979. Contributor of articles and reviews to professional and popular journals, including *American Heritage* and *Phylon.*

WORK IN PROGRESS: A book on ethnic images in film, publication by Jerome Ozer, 1979; a book on slave elites; a book on immigrants in the American South; a film script about a black family.

SIDELIGHTS: Miller writes: "I believe that writing history is a craft worthy of careful attention. Good history should also be good reading, and I like to think that my work at least moves in that direction. My work on *'Dear Master'*, a book based on letters written by a slave family, taught me that no people are inarticulate. People find a way of communicating love, fear, hate, sadness, joy, and loneliness. I also recognized that good history is not a tale of kings and battles; rather, it is understanding the continuity of life as much as the discontinuity, of finding the common folk and letting them inform us of their age."

* * *

MILLER, Walter James 1918-

PERSONAL: Born January 16, 1918, in McKee City, N.J.; son of Walter Theodore (an insurance broker) and Celestia (Simmons) Miller; married Judith Tirsch, July 2, 1961 (marriage ended, 1969); married Bonnie Elizabeth Nelson (a Montessori teacher), July 11, 1969; children: Naomi, Jason, Robin, Jared, Elizabeth. *Education:* Brooklyn College (now of City University of New York), B.A., 1941; Columbia University, M.A., 1952. *Home:* 430 Walnut Ave. S.E., Roanoke, Va. 24014. *Office:* Department of English, New York University, 2 University Pl., New York, N.Y. 10003.

CAREER: Brooklyn Polytechnic Institute, Brooklyn, N.Y., instructor, 1946-53, assistant professor of English, 1953-55; Colorado State University, Fort Collins, assistant professor of English, 1955-56; Brooklyn Polytechnic Institute, assistant professor of English, 1956-58; New York University, New York, N.Y., associate professor, 1958-66, professor of English, 1966—, producer for NYU-Radio and Television, 1967—. Lecturer at Hofstra University, 1968—, founder and director of writer's conference, 1973—; lecturer at other writer's conferences; guest on radio and television programs in Iowa and New York. *Military service:* U.S. Army, Infantry, public relations chief, 1943-46.

MEMBER: International P.E.N. (American Center), Authors Guild of Authors League of America, Modern Language Association of America. *Awards, honors:* Special award from Engineers Council for Professional Development, 1964, for "Master Builders of America."

WRITINGS: (Editor with L.E.A. Saidla, and contributor) *Engineers as Writers: Growth of a Literature,* Van Nostrand, 1953; (general editor and author of foreword) Walter Buehr, *Home Sweet Home in the Nineteenth Century,* Crowell, 1965; (editor and author of introduction and notes) Jules Verne, *Twenty Thousand Leagues Under the Sea,* Washington Square Press, 1965, revised edition, 1970; *The Short Story as a Literary Form,* Simon & Schuster, 1968; (with wife, Bonnie Nelson) *Samuel Beckett's "Waiting for Godot" and Other Works: A Critical Commentary,* Monarch, 1971; (with Nelson) *Eldridge Cleaver's "Soul on Ice": A Critical Commentary,* Monarch, 1971; *Joseph Heller's "Catch-22": A Critical Commentary,* Monarch, 1971; (with Nelson) *Kurt Vonnegut's "Slaughterhouse Five": A Critical Commentary,* Monarch, 1973; *The Annotated Jules Verne: Twenty Thousand Leagues Under the Sea,* Crowell, 1976; *Making an Angel: Poems,* Pylon, 1977; *The Annotated Jules Verne: From the Earth to the Moon,* Crowell, 1978.

Contributor: David Findlay, editor, *Jobs and Careers in Electronics,* Ziff-Davis, 1959 edition, 1958, 1960 edition, 1959, 1961 edition, 1960; H.A. Estrin, editor, *Technical and Professional Writing: A Practical Anthology,* Harcourt, 1963; (author of foreword) Charles L. Barber, *The Story of Speech and Language,* Crowell, 1965; Oscar Williams, editor, *Master Poems of the English Language,* Trident, 1966; (author of foreword) George Moore, *A Mummer's Wife,* Washington Square Press, 1967; (author of foreword) Moore, *The Brook Kerith,* Liveright, 1969; (author of introduction) Homer, *The Odyssey,* Washington Square Press, 1969; (author of introduction) Homer, *The Iliad,* Washington Square Press, 1969; (author of introduction) Sophocles, *Antigone,* Washington Square Press, 1970; (author of introduction) Edwin Corle, *Fig Tree John,* Liveright, 1971; (author of introduction) Burne Hogarth, *Jungle Tales of Tarzan,* Watson-Guptill, 1976.

Work represented in *Fighting Words,* edited by Warfield Lewis, Lippincott, 1944.

Radio and television: (Co-author) "Christmas in Combat," WRBL-Radio, 1944; (co-author) "Music at Midnight" (dramatization of David Ewen's *Men of Popular Music),* WRBL-Radio, 1945; (co-author) "Poetry With and Without Music," two parts, WEVD-Radio, 1961; (co-author) "Literature and the Equality of Women," WBBM-Radio, 1962; "Pleasures of Learning" (series), WNYC-Radio, 1962; (co-author) "Master Builders of America" (series), NBC-TV, 1963-64; "Let It Be Said" (series), WNBC-Radio, 1963; "The Bridge as Fact and Symbol," WNYC-TV, 1963; "Frontiers of Learning: The Studious American" (series), NBC-TV, 1962; "Poetry as a Social Experience," WNYC-FM Radio, 1967; "Consultants-at-Large" (interview series), WNYC-TV, 1967-68; "NYU Audio" (interview series), WEVD-AM & FM Radio, 1968-70; (co-author) "Man and War in the Arts," three parts, WNYC-TV, 1968; "Book Scene" (interview series), WNYC-TV, 1968-70; "Reader's Almanac" (interview series), WNYC-FM Radio, 1970—; (co-author) "Jules Verne," NBC-TV, 1972; "Author! Author!" (interview series), WNYU-FM Radio, 1973—.

Author of teacher's manuals and reader's supplements for Washington Square Press. Contributor to *Explicator Cyclopedia.* Contributor of more than fifteen hundred articles, stories, poems, and reviews to scientific journals and poetry magazines, including *New York Quarterly, Poet Lore,* and *Western Humanities Review,* and newspapers.

WORK IN PROGRESS: *Kurt Vonnegut Talks with Walter James Miller About Writing.*

SIDELIGHTS: Miller comments: "I write because only then can I achieve focus and comprehension. To me, a writer is a person who is miserably incomplete until he writes."

* * *

MILLER, William (Moseley) 1909-

PERSONAL: Born July 20, 1909, in Pascagoula, Miss.; son of Albert Magnus (a sea captain) and Nettie (Maddox) Miller; married Mable Breeland, September 2, 1937; children: Sarah Patsy Miller Knight. *Education:* Attended Harrison-Stone Jackson Junior College, 1929-32, George Washington University, 1933, and Atlanta University, 1958. *Politics:* Democrat. *Religion:* Baptist. *Agent:* Ruth Hagy Brod Literary Agency, 15 Park Ave., New York, N.Y. 10016.

CAREER: U.S. House of Representatives, Washington, D.C., mail carrier, 1933-39, messenger to the doorkeeper, 1939-43, assistant to the Sergeant at Arms, 1943-47, Democratic doorkeeper, 1947-76. Member of the board of governors of the United Givers Fund, 1966-71. *Member:* Masons, Shriners. *Awards, honors:* Named colonel, aide de camp, to the state of Mississippi, 1956, colonel to the state of Kentucky, 1963, colonel to the Louisiana governor, 1965, and lieutenant colonel, aide de camp to the Georgia governor, 1967; elected to the Mississippi Gulf Coast Junior College Hall of Fame, 1971.

WRITINGS: (With Frances Spatz Leighton) *Fishbait: The Memoirs of the Congressional Doorkeeper* (autobiography; Literary Guild selection), Prentice-Hall, 1977.

SIDELIGHTS: When William Miller was a boy, he was dubbed "Fishbait" because of his scrawny build. The nickname stuck, even after Miller became Democratic doorkeeper of the U.S. House of Representatives. As doorkeeper, Miller was chiefly responsible for keeping unauthorized people off the floor of the House, but his duties encompassed far more than that. In his own words, he was "part footman, part chauffeur, part courtier, and part royal clown or hatchet man." Working under his directorship were twenty-six assistant doorkeepers, messengers, pages, telephone operators, and cloakroom employees.

Miller recounts some of his experiences as doorkeeper in *Fishbait: The Memoirs of the Congressional Doorkeeper.* Studded with anecdotes about congressmen, the book has attracted mixed reviews. A critic for *New Republic* called the tone of the book "unremittingly affectionate," and noted that "Fishbait is aware that the public thirsts for tantalizing tales of boozing, womanizing, influence peddling and various high crimes and misdemeanors. He can not quite bring himself to satisfy that need, however, and his stories are for the most part well known and not very instructive."

The opposite tack was taken by a reviewer for the *New York Times Book Review.* "Disguised as an affectionate review of a lifetime in Congress, 'Fishbait' reads more like revenge on the institution that removed him from power in 1975," wrote Jeff Greenfield. He felt that Miller revealed too much about the drunken sprees and lascivious tendencies of congressmen, and termed the book "one of the harshest assaults on parliamentary democracy since the days of Guy Fawkes." A more balanced view was suggested by Anne Chamberlin, who reminded readers that Miller did not create the unsavory world that he describes in *Fishbait:* "It's not really his fault that the world he describes is so unattractive. The enemy is us."

BIOGRAPHICAL/CRITICAL SOURCES: New Orleans Times-Picayune, February 2, 1975; William Miller and Frances Spatz Leighton, *Fishbait: The Memoirs of the Congressional Doorkeeper,* Prentice-Hall, 1977; *Washington Post Book World,* May 1, 1977; *New York Times Book Review,* May 8, 1977; *New Republic,* June 18, 1977; *Economist,* September 24, 1977; *New Yorker,* November 14, 1977.*

* * *

MILLS, Gary B(ernard) 1944-

PERSONAL: Born September 10, 1944, in Marshall, Tex.; son of Harold Garland (a rice planter) and Hazel Cecilia (Rachal) Mills; married Elizabeth Shown (a writer), April 15, 1963; children: Clayton Bernard, Donna Rachal, Daniel Garland. *Education:* Delta State University, B.A., 1967; Mississippi State University, M.A., 1969, Ph.D., 1974. *Religion:* Roman Catholic. *Home:* 543 Haralson Ave., Gadsden, Ala. 35901. *Office:* Department of History, University of Alabama, George Wallace Dr., Gadsden, Ala. 35902.

CAREER: McNeese State University, Lake Charles, La., instructor in history, 1969-72; Mississippi State University, Starkville, instructor in history, 1972-76; University of Ala-

bama, Gadsden, assistant professor of history, 1976—. Consultant to U.S. Army Corps of Engineers. *Member:* American Historical Association, Organization of American Historians, Southern Historical Association, Red River Valley Historical Association, Louisiana Historical Association, Alabama Historical Association, Phi Kappa Phi, Phi Alpha Theta. *Awards, honors:* Robert H. Brown Award from Louisiana Historical Association, 1975, for article, "The Chauvin Brothers"; Louisiana Literary Award, 1978, for *The Forgotten People: Cane River's Creoles of Color.*

WRITINGS: (With wife, Elizabeth Shown Mills) *Melrose,* Association for the Preservation of Historic Natchitoches, 1973; *The Forgotten People: Cane River's Creoles of Color,* Louisiana State University Press, 1977; (with E. S. Mills) *Tales of Old Natchitoches,* Association for the Preservation of Historic Natchitoches, 1978; *Of Men and Rivers,* U.S. Army Corps of Engineers, 1978; (editor) *Civil War Claims in the South,* Polyanthos, 1978; *A Race Apart: Free Negroes in Antebellum Alabama,* Louisiana State University Press, 1979. Contributor to southern history journals and magazines.

WORK IN PROGRESS: A historical novel about a black family dynasty that rises from slavery in colonial Louisiana to become masters of an antebellum plantation system with eighteen thousand acres of land and five hundred slaves of their own (a true story of the family that built Melrose, which is now a national historic landmark).

SIDELIGHTS: Mills writes: "As an historian and writer of the Old South I am particularly concerned with historic interpretations and portrayals of race relations and racial roles. I vehemently disagree with past and contemporary writers who portray Southern blacks as non-achievers and problems in society, rather than contributors to it, and those who interject stereotyped modern attitudes, both Southern and Northern, into their interpretations of racial interaction in the Old South. Through grassroots analyses of minority groups in a variety of contrasting Southern cultures (Latin, Anglo, rural, urban, prosperous, indigent) I strive for a balanced portrayal of the contributions to society that have been made by minorities and a more precise reinterpretation of their historic role.

"Above all, I feel strongly that the end purpose of historical writing is not solely *the edification of professional historians or students* but the *involvement of people,* the development of an appreciation within the masses for the circumstances and the people which have shaped present society. In short, I strive for a more valid reinterpretation of Southern and black history, presented in terms to which both the professional and the layman can relate."

* * *

MILLS, John 1930-

PERSONAL: Born June 23, 1930, in London, England; son of Albert William and Dorothy (Blakeway) Mills; married Jocelyn Thomas (a realtor), June 1, 1961. *Education:* University of British Columbia, B.A., 1964; Stanford University, M.A., 1965. *Religion:* Anglican. *Home:* 1926 West 14th Ave., Vancouver, British Columbia, Canada. *Office:* Department of English, Simon Fraser University, Burnaby, British Columbia, Canada.

CAREER: Worked as fisherman, lumberjack, labourer, and hotel employee in France, Scandinavia, Italy, North Africa, and other countries, 1947-50; labourer in England, France, and Greece, 1950-52; technical writer for Air Trainers Ltd. in Aylesbury, England, and gandy dancer for Canadian Pacific Railway (CPR) in White River, Ontario, 1953; salesman for Grolier Encyclopedia Co. in Northern Ontario and Manitoba, 1953-55; technical writer for Canadian Aviation Electronics (CAE) and Canadair, both in Montreal, Quebec, 1955-56; radio technician for Macroni, Ltd. in Canada, 1956-57; radar technician for Federal Electric, 1957-59; high school teacher, laundry owner, and real estate speculator in Montreal, 1959-61; Simon Fraser University, Burnaby, British Columbia, instructor, 1965-68, assistant professor, 1968-73, associate professor of English, 1973—. *Military service:* British Army, 1950-52; served in Germany. *Awards, honors:* Woodrow Wilson fellowship, 1964; Canada Council arts fellowships, 1968, 1974.

WRITINGS—Novels: *The Land of Is,* Oberon Press, 1972; *The October Man,* Oberon Press, 1973; *Skevington's Daughter,* Oberon Press, 1978. Contributor to magazines, including *West Coast Review, Queen's Quarterly,* and *Fiddlehead.*

WORK IN PROGRESS: A novel based on the "Demeter Case" in Toronto; autobiographical essays.

SIDELIGHTS: Mills writes: "I traveled widely in my early youth, working as a labourer, fisherman, and deckhand in most parts of Europe, especially Scandinavia. I am now glad I did this and do not want to do it again. When I travel now I go as a bourgeois tourist.

"I wrote lugubrious prose and fiction of a pessimistic nature until 1961, then found my own voice after seeing two Truffaut movies—'Four Hundred Blows' and 'Shoot the Piano Player.' I now consider myself a writer of satiric novels of 'artifice.'"

* * *

MILOSLAVSKY, Nikolai Dimitrievich Tolstoy
See TOLSTOY (-MILOSLAVSKY), Nikolai
(Dimitrievich)

* * *

MILOSZ, Czeslaw 1911-
(J. Syruc)

PERSONAL: Surname is pronounced *Mee*-wosh; born June 30, 1911, in Szetejnie, Lithuania; came to United States, 1960; naturalized U.S. citizen; son of Aleksander (a civil engineer) and Weronika (Kunat) Milosz; married Janina Dluska, 1944; children: two sons. *Education:* University of Vilnius, law degree, 1934. *Home:* 978 Grizzly Peak Blvd., Berkeley, Calif. 94708. *Office:* Department of Slavic Languages and Literatures, University of California, 5416 Dwinelle Hall, Berkeley, Calif. 94720.

CAREER: Polish poet, critic, essayist, novelist, and translator. A founder of the catastrophist school of Polish poetry and a leader of the second avante-garde before World War II; worked for Warsaw underground against the Nazis and was a member of the Polish diplomatic service, 1946-50; he reluctantly exiled himself to Paris and continued his writing career, 1951-60; University of California, Berkeley, lecturer, 1960-61, professor of Slavic languages and literatures, 1961—. Founder of literary periodical *Zagary. Member:* American Association for the Advancement of Slavic Studies, P.E.N. Club. *Awards, honors:* Prix Litteraire Europeen, Geneva, 1953, for novel *La Prise du Pouvoir;* Marian Kister Literary Award, 1967; Jurzykowski Foundation Award for creative work, 1968; Institute for Creative Arts fellow, University of California, Berkeley, summer, 1968; Polish P.E.N. Club award for poetry translations, 1974;

Guggenheim fellow, 1976; Litt.D., University of Michigan, 1977; Neustadt International Literary Prize for Literature, 1978.

WRITINGS: Poemat o czasie zastyglym (poetry; title means "A Poem on Time Frozen"), [Vilnius], 1933; (editor with Zbigniew Folejewski) *Antologia poezji spolecznej* (title means "Anthology of Social Poetry"), [Vilnius], 1933; *Trzy zimy* (poetry; title means "Three Winters"), [Vilnius], 1936; (under pseudonym J. Syruc) *Wiersze* (clandestine publication; title means "Poems"), [Warsaw], 1940; (editor) *Piesn niepodlegla* (clandestine collection of resistance poetry; title means "Invincible Song"), Oficyna, 1942; (editor and translator) Jacques Maritain, *Drogami kleski* (clandestine anti-Nazi publication), [Warsaw], 1942; *Ocalenie* (poetry; title means "Salvage"), Czytelnik, 1945.

Zniewolony umysl (essays; title means "The Captive Mind"), Instytut Literacki, 1953, translation by Jane Zielonko published as *The Captive Mind,* Knopf, 1953; *La Prise du pouvoir* (novel), translated from original Polish manuscript by Jeanne Hersch, Gallimard, 1953, original Polish edition published as *Zdobycie wladzy,* Instytut Literacki, 1955, translation by Celina Wieniewska published as *The Seizure of Power,* Criterion, 1955 (published in England as *The Usurpers,* Faber, 1955); *Swiatlo dzienne* (poetry; title means "Daylight"), Instytut Literacki, 1953; *Dolina Issy* (novel; title means "The Valley of Issa"), Instytut Literacki, 1955; (editor and translator) Jeanne Hersch, *Polityka i rzeczywistosc,* Instytut Literacki, 1955; *Traktat poetycki* (poetry; title means "Treatise on Poetry"), Instytut Literacki, 1957; (editor and translator) Daniel Bell, *Praca i jej gorycze* (title means "Work and Its Discontents), Instytut Literacki, 1957; (editor and translator) Simone Weil, *Wybor pism* (selected works) Instytut Literacki, 1958; *Kontynenty* (title means "Continents"), Instytut Literacki, 1958; *Rodzinna Europa* (essays), Instytut Literacki, 1959, translation by Catherine S. Leach published as *Native Realm: A Search for Self-Definition,* Doubleday, 1968; (editor and translator) *Kultura masowa* (title means "Mass Culture"), Instytut Literacki, 1959.

(Editor and translator) *Wegry* (title means "Hungary"), Instytut Literacki, 1960; *Krol Popiel i inne wiersze* (title means "King Popiel and Other Poems"), Instytut Literacki, 1962; *Czlowiek wsrod skorpionow: Studium o Stanislawie Brzozowskim* (title means "A Man Among Scorpions: A Study on St. Brzozowski"), Instytut Literacki, 1962; (editor and translator) *Postwar Polish Poetry: An Anthology,* Doubleday, 1965; *Gucio zaczarowany* (title means "Bobo's Metamorphosis"), Instytut Literacki, 1965; *Wiersze* (poetry; title means "Poems"), Oficyna Poetow i Malarzy, 1967; *Lied vom Weltende* (poetry; title means "A Song for the End of the World"), Kiepenheuer & Witsch, 1967; (translator) Zbigniew Herbert, *Selected Poems,* Penguin, 1968; *Miasto bez imienia* (poetry; title means "City Without a Name"), Instytut Literacki, 1969; *The History of Polish Literature,* Macmillan, 1969; *Widzenia nad Zatoka San Francisco* (title means "Views from San Francisco Bay"), Instytut Literacki, 1969.

Prywatne obowiazki (essays; title means: "Private obligations"), Instytut Literacki, 1972; *Selected Poems,* Seabury, 1973; *Gdzie wschodzi slonce i kedy zapada* (poetry; title means "From Where the Sun Rises to Where it Sets"), Instytut Literacki, 1974; *Utwory poetyckie* (poetry; title means "Poems"), Michigan Slavic Publications, 1976; (editor) *Lettres inedites de O. V. de L. Milosz a Christian Gauss* (correspondence of Milosz's uncle, the French poet Oscar Milosz), Silvaire, 1976; (interviewer) Lidia Ciolkoszowa, editor, Aleksander Wat, *Moj wiek: Pamietnik mowiony* (title means "My Century: An Oral Diary"), Polonia Book Fund, 1977; (translator) *Ksiega Eklezjasty* (title means "The Books of Ecclesiastes"), Tygodnik Powszechny, March-April, 1977; *Emperor of the Earth: Modes of Eccentric Vision,* University of California Press, 1977; (translator from Polish) Alexander Wat, *Mediterranean Poems,* Ardis, 1977; *Ziemia Ulro* (essays; title means "The Land of Ulno"), Instytut Literacki, 1977; *Bells of Winter,* Ecco Press, 1978; (translator) *Ewangelia wedlug sw. Marka* (title means "The Gospel According to St. Mark"), Znak, 1978.

WORK IN PROGRESS: Psalmy (a translation of the Psalms).

SIDELIGHTS: Czeslaw Milosz is considered one of the greatest contemporary Polish poets. Although he gained much of his recognition through his essays in *The Captive Mind,* his creativity is best expressed in his poetry.

During his years at the University of Vilnius, Milosz belonged to a literary group of leftists called Zagary, which prophesied a worldwide cataclysm. They were dubbed the catastrophist school. While avante-garde poets of his time were busy fighting traditional rhythm and rhyme schemes, Milosz and his young associates led the second avante-garde much further with a protest against society, concerning themselves mainly with Poland's problems during post-World War I years. Although Milosz was one of the youngest in this group, his first published work, *Poemat o Czasie Zastyglym* already showed his potential as a major poet. Even the Skamander group, Poland's poetic establishment of the time, had to admit that Milosz had talent.

Milosz remained in Poland during World War II, where he edited, translated, and wrote for the underground. A collection of his poetry, *Ocalenie,* published immediately after the war, shows the change in his style and tone as he expressed the horrors and heroism of war. Milosz disagreed with the compulsory "socialist realism" and the regimentation of cultural life in Poland after the war, and he reluctantly decided to break with his country. Since he wrote exclusively in his native Polish, by exiling himself to France in 1951 he left his audience behind. Despite the language barrier, however, his poetry was soon recognized in the West as well.

For nine years Milosz remained in France. While there he received the Prix Litteraire Europeen for *La Prise du Pouvoir.* In 1960 Milosz came to the University of California at Berkeley where he is still a professor of Slavic languages and literatures.

Critic Zbigniew Folejewski praises the intellectual depth of Milosz's poetry, which he says results from his "intimate contact with Western literature, his deep concern with the moral and political conflicts," and his "striving for purity of expression." There is some disagreement as to which era of Milosz's poems are the finest, but Paul Zweig feels that since his move to the United States "the images . . . that provide nostalgic substance in his later work are answered by a counterpoint of speedways and white California cities . . . [and] above all by the interrogating presence of the American wilderness," thus bringing a new and important element into his writing.

In addition to his own writing, Milosz has translated poems by English, French, Spanish, Lithuanian, and Yiddish poets into Polish. He has also been acclaimed for his translations of writings by Polish poets, especially Zbigniew Herbert, into English. While the translations sometimes betray his unfamiliarity with English idioms, they are generally praised for their consistent excellence.

BIOGRAPHICAL/CRITICAL SOURCES: Saturday Review, June 6, 1953; *Partisan Review,* November, 1953, spring, 1977; *New Yorker,* November 7, 1953; *New Republic,* May 16, 1955; A. Gillon and L. Krzyzanowski, editors, *Introduction to Modern Polish Literature,* Twayne, 1964; *Book Week,* May 9, 1965; G. Goemoeri, *Polish and Hungarian Poetry, 1945 to 1956,* Oxford University Press, 1966; *Eastern European Poetry,* April, 1967; *New York Times,* June 25, 1968; *Book World,* September 29, 1968; *Books Abroad,* winter, 1969, spring, 1970, winter, 1975; *New York Review of Books,* April 4, 1974; *Village Voice,* May 2, 1974; *New York Times Book Review,* July 7, 1974; *Virginia Quarterly Review,* spring, 1975; *Contemporary Literary Criticism,* Volume 5, Gale, 1976; *American Poetry Review,* January, 1977; *Times Literary Supplement,* December 2, 1977, August 25, 1978; *World Literature Today,* winter, 1978, summer, 1978.

* * *

MILSTEIN, Mike M(yron)   1937-

PERSONAL: Born November 8, 1937; son of Martin and Dorothy (Lasky) Milstein; married Linda L. Lee, April 3, 1966; children: Temara Jessie, Avi Seth. *Education:* University of Minnesota, B.S., 1959, M.A., 1960; University of California, Berkeley, Ph.D., 1967. *Home:* Windwood, Hickory Lane, East Aurora, N.Y. 14052. *Office:* Department of Educational Administration, State University of New York at Buffalo, 468 Christopher Baldy Hall, Buffalo, N.Y. 14260.

CAREER: Social studies teacher in public schools in Minneapolis, Minn., 1961-64; State University of New York at Buffalo, assistant professor, 1967-71, associate professor, 1971-76, professor of educational administration, 1976—. Visiting fellow of Anglian Regional Management Centre at North East London Polytechnic, 1973-74. *Member:* American Educational Research Association (chairman of politics of education special interest group), Phi Delta Kappa (vice-president).

WRITINGS: (With Robert E. Jennings) *Factors Underlying Bond Referendum Successes and Failures in Selected Western New York School Districts, 1968-1969* (monograph), Western New York School Development Council, 1970; *State Education Agency Planning and Federally Funded Programs: Perceptions of Selected Groups* (monograph), Improving State Leadership in Education (Denver, Colo.), 1971; (with Jennings) *Educational Policy Making and the State Legislature: The New York Experience,* Praeger, 1973; (editor with James A. Belasco) *Educational Administration and the Behavioral Sciences: A Systems Perspective,* Allyn & Bacon, 1973; (contributor) Troy McKelvey, editor, *Handbook on Metropolitan School Organization,* McCutchan, 1973; (with Jennings and James A. Conway) *Understanding Communities,* Prentice-Hall, 1974; *Impact and Response: Federal Aid and State Education Agencies,* Teachers College Press, 1976; (editor) *Schools, Change and Conflict,* Teachers College Press, 1979. Contributor of more than fifteen articles to education journals.

* * *

MILVERTON, Charles A.
See PENZLER, Otto

* * *

MINER, Dwight Carroll   1904-1978

OBITUARY NOTICE: Born November 4, 1904, in New

York, N.Y.; died August 1, 1978, in Ridgewood, N.J. Educator, specialist in American history, and author. Miner had been a faculty member at Columbia University for forty-six years before his retirement from academic life in 1973. In 1967, he was named Moore Collegiate Professor of History. Miner received numerous awards from appreciative student bodies, including the establishment of a scholarship fund in his name. He was the author of a book on U.S. involvement in the Panama Canal, in addition to a seventeen-volume history of Columbia University. Obituaries and other sources: *Directory of American Scholars,* Volume I: History, 6th edition, Bowker, 1974; *Who's Who in America,* 39th edition, Marquis, 1976; *New York Times,* August 2, 1978.

* * *

MIRON, Murray S(amuel) 1932-

PERSONAL: Born August 7, 1932, in Allentown, Pa.; son of Murray R. and Myrtle (Hurlburt) Miron; married Helen K. Kutuchief (divorced); married Cheryl Adamy, August 6, 1973; children: (first marriage) Melinda S. *Education:* Northwestern University, B.A., 1954; University of Illinois, M.A., 1956, Ph.D., 1960. *Home:* 210 Clarke St., Syracuse, N.Y. 13210. *Office:* Division of Psycholinguistics, Syracuse University, 150 Marshall St., Syracuse, N.Y. 13210.

CAREER: University of Illinois at Urbana-Champaign, Urbana, assistant professor of psychology, 1959-65; Syracuse University, Syracuse, N.Y., associate professor of psychology, 1965-70, professor of psycholinguistics, 1970—, director of Division of Psycholinguistics, 1978—. Member of National Library of Congress steering committee for the implementation of information processing for the blind, National Institute of Mental Health national standardization committee for rehabilitation and disorder codes, and National Institute of Child Health and Human Development Communications Division charter committee; consultant to U.S. Department of Justice.

MEMBER: International Council of Psychologists (fellow), Linguistic Society of America, Acoustical Society of America, American Psychological Association, Psychonomic Society, Academy of Aphasia, Group for the Study of Behavior, Linguistic Circle of New York.

WRITINGS: (Editor with Charles E. Osgood) *Approaches to the Study of Aphasia,* University of Illinois Press, 1963; (with L. S. Hultzen and J.H.D. Allen) *Tables of Transitional Frequencies of English Phonemes,* University of Illinois Press, 1964; *Machine Methods in the Social Sciences,* Institute of Communication Research, 1964; (editor) *Experimental Phoenetics: Selected Articles by Grant Fairbanks,* University of Illinois Press, 1966; (editor with Leon Jakobovits) *Readings in the Psychology of Language,* Prentice-Hall, 1967.

(With J. DeRocher, S. Patten, and D. Pratt) *The Counting of Words,* Defense Language Institute, 1973; (with Osgood and William May) *Cross-Cultural Universals of Affective Meaning,* University of Illinois Press, 1975; *Atlases of Affective Meanings* (on thirty-six languages), University of Illinois Press, 1975; (with Arnold J. Goldstein) *Hostage,* Behaviordelia, 1978; *Reaction to Threat,* Motorola Teleprograms, 1978. Co-author of "Explorations in Semantic Space" (television program), American Psychological Association, 1963. Contributor to psycholinguistic journals. Member of editorial board of *Journal of Psycholinguistic Research.*

WORK IN PROGRESS: The Word Detective: Language Profiles of the Criminal, "reporting on the active case involvement of the author in criminal investigation from the standpoint of psycholinguistics."

SIDELIGHTS: Miron commented: "Ben Johnson observed that 'Language most shows a man: "speak that I may see thee." It springs out of the most retired and inmost part of us, and is the image of the parent of it, the mind. No glass renders a man's form of likeness as true as his speech.' Whether man is at his noblest or his most criminal, his language can be his gauge. This author has specialized in the language of those men who would use language to threaten others.''

* * *

MITCHELL, Loften 1919-

PERSONAL: Born April 15, 1919, in Columbus, N.C.; married Helen March, 1948; children: two. *Education:* Attended City College (now of the City University of New York), 1937-38; Talladega College, B.A., 1943; Columbia University, M.A., 1951; additional study at Union Theological Seminary, and General Theological Seminary. *Home:* 3217 Burris Rd., Vestal, N.Y. 13850. *Office:* Department of Afro-American Studies, State University of New York, Binghamton, N.Y. 13901.

CAREER: Playwright, theatre historian, and novelist; began as actor in New York City during 1930's; social worker for City of New York Department of Welfare; publicity director for Jewish Federation of Welfare Services; assistant for special programs at Harlem Preparatory School; WNCY-Radio, New York City, writer of weekly program "The Later Years," 1950-62; WWRL-Radio, New York City, writer of daily program "Friendly Adviser," 1954; *NAACP Freedom Journal,* New York City, editor for special materials, 1964; Long Island University, New York City, adjunct associate professor of English, 1969; New York University, New York City, adjunct associate professor of English, 1970; State University of New York at Binghamton, lecturer in theatre and Afro-American studies, 1971—. Program director for a senior citizens day center; member of White Council on Aging. *Military service:* U.S. Navy; served during World War II. *Awards, honors:* Guggenheim fellowship, 1958-59; Rockefeller Foundation grant, 1961; Harlem Cultural Council special award, 1969.

WRITINGS: Black Drama: The Story of the American Negro in the Theatre (essays), Hawthorn, 1967; *Harlem, My Harlem* (nonfiction), Emerson Hall, 1973; *The Stubborn Old Lady Who Resisted Change* (novel), Emerson Hall, 1973; *Voices of the Black Theatre,* James T. White, 1975.

Plays: "Blood in the Night," first produced in New York City, 1946; "The Bancroft Dynasty," first produced in New York City, 1948; "The Cellar," first produced in New York City, 1952; *A Land Beyond the River* (first produced in New York City, 1957), Pioneer Drama Service, 1963; (with Irving Burgie) "Ballad for Bimshire" (musical), first produced in New York City, 1963, revised version produced in Cleveland, Ohio, 1964; (with John Oliver Killens) "Ballad of the Winter Soldiers," first produced in New York City, 1964; *Star of the Morning: Scenes in the Life of Bert Williams,* Free Press, 1965; *Tell Pharoah* (first produced in New York City, 1967), Negro Universities Press, 1970; (with Rosetta Lenoire) "Bubbling Brown Sugar" (musical), first produced in New York City, 1975.

Also author of dramas: "The Phonograph"; "Horse's Play"; "And the Walls Came Tumbling Down"; "The Final Solution to the Black Problem in the United States of America; or, The Fall of the American Empire"; "Sojourn to the Southern Wall"; "The World of a Harlem Playwright"; and "The Afro-Philadelphian."

Plays have been represented in anthologies, including *Afro-American Literature: Drama,* edited by William Adams, Peter Conn, and Barry Slepian, Houghton, 1970; *The Black Teacher and the Dramatic Arts,* edited by William R. Reardon and Thomas D. Pawley, Negro Universities Press, 1970; *Black Scenes,* edited by Alice Childress, Doubleday, 1971; *Black Drama Anthology,* edited by Woodie King, Jr. and Ron Milner, New American Library, 1971; *Black Theatre U.S.A.: 1874-1974,* edited by James V. Hatch and Ted Shine, Free Press, 1974.

Also author of film, television, and radio scripts. Contributor to *Oxford Companion to the Theatre* and periodicals, including *Crisis* and *New York Times.*

SIDELIGHTS: Mitchell once explained the beginning of his career in this manner: "I set out to become a playwright, largely because I dared to dream the long dream and others dared to encourage me." He started his work with the theatre while still in high school and joined "the Progressive Dramatizers Group at Salem Church, wrote sketches for it, then worked as an actor for the Rose McClendon Players." Finding opportunities for black actors extremely limited and scarce, Mitchell decided to leave New York City. Doris Abramson says Mitchell recalled that many Negroes who graduated during the Depression were unable financially and academically to attend college, but "Southern Negro colleges, offering athletic scholarships and grants-in-aid, rescued many from the despair into which they had been dumped." Mitchell secured a scholarship from Talladega College in Alabama. En route from Harlem to Talladega, Mitchell said he "saw the first 'colored' and 'White' signs." He added that he "got that sinking feeling that only a black man in these United States can understand. I wondered if I hadn't stepped out of that proverbial frying pan into the equally proverbial, but much hotter, fire."

In March, 1957, Mitchell's "A Land Beyond the River" opened at New York's Greenwich Mews Theatre. The play was originally booked for a ten-week run, but was held over for a year before being taken on tour. One of the major themes of the play is desegregation. Abramson considers the play to be "heavy with message, unashamedly didactic in purpose."

Abramson felt that unlike other black dramatists writing in the twentieth century, Mitchell was writing about "history in the making." She went on to note that Mitchell, "sensing the drama inherent in the early stages in the struggle for desegregated schools . . . focused, in his play, on the experiences of one man who was at the center of that struggle. He did not, however, write a documentary . . . he wrote a fairly conventional play filled with conflict, not just between good Negroes and wicked whites, but between two ways of fighting for a cause." Says Mitchell about his desegregation theme: "We haven't gotten free yet, we got 'integrated'—the double double cross!"

"A Land Beyond the River" was received well critically. Brooks Atkinson said of the play: "Despite the seriousness of the theme, it flares into comedy repeatedly. Mr. Mitchell has not lost his sense of humor in the heart of a crusade." Frances Herridge felt that the play's message was about blacks as "they will win finally . . . not by gunfire or bitterness, but by love and understanding. The implication is that Negroes must set white people a good example, treating them as prodigal sons who will return to brotherhood."

Collections of Loften Mitchell's papers are housed by the State University of New York at Binghamton, Talladega College, and the New York City Library Schomberg Collection.

BIOGRAPHICAL/CRITICAL SOURCES: New York Times, March 29, 1957; *New York Post,* March 29, 1957; *Freedomways,* fall, 1964; *Negro Digest,* June, 1966; *Contemporary Literature,* winter, 1968; Doris E. Abramson, *Negro Playwrights in the American Theatre, 1925-1959,* Columbia University Press, 1969.*

* * *

MITCHELL, Scott
   See GODFREY, Lionel (Robert Holcombe)

* * *

MITCHELL, W.J.T. 1942-

PERSONAL: Born March 24, 1942, in Anaheim, Calif.; son of Thomas Miles (a miner) and Leona (an accountant; maiden name, Gaertner) Mitchell; married Janice Misurell (a composer), August 11, 1968; children: Carmen, Gabriel. *Education:* Michigan State University, B.A., 1964; Johns Hopkins University, M.A., and Ph.D. *Politics:* "Left-Liberal." *Religion:* Agnostic. *Home:* 1331 East 50th St., Chicago, Ill. 60615. *Office:* Department of English, University of Chicago, Chicago, Ill. 60637.

CAREER: Ohio State University, Columbus, assistant professor, 1968-73, associate professor of English, 1973-77; University of Chicago, Chicago, Ill., associate professor of English, 1977—. *Member:* Modern Language Association of America, American Society for Eighteenth Century Studies. *Awards, honors:* American Philosophical Society fellow, 1970; National Endowment for the Humanities fellow, 1977-78.

WRITINGS: Blake's Composite Art, Princeton University Press, 1978. Work represented in anthologies.

Contributor of articles and reviews to language and eighteenth-century studies journals. Co-editor of *Critical Inquiry.*

WORK IN PROGRESS: Word and Image: Essays in Iconology and Poetics, on the interaction of verbal and pictorial structures in the arts.

SIDELIGHTS: Mitchell comments: "The central commitment of my professional life is the theory and practice of criticism, conceived as a method of rigorous intellectual inquiry applicable to all subjects of human concern. I am especially interested in expanding our comprehension of the cognitive nature of artistic works, and overcoming the isolated 'aestheticism' which opposes the arts to practical and scientific matters."

* * *

MITCHELL, William E(dward) 1927-

PERSONAL: Born January 8, 1927, in Wichita, Kan.; son of Edward E. (in business) and Daisy (Watson) Mitchell; married Joyce Slayton (an educational writer), July 4, 1959; children: Edward Slayton, Elizabeth Dix. *Education:* Wichita State University, B.A., 1950; Columbia University, M.A., 1954, Ph.D., 1969. *Home address:* Pleasant Valley Farm, Wolcott, Vt. 05680. *Agent:* Maxine Groffsky, 2 Fifth Ave., New York, N.Y. 10011. *Office:* Department of Anthropology, University of Vermont, Williams Science Hall, Burlington, Vt. 05405.

CAREER: University of Vermont, Burlington, research

associate, 1965-67, assistant professor, 1967-70, associate professor of psychiatry, 1970-73, and anthropology, 1973-78, professor of anthropology, 1978—, head of department, 1978—, leader of anthropological expedition to Papua, New Guinea, 1970-72. Research assistant at Cornell University, 1955-56; research associate of Jewish Family Service of New York, 1957-62. Member of American Museum of Natural History's Jane Belo Expedition to New Guinea, 1967. Lecturer at Cooper Union for the Advancement of Science and Art, 1961; project director for Hope Foundation, 1962-65; convenor of Forum on Children's Rights, 1976-77. *Military service:* U.S. Navy, 1945-46.

MEMBER: American Anthropological Association, American Ethnological Association, American Association for the Advancement of Science, American Association of University Professors, Society for Medical Anthropology, Society for Visual Anthropology, Association for Applied Anthropology, Association for Social Anthropology in Oceania, Royal Anthropological Institute of Great Britain and Ireland, Lamoille County Mental Health Association (president, 1971-72).

WRITINGS: (With Hope Jensen Leichter) *Kinship and Casework: Family Networks and Social Intervention,* Russell Sage, 1967, 2nd edition, Teachers College Press, 1978; *The Bamboo Fire: An Anthropologist in New Guinea,* Norton, 1978; *Mishpokhe: A Study of New York City Jewish Family Clubs,* Mouton, 1978. Contributor to anthropology, natural history, and mental health journals.

WORK IN PROGRESS: Transformations of Evil: Ethnotherapy of the Taute Wape (tentative title); a documentary film on Wape curing cults.

SIDELIGHTS: Mitchell told *CA:* "The question that guides much of my research and writing is the relation between what is culturally defined as 'good' and 'bad.' I am intrigued by the behavioral dialectics set up by these polarized opposites, in how they inter-relate and define one another and, especially, in how societies attempt to eradicate or transform those negative actions that threaten the 'good life.' Related to this interest is a deep concern regarding the tendency for western behavioral science to project its own cultural classifications, for example, 'law,' 'medicine,' and 'religion,' upon exotic cultures to organize moral and social data. In my current work I am formulating an alternative paradigm centered on the concept of 'ethnotherapy' that permits a society's moral beliefs and actions to be phrased in terms of its own institutions with a minimum of cultural distortion.

"*The Bamboo Fire,* my most recent book, is an autobiographical account of fieldwork among a New Guinea tribe in the remote Sepik River Basin. It was written with two purposes in mind. One was to personally 'exorcise' the intensely emotional fieldwork experience, and the other to present a vivid portrait of an anthropologist in action by describing the strange and frustrating—but compelling—experience of living with and studying a primitive society."

Mitchell made a record album, "The Living, Dead, and Dying: Music of the New Guinea Wape," released by Folkways, 1978.

* * *

MOLLEGEN, Anne Rush
See SMITH, Anne Mollegen

MOLLOY, John T. 1937(?)-

PERSONAL: Married. *Residence:* Pennsylvania. *Address:* c/o Follett Publishing Co., 1010 West Washington Blvd., Chicago, Ill. 60607.

CAREER: Author and clothing consultant. Founder of Dress for Success, Inc.

WRITINGS: Dress for Success, Peter H. Wyden, 1975; *The Woman's Dress for Success Book,* Follett, 1977. Also author of syndicated column, "Dress for Success" (formerly "Making It"), appearing in twenty-eight newspapers, including *Detroit Free Press, Philadelphia Inquirer, Milwaukee Journal, Miami News, Seattle Times,* and *Knoxville Journal.*

SIDELIGHTS: Often referred to as a "wardrobe engineer," Molloy believes that clothing plays a large part in a person's ability to be successful. One of Molloy's theories is that women will accomplish more on a job if they adopt a specific uniform. He recommends a conservative blue suit with skirt and white blouse. Molloy also suggests pumps as opposed to boots and believes an attache case is a plus.

But despite its best-seller status, many of *The Woman's Dress for Success Book*'s proposals have met with adamant objection from its female readers. "The typical woman's reaction is generally, 'It's terrible! Oh, my God, are you *kidding?* John, do you really *mean* this?,'" Molloy said. "But most of these women eventually wind up becoming believers."

BIOGRAPHICAL/CRITICAL SOURCES: New York Times Book Review, March 12, 1978.*

* * *

MONET, Dorothy 1927-

PERSONAL: Born May 11, 1927, in New York, N.Y.; daughter of Francisco (a journalist) and Anna (Monet) Manniello; married Jacques Palaci, June 11, 1953 (divorced, October, 1960); married Robert E. Simon, Jr. (in real estate), May 11, 1973; children: (first marriage) Christina Monet. *Education:* Attended Cooper Union College, 1943-45, and Art Students League, 1945-49. *Politics:* "Left wing." *Religion:* "Born Catholic." *Home and office:* 15 West 81st St., New York, N.Y. 10024. *Agent:* Curtis Brown Ltd., 575 Madison Ave., New York, N.Y. 10022.

CAREER: Full-time illustrator for national and international magazines and advertising campaigns; free-lance writer. Co-founder of Women Strike for Peace; active in civil rights and peace movements. *Member:* Authors Guild of Authors League of America, Dramatists Guild. *Awards, honors:* National Endowment for the Arts fellowship, 1978.

WRITINGS: Squandering (novel), Holt, 1971.

Author of plays, "The Wrastling and the Fall," and "Cyrienne." Author of television documentary films, "Mary Cassatt," and "When the World Was Wide." Contributor of illustrations to popular magazines, including *Ladies Home Journal, McCall's,* and *Good Housekeeping.*

WORK IN PROGRESS: Chased Illusions (tentative title), a novel; "Colette's Colette," a television documentary; "Shakespeare for Newcomers," a series for public television.

AVOCATIONAL INTERESTS: Art history, Japanese art and literature, psychology.

MONJO, F(erdinand) N. 1924-

CAREER: Writer and editor. Awards, honors: National Book Award, 1974, for Poor Richard in France.

WRITINGS: Indian Summer (illustrated by Anita Lobel), Harper, 1968; The Drinking Gourd (illustrated by Fred Brenner), Harper, 1970; The One Bad Thing About Father (illustrated by Rocco Negri), Harper, 1970; Pirates in Panama (illustrated by Wallace Tripp), Simon & Schuster, 1970; (translator with Nina Ignatowicz) Reiner Zimnik, The Crane, Harper, 1970; The Jezebel Wolf (illustrated by John Schoenherr), Simon & Schuster, 1971; The Vicksburg Veteran (illustrated by Douglas Gorsline), Simon & Schuster, 1971; Rudi and the Distelfink (illustrated by George Kraus), Windmill Books, 1972; The Secret of the Sachem's Tree (illustrated by Margot Tomes), Coward, 1972; Slater's Mill (illustrated by Laszlo Kubinyi), Simon & Schuster, 1972; (editor) Patricia Lauber, Clarence and the Burglar (illustrated by Paul Galdone), Coward, 1973; Me and Willie and Pa: The Story of Abraham Lincoln and His Son Tad (illustrated by Gorsline), Simon & Schuster, 1973; Poor Richard in France (illustrated by Brinton Turkle), Holt, 1973.

Grand Papa and Ellen Aroon: Being an Account of Some of the Happy Times Spent Together by Thomas Jefferson and His Favorite Granddaughter (illustrated by Richard Cuffari), Holt, 1974; King George's Head Was Made of Lead (illustrated by Tomes), Coward, 1974; The Sea Beggar's Son (illustrated by C. Walter Hodges), Coward, 1974; Letters to Horseface: Being the Story of Wolfgang Amadeus Mozart's Journey to Italy, 1769-1770 (illustrated by Don Bolognese and Elaine Raphael), Viking, 1975; Gettysburg: Tad Lincoln's Story (illustrated by Gorsline), Dutton, 1976; The Porcelain Pagoda (illustrated by Richard Egielski), Viking, 1976; Willie Jasper's Golden Eagle (illustrated by Gorsline), Doubleday, 1976; Zenas and the Shaving Mill (illustrated by Cuffari), Coward, 1976; A Namesake for Nathan, Coward, 1977.

SIDELIGHTS: Critics generally agree that Monjo's books make historical events come alive for young readers. His award-winning Poor Richard in France gave an account of Benjamin Franklin's journey to France as described by Franklin's seven-year-old grandson. A reviewer for Publishers Weekly commented, "The story draws a refreshingly human and endearing portrait of 'Le grand Docteur Franklin. . . .' Altogether a lively story." In reviewing the book for the Bulletin of the Center for Children's Books, Zena Sutherland wrote: "Three cheers for the team of Monjo and [Brinton] Turkle, who have produced an easy-to-read history book that is as engaging as it is informative. . . . Seven-year-old Benny's comments are lively and humorous, and in a perfectly natural way they give a good bit of information about Franklin and about the rebellion against the British."

The author's Letters to Horseface related fourteen-year-old Mozart's tour of Italy through fictitious letters to his sister, Nannerl (affectionately nicknamed 'Horseface'). Monjo reconstructed "the trip through young Mozart's mind, and he has done a remarkable job. The letters read as though they actually came from Wolfgang's pen. . . . [The letters] are light-hearted, and a great deal of information is served up in a painless manner," observed a reviewer for the New York Times. A critic for Publishers Weekly noted that Monjo "is very good at evoking personalities, times and places. His text, based on thorough research, is enhanced by airy, authentic pictures. . . . The book is a fascinating glimpse at the travels and triumphs of [Mozart] as he was accompanied by his father on a tour from Salzburg to Milan.''

BIOGRAPHICAL/CRITICAL RESOURCES: Publishers Weekly, October 8, 1973, November 17, 1975; Mary Gloyne Byler, American Indian Authors for Young Readers, Association on American Indian Affairs, 1973; Bulletin of the Center for Children's Books, March, 1974; New York Times Book Review, November 16, 1975; Children's Literature Review, Volume 2, Gale, 1976.*

*   *   *

MONTGOMERY, Charles F(ranklin) 1910-1978

PERSONAL: Born April 14, 1910, in Austin Twp., Ill.; married; children: Charles F., William P. Education: Harvard University, B.A., 1932. Address: 232 Bradley St., New Haven, Conn. 06510.

CAREER: New York Herald Tribune, New York, N.Y., member of education and promotion departments, 1932-40; dealer in American antiques, 1940-51; Henry Francis du Pont Winterthur Museum, Winterthur, Del., executive secretary and associate curator, 1951-54, director, 1954-61, senior resident fellow, 1962-70; Yale University, New Haven, Conn., professor of art history and curator of Mabel Brady Garvan and Related Collection of American Arts, 1970-78. University of Delaware, lecturer, 1952-67, adjunct professor, beginning 1967; visiting lecturer, University of Pennsylvania, 1965. Member of Independence Hall Furnishing Committee, 1955-58, and consultative committee, Art Quarterly, beginning 1958. Member: International Council of Museums, American Antiquarian Society, American Association of Museums, American Studies Association, Society of Architectural Historians, National Trust for Historic Preservation, Early American Industries Association, College Art Association of America, Furniture History Society, Walpole Society (secretary, 1958-64). Awards, honors: M.A. from University of Delaware, 1954, and Yale University, 1970.

WRITINGS: American Furniture: The Federal Period, Viking, 1966; (compiler) A List of Books and Articles for the Study of the Arts in Early America, [Winterthur, Del.], 1970; A History of American Pewter, Praeger, 1973; (general editor with Patricia E. Kane) American Art, 1750-1800: Towards Independence (collection of essays), New York Graphic Society, 1976. Contributor of articles to museum publications and to professional journals.

SIDELIGHTS: As curator of the Mabel Brady Garvan and Related Collections of American Art at Yale University, Montgomery organized an exhibition of American art that was sent to the Victoria and Albert Museum in London, England. In 1976, the exhibition entitled "American Art, 1950-1800: Towards Independence" opened at the museum and was hailed as a major contribution from the art world towards the celebration of the American bicentennial. During its eight-week stay at the London museum, the exhibition was seen by more than sixty-thousand viewers.

Montgomery also made contributions to American education and was considered a pioneer in the area of forming curriculum programs for students interested in becoming museum curators. During his years at the Henry Francis du Pont Winterthur Museum, Montgomery initiated the first masters program for the training of museum curators in the United States. Montgomery was considered a leading authority on American decorative art.

OBITUARIES: New York Times, February 22, 1978; AB Bookman's Weekly, May 8, 1978.*

(Died February 21, 1978, in New Haven, Conn.)

MONTGOMERY, David 1927-

PERSONAL: Born December 1, 1927, in Bryn Mawr, Pa.; son of Horace Binney and Louise (Tyler) Montgomery; married Martel Wilcher, April 26, 1952; children: Claude D., Edward B. *Education:* Swarthmore College, B.A., 1950; University of Minnesota, M.A., 1960, Ph.D., 1962. *Home:* 1404 Wightman St., Pittsburgh, Pa. 15217. *Office:* Department of History, University of Pittsburgh, Pittsburgh, Pa. 15260.

CAREER: Machinist, 1951-60; University of Pittsburgh, Pittsburgh, Pa., 1962—, began as assistant professor, currently professor of history. Senior lecturer at University of Warwick, 1967-69; Lockwood Professor at State University of New York at Buffalo, 1977-78. *Military service:* U.S. Army, 1946-47; became staff sergeant. *Awards, honors:* Social Science Research Council grant, 1967; American Council of Learned Societies grant, 1970; Guggenheim fellowship, 1972-73.

WRITINGS: *Beyond Equality: Labor and the Radical Republicans, 1862-1872,* Knopf, 1967; *Workers' Control in America: Studies in the History of Work, Technology, and Labor Struggles,* Cambridge University Press, 1978; *Fall of the House of Labor: A History of the American Working Class, 1860-1920,* Cambridge University Press, in press. Contributor to history journals. Editor of *International Labor and Working-Class History;* member of editorial board of *Journal of American History, Labor History,* and *Labour/Le Travailleur.*

SIDELIGHTS: Montgomery told *CA:* "Comparative labor history is a major interest. I have been a participant regularly in the social history roundtables of the Maison des Sciences de l'Homme in Paris."

* * *

MOORE, Geoffrey H(oyt) 1914-

PERSONAL: Born February 28, 1914, in Pequannock, N.J.; son of Edward H. (a builder) and Marian (Leman) Moore; married Ella Goldschmid, July 12, 1938 (died, June, 1975); married Melita Holly, September 28, 1975; children: Stephen, Peter, Kathleen Moore Holness, Pamela Moore Pelligrino. *Education:* Rutgers University, B.S., 1933, M.S., 1937; Harvard University, Ph.D., 1947. *Home:* 1171 Valley Rd., New Canaan, Conn. 06840. *Office:* National Bureau of Economic Research, 261 Madison Ave., New York, N.Y. 10016.

CAREER: National Bureau of Economic Research, New York, N.Y., member of research staff, 1939-48, associate director of research staff, 1939-48, associate director of research, 1948-65, director of research, 1965-68; U.S. Department of Labor, Washington, D.C., commissioner of labor statistics, 1969-73; National Bureau of Economic Research, vice-president in research, 1973-75, director of business cycle research, 1975—. Instructor at Rutgers University, 1939-42; associate professor at New York University, 1947-48; visiting lecturer at Columbia University, 1953-54. Senior research fellow at Hoover Institution on War, Revolution and Peace, 1973-78; adjunct scholar at American Enterprise Institute, 1975—.

WRITINGS: *Business Cycle Indicators,* Volume I: *Contributions to the Analysis of Current Business Conditions,* Volume II: *Basic Data on Cyclical Indicators,* Princeton University Press, 1961; (with Philip A. Klein) *The Quality of Consumer Instalment Credit,* National Bureau of Economic Research, 1967; (with Julius Shiskin) *Indicators of*

Business Expansions and Contractions, National Bureau of Economic Research, 1967; *The Cyclical Behavior of Prices,* Bureau of Labor Statistics, 1971; *How Full Is Full Employment?, and Other Essays on Interpreting the Unemployment Statistics,* American Enterprise Institute, 1973; *Keys to the Business Cycle,* American Management Association, 1979; (with Klein) *Monitoring Business Cycles at Home and Abroad,* National Bureau of Economic Research, 1979; *Business Cycles, Inflation, and Forecasting,* National Bureau of Economic Research, 1979. Contributor to *Contemporary Economic Problems,* American Enterprise Institute, 1976, 1977, 1978.

SIDELIGHTS: Moore believes "the time has come to establish a center for international business cycle research to investigate booms and recessions, inflation, and growth. Its objective would be to provide factual information and objective interpretations of these phenomena, presented in a simple straightforward style. I hope to get this started soon at a university in or near New York."

AVOCATIONAL INTERESTS: Tennis, sailing, gardening.

* * *

MOORE, Jerome (Aaron) 1903-

PERSONAL: Born August 9, 1903, in Rio Vista, Tex.; son of James Aaron (a physician) and Nannie Mae (a teacher; maiden name, Church) Moore; married Ruby Pearl Scott, September 8, 1928; children: Jerome Aaron II. *Education:* Texas Christian University, B.A., 1923, M.A., 1927; further graduate study at University of Texas, 1927-28, Sorbonne, University of Paris, 1929, and University of Geneva, 1932; University of Pennsylvania, Ph.D., 1937. *Home:* 5613 Walla Ave., Fort Worth, Tex. 76133.

CAREER: Ordained minister of Christian Church (Disciples of Christ), 1923; pastor of Christian churches in Shreveport, La., 1923-24; high school teacher of English and history in Corsicana, Tex., 1924-25; Texas Woman's University, Denton, instructor, 1928-29, assistant professor, 1929-34, associate professor, 1934-40, professor of Spanish, 1940-43, co-founder of summer school in Saltillo, Mexico, 1941, director and business manager of Saltillo school, 1941-43; Texas Christian University, Fort Worth, professor of Spanish, 1943-70, head of department of foreign languages, 1944-58, dean of College of Arts and Sciences, 1943-70, dean of university, 1970-73, dean emeritus, 1973—, secretary of board of trustees, 1947-73. President of Texas Council of Church-Related Colleges, 1948-49; life member of Texas Good Neighbor Commission; president of Fort Worth Good Neighbor Council, 1956-57.

MEMBER: American Association of Teachers of Spanish and Portuguese, Southern Association of Schools and Colleges (member of executive committee, 1960-62), South Central Modern Language Association, Texas Foreign Language Association, Texas Foreign Language Association (life member), Association of Texas Colleges and Universities (first vice-president, 1948-49, 1954-55; president, 1955-56), Phi Beta Kappa, Alpha Chi, Pi Kappa Delta, Phi Sigma Iota. *Awards, honors:* Named honorary consul of Mexico in Fort Worth, Tex., 1951-53; D.H.L. from University of the Americas (Mexico), 1963; LL.D. from Texas Christian University, 1968; annual good neighbor award from Fort Worth chapter of International Good Neighbor Council, 1973.

WRITINGS: *The Romancero in the Chronicle-Legend Plays of Lope de Vega,* University of Pennsylvania, 1940; *Texas Christian University: A Hundred Years of History,* Texas Christian University Press, 1974.

WORK IN PROGRESS: Continuing research on the history and people of Texas Christian University.

AVOCATIONAL INTERESTS: International travel.

BIOGRAPHICAL/CRITICAL SOURCES: John H. Hammond, *Jerome A. Moore: A Man of TCU*, Texas Christian University Press, 1974.

*   *   *

MOORE, Richard B.   1893(?)-1978

OBITUARY NOTICE: Born c. 1893 in Barbados, West Indies; died in 1978 in Barbados. Bookseller, speaker, and author of a book on the origins of the term "negro." Moore came to the United States during the early part of the twentieth century and became involved with the Communist party in the 1920's and 1930's. For over twenty years, he was the proprieter of the Frederick Douglass Bookshop in New York City. His main collection of books, mostly on racial issues, was given to the University of the West Indies by the Lions Club of Barbados. In his later years, Moore wrote pamphlets and made speaking engagements in the Caribbean. Obituaries and other sources: *AB Bookman's Weekly,* November 6, 1978.

*   *   *

MOORE, Ruth Nulton   1923-

PERSONAL: Born June 19, 1923, in Easton, Pa.; daughter of Jacob Wesley (a dentist) and Stella (Houck) Nulton; married Carl L. Moore (a professor of accounting and writer), June 15, 1946; children: Carl Nulton, Stephen Eric. *Education:* Bucknell University, A.B., 1944; Columbia University, M.A., 1945; further graduate study at University of Pittsburgh, 1946. *Politics:* Republican. *Religion:* Protestant. *Home:* 3033 Center St., Bethlehem, Pa. 18017. *Agent:* McIntosh & Otis, Inc., 475 Fifth Ave., New York, N.Y. 10017.

CAREER: Teacher of English and social studies in public schools in Easton, Pa., 1946-50; high school teacher of English and social studies in Detroit, Mich., 1952; free-lance writer, 1965—.

WRITINGS—All for children: Frisky the Playful Pony, Criterion, 1966; *Hiding the Bell*, Westminster, 1968; *Peace Treaty*, Herald Press, 1977; *The Ghost Bird Mystery*, Herald Press, 1977; *Mystery of the Hidden Treasure*, Herald Press, 1978; *Tomas and the Talking Birds*, Herald Press, 1978; *Wilderness Journey*, Herald Press, 1979. Contributor of stories and poems to *Jack and Jill* and *Children's Activities.*

WORK IN PROGRESS: Mystery at the Don Cesar and *Moccasins for the Major,* both for children.

SIDELIGHTS: Ruth Moore writes: "I give talks to school children about writing fiction and poetry. I have held poetry seminars for elementary grades and speak about writing children's books to teacher-training classes in our local colleges. I like to travel throughout the country, visiting historical sites and exploring deeply into my country's past and hiking in the mountains of northeastern Pennsylvania where we have a small farm."

AVOCATIONAL INTERESTS: Canoeing, fishing, collecting American Indian artifacts.

BIOGRAPHICAL/CRITICAL SOURCES: Lehigh Valley Monthly, August, 1977.

*   *   *

MORAWSKI, Stefan T(adeusz)   1921-

PERSONAL: Born October 20, 1921, in Cracow, Poland; son of Karol (a court inspector of accounts) and Franciszka Spira; married Anna Zelazny, January 20, 1947 (divorced, 1952); married Helena Opoczynska (a documentalist), May 4, 1957; children: (first marriage) Ewa Morawska Mezynska. *Education:* University of Warsaw, M.A. (philosophy), 1945, Ph.D., 1948; University of Sheffield, B.A. (English literature and culture) 1947; University of Cracow, M.A. (English philosophy), 1948. *Politics:* None. *Religion:* "Not practicing." *Home:* Aleja Waszyngtona, 20m 21, 03-910, Warsaw, Poland. *Office:* Institute of Arts, Polish Academy of Sciences, Dluga 26/28, Warsaw, Poland.

CAREER: Lecturer in Cracow high schools, 1947-52; State Institute of Art, Warsaw, Poland, assistant professor, 1953-58; University of Warsaw, Warsaw, associate professor, 1954-62, professor of aesthetics, 1964-68, philosophy faculty, vice-dean, 1960-62, dean, 1965-67, head of the chair of aesthetics, 1962-68; visiting professor in United States, 1970-73; Institute of Arts, Polish Academy of Sciences, Warsaw, research professor, 1970—. Member of advisory staff of *Polish Art Studies.* Honorary staff member of *Journal of Aesthetics and Art Criticism* and of *Knizevna Kritika,* Belgrade. *Member:* International Society of Aestheticians, International Society of Semiotics, Polish Semiotic Society, Polish Philosophy Society, Greek Philosophy Society.

WRITINGS: Rozwoj mysli estetycznej od Herdera do Heinego (title means "On the History of German Art Theories from Herder till Heine"), Scientific Publishers (Warsaw), 1957; *Studia z historii mysli estetycznej XVIII i XIX wieku* (title means "Studies in the English, French and Polish Aesthetics in the Eighteenth and Nineteenth Centuries") Scientific Publishers, 1961; *Miedzy tradycja a wizja przyszlosci* concerns the recent Soviet aesthetics), Book and Knowledge Publishers, (Warsaw), 1964; *Absolut i forma: Studium o egzystencjalistycznej estetyce Andre Malraux* (title means "The Absolute and the Form: A Treatise on the Existential Aesthetics of Andre Malraux"), Literature Publishers (Cracow), 1966; *O przedmiocie i metodzie estetki* (title means "On the Subject and the Method of Aesthetics"), Book and Knowledge Publishers, 1973; *Inquiries Into the Fundamentals of Aesthetics,* M. I. T. Press, 1974; (with Lee Baxandall) *Marx and Engels on Literature and Art,* International General, 1974. Co-editor of *Estetyka,* 1960-64, *Studia Aestetica,* 1964-68.

WORK IN PROGRESS: On Anarchism, Aesthetics and Art From Proudhon and Courbet Until the Present; George Lukacs, a monograph; *The Crisis of Aesthetics and the Neo-Avant-garde,* to be published in German by Fink Verlag (Munich).

SIDELIGHTS: "The philosophy of art," Morawski told *CA,* "remains my chief subject. Since 1970, I have moved to what I call anti-aesthetics, corresponding to the anti-art movement of our day. My second subject is the history of aesthetic ideas from the eighteenth century until now.

"It is always hard to answer how I began my writing career. It was most surely a propensity backed by some capacities and by circumstances. I tried to write poetry and short stories. I painted a little, but found the proper expression of my creative powers in philosophical reflections upon art. No doubt I am anchored in the Polish culture. I had excellent teachers in philosophy (the world-known Warsaw analytical school); I drew on the riches of Polish literature, theatre, fine arts and music. I know several foreign languages and I am rather well acquainted with the international achievements in philosophy and arts, but they were assimilated by me against my native background. I am surely no exceptional case—it usually occurs that the foreign influences are moulded into a native stock. I couldn't say that any particular writer was a model for me.

"To whom do I write? Principally for the artist and the philosopher but also for all the so called 'intelligentsia,' especially for the students at high schools. But the response is rare, the discussions are almost nonexistent. The satisfaction is already there when after one or two years I reread my work and find that to some extent it stands the test of the time."

Morawski was a member of the Polish Socialist party from 1944 to 1948, and the Polish Workers' party from 1949 to 1968. He also participated in the Warsaw uprisings of 1944. He explained to *CA:* "My orientation is Marxist-critical and towards the Marxist tradition. Since I was expelled from the Polish Workers' party in 1948, I have become a totally independent scholar. My critical and inquisitive *esprit* and open-mindedness could not be reconciled with any of the dogmas the party started in the late fifties."

Some of Morawski's works have been translated in French, Spanish, and Italian.

*   *   *

MORIARTY, Christopher   1936-

PERSONAL: Born March 14, 1936, in Dublin, Ireland; married; children: two. *Politics:* None. *Religion:* Christian. *Home:* 9 Richmond Ave., Monkstown, County Dublin, Ireland.

CAREER: Ecologist and writer. *Member:* Dublin Naturalists' Field Club (past president).

WRITINGS: Food of Perch (Perca Fluviatilis, L.) and Trout (Salmo Trutta, L.) in an Irish Reservoir, Hodges, Figgis & Co., 1963; *A Guide to Irish Birds,* Mercier Press, 1967; *A Natural History of Ireland,* Mercier Press, 1971; *Studies of the Eel Anguilla Anguilla in Ireland,* Stationery Office (Dublin, Ireland), 1975; *Eels,* Universe Books, 1978.

WORK IN PROGRESS: Continuing research on eels.

*   *   *

MORRELL, David C.   1929-

PERSONAL: Born November 6, 1929, in London, England; son of William (in commerce) and Violet (Cameron) Morrell; married Joyce Eaton-Taylor (a nurse), May 30, 1953; children: Margaret, William, Anthony, Thomas, Elizabeth. *Education:* Attended St. Mary's Hospital Medical School, University of London, 1947-52. *Religion:* Roman Catholic. *Home:* 27 Rodney Rd., New Malden, Surrey KT3 5AB, England. *Office:* Medical School, St. Thomas' Hospital, London S.E.1, England.

CAREER: General practitioner of medicine in Hoddesdon, England, 1957-63; University of Edinburgh, Edinburgh, Scotland, lecturer in general practice, 1963-67; St. Thomas' Hospital, Medical School, London, England, senior lecturer, 1967-72, professor of general practice, 1972—. Chairman of special advisory committee on general practice, University of London. *Military service:* Royal Air Force, Medical Branch, 1954-57. *Member:* Royal College of Physicians (fellow), Royal College of General Practitioners (fellow; member of board of examiners), Royal Society of Medicine (fellow), Association of University Teachers of General Practice (chairman).

WRITINGS: The Art of General Practice, E. & S. Livingstone, 1966; *An Introduction to Privy Medical Care,* Chur-

chill Livingstone, 1976; (editor with M. Marisler and J. Cormack), *Practice: A Handbook of Privy Medical Care,* Kluwer-Harrap Handbooks, 1976. Contributor to medical journals.

WORK IN PROGRESS: Research on education for general practice, health education, and filling demands for private medical care.

SIDELIGHTS: Morrell writes: "My main vocational drive is in the development of general practice in the United Kingdom. This includes identifying the characteristics of private care in the United Kingdom, education for this field of work, and the delivery of care. The Christian religion is a major factor in my motivation."

*   *   *

MORRIS, Eric   1940-

PERSONAL: Born October 29, 1940, in Cardiff, Wales; son of Clifford and Phyllis (a boutique owner; maiden name, Furlow) Morris; married Pamela Anne Hunter (a teacher), January 25, 1962; children: Christopher David, Leah Anne. *Education:* St. David's University College, University of Wales, B.A. (honors), 1962; University College, Cardiff, University of Wales, diploma in education, 1963; University of Leicester, M.A., 1968. *Politics:* Social Democrat. *Religion:* Church of England. *Home:* 9 Stockwood Rise, Camberley, Surrey, England. *Office:* Department of War Studies and International Affairs, Royal Military Academy, Sandhurst, Camberley, England.

CAREER: High school history master in Birmingham, England, 1963-65, and at private school in Tamworth, England, 1965-66; University of Liverpool, Liverpool, England, lecturer in international relations and military history, 1967-70; currently associated with Royal Military Academy, Sandhurst, Camberley, England. Visiting lecturer at University of Wales College at Aberystwyth, 1968-71. *Member:* International Institute for Strategic Studies, Royal United Service Institution.

WRITINGS: Blockade Berlin and the Cold War, Hamish Hamilton, 1974, Stein & Day, 1975; *Tanks: An Illustrated History,* Octopus Press, 1975; *Weapons/Warfare,* Octopus Press, 1976; *The Russian Navy: Myth and Reality,* Stein & Day, 1977. Contributor to *Army Quarterly.*

WORK IN PROGRESS: Research on the U.S. Navy in the twentieth century, U.S. operations at Corregidor, 1941-42, and carrier operations in the Pacific, 1941-65.

SIDELIGHTS: In 1976 Morris made a lecture tour of the midwestern United States.

*   *   *

MORRIS, Nobuko
   See ALBERY, Nobuko

*   *   *

MORRIS, Sarah M(iller)   1906-

PERSONAL: Born January 17, 1906, in Peoria, Ill.; daughter of Sumner Marcy (a physician) and Sarah Celeste (a teacher; maiden name, French) Miller; married second husband, David Morris (a professor), August 15, 1959 (died, 1965); children: (first marriage) Emmett, Betsy. *Education:* Attended Bradley University, 1923-25; Northwestern University, B.S., 1927; Columbia University, M.A. (administration), 1950; University of Northern Colorado, Ph.D., 1954; University of Colorado, M.A. (English), 1954. *Politics:*

Republican. *Religion:* Unitarian-Universalist. *Home:* 415 South Howes, Apt. 810, Fort Collins, Colo. 80521. *Agent:* Roy Porter, Porter, Gould & Dierks, 215 West Ohio, Chicago, Ill. 60610.

CAREER: Northwestern University, Evanston, Ill., in personnel, 1927-30; high school personnel director in Peoria, Ill.; Colorado State University, Fort Collins, instructor, 1954-58, assistant professor, 1958-71, associate professor of English, 1971—. Employed as personnel director in a munitions factory during World War II, and as a recruiter for United Service Organizations. Public lecturer. Member of local symphony board; past member of national board of directors of Young Women's Christian Association (YWCA).

WRITINGS: Grief and How to Live with It, Grosset, 1972; *Coping With Crisis,* Chicago Review Press, 1978.

WORK IN PROGRESS: Widowers and Widows: Their Psychological and Personal Problems.

SIDELIGHTS: Sarah Morris writes: "Having a doctor's degree in psychology, I looked for psychological help when my husband died. I wanted to know how best to handle my emotions in order to resolve the grief. I found nothing in popular magazines or books. However, I found what I was looking for in psychiatry. I read everything I could find and then wrote my book on grief. It is based on sound psychology but is written in simple terms so that laymen can understand it. It is a bridge between sound psychology and the people who need the information."

BIOGRAPHICAL/CRITICAL SOURCES: Review, May 24, 1978.

*   *   *

MORRISON, Tony   1936-

PERSONAL: Born July 5, 1936, in Gosport, England; son of Reginald Thomas and Marjorie Morrison; married Elizabeth Marion Davies (a photographer), July 30, 1965; children: Kimball David Bertrand, Rebecca Elizabeth. *Education:* University of Bristol, B.Sc., 1959. *Home:* 48 Station Rd., Woodbridge, Suffolk IP12 4AT, England. *Agent:* Anita Diamant, Writer's Workshop, Inc., 51 East 42nd St., New York, N.Y. 10021. *Office:* 8 Upper Grosvenor St., London W.1, England.

CAREER: Filmmaker and zoologist, University of Bristol transcontinental world expedition by jeep, 1960-61; special cameraman on location in Jordan, Lebanon, and Iran for Television Explorations Ltd., 1962; co-founder of Nonesuch Expeditions Ltd. (film production company), 1963; Tony Morrison Productions Ltd. (producers of history and natural history films), London, England, founder and co-director, 1963—; director of Insight Data Ltd., 1977—. Also freelance writer and photographer. *Member:* International Council for Bird Preservation, Royal Geographical Society (fellow), Fauna Preservation Society, Flamingo Group, Smithsonian Institution.

WRITINGS: (With Mark Howell) *Steps to a Fortune,* Bles, 1966; *Animal Migration,* Hamlyn, 1972; *Land Above the Clouds,* Deutsch, 1974; (contributor) *Peoples of the Earth,* Grolier, 1974; (contributor) Robert Targett, editor, *Our Magnificent Wildlife,* Reader's Digest Press, 1975; *The Andes,* Time-Life, 1976; *Pathways to the Gods: The Mysterious South American Lines,* Harper, 1978.

SIDELIGHTS: Morrison has traveled extensively, both on assignment for BBC-TV productions and more recently with his wife, in the areas of southern Bolivia and the Chilean

Atacama. He has trekked through most of South America, including those regions usually unvisited: Surinam, French Guiana and the interiors of Venezuela and Brazil. Also he has made a descent of the upper Amazon by raft. He writes: "Concerning the Andean desert areas: they are for the Andes, a unique habitat. Few animals occur there and even fewer people go to see them as the natural hostility of the environment provides protection. For those reasons, they are worth studying."

*   *   *

MORTON, Harry   1925-

PERSONAL: Born July 20, 1925, in Gladstone, Manitoba, Canada; son of William (a farmer) and Mary (Manwaring) Morton; married Peggy Stuttard (a researcher), December 11, 1944; children: Carol Morton Johnston, Frances Morton Corkery, Elizabeth, Dorothy. *Education:* University of Manitoba, B.A., 1947, B.Ed., 1964; Cambridge University, B.A. (honors), 1948, M.A., 1954; University of Otago, Ph.D., 1978. *Politics:* Independent. *Religion:* Anglican. *Home:* 193 Signal Hill Rd., Dunedin, New Zealand. *Office:* Department of History, University of Otago, Dunedin, New Zealand.

CAREER: Farmer, 1948-60; English and history teacher in secondary schools in Manitoba, Canada, 1960-66; school principal in Manitoba, 1961-66; University of Otago, Dunedin, New Zealand, lecturer, 1966-68, associate professor of American colonial and Canadian history, 1966—, senior lecturer, 1968-77. *Military service:* Royal Canadian Air Force, flying officer, 1942-45. *Member:* Otago Officers Club, University Club. *Awards, honors:* Sir James Wattie Literary Award from Wattie Industries Ltd., 1976, for *The Wind Commands.*

WRITINGS: And Now New Zealand, John McIndoe, 1969; *The Wind Commands,* Wesleyan University Press, 1975; *Which Way New Zealand?,* John McIndoe, 1976.

WORK IN PROGRESS: A book on whaling.

SIDELIGHTS: Morton writes: "My main concern as a writer is that creation of wealth seems to be diminishing in inverse ratio to its distribution, and so I fear for the future of those who are disadvantaged by ill health or age."

Morton also told *CA* that "*The Wind Commands* is a history of the technical and personnel problems of sailing ships in the Pacific Ocean."

*   *   *

MORTON, W(illiam) Scott   1908-

PERSONAL: Born July 28, 1908, in Edinburgh, Scotland; came to the United States in 1957; son of William Stewart (a businessman) and Mary (Stevenson) Morton; married Alice Gleysteen, July 10, 1936 (separated); children: Michael Scott, Gail Morton Hampson, Alastair Scott, Keith Scott. *Education:* Cambridge University, B.A. (honors), 1930, M.A., 1960; University of Edinburgh, B.D., 1933, Ph.D., 1964. *Residence:* New York, N.Y. *Office:* Office of the President, Bloomfield College, Bloomfield, N.J. 07003.

CAREER: Ordained minister of Church of Scotland, 1933; pastor of churches in Manchuria, 1933-41, China, 1933-38, and in Japan, 1939-41; pastor of Presbyterian churches in Scotland, 1946-57, and Pittsburgh, Pa., 1957-63; New York University, New York, N.Y., director of University Christian Foundation, 1963-65; Seton Hall University, South Orange, N.J., assistant professor, 1965-66, associate professor, 1966-72, professor of history, 1972-74, professor emeritus, 1974-78, faculty member with World Campus Afloat, 1975. Assistant to the president of Bloomfield College. *Military service:* Royal Air Force, chaplain, 1942-46. *Member:* Association for Asian Studies, Scottish Youth Hostels Association (co-founder), Columbia University Seminar on Oriental Thought and Religion.

WRITINGS: Japan: Its History and Culture, Crowell, 1970; *The Japanese: How They Live and Work,* Praeger, 1973; (contributor) Seymour Kurtz, editor, *World Book of Antiquities,* Crown, 1975.

WORK IN PROGRESS: A cultural history of China; a comparative history of the Chinese and Roman empires.

SIDELIGHTS: Morton traveled all around the world with the World Campus Afloat. His foreign languages include Latin, Greek, French, German, Chinese, and Japanese, and his books have been published in England, Germany and Japan. *Avocational interests:* Golf.

*   *   *

MOSS, Robert F 1942-

PERSONAL: Born October 1, 1942, in New York; son of Bernard B. (an engineer) and Madeleine (a high school teacher; maiden name, Morgan) Moss. *Education:* Reed College, B.A., 1964; Columbia University, M.A., 1965, Ph.D., 1972. *Home:* 39 Fifth Ave., New York, N.Y. 10003. *Agent:* Barbara Lowenstein, 250 West 57th St., New York, N.Y. 10019. *Office:* Camden College of Arts and Sciences, Rutgers University, Camden, N.J. 08102.

CAREER: Bantam Books, Inc., New York City, assistant editor, 1966-67; City University of New York, Hunter College, New York City, instructor in English, 1969-71, City College, New York City, instructor, 1970, Brooklyn College, Brooklyn, N.Y., instructor in English, 1971-72; Rutgers University, Camden College of Arts and Sciences, Camden, N.J., assistant professor of English, 1972—. *Member:* Modern Language Association of America.

WRITINGS: Karloff and Company, Pyramid Publications, 1973; *Charlie Chaplin,* Pyramid Publications, 1975; (with Barbara Bauer) *Judge Horton and the Scottsboro Boys,* Ballantine, 1976; *The Adolescent Spirit in Rudyard Kipling,* Firma KLM, 1979. Contributor of more than forty stories, articles, and reviews to magazines and newspapers, including *Saturday Review, New Republic, Film Quarterly, Cottonwood Review, Los Angeles Times, New York Times,* and *Nation.*

WORK IN PROGRESS: A novel and a screenplay; *The Films of Carol Reed,* for Twayne.

SIDELIGHTS: Moss writes: "I have tried to establish a solid footing in the world of free-lance writing, while simultaneously pursuing a traditional academic career. I have a Ph.D. in English and the professional history that usually goes with it—chiefly a string of teaching jobs at the rank of instructor and assistant professor and publication credits in various scholarly journals and literary quarterlies. Still, the bulk of my publishing activity has been in popular or quasi-popular periodicals. Since I feel that I have proved my scholarly mettle with my books on Rudyard Kipling and Carol Reed, I am inclined to concentrate on writing that will reach a general audience. My most cherished goal is to succeed in creative work, which, in my case, means fiction and/or screenwriting."

*   *   *

MOSTEL, Kate 1918-

PERSONAL: Born October 8, 1918, in Philadelphia, Pa.; daughter of Hugh John (a stone cutter) and Anna (McCaffery) Harkin; married Samuel Mostel (an actor under name Zero Mostel), July 2, 1944 (died September, 1977); children: Joshua, Tobias. *Education:* Attended secondary school in Philadelphia, Pa. *Home:* 146 Central Park W., New York, N.Y. 10023. *Agent:* Helen Harvey, 405 West 23rd St., New York, N.Y. 10011.

CAREER: Vaudeville dancer, beginning 1927; Philadelphia Ballet Co., Philadelphia, Pa., dancer, 1935-40; Radio City Music Hall, New York, N.Y., member of "Rockettes," 1941-43; actress, 1950—. *Military service:* Women's Army Auxiliary Corps, 1943; received honorable discharge.

WRITINGS: (With Madeline Lee Gilford, Jack Gilford, Lucie Prinz, and husband, Zero Mostel) *170 Years of Show Business,* Random House, 1978.

SIDELIGHTS: Kate Mostel told *CA:* "I wrote *170 Years of Show Business* because my collaborator made me! I won't write anything else, until she makes me again."

Though the book was completed after Zero Mostel's death, it "is no lugubrious, tear-jerking memorial work," according to reviewer Richard F. Shepard, "but a very lively, chatty and good-natured recollection of lives [the Gilfords' and the Mostels'] that are interesting and quite human, warts (not many) and all.

"There are, refreshingly, no hair-raising revelations of life among the arty or the powerful, no chi-chi exposes or snide sniping," continued Shepard. "This is not a deep book. It is a souffle of reminiscence, often disorganized and conversationally written, but it has the amiability of a letter from home.... Kate and Madeline tell about themselves, how they came to show business and how they met their husbands. They are attractive and bright people with an earthy indisposition to pretension.... The entire book is a scrapbook about four nice people."

BIOGRAPHICAL/CRITICAL SOURCES: New York Times, May 26, 1978.

*   *   *

MOULIER, (Antoine) Fernand 1913-

PERSONAL: Born November 22, 1913, in La Tour-d'Auvergne, France; son of Andronic (a magistrate) and Marie (Broquin) Moulier; married Christine Pagezy, October 27, 1959; children: Philippe. *Education:* University of Lille, licence, 1931; further study at New College, Oxford, 1931-32. *Religion:* Catholic. *Home:* 4448 Hawthorne St. N.W., Washington, D.C. 20016. *Office:* Agence France-Presse, 914 National Press Bldg. N.W., Washington, D.C. 20004.

CAREER/WRITINGS: Excelsior, Paris, France, London bureau chief, 1934-39; French Independent Agency, London, England, co-founder and manager, 1939-44; Agence France-Presse, Paris, director of information, 1944-70, U.S. manager in Washington, D.C., 1970—. Notable assignments include coverage of the final days of World War II in Europe, the signature of the armistice in Berlin and Geneva, and all major international conferences since the war. Correspondent in Peking, China, 1949. Contributor to some four thousand newspapers around the world. *Wartime service:* Correspondent with U.S. Army, 1939-44. *Member:* Overseas Writers Club, National Press Club, Reform Club (London). *Awards, honors:* Officer of the Legion d'Honneur.

SIDELIGHTS: Moulier told *CA* that he has traveled all over the world, and that his principal current interest is American domestic politics.

MPHAHLELE, Ezekiel 1919-
(Bruno Eseki)

PERSONAL: Born in Marabastad Township, Pretoria, South Africa; son of Moses (a messenger) and Eva (a domestic; maiden name, Mogale) Mphahlele; married Rebecca Mochadibane (a social worker), 1945; children: Anthony, Teresa Kefilwe, Motswiri, Chabi Robert, Puso. *Education:* Attended Adams Teachers Training College, Natal, 1939-40; University of South Africa, B.A. (with honors), 1949, M.A., 1956; University of Denver, Ph.D., 1968. *Address:* P.O. Box 120, 0736, South Africa.

CAREER: Secondary school teacher of English and Afrikaans in Johannesburg, South Africa, 1945-52; *Drum* magazine, Johannesburg, fiction editor, 1955-57; University of Ibadan, Ibadan, Nigeria, lecturer in English literature, 1957-61; International Association for Cultural Freedom, Paris, France, director of African programs, 1961-63; Chemchemi Creative Centre, Nairobi, Kenya, director, 1963-65; University College, Nairobi, lecturer, 1965-66; University of Denver, Denver, Colo., visiting lecturer, 1966-68, associate professor of English, 1970-74; University of Zambia, Lusaka, senior lecturer in English, 1968-70; University of Pennsylvania, Philadelphia, professor of English, 1974-77; education officer in charge of English teaching in African schools, Transvaal, South Africa, 1978—. *Awards, honors: African Arts* magazine prize, 1972, for *The Wanderers.*

WRITINGS: Man Must Live and Other Stories, African Bookman, 1947; (contributor) Prudence Smith, editor, *Africa in Transition,* Reinhardt, 1958; *Down Second Avenue* (autobiography), Faber, 1959, Doubleday, 1971; *The Living and the Dead and Other Stories,* Black Orpheus, 1961; *The African Image* (essays), Faber, 1962, Praeger, 1964, revised edition, Faber, 1972; (editor with Ellis Ayitey Komey) *Modern African Stories* (anthology), Faber, 1964; *In Corner B and Other Stories,* East African Publishing House, 1967; (editor and contributor) *African Writing Today,* Penguin, 1967; *The Wanderers* (autobiographical novel), Macmillan, 1972; *Voices in the Whirlwind and Other Essays,* Hill & Wang, 1972.

Work has been represented in anthologies, including *An African Treasury,* edited by Langston Hughes, Crown, 1960; *Poems From Black Africa,* edited by Hughes, Indiana University Press, 1963; *New African Literature and the Arts I,* edited by Joseph Okpaku, Crowell with Third World Press, 1970; *South African Voices,* edited by Bernth Lindfors, African and Afro-American Studies and Research Center, 1975.

Contributor of essays, short stories and poems, sometimes under pseudonym Bruno Eseki, to *Drum, Africa South, Denver Quarterly, Journal of Modern Afirican Studies, Black World, New Statesman,* and other periodicals. Editor, *Black Orpheus,* 1960-66; member of staff, *Presence Africaine,* 1961-63; member of editorial staff, *Journal of New African Literature and the Arts.*

WORK IN PROGRESS: A Critical Anthology of African Poetry; an autobiography on exile and return to South Africa.

SIDELIGHTS: Mphahlele's transition from life in the slums of South Africa to life as a professor of English at a large American university was an odyssey of struggle both intellectually and politically. He trained as a teacher in South Africa, but was banned from the classroom in 1952 as a result of his protest of the segregationist Bantu Education Act. Although he later returned to teaching, Mphahlele first turned to journalism, criticism, fiction, and essay writing.

After being officially silenced by the government of his homeland and living in self-imposed exile for twenty years, Mphahlele has returned to South Africa. "I want to be part of the renaissance that is happening in the thinking of my people," he told *CA.* "I see education as playing a vital role in personal growth and in institutionalizing a way of life that a people chooses as its highest ideal. For the older people, it is a way of reestablishing the values they had to suspend along the way because of the force of political conditions. Another reason for returning, connected with the first, is that this is my ancestral home. An African cares very much where he dies and is buried. But I have not come to die. I want to reconnect with my ancestors while I am still active. I am also a captive of place, of setting. As long as I was abroad I continued to write on the South African scene. There is a force I call the tyranny of place; the kind of unrelenting hold a place has on a person that gives him the motivation to write and a style. The American setting in which I lived for nine years was too fragmented to give me these. I could only identify emotionally and intellectually with the African-American segment, which was not enough. Here I can feel the ancestral Presence. I know now what Vinoba Bhave of India meant when he said: 'Though action rages without, the heart can be tuned to produce unbroken music,' at this very hour when pain is raging and throbbing everywhere in African communities living in this country."

Mphahlele is recognized world-wide as a leading South African writer. His collection of essays, *The African Image,* reflects his changing and developing attitudes toward the African personality and consciousness, and his expanding reassessmant of the concept of negritude.

On the subject of writing, Mphahlele commented: "In Southern Africa, the black writer talks best about the ghetto life he knows; the white writer best about his own ghetto life. We see each other, black and white, as it were through a keyhole. Race relations are a major experience and concern for the writer. They are his constant beat. It is unfortunate no-one can ever think it is healthy both mentally and physically to keep hacking at the social structure in overcharged language. A language that burns and brands, scorches and scalds. Language that is as a machete with a double edge—the one sharp, the other blunt, the one cutting, the other breaking. And yet there are levels of specifically black drama in the ghettoes that I cannot afford to ignore. So I replay the drama. I have got to stay with it. I bleed inside. My people bleed. But I must stay with it."

BIOGRAPHICAL/CRITICAL SOURCES: New Statesman, April 25, 1959; *Times Literary Supplement,* August 11, 1961; Gerald Moore, *Seven African Writers,* Oxford University press, 1962; *Modern African Studies,* March, 1963; *Encounter,* June, 1963; *Africa Report,* July, 1964; Moore, *The Chosen Tongue,* Longmans, Green, 1969; Ezekiel Mphahlele, *Down Second Avenue,* Doubleday, 1971; Dennis Durden, editor, *African Writers Talking,* Heinmann, 1972; Donald E. Herdeck, *African Writers: A Companion to Black African Writing 1300-1973,* Black Orpheus, 1973; Bernth Lindfors, editor, *South African Voices,* African and Afro-American Studies Center, 1975; Ursula A. Barnett, *Ezekiel Mphahlele,* Twayne, 1976.

*   *   *

MUIR, Frank 1920-

PERSONAL: Surname is pronounced *Mew*-er; born February 20, 1920, in Ramsgate, England; son of Charles and Margaret Muir; married Polly McIrvine, July 16, 1949; children: Jamie, Sally. *Education:* Attended high school in Leyton County, England. *Politics:* "Not committed to a party." *Religion:* Church of England. *Home:* Anners, Thorpe, Egham, Surrey TW20 8UE, England. *Agent:* Hilary Rubenstein, A.P. Watt Ltd., 26 Bedford Row, London WC1R 4HL, England.

CAREER: Free-lance writer for radio and television. Worked as consultant on light entertainment for television for British Broadcasting Corp. (BBC), 1960-64, head of television comedy department, 1964-67; London Weekend Television Ltd., London, England, head of entertainment, 1968-69; University of St. Andrews, St. Andrews, Scotland, rector, 1976—. *Military service:* Royal Air Force, 1940-46. *Member:* Johnson Society (president, 1975-76). *Awards, honors:* LL.D. from University of St. Andrews, 1978.

WRITINGS: (With Patrick Campbell) *Call My Bluff,* Eyre Methuen, 1972; (with Denis Norden) *You Can't Have Your Kayak and Heat It,* Eyre Methuen, 1973; (with Norden) *Upon My Word!,* Eyre Methuen, 1974; *Christmas Customs and Traditions,* Sphere Books, 1975, Taplinger, 1977; *An Irreverent and Thoroughly Incomplete Social History of Almost Everything,* Stein & Day, 1976, published in England as *The Frank Muir Book: An Irreverent Companion to Social History,* Heinemann, 1976; (with Norden) *The My Word Stories,* Stein & Day, 1977; *What-a-Mess,* Doubleday, 1977; (with Norden) *Take My Word for It,* Eyre Methuen, 1978; (with Simon Brett) *Frank Muir Goes Into . . . ,* Robson Books, 1978; *What-a-Mess the Good,* Doubleday, 1978. Writer for television series, "Take It from Here," BBC. Contributor to popular magazines, including *Punch* and *Times Literary Supplement.*

WORK IN PROGRESS: Editing *The Oxford Book of Humorous Prose,* for Oxford University Press.

SIDELIGHTS: Muir writes: "After twenty-five years of writing for radio and television comedy, I am now deeply—and happily—embedded in books. I enjoy talking in public about books. I have made speeches at conventions in Chicago and Atlanta on the perils of authorship and authors' promotion tours.

"I only write humour. Sometimes I write humorous fiction, as in my children's books and the 'My Word' stories, and sometimes I write non-fiction, as in my examination of the ludicrous and laughable elements in our social history. I think this is because I have a very low threshold of boredom. I bore easily and am therefore desperately anxious not to bore others."

BIOGRAPHICAL/CRITICAL SOURCES: Observer, September 19, 1976.

* * *

MUJICA LAINEZ, Manuel 1910-

PERSONAL: Surname is pronounced Moo-he-ka Ly-ness; born September 11, 1910, in Buenos Aires, Argentina; son of Manuel (a lawyer) and Lucia (Lainez) Mujica Farias; married Ana de Alvear, November 14, 1936; children: Diego, Ana, Manuel Florencio. *Education:* Escuela Nacional de San Isidro, Buenos Aires, Argentina, B.A., 1928; studied law at University of Buenos Aires, 1928-30. *Politics:* Conservative. *Religion:* Roman Catholic. *Home:* El Paraiso, 5178 Cruz Chica, Cordoba, Argentina; and O'Higgins 2150, Buenos Aires, Argentina.

CAREER: Novelist, short story writer, journalist, biographer, and art critic. *La Nacion,* Buenos Aires, Argentina, staff member and art critic, 1932-68; National Museum of

Decorative Arts, Buenos Aires, secretary, 1935-45; Argentina Ministry of Foreign Relations, Buenos Aires, general director of cultural relations, 1955-58. *Military service:* Served in Argentine Navy; became commander. *Member:* Argentine Academy of Letters, National Academy of Fine arts, Argentine Society of Writers (vice-president). *Awards, honors:* Argentine Society of Writers Grand Prize of Honor for Literature, 1955; Grand National Prize of Honor for Literature, 1962; First National Prize of Letters, 1963; John F. Kennedy Prize, 1964, for *Bomarzo;* Alberto Gerchunoff Prize; Forti Glori Prize.

WRITINGS—In English: (With Cordova Iturburu and Roger Pla) *Gambartes* (bilingual edition in Spanish and English; English translation by Patrick Orpen Dudgeon), Bonino's Gallery (Buenos Aires), 1954; *Argentina,* English translation by William McLeod Rivera from the original Spanish manuscript, Pan American Union, 1961; *Bomarzo* (novel), Editorial Sudamericana (Buenos Aires), 1962, English translation by Gregory Rabassa published under same title, Simon & Schuster, 1969, 8th Spanish edition, Editorial Sudamericana, 1970.

Other works: *Glosas Castellanas,* Bernabe & Cia (Buenos Aires), 1936; *Don Galaz de Buenos Aires,* [Buenos Aires], 1938; *Miguel Cane (Padre),* C.E.P.A. (Buenos Aires), 1942; *Canto a Buenos Aires* (poetry), Editorial Guillermo Kraft (Buenos Aires), 1943; (editor) *Poetas Argentinos en Montevideo,* Emece Editores (Buenos Aires), 1943; *Vida de Aniceto el Gallo* (biography), Emece Editores, 1943; (author of introduction) Hilario Ascasubi, *Paulino Lucero,* Ediciones Estrada (Buenos Aires), 1945, 2nd edition, 1959; *Vida de Anastasio el Pollo* (biography), Emece Editores, 1948; (author of intorduction) Margarita Drago, *Figuras,* F. A. Columbo (Buenos Aires), 2nd edition, 1948; *Aqui Vivieron* (short stories), Editorial Sudamericana (Buenos Aires), 1949, 4th edition, 1969.

Misteriosa Buenos Aires (short stories), Editorial Sudamericana, 1951, 4th edition, 1971; *Los Idolos* (novel), Editorial Sudamericana, 1953, 2nd edition, 1966; *La Casa* (novel), Editorial Sudamericana, 1954, 4th edition, 1972; *Los Viajeros* (novel), Editorial Sudamericana, 1955, 2nd edition, 1967; *Victoria, 1884-1955,* Ediciones Bonino (Buenos Aires), 1955; *Invitados en El Paraiso* (novel), Editorial Sudamericana, 1957, 2nd edition, 1969.

Russo (critical study), Ediciones El Mangrullo (Buenos Aires), 1963; (compiler) *Lira Romantica Sudamericana,* new edition (Mujica Lainez was not associated with 1st edition), Emece Editores, 1964; *El Unicorno* (novel) Editorial Sudamericana, 1965, 2nd edition, 1969; (author of introduction) Oscar Hermes Villordo, *Oscar Hermes Villordo,* Ediciones Culturales Argentinas (Buenos Aires), 1966; *Vidas del Gallo y el Pollo* (biography), Centro Editor de America Latina, 1966; *Cronicas Reales* (short stories), Editorial Sudamericana, 1967, 2nd edition, 1969; *De Milagros y de Melancolias* (novel), Editorial Sudamericana, 1968, 2nd edition, 1969; (contributor) *Cuentos Recontados,* Editorial Tiempo Contemporanco (Buenos Aires), 1968.

Cecil (autobiographical novel), Editorial Sudamericana, 1972; *Cuentos de Buenos Aires* (anthology), Editorial Huemul (Buenos Aires), 1972; *El Laberinto* (novel), Editorial Sudamericana, 1974; *El Viaje de Los Siete Demonios,* Editorial Sudamericana, 1974; *Antologia General e Introduccion a la Obra de Manuel Mujica Lainez,* Felmar (Madrid), 1976; *Sergio,* Editorial Sudamericana, 1976; *The Complete Works of Manuel Mujica Lainez* (in Spanish), Editorial Sudamericana, 1978. Also author of *Los Cisnes,* Editorial Sudamericana.

WORK IN PROGRESS: A novel, *El Gran Teatro,* for Editorial Sudamericana.

SIDELIGHTS: Although considered to be more than a regional writer, most of Mujica Lainez's fiction focuses on Buenos Aires. His historical interest in the city can be seen in *Misteriosa Buenos Aires,* a collection of forty-two tales each set in a different year and era of Buenos Aires history. *Los Idolos, La Casa, Los Viajeros,* and *Invitados en el Paraiso* compose a cycle of Buenos Aires novels termed the "Saga de la sociedad portena" ("Saga of Buenos Aires Society"). The afflicted characters in these novels react to the perversion of their society by fleeing into worlds where love for objects replaces love for persons (*Los Idolos*), and idolatry of art supersedes interpersonal relationships (*Invitados en el Paraiso*).

Isolation is a recurrent problem in Mujica Lainez's fiction and receives more attention in his best known novel, *Bomarzo.* A denunciation of the man-idealizing values cherished from the Renaissance, it is the strange story of 450-year-old Prince Orsini, Duke of Bomarzo, told from his twentieth-century study. Isolated by his physical deformity, Orsini is compelled "to refine everything into art, including cruelty and murder." A garden of stone monsters becomes a tangible form for the immortality forecast at his birth and Orsini comes to understand, four hundred years later, the evils of his isolated existence.

His only novel to have been translated into English, *Bomarzo* has met generally with favorable criticism from American reviewers. While praising *Bomarzo* as a "skillful novel," David Gallagher contended it is "anachronistic," "a modernist novel eighty years late." Paul Hume, meanwhile, cited the "compelling power of four-fifths of its length," and the force of Mujica Lainez's style that "lies as much in the brilliance of his language as in his knowledge of the period and place about which he writes with an affection that clearly holds him in a special grasp."

Mujica Lainez's interest in "period and place" is reflected in his travels. He has traveled extensively around the world and is fluent in English and French, "fair-good" in Italian.

BIOGRAPHICAL/CRITICAL SOURCES: Time, December 12, 1969; *Washington Post,* December 31, 1969; *New York Times Book Review,* January 11, 1970; *America,* February 7, 1970; *Books,* October, 1970; *Latin American Literary Review,* Volume I, number 1, 1973.

*   *   *

MULLANEY, Thomas E.   1922(?)-1978

OBITUARY NOTICE: Born c. 1922 in Brooklyn, N.Y.; died October 21, 1978, in Flushing, N.Y. Journalist for the *New York Times.* Mullaney began his career with the *Times* in 1942, and became a business reporter in 1946. He was named business and financial editor in 1963, and also began his weekly column, "The Economic Scene." In 1976, he left his position as editor in order to expand his column. Obituaries and other sources: *Washington Post,* October 25, 1978.

*   *   *

MULLER, Marcia   1944-

PERSONAL: Born September 28, 1944, in Detroit, Mich.; daughter of Henry J. (a marketing executive) and Kathryn (Minke) Muller; married Frederick T. Gilson, Jr. (a salesman), August 12, 1967. *Education:* University of Michigan, B.A., 1966, M.A., 1971. *Residence:* San Francisco, Calif. *Agent:* Virginia Barber, 44 Greenwich Ave., New York, N.Y. 10011.

CAREER: Sunset (magazine), Menlo Park, Calif., merchandising supervisor, 1968-69; University of Michigan, Institute for Social Research, Ann Arbor, field interviewer in the San Francisco Bay area, 1971-73; free-lance writer, 1973—. *Member:* Mystery Writers of America, Women in Communications.

WRITINGS: Edwin of the Iron Shoes (Mystery Guild selection), McKay, 1977.

WORK IN PROGRESS: Street Song (tentative title), a novel.

SIDELIGHTS: Marcia Muller comments: "My primary aim in writing my first novel was to use the classical puzzle form of the mystery to introduce a contemporary female sleuth, a figure with surprisingly few counterparts in the world of detective fiction."

*   *   *

MURRAY, Edmund P(atrick)   1930-

PERSONAL: Born July 31, 1930, in Brooklyn, N.Y.; son of Edmund Patrick and Kathleen (a nurse; maiden name, Patterson) Murray; children: Patrick. *Education:* Attended Antioch College, 1949-50, 1952-55. *Politics:* "Latent Democrat." *Religion:* "Lapsed Catholic." *Home and office:* 3 Potter Pl., Weehawken, N.J. 07087. *Agent:* Carl Brandt, Brandt & Brandt, 101 Park Ave., New York, N.Y. 10017.

CAREER: Worked as cub reporter for *Women's Wear Daily,* 1949-50; *Alice News,* Alice, Tex., editor, 1950-52; *Cleveland Plain Dealer,* Cleveland, Ohio, police reporter, 1952-54; *Bridgeport Herald,* Bridgeport, Conn., reporter and labor columnist, 1955-59; Amalgamated Clothing and Textile Workers Union, New York, N.Y., assistant public relations director, 1963-64, 1977-78; Communications Workers of America, Washington, D.C., assistant public relations director, 1964-66; writer. Ministry of Information, Addis Ababa, Ethiopia, media adviser, 1966-72; writer, 1972—. *Awards, honors:* William Carlos Williams Award from *Contact,* 1964, for short story, "The Cuban Situation"; Order of Menelik from Haile Selassie, 1971; journalism awards.

WRITINGS: The Passion Players (novel), Crown, 1968; *Kulubi* (novel), Crown, 1973.

Author of "The Arena" (one-act play), first produced in Yellow Springs, Ohio, at Antioch College, March 19, 1952. Contributor of stories, poems, and articles to magazines and newspapers, including *New Yorker.*

WORK IN PROGRESS: Another novel; research for an experimental novel dealing with suicide; poems and stories.

SIDELIGHTS: Murray writes: "Doctors and lawyers can afford to discuss the arts. When writers get together, they talk about paying the rent and the price of groceries.

"For years I wrote short stories which were highly praised and widely unpublished. What finally made me a novelist was a sequence of rejections from *New Yorker,* one because of 'too much violence for the sake of violence' and the next because 'in the final analysis nothing really happens.'

"At thirty-eight, after two decades of frustration with the short story, my first novel hit paydirt. I thought I would never have to hold down a job again.

"But money melts, and my second novel, set in Ethiopia, was savaged in the *Times* by a reviewer who apparently didn't think white men should be allowed to write about Africa. *Kulubi,* though well-reviewed elsewhere, failed to cover its rather modest advance.

"So now I scrounge for jobs with one hand and try to finish

the third novel with the other. Perhaps not surprisingly, the new book is laced with several dozen homicides.

"Suicide has been another major factor in my writing. (I blunt my fingers at the typewriter to avoid slashing my wrists in the bathtub.) Eventually another novel will come out of that, if I survive.

"Though nearly broke, the only debts I owe are to people like Frank O'Connor, the Irish short story writer with whom I studied at Harvard, and John Farrar, the publisher. I also owe much to friends who find me jobs when I need them most. These people have been the major influences on my work.

"Without their help, and that of several beautiful women, including my mother, who at various times have let me live with them, I could not have survived to write what I have. And will."

BIOGRAPHICAL/CRITICAL SOURCES: Paul B. Henze, *Ethiopian Journey,* Benn, 1977.

* * *

MURRAY, Joan E. 1941-

PERSONAL: Born November 6, 1941, in Ithaca, N.Y.; daughter of Isaiah William (a construction worker and union executive) and Amanda Pearl (Yates) Murray. *Education:* Attended Ithaca College, Hunter College of the City University of New York, New School for Social Research, and French Institute. *Home:* 536 East 79th St., New York, N.Y. 10021.

CAREER: Columbia Broadcasting System (CBS), New York City, secretary-assistant in network press information department, 1960, production assistant and script assistant for "Candid Camera" series, 1963; National Broadcasting Co. (NBC), New York City, hostess, writer, and producer for television program "Women on the Move," 1964; WCBS-TV, New York City, news correspondent, interviewer, and hostess of syndicated radio program, "The Joan Murray Show . . . And There Are Women", 1965; Zebra Associates, Inc., New York City, advertising agency founder and executive vice-president, 1969-76. Lecturer at colleges and universities in the United States and abroad; former member of board of directors of National Center for Voluntary Action and Dance Theatre of Harlem.

MEMBER: National Association for the Advancement of Colored People, National Association of Media Women, National Urban League (member of New York advisory board), American Women in Radio and Television (member of board of directors), National Council of Negro Women, American Federation of Television and Radio Artists, Television Academy of Arts and Sciences. *Awards, honors:* More than seventy-six awards, including *Mademoiselle* award for outstanding achievement, 1969; Media Woman of the Year; certificate of merit from New York Urban League, John Russwurm Award; Mary McLeod Bethune Award; Links distinguished service award; New York State Manpower Education award; New York Women in Communications Matrix award, 1974.

WRITINGS: The News (autobiography), McGraw, 1968; *Le Petit Ecran et Moi* (title means "The Little Screen and Me"), Nouveaux Horizions, 1970.

SIDELIGHTS: Murray's career in radio, television, and film has covered many facets of the media. She was the first black female accredited as a television news correspondent in the United States. As a press assistant and journalist, Murray has covered notable events including the Kennedy-Nixon debates, Premier Khrushchev's American visit, John Glenn's first space flight, and the assassination of Dr. Martin Luther King, Jr. She has worked on documentaries with Carl Sandburg and President Eisenhower and on news programs with Walter Cronkite and Edward R. Murrow.

In addition to her work as a news correspondent and interviewer, Murray has contributed to educational productions including "TV High School" and "What Did You Learn in School Today?" She also produced and narrated recorded interviews dealing with drug abuse and young people titled "To All My Young Brothers and Sisters With Love."

Murray and her twin sister were featured in the first television commercials specifically tailored for the black consumer. Her award winning firm, Zebra Associates, became the largest black-owned and operated agency in the United States and the first such firm to become a member of the American Association of Advertising Agencies.

AVOCATIONAL INTERESTS: Theatre, ballet, ice-skating, small plane flying (participated in Trans-Continental Women's Air Race).

BIOGRAPHICAL/CRITICAL SOURCES: George Gordon and Irving Falk, *Your Career in T.V. and Radio,* Messner, 1966; Hughes and Messner, *Black Magic,* Prentice-Hall, 1967; Murray, *The News,* McGraw, 1968; *Non-Traditional Careers for Women,* Messner, 1973.

* * *

MUSHKAT, Jerome 1931-

PERSONAL: Born May 5, 1931, in Liberty, N.Y.; son of Morris and Fanny Mushkat; married Barbara Sacks (an attorney); children: Linda, Steven. *Education:* Syracuse University, B.A., 1953, M.A., 1954, D.S.S., 1964. *Office:* Department of History, University of Akron, Akron, Ohio 44305.

CAREER: University of Akron, Akron, Ohio, instructor, 1962-64, assistant professor, 1964-68, associate professor, 1968-75, professor of history, 1976—. *Military service:* U.S. Army, 1954-56. *Member:* Organization of American Historians, American Studies Association, American Association of University Professors.

WRITINGS: Tammany: The Evolution of a Political Machine, 1789-1865, Syracuse University Press, 1971; *Aaron Burr: Controversial Politician of Early America* (booklet), SamHar Press, 1974; *George Clinton: New York Governor During Revolutionary Times* (booklet), SamHar Press, 1974. Contributor to history journals.

WORK IN PROGRESS: The Reconstruction of the New York Democracy.

* * *

MYLES, Symon
See FOLLETT, Ken(neth Martin)

N

NADEL, Gerald H. 1944-1977

PERSONAL: Born in 1944; married Marion Schonbrunn; children: Deborah and Laura (twins), Norman. *Education:* Graduate of Rutgers University. *Residence:* Melrose, Mass.

CAREER/WRITINGS: WINS Radio, New York, N.Y., news editor, 1965-71; Fairchild Publications Incorporated, Boston, Mass., bureau chief, 1971-77; Simmons College, Boston, writer-in-residence, 1977. Boston bureau chief of *Women's Wear Daily.* Adjunct professor at Rutgers University, 1965-71. Author of "A Portrait of Port Norris" series, WINS Radio, 1969. Contributor of articles to *New York Times, New Times, New Englander, Boston Herald-American, New York Times,* and *Atlantic.* Contributing editor of *Esquire, Boston* Magazine, and *TV Guide.*

OBITUARIES: New York Times, October 3, 1977.*

(Died September 30, 1977, in Boston, Mass.)

*   *   *

NAGLE, James J. 1909-1978

OBITUARY NOTICE: Born in 1909 in New York City; died November 23, 1978, in New York City. Journalist for the *New York Times.* Nagle, a staff member of the *Times* for fifty-one years, was a financial-business news reporter and a specialist on the food industry. He began his extensive career as a secretary in the paper's commercial department in 1927, and was made reporter in 1946. For several years he reported on the daily trading on the American Stock Exchange. Obituaries and other sources: *New York Times,* November 24, 1978.

*   *   *

NAMIAS, June 1941-

PERSONAL: Born May 17, 1941, in Boston, Mass.; daughter of Foster (an optometrist) and Helen (Needle) Namias; children: Robert Victor Slavin. *Education:* University of Michigan, B.A. (honors), 1962; Harvard University, M.A.T., 1963. *Religion:* Jewish. *Residence:* Cambridge, Mass. *Office:* Newton North High School, Newtonville, Mass.

CAREER: History teacher at high school in Cold Springs Harbor, N.Y., 1963-65, and junior high school in Newton, Mass., 1965-67; Newton North High School, Newtonville, Mass., history teacher, 1969—. *Member:* American Historical Association, Organization of American Historians.

WRITINGS: (Contributor) Carol Ahlum and Jacqueline Fralley, editors, *High School Feminist Studies,* Feminist Press, 1976; *First Generation: In the Words of Twentieth-Century American Immigrants,* Beacon Press, 1978. Contributor of poems to magazines, including *Christian Century, Quest, Boston Phoenix,* and *Women: A Journal of Female Liberation.*

WORK IN PROGRESS: A novel.

SIDELIGHTS: June Namias writes: "Whether fiction, nonfiction, or poetry, my writing comes out of a need to explore. The exploration might be outward or inward, but always has some personal connection. In order to see a piece of work through I find it must seize me and hold me, then I can follow it, and stay with it whatever it needs for its fulfillment.

"First Generation is an important book because it combines the sweep of history with the personal voices of those people who made that history. Working on the book gave me the chance to meet some of the most interesting and vital people I have ever know. Researching it reacquainted me with the wonders of the libraries of Boston and Cambridge."

BIOGRAPHICAL/CRITICAL SOURCES: Waltham News-Tribune, July 26, 1978; *Cambridge Chronicle,* July 27, 1978.

*   *   *

NANNES, Caspar Harold 1906-1978

OBITUARY NOTICE—See index for *CA* sketch: Born May 15, 1906, in Fall River, Mass.; died November 25, 1978, in Washington, D.C. Journalist and author. Nannes worked as a tennis editor and later religious news editor for the *Washington Evening Star.* He received the Religious Public Relations Council Award in 1954 and the W. Dickson Cunningham Sr. tennis award in 1963. After retiring, Nannes worked as a free-lance writer. Obituaries and other sources: *Washington Post,* November 27, 1978.

*   *   *

NARAYAN, R(asipuram) K(rishnaswami) 1906-

PERSONAL: Born October 10, 1906, in Madras, India. *Education:* Maharaja's College (now University of Mysore), received degree, 1930. *Home:* 15 Vivekananda Rd., Yadavagiri, Mysore 2, India. *Agent:* David Higham Associates, 5-8 Lower John St., Golden Square, London W1R 4HA, England.

CAREER: Writer. Owner of Indian Thought Publications in Mysore, India. *Awards, honors:* National Prize of the Indian Literary Academy, 1958; Padma Bhushan, India, 1964; National Association of Independent Schools award, 1965; D.Litt. from University of Leeds, 1967; English-Speaking Union Book Award for *My Days: A Memoir,* 1975.

WRITINGS: Swami and Friends: A Novel of Malgudi, Hamish Hamilton, 1935, Fawcett, 1970, published with *The Bachelor of Arts: A Novel,* Michigan State College Press, 1954; *The Bachelor of Arts: A Novel,* Thomas Nelson, 1937; *The Dark Room: A Novel,* Macmillan, 1938; *Malgudi Days* (short stories), Indian Thought Publications, 1941; *Dodu and Other Stories,* Indian Thought Publications, 1943; *Cyclone and Other Stories,* Indian Thought Publications, 1944; *The English Teacher* (novel), Eyre & Spottiswoode, 1945, published as *Grateful to Life and Death,* Michigan State College Press, 1953; *An Astrologer's Day and Other Stories,* Eyre & Spottiswoode, 1947; *Mr. Sampath* (novel), Eyre & Spottiswoode, 1949, published as *The Printer of Malgudi,* Michigan State College Press, 1957.

The Financial Expert: A Novel, Metheun, 1952, Michigan State College Press, 1953; *Waiting for the Mahatma: A Novel,* Michigan State College Press, 1955; *Lawley Road: Thirty-Two Short Stories,* Indian Thought Publications, 1956; *The Guide* (novel), Viking, 1958; *Next Sunday: Sketches and Essays,* Pearl Publications, 1960; *My Dateless Diary* (essays), Indian Thought Publications, 1960; *The Man-Eater of Malgudi* (novel), Viking, 1961; *Gods, Demons and Others* (short stories), Viking, 1965; *The Vendor of Sweets* (novel), Viking, 1967 (published in England as *The Sweet-Vendor,* Bodley Head, 1967); *A Horse and Two Goats and Other Stories,* Viking, 1970; (translator) *The Ramayana: A Shortened Modern Prose Version of the Indian Epic,* Viking, 1972; *My Days: A Memoir,* Viking, 1974; *The Reluctant Guru,* Hind Pocket Books, 1974; *The Painter of Signs,* Viking, 1976; (translator) *The Mahabharata: A Shortened Prose Version of the Indian Epic,* Viking, 1978. Contributor to *Fiction and the Reading Public in India,* edited by C. D. Narasimhaiah, 1967. Contributor of short stories to *New Yorker.*

SIDELIGHTS: R. K. Narayan is perhaps the best-known Indian writing in English today. His works have met with uniformly favorable criticism, and his books have such a popular appeal that, as Narayan himself noted in a *Books Abroad* interview, they "have been translated into all European languages and Hebrew."

Critics have appreciated his success in combining the English language with his Indian setting, the mythical village of Malgudi, to create a fictional microcosm as universal in scope as Faulkner's Yoknapatawpha County. His ability to present his characters sympathetically and realistically has been likened to that of such writers as Chekhov and Isaac Bashevis Singer. Narayan's subject matter is his native India and its people, and his genres are predominantly novels and short stories which exhibit a comic vision pervading even the most tragic episodes.

In a British Broadcasting Corporation radio interview, Narayan spoke to William Walsh of his use of the English language: "English has been with us [in India] for over a century and a half. I am particularly fond of the language. I was never aware that I was using a different, a foreign, language

when I wrote in English, because it came to me very easily. I can't explain how. English is a very adaptable language. And it's so transparent it can take on the tint of any country." Walsh added that Narayan's English "is limpid, simple, calm and unaffected, natural in its run and tone, and beautifully measured" in a unique fashion which takes on an Indian flavor by avoiding "the American purr of the cumbustion engine . . . [and] the thick marmalade quality of British English."

Other critics have noted the rhythms of Narayan's style and the richness of his narrative. Melvin J. Friedman suggested in a comparison with Isaac Bashevis Singer that "both seem part of an oral tradition in which the 'spoken' triumphs over the 'written,'" and theorized that the similarities between Narayan's fiction and the "Indian epics" echo "Singer's prose" and its "rhythm of the Old Testament." Eve Auchincloss noted that the translation-like quality of the language "adds curious, pleasing flavor."

Narayan's fictional setting is Malgudi, a village very similar to the village of his childhood, Mysore. In Malgudi every sort of human condition indigenous not only to India but to life everywhere is represented. Narayan's continued use of an imaginary village based in fact on his observations of his own home might suggest a comparison with William Faulkner's similar use of Oxford to create the fictional town of Jefferson and Yoknapatawpha County, as many critics have pointed out. "Narayan might . . . be called Faulknerian," wrote Warren French, "because against the background of a squalid community he creates characters with a rare quality that can only be called 'compassionate disenchantment.'" French also noted that both Narayan and Faulkner write frequently of "an unending conflict between individuality and the demands of tradition," typifying their respective geographical settings in such a way as to become universal by extension. Charles R. Larson demonstrated similar parallels but reflected that "while Faulkner's vision remains essentially grotesque, Narayan's has been predominantly comic, reflecting with humor the struggle of the individual consciousness to find peace within the framework of public life." Walsh stressed the universal quality of Malgudi: "Whatever happens in India happens in Malgudi, and whatever happens in Malgudi happens everywhere."

In Narayan's novels and short stories are characters who experience some kind of growth or change, or who gain knowledge through the experiences they undergo. As Walsh observed, Narayan most often focuses on the middle class and its representative occupations, many of which provide Narayan with titles for his books: *The Bachelor of Arts, The English Teacher, The Financial Expert, The Guide, The Sweet-Vendor.* Walsh explained Narayan's typical structural pattern in terms of concentric circles, whereby the village represents the outer circle, the family is the inner circle, and the hero, the focus of each novel, stands at the hub. "His hero is usually modest, sensitive, ardent, wry about himself," wrote Walsh, "and sufficiently conscious to have an active inner life and to grope towards some existence independent of the family." Walsh further observed that the typical progress of a Narayan hero involves "the rebirth of self and the progress of its pregnancy or education," thereby suggesting the Indian concept of reincarnation. "Again and again Narayan gives us the account of an evolving consciousness," wrote Larson, "beginning in isolation and confusion and ending in wholeness (peace within the traditional Hindu faith)" while maintaining a unique freshness of presentation.

Closely related to Narayan's gift for characterization is his ability to present his material in such a sympathetic manner that many critics have written at length of his comic vision in his treatment of his characters' failures and disappointments. French declared: "Although he satirizes the foibles of his characters, he never condescends to them or makes them targets for abuse. . . . Narayan is too sophisticated an artist to rail at people for being what they have to be." Walsh wrote of Narayan's "forgiving kindness" and labeled his novels "comedies of sadness . . . lighted with the glint of mockery of both self and others." Paul Zimmerman focused on the "affectionate amusement" with which Narayan treats his heroes, and Anthony Thwaite stated that "R. K. Narayan has achieved . . . an observation that is always acute, a humor that is never condescending, and a delicate sympathy that never becomes whimsical."

Without exception critics have been unusually favorable in their remarks concerning Narayan's expertise in realistically and sensitively creating universals from an imaginary setting which extend not only to India itself but ultimately to the experiences of living anywhere. Again and again critics take note of his effective combination of his Indian sensitivity and the English language to achieve a literary statement of non-geographic scope. Herbert Lomas paraphrased Graham Greene's assessment that "R. K. Narayan's one of the glories of English Literature . . . a sage if ever there was one. . . ." John Updike wrote that, through Narayan's remarkable gifts, "the fabled Indian gentleness still permeates the atmosphere evoked by this venerable cherisher of human behavior," and Eve Auchincloss stated that "[So] poised, so balanced a writer is Narayan, his sympathy and amusement so large, that even God's design for an overpopulated India seems defensible."

Narayan's novel, *The Guide,* was adapted by Harvey Breit and Patricia Rinehart and produced Off-Broadway in New York City at the Hudson Theatre, March, 1968.

BIOGRAPHICAL/CRITICAL SOURCES: Listener, March 1, 1962; *Encounter,* October, 1964; *Harper's,* April, 1965; *New York Times,* August 1, 1965; *Books Abroad,* summer, 1965, spring, 1971, spring, 1976; *Journal of Commonwealth Literature,* Number 2, December, 1966; *New Republic,* May 13, 1967; *New York Times Book Review,* May 14, 1967, June 20, 1976; *Times Literary Supplement,* May 18, 1967; *New Statesman,* June 2, 1967; *New York Review of Books,* June 29, 1967; *New Yorker,* October 14, 1967, March 16, 1968, July 5, 1976; *Season of Promise: Spring Fiction,* University of Missouri, 1967; *Literary Criterion,* winter, 1968; *Banasthali Patrika,* January 12, 1969, July 13, 1969; *Christian Science Monitor,* February 19, 1970; *Osmania Journal of English Studies,* Volume VII, number 1, 1970; *Washington Post,* April 14, 1970; *London Magazine,* September, 1970; William Walsh, *R. K. Narayan,* Longman, 1971; *Nation,* June 28, 1975; *Sewanee Review,* winter, 1975; *Newsweek,* July 4, 1976; *Book World,* July 11, 1976, December 5, 1976; *Contemporary Literary Criticism,* Volume 7, Gale, 1977.

*   *   *

NATHAN, Dorothy (Goldeen)   ?-1966

PERSONAL: Born in Portland, Oregon; married Paul Nathan (a contributing editor); children: Janet, Andrew, Carl. *Education:* Graduated from the University of California.

CAREER: Author of books for children.

WRITINGS: Women of Courage, illustrations by Carolyn Cather, Random House, 1964; *The Shy One,* illustrations by Cather, Random House, 1966; *The Month Brothers* (a-dapted from Samuel Marchak's play, "Twelve Months"; illustrations by Uri Shulevitz), Dutton, 1967.

SIDELIGHTS: Published posthumously, Dorothy Nathan's *The Month Brothers* is an adaptation of a Russian play which was based on eastern European folklore. "The story," according to a *Library Journal* review, "has the classic fairy-tale themes and structure, but details of plot are original and imaginative and will intrigue children. . . . There is humor and subtle satire. Illustrations in delicate block-print style, black across the white pages, evoke wintry Russia and vividly dramatize events and characters."

BIOGRAPHICAL/CRITICAL SOURCES: Library Journal, December 15, 1967.

OBITUARIES: New York Times, December 23, 1966; *Publishers Weekly,* January 9, 1967.*

(Died December 22, 1966)

*   *   *

NATHAN, Robert Stuart   1948-

PERSONAL: Born August 13, 1948, in Johnstown, Pa.; son of Alex (a wholesale toy distributor) and Bernice (a corporate treasurer; maiden name, Fadenhecht) Nathan. *Education:* Amherst College, B.A. (cum laude), 1970. *Residence:* New York, N.Y. *Agent:* Elaine Markson Literary Agency, Inc., 44 Greenwich Ave., New York, N.Y. 10011.

CAREER: Valley Review, Hadley, Mass., publisher, 1970-71; Council on the Environment of New York City, director of research, 1971-73; *Juris Doctor* magazine, New York City, associate editor, 1973-74, editor-in-chief, 1974-75, consulting editor, 1975-76; National Public Radio, Washington, D.C., New York bureau chief and national public affairs correspondent, 1975-76, White House correspondent, 1977; novelist and journalist, 1976—. *Member:* Authors Guild.

WRITINGS: Amusement Park (novel), Dial, 1977; *Rising Higher* (novel), Dial, 1979. Contributor of articles and reviews to popular magazines, including *Harper's, New Republic,* and *Politics Today,* and to newspapers.

WORK IN PROGRESS: Another novel; a play about a disintegrating family.

SIDELIGHTS: The purpose of a novel is to tell a story, Robert Stuart Nathan emphasized to an interviewer for *Library Journal.* He explained that this principle guided him when he wrote *Amusement Park,* and will govern his future novels as well. He went on to comment about the theme of *Amusement Park:* "If there are 'messages' in my novel, they exist only by virtue of the fact that writers will more or less always let you know what they believe in. The mechanical grandiosity of amusement parks—the meshing of fantasy with technology—fascinates me, and struck me as the right modern setting against which to place characters peculiarly caught up in the American dreams and obsessions of their time: money and power and the striving for, and impossibility of, ideal love. These are my concerns, the ingredients of my recipe, and I suspect they'll remain so. All this aside, again, I primarily wanted to tell a story."

Nathan told *CA:* "I consider myself primarily an entertainer, a storyteller. When a novel serves primarily as a writer's soapbox, it seems to me that it is bound to fail. Inevitably, of course, a writer's view of his fellow man, his political opinions, and his sense of morality will reveal themselves, one way or another, in the work itself. But the stuff of fiction is composed of characters and a story.

"I am unable to give the 'reason' I write, for I am not sure anything so simple as a reason exists.

"The question of 'experimental' novels always strikes me as a bit redundant. Every novel is an experiment for its author. Novels which deviate from conventional narrative form, in rendering characters or dialogue or story, fall into the same category—experiments for their authors. Ultimately 'experimental' is a term more useful to critics than novelists, who, after all, are more interested in doing their work than describing it."

BIOGRAPHICAL/CRITICAL SOURCES: Library Journal, October 1, 1977.

* * *

NEAL, Larry
See NEAL, Lawrence (P.)

* * *

NEAL, Lawrence (P.) 1937-
(Larry Neal)

PERSONAL: Born September 5, 1937, in Atlanta, Ga.; son of Woodie and Maggie Neal; married Evelyn Rodgers. *Education:* Lincoln University, B.A., 1961; University of Pennsylvania, M.A., 1963. *Politics:* Black Nationalist. *Religion:* Yoruba. *Home:* 12 Jumel Terrace, New York, N.Y. 10032.

CAREER: Writer. City College (now of the City University of New York), New York, N.Y., instructor in English, 1968-69; Wesleyan University, Middleton, Conn., writer-in-residence, 1969-70; Yale University, New Haven, Conn., fellow, 1970-75. Education director of Panther Party. *Awards, honors:* Guggenheim Fellow.

WRITINGS—Under name Larry Neal: (Editor with LeRoi Jones) *Black Fire: An Anthology of Afro-American Writing,* Morrow, 1968; *Black Boogaloo: Notes on Black Liberation,* Journal of Black Poetry Press, 1969; (with Imamu Baraka and A. B. Spellman) *Trippin': A Need for Change,* New Ark, 1969; *Hoodoo Hollerin' Bebop Ghosts,* Howard University Press, 1974. Also author of *Analytical Study of Afro-American Culture,* 1977.

Work represented in many anthologies, including *Soulscript: Afro-American Poetry,* edited by June Jordan, Doubleday, 1970; *The Black Poets,* edited by Dudley Randall, Bantam, 1971; and *New Black Voices,* edited by Abraham Chapman, New American Library, 1972. Contributor to periodicals, including *Black Dialogue, Cheyney Review, Journal of Black Poetry, Pride, Ebony, Essence, Liberation, Negro Digest,* and *New York Times.* Art editor of *Liberator,* 1964-66; co-editor of *Cricket* and editor of *Pride.*

SIDELIGHTS: Neal's writings reflect his concern and interest in the black arts movement which he described as "primarily concerned with the cultural and spiritual liberation of Black America." Neal wrote that the literature of the movement was not "protest literature," which he said was "a plea to white America for . . . human dignity," but literature for the black community. "We must address each other," Neal said. "We must touch each other's beauty, wonder, and pain." Neal believes black writers "carry the past and future memory of the race, of the Nation. They represent our various identities. They link us to the dependent, more profound aspects of our ancestry." "We are black writers," Neal said, "the bearers of the ancient tribal tradition."

Black Fire: An Anthology of Afro-American Writing was reviewed by Peter Berek as "a polemic anthology of essays, poems, stories, and plays by some seventy contemporary Afro-American writers, and the editors [Neal and LeRoi

Jones], by implication, set for themselves and their authors an enormous and revolutionary task: both to define a black esthetic and to illustrate scope and vitality."

BIOGRAPHICAL/CRITICAL SOURCES: Negro Digest (now *Black World*), January, 1968; *Saturday Review,* November 30, 1968; Lawrence Neal and LeRoi Jones, editors, *Black Fire: An Anthology of Afro-American Writing,* Morrow, 1968; *Ebony,* August, 1969.*

* * *

NEARING, Penny 1916-
(Anne Maguire)

PERSONAL: Name originally Meryl Lucile Munn, born in 1916, in Waterport, N.Y.; daughter of W. Clayton and Florence (Plowman) Munn; married Henry Nearing (an engineer), 1939; children: Susan, Nancy. *Education:* Cornell University, A.B., 1938. *Home:* 50 Clearview, Spencerport, N.Y. 14559.

CAREER: Writer, 1938—. *Member:* Mystery Writers of America, Genesee Valley Writers, Algonquin North Writers.

WRITINGS—Novels; all under pseudonym Anne Maguire: *The Folly of Pride,* Avalon, 1974; *Nurse at Towpath Lodge* (for young adults), Bouregy, 1976; *Substitute Nurse,* Avalon, 1979. Contributor of stories to magazines, including *American Girl* and *Christian Home.*

WORK IN PROGRESS: Two novels for young adults, a mystery set in Cree Indian country near Moosenee and one set in Great Lakes Country.

SIDELIGHTS: Nearing commented: "I write for young adults for the same reason I set my books in the Great Lakes plains and the Erie Canal region. There is an honesty and clear vision in this age group and geographical location that shouldn't be parted."

* * *

NEEDHAM, Rodney 1923-

PERSONAL: Born May 15, 1923, in England; married wife, Claudia; children: Tristan R. A., Guy R. M. *Education:* Oxford University, received B.Litt., M.A., D.Phil., and D.Litt., 1970. *Office:* Department of Anthropology, All Souls College, Oxford University, Oxford, England.

CAREER: Staff member at Oxford University, All Souls College, Oxford, England. *Military service:* Indian Army, 1st Gurkha Rifles, 1942-47; became captain. *Awards, honors:* Monograph prize from American Academy of Arts and Sciences, 1960; Rivers Memorial Medal, 1971.

WRITINGS: Structure and Sentiment: A Test Case in Social Anthropology, University of Chicago Press, 1962; *Belief, Language, and Experience,* University of Chicago Press, 1972; *Remarks and Inventions: Skeptical Essays About Kinship,* Harper, 1974; *Primordial Characters,* University Press of Virginia, 1978; *Symbolic Classification,* Goodyear Publishing, 1978.

Editor: *A Bibliography of Arthur Maurice Hocart,* Blackwell Scientific Publications, 1967; (and author of introduction) Charles Staniland Wake, *The Development of Marriage and Kinship,* University of Chicago Press, 1967; Claude Levi-Strauss, *The Elementary Structures of Kinship,* Beacon Press, 1969; (with Francis Korn) *Levi-Strauss on the Elementary Structures of Kinship: A Concordance to Pagination,* Clowes, 1969; Hocart, *Kings and Councillors: An Essay in the Comparative Anatomy of Human Society,*

University of Chicago Press, 1970; *Rethinking Kinship and Marriage,* Barnes & Noble, 1971; (and author of introduction) *Right and Left: Essays on Dual Symbolic Classification,* University of Chicago Press, 1973; Arthur Maurice Hocart, *The Life-Giving Myth and Other Essays,* 2nd edition (Needham was not associated with the earlier edition), Harper, 1973; Carl N. Starcke, *The Primitive Family,* University of Chicago Press, 1976.

Translator—All from the French: (With wife, Claudia Needham) Robert Hertz, *Death, and, The Right Hand,* Cohen & West, 1960; Arnold van Gennep, *The Semi-Scholars,* Routledge & Kegan Paul, 1961; Claude Levi-Strauss, *Totemism,* Beacon Press, 1963; Emile Durkheim and Marcel Mauss, *Primitive Classification,* University of Chicago Press, 1967.

Contributor of nearly three hundred articles and reviews to scholarly journals.

WORK IN PROGRESS: Indonesian Ethnography; Comparative Study of Symbolism; The Governance of Passion.

AVOCATIONAL INTERESTS: Music (Bach, Schoenberg).

BIOGRAPHICAL/CRITICAL SOURCES: Spectator, March 21, 1969; *Times Literary Supplement,* June 9, 1972; February 2, 1973.

* * *

NEKRICH, Aleksandr M(oisei) 1920-

PERSONAL: Born March 3, 1920, in Baku, Soviet Union; came to the United States in 1976; son of Moisei I. (a journalist) and Funny K. (a teacher; maiden name, Mitlin) Nekrich. *Education:* Attended Moscow State University, 1937-41; U.S.S.R. Academy of Sciences, D.H.S., 1963. *Home:* 505 Pleasant St., Belmont, Mass. 02178. *Office:* Russian Research Center, Harvard University, 1737 Cambridge St., Cambridge, Mass. 02138.

CAREER: U.S.S.R. Academy of Sciences, Institute of World History, Moscow, senior scholar, 1950-76; Harvard University, Cambridge, Mass., fellow of Russian Research Center, 1976—. *Military service:* Soviet Army, 1942-45; became captain; received two Orders of the Red Star. *Awards, honors:* Ford Foundation grant, 1977—; National Endowment for the Humanities grant, 1978.

WRITINGS—In English: 1941, 22 iunya, Nauka Publishers, 1965, translation by V. Petrov published as *Soviet Historians on German Invasion (June 22, 1941),* University of South Carolina Press, 1968; *The Punished Peoples,* Norton, 1978.

Other: *Politika angliiskogo imperialisma v Europe (oktyabr 1938-sentyabr 1939)* (title means "The Policy of British Imperialism in Europe, October, 1938, to September, 1939"), U.S.S.R. Academy of Sciences, 1955; (with L. V. Posdeeva) *Gosudarstvenniy stroi i politicheskiye partii Velikobritanii* (title means "The State System and Political Parties of Great Britain"), U.S.S.R. Academy of Sciences, 1958; *Voina, kotoruya nazvali "Strannoy"* (title means "The War Which Was Called Phony"), U.S.S.R. Academy of Sciences, 1961; *Vneshnyaya Politika Anglii 1939-1941* (title means "British Foreign Policy, 1939-41"), U.S.S.R. Academy of Sciences, 1964; *Vsemirnaya istoria* (title means "World History"), Volumes VIII-X, 1917-45, Mysl Publishing House, 1965; (contributor) V.V. Kurasov, editor, *S.S.S.R. i O.O.N.* (title means "The U.S.S.R. and the U.N."), Nauka Publishers, 1968; (contributor) *Istoria vneshnei politiki S.S.S.R.* (title means "History of U.S.S.R. Foreign Policy"), Volume I, Nauka Publishers, 1969; *For-*

sake Fear (memoirs; in Russian), Overseas Exchange Publishers, in press. Contributor to *Diplomatic Dictionary* and *Bolshaya Sovetskaya Entsyklopedia.* Contributor of more than sixty articles to journals in the Soviet Union and abroad.

WORK IN PROGRESS: The Sunset of the Stalin Era, 1944-55, publication expected in 1980.

SIDELIGHTS: Nekrich writes that in the book *Soviet Historians on German Invasion,* he "criticized errors committed by the Communist Party on the eve of and in the beginning of the war. In June of 1967, for my refusal to acknowledge my 'errors,' I was expelled from the Party. I was ostracized and finally left the Soviet Union in 1976." His books have been published in Rumania, France, Austria, Italy, Poland, Czechoslovakia, Hungary, and Yugoslavia.

BIOGRAPHICAL/CRITICAL SOURCES: V. Petrov, *Soviet Historians and the German Invasion,* University of South Carolina Press, 1968; *Critique,* number 7, 1976-77.

* * *

NELSON, Benjamin N. 1911-1977

PERSONAL: Born February 11, 1911, in New York, N.Y.; son of Mark and Mary (Finesmith) Nelson; married Marie Alma Louise Poole Coleman, November 30, 1959. *Education:* City College (now of the City University of New York), B.A., 1931; Columbia University, M.A., 1933, Ph.D., 1944. *Home:* 29 Woodbine Ave., Stony Brook, N.Y. 11790. *Office:* New School for Social Research, 65th Fifth Ave., New York, N.Y. 10003.

CAREER: University of Chicago, Chicago, Ill., assistant professor of social science and history, 1945-48; University of Minneapolis, Minneapolis, Minn., co-chairman of department of social science and chairman of European heritage sequence of humanities program, 1948-56; Hofstra University, Hempstead, N.Y., professor of history and social science and chairman of department, 1956-59; State University of New York at Oyster Bay and Stony Brook, professor of sociology and anthropology and chairman of department, 1959-66; New School for Social Research, New York, N.Y., professor of sociology and history (graduate faculty), 1966-77. Permanent fellow in University Faculty Seminar; intern in contemporary civilization at Carnegie Institute, 1962; Alexander White Visiting Professor at University of Chicago, 1970; visiting professor at Columbia University, 1970-71; Philip Merlan Memorial Lecturer at Scripps College, 1973. *Member:* International Society for the Comparative Study of Civilization (president), International Sociological Association, American Academy of Arts and Science, American Anthropology Association, American Sociology Association, American History Association, Medieval Academy of America, American Philosophy Association, Society for Scientific Study of Religion, Society for the Arts, Religion, and Contemporary Cultures (director). *Awards, honors:* Guggenheim fellow at Columbia University, 1944-45, 1949.

WRITINGS: The Idea of Usury: From Tribal Brotherhood to Universal Otherhood, Princeton University Press, 1949, revised edition, University of Chicago Press, 1969; *Freud and the Twentieth Century,* Meridian Books, 1957; (editor with John Hine Mundy) *Medieval Life and Thoughts* (essays), Biblo & Tannen, 1965; (contributor) R. S. Cohen and M. W. Wartofsky, editors, *Boston Studies in the Philosophy of Science,* Humanities Press, 1968; (contributor) *Beyond the Classics,* Harper, 1973.

Also author of *Personality-Work-Community: An Introduction to Social Science,* 1961, and other works. Senior consultant editor of "Harper Torchbooks," 1967-77. Member of editorial board of *Social Research,* 1966-71.

WORK IN PROGRESS: A collection of papers, translated into German.

OBITUARIES: New York Times, September 20, 1977; *AB Bookman's Weekly,* February 6, 1978.*

(Died September 17, 1977, in West Germany)

* * *

NELSON, George   1908-

PERSONAL: Born in 1908, in Hartford, Conn. *Education:* Yale University, B.A., 1928, B.F.A., 1931. *Residence:* New York, N.Y. *Office:* George Nelson & Co., Inc., 251 Park Ave. S., New York, N.Y. 10010.

CAREER: Time, Inc., New York City, associate editor of *Architectural Forum,* 1935-43, co-managing editor, 1943-44, head of Fortune-Forum Experimental Department, 1944-45, consultant, 1944-49; George Nelson & Co., Inc., New York City, president, 1947—. Partner of Nelson & Chadwick (architects), 1956—. Visiting distinguished professor at Pratt Institute, 1975-76; visiting critic at Harvard University, 1972-73; lecturer at colleges and universities in the United States, Canada, Japan, and Italy, including Yale University, 1931-32, Columbia University, 1942-45, University of California, Los Angeles, and University of Chicago. Member of board of directors of International Design Conference, 1965—. Member of New York State Council on Architecture, 1968-75 (adviser, 1967), Conseil Superieur de la Creation Esthetique Industrielle of Ministere du Developpement Industriel et Scientifique, 1968-75, and Kennedy Memorial Library committee, 1964; member of comite de patronage of Centre de Creation Industrielle Paris, 1970; member of visiting committee of Boston Museum School of Fine Arts, 1965. Member of President's Committee on Employment for the Handicapped, 1965.

MEMBER: American Institute of Architects (fellow), Industrial Designers Society of America (fellow; member of board of directors, 1969-76). *Awards, honors:* Fellow of American Academy in Rome, 1932; Benjamin Franklin Fellow of Royal Society of Arts; industrial arts medal from American Institute of Architects, 1964; award from Industrial Designers Society of America, 1974; Elsie de Wolfe Award from American Society of Industrial Designers, 1975.

WRITINGS: Industrial Architecture of Albert Kahn, Architectural Book Publishing, 1940; (with Henry Wright) *Tomorrow's House,* Simon & Schuster, 1945; (editor) *Living Spaces,* Whitney Library of Design, 1952; (editor) *Storage,* Whitney Library of Design, 1952; (editor) *Display,* Whitney Library of Design, 1953; (editor) *Chairs,* Whitney Library of Design, 1953; *Problems of Design,* Whitney Library of Design, 1957; *The Design Collection,* Museum of Modern Art, 1970; *How to See,* Little, Brown, 1977. Contributor of more than fifty articles to professional journals and popular magazines, including *Life, Harper's, House and Garden, Playboy,* and *Saturday Review.*

WORK IN PROGRESS: Another book on design, for Whitney Library of Design.

BIOGRAPHICAL/CRITICAL SOURCES: Architectural Record, December, 1957; *Zodiac 8,* 1961; *Cree,* 1972; *Design Quarterly,* Number 98-99, 1976.

NELSON, Peter
See SOLOW, Martin

* * *

NESBITT, Rosemary (Sinnett)   1924-

PERSONAL: Born October 12, 1924, in Syracuse, N.Y.; daughter of Matthew A. (an accountant) and Mary L. (Kane) Sinnett; married George R. Nesbitt, June 18, 1955 (died November 9, 1971); children: Mary, Anne, George, Elizabeth. *Education:* Syracuse University, B.S., 1947, M.A., 1952. *Politics:* Democrat. *Religion:* Roman Catholic. *Home:* 119 West Fourth St., Oswego, N.Y. 13126. *Office:* Department of Theatre, State University of New York College at Oswego, Oswego, N.Y. 13126.

CAREER: Wells College, Aurora, N.Y., instructor in speech, 1950-52; Syracuse University, Syracuse, N.Y., instructor in speech, 1952-57; State University of New York College at Oswego, professor of theatre, 1965—, director of Children's Theatre, 1968—. City historian for Oswego, N.Y. Member of board of directors of local Young Men's Christian Association, 1963-65, and Newman Foundation.

MEMBER: National League of American Penwomen, American Association of University Women, Oswego County Historical Society (member of board of trustees), State University of New York Theatre Association. *Awards, honors:* Named woman of the year in cultural development by *Syracuse Post Standard,* 1972; George Washington Gold Medal from Freedoms Foundation, 1975, for "The Great Rope"; named distinguished teaching professor, 1977.

WRITINGS: The Great Rope (juvenile), Lothrop, 1968; *Colonel Meacham's Giant Cheese* (juvenile), Garrard, 1971.

Adaptor; children's plays; all first produced in Oswego, N.Y., at Waterman Theatre of the State University of New York: "Cinderella" (three-act), May 21, 1971; "The Wizard of Oz" (two-act), April 27, 1972; "Pinocchio" (two-act), March 2, 1973; "A Christmas Carol" (one-act), December 14, 1974; "The Great Rope" (three-act), April 24, 1975; "A Christmas Festival" (two-act), December 14, 1976; "Mary Poppins" (two-act), December 16, 1977; "Alice in Wonderland" (one-act), July 31, 1978.

WORK IN PROGRESS: Research on local history during the French and Indian War and the American Revolution.

SIDELIGHTS: Rosemary Nesbitt writes: "The motivation for my writing began a long time ago. My father emphasized in our home the importance of local history in understanding the development of this country. As I grew older it became painfully apparent that little of this was being done by other parents, and much less, the schools. Then, when I married, I discovered that my husband's family had a rich heritage of participation in the developing history of New York State. These two things made it clear to me that it was time someone began writing about what had happened locally as America was being born. Children have difficulty identifying with Washington or Lincoln in a personal way because these figures are too large and too remote. However, if it is pointed out to them that their own grandfathers joined in alongside these men to fight for freedom, I think it is much easier for children to understand what America is all about. This country was founded on the principle of *individual* commitment to an idea. I have made it my business to write about those individual contributions in my area. *The Great Rope* deals with the true story of my children's great-great-great-great-

great grandfather, who as a boy of twelve, participated in an unusual and exciting way in the Battle of Oswego during the War of 1812.

"My major area of vocational interest is theatre. I spent three years off and on in Europe and the British Isles studying theatre and theatre history. I have also spent many years traveling in the United States and Mexico in further pursuit of my vocation. One of my specialties is offering performance work in Greek theatre, including ancient forms of Greek chant."

* * *

NEWBOUND, Bernard Slade 1930-
(Bernard Slade)

PERSONAL: Born May 2, 1930, in St. Catharines, Ontario, Canada; came to United States, 1963; son of Fred (a mechanic) and Bessie (Walbourne) Newbound; married Jill Foster Hancock (an actress), July 25, 1953; children: Laurel, Christopher. Education: Educated in England and Wales. Religion: "None." Home: 345 North Saltair Ave., Los Angeles, Calif. 90049. Agent: Jack Hutto, Harvey & Hutto, Inc., 110 West 57th St., New York, N.Y. 10011.

CAREER: Writer. Worked as actor in more than two hundred stage productions in Ontario, 1948-58; television writer for Columbia Pictures, Los Angeles, Calif., 1964-75. Member: Writers Guild of America (West), Dramatists Guild. Awards, honors: Drama Desk Award, American Academy of Humor Award, and nomination for Antoinette Perry Award from American Theatre Wing, all 1975, all for "Same Time, Next Year."

WRITINGS—All plays; all under name Bernard Slade: "Simon Gets Married" (three-act comedy), first produced in Toronto, Ontario, at Crest Theatre, 1959; "A Very Close Family" (three-act drama), first produced in Winnipeg, Manitoba, at Manitoba Theatre Centre, 1961; Same Time, Next Year (two-act comedy; first produced in Boston at Colonial Theatre, February, 1975; produced in New York City at Brooks Atkinson Theatre, March 13, 1975), Dell, 1975, with stage directions, Samuel French, 1976; "Tribute" (two-act comedy-drama), first produced in Boston at Colonial Theatre, April 6, 1978; produced in New York City at Brooks Atkinson Theatre, June 1, 1978.

Also author of teleplays for Canadian Broadcasting Corp., including "The Prizewinner," "Men Don't Make Passes," and "The Oddball." Creator of eight television series and author of more than one hundred television scripts for numerous series, including "Bewitched." Author of screenplays, including "Stand Up and Be Counted," Columbia, and "Same Time, Next Year," Universal.

WORK IN PROGRESS: "Romantic Comedy," a two-act play; a screenplay adaptation of "Tribute."

SIDELIGHTS: Slade told CA: "I was strongly influenced by the romantic comedies of Philip Barry, John Van Druten, S. N. Behrman, and Noel Coward. I try to write plays that combine comedy with situations and characters that touch the audience emotionally. I deal in the area of comedy because I find listening to two thousand people roaring their heads off enormously satisfying. Besides, nobody has ever convinced me that life isn't a comedy."

Though both "Same Time, Next Year" and "Tribute" have been extremely successful plays, Slade seems to be unaffected by all the acclaim. "Each play creates totally different problems," he said. "That's what's so fascinating—and so frustrating—about playwriting. Even after you've acquired a

certain expertise, there's no formula for the texture, the chemistry, or whatever it is, that makes a play work."

"Same Time, Next Year," has been produced in London, Paris, Madrid, Stockholm, Copenhagen, Athens, Rome, Rio de Janeiro, Caracas, Germany, Australia, Mexico, and Japan.

AVOCATIONAL INTERESTS: Tennis.

BIOGRAPHICAL/CRITICAL SOURCES: New York Times, April 13, 1975, May 28, 1978; Newsday, April 13, 1975; New York Post, April 19, 1975, June 2, 1978; Los Angeles Times, April 20, 1975; McLean's, July 1975; Canadian, July 26, 1975; Esquire, December, 1975; New York magazine, June 12, 1978.

* * *

NEWMAN, Thelma R(ita) 1925-1978

OBITUARY NOTICE—See index for CA sketch: Born April 24, 1925, in Brooklyn, N.Y.; died October 9, 1978. Expert in fields of crafts and plastics. Newman traveled to such places as Africa and Asia in search of different craft techniques. Her books include Quilting, Patchwork, Applique and Trapunto, Contemporary African Arts and Crafts, and Wax as an Art Form. Her books on plastics include Plastics as an Art Form and Plastics as Design Form. Obituaries and other sources: Publishers Weekly, October 30, 1978.

* * *

NGUGI, James T(hiong'o) 1938-
(Ngugi wa Thiong'o)

PERSONAL: Born in 1938, in Limuru, Kenya; married; children: five. Education: Makerere University, B.A., 1963; University of Leeds, B.A., 1964. Address: c/o William Heinemann Ltd., 15 Queen St., London W1X 8BE, England.

CAREER: Teacher in East African schools, 1964-70; Northwestern University, Evanston, Ill., visiting lecturer, 1970-71; currently senior lecturer and chairman of department of literature at University of Nairobi, Kenya.

WRITINGS: The Black Hermit (play; first produced in Nairobi in 1962), Makerere University Press, 1963, Humanities, 1968; Weep Not, Child (novel), Heinemann, 1964, P. Collier, 1969; The River Between (novel), Humanities, 1965; A Grain of Wheat (novel), Heinemann, 1967, 2nd edition, Humanities, 1968; This Time Tomorrow (play; includes "The Rebels" and "The Wound in the Heart"; produced and broadcast in 1966), East African Literature Bureau, 1970; (under name Ngugi wa Thiong'o) Homecoming: Essays on African and Caribbean Literature, Culture, and Politics (nonfiction), Heinemann, 1972, Lawrence Hill, 1973; Secret Lives (novel), Heinemann, 1974, Lawrence Hill, 1975. Also author, under name Ngugi wa Thiong'o, of Petals of Blood, 1977.

Work represented in anthologies, including: Modern African Short Stories, edited by E. A. Komey and Ezekiel Mphahlele, Faber, 1964; A Selection of African Prose, edited by W. H. Whiteley, Oxford University Press, 1964; Pan African Short Stories, edited by Neville Denny, Nelson, 1965; Africa in Prose, edited by Oscar Ronald Dathorne and Willfried Feuser, Penguin, 1969. Contributor of stories to Transition and Kenya Weekly News.

Editor of Zuka, Penpoint, and Sunday Nation (Nairobi).

SIDELIGHTS: According to Charles R. Larson, James Ngugi is "the first important novelist from East Africa." His works have been praised as a representative statement of the effects of the Mau Mau rebellion and hard-won freedom on a nation previously ruled by colonialism. A related theme successfully expressed throughout much of Ngugi's writings is the contrast between the traditional tribal beliefs of the Kenyan people and the burgeoning Christianity, a contrast which creates divisiveness within village communities and which can only be rectified by personalizing Christianity to the individual needs of an individual country. Ngugi's subject matter is his native Kenya and its people, and his modes of expression are drama, short stories, and novels which exhibit a chronologically maturing use of irony and subtle characterization.

Ngugi's first novel, *Weep Not, Child,* deals with the Mau Mau rebellion of the 1950's, and his third novel, *A Grain of Wheat,* concerns the aftermath of the war and its effects on Kenya's people. Although critics dealt somewhat harshly with the stylistic immaturity of the first novel, most commented favorably on the universality of its theme of the reactions of people to the stresses and horrors of war and to the inevitable changes brought to bear on their lives. Larson approved of Ngugi's "presentation of an historical event so recent" that the memory of it by those actually involved was "still very much alive," and additionally claimed that "the novel probes the nature of loyalty to one's clan, one's nation—the rise of nationalism." Ngugi returned to the Mau Mau rebellion and its aftermath in *A Grain of Wheat* and developed the theme of nationalism in depth. According to Nadine Gordimer, the underlying question of the novel is: "How fit is one for peace, when one has made revolution one's life?" Thomas R. Knipp praised Ngugi for successfully probing the question of violence and its ultimate effects and pointed out that "it is forgiveness not freedom that becomes the basis for what muted hope there is" following a civil war in which families are destroyed by conflicting loyalties.

Several critics mentioned Ngugi's obvious stylistic maturation from his first novel to his third. Eustace Palmer found many sentences in *Weep Not, Child* rather "clumsy," while acknowledging that Ngugi's use of simple sentence structure provided a realistic mirror of the simplicity of the native villagers themselves and that the "biblical aura is most appropriate for the description of the sufferings of a people in bondage" to British rule. Peter Nazareth also noted the "biblical simplicity" of the language and declared that such a technique was useful in reflecting both the colloquial speech patterns of the natives and the war environment of the time. However, Thomas R. Knipp theorized that the simplicity of the syntax resulted in characters "not fully rounded and complex" but rather "almost allegorical" in the morality play sense of being representative "of the author's attitudes."

By contrast, most reviewers found *A Grain of Wheat* to be the culmination of the promise of Ngugi's first novel. Although he used many of the same techniques and structures, he used them more effectively and with greater facility in conjunction with more complex structural techniques such as multiple points of view and flashbacks. Larson praised Ngugi's use of "the lyrical collective consciousness . . . often combined with a quasi-documentary technique . . . at strategic points," and also found the shifting points of view to be "a mirror of the chaos" following the Mau Mau revolt. Knipp focused on Ngugi's more mature use of irony in a crucifixion scene which makes "a bitterly ironic comment on salvation in a world where no one is saved."

The River Between, Ngugi's second novel, is a fictionalized account of the conflicts resulting from the imposition of Christianity upon the people of Kenya. The Honia River symbolizes the union of the opposing factions represented by Christianity on one side of the river and by traditional tribal rites on the other side, according to Lloyd Williams. "[Ngugi] knows that religion can be meaningful to a people only if it relates to them in their daily lives," Williams wrote, "only if it rises out of the important aspects of their past and speaks directly to their experiences in the present." Palmer praised the book's stylistic maturity, its use of "the complex rhythms of English," and Ngugi's developing "powers of characterization."

Ngugi has been lauded as the most articulate spokesman of his people and as an impartial chronicler of Kenya's modern history. His books are appreciated for their attempt to present fairly and without indictment the white man's position in the events preceding and during the Mau Mau rebellion. Knipp wrote that Ngugi "quietly understates the irony that the presence of the white man is responsible for both the violently self-destructive conflicts within traditional society and the curative and purgative blessings of western education."

BIOGRAPHICAL/CRITICAL SOURCES: Books Abroad, autumn, 1967; spring, 1968; Martin Tucker, *Africa in Modern Literature: A Survey of Contemporary Writing in English,* Ungar, 1967; *Michigan Quarterly Review,* fall, 1970; *African Literature Today,* Africana, 1970; Charles R. Larson, *The Emergence of African Fiction,* Indiana University Press, 1972; Eustace Palmer, *An Introduction to the African Novel,* Africana, 1972; *Contemporary Literary Criticism,* Gale, Volume 3, 1975, Volume 7, 1977; *Iowa Review,* spring/summer, 1976; *New York Times,* May 10, 1978.*

* * *

NGUYEN Ngoc Bich   1937-

PERSONAL: Born July 26, 1937, in Hanoi, Vietnam; came to United States, 1975; son of Nguyen Ngoc Bich (a province governor) and Nguyen Thi Suu; married Dao Thi Hoi (an educator), January 25, 1969. *Education:* Princeton University, B.A., 1958; graduate study at Columbia University, 1959-65; also attended University of Vienna, University of Munich, Kyoto University, and Foreign Service Training Center, Saigon, Vietnam. *Politics:* "Nationalist." *Religion:* "Ancestor worship." *Home:* 6103 Amherst Ave., Springfield, Va. 22150. *Office:* 1819 H St. N.W., Suite 500, Washington, D.C. 20006.

CAREER: U.S. Department of Commerce, Joint Publications Research Service, New York, N.Y., translator and editor, 1959-66; Embassy of Vietnam, Washington, D.C., director of Information Office, 1966-72; Mekong University, Saigon, Vietnam, vice-chancellor in charge of development and director of Vietnamese Studies Center, 1972-75. Director-general of Overseas Information Agency and director of Press Center in Saigon, 1974-75; director-general of Vietnam Presse (national news agency of Republic of Vietnam), 1975; counselor for Interagency Task Force Headquarters at Indiantown Gap, Pa., 1975. National Center for Vietnamese Resettlement, Washington, D.C., chief editor of *Lua Viet* and *Viet Center Bulletin,* 1975—. Teacher at Arlington Career Center, 1976—. Secretary-general of Buddhist Congregational Church of America. Lecturer on Vietnamese civilization and culture; has appeared on national television programs and at colleges, universities, and other public gatherings throughout the United States.

MEMBER: Social Sciences Association of Vietnam. *Awards, honors:* Fulbright scholar, 1956-58; Columbia University Presidential fellow, 1962-63; Distinguished Lecturer citation from U.S. Air Force, 1970 and 1972; scroll of appreciation from Foreign Service Institute, 1971.

WRITINGS: The Poetry of Vietnam, Asia Society, 1969; (editor and translator) Nguyen Nang Dac and Nguyen Quang Nhac, *Vietnamese Architecture,* Embassy of Vietnam, 1970; *North Vietnam: Backtracking on Socialism,* Vietnam Council on Foreign Relations, 1971; (editor with Nguyen Dinh Hoa, William Hegherbon, and Vo Dinh, and contributor) *Some Aspects of Vietnamese Culture,* Southern Illinois University Press, 1972; *An Annotated Atlas of the Republic of Vietnam,* Embassy of Vietnam, 1973; *The Asian Student,* Asia Foundation, 1973; (translator from Vietnamese) Pham Duy, *Songs of Joy,* DuCa Publishers, 1973; (contributor of translations from Vietnamese) Dorothy B. Shimers, editor, *Voices of Modern Asia,* New American Library, 1973; (translator from Vietnamese) Cao Tieu, *The Music of Verses,* Boi Ngoc Publishers, 1974; (editor with Burton Raffel and W. S. Merwin, and translator) *A Thousand Years of Vietnamese Poetry,* Knopf, 1975; *15 ca-khuc mung Gaing-sinh* (title means "Fifteen Christmas Carols"; bilingual edition), National Center for Vietnamese Resettlement, 1975; *Loi nhac Xuan va Tet* (title means "Spring Songs from Vietnam"; bilingual edition), National Center for Vietnamese Resettlement, 1976. Contributor to *New International Yearbook.* Contributor of translations of Vietnamese poetry to *Hudson Review, Antioch Review, Texas Quarterly,* and other journals; contributor of articles to literary journals. Chief editor of *Chuong Viet,* 1965-67, 1971-72, *Troi Nam, Vietnam Bulletin,* and *Vietnam Information Series,* all 1967-71, and *Tin tuc Hoi huong,* 1973-74.

WORK IN PROGRESS: Nguyen Du, 1765-1820: Selected Works; The Poetry of the Ly and Tran Dynasties, 1010-1400; research on Vietnamese cultural history and Buddhist studies.

SIDELIGHTS: Nguyen Ngoc Bich writes: "I have in my life only one basic purpose, to serve as a bridge between East and West and more specifically, between Vietnam and the English-speaking world. Wars may be won and lost, depending on the whims of history (historical 'laws' notwithstanding), but culture, I believe, abides. In the end, national culture may be the last redeeming feature of mankind. The world will be beautiful or ugly depending on whether it will have enough room for national cultures or whether it will merge into a formless, valueless, and morally guideless mess." The languages he has studied include Japanese, Chinese, German, Italian, Spanish, Portuguese, Russian, Latin, Greek, and Korean.

* * *

NICHOLAS, Leslie 1913-

PERSONAL: Born December 22, 1913, in Philadelphia, Pa.; son of Samuel (a physician) and Esther (a pharmacist; maiden name, Trallis) Nicholas. *Education:* Temple University, B.S., 1935, M.D., 1937; postdoctoral study at University of Pennsylvania, 1940-43. *Home:* 1919 Chestnut St., Philadelphia, Pa. 19103. *Office:* 1521 Locust St., Philadelphia, Pa. 19102.

CAREER: Dermatologist associated with Doctor's Hospital, 1940—, Graduate Hospital, 1940-65, Kensington-Maimonides Hospital, 1949-61, St. Luke's Hospital, 1950—, and Hahnemann Hospital, Philadelphia, Pa., 1952—; dermatologist in private practice, 1946—; Hahnemann Medical College, Philadelphia, associate professor, 1952-59, professor of dermatology, 1959-65, clinical professor, 1965-72, professor

of medicine, 1972—. Consultant on dermatology-pathology to the Veterans Administration, 1946-50; lecturer at the University of Pennsylvania division of graduate medicine, 1949-67; venereal disease program specialist at Philadelphia Department of Public Health, 1965-72. *Military service:* U.S. Army, 1943-46; became major. *Member:* American Academy of Dermatology, American Venereal Disease Association (president, 1977-78), Hellenic Union of Dermatology (honorary member), Jugoslavian Society of Dermato-Venereology (honorary member), Philadelphia Dermatological Society (president, 1962-63).

WRITINGS: (Editor) *Sexually Transmitted Diseases,* C. C Thomas, 1973; *How to Avoid Social Diseases,* Stein & Day, 1973. Member of editorial board of *Sexually Transmitted Disease.*

* * *

NICHOLS, Maggie
See NICHOLS, Margaret

* * *

NICHOLS, Margaret 1931-
(Maggie Nichols)

PERSONAL: Born June 9, 1931, in Chicago, Ill.; daughter of Milton A. (in building management) and Hazel (an elementary school principal; maiden name, Hartwell) Gethman; married Mike Nichols (a film producer), March 6, 1966. *Education:* Antioch College, B.A., 1954; graduate study at University of New Mexico, 1955-57. *Residence:* New York, N.Y. *Office: Field and Stream,* 1515 Broadway, New York, N.Y. 10036.

CAREER: Field and Stream, New York, N.Y., assistant managing editor, 1961—. *Member:* Society of Woman Geographers, Outdoor Writers Association of America, Outdoor Women, Photo Administrators, National Organization for Women, National Wildlife Association, National Audubon Society.

WRITINGS—Under name Maggie Nichols: *Wild, Wild Women: A Complete Woman's Guide to Enjoying the Great Outdoors,* Berkley Publishing, 1978. Author of "Especially for Women," a column in *Field and Stream,* 1973-76. Contributor to magazines, including *Scouting* and *Woman's Day.*

WORK IN PROGRESS—Under name Maggie Nichols: A humorous travel book; a mystery novel; a suspense novel; a collection of short stories.

SIDELIGHTS: Maggie Nichols writes: "Being blessed with one of those wonderful and rare jobs that lets you do things you really enjoy and call them work, I was able to collect a lot of experiences and practical knowledge of a very wide range of outdoor activities, which I shared in my writing for *Field and Stream.* I later decided to share them in book form with others who, like myself, spend large parts of their lives in a city or urbanized area, and long for some touch of the wild to keep them in balance.

"Although there is a good deal of how-to in the book, it is more of a 'why-to,' full of anecdotes as well as advice. In all my work, I try to entertain first, and inform (if information is the point) through the story wherever possible. I like to laugh, and I like to make others laugh (or smile) in whatever I write.

"I travel a lot, both for work and for pleasure, often in the Great Outdoors—backpacking the Appalachian Trail in Virginia or the San Jacinto Mountains in California, for example, or houseboating and canoeing in Minnesota, fishing in Lake Mead or the Virgin Islands, or hiking near my New York City home.

"I also enjoy living in the city, and spend much leisure as well as work time there. My strong belief that modern people need to be able to enjoy and be comfortable in both worlds—city and wild—is partly what led me to write my book on the outdoors for women (and other non-outdoor people), and will certainly be part of other things I write.

"In addition to my work as a writer and editor, I am also a photographer, which I do partly as part of my profession, and partly as an outdoor sport."

*   *   *

NICHOLSON, Joe
See NICHOLSON, Joseph Hugh, Jr.

*   *   *

NICHOLSON, Joseph Hugh, Jr. 1943-
(Joe Nicholson)

PERSONAL: Born July 13, 1943, in New York, N.Y.; son of Joseph Hugh (a newspaper editor) and Virginia (a teacher; maiden name, Collins) Nicholson. *Education:* Holy Cross College, B.S., 1965; graduate study at Fordham University, 1967-68, and St. John's University, Jamaica, N.Y., 1968-69. *Politics:* "Progressive and democratic." *Religion:* Agnostic. *Home:* 307 Mott St., Apt. 4-C, New York, N.Y. 10012. *Agent:* Knox Burger Associates Ltd., 39½ Washington Sq. S., New York, N.Y. 10012. *Office:* New York Post, 210 South St., New York, N.Y. 10002.

CAREER: Associated Press (AP), New York City, foreign correspondent and member of editorial staff, 1968-70; *New York Post,* New York City, investigative reporter, feature writer, rewriteman, legislative and foreign correspondent, 1971—. *Military service:* U.S. Naval Reserve, active duty, 1965-67; became lieutenant. *Member:* New York Press Club. *Awards, honors:* Citation for excellence in foreign reporting from Overseas Press Club, 1973, for article, "Inside Cuba"; nominated for Pulitzer Prize in nonfiction, 1974, for *Inside Cuba.*

WRITINGS—All under name Joe Nicholson: *Inside Cuba* (nonfiction; with own photographs), Sheed, 1974. Contributor of articles to national magazines, including *Harper's, Commonweal, Nation, New York,* and *Washington Monthly,* and newspapers.

WORK IN PROGRESS: A novel, *Search Pattern.*

SIDELIGHTS: Nicholson told *CA:* "While seventeen of the eighteen reviews I saw were laudatory, a few reviewers felt I was too soft on Communism. The Communist regime in Havana, however, felt I was too hard on Communism. When the *New York Times Magazine* commissioned me to return to write an article for them, the Cubans refused to give me a visa to return, and so the magazine had to turn the assignment over to another writer who could gain entry. One Cuban diplomat told me that his government was particularly offended by my description of Fidel Castro as 'cowardly' in his treatment of Cuban homosexuals.

"My near-complete novel *Search Pattern* is the story of a love triangle involving a young Navy officer, a sailor, and the daughter of the squadron Commodore, as seen through the diary of the young officer. It is set in the late 1960's, against a background of moral conflicts created by the Vietnam war, and ends with a court-martial and death."

Nicholson has visited forty countries on four continents, and speaks Spanish and Italian.

*   *   *

NICHTER, Rhoda 1926-

PERSONAL: Born June 22, 1926, in Brooklyn, N.Y.; daughter of Joseph (a tinsmith) and Celia Samuels; married Murray Nichter (a certified public accountant), June 26, 1948; children: Shelli, Judi. *Education:* Attended Brooklyn College (now of the City University of New York), 1943-46. *Politics:* "Apolitical." *Religion:* Jewish. *Home:* 7 Maxine Ave., Plainview, N.Y. 11803.

CAREER: Financial administrator, 1946-50; writer and lecturer, 1970—. Founder and president of Greater New York Council Against Public Smoking; founder and vice-president of Group Against Smoking Pollution of Long Island; founder and coordinator of I Quit Club (support program); vice-chairman of Long Island Interagency Council on Smoking and Health. Conducts smoking education programs for school students, nurses, and teachers; guest on radio and television programs. *Member:* Women's American Organization for Rehabilitation through Training (ORT; president, 1967-69).

WRITINGS: Yes, I Do Mind if You Smoke! ("humorous survival guide for nonsmokers"), Ashley Books, 1978. Author of "GPCA Council on Smoking and Health," a column in *Greater Plainview Community Association Newsletter,* and "Dear Rhoda," a column in *The Greater New York Council Against Public Smoking Newsletter.* Contributor to magazines and newspapers.

WORK IN PROGRESS: A book on how to quit smoking and how to help a loved one quit smoking.

SIDELIGHTS: Rhoda Nichter writes: "I have seen too many friends and relatives die or become incapacitated as a result of the insidious habit of smoking. We must do everything in our power to reverse the social acceptability of smoking to discourage the next generation from starting to smoke. Concerned citizens like myself are like David fighting Goliath (the tobacco industry).

"As an ex-smoker, I have developed a unique smoking cessation program at St. Francis Hospital in which the smoker is supported in complete withdrawal from nicotine for five consecutive days, with further support in follow-up meetings at regular intervals. We deal with the weight-gain worry as well.

"As a nonsmoker who found that I am adversely affected by ambient tobacco smoke, I became involved in protecting the health and rights of nonsmokers via education, legislation, and polite social action. My book is based upon the real-life problem of second-hand smoke faced by people in all walks of life, along with practical solutions."

AVOCATIONAL INTERESTS: Collecting paintings (antique and contemporary), antiques, old postal greeting cards (especially Valentines), opera, theater (professional and amateur).

*   *   *

NICKLESS, Will 1902-

PERSONAL: Born April 4, 1902, in Brentwood, Essex, England; son of William Thomas and Ada (Baylis) Nickless; married Nellie Agnes Carter, 1927; children: Will. *Education:* Attended St. Martins School of Art. *Home:* Heathfield Hall, Town Row Green, Rotherfield, Sussex, England.

CAREER: Free-lance illustrator for technical periodicals, 1920-25; free-lance illustrator for magazines and advertising firms, 1925—. Painter; lecturer on illustrators of Dickens's work. Advertising consultant.

WRITINGS: The Little Fly and Other Verses, Virgin Press, 1957; *Owlglass* (self-illustrated), 1964, John Day, 1966; *The Nitehood* (self-illustrated), Oliver & Boyd, 1966; *Molepie* (self-illustrated), John Baker, 1967; *Dotted Lines,* John Baker, 1968. Also author of a collection of poems, entitled *A Guide to the Tower.*

Illustrator of numerous books, including: Hans Christian Andersen, *The Ugly Duckling,* Houghton, 1948; Frank Knight, *Stories of Famous Sea Adventures,* Oliver & Boyd, 1966, Westminster, 1967; Allan Cooper, *Fishes of the World,* Grosset, 1971; Neil Grant, *David Livingstone,* F. Watts, 1974.

WORK IN PROGRESS: Making violins and violas.

BIOGRAPHICAL/CRITICAL SOURCES: Times Literary Supplement, February 16, 1968.

*   *   *

NICOSIA, Francesco M(ichael)   1933-
(Franco M. Nicosia)

PERSONAL: Born January 21, 1933, in Milan, Italy; came to the United States in 1957, naturalized citizen, 1961; son of Emmanuele (a mathematician) and Marcella (a teacher; maiden name, Borrini) Nicosia. *Education:* University of Rome, Dott. in Econ. e Comm., 1974; University of California, Berkeley, Ph.D., 1962. *Office:* Graduate School of Business, University of California, Berkeley, Calif. 94720.

CAREER: University of Rome, Rome, Italy, assistant professor of management and marketing, 1950-57; University of California, Berkeley, assistant professor, 1962-64, associate professor, 1965-68, professor of business administration, 1968—, director of consumer research program, 1962—, head of marketing and international business program, 1967-70. Marketing researcher for Milan's La Centrale, 1950-57; partner of Frederickson-Nicosia (consultants), 1961-70; marketing associate of Teknekron, 1970—. Lecturer for schools and business organizations in the United States and abroad. *Member:* American Economic Association, American Association of Public Opinion Research (head of public relations committee; member of executive council, 1973-77), American Psychological Association (fellow), American Marketing Association (member of San Francisco board of directors, 1963-64, 1968-69, 1974-75; president-elect, 1975-76; president, 1976-77), Institute of Management Science.

WRITINGS—Under name Franco M. Nicosia: *Tecnica Amministrativa delle Imprese di Servizi Pubblici* (title means "Marketing and Management of Public Utilities"), Edizioni Ateneo (Rome), 1960; *Consumer Decision Processes: Marketing and Advertising Implications,* Prentice-Hall, 1966; *Advertising, Management, and Society: A Business Point of View,* McGraw, 1974; (editor with Yoram Wind) *Behavioral Models for Market Analysis,* Dryden, 1977; (with Charles Dirksen and Arthur Kroeger) *Advertising: Principles, Cases and Problems,* Irwin, 5th edition, 1977. Contributor to business and marketing journals. Consulting editor for Wadsworth.

WORK IN PROGRESS: Marketing Research: A Behavioral Approach, for Wadsworth.

*   *   *

NICOSIA, Franco M.
See NICOSIA, Francesco M(ichael)

NIEDERLAND, William G(ugliemo)   1904-

PERSONAL: Born August 29, 1904, in Schippenbeil, Germany; came to the United States in 1940, naturalized citizen, 1945; son of Abraham (a rabbi) and Rosa (Mindes) Niederland; married Jacqueline Rosenberg, July 20, 1953; children: James, Daniel, Alan. *Education:* University of Wuerzburg, M.D., 1929; University of Genoa, M.D., 1935; New York Institute of Psychoanalysis, certified psychoanalyst, 1953. *Home and office:* 108 Glenwood Rd., Englewood, N.J. 07631.

CAREER: German State Government, Duesseldorf, Germany, public health officer, 1930-32; Sanatorium Rheinburg, Gailingen, Germany, medical director, 1932-34; practicing physician in Milan, Italy, 1935-39; ship's doctor on vessels in the Philippines and on round-the-world trips, 1939; private medical practice in New York City, 1941-46; University of Tampa, Tampa, Fla., associate professor of psychology, 1946-47; Mount Sinai Hospital, New York City, staff psychiatrist, 1948-51; private psychiatric and psychoanalytic practice in New York City, 1952-74, and Englewood, N.J., 1974—. State University of New York Downstate Medical Center, Brooklyn, N.Y., clinical instructor, 1953-58, associate professor of psychiatry, 1958-71, training psychoanalyst, 1958-72, professor emeritus, 1978—. Chief consulting psychiatrist to Altro Health and Rehabilitation Services, 1958-76; consulting psychiatrist at Hackensack General Hospital, 1975—. *Military service:* British Merchant Marine, ship's doctor and surgeon, 1939-40.

MEMBER: International Psychoanalytic Association, American Psychiatric Association (fellow), American Psychoanalytic Association, Psychoanalytic Association of New York (president, 1971-73), New Jersey Psychoanalytic Society. *Awards, honors:* Cultural achievement medal from University of Tampa, 1948; annual research award from Michigan Neurological and Psychiatric Society, 1970; honor scroll from New York Psychoanalytic Association, 1975; honor citation for leadership and services in community psychiatry from State of New York, 1976.

WRITINGS: Man-Made Plague: A Primer on Neurosis, Renbayle House, 1949; (with H. Krystal) *Psychic Traumatization,* Little, Brown, 1971; *The Schreber Case: Profile of a Paranoid Personality,* Quadrangle, 1974. Contributor of about two hundred articles to scientific journals in the United States, Italy, and Germany. Member of editorial board of *Psychoanalytic Quarterly,* 1959—.

WORK IN PROGRESS: Psychogeography: The Birth of a New Science; continuing research on the origin and essence of creativity.

SIDELIGHTS: Niederland comments: "My scientific studies and findings indicate that ongoing creativity adds not only to progress and improvement in the general sense, but also to that of the individual's own spiritual advance and achievement, and even to his longevity. Investigating the 'dark roots of creativity,' one arrives at a better understanding of one's own creativeness, the conflicts and problems connected with it, and that leads to an increase of one's creative strivings and capacities, especially in relation to aging and the aging process."

Niederland is also the "originator of the 'Survivor Syndrome,' a new clinical entity so named and scientifically described by me in several professional journals. This syndrome is frequently encountered and has been clinically observed by me in survivors of social and natural catastrophies, i.e., survivors of concentration camps and other types of political and racial persecution as well as survivors of floods, fires, earthquakes, etc.''

BIOGRAPHICAL/CRITICAL SOURCES: New York Times, February 28, 1972; *Science News,* February 7, 1978; *Los Angeles Times,* March 11, 1978.

* * *

NIEH, Hualing 1925-

PERSONAL: Born January 11, 1925, in Hupei, China; came to the United States in 1964, naturalized citizen, 1974; daughter of Kuang and Kuo-yin (Sun) Nieh; married Paul Engle (a poet), May 14, 1971; children: Wei-Wei Wang Rupprecht, Lan-lan Wang King. *Education:* National Central University, Nanking, China, B.A., 1948; University of Iowa, M.F.A., 1966. *Home:* 1104 North Dubuque, Iowa City, Iowa 52240. *Office:* International Writing Program, University of Iowa 472 EPB, Iowa City, Iowa 52242.

CAREER: Free China Fortnightly, Taiwan, literary editor, 1949-60; National Taiwan University, Taipei, associate professor of Chinese and English, 1961-64; Tunghai University, Taichung, Taiwan, associate professor of Chinese, 1962-64; University of Iowa, Iowa City, associate director of international writing program, 1967-77, director, 1977—, professor of letters, 1976—. *Member:* Association of Asian Studies.

WRITINGS: (Translator with husband, Paul Engle) *Poems of Mao Tse-Tung,* Simon & Schuster, 1972; *A Critical Biography of Shen Ts'ung-Wen,* Twayne, 1972; *Literature of the Hundred Flowers,* Columbia University Press, 1979.

In Chinese: *The Jade Cat* (short stories), Ming Hua Book Co. (Taiwan), 1958; *A Small Flower* (short stories), Book World Co. (Taiwan), 1962; *The Lost Golden Bell* (novel), Book World Co., 1963; *The Dream Valley* (essays), Cheng Wen Press (Hong Kong), 1965; *Two Women of China* (novel), Union Press (Hong Kong), 1976; *Stories of the Seventies,* Seventies Publishing Co. (Hong Kong), 1979; *After Thirty Years* (essays), Ocean Literature Press (Hong Kong), 1979.

Translator into Chinese: Henry James, *Madame De Mauves,* Literature Magazine, 1959; *Selected American Short Stories,* Ming Hua Book Co., 1963.

WORK IN PROGRESS: Translating the poetry of Chinese emperors and empresses into English for publication.

* * *

NIEMOLLER, Ara
See LLERENA, Mario

* * *

NIJINSKY, Romola Flavia 1891-1978

OBITUARY NOTICE: Born in 1891 in Budapest, Hungary; died June 8, 1978, in Paris, France. Dancer, lecturer, and author. Nijinsky had a brief career as a dancer, and later lectured about dance at universities in the United States, U.S.S.R., and Japan. She was the author of two biographies of her husband, dancer Vaslav Nijinsky, and the editor of his published papers. Obituaries and other sources: *The Author's and Writer's Who's Who,* 6th edition, Burke's Peerage, 1971; *New York Times,* August 4, 1978.

* * *

NISBETT, (Thomas) Alec 1930-

PERSONAL: Born May 7, 1930, in Coventry, Warwickshire, England; son of Sidney and Clarice (Bryant) Nisbett;

married Jean Connigale, June 24, 1950; children: Caroline, Sarah, Guy. *Education:* University of Birmingham, B.Sc., 1953. *Politics:* ''Agnostic.'' *Religion:* ''Floating.'' *Home:* 2 Oval Rd., London NW1 7EB, England. *Office:* BBC-TV, Kensington House, Richmond Way, London W14 OAX, England.

CAREER: Mathematical physicist. British Broadcasting Corp. (BBC), London, England, radio studio manager, 1953-61, radio producer for Overseas Services, 1961-63, transferred to BBC-TV, 1963, production assistant for ''Tonight'' show, 1963-64, staff member of Science and Features Department, 1964—, producer of short series, 1965-69, writer of documentaries, 1969—, senior producer, 1973—; producer and director of many television documentaries, including ''The Weather Machine,'' 1974, and ''Key to the Universe,'' 1976. Visiting expert for a film workshop, India, 1977. *Military service:* Royal Air Force, National Service, 1948-50. *Member:* British Association of Film and Television Arts. *Awards, honors:* Film award from the British Association for the Advancement of Science, and Bronze Prix Futura, Berlin, both 1971, both for ''The Insect War''; Glaxo traveling fellowship from the Association of British Science Writers, 1973, for ''Cancer: Meeting the Challenge.''

WRITINGS: The Technique of the Sound Studio, Hastings House, 1962, 4th edition, 1979; *Science Fairs,* English Universities Press, 1970; *The Use of Microphones,* Hastings House, 1974; *Konrad Lorenz,* Dent, 1976, published as *Konrad Lorenz: A Biography,* Harcourt, 1977.

Documentary teleplays; all as producer and director; all for British Broadcasting Corp. (BBC-TV): ''Cancer Now,'' 1969; ''After the Iron Age,'' 1970; ''Virus,'' 1970; ''The Insect War,'' 1970; ''The Man Who Talks to Frogs,'' 1970; ''A Nice Sort of Accident,'' 1971; ''The Crab Nebula,'' 1971; ''The Missing Link,'' 1972; ''How They Sold Doomsday,'' 1972; ''Cancer: Meeting the Challenge,'' 1972; ''Crime Lab,'' 1973; ''Red Sea Coral and the Crown of Thorns,'' 1973; ''In Search of Konrad Lorenz,'' 1973; (with Robin Bootle) ''The Rise and Fall of DDT,'' 1974, ''The Trobriand Experiment,'' 1975; ''The Message in the Rocks,'' 1978; ''Bags of Life,'' 1978.

Contributor to magazines, including *New Scientist, Listener, Tape,* and *Hi-Fi News and Record Review.*

WORK IN PROGRESS: More documentaries for BBC-TV and Public Broadcasting Service (PBS-TV).

SIDELIGHTS: In 1973 Alec Nisbett traveled to several German and Austrian villages to interview Konrad Lorenz, the founding father of ethology (the comparative study of the behavior of different species). Nisbett talked with and filmed the famous scientist, and then used this material to write *Konrad Lorenz: A Biography.* General assessments of the book, which covers Lorenz's life, his ideas, and the field of ethology as a whole, have been largely favorable. Alden Whitman praised it as ''a clear and authoritative biography and one that is bound to edify any reader with a sense of curiosity,'' while Stephen Jay Gould declared it to be ''an eminently fair and readable'' biography.

Most commentators have observed that the lack of a critical perspective is the chief drawback of *Konrad Lorenz.* A *Time* reviewer noted: ''Nisbett seems to have been overawed by his subject. As a result, he has failed to write a critical study of Lorenz and his work. Instead, he has produced an informative *Festschrift.*'' Peter Gardner made a similar point when he wrote of the biography, ''In its zeal to incorporate a multiplicity of viewpoints on Konrad Lorenz's character, work, ideas, and influence, it is cautious, at times, to the point of indecisiveness." On the same subject, Gould remarked, "Nisbett probes all the dubious aspects of Lorenz's life and works with a peculiarly English sense of fairness, but his verdicts range only from approval to excuse."

Opinions differ as to the adequacy of Nisbett's discussion of the Nazi sentiments which Lorenz espoused in the early 1940's. Anthony Storr believed that "Nisbett is rightly critical of Lorenz's ill-judged flirtation with the Nazis," but feeling the author was too protective of his subject in this case, G. E. Allen contended that "Nisbett . . . argues in the most contorted vein that Lorenz was politically naive." Nisbett treated the Nazi issue too lightly, Gould felt: "Nisbett faces this issue squarely but dismisses it as 'an episode which is small by comparison with so great a life's work.'" In contrast, Whitman considered Nisbett's handling of the incident to be "thorough and tactful"; he thought that the biographer "arrives at a split decision. He doubts that his man was a racist but concedes his use of Nazi terminology in an essay that could be read as an attack on the Jews or as a justification for 'fully superior persons.'"

Of the treatment of Lorenz's scientific work, Allen pointed out that "whenever Lorenz proved to be wrong about a specific issue . . . Nisbett emphasizes that 'whether right or wrong . . . Lorenz has played his usual role of stimulus to others.' While in individual instances such an argument may be true, used too often, it says nothing that is very illuminating." Gould commented that "Nisbett, though accurate and thorough in his discussion of Lorenz' scientific work, barely discusses the deeper issues of Darwinian theory and the meaning of similarity. He follows Lorenz's regrettable tendency to describe animal behavior in human terms."

Nisbett told CA: "I set out to write 'a sympathetic but critical' study of Konrad Lorenz, to relate the flow of an extraordinary scientist's seminal and often controversial ideas to his personal history. I was motivated not by hero worship but by a desire first to understand and then to interpret an enigma. As to whether his own conclusions are right or wrong, in some cases I have surely made it clear that I believe him to be profoundly wrong—for example, in the matter of human domestication. In other cases I suggest that he is wrong in detail, but so what? Newton was wrong, too, in detail, as Einstein demonstrated. I gave my opinions with some diffidence, admittedly, for I believed it more important to give such facts as I could ascertain, together with Lorenz's defense when under attack, and to let the reader—and later, history—make the judgment. I suspect that history may take a different view from that of Lorenz's harsher critics, who by their association become mine, too.

"But the book on Lorenz has been a very small part of my work, and is not, I would say, central to it. More generally, I regard science as an intellectual and cultural activity comparable to the arts. My other films and books reflect this attitude and often more explicitly try to provide a 'consumer's guide' to particular topics, giving background information which improves the 'political' understanding of complex subjects." Nisbett went on to note that his experiences as a writer, director, and producer have fueled his own thinking about human beings and their concept of territory: "In my biography of Lorenz, I self-indulgently allowed myself a few extrapolations from his ideas—offering a suggestion that we humans can sustain much higher population densities than other territorial animals because our concept of territory is based on our individual capacities and interests. When I wrote *The Technique of the Sound Studio* in 1962, I discovered that as an author on that subject at my chosen level I

was the sole occupant of the English speaking world. What a sense of space that gave!

"Similarly, when I wrote on Lorenz himself, I joined a small, worldwide community that is noted for its infighting, as reviews (particularly in the United States), have demonstrated. Within the BBC I belong to yet another group (of science writer/directors) of such a quality that it has little serious competition anywhere in the world except from its own exiles. Delightfully (and amazingly for such a vast and reputedly bureaucratic organization), the freedoms given to its membership are much greater than the constraints. All of which illustrates my further thesis that cities work because they permit the existence of myriads of spatially overlapping, but otherwise distinct villages of the mind. I am not at all sure that Lorenz would like that idea!"

In the course of filming his documentaries, Nisbett has visited thirty-one countries. Some of his books have been translated into Russian, Spanish, French, Italian, and Japanese.

BIOGRAPHICAL/CRITICAL SOURCES: New York Times Book Review, February 27, 1977; *Saturday Review,* March 5, 1977; *Time,* March 14, 1977; *Washington Post Book World,* April 3, 1977; *New York Times,* April 30, 1977; *Natural History,* June-July, 1977.

* * *

NIVEN, Alastair 1944-

PERSONAL: Born February 25, 1944, in Edinburgh, Scotland; son of Harold Robertson (a civil servant) and Elizabeth (Mair) Niven; married Helen Trow (a university administrator), August 22, 1970. *Education:* Gonville & Caius College, Cambridge, B.A., 1966, M.A., 1969; University of Ghana, M.A., 1968; University of Leeds, Ph.D., 1972. *Home:* 16 Bridge St., Berkhamsted, Hertfordshire, England. *Office:* Africa Centre, 38 King St., London WC2E 8JT, England.

CAREER: University of Ghana, Legon, lecturer in English, 1968-69; University of Leeds, Leeds, England, lecturer in English, 1969-70; University of Stirling, Stirling, Scotland, lecturer in English studies, 1970-78; Africa Centre, London, England, director-general, 1978—. *Member:* Royal Commonwealth Society, Association for Commonwealth Literature and Language Studies (member of executive committee, 1975—). *Awards, honors:* Commonwealth fellow at University of Ghana, 1966-68.

WRITINGS: (Editor) *The Commonwealth Writer Overseas,* Didier, 1976; *D. H. Lawrence: The Novels,* Cambridge University Press, 1978; *The Yoke of Pity: The Fiction of Mulk Raj Anand,* Arnold Heinemann, 1978; *Truth Into Fiction: Raja Rao's "The Serpent and the Rope",* Writers' Workshop (Calcutta, India), 1978; *William Golding's "Lord of the Flies",* Alexander's Notes, 1979; *West African Literature in English,* Macmillan, 1979.

Contributor: *Common Wealth,* edited by Anna Rutherford, Akademisk Boghandel (Aarhus, Denmark), 1971; *Readings in Commonwealth Literature,* edited by William Walsh, Oxford University Press, 1973; *D. H. Lawrence,* edited by Damien Grant, British Council in Japan, 1977; *Awakened Conscience,* edited by C. D. Narasimhaiah, Sterling (New Delhi, India).

Contributor to magazines. Co-editor of *Journal of Commonwealth Literature,* 1979—.

WORK IN PROGRESS: Studying African literature in English.

SIDELIGHTS: Niven writes: "Literature is an international means of communication. My main interest is seeing that people of different cultures talk to each other."

AVOCATIONAL INTERESTS: Travel (Africa, Europe, India).

* * *

NOAH, Joseph W(atson) 1928-

PERSONAL: Born March 1, 1928, in Greensboro, N.C.; son of Lawrence Raymond (in railroad work) and Nell (Johnson) Noah; married Betty Richardson, June 1, 1948; children: Robert W., Judy Ann Noah Johnson, Susan Lynn. *Education:* North Carolina State University, B.I.E., 1951; Stanford University, M.S., 1955. *Religion:* Protestant. *Home:* 9003 Stoneleigh Court, Fairfax, Va. 22031. *Office:* J. Watson Noah, Inc., 5205 Leesburg Pike, Suite 510, Falls Church, Va. 22041.

CAREER: RAND Corp., Santa Monica, Calif., staff member, 1958-63; Center for Naval Analyses, Arlington, Va., manager of economics and cost analysis division, 1966—; Planning Research Corp., Washington, D.C., manager of resource and cost analysis department, 1966-70; J. Watson Noah, Inc. (research, engineering, and economics firm), Falls Church, Va., president, 1972—. Member of board of directors of Council on Alcoholism for Fairfax County. *Military service:* U.S. Marine Corps, 1946-48. U.S. Air Force, 1951-58; became captain. U.S. Air Force Reserve, 1951-58; became major. *Member:* Operations Research Society of America, Tau Beta Pi.

WRITINGS: (Contributor) *Defense Management,* Prentice-Hall, 1967; *Wings God Gave My Soul,* Baptie Studios, 1974; (contributor) *Geoscience Instrumentation,* Wiley, 1974; *A World of Scarcities,* Associated Business Programmes, 1976.

WORK IN PROGRESS: Cripes A' Mighty, a revised edition of *Wings God Gave My Soul.*

SIDELIGHTS: Noah told *CA:* "I plan to visit 375 small airports in the Midwest during the next year, to gather material that may be interesting for an aviation-related book."

* * *

NOBILE, Umberto 1885-1978

OBITUARY NOTICE: Born January 21, 1885, in Lauro, Italy; died July 29, 1978, in Rome, Italy. Italian Air Force general, aviator, dirigible expert, adventurer, polar explorer, educator, and author of books on his flying experiences. Nobile was one of the first men to fly over the North Pole when he piloted the dirigible *Norge* over the area on May 12, 1926. Two years later, Nobile organized another expedition to the Arctic but it ended in disaster when the dirigible crashed on the voyage back to Norway. Eight crew men died and Roald Amundsen, the discoverer of the South Pole, disappeared. Nobile was charged by a commission of inquiry with a navigational error that resulted in the crash. After World War II, he was finally exonerated of the blame and was reinstated in the Italian Air Force. Nobile taught aeronautics in the Soviet Union, the United States, and Italy. Obituaries and other sources: *New York Times,* July 31, 1978.

* * *

NORBERG-SCHULZ, Christian 1926-

PERSONAL: Born May 23, 1926, in Oslo, Norway; son of Christian (a professor) and Laura (Lunde) Norberg-Schulz; married Anna Maria De Dominicis (a teacher), February 19, 1955; children: Erik, Elizabeth, Emanuel. *Education:* Eidgenossische Technische Hochschule, diploma in architecture, 1949; Technical University of Trondheim, Dr.Techn., 1963. *Religion:* Roman Catholic. *Home:* Slemdalsveieu 100, Oslo, Norway. *Office:* Oslo School of Architecture, St. Olavsgate 4, Oslo, Norway.

CAREER: Oslo Architects' Association, Oslo, Norway, chairman, 1963-65; Oslo School of Architecture, Oslo, assistant professor, 1951-66, professor of architecture, 1966—. Visiting professor at Massachusetts Institute of Technology, 1973-74, and University of Dallas, 1978. Member of council of Oslo's National Gallery and Oslo Museum of Modern Art. *Military service:* Norwegian Army, 1950-51; became second lieutenant. *Member:* Norwegian Architects' League. *Awards, honors:* D.H.C. from Technical University of Hannover, 1978.

WRITINGS: Intentions in Architecture, M.I.T. Press, 1963; *Existence, Space, and Architecture,* Praeger, 1971; *Baroque Architecture,* Abrams, 1972; *Late Baroque and Rococo Architecture,* Abrams, 1973; *Meaning in Western Architecture,* Praeger, 1975; *Mellom jord og himmel* (title means "Between Earth and Sky"), Universitetsforlaget, 1978; *Genius Loci* (title means "Spirit of Place"), Electa, 1979; *Meaning and Place* (essays), Academy Editions, 1979. Chief editor of *Byggekunst* (Norwegian architects' journal), 1963-78. Co-director of Lotus International.

WORK IN PROGRESS: History of Modern Architecture in Norway, to be published by Gyldendal; *Phenomenology of Modern Architecture.*

SIDELIGHTS: Norberg-Schulz comments that his greatest interest, inspired by Rilke, Heidegger, and many years in Italy, is "the importance of *place* to human life." He writes: "When anything happens we say that it 'takes place.' This shows that 'place' forms a constituent part of the very structure of human existence. To *dwell,* in the true sense of the word, means 'to become friends with the *genius loci* or 'spirit of place.'"

AVOCATIONAL INTERESTS: Classical music.

* * *

NORMAN, Kerry
See Le PELLEY, Guernsey

* * *

NORTH, Elizabeth 1932-

PERSONAL: Born August 20, 1932, in Hampshire, England; daughter of Dudley (an admiral in the Royal Navy) and Eileen (Graham) North; married David Howard (divorced, 1973); married Brian Thompson (a novelist and television writer); children: Philippa, Sophie, Joanna, Thomas; three stepchildren. *Education:* University of Leeds, B.A. (honors), 1973. *Politics:* "Left of centre." *Religion:* Church of England. *Home:* 7 Spring Mount, Harrogate, Yorkshire, England. *Agent:* Murray Pollinger, Longacre, London W.C.2, England.

CAREER: Writer. Has taught English at several colleges of education; creative writing teacher for Workers Educational Authority.

WRITINGS: The Least and Vilest Things, Gollancz, 1971; *Summer Solstice,* Knopf, 1972; *Pelican Rising,* Gollancz, 1975; *Enough Blue Sky,* Gollancz, 1977; *Everything in the Garden,* Gollancz, 1978. Author of radio plays, 1968-69.

WORK IN PROGRESS: Diary of a Small Mind, a novel set in contemporary Yorkshire.

AVOCATIONAL INTERESTS: Gardening, playing contract bridge.

* * *

NORTHOUSE, Cameron (George)   1948-

PERSONAL: Born March 11, 1948, in Omaha, Neb.; son of George Northouse, Jr. and Ruby (Dwyer) Taylor; married Donna George (a teacher), August 16, 1969. *Education:* University of Nebraska at Omaha, B.A., 1971, M.A., 1972; University of South Carolina, Ph.D., 1975. *Home:* 2713 Knight St., Dallas, Tex. 75219.

CAREER: University of South Carolina, Columbia, S.C., instructor, 1975-76; *New London Press,* Dallas, Tex., editor, 1976—. Humanities adviser, Dallas Theater Center, 1978.

WRITINGS: (With Thomas Walsh) *John Osborne: A Reference Guide,* G. K. Hall, 1974; (with Walsh) *Sylvia Plath and Anne Sexton: A Reference Guide,* G. K. Hall, 1974; *Twentieth-Century Opera in England and the United States,* G. K. Hall, 1976; *John Barth, Jerzy Kosinski, and Thomas Pynchon: A Reference Guide,* G. K. Hall, 1978; (editor) *Articles on English Literature: A Comprehensive Bibliography, 1900-1975,* Volume I, New London Press, 1978; (with Nicholas Dalley) *Mark Medoff: An Interview,* New London Press, 1978; (editor) *Concept: An Anthology of Contemporary Writing,* New London Press, 1978. Contributor to *Conversations With Writers II* and *Dictionary of Literary Biography.* Editor, *Texas Arts Journal* and *Reference Book Review.*

WORK IN PROGRESS: An encyclopedia of American drama.

* * *

NORTON, Alan (Lewis)   1926-

PERSONAL: Born November 17, 1926, in Oldbury, England; son of Arthur Christopher (a silversmith) and Doris (a shopkeeper; maiden name, Lewis) Norton; married Susanne Muller (a lecturer), January, 1951; children: Paul Michael, Andrew Peter. *Education:* Selwyn College, Cambridge, B.A., 1951, M.A. (history), 1956; graduate study at Institute of Education, London, 1952; University of Birmingham, M.Soc.Sci., 1965. *Home:* 3 Green Meadow Rd., Birmingham, England. *Office:* Institute of Local Government Studies University of Birmingham, Birmingham B15 2TT, England.

CAREER: Her Majesty's Overseas Civil Service, Warri, Ibadan, and Benin, Western nigeria, senior education officer and inspector of education, 1952-60; County Borough of Barnsley, Yorkshire, England, assistant for further education, 1961-64; University of Birmingham, Birmingham, England, senior research assistant, 1965-66, lecturer, 1966-73, senior lecturer in local government and administration, 1973—. Affiliated with World Bank Consultancy on Housing Management in Nairobi, 1975-76; expert adviser on Training for Urban Management, 1976-78; consultant to the Municipality of Istanbul with Technical Co-Operation Service Organization for Economic Co-Operation and Development, 1977-78. *Military service:* British Army, 1943-47; became sergent. *Member:* International Political Science Association, Royal Institute of Public Administration, Political Studies Association of the United Kingdom, British Educational Administration Society.

WRITINGS: (With Margaret Harrison) *Local Government Administration in England and Wales,* Volume V: *Management of Local Government,* H.M.S.O., 1967; (with Joyce R. Long) *Setting Up the New Local Authorities,* Charles Knight, 1972; (with Long) *Community Land Legislation and Its Implementation,* Institute of Local Government Studies, University of Birmingham, 1975; (editor with G. W. Jones) *Political Leadership in Local Authorities,* Institute of Local Government Studies, University of Birmingham, 1978. Contributor to public administration and public service journals. Founder and editor of *Local Government Studies,* 1971.

WORK IN PROGRESS: Management of the Metropolis, completion expected in 1980; research on collaboration between health and local authorities; studying contributions of international agencies to urban management, and case studies on practical management in European centers.

SIDELIGHTS: Norton writes: "My main public endeavor has been to contribute to the quality of local government and administration, not only through research but also through diffusion of learning between local governmental bodies, nationally and internationally. My current aim is to analyze contemporary practice and contribute to the setting of higher norms in local administration. My work in Istanbul, sponsored by OECD, has catalyzed my thinking in this field. I try to bridge organizational sociology, psychology, and political science insofar as they relate to urban government.

"I have a passionate attachment to the countries around the Aegean—both Greece and Turkey, with an elementary knowledge of their languages. I read French, German, and some Italian, and attach much value to my connections with European scholars, but it is in Istanbul that my historical and modern interests cross.

"I am a cultural nomad, deeply enjoying classical European music, painting, and architecture, but also with a strong instinctive reaction to the music and art of the Levant. My ambition here is to find an adequate literary medium, not to synthesize, but to show the inter-dependency and complementarity of contrasting cultures, both through time and space. But the urgency of modern urban problems makes it seem self-indulgent to take historical or purely analytical approach to these matters when one feels one can intervene effectively through consulting work, and hope to achieve modest improvements—or at least hold back a little the forces of disintegration which are destroying so much of what is valuable in our cultures."

* * *

NOTEHELFER, F(red) G(eorge)   1939-

PERSONAL: Born April 13, 1939, in Tokyo, Japan; came to the United States in 1947; son of John Karl (a clergyman) and Rose (a missionary; maiden name, Henner) Notehelfer; married Margaret Ann deLotbiniere-Harwood, December 30, 1966. *Education:* Harvard University, B.A., 1962; Princeton University, Ph.D., 1968. *Politics:* Democrat. *Religion:* Protestant. *Home:* 3236 Coolidge Ave., Los Angeles, Calif. 90066. *Office:* Department of History, University of California, Los Angeles, Calif. 90024.

CAREER: Princeton University, Princeton, N.J., lecturer in history, 1966-69; University of California, Los Angeles, assistant professor, 1969-71, associate professor of history, 1971—. Visiting professor at Doshisha University, 1971-72. Artist (painter). Member of steering committee of Southern California Japan Seminar. *Member:* International House of Japan, American Historical Association, Association for Asian Studies, Phi Beta Kappa. *Awards, honors:* Fulbright senior fellowship for Japan, 1971.

WRITINGS: Kotoku Shusui: Portrait of a Japanese Radical, Cambridge University Press, 1971.

WORK IN PROGRESS: A biography of Leroy Lansing Janes, an early American educator in Japan; a study of Japan's first modern pollution incident: the Ashio Copper Mine problem.

* * *

NOURISSIER, Francois 1927-

PERSONAL: Born May 18, 1927, in Paris, France; son of Paul and Renee (Heens) Nourissier; married M.-T. Sobesky, 1949 (divorced, 1958); married Cecile Muhlstein (a painter), 1962; children: (first marriage) Alain, Gilles; (second marriage) Paulina. *Education:* Attended Ecole des Sciences Politiques, Paris, 1945-48; Sorbonne, University of Paris, licence es lettres, 1948. *Home:* 23, rue Henri-Heine, 75016 Paris, France. *Agent:* Grasset, 61, rue des Saints-Peres, 75006 Paris, France.

CAREER: Secours Catholique Institut, Paris, France, staff member, 1949-51; Chalet International des Etutiants Combloux, Savoie, France, director, 1951-52; Editions Denoel, Paris, secretary-general, 1951-55; *La Parisienne,* Paris, editor-in-chief, 1955-58; Editions Grasset, Paris, literary adviser, 1958—. Critic, *Les Nouvelles Litteraires,* 1962-72; cinema critic, *L'Express,* 1970-72; literary critic for *Le Point,* 1972-78, for *Le Figaro,* 1975—, and for *Figaro-Magazine,* 1978—. *Awards, honors:* French Academy prize, 1966; "Golden Pen" from Figaro Litteraire, 1968, for *Le Maitre de maison;* Feminz Prize, 1970; Prince Pierre of Monaco prize, 1975; elected to l'Academie Goncourt, 1977.

WRITINGS—In English: *Les Francais,* Editions Rencontre (Lausanne), 1968, translation by Adrienne Foulke published as *The French,* Knopf, 1968; (with Henri Cartier-Bresson) *Vive la France* (text by Nourissier; photographs by Cartier-Bresson), Laffont, 1970, translation by Ray Forty published as *Cartier-Bresson's France,* Thames & Hudson, 1970, Viking, 1971.

Other works: *L'Homme humilie: Sort des refugies et personnes deplaciees, 1912-1950* (title means "Humiliated Men: Fate of Refugees and Displaced Persons"), Spes (Paris), 1950; *L'Eau grise* (novel; title means "Gray Water"), Plon, 1951; *Enracinement des immigres* (title means "The Rooting of Immigrants"), Bloud & Gay, 1951; *La Vie parfaite* (novel; title means "The Perfect Life"), Plon, 1952; *F. Garcia Lorca,* L'Arche, 1955, 2nd edition, 1962; *Les Orphelins d'Auteuil* (novel; title means "The Orphans of Auteuil"), Plon, 1956; *Le Corps de Diane* (novel; title means "Diane's Body"), Julliard, 1957; *Bleu comme la nuit* (novel; title means "Blue as the Night"), Grasset, 1958; *Portrait d'un indifferent* (essay; title means "Portrait of an Unconcerned Person"), Fasquelle, 1958.

(With Paul Strand) *Les Hebrides* (text by Nourissier; photographs by Strand), Clairefontaine (Lausanne), 1962; *Un Petit Bourgeois* (autobiography), Grasset, 1963; *Une Histoire francaise* (novel; title means "A French Story"), Grasset, 1965; *Le Maitre de maison* (novel; title means "The Lord of the Manor"), Grasset, 1968; (with Paul Morand) *La Suisse que j'aime* (travel description; title means "The Switzerland I Love"), Editions Sun, 1968; *La Creve* (novel; title means "The Pit"), Grasset, 1970; *Allemande* (novel; title means "A German Dance"), Grasset, 1973; *Lettre a mon chien* (essay; title means "Letter To My Dog"), Gallimard, 1975; *Lettre ouverte a Jacques Chirac* (essay; title means "Open Letter to Jacques Chirac"), A. Michel, 1976; *Le Musee de l'homme* (autobiography; title means "My Coming of Age"), Grasset, 1979.

SIDELIGHTS: Nourissier told *CA:* "My career has been divided between two activities: creation (my books) and criticism (my work in journalism). This double activity was sanctioned in 1977 by my election to l'Academie Goncourt, which is comprised of ten authors who annually award the most important prize in France and, one could say, in Europe." According to Marc Slavin, in awarding the Goncourt Prize the Goncourt Academy holds "French publishing in suspense every fall, and their verdict automatically promotes the winner to the top of the best-seller list."

On one level, Nourissier's *The French* may have suffered because of its untimeliness. "This generation now watches in amazement as twenty million young people under twenty propel the whole country toward psychological rejuvenation and a fresh historical outlook," he wrote, and these pre-May 1968 lines were made obsolete as students barricaded Paris streets and workers seized factories for the first time since 1936. Michael Harrington objected to Nourissier's proposition that (in Herrington's words) "bad times make people restless and good times render them content," and noted: "Nourissier rightly understood that the demographic shift toward youthfulness was a major force in French society. But he wrongly took this transition as a portent of a happy Gaullist future and not as a precursor of revolution. . . . If the revolution of May had not come, I would have found Nourissier's book plausible, if not profound. . . . Now the main usefulness of *The French* is as a statement of the conventional wisdom which must be measured against events which it did not anticipate."

While critic Anthony Lejeune contended *The French* was "out of date" soon after its publication, others chose to look at the book for possible explanations of the May riots. "It is of some value to approach Nourissier's book in order to find out why he, like everyone else in France, didn't notice the coming of the revolution," Herrington wrote. *Time* magazine agreed: "Now that at least part of the generation has fulfilled his hope [Nourissier's hope 'for vigor, depth, distrust and passion'], the reader can examine Nourissier's catalogue of France's ills for the probable causes of the recent explosion." Jean-Francois Revel, meanwhile, appeared impressed with the wide range of Nourissier's focus and was never compelled to mention the riots in his *New York Times Book Review* article. "The author covers all sections of French life," he declared, "family and politics, economy and culture, demography and militarism, rural wilderness and urban slums, their collective psychology and their variety. It is his keen sense of variety that keeps the author from being dogmatic."

Revel's reservation about *The French,* an attitude shared by Lejeune, is "that he investigates every phenomenon as if it were peculiar to France alone." Yet Nourissier also does much to inspect French criticisms of France that are, in his words, "conceived in terms of a flattering Platonic idea of the country; they refer to an ideal France that unquestionably exists but is being perverted or being brought into disrepute by the government or democracy or reactionaries or fools or whatever. . . . It is precisely this notion of an ideal France that we must get rid of, this national unreality that we must chasten once and for all." This French mystique is attacked by Nourissier as France's "key delusion," around which many others revolve.

France is again Nourissier's subject in his other book translated into English, *Cartier-Bresson's France.* His prose, along with Henri Cartier-Bresson's photographs, reveal "no *France-imaginaire* of public relations or tourism," remarked Lincoln Kerstein. "It is the real France, with its living past and mortal present. . . . As a world citizen, Nourissier knows how ugly are Osaka, Brooklyn, Chicago and Milan; he also despairs the loss of the Seine-side. . . . Nourissier's observations on the May days of 1968, set against the pictures, serve as an epic minifilm which no *cinema-verite* has yet canonized. . . . Its text and photographs do not dilute what is disgusting, tasteless, horrifying, wasteful. But it does glorify that *bon gout,* the fierce stoicism of traditional morality where it once measured more, where it yet means much.'' Though the book has been criticized for its ''annoying feature'' of uncaptioned photographs, Nourissier ''has done his best, which is indeed very good, to explain his country to the reader not familiar with it.''

Nourissier's books have been translated into eight languages.

BIOGRAPHICAL/CRITICAL SOURCES: Best Sellers, July 1, 1968, February 1, 1971; *Time,* July 12, 1968; *New Republic,* July 20, 1968; *New York Times,* August 8, 1968; *Christian Science Monitor,* September 5, 1968; *New York Times Book Review,* August 18, 1969, December 15, 1968; *Virginia Quarterly Review,* winter, 1969; *Punch,* February 25, 1970; *Books,* March, 1970; *L'Express,* October 12-18, 1970; Bersani, Autrand, Lecarme, and Vercier, *La Litterature en France depuis 1945,* Bordas, 1970; *Nation,* March 15, 1971; Jacques Brenner, *Histoire de la litterature francaise, de 1940 a nos jours,* Fayard, 1978; Francois Nourissier, *Le Musee de l'homme,* Grasset, 1979.

O

OAKLEY, Josephine 1903(?)-1978

OBITUARY NOTICE: Born c. 1903 in Kansas; died August 18, 1978, in Topeka, Kan. Editorial staff member and education association leader. Oakley was a former director of the teacher placement bureau of the Kansas State Teachers Association and director of the Kansas State Reading Circle. She also worked in the editorial departments of both the *Reader's Digest* and the *Saturday Evening Post,* where she served as assistant to the managing editor for seventeen years. Obituaries and other sources: *Publishers Weekly,* September 24, 1978.

* * *

O'BRIEN, Francis J(oseph) 1903-

PERSONAL: Born August 29, 1903, in Wheeling, W.Va.; son of Charles Aloysius and Katherine A. (Hasenauer) O'Brien; married Mary Margaret Ziegler, August 21, 1935; children: Charles Francis, Thomas Joseph, Margaret Louise O'Brien Murphy. *Education:* St. Vincent College, A.B., 1931; graduate study at New York University. *Politics:* Republican. *Religion:* Roman Catholic. *Home:* 2040 South Glenwood, Springfield, Ill. 62705. *Office:* Franklin Life Insurance Co., Springfield, Ill. 62713.

CAREER: Fidelity Investment Association, Wheeling, W.Va., director of sales promotion, 1934-40; Franklin Life Insurance Co., Springfield, Ill., director of sales promotion, 1940-47, vice-president, 1947-68, member of board of directors, 1950-68. Active in civic and community organizations. Director of Springfield Municipal Opera, 1955-56, and Springfield Public Libraries, 1949-56 (president of board of directors, 1954-64); director of board of lay trustees of Springfield Junior College, 1959.

MEMBER: Life Insurance Advertisers Association (member of board of directors), Abraham Lincoln Association (vice-president, 1960-65), Illinois Chamber of Commerce, Springfield Chamber of Commerce (member of board of directors), Springfield Advertising Club, Springfield Association of Life Underwriters, Knights of Columbus, Rotary International, Island Bay Yacht Club, Sangamo Club. *Awards, honors:* LL.D. from St. Vincent College, 1962; exhibit awards from Life Insurance Advertisers Association.

WRITINGS: (Editor) *Sixty Years of Distinguished Service,* Franklin Life Insurance Co., 1944; *Europe as We Saw It,*

Frye Printing, 1962; *The Fabulous Franklin Story,* Rand McNally, 1971. Also author of *Distinguished Service Since 1884,* 1947. Contributor to insurance periodicals. Editor of *Franklin Field,* 1940-68.

WORK IN PROGRESS: Research for a revision of *The Fabulous Franklin Story.*

AVOCATIONAL INTERESTS: Travel (Europe, Central America, the Mediterranean, the South Pacific, India).

* * *

O'CALLAGHAN, Joseph F(rancis) 1928-

PERSONAL: Born November 23, 1928, in Philadelphia, Pa.; son of William John (an administrator) and Helen (O'-Sullivan) O'Callaghan; married Anne Drummey (a religious education coordinator), June 15, 1957; children: William, Catherine, Anne, Joseph. *Education:* La Salle College, B.A., 1950; Marquette University, M.A., 1952; Fordham University, Ph.D., 1957. *Politics:* Democrat. *Religion:* Roman Catholic. *Home:* 30 Park Hill Ave., Norwalk, Conn. 06851. *Office:* Department of History, Fordham University, Bronx, N.Y. 10458.

CAREER: Fordham University, Bronx, N.Y., instructor, 1954-59, assistant professor, 1959-63, associate professor, 1963-70, professor of history, 1970—. Visiting assistant professor at Columbia University, 1963-64, and St. Joseph's Seminary, Yonkers, N.Y., 1968—. *Member:* American Catholic Historical Association, Mediaeval Academy of America, Academy of American Research Historians for Medieval Spain, Society to Advance the Retarded (Norwalk, Conn.), Norwalk Montessori Association. *Awards, honors:* Institute of International Education fellowship for Spain, 1955-56; Fulbright fellowship for Spain, 1961-62; *consejero de honor* from Instituto de Estudios Manchegos, 1962; National Endowment for the Humanities fellowship, summer, 1971.

WRITINGS: (Editor and contributor) *Studies in Medieval Cistercian History Presented to Professor Jeremiah F. O'-Sullivan,* Cistercian Publications, 1971; (translator) John C. Olin, editor, *The Autobiography of Saint Ignatius Loyola,* Harper, 1974; *A History of Medieval Spain,* Cornell University Press, 1975; *The Spanish Military Order of Calatrava and Its Affiliates,* Variorum Reprints, 1975. Contributor to *Encyclopaedia Britannica, Encyclopedia Americana,* and *New Catholic Encyclopedia.* Contributor of more than a dozen articles and reviews to history and hispanic studies journals.

WORK IN PROGRESS: The Cortes of Leon-Castile, 1188-1350.

BIOGRAPHICAL CRITICAL SOURCES: Choice, July-August, 1975; *Times Literary Supplement*, November 7, 1975; *Hispanic American Historical Review*, February, 1976; *Americas*, April, 1976; *American Historical Review*, June, 1976.

*   *   *

O'DONNELL, (Philip) Kenneth   1924-1977
(Kenneth P. O'Donnell)

PERSONAL: Born March 24, 1924, in Worcester, Mass.; son of Kenneth O'Donnell (a college football coach); married wife, Helen (a court clerk; divorced); married Asta Hanna Helga Steinfatt (a teacher), April 30, 1977; children: (first marriage) Kenneth Philip, Jr., Kevin M., Mark F., Helen, Kathleen O'Donnell Schlichenmaier. *Education:* Graduated from Harvard University, 1949; also attended Boston College.

CAREER: Public relations consultant for private industry, Boston, Mass.; helped manage John F. Kennedy's senate campaigns, 1952 and 1958, and his presidential campaign, 1960; J. F. Kennedy's senate staff, Massachusetts state representative, 1952-57, assistant in Washington, D.C., 1958-60; administrative assistant to Robert F. Kennedy, counsel of the Senate Rackets Committee, 1957; appointments secretary to President J. F. Kennedy, 1961-63; aide to President Lyndon B. Johnson, 1963-65; owner of own public relations and management consulting firm, Boston, 1965-77; manager of R. F. Kennedy's presidential primaries campaign, 1968. Candidate for Democratic nomination for governor of Massachusetts in 1966 and 1970; assistant in Hubert Humphrey's presidential campaign, 1968; member of the Kennedy Library Foundation. *Military service:* U.S. Army Air Forces, World War II, bombardier in a B-17 squadron; received Distinguished Flying Cross and Air Medal with four Oak Leaf Clusters.

WRITINGS—Under name Kenneth P. O'Donnell: (With David F. Powers and Joe McCarthy) *"Johnny, We Hardly Knew Ye": Memories of John Fitzgerald Kennedy,* Little, Brown, 1972.

SIDELIGHTS: As Robert Kennedy's roommate and friend at Harvard University, Kenneth O'Donnell had the opportunity to meet John Kennedy when he was first campaigning for state representative in 1946. O'Donnell's long association with the political careers of the Kennedy brothers, starting with John's Senate race in 1952, culminated in his being named appointments secretary at the White House. Although O'Donnell's title was appointments secretary, his duties went far beyond that office, for he was one of President Kennedy's closest friends and most trusted advisers. Privy to nearly all the Kennedy White House secrets, O'Donnell offered his counsel during such crises as the Bay of Pigs invasion and the Cuban missile confrontation. Haynes Johnson described O'Donnell as "the perfect aide, tight-lipped, self-effacing, shrewd, tough, totally loyal and never hesitant to say exactly what he thought. He had in that sense, the most valuable asset of a presidential adviser—like Harry Hopkins under Franklin Roosevelt, he dared to say no to the President's face."

Tragically, O'Donnell witnessed the assassinations of both the men whose political careers he had worked so hard to

further. Many have expressed admiration for O'Donnell because he refused to be simply a relic of the Kennedy era. He served in the White House during Lyndon Johnson's administration, and ran twice unsuccessfully for the Massachusetts Democratic gubernatorial nomination. An article which O'Donnell wrote for *Life* magazine in 1970 created a controversy when it appeared. In it O'Donnell asserted that Kennedy had intended to issue an order after the 1964 presidential election to withdraw all American troops from Vietnam. In addition, the former White House aide avowed that Kennedy had chosen Johnson as his running mate in 1960 because he preferred having Mike Mansfield as senate majority leader. His contentions have never been proved.

O'Donnell's account of the Kennedy years is given in his book, *"Johnny, We Hardly Knew Ye": Memories of John Fitzgerald Kennedy.* Reviewers found its depiction of John Kennedy too glowing. Phoebe Adams noted that the authors "remember, predictably, that Kennedy was never wrong (momentarily misguided, perhaps—never wrong)." The book is a "too facile celebration of J.F.K.," Melvin Maddocks declared. Nonetheless, both Adams and Maddocks found that much of the information given in *"Johnny, We Hardly Knew Ye"* was enlightening. Maddocks called it "a valuable collection of footnotes," while Adams praised the book as "a mass of detail, funny, trivial, touching, surprising." The tone of *"Johnny, We Hardly Knew Ye"* also impressed Adams: "Above all, there is a recreation of the optimism and excitement that Kennedy was able to generate, and a superbly lively portrait of a politician in action."

BIOGRAPHICAL/CRITICAL SOURCES: Best Sellers, December 15, 1972; *Atlantic Monthly*, January, 1973; *Time,* January 8, 1973; *New York Times Book Review*, September 10, 1977; *Christian Science Monitor*, February 7, 1973; *Choice,* March, 1973; *Saturday Review,* March, 1973.

OBITUARIES: New York Times, September 10, 1977; *Washington Post,* September 10, 1977; *Time,* September 19, 1977; *Newsweek,* September 19, 1977.*

(Died September 9, 1977, in Boston, Mass.)

*   *   *

O'DONNELL, Kenneth P.
See O'DONNELL, (Philip) Kenneth

*   *   *

O'FAOLAIN, Julia
(Julia Martines)

PERSONAL: Surname is pronounced O'Fay-lawn; born in London, England; daughter of Sean (a writer) and Eileen (Gould) O'Faolain; married Lauro Martines (a teacher and an historian); children: Lucien Christopher. *Education:* University College, Dublin, received B.A. and M.A.; graduate study at Universita di Roma and Sorbonne, University of Paris. *Residence:* London, England. *Agent:* Curtis Brown Ltd., 575 Madison Ave., New York, N.Y. 10022.

CAREER: Writer, translator, and language teacher.

WRITINGS: (Translator, under name Julia Martines) Gene Brucker, editor, *Two Memoirs of Renaissance Florence: The Diaries of Buonaccorso Pitti and Gregorio Dati,* Harper, 1967 (translator, under name Julia Martines) Piero Chiara, *A Man of Parts,* Little, Brown, 1968; *We Might See Sights! and Other Stories,* Faber, 1968; *Godded and Codded,* Faber, 1970, published as *Three Lovers,* Coward, 1971; (editor with husband, Lauro Martines) *Not in God's Image: Women in History From the Greeks to the Victorians* (nonfiction), Harper, 1973; *Man in the Cellar* (short stories), Faber, 1974; *Women in the Wall* (novel; New Fiction Society Selection in England), Viking, 1975.

Work represented in anthologies, including *London Magazine Stories*, edited by Alan Ross, London Magazine Editions, 1967, 1969, 1971; *Winter's Tales*, edited by A. D. Maclean, Macmillan, 1973; *Bitches and Sad Ladies*, edited by Pat Rotter, Harper Magazine Press, 1975. Contributor of short stories and reviews to *New Yorker, Kenyon Review, Texas Quarterly, London Magazine, New Review, Mademoiselle, Saturday Evening Post, Vogue, Critic, Cornhill Magazine, Nova, Cosmopolitan, London Times, Irish Press, New York Times, Washington Post, Hibernia*, and ''Kaleidoscope,'' a British Broadcasting Corporation radio program.

WORK IN PROGRESS: ''I am writing a novel but prefer—superstitiously—not to discuss it.''

SIDELIGHTS: When O'Faolian's *Three Lovers* appeared in 1970, the inevitable comparisons between her novel and the work of her famous father were made. J. R. Franks dismissed the issue simply by saying: ''Yes, Julia O'Faolain is Sean's daughter. No, she does not write like her father. And maybe, if [*Three Lovers*] is a fair harbinger, she'll become the family-member whose name is used for identification.'' His opinion was echoed by Sally Beauman who noted that O'Faolain ''writes firmly, with a voice all her own.'' Praising the author's ''well planned, intelligent, concise'' style, Beauman found O'Faolain's writing ''more pointed than [that of] her father, with a cold female eye for the egocentricities of masculine behavior.''

O'Faolain's interest in the history of women is expressed in *Not in God's Image. Economist* stated that ''as a sourcebook on the history of women, [this book] stands in a class of its own.... The authors deal skillfully with the constant larding of hypocrisy, ranging from recipes for damaged maidenhoods to advice on concealing intellect.'' Mary Ellmann praised the book for being ''distinguished by genuine scholarship. Its feminist sympathy is apparent . . . but it pursues the point by hard work, not by swishy emotionalism. And what a picture unfolds!''

Women in the Wall showed O'Faolain's continued interest in women in history. According to Lalage Pulvertaft, by adapting such characters as Queen Radegund and St. Agnes, O'Faolain tampered with history to ''try to answer fundamental questions about women's role in society.'' Michael Wilding noted that O'Faolain tackled the considerable ''formal problems of presenting, with both wit and sympathy, sexually aware, Irish catholic, sub-hysterical femininity'' so successfully that ''from experience and empathy a contrivance-free authenticity is deftly established.'' Alan Ross evaluated her talent saying, ''Julia O'Faolain has all the essential gifts—a sense of high comedy, fastidiousness of language and of feeling, intellectual control over widely-ranging scraps of knowledge—and she uses them with the lightest of touches.''

O'Faolain's work as a translator and her travels in Europe and the United States have allowed her to study people of different cultures. Roger Garfitt called O'Faolain one of ''the very few Irish writers who [is] truly international in range.'' By choosing ''to work from within the contemporary flux of modes and passions,'' O'Faolain allows her characters to ''escape that terminal haunting that gives most Irish fiction its unease,'' according to Garfitt. He concluded, ''There is a power of mind behind her work, as well as an irreverently perceptive eye, that catches the intensity of human drives, the essential seriousness of the effort to live, without swallowing any of the trends in self-deception.''

O'Faolain divides her time between California, where she teaches, and Europe. ''We have a house in London but try to get to France and Italy and for brief visits to Ireland as often as possible,'' O'Faolain told *CA.*

BIOGRAPHICAL/CRITICAL SOURCES: Listener, June 20, 1968, September 26, 1974; *London Magazine,* September, 1968, November, 1970, October/November, 1974; *Best Sellers,* May 1, 1971; *New York Times Book Review,* May 9, 1971; *Book World,* June 13, 1971; *Saturday Review,* July 3, 1971; *Christian Century,* June 27, 1973; *Choice,* December, 1973, October, 1975; *Economist,* February 17, 1973; *New York Review of Books,* November 1, 1973; Douglas Dunn, editor, *Two Decades of Irish Writing,* Dufour, 1975; *Times Literary Supplement,* April 4, 1975; *New Republic,* May 10, 1975; Patrick Rafroidi and Maurice Harmon, editors, *The Irish Novel in Our Times,* Volume III, Publications de l'-Universite de Lille, 1975-76; *Contemporary Literary Criticism,* Volume 6, Gale, 1976.

*　　*　　*

OGDEN, Gina 1935-

PERSONAL: Born August 9, 1935, in Boston, Mass.; daughter of John (an artist) and Virginia (Wilson) Lavalle; divorced; children: Philip, Cathy. *Education:* Smith College, B.A., 1957; Goddard College, M.A., 1975. *Home and office:* Counseling Center, Hamilton School, Sheffield, Mass. 01257.

CAREER: Expansion, Inc., Bedford, Mass., family therapist, 1974-75; Hamilton School, Counseling Center, Sheffield, Mass., Co-director, 1975—. Professionally-qualified family therapist, sex therapist, and trainer of therapists. Adjunct member of faculty at Lesley College, 1976—, and Antioch College/New England, 1977—. *Member:* American Association of Marriage and Family Counselors (clinical member), Association of Sex Educators, Counselors and Therapists.

WRITINGS: (With Anne Zevin) *When a Family Needs Therapy,* Beacon Press, 1976. Editor of *Premiere,* 1966-67.

SIDELIGHTS: Ogden writes: ''The writing of *When a Family Needs Therapy* was an effort to de-mystify some of the principles of family therapy and to make them more available to those doing the bulk of family therapeutic intervention: the clergy, school personnel, and family members themselves. I am a family therapist and sex therapist by profession, but in the summers I am a counselor at Camp Discovery, Cape Breton Island, Nova Scotia. There I grow a garden to feed us all, and have time and space to be outdoors and be healthy. Somewhere in this garden is another book—a therapy book about being healthy, not about being sick.''

*　　*　　*

O'GORMAN, Edward Charles 1929-
(Ned O'Gorman)

PERSONAL: Born September 26, 1929, in New York, N.Y.; married; children: Richard. *Education:* St. Michael's College, A.B.; Columbia University, A.M. *Home and office:* 60 West 66th St., New York, N.Y. 10023. *Agent:* Harold Matson Company, 22 East 40th St., New York, N.Y. 10016.

CAREER: Jubilee, New York City, editor, 1962-65; U.S. State Department, Washington, D.C., American studies specialist in Chile, Argentina, and Brazil, 1965; Children's Storefront School, New York City, founder and director, 1966—. Has taught at Brooklyn College, New School for Social Research, and Manhattan College. *Member:* Metropolitan Opera. *Awards, honors:* Guggenheim fellowships, 1956, 1962; Lamont Poetry Selection award, 1958, for *The Night of the Hammer.*

WRITINGS—Under name Ned O'Gorman: *The Night of the Hammer: Poems,* Harcourt, 1959; *Adam Before His Mirror* (poetry), Harcourt, 1961; *The Buzzard and the Peacock: Poems,* Harcourt, 1964; *The Harvesters' Vase: Poems,* Harcourt, 1968; (editor) *Prophetic Voices: Ideas and Words on Revolution,* Random House, 1969; *The Storefront: A Community of Children on 129th Street and Madison Avenue* (nonfiction), Harper, 1970; *The Blue Butterfly* (juvenile), Harper, 1971; *The Flag the Hawk Flies* (poetry), Knopf, 1972; *The Wilderness and the Laurel Tree: A Guide for Teachers and Parents on the Observation of Children,* Harper, 1972; *The Children Are Dying,* New American Library, 1978. Contributor of articles and poetry to various magazines, including *Harper's Bazaar* and *Atlantic Monthly.*

WORK IN PROGRESS: A book on his family; a book on Rome; another volume of poetry.

SIDELIGHTS: The Night of the Hammer, O'Gorman's first collection of poetry, a Lamont Poetry Selection award winner, elicited this response from *Kirkus Review:* "O'Gorman . . . has a gift for rich imagery and a strange juxtaposition of words, without the liability of obscurity." Two years later, Samuel Hazo wrote in *Commonweal:* "His first book . . . set the tone of his real poetic talent, and his second book, *Adam Before His Mirror,* confirms it. . . . What strikes me as the chief of O'Gorman's talents is the spontaneity and range of his imagination. . . . And he has an unmistakable lyrical talent that is uniquely his own. In addition, he has all the craft to realize a sensibility that shows itself able to remain fresh."

Although some critics complained of "extravagant phrases" and imprecise imagery, recognition has been generally very favorable, with an appreciation of the religious quality of O'Gorman's work. Josephine Jacobson noted of *The Harvesters' Vase,* O'Gorman's fourth book, "All of these poems are religious, few of their subjects are. The religious sensibility runs in the poetry like blood or sap or electricity—inside." And *Saturday Review* called O'Gorman "a religious poet of genuine passion and power." In an article for *Atlantic Monthly,* the poet acknowledged the strong influence of the Catholic Church in his life: "It was always there. I cannot remember a moment in my life when I did not know its presence about me. It was alpha and omega from the start. In the midst of the greatest delights, in the collapsing world of my family and in the rich new world that brushed my spirit when I was a boy and began to think of poetry, the Church took up its stride beside me." Of the recent changes in the Church, he said, "I am delighted with much that has gone but I am not delighted with the wasteland that has taken its place. My childhood's Church was no wasteland."

O'Gorman's concern with social injustice is evident in *Prophetic Voices: Ideas and Words on Revolution,* a book he compiled of writings solicited from more than twenty contributors. Not content just to express his feelings in books, however, in 1968 he rejected an offer to be poet in residence at City College of New York, refusing to sign the required oath of loyalty to the United States Constitution and the

State of New York. He explained to the *New York Times* that he could not sign the oath because "the black people with whom I work have been served destructively and viciously by the Constitution of the land."

The black people with whom O'Gorman works are the people of Harlem. In 1966 he established the Storefront School for children of the area and the Addie Mae Collins Library, named for one of the four young girls killed when a Birmingham church was bombed in 1963 and stocked mostly by contributions from the poet's friends.

"In my childhood," O'Gorman told *New Yorker,* "all the powers to nourish life were present, and none of the powers of destruction. But here, for these children, it's usually the opposite. The whole theory of the storefront was to build a place where the senses of the children could thrive. No, that's too strong a word. A place where the senses of the children could at least *exist.* I wanted to help build a place of possibilities, of hope and tranquillity, based on the poetic imagination. The storefront's a happy place—most of the kids are happy when they're here."

O'Gorman's "liberation camp," now privately supported without any federal, city, or state aid, accepts any child who wishes to come there, providing breakfast and lunch to each. In a 1975 article in *New York Times,* O'Gorman made a plea for better laws to protect these children from tyranny and neglect: "What we all must seek is a way to speak for the children of the oppressed, a way to become their surrogate will to live." He urged the building of a "community of healing in Harlem" which could, with more forceful laws, offer these children the choice of "becoming so strong there and so filled with hope that the past and its wounds would be cured, the present would be teeming with joy and the future filled with promise."

BIOGRAPHICAL/CRITICAL SOURCES: Kirkus Review, December 1, 1958; *Commonweal,* April 1, 1961, June 21, 1968; *Saturday Review,* May 6, 1961; *New Yorker,* December 2, 1967; *New York Times Book Review,* April 28, 1968; *Virginia Quarterly Review,* Volume 44, number 3, 1968; *Book World,* July 29, 1968; *New York Review,* August 1, 1968; *New York Times,* August 5, 1968; *Atlantic Monthly,* June, 1973; *New York Times Magazine,* June 1, 1975.

*   *   *

O'GORMAN, Ned
See O'GORMAN, Edward Charles

*   *   *

OLIVOVA, Vera 1926-

PERSONAL: Born November 13, 1926, in Prague, Czechoslovakia; daughter of Ladislav (a postal officer) and Vincencie (Vaeterova) Pav; married Pavel Oliva (a university professor), June 23, 1949; children: Hana, Ivan. *Education:* Charles University, Ph.D., 1951, C.Sc., 1957. *Home:* Na Micance 18, Prague 6, Czechoslovakia.

CAREER: Charles University, Prague, Czechoslovakia, assistant professor, 1951-63, associate professor of history, 1964-70, special worker in department of ethnography, 1972—. *Member:* International Council of Sport and Physical Education (corresponding member).

WRITINGS—In English: *Ceskoslovensko v rozrusene Evrope,* Melantrich (Prague), 1968, translation by George Theiner published as *Doomed Democracy: Czechoslovakia in a Disrupted Europe, 1914-38,* Sidgwick & Jackson, 1972.

Other: *Ceskoslovensko-sovetske vztahy v letech, 1918-1922*

(title means "Czechoslovak-Soviet Relations, 1918-1922"), Nase (Prague), 1957; *Z delnickych boju v letech, 1921-23* (title means "The Struggles of the Working Class, 1921-23"), Pace (Prague), 1960; (with husband, Pavel Oliva) *Spartakus: Povstani Spartakovo a spartakovska tradice* (title means "Spartacus: The Uprise of Spartacus and the Spartacus Tradition"), Olympia (Prague), 1960; *Politika ceskoslovenski burzoasie v letechm, 1921-1923* (title means "The Politics of the Czechoslovak Bourgeoisie, 1921-1923"), Ceskoslovenska akademie ved, 1961; *Ceskoslovenski dejiny* (title means "Czechoslovak History"), Volume IV: *1918-1938*, Statni pedagogicke nakladatekstvi, 1967; *Ohlas velke rijnove socialisticke revoluce v ceskem a slovenskem tisku* (title means "The October Revolution in the Czech and Slovak Press"), CTK (Prague), 1967; *Dokumenty ke vzniku Ceskoslovenska* (title means "Documents on the Orgin of Czechoslovakia"), CTK, 1968; *Rok 1938 v ceskoslovenskem tisku* (title means "The Year 1938 in the Czechoslovak Press"), CTK, 1968; *Lide a hry* (title means "Men and Games"), Olympia, 1979. Contributor to scholarly journals.

WORK IN PROGRESS: Ceskoslovensko a Nemecko (title means "Czechoslovakia and Germany, 1918-1938").

SIDELIGHTS: After 1968-69, Vera Olivova was not allowed to continue her work in modern history. In 1972, she started new research, in the department of ethnography, dealing with the history of festivities, sports, and pastimes.

* * *

OLSEN, Richard E(llison) 1941-

PERSONAL: Born February 2, 1941, in New York, N.Y.; son of Harold Burgher (an investment analyst) and Gladys (Ellison) Olsen; married Tina Garber (a teacher), 1978. *Education:* Union College, Schenectady, N.Y., B.S., 1962; Brown University, M.A., 1969, Ph.D., 1971. *Residence:* New York, N.Y. *Office:* Department of Philosophy, Adelphi University, Garden City, N.Y. 11530.

CAREER: U.S. Public Health Service, senior assistant health service officer in Las Vegas, Nev., 1963-64, and in Rockville, Md., 1964-65; Mobil Oil Corp., New York, N.Y., linear program analyst, 1966-67; University of Washington, Seattle, lecturer in philosophy, 1971; Adelphi University, Garden City, N.Y., assistant professor, 1971-76, associate professor of philosophy, 1976—. *Member:* American Philosophical Association, Philosophy of Science Society, Marxist Activist Philosophers. *Awards, honors:* National Endowment for the Humanities grant, 1977.

WRITINGS: Karl Marx, Twayne, 1978. Contributor to *Philo-Research Archives.*

WORK IN PROGRESS: The Primal Horde, a novel; research on the development of modern science as an expression of the growth of an indigenous urban elite, with a book expected to result.

SIDELIGHTS: Olsen writes: "Aside from professional requirements, I do research out of curiosity, and write to clarify my feelings and thoughts for myself. I prefer writing fiction, but so far have had little luck with it. I am interested in a variety of things, perhaps too many—metaphysics, science, literature, Mayan archaeology, and Buddhist thought. I have traveled in Asia and Central America, and lived as a monk for a short time in a Buddhist monastery in Thailand."

* * *

ORBEN, Robert 1927-

PERSONAL: Born March 4, 1927, in New York, N.Y.; son of Walter and Marie Orben; married wife Jean. *Home:* 1200 North Nash St., Arlington, Va. 22209. *Office:* 2510 Virginia Ave. N.W., Washington, D.C. 20037.

CAREER: Writer and consultant, 1946—. Comedy writer for Jack Paar, 1962-63, Red Skelton, 1964-70, and Dick Gregory; speechwriter for President Gerald Ford, 1974-76, director of White House speechwriting department, 1976-77; lecturer to business and college audiences. President of Comedy Center, Inc., 1971-73.

WRITINGS: The Best of Current Comedy, Wehman Brothers, 1962; (editor) Dick Gregory, *From the Back of the Bus,* Dutton, 1962; *If You Have to Be a Comic,* Orben Publications, 1963; *The Joke-Teller's Handbook,* Doubleday, 1966; *The Ad-Libber's Handbook: Two Thousand New Laughs for Speakers,* Doubleday, 1969; *The Encyclopedia of One-Liner Comedy,* Doubleday, 1971. Also author of more than forty humor books.

Contributor to magazines. Editor of *Orben's Current Comedy,* 1958—, and *Orben's Comedy Fillers,* 1971—.

WORK IN PROGRESS: A book of speech humor.

SIDELIGHTS: Orben's periodicals provide comedy material for public speakers, entertainers, and leaders in business, politics, and community affairs. His publications include special features aimed at physicians, clergymen, and members of other individual professions.

BIOGRAPHICAL/CRITICAL SOURCES: Changing Times, December, 1971; *Wilmington Evening Journal,* April 7, 1977; *New York Times,* June 5, 1977; *Nation's Business,* January, 1978.

* * *

ORD, John E. 1917-

PERSONAL: Born January 1, 1917, in Nephi, Utah; son of George V. (a pharmacist) and Loretta (Russell) Ord; married Faun Mellor (an elementary school teacher), May 29, 1941; children: Craig, Sandra Ord Stubben, Bonnie Ord Lyons, Mary Ord Mildenhall. *Education:* Utah State University, B.S., 1940; University of Utah, M.S., 1949; Stanford University, Ed.D., 1958. *Politics:* Republican. *Religion:* Church of Jesus Christ of Latter-day Saints (Mormons). *Home:* 2220 North Oakcrest Lane, Provo, Utah 84601. *Office:* Department of Elementary Education, Brigham Young University, 219 MCK, Provo, Utah 84601.

CAREER: Elementary school teacher in Farmington, Utah, 1946-47, and principal, 1948-52; elementary school consultant in Woodland, Calif., 1954-57; Brigham Young University, Provo, Utah, associate professor of elementary education, 1957—. Educational adviser to University of Tehran, 1959-61. *Military service:* U.S. Army Air Forces. *Member:* National Education Association, Utah Education Association, Phi Delta Kappa.

WRITINGS: Elementary School Social Studies for Today's Children, Harper, 1972.

WORK IN PROGRESS: Research on databank and Utah history.

* * *

ORGILL, Douglas 1922-
(J. D. Gilman, a joint pseudonym)

PERSONAL: Born August 10, 1922, in Walsall, England; son of William Henry (an industrialist) and Madeline (Platt) Orgill; married Margaret Chance Walker (a journalist); children: Richard, Andrew. *Education:* Attended Royal Military College, Sandhurst, 1943; Keble College, Oxford, M.A., 1948. *Agent:* Ursula Winant, Winant Towers, 14 Cliffords Inn, London E.C.4, England. *Office: Daily Express,* Fleet St., London E.C.4, England.

CAREER: Newcastle Journal, Newcastle-upon-Tyne, England, reporter, 1949-50, sub-editor, 1950-52, leader writer, 1952-53; *Daily Mail,* London, England, sub-editor, 1953-59, deputy chief sub-editor, 1957-59; *Daily Express,* London, chief sub-editor, 1966-73, special writer, 1973—. *Military service:* British Army, 1944-46; served in Italy and Austria and with Arab Legion. *Member:* Royal United Services Institute for Defence Studies, Savage Club.

WRITINGS: The Death Bringers (novel), P. Davies, 1962, published as *Journey into Violence,* Morrow, 1963; *Ride a Tiger* (novel), P. Davies, 1963, published as *The Cautious Assassin,* Morrow, 1964; *The Days of Darkness* (novel), P. Davies, 1965; *Man in the Dark* (novel), Morrow, 1965; *The Gothic Line: The Autumn Campaign in Italy, 1944,* Norton, 1967; *The Astrid Factor* (novel), Walker & Co., 1968.

The Tank: Studies in the Development and Use of a Weapon, Heinemann, 1970; *T-34: Russian Armor,* Ballantine, 1971; *Armoured Onslaught: August, 1918,* Ballantine, 1972; *Lawrence* (biography of T. E. Lawrence), Ballantine, 1973; *The Jasius Pursuit* (novel), St. Martin's, 1973; *German Armour,* Ballantine, 1974; (with Jack Fishman; under joint pseudonym J. D. Gilman) *KG200* (novel), Simon & Schuster, 1977. Contributor to *Purnell's History of the Second World War.* Contributor to British newspapers and to a professional journal.

WORK IN PROGRESS: The Sixth Winter, a novel, publication expected in 1979; *Cavalry,* nonfiction.

SIDELIGHTS: Orgill commented: "I work in two fields: as a novelist and as a historian.

"I believe that *as a novelist* my task is, in essence, to tell a story: to place a number of characters into situations which they cannot wholly control, and then observe the degree of success or failure with which they struggle to overcome them. For me, two things matter: the characters must engage the reader's sympathy, and the situations, while sometimes bizarre, must never become unbelievable.

"I believe that *as a historian* my first and absolute duty is accuracy: any interpretation of historical events based on inaccuracy is a house built on sand. My next duty is an attempt, sometimes intuitively, to try to understand why men did what they did, to what extent they had any choice at all, and what material and other factors influenced them in their decisions."

AVOCATIONAL INTERESTS: Entomology, military history, travel.

* * *

OWENS, Virginia Stem 1941-

PERSONAL: Born March 4, 1941, in Houston, Tex.; daughter of Clarence Lamar (in U.S. Air Force) and Esther (a secretary; maiden name, Adams) Stem; married David Clinton Owens (a clergyman), December 26, 1959; children: Alyssa, Amy. *Education:* North Texas State University, B.A., 1965; University of Kansas, M.A., 1969; Iliff School of Theology, M.A.R., 1975. *Politics:* None. *Religion:* United Presbyterian. *Residence:* Elbert, Colo. 80106. *Agent:* Ray Peekner, 2625 North 36th St., Milwaukee, Wis. 53210.

CAREER: Northeast Missouri State University, Kirksville,

instructor in English, 1969-70; writer, 1970—. Also worked as beekeeper, houseparent for mentally-retarded boys, researcher, and library cataloger.

WRITINGS: Assault on Eden (nonfiction), Eerdmans, 1977. Contributor to magazines, including *Theology Today, One World,* and *Mother Earth News.*

WORK IN PROGRESS: Studying Christian exploitation of mass media.

SIDELIGHTS: Virginia Owens writes: "I've never wanted to do anything but write—except for reading. Unfortunately, I never had anything to write about until my nebulous and somewhat insubstantial life coalesced in the cosmic drama of Christ. I was at one time involved in radical politics, the women's movement, ecology activism, etc. Now I have no causes, although I retain my horror of our technological society. At this point I have no desire to influence either society or individuals. I'm only interested in how the story turns out.

"I have an east Texas background rich in the oral tradition of story-telling. Thanks to affluence and television, that will not survive my generation. *Sic transit gloria.* My family is very important to me, almost mythologically so. We are like secret refugees from some unarticulated homeland."

* * *

OWSLEY, Harriet Chappell 1901-

PERSONAL: Born July 26, 1901, in Waco, Tex.; daughter of Charles Arthur (a teacher) and Clementine (Fason) Chappell; married Frank Lawrence Owsley (a professor of history), July 24, 1920 (died, 1956); children: Frank Lawrence, Jr., Margaret Owsley Seigenthaler. *Education:* Attended Birmingham-Southern College, 1919-20, and Vanderbilt University, 1921-23; George Peabody College for Teachers, B.S., 1925. *Religion:* Methodist. *Home:* 120 Mockingbird Rd., Nashville, Tenn. 37205. *Office:* "The Papers of Andrew Jackson," Route 4, Hermitage, Tenn. 37076.

CAREER: Tennessee State Library and Archives, Nashville, director of manuscript section, 1958-70; "The Papers of Andrew Jackson," Hermitage, Tenn., co-editor, 1971—. *Member:* Society of American Archivists, Southern Historical Association. *Awards, honors:* Fulbright fellowship for England, 1956-57.

WRITINGS: (Editor) Frank Lawrence Owsley, *King Cotton Diplomacy,* revised edition (Harriet Owsley was not associated with 1st edition), University of Chicago Press, 1959; (editor) *The South: Old and New Frontiers; Selected Essays of Frank Lawrence Owsley,* University of Georgia Press, 1969; (editor) *Guide to Processed Manuscripts in the Tennessee Historical Society,* Tennessee Historical Commission, 1969; (editor with Sam B. Smith,) *The Papers of Andrew Jackson,* University of Tennessee Press, 1978. Contributor to regional history journals and to *American Archivist.*

SIDELIGHTS: Owsley wrote: "My latest article, 'The Marriages of Rachel Donelson,' contains documentary evidence that Rachel and Andrew Jackson thought that a divorce had been granted to Rachel before their marriage in Natchez about 1791. The Virginia legislature had passed an enabling act and not a divorce in 1790, and the final divorce was not granted until 1793. After receiving this information a license was obtained in January, 1794, and Rachel and Andrew were remarried in Nashville.

"My interest in southern history came as a result of my work with my husband, Frank Lawrence Owsley. As early as

1927, when he received a Guggenheim Fellowship for work in England and France, I worked with him and it was because of my plans to work with him that Vanderbilt University gave us a grant from the Rockefeller-Spellman funds. In the late 1930's, we began work on *Plain Folk of the Old South*. I compiled the statistics for that volume and we published, as co-authors, several articles based on this research in the *Journal of Southern History*. Finally in 1956 when *King Cotton Diplomacy* went out of print, Frank decided to write a more comprehensive history of Civil War diplomacy instead of republishing *King Cotton Diplomacy*. In this undertaking we were working together as joint authors. Frank was given a Fulbright Fellowship and I was given grants-in-aid by the University of Alabama. After Frank's death in England in 1956 I was given a Fulbright Research grant to continue this work. When the offer came to take charge of manuscripts at the Tennessee State Library and Archives I decided to revise and reissue *King Cotton Diplomacy* rather than continue the larger work that we were doing together. Since 1956 my work has been on my own. I have published a number of historical articles and edited several volumes.''

P

PACE, C(harles) Robert 1912-

PERSONAL: Born September 7, 1912, in St. Paul, Minn.; son of Charles Nelson (a clergyman) and Lenore (Lee) Pace; married Rosella Gaarder (a poet), December 18, 1937; children: Rosalind, Jenifer. *Education:* DePauw University, B.A., 1933; University of Minnesota, M.A., 1935, Ph.D., 1937. *Home:* 3653 Woodcliff Rd., Sherman Oaks, Calif. 91403. *Office:* Department of Education, University of California, 405 Hilgard Ave., Los Angeles, Calif. 90024.

CAREER: University of Minnesota, Minneapolis, researcher, 1937-40; American Council on Education, Washington, D.C., researcher, 1940-43; U.S. Department of the Navy, Washington, D.C., researcher, 1943-47; Syracuse University, Syracuse, N.Y., researcher, 1947-61, associate professor of education, 1947-52, professor of psychology, 1952-61, head of department and director of research center, 1952-61; University of California, Los Angeles, professor of higher education, 1961—. Fellow of Center for Advanced Study in the Behavioral Sciences, 1959-60.

MEMBER: American Psychological Association, American Educational Research Association, American Association for Public Opinion Research, American Association for Higher Education, Association for the Study of Higher Education (president, 1976-77).

WRITINGS: They Went to College, University of Minnesota Press, 1941; (with Maurice Troyer) *Evaluation in Teacher Education,* American Council on Education, 1944; *The Junior Year in France: An Evaluation,* Syracuse University Press, 1959; *College and University Environment Scales,* Educational Testing Service, 1963, revised edition, 1969; (with Frank Bowles and James Stone) *How to Get Into College,* Dutton, 1968; *Education and Evangelism,* McGraw, 1972; (editor) *New Directions for Higher Education,* Jossey-Bass, 1973; *The Demise of Diversity?,* Carnegie Commission on Higher Education, 1974.

*   *   *

PACHECO, Ferdie 1927-

PERSONAL: Born December 8, 1927, in Tampa, Fla.; son of Joseph B. (a pharmacist) and Consuelo (Jimenez) Pacheco; married second wife, Karen Louise (a flamenco dancer), September 7, 1969; children: Evelyn, Dawn, Ferdie, Jr., Tina. *Education:* Springhill College, B.S. (biology), 1948; University of Florida, B.S. (pharmacy), 1951; University of Miami, M.D., 1958. *Home:* 4151 Gate Lane, Miami, Fla. 33137. *Agent:* Betty Clark, International Creative Management, 40 West 57th St., New York, N.Y. 10019. *Office:* 946 Northwest Second Ave., Miami, Fla. 33136.

CAREER: Medical doctor in general practice, Miami, Fla., 1958—. Sports commentator for Columbia Broadcasting System (CBS-TV). Paintings have been exhibited by Gallery Art Group, Inc. *Military service:* U.S. Air Force, 1951-54. *Member:* American Medical Association, Florida Medical Association, Dade County Medical Association.

WRITINGS: Fight Doctor, Simon & Schuster, 1977. Contributor to periodicals.

WORK IN PROGRESS: Four novels, *Sweet Sam and the Doctor Man, Redeye Dilemma, Triple Play,* and *The Lector* (a historical novel about the cigar industry in Tampa); a vegetarian diet book; another book, *Tales of the Fifth Street Gym.*

SIDELIGHTS: Pacheco first became interested in boxing when he was eight years old and Jack Dempsey presented him with a pair of miniature boxing gloves. By the time he was an intern at Mt. Sinai Medical Center in Miami Beach, Pacheco was a full-fledged fan, attending fights regularly. In the early 1960's, Chris and Angelo Dundee (the promoter and the trainer) enlisted him as a cornerman for their Cuban fighters. In 1962, they sent him a new fighter/patient, Muhammad Ali, then still known as Cassius Clay. Since then, Pacheco has been the doctor of eight champions, including Jimmy Ellis and Luis Manuel Rodriquez.

In *Fight Doctor,* Pacheco examined the connection between the medical profession and the world of boxing, focusing particularly on his own relationships with boxers. The most famous of these, Muhammad Ali, received the most attention, and Pacheco provided readers with an abundance of inside information about the champion. Most sports writers who reviewed the book were thoroughly satisfied with it. Phil Jackman pointed out that *Fight Doctor* is "not one of those behind-the-scenes, gossipy numbers." "The book is as good as any I've read on the inside world of boxing and of World Champion Muhammad Ali," wrote Joel Ehrenberg.

Pacheco's story, "Sweet Sam's Sad Song," is being adapted by Twentieth Century-Fox as a two-hour television special.

AVOCATIONAL INTERESTS: Painting, drawing cartoons, collecting antique cars, jazz records, military headgear and paraphernalia. Also a military historian.

BIOGRAPHICAL/CRITICAL SOURCES: Washington Post, March 9, 1976; *Miami Herald Tropic,* September 19, 1976; *Esquire,* June, 1977; *Baltimore Evening Sun,* November 10, 1977; *Miami Beach Sun Reporter,* November 12-13, 1977.

* * *

PAGE, Joseph A(nthony) 1934-

PERSONAL: Born April 13, 1934, in Boston, Mass.; son of Joseph E. (an attorney) and Eleanor M. (a teacher; maiden name, Santosuosso) Page. *Education:* Harvard University, A.B., 1955, LL.B., 1958, LL.M., 1964. *Agent:* Carl Brandt, Brandt & Brandt, 101 Park Ave., New York, N.Y. 10017. *Office:* Law Center, Georgetown University, 600 New Jersey Ave. N.W., Washington, D.C. 20001.

CAREER: National Association of Claimants Counsel of America, Watertown, Mass., assistant editor-in-chief of *NACCA Law Journal,* 1960-63; University of Denver, Denver, Colo., assistant professor of law, 1964-68; Georgetown University, Washington, D.C., associate professor, 1968-73, professor of law, 1973—. Member of bars of Massachusetts and District of Columbia. *Military service:* U.S. Coast Guard Reserve, 1958-67; became lieutenant.

WRITINGS: The Revolution That Never Was: Northeast Brazil, 1955-1964, Grossman, 1972; (with Mary Win O'Brien) *Bitter Wages: The Nader Report on Disease and Injury on the Job,* Grossman, 1973; *The Law of Premises Liability,* Anderson, 1976. Contributor of articles and reviews to law journals, popular magazines, and newspapers, including *New Republic, Nation, Atlantic,* and *Progressive.*

WORK IN PROGRESS: A biography of Juan D. Peron.

SIDELIGHTS: Page writes: "My schizophrenic literary life continues to shuttle back and forth between the law and Latin America, with no apparent link between the two. The Peron biography has turned out to be a much more complex and endless task than I had anticipated. I hope to capture the ambiguous essence of this remarkable individual.

"I have also engaged in consumer advocacy in the fields of cosmetic and over-the-counter drug safety, and from time to time have collaborated with various Nader groups."

* * *

PAGE, Thomas 1942-

PERSONAL: Born July 16, 1942, in Washington, D.C.; son of Thomas and Susan Page; married wife, Monika; children: Serena. *Education:* Attended University of North Carolina, Elon College, B.A.; Columbia University, M.F.A. *Agent:* WB Agency, 145 East 52nd St., New York, N.Y. 10022.

CAREER: Writer. Worked in New York, N.Y., as copywriter.

WRITINGS: The Hephaestus Plague, Putnam, 1973; *The Spirit,* Rawson Associates, 1977; *Sigmet Active,* New York Times Books, 1978.

* * *

PALMER, Juliette 1930-

PERSONAL: Born May 18, 1930, in Romford, Essex, England; daughter of Sidney Bernard (a representative) and Edna (a clerk; maiden name, Harris) Woolley; married Dennis Palmer (a civil engineer), April 12, 1952; children: Albertine. *Education:* South-East Essex School of Art, diploma, 1950; University of London, diploma, 1951. *Religion:* "Humanist." *Home:* Melmott Lodge, The Pound, Cookham, Maidenhead, Berkshire, England.

CAREER: Worked as teacher of arts and crafts, 1952-57; display designer for Metal Box Co., 1957-58; representative of Fleet Street Commercial Art Studio, 1959; free-lance illustrator of children's books, 1959-64; author and illustrator, 1970—.

WRITINGS—Self-illustrated; all published by Macmillan: *Cockles and Shrimps,* 1973; *Mountain Wool,* 1973; *Swan Upping,* 1974; *Stow Horsefair,* 1976; *Barley Sow, Barley Grow,* 1978. Also illustrator of more than thirty children's books.

WORK IN PROGRESS: Barley Ripe, Barley Mow.

SIDELIGHTS: Palmer told *CA:* "The books I choose to create are about people working closely with nature, utilizing respectfully the natural treasure of their environment. I want children to appreciate and wonder at the ingenuity of man. In these days of instant puddings and packet crisps they might so easily miss the connection."

* * *

PANATI, Charles 1943-

PERSONAL: Born March 13, 1943, in Baltimore, Md.; son of Charles and Mary Panati. *Education:* Villanova University, B.S., 1965; Columbia University, M.S., 1966. *Religion:* Roman Catholic. *Residence:* New York, N.Y. *Agent:* Ellen Levine, Curtis Brown Ltd., 575 Madison Ave., New York, N.Y. 10022.

CAREER: Columbia University, New York City, associate physicist at Medical Center, 1966-68; RCA Corp., Clark, N.J., head physicist, 1968-71; *Newsweek,* New York City, science editor, 1971-77; writer, 1977—. Television broadcaster for Newsweek Broadcasting Service, 1972-75; consulting physicist. *Member:* American Institute of Physics, American Association for the Advancement of Science, New York Academy of Sciences.

WRITINGS: Supersenses: Our Potential for Parasensory Experience (nonfiction), Quadrangle, 1974; (editor) *The Geller Papers: Scientific Observations on the Paranormal Powers of Uri Geller* (nonfiction), Houghton, 1976; *Links* (novel), Houghton, 1978; *The Book of Breakthroughs: Everything You Must Know About the Astonishing Advances in Science, Medicine and Technology To Come in Your Life Time* (nonfiction), Houghton, 1979.

Television scripts for National Broadcasting Co. (NBC): "In Search of Astral Bodies," 1976; "In Search of Life After Death," 1976. Contributor to popular magazines, including *Family Circle, Redbook, Reader's Digest,* and *New York.*

WORK IN PROGRESS: Two novels.

SIDELIGHTS: Panati comments: "I set out to be a research physicist and somehow ended up a writer. I'm still learning to write—especially fiction—and will be at it till the end."

Panati described *Supersenses* as "a survey of recent U.S. research into such phenomena as telepathy, faith healing, clairvoyancy, and psychokinesis." His novel, *Links,* "is based on actual experiments in mutual hypnosis conducted at the University of California in the late 1960's. The experiments backfired and destroyed the lives of several people."

Links is being adapted for a United Artists movie.

* * *

PANETTA, George 1915-1969

PERSONAL: Born August 6, 1915, in New York, N.Y.;

son of Domenick (a tailor) and Angelina (Panetta) Panetta; married Evelyn Rinder, May 15, 1938; children: one son. *Education:* Attended City College (now of the City University of New York), 1934-36. *Residence:* Brooklyn, N.Y.

CAREER: Was an advertising copywriter before becoming a fiction writer and a playwright. *Member:* Dramatists Guild. *Awards, honors: Village Voice* Off-Broadway (Obie) Award for best comedy, 1957-58, for "Comic Strip."

WRITINGS—Fiction: *We Ride a White Donkey,* Harcourt, 1944; *Jimmy Potts Gets a Haircut,* illustrations by Reisie Lonette, Doubleday, 1947; *Sea Beach Express,* illustrations by Emily McCully, Harper, 1966; *A Kitchen Is Not a Tree,* illustrations by Joe Servello, Norton, 1970; *The Shoeshine Boys,* illustrations by Servello, Grosset, 1971.

Plays: *Viva Madison Avenue!* (first produced in New York City at the Longacre Theatre, April 6, 1960), Harcourt, 1957; *Comic Strip* (three-act; first produced in New York City at the Barbizon-Plaza, May 14, 1958), Samuel French, 1958; *Kiss Mama* (two-act), Samuel French, 1965. Also author of "King of the Whole Damn World!"

SIDELIGHTS: All of George Panetta's stories reflect his Italian-American background. His last book, *The Shoeshine Boys,* was critiqued in the *New York Times Book Review:* "This book presents, without antiseptic distortion, poverty, death, adult failure, and against these realities the special love, trust, and strength of spirit that children want to read about and want to feel exists. Goerge Panetta's style is direct, spare, and without condescension. Since MacDougall is black and Tony an Italian, the story demonstrates the values of brotherhood, but where many books preach, this one breathes."

BIOGRAPHICAL/CRITICAL SOURCES: Olga Peragallo, *Italian-American Authors and Their Contribution to American Literature,* Vanni, 1949; *New York Times Book Review,* May 2, 1971. Obituaries: *New York Times,* October 17, 1969.*

(Died October 16, 1969)

*   *   *

PANIKKAR, Raimundo   1918-

PERSONAL: Born November 3, 1918, in Barcelona, Spain; citizen of India; came to the United States in 1967; son of Ramuni (a chemist) and Carmen (Allemany) Panikkar. *Education:* University of Barcelona, B.A. and B.Sc. (both premio extraordinario), 1935, M.Sc., 1941; University of Madrid, M.A. (premio extraordinario), 1942, Ph.D. (premio extraordinario), 1946, D.Sc., 1958; Lateran University, Th.L. (summa cum laude), 1954, Th.D. (magna cum laude), 1961; also attended University of Bonn. *Office:* Department of Religious Studies, University of California, Santa Barbara, Calif. 93106.

CAREER: Paniker, S.A. (chemical company), Barcelona, Spain, vice-manager, 1940-45; Theological Seminary, Madrid, Spain, professor of Indian culture and comparative cultures, 1946-51; University of Madrid, Madrid, Spain, professor of philosophy of history, 1952-53; researcher at University of Mysore and University of Varanasi, both India, 1955-60; International University for Social Studies, Rome, Italy, professor of Indian culture, 1962-63; Banaras Hindu University, Varanasi, Uttar Pradesh, India, senior research fellow, 1964-66; Harvard University, Divinity School, Cambridge, Mass., visiting professor of comparative religion, 1967-71; University of California, Santa Barbara, professor of comparative philosophy of religion and

history of religions, 1971—. Research director of Instituto Luis Vives de Filosofia—Consejo Superior de Investigaciones Cientificas, 1942-57; assistant professor at University of Madrid, 1943-44; professor at Madrid Institute of Social Sciences, 1950-51; honorary professor at University of Rome, 1963—, and United Theological College, Bangalore, India, 1970—; Teape Lecturer at Cambridge University, 1966; visiting professor at University of Montreal, 1968; Henry Luce Visiting Professor in World Christianity at Union Theological Seminary, New York, N.Y., 1970; William Noble Lecturer at Harvard University, 1973; Cummings Lecturer at McGill University, 1975; guest lecturer at more than ninety universities all over the world.

Secretary general of International Congress of Philosophy, 1947-50; Asian delegate to UNESCO Conseil International de la philosophie et des sciences humaines, 1973—; lecturer for Indian Council of Cultural Relations in Latin and South America, 1974; UNESCO delegate to New Delhi and Buenos Aires. Member of academic council of Ecumenical Institute for Advanced Theological Study, 1965—; member of international board of directors of Institute for Religion and Social Change, 1968—; vice-president of Teilhard Centre for the Future of Man, 1970—; counselor to advisory committee of Centro Latinoamericano de Investigaciones Comparadas de las Culturas de Oriente y Occidente, 1974—.

MEMBER: International Association for the History of Religions (India), International Society for the Comparative Study of Civilizations, Institut International de Philosophie, International Husserl and Phenomenological Research Society, Societe Internationale pour l'etude de la Philosophie Medievale, American Society for the Study of Religion, American Academy of Religion, American Oriental Society, Indian Theological Association (vice-chairman, 1969-72), Societa Italiana di Storia della Religioni, Forschungskreis fuer Symbolik (founder and member of board of directors, 1962—), Associazione per lo Sviluppo delle Scienze Religiose in Italia, Presence de Gabriel Marcel. *Awards, honors:* Menendez and Pelayo Prize in Humanities from Consejo Superior de Investigaciones Cientificas, 1946, for *El Concepto de Naturaleza;* Spanish National Prize of Literature, 1961, for *La India: Gente, Cultura, Creencias.*

WRITINGS—In English: *The Unknown Christ of Hinduism,* Darton, Longman & Todd, 1964: *The Trinity and World Religions: Icon, Person, Mystery,* Christian Literature Society, 1970, revised edition published as *The Trinity and the Religious Experience of Man: Icon, Person, Mystery,* Orbis, 1973; *Worship and Secular Man: An Essay on the Liturgical Nature of Man, Considering Secularization as a Major Phenomenon of Our Time and Worship as an Apparent Fact of All Times; A Study Towards an Integral Anthropology,* Orbis, 1973; *The Vedic Experience, Mantramanjari: An Anthology of the Vedas for Modern Man and Contemporary Celebration,* University of California Press, 1977; *Myth, Faith and Hermeneutics,* Paulist/Newman, in press; *Inter-Religious Dialogue,* Paulist/Newman, in press.

Other writings: *F. H. Jacobi y la Filosofia del sentimiento,* Sapientia (Buenos Aires), 1948; *El concepto de naturaleza: Analisis historico y metafisico de un concepto,* Consejo Superior de Investigaciones Cientificas, 1951, 2nd edition, 1972; *La India: Gente, Cultura, Creencias,* Rialp (Madrid), 1960; *Patriotismo y Cristiandad,* Rialp, 1961; *Ontonomia de La Ciencia: Sobre el sentido de la ciencia y sus relaciones con la Filosofia,* Gredos (Madrid), 1961; *Humanismo y Cruz,* Rialp, 1963; *L'incontro delle religioni del mondo contemporaneo: Morfosociologia dell'Ecumenismo,* Edizioni Internazionali Sociali (Rome), 1963; *Die vielen goetter und der eine Herr: Beitraege oekumenischen Gespraech der Weltreligionen*, O. W. Barth, 1963; *Religione e Religioni* (title means "Religion and Religions"), Morcelliana, 1964; *Kultmysterium in Hinduismus und Christentum: Ein Beitrag zur vergleichenden Religionstheologie*, Karl Alber, 1964; *Maya e Apocalisse: L'incontro dell'Induismo e del Cristianesimo*, Abete (Rome), 1966; *Kerygma und Indien: Zur heilsgeschichtlichen Problematik der Christlichen Begegnung mit Indien*, Reich Verlag, 1967; *Offenbarung und Verkuendigung: Indischen Briefe* (title means "Indian Letters"), Herder, 1967; *Tecnica y Tiempo: La Tecnocronia*, Columba, 1967; *La gioia pasquale*, La Locusta, 1968; *L'homme qui devient Dieu: La foi dimension constitutive de l'homme*, Aubier (Paris), 1969; *La presenza di Dio*, La Locusta, 1970; *El silencio del Dios: Un mensaje del Buddha al mundo actual*, Guadiana, 1970; *Dimensioni mariane della vita*, La Locusta, 1972; *Cometas: Fragmentos de un diario espiritual de la postguerra*, Euramerica, 1972; *Spiritualita indu: Lineamenti* (also see below; previously published in *La Perfeccion Cristiana*), Brecia, 1975.

Contributor: J. Neuner, editor, *Christian Revelation and World Religions*, Burns & Oates, 1967; *A Challenge to the European University*, World Council of Churches, 1967; *Christianity*, Punjabi University, 1969; Stephen Verney, editor, *People and Cities*, Collins, 1969; R. J. Zwiwerblowsky and C. Jouco Bleeker, editors, *Types of Redemption*, E. J. Brill, 1970; George Devine, editor, *New Dimensions in Religious Experience*, Alba, 1970; Raymond Klibansky, editor, *Contemporary Philosophy: A Survey*, La Nuova Italia Editrice, 1971; Joseph Whelan, editor, *The God Experience: Essays in Hope*, Volume II, Newman Press, 1971; *Evangelization, Dialogue, and Development*, Documenta Missionalia, 1972; J. M. Robinson, editor, *Religion and the Humanizing of Man*, Council on the Study of Religion, 1972; G. Gispert-Sauch, editor, *God's Word Among Men*, Vidyajyoti, 1973.

Contributor to numerous books in other languages, including: Baldomero Jimenez Duque and Luis Sala Balust, editors, *La Perfeccion Cristiana*, Volume III: *La Espiritualidad Comparada*, Flors (Barcelona), 1969; L. Reinisch, editor, *Vom Sinn der Tradition*, C. H. Beck (Munich), 1970; A. Vargas-Machuca, editor, *Teologia y mundo contemporaneo*, Universidad Pontificia de Comillas (Madrid), 1975; E. Castelli, editor, *Hermeneutique de la secularisation*, Aubier (Paris), 1976; R. Caporale, editor, *Vecchi e huovi Dei*, Valentino (Torino), 1976. Also contributor to *Diccionario Salvat*. Contributor to journals in English and in several European languages. Co-founder and vice-director of *Arbor*, 1944-52; member of editorial board, *Concilium, Jeevadhara, International Jahrbuch fuer interdizizplinaere Forschung, Journal of Ecumenical Studies, Listening*.

WORK IN PROGRESS: Krishnamandala, "a study on pure awareness as the central and often forgotten element of human consciousness."

SIDELIGHTS: Panikkar writes that his "philosophical life can be summed up under two headings: *existential risk* and *intellectual burden*." The existential risk refers to his acceptance of "the risk of conversion" and a mingling of his cultural (Indian) heritage. He maintains that "the mutual understanding of the different traditions of the world may be accomplished only by sacrificing one's life in the attempt to sustain the existing tensions without becoming schizophrenic and to maintain the polarities without personal or cultural paranoia." The expression of such experiences is his intellectual burden: "Can the pluralism of one's own experiments and experiences find an understandable expression?"

Panikkar believes religions to be at the base of culture. He writes that "to reduce man to a bundle of psychological or economical needs will not do. Unless we come to a religious understanding, we are going to perpetuate destructive tensions, both cultural and ideological."

*   *   *

PAPASHVILY, George   1898-1978

PERSONAL: Born August 23, 1898, in Kobiankari, Georgian Soviet Socialist Republic; came to United States, 1923; naturalized U.S. citizen, 1944; married Helen Waite (an author). *Address:* RD 4, Quakertown, Pa. 18951.

CAREER: Writer and sculptor. Worked as well digger, taxi driver, dishwasher, painter, factory worker, movie extra, and farmer. Exhibitions of sculptings held at National Academy in New York, N.Y., National College of Fine Arts in Washington, D.C., Boston Museum of Fine Arts in Boston, Mass., and numerous other museums and galleries. *Military service:* Served in Russian Army during World War I; served in Georgian National Army during Russian Revolution; served in U.S. Coast Guard. *Member:* Artists Equity Association, Audubon Artists, Philadelphia Art Alliance.

WRITINGS—All with wife, Helen Papashvily: *Anything Can Happen* (Book-of-the-Month Club selection), Harper, 1945; *Yes and No Stories: A Book of Georgian Folk Tales*, illustrations by Simon Lissom, Harper, 1946; *Thanks to Noah*, illustrations by Jack Wilson, Harper, 1951; *Dogs and People*, illustrations by Marguerite Kirmse, Lippincott, 1954; (contributor) *Russian Cooking*, Time-Life, 1969; *Home and Home Again*, Harper, 1973.

SIDELIGHTS: George Papashvily is best remembered for his book, *Anything Can Happen*, the true account of one immigrant's discovery of America and his adjustment to the "strange" customs of his chosen land. The book reportedly sold 600,000 copies, was translated into fifteen foreign languages, and was adapted for motion pictures in 1952. Reviews of the book included Harold Fields's comments in *Saturday Review of Literature:* "Mr. Papashvily's book is an interesting, psychological case-study in the adjustment of the alien, written in terms of personal experiences—each one of which is viewed, in retrospect, with rich enjoyment and humor that the author felt. His humor proves contagious: it communicates itself to the reader and leaves him smiling at the happy ending to this tale of tribulation and bewilderment." The *Springfield Republican* added: "*Anything Can Happen*, with its charming violence to English and its ridiculous adventures can be read for sheer entertainment. None better can be found nowadays. But it is also a deeply satisfying American document which can teach while it delights us."

BIOGRAPHICAL/CRITICAL SOURCES: New York Times, December 31, 1944; *Springfield Republican*, December 31, 1944; George Papashvily and Helen Papashvily, *Anything Can Happen*, Harper, 1945; *Saturday Review of Literature*, January 13, 1945; *American Artist*, October, 1955; G. Papashvily and H. Papashvily, *Home and Home Again*, Harper, 1973.

Obituaries: *New York Times*, March 31, 1978; *Time*, April 10, 1978; *Current Biography*, May, 1978.*

(Died March 29, 1978, in Cambria, Calif.)

PAPASHVILY, Helen (Waite) 1906-

PERSONAL: Born December 19, 1906, in Stockton, Calif.; daughter of Herbert (a contractor) and Isabella Findlay (Lochead) Waite; married George Papashvily (an author). *Education:* Attended the University of California, Berkeley. *Address:* R D 4, Quakertown, Pa. 18951.

CAREER: Author. Has done bibliographical research, collected books for private libraries, and worked in several bookstores, owning and managing the Moby Dick Bookshop, Allentown, Pa., 1939-50.

WRITINGS: All the Happy Endings: A Study of the Domestic Novel in America, the Women Who Wrote It, the Women Who Read It, in the Nineteenth Century, Harper, 1956; *Louisa May Alcott,* illustrations by Bea Holmes, Houghton, 1965.

With husband, George Papashvily: *Anything Can Happen* (Book-of-the-Month Club selection), Harper, 1945; *Yes and No Stories: A Book of Georgian Folk Tales,* illustrations by Simon Lissim, Harper, 1946; *Thanks to Noah,* illustrations by Jack Wilson, Harper, 1951; *Dogs and People,* illustrations by Marguerite Kirmse, Lippincott, 1954; (with the editors of Time-Life Books) *Russian Cooking,* Time-Life Books, 1969; *Home and Home Again,* Harper, 1973.

SIDELIGHTS: Helen Papashvily is credited with writing down her husband George's experiences as an immigrant in America, which later developed into their best seller, *Anything Can Happen.* Originally, one sketch appeared in *Common Ground,* and at the suggestion of an editor at Harper, the material was expanded into a book.

Mrs. Papashvily has also written several books of her own. Of *All the Happy Endings,* the *New York Times* wrote, "The author . . . is fortunately more interested in the social aspects of the fiction she describes than in discovering forgotten literary gems, and therein lies the value of her book. She writes with clarity and vigor and she has provided a chart through a sentimental wilderness that few nowadays would have the temerity to enter. It is a book worth the prayerful consideration of all who are concerned with the world of women." Added *Saturday Review:* "Like most theses, Mrs. Papashvily does not tell the whole story of the domestic novel or of the social revolution it helped bring about. She slurs over some of the writers and novels that do not conform to her pattern. But on the whole she has made an important contribution to our understanding of the nineteenth century and its women. Happily she is entertaining to boot." The *Christian Science Monitor* noted that the book "is endlessly informative, and as accurate as could be expected of a book with so much detail. In the last forty years it has been the fashion to make a jest of those earlier novels, and Mrs. Papashvily cannot quite resist that tone though she gives them a serious sociological purpose. For the most part her tone is crisp, even a little acid about woman's situation in a man's world. Her readers, who recall her writing in *Anything Can Happen,* are prepared for the light touch. . . ."

BIOGRAPHICAL/CRITICAL SOURCES: George and Helen Papashvily, *Anything Can Happen,* Harper, 1945; *New York Times,* October 21, 1956; *Christian Science Monitor,* October 22, 1956; *Saturday Review,* November 10, 1956; G. and H. Papashvily, *Home and Home Again,* Harper, 1973.*

*   *   *

PARELIUS, Ann Parker 1943-

PERSONAL: Born January 24, 1943, in New York, N.Y.; daughter of Louis and Florence (Michaels) Parker; married Robert James Parnelius (a sociologist), June 26, 1964; children: Jesse, Amy. *Education:* Hunter College of the City University of New York, B.A., 1963; University of Chicago, M.A., 1965, Ph.D., 1967. *Office:* Department of Sociology, Rutgers University, New Brunswick, N.J. 08903.

CAREER: Rutgers University, New Brunswick, N.J., assistant professor, 1967-76, associate professor of sociology, 1976—. *Member:* American Sociological Association, Society for the Study of Social Problems, American Association of University Professors, Sociologist for Women in Society, Women's Equity Action League, League of Women Voters, Eastern Sociological Society, Phi Beta Kappa. *Awards, honors:* National Science Foundation fellowship, 1963-66. Woodrow Wilson fellowship, 1966.

WRITINGS: (With husband, Robert J. Parelius) *Sociology of Education,* Prentice-Hall, 1978. Contributor to sociology and education journals.

WORK IN PROGRESS: Research on sociology of age, sociology of education, sociology of sex-roles, and sociology of the family.

*   *   *

PARELIUS, Robert J. 1941-

PERSONAL: Surname is pronounced Pah-*ree*-lee-us; born May 1, 1941, in Portland, Ore.; son of Martin Wells (a lumber wholesaler) and Jessie (LePage) Parelius; married Ann Parker (a professor); children: Jesse Martin, Amy Elizabeth. *Education:* University of Oregon, B.A. (summa cum laude), 1963; University of Chicago, M.A., 1965, Ph.D., 1967. *Office:* Department of Sociology, Douglass College, Rutgers University, New Brunswick, N.J. 08903.

CAREER: Institute of Juvenile Research, Chicago, Ill., junior research associate, 1964-66; Rutgers University, Douglass College, New Brunswick, N.J., associate professor of sociology, 1967—. Visiting assistant professor at University of Oregon, 1968-69. Chairperson, Human Care Systems Principal Area of Specialization, 1976—. Chairperson of human rights commission of Highland Park, 1977. *Member:* American Association for Higher Education, American Educational Research Association, American Sociological Association. *Awards, honors:* Rutgers Research Council fellowship, 1971-72, grants, 1971-72 and 1975-76.

WRITINGS: (With wife, Ann P. Parelius) *The Sociology of Education,* Prentice-Hall, 1978. Contributor of articles to various professional and education journals.

WORK IN PROGRESS: Research on "the feasibility of community service as an alternative to expulsion or legal sanctions for serious school offenders" and on "faculty culture and the quality of undergraduate instruction."

SIDELIGHTS: Parelius writes that "*The Sociology of Education* was written in order to provide students with a comprehensive, understandable, scholarly synthesis of previous work as well as to present our own distinctive analyses of many important issues."

*   *   *

PARKER, Beulah 1912-

PERSONAL: Born January 21, 1912, in Chicago, Ill.; daughter of Harrison and Edith (Stubbs) Parker; married H. Leland Vaughan, January 21, 1954 (deceased); children: Nicholas W. (stepson). *Education:* Bryn Mawr College, A.B., 1933; Columbia University, M.D., 1943. *Home:* 307

Western Dr., Richmond, Calif. 94701. *Office:* 2811 College Ave., Berkeley, Calif. 94705.

CAREER: Resident in psychiatry at Langley Porter Clinic, San Francisco, Calif., 1945-47, and Yale Psychiatric Institute, New Haven, Conn., 1951-53; private practice of psychiatry in Berkeley, Calif., 1946—; lecturer at University of California, San Francisco, 1954—. *Member:* American Psychiatric Association (fellow), San Francisco Psychoanalytic Society.

WRITINGS: My Language Is Me, Basic Books, 1962; *Mental Health In-Service Training,* International Universities Press, 1968; *A Mingled Yarn,* Yale University Press, 1972. Contributor to medical journals.

SIDELIGHTS: Beulah Parker summarized two of her three books: "*A Mingled Yarn* is the true account of life in a family where one of the children eventually became schizophrenic. It is written in fictionalized style and shows the development of attitudes and communication styles in the family, starting with early founders in colonial days. *My Language Is Me* is a quasiverbative account of psychotherapy with a disturbed adolescent boy, whose creative way of expressing his conflicts illuminates problems shared by all young people as well as those called 'disturbed.' A running account of the dialogue between him and the psychotherapist is broken by occasional chapters of interpretation and discussion which can be omitted by those who would like to read the material as the story of two people trying to unravel the boy's code language."

*　　*　　*

PARKES, Colin Murray 1928-

PERSONAL: Born March 26, 1928, in London, England; son of Eric William and Gwyneth Anne Parkes; married wife, Patricia Margaret (a novelist), June 20, 1958; children: Elizabeth, Jennifer, Caroline. *Education:* Westminster Medical School, London, M.B. and B.S., both 1951; Institute of Psychiatry, London, D.P.M., 1959, M.D., 1962. *Religion:* "Humanist." *Home:* High Mare, South Rd., Chorleywood, Hertfordshire, England. *Agent:* Frazer & Dunlop, 91 Regent St., London W.1, England. *Office:* Department of Psychiatry, London Hospital, London E.1, England.

CAREER: Westminster Hospital, London, England, house physician, 1951-52; Westminster Children's Hospital, London, house physician, 1952; Kettering General Hospital, senior house physician, 1952-54; Maudsley Hospital, London, senior house physician, 1956-57, registrar, 1957-60, member of research staff of Medical Research Council's social psychiatry unit, 1960-62; Tavistock Institute of Human Relations, London, member of research staff in family psychiatry, 1962-75, honorary consultant psychiatrist, 1970-75; London Hospital, London, senior lecturer in psychiatry, 1975—. Project director at Harvard University's Laboratory of Community Psychiatry, 1965-69; honorary consultant psychiatrist at St. Christopher's Hospice, Sydenham, 1966—. *Military service:* Royal Air Force, medical officer, 1954-56; became flight lieutenant.

MEMBER: Royal College of Psychiatry (fellow), Cruse: Organization for the Widowed (chairman of council), Association for the Study of Animal Behaviour. *Awards, honors:* Silver award from British Medical Association film competition, 1977, for "The Life That's Left."

WRITINGS: (Contributor) E. J. Anthony and C. Koupernik, editors, *International Yearbook of Child Psychiatry and Allied Professions,* Volume I, Wiley, 1970; (contributor)

Robert Gosling, editor, *Support, Innovation and Autonomy,* Tavistock Publications, 1973; (contributor) B. Schoenberg, editor, *Bereavement: Its Psychosocial Aspects,* Columbia University Press, 1974; (with Ira O. Glick and Robert S. Weiss) *The First Year of Bereavement,* Wiley, 1975; (contributor) J. G. Howell, editor, *Modern Perspectives in the Psychiatric Aspects of Surgery,* Brunner, 1976; (contributor) E. R. Prichard, B.A. Orcutt, and other editors, *Social Work With the Dying Patient and the Family,* Columbia University Press, 1977. Also author of *Bereavement: Studies of Grief in Adult Life.* Author of motion picture, "The Life That's Left." Contributor of about twenty-five articles to medical journals. Advisory editor of *Social Science and Medicine* and *Omega.*

WORK IN PROGRESS: The Stress of Illness (tentative title), to examine the implications of regarding doctors as agents of change; studies to evaluate services for the dying and the bereaved.

SIDELIGHTS: Parkes writes: "My dissatisfaction with standards of care led to a series of studies of the psychological aspects of death, bereavement, and crippling illness. Now I am teaching professionals and developing services for families in crisis." *Avocational interests:* Choral singing (tenor), wine making.

*　　*　　*

PARKINSON, Cornelia M. 1925-
(Day Taylor, joint pseudonym)

PERSONAL: Born October 8, 1925, in Casey, Ill.; daughter of Fred (a telephone lineman and salesman) and Nelle (a seamstress; maiden name, Price) McNary; married Richard W. Parkinson (a professor); children: Cassandra S. Parkinson Adams, Claudia S., Cornelia M. Parkinson Iles. *Education:* Attended public high school. *Residence:* Reynoldsburg, Ohio. *Agent:* David Stewart Hull, James Brown Associates, 25 West 43rd St., New York, N.Y. 11101.

CAREER: First Presbyterian Church, Reynoldsburg, Ohio, church secretary, 1956-58; Reynoldsburg Public Schools, Reynoldsburg, executive secretary to the superintendent, 1958-62; free-lance writer and photographer, 1966—.

WRITINGS—Under joint pseudonym Day Taylor: (With Sharon Salvato) *The Black Swan* (novel), Dell, 1978. Contributor of articles, short stories, and photos to *Bride's, Computer World, Mankind, True Romance, Modern Romances, Sexology, Health, Grit, Hearthstone,* and *Editor and Publisher.*

WORK IN PROGRESS: Dawn of the Damned, a sequel to *The Black Swan,* set in Reconstruction times, with Sharon Salvato; *History of Reynoldsburg, Ohio.*

SIDELIGHTS: Parkinson told *CA:* "In my middle-class family the use of the mind was held to be very important, and intellectual achievement was closely watched and encouraged. I entered and won a number of scholarship contests because for me it was fun, as well as a way to compete for 'best.' This spirit of aiming at the best has helped me in writing, as in life. I consider writing the most fun of any work I've ever done.

"Why do I write? I started when I was twelve years old, sitting on the broad branch of a pear tree in our yard in Williamsport, Ohio, writing about beautiful blonde heroines with long, tanned legs. By the time I was fourteen I had completed a juvenile book; another by fifteen; and by age sixteen I had written a novel with an adult theme. When I was quite a bit older, I wrote stories and confessions and uplift stuff to get something off my mind, or to help someone who needed it. I write because I can't not write. I'm uncomfortable and guilty and aimless when I'm not writing. I feel as if whatever talent I have is something I should be using—back to the intellectual achievement notion, you see. I feel as if writing is my job and I ought to be doing it, and I want to do it because I find it extremely fulfilling. There is no other work I like—or do—as well (in my own mind, at least) as writing.''

When asked by *CA* whether collaborating on a novel creates any difficulties, she explained: "Sharon Salvato and I first plot the material to be written, then one of us writes the first draft. Then she hands it to the other person, who rewrites. We do this until each chapter has been written over about five times. Yes, there were some chapters we didn't need to tinker with; they were fine as written. We had very little difficulty in collaboration because it was not my personality, or her personality, that was important, but the book. Every disagreement was settled with the benefit of the book in mind. It would be hard to say how much time we spent in research. Our basic research took the two of us a solid month. After we began to write, we continued to research nearly every week, depending on the subject being written about. We wrote the first version of 1500 pages in just 369 days. This meant that two women worked many fifty- to sixty-hour weeks during that year. My partner felt that style might be a problem; but since I've written all sorts of articles and stories, I can use whatever style seems to fit the work. My natural, easy style is sort of light and flippant—if it fits—but I shift easily to a more formal style.''

*   *   *

PARNALL, Peter 1936-

PERSONAL: Born in Syracuse, N.Y.; married; children: one son. *Education:* Attended Cornell University and Pratt Institute School of Art. *Residence:* New Milford, N.J.

CAREER: Author and illustrator of books for children; art director for a travel magazine; worked for five years as an art director for an advertising agency; free-lance designer. *Awards, honors:* New York Times named *A Dog's Book of Bugs* by Elizabeth Griffen and *Knee-Deep in Thunder* by Sheila Moon as the best illustrated children's books of the year in 1967, and *Malachi Mudge* by Edward Cecil for the same honor in 1968; Christopher Award for children's book, 1971, for *Annie and the Old One* by Miska Miles; the American Institute of Graphic Arts Children's Book Show selected *When the Porcupines Moved In* by Cora Annett for the 1971-1972 exhibition and *Year on Muskrat Marsh* by Berniece Freschet for the 1973-1974 exhibition; *Annie and the Old One* by Miles and *The Desert Is Theirs* by Byrd Baylor received the Brooklyn Art Books for Children Citation in 1973 and 1977 respectively; *Hawk, I'm Your Brother* by Baylor was named a Caldecott Medal Honor Book in 1977.

WRITINGS—All self-illustrated: *The Mountain,* Doubleday, 1971; *The Great Fish,* Doubleday, 1973; *Alfalfa Hill,* Doubleday, 1975; *A Dog's Book of Birds,* Scribner, 1977.

Illustrator: Wayne Short, *The Cheechakoes,* Random House, 1964; Mary Francis Shura, *A Tale of Middle Length,* Atheneum, 1966; Elizabeth Griffen, *A Dog's Book of Bugs,* Atheneum, 1967; Sheila Moon, *Knee-Deep in Thunder,* Atheneum, 1967; Edward Cecil, *Malachi Mudge,* McGraw, 1968; Frank Lee DuMond, *Tall Tales of the Catskills,* Atheneum, 1968; Jean Craighead George, *The Moon of the Wild Pigs,* Crowell, 1968; Murray Goodwin, *Under-*

ground Hideaway, Harper, 1968; Walt Morey, *Kavik the Wolf Dog,* Dutton, 1968; Patricia Coffin, *The Gruesome Green Witch,* Walker & Co., 1969; Miska Miles, *Apricot ABC,* Little, Brown, 1969; Peggy Parish, *A Beastly Circus,* Simon & Schuster, 1969.

Aileen Lucia Fisher, *But Ostriches,* Crowell, 1970; George Mendoza, *The Inspector,* Doubleday, 1970; Jan Wahl, *Doctor Rabbit,* Delacorte, 1970; Cora Annett, *When the Porcupine Moved In,* F. Watts, 1971; Angus Cameron, *The Nightwatchers,* Four Winds Press, 1971; Mendoza, *Big Frog, Little Pond,* McCall, 1971; Mendoza, *Moonfish and Owl Scratchings,* Grosset, 1971; Miles, *Annie and the Old One,* Little, Brown, 1971; Wahl, *The Six Voyages of Pleasant Fieldmouse,* Delacorte, 1971; Margaret Hodges, *The Fire Bringer,* Little, Brown, 1972; Mary Anderson, *Emma's Search for Something,* Atheneum, 1973; Mary Ann Hoberman, *A Little Book of Little Beasts,* Simon & Schuster, 1973; Laurence P. Pringel, *Twist, Wiggle, and Squirm: A Book about Earthworms,* Crowell, 1973; Miriam Schlein, *The Rabbit's World,* Four Winds Press, 1973; Byrd Baylor, *Everybody Needs a Rock,* Scribner, 1974; Berniece Freschet, *Year on Muskrat Marsh,* Scribner, 1974; Keith Robertson, *Tales of Myrtle the Turtle,* Viking, 1974.

Baylor, *The Desert Is Theirs,* Scribner, 1975; Sally Carrighar, *The Twilight Seas,* Weybright & Talley, 1975; Millard Lampell, *The Pig with One Nostril,* Doubleday, 1975; Alice Schick, *The Peregrine Falcons,* Dial Press, 1975; Baylor, *Hawk, I'm Your Brother,* Scribner, 1976.

SIDELIGHTS: Parnall spent his childhood in the country where he developed a fondness for animals. His interest in wildlife inspired him to become a veterinarian. Parnall enrolled in Cornell University to qualify for a position in the science of animal care, but he soon realized his preference for drawing animals was stronger than his desire to study them.

Parnall left college and wandered from job to job throughout the southwestern United States. The wayfaring young man eventually returned to New York to study advertising at Pratt Institute. It wasn't long, however, before Parnall dropped out of the academic environment to pursue a career as an art director. After working several years in the advertising industry, Parnall developed his own illustrative style, but at the same time became disillusioned with the field and the people in it.

By the 1960's Parnall turned to illustrating books for children. The illustrator is still deeply interested in animals, and often finds inspiration for many of his works by taking long walks to watch deer and other wild creatures.

BIOGRAPHICAL/CRITICAL SOURCES: Lee Kingman, editor, *Illustrators of Children's Books, 1957-1966,* Horn Book, 1968; *Saturday Review,* September 18, 1971; Doris De Montreville and Donna Hill, *Third Book of Junior Authors,* H. W. Wilson, 1972; *New York Times Book Review,* January 2, 1972; *Booklist,* November 15, 1975; *Bulletin of the Center for Children's Books,* February, 1976.*

*   *   *

PARRIS, Guichard 1903-

PERSONAL: Born March 3, 1903, in the French West Indies; came to the United States in 1917, naturalized citizen, 1919; son of Esau Clairemond (a sailor) and Laure (a dressmaker; maiden name, Bolivar) Parris; married Willie Ferron (a social worker), September 8, 1934; children: Louise J. Parris Manly, Frederick, Mary. *Education:* Amherst College, A.B. (honors), 1927; Columbia University, M.A., 1932, further studies, 1936-38. *Politics:* Democrat. *Religion:* Roman Catholic. *Home:* 501 West 123rd St., New York, N.Y. 10027. *Office:* Underwood, Jordan Associates, 230 Park Ave., New York, N.Y. 10017.

CAREER: Livingstone College, Salisbury, N.C., instructor in chemistry, 1930-31; Lincoln University, Jefferson City, Mo., assistant professor of French literature, 1933-34; University of Atlanta, Atlanta, Ga., assistant professor of French literature, 1935-36; National Youth Administration, New York, N.Y. (and Boston, Mass.), member of administrative staff, 1939-43; National Urban League, New York City, director of public relations, 1944-68; Underwood, Jordan Associates, New York City, public relations consultant, 1968—. Member of board of managers of Hospital for Special Surgery of New York; member of advisory committee of New York Public Library's Schomberg Collection; member of national board of directors of Catholic Big Brothers of America. President of Catholic Interracial Council, 1952-58.

MEMBER: National Press Club, Public Relations Society of America (past member of local board of directors), Phi Beta Kappa. *Awards, honors:* Distinguished service medal from New York City Chapter of Public Relations Society of America, 1968.

WRITINGS: (With Lester Brooks) *Blacks in the City,* Little, Brown, 1971. Contributor to *Columbia Review* and *Opportunity.*

WORK IN PROGRESS: Editing *De la litterature des Negres,* by Henri Gregoire, originally published in Paris in 1808.

SIDELIGHTS: Parris writes: "I am interested in research and writing on the intellectual history and the culture of Blacks in the modern world, especially the eighteenth and early nineteenth centuries, both in West Africa and the New World."

*   *   *

PARRISH, Robert (Reese) 1916-

PERSONAL: Born January 4, 1916, in Columbus, Ga.; son of R. Gordon (a salesman) and Laura Virginia (an actress; maiden name, Reese) Parrish; married Kathleen Thompson (a story analyst), September 18, 1943; children: Peter Joseph, Kathleen Anne. *Education:* Attended University of Southern California, 1936. *Residence:* London, England. *Agent:* Don Congdon, Harold Matson Co., Inc., 22 East 49th St., New York, N.Y. 10016.

CAREER: Worked as film editor, 1934-50; motion picture director, 1950—; author, 1976—. Associated with numerous production companies, including United Artists, Universal, Columbia, and Twentieth Century-Fox. Director of motion pictures, including "Cry Danger," 1951, "The Purple Plain," 1952, "Fire Down Below," 1957, "The Wonderful Country," 1958, "Up From the Beach," 1965, and "Casino Royale," 1967. Founded Trimark Productions, Inc., 1955. Consultant to Penguin Books and to Goldcrest Films. *Military service:* U.S. Navy. *Member:* Academy of Motion Picture Arts and Sciences, Directors' Guild of America, American Cinema Editors, Authors Guild, Society of Authors, England. *Awards, honors:* Academy Award for film editing from Academy of Motion Picture Arts and Sciences, 1947, for "Body and Soul"; nomination for Academy Award for film editing, 1949, for "All the King's Men."

WRITINGS: Growing Up in Hollywood, Harcourt, 1976. Contributor to periodicals, including *Punch, Washingtonian,* and *Positif.*

WORK IN PROGRESS: An adaptation of Robert Louis Stevenson's *The Beach of Falesa* for film.

*   *   *

PATTISON, Walter Thomas 1903-

PERSONAL: Born January 5, 1903, in Chicago, Ill.; son of George Henry (an oil jobber) and Alice (McClure) Pattison; married Marion L. Henry, December 17, 1940; children: Sarah (Mrs. Garrie Tufford), Deborah (Mrs. Paul Alper), George Henry, Martha. *Education:* Harvard University, B.S., 1925, M.A., 1926, Ph.D., 1932. *Politics:* Democrat. *Religion:* Humanist. *Home:* 1707 Lindig St., St. Paul, Minn. 55113.

CAREER: University of Minnesota, Minneapolis, instructor in Romance languages, 1926-28; Wesleyan University, Middletown, Conn., assistant professor of Romance languages, 1928-38; University of Minnesota, associate professor, 1938-47, professor of Romance languages, 1947-70, head of department, 1954-60, 1966-67, head of department of Spanish and Portuguese, 1968-70; writer, 1970—. Visiting professor at University of Wisconsin, Madison, 1948, Universidad de San Carlos, 1949, and University of California, Los Angeles, 1951. *Member:* American Institute of Archaeology, American Association of Teachers of Spanish and Portuguese. *Awards, honors:* Guggenheim fellowship, 1957-58.

WRITINGS: Representative Spanish Authors, Oxford University Press, 1942, 3rd edition (with Donald W. Bleznick), 1971; *La fuente de las calaveras,* Crofts, 1944; *The Life and Works of Raimbaut d'Orange,* University of Minnesota Press, 1951; *Benito Perez Galdos and the Creative Process,* University of Minnesota Press, 1954; *College Spanish,* Oxford University Press, 1960; *El naturalismo espanol,* Gredos, 1966; *Emilia Pardo Bazan,* Twayne, 1971; *Benito Perez Galdos,* Twayne, 1975. Contributor to language journals.

WORK IN PROGRESS: A comparison of ancient Iberian inscriptions with the Basque language; a book, *Etapas preliminares de Gloria.*

SIDELIGHTS: Pattison told *CA:* "Much of my work is addressed to scholars only, but *Emilio Pardo Bazan* and *Benito Perez Galdos* are aimed at a wider group. I would say that I have a restless mind, jumping from Old Provencal to nineteenth-century Spanish literature, to the ancient Iberian language." *Avocational interests:* Fishing and skiing.

*   *   *

PATTON, Oliver B(eirne) 1920-

PERSONAL: Born December 24, 1920, in Washington, D.C.; son of Milton Humes (a U.S. Army colonel) and Anne (Richardson) Patton; married Anne Connors, August 7, 1945; children: Oliver II, Shelby, Anya Patton Ward, Ellen, Sarah. *Education:* Attended West Virginia University, 1939-41; U.S. Military Academy, B.S., 1944; University of Pennsylvania, M.A., 1953. *Politics:* Independent. *Religion:* Episcopalian. *Home:* 4817 Morgan Dr., Chevy Chase, Md. 20015. *Agent:* Jim Trupin, Suite 4A, 124 East 84th St., New York, N.Y. 10028. *Office:* U.S. Capitol Historical Society, 200 Maryland Ave., Washington, D.C. 20515.

CAREER: U.S. Army, 1939-74, retiring as brigadier general; U.S. Capitol Historical Society, Washington, D.C., executive secretary, 1974—. During World War II served in England, Belgium and Germany; counter intelligence unit commander, Germany, 1946-49; served in Korea, 1950-51;

instructor in English, U.S. Military Academy, 1953-56; staff and executive officer, Germany, 1957-60; served in Viet Nam as assistant chief of staff, U.S. Intelligence, 1968-69; adviser to Imperial Iranian ground forces, 1971-72; deputy assistant, chief of staff, U.S. Intelligence, Washington, D.C., 1972-74. Member of U.S. Council on Abandoned Military Posts. *Member:* Company of Military Historians, Exchange Club of Capitol Hill, U.S. Military Academy Association of Graduates, West Point Society of Washington, Beta Theta Pi. *Awards, honors*—Military: Legion of Merit with two Oak Leaf Clusters; Bronze Star with "V" and two Oak Leaf Clusters; Air Medal; Purple Heart Medal with two Oak Leaf Clusters; Army Distinguished Service Medal; Presidential Unit Citation (Korea); Cross of Gallantry with Palm, Cross of Gallantry with Gold Star (Viet Nam).

WRITINGS: The Hollow Mountains (novel), Popular Library, 1976; *My Heart Turns Back* (novel), Popular Library, 1978. Contributor of articles to several publications, including *Military Review* and *Catholic Digest.*

WORK IN PROGRESS: Western Wind, a sequel to *The Hollow Mountains,* dealing with the American raids into Mexico in the 1870's, for Popular Library; research on a fourth novel about the clandestine mission of a U.S. Army lieutenant dispatched as an observer to the 1877 Russo-Turkish War.

SIDELIGHTS: Patton writes: "Had I not gotten an appointment to West Point, I expect I would have tried writing as a profession back in 1941. Now, some thirty years later, I have simply returned to a long-deferred ambition.

"I started my first novel, *The Hollow Mountains,* some years before I retired from the army, and worked on it sporadically until 1974 when I quit active military service and joined the U.S. Capitol Historical Society. In addition to many other attractive features, the job gives me my nights and weekends to write, so when I took it up, I also returned to work on *The Hollow Mountains.* That book is about the army, but the army of a hundred years ago whose description happily requires no clearance by the Department of Defense.

"I was attracted to that era by its remarkable similarities to our army's more recent undeclared wars. Our difficulties with the Apache Indians in 1876 indicate we have not since encountered any more capable guerrilla fighters. In addition, the nature of our small, Indian-fighting army is fascinating. By some quirk, it created for itself a microcosm of a rigid Victorian society and carried that oddity to the limits of the American frontier of the 1870's. These things—the nature of the army of that time and its enemies in Arizona—became the elements of *The Hollow Mountains.*

"There were many Irish immigrants at this time and so are the principals of my second book, *My Heart Turns Back.* In this novel, Brigid O'Donnel went West with the army only because she needed a job. The army horrified her and many other Americans, too. Senator John Logan said in 1876, 'The Congress has never declared war on the Indians. . . . If the Senate will not recognize glory in Indian warfare . . . there will not be any glory in Indian warfare.' His edict has a contemporary ring. I think the way in which the ordinary troopers and infantrymen of the frontier army handled that view of their war is fascinating.

"My third novel will continue this examination of our frontier army and the striking parallels between it and our army of the last decade. It is concerned with the effect on the troopers in Texas of an American president who almost started a second war with Mexico by political foot-work.

"My wife, quoting another chronicler of our frontier army, says I may be the last casualty of the Indian Wars, but my interest in those wars is honestly come by. I grew up on little army posts which seemed preserved in amber from an earlier time in an Army that was 'all volunteer,' though many said that was because its members could find no more respectable work. Splendid historians are now documenting our frontier army with precision, but I think it takes fiction with a dash of fact to tell that story so more people will listen.

"I hope I can keep on doing it."

*　　*　　*

PAUCK, Wilhelm 1901-

PERSONAL: Born January 31, 1901, in Laasphe, Germany; came to the United States in 1925; son of Wilhelm (a physicist) and Maria (Hofmann) Pauck; married Olga C. Gumbel-Dietz, May 1, 1928 (died January 14, 1963); married Marion Hausner (a writer), November 21, 1964. *Education:* University of Berlin, Lic. Theol., 1925. *Politics:* Democrat. *Religion:* United Church of Christ. *Home:* 1742 Willow Rd., Apt. 404, Palo Alto, Calif. 94304. *Office:* Department of Religious Studies, Stanford University, Stanford, Calif. 94305.

CAREER: Chicago Theological Seminary, Chicago, Ill., instructor, 1926-28, assistant professor, 1928-31, professor of church history, 1931-39; University of Chicago, Chicago, Ill., professor of history, 1939-53; Union Theological Seminary, New York, N.Y., professor of church history, 1953-60, Charles A. Briggs Graduate Professor of Church History, 1960-67; Vanderbilt University, Nashville, Tenn., distinguished professor of church history, 1967-72; Stanford University, Stanford, Calif., visiting professor of religious studies and history, 1972—.

MEMBER: American Academy of Arts and Sciences (fellow), American Society of Church History (president, 1936), American Theological Society (president, 1962-63). *Awards, honors:* D.Th. from University of Giessen, 1933; Litt.D. from Upsala College, 1964, and Thiel College, 1967; D.D. from Gustavus Adolphus College, 1967, and University of Edinburgh, 1968.

WRITINGS: Das Reich Gottes auf Erden (title means "The Kingdom of God on Earth"), De Gruyter, 1928; *Karl Barth: Prophet of a New Christianity?,* Harper, 1931; *The Heritage of the Reformation,* Free Press, 1961; (editor and translator) *Luther: Lectures on Romans,* Westminster, 1961; *Harnack and Troeltsch: Two Historical Theologians,* Oxford University Press, 1968; (with wife, Marion Pauck) *Paul Tillich,* Harper, Volume I: *His Life,* 1976, Volume II: *His Thought,* 1979. Co-editor of *Church History,* 1939-53.

BIOGRAPHICAL/CRITICAL SOURCES: Jaroslav Pelikan, editor, *Interpreters of Luther,* Fortress, 1968; *New York Times,* December 19, 1976.

*　　*　　*

PAUL VI, Pope 1897-1978

PERSONAL: Born Giovanni Battista Enrico Antonio Maria Montini, September 26, 1897, in Concesio, Italy; son of Giorgio (an attorney and newspaper editor) and Giudetta (Alghisi) Montini. *Education:* Attended Lombard Seminary, University of Rome, Pontifical Gregorian University, and Pontifical Ecclesiastical Academy. *Address:* Palazzo Apostolico Vaticano, Vatican City, Italy.

CAREER: Ordained Roman Catholic priest, 1920; secretary to apostolic nunciature, Warsaw, Poland, 1923; document writer, Secretariat of State, Vatican, 1924; national spiritual adviser, Italian Federation of Catholic University Students, 1925-35; professor of history and pontifical diplomacy, 1931-37; adviser to Pope Pius XII, 1944-52; appointed substitute secretary of state for ordinary (internal) affairs, 1952; consecrated archbishop of Milan, 1954; created cardinal, 1958; elected pope, June 21, 1963, papal reign, 1963-78.

WRITINGS: Ecclesiam Suam (encyclical letter; title means "The Paths of the Church"), America Press, 1964; *Dialogues: Reflections on God and Man,* Simon & Schuster, 1965; *On the Development of Peoples* (encyclical letter; original Latin title, *Populorum Progressio),* Paulist/Newman, 1967; *Humanae Vitae* (encyclical letter; title means "On Human Life"), Paulist/Newman, 1968. Also author of several other encyclical letters and reports and proceedings of the Second Vatican Council.

SIDELIGHTS: Pope Paul VI was the 262nd successor to the seat of St. Peter in Rome. A priest with minimal experience as a pastor, Paul became the supreme pastor to the world's Roman Catholics in 1963. He came to the papacy with the title of liberal and left with the description of a conservative who, in matters of priestly celibacy and birth control, followed strict Catholic traditions.

As a young boy, Paul's life was riddled with illness. He suffered from a heart ailment in his early childhood years and, at one point during a school term, was forced to study with a tutor from his sickbed. Later, when he accepted his first diplomatic mission for the Vatican to Poland, he returned quickly to Rome because he could no longer endure the severe Polish winter. Even though his health prevented him from attending classes at the seminary, Paul was ordained on May 19, 1920. In addition, Paul became a first-rate scholar, taking on a full-load of classes while working at the Vatican. There he soon caught the eye of members of the curia as a probable candidate for their diplomatic ranks.

Perhaps Paul's most important contribution to the papacy came in the area of ecumenism. During his fifteen-year papacy, Paul opened communication channels with non-Christian peoples and with other Christian denominations. During his 1964 trip to the Holy Land, Paul met with the spiritual leader of Eastern Orthodoxy, Patriarch Athenagoras I, on the Mount of Olives. Their meeting began a series of exchanges between the two religious leaders that resulted in the annulment of excommunications passed by both churches in 1054. Many sources have called this incident "the finest moment of Paul's papacy." Likewise, Paul met with the archbishop of Canterbury in 1966. This event was the first meeting between the two leaders of these Christian churches since King Henry VIII's break with Rome during the sixteenth century.

In order to carry out these diplomatic missions, Paul became the most-traveled pope in Roman Catholic history. He traveled to sixteen countries on six continents, including India, Uganda, Colombia, and the United States. The message that he often took to these countries was one of world peace and an end to the sufferings of the poor in Third World nations. In addition to his efforts for world peace, Paul will probably be remembered for his work on behalf of the poor. In 1967, he issued the encyclical *Populorum Progressio* ("On the Development of Peoples"), in which he called for an end to the "dehumanizing value system that allowed rich countries to exploit poor countries." Private property, he stated, "does not constitute for anyone an absolute and unconditional right. No one is justified in keeping for his exclusive use what he does not need, when others lack necessities."

As expected, Paul's encyclical met with strong criticism from the *Wall Street Journal,* which called it "warmed-over socialism," and *Time* magazine, which said that the encyclical "had the strident tone of an early 20th-century Marxist polemic."

Following in this tradition, Paul proceeded to reform the papacy and curia by dismissing with the rich, medieval ceremonies and the extravagant dress of cardinals. He internationalized the college of cardinals by appointing bishops from Asia, Africa, and Latin America. He also established seventy-five as the age of retirement for bishops and told cardinals that they could not vote in papal elections if they had reached the age of eighty. In addition, Paul established the Synod of Bishops which potentially gave the bishops some share in the papal decision-making process.

Liturgical reform was also on Paul's list of priorities and he vernacularized the language of the mass and allowed popular music in church services. He loosened the strict, traditional interpretation of sin and abolished numerous Catholic practices, such as the prohibition of eating meat on Fridays. However, he did continue to uphold traditional devotion to Mary, the mother of Jesus.

As progressive as he was in the areas of social reform, Paul was just as conservative in the matters of family life, priestly celibacy, and birth control and abortion. Advised by some bishops to take a strong stand against artifical methods of birth control, Paul issued the controversial encyclical *Humanae Vitae* ("On Human Life"). Many Catholics expected Paul to be progressive in the area of birth control because of his awareness of the problems of population explosion and the world's poor. Instead, Paul stated in the encyclical that church approval of artificial means of birth control would open "a wide and easy road toward conjugal infidelity and the general lowering of morality." "Every marriage," he stated, "must remain open to the transmission of life." The encyclical caused a split within the church. Many priests openly denounced the document and Western bishops did not conceal their disappointment in the pope's decision. Although he always considered dissent healthy, Paul suffered personal anguish at the criticism of this encyclical. Unfortunately, in many cases, this is the issue that will be linked with Paul's papacy.

Personally, Paul was a man who enjoyed classical music in his apartments at the Vatican. He was fluent in French and Italian, and knew Portuguese, Spanish, German, and English, in addition to Latin and other classical languages. He considered himself a disciple of the French Thomistic philosopher Jacques Maritain. Paul also enjoyed modern art and redecorated the papal residence with such art pieces. He established a collection of modern art in the Vatican Museum. Once Paul remarked, "My predecessor Julius II also favored contemporary artists. One of them happened to be Raphael."

Politically, Paul was anti-fascist and anti-communist. He differed from his mentor Pius XII in his determination to successfully establish diplomatic relations with Communist nations. During the years of Mussolini's regime, Paul was spiritual adviser for a Catholic student group which participated in anti-fascist activities. Under pressure from the government, Paul took the group to the catacombs rather than disband their meetings. He told them, "If today we cannot go forward with flags unfurled, we will work in silence."

Initially Pope Paul VI will be remembered as the pope who held the Roman Catholic church together during one of its most turbulent periods. Concerned about both conservative and liberal members of the church, Paul was successful in preventing a potential schism in this Christian religion. Conservative in matters of morality, faith, and doctrine and progressive in social reform, Paul was considered to have held a well-steered course between "two dangerous deviations." Judged to be too liberal by conservatives and too conservative by liberals, Paul was nevertheless described by both as an active pope with a long list of achievements. Even as he lay dying, Paul was still concerned about the world and asked for pardon of "all those to whom I have not done good." He concluded: "I close my eyes on this sad, dramatic and magnificent world, calling God's charity down on it once more."

BIOGRAPHICAL/CRITICAL SOURCES: Pope Paul VI in the Holy Land, translation by Aileen O'Brien, Herder & Herder, 1964; *Newsweek,* August 7, 1967, September 2, 1968, August 21, 1978; *Time,* August 30, 1968, November 22, 1968, August 21, 1978; *New Statesman,* November 22, 1968; *Christianity Today,* August 22, 1969; *McCall's,* February, 1974; *Four Popes: Keepers of the Faith Since 1958,* souvenir issue number 12, Ideal Publishing Corp., 1978.

OBITUARIES: Washington Post, August 7, 1978; *New York Times,* August 7, 1978.*

(Died August 6, 1978, in Castel Gandolfo, Italy)

*   *   *

PAYNE, Basil 1928-

PERSONAL: Born June 22, 1928, in Dublin, Ireland; married Monessa Keating; children: Cyprian, Norbert and Lucy (twins), Gregory, Bernard, Michael, Christopher. *Education:* Attended National University of Ireland. *Home:* Cortona, 137 Rathfarnham Rd., Dublin 14, Ireland.

CAREER: Poet and writer. Former drama critic for *Irish Times* and *Irish Press;* Radio Telefis Eireann, Dublin, Ireland, scriptwriter, editor, and critic, 1963-73; Glassboro State College, Glassboro, N.J., poet-in-residence, beginning 1974. Lecturer at Trinity College, Dublin, summers, 1970-73, and National University of Ireland University College in Dublin, 1970-73. Has given poetry readings and lectures in Ireland and England, France, Switzerland, Yugoslavia, Canada, and the United States. *Awards, honors:* Guinness Poetry Prize from Cheltenham Festival.

WRITINGS: Sunlight on a Square (poems), John Augustine, 1962; (editor and translator from the German) Hans Carossa, *Elegy for the Western World* (poem), University of Dublin Press, 1965; *Love in the Afternoon* (poems), Gill & Macmillan, 1971; (translator from the German) Karl Gustave Gerold, *Collected Poems,* Dolmen, 1972; *Another Kind of Optimism* (poems), Gill & Macmillan, 1974; *Voyage a Deux,* Perret-Gentil, 1974.

Plays and films: "The Onlooker" (dramatic poem for radio), Radio Telefis Eireann, 1969; "In Dublin's Quare City" (dramatic collage), first produced in Dublin, Ireland, at National Theatre, September, 1973. Also author of radio play, "Don't Call Me Honey," and two films, "A Boy and a Ball," and "Missing Believed Dead."

Work represented in eight anthologies, including *Poems From Ireland,* edited by William Cole, Crowell, 1972, *Young Winters Tales,* Macmillan (England), 1973, and *A Patrick Kavanagh Anthology,* 1973. Contributor of poems, stories, and reviews to magazines in Ireland, England, Scotland, Germany, Switzerland, Yugoslavia, and the United States, including *Irish Writing, New Irish Writing,* and *Dublin.*

WORK IN PROGRESS: Poetry.

PEALE, Norman Vincent 1898-

PERSONAL: Born May 31, 1898, in Bowersville, Ohio; son of Charles Clifford (a physician and minister) and Anna (DeLaney) Peale; married Loretta Ruth Stafford, June 20, 1930; children: Margaret Ann (Mrs. Paul F. Everett), John Stafford (an ordained minister and philosophy professor), Elizabeth Ruth (Mrs. John M. Allen). *Education:* Ohio Wesleyan University, B.A., 1920; Boston University, M.A., 1924, S.T.B., 1924. *Politics:* Republican. *Home:* 1030 Fifth Ave., New York, N.Y. 10028; and "Quaker Hill," Pawling, N.Y. 12564. *Office:* 1025 Fifth Ave., New York, N.Y. 10028.

CAREER: Reporter for *Morning Republican,* Findlay, Ohio, 1920, and *Detroit Journal,* Detroit, Mich., 1920; ordained to the Methodist ministry, 1922; pastor in Berkeley, R.I., 1922-24, Brooklyn, N.Y., 1924-27, Syracuse, N.Y., 1927-32; Marble Collegiate Reform Church, New York, N.Y., pastor, 1932—; writer, 1937—. Chaplain, American Legion, Kings County, N.Y., 1925-27. Host of a weekly radio program on station WOR, and television programs, "What's Your Trouble," and "Guideposts Presents Norman Vincent Peale." President of the National Temperance Society, the Protestant Council, 1965-69, and the Reformed Church of America, 1969-70; member of the executive committee of the Presbyterian Ministers Fund for Life Insurance; member of the Mid-Century White House Conference on Children and Youth, and the President's Commission for Observance of the Twenty-fifth Anniversary of the United Nations. Trustee of Ohio Wesleyan University and Central College. Lecturer on public affairs and personal effectiveness.

MEMBER: American Foundation of Religion and Psychiatry (president), Episcopal Actors Guild, American Authors Guild, Sons of the American Revolution, Ohio Society of New York (president, 1952-55), Alpha Delta, Phi Gamma Delta, Rotary Club, Masons, Metropolitan Club, Union League. *Awards, honors:* Freedoms Foundation award, 1952, 1955, 1959, 1973, 1974; Horatio Alger award, 1952; American Education award, 1955; Government Service Award for Ohio, 1956; National Salvation Army Award, 1956; Distinguished Salesman's Award from New York Sales Executives, 1957; Salvation Army Award, 1957; International Human Relations Award from the Dale Carnegie Club International, 1958; Clergyman of the Year Award, 1964; Paul Harris Fellow Award from Rotary International, 1972; Distinguished Patriot Award from Sons of the American Revolution, 1973; Order of Aaron and Hur, Chaplains Corps, U.S. Army, 1975. D.D. from Syracuse University, 1931, Ohio Wesleyan University, 1936, Duke University, 1938, and Central College, 1964; L.H.D. from Lafayette College, 1952, and University of Cincinnati, 1968; LL.D. from William Jewell College, 1952, Hope College, 1962, and Brigham Young University, 1967; S.T.D. from Millikin University, 1958; Litt.D. from Jefferson Medical College, 1955, Iowa Wesleyan University, 1958, and Eastern Kentucky State College, 1964.

WRITINGS: The Art of Living, Abingdon, 1937, new edition published as *The New Art of Living,* Worlds Work, 1975; *You Can Win,* Abingdon, 1938; (with Smiley Blanton) *Faith Is the Answer: A Psychiatrist and a Pastor Discuss Your Problems,* Abingdon-Cokesbury, 1940, enlarged and revised edition, Guideposts Associates, 1955; *A Guide to Confident Living,* Prentice-Hall, 1948, reprinted, Fawcett, 1975; (editor) *Guideposts: Personal Messages of Inspiration and Faith,* Prentice-Hall, 1948; (with Blanton) *The Art of*

Real Happiness, Prentice-Hall, 1950, revised edition, Fawcett, 1976; (editor) *New Guideposts,* Prentice-Hall, 1951; *The Power of Positive Thinking,* Prentice-Hall, 1952, reprinted, Fawcett, 1976, abridged edition published as *The Power of Positive Thinking for Young People,* Prentice-Hall, 1954; (editor) *The Guideposts Anthology,* Guideposts Associates, 1953; (author of introduction) *Guideposts* editors, *What Prayer Can Do,* Doubleday, 1953; (editor) *Faith Made Them Champions,* Guideposts Associates, 1954; (author of introduction) *The Sermon on the Mount,* World Publishing, 1955; *Inspiring Messages for Daily Living,* Prentice-Hall, 1955; *The Coming of the King: The Story of the Nativity* (juvenile), Prentice-Hall, 1956; *He Was a Child* (juvenile), Prentice-Hall, 1957; *Stay Alive All Your Life,* Prentice-Hall, 1957; (editor) *Unlock Your Faith-Power,* Guideposts Associates, 1957; (editor) *Guideposts to a Stronger Faith,* Guideposts Associates, 1959; *The Amazing Results of Positive Thinking,* Prentice-Hall, 1959.

(Author of foreword) Blanton, *The Healing Power of Poetry,* Crowell, 1960; *The Tough-Minded Optimist,* Prentice-Hall, 1961, revised edition published as *Positive Thinking for a Time Like This,* 1975; *Adventures in the Holy Land,* Prentice-Hall, 1963; *Sin, Sex, and Self-Control,* Doubleday, 1965; *Jesus of Nazareth: A Dramatic Interpretation of His Life From Bethlehem to Calvary,* Prentice-Hall, 1966; *The Healing of Sorrow,* Doubleday, 1966; *Enthusiasm Makes the Difference,* Prentice-Hall, 1967; (editor) *Norman Vincent Peale's Treasury of Courage and Confidence,* Doubleday, 1970; *Bible Stories* (juvenile), F. Watts, 1973; *You Can If You Think You Can,* G. K. Hall, 1974; *The Story of Jesus* (juvenile), Gibson, 1976; *The Positive Principle Today: How to Renew and Sustain the Power of Positive Thinking,* Prentice-Hall, 1976.

Author of newspaper columns, "Positive Thinking," and "Confident Living"; contributor to various secular and religious periodicals, including *Reader's Digest* and *Christian Herald.* Co-editor of *Guideposts,* an inspirational magazine.

SIDELIGHTS: For more than half a century, Norman Vincent Peale has used nearly every medium available to communicate to Americans his message of self-help through positive thinking and prayer.

Peale's dynamic sermons have helped to increase membership in every church with which he has been associated. As minister for three years in a Brooklyn, New York congregation, Peale managed to collect enough funds to build a new church, as well as to raise membership from forty to nearly nine hundred. He became pastor of the Marble Collegiate Church in New York City in 1932, preaching to a membership of just five hundred. Peale holds the same position today, but his sermons are now heard by overflow crowds of more than four thousand people, accommodated through the use of closed circuit television.

Peale's message can be read in his monthly magazine, *Guideposts.* Beginning after World War II as a four-page spiritual newsletter for businessmen, it has now risen to twenty-first in readership among all U.S. magazines, with a circulation of two and one half million. Peale and his wife co-edit the magazine, and he contributes one article per issue.

In addition to his lectures and personal appearances, Peale began a weekly radio program in 1935, sponsored by the National Council of Churches. By the 1950's, an estimated audience of five million were tuning in to "The Art of Living," heard over 125 stations throughout the country. As recently as 1974, Peale's television program was viewed on as many as fifty major stations with high ratings. Critics attributed his renewed popularity to such national problems as Watergate and the energy crisis, and America's need to be told that problems can be overcome and dreams can be realized once again. "My principal emphasis has always been on God," Peale told the *Cleveland Press.* "Positive thinking is the way we bring God into our everyday life."

But perhaps Peale has reached a wider audience through his books. His first few attempts, written prior to World War II were not successful. They advocated escape from the problems of the world rather than facing them and fighting to erase them. His first best seller was his fourth book, *A Guide to Confident Living,* which went through twenty-five printings in four years. In this book and in the ones to follow, religion was no longer a means of escape, but a powerful force enabling man to achieve success against all odds. *The Power of Positive Thinking,* Peale's most successful book, rediscovered the power of suggestion over the human mind, stressing the cultivation of a positive attitude as the key to happiness. The book soared to the top of the *New York Times* best seller list, where it remained for three years, breaking the previous all-time record set by Lloyd Douglas' novel, *The Robe.* Although reviewers criticized its simple formulas and shaky theology, sales of the book have now topped three million copies. *The Power of Positive Thinking* has been translated into thirty-three languages, and in 1953, the author recorded excerpts of it for RCA Victor. Its success made Peale one of the most sought-after clergymen in the United States.

Peale's books have been a direct result of his experiences in guiding his parishoners. He was one of the first clergymen to see a relationship between religion and psychiatry, and to do pastoral counseling with a psychiatrist. With the aid of psychiatrist Dr. Smiley Blanton, Peale initiated a religio-psychiatric outpatient clinic in the 1930's, the forerunner of the American Foundation of Religion and Psychiatry, established as a nonprofit organization in 1951. With a large staff of clergymen representing all religious denominations as well as professional psychologists and social workers, the organization treats approximately six hundred patients a week in its New York City headquarters. It also has branches in Harlem, Chicago, and Green Bay, Wisconsin.

In 1941, Peale served as technical adviser for the Warner Brothers film, "One Foot in Heaven," concerning the life of a minister. Arthur Gordon's biography of Peale, *Minister to Millions,* was produced in 1963 by United Artists. "One Man's Way" starred Don Murray, Diana Hyland, and William Windom.

BIOGRAPHICAL/CRITICAL SOURCES: American Magazine, June, 1949; *Forbes,* 1952; *Newsweek,* December 28, 1953; *Reader's Digest,* February, 1954; *Time,* November 1, 1954; *Quarterly Journal of Speech,* December, 1954; *Good Housekeeping,* January, 1956; Arthur Gordon, *Norman Vincent Peale: Minister to Millions,* Prentice-Hall, 1958; Elisabeth L. Davis, *Fathers of America,* Revell, 1958; Clarence Westphal, *Norman Vincent Peale: Christian Crusader,* Denison, 1964; *Publishers Weekly,* January 14, 1974, July 12, 1976; *Cleveland Press,* March 9, 1974; *Journal of Popular Culture,* Summer, 1975.*

*   *   *

PECK, Richard E(arl) 1936-

PERSONAL: Born August 3, 1936, in Milwaukee, Wis.; son of Earl Mason (a machinist) and Mary (Fry) Peck; married Donna Krippner, August 13, 1970; children: Mason, Laura. *Education:* Carroll College, Waukesha, Wis., B.A., 1961;

University of Wisconsin, Madison, M.S., 1962, Ph.D., 1964. *Home:* 3 Crest Lane, Swarthmore, Pa. 19081. *Agent:* Barbara Rhodes Literary Agency, 143 West End Ave., New York, N.Y. 10023. *Office:* Department of English, Temple University, Broad & Montgomery, Philadelphia, Pa. 19122.

CAREER: University of Virginia, Charlottesville, assistant professor of English, 1964-67; Temple University, Philadelphia, Pa., assistant professor, 1967-68, associate professor, 1968-77, professor of English, 1977—. *Military service:* U.S. Marine Corps, helicopter pilot, 1954-59; became captain. *Member:* Screen Writers Guild of America (West), Dramatists Guild, Players Club of Swarthmore (director, 1976—; member of board of governors, 1977—; production director, 1978—). *Awards, honors:* Ruth Wallerstein Award from Carroll College, Waukesha, Wis., 1961, for poetry; *Final Solution* nominated by Science Fiction Research Association for John Campbell Award as best American science fiction novel, 1973.

WRITINGS: (Editor) *Nathaniel Hawthorne, Poems,* University Press of Virginia, 1967; (editor) Floyd Stovall, *Poems,* privately printed, 1967; *Final Solution* (novel), Doubleday, 1973; *Something for Joey* (novel; based on teleplay by Jerry McNeely), Bantam, 1978.

Plays: *Don't Trip Over the Money Pail* (three-act play; first produced in Ridley Park, Pa., at The Barnstormers, April 1, 1976), privately printed, 1977; "The Cubs Are in Fourth Place and Fading" (three-act), first produced in Swarthmore, Pa., at The Players Club of Swarthmore, December 1, 1977; "Prodigal Father" (three-act), first produced in Swarthmore at the Players Club of Swarthmore, November 30, 1978.

Film and television: "Tutte le Strade Portano a Roma" (title means "All Roads Lead to Rome"), 1975. Author of script for "Owen Marshall," 1972, and story for "Indict and Convict," 1973.

Short story represented in anthology, *Best SF: 1971,* edited by Harrison and Aldiss, Putnam, 1972.

WORK IN PROGRESS: A novel; two plays (comedies); two screenplays.

SIDELIGHTS: Peck writes: "I spent two years in Rome as director of Temple University's center there, picked up basic Italian, and visited about eighteen countries. My recent writing has focused on plays (comedies, principally), with several successful productions and others pending. Drama interests me most because of its immediacy and constant freshness (each single performance is 'new'), and comedy because it earns an unfeigned emotional response. It is also more serious than portentous 'serious drama'—an opinion that is obviously valid to some but cannot be made persuasive to others. I intend to continue with two plays a year, probably a novel a year, short stories as they occur ... no more poetry."

*   *   *

PECK, Robert Newton   1928-

PERSONAL: Born in 1928, in Vermont; son of Haven (a farmer) and Lucy Peck; married Dorothy Anne Houston, 1958; children: Christopher Haven, Anne Houston. *Education:* Attended Rollins College. *Home:* 500 Sweetwater Club Circle, Longwood, Fla. 32750.

CAREER: Farmer and writer. Director of Rollins College Writers Conference, 1978—.

WRITINGS: Juvenile; all fiction, except as noted: *A Day*

No Pigs Would Die, Knopf, 1972; *Path of Hunters: Animal Struggle in a Meadow,* Knopf, 1973; *Millie's Boy,* Knopf, 1973; *Soup,* Knopf, 1974; *Fawn,* Little, Brown, 1975; *Wild Cat,* Holiday House, 1975; *Bee Tree and Other Stuff* (poems), Walker & Co., 1975; *Soup and Me,* Knopf, 1975; *Hamilton,* Little, Brown, 1976; *Hang for Treason,* Doubleday, 1976; *Rabbits and Redcoats,* Walker & Co., 1976; *King of Kazoo* (musical), Knopf, 1976; *Trig,* Little, Brown, 1977; *Last Sunday,* Doubleday, 1977; *The King's Iron,* Little, Brown, 1977; *Patooie,* Knopf, 1977; *Soup for President,* Knopf, 1978; *Mr. Little,* Doubleday, 1978; *Eagle Fur,* Knopf, 1978; *Trig Sees Red,* Little, Brown, 1978; *Basket Case,* Doubleday, 1979; *Hub,* Knopf, 1979; *Clunie,* Knopf, 1979; *Soup's Drum,* Knopf, 1980.

Teleplays: "Soup" (based on own novel of the same name), American Broadcasting Companies (ABC-TV), 1978.

WORK IN PROGRESS: Justice Lion, a novel, set in Vermont during Prohibition, with the theme of "man versus government."

SIDELIGHTS: Most of Robert Newton Peck's books reach back into the past—either to his boyhood on a Vermont farm in the 1920's, or a few centuries earlier to life in Vermont during the Revolutionary War. *A Day No Pigs Would Die,* Peck's first novel, describes the coming of age of a rural youth who is compelled to help butcher his pet pig. A reviewer for *Christian Science Monitor* found the book, with its mixture of gory butcherings and quaint rural scenes, to be "sometimes sickening, often entrancing." Marilyn Sachs considered *A Day No Pigs Would Die* to be "moving and engaging" but was disappointed in Peck's next reminiscent book, *Soup.* "Several of the stories were funny, and one or two are touching but by and large there is a strained quality to the writing and a hearty wholesomeness to the book that is disappointing," wrote Sachs about *Soup.* Peck also drew upon his childhood memories to write *Soup and Me* and *Bee Tree and Other Stuff.*

Fort Ticonderoga serves as the setting for three of Peck's historical novels, *Fawn, Hang for Treason,* and *Rabbits and Redcoats. Fawn* is about the Anglo-French battle for Fort Ticonderoga in 1758. The protagonist is a young boy whose father is a French missionary and whose mother is a Mohawk squaw. *Hang for Treason* shifts to Fort Ticonderoga in 1775, when tensions ran high between American patriots and British loyalists. In this novel the main character is a young American boy who joins Ethan Allen's Green Mountain Boys despite the fact that his father is a Tory. Martin Levin commented that Peck "approaches Revolutionary history with a lively, ebullient style that nonetheless suggests some of the pain and confusion of divided loyalties." Yet another version of the Battle of Fort Ticonderoga is contained in *Rabbits and Redcoats,* but Willard M. Wallace did not find it as satisfactory as *Hang for Treason:* "The dialogue among the three boys rings true. Less convincing is the benign portrayal of Ethan Allen and quite unconvincing is that of Benedict Arnold.... It is regrettable that though writing for a younger group, Mr. Peck did not retain the more valid conception of these two characters as portrayed in his recent 'Hang for Treason.'"

The realism of Peck's books has attracted the attention of several reviewers. "Earthy," and "vivid" are terms frequently used to describe his work. For instance, a critic for *Christian Science Monitor* wrote of *A Day No Pigs Would Die:* "In showing just how earthy farm life is and how stoic a farmer and his children must be Mr. Peck spares us nothing. Vivid animal mating scenes, butcherings, a cruel economy that forces a boy to help slaughter his beloved pig and his father to insist that he does—we get the lot.'' A similar tone prevails in *Wild Cat,* which was called a ''harsh, brutal, detailed moralistic naturalistic'' story by Eden Ross Lipson. Most commentators hasten to point out, however, that combined with the earthiness in Peck's books is a sensitivity and awareness of the beauty as well as the cruelty of life.

Commenting about some of the negative criticism of his books, Peck told *CA:* ''As a Vermont redneck author, I get tired of urbane reviewers who think that pork chops in a supermarket are made by DuPont, out of soybeans. We farmers lead a physical life. My father and I killed pigs. Yet we performed our work without hatred or vitriol.'' He added: ''It's fun to write for television. Sure beats killing hogs.''

BIOGRAPHICAL/CRITICAL SOURCES: Christian Science Monitor, January 17, 1973; *Newsweek,* March 12, 1973; *New York Times Book Review,* May 13, 1973, May 5, 1974, February 2, 1975, May 4, 1975, April 4, 1976, May 2, 1976; *National Review,* July 20, 1973; *Best Sellers,* February 15, 1975, April, 1976, December, 1977.

* * *

PENDERWHISTLE, Judith Blair 1952-

PERSONAL: Born April 1, 1952, in Wild Tire, Ky.; daughter of Laszlo Reuben (a sandwich designer) and Judith Alma (a lunchmeat distributor; maiden name, Rolfe) Gonzago; married Herman Fang (a worm farmer), 1976 (divorced); married Rudy Penderwhistle (a hockey referee), 1978; children: Warren, Omar. *Education:* Educated in Veresdaho, Luxembourg. *Politics:* ''Write-ins only.'' *Religion:* ''Sometimes I pray.'' *Home:* 221 Lewiston Rd., Grosse Pointe Farms, Mich. 48236.

CAREER: Worked as waitress at Laszlo's Deli, 1970-73; part-time singer in Luxembourg, 1974-75; free-lance writer, 1975—. *Member:* Waitresses for Hourly Wages (WHW; president, 1970-72); Foreign Authors Society. *Awards, honors:* Bronze Apron from Waitresses for Hourly Wages, 1970, 1972; Golden Passport Award from Foreign Authors Society, 1976, for *If This Is Germany, I Must Be German,* and 1978, for *No Lettuce.*

WRITINGS: The Fury of Love's Sweet and Savage Tenderness, Busswriderres Verlag, 1976; *If This Is Germany, I Must Be German,* Organized Books, 1976; *No Shoulders for Nugent,* Organized Books, 1977; *Spice Is the Variety of Life,* Quiche, Lorraine, & Co., 1978; *No Lettuce* (poems), Big Verse Books, 1978; *Breathy Whispers of Dawn,* Orgone Books, 1979.

WORK IN PROGRESS: More ''gothic literature,'' *The Crime of Glenda's Lust, Forbidden Anxiety,* and *Clutch the Trend;* an autobiographical travelogue, *The Water Tastes Funny.*

SIDELIGHTS: Penderwhistle told *CA:* ''Having spent equal portions of my early adult years in both my father's deli and in Luxembourg, I have been afforded the rare privilege of seeing what few other people my age have seen. My recollections of those years are a collage of pastrami, strange and exotic streets, sesame seed buns, and eerie cafes. How fortunate I was to have grown up in such a diverse environment.

''Of course, I've not been selfish with my life. Most of my books are attempts to share my life with my fellow readers. I'd admit that I experience a bit of envy regarding my readers though. Many were the days when I would lament for the lack of meaningful books to read. Little did I realize, I was under my own nose all the time!

''Well, I will confess that I've made great strides as a writer. It is sometimes difficult for me to reread my early books (even *If This Is Germany, I Must Be German,* for which I still receive countless fan letters), but I bet I've read the last few novels at least ten times each. Hey, I guess I'm my own favorite writer.

''I also see myself expanding my range. I'm starting to drift away from my lonely-waitress-in-Luxembourg-meets-deliowner plots. But I'll still be giving my readers what they want: an alternative to their dull existence.''

AVOCATIONAL INTERESTS: Repairing water pics, weight lifting.

* * *

PENZLER, Otto 1942-
(Irene Adler, Lucy Ferrier, Stephen Gregory, Charles A. Milverton)

PERSONAL: Born July 8, 1942, in Hamburg, Germany; came to United States, 1947; son of Otto (a chemist) and Jeanette (a secretary; maiden name, Kunmann) Penzler; married Evelyn Barbara Byrne (a teacher; divorced). *Education:* Attended University of Michigan. *Home and office:* 129 West 56th St., New York, N.Y. 10019. *Agent:* Sterling Lord Agency, 660 Madison Ave., New York, N.Y. 10021.

CAREER: New York Daily News, New York City, copyboy, 1963, editorial assistant, 1963-64, sportswriter, 1964-69; American Broadcasting Co. (ABC), New York City, senior sports publicist for television, 1969-73, newswriter, 1973, editor of corporate newsletter, ''Happenings,'' 1973-75; writer, 1971—. Founded Mysterious Press, 1976. Lecturer at various universities, 1975—. *Military service:* U.S. Army Reserve, 1964-70. *Member:* Mystery Writers of America (member of board of directors), Writers Guild of America, East, and several ''Sherlock Holmes organizations,'' including Baker Street Irregulars, Priory Scholars, and Scandalous Bohemians. *Awards, honors:* Edgar Allan Poe Award from Mystery Writers of America, 1977, for *Encyclopedia of Mystery and Detection.*

WRITINGS: (Co-editor with Evelyn B. Byrne) *Attacks of Taste,* Gotham Book Mart, 1971; (with Chris Steinbrunner, Marvin Lachman, Francis M. Nevins, Jr., Charles Shibuk; co-editor with Steinbrunner and Shibuk) *Detectionary,* privately printed, 1972, revised edition, Overlook Press, 1977; (with Jim Benagh) *ABC's Wide World of Sports Encyclopedia,* Stadia Sports/Dell, 1973, revised edition, 1974; (author of introduction) Barry Perowne, *Raffles Revisited,* Harper, 1974; (with Steinbrunner) *Encyclopedia of Mystery and Detection,* McGraw, 1976; (editor) *Whodunit? Houdini?: Thirteen Tales of Magic, Murder, Mystery,* Harper, 1976; (contributor) John Ball, editor, *The Mystery Story,* Publisher's Inc./University of California Press, 1976; (contributor) Matthew J. Bruccoli and C. E. Frazer Clark, Jr., editors, *Pages: The World of Books, Writers, and Writing,* Volume I, Gale, 1976; (contributor) Dilys Winn, editor, *Murder Ink,* Workman Publishing, 1977; *The Private Lives of Private Eyes, Spies, Crimefighters, and Other Good Guys,* Grosset, 1977; (editor) *The Great Detectives,* Little, Brown, 1978; (author of introduction) Christianna Brand, *Green for Danger,* Publisher's Inc./University of California Press, 1978.

Juveniles; all published by Troll Associates: *Sports Car Racing,* 1975; *Demolition Derby,* 1975; *Great Stock Car*

Racing, 1975; *Daredevils on Wheels*, 1975; *Danger! White Water*, 1976; *Hang Gliding: Riding the Wind*, 1976; *Hunting the Killer Shark*, 1976; (under pseudonym Irene Adler) *Ballooning: High and Wild*, 1976; (under pseudonym Lucy Ferrier) *Diving the Great Barrier Reef*, 1976; (under pseudonym Stephen Gregory) *Bobsledding: Down the Chute!*, 1976.

Book reviewer and interviewer for *Ellery Queen's Mystery Magazine*, 1975—. Contributor to periodicals, including *People*, *TV Guide*, and *Games*. Contributing editor for *Contemporary Authors*, 1976—.

WORK IN PROGRESS: Editor of *The Encyclopedia of Television*, for McGraw; (with Chris Steinbrunner) *SF: The Encyclopedia of Science Fiction and Fantasy*, for McGraw; editor and creator of *Widow's Pique*, by Harlan Ellison, Isaac Asimov, and others, for Harper; co-editor with Michele B. Slung of *One Clue Beyond*; editor of *The Great Crooks* and *More Great Detectives*; (under pseudonym Charles A. Milverton) *The Family That Preys Together*, an examination of the Charles Manson family, for Grosset.

SIDELIGHTS: Penzler told *CA*: "My professional life is now shrouded in mystery, but it was not always so; it used to be a sporting life. After being sports editor of *Michigan Daily*, the University of Michigan's newspaper, I decided that a career in that field was a lot better than working for a living, so I got a job at *New York Daily News* and soon had my dream fulfilled (a compromise dream, since I had always *really* wanted to be a professional baseball player). While earning forty-two dollars a week, I started to collect rare books with a sophistication that would have dismayed a nine-year old. I collected 'English and American literary first editions and manuscripts,' not fully appreciating the fact that one needed several millions of dollars to do it correctly. The collection reflected my reading tastes: nineteenth-century Victorian novels, English romantic poets, and the best detective fiction, which soon became my specialty. Buying books beyond my means became a habit (literally going two days without food in order to buy a book) and the collection is now universally regarded as one of the finest collections of mystery and detective fiction in private hands. This collection forms the backbone of my research library and is largely responsible for the many books and articles that I've produced which involve this type of literature.

"The affection for detective stories has a sound philosophical base (although I certainly didn't realize it in my early years)—a somewhat conservative and old-fashioned view of right and wrong, good and evil, and modes of behavior. The detective story rewards virtue and punishes sin, with the detective generally serving the God-like role of final judge.

"Mysterious Press was founded because of the belief that the standards of morality established in detective stories will always exist, despite doomsday philosophers, and that mysteries will therefore endure as well. A genuine affection for books—both for their content and as physical objects—inspired the creation of the publishing house. As president of the company, I make all decisions about a book's production and therefore publish the kind of book I would like to see others publish. The press has been successful only because of the cooperation of some of the finest writers in this honorable genre (they gave me the opportunity to publish their books) and because of the many collectors and afficionados who have supported it.

"My working time (generally a minimum of twelve hours a day, six days a week) is divided evenly (more or less) between editing and writing (about mysteries) and Mysterious

Press. It is fair to say that I detest work of any kind and am delighted (and lucky) that none of the things I do can be regarded as anything other than pleasure."

BIOGRAPHICAL/CRITICAL SOURCES: New York Times, April 25, 1976; *Punch*, December 22, 1976; *Book Collectors Market*, March-June, 1977; *New York Daily News*, June 12, 1977; *Books West*, Volume 1, number 8, 1978.

* * *

PERRY, T. Anthony 1938-

PERSONAL: Born December 24, 1938, in Maine; married Sydney Alderman Perry (a teacher); children: Rachel, Sarah, Michael, Danya, Joshua. *Education:* Bowdoin College, B.A. (summa cum laude), 1960; graduate study at University of Bordeaux, 1960-61; Yale University, Ph.D., 1966; postdoctoral study at Hebrew University of Jerusalem, 1969-71. *Office:* Romance Languages U-57, University of Connecticut, Storrs, Conn. 06268.

CAREER: Williams College, Williamstown, Mass., instructor in Romance languages, 1964-65; Smith College, Northampton, Mass., assistant professor of Romance languages, 1965-67; University of Connecticut, Storrs, associate professor of Romance languages, 1967—. *Member:* Modern Language Association of America. *Awards, honors:* Fulbright fellow at University of Bordeaux, 1960; Woodrow Wilson fellow, 1961; National Endowment for the Humanities grant, 1970.

WRITINGS: Art and Meaning in Berceo's "Vida de Santa Oria", Yale University Press, 1968; (editor) Leon Hebreu, *Dialogues d'amour*, University of North Carolina, 1974. Also author of *Erotic Spirituality From Ebreo to John Donne*, and *Montaigne: Structure d'une conscience*, 1978.

* * *

PERSKY, Mordecai 1931-
(Mort Persky)

PERSONAL: Born October 28, 1931, in Savannah, Ga.; son of Nathan (a merchant) and Esther (Surasky) Persky; married Janet P. Holley, October 28, 1953 (divorced, 1962); married Yolanda P. Kelley, 1964 (divorced, 1974); children: Lisa. *Education:* University of South Carolina, A.B., 1953. *Politics:* Democrat. *Religion:* "Believe in God." *Home:* 210 East Walton Pl., Apt. 1E, Chicago, Ill. 60611. *Office:* 919 North Michigan Ave., Chicago, Ill. 60611.

CAREER/WRITINGS—Under name Mort Persky: *Aiken Standard and Review*, Aiken, S.C., sports writer, 1952-53; WAKN-Radio, Aiken, writer and announcer, 1953; *Augusta Herald*, Augusta, Ga., sports writer, 1953-54; *Atlanta Constitution*, Atlanta, Ga., sports writer, 1954-56; *Augusta Herald*, editor and reviewer, 1956-58; *Miami Herald*, Miami, Fla., editor, 1958-62; *New York Herald Tribune*, New York City, Sunday layout editor, 1962-64; *Detroit Free Press*, Detroit, Mich., 1964-70, began as Sunday editor, became assistant managing editor; *Philadelphia Inquirer*, Philadelphia, Pa., assistant to executive editor, 1970-71; *Family Weekly* magazine, New York City, editor-in-chief, 1971-76; *Philadelphia Daily News*, Philadelphia, managing editor, 1976-77; Playboy Enterprises, Inc., Chicago, Ill., editorial director for new publications, 1978—.

* * *

PERSKY, Mort
See PERSKY, Mordecai

PESHKIN, Alan 1931-

PERSONAL: Born January 6, 1931, in Chicago, Ill.; son of Morris and Harriet (Casty) Peshkin; married Maryann Rotberg, August 15, 1953; children: Nancy, David, Julie. *Education:* University of Illinois, B.A., 1952, M.Ed., 1954; University of Chicago, Ph.D., 1962. *Home:* 704 South Prospect St., Champaign, Ill. 61820. *Office:* College of Education, University of Illinois, Urbana, Ill. 60801.

CAREER: High school social studies teacher in Barrington, Ill., 1954-57; University of Chicago, Chicago, Ill., administrator and adviser for Pakistan education project in Karachi and Dacca, 1958-61; University of Wisconsin, Madison, assistant professor of education, 1962-64; Northern Nigeria Teacher Education Project, Maiduguri, coordinator, 1965-66; University of Illinois, Urbana, associate professor, 1967-69, professor of comparative education, 1969—, head of department of educational policy studies, 1975—, director of African studies, 1969-71. *Member:* Comparative Education Society, Council on Anthropology and Education. *Awards, honors:* Guggenheim fellowship, 1973-74.

WRITINGS: The Kanuri Schoolchildren: Education and Social Mobilization in Nigeria, Holt, 1972; *Growing Up American: Schooling and the Survival of Community,* University of Chicago Press, 1978. Contributor to learned journals.

WORK IN PROGRESS: The Imperfect Union: School Consolidation and Community Conflict.

SIDELIGHTS: Peshkin writes: "My work is basically ethnographic in nature. It focuses on the relationship between school and community in different settings and considers particularly the non-educative (that is, communal) functions of schooling."

*   *   *

PETERS, Ted
See PETERS, Theodore F(rank)

*   *   *

PETERS, Theodore F(rank) 1941-
(Ted Peters)

PERSONAL: Born April 3, 1941, in Wayne, Mich.; son of Theodore F. (an engineer) and Lilian (Tesch) Peters; married Jenny Raidt; children: Paul, Kathy Kim, Elizabeth. *Education:* Michigan State University, B.A., 1963; Trinity Lutheran Seminary, Columbus, Ohio, M.Div., 1967; further graduate study at University of Heidelberg, 1967-68; University of Chicago, M.A., 1970, Ph.D., 1973. *Home and office:* Pacific Lutheran Theological Seminary, 2770 Marin Ave., Berkeley, Calif. 94708.

CAREER: Ordained Lutheran minister, 1970; pastor of Lutheran church in Chicago, Ill., 1970-72; Newberry College, Newberry, S.C., assistant professor of religion and philosophy, 1972-76; Loyola University, New Orleans, La., associate professor of religious studies, 1976-78; Pacific Lutheran Theological Seminary, Berkeley, Calif., associate professor of systematic theology, 1978—. Pastor of Lutheran churches in Newberry, S.C., 1973-74, Diamond Point, N.Y., summers, 1975—, and New Orleans, La., 1976-77. Adjunct instructor at Lutheran Theological Southern Seminary, 1973-75, and Notre Dame School of Theology (New Orleans, La.), 1977; associate professor at Graduate Theological Union, 1978—; lecturer at colleges and seminaries; guest on television and radio programs.

MEMBER: World Future Society, American Academy of Religion, Association of Baptist Professors of Religion, College Theology Society, South Carolina Society for Philosophy (president, 1975-76). *Awards, honors:* National Endowment for the Humanities grant, summer, 1975.

WRITINGS—All under name Ted Peters: *UFOs: God's Chariots?—Flying Saucers in Politics, Science, and Religion,* John Knox, 1977; *Futures: Human and Divine,* John Knox, 1978; *Theology in the Twentieth Century: An Ecumenical Survey,* Augsburg, in press. Contributor of more than thirty articles and reviews to theology journals and religious magazines.

WORK IN PROGRESS—Under name Ted Peters: *The Christian Doctrine of Eschatology,* publication by John Knox expected in 1981.

SIDELIGHTS: Peters commented: "The surface of modern Western culture is painted over with the hues of natural science, confidence in technology, and secular self-understanding. But hidden deep within there is a hollowness or emptiness, a yearning for a secure and transcendent ground of meaning and value. Unable to retrieve the ancient roots of the religious past that once gave life its depth, we moderns contend that we have outgrown it. But have we? We cast about looking in vain for substitutes—looking for idols—in whom we can rest our faith that our way of life has some ultimate value and meaning.

"Unidentified Flying Objects, surprisingly, present us with an extreme but valid example of such idols. Believed by many to have the qualities of transcendence—i.e., believed to be machines which have traversed the infinite distances of outer space and are piloted by creatures of such advanced intelligence that they have achieved immortality through medical science—they represent supra-terrestrial technology coming to save earthbound humanity from self-destruction. This is the theme of *UFOs: God's Chariots?*

"In broader academic and university circles, it is not the UFO but rather scientific humanism that has become the idol. Scientific futurists also fear the self-destruction of humanity feared by the UFO cultists, but the futurists specify the mode of self-destruction, i.e., through nuclear holocaust, pollution poisoning, starvation due to economic collapse. What will save us they firmly believe is the creative potential of man; man, the same creature who created the technological hazards in the first place. This problem is analyzed in *Futures: Human and Divine.*

"There is only one true foundation for value and confidence in the meaningfulness of our way of life, and that is God. We can best face the truth of our predicament, namely, that the root of the problem lies within *us,* when we face it in the context of divine forgiveness and the promise of ultimate redemption. This makes idols unnecessary. My writing aims at bringing this ancient Christian message of God's forgiving love to bear on the contemporary struggle to make sense out of human experience."

*   *   *

PHARES, Donald 1942-

PERSONAL: Born October 10, 1942, in Malden, Mass.; son of E. Carroll and Violet (Margeson) Phares; children: Scott, Mark, Sean. *Education:* Northeastern University, A.B. (honors), 1965; Syracuse University, M.A., 1967, Ph.D., 1970. *Residence:* St. Louis, Mo. *Office:* Department of Economics, University of Missouri, St. Louis, Mo. 63121.

CAREER: Le Moyne College, Syracuse, N.Y., instructor in statistics, 1968-69; University of Missouri, St. Louis, assistant professor, 1969-73, associate professor of economics, 1973—, fellow of Center for Metropolitan Studies, 1969—. Consultant to Standard & Poor's Corp., Urban Institute, Ford Foundation, and RAND Corp. *Member:* American Economic Association, American Real Estate and Urban Economics Association, Association for Evolutionary Economics, Association for the Study of the Grants Economy, National Tax Association, Public Choice Society, Western Regional Science Association. *Awards, honors:* Ford Foundation grant, 1973-75.

WRITINGS: (With John Callahan and William Wilken) *Reform, Relief, Redistribution,* Massachusetts Teachers Association, 1973; *State-Local Tax Equity: An Empirical Analysis of the Fifty States,* Lexington Books, 1973; (with James Little and Hugh O. Nourse) *The Neighborhood Succession Process,* Office of Policy Development and Research, U.S. Department of Housing and Urban Development, 1975; (with David Greytak and Elaine Morley) *Municipal Output and Performance in New York City,* Lexington Books, 1976; *A Decent Home and Environment: Housing Urban America,* Ballinger, 1977.

Contributor: Kenneth Bolding and other editors, *Transfers in an Urbanized Economy,* Wadsworth, 1973; Hugh O. Nourse, editor, *The Effect of Public Policy on Housing Markets,* Heath, 1973; *Substate Regionalism and the Federal System,* Volume IV: *Governmental Functions and Processes: Local and Areawide,* U.S. Advisory Commission on Intergovernmental Relations, 1974; *The Contemporary Neighborhood Succession Process,* Institute for Urban and Regional Studies, Washington University (St. Louis, Mo.), 1975; Richard Rachin and Eugene Czajkoski, editors, *Drug Abuse Control: Administration and Politics,* Lexington Books, 1975; Harold Rose and Gary Gappert, editors, *The Social Economy of Cities,* Sage Publications, 1975. Contributor of about fifteen articles to scholarly journals. Co-editor of *Journal of the American Real Estate and Urban Economic Association,* June, 1973.

WORK IN PROGRESS: Revising *State-Local Tax Equity,* publication by Lexington Books expected in 1979; *Heroin, Society, and Public Policy: The Infernal Triangle.*

* * *

PHILLIPS, Leon
See GERSON, Noel Bertram

* * *

PIANO, Celeste
See LYKIARD, Alexis (Constantine)

* * *

PICKARD, Tom 1946-

PERSONAL: Born in 1946, in Newcastle-upon-Tyne, Northumberland England; married wife, Constance; children: one son, one daughter. *Education:* Attended secondary schools in Newcastle-upon-Tyne, England.

CAREER: Poet, novelist, and playwright. Worked in Newcastle-upon-Tyne, England, for a seed merchant, 1962-63, for a construction company, 1963, and for a wine merchant, 1964; Mordern Tower Book Room, Newcastle-upon-Tyne, co-founder and manager, 1963-72; Ultima Thule Bookshop, Newcastle-upon-Tyne, co-founder and manager, 1969-73. *Awards, honors:* Northern Arts Minor Award, 1965; Arts Council grant, 1969, 1973.

WRITINGS: High on the Walls (poetry), Fulcrum Press, 1967, Horizon Press, 1968; *New Human Unisphere* (poetry), Ultima Thule Bookshop, 1969; *An Armpit of Lice* (poetry), Fulcrum Press, 1970; *The Order of Chance* (poetry), Fulcrum Press, 1971; (editor) Tony Jackson, *The Lesser Known Shagg,* Ultima Thule Bookshop, 1971; *Guttersnipe* (novel), City Lights Books, 1971; *Dancing Under Fire* (poetry), Middle Earth Books, 1973. Also author of "Squire" (television play), 1974.

SIDELIGHTS: Tom Pickard's poetry is generally considered regional in its portrayal of life in Newcastle-upon-Tyne. John Horder praised his highly individual style; Alan Brownjohn focused on Pickard's "peculiar mixture of whimsy, emotional violence and modish regionalism"; and Douglas Dunn pointed to "the pristine excellence" of Pickard's poems.

BIOGRAPHICAL/CRITICAL SOURCES: Times Literary Supplement, July 13, 1967; *Spectator,* October 27, 1967; *New Statesman,* June 18, 1971; *Encounter,* January, 1972.*

* * *

PICKENS, Robert S. 1900(?)-1978

OBITUARY NOTICE: Born c. 1900 in Lenoir, N.C.; died November 12, 1978, near Ashburn, Va. Journalist, farmer, and author of a book on the political atmosphere in Asia during the 1930's. As a newspaperman Pickens was affiliated with several papers, including the *Atlanta Constitution* and the *Chicago Tribune.* He also covered the Hoover administration for the Associated Press. During the middle thirties Pickens moved to a farm in Loudoun County, Va., where he was reputed to have grown prize-winning lilies. Obituaries and other sources: *New York Times,* November 13, 1978; *Washington Post,* November 14, 1978.

* * *

PICKER, Fred 1927-

PERSONAL: Born February 28, 1927, in New York, N.Y.; son of Harold David (in the wine business) and Edna (a clothing designer; maiden name, Marqusee) Picker. *Education:* Attended University of Vermont, 1951. *Home and office address:* Dummerston, Vt. 05346.

CAREER: Fromm & Sichel, Inc., New York, N.Y., in sales, 1952-55; Foothills Realty, New City, N.Y., builder, 1955-70; Zone VI Studios (photography studios), White Plains, N.Y., photographer, 1970-74, also director of Zone VI Workshop; free-lance writer and photographer, 1974—. Member of board of directors of Vermont Council on the Arts. Consultant to Polaroid Corp., 1976—. *Military service:* U.S. Army Air Forces, 1945-47.

*WRITINGS—*All illustrated with own photographs: *Rapa Nui (Easter Island),* Paddington Press, 1973; *Zone VI Workshop,* Amphoto, 1973; *The Fine Print,* Amphoto, 1975; *The Iceland Portfolio* (foreword by Ben Maddow), Amphoto, 1976. Contributor to magazines. Author of *Zone VI Newsletter.*

WORK IN PROGRESS: The Vision of Robert Frost.

AVOCATIONAL INTERESTS: Sailing, skiing (former instructor), gardening, horses, travel (including Easter Island and Iceland).

* * *

PIEKALKIEWICZ, Jaroslaw A. 1926-

PERSONAL: Born July 24, 1926, in Poznan, Poland; son of

Wlodzimierz (an electrical engineer) and Kazimiera (Tolloczko) Piekalkiewicz; married Maura Brennan, July 13, 1957; children: Ellen Zofia, Andrew Michael. *Education:* Trinity College, Dublin, B.A. (honors), 1958; Indiana University, Ph.D., 1963. *Politics:* Democrat. *Home:* 1013 West 20th St., Lawrence, Kan. 66044. *Office:* Department of Political Science, University of Kansas, Lawrence, Kan. 66045.

CAREER: Indiana University, Bloomington, lecturer in government, 1963; University of Kansas, Lawrence, assistant professor, 1963-68, associate professor, 1968-73, professor of political science and Slavic and Soviet studies, 1973—, assistant director of Slavic and Soviet area, 1966-67, director of graduate studies in political science, 1973-74, resident director of exchange program with Poznan, Poland, 1971-72. Senior researcher at Czechoslovak Academy of Sciences, 1968-69, and University of Warsaw, 1975-76. *Military service:* Polish Underground Army, 1941-45, prisoner of war in Germany, 1944-45; received Cross of Valor. British Army, Polish Second Corps, 1945-48; became sergeant.

MEMBER: American Political Science Association, American Association for the Advancement of Slavic Studies, American Association of University Professors, Central Slavic Conference, Kansas Political Science Association, Trinity College Association. *Awards, honors:* International Exchanges and Research Board fellowship, 1975-76; Fulbright-Hays fellowship, 1975-76.

WRITINGS: (Contributor) W. W. Wagner, editor, *Polish Law Throughout the Ages,* Hoover Institution Press, 1970; (editor with Edward Czerwinski) *The Soviet Invasion of Czechoslovakia: Its Effects on Eastern Europe,* Praeger, 1972; *Public Opinion Polling in Czechoslovakia, 1968-69: An Analysis of Surveys Conducted During the Dubcek Era,* Praeger, 1972; *Communist Local Government: A Study of Poland,* Ohio University Press, 1975; (contributor) George W. Simmonds, editor, *Nationalism in the U.S.S.R. and Eastern Europe in the Era of Brezhnev and Kosygin,* University of Detroit Press, 1977. Also editor of *The New Social Stratification and Political Power in East-Central Europe,* and co-author of *The Politics of Ideocracy. Contributor to East European studies journals.*

SIDELIGHTS: Piekalkiewicz has traveled to Western and Eastern Europe often since 1961, and speaks Polish, Czech, Slovak, Russian, French, German, and Italian. He writes: "My interests are the politics of East-Central Europe, communist political systems, and ideocracies."

*   *   *

PINTAURO, Joseph 1930-

PERSONAL: Born November 22, 1930, in New York; son of Agnello (a carpenter) and Carmela (Yovino) Pintauro. *Education:* Manhattan College, B.B.A., 1953; Fordham University, M.A., 1954; further graduate study at Niagara University, 1954-58; St. Jerome's College, earned B.A. degree. *Politics:* Democrat. *Home address:* P.O. Box 531, Sag Harbor, N.Y. 11963. *Agent:* Curtis Brown Ltd., 575 Madison Ave., New York, N.Y. 10022. *Office:* 55 Morton St., New York, N.Y. 10014.

CAREER: Ordained Roman Catholic priest, 1958; pastor of Roman Catholic churches until 1966; laicized in 1966; Young & Rubicam (advertising agency), New York, N.Y., writer, 1968-75; free-lance writer, 1975—; actor, 1975—. Lecturer. *Member:* Broadcast Music, Inc.

WRITINGS: The Trilogy of Belief, Harper, Volume I: *To Believe in God,* 1968, Volume II: *To Believe in Man,* 1970,

Volume III: *To Believe in Things,* 1971; *One Circus, Three Rings, Forever and Ever Hooray!,* Harper, 1969; *The Rainbow Box: A Book for Each Season and a Peace Poster,* Volume I: *A Box of Sun: Summer,* Volume II: *The Peace Box: Winter,* Volume III: *The Rabbit Box: Spring,* Volume IV: *The Magic Box: Autumn,* Harper, 1970; *Kites at Empty Airports,* Perennial Education, 1972; *Earthmass,* Harper, 1973.

Author of plays, "Cacciatore" (three one-acts), "The Orchid Man and the Black Swan" (three-act), first produced at Circle Repertory Workshop, and "The Hunt of the Unicorn," first produced at Circle Repertory Workshop. Also author of films.

WORK IN PROGRESS: Poems; a novel for Simon & Schuster tentatively entitled *Cold Hands.*

SIDELIGHTS: Pintauro wrote "Wallace Stevens is a strong influence. I am very interested in primal psychology. My characters hammer at each other till all emotions are spent. In the crossover from religion to reality, I became fascinated by romance, the picture of life we create in our minds, against the backdrop of life as it is outside us—sexuality, roles, tricks of the mind that cast us in these private dramas. I like to act (Bergoff and Warren Robertson coached me) and dance (Joffrey). I dream of directing one of my films."

AVOCATIONAL INTERESTS: The street people of New York, Italian-Americans, Italy, film, songwriting, playing the guitar and singing original poems, reading.

*   *   *

PIPER, Roger
See FISHER, John (Oswald Hamilton)

*   *   *

PIZZEY, Erin 1939-

PERSONAL: Born February 19, 1939, in Tsingtao, China; separated; children: Ueo, Amos. *Education:* Educated in convent schools. *Politics:* "Apolitical." *Home:* 397 Goldhawk Rd., London W.6, England. *Agent:* Andrew Nurnberg, Clerkenwell House, 45-47 Clerkenwell Green, London EC1R 0HT, England. *Office:* 369 Chiswick High Rd., London W.4, England.

CAREER: Founder and chairwoman of Chiswick Women's Aid, London, England.

WRITINGS: Scream Quietly or the Neighbours Will Hear, Penguin, 1974. Also author of *Infernal Child,* Gollancz. Contributor to magazines.

WORK IN PROGRESS: The Watershed, "about the aftermath of the women's liberation movement in the lives of women."

SIDELIGHTS: Erin Pizzey comments: "I am concerned about the need to understand human relationships. I work mostly with violent relationships and the needs of the women, children, and men which have to be met. All my writing reflects this search and helps me think ahead to how we can see the family in the future."

*   *   *

PLAIN, Belva 1919(?)-

PERSONAL: Married Irving Plain (a physician); children: three. *Education:* Graduated from Barnard College. *Residence:* South Orange, N.J. *Agent:* Dorothy Olding, Harold Ober Associates, Inc., 40 East 49th St., New York, N.Y. 10017.

CAREER: Writer.

WRITINGS: Evergreen (novel; Literary Guild selection), Delacorte, 1978. Contributor of several dozen short stories to periodicals, including *McCall's, Good Housekeeping, Redbook,* and *Cosmopolitan.*

WORK IN PROGRESS: A novel, "a family story, not ethnic, that takes place in England and New York."

SIDELIGHTS: Plain writes: "The seed of *Evergreen* was planted when my own nice suburban middle-class children first thought of asking who their forebears were. But it was not until my children began presenting me with grandchildren that their questions merged in my mind with the whole mystique of the past and finally took shape in this, my first novel.

"I had always been curious about my own grandmother, who came here from Europe alone at the age of sixteen. Such courage! I think of her still saying a final goodbye and sailing toward an unknown world so long ago. She never saw her people again.

"Of course, all that is a common American adventure: the loneliness, the struggles and failures—and sometimes, the rise to shining affluence. In such ways *Evergreen* is everybody's story whether he be of Irish, Italian, Polish, or any other stock. Yet there is a special Jewish aspect to the book, too. I was and am weary of reading the same old story, told by Jewish writers, of the same old stereotypes: the possessive mothers, the worn-out fathers and all the rest of the neurotic, rebellious, unhappy, self-hating tribe. I admit that I wanted to write a *different* novel about Jews, and a truer one."

BIOGRAPHICAL/CRITICAL SOURCES: New York Times Book Review, July 30, 1978.*

* * *

PODENDORF, Illa E.

EDUCATION: Drake University, B.S., 1934, University of Iowa, M.S., 1942. *Residence:* Chicago, Ill.

CAREER: University of Chicago Laboratory School, Chicago, Ill., chairman of science department, beginning 1954; author of nonfiction science books for children. Has lectured extensively on teaching science. *Member:* American Association for the Advancement of Science, National Science Teachers Association, Central Association of Science and Math Teachers, Council of Elementary Science Instructors.

WRITINGS—"True Book" series; all published by Childrens Press, except as indicated: *The True Book of Science Experiments,* illustrations by Mary Salem, 1954; . . . *Pebbles and Shells,* illustrations by Mary Gehr, 1954, published as *My Easy-to-Read True Book of Pebbles and Shells,* Grosset, 1960; . . . *Insects,* illustrations by Chauncey Maltman, 1954; . . . *Trees,* illustrations by Richard Gates, 1954, published as *My Easy-to-Read True Book of Trees,* Grosset, 1960; . . . *Pets,* illustrations by Bill Armstrong, 1954, published as *My Easy-to-Read True Book of Pets,* Grosset, 1960; . . . *Animal Babies,* illustrations by Pauline Adams, 1955; . . . *Seasons,* illustrations by Gehr, 1955; . . . *Sounds We Hear,* illustrations by Maltman, 1955; . . . *Weeds and Wild Flowers,* illustrations by Gehr, 1955; . . . *Animals of the Sea and Shore,* illustrations by Maltman, 1956, revised edition, 1970; . . . *More Science Experiments,* illustrations by Maltman, 1956; . . . *Rocks and Minerals,* illustrations by George Rhoads, 1958, published as *My Easy-to-Read True Book of Rocks and Minerals,* Grosset, 1959; . . . *Space,* illustrations by Robert Borja, 1959, published as *My Easy-*

to-Read Book of Space, Grosset, 1960; . . . *Jungles,* illustrations by Katherine Grace, 1959; . . . *Plant Experiments,* illustrations by B. Armstrong, 1960; . . . *Animal Homes,* illustrations by John Hawkinson, 1960; . . . *Weather Experiments,* illustrations by Felix Palm, 1961; . . . *Magnets and Electricity,* illustrations by Borja, 1961; . . . *Spiders,* illustrations by Betsy Warren, 1962; . . . *Energy,* illustrations by George Wilde, 1963, revised edition, 1971.

Other writings; all published by Childrens Press, except as noted: (Editor) Margaret R. Friskey, *Johnny and the Monarch,* 1946; (with Bertha M. Parker) *Animal World,* illustrations by Gregory Orloff, Row, Peterson, 1949; (with Parker) *The Plant World,* illustrations by Louise Fulton, Row, Peterson, 1949; (with Parker) *Domesticated Plants,* illustrations by Arnold W. Ryan, Row, Peterson, 1959; *101 Science Experiments,* illustrations by Borja, 1960; *Discovering Science on Your Own,* illustrations by Borja, 1962; *Animals and More Animals,* illustrations by Elizabeth Rice, 1970; *Toby on the Move,* illustrations by Roger Herrington, 1970; *Food Is for Eating,* illustrations by Margrit Fiddle, 1970; *Many Is How Many?,* illustrations by Jack Haesly, 1970; *Things Are Made to Move,* illustrations by Jane Ike, 1970; *Things Are Alike and Different,* illustrations by J. Hawkinson, 1970; *Sounds All About,* illustrations by Darrell Wiskur, 1970; *Shapes: Sides, Curves, and Corners,* illustrations by Frank Rakoncay, 1970.

Predicting With Plants, illustrations by Tom Dunnington, 1971; *Shadows and More Shadows,* illustrations by D. Wiskur, 1971; *Magnets,* illustrations by Jim Temple, 1971; *Living Things Change,* illustrations by D. Wiskur, 1971; *How Big Is a Stick?,* illustrations by Richard Mlodock, 1971; *Every Day Is Earth Day,* illustrations by Hawkinson, 1971; *Color,* illustrations by Wayne Stuart, 1971; *Who, What, and When,* illustrations by Sharon Elzaurdia, 1971; *Change and Time,* illustrations by Frances Eckart, 1971; *Tools for Observing,* illustrations by Donald Charles, 1971; *Touching for Telling,* illustrations by Florence Frederick, 1971; *Things to Do With Water,* illustrations by Larry Winbor, 1971; *Plant and Animal Ways,* Standard Educational Corp., 1974.*

* * *

POHLE, Robert W(arren), Jr. 1949-
(James Farnsworth, Devon Lee, E. F. Miller)

PERSONAL: Surname is pronounced *Poe*-lee; born July 23, 1949, in Ridley Park, Pa.; son of Robert Warren Pohle (an automobile dealer) and Mae (a writer; maiden name, Bonsall-Moore) Pohle McKinley; married Rebecca Murray Donaldy (an actress and writer), December 28, 1974. *Education:* Attended Southwark School, 1967-68, and School of Visual Arts, New York, N.Y., 1968-71, 1975. *Politics:* Democrat. *Home and office:* 230 East Park Ave., #26, Lake Wales, Fla. 33853.

CAREER: Book Caravan, Lake Wales, Fla., owner, 1972-73, 1977—. Also worked as newspaper photographer, circus clown, teacher of handicapped children, film extra, and professional puppeteer. Guest lecturer at Lake Wales Depot Museum. *Member:* International Gypsy Lore Society, Sherlock Holmes Society of London, Buddhist Society of London.

WRITINGS: (With D. C. Hart) *Sherlock Holmes on the Screen: The Motion Picture Adventures of the World's Most Popular Detective,* A. S. Barnes, 1977; *Doom of Three Planets* (science fiction novel), Manor, 1978; (with wife, Rebecca D. Pohle and mother, Mae McKinley; under pseudonym E. F. Miller) *Nine Lives* (Irish Civil war novel),

Manor, 1978; (under pseudonym James Farnsworth) *Lash of Vengeance* (western novel), Manor, 1978; (with McKinley; under pseudonym James Farnsworth) *The Fledgling Outlaw* (western novel), Manor, 1978; *Last Rider From Lonesome Canyon* (western novel), Manor, in press; (with R. D. Pohle; under pseudonym Devon Lee) *Dark Intrigue* (romantic novel), Kim/MacFadden, in press. Contributor to British, Irish, and American magazines, including *Baker Street Miscellanea, Modern Maturity,* and *Fling,* and newspapers.

WORK IN PROGRESS: Another book; research on Thomas Edison and on actor Christopher Lee.

SIDELIGHTS: Pohle writes: "I traveled widely in the British Isles, 1971-73, looking for gypsies, megaliths, and other survivals of ancient times. I dabble in Romani, Irish Gaelic, and Spanish. My lifelong interest in Ireland dates back to stories of my grandfather and early childhood.

"I am especially interested in occult lore, including that concerning Arthurian Britain and the Irish *Sidhe* (Fairies). I am fascinated with the folk traditions that lurk behind surface appearances. Geneology also intrigues me, and I trace a remote family relationship to King Edmund II of England. Mysticism fascinates me, and I ransack the works of J. Krishnamurti, G. I. Gurdjieff, H. P. Blavatsky, D. T. Suzuki, and Idries Shah with enthusiasm if not complete belief. I am also interested in the American past, particularly the Jacksonian period. I avidly read Mark Twain, Ernest Haycox, and Edgar Rice Burroughs, and my novels have been heavily influenced by the latter two. Among film directors, my favorites include Jean Renoir, John Ford, and Roy William Neill. My model as a film historian is my former teacher William K. Everson.

"I write because, as Anne Murray sings in 'Children of My Mind,' it is 'the thing that makes me whole.' If anything I have written enables a reader to find a few minutes release from his daily troubles, then I feel quite content.

"With my sisters Terry and Mimi (also a writer) I spent my childhood creating imaginary civilizations a la the Brontes, and was composing fiction before I could read, let alone write!"

AVOCATIONAL INTERESTS: Sitting in the sun, political, theological, and literary arguments, painting, drawing, cartooning, chess, collecting books (especially on Sherlock Holmes, films, and history).

* * *

POLANYI, Michael 1891-1976

PERSONAL: Born March 12, 1891, in Budapest, Hungary; son of Michael (a civil engineer) and Cecile (Wohl) Polanyi; married Magda Elizabeth Kemeny (a chemical engineer), February, 1921; children: Michael George, John Charles. *Education:* University of Budapest, M.D., 1915; University of Berlin, D.Sc., 1919. *Politics:* Conservative. *Religion:* Church of England. *Home:* 22 Upland Park Rd., Oxford, England. *Office:* Merton College, Oxford, England.

CAREER: Lecturer in physico-chemistry at Technical University, Karlsruhe, Germany; University of Berlin, Berlin, Germany, assistant professor, 1923; Kaiser Wilhelm Institute for Physical Chemistry under Haber, Berlin-Dahlem, department head, 1923; University of Manchester, Manchester, England, professor of physical chemistry, 1932-48, professor of social sciences, 1948-58; Oxford University, Merton College, Oxford, England, senior research fellow in philosophy, 1958-61; writer, 1961-76. Gifford Lecturer at University of Aberdeen, 1951-52. Member of Centre de la

Recherche Scientific in Paris. Life member of Kaiser Wilhelm Gesellschaft. *Awards, honors:* Nine honorary degrees; Lecomte du Nouy Award, 1959; Nuffield Gold Medal from Royal Society of Medicine, 1970.

WRITINGS: Atomic Reactions, William & Norgate, 1932; *U.S.S.R. Economics,* Manchester University Press, 1936; *The Rights and Duties of Science,* Manchester School, 1939; *Contempt of Freedom,* Watts & Co., 1940; *Full Employment and Free Trade,* Cambridge University Press, 1945; *Science, Faith, and Society,* Oxford University Press, 1946; *Unemployment and Money* (handbook for film), Gaumont British, 1948.

The Logic of Liberty, University of Chicago Press, 1951; *Beauty, Elegance, and Reality in Science,* Butterworth & Co., 1957; *Personal Knowledge,* University of Chicago Press, 1958; *The Study of Man,* University of Chicago Press, 1959; *Beyond Nihilism,* Cambridge University Press, 1960; *The Tacit Dimension,* Doubleday, 1966; *Knowing and Being,* University of Chicago Press, 1969; *Meaning,* University of Chicago Press, 1975.

Author of film "Full Employment and Money," Gaumont British, 1950. Contributor to scholarly and popular magazines in England, Germany, and the United States, including *Nation, New Statesman,* and *Encounter.*

SIDELIGHTS: Magda Polanyi writes that it was the invitation to deliver the Gifford Lectures in Aberdeen that changed her husband's direction from strictly scientific work to the study of philosophy, which remained his only interest until his death.

BIOGRAPHICAL/CRITICAL SOURCES: Essays to Michael Polanyi on His Seventieth Birthday, Routledge & Kegan Paul, 1961; Richard Gelwick, *Michael Polanyi,* Oxford University Press, 1977.

(Died February 22, 1976)

[Sketch verified by wife, Magda Polanyi]

* * *

POLITZER, Heinz 1910-1978

OBITUARY NOTICE—See index for *CA* sketch: Born December 31, 1910, in Vienna, Austria; died July 30, 1978. Educator, editor, translator, and author. Politzer is best known for his work, *Franz Kafka: Parable and Paradox,* to which he devoted over thirty years of research. In addition, he edited two other works on Kafka, both entitled *Franz Kafka.* Politzer's books on German and Austrian literature include *Martin Buber, Humanist and Teacher.* He also wrote poetry. Obituaries and other sources: *Directory of American Scholars,* Volume III: *Foreign Languages, Linguistics, and Philology,* 6th edition, Bowker, 1974; *The Writers Directory, 1976-78,* St. Martin's, 1976; *New York Times,* August 4, 1978.

* * *

POLLACK, Peter 1911-1978

PERSONAL: Born in Wing, N.D., March 21, 1911. *Education:* Attended Art Institute of Chicago and Bauhaus (now Institute of Design). *Home:* 1001 Bayou Pl., Sarasota, Fla. 33579.

CAREER: Photographer, lecturer, and writer. South Side Community Art Center, Chicago, Ill., director, 1939-42; Art Institute of Chicago, Chicago, curator of photography, 1945-57; director of American Federation of Arts, 1962-64; honorary curator of photography of Worcester Art Museum, 1964-

78; W. J. Sloane, New York, N.Y., director of art, 1965-70; director of photography, Harry N. Abrams, Inc., 1970-78. Photographs exhibited at Art Institute of Chicago, Worcester Art Museum, and Whitney Museum of American Art. Former field director of American Red Cross in Iran and Egypt.

WRITINGS: The Picture History of Photography From the Earliest Beginnings To the Present Day, Abrams, 1958, revised edition, 1970; *Understanding Primitive Art: Sula's Zoo,* Abrams, 1968; *Fletcher Martin: A Thirty Year Retrospective,* [Binghamton, N.Y.], 1968; *Alfred Maurer and the Fauves: The Lost Years Rediscovered,* [New York, N.Y.], 1973. Editor of series of facsimile editions, Amphoto Press, 1971-78.

OBITUARIES: New York Times, May 16, 1978.*

(Died May 13, 1978, in Sarasota, Fla.)

* * *

POLSENO, Jo

EDUCATION: Whitney Art School, A.F.A.; also attended Ecole des Beaux Arts, Marseilles, France.

CAREER: Author and illustrator of children's books.

WRITINGS—All self-illustrated: *Secrets of Redding Glen: The Natural History of a Wooded Valley,* Golden Press, 1973; *Secrets of a Cypress Swamp: The Natural History of Okefenokee,* Golden Press, 1976; *This Hawk Belongs to Me,* McKay, 1976.

Illustrator: Cora Cheney, *Plantation Doll,* Holt, 1955; Mrs. Mickey Klar Marks, *Fine Eggs and Fancy Chickens,* Holt, 1956; Lorena A. Hickok, *Story of Helen Keller,* Grosset, 1958; Alf Evers, *Open the Door,* F. Watts, 1960; Elizabeth C. Walton, *Treasure in the Sand,* Lothrop, 1960; Joy Lonergan, *When My Father Was a Little Boy,* F. Watts, 1961; William Wise, *The House with the Red Roof,* Putnam, 1961; Teri Martini, *What a Frog Can Do,* Reilly & Lee, 1962; Mark Twain, *The Adventures of Tom Sawyer,* Grosset, 1963; Anita Klever, *Stories Jesus Told,* Rand McNally, 1967; Marian Potter, *Copperfield Summer,* Follett, 1967; Scott Corbett, *Cop's Kid,* Little, Brown, 1968; Elizabeth P. Kerby, *The Conquistadors,* Putnam, 1969; Clyde R. Bulla, *New Boy in Dublin: A Story of Ireland,* Crowell, 1969; Roland Bertol, *Charles Drew,* Crowell, 1970; Berniece Freschet, *The Flight of the Snow Goose,* Crown, 1970; Lucy Salamanca, *Lost in the Everglades,* Golden Press, 1971; Roma Gans, *Bird Talk,* Crowell, 1971; Victoria Cox, *Nature's Flying Janitor,* Golden Press, 1974; Alice Thompson Gilbreath, *Nature's Squirt Guns, Bubble Pipes, and Fireworks: Geysers, Hot Springs, and Volcanoes,* McKay, 1977.

SIDELIGHTS: Secrets of a Cypress Swamp drew praise from a *Publishers Weekly* reviewer who wrote: "Jo Polseno, a gifted painter, adds to his laurels with this exploration of the flora and fauna of an exotic part of the world.... The exquisite paintings make even a swamp rat attractive.... Here is a worthy followup to the artist's previous success, 'Secrets of Redding Glen.'" Susan Sprague added in *School Library Journal:* "Polseno sustains a near poetic mood throughout. Lovely to read and look at."

BIOGRAPHICAL/CRITICAL SOURCES: Publishers Weekly, July 19, 1976; *School Library Journal,* November, 1976.*

PORISS, Martin 1948-

PERSONAL: Born March 29, 1948, in Hartford, Conn.; son of Edward I. (a dentist) and Beatrice (a piano teacher; maiden name, Glazer) Poriss. *Education:* Harvard University, A.B., 1970. *Home:* 110 Beverly Dr., Ben Lomond, Calif. 95005. *Agent:* Edward J. Acton, Inc., 17 Grove St., New York, N.Y. 10014. *Office address:* P.O. Box 5, Ben Lomond, Calif. 95005.

CAREER: Consumer reporter on "Today Show," National Broadcasting Co.; writer. Also involved in real estate and investment work.

WRITINGS: How to Live Cheap But Good, McGraw, 1971; *The Unhandywoman's Fix-It Book,* Dell, 1973. Author of "Living Cheap But Good," a column syndicated by *Chicago Tribune,* 1973.

WORK IN PROGRESS: How to Get Your Kid Ahead, on education; *How to Make Your Nest-Egg Hatch;* "American," a screenplay.

* * *

PORLOCK, Martin
See MacDONALD, Philip

* * *

PORTER, Judith D(eborah) R(evitch) 1940-

PERSONAL: Born March 26, 1940, in Philadelphia, Pa.; daughter of Eugene (a physician) and Esther (Tulchinsky) Revitch; married Gerald Joseph Porter (a college professor), June 26, 1960; children: Daniel, Rebecca, Michael. *Education:* Attended Vassar College, 1958-60; Cornell University, B.A., 1962, M.A., 1963; Harvard University, Ph.D., 1966. *Religion:* Jewish. *Home:* 161 Whitemarsh Rd., Ardmore, Pa. 19003. *Office:* Department of Sociology, Bryn Mawr College, Bryn Mawr, Pa. 19010.

CAREER: Bryn Mawr College, Bryn Mawr, Pa., lecturer, 1966-67, assistant professor, 1967-73, associate professor of sociology, 1973—. Member of Haverford Township Democratic Committee, 1976—. *Member:* American Sociological Association, Society for the Scientific Study of Religion, Society for the Study of Social Issues, Eastern Sociological Association, Phi Beta Kappa, Phi Kappa Phi. *Awards, honors:* Ford Foundation fellowship, 1973-74.

WRITINGS: Black Child, White Child: The Development of Racial Attitudes, Harvard University Press, 1971. Contributor to sociology journals. Member of editorial board of *Sociological Inquiry.*

WORK IN PROGRESS: A cross-cultural study of sex role socialization; a study of psychosocial effects of skin diseases.

SIDELIGHTS: Judith Porter writes: "My field is race relations, specifically the development of racial attitudes and the effect of prejudice on self-esteem. Travels in Africa and residence in South Africa for an academic sabbatical have helped to crystallize these interests. My initial work in the area of race relations involved a study of racial attitudes of young children. Even at an early age, white children were found to express clearly negative attitudes toward blacks, and black children were aware of these cultural attitudes and often responded with self-evaluation. These responses varied, however, by factors such as social class, age, sex, and degree of interracial contact. This study led to my current interest in the formation of sex-role attitudes in children, and to my continuing interest in the effects of cultural and structural forces on self-esteem."

PORTER, Sheena 1935-

PERSONAL: Born September 19, 1935; married, 1966; children: Katharine. *Residence:* Shrewsbury, England.

CAREER: Worked as a librarian, 1954-64; writer. Has also worked as a member of children's books editorial staff, Oxford University Press. *Awards, honors:* Carnegie Medal, 1964, for *Nordy Bank*.

WRITINGS—All published by Oxford University Press: *The Bronze Chrysanthemum*, 1961; *Hills and Hollows*, 1962; *Jacob's Ladder*, 1963; *Nordy Bank*, 1964; *The Knockers*, 1965; *Deerfold*, 1966; *The Scapegoat*, 1968; *The Hospital*, 1973.*

*   *   *

PORTER, Sylvia F(ield) 1913-

PERSONAL: Born June 18, 1913, in Patchogue, N.Y.; daughter of Louis and Rose (Maisel) Feldman; married Reed R. Porter, 1931 (divorced); married G. Summer Collins, 1943 (died January, 1977); children: Cris Sarah; Summer Campbell Collins (stepson). *Education:* Hunter College (now of the City University of New York), B.A. (magna cum laude), 1932; graduate study at New York University. *Home:* 2 Fifth Ave., New York, N.Y. 10011. *Office:* 30 East 42nd St., New York, N.Y. 10017.

CAREER: Writer. Worked as editor of *Reporting on Governments* (weekly newsletter); writer with *New York Post*, New York City, 1935-77, and with *New York Daily News*, 1977—; Field Newspaper Syndicate, New York City, nationally syndicated daily columnist. Member of the board of governors of the American National Red Cross, 1968-1973; chairperson of President Gerald R. Ford's Non-partisan Citizens' Action Committee. *Member:* Phi Chi Theta (national honorary member), Phi Beta Kappa.

AWARDS, HONORS: National Headliner's Club medal, 1943, for "best financial and business reporting of 1942"; award from the New York Newspaper Women's Club, 1945, 1947, 1951, and 1962, for "the best column written by a woman in any field"; named one of the twenty-five outstanding women in America by the First Assembly of American Women of Achievement, 1951; medallion from the General Federation of Women's Clubs, 1960, for "outstanding achievement in the field of finance"; named outstanding woman of the year in the field of journalism by *Who's Who of American Women*, 1960; Meritorious Public Service Certificate from the Internal Revenue Service, 1964, for "an outstanding contribution to the greater understanding of the federal tax laws"; Spirit of Achievement award from the Albert Einstein College of Medicine, 1966; named free enterprise writer of the year by the National Management Association, 1966; Top Hat award from the National Federation of Business and Professional Women's Clubs, 1967; named one of the 100 American women of accomplishment by *Harper's Bazaar*, 1967; Hunter College Centennial medal, 1970, for noteworthy achievement; named woman of the year in communications by the Advertising Club of New York, 1970; named one of America's seventy-five most important women by the *Ladies Home Journal*, 1971; elected to the Hall of Fame of the Alumni Association of Hunter College, 1973; Woman of the Year 1975 award from the *Ladies Home Journal*; Missouri Honor Award from the University of Missouri, 1975, for distinguished service in journalism; named one of the ten outstanding living journalists of the past fifty years by the New York Chapter of Sigma Delta Chi and elected to its Hall of Fame, 1975; William Allen White award, 1978, for journalistic merit.

D.Sc. from Bryant College, 1952; LL.D. from Hood College, 1958, Western College for Women, 1965, University of Portland, 1971, and Smith College, 1976; D.Litt. from Bates College, 1959, Allegheny College, 1973, Indiana State University, Evansville, 1974, and Monmouth College, 1974; D.B.A. from Catawba College, 1961; D.H.L. from Russell Sage College and Tufts University, both 1964; honorary degree from Fort Lauderdale University, 1966.

WRITINGS: How to Make Money in Government Bonds, Harper & Brothers, 1939; *If War Comes to the American Home: How to Prepare for the Inevitable Adjustment*, R. M. McBride, 1941; *The Nazi Chemical Trust in the United States*, The National Policy Committee, 1942; (with Jacob Kay Lasser) *How to Live Within Your Income*, Simon & Schuster, 1948; (with Lasser) *Money and You*, Science Research Associates, 1949; *How to Get More for Your Money*, World Publishing Co., 1961; (with Lasser) *Managing Your Money*, Holt, 1953, revised edition, 1963; *Sylvia Porter's Money Book: How to Earn It, Spend It, Invest It, Borrow It, and Use It to Better Your Life*, Doubleday, 1975, updated edition, Avon, 1976. Also author of *Sylvia Porter's Income Tax Guide*, published annually. Member of the board of editors of *The World Book Encyclopedia Yearbook*. Contributing editor to *Ladies Home Journal*.

SIDELIGHTS: In his review of *Sylvia Porter's Money Book*, Leonard Sloane described Porter as a person "who has spent a lifetime combining the principles of economics with everyday common sense and bringing them to the public." He lauded her book for "its emphasis on simplification, clarity, and ease of understanding." However, Sloane was careful to temper his praise with a warning: "Advice on such a broad scale through a book like this, though, may not necessarily be the best advice for every reader in every circumstance. Reading this book with that caveat in mind, many individuals could discover some thing or things in it that will help with their own money problems."

Although general assessments of the book were favorable, commentators also pointed out drawbacks in the manual. *Saturday Review* claimed that "Ms. Porter's investment advice is confusing and somewhat dated," while Susan Lee felt *Sylvia Porter's Money Book* was marred by prejudices about women, class, and the American economic system. Among other criticisms, Lee contended that Porter's guidelines for alimony and child support payments were unrealistically high, and that her suggestions on budgeting and family investments were made without consideration for the wife's credit rating. Nonetheless, Lee still believed the book to be a valuable reference source: "*Sylvia Porter's Money Book* has 1,105 pages of useful and readable information about how people should organize their lives financially. This includes planning budgets, determining work choices, making decisions about insurance, banks, houses, and credit, and buying almost anything."

BIOGRAPHICAL/CRITICAL SOURCES: New York Times, June 21, 1975; *Saturday Review*, July 12, 1975; *Money*, August, 1975; *Ms.*, March, 1976; *Across the Board*, July, 1978; *Washington Post Book World*, November 28, 1978.

*   *   *

PORTNOY, Howard N. 1946-

PERSONAL: Born September 10, 1946, in Pittsburgh, Pa.; son of Joseph (a stockbroker) and Minnie (a bookkeeper; maiden name, Shugerman) Portnoy; married Susan Beth Chansky (an insurance executive), August 10, 1969. *Education:* Duquesne University, B.A., 1969; graduate study at

Brooklyn College of the City University of New York, 1971-73; New York University, M.A., 1973, doctoral study, 1973—. *Residence:* New York, N.Y. *Agent:* Julian Bach Literary Agency, Inc., 3 East 48th St., New York, N.Y. 10017.

CAREER: Teacher of English, science, and mathematics; full-time writer.

WRITINGS: Hot Rain (novel), Putnam, 1977. Restaurant critic for *Brooklyn Courier-Life.* Contributing editor of *Junction.*

WORK IN PROGRESS: Another novel.

SIDELIGHTS: Portnoy writes: "I am driven to write by a passion I believe we all possess for telling stories. This passion finds expression, in fact, in most of us during childhood; little kids seem to be able to ramble on—sometimes for hours on end—'inventing,' as they go, experiences and situations they have supposedly been involved in.

"As we grow up, older members of the species tell us that we have to turn our attention toward more serious matters—to 'face reality,' as they say. Those who don't listen, or who simply never tire of 'making things up,' become professional writers."

* * *

POTTER, Sulamith Heins 1944-

PERSONAL: Born February 8, 1944, in Chicago, Ill.; daughter of Maurice Haskell (a mathematician) and Hadassah (Wagman) Heins; married Jack Michael Potter (an anthropologist), September 20, 1970; children: Elizabeth Rachel, Noah Daniel. *Education:* Attended London School of Economics and Political Science, London, 1965-66; University of California, Berkeley, B.A., 1967, M.A., 1970, Ph.D., 1975. *Politics:* "Former student radical." *Home:* 485 Kentucky Ave., Berkeley, Calif. 94707.

CAREER: California State University, Hayward, lecturer in anthropology, 1970-71, lecturer in human development, 1974-76; full-time writer, 1976—. *Member:* American Anthropological Association, National Organization for Women, Phi Beta Kappa.

WRITINGS: Family Life in a Northern Thai Village: A Study in the Structural Significance of Women, University of California Press, 1978.

WORK IN PROGRESS: An introductory text, tentatively entitled *The Anthropological Imagination,* with husband, Jack M. Potter, for Oxford University Press.

SIDELIGHTS: Potter writes: "As soon as I knew what anthropology was, I knew I wanted to be an anthropologist. I felt drawn to live in a society utterly unlike my own, and to try to understand and explain it. My book is the result of this endeavor. I try to write as clearly and directly as I can, without slipping into jargon." *Avocational interests:* Indian cooking, the novels of Jane Austen.

* * *

POUGH, Frederick Harvey 1906-

PERSONAL: Born June 26, 1906, in Brooklyn, N.Y.; son of Francis H. and Alice H. (Beckler) Pough; married Eleanor C. Hodge, October 14, 1938 (died, May, 1966); children: Frederick Harvey, Barbara Hodge. *Education:* Harvard University, S.B., 1928, Ph.D., 1935; Washington University, St. Louis, Mo., M.S., 1932; also attended University of Heidelberg. *Home address:* P.O. Box 7004, Reno, Nev. 89510.

CAREER: American Museum of Natural History, New York, N.Y., assistant curator of mineralogy, 1935-40, acting curator, 1941, curator, 1942-44, curator of physical geology and mineralogy, 1942-52, consulting mineralogist, 1953-64; Santa Barbara Museum of National History, Santa Barbara, Calif., director, 1965-66; consulting mineralogist, 1966—. Employed on Manhattan Project, 1942-43. Gem consultant to *Jewelers Circular-Keystone. Member:* Geological Society of America, Mineralogical Society of America (fellow), Mineralogical Society of Great Britain, New York Harvard Club, Explorers Club. *Awards, honors:* Bronze medal from Royal Geographical Society (Belgium), 1948; Derby Medal from Brazilian Geological Survey, 1950; named mineralogist of the year by American Federation of Mineralogical Societies, 1966.

WRITINGS: (Contributor) Donald McNeil, editor, *The Jeweler's Dictionary,* Chilton Press, 1945, 3rd edition, 1976; *The History of Granite* (pamphlet), Barre Guild, 1950(?); *All About Volcanoes and Earthquakes* (juvenile), Random House, 1953; *A Field Guide to Rocks and Minerals,* Houghton, 1953, 4th edition, 1976; *Our Earth: What It Is* (juvenile), Whitman Publishing, 1961; *The Story of Gems and Semiprecious Stones* (juvenile), Harvey House, 1967. Contributor to *American Heritage Dictionary* and *Random House New College Dictionary.* Also author of *Geology Book of Knowledge.* Contributing editor of *Compton's Encyclopedia* and *Lapidary Journal.*

WORK IN PROGRESS: Studying mineral paragenesis, to amplify the occurrence section of *A Field Guide to Rocks and Minerals.*

SIDELIGHTS: Pough writes that he has traveled widely, conducting tours of specialists in gemology and mineralogy. His special areas of interest are gems, which have been a specialty for forty years, and volcanology. In 1943 he was sent to Mexico by the American Museum of Natural History to study and make a photographic record of the volcanic eruption of Paricutin. His books have been published in French, Spanish, Hindi, Persian, Bengali, Italian, Arabic, and Portuguese.

BIOGRAPHICAL/CRITICAL SOURCES: Coronet, June, 1949.

* * *

POWELL, Elwin H(umphreys) 1925-

PERSONAL: Born November 18, 1925, in Los Angeles, Calif.; son of Charles D. (an electrician) and Jenny (Rex) Powell; married Juanita Tisdale, January 27, 1956 (died September 15, 1972); children: James E., Stephen R. *Education:* University of Texas, B.A., 1949, M.A., 1951; Tulane University, Ph.D., 1956; postdoctoral study at London School of Economics and Political Science, 1957. *Home:* 124 Jewett Parkway, Buffalo, N.Y. 14214. *Office:* Department of Sociology, State University of New York at Buffalo, Buffalo, N.Y. 14214.

CAREER: University of Tulsa, Tulsa, Okla., assistant professor of sociology, 1954-57; State University of New York at Buffalo, associate professor, 1958-72, professor of sociology, 1972—. Director of Research for Justice. *Military service:* U.S. Navy, 1944-46. *Member:* American Sociological Association, American Society of Criminology.

WRITINGS: Design of Discord: Studies of Anomie, Oxford University Press, 1970.

WORK IN PROGRESS: Research on criminology as the science of social control; a study of suicide, the city and war as forms of self destruction arising out of social disorganization; the role of intelligence agencies in maintaining the structure of society.

* * *

PRICE, Don C(ravens) 1937-

PERSONAL: Born February 28, 1937, in Washington, D.C.; son of Don K. and Margaret Helen (Gailbreath) Price; married Nancy Gray Thompson (an archaeologist), June 10, 1970. *Education:* Amherst College, B.A., 1958; Harvard University, A.M., 1960, Ph.D., 1968. *Politics:* Liberal. *Religion:* Christian. *Office:* Department of History, University of California, Davis, Calif. 95616.

CAREER: Johns Hopkins University, School of Advanced International Studies, Washington, D.C., assistant professor of Asian studies, 1967-68; Yale University, New Haven, Conn., assistant professor of history, 1968-72; University of California, Davis, associate professor of history, 1973—. *Member:* Association for Asian Studies.

WRITINGS: Russia and the Roots of Chinese Revolution, Harvard University Press, 1974.

WORK IN PROGRESS: An intellectual biography of Sung Chiao-Jen.

SIDELIGHTS: Price writes: "I am interested in the relation between people's motivations and the way they understand them, and how these vary, from culture to culture, and from one time to another. For me, the continuities and contrasts in the transition from tradition to modernity in China are an especially fascinating subject.

"In my first book I argued that the Chinese revolution has been distinguished less by its nationalism than by a sort of Confucian supranational moralism, which accounts for the degree of Russian influence in the Chinese revolution. In my current research, I am trying to relate the personal psychological crises of a Confucian revolutionary to his political thought and, I hope, to the nature of modern Chinese politics in general.

AVOCATIONAL INTERESTS: Classical guitar, tennis, softball.

* * *

PRINCE, J(ack) H(arvey) 1908-
(Jon Clinton, Dean Wardell)

PERSONAL: Born November 10, 1908, in London, England. *Education:* Northampton College of Advanced Technology, F.B.O.A., F.S.M.C., 1929. *Home:* 1/15 Dudley St., Balgowlah, New South Wales 2093, Australia.

CAREER: Lecturer in ophthalmology, British Optical Association; Ohio State University, Columbus, 1952-66, began as instructor, became assistant professor, later became associate professor of ophthalmology; writer and illustrator, 1966—. Scientific adviser to professional organizations in the United States. *Member:* Fellowship of Australian Writers, Zoological Society (London; fellow), Royal Zoological Society of New South Wales (member of council), Nature Conservation Council of New South Wales (member of council), Sigma Xi. *Awards, honors:* Research medal from British Optical Association, 1958.

WRITINGS: Ocular Prosthesis, E. & S. Livingstone, 1946; *Visual Development,* E. & S. Livingstone, 1949; *Recent Advances in Ocular Prosthesis,* E. & S. Livingstone, 1950; *Comparative Anatomy of the Eye,* C. C Thomas, 1956; (with Diesem, Ruskell, and Eglitis) *Anatomy and Histology of the Eye and Orbit in Domestic Animals,* C. C Thomas, 1960; *Visual Acuity and Reading in Relation to Letter and Word Design,* Ohio State University Press, 1960; *Comparative Legibility of Highway and Advertising Signs Under Dynamic Conditions,* Ohio State University Press, 1962; (contributor) Arnold Sorsby, editor, *Modern Ophthalmology,* Butterworth & Co., 1962; *Spectral Absorption of the Retina and Choroid From 340 to 1700 Millimicrons,* Ohio State University Press, 1962; (co-editor) *The Rabbit in Eye Research,* C. C Thomas, 1964; *Aging and Pathology of the Retina,* C. C Thomas, 1965; *Small Boats,* Angus & Robertson, 1968; *Animals in the Night: Senses in Action After Dark* (juvenile), Angus & Robertson, 1968, Thomas Nelson, 1971; *Better Life After Fifty,* A. H. & A. W. Reed, 1969.

(Contributor) *Duke's Physiology of the Domestic Animals,* Cornell University Press, 1970, revised edition, 1977; *You and Your Eyes,* A. H. & A. W. Reed, 1970; *The Universal Urge,* Thomas Nelson, 1972; *Weather and the Animal World* (juvenile), Thomas Nelson, 1974; *How to Judge People,* Rydge Publications, 1974; *Languages of the Animal World,* Thomas Nelson, 1975; *Diet for Good Health,* Rigby Ltd., 1975, revised edition, 1977; *Everyday Health Problems and How to Deal With Them,* Rigby Ltd., 1975; *All About Headaches,* Rigby Ltd., 1975; *Plants That Eat Animals,* Thomas Nelson, 1978; (with Jack Murphy) *The Lady Bowler,* Reed & Rigby, 1978; *How Your Body Works,* Rigby Ltd., 1979; *Preventing Strokes,* Rigby Ltd., 1979. Also author of *How Animals Hunt, How to Get Along With Everyone, Headaches Are Only a Symptom, Motion in Animals, Going Below, All from One Cell, About Fish,* and *Finding Australian Birds.*

Under pseudonym Jon Clinton: *Buying Australian Shares,* A. H. & A. W. Reed, 1968, 3rd edition, 1970; *Investment in Australia, New Zealand, and Asia,* A. H. & A. W. Reed, 1969; *Reducing Your Income Tax,* A. H. & A. W. Reed, 1970, 9th edition, 1978; *Buying New Zealand Shares,* A. H. & A. W. Reed, 1971; *How You Can Save Tax,* Rydge Publications, 1972; *Today's Ways to Minimise Income Tax, Gift Duty, and Death Duties,* Rydge Publications, 1974; *Living and Having More; Dying and Paying Less,* Rydge Publications, 1976.

Under pseudonym Dean Wardell: *Instant Handywoman,* Rigby, 1975, revised edition, 1977; *Furniture Restoration,* Rigby, 1977; *Property Protection,* Rigby, 1979. Contributor of more than three hundred articles on zoology and outdoor sports to magazines. Honorary editor of *Koolewong.*

SIDELIGHTS: Prince has traveled in Canada, New Zealand, Europe, and most of South America. *Avocational interests:* Art, literature, music, politics, walking.

* * *

PRITCHARD, John Wallace 1912-
(Ian Wallace)

PERSONAL: Born December 4, 1912, in Chicago, Ill.; son of William Arthur (in advertising) and Hallie (Kohlhas) Pritchard; married Elizabeth Paul, June 17, 1938; children: John William (deceased), Alan Paul. *Education:* University of Michigan, A.B. (honors), 1934, M.A., 1939, further graduate study, 1949-51; Wayne State University, Ed.D., 1957. *Residence:* Beaverdam Valley, near Asheville, N.C.

CAREER: Board of Education, Detroit, Mich., psychologist, 1934-42, chief of publications, 1942-74, divisional director, 1966-74, civil defense coordinator for Detroit public schools, 1950-60; writer, 1974—. Part-time member of faculty at Wayne State University, 1955-74. Past head of Detroit mayor's evacuation planning committee; civil defense consultant to state of Michigan and to federal government. *Military service:* U.S. Army, clinical psychologist, 1944-47; served in France; became captain. *Member:* Philosophy of Education Association (fellow), Science Fiction Writers of America, National Retired Teachers Association, Authors Guild, League of Women Voters, Detroit Schoolmen's Club, Detroit Fact-Finders Club, Phi Sigma Kappa. *Awards, honors:* Distinguished service award from Michigan Congress of Parents and Teachers, 1975.

WRITINGS: (With Marquis E. Shattuck and Alden D. Kumler) *Frank Cody: A Realist in Education* (biography), Macmillan, 1943; (with Lee B. Durham and Mabel Chamberlain) *Other Americans* (biographies), Detroit Board of Education, 1948; (editor with C. C. Barnes, Stanley Dimond, Elsie Beck, Elmer Pflieger, and Edith Forster) *Detroit, Wayne County, and Michigan,* Detroit Board of Education, 1950, 3rd edition, 1972; *Every Crazy Wind* (novel), Dodd, 1952; (editor with Beck) *Detroit: A Manual for Citizens,* Detroit Board of Education, 1958, revised edition, 1968; (editor with Beck) *Labor-Management Dynamics,* Detroit Board of Education, 1961; (with Paul H. Voelker) *Off to Work,* Stanwix, 1962; (editor with Beck) *Detroit at Work,* Detroit Board of Education, 1966; (editor with Forster and Beck) *Exploring Greater Detroit,* Detroit Board of Education, 1955; (editor with Ollie McFarland) *Afro-America Sings,* Detroit Board of Education, 1971.

Science fiction novels, under pseudonym Ian Wallace: *Croyd,* Putnam, 1967; *Dr. Orpheus,* Putnam, 1968; *Deathstar Voyage,* Putnam, 1969; *The Purloined Prince,* McCall, 1971; *Pan Sagittarius,* Putnam, 1973; *A Voyage to Dari,* DAW Books, 1974; *The World Asunder,* DAW Books, 1976; *The Sign of the Mute Medusa,* Popular Library, 1977; *Z-Sting,* DAW Books, 1978; *Heller's Leap,* DAW Books, 1979.

SIDELIGHTS: Pritchard writes: "I wrote my first poem for publication at the age of eleven (it was my grandfather's periodical); since then, I have never stopped writing. A great deal of it has been sour indeed; fortunately, that went unpublished. I would shelve it, and take another look at it a year or two later, and either revise it drastically or junk it—on somebody's good theory that if you still are satisfied with what you wrote two years ago, you aren't growing. Some of it has crept into later work.

"Writing is for me an absorbing pleasure; and in view of my income from another career, I have never been tempted to write what I considered a potboiler. My favorite storytelling medium is the novel; I like scope to develop and probe the story, people, motives, and techniques. During forty pre-retirement years, I formed the habit of beginning to write about mid-evening and staying at it until well after midnight; now that all my days are free, that old habit stays: I am a night owl.

"My first novel, in 1952, was not science fiction; I'd call it psychofiction. During the next fifteen years I wrote and rewrote more than a few novels which were never published. When I tried science fiction in 1966, it worked well almost instantly; it seems to be my medium. While I was changing mediums, for luck I also changed my author's name to Ian Wallace by Scotchifying my first name, keeping my middle name, and dropping my surname (that hurt).

"Without commenting on what other science fiction writers try to do, I'll briefly tell what I try to do. I aim my books at well-educated or self-educated minds. For them, I try to write pleasurable, frequently startling, coherently designed stories, taking advantage of fantasy to enlarge their scope in many dimensions, but disciplining the tales with logic and with scientific or philosophic theory. I try to portray humans living at the highest levels of their humanity, entailing many-sided intelligence, emotion intelligently guided and expressed, and humane fellow-feeling for all the different kinds of humans (including some weird-bodied instances on other planets); that, for me, is both a moral issue and a taste preference.

"A special pleasure in this kind of writing (and, I hope, in its reading) is its receptiveness to every mental and physical aspect of my background. As to the mental aspects, I'll mention human and animal psychology, anthropology, archaeology, biology, geology, astrophysics, philosophy. I've been significantly influenced by French literature and experiences (I've lived in France), by wartime army experiences, by the amusing complexities of bureaucracy in government and big business (the point for my characters is to beat a bureaucracy by swinging from branch to branch), and by innumerable worthwhile writers in the history of the humanities (may they indulgently pardon my shortcomings).

"It is a special satisfaction when a foreign publisher chooses to reissue something of mine in his land and its language. Thus far, five of my novels have been republished in foreign countries, including England, Germany, and Italy.

"Among the endless suggestions which can be offered to younger writers, I'll mention the following. Be sure that the ideas behind your piece are good and coherently interwoven. Maintain integrity in your writing: don't be a charlatan even when that means big money. Write your piece, reread, edit, reread, edit, rewrite, maybe many times; be sure it's right for you, and that it is presented in a manner which can catch and hold the interest of your intended audience. These comments apply to the whole range of writing from fiction through poetry and essays to technical stuff, if you want to publish it. There ought to be writer's conscience in publishing—it affects minds. And—never be discouraged by rejection slips, even unto eternity."

*   *   *

PROUJAN, Carl 1929-

PERSONAL: Born February 15, 1929, in New York, N.Y.; son of Mathieu M. and Clara (Fish) Immerman; married Sonia Christine Candalas (a registered nurse), January 23, 1954; children: David, Lisa, Suzanne. *Education:* Attended Reed College, 1947-50; City College (now of the City University of New York), B.S., 1957. *Home:* 4 Roman Ter., Congers, N.Y. 10920. *Agent:* Maximilian Becker, 115 East 82nd St., New York, N.Y. 10028. *Office:* 167 South Mountain Rd., New City, N.Y. 10956.

CAREER: Pfister Chemical Works, Ridgefield, N.J., research chemist, 1957-59; Academic Press, New York City, chemistry editor, 1959-61; Harper & Row Publishers, Inc., New York City, medical textbook editor, 1961-62; Scholastic Magazines, Inc., New York City, associate editor of *Science World,* 1962-66, managing editor, 1967-68, editor, 1968-73, editorial director of science department, 1973-78; freelance writer, 1978—. *Military service:* U.S. Army, Medical Corps, 1951-53. *Awards, honors:* Gold Cindy from Information Film Producers of America, 1975, for filmstrip series "Human Issues in Science"; gold medals from Virgin Islands International Film Festival, 1975, 1976, for filmstrip series "Adventures in Science."

WRITINGS: Secrets of the Sea, Aldus Books, 1971.

Filmstrips: (Editor) "Human Issues in Science," Scholastic Magazines, 1975; "Adventures in Science," Scholastic Magazines, 1976. Author of filmstrips for National Air and Space Museum, Smithsonian Institution, 1978.

WORK IN PROGRESS: Goodby Suzi, Hello Charlie, "a novel of a man's search for himself."

* * *

PUGH, Charles 1948-

PERSONAL: Born February 28, 1948, in Chicago, Ill.; son of Trez Van (a truck driver) and Pernella (Lewis) Pugh; married Barbara Reed (an assistant administrator of a health care facility), July 29, 1967; children: Charles, Jr., Lenard. *Education:* Wright College, A.A., 1968; University of Illinois at Chicago Circle, B.A., 1970. *Home:* 235 West Scott St., Chicago, Ill. 60610. *Office:* DuSable High School, 4934 South Wabash Ave., Chicago, Ill. 60609.

CAREER: Continental Illinois National Bank & Trust Co., Chicago, Ill., reconciler, 1965-71; high-school teacher of English, 1971-73; DuSable High School, Chicago, Ill., teacher of English, 1973—. Assistant dean of admissions at DeVry Institute of Technology, 1975; tutor for Christian Action Ministry Academy. *Member:* Black Writer's Conference, University of Illinois Alumni Association.

WRITINGS: (With wife, Barbara Pugh) *The Dream of the Mask and Spear* (poetry), Triton Press, 1975; *The Hospital Plot* (novel), Ashley Books, 1978.

WORK IN PROGRESS: The Great Paper Shuffle, "a tragi-comedy" about the Chicago public school system.

SIDELIGHTS: Pugh comments: "As a 'griot' (storyteller and historian), it is up to me to interpret and record the Black experience, *not* in the stereotypic tradition of street violence, sex, dope, and con games, but as something warm, instructive, and wholesome.

"The theme of my first novel is twofold: man's inhumanity to man, and the search for Black identity in America. *The Hospital Plot* is the story of a Chicago-based medical organization conspiring to commit genocide against the Black race. In my book, I attempt to portray a beautiful, searching Black soul, and warn against a growing threat of the systematic extermination of Blacks."

* * *

PURDY, A(lfred) W(ellington) 1918-
(Al Purdy)

PERSONAL: Born December 30, 1918, in Wooler, Ontario, Canada; son of Alfred Wellington (a farmer) and Eleanor Louisa (Ross) Purdy; married Eurithe Mary Jane Parkhurst, November 1, 1941; children: Alfred Alexander. *Education:* Attended Trenton Collegiate Institute and Albert College. *Politics:* New Democratic Party, "i.e., labour or socialist." *Religion:* "Nil." *Home and office:* R.R. 1, Ameliasburgh, Ontario, Canada K0K 1A0.

CAREER: Writer. Worked in factories until about 1960. Visiting associate professor at Simon Fraser University, Burnaby, British Columbia, 1971; writer-in-residence at Loyola University, Montreal, Quebec, 1973-74, University of Manitoba, Winnipeg, 1975-76, and University of Western Ontario, London, 1977-78. Conducted creative writing classes at Banff Center School of Fine Arts, summers, 1972-74. Has served on the Judging Committee of the Canada Council for junior and senior arts grants and the awards committee for the Governor General's literary awards. *Mili-*

tary service: Royal Canadian Air Force, six years service during World War II. *Member:* League of Canadian Poets. *Awards, honors:* Canada Council fellowships, 1965, 1968-69, 1971; President's Medal, University of Western Ontario, 1964, for "The Country North of Belleville"; Governor General's Literary award, 1966, for *The Cariboo Horses;* Centennial Medal, Canadian Federal Government, 1967, for outstanding service; Senior Literary award, Canada Council, 1973; A.J.M. Smith Award, 1974, for *Sex and Death;* elected to Academy of Canadian Writers, 1977; Jubilee Medal, 1978.

WRITINGS—Poetry, except as noted: *The Enchanted Echo,* Clarke & Stuart, 1944; *Pressed on Sand,* Ryerson, 1955; *Emu, Remember!,* University of New Brunswick Press, 1956; *The Crafte So Longe to Lerne,* Ryerson, 1959; *Poems for All the Annettes,* Contact Press, 1962; *The Blur in Between: Poems, 1960-61,* Emblem Books, 1963; *The Cariboo Horses,* McClelland & Stewart, 1965; *North of Summer: Poems from Baffin Island,* McClelland & Stewart, 1967; *The Winemakers Beat: Etude,* Fiddlehead Press, 1968; *Wild Grape Wine,* McClelland & Stewart, 1968; *Spring Song,* Fiddlehead Press, 1968; *Inter ruption,* Fiddlehead Press, 1968; *Poems for All the Annettes: Selected Poems Prior to 1965,* House of Anansi, 1968; *Love in a Burning Building,* McClelland & Stewart, 1970; *The Quest for Ouzo,* M. Kerrigan Almey, 1970; *Selected Poems,* McClelland & Stewart, 1972; *Hiroshima Poems,* Crossing Press, 1972; *On the Bearpaw Sea,* Blackfish Press, 1973; *Sex and Death,* McClelland & Stewart, 1973; *Scott Hutcheson's Boat,* Bailey and McKinnon, 1973; *In Search of Owen Roblin,* McClelland & Stewart, 1974; *Sundance at Dusk,* McClelland & Stewart, 1976; *The Poems of Al Purdy,* McClelland & Stewart, 1976; *A Handful of Earth,* Black Moss Press, 1977; *No Other Country* (articles and essays), McClelland & Stewart, 1977; *At Marsport Drugstore,* Paget Press, 1977; *No Second Spring,* Black Moss Press, 1978; *Being Alive: Poems 1958-78,* McClellan & Stewart, 1978; *Moths in the Iron Curtain,* Paget Press, 1978.

Editor: *The New Romans: Candid Canadian Opinions of the United States,* St. Martin's, 1968; *Fifteen Winds: A Selection of Modern Canadian Poems,* Ryerson, 1969; Milton Acorn, *I've Tasted My Blood: Poems 1956-1968,* Ryerson, 1969; *Storm Warning: The New Canadian Poets,* McClelland & Stewart, 1971; *Storm Warning II,* McClelland & Stewart, 1976; Andrew Suknaski, *Wood Mountain Poems,* Macmillan, 1976.

Work represented in anthologies, including *Five Modern Canadian Poets,* edited by Eli Mandel, Holt, 1970; *The Norton Anthology of Modern Poetry,* edited by Richard Ellman and Robert O'Clair, Norton, 1973; *Twentieth Century Poetry and Poetics,* edited by Gary Geddes, Oxford University Press, 1973; *Canadian Poetry: The Modern Era,* edited by John Newlove, McClelland & Stewart, 1977. Contributor of original and adapted material to Canadian Broadcasting Corporation, both radio and television, 1956—, including "Poems for Voices," 1970. Contributor of poems, reviews, articles, and essays to numerous publications, including *Canadian Literature, Fiddlehead, Saturday Night, Maclean's Magazine,* and *Canadian Forum.*

SIDELIGHTS: Purdy told *CA:* "*Poems for All the Annettes,* 1962, is the most important book of mine from a personal development viewpoint. It might be called a 'watershed' in some sense, in that the poems were very different from what went before. I don't like the idea of writers yammering on endlessly about writing. If people are interested in a writer's writing, then they should read it, because it's undoubtedly more important than narcissistic trivia about writing.''

Peter Stevens observed that Purdy ''does not justify his poetry in long articles'' and praised the poet's ''fresh no-nonsense approach.'' Many critics have followed Purdy's development as a poet, but Mike Doyle gave this assessment: ''Purdy has proved . . . that a boy from Hicksville with the worst, most platitudinous and tum-ti-tum sense of poetry can become a subtle and sensitive craftsman.''

Stevens saw *The Cariboo Horses* as the result of Purdy's ''long struggle . . . to hammer out for himself a poetic idiom.'' Like Doyle, Stevens detected such obvious changes in Purdy's work that he divided the poet's career into three periods for study. The first books written in the mid-to-late fifties were a ''beginning . . . exploratory stage'' followed by a ''central poetic upheaval still retaining some unresolved uncertainties.'' The 1965 publication of *The Cariboo Horses* marked the ''emergence of a truly individual poet,'' according to Stevens's view.

While Stevens was busy classifying Purdy's career, Margaret Atwood was at work classifying the man. While acknowledging Purdy as one of Canada's ''most versatile and prolific poets,'' Atwood noted limitations, especially padding and repetition, in some of his work. One possible key to Purdy's success is, in Atwood's opinion, his ability to separate his personality into its various components and play those ''over-lapping self-created versions'' against each other. Atwood saw the three distinct sides of Purdy as being ''A.W., the intellectual . . . Alfred Wellington, a sentimentalist . . . and plain Al, who sneers at A.W.'s pretensions, questions Alfred Wellington's motives, and puts down the reader when either of the others has sucked him in.''

Doyle recalled George Bowering's comment about Purdy as the poet who thirty years before had created *The Enchanted Echo:* ''He seemed to think that the poet had to be a sort of Emily Dickinson, maybe with a moustache.'' Later Bowering recognized that Purdy ''employs his personality, familiar (familiar as hell, Purdy would say) to his readership, as the main organizing principle of his poetry.''

When Eli Mandel reviewed *The Crafte So Longe to Lerne,* noted Stevens, he saluted Purdy as ''clearly another beginning for Canadian poetry.'' In addition to his contribution as a writer, Purdy has actively promoted Canadian literature and given it international exposure through readings and lectures. Travel has become important to Purdy's actual creative process, for, as he told Gary Geddes, ''somehow or other one uses up one's past.'' Doyle noted that Purdy ''self-admittedly . . . goes looking for poems the way another man would go on safari.''

''I like to think of a continual becoming . . . a changing . . . a moving,'' Purdy told Geddes. His philosophy is evident in his poetry of the past three decades. Throughout that poetry, Stevens noted that Purdy returns to the ''theme of permanence and art's relation to it'' with his ''development as a poet'' governed by his ''balancing of [the] opposing forces of romanticism and realism.''

Critical acclaim such as that from Mandel led Doyle to ask why Purdy is ''so significant a poet for Canada today.'' In answering his question, Doyle discovered certain parallels between country and poet. ''To an outsider Canada must present a somewhat puzzling international image: innocent yet canny, straightforward yet oblique, open and yet shut in, eclectic and yet groping for a single image of itself,'' wrote

Doyle, who continued, ''Purdy . . . seems as much as anyone writing today to sense what it is, the Canadian thing.''

Purdy's *The New Romans: Candid Canadian Opinions of the United States* represented a digression from his poetry. Although Purdy has edited several books, this volume has probably received more attention both in Canada and the United States. Donald Zoll said Purdy selected essays from ''a curious assemblage of angry young poets, aging *literati* and 'pop' journalists.'' Yet Zoll found the book's interest and value in ''its possible use as a bit of evidence in the task of unscrambling the 'Canadian mind' '' despite ''little curiosity'' shown by most Americans on that subject. ''There is no doubt that the emotional, moralistic, and frequently chauvinistic vituperations of many of the contributors . . . represent a sizable portion of current Canadian public opinion,'' he continued.

Stevens summed up Purdy's unique position in Canadian literature: ''Here is the poet who by defining himself in relation to this country and the world has told us something about all of us. If Purdy didn't exist, it would have been necessary for Canadians to invent him.''

BIOGRAPHICAL/CRITICAL SOURCES: Canadian Literature, spring, 1966, summer, 1969, winter, 1970, winter, 1972, spring, 1973, winter, 1973, summer, 1974; *Canadian Forum,* November, 1968; *Poetry,* June, 1969; *Modern Age,* summer, 1969; *Queen's Quarterly,* winter, 1969; *Maclean's Magazine,* January, 1971; *Journal of Canadian Studies,* May, 1971; *Saturday Night,* August, 1971, July, 1972, September, 1972, December, 1973; *Contemporary Literary Criticism,* Gale, Volume 3, 1975, Volume 6, 1976.

*   *   *

PURDY, Al
   See PURDY, A(lfred) W(ellington)

*   *   *

PUXON, Grattan   1939-

PERSONAL: Born January 7, 1939, in England; son of Francois M. (a lawyer) and Freda Evans (Atkinson) Puxon; married Sanije Ibraim, January 15, 1972. *Education:* Attended Northeast Essex Technical College. *Agent:* Intercontinental Literary Agency, 45 Chandos Pl., London W.C.2, England. *Office:* 61 Blenheim Cres., London W.11, England.

CAREER: Essex County Standard, Colchester, England, reporter, 1955-59; National Press Services, Dublin, Ireland, free-lance journalist, 1960-63; free-lance writer, 1963—. Chairman of Dublin Itinerant Settlement Committee, 1964; general secretary of England's Gypsy Council, 1966; joint general secretary of World Romani Congress, 1971, general secretary, 1978. *Member:* Romani Institute, Indian Institute of Romani Studies.

WRITINGS: The Victims, Aisti Eireannacha, 1967; *On the Road,* National Council for Civil Liberties (England), 1968; (with Donald Simon Kenrick) *The Destiny of Europe's Gypsies,* Heinemann, 1972, Basic Books, 1973; *Roma: Europe's Gypsies,* Minority Rights Group, 1973, revised edition, 1975.

WORK IN PROGRESS: A book on the history of the Romani national movement, 1872-1978.

SIDELIGHTS: Times Literary Supplement, November 17, 1972; *New York Review of Books,* June 14, 1973; *Books and Bookmen,* August, 1973.

Q

QUICK, Philip
See STRAGE, Mark

* * *

QUIN-HARKIN, Janet 1941-

PERSONAL: Born September 24, 1941, in Bath, England; came to the United States in 1966; daughter of Frank Newcombe (an engineer) and Margery (a teacher; maiden name, Rees) Lee; married John Quin-Harkin (an airline sales manager), November 26, 1966; children: Clare, Anne, Jane, Dominic. *Education:* University of London, B.A. (honors), 1963; graduate study at University of Kiel and University of Freiburg. *Religion:* Roman Catholic. *Home:* 74 Brandon Rd., Conroe, Tex. 77301.

CAREER: British Broadcasting Corp. (BBC), London, England, studio manager in drama department, 1963-66; teacher of dance and drama, 1971—. Founder and director of San Rafael Children's Little Theater. *Member:* Associated Authors of Children's Literature. *Awards, honors: Peter Penny's Dance* was named outstanding book by *New York Times* and best book of the year by *School Library Journal* and Children's Book Showcase, all in 1976.

WRITINGS: (Contributor) Lawrence Carillo and Dorothy McKinley, editors, *Chandler Reading Program,* five volumes, Noble & Noble, 1967-72; *Peter Penny's Dance* (juvenile), Dial, 1976; *Benjamin's Balloon* (juvenile), Parents' Magazine Press, 1979; *Septimus Bean and His Amazing Machine* (juvenile), Parents' Magazine Press, 1979. Author of several documentaries and of four radio plays and scripts, including "Dandelion Hows," for British Broadcasting Corp., 1966. Contributor to education journals, *Scholastic,* and *Mother's Manual.*

WORK IN PROGRESS: Two juvenile novels, one on the past, the other on refugees in World War II.

SIDELIGHTS: Janet Quin-Harkin comments: "I am particularly interested in travel. Since the first time I crossed Europe alone at the age of thirteen, I feel restless if I don't wander every few months. I have visited most parts of the globe, including a three-month stay in Greece and a year in Australia. I have made four trips to India, which I find fascinating. My love of travel is reflected in everything I write. My characters can never stay in one place.

"I enjoy writing for children because it is a positive medium. You can be optimistic, indulge in fantasy, and have a happy ending. What's more, you don't have to introduce sex and violence to make it sell. Also, in common with many writers for children, I don't think I ever grew up. When I write a book with an eleven-year-old heroine, that child is ME. I still get a very childlike delight from new experiences, from beautiful scenery, from being in the midst of nature. Children are such fine, uncomplicated beings. They accept that the world is full of magic and wonder and do not try to find the scientific proof behind it. Think of the opening of *Stuart Little.* No child questions why Mrs. Little's second son should happen to have been born a mouse. This uncritical acceptance is what I enjoy about writing fantasy. As long as the fantasy world is true to itself, once established, it can behave in any way under the sun."

R

RACHLIN, Nahid

PERSONAL: Born in Abadan, Iran; came to the United States in 1962, naturalized citizen, 1969; daughter of Manoochehr (a lawyer) and Mohtaram Bozorgmehri; married Howard Rachlin (a professor of psychology); children: Leila. Education: Lindenwood College, B.A. Home: 501 East 87th St., New York, N.Y. 10028. Agent: John Ware, 392 Central Park W., New York, N.Y. 10025.

CAREER: Writer. Children's Hospital, Boston, Mass., research assistant, 1968-69. Awards, honors: Bennett Cerf Award from Columbia University, 1974, for short story, "Ruins"; Doubleday-Columbia fellowship for creative writing, 1974-75; Wallace Stegner fellowship, 1975-76.

WRITINGS: Foreigner (novel), Norton, 1978. Contributor of stories to popular magazines and literary journals, including Redbook, Shenandoah, and Four Quarters.

WORK IN PROGRESS: A novel, tentatively entitled Judd and Judith, for Norton.

SIDELIGHTS: Nahid Rachlin comments: "I have always written fiction rather than nonfiction because I feel that only fiction can convey the complexity of character and situation that I see around me. I think that the purpose of fiction in society is to provide models for alternate courses of life—not so much as a guide for action but as a vehicle for understanding people. Foreigner, my first published novel, for instance, seems autobiographical because of many parallels in the protagonist's life and my own life (a young woman coming to the U.S., marrying an American and then returning home for a visit).

"My new novel (working title, Judd and Judith) is entirely different from the other, in that it has American settings and characters and is about an obsessive relationship between a brother and a sister that leads to his murdering her. The core of this novel came out of my fascination with a true case that occurred in California. I kept thinking what it was about the relationship between the privileged and good-looking brother and sister who seemed very close to each other which led to such a drastic outcome."

*　　*　　*

RADLAUER, Ruth (Shaw) 1926-

PERSONAL: Born August 18, 1926, in Midwest, Wyo.; daughter of Tracy Nichols (an industrial relations person) and Ruth (a real estate agent; maiden name, Preston); married Edward Radlauer (a writer), June 28, 1947; children: David, Robin, Dan. Education: Attended University of California, Los Angeles, 1944-47, 1948-50. Residence: La Habra, Calif. Office address: P.O. Box 1637, Whittier, Calif. 90609.

CAREER: Elementary teacher in Norwalk, Calif., 1950-51; substitute teacher in elementary schools in Norwalk, La Habra, and East Whittier, all Calif., 1953-69; special education teacher in La Puente, Calif., 1966-67; adult education teacher of parent education and creative writing, Whittier Union High School District, Calif., 1968-71; Elk Grove Books (a division of Childrens Press), Whittier, Calif., editor, 1971—. Member: Authors Guild, Writers' Club of Whittier.

WRITINGS: Fathers at Work, Melmont, 1958, published as About Men at Work, 1967; Women at Work, Melmont, 1959; Of Course, You're a Horse, Abelard, 1959; Mothers Are That Way, Abelard, 1960; About Four Seasons and Five Senses, Melmont, 1960; (self-illustrated) Good Times Drawing Lines, Melmont, 1961; Good Times With Words, Melmont, 1963; Stein, The Great Retriever, Bobbs-Merrill, 1964; (with Marjorie Pursel) Where in the World Do You Live?, Franklin Publications, 1965; From Place to Place, Franklin Publications, 1965; Food From Farm to Family, Franklin Publishing, 1965; Clothes From Head to Toe, Franklin Publishing, 1965; What Can You Do With a Box?, Childrens Press, 1973; Yellowstone National Park, Childrens Press, 1975; Yosemite National Park, Childrens Press, 1975; Everglades National Park, Childrens Press, 1975; Great Smoky Mountains National Park, Childrens Press, 1976; Mesa Verde National Park, Childrens Press, 1976; Grand Canyon National Park, Childrens Press, 1977; Rocky Mountain National Park, Childrens Press, 1977; Glacier National Park, Childrens Press, 1977; Olympic National Park, Childrens Press, 1977; Acadia National Park, Childrens Press, 1978; Mammoth Cave National Park, Childrens Press, 1978; Zion National Park, Childrens Press, 1978.

With husband, Edward Radlauer: About Missiles and Men, Melmont, 1959; About Atomic Power for People, Melmont, 1960; Atoms Afloat: The Nuclear Ship Savannah, Abelard, 1963; What Is a Community?, Elk Grove Press, 1967; Get Ready for School, Elk Grove Press, 1967; Whose Tools Are These?, Elk Grove Press, 1968; Water for Your Communi-

ty, Elk Grove Press, 1968; *Father Is Big,* Bowmar, 1968; *Colors,* Bowmar, 1968; *Evening,* Bowmar, 1968; *Quarter Midget Challenge,* Childrens Press, 1969; *Horses,* Bowmar, 1968, revised edition, 1975; *Horses Pix Dix: A Picture Dictionary,* Bowmar, 1970; *Buggy-Go-Round,* F. Watts, 1971; *On the Drag Strip,* F. Watts, 1971; *Scramble Cycle,* F. Watts, 1971; *Chopper Cycle,* F. Watts, 1972; *Horsing Around,* F. Watts, 1972; *On the Sand,* F. Watts, 1972; *Bonneville Cars,* F. Watts, 1973; *Motorcycle Mutt,* F. Watts, 1973; *On the Water,* F. Watts, 1973; *Salt Cycle,* F. Watts, 1973; *Foolish Filly,* F. Watts, 1974; *Racing on the Wind,* F. Watts, 1974; *Gymnastics School,* F. Watts, 1976.

WORK IN PROGRESS: Hawaii Volcanoes National Park; Haleakala National Park.

SIDELIGHTS: Ruth Radlauer told *CA:* "I had access to a typewriter when I was seven years old, so I started writing plays which were adaptations of *Cinderella* and the like. I did not set out to be a writer until after I'd taught first grade. I couldn't find the books I wanted for my class, especially in the field of social studies. While I preferred to write fantasy or humor in verse, I got my start in social studies books for primary grades.

"When the State of California adopted a series of my books, my sometime collaborator, Ed Radlauer, began to look upon our writing more seriously. As a school administrator, Ed saw a great need, and we set out to supply it: reading material with a high impact of colorful reality and interest, written with a reluctant or non-bookish reader in mind. This led to our 'Reading Incentive Series' and other similar books on subjects like motorcycles, horses, drag racing, and minibikes."

AVOCATIONAL INTERESTS: Horses, music, hiking, sewing.

* * *

RADOFF, Morris Leon 1905-1978

OBITUARY NOTICE: Born January 10, 1905, in Houston, Tex.; died December 2, 1978, in St. Margaret's, Md. Archivist, records administrator, and author. For twenty-two years Radoff served as Maryland's state archivist and head of records. He authored books on the state's historic buildings, including *The State House at Annapolis,* and edited *The Old Line State, a History of Maryland.* In addition, Radoff contributed articles to numerous professional journals. Obituaries and other sources: *Directory of American Scholars,* Volume I: *History,* 6th edition, Bowker, 1974; *Washington Post,* December 3, 1978.

* * *

RAGUIN, Yves (Emile) 1912-

PERSONAL: Born November 9, 1912, in Ste. Catherine de Fierbois, France; son of Narcisse Stanislas and Jeanne (Guinault) Raguin. *Education:* Sorbonne, University of Paris, Licence es Lettres, 1934; attended Lyon-Fourviere, Lyon, France, 1939-42; Institut Catholique, Licentiate in Theology, 1943; Ecole des Langues Orientales Vivant, University of Paris, diplome (Chinese studies), 1946; additional study at Harvard-Yenching Institute, 1946-48. *Home and office address:* Ricci Institute for Chinese Studies, Hangchow Nan-lu, Section I, Lane 71, No. 9, Taipei 100, Taiwan.

CAREER: Ordained Roman Catholic priest of Society of Jesus (S.J.), 1942; Aurora University, Shanghai, China, teacher of English and French, 1950-51; Jesuit Mission Printing Office, T'u-se-wei, China, revisor of Chinese publications, 1952-53; researcher for Chinese dictionary project in Taichung, Taiwan, 1953-59; National University, Saigon, Vietnam, assistant professor of Chinese history, 1959-64; Dalat University, Dalat, Vietnam, assistant professor of philosophy of Buddhism, 1959-64; Ricci Institute for Chinese Studies, Taipei, Taiwan, researcher, 1965—; Fu-Jen Catholic University, Taipei, 1968—, began as assistant professor, currently professor of Chinese religions. Has also taught in religious institutions in Manila and Vietnam. Visiting faculty member, University of San Francisco, summer, 1976.

WRITINGS: Sheng Ao-szu-ting (title means "St. Augustin"), translated by Paul Ch'Eng, Kuangchi Press, 1960; *Chemins de la contemplation,* Desclee De Brouwer, 1970, translation by Paul Barrett published as *Paths to Contemplation,* Abbey Press, 1974; *Prier a l'heure qu'il est,* Vie Chretienne (Paris), 1971, translation by John Beevers published as *How to Pray Today: A Book of Spiritual Reflections,* Abbey Press, 1974; *Celibat pour notre temps,* Vie Chretienne, 1972, translation by Mary Humbert Kennedy published as *Celibacy for Our Times,* Abbey Press, 1974; *The Lion Head Mountain: A Guide,* Chinese Language Institute, Fu-Jen Catholic University, 1972; *Missionary Spirituality,* East Asian Pastoral Institute (Manila), 1973, enlarged edition published as *I Am Sending You: Spirituality of the Missioner,* 1973; *Bouddhisme/Christianisme* (title means "Buddhism/Christianity"), Editions de l'Epi (Paris), 1973; *La Profondeur de Dieu,* Desclee De Brouwer, 1973, translation by Kathleen England published as *The Depth of God,* Abbey Press, 1975; *Huo-p'o-ti china-kuan* (title means "Lively Contemplation"), Kuangchi Press, 1973; *L'Esprit sur le monde* (title means "The Spirit Over the World"), Desclee De Brouwer, 1975; *Dictionnaire Francais de la Langue Chinoise* (title means "French Dictionary of the Chinese Language"), Ricci Institute, 1976; (contributor) Heinrich Dumoulin and John C. Maraldo, editors, *Buddhism in the Modern World,* Macmillan, 1976.

Contributor to proceedings of East Asian Jesuit Secretariat Conference, and of articles to journals, including *Cistercian Studies, Sursum Corda, Kerygma,* and *Axes* (Paris).

WORK IN PROGRESS: A book on the experience of God; research on Chinese religions and on Eastern and Western mysticism.

SIDELIGHTS: Yves Raguin told *CA:* "I would like to help East and West to meet on a mutual understanding of the deepest human and religious experience. I am looking for a deeper understanding of other religious and especially mystical experience."

* * *

RAIMY, Victor 1913-

PERSONAL: Born March 17, 1913, in Buffalo, N.Y.; son of Christian and Alberta (Wiedeman) Raimy; married Ruth Vendig (a psychologist), July 29, 1938; children: Eric. *Education:* Antioch College, B.A., 1935; Ohio State University, Ph.D., 1943. *Politics:* Democrat. *Home:* 1333 King Ave., Boulder, Colo. 80302. *Office:* Department of Psychology, University of Colorado, Boulder, Colo. 80302.

CAREER: University of Pittsburgh, Pittsburgh, Pa., assistant professor of psychology, 1946; Ohio State University, Columbus, associate professor, 1946-48; University of Colorado, Boulder, associate professor, 1948-50, professor of psychology, 1950—, chairman of department, 1954-62. Consultant to Veterans Administration. *Military service:* U.S.

Navy, 1943-46; became lieutenant. *Member:* American Psychological Association (member of board of directors, 1963-69; president of Division of Clinical Psychology, 1962-63; president of Division of Psychotherapy, 1970-71), American Association for the Advancement of Science.

WRITINGS: Studying the School Child, Holt, 1939; (editor) *Training in Clinical Psychology,* Prentice-Hall, 1950; *The Self-Concept in Counseling,* Libraries, Ohio State University, 1971; *Misunderstandings of the Self,* Jossey-Bass, 1975.

SIDELIGHTS: Raimy writes: "My primary vocational interest is in the practice of and research on psychotherapy from a cognitive standpoint."

*   *   *

RAMKE, Bin 1947-

PERSONAL: Born February 19, 1947, in Port Neches, Tex.; son of Lloyd Binford (an engineer) and Melba (Guidry) Ramke; married Linda Keating (a textiles artist), May 31, 1967. *Education:* Louisiana State University, B.A., 1970; University of New Orleans, M.A., 1971; Ohio University, Ph.D., 1975. *Politics:* "Only among close friends." *Religion:* "Poetry." *Home:* 2000 Wynnton Rd., Apt. N-62, Columbus, Ga. 31906. *Office:* Department of Languages-Humanities, Columbus College, Columbus, Ga. 31907.

CAREER: Columbus College, Columbus, Ga., assistant professor of English, 1975—. *Member:* Modern Language Association of America. *Awards, honors:* Yale Younger Poets Award from Yale University Press, 1977, for *The Difference Between Night and Day.*

WRITINGS: Any Brass Ring (poetry chapbook), Ohio Review, 1977; *The Difference Between Night and Day* (poems), Yale University Press, 1978. Assistant editor of *Ohio Review,* 1973-75.

WORK IN PROGRESS: White Monkeys, poems.

SIDELIGHTS: Ramke writes: "My early interest and training was in mathematics and physics. Curiously, my movement away from those disciplines ten years ago paralleled the major movements *within* them during the same time—toward cosmology, toward the large unanswerable, the first and last questions: toward a concern for a *logos.* I still admire accuracy, discipline, precision, and seek those qualities in my own work. And yet *The Difference Between Night and Day* is a book about where to stand, not in order to move the world, but to be moved by it. However, it is a first book, and parts of it may well be an embarrassment to me in twenty years. Until then, I shall stand by it."

*   *   *

RANDOLPH, Ellen
See ROSS, W(illiam) E(dward) D(aniel)

*   *   *

RASKIN, Jonah 1942-

PERSONAL: Born January 3, 1942, in New York, N.Y.; son of Sam (a lawyer) and Mildred (a teacher; maiden name, Quitkin) Raskin; married Angela Massimo (a legal worker), July 26, 1977; children: Timothy Patrick. *Education:* Columbia University, A.B., 1963, M.A., 1964; University of Manchester, Ph.D., 1967. *Home:* 235 Barham, Santa Rosa, Calif. 95401.

CAREER: State University of New York at Stony Brook, assistant professor of English, 1967-72; *University Review,*

New York, N.Y., editor, 1972-74; Hoffman Institute, Mexico City, Mexico, assistant director, 1975-76; writer, 1976—. *Awards, honors:* Grant from Rabinowitz Foundation, 1974-76.

WRITINGS: The Mythology of Imperialism, Random House, 1971; (editor) *The Weather Eye* (political-cultural analysis), University Square Press, 1974; *Out of the Whale* (autobiography), Links Books, 1974; *Puerto Rico: The Flame of Resistance,* People's Press (San Francisco, Calif.), 1977; *Underground* (fiction), Bobbs-Merrill, 1978; *B. Traven: The Man Who Loved Mystery,* Lawrence Hill, 1979.

WORK IN PROGRESS: Drought, a study of the California drought, 1976-77.

SIDELIGHTS: Raskin told *CA:* "I write because I must. It's an addiction, an affliction, and a love affair. By surrendering to it I lose myself, forget the past, and move into a new identity. Thus, writing is self-creation and re-creation.

"My life in England awakened me to the past, to empire and ruins, to feudal lords and the working man who hated the blacks almost as much as he hated the boss. In Mexico, on the other hand, I awakened to the primitive, to conquest and decay, to Indian women who loved their land almost as much as they loved their own children."

AVOCATIONAL INTERESTS: Fishing, cooking.

BIOGRAPHICAL/CRITICAL SOURCES: Jonah Raskin, *Out of the Whale,* Links Books, 1974; *New York Times Book Review,* May 7, 1978.

*   *   *

RAVEN, Simon (Arthur Noel) 1927-

PERSONAL: Born December 28, 1927, in London, England; son of Arthur Godart and Esther Kate (Christmas) Raven; married Susan Mandeville Kilner, 1951 (divorced, 1957); children: Adam. *Education:* King's College, Cambridge, B.A., 1951, M.A., 1955. *Address:* c/o Blond & Briggs Ltd., 56 Doughty St., London WC1N 2LS, England.

CAREER: Researcher, 1951-52; writer, critic, dramatist, 1957—. *Military service:* British Army, 1946-48, 1953-57; became captain. *Member:* Horatian Society, Marylebone Cricket Club, Butterflies Cricket Club.

WRITINGS—All published by Anthony Blond, except as noted: *The Feathers of Death* (novel), 1959, Simon & Schuster, 1960; *Brother Cain* (novel), 1959, Simon & Schuster, 1960; *Doctors Wear Scarlet* (novel), 1960, Simon & Schuster, 1961; (editor) Gerald Kersh, *The Best of Gerald Kersh,* Heinemann, 1960; *The English Gentleman: An Essay in Attitudes,* 1961, published as *The Decline of the Gentleman,* Simon & Schuster, 1962; *Close of Play* (novel), 1962; *Boys Will Be Boys* (essays), 1963; *Royal Foundation and Other Plays,* 1965; *The Fortunes of Fingel,* Blond & Briggs, 1976.

"Alms for Oblivion" series; all novels; all published by Anthony Blond, except as noted: *The Rich Pay Late,* 1964, Putnam, 1965; *Friends in Low Places,* 1965, Putnam, 1966; *The Sabre Squadron,* 1966, Harper, 1967; *Fielding Gray,* 1967; *The Judas Boy,* 1968; *Places Where They Sing,* 1970; *Sound the Retreat,* 1971; *Come Like Shadows,* Blond & Briggs, 1972; *Bring Forth the Body,* Blond & Briggs, 1974; *The Survivors,* Blond & Briggs, 1976.

Teleplays: "Royal Foundation," British Broadcasting Corp. (BBC-TV), 1961; "The Scapegoat," BBC-TV, 1964; "Sir Jocelyn, The Minister Would Like a Word," BBC-TV,

1965; "The Gaming Book," American Broadcasting Co. (ABC-TV), 1965; "Advise and Dissent," 1965; "A Soiree at Bossoni's Hotel," 1966; "A Pyre for Private James," 1966; "Huxley's Point Counterpoint," BBC-TV, 1968; "Trollope's The Way We Live Now," BBC-TV, 1969; "The Human Element" (based on novel by Somerset Maugham), 1970; "The Pallisers" (twenty-six episode series based on the Palliser novels by Anthony Trollope), ABC-TV, 1974; "An Unofficial Rose" (based on novel by Iris Murdoch), 1974.

Radio plays: "Loser Pays All," 1961; "A Present From Venice," 1961; "The Gate of Learning," 1962; "A Friend in Need," 1962; "The Doomsday School," 1963; "The High King's Tomb," 1964; "Panther Larkin," 1964; "The Melos Affair," 1965; "Triad" (trilogy based on Thucydides' *History of the Peloponnesian War*), 1965-68; "The Last Expedition," 1967; "The Tutor," 1967; "The Prisoners in the Cave," 1968.

Other: "The Sconcing Stoup" (broadcast by BBC, 1964), published in *New Radio Drama,* BBC Publications, 1966; "The Case of Father Brendan," produced in London, 1968; "Unman, Wittering, and Zigo" (screenplay based on play by Giles Cooper), Paramount, 1971.

SIDELIGHTS: In 1964, Raven came out with *The Rich Pay Late,* the first installment in a projected series of ten novels. "Alms for Oblivion," Raven's novel sequence, was designed "to cover the English upper middle class scene since the war," according to Kerry McSweeney. Mc-Sweeney also quoted the author's intentions of having each book present a self-contained plot, though "the ten major characters [would be] all loosely connected with one another by birth or upbringing." Raven's theme for "Alms for Oblivion," as he saw it, was "that human effort and goodwill are persistently vulnerable to the malice of time, chance, and the rest of the human race."

The series, completed with the 1975 publication of *The Survivors,* received mixed reviews from both British and American critics, though several compared Raven's satiric style to that of Evelyn Waugh and Anthony Powell. John Raymond, for one, made that observation in his review of *Fielding Gray,* but he also noted that Raven effectively dealt with "the old old public-school love story with melodramatic consequences" despite its "familiar mixture" limitations. "The writer invests his book with so much witty savagery and unflagging invention and such display of comic and cretinous character that one gallops through it in no time at all," wrote Raymond.

Commonweal's Max Cosman called Raven a "combination of Graham Greene, Lawrence Durrell, and A. Conan Doyle." Speaking of *Doctors Wear Scarlet,* one of Raven's earlier books, Cosman pointed out the "deftness of [Greene's] entertainments, something of the erotic wickedness of [Durrell's] Alexandria, and a fair dash of the old-fashioned literary quality which is so endearing in [Doyle's] works" in Raven's novel. Yet, Cosman found that book "enlivened from time to time by present scatologisms that Doyle would never of course have countenanced."

In a personal column for *Spectator,* aptly entitled "Reflections of a Middle-Aged Novelist," Raven set forth his philosophy of writing with some references to other popular writers. "I have been writing novels, and thereby keeping myself off the street, for the last ten years," wrote Raven, "and as I have come to understand it, the nub of the matter is this: the primary object of a novelist must be to keep his reader reading." A successful novel must have, in Raven's

opinion, conflict, "competition, effort and achievement, on whatever level . . . physical, emotional, mental, or moral dispute." Yet Raven lamented the lack of genuine conflict in most modern novels and confessed that he found such writing easy to put down. He offered these comments of explanation: "In short, what is destroying the quality of the novel, just as it is destroying the quality of life itself, is egalitarian dogma; for the chief fascination of novels, as of life, lies in the perception, and the celebration of human inequalities."

Unlike many of his contemporaries, Raven does not use his writing as a means of protest. In reply to *London Magazine*'s question on the writer as artist and polemicist, Raven noted: "It is not the writer's business to organize public opinion or anything else; it is his business to produce written work. . . . It is the artist's function to give pleasure, not to convert."

Kerry McSweeney noted that one of Raven's characters, Fielding Gray, expressed Raven's "disarmingly modest" evaluation of his own work in the novel *Places Where They Sing:* "I never said I was an artist. I am an entertainer . . . I arrange words in pleasing patterns in order to make money. I try to give good value—to see that my patterns are well-wrought—but I do not delude myself by inflating the nature of my function. I try to be neat, intelligent and lucid: let others be 'creative' or 'inspired'."

BIOGRAPHICAL/CRITICAL SOURCES: Spectator, January 30, 1959, October 23, 1959, November 24, 1961, March 6, 1966, October 14, 1966, September 22, 1967, January 24, 1969, March 7, 1970, October 23, 1971, October 28, 1972, November 2, 1974, June 12, 1976, December 18, 1976; *New Statesman,* January 31, 1959, December 1, 1961, October 2, 1964, October 15, 1965, October 14, 1966, September 15, 1967, February 27, 1970, October 22, 1971, October 6, 1972, October 27, 1972, November 1, 1974, June 11, 1976; *Times Literary Supplement,* October 23, 1959, December 15, 1961, October 8, 1964, October 14, 1965, June 16, 1966, October 13, 1966, September 14, 1967, October 3, 1968, February 26, 1970, October 22, 1971, October 27, 1972, November 1, 1974, June 11, 1976, December 10, 1976; *Kirkus Reviews,* December 1, 1959, March 15, 1961, March 1, 1966.

Yale Review, March, 1960; *New York Herald Tribune Book Review,* October 2, 1960, May 27, 1962; *Manchester Guardian,* November 11, 1960, November 24, 1961, October 13, 1966, September 21, 1967, October 3, 1968; Simon Raven, *The English Gentleman: An Essay on Attitudes,* Anthony Blond, 1961; *Commonweal,* June 16, 1961; *San Francisco Chronicle,* May 27, 1962; *Best Sellers,* April 1, 1965; *New York Times Book Review,* April 4, 1965, April 3, 1966; *Newsweek,* April 5, 1965; *New York Review of Books,* April 22, 1965; *Book Week,* May 1, 1966; *Books and Bookmen,* July, 1966, December, 1966, November, 1968, August, 1969, June, 1970, December, 1970, November, 1971, November, 1972, January, 1973, January, 1977; *Punch,* October 19, 1966, September 20, 1967, October 3, 1968; Simon Raven, *Fielding Gray,* Antony Blond, 1967; *Saturday Review,* May 27, 1967; *Listener,* September 14, 1967, September 26, 1968, February 26, 1970, October 28, 1971, November 30, 1972, November 21, 1974, June 10, 1976, December 16, 1976; *Observer Review,* September 10, 1967, September 22, 1968, February 22, 1970, October 17, 1971, October 22, 1972, November 10, 1974, May 4, 1975, June 6, 1976, November 14, 1976; *London Magazine,* August 8, 1968.

Simon Raven, *Places Where They Sing,* Anthony Blond, 1970; *Queen's Quarterly,* spring, 1971; *Guardian Weekly,* January 9, 1977.

READ, Hadley 1918-

PERSONAL: Born December 4, 1918, in Stanhope, Iowa; son of Benjamin (a farmer) and Lillian (Sickinger) Read; married Margaret Kumlien (a writer and painter), August, 1940; children: Gregory Charles, Mary Ellen Read Beth, Phillip (deceased). *Education:* Iowa State University, B.S., 1939, M.S., 1941. *Politics:* Independent. *Religion:* Methodist. *Home:* 605 South Edwin, Champaign, Ill. 61820. *Office:* Department of Agricultural Communications, University of Illinois, 55 Mumford Hall, Urbana, Ill. 61801.

CAREER: Iowa State University, Ames, assistant editor, 1944-47; University of Illinois at Urbana-Champaign, Urbana, professor of agricultural communications and head of department, 1947-75, professor emeritus, 1975—. Consultant to U.S. Department of State. *Member:* American Association of Agricultural College Editors, Alpha Zeta, Gamma Sigma Delta, Delta Sigma Rho.

WRITINGS: Communication: Methods for All Media, University of Illinois Press, 1972; *Phillip: In Search of Meaning,* Interstate, 1972; *Partners With India: Building Agricultural Universities,* College of Agriculture, University of Illinois, 1974; *Morning Chores and Other Times Remembered,* University of Illinois Press, 1977.

WORK IN PROGRESS: SIDS: Slayer of My Three Children, about a mother who lost three children to Sudden Infant Death Syndrome.

SIDELIGHTS: Read writes: ''As my past writings indicate, I am interested in a wide range of subject areas. The communication book is a textbook. *Phillip* is about our son who died of cancer. *Partners* is about the work of U.S. universities in India. *Morning Chores,* written in prose poem style, is about growing up on an Iowa farm during the Depression.''

*   *   *

REAGEN, Michael V. 1942-

PERSONAL: Born July 27, 1942, in Jersey City, N.J.; son of Vincent Thomas (in insurance) and Jeanette (Jameson) Reagen; married Susan Carol Koplinka (a registered nurse), September 10, 1966; children: Jane, Erin, Jennifer. *Education:* Fordham University, B.S., 1964; University of Illinois, M.S., 1965; Syracuse University, Ph.D., 1972; also attended Wayne State University. *Politics:* Republican. *Religion:* Roman Catholic. *Home:* 209 Lockwood Rd., Syracuse, N.Y. 13214. *Office:* Office of the County Executive, Onondaga County Civic Center, Syracuse, N.Y. 13202.

CAREER: Maria Regina College, Syracuse, N.Y., assistant to the president and assistant dean, 1966-69; Syracuse University, Syracuse, program administrator at Continuing Education Center for the Public Service, 1969-72, directing research fellow of Syracuse University Research Corp. and director of Policy Institute, 1972-74, director of Institute for Drug Education, 1971-72; president of Associated Organizational Consultants, Inc., 1974; Onondaga County, Syracuse, county administrator, 1972—, administrator for human services, 1976—. Visiting lecturer at State University of New York College at Oswego, summer, 1970, U.S. Army Chaplain's School, 1971-72, Central New York Police Academy, 1971-75, and Onondaga Community College, 1975; senior instructor at Institute for Local Public Service, 1974-77; adjunct member of faculty at Syracuse University, 1971—; director of seminars. Creator, producer, and host of ''Dialog,'' on WFBL-Radio, 1966-68; executive producer of ''Syracuse University Forum,'' on WNYS-TV, 1969-70. Established local Emergency Medical Services Advisory

Board, Human Services Cabinet, Advisory Board for Services to Handicapped Persons, Inter-Agency Task Force on Services to Handicapped Persons, and Human Services Advisory Board; head of New York Human Services Task Force, 1977. Head of local mayor's Temporary Commission on Narcotics Abuse and Addiction, 1970-71, and Syracuse Drug Abuse Commission, 1971-72; co-chairman of Onondaga-Syracuse Criminal Justice Coordinating Committee, 1976-77; member of executive committee of Syracuse Neighborhood Health Center, 1976-77; member of board of directors of Onondaga Republican Citizens Committee and Syracuse Urban League, 1976-77; member of advisory board of Syracuse Model Cities Agency, 1969-70, and Onondaga County Correctional Facility, 1973-75. Consultant to Ford Foundation, Kettering Foundation, and Institute for Juvenile Justice.

MEMBER: International Association of Chiefs of Police, American Association of University Professors, Association for Education in Journalism, American Society for Public Administration (regional president, 1974-75), American Academy of Political and Social Science, National Association for the Control of Dangerous Drugs and Narcotics, National Council on Crime and Delinquency, New York State Criminal Justice Educators Association, Beta Gamma Sigma, Alpha Delta Sigma (vice-president, 1964), Alpha Beta Kappa, Alpha Kappa Psi (president, 1964), Snooks Pond Association, Onondaga County Republican Club. *Awards, honors:* Leadership citation from Onondaga County Probation Officers Association, 1978.

WRITINGS: (Editor with Robert I. Iversen, and contributor) *Readings for the Maxwell International Development Seminar,* Syracuse University, 1970; (editor with L. L. Smith, and contributor) *Management Development for Urban Administration,* Syracuse University, 1970; (editor) *Readings for the Institute for Drug Education at Syracuse,* Continuing Education Center for the Public Service, Syracuse University, 1971; (editor with Doris Chertow) *The Challenge of Modern Church-Public Relations,* American Foundation for Continuing Education, Syracuse University, 1972; (editor) *Readings on Drug Education,* Scarecrow, 1972; (with Smith, Stanley Hunterton, and LeeAnn Sumnicht) *Busing: Ground Zero in School Desegregation,* Syracuse University Research Corp., 1972; (with Donald M. Stoughton and Warren R. Darby) *A Manual for Student Service Officers of the New York City School System,* Syracuse University Research Corp., 1972. Also author of *School Behind Bars,* Syracuse University Research Corp., and *Readings for Student Service Personnel of the New York City School System,* Syracuse University Research Corp. (with Gerald M. Pops).

Speechwriter for public officials. Co-author of ''On Campus,'' a column syndicated to sixteen New York state newspapers, 1968-69. Contributor of more than thirty articles to a wide variety of magazines and newspapers, including *Linage, Central New Yorker, Catholic Miss,* and *Public Relations Digest.*

WORK IN PROGRESS: Community Based Corrections: An Introductory Text, for C. W. Anderson Co.; *The Public's Future Safety,* with Lee Porter and Donald M. Stoughton, for C. C Thomas.

SIDELIGHTS: Reagen's emphasis, as an appointed official of county government, has been formulating and implementing public policy in human and criminal justice services. These services include agencies responsible for health, mental health, social well-being, and veterans' affairs. He has also concerned himself with child guidance centers and youth services, and with efforts to de-institutionalize youthful offenders.

AVOCATIONAL INTERESTS: Tennis, motorcycling.

* * *

REAMY, Tom 1935-1977

PERSONAL: Born January 25, 1935, in Woodson, Tex.; son of Oliver Earl (a farmer) and Callie Gertrude (Pitts) Reamy. *Education:* Attended McMurry College, 1953-54, and Odessa Junior College, 1954-55. *Home address:* P.O. Box 162, Woodson, Tex. 76091. *Agent:* Virginia Kidd, P.O. Box 278, Milford, Pa. 18337.

CAREER: Movie projectionist, bank teller, finance company collector, and dispatcher, 1955-57; Collins Radio Inc. (aerospace industry), Dallas, Tex., technical illustrator, 1957-70; Mandala Productions (film company), Hollywood, Calif., art director and scene designer, 1970-72; Nickelodeon Graphics, Kansas City, Mo., co-owner and operator, 1975-77. Held positions involved with various screenplays, including actor in "Adventures of Gary," 1969, actor in "The Goddaughter," 1971, assistant director, scene designer, and actor in "Sadie," 1972, scriptwriter, assistant director, and actor in "The Mislaid Genie," 1972, and property manager of "Flesh Gordon," released by Mammoth Films, 1974. *Member:* Science Fiction Writers of America, Dallas Area Science Fiction Society (vice-president, 1960-70), Kansas City Science Fiction Society. *Awards, honors:* Science Fiction Writers of America Nebula Award for best novella, 1975, for "San Diego Lightfoot Sue"; John W. Campbell Award for best new writer, 1976; three-time Hugo Award nominee for *Trumpet.*

WRITINGS: (Editor and designer) *MidAmericon Program Book,* Science Fiction Conventions of Kansas City, Inc., 1976; *Blind Voices* (science fiction), Putnam, 1978; *San Diego Lightfoot Sue and Other Stories* (science fiction; short stories), introduction by Harlan Ellison, Heritage Press, in press. Also author and director of screenplay "Fugue," 1970. Editor of *Trumpet,* 1964-73; co-editor of *Nickelodeon,* 1976-77; art director of *Delap's F & SF Review,* 1976-77 and *Shayol,* 1977.

SIDELIGHTS: Blind Voices is being considered for a major feature-length film.

BIOGRAPHICAL/CRITICAL SOURCES: Empire SF, February, 1977; *Shayol,* Number 1, November, 1977.

(Died November 5, 1977, in Kansas City, Mo.)

[Sketch verified by literary agent, Virginia Kidd]

* * *

REBETA-BURDITT, Joyce

CAREER: ABC-TV, New York City, currently programming executive.

WRITINGS: The Cracker Factory (novel), Macmillan, 1977.

SIDELIGHTS: Like Cassie Barrett, the protagonist in *The Cracker Factory,* Joyce Rebeta-Burditt knows firsthand what it means to survive a nervous breakdown and come to terms with a humiliating and frightening addiction to alcohol. Her novel is largely the autobiographical story of her struggle up from the desperation and alienation of alcoholism to sobriety, sanity, and self-acceptance.

Sheila Ballantyne commented that the scenes in the mental ward ("the cracker factory") "often read like Insanity-as-Sit-Com; there's a laugh a minute. But Cassie's humor is her strongest weapon, and on a deeper level the book is a serious and moving one. Cassie is a survivor and, while her manner often appears glib, she has insight to burn."

BIOGRAPHICAL/CRITICAL SOURCES: New York Times Book Review, April 17, 1977.*

* * *

REDDER, George
See DRUMMOND, Jack

* * *

REES, Robert A(lvin) 1935-

PERSONAL: Born November 17, 1935, in Los Angeles, Calif.; son of Alvin Clayton and Ona Marie (Hardin) Rees; married Ruth Stanfield (a musician), April 1, 1961; children: Jennifer, Robert S., Julianna, Maddox. *Education:* Universite Laval, certificate, 1959; Brigham Young University, B.A., 1960; University of Wisconsin, Madison, M.A., 1962, Ph.D., 1966. *Politics:* Independent. *Religion:* Church of Jesus Christ of Latter-day Saints (Mormon). *Home:* 10316 Cheviot Dr., Los Angeles, Calif. 90064. *Office:* Department of the Arts, Extension, University of California, 10995 LeConte Ave., Los Angeles, Calif. 90024.

CAREER: University of Wisconsin, Madison, executive secretary, 1964-66; University of California, Los Angeles, assistant professor of English, 1966-74, director of department of humanities and communications for Extension, 1974-77, director of department of the arts for Extension, 1977—. Visiting associate professor at California State University, Northridge, 1967, and California State University, Los Angeles, 1969; adjunct professor at Pepperdine University, 1974—. Professional associate of PEDR (research and development firm), 1973-74; research director at Center for Educational Leadership, 1973-74. Member of board of trustees and executive committee of Dialogue Foundation, 1971-76.

WRITINGS: (Editor with Barry Menikoff) *The Short Story: An Introductory Anthology,* Little, Brown, 1969, 2nd edition, 1974; (editor with Earl N. Harbert, and contributor) *Fifteen American Authors Before 1900: Bibliographic Essays on Research and Criticism,* University of Wisconsin Press, 1971; (editor with Alan Sandy) Washington Irving, *The Adventures of Captain Bonneville,* Twayne, 1977. Contributor of about fifteen articles and reviews to literature journals. Book review editor of *Dialogue: A Journal of Mormon Thought,* 1969-71, editor, 1971-76.

WORK IN PROGRESS: With Carl Johnson, *A Systematic Approach to Preparing for College, Graduate, Professional School Exams.*

SIDELIGHTS: Rees told *CA:* "I am interested in broad based studies in the arts and humanities. My current research involves the arts and religion, with an emphasis on forms of worship."

* * *

REEVES, Paschal 1917-1976

PERSONAL: Born September 8, 1917, in Birmingham, Ala.; son of W. P. (a Baptist minister) and Margaret (Webb) Reeves; married Suzanne Louise Smith, December 17, 1960; children: Paschal III, Margaret Louise. *Education:* University of Alabama, B.A., 1939, also earned M.A.; Southern Baptist Theological Seminary, earned Th.M.;

Duke University, earned M.A. and Ph.D. *Politics:* Democrat. *Religion:* Baptist.

CAREER: Member of English faculty at University of Georgia, Athens. *Military service:* U.S. Army; became captain; received Purple Heart.

WRITINGS: Thomas Wolfe's Albatross: Race and Nationality in America, University of Georgia Press, 1968; (editor) *The Merrill Checklist of Thomas Wolfe,* C. E. Merrill, 1969; *The Merrill Studies in Look Homeward Angel,* C. E. Merrill, 1970; (editor with Richard S. Kennedy) *Notebooks of Thomas Wolfe,* two volumes, University of North Carolina Press, 1970; (editor) *Thomas Wolfe and the Glass of Time,* University of Georgia Press, 1971; *The Merrill Guide to Thomas Wolfe,* C. E. Merrill, 1972; (editor and author of introduction) *Thomas Wolfe: The Critical Reception,* David Lewis, 1974.

(Died July 16, 1976, in Atlanta, Ga.)

[Sketch verified by wife, Suzanne S. Reeves]

*   *   *

REICH, Bernard 1941-

PERSONAL: Born December 5, 1941, in Brooklyn, N.Y.; son of Moe and Rosalyn (Hartglass) Reich; married Madelyn Sue Ingber, June 16, 1963; children: Barry, Norman, Michael, Jennifer. *Education:* City College of the City University of New York, B.A. (cum laude), 1961; University of Virginia, M.A., 1963, Ph.D., 1964. *Religion:* Jewish. *Home:* 13800 Turnmore Rd., Wheaton, Md. 20906. *Office:* Department of Political Science, George Washington University, Washington, D.C. 20052.

CAREER: George Washington University, Washington, D.C., assistant professor, 1964-67, 1968-70, associate professor, 1970-76, professor of political science and international affairs, 1976—, head of department of political science, 1976—. Visiting assistant professor at University of Virginia, spring, 1969; visiting professor at Baltimore Hebrew College, 1975—; member of adjunct faculty at U.S. Defense Intelligence School, 1975—; professorial lecturer at Johns Hopkins University, 1978—; lecturer at National War College, Foreign Service Institute, U.S. Military Academy, U.S. Naval Academy, Inter-American Defense College, and foreign colleges and universities. Visiting research associate at Tel Aviv University, 1971-72. Participant in international seminars; testified before U.S. Congress; consultant to U.S. Department of State and Research Analysis Corp.

MEMBER: International Institute for Strategic Studies, Middle East Institute, Middle East Studies Association (fellow), Phi Beta Kappa, Delta Phi Epsilon. *Awards, honors:* Fulbright grant, summer, 1965, for Egypt; National Science Foundation fellowship, 1971-72, for Israel.

WRITINGS: (Contributor) Tareq Ismael, editor, *Governments and Politics of the Contemporary Middle East,* Dorsey, 1970; *Israel in Paperback* (bibliography), Middle East Studies Association, 1971; *Israel and the Occupied Territories,* U.S. Department of State, 1974; (with Arnon Gutfeld) *Arzot Habrit Vehasechsuch Yisraeli-Aravi* (title means "The United States and the Israeli-Arab Conflict"), Maarachot (Tel Aviv), 1977; *Quest for Peace: United States-Israel Relations and the Arab-Israeli Conflict,* Transaction Books, 1977; (and editor with David Long) *Government and Politics of the Middle East,* Westview, 1979.

Also contributor of chapters published in books in his field. Author of technical reports. Contributor to *Concise Ency-*

clopedia of the Middle East and *Area Handbook for Lebanon.* Contributor of about fifteen articles to scholarly journals. Member of board of advisory editors of *Middle East Journal,* 1977—; consulting editor of *New Middle East,* 1971-73.

WORK IN PROGRESS: Articles and chapters for several books on United States—Middle East policy and on Israeli politics.

*   *   *

REID, John T(urner) 1908-1978

PERSONAL: Born April 21, 1908, in Vallejo, Calif.; son of John Glover (an engineer) and Annie (a nurse; maiden name, Turner) Reid; married Dorcas Worsley, June 3, 1933 (divorced, 1947); married Marian Hamilton, May 17, 1947; children: Margaret Anne Reid O'Connell, Sarah. *Education:* Stanford University, B.A. (cum laude), 1930, M.A., 1931, Ph.D., 1936. *Politics:* Democrat. *Home:* 1045 Northeast Fourth St., Gainesville, Fla. 32601.

CAREER: Duke University, Durham, N.C., assistant professor of Spanish and Spanish-American literature, 1938-41; U.S. Foreign Service, Washington, D.C., special assistant to ambassador in Quito, Ecuador, 1942-44, cultural attache at embassy in Havana, Cuba, 1943-45; University of California, Los Angeles, assistant professor of Spanish and Spanish-American literature, 1946-49; U.S. Foreign Service, public affairs officer at embassy in Caracas, Venezuela, 1949-51; U.S. Department of State, Washington, D.C., area officer, 1951-52, inspector in Germany, 1953; U.S. Foreign Service, cultural attache at embassies in Madrid, Spain, 1953-58, New Delhi, India, 1958-65, and Buenos Aires, Argentina, 1965-66; U.S. Information Agency, Washington, D.C., language and area training officer, 1966-70; University of Florida, Gainesville, assistant professor, 1970-71, associate professor of Spanish, 1972-78. Visiting professor at University of New Mexico, 1949. Head of board of directors of U.S. Educational Foundation (India), 1958-63; executive fellow of Brookings Institution, 1963-64.

MEMBER: International P.E.N., American Association of Teachers of Spanish and Portuguese, Phi Beta Kappa, Sigma Delta Pi (president, 1938-40).

WRITINGS: Modern Spain and Liberalism: A Study in Literary Contrasts, Stanford University Press, 1937; (with E. H. Hespelt and others) *An Outline History of Spanish American Literature,* F. S. Crofts & Co., 1942, new edition, Appleton, 1965; (editor with Hespelt and others) *An Anthology of Spanish American Literature,* 1946, new edition, Appleton, 1968.

Trece ensayos sobre literatura de los Estados Unidos, Tip La Nacion, 1952; *Democracy,* U.S. Information Service, 1960; *Bridges of Understanding,* U.S. Information Service, 1961; *Indian Influences in American Literature and Thought,* Indian Council for Cultural Relations, 1965; *Spanish American Images of the United States, 1790-1960,* University Presses of Florida, 1977.

Also author of *La cultura en una democracia industrializada,* 1954, *The United States in the Spanish American Mind, Literary Nationalism in Spanish America,* and *Artistic Nationalism in Spanish America.*

Editor of *Thoreau and India,* 1962, and *New Directions in the American University,* 1963. Also editor of *Atlantico,* 1955-58, and *American Review,* 1960-63; assistant editor of *Hispania,* 1938-44.

SIDELIGHTS: Reid wrote: "In my writing I have tried to

combine literary scholarship with social concerns." *Avocational interests:* Collecting stamps, poetry, gardening, cooking.

(Died November 11, 1978, in Oaxaca, Mexico)
[Sketch verified by wife, Marian Hamilton]

* * *

REIGSTAD, Paul (Matthew) 1921-

PERSONAL: Born November 12, 1921, in Minneapolis, Minn.; son of Olin Spencer (a clergyman) and Amanda Sophie (Fjelstad) Reigstad; married Marjorie Jane Gullickson, June 24, 1950; children: Emily, Katharine. *Education:* St. Olaf College, B.A., 1943; University of New Mexico, M.A., 1956, Ph.D., 1958. *Religion:* Lutheran. *Home:* 11409 66th Ave. E., Puyallup, Wash. 98371. *Office:* Department of English, Pacific Lutheran University, Tacoma, Wash. 98447.

CAREER: English teacher in public schools in East Grand Forks, Minn., 1948-50, and Fergus Falls, Minn., 1950-54; Pacific Lutheran University, Tacoma, Wash., assistant professor, 1958-62, associate professor, 1962-66, professor of English, 1966—, Regency Professor, 1977-78, chairman of department, 1967-71, chairman of Division of Humanities, 1970-74. *Member:* Modern Language Association of America. *Awards, honors:* Scandinavian-American Foundation fellowship, 1966.

WRITINGS: Roelvaag: His Life and Art, University of Nebraska Press, 1972. Contributor to journals.

WORK IN PROGRESS: The Scandinavian Immigrant Experience.

* * *

REISS, Alvin H(erbert) 1930-

PERSONAL: Born June 15, 1930, in Brooklyn, N.Y.; son of Samuel (a manufacturer) and Anne (Elowsky) Reiss; married Ellen Komoroff (a travel agent), August 26, 1956; children: Steven, Robert, Michael. *Education:* University of Wisconsin (now University of Wisconsin—Madison), B.A., 1952, M.A., 1953. *Home:* 110 Riverside Dr., New York, N.Y. 10024. *Office:* 408 West 57th St., New York, N.Y. 10019.

CAREER: Gordon Pollack Productions, New York City, assistant producer, 1955-56; Larry Gore Publicity, New York City, writer, 1956-57; Lobsenz Public Relations, New York City, media director, 1957-62; *Arts Management,* New York City, editor and publisher, 1962—. Adjunct assistant professor at Adelphi University and director of management program for the arts, both 1975—. Host of "Arts Forum" on WNYC-Radio, 1968—. Program director for Albert Dorne Memorial Foundation, 1968-71; director of Performing Arts Management Institute, 1971—. *Military service:* U.S. Army, Counterintelligence Corps, 1953-55. *Member:* Association of American Dance Companies (member of board of directors; past vice-president), National Guild of Community Schools of the Arts (member of board of directors), American Society of Journalists and Authors (past member of board of directors), Authors Guild of Authors League of America, Symphony for the United Nations (member of board of directors).

WRITINGS: The Arts Management Handbook, Law-Arts Publishers, 1970, revised edition, 1974; *Culture and Company,* Twayne, 1972; *The Arts Management Reader,* Dekker, 1979. Author of "Business and the Arts," a column in *Cul-*

tural Affairs, 1967-70. Contributor to newspapers and magazines, including *New York Times, Esquire, American Way, Coronet, Family Health, Art News, Mainliner,* and *Cue.*

WORK IN PROGRESS: A satirical book; writing and composing a musical play entitled "The Legend of Paul Bunyan."

SIDELIGHTS: Reiss told *CA* that his work involves "frequent lecturing before arts, business, and civic groups throughout the country and the development of seminars and symposia. Many of the above are designed to involve new audiences in working relationships with the arts. Also, I do public readings of my satire from time to time. I consult with corporations on the development of special projects in the arts and in other areas of public interest. Through much of my work and my articles and books I have been able to demonstrate that programs in the public interest frequently benefit the doer as much as they benefit the recipient."

* * *

RELGIS, Eugene 1895-

PERSONAL: Surname originally Siegler; name legally changed in 1920; born March 2, 1895, in Yassy, Romania; immigrated to Uruguay, 1947; son of David (an economist) and Sofia (Wachtel) Siegler; married Ana Taubes, January 15, 1921; children: Alexander. *Education:* University of Bucharest, degree in architecture, 1915, degree in letters and philosophy, 1916. *Home and office:* Calle Gaboto 903, Apt. 7, Montevideo, Uruguay.

CAREER: Writer, 1912—. Worked as librarian in Montevideo, Uruguay, and Bucharest, Romania, 1922-46; lecturer in various colleges and universities, 1922-65, including Faculty of Humanities and Sciences, Montevideo, 1949-56, Colegio Libre de Estudios Superiores, Buenos Aires, Argentina, 1952, and Ministry of Culture, Rio de Janeiro, Brazil, 1953. Honorary member of Hebrew University of Jerusalem. *Member:* P.E.N. (Writers in Exile Section). *Awards, honors:* Award from New History Society, 1933; awards from Wars Resisters International, 1948-51; candidate for Nobel Peace Prize, 1956; awards from Ministry of Education and Culture, Montevideo, 1956, 1958.

WRITINGS—In English: The Principles of Humanism, preface by Albert Einstein, Oriole Press, 1933, 4th edition published as *Que es el humanitarismo?: Principios y accion* (title means "What Is Humanitarism: Principles and Action"), Editiones Humanidad, 1954, 5th edition, 1969; *Muted Voices,* translated from the French edition by Rose Freeman-Ishill, Oriole Press, 1938, reprinted, Gordon Press, 1973.

Other works: *Petru Arbore* (title means "Peter Arbore"), Editura Umanitatea, 1924; *Cosmometapolis,* translated by Rose Arp from the original Romanian manuscript, Mignolet & Storz (Paris), 1935, revised and augmented edition published in Spanish under same title, Ediciones Humanidad, 1950; *Georg Fr. Nicolai: Un sabio y un hombre del porvenir* (title means "Georg Fr. Nicolai: A Wise and Future Man"), Editiones Reconstruir, 1949, 2nd edition, Cajica, 1965.

Romain Rolland (essays), Ediciones Humanidad, 1951; *Stefan Zweig, cazador de almas* (title means "Stefan Zweig, the Hunter of Souls), Ediciones Medina, 1952; *De mis peregrinaciones europeas* (title means "European Pilgrimages"), Ediciones Hachette (Buenos Aires), 1953; *Historia sexual de la humanidad* (title means "A Sexual History of Mankind"), translated by Tito Livio Bancescu from the original Romanian manuscript, Editorial Americales, 1953,

3rd edition, Editorial Cevoit, 1964; *El hombre libre frente a la barbarie totalitaria: Un Caso de conciencia; Romain Rolland* (title means "The Free Man in the Face of Totalitarian Barbarity: A Case of Conscience; Romain Rolland"), University of Montevideo, 1954; *Profetas y poetas: Valores Permanentes y temporarios del judaismo* (title means "Prophets and Poets"), Editorial Candelabro, 1955; *El humanitarismo* (title means "Humanitarianism"), translation by Eloy Muniz and Alicia Rincon from the French manuscript, Editorial Americalee, 1956; *Diario de Otono* (title means "Autumn Diary"), Editorial Americalee, 1956; (with Lotar Radaceanu) *Humanitarismo y socialismo* (title means "Humanitarianism and Socialism"), Ediciones Humanidad, 1957; *Melodias del silencio: Poemas en prosa* (title means "Melodies of Silence: Prose Poems"), Ediciones J. Herrera y Reissig, 1957; *Perspectivas culturales en Sudamerica* (title means "Cultural Perspectives in South America"), University of Montevideo, 1958; *La columna entre ruinas* (title means "The Column Among the Ruins"), Editorial Americalee, 1958; *Albores de libertad* (title means "Daybreak of Liberty"), Editorial Reconstruir, 1959; *El espiritu activo* (essays; title means "The Active Spirit"), Ediciones Humanidad, 1959.

Las amistades de Miron (letters; title means "Miron's Friends"), Ediciones Humanidad, 1960; *En un lugar de los Andes y otros poemas* (title means "In a Place in the Andes, and Other Poems"), Ediciones J. Herrera y Reissig, 1960; *Sendas en spiral* (title means "Spiral Roads"), Ediciones Humanidad, 1960; *Doce capitales: Peregrinaciones Europeas* (title means "Twelve Capitals: European Pilgrimages"; includes "Bulgaria desconocida," "De mis peregrinaciones europeas," and "Sendas en spiral"), Ediciones Humanidad, 1961; *La paz del hombre* (title means "The Peace of Man"), Ediciones Humanidad, 1961; *Testigo de mi tiempo* (title means "Witness of My Time"), Ediciones Humanidad, 1961; *Corazones y motores* (title means "Hearts and Motors"), translated by Pablo R. Troise from original Romanian manuscript, Ediciones Humanidad, 1963; *Sol naciente* [and] *El triunfo del no ser* (title means "Sunrise" and "The Triumph of Not to Be"), translated from original Romanian manuscript, Ediciones Humanidad, 1963; *Invitacion de Eugen Relgis a la encuesta America-Europa,* Tierra y Libertad, 1968; *Eneusta America-Europa* (title means "Inquire America-Europe"), [Mexico], 1968; *Hojas de mi calendario* (title means "Sheets of My Calendar"), Ediciones Humanidad, 1970; *Obras* (collection of four books of poetry), Ediciones Humanidad, 1977. Contributor to Central and South American journals and newspapers, including *El Plata,* 1950-65, and *Revista National,* 1950-68.

SIDELIGHTS: Correspondence between Eugene Relgis and his international friends and associates, which number over twenty thousand letters, have been given to the libraries of Hebrew University of Jerusalem and the International Institute of Social History in Amsterdam. Other papers written by Relgis are preserved in the library of Swarthmore College, the National Library of Montevideo, the Central Library of the Academy in Bucharest, and several other international institutes.

* * *

RENAULT, Mary
    See CHALLANS, Mary

* * *

RENSBERGER, Boyce   1942-
PERSONAL: Born September 7, 1942, in Indianapolis,

Ind.; son of Earl A. (a carpenter) and Nina J. (Fehrman) Rensberger; married Judith Condit, August 20, 1966; children: Erik, Joel. *Education:* University of Miami, Coral Gables, Fla., B.S., 1964; Syracuse University, M.S., 1966. *Residence:* Montclair, N.J. *Agent:* Betty Marks, 51 East 42nd St., New York, N.Y. 10017. *Office: New York Times,* 229 West 43rd St., New York, N.Y. 10036.

CAREER: Detroit Free Press, Detroit, Mich., science writer, 1966-71; *New York Times,* New York, N.Y., science writer, 1971—. *Awards, honors:* Meeman Foundation-Scripps-Howard conservation award, 1970; award from Deadline Club, 1977.

WRITINGS: The Cult of the Wild, Doubleday, 1977. Contributor to national magazines, including *Penthouse, Sports Afield, Mademoiselle,* and *International Wildlife.*

WORK IN PROGRESS: Human Evolution.

SIDELIGHTS: Rensberger writes: "A significant aim has been to present science to the non-scientist, through whatever medium, in a way that exploits the capacity to be fascinated.

"I have a major personal interest in Africa as the cradle of mankind and as the place where the broadest range of human cultures—from the Stone Age to the Space Age—can be found."

* * *

RHEIN, Phillip H(enry)   1923-
PERSONAL: Born August 10, 1923, in Belleville, Ill.; son of Hugo (a banker) and Maybel (Stoltz) Rhein; married Ruth Veile, June 17, 1950; children: Jeffrey P., Tricia L. *Education:* Washington University, A.B., 1950, M.A., 1952; University of Michigan, Ph.D., 1960. *Home:* 4936 Darlington Dr., Nashville, Tenn. 37211. *Office address:* P.O. Box 1567, Station B, Vanderbilt University, Nashville, Tenn. 37235.

CAREER: Valparaiso University, Valparaiso, Ind., assistant professor of English and German, 1953-60; Vanderbilt University, Nashville, Tenn., assistant professor, 1960-64, associate professor, 1964-70, professor of comparative literature and German, 1970—, chairman of comparative literature program, 1966-70, chairman of department of Germanic and Slavic languages and literatures, 1976—. Lecturer; consultant to Tennessee Committee for the Humanities and to Virginia Military Institute, 1972, and Florida Junior College, 1974. *Member:* Modern Language Association of America, American Comparative Literature Association, American Association for the Advancement of Slavic Studies, Southern Atlantic Modern Languages Association, Phi Beta Kappa, Delta Phi Alpha.

WRITINGS: The Urge to Live (nonfiction), University of North Carolina Press, 1964; *Camus,* Twayne, 1970; (contributor) Siegfried Mews, editor, *Studies in German Literature of the 19th and 20th Centuries,* University of North Carolina Press, 1970; (contributor) Raymond Gay-Crosier, editor, *Camus 1970,* Universite de Sherbrooke, 1970; *Camus,* Hippocrene, 1972; (with H. J. Schulz) *Comparative Literature: The Early Years,* University of North Carolina Press, 1973; (contributor) Wolodymyr T. Zyla, editor, *Camus,* Texas Tech University Press, 1976. Contributor of reviews and essays to journals, including *South Atlantic Bulletin, Humanities Journal,* and *Dictionnaire Internationale des termes litteraires.*

WORK IN PROGRESS: Articles, "The Comparable Art of Albrecht Duerer and Guenter Grass," "The What and the Why of Humanities,'' and *Western Humanities*, a series of essays on the integration of the arts; *Alfred Kubin*, a monograph.

* * *

RHODES, William C(onley) 1918-

PERSONAL: Born November 14, 1918, in New Orleans, La.; son of William Conley (a sales executive) and Nell Elizabeth (Von der Haav) Rhodes; married M. Estelle Smith (in paralegal work), April 6, 1942; children: William C. III, Joseph Carl, Naomi Estelle, Trisha Lynn. *Education:* Emory University, A.B., 1948, M.A., 1949; Ohio State University, Ph.D., 1954. *Home:* 1815 East Stadium Blvd., Ann Arbor, Mich. 48104. *Office:* 130 South First St., University of Michigan, Ann Arbor, Mich. 48109.

CAREER: Emory University, Atlanta, Ga., in hospital administration, 1946-49; Georgia Department of Public Health, Atlanta, psychologist, 1949-56; George Peabody College for Teachers, Nashville, Tenn., assistant professor, 1956-58, associate professor, 1958-60, professor of psychology, 1960-66; National Institute of Mental Health, Washington, D.C., assistant director of Division of Children, 1966-68; University of Michigan, Ann Arbor, professor of psychology, 1968—. *Military service:* U.S. Army, Medical Administration Corps, 1941-46; became major. *Member:* Sigma Xi.

WRITINGS: A Study of Child Variance: Conceptual Project in Emotional Disturbance, University of Michigan Press, Volume I: *Conceptual Models*, 1972, Volume II: *Interventions*, 1973, Volume III: *Service Delivery Systems*, 1974, Volume IV: *The Future*, 1974, Volume V: *Exercise Book*, 1975; *Behavioral Threat and Community Response: A Community Psychology Inquiry*, Behavioral Publications, 1972; *Handboek van de hulpverlening* (title means ''Handbook of Intervention''), edited by Jaap Valk, Joep Dumont, and Ko Kok, two volumes, Lemniscaat Rotterdam, 1976; (with James Paul) *Emotionally Disturbed and Deviant Children*, Prentice-Hall, 1977; *Disturbance and Deviance in Children*, Prentice-Hall, 1978.

Contributor: J. D. Gowan and G. D. Demos, editors, *The Guidance of Exceptional Children*, McKay, 1965; Peter Knoblock, editor, *Educational Programming for the Emotionally Disturbed Child*, Syracuse University Press, 1965; Herbert Quay, editor, *Juvenile Delinquency Research and Theory*, Van Nostrand, 1965; Nicholas Long, William C. Morse, and Ruth Newman, editors, *Conflict in the Classroom*, Wadsworth, 1965; Eli M. Bower and William G. Hollister, editors, *Behavioral Science Frontiers in Education*, Wiley, 1967; Jerome Hellmuth, editor, *Educational Therapy*, Volume I, Special Child Publications, 1967; Paul Graubard, editor, *Children Against Schools*, Follett, 1969; Charles Speilberger and Ira Iscoe, editors, *Community Psychology: Perspectives and Research*, Appleton, 1969; Henry Dupont, editor, *Educating Emotionally Disturbed Children*, Holt, 1969; Daniel Adelson, editor, *Community Psychology Perspective on Community Mental Health*, Chandler Publishing, 1969.

C. S. Stone and Bruce Schertzer, editors, *The Guidance Monograph Series*, Houghton, 1970; Stuart Golann and Carl Eisdorfer, editors, *Handbook of Community Psychology and Mental Health*, Appleton, 1972; Herbert C. Quay and John S. Werry, editors, *Psychopathological Disorders of Childhood*, Wiley, 1972, revised edition, 1978; H. W. Harshman, editor, *Educating the Emotionally Disturbed Child*, Crowell, 1972; Graubard, editor, *Education of the Dis-*

turbed, Delinquent Child, World Publishing, 1977; A. J. Pappanikou and James Paul, editors, *Mainstreaming Emotionally Disturbed Children*, Syracuse University Press, 1977; Paul, Donald Stedman, and G. R. Neufeld, editors, *Deinstitutionalization*, Syracuse University Press, 1977; Judith S. Mearig and other editors, *Working for Children: Ethical Issues Beyond Professional Guidelines*, Jossey-Bass, 1978.

Contributor to psychology and education journals, including *Community Mental Health Journal*, *Behavioral Disorders*, and *Health Values: Achieving High Level Wellness*.

WORK IN PROGRESS: Research on the psychology of euthanasia in Germany during and prior to World War II.

SIDELIGHTS: Rhodes comments: ''My career has been motivated by a desire to dedicate my life to human service. My books arise from that motivation plus my interest in probing man's relationship to and creation of his world. There has always been a strong spiritual force in my life guiding my direction and choice of that part of the world I see.''

* * *

RIBEIRO, Joao Ubaldo (Osorio Pimentel) 1941-

PERSONAL: Name pronounced Zho-*un*-o Oo-*Bahl*-do Ri-*bay*-ro; born January 23, 1941, on Island of Itaparica, All Saints Bay, Bahia, Brazil; son of Manoel (a professor, politician, and author) and Maria Felippa (a law student and lecturer; maiden name, Osorio Pimentel) Ribeiro; married Maria Beatriz Gordilho Moreira Caldas, 1962 (divorced); married Monica Maria Roters (divorced); children: (second marriage) Emilia Roters, Manuela Roters. *Education:* Federal University of Bahia, Brazil, LL.B., 1962; University of Southern California, M.S., 1965. *Politics:* ''I believe that the only solution for the wretched plight of Brazil lies in some form of socialism, but I abhor Soviet socialism and would hate to live in China.'' *Religion:* ''Brought up as a Catholic; now an avid reader of the Gospels and Descartes.'' *Home:* Rua Espirito Santo, 118, Apt. 501, 40000 Salvador, Bahia, Brazil. *Office: Tribuna da Bahia*, Rua Djalma Dutra, 121, 40000 Salvador, Bahia, Brazil. *Agent:* Carmen Balcells, Agencia Literaria, Diagonal 580, Barcelona, 21, Spain.

CAREER: Professor of political science at the Federal University of Bahia, Bahia, Brazil; editor-in-chief of *Tribuna da Bahia* newspaper, Salvador, Bahia, Brazil. *Awards, honors: Setembro nao tem sentido* named one of five best novels of year by *Jornal de Brasil*, 1968; Jabuti Prize.

WRITINGS—All novels, except as noted: *Setembro nao tem sentido*, Jose Alvaro, 1968; *Sargento Getulio*, Civilizacao Brasileira, 1971, translation by author published as *Sergeant Getulio*, Houghton, 1978; *Vencecavalo e o outro povo* (collection of novellas), Artenova, 1974. Short stories are represented in many anthologies and journals. Author of unpublished plays.

WORK IN PROGRESS: A novel, *Vila Real*, about the landless people in Brazil; a collection of short stories which have appeared previously in magazines.

SIDELIGHTS: Sergeant Getulio was a best seller in Brazil, although Joao Ribeiro suspects that ''nobody could understand a word in it.'' The title character is a mercenary who has been assigned to kidnap and deliver a prisoner in the remote Brazilian state of Sergipe. Even after his boss retracts the orders, the dutiful Getulio is determined to complete his mission, and he slaughters the troops that try to prevent him from reaching his goal. In the process, Getulio is transformed from a savage gunman for hire into a sort of moral hero.

Ribeiro's English translation of *Sergeant Gestulio* has been acclaimed by reviewers. Because of hostile government authorities, the English copy of the book has not been distributed in Brazil; Ribeiro's own copy was smuggled into the country by a friendly American. Larry Rohter felt that American readers would be able to comprehend *Sergeant Gestulio* because it "reads like a Western—and a brilliant though frightfully gory one at that." Despite the violence in the book, Rohter noted: "Ribeiro here seems concerned primarily with moral issues. But he also happens to be a novelist with a taste for vivid landscapes, crisp dialogue and dramatic confrontations, so what emerges is a work that enlightens and entertains." Joining in the praise of *Sergeant Getulio*, Barbara Probst Solomon commented: "I read the book once; something poetic and passionate in the tone haunted me, and I read it a second time. I remained moved by its intense narrative of events I only partially understood."

Ribeiro felt that it would be arrogant to give *CA* any details about himself, and chose instead to comment on the vast differences between the cultures of Brazil and the United States: "I am not fascinating. I am lonely and frustrated. I live in a nation of 110 million people. Most of those people are presently living in conditions that would be unbelievable to you. I have a culture and a heritage. I have a language. I have seen your movies and and have learned your songs. You know nothing about mine. I know little sounds that are unknown to you, and you know little sounds that are unknown to me. I belong in the same tradition as you do; I am Western and came from Iberia and Africa and America. But also I am Brazilian and you are American. Let us try to understand each other."

AVOCATIONAL INTERESTS: Reading, studying biology.

BIOGRAPHICAL/CRITICAL SOURCES: Washington Post, March 9, 1978; *New York Times Book Review,* April 9, 1978.

*   *   *

RICART, Josep Gudiol i
See GUDIOL i RICART, Josep

*   *   *

RICH, John H., Jr. 1917-

PERSONAL: Born August 5, 1917, in Cape Elizabeth, Me.; son of John H. and Alma E. (Glidden) Rich; married Doris Lee Halstead, September 2, 1954; children: Barbarine, John III, Whitney, Nathaniel. *Education:* Bowdoin College, A.B., 1939; graduate study at Columbia University, 1954-55. *Home:* 5-16-49 Roppongi, Minato-ku, Tokyo 106, Japan. *Office:* AIU Bldg., 1-1-3 Marunouchi, Chiyoda-ku, Tokyo 100, Japan.

CAREER/WRITINGS: Daily Kennebec Journal, Augusta, Me., reporter, 1939-40; *Portland Press Herald,* Portland, Me., reporter, 1940-41; International News Service, New York City, reporter in Far East, 1945-50; National Broadcasting Co. (NBC), New York City, began as reporter in Far East and Europe, became senior Asian correspondent. Vice president of RCA Corp., 1974—. *Member:* Overseas Press Club, Foreign Correspondents Club of Japan (president, 1970-71). *Awards, honors:* Fellowship from Council on Foreign Relations, 1954-55; Double Peabody Award, 1972,

for radio and television reporting; Sigma Delta Chi award, 1972, for radio reporting; Overseas Press Club awards, 1972, for best radio documentary and best reporting from Asia in any medium.

*   *   *

RICHARD, Lee
See Le PELLEY, Guernsey

*   *   *

RICHARDS, Guy 1905-1979

OBITUARY NOTICE—See index for *CA* sketch: Born May 18, 1905, in New York, N.Y.; died January 3, 1979, in Manhattan, N.Y. Journalist and author of novels and books on Czarist Russia. In 1927 Richards was a member of the Whitney South Seas Expedition to New Guinea and the Solomon Islands. Later he worked as a reporter for the *New York Sun,* the *New York Daily News,* and the *New York Journal-American.* He received two Page One Awards from the New York Newspaper Guild and an Order of Silurians Prize. Obituaries and other sources: *New York Times,* January 5, 1979.

*   *   *

RICO, Don 1917-

PERSONAL: Born September 26, 1917, in Rochester, N.Y.; son of Allesandro (a shoe worker) and Josephine (Bartholomay) Rico; married Michal Hart (an actress), September 28, 1962; children: Dianne, Don III. *Home:* 1332 North Curson, Hollywood, Calif. 90046. *Agent:* Twentieth Century Artists Agency, 13273 Ventura Blvd., North Hollywood, Calif. 91604.

CAREER: Artist, editor, and writer. Editor for Marvel Comics Group, New York, N.Y., 1939-57, 1977—. Originator of "Blackout," "Gary Stark," and "Stevie Starlight" comic strips. Teacher at University of California, Los Angeles, 1973—. *Member:* Writers Guild of America, Dramatists Guild.

WRITINGS—All novels: *Last of the Breed,* Lancer Books, 1965; *Daisy Dilemma,* Lancer Books, 1967; *Bed of Lesbos,* Brandon House, 1968; *Lorelei,* Belmont-Tower, 1969; *Passion Flower Puzzle,* Lancer Books, 1969; *Man From Pansy,* Lancer Books, 1970; *Nightmare of the Eyes,* Lancer Books, 1970; *The Golden Circle,* Avon, 1975.

"Casey Grant Caper" series; all published by Paperback Library: *The Ring-A-Ding Girl,* 1969; *The Swinging Virgin,* 1969; *So Sweet, So Deadly,* 1970.

Illustrator of "Captain America," "Human Torch," "Silver Streak," "Dare Devils," "Johnny Jones," and "Golden Archer" comic strip series. Also author of scripts for "Adam 12" television series for Universal Pictures and "Bloody Mary" for Translor. Editor of VII Arts Press.

WORK IN PROGRESS: Stories for the "Captain America" comic strip series; *How To Be a Music Publisher,* written in collaboration with Walter Hurst.

SIDELIGHTS: Rico told *CA:* "I believe in truth and in reflecting the life around me. I have always loved language and words and story-telling."

*   *   *

RIFFE, Ernest
See BERGMAN, (Ernst) Ingmar

RINGER, Robert J.

PERSONAL—Education: Attended Ohio State University. *Office address:* P.O. Box 25235, West Los Angeles, Calif. 90025.

CAREER: Writer, 1975—. Worked as shirt designer and real estate broker.

WRITINGS: Winning Through Intimidation, privately printed, 1973, Los Angeles Book Publishers Co., 1974; *Looking Out for #1,* Los Angeles Book Publishers Co., 1977.

SIDELIGHTS: ''No other living person has the right to decide what is moral (right or wrong) for you,'' Ringer wrote in *Looking Out for #1.* He warns against standing on principles, being altruistic, participating in causes, and feeling guilty about one's actions. ''In *Looking Out for #1,*'' Ringer told *CA,* ''I emphasize, time and again, that no individual has the right to forcibly interfere with anyone else; no one has the right to aggress on the rights of any other person.''

Ringer favors ambitious behavior. ''Ambitious people should see the world as it is—overpopulated, polluted, headed for the worst depression of all time—and get to the well before it dries up forever.''

Consistent in his philosophy, Ringer told *CA* that he wrote both his books only for the purpose of making money. ''This is the kind of honesty that has given me ten million readers on my first two books.''

Ringer also told *CA* that his books do not encourage the reader to succeed through intimidation and arrogance, implying that his intention is ''quite the opposite, if anything.''

BIOGRAPHICAL/CRITICAL SOURCES: Time, September 15, 1975; *Newsweek,* July 25, 1977.

* * *

RISS, Richard 1952-

PERSONAL: Born May 22, 1952, in Rochester, N.Y.; son of Walter (a professor of neuroanatomy) and Barbara (a piano teacher; maiden name, Johnson) Riss. *Education:* University of Rochester, B.A., 1974; graduate study at Regent College, Vancouver, British Columbia, 1975-77. *Home:* 3 Addison Lane, Greenvale, N.Y. 11548.

CAREER: Inter-Varsity Christian Fellowship, Rochester, N.Y., associate member of staff, 1974-75; Pinecrest Retreat Center, Setauket, N.Y., member of staff, 1977—. *Awards, honors:* Gold medal from Long Island Mathematics Fair, 1970, for a paper on a new set of mathematical functions.

WRITINGS: The Evidence for the Resurrection of Jesus Christ, Bethany Fellowship, 1977.

WORK IN PROGRESS: The Charismatic Movement of 1830 and the Catholic Apostolic Church; The Evidence for the Trustworthiness of the Scriptures; The Evangelical Awakening of 1948; research on the Latter Rain Movement of 1948.

SIDELIGHTS: Riss comments: ''*The Evidence for the Resurrection of Jesus Christ* was originally written as a paper for a course, Concepts of the Soul, taught by Richard Taylor at University of Rochester in 1973. It was written in order to demonstrate to the satisfaction of a secular professor of philosophy that Christianity is intellectually defensible. He recommended that it be published, and said, 'My conclusion, after reading your work, was that it does indeed prove something—namely, that in the areas of philosophy

and religion, and doubtless others too, one can prove anything.'''

* * *

RITCHIE, Andrew Carnduff 1907-1978

OBITUARY NOTICE: Born September 18, 1907, in Bellshill, Scotland; died in 1978 in Connecticut. Museum and art gallery director, educator, and author of books on painting and sculpture. Ritchie was the director of the department of painting and sculpture at the New York Museum of Modern Art from 1949 to 1957. He was also the director of the Yale University Art Gallery for over fifteen years. Ritchie taught classes in art at several universities and galleries throughout the United States. He received numerous decorations from other nations, including France, the Netherlands, and Germany. Obituaries and other sources: *Who's Who in America,* 39th edition, Marquis, 1976; *AB Bookman's Weekly,* November 6, 1978.

* * *

ROBBINS, Thomas Eugene 1936-
(Tom Robbins)

PERSONAL: Born in 1936, in Blowing Rock, N.C.; son of Katherine (Robinson) Robbins; married second wife, Terrie (divorced); children: (second marriage) Fleetwood Starr (son). *Education:* Attended Washington and Lee University, 1950-52, Richmond Professional Institute (now Virginia Commonwealth University), and University of Washington. *Residence:* LaConner, Wash. *Agent:* Phoebe Larmore, 6626 Franklin Ave., Hollywood, Calif. 90028.

CAREER: Copy editor at *Richmond Times-Dispatch,* Richmond, Va.; copy editor and art critic at *Seattle Times,* Seattle, Wash.; went to East Village in New York City and researched a book on Jackson Pollock that has never been written; copy editor at *Seattle Post-Intelligencer,* Seattle; full-time writer. *Military service:* U.S. Air Force.

*WRITINGS—*All under name Tom Robbins: *Guy Anderson* (biography), Gear Works Press, 1965; *Another Roadside Attraction* (novel), Doubleday, 1971; *Even Cowgirls Get the Blues* (novel), Houghton, 1976.

WORK IN PROGRESS: A novel, *Woodpecker Rising.*

SIDELIGHTS: Crammed with metaphors, hyperbole, and puns, Tom Robbins's novels are noted for their wildly imaginative style and for their meandering, bizarre plots. His first novel, *Another Roadside Attraction,* describes the clamor which ensues when the mummified body of Jesus Christ is discovered adorning a roadside zoo and hot dog stand. The book features such unlikely characters as an aristocratic baboon, a talking watermelon, and a clairvoyant restaurant proprietor. Robbins's next book, *Even Cowgirls Get the Blues,* is every bit as offbeat as the first. Thomas LeClair described it as ''a Whole Earth narrative, a laid back 'Tristram Shandy,' a barbershop quartet of Vonnegut, Brautigan, Pynchon and Ishmael Reed doing a hymn to the White Goddess, a meditation on the rule of thumb, a manifesto for magic, and a retelling of 'Another Roadside Attraction.''' Both books have been extraordinarily popular with college students.

Basically optimistic, Robbins told an interviewer: ''I'm a real fan of the human race. No other animal even cares about ecology. No deer in the woods gives a damn about other deer. A killer whale would eat all the salmon in sight.

''No other animal has a sense of humor, the highest wisdom in the world. And we're the only animal that falls in love.

The absurd extent to which human beings go when they're in love justifies their existence.''

This philosophy is reflected in Robbins's books. Seeking to explain why college students are attracted to his novels, Robbins speculated: "Perhaps they turn to my work because it deals with joy and happiness without averting its eyes. It isn't pollyanna-ish, it doesn't bury its head in the sand. It looks the beast of totalitarianism right in the chops and still opts for joy and the possibilities of happiness.''

Despite the light and playful tone of his writing, Robbins has insisted that "for all my silliness, I feel that I'm a philosophical writer. I believe in fun, but I'm very serious about the issues I deal with.'' Ann Cameron discerned a serious message in *Even Cowgirls Get the Blues;* she felt that its characters "make us realize that even the pain and death of a culture or a planet are tolerable. . . . What is intolerable is to live without—without what? Magic and poetry, Robbins says. . . . This glorious and extravagant novel reminds us that we live to create as well as to observe.''

Mitchell S. Ross, however, found nothing of philosophical significance in Robbins's works. Lumping Robbins with other "paperback literati" such as Vonnegut, Pynchon, Brautigan, Pirsig, and Castaneda, Ross declared: "With the paperback literati we are asked to witness representations of human relations which do not correspond to our own. This fills their books with literary fireworks; it leaves room for the suggestion of profundity; it permits the characters to spout all sorts of heavy, bogus wisdom—and it leaves the center of the book hollow.''

AVOCATIONAL INTERESTS: Yoga, volleyball.

BIOGRAPHICAL/CRITICAL SOURCES: New York Times Book Review, May 23, 1976; *Nation,* August 28, 1976; *Charleston News and Courier,* Charleston, S.C., June 19, 1977; *Crawdaddy,* August, 1977; *Contemporary Literary Criticism,* Volume 9, Gale, 1978; *Bookviews,* February, 1978; *New York Times Magazine,* February 12, 1978.*

*   *   *

ROBBINS, Tom
    See ROBBINS, Thomas Eugene

*   *   *

ROBERTS, Arthur Sydney   1905(?)-1978

OBITUARY NOTICE: Born c. 1905 in Liverpool, England; died September 27, 1978, in Orange Park, Fla. Journalist. Roberts began his career as a police reporter for the *Savannah News* in 1927. He joined the Associated Press in 1935 and served as a regional reporter in the South and as a member of the Washington bureau. In 1944, Roberts became an editor for the wire service and retired as night editor in 1970. Obituaries and other sources: *Washington Post,* September 29, 1978.

*   *   *

ROBERTS, Bill   1914(?)-1978

OBITUARY NOTICE: Born c. 1914; died November 18, 1978, in Cleveland, Ohio. Artist and editorial cartoonist for the *Cleveland Press* whose work appeared on the front page of the Saturday paper for twenty years. Obituaries and other sources: *New York Times,* November 20, 1978.

*   *   *

ROBERTS, Dan
    See ROSS, W(illiam) E(dward) D(aniel)

ROBERTS, Joe
    See SALTZMAN, Joseph

*   *   *

ROBERTS, Thom(as Sacra)   1940-
    (Thomas Lawrence)

PERSONAL: Born December 4, 1940, in Wichita, Kan.; son of Thomas Noble (a geologist) and Catherine (Whitenton) Roberts; married Jeanne K. Paton, May 17, 1975; children: Wyatt Paul, Bryan Richard, Adam Noble. *Education:* University of Colorado, B.A., 1966. *Home and office address:* Upper Byrdcliffe, Woodstock, N.Y. 12498.

CAREER: Innsmont Center for Children, Denver, Colo., teacher, 1968-69; *Humpty Dumpty's Magazine,* New York, N.Y., editor, 1969-72; free-lance writer and editor in Europe, 1972-75; Institute of Children's Literature, Redding Ridge, Conn., instructor and editor, 1975-78. Builder of homes from recycled materials, 1970—.

WRITINGS—All for children: (Under pseudonym Thomas Lawrence) *Robber Raccoon,* Grosset, 1971; *The Magical Mind Adventure of Hannah and Coldy Coldy,* Knopf, 1971; *Pirates in the Park,* Crown, 1973; (editor) Albert Bigelow Paine, *The Hollow Tree,* Avon, 1973; (editor) Paine, *The Snowed-In Book,* Avon, 1974; *The Barn,* McGraw, 1975; *Summerdog* (novel based on film), Avon, 1978. Contributor to magazines, sometimes under pseudonym Thomas Lawrence.

WORK IN PROGRESS—For children: *Woodstock Gypsies; The Atlantic Free Balloon Race.*

SIDELIGHTS: Roberts writes: "I have tried writing for adults; however, I prefer writing for children. Children are infinitely more critical than adults are, but they're more appreciative, too. I have lived in England and Germany, and all over the United States; all of this has contributed to my writing. If there's such a thing as inspiration, most of it has come from children and travel—and from getting up religiously at 4:00 A.M. every day—to write.''

*   *   *

ROBERTSON, David (Allan, Jr.)   1915-

PERSONAL: Born July 30, 1915, in Chicago, Ill.; son of David Allan (an educator) and Anne (Knobel) Robertson; married Beridge Ruth Leigh-Mallory, June 18, 1940 (died September 7, 1953); married Victoria Adams Bryer (an artist), October 10, 1964; children: Anne (Mrs. Robert Spencer), Susan, Allan, Struan, Isabel, Samuel. *Education:* Princeton University, B.A., 1936, M.A., 1939, Ph.D., 1940; graduate study at Trinity College, Cambridge, 1937-38. *Home:* 79 Spring Lane, Englewood, N.J. 07631. *Office:* Department of English, Barnard College, Columbia University, New York, N.Y. 10027.

CAREER: Columbia University, Barnard College, New York, N.Y., instructor, 1940-47, assistant professor, 1947-50, associate professor, 1950-56, professor of English, 1956-68, McIntosh Professor, 1968—, chairman of department, 1956-59, 1964-67. Member of College Entrance Examination Board's Commission on English, 1959-64; member of advisory councils for Princeton University; member of board of trustees of Dwight-Englewood School. *Military service:* U.S. Naval Reserve, active duty, 1942-46; became lieutenant. *Member:* Modern Language Association of America, Phi Beta Kappa, Century Association, American Alpine Club. *Awards, honors:* Howard Foundation fellowship, 1953-54.

WRITINGS: *George Mallory*, Faber, 1969; (contributor) *Nature and the Victorian Imagination*, University of California Press, 1977; *Sir Charles Eastlake and the Victorian Art World*, Princeton University Press, 1978. Editor of *English Institute Essays*, Columbia University Press, 1947-49. Contributor of articles and reviews to academic journals. Co-editor of *American Alpine Journal*, 1947-52; member of advisory board of *Victorian Studies*, 1959-66, 1975—.

WORK IN PROGRESS: Studying Victorian travelers in the Himalayas.

SIDELIGHTS: Robertson writes: "Mallory participated in the first three Everest expeditions and died on the mountain in 1924. *George Mallory*, however, is not an 'expedition book'; it has to do with all of Mallory's life, including his climbs."

About the subject of his book *Sir Charles Eastlake and the Victorian Art World*, Robertson commented: "Eastlake (1793-1865) rose to extraordinary eminence in the art world of his time: president of the Royal Academy, secretary of the Fine Arts Commission, keeper and then first director of the National Gallery in London."

*   *   *

ROBERTSON, Mary Elsie   1937-

PERSONAL: Born April 28, 1937, in Charleston, Ark.; daughter of Thomas Winfield (a rural mail carrier) and Esther (a teacher; maiden name, Scherer) Robertson; married Peter Marchant (a college professor), October 28, 1961; children: Jennifer Esther, Piers Adam. *Education:* University of Arkansas, earned B.A., M.A., 1959; University of Iowa, M.F.A., 1961. *Politics:* Democrat. *Religion:* Society of Friends (Quakers). *Home:* 113 Adams St., Brockport, N.Y. 14420. *Agent:* Don Congdon, Harold Matson Co., Inc., 22 East 40th St., New York, N.Y. 10016.

CAREER: Pennsylvania State University, State College, instructor, 1965-66; St. John Fisher College, Rochester, N.Y., lecturer, 1974-77; writer. *Awards, honors:* First prize from *Mademoiselle's* fiction contest, 1958, for "Homecoming."

WRITINGS: *Jordan's Stormy Banks and Other Stories*, Atheneum, 1961; *Jemimalee*, McGraw, 1977. Contributor of stories to literary journals and popular magazines, including *Seventeen, Stand, Texas Quarterly*, and *Mississippi Review*.

WORK IN PROGRESS: Short stories; a novel entitled *Mothers, Brothers, Sisters, Lovers*; a book for children, *Tarantula and Red Chigger Forever*.

AVOCATIONAL INTERESTS: Gardening, jogging, listening to music (especially Baroque).

*   *   *

ROBINSON, Budd
See ROBINSON, David

*   *   *

ROBINSON, David   1915-
(Budd Robinson)

PERSONAL: Born April 15, 1915, in New York, N.Y.; married Celia Krebs (an artist), May 27, 1939; children: Denis H. *Education:* City College (now of the City University of New York), B.A., 1935. *Residence:* Canoga Park, Calif. *Office:* 1633 Beverly Blvd., Los Angeles, Calif. 90026.

CAREER: Writer, 1945—. Also worked as drill press operator, salesman, mechanical inspector, cab driver, employment interviewer, claims examiner, and radio technician. *Military service:* U.S. Navy, 1943-45. *Member:* Writers Guild of America (West).

WRITINGS: *The Confession of Alma Quartier* (novel), New American Library, 1962; *The Confession of Andrew Clare* (novel), Gallimard, 1964, McKay, 1968; (under name Budd Robinson; with Rod Amateau) *Where Does It Hurt?* (novel), Sphere Books, 1970.

Plays: "The Torch Grows Dim" (three-act), first produced in Los Angeles, Calif., at Dance Theatre, December, 1948; "Seven Flights to Happiness" (three-act), first produced in Los Angeles, Calif., at Sutro Theatre, December, 1959; "Who Killed Napoleon?" (two-act), first produced in Sacramento, Calif., 1965.

Films: (Co-author) "Monsoon," United Artists, 1951; (co-author) "Where Does It Hurt?," Cinerama, 1972. Also author of television scripts. Contributor of stories to literary magazines.

WORK IN PROGRESS: Nonfiction, under name Budd Robinson.

SIDELIGHTS: Robinson writes: "My first interest was music; I had no training, but finally did secure a brief 'scholarship' in composition with Aaron Copland in 1937. I worked at musical composition until about 1942. The war and other minor events interrupted this. After the war I began to write plays, then drifted into film writing and short stories, and tried my hand at one or two novels. I have worked in all fictional media except radio. My preference is film writing; however, complete authority in that area is almost impossible. Otherwise, to me it is the ideal medium for a writer, the most challenging, the most powerful, the most effective, and at the same time the most subtle. This has been said before: were Shakespeare alive today, he would be a film writer, because film has the greatest appeal to the greatest cross-section of audience. In the last year or two I have returned to musical composition, along with my literary career, and have produced three new compositions of some (hopefully) stature."

*   *   *

ROBINSON, Ira E(dwin)   1927-

PERSONAL: Born December 23, 1927, in New York, N.Y.; son of Samuel (a businessman) and Lenora (a teacher; maiden name, Miller) Robinson; married Arlene Triechel, December, 1961 (divorced); children: Edward, Benjamin. *Education:* Davis-Elkins College, B.A., 1950; attended Ohio State University, 1952-55; University of Minnesota, Ph.D., 1964; Ohio University, M.A., 1972. *Religion:* Jewish. *Home:* 109 Georgetown Dr., Athens, Ga. 30605. *Office:* Department of Sociology, University of Georgia, Athens, Ga. 30601.

CAREER: Ohio State University, Columbus, instructor in psychology, 1952-54, counselor, 1952-53; Chillicothe Hospital, Chillicothe, Ohio, psychologist, 1954-55; Columbus State School, Columbus, clinical psychologist, 1955-56; Minneapolis-Honeywell Regulator Co., Minneapolis, Minn., sociologist, human factors engineer, and consultant, 1960-62; University of Georgia, Athens, 1962—, began as assistant professor, currently associate professor of sociology. Instructor at Macalester College, 1959-61; research associate at Dartmouth College, summer, 1965. Member of president's committee on employment of the handicapped, 1974-77.

MEMBER: American Sociological Association, American Association of University Professors, Society for the Study of Symbolic Interaction, Society for the Study of Social Problems, Southern Sociological Society.

WRITINGS: (With D. K. Darden and W. R. Darden) *Case in Crises,* Austin Press, 1972; (contributor) *Toward a Comprehensive Theory of Suicide in Research in Comprehensive Psychiatry: A Festschrift for Ralph M. Patterson,* Ohio State University Press, 1972; (contributor) H. C. Lindgren, editor, *Contemporary Research in Social Psychology,* Wiley, 2nd edition (Robinson was not included in 1st edition), 1973; (contributor) J. L. Delora and J. S. Delora, editors, *Intimate Life Styles,* Goodyear Publishing, 1975. Contributor of more than twenty-five articles to psychology and sociology journals. Advisory editor of *Creativity, Human Potential and Human Ecology.*

WORK IN PROGRESS: A book on race relations.

* * *

ROBINSON, Paul 1940-

PERSONAL: Born October 1, 1940, in San Diego, Calif.; son of Joseph Cook (a school principal) and Beryl (a teacher; maiden name, Lippincott) Robinson; children: Susan Marie. *Education:* Yale University, B.A., 1962; graduate study at Free University of Berlin, 1962-63; Harvard University, Ph.D., 1968. *Home:* 550 Battery St., #1707, San Francisco, Calif. 94111. *Office:* Department of History, Stanford University, Stanford, Calif. 94305.

CAREER: Stanford University, Stanford, Calif., assistant professor, 1967-73, associate professor of history, 1973—, director of Berlin studies program, 1976—. *Member:* American Historical Association, Phi Beta Kappa. *Awards, honors:* Guggenheim fellow, 1970-71.

WRITINGS: The Freudian Left, Harper, 1969; (editor with David M. Kennedy) *Social Thought in America and Europe,* Little, Brown, 1970; *The Modernization of Sex: Havelock Ellis, Alfred Kinsey, William Masters, and Virginia Johnson,* Harper, 1976. Contributor of articles and reviews to magazines, including *New Republic, Partisan Review, Atlantic,* and *Salmagundi,* and newspapers.

WORK IN PROGRESS: A multi-volume work on opera and the history of ideas, beginning with a volume on Giuseppe Verdi.

SIDELIGHTS: Robinson told *CA:* "In my recent work, *Opera and History,* I am interested in the connections between the history of opera and the history of thought—with showing how the great European operas from Mozart to Strauss reflect the general evolution of European thought and culture from the late eighteenth to the early twentieth century.

"My association with Berlin goes back to 1962, and I have spent nearly two years, all told, living in the city. Most recently I was in charge of a small program for undergraduates that Stanford maintains in Berlin. Through it thirty or forty Stanford students spend between three and six months living and studying in the city. Berlin is, of course, one of the great cities of the world, politically intense, and boasting an extraordinarily rich cultural life. It has become as much home for me as San Francisco.

"Beyond my teaching responsibilities (which lie primarily in the area of modern European intellectual history) and my scholarly writing, I have a general interest in the quality of intellectual and personal life. Thus in my more journalistic writings, I've addressed such diverse issues as television,

homosexuality, intellectual fads (such as Michel Foucault), and singing. I would describe myself as a political radical and a cultural conservative."

* * *

ROBISON, David V. 1911(?)-1978

OBITUARY NOTICE: Born c. 1911; died November 30, 1978, in Woodstock, N.Y. Playwright, writer for television and films, musical conductor, and educator. Robison spent twenty-five years in California writing for radio, television, and motion pictures. He earned a masters degree in musicology from Columbia University and later taught music at Fisk University and Columbia University. Robison was the author of the Broadway comedy "Promenade, All!" He was a former assistant conductor of the San Fernando (Calif.) Symphony Orchestra and chairman of a Woodstock chamber-music series. Robison was also an executive officer of the National Audubon Society. Obituaries and other sources: *New York Times,* December 5, 1978.

* * *

ROBLES, Emmanuel 1914-

PERSONAL: Born May 4, 1914, in Oran, Algeria; son of Manuel (a mason) and Helene (a laundress; maiden name, Ruvira) Robles; married Paulette Puyade, April 22, 1939 (died May 7, 1974); children: Jacqueline Robles Macek. *Education:* Attended Ecole Normale, Algiers, 1931-34, and University of Algiers, 1938-39. *Home:* 6 Rue Edouard-Detaille, Boulogne-sur-Seine, France.

CAREER: Radio Algeria, Algiers, literary critic, 1947-58; full-time writer, 1958—. Member of Academie Goncourt. *Military service:* French Air Force, 1939-46. *Member:* P.E.N. *Awards, honors:* Chevalier de la Legion d'Honneur, 1963.

WRITINGS—In English: *Montserrat* (three-act play; first produced in Paris at Theatre Montparnasse, April 23, 1948), Charlot, 1949, adaptation by Lillian Hellman published as *Montserrat: A Play in Two Acts,* Dramatists Play Service, 1950, French edition reprinted, Le Livre de poche, 1974; *Cela s'appelle L'aurore* (novel), Editions du Seuil, 1952, translation by Therese Pol published as *Dawn on Our Darkness,* Messner, 1954; *Federica* (novel), Editions du Seuil, 1954, translation by Joyce Emerson published as *Flowers for Manuela,* Redman, 1956; *Les Couteaux* (novel), Editions du Seuil, 1956, translation by Geoffrey Sainsbury published as *Knives,* Collins, 1958; *Le Vesuve* (novel), Editions du Seuil, 1961, translation by Milton Stansbury published as *Vesuvius,* Prentice-Hall, 1970; *Three Plays* (contains "Plaidoyer pour un rebelle," "L'Horloge," and "Porfirio" [also see below]), translated and introduced by James A. Kilker, Southern Illinois University Press, 1977.

Other works; all published by Editions du Seuil, except as indicated: *L'Action,* 1938; *La Vallee du paradis* (title means "The Valley of Paradise"), 1941; *La Marie des quatre vents* (title means "Marie of the Four Winds"), Charlot, 1942; *Travail d'homme* (title means "Work of Man"), Charlot, 1942; *Nuits sur le monde* (short stories; title means "Nights on the World"), Charlot, 1944; *Les Hauteurs de la ville* (title means "Heights of the City"), Charlot, 1948.

La Mort en face (short stories; title means "Opposite Death"), 1951; *La verite est morte* (drama; title means "Truth Is Dead"; first produced in Paris by Comedie francaise, November 29, 1953), 1952; (translator from the Spanish) Ramon Sender, *Le Roi et la Reine* (title means "The

King and Queen''), 1955; *L'Horloge, suivi de Porfirio* (plays; contains ''Porfirio,'' first produced in Algiers at Salle Valentin, March 25, 1953; ''L'Horloge'' [title means ''The Clock''], first produced in Paris at Theatre des Buttes-Chaumont, April 10, 1965); *L'Homme d'avril* (short stories; title means ''April Man''), 1959.

Jeunes saisons (title means ''Young Seasons''), Editions Baconnier, 1961; *La Remontee du fleuve* (title means ''The Rising of the River''), 1964; *Plaidoyer pour un rebelle; suivi de Mer libre* (plays; contains ''Mer libre'' [title means ''Free Sea''], first produced by Television francaise, October 5, 1965; ''Plaidoyer pour un rebelle'' [title means ''Case for a Rebel''], first produced in Brussels at Theatre royal du Parc, April 13, 1966), 1965; *La Croisiere* (title means ''The Cruise''), 1968; *Un Printemps d'Italie* (title means ''An Italian Spring''), 1970; *Saison violente* (title means ''Violent Season''), 1974; *Un amour san fin suivi de Les Horloges de Prague* (poems; title means ''An Endless Love and The Clocks of Prague''), 1976; *Les Sirenes* (title means ''The Sirens''), 1977. Also author of a newspaper report, ''Le Chile d'Allende,'' for *Le Canard Enchaine.*

WORK IN PROGRESS: A novel; an adaption of Emile Zola's *Le Fortune des Rougon* for French television.

SIDELIGHTS: Robles writes: ''Events such as the arrival to power of the Nazis in 1933, the Spanish Civil War, World War II, and the Algerian war of liberation influenced my spirit and work profoundly, and inspired such books as *Les Hauteurs de la Ville, La Mort en face, Montserrat, Le Vesuve,* and *Un Printemps d'Italie.*

''My passion for traveling has taken me, as a reporter or lecturer, to such diverse countries as Japan and South America, the United States and Black Africa, and China and the Soviet Union. This passion is linked to the idea that traveling permits one not only to enlarge one's knowledge of men and the world, but also to deepen one's understanding of oneself. From my stay in Japan I brought back the short story, 'L'Homme d'avril,' and my four months in Mexico (working on a film with Luis Bunuel) inspired *Les Couteaux.*

''Born in Algeria of Spanish descent and French culture, I am aware of being a part of a very old civilization which filled my thoughts and influenced my way of feeling, of loving, of perceiving life and death. Centuries ago, that civilization exalted in the grandeur of man; taught how, with lucidity and zest for life, he could control his own destiny. Yes, fatality is a part of being mortal, as is the misery of our condition, but there is also that sun under which I was born that speaks to me always with a feeling of peace—even of possible happiness.

''My books most often are inspirational. It is man, with his destiny so unique in an incomprehensible universe, man with his struggle of being which is at the center of my literary creation. The wars that I have seen, the travels that I have made, the distressing situations that I have encountered have instilled in me respect for the individual and the feeling of human solidarity which are both, it seems to me, the essential traits of my characters, committed to helping our world become less unjust, our earth more habitable.''

BIOGRAPHICAL/CRITICAL SOURCES: Jean-Louis Depierris, *Entretiens avec Emmanuel Robles,* Editions du Seuil, 1967; Fanny Landi-Benos, *Emmanuel Robles ou les raisons de vivre,* Oswald, 1969; Georges A. Astre, *Emmanuel Robles ou l'Homme et son espoir,* Editions Periples, 1972; Micheline Rozier, *Emmanuel Robles ou la rupture du Cercle,* Naaman, 1973.

ROBLES, Mireya 1934-

PERSONAL: Born March 12, 1934, in Guantanamo, Cuba; came to the United States in 1957, naturalized citizen, 1962; daughter of Antonio and Adelaida (Puertas) Robles. *Education:* Russell Sage College, B.A., 1966; State University of New York at Albany, M.A., 1968; State University of New York at Stony Brook, Ph.D., 1975. *Home:* 87 South Highland Ave., #B-25, Ossining, N.Y. 10562.

CAREER: Russell Sage College, Troy, N.Y., instructor in Spanish, 1963-73; Briarcliff College, Briarcliff Manor, N.Y., assistant professor, 1973-74, associate professor of Spanish, 1974-77; poet and writer, 1977—. Guest on television and radio programs in Spain and the United States; has given poetry readings and a book exhibition in New York City. Panel member of First Congress of Cuban Literature, 1973, Conference on Women Writers from Latin America, 1975, Congress of Inter-American Women Writers, 1976, and Conference of Inter-American Women Writers, 1978.

MEMBER: Centro Cultural Literario e Artistico (Portugal; honorary member). *Awards, honors:* First prize from Iberoamerican Poets and Writers Guild of New York, 1971, for *Tiempo artesano;* gold medal from L'Academie Internationale de Lutece, 1974, for essays, stories, and poems; first prize from Circulo de Escritores y Poetas Iberoamericanos de New York, 1974, for ''La relatividad de la realidad''; second prize from *Silarus Literary Review,* 1973, for short story, ''Hidra,'' and University of Maine at Orono, 1973, for short story, ''Trisagio de la muerte.''

WRITINGS: Petits Poemes (title means ''Little Poems''; translated into French by Henri de Lescoet), Profils Poetiques, 1969; *Tiempo artesano* (poems), Editorial Campos, 1973, bilingual edition, translated by Angela de Hoyos published as *Time the Artesan/Tiempo artesano,* Dissemination Center for Bilingual Bicultural Education, 1975; (translator from the English) de Hoyos, *Levantate Chicano/Arise Chicano and Other Poems* (bilingual edition), Backstage Books, 1975; (author of prologue) de Hoyos, *Chicano Poems,* Backstage Books, 1975; *En esta aurora* (poems; title means ''In This Dawn''), Cuadernos del Caballo Verde, Universidad Veracruzana, 1976; (translator from the English) *Selecciones* (title means ''Selections''), Universidad Veracruzana, 1976.

Work represented in anthologies, including *Voces de manana* (title means ''Voices of Tomorrow''), edited by Zenia S. da Silva, Harper, 1973. Contributor of more than a hundred seventy-five articles, stories, poems, translations, and reviews to journals all over the world, including *Opinion, Poet, Star West, International Poetry Review,* and *Thesaurus,* and to newspapers.

WORK IN PROGRESS: A novel.

SIDELIGHTS: Mireya Robles comments: ''I write because I have to. My main aspiration: not to have to waste my time in stupid jobs that have nothing to do with my only vocation, writing.''

Her work has been published all over Europe, Latin America, and India. She has visited Spain, Portugal, Italy, France, Switzerland, Morocco, Greece, Argentina, and Mexico.

BIOGRAPHICAL/CRITICAL SOURCES: Diario las americas, February 13, 1971, February 10, 1973; *Envios,* Number 5, 1973; *El Diario la prensa,* September 9, 1974, June 16, 1975; *Explicacion de textos literarios,* Volume IV, number 2, 1975-76; *Opinion,* August-September, 1976; *Hispania,* December, 1976.

ROCKEFELLER, John Davison III   1906-1978

PERSONAL: Born March 21, 1906, in New York, N.Y.; son of John D(avison), Jr. and Abby Green (Aldrich) Rockefeller; married Blanchette Ferry Hooker, November 11, 1932; children: Sandra Ferry, John D. IV, Hope Aldrich, Alida Davison. *Education:* Princeton University, B.S., 1929. *Politics:* Republican. *Religion:* Baptist. *Residence:* Fieldwood Farms, Tarrytown, N.Y.; and New York, N.Y. *Office:* 30 Rockefeller Plaza, New York, N.Y.

CAREER: Foundation executive and philanthropist. Rockefeller Foundation, became trustee, 1931, chairman of board of trustees, 1952-71; director of Rockefeller Center, 1932-63; Rockefeller Brothers Fund, became trustee and president, 1940, became chairman of Performing Arts Panel, 1963; became director of Rockefeller Brothers, Inc., 1946; president of John D. Rockefeller III Fund, Inc. Member of board of trustees of Colonial Williamsburg, Inc., and director of Williamsburg Restoration, Inc., 1934-39, chairman of both, 1939-51; Lincoln Center for the Performing Arts, president, 1956-61, chairman of the board, 1961-70. Director of Boy's Bureau of Community Service Society, New York City, 1930-40; director of British War Relief Society, 1940-45; director of United China Relief, 1941-45; American Red Cross, became assistant, 1942, then director; American Youth Hostels, director, 1946, president, 1947-51; became director of American International Association for Economic and Social Development, 1946; chairman of Greater New York Fund drive, 1949; became director of New York Life Insurance Co., 1949; became president of Japan Society, Inc., 1952; became director of Phelps Memorial Hospital, Tarrytown, N.Y., 1952; director of New York World's Fair Corp., 1964-65; became chairman of the U.S. Commission of Population Growth and the American Future, 1970; chairman of National Committee for the Bicentennial Era, 1975. Junior secretary at conference sponsored by Institute of Pacific Relations, Kyoto, Japan, 1929; consultant to John Foster Dulles's mission to Japan, 1951; adviser to the U.S. delegation at the Conference for Conclusion and Signature of the Treaty of Peace With Japan, 1951. Became trustee of American Museum of Natural History, 1933; became trustee of Princeton University, 1937. *Military service:* U.S. Navy, 1942-45; became lieutenant commander.

MEMBER: American Academy of Political and Social Sciences, American Association of Museums, Citizens Committee for Reorganization of the Executive Branch of the Government, Council in Foreign Relations, Foreign Policy Association, Academy of Political Science of New York, New York State Chamber of Commerce, New York Zoological Society, Westchester County Conservation Society, Historical Society of the Tarrytowns, Metropolitan Museum of Art, Museum of Modern Art, Century Club, Metropolitan Club, River Club, University Club, Broad Street Club, Sleepy Hollow Country Club. *Awards, honors:* Received Order of Auspicious Star, 1947, from Chinese National Government; received Order of the British Empire, 1948; special Tony Award of the American Theatre Wing, 1960; Gold Medal from Broadway Association, 1962; Gold Baton Award from American Symphony Orchestra League, 1962-63; citation from Concert Artists Guild, 1964; Handel Medallion from New York City, 1964.

WRITINGS: The Second American Revolution: Some Personal Observations (nonfiction), Harper, 1973. Contributor of articles to periodicals, including *New York Times, Life,* and *Rotarian.*

SIDELIGHTS: John D. Rockefeller III, as the oldest grandson of the oil industrialist, was a philanthropist best known for his patronage of the arts and his concern with population planning. Until 1971, he was chairman of the Rockefeller Foundation, which was formed by his father in 1913 in order to support research and various projects to alleviate the fundamental causes of social problems.

Rockefeller's travels throughout the world facilitated his understanding of the particular problems of other countries. "If our country is going to meet its obligations of world leadership," he once said, "our people will have to get abroad and see the world." In 1946, the Rockefeller family made an outstanding contribution to world understanding by donating $8 million to purchase the land in Manhattan where the United Nations is headquartered.

The philanthropist's collection of Asian and American art, while not particularly extensive, is regarded as a superb collection. Pieces from China, Japan, Indochina, Afghanistan, India, Pakistan, Cambodia, and Thailand are included. The oldest piece, a Chinese ritual bronze, dates from the Shang Dynasty. The collection was recently given to the Asian Society, which is planning a new building to house the art.

AVOCATIONAL INTERESTS: Art collecting, woodchopping, landscaping, horseback riding, golfing, and sailing.

BIOGRAPHICAL/CRITICAL SOURCES: New Yorker, November 4, 1972. Obituaries: *New York Times,* July 11, 1978; *Time,* July 24, 1978.*

(Died July 10, 1978, in Mount Pleasant, N.Y.)

*   *   *

ROCKWELL, Norman   1894-1978

OBITUARY NOTICE: Born February 3, 1894, in New York, N.Y.; died November 8, 1978, in Stockbridge, Mass. Artist, illustrator, and author of autobiography *My Life as an Illustrator.* Rockwell, who illustrated more than three hundred covers of the *Saturday Evening Post,* was said to have "painted America as millions of Americans would like it to be." His paintings were of ordinary people and he painted them with affection and idealizing realism. Rockwell was a stickler for detail: before working on a painting of Martha Washington, he visited Valley Forge; and he bought old clothes in Hannibal, Mo., for his models while working on the illustrations of Tom Sawyer and Huckleberry Finn. While studying at the Art Students League, Rockwell began illustrating a series of childrens' books. In 1912, he went to work for *Boy's Life* magazine, and four years later embarked on a career with the *Saturday Evening Post* that was to last more than forty years and make him one of America's most beloved artists. According to a former *Post* editor, Rockwell's covers produced an extra 50,000 to 75,000 sales per issue, and Rockwell illustrated a cover about every seven weeks. He was often criticized by the art elite for producing what they called "photographic corn." A modest man and humble artist, Rockwell once remarked that his worst enemy was the idea of "stretching my neck like a swan and forgetting that I'm a duck." Obituaries and other sources: *Current Biography,* Wilson, 1945; *Who's Who in American Art,* 12th edition, Bowker, 1976; *Who's Who in America,* 40th edition, Marquis, 1978; *New York Times,* November 10, 1978; *Washington Post,* November 10, 1978.

*   *   *

RODDA, Peter (Gordon)   1937-
(Richard Tudhope)

PERSONAL: Born August 5, 1937, in Piet Retief, South

Africa; son of Gordon Thomas (a trader) and Ivy (Brokensha) Rodda; married Barbara Bruce, April 7, 1964 (divorced, 1974); children: Christopher. *Education:* University of Natal, B.A. (honors), 1958; Rhodes University, M.A. (with distinction), 1967. *Politics:* "Libertarian socialist." *Religion:* None. *Home:* 16 Keith Grove, London W.12, England.

CAREER: High school English teacher in Natal, South Africa, 1960-61; Rhodes University, Grahamstown, South Africa, 1962-67, began as junior lecturer, became lecturer in English; University of South Africa, Pretoria, lecturer in English, 1968-69; teacher of English in London, England, 1970—. *Member:* Theatre Writers Union.

WRITINGS—Plays: "The Time of Breaking" (one-act), first produced in London, England, at International Arts Centre, 1975; "Tiger's Night" (one-act), first produced in London, England, 1977.

Work anthologized in *Quarry 76* and *English Studies in Africa.* Author of poems, published in South Africa under pseudonym Richard Tudhope.

WORK IN PROGRESS: A full-length play on murdered black leader, Steve Biko, for Temba Theatre Co.

SIDELIGHTS: Rodda writes: "As an isolated child on a remote trading station in Swaziland, I devoured printed words gluttonously, and have ever since. It was my childish ambition to write a book—presumably a novel, but my attempts to write fiction have all aborted. Brief imprisonment without charge in solitary confinement for political interrogation in 1964 and a 'nervous breakdown' had parallels in my first play 'The Time of Breaking.'"

*   *   *

ROETHKE, Theodore (Huebner)   1908-1963

PERSONAL: Born May 25, 1908, in Saginaw, Mich.; son of Otto Theodore (a floriculturalist and greenhouse owner) and Helen Marie (Huebner) Roethke; married Beatrice Heath O'Connell, January 3, 1953. *Education:* University of Michigan, A.B. (magna cum laude), 1929, M.A., 1936; graduate study at Harvard University, 1930-31. *Home:* 3802 East John, Seattle, Wash. 98112.

CAREER: Lafayette College, Easton, Pa., instructor in English, 1931-35, director of public relations, 1934-35, also varsity tennis coach; Michigan State College (now University), East Lansing, instructor in English, 1935; Pennsylvania State University, University Park, instructor, 1936-39, assistant professor of English, 1939-43, 1947, also varsity tennis coach; Bennington College, Bennington, Vt., assistant professor of English, 1943-46; University of Washington, Seattle, associate professor, 1947-48, professor of English, 1948-62, poet-in-residence, 1962-63. Fulbright lecturer in Italy, 1955. *Member:* National Institute of Arts and Letters, Phi Beta Kappa, Phi Kappa Phi, Chi Phi.

AWARDS, HONORS: Guggenheim fellowship, 1945, 1950; Eunice Tietjens Memorial Prize, 1947; Levinson Prize, 1951, for poetry published in *Poetry;* Fund for the Advancement of Education fellowship, National Institute and American Academy Award in Literature, nomination for honorary membership in International Mark Twain Society, and National Institute of Arts and Letters grant, all 1952; Ford Foundation Grant, 1952, 1959; Pulitzer Prize in poetry, 1954, for *The Waking: Poems 1933-53;* Borestone Mountain Award, 1958; Bollingen Prize in poetry from Yale University Library, 1958 for *Words for the Wind;* National Book Award, 1959, for *Words for the Wind,* and 1965, for *The Far*

Field; Edna St. Vincent Millay Award, Longview Award, and Pacific Northwest Writers Award, all 1959; D.Litt., University of Michigan, Shelley Memorial Award for poetry, and Poetry Society of America Prize, all 1962.

WRITINGS—All poems, except as noted: *Open House,* Knopf, 1941; *The Lost Son and Other Poems,* Doubleday, 1948; *Praise to the End!,* Doubleday, 1951; *The Waking: Poems 1933-1953,* Doubleday, 1953; *Words for the Wind: The Collected Verse of Theodore Roethke,* Secker & Warburg, 1957, Doubleday, 1958; *I Am! Says the Lamb,* Doubleday, 1961; *Party at the Zoo* (juvenile), Crowell, 1963; *Sequence, Sometimes Metaphysical, Poems,* Stone Wall Press, 1963; *The Far Field,* Doubleday, 1964; (contributor) Anthony Ostroff, editor, *The Contemporary Poet as Artist and Critic* (essays), Little, Brown, 1964; *On the Poet and His Craft: Selected Prose,* edited by Ralph J. Mills, Jr., University of Washington Press, 1965; *The Collected Poems of Theodore Roethke,* Doubleday, 1966; *The Achievement of Theodore Roethke: A Comprehensive Selection of His Poems,* edited by William J. Martz, Scott, Foresman, 1966; *Selected Letters of Theodore Roethke,* edited by Mills, University of Washington Press, 1968; *Theodore Roethke: Selected Poems,* selected by wife, Beatrice Roethke, Faber, 1969; *Straw for the Fire* (selections from notebooks), edited by David Wagoner, Doubleday, 1972; *Dirty Dinkey and Other Creatures: Poems for Children,* edited by B. Roethke and Stephen Lushington, Doubleday, 1973.

SIDELIGHTS: Theodore Roethke was hardly one who would have been expected to become a major American poet. Though as a child he read a great deal and as a high school freshman he had a Red Cross campaign speech translated into twenty-six languages, he strove to be accepted by peers who felt "brains were sissys." The insecurity that led him to drink to be "in with the guys" continued at the University of Michigan, where he adopted a tough, bear-like image (he weighed well over 225 pounds) and even developed a fascination with gangsters. Eccentric and nonconformist—he later called himself "odious" and "unhappy"—Roethke yearned for a friend with whom he could talk and relate his ambitions. "His adolescence must have been a hell of a bright awareness," speculated Rolfe Humphries, "frustrated because he did not know what to do with it, and it was constantly sandpapered by those around him."

Roethke's awareness evolved at Michigan into a decision to pursue teaching—and poetry—as a career. The fascination with nature he explored so deeply in his later poetry compelled him to write in an undergraduate paper: "When I get alone under an open sky where man isn't too evident—then I'm tremendously exalted and a thousand vivid ideas and sweet visions flood my consciousness." In addition to the stories, essays, and criticism commonly expected of English students, Roethke began writing poetry at this time. "If I can't write, what can I do," he said, and though Richard Allen Blessing claimed he "wrote a reasonably good prose," it still would "have taken a keen eye to detect the mature poet beneath the layers of undergraduate baby fat." The direction towards his eventual career cleared somewhat when Roethke dropped out "in disgust" after a brief stint as a University of Michigan law student: "I didn't wish to become a defender of property or a corporation lawyer as all my cousins on one side of the family had done." The attitude evident in this decision supported biographer Allan Seager's conclusion that it was more than an unsuppressible awareness of life that led him to choose poetry as a career: "It would be flattering to call it courage; more accurately it seems to have been an angry, defiant, Prussian pigheadedness that was leading him to his decision.''

The first fifteen years of Roethke's writing career, from his beginnings as an undergraduate to the publication of *Open House,* formed a "lengthy and painful apprenticeship" for the young writer. In cultivating his poetic expression, Roethke relied heavily upon T. S. Eliot's belief that "the only way to manipulate any kind of English verse, [is] by assimilation and imitation." With this model in mind, Roethke himself once wrote "imitation, conscious imitation, is one of the great methods, perhaps THE method of learning to write.... The final triumph is what the language does, not what the poet can do, or display." In her book *The Echoing Wood of Theodore Roethke,* Jenijoy La Belle summarized Roethke's major challenge as a "conscious imitator": "The modern poet should move away from the Romantic concept of personal expression.... He must, in effect, march through the history of poetry—rewrite the poems of the past—that he may come out at the end of his journey a poet who has absorbed the tradition and who thus may take one step forward and add to that tradition.''

Roethke's task was no easy one. In addition to debts to such contemporaries as W. H. Auden, Louise Bogan, Babette Deutsch, and William Carlos Williams, his extensive and varied poetic tradition included William Wordsworth, William Blake, Christopher Smart, John Donne, Sir John Davies, Walt Whitman, William Butler Yeats, T. S. Eliot, and Dante.

Along with these influences, the source of much of Roethke's poetry was the notes he dutifully kept throughout his life. A measure of the devotion given to his craft can be found in his statement "I'm always working," and indeed his pockets were seemingly always filled with jottings of striking thoughts and conversations. His less spontaneous reflections found a place in the workbench of his poetry—his notebooks. Though Roethke is not generally considered a prolific writer, a more accurate account of the time and effort spent developing his verse is apparent in this extensive accumulation of criticism (of himself and others), abstract thoughts, reflections on childhood, and, of course, poetry. In his biography of Roethke, *The Glass House,* Allan Seager estimated that only three percent of the lines of poetry in the more than two hundred notebooks was ever published.

The introspective Roethke announced his bold "intention to use himself as the material for his art" through the title of his first published volume, *Open House.* Not surprisingly, however, the book reflected the imitative and traditional elements of his "conscious imitation" apprenticeship. W. D. Snodgrass found it "old-fashioned and prerevolutionary. The poems are open and easily graspable; the metric quite regular and conventional." This "truly cautious" volume, remarked Blessing, is "a loose arrangement of poems ... tacked together for the most part by the limitations of Roethke's early poetic techniques and by the shape of his personality.... At best, he achieves an effect something like that frigidly controlled hysteria that one often feels in Emily Dickinson.''

Regardless of the limitations evident in *Open House,* Seager pointed out that "most of the reviews were good and those that contained adverse criticisms tacitly acknowledged that this was the work of a genuine poet and not a beginner." Marveling at Roethke's "rare" ability to "remember and to transform the humiliation ['of feeling physically soiled and humiliated by life'] into something beautiful," W. H. Auden

called *Open House* "completely successful." In another review of the book, Elizabeth Drew felt "his poems have a controlled grace of movement and his images the utmost precision; while in the expression of a kind of gnomic wisdom which is peculiar to him as he attains an austerity of contemplation and a pared, spare strictness of language very unusual in poets of today.''

Roethke kept both Auden's and Drew's reviews, along with other favorable reactions to his work. As he remained sensitive to how peers and others he respected should view his poetry, so too did he remain sensitive to his introspective drives as the source of his creativity. Understandably, critics picked up on the self as the predominant preoccupation in Roethke's poems. "We have no other modern American poet of comparable reputation who has absorbed so little of the concerns of the age into his nerve-ends," said M. L. Rosenthal, and, as a result, many have cited this "limited" concern as a major weakness in his poetry. Others, however, interpreted Roethke's introspection more positively, claiming it is the essence of his work. Ralph J. Mills called this self-interest "the primary matter of artistic exploration and knowledge, an interest which endows the poems with a sense of personal urgency, even necessity." Stanley Poss, too, heralded Roethke as "a test case of the writer whose interest in himself is so continuous, so relentless, that it transforms itself and becomes in the end centrifugal. With hardly a social or political bone in his body he yet touches all our Ur-selves, our fear and love of our fathers, ... our relish of the lives of plants and animals, our pleasures in women who have more sides than seals, our night fears, our apprehensions of Immanence.''

Whether or not this introspection is a weakness or the essence of his poetry, the intensity he devoted to teaching demonstrates an obvious concern outside the self. An immensely popular professor, Roethke succeeded in driving his students to share his enthusiasm for poetry. Not only was he well liked, often extending classroom sessions into the local bar, he was unique, as demonstrated by a popular anecdote from one of his classes at Michigan State: To stimulate his class in an assignment of the description of physical action, Roethke told his students to describe the act he was about to perform. He then crawled outside through a classroom window and inched himself along the ledge, making faces into each of the surrounding windows.

Such actions corresponded with what Roethke, a very demanding teacher, expected from his students' poetry. Oliver Everette recalled him exclaiming, "You've got to have rhythm. If you want to dance naked in an open barndoor with a chalk in your navel, I don't care! You've got to have rhythm." Another student remembered him saying, "Please let me see evidences of an active mind. Don't be so guarded—let your mind buzz around." And, Roethke impressed poet David Wagoner with the line "motion is equal to emotion." Wagoner along with poets Richard Hugo and James Wright form an impressive trio of ex-Roethke students.

Despite his efforts, Roethke held no dream of developing his students into outstanding poets. In a 1943 letter to Leonie Adams he admitted "one cannot be too grandiose about the results [of teaching]: after all, there are only from five to fifteen with real talent for writing poetry in any one generation." Roethke's hopes for his students were much more practical: "A bright student can be taught to write cleanly; he can learn—and this is most important—much about himself and his own time.''

This energetic pursuit of both a teaching and a writing career at times understandably affected his outlook. Part of his frustration stemmed from the amount of time teaching entailed. "I'm teaching well," he wrote in 1947, "—if I can judge by the response—but haven't done one damned thing on my own. It's no way to live—to go from exhaustion to exhaustion." Later, the fatigue seemed even more crucial to him. "I think I can say there's a real need for me to get out of teaching for a time," he wrote William Carlos Williams in 1949. "I'm getting caught up in it: too obsessed with making dents in these little bitches. The best ones keep urging me to quit: not worth it, etc. etc."

There were times when Roethke was unable to maintain any semblance of balance. His well-publicized mental breakdowns were, at least in part, the result from his going "from exhaustion to exhaustion." Allan Seager explained the apparent inevitability of first attack (1935): "There was no great mystery about his going to the hospital—he had nearly ruined himself in a mad attempt to go without sleep, work hard on everything, eat only one or two meals a day because he was so intent on 'this experiment' he was making in his classes." Roethke himself told Rolfe Humphries (with what Seager noted is a "perfectly rational" explanation) that the reason for his illness, which eventually brought him to the Mercywood Sanitarium in Ann Arbor, "was his own stupidity in trying to live 'a pure and industrious life all of a sudden.'"

Though the second of his breakdowns did not occur until 1945, they became increasingly more frequent in the ensuing decade; by 1958, he was attending therapy sessions six times a week. In all probability he was dismissed from Michigan State because his breakdown was viewed as an unacceptable failing (the letter read "we have decided that it will be better both for you and the College if your appointment for the coming year is not renewed"), but in later years his mental problems were recognized as an unfortunate but accepted part of his personality. When a perspiring Roethke entered the first class of the 1957-58 University of Washington school year by flinging "himself against the blackboard in a kind of crucified pose, muttering incoherently," the plea to the police was a compassionate but urgent "this is a very distinguished man and he is ill. All we want you to do is take him to a sanitarium."

Despite some suspicions of his worth which followed such incidents, Roethke remained an invaluable and highly esteemed member of the Washington faculty. In 1959, a Washington state legislator concerned about Roethke's sick leaves approached university vice-president Frederick Thieme and asked, "Who's this professor you've got down there that's some kind of nut?" This prompted English Department chairman Robert Heilman's unequivocal defense of Professor Roethke describing his illness, the university's obligation to its teachers, his distinguished writing, his teaching success, and his overall service to the university. It read, in part: "Roethke has a nervous ailment of the 'manic-depressive' type. Periodically he goes into a 'high' or 'low' state in which he is incapable of teaching.... His illnesses are well-known throughout the University and the local community. I have always been pleased that they have been accepted as the terribly sad lot of an extraordinarily gifted man....[In] teaching, developing interest in a great literary form, training writers who themselves go on to become known, and doing his own distinguished writing which has won all kinds of acclaim—Roethke is performing what I call a *continuing service to the University*, which goes on whether he is sick or well."

Although Seager admitted the cause of Roethke's problems "may have lain in the chemistries of his blood and nerves," some have claimed that they were attributable to his intense self-exploration and that he was able to see into himself more clearly because of his illnesses. Kenneth Burke has shown that by willingly immersing himself in the conflicts of his childhood Roethke precipitated his second breakdown; one psychiatrist has said "I think his troubles were merely the running expenses he paid for being his kind of poet." Not denying the personal tragedy of Roethke's illness, Rosemary Sullivan maintained "he was able to see in his experience a potential insight into other thresholds of consciousness." These views correspond with Roethke's premise on the search for truth: "To go forward (as a spiritual man) it is necessary first to go back." In *The Lost Son* he explored this pattern in the title poem and in its three companion pieces, as Sullivan explained: "They are desperate poems, each beginning in negative, life-denying solipsism which is gradually and painfully transcended until the poet achieves an exultant experience of wholeness and relation." In the same vein, Roethke probed the darkness of his childhood in "The Greenhouse Poems" of *The Lost Son*.

The roots of the greenhouse sequence lay in the extensive greenhouses owned by Roethke's father and uncle. For Roethke, whom Seager described as "thin, undersized and sickly as a boy, obviously intelligent but shy and diffident as well," the greenhouses became a source of ambivalence: "They were to me, I realize now, both heaven and hell, a kind of tropics created in the savage climate of Michigan, where austere German Americans turned their love of order and their terrifying efficiency into something beautiful." Associated with the greenhouse in measuring the effects of childhood was his father, a German American, who died when Roethke was fourteen. Sullivan explained the paradoxical father-son relationship: "Otto Roethke presented an exterior of authoritarian order and discipline [but] in the greenhouse he gave expression to a deep sensitivity to the beauty of nature." The apparent tendency of Otto to hide this "vulnerable core," Sullivan added, prevented Roethke from understanding his father. Feeling "angered and abandoned," Roethke implicated himself in his father's death, a death that prevented any gradual reconciliation between them. Sullivan further theorized that "from the consequent sense of his own inadequacy Roethke seems to have acquired the burdens of fears and guilts which haunted him all his life." Certainly his writings—from essays written at the University of Michigan to the poem "Otto" in *The Far Field*—uphold Seager's comment that "all his life the memory loomed over him."

By scrutinizing the plants, flowers, and creatures, Roethke attempted to tie the world of the greenhouse to the "inner world" of man. "The sensual world of the greenhouse is the first garden from which we have all emerged," explained Richard Blessing, "and the attempt to make meaning of it, to recall the energies of that place occupies us all in the lonely chill of our adult beds." James G. Southworth agreed that the search through the past is a painful one, as demonstrated in the opening lines of "Cuttings (later)": "This urge, wrestle, resurrection of dry sticks, / Cut stems struggling to put down feet, / What saint strained so much, / Rose on such lopped limbs to new life?" Ultimately the message spelled from the greenhouse sequence, as interpreted by Blessing, "reads that life is dynamic, not static; that the energy of the moment from the past preserves it, in part, in the present; that experience is a continuum, not a collection of dead instant preserved and pinned on walls we have left behind."

While *The Lost Son* focused on a child's struggle for identity, Roethke made great advances in establishing his own identity as a poet during this time. Michael Harrington felt "Roethke found his own voice and central themes in *The Lost Son*" and Stanley Kunitz saw a "confirmation that he was in full possession of his art and of his vision." Blessing echoed this praise when he wrote: "To my mind, the transformation of Theodore Roethke from a poet of 'lyric resourcefulness, technical proficiency and ordered sensibility' to a poet of 'indomitable creativeness and audacity . . . difficult, heroic, moving and profoundly disquieting' is one of the most remarkable in American literary history."

Praise to the End! followed much the same pattern set in *The Lost Son* by continuing "his most heroic enterprise," the sequence of interior monologues initiated in the title poem of *The Lost Son*. Roethke himself offered these suggestions on how to read the new book: "You will have no trouble if you approach these poems as a child would, naively, with your whole being awake, your faculties loose and alert. (A large order, I daresay!) *Listen* to them, for they are written to be heard, with the themes often coming alternately, as in music, and usually a partial resolution at the end. Each poem . . . is complete in itself; yet each in a sense is a stage in a kind of struggle out of the slime; part of a slow spiritual progress; an effort to be born, and later, to become something more."

Admittedly simplifying the two sections of *Praise to the End!*, Karl Malkoff classified the poems of the first as emphasizing "the struggle to be born, [and] those of the second, the effort, perhaps even more strenuous, to become something more." In his article, "The Poetry of Theodore Roethke," Southworth traced the journey undergone in the second half and held that while Roethke does not resolve his personal problems in these poems, there is a pattern of emerging awareness for the subconscious probing poet. From the sequence's first poem, "The Lost Son," Southworth saw the confusion in the lines "Which is the way I take; / Out of what door do I go, / Where and to whom?" relieved by an awareness of the living plants and animals of the greenhouse. Roethke then, through introspection, leaves his past with a new awareness of the self and concludes the final section of the poem "Praise to the End!" with the lines "My ghosts are all gay. / The light becomes me." "From this point forward," observed Southworth, "the poems communicate a sense of restrained ecstasy that is unique in contemporary poetry. The poet has plumbed the depths of his subconciousness, has rid himself of concern for the dead, and has come to realize that excessive thinking without embracing life can be sterile. . . . In order to find the meaning in life, one must accept life to the full, not be too much concerned . . . by those who are not reaching upward. . . . [The book's final poems,] 'I cry Love! Love!' and 'O, Thou Opening, O' continue the achievement of the poet in his struggle to the point where he can face the past squarely and realize that the one true significance in life is in living and loving."

After the intense explorations of *The Lost Son* and *Praise to the End!* "it is not surprising," as W. D. Snodgrass pointed out, "that Roethke might at this point need to step back and regather his forces. He did just that in the group of 'New Poems' in *The Waking*. . . . Here Roethke returned to the more open lyricism of his earlier verse and gave us, again, several markedly successful poems."

Roethke's marriage, his readings in philosophy and religion, and his feelings of anxiety and illness are, according to Malkoff, the most important events projected in the "New Poems" of *Words for the Wind*. His love poems, which first appeared in *The Waking* and earned their own section in the new book, "were a distinct departure from the painful excavations of the monologues and in some respects a return to the strict stanzaic forms of the earliest work," said Stanley Kunitz. Ralph Mills described "the amatory verse" as a blend of "consideration of self with qualities of eroticism and sensuality; but more important, the poems introduce and maintain a fascination with something beyond the self, that is, with the figure of the other, or the beloved woman." Roethke's "surrender to sensualism," claimed Robert Boyers, is not permanent: "He eventually discovers that the love of woman is not the ultimate mode for him." James McMichael reasoned why: "The love poems stress that his simple biological attraction for women, both because it is mindless and because she seems to him more mindless than himself, is the most necessary step on the journey [out of the self]."

As Malkoff noted, Roethke is not a consistent poet. "He moves from utter despair, to resignation, to mystic faith beyond mysticism and back to despair. We shall not find in his poems the development of a systematic philosophy; there emerges rather the complex figure of a man directly confronting the limitations of his existence with none of life's possibilities . . . excluded." *Words for the Wind* wavers in this way when, in Kunitz's words, "the love poems gradually dissolve into the death poems." The book does conclude with "The Dying Man" and "Meditations of an Old Woman," but these poems are more than gloomy contemplations of death: Blessing believed "The Dying Man" (dedicated to Roethke's spiritual father, Yeats) "remains a poem about the creative possibilities inherent in the very shapelessness of death"; Malkoff thought "Meditations of an Old Woman" "provides a kind of frame of reference for the consideration of life, and which often reappearing, is never far from the poem's surface. . . . [Ultimately,] *Words for the Wind,* read from cover to cover, is the spiritual autobiography of a man whose excessive sensitivity to his experience magnifies rather than distorts man's universal condition."

Roethke earned much of this magnified vision with an understanding of the mysticism that pervades *Words for the Wind* and *The Far Field*. Heavily influenced by Evelyn Underhill's *Mysticism*, many of his later poems follow her psychological progression, as outlined by Sullivan: "They begin with the painful apprehension of personal insufficiency, aggravated by the awareness of the possibility of a deeper reality. This is followed by a desire for purification through self-castigation and mortification, which Underhill calls the painful descent into the 'cell of knowledge.' This leads to illumination, a sudden breakthrough to a heightened visionary joy in the awakening of transcendental consciousness. These are only the first three, as it were, secular stages of mystical insight; he never laid claim to the last stages which lead to union with Absolute Being."

William Heyen emphasized that Roethke was not one who dedicated "his life to educating himself to achieve union with God. Rather, Roethke was an artist who experienced moments of deep religious feeling and almost inexpressible illumination. His choice was not traditional Christianity or atheism, but a reliance upon the mystic perceptions of his own imagination." In "Sequence, Sometimes Metaphysical," for example, Roethke defined his focus as "a hunt, a drive toward God; an effort to break through the barrier of rational experience." McMichael, however, found a paradox involved in such an effort: "The more he thinks about that thing [something other than himself] the less likely he is to know it as it really is; for as soon as he begins to acquire for him any of the qualities that his conceptual faculty is ready to impose upon it, his intuition and love of it are lost.'' Roethke does reach points of ecstasy in his poems, though, and Heyen defended him against critics who have charged that his joy is superficial and too easily attained: ''It is important to realize that the happiness achieved in any Roethke poem . . . is not one based on reason. . . . Armed with his study of Underhill and the mystics she discusses Roethke has found his rationale . . . he can rock irrationally between light and dark, can go by feeling where he has to go.''

Admittedly in retrospect, Seager reflected on the years preceeding *The Far Field* and Roethke's death: ''The last years of Ted's life, as we look back on them knowing they were the last, seem to have a strange air of unconscious preparation. As the fabric of his body begins to give way, the best part of his mind, his poetry, . . . strives toward a mystical union with his Father. But this was unconscious. I don't think he was at all aware that he was getting ready to go. He had too much work in hand, too much projected, yet the last poems seem prophetic: they read like last poems.'' (Roethke told Ralph Mills, however, ''a year before his death, that this might well be his final book.'') Perceiving a similar pattern in *The Far Field*, W. D. Snodgrass wrote that ''these poems, recording that withdrawal [as in 'The Longing'], also, I think suffer from it. The language grows imprecise with pain. . . . Metrically, too, one has a sense of discouragement and withdrawal. . . . More and more, Roethke's late poems seem to have lost their appetite, their tolerance for that anguish of concreteness.'' Why Roethke's poems might have lost their concreteness was interpreted by Sullivan, who believed the despair in his poetry rooted in his search for assurances. Since the mind cannot understand the mystery of being, Sullivan continued, Roethke learns to reject his self-destructive impulses and celebrates ''the capacity to rest in mystery without feeling the need to reach after certainties.''

The Far Field contained two sequences representing earlier themes and images, as well as ''North American Sequence'' and ''Sequence, Sometimes Metaphysical.'' According to Sullivan, Roethke wished to be remembered by the last poems in the latter sequence. Roethke himself wrote that ''in spite of all the muck and welter, the dreck of these poems [in 'Sequence, Sometimes Metaphysical'], I count myself among the happy poets: I proclaim once more a condition of joy.'' Indeed for those distressed by the tragic self-implications of his statement—''There is nothing more disconcerting than when a rich nature thins into despair''—these last poems, in celebrating the richness of nature and the poet's ''capacity to face up to genuine mystery,'' erase the despair. His last lines read: ''And everything comes to One, / As we dance on, dance on, dance on.''

Roethke's death, of a heart attack while swimming in a friend's pool, was ''an incalculable loss to American Literature,'' wrote Ralph Mills. While the poet was drinking much and suffering in his later years from a combination of ailments, including arthritis, bursitis, and periods of manic excitement, his poetry was reaching its peak and earned this praise from James Dickey: ''Roethke seems to me the finest poet now writing in English. I [say] this with a certain fierceness, knowing that I have to put him up against Eliot, Pound, Graves, and a good many others of high rank. I do it cheerfully, however. . . . I think Roethke is the finest poet not so much because of his beautifully personal sense of form . . . but because of the way he sees and feels the aspects of life which are compelling to him.''

The publication of *Collected Poems* in 1966 brought renewed interest in Roethke and prompted illuminating overviews of his work. David Ferry felt ''there are many things wrong with the poetry of Theodore Roethke. . . . His seriousness is frequently too solemnly serious, his lyrical qualities too lyrically lyrical. His mystical vein often seems willed, forced. . . . And yet Roethke is a very interesting and important poet. For one thing there is . . . the brilliance there [in *Praise to the End!*] with which he uses imitations of children's voices, nursery rhymes, his beautiful sense of the lives of small creatures, the shifting rhythms and stanza forms. . . . [And, in *The Far Field*] there are signs . . . of a new and promising expansiveness and tentativeness. . . . For the reader, the pity is not to be able to see where this would have taken him.'' In a *Sewanee Review* critique Karl Malkoff wrote: ''Though not definite, *Roethke: Collected Poems* is a major book of poetry. It reveals the full extent of Roethke's achievement: his ability to perceive reality in terms of the tensions between inner and outer worlds, and to find a meaningful system of metaphor with which to communicate this perception. . . . It also points up his weaknesses: the derivative quality of his less successful verse, the limited areas of concern in even his best poems. The balance, it seems to me, is in Roethke's favor. . . . He is one of our finest poets, a human poet in a world that threatens to turn man into an object.''

Roethke was altogether human, both in creating ''the most exhaustive, vital, and vivid reports we have of a soul in the several agonies normally recorded in one human life,'' and in impressing ''his friends and readers profoundly as a human being.'' His appreciation for all life is evident in his statement, ''If I have a complex, it's a full-life complex.'' Roethke lived energetically, most notably through a devotion to his teaching and through the introspection necessary to his poetry. At the same time, it is generally acknowledged that he paid for his tremendous mental and physical energy with his breakdowns. Thus, as Snodgrass said, one can view Roethke's career ''with an astonished awe, yet with sadness.''

BIOGRAPHICAL/CRITICAL SOURCES—Books: Dorothy Nyron, editor, *A Library of Literary Criticism*, Ungar, 1960; Edward Buell Hungerford, editor, *Poets in Progress: Critical Prefaces to Ten Contemporary Americans*, Northwestern University Press, 1962; Babette Deutsch, *Poetry in Our Time*, Doubleday, 1963; Ralph J. Mills, *Theodore Roethke*, University of Minnesota Press, 1963; Richard Kostelanetz, editor, *On Contemporary Literature: An Anthology of Critical Essays*, Avon, 1964; Mills, *Contemporary American Poetry*, Random House, 1965; Arnold Stein, editor, *Theodore Roethke: Essays on the Poetry*, University of Washington Press, 1966; Karl Malkoff, *Theodore Roethke: An Introduction to the Poetry*, Columbia University Press, 1966; Kostelanetz, compiler, *The Young American Writers: Fiction, Poetry, Drama, and Criticism*, Funk, 1967; M. L. Rosenthal, *The New Poets: American and British Poetry Since World War II*, Oxford University Press, 1967; Allan Seager, *The Glass House: The Life of Theodore Roethke*, McGraw, 1968; Ursula Genug Walker, *Notes on Theodore Roethke*, University of North Carolina Press, 1968; Hyatt H. Waggoner, *American Poets From the Puritans to the Present*, Houghton, 1968; James Dickey, *Babel to Byzantium: Poets and Poetry Now*, Farrar, Strauss, 1968.

Jerome Mazzaro, editor, *Modern American Poetry, Essays in Criticism*, McKay, 1970; William Heyen, compiler, *Profile of Theodore Roethke*, C. E. Merrill, 1971; James R. McLeod, *Roethke: A Manuscript Checklist*, Kent State

University Press, 1971; Nathan A. Scott, *The Wild Cry of Longing,* Yale University Press, 1971; Warren French, editor, *The Fifties: Fiction, Poetry, Drama,* Everett/Edwards, 1971; *Contemporary Literary Criticism,* Gale, Volume 1, 1973, Volume 3, 1975, Volume 8, 1978; McLeod, *Theodore Roethke: A Bibliography,* Kent State University Press, 1973; John Vernon, *The Garden and The Map: Schizophrenia in Twentieth Century Literature and Culture,* University of Illinois Press, 1973; Richard Allen Blessing, *Theodore Roethke's Dynamic Vision,* Indiana University Press, 1974; Rosemary Sullivan, *Theodore Roethke: The Garden Master,* University of Washington Press, 1975; Jenijoy LaBelle, *The Echoing Wood of Theodore Roethke,* Princeton University Press, 1976.

Periodicals: *Saturday Review,* April 5, 1941, August 19, 1949, August 31, 1963, January 2, 1965, July 31, 1965, December 31, 1966, June 22, 1968, March 11, 1972; *Kenyon Review,* autumn, 1941, winter, 1954, autumn, 1965, November, 1966; *New Republic,* July 14, 1941, July 16, 1956, August 10, 1959, January 23, 1965, August 27, 1966, September 21, 1968, March 4, 1972, February 9, 1974; *New Yorker,* May 15, 1948, February 16, 1952, September 24, 1966; *Herald Tribune Book Review,* July 25, 1948, December 2, 1951; *Poetry,* January, 1949, June, 1959, October, 1960, April, 1962, November, 1964, March, 1966, January, 1967, August, 1969, March, 1973; *Sewanee Review,* January, 1950, summer, 1967, summer, 1968, autumn, 1973; *New York Times Book Review,* December 16, 1951, May 16, 1954, November 9, 1958, August 5, 1964, July 18, 1965, July 17, 1966, September 29, 1968, April 9, 1972; *Nation,* March 22, 1952, November 14, 1953, March 21, 1959, September 28, 1964; *Western Review,* winter, 1954; *College English,* May, 1957, March, 1960, February, 1966; *Newsweek,* March 17, 1958, August 12, 1963; *Encounter,* April, 1958; *Northwestern University Review,* fall, 1958; *Chicago Review,* winter, 1959; *Hudson Review,* spring, 1959, winter, 1964/65, winter, 1966/67; *Virginia Quarterly Review,* spring, 1959, winter, 1967, autumn, 1968, autumn, 1972; *Yale Review,* June, 1959, winter, 1965, winter, 1967; *American Scholar,* summer, 1959.

Speech Monographs, March, 1963; *Time,* August 9, 1963; *American Literature,* May, 1964, November, 1974; *Shenandoah,* autumn, 1964; *Southern Review,* summer, 1965, winter, 1967, winter, 1969, spring, 1965; *Midwest Quarterly,* autumn, 1965, January, 1966; *Western Humanities Review,* winter, 1966, autumn, 1975; *New York Review of Books,* September 22, 1966; *Michigan Quarterly Review,* fall, 1967; *Listener,* June 27, 1968, August 22, 1968; *Atlantic,* November, 1968; *Minnesota Review,* Volume 8, 1968; *Commonweal,* February 21, 1969; *Texas Studies in Literature and Language,* winter, 1969, winter, 1973, winter, 1975; *Earlham Review,* spring, 1970; *Modern Poetry Studies,* July, 1970; *Northwest Review,* summer, 1971; *Tulane Studies in English,* Volume 20, 1972; *American Poetry Review,* January/February, 1974; *Journal of Modern Literature,* July, 1974.*

(Died August 1, 1963, on Bainbridge Island, Wash.)

*   *   *

ROLL, William George, Jr. 1926-

PERSONAL: Born July 3, 1926, in Bremen, Germany; U.S. citizen; son of William George and Gudrun (Agerholm) Roll; married Muriel Gold, June 22, 1950; children: Lise Renata, Leif Agerholm, William George III. *Education:* University of California, Berkeley, B.A., 1949; Oxford University, B.Litt., 1960. *Home:* 3509 Rugby Rd., Durham, N.C.

CAREER: Duke University, Durham, N.C., research associate at Parapsychology Laboratory, 1958-60, project director, 1960; associated with Psychical Research Foundation, Inc., Durham, 1961—. President of Oxford University Society for Psychical Research, 1952-57. *Military service:* Danish Resistance Forces, 1943-45. *Member:* American Association for the Advancement of Science, American Society for Psychical Research, Parapsychological Association (charter member; member of council, 1957-61, 1963-65, 1975-78; president, 1964), Society for Psychical Research (England). *Awards, honors:* Grants from Oxford University, 1951, 1952, Society for Psychical Research (England), 1953, and Parapsychology Foundation, Inc., 1954-56; Louis K. Anspacher fellowship, 1957-58.

WRITINGS: (Contributor) John White, editor, *The Highest State of Consciousness,* Anchor Books, 1970; *The Poltergeist,* Doubleday, 1972; (editor with J. D. Morris and R. L. Morris, and contributor) *Research in Parapsychology,* Scarecrow, 1973, new edition, 1976; *Theory and Experiment in Psychical Research,* Arno, 1975; (contributor) Stanley R. Dean, editor, *Psychiatry and Mysticism,* Nelson-Hall, 1975; (contributor) Hoyt Edge and James Wheatley, editors, *Philosophical Dimensions of Parapsychology,* C. C Thomas, 1976; (contributor) Rhea White, editor, *Surveys in Parapsychology,* Scarecrow, 1976; (contributor) Benjamin B. Wolman, editor, *Handbook of Parapsychology,* Van Nostrand, 1976.

Contributor of more than fifty articles and reviews to psychology and parapsychology journals, and to *Nature.* Co-editor of *Journal of Parapsychology,* 1958-60; editor of *Theta,* 1963; co-editor of *Proceedings of the Parapsychological Association,* 1964, 1970-71, editor, 1965-69.

WORK IN PROGRESS: Another book on poltergeists; survival research.

SIDELIGHTS: Roll is interested in a psi structure as it relates to the survival question.

*   *   *

ROLLO, Vera Foster 1924-

PERSONAL: Born December 20, 1924, in Raleigh, N.C.; daughter of Joseph Milton (an attorney) and Hilda (Graf) Prevette; married Eric Foster (marriage ended); married Anthony L. Rollo (divorced); children: (first marriage) Michael, Sally. *Education:* University of Maryland, B.A., 1972, M.A., 1976. *Religion:* Methodist. *Home and office:* 9205 Tuckerman St., Lanham, Md. 20801. *Agent:* Ann Buchwald, P.O. Box 1125, Washington, D.C. 20014.

CAREER: Flight instructor in Florida, winters, 1946-49, and Washington, D.C., summers, 1946-49; Civil Aeronautics Administration, Washington, D.C., secretary and flight training specialist, 1949-50; *American Aviation,* Washington, D.C., light plane editor, reporter, and feature writer, 1950-51; taught aviation courses at an air base, airports in Maryland, and her own ground school, 1952-56; ACF Industries, Riverdale, Md., editor of technical manuals, 1956-57; National Insurance Underwriters (aircraft insurors), St. Louis, Mo., accident analyst at Civil Aeronautics Board in Washington, D.C., 1959-60; *Chesapeake Times,* Bowie, Md., worked in advertising sales and as reporter, 1962-64; Maryland Historical Press, Lanham, publisher, editor, and writer, 1965—. Associate editor of University Press of America, 1976-77. Assistant professor and coordinator of aviation business management at Wilmington College, 1977-78. Professional ratings include commercial pilot, civilian flight instructor, ground instructor, Link operator, and multi-engine land and sea ratings. *Military service:* Civil Air Patrol, check pilot, 1976—.

MEMBER: American Historical Association, American Aviation Historical Society, Educational Salesmen's Association, Maryland Historical Society, Delaware Society of History, Prince George's County Historical Society, Phi Alpha Theta, Ninety-Nines (women pilots).

WRITINGS: Your Maryland, Maryland Historical Press, 1965, 3rd edition, 1976; *Maryland Personality Parade,* Volume I, Maryland Historical Press, 1967, 2nd edition, 1970; *Ask Me About Maryland* (geography), Maryland Historical Press, 1968, revised edition, 1976; *Maryland's Constitution and Government,* Maryland Historical Press, 1969, supplement, 1977; *The Negro in Maryland,* Maryland Historical Press, 1972; (with Henry Harford) *Last Proprietor of Maryland,* Harford County Committee, Bicentennial Commission of Maryland, 1976. Also author of *Lanham United Methodist Church: A History,* 1969, and editor of *Bits and Pieces About Maryland,* by D. B. Artes, 1974.

Writer of a column in *Prince George's County Post,* 1960-65, "Aviation News" column in *Suburban Times,* 1962-64, and "The Seabrook Report" column in *Laurel News,* 1964-67. Contributor of articles to aviation magazines and to *Chesapeake Times.*

WORK IN PROGRESS: A book on aviation law; a book on contemporary Maryland.

SIDELIGHTS: Vera Rollo writes: "I am one of the first few women to earn a civilian flight instructor's certificate (1945). I continue to fly on business and with the Civil Air Patrol in the Maryland Wing."

Of her work with the Maryland Historical Press, Rollo comments: "Maryland Historical Press was established as a prime source of materials dealing with the state of Maryland. It has been a challenge and a rewarding experience to fill this need as editor and publisher. Dealing with school systems and with other historical researchers has been both lucrative and entertaining."

Rollo has also conducted historical research in England.

* * *

ROM, M. Martin 1946-

PERSONAL: Born March 2, 1946, in Detroit, Mich.; son of Jack (a physician) and Thelma (Meyer) Rom; married Barbara Miller (an attorney), July 12, 1970. *Education:* University of Michigan, B.A. (magna cum laude), 1967. *Home:* 5136 Corners Dr., West Bloomfield, Mich. 48033. *Office:* Martin Rom Co., Inc., 30400 Telegraph Rd., Suite 357, Birmingham, Mich. 48010.

CAREER: MultiVest, Inc., Fort Lauderdale, Fla., founder, chief executive officer, and chairman of board of directors, 1969-76; The Martin Rom Co., Inc., Birmingham, Mich., president, 1976—. Vice-chairman of Sports Illustrated Courts Clubs, Inc. Member of advisory committee of U.S. Commodity Futures Trading Commission and Bureau of National Affairs housing and development reporter. *Member:* National Association of Securities Dealers, National Association of Realtors (member of board of directors), Real Estate Securities and Syndication Institute (president, 1975), Realtors Ligislative Committee, Phi Beta Kappa.

WRITINGS: Nothing Can Replace the U.S. Dollar . . . and It Almost Has! (selection of Dun & Bradstreet Book Club and Investors Book Club), Crowell, 1975.

SIDELIGHTS: Rom told *CA:* "Since my book was pub-

lished in 1975, I have continued to be disturbed regarding events in the domestic and international economies. Most of the events predicted in my book have now come to pass, including a record high price for gold, chaos in the international money markets, high interest rates, and a renewal of double digit inflation. I am currently contemplating writing a new book concerning the current events in the economy with predictions and investment strategy for the next several years, but have not yet made a decision in that regard."

BIOGRAPHICAL/CRITICAL SOURCES: Detroit Free Press, October 19, 1975.

* * *

ROONEY, Miriam Theresa

PERSONAL: Born in Charlestown, Mass. *Education:* Attended Harvard University, 1926-28; Catholic University of America, A.B., 1930, A.M., 1932, Ph.D., 1937; George Washington University, J.D., 1942. *Home:* 66 Myrtle Ave., Millburn, N.J. 07041. *Office:* 20 East 72nd St., New York, N.Y. 10021.

CAREER: Boston Public Library, Boston, Mass., assistant cataloger, 1924-28; U.S. Department of State, Washington, D.C., 1928-48, began as drafting officer, became assistant to legal officer; Catholic University of America, Washington, D.C., associate professor of law and law librarian, 1948-51; Seton Hall University, South Orange, N.J., professor of international law and jurisprudence, 1950-68, dean of School of Law, 1950-61. Admitted to Bars of District of Columbia, 1942, U.S. Supreme Court, 1945, New Jersey, 1962, and U.S. Customs Court, 1971. Fulbright professor in Vietnam, 1965-66, 1967-68. Representative of World Peace Through Law at the United Nations.

MEMBER: International Association for Philosophy of Law and Social Philosophy (American section), International Law Association (American branch), International Bar Association, International Federation of Women Lawyers, Inter American Bar Association, National Association of Women Lawyers, American Bar Association, American Foreign Law Association, American Society for Political and Legal Philosophy, American Catholic Philosophical Association, Mediaeval Academy of America, Federal Bar Association, Selden Society.

AWARDS, HONORS: Outstanding Woman award from the National Association of Women Lawyers, 1962; Alumni Achievement for Law award from Catholic University of America, 1962 and 1973; Pax Urbis ex Jure gold medal from World Peace Through Law Center, 1971; gold medal from International Community Services, London, 1972; cross "Pro Ecclesia et Pontifice" from Pope Paul VI, 1976; L.H.D. from Caldwell College, 1977.

WRITINGS: Lawlessness, Law, and Sanction, Catholic University of America Press, 1937; (author of introduction) Maurice Hauriou, Georges Renard, and Joseph T. Delos, *The French Institutionalists,* Harvard University Press, 1970. Section editor and contributor to *The New Catholic Encyclopedia.* Contributor of about a hundred articles and reviews on philosophy of law to journals in the United States and Europe.

WORK IN PROGRESS: Studying medieval and contemporary American philosophy of law.

SIDELIGHTS: Miriam Rooney comments: "Having done considerable research on the long history of legal thought, I became concerned about the falling away (at intervals through the centuries) from ethical, or moral, or religious and spiritual sources, particularly in the interpretation of *justice,* and the law as an instrument of justice. My life-long dedication has therefore been 'Instaurare legum in Christo.'"

*   *   *

ROOSE, Ronald 1945-

PERSONAL: Born December 24, 1945, in Daytona Beach, Fla.; son of Lawrence J. (a physician) and Roslyn (a painter; maiden name, Vlosky) Roose. *Education:* University of Wisconsin, Madison, B.A., 1966. *Home:* 463 West St., New York, N.Y. 10014. *Agent:* Erica Spellman, International Creative Management, 40 West 57th St., New York, N.Y. 10019.

CAREER: Free-lance film editor in New York and California, 1967—. Work includes "Little Big Man," "The Godfather," "Bang the Drum Slowly," "Serpico," and "The Wiz."

WRITINGS: Gallivant (novel), Dial, 1979.

WORK IN PROGRESS: A novel about the film industry.

SIDELIGHTS: Roose comments: "My writing reflects, for the most part, people and situations I have felt a personal involvement with. *Gallivant* is the story of two young men who leave the Lower East Side of New York in 1908 to take part in the last American gold rush. Although the setting and time are far different from what I have known, the characters and their search are subjects I pondered for quite some time before the idea of writing a book even occurred to me. So too, my next novel will be about a part of the film industry in which I have worked for many years."

*   *   *

ROPER, Susan Bonthron 1948-
(Susan Brand)

PERSONAL: Born May 21, 1948, in Philadelphia, Pa.; daughter of William Robert (a certified public accountant) and Jane (Hand) Bonthron; married Robert Roper (a writer), March 17, 1975; children: Caitlin Bonthron. *Education:* Swarthmore College, B.A., 1970. *Residence:* Redwood City, Calif. *Agent:* Maggie Curran, International Creative Management, 40 West 57th St., New York, N.Y. 10019.

CAREER: Wallingford Arts Center, Wallingford, Pa., ballet teacher, 1970-71; potter, 1971—. Plays acoustic bass and sings with "Spider Creek."

WRITINGS: (Under pseudonym Susan Brand) *Shadows on the Tor* (romantic suspense novel), Simon & Schuster, 1977.

WORK IN PROGRESS: The Magical Voice of Dulcie Rainsong, a juvenile; *Black Jaguar* (tentative title), a romantic suspense novel.

SIDELIGHTS: Susan Roper comments: "I live in a beautiful locale in the Santa Cruz mountains and I began to write because I wanted to supplement my income from pottery without having to commute elsewhere to work. I keep on writing because I enjoy it, and I try to live a simple life." *Avocational interests:* Travel (Haiti, France, England, Ireland, Scotland, Italy, Belgium, Mexico, Guatemala, Belize, and Costa Rica), raising organic vegetables, reading, practicing tai-chi.

*   *   *

ROSEN, George 1910-1977

PERSONAL: Born June 23, 1910, in New York, N.Y.; son of Morris and Rose (Hendleman) Rosen; married Beate Caspari (an opthalmologist), July 6, 1933; children: Paul Peter, Susan Joan Rosen Kosglow. *Education:* City College (now of the City University of New York), B.S., 1930; University of Berlin, M.D., 1935; Columbia University, Ph.D., 1944, M.P.H., 1947. *Home:* 1480 Ridge Rd., North Haven, Conn. 06510. *Office:* 333 Cedar St., New Haven, Conn. 06510.

CAREER: Beth-El Hospital, Brooklyn, N.Y., intern, 1935-36; practicing physician, New York City, 1937-42; New York City Health Department, health officer, 1947-49, director, bureau of public health education, 1949-50; Health Insurance Plan of Greater New York, New York City, associate medical director, 1950-57. Columbia University, New York City, lecturer, 1949-50, professor of health education, 1951-69; Yale University, New Haven, Conn., professor of history of medicine, epidemiology, and public health, 1969-77. Visiting lecturer at Harvard University, 1956-60; Victor Robinson Memorial lecturer at Temple University, 1958; Fielding H. Garrison lecturer at American Association for the History of Medicine, 1961; Beaumont lecturer at Yale University, 1962 and 1964; Benjamin Rush lecturer at American Psychiatric Association, 1967; Hideyo Noguchi lecturer at Johns Hopkins University, 1968. Consultant to National Institutes of Health, 1959-64. *Military service:* U.S. Medical Corps, 1943-46; became medical intelligence officer.

MEMBER: International Academy of the History of Medicine (president), American Association for the History of Medicine (vice-president, 1962-64; president, 1964-66), American Public Health Association, American Sociological Association (fellow), Society of the Social History of Medicine, Association of Teachers of Preventive Medicine, New York Academy of Medicine (fellow). *Awards, honors:* Grant Squires Award from Columbia University, 1945; William H. Welch Medal from American Association for the History of Medicine, 1961; Elizabeth Serverance Prentiss Award from Cleveland Health Museum, 1964; Edgar C. Hayhow Award from American College of Hospital Administrators, 1964; Hafner Award from American Association for the History of Medicine and Medical Library Association, 1966.

WRITINGS: The Reception of William Beaumont's Discovery in Europe, foreword by John F. Fulton, Schuman's, 1942; *The History of Miners' Diseases: A Medical and Social Interpretation,* introduction by Henry E. Sigerist, Schuman's, 1943; *The Specialization of Medicine With Particular Reference to Ophthalmology,* Froben Press, 1944, reprinted, Arno Press, 1972; *Fees and Fee Bills: Some Economic Aspects of Medical Practice in Nineteenth Century America,* Johns Hopkins Press, 1946; (editor with wife, Beate Caspari-Rosen) *400 Years of a Doctor's Life,* Schuman, 1947; (translator and editor) *Einstein: His Life and Times,* Knopf, 1947; *A History of Public Health,* MD Publications, 1958; *Madness in Society: Chapters in the Historical Sociology of Mental Illness,* University of Chicago Press, 1968; (compiler) *From Medical Police to Social Medicine: Essays on the History of Health Care,* Science History Publications, 1974.

Contributor of articles to medical and historical journals, including *Journal of the History of Medicine and Allied Sciences.* Editor, *Ciba* symposia, 1938-44, and *Journal History of Medicine,* 1946-52; *American Journal of Public Health,* member of editorial board, 1948-57, board chairman, 1957, editor, 1957-73.

BIOGRAPHICAL/CRITICAL SOURCES: New York Times Book Review, July 21, 1968; *Observer*, February 4, 1968; *American Historical Review*, February, 1969; *American Journal of Sociology*, Volume 74, 1969; *Times Literary Supplement*, January 9, 1969; *Choice*, 1973.

OBITUARIES: New York Times, August 6, 1977; *AB Bookman's Weekly*, October 17, 1977.*

(Died July 28, 1977, in Oxford, England)

*　*　*

ROSENBERG, Maurice 1919-

PERSONAL: Born September 3, 1919, in Oswego, N.Y.; son of Samuel L. (in business) and Diana (a teacher; maiden name, Lishansky) Rosenberg; married Ruth Myers, December 7, 1941 (died November 9, 1945); married Gloria Jacobson (a teacher), December 19, 1948; children: David, Joan, Richard. *Education:* Syracuse University, A.B., 1940; Columbia University, LL.B., 1947. *Religion:* Jewish. *Home:* 10 Hunting Ridge Rd., White Plains, N.Y. 10605. *Office:* School of Law, Columbia University, 435 West 116th St., New York, N.Y. 10027.

CAREER: New York Court of Appeals, law clerk in Albany and New York City, 1947-49; Cravath, Swaine & Moore, New York City, associate attorney, 1949-53; Austrian, Lance & Stewart, New York City, associate attorney, 1953-56; Columbia University, New York City, associate professor, 1956-58, professor, 1958—, Harold R. Medina Professor of Law, 1975—, executive director of project for effective justice, 1956-64. Executive director of Walter E. Meyer Research Institute of Law, 1965-71; chairman, Advisory Council on Appellate Justice, 1971-75; special assistant to U.S. attorney-general, 1976-77; chairman, Council on Role of Courts in American Society, 1978—; served on organizing committees and as faculty member for National Judicial College and Federal Judicial Center; consultant to government agencies and private foundations. *Military service:* U.S. Army, 1941-45; became staff sergeant.

MEMBER: American Bar Association, American Academy of Arts and Sciences, Association of American Law Schools (president-elect, 1972; president, 1973), American Judicature Society (vice-president, 1973-75), Association of the Bar of the City of New York, Cosmos Club, Century Association. *Awards, honors:* Herbert Harley Award from American Judicature Society, 1972.

WRITINGS: (With J. B. Weinstein, Hans Smit, and Harold Korn) *Elements of Civil Procedure*, Foundation Press (Mineola, N.Y.), 1960, 3rd edition, 1977; (with E. E. Cheatham, E. N. Griswold, and W.L.M. Reese) *Conflict of Laws*, Foundation Press, 5th edition (Rosenberg was not associated with earlier editions), 1964, 7th edition (with Reese only), 1978; *The Pretrial Conference and Effective Justice*, Columbia University, 1964; (with P. D. Carrington and D. J. Meador) *Justice on Appeal*, West Publishing, 1976. Contributor to law journals and popular magazines, including *Nation*.

WORK IN PROGRESS: Law and Social Research, with L. E. Ohlin, publication forthcoming; a book on improving the law by improving communications, completion expected in 1981.

SIDELIGHTS: Rosenberg comments: "My primary vocational interest is to improve the law and the delivery of justice in this country by improving the processes, personnel, and structures of the courts (federal and state); and by clarifying the messages the law transmits to persons in and out of the court system."

AVOCATIONAL INTERESTS: Comparing cultures (including languages and art).

*　*　*

ROSENFELD, Isadore 1926-

PERSONAL: Born September 7, 1926, in Montreal, Quebec, Canada; came to the United States in 1958, naturalized citizen, 1963; son of Morris and Vera Rosenfeld; married Camilla Master; children: Arthur, Stephen, Hildi, Herbert. *Education:* McGill University, B.Sc., 1947, M.D.C.M., 1951, diploma in internal medicine, 1956. *Politics:* Democrat. *Religion:* Jewish. *Home:* 510 Park Ave., New York, N.Y. *Agent:* Robert Lantz, 114 East 55th St., New York, N.Y. 10022. *Office:* 125 East 72nd St., New York, N.Y. 10021.

CAREER: Royal Victoria Hospital, Montreal, Quebec, junior rotating intern, 1951-52, junior assistant resident in medicine, 1952-53; Johns Hopkins Service, Baltimore, Md., assistant resident in Baltimore city hospitals, 1953-54; Jewish General Hospital, Montreal, Quebec, Mona B. Scheckman Research Fellow in Cardiology, 1954-55; Mount Sinai Hospital, New York, N.Y., fellow in cardiology, 1955-56; currently in private practice of medicine in New York, N.Y. Clinical assistant professor of medicine at Cornell University, 1964-71, clinical associate professor, 1971—. Certified specialist in Cardiology College of Physicians and Surgeons (Quebec); associate attending physician at New York Hospital. President of Rosenfeld Heart Foundation; director of Weitzman Institute of Science. Member of board of scientific advisers of American Health Foundation; member of board of directors of World Rehabilitation Fund, Inc., 1975—, and American Associates of Ben-Gurion University of the Negev, 1977—; member of board of trustees of Sackler School of Medicine, Ben-Gurion University, 1977—; member of advisory board of Leeds Castle Foundation; member of international advisory council of Imperial Medical Complex of Iran, 1975. Member of National Heart Institute Task Force on Arteriosclerosis, 1970, 1971; member of National Task Force on Hypertension, 1975-77. Juror for Lasker Scientific Awards, 1972—.

MEMBER: American College of Physicians (fellow), American College of Chest Physicians (fellow), American College of Cardiology (fellow), American Heart Association (fellow of Council on Epidemiology), American Physicians Fellowship for Israel (chapter president, 1973-75; national president, 1973-74; honorary national president, 1975—), American Therapeutic Society, American Public Health Association, Harvey Society, American Friends of McGill University (member of board of trustees), Royal College of Physicians (Canada; fellow), New York Cardiological Society (fellow), New York Heart Association, New York Academy of Sciences, New York Academy of Medicine, New York County Medical Society (censor, 1975-78). *Awards, honors:* Sir Edward Beattie Scholarship from McGill University, 1955-56; honorary surgeon of New York City Police Department.

WRITINGS: (With Arthur M. Master, R. P. Lasser, and E. Donoso) *The Electrocardiogram and Chest Roentgenogram in Diseases of the Heart*, Lea & Febiger, 1963; (author of foreword) Richard G. Margoles, *A Doctor's Eat-Hearty Guide for Good Health and Long Life*, Parker Publishing, 1974; *The Complete Medical Exam: What Your Doctor Knows Is Critical; What YOU Know Is Crucial*, Simon & Schuster, 1978; (contributor) *Ann Landers Encyclopedia*, Doubleday, 1978. Contributor of more than fifty articles to medical journals. Member of editorial board of *Preventive Medicine*, 1977—; editorial consultant for *Journal of Electrocardiology*, 1973—.

WORK IN PROGRESS: "A layman's guide to medical treatment," publication by Simon & Schuster expected in 1980.

SIDELIGHTS: Rosenfeld told *CA:* "*The Complete Medical Exam* was my first foray into the world of non-professional writing. I felt it was necessary because I believe the best informed patient gets the best medical care, and that the era of double-talk from doctor to patient is over, and none too soon. But how to find the time, in the midst of an 18 hour day practicing medicine, to write a book that (a) patients would read, understand, and enjoy; and (b) somebody would publish. It took me two years of weekend writing, editing and re-writing alone. No ghost writer, no chapters written by guest editors. I just closed my eyes and dictated a typical office visit by a patient coming for a check-up, complete with the pathos and the humor of everyday situations.

"When I first broached the subject of my proposed book, a publisher turned it down sight unseen. But my motivation was not royalties or income. I felt this was a book that needed to be written. When I finished the same publisher who turned it down bought it with enthusiasm, and has guided it into its fourth printing and a very gratifying paperback sale. The point of all this is that you don't have to stop whatever else you're doing in order to write a book. Also, if you're convinced that an idea is good, you mustn't be discouraged by a rejection. Chances are that those who turn you down know less about what the reading public wants and needs than you do.

"My countless hours on weekends, far from taking me away from my family, have motivated my children to take writing courses at college. Coincident with the appearance of my own work, my son, a college junior, contributed the article on snakes in *Ann Landers Encyclopedia*."

*　　　*　　　*

ROSOW, Jerome M(orris)　1919-

PERSONAL: Born December 2, 1919, in Chicago, Ill.; son of Morris (a tailor) and Mary (Cornick) Rosow; married Rosalyn Levin (an artist), September 28, 1941; children: Michael, Joel. *Education:* Wright Junior College, A.A., 1942; University of Chicago, B.A. (cum laude), 1942. *Religion:* Jewish. *Home:* 117 Fox Meadow Rd., Scarsdale, N.Y. 10583. *Office:* Work in America Institute, 700 White Plains Rd., Scarsdale, N.Y. 10583.

CAREER: U.S. Government, Washington, D.C., in personnel and policy, 1942-53; Creole Petroleum, Caracas, Venezuela, personnel executive, 1953-55; Exxon Corp., New York, N.Y., executive in personnel and employee relations, 1955-65; Esso Europe, London, England, manager in employee relations, 1966-69; U.S. Department of Labor, Washington, D.C., assistant secretary of labor, 1969-71; Exxon Corp., manager in public affairs and planning, 1971-77; Work in America Institute, Scarsdale, N.Y., president, 1977—. Chairman of Advisory Committee on Federal Policy, 1971—; adviser to Presidents Johnson, Nixon, Ford, and Carter; member of business and industry advisory committee for Organization for Economic Co-Operation and Development. Member of study team for "Education and Work in the People's Republic of China," 1978. *Military service:* U.S. Army, 1942-45; became chief warrant officer. *Member:* Industrial Relations Research Association (president, 1979).

WRITINGS: (Editor) *American Men in Government*, Schnapper Press, 1949; (editor) *The Worker and the Job*, Prentice-Hall, 1974; (contributor) *Bargaining Without Boundaries*, University of Chicago Press, 1974; (editor with Clark Kerr) *Work in America: The Decade Ahead*, Van Nostrand, 1979. Contributor to academic journals, popular magazines, and newspapers, including *Saturday Review of Literature*.

*　　　*　　　*

ROSS, Clarissa
　　See ROSS, W(illiam) E(dward) D(aniel)

*　　　*　　　*

ROSS, Dan
　　See ROSS, W(illiam) E(dward) D(aniel)

*　　　*　　　*

ROSS, Dana
　　See ROSS, W(illiam) E(dward) D(aniel)

*　　　*　　　*

ROSS, Helen　1890(?)-1978

OBITUARY NOTICE: Born c. 1890 in Independence, Mo.; died August 9, 1978, in Washington, D.C. Child psychoanalyst, educator, columnist, and author of books on psychoanalysis and child development. After studying with Anna Freud and Helene Deutsche at the Vienna Institute of Psychoanalysis during the 1930's, Ross served as administrative director of the Chicago Institute for Psychoanalysis (1941-56) and taught child development and analysis in various schools, including the Washington Psychoanalytic Institute (1966-78). Her book, *Fears of Children*, has been published in more than twelve languages. Obituaries and other sources: *Washington Post*, August 11, 1978.

*　　　*　　　*

ROSS, Mabel (Irene) H(ughes)　1909-

PERSONAL: Born November 15, 1909, in Lawson, Md.; daughter of John Edward (a railroad worker) and Fay (a waitress; maiden name, Jones) Hughes; married John Edward Ross (a physician), May 6, 1929; children: Ernest Edward. *Education:* Attended Chapman College, 1927-30; Butler University, A.B., 1943; Christian Theological Seminary, Indianapolis, Ind., B.D., 1947; also studied at Yale University. *Religion:* Christian Church. *Home:* 82-831 Ave. 54, Thermal, Calif. 92274.

CAREER: Employed as dietician's assistant, 1940-47; Southern Baptist Hospital, New Orleans, La., dietician, 1948-49; United Christian Missionary Society, Indianapolis, Ind., missionary and teacher in the Belgian Congo (now Zaire), 1950-71; writer and researcher, 1972—.

WRITINGS: (With Barbara K. Walker) "*On Another Day* ...": *Tales Told Among the Nkundo of Zaire*, Archon, 1979. Contributor to *Instructor* and *Humpty Dumpty*.

WORK IN PROGRESS: Filmstrips and retellings of folk tales from Zaire.

SIDELIGHTS: Commenting on her book of African folktales, Mabel Ross wrote: "I was inspired to collect folktales in 1972 by Barbara K. Walker and have been involved with folktales ever since. [Because] I had already spent twenty-one years among the Nkundo people, I knew their language quite well. Besides they knew me, trusted me and were willing to share their wealth of tales and culture with me."

ROSS, Marilyn
See ROSS, W(illiam) E(dward) D(aniel)

* * *

ROSS, Marilyn Heimberg 1939-
(Marilyn Markham Heimberg)

PERSONAL: Born November 3, 1939, in San Diego, Calif.; daughter of Glenn J. (in business) and Dorothy (a real estate broker; maiden name, Sudder) Markham; married T. M. Ross (an advertising executive), May 25, 1977; children: Scott, Steven, Kevin, Laurie. *Education:* Attended San Diego State University, 1957-58. *Religion:* Church of Religious Science. *Address:* P.O. Box 9512, San Diego, Calif. 92109.

CAREER: South Bay Trade Schools, Inc., San Diego, Calif., director of marketing, 1969-74; writer and independent marketing consultant, 1974—. Instructor at San Diego Community College, 1975-77. Member of board of directors of Research Electronics Co. *Member:* World Leisure and Recreation Association, Authors Guild, Authors League of America, National Federation of Press Women, National Genealogical Society. *Awards, honors:* First place award for nonfiction from Southern Division of California Press Women, 1977, for "Business Bites Back."

WRITINGS: (Under name Marilyn Markham Heimberg) *Discover Your Roots: A New, Easy Guide for Tracing Your Family Tree,* Communication Creativity, 1977; *Finding Your Roots,* Dell, 1978; *Creative Loafing: A Shoestring Guide to New Leisure Fun,* Communication Creativity, 1978. Contributor to magazines.

WORK IN PROGRESS: Creative Loafing Vacations, publication by Communication Creativity expected in 1980.

SIDELIGHTS: Marilyn Ross writes: "To me, communication is a vital fact of life. It is the catalyst that helps us understand ourselves and others better. I intend to use the written and spoken word to enlighten and entertain on a broad scope. It is important to me that others be encouraged to enjoy the abundance in life that I have discovered. Towards this goal, I lecture and consult on various aspects of writing and publishing, and find great personal satisfaction in assisting promising writers."

* * *

ROSS, Mitchell S(cott) 1953-

PERSONAL: Born December 7, 1953, in Detroit, Mich.; son of Aaron R. (a shoe retailer) and Raquel (Moss) Ross. *Education:* Attended University of Michigan, 1971, 1973. *Residence:* Southfield, Mich.

CAREER: Writer, 1974—. Worked as shoe salesman.

WRITINGS: The Literary Politicians (essays), Doubleday, 1978. Also author of *Memoirs of Liberated America,* 1979. Contributor to periodicals, including *Atlantic, National Review, New Republic, New York Times Magazine.*

SIDELIGHTS: The Literary Politicians is a collection of essays on several American writers who Ross believes reveal their political stances through their writings; the author himself claimed, "I just wanted to write a book about the intermingling of politics and literature, and I wanted to discuss varieties of writers." Christopher Lehmann-Haupt commented that, apparently, "a literary politician is anyone Mr. Ross wishes to characterize as such, so that he may deliver himself of certain rounded judgments on individuals who have loomed large on the American scene in recent years."

Lehmann-Haupt observed that Ross "has created the unfortunate impression that he is simply showing off," and found that *The Literary Politicians* did not attain the literary heights it aspired to. Asking "where are the great humane studies and vivid polemics of yesteryear?," the critic concluded that "putting these seven essays in a single volume seems to have served no larger purpose than to show that the author has done his homework and can quote with reverence or scorn those passages he either admires or abominates."

Describing the book as having the tone of "a brilliant but extremely beligerant honors thesis," *Washington Post* reviewer Larry McMurtry wrote: "I am not sure that Mitchell Ross ever arrives at a consistent notion of what he wants to do with this diverse group of writers. Basically, I would judge, he just likes to read them, and feels that their excellence has gone unappreciated, thanks to the effete modernism of the universities." McMurtry noted that the "author can't stop pouting over the fact that his brilliance is not being given its due."

Both Lehmann-Haupt and McMurtry believe Ross has shown promise as a writer, however. "Mr. Ross does draw fast and hit an occasional target," judged Lehmann-Haupt. "So perhaps if he steadies his aim, he will write a worthwhile book one of these days." McMurtry declared that "Ross has a very promising future—one hopes that his enthusiasm for his subjects never wanes."

BIOGRAPHICAL/CRITICAL SOURCES: Chicago Tribune, January 8, 1978; *New York Times Book Review,* January 15, 1978; *New York Times,* January 17, 1978; *Washington Post,* February 6, 1978; *Detroit Free Press,* March 26, 1978.

* * *

ROSS, W(illiam) E(dward) D(aniel) 1912-
(Dan Ross; Leslie Ames, Rose Dana, Ruth Dorset, Ann Gilmer, Ellen Randolph, Dan Roberts, Clarissa Ross, Dana Ross, Marilyn Ross, Jane Rossiter, Tex Steel, Rose Williams, pseudonyms)

PERSONAL: Born November 16, 1912, in Saint John, New Brunswick, Canada; son of William Edward (a military man) and Laura Frances (an actress; maiden name, Brooks) Ross; married Charlotte Edith MacCormack (died, 1958); married Marilyn Ann Clark (an editor), July 2, 1960. *Education:* Attended Provincetown Theatre School, New York, N.Y., 1934; further study at University of Chicago, University of Oklahoma, Columbia University, and University of Michigan. *Politics:* None. *Religion:* Anglican. *Home:* 80 Horton Rd., East Riverside, Saint John, New Brunswick, Canada E2H IP8. *Agent:* Robert P. Mills, 156 East 52nd St., New York, N.Y. 10022.

CAREER: Worked as traveling actor and actor manager with own company, 1930-48; film distributor for own company, for Paramount, and for Monogram Films, 1948-57; full-time writer, 1957—. Member of panel of judges for Gibson National Literary Award, given for best first novel yearly in Canada. *Wartime service:* Served with British Entertainment Services during World War II. *Member:* Canadian Authors Association (former president), Mystery Writers of America, Authors Guild, Authors League of America, Western Writers of America, Society of Authors (United Kingdom), Christian Press, Riverside Country Club. *Awards, honors:* Dominion Drama Festival Prize for Playwrighting, 1934; D.Litt. from London University, 1975; Queen Elizabeth Silver Jubilee Medal, 1978, for contributions to popular fiction.

WRITINGS: Alice in Love, Popular Library, 1965; *Fog Island*, Paperback Library, 1965, published under pseudonym Marilyn Ross, Popular Library, 1977; *Journey to Love*, Bouregy, 1967; *Love Must Not Waver*, R. Hale, 1967; *Winslow's Daughter*, Bouregy, 1967; *The Ghost of Oaklands*, Arcadia House, 1967; *The Third Spectre*, Arcadia House, 1967, published under name Dan Ross, Macfadden-Baitell, 1969; *Our Share of Love*, R. Hale, 1967; *Dark Villa of Capri*, Arcadia House, 1968; *The Twilight Web*, Arcadia House, 1968; *Behind Locked Shutters*, Arcadia House, 1968, published under name Dan Ross, Manor, 1975; *Dark of the Moon*, Arcadia House, 1968; *Let Your Heart Answer*, Bouregy, 1968; *Christopher's Mansion*, Bouregy, 1969; *Luxury Liner Nurse*, R. Hale, 1969; *The Need to Love*, Avalon, 1969.

Sable in the Rain, Lenox Hill, 1970; *The Web of Love*, R. Hale, 1970; *An Act of Love*, Bouregy, 1970; *Magic Valley*, R. Hale, 1970; *This Man I Love*, R. Hale, 1970; *The Whispering Gallery*, Lenox Hill, 1970, published under name Dan Ross, Manor, 1977; *Beauty Doctor's Nurse*, Lenox Hill, 1971; *The Yesteryear Phantom*, Lenox Hill, 1971; *King of Romance*, R. Hale, 1971; *The Room Without a Key*, Lenox Hill, 1971; *Music Room*, Dell, 1971; *Wind Over the Citadel*, Lenox Hill, 1971; *Rothhaven*, Avalon, 1972; *The House on Mount Vernon Street*, Lenox Hill, 1972; *Mansion on the Moors*, Dell, 1974; *Nightmare Abbey*, Berkeley, 1975; *One Louisburg Square*, Belmont-Tower, 1975; *Witch of Goblin's Acres*, Belmont-Tower, 1975; *Dark Is My Shadow*, Manor, 1976; *Summer's End*, Fawcett World, 1976; *House on Lime Street*, Bouregy, 1976; *Pattern of Love*, Bouregy, 1977; *Shadows Over Garden*, Belmont-Tower, 1978; *Return to Barton*, Avalon, 1978.

Under name Dan Ross: *The Castle on the Cliff*, Bouregy, 1967; *Nurse in Love*, Avalon, 1972.

Under pseudonym Leslie Ames: *Bride of Donnybrook*, Arcadia House, 1966; *The Hungry Sea*, Arcadia House, 1967; *The Hidden Chappel*, Arcadia House, 1967; *The Hill of Ashes*, Arcadia House, 1968; *King's Castle*, Lenox Hill, 1970.

Under pseudonym Rose Dana: *Citadel of Love*, Arcadia House, 1965; *Down East Nurse*, Arcadia House, 1967; *Nurse in Jeopardy*, Arcadia House, 1967; *Labrador Nurse*, Arcadia House, 1968; *Network Nurse*, Arcadia House, 1968; *Whitebridge Nurse*, Arcadia House; *Department Store Nurse*, Lenox Hill, 1970.

Under pseudonym Ruth Dorset: *Front Office Nurse*, Arcadia House, 1966; *Hotel Nurse*, Arcadia House, 1967; *Nurse in Waiting*, Arcadia House, 1967.

Under pseudonym Ann Gilmer: *The Fog and the Stars*, Avalon, 1963; *Winds of Change*, Bouregy, 1965; *Private Nurse*, Bouregy, 1969; *Nurse on Emergency*, Bouregy, 1970; *Skyscraper Nurse*, Bouregy, 1976.

Under pseudonym Ellen Randolph: *Personal Secretary*, Avalon, 1963; *The Castle on the Hill*, Avalon, 1964.

Under pseudonym Dan Roberts: *The Well Fargo Brand*, Arcadia House, 1964; *The Cheyenne Kid*, Arcadia House, 1965; *Durez City Bonanza*, Arcadia House, 1965; *Outlaw's Gold*, Arcadia House, 1965; *Stage to Link City*, Arcadia House, 1966; *Wyoming Range War*, Arcadia House, 1966; *Yuma Brand*, Arcadia House, 1967; *Lawman of Blue Rock*, Arcadia House, 1967; *The Dawn Riders*, Arcadia House, 1968.

Under pseudonym Clarissa Ross: *Mistress of Ravenswood*, Arcadia House, 1966; *The Secret of Mallet Castle*, Arcadia

House, 1966; *Fogbound*, Arcadia House, 1967, published under name Dan Ross, Manor, 1976; *Let Your Heart Answer*, Valentine, 1968; *Secret of the Pale Lover*, Magnum, 1969; *Beware the Kindly Stranger*, Lancer, 1970; *Gemini in Darkness*, Magnum, 1970; *Glimpse into Terror*, Magnum, 1971; *The Spectral Mist*, Magnum, 1972; *Phantom of Glencourt*, Magnum, 1972; *Whispers in the Night*, Bantam, 1972; *China Shadow*, Avon, 1974; *Drafthaven*, Avon, 1974; *Ghost of Dark Harbor*, Avon, 1974; *A Hearse for Dark Harbor*, Avon, 1974; *Dark Harbor Hunting*, Avon, 1975; *Evil of Dark Harbor*, Avon, 1975; *Terror At Dark Harbor*, Avon, 1975; *Durrell Towers*, Pyramid, 1976; *Jade Princess*, Pyramid, 1977; *Moscow Mists*, Avon, 1977; *A Scandalous Affair*, Belmont-Tower, 1978; *Kashmiri Passions*, Warner Brothers, 1978; *Istanbul Nights*, Jove, 1978; *Flame of Love*, Belmont-Tower, 1978.

Under pseudonym Dana Ross: *Demon of Darkness*, Paperback Library, 1975; *Lodge Sinister*, Paperback Library, 1975; *This Shrouded Night*, Paperback Library, 1975; *The Raven and the Phantom*, Paperback Library, 1976.

Under pseudonym Marilyn Ross: *The Locked Corridor*, Paperback Library, 1965; *Beware My Love!*, Paperback Library, 1965; *Dark Shadows*, Paperback Library, 1968; *The Foe of Barnabas Collins*, Paperback Library, 1969.

Barnabas, Quentin and Dr. Jekyll's Son, Paperback Library, 1971; *Phantom of Fog Island*, Warner, 1971; *Dark Stars Over Seacrest*, Paperback Library, 1972; *The Long Night of Fear*, Warner, 1972; *Mistress of Moorwood Manor*, Warner, 1972; *Night of the Phantom*, Warner, 1972; *The Sinister Garden*, Warner, 1972; *Witch of Bralhaven*, Warner, 1972; *Phantom of the Swamp*, Paperback Library, 1972; *Behind the Purple Veil*, Warner, 1973; *Don't Look Behind You*, Warner, 1973; *Face In the Shadows*, Warner, 1973; *House of Ghosts*, Warner, 1973; *Marta*, Warner, 1973; *Step Into Terror*, Warner, 1973; *The Amethyst Tears*, Ballantine, 1974; *A Garden of Ghosts*, Popular Library, 1974; *Loch Sinister*, Popular Library, 1974; *The Vampire Contessa*, Pinnacle, 1974; *Witches Cove*, Warner, 1974.

Cameron Castle, Warner, 1975; *Dark Towers of Fog Island*, Popular Library, 1975; *Fog Island Secret*, Popular Library, 1975; *The Ghost and the Garnet: Birthstone No. One*, Ballantine, 1975; *Ghost Ship of Fog Island*, Popular Library, 1975; *Phantom of the Thirteenth Floor*, Popular Library, 1975; *Ravenhurst*, Popular Library, 1975; *Satan's Island*, Warner, 1975; *Shadow Over Emerald Castle*, Ballantine, 1975; *The Widow of Westwood*, Popular Library, 1976; *Brides of Saturn*, Berkeley, 1976; *The Curse of Black Charlie*, Popular Library, 1976; *Haiti Circle*, Popular Library, 1976; *Phantom Wedding*, Popular Library, 1976; *Shadow Over Denby*, Popular Library, 1976; *Stewarts of Stormhaven: Cellars of the Dead*, Popular Library, 1976; *Temple of Darkness*, Ballantine, 1976; *Waiting in the Shadows*, Popular Library, 1976; *Cauldron of Evil*, Popular Library, 1977; *Death's Dark Music*, Popular Library, 1977; *Mask of Evil*, Popular Library, 1977; *Phantom of the Snow*, Popular Library, 1977; *This Evil Village*, Popular Library, 1977; *This Frightened Lady*, Popular Library, 1977; *Delta Flame*, Popular Library, 1978; *Rothby*, Popular Library, 1978; *The Twice Dead*, Fawcett, 1978; *Horror of Fog Island*, Popular Library, 1978.

Under pseudonym Jane Rossiter: *Backstage Nurse*, Avalon, 1963; *Love Is Forever*, Avalon, 1963; *Summer Star*, Avalon, 1964.

Under pseudonym Rose Williams: *Five Nurses*, Arcadia House, 1964; *Nurse in Doubt*, Arcadia House, 1965; *Nurse*

Diane, Arcadia House, 1966; *Nurse in Spain,* R. Hale, 1967; *Nurse in Nassau,* Arcadia House, 1967; *Airport Nurse,* Arcadia House, 1968.

Also writes under pseudonym Tex Steel. Contributor of short stories to *Saint Mystery Magazine, Mike Shayne Mystery Magazine,* and other periodicals.

WORK IN PROGRESS: Three novels, *Wine of Passion, Roman Shades,* and *Dark Lane.*

SIDELIGHTS: Under a long list of pseudonyms Ross has published close to three hundred books that include Gothic romance, mystery, and western novels. His popularity has been broad: *China Shadow* was on the *New York Times* best seller list in 1975. A series of gothic romances, including *Dark Shadows* and *Barnabus Quentin and Dr. Jekyll's Son,* was the basis for a well-received afternoon television soap opera in the late 1960's.

Ross told *CA:* "I am a professional writer dedicated to bettering the lot of my group and interested in turning out as many readable books as possible. I consider the Gothic genre which dates to Wilkie Collins's *Woman in White* and before, to be the first version of what we know as the mystery story. I like its quality and clarity. My advice to would-be writers is read the best of the classic writers, then read everything, find out what appeals to you most and concentrate on that area."

*   *   *

ROSSITER, Jane
See ROSS, W(illiam) E(dward) D(aniel)

*   *   *

ROTTENSTEINER, Franz   1942-

PERSONAL: Born January 18, 1942, in Waidmannsfeld, Austria; son of Franz and Hedwig (Buchleitner) Rottensteiner. *Education:* University of Vienna, Ph.D., 1968. *Religion:* Atheist. *Home:* Marchettigasse 9/17, A-1060 Vienna, Austria.

CAREER: Austrian Institute for Building Research, Vienna, Austria, librarian, 1970—. Literary agent for Polish writer, Stanislaw Lem. *Military service:* Austrian Army, 1969-70.

WRITINGS: (Editor) *View From Another Shore: European Science Fiction,* Seabury, 1973, original German edition published as *Blick vom anderen Ufer,* Suhrkamp Verlag, 1977; *The Science Fiction Book,* Seabury, 1975; (editor) *Polaris,* Volume I, Insel Verlag, 1973, Volume II, Insel Verlag, 1974, Volume III, Insel Verlag, 1975, Volume IV, Suhrkamp, 1978; *The Fantasy Book,* Macmillan, 1978.

In German: (Editor) *Die Ratte im Labyrinth* (title means "The Rat in the Labyrinth"), Insel Verlag, 1971; (editor) *Insel Almanach auf das Jahr 1972* (title means "Insel Almanac for the Year 1972"), Insel Verlag, 1971; (editor with Marek Wydmuch) *Gespenstergeschichten aus Polen* (title means "Ghost Stories From Poland"), Fischer, 1978; (editor) *Gespenstergeschichten aus Oesterreich* (title means "Ghost Stories From Austria"), Fischer, 1979; (editor) *Quarber Merkur,* Suhrkamp Verlag, 1979.

Work anthologized in *SF: The Other Side of Realism,* edited by Thomas D. Clareson, Bowling Green University Popular Press, 1971; *Science Fiction,* edited by Eike Barmeyer, Wilhelm Fink, 1972; *SF: A Critical Guide,* edited by Patrick Parrinder, Longman, 1979.

Editor of "Science Fiction of the World," fifteen volumes,

Insel Verlag, 1971-75, and "Fantastic Novels," Zsolnay Verlag. Contributor to *Science-Fiction Studies.*

WORK IN PROGRESS: Editing science fiction and fantasy anthologies.

SIDELIGHTS: Rottensteiner writes: "I conduct research into various aspects of fantastic literature and science fiction, as well as editing, agenting, and sometimes translating, both in English and German. I am of the opinion that fantasy and science fiction are literary genres with a great potential, but that this potential has rarely ever been fulfilled by the practitioners in the field, most of whom are quite incompetent, and that it is of vital importance to separate the few essential works from the trash."

*   *   *

RUBICON
See LUNN, Arnold

*   *   *

RUBIN, Ernest   1915-1978

OBITUARY NOTICE: Born May 14, 1915, in New York, N.Y.; died November 12, 1978, in Washington, D.C. Statistician, economist, educator, and author. Rubin served as director of the Eastern Europe division of the Bureau of International Commerce from 1961 to 1973, during which time he participated in many trade missions abroad. He co-authored *Immigration and the Foreign Born* and was an editor for *American Statician* from 1954 to 1973. Obituaries and other sources: *Who's Who in Government,* Marquis, 1972; *Who's Who in World Jewry,* Pitman, 1972; *American Men and Women of Science: The Social and Behavioral Sciences,* 12th edition, Bowker, 1973; *Washington Post,* November 15, 1978.

*   *   *

RUGH, Roberts   1903-1978

OBITUARY NOTICE: Born in 1903 in Springfield, Ohio; died November 10, 1978, in Bethesda, Md. Biologist, radiologist, educator, and author of books on embryology. He spent over twenty years at Columbia University researching the effect of radiation on embryos and after his retirement in 1971 he joined the bureau of radiological health at the National Institutes of Health. In addition to his more technical books, Rugh also wrote *From Conception to Birth: The Drama of Life's Beginnings* for the general reader. Obituaries and other sources: *American Men and Women of Science: The Physical and Biological Sciences,* 12th edition, Bowker, 1971-73; *Who's Who in the East,* 14th edition, Marquis, 1973; *Washington Post,* November 13, 1978.

*   *   *

RUPP, Leila J(ane)   1950-

PERSONAL: Born February 13, 1950, in Plainfield, N.J.; daughter of Walter H. (a chemical engineer) and Sidney (Stanton) Rupp. *Education:* Bryn Mawr College, A.B., 1972, Ph.D., 1976; graduate study at University of North Carolina at Chapel Hill, 1972-73. *Home:* 199 East Como Ave., Columbus, Ohio 43202. *Office:* Department of History, Ohio State University, 230 West 17th Ave., Columbus, Ohio 43210.

CAREER: University of Pennsylvania, Philadelphia, Pa., visiting lecturer, 1976-77; Ohio State University, Columbus, Ohio, assistant professor of history and women's studies, 1977—. *Member:* American Historical Association, National Women's Studies Association, Berkshire Conference of Women Historians. *Awards, honors:* National Endowment for the Humanities grant, summer, 1977.

WRITINGS: Mobilizing Women for War: German and American Propaganda, 1939-45, Princeton University Press, 1978; (editor with Barbara Miller Lane) *Nazi Ideology Before 1933: A Documentation*, University of Texas Press, 1978.

WORK IN PROGRESS: Research on American feminism, 1945-60.

SIDELIGHTS: Rupp told *CA:* "Women's history has a great deal to tell us about the shape of our lives today. My current research on American feminism since 1945 convinces me that we have to rethink our assumptions about the death of feminism in 1920 and its rebirth in the 1960's. Certainly the study of women's history quickly disabuses one of any notion of simple progress in history."

*   *   *

RUSHING, William A. 1930-

PERSONAL: Born April 3, 1930, in Murfreesboro, Tenn.; son of William A. (a barber) and Myrtle Marie Rushing; married Kay Frances Dunsmore, December 26, 1958; children: Todd Winslow, Claudia Ann. *Education:* University of Colorado, B.A., 1956, M.A., 1958; University of North Carolina, Ph.D., 1961. *Religion:* None. *Home:* 109 Blackburn Dr., Nashville, Tenn. 37205. *Office:* Department of Sociology/Anthropology, Vanderbilt University, Nashville, Tenn. 37235.

CAREER: Florida State University, Tallahassee, Fla., assistant professor of sociology, 1961-63; University of Wisconsin—Madison, assistant professor of sociology, 1963-64; Washington State University, Pullman, associate professor of sociology, 1964-68; Vanderbilt University, Nashville, Tenn., associate professor, 1968-69, professor of sociology, 1969—, chairman of department of sociology/anthropology, 1975—. Head of section of sociological studies for Tennessee Mid-South Regional Medical Program, Nashville, 1968-72. *Military Service:* U.S. Air Force, 1949-52. *Member:* American Sociological Association, Society for the Scientific Study of Social Problems, Southern Sociological Society, Phi Beta Kappa.

WRITINGS: The Psychiatric Professions: Power Conflict and Adaptation in a Psychiatric Setting, University of North Carolina Press, 1964; *Class Culture and Alienation: A Study of Farmers and Farm Workers*, Lexington Books, 1972; *Community Physicians and Inequality: A Sociological Analysis of the Maldistribution of Physicians*, Lexington Books, 1975.

*   *   *

RUSSELL, Pamela Redford 1950-

PERSONAL: Born June 11, 1950, in Long Beach, Calif.; daughter of George Martin and Helen (Brewen) Russell. *Education:* Attended University of California, Los Angeles, 1972-74. *Residence:* Studio City, Calif. *Agent:* Robinson/Weintraub, 554 South San Vicente, Los Angeles, Calif. 90048.

CAREER: Fashion model in New York, N.Y. and Los Angeles, Calif., 1970-72; Columbia Broadcasting System, Los Angeles, page, 1972-75; MTM Enterprises, Los Angeles, writer for "The Mary Tyler Moore Show," 1975; free-lance writer, 1975—.

WRITINGS: The Man Who Loved John Wilkes Booth (novel), Putnam, 1978.

WORK IN PROGRESS: Summer Gossamer, a novel.

SIDELIGHTS: Pamela Russell comments: "I wrote my first short story when I was nine years old. I have had many jobs in my life, some that were fascinating and some that merely paid the rent, but there is only one thing I have ever truly been—a writer. I cannot imagine living and not writing. It is the mirror that I hold up to my existence."

*   *   *

RUSSELL TAYLOR, Elisabeth 1930-

PERSONAL: Born May 14, 1930, in London, England; daughter of Charles (a physician) and Peggy (a pianist; maiden name, Davidson) Lewsen; divorced. *Education:* Attended Sorbonne, University of Paris, 1951-53. *Politics:* Socialist. *Home:* 21 Steeles Rd., London N.W.3, England. *Agent:* Bolt & Watson Ltd., 8-12 Queen Anne's Gate, London S.W.1, England.

CAREER: Assicurazione Generale (insurance company), Johannesburg, South Africa, translator of legal documents from French, 1953-55; dealer in antiques and objets d'art in Israel, 1955-56, and in London, England, 1957-63; interior decorator in London, 1957-68; British Broadcasting Corp. (BBC), London, broadcaster on domestic, sociological, and political subjects, 1963-65; free-lance journalist, 1957—; agent for British sculptors, and organizer of sculpture exhibitions in Canada, 1966-70; writer, 1970—.

WRITINGS: Wish You Were Here (nonfiction), Wildwood House, 1976; *London Lifelines* (nonfiction), Wildwood House, 1977; *Critical Bibliography of Work in English on the Life and Work of Marcel Proust*, Garland Publishing, in press. Also author of *Caesar's Trencher, The Next Amusement,* and *Winter Walks in Paris.*

Books for children: *The Gifts of the Tarns,* Collins, 1977; *Tales From Barleymill,* Abelard, 1978; *The Loadstone,* Abelard, 1978. Also author of *The Banana Skin Tree, The Fall and Rise of the City of Bentor, The Hermit of Silene,* and *Turkey in the Middle.* Contributor of articles and photographs to magazines, including *Queen, House Beautiful,* and *Amateur Gardening.*

WORK IN PROGRESS: Time Still, "an evocation of Proust's geography as it relates to his work"; an untitled book consisting of "a series of landscape photographs in colour taken from stone walls, peeling wood surfaces such as rotting boats, and torn posters—fragments of things I come across on walks. The results are figurative—discernible land and seascapes."

SIDELIGHTS: Elisabeth Russell Taylor writes: "My particular interests are primitive Italian painting, Impressionism, and Surrealism. I lived in Paris for two years in the 1950's and subsequently have visited there yearly. I am widely traveled in North America, Europe, and the Middle East. I favor the bicycle over the car and 'homemade' over 'shop-bought.' My ambition to cycle round the world is thwarted only by unlimited fears. About her books, she adds: "*Time Still* depends on my knowledge of the painters who influenced Proust and the special qualities of the locations that prompted his descriptions of fictitious places."

AVOCATIONAL INTERESTS: Lieder and chamber music, English and French literature, *cordon bleu* cooking, gardening.

RUTTLE, Lee 1909-

PERSONAL: Born May 8, 1909, in Providence, R.I.; son of James Patrick (a clerk) and Mary (Stanton) Ruttle; married Caroline Chew (a dancer), May 28, 1938. *Education:* Attended New York University and University of California, Oakland, 1946. *Politics:* "Changes with the wind, liberal (conservative)." *Religion:* "I believe in God and man." *Home:* 206 Hermosa Ave., Oakland, Calif. 94618.

CAREER: Co-director of a Chinese puppet theater group, 1931-39; owner of his own public relations and advertising business, 1940-43, and 1946-76; writer. Has worked as professional actor, stagehand, and publicist, and director of amateur theatricals. *Military service:* U.S. Marine Corps, 1928-29, 1943-45; served in Pacific theater; received three battle stars. California Military Reserve, 1952-64; became lieutenant colonel. *Member:* San Francisco Press Club, First Marine Division Association, Marine Memorial Club (life member).

WRITINGS: The Private War of Dr. Yamada (novel), San Francisco Book Co., 1978.

Work anthologized in *Scoop,* San Francisco Press Club. Special correspondent for *Pacific Citizen.* Contributor of articles and stories to magazines, including *Leatherneck, Our Navy,* and *Cross Roads,* and newspapers.

WORK IN PROGRESS: Two novels, *Windward Passage* and *Return to Nara;* three other novels.

SIDELIGHTS: Ruttle comments: "I recalled reading *All Quiet on the Western Front* by Erich Remarque, and wished to do for the Japanese soldier of World War II what Remarque had done for the German soldier of World War I. This was my motivation for writing *The Private War of Dr. Yamada.* Additionally, my first experience in combat (Peleliu, 1944) impressed upon me the futility of war."

* * *

RUZICKA, Rudolph 1883-1978

OBITUARY NOTICE: Born June 29, 1883, in Bohemia; died July 20, 1978, in Hanover, N.H. Graphic artist, designer, typographer, and author. Best known for his achievements as a print engraver, book illustrator, and designer of fine books, Ruzicka also designed the "Fairfield," "Fairfield Medium," and "Primer" typefaces which are still used in book production. He wrote *Thomas Bewick, Engraver,* 1943, and *Studies in Type Design,* 1968. Obituaries and other sources: *American Artist,* December, 1967; *Illustrators of Books for Young People,* 2nd edition, Scarecrow, 1975; *Who's Who in America,* 40th edition, Marquis, 1978; *Publishers Weekly,* August 7, 1978; *AB Bookman's Weekly,* October 23, 1978.

* * *

RYAN, Bryce F(inley) 1911-

PERSONAL: Born February 16, 1911, in Youngstown, Ohio; son of William D. (a clergyman) and Julia (Grinnel) Ryan; married Margaret Warnken (divorced, 1952); married Beatrice Mitchell (died, 1977); children: Bruce; Arthur T. Bunce, Bayne R. Bunce (stepchildren). *Education:* University of Washington, Seattle, A.B., 1932; University of Texas, M.A., 1933; Harvard University, M.A., 1937, Ph.D., 1940. *Politics:* Democrat. *Religion:* Christian. *Home:* 6141 West Suburban Dr., Miami, Fla. 33156. *Office:* Department of Sociology, University of Miami, Coral Gables, Fla. 33124.

CAREER: Iowa State University, Ames, assistant professor of sociology, 1937-43; United Nations Relief and Rehabilitation Administration, Germany, chief reports analyst, 1944-46; Rutgers University, New Brunswick, N.J., assistant professor of sociology, 1946-48; University of Ceylon, Colombo, professor of sociology and chairman of department, 1948-52; University of Miami, Coral Gables, Fla., professor of sociology, 1955-76, professor emeritus, 1976—, chairman of department, 1955-76. Consultant to the Rockefeller Foundation, 1950-52; Ford Foundation visiting professor at National University of Colombia, 1963. *Member:* American Sociological Association, Southern Sociological Society, Omicron Delta Kappa.

WRITINGS: (With J. Riley and others) *The Student Looks at His Teacher,* Rutgers University Press, 1950; *Caste in Modern Ceylon,* Rutgers University Press, 1953; *Sinhalese Village,* University of Miami Press, 1958; *Social and Cultural Change,* Ronald, 1969; *Social and Cultural Dynamics,* Ronald, 1978. Contributor to sociology journals.

WORK IN PROGRESS: Research on social trends and dynamics, with special reference to futurology.

* * *

RYAN, Paul B(rennan) 1913-

PERSONAL: Born April 19, 1913, in Burlington, Vt.; son of Leo T. and Mary Elizabeth (Brennan) Ryan; married Margaret Alice Hughes; children: Holly Elizabeth Ryan Kaufman. *Education:* U.S. Naval Academy, B.S., 1936; Stanford University, A.M. (international relations), 1964; San Jose State University, M.A. (history), 1965. *Office:* Hoover Institution on War, Revolution and Peace, Stanford, Calif. 94305.

CAREER: U.S. Navy, career officer, 1932-62, 1969-72, retiring as captain; ship's officer on battleships and cruisers, 1936-40, submarine service, 1941-45, commanding officer in Far East, 1945-48, naval attache in Cuba, 1950-52, commanding officer of Fleet ship in Mediterranean and Atlantic, 1955; naval attache in Ottawa, Ontario, 1956-59, worked in Pentagon's Office of International Security Affairs, 1960-62; management education specialist in aerospace industry for Apollo Program, 1966-68; deputy director of naval history for U.S. Department of the Navy, 1969-72; Stanford University, Hoover Institution on War, Revolution and Peace, Standford, Calif., naval historian, 1972—. Member of Naval Historical Foundation; president of U.S. Commission for Maritime History.

MEMBER: North American Society for Oceanic History, Organization of American Historians, U.S. Naval Institute, Phi Kappa Phi. *Awards, honors*—Military: Legion of Merit; Navy Commendation Medal.

WRITINGS: (With Thomas A. Bailey) *The Lusitania Disaster,* Free Press, 1975; *The Panama Canal Controversy: U.S. Diplomacy and Defense Interests,* Hoover Institution, 1977; (with Bailey) *Hitler vs. Roosevelt: Their Undeclared Naval War,* Free Press, 1979; (contributor) Paolo Coletta, editor, *The Secretaries of the Navy,* U.S. Naval Institute, 1979; *U.S. National Strategy and the Role of Sea Power,* Hoover Institution Press, in press. Contributor of articles and reviews to military journals and newspapers.

SIDELIGHTS: Ryan writes: "Most of my work turns on the linkage between international relations and sea power. My life in the Navy allowed me to see first-hand how national strategic interests frequently are shaped by a nation's maritime capabilities. On shore duty in the Pentagon's Division of International Security Affairs, I observed the development of diplomatic and defense policies, and the strategic implications that they held for the U.S. Armed Forces, particularly the Navy. Consequently my writings, while historical in structure, reflect my interest in diplomacy and navies.''

*   *   *

RYBAK, Nathan   1913-1978(?)

OBITUARY NOTICE: Born in 1913 in the Ukraine; died c. 1978 in Kiev, Ukrainian S.S.R. Deputy chairman of the Soviet Peace Committee and author of several books, including *The Pereyaslav Rada* and *Honore de Balzac's Mistake.* Obituaries and other sources: *AB Bookman's Weekly,* January 8, 1979.

S

SACHAR, Louis 1954-

PERSONAL: Surname is pronounced *Sack*-er; born March 20, 1954, in East Meadow, N.Y.; son of Robert J. (in sales) and Ruth (a real estate broker; maiden name, Raybin) Sachar. *Education:* University of California, Berkeley, B.A., 1976; graduate study at Hastings College of Law, 1977—. *Home:* 151 Henry St., San Francisco, Calif. 94114.

CAREER: Beldoch Industries (manufacturers of women's sweaters), Norwalk, Conn., shipping manager, 1976-77; writer, 1977—.

WRITINGS: Sideways Stories From Wayside School (juvenile), Follett, 1978.

WORK IN PROGRESS: A novel; revising a children's novel, for Follett.

SIDELIGHTS: Sachar told *CA* how he began his writing career: "I was wandering around the Berkeley campus trying to find some kind of course to take. I had taken four quarters of Russian and had been to the first three days of Russian 5. I thought someday I'd be able to read Tolstoi and Dostoevski in the original. I'd even bought a Russian book of Chekhov short stories that I planned to start reading one day, but first I had to find the right Russian-English dictionary. A classmate stood up and read to us an amusing anecdote he'd written in Russian. I knew it was amusing because everyone else in the class was laughing. I guess I never progressed too much after Russian 3. So I was wandering about trying to find another course as people were handing out various political and religious leaflets. A little blonde girl gave me a piece of paper that said, "Help!!!! Our elementary school needs teachers' aides. Earn three units of credit. Come to Hillside School, 7:30 Tuesday." With much reluctance I ended up doing it. I've now written two children's books. If that blonde girl hadn't handed me that piece of paper I'd still be an unpublished writer, trying to be another Tolstoi or Dostoevski."

AVOCATIONAL INTERESTS: Watching the San Francisco Giants, playing rugby.

*   *   *

SAGARIN, Mary 1903-

PERSONAL: Born in 1903, in Massachusetts. *Education:* Attended high school in Schenectady, N.Y. *Residence:* Brooklyn, N.Y.

CAREER: Worked as writer and office worker; executive secretary with American Federation of Television and Radio Artists until 1966; writer, 1966—.

WRITINGS—For teenagers: *Equal Justice Under Law: Our Court System and How It Works,* Lothrop, 1966; *Washington Alphabet: Seven Agencies That Regulate Business,* Lothrop, 1968; *John Brown Russwurm: The Story of "Freedom's Journal," Freedom's Journey,* Lothrop, 1970. Contributor to confession magazines.

SIDELIGHTS: Mary Sagarin writes: "I was one of eleven children of Jewish-Russian immigrant parents. I was imbued with a love of the classics, of languages, and with a sense of history and of political movements. My plans to go on to college were cut short by the death of my parents when I was fifteen, when I was left with four younger brothers to support.

"We lived, rather precariously, on my earnings as an office worker and writer of 'confession' stories for many years.

"I have been interested in race relations since my high school days, and I welcomed the opportunity to write the biography of John Brown Russwurm, America's first black college graduate and founder of *Freedom's Journal,* the first newspaper to be published by blacks in this country. I am still active in the fight for civil rights and in the peace movement, although my chief pleasure in life as I grow older is reading (and rereading)."

AVOCATIONAL INTERESTS: Graphology.

*   *   *

SAID, Abdul Aziz 1930-

PERSONAL: Born September 1, 1930, in Amouda, Syria; came to the United States in 1950, naturalized citizen, 1962; son of Said and Shamsah (Khacho) Ishak; married Elizabeth Miller, 1964; children: Riyad, Jamil. *Education:* American University, B.S., 1954, M.A., 1955, Ph.D., 1957. *Home:* 5045 Garfield St. N.W., Washington, D.C. 20016. *Office:* School of International Service, American University, Washington, D.C. 20016.

CAREER: American University, Washington, D.C., instructor, 1957, assistant professor, 1957-60, associate professor, 1960-63, professor of international relations, 1963—. Lecturer for U.S. State Department Foreign Service Institute. President of Center for Mediterranean Affairs. *Member:* International Studies Association.

WRITINGS: (With Charles O. Lerche, Jr.) *Concepts of International Politics,* Prentice-Hall, 1963, 3rd edition, 1979; (with Daniel Collier) *Revolutionism,* Allyn & Bacon, 1968; *The African Phenomenon,* Allyn & Bacon, 1968; (editor) *Theory of International Relations: The Crisis of Relevance,* Prentice-Hall, 1968; (editor) *America's World Role in the Seventies,* Prentice-Hall, 1970; (editor) *Protagonists of Change: Subcultures in Development and Revolution,* Spectrum Books, 1971; (editor with L. R. Simmons) *The New Sovereigns: Multinational Corporations as World Powers,* Prentice-Hall, 1974; (editor with Simmons) *Drugs, Politics, and Diplomacy,* Sage, 1974; (editor) *Whose National Interest?: Ethnic and American Foreign Policy,* Praeger, 1978; (editor) *Human Rights and World Order,* Praeger, 1978. Associate editor, *Society.*

*   *   *

SALK, Erwin Arthur 1918-

PERSONAL: Born June 24, 1918, in Chicago, Ill.; son of Harry (a mortgage banker) and Gertrude (Kaplan) Salk; married Evelyn Sugg; children: Justin, Anthony, Jonathan. *Education:* University of Chicago, B.A., 1939, M.A., 1941. *Home:* 1110 Sheridan Rd., Evanston, Ill. 60201. *Agent:* Joan Daves, 515 Madison Ave., New York, N.Y. 10022. *Office:* Salk, Ward & Salk, 11 South LaSalle St., Chicago, Ill. 60603.

CAREER: Chief of wages, hours, and working conditions for Japanese nation, 1944-46; UNESCO, Paris, France, staff member, 1945-46, section chief, 1946-48; Salk, Ward & Salk, Inc., Chicago, Ill., president, 1957—. President of Salk Insurance Agency and Management Co., Inc., Ermel Appraisal and Analysis, Inc., and A.M.I. Real Estate Corp. Professor and member of board of trustees at Columbia College, Chicago, Ill.; lecturer at Loop College. National founder and organizer of Business Executives Move for Vietnam Peace; vice-president of Jewish Council on Urban Affairs; past chairman of executive committee of Evanston Community Relations Commission; member of executive board and past chairman of housing committee of Chicago Conference on Religion and Race. Member of board of directors of Independence Bank of Chicago and DuSable Museum of African American History; member of board of trustees of Amistad Research Center at Dillard University.

MEMBER: Mortgage Bankers Association of America, Association for the Study of Afro-American Life and History (member of executive council), National Council for U.S.-China Trade, U.S.-China Peoples Friendship Association (sponsor; chairman of finance committee), B'nai B'rith (past local president), Lambda Alpha (Ely chapter). *Awards, honors:* American Friendship Award from American Friendship Committee, 1966.

WRITINGS: A Layman's Guide to Negro History, McGraw, 1967, revised edition published as *Missing Pages in U.S. History: A Guide to Afro-American Life and History,* in press; *Two Giants of the Twentieth Century: The Story of an Exhibit and a Bibliography,* Columbia College Press, 1977. Contributor to *Encyclopedia International.* Contributor to banking, investment, and Afro-American studies journals.

WORK IN PROGRESS: "Songs of Struggle," a recording on social protest by American minorities.

SIDELIGHTS: Salk comments: "I have an interest in China's economy, development, and foreign policy, with emphasis on U.S.-China trade potential. I visited the People's Republic of China in 1974. I lecture on this topic to business and academic groups; I also lecture on the military economy, education in the schools, black history, the history of minorities, housing, and urban affairs, and real estate.

"'Missing Pages in U.S. History,' a course I teach at Columbia College, covers blacks, Chicanos, native Americans, Asian-Americans, white Appalachians, women, the labor movement, et cetera, and deals with people, places, and events that have been neglected, often deliberately omitted from texts and school curricula."

AVOCATIONAL INTERESTS: International travel.

*   *   *

SALTZMAN, Joe
See SALTZMAN, Joseph

*   *   *

SALTZMAN, Joseph 1939-
(Joe Saltzman; Joseph Laertes, Joe Michaels, Joe Roberts, pseudonyms)

PERSONAL: Born October 28, 1939, in Los Angeles, Calif.; son of Morris and Ruth (Weiss) Saltzman; married Barbara Dale Epstein (a journalist and editor), July 1, 1962; children: Michael Stephen Ulysses, David Charles Laertes. *Education:* University of Southern California, B.A., 1961; Columbia University, M.A., 1962. *Home:* 2116 Via Estudillo, Palos Verdes Estates, Calif. 90274. *Office:* School of Journalism, University of Southern California, University Park, Los Angeles, Calif. 90008.

CAREER: Los Angeles Examiner, Los Angeles, Calif., general assignment reporter, 1960-61; *San Fernando Valley Times Today,* San Fernando, Calif., general assignment reporter and mid-Valley bureau chief, 1962-64; *Palisadian Post* (weekly newspaper), Pacific Palisades, Calif., news editor, 1964; CBS-KNXT Television, Los Angeles, staff reporter-writer, 1964-65, senior staff news writer-editor-producer, 1965-66, senior writer-producer, 1967-73, senior producer, 1973-74; free-lance writer, producer, and editor, 1974—; University of Southern California, Los Angeles, assistant professor, 1974-76, associate professor of journalism, 1976—, School of Journalism, director of undergraduate studies. Owner-editor of Roberts Reviewing Service, 1967—. Producer of a ninety-minute documentary on urban blacks in Los Angeles, 1968, and of "Why Me," a sixty-minute documentary on breast cancer, 1974. *Member:* National Academy of Television Arts and Sciences, Writers Guild of America West, Greater Los Angeles Press Club, Phi Beta Kappa, Sigma Delta Chi, Alpha Epsilon Rho. *Awards, honors:* Seymour Berkson fellow, 1961-62; Robert E. Sherwood fellow and Pulitzer Traveling fellowship, both 1962-63; has received more than fifty local and national broadcasting and journalism awards, including Edward R. Murrow Award from the Radio-Television News Association, 1969, for best television documentary "Black on Black"; award for distinguished achievement in broadcast journalism, 1972; Alfred I. DuPont Award from Columbia University, 1973-74; distinguished journalism citation from Scripps Howard Foundation, 1974-75, for outstanding public service reporting.

WRITINGS—Television documentaries; all for CBS-TV: "Black on Black" (on urban Blacks), 1968; "The Unhappy Hunting Ground" (on urban Indians), 1971; "The Junior High School," 1971; "The Very Personal Death of Elizabeth Schell Holt-Hartford," 1972; "Rape," 1972; "Why Me?" (on breast cancer), 1974.

Columnist, under pseudonyms Joe Michaels and Joe Roberts, with weekly columns appearing in more than forty community and metropolitan newspapers and in magazines. Contributor of articles to magazines, including *Reporter, Look, Esquire, Saturday Evening Post, Saturday Review, Frontier,* and *TV Guide.*

SIDELIGHTS: Saltzman told *CA:* "I became a journalist to inform, educate, and reveal various truths to the public. I have always seen teaching as a logical extension of that role. Teaching journalism is more rewarding and satisfying than anything else I can imagine doing.

"I am doing what I want to do—head of broadcasting at University of Southern California, television and media consultant; free-lance magazine and newspaper writer, and the owner-editor of Roberts Reviewing Service."

* * *

SANDERS, Lawrence 1920-

PERSONAL: Born in 1920, in Brooklyn, N.Y. *Education:* Wabash College, B.A., 1940. *Residence:* Pompano Beach, Fla. *Address:* c/o G. P. Putnam's Sons, 200 Madison Ave., New York, N.Y. 10016.

CAREER: Macy's department store, New York City, staff member, 1940-43; worked for various magazines as an editor and as a writer of war stories, men's adventure stories, and detective stories; feature editor for *Mechanix Illustrated,* New York City; editor for *Science and Mechanics,* New York City; Magnum-Royal Publications, New York City, free-lance writer for men's magazines, 1967-68; novelist, 1969—. *Military service:* U.S. Marine Corps, 1943-46; became sergeant. *Awards, honors:* Mystery Writers of America Edgar award for best first mystery novel, 1970, for *The Anderson Tapes.*

WRITINGS—All novels; all published by Putnam, except as noted: (With Richard Carol) *Handbook of Creative Crafts* (nonfiction), Pyramid Books, 1968; *The Anderson Tapes,* 1970; *The Pleasures of Helen,* 1971; *Love Songs,* 1972; *The First Deadly Sin,* 1973; *The Tomorrow File,* 1975; *The Tangent Objective,* 1976; *The Marlow Chronicles,* 1977; *The Second Deadly Sin,* 1977; *The Tangent Factor,* 1978. Also author of several "purse books" for Dell. Contributor of over one hundred stories and articles to various publications.

WORK IN PROGRESS: Another novel, to be published under a pseudonym.

SIDELIGHTS: "I learned my trade as a novelist," Sanders has said, "by working as an editor of pulp magazines" and writing "gag lines for cheesecake magazines." After editing various men's magazines, *Mechanix Illustrated,* and *Science and Mechanics,* he "got to the point where a lot of editors get—I said to myself that I could write the stuff better myself. And so I wrote *The Anderson Tapes*—my first novel—at age fifty."

The Anderson Tapes is the story of a Mafia-backed effort to rob an entire luxury apartment building. Foreshadowing the role electronics played in Watergate, this plot is thwarted when several governmental agencies tap "everything from a candy-store pay phone to Central Park itself." Christopher Lehmann-Haupt speculated that only those "fashionably paranoic and willing to believe that the whole world is plugged into a tape recorder" could easily enjoy this novel. Nonetheless, *The Anderson Tapes* was a best seller upon publication and was made into a Columbia motion picture soon thereafter.

Since becoming a full-time novelist, Sanders has settled down from the post-*Anderson Tape* days when he was "shoveling down martinis at night and waking up on Tums." "I've been working my tail off and enjoying it," he says. "I usually write about five pages a night, and it adds up." In one span Sanders produced three novels within a year, including *The Second Deadly Sin* and a story of one man's struggle to unite Africa, *The Tangent Factor.*

The Tangent Factor "depicts how one man imposes his will on whole nations, and the basic thesis is that it is not done merely through strength of character but through treachery, manipulation and carefully calculated violence," wrote Joseph McLellan. Despite objecting to its "unpleasant aftertaste," critic Thomas Lask admitted the "narrative is lean, fat free and highly readable. . . . It's hard not to admire his [Sanders's] skill."

Sanders now lives in Florida and continues to share his life with his "constant and beloved" companion of thirty years, Fleurette Ballou. Though he has expressed a desire to "try to slow down to only two books a year," he readily admits: "I'm obsessed with writing. I have no hobbies. I don't fish. I'm not interested in sports. I don't even own a car. When I'm writing, my fantasies become more important than my personal life. I'm a Walter Mitty—living out my years through my characters."

BIOGRAPHICAL/CRITICAL SOURCES: New York Times, February 20, 1970, August 25, 1977, March 24, 1978; *Time,* April 27, 1970; *Publishers Weekly,* August 2, 1976; *New York Times Book Review,* August 21, 1977, October 9, 1977; *People,* November 28, 1977; *Washington Post,* May 4, 1978.*

* * *

SANDFORD, Nell Mary 1936-
(Nell Dunn)

PERSONAL: Born in 1936, in London, England; married Jeremy Sandford (a writer), 1956; children: three. *Education:* Educated at a convent school. *Home:* 10 Bell Lane, Twickenham, Middlesex, England.

CAREER: Writer. Has also worked in a candy factory, a butter factory, and in a night club, all in Clapham, England, to gather background materials for her writing. *Awards, honors:* John Llewellyn Rhys Memorial Prize for short story collection, *Up the Junction,* 1964.

WRITINGS—Under pseudonym Nell Dunn: *Up the Junction* (short stories), MacGibbon & Kee, 1963, Lippincott, 1966; *Talking to Women* (interviews), MacGibbon & Kee, 1965; *Poor Cow* (novel), Doubleday, 1967; (with Susan Campbell) *Freddy Gets Married* (juvenile), MacGibbon & Kee, 1969; *The Incurable* (novel), Doubleday, 1971; (with Adrian Henri) *I Want* (novel), J. Cape, 1972; *Tear His Head Off His Shoulders* (novel), J. Cape, 1974, Doubleday, 1975; *Living Like I Do,* Lorrimer Publishing Ltd., 1976.

Also author, with Kenneth Loach, of a screenplay, "Poor Cow," adapted from her novel of the same title, National General, 1968.

SIDELIGHTS: Writing on *Up the Junction,* Edgar Z. Friedenberg noted the success of Dunn's "use of ethnology" in her accounts of "lower-depths poverty." "Poverty of intellect and emotional range—though not emotional intensity—is depicted here in terms even more horrifying than lack of possessions," wrote Friedenberg, who also pointed to the absence of "a tolerable social milieu" as the probable determining factor in the inability "to tell good quality from bad."

Jillings observed that "the over-40s seem to live in hair curlers and memories of their dead or deserted husbands or lovers. . . . The poor diet, the air pollution, and the monotony of life up the junction . . . provide the setting for crime and road accidents."

V. S. Pritchett found that Dunn's realistic dialogue in *Poor Cow* provided an accurate mirror of "contemporary London speech in low life." Again, there is no authorial intrusion, Pritchett noted, resulting in a faithful picture of "the exposed, unsupported, morally anonymous condition of people who have nothing that can really mean much to them except the vagaries of the sexual itch, what the telly says, and what is lit up in the supermarkets and pubs." However, it was Edwin Morgan's feeling that Dunn "sits rather uneasily with the documentary brilliance" of various episodes, although he conceded that "praise must be given to the many felicities of uneducated dialogue and the exact evocation of places and objects which Miss Dunn has mastered." *Punch* labeled *Poor Cow* "just taking the lid off a slum and leaving it at that," while R. Z. Sheppard acknowledged the "vitality and distinctive tone" of "this greasy slice of English life."

BIOGRAPHICAL/CRITICAL SOURCES: Village Voice, April 20, 1967; *Punch,* April 26, 1967, January 31, 1968; *New Statesman,* April 28, 1967; *Observer Review,* April 30, 1967, May 9, 1971; *Times Literary Supplement,* May 4, 1967; *New York Review of Books,* May 18, 1967, January 18, 1968; *Books and Bookmen,* June, 1967; *New York Times Book Review,* October 29, 1967; *Book World,* November 5, 1967; *New Yorker,* November 11, 1967; *Commonweal,* February 16, 1968; *Esquire,* May, 1968; *Listener,* November 14, 1968; *Yale Review,* spring, 1968.*

* * *

SANDON, Henry 1928-

PERSONAL: Born August 4, 1928, in London, England; married Barbara Starkey, August 2, 1956; children: David, Peter, John. *Education:* Guildhall School of Music, A.R.C.M. *Office:* Dyson Perrins Museum, Worcester, England.

CAREER: Music master at private grammar school in Worcester, England, lay clerk at Worcester Cathedral Choir, Worcester, England, and conductor, singer, and lecturer all over England, 1953-66; Dyson Perrins Museum, Worcester, England, curator, 1966—. Lecturer at University of Birmingham, 1953—. Curator of Royal Porcelain Works, 1966—. *Military service:* British Army, 1946-48. *Member:* Commemorative Collectors Society (vice-chairman), English Ceramic Circle, Choir Benevolent Fund (member of managing committee), London College of Music (fellow).

WRITINGS: British Pottery and Porcelain, Gifford, 1969, revised edition, 1979; *Worcester Porcelain, 1751-1793,* Barrie & Jenkins, 1969; *Coffeepots and Teapots,* John Bartholomew, 1973; *Royal Worcester Porcelain From 1862,* Barrie & Jenkins, 1973; *Flight and Barr Worcester Porcelain, 1783-1840,* Antique Collectors Club, 1978.

WORK IN PROGRESS: A biography of Doris Lindner; *Grainger Worcester Porcelain; Chamber Pots and Bourdeloues.*

SIDELIGHTS: Sandon writes: "My early life was spent as a professional musician. A growing interest in archaeology led to a passion for ceramics and a change of career. Archaeological excavations have provided information that has led to a complete rethink on eighteenth-century English porcelain, the import of a number of my books."

SANTINI, Rosemarie

PERSONAL: Born in New York, N.Y. *Education:* Attended Hunter College of the City University of New York. *Address:* P.O. Box 117, Village Station, New York, N.Y. 10014. *Agent:* William Morris Agency, 1350 Avenue of the Americas, New York, N.Y. 10019.

CAREER: Writer. Teacher of fiction and nonfiction workshops in New York, N.Y. *Member:* Forum, Poets and Writers.

WRITINGS: Forty-One Grove Street (novel), Curtis Books, 1973; *The Sex Doctors* (nonfiction), Pinnacle Books, 1975; *The Secret Fire: A New View of Women and Passion,* Playboy Press, 1977, reprinted as *The Santini Report,* Playboy Press, 1977; *Abracadabra* (novel), Playboy Press, 1978. Contributor to periodicals, including *Penthouse, Essence, Playboy,* and *Family Circle,* and to newspapers, including *New York Daily News.*

WORK IN PROGRESS: "The Gentle Wind," a three-act play; a novel, *Jade.*

SIDELIGHTS: Rosemarie Santini writes: "I wish to investigate the matters of the heart—whether personal or cultural—and explore just how and when our human society loses its dreams and gives up its inspiration and aspirations. I identify closely with the French writers like Colette, F. du Plessix Gray, and de Beauvoir, rather than American writers, with the only exception of Joan Didion, who I think is our genius. However, the rhythms of my work are Italian rhythms—the language of my birth." She has written often on the Italian-American theme, particularly on Italian-American women.

* * *

SARVEPALLI, Gopal 1923-

PERSONAL: Born April 23, 1923, in Madras, India; son of Radhakrishnan (a teacher) and Sivakamamma Sarvepalli. *Education:* Presidency College, M.A., 1942; Balliol College, Oxford, M.A., 1947, D.Phil., 1957. *Politics:* Liberal. *Religion:* Hindu. *Home:* 30 Edward Elliot Rd., Madras 600 004, India. *Office:* Centre for Historical Studies, Jawaharlal Nehru University, New Delhi 110 057, India.

CAREER: Andhra University, Waltair, India, lecturer, 1948-49, reader in history, 1949-52; National Archives, Delhi, India, assistant director, 1952-54; Ministry of External Affairs, Delhi, India, director of Historical Division, 1954-66; Oxford University, Oxford, England, reader in history, 1966-71; Jawaharlal Nehru University, New Delhi, India, professor of history, 1971—. *Member:* Indian History Congress (president, 1978), Royal Historical Society (fellow).

WRITINGS: Permanent Settlement in Bengal, Allen & Unwin, 1949; *The Viceroyalty of Lord Ripon,* Clarendon Press, 1953; *The Viceroyalty of Lord Irwin,* Clarendon Press, 1957; *British Policy in India, 1858-1905,* Cambridge University Press, 1965; *Modern India,* Historical Association (London, England), 1967; *Jawaharlal Nehru: A Biography,* Volume I, J. Cape, 1975. General editor of "Selected Works of Jawaharlal Nehru," Orient Longman, 1972—.

WORK IN PROGRESS: Jawaharlal Nehru: A Biography, Volumes II and III, for J. Cape; editing selected writings of Nehru.

SIDELIGHTS: Sarvepalli comments: "My main interest is in the history of South Asia, the reaction of the countries of this region to imperialism and their efforts after the withdrawal of imperialism. I have my roots in two countries, India and Britain, am equally proud of both, and am intellectually and emotionally involved in their interaction.''

* * *

SAUER, Julia Lina 1891-

PERSONAL: Born in 1891, in Rochester, N.Y. *Education:* Attended the University of Rochester, and New York State Library School. *Residence:* Rochester, N.Y.; and North Mountain, Nova Scotia.

CAREER: Writer. Worked as children's librarian at Rochester Public Library, Rochester, N.Y. *Awards, honors:* Runner-up for the Newbery Medal, 1944, for *Fog Magic*, and 1952, for *The Light at Tern Rocks.*

WRITINGS: (Editor) *Radio Roads to Reading: Library Book Talks Broadcast to Girls and Boys*, H. W. Wilson, 1939; *Fog Magic*, Viking, 1943, new edition, Pocket Books, 1977; *The Light at Tern Rock* (illustrated by Georges Schreiber), Viking, 1951; *Mike's House* (illustrated by Don Freeman), Viking, 1954, new edition, 1970.

SIDELIGHTS: Speaking of Julia Sauer's *Fog Magic*, a *Book Week* critic commented, ''This is not a book for every child, but to the right child it will bring beauty, magic, tenderness, and a brave philosophy of living. . . .'' The *Christian Science Monitor* called it ''an exquisite book, one that has great rewards for the imaginative reader.'' Added *Saturday Review of Literature:* ''Sometimes a book comes along that creates a sort of nostalgia in adults; a longing to go back to a time when it would have had free entry into their mind and imagination. Such a book is *Fog Magic.* . . . There is nothing about this book that is 'creepy' or unhealthy. Miss Sauer's feeling for Nova Scotia and its people gives the past as well as the present warmth and humor and reality.''

In a review of *The Light at Tern Rock*, a *New York Times* critic wrote, ''This is a quiet story, lacking in action, and will be chiefly appreciated by thoughtful readers who are receptive to its poetic sense of the sea.'' Noted *Saturday Review of Literature*, ''As in her *Fog Magic*, Miss Sauer's wording sets an atmosphere that is strongly reinforced here in Georges Scribner's beautiful drawings.''

BIOGRAPHICAL/CRITICAL SOURCES: Saturday Review of Literature, November 13, 1943; *Christian Science Monitor*, November 15, 1943; *Book Week*, November 21, 1943; *Saturday Review of Literature*, November 10, 1951; *New York Times*, December 2, 1951.*

* * *

SAUL, John (W. III) 1942-

PERSONAL: Born February 25, 1942, in Pasadena, Calif.; son of John W., Jr. and Elizabeth (Lee) Saul. *Education:* Attended Antioch College, 1959-60, Montana State University, 1961-62, and San Francisco State College (now University), 1963-65. *Politics:* ''Mostly Democrat.'' *Religion:* ''Sort of Swedenborgian.'' *Residence:* Bellevue, Wash. *Agent:* Jane Rotrosen, 318 East 51st St., New York, N.Y. 10022.

CAREER: Writer. Spent several years traveling about the United States, writing and supporting himself by odd jobs; worked for a drug and alcohol program in Seattle, Wash.; director of Tellurian Community, Inc., 1976-78; Seattle Theater Arts, Seattle, director, 1978—.

WRITINGS: Suffer the Children, Dell, 1977; *Punish the Sinners*, Dell, 1978.

WORK IN PROGRESS: Night Waves (working title), for Dell; *The Unwanted* (working title).

SIDELIGHTS: Saul attributes his successful writing career to ''a good agent, a good editor, and a good typewriter, as well as the good ideas and good criticisms of a good friend. Also, a good lawyer and a good accountant. And, as my father says, 'A hundred years from now, what the hell difference will it make?' But it's fun . . . it's lots of fun!''

* * *

SAVARIN
See COURTINE, Robert

* * *

SAWYER, Ralph Alanson 1895-1978

OBITUARY NOTICE: Born January 5, 1895, in Atkinson, N.H.; died December 6, 1978, in Ann Arbor, Mich. Physicist, educator, and author best known for being in charge of the atomic bomb tests at Bikini Atoll in the Pacific Ocean in 1946. Sawyer did research in radiometry and spectographic analysis at the University of Michigan and during his years as director of the Memorial Phoenix Project he worked to develop peaceful uses of nuclear energy. He was the author of *Experimental Spectroscopy* as well as many articles for scientific journals. Obituaries and other sources: *Who's Who in America*, 39th edition, Marquis, 1976; *The International Who's Who*, Europa, 1978; *New York Times*, December 7, 1978.

* * *

SAXTON, Martha 1945-

PERSONAL: Born September 3, 1945, in New York, N.Y.; daughter of Mark (a writer and editor) and Josephine (an editor; maiden name, Stocking) Saxton; married Enrico Ferorelli (a photographer), July 11, 1977. *Education:* University of Chicago, B.A., 1967. *Residence:* New York, N.Y. *Agent:* Lois Wallace, Wallace & Sheil, Inc., 118 East 61st St., New York, N.Y. 10021.

CAREER: Massachusetts Historical Society, Boston, editorial assistant, 1967-68; Rand McNally & Co., New York City, editorial assistant, 1969; Literary Guild, New York City, editor, 1970-73; free-lance writer, 1973—. *Member:* Authors Guild of Authors League of America.

WRITINGS: (With Rupert Holmes) *The Forties*, edited by Jeffrey Weiss, Links Books, 1975; *The Fifties*, edited by Weiss, Links Books, 1975; *Jayne Mansfield and the American Dream*, Houghton, 1975; *The Twenties*, edited by Weiss, Links Books, 1976; (with Gordon Williams) *Love Songs*, Music Sales, 1976; *Louisa May Alcott*, Houghton, 1977. Contributor to periodicals, including *Quest, New Yorker, American Heritage*, and *Viva*.

SIDELIGHTS: Martha Saxton comments: ''Good biography, like good fiction, seems to me the best way to understand as completely as possible another person's point of view. History and travel are the other two ways I prefer for changing perspective. I read and write history, and travel as often as possible. I spend some time every year in my husband's native Italy.''

AVOCATIONAL INTERESTS: Playing the piano, jogging.

* * *

SCAGLIONE, Cecil F(rank) 1934-

PERSONAL: Born December 2, 1934, in North Bay, Ontario, Canada; son of Frank (a railroad sectionhand) and Rose

(Aubin) Scaglione; married Mary Margaret Stewart (a photographer), November 11, 1954; children: Cris, Michael, Patrick. *Education:* Attended North Bay College, 1947-52, and Ryerson Technological Institute, 1955-56. *Religion:* Roman Catholic. *Home:* 8712 Big Rock Rd., Santee, Calif. 92071. *Office: San Diego Union,* 350 Camino de la Reina, San Diego, Calif. 92108.

CAREER: Ontario Northland Railway, North Bay, Ontario, part-time sectionhand, 1948-54; T. Eaton Co., North Bay, worked in sales and advertising department, 1954-55; *Toronto Telegram,* Toronto, Ontario, financial department, copy editor, reporter, and feature writer, 1955; Canada Packers, Toronto, assistant office manager, 1955-56; *Sarnia Observer,* Sarnia, Ontario, general assignment reporter and feature writer, 1956-57; *Kitchener-Waterloo Record,* Kitchener-Waterloo, Ontario, church editor and military writer, 1957-61; *Windsor Star,* Windsor, Ontario, night editor, feature writer, and reporter, 1961-67; *Detroit News,* Detroit, Mich., assistant picture editor and swing man on telegraph, cable, and copy desk, 1967-71; *San Diego Union,* San Diego, Calif., reporter, South San Diego County bureau chief, and financial writer, 1971—. Feature writer for *Canadian Register.* Founder and chairman of annual Quill Award; vice-president of Special Information Services, Inc. *Member:* Sindicato Nacional de Redactores de la Prensa (National Guild of Mexican Newsmen), Independent Order of Foresters, Ontario Federation of Italian Clubs (founder, secretary), San Diego Press Club (president), Detroit Press Club, Sigma Delta Chi. *Awards, honors:* Humorous writing award from *Canadian* newspaper, 1962 and 1966, for feature writing of a series; Canadian Centennial grant to write *The Tomato Capital,* 1966; Herbert J. Davenport fellowship for business and economics writers, 1977; San Diego Press Club journalism awards for best daily living story and freelance story, 1977-78.

WRITINGS: The Tomato Capital, Heinz-Leamington Post, 1967. Also author, with Igor Labanov, of *Hospital Office Procedure,* Career Publishing. Contributor of articles to *Flying, Modern Purchasing, Civic Administration, Canadian Restaurant and Hotel, Men's Wear, Business Forum, Financial Post, California, Travel/Holiday,* and other periodicals and newspapers. Founder and editor-in-chief, *Aeromexico* magazine.

WORK IN PROGRESS: California Almanac.

SIDELIGHTS: Scaglione told *CA* that while he is a newsman by profession, it is in his other writing, which he tries to keep as "eclectic as possible in form and field," that he best exercises his creative abilities. *Avocational interests:* Travel, reading, cooking, music, photography, and sports.

* * *

SCHICK, Alice 1946-

PERSONAL: Born June 20, 1946, in New York, N.Y.; daughter of Michael and Muriel (Steier) Raffer; married Joel Schick (an illustrator), June 22, 1967; children: Morgan. *Education:* Northwestern University, B.A., 1968. *Home and office address:* P.O. Box 101, Monterey, Mass. 01245. *Agent:* Writers House, Inc., 132 West 31st St., New York, N.Y. 10001.

CAREER: Holt, Rinehart & Winston, Inc., New York, N.Y., editor, 1969-70; writer, 1971—. Member of board of trustees of Monterey's library. *Member:* Authors Guild, Authors League of America, American Association of Zoological Parks and Aquariums, Phi Beta Kappa, Friends of the Zoo (New York City). *Awards, honors:* Awards for out-

standing science books for children from joint committee of National Science Teachers Association and Children's Book Council, 1976, for *The Siamang Gibbons: An Ape Family,* and 1977, for *Serengeti Cats.*

WRITINGS—Children's books: *Kongo and Kumba: Two Gorillas,* Dial, 1974; *The Peregrine Falcons,* Dial, 1975; *The Siamang Gibbons: An Ape Family,* Westwind Press, 1976; (with Marjorie Allen) *The Remarkable Ride of Israel Bissell as Related by Molly the Crow,* Lippincott, 1976; (with husband, Joel Schick) *Santaberry and the Snard,* Bookstore Press, 1976; *Serengeti Cats,* Lippincott, 1977; (with J. Schick) *Viola Hates Music,* Lippincott, 1977; (with J. Schick) *Just This Once,* Lippincott, 1978; (with Sara Ann Friedman) *Zoo Year,* Lippincott, 1978.

WORK IN PROGRESS: The Penguin Child and the Albatross Child, a picture book for children; a nonfiction book about tigers; a comic novel about communications research with apes; picture book adaptations of *Frankenstein* and *Dracula.*

SIDELIGHTS: Alice Schick writes: "My writing is an attempt to communicate my interest in and love and concern for animals. Most of my books are about wildlife because I hope to inspire readers to save wild places and their inhabitants. But I'm interested in domestic animals as well, at least in an avocational way: we live with six former stray cats. I'm involved in obedience training my Samoyed dog, and I'm a great fan of thoroughbred horse racing."

* * *

SCHILLER, Craig 1951-
(Mayer Schiller)

PERSONAL: Born June 22, 1951, in Brooklyn, N.Y.; son of Syd Schiller (an owner of a decorating company) and Lila Miller (a librarian); married Yehudis Cohen; children: Casriel, Moshe, Yecheskel. *Education:* Educated in Hebrew schools. *Politics:* Conservative. *Religion:* Orthodox Jewish. *Home:* 2 Walter Dr., Monsey, N.Y. 10952.

CAREER: Yeshiva High School at Queens, New York, N.Y., teacher of Talmud, 1977—.

WRITINGS: The Guilty Conscience of a Conservative, Arlington House, 1978; (under pseudonym Mayer Schiller) *The Road Back,* Feldheim, 1978; *God, State, and Man,* Arlington House, 1979.

SIDELIGHTS: Schiller told *CA:* "I view western civilization as being in a state of almost total decadence and imminent disintegration. I feel that the coming dark ages of relativism, ideology, Third World-ism and government by Carter, Koch and the *New York Times* will force all those who believe in value, truth, God, country, family, etc., to lead a remnant-like existence. I am not disheartened however, for I feel, along with T. S. Eliot, that there are 'no lost causes, for there are no gained causes.'

"My basic commitments are to God and my faith (Jewish) which is eternally binding, true and forever relevant, and feel an allegiance to all those who profess a belief in eternal norms and orthodoxies and to the United States, which has had its share of true heroes from Nathan Hale to Douglas McArthur and has provided ample backdrop for the virtue of patriotism to flourish."

* * *

SCHILLER, Mayer
See SCHILLER, Craig

SCHLAMM, William S. 1904-1978

OBITUARY NOTICE: Born June 10, 1904, in Przemysl, Austria-Hungary (now in Poland); died September 1, 1978, in Salzburg, Austria. Editor and author. Schlamm, a former Communist turned staunch conservative, immigrated to the United States before World War II and did not return to Europe until the early 1970's. He was an editor of *Fortune, National Review* (which he helped create), and *Zeibuehne.* Obituaries and other sources: *The Author's and Writer's Who's Who,* 6th edition, Burke's Peerage, 1971; *Time,* October 2, 1978.

* * *

SCHLANT, Ernestine 1935-

PERSONAL: Born August 14, 1935, in Passau, Germany; divorced; children: one. *Education:* Emory University, Ph.D., 1965. *Office:* Department of German, Montclair State College, Upper Montclair, N.J. 07834.

CAREER: Spelman College, Atlanta, Ga., instructor in French, 1963-65; State University of New York at Stony Brook, assistant professor of German, 1965-69; Cinema Arts, Inc., New York, N.Y., assistant film producer, 1969-71; Montclair State College, Upper Montclair, N.J., associate professor of German, 1971—. *Member:* American Association of University Professors. *Awards, honors:* Woodrow Wilson fellow, 1963-65; National Endowment for the Humanities grant, summer, 1972.

WRITINGS: (With Irmgard Feix) *Gespraeche, Diskussionen, Aufsaetze,* Holt, 1969; *Die Philosophie Hermann Brochs,* Francke, 1971; (with Feix) *Literatur und Umgangssprache,* Holt, 1971; (translator) Gerhard Habermann, *Maksim Gorki,* Ungar, 1971; (editor with Feix) *Junge deutsche Prosa,* Holt, 1974. Contributor to professional journals.

* * *

SCHLOSSMAN, Steven L(awrence) 1947-

PERSONAL: Born July 23, 1947, in New York, N.Y.; son of Ralph R. and Tillie (Gross) Schlossman; married Stephanie Wallach (an academic administrator), July 8, 1973. *Education:* Queens College of City University of New York, B.A., 1968; University of Wisconsin—Madison, M.A., 1971; further graduate study at University of California, Berkeley, 1975-76; Columbia University, Ph.D., 1976. *Home:* 93 Longwood Ave., #3, Brookline, Mass. 02146. *Office:* Radcliffe Institute, 3 James St., Cambridge, Mass. 02138.

CAREER: University of Chicago, Chicago, Ill., assistant professor of education, 1974—. Research associate at Radcliffe Institute, 1977-79. *Military service:* U.S. Army Reserve, 1969-74. *Member:* History of Education Society.

WRITINGS: Love and the American Delinquent: The Theory and Practice of "Progressive" Juvenile Justice, 1825-1920, University of Chicago Press, 1977. Contributor of articles and reviews to education and history journals.

WORK IN PROGRESS: For Mother's Sake?: Fads and Follies in Educating Parents (tentative title), on the history of child rearing.

* * *

SCHNEIDER, Laurence Allen 1937-

PERSONAL: Born May 24, 1937, in St. Louis, Mo. *Education:* Washington University, St. Louis, Mo., B.A., 1958; University of California, Berkeley, M.A., 1960, Ph.D., 1968. *Office:* Department of History, State University of New York at Buffalo, Buffalo, N.Y. 14620.

CAREER: State University of New York at Buffalo, assistant professor, 1966-71, associate professor of history, 1971—. *Awards, honors:* Fellowships from National Endowment for the Humanities, 1969, Social Science Research Council, 1973, and National Science Foundation, 1978.

WRITINGS: Ku Chieh-kang and China's New History, University of California Press, 1971; *A Madman of Ch'u: The Chinese Myth of Loyalty and Dissent,* University of California Press, 1979.

WORK IN PROGRESS: The Development of Modern Science in Twentieth-Century China.

* * *

SCHULZ, Juergen 1927-

PERSONAL: Born August 18, 1927, in Kiel, Germany; son of Johannes Martin (an engineer) and Ilse (a professor of crafts; maiden name, Lebenbaum) Schulz; married Justine Hume, September, 1951 (divorced, 1968); married Anne Markham (an art historian), April, 1969; children: Christoph (deceased), Ursula, Catherine, Jeremy. *Education:* University of California, Berkeley, B.A., 1950; Courtauld Institute of Art, London, Ph.D., 1958. *Politics:* Democrat. *Religion:* "None." *Home:* 192 Bowen St., Providence, R.I. 02906. *Office:* Department of Art, Brown University, Providence, R.I. 02912.

CAREER: San Francisco Chronicle, San Francisco, Calif., reporter, 1950-51; United Press International, London, England, copy editor, 1952-53; University of California, Berkeley, 1958-68, began as instructor, worked as assistant professor, became associate professor of art history; Brown University, Providence, R.I., professor of art history, 1968—. *Military service:* U.S. Army, 1945-48; became staff sergeant.

MEMBER: College Art Association of America, Society of Architectural Historians, Renaissance Society of America, Verein zur Foerderung des Kunsthistorischen Institutes in Florenz. *Awards, honors:* Guggenheim fellow, 1966-67; named grande ufficiale of Ordine della Stella della Solidarieta della Repubblica Italiana, 1969.

WRITINGS: Venetian Painted Ceilings of the Renaissance, University of California Press, 1968; *Printed Plans and Panoramic Views of Venice, 1486-1797,* Fondazione Giorgio Cini, 1972; *Venezia nel 1500: La grande veduta di Jacopo dei Barbari e le cartografia moralizzata,* Neri Pozza, 1977. Contributor of articles and reviews to academic journals. Book review editor of *Art Bulletin.*

WORK IN PROGRESS: An urban and architectural history of Venice.

* * *

SCHUMACHER, Ernst Friedrich 1911(?)-1977

PERSONAL: Born in Bonn, Germany; British citizen; married first wife, 1960 (deceased); married second wife, 1962; children: eight. *Education:* Attended Columbia University and Oxford University. *Residence:* London, England.

CAREER: Economist and author. Confined and required to work on farms during World War II; after his release, he worked with Lord Beveridge on the theories for Britain's welfare state; served on Britain's National Coal Board as economic adviser, 1950-70. Founder, Intermediate Technology Development Group in London, 1966; assistant lecturer, Columbia University. Consultant in Asia.

WRITINGS: Britain's Coal: A Study Conference Organized by the National Union of Mineworkers, Victoria House Printing Co., 1960; *Roots of Economic Growth,* Grandhian Institute of Studies, 1962; *Small Is Beautiful: Economics as if People Mattered,* Harper & Row, 1973; *A Guide for the Perplexed,* Harper & Row, 1977. Also author of several published pamphlets and reports. Contributor of articles to *London Times, Observer,* and *Economist.*

SIDELIGHTS: Martin Weil, staff writer for the *Washington Post,* wrote: "Dr. Schumacher's emphasis on the value of small-scale technology has become increasingly influential both in underdeveloped nations and among ecologists and advocates of decentralization in the more developed countries.... Dr. Schumacher's specific proposals for technology on a smaller and more human scale, once ridiculed, have found an expanding audience."

Small Is Beautiful, a best seller that made the author something of a folk hero, encourages human fulfillment and indicates ways of obtaining that goal. A *Time* magazine reviewer wrote, "In his 1973 book, Schumacher maintained that continous growth was not necessarily desirable; that small, energy-saving units of production could often best serve human needs."

"In that book, subtitled 'Economics as Though People Mattered,' Schumacher flayed what he called 'the religion of economics," remarked Harvey Cox in the *New York Time Book Review.* Schumacher gave his advice on what a person could do to begin the reversal he was advocating. His advice was given in the form of a quotation from a contemporary Catholic philosopher on prudence. Cox explained: "Prudence is one of the classical virtues, the one based on the realization that doing good presupposes knowledge of reality, that just 'meaning well' is never enough. Schumacher himself added that prudence can never be achieved 'except by an attitude of "silent contemplation" of reality.' The answer to the ... question 'What can I actually do?' is, according to Schumacher,' Work to put our own house in order.'"

A Guide for the Perplexed "begins literally where the last one [*Small Is Beautiful*] ended." Cox commented: "I found parts of it wise, much of it hard to follow, and some of it not at all convincing. 'A Guide for the Perplexed' is a call, more like a plea, for a radical turn toward self-awarness.... The longest chapter is devoted to an extensive, though somewhat random, survey of the religious and philosophical literature endorsing self-knowledge.... He [Schumacher] feels very strongly that the modern experiment of living without religion has failed, and without a certain kind of self-knowledge all our knowledge of the outside world will be worse than useless."

BIOGRAPHICAL/CRITICAL SOURCES: Economist, June 23, 1973; *Guardian Weekly,* June 30, 1973; *Times Literary Supplement,* September 28, 1973; *Books and Bookman,* January, 1974; *National Review,* December 24, 1976; *Kirkus Reviews,* July 1, 1977; *Observer,* September 25, 1977; *New York Times Book Review,* October 2, 1977; *Christian Century,* October 12, 1977.

OBITUARIES: New York Times, September 6, 1977; *Washington Post,* September 7, 1977; *Newsweek,* September 19, 1977; *Times,* September 19, 1977; *AB Bookman's Weekly,* November 21, 1977.*

(Died September 4, 1977, in Zurich, Switzerland)

SCHUTZ, Anton Friedrich Joseph   1894-1977

PERSONAL: Born April 19, 1894, in Berndorf, Germany; came to United States in 1924, naturalized in 1930; son of Anton Valentine and Elizabeth (Struth) Schutz; married Mimi Gross, August 30, 1920; married Christa Trapp, July 13, 1961; children: (first marriage) Herbert, Beatrice A. Warlam Schutz; (second marriage) Anton Villars, Christina Villars and Linda Francis (twins). *Education:* Attended Munich Academy of Fine Arts, 1919-23; University of Munich, M.E., 1920; further study at Art League of New York, 1924-25. *Home:* 4 Heathcote Rd., Scarsdale, N.Y. 10583. *Office:* 140 Greenwich Ave., Greenwich, Conn. 06830.

CAREER: Etcher and writer. New York Graphic Society, New York, N.Y., founder, 1925, president, 1925-66, director and consultant, 1966-77. "UNESCO Art Popularization Series," founder, 1953, publisher and co-editor, participating in numerous missions gathering materials in countries, including India, Bulgaria, Ceylon, Egypt, Israel, Japan, and Mexico, 1953-61. Past president, Inter-American Graphic Ltd. Own work represented in collections at Library of Congress, British Museum, Bibliotheque Nationale, and other national and international collections. *Military service:* German Army, 1914-18; became lieutenant of engineers; received first and second class Iron Cross (Germany), Iron Half Moon (Turkey), and Croce Laterane (Vatican). *Member:* Society of American Graphic Artists, Chicago Society of Etchers.

WRITINGS: New York in Etchings (a portfolio of skyscraper scenes), Bard Brothers, 1939; *My Share of Wine: The Memoirs of Anton Schutz,* New York Graphic Society, 1972.

BIOGRAPHICAL/CRITICAL SOURCES: American Artists, 1966; *Choice,* 1966; Anton Schutz, *My Share of Wine: The Memoirs of Anton Schutz,* New York Graphic Society, 1972.

OBITUARIES: New York Times, October 7, 1977.*

(Died October 6, 1977, in White Plains, N.Y.)

*   *   *

SCHUYLER, George Samuel   1895-1977

PERSONAL: Born February 25, 1895, in Providence, R.I.; son of George (a chef) and Eliza (Fischer) Schuyler; married Josephine E. Lewis (a painter), January 6, 1928 (deceased); children: Philippa (deceased). *Education:* Educated in Syracuse, N.Y. *Home:* 270 Convent Ave., New York, N.Y. 10031.

CAREER: Clerk for U.S. Civil Service, 1919-20; co-founder and associate editor, *Messenger* magazine, 1923-28; *Pittsburgh Courier,* Pittsburgh, Pa., columnist, chief editorial writer, and associate editor, 1924-66, special correspondent to South America and West Indies, 1948-49, French West Africa and Dominican Republic, 1958; analysis editor, *Review of the News,* 1967-77. Special correspondent to Liberia, *New York Evening Post,* New York, N.Y., 1931; business manager, *Crisis* magazine, 1937-44; literary editor, *Manchester Union Leader,* Manchester, N.H. Special publicity assistant, National Association for the Advancement of Colored People (NAACP), 1934-35. Member of international committee of Congress for Cultural Freedom, and U.S. delegation to Berlin and Brussels meetings, 1950. President of Philippa Schuyler Memorial Foundation. *Military service:* U.S. Army, 1912-18; became first lieutenant. *Member:* American Writers Association (vice-president), American Asian Educational Exchange, American African Affairs

Association, Author's Guild. *Awards, honors:* Citation of Merit award from Lincoln University School of Journalism, 1952; American Legion award, 1968; Catholic War Veterans Citation, 1969; Freedoms Foundation at Valley Forge award, 1972.

WRITINGS: Black No More: Being an Account of the Strange and Wonderful Workings of Science in the Land of the Free, A.D. 1933-1940 (novel), Macaulay, 1931, reprinted, Negro Universities Press, 1969; *Slaves Today: A Story of Liberia,* Brewer, Warren & Putnam, 1931, reprinted, McGrath, 1969; *Black and Conservative: The Autobiography of George S. Schuyler,* Arlington House, 1966. Contributor, Spadeau Columns, Inc., 1953-62, North American Newspaper Alliance, 1965-77. Contributor to the annals of the American Academy of Political Science, and of articles to *Nation, Reader's Digest, American Mercury, Common Ground, Freeman, Americans, Christian Herald American,* and other works. Contributing editor to *American Opinion.*

SIDELIGHTS: Schuyler was a satirist on race relations, and known for upholding the opposite stance than popularly held on the subject. His shifting views attacked Marcus Garvey and his back-to-Africa movement, and civil rights leaders such as Martin Luther King and his practice of non-violence. Black historian John Henrik Clarke said: "I used to tell people that George got up in the morning, waited to see which way the world was turning then struck out in the opposite direction.

"He was a rebel who enjoyed playing that role," continued Clarke. Schuyler put his wit and sarcasm to work with the publication of *Black No More,* a satirical novel that gave the fictitious solution to the race problem. Through glandular treatments, blacks could take a cream that would eventually turn them white and they would disappear into white society.

This novel and other work by Schuyler was initially highly rated by various black leaders, regardless of the ridicule that was present in his work and was directed toward some of these spokeman. Rayford W. Logan, chairman of the department of history at Howard University, stated that "he could cut deeply and sometimes unfairly, but he was interesting to read."

However, in the early 1960's, when the civil rights movement began to gain momentum, civil rights leaders became less enthusiastic about Schuyler, whose positions moved farther right and seemed reactionary to most blacks. This era of civil rights proved to be too powerful for Schuyler, and he was soon overtaken completely. "His outlets became more and more limited ...," remarked George Goodman, Jr., though "he nonetheless continued to champion conservative issues such as the presence of U.S. troops in Southeast Asia...."

BIOGRAPHICAL/CRITICAL SOURCES: Black and Conservative: The Autobiography of George S. Schuyler, Arlington House, 1966; *Books and Bookmen,* Volume 16, 1971; *Black World,* Volume 21, 1971.

OBITUARIES: New York Times, September 7, 1977; *Washington Post,* September 9, 1977; *AB Bookman's Weekly,* November 21, 1977.*

(Died August 31, 1977, in New York, N.Y.)

*   *   *

SCHWARZENEGGER, Arnold 1947-

PERSONAL: Born in Graz, Austria; came to United States in 1968. *Education:* Attended Santa Monica City College

and University of California, Los Angeles. *Office:* 207 Ashland Ave., Santa Monica, Calif. 90405.

CAREER: Bodybuilder, athlete, and actor. Producer of Mr. Olympia/Mr. International competition, 1975—; television commentator for bodybuilding events, Wide World of Sports, ABC-TV. Appeared in documentary, "Pumping Iron," 1977, and, as an actor in motion pictures, "Stay Hungry," 1976, and "The Villains," 1979. Former health club owner and instructor in Munich, Germany. *Military service:* Austrian Army, 1965. *Awards, honors:* Winner of sixteen titles, including Mr. Olympia, Mr. Universe, and Mr. World, as an amateur and as a professional bodybuilder; Hollywood Foreign Press Association Golden Globe Award for performance in "Stay Hungry."

WRITINGS: (With Douglas Kent Hall) *Arnold: The Education of a Body Builder,* Simon & Schuster, 1977.

SIDELIGHTS: Arnold Schwarzenegger, nicknamed "The Austrian Oak," is the epitome of a successful bodybuilder. In 1970, he won all three major titles of Mr. Universe, Mr. World, and Mr. Olympia, a feat that no one had yet accomplished. Charles Gaines, in his book *Pumping Iron: The Art and Sport of Bodybuilding,* described Schwarzenegger as "the best bodybuilder alive, and very possibly the most perfectly developed man in the world."

Schwarzenegger began training for bodybuilding at the age of fifteen and has been fiercely dedicated to it ever since. In *Arnold: The Education of a Bodybuilder,* he described his experiences with bodybuilding: "During the early years I didn't care how I felt about anything except bodybuilding. It consumed every minute of my days and all my best effort." Schwarzenegger's regimen was strenuous and he added to it his intense desire to perfect his body and to win: "When I was ten years old I got this thing that I wanted to be the best in swimming, so I started swimming. I won championships, but I felt I couldn't be the best. I tried it in skiing, but there I felt that I didn't have the potential. I played soccer, but I didn't like that too well because there I didn't get the credit alone if I did something special. Then I started weight lifting through other sports.... I won the Austrian championship in 1964 but I found out I was just too tall. So I quit that and went into bodybuilding. Two years later I found out that that's it—that's what I can be best in."

When asked about the popular image of bodybuilders as being too narcissistic, Schwarzenegger replied: "People think it is strange if you stare in the mirror at your own body. If you're a writer, you're into writing. If you're a body builder, you're into your body." Schwarzenegger also stated that pumping iron is only one of the methods to becoming a successful bodybuilder: "If you can only lift, and not move, then your body is not perfect. You have to concentrate on speed, power, and flexibility at the same time. This way, I perfect my body both visually and physically." In fact, Schwarzenegger has taken ballet lessons to learn graceful movements and poses.

Summing up his views on bodybuilding, the former six-time winner of the title of Mr. Olympia wrote: "I've retired from bodybuilding but I haven't quit. I have only stopped competing. I would describe myself as sort of the leader of the bodybuilders.... And I'm also the most experienced bodybuilder, the one who has had the success.... I think bodybuilders see me as a person who loves bodybuilding and is really trying to help it as a sport.... Whatever else I do, I want to always be a kind of ambassador, a preacher for bodybuilding."

BIOGRAPHICAL/CRITICAL SOURCES: Charles

Gaines and George Butler, *Pumping Iron: The Art and Sport of Bodybuilding,* Simon & Schuster, 1974; *Newsweek,* March 17, 1965, May 17, 1976, October 18, 1976; Arnold Schwarzenegger and Douglas Kent Hall, *Arnold: The Education of a Body Builder,* Simon & Schuster, 1977.

* * *

SCHWEITZER, Byrd Baylor
See BAYLOR, Byrd

* * *

SCHWENDEMAN, J(oseph) R(aymond) 1897-

PERSONAL: Born May 11, 1897, in Waterford, Ohio; son of Francis (a farmer and contractor) and Margaret (a teacher; maiden name, Tornes) Schwendeman; married Eithnea O'Donnell (a teacher; died February 18, 1978); children: Elaine Mary, Marion, Gerald, Joseph Raymond, Jr., Francis, Elizabeth Ann. *Education:* Ohio University, B.S., 1926; Clark University, M.A., 1927, Ph.D., 1941; also attended University of Minnesota, 1927-28. *Politics:* Democrat. *Religion:* Roman Catholic. *Home:* 3512 Greentree Rd., Lexington, Ky. 40502. *Office:* State Educators, P.O. Box 705, Lexington, Ky. 40501.

CAREER: Elementary school teacher in East Salem, Ohio, 1915-18; railway mail clerk in Pittsburgh, Pa., 1918-20; elementary school teacher in Rainbow, Ohio, 1920-24; Moorhead State College, Moorhead, Minn., professor of geography and head of department, 1928-44; University of Kentucky, Lexington, professor of geography and head of department, 1944-67, professor emeritus, 1967—; Eastern Kentucky University, Richmond, distinguished professor of geography and co-director of Geographic Studies and Research Center, 1967—. Chief of U.S. Weather Bureau, 1934-44. Writer for State Educators. Professor at St. John College (Collegeville, Minn.), 1941; member of summer faculty at Columbia College (Dubuque, Iowa), 1927, South Dakota State University, Spearfish, 1928, Ohio University, 1941, State University of New York College at New Paltz, 1963, and University of Oregon, 1966. Member of United Nations Scientific Conference, 1949; member of Catholic Commission on Cultural and Intellectual Affairs. *Military service:* U.S. Army Air Forces, instructor and weather observer, 1941-44.

MEMBER: National Council of Geography Teachers, National Geographic Society, Association of American Geographers (southeastern president, 1949-51), American Geographic Society, American Association for the Advancement of Science (fellow), Kiwanis. *Awards, honors:* Distinguished service citation from Association of American Geographers, 1967, for *Directory of College Geography.*

WRITINGS: Geography of Minnesota, American Book Co., 1933; (editor with Irwin Sanders and others, and contributor) *Societies Around the World,* Dryden, 1948, revised edition, 1956; (contributor) *World Political Geography,* Crowell, 1948; (contributor) *Geography of Kentucky,* Harlow Publishing, 1958, 3rd edition published as *Geography of Kentucky: An Environmental and Social Science,* 1970, 5th edition, 1980; (with Jerry A. Rickett) *Climate Characteristics of the Richmond, Kentucky Area,* Geographical Studies and Research Center, Eastern Kentucky University, 1976. Also contributor to *Regional Geography of the Midwest,* edited by Russell H. Fifield and G. Etzel Pearcy, 1956.

Author of "Geography of Kentucky and Its Resources" (filmstrip series, with manual), Associated Educators, 1961; "Historical Geography of Kentucky" (filmstrip series, with

manual), State Educators, 1978, updated version, 1979. Contributor to *Encyclopaedia Britannica* and *World Book Encyclopedia.* Contributor to scientific journals. Editor of *Directory of College Geography,* 1949—.

WORK IN PROGRESS: "Resource Use and the Environment: Past to Present," a filmstrip, with manual, for State Educators.

SIDELIGHTS: Schwendeman writes that he was raised in a pioneer setting, on a one-hundred-sixty-acre farm in Rainbow, Ohio, with eight brothers and sisters in a religious environment. He was educated in a one-room schoolhouse and became interested in reading from his family's extensive home library.

Schwendeman and his wife conducted annual travel-study tours of western Europe and North America from 1928 to 1960. They also organized and conducted an ascent of the volcano Orizaba in order to discover the reason for such a snow cap under a tropical sun. Schwendeman is the inventor of the world map projection, "Geomatic."

* * *

SCOTT, Jody

PERSONAL: Born in Chicago, Ill.; daughter of Joseph Edward (in business) and Ann Pierce (Pritchard) Huguelet; divorced; children: Dylan Thompson Wood. *Religion:* "Zenmaster." *Home:* 17267 10th Ave. N.W., Seattle, Wash. 98177.

CAREER: Writer and real estate agent. Also worked as counselor, editor, chemist, artist, model, medicine show barker, filmmaker, market research analyst, and president of Scojaf Inc.

WRITINGS: Passing for Human (science fiction novel), Daw Books, 1977. Contributor to *Escapade, Fantasy,* and *If.*

WORK IN PROGRESS: Kiss the Whip, a novel.

AVOCATIONAL INTERESTS: Scuba diving, travel (hitchhiked all over the United States and Europe).

* * *

SCOTT, Paul (Mark) 1920-1978

PERSONAL: Born March 25, 1920, in Palmers Green, England; married Nancy E. Avery, 1941; children: Carol, Sally. *Education:* Attended public schools in England. *Agent:* David Higham Associates, 5-8 Lower John St., Golden Sq., London W1R 4HA, England.

CAREER: Novelist. Company secretary, Falcon Press and Grey Walls Press, both London, England, 1946-50; director of David Higham Associates (literary agents), London, 1950-60; free-lance writer, 1960-78. *Military service:* British Army, served in India and Malaya, 1940-46. *Member:* Royal Society of Literature (fellow). *Awards, honors:* Eyre & Spottiswoode Literary fellowship, 1951; Arts Council grant, 1969.

WRITINGS—Novels: Johnnie Sahib, Eyre & Spottiswoode, 1952; *Six Days in Marapore,* Morrow, 1953 (published in England as *The Alien Sky,* Eyre & Spottiswoode, 1953); *A Male Child,* Eyre & Spottiswoode, 1956, Dutton, 1957; *The Mark of the Warrior,* Morrow, 1958; *The Love Pavilion,* Morrow, 1960 (published in England as *The Chinese Love Pavilion,* Eyre & Spottiswoode, 1960); *The Birds of Paradise,* Morrow, 1962; *The Bender,* Morrow, 1963 (published in England as *The Bender: Pictures From an Exhibition of Middle Class Portraits,* Secker & Warburg,

1963); *The Corrida at San Felieu,* Morrow, 1964; *The Jewel in the Crown* (first novel in tetralogy; also see below), Morrow, 1966; *The Day of the Scorpion* (second novel in tetralogy; also see below), Morrow, 1968; *The Towers of Silence* (third novel in tetralogy; also see below), Heinemann, 1971, Morrow, 1972; *A Division of Spoils* (fourth novel in tetralogy; also see below), Morrow, 1975; *The Raj Quartet* (tetralogy; includes *The Jewel in the Crown, The Day of the Scorpion, The Towers of Silence, A Division of Spoils*), Morrow, 1976; *Staying On,* Morrow, 1977.

Contributor to *Essays by Divers Hands,* Oxford University Press, 1970. Also contributor of articles to British newspapers and periodicals, including *Country Life* and the *London Times.*

SIDELIGHTS: Paul Scott was perhaps best known as the chronicler of the decline of the British occupation of India. His most famous works are those of *The Raj Quartet.* They center on a single dramatic event, the rape of an English woman by several Indians, but proceed to describe life for both the British and the Indian under the British raj, or rule. This seemed to be characteristic of Scott's novels; or "as more than one reviewer pointed out he dealt less with events than with the situation created by these events."

Scott's novels have consistently drawn positive reviews. A *Punch* reviewer once described Scott as "a professional novelist of the expansive, humane, nineteenth-century type, though with mid-twentieth-century sensibilities. . . . Mr. Scott has two great qualities that are rarely found together, excitement with material and control. His work is packed, not crammed."

A *Times Literary Supplement* critic in his review of *The Day of the Scorpion* wrote: "The characters, while they successfully represent aspirations and conflicts which are bigger than themselves, never cease to be individuals. The conversations have subtlety and a quality of plenteousness which is none the less welcome for being out of fashion. Above all, the reader is impressed, and given confidence, by the feeling which Mr. Scott can generate of a writer who has thoroughly mastered his material, and who can, because of this, work through a maze of fascinating detail without for a moment losing sight of distant, and considerable objectives." A *Listener* critic agreed: "Paul Scott's is one of those rare books that express not only themselves but something of the essence of their genre. Prose fiction does many things, but nothing more characteristic than the intricate relating of private lives to public issues. When this is done with the subtlety, wisdom and grace of *The Day of the Scorpion,* the triumph is more than a personal one for the author. It vindicates a whole tradition of literary endeavour."

John Leonard of the *New York Times Book Review* commented that the strength of Scott's last novel, *Staying On,* lay in "its portrayal of hitherto unsuspected dignity, of depths of feeling hiding in the ordinary." In contrast, Malcolm Muggeridge noted that he had difficulty in trying "to work up sympathy with any of the characters to care about what happened to them."

The last novel in *The Raj Quartet* led Webster Schott to write: "Sometimes [Scott] seemed to be writing mostly history. Other times a study of racist psychology. And now and then an outrageously long love letter to a land and people unable to decide whether they liked or loathed what fate had dealt them."

Scott once said that he preferred "to write about people in relation to their work, which strikes me as a subject no less important than their private lives." Although during his years in the army he wrote poetry and plays, all of his published works are novels; he viewed the novel as the ultimate form of literature. "He was no miniaturist. He required a broad canvas, he never wrote a short story, for example," commented Thomas Lask. In addition, Jean G. Zorn observed: "The world of Scott's Indian novels is so extraordinarily vivid in part because it is constructed out of such accuracies of detail as the proper name or the precise sum that a retired colonel's widow could expect to receive as a pension. Scott's vision is both precise and painterly."

BIOGRAPHICAL/CRITICAL SOURCES: Observer Review, September 1, 1968; *Punch,* September 4, 1968; *Listener,* September 5, 1968; *Times Literary Supplement,* September 12, 1968; *Books and Bookmen,* November, 1968; *New York Times Book Review,* November 10, 1968, July 26, 1977, August 21, 1977; *Best Sellers,* March 1, 1969; *Contemporary Literary Criticism,* Volume 9, Gale, 1978. *Obituaries: New York Times,* March 3, 1978.*

(Died March 1, 1978, in London, England)

* * *

SCULL, Andrew 1947-

PERSONAL: Born May 2, 1947, in Edinburgh, Scotland; came to United States in 1969; son of Allan Edward (a civil engineer) and Marjorie (a college teacher; maiden name, Corrigan) Scull; married Nancy Principi (a teacher), August 16, 1970; children: Anna Theresa. *Education:* Balliol College, Oxford, B.A. (first class honors), 1969; Princeton University, M.A., 1971, Ph.D., 1974. *Religion:* "Voltairean." *Agent:* A. D. Peters, 10 Buckingham St., London W.C.2, England. *Office:* Department of Sociology, University of California at San Diego, La Jolla, Calif.

CAREER: University of Pennsylvania, Philadelphia, lecturer, 1973-74, assistant professor of sociology, 1974-78; University of California at San Diego, La Jolla, associate professor of sociology, 1978—. Visiting fellow at University of London, 1977, and Princeton University, 1978-79. *Member:* American Sociological Association. *Awards, honors:* American Council of Learned Societies fellow, 1976-77.

WRITINGS: Decarceration: Community Treatment and the Deviant; a Radical View, Prentice-Hall, 1977; *Museums of Madness: The Social Organization of Insanity in Nineteenth-Century England,* Allen Lane, 1979; (with Steven Lukes) *Durkheim and the Law,* Martin Robertson, 1979.

Contributor: Robert A. Scott and Jack D. Douglas, editors, *Theoretical Perspectives on Deviance,* Basic Books, 1972; D. Greenberg, editor, *Corrections and Punishment: Structure, Function, and Process,* Sage Publications, 1977; A. D. King, editor, *Buildings and Society: Essays on the Social Development of the Built Environment,* Routledge & Kegan Paul, 1979. Contributor of articles and reviews to sociology journals.

WORK IN PROGRESS: Psychiatry and Neurology in Nineteenth-Century America; Crime, Punishment, and Social Structure in Eighteenth- and Nineteenth-Century England.

SIDELIGHTS: Scull's first book, *Decarceration: Community Treatment and the Deviant, a Radical View* has drawn diverse reviews. A critic for *Working Papers for a New Society* stated that the book offers "not only the best overview of this decade's 'reforms' but also the best analysis of how the reforms have failed." However, he also observed that "Scull provides conservatives with a lot of ammunition, and if they can get past the 'radical' in his title, they may find his ideas confirming their own prejudices."

Kim Hopper of the *Health-PAC Bulletin* described Scull as "an able and effective historian, a shrewd critic, and a clear, compelling writer." Hopper also called *Decarceration* "closely documented and carefully argued ... [a book] without parallel in the recent literature on psychiatric and penal institutions."

BIOGRAPHICAL/CRITICAL SOURCES: Manchester Guardian, May 23, 1977; *Health-PAC Bulletin,* September-October, 1977; *Working Papers for a New Society,* May-June, 1978.

* * *

SEARCY, Margaret Zehmer 1926-

PERSONAL: Born October 26, 1926, in Raleigh, N.C.; daughter of John Adrain (in engineering sales) and Agnes Tyler (Johnson) Zehmer; married Joseph Alexander Searcy (a real estate broker), June 23, 1948; children: Margaret Tyler, Joseph Alexander III, Elizabeth Baskerville. *Education:* Duke University, B.A., 1946; University of Alabama, M.A., 1959; further graduate study at University of the Americas. *Religion:* Presbyterian. *Home:* 1 Oaklana, Tuscaloosa, Ala. 35401. *Office:* Department of Anthropology, University of Alabama, University, Ala. 35486.

CAREER: University of Alabama, University, instructor in anthropology, 1964—. Visiting lecturer at University of South Dakota. Public lecturer and consultant. *Member:* American Anthropological Association, Guild of Professional Writers for Children (chairwoman), Alabama Academy of Science (past vice-president), Alabama Archaeological Society (past president), Alpha Kappa Delta. *Awards, honors:* University of Alabama faculty grant, 1969; grants from Alabama Consortium for Higher Education, 1973, for study in Mexico, and 1973, for study in Guatemala; Charlton W. Tebeau Literary Award from Florida Historical Society, 1975, for *Ikwa of the Temple Mounds.*

*WRITINGS—*All for children: *Ikwa of the Temple Mounds,* University of Alabama Press, 1974; *Tiny Bat and the Ball Game,* Portals Press, 1978; *Alli Gator Gets a Bump on His Nose,* Portals Press, 1978; *The Race of Flitty Humming Bird and Flappy Crane,* Portals Press, 1978. Contributor to professional journals.

WORK IN PROGRESS: Wolf Dog of the Copena Indians.

SIDELIGHTS: Both *Ikwa of the Temple Mounds* and *The Race of Flitty Humming Bird and Flappy Crane,* have been adapted for presentation by Alabama Public Television in 1978. Searcy writes that her Portals Press books, part of the "Fact and Fantasy Series," are "based upon Southeastern Indian myths. The series is designed to acquaint the reader with southeastern flora and fauna while helping to eliminate problems for the child who is 'different.' All of my books are designed to present some positive aspects of a culture."

* * *

SECREST, Meryle
See BEVERIDGE, Meryle Secrest

* * *

SEFLER, George Francis 1945-

PERSONAL: Born April 4, 1945, in Chicago, Ill. *Education:* DePaul University, A.B. (summa cum laude), 1966; Georgetown University, Ph.D., 1970. *Office:* Department of Philosophy, Mansfield State College, Mansfield, Pa. 16933.

CAREER: Georgetown University, Washington, D.C., instructor in philosophy, summer, 1969; Mansfield State College, Mansfield, Pa., 1969—, began as assistant professor, became associate professor of philosophy. *Member:* American Philosophical Association, Society for Phenomenology and Existentialism. *Awards, honors:* National Endowment for the Humanities grant, summer, 1976.

WRITINGS: Language and the World: A Methodological Synthesis Within the Writings of Martin Heidegger and Ludwig Wittgenstein, Humanities Press, 1974. Contributor to philosophy and theology journals.

WORK IN PROGRESS: A philosophical basis for contemporary man's loneliness.

SIDELIGHTS: Sefler writes: "My professional motivation is to show to a broad, intellectually-concerned audience the value of philosophy for enhancing the quality of human experience." *Avocational interests:* Magic, music.

* * *

SEIDMAN, Ann (Willcox) 1926-

PERSONAL: Born April 30, 1926, in New York, N.Y.; daughter of Henry (an engineer) and Anita (an artist; maiden name, Parkhurst) Willcox; married Robert B. Seidman (a professor of law), June 4, 1945; children: Jonathan, Judy Ann Seidman Parsons, Katha Rose, Jay Willcox, Neva Lynn Seidman Makgetla. *Education:* Smith College, B.A., 1947; Columbia University, M.A., 1953; University of Wisconsin—Madison, Ph.D., 1968. *Home:* 7 Dartmouth Place, Boston, Mass. 02116. *Office:* Department of Sociology, Brown University, Providence, R.I. 02912.

CAREER: University of Bridgeport, Bridgeport, Conn., lecturer in economics, 1958-62; University of Ghana, Legon, lecturer in economics, 1962-66; University of Dar es Salaam, Dar es Salaam, Tanzania, senior lecturer in economics, 1968-70; University of Wisconsin—Madison, lecturer in economics, 1970-72; University of Zambia, Lusaka, professor of economics and chairman of department, 1972-74; University of Massachusetts, Boston Campus, visiting associate professor of economics, 1974-75; Clark University, Worcester, Mass., affiliate professor of economics, 1975-78; Brown University, Providence, R.I., Nancy Duke Lewis Professor of Economics, 1978—. Visiting professor at University of Massachusetts—Amherst, 1977-78. Project director at Wellesley Center for Research on Women, 1975-76. Member of Massachusetts governor's Commission on the Status of Women; consultant to United Nations.

MEMBER: African Studies Association, Association of Concerned African Scholars, American Association of University Professors, Southern African Research Association, Phi Beta Kappa.

WRITINGS: (With R. H. Green) *Unity or Poverty?: The Economics of Pan-Africanism,* Penguin, 1968; *An Economics Textbook for Africa,* Methuen, 1968; *Comparative Development Strategies in East Africa,* East African Publishing House, 1972; *Planning for Development in Subsaharan Africa,* Praeger, 1974; (editor) *National Resources and National Welfare: The Case of Copper,* Praeger, 1976; (with daughter, Neva Seidman) *South Africa and U.S. Multinational Corporations,* Lawrence Hill, 1977; (editor) *Women and Work: A Pilot Study of Women in Paid Jobs,* Westview Press, 1978; *Ghana's Development Experience,* East African Publishing, 1978. Member of editorial advisory board of *Contemporary Crisis, African Law Journal,* and *Journal of Southern African Studies.*

WORK IN PROGRESS: With daughter, Neva Seidman Makgetla, *Transnational Corporate Involvement in South Africa; Economic Development in Southern Africa;* studying the New England economy and women workers.

SIDELIGHTS: Seidman told *CA:* "My books have mainly dealt with problems and possibilities of planning for development in Africa, based on almost a decade of research and teaching in universities on that continent. I have been particularly concerned with the necessity of formulating longterm industrial strategies, based on national resources, to transform inherited, externally dependent economies into balanced, integrated structures capable of providing increasingly productive employment opportunities for all their inhabitants.

"Following my years of teaching in Tanzania and Zambia, I became especially concerned with the role of transnational corporations and their tendency to invest in advanced industrial development primarily in the racist stages of southern Africa. Their activities have been a significant impediment to more balanced integrated development in the independent African states.

"At the same time, I have become more aware of the fact that development strategies have not infrequently disadvantaged women, and have begun to focus more of my research on these issues. I have become convinced that the problems confronting women in the United States are interrelated with those affecting women in the Third World; and that much more exchange of information and analysis would benefit women everywhere."

AVOCATIONAL INTERESTS: Sailing, skiing, travel (eastern and western Europe, Mexico, Chile; extensive travel throughout Africa).

* * *

SELDEN, Mark 1938-

PERSONAL: Born June 18, 1938, in Brooklyn, N.Y.; son of Paul and Ruth (Tancer) Selden; married Kyoko Iriye (a teacher, writer, and translator), May 25, 1963; children: Lili, Ken, Yumi. *Education:* Amherst College, B.A., 1959; Yale University, Ph.D., 1967. *Home:* 6919 Columbia St., St. Louis, Mo. 63130. *Office:* Department of History, Washington University, St. Louis, Mo. 63130.

CAREER: Washington University, St. Louis, Mo., assistant professor, 1967-72, associate professor of history, 1972—, co-director of international development program, 1976-77. Visiting research fellow at Institute of Developing Economies (Tokyo), 1973-74, 1977-78.

WRITINGS: The Yenan Way in Revolutionary China, Harvard University Press, 1971; (editor) *America's Asia: Dissenting Essays on Asian-American Relations,* Pantheon, 1971; (editor) *Open Secret: The Kissinger-Nixon Doctrine in Asia,* Harper, 1972; (editor) *Remaking Asia: Essays on the American Uses of Power,* Pantheon, 1974; (editor) *Korea North and South: The Deepening Crisis,* Monthly Review Press, 1978; *The People's Republic of China,* Monthly Review Press, 1978. Contributor to magazines in the United States and abroad, including *Monthly Review* and *Nation.* Editor of *Bulletin of Concerned Asian Scholars,* 1970-72.

WORK IN PROGRESS: Research on socialist revolution and development in the third world and on multinational enterprise and American power.

SIDELIGHTS: Selden writes: "My goal as a writer is to chronicle the struggle of people striving for revolutionary change, to elucidate their aspirations and dreams, and to clarify the international and domestic forces which hold them in bondage. I operate frequently at the intersection of American corporate, military, and state power and the aspirations of third world peoples for independence, self-reliance, and socialist development in an effort to penetrate the myths which conceal and perpetuate illegitimate power."

* * *

SENN, Milton J(ohn) E(dward) 1902-

PERSONAL: Born March 23, 1902, in Milwaukee, Wis.; son of John (a merchant) and Louise (Rosenkranz) Senn; married Blanche Forsythe, September 8, 1933; children: Corelyn Senn Midelfort. *Education:* University of Wisconsin, Madison, B.S., 1925, M.D., 1927. *Politics:* Democrat. *Religion:* Unitarian-Universalist. *Home:* 275-A Heritage Village, Southbury, Conn. 06488. *Office:* Child Study Center, Yale University, 333 Cedar St., New Haven, Conn. 06510.

CAREER: Washington University, St. Louis, Mo., fellow and instructor in pediatrics, 1927-32; Cornell University, New York Hospital, New York, N.Y., associate professor, 1932-47, professor of pediatrics and psychiatry, 1947-48; Yale University, New Haven, Conn., Sterling Professor of Pediatrics and Psychiatry and director of Child Study Center, 1948-70, professor emeritus, 1970—. Member of board of trustees of Field Foundation, 1942—, and Foundation for Child Development, 1946-77.

MEMBER: American Orthopsychiatric Association, American Academy of Pediatrics, New York Academy of Medicine, Yale Club (New York City). *Awards, honors:* M.A. from Yale University, 1948; Aldrich Award from American Academy of Pediatrics, 1964; Gavin Award from American Psychiatric Association, 1965.

WRITINGS: (With Claire Hartford) *The Firstborn: Experiences of Eight American Families,* Harvard University Press, 1968; (with Albert J. Solnit) *Problems in Child Behavior and Development,* Lea & Febiger, 1968; *Insights on the Child Development Movement in the U.S.A.* (monograph), University of Chicago Press, 1975; *Speaking Out for America's Children,* Yale University Press, 1977.

WORK IN PROGRESS: An oral history of the American child guidance movement.

SIDELIGHTS: Senn writes: "Concern over the plight of America's children, and the frequent lack of implementation of research for their benefit prompted me to do research (via the oral history technique) which led to my last two publications. My first two books resulted from work with normal children and families, as well as those in psycho-social difficulties."

BIOGRAPHICAL/CRITICAL SOURCES: A. J. Solnit and Sally Provence, *Modern Perspectives in Child Development,* International Universities Press, 1963.

* * *

SERAFIAN, Michael
See MARTIN, Malachi

* * *

SERB, Ann Toland 1937-

PERSONAL: Born January 11, 1937, in Woburn, Mass.; daughter of Joseph Anthony (a market researcher) and Ann (a comptometer operator; maiden name, Fallon) Toland; married Thomas Serb (in public relations), October 18, 1958;

children: Tom, Mary, Ann, Joseph, Robert, Steven, Christopher, William. *Education:* Attended Loyola University and DePaul University, 1954-58; Mundelein College, B.S., 1958. *Politics:* "Chronic ticket-splitter." *Religion:* Roman Catholic. *Home and office:* 1429 West Chase St., Chicago, Ill. 60626.

CAREER: A. C. Nielson Co., Chicago, Ill., office worker, 1956-58; St. Jerome Grammar School, Chicago, junior high school teacher, 1958; writer, 1972—.

WRITINGS: (Contributor) Marcy Cavanagh Sneed and others, editors, *Human Life: Our Legacy and Our Challenge,* McGraw, 1976; (with Joan W. Anderson) *Love, Lollipops, and Laundry,* Our Sunday Visitor, 1976; *Mother-in-Law,* Carillon Books, 1978; (with Anderson) *Stop the World . . . Our Gerbils Are Loose,* Doubleday, 1979. Author of "Just a Minute, Lord," a column in *Family Digest* and *Parish Monthly.* Contributor of more than two hundred articles to magazines, including *Catholic Digest* and *Family Weekly.*

WORK IN PROGRESS: Two books, a nonfiction handbook on living away from home for the first time, and a historical novel about a turn-of-the-century immigrant girl.

SIDELIGHTS: Serb told *CA:* "I write for the family woman primarily, one of the most ignored groups today. She may have an outside career, yet her major interest is still home, husband, and children. This means dealing with jelly on the table, battles over curfew, and all the myriad joys and sorrows that are part of every family's life. My career began the day I faced four grammar-school kids on vacation, combined with two pre-schoolers, a toddler, and an infant—and realized that women all over the country also faced the challenge of summer. This triggered my first family humor piece, which sold immediately and addicted me to this new profession.

"Since then, everything has been grist for my personal literary mill. The only thing that makes me different from millions of other women is the realization that our experiences are indeed universal, and the knowledge that readers love to make this discovery.

"Surprisingly, men and children of various ages also have enjoyed my woman-oriented articles—probably because it helps them understand maternal reactions, and they too recognize themselves within each piece.

"Sometimes writing is a joy; often it is agony; always, when something is finally well-done, it becomes a victory. I'd compare it to my other profession of family life."

* * *

SEUPHOR, Michel
See ARP, Jean

* * *

SEYMOUR, Whitney North, Jr. 1923-

PERSONAL: Born July 7, 1923, in Huntington, W. Va.; son of Whitney North (a lawyer) and Lola (Vickers) Seymour; married Catryna Ten Eyck (a writer and artist), November 16, 1951; children: Tryntje (daughter), Gabriel (daughter). *Education:* Princeton University, B.A. (magna cum laude), 1947; Yale University, LL.B., 1950. *Politics:* Republican. *Religion:* Episcopalian. *Home:* 290 West 4th St., New York, N.Y. 10014. *Office:* One Battery Park Plaza, New York, N.Y. 10004.

CAREER: Admitted to the Bar of New York State, 1950; Simpson, Thacher & Bartlett (law firm), New York City,

associate, 1950-53; assistant U.S. attorney for southern district of New York, 1953-56; Simpson, Thacher & Bartlett, associate, 1956-59; New York State Commission of Governmental Operations, New York City, chief counsel, 1959-60; chief counsel for Special Unit of New York State Commission of Investigation, 1960-61; Simpson, Thacher & Bartlett, partner, 1961-70; New York state senator in Albany, 1966-68; U.S. attorney for southern district of New York, 1970-73; Simpson, Thacher & Bartlett, partner, 1973—. Vice-chairman of local committee for modern courts; member of board of directors and co-founder of Natural Resources Defense Council and South Street Seaport; member of Citizens' Committee for Children; co-founder of National Citizens' Emergency Committee to Save Our Public Libraries. Vice-president of Art Commission of the City of New York; member of board of trustees of New York Public Library. *Military service:* U.S. Army, Artillery; served in Pacific theater; became captain.

MEMBER: American Judicature Society (past member of board of directors), American College of Trial Lawyers, American Bar Foundation (fellow), New York State Bar Association (president, 1974-75), New York County Lawyers Association (past member of board of directors), New York Bar Foundation (fellow), Association of the Bar of the City of New York (past member of executive committee), Phi Beta Kappa, Phi Delta Phi, Order of Coif. *Awards, honors:* LL. D. from New York Law School, 1972.

WRITINGS: (Editor) *Small Urban Spaces: The Philosophy, Design, Sociology, and Politics of Vest-Pocket Parks and Other Small Urban Open Spaces,* New York University Press, 1969; *The Young Die Quietly: The Narcotics Problem in America,* Morrow, 1972; *Why Justice Fails,* Morrow, 1973; *United States Attorney,* Morrow, 1975; *Fighting for Public Libraries,* Doubleday, 1979. Contributor to magazines.

SIDELIGHTS: When Seymour was assistant U.S. attorney for the southern district of New York, he participated as chief appellate attorney in the prosecution of Frank Costello. Later, as a state senator, he became involved in legislation on housing, then returned to investigating and prosecuting federal crimes in the areas of narcotics, white-collar crime, and official corruption, and also became interested in civil enforcement actions in the fields of the environment, civil rights, and consumer fraud.

He writes: "I view writing for publication as an opportunity to achieve public awareness of contemporary problems and needs I have seen as a lawyer, public official, and concerned citizen. I hope my books have helped produce some constructive change, and have provided encouragement to younger people to get out and *do* something about things they believe are wrong."

* * *

SHAFFER, Helen B. 1909(?)-1978

OBITUARY NOTICE: Born c. 1909, in Washington, D.C.; died July 18, 1978, in Washington, D.C. Journalist best known for her work for Editorial Research Reports (ERR). While with ERR, Shaffer's writings were featured in more than three hundred twenty newspapers. Shaffer also worked as culture critic for *Washington Daily News* and later became that paper's assistant city editor. Obituaries and other sources: *Washington Post,* July 19, 1978.

SHAPIRO, Irwin 1911-

PERSONAL: Born in 1911, in Pittsburgh, Pa. *Education:* Attended Carnegie Institute of Technology (now Carnegie-Mellon University), and Art Students League. *Residence:* Flushing, N.Y.

CAREER: Has worked as a typist, shoe salesman, bookstore clerk, group worker in a country school, manuscript reader for motion picture companies, lathe hand in a machine shop, and seaman, as national affairs editor of *Scholastic* magazine and *Facts on File*, and as a member of the staff of a theater and film magazine; author of books for children, movie scripts, and criticism. *Awards, honors:* Julia Ellsworth Ford Foundation award, 1947, for *Joe Magarac and His U.S.A. Citizen Papers.*

WRITINGS: How Old Stormalong Captured Mocha Dick (illustrated by Donald McKay), Messner, 1942; *The Gremlins of Lieut. Oggins* (illustrated by McKay), Messner, 1943; *Steamboat Bill and the Captain's Top Hat* (illustrated by McKay), Messner, 1943; *Yankee Thunder: The Legendary Life of Davy Crockett* (illustrated by James Daugherty), Messner, 1944; *Casey Jones and Locomotive No. 638* (illustrated by McKay), Messner, 1944; *John Henry and the Double Jointed Steam-Drill* (illustrated by Daugherty), Messner, 1945; *Joe Magarac and His U.S.A. Citizen Papers* (illustrated by Daugherty), Messner, 1948.

(Reteller) *Walt Disney's Davy Crockett, King of the Wild Frontier*, Simon & Schuster, 1955; *J. Fred Muggs* (illustrated by Edwin Schmidt), Simon & Schuster, 1955; *Presidents of the United States* (illustrated by Mel Crawford), Simon & Schuster, 1956; *Daniel Boone* (illustrated by Miriam S. Hurford), Simon & Schuster, 1956; (reteller with Margaret Soifer) *Golden Tales from the Arabian Nights* (illustrated by Gustaf Tenggren), Simon & Schuster, 1957; *Lassie Finds a Way: A New Story of the Famous Dog* (illustrated by Hamilton Greene), Simon & Schuster, 1957; *Cleo*, Simon & Schuster, 1957; *Circus Boy* (illustrated by Joan W. Anglund), Simon & Schuster, 1957; (reteller) *Walt Disney's Old Yeller* (illustrated by Edwin Schmidt and E. Joseph Dreany), Simon & Schuster, 1957; (adapter) *The Golden Book of America: Stories from Our Country's Past*, Simon & Schuster, 1957; *Tall Tales of America* (illustrated by Al Schmidt), Golden Press, 1958; (with John B. Lewellen) *The Story of Flight, From the Ancient Winged Gods to the Age of Space* (illustrated by Harry McNaught), Golden Press, 1959, published as *The Golden Book of Aviation, From the Ancient Winged Gods to the Age of Space*, 1961; *The Story of Yankee Whaling*, Golden Press, 1959.

The Golden Book of California From the Days of the Spanish Explorers to the Present, Golden Press, 1961; *Jonathan and the Dragon* (illustrated by Tom Vroman), Golden Press, 1962; *Heroes in American Folklore* (illustrated by Daugherty and McKay), Messner, 1962; (adapter) *The Golden Book of the Renaissance*, Golden Press, 1962; *Gretchen and the White Steed* (illustrated by Herman Vestal), Garrard, 1972; *Sam Patch, Champion Jumper* (illustrated by Ted Schroeder), Garrard, 1972; *Willie's Whizmobile* (illustrated by Paul Frame), Garrard, 1973; *Twice Upon a Time* (illustrated by Adrienne Adams), Xerox Family Education Services, 1973; *Uncle Sam's 200th Birthday Parade* (illustrated by Frank Brugos), Golden Press, 1974; *Dan McCann and His Fast Sooner Hound* (illustrated by Mimi Korach), Garrard, 1975; *Paul Bunyan Tricks a Dragon* (illustrated by Raymond Burns), Garrard, 1975; *Smokey Bear's Camping Book* (illustrated by Crawford), Golden Press, 1976.

Editor: Stephen Crane, *The Red Badge of Courage*, Pendulum Press, 1973; Herman Melville, *Moby Dick*, Pendulum Press, 1973; Mark Twain, *Tom Sawyer*, Pendulum Press, 1973.

SIDELIGHTS: Although he studied painting, Irwin Shapiro's interest in American folklore turned him to writing. His first book, *How Old Stormalong Captured Mocha Dick*, was reviewed by a *New York Times* critic who wrote, "children won't know which is funnier, the yarn or its pictures. They are perfectly matched, and the book is the freshest, most rollicking one that boys, wanting to laugh, will have found in a long time." Another early book, *Yankee Thunder: The Legendary Life of Davy Crockett*, drew this reaction from a *Horn Book* reviewer: With little dependence on history, but much on a rollicking imagination, Irwin Shapiro has embellished the folk tales, preserved in old almanacs and songs, and has re-created a lusty hero, already enshrined in American tradition. No pictures could be more completely in the fun-making spirit than those of James Daugherty, with their hint of Daniel Boone's vigor and strength, as well as Davy Crockett's boisterous thunder."

BIOGRAPHICAL/CRITICAL SOURCES: New York Times, November 15, 1942; *Horn Book*, May, 1944, February, 1974.*

* * *

SHAPIRO, Milton J. 1926-

PERSONAL: Born in 1926, in Brooklyn, N.Y. *Education:* Attended City College (now City College of the City University of New York). *Residence:* London, England.

CAREER: Writer. Has also worked as a sportswriter and movie critic for a newspaper in New York City, as a sports editor for *National Enquirer*, and as executive editor of *Gunsport*. *Military service:* Served in U.S. Army Air Forces during World War II.

WRITINGS—All published by Messner: *The Sal Maglie Story*, 1957; *Jackie Robinson of the Brooklyn Dodgers*, 1957; *The Roy Campanella Story*, 1958; *The Warren Spahn Story*, 1958; *The Phil Rizzuto Story*, 1959; *The Mel Ott Story*, 1959; *The Willie Mays Story*, 1960; *The Gil Hodges Story*, 1960; *The Hank Aaron Story*, 1961; *A Beginner's Book of Sporting Guns and Hunting*, 1961; *The Whitey Ford Story*, 1962; *Mickey Mantle, Yankee Slugger*, 1962; *The Dizzy Dean Story*, 1963; *The Don Drysdale Story*, 1964; *Laughs from the Dugout*, 1966; *The Year They Won the Most Valuable Player Award*, 1966; *Champions of the Bat: Baseball's Greatest Sluggers*, 1967; *Heroes of the Bullpen: Baseball's Greatest Relief Pitchers*, 1967; *Heroes Behind the Mask: America's Greatest Catchers*, 1968; *The Day They Made the Record Book*, 1968; *Baseball's Greatest Pitchers*, 1969; *All Stars of the Outfield*, 1970; *The Pro Quarterbacks*, 1971; *A Treasury of Sports Humor*, 1971; *The Screaming Eagles: The 101st Airborne Division in World War II*, 1976; *Behind Enemy Lines: American Spies and Saboteurs in World War II*, 1978.

SIDELIGHTS: Milton J. Shapiro's early books were all biographies of great baseball players. The *Christian Science Monitor* called *Jackie Robinson of the Brooklyn Dodgers* "an excellent contribution," adding, "The real heartwarming story in this book is the acceptance and the success with which Robinson himself met the challenge." In a review of *The Phil Rizzuto Story*, a *Kirkus* critic observed: "Milton Shapiro not only writes confidently of the man as an athlete, but, as in his previous books, portrays his subject with dramatic insight.... Of interest to fans and to all readers who are attracted by accounts of contemporary valor."

In the late 1960's, Shapiro's books concentrated on collective, rather than individual, biographies. Of *Heroes Behind the Mask: America's Greatest Catchers,* a critic for *Young Reader's Review* commented: "The book is interestingly written, fast-paced, and provides considerable action. The author does not try to force each of the capsule biographies into a set form but adapts the approach to the particular case...." A *Young Reader's Review* critic said of *The Day They Made the Record Book:* "There is drama a plenty in these stories without need to dress up the facts, and the author sticks to the facts, and so enhances the drama.... Today's youngsters will enjoy reading about the 'legendary' feats here presented: Don Larsen's perfect series no-hitter, Roger Maris' home run hitting, Joe DiMaggio's hitting streak, and Maury Will's one hundred four stolen bases.... The author emphasizes the record making feat, but also tells about the subsequent careers and the personalities of these players."

BIOGRAPHICAL/CRITICAL SOURCES: Christian Science Monitor, November 21, 1957; *Booklist,* June 15, 1959, November 1, 1960; *Kirkus,* March 1, 1959; *Young Reader's Review,* May, 1968, December, 1968.

* * *

SHAPLEY, John 1890(?)-1978

OBITUARY NOTICE: Born c. 1890 in Jasper County, Mo.; died September 8, 1978, in Washington, D.C. Art historian, educator, and author. While still a student, Shapley helped to found the College Art Association as well as the *Art Bulletin,* which he edited for twenty years and helped to finance during the depression. Shapley was best known as director of the Carnegie Corporation project that supplied a collection of art history study materials to nearly two hundred high schools and colleges in the United States and England. He was a contributor to *A Survey of Persian Art, Encyclopaedia Britannica, Dictionary of Religion and Ethics,* and many other scholarly publications. Obituaries and other sources: *Who's Who in American Art,* Bowker, 1973; *Washington Post,* September 13, 1978.

* * *

SHARMA, Jagdish Prasad 1934-

PERSONAL: Born January 4, 1934, in Kota, India; came to the United States in 1962, naturalized citizen, 1977; son of Chandra Bhan (a farmer) and Dwala (Devi) Sharma; married Miriam Fine (a university director of ethnic studies), February 2, 1962; children: Arun David, Nitasha Tamar. *Education:* Agra University, B.A., 1955; London School of Oriental and African Studies, B.A. (honors), 1959, Ph.D., 1962. *Politics:* "No affiliation." *Religion:* Hindu. *Home:* 3092 Lanikaula St., Honolulu, Hawaii 96822. *Office:* Department of History, University of Hawaii, Honolulu, Hawaii 96822.

CAREER: University of Virginia, Charlottesville, visiting assistant professor of Indian history, 1963-64; American University, Washington, D.C., visiting assistant professor of Indian history, 1964; University of Hawaii, Honolulu, assistant professor, 1964-68, associate professor, 1968—. Lecturer at Columbia University, summer, 1963, assistant professor, summer, 1966. Broadcaster for British Broadcasting Corp. India Programme, 1956-62. *Member:* American Oriental Society (life member), Association for Asian Studies (life member), Royal Asiatic Society (life fellow), India Association of Hawaii (president, 1964, 1966-67).

WRITINGS: Republics in Ancient India, circa 1500-500 B.C., E. J. Brill, 1968; (contributor) Donald E. Smith, editor, *Religion and Political Modernization,* Yale University Press, 1974; (co-author) *Dream Symbolism in the Shramanic Tradition: Two Psychoanalytical Studies,* Firma KLM (Calcutta), 1978; (editor) *Men and Ideas in India,* Firma KLM (Calcutta), 1978. Contributor of articles and reviews to scholarly journals.

WORK IN PROGRESS: Jaina Heroes and Jainism; editing *Minozities in Indian Society and History* and *Men and Ideas in Traditional India.*

SIDELIGHTS: Sharma writes: "There has been such a dearth of books on ancient Indian republics that I had to write on that subject. A second volume will deal with republics during 500 B.C.-500 A.D., keeping in mind Greek and Roman works on the subject. It will also include a discussion of the last days and death of Alexander the Great. In a democratic century we must not forget our republican past, even if it was of a different kind.

"My study of Jainism is inspired by lack of western knowledge of the subject and is carried out in a comparative manner. Scholars must write in such a way that general readers may benefit from and enjoy it."

AVOCATIONAL INTERESTS: Travel (Japan, Iceland, the South Pacific), lecturing, palmistry.

* * *

SHARP, Ann Margaret 1942-

PERSONAL: Born May 31, 1942, in Brooklyn, N.Y.; daughter of Edward Charles (a transit supervisor) and Dolores (a secretary) Shoub; married Frank Vincent Sharp (an educational director at a zoo), December 17, 1966; children: Brendan Vincent. *Education:* College of New Rochelle, B.A., 1963; Catholic University of America, M.A., 1966; further graduate study at Union Theological Seminary, Richmond, Va., 1966-67, and University of New Hampshire, 1968-70; University of Massachusetts, Ed.D., 1973. *Home:* 160 Gordonhurst Ave., Upper Montclair, N.J. *Office:* Institute for the Advancement of Philosophy for Children, Montclair State College, Upper Montclair, N.J. 07043.

CAREER: Fayetteville State College, Fayetteville, N.C., instructor in history, 1965-66; Virginia Union University, Richmond, assistant professor of history, 1966-67; Notre Dame College, Manchester, N.H., assistant professor of humanities and history, 1967-70; Montclair State College, Upper Montclair, N.J., assistant professor of educational philosophy, 1973—, assistant director of Institute for the Advancement of Philosophy for Children, 1974—.

MEMBER: American Philosophical Association, Philosophy of Education Society, American Educational Research Association, American Educational Studies Association, History of Education Society, Middle Atlantic Philosophy of Education Society. *Awards, honors:* National Endowment for the Humanities grants, 1974—; Rockefeller Foundation grant, 1978-81.

WRITINGS: (Contributor) Francesco Cordasco and William W. Brickman, editors, *A Bibliography of American Educational History: An Annotated and Classified Guide,* AMS Press, 1975; (with Matthew Lipman and Frederick J. Oscanyan) *Instructional Manual to Accompany Harry Stottlemeier's Discovery,* Institute for the Advancement of Philosophy for Children, Montclair State College, 1975, revised edition published as *Philosophical Inquiry: Instructional Manual to Accompany Harry Stottlemeier's Discovery,* 1978; (with Lipman and Oscanyan) *Philosophy in the Class-*

room, Institute for the Advancement of Philosophy for Children, Montclair State College, 1977; (with Lipman and Oscanyan) *Ethical Inquiry: Instructional Manual to Accompany Lisa,* Institute for the Advancement of Philosophy for Children, Montclair State College, 1977; (with Lipman) *Growing Up With Philosophy,* Temple University Press, 1978. Contributor to history, humanities, education, and philosophy journals.

WORK IN PROGRESS: Moral Education and Philosophical Inquiry; The Educational Thought of Georg Simmel, completion expected in 1980; *The Educational Philosophy of Friedrich Nietzsche;* editing Simone Weil's *Philosophical Essays.*

SIDELIGHTS: Ann Sharp writes: "I am primarily interested in education of the young and the relationship of philosophy to education. My writings on Nietzsche, Simone Weil, my interest in teacher education, and my work in the Institute for the Advancement of Philosophy for Children are all centered in this basic interest."

* * *

SHAVIN, Norman 1926-

PERSONAL: Born March 2, 1926, in Chattanooga, Tenn.; son of Isadore J. and Dora (Pickelni) Shavin; married Phyllis Grumet (an interior decorator), April 15, 1951; children: Julie, Mark, Dana. *Education:* Attended University of Chattanooga, 1943-46; Indiana University, A.B., 1949, graduate study, 1950; graduate study at University of Louisville, 1951-52. *Office:* Special Projects Division, Perry Communications, Inc., 2181 Sylvan Rd. SW, Atlanta, Ga. 30344.

CAREER: Chattanooga Times, Chattanooga, Tenn., copyboy, then copydesk editor, 1949; *Louisville Times,* Louisville, Ky., picture editor, copy editor, columnist, amusements critic, and education specialist, 1950-55; *Jackson State-Times,* Jackson, Miss., Sunday editor, 1955-56; *Atlanta Journal,* Atlanta, Ga., radio-television editor, 1956-60; *Atlanta Journal-Constitution,* Atlanta, Sunday editor, 1960-62; *Atlanta Constitution,* Atlanta, editorial page columnist, 1963-67; U.S. Peace Corps, Washington, D.C., assistant to regional director in Atlanta, 1967-70; *Atlanta* Magazine, Inc., Atlanta, editor, then editor and associate publisher of *Atlanta* Magazine, 1970-77, editor and publisher, 1978; Perry Communications, Inc., Atlanta, director of special projects division, 1978—. President of Capricorn Corporation (book publishers and consultants); magazine consultant in various cities. Instructor in basic adult education at Emory University; has taught courses in journalism at Millsaps College and Georgia State University; lecturer to various organizations and associations. Moderator for local television talk show. Member of board of directors of Atlanta Urban Corps, 1965-67, Atlanta Metropolitan Area Planning Commission, 1971-72, and The Link (counseling center), 1973—; appointed member of Atlanta Civic Design Commission, 1971-73; member of advisory committee of Emory University School of Medicine. *Military service:* U.S. Navy, 1944-45.

MEMBER: American Association of Chamber Magazines (president, 1975-76), Atlanta Press Club (president, 1975-76). *Awards, honors:* National Civil War Commission Award, 1961, and Georgia Press Association Award, 1962, for "The Atlanta Century"; George Washington Honor Medal Award, 1971, for "Debts Owed Some Youth" (editorial); Mississippi State Associated Press Awards for public service, best newspaper column, and creation of best newspaper section, 1956; local award for documentary, "The Secret of *Gone With the Wind.*"

WRITINGS: (With Mike Edwards) *The Atlanta Century: March 1860 to May 1865* (historically researched series in weekly newspaper style of the Civil War period, first published in *Atlanta Journal-Constitution*), I/D Publishing, 1965. Also author, with Bruce Galphin, of *Atlanta: A Celebration,* 1978, and, with Martin Shartar, of *The Wonderful World of Coca-Cola,* 1978. Author of numerous booklets and other materials on Georgia and American history, including "Old Atlanta," "Illustrated Stores of the Century," and "The Million Dollar Legends: Margaret Mitchell and *Gone With the Wind.*" Also author of "Two-Bits," "Georgia Minute," and "Confederate Diary," television series; "McGill: They Call Him Pappy," "The Secret of *Gone With the Wind*" (with Martin Shartar), television documentaries; and "Our Noble Heritage," radio series. Syndicated weekly newspaper columnist, 1967-69. Free-lance contributor to magazines, newspapers, and to television and radio programs.

WORK IN PROGRESS: Books tentatively titled *The Perry Guide to Atlanta* (a guidebook), *Tales From the Teacher's Lounge, A Funny Thing About Georgia, Old Georgia* (a picture/photo book), *Letters of the Greats* (important letters by famous people in their own hand), and *My Father's Diary;* research for a play, tentatively titled "Listen, God."

SIDELIGHTS: Shavin told *CA:* "Several influences motivated my decision to spend twenty-five years in this painful passion called writing; painful, because it is lonely labor, and as hurtful as raking skin from your body; passion, because it *is* a loving affair made joyous when you have selected the right words to march like obedient sentinels in the precise order so that the sum—if you're talented, or lucky, or both—creates in the reader some added knowledge, a sense of joy, insight, a laugh, a sadness of recognition.

"The first influence came in boyhood when the library reading room was my baby-sitter. The second was growing up in the midst of Civil War battlefields in Chattanooga; they were my playgrounds, and reading the markers of historic events made them alive. The third was a ninth-grade English teacher, who conveyed her passion for the word-magic of Shakespeare and Milton. The fourth influence was an 11th grade football coach who also taught American history in so dull a fashion (I swear he thought 1492 was a football signal) that I knew history had to be more interesting than that, and could be made more fascinating. The fifth was a college teacher who gave me an 'A' on an essay about suicide and remarked that I had a talent for writing, and the sixth, a splendid Latin teacher who made it come alive.

"A diary kept during my Navy time, and that first check for a free-lance piece to a national magazine—$15 for 1,000 words of humor titled 'The Most Forgettable Man I Ever Met'—those events helped cinch the desire to live by the two fingers I use to type. (The other eight crouch underneath, unused, in blissful ignorance of the punching which two index fingers have endured over the years.)

"To be paid for stringing together words—the same words that everybody uses—struck me as miraculous. It still does. It ensnared me. And since I'm still learning to write, I find that whatever success I have had makes the writing harder. One's own expectations rise with each plateau reached, and the reader has a right to demand better of you than last he read of you. That's terrifying.

"I write with some facility, and rewrite with care. I write to inform and amuse (if possible), as well as to respond to the passion to share ideas.

"Aspiring writers aspire more than they perspire. They want

to *be*—to *arrive*—but often do not wish to pay the price of *becoming*. Occasionally I have taught classes to would-be writers (I didn't say writing can be taught, but it *can* be learned). I'd open each session with a question: 'How many of you really want to write?' Everybody's hand shot up. Then I'd say, 'Then why don't you go home and *do* it?' And nobody would move. Right there I knew I was in trouble. And one of those troubles in this nation of 230 million is there are 250 million avowed writers. Except that only a pitiful handful want to pay the freight. Or the fright.

"Advice? Read, read, read. Listen for the music in the words. Ask yourself, where comes the harmony in those words? Write, write, write. If you *must* write, nothing can stop you. But be prepared for frustration, agony—and occasional joy. Voltaire was right when he said, 'He who has a pen has war'—with himself, editors, the public, and, above all, peace of mind.''

Shavin is the creator of two devices used in public schools in seven states to assist teachers and students in enjoying the learning of history, the "Stamp-'n- Map Game," and "The Name of the Game." An avid traveler, Shavin has recently toured West Germany, Hungary, Israel, Austria, England, Japan, Hong Kong, Taiwan, Mexico, North Africa, Italy, Alaska, Hawaii, and most of the Caribbean Islands.

*   *   *

SHAW, Gaylord   1942-

PERSONAL: Born July 22, 1942, in El Reno, Okla.; son of Charley and Ruth Shaw; married Judy Howard, August 27, 1960; children: Randall, Kristine. *Education:* Attended Cameron College, 1960-62, and University of Oklahoma, 1962-64. *Home:* 19 Oak Ridge Dr., Castle Rock, Colo. *Office:* 1415 Larimer Square, Suite 300, Denver, Colo.

CAREER/WRITINGS: Lawton Constitution-Press, Lawton, Okla., police reporter, 1960-62; Associated Press, statehouse correspondent in Oklahoma City, 1962-66, Washington bureau deskman, 1966-67, investigative reporter and supervising editor, special assignments team, 1967-71, White House correspondent, 1971-75; *Los Angeles Times,* Los Angeles, Calif., Washington bureau staff writer, 1975-78, Denver bureau chief, 1978—. Notable assignments include coverage of the assassination of Martin Luther King, 1968, national Democratic and Republican political conventions, 1968, 1972, 1976, the presidencies of Richard M. Nixon and Gerald Ford, the Nixon impeachment proceedings, 1974, and an eighteen-month investigation of unsafe conditions at government and private dams throughout the United States. *Awards, honors:* Worth Bingham Award for Distinguished Reporting, 1968; Merriman Smith/White House Correspondents Association award for presidential coverage, 1974; Pulitzer Prize for investigative reporting and Sigma Delta Chi distinguished service award, both 1978, both for investigative reporting on conditions of U.S. private and government dams.

SIDELIGHTS: Shaw's investigation of government and private dams began shortly after the collapse of Idaho's Teton dam on June 7, 1976. This accident resulted in the death of at least ten people. Shaw followed up on the disaster by calling the Bureau of Reclamation for field reports on the construction of Teton dam. At first, the agency seemed willing to pen their information to him, but he was soon told that the reports were not public documents. Shaw's follow-up story caused the bureau to reconsider its decision and Shaw was finally allowed access to the Teton reports and hundreds of others. His conclusion was submitted in writing to Los Angeles Times editor for consideration: "We are flirting with disaster as far as dams are concerned.... A catastrophe far greater than Teton will rivet attention on the problem.... I propose that we undertake a major project on dam safety.'' The project began and it yielded a wealth of information about unsafe conditions of dams across the country. The results of the report were beneficial to both Shaw and the United States: a Pulitzer Prize for his reporting and the release of funds for an investigation into the latest dam accident at the Toccoa Falls dam in Georgia, an accident which killed thirty-six people.

When asked about the advice that he might give to aspiring journalists, Shaw wrote: "First, build a solid foundation through study of political and social sciences and economics; second, learn to write clearly and simply; third, be persistent in the pursuit of interviews and documents; fourth, be patient—good stories and assignments don't fall in your lap automatically. I'm certain tomorrow's journalists will find what I have—the most satisfying profession, bar none.''

*   *   *

SHAW, Harry (Lee, Jr.)   1905-

PERSONAL: Born February 19, 1905, in Fountain Inn, S.C.; son of Harry Lee (a physician) and Jane Bayard (Wilson) Shaw; married Marie Louise Ragsdale, August 12, 1931 (divorced); married Jocelyn Thomas (an environmentalist), October 30, 1953; children: (first marriage) Harry Lee III, Edward S., Stephen Willard; (second marriage) Jill, Gray. *Education:* Davidson College, A.B., 1926; University of South Carolina, M.A., 1927; further graduate study at New York University, 1928-31. *Politics:* Republican. *Religion:* Episcopalian. *Home:* 476 Old Mill Rd., Fairfield, Conn. 06430.

CAREER: University of South Carolina, Columbia, instructor in English, 1927-28; New York University, New York City, instructor, 1928-39, assistant professor of English, 1939-42; *Look,* New York City, associate editor and director of editorial research, 1942-43, managing editor, 1943-44, editorial director, 1944-47; Harper & Brothers (now Harper & Row Publishers, Inc.), New York City, editor in charge of humanities, 1947-52; Tupper & Love, Inc., Atlanta, Ga., executive vice-president and managing editor, 1952-53; E. P. Dutton & Co., Inc., New York City, senior editor, 1953-57, vice-president, 1955-57; Henry Holt & Co. (now Holt, Rinehart & Winston, Inc.), New York City, editor-in-chief of General Book Division, 1957-60, manager of division, 1958-60; Barnes & Noble, Inc., New York City, consulting editor, 1961-63, director of publications, 1963-64; W. W. Norton & Co., Inc., New York City, consulting editor, 1964-75; writer, 1975—. Director of New York City federal writer's project, 1939. director of University of Colorado's Western Writers' Conference, summers, 1947-48; lecturer at Columbia University, 1948-52; lecturer at writers' workshops.

MEMBER: Phi Beta Kappa, Omicron Delta Kappa, Sigma Upsilon, Pi Kappa Phi. *Awards, honors:* Litt. D. from Davidson College, 1969.

WRITINGS: Writing and Rewriting: A Handbook of Good Usage (college text), Harper, 1937, 5th edition, 1973, high school adaptation by Marquis E. Shattuck published as *Harper's Handbook of English,* 1942; *A Complete Course in Freshman English,* Harper, 1940, workbook, 1941, 8th edition, 1979; (editor with Douglas Bement) *Reading the Short Story,* Harper, 1941, 2nd edition, 1954; (editor) *A Collection of Readings for Writers,* Harper, 1946, 5th edition published as *Creative Readings for Writers,* 1959, 6th edition, 1967;

(editor with Ruth Davis) *Americans One and All* (stories), Harper, 1947; (editor with William Henry Davenport) *Dominant Types in British and American Literature*, Harper, 1949.

(With Virginia Shaffer) *McGraw-Hill Handbook of English*, McGraw, 1952, 4th edition (sole author), 1978; (with George Steward Wykoff) *The Harper Handbook of College Composition*, Harper, 1952, 4th edition, 1969; (editor) *Expository Readings for Writers*, Harper, 1959; *Spell It Right!*, Barnes & Noble, 1961, 2nd edition, 1965; *Errors in English and Ways to Correct Them*, Barnes & Noble, 1962, 2nd edition, 1970; *Punctuate It Right!*, Barnes & Noble, 1963; (with Richard H. Dodge) *The Shorter Handbook of College Composition*, Harper, 1965.

Dictionary of Literary Terms, McGraw, 1972; *Say It Right!*, Barnes & Noble, 1972; *Twenty Steps to Better Writing*, Littlefield, Adams, 1975; *Dictionary of Problem Words and Expressions*, McGraw, 1975; *Concise Dictionary of Literary Terms*, McGraw, 1976; *Thirty Ways to Improve Your Grades*, McGraw, 1976; *Talk Your Way to a Better Job*, Littlefield, 1979. Contributor to national magazines.

WORK IN PROGRESS: Fifth edition of *The Harper Handbook of College Composition*.

SIDELIGHTS: Shaw comments: "During several decades as a teacher, writer, editor, and publisher, I have become more and more convinced that Americans write astonishingly well—considering the amount of time they spend doing it and the gross inadequacy of the instruction and practice they have had in writing from primary grades to graduate school. Someday we may all become aware of two facts: nothing is more important to a responsible citizen than the ability to communicate clearly and effectively to fellow citizens in both speech and writing; and there is no such thing as good writing, there is only good *rewriting*."

* * *

SHAW, Robert 1927-1978

OBITUARY NOTICE—See index for *CA* sketch: Born August 9, 1927, in England; died August 28, 1978, near Tourmakeady, Ireland. Actor and author. Shaw was best known for his performances in films, including "A Man for All Seasons," "The Sting," "Jaws," and "The Deep." Among his five novels are *The Hiding Place, The Flag,* and *The Man in the Glass Booth.* Shaw later adapted *The Man in the Glass Booth* successfully for the stage with Harold Pinter as the director. The novel was also adapted as a critically acclaimed motion picture. Obituaries and other sources: *The Biographical Encyclopaedia and Who's Who of the American Theatre,* James Heineman, 1966; *Celebrity Register,* 3rd edition, Simon & Schuster, 1973; *Who's Who in the World,* 2nd edition, Marquis, 1973; *The Writers Directory, 1976-78,* St. Martin's, 1976; *Who's Who in the Theatre,* Pitman, 1977; *Who's Who,* 130th edition, St. Martin's, 1978; *Detroit News,* August 29, 1978; *Washington Post,* August 29, 1978; *Time,* September 11, 1978; *Current Biography,* October, 1978.

* * *

SHECTER, Ben 1935-

PERSONAL: Born April 28, 1935, in New York, N.Y. *Education:* Attended City College (now of the City University of New York), and Yale University. *Residence:* New York, N.Y. *Address:* c/o Harper & Row, 10 East 53rd St., New York, N.Y. 10022.

CAREER: Started working in the field of window display; became a costume and scenic designer for opera, ballet, theater, and television, 1962; author and illustrator of books for children. His works have been exhibited by the American Institute of Graphic Arts. *Military service:* U.S. Army, 1958-60. *Awards, honors: The Hating Book* by Charlotte Zolotow was named by *House Beautiful* as one of the ten best children's books for 1969.

WRITINGS: Emily, Girl Witch of New York (self-illustrated), Dial, 1963; *Jonathan and the Bank Robbers* (self-illustrated), Dial, 1964; *Partouche Plants a Seed,* Harper, 1966; *Conrad's Castle* (self-illustrated), Harper, 1967; *Inspector Rose* (self-illustrated), Harper, 1969; *If I Had a Ship* (self-illustrated), Doubleday, 1970; *Someplace Else* (self-illustrated), Harper, 1971; *Across the Meadow* (self-illustrated), Doubleday, 1972; *Game for Demons,* Harper, 1972; *Stone House Stories* (self-illustrated), Harper, 1973; *The Whistling Whirligig* (self-illustrated), Harper, 1974; *The Toughest and Meanest Kid on the Block,* Putnam, 1975; *Molly Patch and Her Animal Friends,* Harper, 1975; *The Stocking Child,* Harper, 1976; *Hester the Jester,* Harper, 1977; *The Hiding Game* (self-illustrated), Parents Magazine Press, 1977; *A Summer Secret,* Harper, 1977.

Illustrator: Joan M. Lexau, *Millicent's Ghost,* Dial, 1962; Miriam Anne Bourne, *Emilio's Summer Day,* Harper, 1966; Nancy Brelis, *The Mummy Market,* Harper, 1966; Charlotte Zolotow, *If It Weren't for You,* Harper, 1966; Barbara Borack, *Grandpa,* Harper, 1967; Janet Chenery, *The Toad Hunt,* Harper, 1967; Lexau, *Every Day a Dragon,* Harper, 1967; Nathaniel Benchley, *A Ghost Named Fred,* Harper, 1968; Mary Church, *John Patrick's Amazing Morning,* Doubleday, 1968; Zolotow, *My Friend John,* Harper, 1968; Aileen Lucia Fisher, *Clean as a Whistle,* Crowell, 1969; Zolotow, *The Hating Book,* Harper, 1969; Sandra Hochman, *The Magic Convention,* Doubleday, 1971; Marjorie Weinman Sharmat, *Getting Something on Maggie Marmelstein,* Harper, 1971; Zolotow, *A Father Like That,* Harper, 1971; Millicent Selsam, *More Potatoes,* Harper, 1972; Robert Wahl, *What Will You Do Today, Little Russell?,* Putnam, 1972; Felice Holman, *The Escape of the Giant Hogstalk,* Scribner, 1974; Zolotow, *The Summer Night,* Harper, 1974; Nancy Jewell, *Cheer Up, Pig!,* Harper, 1975; Sharmat, *Maggie Marmelstein for President,* Harper, 1975; Charlotte Herman, *The Difference of Ari Stein,* Harper, 1976; Sharmat, *Mooch the Messy,* Harper, 1976.

SIDELIGHTS: Raised in Brooklyn, N.Y., Ben Shecter had easy access to museums, libraries, and numerous cultural events. This background, plus the advantage of having an encouraging and understanding father, filled young Shecter with dreams of becoming a set designer for stage productions.

A chance meeting with Franco Zeffirelli at a party led to an introduction to Gian Carlo Menotti. As a result of that introduction, Shecter went to Italy in the summer of 1962 to attend the Spoleto Festival of Two Worlds and began his career as a scenic designer. About the same time, Shecter did a series of drawings about a little girl in a haunted house which served as the basis for Joan Lexau's book *Millicent's Ghost* and introduced Shecter to the world of book illustration.

Shecter eventually began to write as well as illustrate books for children. In *Someplace Else,* the author-illustrator told the story of an eleven-year-old boy adjusting to a move to a new neighborhood. "The author writes with rare humor and affection, etching incidents so clearly one feels that the story must stem from his own experience. And one feels fortunate in being able to share them," noted a critic for *Book World.*

BIOGRAPHICAL/CRITICAL SOURCES: Book World, November 7, 1971.*

* * *

SHEEKMAN, Arthur 1901-1978

PERSONAL: Born February 5, 1901, in Chicago, Ill.; married Gloria Stuart (an actress); children: Sylvia Vaughn Sheekman Thompson. Education: Attended University of Minnesota.

CAREER: Worked as reporter for St.Paul News and as columnist and art critic for Chicago Times before becoming motion picture screenwriter. Producer of plays. Member: Writers Guild of America (secretary, 1948; representative to Motion Picture Council and Motion Picture Relief Fund). Awards, honors: Writers Guild nomination, 1953, for "Call Me Madam."

WRITINGS: (Editor and author of introduction) The Groucho Letters: Letters From and to Groucho Marx, Simon & Schuster, 1967.

Screenplays: (With Frank Partos and Charles Brackett) "Rose of the Rancho" (adapted from the play by Richard Walton Tully and David Belasco), Paramount, 1936; (with Nat Perrin) "Dimples," Twentieth Century-Fox, 1936; (with William Conselman and Perrin) "Stowaway," Twentieth Century-Fox, 1936; (with Charlie Melson) "The Gladiator" (adapted from the novel by Philip Wylie), Columbia, 1938; "Blue Skies," Paramount, 1945; "Dear Ruth" (adapted from the play by Norman Krasna), Paramount, 1946; (author of additional dialogue) "The Well Groomed Bride," Paramount, 1946; (with Frank Wead) "Blaze of Noon" (adapted from the novel by Ernest K. Gann), Paramount, 1947; "Trouble With Women," Paramount, 1947; "Welcome Stranger," Paramount, 1947; (with P. J. Wolfson) "Saigon," Paramount, 1948; (with Roy Chanslor) "Hazard" (adapted from the novel by Chanslor), Paramount, 1948.

(With Richard N. Nash) "Dear Wife," Paramount, 1950; "Mr. Music" (adapted from the play, "Accent on Youth," by Samson Raphaelson, Paramount, 1950; "Young Man With Ideas," Metro-Goldwyn-Mayer, 1952; "Call Me Madam" (adapted from the musical comedy by Howard Lindsay and Russel Crouse), Twentieth Century-Fox, 1953; (with Krasna and Robert Carson) "Bundle of Joy" (re-make of film "Bachelor Mother"), RKO, 1956; (with John Patrick) "Some Came Running" (adapted from the novel by James Jones), Metro-Goldwyn-Mayer, 1958; (with William L. Driskill) "Ada" (adapted from the novel, Ada Dallas, by Wirt Williams), Metro-Goldwyn-Mayer, 1961.

SIDELIGHTS: Sheekman was one of the founders of the Screen Writers Guild in the 1930's. He also maintained a long friendship with Groucho Marx.

OBITUARIES: New York Times, January 14, 1978.*

(Died January 12, 1978, in Santa Monica, Calif.)

* * *

SHER, Gerson S(amuel) 1947-

PERSONAL: Born July 31, 1947, in Hackensack, N.J.; son of Philip Herschel (a certified public accountant) and Rita (a social worker; maiden name, Leight) Sher; married Margery Leveen (a day-care center director), June 29, 1969; children: Jeremy Daniel. Education: Yale University, B.A., 1969; Princeton University, Ph.D., 1975. Politics: "Closet Socialist." Religion: Jewish. Home: 1613 Valencia Way, Reston,

Va. 22090. Office: National Academy of Sciences, Washington, D.C. 20418.

CAREER: National Academy of Sciences, Washington, D.C., professional associate of Commission on International Relations and administrator of East-West scientific exchanges, 1973—. Visiting assistant professor at Duke University, spring, 1979. Military service: New Jersey National Guard, 1969-73. U.S. Army Reserve, 1973-75. Member: American Political Science Association, American Association for the Advancement of Slavic Studies, Phi Beta Kappa. Awards, honors: Woodrow Wilson fellowship, 1969-70.

WRITINGS: (Translator) Svetozar Stojanovic, Between Ideals and Reality, Oxford University Press, 1973; Praxis: Marxist Criticism and Dissent in Socialist Yugoslavia, Indiana University Press, 1977; (editor) Marxist Humanism and Praxis, Prometheus Books, 1978.

* * *

SHETTER, William Z(eiders, Jr.) 1927-

PERSONAL: Born August 17, 1927, in Allentown, Pa.; married, 1953. Education: University of Pennsylvania, A.B., 1951; University of California, Berkeley, M.A., 1953, Ph.D., 1955. Office: Department of Germanic Languages, Indiana University, Bloomington, Ind. 47401.

CAREER: University of Wisconsin, Madison, instructor, 1956-59, assistant professor of German, 1959-61; Bryn Mawr College, Bryn Mawr, Pa., assistant professor, 1962-64, associate professor of German, 1964-65; Indiana University, Bloomington, associate professor, 1965-71; professor of Germanic languages, 1971—. Military service: U.S. Army, 1945-46. Member: Modern Language Association of America, Linguistic Society of America, Society for Netherlands Literature. Awards, honors: Fulbright fellow at University of Leiden, 1955-56; Fulbright research grant from University of Groningen, 1961-62.

WRITINGS: Introduction to Dutch: A Practical Grammar, Nijhoff, 1958, 4th edition, 1947; (with Robert Byron Bird) Dutch: Een Goed Begin—A Contemporary Dutch Reader, two volumes, Nijhoff, 1963; The Pillars of Society: Six Centuries of Civilization in the Netherlands, Nijhoff, 1971.

* * *

SHIELDS, Carol 1935-

PERSONAL: Born June 2, 1935, in Oak Park, Ill.; daughter of Robert E. and Inez (Selgren) Warner; married Donald Hugh Shields (a professor), July 20, 1957; children: John, Anne, Catherine, Margaret, Sara. Education: Hanover College, B.A., 1957; University of Ottawa, M.A., 1975. Politics: New Democratic Party. Religion: Protestant. Home: 582 Driveway, Ottawa, Ontario, Canada K1S 3N5. Agent: Virginia Barber Literary Agency, Inc., 44 Greenwich Ave., New York, N.Y. 10011.

CAREER: Canadian Slavonic Papers, Ottawa, Ontario, editorial assistant, 1972-74; free-lance writer, 1974—. Awards, honors: Winner of young writers' contest sponsored by Canadian Broadcasting Corp., 1965; Canada Council grants, 1972, 1974, 1976; fiction prize from Canadian Authors Association, 1976, for Small Ceremonies.

WRITINGS: Others (poetry), Borealis Press, 1972; Intersect (poetry), Borealis Press, 1974; Susanna Moodie: Voice and Vision, Borealis Press, 1976; Small Ceremonies (novel), McGraw, 1976; The Box Garden (novel), McGraw, 1977.

WORK IN PROGRESS: Another novel; a non-fiction book on an Ottawa, Canada, court case.

SIDELIGHTS: Shields told *CA:* "I am interested in reality, with the texture of ordinary life, and the way people appear and relate. I like to write about survivors."

* * *

SHIFFRIN, Nancy 1944-

PERSONAL: Born April 6, 1944, in New York, N.Y.; daughter of Martin (a teacher) and Minna (a legal secretary) Shiffrin. *Education:* International College, Los Angeles, M.A., 1977. *Residence:* Los Angeles, Calif. *Agent:* Sanford J. Greenburger Associates, Inc., 825 Third Ave., New York, N.Y. 10022.

CAREER: Hollywood-Sunset Free Clinic, Hollywood, Calif., counseling director, 1973-74; County of Los Angeles, Los Angeles, Calif., worker with disturbed and delinquent children, 1974-76; writer. Teacher of West Los Angeles College, 1978. Public speaker and conductor of poetry therapy seminars. *Awards, honors:* Award from Academy of American Poets, 1972, for "Hot Liquid" and "Games."

WRITINGS: Encounter, Major Books, 1976; *Anger,* Major Books, 1976; *Acupressure,* Major Books, 1977; *Your Bedside Book of Dreams,* Major Books, 1977; (with Morris Netherton) *Past Lives Therapy,* Morrow, 1978; *Defying Death,* Grosset, 1979. Contributor of stories, articles, and poems to a wide variety of magazines, including *Human Behavior, New Woman,* and *Viva.*

SIDELIGHTS: Shiffrin told *CA:* "W. H. Auden once said, 'It's a privilege to live by one's gifts.' That speaks for me. I love to write and would not want to live my life any other way."

* * *

SHIFLET, Kenneth E(lwood) 1918-1978

OBITUARY NOTICE—See index for *CA* sketch: Born February 2, 1918, in Penn Yan, N.Y.; died November 14, 1978, in Washington, D.C. Military officer, educator, and author. Shiflet was best known for his service in Africa, Sicily, and Italy during World War II and for his membership on General Westmoreland's staff during the Vietnam War. Although he did not begin to write until after World War II, Shiflet produced two novels, *The Valiant Strain* and *The Convenient Coward,* and several short stories for periodicals such as *Esquire* and *Cosmopolitan.* Obituaries and other sources: *Washington Post,* November 16, 1978.

* * *

SHIH, Chung-wen

PERSONAL: Born in Nanking, China; came to the United States in 1948, naturalized citizen, 1960; daughter of Chokiang and Chia-pu (Fang) Shih. *Education:* St. Johns University, Shanghai, China, B.A., 1945; Duke University, M.A., 1949, Ph.D., 1955; postdoctoral study at Harvard University, 1960-61. *Home:* 2500 Virginia Ave. N.W., #602-S, Washington, D.C. 20037. *Office:* Department of East Asian Languages and Literatures, George Washington University, Washington, D.C. 20052.

CAREER: King's College, Briarcliff Manor, N.Y., assistant professor of English, 1955-56; University of Bridgeport, Bridgeport, Conn., assistant professor of English, 1956-60; Stanford University, Stanford, Calif., assistant professor of Chinese, 1961-64; George Washington University, Washing-

ton, D.C., associate professor, 1965-71, professor of Chinese, 1971—, head of department of East Asian languages and literatures, 1971—. *Awards, honors:* American Association of University Women, fellowship, 1964-65; Social Science Research Council fellowship, 1976-77.

WRITINGS: Injustice to Tou O, Cambridge University Press, 1972; *The Golden Age of Chinese Drama: Yuan Tsachu,* Princeton University Press, 1976. Contributor to *China Quarterly.*

WORK IN PROGRESS: Historical Records, on first-century China; *Twentieth-Century Chinese Drama.*

* * *

SHIMIN, Symeon 1902-

PERSONAL: Born November 1, 1902, in Astrakhan, Russia; came to United States, 1902; naturalized citizen, 1927; separated; children: Tonia, Toby. *Education:* Studied with George Luks, 1920-22, and at Cooper Union. *Residence:* New York, N.Y.

CAREER: Writer, illustrator, and painter. Exhibited drawings from *The Paint Box Sea* and *The Pair of Shoes* at Portland Museum, Portland, Ore. *Awards, honors:* Received award for a painting in the Department of Justice Building in Washington, D.C., 1939; Purchase Award from the Walter Chrysler Museum, First Provincetown Festival; certificate of excellence from American Institute of Graphic Arts, 1955 and 1957; two Christopher Awards; has received numerous citations, including a citation from U.S. Treasury Department for a war poster, citation for merit from Society of Illustrators, 1964, and children's books citation from Brooklyn Museum-New York Public Library.

WRITINGS—All self-illustrated: *I Wish There Were Two of Me,* Warne, 1976; *A Special Birthday,* McGraw, 1976.

Illustrator of over forty books, including: Joseph Krumgold, *Onion John,* Crowell, 1959; R. Wilson, *Outdoor Wonderland,* Lothrop, 1961; Aileen Fisher, *Listen Rabbit,* Crowell, 1964; B. Schweitzer, *One Small Blue Bead,* Macmillan, 1965; G. Cretan, *All Except Sammy* (Junior Literary Guild selection), Little, Brown, 1966; Millicent Selsam, *All Kinds of Babies,* Scholastic Book Services, 1967; Aline Glasgow, *The Pair of Shoes,* Dial, 1970; Doris H. Lund, *The Paint Box Sea,* McGraw, 1972.

SIDELIGHTS: Shimin is primarily self-taught. At fifteen he was apprenticed to a commercial artist; 1929 and 1930 were spent in France and Spain, studying El Greco and Goya, as well as other old masters and contemporary painters. He wrote that his aim in illustrating is "to develop a style that will express unmistakably [his] preoccupation with the contemporary scene." His favorite book illustrations are *One Small Blue Bead, Dance in the Desert, A Special Birthday,* and *I Wish There Were Two of Me.*

Shimin explained to an interviewer that he did not plan to be an artist: "I always wanted to be a musician. I never drew as a child. I never thought about drawing. I didn't know what *a painter* meant nor what *painting* meant. Then one day—the next day or the next week of my childhood, it seems—I drew. And I have never stopped drawing!"

Concerning his work routine, Shimin said: "I don't work steadily at book illustration. I illustrate for a time and then stop to devote myself to painting. . . . In doing book illustrations, I always use live models since I am a figurative artist. I do dozens of drawings from each sketch, working and reworking until I am satisfied—until I feel the illustrations are perfect. I work in watercolor; recently I've been illustrating in acrylics. I like to allow about six weeks to do a book. I absolutely hate deadlines!''

Shimin added: ''Art means everything to me. It is my life. It is me. . . . I like all kinds of art if it is done with conviction.''

BIOGRAPHICAL/CRITICAL SOURCES: Lee B. Hopkins, *Books Are by People,* Citation Press, 1969.

* * *

SHIPLETT, June Lund 1930-

PERSONAL: Born June 17, 1930, in Mayfield Heights, Ohio; daughter of Arthur Ellsworth (a factory worker) and Gladys Margaret (Eames) Lund; married Charles Eugene Shiplett (a lift truck operator), January 7, 1950; children: Maureen (Mrs. Robert Segal), Geraldine Shiplett Sease, Yvonne, Laura. *Education:* Attended high school in Mayfield Heights, Ohio. *Religion:* Christian. *Residence:* Mentor-on-the-Lake, Ohio. *Agent:* Michael Larsen/Elizabeth Pomada, 1029 Jones St., San Francisco, Calif. 94109.

CAREER: Ohio Bell Telephone, Mayfield Heights, switchboard operator, 1948-50; Answering Service, Inc., Mayfield Heights, switchboard operator, 1967-74; Professional Answering Service, Mentor, Ohio, switchboard operator, 1974-77; writer, 1977—.

WRITINGS: The Raging Winds of Heaven (historical romance), New American Library, 1978; *The Long Way Home* (historical romance), Pocket Books, 1979.

WORK IN PROGRESS: Two sequels to *The Raging Winds of Heaven,* for New American Library; a novel set in Texas shortly after the Civil War.

SIDELIGHTS: June Shiplett writes: ''My motivation is strictly to entertain. There are enough people in the world trying to put across messages, but I don't think there are enough books written solely for entertainment. The world revolves around love, no matter how much some people try to say differently, and truly good love stories with romance and adventure are hard to come by, especially those that take place in the United States. With my writing I hope to make people aware that this country's history can be as exciting and romantically adventurous as were the French Revolution and the Crusades.

''Too many of today's historical romances are not true historical romances. Because a few excellent authors included sex in the love scenes they wrote and the books ended up on the bestseller lists, publishers and some writers have decided all that's needed to sell a book is a time period somewhere in the eighteenth or nineteenth century and sex. Of all the historical romances written, only those with good plots and a strong love story have reached the bestseller lists, regardless of the amount of sex in the books.

''Although I do not write historical romance exclusively, I prefer it, perhaps because I love history. Research is part of the fun of writing, and it's surprising what new incidents we can learn about. It took me thirteen years from the time I first decided to write a book to the day my first novel appeared on the bookstands. A long time, but well worth it. I only hope I can continue to write about love in all its aspects.

''From my biography it sounds as if I came from an environment far removed from the arts, but statements are many times misleading. My grandfather, Harry Gordon Eames, was an old-time vaudevillian, my brother was in show business when he was quite young, I was exposed to music and drama at an early age, and both my parents were avid read-

ers. From the moment I learned to read I've been in love with words, so I guess writing was natural for me. Since the type of books I write is the type of books I like to read, my only hope is that others will enjoy them too.''

* * *

SHIPPY, Richard W. 1927-

PERSONAL: Born May 7, 1927, in Kalamazoo, Mich.; son of James M. and Emma (Williams) Shippy; married Joanne Louise Griffin (a counselor), September 23, 1950; children: Kathleen, Kevin, Brian, Drew. *Education:* Attended University of Kentucky, 1944; Northwestern University, B.S., 1951. *Politics:* Democrat. *Religion:* None. *Home:* 1056 Garman Rd., Akron, Ohio 44313. *Office:* Akron Beacon Journal, 44 East Exchange, Akron, Ohio 44328.

CAREER/WRITINGS: Akron Beacon Journal, Akron, Ohio, film, drama, and television critic. *Military service:* Served in U.S. Army.

SIDELIGHTS: Asked by *CA* what motivated him, Shippy replied: ''Motivation? How about a genuine respect for the English language.''

Shippy also told *CA* he wrote ''political speeches for radic-lib candidates who promised to vote for Richard Nixon's impeachment.''

* * *

SHORTALL, Leonard W.

PERSONAL: Born in Seattle, Wash.; married; children: three. *Education:* Attended University of Washington. *Address:* c/o Golden Press, Western Publishing Co., Inc., 1220 Mound Ave., Racine, Wis. 53404.

CAREER: Illustrator; also worked in the field of advertising. *Awards, honors:* Garden State Children's Book Award, 1977, for *Encyclopedia Brown Lends a Hand* by Donald J. Sobol.

WRITINGS—All self-illustrated; all published by Morrow, except as noted: *Country Snowplow,* 1960; *John and His Thumbs,* 1961; *Sam's First Fish,* 1962; *Davey's First Boat,* 1963; *Danny on the Lookout,* 1964; *Ben on the Ski Trail,* 1965, reprinted, Western Publishing, 1976; *The Hat Book,* Golden Press, 1965; *Steve's First Pony Ride,* 1966; *Eric in Alaska,* 1967; *Andy, the Dog Walker,* 1968; *Peter in Grand Central Station,* 1969; *Jerry the Newsboy,* 1970; *Tod on the Tugboat,* 1971; *Tony's First Dive,* 1972; *Just-in-Time Joey,* 1973; *One Way: A Trip With Traffic Signs,* Prentice-Hall, 1975; *A Little Toad to the Rescue,* Golden Press, 1977.

Illustrator: Jerrold Beim, *Andy and the School Bus,* Morrow, 1947; Beim, *Country Fireman,* Morrow, 1948; Mabel Louise Robinson, *Back-Seat Driver,* Random House, 1949; Lilian Moore and Leone Adelson, *Old Rosie, the Horse Nobody Understood,* Random House, 1952; Moore and Adelson, *Terrible Mr. Twitmeyer,* Random House, 1952; Caary Paul Jackson, *Spice's Football,* Crowell, 1955; Robinson, *Skipper Riley,* Random House, 1955; Patricia Gray, *Heads Up,* Coward, 1956; Robinson, *Riley Goes to Obedience School,* Random House, 1956; Jeanne McGahey Hart, *Gloomy Erasmus,* Coward, 1957; Beim, *Country Mailman,* Morrow, 1958; Doris Faber, *Wonderful Tumble of Timothy Smith,* Knopf, 1958; Jean Fritz, *How to Read a Rabbit,* Coward, 1959; Patricia Lauber, *Adventure at Black Rock Cave,* Random House, 1959.

Illustrator: P. Lauber, *Champ: Gallant Collie,* Random House, 1960; Mary Stolz, *A Dog on Barkham Street,* Harper, 1960, reprinted, Dell, 1973; Fritz, *Tap, Tap, Lion—1, 2, 3,* Coward, 1962; Eve Rouke, *Never in a Hurry,* Guild Press, 1962; Eleanor Clymer, *Harry, the Wild West Horse,* Atheneum, 1963; Moore and Adelson, *Mr. Twitmeyer and the Poodle,* Random House, 1963; Stolz, *The Bully of Barkham Street,* Harper, 1963; Harold W. Felton, *Pecos Bill and the Mustang,* Prentice-Hall, 1965; Lauber, *Clarence Turns Sea Dog,* Random House, 1965; Daniel Mannix, *The Outcasts,* Dutton, 1965; Osmond Molarsky, *Piper, the Sailboat That Came Back,* Graphic Society Publishers, 1965; Dorothy Edwards Shuttlesworth, *ABC of Buses,* Doubleday, 1965; Jean Bothwell, *The Mystery Clock,* Dial, 1966; James W. English, *Tops in Troop 10,* Macmillan, 1966; Adelaide Holl, *Colors Are Nice,* Golden Press, 1966; Pauline L. Jensen, *Thicker Than Water,* Bobbs-Merrill, 1966; Elizabeth Vreeken, *One Day Everything Went Wrong,* Follett, 1966; J. Bothwell, *The Mystery Box,* Dial, 1967; Beth Brown, editor, *The Wonderful World of Horses,* Harper, 1967; Naomi Buchheimer, *I Know a Teacher,* Putnam, 1967; Cliff Faulknor, *The In-Betweener,* Little, Brown, 1967; Peter Paul Hilbert, *Zoo on the First Floor,* Coward, 1967; Thoeger Birkeland, *When the Cock Crows,* Coward, 1968; Christine Govan, *Phinny's Fine Summer,* World Publishing, 1968; Carol J. Farley, *Sergeant Finney's Family,* F. Watts, 1969; Wilfred McCormick, *Fullback in the Rough,* Prentice-Hall, 1969; Barbara Rinkoff, *Harry's Homemade Robot,* Crown, 1969; Emily West, *Mr. Alexander and the Witch,* Viking, 1969.

Illustrator: Patricia A. Anthony, *Animals Grow,* Putnam, 1970; C. Govan, *The Trash Pile Treasure,* World Publishing, 1970; Keo Felker Lazarus, *The Gismo,* Follett, 1970; Lois Duncan, *Hotel for Dogs,* Houghton, 1971; Sonia Levitin, *Rita, the Weekend Rat,* Atheneum, 1971; Rinkoff, *The Case of the Stolen Code Book,* Crown, 1971; Mary Jo Stephens, *Zoe's Zodiac,* Houghton, 1971; Thomas E. Tinsley, *Plants Grow,* Putnam, 1971; Hilary Beckett, *Rafael and the Raiders,* Dodd, 1972; Lee Kingman, *Georgina and the Dragon,* Houghton, 1972; Alison Prince, *The Red Jaguar,* Atheneum, 1972; Thomas Biddle Perera, *Louder and Louder,* F. Watts, 1973; Seymour Simon, *A Building on Your Street,* Holiday House, 1973; Barbara Shook Hazen, *Animal Manners,* Golden Press, 1974; David Protheroe, *More Social Science Projects You Can Do,* Prentice-Hall, 1974; Carolyn Lane, *The Winnemah Spirit,* Houghton, 1975; Martha Shapp, *Let's Find Out What Electricity Does,* revised edition, F. Watts, 1975; Stan Applebaum and Victoria Cox, *Going My Way?,* Harcourt, 1976; Wanda Cheyne, *Animal Crackers,* Rand McNally, 1976; Molly Cone, *Mishmash and the Venus Flytrap,* Houghton, 1976; Kathleen Savage and Margaret Siewert, *Bear Hunt,* Prentice-Hall, 1976.

Illustrator of "Encyclopedia Brown" series; written by Donald J. Sobol; published by Thomas Nelson: *Encyclopedia Brown, Boy Detective,* 1963; *. . . Finds the Clues,* 1966; *. . . Keeps the Peace,* 1969; *. . . Saves the Day,* 1970; *. . . Tracks Them Down,* 1971; *. . . Shows the Way,* 1972; *. . . Takes the Case,* 1973; *. . . Lends a Hand,* 1974; *. . . and the Case of the Dead Eagles,* 1975.

Also illustrator for several national magazines, including *Woman's Day, Redbook,* and *Farm Journal.**

*   *   *

SHORTER, Aylward 1932-
(Muganwa Nsiku Jensi)

PERSONAL: Born May 2, 1932, in London, England; son of Alan Wynn (an Egyptologist) and Joan (Dove) Shorter.

Education: Queen's College, Oxford, B.A. (second class honors), 1955, diploma (distinction), 1964, D.Phil., 1971; attended Pontifical Gregorian University, 1962-63. *Home and office:* Kipalapala Senior Seminary, Box 325, Tabora, Tanzania.

CAREER: Entered Society of Missionaries of Africa (White Fathers); ordained Roman Catholic priest, 1962; Gaba Pastoral Institute, Uganda, lecturer in social anthropology, 1968-77; Kipalapala Senior Seminary, Tabora, Tanzania, lecturer in African theology and African religions, 1977—. Part-time lecturer at Makerere University, 1969-73, moderator in theology, 1972-75; Downside Visiting Lecturer in African Religions at University of Bristol, 1977—. Consultant for Secretariat for Non-Christians (Vatican), 1973—. *Military service:* British Army, King's African Rifles, 1951-52; became lieutenant.

MEMBER: Royal Anthropological Institute of Great Britain and Ireland (fellow). *Awards, honors:* Nuffield sociological scholarship, 1964.

WRITINGS: Nyungu-ya-Mawe: Leadership in Nineteenth-Century Tanzania, East African Publishing House, 1969; (with Njelu Mulugala) *Nyungu-ya-Mawe: Mtawala Shujaa wa Kinyamwezi,* East African Literature Bureau, 1971; (with Eugene Kataza) *Missionaries to Yourselves: African Catechists Today,* Geoffrey Chapman, 1972; *The Theology of Mission,* Mercier Press, 1972; *Chiefship in Western Tanzania,* Clarendon Press, 1972; (translator) Michael Kayoya, *My Father's Footprints,* East African Publishing House, 1973; *African Culture and the Christian Church,* Geoffrey Chapman, 1973; *East African Societies,* Routledge & Kegan Paul, 1974; *Prayer in the Religious Traditions of Africa,* Oxford University Press (East Africa), 1975; *African Christian Theology,* Geoffrey Chapman, 1975; (with Benezeri Kisembo and Laurenti Magesa) *African Christian Marriage,* Geoffrey Chapman, 1977; (editor) *Church and Marriage in Eastern Africa,* Gaba Pastoral Institute, 1977; also editor of *African Christian Spirituality.* Contributor to African studies and theology journals, once under pseudonym Muganwa Nsiku Jensi.

WORK IN PROGRESS: Priest in the Village: Experiences of African Community.

SIDELIGHTS: Shorter writes: "The motivation for my interest in African religion and anthropology was provided by my army experience in East Africa, 1951-52, and by fieldwork for my doctorate in anthropology in Tanzania, 1964-70."

*   *   *

SIEGEL, Eli 1902-1978

OBITUARY NOTICE—See index for *CA* sketch: Born August 16, 1902, in Dvinsk, Latvia; died November 8, 1978, in New York, N.Y. Literary critic and poet best known as the founder of aesthetic realism, a concept defined by Siegel as "the art of liking the world and oneself at the same time, by seeing the world and oneself as aesthetic opposites." He wrote criticism, including volumes on William Carlos Williams and Henry James. His poetry books include *Hot Afternoons Have Been in Montana* and *Hail, American Development.* Obituaries and other sources: *Who's Who in World Jewry,* Pitman, 1972; *Contemporary Poets,* 2nd edition, St. Martin's, 1975; *The Writers Directory, 1976-78,* St. Martin's, 1976; *Who's Who in America,* 40th edition, Marquis, 1978; *New York Times,* November 10, 1978.

SIEGELMAN, James Howard   1951-
(Jim Siegelman)

PERSONAL: Born January 31, 1951, in Cleveland, Ohio; son of Leonard P. (in business) and Arline P. (an artist) Siegelman. *Education:* Harvard University, B.A. (cum laude), 1973; graduate study at Trinity College, Cambridge, 1973-74. *Residence:* New York, N.Y.

CAREER: Free-lance writer, communication researcher, editor, illustrator, and magazine design consultant, 1969—. Member of "Cambridge Footlights" (musical comedy revue), 1973-74. *Awards, honors:* Lieutenant Charles Henry Fiske III Fellowship for Trinity College, Cambridge, 1973-74; runner-up in the satire category of Annual Writers awards from *Playboy* magazine, 1975.

WRITINGS—Under name Jim Siegelman: (With Jerry Ames) *The Book of Tap: Recovering America's Long Lost Dance,* McKay, 1977; (with Flo Conway) *Snapping: America's Epidemic of Sudden Personality Change,* Lippincott, 1978. Contributor to *Encyclopedia of Dance and Ballet.* Author of "The Presspasser," a column distributed by Universal Press Syndicate to twenty-six newspapers, 1972-73. Special feature writer for *Detroit News,* 1974. Staff editor and writer for *Playboy,* 1973, and for *Harper's Weekly,* 1974-76. Member of *Harvard Lampoon* staff, 1969-73, president, 1971.

WORK IN PROGRESS—Under name Jim Siegelman: nonfiction and fiction books; communication research projects; a television documentary and mini-series; a musical.

SIDELIGHTS: Siegelman writes: "I'm interested in ideas and information, and in making new work in the hard sciences, communication, philosophy, literature, dance, and music accessible and, wherever possible, entertaining to the general reader."

Siegelman supplied some descriptions of his books. He explained that *Snapping: America's Epidemic of Sudden Personality Change* is "an investigation of the impact on human awareness, behavior, and personality of the communication techniques employed by America's religous cults and mass-marketed self-help therapies, and an exploration of how information and experience, in general, may bring about drastic alterations of the fundamental workings of the brain." *The Book of Tap: Recovering America's Long Lost Dance* is "a comprehensive, illustrated history of America's only indigenous dance form."

AVOCATIONAL INTERESTS: Classical and jazz musician.

*   *   *

SIEGELMAN, Jim
See SIEGELMAN, James Howard

*   *   *

SIGELSCHIFFER, Saul   1902-

PERSONAL: Born October 16, 1902, in New York, N.Y.; son of Hyman L. (in insurance) and Lena (Klinger) Sigelschiffer; married Rita Weiss (a teacher), July 5, 1936; children: Tamar (Mrs. Michael Naaman). *Education:* City College (now of the City University of New York), B.A., 1924; New York University, J.D., 1928, J.S.D., 1934. *Religion:* Orthodox Judaism. *Home:* 36 Carwall Ave., Mount Vernon, N.Y. 10552.

CAREER: Elementary school teacher in New York City, 1924-28; junior high school teacher of languages and social

sciences, 1926-35, high school teacher of history, 1935-40; principal of elementary school in New York City, 1940-48, and junior high school, 1948-72. Yeshiva University, New York City, instructor, 1948-58, professor of education and coordinator of department of religious education, 1958-65.

WRITINGS: The American Conscience: The Drama of the Lincoln-Douglas Debates (History Book Club selection), Horizon Press, 1973.

SIDELIGHTS: Sigelschiffer writes: "When Abraham Lincoln was asked by his friend, Jesse W. Fell, to write his autobiography as an aid to his presidential possibilities, he wrote: 'There is not much of it, for the reason, I suppose, that there is not much of me.'

"I borrow Lincoln's words in writing about myself because I have written just one book. I imagine other things about myself may not be of much interest.

"My book is about a phase of Lincoln's career which is not well-known to the general public—his debates with Stephen A. Douglas, the 'Little Giant,' which were so fateful to the course of United States history and to the careers of both men.

"As a teacher of high school history, I became interested in these debates because of their scant treatment in the history books. When I searched for a book on the subject, I found none. There were the texts of the debates, articles and treatises which dealt with one or more aspects, and biographies and general historical works which gave partial accounts. An overall view and the great drama of the event were lacking.

"I therefore determined to write a book for the student, the scholar, the teacher, and the educated layman that would tell the complete story. I spent more than a decade in research, including visits to the sites of the debates and interviews with local people and authorities.

"My chief interests, aside from my professional work, have been the Jewish people and the land of Israel, where I have a home in the village of Hofit and spend part of each year."

AVOCATIONAL INTERESTS: Tennis—Sigelschiffer is a life umpire of U.S. Tennis Association, and has officiated at U.S. national championships and at Wimbledon.

*   *   *

SILONE, Ignazio   1900-1978

OBITUARY NOTICE—See index for *CA* sketch: Born May 1, 1900, in Pescina, Italy; died, 1978, in Geneva, Switzerland. Politician and writer. Silone helped found the Italian Communist party in 1921. However, by the 1930's, he had become disenchanted with Communist policy. When Mussolini gained power, he exiled Silone to Switzerland. Silone's most well-known works, *Fontamara* and *Bread and Wine,* are both regarded as extremely anti-fascist pieces. In *Bread and Wine* the author examined the ambiguity of the Italian peasant's inability to comprehend Communism. His writing style was marked by poetic imagery contained within a simple style. Obituaries and other sources: *Encyclopedia of World Literature in the Twentieth Century,* updated version, Ungar, 1967; *Cassell's Encyclopaedia of World Literature,* revised edition, Morrow, 1973; *Who's Who in the World,* 2nd edition, Marquis, 1973; *Who's Who in Twentieth Century Literature,* Holt, 1976; *The International Who's Who,* Europa, 1978; *Who's Who,* 130th edition, St. Martin's, 1978; *Time,* September 4, 1978; *AB Bookman's Weekly,* November 6, 1978.

SILVESTRI, Richard 1944-

PERSONAL: Born June 11, 1944, in New York, N.Y.; son of Anthony Joseph and Connie (Constantino) Silvestri; married Susan Cowles (a speech therapist), April 8, 1972. *Education:* City College of the City University of New York, B.S., 1967; Kent State University, M.A., 1969, Ph.D., 1973. *Home:* 590 Doremus Ave., Glen Rock, N.J. 07452. *Agent:* Lisa Collier, Collier Associates, 280 Madison Ave., New York, N.Y. 10016. *Office:* Comprehensive Counseling Center, 5 Sicomac Rd., North Haledon, N.J. 07508.

CAREER: Worked as psychologist (as alternate service to military duty), Apple Creek State Hospital, Apple Creek, Ohio; Comprehensive Counseling Center, North Haledon, N.J., director, 1973—. Private practice in clinical psychology, 1973—. Assistant professor at William Paterson College, 1973—. Adviser to Murray House (for the retarded). *Member:* American Psychological Association, National Register of Health Care Providers, New Jersey Psychological Association.

WRITINGS: CT: The Astounding New Confrontation Therapy, Morrow, 1978. Contributor to psychology journals.

WORK IN PROGRESS: Confrontation Therapy for Children.

SIDELIGHTS: Silvestri writes: "Most psychological problems—including many of the ones I see in my practice—could be treated quickly and effectively by the average person with a minimum of training. If there is any doubt about the essential truth of this, consider the self-help groups: Alcoholics Anonymous, Parents Without Partners, Overeaters Anonymous. In each case these programs are the treatment of choice. Self-help skills, along with the dismantling of the psychotherapist's mystique, should be taught, starting with the earliest grades. It would be nice to see this happen with the other professions as well."

*   *   *

SIMMEL, Johannes M(ario) 1924-

PERSONAL: Born April 7, 1924, in Vienna, Austria; son of Walter (a chemist) and Helena (a teacher; maiden name, Schneider) Simmel; married Helena Maass (a reporter), March 19, 1970. *Education:* Graduated from Political Science and Research Institute, Vienna. *Home and office:* Sun Tower, Monte Carlo, Monaco. *Politics:* Social democrat.

CAREER: Chemist, 1944-45; writer, 1945—. Interpreter for U.S. Government in Vienna, Austria, 1945-47; editor and reporter for numerous German newspapers, 1947-60; film-script writer in Germany, 1950; *Quick* magazine, Munich, Germany, chief reporter and ghost writer, 1951-61. *Member:* Authors Guild of America, Verband Deutscher Schriftsteller. *Awards, honors:* First Prize from Mannheim National Theatre, 1960, for "Der Schulfreund"; recipient of numerous awards for screenplays.

*WRITINGS—*All novels, except as noted: *Ein Autobus gross wie die Welt* (juvenile), Jungbrunnen Verlag, 1949, reprinted, Droemer Knaur, 1977; *Weinen ist streng Verboten* (juvenile), Jungbrunnen Verlag, 1950, reprinted, Droemer Knaur, 1977; *Meine Mutter darf es nie erfahren* (juvenile), Jungbrunnen Verlag, 1951, reprinted, Droemer Knaur, 1977; *Es muss nicht immer Kaviar sein,* Schweizer Verlagshaus, 1959, translation by James Cleugh published as *It Can't Always Be Caviar,* Doubleday, 1965, published as *The Monte Cristo Cover-Up,* Popular Library, 1976; *Der Schulfreund* (play), Rowohlt Verlag, 1960; *The Wind and the Rain,* Popular Library, 1978.

Published by Paul Zsolnay Verlag: *Begegnung im Nebel* (collection of short stories), 1947; *Mich Wundert dass ich so froehlich bin,* 1948; *Das geheime Brot,* 1950; *Ich gestehe alles,* 1952, translation published as *I Confess,* Popular Library, 1977; *Gott schuetzt die Liebenden,* 1954; *Affaire Nina B.,* 1957, translation published as *The Affair of Nina B.,* Popular Library, 1978.

Published by Droemer Knaur: *Bis zur bitteren Neige,* 1962, translation by Rosemary Mays published as *To the Bitter End,* Popular Library, 1970, published as *The Berlin Connection,* Popular Library, 1977; *Liebe ist nur ein Wort,* 1963, translation by Mays published as *Love Is Just a Word,* McGraw, 1969; *Lieb Vaterland Magst Ruhig sein,* 1965, translation by Richard Winston and Clara Winston published as *Dear Fatherland,* Random House, 1969, published as *Double Agent: Triple Cross,* Popular Library, 1977; *All Menschen werden Brueder,* 1967, translation by Mays published as *Cain '67,* McGraw, 1971, published as *Cain Conspiracy,* Popular Library, 1976; *Und Jimmy ging zum Regenbogen,* 1969; *Der Stoff aus dem die Traeume sind,* 1972; *Die Antwort kennt nur der Wind,* 1974; *Niemand ist eine Insel,* 1976; *Hurra Wir leben noch* (title means "Halleluja, We're Still Alive"), 1978.

Also author of numerous television plays and of thirty-six screenplays for international productions, 1948-65. Contributor of articles to many newspapers.

SIDELIGHTS: Johannes Simmel told *CA* he is a proud social democrat whose books relate to current issues, such as the revival of Nazism, the lost generation, divided Berlin, mentally disabled children, and "the wave of drugs and alcohol which is drowning us." He described his latest novel, *Hurra Wir leben noch* ("Halleluja, We're Still Alive") as the humorous but thought-provoking story of a man and his experiences over the past thirty "chaotic" years.

Simmel called himself an analyst of our times who gears his novels toward everyone from the laborer to the intellectual. He observed that it is because of this formula that his books have become an international success.

Reviewing *Dear Fatherland,* C. Bryan wrote in the *New York Times Book Review* that "what marks it as the maturation of the realistic spy adventure is the barely restrained anger of its author." A *New Statesman* reviewer considered the characters of the novel, however, to be "too naively drawn to support the intellectual strain of the manoeuvres in which they engage."

Simmel reported that his books have been translated into eighteen languages and forty-five million copies have been sold. Mergar Memorial Library of Boston University houses a collection of his original works.

BIOGRAPHICAL/CRITICAL SOURCES: New York Times Book Review, April 13, 1969; *New Statesman,* August 15, 1969.

*   *   *

SIMMONDS, A(ndrew) J(effrey) 1943-

PERSONAL: Born February 6, 1943, in Preston, Idaho; son of Grant (a farmer) and Cleo (Coburn) Simmonds; married Jeannie Martha Foersterling (a librarian), May 20, 1977; children: Andrew Charles. *Education:* Utah State University, B.S., 1965, M.A., 1966. *Politics:* Republican. *Religion:* Episcopalian. *Home address:* Black Jack-on-the-Flats, Trenton, Utah 84338. *Office:* Library, Utah State University, Logan, Utah 84322.

CAREER: Utah State University, Logan, special collections librarian and university archivist, 1966—. *Member:* Society of American Archivists, Conference of Intermountain Archivists (member of governing council, 1973-75), Utah State Historical Society, Cache Valley Historical Society (president, 1974-75).

WRITINGS: (Editor) *Name Index to the Library of Congress Collection of Mormon Diaries,* Western Text Society, 1970; *On the Big Range: A Centennial History of Cornish and Trenton, Utah, 1870-1970,* Utah State University Press, 1970; (editor) Lars Frederickson, *History of Weston, Idaho,* Western Text Society, 1972; *The Gentile Comes to Cache Valley: A Study of the Logan Apostasies of 1874 and the Establishment of Non-Mormon Churches in Cache Valley, 1873-1913,* Utah State University Press, 1976; (contributor) Douglas D. Alder, editor, *Cache Valley: Essays on Her Past and People,* Utah State University Press, 1976. Author of "Looking Back," a column in *Valley,* 1975—. Contributor of articles and reviews to western history journals. Contributing editor of *Valley.*

WORK IN PROGRESS: Reluctant Gentile: The Life and Times of A. M. Simmonds, 1844-1925, completion expected in 1980; *History of Cache Valley, Utah-Idaho,* completion expected in 1982.

SIDELIGHTS: Simmonds writes: "I am a localist with major interests in the history of my home area, Cache Valley. The valley lies astride the Utah-Idaho border, about seventy-five miles north of Salt Lake City.

"I am a sixth-generation 'Cachian' and one of the small minority in the valley who are native non-Mormons. It is the 'whys' of my ancestors' alienation from the Mormon church that I trace in *The Gentile Comes to Cache Valley.*

"My home is a farm which I work in addition to my profession as an archivist. Parts of the land have belonged only to the Indians and my family. This association with place colors my whole being and, I trust, makes me a better local historian."

AVOCATIONAL INTERESTS: Genealogical research, painting, carpentry.

*   *   *

SIMMONS, Mary Kay 1933-

PERSONAL: Born October 24, 1933, in New York; daughter of Louis Garner (a manufacturer) and Bernadine (Hogan) Simmons; children: two. *Politics:* "Democrat in America." *Religion:* Roman Catholic. *Residence:* Dublin, Ireland. *Address:* c/o Pocket Books, Simon & Schuster Bldg., 1230 Ave. of the Americas, New York, N.Y. 10020.

CAREER: Has worked as actress, drama teacher, junior account executive, paid political campaigner, and stringer; writer. *Member:* American Society of Composers, Authors, and Publishers, National Association of Journalists and Writers, Mystery Writers of America, Authors Guild.

WRITINGS—Gothic and romantic suspense novels; all published by Dell, except as noted: *The Hermitage,* 1970; *The Captain's House,* 1970; *The Year of the Rooster,* Delacorte, 1971; *Megan,* 1971; *The Diamonds of Alcazar,* 1972; *The Willow Pond,* 1972; *Cameron Hill,* 1972; *The Gypsy Grove,* 1974; *The Girl With the Key,* 1974; *Saracen Gardens,* 1974; *Flight From Rivers Edge,* 1975; *Haggard's Cove,* 1975; *The Kill Cross,* 1975; *Smuggler's Gate,* 1976; *The Clock Face,* 1976; *Dark Holiday,* 1976; *Fire in the Blood,* Pocket Books, 1977; *Domino,* Pocket Books, 1978. Author of song lyrics and a libretto for an opera.

WORK IN PROGRESS: The Cornishman (tentative title), for Pocket Books; an Irish saga.

AVOCATIONAL INTERESTS: Politics, reading, travel, puzzles of all kinds, all music, history, vegetable gardening.*

*   *   *

SIMON, Paul 1928-

PERSONAL: Born November 29, 1928, in Eugene, Ore.; son of Martin Paul (a minister) and Ruth (Troemel) Simon; married Jeanne Hurley (an attorney), April 21, 1960; children: Sheila, Martin. *Education:* Attended University of Oregon, 1945-46, and Dana College, 1946-48. *Residence:* Carbondale, Ill. 62901. *Office:* 227 Cannon Building, Washington, D.C. 20515.

CAREER: Troy Tribune, Troy, Ill., publisher, 1948-66; member of Illinois House of Representatives, 1955-63; senator in Illinois, 1963-69; lieutenant governor of Illinois, 1969-72; Sangamon State University, Springfield, Ill., professor of public affairs, 1973-74; U.S. House of Representatives, Washington, D.C., congressman from 24th Illinois district, 1975—. *Military service:* U.S. Army, Counterintelligence Corps, 1951-53. *Member:* Lions International, National Association for the Advancement of Colored People, National Urban League, American Legion, Veterans of Foreign Wars, Lutheran Human Relations Association, Sigma Delta Chi. *Awards, honors:* Award for distinguished reporting of state and local government, American Political Science Association, 1957; LL.D. from Dana College, 1965, Concordia Teachers College, 1968, Lincoln Christian College, 1969, and Loyola University, 1969; D.Litt. from McKendree College, 1965; D.C.L. from Greenville College, 1968; John F. Kennedy Institute of Politics fellow at Harvard University, 1973; named best legislator seven times by Independent Voters of Illinois.

WRITINGS: Lovejoy: Martyr to Freedom, Concordia, 1964; *Lincoln's Preparation for Greatness,* University of Oklahoma Press, 1965; *A Hungry World,* Concordia, 1966; (with wife, Jeanne Hurley Simon) *Protestant-Catholic Marriages Can Succeed,* Association Press, 1967; *The Ombudsman in Illinois: An Experiment in Government,* Springfield, 1970; *You Want to Change the World? So Change It!,* Thomas Nelson, 1971; (with brother, Arthur Simon) *The Politics of World Hunger: Grass-Roots Politics and World Poverty,* Harper Magazine Press, 1973. Wrote weekly columns "Sidelights From Springfield," distributed to over three hundred newspapers, 1955-72, and "P.S./Washington," 1975—. Contributor of articles to periodicals including *Harper's, Saturday Review, New Republic,* and *Columbia Journalism Review.*

SIDELIGHTS: Paul Simon's accomplishments began at an early age. At sixteen he entered the University of Oregon to study journalism. Three years later he left school to buy a defunct weekly newspaper. With the help of a $3,600 loan underwritten by the local Lions Club, he purchased the *Troy Tribune,* thus becoming the youngest editor-publisher in the country. He used his paper to expose syndicate gambling connections with government officials in Madison County, Ill., and because of this work he was called to testify before the U.S. Senate's Crime Investigating Committee in 1951.

During his career as an Illinois representative, Simon married Jeanne Hurley, who was also serving in the Illinois House of Representatives at that time. They were the first and only husband-wife team in the history of the Illinois general assembly. In his general assembly career Simon won passage of forty-six major pieces of legislation, including a law establishing the high school equivalency (G.E.D.) test in that state, a law creating the Illinois Arts Council, and the state's first "open meeting" law. He is known as a progressive on social issues and a watchdog on public expenditures. Simon's frank discussions of corruption in government have earned him the Benedict Arnold Award, a spoofing honor, from his fellow state senators.

Simon's book, *The Politics of World Hunger,* written with his brother, a Lutheran minister, discusses the history of the U.S. foreign aid programs and the problems of developing nations. While Bruce Barr felt that the Simon brothers' inexperience in the science of agronomy rendered their suggestions for better world production unfeasible, T. P. Melady praised the book as a "treasure house of information on the economic problems of developing peoples."

Simon told *CA:* "One of the problems that has concerned me most during more than two decades in office has been the question of public confidence in elected officials. I have made a complete and detailed disclosure of my personal income, assets, and liabilities every year since 1955, because I think disclosure is the best way to deal with conflict of interest problems that arise during public service. We need stronger disclosure laws at both the federal and state level.

"Another principal issue I've been dealing with for a number of years is the twin problem of world population and hunger. Doing something about overpopulation and scarcity of food is the major problem we face for the remainder of this century. When John F. Kennedy took office in 1961, he set two goals for this nation: putting a man on the moon and wiping hunger from the face of the earth. The more glamorous of the two we have achieved. But we have a long way to go on the more important of the two challenges."

BIOGRAPHICAL/CRITICAL SOURCES: Harper's, September, 1964; *America,* September 29, 1973; *National Review,* November 9, 1973; *Critic,* January/February, 1974.

* * *

SIMON, William E(dward) 1927-

PERSONAL: Born November 27, 1927, in Paterson, N.J.; son of Charles (an insurance broker) and Eleanor (Kearns) Simon; married Carol Girard, 1950; children: two sons, five daughters. *Education:* Lafayette College, B.A., 1952. *Residence:* New Vernon, N.J. *Office:* Booz Allen & Hamilton, Inc., 245 Park Ave., New York, N.Y. 10017.

CAREER: Union Securities, New York City, 1952-57, began as staff member, assistant vice president and manager of municipal trading department, 1955-57; Weeden & Co., New York City, vice-president, 1957-64; Salomon Brothers, New York City, senior partner, 1964-72; Federal Energy Office, Washington, D.C., chairman, 1973-74; U.S. Treasury Department, Washington, D.C., deputy secretary, 1973-74, secretary of treasury, 1974-77; Booz Allen & Hamilton, Inc., New York City, senior adviser, 1977—. Senior consultant, Blyth Eastman Dillon & Co., Inc. Chairman of National Energy Foundation; chairman of Wilson Council, Woodrow Wilson International Center for Scholars; finance chairman of American Institute for Public Service; president of John M. Olin Foundation. Member of public review board, Arthur Anderson & Co.; member of international advisory board, Center for Public Resources; member of board of overseers, Hoover Institution on War, Revolution and Peace, Stanford University. Member of board of directors of International Rescue Committee, Alternative Educational Foundation, Inc., Xerox Corp., Olin Corp., Dart Industries, Bessemer Securities, Interpublic Group of Companies, INA Corp., Citibank/Citicorp., and Damon Runyon-Walter Winchell Cancer Fund. Member of board of trustees of United States Council of International Chamber of Commerce, National Executive Service Corps, Georgetown University, Lafayette College, Hudson Institute, and Freedom House. *Member:* U.S. Olympic Committee (national chairman of fund raising committee; treasurer), Securities Industry Association (former director), Association of Primary Dealers in U.S. Government Securities (founder; former president).

WRITINGS: A Time for Truth, Reader's Digest Press, 1978. Author of government documents on inflation, tax cuts, and food stamps.

SIDELIGHTS: In *A Time for Truth* William E. Simon discourses on his conservative philosophy. Denouncing government regulation and spendthrift congressmen as the causes of most economic problems, Simon predicts that Americans will witness the downfall of democracy if they do not protect their historic free enterprise system. According to Simon, the chief propagators of the anticapitalist trend in the United States are liberal intellectuals in foundations, in the media, and in academic institutions. He recommends that business stop supporting liberal news organizations and those universities which do not introduce students to conservative principles as well as collectivist theory.

"Frightening" was the word James Tobin used to describe Simon's attack on academic institutions. He elaborated: "Mr. Simon's wholly undocumented assertion that teaching in American colleges and universities is just ideological indoctrination is ignorant slander of teachers and students." Tobin considered the former secretary of treasury's views to be neither original nor profound: "Mr. Simon is only the latest capitalist to complain that democracy and free speech bite the hand that feeds them.... It is superficial to attribute the anticapitalist trends he detects to the malice, error, ignorance, irresponsibility and ingratitude of a few intellectuals."

Edwin Warner's assessment of *A Time for Truth* was more favorable. He remarked that "Simon's harsh, free enterprise medicine is easy to take because it is spiced with considerable wit, especially at the expense of dissembling politicians." Warner believes that Simon's book and Irving Kristol's *Two Cheers for Capitalism* signal "a certain shift in conservative thinking. They are not so much polemical assaults on the left as probing critiques of their own faith. Such candid self-examination may give liberals genuine cause for alarm."

BIOGRAPHICAL/CRITICAL SOURCES: New York Times, December 5, 1973, August 5, 1978; *New York Times Book Review,* June 11, 1978; *Time,* June 26, 1978.

* * *

SIMONS, Joseph 1933-

PERSONAL: Born February 3, 1933, in Janesville, Wis.; son of Joseph B. (an accountant) and Helen (Farrington) Simons; married Jeanne Reidy (a teacher), May 22, 1969. *Education:* University of Notre Dame, B.S., 1957, M.S., 1961, Ph.D., 1967. *Office:* Department of Behavioral Sciences, Santa Rosa Junior College, Santa Rosa, Calif. 95401.

CAREER: University of Notre Dame, Notre Dame, Ind., dean of students, 1965-67, assistant professor of psychology, 1967-69; Santa Rosa Junior College, Santa Rosa, Calif., teacher of psychology, 1969—. Private practice of psychology. *Member:* American Psychological Association.

WRITINGS: Retreat Dynamics, Fides, 1967; *Risk of Loving,* Seabury, 1968; *Wisdom Child,* Herder & Herder, 1969; *Risk of Freedom,* Seabury, 1970; *The Human Art of Counseling,* Seabury, 1971; *Living Together,* Nelson-Hall, 1978; *The Search for Self,* Heath, in press.

WORK IN PROGRESS: An introductory psychology textbook.

SIDELIGHTS: Simons writes: "My entire life as a professional writer has been dedicated to my personal attempts to translate the jargon of psychology into the language of daily experiences. Out of such efforts has come an appreciation for life I would never have achieved in any other way. I feel pleased my work has been successful. However, I now know that even without publication success, my writing has adequately rewarded me with many fulfilling insights and experiences."

*   *   *

SINGER, Sarah 1915-

PERSONAL: Born July 4, 1915, in Brooklyn, N.Y.; daughter of Samuel (a merchant) and Rose (Dunetz) White; married Leon Singer (a dentist), November 23, 1938; children: Jack, Rachel. *Education:* New York University, B.A., 1934; also attended New School for Social Research, 1964 and 1965. *Religion:* Jewish. *Home:* 38 Stephan Marc Lane, New Hyde Park, N.Y. 11040.

CAREER: Poet, 1955—. Teacher at Hillside Hospital, Queens, N.Y., 1966-74. *Member:* Poetry Society of America (vice-president, 1974—), National League of American Pen Women (local poetry chairman, 1959—). *Awards, honors:* Stephen Vincent Benet Award from *Poet Lore,* 1968, for narrative poem "The Kid and the Devil," and 1971, for narrative poem "After the Beginning"; James Joyce Award from Poetry Society of America, 1972, for "Girl of Sumer"; Consuelo Ford Memorial Award, 1973, for lyric poem "Suffer the Little Children"; Gustav Davidson Award, 1974, for sonnet sequence "In Sickness and in Health"; award, 1975, for "Mrs. Hall"; Celia B. Wagner Memorial Award, 1976, for sonnet sequence "Let There Be Light"; Marion Doyle Memorial Award from National League of American Pen Women, 1976, for *After the Beginning;* drama award, 1977, for one-act play "Ride a Cockhorse"; poetry award, 1977, for "The Quarrel"; first prize in modern rhymed poetry category from National League of American Pen Women, 1978, for "Mrs. Hall"; Dellbrook Award from Dellbrook-Shenandoah Writers' Conference, 1978, for "Jacob and the Sisters."

WRITINGS: After the Beginning (poems), William Bauhan, 1975.

Plays: "Ride a Cockhorse" (one-act), first produced in New York City at the Institute for Advanced Studies in the Theatre Arts, January, 1966. Also author of "Thy Neighbor's Wife," (five scenes), neither published nor produced.

Contributor of poems to magazines. Consulting editor for *Poet Lore.*

WORK IN PROGRESS: Let There Be Light (tentative title), a book of poems.

SIDELIGHTS: Sarah Singer writes: "I write because I must. I am particularly interested in portraying people, their loves and hates, and their reactions to their own peculiar circumstances. Each is a living poem I try to translate into a poem composed of words and stanzas.

"Poetry for me is metaphor and music. It does not necessar-

ily have to rhyme, but it must leave no doubt in the reader's mind that it is verse, not prose. I do not go along with much of today's 'non-poetry' or prose poetry. The terms are contradictions in themselves.

"I have been a teacher as well as a poet. I have taught poetry and conducted writing workshops in a mental hospital, and have found mental patients to be particularly responsive to imagery and music."

*   *   *

SIZEMORE, Chris(tine) Costner 1927-
(Evelyn Lancaster)

PERSONAL: Born April 4, 1927, in Edgefield, S.C.; daughter of Acie (a county employee) and Zueline (Hastings) Costner; married Ralph White, December 18, 1946 (divorced, 1952); married Don Sizemore (an electrician), December 19, 1953; children: (first marriage) Taffy White Fecteau; (second marriage) Bobby. *Education:* Attended public school in Edgefield, S.C. *Politics:* Democrat. *Religion:* Methodist. *Home:* 2616 Armada St., Herndon, Va. 22070.

CAREER: Worked as a long distance telephone operator in Augusta, Ga., 1943-45; Chris' House of Cloth, Manassas, Va., owner, designer, and tailoring teacher, 1963-66; manager of ladies' specialty shops in Virginia, Maryland, and Washington, D.C., 1966-72; writer. *Member:* Northern Virginia Mental Health Association.

WRITINGS: (Under pseudonym Evelyn Lancaster, with James Poling) *Final Face of Eve,* McGraw, 1958; (with Elen Sain Pittillo) *I'm Eve,* Doubleday, 1977. Contributor of poetry to several newspapers.

WORK IN PROGRESS: Eve's Reflections, a book of poetry by other personalities as well as her own; *Tears and Laughter,* an account of her experiences and adjustments since revealing her identity; "Why Me," a play about multiple personality.

SIDELIGHTS: Richard Lingeman of the *New York Times* stated that *I'm Eve* is "a valuable mine of material on the genesis of mental illness and the mystery of personality, of the enemies we have within who sometimes seize control of our behavior." In the opening comments of her book, Chris Sizemore wrote: "This book was born because of my conviction that the true facts of my life were not known, and that I had a story to tell; because the world had the impression that I had recovered from my dissociative problem, multiple personality. I have known twenty-two personalities and have lived to tell of their demise."

The impression that the world had of her came mainly from three sources: the two books, *The Three Faces of Eve* and *The Final Face of Eve,* and the 1957 film, "The Three Faces of Eve," which starred Joanne Woodward. "Eve" or Sizemore, according to these sources, had only three personalities and was cured after psychiatric treatment. In reality, Sizemore had experienced some twenty-two distinct personalities and only now does she consider the possibility that the past has been laid to rest. She simply states that she has "a gut feeling that it is finally over." Perhaps proof of her feeling is evidenced by the way in which Sizemore handled the death of her father over a year ago. No new personality emerged to cope with this situation; Sizemore dealt with it "alone." This is important because death is considered to be one cause of her multiple personality problem. The first time Sizemore remembered "being aware" of another personality occurred when she witnessed the body of a drowned man being retrieved from an irrigation ditch near her home. In her book, she wrote: "The two men were slowly dragging the awkward body through the water to the bank beside the road. But there was someone else in the picture now, someone who had not been there when Christine closed her eyes. On the bridge looking directly down upon the scene in the water stood a little girl . . . the first thing Christine noticed was that her bright blue eyes were calm and unafraid." It is thought that Sizemore used multiple personalities as coping mechanisms to deal with situations that she could not accept.

Sizemore began writing her own story with the encouragement of her present psychiatrist, Dr. Tony Tsitos, and the support of her cousin and co-author, Elen Sain Pattillo. Published in 1977, *I'm Eve* was used as a form for therapy for Sizemore. Another aid in working through her dissociative problem was the emergence from her past life of hiding. Her former psychiatrist, Dr. Corbett Thigpen, thought it best that Sizemore hide her identity from both the medical profession and, more importantly, from the general public. He advised her not to see the film which was based on her life. According to the *New York Times,* Thigpen profited from her anonymous existence: he wrote the book, *The Three Faces of Eve,* and when "the movie rights to his book were sold, Dr. Thigpen persuaded Chris to sign a release that gave him the rights to her story 'forever.'"

When asked by *Newsday* to comment on the other personalities, Sizemore stated: "I liked Eve Black the most. She was honest. Not admirable in her traits. But she was honest to herself. . . . I liked the Bell Lady. She was generous and civic-minded and she considered the importance of the marriage and the children." Finally Sizemore said: "And I like myself. I'm not the greatest person in the world, but I can live with my principles. . . . I have my own identity now, and it's exciting."

AVOCATIONAL INTERESTS: Painting, writing poetry, rock hunting, classical music.

BIOGRAPHICAL/CRITICAL SOURCES: Corbett Hillsman Thigpen and H. M. Cleckley, *The Three Faces of Eve,* McGraw, 1957; Chris Sizemore, under pseudonym Evelyn Lancaster, and James Poling, *Final Face of Eve,* McGraw, 1958; *Washington Post,* September 14, 1975; Sizemore and Elen Sain Pittillo, *I'm Eve,* Doubleday, 1977; *Kirkus Reviews,* May 15, 1977; *New York Daily News,* July 25, 1977; *Women's Wear Daily,* July 25, 1977; *Los Angeles Times,* August 12, 1977; *Newsday,* August 17, 1977; *New York Times,* August 20, 1977; *People,* September 12, 1977; *London Daily Express,* September 16, 1977; *Saturday Evening Post,* March, 1978.

*   *   *

SLACK, Robert C(harles) 1914-

PERSONAL: Born January 12, 1914, in Pittsburgh, Pa.; son of T. Franklin and Ethel (Weckbecker) Slack; married Jeanne Getter, April 4, 1942; children: Carolyn, John, Thomas. *Education:* University of Pittsburgh, B.A., 1935, M.A., 1941, Ph.D., 1953. *Politics:* Conservative. *Religion:* Protestant. *Home:* 226 West Swissvale Ave., Pittsburgh, Pa. 15218. *Office:* Department of English, Carnegie-Mellon University, Pittsburgh, Pa. 15213.

CAREER: High school English teacher in Freeland, Pa., and Bridgeville, Pa., 1937-41; Carnegie-Mellon University, Pittsburgh, Pa., instructor, 1946-49, assistant professor, 1949-55, associate professor, 1955-67, professor of English, 1967—. Consultant to Westinghouse Electric. *Military service:* U.S. Army, Signal Corps, 1941-46; became captain.

Member: Modern Language Association of America, National Council of Teachers of English, Society of Technical Writers and Publishers, Conference on College Composition and Communication (member of executive committee, 1964-66), Pennsylvania Council of Teachers of English, Theta Chi, Pi Tau Phi, Sigma Kappa Phi.

WRITINGS: (Editor and contributor) *Bibliographies of Studies in Victorian Literature for the Ten Years, 1955-1964,* University of Illinois Press, 1967; (editor and author of introduction) Thomas Hardy, *Jude the Obscure,* Random House, 1967; (editor) *English Literature,* four volumes, Noble & Noble, 1968-69; (with Beekman W. Cottrell) *Write On!: A Preparation for College Composition,* Glencoe Press, 1971, 2nd edition published as *Writing,* 1978. Contributor of about twenty articles to scholarly journals. Editor of *Victorian Bibliography,* 1959-65.

WORK IN PROGRESS: An introductory approach to literature, publication by Glencoe Press expected in 1980; poems and short stories.

SIDELIGHTS: Slack writes: "Some of my published work is scholarly-critical (my major literary interest is in the Romantics and Victorians); some reflects my engagement in curricular development, seeking more effective ways to teach writing and literature. A few poems have been accepted for publication, and I am proud of these. I hope to add more poetry and some fiction to my list in the near future. I have also had a strong interest in music all along the way—from the days when I wrote arrangements for a large band and almost went into the field professionally." *Avocational interests:* European travel.

*   *   *

SLADE, Bernard
See NEWBOUND, Bernard Slade

*   *   *

SLATER, Peter Gregg 1940-

PERSONAL: Born June 3, 1940, in New York, N.Y.; son of Nathaniel (a comptroller) and Regina (a craftsperson; maiden name, Stern) Slater; married Victoria Custer, June 16, 1963; children: Randall Allen. *Education:* Cornell University, B.A., 1962; Brown University, M.A., 1965; University of California, Berkeley, Ph.D., 1970. *Politics:* "Moderate version of 1960's New Left." *Religion:* "Archsecularist." *Home:* 9 Ganung Dr., Ossining, N.Y. 10562. *Office:* Department of History and Political Science, Mercy College, 555 Broadway, Dobbs Ferry, N.Y. 10522.

CAREER: University of California, Berkeley, acting instructor in history, 1966-67; Dartmouth College, Hanover, N.H., instructor, 1968-70, assistant professor of history, 1970-77; Mercy College, Dobbs Ferry, N.Y., associate professor of history and head of department, 1977—. Visiting assistant professor at Cornell University, summer, 1972. *Member:* American Historical Association, American Studies Association, New England Historical Association, Phi Beta Kappa, Phi Alpha Theta. *Awards, honors:* Woodrow Wilson fellow, 1962-63.

WRITINGS: Children in the New England Mind: In Death and in Life, Shoe String, 1977. Contributor to history and literature journals.

WORK IN PROGRESS: Research on Cotton Mather and his family and on Joseph Wood Krutch's *The Modern Temper.*

SIDELIGHTS: Slater comments: "I believe that the best

type of historical writing combines precise analysis with imaginative evocation. The history books which I most admire are in this mode: Perry Miller's *New England Mind,* Richard Hofstadter's *The American Political Tradition,* George Dangerfield's *The Era of Good Feeling,* and Henry May's *The End of American Innocence.*''

AVOCATIONAL INTERESTS: Running (''not jogging'').

*   *   *

SLOANE, Howard N(orman) 1932-

PERSONAL: Born July 24, 1932, in New York, N.Y.; son of Howard N. (in advertising) and Lucille (Lipsett) Sloane; married Davina Hecht, August 15, 1954 (divorced, 1974); married Judith Ann Crandall (a psychologist), December 27, 1976; children: Gary Kenneth, Jeffrey Steven, Wendy Sarah. *Education:* Dartmouth College, B.A., 1954; Pennsylvania State University, M.S., 1955, Ph.D., 1959. *Politics:* Democrat. *Religion:* Jewish. *Home:* 1491 Sandpiper Way, #35, Salt Lake City, Utah 84117. *Office:* Department of Educational Psychology, University of Utah, 308-MBH, Salt Lake City, Utah 84112.

CAREER: New Jersey State Hospital, Greystone Park, psychiatric aide, summer, 1953; Belmont Hospital, Sutton, England, nursing assistant, summer, 1954; Veterans Administration Hospital, Roanoke, Va., psychology intern, 1955-56; Southern Illinois University, Carbondale, lecturer in psychology, 1958-60; Johns Hopkins University, Baltimore, Md., assistant professor of biochemistry, 1962-64; University of Washington, Seattle, research assistant professor of developmental psychology, 1964-65; University of Illinois, Urbana, research assistant professor of psychology, 1965-66; University of Utah, Salt Lake City, associate professor, 1966-69, professor of educational psychology, 1969—, head of instructional psychology program, 1972-77, 1978—. Cofounder and co-director of Camp Westland (remedial reading and behavior problem camp), 1974-75. Member of board of directors of Behavior Systems Corp., 1968-76, Animalated Advertising, Inc., 1975-76, and Learning Technology Corp.; head of board of trustees of Behavior Modification Training Center, Inc., 1968-72. Speaker; participant in workshops; consultant to Technical Assistant Development System, Bureau of Indian Services, and Bureau of Education of the Handicapped.

MEMBER: American Psychological Association, American Educational Research Association, Institute for Professional Training and Development (member of national board of advisors), Society for Research in Child Development, Association for Behavior Analysis, Utah Psychological Association, Utah Association for the Advancement of Behavior Therapy. *Awards, honors:* National Institutes of Health fellowship, 1960-62; Danforth Foundation grant, 1971-72.

WRITINGS: (With Robert Clark and Charles I. Foltz) *''Teachall'' Learning Programs: Introductory Set,* Publishers Co., 1962; (editor with B. D. MacAulay, and contributor) *Operant Procedures in Remedial Speech and Language Training,* Houghton, 1968; (editor with George Semb and others) *Behavior Analysis and Education, 1972,* University of Kansas Department of Human Development, 1973; (with David R. Buckholdt) *Classroom and Instructional Management,* Central Midwest Regional Education Laboratory, 1974; (with Donald A. Jackson) *A Guide to Motivating Learners,* Educational Technology Publications, 1974; (with Jackson and Gabriel M. Della-Piana) *How to Establish a Behavior Observation System,* Educational Technology

Publications, 1975; *Classroom Management: Remediation and Prevention,* Wiley, 1976; *Stop That Fighting,* Telesis, 1976; *Dinner's Ready,* Telesis, 1976; *No More Whining,* Telesis, 1976; *Not 'Til Your Room's Clean,* Telesis, 1976; *Because I Said So,* Telesis, 1976; (with Buckholdt, Judith A. Crandall, and William R. Jensen) *Structured Teaching,* Research Press, 1979.

Contributor: I. A. Berg and L. A. Pennington, editors, *An Introduction to Clinical Psychology,* Ronald, 3rd edition (Sloane was not included in earlier editions), 1966; George A. Fargo, Charles Behrns, and Patricia Nolen, editors, *Behavior Modification in the Classroom,* Wadsworth, 1970; Wesley C. Becker, editor, *An Empirical Basis for Change in Education,* Science Research Associates, 1971; Eugene A. Ramp and Bill L. Hopkins, editors, *A New Direction for Education: Behavior Analysis, 1971,* Department of Human Development, University of Kansas, 1971; *Educational Psychology: A Contemporary View,* CRM, 1972; Barbara C. Etzel, Judith M. Leblanc, and Donald M. Baer, editors, *New Developments in Behavioral Research: Theory, Methods and Applications,* Erlbaum Associates, 1977.

Contributor to journals in psychology and the behavioral sciences. Guest editor of *Journal of Experimental Child Psychology, Journal of Abnormal and Social Psychology,* and *Behavior Therapy;* past member of board of editors of *Journal of Applied Behavior Analysis.*

WORK IN PROGRESS: Quit Misbehaving, for New American Library.

SIDELIGHTS: Sloane's work has taken him to India, Bolivia, and Venezuela. He writes: ''I am interested in the application of psychology to various areas—including the family, clinical areas, social problems, education, and business. I want to make what we know available to the general public.''

*   *   *

SLOMAN, Larry 1948-

PERSONAL: Born July 9, 1948, in New York, N.Y.; son of Jack (in sales) and Lilyan (a bookkeeper; maiden name, Damsky) Sloman. *Education:* Queens College of the City University of New York, B.A. (magna cum laude), 1969; University of Wisconsin, Madison, M.S., 1972. *Politics:* ''Surrealist.'' *Religion:* Jewish. *Home address:* P.O. Box 280, Village Station, New York, N.Y. 10014. *Agent:* John Brockman Associates, Inc., 200 West 57th St., New York, N.Y. 10019. *Office:* Ratso Productions, P.O. Box 280, Village Station, New York, N.Y. 10014.

CAREER: Worked various jobs, including postal worker, copywriter, and trainee at the National Institute of Mental Health; *Avant-Garde,* New York City, articles editor, 1973; staff member of Ratso Productions, New York City. *Member:* Phi Beta Kappa.

WRITINGS: On the Road With Bob Dylan: Rolling With the Thunder, Bantam, 1978; *Reefer Madness: The History of Marijuana in the United States,* Bobbs-Merrill, 1978. Contributor to magazines, including *Rolling Stone, High Times,* and *Crawdaddy.*

WORK IN PROGRESS: A book on the 1978-79 season of the New York Rangers hockey team.

SIDELIGHTS: Sloman comments: ''I write because I have to; otherwise life would be too boring. My style, which is based on direct encounters with the empirical world, is predicated on the assumption that the members of the environment under discussion (i.e., a rock tour, a hockey team, dope smokers, shopping bag ladies) are often the most eloquent spokespeople in describing that environment. I give them a voice with dignity.''

* * *

SLOMOVITZ, Philip 1896-

PERSONAL: Born December 5, 1896, in Nowogrodek, Russia; came to United States in 1910; naturalized; son of Samuel and Malko Slomovitz; married wife, Anna, 1925; children: Gabriel, Carmi. *Education:* University of Michigan, B.A., 1918. *Home:* 22300 Lucerne, Southfield, Mich. 48075. *Office: Detroit Jewish News*, 17515 West Nine Mile Rd., Suite 865, Southfield, Mich. 48075.

CAREER/WRITINGS: Detroit News, Detroit, Mich., on staff of editorial department, 1918-20; *Palestine Pictorial*, New York, N.Y., editor, 1925-27; *Jewish Herald Chronicle*, Detroit, columnist, 1927-29; *Detroit Jewish News*, Southfield, Mich., founder, editor, publisher, and columnist, 1942—; United Nations correspondent, 1945—. Notable assignments include coverage of establishment of Israel, 1947-48, and Israel's admission to United Nations. Contributor to *Jewish Encyclopedia, Universal Jewish Encyclopedia*, and numerous magazines and periodicals, including *Commonweal* and *Christian Century*. Member of American section of Bar Ilan University, Israel; member of board of governors of Dropsie University.

MEMBER: World Jewish Congress, World Zionist Congress, American Jewish Press Association (founding president), Jewish Publication Society of America, Jewish War Veterans of the United States, Zionist Organization of America, Overseas Press Club, Jewish Telegraphic Agency (vice president), Society of Occident and Orient (former prefect), Sigma Delta Chi. *Awards, honors:* Smolar Award for Excellence in Journalism from Council of Jewish Federations and Welfare Funds, Inc.; St. Cyprian Award, American Jewish Tercentenary; American Technion Society Einstein Award for outstanding service to the society, 1977; Philip Slomovitz Chair for the Hebrew Language established in his honor at the Technion-Israel Institute of Technology, 1977.

* * *

SMART, Elizabeth 1913-

PERSONAL: Born December 27, 1913, in Ottawa, Ontario, Canada; daughter of Russel S. (a barrister) and Emma Louise (Parr) Smart; children: Georgina, Christopher, Sebastian, Rose. *Education:* Attended King's College, London. *Home:* The Dell, Flixton, Bungay, Suffolk, England.

CAREER: Writer. Worked for *House and Garden* and *Queen* in London, England; also worked as advertising copywriter.

WRITINGS: By Grand Central Station I Sat Down and Wept, Nicholson & Watson, 1945, Popular Library, 1976; *A Bonus* (poems), Polytantric Press, 1977; *The Assumption of the Rogues and Rascals*, J. Cape, 1978.

WORK IN PROGRESS: Dig a Grave and Let Us Bury Our Mother; A First and Last Garden.

* * *

SMITH, Anne Mollegen 1940-
(Anne Rush Mollegen)

PERSONAL: Maiden name is pronounced *Moll*-e-jen; born July 28, 1940, in Meridian, Miss.; daughter of Albert Theodore (an Episcopal theologian) and Ione (a teacher; maiden name, Rush) Mollegen; married David F. Smith (an editor), November 3, 1962; children: Amanda Wetherbee. *Education:* Smith College, B.A., 1961. *Home:* 451 West 24th St., New York, N.Y. 10011. *Office: Redbook*, 230 Park Ave., New York, N.Y. 10017.

CAREER: Ladies Home Journal, New York City, staff correspondent, 1961-62; *China Post*, Taipei, Taiwan, feature editor, 1965; *Redbook*, New York City, associate editor, 1967-73, fiction editor, 1973-77; *Your Place*, New York City, managing editor, 1977-78; *Redbook*, managing editor, 1978—. *Member:* American Society of Magazine Editors, National Organization for Women, Women's Media Group (president, 1978), Smith College Club of New York. *Awards, honors:* National Magazine Award from School of Journalism at Columbia University and American Society of Magazine Editors, 1975, for editorial achievement in fiction.

WRITINGS: (Editor) *Redbook's Famous Fiction, Number I*, Redbook Publishing, 1977. Contributor of articles and poems (sometimes under name Anne Rush Mollegen) to *Writer* and to literary magazines.

SIDELIGHTS: Smith writes: ''I think of myself as an editor first, as a writer very much second to that. These priorities make me comfortable in my editing, since there is no question of competing with my own writers.''

* * *

SMITH, Courtland L(ester) 1939-

PERSONAL: Born November 8, 1939, in Hartford, Conn.; son of Lester Courtland (a mechanical engineer) and Nuala (a teacher; maiden name, Rommel) Smith; married Linda Varsell (a poet and teacher), June 21, 1961; children: Kip, Jonathan, Rebecca. *Education:* Rensselaer Polytechnic Institute, B.M.E., 1961; University of Arizona, Ph.D., 1968. *Home:* 471 Northwest Hemlock Ave., Corvallis, Ore. 97330. *Office:* Department of Anthropology, Oregon State University, Corvallis, Ore. 97330.

CAREER: United Aircraft Corp., Pratt & Whitney Division, East Hartford, Conn., test engineer, 1961-62; Carnegie-Mellon University, Pittsburgh, Pa., assistant professor of business administration, 1968-69; Oregon State University, Corvallis, assistant professor, 1969-72, associate professor of anthropology, 1972—. Member of Citizens for a Clean Environment, 1974-75. Member of Western Interstate Commission on Higher Education task force on mental health problems, 1971-73. *Military service:* U.S. Army, Transportation Corps, 1962-64; became first lieutenant.

MEMBER: Society for Applied Anthropology (fellow), American Association for the Advancement of Science (fellow), American Anthropological Association (fellow), Oregon Academy of Science. *Awards, honors:* Grants from National Endowment for the Humanities, 1970-71, Office of Water Resource Research, 1970-72, National Oceanic & Atmospheric Administration, 1972-73, 1973-74, 1974-75, and Woods Hole Oceanographic Institution, 1975-76.

WRITINGS: (Contributor) William G. McGinnies and Bram J. Goldman, editors, *Arid Lands in Perspective*, University of Arizona Press, 1969; *The Salt River Project: A Case Study in Cultural Adaptation to an Urbanizing Community*, University of Arizona Press, 1972; (contributor) Donald R. Field, James C. Baron, and Burl F. Long, editors, *Water and the Community*, Ann Arbor Science Publishers, 1974; *Salmon Fishers of the Columbia*, Oregon State University Press, 1978. Contributor of about twenty articles and reviews to professional journals and regional magazines, including *Northwest* and *Portland*.

WORK IN PROGRESS: Research on simulating the evolution of human society and simulating the impact of fisheries on Oregon coastal communities.

SIDELIGHTS: Smith writes: "I enjoy writing. It is important in communicating research results, and influencing public perception of resource problems." *Avocational interests:* Skiing, hiking, sports.

* * *

SMITH, Craig R(alph) 1944-

PERSONAL: Born October 3, 1944, in San Diego, Calif.; son of Ralph E. (a teacher) and Anna T. (a religious worker; maiden name, Postic) Smith. *Education:* University of California, Santa Barbara, B.A., 1966; Queens College of the City University of New York, M.A., 1967; Pennsylvania State University, Ph.D., 1969. *Religion:* Roman Catholic. *Office:* Department of Communication Arts, University of Alabama, #3, 414-A, Birmingham, Ala. 35294.

CAREER: San Diego State University, San Diego, Calif., assistant professor of communication, 1969-73; University of Virginia, Charlottesville, associate professor of communication, 1973-76; University of Alabama, Birmingham, associate professor of communication arts and head of department, 1976—. Newswriter and researcher for Columbia Broadcasting System, 1968, 1972; speechwriter for President Gerald R. Ford, 1976. Member of executive committee of Republican party. *Member:* International Communication Association, American Communications Association, Speech Communication Association of America.

WRITINGS: The Bases of Argument: Ideas in Conflict, Bobbs-Merrill, 1971; *Orientations to Speech Criticism,* Science Research Associates, 1976. Contributor of about a dozen articles to speech and rhetoric journals.

WORK IN PROGRESS: Persuasion as a Force in American History, completion expected in 1980; research on Daniel Webster as a speaker.

SIDELIGHTS: Smith comments: "All we can do is make our own worlds. The best way to do that is to equip ourselves with rhetorical skills. The Sophists were correct: living is creating, and creating means the better illusion. Truth is a debilitating notion to a writer. It leads to authoritarianism and a lack of freedom."

* * *

SMITH, Curt 1951-

PERSONAL: Born March 20, 1951, in Bath, N.Y.; son of Howard Frederick (a guidance counselor) and Guendolen (a librarian; maiden name, Stuart) Smith; married Linda Kuhn (a librarian), June 22, 1974. *Education:* Attended Allegheny College, 1969-71; State University of New York College at Geneseo, B.A. (magna cum laude), 1973. *Politics:* Republican. *Religion:* Presbyterian. *Home:* 3 Stryker Lane, Clinton, N.Y. 13323. *Office:* Office of Communications, Hamilton College, Clinton, N.Y. 13323.

CAREER: Rochester Democrat & Chronicle, Rochester, N.Y., reporter and feature writer, 1973-75; Hamilton College, Clinton, N.Y., director of public relations, 1975—. *Member:* American Association of Public Relations Directors, National Association of Sportswriters and Sportscasters, Central New York Public Relations Council, Sigma Delta Chi. *Awards, honors:* Award from St. Bonaventure-

New York Times, 1973, for stories on Floyd Patterson and Roberto Clemente; four national awards from Council for the Advancement and Support of Education, 1976-77, for writing, layout, and design.

WRITINGS: America's Dizzy Dean (Sports Illustrated Book-of-the-Month Club selection), Bethany Press, 1978. Contributor of stories and articles to baseball magazines, *Library Journal, Upstate,* and newspapers.

WORK IN PROGRESS: A book about baseball's greatest rivalries; a book "about the hurt and poignancy of someone armed with values from the 1950's in the America of the late 1970's."

SIDELIGHTS: Smith writes: "There are, I suspect, few Americans of my age (twenty-seven) and social persuasion (conservative middle American) who turn to writing as a full-time career. I feel a special responsibility, therefore, to articulate the beliefs of America's old and imperiled culture, and a special kinship with America's good, quiet people. This empathy is reflected in most of my in-depth works, in my literary subjects chosen (baseball, America's loss of self-reliance, permissive morality) and in people I choose to write about (Dizzy Dean, Richard Nixon, Floyd Patterson). While some self-styled 'better people' find this type of literature neither fashionable nor chic, it is what I know best—and take most pride in crafting."

BIOGRAPHICAL/CRITICAL SOURCES: Geneseo Scene, spring, 1978; *Allegheny College Bulletin,* April, 1978; *Utica Observer-Dispatch,* March 30, 1978; *Syracuse Herald American,* May 8, 1978; *St. Louis Post-Dispatch,* May 21, 1978; *Chicago Tribune,* May 21, 1978; *Buffalo News,* June 18, 1978.

* * *

SMITH, Gene 1929-

PERSONAL: Born May 9, 1929, in New York, N.Y.; son of Julius S. (a lawyer) and Sara (Reisher) Smith; married Jayne Barry (a horse breeder), February 14, 1967; children: Jessica Barry. *Education:* University of Wisconsin, Madison, B.S., 1952.

CAREER: Newark Star-Ledger, Newark, N.J., reporter, 1956-57; *New York Post,* New York, N.Y., reporter, 1957-60; free-lance writer, 1960—. *Military service:* U.S. Army, 1952-54. *Member:* Society of American Historians.

WRITINGS: The Life and Death of Serge Rubinstein, Doubleday, 1962; *When the Cheering Stopped: The Last Years of Woodrow Wilson,* Morrow, 1964; *Still Quiet on the Western Front: Fifty Years Later,* Morrow, 1966; *The Shattered Dream: Herbert Hoover and the Great Depression,* Morrow, 1970; *The Winner* (juvenile), Cowles, 1970; *The Visitor* (juvenile), Cowles, 1971; (co-editor with Jayne Barry Smith) *The Police Gazette,* Simon & Schuster, 1972; *Maximilian and Carlota,* Morrow, 1973; *The Hayburners* (juvenile), Delacorte, 1974; *The Horns of the Moon,* Charterhouse, 1973; *High Crimes and Misdemeanors: The Impeachment and Trial of Andrew Johnson,* Morrow, 1977.

Contributor to magazines, including *Saturday Evening Post, Saturday Review, Reader's Digest,* and *Horizon.*

WORK IN PROGRESS: A historical novel.

SIDELIGHTS: Smith writes: "One does what one can. If one is going to write, one will do it. It is generally best to discuss it as little as possible. If you talk too much, the book never gets written. *Avocational interests:* Breeding horses.

SMITH, John F(erris) 1934-

PERSONAL: Born November 20, 1934, in Flint, Mich.; son of Joseph (a laborer) and Agnes (Ferris) Smith; married: Mary Grace Miller (an editor), June 8, 1957; children: Sarah E., Priscilla J. *Education:* University of Michigan, B.A., 1956; Episcopal Theological School, B.D., 1959. *Home and office:* Groton School, Groton, Mass. 01450.

CAREER: Ordained Episcopal priest, 1959; pastor of Episcopal churches in Detroit, Mich., 1959-61; Boston University, Boston, Mass., chaplain, 1961-78, member of humanities faculty, 1970-75; Groton School, Groton, Mass., chaplain, 1978—. *Awards, honors:* Underwood Fellowship from Danforth Foundation, 1975-76.

WRITINGS: The Bush Still Burns, Sheed, 1978. Author of a weekly column in Boston University's *Daily Free Press.*

WORK IN PROGRESS: A novel; a collection of columns and meditations.

SIDELIGHTS: Smith comments: "I am interested in reflecting on contemporary culture from a theological point of view, particularly on social and political issues, pointing out the profound spiritual implications of those issues.

"My seventeen years as a college chaplain brought me into contact with hundreds of young people (and others) who were moved by the events of the sixties and the seventies. Some of them were destroyed, others made stronger by the terrible realities of those times. My writing in spirituality comes out of that wonderful and dreadful experience. Thus I tend to challenge conventional notions of spirituality which direct themselves to the discovery of God in what people call a transcendent way. Thus I want to struggle against 'monastic' spirituality, as it is defined usually by a non-monastic world, and 'Eastern' spirituality, as it is defined usually by a non-Eastern world. People are sometimes surprised to find my writing so gritty, so concentrated on the ordinary, so opposed to 'uplift.' That's the way it is. We can't discover ourselves or our history, or our God, in any world but the one in which we live. I believe that discovery is not only rewarding, but it is also essential if we are to emerge from the slough of nihilism and banality in which we find ourselves."

AVOCATIONAL INTERESTS: Running, playing clarinet, photography.

*   *   *

SMITH, Lendon H(oward) 1921-

PERSONAL: Born June 3, 1921, in Portland, Ore.; son of Lendon Howard (a physician) and Hilda M. Smith; married Juliet Starhelm, July 10, 1948; children: Tracy, Nancy Hoffman, Eric, Duncan, Timothy. *Education:* Reed College, B.A., 1945; University of Oregon, M.D., 1946. *Politics:* Democrat. *Religion:* Episcopalian. *Home:* 2233 Southwest Market St., Portland, Ore. 97201. *Agent:* Aaron M. Priest Literary Agency, 150 East 35th St., New York, N.Y. 10016. *Office:* 1561 Southwest Market St., Portland, Ore. 97201.

CAREER: Private practice in pediatrics in Portland, Ore., 1951—. *Military service:* U.S. Army, psychiatrist, 1947-49. *Member:* Multnomah County Medical Society.

WRITINGS: The Children's Doctor, Prentice-Hall, 1969; *The Encyclopedia of Baby and Child Care,* Prentice-Hall, 1972; *New Wives' Tales: Conversations With Parents About Today's Pediatrics,* Prentice-Hall, 1974; *Improving Your Child's Behavior Chemistry,* Prentice-Hall, 1976; *Feed Your Kid Right,* McGraw, 1979. Writer for "The Children's Doctor," on ABC-TV, 1967-69.

SIDELIGHTS: Smith comments that his books are designed to provide "cheerful supportive information for worried parents."

*   *   *

SMITH, R(obert) Philip 1907-

PERSONAL: Born September 21, 1907, in Brockton, Mass.; son of Thomas F.B. (a Presbyterian minister) and Elizabeth (Laughlin) Smith; married Delene Pipes, 1932 (divorced, 1961); married Geraldine Martin, January 12, 1963; children: Sharon E. Smith Hillberg, Steven Buchanan, Roberta C., Rebecca E. *Education:* University of Kansas, A.B., 1930, B.S., 1932, M.D., 1934. *Home:* 7184 Estrellas de Mar, Carlsbad, Calif. 92008. *Agent:* Zetta Castle, Costa Del Mar Rd., Carlsbad, Calif. 92008. *Office:* La Costa Health Spa, Costa Del Mar Rd., Carlsbad, Calif. 92008.

CAREER: University of Kansas, Kansas City, resident in obstetrics and gynecology at university hospital, 1935-39, head of department of gynecological endocrinology clinical and laboratory research, 1936-39, instructor in obstetrics and gynecology, 1938-39; Providence Hospital School of Nursing, Seattle, Wash., instructor in obstetrics and gynecology, 1941-43; University of Washington, Seattle, Department of Nursing Education, instructor in obstetrics and gynecology, 1943-46, Medical School, clinical professor in department of obstetrics and gynecology, 1946-65; La Costa Health Spa, Carlsbad, Calif., medical director, 1965—. Speaker on dieting, nutrition, and other health topics. Consultant to United States Public Health Hospital, Seattle, and Scripps Clinic and Research Foundation, La Jolla, Calif. Diplomate, American Board of Gynecology; fellow, American College of Surgeons. Member of Seattle Civic Commission; former member and past president of Seattle Park Board; former chairman of Seattle Seafair and Seattle Open Golf Tournament; former vice-president of Greater Seattle Inc. *Military service:* U.S. Army, 1941-43; became captain. *Member:* American Medical Association, Southwest Gynecological Association, California Medical Association, San Diego County Medical Association, San Diego Gynecological Society, Greater San Diego Sports Association, Pacific International Yachting Association (former commodore), Pacific Coast Yachting Association (former commodore), Cruising Club of America, Century Club (San Diego; vice-president). *Awards, honors:* First prize in International Festival, Cortina, Italy, 1952, for documentary film, "Gossip Goes to Honolulu."

WRITINGS: The La Costa Diet and Exercise Book, Grosset & Dunlap, 1977. Contributor of articles to medical journals.

WORK IN PROGRESS: Research in nutrition and its effect on stress; work on existing knowledge about trace minerals and their effectiveness on human health.

SIDELIGHTS: Smith, in an article for *Palm Springs Life,* revealed his reasons for writing *The La Costa Diet and Exercise Book:* "I wrote the book primarily for the people who come to La Costa to have something to take home with them to follow. I also made it comprehensive enough for those who can't afford the spa to be able to follow the regimen at home."

The La Costa Spa, along with other famous spas, is quite naturally visited by public figures. Dr. Smith describes these people as the most willing to stay on the regimen. "Professional people are the most dedicated. Movie and tv stars, senators, congressmen and the like, base their livelihood on fitness and appearance. . . .Carol Burnett is a good example.

She frequents the spa several times a year and is a favorite of the staff."

AVOCATIONAL INTERESTS: Skiing, fishing, yachting, and golf.

BIOGRAPHICAL/CRITICAL SOURCES: Palm Springs Life, June, 1978.

*   *   *

SMITH, Richard 1941-

PERSONAL: Born in 1941; divorced. Education: Attended Orange County Community College. Address: c/o Workman Publishing Co., Inc., 231 East 51st St., New York, N.Y. 10022.

CAREER: Worked various jobs, including driver for Pepsi-Cola Co., executive trainee and later women's underwear buyer at Alexander's department store, Manhattan, N.Y., and publicity director; full-time humorous writer.

WRITINGS: The Dieter's Guide to Weight Loss During Sex, Workman Publishing, 1978. Contributor to periodicals.

WORK IN PROGRESS: A sequel to The Dieter's Guide to Weight Loss During Sex; a Jewish Gothic novel; a novel about a man who is terrified of women.

SIDELIGHTS: Richard Smith's tongue-in-cheek diet and sex manual, The Dieter's Guide to Weight Loss During Sex, was an outgrowth of a poster that Smith created in 1974. The poster, called "The Sensuous Guide to Weight Loss During Sex," was a smash hit, selling tens of thousands of copies, and his book has been equally popular. A lover of pizza and halvah, Smith keeps in shape by running rather than by the weight loss method advocated in his book.

BIOGRAPHICAL/CRITICAL SOURCES: New York Times Book Review, July 2, 1978.*

*   *   *

SMITH, Richard C(hristopher) 1948-

PERSONAL: Born December 10, 1948, in Anthony, Kan.; son of Clarence M. (a teacher and farmer) and Mary (Crampton) Smith; married Carol A. Patry (a seamstress), June 22, 1971; children: Amy Rebecca, Aaron Christopher, Roxanne. Education: Attended Kansas School of Business, 1967-68, Wichita State University, 1968-69, and Friends University, 1969-70. Religion: Roman Catholic. Home address: R.R.1, Amorita, Okla. 73719.

CAREER: Farm foreman in Amorita, Okla., 1974-76; Smith Custom Hay, Amorita, Okla., owner-manager, 1976; free-lance writer, 1976—. Lecturer at colleges and high schools. Military service: U.S. Army Reserve, 1970—; present rank, sergeant. Member: National Amateur Press Association, American Poet's Fellowship Society, Kansas Authors Club, Kansas Writers Guild. Awards, honors: Grant from American Poet's Fellowship Society, 1976.

WRITINGS: Something From Inside Me, privately printed, 1970; (with Frank Crampton) Magnolia Blossoms and Sunflower Seeds, Prairie Poet Books, 1975; (editor) Kansas Writer's Market 1977, Golden Grain Press, 1976.

SIDELIGHTS: Smith writes: "I am extremely concerned with the push of writers into the large cities to establish themselves, to learn, make contacts, and promote their writing. I want to bring the knowledge to the writer, wherever he or she lives. National writer's books cater to the east or west or nation as a whole, leaving many unanswered questions. My third book exposes the little markets and answers many of the questions a writer must ask, in Kansas."

SMITH, W. Eugene 1918(?)-1978

OBITUARY NOTICE: Born c. 1918; died October 15, 1978, in Tucson, Ariz. Journalist best known for his book Minamata, a photographic documentation of a Japanese village whose inhabitants contracted mercury poisoning. During the research period for Minamata, Smith was attacked and nearly blinded by men believed to have been hired by the industry responsible for the poisoning. Smith was also well known for his coverage of World War II in which he covered thirteen invasions and was wounded at Okinawa. Obituaries and other sources: Washington Post, October 20, 1978; Newsweek, October 30, 1978; Time, October 30, 1978.

*   *   *

SMITH, (Francis) Wilson 1922-

PERSONAL: Born January 23, 1922, in Malden, Mass.; son of Francis Marion (a clergyman) and Daisyolah (Wilson) Smith; married Kathryn Reed (a volunteer worker), August 27, 1949; children: Sheryl Reed, Deborah Wilson. Education: Amherst College, A.B., 1947; University of California, Berkeley, M.A., 1948; Columbia University, Ph.D., 1955. Residence: Davis, Calif. Office: Department of History, University of California, Davis, Calif. 95616.

CAREER: Princeton University, Princeton, N.J., instructor in history, 1953-58; Johns Hopkins University, Baltimore, Md., assistant professor, 1958-61, associate professor of history and education, 1961-64; University of California, Davis, professor of history, 1964—. Member of summer faculty at University of Iowa, 1958, University of California, Los Angeles, 1960, and Harvard University, 1965. Member of the Examining Committee, American History and Social Studies Achievement Test, of the College Entrance Examination Board, 1969-72. Military service: U.S. Army, 1942-46; became staff sergeant; received Bronze Star.

MEMBER: American Historical Association (head of committee on teaching, 1966-68), Organization of American Historians, American Studies Association, American Association of University Professors (chapter president, 1965-66), History of Education Society (member of board of directors, 1963-66), Historical Society of Pennsylvania, New York Historical Society. Awards, honors: Albert J. Beveridge Award, honorable mention, from American Historical Association, 1955, for doctoral dissertation, "Professors and Public Ethics"; Social Science Research Council grants, 1958, 1960-61.

WRITINGS: Professors and Public Ethics: Studies of Northern Moral Philosophers Before the Civil War, Cornell University Press, 1956; (editor with Richard Hofstadter) American Higher Education: A Documentary History, two volumes, University of Chicago Press, 1961; (editor) Cities of Our Past and Present, Wiley, 1964; (contributor) Harold Hyman and Leonard Levy, editors, Freedom and Reform: Essays for Henry Steele Commager, Harper, 1967; (editor) Theories of Education in Early America, 1655-1819, Bobbs-Merrill, 1973; (contributor) Stanley Elkins and Eric McKitrick, editors, The Hofstadter Aegis, Knopf, 1974; (editor) Essays in American Intellectual History, Dryden, 1975. Contributor to Encyclopedia of Education. Contributor of articles and reviews to scholarly journals. Associate editor of The Concise Dictionary of American Biography, 1964; member of editorial board of History of Education Quarterly, 1966—.

WORK IN PROGRESS: Research on history of American higher education, "especially on the network of college-educated people in public life during the early nineteenth century."

* * *

SNOW, Edgar Parks 1905-1972

PERSONAL: Born July 19, 1905, in Kansas City, Mo.; son of James Edgar (a printer and editor) and Anna Catherine (Edelman) Snow; married Helen Foster (a writer under pseudonym Nym Wales), 1932 (divorced, 1949); married Lois Wheeler, 1949; children: Christopher, Sian (daughter). *Education:* Attended Junior College of Kansas City (now Metropolitan Junior College—Kansas City), 1923-24, University of Missouri, 1924-26, and Columbia University, 1926-27.

CAREER: Worked as printer's devil in his father's print shop during summers in high school; *Kansas City Star,* Kansas City, Mo., correspondent, 1927; *New York Sun,* New York City, reporter, 1928; began world travels to Central America, Hawaii, and Far East, 1928; *China Weekly Review,* Shanghai, China, assistant editor, 1929; *Chicago Tribune,* Chicago, Ill., correspondent, 1929-30; staff correspondent for Consolidated Press Association, 1930-34; *New York Sun,* correspondent, 1930-38; *London Daily Herald,* London, England, staff correspondent, 1933-37, chief correspondent in Far East, 1937-41; returned to America, 1941; *Saturday Evening Post,* Indianapolis, Ind., world correspondent, 1941-53, associate editor, 1943-52. Lectured at Yenching University (now Peking University), Peking, China, in the early 1930's.

WRITINGS: Far Eastern Front, H. Smith & R. Haas, 1933; *Red Star Over China,* Gollancz, 1937, Random House, 1938, revised and enlarged edition, Grove, 1968; *Living China: Modern Chinese Short Stories,* Reynal, 1937; (with Norman D. Hanwell) *Wai kuo chi che hsi pei yin shiang chi,* [China], 1937, published as *Mei-huo chi che Chung-kuo hung ch'u yin hsiang chi,* [China], 1949; *Chung-kuo ti hung ch'u,* [China], 1938.

The Battle for Asia, Random House, 1941 (published in England as *The Scorched Earth,* Gollancz, 1941); (author of introduction) Maung Thein Pe, *What Happened in Burma: The Frank Revelation of a Young Burmese Revolutionary Leader Who Has Recently Escaped From Burma to India,* Kitabistan, 1943; *People on Our Side* (Book-of-the-Month Club selection), Random House, 1944 (published in England as *Glory and Bondage,* Gollancz, 1945); *The Pattern of Soviet Power,* Random House, 1945; *Stalin Must Have Peace,* Random House, 1947.

Random Notes on Red China, Harvard University Press, 1957; *Journey to the Beginning,* Random House, 1958; *The Other Side of the River,* Random House, 1962, excerpts published as *China, Russia, and the U.S.A.: Changing Relations in a Changing World,* Marzani & Munsell, 1963, excerpts with new introduction published as *War and Peace in Vietnam,* Marzani & Munsell, 1963, published with a new preface as *Red China Today: The Other Side of the River,* Penguin, 1970, published as *Red China Today,* Random House, 1971, revised and updated edition published as *Red China Today,* Vintage Books, 1971; *Mei-huo yu hao jen shih S su-no fang Hua wen chang,* [China], c. 1971; *The Long Revolution,* Random House, 1972. Co-author of *Smash Hitler's International,* c. 1942. Contributor of numerous articles to newspapers and magazines including *Asia, Current History, Fortune,* and *Look.*

SIDELIGHTS: An American journalist and writer, Edgar Parks Snow is best known for acquainting the Western world with the Communist movement in China. For years he had "the distinction of being the only American writer who [could] regularly get a visa to enter mainland China."

Snow's career as a foreign correspondent began at age twenty-three when he decided to seek adventure abroad. After visiting Hawaii and Central America, Snow wandered into the Far East and remained in China for the next twelve years. During this time he was able to see much of the country. In 1929 he was invited by Dr. Sun Fo, Minister of Railways and son of the late Dr. Sun Yat-sen, to travel the entire system of government railways in China and Manchuria, and from the information he collected he wrote a series of guide books on China.

Over the years Snow also traveled to the Philippines, Japan, Manchuria, India, the Dutch Indies, Baluchistan, and Siberia, and wrote many firsthand reports of major news events. These included stories on the Northwest famine, the Sino-Russian hostilities in Manchuria during 1929 and 1930, the agrarian revolt in Indo-China in 1930, a head-hunters uprising in Formosa, and Tharawaddy uprisings against British rule in Burma.

During the 1930's Snow, his wife Helen, and Rewi Alley drew up plans for the Chinese Industrial Co-operatives (Indusco). These were designed as a means of quickly rebuilding industry lost during World War II. Helen Snow described the co-operatives in her book *China Builds for Democracy,* written under the pseudonym Nym Wales.

In 1936 Snow scored "a world scoop" when he traveled with the Chinese Red Army for five months into Soviet China. His photographs and articles in the *London Daily Herald* and the *Saturday Evening Post* broke a news blockade that had existed in this area for nine years. His book *Red Star Over China,* also based on these travels, is an account of the rising power of Communist leaders in China, the Red army, and China's war tactics and objectives. This book was an international best-seller which critics praised as "a vitally important historical and political volume, rich in present significance and even more wealthy for future reference."

Edgar Snow interviewed many famous men such as Winston Churchill, Harry Truman, Chiang Kai-shek, Gandhi, Nehru, and Chou En-lai, but he gained the most recognition for his talks with Mao Tse-tung. The first time they met was after the Long March in 1936 when Mao was "a lean and hunted Red-bandit with a price of 250,000 silver dollars on his head." Much of their conversation, which took place during several days and nights in a cave near Mongolia, is contained in the prophetic *Red Star Over China.* As their friendship continued to grow over the next thirty years, Snow wrote further reports of Mao in *The Long Revolution* and in many articles. Snow often gained noteworthy information during his talks with Mao, such as in 1971 when he was the first to hint that the Chinese leader would welcome a visit by President Nixon.

Although Snow was not a Communist himself, he sympathized with the Communist movement in China, which he believed was "an attempt by the Chinese to rid themselves not only of foreign imperialistic designs but also of centuries of old oppression by bureaucratic officialdom, greedy bankers, and others." After World War II, Cold War politics did not cater to friendly feelings toward the Chinese, so Snow was blacklisted in the United States for the last years of his life, having to live on free-lance sales to foreign journals. When the United States was at last beginning to prepare for a reversal of policy toward the People's Republic of China, Snow was in Switzerland dying of cancer. Since it was

Snow's friendship with Mao Tse-tung that helped to open the way for this new foreign policy, Dr. E. Grey Dimond wrote to President Nixon on behalf of Lois Wheeler Snow and "suggested that it would be a major act of justice and conciliation if . . . he reached out personally, brought Snow home, and sent him to the National Institutes of Health. The President's sole response was a letter to Snow, expressing regrets and wishing a speedy recovery. . . . Ironically, when Snow died while abroad in 1972, he was buried in Switzerland at almost the very moment of President Nixon's triumphant arrival in Shanghai."

In *Journey to the Beginning* Snow wrote: "part of me would always remain with China's tawny hills, her terraced emerald fields, her island temples seen in the early morning mist, a few of her sons and daughters who had trusted or loved me, her bankrupt cheerful civilized peasants who had sheltered and fed me, her brown, ragged, shining-eyed children, the equals and the lovers I had known, and above all the lousy, unpaid, hungry, despised, peasant foot-soldier who in the mysterious sacrifice of his own life alone now gave value to all life and put the stamp of nobility upon the struggle of a great people to survive and to go forward.

"Yes, I was proud to have known them, to have straggled across a continent with them in defeat, to have wept with them and still to share a faith with them. But I was not and could never be one of them. A man who gives himself to be the possession of an alien land . . . lives a Yahoo life. . . . I was an American."

Snow felt that even after he died he would belong partly in China and partly in the United States. His remains now rest in a garden at Peking University and also near "the Hudson River, before it enters the Atlantic to touch Europe and all the shores of mankind of which I felt a part."

BIOGRAPHICAL/CRITICAL SOURCES: London Times, December 10, 1936, December 12, 1936; *New York Times,* December 10, 1936; *Asia,* February, 1937; *Saturday Review of Literature,* January 1, 1938, March 1, 1941; *Publishers Weekly,* February 12, 1938; *Saturday Evening Post,* May 31, 1941; *Time,* December 17, 1945, February 28, 1972, September 20, 1976; *New Republic,* March 3, 1947, February 27, 1965, January 26, 1974, September 25, 1976; *Newsweek,* April 12, 1971; *Saturday Review,* May 17, 1975; Lois Wheeler Snow, *Death With Dignity: When the Chinese Came,* Random House, 1975; *Pacific Historical Review,* November, 1976; *New Yorker,* November 29, 1976.

OBITUARIES: New York Times, February 16, 1972; *Washington Post,* February 16, 1972; *Nation,* February 28, 1972; *Time,* February 28, 1972; *Current Biography,* April, 1972.*

(Died February 15, 1972, in Switzerland)

*   *   *

SNOW, Kathleen   1944-

PERSONAL: Born April 15, 1944, in Lexington, Ky.; daughter of Charles E. Snow (a professor and anthropologist) and Katherine (a professor and speech pathologist; maiden name, Meyer) Snow Egan. *Education:* Grinnell College, B.A., 1965. *Home:* 410 East 65th St., Apt. 4-J, New York, N.Y. 10021. *Agent:* Meredith Bernstein, Henry Morrison, Inc., 58 West 10th St., New York, N.Y. 10011. *Office:* Yankelovich, Skelly & White, 575 Madison Ave., New York, N.Y. 10022.

CAREER: Analog (science fiction magazine), New York City, editorial assistant, 1966-68; N.W. Ayer & Son (adver-

tising agency), New York City, copywriter, 1969-73; freelance writer and copy editor, 1973-74; *Where* (entertainment guide), New York City, editor, 1974-75; Yankelovich, Skelly & White, New York City, secretary, 1975—. Founding member of Committee for a Responsive Park Commission (Palisades Park). *Awards, honors:* Award from American Institute of Graphic Arts, 1969, for a newspaper advertisement.

WRITINGS: Night Waking (suspense novel), Simon & Schuster, 1978. Contributor to *Harper's.*

WORK IN PROGRESS: A suspense novel.

SIDELIGHTS: Kathleen Snow writes: "To solve my basic problem—the loneliness of the long distance writer—I became a professional writing-course taker. I also helped form a writing group with three women in 1976. We have been meeting every two weeks ever since, reading our manuscripts, offering advice and encouragement. In the end, though, a book is never finished, just abandoned."

*   *   *

SOHL, Jerry   1913-
(Nathan Butler, Sean Mei Sullivan)

PERSONAL: Born December 2, 1913, in Los Angeles, Calif.; son of Fred J. (a pharmacist) and Florence (a masseuse; maiden name, Wray) Sohl; married Jean Gordon, October 28, 1942; children: Allan, Martha Jane, Jennifer. *Education:* Attended Central College of Arts and Sciences, Chicago, Ill., 1932-34. *Politics:* Democrat. *Religion:* Unitarian-Universalist. *Home:* 3020 Ash Court, Thousand Oaks, Calif. 91360. *Agent:* Pat Myrer, McIntosh & Otis, Inc., 475 Fifth Ave., New York, N.Y. 10017.

CAREER: Daily Pantagraph, Bloomington, Ill., photographer, 1945-53, police reporter, 1947-49, critic, 1949-52, reviewer, 1949-53, telegraph editor, 1953-58; free-lance writer, 1958—. Also worked as concert pianist. *Military service:* U.S. Army Air Forces, 1942-45; became sergeant. *Member:* Science Fiction Writers of America (charter member), Mystery Writers of America, Writers Guild of America (West).

WRITINGS—All science fiction, except as noted: *The Haploids,* Rinehart, 1952; *The Transcendent Man,* Rinehart, 1953; *Costigan's Needle,* Rinehart, 1953; *The Altered Ego,* Rinehart, 1954; *Point Ultimate,* Rinehart, 1955; *The Mars Monopoly,* Ace Books, 1956; *Prelude to Peril* (mystery), Rinehart, 1957; *The Time Dissolver,* Avon, 1957; *The Odious Ones,* Rinehart, 1959; *One Against Herculum,* Ace Books, 1959; *Night Slaves,* Gold Medal, 1965; *The Lemon Eaters* (novel), Simon & Schuster, 1967; *The Anomaly,* Curtis Books, 1971; *The Spun Sugar Hole* (novel), Simon & Schuster, 1971; *The Resurrection of Frank Borchard* (novel), Simon & Schuster, 1973; *Underhanded Chess,* Hawthorne, 1973; *Underhanded Bridge,* Hawthorne, 1975; *I, Aleppo,* Laser, 1976.

Under pseudonym Nathan Butler—All novels: *Dr. Josh,* Gold Medal, 1973; *Mamelle,* Gold Medal, 1974; *Blow-Dry,* Gold Medal, 1976; *Mamelle, the Goddess,* Gold Medal, 1977.

Under pseudonym Sean Mei Sullivan: *Supermanchu* (adventure novel) Ballantine, 1974.

Screenplays: "Twelve Hours to Kill," Twentieth Century-Fox, 1960; "Die, Monster, Die," American International, 1963; "Night Slaves" (for television; based on his novel), American Broadcasting Co., 1970.

Staff writer for "Star Trek," "Alfred Hitchcock Presents,"

and "The New Breed." Also wrote scripts for "Naked City," "Twilight Zone," "Outer Limits," "Route 66," "M-Squad," "G.E. Theater," "Markham," "Border Patrol," "The Invaders," "Target: The Corruptors," and "Man From Atlantis."

Contributor to popular magazines, including *Playboy*, and science fiction magazines, including *Galaxy*, *If*, and *Science Fiction and Fantasy*.

WORK IN PROGRESS: Herzog's Planet, a science fiction novel; *Kaheesh*, mystery novel; a long novel about northern California Indians.

SIDELIGHTS: Sohl writes: "The written word will always be superior to the vapidity of television or film; I see no reason why each should not support and enhance the other, however, just as rock enhances classical music and vice versa. I will continue to address myself to the work of entertainment and making people examine their values in the process. We have not yet begun to use all our resources, particularly the brain. We should not be afraid of those who use theirs, for they are lighting the way."

*   *   *

SOLOW, Martin 1920-
(Peter Nelson)

PERSONAL: Born May 19, 1920, in Brooklyn, N.Y.; son of John (a cutter) and Ruth (Nelson) Solow; married Rita Newman (a teacher), 1943; children: Ellen Solow Holzman, Peter, Michael, Steven. *Education:* Franklin and Marshall College, A.B., 1942. *Politics:* Independent. *Religion:* Jewish. *Home:* 24 Hemlock Lane, Roslyn Heights, N.Y. 11577. *Agent:* Julia Coopersmith Literary Agency, 10 West 15th St., New York, N.Y. 10011. *Office:* Martin Solow Creative Service, Inc., 488 Madison Ave., New York, N.Y. 10022.

CAREER: Congress of Industrial Organizations, Washington, D.C., assistant editor, 1946-47; *District 65* (newspaper), New York City, managing editor, 1947-49; free-lance writer, 1949-52; *Nation*, New York City, assistant publisher, 1952-56; free-lance writer, 1956-58; Solow/Wexton, New York City, president and creative director, 1958-73; Kenyon & Eckhardt, New York City, vice-president and copy chief, 1973-74; Martin Solow Creative Service, Inc., New York City, president, 1974—. *Military service:* U.S. Army, 1942-46; became technical sergeant. *Member:* New York Copy Club (past president). *Awards, honors:* More than a hundred advertising awards, including the annual media award from the National Conference of Christians and Jews, Clio awards, and Gold Key awards.

WRITINGS: Effective Advertising, Grosset, 1963; *Second Love* (novel), Dell, 1973. Contributor of articles and reviews (sometimes under pseudonym Peter Nelson) to popular magazines and newspapers, including *Nation*, *Esquire*, and *Coronet*.

WORK IN PROGRESS: I Never Saw the World's Fair, a semi-autobiographical novel about "a nineteen-year-old Jewish kid from Brooklyn who winds up working for an uncle in a retail store in Hazard, Kentucky, then hitchhikes through the South"; *Thirty Seconds Over America*, on the impact of television commercial advertising on American society, publication by Prentice-Hall expected in 1980.

SIDELIGHTS: Solow told *CA:* "I started to write fiction in high school and college. I got sidetracked by the army, and afterwards by wanting to help 'save the world.' Now I am trying to fight my way back to fiction while making a living writing advertising copy—very tough."

Solow explained that *Second Love* "was frankly written as a response to *Love Story*. It is the *Love Story* for the Geritol generation, about a middle-aged man who loses his wife and a couple of children, then tries to find happiness in a new marriage. It ends sadly, alas! The man dies—a dramatic switch!"

An advertising campaign that Solow created in 1962, "The Beloved Herring Maven," is credited with thrusting the Yiddish word *maven* into ordinary English usage.

*   *   *

SOMIT, Albert 1919-

PERSONAL: Born October 25, 1919, in Chicago, Ill.; son of Samuel and Mary (Rosenblum) Somit; married Leyla D. Shapiro, August 31, 1947 (divorced, August, 1978); children: Scott H., Jed L. *Education:* University of Chicago, A.B., 1941, Ph.D., 1947. *Office:* Department of Political Science, State University of New York at Buffalo, 503 Capen Hall, Buffalo, N.Y. 14260.

CAREER: New York University, New York, N.Y., director of graduate program in government, 1952-54, deputy director of Office of Educational Services, 1958-59; U.S. Naval War College, Newport, R.I., Nimitz Professor of Political Philosophy, 1961-62; New York University, Graduate School of Public Administration, director of doctoral program, 1962-66; State University of New York at Buffalo, professor of political science, 1966—, head of department, 1966-69, executive vice-president, 1970—. Fellow at Netherlands Institute for Advanced Study, 1978-79. Member of directing group of Organization for Economic Co-operation & Development's Programme on Institutional Management in Higher Education. *Military service:* U.S. Army, 1950-52; became first lieutenant.

WRITINGS: (With Joseph Tanenhaus) *American Political Science: A Profile of a Discipline*, Atherton, 1964; (with Tanenhaus) *The Development of American Political Science: From Burgess to Behavioralism*, Allyn & Bacon, 1967; *Political Science and the Study of the Future*, Dryden, 1973; *Biology and Politics: Recent Explorations*, Maison des Science de l'Homme, 1976.

*   *   *

SONTAG, Frederick H(erman) 1924-

PERSONAL: Born April 29, 1924, in Breslau, Germany; came to the United States in 1937, naturalized citizen, 1943; son of Hugo (a banker) and Lotte (a book executive; maiden name, Laband) Sontag; married Edith Virginia Frances Sweeney (an executive), February 8, 1958. *Education:* Colby College, A.B., 1946; graduate study at Columbia University, 1947-48. *Religion:* Anglo Catholic. *Home and address:* 764 Scotland Rd., South Orange, N.J. 07079; (summers) P.O. Box 207, Seal Harbor, Maine 04675.

CAREER: Earl Newsom & Co., New York City, public relations counsel, 1947-48; Citizens Foundation, Syracuse, N.Y., director, 1948-50; *Business Week*, New York City, central New York correspondent, 1950-51, director of public relations, 1951-55; National Council of the Episcopal Church, New York City, program planning associate in broadcasting, 1956-61; U.S. House of Representatives, Washington, D.C., executive director of committee for Increased Minority Staffing, 1961-69; Study of American Political Parties, South Orange, N.J., co-director, 1969-73, director, 1973—. Visiting lecturer at Colby College, 1975; lecturer at Harvard University, Columbia University,

Brookings Institution, and Woodrow Wilson International Center of Scholars; member of board of advisers of Husson College. Associate of Anna M. Rosenberg Associates, 1957-60; analyst and commentator for Maine Public Broadcasting Network, 1973-75; member of New Jersey Conference on the Promotion of Better Government; consultant to Civic Service, Inc., 1957—, 1960 Winter Olympics, and to U.S. International Trade Commission, 1975-77.

MEMBER: Public Relations Society of America, American Association of Political Consultants (member of board of directors), American Political Science Association, Overseas Press Club of America, Phi Delta Theta, Phi Gamma Mu. *Awards, honors:* Certificate of achievement from American Public Relations Association, 1952, 1954, Silver Anvil Award, 1953; special achievement award from U.S. International Trade Commission, 1976.

WRITINGS: (With John S. Saloma III) *Parties: The Real Opportunity for Effective Citizen Politics,* Knopf, 1972. National correspondent for *American Church News, Witness, Living Church,* and *Scroll.* Contributor to newspapers. Member of editorial advisory board of *Sage Electoral Studies Yearbook.*

* * *

SOREL, Julia
    See DREXLER, Rosalyn

* * *

SOUERWINE, Andrew H(arry) 1924-

PERSONAL: Born February 29, 1924, in Slatington, Pa.; son of Harry W. (in retail grocery) and Katie E. (Anthony) Souerwine; married Jane Day (a teacher and coach), August 27, 1949; children: David A., Andrew D. *Education:* Ursinus College, B.A., 1947; University of Pennsylvania, M.A., 1948; University of Connecticut, Ph.D., 1954. *Home:* 265 Dale Rd., Wethersfield, Conn. 06109. *Office:* Department of Management and Administrative Sciences, University of Connecticut, 39 Woodland St., Hartford, Conn. 06105.

CAREER: Trinity College, Hartford, Conn., assistant professor of psychology, 1949-58, head of department, 1952-58; Travelers Insurance Co., Hartford, Conn., staff psychologist, 1958-67, director of management conferences, 1959, director of career planning and development, 1966; University of Connecticut, Hartford, associate professor, 1967-71, professor of business administration, 1971—, director of masters program, 1967-77. Adjunct member of faculty at University of Hartford, 1959-61, and Hartford College for Women, 1960-62; lecturer at University of Connecticut, 1963-67. Part-time research associate of Psychological Corp., Personnel Testing Laboratories, and George Fry & Associate, 1950-57. Director of Community Council of the Greater Hartford Region, 1977—; member of advisory board of Young Men's Christian Association Counseling Service, 1971—; member of board of directors of Bristol Brass Corp. and Accurate Forging, Inc., both 1978—. *Military service:* U.S. Army, 1943-46.

MEMBER: American Psychological Association, American Society for Training and Development, Eastern Psychological Association, Connecticut Psychological Society, Connecticut Valley Association of Psychologists (president, 1957), Beta Gamma Sigma, Pi Gamma Mu, Tau Kappa Alpha, Alpha Psi Omega.

WRITINGS: (Contributor) Dale S. Beach, editor, *Managing People at Work: Readings in Personnel,* Macmillan,

1971, 2nd edition, 1975; *Career Strategies: Planning for Personal Achievement,* American Management Association, 1978. Contributor of about thirty articles and reviews to education, business, and management journals.

WORK IN PROGRESS: "A realistic look at leadership in organizations"; a career-planning workbook for professionals.

SIDELIGHTS: Souerwine writes: "My materials are written from a base of extensive consulting experience with business people at all levels within the organizations. Research and theory concepts are translated into the practical issues and careers of present-day workers and managers. *Career Strategies* is written from that perspective and provides people presently employed with concepts and processes to take a closer look at jobs, at organizations, at bosses, and especially at themselves. It is an outgrowth of over fifteen years of experience of working with young career people and understanding the unique problems that they face as they attempt to establish themselves in their careers.

"An important aspect of career strategy is the quality of the leadership environment in which the planning is done. That is why I am turning some of my energies to a more careful look at those leadership dimensions which seem to be essential to provide for a productive and maturing career."

* * *

SOUTHWORTH, Louis
    See GREALEY, Thomas Louis

* * *

SOYER, Raphael 1899-

PERSONAL: Born December 25, 1899, in Borisogliebsk, Russia; came to United States in 1912, naturalized citizen, 1917; son of Abraham (a teacher and writer) and Bella (Schneyer) Soyer; married Rebecca Letz (a teacher), February 8, 1931; children: Mary Soyer Lieber. *Education:* Attended Cooper Union College, 1916-17, National Academy of Design, 1918-20, and Art Students League, 1921. *Home:* 88 Central Park W., New York, N.Y. 10023. *Office:* 54 West 74th St., New York, N.Y. 10023.

CAREER: Artist, 1921—. Taught at Art Students League, National Academy Art School, American Artists School, and New School for Social Research. Work exhibited nationally and internationally, including Corcoran Museum and Whitney Museum of Art; solo shows of his work since 1929. *Member:* Artists Equity Association, American Art Group, Society of Painters, Sculptors, and Gravers, National Institute of Arts and Letters (member of council), National Academy of Design (associate), American Academy of Arts and Letters. *Awards,. honors:* Art awards include an award from International Exhibition in Pittsburgh, Pa., 1959.

WRITINGS: An Artist's Pilgrimage, Crown, 1962; *Homage to Thomas Eakins,* Yoseloff, 1968; *Self Revealment,* Random House, 1971; *An Artist's Diary,* New Republic, 1977.

BIOGRAPHICAL/CRITICAL SOURCES: New York Times, November 6, 1977.

* * *

SPACKMAN, W(illiam) M(ode) 1905-

PERSONAL: Born May 20, 1905, in Coatesville, Pa.; son of George Harvey (an executive) and Alice Pennock (Mode)

Spackman; married Mary Ann Matthews, September 4, 1929; children: Peter Matthews, Harriet (Mrs. Bruce St. John Newell). *Education:* Princeton University, A.B. (cum laude), 1927, M.A., 1933; Balliol College, Oxford, B.A., 1930. *Religion:* Society of Friends (Quakers). *Home:* 38 Dodds Lane, Princeton, N.J. 08540. *Agent:* International Creative Management, 40 West 57th St., New York, N.Y. 10019.

CAREER: New York University, New York City, instructor in classics, 1930-31; copy-writer and account executive in public relations agencies in New York City, 1935-38; University of Colorado, Boulder, director of public information, 1939-44, assistant professor of classics, 1948-53; writer. *Military service:* U.S. Navy, Russian-speaking agent, 1944. *Awards, honors:* Rhodes scholar, 1927-30; Rockefeller fellow in opinion research, 1940-41; various national awards for educational radio programs.

WRITINGS: Heyday (novel), Ballantine, 1953; *On The Decay of Humanism* (essays), Rutgers University Press, 1967; *An Armful of Warm Girl* (novel), Knopf, 1978; *Portraits of the Painter* (novel), Knopf, 1979. Contributor to *Parnassus, Canto,* and *Esquire.*

SIDELIGHTS: Spackman comments briefly: "My only real literary interest is the high-style novel. The 'novel of ideas' and the *engage* never seem to me to come to life. My critical articles are heavily slanted toward technique (as against the 'meaning-boys')."

Spackman designed and built two Queen Anne houses for himself, including rough carpentry and panelling, remodeled a later modern house, and remodeled a large seaside villa in France.

AVOCATIONAL INTERESTS: Architecture.

BIOGRAPHICAL/CRITICAL SOURCES: New York Times, April 10, 1978.

*   *   *

SPALDING, R(onald) W(olcott) 1904-

PERSONAL: Born December 31, 1904, in Battle Creek, Mich.; son of Arthur Whitefield (a writer and teacher) and Maud (a teacher; maiden name, Wolcott) Spalding; married Helen Louise McElmurry (a registered nurse), August 21, 1930; children: Arthur W., Elaine (Mrs. Donald Halenz), Carole (Mrs. Larry Colburn), Sylvia Spalding Davis. *Education:* Columbia Union College, pre-med certificate, 1929; Loma Linda University, Dr. Med., 1934. *Religion:* Seventh-day Adventist. *Home:* 226 Kimber Lane, Berrien Springs, Mich. 49103.

CAREER: Baroness Erlanger Hospital, Chattanooga, Tenn., intern, 1934-35; private practice of family medicine in Gobles, Mich., 1936-56; Michigan Conference of Seventh-day Adventists, Lansing, physician, 1956-61; private practice in Gobles, Mich., 1961-70; Bacolod Adventist Hospital, Bacolod City, Philippines, physician, 1970-71; Mountain View College, Malaybalay, Philippines, teacher of Christian home and Christian marriage, 1971-72; private practice in Gobles, Mich., 1972-74; Andrews University, Berrien Springs, Mich., family physician at Medical Center, 1974-76; writer, 1976—.

WRITINGS: Where Did I Come From? (juvenile), Philippine Publishing House, 1974; (with sister, Elizabeth Spalding McFadden) *A Fire in My Bones: The Biography of A. W. Spalding, 1877-1953,* Pacific Press Publishing Association, 1979. Author of "Youth Asks—The Doctor Answers," a column in *Listen,* 1968-70. Contributor to *Life and Health* and *Review and Herald.*

WORK IN PROGRESS: Where Did the Baby Come From?, a revision of the Philippine *Where Did I Come From?,* written for the American culture.

SIDELIGHTS: Spalding writes: "In my early twenties I became assistant editor on my college paper. About that time I became interested in a student nurse because her life goal was to become a missionary nurse. We planned a doctor-nurse team for overseas work. Not until we had sent two daughters to the Far East did we attain our goal. I was called to relieve an American physician in the Philippines while he was on a one-year furlough. At the end of that year I was invited to introduce two classes on the Christian home and Christian marriage into the college curriculum of Mountain View College. While there my first book was written, later being published in Manila.

"My philosophy: Love is life. To give is to live. As my God is love (1 John 4:8, 16) I know that He created human love so that I (and all my brothers and sisters—all human beings) might experience and begin to understand what He means when He says 'I have come that they might have life and that they might have it more abundantly' (John 10:10).

"Prevention needs no cure. Perfect love can prevent unhappiness and fear (1 John 4:18), especially within the home. The better we can come to understand the richness, the contentment, and the joy of love as God would have us understand and practice it, the better we can come to understand God's perfect plan for our never-ending peace and happiness. My medical practice of forty years taught me that God's way, the way of unselfish love, is the only way to find the goal of every man and woman—happiness and contentment. Only in God can joy everlasting be found. May what I write contribute toward showing the way to the finding of the end of that rainbow, the finding of God's unending love."

*   *   *

SPIEGEL, Robert H. 1922-

PERSONAL: Born February 20, 1922, in Odebolt, Iowa; son of Harvey H. and Adad (Harter) Spiegel; married Dorothy Kerr, August 3, 1946; children: Ronald, Richard, Craig. *Education:* Drake University, B.A., 1943. *Religion:* Methodist. *Home:* 1109 Woodland Way, Madison, Wis. 53711. *Office: Wisconsin State Journal,* 1901 Fish Hatchery Rd., Madison, Wis. 53701.

CAREER/WRITINGS: Des Moines Register and Tribune, Des Moines, Iowa, reporter, 1946-63; *Mason City Globe-Gazette,* Mason City, Iowa, editor, 1963-74; *Wisconsin State Journal,* Madison, Wis., editor and columnist, 1974—. Notable assignments include coverage of national political conventions since 1956. Has served as frequent leader of American Press Institute seminars. President and campaign chairman for United Way in Mason City. *Military service:* U.S. Army, Security Agency, 1943-46; became first lieutenant. *Member:* Madison Press Club, Sigma Delta Chi. *Awards, honors:* Headliner Award, 1951, for a series on city government; three Iowa Associated Press newswriting sweepstakes awards, 1953, 1956, 1959; Sidney Hillman Foundation Award, 1956, for a series on segregated housing; Des Moines Education Association distinguished service award, 1962; Madison, Wis., Newspaperman of the Year Award, 1975.

*   *   *

SPILKA, Mark 1925-

PERSONAL: Born August 6, 1925, in East Cleveland,

Ohio; son of Harvey Joseph (a lawyer) and Zella (a poet; maiden name, Fenberg) Spilka; married Ellen Potter, May 6, 1950 (divorced December 14, 1965); married Ruth Dane Farnum (a weaver), January 18, 1975; children: Jane, Rachel, Aaron; (stepchildren) Betsy, Polly. *Education:* Brown University, B.A., 1949; Indiana University, M.A., 1953, Ph.D., 1956. *Home:* 294 Doyle Ave., Providence, R.I. 02906. *Office:* Department of English, Brown University, Providence, R.I. 02912.

CAREER: American Mercury, New York, N.Y., editorial assistant, 1949-51; University of Michigan, Ann Arbor, instructor, 1954-58, assistant professor of English, 1958-63; Brown University, Providence, R.I., associate professor, 1963-67, professor of English, 1967—, head of department, 1968-73. Visiting professor at Indiana University, autumn, 1961, summer, 1976, Hebrew University of Jerusalem, spring, 1972, and University of Tulsa, summer, 1975. *Military service:* U.S. Army Air Forces, 1944-46; became sergeant. *Member:* Modern Language Association of America (president of conference of editors of learned journals, 1974-75), American Association of University Professors. *Awards, honors:* Fellow of Indiana School of Letters, 1963; Guggenheim fellow, 1967-68; director of National Endowment for the Humanities summer seminar, 1974, fellow, 1978-79.

WRITINGS: The Love Ethic of D. H. Lawrence, Indiana University Press, 1955; *Dickens and Kafka: A Mutual Interpretation,* Indiana University Press, 1963; (editor) *D. H. Lawrence: A Collection of Critical Essays,* Prentice-Hall, 1963; (editor) *Toward a Poetics of Fiction,* Indiana University Press, 1977. Editor of *Novel: A Forum on Fiction,* 1967—.

WORK IN PROGRESS: Virginia Woolf's Quarrel With Grieving, which will be published separately or as part of a longer study on the taboo on tenderness in modern fiction, to be called *New Literary Quarrels With Tenderness.*

SIDELIGHTS: Spilka told *CA:* "I hold the dubious distinction of receiving in 1953 the world's first master's degree in literary criticism from the School of Letters (now defunct) at Indiana University. My mentors there were Leslie Fiedler, Francis Fergusson, and the philosophical anthropologist David Bidney. From Fiedler I learned to combine my penchant for New Critical exegesis with psychological speculations and a certain measure of artistry. From Fergusson I learned how to diagnose dramatic actions in fiction. From Bidney I learned to look for definitions of human nature by which writers' works and worlds were governed. Most of my published criticism reflects these lessons."

BIOGRAPHICAL/CRITICAL SOURCES: Saturday Review, July 13, 1963; *Times Literary Supplement,* January 16, 1964.

*   *   *

SPRING, David 1918-

PERSONAL: Born April 29, 1918, in Toronto, Ontario, Canada; came to the United States in 1949, naturalized citizen, 1963; son of Joseph (a pharmacist) and Miriam (Gold) Spring; married Eileen Jeffries (a writer), June 14, 1948. *Education:* University of Toronto, B.A., 1939; Harvard University, A.M., 1940, Ph.D., 1948. *Politics:* Democrat. *Home:* 5605 Wexford Rd., Baltimore, Md. 21209. *Office:* Department of History, Johns Hopkins University, Baltimore, Md. 21218.

CAREER: University of Toronto, Toronto, Ontario, lec-

turer in history, 1946-49; Johns Hopkins University, Baltimore, Md., assistant professor, 1949-56, associate professor, 1956-62, professor of history, 1962—. Visiting professor at University of Leicester, 1968-69. *Military service:* Canadian Army, 1942-44. Royal Canadian Navy, 1944-46. *Member:* American Historical Association, Economic History Association, Royal Historical Society, Maryland Audubon Society (head of conservation, 1964—), Phi Beta Kappa. *Awards, honors:* Ford Foundation fellowship, 1952-53; Guggenheim fellowship, 1957-58; National Endowment for the Humanities fellowship, 1977-78.

WRITINGS: The English Landed Estate in the Nineteenth Century, Johns Hopkins Press, 1963; (editor) John Bateman, *The Great Landowners of Great Britain,* Leicester University Press, 1971; (editor) *Ecology and Religion in History,* Harper, 1974; *The First Industrial Revolution,* Macmillan, 1975; (editor) *European Landed Elites in the Nineteenth Century,* Johns Hopkins Press, 1977. Contributor to history journals.

WORK IN PROGRESS: A book on Jane Austen and her society; a book on the English landed elite from the eighteenth century to the present.

SIDELIGHTS: Spring comments: "My study of the English landed elite sums up a lifetime's work. The English landed elite provided the core of what was the greatest governing class since the Roman. It is a story of decline and fall." *Avocational interests:* Walking, birdwatching.

*   *   *

SPRINGER, Nesha Bass 1930-

PERSONAL: Born April 19, 1930, in Boston, Mass.; daughter of Harris (a physician) and Sylvia (Gale) Bass; married Robert P. Springer (an attorney), September 23, 1951; children: Nancy Springer Westendorf, Mark Bass, Carrie Kasen, Stephen Richard. *Education:* Mt. Holyoke College, B.A., 1951; Boston University, M.Ed., 1972. *Politics:* Democrat. *Religion:* Jewish. *Home:* 28 Russell Circle, Natick, Mass. 01760.

CAREER: Suburban World, Inc., Needham, Mass., reporter and author of column in *Suburban Free Press,* 1970-78; researcher and free-lance writer, 1978—.

WRITINGS: (With Beatrice Marden Glickman) *Who Cares for the Baby?: Choices in Child Care,* Schocken, 1978. Also author of children's books. Contributor of articles and stories to magazines.

WORK IN PROGRESS: A nonfiction book, with Beatrice Marden Glickman.

SIDELIGHTS: Nesha Springer writes: "I am concerned about the conflicts in the needs of working mothers and their babies, and the origin, development, and amelioration [of these needs] through individual choice based on informed judgment and personal circumstance. I am also concerned about the other similar critical and growing problems in other stages of life. I am working on a book about healthy, vital old people in all walks of life. It will deal with ordinary men and women seventy-five and older. Its purpose is to help others make the choices available to them."

*   *   *

SPULER, Bertold 1911-

PERSONAL: Born December 5, 1911, in Karlsruhe, West Germany; son of Rudolf (an ophthalmologist) and Natalena (Lindner) Spuler; married Gerda Roehrig, October 22, 1937;

children: Christof, Thomas, Hanna Spuler Lemm. *Education:* Attended University of Heidelberg, 1930-31, University of Munich, 1931-33, and University of Hamburg, 1932; University of Breslau, Dr. Phil., 1935. *Home:* Mittelweg 90, D2 Hamburg 13, West Germany. *Office:* Department of Oriental Culture and History, Rothenbaumchaussee 36, D2 Hamburg 13, West Germany.

CAREER: University of Berlin, Berlin, West Germany, assistant professor of East European history, 1935-37; University of Goettingen, Goettingen, West Germany, lecturer, 1937-42; University of Munich, Munich, West Germany, professor of Oriental studies, 1942-46; University of Goettingen, professor of Oriental studies, 1946-48; University of Hamburg, Hamburg, West Germany, professor of Oriental studies, 1948—. *Military service:* German Army, 1940-44.

MEMBER: Academy of Sciences and Letters (Bordeaux, France), Finnish Oriental Society, Deutsche Morgenlandische Gesellschaft, Deutsche Gesellschaft fuer Aseuropa Kunde. *Awards, honors:* Dr. theology, University of Berne, 1962; Dr. es lettres, University of Bordeaux, 1965.

WRITINGS—In English: *The Muslim World: A Historical Survey,* text edition, Humanities, 1960, Volume I: *Age of the Caliphs,* Volume II: *The Mongol Period; Les Mongols dans l'histoire,* Payot, 1961, translation by Geoffrey Wheeler published as *The Mongols in History,* Praeger, 1971; *Geschichte der Mongolen, nach oestlichen und europaeischen Zeugnissen des 13 und 14 Jahrhunderts,* Artemis (Zurich), 1968, translation by Helga Drummond and Stuart Drummond published as *History of the Mongols: Based on Eastern and Western Accounts of the Thirteenth and Fourteenth Centuries,* University of California Press, 1972; *Rulers and Government of the World,* Volume II: *1492-1929,* Volume III: *1930-1975,* Bowker, 1977.

Other works: *Die europaeische Diplomatie in Konstantinopel* (title means "European Diplomacy in Constantinople"), Priebatsch Breslan, 1935; *Die Mongolen in Iran: Politik, Verwaltung und Kultur der Ilchunzeit, 1220-1350* (title means "The Mongols in Iran: Politics, Administration and Culture Under the Ilkhans, 1220-1350"), J. C. Hinrichs, 1939, 3rd edition, Deutsche Akademie, 1968; *Idel-Ural, Voelker und Staaten zwischen Wolga und Ural* (title means "Idel-Ural: Peoples and Empires Between Volga and Ural"), O. Stollberg, 1942; *Die goldene Horde: Die Mongolen in Russland, 1223-1502* (title means "The Golden Horde: The Mongols in Russia, 1223-1502"), Harrassowitz, 1943, 2nd edition, 1965; *Die Gegenwartslage der Ostkirchen in ihrer voelkischen und staatlichen Umwelt* (title means "The Present Situation of the Eastern Churches in Their National and Political Environment"), Metopen, 1948, 2nd edition, 1969.

Minister Ploetz Regenten und Regierunge der Welt, Ploetz, 1953, 3rd edition, 1972, Volume II-III: *1892-1970;* (with Ludwig Forrer) *Der Vordere Orient in islamischer Zeit* (title means "The Near East During the Islamic Period"), A. Francke, 1954; (with Heinrich Ferdinand Wuestenfeld and Gustave Mahler) *Vergleichungs-Tabellen zur muslimischen und iranischen Zeitrechnung* (title means "Comparative Table of Muslim, Iranian, and Oriental Christian Calenders"), Deutsche Morgenlandische Gesellschaft, 1961, 3rd edition; (with J. M. Hornus) *Relations exterieures de l'-Eglise orthodoxe orientale* (title means "International Relations of the Eastern Churches"), [Paris], 1965; *Die Gegenwartslage der Oskirehen in ihrer voelkischen und staatlichen Umwelt,* Metopen, 1968; *Die Kultur des Islams* (title means "Islamic Culture"), Athenaion, 1971; (with Janine Sourdel-

Thomine) *Die Kunst des Islam* (title means "The Art of Islam"), Propylaen, 1973.

Contributor of articles to journals in his field. Co-editor, *Jahrbuecher fuer Geschichte Osteuropus,* 1935-37, and *Das Historisch-Politische Buch,* 1953—; editor, *Der Islam,* 1949—, *Handbuch der Orientalistik,* 1952—, and *Studien zur Sprache, Geschichte und Kultur des Islamischen Orients,* 1965—.

WORK IN PROGRESS: History of Iran During the Seldjukid Period.

SIDELIGHTS: Spuler is fluent in many languages, including French, English, Russian, Polish, Arabic, Turkish, Persian, and Italian.

* * *

SPURR, Stephen Hopkins 1918-

PERSONAL: Born February 14, 1918, in Washington, D.C.; son of Josiah Edward and Sophie Clara (Burchard) Spurr; married Patricia Chapman Orton, August 18, 1945; children: Daniel Orton, Jean Burchard. *Education:* University of Florida, B.S. (highest honors), 1938; Yale University, M.F. (cum laude), 1940, Ph.D., 1950. *Religion:* Unitarian-Universalist. *Home:* 4007 Sierra Dr., Austin, Tex. 78731. *Office:* Lyndon B. Johnson School of Public Affairs, University of Texas, Austin, Tex. 78712.

CAREER: Harvard University, Cambridge, Mass., instructor, 1940-45, assistant professor of forestry, 1945-50, acting director of Harvard Forest, 1943-45; University of Minnesota, Minneapolis, associate professor of forestry, 1950-52; University of Michigan, Ann Arbor, professor of silviculture and natural resources, 1952-71, dean of School of Natural Resources, 1962-65, dean of Horace H. Rackham School of Graduate Studies, 1964-71, vice-president, 1969-71; University of Texas, Austin, professor of botany and public affairs, 1971—, president, 1971-74. Visiting scholar at Center for Advanced Studies in Behavioral Sciences, 1966-67. Inventor of photogrammetric devices. Head of Council of Graduate Schools, 1969-71, and Graduate Record Examination Board; member of Commission on Non-Traditional Study, 1971, and National Board of Graduate Education, 1971-75. Member of board of trustees of Educational Testing Service, Carnegie Foundation for the Advancement of Teaching, Carnegie Council on Policy Studies in Higher Education, and Institute of International Education.

MEMBER: Society of American Foresters (fellow; member of council; vice-president; president-elect), Ecological Society of America, Organization for Tropical Studies (president, 1968-69), Council of Biology Editors (member of executive committee), Nature Conservancy (member of board of trustees), New Zealand Institute of Foresters (honorary member), Michigan Academy of Science, Arts and Letters (president, 1968-69), University of Michigan Society of Fellows (senior fellow), Phi Beta Kappa, Sigma Xi, Phi Eta Sigma, Phi Kappa Phi. *Awards, honors:* National Science Foundation fellowship, 1957-58; Fulbright scholarship for New Zealand and Australia, 1960; D.Sc. from University of Florida, 1971; Wilbur L. Cross Medal from Yale University, 1978.

WRITINGS: Aerial Photographs in Forestry, Ronald, 1948; *Forest Inventory,* Ronald, 1952; *Photogrammetry and Photo-Interpretation,* Ronald, 1960; *Forest Ecology,* Ronald, 1964, 2nd edition, 1973; *Academic Degree Structures,* McGraw, 1970; *American Forest Policy in Development,* University of Washington Press, 1976; *Forests for the Fu-*

ture, Wiley, 1980. Founding editor of *Forest Science,* 1955-60.

SIDELIGHTS: Spurr told *CA*: "As the earth's stored accumulations of fossil hydrocarbons are used up, we must inevitably place more and more reliance upon the current production of biomass—mainly wood and agricultural residues."

*   *   *

STADELMAN, S(ara) L(ee) 1917-
(Sara Lee Harris)

PERSONAL: Born May 4, 1917, in Brooklyn, N.Y.; moved to Sarnia, Ontario, Canada in 1969; naturalized Canadian citizen in 1974; daughter of Harry Leopold (a salesman) and Minnie (Cohen) Harris; married Richard Ryerson Stadelman (an architect), December 28, 1945 (died June 24, 1969); children: Kris Ryerson (son), Catherine. *Education:* Attended Columbia University, 1934-36, 1953, and Bennington School of the Dance, 1941; Neighborhood Playhouse, graduate, 1942; attended Pasadena Playhouse, 1946, Yale University School of the Drama, 1955-56, and Immaculate Heart College, 1957; Mercy College (now Mercy College of Detroit), B.A., 1960; graduate studies, University of Windsor, 1960-61. *Home and office:* Moving Word Centre, R.R. 1, Palmer Rapids, Ontario, Canada K0J 2E0.

CAREER: Early career as an actress on Broadway, 1942, 1944-45, included featured roles in "Snafu," "Skin of Our Teeth," "Sons and Soldiers," and "Boy Meets Girl"; actress with United Service Organizations (USO) in United States, and part of first professional acting troupe to perform in European and North African combat zones, featured in "Boy Meets Girl," "The Male Animal," "You Can't Take It with You," and "Out of the Frying Pan," 1943; founder and producer-director of the first professional stock company in the state of Nevada, The Bird Cage Theater, Las Vegas, 1947-49, acted there in "Joan of Lorraine," "The Glass Menagerie," and "The Heiress"; Immaculate Heart College, Los Angelés, Calif., instructor of dance, 1956-57; originator of theatre form Choreologia, 1958; Catholic University of America, Washington, D.C., guest artist, 1958; Mercy College (now Mercy College of Detroit), Detroit, Mich., instructor in speech and drama and director of children's theatre, 1959-60; Marygrove College, Detroit, instructor in speech and drama, 1962-63; Performing Arts Workshop, Detroit and Whitehall, Mich., director, 1963-68; Moving Word Centre, Palmer Rapids, Ontario, director, 1969—. Disk jockey, counter-voice to "Sally," the German radio propagandist, Italy, 1943; news commentator, WNYC radio, 1944; writer and host, "Time for Everyone," Las Vegas Public Library weekly radio program, KENO radio, 1946; writer and announcer, Red Cross radio show, KENO radio, 1946-47; producer, director, and choreographer of pageant "Vegas in Calico," 1948; produced in Choreologia form several works by other authors, 1958-65; writer, director, and performer of more than sixty productions and multimedia lecture-demonstrations in the United States, Canada, and Mexico, 1963-78. Artist-in-residence at Marygrove College, 1961, St. Mary's Academy (Windsor, Ontario), spring, 1964, Mercy College (Omaha, Neb.), fall, 1964, Seton Hill College, 1966, Madonna House (Combermere, Ontario), 1966, Aquinas College, spring, 1967, St. Mary's Academy (Combermere), 1968, and Scollard Hall (North Bay, Ontario), 1974.

MEMBER: Canadian Women and Religion. *Awards, honors:* Special Service Award, U.S. Government, 1947, for USO work; City of Las Vegas Award, 1948, for "Vegas in Calico"; Huntington Drama Festival Award, University of Southern California, 1956, for play "No Time for Tea"; Cabrini Literary Award, first prize for short story, 1957, for "Summertime and Wintertime"; teaching fellowship, University of Windsor, 1960-61; Senior Filmmaker's Grant, Ontario Arts Council, 1976, for "Catherine's Song."

WRITINGS—Plays: "No Time for Tea," first produced in Los Angeles at Stop Gap Theatre, University of Southern California, January 10, 1957; "Teresa of Avila," first produced in Los Angeles at Immaculate Heart College, May 24, 1957; "The New Canticle," first produced in Washington, D.C., at Catholic University of America, 1959; "No Hasty Flight," first produced in Windsor, Ontario, at St. Mary's Academy, April 24, 1964; "Western Testament," first produced in Omaha, Neb., at Civic Music Hall, October 23-25, 1964; "Maranatha," first produced in Greensboro, N.C., at Notre Dame High School, March, 1966; "Touch the Mountain," first produced in Greensburgh, Pa., at Seton Hill College, April, 1966; "A New Song for Prisoners," first produced in Muskegon, Mich., at St. Paul's Episcopal Church, September 23, 1966; "The Passion of Jocasta," first produced in Grand Rapids, Mich., at St. Cecilia Auditorium, April 13, 1967; "Innocent Until," first produced in Ottawa, Ontario, at Unitarian Church, 1971; "Dialogue a St. Pierre," (written in French), first produced in St. Pierre et Miquelon at Cathedral of St. Pierre et Miquelon, 1971; "Eve of Genesis," first produced in Montreal, Quebec, for cable television broadcast, 1972; "Memoirs of a Master-Builder," first produced in Antigonish, Nova Scotia, at St. Ninan's Cathedral, spring, 1974; "Autobiography of an Artist Before and After Pentecost," first produced in Ottawa, Ontario, at Canadian Religious Conference, 1974.

Works adapted for performance: D. H. Lawrence, "The Princess" (short story adapted to one-act play), first produced in Los Angeles at University of Southern California, January 10, 1957; Ruth Russell Davis, "Chiara" (poems adapted to one-act play), first produced in Detroit, Mich., at Detroit Institute of Arts, November, 1963; William Shakespeare, "The Dark Lady Within" (sonnets adapted to one-act play), first produced in Detroit at Marygrove College, 1962; Sister Stanislaus, I.H.M., "November to November" (poems adapted to one-act play), first produced in Detroit at Performing Arts Workshop, November, 1965.

Other: "Snowball!" (filmscript), Moving Word Centre, 1970; "Catherine's Song" (filmscript), Moving Word Centre, 1975; *After the Ascension* (poems), privately printed, 1976. Also author of a one-act play for television, "Shining Secret," an autobiographical collection, "Why Should I Honor Your Gods of the Drama?," and short stories. Contributor of articles, reviews, and poetry (some under name Sara Lee Harris) to *Chelsea Journal, Catholic Theatre,* and *Sign.* Contributing editor, *Drama Critique,* 1959-60.

WORK IN PROGRESS: A collection of poetry, *Grave Statements;* a novel, *The General's Wife;* a screenplay on Marie Guyart (Marie de l'Incarnation); two plays, "Pia dei Tolomei" and "Alien Kingdom"; short stories.

SIDELIGHTS: Sara Lee Stadelman is the originator of Choreologia, a theatre form in which the actor uses speech (or song) and stylized movement simultaneously. She developed Choreologia, she says, "because epic themes demand epic treatment." Stadelman points out that her work is not the conventional dance drama which interprets words or phrases or emotions (in fact she has little use for interpretive dance, and does not want to be called a dancer). "In Choreologia no gesture is ever made without interior motivation,'' she explains. Joseph K. Hogan says: ''Choreologia is like a modern abstract painting which is good art. The painter takes off all the surrounding materials of an object in order to focus the viewer's attention on what the essence or mood of the object is. So in choreologia, Sara Lee in communicating truth, especially a religious truth as she does so often in her plays, strips off all the unnecessary appendages and props which are common in naturalistic drama and by the use and blend of movement, music and acting produces truth in a new manner and [with] greater freedom.'' Her choreography shows the influence of her teachers Martha Graham and Louis Horst, as well as ballet, in an unusual blend. ''I teach my actors to dance, and my dancers to act, although I find the latter more difficult,'' she told *CA*.

Her productions have stirred up controversy and won critical acclaim. Drama critic Louis Cook called her production of Euripedes' ''Trojan Women'' in Choreologia ''one of the most effective and unique dramatic presentations of the Detroit season, either amateur or professional.''

Stadelman created the first dramatization in theatrical history of the sonnets of William Shakespeare. Her presentation, entitled ''The Dark Lady Within,'' is registered as the first such production by the British Museum and the New York Public Library Theatre Section. The original production of ''The Dark Lady Within'' was called ''ingenious, delightful'' by Cook, who added, ''Mrs. Stadelman makes Albee look like a sissy, and Ionesco tongue-tied.'' Her religious productions have often been controversial because of her unsentimental portrayal of saints, and because the works were sometimes performed in churches. Stadelman feels that controversy arises because ''some people see my work as an attack on a life style—as a criticism of poor art, sentimental thinking, and shallow religiosity.'' At times she can say, ''I have a peculiar genius—narrow, but quite deep,'' and at other times is embarrassed by the word ''genius.'' ''I am not a great scholar, but I have a formidable power of observation and a prophetic instinct.'' She has tried to avoid success as bringing ''too much identity,'' and has chosen a life of faith and poverty.

Movie critic Juliet O'Neill calls ''Catherine's Song'' ''a religious-feminist film . . . [which] contains a bizarre dialogue between a 14th century nun, St. Catherine . . . and a contemporary woman. . . . St. Catherine was a radical nun and it is the radicalization of Christian women that Ms. Stadelman seeks.'' Of her poems *After the Ascension* a *Chelsea Journal* reviewer says: ''A unique little book has appeared which in its simplicity might go unnoticed by many. Yet . . . the book contains an unexpected power.'' Critic H. Raff remarks that ''our culture does not easily take to the condensed brevity of these gestures, which, like the art form of the dance, cut through our traditional expectations of continuity and our assumptions about the nature of 'realistic' representation.''

BIOGRAPHICAL/CRITICAL SOURCES: New York Times, May 5, 1943, June 23, 1943; *Detroit Free Press*, October 30, 1961, January 21, 1962; *Sign*, July, 1962; *Catholic Theatre*, November, 1962, April, 1965, December, 1965, October, 1966; *Restoration*, February, 1967, March, 1967; *Ottawa Citizen*, October 7, 1975; *Chelsea Journal*, September/October, 1977.

* * *

STAHL, Gustav Richard 1888(?)-1978

OBITUARY NOTICE: Born c. 1988; died July 17, 1978, in New York, N.Y. Editor. Formerly an executive secretary of the National Bureau of Economic Research, Stahl was best known as editor of *Supervision*, an industrial relations magazine. Obituaries and other sources: *New York Times*, July 18, 1978.

* * *

STANKE, Alain 1934-

PERSONAL: Born June 11, 1934, in Kaunas, Lithuania; came to Canada; married Josette Ghedin (an aesthetician); children: Daniel, Brigitte, Claudie, Sophie. *Education:* Attended Institut Universitaire and Montreal University. *Office:* Editions Internationales Alain Stanke, Montreal, Quebec, Canada H3H 2N4.

CAREER: Editions La Presse, Montreal, Quebec, general director, 1971-75; Editions Internationales Alain Stanke, Montreal, president, 1975—; journalist and radio and television announcer. *Member:* Canadian Union of French Speaking Journalists (director). *Awards, honors:* Wilderness Award for best humanitarian film of the year, 1967, for ''Cent Ans Deja.''

WRITINGS—All published by L'Editions de L'Homme, except as noted: (Editor) J. Arthur Taillefer, *Un Pretre et son peche*, 1961, translation published as *A Priest and His Sin;* (with Marie Jose Beaudoin) *Le Rage des ''goof balls''*, 1962; (editor) *Toges, bistouris, matraques et soutanes*, 1962; (editor) *Pourquoi et comment cesser de fumer*, illustrations by Jean Dubuc, 1965; *Cents ans deja* (screenplay); *Les Greffes du coeur*, 1968; *''J'aime encore mieux le jus de betterave!'': Souvenirs d'un enfant de guerre* (autobiography), 1969; (with Jean-Louis Morgan) *''Ce Combat qui n'en finit plus . . .''* 1970; (with Morgan) *Pax: Lute a finir avec la pegre*, Editions La Presse, 1972; *Guide des vacances inusitees*, Editions La Presse, 1974; *So Much to Forget*, Vanguard, 1977. Also author of *Un Mois chez les damnes, Le Journalisme mene a tout,* and *Rampa, imposteur ou initie?*

* * *

STAPLETON, Ruth Carter 1929-

PERSONAL: Born August 7, 1929, in Archery, Ga.; daughter of Earl (a grocer, farm machinery salesman, and politician) and Lillian (a nurse; maiden name, Gordy) Carter; married Robert Stapleton (a veterinarian), November 14, 1948; children: Lynn, Scott, Patti, Michael. *Education:* Attended Georgia State College for Women, 1946-48, Methodist College, and University of North Carolina. *Religion:* Southern Baptist. *Home:* 329 DeVane, Fayetteville, N.C. 28305. *Office:* 655 Deep Valley Dr., Suite 190, Rolling Hills Estates, Calif. 90274.

CAREER: Spiritual therapist and author. Operates Behold, Inc. (nonprofit corporation). Leader of workshops and retreats throughout the world. High school English teacher in Fayetteville, N.C.

WRITINGS—Nonfiction: *The Gift of Inner Healing*, Word, Inc., 1976; *Experiencing Inner Healing*, Word, Inc., 1977; (with Robert Cochran) *How Do You Face Disappointments?*, Creation House, 1977; *Brother Billy*, Harper, 1978.

Author of quarterly newsletter, ''Behold and Be Whole.'' Has recorded cassettes, including ''Living With Jesus Within,'' ''In Cahoots With the Holy Spirit,'' ''From the Valley to a Velvet Victory,'' and ''With Jesus You Can't Go Wrong.''

SIDELIGHTS: Stapleton has combined ''eloquence and charismatic appeal'' to become one of the most popular religious leaders today. Her particular brand of spiritual therapy seems to owe as much to self-help movements as it does to theology, although she told Jessamyn West that "the psychiatric therapy part is a drop in the bucket compared to the flood of healing that comes from the Holy Spirit."

Stapleton described her nondenominational religion to Claire Safran as a "religion of all mankind," and she works with Catholics as well as with Protestants. While some more traditional clergy have been doubtful of her therapy's theological substance, few would argue that she is ineffective as a spiritual healer.

In her best-selling books, Stapleton talks about "the healing of memories" by "faith-imagination therapy." A reporter for *Newsweek* wrote: "She teaches that physical and emotional problems afflicting adults result from the 'negative memories' of early childhood traumas buried in the subconscious. Guided by Ruth's own meditations, people learn to visualize those early traumas and then to imagine the presence of Jesus as 'the principle of universal love.' Once Jesus is allowed to heal their painful memories, people are freed from the grip of the past and restored to self-assurance as accepted children of the Heavenly Father."

Stapleton and her husband have recently established a retreat center called "Holovita" ("Whole Life") on a thirty-acre ranch outside of Dallas.

BIOGRAPHICAL/CRITICAL SOURCES: Time, April 26, 1976, July 19, 1976; *Redbook,* October, 1976; *McCalls,* April, 1977; *Newsweek,* November 14, 1977, July 17, 1978; *New York,* March 27, 1978.

*   *   *

STEEL, Danielle

PERSONAL: Born in New York, N.Y. *Education:* Educated in France. *Residence:* New York, N.Y. *Address:* c/o Dell Publishing Co., Inc., 1 Dag Hammarskjold Plaza, 245 East 47th St., New York, N.Y. 10017.

CAREER: Writer.

WRITINGS—Novels: *Going Home,* Pocket Books, 1973; *Passion's Promise,* Dell, 1977; *The Promise* (based on a screenplay by Garry Michael White), Dell, 1978; *Now and Forever,* Dell, 1978; *Season of Passion,* Dell, 1979; *Summer's End,* Dell, 1980. Contributor of articles and poetry to numerous periodicals, including *Viva, California Living, San Francisco, Good Housekeeping, McCall's, Ladies Home Journal,* and *Cosmopolitan.*

*   *   *

STEEL, Tex
See ROSS, W(illiam) E(dward) D(aniel)

*   *   *

STEIN, Jerome L(eon)   1928-

PERSONAL: Born November 14, 1928, in Brooklyn, N.Y.; son of Meyer and Ida (Shapiro) Stein; married Hadassah Levow (a medical librarian), August 27, 1950; children: Seth, Gil, Ilana. *Education:* Brooklyn College (now of the City University of New York), B.A. (summa cum laude), 1949; Yale University, M.A., 1950, Ph.D., 1955. *Home:* 77 Elton St., Providence, R.I. 02906. *Office:* Department of Economics, Brown University, Providence, R.I. 02912.

CAREER: Brown University, Providence, R.I., instructor, 1953-56, assistant professor, 1956-60, associate professor, 1960-62, professor of economics, 1962-70, Eastman Professor of Political Economy, 1970—. Visiting professor at He-

brew University, Jerusalem, 1965-66, 1972-73. Member of Social Science Research Council grants committee, 1967—, chairman, 1971—. *Member:* American Economic Association. *Awards, honors:* Ford Foundation fellow, 1961-62; Social Science Research Council grant, 1965-66; Guggenheim fellow, 1972-73.

WRITINGS: The Nature and Efficiency of the Foreign Exchange Market: Essays in International Finance, Princeton University Press, 1962; (with G. M. Borts) *Economic Growth in a Free Market,* Columbia University Press, 1964; *Money and Capacity Growth,* Columbia University Press, 1971; (editor) *Monetarism,* North-Holland Publishing, 1976. Associate editor of *Journal of Finance,* 1964-70; member of board of editors of *American Economic Review.*

*   *   *

STEINBACK, Alexander Alan   1894-1978

OBITUARY NOTICE: Born February 2, 1894, in Baltimore, Md.; died November 12, 1978, in Hollywood, Fla. Rabbi, poet, and author of books on philosophical themes. Steinback served as rabbi in Virginia, West Virginia, and for thirty-two years in Brooklyn, N.Y. In 1970 he received the Frank L. Weil Award for Distinguished Contributions to the Advancement of Jewish Culture in America from the Jewish Welfare Board. He wrote nine books. Obituaries and other sources: *Who's Who in World Jewry,* Pitman, 1972; *New York Times,* November 15, 1978.

*   *   *

STEINER, Wendy   1949-

PERSONAL: Born March 20, 1949, in Winnipeg, Manitoba, Canada; came to the United States in 1970; daughter of William Harrison (an educational psychologist) and Ida (Abramson) Lucow; married Peter Steiner (a professor of Slavic language and literature), February 2, 1973. *Education:* McGill University, B.A., 1970; Yale University, M.Phil., 1972, Ph.D., 1974. *Home:* Riverloft Apartments, 331, 2300 Walnut St., Philadelphia, Pa. 19103. *Office:* Department of English, University of Michigan, Haven Hall, Ann Arbor, Mich. 48109.

CAREER: Yale University, New Haven, Conn., assistant professor of English, 1974-76; University of Michigan, Ann Arbor, assistant professor of English, 1976—. *Member:* Modern Language Association of America, Semiotic Society of America (member of executive board, 1978-80). *Awards, honors:* Woodrow Wilson fellowship, 1970-71; Josephine Keal fellowship from University of Michigan, 1978-79.

WRITINGS: Exact Resemblances to Exact Resemblance: The Literary Portraiture of Gertrude Stein, Yale University Press, 1978.

WORK IN PROGRESS: A book on the relation between modern painting and literature; editing proceedings of International Conference on the Semiotics of Art, Indiana University Press, 1979-80.

SIDELIGHTS: Steiner told *CA:* "Gertrude Stein interested me as a problem in criticism because she strikes everyone intuitively as crucial to modernism, yet defies conventional literary-critical explanation. She seemed a perfect case—and a very deserving one—to examine in the light of structuralist and semiotic methodology, and I have been amply rewarded for this attention with surprising insights into Stein, modern literature in general, and the very methodologies that I was so interested in applying. Out of this work has come my current preoccupation with the relation between modern painting and literature, for Stein and cubism were closely connected. This new topic, involving concrete poetry, nonsense in the two arts, William Carlos Williams and Brueghel, imagism, vorticism, and other modern schools, will be my next full-length study.''

* * *

STEINERT, Marlis G(ertrud)

PERSONAL: Born in Basel, Switzerland; daughter of Peter (an industrialist) and Maria Degener (Boening) Dalmer; married Otto Steinert (deceased); children: Stefan. *Education:* Attended University of Heidelberg and University of Berlin; University of Saarbruecken, Ph.D., 1956. *Religion:* Protestant. *Home:* Ave. Adrien Jeandin, Thonex-Geneva, Switzerland. *Office:* Graduate Institute of International Studies, 132 Rue de Lausanne, Geneva, Switzerland.

CAREER: Carnegie Endowment, European Center, Geneva, Switzerland, research assistant, 1955-58; associated with Foundation Nationale des Sciences Politques, Paris, France, 1958-60; Carnegie Endowment, research assistant, 1961-62; Graduate Institute of International Studies, Geneva, associate professor and research associate, 1969-71, professor of contemporary history and international relations, 1972—, director of doctoral program, 1977—. *Member:* European Association for Japanese Studies, Association of European History, Swiss Historical Association, Swiss-Japanese Association, Association of Professors of the University of Geneva.

WRITINGS: (Translator) Alfred Grosser, *Die Bonner Demokratie* (title means ''The Democracy of Bonn''), Rauch Verlag, 1960; *Die dreiundzwanzig Tage der Regierung Doenitz*, Econ Verlag, 1967, translation by Richard Barry published as *Twenty-Three Days: The Final Collapse of Nazi Germany*, Walker & Co., 1969, published in England as *Capitulation 1945: The Story of the Doenitz Regime*, Constable, 1969; *Hitlers Krieg und die Deutschen: Stimmung und Haltung der Bevoelkerung im Zweiten Weltkrieg*, Econ Verlag, 1970, translation by Thomas E. DeWitt published as *Hitler's War and the Germans: Public Mood and Attitude during the Second World War*, Ohio University Press, 1977; *L'Allemagne national-socialiste, 1933-1945* (title means ''National Socialist Germany, 1933-1945''), Editions Richelieu, 1972; *Les origines de la seconde guerre mondiale* (title means ''The Origins of the Second World War''), Presses universitaires de France, 1974; *Le Japon face au monde contemporain* (title means ''Japan in the Contemporary World''), Asian Documentation and Research Center, 1975; (contributor) Institut Universitaire des Hautes Etudes Internationales, editors, *International Relations in a Changing World*, Sijthoff, 1977. Contributor to international studies journals.

WORK IN PROGRESS: A study of Japanese foreign policy; studying external relations of the European Economic Community.

SIDELIGHTS: Marlis Steinert comments: ''I am of German nationality, but I teach in French and English; I write in German and French and have started to write in English. My interest is contemporary history and international relations, which implies intensive traveling.

''Writing now is only a secondary task since most of my time is devoted to teaching and administrative work. Most of my interests cover the wide range of nineteenth-century history up to international relations in our time. These are the dominant factors of my activities. My thesis treated the economic, social, and political thoughts of Michel Chevalier, adviser to Napoleon III; I then turned to international conflict studies, research, and publications concerning national socialist Germany as well as teaching and research in international relations.

''At the core of my interests is the question of what happens to people and nations in a certain historical constellation; what are the main features and currents of the international system. I am also very much concerned with the influence of public opinion toward the foreign policy process. *Hitler's War and the Germans* illustrates this concern in showing what are the fundamental attitudes of the Germans, where are the limits of propaganda, etc.

''My teachings are mostly concerned with the history and the relations between Europe, the United States, and Japan. I am focusing on the similarities and the disparities in this trilateral relationship.''

* * *

STELZIG, Eugene Louis 1943-

PERSONAL: Born August 18, 1943, in Bischofshofen, Austria; came to the United States in 1961, naturalized citizen, 1966; son of Josef R. (a police officer) and Susanna (Fuereder) Stelzig; married Elsge Hilly van Munster, December 31, 1968. *Education:* University of Pennsylvania, B.A., 1966; King's College, Cambridge, B.A., 1968, M.A., 1970; Harvard University, M.A., 1969, Ph.D., 1972. *Politics:* Independent. *Religion:* ''Lapsed Catholic.'' *Home:* 3294 Polebridge Rd., Geneseo, N.Y. 14454. *Office:* Department of English, State University of New York College at Geneseo, Geneseo, N.Y. 14454.

CAREER: State University of New York College at Geneseo, assistant professor of English, 1972—. Member of Woodrow Wilson Fellowship Foundation. *Member:* Modern Language Association of America, Phi Beta Kappa. *Awards, honors:* Woodrow Wilson fellowship, 1966-77; National Endowment for the Humanities fellow at Indiana University, 1978-79.

WRITINGS: *All Shades of Consciousness: Wordsworth's Poetry and the Self in Time*, Mouton, 1975. Also author of ''A Little Fire in a Wild Field: Collected Poems.'' Contributor of articles and poems to professional journals and literary magazines.

WORK IN PROGRESS: *Paralogues*, poems; research for a book on the confessional imagination in the major fiction of Hermann Hesse, *Hermann Hesse's Fictions of the Self: A Study in Eigensinn and the Confessional Imagination*.

SIDELIGHTS: Stelzig comments: ''I define myself as essentially a poet and writer who, like Kafka, is doomed not to have his work accepted in his lifetime, and probably never. The modern poet is not allowed any 'presence' in the modern world; above all he is the *persona non grata*, the nonexistent artist who has been pre-empted and excluded by all other arts and sciences. Thus my dictum, from an unpublished poem: 'the modern poet lives in a kingdom of his own despair; he doesn't need any company there.' I'm just one of Kafka's many contemporary offspring. I live in silence; silence lives in me.''

* * *

STERN, Gerald 1925-

PERSONAL: Born February 22, 1925, in Pittsburgh, Pa.; son of Harry and Ida (Barach) Stern; married Patricia Miller (an artist), September 12, 1952; children: Rachael, David.

Education: University of Pittsburgh, B.A., 1947; Columbia University, M.A., 1949. *Home address:* R.D.4, Box 207-A, Easton, Pa. 18042.

CAREER: Lake Grove School, Lake Grove, N.Y., English teacher and principal, 1951-53; Victoria Drive Secondary School, Glasgow, Scotland, English teacher, 1953-54; Temple University, Philadelphia, Pa., instructor in English, 1957-63; Indiana University of Pennsylvania, Indiana, associate professor of English, 1963-67; Somerset County College, Somerville, N.J., professor of English, 1968—. Visiting poet at Sarah Lawrence College, spring, 1978, and University of Pittsburgh, fall, 1979. Conducts poetry workshops; gives readings at colleges, universities, theaters, and art centers. Consultant in literature to Pennsylvania Council on the Arts. *Military service:* U.S. Army Air Corps, 1946-47. *Member:* Modern Language Association, P.E.N., New Jersey Poets & Writers. *Awards, honors:* Creative writing grant from National Endowment for the Arts, 1976; Lamont Poetry Selection, 1977, for *Lucky Life;* nomination for National Book Critics Circle Award, 1978, for *Lucky Life.*

WRITINGS: Pineys (poem), Rutgers University Press, 1971; *Rejoicings* (poems), Fiddlehead Poetry Books, 1973; *Lucky Life* (poems), Houghton, 1977. Contributor to poetry journals and popular magazines, including *New Yorker, Nation, Paris Review, Poetry Now, American Poetry Review,* and *Poetry.*

SIDELIGHTS: Stern writes: "If I had to explain my art I would talk about it in terms of staking out a place that no one else wanted, because it was not noticed, because it was abandoned or overlooked. I am talking about something of immense importance—and not just to me—but most others would not see it that way; they would see something else. On a most literal level, I am talking about weeds, and waste places and lovely pockets, and in my poems I mean it on a literal as well as on a psychological and symbolic level. That is, I am writing about actual places and ascribing value to them; but of course, I am thinking also of what those places stand for, and might stand for, in the reader's or listener's mind if I awakened his lost places. In one sense there is a battle—or at least a dialogue—going on between light and dark, present and past, city and country, civilization and savagery, power and lack of it, and I would seem to favor the latter. But I don't write from a philosophical point of view; and furthermore I am seized by the contradictions, and I have irony; but most of all I have affection for both sides, if I may call them sides, and I move towards reconciliation and forgiveness. I am moved a lot by Jewish mysticism and Chasidism and by the historic idea of the Jew—from a poetic and mythic point of view. A lot of my poems have as a setting nature, or the garden, but I am in no sense of the word a nature poet; I am equally at home in the city and the country and go where my spirit takes me, whether it be upper Broadway or the Delaware River."

Leonard Michaels found Stern's poetry to be "very subtle at times and often marvelous," and further contended that he is "a very brilliant moving poet." Hayden Carruth was also appreciative of Stern's work. He wrote: "It is extremely difficult to bring off the kind of poem Stern writes, doomsday among the tricycles and kittens. Most poets who try end up with trite magazine verse, predictabilities of faded irony. But Stern succeeds. His low-voiced, prosy syntax gives us direct statements, simple and true, moving almost monotonously toward the hysterical outbreak of silence, the twisted smile. But he draws back; he doesn't push to that catastrophe—not quite. Instead he resumes, again and again, poem after poem. . . ."

BIOGRAPHICAL/CRITICAL SOURCES: *New York Times,* October 9, 1977; *Georgia Review,* spring, 1978; *Harper's,* June, 1978.

*   *   *

STERNBERG, Josef von   1894-1969

PERSONAL: Born Jonas Sternberg, May 29, 1894, in Vienna, Austria; name changed; came to United States, 1901 (?); son of Maurice and Serafine (Singer) Sternberg; married wife, Mary, October 2, 1948; children: Catherine, Nicholas. *Education:* Attended high schools in Vienna, Austria and New York. *Home:* 10516 Lindbrook Dr., Los Angeles, Calif. 90024. *Agent:* Kurt Hellmer, 52 Vanderbilt Ave., New York, N.Y. 10017.

CAREER: Screenwriter and director of motion pictures. Associated with Paramount Pictures, 1927-35. Director of motion pictures, including "The Blue Angel," 1930, "Morocco," 1930, "Shanghai Express," 1932, "The Devil Is a Woman," 1935, "Crime and Punishment," 1935, "Jet Pilot," 1957. Lecturer in motion pictures at numerous universities, including University of Southern California, 1947, and University of California, Los Angeles, 1965. *Military service:* U.S. Army; became corporal. *Member:* Academy of Arts, Berlin.

WRITINGS: Fun in a Chinese Laundry (autobiography), Macmillan, 1965.

Screenplays; all as director unless otherwise indicated: "The Salvation Hunters," United Artists, 1925; (screenwriter only) "The Street of Sin," Paramount, 1928; "Dishonored," Paramount, 1932; (with Jules Furthman, Karl Vollmoeller, and Geza Herczeg) "The Shanghai Gesture" (adapted from the play by John Colton), United Artists, 1941; "Ana-Ta-Han," produced in Japan, 1954.

Contributor to *Esquire.*

SIDELIGHTS: It has only been within the last ten years that Sternberg has received recognition as one of the most innovative filmmakers in American cinema. Although his last film was in 1957, and the peak of his creativity was during the 1930's, Sternberg's abilities were always overshadowed by the persona of Marlene Dietrich, his most frequently used actress.

He was already an accomplished director when he was sent to Germany to direct "The Blue Angel," a film intended to re-establish silent star Emil Jannings as an actor with potential in sound films. Sternberg had not yet cast the part of the femme fatale who drives an aging professor (played by Jannings) to suicide, when he wandered into a cabaret one night. He spotted Dietrich as one of the performers and immediately cast her in the part. The film brought both Sternberg and Dietrich a great deal of recognition and when he returned to the United States, she came, too. Oddly enough, Jannings performance was considered a disappointment and he never regained the stature he'd enjoyed as an actor in silent films.

After Sternberg and Dietrich arrived in the United States, they began the series of films upon which both their reputations rest. From 1930 to 1935, they made six films together: "Morocco," "Dishonored," "Shanghai Express," "The Scarlett Empress," "Blonde Venus," and "The Devil Is a Woman." Each of the films is distinguished by Sternberg's use of lighting to enhance Dietrich's mystique.

Unfortunately, Sternberg undermined his own abilities by using his considerable skills with lighting to such an extent that critics recognized only Dietrich's beauty, not that which emphasized it. For years he was known as "the one who directed Dietrich." Only when he was resurrected by Andrew Sarris as one of the "Pantheon" directors, along with Orson Welles, Charlie Chaplin, and a dozen other film greats, did other critics take note of his artistry.

Sternberg reacted bitterly to his lack of recognition. Even Dietrich, who never hesitated to give full credit to Sternberg for developing her screen persona, fell victim to his disillusionment. He saw her very insistence on his creative abilities as a way of casting doubt on them while reaffirming her own modesty.

Sternberg, however, did enjoy success as a filmmaker aside from his collaborations with Dietrich, notably with "Crime and Punishment" and "The Shanghai Gesture," but they have been obscured by time and the ceaseless image of the infamous "Blonde Venus." In 1954, he made "Ana-Ta-Han" in Japan, a film which has only recently been acknowledged by critics as one of Sternberg's most creative ventures. He followed "Ana-Ta-Han" with two forgotten films for then-producer Howard Hughes, after which he retired to his "ivory tower of steel and glass" where he painted and studied art.

Sternberg left behind a unique canon in film history for he was neither a storyteller nor a realist. As Sarris noted, "His plots seem farfetched, his backgrounds bizarre, and his character motivations obscure, at least by conventional standards of storytelling." He was more concerned with emotional crises. His films inevitably have "moments of truth" for the lead characters. As Sarris wrote, "His characters generally make their entrance at a moment in their lives when there is no tomorrow." But, "they will struggle a short time longer ... to discover the truth about themselves and those they love."

BIOGRAPHICAL/CRITICAL SOURCES: Theatre Arts, November, 1950, August, 1953; *Newsweek,* March 29, 1965; Josef von Sternberg, *Fun in a Chinese Laundry,* Macmillan, 1965; Andrew Sarris, *The American Cinema: Directors and Direction, 1929-1968,* Dutton, 1968; Homer Dickens, *The Films of Marlene Dietrich,* Citadel, 1970; John Baxter, *The Cinema of Josef von Sternberg,* A. S. Barnes, 1971.

OBITUARIES: New York Times, December 23, 1969.*

(Died December 22, 1969, in Hollywood, Calif.)

*   *   *

STERNFELD, Robert   1917-

PERSONAL: Born November 26, 1917, in Montgomery, Ala.; son of Julius (a lawyer) and Ida (Weiler) Sternfeld; married Isabelle Brown, August 30, 1939; children: Robert W., John M. *Education:* University of Illinois, A.B., 1938; University of Chicago, A.M., 1939, Ph.D., 1948. *Home address:* Crane Neck Rd., Setauket, N.Y. 11733. *Office:* Department of Philosophy, State University of New York at Stony Brook, Stony Brook, N.Y. 11794.

CAREER: University of Illinois, Urbana, instructor in philosophy, 1946-49; University of Kansas, Lawrence, assistant professor of philosophy, 1949-58; State University of New York at Stony Brook, Stony Brook, professor of philosophy, 1958—. *Military service:* U.S. Army, 1942-46; became first lieutenant. *Member:* American Philosophical Association.

WRITINGS: Frege's Logical Theory, Southern Illinois University Press, 1966; (with Harold Zyskind) *The Voiceless University,* Jossey-Bass, 1970; (with Zyskind) *Plato's "Meno": A Philosophy of Man as Acquisitive,* Southern Illinois University Press, 1978.

WORK IN PROGRESS: A study of the concept of freedom.

SIDELIGHTS: Sternfeld remarks: "My most difficult and persistent problem is to attain an adequate understanding. Such understanding, as many thinkers have noted, is one of life's greatest pleasures.

"My interests originally centered upon twentieth-century thought, but has expanded back to Plato and to problems in ethics and political philosophy. In the study of Plato's *Meno,* I have found an old conception of freedom. It is the fittingness of the opinion one uses in action to project oneself into the world—the fittingness of that opinion with the events which actually do occur. Whitehead's statement that 'the essence of freedom is the practicability of purpose' is another way of expressing this same thought."

*   *   *

STEVENS, Rolland E(lwell)   1915-

PERSONAL: Born April 7, 1915, in St. Louis, Mo.; son of Clair E. (in sales) and Viola (Foelsch) Stevens; married Dorothy Zulauf, August 30, 1941; children: Barbara K. Stevens Osgood, Trudi K. Stevens Fontenot. *Education:* Washington University, St. Louis, Mo., A.B., 1939; University of Illinois, B.S. in L.S., 1940, M.S. in L.S., 1942, Ph.D., 1951. *Home:* 305 Burkwood Court W., Urbana, Ill. 61801. *Office:* Graduate School of Library Science, University of Illinois, Urbana, Ill. 61801.

CAREER: University of Rochester, Rochester, N.Y., assistant to library director, 1946-48; Ohio State University, Columbus, acquisitions librarian, 1950-53, assistant director of library, 1953-60, associate director, 1960-63; University of Illinois, Urbana, professor of library science, 1963—. *Military service:* U.S. Army, 1942-46; became staff sergeant. *Member:* American Library Association (chairman of Library Research Round Table, 1972-73), Eta Sigma Phi, Phi Beta Kappa, Beta Phi Mu. *Awards, honors:* Good teaching award from Beta Phi Mu, 1968.

WRITINGS: (Editor) *University Archives,* Graduate School of Library Science, University of Illinois, 1965; (editor) *Research Methods in Librarianship: Historical and Bibliographical Methods in Library Research,* Graduate School of Library Science, University of Illinois, 1971; *Reference Books in the Social Sciences and Humanities,* Stipes, 1966, 4th edition, 1977. Editor of "ACRL Monographs," for Association of College and Research Libraries, 1956-60. Associate editor of *Library Resources and Technical Services,* 1960-63.

WORK IN PROGRESS: A reference work on current problems; research on information-seeking behavior of humanists.

SIDELIGHTS: Stevens told *CA:* "Currently available writing on solving reference problems refers to facts and events occuring a year ago or more; hence, recorded in almanacs and other reference books. But many questions reaching the library concern information and recent events that have not yet been recorded in reference books. The book on which I am currently working explores avenues of finding answers to these problems which concern recent facts and events: newspapers, journals, current statistics, etc. Similarly, research in the information-seeking behavior of humanists has been neglected, although much has been written about such behavior by scientist and technologists, and some has been written lately about information-seeking behavior among social scientists. Yet, the methods and techniques by which humanists operate, how they perform their research and how they keep abreast of literature in their field, all are probably quite different from the methods and techniques of scientists and social scientists and, therefore, ought to be subjected to close scrutiny and description.''

AVOCATIONAL INTERESTS: Bridge, gardening, golf, woodworking.

BIOGRAPHICAL/CRITICAL SOURCES: Library Quarterly, January, 1953; *College and Research Libraries,* January, 1954, May, 1963.

*   *   *

STEWART, Donald Ogden 1894-

PERSONAL: Born November 30, 1894, in Columbus, Ohio; son of Gilbert Holland (a lawyer and judge) and Clara (Landon) Stewart; married Beatrice Ames, July 24, 1926 (divorced September 8, 1938); married Ella Winter (a writer), March 4, 1939; children: (first marriage) Ames Ogden, Donald Ogden, Jr. *Education:* Yale University, A.B., 1916. *Home:* 103 Frognal, London N.W.3, England. *Agent:* Anne Powys-Libby, Horsted Keynes, Sussex, England.

CAREER: Vanity Fair, New York, N.Y., writer of humorous pieces, 1921-29; playwright; screenwriter, 1928-51. Actor on stage and in films, including "Holiday," 1928, "Rebound," 1928, and "Not So Dumb," 1930. *Military service:* U.S. Naval Reserve Force, 1917-19; instructor in navigation, naval ordnance, and signals; became chief quartermaster. *Awards, honors:* Academy of Motion Picture Arts and Sciences Academy Award (Oscar) nomination, 1930-31, for "Laughter"; Academy Award for best screenplay, 1940, for "The Philadelphia Story."

WRITINGS: A Parody Outline of History, Wherein May Be Found a Curiously Irreverent Treatment of American Historical Events, Imagining Them as They Would Be Narrated by America's Most Characteristic Contemporary Authors (humorous parodies), George H. Doran, 1921; *Perfect Behavior: A Parody Outline of Etiquette* (satirical anecdotes), George H. Doran, 1922, reprinted, Dover, 1964; *Aunt Polly's Story of Mankind,* George H. Doran, 1923; *Mr. and Mrs. Haddock Abroad* (novel), George H. Doran, 1924, reprinted, Southern Illinois University Press, 1975, original edition published as *Mr. and Mrs. Haddock in Paris, France,* Harper & Brothers, 1926; *The Crazy Fool,* A. & C. Boni, 1925; *Father William: A Comedy of Father and Son,* Harper & Brothers, 1929; (editor) *Fighting Words,* Harcourt, 1940; (contributor) Henry Darcy Curwen, editor, *Exeter Remembered,* Phillips Exeter Academy Press, 1965; *By A Stroke of Luck: An Autobiography,* Paddington Press, 1975.

Plays: *Rebound: A Comedy in Three Acts* (first produced November, 1928; produced on Broadway at Plymouth Theatre, February 3, 1930), Samuel French, 1931; (author of book) "Fine and Dandy" (musical), first produced in New York at Erlanger Theatre, September 23, 1930; "How I Wonder," first produced Off Broadway at Hudson Theatre, September 30, 1947; "The Kidders," first produced in the West End at Arts Theatre, November 12, 1957; "Honor Bright," first produced in the West End at Lyric Theatre, June 17, 1958. Also author of unproduced play, "Emily Brady."

Screenplays; either author or collaborator; all released by Metro-Goldwyn-Mayer, except as noted: "Laughter," Paramount, 1930; (with John Balderston) "Smiling Through," 1932; "White Sister" (based on novel by F. Marion Craw-

ford), 1933; "Going Hollywood," 1933; (with Ernest Vajdaand Claudine West) "The Barretts of Wimpole Street," 1934; (with Herman J. Mankiewicz) "Another Language," 1935; (with Horace Jackson) "No More Ladies," 1935; (with Balderston and Wells Root) "Prisoner of Zenda" (based on novel by Anthony Hope), United Artists, 1938; (with Sidney Buchman) "Holiday," Columbia, 1938; (with Vajda and West) "Marie Antionette," 1938; "Night of Nights," Independent, 1939; (with Delmer Davis) "Love Affair," RKO, 1939.

(With Dalton Trumbo) "Kitty Foyle," RKO, 1940; "The Philadelphia Story," 1940; "That Uncertain Feeling," United Artists, 1941; (with Elliott Paul) "A Woman's Face," 1941; (with others) "Tales of Manhattan," Twentieth Century-Fox, 1942; "Keeper of the Flame" (based on the novel by I.A.R. Wylie), 1942; (with others) "Forever and a Day," RKO, 1944; "Without Love," 1945; "Life Without Father," Warner Bros., 1947; (with Sonja Levien) "Cass Timberlaine" (based on the novel by Sinclair Lewis), 1947; "Edward My Son," 1949; "Malaya," 1950.

SIDELIGHTS: Stewart rose to prominence in the 1930's as the author of numerous popular films, including "The Philadelphia Story," for which he shared an Academy Award for best screenplay with Dalton Trumbo. Prior to his success in Hollywood, Stewart had received some recognition as a humorist. His first book, A *Parody Outline of History,* was surprisingly well received. Simultaneously, Stewart was contributing funny pieces to magazines. But in spite of the acclaim he'd received, Stewart quit writing for magazines in favor of a career as a playwright.

Stewart received only moderate success as a playwright, though, and in 1930, he moved to Hollywood. There, besides his huge popularity as a screenwriter, he gained a reputation as "the life of the party." As one critic put it, Stewart "had it all."

But Stewart wasn't all that pleased with his work. He often felt the desire to do serious writing, to get away from comedy and humor. In the 1930's, his work involved outlining a play in which a Communist was included among the characters. While doing some background research on Communism, however, Stewart was swayed by John Strachey's *The Coming Struggle for Power* and he soon became an enthusiastic anti-Fascist.

As president of the Hollywood branch of the League of American Writers, Stewart was instrumental in raising funds for exiled authors. He also helped collect medical aid for Loyalist Spain. He had alienated several of his friends with his new political interest, but he still maintained his status as one of the finer screenwriters.

Nonetheless, Stewart was victimized by the paranoia of McCarthyism which swept through the film industry following World War II. Throughout his career, Stewart had enjoyed associations with many other prominent literary figures, including Robert Benchley, F. Scott Fitzgerald, Dashiell Hammett, and Dalton Trumbo. By 1940, he had established himself as an influential member of the film world and had served as president of both the League of American Writers and the Hollywood Anti-Nazi League. Unfortunately, Stewart's participation within these organizations brought about his eviction from filmmaking.

Stewart's avid faith in Communism led to him seeing Stalin as a worthy representative of that political movement. Stewart's belief in Stalin, according to a *New Yorker* reviewer, was to be the "sole regret in his zigzag career." Accused of using the Hollywood Anti-Nazi League as a Communist front, Stewart was blacklisted along with Hammett, Trumbo, and numerous others. He moved to England soon afterward.

Oddly enough, Stewart's autobiography, *By a Stroke of Luck*, was seen by some critics as less than a thorough account of the turbulent period in his life. One critic, Deborah Elliot, claimed the book "shies away from delving deeply into the Red Scare that eventually forced Stewart to leave the country." Similarly, a *New Yorker* reviewer found that "the chapters recalling the frivolous high life he foreswore are more diverting than those about his earnest era."

BIOGRAPHICAL/CRITICAL SOURCES: Film Comment, winter, 1970-71; *New York Times Book Review*, December 14, 1975; *Booklist*, December 15, 1975; Donald Ogden Stewart, *By A Stroke of Luck: An Autobiography*, Paddington Press, 1975; *Library Review*, Volume 25, 1975; *Times Literary Supplement*, December 19, 1975; *Publishers Weekly*, August 25, 1975; *New Yorker*, January 5, 1976; *Choice*, March, 1976; *Virginia Quarterly Review*, Volume 52, 1976.

* * *

STEWART, Douglas (Alexander)   1913-

PERSONAL: Born May 6, 1913, in Eltham, New Zealand; son of Alexander (a solicitor) and Mary (Fitzgerald) Stewart; married Margaret Coen (an artist), December 5, 1946; children: Meg. *Education:* Attended Victorian University of Wellington, 1930. *Home:* 2 Banool Ave., St. Ives, New South Wales 2075, Australia. *Agent:* Curtis Brown Ltd., P.O. Box 19, Paddington, New South Wales 2021, Australia.

CAREER: Writer. Literary adviser for Angus & Robertson, 1960-71. Member of advisory board of Commonwealth Literary Fund, 1955-70. *Awards, honors:* Member of Order of the British Empire, 1960; Britannica Australia Award, 1968.

WRITINGS—Books of poems: *Green Lions*, Whitcombe & Tombs, 1937; *The White Cry*, Dent, 1939; *Elegy for an Airman*, F. C. Johnson, 1940; *Sonnets to the Unknown Soldier*, Angus & Robertson, 1941; *The Dosser in Springtime*, Angus & Robertson, 1946; *Glencoe* (ballad cycle), Angus & Robertson, 1947; *Sun Orchids*, Angus & Robertson, 1952; *The Birdsville Track and Other Poems*, Angus & Robertson, 1955; *Rutherford and Other Poems*, Angus & Robertson, 1962; *The Garden of Ships*, Wentworth Press, 1962; *Douglas Stewart*, Angus & Robertson, 1963, reprinted as *Douglas Stewart: Selected Poems*, 1969; *Collected Poems, 1936-1967*, Angus & Robertson, 1967; *Douglas Stewart Reads from His Own Work*, with phonograph record, University of Queensland Press, 1971; *Selected Poems*, Angus & Robertson, 1973. Also author of *The Dryad and Other Poems* and *Poems*.

Plays: *Ned Kelly*, Angus & Robertson, 1943; *The Golden Lover and The Fire on the Snow* (radio plays; former first produced, January 24, 1943; latter first produced, June 6, 1941), Angus & Robertson, 1944; *Shipwreck*, Shepherd Press, 1947; *Four Plays* (contains "The Fire on the Snow," "The Golden Lover," "Ned Kelly," and "Shipwreck"), Angus & Robertson, 1958; *Fisher's Ghost* (historical comedy; first produced in Sydney, Australia, 1961), Wentworth Press, 1960. Author of "An Earthquake Shakes the Land" (radio play), first produced, 1944.

Short stories: *A Girl with Red Hair and Other Stories*, Angus & Robertson, 1944.

Nonfiction: *Personal Religion and the Future of Europe*,

S.C.M.P., 1941, 2nd edition, 1941; *The Flesh and the Spirit: An Outlook on Literature*, Angus & Robertson, 1948, reprinted, Folcroft, 1970; *The Seven Rivers*, Angus & Robertson, 1966; *Australia Fair*, Ure Smith, 1974; *Norman Lindsay: A Personal Memoir*, Thomas Nelson, 1975; *The Broad Stream: Aspects of Australian Literature*, Angus & Robertson, 1975; *Norman Lindsay's Cats*, Macmillan (Australia), 1975. Also author of *A Man of Sydney: An Appreciation of Kenneth Slessor*, 1977.

Editor: *Australian Poetry*, Angus & Robertson, 1941; *Coast to Coast: Australian Stories*, Angus & Robertson, 1945; (with Nancy Keesing) *Australian Bush Ballads*, Angus & Robertson, 1955; (editor of revision, with Keesing) A. B. Patterson, *Old Bush Songs and Rhymes of Colonial Times*, Angus & Robertson, 1957; *Voyager Poems*, Jacaranda, 1960; Joseph Tischler, *The Book of Bellerive*, Jacaranda, 1961; *Modern Australian Verse*, Angus & Robertson, 1964, 2nd edition, 1971; *Poetry in Australia*, two volumes, Angus & Robertson, 1964, University of California Press, 1965; Hugh McCrae, *Selected Poems*, Angus & Robertson, 1966; *The Lawson Tradition*, Angus & Robertson, 1967; *Short Stories of Australia: The Lawson Tradition*, Angus & Robertson, 1967; (with Keesing) *The Pacific Book of Bush Ballads*, Angus & Robertson, 1967; (with Keesing) *Bush Songs, Ballads, and Other Verse*, Discovery Press, 1968; *The Wide Brown Land: A New Selection of Australian Verse*, Pacific Books, 1971; (with Beatrice Davis) *Best Australian Short Stories*, Lloyd O'Neil, 1971.

BIOGRAPHICAL/CRITICAL SOURCES: Nancy Keesing, *Douglas Stewart*, Oxford University Press, 1965; Clement Semmler, *Douglas Stewart*, Twayne, 1974.

* * *

STEWIG, John Warren   1937-

PERSONAL: Born January 7, 1937, in Waukesha, Wis.; son of John G. and Marguerite W. Stewig. *Education:* University of Wisconsin, Madison, B.S., 1958, M.S., 1962, Ph.D., 1967. *Religion:* Episcopalian. *Home:* 2908 North Stowell Ave., Milwaukee, Wis. 53211. *Office:* University of Wisconsin, 393 Enderis Hall, Milwaukee, Wis. 53201.

CAREER: Elementary school teacher in Monona Grove, Wis., 1958-64; Purdue University, West Lafayette, Ind., assistant professor, 1967-72, associate professor of curriculum and instruction, 1972-77; University of Wisconsin, Milwaukee, professor of language arts, 1977—. Faculty member and workshop leader at colleges and universities in the United States and Canada, including Indiana University, School of the Ozarks, and University of Victoria; speaker at schools and professional gatherings. Worked as music teacher at a hospital school for school-age patients. Member of Wisconsin Statewide Literacy Assessment Advisory Committee, 1974; member of advisory board of Madison Cooperative Children's Book Center, 1974-78.

MEMBER: International Reading Association, Association for Childhood Education International, National Council of Teachers of English, Wisconsin Council of Teachers of English (member of board of directors, 1977-79), Milwaukee Association for the Education of Young Children, English Association of Greater Milwaukee (member of board of directors, 1973—). *Awards, honors:* Grant from U.S. Office of Education, 1973.

WRITINGS: Spontaneous Drama: A Language Art, C. E. Merrill, 1973; *Exploring Language With Children*, C. E. Merrill, 1974; *Read to Write: Using Literature as a Springboard to Children's Composition*, Hawthorn, 1975; *Chil-

dren's Language Acquisition, Department of Public Instruction (Madison, Wis.), 1976; *Sending Messages* (juvenile), Houghton, 1978; (editor with Sam L. Sebesta, and contributor) *Using Literature in the Elementary Classroom* (monograph), National Council of Teachers of English, 1978; *Using Literature With Children,* Rand McNally, 1980.

Contributor: Joe L. Frost, editor, *The Elementary School: Principles and Problems,* Houghton, 1969; Martha King and others, editors, *The Language Arts in the Elementary School: A Forum for Focus,* National Council of Teachers of English, 1973; Linda Western, editor, *Children's Literature,* Extension, University of Wisconsin, Madison, 1975; Walter Petty and Patrick Flynn, editors, *Creative Dramatics in the Language Arts Classroom,* State University of New York at Buffalo, 1976; Bernice Cullinan and others, editors, *Literature for the Young Child,* National Council of Teachers of English, 1977.

Editor of "Instructional Strategies," a column in *Elementary English,* 1972-73. Contributor of more than thirty articles and reviews to language arts, library, and theater journals.

SIDELIGHTS: Stewig wrote: "Scholars have shown through research what perceptive teachers have observed for years: children come to school with impressive abilities to use language. The school's task is to help them improve the natural language skills they already possess. This has to be done apart from traditional, analytic/evaluative exercises which have pervaded the curriculum for too long. My writing for teachers is concerned with this common theme: there are imaginative ways to enhance children's language, without forsaking the structure and sequence which creative approaches too often ignore. I have written about each of the language arts: listening, speaking, reading and writing. A particular interest has been showing teachers how to make creative drama integral to all of these language arts. My focus is on providing imaginative activities, set within a framework (rationale) which would help teachers understand why the activities are crucial for children. Too frequently creativity is seen as complete freedom: nothing could be further from the truth. I have written at length about how to use the language of writers for children, and children's own language, to plan curricula that are responsive to children's needs, and challenging in ways too often left untapped. A recent effort is *Sending Messages,* a juvenile title, which helps children understand some ways adults use language in society. To be truly literate, we need to understand the processes involved as adults use language. This book speaks to children on their level about this rather complex activity."

BIOGRAPHICAL/CRITICAL SOURCES: Wesley Shibles, *Metaphor: An Annotated Bibliography and History,* Language Press, 1971.

*   *   *

STIRLING, Monica   1916-

ADDRESS: c/o Harcourt, Brace, & Jovanovich Inc., 757 Third Ave., New York, N.Y. 10017.

CAREER: Writer. War correspondent in France for *Atlantic Monthly,* 1944. *Awards, honors:* Metro-Goldwyn award, 1946.

WRITINGS—Novels: *Lovers Aren't Company,* Little, Brown, 1949; *Dress Rehearsal,* Gollancz, 1951, Simon & Schuster, 1952; *Ladies With a Unicorn,* Gollancz, 1953, Simon & Schuster, 1954; *Boy in Blue,* Coward, 1955; *Some Darling Folly,* Coward, 1956; *Sigh for a Strange Land,* Gol-

lancz, 1958, Little, Brown, 1959; *A Sniper in the Heart,* Gollancz, 1960; *The Summer of a Dormouse,* Harcourt, 1967.

Biographies: *The Fine and the Wicked: The Life and Times of Ouida,* Gollancz, 1957, Coward, 1958; *Madame Letizia: A Portrait of Napoleon's Mother,* Harper, 1961 (published in England as *A Pride of Lions: A Portrait of Napoleon's Mother,* Collins, 1961); *The Wild Swan: The Life and Times of Hans Christian Andersen,* Harcourt, 1965.

Juvenile books: *The Little Ballet Dancer,* Lothrop, 1952; *The Cat from Nowhere,* Harcourt, 1969.

Short stories: *Adventurers Please Abstain: Short Stories,* Gollancz, 1952; *Journeys We Shall Never Make: Short Stories,* Gollancz, 1957.

SIDELIGHTS: Stirling's novel, *Boy in Blue,* revolved around the love affairs of Laurent Tenant, a French composer in love with two women. Nora Magid reviewed the novel in *Commonweal* saying: "Monica Stirling is a relatively recent comer in a procession that extends back at least to Jane Austen. She writes a neat and delicate prose, as deliberate as it seems artless. The plot in *The Boy in Blue* is slight, but the exposition, the dialogue, the symbols, are all calculated components in an elaborately structured comedy of manners."

A second love triangle set in France formed the plot for Stirling's *Some Darling Folly,* called by many critics her best novel. Patricia Hodgart termed it "a minor triumph of good sense and coolness," adding, "It is, indeed, no more than a triangle, but one of very graceful proportions." *Times Literary Supplement* reported: "It is a considerable achievement to write a convincing story about modern people living in another country and speaking a language other than the author's. Miss Monica Stirling does this with great naturalness in *Some Darling Folly.*"

Stirling also made use of her familiarity with Italy in several of her novels. *Ladies With a Unicorn* went beyond her familiar love triangle plots to include two additional parties, for it is the story of four women in love with the same man, an Italian film director. "Miss Stirling's novel is worth reading," wrote William Murray in *Saturday Review,* "if only because she writes with tenderness and an unusual skill for accurately recreating the sights and sounds of life in modern Rome." John Nerber's review in the *New York Times* noted that the "author's sense of irony blends rather naturally with a wise and tender understanding of human nature."

It was, in fact, a novel set in Italy with which Monica Stirling made her literary debut in 1949. *Lovers Aren't Company* was not considered exceptional by most critics even though some agreed that the novel showed "promise." W. F. Weaver called Miss Stirling's writing "meticulous and accurate"—descriptions that often accompany reviews of her books.

The effects of Eastern European political upheavals and revolutions on ordinary citizens were sympathetically portrayed by Stirling in *Sigh for a Strange Land.* Mary Ross wrote in the *New York Herald Tribune Book Review* that "to call this novel a tale of refugees would conjure up something very different from its almost lyric, often humorous temper. . . . Largely unspecified as to time and place, unconcerned with documentation or ideology or recrimination, this highly original little story is an affirmation of the vitality of the human spirit." *Time* reported that the novel comments on "man's inhumanity to man and fleetingly embodies the Simone Weil text it takes for its theme: 'At the bottom of the heart of every human being . . . there is something that goes on indomitably expecting, in the teeth of all experience . . . that good and not evil will be done to him.'''

As a biographer, Monica Stirling has published three books, all of which have met with success. Her first biography, *The Fine and the Wicked: The Life and Times of Quida*, told the life story of the French-English writer Maria Louise Rame. ''[It is] a true contribution to the history of literature, in its re-creation of time and taste, and of a writing talent, which do not deserve to be forgotten,'' wrote L. G. Offord in the *San Francisco Chronicle*. Edward Wagenknecht shared this idea in the *Chicago Sunday Tribune*: ''In this very well written book, crammed with references to modern literature and art, she has told her story against the background of her time.''

Times Literary Supplement called Stirling's third biography, *The Wild Swan: The Life and Times of Hans Christian Andersen*, ''a brilliant and clever retelling of Andersen's life story with special reference to its European background,'' adding: ''Miss Stirling succeeds in giving this background both depth and perspective; even the story of Andersen's childhood, schooldays, and formative years, though told by himself time and again, and retold repeatedly by others, acquires a new freshness in Miss Stirling's account. . . .'' Harry T. Moore noted that Stirling ''keeps interest alive by dramatizing Andersen's travels,'' and ''provides many engaging anecdotes of his experiences with the political and literary-artistic royalty he encountered.'' ''Along with its purely biographical aspects,'' concluded Moore, ''the volume presents a lively picture of nineteenth-century European life. . . .''

Stirling's novel *The Summer of a Dormouse* was published not long after the Andersen biography, and many critics noted the relationship. *Times Literary Supplement* observed: ''Monica Stirling's tale of a chic psychiatric clinic in Bavaria . . . is presumably meant to be something of a modern fairy story. . . . Among the many literary allusions Hans Andersen predominates, and it may be that the author is working a vein of interest aroused by her recent biography of him.''

''Entering . . . [the world of the mentally ill] is naturally affecting,'' wrote Stephen Wall in *The Observer Review*, ''but Miss Stirling allows us to do so on too easy terms. Nothing compromises a character's dignity more—let alone a patient's—than letting him become lovable.'' Carmen P. Collier concluded: ''Although the reader is aware that not all of the patients are curable . . . and that evil does exist in people and in institutions, he is conscious always of existing beauty in life. . . .''

Several of Stirling's works have been translated into French and German, including *Madame Letizia* and *The Wild Swan*.

BIOGRAPHICAL/CRITICAL SOURCES: New York Times, May 15, 1949, January 24, 1954; *New York Herald Tribune Book Review*, December 14, 1952, November 4, 1956, March 8, 1959, February 18, 1962; *Chicago Sunday Tribune*, February 15, 1953, September 11, 1955, February 16, 1958; *Saturday Review*, April 4, 1953, February 13, 1954, February 28, 1959, January 8, 1966; *Commonweal*, October 21, 1955; *Manchester Guardian*, September 21, 1956; *Times Literary Supplement*, October 5, 1956, September 15, 1961, November 18, 1965, September 21, 1967; *San Francisco Chronicle*, February 16, 1958; *Time*, March 2, 1959, December 24, 1965; *The Observer Review*, July 16, 1967; *Books and Bookmen*, September, 1967; *New York Times Book Review*, October 22, 1967; *Best Sellers*, November 1, 1967; *Center for Children's Books Bulletin*, March, 1970.*

STOBBS, William 1914-

PERSONAL: Born June 27, 1914, in South Shields, England; married wife, Brenda, 1938; children: two sons. *Education:* Attended the King Edward VI School of Art, 1933-38; Durham University, B.A., 1938, M.A., 1945.

CAREER: London School of Printing and Graphic Arts, London, England, head of design department, 1948-58; Maidstone College of Art, Kent, England, principal, 1958—; artist and illustrator of children's books. *Member:* Society of Industrial Artists. *Awards, honors:* Kate Greenaway Medal, 1959, for *Kashtanka* and *A Bundle of Ballads*.

WRITINGS—All self-illustrated picture books: (Reteller) *The Story of the Three Bears*, McGraw, 1965; (reteller) *The Story of the Three Little Pigs*, McGraw, 1965; *The Golden Goose*, Bodley Head, 1966, McGraw, 1967; (with Amabel Williams-Ellis) *Life in England*, Blackie & Son, 1968; *Henny Penny*, Bodley Head, 1968, Follett, 1970; (with Williams-Ellis) *Georgian England*, Blackie & Son, 1969; *A Mini Called Zak*, Bodley Head, 1973; *A Is an Apple Pie*, Bodley Head, 1974; *A Rolls Called ARK*, Bodley Head, 1974; (reteller) *Puss in Boots*, McGraw, 1975; *The Derby Ram*, McGraw, 1975; *Old Mother Wiggle Waggle*, Bodley Head, 1975; *Johnny-Cake*, Viking, 1975; (reteller) *The Country Mouse and the Town Mouse*, Pelham Books, 1976; *A Car Called Beetle*, Bodley Head, 1976; *A Gaping Wide-Mouthed Frog*, M. Joseph, 1977.

Illustrator: Ronald Syme, *Hakluyt's Sea Stories*, Heinemann, 1948; David W. MacArthur, *Traders North*, Collins, 1951, Knopf, 1952; Syme, *Balboa: Finder of the Pacific*, Morrow, 1952; Syme, *Champlain of the St. Lawrence*, Morrow, 1952; Syme, *Columbus: Finder of the New World*, Morrow, 1952; Syme, *I, Gordon of Khartoum*, Burke Publishing, 1953; Syme, *La Salle of the Mississippi*, Morrow, 1953; Syme, *Magellan: First Around the World*, Morrow, 1953; Syme, *John Smith of Virginia*, Morrow, 1954; Syme, *Gipsy Michael*, Hodder & Stoughton, 1954; Ronald Welch, *Knight Crusader*, Oxford University Press, 1954; Syme, *They Came to an Island*, Hodder & Stoughton, 1955; Syme, *Henry Hudson*, Morrow, 1955 (published in England as *Hudson of the Bay*, Hodder & Stoughton, 1955); Lois Lamplugh, *Nine Bright Shiners*, J. Cape, 1955; Syme, *Ice Fighter*, Hodder & Stoughton, 1956; Syme, *Isle of Revolt*, Hodder & Stoughton, 1956; Tyler Whittle, *Runners of Orford*, J. Cape, 1956; R. L. Delderfield, *Adventure of Ben Gunn*, Hodder & Stoughton, 1956; Elizabeth Grove, *Wintercut*, Verry, 1957; Mary E. Patchett, *Caribbean Adventures*, Lutterworth, 1957; Syme, *De Soto: Finder of the Mississippi*, Morrow, 1957.

Illustrator: Syme, *Cartier: Finder of the St. Lawrence*, Morrow, 1958; Syme, *Forest Fighters*, Hodder & Stoughton, 1958; David S. Daniell, *Hunt Royal*, Verry, 1958; Syme, *The Man Who Discovered the Amazon*, Morrow, 1958 (published in England as *River of No Return*, Hodder & Stoughton, 1958); Syme, *The Spaniards Came at Dawn*, Hodder & Stoughton, 1959; Syme, *Vasco Da Gama: Sailor Toward the Sunrise*, Morrow, 1959; Syme, *On Foot to the Arctic: The Story of Samuel Hearne*, Morrow, 1959 (published in England as *Trail to the North*, Hodder & Stoughton, 1959); Ruth Manning-Sanders, compiler, *A Bundle of Ballads*, Oxford University Press, 1959, Lippincott, 1961; Daniell, *Mission for Oliver*, Verry, 1959; Anton Chekov, *Kashtanka*, Oxford University Press, 1959, Walck, 1961; Daniell, *The Boy They Made King*, J. Cape, 1959.

Illustrator: Frederick Grice, *Aidan and the Strollers*, J. Cape, 1960; Hilda Lewis, *Here Comes Harry*, Oxford University Press, 1960, Criterion, 1961; Welch, *Escape From France*, Oxford University Press, 1960, Criterion, 1961; Syme, *Buccaneer Explorer*, Hodder & Stoughton, 1960; Lamplugh, *Pigeongram Puzzle*, Verry, 1960; Syme, *Captain Cook: Pacific Explorer*, Morrow, 1960; Lamplugh, *Midsummer Mountains*, Verry, 1961; Madeleine Polland, *Boern the Proud*, Constable, 1961, Holt, 1962; Henry Treece, *The Golden One*, Bodley Head, 1961, Criterion, 1962; Daniell, *Battles and Battlefields*, B. T. Batsford, 1961; William Mayne, *Summer Visitors*, Oxford University Press, 1961; Welch, *For the King*, Oxford University Press, 1961; Syme, *First Man to Cross America: The Story of Cabeza de Vaca*, Morrow, 1961; Syme, *Francis Drake: Sailor of the Unknown Seas*, Morrow, 1961; Joan E. Cass, *The Cat Show*, Abelard, 1962; Cass, *The Cat Thief*, Abelard, 1962; Syme, *Walter Raleigh*, Morrow, 1962; Welch, *Mohawk Valley*, Oxford University Press, 1962; Polland, *The White Twilight*, Constable, 1962; Ronald D. Storer, reteller, *King Arthur and His Knights*, Oxford University Press, 1962; Ian Serraillier, *Gorgon's Head: The Story of Perseus*, Walck, 1962; Anita Hewett, *The Little White Hen*, Oxford University Press, 1962, McGraw, 1963; Manning-Sanders, *The Smugglers*, Oxford University Press, 1962.

Illustrator: Serraillier, *Way of Danger: The Story of Theseus*, Walck, 1963; Rene Guillot, *Rex and Mistigri*, Bodley Head, 1963; Syme, *Francisco Pizarro: Finder of Peru*, Morrow, 1963; Polland, *The Queen's Blessing*, Constable Young Books, 1963; R. J. Unstead, *Royal Adventurers*, Odhams Books, 1963; Daniell, *Polly and Oliver Pursued*, Verry, 1964; Syme, *Alexander Mackenzie: Canadian Explorer*, Morrow, 1964; Syme, *Invaders and Invasions*, Batsford, 1964, Norton, 1965; Serraillier, *Clashing Rocks: The Story of Jason*, Walck, 1964; Syme, *Francisco Coronado and the Seven Cities of Gold*, Morrow, 1965; Syme, *Sir Henry Morgan, Buccaneer*, Morrow, 1965; Jean MacGibbon, *A Special Providence*, Coward-McCann, 1965; Lamplugh, *Vagabond's Castle*, Verry, 1965; *Jack and the Beanstalk*, Delacorte, 1966; Audrey E. Lindop, *The Adventures of the Wuffle*, Methuen, 1966, McGraw, 1968; Syme, *William Penn: Founder of Pennsylvania*, Morrow, 1966; Syme, *Quesada of Colombia*, Morrow, 1966; Williams-Ellis, *Round the World Fairy Tales*, Warne, 1966; Williams-Ellis, *Old World and New World Fairy Tales*, Warne, 1966; Cass, *The Canal Trip*, Abelard, 1966; Serraillier, *Fall From the Sky*, Walck, 1966.

Illustrator: *Monkeys and Magicians*, Blackie & Son, 1967; Treece, *Westward to Vinland*, S. G. Phillips, 1967; Syme, *Garibaldi: The Man Who Made a Nation*, Morrow, 1968; Mollie Clarke, *The Three Brothers*, Follett, 1967; Unstead, *Some Kings and Queens*, Follett, 1967; Unstead, *Royal Adventurers*, Follett, 1967; Geoffrey Trease, *White Nights of St. Petersburg*, Vanguard, 1968; Peter C. Asbjoernsen, *The Three Billy Goats Gruff*, McGraw, 1968; Syme, *Captain John Paul Jones*, Morrow, 1968; Williams-Ellis, *Early and Medieval Times*, Blackie & Son, 1968; Jane H. Yolem, *Greyling*, World Publishing, 1968; Williams-Ellis, *Tudor England*, Blackie & Son, 1968; Syme, *Bolivar: The Liberator*, Morrow, 1968; Cass, *The Cats Go to Market*, Abelard, 1969; Syme, *Amerigo Vespucci: Scientist and Sailor*, Morrow, 1969; Naomi Mitchison, *African Heroes*, Farrar, Straus, 1969; Syme, *Frontenac of New France*, Morrow, 1969.

Illustrator: Brothers Grimm, *Rumpelstiltskin*, Bodley Head, 1970; Joseph Jacobs, *The Magpie's Nest*, Follett, 1970; George MacDonald, *The Princess and the Goblin* [and] *The Princess and the Curdie*, American Education Publications,

1970; Syme, *Vancouver: Explorer of the Pacific Coast*, Morrow, 1970; Syme, *Benedict Arnold: Traitor of the Revolution*, Morrow, 1970; Cass, *The Cats' Adventure with Car Thieves*, Abelard, 1971; Jacobs, *The Crock of Gold*, Follett, 1971; Manning-Sanders, *Gianni and the Ogre*, Dutton, 1971; Syme, *Zapata: Mexican Rebel*, Morrow, 1971; Syme, *Toussaint: The Black Liberator*, Morrow, 1971; Rex Warner, *Athens at War*, Dutton, 1971; Compton Mackenzie, *Theseus*, Aldus Books, 1972; Elizabeth Poston, compiler, *The Baby's Song Book*, Crowell, 1972; Mackenzie, *Jason*, Aldus Books, 1972; Mackenzie, *Achilles*, Aldus Books, 1972; William Cole, compiler, *Poems From Ireland*, Crowell, 1972; Syme, *John Cabot and His Son, Sebastian*, Morrow, 1972.

Illustrator: Charles Perrault, *The Little Red Riding Hood*, Walck, 1973; Syme, *Verrazano: Explorer of the Atlantic Coast*, Morrow, 1973; Syme, *Marquette and Joliet: Voyagers on the Mississippi*, Morrow, 1974; Williams-Ellis, *Fairy Tales From Here and There*, British Book Center, 1977; Williams-Ellis, *Fairy Tales From Everywhere*, British Book Center, 1977; Williams-Ellis, *Fairy Tales From East and West*, British Book Center, 1977; Williams-Ellis, *Fairy Tales From Near and Far*, British Book Center, 1977.

SIDELIGHTS: William Stobbs credits his extensive training in art history with influencing the traditional form of his drawings. He has also cited Renaissance and Chinese drawing, and artists such as Caravaggio, Picasso, and Rembrandt as influential forces.

Stobbs feels that an illustration should enhance the printed word and not be merely a repetition of facts into drawings. His illustrations, for the most part historical or maritime in theme, are strong and vigorous, and male images are characteristically square, tough, wood-hewn figures.

BIOGRAPHICAL/CRITICAL SOURCES: John Ryder, *Artists of a Certain Line*, Bodley Head, 1960.*

*   *   *

STONE, Donald D(avid)   1942-

PERSONAL: Born January 17, 1942, in Los Angeles, Calif.; son of David A. (a realtor) and Pauline (Garnes) Stone. *Education:* University of California, Berkeley, B.A., 1963; Harvard University, M.A., 1964, Ph.D., 1968. *Home:* 60 West 66th St., New York, N.Y. 10023. *Office:* Department of English, Queens College of the City University of New York, Flushing, N.Y. 11367.

CAREER: Queens College of the City University of New York, Flushing, N.Y., assistant professor, 1968-72, associate professor of English, 1972—. *Member:* Modern Language Association of America. *Awards, honors:* Woodrow Wilson fellowship, 1963; Guggenheim fellowship, 1977.

WRITINGS: Novelists in a Changing World: Meredith, James, and the Transformation of English Fiction in the 1880's, Harvard University Press, 1972. Contributor of articles and reviews to literature journals. Member of advisory board of *Nineteenth-Century Fiction*, 1976—.

WORK IN PROGRESS: Studies in the Romantic Impulse in Victorian Fiction, publication by Harvard University Press expected in 1980.

SIDELIGHTS: Stone writes: "My chief interests are a reverence for artistic achievement, a love of nature, and a love of teaching. My literary criticism is rooted in my interest in cultural history: I tend to look at literature in its historical context, and at history in terms of its cultural achievement." *Avocational interests:* Travel, Victorian novels, opera, and painting.

STOOKEY, Robert W(ilson) 1917-

PERSONAL: Born July 20, 1917, in Maquoketa, Iowa; son of Robert Marshall (a teacher) and Beatrice (Wilson) Stookey; married Louise Auch, April 6, 1946. Education: Sorbonne, University of Paris, diploma, 1938; University of Nebraska, B.A., 1938, M.A., 1940; University of Texas, Ph.D., 1972. Politics: Liberal. Religion: Presbyterian. Home: 3304 White Pine Dr., Austin, Tex. 78757. Office: Center for Middle Eastern Studies, University of Texas, Austin, Tex. 78712.

CAREER: U.S. Foreign Service, Washington, D.C., third secretary and vice consul in Tangier, Morocco, 1946-49, vice consul in Nairobi, Kenya, 1949-52, second secretary in Ankara, Turkey, 1952-53, involved in Arabic language and area training in Washington, D.C. and in Beirut, Lebanon, 1953-55, principal officer in Basra, Iraq, 1955-57, regional affairs officer in Cairo, Egypt, 1957-59, Department of State, foreign relations officer, 1959-61, and officer in charge of Sudan affairs, 1963-66, charge d'affaires in Taizz, Yemen, 1961-63, supervisory political officer in Jidda, Saudi Arabia, 1966-68; retired from U.S. Government service, 1968; University of Texas at Austin, research associate at Center for Middle Eastern Studies, 1973—. Fulbright-Hays senior research scholar in Yemen, 1973. Military service: U.S. Army, Field Artillery, 1941-46; became major; received Bronze Star.

WRITINGS: America and the Arab States: An Uneasy Encounter, Wiley, 1975; (with James A. Bill) Politics and Petroleum: The Middle East and the United States, King's Court Communications, 1975, new edition published as With or Without Oil: The Middle East and the United States, 1979; Yemen: The Politics of the Yemen Arab Republic, Westview Press, 1978; (translator) Jacques Berque, Cultural Expression in Arab Society Today, University of Texas Press, 1978. Contributor to Middle East journals.

WORK IN PROGRESS: Editing with Carl Leiden, Political Parties of the Middle East, for Greenwood Press.

SIDELIGHTS: Stookey told CA: "The privilege I have had of studying Middle Eastern politics both from within as an active participant, and from the sidelines as a scholar, is a precious one given to rather few. We Americans have critically important interests in this part of the world, and can safeguard them only through wise policies rooted in sympathetic understanding by our public of the peoples of this turbulent and disconcerting region. In our relations with the Middle East we have blundered into some booby traps in the past; if my writing helps us to avoid some of those that lie ahead, my labor will be amply rewarded."

Reviewing America and the Arab States, Alan Hornton described the book as "excellent." He wrote that it's "outstanding quality is balance," especially with respect to the Arab-Israeli conflict. To Hornton, it is apparent that Stookey has attempted "to be dispassionate yet understanding, to come as close as possible to a non-partisan perception of reality." While his style "will not inveigle many casual readers into a lifelong interest" in Middle East affairs, "the prose is straightforward and efficient."

BIOGRAPHICAL/CRITICAL SOURCES: Middle East Journal, Volume 30, number 3, 1976.

*   *   *

STOPPARD, Tom 1937-

PERSONAL: Original name, Tom Straussler; born July 3, 1937, in Zlin, Czechoslovakia; son of Eugene Straussler (a physician) and Martha Stoppard; married Jose Ingle, 1965 (divorced, 1972); married Miriam Moore-Robinson (a physician), 1972; children: (first marriage) two sons; (second marriage) two children. Education: Educated in Europe and England. Home: Fernleigh, Wood Lane, Iver Heath, England. Agent: Kenneth Ewing, Fraser & Dunlop Ltd., 91 Regent St., London WC1 4AE, England.

CAREER: Playwright, novelist, radio and television script writer. Western Daily Press, Bristol, England, reporter and critic, 1954-58; Evening World, Bristol, reporter, 1958-60; free-lance reporter, 1960-63. Director of play, "Born Yesterday," in London, England, at Greenwich Theatre, 1973. Awards, honors: Ford Foundation grant to Berlin, 1964; John Whiting Award, 1967; Evening Standard drama award for most promising playwright, 1967, for best play of the year for "Jumpers," 1972, and for best comedy of the year for "Travesties," 1974; Prix Italia, 1968; Antoinette Perry (Tony) Award for best play for "Rosencrantz and Guildenstern Are Dead," 1968, 1976; New York Drama Critics Circle Award for best play for "Rosencrantz and Guildenstern Are Dead," 1968, and for best play for "Travesties," 1976.

WRITINGS: Lord Malquist and Mr. Moon (novel), Anthony Blond, 1966, Knopf, 1968.

Plays: Rosencrantz and Guildenstern Are Dead (three-act; first produced at Edinburgh Festival at Cranston Street Hall, August 24, 1966; produced on the West End at Old Vic Theatre, April 12, 1967; produced on Broadway at Alvin Theatre, October 16, 1967), Samuel French, 1967; Enter a Free Man (broadcast as "A Walk on the Water" in England for BBC-TV, 1963; broadcast as "A Walk on the Water" in Hamburg, 1964; broadcast as "The Preservation of George Riley," 1964; first produced in London, 1968; produced in Olney, Maryland, at Olney Theatre, August 4, 1970; produced Off-Broadway at St. Clements Theatre, December 17, 1974), Faber, 1968, Grove, 1972; Tango (based on the play by Slawomir Mrozek; produced in London, 1966; produced on the West End at Aldwych Theatre, May 25, 1968), J. Cape, 1968; The Real Inspector Hound (one-act; first produced on the West End at Criterion Theatre, June 17, 1968; produced in Providence at Brown University Summer Theatre, August 2, 1970), Samuel French, 1968.

After Magritte (one-act; first produced in London at Green Banana Restaurant, April 9, 1970; produced Off-Broadway at Theatre Four, April 23, 1972), Faber, 1971, Grove, 1972; Jumpers (first produced on the West End at Old Vic Theatre, February 2, 1972; produced in Washington, D.C., at Kennedy Center, February 18, 1974; produced on Broadway at Billy Rose Theatre, April 22, 1974), Grove, 1972; Travesties (produced on the West End at Aldwych Theatre, June 10, 1974; produced on Broadway at Ethel Barrymore Theatre, October 30, 1974), Grove, 1975; Dogg's Our Pet (produced in London, 1971), published in Six of the Best, Inter-Action Imprint, 1976; Dirty Linen and New-Found-Land (produced in London, 1976; produced on Broadway at John Golden Theatre, January 11, 1977), Grove, 1976; Every Good Boy Deserves Favor [and] The Professional Foul (the latter produced as screenplay for Public Broadcasting Service, April 26, 1978), Grove, 1978.

Unpublished plays: "The Gamblers," produced in Bristol, England, 1965; "The House of Bernarda" (based on the play by Garcia Lorca), produced in London at Greenwich Theatre, March, 1973. Also author of "Home and Dry," and "Riley."

Screenplays: "Despair" (adapted from novel by Vladimir Nabokov), 1978.

Television plays; all for BBC-TV, except as noted: (Adaptor) "A Separate Peace," 1966, published in *Playbill 2*, edited by Alan Durband, Hutchinson, 1969; "Teeth," 1967; "Another Moon Called Earth," 1967; "Neutral Ground," 1968; "The Engagement," National Broadcasting Company, (NBC-TV), for "Experiment in Television," 1970; "One Pair of Eyes," 1972; (with Clive Exton) "Eleventh House," 1975; (with Exton) "Boundaries," 1975; "Three Men in a Boat" (based on the novel by Jerome K. Jerome), 1975.

Radio plays; all for British Broadcasting Corporation (BBC): "The Dissolution of Dominic Boot," 1964; "M Is for Moon Among Other Things," 1964; *Albert's Bridge and If You're Glad I'll Be Frank: Two Plays for Radio* (the former produced, 1965; the latter produced, 1967, produced as one-act play in Washington, D.C., at Saint Albans Repertory Theatre, June 24, 1969), Faber, 1969; *Artist Descending a Staircase and Where Are They Now?: Two Plays for Radio* ("Where Are They Now?" 1970; "Artist Descending a Staircase," 1972), Faber, 1973.

Contributor of short stories to *Introduction 2,* edited by Francis Hope, Faber, 1964. Reviewer for *Scene* magazine, 1962.

SIDELIGHTS: "Basically, I like them as people. Shakespeare suggests they're black conspirators in alliance with the King. But to me they seem like just men thrust into a situation they know little about, then killed for reasons they know nothing about, not having sinned against God or anyone." This was Tom Stoppard's assessment of his title characters in his phenomenally successful "Rosencrantz and Guildenstern Are Dead" as he revealed it to *Newsweek* writer Irwin Goodwin. "I feel like three cherries have come up on my slot machine," Stoppard said of the unexpected critical and financial rewards his play had amassed.

Stoppard's delight at his play's debut was justified, for his writing now commands the sort of attention which led Clive Barnes to place Stoppard "among the finest English-speaking writers of our stage." "Rosencrantz and Guildenstern LIVE!" reported Barnes. "I'm beginning to feel like a popular Argentinian corned-beef millionaire," Stoppard told a *Look* critic, who pointed out that this treatment of "*Hamlet*'s two most forgettable figures" included "an original play-within-a-play, complete with metaphysics, existential absurdity and snappy vaudeville-style patter."

Interwoven with Shakespeare's blank verse, "Rosencrantz and Guildenstern" is nevertheless an original and imaginative attempt to explain the *raison d'etre* of the title characters within an existential framework. In the tradition of Pirandello, Beckett, and Pinter, Stoppard deals thematically with the question of "free will versus predestination," noted John Simon, and with the question of whether life's meaning is actually to be answered in death rather than in life. It was Jeremy Kingston's feeling that Rosencrantz and Guildenstern "define themselves by choosing to die" rather than by existing as "the littlest wheels in the machinery of other people's lives." Charles Marowitz called the play "a blinding metaphor about the absurdity of life," and a *Time* reviewer compared Rosencrantz and Guildenstern with "the two tramps who wait for Godot."

The bulk of Stoppard criticism has pointed to the syntactic brilliance of his dialogue as the unique characteristic of his work. Through the use of stichomythia, puns, and other rhetorical devices, "Stoppard's lines pant with inner panic" in "Rosencrantz and Guildenstern," noted *Time.* Like Beckett, Stoppard often juxtaposes stichomythia with "periodic

bursts of busy activity across the calmer, reflective passages" while his dialogue provides a realistic mirror of Shakespeare's language, observed Kingston. Tom Prideaux echoed this assessment and added that Stoppard's achievement in "Rosencrantz and Guildenstern" lay in his recreation of Shakespeare's "comic word play" rather than in any futile attempt to recreate his poetry in this "elaborate club sandwich of Shakespeare and Stoppard." *Newsweek* called attention to the "Wonderlandish language games" played by these "Elizabethan Ritz Brothers" who, noted *Village Voice*'s Michael Smith, ultimately "talk themselves out of existence." About his style, Stoppard told Giles Gordon: "It's taken me a long time to shake the illusion that everything I write is self-evident, that it's self-evident in the way it is intended to be performed, spoken, moved and so on. Not at all! I write with a very dominant sense of rhythm in the dialogue, and to me the orchestration of that dialogue has a kind of inevitability.... I'm hooked on style." It was Bruce Cook's feeling that Stoppard's international upbringing resulted in a "version of English [that] seems always to have something of a foreign language—that sense of freshness and verbal discovery, of sport with words."

Other critics have discussed Stoppard's displays of verbal genius as they appear in his very successful "Travesties," a play based on a 1917 meeting in Zurich of three reactionaries: Lenin, James Joyce, and Tristan Tzara. In a manner similar to that in "Rosencrantz and Guildenstern," Stoppard uses plot line and characterization from Oscar Wilde's "The Importance of Being Earnest" to parallel and emphasize his own plot structure. John Beaufort called the play "a dazzling skyrocket ... a breathtaking word flight into the Wilde blue yonder of Tom Stoppard's imagination." Jack Kroll discussed the play in terms of Stoppard's stylistic debts to other writers, such as his use of stream of consciousness in the manner of James Joyce and his comedic play with limericks in the manner of Oscar Wilde. "I fall into comedy like a man falling into bed," Stoppard told Kroll, to which Kroll added that "underneath the mattress is a hard board—Stoppard's lust for ideas." Again, Stoppard's characters operate within an existential framework of despair and absurdity.

Various reviewers have attempted to analyze and define Stoppard's philosophical position as he presents and develops it within his plays. Most often his ideas are considered from an existentialist perspective and encompass such concepts as man's alienation and consequent anguish. According to T. E. Kalem, Stoppard "chain-smokes ideas like cigarettes and emits the smoke with puffs of mirth" in his treatment of "the abyss of non-belief" in which "man [is] devoid of metaphysical absolutes" and so cannot act effectively. David J. Gordon observed that, with Stoppard, nothing is sacred, for he takes standard situations and turns them to his own literary advantage: "Old-fashioned melodrama, drawing-room comedy, ladies' magazine fiction, westerns, vaudeville, cinema, but especially absurdist literature ... are grist to his parodic mill." Kroll stated that "Stoppard's special trick is finding the sweet, sad craziness hidden in real behavior," and Jack Richardson declared him to be "the best playwright around today, the only writer ... capable of making the theater a truly formidable and civilized experience again."

BIOGRAPHICAL/CRITICAL SOURCES: Observer Review, April 16, 1967, December 17, 1967, June 23, 1968; *Punch,* April 19, 1967; *Illustrated London News,* April 22, 1967; *Village Voice,* May 4, 1967, October 26, 1967, May 2, 1974; *New Yorker,* May 6, 1967, October 28, 1967, May 4,

1968, May 6, 1972, March 4, 1974, May 6, 1974, January 6, 1975, January 24, 1977; *Newsweek,* August 7, 1967, August 31, 1970, March 4, 1974, January 8, 1975, November 10, 1975; *New York Times,* October 18, 1967, October 29, 1967, March 24, 1968, May 8, 1968, June 19, 1968, July 8, 1968, October 15, 1968, April 23, 1974; *National Observer,* October 23, 1967; *Time,* October 27, 1967, August 9, 1968, March 11, 1974, May 6, 1974; *Nation,* November 6, 1967, May 11, 1974, May 18, 1974; *Commonweal,* November 10, 1967; *Vogue,* November 15, 1967, April 15, 1968; *Reporter,* November 16, 1967; *National Review,* December 12, 1967; *Look,* December 26, 1967; *Commentary,* December, 1967, June, 1974; *Hudson Review,* Volume XX, number 4, winter, 1967-68, Volume XXI, number 2, summer, 1968; *Life,* February 9, 1968; *Times Literary Supplement,* March 21, 1968; *Listener,* April 11, 1968, April 18, 1968, June 20, 1974; *Atlantic,* May, 1968; *Playboy,* May, 1968; *New Republic,* June 15, 1968, May 18, 1974, November 22, 1975; *New York Times Book Review,* August 25, 1968; *London Magazine,* August, 1968; *Drama,* summer, 1968, fall, 1969, summer, 1972, winter, 1973, autumn, 1974; *Transatlantic Review,* summer, 1968; *Yale Review,* autumn, 1968; Robert Brustein, *The Third Theatre,* Knopf, 1969; *Washington Post,* May 11, 1969, June 25, 1969, July 9, 1969.

Plays and Players, July, 1970; John Russell Taylor, *The Second Wave: British Drama for the Seventies,* Hill & Wang, 1971; *Stage,* February 10, 1972; *Saturday Review of the Society,* August 26, 1972; *Contemporary Literary Criticism,* Gale, Volume 1, 1973, Volume 3, 1975, Volume 4, 1975, Volume 5, 1976, Volume 8, 1978; *New York Magazine,* March 11, 1974, May 13, 1974, August 26, 1974; *Wall Street Journal,* March 11, 1974, November 3, 1975; *New York Post,* April 23, 1974; *Women's Wear Daily,* April 24, 1974; *Christian Science Monitor,* April 25, 1974, November 6, 1975; *Show Business,* April 25, 1974; *New Statesman,* June 14, 1974; *Spectator,* June 22, 1974; *Encounter,* September, 1974; Christopher William Edgar Bigsby, editor, *Writers and Their Work,* Longman, 1976; *Saturday Review,* January 8, 1977.*

* * *

STOREY, David (Malcolm) 1933-

PERSONAL: Born July 13, 1933, in Wakefield, Yorkshire, England; son of Frank Richmond (a coal miner) and Lily (Cartwright) Storey; married Barbara Rudd Hamilton, 1956. *Education:* Slade School of Art, diploma, 1956. *Home:* 2 Lyndhurst Gardens, London NW3, England. *Agent:* International Famous Agency, 11/12 Hanover St., London W1, England.

CAREER: Novelist and playwright. Worked as teacher, farm worker, postman, tent erector, and bus conductor; player for Leeds Rugby League Club, 1952-56; director of television productions "Portrait of Margaret Evans" and "Death of My Mother," 1963; associate artistic director of Royal Court Theatre, London, England, 1972-74; currently fellow at University College, London. *Awards, honors:* Macmillan Award, 1959, for *This Sporting Life;* John Llewelyn Rhus Memorial Prize, 1961, and Somerset Maugham Award, 1963, both for *Flight Into Camden;* drama award from *Evening Standard,* 1967, for most promising playwright; award from London Theatre Critics, 1970, Writer of the Year award from Variety Club of Great Britain, 1971, award from New York Drama Critics Circle, 1974, all for "The Contractor"; drama award from *Evening Standard,* 1970, award from New York Drama Critics Circle, 1971, and nomination for Antoinette Perry (Tony) Award from

League of New York Theatres and Producers, 1971, all for "Home"; award from New York Drama Critics Circle and nomination for Tony Award, both 1973, both for "The Changing Room"; Geoffrey Faber Memorial Award, 1973, for *Pasmore;* Obie drama award from *Village Voice,* 1974; Booker Prize for Fiction, 1976, for *Saville.*

WRITINGS—Novels: *This Sporting Life,* Macmillan, 1960; *Flight Into Camden,* Longmans, Green, 1960, Macmillan, 1961; *Radcliffe,* Longmans, Green, 1963, Coward, 1964; *Pasmore,* Longmans, 1972, Dutton, 1974; *A Temporary Life,* Allen Lane, 1973, Dutton, 1974; *Saville,* J. Cape, 1976, Harper, 1977.

Plays: *The Restoration of Arnold Middleton* (three-act; first produced in Edinburgh, Scotland, at Traverse Theatre, November, 1966; produced on West End at Criterion Theatre, 1967), J. Cape, 1967, Samuel French, 1968; *In Celebration* (two-act; first produced in London at Royal Court Theatre, April 22, 1969; produced in New York City at Sutton East Theatre, 1977), J. Cape, 1969, Grove, 1975; *The Contractor* (three-act; first produced in London at Royal Court Theatre, October 20, 1969; produced on West End at Fortune Theatre, April 6, 1970; produced in New York City, October, 1973), J. Cape, 1970, Random House, 1970; *Home* (two-act; first produced in London at Royal Court Theatre, June 17, 1970; produced on Broadway at Morosco Theatre, November 17, 1970), J. Cape, 1970, Random House, 1971; *The Changing Room* (three-act; first produced in London at Royal Court Theatre, November 9, 1971; produced on Broadway at Morosco Theatre, March 6, 1973), J. Cape, 1972, Random House, 1972; *Cromwell* (first produced in London at Royal Court Theatre, 1973), J. Cape, 1973; *Life Class* (first produced in London, 1974), J. Cape, 1975; "Night," 1976; "Mother's Day," 1976.

Other: "This Sporting Life" (screenplay; adapted from the novel), Continental, 1963; (contributor) *Writers on Themselves,* BBC Publications, 1964; "Home" (teleplay; adapted from the play), Public Broadcasting Service, 1971; "Grace" (teleplay), for television series "Play for Today," British Broadcasting Corporation, 1974; *Edward,* (juvenile), Allen Lane, 1973; "In Celebration" (screenplay; adapted from the novel), American Film Theatre, 1975.

SIDELIGHTS: Critics and Storey himself have noted his preference for the dramatic form as opposed to the novel. John Russell Taylor commented that Storey's adaptation of *The Sporting Life* revealed an understanding of "the advantages of the dramatic media for directing an audience's responses through angling and selection, in a way which is much more difficult in the more expansive medium of the novel." In the same article, Storey compared writing a novel with "launching an unmanned ship" and added that "a play is like a properly crewed ship: you can modify from moment to moment, take account of the climate of feeling at any particular performance, test out ideas and if they don't work as you want them to, change them."

In an interview with Ronald Hyman, Storey observed that with a novel it is unnecessary to maintain focus on every character, while the dramatic form demands that visible characters be justifiably engaged "even if they are passive—they've got to be engaged in a way that's just as important, as informative, as the people who are talking."

Basic to an understanding of Storey's themes and characters is a consideration of his pre-literary experiences. His four years as a professional rugby player provided the background for *This Sporting Life* and for *The Changing Room;* a stint as a tent erector inspired the stage action of *The Con-*

tractor; *Flight Into Camden* is based on his years in art school.

In a *Listener* article, Storey described the weekly four-hour train journey from his London art endeavors to the Leeds rugby field as a "life . . . neatly divided into half," thereby recalling the philosophical and physical tension vital to his writings. "I seemed, through these two activities," wrote Storey, "to be trying to resolve two sides of my temperament which were irreconcilable—the courtship of a self-absorbed, intuitive kind of creature with a hard, physical, extroverted character: the one the very antithesis of the other." He related the despair he felt at being "continually torn between the two extremes of my experience, the physical and the spiritual, with the demand to be effective in both." Storey told an interviewer that he combined the two extremes in *Radcliffe* with two major characters reflecting both sides of his own personality.

AVOCATIONAL INTERESTS: Painting.

BIOGRAPHICAL/CRITICAL SOURCES: James Gindin, *Postwar British Fiction: New Accents and Attitudes,* University of California Press, 1962; *Listener,* August 1, 1963; John Russell Taylor, *The Second Wave: British Drama for the Seventies,* Hill & Wang, 1971; Ronald Hayman, *Playback,* Davis-Poynter Ltd., 1973; Taylor, *David Storey,* Longman, 1974; *Contemporary Literary Criticism,* Gale, Volume 2, 1974, Volume 4, 1975, Volume 5, 1976, Volume 8, 1978.*

*   *   *

STORM, Hyemeyohsts 1935-
(Golden Silver)

PERSONAL: Given name is pronounced Hy-*am*-ee-yosts; born May 23, 1935, in Lame Deer, Mont.; son of Arthur Charles (a carpenter) and Pearl (Eastman) Storm; married wife, Mary Ann; married second wife, Sandra Karen; children: Veronica, Michie, Rocky, Antonette. *Education:* Attended Eastern Montana College. *Address:* c/o Harper & Row Publishers, Inc., 10 East 53rd St., New York, N.Y. 10022.

WRITINGS: Seven Arrows (novel), Harper, 1972; *The Song of Heyoehkah,* Harper, 1979. Also author of a book of short stories, *Reliability Mirrors,* and a play, "The Beaded Path."

WORK IN PROGRESS: The Magii Ship, under pseudonym Golden Silver.

SIDELIGHTS: "There are few books that have a genuine hypnotic effect on the reader," wrote Charles Larson of American Indian Hyemeyohsts Storm's novel, *Seven Arrows.* "Fewer still are those occasions in our reading lives when we come across a work with magical properties so enchanting that we immediately sense that we will be haunted by it the rest of our lives. *Seven Arrows* . . . is such a book. . . . It is the most extraordinary book I have ever read. I think that it is going to force us to reconsider some of our basic conceptions of American literature. I know that it is going to make us stand up and look at the American Indian artist in a way that we have never regarded him before."

BIOGRAPHICAL/CRITICAL SOURCES: Saturday Review, July 1, 1972; *Harper's,* November, 1972; *Natural History,* November, 1972; *Newsweek,* January 15, 1973; *Books Abroad,* winter, 1973; *Contemporary Literary Criticism,* Volume 3, Gale, 1975.

STOUT, George L(eslie) 1897-1978

PERSONAL: Born October 5, 1897, in Winterset, Iowa; son of Abraham Lincoln and Lulu May (McBride) Stout; married Margaret Hayes, June 11, 1924; children: Robert Hayes, Thomas McBride.

Education: Attended Grinnell College, 1915-17; University of Iowa, B.A., 1921; Harvard University, A.M., 1928. *Home:* 350 Sharon Park Dr., C-23, Menlo Park, Calif. 94025.

CAREER: State University of Iowa, Iowa City, instructor in department of graphic and plastic arts, 1921-24; University of Pittsburgh, Pittsburgh, Pa., lecturer, 1925-26; Fogg Museum of Art, Cambridge, Mass., research fellow, 1929-33, head of department of conservation, 1933-47; Worcester Art Museum, Worcester, Mass., director, 1947-54; Isabella Stewart Gardner Museum, Boston, Mass., director, 1955-70. *Military service:* U.S. Army, 1917-19; U.S. Naval Reserve, 1943-46; became lieutenant commander. *Member:* International Institute for Conservation of Historic and Artistic Works (honorary fellow), American Antiquarian Society, American Academy of Arts and Sciences. *Awards, honors:* Carnegie fellow at Harvard University, 1926-28; Litt. D., Clark University, 1955.

WRITINGS: (Editor) Roland Rood, *Color and Light in Painting,* Columbia University Press, 1941; *The Care of Pictures,* Columbia University Press, 1948, revised edition, Dover, 1966; (with Rutherford J. Gettens) *Painting Materials: A Short Encyclopaedia,* Dover, 1966; *Treasures From the Isabella Stewart Gardner Museum,* Crown, 1969. Managing editor, *Technical Studies in the Field of the Fine Arts,* 1932-42.

OBITUARIES: Washington Post, July 6, 1978.*

(Died July 1, 1978, in Palo Alto, Calif.)

*   *   *

STOWERS, Carlton 1942-

PERSONAL: Born April 14, 1942, in Brownwood, Tex.; son of Ira (in sales) and Fay (a secretary; maiden name, Stephenson) Stowers; married Lynne Livingston, November 30, 1975; children: Anson, Ashley. *Education:* Attended University of Texas, 1961-63. *Religion:* Episcopalian. *Home address:* Route 1, Box 834, Cedar Hill, Tex. 75104. *Agent:* Bill Adler, 1230 Sixth Ave., New York, N.Y. 10020. *Office: Dallas Morning News,* Communications Center, Dallas, Tex. 75104.

CAREER: Associated with *Amarillo Daily News,* Amarillo, Tex., 1966-69, and *Lubbock Avalanche Journal,* Lubbock, Tex., 1970-73; free-lance writer, 1974-76; *Dallas Morning News,* Dallas, Tex., sportswriter and columnist, 1976—. *Member:* Professional Football Writers Association, Texas Sportswriters Association. *Awards, honors:* State awards for newspaper journalism include citations from Texas Headliners Club, Texas Sportswriters Association, Texas UPI Editors Association.

WRITINGS: The Randy Matson Story, Tafnews, 1971; *Spirit,* Berkley, 1973; (with Wilbur Evans) *Champions,* Strode, 1978; *The Overcomers,* Word Books, 1978; (with Trent Jones) *Where the Rainbows Wait,* Playboy Press, 1978; (editor) *Happy Trails to You* (autobiography of Roy Rogers and Dale Evans), Word Books, 1979. Contributor to magazines, including *Good Housekeeping, Sports Illustrated, People,* and *TV Guide.*

WORK IN PROGRESS: Like Father, Like Son, a book on sons of sports celebrities.

SIDELIGHTS: Stowers comments: "I do my books and magazine work in what spare time I can find after fulfilling my responsibilities as a sportswriter and columnist assigned to cover the Dallas Cowboys. Much of my free-lance writing is of a non-sport nature, which gives me some relief from the daily routine my job demands."

* * *

STRABOLGI, Bartolomeo
See TUCCI, Niccolo

* * *

STRAGE, Mark 1927-
(Joseph Hazlitt, Philip Quick)

PERSONAL: Born October 27, 1927, in Harbin, Manchuria, came to the United States in 1939, naturalized citizen, 1945; son of Michael (an engineer) and Sophie Strage; married Tatiana N. Glaskowsky (an editor), June 6, 1953; children: Amy, Michael, Claudia. Education: Columbia University, B.A., 1950. Home: 448 Riverside Dr., New York, N.Y. 10027. Agent: William Morris Agency, 1350 Ave. of the Americas, New York, N.Y. 10019.

CAREER: Overseas News Agency, New York City, correspondent in Rome, Berlin, Athens, and Tel Aviv, 1948-51; Pageant, New York City, editor, 1952-56; American Cyanamid Co., New York City, assistant director of public relations, 1957-63; Warner-Lambert Co., Morris Plains, N.J., director of public relations, 1963-67; free-lance writer, 1967—. Military service: U.S. Army, 1946-47.

WRITINGS: Cape to Cairo (nonfiction), Harcourt, 1973; Women of Power (nonfiction), Harcourt, 1976. Contributor to magazines, sometimes under pseudonyms Joseph Hazlitt and Philip Quick.

WORK IN PROGRESS: "A book on aspects of male sexuality," publication by Morrow expected in 1979.

SIDELIGHTS: Strage told CA: "So far, I have tended to choose subjects which interest me, if only because the research takes five or six times as long as the actual writing. One reason for this disproportion, I suspect, is that I hate the act of writing—no more masochistic pastime has ever been devised—and I only do it so I can go on to dig into the next project."

* * *

STRAUSS, Walter A(dolf) 1923-

PERSONAL: Born May 14, 1923, in Mannheim, Germany; came to the United States in 1936, naturalized citizen, 1944; son of Ludwig (a businessman) and Fanny (Haas) Strauss; married Lilo Teutsch, September 8, 1946 (divorced, September, 1966); married Nancy R. Shirley (a teacher), October 18, 1966; children: Robert D., Joan E., Charles L., Philip R., Matthew C. Education: Emory University, B.A., 1944; Harvard University, M.A., 1948, Ph.D., 1951. Religion: Jewish. Home: 2861 Berkshire Rd., Cleveland Heights, Ohio 44118. Office: Department of Modern Languages and Literatures, Case Western Reserve University, Cleveland, Ohio 44106.

CAREER: Harvard University, Cambridge, Mass., instructor in Romance languages and general education, 1951-54; Emory University, Atlanta, Ga., assistant professor, 1954-58, associate professor, 1958-62, professor of Romance languages, 1962-70; Case Western Reserve University, Cleveland, Ohio, Treuhaft Professor of the Humanities, 1970—. Member of Intelligence Department, U.S. War Depart-

ment, 1946-47. Military service: U.S. Army, 1944-46. Member: Modern Language Association of America, Dante Society, American Association of University Professors. Awards, honors: Guggenheim fellow, 1962-63; Bollingen Foundation grant, 1962-63; National Endowment for the Humanities grant, summer, 1977.

WRITINGS: Proust and Literature, Harvard University Press, 1957; Descent and Return, Harvard University Press, 1971.

WORK IN PROGRESS: Franz Kafka: The Later Years, 1917-1924; Paris-Vienna, 1900-1914 (tentative title), completion expected in 1981.

SIDELIGHTS: Strauss comments: "I have a strong interest in all aspects of literature, and in the intersection of literature and ideas."

His languages include Greek, Latin, French, German, Italian, and Spanish, and travels include England, France, Germany, Italy, Austria, the Netherlands, Belgium, Spain, Greece, Israel, and Czechoslovakia.

AVOCATIONAL INTERESTS: Music, fine arts, philosophy.

* * *

STRAUSS, Walter L(eopold) 1928-

PERSONAL: Born April 23, 1928, in Nuremberg, Germany; came to the United States in 1936, naturalized citizen, 1949; son of Justin (a toy manufacturer) and Adolfine (Lowenthal) Strauss; married Lore Seidenberger (a modern dancer), 1950; children: Claudia, Thomas, Michael, Daniel. Education: Pratt Institute, received degree in chemical engineering; attended University of Wyoming, 1950, and University of Minnesota, 1952; New School for Social Research, M.A., 1974. Home address: Marlborough Rd., Scarborough, N.Y. 10510. Office: 24 West 40th St., New York, N.Y. 10017.

CAREER: Abaris Books, Inc., New York, N.Y., editor-in-chief, 1974—. Visiting professor at State University of New York at Binghamton, 1977. Member of Briarcliff Manor government committee. Military service: U.S. Army, 1950-51; became second lieutenant; received Bronze Star. Member: College Art Association of America.

WRITINGS: The Human Figure: Albrecht Duerer's Dresden Sketchbook, Dover, 1972; Albrecht Duerer's Complete Engravings, Woodcuts, and Dry-Points, Dover, 1972; The Chiaroscuro Woodcuts of the German and Netherlandish Masters of the Sixteenth Century, New York Graphic Society, 1973; The German Single-Leaf Woodcut, 1500-1550, four volumes, Hacker, 1974; The Book of Hours of Emperor Maximilian I, Abaris, 1974; The Complete Drawings of Albrecht Duerer, six volumes, Abaris, 1975; The German Single-Leaf Woodcut, 1550-1600, three volumes, Abaris, 1975; (editor) Tribute to Wolfgang Stechow, Pratt Institute, 1976; Hendrick Goltzius, Master Engraver, two volumes, Abaris, 1977; The Intaglio Prints of Albrecht Duerer and Their Preparatory Drawings, Kennedy Galleries, 1977; The Iconography of Astrology, Dover, 1977; Albrecht Duerer Woodcuts and Woodblocks, Abaris, 1977; (with Dorothy Alexander) The German Single-Leaf Woodcut of the Seventeenth Century, Abaris, 1977; The Painter's Manual: Albrecht Duerer's "Unterweisung der Messung", Abaris, 1977; (with Marjon van der Meulen) The Documents of Rembrandt, Abaris, 1978. Also contributor to Thayer's Life of Beethoven, edited by Elliot Forbes, Princeton University Press. Contributor of articles and reviews to art journals. Editor of Print Review.

WORK IN PROGRESS: Editing a series of basic philosophical works in new translations and an encyclopedic handbook of the opera.

SIDELIGHTS: Strauss told *CA:* "My main interest is in the history of art and in its philosophical foundation."

Strauss has a reading knowledge of Russian, Dutch, and Spanish.

AVOCATIONAL INTERESTS: Travel (Central Europe, Japan, the Persian Gulf).

*   *   *

STREATFEILD, Noel 1897-

PERSONAL: Born in December, 1897, in Amberley, Sussex, England; daughter of William Champion (a bishop) and Janet Mary (Venn) Streatfeild. *Education:* Attended Royal Academy of Dramatic Art, London. *Address:* 51 Elizabeth St., Eaton Square, London S.W.1, England.

CAREER: Began as an actress with a Shakespearean repertory company in England; later appeared in a variety of theatrical productions in South Africa and Australia; writer, 1930—; became a book critic for *Elizabethan* magazine; presented book talks for BBC radio. *Awards, honors:* Carnegie Medal, 1938, for *The Circus Is Coming;* Emmy award for "Ballet Shoes."

WRITINGS—Fiction: *The Wicharts,* Heinemann, 1931, Brentano's, 1932; *Parson's Nine,* Heinemann, 1932, Doubleday, Doran, 1933; *Tops and Bottoms,* Doubleday, Doran, 1933; *Children's Matinee* (plays; illustrated by Ruth Gervis), Heinemann, 1934; *Shepherdess of Sheep,* Heinemann, 1934, Reynal & Hitchcock, 1935; *Creeping Jenny,* Heinemann, 1936; *It Pays to Be Good,* Heinemann, 1936; *Wisdom Teeth* (three-act play), Samuel French, 1936; *Caroline England,* Heinemann, 1937, Reynal & Hitchcock, 1938; *The Circus Is Coming* (illustrated by Steven Spurrier), Dent, 1938, revised edition, illustrated by Clarke Hutton, 1960; *Dennis the Dragon,* Dent, 1939; *Luke,* Heinemann, 1939.

The House in Cornwall (illustrated by D. L. Mays), Dent, 1940; *The Secret of the Lodge* (illustrated by Richard Floethe), Random House, 1940; *The Winter Is Past,* Collins, 1940; *The Stranger in Primrose Lane* (illustrated by Floethe), Random House, 1941 (published in England as *Children of Primrose Lane* [illustrated by Marcia Lane Foster]), Dent, 1941; *I Ordered a Table for Six,* Collins, 1942; *Harlequinade* (illustrated by Hutton), Chatto & Windus, 1943; *Myra Carrel,* Collins, 1944; *Saplings,* Collins, 1945; *Party Frock* (illustrated by Anna Zinkeisen), Collins, 1946; *Grass in Piccadilly,* Collins, 1947.

Mothering Sunday, Coward, 1950, reprinted, Morley-Baker, 1969; *Osbert* (illustrated by Susanne Suba), Rand McNally, 1950; *The Theater Cat* (illustrated by Suba), Rand McNally, 1951; *Aunt Clara,* Collins, 1952; (with Roland Pertwee) *Many Happy Returns* (two-act play), English Theatre Guild, 1953; *Judith,* Collins, 1956; *The Grey Family* (illustrated by Pat Marriott), Hamish Hamilton, 1957; *Wintle's Wonders* (illustrated by Richard Kennedy), Collins, 1957; *Bertram* (illustrated by Margery Gill), Hamish Hamilton, 1959; *Christmas with the Chrystals,* Basil Blackwell, 1959.

Look at the Circus (illustrated by Constance Marshall), Hamish Hamilton, 1960; *New Town: A Story about the Bell Family* (illustrated by Shirley Hughes), Collins, 1960; *The Silent Speaker,* Collins, 1961; *Apple Bough* (illustrated by Gill), Collins, 1962; *Lisa Goes to Russia* (illustrated by Ger-

aldine Spence), Collins, 1963; *The Children on the Top Floor* (illustrated by Jillian Willett), Collins, 1964, Random House, 1965; *Let's Go Coaching* (illustrated by Peter Warner), Hamish Hamilton, 1965; *The Growing Summer* (illustrated by Edward Ardizzone; Junior Literary Guild selection), Collins, 1966, published as *The Magic Summer,* Random House, 1967; *Caldicott Place* (illustrated by Betty Maxey; Junior Literary Guild selection), Collins, 1967, published as *The Family at Caldicott Place,* Random House, 1968; *Gemma* (illustrated by Maxey), May Fair Books, 1968; *Gemma and Sisters* (illustrated by Maxey), May Fair Books, 1968.

Thursday's Child (illustrated by Peggy Fortnum), Random House, 1970; *When the Siren Wailed* (illustrated by Gill), Collins, 1974, American edition illustrated by Judith Gwyn, Random House, 1976; *Ballet Shoes for Anna* (illustrated by Mary Dinsdale), Collins, 1976; *Gran-Nannie* (illustrated by Charles Mozley), M. Joseph, 1976.

"Shoes" series: *Ballet Shoes: A Story of Three Children on the Stage* (illustrated by Gervis), Dent, 1936, reprinted, 1962, published as *Ballet Shoes* (illustrated by Floethe), Random House, 1937; *Tennis Shoes* (illustrated by Mays), Dent, 1937, reprinted, 1965, American edition illustrated by Floethe, Random House, 1938; *Circus Shoes* (illustrated by Floethe), Random House, 1939; *Curtain Up,* Dent, 1944, published as *Theater Shoes; or, Other People's Shoes* (illustrated by Floethe), Random House, 1945; *Party Shoes* (illustrated by Zinkeisen), Random House, 1947; *Movie Shoes* (illustrated by Suba), Random House, 1949 (published in England as *Painted Garden,* Collins, 1949), new edition illustrated by Hughes, Penguin, 1961; *Skating Shoes* (illustrated by Floethe), Random House, 1951 (published in England as *White Boots,* Collins, 1951), illustrated by Milein Cosman, Penguin, 1976; *Family Shoes* (illustrated by Floethe), Random House, 1954 (published in England as *The Bell Family* [illustrated by S. Hughes], Collins, 1954); *Dancing Shoes* (illustrated by Floethe), Random House, 1958; *New Shoes* (illustrated by Vaike Low), Random House, 1960; *Traveling Shoes* (illustrated by Reisie Lonette), Random House, 1962.

Also author of the "Baby Books" series, published by A. Barker, 1959—.

Nonfiction: *The Picture Story of Britain* (illustrated by Ursula Koering; edited by Helen Hoke), Bell Publishing, 1951; *The Fearless Treasure: A Story of England From Then to Now* (illustrated by Dorothea Braby), M. Joseph, 1953; *The First Book of the Ballet* (illustrated by Moses Soyer), F. Watts, 1953, revised edition, illustrated by Stanley Houghton and Soyer, Edmund Ward, 1963; *The First Book of England* (illustrated by Gioia Fiammenghi), F. Watts, 1958; *Magic and the Magician: E. Nesbit and Her Children's Books,* Abelard, 1958; *Queen Victoria* (illustrated by Robert Frankenberg), Random House, 1958; *The Royal Ballet School,* Collins, 1959.

A Vicarage Family: An Autobiographical Story (illustrated by Mozley), F. Watts, 1963; *The Thames: London's River* (illustrated by Kurt Wiese), Garrard, 1964; *Away From the Vicarage* (autobiographical), Collins, 1965; *On Tour: An Autobiographical Novel of the 20's,* F. Watts, 1965; *The First Book of the Opera* (illustrated by Hilary Abrahams), F. Watts, 1966 (published in England as *Enjoying Opera,* Dobson, 1966); *Before Confirmation,* Heinemann, 1967; *The First Book of Shoes* (illustrated by Jacqueline Tomes), F. Watts, 1967; *Beyond the Vicarage* (autobiographical), Collins, 1971, F. Watts, 1972; *The Boy Pharaoh: Tutankha-*

men, M. Joseph, 1972; *A Young Person's Guide to the Ballet* (illustrated by Georgette Bordier), Warne, 1975.

Editor: *The Years of Grace*, Evans Brothers, 1950, revised edition, 1956; *By Special Request: New Stories for Girls*, Collins, 1953; *Growing Up Gracefully* (illustrated by John Dugan), A. Barker, 1955; *The Day Before Yesterday: First-hand Stories of Fifty Years Ago* (illustrated by Dick Hart), Collins, 1956; *Confirmation and After*, Heinemann, 1963; Merja Otava, *Priska* (translated by Elizabeth Portch), Benn, 1964; Marlie Brande, *Nicholas* (translated by Elisabeth Boas), Follett, 1968; M. Brande, *Sleepy Nicholas*, Follett, 1970; *The Noel Streatfeild Summer Holiday Book* (illustrated by Sara Silcock), Dent, 1973; *The Noel Streatfeild Easter Holiday Book* (illustrated by Silcock), Dent, 1974.

Also editor of *Noel Streatfeild's Ballet Annual*, 1959—.

SIDELIGHTS: Noel Streatfeild's theatrical background served as the basis for many of her books for children. *Ballet Shoes* was the author's first attempt at writing a children's story and was highly acclaimed in both the United States and England. The book followed the stage training of three girls attending the Academy of Dancing in London. "Ostensibly, this is a book for children. But it is so full of knowledge of an unknown craft that older readers will find it instructive. . . . Miss Streatfeild is such an amusing and charming writer that it has a quality of its own," noted a critic for the *Chicago Daily Tribune*. A reviewer for the London *Times Literary Supplement* commented that "every step of their [the three girls'] progress is pleasant, amusing and very interesting, dealing as it does with facts that should prove very helpful to small aspirants for life behind the footlights."

The author often did extensive research when writing about subjects with which she was unfamiliar. Miss Streatfeild traveled with a circus for several months to capture just the right atmosphere to write her book, *Circus Shoes*. In reviewing the book, a *New York Times* reviewer noted, "The gradual development of characters is as amusing and interesting as is this account of that world compounded of glitter, hard work and loyalty . . . a vivid and entertaining book. . . ."

One of Miss Streatfeild's later books for children was *The Family at Caldicott Place*. "As romantic as a valentine, the story avoids base sentimentality because of the author's light, graceful style and her signal ability to create characters that come alive," described Zena Sutherland in an article for *Saturday Review*. A *Book World* critic observed, "A seasoned English storyteller, she [Miss Streatfeild] involves the reader at once in the efforts of the Johnstone family. . . . It makes a fine, cozy story for an evening's reading."

The author wrote about her own family in *A Vicarage Family*. Although autobiographical in nature, Miss Streatfeild's book was not a carbon copy of her life. In the dedication of her book, the author explained, "It is because of my awareness that my portraits of the rest of my family are probably faulty that I have used no real names. The thin shield of anonymity helped me to feel unselfconscious in drawing them, and in approaching the facts of my own life. . . ." Miss Streatfeild continued her autobiographical story in *On Tour* and *Beyond the Vicarage*. In reviewing the latter book, a critic for the *Bulletin of Center for Children's Books* noted, "The story is vivid both as a personal document and as a picture of wartime England; the characters are vividly alive, the events dramatic, the writing style rich and humorous."

In *A Young Person's Guide to Ballet*, the author gave a nonfiction account of the field to which she became attracted as a child. A reviewer for *Publishers Weekly* observed, that Streatfeild is an expert on her subject. Through her simple, precise text, we learn how much discipline and sweat is required to create the illusion that ballet movements are as easy and natural as breathing. . . . Skillful sketches and photos, along with period illustrations, add to the value of the outstanding contender for shelf-space."

Many of Miss Streatfeild's books have been heard on BBC radio and her story, *The Magic Summer*, was made into a television film. In 1976, *Ballet Shoes* was made into a television play and was televised in England and the United States.

BIOGRAPHICAL/CRITICAL SOURCES: Times Literary Supplement, November 21, 1936; *Chicago Daily Tribune*, January 9, 1937; *New York Times*, July 30, 1939; Noel Streatfeild, *Vicarage Family: An Autobiographical Story*, F. Watts, 1963; Barbara Ker Wilson, *Noel Streatfeild*, Walck, 1964; Streatfeild, *Away from the Vicarage*, Collins, 1965; Streatfeild, *On Tour: An Autobiographical Novel of the 20's*, F. Watts, 1965; *Saturday Review*, November 9, 1968; *Book World*, April 20, 1969; Streatfeild, *Beyond the Vicarage*, Collins, 1971, F. Watts, 1972; *Bulletin of the Center for Children's Books*, September, 1972; *Publishers Weekly*, May 26, 1975.

*   *   *

STRICKLAND, Joshua 1896-

PERSONAL: Born October 18, 1896, in Auckland, New Zealand; came to the United States in 1973; son of Ernest T. (a sheep rancher) and Gladys (a midwife; maiden name, Treveylan) Strickland; married Millicent Crookes-Hemings, June 10, 1918 (died December 11, 1970); married Louisa M. Pearl (a dancer), June 28, 1971; children: Joshua, Jr., Arthur, Ernest, William, Pierce, Treveylan, Phillip, Gertrude (Mrs. Thomas Gold), Norman, Harold, Robert. *Education:* Cambridge University, M.A., 1921. *Residence:* New York, N.Y.

CAREER: Strickland Lines Ltd., Mombasa, Kenya, president, 1923-51; Habib & Narinian, Murbat, Oman, partner, 1952-67; free-lance writer, 1967—. Member of board of directors of Anglo-Iranian Trust. Chairman of East Africa Red Cross, 1949-56. *Military service:* British Naval Air Service, 1915-17; became commander; received Distinguished Service Order. Royal Navy, 1939-45; became captain. *Member:* Philologists Union, League of African Amity, Clarendon Club, Kent Shooting Club.

WRITINGS: Superworlds, Grosset, 1975; *Aliens on Earth*, Grosset, 1977.

WORK IN PROGRESS: Writing the text for a musical play about Oman; translating an epic poem of a Tuareg tribe of the Kinshasa Basin, and a collection of stories about differential equations, for young people.

SIDELIGHTS: Strickland comments: "I became a writer several years ago after I retired from business, because I found myself unemployable. If someone would give me a ship to sail or a consignment of munitions to peddle to the Arabs, I'd never touch a typewriter again. It's dreadfully boring work that causes the abdomen to become flaccid and the brain to become rigid. As nothing worthwhile can be translated into words, one finds oneself merely fumbling with reality. I except poets. Unfortunately, I am not a poet." Strickland lives on a boat, and reports that he is "usually on the move."

STRIEBER, Whitley 1945-

PERSONAL: Born June 13, 1945, in San Antonio, Tex.; son of Karl (a lawyer) and Mary (Drought) Strieber; married Anne Mattocks (a teacher), November 20, 1970. *Education:* University of Texas, B.A., 1968; London School of Economics and Political Science, certificate, 1968. *Home:* 300 Cognewaugh Rd., Cos Cob, Conn. 06830. *Agent:* Charles Neighbors, Inc., 240 Waverly Pl., New York, N.Y. 10014.

CAREER: Cunningham & Walsh Advertising, New York, N.Y., account supervisor and vice-president, 1973—. *Member:* Authors Guild, Authors League of America, Writers Guild, Poets and Writers.

WRITINGS: The Wolfen (novel), Morrow, 1978. Author of screen adaptation for "The Wolfen," Orion Productions, 1978.

WORK IN PROGRESS: Another novel.

SIDELIGHTS: Strieber designs games based on various periods of history, including "a game about the late middle ages entitled 1480: Age of Exploration and one covering the Hellenistic Age called Seven Against History. These are multiplayer games played by mail that move in real time. 1480 has been under way for three years, and has about thirty players."

He wrote: "I write to entertain myself and others; for me this is the most meaningful function of fiction, although from a cultural standpoint I recognize that it is not the most important. Contemporary fiction seems to me to have divided between frenetic commercial brouhaha and arid intellectualism. I wonder if it isn't possible to provide the public with high entertainment and prose of value at the same time. Certainly it would be no new achievement, having been the standard of Anglo-Saxon letters since the time of Chaucer, and indeed long before and after. To do it is my constant ambition."

AVOCATIONAL INTERESTS: Computers and designing computer games; "has participated in archaeological projects in Central America, and is at present involved with the attempt to authenticate the Holy Shroud that has been undertaken by a scientific group."

*   *   *

STRYKER-RODDA, Harriet 1905-

PERSONAL: Born March 18, 1905, in Brooklyn, N.Y.; daughter of Harry Boardman and Ruth (Robson) Mott; married Kenn Stryker-Rodda (an editor and genealogist), December 29, 1924; children: Paul Mott, E. Natton (deceased), Andrea. *Education:* New York University, B.A., 1947. *Home and office:* 421 Summit Ave., South Orange, N.J. 07079.

CAREER: Professional genealogist, 1940—, certified, 1966. Executive secretary at New York University, 1937-46. Curator of manuscripts and assistant librarian for Long Island Historical Society, 1952-68.

MEMBER: National Genealogical Society, Daughters of the American Revolution, Daughters of the American Colonists, Daughters of Colonial Wars, Colonial Dames of the Seventeenth Century, New England Women, New York Genealogical and Biographical Society, Genealogical Society of New Jersey, New Jersey Historical Society, New Jersey League of Historical Societies, Pennsylvania Genealogical Society, Long Island Historical Society, Staten Island Historical Society, Van Kouwenhoven Family Association, Wyckoff Family Association, Pi Lambda Theta, Flagon and

Trencher. *Awards, honors:* First place award from Heart of America Genealogical Society, 1977, for *Ancestors and Descendants of Frank Lusk Babbott, Jr., M.D.*

WRITINGS: Price-Goldsmith-Lowenstein and Related Families, privately printed, 1967; *Ancestors and Descendants of Eugene Waterman Mason,* privately printed, 1968; *Descendants of James Angus, 1751-1806,* privately printed, 1969; *Descendants of John Jacob Bauer, 1796-1858,* privately printed, 1969; *Preservation of Manuscripts in the Local Historical Society,* New Jersey League of Historical Societies, 1969, revised edition, 1976.

Hayward-Howard and Littlefield, privately printed, 1970; *Ancestors and Descendants of Frank Lusk Babbott, Jr., M.D.,* Polyanthos, 1974; *Index to Onderdonk's Revolutionary Incidents of Long Island,* Polyanthos, 1974; *Partial Ancestry of Charles Pratt, 1830-1891,* Polyanthos, 1974; *Some Early Records of Morris County, New Jersey, 1740-1799,* Polyanthos, 1975; *Watts: Ancestry and Descendants of Ridley Watts,* Polyanthos, 1976; *How to Climb Your Family Tree: Genealogy for Beginners,* Lippincott, 1977. Contributor to history and genealogy journals. Editor of *News* (of New Jersey League of Historical Societies), 1973—; publications editor of *Flagon and Trencher: Descendants of Colonial Tavernkeepers,* Volumes I-III.

WORK IN PROGRESS: Family History of George Comyns Thomas, Jr. of Elizabeth, N.J. 1664-1978, Replica (Elizabeth, N.J.); genealogical research; research on two manuscripts for librarians, one on handwriting and one on genealogy.

SIDELIGHTS: Harriet Stryker-Rodda writes: "I have been teaching beginning genealogists in lecture series and seminars for over forty years, emphasizing the proper learning of the techniques needed and the necessity for thoroughness in research, documentation, analysis, and synthesis. I have developed and used successfully lectures aimed at the importance of women as the link in families, urging them to preserve and transmit family information and traditions that should not be lost or should be reclaimed."

*   *   *

STUART, Lyle 1922-

PERSONAL: Original name Lionel Simon; name legally changed; born August 11, 1922, in New York, N.Y.; son of Alfred and Theresa Simon; married Mary Louise Strawn, September 7, 1946 (died, August, 1969); children: Sandra Lee, Rory John. *Politics:* "Revolutionary." *Religion:* Atheist. *Home:* 1530 Palisade Ave., Fort Lee, N.J. 07024. *Office:* 120 Enterprise Ave., Secaucus, N.J. 07094.

CAREER: Writer and publisher. Former editor of *Mad* magazine; founder of *The Independent,* 1951. Founder of Lyle Stuart, Inc. (publishers), 1956. Member of board of directors of North Bergen Public Library. *Member:* Authors League of America (member of executive committee of pulp writers section).

WRITINGS: God Wears a Bow Tie, Greenberg, 1949; (with M. J. Rivise) *Inside Western Union,* Sterling, 1950; *The Secret Life of Walter Winchell,* Boars Head, 1953; (with Arthur Coca) *The Pulse Test,* Lyle Stuart, 1956; *Mary Louise,* Citadel, 1972; *Casino Gambling for the Winner,* Lyle Stuart, 1978. Contributor to periodicals, including *World at War, Writer,* and *Seven Days.*

SIDELIGHTS: Stuart wrote *The Secret Life of Walter Winchell* in retaliation for the columnist's harsh criticism of singer Josephine Baker. One thing led to another and eventually Stuart won enough money in a court settlement to form his own publishing company.

With the publishing of both *The Sensuous Man* and *The Sensuous Woman*, Stuart initiated the trend towards sex-related books. "We were pioneers," he said. "Everybody does sex books now—everybody. But we started the sex revolution in publishing." And he continues to specialize in the controversial.

Despite his success as a publisher, Stuart would rather write. "I suppose if I had a choice I would have preferred to have been a novelist than a publisher," he said. "I mean then you're not just talking to the other person, one to one, you're talking to the whole world. And that's fun."

AVOCATIONAL INTERESTS: Gambling.

BIOGRAPHICAL/CRITICAL SOURCES: Publishers Weekly, May 29, 1978; *Washington Post,* September 6, 1978.

* * *

STUART, W. J.
See MacDONALD, Philip

* * *

STUART, Warren
See MacDONALD, Philip

* * *

STURGEON, Theodore Hamilton 1918-
(Frederick R. Ewing, E. Hunter Waldo)

PERSONAL: Birth-given name, Edward Hamilton Waldo; name legally changed; born February 26, 1918, in St. George, Staten Island, N.Y.; son of Edward (a retail paint businessman) and Christine (a teacher and writer; maiden name, Hamilton) Waldo; married Dorothy Fillingame (divorced, 1945); married Mary Mair (a singer), 1949 (divorced, 1951); married third wife, Marion, 1951; married Wina Bonnie Golden (a television personality), 1969; children: Patricia, Cynthia, Robin, Tandy, Noel, Timothy, Andros. *Education:* Attended Pennsylvania State Nautical School. *Religion:* Episcopal. *Agent:* Robert Mills Ltd., 156 East 52nd St., New York, N.Y. 10022.

CAREER: Has worked as an engine room wiper at sea, speech writer, bulldozer operator in Puerto Rico, copy editor, resort hotel manager in West Indies, literary agent, and writer, 1938—. *Member:* Writers Guild of America. *Awards, honors: Argosy* magazine story award, 1949, for "Bianca's Hands"; International Fantasy award, 1954, for *More Than Human;* guest of honor at Twentieth World Science Fiction Convention, 1962; Nebula award, 1970, and Hugo award, 1971, both for "Slow Sculpture."

WRITINGS: Without Sorcery (short stories), introduction by Ray Bradbury, Prime Press, 1948; *The Dreaming Jewels* (science fiction novel), Greenberg, 1950, published as *The Synthetic Man,* Pyramid, 1961; *More Than Human* (science fiction novel), Farrar, Straus, 1953; *E Pluribus Unicorn* (short stories), Abelard, 1953; *Caviar* (short stories), Ballantine, 1955; *A Way Home* (short stories), Funk, 1955 (published in England as *Thunder and Roses,* M. Joseph, 1957); *The King and Four Queens* (western; based on story by Margaret Fitt), Dell, 1956; (under pseudonym Frederick R. Ewing) *I, Libertine,* Ballantine, 1956; *A Touch of Strange* (short stories), Doubleday, 1958; *The Cosmic Rape* (science fiction novel), Dell, 1958; *Aliens 4* (short stories), Avon, 1959.

Beyond, Avon, 1960; *Venus Plus X* (science fiction novel), Pyramid, 1960; *Some of Your Blood,* Ballantine, 1961; *The Unexpected* (short stories; compiled by Leo Margulies), Pyramid, 1961; *Voyage to the Bottom of the Sea* (novel based on screenplay by Irwin Allen and Charles Bennet), Pyramid, 1961; *Two Complete Novels* (contains "And My Fear is Great" and "Baby Is Three"), Galaxy, 1965; *The Joyous Invasions* (short stories), Gollancz, 1965; (contributor) Harlan Ellison, editor, *Dangerous Visions,* Berkeley, 1967; (with Ray Bradbury and Oliver Chadwick Symmes) *One Foot and the Grave* (short stories), Avon, 1968; *Starshine* (short stories), Gollancz, 1968.

Sturgeon in Orbit (short stories), Gollancz, 1970; *Sturgeon Is Alive and Well* (short stories), Putnam, 1971; *The Worlds of Theodore Sturgeon* (short stories), Ace Books, 1972; *To Here and the Easel* (short stories), Gollancz, 1973; *Sturgeon's West,* Doubleday, 1973; (contributor) Reginald Bretnor, editor, *Science Fiction: Today and Tomorrow,* Harper, 1974; *Case and the Dreamer* (short stories), Doubleday, 1974.

Also author of plays. Contributor of scripts to television series, including "Star Trek," "The Invaders," and "Wild, Wild West." Contributor of articles and stories, sometimes under pseudonym E. Hunter Waldo, to magazines, including *Astounding Science Fiction, Unknown, Galaxy, Weird Tales, Argosy, Venture Science Fiction,* and *Thrilling Wonder Stories.* Regular science fiction book reviewer for *National Review.*

SIDELIGHTS: Sturgeon's stepfather, whose name the writer adopted, was a rather stern and scholarly teacher. Unfortunately, the younger Sturgeon's consuming interest was not in his studies, but in gymnastics instead. He served as the captain of his school team for a time, but was forced to give the sport up after a bout with rheumatic fever. His dream of a career with the circus shattered, Sturgeon turned to wearing "weird outfits just to be annoying." As an antidote to his step-son's lack of scholarly interest, the elder Sturgeon subjected Theodore to regular sessions of reading in the home library. The immediate intent was to supplement the studies Theodore avoided at school, but the long term result was a sound literary background for the writer-to-be.

After graduation from high school with a less than illustrious record, Sturgeon undertook nautical studies to prepare himself for a life at sea. He did not complete the course, but went to sea as an engine room wiper. It was then that Sturgeon began his career as a writer. Science fiction historian Sam Moskowitz wrote that Sturgeon "had thought of a 'foolproof' way of cheating the American Railway Express Agency, but lacked the immoral courage to test it himself. Instead, he cast the mischief in the form of a short-short story which he sold to McClure's Syndicate in 1937." Sturgeon's first story and the others he wrote during the next two years were not fantasy or science fiction.

In 1939, at the urging of a friend, Sturgeon tried his hand at writing fantasy. His first story was accepted by *Unknown* magazine and Sturgeon became a full-time writer. Despite periods of difficulty in his personal and professional life, Sturgeon found new markets for his writing largely through his work as a literary agent. His stories began to appear in magazines such as *Astounding Science Fiction, Weird Tales,* and *Thrilling Wonder Stories.*

Although Sturgeon is primarily a short story writer, his first full-length novel was published in 1951. *The Dreaming Jewels* was received with mixed reviews. His second novel met with greater success. *More Than Human* deals with psychic phenomena within the framework of Gestalt philosophy. The book was awarded the International Fantasy Award and firmly established Sturgeon's success as a writer of fantasy. Moskowitz wrote of Sturgeon's attitude toward financial success. "If ever an author epitomized the skittishness and sensitivity attributed to the 'artist,' it is Theodore Sturgeon. While he appreciated the need for money, his primary motivation was not the dollar. Despite the knowledge that he could sell *anything* of a fantastic nature he cared to write . . . , it was typical of him to take a couple of months off to write a three-act play *free* for a small-town theater, with the review in a local weekly his sole reward."

In addition to his somewhat unorthodox attitude about financial matters, Sturgeon is also noted for his use of unusual themes and subjects in his writing. Before his reputation was firmly established, Sturgeon's stories were sometimes considered too perverse or disgusting for publication. One of Sturgeon's early stories, "Bianca's Hands," was rejected for this reason but later won the *Argosy* magazine story award.

Venus Plus X is another of Sturgeon's works which evokes strong reaction to its unusual subject. The novel is considered by David Ketterer and other students of science fiction to be one of the few science fiction works to successfully employ a utopian motif. Sturgeon's utopian society is called Ledom (model spelled backwards). The twist in the story is that in order to maintain their utopia, the inhabitants submit to operations to render themselves hermaphroditic.

Sturgeon, himself a regular science fiction book reviewer for *National Review,* is mildly amused at the hesitancy of many reviewers and critics to take fantasy and science fiction seriously. Perhaps a representative statement was made by a reviewer for the *New York Herald Tribune* about one of Sturgeon's own novels. The reviewer wrote: "One fears to toss about words like 'profundity' and 'greatness' in connection with the literature of entertainment. . . ." The prevailing attitude is that science fiction and fantasy must all be hack writing and trash. Sturgeon maintains that science fiction "has been around since Ezechiel (the Old Testament prophet) saw that flying saucer," and he adds an axiom that has become known as Sturgeon's Law: "90% of everything is trash."

BIOGRAPHICAL/CRITICAL SOURCES: New York Times, September 24, 1950, November 22, 1953; *New York Herald Tribune,* November 23, 1953; *Magazine of Fantasy and Science-Fiction,* September, 1962; Sam Moskowitz, *Explorers of the Infinite,* World Publishing, 1963; Moskowitz, *Seekers of Tomorrow,* World, 1965; David Ketterer, *New Worlds for Old,* Indiana University Press, 1974.*

* * *

SULLIVAN, Sean Mei
See SOHL, Jerry

* * *

SULLIVAN, Thomas Joseph, Jr. 1947-
(Tom Sullivan)

PERSONAL: Born March 27, 1947, in Boston, Mass.; son of Thomas Joseph and Marie (Kelly) Sullivan; married Patricia Steffen, May 17, 1969; children: Blythe Patrice, Thomas Joseph III. *Education:* Attended Providence College, 1965-67, and Harvard University, 1969. *Politics:* Republican. *Religion:* Roman Catholic. *Home address:* P.O. Box 7000-17, Redondo Beach, Calif. 90277.

CAREER: Singer and songwriter. Gives public lectures. Member of board of directors of Los Angeles Braille Institute and Up with People (Tucson). Delegate to Republican National Convention, 1976; member of President Ford's committee on job opportunities for the handicapped.

WRITINGS—Under name Tom Sullivan: (With Derek Gill) *If You Could See What I Hear* (autobiography), Harper, 1975; *Adventures in Darkness* (autobiography for young adults), McKay, 1976. Has written for (and performed on) "M.A.S.H.," CBS-TV, "Airport 77," and "Park Ride."

WORK IN PROGRESS: A series of books on the senses, for small children.

SIDELIGHTS: Sullivan writes: "My foremost interest in life is to live each day to its fullest, using every gift given to me to its potential. Because of an inconvenience (blindness) it seems I have spent a good deal of my life struggling against the labels that society puts on any minority group, thereby placing limits on that group. I have, as my books point out, done a lot of crazy things, just to prove I could do them. Then, in my middle twenties an incident happened which gave me the incentive to write my own story.

"I have a vital interest in the well-being of our country, and am becoming more and more active in politics, handicapped education, and giving motivational lectures to many organizations around the world. In short, where there is a need before me I try to do my part.

"If I were to sum up my own personal philosophy, it would be that yesterday is only a memory, tomorrow is a dream, but we must live well for this moment—focus our attention on the now, the present, what is happening today."

* * *

SULLIVAN, Tom
See SULLIVAN, Thomas Joseph, Jr.

* * *

SUMMER, Charles Edgar 1923-

PERSONAL: Born June 13, 1923, in Newton, Miss.; son of Charles Edgar (a banker) and Emily (O'Rourke) Summer; married Carol Carlisle, February 21, 1968. *Education:* College of William & Mary, B.A., 1947; University of Pennsylvania, M.B.A., 1949; Columbia University, Ph.D., 1957. *Home:* 2342 43rd Ave. E., Seattle, Wash. 98112. *Office:* Department of Management, University of Washington, Seattle, Wash. 98195.

CAREER: Texaco, Inc., New York City, economist, 1949-52; Booz, Allen & Hamilton, New York City, consultant, 1952-54; Columbia University, New York City, associate professor, 1957-64, professor, 1964-67; University of Lausanne, Lausanne, Switzerland, professor, 1967-69; associated with University of Washington, Seattle, 1969—. *Military service:* U.S. Army Air Forces, 1943-46; became first lieutenant. *Member:* Academy of Management (past president), Phi Beta Kappa.

WRITINGS: Factors in Effective Administration, Columbia University Graduate School of Business, 1958; (with David Hampton and Ross Webber) *Organizational Behavior,* Scott, Foresman, 1977; (with J. J. O'Connell and Newman Perry) *The Managerial Mind,* Irwin, 1977. Editor of a series on policy for Little, Brown.

WORK IN PROGRESS: The Logic and Ethics of Policy (tentative title), for Little, Brown.

SURAN, Bernard G(regory) 1939-

PERSONAL: Born May 10, 1939, in Charleroi, Pa.; son of Frank Steven (an engineer) and Emera (an actress; maiden name, Sabaday) Suran; married wife, Mary Elizabeth (a clinical psychologist), November 29, 1969; children: Gregory, William Steven, Elizabeth Jane. *Education:* John Carroll University, B.S. (psychology and sociology), 1961; Aquinas Institute, B.A. (philosophy), 1963, M.A. (philosophy), 1965, Ph.L., 1965; Loyola University, Chicago, Ill., M.A. (psychology), 1966, Ph.D., 1970. *Home:* 6533 Blackhawk Trail, Indianhead Park, Ill. 60525. *Office:* 600 North McClurg St., #1802-A, Chicago, Ill. 60611.

CAREER: Marquette University, Milwaukee, Wis., assistant professor of psychology, 1970-71; Northwestern University, School of Medicine, Chicago, Ill., assistant professor, 1971-77, associate professor of psychology, 1977—. Chief psychologist at Children's Memorial Hospital, 1971-76; private practice of clinical psychology, 1971—. *Military service:* U.S. Army Reserve, 1961-70; became captain. *Member:* American Psychological Association, Society of Pediatric Psychology, Association for Precision Teaching, Midwest Psychological Association, Illinois Psychological Association.

WRITINGS: Playboy in Profile, Aquinas Institute Press, 1966; *Oddballs: A Study of the Social Maverick,* Nelson-Hall, 1978; *Special Children,* Scott, Foresman, 1979. Contributor of about twenty-five articles to psychology and philosophy journals.

WORK IN PROGRESS: A fictionalized account of the psychological crises in the life of an adolescent male; research on the male mid-life crisis.

SIDELIGHTS: Suran writes: "As a practicing psychotherapist for the past ten years, I am most interested in the sources of inspiration and the obstacles to growth that affect the individual human condition. I am becoming increasingly interested in the impact of activist feminism on male ego structures and the development of new formats of parity between man and woman in intimate relationships. My philosophical preference is existential; my belief system is pragmatic and relativist; my style of therapy is gestaltist and confronting."

*   *   *

SWALES, Martin 1940-

PERSONAL: Born November 3, 1940, in Victoria, British Columbia, Canada; son of Percy Johns (an engineer) and Doris (Davies) Swales; married Erika Meier (a university teacher), September 23, 1967; children: Christopher, Catherine. *Education:* Christ's College, Cambridge, B.A., 1961; University of Birmingham, Ph.D., 1963. *Politics:* "Liberal Scepticism." *Religion:* "Tentative Christian." *Home:* 11 De Freville Ave., Cambridge CB4 1HW, England. *Office:* Department of German, University College, University of London, Gower St., London WC1E 6BT, England.

CAREER: University of Birmingham, Birmingham, England, lecturer in German, 1964-70; University of Toronto, Toronto, Ontario, associate professor of German, 1970-72; University of London, King's College, London, England, reader in German, 1972-75; University of Toronto, professor of German, 1975-76; University of London, University College, professor of German, 1976—. *Member:* British Comparative Literature Association, Goethe Society (England), Modern Humanities Research Association, Association of Teachers of German (United Kingdom).

WRITINGS: Arthur Schnitzler: A Critical Study, Oxford University Press, 1971; *The German Novelle,* Princeton University Press, 1977; *The German Bildungsroman,* Princeton University Press, 1978; *Thomas Mann,* Heinemann, in press. Contributor to language and German studies journals.

SIDELIGHTS: Swales comments: "My work derives its chief impetus from a sense of the 'foreign-ness' of German literature and culture to me as an English-speaking reader. I believe that this 'foreign-ness' generates, not alienation, but creative estrangement. It is my hope that I see things German with a certain clarity and cogency—precisely because I cannot take them for granted."

*   *   *

SWEET, Jeffrey 1950-

PERSONAL: Born May 3, 1950, in Boston, Mass.; son of James Stouder (a writer) and Vivian (a violinist; maiden name, Roe) Sweet. *Education:* New York University, B.F.A., 1971. *Home:* 344 West 12th St., Apt. 6-A, New York, N.Y. 10014. *Agent:* Susan Schulman, 165 West End Ave., New York, N.Y. 10023.

CAREER: Free-lance writer, 1967—. Editorial assistant for Scholastic Magazines, 1970-71, and W. W. Norton & Co., Inc., 1974-75; librarian for Russell Sage Foundation, 1977-78. Director of special projects for Encompass Theatre. *Member:* Broadcast Music, Dramatists Guild (actors studio playwrights' unit).

WRITINGS: Something Wonderful Right Away: An Oral History of the Second City and the Compass Players, Avon, 1978.

Plays: "Porch" (one-act), first produced in Washington, D.C., at Arena Stage, February 5, 1977; "Hard Feelings" (three-act), first produced in New York, N.Y., at Actors Studio, May 23, 1978. Work represented in *The Best Short Plays 1976,* edited by Stanley Richards, Chilton, 1976.

Contributor of articles and stories to popular magazines, including *Ellery Queen, Newsday, Gallery,* and *Chicago.* Associate editor of *Dramatists Guild Quarterly.*

WORK IN PROGRESS: A book on the Committee, a theater based in San Francisco during the 1960's; several plays.

SIDELIGHTS: Sweet writes: "Most of my work revolves around the theatre, writing for or about it. I'm particularly interested in the relationship between the theatre and the community from which it springs. If I hadn't become a playwright, I probably would have become a sociologist.

"The greatest single influence on my work and the philosophy from which it springs probably has been the improvisational theatre movement, as developed by such figures as Viola Spolin, Paul Sills, David Shepherd, Alan Myerson, Mike Nichols, Elaine May, Del Close, and others. Implicit in this movement is the idea of theatre as the forum of the concerns of the community as opposed to the self-absorbed fantasies of a professional elite. It was to explore the improvisational theatre movement that I wrote *Something Wonderful Right Away.*

"I also write musical comedy (I'm a composer-lyricist and have studied with Lehman Engel and Paul Simon) and expect to get into film one of these days (having studied with Martin Scorcese at New York University and at the American Film Institute)."

AVOCATIONAL INTERESTS: Reading, playing piano, going to the theatre and movies, "having long, involved conversations on all manner of nonsense."

SWIFT, David
    See KAUFMANN, John

*   *   *

SYRUC, J.
    See MILOSZ, Czeslaw

*   *   *

SZATHMARY, Louis (Istvan) II   1919-

PERSONAL: Surname is pronounced Southmaree; born June 2, 1919, in Rakospalota, Hungary; came to United States in 1951, naturalized in 1963; son of Louis Istvan (an army officer) and Irene Aranka (Strausz) Szathmary; married Magda Mandak, June 20, 1953 (divorced May 8, 1960); married Sadako Tanino (a company executive), May 9, 1960; children: Magda (Mrs. Kirk Bennett). *Education:* University of Budapest, M.A., 1940, Ph.D., 1944. *Religion:* Calvinist. *Home and office:* 2218 North Lincoln Ave., Chicago, Ill. 60614.

CAREER: New England Province Jesuits, Manresa Island, Conn., chef, 1952-55; Mutual Broadcasting System, New York, N.Y. executive chef, 1955-58; Reddi Fox Inc., Darien, Conn. plant superintendent, 1958-59; Armour & Co., Chicago, Ill., new product development manager, 1958-63; The Bakery Restaurant, Chicago, owner/chef, 1963—; Louis Szathmary Associates, Chicago, president, 1964—. President of Lou'Or Inc. and Transworldtaste Inc. Adjunct professor, Pennsylvania State University. Member of board of governors of National Space Institute; member of board of directors of Friends of the Chicago Public Library and Japan America Society. Trustee of Chicago Academy of Sciences. *Member:* World Institute of Chefs (London; Western Hemisphere vice-president, 1963-67). Confrerie de la Chaine des Rotisseurs (Paris), National Restaurant Association, American Academy of Chefs, Society of Professional Management Consultants, Council on Hotel, Restaurant and Institutional Education, Institutional Food Editorial Council, Screen Writers Guild, Grolier Club, Chicago Press Club, Catering Executive Club, Illinois Athletic Club. *Awards, honors:* Named man of the year by Pennsylvania State Hotel and Restaurant Society, 1976.

WRITINGS: Sears Gourmet Cooking, edited by Arthur E. Kreatschman, Sears, Roebuck, 1969; *The Chef's Secret Cookbook,* foreword by Jean Hewitt, Quadrangle, 1971; *American Gastronomy,* Regnery, 1974; *The Chef's New Secret Cookbook,* Regnery, 1976.

Compiler and author of introduction; all published by Arno: *Along the Northern Border: Cookery in Idaho, Minnesota, and North Dakota,* 1973; *Cool, Chill, Freeze: A New Approach to Cookery,* 1973; *Fifty Years of Prairie Cooking,* 1973; *Midwestern Home Cooking,* 1973; *Southwestern Cookery: Indian and Spanish Influences,* 1973; *Home Cookery: Ladies' Indispensable Companion; Cookery in Northeastern Cities,* 1973. Columnist for newspapers and magazines, including *Chicago Sun Times, Chicago Daily News, Travel/Holiday* and *Family Heritage.* Contributor of articles to *Cornell Hotel and Restaurant Administration Quarterly,* 1965-73.

SIDELIGHTS: Cookbooks from Szathmary's collection have been on exhibit at the Grolier Club, several universities, and in New York.

BIOGRAPHICAL/CRITICAL SOURCES: Kirkus Reviews, August 15, 1971; *Best Sellers,* December 1, 1971; *New York Times Book Review,* December 12, 1971; *AB Bookman's Weekly,* December 20, 1971.

T

TATE, Jackson R. 1899(?)-1978

OBITUARY NOTICE: Born c. 1899; died July 20, 1978, in Orange Park, Fla. U.S. Navy rear admiral and author. During 1945 Tate was stationed in Moscow where he had an affair with Russia's leading motion picture star, Zoya Fyodorova. After the war in Europe ended, Stalin ordered Tate to leave the country. It was not until 1973 that Tate learned the actress had given birth to their daughter, Victoria Fyodorova, in January, 1946, and then been exiled to Siberia for eight years as a spy because of her affair with him. When Tate learned of his daughter's existence, he pleaded with the Soviet government for two years before she was allowed to visit him in America. Victoria, also an actress, was married during her visit to the United States. Tate wrote the book on which the movie "Hell's Divers," starring Clark Gable, was based. Obituaries and other sources: *New York Times,* July 21, 1978; *Washington Post,* July 21, 1978; *Newsweek,* July 31, 1978; *Time,* July 31, 1978.

* * *

TAYLOR, Day
See PARKINSON, Cornelia M.

* * *

TAYLOR, Eleanor Ross 1920-

PERSONAL: Born June 30, 1920, in North Carolina; daughter of Fred E. and Jennie (Lilly) Ross; married Peter Taylor (a writer), June 4, 1943; children: Katherine, Peter. *Education:* University of North Carolina at Greensboro, B.A., 1940; additional study at Vanderbilt University, 1942-43. *Home:* 1841 Wayside Pl., Charlottesville, Va. 22903.

CAREER: High school teacher of English in North Carolina schools, 1940-42, 1944-45; worked in various public libraries in North Carolina and Tennessee, 1943-44; University of North Carolina, Greensboro, reserve librarian, 1945-46; University of Virginia, Charlottesville, teacher of poetry writing, 1977. *Awards, honors:* National Book Award nomination, 1960, for *Wilderness of Ladies;* D. Litt. from University of North Carolina at Greensboro, 1976.

WRITINGS: Wilderness of Ladies (poetry), McDowell, Obolensky, 1960; *Welcome Eumenides* (poetry), Braziller, 1972. Contributor of poems to journals, including *Sewanee Review* and *Southern Poetry Review.* Poetry editor, *Shenandoah* magazine, 1977.

WORK IN PROGRESS: A third collection of poems, nearly completed; a book of fiction.

SIDELIGHTS: Eleanor Ross Taylor's poems spring from her experiences as a Southerner and as a woman. Her first book, *Wilderness of Ladies,* attracted a small but loyal band of admirers, including Randall Jarrell. Adrienne Rich observed that many of the poems in this collection of verse "speak of the underground life of women, the Southern white Protestant woman in particular, the woman-writer, the woman in the family, coping, hoarding, preserving, observing, keeping up appearances, seeing through the myths and hypocrisies, nursing the sick, conspiring with sister-women, possessed of a will to survive and to see others survive."

Twelve years elapsed between the publication of *Wilderness of Ladies* and *Welcome Eumenides.* In the ensuing years the women's liberation movement had gained ground, which helped to create a larger audience for Taylor's poetry. *Welcome Eumenides* received accolades from a number of critics. Erica Jong found her depictions of women striking: "In her poems about women, she often seems to be concerned with the stripping away of outward roles that hide a woman's true identity even from herself." But Taylor's poems were not extolled merely because they were topical; commentators also admired her poetic techniques. A reviewer for *Virginia Quarterly Review* noted that "there is an intense reality in her images, a firmness and strength in her style." Taylor's poems "set their own standard for honesty and wit, for rueful downrightness, for sparkle and restraint few other poets reach," Robert Mazzocco wrote.

Seeking to describe Taylor's verse and the poet herself, Mazzocco arrived at this explanation: "Mrs. Taylor is a little like a Southern belle who has uncharacteristically read all the big books, thought all the gray thoughts, who is a bit fearful perhaps of expressing grief or depth of the cruel chemical wit of which she is capable, yet who, against 'cyclonic gust and chilly rain,' expresses them forthrightly anyway."

BIOGRAPHICAL/CRITICAL SOURCES: New York Times Book Review, July 2, 1972; *Virginia Quarterly Review,* autumn, 1972; *Parnassus,* fall/winter, 1974; *New York Review of Books,* April 3, 1975; *Contemporary Literary Criticism,* Gale, Volume 5, 1976.*

* * *

TAYLOR, Eugene Jackson 1913-1978

OBITUARY NOTICE: Born June 26, 1913, in Wichita,

Kan.; died December 2, 1978, in Schenectady, N.Y. A writer closely associated with the former medical columnist Howard A. Rusk, Taylor collaborated with Rusk on books, including *New Hope for the Handicapped, Living With a Disability,* and *Rehabilitative Medicine.* He was an officer in several rehabilitation organizations. Obituaries and other sources: *New York Times,* December 4, 1978; *Who's Who in America,* 40th edition, Marquis, 1978.

*   *   *

TAYLOR, John 1925-

PERSONAL: Born August 22, 1925, in Lancastershire, England; son of Richard Henry (a teacher) and Margaret (a teacher; maiden name, Lowe) Taylor; married Ella Mac-Donald (a medical practitioner), April 2, 1955; children: Richard Cameron, Donald John. *Education:* Balliol College, Oxford, M.A., 1950. *Politics:* "Slightly left of centre." *Religion:* Church of England. *Home:* Storey Cottage, Kirkby Overblow, Harrogate, Yorkshire, England. *Office:* School of History, University of Leeds, Leeds 2, Yorkshire, England.

CAREER: University of Leeds, Leeds, England, lecturer, 1950-65, senior lecturer, 1965-70, reader in medieval history, 1970—. Associate professor at Princeton University, 1961-62. *Military service:* British Army, Royal Artillery, 1943-47; served in India; became lieutenant. *Member:* Royal Historical Society, Yorkshire Archaeological Society, Leeds Philosophical and Literary Society (past president).

WRITINGS: The Universal Chronicle of Ranulph Higden, Oxford University Press, 1966; (with R. B. Dobson) *Rymes of Robyn Hood,* University of Pittsburgh Press, 1976. Contributor to history, archaeology, philosophy, and literary journals. Editor of record series of Yorkshire Archaeological Society and of proceedings of Leeds Philosophical and Literary Society.

WORK IN PROGRESS: Parliamentary Texts of the Later Middle Ages, with Nicholas Pronay, publication by Oxford University Press expected in 1980; an edition of *Modus Tenendi Parliamentum,* the only treatise on Parliament to be written in medieval England.

SIDELIGHTS: Taylor writes: "I am interested in the historical literature of the later Middle Ages, including chronicles, ballads, and legal texts. What contemporaries thought about events at the time when they were happening is an important aspect of history, and this type of historical literature gives an indication of their thought. It has been said that 'there is no more significant pointer to the character of a society than the history it writes,' and *The Universal Chronicle of Ranulf Higden* illuminates many important aspects of the outlook of fourteenth-century England. The ballads of Robin Hood illustrate one aspect of the popular thought of medieval and modern times, while the *Modus Tenendi Parliamentum* (written ca. 1321), which describes Parliament as a representative assembly, illustrates the manner in which lawyers and parliamentary officials regarded Parliament during the later Middle Ages. The ideas about Parliament, social justice, and historical development that are embodied in these texts played a part in the outcome of events."

AVOCATIONAL INTERESTS: Walking.

*   *   *

TAYLOR, Paul B(eekman) 1930-

PERSONAL: Born December 31, 1930, in London, England; son of Edith (Annesley) Taylor; married Alexandra

Fatio, May 10, 1958 (divorced October 19, 1977); married Rose-Marie Beauverd (a teacher), January 4, 1978; children: Andrea, Maurice, Nora, Paul Guillaume, Gareth. *Education:* Brown University, A.B., 1954, Ph.D., 1960; Wesleyan University, M.A., 1958; postdoctoral study at University of Oslo, 1960-61. *Home:* 35, Cret de la Neige, 1227 Carouge, Geneva, Switzerland. *Agent:* Curtis Brown, Ltd., 575 Madison Ave., New York, N.Y. 10022. *Office:* Department of English, University of Geneva, 1211 Geneva 4, Switzerland.

CAREER: Brown University, Providence, R.I., assistant professor of English, 1961-64; University of Iceland, Reykjavik, Iceland, professor of English, 1964-65; University of Geneva, Geneva, Switzerland, professor of medieval English, 1965—. *Military service:* U.S. Army, 1954-57; became sergeant. *Member:* Modern Language Association of America, Mediaeval Academy of America, Early English Text Society. *Awards, honors:* Fulbright fellowship, University of Oslo, 1960-61; National Translation Center fellowship, 1967-69.

WRITINGS: (Editor and translator with W. H. Auden) *The Song of the Sybil,* Windover Press, 1967; (translator from the Icelandic with Auden) *The Elder Edda,* Random House, 1969; (editor with P. H. Salus) *For W. H. Auden,* Random House, 1972; (translator with Auden) *Poems From the Old Norse,* in press. Contributor of articles on Germanic philology and literature in *English Studies, Neuphilologische Mitteilungen, Philological Quarterly,* and other journals.

WORK IN PROGRESS: A study of Chaucer's theory of language.

SIDELIGHTS: Taylor writes: "My major interest has always been Germanic language and literature, particularly as an expression of early cultural attitudes. I have studied theories of language use, particularly in Old Icelandic and Old English literature. This interest in language derives primarily from early studies with G. I. Gurdjieff in New York and in Paris (1948-49), and was stimulated by my collaboration with W. H. Auden (1966-72)."

*   *   *

TAYLOR, Paul S(chuster) 1895-

PERSONAL: Born June 9, 1895, in Sioux City, Iowa; son of Henry James (an attorney) and Rose Eugenia (Schuster) Taylor; married Katharine Page Whiteside, May 15, 1920 (divorced, 1935); married Dorothea Lange, December 6, 1935 (died, 1965); children: (first marriage) Ross Whiteside (deceased), Katharine Page Taylor Loesch, Margot Agnes Taylor Fanger. *Education:* University of Wisconsin, Madison, A.B., 1917; University of California, Berkeley, M.A., 1920, Ph.D., 1922. *Politics:* Democrat. *Home:* 1163 Euclid Ave., Berkeley, Calif. 94708. *Office:* Department of Economics, University of California, 275 Barrows Hall, Berkeley, Calif. 94720.

CAREER: University of California, Berkeley, instructor, 1922-24, assistant professor, 1924-29, associate professor, 1929-39, professor of economics, 1939-62, professor emeritus, 1962—, head of department, 1952-56, head of Institute of International Studies, 1956-62. Visiting professor at University of Alexandria, 1962-63. President of California Rural Rehabilitation Corp., 1936-43. Field director of Rural Rehabilitation Division of California Emergency Relief Administration, 1935; regional labor adviser to Resettlement Administration, 1935-36; member of advisory council of California Department of Employment, 1935-42; member of California Board of Agriculture, 1940-44; research director for California Labor Federation, 1970; consultant to U.S. Department of the Interior, Export-Import Bank, Stanford Research Institute, U.S. Agency for International Development, and United Nations. *Military service:* U.S. Marine Corps, American Expeditionary Forces, 1917-19; served in France; became captain; received Purple Heart.

MEMBER: American Economic Association, Academia Nacional de Ciencias (Mexico; honorary corresponding member), Phi Beta Kappa, Chi Phi, Phi Alpha Delta, Delta Sigma Pi, Delta Sigma Rho, Cosmos Club, Faculty Club (University of California, Berkeley). *Awards, honors:* Guggenheim fellowship for Latin America, 1931; LL.D. from University of California, Berkeley, 1965; Henry Wagner Award from California Historical Society, 1977, for work in California history.

WRITINGS: The Sailors' Union of the Pacific, Ronald, 1923, reprinted, Arno, 1971; *Mexican Labor in the United States,* three volumes, University of California Press, 1928-34, reprinted in two volumes, Johnson Reprint, 1966; *A Spanish-Mexican Peasant Community: Arandas in Jalisco, Mexico,* University of California Press, 1933; *An American-Mexican Frontier: Nueces County, Texas,* University of North Carolina Press, 1934, reprinted, Russell & Russell, 1971; (with wife, Dorothea Lange) *An American Exodus,* Reynal, 1939, revised edition, Yale University Press, 1969; *Adrift on the Land,* Public Affairs Committee, Inc., 1940; *Principles and Practices of Community Development,* Institute of International Studies, University of California, Berkeley, 1960; *Georgia Plan, 1732-1752,* Institute of Business and Economic Research, University of California, Berkeley, 1971; (contributor) Arthur F. Corwin, editor, *Immigrants—And Immigrants: Perspectives on Mexican Migration to the United States,* Greenwood Press, 1978. *Work in Progress:* Research on excess land and residency requirements of U.S. reclamation law.

SIDELIGHTS: Taylor told *CA:* "My interest in land tenure was stimulated by fifteen months service with the American Expeditionary Forces. The Bolshevik revolution of 1917 released German troops on the Eastern Front to attack the Allies on the Western Front. We stopped them at Chateau-Thierry-Bouresches-Belleau Wood, where I was gassed. When I researched the Mexican migration of 1927-32, I saw the effects of the Mexican revolution in both the United States and Mexico. The Russian slogan was "Peace, Bread, and the Land"; the Mexican slogan was "Land and Liberty." In 1958 I spent two weeks evaluating General Douglas MacArthur's land reform in Japan. I researched the land reform program in Vietnam in 1958 and 1967. Incidentally, one of the important reasons for our failure in Vietnam was our failure to press for land reform in that country. The Viet Cong thus had two main charges against us: We were foreigners splitting their country, and we were backing a landlord-based government."

Taylor also commented about his research methods: "I have always sought to do my research at ground level, whether literally in the fields for contemporary research in the United States, Asia, Latin America, or elsewhere. In historical research I sought ground level sources in the sense of original documents of the time and subject. In other words, I wanted primary rather than secondary sources."

BIOGRAPHICAL/CRITICAL SOURCES: Suzanne B. Riess, *Paul Schuster Taylor, California Social Scientist: An Interview,* three volumes, Bancroft Library, University of California, Berkeley, 1973.

TAYLOR, Robert 1925-

PERSONAL: Born January 19, 1925, in Newton, Mass.; son of Frank M. (in sales) and Elsie (Sundling) Taylor; married Brenda Kathleen Slattery, June 20, 1964; children: Gillian, Douglas. *Education:* Colgate University, A.B., 1946; graduate study at Brown University, 1948. *Agent:* Boston Literary Agency, Manchester, Mass. *Office:* Boston Globe, Boston, Mass. 02107.

CAREER: Boston Herald, Boston, Mass. critic (art, music, film, and theater), 1948-66; Institute of Contemporary Art, Boston, director of publications, 1967; *Boston Globe,* Boston, arts editor, 1967—. Lecturer at Wheaton College Norton, Mass., 1961—; arts associate at Boston University, 1972-74. *Military service:* U.S. Navy, radarman, 1943-46. *Member:* National Book Critics Circle, St. Botolph Club.

WRITINGS: In Red Weather (novel), Holt, 1961. Author of "Fifty Winches" in *New Boston Review,* 1975—. Contributor to magazines, including *Atlantic,* and newspapers.

WORK IN PROGRESS: Two novels, *A Season in Venice,* and *Jackdaw.*

*   *   *

TAYLOR, Robert B(artley) 1926-

PERSONAL: Born October 15, 1926, in Pendleton, Ore.; son of Robert B. (a farmer and administrator) and Anna (Geiss) Taylor; married Floris Mae Bringedahl, 1949; children: Mark L., Linnea Taylor Carrick, Gwen Taylor Jorgensen. *Education:* Wheaton College, Wheaton, Ill., B.S., 1949; University of Oregon, M.S., 1951, Ph.D., 1960. *Politics:* Republican. *Religion:* Presbyterian. *Home:* 1625 Hudson Ave., Manhattan, Kan. 66502. *Office:* Department of Sociology, Anthropology, and Social Work, Kansas State University, Manhattan, Kan. 66502.

CAREER: Wheaton College, Wheaton, Ill., instructor in anthropology, 1951-54; Kansas State University, Manhattan, instructor, 1957-67, associate professor, 1967—. Visiting assistant professor at University of New Mexico, 1959-60. *Member:* American Anthropological Association (fellow), Society for Applied Anthropology.

WRITINGS: Cultural Ways: A Compact Introduction to Cultural Anthropology, Allyn & Bacon, 1969, 3rd edition, 1979; *Introduction to Cultural Anthropology,* Allyn & Bacon, 1973. Contributor to anthropology and sociology journals.

WORK IN PROGRESS: Cultural Change in Colonial Mesoamerica.

*   *   *

TAYLOR, William 1930-

PERSONAL: Born May 31, 1930, in Grayford, Kent, England; son of Herbert (a postal official) and Maud Ethel (Peyto) Taylor; and married Rita Hague (a teacher), December 30, 1954; children: Anne Catherine, Rosemary Caroline, Richard William James. *Education:* London School of Economics and Political Science, London, B.Sc., 1952; Westminster College, P.G.C.E., 1953; Institute of Education, London, Dipl. Ed., 1954, Ph.D., 1960. *Office:* Institute of Education, Bedford Way, London WC1H OAL, England.

CAREER: Teacher at schools in Kent, England, 1954-59, deputy principal of Slade Green Secondary School, 1956-59; St. Luke's College, Exeter, England, senior lecturer, 1959-61; Bede College, Durham, England, head of education department, 1961-64; Oxford University, Oxford, England, tutor in education, 1964-66; University of Bristol, Bristol, England, professor of education, 1966-73; University of London, London, England, director of Institute of Education, 1973—. President of English New Education Fellowship, 1977—; chairman of educational advisory council of Independent Broadcasting Authority, 1974—, Universities Council for the Education of Teachers, 1975—, and education advisory committee of UK National Commission for UNESCO, 1975—. Consultant to Organization for Economic Co-operation & Development (OECD) and UNESCO. *Awards, honors:* Commonwealth fellow, Australian States, 1975; honorary doctor of science from University of Aston at Birmingham, 1977; honorary fellow of the College of Preceptors, 1977; New Zealand University prestige fellowship, 1977.

WRITINGS: The Secondary Modern School, Faber, 1963; (editor) *Towards a Policy for the Education of Teachers,* Butterworth & Co., 1969; *Society and the Education of Teachers,* Faber, 1969; (editor with George Baron) *Educational Administration and the Social Sciences,* Athlone Press, 1969; *Heading for Change,* Routledge & Kegan Paul, 1972; *Policy and Planning for Post Secondary Education: A European Overview,* Council of Europe, 1972; (editor) *Research Perspectives in Education,* National Foundation for Educational Research 1973; (editor with R. Farquahar and R. Thomas) *Educational Administration in Australia and Abroad,* University of Brisbane Press, 1975; *Research and Reform in Teacher Education,* National Foundation for Educational Research, 1978.

Contributor: W. R. Niblett, editor, *How and Why Do We Learn?,* Faber, 1965; J. W. Tibble, editor, *The Study of Education,* Routledge & Kegan Paul, 1966; M. Craft and others, editors, *Linking Home and School,* Longmans, Green, 1967; R. Oxtoby, *Staff-Student Relations,* World University Service, 1967; W. G. Walker, G. Baron, and D. Cooper, editors, *Educational Administration: International Perspectives,* Rand McNally, 1968; W. Taylor and Baron, *Educational Administration and the Social Sciences,* Athlone Press, 1969; M. Bressler and M. M. Tumin, editors, *Evaluation of the Effectiveness of Educational Systems,* U.S. Department of Health, Education, and Welfare, Bureau of Research, 1969; Taylor, editor, *Towards a Policy for the Education of Teachers,* Butterworth & Co., 1969; B. W. Allen, editor, *Headship in the Seventies,* Basil Blackwell, 1970.

F. H. Klassen and J. Collier, editors, *Crisis and Change in Teacher Education,* International Council on Education for Teaching, 1971; R. Hooper, editor, *The Curriculum: Context, Design and Development,* Oliver & Boyd, 1971; G. Chanan, editor, *Research Forum on Teacher Education,* NFER Publishing, 1972; Klassen, editor, *Innovations in Teacher Education,* International Council on Education for Teaching, 1972; D. J. McCarty and others, editors, *New Perspectives on Teacher Education,* Jossey-Bass, 1973; Taylor, editor, *Research Perspectives in Education,* Routledge & Kegan Paul, 1973; H. J. Butcher and H. B. Pont, editors, *Educational Research in Britain,* University of London Press, 1973; M. G. Hughes, editor, *Administering Education: International Challenge,* Athlone Press, 1975; Taylor and others, editors, *Educational Administration in Australia and Abroad,* University of Queensland Press, 1975; R. S. Peters, editor, *The Role of the Head,* Routledge & Kegan Paul, 1976; D. W. Piper and R. Glatter, editors, *The Changing University,* NFER Publishing, 1977.

Contributot to periodicals in his field, including *Sociological*

Review, Times Educational Supplement, Teacher, and *Trends in Education,* and to *Encyclopaedia Brittanica.*

WORK IN PROGRESS: A sequel to *Society and the Education of Teachers* dealing with the development of teacher education since 1969; a book on problems of contraction in education.

SIDELIGHTS: William Taylor told *CA:* "Nearly all my books reflect my own experience in the world of education and represent an attempt to understand more fully the activity in which I am engaged." *Avocational interests:* Walking, travel (Australia, New Zealand, Canada).

*   *   *

TENNYSON, Charles Bruce Locker   1879-1977

PERSONAL: Born November 8, 1879, in London, England; son of Lionel and Eleanor Bertha Mary (Locker) Tennyson; married Ivy Gladys Pretious, 1909 (died, 1958); children: Hallam, two other sons (killed in action, 1941 and 1945). *Education:* King's College, Cambridge, M.A.

CAREER: Called to the Bar of Gray's Inn, 1906; British Office of Works, junior equity counsel, 1909-11; British Colonial Office, assistant legal adviser, 1911-19; Federation of British Industries, deputy director, beginning 1919; Dunlop Rubber Co., secretary, 1928-48. British delegate at New Hebrides Conference, 1914. Chairman, Board of Trade Utility Furniture Committee, 1943, Furniture Production Committee, 1944. President, Union of Educational Institutions, 1948; chairman of council, Bedford College, London, 1946-53. *Member:* Royal College of Art (honorary fellow), Royal Society of Literature (fellow). *Awards, honors:* Honorary fellow, King's College, Cambridge; Companion of the Order of St. Michael and St. George, 1915; LL.D., Cambridge University; D.Litt., University of Leicester; Order of the British Empire, 1945.

WRITINGS: Cambridge From Within, Jacobs, 1913; *Alfred Tennyson* (biography), Macmillan, 1949; *Life's All a Fragment* (memoirs of Charles D. Fisher, John D. Snaith, Roy F. Truscott, Penrose Tennyson, and Julian Tennyson), Cassell, 1953; *Six Tennyson Essays,* Cassell, 1954; (editor) *Alfred Tennyson, "The Idylls of the King" and "The Princess,"* Collins, 1956; *Stars and Markets* (autobiography), Chatto & Windus, 1957; *The Somersby Tennysons,* Victorian Studies, 1963; (editor) A. Tennyson, *"The Devil and the Lady" and Unpublished Early Poems,* Indiana University Press, 1964; (editor) *Some Unpublished Poems by Arthur Henry Hallam,* West Virginia University Library, 1965; (with Christine Fall) *Alfred Tennyson: An Annotated Bibliography,* University of Georgia Press, 1967; (editor with Hope Dyson) *Dear and Honored Lady: The Correspondence Between Queen Victoria and Alfred Tennyson,* Macmillan (London), 1969, Farleigh Dickinson University Press, 1971; (compiler and editor, with son, Hallam Tennyson) *Victorian Poetry, 1830-1890,* Ginn, 1971; (with Dyson) *The Tennysons: Background to Genius,* Macmillan, 1974; (editor) A. Tennyson, *Unpublished Early Poems,* Folcroft, 1974.

SIDELIGHTS: Charles Tennyson's best known writing was *Alfred Tennyson,* his 1949 biography of his grandfather. More recently, Tennyson and Hope Dyson received praise as editors of *Dear and Honored Lady: The Correspondence Between Queen Victoria and Alfred Tennyson. Times Literary Supplement* wrote: "On the title page of [this book] Mrs. Hope Dyson and Sir Charles Tennyson claim merely to have 'edited' the correspondence itself is slender enough, and they have wisely decided to supply a reasonably full biographical setting. . . . Illuminated by the narrative, the letters and other documents are always interesting and sometimes moving.''

Alethea Hayter, in her review of *The Tennysons: Background to Genius,* remarked: "But . . . this delightful book about them [the Tennysons], though it does not gloss over their melancholy and indolence, dwells much more on their extremely amusing oddities and enjoyments, and their remarkable talents. . . . It would not be fair to treat this book simply as a anthology of amusing oddities, though it certainly is that. This would be to ignore the tragic figure who overshadows four of its earlier chapters—the Reverend George Tennyson, the poet's father. . . . This darker undercurrent flows on beneath the bright bubbles of anecdotes about George Tennyson's children.''

BIOGRAPHICAL/CRITICAL SOURCES: Charles Tennyson, *Stars and Markets,* Chatto & Windus, 1957; *Observer,* February 1, 1970; *Times Literary Supplement,* January 8, 1970, March 14, 1975; *New Statesman,* December 6, 1974.

OBITUARIES: AB Bookman's Weekly, September 12, 1977.*

(Died June 22, 1977, in England)

* * *

TERRIEN, Samuel Lucien   1911-

PERSONAL: Born March 27, 1911, in Saumur, France; came to the United States in 1935, naturalized citizen, 1943; son of Georges G. H. and Helene J. (Perrin) Terrien; married Sara Margaret Frantz, July 1, 1938; children: George Blaise, Cecile Jeanne, Alys Margareta, Beatrice Elinor. *Education:* Attended Sorbonne, University of Paris and Faculte Protestante Theology, both 1928-32; Ecole du Louvre, diplome, 1932; Ecole Francaise de Jerusalem, diplome, 1934; Union Theological Seminary, New York, N.Y., Th.D., 1941. *Home address:* Church Hill Rd., Washington Depot, Conn. 06794.

CAREER: College of Wooster, Wooster, Ohio, instructor in French literature, 1936-40; Union Theological Seminary, New York, N.Y., instructor, 1941-43, assistant professor, 1943-47, associate professor, 1947-53, Auburn Professor of Old Testament, 1953-64, Davenport Professor of Hebrew and cognate languages, 1964-76, professor emeritus, 1976—; writer, 1976—. Adjunct professor at Columbia University, 1964-76. Ordained Presbyterian minister, 1943; pastor of French Evangelical Church, 1977—.

WRITINGS: The Psalms and Their Meaning for Today, Bobbs-Merrill,1952; *Job: Poet of Existence,* Bobbs-Merrill, 1957; *Lands of the Bible,* Golden Press, 1958; *Le Livre de Job: Commentaire* (title means "The Book of Job: A Commentary", Delachaux et Niestle, 1963; *The Power to Bring Forth,* Fortress, 1969; *The Elusive Presence: Prolegomenon to an Ecumenical Theory of the Bible,* Harper, 1978. Associate editor of *Interpreter's Bible,* 1952-57, and *Interpreter's Dictionary of the Bible,* 1962. Also author of *Introduction and Exegesis of Job,* 1954, and *The Bible and the Church,* 1963.

WORK IN PROGRESS: A Biblical Theology of Womanhood; The Psalms: Commentary in Three Volumes.

* * *

THEVENIN, Denis
See DUHAMEL, Georges

THIONG'O, Ngugi wa
See NGUGI, James T(hiong'o)

* * *

THOENE, Peter
See BIHALJI-MERIN, Oto

* * *

THOMAS, Alan (Cedric)   1933-

PERSONAL: Born April 20, 1933, in Doddington, England; son of Harry (a mining prospector) and Frances (an actress; maiden name, Dickeson) Thomas; married Clare O' Gorman (a librarian); children: Neil, Harry. *Education:* Carleton University, B.A., 1963; University of Toronto, M.A., 1964, Ph.D., 1970. *Politics:* Socialist. *Religion:* None. *Home:* 78 Willcocks St., Toronto, Ontario, Canada M5S 1C8. *Office:* Department of English, Scarborough College, University of Toronto, Toronto, Ontario, Canada.

CAREER: Northern Echo, Darlington, England, journalist, 1955-56; miner and prospector in northern Canada, 1956-58; *Montreal Gazette,* Montreal, Quebec, journalist, 1958; *Ottawa Citizen,* Ottawa, Ontario, journalist, 1959-60; University of Toronto, Toronto, Ontario, lecturer, 1967-70, assistant professor, 1970-75, associate professor of English, 1975—. *Awards, honors:* Ohio State Award for Educational Television, 1975, for "Voices From the Ranks" in the series "The Victorians."

WRITINGS: Time in a Frame: Photography and the Nineteenth Century Mind, Schocken, 1977. Also author of "The Victorians," Ontario-TV, 1975-76.

WORK IN PROGRESS: Scripts for "Early Canadians," on Ontario-TV; book on photography and the Canadian Indian.

* * *

THOMAS, Kenneth Bryn   ?-1978

OBITUARY NOTICE: Died September 22, 1978, in England. Anesthesia specialist, medical historian, lecturer, and author. He wrote several books and articles on medical subjects, including *Curare: Its History and Usage, The Development of Anesthetic Apparatus,* and *James Douglas of the Pouch and His Pupil, William Hunter.* Obituaries and other sources: AB *Bookman's Weekly,* November 6, 1978.

* * *

THOMAS, Vaughan   1934-

PERSONAL: Born July 3, 1934, in Wales; son of Harold (in business) and Gwendoline (Jones) Thomas; married Christina Haddon (a secretary), March 5, 1954; children: Garth Haddon, Kim Christina. *Education:* Loughborough College, diploma (first class honors), 1966; University of Nottingham, teaching certificate, 1966; Loughborough University of Technology, M.Sc., 1968; University of Surrey, Ph.D., 1971; Liverpool Polytechnic, diploma, 1974. *Home:* 41 Warren Dr., Wallasey, Merseyside, England. *Office:* Department of Physical Education, Liverpool Polytechnic, Byron St., Liverpool L3 3AF, England.

CAREER: Liverpool Polytechnic, Liverpool, England, head of department of physical education, 1971—. Chairman of Liverpool Sports Council. Consultant to government and industry. *Military service:* Royal Air Force, physical education teacher, 1952-64. *Member:* Physical Education Association (fellow), British Association of Sport and Medicine,

Society of Sports Sciences, Association of Polytechnic Physical Education Lecturers (chairman), British Institute of Management (associate member).

WRITINGS: Science and Sport, Faber, 1970, Little, Brown, 1972; *Basketball: Techniques and Tactics,* Faber, 1972; *Exercise Physiology,* Crosby Lockwood, 1975; *Bettery Physical Fitness,* Kaye & Ward, 1979. Contributor to journals.

SIDELIGHTS: Thomas writes: "I believe in balanced personal excellence (mental, physical, aesthetic, social, emotional). I have been an international standard competitor at track and field, basketball, and cycling. I am currently interested in preparing for the Olympics in archery."

AVOCATIONAL INTEREST: Musician (piano, guitar, chrominica), building (built his own home).

*   *   *

THOMPSON, David H(ugh)   1941-

PERSONAL: Born in New Haven, Conn.; son of Kenneth (a research pharmacist) and Helen Thompson; married Mary Berliner; children: Christopher, Loren. *Education:* Stanford University, A.B. (honors), 1963; University of Wisconsin—Madison, Ph.D., 1974. *Home:* 7105 Hickory Rd., West Bend, Wis. 53095.

CAREER: Worked as photographer, 1970-74; University of Wisconsin, Washington County Center, West Bend, assistant professor of biology, 1974-78; environmental consultant, 1978—. Part-time research biologist at Waterways Experiment Station, for U.S. Army Corps of Engineers, 1977-78; investigator for project funded by National Audubon Society; teacher of workshops on bird identification and conductor of field studies on birds. Member of conservation committee of Colonial Waterbird Group, 1977—.

WRITINGS: The Penguin: Its Life Cycle (self-photographed), Sterling, 1974; (contributor) Bruce Parker, editor, *Terrestrial Biology,* American Geophysical Union, 1978. Contributor of photographs to books, including *The Marvels of Animal Behavior* and *Animal Behavior.*

SIDELIGHTS: Thompson told *CA:* "I got started in photography when my father gave me a camera to take to Antarctica. The camera became my principal form of recreation and I quickly taught myself how to use it. I specialize in taking good photographs which illustrate some biological concept and which have a scientifically accurate caption." *Avocational interests:* Piloting.

*   *   *

THOMPSON, Earl   1931(?)-1978

OBITUARY NOTICE: Born c. 1931; died November 9, 1978, in Sausalito, Calif. Thompson wrote three novels, *A Garden of Sand* (which received a National Book Award nomination), *Tattoo,* and *Caldo Largo.* Obituaries and other sources: *Publishers Weekly,* November 27, 1978.

*   *   *

THOMSON, June   1930-

PERSONAL: Born June 24, 1930, in Kent, England; daughter of Alfred (a mail carrier) and Lily (a shopkeeper; maiden name, Marshall) Manders; divorced; children: Mark, Paul. *Education:* Bedford College, London, B.A. (honors), 1952. *Home:* Spring Cottage, Oakley Rd., Wix, Manningtree, Essex, England. *Agent:* Leslie Gardner, London Management, 235/241 Regent St., London W1A 2JT, England.

CAREER: Teacher in elementary schools in Stoke-on-Trent, England, and Lardar, England, 1953-67; high school teacher of English in St. Albans, England, 1967-73; lecturer in English at teacher training college near Watford, Hertfordshire, England, 1973-77; writer, 1978—. Member of management committee of St. Albans Young People's Arts Centre. *Member:* Crime Writers Association.

WRITINGS—All detective novels: Not One of Us Harper, 1971; *Death Cap,* Constable, 1973, Doubleday, 1977; *The Long Revenge,* Constable, 1974, Doubleday, 1975; *Case Closed* Doubleday, 1977; *A Question of Identity,* Doubleday, 1977; *The Habit of Loving* Doubleday, 1979, published in England as *Deadly Relations,* Constable, 1979.

Work anthologized in *Winter Crimes,* Number Ten, Macmillan (England), 1978.

WORK IN PROGRESS: Another novel about Detective Inspector Rudd.

SIDELIGHTS: June Thomson's novels have been published in Italy, Germany, and France. She writes: "I write detective fiction for the same reason I enjoy reading it: the fascination of a mystery or a puzzle. It also gives me the opportunity to examine characters and relationships in extremis, as it were. The country setting, close and closed, has its own loyalties and tensions. Being country-bred, I feel I understand this kind of community."

AVOCATIONAL INTERESTS: Gardening, cooking.

BIOGRAPHICAL/CRITICAL SOURCES: Jury, summer, 1978.

*   *   *

THORNTON, Richard C.   1936-

PERSONAL: Born March 22, 1936, in Camden, N.J. *Education:* Attended Yale University, 1955-56; Colgate University, B.A., 1961; University of Washington, Seattle, Ph.D., 1966. *Home:* 7016 Benjamin St., McLean, Va. 22101. *Office:* Institute for Sino-Soviet Studies, George Washington University, Washington, D.C. 20052.

CAREER: University of Washington, Seattle, research associate at Far Eastern and Russian Institute, 1966-67; George Washington University, Washington, D.C., 1967—, currently professor of history and international affairs. *Military service:* U.S. Air Force, Mandarin Chinese translator, 1955-59. *Member:* Phi Beta Kappa.

WRITINGS: (Contributor) Milorad M. Drachkovitch, editor, *The Comintern: Historical Highlights,* Praeger, 1966; *The Comintern and the Chinese Communists, 1928-31,* University of Washington Press, 1969; (contributor) Trager and Henderson, editors, *Communist China, 1949-69: A Twenty-Year Assessment,* New York University Press, 1970; *Bear and Dragon: Sino-Soviet Relations, 1949-1971,* American-Asian Educational Exchange (New York), 1972; (contributor) Norton L. Dodge, editor, *Soviets in Asia,* Cremona Foundation (Mechanicsville, Md.), 1972; *China: The Struggle for Power, 1917-1972,* Indiana University Press, 1973; (contributor) Roy C. Macredis and Bernard E. Brown, editors, *Comparative Politics: Notes and Readings,* Dorsey, 1977. Also contributor to *Chugokuwa Donaruka* (title means "China's Future"), edited by Toji Kuwabara and Tsuneari Fukuda, 1976. Contributor to academic journals.

SIDELIGHTS: Thornton is competent in modern Russian, Chinese, German, and French.

THUROW, Lester C(arl) 1938-

PERSONAL: Born May 7, 1938, in Livingston, Mont.; son of Willis Carl (a clergyman) and Alice (Hickman) Thurow; married Emily Fooks (died, May, 1972); married Gretchen Pfuetze (a computer programmer); children: Torben, Ethan. *Education:* Williams College, B.A. (magna cum laude), 1960; Balliol College, Oxford, M.A. (first class honors), 1962; Harvard University, earned M.A., Ph.D., 1964. *Home address:* R.D.2., Sandy Pond Rd., Lincoln, Mass. 02173. *Office:* Sloan School of Management, Massachusetts Institute of Technology, Cambridge, Mass. 02139.

CAREER: Harvard University, Cambridge, Mass., assistant professor of economics, 1965-68, research associate of Kennedy School of Government, 1968—, member of Institute of Politics, 1971—. Professor at Massachusetts Institute of Technology. Weekly commentator on WGBH-TV, 1969-75. Staff economist for President's Council of Economic Advisers, 1964-65; has testified before U.S. Congress and its committees; consultant to government agencies and private corporations. *Member:* Phi Beta Kappa. *Awards, honors:* Rhodes scholar, 1962; David A. Wells Prize from Harvard University, 1967-68, for *Poverty and Discrimination*.

WRITINGS: (Editor and contributor) *Fiscal Policy: Experiment for Prosperity*, Prentice-Hall, 1967; *Poverty and Discrimination*, Brookings Institution, 1969; *Investment in Human Capital*, Wadsworth, 1970; *The Impact of Taxes on the American Economy*, Praeger, 1971; (with Robert Heilbroner) *The Economic Problem*, Prentice-Hall, 1974, 4th edition, 1978; *Generating Inequality: The Distributional Mechanisms of the Economy*, Basic Books, 1975; *The Political Economy of Income Redistribution Policies*, U.S. Information Agency, 1977.

Contributor: R. A. Gordon, editor, *Toward a Manpower Policy*, Wiley, 1967; Gerald Somers, editor, *The Education and Training of Racial Minorities*, University of Wisconsin Press, 1968; Paul Streeten, editor, *Unfashionable Economics: Essays in Honor of Thomas Balogh*, Weidenfeld & Nicolson, 1969; Anthony H. Pascal, editor, *Thinking About Cities*, Dickenson, 1970; K. R. Griffin, editor, *Development Finance in Latin America*, Macmillan, 1971; Ray Marshall and Richard Perlman, editors, *An Anthology of Labor Economics: Readings and Commentary*, Wiley, 1972; K. Boulding and M. Pfaff, editors, *Redistribution to the Rich and Poor: The Grants Economies of Income Distribution*, Wadsworth, 1972; Lloyd Ulman, editor, *Manpower Programs in the Policy Mix*, Johns Hopkins Press, 1973; Ulman and Margaret Gordon, editors, *Higher Education and the Labor Force*, McGraw, 1973; Ronald Grieson, editor, *Urban Economics*, Little, Brown, 1973; Andrew Weintraub, Schwartz, and Aronson, editors, *The Economic Growth Controversy*, International Arts & Sciences Press, 1973; *Inflation, Unemployment, and Social Justice*, Academy for Contemporary Problems, 1973; O. S. Oldman and F. P. Schoettle, editors, *State and Local Taxes and Finance*, Foundation Press, 1974; Willett and Tollison, editors, *Political Economy and Public Policy*, Cornell University Press, 1974; Lee Rainwater, editor, *Inequality and Justice*, Adler's Publishing, 1974; Mary Jo Bane and Donald Levine, editors, *The Inequality Controversy*, Basic Books, 1975.

Agenda for a New Urban Era, American Society of Planning Officials, 1976; Havrilesky and Boorman, editors, *Banking*, AHM Publishing, 1976; Hellesoe and Henon, editors, *Great Debates*, Goodyear Publishing, 1976; Ashline, Pezzulo, and Norris, editors, *Education, Inequality, and National Policy*, Heath, 1976; *Increasing Understanding of*

Public Policy and Problems, Farm Foundation, 1976; Otto Eckstein, editor, *Parameters and Policies in the U.S. Economy*, North-Holland Publishing, 1976; Biderman and Drury, editors, *Measuring Work Quality for Social Reporting*, Halstead Press, 1976; Michael B. Weis, editor, *Beyond Civil Rights: The Right to Economic Security*, Notre Dame Center for Civil Rights, 1976; Thomas F. Powers, editor, *Education for Careers*, Pennsylvania State University Press, 1977; John Carn, editor, *Full Employment and Economic Justice*, U.S. Catholic Conference, 1977; Richard Auster, editor, *American Re-Evolutionary Papers*, University of Arizona Press, 1977; Jack Rothman, editor, *Issues in Race and Ethnic Relations*, F. T. Peacock, 1977; Dunkin, Bernat, and Brown, editors, *Markets and Morals*, new text edition, Princeton University Press, 1977. Also contributor to *Beyond the New Deal: Democrats Look to the Future*, 1976, to *Introduction to Science Technology and Public Policy in the United States*, edited by Joel Goldham, Gordon & Breach, to *Energy*, and to *Ethnic Groups*.

Contributor of more than sixty articles to professional journals and popular magazines, including *Nation, Newsweek, Skeptic, Challenge, Dissent, Daedalus,* and *New Times,* and newspapers.

WORK IN PROGRESS: The Importance of Disequilibrium; The Incidence of Government Expenditures.

* * *

TIRRO, Frank (Pascale) 1935-

PERSONAL: Born September 20, 1935, in Omaha, Neb.; son of Frank and Mary (Spensieri) Tirro; married Charlene Rae Whitney, August 16, 1961; children: John Andrew, Cynthia Anne. *Education:* University of Nebraska, B.M.E., 1960; Northwestern University, M.M., 1961; University of Chicago, Ph.D., 1974. *Politics:* Republican. *Religion:* Lutheran. *Home:* 3816 Pickett Rd., Durham, N.C. 27705. *Office:* Department of Music, Duke University, Durham, N.C. 27708.

CAREER: University of Chicago, Chicago, Ill., music teacher at Laboratory Schools and chairman of department, 1961-70; University of Kansas, Lawrence, visiting lecturer in music, 1972-73; Duke University, Durham, N.C., assistant professor, 1973-74, associate professor of music and chairman of department, 1974—, director of Southeastern Institute of Medieval and Renaissance Studies, 1977—. Also played clarinet with Lincoln Symphony Orchestra and with jazz groups.

MEMBER: International Musicological Society, International Society for Jazz Research, American Musicological Society (member of council, 1978-80), College Music Society, Mediaeval Academy of America, Renaissance Society of America, Music Library Association, Society for Ethnomusicology. *Awards, honors:* Vreeland award from the University of Nebraska, 1960, for ballet, "Masque of the Red Death"; award from National Federation of Music Clubs, 1961, for "Sonata for Clarinet and Piano"; grant from American Council of Learned Societies, 1968; awards from American Society of Composers, Authors and Publishers, 1970, 1971, and 1973, for professional activities as a standard composer; fellowship from Harvard University, 1971-72.

WRITINGS: (Contributor) H. Alan Robinson and Ellen Lamar Thomas, editors, *Fusing Reading Skills and Content*, International Reading Association, 1969; *Jazz: A History*, Norton, 1977; *The Jazz Combo: From ODJB to MJQ*, University of Illinois Press, 1979; *Renaissance Music Manuscripts in the Archive of San Petronio in Bologna*, American Institute of Musicology, in press; (with Mary Ann Witt, Charlotte Brown, and others) *The Humanities: Cultural Roots and Continuities,* Heath, in press.

Compositions: *American Jazz Mass,* Summy-Birchard, 1960; *Sing a New Song,* World Library Publications, 1966; *Church Sonata for Organ,* World Library Publications, 1967; *Melismas for Carillon,* World Library Publications, 1967; *American Jazz Te Deum,* World Library Publications, 1970.

Contributor to *Dictionary of Contemporary Society* and *Grove's Dictionary of Music and Musicians.* Contributor to music journals. Editor, *Medieval and Renaissance Studies* (proceedings of Southeastern Institute of Medieval and Renaissance Studies), 1978-82.

WORK IN PROGRESS: Music of the Renaissance; History of Jazz; Music Theory.

SIDELIGHTS: Frank Tirro told *CA:* "My life at present is a fascinating conglomerate of related but contrasting activities: researching and writing about music of the early sixteenth century; playing jazz in the parks of Raleigh and Durham; teaching counterpoint; administering opera festivals and post-doctoral seminars in history; and, more occasionally than before, writing music of my own. Each activity, in a sense, robs from the others, but each also reinforces the others by providing release, new perspectives, and goal-oriented variety. My large blocks of time tend to divide mornings for study, afternoons for office and teaching, and evenings for family; and the academic year, in contrast with summers, leans more heavily toward teaching and administration where the latter provides more time for research and writing. The university environment provides stimulating contact with artists and scholars as well as intellectually talented students, and the university life is now allowing me to look forward to a summer in Bologna, Italy, next year and a full year in Cambridge, England, in 1980-1981."

*   *   *

TITLER, Dale M(ilton) 1926-

PERSONAL: Born August 25, 1926, in Altoona, Pa.; son of Guy Edwin (a railroad engineer) and Helen Catherine (Bockel) Titler; married Helen Ruth Burt (an executive secretary in law enforcement), June 14, 1952; children: Dale Milton, Jr., Barbara Gail, Helen Catherine. *Education:* Attended Pennsylvania State College, 1947-48, and University of Southern Mississippi, 1974-75. *Politics:* "Conservative hawk." *Religion:* Protestant. *Office:* P.O. Box 7361, Mississippi City Station, Gulfport, Miss. 39501.

CAREER: U.S. Air Force, civilian senior academic instructor of pilot trainees in Marianna, Fla., 1951-60, instructor in fire protection at Greenville Air Force Base in Greenville, Miss., 1960-63, instructor in electronics and military personnel training at Keesler Air Force Base in Biloxi, Miss., 1964-78, KTTC center historian, 1978—. *Military service:* U.S. Army Air Forces, 1945-46.

WRITINGS: Ye Chart of True Locations of Sunken Vessels, Honest and Pirate, privately printed, 1954; *Billy Bowleg's Owne Charte,* privately printed, 1956; *Wings of Mystery: True Stories of Aviation History,* Dodd, 1966; *The Day the Red Baron Died,* Walker & Co., 1970; *Wings of Adventure,* Dodd, 1972; (editor) Curtis Kinney, *I Flew a Camel,* Dorrance, 1972; *Unnatural Resources: True Stories of American Treasure* (juvenile), Prentice-Hall, 1973; *Haunted Treasures* (juvenile), Prentice-Hall, 1976.

TITTLER, Robert 1942-

PERSONAL: Born December 7, 1942, in New York, N.Y.; son of I. A. (a scientist) and S. I. Tittler; married Anne Kelso, 1966; children: Andrew, Rebecca. *Education:* Oberlin College, B.A., 1964; New York University, M.A., 1965, Ph.D., 1971. *Residence:* Montreal, Quebec, Canada. *Office:* Department of History, Concordia University, 7141 Sherbrooke St. W., Montreal, Quebec, Canada H4B 1R6.

CAREER: Concordia University, Montreal, Quebec, assistant professor, 1969-74, associate professor of history, 1974—, head of department at Loyola College, 1976-78. Reader for University of London's Institute of Historical Research, 1968-69, 1975—. *Member:* Conference on British Studies, Past and Present Society, American Historical Association.

WRITINGS: Nicholas Bacon: The Making of a Tudor Statesman, Ohio University Press, 1976. Contributor to history and law journals.

WORK IN PROGRESS: Editing *The Tudors in Mid-Passage,* with S. J. Loach, publication by Macmillan expected in 1980; editing "Roberts Household Accounts, 1568-82," for Sussex Record Society.

SIDELIGHTS: Tittler writes: "I try to maintain a research involvement in Tudor history despite my isolation from the sources and co-workers in the field. My particular scholarly interests are urban development and the reign of Mary Tudor, but I am also interested in university administration in North America."

*   *   *

TITTMANN, George Fabian 1915-1978

OBITUARY NOTICE—See index for *CA* sketch: Born Febuary 27, 1915, in St. Louis, Mo.; died August 26, 1978, in Berkeley, Calif. Episcopal minister and author. Tittmann served both with missionaries and churches. *He wrote Whisper From the Dust, What Manner of Love?,* and *Is Religion Enough?* Tittmann had also gained a reputation in the Berkeley area for his prowess at tennis. Obituaries and other sources: *Washington Post,* August 30, 1978.

*   *   *

TKACIK, Arnold J(ohn) 1919-

PERSONAL: Born November 20, 1919, in Parchovany, Czechoslovakia; came to the United States in 1928, naturalized citizen in 1942; son of John J. (a laborer) and Mary (Sabol) Tkacik; married Helen Zysk (a Montessori teacher), September 16, 1976. *Education:* St. Benedict's College, Atchison, Kan., B.A., 1943; Biblical Institute, Rome, Italy, S.S.L., 1952; Governors State University, M.A., 1975. *Religion:* Roman Catholic. *Home:* 1644 North Nagle, Chicago, Ill. 60635. *Office:* Department of External Training Programs, Illinois College of Podiatric Medicine, 1001 North Dearborn, Chicago, Ill. 60610.

CAREER: St. Benedict's College and School of Theology, Atchison, Kan., associate professor of Bible, 1953-64, chairman of department of religious studies, 1965-70; University of Kansas, Lawrence, associate professor of Biblical literature, 1967-71; Illinois Benedictine College, Lisle, associate professor of Biblical Literature, 1972-73; Illinois College of Podiatric Medicine, Chicago, coordinator of external training programs, 1977—. Summer director of graduate theology at St. Mary College, Morago, Calif., 1965-68. Member of Austin Mental Health Planning Council, Chicago-Read Citizens Advisory Board, Loretto Hospital Outpatient Mental

Health Clinic Advisory Board. *Member:* American Benedictine Academy, Society of Biblical Literature, Catholic Biblical Association, Religious Research Association, Association for Humanistic Psychology, Institutes of Religion and Health. *Awards, honors:* Eli Lilly fellowship, 1964-65.

WRITINGS: Commentary of the Book of Ezekiel in the Jerome Biblical Commentary, Prentice-Hall, 1968. Apocrypha editor of *New English Bible,* Oxford Study Edition, Oxford University Press, 1976. Contributor to theology journals. Associate editor of *American Benedictine Review,* 1967-72.

WORK IN PROGRESS: Studying the impact of religion on contemporary society.

SIDELIGHTS: Tkacik writes: "I studied the origins of the Judaeo-Christian tradition and its literature at Ecole Biblique et Archeologique Francaise in Jerusalem, and visited archaeological and historical sites for that purpose. At present I am investigating the contribution of traditional religions to the growth and development of the human person in contemporary society."

* * *

TOBACH, Ethel 1921-

PERSONAL: Born November 7, 1921, in Russia; daughter of Ralph and Fannie (Schechterman) Wiener. *Education:* Hunter College (now of the City University of New York), B.A., 1949; New York University, M.A., 1952, Ph.D., 1957. *Residence:* New York, N.Y. *Office:* American Museum of Natural History, Central Park W., New York, N.Y. 10024.

CAREER: American Museum of Natural History, New York, N.Y., associate curator, 1946-69, curator of department of animal behavior, 1969—. Adjunct associate professor at Yeshiva University, 1957-61; assistant professor at New York University, 1961-65, adjunct professor, 1976—; adjunct professor at Hunter College and City College, both of the City University of New York, 1969—; lecturer at University of Oklahoma, 1978.

MEMBER: American Psychological Association (fellow; member of council of representatives), Animal Behavior Society (fellow), American Association for the Advancement of Science (fellow), Psychonomic Society, Society for Neurosciences, American Orthopsychiatric Association (fellow), Association for the Advancement of Psychology (member of board of trustees, 1977-81), Eastern Psychological Association (member of board of directors, 1978-81), New York Academy of Sciences (fellow; chairman of psychology section, 1973), Phi Beta Kappa, Sigma Xi. *Awards, honors:* Career development awards from U.S. Public Health Service, 1964-69, 1969-74; member of Hunter College Hall of Fame, 1975; D.Sc. from Southampton College, 1975.

WRITINGS: (Editor) *Development of Evolution of Behavior: Essays in Memory of T. C. Schneirla,* W. H. Freeman, 1970; (editor) *Selected Writings of T. C. Schneirla,* W. H. Freeman, 1971; *The Biopsychology of Development,* Academic Press, 1971; *The Four Horsemen: Racism, Sexism, Militarism, and Social Darwinism,* Behavioral Publications, 1973; *Genetic Destiny: Scientific Controversy and Social Conflict,* AMS Press, 1976; *Genes and Gender,* Volume I, Gordian, 1978.

WORK IN PROGRESS: Bibliography of Animal Behavior; Volumes II and III of *Genes and Gender;* editing *Reader in Behavioral Evolution.*

TODD, Ruthven 1914-
(R. T. Campbell)

PERSONAL: Born June 14, 1914, in Edinburgh, Scotland; came to United States in 1948, naturalized citizen, 1959; son of W. J. W. (an architect) and Christian (Craik) Todd; children: Christopher. *Education:* Attended Fettes College and Edinburgh College of Art. *Agent:* Harold Ober Associates, 40 East 49th St., New York, N.Y. 10017.

CAREER: Began career as a painter; later worked as a shepherd and farm laborer on the Isle of Mull for two years, writing poetry in his spare time; has also worked in an art gallery, in a literary agency, as an assistant editor for the *Scottish Bookman,* and for *Horizon* magazine in Edinburgh; in London, worked as a teacher, in a pottery gallery, as a copywriter, in a bookstore, and for the Civil Defense during World War II; in the United States, operated The Weekend Press, New York, 1950-54, taught creative writing at Iowa State University, and was a visiting professor at the State University of New York in Buffalo, 1972; began writing novels professionally during World War II. *Awards, honors:* Received a citation from the National Institute of Arts and Letters in 1954 for his "loving devotion to natural history"; Guggenheim Fellowship, 1960, 1967; Chapelbrook Fellowship, 1968; Ingram Merrill Foundation Fellowship, 1970.

WRITINGS—Poems: (With others) *Proems: An Anthology of Poems,* Fortune Press, 1938; (with others) *Poets of Tomorrow: First Selection,* Hogarth Press, 1939; *Until Now,* Fortune Press, 1941; *The Acreage of the Heart,* W. Maclellan, 1944; *The Planet in My Hand: Twelve Poems,* privately printed, 1944, Grey Walls Press, 1946; *In Other Worlds: Twelve Poems,* Piper's Press, 1951; *A Mantelpiece of Shells,* Bonacio & Saul, 1954; *Garland for the Winter Solstice: Selected Poems,* Dent, 1961, Little, Brown, 1962; *McGonagall Remembers Fitzrovia in the 1930's,* M. Parkin Fine Arts, 1973; *Lament of the Cats of Rapallo,* J. Roberts Press, 1973.

Novels: *Over the Mountain,* Knopf, 1939; *The Lost Traveller,* Grey Walls Press, 1944, reprinted, Dover, 1968; (under pseudonym R. T. Campbell) *Unholy Dying,* Westhouse, 1945; (under Campbell pseudonym) *Take Thee a Sharp Knife,* Westhouse, 1946; (under Campbell pseudonym) *Adventure With a Goat* (includes "Adventure with a Goat" and "Apollo Wore a Wig"), Westhouse, 1946; (under Campbell pseudonym) *Bodies in a Bookshop,* Westhouse, 1946; (under Campbell pseudonym) *The Death Cap,* Westhouse, 1946; (under Campbell pseudonym) *Death for Madame,* Westhouse, 1946; (under Campbell pseudonym) *Swing Low, Swing Death,* Westhouse, 1946; *Loser's Choice,* Hermitage House, 1953.

For children: *First Animal Book,* P. Lunn, 1946; *Space Cat* (illustrated by Paul Galdone), Scribner, 1952; *Trucks, Tractors, and Trailers* (illustrated by Lemuel B. Line), Putnam, 1954; *Space Cat Visits Venus* (illustrated by Galdone), Scribner, 1955; *Space Cat Meets Mars* (illustrated by Galdone), Scribner, 1957; *Space Cat and the Kittens* (illustrated by Galdone), Scribner, 1958; *Tan's Fish* (illustrated by Theresa Sherman), Little, Brown, 1958.

Other: *The Laughing Mulatto: The Story of Alexandre Dumas,* Rich & Cowan, 1940; *Tracks in the Snow: Studies in English Science and Art* (essays), Grey Walls Press, 1946, Scribner, 1947, reprinted, Norwood Editions, 1976; *The Tropical Fish Book,* Fawcett, 1953; *William Blake the Artist,* Studio Vista, 1971.

Editor: Alexander Gilchrist, *Life of William Blake,* Dutton,

1942, revised edition, Dent, 1945; Christopher Smart, *A Song to David, and Other Poems,* Grey Walls Press, 1947; William Blake, *Songs of Innocence and of Experience,* United Book Guild, 1947; Blake, *America: A Phrophesy,* United Book Guild, 1947; Richard and Samuel Redgrave, *A Century of British Painters,* Phaidon Press, 1947; Blake, *Poems, Selected and Introduced,* Grey Walls Press, 1949; Blake, *Selected Poetry,* Dell, 1960; *Blake's Dante Plates,* Book Collecting and Library Monthly, 1968.

SIDELIGHTS: Ruthven Todd's roots are diverse, as he claims Scottish, English, Irish, Spanish, and French ancestry. He is related to such well-known literary figures as Sir Walter Scott, Henry Mackenzie, George Lillie Craik, and Sir Henry Craik.

Mixed reviews appeared with the publication of Todd's allegorical novel, *Over the Mountain.* "It is a subtle book, subtly planned," wrote the *New York Times.* "It is full of strong and original situations, many of them saturated with grim humor, most of them the outcome of Michael's insistence on candor and nearly all of them resulting in a battle royal and a run for life." "If it says nothing new about fascism," added *Saturday Review of Literature,* "which would be a tall order, anyhow—it presents some original devices which the current dictators have fortunately overlooked, and if it never cuts very deep, it moves fast and is consistently entertaining." On the other hand, the comments of *New Republic* included, "One cannot help feeling that the whole mechanism of Mr. Todd's satire is unnecessarily complicated." The *Times Literary Supplement* observed: "This is a theme that has already been tackled so superbly that it is hazardous for a new writer to embark upon it, and Mr. Todd has not been particularly successful in his attempt."

Space Cat was the first book for children which combined the talents of Ruthven Todd and Paul Galdone. A *New York Times* critic commented: "The visit to the moon is the best and most imaginative part of the story, sounding real and serious, and also lively. Paul Galdone's illustrations are witty and solid." Added the *San Francisco Chronicle,* "It is possible that *Space Cat* is more entertaining when considered as satire on current science fiction than as a child's book."

Mantelpiece of Shells was Todd's first book of poetry published in America. In reviewing the work, a *San Francisco Chronicle* critic wrote: "Todd writes with a simple lyricism that first of all sings. Using conventional forms, Todd's songs range widely in subject from simple subjects and objects of nature, to love, to art. Perhaps the most interesting poems in *A Mantelpiece of Shells* are those that present the essence of various modern artists: Miro, Ernst, Moore, Gris, Calder." *Saturday Review* added: "The poems which make up *A Mantelpiece of Shells* are notable for their quiet distinction, for their combination of wit and imagination with a disciplined restraint in technique. This difficult juxtaposition Mr. Todd manages with an urbane dexterity. His work has a high polish and a rather clipped austerity which cloaks but does not conceal the warmth of emotion beneath. An occasional professional solemnity is counteracted by the twinkle in the poet's eye." *Poetry* commented: "Pride masquerading as humility has been so prominent in contemporary literature that Todd's real humility seems very rare, very refreshing. It's a humility that need not be humble but simply itself, half playful, half contrite, aspiring to less than superexcellence. One's impression is that none of Todd's poems is more than three-quarters serious, no matter how deep or desperate the experience it conveys."

BIOGRAPHICAL/CRITICAL SOURCES: Times Liter-ary Supplement, March 18, 1939; *Saturday Review of Literature,* March 25, 1939, May 12, 1955; *New York Times,* March 26, 1939, November 16, 1952; *New Republic,* April 19, 1939; *San Francisco Chronicle,* November 16, 1952, April 10, 1955; *Poetry,* June, 1955.*

* * *

TOKER, Franklin K(arl) B(enedict) S(erchuk) 1944-

PERSONAL: Born April 29, 1944, in Montreal, Quebec, Canada; came to the United States in 1964; son of Maxwell Harris (a dental surgeon) and Ethel (Serchuk) Toker; married Ellen Judith Burack (a museum administrator), September 3, 1972. *Education:* McGill University, B.A., 1964; Oberlin College, A.M., 1966; Harvard University, Ph.D., 1972. *Politics:* "Jeffersonian." *Residence:* Squirrel Hill, Pittsburgh, Pa. *Office:* Department of Architecture, Carnegie-Mellon University, Pittsburgh, Pa. 15213.

CAREER: Soprintendenza ai Monumenti (historic buildings commission), Florence, Italy, archaeological director of excavation of Florence Cathedral, 1969-74; Carnegie-Mellon University, Pittsburgh, Pa., visiting professor, 1974-76, associate professor of history of architecture, 1976—. *Member:* International Center for Medieval Art, College Art Association of America (life member), Society of Architectural Historians, National Trust for Historic Preservation. *Awards, honors:* Alice David Hitchcock Book Award from Society of Architectural Historians, 1971, for *The Church of Notre-Dame in Montreal.*

WRITINGS: (Contributor) James Ackerman, editor, *Guiseppe Zocchi's Views of Florence,* Walker & Co., 1967; *The Church of Notre-Dame in Montreal,* McGill-Queen's University Press, 1970; (with Guido Morozzi and J. A. Herrmann) *S. Reparata: L'Antica Cattedrale Fiorentina* (title means "St. Reparata: The Ancient Cathedral of Florence"), Bonechi, 1974. Contributor to art and architecture journals.

WORK IN PROGRESS: Multi-volume works on the excavation of Florence Cathedral; a history of the architectural profession; research on medieval housing and urbanism in Siena, Italy.

SIDELIGHTS: Toker comments: "I write about scholarly material and use scholarly method, but I write as an *author,* with the aim of provoking and enlivening rather than deadening a scholarly audience. I am contemptuous of technical jargon in other fields, and try to keep it out of my works." *Avocational interests:* Foreign languages, travel, painting, writing fiction.

* * *

TOKLAS, Alice B(abette) 1877-1967

PERSONAL: Born April 30, 1877, in San Francisco, Calif.; daughter of Ferdinand (a merchant) and Emma (Levinsky) Toklas. *Education:* Attended University of Washington, 1893-95; studied music privately. *Residence:* Paris, France.

CAREER: Writer; owner and publisher of Plain Edition, a press devoted to publishing the works of Gertrude Stein.

WRITINGS: The Alice B. Toklas Cook Book, Harper, 1954; (translator from the French) Anne Bodart, *The Blue Dog, and Other Fables for the French,* Houghton, 1956; *Aromas and Flavors of Past and Present,* introduction and notes by Poppy Cannon, Harper, 1958; (author of introduction) Beryl Barr and Barbara Turner Sachs, *The Artists' and Writers' Cookbook,* Contact Editions, 1961; *What Is Remembered* (memoirs), Holt, 1963; *Staying on Alone: Letters of Alice B. Toklas,* edited by Edward Burns, Liveright,

1973. Also contributor of articles and reviews to *New York Times Book Review, Atlantic, New Republic,* and *Yale Literary Magazine.*

SIDELIGHTS: For almost forty years, Alice B. Toklas shared her life with the writer Gertrude Stein. In the early days of the modernist movement such painters and writers as Pablo Picasso, Henri Matisse, Guillaume Apollinaire, Sherwood Anderson, Ernest Hemingway, and F. Scott Fitzgerald often gathered at their salon at 27, rue de Fleurus in Paris. On these Saturday evenings, while Stein held court with the men, Toklas would entertain the women with gossip and talk of recipes and fashion. Janet Flanner reminisced about these gatherings: "Alice was a very entertaining purveyor of news. She gave it to you adding item to item, as if she were detailing the recipe for a fruitcake. You always knew where Gertrude was in the room, because she would let out her whoops of laughter; curiously, I don't remember ever hearing Alice laugh, although she had an acute and sharp sense of humor, which, since it was bordered with wit, was quiet in tone. Her conversation had its own pattern—she obtained a variety of effects by setting forth the opposite of what anyone else might have said. Her voice was soft, her California accent agreeable, her vocabulary precise, rhythmic, and possessed of its own sense of speed, with allegro touches."

However overshadowed by Stein's accomplishments Toklas might have seemed, it was she who organized their lives by running the household, cooking, typing Stein's manuscripts, offering critical suggestions and praise, and even screening the friends and visitors the two would have. Toklas's prejudices against Ernest Hemingway (whom she thought "crude") and the painter Pavel Tchelitchew led to the break-up of their friendships with Stein. As their friend Bernard Fay wrote, "Between the two women, one seemingly stronger and the other more frail, one affirming her genius and the other venerating it, one speaking and the other listening, only a blind man could ignore that the most vigorous one was Alice, and that Gertrude, for her behavior as much as for her work and publications, leaned on her, used her and followed her advice."

It was Toklas who, while she was typing the manuscript of Stein's *Geography and Plays,* discovered the line that would become Stein's trademark—"Rose is a rose is a rose is a rose is a rose." As Linda Simon recounted the episode, Toklas said: "It was I who found it . . . and insisted upon putting it as a device on the letter paper, on the table linen and anywhere that she would permit that I would put it. I am very pleased with myself for having done so." "Indeed, she should have been," Simon commented. "The 'device' became Gertrude's trademark, indelibly impressed on twentieth-century literary consciousness, and a symbol of Gertrude's own blossoming."

When Stein was having difficulty getting her work published due to its inaccessible nature, Toklas started her own press, Plain Edition, for which she served as publisher, director, and managing editor. The press was devoted to publishing only Stein's work: the first book to be published by Plain Edition was the novel *Lucy Church Amiably* in 1931.

Not only did Toklas shepherd Stein's works through publication, she also figured prominently in many of the works themselves. Stein's rhapsodic love poems were written about her. In *The Autobiography of Alice B. Toklas,* Stein wrote her own autobiography using Toklas as the narrator. Stein had always depended on Toklas to remember details of stories, and in *The Autobiography,* Simon wrote, "the stories were written as though Alice dictated them, with her deadpan humor and acerbic comments. So closely did Gertrude capture Alice's style that friends could almost hear her gritty voice delivering gossip with mischievous pleasure."

After Stein's death in 1946, Toklas devoted her remaining years to preserving her memory. Carl Van Vechten, an old friend, was appointed Stein's literary executor, and with his help and that of another friend, Thornton Wilder, Toklas lived to see eight volumes of Stein's unpublished works printed by Yale University Press. Toklas guarded Stein's literary reputation fiercely and was disheartened by several mildly critical biographies of Stein written by friends.

In order to support herself, Toklas turned to writing. Her first two books were combination cookbooks and memoirs. The British edition of *The Alice B. Toklas Cook Book* included the infamous recipe for hashish fudge, which was the entry of a painter friend. Toklas was reportedly horrified to learn that readers assumed that she and Stein had been in the habit of indulging in hashish.

Toklas's book of memoirs, *What is Remembered,* "depends more on the effects of an original personality—on style and tone—than on content," Jean Holzhauer noted. "Though it is not an analytical or profoundly relevatory book," critic Gene Baro wrote, "*What Is Remembered* is an important interpretation of the personalities and relationships that centered upon the households in the rue de Fleurus, at Bilignin, and in the rue Christine. Miss Toklas tells a story well, which is to say sparely. There are pages where she delivers an anecdote a paragraph. She has a ready eye for the ludicrous, for the bizarre detail that adds resonance to a scene." While the reviewer for *Time* was dismayed that in the collection of letters published posthumously Toklas seemed "to have disappeared virtually without a trace into Gertrude Stein's life," Harold Leibowitz commented that she is revealed "as a remarkable woman in her own right. There is never any self-pity, only an eloquent tenderness and a deep nostalgia for the 'old happy days.'"

BIOGRAPHICAL/CRITICAL SOURCES—Selected books: Carl Van Vechten, *Sacred and Profane Memories,* Knopf, 1932; Van Vechten, editor, *Selected Writings of Gertrude Stein,* Random House, 1946; W. G. Rogers, *When This You See Remember Me,* Rinehart, 1948; Donald Sutherland, *Gertrude Stein: A Biography of Her Work,* Yale University Press, 1951; Alice B. Toklas, *What Is Remembered,* Holt, 1963; Richard Bridgman, *The Colloquial Style in America,* Oxford University Press (New York), 1966; Joseph Barry, *The People of Paris,* Doubleday, 1966; Kay Boyle and Robert McAlmon, *Being Geniuses Together,* Doubleday, 1968; Ernest Earnest, *Expatriates and Patriots: American Artists, Scholars and Writers in Europe,* Duke University Press, 1968; Janet Flanner, *Paris Was Yesterday,* Viking, 1972; Edward Burns, editor, *Staying on Alone: Letters of Alice B. Toklas,* Liveright, 1973; James Mellow, *A Charmed Circle,* Praeger, 1974; Linda Simon, *The Biography of Alice B. Toklas,* Doubleday, 1977.

Selected periodicals: *Time,* March 22, 1963; *Critic,* April, 1963; *New York Times Book Review,* April 14, 1963, February 3, 1974; *Commonweal,* May 10, 1963; *Newsweek,* January 7, 1974; *Christian Science Monitor,* January 23, 1974; *New Yorker,* December 15, 1975.

OBITUARIES: New York Times, March 8, 1967; *Time,* March 17, 1967; *Newsweek,* March 20, 1967; *Publishers Weekly,* March 20, 1967; *Antiquarian Bookman,* March 27, 1967; *Books Abroad,* spring, 1968; *Britannica Book of the Year,* 1968.*

(Died March 7, 1967, in Paris, France)

TOLSTOY (-MILOSLAVSKY), Nikolai (Dimitrievich) 1935-

PERSONAL: Born June 23, 1935, in Maidstone, England; son of Dimitri Mihailovich (a barrister) and Mary O'Brian (Wicksteed) Tolstoy-Miloslavsky; married Georgina Katherine Brown, October 9, 1971; children: Alexandra, Anastasia, Dimitri. *Education:* Attended Royal Military Academy, Sandhurst, 1954; Trinity College, Dublin, M.A. (honors), 1961. *Politics:* "Monarchist (legitimist and Jacobite)." *Religion:* Russian Orthodox. *Home address:* Cricket Court, Cricket Malherbie, near Ilminster, Somerset, England. *Agent:* Jonathan Clowes Ltd., 19 Jeffrey's Pl., London N.W.1, England.

CAREER: Writer, 1968—. *Military service:* British Army, 1953-54.

WRITINGS: The Founding of Evil Hold School (juvenile), W. H. Allen, 1968; *The Secret Betrayal, 1944-1947,* Scribner, 1978 (published in England as *Victims of Yalta,* Hodder & Stoughton, 1978); *The Half-Mad Lord* (biography), J. Cape, 1978, Holt, 1979; *Stalin's Secret War,* Holt, in press. Contributor to *Bulletin of the Board of Celtic Studies* and *Transactions of the Honourable Society of Cymmrodorion.*

WORK IN PROGRESS: A biography of George Hanger; a book on pagan survival in the England of the Dark Ages.

SIDELIGHTS: Count Tolstoy writes: "My prime interest has always been in history of all periods and in the widest sense, including the subdivision now known as sociology. My aim is to amuse and, I hope, enlighten. When writing *The Secret Betrayal,* I was spurred on through many difficult years by a determination to honor and vindicate the memory of so many of my unfortunate compatriots who suffered appalling barbarities and indignities, whilst 'radical chic' progressive writers in the West praised their persecutors and exulted over the sufferings of millions of their fellow humans. My family has lived a privileged existence for many centuries; I suppose it is time to repay the debt."

*　　　*　　　*

TOMASEVIC, Nebojsa 1929-

PERSONAL: Surname is pronounced To-*ma*-she-vich; born November 9, 1929, in Kosovska Mitrovica, Yugoslavia; son of Petar and Milica (Rajkovic) Tomasevic; married Madge Phillips (a university lecturer), April, 1958; children: Una, Stela. *Education:* Attended University of Belgrade, 1948-52, and University of Exeter, 1953-55, received diploma in English language and literature. *Office:* c/o *Yugoslav Review,* Terazije 31/I, Belgrade, Yugoslavia.

CAREER: Active member of partisan group, 1943-45; Yugoslav Foreign Office, member of staff, 1945-59, with Yugoslav Embassy in London, England, 1954-58; staff member of Secretariat for Information, 1959-63; *Yugoslav Review,* Belgrade, Yugoslavia, chief editor, 1963-72; Revija (publishing house), Belgrade, director, 1973—.

WRITINGS: Naivci o sebi, Jugoslovenska revija, 1973, translation by Madge Phillips Tomasevic, Kordija Kveder, and Milica Hrgovic published as *Yugoslav Naive Art: Eighty Self-Taught Artists Speak About Themselves and Their Work,* International Learning Systems, 1976; *Magicni svet Ivana Generalica,* Jugoslovenska revija, 1975, translation by John Shepley published as *The Magic World of Ivan Generalic,* Rizzoli, 1977; *Joze Tisnikar, svet vaskrslih mrtvaca,* Jugoslovenska revija, 1978, translation by Kveder published as *Joze Tisnikar, Painter of Death,* Two Continents Publishing Group, 1978; *Naivni slikari Jugoslavije,*

Jugoslovenska knjiga, 1978, translation by M. P. Tomasevic published as *Naive Painters of Yugoslavia,* Two Continents Publishing Group, 1978.

WORK IN PROGRESS: The World of Gipsies.

SIDELIGHTS: Nebojsa Tomasevic told *CA:* "Although I have been a lover and collector of naive art since the late fifties, I have tried to discuss it in my books primarily from the sociological standpoint or in close association with the personality of a particular artist, rather than dwell on its aesthetic aspects. This approach seems to have made the books more interesting for a large number of readers who are rather intimidated by the usual esoteric art-critic jargon. One of the pleasures of doing these books has been meeting and getting to know the artists in their homes in all parts of the country. In most books I have preferred to let the artists speak for themselves, so that the reader can hear the authentic voice rather than a literary rehashing of peasant speech. Unfortunately, the regional speech varieties which add charm to the original Serbo-Croatian or Slovenian text are inevitably lost in translation."

Tomasevic's books have been translated into Italian, Dutch, French, German, Japanese, Norwegian, Swedish, and Danish.

*　　　*　　　*

TOOK, Belladonna
See CHAPMAN, Vera

*　　　*　　　*

TORGERSEN, Paul Ernest 1931-

PERSONAL: Born October 13, 1931, in New York, N.Y.; son of Einar and Francis (Hansen) Torgersen; married Dorothea Zuschlag, September 11, 1954; children: Karen Elizabeth, Janis Elaine, James Einar. *Education:* Lehigh University, B.S., 1954; Ohio State University, M.S., 1956, Ph.D., 1959. *Home:* 1510 Palmer Dr., Blacksburg, Va. 24060. *Office:* College of Engineering, Virginia Polytechnic Institute and State University, Blacksburg, Va. 24061.

CAREER: Ohio State University, Columbus, instructor in engineering, 1956-59; Oklahoma State University, Stillwater, assistant professor, 1959-63, associate professor of engineering, 1963-67; Virginia Polytechnic Institute and State University, Blacksburg, professor of engineering, 1967—, head of department of industrial engineering, 1967-70, dean of College of Engineering, 1970—. Member of Montgomery-Floyd Counties Library Board. *Military service:* U.S. Air Force, 1953-55; became first lieutenant. *Member:* American Institute of Industrial Engineering (vice-president in publications, 1972—), American Society for Engineering Education (head of Industrial Engineering Division, 1966-67), Alpha Pi Mu (member of regional board of directors, 1962-70). *Awards, honors:* H. B. Maynard Book of the Year Award from the American Institute of Industrial Engineers, 1972, for *Industrial Operations Research.*

WRITINGS: (With W. J. Fabrycky) *Operations Economy: Industrial Applications of Operations Research,* Prentice-Hall, 1966; *A Concept of Organization,* Van Nostrand, 1969; (with I. T. Weinstock) *Management: An Integrated Approach,* Prentice-Hall, 1972; (with Fabrycky and P. M. Ghare) *Industrial Operations Research,* Prentice-Hall, 1972; (with Marvin H. Agee and Robert E. Taylor) *Quantitative Analysis for Management Decisions,* Prentice-Hall, 1976. Member of editorial board of American Institute of Industrial Engineering, 1967-70, and vice president of publications, 1973-75.

TOSCHES, Nick 1949-

PERSONAL: Born October 23, 1949, in Newark, N.J.; son of Nick (a bartender) and Muriel Ann (Wynn) Tosches. *Education:* Attended high school in South Orange, N.J. *Agent:* Russ Galen, Scott Meredith Literary Agency, Inc., 845 Third Ave., New York, N.Y. 10022.

CAREER: Writer, 1968—.

WRITINGS: Country, Stein & Day, 1977; *Broads and Money* (novel), Venus, 1978. Contributor of articles, stories, and poems to popular magazines, including *Playboy, Penthouse, Rolling Stone,* and *Oui,* and newspapers.

WORK IN PROGRESS: Career of Evil, a novel based on the last ten years of Blackbeard's life.

* * *

TOURNIER, Paul 1898-

PERSONAL: Born May 12, 1898, in Geneva, Switzerland; son of Louis (a clergyman) and Alisabeth (Ormond) Tournier; married Nelly Bouvier, October 4, 1924; children: Jena-Louis, Gabriel. *Education:* University of Geneva, M.D., 1923. *Religion:* "Reformed." *Home and office:* Chemin Ormond 50, 1256 Troinex, Geneva, Switzerland.

CAREER: Physician in private practice; writer. *Military:* Physician in Swiss Army, 1939-45.

WRITINGS—All published by Delachaux & Niestle, except as noted: (With Philippe Mottu and Charles F. Ducommun) *Pierres d'angles de la reconstruction nationale,* 1941; *Medecine de la personne,* 1945, translation by Edwin Hudson published as *The Healing of Persons,* Harper, 1965, published as *Tournier's Medicine of the Whole Person,* Word Books, 1973; (with Jacques Ellul and Rene Gillouin) *L'Homme mesure de toute chose,* Centre protestant d'etudes, 1947; *Desharmonie de la vie moderne,* 1947; *Les Forts et les faibles,* 1948, translation by Hudson published as *The Strong and the Weak,* Westminster Press, 1963; *Le Personnage et la personne,* translation by Hudson published as *The Meaning of Persons,* Harper, 1957; *Bible et medecine,* translation by Hudson published as *A Doctor's Casebook in the Light of the Bible,* Harper, 1960; *Vrai ou fausse culpabilite,* 1958, translation by Arthur W. Heathcote and others published as *Guilt and Grace: A Psychological Study* (also see below), Harper, 1962; *De la solitude a la communaute,* translation by John S. Gilmour published as *Escape From Loneliness,* Westminster Press, 1962.

Des cadeaux pourquoi?, Labor et fides, 1961, translation by Gilmour published as *The Meaning of Gifts,* John Knox Press, 1963; *Les Saisons de la vie* (also see below), Labor et fides, 1961, translation by Gilmour published as *The Seasons of Life,* John Knox Press, 1963; *Tenir tete ou ceder* (also see below), Labor et fides, 1962, translation by Gilmour published as *To Resist or to Surrender,* John Knox Press, 1964; *Difficultes conjugales: Pour les surmonter, il faut chercher a se comprendre,* Labor et fides, 1962, translation by Gilmour published as *To Understand Each Other* (also see below), John Knox Press, 1967; *Le Secret,* Labor et fides, 1963, translation by Joe Embry published as *Secrets,* John Knox Press, 1965; *Solitude de l'homme moderne,* Westminster Press, 1964; *L'Aventure de la vie,* translation by Hudson published as *The Adventure of Living,* Harper, 1965; *Desharmonie de la vie moderne,* translation by John Doberstein and Helen Doberstein published as *The Whole Person in a Broken World,* Collins & World, 1965.

Technique et foi, translation by Hudson published as *The Person Reborn* (also see below), Harper, 1966; *L'Homme et son lieu: Psychologie et foi,* 1966, translation by Hudson published as *A Place for You: Psychology and Religion,* Harper, 1968; *Dynamique de la guerison,* 1968; *Problemes de vie* (includes *Les Saisons de la vie, Des cadeaux, pourquoi?,* and *Tenir tete du ceder*), Labor et fides, 1970; *Apprendre a vieiller,* 1971, translation by Hudson published as *Learning to Grow Old,* Harper, 1972; *Quel nom lui donnerez-vous?,* Labor et fides, 1974, translation by Hudson published as *The Naming of Persons,* Harper, 1975 (published in England as *What's in a Name?,* SCM Press, 1975); *A Tournier Companion* (extracts from author's works), SCM Press, 1976; *The Best of Paul Tournier* (includes *Guilt and Grace, The Meanings of Persons, The Person Reborn,* and *To Understand Each Other*), Iverson-Norman, 1977; *The Violence Inside,* SCM Press, 1978. Also editor of *Surmenage et repos,* 1963, translation by James H. Farley published as *Fatigue in Modern Society.*

WORK IN PROGRESS: A book about women's mission.

SIDELIGHTS: Tournier's books have been translated into thirteen additional languages, including Finnish, Dutch, Norwegian, Greek, Chinese, and Spanish.

BIOGRAPHICAL/CRITICAL SOURCES: Times Literary Supplement, November 11, 1965; *Christianity Today,* May 11, 1973; *Christian Century,* August 29, 1973, August 17, 1977.

* * *

TREE, Gregory
See BARDIN, John Franklin

* * *

TREMAYNE, Peter
See ELLIS, Peter Berresford

* * *

TRIGOBOFF, Joseph 1947-

PERSONAL: Born August 3, 1947, in Brooklyn, N.Y.; son of Leo (an assistant principal) and Rose (a secretary; maiden name, Taub) Trigoboff. *Education:* Long Island University, B.A., 1969; Adelphi University, M.A., 1973. *Politics:* "Neo-proto-conservatism." *Religion:* Orthodox Judaism. *Home:* Lincoln Towers Apartments, 142 West End Ave., New York, N.Y.

CAREER: Teacher in public schools, New York, N.Y., 1970—; writer, 1970—.

WRITINGS: Streets, Windy Row Press, 1970; *Abu,* Lothrop, 1975; *Abu and Itzhak,* Ravensburger, 1977.

WORK IN PROGRESS: A novel about smugglers.

SIDELIGHTS: Trigoboff told *CA:* "My viewpoint is notoriously fickle. As everyone in the literary world knows, my politics and 'world view' is constant only in its inconsistancy. My current literary goal is to become a politician, go to jail, and then write a best seller based on my memoirs."

* * *

TRING, A. Stephen
See MEYNELL, Laurence Walter

* * *

TROHAN, Walter (Joseph) 1903-

PERSONAL: Born July 4, 1903, in Mt. Carmel, Pa.; son of E. Henry (a wholesale grocer) Bernice (Skindzier) Trohan;

married Carol Rowland, March 12, 1929; children: Carol (Mrs. Wayne A. Glover), Walter Joseph, Jr., Nancy (Mrs. Robert Dollar). *Education:* University of Notre Dame, B.A., 1926. *Politics:* Independent. *Religion:* Roman Catholic. *Home:* 5711 Phelps Luck Dr., Columbia, Md. 21045.

CAREER: City News Bureau, Chicago, Ill., reporter, 1927-29; *Chicago Tribune,* Chicago, Ill., reporter, 1929-34, Washington correspondent, 1934-48, Washington bureau chief, 1948-68, columnist, 1968-72; free-lance writer, 1972—. Past member of board of trustees of Lincoln Christian College. *Member:* Gridiron Club (president, 1937), Bohemian Club, George Town Club. *Awards, honors:* Edward Scott Beck Editorial Award, 1948, and 1950; member of Delta Sigma Chi Journalistic Hall of Fame, 1976—; Litt. D. from Lincoln Christian College.

WRITINGS: Jim Farley's Story, McGraw, 1948; *Political Animals,* Doubleday, 1975. Contributor to magazines.

WORK IN PROGRESS: Research on the American Civil War and on Philip Sheridan.

SIDELIGHTS: Trohan comments: "I was induced to write out of friendship. Doubleday importuned me to write my memoirs for ten years, and I finally consented in order to promise funds for a diabetic grandson. I am being urged to write further, but so far have resisted."

* * *

TRUAX, R. Hawley 1889(?)-1978

OBITUARY NOTICE: Born c. 1889 in Cleveland, Ohio; died November 24, 1978, in New York, N.Y. Lawyer, real estate executive, magazine executive, and poet. A former chairman of the board of directors of *New Yorker* and a director for forty-six years, Truax was legendary as the intermediary between the editorial and business sides of the magazine. He was also a published poet. Obituaries and other sources: *New York Times,* November 27, 1978; *New Yorker,* December 4, 1978.

* * *

TRUDEAU, G(arretson) B(eekman) 1948-
(Garry B. Trudeau)

PERSONAL: Born in New York, N.Y. *Education:* Yale University, received degree, 1970, received M.F.A. *Residence:* New Haven, Conn. *Office:* c/o Universal Press Syndicate, 6700 Squibb Rd., Mission, Kan. 66202.

CAREER: Cartoonist and writer. Operates graphics studio in New Haven, Conn. *Awards, honors:* Pulitzer Prize for editorial cartooning, 1975; D.H.L. from Yale University, 1976; Academy Award nomination and Cannes Film Festival special jury prize, both 1977, both for the animated film, "A Doonesbury Special."

WRITINGS: Doonesbury, foreword by Erich Segal, American Heritage Press, 1971; *Still a Few Bugs in the System,* Holt, 1972, selections published as *Even Revolutionaries Like Chocolate Chip Cookies* and as *Just a French Major From the Bronx,* Popular Library, 1974; *The President Is a Lot Smarter Than You Think,* Holt, 1973; *But This War Had Such Promise,* Holt, 1973, selections published as *Bravo for Life's Little Ironies,* Popular Library, 1975; (under name Garry Trudeau) *Doonesbury: The Original Yale Cartoons,* Sheed, 1973; *Call Me When You Find America,* Holt, 1973; (with Nicholas von Hoffman) *The Fireside Watergate,* Sheed, 1973; *Guilty, Guilty, Guilty!,* Holt, 1974; (under name Garry Trudeau) *Joanie,* afterword by Nora Ephron, Sheed, 1974; (under name Garry Trudeau) *Don't Ever*

Change Boopsie, Popular Library, 1974; *Dare to Be Great, Ms. Caucus,* Holt, 1975; *"What Do We Have for the Witnesses, Johnnie?",* Holt, 1975; *The Doonesbury Chronicles,* introduction by Garry Wills, Holt, 1975; (under name Garry Trudeau) *We'll Take It From Here, Sarge,* afterword by Chuck Stone, Sheed, 1975; (under name Garry Trudeau) *I Have No Son,* Popular Library, 1975; *Wouldn't a Gremlin Have Been More Sensible?,* Holt, 1975.

(With von Hoffman) *Tales From the Margaret Mead Taproom: The Compleat Gonzo Governorship of Doonesbury's Uncle Duke,* Sheed, 1976; *"Speaking of Inalienable Rights, Amy . . .",* Holt, 1976; *You're Never Too Old for Nuts and Berries,* Holt, 1976; *An Especially Tricky People,* Holt, 1977; (with David Levinthal) *Hitler Moves East: A Graphic Chronicle, 1941-43,* Sheed, 1977; (under name Garry B. Trudeau) *As the Kid Goes for Broke,* Holt, 1977; *Stalking the Perfect Tan,* Holt, 1978; (under name Garry Trudeau) *Any Grooming Hints for Your Fans Rollie,* Holt, 1978; *Doonesbury's Greatest Hits,* introduction by William F. Buckley, Holt, 1978. Also author, with von Hoffman, of *Trout Fishing in the Reflecting Pool,* Popular Library.

Author and artist for cartoon strip "Doonesbury," under name Garry Trudeau, syndicated by Universal Press Syndicate and appearing in more than 500 newspapers, 1970—. Creator of animated film, "A Doonesbury Special," 1977. Contributor of articles to *Rolling Stone, New York,* and *New Republic.* Editor, "Cartoons for New Children" series for Sheed.

SIDELIGHTS: Trudeau's immensely popular daily cartoon strip, "Doonesbury," began as a strip he did for the Yale newspaper when he was an undergraduate there. Originally named "Bull Tales," the strip featured such Yale notables as B.D. (based on the school's football hero Brian Dowling), and a thinly disguised caricature of Yale president Kingman Brewster. Then, as now, the main character was Michael Doonesbury, whose name is a combination of "doone" (a slang term meaning "good-natured fool") and the last syllable of Pillsbury (a former roommate of Trudeau's). When the strip was acquired by Universal Press Syndicate in 1970, the expletives were deleted, naked co-eds were clothed, and the name was changed to "Doonesbury."

Humorist Art Buchwald has called "Doonesbury" "not only the best comic strip, but the best satire that's come along in a long time." Dominique Paul Noth commented that Jules Feiffer's "social dialog cartoons" are the direct antecedent of Trudeau's creations. Garry Wills, in the introduction to *The Doonesbury Chronicles,* concurred with that often made comparison, but noted that "Feiffer's characters are stranded in a desert of themselves, while Trudeau's people interact."

Trudeau has, Noth wrote, "an uncanny radar that sweeps up material across the American scene. While many readers presume a leftish bent to his views, Trudeau has taken on the sacred cows and semantic bull of both sides. He has poked fun at both Nixon and the press, activists and reactionaries. He has looked with a strange mixture of sadness, love and humor at his own generation."

Perhaps the strip's most popular character has been the newly liberated Ms. Joanie Caucus who, in the course of the strip, left her husband and children, joined the Walden commune (home of many "Doonesbury" regulars), and eventually became a lawyer. In an early strip, Joanie explained that she finally knew her marriage was over when, after cooking dinner for her husband and his friends, "Clinton leaned back in his chair, and said with a big, stupid grin,

'My wife, I think I'll keep her!' I broke his nose." When Joanie was applying to law schools, several actual schools sent word that she had been accepted. Trudeau receives so many letters addressed to her that, he said, "my mailman thinks I'm living with this woman."

The humor of "Doonesbury" is topical and often political. The most controversial strips have been on Watergate. Although Trudeau's targets included Senator Sam Ervin's Watergate committee ("The chair opens up the floor to innuendo and hearsay."), the Nixon administration was more often the subject of his sometimes caustic humor. In one strip, Mark Slackmeyer, the radical activist disc jockey, pronounces then-Attorney General John Mitchell "guilty, guilty, guilty" of Watergate-related charges, and several newspapers, including the *Washington Post,* refused to run the strip. In response to the outrage of "Doonesbury" fans, the *Post* ran an editorial explaining its reasons for deleting that episode of the strip. It stated: "If anyone is going to find any defendent guilty, it's going to be the due process of justice, not a comic-strip artist. We cannot have one standard for the news pages and another for the comics." Some newspapers responded to the controversial humor of "Doonesbury." by moving the strip from the cartoon page to the editorial page.

Some public officials have seen the humor in "Doonesbury" even when it's been at their own expense. Gerald Ford ("Snowbunny"), William Simon ("His Exchequership"), and John Ehrlichman have all requested and received the originals of strips in which they were caricatured. Ford once quipped to a gathering of radio and televison correspondents: "There are only three major vehicles to keep us informed as to what is going on in Washington. The electronic media, the print media, and 'Doonesbury' . . . not necessarily in that order."

Trudeau defended the strip's satirical view of contemporary American life in a speech before a gathering of newspaper editors. He said: "The particular sociological outlook of 'Doonesbury' is specific enough to leave more than a few readers irate, and I am frequently compelled to answer the question of whether or not this strip is a fair commentary on the present social scene. It does, however, seem to me that what is lacking in such a question is a fundamental understanding of the nature of comedy. The derivatives of humor on comic strips have always been based on hyperbole, exaggeration and overstatement. Satire has always been formulated through the expansion and refraction of the truth. Cartoonists *do* concern themselves with truth, but if they delivered it straight, they would totally fail in their role as humorists. Therefore, I feel no obligation to be 'fair' in any absolute sense to a subject simply because certain individuals are sensitive to it."

Trudeau has a well-known penchant for privacy and denies all requests for interviews. "If I have anything to say," he has explained, "I say it in the strip."

BIOGRAPHICAL/CRITICAL SOURCES: Columbia Journalism Review, November, 1974; *Newsweek,* January 13, 1975; *Milwaukee Journal,* May 20, 1975; *Time,* February 6, 1976.*

* * *

TRUDEAU, Garry B.
   See TRUDEAU, G(arretson) B(eekman)

TRUFFAUT, Francois 1932-

PERSONAL: Born February 26, 1932, in Paris, France; son of Roland (an architect) and Janine (de Monferrand) Truffaut; married Madeleine Morgenstern, October 29, 1957 (divorced); children: Laura, Eva. *Education:* Educated in Paris, France. *Office:* Films du Carrosse, 5 rue Robert-Estienne, 75008 Paris, France.

CAREER: Film journalist and writer; screenwriter, director, and producer of motion pictures; actor. Worked as messenger, shop assistant, storekeeper, clerk, welder, cinema manager, and film department employee for French Ministry of Agriculture, 1946-54; film critic for *Cahiers du Cinema* and for *Arts,* 1954-62; researcher for Roberto Rossellini, 1956. Actor in motion pictures, including "L'Enfant Sauvage," 1969, "La Nuit americaine," 1973, "Close Encounters of the Third Kind," 1977, and "La Chambre Verte," 1978. *Military service:* French Army, 1949-51.

AWARDS, HONORS: Prix des Jeunes Spectateurs for direction from Brussels Film Festival and gold medal from Mannheim, both 1958, both for "Les Mistons"; grand prize for best director from Cannes Film Festival, Swiss Film Press Association award, director's prize from Belgium Film Festival, prize from World Festival at Acapulco, Grand Prix of the International Catholic Film Office, and best foreign film award from New York Film Critics, all 1959, all for "Les Quatre Cents Coups"; German Photography Prize and French New Critics Prize, both 1960, both for "Tirez sur le pianiste"; Director's Prize from Acapulco Film Festival, Director's Prize from Mar del Plata Film Festival, prize for best French film from l'Academie du Cinema, Critics Prize from Carthage Film Festival, and awards from film festivals in Italy, Denmark, Mexico, Venezuela, and Colombia, all 1961, all for "Jules et Jim"; Melies Prize and Grand Prize du Cinema, both 1968, and Louis Delluc Prize, 1969, all for "Baisers voles"; Academy Award for best foreign language film from Academy of Motion Picture Arts and Sciences and Stella Award for best film and for best director from British Society of Film and Television Arts, all 1973, all for "La Nuit americaine"; Grand Prize of French Cinema, 1976, and Georges Melies Prize, 1977, both for "L'Histoire d'Adele H."; and countless other film awards.

WRITINGS: (With Marcel Moussy) *Les Quatre Cents Coups* (novelization of screenplay), Gallimard, 1959; (author of introduction) Henri-Pierre Roche, *Jules and Jim,* translation by Patrick Evans, Avon, 1963; *Le Cinema selon Hitchcock* (collection of interviews with Alfred Hitchcock), Robert Laffont, 1966, translation published as *Hitchcock,* Simon & Schuster, 1967; (editor) Andre Bazin, *Jean Renoir,* Simon & Schuster, 1973; *La Nuit americaine et le Journal de Fahreheit 451,* Seghers, 1974; (editor) Bazin, *Le Cinema de la cruaute,* Flammarion, 1975; (editor and author of introduction) Bazin, *Le Cinema de l'occupation et de la resistence,* editions 10-18, Flammarion, 1975; *Les Films de ma vie* (collection of reviews), Flammarion, 1975, translation by Leonard Mayhew published as *The Films of My Life,* Simon & Schuster, 1978.

Published screenplays: *Jules and Jim,* Simon & Schuster, 1968; *The Four Hundred Blows,* Grove, 1969; *The Adventures of Antoine Doinel: Four Autobiographical Screenplays,* Simon & Schuster, 1972; *The Wild Child,* translation by Linda Lewin and Christine Memery, Washington Square Press, 1973; *Day for Night,* translation by Sam Flores, Grove, 1975; *The Story of Adele H.,* Grove, 1975; *Small Change,* Grove, 1977.

Screenplays and director: "Une visite," 1954; "Les Mistons'' (released in U.S. as ''The Mischief Makers''), 1957; (with Jean-Luc Godard) ''Une Histoire d'eau,'' 1958; (with Marcel Moussy) ''Les Quatre Cents Coups'' (released in U.S. as ''The Four Hundred Blows''), 1959; (with Moussy) ''Tirez sur le pianiste'' (released in U.S. as ''Shoot the Piano Player''; adapted from the novel by David Goodis, *Down There),* 1960; (with Jean Gruault) ''Jules et Jim'' (adapted from the novel by Henri-Pierre Roche), 1961; ''Antoine et Colette,'' 1962; (with Jean-Louise Richard) ''La Peau douce'' (released in U.S. as ''The Soft Skin''), 1964; (with Richard) ''Fahrenheit 451'' (adapted from the novel by Ray Bradbury), 1966; (with Richard) ''La Mariee etait en noir'' (released in U.S. as ''The Bride Wore Black''; adapted from the novel by William Irish), 1967; (with Claude de Givray and Bernard Revon) ''Baisers voles'' (released in U.S. as ''Stolen Kisses''), 1966; (co-author) ''La Sirene du Mississippi'' (released in U.S. as ''Mississippi Mermaid''), 1969.

(With Gruault) ''L'Enfant sauvage'' (released in U.S. as ''The Wild Child''; adapted from a book by Jean-Marc-Gaspard Itard), 1970; (with Givray and Revon) ''Domicile conjugal'' (released in U.S. as ''Bed and Board''), 1970; (with Gruault) ''Les Deux Anglaises et le continent'' (released in U.S. as ''Two English Girls''; adapted from the novel by Roche), 1973; (co-author) ''Une Belle Fille comme moi'' (released in U.S. as ''Such a Gorgeous Kid Like Me''), 1972; (with Suzanne Schiffman and Richard) ''La Nuit americaine'' (released in U.S. as ''Day for Night''), 1973; (with Gruault and Schiffman) ''L'Histoire d'Adele H.'' (released in U.S. as ''The Story of Adele H.''; adapted from the biography by Frances Vernor Guille, *Le Journal d'Adele Hugo),* 1976; (with Schiffman) ''L'Argent de poche'' (released in U.S. as ''Small Change''), 1976; (with Michel Fermaud and Schiffman) ''L'Homme qui aimait les femmes'' (released in U.S. as ''The Man Who Loved Women''), 1977; (with Gruault) ''La Chambre verte'' (released in U.S. as ''The Green Room''; adapted from the short story by Henry James), 1978; (co-author) ''L'Amour en fuite'' (released in U.S. as ''Love on the Run''), 1978.

Other screenplays: ''Tire au Flanc,'' 1962; ''Mata-Hari,'' 1964.

Contributor to periodicals, including *Atlantic, Arts, Cahiers du Cinema, Harper's,* and *Travail et Culture.*

SIDELIGHTS: Truffaut began his film career as a critic for *Cahiers du Cinema* where he developed a reputation as a sarcastic opponent of successful producers. One of these producers, Truffaut's father-in-law Ignace Morgenstern, was so aggravated that he offered to finance Truffaut's next film undertaking, hoping that Truffaut would accept the offer and create such an embarrassing film that he would desist from criticizing the proven successes in the film industry. Later, Truffaut accepted the challenge but the results were hardly what Morgenstern expected.

Truffaut had already made one short film with documentary filmmaker Alain Resnais, entitled ''Une Visite.'' After serving as a researcher for filmmaker Roberto Rossellini, Truffaut made a second short, ''The Mischief Makers.'' The film was a surprise to critics who, like Morgenstern, expected Truffaut to humiliate himself. Critic John Russell Taylor wrote that ''whatever might have been anticipated from a wild young critic of revolutionary tendencies, it was hardly this: a quiet, graceful, even, one might say, romantic evocation of childhood and far-off innocence.''

In 1959, Truffaut proved that the success of ''The Mischief Makers'' was no fluke. With the release of the Morgenstern-

financed ''The Four Hundred Blows,'' Truffaut seized international fame as the spokesman of the French ''new wave.'' Truffaut's film of delinquent Antoine Doinel procured numerous awards and, along with Resnais's ''Hiroshima, Mon Amour'' and Jean-Luc Godard's ''Breathless'' (for which Truffaut provided the basic idea), was hailed as part of a new era in cinema.

Truffaut returned to his semi-autobiographical character, Antoine Doinel, in four later movies. He contributed ''Antoine and Collette'' to the omnibus film, ''Love at Twenty.'' In ''Stolen Kisses,'' Truffaut once again placed Doinel in full-length format and the result was a critical success. ''Stolen Kisses'' chronicled Doinel's adventures as a hotel night clerk and private detective after his discharge from the army. Regarded by many as one of Truffaut's finest comedies, ''Stolen Kisses'' received lavish praise from Vincent Canby who wrote that ''to define it may make it sound like a religious experience, which of course it is—but in a wonderfully unorthodox, cockeyed way.'' A later film, ''Bed and Board,'' was similarly successful at following Doinel's marital crises. ''Antoine comes very close to being an outright rat,'' wrote Canby, ''but, happily, he fails at this as he does at just about everything else he undertakes with such intensity.'' ''Love on on the Run'' is the most recent segment of the Doinel series.

The subject of children also proved popular with Truffaut and he returned to it in two later films, ''The Wild Child'' and ''Small Change.'' Explaining why he used children as subjects, Truffaut said: ''Even as a child, I loved children. I have very strong ideas about the world they inhabit. Morally, the child is like a waif—outside society. In the early life of a child, there is no notion of accident . . . while in the world of the adult everything is allowed.'' ''Small Change,'' released in 1976, is probably Truffaut's last film about children. With the film's box-office success, he was inundated with scripts about children and reviews that claimed him ''as a marvelous director of children.'' But Truffaut was not inclined to being typecast as a children's director. He recently told a *Take One* interviewer, ''No more films about children!''

Truffaut is as well known for his homages to cinema as he is for his Doinel and children's films. ''Shoot the Piano Player'' and ''Day for Night'' both show an affection for the medium. ''Shoot the Piano Player'' was Truffaut's response to critics expecting another film like ''The Four Hundred Blows.'' ''With my second film I felt myself being watched, waited for by this public,'' he said, ''and I really wanted to send them all packing.'' The story of a pianist's involvement with mobsters was hardly what had been expected from Truffaut. ''I had a number of projects for films with children,'' he recalled, ''I put them all aside since I didn't want to seem to be exploiting a trick that worked well before. This time I wanted to please the real film nuts and them alone, while leading astray a large part of those who liked 'The Four Hundred Blows.' ''

Truffaut's ''Day for Night'' was another film for those who shared his affection for the cinema. Critic Jay Carr called it ''one of the fondest compliments the movies have ever been paid—a tribute to all the dream spinners by one of the best.'' The popular film about the joys and frustrations of filmmaking summed up both sides of life on the set. ''Shooting a film is like taking a stagecoach ride in the Old West,'' claims the director character (played by Truffaut) in ''Day for Night.'' ''First you hope to have a nice trip. Then you just hope to reach your destination.''

Like children and the Doinel character, women also occupy an important position in the Truffaut canon. Films such as "Jules and Jim" and "The Soft Skin" betray Truffaut's early perception of women. Driven by an inability to communicate their emotions, Truffaut's women resolve their plights by committing suicide ("Jules and Jim") and by succumbing to madness ("The Story of Adele H."). The female character in "The Bride Wore Black" reacts to her fiance's murder by murdering his killers, and the woman in "The Soft Skin" murders her unfaithful husband.

By comparison, the women in "The Man Who Loved Women" are quite different. Critic Annette Insdorf commented that in "'The Man Who Loved Women,' each of the women can generously take or lucidly leave love, thus illustrating Truffaut's growing appreciation for 'sane' women." Insdorf also suggested that Truffaut was a feminist director. "'The Man Who Loved Women' is perhaps a feminist film, in my own way," Truffaut responded. "But I would not actually praise women in a film today. It is too fashionable." Fearing an abundance of scripts about women, Truffaut also said that "now it's time for women to make feminist films, not me. . . . It is women who should depict the new roles they are playing in society."

In addition to his role as a filmmaker, Truffaut has made contributions to cinema as a critic. His auteur theory has long been the subject of debate in American film circles. Through his writings, he has brought attention to formerly unrecognized directors such as Nicholas Ray and Raoul Walsh. *Hitchcock,* Truffaut's collection of interviews with the filmmaker, was referred to as "an insight into the old suspense master's creative habits" by a *Variety* reviewer. "Anyone can be a film critic," Truffaut wrote in *Harper's.* "The apprentice need not possess a tenth of the knowledge that would be demanded of a critic of literature, music, or painting." He also qualified his accomplishments as a filmmaker: "Cinematic success is the result not necessarily of good brainwork but of a harmony of existing elements in ourselves that we may not have even been conscious of: a fortunate fusion of subject and our deeper feelings, an accidental coincidence of our own and the public's preoccupations at a certain moment of life."

BIOGRAPHICAL/CRITICAL SOURCES: New Yorker, February 20, 1960; John Russell Taylor, *Cinema Eye, Cinema Ear,* Hill & Wang, 1964; *Best Sellers,* January 15, 1968; *Film Quarterly,* summer, 1968, spring, 1971, winter, 1973-74; *Variety,* November 20, 1968; *New York Times,* March 3, 1969, January 22, 1971; Leo Braudy, editor, *Focus on Shoot the Piano Player,* Prentice-Hall, 1972; *Time,* October 15, 1973; *Newsweek,* January 5, 1976; *Harper's,* October, 1977; *Take One,* January, 1978.*

* * *

TUCCI, Niccolo 1908-
(Bartolomeo Strabolgi)

PERSONAL: Born May 1, 1908, in Lugano, Switzerland, "but raised in Florence, Italy, therefore a Florentine. Also (through my mother) a Russian, a Parisian, an Interplanetarian. Came frequently to the United States, was naturalized citizen in 1953, after an eight-year lawsuit (*Tucci* vs. *United States*) as 'a greater friend of Plato than of himself' (see opinion of Judge Jerome Frank of Circuit Court of New York, 1953), and also as the first conscientious objector to all future wars on scientific rather than religious grounds"; married Laura Rusconi, 1936; children: two.

EDUCATION: "Studied with private German tutors until 1914, when I became precociously illiterate (the first such case observed in a precociously literate child, and described as 'cultural shell-shock'). After learning the ABC's again, I became entirely self-taught, despite constant brainwashing by parents and teachers. I read a great deal in four languages, wandered aimlessly through many German universities without doing any work, and was at Amherst College (1931-32) without doing any work. Then I went back to Italy and Germany where I witnessed Hitler's rise to power and decided that Europe was finished and America my only hope. I emigrated to Berkeley, California, with a grant, became a resident worked on a Ph.D., but, unfortunately, also read the Treaty on Pedagogy by Giovanni Gentile (official philosopher of fascism but also, earlier, a great scholar and author of a beautiful book on freedom of thought). Gentile called upon all Italians to prove their philosophical maturity in the supreme sacrifice of war, ANY war, no matter how absurd, in obedience to whatever Mussolini, the greatest of thinkers in all history, had decided. I obeyed, left everything, returned as a penniless, jobless sailor on a freighter, ready for the supreme sacrifice, and was called a damn fool by everybody, including Giovanni Gentile.

"I had a second cultural shell-shock (without a war this time), but instead of becoming illiterate, I became much too literate and received a doctorate in political science at the University of Florence, defending Mussolini's 'Doctrine' that international treatises were worthless scraps of paper, and his word alone the everlasting international law. It must be said, to the everlasting credit of some university professors under fascism, that they tried to deny me my doctorate but failed." *Home and office:* 25 East 67th St., New York, N.Y. 10021.

CAREER: "I graduated, then entered Mussolini's press and propaganda ministry, became head of the German-language radio station, invited German Jews to air their political views. I was reprimanded but not fired because my allegorical fairy tales in German had made me a great favorite with German audiences. I refused many offers from German publishers, resigned from my post (1936), managed to get an anti-Nazi Italian called Gasbarra to replace me, but went on broadcasting my fairy tales in French (my own translation) and English (translation by a nun, Mother Mary St. John, sister of Bertrand Russell).

"In 1936, as ghost writer for an Austrian statesman and translator of Mussolini's speeches into German, I caused a minor storm in the highest diplomatic teapots of Italy and Austria, because I had gravely altered Mussolini's text. But two days later, the infallible law-giver had changed his policies and the incident was forgotten. (Mussolini knew not more than seventeen words of German; had he known twenty-six, he would never have read my version of his speech. This kind of vanity led to serious misunderstandings when he insisted on seeing Hitler without interpreters.)

"December, 1936: I was kicked upstairs and east—all the way to Japan—as professor of fascist culture at the Imperial University of Tokyo, but on the eve of my departure I found myself kicked back downstairs and west—all the way to New York (this was due to pressure by my namesake—no relative, thank God—the Orientalist Tucci, who, in 1938, distinguished himself for writing in defense of the Aryan Italian race, on the 'Misdeeds of the Jews in Tibet, India, and Japan')!

"January—July, 1937: In New York, I was fascist propagandist and Dante lecturer at the Italy-American Society, a cultural organization endowed by the usual scatterbrain endowagers so well portrayed in Ruth Draper's *Italian Lesson*, but controlled by the fascist government (see Albert Einstein's *Correspondence avec Michele Besso, 1903-1955*, published by Hermann Editeurs des Sciences et des Arts, Paris). The last Dante lecturer there, a distinguished Roman poet, Lauro de Bosis, engaged to marry Ruth Draper, had defected in 1930. He died a glorious death flying low over Rome for a whole day dropping anti-fascist leaflets everywhere. Before leaving France in his old airplane (he hardly knew how to fly), he had written the beautiful *Story of My Death*. Like de Bosis until 1930, I, in 1937, still believed in the supreme power of poetry over politics to bring Mussolini back to his senses. How silly this hope was I understood only in October, 1937, in long discussions with my friend Enrico Fermi, during our return to Italy on the S.S. *Vulcania*. Back in New York as a penniless immigrant in 1938, I then became active in anti-fascist propaganda and ghost-wrote for a dishonest, unimaginative playwright. Rescued from this job by my friend Sidney Howard, I was promised assistance in producing my own play, 'Posterity for Sale.' Sidney Howard's sudden death put an end to my hopes. The play was produced by the American Place Theatre in 1967.

"In 1941, I became assistant director of the Bureau of Latin American Research, a branch of Nelson Rockefeller's Coordinating Office, and of the State Department. I wrote anti-fascist articles, ghost-wrote for higher government officials who shall remain unnamed, and wrote stories for Walt Disney without ever receiving credit.

"In 1944, I became a free-lance writer for various magazines. . . . In 1965, I was writer-in-residence at Columbia University, and in 1973, I founded a theatrical company called The Wide Embrace with E. G. Marshall, Kevin McCarthy, David Amram, Kurt Vonnegut, Maria Tucci, Deborah S. Pease, Ruby Dee, Estelle Parsons, and others."

AWARDS, HONORS: "Awards not listed because they have nothing to do with talent, only with tax deduction for foundations, and with public relations for publishers. But I do list as my honors the following: A letter from James Joyce in 1924, praising me for my Italian fairy tales; a letter from E. B. White to William Shawn in 1956, saying, 'One Tucci piece a year, and the *New Yorker* is in the clear'; being quoted at length by W. H. Auden in *The Dyer's Hand and Other Essays* (pg. 197)."

WRITINGS: Il Segreto (autobiography), Garzanti, 1956; *Before My Time* ("pre-autobiography"), Simon & Schuster, 1962; *Unfinished Funeral* (novel), Simon & Schuster, 1964; *Gli Atlantici* (autobiography), Garzanti, 1968; *Confessioni Involontarie* (autobiography), Mondadori, 1977; *The Sun and the Moon* (novel), Knopf, 1977. Also author of plays, including "Nixon: Man for One Season," "Murder in the Oval Room," "Bullshit in the China Cabinet," "La Plume de ma te detente," "Nixon in the Egosphere," "Oedipus President," and "Posterity for Sale." Contributing correspondent to *New Yorker*, 1947—. Contributor to periodicals, including *Harper's Bazaar, Harper's, Atlantic, New Republic, Nation, Politics, Village Voice*, and, under pseudonym Bartolomeo Strabolgi, *Commonweal*.

WORK IN PROGRESS: "Several other volumes of my preposthumous autobiography."

SIDELIGHTS: Tucci comments: "Given the fact that whatever a non-writer writes about a writer's life is both *inaccurate* and *damaging*, I found myself compelled to squeeze into a few lines what it had taken me more than half a century and many thousands of pages to reduce to a bare minimum; namely my basic autobiography, which is also the

autobiography of an age. Writers ARE spokesmen for their age or they are nothing.

"I am not pleased with the result. It sounds like an extorted confession. But as the compilers of lists have a right to satisfy the imbecilic curiosity of the public, I was trapped between doing my homework for lawyers or for compilers of lists, and quite frankly, I much prefer the latter. I'd rather sign an extorted confession with no room for self-defense, than a lawyer's brief, let alone read one. So this is my confession: yes I *did* waste the best years of my life serving and praising one of the greatest imbeciles and criminals of the century, knowing that he was both, but 'hoping for the best.' And yes, I *did* say that his critics were traitors, because 'all dirty laundry must be washed at home,' and yet I knew that water and soap were forbidden by law, lest the enemy get wind of the truth. Some wind! And did we stink!

"Yet, instead of feeling guilty, I feel totally forgiven and even overjoyed. Why? Because, when I lost my fascist faith, I also died. Not in glory, like Lauro De Bosis, but in shame. What saved me was my death. I did not waste it all in one gesture, I lived it out to the last breath: that was the end of literature for me, and the beginning of science. I dissected that first dead body of mine and many more to come, as we all should in life, every single time we die, practicing strict 'rebirth control,' because the purpose of rebirth is to repeat a crime that didn't pay, and make it pay. With the help of American publishers (and of Communist parties in Europe) it does. The profits are enormous. But the second life of these criminals is even shorter that the first one. The classics of the checkbook become writers of stubs overnight. No one can learn anything from them, no one can be amused by their mistakes, and that is why they cannot be forgiven. Our mistakes can only be forgotten by others, if we remember them so well, that we can speak amusingly about them. This alone, this joy of the clean word, is a sign of rebirth, but it cannot bear fruits five minutes after the seed has been planted and then covered by manure.

"My advice is: first learn to write as if you were already dead and then you will discover that you can write as if you were still alive (not now, of course, but centuries after your last death). Teachers of writing courses please note."

*　　　*　　　*

TUDHOPE, Richard
See RODDA, Peter (Gordon)

*　　　*　　　*

TUDOR, Tasha 1915-

PERSONAL: Original name, Starling Burgess; name legally changed; born August 28, 1915, in Boston, Mass.; daughter of W. Starling Burgess (a yacht designer) and Rosamond Tudor (a portrait painter); married Thomas Leighton McCready, Jr., 1938 (divorced); married Allan John Woods; children: (first marriage) Bethany Wheelock, Seth Tudor, Thomas Strong, Efner Strong. *Education:* Studied at the Boston Museum Fine Arts School. *Residence:* Marlboro, Vt.

CAREER: Author and illustrator of children's books, 1938—. *Awards, honors:* Runner-up for the Caldecott Medal, 1945, for *Mother Goose*, and 1957, for *1 Is One*; Regina Medal, 1971.

WRITINGS—All self-illustrated; all published by Oxford University Press, except as noted: *Pumpkin Moonshine*, 1938, enlarged edition, Walck, 1962; *Alexander the Gander*,

1939, enlarged edition, Walck, 1961; *The County Fair*, 1940, enlarged edition, Walck, 1964; *A Tale for Easter*, 1941; *Snow Before Christmas*, 1941; *Dorcas Porkus*, 1942, enlarged edition, Walck, 1963; *The White Goose*, 1943; *Linsey Woolsey*, 1946; *Thistly B*, 1949; *The Dolls' Christmas*, 1950; *Amanda and the Bear*, 1951; *Edgar Allan Crow*, 1953; *A Is for Annabelle*, 1954; *1 Is One*, 1956; *Around the Year*, 1957; *Becky's Birthday*, Viking, 1960; (with others) *My Brimful Book*, edited by Dana Bruce, Platt, 1960; *Becky's Christmas*, Viking, 1961; *First Delights: A Book About the Five Senses*, Platt, 1966; *The Tasha Tudor Book of Fairy Tales*, Platt, 1969; *Corgiville Fair*, Crowell, 1971; *A Time to Keep: The Tasha Tudor Book of Holidays*, Rand McNally, 1977; *Tasha Tudor's Sampler: A Tale for Easter, Pumpkin Moonshine, [and] The Dolls' Christmas*, McKay, 1977.

Editor: (Self-illustrated) *Book of Fairy Tales*, Platt, 1961; (self-illustrated) *Wings From the Wind: An Anthology of Poems*, Lippincott, 1964; *Tasha Tudor's Favorite Stories*, Lippincott, 1965; *Take Joy! The Tasha Tudor Christmas Book*, Lippincott, 1966.

Illustrator: Mother Goose, *Seventy-Seven Verses*, Walck, 1944; Hans Christian Andersen, *Fairy Tales from Hans Christian Andersen*, Walck, 1945; Robert Louis Stevenson, *Child's Garden of Verses*, Oxford University Press, 1947; Juliana Horatia Ewing, *Jackanapes*, Oxford University Press, 1947; *First Prayers*, Oxford University Press, 1952; Thomas Leighton McCready, Jr., *Biggity Bantam*, Farrar, 1954; McCready, *Pekin White*, Farrar, 1955; *First Graces*, Oxford University Press, 1955; McCready, *Mr. Stubbs*, Farrar, 1956; McCready, *Increase Rabbit* (Junior Literary Guild selection), Farrar, 1958; *And It Was So*, Westminster Press, 1958; McCready, *Adventures of a Beagle*, Farrar, 1959; Rumer Godden, *Doll's House*, Viking, 1962; Frances H. Burnett, *Secret Garden*, Lippincott, 1962; Burnett, *Little Princess*, Lippincott, 1963; Louisa May Alcott, *A Round Dozen: Stories*, Viking, 1963; Bible, *The Twenty-Third Psalm*, St. Onge, 1965; Kenneth Grahame, *The Wind in the Willows*, World Publishing, 1966; Henry A. Shute, *The Real Diary of a Real Boy*, R. R. Smith, 1967; *More Prayers*, Walck, 1967; *First Poems of Childhood*, Platt, 1967; Shute, *Brite and Fair*, Noone House, 1968; Alcott, *Little Women*, World Publishing, 1969; Clement C. Moore, *The Night Before Christmas*, Rand McNally, 1975; Efner Tudor Holmes, *The Christmas Cat*, Crowell, 1976.

SIDELIGHTS: Tasha Tudor claims her love of drawing was inherited from her mother, a portrait painter. As a child, she enjoyed the books of Beatrix Potter, Randolph Caldecott, and Walter Crane, and was influenced by the works of Edmund Dulac, Arthur Rackham, and Hugh Thomson, among others. Her illustrations, done mostly in water color and pencil, are reminiscent of Kate Greenaway.

She has lived most of her life in the countryside of the northeastern United States. She now owns 160 acres in Vermont, living there in the manner of the nineteenth century. Four years ago, her sons Seth and Tom built a reproduction of an old farmhouse, set in a pine clearing unreachable by an ordinary car. Electricity was installed in the unpainted, clapboard house two years ago, but water must still be fetched in buckets from the barn. Tasha Tudor raises all of her food, including cheese and butter. She makes her own candles, spins yarn, and weaves cloth made from her own flax. She wears long calico dresses and no shoes, to save on shoe leather. A menagerie of animals lives with her—ducks, geese, goats, chickens, dogs, and cats.

Tudor and some of her friends who enjoy the life-style of the nineteenth century have formed a group called the Stillwaters. Their aim is to revive the kind of life reminiscent of that era. "We are great venerators of nature," she explained in a recent *New York Times* article, and "believe in peaceful living, in live and let live, and discipline for children."

Tasha Tudor raised and educated her children on the money she earned from the sale of her books. Her first book, *Pumpkin Moonshine*, was written as a Christmas gift for a niece. A *New York Times* critique of *Snow Before Christmas* remarked, "The pictures are charming in color and spirit, and Tasha Tudor has succeeded in capturing that feeling of anticipation in which, for the child, lies in the joy of the Christmas season." Commenting on *Dorcas Porkus*, the *New York Times* wrote: "As always in Tasha Tudor's books, the story is simplicity itself, yet it has lively action and eventfulness in line with a little child's interests. The drawings on every page add distinction and atmosphere and make the setting very convincing.... These little stories are never dull nor perfunctory, for the artist-author has touched them with the magic of the changing seasons ... of firelight and candlelight, cozy kitchens and shady orchards, all homely delights which belong by right to childhood and contribute to joy." Of *1 Is One*, the *Chicago Sunday Tribune* observed, "All the pictures—alternating black and white with delicate pastel colors—have a warm, old fashioned flavor which will captivate the ages."

BIOGRAPHICAL/CRITICAL SOURCES: New York Times, December 14, 1941, October 25, 1942, July 5, 1977; *Chicago Tribune*, November 11, 1956.*

* * *

TULL, Donald S(tanley) 1924-

PERSONAL: Born October 28, 1924, in Cross Timbers, Mo.; son of Raymond Edgar and Ethel (Stanley) Tull; married Marjorie Dobbie (a teacher), May 15, 1948; children: Susan Tull Beyerlein, David, Brooks. *Education:* University of Chicago, S.B., 1948, M.B.A., 1949, Ph.D., 1956. *Home:* 2580 Highland Oaks, Eugene, Ore. 97405. *Office:* Department of Marketing, Transportation, and Business Environment, University of Oregon, Eugene, Ore. 97403.

CAREER: North American Aviation, Downey, Calif., manager of administration, 1954-61; California State University, Fullerton, professor of marketing and quanitative methods, 1961-66, dean of business and economics, 1966-67; University of Oregon, Eugene, professor of marketing, 1967—. Senior Fulbright Professor at University of Skopje, 1974-75. Lecturer in the United States and abroad. Member of advisory committee of U.S. Bureau of the Census, 1976-79; consultant to business corporations. *Military service:* U.S. Naval Reserve, active duty, 1943-46; became lieutenant junior grade. *Member:* American Marketing Association, American Economic Association, American Statistical Association, American Association of University Professors (local president).

WRITINGS: (With Paul E. Green) *Research for Marketing Decisions*, Prentice-Hall, 1966, 4th edition, 1978; (with Gerald S. Albaum) *Survey Research: A Decisional Approach*, Intext Educational, 1973; (with Del I. Hawkins) *Marketing Research: Measurement and Method*, Macmillan, 1976, 2nd edition, 1979.

WORK IN PROGRESS: Marketing Management, publication by Irwin expected in 1981; *Principles of Marketing*, Irwin, 1982.

AVOCATIONAL INTERESTS: European travel.

TULLIS, F. LaMond 1935-

PERSONAL: Born February 10, 1935. Education: Brigham Young University, B.A., 1961, M.A., 1964; Harvard University, M.P.A., 1965, Ph.D., 1969. Religion: Church of Jesus Christ of Latter-day Saints (Mormons). Home: 5046 West 11200th N., Highland, Utah 84003. Office: 374 Maeser Building, Brigham Young University, Provo, Utah 84602.

CAREER: Arizona State University, Tempe, assistant professor of political science, 1968-69; Brigham Young University, Provo, Utah, assistant professor, 1969-70, associate professor, 1970-75, professor of political science, 1975—, chairman of department of government, 1978—. Member of Highland City Council, 1978—. Conducted field research in Bolivia, Peru, Colombia, Panama, Guatemala, Mexico, Brazil, Uruguay, Argentina, Chile, and Paraguay, 1967-76. Consultant to Agency for International Development. Member: Phi Kappa Phi, Pi Sigma Alpha, Sigma Delta Pi. Awards, honors: Social Science Research Council and American Council of Learned Societies fellowship, 1967, for study in Andean South America.

WRITINGS: (Contributor) R. Joseph Monsen, Jr. and Mark W. Cannon, editors, The Makers of Public Policy: American Power Groups and Their Ideologies, McGraw, 1965; Lord and Peasant in Peru: A Paradigm of Political and Social Change, Harvard University Press, 1970; Politics and Social Change in Third World Countries, Wiley, 1973; Modernization in Brazil (monograph), Brigham Young University Press, 1973. Contributor to academic journals.

WORK IN PROGRESS: Religion and Social Mobilization in Latin America; studying agriculture and food production in third-world countries, ethnicity and ethnic conflict, and the Mormon experience in Latin America. Avocational interests: Travel (Latin America).

BIOGRAPHICAL/CRITICAL SOURCES: Comparative Politics, April, 1976.

* * *

TURNER, Edward R(euben) A(rthur) 1924-

PERSONAL: Born August 21, 1924, in Newport, Monmouth, England; son of Charles (a tailor) and Ethel Turner; children: Penelope Jane, Clive Hampton Charles, Helen Kate. Education: Christ's College, Cambridge, M.A., 1951, Ph.D., 1961. Home: Glebe Cottage, Shillingford, St. George, Exeter, England.

CAREER: Brighton College, Sussex, England, head of biology department, 1952-58; University of Exeter, School of Education, Exeter, England, 1958—, began as teacher of environmental studies and head of department, currently director of studies for American students. Military service: British Army, 1946-48; became sergeant.

WRITINGS—All for children, except as noted: (Editor) Animal Behaviour, Basil Blackwell, 1967; (with George Martin) Handbook of Environmental Studies (for teachers), Blond Educational, 1971; (with son, Clive Turner) Frogs and Toads, Priory Press, 1974; (with C. Turner) Bats, Priory Press, 1974; (with C. Turner) Snakes and Lizards, Priory Press, 1974.

WORK IN PROGRESS: Studying architectural evolution and architecture of Exeter, England.

SIDELIGHTS: Turner writes: "By founding a department of environmental studies in late career a strong interest developed in a variety of subjects, particularly architecture, archaeology, and fine art. As a biologist I was irresistably drawn to examine architecture in the light of an evolutionary process—hence, the current writing on 'A Biologist Looks at Architecture.' This book is an attempt to combine two disciplines not traditionally connected."

AVOCATIONAL INTERESTS: Travel, golf, gardening, construction work, "one of the worst classical guitarists in southwest England, marginally, but arguably, better as a painter on a good day."

* * *

TWADDELL, W(illiam) F(reeman) 1906-

PERSONAL: Born March 22, 1906, in Rye, N.Y.; son of William Powell (a musician) and Emily May (Fawcett) Twaddell; married Helen Treadway Johnson, December 21, 1930; children: Stephen Treadway, James Freeman, William Hartshorne. Education: Duke University, A.B., 1926; Harvard University, M.A., 1927, Ph.D., 1930. Politics: Independent. Religion: None. Home: 78 Oriole Ave., Providence, R.I. 02906.

CAREER: University of Wisconsin, Madison, instructor, 1929-31, assistant professor, 1931-34, associate professor, 1935-37, professor of German, 1937-46; Brown University, Providence, R.I., professor of Germanic languages, 1946-71, professor emeritus, 1971—, chairman of department of linguistics, 1960-68. Fulbright lecturer in Egypt, 1954-55, and the Philippines, 1968; visiting professor at University of Hamburg, summer, 1955, Princeton University, 1957-58, University of Michigan, Stanford University, and University of Indiana. Consultant to U.S. Information Agency.

MEMBER: Modern Language Association of America (member of executive council, 1967-71), Linguistic Society of America (president, 1957), American Academy of Arts and Sciences, Institut fuer deutsche Sprache (member of council), Phi Beta Kappa, Phi Delta Theta. Awards, honors: Fellowship from Princeton University's Humanities Council, 1957-58; Litt. D. from Duke University, 1964.

WRITINGS: On Defining the Phoneme (monograph), Waverly, 1935; (with Helmut Rehder) Conversational German for Beginning and Refresher Courses, Holt, 1944; (with Rehder) German, Holt, 1947, 3rd edition, 1960; The English Verb Auxiliaries, Brown University Press, 1960, 2nd edition, 1963; Foreign Language Instruction at the Second Level, Holt, 1963; (with Rehder and Ursula Thomas) Verstehen und Sprechen, Holt, 1970, revised edition, 1970; (with Rehder and R.M.S. Heffner) Goethe, Faust, student's edition, 2 volumes, University of Wisconsin Press, 1975; (with Thomas) Lesestoff Nach Wahl, Volume I: Einfuhrung, Volume II: Physik und Chemie, Volume III: Mensch und Gesellschaft, Volume IV: Biologie, Volume V: Literatur, Volume VI: Teacher's Manual, University of Wisconsin Press, 1977; (translator from the German) Conrad F. Meyer, The Saint, Brown University Press, 1977. Contributor to learned journals.

* * *

TYLER, Converse 1903(?)-1978

OBITUARY NOTICE: Born c. 1903 in Atlantic City, N.J.; died September 22, 1978, in Silver Spring, Md. Public relations official and playwright. Tyler was most recently employed by the American Red Cross. Previously he was on the public information staff of Admiral Richard Byrd's second Antarctic expedition and was the play-reading division chief of the National Theatre Project during the 1930's. He wrote several plays. Obituaries and other sources: Washington Post, September 23, 1978.

U

UHNAK, Dorothy 1933-

PERSONAL: Born in 1933, in Bronx, N.Y.; married Tony Uhnak (an electrical engineer); children: Tracy. *Education:* Attended City College (now of the City University of New York); John Jay College of Criminal Justice of the City University of New York, B.S., 1968. *Residence:* Queens, N.Y. *Address:* c/o Simon & Schuster, Simon & Schuster Building, 1230 Avenue of the Americas, New York, N.Y. 10020.

CAREER: New York City Transit Police, New York, N.Y., 1953-67, began as policewoman, became detective second grade; full-time writer, 1967—. Former counselor-group leader for Rivington Street settlement house, the Family Welfare Shelter, and an East Bronx settlement house. *Awards, honors:* Outstanding Police Duty Medal from the New York City Transit Police, 1955, for heroism above and beyond the call of duty; Edgar for the best first mystery from the Mystery Writers of America, 1968, for *The Bait.*

WRITINGS—Novels; all published by Simon & Schuster: *Policewoman: A Young Woman's Initiation Into the Realities of Justice* (semi-autobiographical), 1964; *The Bait,* 1968; *The Witness,* 1969; *The Ledger,* 1970; *Law and Order* (Literary Guild selection), 1973; *The Investigation* (Literary Guild selection), 1977.

WORK IN PROGRESS: A novel, *The Crime.*

SIDELIGHTS: The authenticity of Dorothy Uhnak's novels has been unanimously praised by critics. It is small wonder: the books all reflect her fourteen years of experience in the New York City Transit Police. While serving as a policewoman and detective, Uhnak routinely dealt with thieves, muggers, and rapists. On one occasion she disarmed an attacker who was holding a gun to her forehead, an act of bravery for which she received an Outstanding Police Duty Medal. Many commentators believe the heroine of three of Uhnak's novels, Christie Opara, Detective Second Grade on the New York District Attorney's Special Investigation Squad, is closely modeled after the author. A *Washington Post* reviewer has stated that Opara "is a mirror image of her creator and is true, both environmentally and emotionally, to the life of a policewoman." According to Margo Jefferson, Uhnak's experience as a cop lends believability not only to her portrayal of Christie Opara but also to her depiction of the criminal world in general: "Dorothy Uhnak's strength lies in her firm, unsentimental knowledge of the harsh world of crime, police work and city politics."

Uhnak's flair for realism sometimes makes it difficult to distinguish fact from fiction. In struggling to pinpoint the genre of her first book, *Policewoman,* commentators alternately described it as "semi-documentary," "a semi-autobiographical novel," and "nonfiction." Uhnak herself referred to *Policewoman* as "fictionalized fact." The boundary between actuality and literary fabrication becomes even less distinct in Uhnak's most recent novel, *The Investigation.* Reviewers noted that the situation set forth in the book, in which a young woman with gangland connections is accused of killing her two children, closely parallels the Alice Crimmins murder case that occurred in New York City in 1965. "One would have to be a cretin, or to have been living on Mars the last five years, not to recognize similarities between Alice Crimmins and Kitty Keeler, the central figure in Dorothy Uhnak's new novel," John Leonard remarked. Uhnak, however, has repeatedly asserted that her book is not patterned after the real crime. She told an interviewer, "I can honestly say that Kitty Keeler is not Alice Crimmins." Because of the resemblance between the plot and the circumstances surrounding the Crimmins case, *The Investigation* has regenerated a long-standing debate on the morality of the fictional reconstruction of crime.

Concerning her creative processes, Uhnak once told an interviewer: "I'm an instinctive writer, and I didn't want anyone tampering with my style. I write about very hard situations and in a strong way. In my novels I'm concerned with people who just happen to be policemen. What people say and do is what interests me."

Uhnak's books on policewoman Christie Opara were the basis for a television series, "Get Christy Love." Paramount has acquired the movie rights for *Law and Order* and *The Investigation.*

AVOCATIONAL INTERESTS: Animals, bicycling, and swimming.

BIOGRAPHICAL/CRITICAL SOURCES: Saturday Review, March 28, 1964; *New York Times Book Review,* April 28, 1968, December 1, 1968, December 14, 1969, August 21, 1977, September 25, 1977; *New York Times,* March 8, 1971, August 1, 1977, October 5, 1977; *Newsweek,* March 22, 1971, August 22, 1977; *Washington Post,* March 27, 1971; *Akron Beacon Journal,* April 29, 1973; *People,* October 24, 1977.*

UHR, Carl George 1911-

PERSONAL: Born October 20, 1911, in Karlstad, Sweden; came to the United States in 1929, naturalized U.S. citizen, 1937; son of Josef A. E. (an engineer) and Agnes C. (Olson) Uhr; married Miriam Goldstein (deceased); married Patricia Jean Robbins (a writer, under name Patricia Robbins Beatty). *Education:* Reed College, B.A., 1934; University of California, Berkeley, M.A., 1939, 1943, Ph.D., 1950. *Politics:* Democrat. *Home:* 5085 Rockledge Dr., Riverside, Calif. 92506. *Office:* Department of Economics, University of California, Riverside, Calif. 92521.

CAREER: University of San Francisco, San Francisco, Calif., assistant professor of economics, 1947-51; director of Research of Study Commission on Unemployment Insurance, 1951-54; University of California, Riverside, assistant professor, 1954-58, associate professor, 1958-63, professor of economics, 1963—, head of department, 1959-60, 1964-66, also director of education abroad program, 1966-68. National research professor at Brookings Institution, 1957-58; visiting professor at Swedish School of Economics (Finland), 1961-62, 1966, University of Lund, 1966-68, and University of Melbourne, 1972. Consultant to Social Security Administration. *Wartime service:* Regional economist based in San Francisco, 1943-47.

MEMBER: American Economic Association, History of Economics Society (president, 1977-78), Royal Economic Society, Western Economic Association. *Awards, honors:* Brookings Institution National Research professorship award, 1957-58; Fulbright grants for Finland, 1961, 1962, and 1966, and Australia, 1970.

WRITINGS: Economic Doctrines of Knut Wicksell, University of California Press, 1960; *Sweden's Employment Security Program and Its Impact on the Country's Economy* (monograph), Benefits and Insurance Research Center, California Institute of Technology, 1960; (with Michael Theodore Wermel) *Financial Prospects for the California Unemployment Insurance Program in the 1960's* (monograph), Senate of the State of California, 1961; *Development of Capital Theory and Enterprise Economics from Medieval Times* (textbook), Random House, 1962; *Anders Chydenius, 1729-1803: A Finnish Predecessor to Adam Smith,* Swedish School of Economics, 1964; *Economics in Brief* (monograph), Random House, 1966; *Sweden's Social Security System: An Appraisal of Its Economic Impact in the Postwar Period,* U.S. Department of Health, Education & Welfare, 1967; *Economic Doctrines of David Davidson,* University of Uppsala Press, 1975. Contributor of nearly fifty articles to professional journals.

WORK IN PROGRESS: Studying the writings of nineteenth-century mathematical economist, Heinrich von Mangoldt; research on capital theory and theory of economic growth.

SIDELIGHTS: Uhr speaks Swedish, Norwegian, Danish, German, French, and reads Finnish.

* * *

UMSTEAD, William Lee 1921-

PERSONAL: Born July 23, 1921, in Durham, N.C.; son of William Lee (a tobacconist) and Sally (Breeze) Umstead; married June Myers, February 18, 1949; children: William Lee III, Eric, Robin. *Education:* Attended George Washington University, 1939-43. *Home:* 5 Heatherbloom Rd., White Plains, N.Y. 10605. *Office:* New York News, 220 East 42nd St., New York, N.Y. 10017.

CAREER/WRITINGS: International News Service, Washington, D.C., reporter and editor, 1941-58; United Press International, Washington, D.C., night editor, 1958-67; *New York News,* New York City, news editor in Washington D.C., 1967-69, night managing editor in New York City, 1969—. Notable assignments include coverage of the Adlai Stevenson campaign, 1952, national political conventions since 1952, and the House of Representatives, 1952-54, and the direction of *Daily News* polls since 1972. *Military service:* U.S. Air Force, 1943-45; became staff sergeant; received Purple Heart, Air Medal with two oak leaf clusters, and seven battle stars. *Member:* National Press Club.

* * *

UNGS, Thomas D(ale) 1928-

PERSONAL: Born October 3, 1928, in Dyersville, Iowa; son of Charles (in business) and Leona (Holscher) Ungs; married Theresa Mae Lamm (a registered nurse), August 13, 1955; children: Susan Mary, Elizabeth, Andrea, Lisa, Matthew. *Education:* University of Iowa, B.A., 1951, M.A., 1952, Ph.D., 1957. *Politics:* Democrat. *Religion:* Roman Catholic. *Home:* 3525 Bluff Point Dr., Knoxville, Tenn. 37920. *Office:* Department of Political Science, University of Tennessee, Knoxville, Tenn. 37916.

CAREER: University of North Dakota, Grand Forks, assistant professor of political science, 1957-60; Wichita State University, Wichita, Kan., assistant professor, 1960-64, associate professor of political science, 1964-68; Kent State University, Kent, Ohio, professor of political science and chairman of department, 1968-71; University of Tennessee, Knoxville, professor of political science, chairman of department, and director of Bureau of Public Administration, all 1971—. *Military service:* U.S. Army, 1952-54. *Member:* American Political Science Association, American Society for Public Administration, American Association of University Professors, Law and Society Association, Southern Political Science Association, Tennessee Political Science Association (president, 1977-78), Pi Sigma Alpha.

WRITINGS: (With Dan Nimmo) *American Political Patterns: Conflict and Consensus,* Little, Brown, 1966, 4th edition, in press; (contributor) Nimmo and C. M. Bonjean, editors, *Political Attitudes and Public Opinion,* McKay, 1972. Also author of *Consensus and American Politics.* Contributor to political science, social science, and law journals.

* * *

UPJOHN, Everard M(iller) 1903-1978

OBITUARY NOTICE—See index for *CA* sketch: Born November 7, 1903, in Scranton, Pa.; died November 3, 1978, in Hightstown, N.J. Educator and author best known for his key role in shaping and revising humanities and art history courses at Columbia University. Upjohn also developed the arts program at the University of Minnesota during the early 1930's. His writings include *Richard Upjohn, Architect and Churchman* and *History of World Art.* Obituaries and other sources: *Who's Who in American Art,* Bowker, 1973; *Directory of American Scholars,* Volume I: *History,* 6th edition, Bowker, 1974; *Who's Who in America,* 40th edition, Marquis, 1978; *New York Times,* November 8, 1978.

* * *

UPTON, Arvin 1914-

PERSONAL: Born April 8, 1914, in Upton, Ky.; son of Arvin Edward and Jennie (Ferrill) Upton. *Education:* Western Kentucky University, A.B., 1933; Harvard University, J.D., 1940. *Politics:* Democrat. *Religion:* Episcopalian. *Home and office:* 1239 31st St. N.W., Washington, D.C. 20007. *Agent:* Patricia Falk Feeley, 52 Vanderbilt Ave., New York, N.Y. 10017.

CAREER: Admitted to the Bar of Kentucky, 1939, and the Bar of Washington, D.C., 1953; executive assistant in child welfare for Kentucky Department of Welfare, 1936-39; Ogden, Galphin, Tarrant & Street (law firm), Louisville, Ky., attorney, 1940-43; assistant executive director of Foreign Liquidation Commission, 1946-47; Hammond, Harvey, Braxton Co., New York City, associate, 1947-48; U.S. Air Force, associate general counsel, 1950-52, deputy general counsel, 1952-53, special consultant to secretary of the Air Force, 1953; LeBoeuf, Lamb, Leiby & MacRae, Washington, D.C. and New York City, senior partner in Washington, 1953-75; writer, 1975—. Secretary of Atomic Power Development Association, Inc.; chairperson of D.C. Health & Welfare Council; first vice-president of Episcopal Home for Children; president of Pastoral Institute of United Community Services of Washington. *Military service:* U.S. Army, 1943-46; became major. *Member:* American Bar Association, Bar Association of Washington, D.C., International Nuclear Law Association, City Club (Georgetown), Harvard Club (New York City), Metropolitan Club (Washington). *Awards, honors:* Air Force exceptional civilian service award, 1953.

WRITINGS: Lorenzino (novel), Norton, 1977.

WORK IN PROGRESS: Truth and Consequences (tentative title), a novel set in Washington, D.C., 1949-52.

SIDELIGHTS: Upton told *CA:* "I always wanted to write but was too busy with a conventional career until recently. Art is the only thing that makes human life and society tolerable. My first novel drew on my personal experiences very indirectly."

* * *

UPTON, Joseph C(heshire) N(ash) 1946-

PERSONAL: Born January 4, 1946, in Washington, D.C.; son of Thomas Graydon and Ann (Nash) Upton; married Susanna Stillman Taylor (a teacher), July 9, 1972 (divorced). *Education:* Harvard University, B.A., 1969; graduate study at University of Rhode Island, 1970. *Home:* 817 Bulls Neck Rd., McLean, Va. 22101; and Vinalhaven, Me. 04863.

CAREER: Owner and operator of fishing vessels for fisheries in Washington, Alaska, and Maine, 1970—. Fishing gear designer, 1971; consultant to United Nations. *Member:* Friends of the Earth.

WRITINGS: Alaska Blues (nonfiction), Alaska Northwest Publishing, 1977. Contributor to fishermen's journals and newspapers.

WORK IN PROGRESS: A book about the Gulf of Maine herring fishery; a book about alternative energies and present policy.

SIDELIGHTS: Upton writes: "My career, as such, is one of operating my boat in a fishery for about six months of the year and spending the rest of the time in writing, citizen action stuff, or alternate sources of energy work. In addition to this I am trying to design and, if it looks feasible, get financing for a seventy-five-foot steam and sail fishing schooner for southeastern Alaska, to demonstrate the feasibility of using renewable resources for fuel.

"I thought of writing full time, but fishing commercially for

part of the year seems to be a good balance for now. In the fall I just want to tie up my boat and settle down and write, and in the spring it excites me to set my boat and gear together and face the new season."

* * *

UTKE, Allen R(ay) 1936-

PERSONAL: Born February 5, 1936, in Moline, Ill.; son of Harold E. and Alexis N. (Anderson) Utke; married Jean Ann Rinell, September 14, 1957 (divorced June 7, 1971); married Janice Lynn Verbruggen, June 16, 1972; children: Steven Mark, Sharon Lee, Michael Kevin. *Education:* Augustana College, Rock Island, Ill., B.A., 1958; Iowa State University, M.S., 1961, Ph.D., 1963. *Politics:* Independent. *Religion:* Lutheran. *Home:* 1648 Western St., Oshkosh, Wis. 54901. *Office:* Department of Chemistry, University of Wisconsin, Oshkosh, Wis. 54901.

CAREER: Pittsburgh Plate Glass Co., Corpus Christi, Tex., senior research chemist, 1963-64; University of Wisconsin, Oshkosh, assistant professor, 1964-69, associate professor of chemistry, 1969—. Organizer of seminars and workshops; delegate to Wisconsin Council of Churches convention. *Member:* Sigma Xi, Alpha Chi Sigma, Phi Lambda Epsilon.

WRITINGS: Bio-Babel: Can We Survive the New Biology?, John Knox, 1978. Contributor to local magazines and *Friar.*

WORK IN PROGRESS: Everything You Should Have Known About Energy But Always Neglected to Ask; Come, Let Us Bottle God!, completion expected in 1981.

SIDELIGHTS: Utke writes: "In 1968, I read *The Biological Time Bomb* by Gordon Rattray Taylor, after rather casually purchasing the book while on a trip. The book had caught my eye because it was a best-seller, and because it dealt with DNA, biochemistry, and the interface between chemistry and biology. The book was subsequently to change my life, for I found it to be greatly disturbing, in addition to being deeply interesting. I hadn't realized that science had made so much progress in the 1950's and 1960's toward possibly being able to alter man physically and mentally, and control the evolutionary process itself. And I found Taylor's warnings about what it could all eventually mean to be frightening as well as simply thought-provoking.

"In 1971 I attended a Chautauqua-type short course on the societal implications of genetics, held at Field Museum in Chicago. The course, and data which I soon obtained from using the exercise it offered, convinced me that there was a great need for more societal thought about the 'new biology' and the possible societal consequences which it could produce.

"The 'biological revolution' took almost a quantum leap forward in the early 1970's with the sudden, largely-unexpected emergence of a series of dramatically new developments which even people like Taylor had not foreseen. Those included such things as the first successful genetic engineering experiment performed on human cells, the initiation of recombinant DNA research at Stanford University, the synthesis of the first fully-functional gene, et cetera. Such developments convinced me that the 'biological revolution' had entered a new, accelerated stage, and that earlier books on the subject were now outdated.

"The late 1960's and early 1970's were also periods of great transition and even turmoil in education, government, and science. Laymen were feeling less confident about the supposed benefits of science and technology. Students were demanding 'relevance' in the curriculum, many educators were initiating coursework and research in futurism and futuristics, the government was establishing an office of technology assessments, activists were demanding 'conscience and responsibility' from scientists, and even scientists themselves were recommending a greater societal role for themselves, more social concern and involvement, greater interdisciplinary efforts, and a greater effort to educate the layman in scientific principles and issues.

"Thus, I began to see both a challenge and a responsibility in the 'new biology.' My goal in writing is to draw attention to missed opportunities and responsibilities, including effective communication of the nature of science and theology to the layman, effective and meaningful engagement in social action, attempts to delineate and mold the future of society, alleviation of the 'future shock' that seems to permeate society today, and attempts to modernize and revitalize the God concept and make it more meaningful for twentieth-century man, and hopefully to help direct both science and religion toward the extremely important interface that exists between them."

AVOCATIONAL INTERESTS: All sports (especially tennis and basketball), travel (including Mexico, England, Italy, and Greece).

*   *   *

UTLEY, Freda 1898-1978

PERSONAL: Born January 23, 1898, in London, England; came to United States, 1939; naturalized U.S. citizen, 1950; daugher of William Herbert and Emily (Williamson) Utley; married Arcadi Berdichevsky, 1928; children: Jon Basil. *Education:* King's College, London, B.A. (first class honors), 1923; graduate study at Westfield College, London, 1924-25; London School of Economics and Political Science, London, M.A. (with distinction), 1925. *Residence:* Washington, D.C.

CAREER: Author, journalist, lecturer. University of London, London School of Economics and Political Science, London, England, research fellow, 1926-28; *Manchester Guardian,* special correspondent in Japan, 1928-29; Institute of World Economy and Politics, Moscow, U.S.S.R., senior scientific researcher, 1930-36; *London News Chronicle,* China War correspondent, 1938; Starr, Park & Freeman, Inc., New York, N.Y., economic adviser, 1940-44; *Readers Digest,* correspondent in China, 1944-45, and in Germany, 1948; correspondent for *Pathfinder* and *Freeman,* 1952-53. Director of America-China Policy Association, Inc. Member of department of politics advisory council, Princeton University, 1941-47; consultant to Chinese Supply Commission, 1944-45. Guest on radio and television shows, including "Invitation to Learning," "Author Meets the Critics," and "Court of Current Issues."

WRITINGS: (Translator) W. Astrov, A. Slepkov, and J. Thomas, editors, *An Illustrated History of the Russian Revolution,* International Publishers, 1928; *Lancashire and the Far East,* Allen & Unwin, 1931; *Japan's Feet of Clay,* Norton, 1937; *Japan Can Be Stopped!,* London News Chronicle Publications Department, 1937; *Japan's Gamble in China,* Secker & Warburg, 1938; *China at War,* Faber, 1939; *The Dream We Lost: Soviet Russia Then and Now,* John Day, 1940, revised edition published as *Lost Illusion,* Allen & Unwin, 1949, Regnery, 1959; *Last Chance in China,* Bobbs-Merrill, 1947; *The High Cost of Vengeance,* Regnery, 1949; *The China Story,* Regnery, 1951; *Will the Middle East Go*

West?, Regnery, 1957; *Odyssey of a Liberal: Memoirs,* Washington National Press, 1970.

SIDELIGHTS: Utley was a Socialist leader in London before joining the British Communist party after the 1926 General Strike. Later, when she had given up all hope that her husband, a Russian Jew, survived Soviet imprisonment, she wrote *The Dream We Lost*—her account of the six years she and her husband spent together in the Communist country. "I failed in my youth to perceive that Communism is a substitute for religion," she reflected in 1948. "The instinctive desire for a religion was the compelling force leading me step by step into the Communist trap." In 1970, Utley offered further insight into her Communist activities: "My own case proves that it is not necessarily, or even primarily, poverty or lack of opportunity which makes Communists, since it was only after I began to earn a good income that I joined the Communist Party."

While concern for her husband's life forced her to keep secret her hatred for the "Stalinist tyranny," Utley published several books on China and Japan before *The Dream We Lost. China at War* summarized her experiences as war correspondent for the *London News Chronicle.* Her study of contemporary Japan, *Japan's Feet of Clay,* was banned there while receiving favorable reviews in the United States. W. H. Mallory felt "it is a pity that the Japanese cannot read Dr. Utley's work, for there is enough basis for her criticisms to make them useful." Eventually, "finding it more and more difficult to hold either my tongue or pen concerning the Soviet Union and Communism," she released *The Dream We Lost* in 1940.

The "thorny and indominatable" Utley was often the center of controversy. Her pre-World War II warnings about Japan and the U.S.S.R. brought many admirers, but also the threat of deportation. Only after several influentials came to her defense, including Congressman Jerry Voorhis, was she permitted to remain in the United States.

Utley lost no ability to probe the disputable in the 1950's. R. L. Walker explained some circumstances surrounding *The China Story:* "[She was] one of the key witnesses against Owen Lattimore in the Tydings Committee investigation [in 1950] of Senator Joseph R. McCarthy's charges of Communist influence in the U.S. Department of State. Since this is her answer to Lattimore's *Ordeal By Slander,* it must in all fairness be read by those who have read that volume." In *Will the Middle East Go West?* she "marshalled her considerable knowledge of Communism and the Far East, and [wrote] . . . a timely warning to the Arabs and the West." Herschel Williams outlined her message: "In a clear-cut presentation Miss Utley sets forth an Arab-China 'deadly parallel' which, if recognized by the American people and their leaders, she feels might yet prevent the Arab world from taking the same route to Communism that China has traveled."

Pearl Buck once explained Utley's character as the misfortune of having "a brilliant mind, rigorously truthful in its working, though born unhappily in the body of a woman." John Chamberlain, meanwhile, admitted "this judgment may have some value," but "the fact is that Freda Utley's running battle with the four of five Establishments under which she was doomed to live in various parts of the world had little to do with her sex. . . . Her troubles have all derived from a continually renewed temperament and the tentative mind of the scientist who insists that judgments must be held lightly lest one be locked into hypotheses long after they have failed to meet the tests of experience."

Utley detailed her stormy career in her 1970 memoirs, *The Odyssey of a Liberal*. Her portraits of the times and personalities of half a century met applause from Russell Kirk. "Indeed, she has known our time and its afflictions as have few other people," Kirk wrote. "Her sketches of Bloomsbury existence in the twenties, of Russian existence under Stalin, . . . of China devastated by war and ideology, of Greenwhich Village in the forties, and of Washington intrigue more recently . . . are the work of an involved observer pitilessly realistic and penetrating."

In particular interest to Utley was Bertrand Russell, whom she revered as "a philosopher and a humanitarian," thus allowing her to dismiss his "terrific sexual urges which were the accompaniment of his genius." Among other notables, Utley scrutinized Pearl Buck, Virginia Woolf, Chiang Kai-Shek, and George Bernard Shaw, who, according to Henry C. Wolfe, "emerges from the letters as a not very admirable human being."

Reviewers had several objections to Utley's memoirs while praising the whole of her "stormy chronicle." Kirk noted the "book is set in lamentable small type and blemished by misprints. Yet it ought to be read widely." Chamberlain criticized Utley's criticism of others: "Though her portraits are just for the most part, Freda Utley is not consistent in her ability to forgive. . . . But this double standard of forgiveness is only a minor blot on her book. If she had been other than she is, she would never have gone into hell to return with such a searing documentary as *The Dream We Lost*. And she would never have had the life that has resulted in the rich pages of her *Odyssey of a Liberal* (meaning, of course, a liberal in the old-fashioned sense)."

An old-fashioned liberal? At one time Utley herself was not sure of an appropriate label: "I do not know whether in the parlance of our time I am now a liberal or a conservative, a progressive or a reactionary." But she did offer a tempered definition of herself in the light of that "much-abused word" in the preface to *The Odyssey of a Liberal*: "The belief that we can ourselves create a better world makes life purposeful and worth living—however dim the hope becomes as we grow old. Thus, I suppose I am still a liberal within the original meaning of that much-abused word, although having learned through experience more than is dreamed of in the philosophy of most Western liberals, I no longer share their faith in the inevitability of progress and the perfectibility of man through the creation of a better material environment."

BIOGRAPHICAL/CRITICAL SOURCES: New York Times, April 18, 1937, May 16, 1948, May 13, 1951, December 8, 1957; *Saturday Review of Literature*, September 28, 1940, May 1, 1948; *Herald Tribune Book Review*, May 20, 1951, December 29, 1957; Freda Utley, *Odyssey of a Liberal: Memoirs*, Washington National Press, 1970; *National Review*, February 10, 1970; *Saturday Review*, March 28, 1970; *New York Times Book Review*, April 19, 1970; *Choice*, May, 1970; *Modern Age*, summer, 1970; *Esquire*, October, 1970.

OBITUARIES: New York Times, January 23, 1978; *Washington Post*, January 25, 1978; *Time*, February 6, 1978.*

(Died January 22, 1978, in Washington, D.C.)

V

VALENS, Evans G.

WRITINGS: A Long Way Up: The Story of Jill Kinmont, Harper, 1966; (with Berenice Abbott) *Attractive Universe: Gravity and the Shape of Space* (juvenile), Collins & World, 1969; *The Other Side of the Mountain,* Warner Books, 1975; *The Other Side of the Mountain II,* Warner Books, 1978.

SIDELIGHTS: Valens's writings have been largely devoted to chronicling the life of Jill Kinmont, a skier who suffered severe injuries in an accident. Kinmont, who was slated as an American hopeful in the 1956 Olympics, emerged from her mishap with paralysis of motor and sensory capabilities. Her struggle to cope with her disabilities and adapt is an admirable one and she eventually became sufficiently independent to become a teacher. Further hardships and traumas have been the subject of succeeding books.

Both *The Other Side of the Mountain* and its sequel have been adapted for film.*

* * *

Van WEDDINGEN, Marthe 1924-
(Claire Dumas)

PERSONAL: Born July 12, 1924, in Herck-la-Ville, Belgium; daughter of Emile (a lawyer) and Germaine (Strauven) Van Weddingen. *Education:* Free University of Brussels, received degree in law. *Politics:* None. *Religion:* None. *Home and office:* Domaine de la Mirayette, Le Luc, France 83340.

CAREER: Solicitor in law courts in Brussels, Belgium, 1955-69; writer, 1975—. *Awards, honors:* Prix de l'Ete from the city of Cannes, France, 1975, for *L'Herbe chaude.*

WRITINGS—Under pseudonym Claire Dumas: *L'Herbe chaude* (novel), Grasset, 1975, translation by Jennifer Malkin published as *The Stranger,* Ballantine, 1977; *Un Ete d'orages* (novel; title means "A Stormy Summer"), Grasset, 1978.

Author of radio play, "Banlieue" (title means "Suburb"), aired on French radio, September 23, 1978.

WORK IN PROGRESS: A novel, *La Grande Fatigue* (title means "The Great Fatigue"), for Grasset.

SIDELIGHTS: Van Weddingen told *CA:* "Writing has always been essential to me. I think I can't live happily without reading and writing. Even as a child I wrote a lot: diaries, letters, short stories. During my career as a solicitor I was short of free time, but as soon as I came to live in the south of France, a very peaceful place, I wrote again and, for the first time, thought about being published.

"I was a career woman and now I live in the country and don't meet many people. This gives me, I think, a particular view on the two kinds of lives women can have: working or staying at home. The two novels I wrote, and the play as well, reflect this experience.

"I want to write novels about love, friendship, nature, solitude, disillusionment and fright; about women, what they are, and what they are trying to be; about men and the lives of couples. I want to write about obsessions, happiness, personal life, liberty, death, and truth. I don't care about religion or politics. I care about human beings and animals, about nature and the sun, about life—what it is and what it could be—and about our duties and powers with respect to ourselves, our happiness, and our personal values and liberty.

"I believe in imagination. The first fight—and the delight!—of a writer is to create a world that doesn't exist, and that readers will recognize and accept as real.

"I enjoyed the fact that *L'Herbe chaude* was adapted for French television (September 27, 1978). It was a very rich experience for me. I also took great interest in the writing of the radio play 'Banlieue.' It is a totally different kind of writing. I enjoyed it."

* * *

VASSILIKOS, Vassilis 1933-

PERSONAL: Born November 18, 1933, in Kavala, Greece; son of Nicolas and Katy (Zaphizion) Vassilikos; married Dimitra Atsedes (a painter and pianist), June 29, 1960. *Education:* Attended Anatolia College, 1946-52; University of Salonika, diploma in law, 1956. *Politics:* Communist. *Religion:* Greek Orthodox. *Home:* Solomonitov 52-54, Athens 509, Greece. *Agent:* Eric Linder, A.L.I., Corso Mettestti 3, Milano, Italy.

CAREER: Assistant director of documentary films, 1961; *Tachydromos* (weekly magazine), Athens, Greece, freelance reporter, 1962-63; full-time writer, 1963—. *Awards, honors:* Grant from Ford Foundation, 1960.

WRITINGS—In English: *To phyllo; To pegadi; T'ag-*

geliasma: A Trilogy, three volumes, Vivliopoleion tes Hestias, 1961, translation by Edmund Keeley and Mary Keeley published as *The Plant; The Well; The Angel: A Trilogy,* Knopf, 1964; *Hoi photographies,* Bibliopoleon tes Hestias, 1964, translation by Mike Edwards published as *The Photographs,* Harcourt, 1971; *Zeta,* Ekdoseis Themelio, 1966, translation by Marilyn Calmann published as *Z,* Farrar, Straus, 1968; *Outside the Walls* (collection of newspaper articles), translated by Edwards, Harcourt, 1973; *The Harpoon Gun,* translated by Barbara Bray, Harcourt, 1973; *O monarchis,* translation published as *The Monarch,* Bobbs-Merrill, 1976.

Other: *He diegese tou Iasona,* Oikos G. Phexe, 1962; *He mythologia tes Amerikes,* Vivliopoleion tes Hestias, 1963, 2nd edition, 1970; *Ektos ton teichon,* Ekdoseis Themelio, 1966; *Thymata eirenes,* Vivliopolein tes Hestias, 1970; *Kapheneion Emigkrek ho Hagios Klaudios,* Ekdoseis Themelio, 1972, 2nd edition, Pleias, 1973; *Synantese me ton helio,* Ekdoseis, 1972; (translator) Regis Debray, *Mathainontas ap' tous Toupamaros,* Ekdoseis, 1972; *Anamneseis apo ton Cheirona kai alles histories,* Vivliopoleion tes Hestias, 1975.

SIDELIGHTS: One of the premier Greek novelists, Vassilikos's approach to writing is similar to James Joyce's. "Vassilikos is an original," wrote George Giannaris: "He breaks words down into their original meaning, and through the etymologies and anagrammatisms he injects a dose of humor which contributes to a pleasant reading of the 'printed' word." Despite being "pleasant reading," Vassilikos's style requires patience on the reader's part. His "narrative is difficult to follow," noted Giannaris, "but if the reader is able to do so, he will enjoy the black humor and manner in which the human condition is ridiculed. . . ."

Again, like Joyce, Vassilikos often employs heavy symbolism in his work. This is never more evident than in his novel, *The Photographs.* It is the story of a man, Lazarus, who lives in Necropolis ("Dead City"). Lazarus, it may be remembered, is one of the characters in the Bible who returns from the dead. And to further mask things, Lazarus turns into a cat!

A consistent element in Vassilikos's writings is politics. *The Harpoon Gun,* a collection of short stories and two novels, is built around the subject of exile. *The Harpoon Gun,* wrote Edwin Jahiel, "is not entertainment or a stylistic exercise. . . . It is essentially a treatise on sociopolitical conditions, but of such a specifically Greek nature that allusions, references, and 'personnages a cle' will be fully appreciated only by those readers . . . who are able to become involved in the protracted dialectics of the Resistance."

Perhaps Vassilikos's best known work in the United States is *Z.* Like *The Harpoon Gun* (which it preceded), *Z* is concerned with politics and exile as a reaction to it. *Z* is the story of Greek Socialist figure Lambrakis's murder. As Peter Sourian observed, "At the end of that book, the fates of those involved in the affair are told: evil was handsomely rewarded and ordinary decency carried a heavy price." Sourian continues by stating: "One price can be exile, a Greek solution to political questions. . . . Vassilikos himself, since *Z* was banned by the present Government, has lived in exile from his own country. . . ."

An alternative to exile is proposed in *The Monarch.* Kimon Friar wrote that "an individual integrity is insisted on as blossoming apart from the inroads of historical necessity. There is an acceptance of a new order of life wherein the masses may be freed of exploitation but where the individual

also may retain his unique freedom, a planned economy that establishes a give and take between these two equal forces. . . ."

One of Vassilikos's merits is that he doesn't allow his artistic goals to conflict. "Vassilikos almost always remembers that he is first of all a novelist," wrote Robert J. Clements. "He accepts experimental techniques as compatible with his didactic purpose and as by no means an intrusion of form into content."

BIOGRAPHICAL/CRITICAL SOURCES: Saturday Review/World, November 16, 1968; *Book World,* May 9, 1971; *New York Times Book Review,* May 6, 1973, August 15, 1976; *Books Abroad,* spring, 1974, summer, 1976, autumn, 1976; *Contemporary Literary Criticism,* Gale, Volume 4, 1975, Volume 8, 1978.

*   *   *

VAUGHAN, Alan   1936-

PERSONAL: Born December 28, 1936, in Akron, Ohio; son of Robert Lorn (an engineer) and Millie (Denny) Vaughan; married Iris Collins, April 15, 1967 (divorced, 1971); married Diane Dudley (a secretary), June 20, 1975; children: (second marriage) Lauren Roberta. *Education:* University of Akron, A.B., 1958; graduate study at Rutgers University, 1958-59, New School for Social Research, 1966-67, and College of Psychic Studies, London, England, and University of Freiburg, both 1967-68. *Home and office:* New Ways of Consciousness Foundation, 1801 Franklin, #402, San Francisco, Calif. 94109. *Agent:* Michael Larsen/Elizabeth Pomada, 1029 Jones St., San Francisco, Calif. 94109.

CAREER: National Enquirer, New York, N.Y., researcher and cartoon editor, 1963; International Nickel, New York City, information specialist, 1964-65; American Book Co., New York City, science editor of college textbooks, 1965-67; Van Nostrand Reinhold Co., New York City, science editor of college textbooks, 1968-69; *Psychic* (now *New Realities*), San Francisco, Calif., Eastern editor, 1969-72, co-editor, 1973, articles editor, 1973-75, editor, 1976-77; New Ways of Consciousness Foundation, San Francisco, Calif., president, 1978—. Staff instructor at Psychic Integration Institute; faculty member at Sonoma State College, 1973-74, and Institute for the Study of Consciousness, 1974-75; lecturer at seminars, conferences, and colleges. Member of board of directors of Central Premonitions Registry, 1968—. Appeared on national television and radio programs, including Merv Griffin's, David Frost's, and Phil Donohue's shows, and programs in Canada, England, and Italy. *Military service:* U.S. Army, 1959-62.

MEMBER: Parapsychological Association (associate member). *Awards, honors:* Grant from Parapsychology Foundation, 1967-68; honorary doctorate from El Instituto de Ciencias Parapsicologias Hispano-Americano, 1977.

WRITINGS: Patterns of Prophecy, Hawthorne, 1973; (with Montague Ullman and Stanley Krippner) *Dream Telepathy,* Macmillan, 1973; (with James Bolen) *Psychics,* Harper, 1972; (contributor) Martin Ebon, editor, *They Knew the Unknown,* New American Library, 1973; (contributor) Edgar D. Mitchell and other editors, *Psychic Exploration,* Putnam, 1974; *Incredible Coincidence: The Baffling World of Synchronicity,* Lippincott, 1979. Contributor of more than fifty articles and interviews to *Psychic* and *Parapsychology Review.*

WORK IN PROGRESS: Who Are You and What Are You

Doing Here?, completion expected in 1980; *Chance Encounters of the Stars*, interviews; *Chances Are, Chance Will Help*.

SIDELIGHTS: Vaughan writes: "The transition from a skeptical science textbook editor to a parapsychologist and practicing psychic was a painful one. I had to give up the cherished ideas of traditional science to discover the more important, underlying realities of consciousness and its psychic effects. The research leading to *Patterns of Prophecy* opened up my own prophetic talent, and enabled me to teach others how to develop their latent psi gifts. To write about something, I have had to experience it. That is the only way I could carefully observe the psychological and emotional factors in psychic experience. It has led me to some strange experiences: from dream premonitions of Robert Kennedy's assassination, to healing of others by consciousness focusing, to influencing delicate machinery by psychokinesis, to experiencing incredible coincidences and even coming into contact with apparent alien life forms (not little green men, but little orange-red spots that flit about and play games).

"Writing *Incredible Coincidence* was an incredible experience of chance (?) coincidence. As I focused my mind on each chapter, a chance event leapt into my life to provide an example. I felt the book had a magical life of its own. It forced me to consider that Consciousness is Creator: that we create our lives moment-by-moment by creating space and time; and that by believing in the miraculous, we experience the miraculous—especially when the miraculous arrives in the form of an apparent chance coincidence.

"The major upshot was to realize that predicting events is less important than making the events we want to happen materialize by focusing our consciousness on them (and adding some elbow grease). That is why I founded the New Ways of Consciousness Foundation to solve problems with consciousness techniques. The first problem is finding money for consciousness research. I have adapted the motto of my first mentor, Eileen Garrett, the medium and founder of the Parapsychology Foundation, which started me in the career of consciousness research: 'Find the money, and the work will get done.'

"My basic premise, drawn from a decade of work in parapsychology, is this: You were born into this life for a purpose. Your inner self knows that purpose. By unlocking the secrets of your inner self, you will find out who you are and what you are doing here. Once you discover that, then it will become easier to do what you are meant to do. If you do it well, then you will achieve excellence.

"Each of us has a unique consciousness and a unique task in life. We also have unique problems to solve. But only *our* consciousness has the answers to *our* problems. Your inner self has the wisdom of the universe locked up within it. By finding the key to unlock that wisdom, you will enrich your life."

BIOGRAPHICAL/CRITICAL SOURCES: David Wallechinsky and Irving Wallace, *The People's Almanac,* Doubleday, 1975.

*   *   *

VAUGHAN, Carter A.
See GERSON, Noel Bertram

*   *   *

VERNEY, Peter (Vivian Lloyd)   1930-
PERSONAL: Born November 13, 1930, in London, En-

gland; son of Gerald Lloyd (a major-general in British Army) and Joyce Sybil (Smith) Verney; married Caroline Evelyn Harford, July 14, 1959; children: Harry, Louisa, Henrietta. *Education:* Trinity College, Dublin, B.Agr. and M.A., both 1953. *Home:* Chantry, Bisley, Stroud, Gloucestershire, England. *Agent:* A.P. Watt, 26 Bedford Row, London W.C.1, England.

CAREER: Served with British Army in Egypt, Cyprus, Germany, Great Britain, and Norway, 1954-70, became major; writer, 1970—.

WRITINGS: The Standard Bearer: The Story of Sir Edmund Verney, Knight-Marshal to King Charles I, Hutchinson, 1963; *The Micks: The Story of the Irish Guards,* P. Davies, 1970; *The Battle of Blenheim,* Hippocrene Books, 1976; *The Gardens of Scotland,* Batsford, 1976; *Here Comes the Circus,* Paddington Press, 1978; *Anzio: An Unexpected Fury, 1944,* Batsford, 1978; *The Earthquake Handbook,* Paddington Press, 1979. Contributor to magazines, including *Monarchist* and *Countryman,* and newspapers.

WORK IN PROGRESS: Historical novels, set in the eighteenth century.

SIDELIGHTS: Verney writes: "The world of military history can be drab and deathly dull. Yet the drama, the intensity of emotions, the elemental story behind military actions, have a potential all their own. It is this that I am trying to create in my writings. The past wars, particularly the last one, have a fascination for a younger generation. Why, why, why could you go on killing each other, they ask themselves. What was it like to be there and to be scared and frightened almost out of your wits? And yet there was a certain glamour about it all, occasionally even a nobleness of spirit. Some people were brave, some not so brave, yet they were all human beings—and how did they feel? That is what I'm trying to recreate and to pass on."

*   *   *

VERNON, Edward
See COLEMAN, Vernon

*   *   *

VINES, Alice Gilmore   1923-
PERSONAL: Born March 24, 1923, in Anderson, Ind.; daughter of Amos D. and Madonna (Stanley) Gilmore; married Ralph Vines (a writer), August 9, 1942; children: Linell, Gail. *Education:* University of Cincinnati, B.A., and B.S., both 1960, M.A., 1961, Ph.D., 1975. *Home:* 254 Forrer Blvd., Dayton, Ohio 45419. *Office:* Department of History, University of Dayton, 300 College Park Ave., Dayton, Ohio 45469.

CAREER: Secondary school teacher, 1961-67; University of Dayton, Ohio, instructor, 1968-72, assistant professor, 1972-77, associate professor of British history and women's history, 1977—. *Member:* American Historical Association, Conference on British Studies, Historical Association (England), Ohio Academy of History.

WRITINGS: Neither Fire Nor Steel: Sir Christopher Hatton, Nelson-Hall, 1978; *Despite the Odds: A History of British Women,* University of Dayton Press, 1978.

WORK IN PROGRESS: A biography of Margaret MacDonald; editing autobiography of Ishbel MacDonald Peterkin.

SIDELIGHTS: Alice Vines writes: "I am committed to the idea of inter-disciplinary teaching. I am teaching one course with another professor in American history and comparative women's history, and the other with a professor of English, in which we interweave English history and literature from the eighteenth century to the present. My other major interest is in overseas teaching, having helped to originate University of Dayton's overseas semester. I teach every summer in London, and have developed a course on the history of London. I think English history is vital to America's understanding of itself.''

*   *   *

VISCONTI, Luchino   1906-1976

PERSONAL: Born November 2, 1906, in Milan, Italy; son of Guiseppe (in theatre) and Carla (a musician; maiden name, Erba) Visconti. *Education:* Attended college in Genoa, Italy. *Home:* 366 Via Salaria, Rome, Italy.

CAREER: Screenwriter and director of motion pictures; set and costume designer, producer, and director of stage productions. Worked as assistant to Jean Renoir, 1935; director with Morelli-Stoppa Company, 1958-59. Producer and director of stage productions, including "La Vestale," 1954, "Don Carlos," 1958, "Salome," 1961, "La Traviata," 1963. *Military service:* Worked with Italian underground during World War II before imprisonment. *Awards, honors:* First Prize from Venice Film Festival, 1948, for "La Terra Trema"; special jury prize from Venice Film Festival and numerous other international awards, 1961, for "Rocco e i suoi fratelli"; Golden Palm award from Cannes Film Festival, 1963, for "Il gattopardo"; and other film awards.

WRITINGS: Ludwig by Luchino Visconti, edited by Giorgi Ferrara, Cappelli, 1973.

Published screenplays: *Rocco y sus hermanos,* Ayma, 1963; *El gatopardo,* Ayma, 1963; *Vaghe stelle dell'Orsa,* edited by Pietro Blanchi, Cappelli, 1965; *Three Screenplays: White Nights, Rocco and His Brothers, The Job,* translated from the Italian by Judith Green, Orion Press, 1970; *Two Screenplays: La terra trema, Senso,* translated from the Italian by Green, Orion Press, 1970; *Gruppo di famiglia in un interno,* edited by Giorgio Treves, Cappelli, 1975.

Screenplays; all as director: (With A. Pietrangeli, G. Puccini, and G. De Santis) "Ossessione" (released in the U.S. as "Obsession"; adapted from the novel by James M. Cain, *The Postman Always Rings Twice*), ICI Rome, 1942; "La terra trema" (based on a story by Giovanni Verga), Universalia, 1948; (with Suso Cecchi d'Amico and Francesco Rosi) "Bellissima" (released in the U.S. as "The Most Beautiful"), Bellissima Films, 1951; (with d'Amico) "Senso" (released in the U.S. as "Sense"; released in England as "The Wanton Countess"; adapted from a novella by Camilla Boito), Lux Films, 1954; (with d'Amico) "Le notti bianchi" (released in the U.S. as "White Nights"; adapted from the short story by Dostoyevsky), CIAS/Vides, 1957.

(With d'Amico, Pasquale Festa Campanile, Massimo Franciosa, and Enrico Medioli) "Rocco e i suoi fratelli" (released in the U.S. as "Rocco and His Brothers"; adapted from the novel by Giovanni Testori, *Il ponte della ghisolfa*), Titanus/Films Marceau, 1960; "Il lavoro" (released in the U.S. as "The Job"), 1962; (with d'Amico, Campanile, Medioli, and Franciosa) "Il gattopardo" (relased in the U.S. as "The Leopard"; adapted from the novel by Lampedusa), Techirama, 1963; (with d'Amico and Medioli) "Vaghe stelle dell'Orsa" (released in the U.S. as "Sandra"), Vides, 1965; (with d'Amico and Georges Conchon) "Le Straniero" (released in the U.S. as "The Stranger"; adapted from the novel by Albert Camus), Paramount, 1967.

(With Medioli and Nicola Badalucco) "La caduto degli dei" (released in the U.S. as "The Damned"), W-7, 1970; (with Badalucco) "Morte e Venezia" (released in the U.S. as "Death in Venice"; adapted from the novella by Thomas Mann), Alfa Cinematografico, 1971; (with d'Amico and Medioli) "Gruppo di famiglia in un inferno" (released in the U.S. as "Conversation Piece"), Rusconi Film/Gaumont International Sarl, 1975. Also co-author and director of "L'Innocente."

SIDELIGHTS: Although Visconti is often ranked by critics with Michelangelo Antonioni and Federico Fellini in the pantheon of Italian cinema, his standing would be considerably less were he judged solely on what American audiences saw of his work during his lifetime. His earliest films, the cornerstones of his reputation, were either released abroad only after being heavily edited or never released at all.

Many critics regard Visconti's first film, "Ossessione," as his finest effort. An adaptation of James Cain's novel of permissive behavior, *The Postman Always Rings Twice,* "Ossessione" was banned upon release for detailing human emotions in a way which Italian censors found unacceptable. The film was given a brief revival by Mussolini who felt it was artistic but, in 1943, new leaders assumed power and prints of "Ossessione" were confiscated and destroyed. Although he was imprisoned afterward for working with the underground, Visconti managed to save a negative of the film. Unfortunately, "Ossessione" was not shown in the United States until shortly before Visconti's death.

After World War II, Visconti abandoned further film projects in favor of staging plays. He developed a troupe of actors by using the same ones consistently and he called upon many of them when he decided to make his second film.

"La terra trema" suffered almost the same fate as "Ossessione" upon release. It took top honors at the Venice Film Festival in 1948 and was hailed as a breakthrough in bringing the terms "art" and "cinema" closer together. A prelude to the neo-realism of later Italian films, including Vittorio De Sica's "Bicycle Thief," "La terra trema" showed a lone fisherman in a losing battle against the oppression and squalor of a small village. But despite the seemingly accessible subject, the film was an enormous financial disappointment and, like "Ossessione," was rarely shown outside Italy and only recently released in the United States.

The failure of "La terra trema" drove Visconti back to the stage where he had achieved considerable success with his productions of operas featuring Maria Callas. He did return to filmmaking in 1951, with "Bellissima," and although the film was his first to be released in the United States, it lacked the artistic temperament so evident in "Ossessione" and "La terra trema."

If "Bellissima" buoyed Visconti's hopes as a filmmaker, "Senso" brought him back to the futility he'd felt after his first two films. "Senso" was his first color film and critics dwelled on his expressive use of color and framing. Unfortunately, the financiers of the film felt it was far too long and ordered extensive editing for release abroad. When "Senso" was released in England (under the title "The Wanton Countess"), the film had been edited to twenty-five percent of its original length. Visconti refused to recognize the abbreviated version as his own film.

With such a history of financial disasters behind him, Visconti was hard pressed to find producers for further projects. He therefore funded "White Nights" with some of his friends and shot the film within seven weeks. "White Nights" did receive some praise when shown at the Venice

Film Festival in 1956, but was greeted without response when released in the United States in 1961. Visconti's own opinion was that the hectic shooting schedule was sometimes apparent in the finished movie.

Heavy editing plagued Visconti's next film, "Rocco and His Brothers." Despite favorable reviews, the film was often victimized by its own incoherence and it too lost money in the United states. "Rocco and His Brothers" was an enormous critical success, through, and encouraged Visconti to embark on his most ambitious film, "The Leopard."

Visconti was provided with a seven-month shooting schedule and $5 million for "The Leopard," his documentation of the decline of feudalism in Sicily. Like "Rocco and His Brothers" before it, "The Leopard" was an enormous success at various festivals but it too was altered before release in the United States. The same film which won the Golden Palm award from the Cannes Film Festival was deemed "a sad, luxurious failure" by an American film critic after viewing the American version (which was shorter by twenty-five minutes and featured poor dubbing).

After the moderate success of "Rocco and His Brothers" and "The Leopard," Visconti had less difficulty getting his films released in the United States. Ironically, his later films lack the high degree of creativity so evident in his earlier work. His adaptations of famous literary works, "The Stranger" and "Death in Venice," were both cited by critics for their "boring and pretentious" style.

Visconti attempted to return to his earlier form with "Conversation Piece" but the results were disastrous. The film about vanishing aristocracy was called "ludicrous" by one critic, a "mess" by another. Sadly, "Conversation Piece" was Visconti's last film to be released in the United States before his death.

BIOGRAPHICAL/CRITICAL SOURCES: Film Culture, December, 1957; *Films and Filming,* October, 1962; *New York Times,* June 18, 1971; *Women's Wear Daily,* September 26, 1975; *Nation,* October 18, 1975; *New Times,* August 19, 1977.

OBITUARIES: Time, March 29, 1976.*

(Died in 1976, in Rome, Italy)

* * *

VOINOVICH, Vladimir (Nikolaevich) 1932-

PERSONAL: Born September 26, 1932, in Dushanbe, Tadzhik, U.S.S.R.; son of Nikolai Pavlovich (a journalist) and Rosa (a teacher; maiden name, Goichman) Voinovich; married wife, Valentina, 1957 (marriage ended, 1965); married Irina Braude (a teacher), 1965; children: (first marriage) Marina, Pavel; (second marriage) Olga. *Education:* Attended Moscow Pedagogical Institute, 1957-59. *Home:* Cherniachovskii St., House 4, Apt. 66, 125319 Moscow, U.S.S.R. *Agent:* Leonard W. Schroeter, 540 Central Bldg., Seattle, Wash. 98104.

CAREER: Worked as a herdsman on a collective farm when a youth; held a variety of jobs, including factory hand, locksmith, construction worker, railroad laborer, carpenter, aircraft mechanic, and editor of radio programs; went to Moscow and became a writer, 1956; continues to write although he has officially been denied the right to earn his living as an author, 1974—. *Military service:* Soviet Army, 1951-55. *Member:* Union of Soviet Writers (expelled, 1974), P.E.N. (French division), Mark Twain Society (honorary member), Bavarian Academy of Fine Arts.

WRITINGS: My zdes' zhivem (short story; title means "We Live Here"), published in *Novy Mir,* 1961, published in book form, [Moscow], 1963; "Khochu byt'-chestnym" (novella; title means "I Want to be Honest"), published in *Novy Mir,* 1963; "Dva tovarishcha" (novella; title means "Two Friends"), published in *Novy Mir,* 1964; *Vladychitsa* (title means "The Sovereign Mistress"), [Moscow], 1969; *Stepen' doveriia* (historical novel; title means "A Degree of Trust"), [Moscow], 1972; *Povesti* (title means "Novellas"), [Moscow], 1972; *Zhizn' i neobychainye prikliucheniia soldata Ivana Chonkina* (novel), YMCA Press (Paris), 1975, translation by Richard Lourie published as *The Life and Extraordinary Adventures of Private Ivan Chonkin,* Farrar, Straus, 1977; *Ivan'kiada, ili rasskaz o vselenii pisatelia Voinovicha v novuiu kvartiru* (autobiography), Ardis, 1976, translation by David Lapeza published as *The Ivankiad: The Tale of the Writer Voinovich's Installation in His New Apartment,* Farrar, Straus, 1977. Also author of poems, feuilletons, six movie scripts, and two plays produced in the U.S.S.R. based on his novellas, "Khochu byt' chestnym" and "Dva tovarishcha." Contributor of short stories to *Novy Mir,* and of articles to journals.

WORK IN PROGRESS: "Many future plans, but I fear to speak of them."

SIDELIGHTS: "I have been enraged and moved to tears by contemporary Russian prose and poetry, but Vladimir Voinovich is the only Russian writer who makes me laugh out loud," declared Susan Jacoby in *Saturday Review.* Other critics have also relished Voinovich's sense of humor. The *New York Times Book Review* called Voinovich "the first genuine comic writer entirely produced by the Soviet system," while *Newsweek* proclaimed him "the most drolly entertaining of the new Soviet dissident writers." Voinovich's reputation as a comic writer rests on two of his books which have been published in the United States, *The Life and Extraordinary Adventures of Private Ivan Chonkin* and *The Ivankiad.*

Suppressed in Russia, *The Life and Extraordinary Adventures of Ivan Chonkin* was circulated secretly and became an underground success. Peter S. Prescott speculated that Soviet officials found the novel subversive because "it suggests that amiable sloth and native cunning will prevail against bureaucracy," and "it illustrates what Marx never understood: that even under socialism human nature remains an unregenerate constant." The book recounts the tale of a good-natured bumpkin, Private Chonkin, who is ordered by his army officer to remain on a remote collective farm and guard a downed airplane. Headquarters soon forgets him, and Chonkin amuses himself by puttering in the collective's garden and making love to the local postmistress. Despite his simple and placid exterior, Chonkin can be shrewd and even valiant, as his last-ditch effort to prevent himself from being reclaimed by the army demonstrates. Voinovich told an interviewer that Chonkin is not so dull as he appears: "The stupidity that everyone laughs at is not really stupidity when you examine it. My heroes, not only Chonkin but others, too, are very natural people who fall into unnatural situations."

Reflecting on Voinovich's use of satire in *The Life and Extraordinary Adventures of Ivan Chonkin,* Theodore Solotaroff observed, "The choice of a satirical mode was inspired, for it unearthed a first-rate comic talent that had been lurking beneath the sober gritty surface of his early realism and a new and powerful gift for rendering the transactions between reality and fantasy, the ordinary life haunted by the phantoms and phantasmagoria of the police state." In the same vein, Richard R. Lingeman remarked, "This is a very funny book, its humor making a sly and rueful point, as the best satire does, without being grim or heavy-handed." A reviewer for the *New Yorker* disagreed, however, with such assessments of the book, maintaining that "as satire, it is a bit lame and obvious."

Having written a fictional story about one man's war against bureaucracy, Voinovich then proceeded to write a nonfiction account of his own battles with the "phantasmagoria of the police state." The result was *The Ivankiad,* which *Newsweek* described as a "mock epic account of the author's struggle with a powerful publishing bureaucrat over possession of a two-room apartment in the Writers' Housing Cooperative." The theme of this struggle, Anatole Shub explained, is "the contrast between Soviet pretense and reality, theory and practice . . . but the book's delight lies in the human-scale merriment with which Voinovich tells the tale. As in all great satires, the situation is both thoroughly real and utterly preposterous."

Voinovich's battle to gain a larger apartment was only one of many struggles with Soviet bureaucrats. Although his writings were initially well received in the Soviet Union, he fell into official disfavor in the late 1960's. After writing a letter defending Aleksandr Solzhenitsyn in 1974, Voinovich was ousted from the Union of Soviet Writers and forbidden to earn his living as a writer. "I was expelled for trying to write with talent and to live with conscience," Voinovich told *CA.* He explained that his name can no longer be mentioned in Russian encyclopedias and newspapers.

In retaliation, Voinovich has seen fit to lampoon Soviet officialdom with satirical letters. When his telephone service was abruptly severed, Voinovich composed an open letter to the Minister of Communications which began: "It is with deep concern that I bring to your attention the fact that an enemy of the Relaxation of International Tension, the head of the Moscow telephone system, is in hiding somewhere in the field of national economy headed by you." He went on to note, "After all, not even the notorious George Meany has managed to disconnect a single telephone." On another occasion he penned a hilarious epistle to the director of the new Soviet copyright agency. In order to shield Russian authors from Western influences, Voinovich recommended to the director that Moscow's prisons "with the necessary guards and police dogs [be] placed at your disposal."

"There is humor in Soviet life. You only have to have a sense of humor so you can recognize it," Voinovich once assured an inquirer. Buoyed by his comic sense, Voinovich remains undaunted by the persecution he has been subjected to in his native land, and continues to live and to write in Moscow.

Some of Voinovich's poems were set to music and became popular songs in the U.S.S.R. His books have been translated into more than twenty languages.

BIOGRAPHICAL/CRITICAL SOURCES: Vladimir Voinovich, *The Ivankiad,* Farrar, Straus, 1977; *Time,* January 3, 1977; *New York Times Book Review,* January 23, 1977, August 7, 1977; *Newsweek,* February 14, 1977, August 1, 1977; *New Yorker,* March 7, 1977; *New York Times,* March 26, 1977, April 27, 1977; *Saturday Review,* September 17, 1977.

* * *

von BRAND, Theodor C.   1900(?)-1978

OBITUARY NOTICE: Born c. 1900 in Ortenberg, Germany; died July 18, 1978, in Washington, D.C. Research parasitologist, educator, and author of books in his field. He was employed by the National Institutes of Health for twenty-three years. Obituaries and other sources: *Washington Post,* July 19, 1978.

* * *

von HIRSCH, Andrew   1934-

PERSONAL: Born July 16, 1934, in Zurich, Switzerland; came to the United States in 1941, naturalized citizen, 1947; son of Baron Donald (a diplomat) and Katherine (a language pathologist; maiden name, Bachert) von Hirsch. *Education:* Harvard University, A.B., 1956, LL.B., 1960. *Office:* Graduate School of Criminal Justice, Rutgers University, 15 Washington St., Newark, N.J. 07102.

CAREER: Attorney in private practice in New York, N.Y., 1961-63; staff lawyer for various government agencies in New York, 1964-69; legislative counsel to U.S. Senator Charles E. Goodell, in Washington, D.C., 1969-70; Committee for the Study of Incarceration, Washington, D.C., executive director, 1971-74; State University of New York at Albany, visiting associate professor of criminal justice, 1974-75; Rutgers University, Graduate School of Criminal Justice, Newark, N.J. associate professor of criminal justice, 1975—.

WRITINGS: Doing Justice: The Choice of Punishments, Hill & Wang, 1976; *Abolish Parole?,* Ballinger, 1978. Contributor to criminology journals.

WORK IN PROGRESS: Continuing research on sentencing reform, especially issues of fairness and justice in sentencing.

SIDELIGHTS: Von Hirsch told *CA: "Doing Justice* develops a conceptual model for sentencing to replace traditional rehabilitational models. Under the conceptual model, decisions would be based primarily on offenders' *desserts*—that is, the seriousness of their criminal conduct."

* * *

von HOFFMAN, Nicholas   1929-

PERSONAL: Born October 16, 1929, in New York, N.Y.; son of Carl and Anna (a dentist; maiden name, Bruenn) von Hoffman; married Ann Byrne, 1950 (divorced); children: Alexander, Aristodemos, Constantine. *Education:* Attended Fordham Prep School. *Office:* c/o *Washington Post,* 1150 15th St. N.W., Washington, D.C. 20000.

CAREER: Industrial Area Foundation, Chicago, Ill., associate director, 1954-63; *Chicago Daily News,* Chicago, staff member, 1963-66; *Washington Post,* Washington, D.C., staff member and columnist, 1966—. "Point-Counterpoint" commentator on CBS's "60 Minutes."

WRITINGS: Mississippi Notebook, David White, 1964; *The Multiversity: A Personal Report on What Happens to Today's Students at American Universities,* Holt, 1966; *We Are the People Our Parents Warned Us Against,* Quadrangle, 1968; *Two, Three, Many More: A Novel,* Quadrangle, 1969; *Left at the Post,* Quadrangle, 1970; (with Garry Trudeau) *The Fireside Watergate,* Sheed, 1973; (with Trudeau) *Tales From the Margaret Mead Taproom: The Compleat Gonzo Governorship of Doonesbury's Uncle Duke,* Sheed, 1976; *Make-Believe Presidents: Illusions of Power From McKinley to Carter,* Pantheon, 1978. Author of syndicated column. Contributor of numerous articles to periodicals, including *Progressive, Esquire,* and *Harper's Bazaar.* Contributing editor, *New Times,* 1973-.

SIDELIGHTS: In 1966, Ben Bradlee of the Washington Post hired reporter Nicholas von Hoffman. Chalmers M. Roberts assessed his impact on the Post: "Over the next decade his vivid prose, often intentionally provocative, produced more angry letters to the editor than the work of any other single reporter in the paper's history. In the late 1960s and early 1970s he became a favorite of the New Left and of some of the youth cults. At the Post some adored him; others considered him a menace to journalism. His contribution, until he began to fade after the end of the Nixon era, was substantial: by the very power of his words, the details of his reporting, and the outrage of his expressed beliefs he forced uncounted Post readers to examine a life style that repelled them, especially when it became that of their own middle-class offspring."

BIOGRAPHICAL/CRITICAL SOURCES: Washington Post, June 4, 1968, May 9, 1969; Book World, July 2, 1968; New York Times Book Review, October 13, 1968; Newsweek, May 12, 1969; Nation, June 2, 1969; Saturday Review, November 14, 1970; New York Review of Books, November 19, 1970; Commonweal, January 18, 1974; Philadelphia Bulletin, December 12, 1974; Chalmers M. Roberts, The Washington Post: The First 100 Years, Houghton, 1977; Washington Post Book World, October 22, 1978.*

* * *

von STERNBERG, Josef
See STERNBERG, Josef von

* * *

von TRAPP, Maria Augusta 1905-

PERSONAL: Born January 26, 1905, in Vienna, Austria; came to United States in 1939; naturalized U.S. citizen in 1948; daughter of Karl (an engineer) and Augusta (Ranier) Kutschera; married Georg von Trapp (a World War I submarine commander), November 26, 1927 (died May 30, 1947); children: Rosemarie, Eleanor (Mrs. Hugh Campbell), Johannes; stepchildren: Rupert, Agatha, Maria, Werner, Hedwig (deceased), Johanna (Mrs. Ernst I. Winter), Martina (Mrs. Jean Dupiere; deceased). Education: State Teachers College of Progressive Education, Vienna, graduate, 1924; further study at Nonnberg Benedictine Convent, Salzburg, Austria, 1924-26. Religion: Roman Catholic. Residence: Stowe, Vt.

CAREER: Member of Trapp Family Singers, performed in Europe, South America, Central America, the United States, Hawaii, Australia, and New Zealand, 1938-56; founder of Trapp Family Austrian Relief, Inc., 1947; founder and teacher, Trapp Family Music Camp, Stowe, Vt., 1951-56; manager of Trapp Family Lodge, Stowe, until 1956; writer and lecturer. Member: Catholic Women's Club of Stowe, Zonta Club. Awards, honors: Bene Merenti medal (Papal decoration), 1949; Catholic Writers Guild St. Francis de Sales Golden Book Award for best nonfiction, 1950, for The Story of the Trapp Family Singers; LL.D., St. Mary's College, 1957; D. Music, St. Anselme's College, 1966; Honorary Cross First Class for Science and Art, Austrian Government, 1967.

WRITINGS: The Story of the Trapp Family Singers, Lippincott, 1949, new edition published as The Sound of Music: The Story of the Trapp Family Singers, White Lion, 1976; Yesterday, Today, and Forever, Lippincott, 1952; Around the Year With the Trapp Family, illustrations by Rosemarie von Trapp and Nikolaus E. Wolff, Pantheon, 1955; (with Ruth T. Murdoch) A Family on Wheels: Further Adventures

of the Trapp Family Singers, Lippincott, 1959; Maria (autobiography), Creation House, 1972; When the King Was Carpenter, New Leaf, 1976.

WORK IN PROGRESS: Trapp Family Cook Book.

SIDELIGHTS: Born in a train heading for Vienna, Maria von Trapp has been teased about her unusual entrance into the world, especially since her later life has been one of constant travel. The story of her life and that of her family was revealed in The Story of the Trapp Family Singers. A San Francisco Chronicle reviewer called it "astonishingly good. It is an amusing, sometimes serious, always highly personal record of one of the distinguished musical families of our time, and it is also an intimate, friendly, completely engaging story of how an indomitable woman . . . met adversity and triumphed."

Maria von Trapp writes and lectures primarily on her colorful life story. Everyone who has seen either the musical play or screenplay version of "The Sound of Music" knows the romantic beginning of that story: The young novice Maria is sent from an Austrian convent by the Reverend Mother to care for the seven children, ranging in age from four to fourteen, of widower Georg von Trapp, a baron and officer of the Imperial Navy. Although she is reluctant to leave the novitiate to live on the estate of a baron, the provincial Maria tells herself it is God's will and it will only encompass a period of ten months. Almost immediately, she falls in love with the family and they with her. The von Trapps spend much of their time hiking together in the Alps, riding bicycles, and singing Austrian folk songs. Before ten months have passed, instead of asking a princess to become his bride as expected, the baron asks Maria. She accepts.

Left out of "The Sound of Music" is the fact that the von Trapps learn to sing sixteenth, seventeenth, and eighteenth-century music a capella under the guidance of a priest who comes to say mass at the chapel on their estate. They sing solely for their own enjoyment until opera singer Lotte Lehman hears them and persuades the family to enter a contest at the Salzburg Festival. As portrayed in the musical and film, they enter, win first prize, and are given offers to sing at concerts all around Austria, thus beginning their professional career as "The Trapp Family Singers."

Although they could still live comfortably under the rule of Hitler, the von Trapps realize it would be at the price of their freedom. In 1938 they make the difficult decision to leave their friends, possessions, and country behind. In "The Sound of Music," the story ends with the von Trapps climbing over the Alps to freedom. In reality, they leave Austria by train, earn money from giving concerts in various countries, and eventually come to the United States.

Both the musical play and screenplay of "The Sound of Music" were highly successful. Mary Martin saw a German-made movie of the Trapp family and decided that it must become a Broadway musical. Howard Lindsay and Russel Crouse wrote the story based on von Trapp's book, and with lyrics by Oscar Hammerstein II and music by Richard Rodgers, the play opened on Broadway on November 16, 1959, and was a blockbuster success. Starring Mary Martin and Theodore Bikel, its run was 1,443 performances, winning six Antoinette Perry (Tony) awards, including best musical of the season. The play toured for two and a half years, playing to capacity houses everywhere. Over three million copies of the original cast album were sold.

Twentieth-Century Fox's film version was an equal success. Released in 1965, and starring Julie Andrews and Christopher Plummer, the motion picture won five Academy

Awards, including best picture of the year. Its original soundtrack recording sold over eight million copies.

In an interview with Jennifer Small, Maria von Trapp, referring to "The Sound of Music," confided: "I was a wild creature. Julie Andrews and Mary Martin were too gentle—like girls out of Bryn Mawr." The royalties she has received from the stage, film, and recorded versions of "The Sound of Music" have been used for Catholic missionary work, in which she is deeply involved. She has worked with missions in New Guinea and in other underdeveloped regions.

Around the World With the Trapp Family Singers has been translated into nineteen languages.

AVOCATIONAL INTERESTS: Swimming, hiking, horseback riding, cross-country skiing.

BIOGRAPHICAL/CRITICAL SOURCES: Reader's Digest, January, 1948; Maria von Trapp, *The Story of the Trapp Family Singers,* Lippincott, 1949, new edition published as *The Sound of Music: The Story of the Trapp Family Singers,* White Lion, 1976; *San Francisco Chronicle,* December 1, 1949; von Trapp, *Maria,* Creation House, 1972; *TV Guide,* February 28, 1976; *Travel and Leisure,* November, 1977; *Saturday Evening Post,* April, 1978.

* * *

VRBOVSKA, Anca 1905-

PERSONAL: Born November 23, 1905, in Bratislava, Czechoslovakia; came to the United States, 1924, naturalized citizen, 1934; daughter of John Jacques and Kathie (Vrbovska) Schultz; married Dominic Saitta (died, 1962). *Education:* Studied at Bratislava Commercial Academy, 1920; Lyceum, Bratislava, Czechoslovakia, B.A., 1924; further study at Bryn Mawr College, 1928, and at Hunter College and City College (both of the City University of New York), and New York University. *Politics:* "I believe in honesty, regardless of party." *Religion:* None. *Home:* 3601 Surf Ave., Apt. F17, Brooklyn, N.Y. 11224. *Office:* New Orlando Publications, P.O. Box 296, Village Station, New York, N.Y. 10014.

CAREER: Pegasus, New York City, translator and editor, 1951-58; New Orlando Publications, New York City, editor, 1958—. Translator and research editor for *American Dialog,* 1969-73; participant in workshops; guest lecturer. *Member:* International Women's Writing Guild (sponsor), Poetry Society of America, Greenwich Village Poetry Society (president), Les Violetti et Normands (honorary life member), Academia de Ciencas Humanisticas y Relaciones (Mexico; honorary life member), Club des Intellectuels Francais, Musique, Poesie, Theatre, Sciences, Arts, Literature (honorary member), Academia de Ciencas Humanisticas y Relaciones (Dominican Republic; honorary member).

WRITINGS: Cyclone (poems and prose), B.U. Frederick Fritts, 1934; *The Other Selves* (poems), Helenson Press, 1950; *The Gate Beyond the Sun* (poems), New Orlando Publications, 1970; (editor with Alfred Dorn) *From Deborah and Sappho to the Present* (anthology of international women's literature), New Orlando Publications, 1976.

Work represented in anthologies, including *Writing on the Wall,* edited by Walter Lowenfels, Doubleday, 1969, and *For Neruda for Chile,* edited by Lowenfels, Beacon Press, 1973. Contributor of translations, poems, articles, stories, and reviews to periodicals, including *Hungarian World, Dasein,* and *Poet.*

WORK IN PROGRESS: The Sanguine Countess, a historical novel; *Fantastic Bouquet,* a "neo-grotesque" book of stories.

SIDELIGHTS: Anca Vrbovska writes: "Before learning English I worked in factories, restaurants, and Bell Telephone laboratories. At night I attended courses at Hunter College and City College of the City University of New York, and New York University. During the Depression I helped to organize the Writers' and Artists' Union, which later fought for Works Progress Administration writers' and artists' projects. I firmly believe that there is a great need for similar federally-supported writers' and artists' projects on a permanent basis. Some excellent so-far-unrecognized writers and artists live in dire poverty. The National Endowment for the Arts prizes are few and are often awarded to recognized authors. When I applied for a position created in New York City for five hundred artists, dancers, poets, playwrights, and authors, I was told that I didn't qualify because my yearly income was close to twenty-eight hundred dollars! In the *New Yorker,* I saw an advertisement for a necktie costing (only) two thousand dollars.

"We should give useful work to those in the art field, as they did during the WPA era: several hours of work for the community they live in, and the remaining time for their specific art. Some of our greatest American artists, poets, and writers were saved from starvation by WPA: Richard Wright, Zero Mostel, Orson Welles, May Swenson, and myself, to mention a few. Raphael Soyer, Art Young, Adolph Dehn, William Gropper, Hugo Gellert, Phillip Evergood, and Anton Refregier were some of the artists whose paintings and murals enriched the United States.

"We need a constructive art revival that not only reflects the destructive aspects of the atomic and other scientific inventions, but also its vast potential for improving life for humanity, plus outer-space explorations men of courage always envisioned. Let us remember that nations are not remembered because of their wars, but like ancient Greece, because of their artists, playwrights, poets, philosophers, and discoverers. Shelley put it aptly: 'Poets are the unacknowledged legislators of the world.'

"As for my work—based on the tradition of the metaphysical poets, the romantics, classico-romantics, symbolists—I want to and *do* write poetry and prose in a new way. However I may disagree with Ezra Pound, he was an excellent poet, translator, editor, and I accept his credo: 'Make it new,' but I add to that 'reawaken the conscience of those in power; avoid wars; create a decent life for mankind on this small planet—Earth.'

"Since ours is an era of social, economic, and scientific discoveries, for better or worse, I want my novel and collections of stories and poetry to reflect these events that are shaping the destiny of mankind and our globe—interestingly, imaginatively, often with sardonic humor, as did the best authors, poets, and artists in all ages. We must not discard our rich heritage, but use it, the better to express our epoch. To deal only with the past is escape and interment."

BIOGRAPHICAL/CRITICAL SOURCES: Writers' Forum, spring, 1967.

* * *

VUILLEUMIER, Marion 1918-

PERSONAL: Born October 12, 1918, in Worcester, Mass.; daughter of Walter (a bookkeeper) and Mary Ethel (White) Rawson; married Pierre Dupont Vuilleumier (a minister), May 3, 1942; children: Virginia Marion Vuilleumier Hockley, Pierre Dupont, Louis Edward. *Education:* Gordon College, B.A.; graduate study at Boston University, and Bridgewater State College. *Home address:* P.O. Box 111, West Hyannisport, Mass. 02672.

CAREER: Assistant to chief inspector of claims, Liberty Mutual Insurance Co., 1940-42; christian education director, 1951-59; public school teacher, 1959-62; co-director of Craigville Inn and Conference Center, 1960-73; free-lance writer, 1973—. Cape Cod Writers' Conference, executive secretary, 1963—, interviewer for television show, "Books and the World," 1977—. Barnstable Association United Church of Christ, executive director of Cape Cod United Church Apartments, Falmouth, Mass., 1962-70, Mashpee United Church Village, 1970-76, and Mayflower Place, 1977—. *Member:* Authors League of America, Authors Guild, National Federation of Press Women, American Federation of Television and Radio Artists, National Book Critics Circle, Pilgrim Society, Word Guild, Twelve O'Clock Scholars, Massachusetts Society of Mayflower Descendants.

WRITINGS: Earning a Living on Olde Cape Cod, William S. Sullwold, 1968; *Boys and Girls on Olde Cape Cod* (juvenile), William S. Sullwold, 1968; *Indians on Olde Cape Cod,* William S. Sullwold, 1970; *Sketches of Old Cape Cod,* William S. Sullwold, 1972; *Craigville on Old Cape Cod,* William S. Sullwold, 1972; *Churches on Cape Cod,* William S. Sullwold, 1974; *America's Religious Treasures,* Harper, 1976; *Along the Wampanoag Trail* (juvenile), William S. Sullwold, 1976; *Cape Cod in Color,* Hastings House, 1979. Columnist for *Cape Cod Times,* 1970—; feature writer and book reviewer for *Cape Cod Illustrated,* 1972-76. Editor of *Transformation,* 1972—.

WORK IN PROGRESS: Meditations by the Sea.

SIDELIGHTS: Marion Vuilleumier writes that she is "active in creating housing for low- and moderate-income persons." She is also concerned with the decrease in writing skills nationwide. This has caused Vuilleumier to become involved in workshops on communication arts for both children and adults.

W

WAKEFIELD, R. I.
   See WHITE, Gertrude M(ason)

* * *

WAKEFIELD, Walter Leggett 1911-

PERSONAL: Born May 29, 1911, in Ballston Spa, N.Y.; son of Raymond J. and Mary L. (Leggett) Wakefield; married Virginia N. Walters, August 6, 1946 (marriage ended); married Betty D. Doyle, February 8, 1974; children: (first marriage) William Walters. *Education:* Syracuse University, A.B., 1934; Rutgers University, M.A., 1936; Columbia University, Ph.D., 1951. *Home:* 44 Leroy St., Potsdam, N.Y. 13676. *Office:* Department of History, State University of New York College at Potsdam, Potsdam, N.Y. 13676.

CAREER: Syracuse University, Syracuse, N.Y., instructor in history, 1938-42, 1945-49; State University of New York College at Potsdam, professor of history, 1949-74, distinguished teaching professor, 1974-78, professor emeritus, 1978—, head of department of history and political science, 1964-69. *Military service:* U.S. Army, 1942-45; received Bronze Star and Combat Infantry Badge.

WRITINGS: (With Oscar T. Barck and Hugh P. Lefler) *The United States: A Survey of National Development,* Ronald, 1951; (with Austin P. Evans) *Heresies of the High Middle Ages,* Columbia University Press, 1969; *Heresy, Crusade, and Inquisition in Southern France, 1100-1250,* University of California Press, 1974. Contributor to history journals.

WORK IN PROGRESS: Inquisitors and Heretics, 1234-1249 (tentative title), on the early operations of the medieval Inquisition in villages of southern France.

SIDELIGHTS: Wakefield writes: "I had the great good fortune to study with, become a friend of, and collaborate with the late Professor Austin P. Evans of Columbia University, whose interest in religious controversy in the Middle Ages I came to share deeply.

"My teaching at Syracuse University was interrupted by World War II. Afterward, Professor Evans and I worked together on the project which became *Heresies of the High Middle Ages,* the only major collection of sources in English translation for the history of religious dissent in the Middle Ages.

"The same interest led me to a study of attempts to suppress dissent and to a more detailed examination of the interaction of inquisitors and heretics in the first years of the medieval Inquisition in southern France."

AVOCATIONAL INTERESTS: Vegetable and flower gardening, playing poker.

* * *

WALCHARS, John 1912-

PERSONAL: Born May 9, 1912, in Vienna, Austria; came to the United States in 1946, naturalized citizen, 1969; son of Joseph (a laborer) and Adele (Vogler) Walchars. *Education:* Innsbruck University, M.A., 1938; attended Chinese Language School, Peking, China, 1938-40; further study in Zikawe, Shanghai, 1944, and with Jesuit Order of Cleveland, 1947. *Home:* Campion Center, Weston, Mass. 02193.

CAREER: Entered Society of Jesus (Jesuits), 1932; Cranwell School, Lenox, Mass., teacher of French and German, 1938-75; missionary in Kucheng, Hopei, China, 1945-46; writer, lecturer, and spiritual counselor in the United States, England, Ireland, and New Zealand, 1975—. Volunteer interpreter for U.S. peace mission in northern Chinese sector after World War II.

WRITINGS: The Call from Beyond, North Central Publishing, 1960, 2nd edition, 1961; *Splendor and Shadow,* North Central Publishing, 1964, 2nd edition, 1965; *The Unfinished Mystery,* Seabury, 1978, 2nd edition, 1978. Contributor to Roman Catholic magazines in the United States and China.

WORK IN PROGRESS: "A book to stem the colossal permissiveness of our civilization, not by preaching, but by questioning the modern American mind."

SIDELIGHTS: Walchars writes: "The purpose of my writing is to expose the trend of thoughts not in harmony with men's temporal and eternal destiny. Realizing that some of our current publications accommodate too readily the dangerous thinking in vogue, I find it an inescapable consequence of my commitment to wrestle with the prevalent mood of shallow thinking.

"We give to our civilization its due—we know its achievements and we enjoy the fruits of progress. But should we not always be alert for those aberrations on the fringe which can assume major proportions, if unchecked?

"The above concern is exposed in the preface of *The Unfinished Mystery* and examined in the chapter, 'Humanity in Crisis.'

"The malady will not vanish merely through the protestation of wise prophets, but only by an individual awareness of the peril on the part of each. To stimulate in the minds of my readers the awareness of this peril and to counteract its effects is the deepest motivation for my writing. I implement this purpose by direct contact with individuals and groups in every clime. My mission has taken me to every major country in the world." *Avocational interests:* Tennis.

* * *

WALDER, (Alan) David 1928-1978

OBITUARY NOTICE—See index for *CA* sketch: Born November 13, 1928, in London, England; died October 26, 1978, in London. Politician, historian, and novelist. For many years, Walder served as a Conservative member of Parliament. Among his novels are *The Chanak Affair, The Short Victorious War, Bags of Swank,* and *The Fair Ladies of Salamanca.* Obituaries and other sources: *The Author's and Writer's Who's Who,* 6th edition, Burke's Peerage, 1971; *Who's Who,* 130th edition, St. Martin's, 1978; *Publishers Weekly,* December 11, 1978.

* * *

WALDO, E. Hunter
See STURGEON, Theodore Hamilton

* * *

WALDO, Edward Hamilton
See STURGEON, Theodore Hamilton

* * *

WALE, Michael

EDUCATION: Attended school in Bedales, Hampshire, England. *Residence:* London, England. *Agent:* Isobel Davie Ltd., 13 Bruton St., London W1X 8JY, England.

CAREER: Worked as journalist in Kendal, England, for *Westmoreland Gazette,* in Newcastle, England, for *Northern Echo,* in London, England, for *Daily Express,* and in London, England, for *Sun;* free-lance writer. Notable assignments include coverage of the record industry, race riots in Notting Hill, and betting shops. Regular broadcaster (comedy writer and performer) on "Start the Week," and "Scene and Heard"; presented weekly rock music program, "Rockspeak," Radio 1, 1973-75; appeared regularly on teenage program, "London Bridge," London Weekend Television, 1974-75; reporter for "Today," Thames Television, 1975; comedy writer for performers, including David Frost.

WRITINGS: Voxpop (study of the rock music industry), Harrap, 1972; (with Tam Paton) *The Bay City Rollers,* Everest, 1975.

Author of television documentary "The Kinks at the Rainbow," British Broadcasting Corp.

Radio programs: "Death of a Rolling Stone" (documentary), Radio 4; "Donovan" (documentary), Radio 4; "The Betty Witherspoon Show" (series), Radio 2, 1974.

Author of column in *Queens Park Rangers.* Author of recording "Funny Game Football." Also author of live show for "The Osmonds" and adaptation of "Top of the Pops." Contributor to popular magazines and newspapers, including *Financial Times* and *Observer.*

AVOCATIONAL INTERESTS: Sport (playing soccer, exercising race horses), visiting the country.

* * *

WALKOWITZ, Daniel J(ay) 1942-

PERSONAL: Born November 25, 1942, in Paterson, N.J.; son of Sol (a shopkeeper) and Selda (a nurse; maiden name, Margel) Walkowitz; married Judith Rosenberg (a historian and professor), December 26, 1965; children: Rebecca. *Education:* University of Rochester, A.B. (honors), 1964, Ph.D., 1972; graduate study at University of Grenoble, 1965. *Politics:* "Democrat/Socialist." *Religion:* "Secular (cultural, not religious) Jew." *Home:* 710 South Second Ave., Highland Park, N.J. 08904. *Office:* Department of History, New York University, 19 University Pl., New York, N.Y. 10003.

CAREER: Campus Laundry (retail business), Rochester, N.Y., partner, 1961-64; State University of New York College at Brockport, visiting instructor in history, 1967; University of Rochester, Rochester, N.Y., assistant lecturer in history, 1967-69; Rensselaer Polytechnic Institute, Troy, N.Y., instructor in history, 1969-71; Rutgers University, New Brunswick, N.J., assistant professor of history, 1971-78; New York University, New York, N.Y., assistant professor of history, 1978—. Vice-president and project director of Past Time Productions (in film and video development), 1978—; project director for WMHT-TV (Schenectady, N.Y.), 1976-77; consultant to publishers. *Member:* American Historical Association, Organization of American Historians. *Awards, honors:* National Endowment for the Humanities media grants, 1976-77, 1978.

WRITINGS: (Editor with Peter N. Stearns) *Workers in the Industrial Revolution,* Transaction Books, 1974; *Worker City, Company Town,* University of Illinois Press, 1978. Contributor to history journals. Member of editorial board of *Journal of Social History,* 1974—; editorial consultant, *Feminist Studies,* 1977—.

WORK IN PROGRESS: A series of historical dramatic films for television on the industrialization of American society; research on social history and industrial archaeology, the political economy and social history of casual labor, and the docks and dockyard workers in New York City.

SIDELIGHTS: Walkowitz' book, *Worker City, Company Town,* has been made into a film, "Molders of Troy," for Public Broadcasting System, 1979.

Walkowitz wrote: "I see all my work as intensely personal and political, but I feel my writing should not preach; rather, it should create a sense of disjuncture in the reader or viewer. Irony, cynicism, and a profound sense of contradiction can impel critical rethinking of all assumptions—and in a country where the assumptions of the social and economic system are usually not considered, good, accurate, historical analysis should be full of the contradictions of that system."

* * *

WALLACE, Amy 1955-

PERSONAL: Born July 3, 1955, in Los Angeles, Calif.; daughter of Irving (a writer) and Sylvia (a writer; maiden name, Kahn) Wallace. *Education:* Graduated from Berkeley Psychic Institute. *Politics:* "Changes all the time. Generally, though, anarchism." *Religion:* "Ecstatic." *Agent:* Arthur Pine Associates, Inc., 1780 Broadway, New York, N.Y. 10019. *Office address:* P.O. Box 4507, Berkeley, Calif. 94704.

CAREER: Psychic reader; writer.

WRITINGS: (With father, Irving Wallace, and brother, David Wallechinsky) *The People's Almanac Presents the Book of Lists,* Morrow, 1977; (with I. Wallace) *The Two: A Biography,* Simon & Schuster, 1978; (with William Henkin) *The Psychic Healing Book,* Delacorte, 1978.

WORK IN PROGRESS: Book of Lists II.

SIDELIGHTS: In the introduction to *The Book of Lists* Amy Wallace and her co-authors explained how they got the idea for the book: "To begin with, we were always fascinated by lists. Then in 1975, when we prepared *The People's Almanac,* we decided to test the entire appeal of lists—were other people really as interested in them as we were?—by including a light sampling of them.... Readers and media alike found these lists and responded with overwhelming affirmation.... From the time *The People's Almanac* was first published to the present day, readers' letters have poured in, coming by the hundreds from every corner of the continent, and writers of the largest percentage of these letters have wanted to discuss our lists, add to them, and suggest new ones. And that's how *The Book of Lists* was born. Out of our interest. Out of public enthusiasm."

Publishers Weekly quipped: "No cocktail party habitue worth his martini will be able to venture out without his copy of this funny and fascinating book." Commenting on "how not to be listless," *Saturday Review* found *The Book of Lists* "an ideal dipping-into book.... with lots to disbelieve, brood over, and enjoy."

BIOGRAPHICAL/CRITICAL SOURCES: Amy Wallace, Irving Wallace, and David Wallechinsky, *The People's Almanac Presents the Book of Lists,* Morrow, 1977; *Publishers Weekly,* March 21, 1977; *Saturday Review,* April 30, 1977; *Time,* May 2, 1977; *New York Times,* May 6, 1977, March 8, 1978; *New York Times Book Review,* June 19, 1977, March 19, 1978.

*   *   *

WALLACE, David Rains   1945-

PERSONAL: Born August 10, 1945, in Charlottesville, Va.; son of Sebon Rains (a psychologist) and Sarah (Hahn) Wallace; married Elizabeth Ann Kendall (an artist), July 3, 1975. *Education:* Wesleyan University, Middletown, Conn., B.A. (cum laude), 1967; graduate study at Columbia University, 1967-68; Mills College, M.A., 1974. *Politics:* Democrat. *Home:* 4289 Piedmont Ave., Apt. A, Oakland, Calif. 94611.

CAREER: Metropolitan Park District of Columbus and Franklin County, Columbus, Ohio, public information specialist, 1974-78; free-lance writer, 1978—. *Member:* Sierra Club, Nature Conservancy, National Audubon Society, Zero Population Growth.

WRITINGS: The Dark Range: A Naturalist's Night Notebook, illustrations by Roger Bayless, Sierra Club Books, 1978. Contributor to conservation journals and newspapers, including *Clear Creek, Defenders of Wildlife News,* and *Ohio Sierran.*

WORK IN PROGRESS: Idle Weeds, Obscure Places: The Life and Times of a Sandstone Ridge.

SIDELIGHTS: Wallace told *CA:* "My writing arises from a lifelong fascination with this beautiful planet—its winds, waters, rocks, soils, plants, and animals. By dramatizing its ecological functionings—the relationships of living things to their surroundings and to each other—I hope to help people awaken to the fact that we remain very much a part of the biosphere, that we cannot destroy any part of it without destroying part of ourselves. I believe the human body and mind are gifts from the planet, and that we can't cherish the gifts without cherishing the giver."

BIOGRAPHICAL/CRITICAL SOURCES: San Francisco Bay Guardian, November 9, 1978.

*   *   *

WALLACE, Ian
See PRITCHARD, John Wallace

*   *   *

WALLACE, Walter L.   1927-

PERSONAL: Born August 21, 1927, in Washington, D.C.; son of Walter L., Sr. and Rosa Belle (Powell) Wallace; married Barbara Jeffries, November 1, 1958 (divorced April 13, 1963); married Patricia Denton (a teacher), March 28, 1964 (separated); children: Jeffrey Richard, Robin Claire, Jennifer Rose. *Education:* Columbia University, B.A., 1954; Atlanta University, M.A., 1955; University of Chicago, Ph.D., 1963. *Politics:* Independent. *Religion:* None. *Office:* Department of Sociology, Princeton University, Princeton, N.J. 08540.

CAREER: Atlanta University, Spelman College, Atlanta, Ga., instructor in sociology, 1955-57; National Opinion Research Center, Chicago, Ill., associate study director, 1960-62; Northwestern University, Evanston, Ill., 1963-71, began as lecturer, became professor of sociology; Princeton University, Princeton, N.J., professor of sociology, 1971—. Visiting scholar at Russell Sage Foundation, 1968, staff sociologist, 1969—. Fellow of Center for Advanced Study in the Behavioral Sciences, 1974-75. Member of board of trustees of Foundation for Child Development, 1974—; member of executive committee of Assembly of Behavioral and Social Scientists, 1974—. *Military service:* U.S. Army, 1950-52.

MEMBER: American Sociological Association (member of council, 1971-74), American Association for the Advancement of Science, Caucus of Black Sociologists, Sociological Research Association.

WRITINGS: Student Culture, Aldine, 1966; (editor and contributor) *Sociological Theory,* Aldine, 1969; *The Logic of Science in Sociology,* Aldine, 1971; (with James E. Conyers) *Black Elected Officials,* Russell Sage Foundation, 1975. Contributor to professional journals.

*   *   *

WALLS, William J(acob)   1885-1975

PERSONAL: Born May 8, 1885, in Rutherford County, N.C.; son of Edward (a farmer) and Harriet (Edgerton) Walls; married Dorothy L. Jordan (a missionary), December 6, 1956. *Education:* Livingstone College, Salisbury, N.C., A.B., 1908; Hood Theological Seminary, B.D., 1913; graduate study at Columbia University; University of Chicago, M.A., 1941. *Politics:* Independent Republican.

CAREER: Ordained American Methodist Episcopal minister; worked as pastor of American Methodist Episcopal Zion churches; bishop of Zion Church of the United States of America, 1924-75. Chairman of board of religious education at Livingstone College, 1924-68, member of board of trustees, 1941-73. Member of central committee of World Council of Churches, 1948-54; vice-president of National Council of Churches; member of executive board and vice-president of World Methodist Council. *Awards, honors:* LL.D. from Livingstone College, 1942; D.D. from Gammon Theological Seminary and Hood Theological Seminary.

WRITINGS: Joseph Charles Price: Educator and Race Leader, Christopher, 1943; *The Romance of a College: An Evolution of the Auditorium* (address), privately printed, 1963; *The African Methodist Episcopal Church: Reality of the Black Church*, American Methodist Episcopal Zion Publishing, 1974. Also author of *Prophets of Freedom*. Author of pamphlets and booklets. Editor of *Star of Zion*, 1920-24.

(Died April 23, 1975)

* * *

WALTER, Claire 1943-

PERSONAL: Born September 9, 1943, in Bridgeport, Conn.; daughter of Oscar (an engineer) and Louise (a translator; maiden name, Laden) Walter; married Burns E. Cameron (an executive recruiter), April 20, 1974. *Education:* Boston University, A.B., 1965. *Home:* 939 Bloomfield St., Hoboken, N.J. 07030.

CAREER: U.S. Camera & Travel, New York City, assistant editor, 1964-67; *Ski*, New York City, managing editor, 1967-71; Davis Public Relations, New York City, director, ski marketing services, 1971-73; Swissair Co., New York City, sales promotion representative, 1973-75; writer and editor, 1975—. Publicity chairman, Hoboken Environment Committee, 1975—. *Member:* Eastern Ski Writers Association (member of board of directors, 1973-74, 1975-77).

WRITINGS: Women in Sports: Skiing, Harvey House, 1977; *Winners: The Blue Ribbon Encyclopedia of Awards*, Facts on File, 1978; (contributor) *London Daily Mail Skiers Guide*, Ski Specialists Ltd., 1978. Contributor of articles to magazines and newspapers. Editor, *Take-off* (Academy of Aeronautics Newsletter); contributing editor, *New Jersey Monthly, Camera 35, Ski Racing*, and *Skiing Trade Monthly News*.

WORK IN PROGRESS: The Atlas of the World's Airlines and Airlanes, for Facts on File.

SIDELIGHTS: Walter has done extensive coverage of skiing and other winter sports for newspapers and magazines. Her travel writings usually lean towards sports subjects too. Fluent in German and adequate in French, she has traveled widely in Europe, especially the Alpine Mountains.

* * *

WALTERS, C(harles) Glenn 1929-

PERSONAL: Born April 20, 1929, in Americus, Ga.; son of Johnny Bascomb and Eunice Dorothy (Coleman) Walters; married Patricia Mohelnitzky, September 27, 1952; children: Michael, David, Greg, Julie. *Education:* Auburn University, B.S., 1955, M.S., 1957; University of Illinois, Ph.D., 1963. *Religion:* "Practicing non-Catholic." *Home:* 9 High Forest Dr., Heritage Hills, Carbondale, Ill. 62901. *Office:* Department of Marketing, Southern Illinois University, Carbondale, Ill. 62901.

CAREER: Louisiana State University, Baton Rouge, assistant professor, 1961-66, associate professor of marketing, 1966-70, coordinator of marketing, 1969-70; Mississippi State University, Starkville, professor of marketing, 1970-77; Southern Illinois University, Carbondale, professor of marketing and chairman of department, 1977—. *Military service:* U.S. Navy, 1948-52. *Member:* American Marketing Association, Southwestern Marketing Association, Southern Marketing Association, Mid-South Marketing Teacher's Conference, Beta Gamma Sigma.

WRITINGS: Consumer Behavior: An Integrated Framework, Irwin, 1970, 3rd edition, 1978; *Marketing Channels*, Ronald, 1974; *Marketing Channels*, Goodyear Publishing, 1977; *Classics in Marketing*, Goodyear Publishing, 1978; *Classics in Consumer Behavior*, Goodyear Publishing, 1979.

WORK IN PROGRESS: Editing *Readings in Marketing* for CBI-Wadsworth; *Basic Marketing: A Contingency Approach*, for CBI-Wadsworth; research on marketing theory, marketing channels, and consumer behavior.

SIDELIGHTS: Walters writes: "*Consumer Behavior* orginally evolved out of personal research to overcome a deficiency in my marketing background. The book deals with the psychology and sociology of why, when, and where people buy. It was the second text in what is now a primary marketing area. The *Channels* text is a pioneering textbook in marketing. It was the first complete text to be published on this subject. It deals with the movement of products from manufacturer to consumer and integrates the study of marketing institutions."

* * *

WALTON, Richard Eugene 1931-

PERSONAL: Born April 15, 1931, in Pulaski, Iowa; son of Leo Richard and Florence (King) Walton; married Sharon Claire Doty, April 13, 1952; children: Richard (deceased), John, Elizabeth, Margaret, Andrew. *Education:* Purdue University, B.S., 1953, M.S., 1954; graduate study at Victoria University of Wellington, 1953; Harvard University, D.B.A., 1959; postdoctoral study at University of Michigan, 1962-63. *Home:* 109 Beaver Rd., Weston, Mass. 02193. *Office:* School of Business, Harvard University, Boston, Mass. 02163.

CAREER: Purdue University, Lafayette, Ind., faculty member of Krannert Graduate School of Industrial Administration, 1959-68; Harvard University, School of Business, Boston, Mass., faculty member, 1968—, Edsel Bryant Ford Professor of Business, 1970-76, director of Research Division, 1970-76. Member of board of directors of Berol Corp.; member of board of trustees of Marketing Science Institute; consultant to industrial firms and government agencies, including U.S. Department of State. *Military service:* U.S. Army, 1954-56. *Awards, honors:* Ford Foundation grant, 1962-63.

WRITINGS: The Impact of the Professional Engineering Union, Division of Research, Graduate School of Business Administration, Harvard University, 1961; (with R. B. McKersie) *A Behavioral Theory of Labor Negotiations: An Analysis of a Social Interaction System*, McGraw, 1965; *Interpersonal Peacemaking: Confrontations and Third Party Consultation*, Addison-Wesley, 1969.

WORK IN PROGRESS: A book, with Len Schlesinger, on "the theory and practice of work restructuring and the quality of work life activities in industry."

SIDELIGHTS: Walton comments: "I am currently studying ways in which new information technologies can be designed to best fit the needs of the human organizations which employ them."

* * *

WARD, Andrew (Spencer) 1946-

PERSONAL: Born January 7, 1946, in Chicago, Ill.; son of Fredrick Champion (an educator) and Duira (in social services; maiden name, Baldinger) Ward; married Deborah

Huntington (a nurse practitioner), July 27, 1969; children: Jacob Champion. *Education:* Attended Oberlin College, 1964-66, and Rhode Island School of Design, 1966-68. *Home:* 87 Olive St., New Haven, Conn. 06511.

CAREER: Writer. Worked as photographer for Ford Foundation in New Delhi, India, 1968-70; free-lance writer and photographer, 1970-72; Marvelwood School, Cornwall, Conn., art teacher, 1972-74. *Awards, honors:* Atlantic grant from *Atlantic,* 1977, for *Fits and Starts.*

WRITINGS: Fits and Starts: The Premature Memoirs of Andrew Ward, Little, Brown, 1978; *Bits and Pieces* (essays and parodies), Little, Brown, 1980.

Work anthologized in *Best American Short Stories of 1973,* edited by Martha Foley. Contributor to magazines and newspapers, including *Redbook, Fantasy and Science Fiction, Horizon, American Heritage,* and *Inquiry.* Contributing editor of *Atlantic Monthly.*

WORK IN PROGRESS: Two novels; short stories.

SIDELIGHTS: Ward writes: "I consider myself a humorist, a designation which performs the function of forcing my intentions out into the open. My work must pass a simple test; if it fails to get a laugh or raise a smile from my readers (meaning my wife and brother) then it fails to justify itself. This may not seem a particularly lofty test, but I'm not a very lofty fellow, and believe that laughter, at least the laughter that comes with recognition, is our surest barometer of truth. Besides, being a humorist beats being a puzzle cutter, a soda jerk, a machinist, a janitor, a teacher, a photographer, or any of the other professions I've given a try."

BIOGRAPHICAL/CRITICAL SOURCES: New Haven Register, June 5, 1978; *Stamford Advocate,* August 13, 1978.

*   *   *

WARD, Douglas Turner   1930-

PERSONAL: Born May 5, 1930, in Burnside, La.; son of Roosevelt and Dorothy (Short) Ward; married Diana Hoyt Powell, 1966; children: two. *Education:* Attended Wilberforce University, 1946-47, and University of Michigan, 1947-48. *Home:* 222 East 11th St., New York, N.Y. 10003. *Agent:* Gilbert Parker, Curtis Brown Ltd., 575 Madison Ave., New York, N.Y. 10022. *Office:* 60 East 56th St., New York, N.Y. 10022.

CAREER: Playwright, actor, producer, and director; worked as a journalist in New York City, 1948-51; studied acting in New York City, 1955-58; appeared in productions of "The Iceman Cometh," 1959, "A Raisin in the Sun," 1960-62, "One Flew Over the Cuckoo's Nest," 1963, and "Ceremonies in Dark Old Men," 1969; appeared as actor on television and in film; Negro Ensemble Company (NEC), New York City, co-founder, 1965, artistic director, 1967—; producer or director of and actor in plays including "Man Better Man," 1969, and "The River Niger," 1972. *Awards, honors:* Vernon Rice Drama Award, 1966, Obie award, 1966, Lambda Kappa Nu citation, 1968, special Tony award, 1969, and Brandeis University creative arts award, 1969, all for "Happy Ending" and "Day of Absence"; Drama Desk acting citation, 1969; Obie award, 1970, for "The Reckoning."

WRITINGS—Plays: *Happy Ending* [and] *Day of Absence* (comedies; first produced in New York at St. Mark's Playhouse, November 15, 1965), Dramatists Play Service, 1966; *The Reckoning* (first produced at St. Mark's Playhouse, September 13, 1969), Dramatists Play Service, 1970; *Broth-*

erhood (first produced with "Day of Absence" at St. Mark's Playhouse, May, 1970), Dramatists Play Service, 1970; *Two Plays,* Third Press, 1975.

Plays have been represented in anthologies, including *New Black Playwrights,* edited by William Couch, Jr., Louisiana State University Press, 1968; *Black Drama,* edited by William Brasmer and Dominick Consolo, Merrill, 1970; *Contemporary Black Drama,* edited by Clinton Oliver and Stephanie Sills, Scribner, 1971; *Afro-American Literature,* edited by Robert Hayden, David Burrows, and Frederick Lapides, Harcourt, 1971; *Blackamerican Literature,* edited by Ruth Miller, Free Press, 1971.

SIDELIGHTS: Perhaps Ward's greatest contribution to drama, and black drama in particular, is the Negro Ensemble Company (NEC) in New York City, which he co-founded with Robert Hooks and Gerald Krone. The NEC was formed "to provide a showcase for black acting, writing, and administrative talents largely shut out from the world of white audiences, and to develop and expand those talents while building a black audience for them." The NEC was financed by a grant awarded by the Ford Foundation. Ward commented on the importance of the grant to the NEC: "Until now . . . the theatre has more or less defined, created, and controlled the possibilities of Negro stage activity. The Negro Ensemble Company is an example of Negroes' controlling their own possibilities." Two years after the founding of the NEC, John G. O'Connor noted in the *Wall Street Journal* that "from the beginning, the NEC's productions have been notable for their excellent acting, intelligent direction, and imaginative presentation." He also felt that it was "already perhaps the finest acting-producing company in the United States."

Loften Mitchell has described Ward as "a polemicist, blessed with a keen sense of humor." Of Ward's first two plays, "Happy Ending" and "Day of Absence," Mitchell wrote: He has, in effect, taken what could be two slight jokes and made two plays out of them." Mitchell added, "the discovery of the Negro writer's use of humor in 1965-66 can only relate to one obvious fact—that white critics have not really been seeing black drama unfold!"

Howard Taubman reported in a *New York Times* review of "Happy Ending" and "Day of Absence" that "increasingly the Negro is using sardonic laughter to express his resentment at years of forced inferiority and to articulate his passion for change. . . . Douglas Turner Ward chuckles at the white employer-Negro servant relationship and bellows raucously at a Southern city's dependence on its Negro population." According to Loften Mitchell, in "Happy Ending" Ward "points up, quite humorously, the interdependence of groups in America. Whites depend on Negroes for their labor and Negroes use Whites to promote their future. The question the author raises is: When will both groups learn the truth of their interrelationship and interdependence?"

"Day of Absence" is satirically sharper than "Happy Ending." Clive Barnes commented in the *New York Times:* "It ["Day of Absence"] is a very clever, very funny and pertinent play. But what gives it an extra power is Ward's conception of it as a minstrel show in reverse. All the white roles are played by blacks in white-face or rather that minstrel vestigial equilvalent of white-face, and the results are both savage and touching. . . . The conclusion of 'Day of Absence' is almost gentle. Okay, the whites have been given a warning, in a friendly fashion, but the situation is at the very least negotiable."

BIOGRAPHICAL/CRITICAL SOURCES: New York

Times, November 16, 1965, September 14, 1969, March 18, 1970; Loften Mitchell, *Black Drama: The Story of the American Negro Theatre,* Hawthorn, 1967; *Wall Street Journal,* February 19, 1969.*

* * *

WARDELL, Dean
See PRINCE, J(ack) H(arvey)

* * *

WATERS, Ethel 1896-1977

PERSONAL: Born October 31, 1896, in Chester, Pa.; daughter of John Wesley Waters and Louisa Tar Anderson; married Merritt Purnsley, 1914 (divorced); married Edward Mallory (divorced).

CAREER: Actress, singer, and writer. Worked as a maid in Philadelphia, Pa., before making first vaudeville appearance in 1917; played night clubs and leading vaudeville circuits, 1917-27; stage actress, 1927-70; motion picture actress, 1929-59; radio and television performer, 1934-70. *Military service:* California State Militia, 7th Women's Ambulance Corps, 1942; became honorary captain. *Member:* Hollywood Victory Committee (council member, 1942), Actors Equity Association (executive council, 1942-43), Negro Actor's Guild of America (vice-president, 1942-43), American Federation of Television and Radio Artists, American Guild of Variety Artists, American Guild of Musical Artists, Screen Actors Guild. *Awards, honors:* Nominated for Academy Award from Academy of Motion Picture Arts and Sciences, 1949, for "Pinky," and 1952, for "The Member of the Wedding"; Negro Actor's Guild of America plaque, 1949, for "Pinky"; American National Theatre and Academy, St. Genesius Medal, 1951; Joseph Jefferson Award, 1970, for "The Member of the Wedding."

WRITINGS: (With Charles Samuels) *His Eye Is on the Sparrow* (autobiography), Doubleday, 1951; *To Me It's Wonderful* (autobiography), Harper, 1972.

SIDELIGHTS: Like many show business personalities, Ethel Waters rose from the depths of an impoverished childhood to become a celebrity. Yet she was distinguished by an optimism which transcended the many dark moments in a largely prosperous career. "I've stolen food to live on," she once said; "I was a real Dead End kid." When she was seventeen she left her job as a chambermaid to become what she called "a honkeytonk entertainer . . . I used to work from nine until unconscious. I was just a young girl then and when I tried to sing anything but the double meaning songs they'd say 'Oh my God, Ethel, get hot!'" She later sang Negro spirituals at home and continued her religious devotion throughout her life. In recent years, Water crusaded with Billy Graham.

Waters always preferred acting over singing and claimed to have had "no acting technique." "I act instinctively," she said; "That's why I can't play any role that isn't based on something in my life." In "The Member of the Wedding" Waters was described as "superb," "magnificently assured," and "high up among the first ladies of American theatre." One admirer of her acting ability, Oscar Hammerstein, was one of the signatories of a notice praising Waters's 1938 performance in "Mamba's Daughters" as an example of outstanding acting. The notice was a response to the play's lukewarm reviews.

Never unwilling to discuss the hardships of her life, Waters won praise for the candidness of her first autobiography, *His Eye Is on the Sparrow.* On its first page she wrote: "I was never a child. I never felt I belonged. I was always an outsider." Even though Waters reportedly made over a million dollars in her lifetime, she faced financial crises several times in her cyclical career. Though some of her money was spent to help support and educate girls from deprived backgrounds, she admitted: "Where I come from people don't get close enough to money to keep a working acquaintance with it. So, I don't know how to keep it."

BIOGRAPHICAL/CRITICAL SOURCES: Ethel Waters and Charles Samuels, *His Eye Is on the Sparrow,* Doubleday, 1951; Ethel Waters, *To Me It's Wonderful,* Harper, 1972.

OBITUARIES: New York Times, September 2, 1977; *Washington Post,* September 2, 1977.*

(Died September 1, 1977, in Los Angeles, Calif.)

* * *

WATERS, Thomas F(rank) 1926-

PERSONAL: Born May 17, 1926, in Hastings, Mich.; son of Raymond Edward (a clothier) and Ella (Steinke) Waters; married Carol Yonker, June 21, 1953; children: Daniel Frank, Elizabeth Lee, Benton Edward. *Education:* Michigan State University, B.S., 1952, M.S., 1953, Ph.D., 1956. *Home:* 2551 Charlotte St., St. Paul, Minn. 55113. *Office:* Department of Biology, University of Minnesota, 1980 Folwell Ave., St. Paul, Minn. 55108.

CAREER: Michigan Department of Conservation, Vanderbilt, fisheries biologist, 1956-57; University of Minnesota, St. Paul, assistant professor, 1958-61, associate professor, 1961-68, professor of fisheries, 1968—. *Military service:* U.S. Navy, radio technician, 1944-46. *Member:* North American Benthological Society, American Fisheries Society, American Society of Limnology and Oceanography, Ecological Society of America, American Institute of Fishery Research Biologists.

WRITINGS: The Streams and Rivers of Minnesota, University of Minnesota Press, 1977. Contributor to scientific journals.

WORK IN PROGRESS: Research for books on the natural resources of the upper Mississippi River and Lake Superior regions.

SIDELIGHTS: Waters wrote: "I am vitally interested in the preservation of the natural values of rivers and streams—from biological, recreational, aesthetic, social, and historical viewpoints. I conduct scientific research primarily on stream ecology and fisheries, but my avocational and community interests also center on the influence of rivers on the quality of the environment of my own region and the nation."

* * *

wa THIONG'O, Ngugi
See NGUGI, James T(hiong'o)

* * *

WATKIN, Lawrence Edward 1901-

PERSONAL: Born December 9, 1901, in Camden, N.Y.; son of George Edward and Caroline Harriet (Covert) Watkin; married Dorothy Edwards Parke, September 1, 1926; children: Lawrence Parke, Margaret Jean, Anne Caroline. *Education:* Syracuse University, A.B., 1924; Harvard University, A.M., 1925; also attended Columbia University.

Home: 3450 West Benjamin Holt Dr., Stockton, Calif. 95209.

CAREER: Syracuse University, Syracuse, N.Y., instructor in English, 1925-26; Washington and Lee University, Lexington, Va., assistant professor, 1926-38, associate professor of English and composition, 1938-42, founder of little theatre; free-lance screenwriter in Hollywood, Calif., 1945-47; Walt Disney Studio, Hollywood, screenwriter, 1947-65, producer of own screenplay, "The Great Locomotive Chase," 1956; California State University, Fullerton, professor of English, 1965-70, professor emeritus, 1970—; Walt Disney Studio, screenwriter, 1970—. *Military service:* U.S. Naval Reserve, 1942-45; head of aviation training manuals unit; became lieutenant commander. *Member:* Phi Gamma Delta, Sigma Upsilon.

WRITINGS: On Borrowed Time (novel), Knopf, 1937, published as *On Borrowed Time: A Comedy in Two Acts,* Dramatists Play Service, 1964; *Geese in the Forum* (novel), Knopf, 1940; *Gentleman From England* (novel), Knopf, 1941; *Thomas Jones and His Nine Lives* (juvenile), Harcourt, 1941; *Marty Markham* (juvenile; basis for "Spin and Marty" television series), Holt, 1942; *Darby O'Gill and the Little People* (based on the Walt Disney Production of own screenplay), introduction by Walt Disney, Dell, 1959.

Screenplays; all Walt Disney Productions: "On Borrowed Time" (based on his own novel), released by Metro-Goldwyn-Mayer, 1939; "Keeper of the Bees" (based on the novel by Gene Stratton Porter), Columbia, 1947; (author of additional dialogue) "Task Force," Warner Bros., 1949; "Beaver Valley," RKO, 1950; "Treasure Island" (based on the novel by Robert Louis Stevenson), RKO, 1950; "The Story of Robin Hood and His Merrie Men," RKO, 1952; "The Sword and the Rose" (based on *When Knighthood Was in Flower,* a novel by Charles Major), RKO, 1953; "Rob Roy, the Highland Rogue," RKO, 1954; "The Great Locomotive Chase" (based on a historical incident), Buena Vista, 1956; "The Light in the Forest" (based on the novel by Conrad Richter), Buena Vista, 1958; "Darby O'Gill and the Little People," Buena Vista, 1959; "Ten Who Dared" (based on the journal of Major John Wesley Powell), Buena Vista, 1960; "The Biscuit Eater," 1970.

Contributor of scripts to television programs, and of articles to magazines.

WORK IN PROGRESS: More writing projects.*

* * *

WATSON, Aldren A(uld) 1917-

PERSONAL: Born May 10, 1917, in Brooklyn, N.Y.; son of Ernest W. (an artist) and Eva (an artist; maiden name, Auld) Watson; married Nancy Dingman (a writer), August 9, 1941; children: Wendy Watson Harrah, Peter, Clyde (daughter), Linda Watson Wright, Ann Watson Blagden, Nancy Watson Cameron, Caitlin, Thomas. *Education:* Attended Yale University, 1935, and Art Students League (New York). *Home address:* P.O. Box 482, Brattleboro, Vt. 05301.

CAREER: Illustrator (books and advertising) and artist (including commissioned murals), 1939—; also worked as cartographer. Textbook designer for Heath, 1965-66; chief editor of curriculum-oriented material for Silver Burdett, 1966-68. Official artist for National Aeronautics & Space Administration, 1968. Teacher of bookbinding courses; books exhibited in the United States, Canada, and Europe. Field worker for American Friends Service Committee during World War II. Design consultant for publishers and private

corporations. *Member:* Authors Guild of Authors League of America. *Awards, honors:* First prize from Domesday Book Illustration Competition, 1945, for *Moby Dick.*

WRITINGS—Self-illustrated children's books: (With wife, Nancy Dingman Watson) *The Village Blacksmith,* Crowell, 1958, new edition, 1977; *My Garden Grows,* Viking, 1962; (with Ernest William Watson) *The Watson Drawing Book,* Reinhold, 1962; *Hand Bookbinding: A Manual of Instruction,* Reinhold, 1963, 3rd edition, 1975; *The River: A Story Told in Pictures,* Holt, 1963; *Town Mouse, Country Mouse,* Holt, 1966; *A Maple Tree Begins,* Viking, 1970; *Country Furniture,* Crowell, 1974. Also author of *What Does A Begin With?*

Illustrator of more than two hundred books for children and adults, including Frances Frost, *Christmas in the Woods,* Harper, 1942; Clement Clarke Moore, *A Visit From St. Nicholas,* Peter Pauper, 1950; A. White, *Prehistoric America,* Random House, 1951; N. D. Watson, *Annie's Spending Spree,* Viking, 1957; *Mother Goose Nursery Rhymes,* Dutton, 1958; Muehl, *My Name Is . . . ,* Holiday House, 1959; Felton, *Mike Fink: Best of the Keelboatmen,* Dodd, 1960; M. Bartlett, *The Clean Brook,* Crowell, 1961; Bartlett, *Where the Brook Begins,* Crowell, 1961; Constant, *Willie and the Wildcat Well,* Crowell, 1962; N. D. Watson, *Sugar on Snow,* Viking, 1964; Evans, *The Snow Book,* Little, Brown, 1965; N. D. Watson, *Katie's Chicken,* Knopf, 1965; Maria Puccinelli, *Catch a Fish,* Bobbs-Merrill, 1965; Regina Kelly, *The Picture Story and Biography of John Adams,* Follett, 1965; Carolyn Horton, *Cleaning and Preserving Bindings,* American Library Association, 1967; Lilian Moore, *Just Right,* Parents' Magazine Press, 1968; N. D. Watson, *Carol to a Child, and a Christmas Pageant,* World Publishing, 1969; Bernice Kohn Hunt, *A First Look at Psychology,* Hawthorn, 1969; Herbert H. Wong, *Our Terrariums,* Addison-Wesley, 1969; N. D. Watson, *New Under the Stars,* Little, Brown, 1970; William Ivan Martin, *Tatty Mae and Catty Mae,* Holt, 1970; Carleton Coon, *The Hunting Peoples,* Little, Brown, 1971; N. D. Watson, *Tommy's Mommy's Fish,* Viking, 1971; Bernard Middleton, *Restoration of Leather Bindings,* American Library Association, 1972; Murray Hoyt, *30 Miles for Icecream,* Stephen Greene, 1974; Winthrop Dolan, *A Choice of Sundials,* Stephen Greene, 1974; *Where Everyday Things Come From,* Platt, 1974; Frank Rowesome, *The Bright and Glowing Place,* Stephen Greene, 1975; Howard Roger Garis, *Uncle Wiggily's Happy Days,* Platt, 1976; *Uncle Wiggily and the Sugar Cookie,* Platt, 1977; *Uncle Wiggily and the Runaway Cheese,* Platt, 1977.

WORK IN PROGRESS: A book on hand woodworking tools and their use, publication expected in 1980; a book on construction of wooden sailing vessels, pre-1900, publication expected in 1981; illustrating articles for various magazines on tools.

SIDELIGHTS: Watson prepared himself in the traditional manner for a career as a professional artist, by studying painting and drawing, as well as etching, caricature, fashion illustration, and color block printing. But his interests soon broadened and his expertise came to include book illustration, hand bookbinding, type and lettering, and cartography. He designed a new type-face for one of his own books, taught and wrote about bookbinding methods and techniques, and made maps for magazine publication and textbooks.

Watson told *CA:* "Living in rural Vermont, coping with seventy-two inches of snow, bitter cold, routine house maintenance problems, doing and making things for myself, growing a garden, raising animals for milk and meat, repairing buildings—these have influenced my interest in how-to-do-it with as little effort and time as possible. This led me to find out how people did things a generation or more ago, and why they did them.''

On his development as a writer, Watson commented: ''It looks to me now that illustrating and writing are separated by a very thin line. Considering my apparent preoccupation with how things get done, it is perhaps logical I got into writing by accident (as indeed I did) in the interest of exploring how to convey to others in any and every way possible how it can be done. If you think about it, there isn't much difference between writing and illustrating, or drawing. They are both graphic records. And if left alone, kids will both draw pictures and write ideas—with the same pencil and with almost equal clarity of expression. I don't work by any conscious underlying philosophy—I just do what I do. But—I feel that in this 1978 world more people are going to have to learn how to govern and dictate their own lives, how to provide more of their material needs, and food, if the supposed advantages of being the supreme animal are to mean anything.''

*   *   *

WATTS, Emily Stipes   1936-

PERSONAL: Born March 16, 1936, in Champaign, Ill.; daughter of Royal Arthur (a publisher) and Virginia (Schenck) Stipes; married Robert Allan Watts (a publisher), August 30, 1958; children: Benjamin, Edward, Thomas. *Education:* Attended Smith College, 1954-56; University of Illinois, B.A., 1958, M.A., 1959, Ph.D., 1963. *Home:* 1009 West University Ave., Champaign, Ill. 61820. *Office:* Department of English, University of Illinois, 100 English Building, Urbana, Ill. 61801.

CAREER: University of Illinois, Urbana, assistant professor, 1966-72, associate professor, 1972-77, professor of English and director of graduate studies, 1977—. *Member:* Authors Guild, Illinois Writers Association, Phi Beta Kappa, Phi Kappa Phi. *Awards, honors:* Woodrow Wilson fellow, 1958-59; Kappa Alpha Theta fellow, 1960; Guggenheim fellow, 1973-74.

WRITINGS: Ernest Hemingway and the Arts, University of Illinois Press, 1971; *The Poetry of American Women from 1632 to 1945,* University of Texas Press, 1977. Contributor to scholarly journals.

WORK IN PROGRESS: Research on the American novel.

SIDELIGHTS: Watts writes: ''*Ernest Hemingway and the Arts* is as much an exploration of interdisciplinary critical techniques as it is a study of Hemingway's writing. I have hoped to contribute as much to critical methodology as to an understanding of Hemingway. This book was named as a Scholars Library selection by the Modern Language Association, and a portion is currently being translated for publication in Germany.

''*The Poetry of American Women From 1632 to 1945* is an attempt to reintroduce a number of early American women poets to the mainstream of critical concern. The nature and significance of women's poetry within the general context of American poetry have often been ignored and should be considered as critics and scholars seek new ways to understand poetry by Americans—both male and female.''

WEAVER, Ward
See MASON, F(rancis) van Wyck

*   *   *

WEAVER, Warren   1894-1978

OBITUARY NOTICE: Born July 17, 1894, in Reedsburg, Wis.; died November 24, 1978, in New Milford, Conn. Mathematical physicist, educator, and author. For many years Weaver was an executive at the Rockefeller Foundation and the Alfred P. Sloan Foundation, allocating millions of dollars in science and medicine research grants. He won several awards for science and communication, including the Kalinga Prize, an international literary award sponsored by UNESCO, in 1965. In addition to his scientific books, Weaver also wrote *Lady Luck,* a popular book dealing with the theory of probability, and *Alice in Many Tongues,* concerning foreign translations of Lewis Carroll's *Alice in Wonderland.* Weaver owned a large collection of writings by Carroll, which is now housed at the University of Texas. Obituaries and other sources: *Current Biography,* Wilson, 1952; *The International Who's Who,* Europa, 1978; *Who's Who,* 130th edition, St. Martin's, 1978; *Who's Who in America, 40th edition,* Marquis, *1978;* New York Times, *November 25, 1978.*

*   *   *

WEBB, James H(enry), Jr.   1946-

PERSONAL: Born February 9, 1946, in St. Joseph, Mo.; son of James Henry and Vera (Hodges) Webb; married Barbara DuCote (an attorney), June 7, 1968; children: Amy Lorraine. *Education:* Attended University of Southern California, 1963-64; U.S. Naval Academy, B.S., 1968; Georgetown University, J.D., 1975. *Home:* 4712 Little Falls Rd., Arlington, Va. 22207. *Agent:* Collier Associates, 280 Madison Ave., New York, N.Y. 10016. *Office:* Committee on Veterans Affairs, U.S. House of Representatives, Washington, D.C. 20515.

CAREER: Government of Guam, Territorial Planning Commission, Agana, Guam, consultant on military planning, 1974; U.S. House of Representatives, Committee on Veterans Affairs, Washington, D.C., assistant minority counsel, 1977—. Member of Advisory Committee on Outreach of Republican National Committee, 1977—. *Military service:* U.S. Marine Corps, 1968-72; became captain; received Navy Cross, Silver Star, two Bronze Stars, National Achievement Medal, and two Purple Hearts. *Member:* Pacific Asian Studies Association, Disabled American Veterans. *Awards, honors:* Named Outstanding Veteran by Vietnam Veterans Civic Council, 1976.

WRITINGS: Micronesia and U.S. Pacific Strategy, Praeger, 1974; *Fields of Fire,* Prentice-Hall, 1978. Contributor of articles on military subjects to numerous periodicals.

SIDELIGHTS: Webb commented: ''I wrote *Fields of Fire* with a desire to convey certain truths about human nature that become illuminated in a combat environment. Too often our combat literature notes that men discover camaraderie and courage, and are debased by the realization that they are violent and cruel in their unnatural surroundings, and then stops, as if the point has been made.

''Combat to me represents not the discovery of courage, but the limitations of heroism. Most people have the capacity for bravery. But in a war of attrition such as Vietnam, the greatest acts of courage often yielded nothing more than a corpse-strewn ridgeline that would be abandoned immediately after having been attained. Courage in this environment, where day after day a man was required to place his life on the line for no attainable objective, became a waste, and the end result was that it became a precious commodity, to be used sparingly. Unless a man lost his regard for his own life (which sometimes happened), heroic acts became limited to the preservation of the unit and the man's friends. From this comes the natural feeling of isolation and disaffection from those who are not participating in the misery.

"With respect to violence, people do not discover a capacity for cruelty in combat, but rather find that their natural violent tendencies have been afforded a longer leash. If man was not a naturally violent animal, he would have become extinct long before civilization placed rational limits on his behavior. My exposure to combat showed me again and again that most violent acts, including most of those sensationalized by our press, came from good intentions. That which was labeled cruelty, even 'atrocious,' was, with limited exceptions, inherently logical given the circumstances of the alleged culprit. The acts may be wrong, in society's judgment, but if so they were mistakes of judgment, not murder. And, in many cases, I would venture that these alleged 'perpetrators' merely have been exposed to a greater truth than those who judge them. When it boils down to the actual confrontation, there are very few martyrs among us, and very many who would accomplish their own survival, no matter the cost.

"Another truth illuminated by combat is the effect of peer groups on human actions. A collection of people develops its own moral ambience, its own standards of dignity. A group will do things that an individual member would never do, on his own. Further, an individual will often pay almost any price for the respect of his peers. Thus, a group will kill when an individual would not, and an individual will sometimes die because he believes it is expected of him under the circumstances by his peers. Some men will attempt an impossible feat because the alternative—not trying—would destroy the 'pecking order' they have accomplished in the group.

"These truths, stripped bare in combat, are the most powerful driving forces in our culture."

*   *   *

WEINSTOCK, John M(artin) 1936-

PERSONAL: Born January 8, 1936, in Milwaukee, Wis.; son of Gilbert B. (an employment counselor) and Madeleine Milner (Jandell) Weinstock; married Sandra Kathryn Yarne, August 28, 1965 (divorced); children: Christopher Garth, Sigrid Liv. *Education:* University of Wisconsin, Madison, B.S., 1957, Ph.D., 1967; University of Paris, diplome, 1962. *Home:* 1109 West Ninth St., Austin, Tex. 78703. *Office:* Department of Germanic Languages, University of Texas, P.O. Box 7939, Austin, Tex. 78712.

CAREER: University of Texas, Austin, instructor, 1966-67, assistant professor, 1967-71, associate professor of Germanic languages, 1971—. Associate managing editor of *Scandinavian Studies,* 1972-76. *Military service:* U.S. Army Reserve, 1954-62. *Member:* Society for the Advancement of Scandinavian Study (member of advisory committee, 1968-72). *Awards, honors:* American Council of Learned Societies study fellowship, 1968-69; grants from University of Texas Research Institute, Norwegian Foreign Ministry, National Science Foundation, and American Council of Learned Societies, for research and travel.

WRITINGS: (Editor) *Saga og spraak: Studies in Language and Literature,* Jenkins Publishing, 1972; (editor with Robert Rovinsky) *The Hero in Scandinavian Literature,* University of Texas Press, 1974; (editor) *The Nordic Languages and Modern Linguistics,* University of Texas Press, 1978.

WORK IN PROGRESS: A book on the origins and history of skiing.

SIDELIGHTS: Weinstock comments: "My present work on skiing is motivated by a long interest in cross-country skiing and marathoning, plus my years of teaching various Scandinavian subjects (since it is in Scandinavia where the ski underwent its development).

"My skiing background includes annual trips for slalom skiing since college with my first cross-country skiing in Norway during winter of 1968-69, including competition in one thirty kilometer race.

"The ski history book is primarily an ethnological study of the ski, its origins, and its relationship to other early transportation devices such as the snowshoe, mocassin, etc., as well as its development up to the end of the nineteenth century. *Saga og spraak* is a collection of essays in honor of Lee M. Hollander and in the areas of Old Norse, general linguistics, and German literature. *The Hero in Scandinavian Literature* presents the proceedings of a symposium held at the University of Texas in 1972, including lectures, discussions, paintings by James Kacirk, and an introductory article by the editors."

*   *   *

WEISS, Adelle 1920-

PERSONAL: Born July 30, 1920, in New York, N.Y.; daughter of Clifford (an insurance agent) and Helen (Grossman) Nack; married Morris Weiss (an electronics engineer), October 23, 1943; children: Howard, Peter. *Education:* Cooper Union School of Art, A.A., 1943; State University of New York Empire State College, B.S., 1977. *Home and office:* 214 Carol Ave., Pelham, N.Y. 10803.

CAREER: Former owner of hand painting business; part-time art teacher at art and civic centers, and public schools of Greenwich, Conn. Paintings exhibited at centers, schools, and galleries. *Member:* League of Women Voters, Long Island Guild of Contemporary Artists.

WRITINGS: (With Claire V. Roth) *Art Careers,* Walck, 1963; (with Vivienne Elsiner; self-illustrated) *The Newspaper Everything Book,* Dutton, 1975; (with Elsiner; self-illustrated) *A Boat, a Bat, and a Beanie: Things to Make From Newspaper,* Lothrop, 1977.

WORK IN PROGRESS: A book on a new kind of needlework that she created.

SIDELIGHTS: Adelle Weiss writes: "I like to bring young people and adults to an individualized view of the arts as participants and as observers. One of my chief interests is the use of materials in new ways for the sake of beauty and innovation."

*   *   *

WEISSMAN, Dick
See WEISSMAN, Richard

*   *   *

WEISSMAN, Richard 1935-
(Dick Weissman)

PERSONAL: Born January 21, 1935, in Philadelphia, Pa.;

son of David (a hospital superintendent) and Crystal (a teacher) Weissman; married Diane Dechaner, June 3, 1964; children: Jaime, Janelle. *Education:* Goddard College, B.A. (social sciences), 1956; graduate study at Columbia University, 1957-58; University of Colorado, B.A. (music), 1976. *Home:* 2557 Ash St., Denver, Colo. 80207. *Office:* Department of Music, Colorado Women's College, Denver, Colo. 80220.

CAREER: Worked as record producer and studio musician in New York City, 1964-72; American Broadcasting Co., New York City, staff record producer for Command Probe Records, 1968-69; Colorado Women's College, Denver, instructor in music, 1975—. *Member:* American Federation of Musicians, American Society of Composers, Authors and Publishers. *Awards, honors:* Deems Taylor Award from American Society of Composers, Authors and Publishers, 1976, for *Folk Music Sourcebook.*

WRITINGS—Under name Dick Weissman: *Five-String Banjo Method,* three volumes, Big 3 Music Corp., 1973-77; (with Larry Sandberg) *Folk Music Sourcebook,* Knopf, 1976; *Self-Defense and Career Opportunities in the Music Business,* Crown, 1979.

Author of banjo and guitar instruction books and co-author with Dan Fox of *New Age Guitar Method,* 6 volumes, G. Schirmer. Author of recordings, including "The Things That Trouble My Mind," Capital, 1962. Composer of songs and film scores, including music for "The Edge." Contributor of articles and reviews to magazines and newspapers, including *Crawdaddy, Music Retailer, Sing Out,* and *Jazz Review.*

AVOCATIONAL INTERESTS: Politics, social psychology, anthropology.

*   *   *

WELLING, William 1924-

PERSONAL: Born February 20, 1924, in New York, N.Y.; son of Lindsay H. and Lucy Randolph (Blodget) Welling. *Education:* Yale University, B.A., 1950. *Home:* 145 East 27th St., New York, N.Y. 10016.

CAREER: Hamden Chronicle, Hamden, Conn., reporter, 1949-50; *Baltimore Evening Sun,* Baltimore, Md., general assignment and aviation reporter, 1950-54; Glenn L. Martin Co. (now Martin-Marietta), Baltimore Division, Baltimore, technical publicity manager and liaison representative to U.S. Government information offices, 1954-60; PR Associates, Inc., New York, N.Y., account executive and technical publicity manager, 1961-70; HBH Associates, Inc., Park Ridge, N.J., principal, 1970-73; writer, 1973—.

WRITINGS: Collectors' Guide to Nineteenth-Century Photographs, Macmillan, 1976; *Photography in America: The Formative Years, 1839-1900,* Crowell, 1977. Contributor to business, technical, and military journals. U.S. editor of *Urban.*

*   *   *

WELLS, George A(lbert) 1926-

PERSONAL: Born May 22, 1926, in London, England; son of George John Henry (a textile manufacturers agent) and Lilian (Mand) Wells; married Elisabeth Delhey (a teacher), 1959. *Education:* University of London, B.A., 1947, M.A., 1950, Ph.D., 1954, B.Sc., 1963. *Politics:* "No affiliation." *Religion:* None. *Residence:* St. Albans, England. *Office:* Department of German, Birkbeck College, University of London, Malet St., London W.C.1, England.

CAREER: University of London, London, England, University College, lecturer, 1949-64, reader in German, 1964-68, Birkbeck College, professor of German and head of department, 1968—. *Member:* Rationalist Press Association (vice-chairman), Goethe Society (member of council).

WRITINGS: Herder and After: A Study in the Development of Sociology, Mouton, 1959; *The Plays of Grillparzer,* Pergamon, 1969; (editor) Franz Grillparzer, *Die Juedin von Toledo* (title means "The Jewels of Toledo"), Pergamon, 1969; *The Jesus of the Early Christians,* Prometheus Books, 1971; *Did Jesus Exist?,* Prometheus Books, 1975; (editor with D.R. Oppenheimer) F.R.H. Englefield, *Language: Its Origin and Its Relation to Thought,* Scribner, 1975; *Goethe and the Development of Science, 1750-1900,* Sitjhoff, 1978. Contributor to language, philology, and philosophy journals, and to *New Humanist.* Editor of *Question.*

WORK IN PROGRESS: Research on Christian origins and on the history of New Testament criticism.

SIDELIGHTS: Wells writes: "The Grillparzer book and many of my articles on literature are, in part, attempts to combat present-day make-believe, by which I mean writing which purports to be scholarly and informative, but which does not convey clear ideas or consist of coherent argument.

"Of my two books on Jesus, I would claim that the second (of 1975) is the only one in the field which, while written by a non-theologian, fully assimilates present theological scholarship. My motive in writing it was to inform the public of the very sceptical views on early Christianity advanced by theologians in books and articles seldom consulted except by other theologians; and also to press the implications of these views on the theologians themselves.

"Concerning my book on Goethe and the history of science, my interest in the natural sciences (particularly geology) began when I was drafted to the coal mines in 1944. Study of the sciences influenced my outlook by convincing me that knowledge can only be reached from slavish dependence on fact and formulation of hypotheses which can be tested by an appeal to fact. In the natural sciences this is not disputed. I have tried to argue the same attitude in theology and in literature—spheres where it is not so universally accepted."

*   *   *

WELLS, Henry W(illis) 1895-1978

PERSONAL: Born in Sewanee, Tenn.; married Katharine Alleb Powell. *Education:* Amherst College, graduated, 1917; Columbia University, Ph.D., 1924. *Home:* 777 Kappock St., Bronx, N.Y.

CAREER: Writer. Member of graduate department of Columbia University for 40 years, worked as professor of English and comparative literature; secretary of American Society for Theater Research and U.S. Institute for Theater Technology; director of Committee for Refugee Education.

WRITINGS: The Realm of Literature, Columbia University Press, 1927, Kennikat, 1964; *The Judgement of Literature,* Norton, 1928; *Elizabethan and Jacobean Playwrights,* Columbia University Press, 1939, Greenwood Press, 1975; *New Poets From Old: A Study in Literary Genetics,* Columbia University Press, 1940, Russell & Russell, 1964; *Poetic Imagery Illustrated From Elizabethan Literature,* Columbia University Press, 1942; *The American Way of Poetry,* Columbia University Press, 1943; *Edwin J. Pratt: The Man and His Poetry,* Ryerson Press, 1947; *Introduction to Emily Dickinson,* Hendricks House, 1947; *Where Poetry Stands Now,* Ryerson Press, 1948.

(Editor) *One Thousand and One Poems of Mankind: Memorable Short Poems From the World's Chief Literatures,* Tupper and Love, 1953; *Poet and Psychiatrist: Merrill Moore, M.D.; A Critical Portrait With an Appraisal of Two Hundred of His Poems,* Twayne, 1955; *The Classical Drama of India: Studies in Its Values for the Literature and Theatre of the World,* Asia Publishing House, 1963; *Introduction to Wallace Stevens,* Indiana University Press, 1963; (editor) *Six Sanskrit Plays, In English Translation,* Asia Publishing House, 1964; (adapter into modern English) William Langland, *The Vision of Piers Plowman,* Sheed and Ward, 1959, Greenwood Press, 1968; (translator) *Ancient Poetry From China, Japan, and India,* University of South Carolina Press, 1968; (editor with Roger Sherman Loomis, and translator) *Representative Medieval and Tudor Plays,* Books for Libraries Press, 1970; (translator and adapter into English verse) *Classical Triptych: Sakuntala. The Little Clay Cart and Nagananda; New Renderings Into English Verse,* University of Mysore, 1970; (editor with Arthur Christy) *World Literature,* Books for Libraries Press, 1971; *Traditional Chinese Humor: A Study in Art and Literature,* Indiana University Press, 1971; (editor) Po Chue-i, *Translations From Po Chue-i's Collected Works,* translated by Howard S. Levy, Paragon, 1971. Contributor to journals in India, Taiwan, and Japan.

SIDELIGHTS: Although most of Wells's writings are concerned with English literature and drama, he also wrote several articles on Sanskrit drama and the drama of China, India, and Japan. Wells devoted a series of articles to the similarities between Chinese poets and those from England and America.

OBITUARIES: New York Times, March 24, 1978.*

(Died March 22, 1978, in Bronx, N.Y.)

* * *

WERLICH, David P(atrick) 1941-

PERSONAL: Born November 2, 1941, in Minneapolis, Minn.; son of Eugene Gordon (a civil engineer) and Mary Ellen (a decorator; maiden name, Doran) Werlich; married Sandra Januszewski (a retail manager), December 28, 1960; children: David A., Thomas G., Susan E. *Education:* University of Minnesota, B.A., 1963, M.A., 1967, Ph.D., 1968. *Home:* 2018 West Norwood Dr., Carbondale, Ill. 62901. *Office:* Department of History, Southern Illinois University, Carbondale, Ill. 62901.

CAREER: Great Northern Railway, Minneapolis, Minn., clerk, 1959-68; Southern Illinois University, Carbondale, assistant professor, 1968-78, associate professor of history, 1978—. Lecturer at University of Minnesota, 1966-67. *Member:* Conference on Latin American History, Midwest Association of Latin American Studies.

WRITINGS: Peru: A Short History, Southern Illinois University Press, 1978; *Research Tools for Latin American Historians: A Select, Annotated Bibliography,* Garland Publishing, 1979.

WORK IN PROGRESS: Admiral of the Amazon: John Randolph Tucker and His Confederate Colleagues in Peru.

* * *

WERNICK, Saul 1921-

PERSONAL: Born July 8, 1921, in Boston, Mass.; son of Samuel Isaac (an antiques dealer) and Rebecca (Sacks) Wernick; married Rose Toner, April, 1945 (divorced, 1960); married Julia Stratton (a photographer), March 13, 1976; children: (first marriage) Robin Toner; (second marriage) Claudia Nicole. *Education:* Boston University, B.S. and M.A., both 1948; further graduate study at University of Minnesota, 1950-53. *Religion:* Unitarian-Universalist. *Residence:* Rockport, Mass. *Agent:* Aaron M. Priest Literary Agency, 135 East 35th St., New York, N.Y. 10016.

CAREER: Associated with University of Kansas, Lawrence, 1948-50, University of Minnesota, Minneapolis, and Boston University, Boston, Mass.; Bozell & Jacobs Advertising, Inc., Minneapolis, Minn., account executive, 1953-56; Saul Wernick Advertising, Inc., Minneapolis, Minn., president, 1956-62; Hazel Bishop Co., Union, N.J., sales promotion director, 1962-64; William Esty Advertising, New York City, account supervisor, 1964-65; Kenyon & Eckhardt Advertising, Inc., New York City, director of merchandising and marketing and vice-president of company, 1965-68; Synchronex Corp., New York City, executive vice-president, 1968-73; writer, 1973—. Inventor. *Military service:* U.S. Army Air Forces, combat correspondent, 1942-45; served in Pacific theater.

MEMBER: American Legion, Veterans of Foreign Wars, Kappa Tau Alpha. *Awards, honors:* Citation from American Management Association.

WRITINGS—Novels: *Fire Ants,* Charter Books, 1978; *Cain's Touch,* Dell, 1978; *The Nazi,* Dell, 1979. Also author of *Winter Owl,* and Nick Carter mystery novels. Contributor to detective magazines.

SIDELIGHTS: Wernick writes: "I've spent most of my life at a typewriter, even though it's been only in the last three years that I've written novels. I write entertainments, because that's what reaches most of the people, but every one of my novels incorporates my personal philosophies. If I can make a lot of people *think* a little bit more than they did before, I will have accomplished what I want to do.

"A good writer is one who has an obligation to his readers: to pass on what he thinks and sees and feels, and to make them think, even for a short while, about the values he's developed about life and people. But unless his books are read, the writer hasn't been able to do this. A good writer is a craftsman who works and reworks his material and his style until it's polished and he's woven around the skeleton of his story all the things he has to say.

"I was in advertising for many years, and I saw how words and images influence people to spend money on material and often foolish things, and to elect officials to public office, and to adopt life-styles and values that are damaging to them. Okay then. If words can have so great an effect, then why not try to use them to make readers aware of what life is about and should be about, and to get them to think for themselves?"

AVOCATIONAL INTERESTS: Travel (Australia, New Guinea, Netherlands East Indies, Mexico, England, Japan, France), photography, flying (private license), literature, art, painting, firearms, sociology, psychology, anthropology, politics, reading.

* * *

WERTH, Kurt 1896-

PERSONAL: Born September 21, 1896, in Leipzig, Germany; naturalized U.S. Citizen, 1947; married; children: one son. *Education:* Attended Academy for Graphic Arts, Leipzig, Germany. *Address:* 645 West 239th St., Bronx, N.Y. 10463.

CAREER: Artist and illustrator of books and magazines in Germany and United States.

WRITINGS—All retold and self-illustrated: *The Valiant Tailor*, Viking, 1965; *The Cobbler's Dilemma: An Italian Folktale*, McGraw, 1967; *The Monkey, the Lion, and the Snake*, Viking, 1967; *King Thrushbeard*, Viking, 1968; *Lazy Jack*, Viking, 1970; (with Mabel Watts) *Molly and the Giant*, Parents' Magazine Press, 1973.

Illustrator: Rosemary Sprague, *Northward to Albion*, Roy, 1947; Nina Schneider, *Hercules, the Gentle Giant*, Roy, 1947; Alma B. Weber and others, *Coonskin for a General*, Aladdin, 1951; Rosalys Hall, *Merry Miller*, Oxford University Press, 1952; Hall, *No Ducks for Dinner*, Oxford University Press, 1953; Phyllis R. Fenner, editor, *Stories of the Sea*, Knopf, 1953; Charlotte Zolotow, *Quiet Mother and the Noisy Little Boy*, Lothrop, 1953; Priscilla Carden, *Aldo's Tower*, Ariel, 1954; Elizabeth Tate, *Little Teddy and the Big Sea*, Lothrop, 1954; Hall, *Baker's Man*, Lippincott, 1954; Pearl Buck, *Beech Tree*, John Day, 1955; Blossom Budney, *Huff Puff Hickory Hill*, Longman, 1955; Dorothy G. Butters, *Papa Dolphin's Table*, Knopf, 1955; Rachel Varble, *Pepys' Boy*, Doubleday, 1955; Helen Kay, *One Mitten Lewis*, Lothrop, 1955.

Vardine R. Moore, *Picnic Pony*, Lothrop, 1956; Ruth L. Holberg, *Tabitha's Hill*, Doubleday, 1956; Joan Windham, *Saints Upon a Time*, Sheed, 1956; Playsted Wood, *Elephant in the Family*, Nelson, 1957; John B. Lewellyn, *Tee Vee Humphrey*, Knopf, 1957; Ruth D. Leinhauser, *Holiday with Eric*, Washburn, 1957; Phyllis McGinley, *Year Without a Santa Claus*, Lippincott, 1957; Carden, *Boy on the Sheep Trail*, Nelson, 1957; Hall, *Green as Spring*, Longman, 1957; Frederick W. Keith, *Danger in the Everglades*, Abelard, 1957; Geraldine Ross, *Scat, the Witch's Cat*, McGraw, 1958; Hall, *Seven for Saint Nicholas*, Lippincott, 1958; Leinhauser, *Aunt Sharon's Wedding Day*, Washburn, 1958; Joanna Johnston, *Great Gravity the Cat*, Knopf, 1958; Rose L. Mincieli, *Tales Merry and Wise*, Holt, 1958; Frances M. Frost, *Little Naturalist*, McGraw, 1959; Constance F. Irwin, *Jonathan D*, Lothrop, 1959; Ross, *Stop It, Moppit*, McGraw, 1959; Maria Leach, *Thing at the Foot of the Bed*, Collins, 1959.

Patricia M. Martin, *Happy Piper and the Goat*, Lothrop, 1960; Jane A. Hyndham, *Timid Dragon*, Lothrop, 1960; Lilian Moore, *Bear Trouble*, McGraw, 1960; Millicent E. Selsam, *Tony's Birds*, Harper, 1961; Leach, editor, *Noodles, Nitwits, and Numskills*, Collins, 1961; Doris Foster, *Honker Visits the Island*, Lothrop, 1962; Zolotow, *Tiger Called Thomas*, Lothrop, 1963; Polly Curren, *Hear Ye of Boston*, Lothrop, 1964; Leach, editor, *The Luck Book*, World Publishing, 1964; Ruth J. Adams, *Mr. Picklepaw's Popcorn*, Lothrop, 1965; Roberta S. Feuerlicht, *The Legends of Paul Bunyan*, Macmillan, 1965; Lillian Bason, *Isabelle and the Library Cat*, Lothrop, 1966; Albert S. Fleischman, *McBroom Tells the Truth*, Norton, 1966; Ross, *The Elf Who Didn't Believe in Himself*, Steck, 1966; Fleischman, *McBroom and the Big Wind*, Norton, 1967; Maxine W. Kumin, *Faraway Farm*, Norton, 1967; Hall, *Miranda's Dragon*, McGraw, 1968; Fleischman, *McBroom's Ear*, Norton, 1969; Hall, *The Bright and Shining Breadboard*, Lothrop, 1969; Edna M. Preston, *One Dark Night*, Viking, 1969.

Charles M. Daugherty, *Samuel Clemens*, Crowell, 1970; John Hampden, *Endless Treasure*, World Publishing, 1970; Earl S. Miers, *That Jefferson Boy*, World Publishing, 1970; Richard Shaw, *Who Are You Today?*, Warne, 1970; Ruth J. Adams and Guy Adams, *Mr. Pickelpaw's Puppy*, Lothrop, 1970; Boris V. Zakhoder, *How a Piglet Crashed the Christmas Party*, Lothrop, 1971; Hazel H. Wilson, *Herbert's*

Stilts, Knopf, 1972; Fleischman, *McBroom's Zoo*, Grosset, 1972; Fleischman, *McBroom the Rainmaker*, Grosset, 1973; Eva Moore, *Dick Whittington and His Cat*, Seabury, 1974; Joseph Raskin, *The Newcomers: Ten Tales of American Immigrants*, Lothrop, 1974; Hall, *The Three Beggar Kings: A Story of Christmas*, Random House, 1974.

Contributor to *Simplicissimus* and *Querschnitt*. Illustrator of limited editions of German and Russian classics for several German publishers.

SIDELIGHTS: Kurt Werth credits Rembrandt, Daumier, and Slevogt with inspiring his art. Recently his style has become more expressive and modern.*

*   *   *

WEST, Charles Converse 1921- (Barnabas)

PERSONAL: Born February 3, 1921, in Plainfield, N.Y.; son of George Parsons (an engineer) and Florence (Farish) West; married Ruth Floy Carson (a professor of education), September 6, 1944; children: Russell Arthur, Walter Lawrence, Glenn Andrew. *Education:* Columbia University, B.A., 1942; Union Theological Seminary, New York, N.Y., B.D., 1945; Yale University, Ph.D., 1955. *Politics:* "Left of center but moderate." *Home address:* R.D.2, Mountain Rd., Box 173, Ringoes, N.J. 08551. *Office:* Princeton Theological Seminary, Princeton, N.J. 08540.

CAREER: Ordained Presbyterian minister, 1946; commissioned as foreign missionary by Presbyterian Church in the United States of America, Board of Foreign Missions, New York, N.Y., 1946; service in China, 1947-50, fraternal worker in Mainz and Berlin, Germany, 1950-53; Hartford Seminary, Missionary Training Program, Hartford, Conn., instructor, 1955-56; World Council of Churches, Ecumenical Institute, Bossey, Switzerland, associate director, 1956-61; Princeton Theological Seminary, Princeton, N.J., associate professor, 1961-63, Stephen Colwell Professor of Christian Ethics, 1963—. Instructor at Peking National University, 1948; chaplain and instructor at Cheeloo University, 1948-49, and Nanking Theological Seminary, 1949-50; high school teacher in Berlin, Germany, 1951-53; *charge de cours* at University of Geneva, 1956-61; guest professor at Union Theological Seminary (New York, N.Y.), Drew Theological Seminary, Lutheran Theological Seminary (Philadelphia, Pa.), and Silliman University. Chairman of U.S. Commission for Christian Peace Conference, 1965-72; vice-chairman of Christians Associated for Relations with Eastern Europe, 1973—. Worked at Gossner Mission (Germany), 1950-51. *Member:* American Society for Christian Ethics (vice-president, 1972-73; president, 1973-74), Americans for Democratic Action.

WRITINGS: (Under pseudonym Barnabas) *Christian Witness in Communist China*, S.C.M. Press, 1951; *Communism and the Theologians: Study of an Encounter*, Westminster, 1958; (editor with David M. Paton, and contributor) *The Missionary Church in East and West*, S.C.M. Press, 1959; *Outside the Camp: The Christian and the World*, Doubleday, 1959.

(Translator) Johannes Hamel, *A Christian in East Germany*, Association Press, 1960; (editor with Robert C. Mackie) *The Sufficiency of God: Essays in Honor of Dr. W. A. Visser't Hooft*, Westminster, 1962; (contributor) Harvey Cox, editor, *The Church Amidst Revolution*, Association Press, 1966; *Technologists and Revolutionaries* (pamphlet), Committee on Church and Economic Life, National Council of Churches of Christ in the United States of America, 1967;

(contributor) *Une theologie de la revolution?* (title means "A Theology of Revolution?"), Editions Labor et Fides, 1968; *Ethics, Violence, and Revolution,* Council on Religion and International Affairs, 1969.

The Power to Be Human: Toward a Secular Theology, Macmillan, 1971.

WORK IN PROGRESS: Marxist-Christian Dialogue and Encounter; The Problem of Freedom in a Theological and Political Perspective; Theology and Practice of the Christian World Mission.

SIDELIGHTS: West writes: "I suppose the basic themes motivating my ministry, including its writing dimension, might be reduced to two: first, a search for the true form of social justice and a revulsion against the domination of the weak by the strong—which was an early childhood experience refined and given direction by good teaching and parental influence; and second, commitment to the ultimate reality of God at work in Jesus Christ, as the context in which human life is given its direction and purpose—which was a conviction of my maturity, born of deep experience in the ecumenical movement that later came to be expressed in the World Council of Churches. Union Theological Seminary, where I studied, was a crossroads of world Christianity and a school with a social mission to the church in the United States.

"I entered the service of the Board of Foreign Missions of the Presbyterian Church in the conviction that the claim and reality of Christ is universal and challenges believers most deeply to express it in an environment which is not traditionally Christian. I was in China three years—two before the Communist victory there and one year afterward. Concern for China and for the life and witness of the Christian church in Asia has been a continuing subordinate theme in my later career.

"A second aspect of this missionary service was a three-year period in Germany, where my primary engagement was with the life of the Christian church in Eastern Germany under Communist domination. This too has been a continuing aspect of my career, broadened to include study, writing, and engagement with church life in Eastern Europe as a whole, including the Soviet Union, and Marxist theory and practice in intersection with it. This was expressed in my active involvement with the World Council of Churches' ministry to Eastern Europe; in the Christian Peace Conference before 1968; in theological deputations of the National Council of Churches to the Soviet Union in 1962 and 1974; in return visits of Soviet churchmen to this country; and in continuing dialogue with Marxists in Europe and in this country.

"Another continuing theme of my work, at the moment somewhat in abeyance, is a theological understanding of secularization and its implications for religion and ideology. Most recently I have been concerned specifically with the political-ethical focus of this problem. My concern here is to understand politics theologically as a secular enterprise in which concrete concern for human justice goes beyond and corrects all ideological attempts to define human nature in political terms."

*   *   *

WEST, John Anthony 1932-

PERSONAL: Born July 9, 1932, in New York, N.Y.; son of Jack (in business) and Isobel (in business; maiden name, Kline) West; divorced. *Education:* Lehigh University, B.S., 1953. *Politics:* None. *Religion:* "Not formally affiliated." *Office:* 59 Old Lake St., White Plains, N.Y. 10604.

CAREER: Magazine of Fantasy and Science Fiction, New York City, assistant editor, 1955; Franklin Spier, Inc. (advertising agency), New York City, copywriter, 1956; freelance writer, 1956—. *Military service:* U.S. Army, 1953-55. *Member:* Astrological Association of England.

WRITINGS: Call Out the Malicia (stories), Dutton, 1963; *Osborne's Army* (novel), Morrow, 1968; (with Jan Gerhard Toonder) *The Case for Astrology,* Coward, 1971; *Serpent in the Sky: The High Wisdom of Ancient Egypt,* Harper, 1978; *The Only Wheel in Town,* Black Pig Press, 1979.

Plays: "George" (one-act), first produced in London at Hampstead Theatre Club, July, 1960; "Bar-B-Q" (one-act), first produced in London at Soho Poly, July, 1975. Also author of plays produced by British Broadcasting Corp., including "Jarry" (three-act), 1964, and "The Death Ship" (three-act; adapted from the novel by B. Traven), 1971. Author of unproduced play, "Rock Romeo, Rock Juliet."

Contributor to periodicals, including *Atlantic Monthly* and *Penthouse.*

WORK IN PROGRESS: Number: Key to the Cosmos, a study of the Pythagorean number symbolism, and *The Sound of Healing,* a study of a revolutionary healing technique, both for Wildwood House; *The Wizard of Oxbridge,* a novel; *Eladia,* a novel based on a true account of survivors of a harem kept by Grand Inquisitors of Zaragoza in the seventeenth century.

SIDELIGHTS: West writes: "I'm a novelist, playwright, astrologer, and Pythagorean (not necessarily in that order). My nonfiction is largely concerned with serious scholarship in ancient science, philosophy, religion, and art; my training as a novelist and playwright seems to allow me to write lucidly on subjects usually considered abstruse. My novels and plays are generally based on satire, but embody mystical elements or themes. Though unaffiliated with any institutionalized religion, I'm violently anti-materialistic. Though I like to chronicle the downfall of modern civilization—the silliest ever to exist on the face of the earth—I see the possibility of something better arising from its ashes, and, despite the satire, remain an optimist in a curious sense."

*   *   *

WESTERMANN, Claus 1909-

PERSONAL: Born October 7, 1909, in Berlin, Germany; son of Diedrich (a professor) and Katharina (Claus) Westermann; married Anna Kellner, 1935; children: Anna Katharina Westermann Cherdron. *Education:* Attended University of Tuebingen, University of Marburg, and University of Berlin; University of Zurich, Th.D., 1949. *Religion:* Evangelical. *Home:* 6837 St. Leon-Rot, Ketteler Strasse 2, Bundesrepublik, Germany.

CAREER: Worked in Berlin, Germany, as assistant pastor, 1935-1939, pastor, 1945-49; Kirchliche Hochschule Berlin, Berlin, Germany, assistant professor, 1949-54, professor of theology, 1954-58; University of Heidelberg, Heidelberg, Germany, professor of theology, 1959-78, professor emeritus, 1978—. Member of synod of evangelical church. *Military service:* German military, 1939-45. *Member:* Society for Old Testament Studies (honorary member). *Awards, honors:* Dr.h.c. from University of Goettingen.

WRITINGS—In English: Das Loben Gottes in den Psalmen, Vandenhoeck & Ruprecht, 1953, translation by Keith R. Crim published as *The Praise of God in the Psalms,* John Knox, 1965, 5th German edition, 1977; *Tausend Jahre und ein Tag: Unsere Zeit im Alten Testament,* Kreuz-Verlag,

1957, translation by Stanley Rudman published as *A Thousand Years and a Day: Our Time in the Old Testament*, Fortress Press, 1962; (editor) *Probleme alttestamentlicher Hermeneutik*, Kaiser, 1960, translation by James Luther Mays published as *Essays on Old Testament Hermeneutics*, John Knox, 1963, 2nd edition, 1964; *Grundformen prophetischer Rede*, Kaiser, 1960, translation by Hugh Clayton White published as *Basic Forms of Prophetic Speech*, Westminster, 1967, 5th German edition, 1978; *Umstrittene Bible*, Kreuz-Verlag, 1960, translation by Darold H. Beekmann published as *Our Controversial Bible*, Augsburg, 1969; (editor) *Abriss der Bibelkunde: Altes und Neues Testament*, Kreuz-Verlag, 1962, translation by Robert H. Boyd published in two volumes, *Handbook to the Old Testament*, Augsburg, 1967, and *Handbook to the New Testament*, Augsburg, 1969; (editor and translator) *Das Buch Jesaja, Kapitel 40-66*, Vandenhoeck & Ruprecht, 1966, translation by David M. Stalker published as *Isaiah 40-66: A Commentary*, Westminster, 1969; *Das Alte Testament und Jesus Christus*, Calwer Verlag, 1968, translation by Omar Kaste published as *The Old Testament and Jesus Christ*, Augsburg, 1970; *Anfang und Ende in der Bibel*, Calwer Verlag, 1969, translation by Crim published as *Beginning and End in the Bible*, Fortress Press, 1972.

Untranslated works: *So sagt es Lukas* (title means "Thus Does it Say Luke"), Burckhardthaus, 1949; *Sprueche, Prediger, Hoheslied* (title means "Proverbs, Ecclesiastes, Song of Solomon"), Quell-Verlag, 1956; *Jeremia und Klagelieder* (title means "Jeremiah and Lamentations"), Quell-Verlag, 1956; *Der Aufbau des Buches Hiob* (title means "Structure of the Book of Job"), Mohr, 1956; *Gewendete Klage* (title means "Changed Lament"), Buchhandlung des Erziehungsvereins, 1957; *Gottes Engel brauchen keine Fluegel* (title means "Angels of God Do Not Need Wings"), Kaethe Vogt Verlag, 1957; *Verkuendigung des Kommenden: Predigten alttestamentlicher Texte* (title means "He That Cometh: Sermons From the Old Testament"), Kaiser, 1958; *Der Psalter* (title means "The Psalter"), Quell-Verlag, 1959.

Forschung am Alten Testament (title means "Inquiries Into the Old Testament"), Kaiser, Volume I, 1964, Volume II, 1974; (editor with Herbert Breit) *Ausgewaehlte alttestamentliche Texte* (title means "Preparations to Sermons from the Old Testament"), Calwer Verlag, 1966; *Genesis*, Neukirchener, 1966; *Jeremia*, Calwer Verlag, 1967; (editor) *Theologie Grundbegriff* (title means "Theology Basic Concepts"), Kreuz-Verlag, 1967; *Der Segen in der Bibel und im Handeln der Kirche* (title means "Blessing in the Bible and in the Churches"), Kaiser, 1968; (with Paul Philippe and Guenther Bornkamm) *Zuwendung und Gerechtigkeit*, Vandenhoeck & Ruprecht, 1969; *Schoepfund*, Kreuz-Verlag, 1971; (editor with Ernst Jenni) *Theologisches Handwoeterbuch zum Alten Testament* (title means "Theological Handbook to the Old Testament"), Kaiser, Volume I, 1971, Volume II, 1976.

WORK IN PROGRESS: Volume II of *Kommentars zur Genesis; Theologie des Alten Testaments*.

SIDELIGHTS: Westermann told *CA:* "It was one of my intentions to show that the Bible of Christianity is not only the New Testament but the Old Testament and the New Testament together, the one not without the other. I hope to have shown in my exegesis of the Old Testament that we can speak about God not only in the speculative and abstract but far more in a simple and straightforward way."

WESTOFF, Charles Francis 1927-

PERSONAL: Born July 23, 1927, in New York, N.Y.; son of Frank Barnett and Evelyn (Bales) Westoff; married Joan P. Uszynski, September 11, 1948 (divorced, January, 1969); married Leslie Aldridge, August, 1969; children: (first marriage) David, Carol. *Education:* Syracuse University, A.B., 1949, M.A., 1950; University of Pennsylvania, Ph.D., 1953. *Home:* 537 Drake's Corner Rd., Princeton, N.J. 08540. *Office:* Office of Population Research, Princeton University, Princeton, N.J. 08540.

CAREER: University of Pennsylvania, Philadelphia, instructor in sociology, 1950-52; Milbank Memorial Fund, New York City, research associate, 1952-55; Princeton University, Princeton, N.J., research associate of Office of Population Research, 1955-59; New York University, New York City, associate professor and head of sociology department at Washington Square College, 1959-62; Princeton University, professor of sociology, 1962—, Demographic Studies and Sociology, 1972—, head of department, 1965-70, Office of Population Research, associate director, 1962-75, director, 1976—. Vice-chairman of board of directors of Alan Guttmacher Institute. Executive director of Commission on Population Growth and America's Future, 1970-72; consultant to UNESCO.

WRITINGS: (With R. G. Potter, P. C. Sagi, and E. G. Mishler) *Family Growth in Metropolitan America*, Princeton University Press, 1961; (with Potter and Sagi) *The Third Child: A Study in the Prediction of Fertility*, Princeton University Press, 1963; (with Larry L. Bumpass) *The Later Years of Childbearing*, Princeton University Press, 1967; (with Potter) *College Women and Fertility Values*, Princeton University Press, 1967; (with Norman B. Ryder) *Reproduction in the United States: 1965*, Princeton University Press, 1971; (with wife, Leslie A. Westoff) *From Now to Zero: Fertility, Contraception, and Abortion in America*, Little, Brown, 1971; (Co-author) *Toward the End of Growth: Population in America*, Prentice-Hall, 1973; (with Ryder) *The Contraceptive Revolution*, Princeton University Press, 1977; (editor with Wilbur J. Cohen) *Demographic Dynamics in America*, Free Press, 1977. Contributor to sociology, demography, and family planning journals.

WORK IN PROGRESS: Research on the demographic effects of sterilization in the United States and Panama; studying international comparisons of the effects of the education of women on fertility; conducting predictive studies of fertility in the United States.

* * *

WESTON, Susan B(rown) 1943-

PERSONAL: Born October 5, 1943, in Pennsylvania; daughter of Charles E. (a teacher) and Margaret (a proofreader; maiden name, Beck) Brown; married John H. Weston (a life insurance agent), January 7, 1968; children: Stephen D., Nathaniel. *Education:* Columbia University, B.A., 1967, M.A., 1968, Ph.D., 1974. *Home:* 3930 Lanipili Pl., Honolulu, Hawaii, 96816. *Office:* Department of English, University of Hawaii, 1733 Donaghho Rd., Honolulu, Hawaii 96822.

CAREER: University of Hawaii, Honolulu, instructor, 1972-74, assistant professor of English, 1974—. Member of Hawaii Literary Arts Council (vice-president, 1978—).

WRITINGS: Wallace Stevens: An Introduction to the Poetry, Columbia University Press, 1977. Contributor to *Criticism, Phantasm, Iowa Review, Virginia Woolf Quarterly*, and *Poets of Hawaii*.

WORK IN PROGRESS: Research on Galway Kinnell; a novel.

SIDELIGHTS: Susan Weston writes: "Raising two children and writing poetry and supporting my husband in his developing career have kept me well-rounded though spread a bit thin."

* * *

WETMORE, Alexander 1886-1978

OBITUARY NOTICE: Born June 18, 1886, in North Freedom, Wis.; died December 6, 1978, in Montgomery County, Md. Ornithologist, museum executive, and author. Wetmore was associated with the Smithsonian Institution from 1924 until shortly before his death, most notably as secretary of the Institution and as director of the Museum of National History. Wetmore described 189 previously unknown species and subspecies of birds during his career. He wrote numerous articles and several books on ornithology. His book, *A Classification for the Birds of the World,* is known as a classic in its field. Obituaries and other sources: *Current Biography,* Wilson, 1948; *American Men and Women of Science,* 13th edition, Bowker, 1976; *Who's Who in America,* 39th edition, Marquis, 1976; *The International Who's Who,* Europa, 1978; *Washington Post,* December 9, 1978.

* * *

WHARTON, John Franklin 1894-1977

PERSONAL: Born July 28, 1894, in Newark, N.J.; son of Charles Adolphus (a manufacturer) and Lenna Irene (Lyon) Wharton; married Carolin Bumiller (a producer), December 6, 1924 (divorced, 1949); married Betty Ann Fisher (an actress under stage name, Mary Mason), August 30, 1949; children: (first marriage) Joan Franklin (deceased), Barry (daughter). *Education:* Williams College, A.B., 1915; attended New York Law School, 1915-17; Columbia University Law School, LL.B., 1920. *Residence:* New York, N.Y.

CAREER: McCarter & English, Newark, N.J., law clerk, 1915-17; admitted to the Bar of New York State, 1920; Rounds, Hatch, Dillingham & Debevoise, Newark, law clerk, 1920-23; became active in theatrical law, 1923; co-founder and partner, Paul, Weiss, Rifkind, Wharton & Garrison. Playwrights Producing Co., co-founder, 1938, president and general business adviser for twenty-two years; director of American Academy of Dramatic Arts, Legitimate Theatre Exploratory Commission, and Kurt Weill Foundation for Music; trustee of Cole Porter's musical and literary works; chairman of the board, Hiroshima Peace Center Association. Consultant, Board of Economic Warfare, World War II. *Military service:* U.S. Navy, World War I; received medical discharge. Worked with British Ministry of Shipping until conclusion of war. *Member:* American National Theatre and Academy (director), Theatre Development Fund (director), New Dramatists Committee (co-founder; general counsel and director, 1951-60), Ballet Theatre Foundation (director), Institute for Advanced Studies in the Theatre Arts (co-founder and chairman of the board), Little Orchestra Society (director), Citizens for a Quieter Society (co-founder), Citizens for Clean Air (organizer and first chairman), New York City Bar Association, Phi Beta Kappa, Theta Delta Chi. *Awards, honors:* Kelcey Allen award, 1965; named man who did most for theatre by *Variety* magazine, 1966; special Tony award, 1974; special New Dramatists award, 1974; New York City citation for distinguished service, 1975.

WRITINGS: This Road to Recovery: A Primer of Econom-

ics for Bewildered Americans, Morrow, 1934; *The Theory and Practice of Earning a Living,* Simon & Schuster, 1945; *The Explorations of George Burton* (novel), Simon & Schuster, 1951; *Life Among the Playwrights: Being Mostly the Story of the Playwrights Producing Company, Inc.,* photos selected by wife, Betty A. Wharton, Quadrangle, 1974. Contributor of articles on theatre to *Saturday Review, New York Times,* and *Chicago Daily News.*

SIDELIGHTS: At the age of fourteen Wharton decided to pursue a law career when his mother wanted him to be a professional man. "I didn't want to be a doctor," he later explained, "so that's why I became a lawyer." His legal talent combined with his lifelong love for theatre led him to many clients in the theatre world, including Dwight Wiman and Cole Porter. Wharton's relationship with Porter continued over the years and, as sole trustee of his musical and literary property trusts, he devoted considerable effort to make public 250 unused Porter songs.

Wharton made several lasting legal contributions to the theatre. In addition to co-founding the Playwrights Producing Co. so that writers, instead of producers, could control their own material, he devised contracts to allow writers to sell a play's motion picture rights before being produced on stage.

His varied interests spread far beyond the legal and theatrical worlds as he wrote extensively on world peace and on social and economic problems. "The older I get," Wharton once wrote, "the more certain I feel that the continuance of our civilization depends upon our learning the causes of, and the means to control, Man's inhumanity to Man."

OBITUARIES: New York Times, November 25, 1977; *Time,* December 5, 1977.*

(Died November 24, 1977, in New York, N.Y.)

* * *

WHITE, Carol Hellings 1939-

PERSONAL: Born August 10, 1939, in Camden, N.J.; daughter of Richard and Evalyn (a psychic; maiden name, Greene) Hellings; married Nathaniel White (divorced); children: Jeffrey Lawrence. *Home address:* c/o Harrold, R.D.10, Box 660, Greensburg, Pa. 15601.

CAREER: Has worked in real estate, in the recording business, and in urban renewal; astrologer, 1970-75; writer. Teacher and lecturer on astrology. Civil rights activist during the 1960's. *Member:* Astrologers Guild of America, National Council for Geocosmic Research.

WRITINGS: Holding Hands (palmistry for young adults), Putnam, 1978. Contributor to magazines, including *Woman's Day* and astrology journals, and newspapers.

SIDELIGHTS: Carol White's work involves palmistry, cards, clairvoyance, and psychic work, in addition to astrology.

* * *

WHITE, Gertrude M(ason) 1915-
(R. I. Wakefield)

PERSONAL: Born August 5, 1915, in Pawtucket, R.I.; daughter of Frank F. (an attorney) and Gertrude T. (Brown) Mason; married William White (a professor), June 20, 1951; children: Geoffrey M., Roger W. *Education:* Mount Holyoke College, A.B., 1936; Columbia University, M.A., 1937; University of Chicago, Ph.D., 1950. *Politics:* Democrat. *Religion:* Episcopalian. *Home:* 25860 West 14 Mile

Rd., Franklin, Mich. 48025. *Office:* Department of English, Oakland University, Rochester, Mich. 48063.

CAREER: University of Chicago, Chicago, Ill., instructor in English, 1942-43; McGill University, Montreal, Quebec, lecturer in English, 1943-45; Wayne State University, Detroit, Mich., instructor in English, 1946-50; University of Maryland, Overseas Division, Ruislip Air Force Base, Middlesex, England, instructor in English, 1951-53; Oakland University, Rochester, Mich., assistant professor, 1959-63, associate professor, 1963-67, professor of English, 1967—. *Member:* Modern Language Association of America, College English Association.

WRITINGS: (Under pseudonym R. I. Wakefield) *You Will Die Today* (mystery novel), Dodd, 1953; *Wilfred Owen,* Twayne, 1967; (with Joan Rosen) *A Moment's Monument: The Development of the Sonnet,* Scribner, 1972. Contributor to literature and literary journals, including *Walt Whitman Review, Sewanee Review,* and *Criticism.*

WORK IN PROGRESS: Research on Victorian and earlier twentieth-century poetry.

SIDELIGHTS: Gertrude White told *CA:* "Most of what I would say about problems of teaching literature in universities at present has been better said by others. Two things only I want to say for myself: I am interested in literature primarily as an art, not as a vehicle for sociology or psychology, and not as a means of converting the young to any idelogy whatever. It is often difficult to make students—and many colleagues—understand this point of view, but I think it's important to do so. The second matter concerns the preparation of students by the average high school. Thirty-five years ago my traditionally-trained professors at the University of Chicago were complaining because they could count on no common body of knowledge, no common syllabus of readings. Now we complain because we can no longer assume that our students have read anything. They are certainly just as bright as students ever were; but they are more ignorant of literature and culture generally than it is easy to believe university students ever were before."

* * *

WHITE, Glenn M.   1918(?)-1978

OBITUARY NOTICE: Born c. 1918, in Indiana; died November 27, 1978, in San Francisco, Calif. Writer and editor. White was associated with *Ladies' Home Journal* for sixteen years and departed in 1963 as senior associate editor. White was also a medical writer for *Psychiatric Reporter* and wrote *The Ball State Story,* a historical account of that school's growth. Obituaries and other sources: *Washington Post,* December 2, 1978.

* * *

WHITE, Patrick (Victor Martindale)   1912-

PERSONAL: Born May 28, 1912, in London, England; son of Victor Martindale and Ruth (Withycombe) White. *Education:* King's College, Cambridge, B.A., 1935. *Home:* 20 Martin Rd., Centennial Park, Sydney, New South Wales 2021, Australia.

CAREER: Writer. *Military service:* Royal Air Force, 1940-45; intelligence officer. *Awards, honors:* Australian Literary Society gold medal for *Happy Valley,* and for *The Tree of Man,* 1956; Miles Franklin Award for *Voss,* 1958, and for *Riders in the Chariot,* 1962; W. H. Smith & Son literary award for *Voss,* 1959; brotherhood award from National Conference of Christians and Jews, 1962, for *Riders in the Chariot;* Nobel Prize for Literature, 1973.

WRITINGS: The Ploughman and Other Poems, Beacon Press, 1935; *Happy Valley* (novel), Harrap, 1939, Viking, 1940; *The Living and the Dead* (novel), Viking, 1941; *The Aunt's Story* (novel), Viking, 1948; *The Tree of Man* (novel), Viking, 1955; *Voss* (novel), Viking, 1957; *Riders in the Chariot* (novel), Viking, 1961; *The Burnt Ones* (short stories), Viking, 1964; *The Solid Mandala* (novel), Viking, 1966; *The Vivisector* (novel), Viking, 1970; *The Eye of the Storm* (novel), J. Cape, 1973, Viking, 1974; *Poems,* Soft Press, 1974; *The Cockatoos: Shorter Novels and Stories,* J. Cape, 1974, Viking, 1975; *A Fringe of Leaves,* J. Cape, 1976, Viking, 1977.

Plays: "Return to Abyssinia," produced in London, 1947; *Four Plays* (contains "The Ham Funeral," produced in Adelaide, 1961; "The Season at Sarsaparilla," produced in Adelaide, 1962; "A Cheery Soul," produced in Melbourne, 1963; "Night on Bald Mountain," produced in Adelaide, 1964), Eyre & Spottiswoode, 1965, Viking, 1966; "Big Toys," 1977.

Also contributor to *Australian Letters,* Volume I, 1958.

SIDELIGHTS: The works of English-born Patrick White are probably the most complex, structurally and thematically, in present-day Australia, the country where White grew up and which he has adopted as his own. Although most critics acknowledge White's talent and genius, several have written of the difficulty in reading his novels because of the multiplicity of symbols, myths, and allegories: William Walsh discussed White's "choking thickets of imagery"; Robert Phillips called reading White "a bit like over-indulgence in chocolate *mousse"*; Bruce Allen wrote of White's "stylistic crudeness."

White's basic orientation is religious and he takes from a variety of religious attitudes the philosophies he needs to explore his overriding concern: man's search for meaning in an apparently meaningless society. Inherent in White's consideration of spirituality in a mechanical and materialistic world is the concept of man's isolation in a crowded society. He asks, Peter S. Prescott wrote, as a pathologist might, "What pox, what gangrene have we here? What rot will be extruded from this pustule?" Even within the most basic societal structures, man is alienated, alone; man's need for meaning is ultimately to be found in the interior world, the world of the imagination and the soul. Robert Phillips said, "White's thesis . . . is simply this: We are all alone in a chaotic world, and only we ourselves can help ourselves during our brief tenure." Often White's theory of the duality of man is exhibited through characters decayed in body but spiritually whole. George Steiner wrote, "Incontinence, the worn skin, the sour odors of senility, the toothless appetites and spasms of the old . . . lay bare the ignoble, perhaps accidental fact that the spirit is so meanly housed."

White's frequent use of the isolation theme in his fiction is rooted in his personal feelings of alienation and non-acceptance by his fellow countrymen. Several periods of expatriation preceded his ultimate return to Australia, as he explained to Ingmar Bjorksten in 1962: "It was eighteen years before I dared to come back to Australia for the third time. . . . I couldn't do without the countryside out here. I don't believe in a final break with the place one originates from. Only in a temporary break . . . to get perspective. You are shaped by the place you have your roots in; it has become part of you. Outside places don't shape you in the same way. This has nothing to do with nationalism. People are always the same. This is what my compatriots find so difficult to understand." Bjorksten explored another possible cause of White's feelings of alienation: "For a long time he was dismissed as a peculiar, pretentious, and irrelevant by his countrymen, whose restricted vision and whose limited experience of what human life has to offer he exposes time after time, while simultaneously attacking the holy cow that they so deeply revere: an uncritical materialism that never questions itself." White's 1973 Nobel Prize has gained him greater acceptance among the Australians, although he is still more widely read in other countries.

In expressing his theories of alienation and individual spirituality, White often uses Jungian archetypes of the collective unconscious and symbols of religions such as Buddhism and Christianity. A recurring concept involves the mandala, a motif of Buddhist origin. Mandala is the "Sanskrit word for 'magic ring,'" according to Bjorksten, who also explained that "the mandala represents the Buddhist concept of the universe, of completeness in the form of a square with circles inside or outside it." White most often uses the Jungian explanation of the mandala motif to express man's own divinity, with man at the circle's center rather than God, according to Bjorksten. In a 1973 letter, White himself acknowledged both his early indebtedness to Jung and his more recent belief in the possibility of the existence of God: "I have great admiration for [Jung] and his findings, but I also have a belief in a supernatural power of which I have been given inklings from time to time: there have been incidents and coincidences which have shown me that there is a design behind the haphazardness." Peter Beatson discussed White's recent affirmation of God's existence in terms of his recurrent metaphors expressing the cycles of life, death, and ultimate rebirth.

Although the obscurity of White's novels has resulted in some critics' labeling him "unreadable," a majority have received his efforts with warm acceptance. A. Alvarez called White's isolation "an image of great beauty." Shirley Hazzard spoke of his "rich, distinctive language, now stately, now mercurial, always borne on the civilizing tide of irony." Pearl K. Bell wrote of White's "strange and somber poetic truth." And D. Keith Mano remarked: "It's as easy to be irked or bloody bored by Patrick White as it is to be astonished by him. If you cooperate, magnificence can be tedious, or tedium magnificent. White is, without conditional clause, brilliant. And exasperating...."

Harry M. Miller bought the movie rights to *Voss*, and *Variety* reported in 1970 that the film "should be the biggest attempt in the history of Aussie film-making to pitch a quality product at the international market."

AVOCATIONAL INTERESTS: Cooking, gardening, music.

BIOGRAPHICAL/CRITICAL SOURCES—Books: Janette Finch, *A Bibliography of Patrick White*, Libraries Board of South Australia, 1966; A. Alvarez, *Beyond All This Fiddle: Essays 1955-1967*, Random House, 1969; Patricia A. Morley, *The Mystery of Unity: Theme and Technique in the Novels of Patrick White*, McGill-Queen's University Press, 1972; J. R. Dyce, *Patrick White as Playwright*, University of Queensland Press, 1974; *Contemporary Literary Criticism*, Gale, Volume 3, 1975, Volume 4, 1975, Volume 5, 1976, Volume 7, 1977; Peter Beatson, *The Eye in the Mandala*, Paul Elek, 1976; Ingmar Bjorksten, *Patrick White*, University of Queensland Press, 1976.

Articles: *Variety*, July 22, 1970; *Harper's*, September, 1970; *New Leader*, September 7, 1970, January 21, 1974; *Listener*, November 5, 1970; *New Statesman*, September 7, 1973, July 5, 1974; *Times Literary Supplement*, September 21, 1973;

New Republic, January 5, 1974, January 12, 1974, March 22, 1975; *New York Times Book Review*, January 6, 1974, January 19, 1975; *Time*, January 14, 1974; *Newsweek*, January 21, 1974; *New York*, January 21, 1974; *Village Voice*, February 7, 1974; *National Review*, February 15, 1974; *New Yorker*, March 4, 1974; *New York Review of Books*, April 4, 1974; *Commonweal*, May 17, 1974; *Sewanee Review*, spring, 1974, summer, 1975; *Spectator*, June 22, 1974; *Books Abroad*, summer, 1974; *Hudson Review*, summer, 1974; *Prairie Schooner*, fall, 1974; *Saturday Review*, January 25, 1975.*

* * *

WHITE, Philip L(loyd) 1923-

PERSONAL: Born July 31, 1923, in Akron, Ohio; son of Lloyd Putnam and Della (Depew) White; married Meda Miller, April 3, 1958; children: David, Carolyn, Michael, John, Jean Ann. *Education:* Baldwin-Wallace College, B.A., 1947; Columbia University, Ph.D., 1954. *Politics:* Democrat. *Religion:* None. *Home:* 2614 Maria Anna, Austin, Tex. 78703. *Office:* Department of History, University of Texas, Austin, Tex. 78712.

CAREER: City College (now of the City University of New York), New York, N.Y., lecturer in history, 1954-55; University of Texas, Austin, assistant professor of history, 1955-58; University of Nottingham, Nottingham, England, Fulbright lecturer in history, 1958-59; University of Chicago, Chicago, Ill., assistant professor of history, 1959-62; University of Texas, Austin, associate professor, 1962-75, professor of history, 1975—. Member of Austin Charter Study Commission. *Military service:* U.S. Army, 1943-46; became staff sergeant. *Member:* Organization of American Historians, Society for Historians of the Early American Republic, Institute of Early American History and Culture, Texas Association of College Teachers (member of executive board; local president).

WRITINGS: Beekmans of New York in Politics and Commerce, 1647-1877, New York Historical Society, 1956; (editor) *Beekman Mercantile Papers*, three volumes, New York Historical Society, 1956; (with Norman Graebner and G. C. Fite) *History of the American People*, McGraw, 1970, revised edition, 1975; (contributor) A. T. Vaughan and G. A. Billias, editors, *Perspectives in Early American History*, Harper, 1973; *Community Growth in a Frontier Forest: Beekmantown, New York, 1769-1849*, University of Texas Press, 1979.

WORK IN PROGRESS: Research on the nature of nationality and the origins of American nationality; studying the early history of Warren County, Pa.

SIDELIGHTS: White writes: "My two local history studies reflect my strong feeling that the traditional preoccupations of historians with national politics has left much of the vital history of the American people unexamined. I want to be able to characterize life in the small rural communities in which nearly all Americans lived during the early national period. My interest in nationality reflects my belief that the phenomenon of nationality is not as well understood as its importance in human events dictates it should be, and that it will illuminate both the American Revolution and the phenomenon of nationality to consider the interrelation of the two."

* * *

WHITE, Ruth Morris 1902(?)-1978

OBITUARY NOTICE: Born c. 1902; died November 16,

1978, in Bal Harbour, Fla. Actress and writer. White wrote for King Features Syndicate and contributed articles on women in show business to *Variety.* White also completed *Tin Can on a Shingle,* a book on ironclad boats which had been started by her husband. She later wrote *Yankee From Sweden* about John Ericsson who built the battleship *Monitor.* Obituaries and other sources: *New York Times,* November 22, 1978.

* * *

WHITEHEAD, (Walter) Edward 1908-1978

PERSONAL: Born May 20, 1908, in Hampshire, England; came to United States, 1953; married wife Adinah, September 14, 1940; children: Charles, Mrs. Keith Shackelton. *Residence:* Bahamas.

CAREER: Worked in advertising before World War II; head of industrial section of economic information unit of His Majesty's Treasury, 1947-50; advertising manager of Schweppes Ltd., 1950, became sales manager and overseas general manager, member of board of directors, 1952-71, became president of Schweppes (U.S.A.) Ltd., chairman of Schweppes (Canada) Ltd., and president of Rose & Company (U.S.A.) Ltd., retired in 1971. Commentator for WQXR-Radio program, "This Is Britain," 1959-61. Member of Council of International Marketing Programme Ltd., and board of directors of General Cigar Co.; trustee of International Marketing Institute (Harvard), and Cunard Steamship Co.; chairman of British Export Marketing Advisory Committee. *Military service:* Royal Navy Volunteer Reserve, 1937-39; Royal Navy, 1939-46(?); became commander. *Awards, honors:* Named Officer of the British Empire, 1962; Commander of the Order of the British Empire, 1967.

WRITINGS: How to Live the Good Life: The Commander Tells You How, Doubleday, 1977.

SIDELIGHTS: Whitehead was thrust into the international spotlight in May, 1953, when a photograph showing him leaving an airplane was accompanied by the caption, "The man from Schweppes is here." Immediately, Whitehead was equated with the product for which he'd already spent three years helping to market.

Whitehead came to Schweppes in 1950, after deciding against a bureaucratic post within the British government. He quickly rose within the organization and in 1953, he was sent to the United States to help boost sales. Whitehead proved equal to the occasion by negotiating a deal with Pepsi-Cola. In return for bottling their product in England, Pepsi-Cola had agreed to bottle Schweppes in America.

Although the deal was a brilliant business maneuver, the new pact caused the price of Schweppes to plummet to 16¢ per bottle. This in itself would appear to have been a bargain for the Schweppes consumer except that prospective purchasers now doubted the quality of a product whose price could decline so noticeably. A new campaign was undertaken to bolster Schweppes image and Whitehead was chosen as the man to recoup the buying public.

The campaign, of course, was an enormous success and over the years Whitehead could be seen on television mouthing slogans such as, "I claim this land in the name of Schweppes," and "Always keep the bar in your Rolls-Royce as well stocked with Schweppes as the bar at home." By 1965, Schweppes sales had increased by over two-thousand percent and Whitehead was still climbing the corporate ladder.

During the 1960's, Whitehead became popular as a public speaker of sorts. Besides his regular duties with Schweppes, he also found time to give lectures and he even hosted a radio program, "This Is Britain," on which he gave his opinions of his homeland and played music.

Whitehead also possessed a keen perception of economics. He urged Britain to adapt American financial attitudes which he'd applied so cleverly in his own business arrangements. But his role of financial adviser didn't deter from his work for Schweppes. He continued to actively participate in dealings in the United States, Canada, and Great Britain.

But despite his shrewd business maneuvers, Whitehead was always best known for his work in the Schweppes commercials. In fact, his beard, an integral part of the image he portrayed, was insured with famed Lloyd's of London for $10 thousand. Apparently, Whitehead's worth was well known within the Schweppes company. When he abruptly withdrew himself from the commercial aspect of the organization, the advertising department caused such a commotion that Whitehead was persuaded to gradually ease out of the public eye instead of quitting outright.

In 1971, Whitehead finally retired from the company he'd served so well and so diversely. Living in the Bahamas, he devoted his time to a life of leisure while also composing his memoirs.

AVOCATIONAL INTERESTS: Riding, fox hunting, beagling, skiing, swimming, sailing, listening to American jazz.

BIOGRAPHICAL/CRITICAL SOURCES: David Ogilvy, *Confessions of an Advertising Man,* Atheneum, 1964; Tommy Whitehead, *The Beard and I,* McKay, 1965; Edward Whitehead, *How to Live the Good Life: The Commander Tells You How,* Doubleday, 1977.

OBITUARIES: Washington Post, April 19, 1978.*

(Died April 17, 1978, in Petersfield, England)

* * *

WHITMAN, Robert Freeman 1925-

PERSONAL: Born July 9, 1925, in Boston, Mass.; son of Alfred Freeman and Fannie Marie Whitman; married Marina von Neumann, June 23, 1956; children: Malcolm, Laura Mariette. *Education:* Cornell University, A.B., 1949; Harvard University, M.A., 1951, Ph.D., 1956. *Politics:* Democrat. *Religion:* Unitarian-Universalist. *Home:* 5440 Aylesboro Ave., Pittsburgh, Pa. 15217. *Office:* Department of English, University of Pittsburgh, Pittsburgh, Pa. 15260.

CAREER: Princeton University, Princeton, N.J., instructor in English, 1955-60; University of Pittsburgh, Pittsburgh, Pa., assistant professor, 1960-65, associate professor, 1965-67, professor of English, 1967—, head of department, 1967-72. *Military service:* U.S. Army Air Forces, 1943-46; became second lieutenant. *Member:* Modern Language Association of America, Malone Society, American Association of University Professors. *Awards, honors:* National Endowment for the Humanities senior research fellow, 1972-73.

WRITINGS: The Play Reader's Handbook, Bobbs-Merrill, 1966; *Beyond Melancholy: John Webster and the Tragedy of Darkness,* Institut fuer Englisch Sprache und Literatur (Salzburg, Austria), 1973; *Shaw and the Play of Ideas,* Cornell University Press, 1977.

* * *

WHITNEY, Charles Allen 1929-

PERSONAL: Born January 31, 1929, in Milwaukee, Wis.;

son of Charles Smith and Gertrude (Schuyler) Whitney; married Jane Ann Hall, January 27, 1951; children: Elizabeth Ann, David Hall, Thomas Charles, Peter Schuyler, James Andrew. *Education:* Massachusetts Institute of Technology, B.S., 1951; Harvard University, A.M., 1953, Ph.D., 1955. *Religion:* Congregational. *Home:* 527 Boston Post Rd., Weston, Mass. 02193. *Office:* Observatory, Harvard University, Cambridge, Mass. 02138.

CAREER: Harvard University, Cambridge, Mass., research associate, 1956-63; associate professor, 1963-68, professor of astronomy, 1968—. Physicist at Smithsonian Astrophysical Observatory, 1956—. Science consultant for children's television. *Member:* International Astronomical Union, American Astronomical Society, American Academy of Arts and Sciences. *Awards, honors:* National Book Award nomination, 1972, for *The Discovery of Our Galaxy.*

WRITINGS: The Discovery of Our Galaxy, Knopf, 1971; *Whitney's Starfinder,* Knopf, 1974, revised edition, 1977; *The Stars,* Harvard University Press, 1979. Contributor of articles and reviews to scientific journals, popular magazines, and newspapers, including *New Yorker* and *Natural History.* Editor of *Journal of the American Association of Variable Star Observers.*

WORK IN PROGRESS: Biographical research; studies of natural phenomena; "a series of frankly autobiographical prose pieces cast as short stories."

SIDELIGHTS: Whitney comments: "My aim is to bring science—particularly astronomy—into the lap of the general public and to television. My approach is to relate science to the lives of the scientists who made interesting discoveries."

BIOGRAPHICAL/CRITICAL SOURCES: Scientific American, February, 1972; *Time,* July 17, 1972; *Times Literary Supplement,* October 6, 1972.

* * *

WHITNEY, Steve(n) 1946-

PERSONAL: Born October 14, 1946; son of Lambert (an attorney) and Kathryn (an English teacher; maiden name, Erickson) Ochsenschlager. *Education:* Attended University of California, Los Angeles, and Harvard University; Southern Methodist University, B.F.A., 1978. *Residence:* Los Angeles, Calif. *Agent:* Elaine Markson Literary Agency, Inc., 44 Greenwich Ave., New York, N.Y. 10011.

CAREER: Crime reporter in New York City; worked as actor, 1968-74, and stage director, 1970-74; writer. *Member:* Authors Guild of Authors League of America, Players Club, Film Industry Workshop.

WRITINGS: The George Raft File, Drake, 1973; *Vincent Price Unmasked,* Drake, 1974; *Charles Bronson, Superstar,* Dell, 1975; (with Laversen Niels) *It's Your Body: A Woman's Guide to Gynecology* (Woman Today Book Club Selection), Grosset, 1977; *Singled Out* (novel), Morrow, 1978.

Author of "Star Treatment," a film, Libra Films.

WORK IN PROGRESS: Piano Man, a contemporary love story set in the pop music world; *The New Man: An Evaluation of the Changing Roles of Men in American Society; Dancer and Twain.*

SIDELIGHTS: Whitney writes: "The only important thing I have to say about my work in the theatre and how it relates to writing is that it taught me, albeit unconsciously, a lot about scene structure. And perhaps that all the creative arts—theatre, painting, music, writing—are one and the same, only the specific skills required for each one differ."

When asked about his books Whitney added: "It's difficult for any author to really talk about his work. I wrote the Price book and the Raft book with rather constricted formulas, biographical chronology. With the Bronson book, I broke that formula, and the book is probably much more about Hollywood in the mid-1970's than it is about Bronson. *It's Your Body* is a comprehensive view of women's bodies and functions, a sex guide, and a consumer guide which will enable women to better understand what her doctor is doing (or isn't doing). *Singled Out* is a novel of terror about a 1970's phenomenon—mass murder. It is also a story about the triumphs and failures of love, and the danger of showing vulnerability in today's society."

* * *

WHITT, Richard 1944-

PERSONAL: Born December 15, 1944, in Beauty Ridge, Ky.; son of Walter C. and Irene (Hayes) Whitt; married Sharon Lyon, June 8, 1968; children: Hayes, Emily. *Education:* Attended Ashland Community College, 1966-68; University of Kentucky, B.A., 1970. *Home:* Route 8, Frankfort, Ky. 40601. *Office: Courier-Journal,* 730 Shelby St., Frankfort, Ky. 40601.

CAREER/WRITINGS: Middlesboro Daily News, Middlesboro, Ky., reporter, 1970-71; *Daily Courier,* Waterloo, Iowa, reporter, 1971-73; *Times-News,* Kingsport, Tenn., city editor, 1972-76; *Courier-Journal,* Frankfort, Ky., bureau chief, 1977—. Notable assignments include coverage of Beverly Hills fire disaster, bootleggers in eastern Kentucky, and bribery and land frauds in Tennessee. *Military service:* U.S. Navy, 1962-66; received Air Combat Medal. *Awards, honors:* Pulitzer Prize, 1977, for coverage of Beverly Hills fire disaster; named outstanding Kentucky journalist by Sigma Delta Chi, 1977.

WORK IN PROGRESS: "Considering a book on the Beverly Hills supper club fire."

SIDELIGHTS: Whitt told *CA:* "If someday I am able to gain the respect that commands attention from my fellow man, I'd like to stand on a soap box and say, no, scream, the things I felt and saw and did as a hillbilly growing up on Beauty Ridge and in the Navy."

* * *

WHYTE, Martin King 1942-

PERSONAL: Born November 4, 1942, in Oklahoma City, Okla.; son of William Foote (a professor) and Kathleen (King) Whyte; married Veronica Mueller, November 5, 1966; children: Adam, Tracy. *Education:* Cornell University, B.A., 1964; Harvard University, M.A., 1966, Ph.D., 1971. *Home:* 502 Sunset Rd., Ann Arbor, Mich. 48103. *Office:* Department of Sociology, University of Michigan, Ann Arbor, Mich. 48109.

CAREER: University of Michigan, Ann Arbor, assistant professor, 1969-76, associate professor of sociology, 1976—. Director of Universities Service Centre in Hong Kong. *Member:* American Sociological Association, Association for Asian Studies, American Anthropological Association, Phi Beta Kappa.

WRITINGS: Small Groups and Political Rituals in China, University of California Press, 1974; *The Status of Women in Preindustrial Societies,* Princeton University Press, 1978; (with William L. Parish) *Village and Family in Contemporary China,* University of Chicago Press, 1978. Contributor to sociology, China studies, and ethnology journals.

WORK IN PROGRESS: Research on urban social life in contemporary China.

SIDELIGHTS: Whyte writes: "I am concerned about developing ways to carry out more detailed and objective research on social life in contemporary China. To this end I have on three occasions lived for a year in Hong Kong, occupied primarily with interviewing emigres from China, and have made two trips to China myself. I am also interested in comparisons with social life in the Soviet Union, and I speak Russian as well as Chinese."

*   *   *

WIGAL, Donald   1933-

PERSONAL: Surname is pronounced Why-*gal;* born January 16, 1933, in Indianapolis, Ind.; son of Wayne Wendell and Mary Louise (Eder) Wigal. *Education:* University of Dayton, B.S., 1955; University of Notre Dame, M.A., 1965; Dominican House of Studies, River Forest, Ill., certificate in theology, 1961. *Home:* 4 Park Ave., New York, N.Y. 10016. *Agent:* Meredith Bernstein, Henry Morrison, Inc., 58 West 10th St., New York, N.Y. 10011.

CAREER: University of Dayton, Dayton, Ohio, instructor in music, theology, and art, 1962-68; Grey Advertising, New York City, librarian and market researcher, 1968-71; World Horizon Films, Osining, N.Y., director, 1972; Dell Publishing Co., New York City, executive editor of special markets, 1972-76; Alternative Works Inc., president, 1976-78; Lakewood Books, Clearwater, Fla., executive editor, 1978—. Instructor at Antioch College, 1965; guest instructor at Xavier University, 1967, and Mary Rogers College, 1968. *Member:* International Platform Association, National Writers Club, Society of Indexers, American Association of University Professors, Alternative (president, 1975—).

WRITINGS: (With Sharon Fayen) *Screen Experience: An Approach to Film,* Pflaum, 1968; (with Charles Murphy) *A Sense of Life,* Herder & Herder, 1970; *A Presence of Love,* Herder & Herder, 1970; *A Way of Community,* Herder & Herder, 1970; *A Vision of Hope,* Herder & Herder, 1970; (editor) *Drug Education,* Sadlier, 1970; (editor) *Filmmaking for Children,* Pflaum, 1971; *Love Your Kitchen,* Dell, 1975; (editor) *The First One Hundred Years,* Dell, 1975; *Biorhythms,* Q Publications, 1978; *Personal Energy,* Q Publications, 1978. Also author of *The Crossword Lover's Book of Lists* and musical compositions. Author of *Star Date Time Line Chart.* Editor of "Lakewood Books" series, 1978—.

Work anthologized in *Teaching Teens,* 1970; *Effective English,* book 5, Silver Burdett, 1978. Contributor of articles and reviews to film and popular art journals. Contributor of word puzzles to periodicals.

WORK IN PROGRESS: Collecting material on mnemonics; research on the history of New York City's organizations for single people; a practical guide for arthritics; "several collections of puzzles which are on popular culture themes such as movies and celebrities."

*   *   *

WIJASURIYA, D(onald) E(arlian) K(ingsley)   1934-

PERSONAL: Born November 22, 1934, in Kuala Lumpur, Malaysia; son of Joseph Stanislaus (a clerk) and Florence (de Silva) Wijasuriya; married Annette Jayatilaka (a television producer), April 3, 1961; children: Rohan, Rienzi, Renan. *Education:* University of Ceylon, B.A., 1959; Northwestern Polytechnic, London, England, A.L.A., 1962, F.L.A., 1965. *Religion:* Christian. *Home:* 19 Jalan

17/21, Petaling Jaya, Selangor, Malaysia. *Office:* National Library of Malaysia, Wisma Thakurdas/Sachdev, Jalan Raja Laut, Kuala Lumpur, Malaysia.

CAREER: University of Malaya, Lembah Pantai, Kuala Lumpur, assistant librarian, 1964-70, deputy university librarian, 1971-72; National Library of Malaysia, Jalan Raja Laut, Kuala Lumpur, deputy director general, 1972—. External examiner for Mara School of Library Science, 1962-63. *Member:* Malaysian Library Association (vice-president, 1970-71; president, 1972, 1973, 1975), Por Dickson Yacht Club, Subang Royal Golf Club.

WRITINGS: (Editor with Kaw Hun Woon) *Proceedings of the Conference on Scientific and Technical Information Needs for Malaysia and Singapore,* Persatuan Perpustakaan Malaysia, 1972; (with Lim Huck Tee) *Index Malaysiana: An Index to the Journal of the Straits Branch Royal Asiatic Society and the Journal of the Malayan Branch Royal Asiatic Society, 1878-1963,* Malaysian Branch, Royal Asiatic Society, 1970, Supplement I: *An Index to the Journal of the Malaysian Branch of the Royal Asiatic Society and the JMBRAS Monographs, 1964-1973,* 1974; (with Tee and Radha Nadarajah) *The Barefoot Librarian* (nonfiction), Bingley, 1975; (contributor) Teeand Rashidah Begum, editors, *National and Academic Libraries in Malaysia and Singapore,* Persatuan Perpustakaan Malaysia, 1975; (editor with Khoo Siew Mun, Shahaneem Mustafa, and Ch'ng Kim See) *Keperluan mengetahui: Perkembangan perkhidmatan perpustakaan awaw bagi masyarakat* (title means "The Need to Know: Developing Public Library Services for the Community"), Persatuan Perpustakaan Malaysia, 1977. Contributor to *Encyclopaedia of Library and Information Science.* Contributor to library, literature, and Southeast Asian studies journals.

SIDELIGHTS: Wijasuriya commented: *"The Barefoot Librarian* is perhaps the first book about Southeast Asian library developments written by Southeast Asians themselves. It was written out of a sense of irritation that so many writings about Southeast Asia were being written by visiting 'experts,' far too superficially exposed to the region to write meaningfully about it. Reviewers of the book have stated that it is 'incisively written,' 'informed in content,' 'a valuable appraisal' and 'a welcome addition for other readers to the literature of comparative librarianship.'"

*   *   *

WIK, Reynold M.   1910-

PERSONAL: Born March 19, 1910, in Norbeck, S.D.; son of Nicholas (in business) and Emma (a teacher; maiden name, Olson) Wik; married Helen Bryan (a librarian and teacher), August 22, 1942; children: Denis Peter. *Education:* Sioux Falls College, B.A., 1936; University of Minnesota, M.A., 1940, Ph.D., 1949; further graduate study at Harvard University, 1940, University of Chicago, 1941, and Indiana University, 1941-42. *Politics:* Liberal. *Religion:* Baptist. *Home:* 4641 Meldon Ave., Oakland, Calif. 94619.

CAREER: High school teacher of history in Cresbard, S.D., 1936-37, Parker, S.D., 1937-39, Minot, N.D., 1939-41, and Pontiac, Mich., 1942-43; Minot State Teachers College, Minot, assistant professor of history, 1943-45; University of Minnesota, Minneapolis, instructor in history, 1945-46; Northern Iowa University, Cedar Falls, instructor in history, 1946-47; Bethel College, St. Paul, Minn., professor of history, 1947-51; Mills College, Oakland, Calif., May Treat Morrison Professor of History, 1951-75; Sioux Falls College, Sioux Falls, S.D., professor of history, 1976—.

Fulbright lecturer at Free University of Berlin, 1955-56; lecturer at University of California, Berkeley, 1964; visiting distinguished lecturer at Boise State University, 1974, and Georgetown College (Georgetown, Ky.), 1978. Public lecturer on the history of technology. Member of board of trustees of Sioux Falls College, 1971-75. Consultant to galleries and museums.

MEMBER: Society for the History of Technology (past member of advisory council; member of executive council, 1962-65), Agricultural History Society (member of executive committee, 1961-64), American Studies Association (northern California president, 1967-69), Association of American Historians, Pacific Historical Association (member of executive council, 1960-64). *Awards, honors:* Albert J. Beveridge Memorial Prize from American Historical Association, 1950, for *Steam Power on the American Farm;* Guggenheim fellow, 1958-59; Ford Foundation grant, 1954; Social Science Research Council grant, 1956; American Philosophical Society grant, 1964; National Academy of Sciences grant for Japan, 1974; D.H.L. from Sioux Falls College, 1974; National Endowment for the Humanities grant, 1977.

WRITINGS: Steam Power on the American Farm, University of Pennsylvania Press, 1953; (contributor) David Van Tassel and Michael Hall, editors, *Science and Society in the United States,* Dorsey, 1966; (contributor) Melvin Kranzberg and Carroll Pursell, editors, *Technology in Western Civilization,* Volume II, Oxford University Press, 1967; *Henry Ford and Grass-Roots America,* University of Michigan Press, 1972; (contributor) Richard Lowitt and Joseph Wall, editors, *Interpreting Twentieth-Century America: A Reader,* Crowell, 1973; (contributor) Kranzberg and William Davenport, editors, *Technology and Culture,* Schocken, 1973. Contributor of more than fifty articles and reviews to science, agriculture, and history journals, and newspapers. Advisory editor of *Technology and Culture,* 1958—.

WORK IN PROGRESS: Benjamin Holt and the Invention of the Caterpillar Tractor; The Radio and Social Change in America.

SIDELIGHTS: Wik wrote to *CA:* "Since I was raised on a farm in Faluk County, South Dakota, I learned to operate farm machinery. My father, Nicholas, owned a large Reeves steam traction engine which he used for plowing and threshing grain, and I used to observe this engine as a young lad on the farm. After entering the teaching profession and doing historical research, it was natural for me to make a study of rural technology in America. As a result, I wrote *Steam Power on the American Farm,* which has remained the definitive work describing the application of steam power to agriculture.

"Subsequently, I did research in the archives of the Ford Motor Company in Dearborn, Michigan, where I read thousands of letters written to Henry Ford, most of them from rural Americans. Out of this research emerged the book, *Henry Ford and Grass-Roots America,* an account of the Model T car and Henry Ford's life-long interest in American agriculture.

"In 1974, I began research on the invention of the Caterpillar track-type tractor which was developed by Benjamin Holt of Stockton, California. Since this invention became the father of the military tank of World War I and the bulldozer of World War II, and the modern snowmobile, it is of paramount importance in the history of technology. This work will complete what I like to call the 'Wik Trilogy'—three works depicting the evolution of the farm steam engine, the Model T. car, and the Caterpillar tractor.

"My interests tend to focus on the average working man and his reactions to his own experiences in using new machines of great economic importance. These machines eliminated the 'Man With the Hoe,' and emancipated millions from back-breaking manual labor. These pioneers are, in my opinion, real heroes."

AVOCATIONAL INTERESTS: Travel, photography, restoring old Ford automobiles.

*   *   *

WILBOURN, Carole C(ecile)   1940-

PERSONAL: Born March 19, 1940, in New York, N.Y.; daughter of Gus and Harriet (Greenwald) Engel; married David Lee Wilbourn, September 13, 1965 (divorced, 1970); married Paul D. Rowan (a veterinarian), October 2, 1978. *Education:* New York University, B.S., 1965. *Office:* Cat Practice, 230 West 13th St., New York, N.Y. 10011.

CAREER: Cat therapist. Cat Practice, New York, N.Y., co-founder, 1973, and currently consulting associate. Previously worked as substitute teacher in public high schools, and as Playboy bunny, 1965-73. Also participated in various humane activities, including work on a telephone information service about cats.

WRITINGS: Cats Prefer It This Way, Coward, 1976; *The Inner Cat,* Stein & Day, 1978. Contributor of articles to *Ladies Home Journal* and *Cosmopolitan.*

WORK IN PROGRESS: Another book about cats, for publication by McGraw.

SIDELIGHTS: Wilbourn, in her practice of feline psychotherapy, has treated more than 7,000 cats. She told *CA* that she "was very interested in cats and their welfare and want people to understand their cats better." In an interview with *Us* magazine, she revealed some of her professional observations: "[Cats are] affected by pleasure, by pain, by sadness, just like people. . . . Cats get emotional. They really depend and act on the feelings they pick up from their humans. . . . If the human's head is messed up, the cat stands a good chance of being in bad shape, too." What's the best thing that you can do for your cat? Wilbourn advised that you make sure that your cat is aware that you love him.

AVOCATIONAL INTERESTS: Psychology, ballet, jogging, and bicycling.

BIOGRAPHICAL/CRITICAL SOURCES: Us, September 19, 1978.

*   *   *

WILD, Rolf H(einrich)   1927-

PERSONAL: Born May 5, 1927, in Zurich, Switzerland; came to the United States in 1952, naturalized citizen, 1958; son of Heinrich (a photographer) and Elfriede (a photographer; maiden name, Mollet) Wild; married Suzanne Wadewitz, November 7, 1953; children: Patricia, Sylvia. *Education:* Juventus College, Zurich, Switzerland, degree in mechanical engineering, 1949. *Home and office:* 34 Rue Pereire, St. Germain-en-laye, France 78100. *Agent:* JDS Associates, South Norwalk, Conn. 06854.

CAREER: Oerlikon Tool & Arms Corp., Asheville, N.C., staff engineer, 1952-56; Olin Corp., assistant director of arms research and development for Winchester Division in New Haven, Conn., 1956-59, European director of chemicals and industrials in Paris, France, and Dusseldorf, Germany, 1960-68; management consultant in St. Germain-en-laye, France, 1968—.

WRITINGS: Management by Compulsion: The Corporate Urge to Grow, Houghton, 1978.

WORK IN PROGRESS: Compulsions of Democracy, a discussion of the political and institutional motivations for the growth of government; *La Penitence scolaire* (title means "The Ordeal of School"), on the French school system.

SIDELIGHTS: Wild writes: "The destiny of modern man is to a remarkable extent shaped by large organizations over which we have no control. Yet while we worry about their power and their pernicious influence on our lives, these large organizations are really of our own making. They respond to the threats and incentives of their environment and we all help to create this environment. It is our demands for high wages and low cost goods, for protection and better services, for advantages and special privileges that create an environment in which large organizations grow and prosper.

"My first book, *Management by Compulsion,* dealt with the corporate environment—the conditions that make rapid corporate growth not only a logical objective, but often a condition of survival. The book examines the consequences of corporate growth and the effects of this growth on the people within and outside of the corporate structure. It was perhaps inevitable that this should be followed by another book, *Compulsions of Democracy,* on the bureaucratic and political growth urges built into government organizations that have become something akin to supercorporations, selling protection of all kinds to the public. Since government agencies are monopolies they are not subject to the restraints of the marketplace and are thus free to pursue their internal growth urges and institutional aberrations. At the same time the political imperative to give the public what the public wants creates a steady pressure for the enlargement of government services. Nobody particularly wants big government, but we all unwittingly contribute to government growth by clamoring incessantly for more protection.

"A third book, *La Penitence scolaire,* now being written in French in collaboration with my daughters, deals with the activities and aberrations of a large government agency—in this case the French public school system. It describes the experiences of two students as they progress through the system, and the reactions of the parents to the inefficiencies and absurdities of an inbred organization that has become so large that it no longer needs to respond to practical considerations or outside control."

AVOCATIONAL INTERESTS: Photography, landscape painting, aviation, ferroequinology.

*   *   *

WILDE, Meta Carpenter (Doherty)   1907-

PERSONAL: Born November 25, 1907, in Memphis, Tenn.; daughter of Clark White (a cotton planter) and Beulah Redding (Ussery) Doherty; married Fabian Pleas Carpenter, 1925 (divorced); married Wolfgang Edward Rebner (a concert pianist), April 6, 1937 (divorced, 1941); remarried Rebner, 1945 (divorced, 1952); married Arthur Lionel Wilde (a motion picture publicist), September 30, 1969. *Education:* Attended private schools in Memphis, Tenn. *Politics:* Democrat. *Religion:* Humanist. *Home:* 1882 South Pandora Ave., Los Angeles, Calif. 90025. *Agent:* Sanford J. Greenburger Associates, Inc., 825 Third Ave., New York, N.Y. 10022.

CAREER: Classical pianist for radio stations in Memphis, Tenn., and New Orleans, La., 1926; WCBE radio station, New Orleans, program director, 1926-27; worked at various jobs, including model, music librarian, and salesperson, in Hollywood, Calif., 1930-31; Columbia Pictures Industries, Inc., Hollywood, staff member, 1931-33; secretary to director Howard Hawks, 1934-37; script supervisor, 1935-76. Member of Women in Film; president of Script Supervisors Union, 1958-60.

WRITINGS: (With Orin Borsten) *A Loving Gentleman: The Love Story of William Faulkner and Meta Carpenter* (Book-of-the-Month Club alternate selection), Simon & Schuster, 1976.

WORK IN PROGRESS: A book, tentatively entitled *Working Girl, Working Woman,* completion expected in 1979.

SIDELIGHTS: In 1935 Meta Wilde (then Meta Carpenter) and William Faulkner met at the Twentieth Century-Fox studios when they were working on a Howard Hawks film, "The Road to Glory." Faulkner, who loathed Hollywood and his job as a screenwriter, was delighted to meet another person with a Southern background. Although the famous novelist was married and had a family at home in Mississippi, he fell in love with Wilde. Their relationship continued on and off for eighteen years.

As a child, Wilde had spent her summers and holidays on the family plantation in Ussery Ridge, Miss. Her forebears, like Faulkner's, had been slave owners and Confederate soldiers. In an unpublished chapter from *A Loving Gentleman: The Love Story of William Faulkner and Meta Carpenter,* Wilde described how she and Faulkner spent many evenings reminiscing about the South: "Because I had grown up on the same soil from which he [Faulkner] came, had rolled in its rich mud, sprawled on its offerings of fern, clover and wild violet, I could make him forget for hours on end that he was so far from home. . . . Together we re-created our own South. It helped make his life away from Oxford endurable."

Wilde's decision to write a book about her love affair with Faulkner was a difficult one to make. She was well aware that Faulkner had passionately protected his right to personal privacy. But because their liaison was common knowledge in the movie studios, she feared that someone would write a lurid book about the relationship after her death. "There was no option left to me but to write . . . my own account of my years with Bill," she wrote in *A Loving Gentleman.* "One cannot prevent distortions of truth from the grave." Wilde also hoped that her book would provide a more rounded view of Faulkner the man. She told an interviewer: "Many don't want to see any change in the public image of Faulkner as an anti-social, hard-drinking, cynical, bitter, dour, unpleasant, sometimes rude, sometimes crude, man. But this wasn't the William Faulkner I knew. He was a loving, gentle man. My lover, my friend, a great joy in my life. And I think that part of his life should be known to the people who really revere and admire him and read his books."

Although some reviewers decried Wilde's decision to record the details of her intimate relationship with a married man, others felt the subject matter was handled with taste and delicacy. Many scholars welcomed the new perspective that *A Loving Gentleman* provided to Faulkner's personality. Carvel Collins, a professor at Notre Dame who is currently preparing a biography of Faulkner, has reviewed hundreds of letters from Faulkner to Wilde. He found the correspondence to be a valuable aid, and remarked that "obviously William and Meta were very much in love with each other."

Malcolm Cowley's assessment of *A Loving Gentleman* was more ambivalent. "Meta Carpenter, I feel, would have preserved more of her dignity, and Faulkner's, by remaining silent," he declared. "I deplore the book from that point of view, but still, in this shameless age, I confess to having read it with sharp interest and not a little profit. 'A Loving Gentleman' contains fresh information, most of it reliable, about the character, the love life and the working habits of a great novelist."

Wilde told *CA:* "My life in the motion picture industry has been interesting, at times exciting, and certainly rewarding. I have met and been associated with many of the greats in the field—not only actors, but many talented directors, writers, and producers. I feel that I have had a liberal education through my work, travel, and association with so many fine, talented, and creative people."

Faulkner's letters, drawings, and poems to Wilde are on file with the Faulkner Library at the University of Texas and in the Berg Collection at the New York Public Library. *A Loving Gentleman* has been published in French and Spanish.

AVOCATIONAL INTERESTS: Yachting, bicycling, playing the piano, travel (Alaska, Italy, Jamaica, Mexico, England, Germany, the Bahamas).

BIOGRAPHICAL/CRITICAL SOURCES: Meta Carpenter Wilde and Orin Borsten, *A Loving Gentleman: The Love Story of William Faulkner and Meta Carpenter,* Simon & Schuster, 1976; *Los Angeles Magazine,* November, 1976; *The Toronto Sun,* November 28, 1976; *Variety,* December 3, 1976; *San Francisco Chronicle,* December 15, 1976; *New York Times Book Review,* December 19, 1976; *Chicago Daily News,* December 25-26, 1976; *Washington Post,* February 2, 1977; *Hollywood Reporter,* February 25, 1977; *Best Sellers,* April, 1977; *Mississippi Quarterly,* summer, 1977; *Sewanee Review,* July, 1977; *Commonweal,* August 5, 1977.

* * *

WILDER, Amos Niven 1895-

PERSONAL: Born September 18, 1895, in Madison, Wis.; son of Amos Parker and Isabella (Niven) Wilder; married Catharine Kerlin, June 26, 1935; children: Catharine Dix, Amos Tappan. *Education:* Yale University, B.A., 1920, B.D. (cum laude), 1924, Ph.D., 1933; graduate study at Mansfield College, Oxford, 1921-23, and Harvard University, 1929-30. *Home:* 10 Bates St., Cambridge, Mass. 02140.

CAREER: Ordained Congregationalist minister, 1926; pastor of Congregational church in North Conway, N.H., 1925-28; Hamilton College, Clinton, N.Y., associate professor of ethics and Christian evidences, 1930-33; Andover Newton Theological School, Newton Centre, Mass., professor of New Testament interpretation, 1933-43; Chicago Theological Seminary, Chicago, Ill., professor of New Testament, 1943-54; Harvard University, Cambridge, Mass., professor of New Testament, 1954-56, Hollis Professor of Divinity, 1956-63, professor emeritus, 1963—; writer, 1963—. Visiting professor at University of Frankfort, 1951, 1952. *Military service:* American Ambulance Field Service, 1916-17; served in France; received Croix de Guerre. U.S. Army, Field Artillery, 1918-19.

MEMBER: American Academy of Arts and Sciences, Society for the Arts, Literature, and Contemporary Culture, Massachusetts Historical Society, Alpha Delta Phi, Elizabethan Club, Winthrop Club. *Awards, honors:* Belgian-American Foundation fellow at University of Brussels, 1920-21; National Council for Religion in Higher Education

fellow, 1928; D.D. from Hamilton College, 1933, Oberlin College, 1952, Yale University, 1956, and Fairfield University, 1969; Bross Decennial Award from Lake Forest College, 1951, for *Modern Poetry and the Christian Tradition;* L.H.D. from University of Chicago, 1955; Guggenheim fellow, 1958-59; Th.D. from University of Basel, 1960.

WRITINGS: Battle-Retrospect and Other Poems, Yale University Press, 1923, reprinted, AMS Press, 1971; *Arachne* (poems), Yale University Press, 1928; *Eschatology and Ethics in the Teaching of Jesus,* Harper, 1939, revised edition, 1950; *Spiritual Aspects of the New Poetry,* Harper, 1940, reprinted, Books for Libraries, 1968; *The Healing of the Waters* (poems), Harper, 1943; *Modern Poetry and the Christian Tradition: A Study In the Relation of Christianity to Culture,* Scribner, 1952; *Otherworldliness and the New Testament,* Harper, 1954; *New Testament Faith for Today,* Harper, 1955; *Theology and Modern Literature,* Harvard University Press, 1958; *The Language of the Gospel: Early Christian Rhetoric,* Harper, 1964, reprinted as *Early Christian Rhetoric,* Harvard University Press, 1971; *Kerygma, Eschatology and Social Ethics,* Fortress, 1966; *The New Voice: Religion, Literature, Hermeneutics,* Herder, 1969; (editor) *Grace Confounding* (poems), Fortress, 1972; *Theopoetic: Theology and the Religious Imagination,* Fortress, 1976.

WORK IN PROGRESS: Thornton Wilder and His Public.

SIDELIGHTS: Wilder comments: "My main field of scholarly study and teaching has been the New Testament and early Christian origins. But my literary interests have led me to the literary study of the Bible, and to teaching and writing on modern literature. In the Society for the Arts, Literature, and Contemporary Culture, I have long been interested in modern cultural assessment, in association with many gifted artists and qualified critics and social scientists."

* * *

WILKES, Paul 1938-

PERSONAL: Born September 12, 1938, in Cleveland, Ohio; son of Paul Thomas (a carpenter) and Margaret (Salansky) Wilkes. *Education:* Marquette University, B.A., 1960; Columbia University, M.A., 1967. *Home and office:* 45 West 10th St., New York, N.Y. 10011. *Agent:* Theron Raines, Raines & Raines, 488 Fifth Ave., New York, N.Y. 10017.

CAREER: Boulder Daily Camera, Boulder, Colo., staff member, 1964-66; *Baltimore Sun,* Baltimore, Md., writer, 1967-68; Harper & Row, New York City, editor, 1969; freelance writer, 1969—; Harper's Magazine Press, New York City, editor, 1970. Lecturer in feature writing at Brooklyn College, 1973-75; co-founder, Christian Help in Park Slope (CHIPS), 1973-75. *Military service:* U.S. Navy, communications officer, 1961-64; became lieutenant. *Awards, honors:* Best nonfiction awards from Society of Midland Authors and Friends of American Writers, both 1974, both for *Fitzgo: The Wild Dog of Central Park;* by-line award from Marquette University, 1977, for distinguished service in journalism; alumni award from Columbia University Graduate School of Journalism, 1978, for distinguished service to journalism; Alfred I. DuPont-Columbia Survey and Award in Broadcast Journalism, 1978, for "Six American Families."

WRITINGS: Fitzgo: The Wild Dog of Central Park (nonfiction), Lippincott, 1973; *These Priests Stay* (biography), Simon & Schuster, 1973; (with wife, Joy Wilkes) *You Don't Have to Be Rich to Own a Brownstone* (nonfiction), Quadrangle, 1973; *Trying Out the Dream: A Year in the Life of an*

American Family (nonfiction), Lippincott, 1975; *Six American Families* (based on his television documentary series of the same title), Office of Communication, United Church.

Teleplays: "Six American Families" (documentary), Public Broadcasting Service (PBS), 1977; "Men of Iron" (drama), PBS, 1978.

Contributor to numerous periodicals, including *New York Times Magazine, New York, Atlantic, Life,* and *Look.*

SIDELIGHTS: A stray dog which Paul Wilkes adopted served as the inspiration for Wilkes's first book, *Fitzgo: The Wild Dog of Central Park.* "Discreetly down-to-earth, sentimental (in the best sense of the word), warmhearted, and heartwarming," Neil Millar wrote of the story. A reviewer for *Best Sellers* commented, "Anybody who cares at all about dogs will find [this book] charming."

Wilkes's subsequent books have been about sociological topics. *These Priests Stay* consists of a series of biographies on nine Roman Catholic priests and one bishop who contemplated leaving the clergy. Wilkes provides short introductions to each sketch as well as a general introduction to the book. The biographies, remarked Charles Dollen, "are touching and, at times, compelling stories of clergymen who have been through identity crises." He added, however, that the book is "of very limited appeal. It is not large enough to be a statistical sample and it is hardly of much value as a sociological study."

After spending a year in a statistically average American household, Wilkes wrote *Trying Out the Dream,* in which he documents the lives of the pseudonyms Neumeyer family. W. A. Babcock described the book as "a stark, composite picture of a 'typical' American family. Although much of Mr. Wilkes's editorializing turns out to be little more than a statement of the obvious, his character studies of individual family members are often superb." Writing of his emotional involvement with the Neumeyers, a *Newsweek* reviewer stated, "So skillful is Wilkes at presenting this family without a story that I found myself caring for each of them and feeling that at the end of their year I knew them fairly well." More praise for *Trying Out the American Dream* came from Abigail McCarthy, who remarked: "It is as engaging, and has the strong narrative interest of the best magazine fiction . . . the relationship of the Neumeyers to the American dream—the extent to which they embody it—is skillfully sketched."

BIOGRAPHICAL/CRITICAL SOURCES: Christian Science Monitor, June 13, 1973, April 2, 1975; *Best Sellers,* August 1, 1973, March 1, 1974; *Newsweek,* March 24, 1975; *New Republic,* April 26, 1975.

* * *

WILLARD, Barbara Mary 1909-

PERSONAL: Born in 1909, in Hove, Sussex, Eng. *Education:* Attended the Convent of La Sainte Union, Southampton. *Residence:* Forest Edge, Nutley, Sussex, England.

CAREER: Actress; novelist and screenwriter. *Member:* Society of Authors. *Awards, honors:* Guardian Award for Children's Fiction, 1974, for *The Iron Lily.*

WRITINGS: (With Elizabeth H. Devas) *Love in Ambush,* G. Howe, 1930; *Ballerina,* G. Howe, 1932; *Candle Flame,* G. Howe, 1932; *Name of Gentleman,* G. Howe, 1933; *Joy Befall Thee,* G. Howe, 1934; *As Far as in Me Lies,* Thomas Nelson, 1936; *Set Piece,* Thomas Nelson, 1938; *Personal Effects,* Macmillan, 1939; *The Dogs Do Bark,* Macmillan, 1948; *Portrait of Philip,* Macmillan, 1950: *Brother Ass and*

Brother Lion (play; based on the story, *St. Jerome, the Lion and the Donkey,* by Helen J. Waddell), J. G. Miller, 1951; *Proposed and Seconded,* Macmillan, 1951; *Celia Scarfe,* Appleton-Century, 1951; *Echo Answers,* Macmillan, 1952; *One of the Twelve* (one-act play), Samuel French, 1954; *He Fought for His Queen: The Story of Sir Philip Sidney,* Warne, 1954; *The Snail and the Pennithornes* (illustrated by Geoffrey Fletcher), Epworth, 1957; *Winter in Disguise,* M. Jospeh, 1958; *The House With Roots* (illustrated by Robert Hodgson), Constable, 1959, F. Watts, 1960; *Son of Charlemagne* (illustrated by Emil Weiss), Doubleday, 1959.

The Dippers and Jo (illustrated by Jean Harper), Hamish Hamilton, 1960; *Eight for a Secret* (illustrated by Lewis Hart), Constable, 1960, F. Watts, 1961; *The Penny Pony* (illustrated by Juliette Palmer), Hamish Hamilton, 1961, Penguin, 1967; *The Summer With Spike* (illustrated by Anne Linton), Constable, 1961, F. Watts, 1962; *If All the Swords in England* (illustrated by Robert M. Sax), Doubleday, 1961; *Stop the Train!* (illustrated by Harper), Hamish Hamilton, 1961; *Hetty* (illustrated by Pamela Mara), Constable, 1962, Harcourt, 1963; *Duck on a Pond* (illustrated by Mary Rose Hardy), F. Watts, 1962; *The Battle of Wednesday Week* (illustrated by Douglas Hall), Constable Young Books, 1963, published as *Storm From the West,* Harcourt, 1964; *The Suddenly Gang* (illustrated by Lynette Hemmant), Hamish Hamilton, 1963; *Augustine Came to Kent* (illustrated by Hans Guggenheim), Doubleday, 1963; *The Dippers and the High-Flying Kite* (illustrated by Maureen Eckersley), Hamish Hamilton, 1963; *Three and One to Carry* (illustrated by Hall), Constable, 1964; Harcourt, 1965; *A Dog and a Half* (illustrated by Jane Paton), Hamish Hamilton, 1964, Thomas Nelson, 1971; *The Pram Race* (illustrated by Constance Marshall), Hamish Hamilton, 1964.

The Wild Idea (illustrated by Douglas Bissett), Hamish Hamilton, 1965; *Sussex,* Batsford, 1965, Hastings House, 1966; *Charity at Home* (illustrated by Hall), Constable, 1965, Harcourt, 1966; *Surprise Island* (illustrated by Paton), Hamish Hamilton, 1966, Meredith Press, 1969; *The Richleighs of Tantamount* (illustrated by C. Walter Hodges), Constable, 1966, Harcourt, 1967; *Flight to the Forest* (illustrated by Gareth Floyd), Doubleday, 1967 (published in England as *The Grove of Green Holly,* Constable, 1967; *To London! To London!* (illustrated by Antony Maitland), Weybright & Talley, 1968; *The Family Tower,* Harcourt, 1968; (with Frances Howell) *Junior Motorist: The Driver's Apprentice* (illustrated by Ionicus), Collins, 1969, *The Toppling Towers,* Harcourt, 1969; *The Pocket Mouse* (illustrated by Mary Russon), Knopf, 1969; (compiler) *Hullabaloo! About Naughty Boys and Girls* (illustrated by Fritz Wegner), 1969.

The Reindeer Slippers (illustrated by Tessa Jordan), Hamish Hamilton, 1970; *The Lark and the Laurel,* Harcourt, 1970; *Chichester & Lewes* (illustrated by Graham Humphreys), Longman, 1970; *Priscilla Pentecost* (illustrated by Doreen Roberts), Hamish Hamilton, 1970; *The Sprig of Broom* (illustrated by Paul Shardlow), Longman, 1971, Dutton, 1972; (compiler) *"I–": An Anthology of Diarists* (illustrated by John Sergeant), Chatto & Windus, 1972; *A Cold Wind Blowing,* Longman, 1972, Dutton, 1973; *Jubilee!* (illustrated by Hilary Abrahams), Heinemann, 1973; *The Iron Lily,* Longman, 1973, Dutton, 1974; *Harrow and Harvest,* Penguin, 1974; (compiler) *Happy Families* (illustrated by Krystyna Turska), Macmillan, 1974; (editor) *Field and Forest* (illustrated by Faith Jaques), Penguin, 1975; (author of English text) Bunshu Iguchi, *Convent Cat,* Hamish Hamilton, 1975, McGraw, 1976; *Bridesmaid* (illustrated by Paton), Hamish

Hamilton, 1976; *The Miller's Boy* (illustrated by Floyd), Dutton, 1976.

SIDELIGHTS: Willard said once that she writes to enjoy herself, with the hope that others will enjoy reading what she has written. Her best stories are those which concern large, close-knit families. Since she was an only child until age twelve, this kind of writing seems to vicariously fulfill her desire to be part of a large family.

A *Book Week* critic called *Three and One to Carry,* "a well-paced story with natural characters, sprightly style and a plot which hinges believably on a lost document in the ancient village church. The bond of family affections is skillfully underplayed with an astringent touch of realism. Miss Willard's opening chapter is a model of how to establish characters, delineate a situation and get a story under way."

Horn Book's comments on *The Sprig of Broom* included: "In addition to the tantalizing mystery, the book presents history, romance, and a masterful re-creation of life lived long ago. The characters are real and solid, and the story can be read for the engrossing plot and rich background. The author has shown great skill in revealing gradually the information that leads to the solution of the mystery." A *Times Literary Supplement* critic, reviewing *The Sprig of Broom,* wrote: "If the mystery provides the motive force of the story, the main interest lies in the everyday life of a forest community surviving, for the most part undisturbed, away from the affairs of the world. Medley and his wilful, high-spirited love are attractively drawn, but the author's real hero is the forest itself, its changing seasons and moods evoked unobtrusively but always with understanding affection."

A *Cold Wind Blowing* is one of Willard's most recent efforts. The *Times Literary Supplement* review included: "It was Rumer Godden who advised those who read and review children's books to treat them like Persian carpets; design, she said, and colour are important—but what really counts is the perfection of the stitching, for if the stitching is less than perfect, the carpet will soon disintegrate. Barbara Willard is one of the few craftsmen writing for young people today whose stitching can be examined under a magnifying glass and found flawless.... [Her] chronicle grows in stature with every book." Observed *New Statesman:* "Miss Willard's achievement is the mysterious one of her giving her narrative the feel of its period; the language, without being archaic is somehow all of a piece with the story. She's marvellous on the curious wedding of weather and event, on the growth and decline of human passions; and there are big scenes, of a quality that won't easily by forgotten...."

BIOGRAPHICAL/CRITICAL SOURCES: New York Times, June 24, 1951; *San Francisco Chronicle,* July 1, 1951; *Times Literary Supplement,* November 28, 1963, *October 22, 1971, December 8, 1972;* Book Week, *October 31, 1965;* New Statesman, *November 10, 1972;* Children's Literary Review, *Volume 2, Gale, 1976.**

* * *

WILLARD, Charlotte 1914-1977

PERSONAL: Born in 1914, in Miscolz, Hungary; came to United States in 1916; daughter of Edmund and Hermina (Newman) Schwartz; married Howard W. Willard, June 15, 1937 (deceased). *Education:* New York University, B.A.; graduate studies at Columbia University, New School for Social Research, and Hunter College of the City University of New York. *Residence:* New York, N.Y.

CAREER: Seventeen magazine, New York City, managing editor, 1943-45; *Jr. Bazaar* magazine, New York City, executive editor, 1945-46; *Look* magazine, New York City, art editor, 1951-55; *Art in America,* New York City, contributing editor, 1963-69; *New York Post,* New York City, art critic, 1964-69. *Awards, honors:* MacDowell Colony fellowship, 1971-72.

WRITINGS: (Contributor) *The Story Behind the Painting,* Doubleday, 1960; (author of introduction) Moses Soyer, *Moses Soyer,* World Publishing, 1962; *What is a Masterpiece?* (juvenile), Putnam, 1964; *Famous Modern Artists: From Cezanne to Pop Art,* Platt, 1971; *Frank Lloyd Wright: American Architect,* Macmillan, 1972; *Adomas Galdikas: A Color Odyssey,* October House, 1973. Contributor of articles on art to various publications.

OBITUARIES: New York Times, October 23, 1977.*

(Died October 20, 1977. in New York, N.Y.)

* * *

WILLIAMS, J(ohn) Rodman 1918-

PERSONAL: Born August 21, 1918, in Clyde, N.C.; son of John Rodman (a clergyman) and Obessa Lee (Medford) Williams; married Johanna Servaas (a writer), August 6, 1949; children: John, Lucinda, David. *Education:* Davidson College, A.B., 1939; Union Theological Seminary, Richmond, Va., B.D., 1943, Th.M, 1944; Columbia University, Ph.D., 1954. *Home:* 2238 East Vermont Ave., Anaheim, Calif. 92806. *Office:* Melodyland School of Theology, 10 Freedman Way, Anaheim, Calif. 92806.

CAREER: Ordained Presbyterian minister, 1943; Beloit College, Beloit, Wis., assistant professor of philosophy and college chaplain, 1949-52; pastor of Presbyterian church in Rockford, Ill., 1952-59; Austin Presbyterian Theological Seminary, Austin, Tex., associate professor, 1959-65, professor of systematic theology and philosophy of religion, 1965-72; Melodyland School of Theology, Anaheim, Calif., president of college and professor of systematic theology, 1972—. *Military service:* U.S. Naval Reserve, active duty as chaplain, 1944-46; became lieutenant senior grade.

WRITINGS: Contemporary Existentialism and Christian Faith, Prentice-Hall, 1965; *The Era of the Spirit,* Logos International, 1971; *The Pentecostal Reality,* Logos International, 1972; *Ten Teachings,* Creation House, 1974.

WORK IN PROGRESS: The Gift of the Holy Spirit.

SIDELIGHTS: Williams comments: "I am active in the charismatic movement which is occurring in many churches (Protestant, Roman Catholic, Eastern Orthodox) and I am a kind of theological resource person."

AVOCATIONAL INTERESTS: Travel in Europe, Australia, and the Middle East.

* * *

WILLIAMS, Jay 1914-1978

*OBITUARY NOTICE—*See index for *CA* sketch: Born May 31, 1914, in Buffalo, N.Y.; died July 12, 1978, in England. Writer best known for his Danny Dunn series of books for children. Williams also wrote several adult novels that received critical praise. *Tomorrow's Fire* and *The Siege* were both well acknowledged by reviewers for their adherence to the periods in which the respective novels take place. Williams wrote more than sixty books, among which the most popular were *The Counterfeit African, The Good Yeoman,* and several books in the Danny Dunn series, including *Danny Dunn and the Antigravity Paint* and *Danny Dunn and the Automatic House.* As a result of his popular children's books, Williams received more than one thousand letters every year, each of which he answered himself. Obituaries and other sources: *World Authors, 1950-1970,* Wilson, 1975; *The Writers Directory, 1976-78,* St. Martin's, 1976; *New York Times,* July 16, 1978; *Publishers Weekly,* July 24, 1978; *Current Biography,* September, 1978; *AB Bookman's Weekly,* November 6, 1978.

* * *

WILLIAMS, Mona (Goodwyn) 1916-

PERSONAL: Born March 26, 1916, in Vermont; daughter of Wirt (a produce dealer) and Annabel (a teacher; maiden name, Trask) Goodwyn; married Henry Meade Williams (a writer and editor); children: Karen (Mrs. Ben Lyon), Christopher, Lacy (Mrs. John Faia III). *Education:* Attended private school in Northampton, Mass. *Home:* 3572 Lazarro Dr., Carmel, Calif. 93921. *Agent:* Don Congdon, Harold Matson Co., Inc., 22 East 40th St., New York, N.Y. 10016.

CAREER: Writer, 1936—.

WRITINGS—All novels, except as noted: *Here Are My Children,* Mohawk Press, 1932; *Bright Is the Morning,* H. Smith & R. Haas, 1934; *The Marriage,* Putnam, 1958; *The Hot Breath of Heaven,* Putnam, 1961; *The Company Girls,* Gold Medal, 1965; *The Passion of Amy Styron,* Paperback Library, 1965; *Celia,* Dell, 1968; *Voices in the Dark* (poems), Doubleday, 1968; *The Messenger,* Rawson Associates, 1977; *This House Is Burning,* Rawson Associates, 1978. Contributor of articles, fiction, and poems to magazines, including *Writer, McCall's, Ladies Home Journal,* and *Cosmopolitan.*

SIDELIGHTS: Mona Williams's *The Messenger* was praised by Christopher Lehmann-Haupt for its "basic gimmick" and the feeling of "eerie otherworldliness" that it evokes. According to Lehmann-Haupt, this book about a haunted island is so frightening that "a reader doesn't even require candlelight and shadows to be thoroughly nervous." However, he went on to say that Williams does not satisfactorily solve some difficulties: "Despite the appeal of her wholesome and well-drawn characters and the delicate way in which she introduces her island's mysteries, she eventually writes herself into a corner.... Miss Williams ... is left juggling so many improbabilities that she finally fumbles them."

Williams told *CA* about her writing career: "I started writing in my teens and never stopped, although the novels didn't come along until after a long period of publishing short stories and novelettes. I began, as most teenagers do, with poetry, returning to it seriously only once. I've had stories in every slick magazine, perhaps two hundred in all."

The Company Girls was sold to Metro-Goldwyn-Mayer and one of Williams's novelettes, originally published in a popular magazine, was made into the film "Woman's World" by Columbia.

BIOGRAPHICAL/CRITICAL SOURCES: Writer, April, 1969; *New York Times,* April 22, 1977.

* * *

WILLIAMS, Paul (Steven) 1948-

PERSONAL: Born May 19, 1948, in Boston, Mass.; son of Robert Walter (a physicist) and Janet (an editor; maiden name, Rossman) Williams; married Sachiko Kanenobu (a musician), July 29, 1972; children: Kenta, Taiyo (sons).

Education: Attended Swarthmore College, 1965-66. *Agent:* Susan Ann Protter, 156 East 52nd St., New York, N.Y. 10022. *Office:* Entwhistle Books, P.O. Box 611, Glen Ellen, Calif. 95442.

CAREER: Crawdaddy, New York, N.Y., founder, editor, and publisher, 1966-68; Entwhistle Books, Glen Ellen, Calif., co-founder, editor, and publisher, 1968—. Member of Glen Ellen Volunteer Fire Department.

WRITINGS: Outlaw Blues: A Book of Rock Music, Dutton, 1969; *Time Between* (autobiography), Entwhistle Books, 1972; *Pushing Upward* (collected writings), Links, 1973; *Das Energi* (philosophy), Elektra, 1973; *Apple Bay, or Life on the Planet* (autobiography), Warner Paperback, 1976; *Right to Pass,* Berkley-Windhover, 1977; *Coming* (prose-poem), Entwhistle Books, 1977; *Theodore Sturgeon, Storyteller* (chapbook), Pendragon, 1978.

Author of introduction: Philip K. Dick, *Confessions of a Crap Artist,* Entwhistle Books, 1975; Alfred Bester, *The Stars My Destination,* Gregg, 1975; Theodore Sturgeon, *Venus Plus X,* Gregg, 1976; Chester Anderson, *The Butterfly Kid,* Gregg, 1977; Sturgeon, *The Dreaming Jewels,* Gregg, 1978; Robert A. Heinlein, *I Will Fear No Evil,* Gregg, 1978.

Author of columns, including "What Goes On," *Crawdaddy,* 1966-68; "The Sources of the Nile," *San Francisco Express Times,* 1968, and *Crawdaddy,* 1972-75; record review column, *Soho Weekly News,* 1974-75; "Heart of Gold," *Soho Weekly News,* 1975, and *Santa Cruz Good Times,* 1977. Contributor to numerous magazines and newspapers, including *Rolling Stone, Vogue, Gallery, Seventeen,* and *Ariel.* Editor of *Within,* 1962-63, *There Must Be Some Way Out of Here,* 1969, *Friends and Neighbors,* 1969, *Rallying Point,* 1973, *Delta-T,* 1975-77, and *Small Publication,* 1977-78.

WORK IN PROGRESS: Heart of Gold, semi-autobiographical; *State of Mind,* on his personal political vision; a book on the influence of science fiction, with David G. Hartwell.

SIDELIGHTS: Williams writes: "The message of any performance—writing, music, acting—is 'I am.' Modify that slightly and you have 'I am here—this is what it looks like from here.' Which in turn is only of interest to the reader because she (he) recognizes bits and snatches of her own personal 'here' as she's reading. In other words, I write to affirm my own reality and in the hope of affirming and challenging my reader's reality (perception) in the process. So my writing, regardless of subject matter or form, is a kind of talking on paper, in which I am conscious that this will be transformed into someone else, the reader, talking to herself or himself—and maybe saying something different, but that's okay, because when you use my words to make your statement we share a bond of intimacy that goes far beyond what the words seem to mean. I write and as an editor I put forward other people's writings in order to triangulate our subjective reality: I look at the world and you look at it with me and it's like the difference between one eye and two, together we create depth, we create a field of perception, we break through loneliness for a moment, we create and feel the shared universe, mutual reality.

"One small example: In writing about rock music, back in the sixties, my intention was not to judge the records (like a critic) or report on the scene (like a journalist) but to explore (as an essayist) the experience of listening to certain records and feeling the whole world through them. My form has always been the essay; talking on paper; my subject matter has always been transcendence."

WILLIAMS, Rose
See ROSS, W(illiam) E(dward) D(aniel)

* * *

WILLIAMSON, Henry   1895-1977

PERSONAL: Born December 1, 1895, in Bedfordshire, England; son of William Williamson; married twice (divorced twice); children: seven. *Residence:* Berkshire, England.

CAREER: Became a journalist in London after World War I; writer, 1921-74. Served as a broadcaster on farming life in 1930's and was a farmer in Norfolk. *Military service:* British Army, World War I; infantryman and officer. *Member:* National Liberal Club, Savage Club, Chelsea Arts Club. *Awards, honors:* Hawthornden Prize, 1928, for *Tarka the Otter.*

WRITINGS—"The Flax of Dream" series: *The Beautiful Years,* Dutton, 1921, revised edition, 1929; *Dandelion Days,* Dutton, 1922, revised edition, 1930; *The Dream of Fair Women,* Dutton, 1924, revised edition, 1931; *The Pathway,* J. Cape, 1928, Dutton, 1929; tetralogy published as *The Flax of Dream,* Faber, 1936.

"A Chronicle of Ancient Sunlight" series; all published by Macdonald, except as noted: *The Dark Lantern,* 1951; *Donkey Boy,* 1952; *Young Phillip Maddison,* 1953; *How Dear Is Life,* 1954; *A Fox Under My Cloak,* 1955; *The Golden Virgin,* 1957; revised edition, Panther, 1963; *Love and the Loveless: A Soldier's Tale,* 1958; *A Test to Destruction,* 1960, revised edition, Panther, 1964; *The Innocent Moon,* 1961; *It Was the Nightingale,* 1962, *The Power of the Dead,* 1963, revised edition, Panther, 1966; *The Phoenix Generation,* 1965; *A Solitary War,* 1966; *Lucifer Before Sunrise,* 1967; *The Gale of the World,* 1969.

Other works: *The Lone Swallows,* Collins, 1922, Dutton, 1926, revised edition published as *The Lone Swallows and Other Essays of Boyhood and Youth,* Putnam, 1933; *The Peregrine's Saga and Other Stories of the Country Green,* Collins, 1923, published as *Sun Brothers,* Dutton, 1925; *The Old Stag: Stories,* Putnam (London), 1926, Dutton, 1927; *Tarka the Otter: Being His Joyful Water-Life and Death in the Country of the Two Rivers* (novel), Dutton, 1927; *The Linhay on the Downs* (short stories), Mathews & Marrot, 1929; *The Wet Flanders Plain* (war recollections), Dutton, 1929, revised edition, Faber, 1929; *The Ackymals* (short stories), Windsor Press, 1929.

The Patriot's Progress: Being the Vicissitudes of Private John Bullock (novel), Dutton, 1930; *The Village Book* (short stories), Dutton, 1930; *The Wild Red Deer of Exmoor: A Digression on the Logic and Ethics and Economics of Stag-Hunting in England Today,* Faber, 1931; *The Labouring Life* (short stories), J. Cape, 1932, published as *As the Sun Shines,* Dutton, 1933; *The Gold Falcon; or, The Haggard of Love: Being the Adventures of Manfred, Airman and Poet of the World War, and Later, Husband and Father, in Search of Freedom and Personal Sunrise, in the City of New York, and of the Consummation of His Life* (novel; published anonymously), Smith, 1933, revised edition published under own name, Faber, 1947; *The Star-Born,* Faber, 1933, revised edition, 1948, Chivers, 1973; *On Foot in Devon; or, Guidance and Gossip: Being a Monologue in Two Reels* (short stories), Maclehose, 1933; *The Linhay on the Downs and Other Adventures in the Old and New World* (short stories), J. Cape, 1934; *Salar the Salmon* (novel), Faber, 1935; *Devon Holiday,* J. Cape, 1935; (editor) *An Anthology of*

Modern Nature Writing, Thomas Nelson, 1936; *Goodbye West Country,* Putnam (London), 1937, Little, Brown, 1938; (editor) *Richard Jefferies: Selections of His Work,* Faber, 1937; (editor) Richard Jefferies, *Hodge and His Masters,* Methuen, 1937; *The Children of Shallowford* (autobiography), Faber, 1939, revised edition, 1959.

As the Sun Shines: Selections, Faber, 1941; *The Story of a Norfolk Farm* (autobiography), Faber, 1941; *Genius of Friendship: "T. E. Lawrence",* Faber, 1941; (editor) L. R. Haggard, *Norfolk Life,* Faber, 1943; *The Sun in the Sands* (novel), Faber, 1945; *Life in a Devon Village* (short stories), Faber, 1945; *Tales of a Devon Village,* Faber, 1945; (editor) *My Favourite Country Stories,* Lutterworth, 1946; *The Phasian Bird* (novel), Faber, 1948, Little, Brown, 1950; *Scribbling Lark,* Faber, 1949; (editor) *Unreturning Springs: Being the Poems, Sketches, Stories and Letters of James Farrar,* William & Norgate, 1950.

Tales of Moorland and Estuary (short stories), Macdonald, 1953; *A Clear Water Stream* (autobiography), Faber, 1958, Washburn, 1959, revised edition, Macdonald, 1975; *In the Woods* (short stories), St. Albert's Press (Wales), 1960; (contributor) *A First Adventure With Francis Thompson,* St. Albert's Press, 1966; *Collected Nature Stories,* Macdonald, 1970; "The Vanishing Hedgerow" (television play), 1972; *The Scandaroon* (novel), Macdonald, 1972, Saturday Review Press, 1973; *Animal Saga* (short stories) Macdonald and Jones, 1974. Also contributor to *Some Nature Writers and Civilization,* 1960.

SIDELIGHTS: Henry Williamson was not a novelist who also wrote short stories, or an essayist who managed to write an autobiography. He was a writer recognized as a talent in each of those genres and more. In the wide range of Williamson's works, however, there does seem to be one basic, though sometimes underlying, theme with which the author was particularly captivated. This theme is nature and its effects on the characters he created as well as on himself. Williamson's own close association with the country easily provided him with an enormous supply of background information and observations for his writings, and even more so lent authenticity and factuality to his "nature stories."

Many of the nature books which Williamson wrote, particularly those he wrote as a younger man, appeal to children, for he gave his animal characters their own unique personalities. *Sun Brothers,* a collection of eighteen sketches, is a good example of Williamson's technique although it is not considered by critics to be one of his better books. The stories, which Williamson completed and compiled just after World War I, were described by J. O. Swift in the *New York World* as "vivid, splendidly written and [they] grip the heart. The book is full of poetry in prose, color, and a vague, haunting sadness, so common since the war, but is lightened with hope—the hope of Life."

Another publication of a type similar to that of *Sun Brothers* is *The Old Stag.* Perhaps because of its predecessor, *The Old Stag* brought Williamson greater attention from the public and the press. One critic wrote in the *New York Times:* "In literary skill, native equipment and innate interest Henry Williamson is of the elect among nature writers." Another critic said in *Saturday Review of Literature* that the book was "far from exciting," but added "even in its dullest moments the author's deep knowledge and love of his subject is apparent. Such qualifications as are provided by complete sincerity and an exquisite feeling for the details of what may be termed animal psychology, Mr. Williamson's book possesses."

The author's most critically acclaimed animal book was a novel entitled *Tarka the Otter*. The book was written on the experiences of Williamson and the otter he raised. A critic for the *New York Times* said of the novel: "In keen, sympathetic, accurate and comprehensive observation of wild life, Mr. Williamson's nature tales, of which this is the fourth, are not excelled by any English or American writer."

The countryside Williamson described so well in *Tarka the Otter* and many other of his books is Devon, the small country village where Williamson moved in the early 1920's and spent roughly seven years. Williamson recorded the story of his involvement with the stream which ran beside his cottage in *A Clear Water Stream*. S. B. Bellows wrote in the *Christian Science Monitor*: "This is a book that goes far beyond nature-observation, or even nature-sympathy. It is the work of a thinker and an artist, of a man who is trying to understand himself along with the rest of nature, and there are passages of pure literature that will greatly reward the thoughtful seeker for beauty and wisdom."

The Phasian Bird allowed Williamson to point out the necessity of soil conservation in the same manner in which he advocated water conservation in *A Clear Water Stream*. F. F. Van de Water remarked that "if Mr. Williamson is not completely able to make the twin themes of avian biography and soil conservation march in step, I can think of no writer in either field who could have done better." In the *Chicago Sunday Tribune* Bob Becker stated that *The Phasian Bird* "has all the richness of detail, the fast pace and color of [Williamson's] previous outdoor narratives. It's the kind of book that combines authentic natural history with . . . action and suspense."

Williamson recorded the last year he spent at Devon in *Goodbye West Country* and included many recollections of his years spent there and the years of his youth. R. P. Harriss wrote of the book: "To read Henry Williamson is to read nature writing at its best. It is not merely beautiful prose, it is intensely and everlasting factual stuff." In the *New York Times* Anita Moffett said, "The book is an interesting record, perhaps at its best in its observations of the natural world, in actuality of experience conveyed with light and clarity, a world of infinite beauty, strangeness and variety seen through a temperament of unusual sensitivity, fineness and fidelity."

Of Williamson's works one of the largest in scope was *The Flax of Dream*, a tetralogy combining novels written over a period of about eight years. The autobiographically-based novels follow the life of one boy from the English country. Herschel Brickell wrote of the first novel of the series: "*The Beautiful Years* is the story of the childhood of Willie Maddison. . . . It is not an easy feat to make an adult novel out of the first ten years of a hero's life. But this Mr. Williamson has done. On its own merits, the book is likely to take its place in the enduring literature of boyhood."

The second novel in the tetralogy continued the story of the hero into his school years. "Mr. Williamson's style has an original and distinguished quality," commented Helen Berlin about *Dandelion Days*. "His profound feeling for nature makes sometimes lush writing, but is effective in creating an atmosphere of languor and sentimentality to which the mood of the young is so responsive," Berlin observed.

The book completing the series was *The Pathway*. E. C. Beckwith wrote of the novel: "The splendors of Williamson's prose, always brilliant in his novels of the strictly nature genre, here enriched by the power of a poignant human theme rise to heights of magnificence he has never hitherto achieved. An exquisite work of art, this is surely a book that should long endure." A *Springfield Republican* review contained several insights into the novel's strongpoints: "Perhaps the dominant quality of the book is its accurate observation and description. . . . The style is very beautiful. The book's prose is pliant and supple, capable of rising to the heights of sustained intense feeling."

Williamson's own involvement in World War I inspired at least two of his books. War, in Williamson's opinion, is the act of man most distant from the "natural." His books were written to deglamorize war and encourage peace. Harold King described *The Wet Flanders Plain* in this manner: "The book is a series of vignettes, done with that delicate skill of which Mr. Williamson is master. It is deep and tender and moving, and will probably rank with the few really great books of the war. The style is as beautiful as ever, and its rare power of conveying the charm of the English countryside is as successful with the ruin and the gaudy resurrection of the wet Flanders plain." "The book has a spiritual body as well as a material body," reported a critic in the *New York Times*, "and it is the spiritual body which makes it important, and, one ventures to predict, probably lasting, and this in spite of its modest and self-effacing mien. . . . From it seems to emanate something rather rare, and not easy to classify."

"*The Patriot's Progress* is undoubtedly one of the best of the British War books, and Mr. Williamson has proved that he is a writer of the utmost integrity," declared Vernon Bartlett of Williamson's second war book, which followed the story of one soldier's experiences from his enlistment until the end of the war. Herschel Brickell had this to say of Williamson's writing in the novel: "*Patriot's Progress* . . . shows [Williamson] in a changed mood as well as a changed manner. Here he has apparently suppressed the sensitivity that is so marked a quality of his nature books and of his four-part novel as well; he writes with feelings so deeply harrowed, perhaps, that he has them under complete control, and the effect is all the stronger. Mr. Williamson's book . . . is superior because it is written by a man whose business is writing, who knows his job, and who in this instance was powerfully moved before he sat down to write. . . ."

BIOGRAPHICAL/CRITICAL SOURCES: Saturday Review of Literature, January 3, 1925, May 21, 1927, December 21, 1929, July 19, 1930; *New York Tribune*, June 14, 1925; *New York World*, June 21, 1925, March 24, 1928, June 15, 1930; *New York Times*, April 17, 1927, March 4, 1928, December 8, 1929, July 13, 1930, March 27, 1938, October 15, 1950; *Springfield Republican*, April 21, 1929; *New York Herald Tribune Book Review*, September 8, 1929, July 20, 1930, April 10, 1933; *Spectator*, July 14, 1930; I. Waveny Girvan, *A Bibliography and a Critical Survey of the Works of Henry Williamson*, Alcuin Press (Gloucestershire), 1931; Henry Williamson, *The Children of Shallowford*, Faber, 1939, revised edition, 1959; Williamson, *The Story of a Norfolk Farm*, Faber, 1941; *Chicago Sunday Tribune*, November 5, 1950; *Christian Science Monitor*, November 4, 1950, July 30, 1959; Williamson, *A Clear Water Stream*, Faber, 1958, Washburn, 1959; *Times Literary Supplement*, June 27, 1958.

OBITUARIES: New York Times, August 14, 1977; *AB Bookman's Weekly*, October 10, 1977.*

(Died August 13, 1977, in Berkshire, England)

WILLIAMSON, Oliver E(aton) 1932-

PERSONAL: Born September 27, 1932, in Superior, Wis.; son of Scott and Lucille Williamson; married Dolores Celini; children: Scott, Tamara, Karen, Oliver, Dean. *Education:* Massachusetts Institute of Technology, S.B., 1955; Stanford University, M.B.A., 1960; Carnegie-Mellon University, Ph.D., 1963. *Office:* Department of Economics, University of Pennsylvania, Philadelphia, Pa. 19104.

CAREER: U.S. Government, Washington, D.C., project engineer, 1955-58; University of California, Berkeley, assistant professor of economics, 1963-65; University of Pennsylvania, Philadelphia, associate professor, 1965-68, professor of economics, 1968—, professor of law and public policy, 1974—, Charles and William Day Professor of Economics and Social Science, 1977—, head of department of economics, 1971-72, 1976-77, director of Fels Center of Government, 1975-76, director of Center for the Study of Organizational Innovation, 1976—. Visiting professor at University of Warwick, spring, 1973. Senior fellow at Brookings Institution, 1967-71; fellow of Center for Advanced Study in the Behavioral Sciences, 1977-78. Industrial economist for Stanford Research Institute, summer, 1959, operations analyst, summer, 1960. Member of board of directors of Media Networks, Inc., 1973—. Member of defense science board of U.S. Department of Defense, 1975-76, and National Academy of Sciences panel on food safety regulation and societal impact, 1978—; consultant to RAND Corp., U.S. Department of Justice, and National Science Foundation. *Member:* Econometric Society (fellow). *Awards, honors:* Guggenheim fellowship, 1977-78.

WRITINGS: The Economics of Discretionary Behavior: Managerial Objectives in a Theory of the Firm, Prentice-Hall, 1964; (editor with Almarin Phillips, and contributor) *Prices: Issues in Theory, Practice, and Public Policy,* University of Pennsylvania Press, 1968; *Corporate Control and Business Behavior: An Inquiry Into the Effects of Organization Form on Enterprise Behavior,* Prentice-Hall, 1970; *Markets and Hierarchies: Analysis and Antitrust Implications,* Free Press, 1975.

Contributor of nearly sixty articles and reviews to economics and business journals. Associate editor of *Bell Journal of Economics,* 1973-74, co-editor, 1974—; member of editorial board of *Administrative Science Quarterly,* 1968-72, and "Bobbs-Merrill Economics Reprint Series," 1969—.

*   *   *

WILLS, Philip Aubrey 1907-1978

PERSONAL: Born May 26, 1907, in London, England; son of C.P. and Patton (Bethane) Wills; married Katharine Fisher, 1931; children: Christopher, Stephen, Vanessa, Justin. *Education:* Attended private school in Harrow, Middlesex, England. *Religion:* Church of England.

CAREER: Technical manager of British European Airways Corp., 1946-48; founder of George Wills & Sons Ltd., chairman, 1925-78. *Military service:* Air Transport Auxiliary, World War II. *Awards, honors:* Commander of the Order of the British Empire, 1945; coronation medal from British Government, 1953; British Gold Medal for aeronautics, 1960.

WRITINGS: On Being a Bird, preface by Prince Philip, Parrish, 1953, reprinted, David & Charles, 1977; *Where No Birds Fly,* George Newnes, 1961; *Free as a Bird,* J. Murray, 1973. Contributor to magazines.

SIDELIGHTS: Wills was internationally known as a glider pilot. He learned to fly in 1928 and began to specialize in gliding as early as 1932. He held several height and distance records, and was the British team's senior pilot for seven World Gliding Championships. He was World Champion in 1952.

(Died January 17, 1978)

[Sketch verified by wife, Kitty Fisher Wills]

*   *   *

WILSON, Don(ald) 1932-

PERSONAL: Born March 31, 1932, in St. Ignace, Mich.; son of George H. (an under sheriff) and Grace (Albright) Wilson; married Lynn Bennett (a teacher), July 5, 1966; children: Robert, Jeffrey, Douglas. *Education:* Attended Michigan State University, Jordan Seminary, and Salvatorian Seminary; Sacred Heart Seminary of Detroit, B.A., 1957; graduate study at St. John's Theological Seminary, 1957-58; University of Detroit, M.A., (in world history), 1963; University of Michigan, M.A. (in American history), 1965. *Residence:* Plymouth, Mich. *Agent:* Dominick Abel Literary Services, 498 West End Ave., New York, N.Y. 10024.

CAREER: Teacher in high schools in Mackinaw City, Mich., 1959-60; Taylor Center High School, Taylor, Mich., teacher, 1960-78; writer, 1978—. Wilson has also worked variously as a sailor, purser, recreational director, and business manager. *Member:* International Kirlian Research Association.

WRITINGS: Our Mysterious Spaceship Moon, Dell, 1975; *The Force in Your Life,* Universal Press, 1977; *Secrets of Spaceship Moon,* Dell, 1978.

WORK IN PROGRESS: Inside Your World of Words, a systemization of all the usable words in the English language; *This Spaceship Moon,* science fiction based on his two factual moon books; research on the mysteries of Mars for *Mysterious Mars,* a work incorporating the latest findings of recent Viking probes.

SIDELIGHTS: Wilson writes: "Both of my books on moon's mysteries were sparked by the hollow-moon theory of two Russian scientists. If their theory is proven to be correct (and the Apollo evidence seems to back it), it would, of course, be one of the greatest discoveries in the history of mankind. *This Spaceship Moon* (in progress), an intriguing science fiction novel based on this holow-moon theory, envisions a journey to this strange alien world inside our moon. I am also researching the moon myths and history of the cradles of civilization to see if the Van Daniken ancient astronaut theory measures up to the scientific criteria of Dr. Carl Sagan's and Joseph Shklovskii's *Intelligent Life in the Universe.*

"*Inside Your World of Words,* a multi-volume series, will 'systematize' the English language, categorizing all usable words into verbal families, each revolving around its etymological root, and each built into a unique crossword puzzle that will turn the learning of language from drudgery into an exciting adventure.

"I am also gathering material for a sequel to *The Force in Your Life,* in which I probed the essence of life and energy (it is electrical), reintroducing a remarkable system developed by Edmund Shafestbury (the legendary teacher of Winston Churchill, Douglas MacArthur, and Theodore and Franklin Roosevelt, among others), that demonstrates how to accumulate the *natural* electricity of life. This book shows that this electrical essence of living things, the life force, can be mastered, thus producing greater energy and vitality."

BIOGRAPHICAL/CRITICAL SOURCES: Grit, March 26, 1978.

*   *   *

WILSON, William S(mith) 1932-

PERSONAL: Born April 7, 1932, in Baltimore, Md.; son of William S., Jr. (a lawyer) and May A. (a sculptor) Wilson; children: Katherine, Ara, Andrew. *Education:* University of Virginia, B.A., 1953; Yale University, Ph.D., 1961. *Home:* 458 West 25th St., New York, N.Y. 10001.

CAREER: University of Delaware, Newark, instructor in English, 1957-58; Bowdoin College, Brunswick, Maine, instructor in English, 1959-61; Queens College of the City University of New York, Flushing, N.Y., 1961—, currently professor of English.

WRITINGS: Why I Don't Write Like Franz Kafka (stories), Ecco Press, 1977. Work anthologized in *Best Short Stories of 1977,* edited by Martha Foley. Contributor to art magazines and *Antaeus.*

WORK IN PROGRESS: The Effort to Be Born, a novel; *Moonwork,* philosophic criticism ("an interpretation of the Apollo program"); "Aboveboard," a play.

SIDELIGHTS: Wilson told *CA:* "My fiction is no more difficult than contemporary biology or physics or constitutional law. Entertainment does not entertain me. Writing gives me a chance to think, and any audience I might reach would have to want to think about that. Each story has a meaning as explicit and clear as I can make it, but that meaning is constructed by the bearing of all the parts upon each other, and to state it would merely provide another part with other bearings. The meaning of the fiction is in the experience of figuring out how to read it. I am interested in methods of thinking, and in the implications of methods for content, meaning, and value."

BIOGRAPHICAL/CRITICAL SOURCES: Antaeus, autumn, 1975; *New York Times,* December 7, 1977; *New York Times Book Review,* January 1, 1978.

*   *   *

WINGO, Walter (Scott) 1931-

PERSONAL: Born June 1, 1931, in Newport, Ohio; son of James Guerrero (a journalist) and Edna (Scott) Wingo; married Mary Frances Lafayette (a real estate agent), August 15, 1959; children: Scott C., Susan L., Jacqueline L., James H. *Education:* George Washington University, A.B., 1958; graduate study at Columbia University, 1962-63, and University of Missouri, 1977. *Home:* 4655 North 24th St., Arlington, Va. 22207. *Office:* U.S. News & World Report, 2300 N St. N.W., Washington, D.C. 20037.

CAREER: Washington Daily News, Washington, D.C., 1949-62, began as copy boy, became reporter, picture editor, and feature writer; Science Service, Washington, D.C., news editor, 1963-64; *Nation's Business,* Washington, D.C., associate editor, 1964-70; *U.S. News & World Report,* Washington, D.C., associate business editor, 1970—. *Military service:* U.S. Army, 1952-54. *Member:* Society of American Business and Economic Writers (member of board of governors, 1975—), National Association of Business Economists (member of local board of directors, 1975-78), National Press Club, National Economists Club, White House Correspondents Association, Society of Professional Journalists, Society of Government Economists. *Awards, honors:* First prize from Washington Newspaper Guild, 1957, for human interest stories; Ernie Pyle Memorial Award from Scripps-Howard Newspaper Alliance, 1958.

WRITINGS: Pattern for Success, Doubleday, 1967; *Mekka des Managers,* Verlag Moderne Industrie, 1968. Contributor to magazines and newspapers.

WORK IN PROGRESS: Research on business journalism and reading business trends.

AVOCATIONAL INTERESTS: Mathematics, statistics, bicycle racing, chess.

*   *   *

WINKLER, Allan M(ichael) 1945-

PERSONAL: Born January 7, 1945, in Cincinnati, Ohio; son of Henry R. (a professor) and Clare (a teacher; maiden name, Sapadin) Winkler; married Alberta Hemsley (a teacher), June 7, 1967; children: Jennifer Lynn, David Vaughn. *Education:* Harvard University, B.A. (magna cum laude), 1966; Columbia University, M.A., 1967; Yale University, M.Phil., 1972, Ph.D., 1974. *Religion:* Jewish. *Home:* Timothy Dwight College, Yale University, New Haven, Conn. 06520. *Office:* Department of History, Yale University, New Haven, Conn. 06520.

CAREER: U.S. Peace Corps, Washington, D.C., volunteer worker in the Philippines, 1967-69; Yale University, New Haven, Conn., acting instructor, 1973-74, instructor, 1974-75, assistant professor of history, 1975—. Bicentennial Professor of American Studies at University of Helsinki, 1978-79. Organizer and administrator of Toddler Cooperative Day Care Center at Yale University, 1977-78. *Member:* American Historical Association, Organization of American Historians. *Awards, honors:* American Philosophical Society travel grant, 1977; Fulbright grant for Finland, 1978-79; Mellon Fellow at Aspen Institute for Humanistic Studies, 1978.

WRITINGS: The Politics of Propaganda: The Office of War Information, 1942-1945, Yale University Press, 1978. Contributor of more than a dozen articles and reviews to scholarly journals.

WORK IN PROGRESS: A book on the problem of civil defense and the response to atomic energy in the United States, 1945-65, publication expected in 1981.

SIDELIGHTS: Winkler explained that his book is a "study of the American propaganda effort in World War II. It deals with Franklin D. Roosevelt and his relationship with men like Archibald MacLeish, Robert Sherwood, Elmer Davis, and Milton Eisenhower—all top officials in the Office of War Information. It is a lively treatment of the effort to hammer out policy in one phase of the war—and sheds light on problems in other areas of the struggle, too."

AVOCATIONAL INTERESTS: Running (has finished in the Boston marathon), cross-country skiing.

BIOGRAPHICAL/CRITICAL SOURCES: New York Times, June 30, 1978.

*   *   *

WINTERS, Marian 1924-1978

OBITUARY NOTICE: Born April 19, 1924, in New York, N.Y.; died in 1978 in Warwick, N.Y. Actress, playwright, and book author. Winters won an Emmy Award for her play "Animal Keepers." She also won numerous awards for acting. A book Winters wrote in collaboration with Wilbur Pippin will be published posthumously. Obituaries and other sources: *The Biographical Encyclopaedia and Who's Who of the American Theatre,* James Heineman, 1966; *Who's Who in the Theatre,* 16th edition, Pitman, 1977; *Publishers Weekly,* November 20, 1978.

WITHERSPOON, Thomas E. 1934-

PERSONAL: Born August 8, 1934, in Petersburg, Ind.; son of James Eugene (a railroad conductor) and Una Christian (Taylor) Witherspoon; married first wife, Marilyn C., October 18, 1970 (divorced January, 1978); married Jane H. Waddington (a minister), January 10, 1978. *Education:* Vincennes University, A.A., 1957; Indiana University, A.B., 1959; attended Unity School for Ministerial and Religious Studies, 1974-76. *Politics:* Independent. *Home:* 1016 Langsford Rd., Lee's Summit, Mo. 64063. *Office:* Unity School of Christianity, Unity Village, Mo. 64065.

CAREER: Graphic Printing Co., Portland, Ore., editor, 1960-66; *Dayton Journal Herald,* Dayton, Ohio, night city editor, 1966-67; Graphic Printing Co., publisher, 1967-70; *Decatur Daily Review,* Decatur, Ill., city editor, 1971-74; ordained minister by Unity School for Ministerial and Religious Studies, 1976; Unity School of Christianity, Unity Village, Mo., editor, 1976—. Vice-president of Indiana United Press International, 1966. *Military service:* U.S. Navy, 1952-55; served in European theater. *Member:* Rotary International, Lions, Chamber of Commerce. *Awards, honors:* Journalism awards from Inland Daily Press, Hoosier State Press Association, and Indiana Republican Editorial Association; top news story award from Illinois Associated Press, 1974.

WRITINGS: Myrtle Fillmore: Mother of Unity, Unity Books, 1977. Contributing editor of *Unity.* Supervisor of Unity Books and *Wee Wisdom.*

WORK IN PROGRESS: Basic Unity Fundamentals, a textbook; a cassette series on the development of Unity School.

SIDELIGHTS: Witherspoon writes: "Unity School is a ninety-year-old spiritual institution, founded by Charles and Myrtle Fillmore in 1889. Our work is world-wide, teaching Jesus Christ fundamentals, metaphysically interpreted. I am chief editor and responsible for most of our literature, which reaches millions of people through magazines, books, and pamphlets. I travel extensively for Unity School, lecturing and giving sermons."

*   *   *

WOOD, Bari 1936-

PERSONAL: Born in 1936, in Illinois; *Education:* Graduated from Northwestern University. *Residence:* New York, N.Y.

CAREER: Writer. Worked as editor and bibliographer for the American Cancer Society; editor for *Drug Therapy* magazine, New York, N.Y.

*WRITINGS—*Novels: *The Killing Gift,* Putnam, 1975; (with Jack Geasland) *Twins* (Literary Guild selection), Putnam, 1977.

WORK IN PROGRESS: A novel.

SIDELIGHTS: In reviewing *Twins,* most commentators have pointed out the numerous parallels between the plot of the book and a real case which received a large amount of attention from the press in 1975. Cyril and Stewart Marcus were twin brothers, both doctors and drug addicts, whose dead bodies were discovered in their littered Manhattan apartment. The main characters in *Twins* are also twin brothers in medical practice. They, too, are hooked on Seconal and die under mysterious circumstances. Julian Baines dismissed the book as a money-making enterprise: "*Twins* is a good example of the latest American way to make $1 mil-

lion (the price of paperback rights). You take a spectacular newspaper story . . . and ease it into fiction. The actual details of the messy end you keep nudgingly close to the real case, hitching as much of a ride from authenticity as you can, and then work backwards, inventing motive, childhood, and the current market level of sex."

While acknowledging that *Twins* is a "potboiler," Carol Eisen Rinzler felt the storytelling was absorbing: "Wood's and Geasland's reconstruction may well appear hogwash to anyone with a grounding in psychology, but if one is mercifully ignorant of such matters—and if one is able to suspend as well any faculties critical of literature—one is left with a good read of the first order, a gripping, stunningly paced novel, a first-rate entertainment with which to while away a few hours." Ted Morgan disagreed, saying, "Contrary to the usual encomium, this is a book that I could have put down." He went on to declare that "the book as a whole is too gratuitous and mechanical to make one feel anything stronger than a shudder of distaste."

BIOGRAPHICAL/CRITICAL SOURCES: Washington Post Book World, April 24, 1977; *New York Times Book Review,* May 1, 1977; *New Statesman,* July 1, 1977.*

*   *   *

WOOD, Larry
See WOOD, Marylaird

*   *   *

WOOD, Marylaird
(Larry Wood)

PERSONAL: Born in Sandpoint, Idaho; daughter of Edward Hayes and Alice (McNeel) Small; married W. Byron Wood, January 30, 1942 (divorced May, 1975); children: Mary, Marcia, Barry. *Education:* University of Washington, B.A. (magna cum laude), 1938, M.A. (with highest honors), 1940; graduate study at University of California, Berkeley, 1943-44 and 1975-76, University of California, Santa Cruz, 1970-77, Stanford University, 1970-77, University of Wisconsin, Madison, 1971-73, University of Minnesota, Minneapolis, 1972-74, and University of Georgia, 1972-73. *Home:* 6161 Castle Dr., Oakland, Calif. 94611. *Office address:* c/o CSM News Syndicate, Box 4994, Des Moines, Iowa 50306.

CAREER: Public relations executive in Seattle, Wash., and northern California, 1942-70; columnist for *San Francisco Chronicle,* San Francisco, Calif., and *Oakland Tribune,* Oakland, Calif., 1946—; CSM International News Syndicate, Des Moines, Iowa, special correspondent, 1972—; San Diego State University, San Diego, Calif., assistant professor of journalism, 1976—. Notable assignments include coverage of the World Wildlife Fund's International Congress in San Francisco, 1976, and the flight of the Boeing Jetfoil between Hawaii and Hong Kong, as well as CSM Syndicate series "Railroad of the West," "Wildlife Refuges of the West," and "Endangered Species of the United States." Environmental consultant; member of consultants project, University of Maryland. Visiting professor at San Diego State University, 1974-76, University of California, Hayward, 1976-77, University of California, Berkeley, 1976-78, San Jose State University, 1976, and College of the Pacific, 1978—. Trustee of California State Parks Foundation, 1977—.

MEMBER: International Environmental Consultants, International Oceanographic Society, Environmental Consultants of North America, National Press Photographers Association, National School Public Relations Association, National Association of Science Writers, National Wildlife Federation, Public Relations Society of America, Society of American Travel Writers (education chairman), Women in Communications (national board member, 1968-71, regional director, 1969-71), Association for Education in Journalism (member of national executive board of magazine division), Investigative Reporters and Editors, Inc. (charter member), Sierra Club, Audubon Society, Oceans Society, California Writers' Club, Northern California Association (board member and head of public relations), Ocean Sciences Alumni Association (charter member), East Bay Women's Press Club (former president), San Francisco Press Club, Oakland-San Francisco Advertising Club, Seattle YWCA (board member), Oakland YWCA (board member), Camp Fire Girls (board member in Seattle and Oakland), Girl Scouts of America (board member in Seattle and Oakland), Phi Beta Kappa, Pi Lambda Theta, Sigma Delta Chi. *Awards, honors:* Award from Public Broadcasting Service (PBS-TV), 1974, for five-part series, "Waterfronts of the West"; citations from U.S. Forest Service, 1975, and National Park Service, 1976; selected as one of eighteen investigative reporters on the Arizona Investigative Team on Land Fraud, 1977.

WRITINGS—Under name Larry Wood: (Contributor) Harold Benjamin, editor, *English for Social Living,* McGraw-Hill, 1943; *Tell the Town,* University of Washington Press, 1943. Contributor to "Contemporary Issues" series, Maryland State Department of Education, 1978. Regular feature writer for *Christian Science Monitor, Travelday, Mechanix Illustrated, Popular Mechanics, Seattle Times Sunday Magazine,* and *Sea Frontiers.* Contributor to numerous magazines, including *Sports Illustrated, Better Homes and Gardens, Oceans, Time, Life, Off Duty,* and *Parents Magazine.*

SIDELIGHTS: The sea, the woods, and wildlife have always interested Larry Wood and have been the subject of many of her articles. Although her specialties are feature writing and investigative reporting in scientific and environmental fields, she regularly writes stories on other topics, ranging from personality profiles to architecture to finance. She told *CA:* "I've been fortunate enough to have always been able to write about the things I enjoy most. Like most reporters, I especially enjoy the people I meet in my work—the journalists with whom I share an interest in the media and the exciting people who are the subjects of interviews and stories that I write. I work a seven-day week, but I schedule time off for fun and family because my life can adjust to deadlines." Wood's flair for reporting and photography has been passed on to her offspring. She frequently collaborates with her son Barry, a professional photographer, and her daughter Marcia, a professional journalist.

AVOCATIONAL INTERESTS: Bicycling, swimming, scuba, and tennis.

*   *   *

WOOD, Thomas W(esley), Jr. 1920-

PERSONAL: Born March 16, 1920, in Hugo, Okla.; son of Thomas Wesley (a salesman) Wood and Alma (Rogers Wood) Daniel; married Doreen Anderson, June 1, 1950 (divorced, 1966); married Lola Deloris Gray (a free-lance photographer), May 31, 1968; children: John, Thomas (died November 6, 1977). *Education:* University of Tulsa, B.A., 1951, M.A., 1953; Northwestern University, M.S., 1953;

University of Oklahoma, Ph.D., 1966. *Home:* 6310 Asher, Apt. 585, Little Rock, Ark. 72204. *Agent:* Anita Diamant, 51 East 42nd St., New York, N.Y. 10017. *Office:* Department of Journalism, University of Arkansas at Little Rock, 33rd and University, Little Rock, Ark. 72204.

CAREER: Worked on newspaper in Oklahoma, 1948; City News Bureau of Chicago, Chicago, Ill., reporter and rewriteman, 1952-54; *Tulsa Daily World,* Tulsa, Okla., reporter-photographer, feature writer, copyreader, and foreign correspondent, 1954—; *Philadelphia Inquirer,* Philadelphia, Pa., copyreader, 1956; *Chicago Sun Times,* Chicago, Ill., copyreader, 1960. University of Tulsa, Tulsa, Okla., associate professor, 1954-71, professor of history and journalism, 1971-73; Southern Illinois University, Carbondale, associate professor of journalism, 1973-75; American University, Cairo, Egypt, visiting professor, 1977-78; Arkansas University at Little Rock, visiting professor, 1978—. *Military service:* U.S. Army Air Forces, 1942-46; became first sergeant. *Member:* American Association of Educators in Journalism, American Historical Society, New York Overseas Press Club, Cairo Press Association (Egypt), Tulsa Press Club, Pi Alpha Mu (national president, 1956-62), Sigma Delta Chi, Phi Alpha Theta.

WRITINGS: Editing Handbook, University of Tulsa, 1955, 2nd revised edition, 1966; *Reporting Handbook,* University of Tulsa, 1955, 2nd revised edition, 1966; (editor) *History of the University of Tulsa, 1935-58,* Pi Alpha Mu, 1958; *Basic Production Equipment and Processes for Letterpress,* University of Tulsa, 1960; *An Outline History of American Journalism,* Pi Alpha Mu, 1961; (contributor of photographic essays) *Ulysses: Fifty Years,* Indiana University Press, 1974. Contributor to *Encyclopedia of World Biography,* 1973. Foreign correspondent for *Oil and Gas Journal,* 1976-78. Feature writer for *Egyptian Gazette,* 1977-78. Contributor of articles to general and specialized periodicals. Founder and editor of *Lost Generation Journal,* 1973—.

WORK IN PROGRESS: Paris: The Vintage Years; A Brief History of Dar al Hillal: Egypt's Largest Magazine Publishing House; A History of the Egyptian Gazette; fourteen biographies for Gale's *Dictionary of Literary Biography;* further research and several articles on lost generation writers.

SIDELIGHTS: Wood told *CA:* "It is with no hesitation that I say my life is deeply marked by the belief that the reporter and the writer who seek to do more than entertain have the greatest 'calling' possible for man. It easily outstrips the roles of the law enforcer, the priest, the scientist, and all socially sensitive people, including the well meaning lawyer. The detractor might refer to this outburst as a manifestation of the 'Orphan Annie Syndrome' but I hope the more enlightened ones will see that what I revere most is the role of the writer who offers the most honest information he can find and allows readers an opportunity to make a sensible choice in matters.

"Amazement mounts in me each time I realize that my life has been dominated the past twenty-two years by exposure to one book, Frank Luther Mott's *American Journalism: A History of Newspapers in the United States Through 260 Years, 1690 to 1950.* A few of Mott's paragraphs sent me in quest of E. W. Scripps's adless newspapers. This led to my master's work, my doctoral dissertation, and a short career in Chicago newspapering. Three file cabinets in my study now bulge with material relating to lost generation writers who started their careers on American newspapers in Paris between World Wars I and II: the *Herald,* the *Paris Times,* and the *Chicago Tribune European Edition.* I have interviewed or corresponded with more than one hundred of these people. The collection of tapes, photos, letters, manuscripts and the like which I am pulling together is intended to be the heart of lost generation archival holdings at the University of Tulsa.

"Life has an endless fascination for me. Part of my journalistic career was spent with some of the men who had inspired Chicago newspaper characters depicted in the play 'The Front Page.' I feel fortunate that I was born at a time when I could join hands with gods of the past and with the budding ones of the future.

"A newspaper and magazine man for nearly thirty years, I shifted into teaching because of my belief that the world has a greater need for the development of a corps of competent and dedicated communicators than for one reporter. I have now had a hand in the training of more than five thousand communicators. So far, nothing has happened to make me think my belief or energies have been misplaced.

"I am able to work with young people who still have a pristine glow about them, but it disturbs me to find that I am more optimistic than they are. The music and dance of the young emphasize a desperate loneliness and their each-man-needs-his-own-microphone attitude reveals an unwillingness to judge things. It seems, unhappily, that we are working toward a thoughtless egalitarianism in which put downs are grim, but are directed against someone outside the 'equal group.'

"In 1973 I founded the *Lost Generation Journal,* a scholarly magazine issued three times a year in an effort to perpetuate the memory of the people and the era of the lost generation. The publication, a slick, illustrated work primarily dedicated to the writings of surviving members of that golden era in American letters, features a broader look at the era than usually is the case. Emphasis is placed on Americans in Paris between 1919 and 1939, such as Ezra Pound, Gertrude Stein, Ernest Hemingway, James Thurber, William Shirer, Henry Miller, and Janet Flanner. The *Lost Generation Journal* concentrates on Americans who started their careers in writing and the arts while they were residing in Paris. Americans who made it at home (Eugene O'Neill, F. Scott Fitzgerald) or some place else (T. S. Eliot, John Dos Passos) are not ignored but the relationship to Americans and Paris must be shown. An effort is made to go beyond writers, sculptors, and painters through a secondary concentration on musicians, dancers, composers, and actors, as well as to seek out economic, psychological, and political interpretations relating to Americans in Paris during those years. It would be fair to call *LGJ* a specialized general publication which focuses on a twenty-year segment of American arts and letters in an effort to recreate the people and the events of those days."

*   *   *

WOODBURY, Lael J(ay) 1927-

PERSONAL: Born July 3, 1927, in Fairview, Idaho; son of Raymond W. (a merchant) and Wanda (a nurse; maiden name, Dawson) Woodbury; married Laura Young, July 30, 1944 (died, 1949); married Margaret Swenson, December 19, 1949; children: Kippy Woodbury Hancock, Shannon Woodbury Busenbark, Jordan, Lexon. *Education:* Utah State University, B.S., 1952; Brigham Young University, M.A., 1953; University of Illinois, Ph.D., 1954. *Home:* 1303 Locust Lane, Provo, Utah 84601. *Office:* College of Fine Arts and Communications, Brigham Young University, A-410 HFAC, Provo, Utah 84602.

CAREER: Brigham Young University, Provo, Utah, associate professor of dramatic arts, 1954-61, theater business manager, 1956-61; Bowling Green State University, Bowling Green, Ohio, assistant professor of theatre arts, 1961-62; University of Iowa, Iowa City, associate professor of theatre arts, 1962-65; Brigham Young University, professor of dramatic arts, 1965—, head of department, 1966-67, head of department of speech and dramatic arts, 1967-70, head of Academic Enrichment Council, 1973-75, assistant dean of College of Fine Arts and Communications, 1970-72, associate dean, 1972-73, dean, 1973—. Guest professor at Colorado State College, summer, 1962. Producer and director at Ledges Playhouse, summers, 1963-65; member of board of directors of Repertory Dance Theatre, 1977—. Vice-chairman of board of directors of Utah Alliance for Arts Education, 1976—. Member of board of directors of Eagle Marketing Corp. Narrator of professional recordings, including the New Testament and the Book of Mormon; speaker on radio programs.

MEMBER: American Theatre Association (head of national committee on royalties, 1972—), Western Speech Communication Association (head of Drama Division, 1971), Rocky Mountain Theatre Conference (president, 1959).

WRITINGS: Play Production Handbook, Mutual Improvement Association, 1959; *Continually Before the Lord* (monograph), Brigham Young University Press, 1974; *The Origins and Uses of the Sacred Hosanna Shout* (monograph), Brigham Young University Press, 1975; *Mosaic Theatre: The Creative Use of Theatrical Constructs,* Brigham Young University Press, 1976. Contributor of about thirty-five articles and reviews to speech, theater, and education journals. Associate editor of *Mormon Arts,* Volume I, Brigham Young University Press, 1972.

SIDELIGHTS: Lael Woodbury told *CA:* "How long will it take us to subdue the idea that theatre always consists of live actors reciting memorized words? Art advances only when an artist conceives a compeling statement and then chooses the most effective means for conveying it.

"Thus words are best for word concepts, but they are not best when a picture will serve a thousand times better. We seem always to be relearning that music is not the sound of an orchestra, but total sound from whatever source; a painting is not what's within the frame, but everything seen—including the frame and the wall; dance is not the soloist, but everything that moves; and architecture is not bricks and windows, but space—or its absence.

"That's the point of my book, *Mosaic Theatre.* It describes how, using today's precise and flexible technology, one can express certain concepts most artfully."

*   *   *

WOODEN, Kenneth 1935-

PERSONAL: Born October 18, 1935, in Burlington, N.J.; son of Edward F. (a worker) and Grace Theresa (Ward) Wooden; married Martha B. Braun (a nurse), August 30, 1958; children: Grace, Rosemary, Jennifer, John Allen. *Education:* Glassboro State College, B.A. (honors), 1962. *Politics:* Democrat. *Home and office:* 66 Witherspoon St., Princeton, N.J. 08540. *Agent:* Sterling Lord Agency, Inc., 660 Madison Ave., New York, N.Y. 10021.

CAREER: Bricklayer in Burlington, N.J., 1955-56; high school teacher of social studies in Newton, N.J., 1962-66; Institute of Applied Politics, Princeton, N.J., executive director, 1966-73; writer, 1973-76; National Coalition of

Children's Justice, Princeton, N.J., director, 1976—. Member of Commission on Prison Reform in New Jersey, 1970; speaker at colleges and universities. Consultant to "Sixty Minutes," National Right to Read Program, and Gallup Poll. *Military service:* U.S. Army, 1955-57; served in Korea. *Member:* Investigative Reporters and Editors, Authors Guild of Authors League of America. *Awards, honors:* Eagleton fellowship, 1963.

WRITINGS: Weeping in the Playtime of Others, McGraw, 1976. Contributor to *New York Times.*

WORK IN PROGRESS: Child Sex Abuse.

SIDELIGHTS: Wooden wrote: "When I graduated from high school, I was refused employment in a soap factory because I was unable to fill out an application form. I entered Glassboro State College, even though post-entrance exams revealed I had no basic educational skills. I started my teaching career at my old high school—a colleague with some faculty members who had years earlier predicted a life in prison for me.

"Later, my recommendations for a legitimate school system were established by law within the New Jersey prison system. Adult and youthful offenders can now take college courses and obtain degrees. Other prisoners, locked within the prison of illiteracy, are offered reading programs.

"In the mid-sixties, while teaching high school, I formed an organization, the first of its kind in the United States, which eventually became the Institute of Applied Politics. Its purpose was to blend the world of political reality and the arts so that high-school students could better understand government and politics as they developed their own potential.

"During the summer of 1972, I discovered that over fifty percent of all young children incarcerated within New Jersey prisons are there for non-criminal acts. That shocking revelation, coupled with my own lifetime experiences, led me to write *Weeping in the Playtime of Others.* The book was read by Mike Wallace of 'Sixty Minutes,' and subsequently I helped to develop and provide investigative reporting for three of his programs directly related to the contents of that book.

"Now, with the support of Otto Preminger and Carol Burnett, I am designing a strategy to accelerate social reform in children's justice."

BIOGRAPHICAL/CRITICAL SOURCES: San Francisco Sunday Examiner and Chronicle, February 12, 1978.

*   *   *

WOODS, Margaret S(taeger)   1911-

PERSONAL: Born August 21, 1911, in Chehalis, Wash.; daughter of Carl P. and M. Olivia (Waring) Staeger; married Frederick E. Woods, 1937 (marriage ended, 1970); children: Frederick Waring, Pamela Templeton Woods Ryman. *Education:* Washington State University, B.A., 1932; University of Washington, Seattle, M.Ed., 1954. *Religion:* Congregationalist. *Home:* 1208 West Leisure, Coupeville, Wash. 98239. *Office:* Department of Education, Seattle Pacific University, Seattle, Wash. 98119.

CAREER: High school language teacher in Chehalis, Wash., 1932-37; kindergarten teacher in Seattle, Wash., 1956-57; Seattle Pacific University, Seattle, lecturer, 1958-64, assistant professor, 1964-68, associate professor, 1968-75; professor of education, 1975-77, professor emeritus, 1977—. Owner of 7 C's Press (publishing company). Lecturer and director of workshops on creative education,

1955—. Member of board of directors of National Children's Theatre, 1956-58, and Washington Congress of Parents and Teachers, 1960-64. Member of summer faculties of University of Arkansas, University of Hawaii, Portland State University, University of Washington, Western Illinois State University, Southern Illinois University, Montana State University, Pacific Lutheran University, Seattle Pacific University, and Bowling Green State University.

MEMBER: Association for Childhood International, Organisation Mondiale pour l'Education Prescolaire, Educational Leadership of America, Association for Supervision and Curriculum Development (member of board of directors), American Association of Elementary, Kindergarten, and Nursery Educators (president, 1964, 1969), Pi Lambda Theta (life member), Delta Kappa Gamma. *Awards, honors:* Norman Borgerson Award from *Safety Education Journal,* 1964, for article "Let's Play It Safe"; distinguished service award from Zeta Phi Eta, 1967; named woman of the year by Delta Zeta, 1968.

WRITINGS: Thinking, Feeling, Experiencing: Toward Realization of Full Potential, National Education Association, 1962; (with Beryl Trithart) *A Guide for Teaching Creative Dramatics,* DOK Publishers, 1970; *Wonderwork,* DOK Publishers, 1970; *Creativity: Process and Product,* 7 C's Press, 1977; *A Model for Staff Development,* 7 C's Press, 1978; *Storied Ventures,* 7 C's Press, 1978; (editor) *Fabled Foibles,* 7 C's Press, Volume I: *Jack and Jill,* 1977, Volume II: *Humpty Dumpty,* 1978, Volume III: *Three Blind Mice,* 1978, Volume IV: *Wee Willie Winkie,* 1977, Volume V: *E'-eencie We'encie Spider,* 1977. Author of "Creative Teaching Tips," a column in *Keep Up With Elementary Education,* 1967-69.

WORK IN PROGRESS: Wonderwork: Dramatic Experiencing; Creative Dramatics in the Classroom.

SIDELIGHTS: Margaret Woods writes: "I am publishing *Fabled Foibles,* nursery rhymes communicated symbolically. The rights to the coded books are submitted by university students in storytelling; a graphic arts person prepares the copy for publication. They are designed to give the reader an experience in success and help children read in the way they learn naturally to read. Readers must know the nursery rhymes first. With the aid of the code, three-year-olds read them beautifully. Mentally-retarded people are excited about their successes. Normal children are challenged by the code and are motivated to create their own."

*   *   *

WOODYARD, George   1934-

PERSONAL: Born November 18, 1934, in Charleston, Ill.; son of A. Lincoln (a farmer) and Iva (Hanna) Woodyard; married Eleanor A. Tendick, July 31, 1960; children: Shana, Lance, Devon, Kenda. *Education:* Eastern Illinois University, B.S.Ed., 1954; New Mexico State University, M.A., 1955; University of Illinois, Ph.D., 1966. *Home:* 2204 Alabama, Lawrence, Kan. 66044. *Office:* Department of Spanish and Portuguese, University of Kansas, Lawrence, Kan. 66045.

CAREER: University of Kansas, Lawrence, assistant professor, 1966-71, associate professor, 1971-76, professor of Spanish and Portuguese, 1976—, chairman of department, 1974-78, associate dean of graduate school, 1978. *Military service:* U.S. Army, English instructor in Puerto Rico, 1957-59. *Member:* Modern Language Association of America, American Association of Teachers of Spanish and Portuguese, American Association of University Professors.

WRITINGS: (Editor) *The Modern Stage in Latin America: Six Plays,* Dutton, 1971; (editor with Leon F. Lyday) *Dramatists in Revolt: The New Latin American Theatre,* University of Texas Press, 1976; (with Lyday) *A Bibliography of Latin American Theatre Criticism, 1940-1974,* Institute of Latin American Studies, University of Texas, 1976. Editor of *Latin American Theatre Review.*

* * *

WOOLLEY, Herbert B(allantyne)　1917-1978

OBITUARY NOTICE: Born November 19, 1917, in Logan, Utah; died September 24, 1978, in Potomac, Md. Economist, educator, and author. Woolley was an expert in the field of international economics. He wrote *Measuring Transactions Between World Areas* in 1966. Obituaries and other sources: *Who's Who in Government,* Marquis, 1972; *Washington Post,* September 27, 1978.

* * *

WORM, Piet　1909-

PERSONAL: Born September 17, 1909, in Alkmaar, Holland; married Tia Wiegman; children: two daughters. *Education:* Attended Technical School for Architects and Royal Academy of Art, Amsterdam. *Residence:* Amsterdam, Holland.

CAREER: Worked as an architect in South Africa; author and illustrator of books for young people.

WRITINGS—All self-illustrated; in English: *Three Little Horses,* Random House, 1955; *Stories from the Old Testament from Adam to Joseph,* Sheed, 1956; *More Stories from the Old Testament,* Sheed, 1957; *Stories from the New Testament,* Sheed, 1958; *Three Little Horses at the King's Palace,* Random House, 1959; *Three Little Horses Have a Holiday,* Random House, 1963.

Other works: *Het Heldenlied van Jan en Piet,* Uitgeverij De Fontein (Utrecht), 1947; *De Man van Nazareth,* Ven Kempen, 1970.

Illustrator: Valery Larbaud, *Questions Militaires,* A.A.M. Stols, 1944; Josephine Baker, *De Regenboog-Kinderen,* Mulder & Zoon, 1957; J. Baker, *La Tribu Arc-en-Ciel,* Mulder & Zoon, 1957.*

* * *

WORTH, Sol　1922(?)-1977

PERSONAL: Born in New York, N.Y.; married Tobia Lessler; children: Debora Worth Hymes. *Education:* University of Iowa, B.A., 1943. *Residence:* Philadelphia, Pa.

CAREER: Photographer and creative vice-president, Goold Studios, Inc.; Annenberg School of Communications, Philadelphia, Pa., professor of documentary filmmaking and visual communication, 1960-77. Visiting research professor, Mount Sinai Medical School, 1968-72. *Member:* American Anthropological Association (fellow and editor of journal), Society for the Anthropology of Visual Communication (past president). *Awards, honors:* Fulbright scholar at University of Helsinki, 1957.

WRITINGS: (With John Adair) *Through Navajo Eyes: An Exploration in Film Communication and Anthropology,* Indiana University Press, 1972.

OBITUARIES: New York Times, August 31, 1977; *AB Bookman's Weekly,* October 17, 1977.*

(Died August 29, 1977, in Boston, Mass.)

WRIGHT, Burton　1917-

PERSONAL: Born January 31, 1917, in Detroit, Mich.; son of Burton, Sr. and Hazel (Thomas) Wright; married Marie F. Gallivan, January 23, 1952; children: Burton III, Catherine Margaret (deceased). *Education:* Canal Zone College, A.A., 1944; University of Washington, Seattle, B.S., 1947, M.S., 1949; Florida State University, Ph.D., 1972. *Politics:* "Uncommitted." *Religion:* Roman Catholic. *Home:* 640 London Rd., Winter Park, Fla. 32792. *Office:* Department of Sociology, University of Central Florida, Box 25000, Orlando, Fla. 32816.

CAREER: U.S. Navy, 1936-64; during World War II served in Panama Canal Zone, first as radioman first class, then chief radioman; commissioned ensign, served in Pacific, 1944; worked in Recruiting Division of Bureau of Naval Personnel, 1944-60; director of Naval Reserve Recruiting at Naval Reserve Training Command in Omaha, Nebraska, 1960-64; Rollins College, Winter Park, Florida, assistant professor, 1966-69; University of Central Florida, Orlando, associate professor of sociology, 1970—. Assistant professor of naval science, University of Washington, Seattle, 1948-49; assistant professorial lecturer, George Washington University, Washington, D.C., 1950-61; summer instructor at Northwestern University, 1953-57. Consultant to Ford Foundation.

MEMBER: American Sociological Association, American Anthropological Association (fellow), American Psychological Association, Society for the Psychological Study of Social Issues, American Association of University Professors, Southern Sociological Society, North-Central Sociological Society, Florida Sociological Society.

WRITINGS: A Management Guide for Officers-in-Charge of Main Navy Recruiting Stations, U.S. Department of the Navy, 1958; *The Science and Art of Navy Recruiting,* U.S. Department of the Navy, 1958; *The Naval Recruiting Guide,* U.S. Department of the Navy, 1962; *The Team Concept of Naval Reserve Recruiting,* U.S. Department of the Navy, 1963; *Operation Return* (pamphlet), U.S. Department of the Navy, 1964; *An Instructor's Guide for Points of Departure,* Dryden, 1973; (with John P. Weiss and Charles M. Unkovic) *Perspective: An Introduction to Sociology,* with study guide and instructor's guide, Dryden, 1975; (with Vernon Fox) *Criminal Justice and the Social Sciences,* with instructor's guide, Saunders, 1978; *Sociology: An Introduction,* Goodyear Publishing, in press; (with John Weiss) *Social Problems,* Little, Brown, in press.

WORK IN PROGRESS: Continuing research on values.

SIDELIGHTS: Wright commented: "Now on my second career, I have no regrets about my long Navy service; it was both enriching and rewarding. As a sociologist, I fall most closely in what can best be described as the neo-functionalist orientation. However, I recognize the importance of conflict theory. I believe strongly in pursuing an objective and rational analysis of human societies. Much of the trouble of this world arises out of irrationality and subjectivity, *not* objectivity and rationality. My writings reflect this view.

"My principal research interest is in the area of values. In the past years, I have aroused considerable interest in a scientific study of values and my research has spread to Great Britain. This research tends to indicate that values are highly resistant to change and that college students are, in effect, value replicas of their parents, which would seem to negate journalistic assumptions that values change easily or that young people hold widely different values than older persons.

"I write, in part, because I enjoy doing it. But, more than that, it is my deep conviction that sociology has a great deal to offer people wherever they are. It is not that I believe sociology (or any other discipline) to be the saviour of the world. However, I do feel that the rational, objective perspective which sociology brings to human affairs is of great importance. When we look around the world, it is not too difficult to see that a good deal of the world's human troubles arise out of irrationality. If through my writings I manage to convince even only a few persons of this, I will feel that the time and effort was well spent.

"For those who aspire to write textbooks of their own, I have only two pieces of advice. First, you must have something to say and want to say it. Secondly, if your chief purpose in writing is to make money or achieve fame, don't bother to even try. You will probably be unable to produce anything very much worthwhile. And, of course, there is always that final and frequently uttered advice to the effect that the only way to learn to write is . . . to write!"

AVOCATIONAL INTERESTS: Bicycling, reading history and biographies, swimming, chess.

* * *

WRIGHT, Denis (Arthur Hepworth) 1911-

PERSONAL: Born March 23, 1911, in Kingston-upon-Thames, England; son of Arthur Edgar (a surveyor) and Margery Hepworth (Chapman) Wright; married Iona C. Craig (a painter), November 10, 1939. *Education:* St. Edmund Hall, Oxford, B.A. (second class honors), 1929, M.A., 1961. *Religion:* Church of England. *Home:* Duck Bottom, Flint St., Haddenham, Buckinghamshire, England.

CAREER: Gallaher & Co. (tobacco manufacturers), London, England, assistant advertising manager, 1935-39; British Diplomatic Service, vice-consul on economic warfare work in Constantza, Romania, 1939-41, vice-consul-in-charge in Trebizond, Turkey, 1941-43, acting consul-in-charge in Mersin, Turkey, 1943-45, first secretary at embassy in Belgrade, Yugoslavia, 1946-48, superintending trade consul in Chicago, Ill., 1949-51, head of economic relations department at Foreign Office in London, 1951-53, *charge d'affaires* for Iran, 1953, counselor at embassy in Teheran, 1954-55, assistant under-secretary at Foreign Office, 1955-59, ambassador to Ethiopia, 1959-62, assistant under-secretary at Foreign Office, 1962, ambassador to Iran, 1963-71; writer, 1971—. Chairman of Iran Society, 1976—; president of British Institute of Persian Studies, 1978—. Member of board of directors of Standard Bank Chartered Bank, Shell Transport & Trading Co., Mitchell Cotts Group, and Standard & Chartered Banking Group, International Briefing Center at Farnham Castle, all 1971—.

MEMBER: Travellers Club. *Awards, honors:* Companion of Order of St. Michael and St. George, 1954, knight commander, 1961, grand knight cross, 1971; honorary fellow of St. Edmund Hall, Oxford, 1971, and St. Antony's College, Oxford, 1975.

WRITINGS: (With James Morris and Roger Wood) *Persia,* Thames & Hudson, 1969; *The English Amongst the Persians During the Qajar Period, 1787-1921,* Heinemann, 1977.

WORK IN PROGRESS: Research on nineteenth-century Anglo-Iranian relations.

SIDELIGHTS: Wright describes *The English Amongst the Persians During the Qajar Period, 1787-1921* as "an account of Anglo and Russian rivalry in Iran, British interest in Iran as an outer bastion in the defense of India, and British activities in Iran between 1787 and 1921."

* * *

WRONG, Dennis H(ume) 1923-

PERSONAL: Born November 22, 1923, in Toronto, Ontario, Canada; son of Humphrey Hume (a diplomat) and Mary Joyce (Hutton) Wrong; married Elaine Gale, October 24, 1949 (divorced, 1965); married Jacqueline Conrath, March 23, 1966; children: Terence Hume. *Education:* University of Toronto, B.A., 1945; Columbia University, Ph.D., 1956. *Home address:* Drakes Corner Rd., Princeton, N.J. 08540. *Office:* Department of Sociology, New York University, 19 University Pl., New York, N.Y. 10003.

CAREER: University of Toronto, Toronto, Ontario, lecturer in sociology, 1954-56; Brown University, Providence, R.I., assistant professor, 1956-60, associate professor of sociology, 1960-61; New School for Social Research, New York, N.Y., associate professor of sociology, 1961-63; New York University, New York, N.Y., professor of sociology, 1963—. *Member:* American Sociological Association, Eastern Sociological Society.

WRITINGS: American and Canadian Viewpoints, American Council on Education, 1955; *Population,* Random House, 1956; *Population and Society,* Random House, 1961; (editor with Harry Gracey) *Readings in Introductory Sociology,* Macmillan, 1967; (editor) *Max Weber,* Prentice-Hall, 1970; *Skeptical Sociology,* Columbia University Press, 1976; *Power: Its Forms, Bases, and Uses,* Harper, 1979. Contributor to periodicals, including *Commentary, Dissent, New Leader, Times Literary Supplement,* and *Partisan Review.* Editor of *Social Research,* 1962-64, and *Contemporary Sociology,* 1972-74; member of editorial board of *Dissent,* 1967—.

WORK IN PROGRESS: A book on sociological theory.

SIDELIGHTS: Wrong comments: "My main interest is always in theory, particularly from the standpoint of intellectual history and political relevance. I have a strong interest in the contemporary political and intellectual history of Western societies."

* * *

WYATT, Stephen (John) 1948-

PERSONAL: Born April 2, 1948, in Kent, England; son of Geoffrey and Elaine (Clarke) Wyatt. *Education:* Clare College, Cambridge, B.A., 1969, M.A., 1971, Ph.D., 1975. *Home and office:* 13 Olney Rd., London S.E.17, England. *Agent:* Marc Berlin, London Management, 235-241 Regent St., London W1A 2JT, England.

CAREER: University of Glasgow, Glasgow, Scotland, lecturer in drama, 1973-74; University of Lancaster, Lancaster, England, fellow in theater studies, 1975; playwright, 1975—. *Member:* British Actors Equity Association, Theatre Writers Union, Scottish Society of Playwrights. *Awards, honors:* British Arts Council bursary, 1977.

WRITINGS: (Editor with Maggie Steed) *Rare Earth,* Methuen, 1976.

Unpublished plays: "Take Diogenes" (one-act), first produced in London, England, at Little Theatre, February, 1973; "Exit, Pursued by a Bear" (three-act comedy), first produced in Edinburgh, Scotland, at Edinburgh Festival, 1973; "A Visigoth by Any Other Name" (one-act), first produced in Glasgow, Scotland, at Strathclyde Drama

Centre, October 1974; "Come in, Mr. Spartacus, Your Time Is Up!" (one-act), first produced in Edinburgh, at Netherbow Theatre, October, 1974; (co-author) "Secrets of the Amazon," first produced in England, at Belgrade Theatre, February 1975; "Example" (juvenile), first produced in Coventry, England, September, 1975; "Keep the Home Fires Burning," first produced, 1975; "Friends in High Places," first produced, 1976; "Parting Shots From a Hero," first produced in Edinburgh, Scotland, at Edinburgh Festival, August, 1976; (co-author) "Tippity, Flip Flop, Gumdrops and Boost" (juvenile), first produced in Woolwich, England, at Tramshed, April, 1977; (co-author) "After Shave" (musical revue), first produced in London, England, at Apollo Theatre, August, 1977; "Melmoth the Wanderer," first produced in Canterbury, England, at University of Kent Theatre, September, 1977; "The Magic Cabbage" (juvenile), first produced in London, at Unicorn Theatre, February, 1978; "Monster!" (juvenile), first produced in York, England, at York Theatre Royal, July, 1978.

SIDELIGHTS: Wyatt comments: "I am particularly interested in breaking down the often rigid division made between work regarded as serious on one hand and work which by its nature is assumed to be less important or significant—the musical plays for children, revues—and I try to use humour as my principal weapon (I hope it's not a sledge hammer)."

Y

YAHRAES, Herbert 1905-

PERSONAL: Surname is pronounced *Yehr*-us; born November 19, 1905, in Bethlehem, Pa.; son of Herbert C. (a postal superintendent) and Kate (Brinker) Yahraes; married Genevieve Leppert (a newspaperwoman), October 31, 1929; children: Genevieve Yahraes Neff, Katrina N. *Education:* Lafayette College, A.B. (honors), 1927. *Residence:* Stanfordville, N.Y. 12581.

CAREER: Easton Express, Easton, Pa., reporter, 1924-27; American Book Co., New York City, editor, 1927-28; *New Orleans Item,* New Orleans, La., reporter, 1928-29; *Fairlawn-Radburn News,* Fairlawn, N.J., managing editor, 1929-31; Associated Press, New York City, reporter and editor, 1931-39; *PM* (newspaper), New York City, editor of Sunday magazine, 1939-46; free-lance writer, 1946—. *Member:* National Association of Science Writers, Washington Press Club, Harvard Club (New York City), Stanford Lions Club (past president). *Awards, honors:* Nieman Fellow at Harvard University, 1943-44; Albert Lasker Award from Albert and Mary Lasker Foundation, 1949, for medical writing in magazines.

WRITINGS: (With Julius Segal) *A Child's Journey: Forces That Shape the Lives of Our Young,* McGraw, 1978. Author of medical pamphlets, and brochures for New York City's Public Affairs Committee. Contributor to popular magazines, including *Harper's, Scientific American, Popular Science, Psychology Today,* and *McCall's.*

WORK IN PROGRESS: Magazine articles; two family biographies; *Faith Can Indeed Cure You: The Experiences of Prominent Healers.*

SIDELIGHTS: Yahraes writes: "My general aim throughout has been to take difficult subjects in medicine and science and report them in terms for the intelligent layman. My major field of interest for a dozen years has been the reporting of mental health research. The most important problem facing the nation (and the world) is the bringing up of children in such a way as to enchance their mental health and allow them to reach their full capabilities. Hence the Segal-Yahraes book, which reports not opinions, but the results of research by psychologists, psychiatrists, sociologists, and child development authorities."

*   *   *

YATES, Alayne 1929-

PERSONAL: Born June 30, 1929, in Brooklyn, N.Y.; daughter of Carlyle Edgar (a lawyer) and Ethel (an anthropologist; maiden name, Clarke) Yates; married Jose Aruguete (a physician), August 26, 1960 (divorced); married James Warren Neiswonger (a corrections department program director), May 20, 1973; children: Pamela, Donna, Sara, Moses, Eve, Mara, Miriam. *Education:* Radcliffe College, B.A., 1950; University of Illinois, M.D., 1961; postdoctoral study at University of California, Davis, 1973. *Home address:* P.O. Box 773, Blue Jay, Calif. 92317. *Agent:* John Brockman, 200 West 57th St., Suite 1207, New York, N.Y. 10019. *Office:* Department of Psychiatry, Loma Linda University, Loma Linda, Calif. 92354.

CAREER: Army Chemical Center, Army Chemical Center, Md., research psychologist, 1951-54; Galesburg State Research Hospital, Galesburg, Ill., research psychologist, 1954-57; Michael Reese Hospital, Chicago, Ill., intern, 1961-62, resident in pediatrics, 1962-64; private practice of pediatrics in Sandstone, Minn., 1964-70; University of Minnesota, Minneapolis, resident in psychiatry, 1970-72; University of California, Davis, assistant professor of psychiatry and pediatrics, 1972-75; Loma Linda University, Loma Linda, Calif., assistant professor, 1975-76, associate professor of psychiatry and pediatrics, 1976—, director of Division of Child Psychiatry, 1977—. Licensed in Illinois, Minnesota, and California; medical director of Arnold Homes for Children, 1973-75; member of board of directors of Family Services, 1974; consultant to California Youth Authority. *Member:* Academy of Child Psychiatry. *Awards, honors:* Mead Johnson fellow in pediatrics, 1963-64.

WRITINGS: Sex Without Shame, Morrow, 1978. Contributor to medical journals.

WORK IN PROGRESS: A book on the child's development of meaningful relationships; studying pathological narcissism, child abuse, and evaluation of the sex offender.

SIDELIGHTS: Alayne Yates writes: "I feel that we must study and understand children's early sexual development if we are to prevent adult sexual problems. Children have sexual needs and experiences, beginning even in the first year of life; we as parents need to encourage positive erotic growth by smiling and complimenting the child rather than distracting him or turning away."

YEVTUSHENKO, Yevgeny (Alexandrovich) 1933-

PERSONAL: Listed in some sources as Evgenii Aleksandrovich Evtushenko; born July 18, 1933, in Stanzia Zima, Siberia, U.S.S.R.; son of Gangnus (a geologist) and Zinaida (a geologist and singer) Yevtushenko; married Bella Akhmadulina (a poet), 1954 (divorced); married Galina Semyonovna (a literary translator). *Education:* Attended Gorky Literary Institute, 1951-54. *Politics:* Communist. *Religion:* "Revolution."

CAREER: Poet and author. Worked on geological expedition in Kazakhstan, U.S.S.R. *Member:* Gorky Literary Institute, Writer's Union.

WRITINGS—In English; all poetry unless otherwise indicated: (With others) *Red Cats;* City Lights, 1961; *Selected Poems,* translated from the Russian by Robin Milner-Gulland and Peter Levi, Dutton, 1962; *Yevtushenko* (young adult), edited by Milner-Gulland, Penguin, 1962; *Selected Poetry,* Pergamon, 1963; *A Precocious Autobiography,* translated from the Russian by Andrew R. MacAndrew, Dutton, 1963; *Winter Station,* translated from the Russian by Oliver J. Frederiksen, C. Gerber, 1964; *The Poetry of Yevgeny Yevtushenko, 1953-1965,* translated from the Russian and edited by George Reavey, October House, 1964; *Bratskaya GES,* Russian Language Specialties, 1965, translation by Tina Tupikina-Glaessner, Igor Mexhakoff-Koriakin, and Geoffrey Dutton published as *New Works: The Bratsk Station,* Praeger, 1966, published as *The Bratsk Station and Other New Poems,* Praeger, 1967; *The City of Yes and the City of No and Other Poems,* translated from the Russian by Tupilina-Glaessner, Mezhakoff-Koriakin, and Dutton, Sun Books, 1966; *Yevtushenko's Reader: The Spirit of Elbe, A Precocious Autobiography, Poems,* Dutton, 1966; *Poems,* translated from the Russian by Herbert Marshall, Dutton, 1966; *Poems Chosen by the Author,* translated from the Russian by Milner-Gulland and Levy, Collins, 1966, Hill & Wang, 1967; *New Poems,* Sun Books, 1968.

Bratsk Station, The City of Yes and the City of No, and Other New Poems, translated from the Russian by Tupikina-Glaessner, Dutton, and Mezhakoff-Koriakin, Sun Books, 1970; *Flowers and Bullets & Freedom to Kill,* City Lights, 1970; *Stolen Apples,* Doubleday, 1971; *Kazan University and Other New Poems,* translated from the Russian by Dutton and Eleanor Jacka, Sun Books, 1973; *From Desire to Desire,* Doubleday, 1976.

Other poems: *Razvedchiki Gryadushchego* (title means "The Prospectors of the Future"), Sovietsky Pisatel, 1952; *Tretii Sneg* (title means "Third Snow), Sovietsky Pisatel, 1955; *Shosse Entusiastov* (title means "Highway of the Enthusiasts"), Moskovskii Rabochii, 1956; *Obeschanie* (title means "Promise"), Sovietsky Pisatel, 1957; *Luk i lira* (title means "The Bow and the Lyre"), Zara Vostoka, 1959; *Stikhi Raznykh Let* (title means "Poems of Several Years"), Molodaya Gvardia, 1959; *Yabloko* (title means "The Apple"), Sovietsky Pisatel, 1960; *Vzmakh Ruki* (title means "A Wave of the Hand"), Molodaya Gvardia, 1962; *Nezhnost: Novyii Stikhi* (title means "Tenderness: New Poems"), Sovietsky Pisatel, 1962; *Posie Stalina* (title means "After Stalin"), Russian Language Specialties, 1962; *Kater Sviazi* (title means "Torpedo Boat Signalling"), Molodaya Gvardia, 1966; *Kazanskii universitet* (title means "Kazan University"), Tatarskoe knizhnoe izd-vo, 1971.

Plays: "Bratsk Power Station," produced in Moscow, 1968; "Under the Skin of the Statue of Liberty," produced in 1972.

Work represented in numerous anthologies. Contributor to periodicals, including *L'Express* and *Literaturnaya Gazeta.*

SIDELIGHTS: As with few other living poets, Yevtushenko's career sharply illustrates the relationship between poetry and politics. While there exists a long Western tradition of politically engaged poetry, poets in the West have generally remained, as Shelly said in 1840, "the unacknowledged legislators of the world." But in the Soviet Union, the political nature and power of poetry, and literature in general, have been more often recognized. This is evident by the persecution of various writers, including Alexander Solzhenitsyn, who have been considered as subversive or as some political threat.

Yevtushenko has always frankly embraced his political role as a poet by encorporating both public and personal themes in his work as well as by being outspoken on current events. Consequently, his stature among the Soviet literati has fluctuated despite his insistence that he is a loyal, revolutionary Soviet citizen. Following the death of Stalin, the morally outraged tone and revolutionary idealism of Yevtushenko's early poetry were enthusiastically received by young Russians and generally tolerated by the post-Stalin authorities. During the 1950's, Yevtushenko's books were published regularly and in 1960, he was permitted to travel outside the Soviet Union to give poetry readings in Europe and the United States.

Occasionally, however, Yevtushenko overstepped his priveleged bounds and found himself caught up in political controversy. One such situation developed upon the publication of "Babi Yar" in 1960. The title of the poem refers to a ravine near Kiev where 96,000 Jews were killed by Nazis during the German occupation; because the poem attributes anti-Semitism to Russians as well as Germans, Yevtushenko was criticized. He was also reprimanded in 1963 for allowing, without official permission from the state, the publication of "Notes for an Autobiography" in the French newspaper, *L'Express.*

On still other occasions, Yevtushenko has been censored because of his political "indiscretions." In 1968, he wrote a letter condemning the Soviet Union's occupation of Czechoslovakia. The negative response provoked by the letter resulted in a cancellation of a performance of "Bratsk Station." In 1974, he sent a telegram to Soviet official Leonid Breshnev expressing concern for the safety of Solzhenitsyn after his arrest. Shortly after Yevtushenko's letter was received, a major recital of his work was cancelled.

In the West, Yevtushenko's reputation has also been unstable, though often in inverse relation to his reputation at home. In 1968, when he was nominated for an Oxford professorship, Kingsley Amis denounced him as a pawn of the Communist Party; his defenders including Arthur Miller and William Styron, had to prove his integrity with evidence of his protests against the Czechoslovakian invasion. Yet, in 1972, he headlined an enormously successful recital in New York City which also featured James Dickey and Stanley Kunitz.

Despite a flair for publicity and occasional successes at recitals, Yevtushenko's popularity has declined in the United States as his poetry becomes more available. When "Bratsk Station" appeared in 1967, Rosemary Neiswender praised his "technical virtuosity" and Andrew Field dubbed him "the best of the political activists writing editorials in verse form." But two of Yevtushenko's most recent collections of poetry have caused some critics to question his writing ability. J. F. Cotter, in a review of *Stolen Apples,* wrote that

"Yevtushenko is simply not that great a poet." Gerard Grealish was even less kind in his dismissal of *From Desire to Desire.* "Yevtushenko is the Rod McKuen of Russia," Grealish wrote. "Both men have captured the popular mind and neither man can write poetry. It is sad."

Nevertheless, Yevtushenko remains a major literary figure in the post-Stalinist Soviet Union. Comparisons to past Russian poets, including Voznesensky and early Mayakovsky continue to be made, and Yevtushenko persists in speaking out for his art and his political ideals. "It goes without saying that the dogmatists used, still use, and will go on using every opportunity they can find to arrest the process of democratization in our society," wrote Yevtushenko in *A Precocious Autobiography.* "I have no rosy illusions about that."

BIOGRAPHICAL/CRITICAL SOURCES: Olga Carlisle, *Voices in the Snow,* Random House, 1962; Yevgeny Yevtushenko, *A Precocious Autobiography,* Dutton, 1963; Vera Alexandrova, *History of Soviet Literature,* Doubleday, 1963; Edward James Brown, *Russian Literature Since the Revolution,* Collier, 1963; Max Hayward and Leopold Labedz, editors, *Literature and Revolution in Soviet Russia,* Oxford University Press, 1963; *Paris Review,* spring-summer, 1965; Katherine Hunter Blair, *A Review of Soviet Literature,* Ampersand, 1966; *Library Journal,* January 15, 1967; *Life,* February 17, 1967; *Book Week,* February 26, 1967; *America,* November 13, 1971; *Contemporary Literary Criticism,* Gale, Volume 1, 1973, Volume 3, 1975.*

*   *   *

YOORS, Jan   1922(?)-1977

PERSONAL: Born in Belgium; married wife, Marion; children: Vanya and Kore (sons), Lyuba (daughter). *Education:* Attended School of Oriental and African Studies, London, in the 1940's. *Residence:* New York, N.Y.

CAREER: Left home at age twelve to join a western European band of gypsies; became liaison operative between allied intelligence units and gypsies behind German lines, 1940; arrested by the Gestapo and sentenced to solitary confinement, torture, and death, escaped from prison and organized escape routes between Germany and Spain, 1943; came to New York City and practiced tapestry art, 1950; tapestry maker, photographer, and writer, 1950-77. U.S. representative at International Biennial of Contemporary Tapestries, 1962, 1965.

WRITINGS: The Gypsies (nonfiction), Simon & Schuster, 1967; *Crossing* (autobiography), Simon & Schuster, 1971 (published in England as *Crossing: A Journal of Survival and Resistance in World War II,* Weidenfeld & Nicolson, 1972); *The Gypsies of Spain,* Macmillan, 1974.

Books of photographs: *Only One New York,* Simon & Schuster, *1965.*

SIDELIGHTS: Yoors's unique and brightly colored tapestries appeared in exhibitions at the Montclair (N.J.) Art Museum (1956), St. Peter's Abbey in Ghent (1974), and in Chicago (1976). In 1966 and 1967 Yoors traveled and took photographs in the Amazon, the Far East, and the Soviet Union. His first book, *Gypsies,* is an account of the six years he spent living among European nomads. *Crossing* is an autobiographical sequel.

BIOGRAPHICAL/CRITICAL SOURCES: Jan Yoors, *Crossing,* Simon & Schuster, 1971 (published in England as *Crossing: A Journal of Survival and Resistance in World War II,* Weidenfeld & Nicolson, 1972).

OBITUARIES: New York Times, November 29, 1977; AB Bookman's Weekly, *February 6, 1978.**

(Died November 27, 1977, in New York, N.Y.)

*   *   *

YORK, Amanda
See DIAL, Joan

*   *   *

YOUNG, Elisabeth Larsh   1910-

PERSONAL: Born August 3, 1910, in San Francisco, Calif.; daughter of Herbert Gladstone (a banker) and Florence (Lipsher) Larsh; married James Young, August 13, 1937 (died September 20, 1976); children: David, Eve. *Education:* Stanford University, B.A., 1931, M.A., 1933; Coe College, B.A., 1962. *Religion:* Unitarian-Universalist. *Residence:* Cedar Rapids, Iowa. *Office:* c/o Iowa State University Press, South State Ave., Ames, Iowa, 50010.

CAREER: Sunset, San Francisco, Calif., member of editorial staff, 1935-38; California State Chamber of Commerce, San Francisco, member of editorial staff, 1939-40; managing editor, 1940-41; free-lance writer, 1941—. *Member:* Women's International League for Peace and Freedom, League of Women Voters, United Nations Association, Beethoven Music Club.

WRITINGS: (With husband, Jim Young) *Bicycle Built for Two* (travelogue), Binfords & Mort, 1940; *Family Afoot* (travelogue), Iowa State University Press, 1978.

Work anthologized in *Best American Short Stories 1960,* edited by Martha Foley. Contributor of short stories to *Quixote* and *The Husk.*

SIDELIGHTS: Elisabeth Young writes: "Some years ago my interest lay mostly in writing fiction. I now prefer light, entertaining travel writing. But that is not to say that I won't ever return to fiction, or perhaps go on to more serious work."

*   *   *

YOUNG, Mahonri   1911-

PERSONAL: Born July 23, 1911, in New York, N.Y.; son of Mahonri Mackintosh (a sculptor) and Cecila (a pianist; maiden name, Sharp) Young; married Elizabeth Chamberlain, July 23, 1932 (divorced, August, 1940); married Rhoda Satterthwaite, December 7, 1940; children: Mahonri Mackintosh II. *Education:* Dartmouth College, A.B., 1932; New York University, M.A., 1951. *Home address:* Kellis Pond Lane, Bridgehampton, N.Y. 11932.

CAREER: Sarah Lawrence College, Bronxville, N.Y., instructor in history of art, 1941-50; Munson-Williams-Proctor Institute, Utica, N.Y., acting director of community arts program, 1951-53; Columbus Gallery of Fine Arts, Columbus, Ohio, director, 1953-76; writer, 1976—. *Military service:* U.S. Army Air Forces, 1942-46. *Member:* Century Association.

WRITINGS: Old George (novel), Washburn, 1940; *The Paintings of George Bellows,* Watson-Guptill, 1973; *The Eight,* Watson-Guptill, 1973; *Early American Moderns,* Watson-Guptill, 1975; *American Realists: Homer to Hopper,* Watson-Guptill, 1977. Author of columns "Letter from the U.S.A." and "Art Across the U.S.A.," in *Apollo,* 1969—. Contributor to popular magazines, including *Vogue, American Scholar,* and *American Art Journal.*

WORK IN PROGRESS: Urban Realists; American Marine Painters; Emerson Burkhart.

Z

ZIEGLER, Bette 1940-

PERSONAL: Born January 5, 1940, in N.Y.; daughter of Jack J. (in business) and Jean Flaks; married Herman Ziegler (an attorney); children: Scott, Laurie. *Education:* Fairleigh Dickinson University, B.A., 1972. *Politics:* "Hopeful." *Home and office:* 19 Wingate Dr., Livingston, N.J. 07039. *Agent:* Henry Morrison, Inc., 58 West 10th St., New York, N.Y. 10011.

CAREER: Worked as advertising copywriter in New Jersey, 1969-71; *Find-a-Tour* (magazine), East Orange, N.J., editor, 1969-72; free-lance writer, 1973—. Teacher of creative writing in Caldwell, N.J. Active in civie volunteer work. *Member:* Authors Guild of Authors League of America, Dramatists Guild, Poets and Writers.

WRITINGS: An Affair for Tomorrow (novel), Harcourt, 1978; (with Jane Seskin) *Pairings: Older Woman and Younger Man Relationships,* Doubleday, 1979; *Final Set* (novel), Harcourt, 1979.

Plays: "The Guest" (one-act), first produced in Madison, N.J., at Fairleigh Dickinson University, March, 1972; "Second Chance" (one-act), first produced in New York City, at New York Theatre Ensemble, September 28, 1972; "In the Beginning" (three-act), first produced in New York City, at National Academy of Television Arts and Sciences, October, 1975; "The Life Game" (three-act), first produced in New York City at Encompass Theatre, March 16, 1977.

Co-author of television pilot series "Whitmore and Berg" and "Dear Suzy." Contributor of poems to literary magazines and newspapers.

WORK IN PROGRESS: Switching Channels, a novel; filmscripts for television.

SIDELIGHTS: Bette Ziegler writes: "I've always known I was going to write full-time some day. One morning I got up and looked in the mirror and realized that someday was now, and put aside other things I was filling my time with, and enrolled in a local creative writing course filled with other women also waiting for 'someday.'

"This was in 1969-70. The woman's movement was beginning to raise our consciousness. We began to take our work seriously. The group members were very supportive of one another and when it ended I was a full-fledged playwright, whose first work had been performed on the stage. After writing four more plays I had the idea for a novel, and decided to take a sabbatical, fully intending to go back to the play form once this novel was completed. I was in for a surprise. It seemed there were quite a few novels lurking in my head, waiting to be written. I've just completed a second, and have been making notes for a third and fourth.

"The past few years I've become involved with Eastern philosophy and meditation. It's an integral part of my life and it's changed me considerably.

"Teaching is also important to me. I like working with people (old and young) who come from different places and bring very many differing attitudes toward things. It's exciting to see a woman of sixty finally take pen to paper and put down the words she's always been meaning to write, and then to find that this same person has talent and a great many interesting things to say."

AVOCATIONAL INTERESTS: "I love travel, walking on the beach, early morning and evening, being with people I care about, and getting lost in my own world when the work is going well."

*   *   *

ZIMMERMAN, Mary K. 1945-

PERSONAL: Born August 9, 1945, in Clinton, Iowa; daughter of John J. (a university professor) and Gwendolyn (an English teacher; maiden name, Smith) Zimmerman; married Burton P. Halpert (a university professor), April 29, 1972; children: Benjamin Anthony. *Education:* University of Michigan, B.A., 1967; University of Minnesota, M.A., 1971, Ph.D., 1976; postdoctoral study at University of Kansas at Kansas City, 1975-78. *Office:* Department of Behavioral Sciences, School of Medicine, University of Minnesota, Duluth, Minn. 55812.

CAREER: University of Wisconsin, River Falls, instructor in sociology, 1972-74; University of Kansas, Kansas City, adjunct instructor in community health, 1975-78; University of Minnesota, Duluth, assistant professor of behavioral sciences, 1978—. *Member:* American Sociological Association, American Public Health Association, Society for the Study of Social Problems, Society for Epidemiological Research, Sociologists for Women in Society. *Awards, honors:* National Institutes of Health postdoctoral fellowship, 1976-77.

WRITINGS: (Contributor) Betty Dubois and Isabel Crouch, editors, *The Sociology of Languages of American*

Women, Trinity University Press, 1976; *Passage Through Abortion: The Personal and Social Reality of Women's Experiences*, Praeger, 1977; (contributor) Gregory Stone and Harvey Farberman, editors, *Social Psychology Through Symbolic Interaction*, Wiley, 1979. Contributor to *Preventive Medicine* and *Teaching Sociology*.

WORK IN PROGRESS: Research for a book on job stress and high blood pressure among working women; studying teenage pregnancy and the impact of stress on health.

SIDELIGHTS: Mary Zimmerman comments: "I am concerned about the condition of women in American society today, specifically their physical and mental well-being. This concern has deepened as a result of my research work on women's specific problems such as unwanted pregnancy and high blood pressure, and it continues to motivate my research, teaching, and writing. Women in American society are undergoing a time of great transition in their social roles. Unfortunately, some roles have changed more than others, meaning disruption and stress for many. It also has led some women to develop creative and innovative ways of coping."

*   *   *

ZION, Eugene   1913-1975
(Gene Zion)

PERSONAL: Born in New York, N. Y.; married Margaret Bloy Graham (an artist). *Education:* Attended the New School for Social Research; graduated from Pratt Institute. *Residence:* New York, N.Y.

CAREER: Member of the staff of Esquire Publications, 1940-42; art designer for Columbia Broadcasting System, 1944-46, and Conde Nast Publications, 1946-49; free-lance writer and designer, 1949-75. *Military service:* Served in the Army during World War II in the Antiaircraft Artillery Visual Training Aids Section, designing training manuals and filmstrips. *Member:* Authors Guild. *Awards, honors:* Runner-up for the Caldecott Medal, 1952, for *All Falling Down; Really Spring* was listed among the *New York Times*'s choice of best illustrated children's books of the year, 1956.

WRITINGS—All written under name Gene Zion and all illustrated by wife, Margaret Bloy Graham: *All Falling Down*, Harper, 1951; *Hide and Seek Day*, Harper, 1954; *The Summer Snowman*, Harper, 1955; *Harry, the Dirty Dog*, Harper, 1956, new edition, 1976; *Really Spring*, Harper, 1956; *Dear Garbage Man*, Harper, 1957; *Jeffie's Party*, Harper, 1957; *No Roses for Harry*, Harper, 1958, new edition, 1976; *The Plant Sitter*, Harper, 1959, new edition, 1976; *Harry and the Lady Next Door*, Harper, 1960; *The Meanest Squirrel I Ever Met*, Scribner, 1962; *The Sugar Mouse Cake*, Scribner, 1964; *Harry By the Sea*, Harper, 1965, new edition, 1976.

SIDELIGHTS: His wife's sketch of children gathering apples in an orchard was the inspiration for Eugene Zion's first children's book, *All Falling Down*. "It might seem oversimple were it not that the pictures have such charm and offer so many details for further talk," commented a *New York Herald Tribune Book Review* critic. "The scenes are in city or country, and the many moods so happily translated into action are worth the long look. . . ."

As collaborators, Zion and his wife are probably best known for their stories about Harry the dog. The first one, *Harry, the Dirty Dog*, received the following comments from a *New York Times* reviewer: "Harry is sure to be loved; especially by those pre-school children to whom dirt is an ever-delight-

ful thing. The illustrations by Margaret Bloy Graham are bright, animated, and expressive, and are a bold complement to the direct and charming text." Concerning *Plant Sitter*, the *London Times Literary Supplement* observed: "The happy blend of unanswerable logic and wild improbability that is the special gift of American children's writers is as strong as ever."

BIOGRAPHICAL/CRITICAL SOURCES: New York Herald Tribune Book Review, November 11, 1951; *New York Times*, September 16, 1956; *Times Literary Supplement*, May 29, 1959; *New York Times*, December 9, 1975; *Publishers Weekly*, December 29, 1975; *A. B. Bookman's Weekly*, March 22, 1976.*

(Died December 5, 1975)

*   *   *

ZION, Gene
See ZION, Eugene

*   *   *

ZOCHERT, Donald (Paul, Jr.)   1938-

PERSONAL: Surname is pronounced *Zock*-ert; born May 3, 1938, in Oak Park, Ill.; son of Donald P. (an engineer) and Dorothy (Schmidt) Zochert; married Nancy Ann Schoenwolf, 1960; children: Corey, John, Michael. *Education:* Attended University of Illinois, University of Illinois at Chicago Circle, University of Colorado, and Roosevelt University; Elmhurst College, B.A., 1961. *Home:* 511 South Craig Pla., Lombard, Ill. 60148. *Agent:* Ellen Levine, Curtis Brown Ltd., 575 Madison Ave., New York, N.Y. 10022.

CAREER: United Press International, Chicago, Ill., reporter, 1961-66; *Chicago Daily News*, Chicago, Ill., reporter, 1966-78; free-lance writer, 1978—.

WRITINGS: (Editor) *Walking in America*, Knopf, 1974; *Laura: The Life of Laura Ingalls Wilder*, Contemporary Books, 1976; *Murder in the Hellfire Club* (novel), Holt, 1979. Contributor to scholarly journals, including *Isis, James Joyce Quarterly*, and *Western American Literature*.

WORK IN PROGRESS: A biography of Robert Kennicott, a nineteenth-century American naturalist; a history of America through the life of James Clyman; a novel about a woman who wants to know how to live; a collection of articles about American eccentrics.

SIDELIGHTS: Zochert writes: "A long experience in journalism exposed me to public and private emotion, to the notion of time and its indifference, and to the primacy of crucial detail in a way that perhaps no other vocational experience could have. Despite an extended college career—six years to get one lousy B.A.—I consider myself self-educated in the most important particulars. These two circumstances have a decisive influence on my approach to writing. I follow my interests. I try to hold myself apart from conventional 'success' and 'failure' (while acknowledging their practical importance). My deepest satisfaction in writing comes from satisfying myself. If this sounds self-indulgent, it isn't. The act of writing is the most certain self-discovery. The best writing comes out of that discovery—the exercise and definition of one's perceptions, the continual testing of eye, ear, and endurance, the reflections of society and life shot off from the mirrors of one personality.

"In person I am large and lethargic (although easily excited by absurdities). My sense of humor is rather too condemning. I am a good listener."

ZOLLINGER, Norman 1921-

PERSONAL: Born November 8, 1921, in Chicago, Ill.; son of Albert (a manufacturer) and Anne (Kennedy) Zollinger; married Gerrie Harte, September 7, 1946; children: Peter, Ann, Robin. *Education:* Attended Cornell College, Mt. Vernon, Iowa, 1940-42. *Home:* 4608 Sherwood N.E., Albuquerque, N.M. 87109. *Office:* Little Professor Book Center, 6001 Lomas N.E., Albuquerque, N.M. 87110.

CAREER: Bank messenger in Chicago, Ill., 1939-40; AZI, Inc. (manufacturing company), Downers Grove, Ill., president and chairman of board of directors, 1945-71; Little Professor Book Center, Albuquerque, N.M., owner, 1971—. Commissioner and assistant mayor in Downers Grove, 1950-55, president of Community Council, 1965-67. *Military service:* U.S. Army Air Forces, 1942-45; served in European theater; became first lieutenant; received Air Medal with five oak leaf clusters. *Member:* Rio Grande Writers Association (president, 1978), New Mexico Book League (vice-president, 1978).

WRITINGS: Riders to Cibola (novel), Museum of New Mexico Press, 1978.

WORK IN PROGRESS: Medal of Honor, a novel.

SIDELIGHTS: Zollinger writes: "I wrote as a college student and as a young man, and was published in newspapers and college quarterlies. I abandoned writing after World War II for a career in business, and returned to it when I became disenchanted with manufacturing. I moved to New Mexico in 1971 to open a bookstore and complete *Riders to Cibola.*

"My novel is a three generation story of a ranch family in central New Mexico as seen through the eyes of an illegal alien, an orphaned Mexican who holds things together for his adopted family through wars, depressions, and droughts. It is, I hope, straightforward narrative writing. Any messages—there might be a small one on brotherhood and tolerance—come from the characters and the action, not from the author. *Medal of Honor* is perhaps a little more autobiographical. Three midwestern boys grow up in the 1930's and 1940's and go off to World War II. I hope it can illuminate some of the older generations attitudes toward that war, but certainly without glorifying it."

AVOCATIONAL INTERESTS: Skiing, backpacking, tennis.

BIOGRAPHICAL/CRITICAL SOURCES: Library Journal, February 1, 1978; *Albuquerque Journal,* February 9, 1978; *Downers Grove Reporter,* March 15, 1978; *Albuquerque Tribune,* April 28, 1978.

*   *   *

ZUSNE, Leonard 1924-

PERSONAL: Born December 24, 1924, in Liepaja, Latvia; came to the United States in 1957, naturalized citizen, 1968; son of Janis (an electronics engineer) and Anna (Anisimova) Zusne; married Helen C. Horning (a psychologist), January 28, 1965; children: Megan. *Education:* Attended Mainz University, 1947-48; Purdue University, B.S., 1959, M.S., 1961, Ph.D., 1964. *Politics:* Democrat. *Religion:* "No official affiliation." *Home:* 6245 South Knoxville, Tulsa, Okla. 74136. *Office:* Psychology Program, University of Tulsa, Tulsa, Okla. 74104.

CAREER: Clerk and secretary to business and law firms in Caracas, Venezuela, 1949-53; Creole Petroleum Corp., administrative secretary in Lagunillas, Venezuela, 1953-57, and Tia Juana, Venezuela, 1960; University of Tulsa, Tulsa, Okla., assistant professor, 1964-68, associate professor, 1968-75, professor of psychology, 1975—, chairman of department, 1976-78. *Member:* American Psychological Association, American Association for the Advancement of Science, Psychonomic Society, Southwestern Psychological Association, Sigma Xi (local vice-president, 1975-76; president, 1976-77).

WRITINGS: Visual Perception of Form, Academic Press, 1970; *Names in the History of Psychology,* Hemisphere Publishing, 1975. Contributor of more than thirty articles to psychology journals.

WORK IN PROGRESS: Second edition of *Names in the History of Psychology; The Psychology of the Extraordinary,* with Warren H. Jones, publication expected in 1980; *A History of Psychology,* publication expected in 1981.

SIDELIGHTS: Zusne comments: "The existence of an objective and a subjective side of life is not only at the root of all psychology but is the most fundamental distinction that can be made in human life, all other distinctions being based on it. The key to a comprehensive psychology and to all philosophies of life is to be found in this distinction. My planned *History of Psychology* will be built upon this notion."